THE NIV
YOUTH BIBLE

THE NIV YOUTH BIBLE

...ETERNITY STARTS HERE

Hodder & Stoughton
LONDON SYDNEY AUCKLAND

This publication is not included under licences issued by the Copyright Licensing Agency. Photoset by Rowland Phototypesetting Ltd, Bury St Edmunds, Suffolk. Printed in Great Britain for Hodder and Stoughton Ltd, a division of Hodder Headline PLC, 338 Euston Road, London NW1 3BH, by Clays Ltd, St Ives plc.

PREFACE

THE NEW INTERNATIONAL VERSION is a completely new translation of the Holy Bible made by over a hundred scholars working directly from the best available Hebrew, Aramaic and Greek texts. It had its beginning in 1965 when, after several years of exploratory study by committees from the Christian Reformed Church and the National Association of Evangelicals, a group of scholars met at Palos Heights, Illinois, and concurred in the need for a new translation of the Bible in contemporary English. This group, though not made up of official church representatives, was transdenominational. Its conclusion was endorsed by a large number of leaders from many denominations who met in Chicago in 1966.

Responsibility for the new version was delegated by the Palos Heights group to a self-governing body of fifteen, the Committee on Bible Translation, composed for the most part of biblical scholars from colleges, universities and seminaries. In 1967 the New York Bible Society (now the International Bible Society) generously undertook the financial sponsorship of the project—a sponsorship that made it possible to enlist the help of many distinguished scholars. The fact that participants from the United States, Great Britain, Canada, Australia and New Zealand worked together gave the project its international scope. That they were from many denominations—including Anglican, Assemblies of God, Baptist, Brethren, Christian Reformed, Church of Christ, Evangelical Free, Lutheran, Mennonite, Methodist, Nazarene, Presbyterian, Wesleyan and other churches—helped to safeguard the translation from sectarian bias.

How it was made helps to give the New International Version its distinctiveness. The translation of each book was assigned to a team of scholars. Next, one of the Intermediate Editorial Committees revised the initial translation, with constant reference to the Hebrew, Aramaic or Greek. Their work then went to one of the General Editorial Committees, which checked it in detail and made another thorough revision. This revision in turn was carefully reviewed by the Committee on Bible Translation, which made further changes and then released the final version for publication. In this way the entire Bible underwent three revisions, during each of which the translation was examined for its faithfulness to the original languages and for its English style.

All this involved many thousands of hours of research and discussion regarding the meaning of the texts and the precise way of putting them into English. It may well be that no other translation has been made by a more thorough process of review and revision from committee to committee than this one.

From the beginning of the project, the Committee on Bible Translation held to certain goals for the New International Version: that it would be an accurate translation and one that would have clarity and literary quality and so prove suitable for public and private reading, teaching, preaching, memorising and liturgical use. The Committee also sough' to preserve some measure of continuity with the long tradition of translating the Scriptures into English.

In working towards these goals, the translators were united in their commitment to the authority and infallibility of the Bible as God's Word in written form. They believe that it contains the divine answer to the deepest needs of humanity, that it sheds unique light on our path in a dark world, and that it sets forth the way to our eternal well-being.

The first concern of the translators has been the accuracy of the translation and its fidelity to the thought of the biblical writers. They have weighed the significance of the lexical and grammatical details of the Hebrew, Aramaic and Greek texts. At the same time, they have striven for more than a word-for-word translation. Because thought patterns and syntax differ from language to language, faithful communication of the meaning of the writers of the Bible demands frequent modifications in sentence structure and constant regard for the contextual meanings of words.

A sensitive feeling for style does not always accompany scholarship. Accordingly the Committee on Bible Translation submitted the developing version to a number of stylistic consultants. Two of them read every book of both Old and New Testaments twice—once before and once after the last major revision—and made invaluable suggestions. Samples of the translation were tested for clarity and ease of reading by various kinds of people—young and old, highly educated and less well educated, ministers and laymen.

Concern for clear and natural English—that the New International Version should be idiomatic but not idiosyncratic, contemporary but not dated—motivated the translators and consultants. At the same time, they tried to reflect the differing styles of the biblical writers. In view of the international use of English, the translators sought to avoid obvious Americanisms on the one hand and obvious Anglicisms on the other. A British edition reflects the comparatively few differences of significant idiom and of spelling.

As for the traditional pronouns "thou", "thee" and "thine" in reference to the Deity, the translators judged that to use these archaisms (along with old verb forms such as "doest", "wouldest" and "hadst") would violate accuracy in translation. Neither Hebrew, Aramaic nor Greek uses special pronouns for the persons of the Godhead. A present-day translation is not enhanced by forms that in the time of the King James Version were used in everyday speech, whether referring to God or man.

For the Old Testament the standard Hebrew text, the Masoretic Text as published in the latest editions of *Biblia Hebraica*, was used throughout. The Dead Sea Scrolls contain material bearing on an earlier stage of the Hebrew text. They were consulted, as were the Samaritan Pentateuch and the ancient scribal traditions relating to textual changes. Sometimes a variant Hebrew reading in the margin of the Masoretic Text was followed instead of the text itself. Such instances, being variants within the Masoretic tradition, are not specified by footnotes. In rare cases, words in the consonantal text were divided differently from the way they appear in the Masoretic Text. Footnotes indicate this. The translators also consulted the more important early versions—the Septuagint; Aquila, Symmachus and Theodotion; the Vulgate; the Syriac Peshitta; the Targums; and for the Psalms the *Juxta Hebraica* of Jerome. Readings from these versions were occasionally followed where the Masoretic Text seemed doubtful and where accepted principles of textual criticism showed that one or more of these textual witnesses appeared to provide the correct reading. Such instances are footnoted. Sometimes vowel letters and vowel signs did not, in the judgment of the translators, represent the correct vowels for the original consonantal text. Accordingly some words were read with a different set of vowels. These instances are usually not indicated by footnotes.

The Greek text used in translating the New Testament was an eclectic one. No other piece of ancient literature has such an abundance of manuscript witnesses as does the New Testament. Where existing manuscripts differ, the translators made their choice of readings according to accepted principles of New Testament textual criticism. Footnotes call attention to places where there was uncertainty about what the original text was. The best current printed texts of the Greek New Testament were used.

There is a sense in which the work of translation is never wholly finished. This applies to all great literature and uniquely so to the Bible. In 1973 the New Testament in the New International Version was published. Since then, suggestions for corrections and revisions have been received from various sources. The Committee on Bible Translation carefully considered the suggestions and adopted a number of them. These were incorporated in the first printing of the entire Bible in 1978. Additional revisions were made by the Committee on Bible Translation in 1983 and appear in printings after that date.

As in other ancient documents, the precise meaning of the biblical texts is sometimes uncertain. This is more often the case with the Hebrew and Aramaic texts than with the Greek text. Although archaeological and linguistic discoveries in this century aid in understanding difficult passages, some uncertainties remain. The more significant of these have been called to the reader's attention in the footnotes.

In regard to the divine name YHWH, commonly referred to as the *Tetragrammaton*, the translators adopted the device used in most English versions of rendering that name as "Lord" in capital letters to distinguish it from *Adonai*, another Hebrew word rendered "Lord", for which small letters are used. Wherever the two names stand together in the Old Testament as a compound name of God, they are rendered "Sovereign Lord".

Because for most readers today the phrases "the Lord of hosts" and "God of hosts" have little meaning, this version renders them "the Lord Almighty" and "God Almighty". These renderings convey the sense of the Hebrew, namely, "he who is sovereign over all the 'hosts' (powers) in heaven and on earth, especially over the 'hosts' (armies) of Israel." For readers unacquainted with Hebrew this does not make clear the distinction between *Sabaoth* ("hosts" or "Almighty") and *Shaddai* (which can also be translated "Almighty"), but the latter occurs infrequently and is always footnoted. When *Adonai* and *YHWH Sabaoth* occur together, they are rendered "the Lord, the Lord Almighty".

As for other proper nouns, the familiar spellings of the Authorised Version are generally retained. Names traditionally spelled with "ch", except where it is final, are usually spelled in this translation with "k" or "c", since the biblical languages do not have the sound that "ch" frequently indicates in English—for example, in *chant*. For well-known names such as Zechariah, however, the traditional spelling has been retained. Variation in the spelling of names in the original languages has usually not been indicated. Where a person or place has two or more different names in the Hebrew, Aramaic or Greek texts, the more familiar one has generally been used, with footnotes where needed.

To achieve clarity the translators sometimes supplied words not in the original texts but required by the context. If there was uncertainty about such material, it is enclosed in brackets. Also for the sake of clarity or style, nouns, including some proper nouns, are sometimes substituted for pronouns, and vice versa. And though the Hebrew writers often shifted back and forth between first, second and third personal pronouns without change of antecedent, this translation often makes them uniform, in accordance with English style and without the use of footnotes.

Poetical passages are printed as poetry, that is, with indentation of lines and with separate stanzas. These are generally designed to reflect the structure of Hebrew poetry. This poetry is normally characterised by parallelism in balanced lines. Most of the poetry in the Bible is in the Old Testament, and scholars differ regarding the scansion of Hebrew lines. The translators determined the stanza divisions for the most part by analysis of the subject matter. The stanzas therefore serve as poetic paragraphs.

As an aid to the reader, italicised sectional headings are inserted in most of the books. They are not to be regarded as part of the NIV text, are not for oral reading, and are not intended to dictate the interpretation of the sections they head.

The footnotes in this version are of several kinds, most of which need no explanation. Those giving alternative translations begin with "Or" and generally introduce the alternative with the last word preceding it in the text, except when it is a single-word alternative; in poetry quoted in a footnote a slant mark indicates a line division. Footnotes introduced by "Or" do not have uniform significance. In some cases two possible translations were considered to have about equal validity. In other cases, though the translators were convinced that the translation in the text was correct, they judged that another interpretation was possible and of sufficient importance to be represented in a footnote.

In the New Testament, footnotes that refer to uncertainty regarding the original text are introduced by "Some manuscripts" or similar expressions. In the Old Testament, evidence for the reading chosen is given first and evidence for the alternative is added after a semicolon (for example: Septuagint; Hebrew *father*). In such notes the term "Hebrew" refers to the Masoretic Text.

It should be noted that minerals, flora and fauna, architectural details, articles of clothing and jewellery, musical instruments and other articles cannot always be identified with precision. Also measures of capacity in the biblical period are particularly uncertain (see the table of weights and measures following the text).

Like all translations of the Bible, made as they are by imperfect man, this one undoubtedly falls short of its goals. Yet we are grateful to God for the extent to which he has enabled us to realise these goals and for the strength he has given us and our colleagues to complete our task. We offer this version of the Bible to him in whose name and for whose glory it has been made. We pray that it will lead many into a better understanding of the Holy Scriptures and a fuller knowledge of Jesus Christ the incarnate Word, of whom the Scriptures so faithfully testify.

The Committee on Bible Translation

June 1978
(Revised August 1983)

Names of the translators and editors may be secured
from the International Bible Society
1820 Jet Stream Drive, Colorado Springs, CO 80921-3696, U.S.A.

Hello

and welcome to your new Bible

This special edition of the NIV, the most popular modern Bible translation in the world, has been produced with a number of goals in mind:

✔ *to help you gain confidence in reading the Bible for yourself;*

✔ *to introduce you to Jesus, God the Father and the Holy Spirit;*

✔ *to introduce you to some young Christians who are willing to share their ideas, experiences and understanding.*

When reading the additional material, you need to bear a few things in mind:

➼ *it assumes very little or no prior knowledge of the Bible, so if you've never been to church or Sunday school, don't worry, you'll find any explanations you need here;*

➼ *it has been written in bite-sized chunks, so don't be concerned that you need a degree-level education to read the Bible, you don't;*

➼ *for those coming to the Bible looking for answers, we won't tell you all of those. We want you to read the Bible and find out for yourself (for this reason, page numbers are provided to major sections to help you find the Bible text itself);*

➼ *it has been written and edited by real people. While we can't introduce you to the original writers of the Bible, we can enable you to get to know the people that have contributed to the new material so that we can learn together how to live out the amazing message of the Bible. For that reason, this Bible comes with details of how to access an internet forum where you can meet up with other young Christians for discussion, encouragement, prayer requests, answers to prayer, whatever, that's up to you. Why not check it out on: www.NIV-YOUTH-BIBLE.COM*

➼ *it tries to keep a balance between the Christian faith as rooted in the experience of believers and as rooted in God's revelation of himself in the Bible. This balance may be better achieved in some places than others;*

➼ *it contains repetition of key ideas expressed in different ways by different people. We think this is valid as many important ideas are worth repeating and may become clearer second or third time round.*

Before you dive straight in, have a look at the next three pages which provide a whistle-stop tour of what's in this Bible and how to find your way around.

Happy hunting! And we pray that through reading these words you will find the one who is 'the Word'.

Simon Hall

the Bible

The Bible is an amazing book, for lots of reasons. In fact, it's not one book at all, but sixty-six. That makes finding your way around the Bible quite difficult, because the story of God and his people doesn't flow quite as seamlessly as a novel. Here are a few suggestions to help you find your way:

Don't read the Bible like a novel. It wasn't written as such, and trying to read it straight through will probably leave you tired and frustrated. Parts of the Bible *are* like a novel, other parts are like a history book, others more like an encyclopaedia and some are letters. If you don't know where to start, go straight to the Deep End section at the back of this Bible which will give you a choice of 5-day reading plans to get you into the Bible. If you've never read the Bible before it's good to start with the life of Jesus: the gospel of Mark (p. 1002) will take you about an hour to read.

There is an easy way to find your way to particular parts of the Bible because each book has a name, and with a few exceptions, they are divided up into numbered chapters. Each chapter is then divided further into verses. So when you see:

book   chapter ↓   verse
↳ John 3:16 ↵

it means the book of John (p. 1063 of the Bible), the third chapter and the sixteenth verse which begins: 'For God so loved the world . . .' The top of each Bible page will help you to see where you are. If you have trouble finding a book, just turn to the page opposite this one which tells you where to find each book.

> Exceptions: *Some books have the same name and are distinguished as the first, second or third book of the same name. This is true of Kings, Samuel, Chronicles, Corinthians, Thessalonians, Timothy, Peter and John's letters.*
> *Some books have only one chapter: Jude 21 means Jude verse 21 not Jude chapter 21. This is also true of Obadiah, 2 John and 3 John.*

Everybody needs help so don't worry if you find parts of the Bible difficult to understand, you are following in the footsteps of millions! The extra material in this Bible will be a good starting point in learning about the Bible and its message, but be ready to ask someone who might know more.

Books of the Bible
in alphabetical order

Books of the New Testament are in italic

Acts	1092	Judges	242
Amos	916	1 Kings	334
1 Chronicles	400	2 Kings	368
2 Chronicles	436	Lamentations	822
Colossians	1182	Leviticus	102
1 Corinthians	1144	*Luke*	1025
2 Corinthians	1158	Malachi	960
Daniel	883	*Mark*	1002
Deuteronomy	178	*Matthew*	965
Ecclesiastes	668	Micah	930
Ephesians	1173	Nahum	937
Esther	501	Nehemiah	485
Exodus	58	Numbers	133
Ezekiel	830	Obadiah	925
Ezra	473	*1 Peter*	1217
Galatians	1168	*2 Peter*	1222
Genesis	3	*Philemon*	1200
Habakkuk	940	*Philippians*	1178
Haggai	948	Proverbs	635
Hebrews	1201	Psalms	543
Hosea	900	*Revelation*	1233
Isaiah	685	*Romans*	1128
James	1213	Ruth	267
Jeremiah	755	1 Samuel	271
Job	509	2 Samuel	304
Joel	911	Song of Songs	678
John	1063	*1 Thessalonians*	1186
1 John	1225	*2 Thessalonians*	1189
2 John	1229	*1 Timothy*	1191
3 John	1230	*2 Timothy*	1195
Jonah	927	*Titus*	1198
Joshua	216	Zechariah	950
Jude	1231	Zephaniah	944

Books of the Bible

in biblical order

Books of the Old Testament

Books of the New Testament

the extra bits

Here is a handy guide to the additional material. It might be worth keeping a bookmark or sticker at this page for easy reference.

Front section of this Bible

These are the pages immediately following. They are numbered 1 to 66 with F preceding for FRONT! This section tries to answer questions about the Bible itself as a book; provide an overview of the story of the Bible; help you to apply the Bible to your life.

Middle sections in colour

These can easily be found throughout the Bible as they are printed in colour on shiny paper and they look and read very differently to the actual Bible text itself. These pages are numbered 1, 2, 3 and following and when they are mentioned elsewhere, they will have a C preceding for COLOUR! These sections contain material about real people and their attempts to apply the Bible to their lives; Bible studies making suggestions on how to approach Bible reading; a couple of questionnaires completed by Christians you may have heard of.

Back section

These pages are numbered 1, 2, 3 and following with B preceding for BACK! (For a more detailed contents page see B1.) This is a meaty section which provides thirty 5-day reading plans; explanations for key biblical and Christian concepts; Bible references when you want to find a text on a particular issue; a one-year Bible reading plan; a prayer of commitment.

Testing the water

What's in the Bible?

JARGON-BUSTER

Babylon

Canaan

Christian

church

covenant

Daniel

death

Egypt

exile

God

gospel

Israelites

Jesus

Jordan

Joseph

Joshua

Law

Moses

promised land

prophecy

resurrection

Testament

Introduction

One of the most amazing thing about the Bible is the huge variety of material in it. If you're reading through the Bible and wondering exactly what it is you've got, I'm here to explain.

The Bible consists of two main parts: the Old Testament and the New Testament. 'Testament' means 'agreement' or 'covenant' and so the two parts describe the main covenants that God made with his people. These include the giving of the Law to Moses and the Israelites (Exodus 20 and Deuteronomy 5) and, of supreme importance for Christians, the life, death and resurrection of Jesus, which led to a completely new understanding of how people could relate to God (John 1:17). But that's just for starters . . . Within these testaments are individual books, sixty-six in all. These books were written at different times in different styles which are generally recognised as being: law, history, wisdom, prophecy, Gospels, letters, apocalyptic literature.

Within the formal categories, you can make your own personal classifications (if it's helpful). For example, I would classify Song of Songs under 'passion'; Jeremiah under 'prophetic anger' and Kings under 'thriller'. Try it once you're familiar with some of the Bible text.

More detailed breakdown of the Old Testament

LAW: The five books of the Law given to Israel through Moses (often called the Pentateuch, 'The Five Scrolls' or the Torah): Genesis, Exodus, Leviticus, Numbers, Deuteronomy.

These first five books deal with the creation of the world, the calling of Israel as a people, and its early history, including the exodus from Egypt. The story they tell features names such as Noah, Joseph, Moses and ends with the people of Israel about to cross over the Jordan and enter the promised land. One of the most important themes of these books is the giving of the Law to Moses, and its implications for the life of Israel (Leviticus in particular is concerned with the regulation of the life of Israel). Although these books appear at the start of the Bible, unless you are a very able reader or have a very straightforward and easy-read Bible translation, don't start here! Wait until you have read one or more of the Gospels.

HISTORY: Joshua, Judges, Ruth, 1 and 2 Samuel, 1 and 2 Kings, 1 and 2 Chronicles, Ezra, Nehemiah, Esther.

These books reveal God's activity throughout the history of the people of Israel, his chosen people, from their entry into the promised land of Canaan to the return of the people of Jerusalem from exile in the city of Babylon. These are histories with a special perspective; right from the moment Joshua leads the Israelites into Canaan at the start of the book that bears his name, we are being shown God at work. Be warned: there is much blood and sex in this part of the Bible. The Bible doesn't hide bloody reality from us, neither does it pretend that the great heroes of the faith were perfect. Yet these are the stories of Israel, of how God took a bunch of ex-slaves and turned them into a special nation. Try reading from the start of 1 Samuel to the end of 2 Kings like you would a novel.

WISDOM: Job, Psalms, Proverbs, Ecclesiastes, Song of Songs, Lamentations.

These are also earthy books full of realism and passion (the common factor rather than any one literary style). Some of these books have a raw edge about them. If you have never read the Psalms before, you will quickly see why their mixture of pain, anger, joy and praise makes them so popular with Christians. Each of these books stands on its own, although Job, Proverbs, Ecclesiastes and Lamentations are all musings on life, love and death, while Psalms and Song of Songs are written as poetry.

PROPHETS: Major prophets are Isaiah, Jeremiah, Ezekiel, Daniel; minor prophets: Hosea, Joel, Amos, Obadiah, Jonah, Micah, Nahum, Habakkuk, Zephaniah, Haggai, Zechariah, Malachi.

This section of the Old Testament views part of the story of God's people from within through the eyes of individuals - prophets. Instead of the wide political scope of Chronicles, we get very personal revelations to individuals who have been chosen by God, about what God really feels as a result of his people's constant round of disobedience-obedience-disobedience. Try reading one of the 'minor' (shorter) prophets like Amos before tackling the likes of Jeremiah. Daniel isn't really a major prophet (the other three in that category are much longer than all the other prophets), but he's a bit of an anomaly, containing part story, and part 'apocalyptic' material (apocalypse being a vision of the end of the world).

The New Testament
GOSPELS: Matthew, Mark, Luke, John
The New Testament starts with four slightly different accounts of the life, death and resurrection of Jesus. Sometimes people think one Gospel would be better than four and start worrying about why they are different. My response would be that it's a bit like reporting on a

football match. In football, you have one referee and two assistants: while the referee is watching the ball, the assistants are looking out for offsides and fouls and what they each remember from a match will be slightly different from the other's memory. So it is with the Gospels, each story has a different twist: Matthew's is filled with practical teaching, Mark's is action-packed, Luke's is intelligent, John's is deep, very deep. But all these different writers highlight one thing: Jesus is the most important person ever to have lived, because he was . . . well, why don't you read about it!

ACTS: is part two of the Gospel of Luke, and starts off where Luke ends. It provides amazing glimpses into the early church, recording how the good news about Jesus spread from Palestine through Lebanon, Turkey and Greece and on to Italy.

LETTERS: Romans, 1 and 2 Corinthians, Galatians, Ephesians, Philippians, Colossians, 1 and 2 Thessalonians, 1 and 2 Timothy, Titus, Philemon, Hebrews, James, 1 and 2 Peter, 1, 2 and 3 John, Jude.

The New Testament was formed much more quickly than the Old Testament because the length of time it spans is so much shorter. There is a much stronger feel of the here and now about it. That's mainly because of all these special letters written to the new churches by really special people such as Paul.

REVELATION: Apocalypse:
These two long words actually mean the same thing: a vision especially of the end of the world. Don't worry if you find this book difficult to fathom! It's not all double Dutch. It's written in a highly symbolic way that its readers would have understood. If you want to really get into this book, using a commentary would definitely be a good idea.

The Story of the Bible (pp. 3-241):

Creation to Joshua

The Bible begins at the beginning . . . of everything. We learn that although God made the universe as a wonderful, beautiful place (Genesis 1), the first humans messed up badly almost straight away (Genesis 3 and 4). In fact, it got so bad that God decided to start again with people, saving just one family (Genesis 6–9). These stories, and the others in Genesis 1–11, are lost in the mists of time, but the rest of the Bible all happened within the last 4,000 years and can be dated roughly.

About 4,000 years ago, God set in motion the long process of salvation that finally brought us Jesus. It started when he chose one man, Abraham, to be the 'father' of his special people (Genesis 12), the nation of Israel into which Jesus was born. Abraham obeyed God and moved to Canaan, where miraculously he became a father in his (and Sarah's) old age (Genesis 17 and 21). God tested Abraham's faith in the most heart-rending way, but he passed the test (Genesis 22). Abraham's son Isaac had two sons, Esau and Jacob. They were very different, and fell out in a spectacular way (Genesis 27 and 28), not speaking to each other for many years. Genesis 32 and 33 record their reconciliation.

Jacob was father to Joseph, famous for his flashy coat and ability to interpret dreams, but much more important because of his time in Egypt which was engineered by his jealous brothers but planned by God (Genesis 37–50). The descendants of Abraham flourished in this foreign land, but 250 years later the 'Israelites' (Jacob's other name was Israel) were forced into slavery working for the great Pharaohs (Exodus 1). This was not what God wanted! So, as God often does, he chose an unlikely hero, Moses (a nervy, possibly speech-impaired Israelite murderer) to save the day and lead the Israelites out of Egypt. The book of Exodus tells us that the great Pharaoh didn't give up his slaves without a fight, but he didn't realise who he was fighting against (God) and lost, big time (Exodus 3–14).

There then followed a momentous time for the people of Israel. Between Egypt and Canaan there is a desert which is not a nice place to be, and the newly freed slaves realised that life in chains was actually more comfortable than travelling through a desert relying completely on God for provision. They doubted, they rebelled, they worshipped the gods of their former 'employers'. Significantly during this time, Moses received from God the Ten Commandments and the Law (the basis of Israelite society to this day). While the Israelites were busy worshipping their golden calf, Moses was pleading on their behalf with God (Exodus 20 and 32).

Moses led the Israelites through the desert, carrying with them the stone tablets on which the Commandments were written. These, and the box in which they were carried (the ark of the covenant: Exodus 25:10-16), became the centre of the Israelites' worship for centuries to come. God's final generous gesture to Moses before he died was to see the land that God had originally promised to Abraham. But Moses never got to set foot in the promised land (Deuteronomy 34:1-4); the job of ejecting the present occupants was left to a younger man, Joshua.

JARGON-BUSTER
Abraham
ark of the covenant
Canaan
God
Isaac
Israel
Jacob
Jesus
Joseph
judges
Law
Moses
Pharaoh
promised land
Ten Commandments

The seizure of the city of Jericho set the pattern for the whole of Joshua's time as a leader of the Israelites. Just as it seemed that this strange band of nomads had finally met their match in this fortified city, so God told them that he would hand over the city to them if they obeyed him (Joshua 6). The book of Joshua does not make pleasant reading, but it is clear that drastic action (bloodshed and killing) had to be taken if God was going to re-establish his people in the land he had given them. But these mini-wars took their toll and periodically someone was needed to drag the Israelites away from their agriculture to defend the nation. Bring on the judges!

The Story of the Bible (pp. 242-472):

Judges and Kings

JARGON-BUSTER

ark of the covenant

Babylon

Canaan

David

Elijah

God

holy

Israel

Jacob

Jerusalem

Joshua

Judah

Judges

LORD

promised land

prophet

Samuel

Solomon

temple

From the initial invasion of the promised land to the establishment of the kingdom of Israel was probably around four hundred years. These were difficult times. The Israelites that had arrived in Canaan with Joshua were nomads and were struggling to establish settled farming communities while coping with the added problem of marauding neighbours (Judges 2:10-15). God seemed far away and they called out for help. The book of Judges is a collection of stories from the first centuries of the nation of Israel, telling of the leaders who rescued the people from themselves and their enemies. Some of these judges were both particularly heroic and particularly human, like Samson (Judges 13–16) and Gideon (Judges 6–8). Others were the right people at the right time, like Deborah (Judges 4–5). Somehow, despite the lack of any clear national organisation, the twelve tribes of Israel (descendants of Jacob's twelve sons) managed to hold together over four hundred rocky years.

Despite the overall success of the judges, the Israelites weren't too happy with their infrastructure and decided that their enemies were right after all; what they needed was a king. God allowed them their wish on provision that kings were appointed by his prophets: special mouthpieces of God recognised by both God and the people as holy men. One of the most famous of these prophets was Samuel, and he appointed Saul (1 Samuel 9:15-16) and David (1 Samuel 16:1-13) the first two kings of Israel. The

story of Saul, David and Saul's son Jonathan is one of the
most beautiful and moving in the Bible. It's impossible to
do it justice here, so you'll just have to read 1 Samuel
10–1 Kings 11!

JUDGES: HEROIC AND HUMAN

Saul and David (and David's son Solomon) were very
successful so that for over a hundred years the twelve tribes
lived together under the same king. It was the golden age, apart from the wars, assassinations,
adultery, incest, murder, conspiracy, revolution, deceit and more wars that went on.
The first temple was built in the new capital city of Jerusalem (2 Samuel 6,
1 Kings 3:1-3), to house the ark of the covenant. Israel grew through many
victories against and alliances with neighbouring states. She also became complacent
and when Solomon died the kingdom split into two: Israel in the north, and Judah in
the south (1 Kings 12). For two hundred years these two rival kingdoms rubbed up
against each other without actually declaring all out war.

Onto the scene stepped two more star prophets: Elijah (1 Kings 18:18-45) and Elisha
(2 Kings 2:1-9). Unlike Samuel, who was ministering to kings who were fallen but faithful
followers of God, Elijah and Elisha were speaking out God's word at a time when the nation
of Israel was beginning to melt away, being assimilated into the religious and cultural
hotch-potch of the Middle East at that time. There were a few 'good men' who 'did what was
right in the eyes of the LORD' ruling over Israel and Judah, but the Bible depicts an awful
rollercoaster ride for both nations as sincere kings (2 Kings 18:5-8) were succeeded by
charlatans (2 Kings 21:1-6).

God's people were not nice to know. It seemed almost as if God's patience had run out. In
700 B.C. the prophet Isaiah (Isaiah 8) warned Judah of impending doom from Assyria which
they survived/averted. Meanwhile, Israel was invaded and taken over by the Assyrians and the
Israelites deported to far-off lands. A hundred years later
Jeremiah warned Judah again that God's hand of
protection was being lifted from them (Jeremiah
25) and this time they too were exiled, but
under the Babylonians not the Assyrians.

Kings

Exile and Return

The millennium up to and including the time of Jesus was an age of rapidly changing, voracious empires. One empire would become dominant, only to be consumed by another. From the downfall of Jerusalem (587 B.C.) the Israelites did not enjoy very much freedom, apart from a brief period just before the birth of Jesus. Each of the invading empires tried to destroy the local culture and traditions of each place that they invaded, and the most effective way of doing that was by mass deportation. When the Babylonians invaded Judah, they shipped the Jews (the new term coined during the exile for the descendants of the people of Judah) back to Babylon (Jeremiah 52:28-30).

JARGON-BUSTER

Anointed One

Babylonian Empire

Christ

God

Israel

Jerusalem

Jesus

Jew

Judah

love

Messiah

promised land

prophet

temple

Testament

What is known as 'the exile' gave rise to some of the most important prophetic writings of the Old Testament. Despite the prophetic warnings, Israel thought: 'He won't do that, he's God, he loves us.' Yet a parent must discipline his child, and the exile was the most dramatic event in Israel's history after the flood and the exodus. The psalmist captures the mood perfectly:

> By the rivers of Babylon we sat and wept
> when we remembered Zion.
> There on the poplars
> we hung our harps,
> our tormentors demanded songs of joy;
> they said, 'Sing us one of the songs of Zion!'
>
> How can we sing the songs of the LORD
> while in a foreign land?
>
> *(Psalm 137:1-4)*

The prophet Ezekiel, one of the Jews deported to Babylon, struggles with what God wants from his people in order for them to be returned to the promised land. He dreams of a national reawakening (Ezekiel 37) and a new temple (40–42). The amazing thing is that within fifty years of the Jews' mass deportation, the power struggles in Babylon meant that Jews were being offered the chance to go back and rebuild their temple in Jerusalem!

In 539 B.C. the Babylonian Empire was taken over by the Persians and, in the years following, their relatively benign ruler decreed that the temple in Jerusalem should be rebuilt (Ezra 1:1-4). Despite significant opposition from the many new immigrants and old enemies now occupying Judah and Israel, people began to trickle back to Jerusalem to rebuild the city walls, the foundations of the temple, and finally the temple itself (Ezra p. 473 and Nehemiah p. 485) which was dedicated in 515 B.C.

The Messiah

The book of Esther indicates that despite some of the freedoms given to the Jews at that time, they were still a subject race and as such were in constant danger. Over the next four hundred years, leading up to the birth of Christ, this small but tenacious community survived invasions by the Greeks, the Egyptians, the Seleucids and the Romans, as well as a hundred years of self-rule. Throughout that time the Jews held on to some of their great prophecies of old concerning the Messiah, 'the Anointed One'. They waited eagerly for the day God's Chosen One would free them from their oppressors . . .

The Story of the Bible:

Jesus and his followers

The story of how a craftsman from a small village in a most unfashionable neighbourhood became the most important figure in history is one well worth reading. The Jews were waiting for a particular kind of Messiah to rescue them, so they certainly weren't expecting anyone like Jesus. Apart from the odd rumour about his parentage, no-one knew much about Jesus Bar Joseph from Nazareth except that there was always something special about him, in his eyes perhaps, when he came down to the lake for fish. He was from a different class to the fishermen with whom he traded, but they somehow knew that he cared about them more than anyone else ever had.

These fishermen just stopped work and followed him out into the desert (Mark 1:14-19). They had been associating with John the Baptist, so everyone knew no good would come of it (Mark 1:4-11). Yet soon stories were coming from other villages about the miracles that this carpenter had performed. He talked as well, in a way that made people listen (Matthew 7:28-29). He said that the synagogues had made God seem far away from people and that he was actually right there on earth for everyone to know (Matthew 12:28). He said that people could go straight to God for forgiveness, that they needn't pay the temple charges to make sin offerings that were no longer needed (Matthew 9:1-8).

In his home region of Galilee, he became a local hero. He didn't care what the Romans, or Herod the local ruler, or even the Jerusalem-based religious leaders thought of him. He just got on with telling people about the kingdom of God. People would comment that he often seemed happy and sad at the same time. He was a mystery and people flocked to him. He fed thousands when there was no food available by walking for a day in any direction (Luke 9:12-17); he raised a friend from the dead (John 11:1-44); he walked on water (Matthew 14:25-31) and more amazing things.

Jesus rose from the dead

Jesus reached a real 'dead end', and for some people, that was that. He'd gone to Jerusalem for the Passover Feast and had caused a stir in the temple (Mark 11:15-18) so he was asking for it, some thought. His followers were 'knocked for six', dumbfounded, shell-shocked (any number of adjectives could describe their confusion and sadness) after the death on the cross of Jesus of Nazareth. Then, slowly at first, word was passed through the villages of Galilee saying that he was alive (Luke 24:1-12). Some of his followers claimed to have seen him, including one or two of the local fishermen. They talked about God living inside them and fire coming down on their heads (Acts 2); people were raised from the dead (Acts 20); and they taught people things they really listened to. There was fire in their eyes, that was for sure.

There was fire in their eyes, that was for sure.

When the Romans destroyed the temple in Jerusalem and all the Jews spread out throughout the Roman empire, it made matters worse for the authorities. Jesus' followers had a leader who was a Roman citizen and knew how to talk himself out of trouble (Acts 22:25-30) and who spread the news about Jesus far and wide by visiting and 'church planting' and by letter-writing. They killed him (Paul) eventually, but by then he had made new Christians, followers of Jesus Christ, all over Asia Minor. Despite the Romans' attempts to get rid of Jesus' followers, their numbers just kept growing, particularly among non-Jews. There were significant churches in Antioch (Acts 11:19-21) where these followers were called 'Christians' for the first time, Ephesus (Ephesians, p. 1173), Corinth (1 and 2 Corinthians, p. 1144 and p. 1158), Athens (Acts 17:16-33, p. 1113) and eventually even Rome (Romans, p. 1128). There seems to be no stopping them...

The Bible at a glance

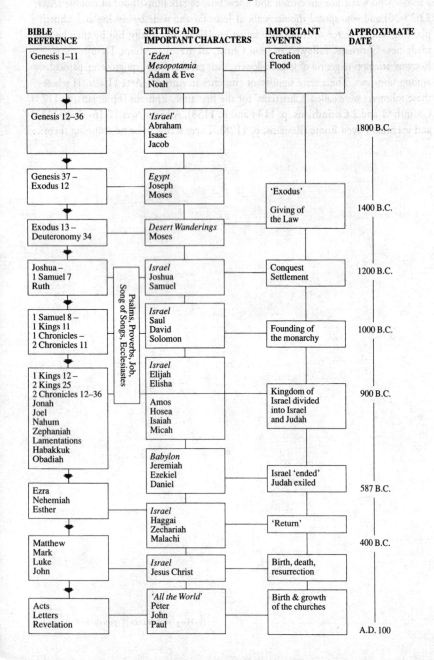

BIBLE REFERENCE	SETTING AND IMPORTANT CHARACTERS	IMPORTANT EVENTS	APPROXIMATE DATE
Genesis 1–11	*'Eden'* *Mesopotamia* Adam & Eve Noah	Creation Flood	
Genesis 12–36	*'Israel'* Abraham Isaac Jacob		1800 B.C.
Genesis 37 – Exodus 12	*Egypt* Joseph Moses	'Exodus' Giving of the Law	1400 B.C.
Exodus 13 – Deuteronomy 34	*Desert Wanderings* Moses		
Joshua – 1 Samuel 7 Ruth	*Israel* Joshua Samuel	Conquest Settlement	1200 B.C.
1 Samuel 8 – 1 Kings 11 1 Chronicles – 2 Chronicles 11	*Israel* Saul David Solomon	Founding of the monarchy	1000 B.C.
1 Kings 12 – 2 Kings 25 2 Chronicles 12–36 Jonah Joel Nahum Zephaniah Lamentations Habakkuk Obadiah	*Israel* Elijah Elisha Amos Hosea Isaiah Micah	Kingdom of Israel divided into Israel and Judah	900 B.C.
Ezra Nehemiah Esther	*Babylon* Jeremiah Ezekiel Daniel	Israel 'ended' Judah exiled	587 B.C.
Matthew Mark Luke John	*Israel* Haggai Zechariah Malachi	'Return'	400 B.C.
	Israel Jesus Christ	Birth, death, resurrection	
Acts Letters Revelation	*'All the World'* Peter John Paul	Birth & growth of the churches	A.D. 100

Psalms, Proverbs, Job, Song of Songs, Ecclesiastes

Route of the
Exodus

SYRIA

MOUNT LEBANON △

MOUNT HERMON △

Sidon

Damascus

Tyre

Sea of Kinnereth

MOUNT CARMEL △

AMMON

Great Sea

Shechem

Jabbok River

Jericho

Heshbon

MOUNT NEBO △

Medeba

Hebron

Dibon

Arnon River

Beersheba

Arad

Hormah

MOAB

Sea of Reeds

Bene Jaakan

DESERT OF ZIN

Baal Zephon

Azmon

Kadesh Barnea (Meribah)

Oboth

Punon

Rameses

DESERT OF SHUR

EDOM

Pithom

Succoth

Bitter Lakes

DESERT OF PARAN

EGYPT

Ezion Geber

Marah

Elim

Dophkah

DESERT OF SIN

Hazeroth

MIDIAN

Rephidim

MOUNT SINAI (HOREB) △

DESERT OF SINAI

Red Sea

| 0 | 20 | 40 | 60 | 80 | Miles |

| 0 | 40 | 80 | 120 | Kilometres |

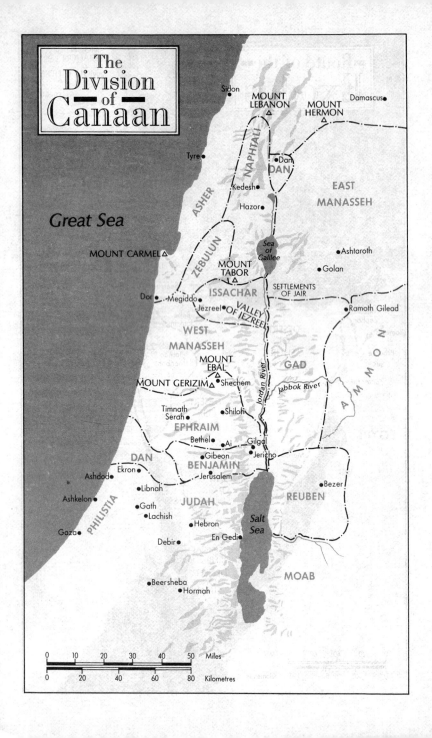

The Division of Canaan

Great Sea

Sidon

MOUNT LEBANON
MOUNT HERMON
Damascus

NAPHTALI

Tyre

Dan
DAN

Kedesh

EAST MANASSEH

Hazor

ASHER

Sea of Galilee

Ashtaroth

MOUNT CARMEL

ZEBULUN

MOUNT TABOR

Golan

Dor
Megiddo

ISSACHAR

SETTLEMENTS OF JAIR

Jezreel

VALLEY OF IEZREEL

Ramoth Gilead

WEST MANASSEH

A
M
M
O
N

MOUNT EBAL
MOUNT GERIZIM
Shechem

GAD

Jordan River

Jabbok River

Timnath Serah
Shiloh

EPHRAIM

Bethel
Ai
Gilgal

DAN

Gibeon
Jericho

Ekron
BENJAMIN

Ashdod
Jerusalem

Bezer

Libnah

Ashkelon

PHILISTIA

Gath
JUDAH
Lachish

REUBEN

Salt Sea

Gaza

Hebron

Debir
En Gedi

MOAB

Beersheba
Hormah

| 0 | 10 | 20 | 30 | 40 | 50 | Miles |
| 0 | 20 | 40 | 60 | 80 | Kilometres |

The Holy Land at the time of Jesus

Mediterranean Sea

Sidon
SYRIA
Damascus
MOUNT HERMON △
Tyre
PHOENICIA
Caesarea Philippi
GALILEE
Ptolemais
Chorazin
Capernaum
Bethsaida
Cana
Magadan
Sea of Galilee
MOUNT CARMEL △
Nazareth
Tiberias
Nain
Gadara
Caesarea
Pella
DECAPOLIS
Sebaste (Samaria)
Shechem
Sychar
SAMARIA
River Jordan
Joppa
Arimathea
Ephraim
PEREA
Philadelphia
Jamnia
Jericho
Emmaus
Azotus
Jerusalem
Bethany
Bethlehem
Ashkelon
Salt Sea (Dead Sea)
JUDEA
Hebron
Gaza
IDUMEA
Beersheba
NABATEA

0   10   20   30   40 Miles
0   20   40   60 Kilometres

Paul's missionary journeys

MACEDONIA
Amphipolis
Philippi
Thessalonica
Neapolis
Berea
Appollonia
THRACE
Larissa
Troas
Assos
LESBOS
Pergamum
ASIA
GALATIA
Antioch
CAPPADOCIA
Athens
Smyrna
Iconium
Corinth
Ephesus
Lystra
Tarsus
Miletus
Perga
Derbe
Attalia
CILICIA
Selucia
Antioch
COS
Patara
RHODES
Salamis
CYPRUS
CRETE
Paphos
Sidon
Damascus
Tyre
Ptolemais
Caesarea
Jerusalem

Aegean Sea

Mediterranean Sea

CYRENAICA
EGYPT

•••••• First journey
——— Second journey
– – – Third journey

0   100   200 Miles
0 100 200 300 Kilometres

Paul's journey to Rome

ITALY
Rome
Three Taverns
Forum of Appius
Puteoli
Adriatic Sea
Black Sea
THRACE
MACEDONIA
Aegean Sea
ASIA
GALATIA
CAPPADOCIA
SICILY
Rhegium
CILICIA
Tarsus
Antioch
Syracuse
Cnidus
Myra
MALTA (Melita)
Phoenix
CRETE
Lasea
CYPRUS
CAUDA
SALMONE
Sidon
Caesarea
Jerusalem

Mediterranean Sea

EGYPT

0   100   200   300 Miles
0 100 200 300 400 500 Kilometres

JARGON-
BUSTER

apostle
Christian
church
God
gospel
Jerusalem
Jesus
Paul
Peter
Scripture
temple
Testament

How did the Bible become the Bible?

The Bible appears to us as a book and is thought of as one book, but upon opening it, we see that it is a collection of books. The word 'Bible' itself comes from a plural word meaning 'books'. It is a collection of religious writings written over an extended period of time (as many as sixteen centuries may have separated the writing of the first book and the last) by different authors.

How was this collection of books put together?

The church uses the word 'canon' to describe the collection of writings that have been included in the Bible. The word literally means 'standard', and suggests that all the books in the Bible have reached a certain standard. Certainly, the people who decided which books would be in the Bible did not choose their own particular favourites. Rather, they tried to work out which books met the standard. But what was this standard?

The Old Testament canon

The Old Testament's standard was to do with standing the test of time. Had some of the writings continued to be important for centuries after they were written, while others were forgotten or discredited? Each of these books was chosen as saying something important about God and his people and each had been through centuries of testing. The first sign of what we call the Old Testament appeared in the second century B.C., although it wasn't until the temple in Jerusalem was destroyed in A.D. 70 that the need for an established collection of scriptures became really important as the Jews spread out across the Roman empire. The main Jewish leaders met together at a place called Jamnia and confirmed the Old Testament canon. Decision-making was not easy: some were against including Esther because God is not mentioned; others were unsure of the adult theme of Song of Songs. However, in the end the so-called council of Jamnia decided to recognise all the scriptures that Jewish tradition had handed down to them, described in Luke as 'the Law of Moses, the Prophets and the Psalms'.

The New Testament canon

When the first Christians met together they would often read the Jewish scriptures, someone would recite stories about Jesus or read part of a letter from one of the major church leaders (called 'apostles'). After about twenty years the church had grown to a size so that people who had met Jesus were in short supply and these letters from apostles were saved as something special. Paul's first letter to the Christians in Thessalonica was one of the first of the New Testament books to be written, about fifteen years after Jesus' death. Christians started to collect the stories about Jesus soon after his death. Mark's Gospel was probably written about thirty years after Jesus' death by Mark, a companion of Peter who simply collated some of Peter's most exciting stories about Jesus.

The books of the New Testament - the specifically Christian part of the Bible - were written over a much shorter period of time and were written about events that had happened relatively recently. Thus, the 'standard' for determining the New Testament canon was slightly different from that applied to the Old Testament books, it concerned authorship and authenticity. Right from the first century Christian leaders had demanded evidence of authorship before they would grant an individual book authority. Thus, books written by the apostles Peter, Philip and Thomas were excluded from the New Testament because there was insufficient evidence of authorship. As before, personal favouritism or bias in choosing books was irrelevant: the letter of James is included in the New Testament on the strength of its authorship by the brother of Jesus, even though many of the Greek Christians who finally agreed the New Testament canon in A.D. 393 would have been uncomfortable with its Jewish leanings.

authorship & authenticity

These are some of the reasons why we can trust what we read in the Old and New Testaments of our Bible. The next article will help us discover further reasons.

JARGON-
BUSTER

Abraham

Christian

David

eternal

heaven

Jerusalem

Jesus

Peter

revelation

Scripture

temple

Testament

Can I trust the Bible?

If you have read the previous two pages you will know a little about how the Bible was put together. Books were chosen according to two main criteria:

each book stood the test of time

Furthermore, the whole Bible has stood the test of time, 4,000 years of testing. Voltaire the eighteenth-century philosopher and ardent atheist declared from exile in Geneva that within a hundred years of his death Christianity would be dead and no-one would ever read the Bible again. One hundred years after his death, the Geneva Bible Society owned Voltaire's old house and was printing Bibles there.

the manuscript evidence

The Bible has more manuscript evidence than any other early writing. There are more copies of the books of the Bible (especially the New Testament) than any of the great Greek or Roman 'classics' (Julius Caesar's *Gallic War* survives in only nine or ten copies while we have over 5,000 copies of the New Testament in the original Greek alone).

There are many more reasons for trusting the books of the Bible:

historicity

The Bible records actual events that occurred in places that do or did exist (see the next couple of points). The Bible is an honest book and tells the truth about its heroes even if that truth is negative. Thus Abraham's deception (Genesis 12) is included; the psalmist's desire for revenge (Psalm 137); King David's murder of Uriah and seduction of Bathsheba (2 Samuel 11) are not left out, nor is Peter's cowardice (Matthew 26:70).

archaeological evidence

Archaeologists are constantly backing up what the Bible says. Traditionally scholars used to think the existence of the pool of Bethesda (for example) was made up by John (John 5:2-3), then it was found in 1888 with its five arches and an inscription attesting to the healing that occurred there.

One of the most pressing evidences for the trustworthiness of the Bible is found within the Bible itself. Many of the biblical writers made accurate predictions about the future:

Ezekiel (26:1–28:19)

predicted the destruction of the city/nation of Tyre to the north of Israel hundreds of years before it happened

Mark (Mark 13:2)

records Jesus' prediction of the downfall of the temple in Jerusalem.

Old Testament predictions

Concerning Jesus (for example) were fulfilled: his birth in Bethlehem (Micah 5:2); his entry into Jerusalem on a donkey (Zechariah 9:9); that he would be rejected and killed (Isaiah 53:3-5) while men gambled for his clothes (Psalm 22:18).

the Bible contains God's words

The Bible itself has its own intrinsic authority because it is God's revelation of himself to us: 'All Scripture is God-breathed' (2 Timothy 3:16). Christians, Paul says, 'have been entrusted with the very words of God' (Romans 3:2) and these words are eternal Jesus tells us: 'Heaven and earth will pass away, but my words will never pass away' (Matthew 24:35). As such, the Bible is eternally trustworthy (John 21:24; Revelation 21:5) and eternally relevant.

God speaks to us through the Bible

Finally and perhaps most important of all, there is the test of the Bible's continued relevance, its efficacy and veracity. Or, in other words, does it work and can we personally know that what it says is true? There are many millions of Christians around the world who eagerly say 'yes' to these questions. These people have seen the Bible working in their own lives, they have experienced its truth for themselves. To say 'yes' with them, you need to dive in and read and live the Bible for yourself. The Bible is not like some recipe book, where you just follow the instructions and everything turns out fine. It is more like food that you can eat, enjoy and take sustenance from (Jeremiah 15:16). To put it another way, the Bible is like a pair of sunglasses: put them on and your view of the world is changed. As you read the Bible you will begin to get an idea of what the world looks like from God's perspective. When you wear God's sunglasses the questions 'does it work?' and 'is the Bible true?' can really be answered.

Why is the Bible so important to Christians?

JARGON-BUSTER

Abraham

Christ

Christian

forgiveness

God

hope

Isaac

Jacob

Jesus

justice

Nazareth

sin

worship

What is it about the Bible that makes it so important that it is trustworthy. Why do so many people read it and so many people write books and notes about it to get other people reading it for themselves? Are we not supposed to be followers of Jesus of Nazareth and not some oversized book? Well, yes. Even Karl Barth, one of the most important theologians of the twentieth century, accused some Christians of what he called 'Bibliolatry': worshipping the gift (the Bible) and not the giver (God). For, Christians worship the incarnate (which means 'made flesh') Word of God, Jesus Christ (John 1:1-18) not the written Word, the Bible. The incarnate Word of God and the written Word of God complement each other. Without giving the Bible too high a place, if you want proof that 'the pen is mightier than the sword' the Bible offers that proof.

'the pen is mightier than the sword'

The Bible changes lives

The Bible has changed the world more than any other book. Millions of people have found God in Jesus in the pages of the Bible, and their lives have been changed. Take a look at the resources pages at the end of this front section for books which give testimony to how God has worked in people's lives through his Word.

The Bible is a force for good in history

Despite what you may have been taught at school, the Bible has been one of the most powerful forces for good in the world, because it has motivated so many people to a higher goal in life than their own comfort.

Certainly the Bible has been used and abused by many Christians over the centuries: the crusades and the inquisition both come to mind for most of us, or more recently the troubles in Northern Ireland. But we remember these events precisely because they stick out in history, going against the grain of the good influence the Bible has had on world events. In the United Kingdom, for example, Christians got slavery abolished, raised the age of consent to sixteen to protect child prostitutes, invented the welfare state and the national health service. The power of the Bible in history is irrefutable.

It is still relevant today

The Bible should still be taken seriously today. The Bible has not 'had its day', the demise of the world's bestselling book is not imminent for many reasons:

THE BIBLE TELLS US WHO WE ARE

The Bible is at the centre of the story of humanity. The stories it contains deal with all the key issues concerning humanity: human identity and human rights, hope, justice, freedom, sin and forgiveness. Also, those who read the Bible can recognise the people of the Bible in the same way that I can recognise relatives in fading black-and-white photographs: these people, even though I never knew them, are my kin, we are part of each other's stories.

THE BIBLE TELLS US ABOUT GOD

What it tells us is a small fraction of everything there is to know about God, but it is enough to keep most humans busy for their time on this earth. Christians treasure the Bible as a lost man treasures a map he has just found. It describes my world and my place in it, plus I get a glimpse of what this world looks like from a bigger perspective. Christians take their knowledge and experience of God to the Bible and say, 'Yes, I know the God of Abraham, Isaac and Jacob!' (Exodus 3:6). Similarly, reading what the Bible (and other Christians) say about God also helps to shape our experience and knowledge of him.

THE BIBLE TELLS US ABOUT HUMAN POTENTIAL

I must admit that I find many people of my own generation both surprising and a little depressing. If I were to ask most of my friends, 'What is the point of your life?', there would be a terrible silence punctuated by an embarrassed giggle, dirty looks or nervous coughing. 'What a funny question!' they would think. Of course it's funny: if we didn't laugh we'd all be crying ourselves into a long, black sleep. The life of Jesus is the most wonderful sign of what being human could be and

Christians are called to become like Christ and will one day participate in Christ's perfection (2 Corinthians 3:18). If you are not a Christian, I suggest you read the story of Jesus and follow him . . .

JARGON-BUSTER

Christian

faith

God

Jesus

love

Paul

Testament

What to do with difficult questions

As you read the Bible you may occasionally come across something that you find hard to deal with. Perhaps a story or idea may seem to contradict something you have read elsewhere in the Bible. Perhaps the Bible will portray a picture of God that does not fit in with your own ideas of what God is like. Perhaps you will not agree with everything you read.

This is fairly normal, so don't feel out on a limb. Having specific questions about parts of the Bible does not mean that you are not a Christian or that you risk forfeiting God's love!

There are a number of things to think about when looking at a difficult passage in the Bible.

Context

Try to look at the difficult bit in context. First read around the passage to see what else the writer is saying. Bible study can become problematic when one or two verses are taken out of context. The other context that you might like to look at is the historical one. This means getting hold of a commentary on the Bible and checking out what was happening at the time. For example someone might say, 'I don't like the Old Testament, it's full of violence and people killing each other in the name of God.' In a biblical context, reading broadly in the Old Testament will let you know that that is not the case. In the historical context, finding out a bit about the history of the time will help put things in perspective. For example, the institution of cities of refuge (Numbers 35) was an

innovative way of reducing some of
that violence.

More than one viewpoint

Remember as you read that one of the things that's
special about the Bible is that it was not all
written by one person. Each writer expresses
their knowledge and experience of God differently.
Therefore the same idea can be expressed in a
number of ways. Paul's expression of the tension
between faith and 'works' (Romans 8) is different
from James' (James 2), and together they tell the
full story.

> 'It's not the parts
> in the Bible
> that I don't
> understand that
> trouble me, but
> the parts that
> I understand
> perfectly well.'

Literally speaking

This may sound obvious, but sometimes we have to understand the language of the
Bible. When Jesus says to his followers that they must hate their parents (Luke 14:26),
he's using a rhetorical device to make his point. Sometimes we need to let the language
have this kind of depth: when we take a passage like this too literally, problems arise
quite quickly! Also, try to remember that the originals were not written in English and
the translation work has been done by fallible men and women who try, in God's
name, to represent the originals in the best and most accurate way possible.

With humility

Finally, remember that you could be wrong. The Bible represents wisdom that people
have handed down and lived by for thousands of years. Just because you don't like
parts of it, it doesn't make all or part of it wrong. As C.S. Lewis once said wisely, 'It's
not the parts in the Bible that I don't understand that trouble me, but the parts that I
understand perfectly well.'

Reading the Bible will always be a challenge. Sometimes it will give you great pleasure,
it may even make you laugh out loud, at other times it will prove more difficult.
Always be ready for the Bible to tell you something you didn't expect to hear.

When Christians disagree

If you are fairly new to reading the Bible, it may be a while before you have confidence to disagree with someone about what a passage is saying. Don't be afraid to disagree or argue (but don't look forward to it too much either!).

> *Here are some helpful ways to help you work through a disagreement*

Set some ground rules

The main reason for this is because people sometimes get too excited about things once the discussion is underway. For example, it is worth saying, 'If one of us gets too angry, or if one of us feels picked on, then we'll stop the discussion.' Ultimately, you may want the option of turning to someone who knows the Bible better for an opinion.

Try and see where the other person is coming from

Often, it's not the Bible people are arguing about, but rather the 'baggage' that they bring to the Bible with them. Try and listen to what they are really saying, ask yourself 'How did they come to see things that way?', try and work out what makes them tick. It might also help to see how things that have happened to us affect the way we view the world and the Bible. Someone may have a very strong opinion about alcohol abuse or sex, for example, but this may be because of things that have happened to them, not because of what the Bible says about alcohol and sex. Be generous with each other (Romans 14:1).

Sometimes you will get a helpful insight into someone's attitudes (some people see a glass as half full and others see it as half empty). Is one of you 'looking for trouble'? Some people just enjoy having an argument (if that is you, beware and remind yourself of Matthew 5:9)!

Watch yourself

You might want to check your own motivations. Why are you having this argument? Do you need to win it? If you and the others in the discussion share the desire to follow Jesus can you lay down the disagreement?

Beware of prejudice

Sometimes prejudices come into play, particularly when Christians from others churches, denominations or traditions get together. I get really upset when people label me as a certain kind of person just because I go to the kind of church I do. Prejudice (it roughly means, 'deciding before knowing') is always a bad idea.

In the end, you may have to agree to differ on a particular passage or point but, ideally, this should not prevent you remaining friends, worshipping together and so on (1 Corinthians 1:10-12). Also, do keep an open mind. Two contradictory things can't both be true. Listen to fellow Christians who disagree with you and think about what they say, but spend time talking to God, reading the Bible, listening to good Bible teaching. Clever people are often wrong (and that could be you)!

Be positive

In the end, we all have to live with these tensions and trying to be positive is helpful. It is good to know the basics that all Christians agree about in order to be Christians. Often the disagreements are about peripheral things anyway. Hundreds of years ago, the church had a serious and long-running debate about how many angels could fit on the head of a pin. In a hundred years some of our arguments may sound just as silly.

> In conclusion: listen to each other,
> love each other and remember: the truth is
> not 'out there' it's in here...

Diving in

If you are a Christian already, or thinking about following Jesus, this section will tell you what we think you absolutely need to know about what you're getting into. Feel free to read straight through or just read the parts that interest you. Also, it's worth remembering that the articles are just the beginning, have a look at the Bible passages that each article refers to for more in-depth food for head, heart and spirit.

Some of these articles are the results of conversations with Christians who have been working through the issues over the years. Where this is the case they have been credited.

you and the Bible

As an individual you are approaching this book as a unique person. You may want to find out what the Bible really says, to explore what Christianity and a relationship with Christ involves. Or you may have become a Christian recently and be experiencing feelings such as peace, joy, excitement, trepidation. You could be a little further down the road and need assurance to nullify some doubts you may be having. You could have reached the stage of serious commitment and want to become an authentic disciple, obedient to God. No matter where you have come from you share a common need to nurture and develop your relationship with God in and through the person of Christ. Wherever you are on the journey of life, on your pilgrimage of faith, in your relationship to God, the Bible will not disappoint you or let you down. It provides practical advice, guidance and direction.

JARGON-BUSTER

believe

Christ

Christian

church

disciple

faith

God

gospel

Hebrew

holiness

Holy Spirit

Jesus

joy

kingdom of God

love

peace

revelation

Scripture

Testament

You, other people and the Bible

God has made us as people intended to live in relationships - not only in the vertical sense with God but also in the horizontal sense with other people. Relationships are never static, they have to be worked at and nurtured and your relationship with God will dry up and wither if neglected. The Bible will help you to build human relationships and help you to know and experience God in a deeper way. No matter how awesome it sounds, never doubt the fact that you are very capable of knowing God, for you are made in his image and part of his Spirit lives in you.

The Bible and today

As you discover the Bible for yourself opportunities for exploring the distance and connections between the world of today and the world of the Bible will become everyday realities.

A story-book and manual

People react differently to print, lines of words on paper. For some, sentences and paragraphs are oppressive and threatening, particularly if they have had a struggle with reading. For some, reading equates with the negative. For others those very same words are an invitation to engage with the text and to let their imagination loose in the creation of vivid and colourful mind-pictures.

Whatever your response to reading, it is important to realise that the Bible is not a textbook. Essentially, the Bible is a story-book: a book that tells the story of a creator God active in human history. It contains the stories of many individuals, groups and nations all of which are part of the story of God becoming real in the person of his Son. The Bible is also a manufacturer's instruction manual written to help us in the process of becoming like Jesus and living in the way God intended. For this is the goal as you read the Bible, to become more like Jesus, not only in the way he lived and behaved and related to his Father. Also, it's not just a question of reading the words, you need to allow the Holy Spirit the space to shape and model you as you read and learn. You should have a sense of expectation as you delve into the contents of the Bible. It has the potential, in the power and outworking of the Holy Spirit, to shape and influence your life and cause you to be an effective Christian in all areas of your life.

Living as a Christian

The story of God, as found in the Bible, helps us to make sense of the world and to understand where humans, created in the image of God, find their place in his overall design. To be a Christian means that you seek to live according to that story in ways that reflect the nature and character of God made real in Christ. A key reason for reading and studying the Bible is that any knowledge and understanding gained will directly influence and shape the way you live out the story. It is a fact that this book will seriously challenge your values, morals, lifestyle, and the things in which you place and find your security. Reading and getting to grips with this book will also make you challenge society's norms. Being a Bible-reading Christian will not guarantee that you will 'fit in' at church. You may find tension and misunderstandings arise over different expressions of church, over what it means to be Christian and how the Bible is understood.

It is a fact that this book will seriously challenge your values

The biblical counter-culture

Reading the Bible is an essential part of the process of understanding what God had in mind when, in his coming, Jesus inaugurated the kingdom of God. A kingdom which is dramatically 'upside down' to prevailing norms and accepted social patterns of behaviour and action. As a Christian you will need to distinguish between 'church' and 'kingdom' for they are not one and the same. The church is called to be a sign of the kingdom. As a Christian you are privileged to be part of the 'avant-garde' of a whole new order pointing to the rule and reign of God. If this is true then Christians face huge challenges that could mean making radical changes and being set at odds to the norms and values of the current worldly culture. The contemporary culture with its values of materialism, consumption, instant satisfaction and 'me' is in direct contrast to the values and lifestyle of the kingdom of God. The agendas of power, status and money are dominant. In contrast, by reading the Bible you will see how Jesus used powerlessness and servanthood and how Christians should do likewise. A sign of your Christian or spiritual growth will be evident when you can honestly begin to examine and critique your culture. Evaluating it in the light of what you are discovering in the Bible will be a challenging experience. Seeing things from God's perspective should increasingly begin to impact upon and change your behaviour and attitudes. From your reading, reflection and prayer, a biblical counter-culture should begin to develop, which needs nurturing in company with other like-minded Christians. Sadly the church or individual churches are not always steeped in that biblical counter-culture, and sometimes the norms of the world are often mirrored in the life and actions of the church. The distinctiveness that is so vital will perhaps only develop as Christians take God's word more seriously than at present and live as citizens of the kingdom in a world which is hostile to the gospel. John Wimber suggested that too many Christians think they are embarking on a cruise liner when they become Christians instead of realising they are enlisting as the crew of a gunboat sailing in enemy waters. It is to be hoped that your reading of God's word will encourage a more radical edge to your life as a disciple of the King of Kings.

Knowledge and personal experience
To grow into the likeness of Jesus demands that he, and your relationship with him, is not assumed or taken lightly. It means becoming an active and enthusiastic learner (Matthew 11:29, 28:20; Acts 2:42; 2 Timothy 2:2). The task you are facing, in partnership with the Holy Spirit, is that of a totally changed mindset, you are learning to see things differently, to think and perceive in an upside down fashion. Engaging the mind in serious thinking has to become the norm to avoid the dangers of froth and superficiality. This discipline may prove to be a steadying anchor when the bad times roll and the days appear grim, grey and joyless.

At the same time however try to maintain a balance between the intellectual and the emotional, allowing your whole being - personality, mind, and senses - to be caught up in the process of discovery and change. Learning involves doing and saying, suggesting that as you put the discoveries from your Bible reading into ACTION and begin to SHARE your relationship with Christ with others you will almost certainly experience growth. This point is illustrated if you think for a moment about life and how important experience is. That handling and working through different experiences enables learning. Part of your growth as an explorer or as a Christian will come as you begin to reflect upon your life experiences in the light of what you read in the Bible. You will come to know when God brings a thought into your mind or when a change of attitude is necessary. (Note that in scripture the word 'know' means more than just knowing a fact or how something works. In the Bible it means to have had personal experience of something. Thus to know Jesus is to have personal, firsthand experience of him.) Reading the Gospels will reveal how Jesus enabled and encouraged the disciples in their learning in which 'doing' and 'reflecting' were inseparable. They probably learnt a great deal from their shared experiences and from exploring the 'why's' and the 'what's' and asking questions in a process that brought theory and practice together.

> to know Jesus is to have firsthand experience of him.

Reading the Bible is NOT about getting as much factual information as you can in your head or becoming obsessed with dates, names, places and events. Neither is it about being able to make long or impressive quotations or sharing your grasp of doctrine or of systematic theology. Perhaps that is why some find reading their Bible boring because they are reading for the wrong motives and in the wrong way. If you read some of the stories in the four Gospels for a moment, can you imagine the disciples ever having been bored or finding themselves longing to get away from Jesus? Approach the reading of this book in an expectant attitude knowing that as you read God will engage with you and surprise you in many different and sometimes unexpected ways.

Absolute truth?

In this post-modern world it is becoming harder to determine truth claims. In the eyes of the world no religion has an exclusive claim to absolute truth. 'You can believe whatever you want to believe and I'll believe what I want to or nothing at all' is a commonly heard response. This prompted me to reread part of the Westminster Confession of Faith of 1648:

> *The authority of the Holy Scripture, for which it ought to be believed and obeyed, dependeth not upon the testimony of any man or church, but wholly upon God, (who is truth itself), the author thereof (2 Peter 1:19, 21; 2 Timothy 3:16; 1 John 5:1; 1 Thessalonians 2:13) . . . The whole counsel of God, concerning all things necessary for his own glory, man's salvation, faith and life, is either expressly set down in scripture, or by good and necessary consequence may be deduced from scripture; unto which nothing at any time is to be added, whether by new revelations of the Spirit, or traditions of men. (2 Timothy 3:15-17; Galatians 1: 8-9; 2 Thessalonians 2:2).*

The Church acknowledges and accepts that this unique and precious book has ultimate authority. Jesus himself said in John 14:6 that he is 'the way, the truth and the life', and in John 17:17 he declared that God's word is truth. Do not be afraid of absolutes in this current climate of relativism. They may be unfashionable and uncomfortable but they are emphatic reminders that God has set boundaries and provided guidelines in order to bring shalom (peace) and wholeness in the context of the kingdom of God.

Getting beneath the text

One further aspect of Bible reading demands attention and relates closely to what you will be reading and the degree to which it impacts upon and changes your life as a disciple. Take time to uncover the meanings of original Hebrew and Greek words and phrases. It might appear tedious and time consuming but it will also prove very worthwhile. It is all too easy just to substitute a particular word with one from the English language which appears to embody a similar meaning. This may not always help when it comes to understanding what the text is really saying. The meaning of the word in the original text and the meaning in our culture may not necessarily be the same or they may have differing applications. There are profound opportunities for learning and growth awaiting discovery in the text. A hurried and superficial reading will miss these riches and your spiritual life will be the poorer. Reading and studying God's word will be a life-changing experience if you are prepared to explore beneath the text and to work in genuine openness.

> Reading and studying God's word will be a life-changing experience if you are prepared to explore beneath the text and to work in genuine openness.

Regular reading

There are many books and guides to reading the Bible on the shelves of Christian bookshops. Several leading Christian publishers produce Bible reading notes to help in cultivating the habit of a daily encounter with scripture. I recall that as a young person I was made to feel quite guilty if I missed a day's reading. Controversial as it may appear to some there are alternatives. It may be far more helpful to timetable three in depth sessions in a week rather than a hurried or snatched few minutes at the beginning or end of each day.

I have a dream

If you remember nothing else of what you have read hold on to this truth. God wants you to discover his truth for yourself and not only to inherit or take on board what someone else has said or written. Tradition has suggested that often we take for granted what others are saying or writing, by virtue of their role and academic qualifications. Perhaps many church sermons work on this principle so that many of God's people use the Sunday sermon as their only spiritual fuel for the whole week. Do not simply accept what you hear or read. Be prepared and eager to challenge or to explore the text and do not just look for answers which match your expectations and feelings. Scripture encourages Christians, Philippians 2:12, to keep on working with 'fear and trembling' to complete their salvation.

Do not simply accept what you hear or read.

A second-hand, passed-down faith or Christian experience is worthless in terms of personal experience and effective mission. Your learning will only shape your life when you adopt or apply something you have learned or discovered for yourself. Hence my dream for you is that you will wrestle with God's word in such a way that your faith will become one that is authentically yours. A faith that is culturally relevant, real and appropriate in the community where you live, where you work, in your school or college and in your family. Discovering things for yourself and building them into your life can be an exciting and risky business. Be prepared for negative reactions from others who may see things differently or who may prefer their comfortable 'foxhole', rejecting any disturbance of or challenge to their current position. God is calling you to an authentic and biblical discipleship which mirrors that modelled by Christ. A discipleship that engages with the world on the basis of a relationship with Jesus characterised by love, faith, prayer, holiness and Spirit-empowered gifts.

Bible Reading Tips

Reading the Bible and understanding its truth and teaching is not meant to be just an intellectual exercise best accomplished by those with academic prowess. It is not to be studied in a vacuum but in the midst of the journey of life, for this book is about real living in a real world. It is also for those who may not be at home with books and may not have 'A' levels or higher intelligence. It is for ordinary people living ordinary lives who want to find God in everyday life.

Reading the same passage in different versions can be very helpful.
It is a good idea to have resources other than this New International Version of the Bible at your side. Use the NIV as your primary source but use others such as The Good News Bible, The Contemporary English Version, The Living Bible and The Message NT & Psalms, (some of these are paraphrases not translations) and the New English Bible. Other helpful sources include, J.B. Phillips NT, The New Revised Standard Version, the Jerusalem Bible and of

course The Authorised Version. Also, don't forget the many aids and resources available to PC users on disc, CD-ROM or on the Internet!

Approach

Have a moment of prayer before you read to invite the Holy Spirit to be active in your reading and understanding. He will bring to your heart and mind those aspects and challenges which God wants you to deal with.

● Determine your motives and expectations before you start reading, use the list here as a checklist (add your own if you wish):

Why do you want to read the Bible?

What are your aims, objectives and motives?

What do you expect to gain:

Knowledge?

Information and facts?

Truth?

Christian growth?

Answers?

Action?

● As you read, do not leave your imagination and emotions behind:

In your imagination try to picture the original scene, the weather, people, noises, houses and buildings, landscape, attitudes, emotions, feelings and the realities.

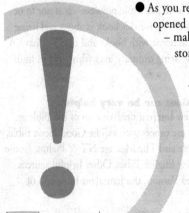

● As you read keep your brain switched on and your heart opened up:

– make a note of WHO is involved in this incident, story or passage

– identify what happened and in what order

– note the words, phrases and concepts that you do not fully understand to look up later or to ask someone about

– do not rush things or skip the harder passages.

– remember that you are beginning a lifelong process and that you will never know it all! If

we did understand it all, then perhaps God would be less than the God described in Scripture!
    – list those words and phrases that resonate with your heart

● Try to retell or rewrite the passage in your own words:
    – be honest, real and earthed, keep things simple, clear and without confusion
    – get behind Christian jargon by trying to use words in normal use
    – do not give yourself information overload

● Ask what is the historical context of this passage?
    Who was the author, why was it written and to whom? What was happening at that time, socially, politically and economically? Why is this passage in the Bible?

Always try to read the passage in its context, even if it means reading a whole chapter or two. Extracting passages from their context is not usually helpful.

● Respond personally to the text (SPACESTEP):
John Mallison's book *The Small Group Leader* contains the following acrostic devised by Terry Fullan. This could be a helpful tool to use when you have completed the reading you have selected.

S	is there a **Sin** to confess?
P	is there a **Promise** to receive?
A	is there an **Attitude** to change or cultivate?
C	is there a **Command** to obey?
E	is there an **Example** to follow or to avoid?
S	is there **Something** for which to give thanks?
T	is there a **Truth** to believe?
E	is there an **Error** to reject?
P	learn to **Pray** the passage.

God did not intend that your experiences of him should primarily be of a 'privatised' nature. Twentieth-century Christianity has often majored on the personal aspects of faith at the expense of what it means to be a community of the people of God. Human beings are designed to function best in the context of relationships and Bible reading is no exception. Any learning outside the caring, supportive and encouraging relationships may be second best. Remember that like many others you too are imperfect, sometimes up and sometimes down, experiencing doubt and failure and in need of reassurance. Read the Bible with other people, either with a mentor or in a Bible study group. Find a mature Christian with whom you can share some reading, ask the hard questions and verbalise what you are learning and discovering.

Ross Snyder writes in describing his 'Depth and Encounter' method of group Bible study: ' The truth of the Bible needs to get into the places where people are living. When we find an important passage we should stay with it long enough to really grasp it . . . Too often we never stop to study precisely any particular verse, never dig and sweat . . . seldom become involved personally in the message of a particular verse . . . never really possess any verse. In group discussion we make pious comments, knowing full well that no-one intends to take them seriously.'

As you move into taking more than a superficial look at the Bible it will become obvious that some of the Old Testament passages seem to conflict strongly with what Jesus said and did. You will need to view the Old Testament in its historical and cultural setting. Then look over and beyond that passage or chapter in order to see how God acted later in the sending of Jesus. If you fail to take such an overview there are dangers of misunderstanding and of arriving at a less than complete Christian understanding. Keep in mind that Jesus is the Key to understanding Scripture. In him the Old Testament prophecies are fulfilled and for Christians Jesus is at the centre of the Bible.

Keep in mind that Jesus is the Key to understanding Scripture.

Bible studies

In different parts of the additional material to this Bible, you will find some examples of how to approach reading the Bible. These contain tried and tested methods to enable you to effectively and creatively engage in life-changing Bible reading and study. What you have just read is by no means an inclusive list for there are many ideas and models around, some of which are best used in groups and others by individuals. None of them are set in tablets of stone, they are simply helpful suggestions from which you can select. In time you will create and develop your own distinctive style and approach, but do try to avoid getting into a rut by using a variety of methods.

These examples will hopefully encourage you, not just in reading the Bible but also in allowing its truth to intersect every aspect of your life and in strengthening and deepening your Christian discipleship.

Responding to change and moving forward	C4
Doing God's will	C5 & 8
Listening to God	C9
Waiting on God	C13 & 16
Justice	C17
Relating to Jesus	C21 & 24
Being Jesus to others	C25 & 28
Spiritual growth	C29
Stocktaking time	C30, 31

Terry Dunnell

JARGON- BUSTER
Christ
Christian
church
death
evil
God
heaven
Jesus
love
sin

What is a Christian?

This is a hard question to answer because there are over a billion Christians in the world and between us we'd probably give a million different answers. However, there is some key stuff that nearly all of us agree on, and it's all here in the book you're holding, so each statement made will have some verses expanding and explaining it.

A Christian knows there's more to life than this

'The fool says in his heart, "There is no God."' (Psalm 14:1, 53:1). Every now and then we get glimpses of something beyond what we know. This may happen when we are standing on top of a mountain or witnessing the birth of a child, it may be something more obviously 'spiritual'. A Christian sees another dimension to life. The starting point for being a Christian is an ability (or at least a willingness) to see beyond the surface, to believe that there is something more. In the Bible that something is called heaven. This is the part of the universe we can't see, but which impacts on us dramatically, because it's the dimension in which God lives (Genesis 28:10-17, Psalm 14:1-2, Matthew 6:19-21). It is the eternity referred to in the sub-title for this particular Bible.

A Christian knows that she and the world are not perfect

A Christian is someone who knows what the word 'sin' means and isn't afraid to admit that sin has polluted her own spirit and everyone else's (Romans 3:23). But this admission does not drag a Christian down to the depths of despair for a Christian knows the balance between the capacity for good in a person and the capacity for evil, and knows the beauty in the world as well as the pain. Ultimately, a Christian trusts in God (Psalm 46:1-3) and owns up to sin courageously as did the psalmist (Psalm 51 for example).

> It's hard to read about Jesus
> without learning about love.

A Christian is loved

Once a Christian has come to realise his own imperfection, he is ready to receive God's love. Most of us don't appreciate what Jesus' life and death mean until we know how much we need God's loving mercy. It's hard to read about Jesus without learning about love. (John 3:16-17, Romans 5:8, 1 John 3:16)

A Christian is free

Jesus said that we can be 'born again'. Only a Christian can beat the system and be truly free, truly human. Owning up to the rubbish in our lives and turning our back on it will result in only one thing: having our relationship with God restored. Freedom from sin and from the need to conform to what others want brings a release that no drug, relationship or orgasm can provide. (Luke 4:16-20, Luke 5:17-26, John 3:1-8, Romans 12:1-2).

A Christian's life is not her own

Christian freedom however comes through submission. The greatest, hardest paradox in the Bible is not that Jesus could be both human and God (John 1:14), but that you can only save your life by sacrificing it. We all know instinctively that the one who made us knows how we should live, but we all have this tendency to try and run our own lives (Luke 15, Romans 6:18, Hebrews 12:9-11).

A Christian lives in the past, present and future at the same time

Christians have an amazing relationship to time, because their God has an amazing relationship to time. God seems to travel through life with us while also remaining outside time. In the same way we are connected to all that has come before us and all that is yet to come. The Bible is important to us because it tells us where we've come from and what God has done (particularly through Jesus). But it doesn't stop there. The Bible also helps us to work out how we should be living now and gives us many word-pictures and predictions about the future, when God will bring the whole universe to new birth. Knowing both our past and our future helps us to live for God in the present. (Jeremiah 29:11-14, Luke 1:1-4, 1 Timothy 3:16)

Eternity starts here...

A Christian has a reason for living

Christians wonder why most people get up in the morning: the family, money, flirting, office politics, TV, clubbing? The list seems worthless compared to the task entrusted to us: healing the world which includes loving the world and reconciling the world to God. The message of Jesus is for everyone and everything, which is good news for our friends round the corner as well as being good news for the ozone layer. It is God's plan to renew the whole of the universe and at this stage of the story we've been asked to be his agents of change. (Matthew 28:18-20, Mark 1:16-20, Acts 17:16-34)

A Christian is not alone

Lots of famous philosophers agree with God that it is really hard to be a person on your own. It's part of our very nature that we are made whole through relating to God and to our brothers and sisters all over the world. The church is a good way of showing the world how Christians can live together (Psalm 133). But beware, no church is perfect, because it will have in it people just like you and me. A good church is somewhere where individual Christians can grow and flourish and get closer to God.

All Christians are equal

Christians are equal in many ways, all of us are made by God (Proverbs 22:2); all are sinful (Romans 3:22-24); all are 'one in Christ Jesus' (see Galatians 3:26-28). Although each individual Christian has a unique personality and life and has different gifts and skills, these 'many parts . . . form one body' (see 1 Corinthians 12).

Deepening your relationship with God

JARGON-BUSTER

Christian

church

confession

forgiveness

God

Holy Spirit

Jesus

Moses

prayer

repentance

sin

Ten Commandments

How do relationships work? Most work best when people spend time together and get to know each other. In time, they learn to trust each other and share things about themselves. If they are a man and a woman they might get married. If they are really good friends they will be able to not see each other for months but still keep the closeness of the friendship when they do meet.

With God it is the same . . .

It's the same because God is a person and we have to get to know him in the same way that we get to know other people: primarily by spending time with him and talking with him. That way (for example) we can learn what he's like, what makes him happy, what he thinks about things. Early in the relationship between God and his people, to be a friend of God was a special privilege given only to Moses (Exodus 33:11). Later, Jesus is a friend to all kinds of people, even tax collectors and sinners (Matthew 11:19) and being God's friend is extended to you and me (John 15:12-17).

With God it is different . . .

A relationship with God is different in one major respect: God doesn't have a body in the same way that we do. Making friends with God is harder than making friends with another human because most of the time God speaks to us through intermediaries: the Bible, friends, preachers and speakers, music . . . It is important to develop these practical ways of building our relationship with God.

God knows us inside-out

One big help is that God has a head start on us: he knows us better than we know ourselves! This has a few consequences: it should make praying and addressing our faults a bit easier. I still remember the times when I had to tell one of my parents about something I'd done wrong. The tension and the shame were unbearable. Fortunately God knows what we've done and what we'd like to talk to him about before we open our mouths. It also means that he knows us better than we know ourselves and knows best in general. This can be a pain sometimes: imagine a human friend who was always right!

Barriers to closeness

Just because God knows each of us intimately, it does not mean that we take the relationship for granted. As with everyday friendships, things can go wrong, misunderstandings occur and barriers go up. In our friendship with God, sin can be a huge barrier (and believe me, we are all sinners by nature even if we haven't broken all ten of the Ten Commandments - Romans 5:12). Regular confession and repentance of our sins and acceptance of God's forgiveness are vital if we want to grow closer to God (1 John 1:8-10) and if we want to become a 'new creation' (2 Corinthians 5:17).

> Regular confession and repentance of our sins and acceptance of God's forgiveness are vital if we want to grow closer to God

Bible reading

So what can we do practically to keep the relationship growing? First, read your Bible and other Christian literature on a regular basis. Reading the Bible is often more like learning about someone than getting to know them properly, but it is possible that at times you will find yourself reading a passage of the Bible and you will know that God is speaking to you through it.

Prayer

Praying (communicating with God) is important, because this gets you closer to the heart of God. Praying includes all means of talking to God: thanking him for things, worshipping him, saying sorry, asking him for things, even just talking to him about your life or having a moan. Most people at some stage in their Christian life find it hard to pray but the Bible promises that the Holy Spirit will assist us (Romans 8:26-27).

An important part of prayer is leaving spaces between the words. It doesn't matter whether you pray out loud or in your head, you still need to stop talking and just listen and wait for 'direct leadings of the Holy Spirit' as Bill Hybels calls it in his book *Too Busy Not to Pray*.

Every now and then something will come into your mind which you weren't expecting and you think, 'what was that?' and it could well be God trying to get through, it could be the Holy Spirit seeking to 'prompt you, tug at you and guide you' (Bill Hybels). God doesn't always shout at us when he's got something to say (1 Kings 19:11-13).

Other people

Finally, God speaks to us through our relationships with other people. Remember that the church is called 'the body of Christ' (1 Corinthians 12:27), which means you should expect to find him speaking in church through the teaching there and through the communion of saints (Christians) who meet and relate there. Don't forget that Jesus promised, 'where two or three come together in my name, there am I with them.' Christian friends will have a lot to teach you, but so will life in general. Always be ready to ask, 'God, what can you teach me though this?'

JARGON-BUSTER

God

Jesus

love

prayer

prophet

Does God have plans for your life?

It's quite a frightening idea: God, the creator of the universe, is watching you. He's keeping an eye on you. And because he knows you and loves you he wants the best for you. That we can all agree on, but the big question is, does God have a master plan for you, including what job you should have and who you should marry (if anyone)?

There's no getting away from the fact that God chooses individuals and lets them know he has something special planned for them. The prophet Jeremiah was specially appointed by God before he was even born (Jeremiah 1:5). That's OK for prophets like Jeremiah, Isaiah or Jesus, but does God really care what we do with our lives?

There are two ways of looking at this. First, God has made humans special because we have the power to choose (Genesis 2:16-17, 19) we have free will. This means (as far as we know) that we are the only creatures that can make decisions in a reasoned way, thinking through all the options, examining the possible consequences before acting. God wants us to be free, to express who we are and to seek him (Isaiah 55:6) and to choose between life and death (Deuteronomy 11:26-28). If we are Christians, we try and make those rational decisions based on what the Bible tells us about God and in terms of what pleases him. I have a friend who says to me, 'I keep asking God what he wants me to do with my life and he keeps saying, "Love the Lord your God with all your heart and with all your soul and with all your mind and with all your strength and love your neighbour as yourself."' (Mark 12:29-31) In a similar vein, if someone comes to see me and says, 'I don't know what to do with my life, what does God want from me?' I will always hand him or her a Bible saying, 'When you've done all that, come back to me.'

Second, God is so interested in your life and mine that he even knows how many hairs there are on our heads (Matthew 10:30). He made you and loves you: isn't it likely that he has a purpose for your life? Of course he does! From the moment you were born God had plans for you. Some people quickly and easily realise what those plans are and lead their whole adult lives accordingly, others, who may not have been best friends with God may not have lived according to his plans. Perhaps you now have a job or partner that God didn't plan for you, or are even living in the 'wrong' country. That's OK, because God is loving and forgiving and will rewrite his purposes for you so that you can start again right where you are. God has plans for you which you should try to find out through prayer and Bible study, but it's not the end of the world (no joke intended) if you fail to work out all God's plans for you as he can use you and will take you wherever he finds you.

In conclusion, the key is to take following Jesus seriously, to take knowing and loving God seriously. The next important step is to trust God, don't be frozen by fear. If you pray, read your Bible, think and then act, trusting in God, he will honour your decision, he will be there with you. He might not always agree with you, but he will always be around, calling you on to the next step of obedience.

Money, sex, power and fame

A very special world-renowned Christian called Richard Foster once wrote a book called, *Money, Sex and Power* (Hodder & Stoughton, new edition 1998) which he said were the three major 'idols' of the late twentieth century. To these three I add a fourth, which seems, in today's world, to consist of a combination of all four: fame.

JARGON-BUSTER
blessing
Christ
church
David
God
idol
Jesus
Jew
Judges
offering
Paul
Scripture
temple
Testament

Let's take a brief look at each and see what today's culture says about each and how that compares with what the Bible teaches.

Money

The pop song 'Money, money, money' is no longer topping the charts but the throw away phrase 'Money makes the world go round' is still top of the clichés and many people believe it. Money makes good TV, the National Lottery programmes in the UK for example, and makes the papers when an anonymous old lady leaves millions to a cat rescue centre or when interest rates do or don't rise, when Anglican bishops discuss what can be done about world debt and the 1.3 billion people (nearly a quarter of the world's population and two-thirds of the world's women) who live in extreme poverty on less than US$1 per day. With only basic education, everybody can learn to count and to recognise different coins and notes, even those from other countries. If only using the stuff wisely were as easy as learning to count!

Mammon

Money is referred to often in the Bible and even has a special name, Mammon. Jesus talks about money a lot, certainly a lot more than sex. Jesus is not an extreme anarchist who wants to abolish money (Mark 12:13-17) and Scripture treats money as something that in itself is neither good nor bad. Money can be used for good: in the Bible for example to pay wages, to purchase and sell land, in buying religious offerings or (2 Kings 12:4-5) repairing the temple; today by funding medical research, giving money to charity, keeping ourselves in food and clothes, in evangelism and so on. There is also a noticeable theme in the Bible of material blessing for those who serve God (Proverbs 8:17-21). But money can also be abused: in the Bible by theft, usury, (excessive interest)by leading people away from God (the rich young ruler in Luke 18:23-24); today in the sale of arms, greed and materialism whereby accumulation of money is all that matters (you can think of further examples I'm sure). Jesus explained that we cannot serve both God and money (Matthew 6:24) and Paul asserted that 'the love of money is a root of all kinds of evil' (1 Timothy 6:10) while Ecclesiastes 5:10-12 condemns modern-day materialism.

Generally, although a summary is not easy, the

world might be a better place if individuals and governments acknowledged that wealth is a blessing from God which should not be selfishly grasped but shared, otherwise it might turn to dust in our hands (Luke 12:13-21, 33-34). As Paul (1 Timothy 6:7) wrote: 'we brought nothing into the world, and we can take nothing out of it.'

Sex

People generally have trouble talking about sex, with the result that most people think that God, who created male and female (sex as in 'gender') and invented sex, doesn't actually like it or want us to like it. Basically, there seem to be two ways of having sex: there is the sex that many thousands of people will be having on a Friday or Saturday night after a few drinks. This is basically masturbation but using someone else's body (this is the 'sexual immorality' about which we are warned in the Bible in

Jesus talks about money a lot, certainly a lot more than sex,

1 Corinthians 6:13, 18 for example). The other way of approaching sex focuses on the biblical idea of 'becoming one flesh' (Genesis 2:24) and 'knowing' the other person. This second kind of sex is what God intended us to have when he created the two different genders, male and female. We know instinctively that this kind of physical intimacy (which rests alongside emotional and spiritual intimacy) builds us up as human beings, whereas the other kind makes us smaller and less human as it focuses more on the act of sex and less on the whole person involved who is expressing themselves through their sexuality. That is why God's intention is for us to be physically intimate only with our marriage partner: sex is a natural expression of love and marriage is the context in which it finds its role (1 Corinthians 7:3-4).

It is in the area of sex that secular society (since the 1960s) most at odds with the teaching of the Bible as it spreads its 'lies' in every way possible. Some of these lies are that:

- you will never be a complete person unless you have sex
- everyone in the world is having brilliant sex apart from you
- who you are is centred on your sexual identity and sexual activity

The Bible counters that:

- gender, male and female, was intended and created by God (Genesis 1:27)
- God intended that men and women should have sex (Genesis 1:28, Matthew 19:4-6)
- sex should be practised within the context of marriage (1 Corinthians 7:9) - don't forget that Jesus was celibate but his sexuality and identity were never compromised
- sex can and should be enjoyed (Proverbs 5:18-20)

Power

The word 'power' will suggest many things: ascendancy, control, authority, influence, military might, girl power, power of life and death and the opposite: helplessness, despair, poverty and hunger. However hard I try, my wordly understanding of the word summons up negative images and associations. Perhaps this is because very few human being have the type of power they want or enough of the power they do have. Many of us have little power to control even our daily lives or emotions as Paul says: 'what I want to do I do not do, but what I hate I do' (Romans 7:15).

> ## Often famous people today are really more 'infamous' than famous!

The biblical understanding of power is more positive: God is the ultimate source of all power and any human power comes from God (Deuteronomy 8:17-18). Although humanity is relatively powerless in God's sight (2 Chronicles 14:11), God does give authority to some: the judges and kings of the Old Testament (1 Kings 16:1-3 for example) and Paul affirms that the authorities are appointed over us by God (Romans 13:1). Such power granted by God to individuals, nations or rulers should be used in God's service in humility and reliance on God (Isaiah 40:29-31; Luke 9:1; Acts 1:8). Also, it is important to remember that Jesus rejected military might and kingly power in favour of service and humility (Matthew 20:25-28 and the Beatitudes in Matthew 7:3-12).

Fame

Fame is quite a new 'idol' for many younger people today, probably because it offers a share of all the above: money, sex and power! Yet, many famous people can confirm that having a share of all these things still leaves a person empty. Sometimes they find that the chase was more exciting than 'arriving', or that their fame vanishes overnight or causes problems and anxiety (many famous people are stalked by fans or lose their privacy completely). Such worldly fame is contrived and 'man/womanmade'. Often famous people today are really more 'infamous' than famous! There are examples of famous people in the Bible, King David for example (1 Chronicles

14:17) and God and Jesus are famous. God's fame rested on his saving actions (Joshua 9:9) and Jesus' fame was connected with his miraculous ministry (Matthew 4:24) and teaching (Mark 1:27-28). The Bible does not therefore reject fame altogether but note that David's fame rests on the mighty things he is able to do in God's name and with God's power (1 Chronicles 14:10) and Jesus' power and fame rest in who he is, the Son of God. Indeed, the Bible tells us that God will judge those who become arrogant as a result of their fame (Isaiah 23:8-9) and Jesus, as we learnt earlier, taught service and humility rather than status and fame (Mark 9:33-35,10:42-45).

> David's fame rests on the mighty things he is able to do in God's name and with God's power

The amazing thing about these 'idols' is that they were created by God for good. The solution for the misuse and abuse of money, sex, power and fame is not to hide them away or to spurn them completely but to read the maker's instructions, - the Bible!

Following Jesus

by Liz West who works with YWAM

The Journey

What I've learned about being a follower of Jesus is that it really is a journey, it has a beginning point - although for some people that isn't a definite moment - and it has a destination towards which we are all moving. It's very important to remember that fact, because we often hit ourselves over the head because we're not doing very well at this particular moment in time. If we think of following Jesus as a journey then what is important is that we are pushing forward. Paul says it well:

> *I press on to take hold of that for which Christ Jesus took hold of me. Brothers, I do not consider myself yet to have taken hold of it. But one thing I do: Forgetting what is behind and straining towards what is ahead, I press on towards the goal to win the prize for which God has called me heavenwards in Christ Jesus.*
> *Philippians 3:12-14*

It is the most satisfying journey to be on, but also the most challenging, and it reveals more of ourselves than anything else we will ever do.

For me the place we are trying to get to is a relationship with God that is unbroken, and that's the goal that we all are striving for. What this implies to me is that we need to grow and mature, we shouldn't just stay safe where we are: getting 'saved' is just the beginning! The process of change starts out with us recognising that God knows better than we do and letting him teach us. We need to learn how to be a child of God, who will sometimes discipline us as well as love us (Hebrews 12:6). That's my heart: I want to be like Jesus so I will do what I can to learn from him.

Passionate about God

Yet I don't think it's all down to us. God knows us and he knows what we can handle at each point in our lives. He will slow down or speed up as we need him to. Our job is to be obedient and to keep following him. Lately I've been struck by how it often starts with knowledge and understanding but things only start taking off when we get passionate about God. The Holy Spirit's job is to teach us all things (John 14:26), which is great, because it means we're allowed to say, 'show me, I don't understand!' Once we understand, then we will get excited and want to follow.

> Try to have a good number of companions with you, because you will all need to carry each other at different times.

One step forward, two steps back

We need to get to know God and spend time doing the things that help that to happen:

> reading the Bible
> opening up to him
> being honest with him
> having the self-discipline to keep going when things get tough

My experience has taught me that following Jesus is like walking up a down escalator: if you're not pushing forwards you're falling back. However, I think failure is an important part of following Jesus. It's OK if we fall over or even take a few steps backwards, we must recognise that we're not perfect and we need to admit that.

Community

We do not grow best alone: the Bible is full of powerful images about how important it is for us to follow Jesus together (Psalm 133, Romans 12, 1 Corinthians 12). Try to have a good number of companions with you on the journey, because you will all need to carry each other at different times.

Finally, I think it's a combination of 'doing' and 'being'. God loves us as we are, in our being, who we are, but he wants us to be doers as well (James 1:22). Let's not have loads of understanding in our heads without it transmitting into our lives and transforming us.

News to Tell

by Andy Hawthorne
of the World Wide Message Tribe

It's good to talk

Right from the word go, one of the very first things you should do is start talking about your faith. Within 24 hours of deciding to follow Jesus you should tell as many people as you can that you're a Christian. From there on, don't stop until the day you die. This life is very short and it's our one opportunity in all eternity to talk about Jesus to people who don't know him. In heaven there will be no-one who doesn't know Jesus: this is our one chance and we need to grasp it. It's not an optional extra for professional evangelists or church leaders, every single one of us is meant to be telling people about Jesus, by our life and by our words.

Practice what you preach

As long as you are trying to live for Jesus you can be an 'evangelist'. If there are loads of areas of your life which you think don't concern Jesus, you are probably doing and will carry on doing lots of stuff that non-Christians know is out of order. Please stop talkig about Jesus, because you just bring disgrace on his name. If - as best as you can - you're living the right kind of life, you're trying to follow Jesus, just speak boldly as much as you possibly can.

It's not just about talking. How we live goes hand-in-hand with what we say. Social action is as much evangelism as talking about Jesus. We speak a lot louder by the way that we live than by the words we speak. That can be a cop out, an excuse not to speak, but we ought to be looking to do both all the time. We ought to be openly living and speaking as Christians.

Team mentality

When I get together with another Manchester United fan I don't find it difficult to talk for ages about my football team. We're not embarrassed, we don't cringe because we both think this football team is utterly brilliant. It's not that hard to convince a Manchester City fan to convert to my team (or at least to have a go), because I'm sure my team is best. In one sense we ought to be really proud of our team, which is a world-wide team, God's chosen team. He hasn't chosen you to sit in the stands, he's chosen you to play in the team. And the team will not play as it should do unless every single player is pulling their weight. We all have different positions to play, but as Christians we are all on the same team. We don't have just 50,000 people watching us, millions of people are looking at us to see if our lives match up to what we say.

Stand up for Jesus

The thing that Christians ought to delight in speaking about the most is Jesus. There's a totally brilliant verse in Luke 12:8 where Jesus says:

I tell you, whoever acknowledges me before men, the Son of Man will also acknowledge him before the angels of God.

When I get to heaven I want the angels to know what I've done, the stand I've made for Jesus. There are some people who will get to heaven and the angels will say, 'Who are you?' What we do for Jesus lasts for ever.

Then one day that person will say, 'Yes, I want to follow Jesus.'

So often we can be a link in the chain. I became a Christian because lots of different people prayed for me, took me to meetings and so on. Most of them never knew that they were part of me becoming a Christian, but they were key in God's purposes. Most of our witnessing is saying the right word or doing something loving, being a bit different to the crowd. Then one day that person will say, 'Yes, I want to follow Jesus.'

LOVE: A Revolution

by David Westlake who works with Tear Fund

Love

Jesus Christ came bringing a whole new way of living, called 'the kingdom of God.' (Mark 1:14-15) The whole of the Gospels are about Jesus showing us his way of living. He came saying that the old ways of life just weren't working and to have a look at this: life according to unconditional love. He calls that 'the kingdom of God': God's way of doing things. Jesus' whole life and death demonstrate a way of living according to love.

Towards social concern

Right at the end of the Bible, in James 1:27, it says this:

> Religion that God our Father accepts as pure and faultless is this: to look after orphans and widows in their distress and to keep oneself from being polluted by the world.

For me, that sums up what authentic Christianity is about. It is about serving the people who are hurting, who are needy, who are poor. That could be someone bullied at work or school, a lonely old lady in your street, someone on the other side of the world who has suffered in a natural disaster.

Call to action

Social concern is a challenge for me. We have to ask ourselves as Christians what we're doing. Are we just creating a cosy little club made up of the people who are just like us, or are we taking the outsider and bringing them inside? Christianity has got to be about being with the poor, it's got to be about 'those who have' serving 'those who have not'. The prevailing culture of feathering one's nest and 'looking after no. 1' has pervaded the church. As at other times in its history the church (the time before the Reformation in Europe for example) and its individual members can fail to be as socially aware and active as I think biblical teaching warrants.

Things will only change when we live in God's world God's way: when we remember the widow and the orphan, when we remember the have nots. That's what it means in Isaiah 58, where God says, the nation will be changed when we pay workers decent wages, take away gossip and slander and lying about people, when we treat people with respect, when we meet people who are powerless and serve them. When the church speaks up for these people then the Holy Spirit will move.

Jesus always seemed to make friends with people that others were putting down: tax collectors who collaborated with the occupying Roman army, 'sinners', prostitutes, outcasts. His treatment of the woman caught in adultery (John 8:1-11) is a good example of his attitude: rather than condemning her he let her know that he loved her, that he was her friend and on her side. He gave her a new future. All of us are challenged to do that. We have opportunities to show people that they matter more than our comfort, whether it's someone who's being picked on because their face just doesn't fit, whether it's just someone who needs help and who's struggling. We've got to live a socially responsible life all day long, every day.

The whole of the Gospels are about Jesus showing us his way of living.

Financial stewardship

We also need to think about our lifestyle. If the kingdom of God is about justice for the poor, building good relationships and loving people who are outside 'the club', then we have to decide how much materialism we want to buy into. How much money do we spend on leisure? How much do we spend on the toys that society tells us we need? How much of that really matters? How much is consistent with being a Christian? How much is a terrible distraction which keeps us from loving people and serving the poor?

Getting to know God

by Mike Pilavachi a leader of Soul Survivor

Talk to God

How do you communicate with God? You talk to him. Talking to him is what prayer's about. We need to get away from the stereotyped ideas of what prayer is - it's simply having a conversation with God. Conversations are meant to be two way things: we don't just tell God about who we are, about our concerns, about what we think of him and how much we love him - that's the worship aspect of prayer - we need just to be with him and hear his voice.

Love God

Our relationship with God is a love relationship, it's wanting to spend time with God. Sometimes I just want to be with God in prayer. Our church is full of couples and people are getting married all the time and they just seem to stare into each others' eyes. That's it in a sense, getting to know God happens as you just spend time with him and with Jesus.

Read God's Word

Also, we can hear God speak. One of the ways that happens - the major way - is through the Bible. You could call it God's love letter to the world, but it's more than that. Is it a love letter? Is it a book of maps? Is it a guidebook? Well, it's a bit of each of these. If you want to know what God's like, don't just ask his friends: find out what he says about himself as well by reading the Bible where he revealed to us who he is. Again, the analogy of a relationship is helpful. When you're thinking about going out with someone, you don't get too far just looking at their legs or whatever, you need to find out from them what they are actually like.

There are different ways of reading the Bible. You can read whole chunks as a story, sometimes it's great just to read one of the Gospels straight through. Other times you can really study a part of the Bible and read what other people think about it in commentaries or Bible reading notes. Sometimes you can just read a verse and meditate on that, coming back to it and chewing it over.

Know Jesus the Word

If you want to know God, it can be helpful to start with Jesus, the Son of God who is both 'the image of the invisible God' (Colossians 1:15) and actually God 'In the beginning was the Word, and the Word was with God, and the Word was God' (John 1:1). To know Jesus, start with the Gospels, because they're the story of Jesus and tell us what he did, what he was like and what he said. Jesus is the image of his father and if you want to know what God the father's like then look at Jesus (Hebrews 1:3). One thing that I used to do when I read the Gospels was to skip over the things that Jesus did just to get to the things he said which I thought were the real thing. Actually, what he did tells us just as much about who he is as what he said.

Worship God

Also, it's worth asking his friends what he's like. It's not that God changes, but everyone appreciates a different aspect of God: 'Oh! From where I'm standing . . . is the thing I love about him.' Worshipping together is a means of expressing our love for God and doing that will deepen your relationship with him. What kind of relationship would you have with a friend if you never told them or showed them that you liked them or if you never spent time with them in other people's company?

the Bible... God's love letter to the world

Become like God the Father and God the Son

So, the more time we spend with God, the more we 'stare into his eyes', the more we have a relationship with him, the more the Holy Spirit will make us like him (Ephesians 4:20-24) and like Jesus his son (2 Corinthians 3:18). Becoming like him isn't necessarily, 'Oh! My face has changed!', it means becoming like him in character and doing his will (John 5:19).

Serve others

To serve is to be like Jesus, to care is to be like Jesus, to forgive is to be like Jesus. As we do these things we will become more like him. As we become more like him, we will do these things more - it's a virtuous circle. If you want to be where Jesus is and who he is, you are going to have to serve the poor, the broken and the needy. While Jesus hangs out in churches, he really spends a lot of his time with the hurting and broken (Matthew 25:44-45).

The problem with suffering

by Michael Flowers

a hand surgeon who has spent many years working with leprosy victims

C.S. Lewis, who wrote the Narnia Chronicles, also wrote two books on the question of why God seems to let people suffer. It is interesting that the first of these books, *The Problem of Pain*, is very dry and academic and looks at the arguments from a fairly detached point of view. The second book was very different. *A Grief Observed* was published shortly after the death from cancer of Lewis' wife and is an emotional cry to God asking him if he notices the suffering in the world. Compared to the first book's more brainy approach, it is all heart. Here we can only cover the intellectual arguments, but be warned that at some point in your life you will have to deal with 'the problem of pain' at first-hand.

The central question all Christians are asked or ask is this: 'If God loves me and is all-powerful, why doesn't he do something about . . . (insert latest disaster, personal or televised)?' This question sounds simple, but it contains lots of assumptions. First, we have to ask what 'God loves me' means, because I don't think it means that I am at the centre of the universe. To say 'God loves me' doesn't mean I can get God to do whatever I want. Secondly, God being all-powerful doesn't mean that everything is his fault. We clearly have free will and (within the limits of our own sinful nature) we can choose whether or not to hurt someone else. If we go against the way the world is made we will end up in trouble but that's not God's fault, it's our own. The truth of the situation is that nearly all suffering is a direct result of our sin, even so-called natural disasters. The whole of creation is fallen, and even that is partly our individual responsibility (Genesis 3:17, Romans 8:22).

However, suffering does not depend directly on what a person deserves, it is not as simple as that. If we look at the teaching of Jesus (Luke 13:1-5), on one occasion he taught that personal calamity (being killed by a tower falling down is mentioned) does not happen to some rather than others because of the degree of their sin: 'do you think they were more guilty than all the others?' In John 9:1-3 Jesus makes clear that troubles need not relate that closely to the circumstances or sin of the person suffering.

If we look not only at Jesus' teaching but at Jesus himself we gain a bit more insight. I remember working in a hospital when a bereaved father came up to me and asked, 'Where was God when my boy died?'. Of course, God is where he was and feeling how he was when his boy died. When God entered human history in the form of the man Jesus and died on a cross he answered that man's question by showing that he experiences suffering with us. We know God loves us because Jesus died for us in agony and we know that God is powerful and can overcome death and suffering and pain because he raised Jesus from death. This is the key to the mystery.

When I was in Bangladesh I went to visit a family making carpets. The whole family would sit on one side of a huge vertical loom, each member adding a different coloured thread in some kind of rhythm. Everyone was singing a song, and this song clearly told them which threads to put where, which was necessary because the family were all on the wrong side of the carpet to see what the pattern was like. When I went round to the other side I met the father of the family, who was leading the song: he could see what the pattern was like and was helping all the other family members to make the carpet. That's true for us: there is a lot in this life that we can't understand, but we need to try to live according to the song, and one day we will find ourselves looking at the carpet from the other side.

So you want to know more

This Bible has got as much extra material in it as we could manage. However, God is limitless, and there are countless books about him, about Christianity, evangelism, the church and so on. Here are a few ideas for where you might want to go next in your exploration of the Bible and the Christian faith. Most of these books will be worth buying as you will be able to refer to them again and again. Others you may be able to borrow from friends or a library. If you find something really helpful in a borrowed book, why not write it out in a blank book or pad of your own to refer to when you need the information or inspiration later. This list is not exhaustive, for further suggestions why not try your local Christian bookshop (the yellow pages will help), or look on the internet at sites like www.bookshop.co.uk. Suggestions for favourite or helpful books can be posted on the Youth Bible forum on the internet (and don't forget, this site will only stay open as long as readers like you use it and find it helpful).

commentaries

A commentary is a book which helps you to understand the Bible more than is sometimes possible just by reading the text alone. You can buy commentaries on individual books, but the best place to start is to get a one-volume commentary on the whole Bible. The best one I've seen is *The NIV Bible Commentary* by Alister McGrath (Hodder & Stoughton) This will help you to understand difficult passages and to see how

each book fits in its historical context.
A helpful and imaginative overview or
 introduction to the Bible is *Crash Course on
the Bible* by Michael Gantt (Hodder &
Stoughton).

book-by-book commentaries

The NIV Application Commentaries
(Zondervan) are very helpful as they
focus both on the original meaning of the
passage and its contemporary application
(they are less academic than some ranges
of commentaries).

dictionaries

Bible dictionaries can be very helpful. Like a
turbo-charged version of the jargonbuster at
the back of this Bible, a Bible dictionary will
help you understand difficult words, as
well as provide information on the ideas,
concepts, people and places found in the
Bible. We recommend the *New Bible
Dictionary* (IVP).

concordances

Concordances are cool in every way except
the name! They are like a ridiculously
detailed index in which you can find all or
some of the words in the Bible and exactly
which verses they appear in. These range
from short paperback concordances
featuring only some words and entries to
more exhaustive reference books featuring
every word and every entry! There should
be concordances for most Bible translations.

handbooks

We also think that the *Lion Handbook* to

the Bible is brilliant: part commentary, part
introduction, it's really helpful for anyone
who wants to get into the Bible.

study Bibles

If the concordance approach appeals then
the *NIV Thematic Study Bible* will be
helpful. This provides information on over
2000 biblical themes (the fatherhood of God
or Jesus' anger for example) together with
the key Scripture references. The *NIV Study
Bible* is helpful in a Bible study situation as
it has helpful background notes and cross
references on the page with the Bible text.
(Both Hodder & Stoughton.)

Bible reading notes

Scripture Union do a series of small booklets
of daily readings, like the 5-day plans.
Disclosure is a fanzine-style package aimed at
young-ish people, *Daily Bread* is more
grown up, *Every Day With Jesus* notes are
popular.

books

The Book of God by Walter Wangerin (Lion)
is a brilliant book: it's a novelisation of the
Bible written in a very accessible and vivid
style. *How to Get into the Bible* by Stephen
Miller (Word) is a good next step for you if
you are still unsure about the Bible. It's
aimed at people that don't know loads about
the Bible and has an easy style.

the Christian life

The Crash Course series of books are written
in an accessible style at an accessible price
and although majoring on information and

fact, they should help you apply your knowledge: *Crash Course on Christian Teaching* is particularly recommended (Hodder & Stoughton). *Mere Christianity* by C.S. Lewis (Fount, HarperCollins) *Live the life* by Mike Pilavachi is an ideal introduction to how to live as a Christian in everyday life (Hodder & Stoughton). *Too Busy Not to Pray* by Bill Hybels (IVP) is a very helpful book on prayer.

evangelism

Questions of Life Nicky Gumbel (linked to the Alpha Course and published by Alpha Kingsway). *How Can I Lead a Friend to Christ* by Michael Green, *Love your Neighbour for God's Sake* by Justyn Rees (Hodder & Stoughton).

testimony

Honestly by Sheila Walsh, *Prison to Praise* by Merlin Carothers and *Run Baby Run* by Nicky Cruz (Hodder & Stoughton) *Wisdom for the Race of Life* by Kriss Akabusi and Stuart Weir (Bible Reading Fellowship).

THE
OLD TESTAMENT

Genesis

The Beginning

1 In the beginning God created the heavens and the earth. ²Now the earth was*a* formless and empty, darkness was over the surface of the deep, and the Spirit of God was hovering over the waters.

³And God said, "Let there be light," and there was light. ⁴God saw that the light was good, and he separated the light from the darkness. ⁵God called the light "day", and the darkness he called "night". And there was evening, and there was morning—the first day.

⁶And God said, "Let there be an expanse between the waters to separate water from water." ⁷So God made the expanse and separated the water under the expanse from the water above it. And it was so. ⁸God called the expanse "sky". And there was evening, and there was morning—the second day.

⁹And God said, "Let the water under the sky be gathered to one place, and let dry ground appear." And it was so. ¹⁰God called the dry ground "land", and the gathered waters he called "seas". And God saw that it was good.

¹¹Then God said, "Let the land produce vegetation: seed-bearing plants and trees on the land that bear fruit with seed in it, according to their various kinds." And it was so. ¹²The land produced vegetation: plants bearing seed according to their kinds and trees bearing fruit with seed in it according to their kinds. And God saw that it was good. ¹³And there was evening, and there was morning—the third day.

¹⁴And God said, "Let there be lights in the expanse of the sky to separate the day from the night, and let them serve as signs to mark seasons and days and years, ¹⁵and let them be lights in the expanse of the sky to give light on the earth." And it was so. ¹⁶God made two great lights—the greater light to govern the day and the lesser light to govern the night. He also made the stars. ¹⁷God set them in the expanse of the sky to give light on the earth, ¹⁸to govern the day and the night, and to separate light from darkness. And God saw that it was good. ¹⁹And there was evening, and there was morning—the fourth day.

²⁰And God said, "Let the water teem with living creatures, and let birds fly above the earth across the expanse of the sky." ²¹So God created the great creatures of the sea and every living and moving thing with which the water teems, according to their kinds, and every winged bird according to its kind. And God saw that it was good. ²²God blessed them and said, "Be fruitful and increase in number and fill the water in the seas,

and let the birds increase on the earth." ²³And there was evening, and there was morning—the fifth day.

²⁴And God said, "Let the land produce living creatures according to their kinds: livestock, creatures that move along the ground, and wild animals, each according to its kind." And it was so. ²⁵God made the wild animals according to their kinds, the livestock according to their kinds, and all the creatures that move along the ground according to their kinds. And God saw that it was good.

²⁶Then God said, "Let us make man in our image, in our likeness, and let them rule over the fish of the sea and the birds of the air, over the livestock, over all the earth,ᵇ and over all the creatures that move along the ground."

²⁷So God created man
    in his own image,
in the image of God
    he created him;
male and female
    he created them.

²⁸God blessed them and said to them, "Be fruitful and increase in number; fill the earth and subdue it. Rule over the fish of the sea and the birds of the air and over every living creature that moves on the ground."

²⁹Then God said, "I give you every seed-bearing plant on the face of the whole earth and every tree that has fruit with seed in it. They will be yours for food. ³⁰And to all the beasts of the earth and all the birds of the air and all the creatures that move on the ground—everything that has the breath of life in it—I give every green plant for food." And it was so.

³¹God saw all that he had made, and it was very good. And there was evening, and there was morning—the sixth day.

2 Thus the heavens and the earth were completed in all their vast array.

²By the seventh day God had finished the work he had been doing; so on the seventh day he restedᵃ from all his work. ³And God blessed the seventh day and made it holy, because on it he rested from all the work of creating that he had done.

Adam and Eve

⁴This is the account of the heavens and the earth when they were created.

When the LORD God made the earth and the heavens—⁵and no shrub of the field had yet appeared on the earthᵇ and no plant of the field had yet sprung up, for the LORD God had not sent rain on the earthᵇ and there was no man to work the ground, ⁶but streamsᶜ came up from the earth and watered the whole surface of the ground—⁷the LORD God formed the manᵈ from the dust of the ground and breathed into his nostrils the breath of life, and the man became a living being.

⁸Now the LORD God had planted a garden in the east, in Eden; and there he put the man he had formed. ⁹And the LORD God made all kinds of trees grow out of the ground—trees that were pleasing to the eye and good for food. In the middle of the garden were the tree of life and the tree of the knowledge of good and evil.

¹⁰A river watering the garden flowed from Eden; from there it was separated into four headwaters. ¹¹The name of the first is the Pishon; it winds through the entire land of Havilah, where there is gold. ¹²(The gold of that land is good; aromatic resinᵉ and onyx are also there.) ¹³The name of the second river is the Gihon; it winds through the entire land of Cush.ᶠ ¹⁴The name of the third river is the Tigris; it runs along the east side of Asshur. And the fourth river is the Euphrates.

¹⁵The LORD God took the man and put

ᵇ26 Hebrew; Syriac *all the wild animals*
ᵃ2 Or *ceased*; also in verse 3   ᵇ5 Or *land*; also in verse 6   ᶜ6 Or *mist*
ᵈ7 The Hebrew for *man* (*adam*) sounds like and may be related to the Hebrew for *ground* (*adamah*); it is also the name Adam (see Gen. 2:20).   ᵉ12 Or *good; pearls*   ᶠ13 Possibly south-east Mesopotamia

him in the Garden of Eden to work it and take care of it. ¹⁶And the LORD God commanded the man, "You are free to eat from any tree in the garden; ¹⁷but you must not eat from the tree of the knowledge of good and evil, for when you eat of it you will surely die."

¹⁸The LORD God said, "It is not good for the man to be alone. I will make a helper suitable for him."

¹⁹Now the LORD God had formed out of the ground all the beasts of the field and all the birds of the air. He brought them to the man to see what he would name them; and whatever the man called each living creature, that was its name. ²⁰So the man gave names to all the livestock, the birds of the air and all the beasts of the field.

But for Adam^g no suitable helper was found. ²¹So the LORD God caused the man to fall into a deep sleep; and while he was sleeping, he took one of the man's ribs^h and closed up the place with flesh. ²²Then the LORD God made a woman from the rib^i he had taken out of the man, and he brought her to the man.

²³The man said,

"This is now bone of my bones
　　and flesh of my flesh;
she shall be called 'woman',^{j}
　　for she was taken out of man."

²⁴For this reason a man will leave his father and mother and be united to his wife, and they will become one flesh.

²⁵The man and his wife were both naked, and they felt no shame.

The Fall of Man

3 Now the serpent was more crafty than any of the wild animals the LORD God had made. He said to the woman, "Did God really say, 'You must not eat from any tree in the garden'?"

²The woman said to the serpent, "We may eat fruit from the trees in the garden, ³but God did say, 'You must not eat fruit from the tree that is in the middle of the garden, and you must not touch it, or you will die.'"

⁴"You will not surely die," the serpent said to the woman. ⁵"For God knows that when you eat of it your eyes will be opened, and you will be like God, knowing good and evil."

⁶When the woman saw that the fruit of the tree was good for food and pleasing to the eye, and also desirable for gaining wisdom, she took some and ate it. She also gave some to her husband, who was with her, and he ate it. ⁷Then the eyes of both of them were opened, and they realised that they were naked; so they sewed fig leaves together and made coverings for themselves.

⁸Then the man and his wife heard the sound of the LORD God as he was walking in the garden in the cool of the day, and they hid from the LORD God among the trees of the garden. ⁹But the LORD God called to the man, "Where are you?"

¹⁰He answered, "I heard you in the garden, and I was afraid because I was naked; so I hid."

¹¹And he said, "Who told you that you were naked? Have you eaten from the tree from which I commanded you not to eat?"

¹²The man said, "The woman you put here with me—she gave me some fruit from the tree, and I ate it."

¹³Then the LORD God said to the woman, "What is this you have done?"

The woman said, "The serpent deceived me, and I ate."

¹⁴So the LORD God said to the serpent, "Because you have done this,

"Cursed are you above all the livestock
　　and all the wild animals!
You will crawl on your belly
　　and you will eat dust
　　all the days of your life.
¹⁵And I will put enmity
　　between you and the woman,
　　and between your offspring^a and hers;
he will crush^b your head,
　　and you will strike his heel."

¹⁶To the woman he said,

---

g20 Or *the man*　　　h21 Or *took part of the man's side*
j23 The Hebrew for *woman* sounds like the Hebrew for *man*.
a15 Or *seed*　　　b15 Or *strike*

i22 Or *part*

"I will greatly increase your pains in
　　childbearing;
　with pain you will give birth to
　　children.
Your desire will be for your husband,
　and he will rule over you."

17To Adam he said, "Because you listened to your wife and ate from the tree
about which I commanded you, 'You must
not eat of it,'

"Cursed is the ground because of you;
　through painful toil you will eat of it
　all the days of your life.
18It will produce thorns and thistles for
　you,
　and you will eat the plants of the
　　field.
19By the sweat of your brow
　you will eat your food
until you return to the ground,
　since from it you were taken;
for dust you are
　and to dust you will return."

20Adam*c* named his wife Eve,*d* because
she would become the mother of all the
living.

21The LORD God made garments of skin
for Adam and his wife and clothed them.
22And the LORD God said, "The man has
now become like one of us, knowing good
and evil. He must not be allowed to reach
out his hand and take also from the tree of
life and eat, and live for ever." 23So the
LORD God banished him from the Garden
of Eden to work the ground from which he
had been taken. 24After he drove the man
out, he placed on the east side*e* of the
Garden of Eden cherubim and a flaming
sword flashing back and forth to guard the
way to the tree of life.

Cain and Abel

4 Adam*a* lay with his wife Eve, and she
became pregnant and gave birth to
Cain.*b* She said, "With the help of the
LORD I have brought forth*c* a man." 2Later
she gave birth to his brother Abel.

Now Abel kept flocks, and Cain worked
the soil. 3In the course of time Cain
brought some of the fruits of the soil as an
offering to the LORD. 4But Abel brought
fat portions from some of the firstborn of
his flock. The LORD looked with favour on
Abel and his offering, 5but on Cain and his
offering he did not look with favour. So
Cain was very angry, and his face was
downcast.

6Then the LORD said to Cain, "Why are
you angry? Why is your face downcast? 7If
you do what is right, will you not be
accepted? But if you do not do what is
right, sin is crouching at your door; it
desires to have you, but you must master
it."

8Now Cain said to his brother Abel,
"Let's go out to the field."*d* And while
they were in the field, Cain attacked his
brother Abel and killed him.

9Then the LORD said to Cain, "Where is
your brother Abel?"

"I don't know," he replied. "Am I my
brother's keeper?"

10The LORD said, "What have you
done? Listen! Your brother's blood cries
out to me from the ground. 11Now you are
under a curse and driven from the ground,
which opened its mouth to receive your
brother's blood from your hand. 12When
you work the ground, it will no longer
yield its crops for you. You will be a
restless wanderer on the earth."

13Cain said to the LORD, "My punishment is more than I can bear. 14Today you
are driving me from the land, and I will be
hidden from your presence; I will be a
restless wanderer on the earth, and whoever finds me will kill me."

15But the LORD said to him, "Not so;*e* if
anyone kills Cain, he will suffer vengeance
seven times over." Then the LORD put a
mark on Cain so that no-one who found
him would kill him. 16So Cain went out
from the LORD's presence and lived in the
land of Nod,*f* east of Eden.

---

c20 Or *The man*　　*d20* *Eve* probably means *living.*　　*e24* Or *placed in front*
a1 Or *The man*　　*b1* *Cain* sounds like the Hebrew for *brought forth* or *acquired.*
c1 Or *have acquired*
d8 Samaritan Pentateuch, Septuagint, Vulgate and Syriac; Masoretic Text does not have *"Let's go out to the field."*
e15 Septuagint, Vulgate and Syriac, Hebrew *Very well*　　*f16* *Nod* means *wandering* (see verses 12 and 14).

¹⁷Cain lay with his wife, and she became pregnant and gave birth to Enoch. Cain was then building a city, and he named it after his son Enoch. ¹⁸To Enoch was born Irad, and Irad was the father of Mehujael, and Mehujael was the father of Methushael, and Methushael was the father of Lamech.

¹⁹Lamech married two women, one named Adah and the other Zillah. ²⁰Adah gave birth to Jabal; he was the father of those who live in tents and raise livestock. ²¹His brother's name was Jubal; he was the father of all who play the harp and flute. ²²Zillah also had a son, Tubal-Cain, who forged all kinds of tools out of*g* bronze and iron. Tubal-Cain's sister was Naamah.

²³Lamech said to his wives,

"Adah and Zillah, listen to me;
    wives of Lamech, hear my words.
I have killed*h* a man for wounding me,
    a young man for injuring me.
²⁴If Cain is avenged seven times,
    then Lamech seventy-seven times."

²⁵Adam lay with his wife again, and she gave birth to a son and named him Seth,*i* saying, "God has granted me another child in place of Abel, since Cain killed him." ²⁶Seth also had a son, and he named him Enosh.

At that time men began to call on*j* the name of the LORD.

From Adam to Noah

5 This is the written account of Adam's line.

When God created man, he made him in the likeness of God. ²He created them male and female and blessed them. And when they were created, he called them "man".*a*

³When Adam had lived 130 years, he had a son in his own likeness, in his own image; and he named him Seth. ⁴After Seth was born, Adam lived 800 years and had other sons and daughters. ⁵Altogether, Adam lived 930 years, and then he died.

⁶When Seth had lived 105 years, he became the father*b* of Enosh. ⁷And after he became the father of Enosh, Seth lived 807 years and had other sons and daughters. ⁸Altogether, Seth lived 912 years, and then he died.

⁹When Enosh had lived 90 years, he became the father of Kenan. ¹⁰And after he became the father of Kenan, Enosh lived 815 years and had other sons and daughters. ¹¹Altogether, Enosh lived 905 years, and then he died.

¹²When Kenan had lived 70 years, he became the father of Mahalalel. ¹³And after he became the father of Mahalalel, Kenan lived 840 years and had other sons and daughters. ¹⁴Altogether, Kenan lived 910 years, and then he died.

¹⁵When Mahalalel had lived 65 years, he became the father of Jared. ¹⁶And after he became the father of Jared, Mahalalel lived 830 years and had other sons and daughters. ¹⁷Altogether, Mahalalel lived 895 years, and then he died.

¹⁸When Jared had lived 162 years, he became the father of Enoch. ¹⁹And after he became the father of Enoch, Jared lived 800 years and had other sons and daughters. ²⁰Altogether, Jared lived 962 years, and then he died.

²¹When Enoch had lived 65 years, he became the father of Methuselah. ²²And after he became the father of Methuselah, Enoch walked with God 300 years and had other sons and daughters. ²³Altogether, Enoch lived 365 years. ²⁴Enoch walked with God; then he was no more, because God took him away.

²⁵When Methuselah had lived 187 years, he became the father of Lamech. ²⁶And after he became the father of Lamech, Methuselah lived 782 years and had other sons and daughters. ²⁷Altogether, Methuselah lived 969 years, and then he died.

²⁸When Lamech had lived 182 years, he had a son. ²⁹He named him Noah*c* and

---

g22 Or *who instructed all who work in*   *h23* Or *I will kill*   *i25* *Seth* probably means *granted.*
j26 Or *to proclaim*
a2 Hebrew *adam*   *b6* *Father* may mean *ancestor*; also in verses 7–26.   *c29* *Noah* sounds like the Hebrew for *comfort.*

said, "He will comfort us in the labour and painful toil of our hands caused by the ground the LORD has cursed." [30]After Noah was born, Lamech lived 595 years and had other sons and daughters. [31]Altogether, Lamech lived 777 years, and then he died.

[32]After Noah was 500 years old, he became the father of Shem, Ham and Japheth.

The Flood

6 When men began to increase in number on the earth and daughters were born to them, [2]the sons of God saw that the daughters of men were beautiful, and they married any of them they chose. [3]Then the LORD said, "My Spirit will not contend with[a] man for ever, for he is mortal;[b] his days will be a hundred and twenty years."

[4]The Nephilim were on the earth in those days—and also afterwards—when the sons of God went to the daughters of men and had children by them. They were the heroes of old, men of renown.

[5]The LORD saw how great man's wickedness on the earth had become, and that every inclination of the thoughts of his heart was only evil all the time. [6]The LORD was grieved that he had made man on the earth, and his heart was filled with pain. [7]So the LORD said, "I will wipe mankind, whom I have created, from the face of the earth—men and animals, and creatures that move along the ground, and birds of the air—for I am grieved that I have made them." [8]But Noah found favour in the eyes of the LORD.

[9]This is the account of Noah.

Noah was a righteous man, blameless among the people of his time, and he walked with God. [10]Noah had three sons: Shem, Ham and Japheth.

[11]Now the earth was corrupt in God's sight and was full of violence. [12]God saw how corrupt the earth had become, for all the people on earth had corrupted their ways. [13]So God said to Noah, "I am going to put an end to all people, for the earth is filled with violence because of them. I am surely going to destroy both them and the earth. [14]So make yourself an ark of cypress[c] wood; make rooms in it and coat it with pitch inside and out. [15]This is how you are to build it: The ark is to be 450 feet long, 75 feet wide and 45 feet high.[d] [16]Make a roof for it and finish[e] the ark to within 18 inches[f] of the top. Put a door in the side of the ark and make lower, middle and upper decks. [17]I am going to bring floodwaters on the earth to destroy all life under the heavens, every creature that has the breath of life in it. Everything on earth will perish. [18]But I will establish my covenant with you, and you will enter the ark —you and your sons and your wife and your sons' wives with you. [19]You are to bring into the ark two of all living creatures, male and female, to keep them alive with you. [20]Two of every kind of bird, of every kind of animal and of every kind of creature that moves along the ground will come to you to be kept alive. [21]You are to take every kind of food that is to be eaten and store it away as food for you and for them."

[22]Noah did everything just as God commanded him.

7 The LORD then said to Noah, "Go into the ark, you and your whole family, because I have found you righteous in this generation. [2]Take with you seven[a] of every kind of clean animal, a male and its mate, and two of every kind of unclean animal, a male and its mate, [3]and also seven of every kind of bird, male and female, to keep their various kinds alive throughout the earth. [4]Seven days from now I will send rain on the earth for forty days and forty nights, and I will wipe from the face of the earth every living creature I have made."

[5]And Noah did all that the LORD commanded him.

[6]Noah was six hundred years old when the floodwaters came on the earth. [7]And

Noah and his sons and his wife and his sons' wives entered the ark to escape the waters of the flood. [8]Pairs of clean and unclean animals, of birds and of all creatures that move along the ground, [9]male and female, came to Noah and entered the ark, as God had commanded Noah. [10]And after the seven days the floodwaters came on the earth.

[11]In the six hundredth year of Noah's life, on the seventeenth day of the second month—on that day all the springs of the great deep burst forth, and the floodgates of the heavens were opened. [12]And rain fell on the earth for forty days and forty nights.

[13]On that very day Noah and his sons, Shem, Ham and Japheth, together with his wife and the wives of his three sons, entered the ark. [14]They had with them every wild animal according to its kind, all livestock according to their kinds, every creature that moves along the ground according to its kind and every bird according to its kind, everything with wings. [15]Pairs of all creatures that have the breath of life in them came to Noah and entered the ark. [16]The animals going in were male and female of every living thing, as God had commanded Noah. Then the LORD shut him in.

[17]For forty days the flood kept coming on the earth, and as the waters increased they lifted the ark high above the earth. [18]The waters rose and increased greatly on the earth, and the ark floated on the surface of the water. [19]They rose greatly on the earth, and all the high mountains under the entire heavens were covered. [20]The waters rose and covered the mountains to a depth of more than twenty feet.[b,c] [21]Every living thing that moved on the earth perished—birds, livestock, wild animals, all the creatures that swarm over the earth, and all mankind. [22]Everything on dry land that had the breath of life in its nostrils died. [23]Every living thing on the face of the earth was wiped out; men and animals and the creatures that move along the ground and the birds of the air were wiped from the earth. Only Noah was left, and those with him in the ark.

[24]The waters flooded the earth for a hundred and fifty days.

8 But God remembered Noah and all the wild animals and the livestock that were with him in the ark, and he sent a wind over the earth, and the waters receded. [2]Now the springs of the deep and the floodgates of the heavens had been closed, and the rain had stopped falling from the sky. [3]The water receded steadily from the earth. At the end of the hundred and fifty days the water had gone down, [4]and on the seventeenth day of the seventh month the ark came to rest on the mountains of Ararat. [5]The waters continued to recede until the tenth month, and on the first day of the tenth month the tops of the mountains became visible.

[6]After forty days Noah opened the window he had made in the ark [7]and sent out a raven, and it kept flying back and forth until the water had dried up from the earth. [8]Then he sent out a dove to see if the water had receded from the surface of the ground. [9]But the dove could find no place to set its feet because there was water over all the surface of the earth; so it returned to Noah in the ark. He reached out his hand and took the dove and brought it back to himself in the ark. [10]He waited seven more days and again sent out the dove from the ark. [11]When the dove returned to him in the evening, there in its beak was a freshly plucked olive leaf! Then Noah knew that the water had receded from the earth. [12]He waited seven more days and sent the dove out again, but this time it did not return to him.

[13]By the first day of the first month of Noah's six hundred and first year, the water had dried up from the earth. Noah then removed the covering from the ark and saw that the surface of the ground was dry. [14]By the twenty-seventh day of the second month the earth was completely dry.

[15]Then God said to Noah, [16]"Come out of the ark, you and your wife and your sons and their wives. [17]Bring out every kind of living creature that is with you— the birds, the animals, and all the

---

b20 Hebrew *fifteen cubits* (about 6.9 metres)   *c20* Or *rose more than twenty feet, and the mountains were covered* creatures that move along the ground—so they can multiply on the earth and be fruitful and increase in number upon it."

¹⁸So Noah came out, together with his sons and his wife and his sons' wives. ¹⁹All the animals and all the creatures that move along the ground and all the birds—everything that moves on the earth—came out of the ark, one kind after another.

²⁰Then Noah built an altar to the LORD and, taking some of all the clean animals and clean birds, he sacrificed burnt offerings on it. ²¹The LORD smelled the pleasing aroma and said in his heart: "Never again will I curse the ground because of man, even though*a* every inclination of his heart is evil from childhood. And never again will I destroy all living creatures, as I have done.

²²"As long as the earth endures,
    seedtime and harvest,
    cold and heat,
    summer and winter,
    day and night
    will never cease."

God's Covenant With Noah

9 Then God blessed Noah and his sons, saying to them, "Be fruitful and increase in number and fill the earth. ²The fear and dread of you will fall upon all the beasts of the earth and all the birds of the air, upon every creature that moves along the ground, and upon all the fish of the sea; they are given into your hands. ³Everything that lives and moves will be food for you. Just as I gave you the green plants, I now give you everything.

⁴"But you must not eat meat that has its lifeblood still in it. ⁵And for your lifeblood I will surely demand an accounting. I will demand an accounting from every animal. And from each man, too, I will demand an accounting for the life of his fellow man.

⁶"Whoever sheds the blood of man,
    by man shall his blood be shed;
    for in the image of God
    has God made man.

⁷As for you, be fruitful and increase in number; multiply on the earth and increase upon it."

⁸Then God said to Noah and to his sons with him: ⁹"I now establish my covenant with you and with your descendants after you ¹⁰and with every living creature that was with you—the birds, the livestock and all the wild animals, all those that came out of the ark with you—every living creature on earth. ¹¹I establish my covenant with you: Never again will all life be cut off by the waters of a flood; never again will there be a flood to destroy the earth."

¹²And God said, "This is the sign of the covenant I am making between me and you and every living creature with you, a covenant for all generations to come: ¹³I have set my rainbow in the clouds, and it will be the sign of the covenant between me and the earth. ¹⁴Whenever I bring clouds over the earth and the rainbow appears in the clouds, ¹⁵I will remember my covenant between me and you and all living creatures of every kind. Never again will the waters become a flood to destroy all life. ¹⁶Whenever the rainbow appears in the clouds, I will see it and remember the everlasting covenant between God and all living creatures of every kind on the earth."

¹⁷So God said to Noah, "This is the sign of the covenant I have established between me and all life on the earth."

The Sons of Noah

¹⁸The sons of Noah who came out of the ark were Shem, Ham and Japheth. (Ham was the father of Canaan.) ¹⁹These were the three sons of Noah, and from them came the people who were scattered over the earth.

²⁰Noah, a man of the soil, proceeded*a* to plant a vineyard. ²¹When he drank some of its wine, he became drunk and lay uncovered inside his tent. ²²Ham, the father of Canaan, saw his father's nakedness and told his two brothers outside. ²³But Shem and Japheth took a garment and laid it across their shoulders; then

a21 Or man, for
a20 Or soil, was the first

they walked in backwards and covered their father's nakedness. Their faces were turned the other way so that they would not see their father's nakedness.

[24]When Noah awoke from his wine and found out what his youngest son had done to him, [25]he said,

"Cursed be Canaan!
  The lowest of slaves
  will he be to his brothers."

[26]He also said,

"Blessed be the LORD, the God of
      Shem!
  May Canaan be the slave of Shem.[b]
[27]May God extend the territory of
      Japheth;[c]
  may Japheth live in the tents of
      Shem,
  and may Canaan be his[d] slave."

[28]After the flood Noah lived 350 years. [29]Altogether, Noah lived 950 years, and then he died.

The Table of Nations

10 This is the account of Shem, Ham and Japheth, Noah's sons, who themselves had sons after the flood.

The Japhethites

[2]The sons[a] of Japheth:
    Gomer, Magog, Madai, Javan, Tubal, Meshech and Tiras.
[3]The sons of Gomer:
    Ashkenaz, Riphath and Togarmah.
[4]The sons of Javan:
    Elishah, Tarshish, the Kittim and the Rodanim.[b] [5](From these the maritime peoples spread out into their territories by their clans within their nations, each with its own language.)

The Hamites

[6]The sons of Ham:
    Cush, Mizraim,[c] Put and Canaan.
[7]The sons of Cush:
    Seba, Havilah, Sabtah, Raamah and Sabteca.
  The sons of Raamah:
    Sheba and Dedan.

[8]Cush was the father[d] of Nimrod, who grew to be a mighty warrior on the earth. [9]He was a mighty hunter before the LORD; that is why it is said, "Like Nimrod, a mighty hunter before the LORD." [10]The first centres of his kingdom were Babylon, Erech, Akkad and Calneh, in[e] Shinar.[f] [11]From that land he went to Assyria, where he built Nineveh, Rehoboth Ir,[g] Calah [12]and Resen, which is between Nineveh and Calah; that is the great city.

[13]Mizraim was the father of
    the Ludites, Anamites, Lehabites, Naphtuhites, [14]Pathrusites, Casluhites (from whom the Philistines came) and Caphtorites.
[15]Canaan was the father of
    Sidon his firstborn,[h] and of the Hittites, [16]Jebusites, Amorites, Girgashites, [17]Hivites, Arkites, Sinites, [18]Arvadites, Zemarites and Hamathites.

Later the Canaanite clans scattered [19]and the borders of Canaan reached from Sidon towards Gerar as far as Gaza, and then towards Sodom, Gomorrah, Admah and Zeboiim, as far as Lasha.

[20]These are the sons of Ham by their clans and languages, in their territories and nations.

The Semites

[21]Sons were also born to Shem, whose older brother was[i] Japheth; Shem was the ancestor of all the sons of Eber.

---

b26 Or *be his slave*   c27 *Japheth* sounds like the Hebrew for *extend.*   d27 Or *their*
a2 *Sons* may mean *descendants* or *successors* or *nations*; also in verses 3, 4, 6, 7, 20–23, 29 and 31.
b4 Some manuscripts of the Masoretic Text and Samaritan Pentateuch (see also Septuagint and 1 Chron. 1:7); most manuscripts of the Masoretic Text *Dodanim*   c6 That is, Egypt; also in verse 13
d8 *Father* may mean *ancestor* or *predecessor* or *founder*; also in verses 13, 15, 24 and 26.
e10 Or *Erech and Akkad—all of them in*   f10 That is, Babylonia   g11 Or *Nineveh with its city squares*
h15 Or *of the Sidonians, the foremost*   i21 Or *Shem, the older brother of*

²²The sons of Shem:

Elam, Asshur, Arphaxad, Lud and Aram.

²³The sons of Aram:

Uz, Hul, Gether and Meshech.*j*

²⁴Arphaxad was the father of*k* Shelah, and Shelah the father of Eber.

²⁵Two sons were born to Eber:

One was named Peleg,*l* because in his time the earth was divided; his brother was named Joktan.

²⁶Joktan was the father of

Almodad, Sheleph, Hazarmaveth, Jerah, ²⁷Hadoram, Uzal, Diklah, ²⁸Obal, Abimael, Sheba, ²⁹Ophir, Havilah and Jobab. All these were sons of Joktan.

³⁰The region where they lived stretched from Mesha towards Sephar, in the eastern hill country.

³¹These are the sons of Shem by their clans and languages, in their territories and nations.

³²These are the clans of Noah's sons, according to their lines of descent, within their nations. From these the nations spread out over the earth after the flood.

The Tower of Babel

11 Now the whole world had one language and a common speech. ²As men moved eastward,*a* they found a plain in Shinar*b* and settled there.

³They said to each other, "Come, let's make bricks and bake them thoroughly." They used brick instead of stone, and bitumen for mortar. ⁴Then they said, "Come, let us build ourselves a city, with a tower that reaches to the heavens, so that we may make a name for ourselves and not be scattered over the face of the whole earth."

⁵But the Lord came down to see the city and the tower that the men were building. ⁶The Lord said, "If as one people speaking the same language they have begun to do this, then nothing they plan to do will be impossible for them. ⁷Come, let us go down and confuse their language so they will not understand each other."

⁸So the Lord scattered them from there over all the earth, and they stopped building the city. ⁹That is why it was called Babel*c*—because there the Lord confused the language of the whole world. From there the Lord scattered them over the face of the whole earth.

From Shem to Abram

¹⁰This is the account of Shem.

Two years after the flood, when Shem was 100 years old, he became the father*d* of Arphaxad. ¹¹And after he became the father of Arphaxad, Shem lived 500 years and had other sons and daughters.

¹²When Arphaxad had lived 35 years, he became the father of Shelah. ¹³And after he became the father of Shelah, Arphaxad lived 403 years and had other sons and daughters.*e*

¹⁴When Shelah had lived 30 years, he became the father of Eber. ¹⁵And after he became the father of Eber, Shelah lived 403 years and had other sons and daughters.

¹⁶When Eber had lived 34 years, he became the father of Peleg. ¹⁷And after he became the father of Peleg, Eber lived 430 years and had other sons and daughters.

¹⁸When Peleg had lived 30 years, he became the father of Reu. ¹⁹And after he became the father of Reu, Peleg lived 209 years and had other sons and daughters.

²⁰When Reu had lived 32 years, he became the father of Serug. ²¹And after he became the father of Serug, Reu lived 207 years and had other sons and daughters.

---

j23 See Septuagint and 1 Chron. 1:17; Hebrew *Mash*.
k24 Hebrew; Septuagint *father of Cainan, and Cainan was the father of*   *l25* *Peleg* means *division*.
a2 Or *from the east*; *or in the east*   *b2* That is, Babylonia
c9 That is, Babylon; *Babel* sounds like the Hebrew for *confused*.
d10 *Father* may mean *ancestor*; also in verses 11–25.
e12,13 Hebrew; Septuagint (see also Luke 3:35, 36 and note at Gen. 10:24) *35 years, he became the father of Cainan.* ¹³*And after he became the father of Cainan, Arphaxad lived 430 years and had other sons and.daughters, and then he died. When Cainan had lived 130 years, he became the father of Shelah. And after he became the father of Shelah, Cainan lived 330 years and had other sons and daughters*

22When Serug had lived 30 years, he became the father of Nahor. 23And after he became the father of Nahor, Serug lived 200 years and had other sons and daughters.

24When Nahor had lived 29 years, he became the father of Terah. 25And after he became the father of Terah, Nahor lived 119 years and had other sons and daughters.

26After Terah had lived 70 years, he became the father of Abram, Nahor and Haran.

27This is the account of Terah.

Terah became the father of Abram, Nahor and Haran. And Haran became the father of Lot. 28While his father Terah was still alive, Haran died in Ur of the Chaldeans, in the land of his birth. 29Abram and Nahor both married. The name of Abram's wife was Sarai, and the name of Nahor's wife was Milcah; she was the daughter of Haran, the father of both Milcah and Iscah. 30Now Sarai was barren; she had no children.

31Terah took his son Abram, his grandson Lot son of Haran, and his daughter-in-law Sarai, the wife of his son Abram, and together they set out from Ur of the Chaldeans to go to Canaan. But when they came to Haran, they settled there.

32Terah lived 205 years, and he died in Haran.

The Call of Abram

12 The LORD had said to Abram, "Leave your country, your people and your father's household and go to the land I will show you.

2"I will make you into a great nation
　and I will bless you;
I will make your name great,
　and you will be a blessing.
3I will bless those who bless you,
　and whoever curses you I will curse;
and all peoples on earth
　will be blessed through you."

4So Abram left, as the LORD had told him; and Lot went with him. Abram was seventy-five years old when he set out from Haran. 5He took his wife Sarai, his nephew Lot, all the possessions they had accumulated and the people they had acquired in Haran, and they set out for the land of Canaan, and they arrived there.

6Abram travelled through the land as far as the site of the great tree of Moreh at Shechem. At that time the Canaanites were in the land. 7The LORD appeared to Abram and said, "To your offspring[a] I will give this land." So he built an altar there to the LORD, who had appeared to him.

8From there he went on towards the hills east of Bethel and pitched his tent, with Bethel on the west and Ai on the east. There he built an altar to the LORD and called on the name of the LORD. 9Then Abram set out and continued towards the Negev.

Abram in Egypt

10Now there was a famine in the land, and Abram went down to Egypt to live there for a while because the famine was severe. 11As he was about to enter Egypt, he said to his wife Sarai, "I know what a beautiful woman you are. 12When the Egyptians see you, they will say, 'This is his wife.' Then they will kill me but will let you live. 13Say you are my sister, so that I will be treated well for your sake and my life will be spared because of you."

14When Abram came to Egypt, the Egyptians saw that she was a very beautiful woman. 15And when Pharaoh's officials saw her, they praised her to Pharaoh, and she was taken into his palace. 16He treated Abram well for her sake, and Abram acquired sheep and cattle, male and female donkeys, menservants and maidservants, and camels.

17But the LORD inflicted serious diseases on Pharaoh and his household because of Abram's wife Sarai. 18So Pharaoh summoned Abram. "What have you done to me?" he said. "Why didn't you tell me she was your wife? 19Why did you say, 'She is my sister,' so that I took her to be my wife? Now then, here is your wife. Take her and go!'' 20Then Pharaoh gave orders about Abram to his men, and they sent him on his way, with his wife and everything he had.

Abram and Lot Separate

13 So Abram went up from Egypt to the Negev, with his wife and everything he had, and Lot went with him. 2Abram had become very wealthy in livestock and in silver and gold.

3From the Negev he went from place to place until he came to Bethel, to the place between Bethel and Ai where his tent had been earlier 4and where he had first built an altar. There Abram called on the name of the LORD.

5Now Lot, who was moving about with Abram, also had flocks and herds and tents. 6But the land could not support them while they stayed together, for their possessions were so great that they were not able to stay together. 7And quarrelling arose between Abram's herdsmen and the herdsmen of Lot. The Canaanites and Perizzites were also living in the land at that time.

8So Abram said to Lot, "Let's not have any quarrelling between you and me, or between your herdsmen and mine, for we are brothers. 9Is not the whole land before you? Let's part company. If you go to the left, I'll go to the right; if you go to the right, I'll go to the left.''

10Lot looked up and saw that the whole plain of the Jordan was well watered, like the garden of the LORD, like the land of Egypt, towards Zoar. (This was before the LORD destroyed Sodom and Gomorrah.) 11So Lot chose for himself the whole plain of the Jordan and set out towards the east. The two men parted company: 12Abram lived in the land of Canaan, while Lot lived among the cities of the plain and pitched his tents near Sodom. 13Now the men of Sodom were wicked and were sinning greatly against the LORD.

14The LORD said to Abram after Lot had parted from him, "Lift up your eyes from where you are and look north and south, east and west. 15All the land that you see I will give to you and your offspring[a] for ever. 16I will make your offspring like the dust of the earth, so that if anyone could count the dust, then your offspring could be counted. 17Go, walk through the length and breadth of the land, for I am giving it to you.''

18So Abram moved his tents and went to live near the great trees of Mamre at Hebron, where he built an altar to the LORD.

Abram Rescues Lot

14 At this time Amraphel king of Shinar,[a] Arioch king of Ellasar, Kedorlaomer king of Elam and Tidal king of Goiim 2went to war against Bera king of Sodom, Birsha king of Gomorrah, Shinab king of Admah, Shemeber king of Zeboiim, and the king of Bela (that is, Zoar). 3All these latter kings joined forces in the Valley of Siddim (the Salt Sea[b]). 4For twelve years they had been subject to Kedorlaomer, but in the thirteenth year they rebelled.

5In the fourteenth year, Kedorlaomer and the kings allied with him went out and defeated the Rephaites in Ashteroth Karnaim, the Zuzites in Ham, the Emites in Shaveh Kiriathaim 6and the Horites in the hill country of Seir, as far as El Paran near the desert. 7Then they turned back and went to En Mishpat (that is, Kadesh), and they conquered the whole territory of the Amalekites, as well as the Amorites who were living in Hazezon Tamar.

8Then the king of Sodom, the king of Gomorrah, the king of Admah, the king of Zeboiim and the king of Bela (that is, Zoar) marched out and drew up their battle lines in the Valley of Siddim 9against Kedorlaomer king of Elam, Tidal king of Goiim, Amraphel king of Shinar and Arioch king of Ellasar—four kings against five. 10Now the Valley of Siddim was full of tar pits, and when the kings of Sodom and Gomorrah fled, some of the

---

[a]15 Or seed; also in verse 16
[a]1 That is, Babylonia; also in verse 9   [b]3 That is, the Dead Sea

men fell into them and the rest fled to the hills. [11]The four kings seized all the goods of Sodom and Gomorrah and all their food; then they went away. [12]They also carried off Abram's nephew Lot and his possessions, since he was living in Sodom.

[13]One who had escaped came and reported this to Abram the Hebrew. Now Abram was living near the great trees of Mamre the Amorite, a brother[c] of Eshcol and Aner, all of whom were allied with Abram. [14]When Abram heard that his relative had been taken captive, he called out the 318 trained men born in his household and went in pursuit as far as Dan. [15]During the night Abram divided his men to attack them and he routed them, pursuing them as far as Hobah, north of Damascus. [16]He recovered all the goods and brought back his relative Lot and his possessions, together with the women and the other people.

[17]After Abram returned from defeating Kedorlaomer and the kings allied with him, the king of Sodom came out to meet him in the Valley of Shaveh (that is, the King's Valley).

[18]Then Melchizedek king of Salem[d] brought out bread and wine. He was priest of God Most High, [19]and he blessed Abram, saying,

"Blessed be Abram by God Most High,
    Creator[e] of heaven and earth.
[20]And blessed be[f] God Most High,
    who delivered your enemies into your
        hand."

Then Abram gave him a tenth of everything.

[21]The king of Sodom said to Abram, "Give me the people and keep the goods for yourself."

[22]But Abram said to the king of Sodom, "I have raised my hand to the LORD, God Most High, Creator of heaven and earth, and have taken an oath [23]that I will accept nothing belonging to you, not even a thread or the thong of a sandal, so that you

will never be able to say, 'I made Abram rich.' [24]I will accept nothing but what my men have eaten and the share that belongs to the men who went with me—to Aner, Eshcol and Mamre. Let them have their share."

God's Covenant With Abram

15 After this, the word of the LORD came to Abram in a vision:

"Do not be afraid, Abram.
    I am your shield,[a]
    your very great reward."[b]

[2]But Abram said, "O Sovereign LORD, what can you give me since I remain childless and the one who will inherit[c] my estate is Eliezer of Damascus?" [3]And Abram said, "You have given me no children; so a servant in my household will be my heir."

[4]Then the word of the LORD came to him: "This man will not be your heir, but a son coming from your own body will be your heir." [5]He took him outside and said, "Look up at the heavens and count the stars—if indeed you can count them." Then he said to him, "So shall your offspring be."

[6]Abram believed the LORD, and he credited it to him as righteousness.

[7]He also said to him, "I am the LORD, who brought you out of Ur of the Chaldeans to give you this land to take possession of it."

[8]But Abram said, "O Sovereign LORD, how can I know that I shall gain possession of it?"

[9]So the LORD said to him, "Bring me a heifer, a goat and a ram, each three years old, along with a dove and a young pigeon."

[10]Abram brought all these to him, cut them in two and arranged the halves opposite each other; the birds, however, he did not cut in half. [11]Then birds of prey came down on the carcasses, but Abram drove them away.

[12]As the sun was setting, Abram fell

---

[c]13 Or *a relative*; or *an ally*   [d]18 That is, Jerusalem   [e]19 Or *Possessor*; also in verse 22
[f]20 Or *And praise be to*
[a]1 Or *sovereign*   [b]1 Or *shield*; / *your reward will be very great*
[c]2 The meaning of the Hebrew for this phrase is uncertain.

into a deep sleep, and a thick and dreadful darkness came over him. 13Then the LORD said to him, "Know for certain that your descendants will be strangers in a country not their own, and they will be enslaved and ill-treated four hundred years. 14But I will punish the nation they serve as slaves, and afterwards they will come out with great possessions. 15You, however, will go to your fathers in peace and be buried at a good old age. 16In the fourth generation your descendants will come back here, for the sin of the Amorites has not yet reached its full measure."

17When the sun had set and darkness had fallen, a smoking brazier with a blazing torch appeared and passed between the pieces. 18On that day the LORD made a covenant with Abram and said, "To your descendants I give this land, from the river*d* of Egypt to the great river, the Euphrates—19the land of the Kenites, Kenizzites, Kadmonites, 20Hittites, Perizzites, Rephaites, 21Amorites, Canaanites, Girgashites and Jebusites."

Hagar and Ishmael

16 Now Sarai, Abram's wife, had borne him no children. But she had an Egyptian maidservant named Hagar; 2so she said to Abram, "The LORD has kept me from having children. Go, sleep with my maidservant; perhaps I can build a family through her."

Abram agreed to what Sarai said. 3So after Abram had been living in Canaan ten years, Sarai his wife took her Egyptian maidservant Hagar and gave her to her husband to be his wife. 4He slept with Hagar, and she conceived.

When she knew she was pregnant, she began to despise her mistress. 5Then Sarai said to Abram, "You are responsible for the wrong I am suffering. I put my servant in your arms, and now that she knows she is pregnant, she despises me. May the LORD judge between you and me."

6"Your servant is in your hands," Abram said. "Do with her whatever you

think best." Then Sarai ill-treated Hagar; so she fled from her.

7The angel of the LORD found Hagar near a spring in the desert; it was the spring that is beside the road to Shur. 8And he said, "Hagar, servant of Sarai, where have you come from, and where are you going?"

"I'm running away from my mistress Sarai," she answered.

9Then the angel of the LORD told her, "Go back to your mistress and submit to her." 10The angel added, "I will so increase your descendants that they will be too numerous to count."

11The angel of the LORD also said to her:

"You are now with child
  and you will have a son.
You shall name him Ishmael,*a*
  for the LORD has heard of your
    misery.
12He will be a wild donkey of a man;
  his hand will be against everyone
  and everyone's hand against him,
and he will live in hostility
  towards*b* all his brothers."

13She gave this name to the LORD who spoke to her: "You are the God who sees me," for she said, "I have now seen*c* the One who sees me." 14That is why the well was called Beer Lahai Roi;*d* it is still there, between Kadesh and Bered.

15So Hagar bore Abram a son, and Abram gave the name Ishmael to the son she had borne. 16Abram was eighty-six years old when Hagar bore him Ishmael.

The Covenant of Circumcision

17 When Abram was ninety-nine years old, the LORD appeared to him and said, "I am God Almighty;*a* walk before me and be blameless. 2I will confirm my covenant between me and you and will greatly increase your numbers."

3Abram fell face down, and God said to him, 4"As for me, this is my covenant with you: You will be the father of many

---

d18 Or *Wadi*
a11 Ishmael means *God hears.*   *b12* Or *live to the east / of*   *c13* Or *seen the back of*
d14 Beer Lahai Roi means *well of the Living One who sees me.*
a1 Hebrew *El-Shaddai*

nations. [5]No longer will you be called Abram;[b] your name will be Abraham,[c] for I have made you a father of many nations. [6]I will make you very fruitful; I will make nations of you, and kings will come from you. [7]I will establish my covenant as an everlasting covenant between me and you and your descendants after you for the generations to come, to be your God and the God of your descendants after you. [8]The whole land of Canaan, where you are now an alien, I will give as an everlasting possession to you and your descendants after you; and I will be their God."

[9]Then God said to Abraham, "As for you, you must keep my covenant, you and your descendants after you for the generations to come. [10]This is my covenant with you and your descendants after you, the covenant you are to keep: Every male among you shall be circumcised. [11]You are to undergo circumcision, and it will be the sign of the covenant between me and you. [12]For the generations to come every male among you who is eight days old must be circumcised, including those born in your household or bought with money from a foreigner—those who are not your offspring. [13]Whether born in your household or bought with your money, they must be circumcised. My covenant in your flesh is to be an everlasting covenant. [14]Any uncircumcised male, who has not been circumcised in the flesh, will be cut off from his people; he has broken my covenant."

[15]God also said to Abraham, "As for Sarai your wife, you are no longer to call her Sarai; her name will be Sarah. [16]I will bless her and will surely give you a son by her. I will bless her so that she will be the mother of nations; kings of peoples will come from her."

[17]Abraham fell face down; he laughed and said to himself, "Will a son be born to a man a hundred years old? Will Sarah bear a child at the age of ninety?" [18]And Abraham said to God, "If only Ishmael might live under your blessing!"

[19]Then God said, "Yes, but your wife Sarah will bear you a son, and you will call him Isaac.[d] I will establish my covenant with him as an everlasting covenant for his descendants after him. [20]And as for Ishmael, I have heard you: I will surely bless him; I will make him fruitful and will greatly increase his numbers. He will be the father of twelve rulers, and I will make him into a great nation. [21]But my covenant I will establish with Isaac, whom Sarah will bear to you by this time next year." [22]When he had finished speaking with Abraham, God went up from him.

[23]On that very day Abraham took his son Ishmael and all those born in his household or bought with his money, every male in his household, and circumcised them, as God told him. [24]Abraham was ninety-nine years old when he was circumcised, [25]and his son Ishmael was thirteen; [26]Abraham and his son Ishmael were both circumcised on that same day. [27]And every male in Abraham's household, including those born in his household or bought from a foreigner, was circumcised with him.

The Three Visitors

18 The LORD appeared to Abraham near the great trees of Mamre while he was sitting at the entrance to his tent in the heat of the day. [2]Abraham looked up and saw three men standing nearby. When he saw them, he hurried from the entrance of his tent to meet them and bowed low to the ground.

[3]He said, "If I have found favour in your eyes, my lord,[a] do not pass your servant by. [4]Let a little water be brought, and then you may all wash your feet and rest under this tree. [5]Let me get you something to eat, so you can be refreshed and then go on your way—now that you have come to your servant."

"Very well," they answered, "do as you say."

[6]So Abraham hurried into the tent to Sarah. "Quick," he said, "get three seahs[b] of fine flour and knead it and bake some bread."

[7]Then he ran to the herd and selected a

---

b5 Abram means exalted father.   *c5 Abraham means father of many.*   *d19 Isaac means he laughs.*
a3 Or O Lord   *b6 That is, probably about 39 pints (about 22 litres)*

choice, tender calf and gave it to a servant, who hurried to prepare it. ⁸He then brought some curds and milk and the calf that had been prepared, and set these before them. While they ate, he stood near them under a tree.

⁹"Where is your wife Sarah?" they asked him.

"There, in the tent," he said.

¹⁰Then the LORD*c* said, "I will surely return to you about this time next year, and Sarah your wife will have a son."

Now Sarah was listening at the entrance to the tent, which was behind him. ¹¹Abraham and Sarah were already old and well advanced in years, and Sarah was past the age of childbearing. ¹²So Sarah laughed to herself as she thought, "After I am worn out and my master*d* is old, will I now have this pleasure?"

¹³Then the LORD said to Abraham, "Why did Sarah laugh and say, 'Will I really have a child, now that I am old?' ¹⁴Is anything too hard for the LORD? I will return to you at the appointed time next year and Sarah will have a son."

¹⁵Sarah was afraid, so she lied and said, "I did not laugh."

But he said, "Yes, you did laugh."

Abraham Pleads for Sodom

¹⁶When the men got up to leave, they looked down towards Sodom, and Abraham walked along with them to see them on their way. ¹⁷Then the LORD said, "Shall I hide from Abraham what I am about to do? ¹⁸Abraham will surely become a great and powerful nation, and all nations on earth will be blessed through him. ¹⁹For I have chosen him, so that he will direct his children and his household after him to keep the way of the LORD by doing what is right and just, so that the LORD will bring about for Abraham what he has promised him."

²⁰Then the LORD said, "The outcry against Sodom and Gomorrah is so great and their sin so grievous ²¹that I will go

down and see if what they have done is as bad as the outcry that has reached me. If not, I will know."

²²The men turned away and went towards Sodom, but Abraham remained standing before the LORD.*e* ²³Then Abraham approached him and said: "Will you sweep away the righteous with the wicked? ²⁴What if there are fifty righteous people in the city? Will you really sweep it away and not spare*f* the place for the sake of the fifty righteous people in it? ²⁵Far be it from you to do such a thing—to kill the righteous with the wicked, treating the righteous and the wicked alike. Far be it from you! Will not the Judge*g* of all the earth do right?"

²⁶The LORD said, "If I find fifty righteous people in the city of Sodom, I will spare the whole place for their sake."

²⁷Then Abraham spoke up again: "Now that I have been so bold as to speak to the Lord, though I am nothing but dust and ashes, ²⁸what if the number of the righteous is five less than fifty? Will you destroy the whole city because of five people?"

"If I find forty-five there," he said, "I will not destroy it."

²⁹Once again he spoke to him, "What if only forty are found there?"

He said, "For the sake of forty, I will not do it."

³⁰Then he said, "May the Lord not be angry, but let me speak. What if only thirty can be found there?"

He answered, "I will not do it if I find thirty there."

³¹Abraham said, "Now that I have been so bold as to speak to the Lord, what if only twenty can be found there?"

He said, "For the sake of twenty, I will not destroy it."

³²Then he said, "May the Lord not be angry, but let me speak just once more. What if only ten can be found there?"

He answered, "For the sake of ten, I will not destroy it."

³³When the LORD had finished speaking with Abraham, he left, and Abraham returned home.

---

c10 Hebrew *Then he*   *d12* Or *husband*
e22 Masoretic Text; an ancient Hebrew scribal tradition *but the LORD remained standing before Abraham*
f24 Or *forgive*; also in verse 26   *g25* Or *Ruler*

Sodom and Gomorrah Destroyed

19 The two angels arrived at Sodom in the evening, and Lot was sitting in the gateway of the city. When he saw them, he got up to meet them and bowed down with his face to the ground. 2"My lords," he said, "please turn aside to your servant's house. You can wash your feet and spend the night and then go on your way early in the morning."

"No," they answered, "we will spend the night in the square."

3But he insisted so strongly that they did go with him and entered his house. He prepared a meal for them, baking bread without yeast, and they ate. 4Before they had gone to bed, all the men from every part of the city of Sodom—both young and old—surrounded the house. 5They called to Lot, "Where are the men who came to you tonight? Bring them out to us so that we can have sex with them."

6Lot went outside to meet them and shut the door behind him 7and said, "No, my friends. Don't do this wicked thing. 8Look, I have two daughters who have never slept with a man. Let me bring them out to you, and you can do what you like with them. But don't do anything to these men, for they have come under the protection of my roof."

9"Get out of our way," they replied. And they said, "This fellow came here as an alien, and now he wants to play the judge! We'll treat you worse than them." They kept bringing pressure on Lot and moved forward to break down the door.

10But the men inside reached out and pulled Lot back into the house and shut the door. 11Then they struck the men who were at the door of the house, young and old, with blindness so that they could not find the door.

12The two men said to Lot, "Do you have anyone else here—sons-in-law, sons or daughters, or anyone else in the city who belongs to you? Get them out of here, 13because we are going to destroy this place. The outcry to the LORD against its

people is so great that he has sent us to destroy it."

14So Lot went out and spoke to his sons-in-law, who were pledged to marry[a] his daughters. He said, "Hurry and get out of this place, because the LORD is about to destroy the city!" But his sons-in-law thought he was joking.

15With the coming of dawn, the angels urged Lot, saying, "Hurry! Take your wife and your two daughters who are here, or you will be swept away when the city is punished."

16When he hesitated, the men grasped his hand and the hands of his wife and of his two daughters and led them safely out of the city, for the LORD was merciful to them. 17As soon as they had brought them out, one of them said, "Flee for your lives! Don't look back, and don't stop anywhere in the plain! Flee to the mountains or you will be swept away!"

18But Lot said to them, "No, my lords,[b] please! 19Your[c] servant has found favour in your[c] eyes, and you[c] have shown great kindness to me in sparing my life. But I can't flee to the mountains; this disaster will overtake me, and I'll die. 20Look, here is a town near enough to run to, and it is small. Let me flee to it—it is very small, isn't it? Then my life will be spared."

21He said to him, "Very well, I will grant this request too; I will not overthrow the town you speak of. 22But flee there quickly, because I cannot do anything until you reach it." (That is why the town was called Zoar.[d])

23By the time Lot reached Zoar, the sun had risen over the land. 24Then the LORD rained down burning sulphur on Sodom and Gomorrah—from the LORD out of the heavens. 25Thus he overthrew those cities and the entire plain, including all those living in the cities—and also the vegetation in the land. 26But Lot's wife looked back, and she became a pillar of salt.

27Early the next morning Abraham got up and returned to the place where he had stood before the LORD. 28He looked down towards Sodom and Gomorrah, towards all the land of the plain, and he saw dense

---

a14 Or *were married to*   *b18* Or *No, Lord; or No, my lord*   *c19* The Hebrew is singular.
d22 Zoar means *small.*

smoke rising from the land, like smoke from a furnace.

²⁹So when God destroyed the cities of the plain, he remembered Abraham, and he brought Lot out of the catastrophe that overthrew the cities where Lot had lived.

Lot and His Daughters

³⁰Lot and his two daughters left Zoar and settled in the mountains, for he was afraid to stay in Zoar. He and his two daughters lived in a cave. ³¹One day the older daughter said to the younger, "Our father is old, and there is no man around here to lie with us, as is the custom all over the earth. ³²Let's get our father to drink wine and then lie with him and preserve our family line through our father."

³³That night they got their father to drink wine, and the older daughter went in and lay with him. He was not aware of it when she lay down or when she got up.

³⁴The next day the older daughter said to the younger, "Last night I lay with my father. Let's get him to drink wine again tonight, and you go in and lie with him so we can preserve our family line through our father." ³⁵So they got their father to drink wine that night also, and the younger daughter went and lay with him. Again he was not aware of it when she lay down or when she got up.

³⁶So both of Lot's daughters became pregnant by their father. ³⁷The older daughter had a son, and she named him Moab;ᵉ he is the father of the Moabites of today. ³⁸The younger daughter also had a son, and she named him Ben-Ammi;ᶠ he is the father of the Ammonites of today.

Abraham and Abimelech

20 Now Abraham moved on from there into the region of the Negev and lived between Kadesh and Shur. For a while he stayed in Gerar, ²and there Abraham said of his wife Sarah, "She is my sister." Then Abimelech king of Gerar sent for Sarah and took her.

³But God came to Abimelech in a dream one night and said to him, "You are as good as dead because of the woman you have taken; she is a married woman."

⁴Now Abimelech had not gone near her, so he said, "Lord, will you destroy an innocent nation? ⁵Did he not say to me, 'She is my sister,' and didn't she also say, 'He is my brother'? I have done this with a clear conscience and clean hands."

⁶Then God said to him in the dream, "Yes, I know you did this with a clear conscience, and so I have kept you from sinning against me. That is why I did not let you touch her. ⁷Now return the man's wife, for he is a prophet, and he will pray for you and you will live. But if you do not return her, you may be sure that you and all yours will die."

⁸Early the next morning Abimelech summoned all his officials, and when he told them all that had happened, they were very much afraid. ⁹Then Abimelech called Abraham in and said, "What have you done to us? How have I wronged you that you have brought such great guilt upon me and my kingdom? You have done things to me that should not be done." ¹⁰And Abimelech asked Abraham, "What was your reason for doing this?"

¹¹Abraham replied, "I said to myself, 'There is surely no fear of God in this place, and they will kill me because of my wife.' ¹²Besides, she really is my sister, the daughter of my father though not of my mother; and she became my wife. ¹³And when God caused me to wander from my father's household, I said to her, 'This is how you can show your love to me: Everywhere we go, say of me, "He is my brother."'"

¹⁴Then Abimelech brought sheep and cattle and male and female slaves and gave them to Abraham, and he returned Sarah his wife to him. ¹⁵And Abimelech said, "My land is before you; live wherever you like."

¹⁶To Sarah he said, "I am giving your brother a thousand shekelsᵃ of silver. This is to cover the offence against you before

---

ᵉ37 *Moab* sounds like the Hebrew for *from father*.   ᶠ38 *Ben-Ammi* means *son of my people*.
ᵃ16 That is, about 25 pounds (about 11.5 kilograms)

all who are with you; you are completely vindicated."

[17]Then Abraham prayed to God, and God healed Abimelech, his wife and his slave girls so they could have children again, [18]for the LORD had closed up every womb in Abimelech's household because of Abraham's wife Sarah.

The Birth of Isaac

21 Now the LORD was gracious to Sarah as he had said, and the LORD did for Sarah what he had promised. [2]Sarah became pregnant and bore a son to Abraham in his old age, at the very time God had promised him. [3]Abraham gave the name Isaac[a] to the son Sarah bore him. [4]When his son Isaac was eight days old, Abraham circumcised him, as God commanded him. [5]Abraham was a hundred years old when his son Isaac was born to him.

[6]Sarah said, "God has brought me laughter, and everyone who hears about this will laugh with me." [7]And she added, "Who would have said to Abraham that Sarah would nurse children? Yet I have borne him a son in his old age."

Hagar and Ishmael Sent Away

[8]The child grew and was weaned, and on the day Isaac was weaned Abraham held a great feast. [9]But Sarah saw that the son whom Hagar the Egyptian had borne to Abraham was mocking, [10]and she said to Abraham, "Get rid of that slave woman and her son, for that slave woman's son will never share in the inheritance with my son Isaac."

[11]The matter distressed Abraham greatly because it concerned his son. [12]But God said to him, "Do not be so distressed about the boy and your maidservant. Listen to whatever Sarah tells you, because it is through Isaac that your offspring[b] will be reckoned. [13]I will make the son of the maidservant into a nation also, because he is your offspring."

[14]Early the next morning Abraham took some food and a skin of water and gave them to Hagar. He set them on her shoulders and then sent her off with the boy. She went on her way and wandered in the desert of Beersheba.

[15]When the water in the skin was gone, she put the boy under one of the bushes. [16]Then she went off and sat down nearby, about a bow-shot away, for she thought, "I cannot watch the boy die." And as she sat there nearby, she[c] began to sob.

[17]God heard the boy crying, and the angel of God called to Hagar from heaven and said to her, "What is the matter, Hagar? Do not be afraid; God has heard the boy crying as he lies there. [18]Lift the boy up and take him by the hand, for I will make him into a great nation."

[19]Then God opened her eyes and she saw a well of water. So she went and filled the skin with water and gave the boy a drink.

[20]God was with the boy as he grew up. He lived in the desert and became an archer. [21]While he was living in the Desert of Paran, his mother got a wife for him from Egypt.

The Treaty at Beersheba

[22]At that time Abimelech and Phicol the commander of his forces said to Abraham, "God is with you in everything you do. [23]Now swear to me here before God that you will not deal falsely with me or my children or my descendants. Show to me and the country where you are living as an alien the same kindness that I have shown to you."

[24]Abraham said, "I swear it."

[25]Then Abraham complained to Abimelech about a well of water that Abimelech's servants had seized. [26]But Abimelech said, "I don't know who has done this. You did not tell me, and I heard about it only today."

[27]So Abraham brought sheep and cattle and gave them to Abimelech, and the two men made a treaty. [28]Abraham set apart seven ewe lambs from the flock, [29]and Abimelech asked Abraham, "What is the

---

[a]3 Isaac means he laughs.   [b]12 Or seed   [c]16 Hebrew; Septuagint the child

meaning of these seven ewe lambs you have set apart by themselves?"

³⁰He replied, "Accept these seven lambs from my hand as a witness that I dug this well."

³¹So that place was called Beersheba,ᵈ because the two men swore an oath there.

³²After the treaty had been made at Beersheba, Abimelech and Phicol the commander of his forces returned to the land of the Philistines. ³³Abraham planted a tamarisk tree in Beersheba, and there he called upon the name of the LORD, the Eternal God. ³⁴And Abraham stayed in the land of the Philistines for a long time.

Abraham Tested

22 Some time later God tested Abraham. He said to him, "Abraham!"

"Here I am," he replied.

²Then God said, "Take your son, your only son, Isaac, whom you love, and go to the region of Moriah. Sacrifice him there as a burnt offering on one of the mountains I will tell you about."

³Early the next morning Abraham got up and saddled his donkey. He took with him two of his servants and his son Isaac. When he had cut enough wood for the burnt offering, he set out for the place God had told him about. ⁴On the third day Abraham looked up and saw the place in the distance. ⁵He said to his servants, "Stay here with the donkey while I and the boy go over there. We will worship and then we will come back to you."

⁶Abraham took the wood for the burnt offering and placed it on his son Isaac, and he himself carried the fire and the knife. As the two of them went on together, ⁷Isaac spoke up and said to his father Abraham, "Father?"

"Yes, my son?" Abraham replied.

"The fire and wood are here," Isaac said, "but where is the lamb for the burnt offering?"

⁸Abraham answered, "God himself will provide the lamb for the burnt offering, my son." And the two of them went on together.

⁹When they reached the place God had told him about, Abraham built an altar there and arranged the wood on it. He bound his son Isaac and laid him on the altar, on top of the wood. ¹⁰Then he reached out his hand and took the knife to slay his son. ¹¹But the angel of the LORD called out to him from heaven, "Abraham! Abraham!"

"Here I am," he replied.

¹²"Do not lay a hand on the boy," he said. "Do not do anything to him. Now I know that you fear God, because you have not withheld from me your son, your only son."

¹³Abraham looked up and there in a thicket he saw a ramᵃ caught by its horns. He went over and took the ram and sacrificed it as a burnt offering instead of his son. ¹⁴So Abraham called that place The LORD Will Provide. And to this day it is said, "On the mountain of the LORD it will be provided."

¹⁵The angel of the LORD called to Abraham from heaven a second time ¹⁶and said, "I swear by myself, declares the LORD, that because you have done this and have not withheld your son, your only son, ¹⁷I will surely bless you and make your descendants as numerous as the stars in the sky and as the sand on the seashore. Your descendants will take possession of the cities of their enemies, ¹⁸and through your offspringᵇ all nations on earth will be blessed, because you have obeyed me."

¹⁹Then Abraham returned to his servants, and they set off together for Beersheba. And Abraham stayed in Beersheba.

Nahor's Sons

²⁰Some time later Abraham was told, "Milcah is also a mother; she has borne sons to your brother Nahor: ²¹Uz the firstborn, Buz his brother, Kemuel (the father of Aram), ²²Kesed, Hazo, Pildash,

---

ᵈ31 *Beersheba* can mean *well of seven* or *well of the oath*.
ᵃ13 Many manuscripts of the Masoretic Text, Samaritan Pentateuch, Septuagint and Syriac; most manuscripts of the Masoretic Text *a ram behind him* ᵇ18 Or *seed*

Jidlaph and Bethuel." [23]Bethuel became the father of Rebekah. Milcah bore these eight sons to Abraham's brother Nahor. [24]His concubine, whose name was Reumah, also had sons: Tebah, Gaham, Tahash and Maacah.

The Death of Sarah

23 Sarah lived to be a hundred and twenty-seven years old. [2]She died at Kiriath Arba (that is, Hebron) in the land of Canaan, and Abraham went to mourn for Sarah and to weep over her.

[3]Then Abraham rose from beside his dead wife and spoke to the Hittites.[a] He said, [4]"I am an alien and a stranger among you. Sell me some property for a burial site here so that I can bury my dead."

[5]The Hittites replied to Abraham, [6]"Sir, listen to us. You are a mighty prince among us. Bury your dead in the choicest of our tombs. None of us will refuse you his tomb for burying your dead."

[7]Then Abraham rose and bowed down before the people of the land, the Hittites. [8]He said to them, "If you are willing to let me bury my dead, then listen to me and intercede with Ephron son of Zohar on my behalf [9]so that he will sell me the cave of Machpelah, which belongs to him and is at the end of his field. Ask him to sell it to me for the full price as a burial site among you."

[10]Ephron the Hittite was sitting among his people and he replied to Abraham in the hearing of all the Hittites who had come to the gate of his city. [11]"No, my lord," he said. "Listen to me; I give[b] you the field, and I give[b] you the cave that is in it. I give[b] it to you in the presence of my people. Bury your dead."

[12]Again Abraham bowed down before the people of the land [13]and he said to Ephron in their hearing, "Listen to me, if you will. I will pay the price of the field. Accept it from me so that I can bury my dead there."

[14]Ephron answered Abraham, [15]"Listen to me, my lord; the land is worth four hundred shekels[c] of silver, but what is that between me and you? Bury your dead."

[16]Abraham agreed to Ephron's terms and weighed out for him the price he had named in the hearing of the Hittites: four hundred shekels of silver, according to the weight current among the merchants.

[17]So Ephron's field in Machpelah near Mamre—both the field and the cave in it, and all the trees within the borders of the field—was legally made over [18]to Abraham as his property in the presence of all the Hittites who had come to the gate of the city. [19]Afterwards Abraham buried his wife Sarah in the cave in the field of Machpelah near Mamre (which is at Hebron) in the land of Canaan. [20]So the field and the cave in it were legally made over to Abraham by the Hittites as a burial site.

Isaac and Rebekah

24 Abraham was now old and well advanced in years, and the LORD had blessed him in every way. [2]He said to the chief[a] servant in his household, the one in charge of all that he had, "Put your hand under my thigh. [3]I want you to swear by the LORD, the God of heaven and the God of earth, that you will not get a wife for my son from the daughters of the Canaanites, among whom I am living, [4]but will go to my country and my own relatives and get a wife for my son Isaac."

[5]The servant asked him, "What if the woman is unwilling to come back with me to this land? Shall I then take your son back to the country you came from?"

[6]"Make sure that you do not take my son back there," Abraham said. [7]"The LORD, the God of heaven, who brought me out of my father's household and my native land and who spoke to me and promised me on oath, saying, 'To your offspring[b] I will give this land'—he will send his angel before you so that you can get a wife for my son from there. [8]If the woman is unwilling to come back with you, then you will be released from this

---

[a]3 Or the sons of Heth; also in verses 5, 7, 10, 16, 18 and 20
[c]15 That is, about 10 pounds (about 4.5 kilograms)
[a]2 Or oldest　　[b]7 Or seed

[b]11 Or sell

oath of mine. Only do not take my son back there." ⁹So the servant put his hand under the thigh of his master Abraham and swore an oath to him concerning this matter.

¹⁰Then the servant took ten of his master's camels and left, taking with him all kinds of good things from his master. He set out for Aram Naharaim*c* and made his way to the town of Nahor. ¹¹He made the camels kneel down near the well outside the town; it was towards evening, the time the women go out to draw water.

¹²Then he prayed, "O LORD, God of my master Abraham, give me success today, and show kindness to my master Abraham. ¹³See, I am standing beside this spring, and the daughters of the townspeople are coming out to draw water. ¹⁴May it be that when I say to a girl, 'Please let down your jar that I may have a drink,' and she says, 'Drink, and I'll water your camels too'—let her be the one you have chosen for your servant Isaac. By this I will know that you have shown kindness to my master."

¹⁵Before he had finished praying, Rebekah came out with her jar on her shoulder. She was the daughter of Bethuel son of Milcah, who was the wife of Abraham's brother Nahor. ¹⁶The girl was very beautiful, a virgin; no man had ever lain with her. She went down to the spring, filled her jar and came up again.

¹⁷The servant hurried to meet her and said, "Please give me a little water from your jar."

¹⁸"Drink, my lord," she said, and quickly lowered the jar to her hands and gave him a drink.

¹⁹After she had given him a drink, she said, "I'll draw water for your camels too, until they have finished drinking." ²⁰So she quickly emptied her jar into the trough, ran back to the well to draw more water, and drew enough for all his camels. ²¹Without saying a word, the man watched her closely to learn whether or not the LORD had made his journey successful.

²²When the camels had finished drinking, the man took out a gold nose ring weighing a beka*d* and two gold bracelets weighing ten shekels.*e* ²³Then he asked, "Whose daughter are you? Please tell me, is there room in your father's house for us to spend the night?"

²⁴She answered him, "I am the daughter of Bethuel, the son that Milcah bore to Nahor." ²⁵And she added, "We have plenty of straw and fodder, as well as room for you to spend the night."

²⁶Then the man bowed down and worshipped the LORD, ²⁷saying, "Praise be to the LORD, the God of my master Abraham, who has not abandoned his kindness and faithfulness to my master. As for me, the LORD has led me on the journey to the house of my master's relatives."

²⁸The girl ran and told her mother's household about these things. ²⁹Now Rebekah had a brother named Laban, and he hurried out to the man at the spring. ³⁰As soon as he had seen the nose ring, and the bracelets on his sister's arms, and had heard Rebekah tell what the man said to her, he went out to the man and found him standing by the camels near the spring. ³¹"Come, you who are blessed by the LORD," he said. "Why are you standing out here? I have prepared the house and a place for the camels."

³²So the man went to the house, and the camels were unloaded. Straw and fodder were brought for the camels, and water for him and his men to wash their feet. ³³Then food was set before him, but he said, "I will not eat until I have told you what I have to say."

"Then tell us," ˌLabanˌ said.

³⁴So he said, "I am Abraham's servant. ³⁵The LORD has blessed my master abundantly, and he has become wealthy. He has given him sheep and cattle, silver and gold, menservants and maidservants, and camels and donkeys. ³⁶My master's wife Sarah has borne him a son in her*f* old age, and he has given him everything he owns. ³⁷And my master made me swear an oath, and said, 'You must not get a wife for my son from the daughters of the Canaanites,

*c*10 That is, North-west Mesopotamia   *d*22 That is, about ⅓ ounce (about 6 grams)
*e*22 That is, about 4 ounces (about 115 grams)   *f*36 Or *his*

in whose land I live, [38]but go to my father's family and to my own clan, and get a wife for my son.'

[39]"Then I asked my master, 'What if the woman will not come back with me?'

[40]"He replied, 'The LORD, before whom I have walked, will send his angel with you and make your journey a success, so that you can get a wife for my son from my own clan and from my father's family. [41]Then, when you go to my clan, you will be released from my oath even if they refuse to give her to you—you will be released from my oath.'

[42]"When I came to the spring today, I said, 'O LORD, God of my master Abraham, if you will, please grant success to the journey on which I have come. [43]See, I am standing beside this spring; if a maiden comes out to draw water and I say to her, "Please let me drink a little water from your jar," [44]and if she says to me, "Drink, and I'll draw water for your camels too," let her be the one the LORD has chosen for my master's son.'

[45]"Before I finished praying in my heart, Rebekah came out, with her jar on her shoulder. She went down to the spring and drew water, and I said to her, 'Please give me a drink.'

[46]"She quickly lowered her jar from her shoulder and said, 'Drink, and I'll water your camels too.' So I drank, and she watered the camels also.

[47]"I asked her, 'Whose daughter are you?'

"She said, 'The daughter of Bethuel son of Nahor, whom Milcah bore to him.'

"Then I put the ring in her nose and the bracelets on her arms, [48]and I bowed down and worshipped the LORD. I praised the LORD, the God of my master Abraham, who had led me on the right road to get the granddaughter of my master's brother for his son. [49]Now if you will show kindness and faithfulness to my master, tell me; and if not, tell me, so I may know which way to turn."

[50]Laban and Bethuel answered, "This is from the LORD; we can say nothing to you one way or the other. [51]Here is Rebekah;

take her and go, and let her become the wife of your master's son, as the LORD has directed."

[52]When Abraham's servant heard what they said, he bowed down to the ground before the LORD. [53]Then the servant brought out gold and silver jewellery and articles of clothing and gave them to Rebekah; he also gave costly gifts to her brother and to her mother. [54]Then he and the men who were with him ate and drank and spent the night there.

When they got up the next morning, he said, "Send me on my way to my master."

[55]But her brother and her mother replied, "Let the girl remain with us ten days or so; then you[g] may go."

[56]But he said to them, "Do not detain me, now that the LORD has granted success to my journey. Send me on my way so I may go to my master."

[57]Then they said, "Let's call the girl and ask her about it." [58]So they called Rebekah and asked her, "Will you go with this man?"

"I will go," she said.

[59]So they sent their sister Rebekah on her way, along with her nurse and Abraham's servant and his men. [60]And they blessed Rebekah and said to her,

"Our sister, may you increase
    to thousands upon thousands;
may your offspring possess
    the gates of their enemies."

[61]Then Rebekah and her maids got ready and mounted their camels and went back with the man. So the servant took Rebekah and left.

[62]Now Isaac had come from Beer Lahai Roi, for he was living in the Negev. [63]He went out to the field one evening to meditate,[h] and as he looked up, he saw camels approaching. [64]Rebekah also looked up and saw Isaac. She got down from her camel [65]and asked the servant, "Who is that man in the field coming to meet us?"

"He is my master," the servant answered. So she took her veil and covered herself.

66Then the servant told Isaac all he had done. 67Isaac brought her into the tent of his mother Sarah, and he married Rebekah. So she became his wife, and he loved her; and Isaac was comforted after his mother's death.

The Death of Abraham

25 Abraham took*a* another wife, whose name was Keturah. 2She bore him Zimran, Jokshan, Medan, Midian, Ishbak and Shuah. 3Jokshan was the father of Sheba and Dedan; the descendants of Dedan were the Asshurites, the Letushites and the Leummites. 4The sons of Midian were Ephah, Epher, Hanoch, Abida and Eldaah. All these were descendants of Keturah.

5Abraham left everything he owned to Isaac. 6But while he was still living, he gave gifts to the sons of his concubines and sent them away from his son Isaac to the land of the east.

7Altogether, Abraham lived a hundred and seventy-five years. 8Then Abraham breathed his last and died at a good old age, an old man and full of years; and he was gathered to his people. 9His sons Isaac and Ishmael buried him in the cave of Machpelah near Mamre, in the field of Ephron son of Zohar the Hittite, 10the field Abraham had bought from the Hittites.*b* There Abraham was buried with his wife Sarah. 11After Abraham's death, God blessed his son Isaac, who then lived near Beer Lahai Roi.

Ishmael's Sons

12This is the account of Abraham's son Ishmael, whom Sarah's maidservant, Hagar the Egyptian, bore to Abraham.

13These are the names of the sons of Ishmael, listed in the order of their birth: Nebaioth the firstborn of Ishmael, Kedar, Adbeel, Mibsam, 14Mishma, Dumah, Massa, 15Hadad, Tema, Jetur, Naphish and Kedemah. 16These were the sons of

Ishmael, and these are the names of the twelve tribal rulers according to their settlements and camps. 17Altogether, Ishmael lived a hundred and thirty-seven years. He breathed his last and died, and he was gathered to his people. 18His descendants settled in the area from Havilah to Shur, near the border of Egypt, as you go towards Asshur. And they lived in hostility towards*c* all their brothers.

Jacob and Esau

19This is the account of Abraham's son Isaac.

Abraham became the father of Isaac, 20and Isaac was forty years old when he married Rebekah daughter of Bethuel the Aramean from Paddan Aram*d* and sister of Laban the Aramean.

21Isaac prayed to the LORD on behalf of his wife, because she was barren. The LORD answered his prayer, and his wife Rebekah became pregnant. 22The babies jostled each other within her, and she said, "Why is this happening to me?" So she went to enquire of the LORD.

23The LORD said to her,

"Two nations are in your womb,
    and two peoples from within you will
        be separated;
one people will be stronger than the
        other,
    and the older will serve the younger."

24When the time came for her to give birth, there were twin boys in her womb. 25The first to come out was red, and his whole body was like a hairy garment; so they named him Esau.*e* 26After this, his brother came out, with his hand grasping Esau's heel; so he was named Jacob.*f* Isaac was sixty years old when Rebekah gave birth to them.

27The boys grew up, and Esau became a skilful hunter, a man of the open country, while Jacob was a quiet man, staying

a1 Or had taken   b10 Or the sons of Heth   c18 Or lived to the east of
d20 That is, North-west Mesopotamia
e25 Esau may mean hairy; he was also called Edom, which means red.
f26 Jacob means he grasps the heel (figuratively, he deceives).

among the tents. [28]Isaac, who had a taste for wild game, loved Esau, but Rebekah loved Jacob.

[29]Once when Jacob was cooking some stew, Esau came in from the open country, famished. [30]He said to Jacob, "Quick, let me have some of that red stew! I'm famished!" (That is why he was also called Edom.[g])

[31]Jacob replied, "First sell me your birthright."

[32]"Look, I am about to die," Esau said. "What good is the birthright to me?"

[33]But Jacob said, "Swear to me first." So he swore an oath to him, selling his birthright to Jacob.

[34]Then Jacob gave Esau some bread and some lentil stew. He ate and drank, and then got up and left.

So Esau despised his birthright.

Isaac and Abimelech

26 Now there was a famine in the land—besides the earlier famine of Abraham's time—and Isaac went to Abimelech king of the Philistines in Gerar. [2]The LORD appeared to Isaac and said, "Do not go down to Egypt; live in the land where I tell you to live. [3]Stay in this land for a while, and I will be with you and will bless you. For to you and your descendants I will give all these lands and will confirm the oath I swore to your father Abraham. [4]I will make your descendants as numerous as the stars in the sky and will give them all these lands, and through your offspring[a] all nations on earth will be blessed, [5]because Abraham obeyed me and kept my requirements, my commands, my decrees and my laws." [6]So Isaac stayed in Gerar.

[7]When the men of that place asked him about his wife, he said, "She is my sister," because he was afraid to say, "She is my wife." He thought, "The men of this place might kill me on account of Rebekah, because she is beautiful."

[8]When Isaac had been there a long time, Abimelech king of the Philistines looked down from a window and saw Isaac caressing his wife Rebekah. [9]So Abimelech summoned Isaac and said, "She is really your wife! Why did you say, 'She is my sister'?"

Isaac answered him, "Because I thought I might lose my life on account of her."

[10]Then Abimelech said, "What is this you have done to us? One of the men might well have slept with your wife, and you would have brought guilt upon us."

[11]So Abimelech gave orders to all the people: "Anyone who molests this man or his wife shall surely be put to death."

[12]Isaac planted crops in that land and the same year reaped a hundredfold, because the LORD blessed him. [13]The man became rich, and his wealth continued to grow until he became very wealthy. [14]He had so many flocks and herds and servants that the Philistines envied him. [15]So all the wells that his father's servants had dug in the time of his father Abraham, the Philistines stopped up, filling them with earth.

[16]Then Abimelech said to Isaac, "Move away from us; you have become too powerful for us."

[17]So Isaac moved away from there and encamped in the Valley of Gerar and settled there. [18]Isaac reopened the wells that had been dug in the time of his father Abraham, which the Philistines had stopped up after Abraham died, and he gave them the same names his father had given them.

[19]Isaac's servants dug in the valley and discovered a well of fresh water there. [20]But the herdsmen of Gerar quarrelled with Isaac's herdsmen and said, "The water is ours!" So he named the well Esek,[b] because they disputed with him. [21]Then they dug another well, but they quarrelled over that one also; so he named it Sitnah.[c] [22]He moved on from there and dug another well, and no-one quarrelled over it. He named it Rehoboth,[d] saying, "Now the LORD has given us room and we will flourish in the land."

[23]From there he went up to Beersheba. [24]That night the LORD appeared to him and said, "I am the God of your father

---

[g]30 *Edom* means *red.*
[a]4 Or *seed.*   [b]20 *Esek* means *dispute.*   [c]21 *Sitnah* means *opposition.*   [d]22 *Rehoboth* means *room.*

Abraham. Do not be afraid, for I am with you; I will bless you and will increase the number of your descendants for the sake of my servant Abraham."

25Isaac built an altar there and called on the name of the LORD. There he pitched his tent, and there his servants dug a well.

26Meanwhile, Abimelech had come to him from Gerar, with Ahuzzath his personal adviser and Phicol the commander of his forces. 27Isaac asked them, "Why have you come to me, since you were hostile to me and sent me away?"

28They answered, "We saw clearly that the LORD was with you; so we said, 'There ought to be a sworn agreement between us'—between us and you. Let us make a treaty with you 29that you will do us no harm, just as we did not molest you but always treated you well and sent you away in peace. And now you are blessed by the LORD."

30Isaac then made a feast for them, and they ate and drank. 31Early the next morning the men swore an oath to each other. Then Isaac sent them on their way, and they left him in peace.

32That day Isaac's servants came and told him about the well they had dug. They said, "We've found water!" 33He called it Shibah,e and to this day the name of the town has been Beersheba.f

34When Esau was forty years old, he married Judith daughter of Beeri the Hittite, and also Basemath daughter of Elon the Hittite. 35They were a source of grief to Isaac and Rebekah.

Jacob Gets Isaac's Blessing

27 When Isaac was old and his eyes were so weak that he could no longer see, he called for Esau his older son and said to him, "My son."

"Here I am," he answered.

2Isaac said, "I am now an old man and don't know the day of my death. 3Now then, get your weapons—your quiver and bow—and go out to the open country to hunt some wild game for me. 4Prepare me the kind of tasty food I like and bring it to

me to eat, so that I may give you my blessing before I die."

5Now Rebekah was listening as Isaac spoke to his son Esau. When Esau left for the open country to hunt game and bring it back, 6Rebekah said to her son Jacob, "Look, I overheard your father say to your brother Esau, 7'Bring me some game and prepare me some tasty food to eat, so that I may give you my blessing in the presence of the LORD before I die.' 8Now, my son, listen carefully and do what I tell you: 9Go out to the flock and bring me two choice young goats, so that I can prepare some tasty food for your father, just the way he likes it. 10Then take it to your father to eat, so that he may give you his blessing before he dies."

11Jacob said to Rebekah his mother, "But my brother Esau is a hairy man, and I'm a man with smooth skin. 12What if my father touches me? I would appear to be tricking him and would bring down a curse on myself rather than a blessing."

13His mother said to him, "My son, let the curse fall on me. Just do what I say; go and get them for me."

14So he went and got them and brought them to his mother, and she prepared some tasty food, just the way his father liked it. 15Then Rebekah took the best clothes of Esau her older son, which she had in the house, and put them on her younger son Jacob. 16She also covered his hands and the smooth part of his neck with the goatskins. 17Then she handed to her son Jacob the tasty food and the bread she had made.

18He went to his father and said, "My father."

"Yes, my son," he answered. "Who is it?"

19Jacob said to his father, "I am Esau your firstborn. I have done as you told me. Please sit up and eat some of my game so that you may give me your blessing."

20Isaac asked his son, "How did you find it so quickly, my son?"

"The LORD your God gave me success," he replied.

---

e33 *Shibah* can mean *oath* or *seven.*   f33 *Beersheba* can mean *well of the oath* or *well of seven.*

²¹Then Isaac said to Jacob, "Come near so I can touch you, my son, to know whether you really are my son Esau or not."

²²Jacob went close to his father Isaac, who touched him and said, "The voice is the voice of Jacob, but the hands are the hands of Esau." ²³He did not recognise him, for his hands were hairy like those of his brother Esau; so he blessed him. ²⁴"Are you really my son Esau?" he asked.

"I am," he replied.

²⁵Then he said, "My son, bring me some of your game to eat, so that I may give you my blessing."

Jacob brought it to him and he ate; and he brought some wine and he drank. ²⁶Then his father Isaac said to him, "Come here, my son, and kiss me."

²⁷So he went to him and kissed him. When Isaac caught the smell of his clothes, he blessed him and said,

"Ah, the smell of my son
  is like the smell of a field
  that the LORD has blessed.
²⁸May God give you of heaven's dew
  and of earth's richness—
  an abundance of grain and new wine.
²⁹May nations serve you
  and peoples bow down to you.
Be lord over your brothers,
  and may the sons of your mother bow
    down to you.
May those who curse you be cursed
  and those who bless you be blessed."

³⁰After Isaac finished blessing him and Jacob had scarcely left his father's presence, his brother Esau came in from hunting. ³¹He too prepared some tasty food and brought it to his father. Then he said to him, "My father, sit up and eat some of my game, so that you may give me your blessing."

³²His father Isaac asked him, "Who are you?"

"I am your son," he answered, "your firstborn, Esau."

³³Isaac trembled violently and said,

"Who was it, then, that hunted game and brought it to me? I ate it just before you came and I blessed him—and indeed he will be blessed!"

³⁴When Esau heard his father's words, he burst out with a loud and bitter cry and said to his father, "Bless me—me too, my father!"

³⁵But he said, "Your brother came deceitfully and took your blessing."

³⁶Esau said, "Isn't he rightly named Jacob?ᵃ He has deceived me these two times: He took my birthright, and now he's taken my blessing!" Then he asked, "Haven't you reserved any blessing for me?"

³⁷Isaac answered Esau, "I have made him lord over you and have made all his relatives his servants, and I have sustained him with grain and new wine. So what can I possibly do for you, my son?"

³⁸Esau said to his father, "Do you have only one blessing, my father? Bless me too, my father!" Then Esau wept aloud.

³⁹His father Isaac answered him,

"Your dwelling will be
  away from the earth's richness,
  away from the dew of heaven above.
⁴⁰You will live by the sword
  and you will serve your brother.
But when you grow restless,
  you will throw his yoke
  from off your neck."

Jacob Flees to Laban

⁴¹Esau held a grudge against Jacob because of the blessing his father had given him. He said to himself, "The days of mourning for my father are near; then I will kill my brother Jacob."

⁴²When Rebekah was told what her older son Esau had said, she sent for her younger son Jacob and said to him, "Your brother Esau is consoling himself with the thought of killing you. ⁴³Now then, my son, do what I say: Flee at once to my brother Laban in Haran. ⁴⁴Stay with him for a while until your brother's fury subsides. ⁴⁵When your brother is no longer

---

ᵃ36 *Jacob* means *he grasps the heel* (figuratively, *he deceives*).

angry with you and forgets what you did to him, I'll send word for you to come back from there. Why should I lose both of you in one day?"

⁴⁶Then Rebekah said to Isaac, "I'm disgusted with living because of these Hittite women. If Jacob takes a wife from among the women of this land, from Hittite women like these, my life will not be worth living."

28 So Isaac called for Jacob and blessed*ᵃ* him and commanded him: "Do not marry a Canaanite woman. ²Go at once to Paddan Aram,*ᵇ* to the house of your mother's father Bethuel. Take a wife for yourself there, from among the daughters of Laban, your mother's brother. ³May God Almighty*ᶜ* bless you and make you fruitful and increase your numbers until you become a community of peoples. ⁴May he give you and your descendants the blessing given to Abraham, so that you may take possession of the land where you now live as an alien, the land God gave to Abraham." ⁵Then Isaac sent Jacob on his way, and he went to Paddan Aram, to Laban son of Bethuel the Aramean, the brother of Rebekah, who was the mother of Jacob and Esau.

⁶Now Esau learned that Isaac had blessed Jacob and had sent him to Paddan Aram to take a wife from there, and that when he blessed him he commanded him, "Do not marry a Canaanite woman," ⁷and that Jacob had obeyed his father and mother and had gone to Paddan Aram. ⁸Esau then realised how displeasing the Canaanite women were to his father Isaac; ⁹so he went to Ishmael and married Mahalath, the sister of Nebaioth and daughter of Ishmael son of Abraham, in addition to the wives he already had.

Jacob's Dream at Bethel

¹⁰Jacob left Beersheba and set out for Haran. ¹¹When he reached a certain place, he stopped for the night because the sun had set. Taking one of the stones there, he put it under his head and lay down to sleep. ¹²He had a dream in which he saw a stairway*ᵈ* resting on the earth, with its top reaching to heaven, and the angels of God were ascending and descending on it. ¹³There above it*ᵉ* stood the Lord, and he said: "I am the Lord, the God of your father Abraham and the God of Isaac. I will give you and your descendants the land on which you are lying. ¹⁴Your descendants will be like the dust of the earth, and you will spread out to the west and to the east, to the north and to the south. All peoples on earth will be blessed through you and your offspring. ¹⁵I am with you and will watch over you wherever you go, and I will bring you back to this land. I will not leave you until I have done what I have promised you."

¹⁶When Jacob awoke from his sleep, he thought, "Surely the Lord is in this place, and I was not aware of it." ¹⁷He was afraid and said, "How awesome is this place! This is none other than the house of God; this is the gate of heaven."

¹⁸Early the next morning Jacob took the stone he had placed under his head and set it up as a pillar and poured oil on top of it. ¹⁹He called that place Bethel,*ᶠ* though the city used to be called Luz.

²⁰Then Jacob made a vow, saying, "If God will be with me and will watch over me on this journey I am taking and will give me food to eat and clothes to wear ²¹so that I return safely to my father's house, then the Lord*ᵍ* will be my God ²²and*ʰ* this stone that I have set up as a pillar will be God's house, and of all that you give me I will give you a tenth."

Jacob Arrives in Paddan Aram

29 Then Jacob continued on his journey and came to the land of the eastern peoples. ²There he saw a well in the field, with three flocks of sheep lying near it because the flocks were watered from that well. The stone over the mouth of the well was large. ³When all the flocks

---

ᵃ1 Or *greeted*   *ᵇ2* That is, North-west Mesopotamia; also in verses 5, 6 and 7   *ᶜ3* Hebrew *El-Shaddai*
ᵈ12 Or *ladder*   *ᵉ13* Or *There beside him*   *ᶠ19* *Bethel* means *house of God.*
ᵍ20,21 Or *Since God . . . father's house, the* Lord   *ʰ21,22* Or *house, and the* Lord *will be my God,* ²²*then*

were gathered there, the shepherds would roll the stone away from the well's mouth and water the sheep. Then they would return the stone to its place over the mouth of the well.

4Jacob asked the shepherds, "My brothers, where are you from?"

"We're from Haran," they replied.

5He said to them, "Do you know Laban, Nahor's grandson?"

"Yes, we know him," they answered.

6Then Jacob asked them, "Is he well?"

"Yes, he is," they said, "and here comes his daughter Rachel with the sheep."

7"Look," he said, "the sun is still high; it is not time for the flocks to be gathered. Water the sheep and take them back to pasture."

8"We can't," they replied, "until all the flocks are gathered and the stone has been rolled away from the mouth of the well. Then we will water the sheep."

9While he was still talking with them, Rachel came with her father's sheep, for she was a shepherdess. 10When Jacob saw Rachel daughter of Laban, his mother's brother, and Laban's sheep, he went over and rolled the stone away from the mouth of the well and watered his uncle's sheep. 11Then Jacob kissed Rachel and began to weep aloud. 12He had told Rachel that he was a relative of her father and a son of Rebekah. So she ran and told her father.

13As soon as Laban heard the news about Jacob, his sister's son, he hurried to meet him. He embraced him and kissed him and brought him to his home, and there Jacob told him all these things. 14Then Laban said to him, "You are my own flesh and blood."

Jacob Marries Leah and Rachel

After Jacob had stayed with him for a whole month, 15Laban said to him, "Just because you are a relative of mine, should you work for me for nothing? Tell me what your wages should be."

16Now Laban had two daughters; the name of the older was Leah, and the name of the younger was Rachel. 17Leah had weak*a* eyes, but Rachel was lovely in form, and beautiful. 18Jacob was in love with Rachel and said, "I'll work for you seven years in return for your younger daughter Rachel."

19Laban said, "It's better that I give her to you than to some other man. Stay here with me." 20So Jacob served seven years to get Rachel, but they seemed like only a few days to him because of his love for her.

21Then Jacob said to Laban, "Give me my wife. My time is completed, and I want to lie with her."

22So Laban brought together all the people of the place and gave a feast. 23But when evening came, he took his daughter Leah and gave her to Jacob, and Jacob lay with her. 24And Laban gave his servant girl Zilpah to his daughter as her maidservant.

25When morning came, there was Leah! So Jacob said to Laban, "What is this you have done to me? I served you for Rachel, didn't I? Why have you deceived me?"

26Laban replied, "It is not our custom here to give the younger daughter in marriage before the older one. 27Finish this daughter's bridal week; then we will give you the younger one also, in return for another seven years of work."

28And Jacob did so. He finished the week with Leah, and then Laban gave him his daughter Rachel to be his wife. 29Laban gave his servant girl Bilhah to his daughter Rachel as her maidservant. 30Jacob lay with Rachel also, and he loved Rachel more than Leah. And he worked for Laban another seven years.

Jacob's Children

31When the LORD saw that Leah was not loved, he opened her womb, but Rachel was barren. 32Leah became pregnant and gave birth to a son. She named him Reuben,*b* for she said, "It is because the

---

a17 Or delicate
b32 Reuben *sounds like the Hebrew for* he has seen my misery; *the name means* see, a son.

LORD has seen my misery. Surely my husband will love me now."

33She conceived again, and when she gave birth to a son she said, "Because the LORD heard that I am not loved, he gave me this one too." So she named him Simeon.c

34Again she conceived, and when she gave birth to a son she said, "Now at last my husband will become attached to me, because I have borne him three sons." So he was named Levi.d

35She conceived again, and when she gave birth to a son she said, "This time I will praise the LORD." So she named him Judah.e Then she stopped having children.

30 When Rachel saw that she was not bearing Jacob any children, she became jealous of her sister. So she said to Jacob, "Give me children, or I'll die!"

2Jacob became angry with her and said, "Am I in the place of God, who has kept you from having children?"

3Then she said, "Here is Bilhah, my maidservant. Sleep with her so that she can bear children for me and that through her I too can build a family."

4So she gave him her servant Bilhah as a wife. Jacob slept with her, 5and she became pregnant and bore him a son. 6Then Rachel said, "God has vindicated me; he has listened to my plea and given me a son." Because of this she named him Dan.a

7Rachel's servant Bilhah conceived again and bore Jacob a second son. 8Then Rachel said, "I have had a great struggle with my sister, and I have won." So she named him Naphtali.b

9When Leah saw that she had stopped having children, she took her maidservant Zilpah and gave her to Jacob as a wife. 10Leah's servant Zilpah bore Jacob a son.

11Then Leah said, "What good fortune!"c So she named him Gad.d

12Leah's servant Zilpah bore Jacob a second son. 13Then Leah said, "How happy I am! The women will call me happy." So she named him Asher.e

14During wheat harvest, Reuben went out into the fields and found some mandrake plants, which he brought to his mother Leah. Rachel said to Leah, "Please give me some of your son's mandrakes."

15But she said to her, "Wasn't it enough that you took away my husband? Will you take my son's mandrakes too?"

"Very well," Rachel said, "he can sleep with you tonight in return for your son's mandrakes."

16So when Jacob came in from the fields that evening, Leah went out to meet him. "You must sleep with me," she said. "I have hired you with my son's mandrakes." So he slept with her that night.

17God listened to Leah, and she became pregnant and bore Jacob a fifth son. 18Then Leah said, "God has rewarded me for giving my maidservant to my husband." So she named him Issachar.f

19Leah conceived again and bore Jacob a sixth son. 20Then Leah said, "God has presented me with a precious gift. This time my husband will treat me with honour, because I have borne him six sons." So she named him Zebulun.g

21Some time later she gave birth to a daughter and named her Dinah.

22Then God remembered Rachel; he listened to her and opened her womb. 23She became pregnant and gave birth to a son and said, "God has taken away my disgrace." 24She named him Joseph,h and said, "May the LORD add to me another son."

---

c33 Simeon probably means one who hears.
d34 Levi sounds like and may be derived from the Hebrew for attached.
e35 Judah sounds like and may be derived from the Hebrew for praise.
a6 Dan here means he has vindicated.   b8 Naphtali means my struggle.
c11 Or "A troop is coming!"   d11 Gad can mean good fortune or a troop.   e13 Asher means happy.
f18 Issachar sounds like the Hebrew for reward.   g20 Zebulun probably means honour.
h24 Joseph means may he add.

Jacob's Flocks Increase

25After Rachel gave birth to Joseph, Jacob said to Laban, "Send me on my way so that I can go back to my own homeland. 26Give me my wives and children, for whom I have served you, and I will be on my way. You know how much work I've done for you."

27But Laban said to him, "If I have found favour in your eyes, please stay. I have learned by divination that*i* the LORD has blessed me because of you." 28He added, "Name your wages, and I will pay them."

29Jacob said to him, "You know how I have worked for you and how your livestock has fared under my care. 30The little you had before I came has increased greatly, and the LORD has blessed you wherever I have been. But now, when may I do something for my own household?"

31"What shall I give you?" he asked.

"Don't give me anything," Jacob replied. "But if you will do this one thing for me, I will go on tending your flocks and watching over them: 32Let me go through all your flocks today and remove from them every speckled or spotted sheep, every dark-coloured lamb and every spotted or speckled goat. They will be my wages. 33And my honesty will testify for me in the future, whenever you check on the wages you have paid me. Any goat in my possession that is not speckled or spotted, or any lamb that is not dark-coloured, will be considered stolen."

34"Agreed," said Laban. "Let it be as you have said." 35That same day he removed all the male goats that were streaked or spotted, and all the speckled or spotted female goats (all that had white on them) and all the dark-coloured lambs, and he placed them in the care of his sons. 36Then he put a three-day journey between himself and Jacob, while Jacob continued to tend the rest of Laban's flocks.

37Jacob, however, took fresh-cut branches from poplar, almond and plane trees and made white stripes on them by peeling the bark and exposing the white inner wood of the branches. 38Then he placed the peeled branches in all the watering troughs, so that they would be directly in front of the flocks when they came to drink. When the flocks were in heat and came to drink, 39they mated in front of the branches. And they bore young that were streaked or speckled or spotted. 40Jacob set apart the young of the flock by themselves, but made the rest face the streaked and dark-coloured animals that belonged to Laban. Thus he made separate flocks for himself and did not put them with Laban's animals. 41Whenever the stronger females were in heat, Jacob would place the branches in the troughs in front of the animals so that they would mate near the branches, 42but if the animals were weak, he would not place them there. So the weak animals went to Laban and the strong ones to Jacob. 43In this way the man grew exceedingly prosperous and came to own large flocks, and maidservants and menservants, and camels and donkeys.

Jacob Flees From Laban

31 Jacob heard that Laban's sons were saying, "Jacob has taken everything our father owned and has gained all this wealth from what belonged to our father." 2And Jacob noticed that Laban's attitude towards him was not what it had been.

3Then the LORD said to Jacob, "Go back to the land of your fathers and to your relatives, and I will be with you."

4So Jacob sent word to Rachel and Leah to come out to the fields where his flocks were. 5He said to them, "I see that your father's attitude towards me is not what it was before, but the God of my father has been with me. 6You know that I've worked for your father with all my strength, 7yet your father has cheated me by changing my wages ten times. However, God has not allowed him to harm me. 8If he said, 'The speckled ones will be your

---

i27 Or possibly have become rich and

wages,' then all the flocks gave birth to speckled young; and if he said, 'The streaked ones will be your wages,' then all the flocks bore streaked young. ⁹So God has taken away your father's livestock and has given them to me.

¹⁰"In the breeding season I once had a dream in which I looked up and saw that the male goats mating with the flock were streaked, speckled or spotted. ¹¹The angel of God said to me in the dream, 'Jacob.' I answered, 'Here I am.' ¹²And he said, 'Look up and see that all the male goats mating with the flock are streaked, speckled or spotted, for I have seen all that Laban has been doing to you. ¹³I am the God of Bethel, where you anointed a pillar and where you made a vow to me. Now leave this land at once and go back to your native land.'"

¹⁴Then Rachel and Leah replied, "Do we still have any share in the inheritance of our father's estate? ¹⁵Does he not regard us as foreigners? Not only has he sold us, but he has used up what was paid for us. ¹⁶Surely all the wealth that God took away from our father belongs to us and our children. So do whatever God has told you."

¹⁷Then Jacob put his children and his wives on camels, ¹⁸and he drove all his livestock ahead of him, along with all the goods he had accumulated in Paddan Aram,ᵃ to go to his father Isaac in the land of Canaan.

¹⁹When Laban had gone to shear his sheep, Rachel stole her father's household gods. ²⁰Moreover, Jacob deceived Laban the Aramean by not telling him he was running away. ²¹So he fled with all he had, and crossing the River,ᵇ he headed for the hill country of Gilead.

Laban Pursues Jacob

²²On the third day Laban was told that Jacob had fled. ²³Taking his relatives with him, he pursued Jacob for seven days and caught up with him in the hill country of Gilead. ²⁴Then God came to Laban the Aramean in a dream at night and said to him, "Be careful not to say anything to Jacob, either good or bad."

²⁵Jacob had pitched his tent in the hill country of Gilead when Laban overtook him, and Laban and his relatives camped there too. ²⁶Then Laban said to Jacob, "What have you done? You've deceived me, and you've carried off my daughters like captives in war. ²⁷Why did you run off secretly and deceive me? Why didn't you tell me, so that I could send you away with joy and singing to the music of tambourines and harps? ²⁸You didn't even let me kiss my grandchildren and my daughters good-bye. You have done a foolish thing. ²⁹I have the power to harm you; but last night the God of your father said to me, 'Be careful not to say anything to Jacob, either good or bad.' ³⁰Now you have gone off because you longed to return to your father's house. But why did you steal my gods?"

³¹Jacob answered Laban, "I was afraid, because I thought you would take your daughters away from me by force. ³²But if you find anyone who has your gods, he shall not live. In the presence of our relatives, see for yourself whether there is anything of yours here with me; and if so, take it." Now Jacob did not know that Rachel had stolen the gods.

³³So Laban went into Jacob's tent and into Leah's tent and into the tent of the two maidservants, but he found nothing. After he came out of Leah's tent, he entered Rachel's tent. ³⁴Now Rachel had taken the household gods and put them inside her camel's saddle and was sitting on them. Laban searched through everything in the tent but found nothing.

³⁵Rachel said to her father, "Don't be angry, my lord, that I cannot stand up in your presence; I'm having my period." So he searched but could not find the household gods.

³⁶Jacob was angry and took Laban to task. "What is my crime?" he asked Laban. "What sin have I committed that

---

ᵃ18 That is, North-west Mesopotamia   ᵇ21 That is, the Euphrates you hunt me down? [37]Now that you have searched through all my goods, what have you found that belongs to your household? Put it here in front of your relatives and mine, and let them judge between the two of us.

[38]"I have been with you for twenty years now. Your sheep and goats have not miscarried, nor have I eaten rams from your flocks. [39]I did not bring you animals torn by wild beasts; I bore the loss myself. And you demanded payment from me for whatever was stolen by day or night. [40]This was my situation: The heat consumed me in the daytime and the cold at night, and sleep fled from my eyes. [41]It was like this for the twenty years I was in your household. I worked for you fourteen years for your two daughters and six years for your flocks, and you changed my wages ten times. [42]If the God of my father, the God of Abraham and the Fear of Isaac, had not been with me, you would surely have sent me away empty-handed. But God has seen my hardship and the toil of my hands, and last night he rebuked you."

[43]Laban answered Jacob, "The women are my daughters, the children are my children, and the flocks are my flocks. All you see is mine. Yet what can I do today about these daughters of mine, or about the children they have borne? [44]Come now, let's make a covenant, you and I, and let it serve as a witness between us."

[45]So Jacob took a stone and set it up as a pillar. [46]He said to his relatives, "Gather some stones." So they took stones and piled them in a heap, and they ate there by the heap. [47]Laban called it Jegar Sahadutha,[c] and Jacob called it Galeed.[d]

[48]Laban said, "This heap is a witness between you and me today." That is why it was called Galeed. [49]It was also called Mizpah,[e] because he said, "May the LORD keep watch between you and me when we are away from each other. [50]If you ill-treat my daughters or if you take any wives

besides my daughters, even though no-one is with us, remember that God is a witness between you and me."

[51]Laban also said to Jacob, "Here is this heap, and here is this pillar I have set up between you and me. [52]This heap is a witness, and this pillar is a witness, that I will not go past this heap to your side to harm you and that you will not go past this heap and pillar to my side to harm me. [53]May the God of Abraham and the God of Nahor, the God of their father, judge between us."

So Jacob took an oath in the name of the Fear of his father Isaac. [54]He offered a sacrifice there in the hill country and invited his relatives to a meal. After they had eaten, they spent the night there.

[55]Early the next morning Laban kissed his grandchildren and his daughters and blessed them. Then he left and returned home.

Jacob Prepares to Meet Esau

32 Jacob also went on his way, and the angels of God met him. [2]When Jacob saw them, he said, "This is the camp of God!" So he named that place Mahanaim.[a]

[3]Jacob sent messengers ahead of him to his brother Esau in the land of Seir, the country of Edom. [4]He instructed them: "This is what you are to say to my master Esau: 'Your servant Jacob says, I have been staying with Laban and have remained there till now. [5]I have cattle and donkeys, sheep and goats, menservants and maidservants. Now I am sending this message to my lord, that I may find favour in your eyes.'"

[6]When the messengers returned to Jacob, they said, "We went to your brother Esau, and now he is coming to meet you, and four hundred men are with him."

[7]In great fear and distress Jacob divided the people who were with him into two

---

[c]47 The Aramaic *Jegar Sahadutha* means *witness heap.*
[e]49 *Mizpah* means *watchtower.*
[a]2 *Mahanaim* means *two camps.*

[d]47 The Hebrew *Galeed* means *witness heap.*

36

groups,[b] and the flocks and herds and camels as well. [8]He thought, "If Esau comes and attacks one group,[c] the group[c] that is left may escape."

[9]Then Jacob prayed, "O God of my father Abraham, God of my father Isaac, O Lord, who said to me, 'Go back to your country and your relatives, and I will make you prosper,' [10]I am unworthy of all the kindness and faithfulness you have shown your servant. I had only my staff when I crossed this Jordan, but now I have become two groups. [11]Save me, I pray, from the hand of my brother Esau, for I am afraid he will come and attack me, and also the mothers with their children. [12]But you have said, 'I will surely make you prosper and will make your descendants like the sand of the sea, which cannot be counted.'"

[13]He spent the night there, and from what he had with him he selected a gift for his brother Esau: [14]two hundred female goats and twenty male goats, two hundred ewes and twenty rams, [15]thirty female camels with their young, forty cows and ten bulls, and twenty female donkeys and ten male donkeys. [16]He put them in the care of his servants, each herd by itself, and said to his servants, "Go ahead of me, and keep some space between the herds."

[17]He instructed the one in the lead: "When my brother Esau meets you and asks, 'To whom do you belong, and where are you going, and who owns all these animals in front of you?' [18]then you are to say, 'They belong to your servant Jacob. They are a gift sent to my lord Esau, and he is coming behind us.'"

[19]He also instructed the second, the third and all the others who followed the herds: "You are to say the same thing to Esau when you meet him. [20]And be sure to say, 'Your servant Jacob is coming behind us.'" For he thought, "I will pacify him with these gifts I am sending on ahead; later, when I see him, perhaps he will receive me." [21]So Jacob's gifts went on ahead of him, but he himself spent the night in the camp.

Jacob Wrestles with God

[22]That night Jacob got up and took his two wives, his two maidservants and his eleven sons and crossed the ford of the Jabbok. [23]After he had sent them across the stream, he sent over all his possessions. [24]So Jacob was left alone, and a man wrestled with him till daybreak. [25]When the man saw that he could not overpower him, he touched the socket of Jacob's hip so that his hip was wrenched as he wrestled with the man. [26]Then the man said, "Let me go, for it is daybreak."

But Jacob replied, "I will not let you go unless you bless me."

[27]The man asked him, "What is your name?"

"Jacob," he answered.

[28]Then the man said, "Your name will no longer be Jacob, but Israel,[d] because you have struggled with God and with men and have overcome."

[29]Jacob said, "Please tell me your name."

But he replied, "Why do you ask my name?" Then he blessed him there.

[30]So Jacob called the place Peniel,[e] saying, "It is because I saw God face to face, and yet my life was spared."

[31]The sun rose above him as he passed Peniel,[f] and he was limping because of his hip. [32]Therefore to this day the Israelites do not eat the tendon attached to the socket of the hip, because the socket of Jacob's hip was touched near the tendon.

Jacob Meets Esau

33 Jacob looked up and there was Esau, coming with his four hundred men; so he divided the children among Leah, Rachel and the two maidservants. [2]He put the maidservants and their children in front, Leah and her children next, and Rachel and Joseph in the rear. [3]He himself went on ahead and bowed down to the ground seven times as he approached his brother.

[4]But Esau ran to meet Jacob and

---

[b]7 Or *camps*; also in verse 10   [c]8 Or *camp*   [d]28 *Israel* means *he struggles with God.*
[e]30 *Peniel* means *face of God.*   [f]31 Hebrew *Penuel*, a variant of *Peniel*

embraced him; he threw his arms around his neck and kissed him. And they wept. [5]Then Esau looked up and saw the women and children. "Who are these with you?" he asked.

Jacob answered, "They are the children God has graciously given your servant."

[6]Then the maidservants and their children approached and bowed down. [7]Next, Leah and her children came and bowed down. Last of all came Joseph and Rachel, and they too bowed down.

[8]Esau asked, "What do you mean by all these droves I met?"

"To find favour in your eyes, my lord," he said.

[9]But Esau said, "I already have plenty, my brother. Keep what you have for yourself."

[10]"No, please!" said Jacob. "If I have found favour in your eyes, accept this gift from me. For to see your face is like seeing the face of God, now that you have received me favourably. [11]Please accept the present that was brought to you, for God has been gracious to me and I have all I need." And because Jacob insisted, Esau accepted it.

[12]Then Esau said, "Let us be on our way; I'll accompany you."

[13]But Jacob said to him, "My lord knows that the children are tender and that I must care for the ewes and cows that are nursing their young. If they are driven hard just one day, all the animals will die. [14]So let my lord go on ahead of his servant, while I move along slowly at the pace of the droves before me and that of the children, until I come to my lord in Seir."

[15]Esau said, "Then let me leave some of my men with you."

"But why do that?" Jacob asked. "Just let me find favour in the eyes of my lord."

[16]So that day Esau started on his way back to Seir. [17]Jacob, however, went to Succoth, where he built a place for himself and made shelters for his livestock. That is why the place is called Succoth.[a]

[18]After Jacob came from Paddan Aram,[b] he arrived safely at the[c] city of Shechem in Canaan and camped within sight of the city. [19]For a hundred pieces of silver,[d] he bought from the sons of Hamor, the father of Shechem, the plot of ground where he pitched his tent. [20]There he set up an altar and called it El Elohe Israel.[e]

Dinah and the Shechemites

34 Now Dinah, the daughter Leah had borne to Jacob, went out to visit the women of the land. [2]When Shechem son of Hamor the Hivite, the ruler of that area, saw her, he took her and raped her. [3]His heart was drawn to Dinah daughter of Jacob, and he loved the girl and spoke tenderly to her. [4]And Shechem said to his father Hamor, "Get me this girl as my wife."

[5]When Jacob heard that his daughter Dinah had been defiled, his sons were in the fields with his livestock; so he kept quiet about it until they came home.

[6]Then Shechem's father Hamor went out to talk with Jacob. [7]Now Jacob's sons had come in from the fields as soon as they heard what had happened. They were filled with grief and fury, because Shechem had done a disgraceful thing in[a] Israel by lying with Jacob's daughter—a thing that should not be done.

[8]But Hamor said to them, "My son Shechem has his heart set on your daughter. Please give her to him as his wife. [9]Intermarry with us; give us your daughters and take our daughters for yourselves. [10]You can settle among us; the land is open to you. Live in it, trade[b] in it, and acquire property in it."

[11]Then Shechem said to Dinah's father and brothers, "Let me find favour in your eyes, and I will give you whatever you ask. [12]Make the price for the bride and the gift I am to bring as great as you like, and I'll

---

[a]17 *Succoth* means *shelters.*   [b]18 That is, North-west Mesopotamia   [c]18 Or *arrived at Shalem, a*
[d]19 Hebrew *hundred kesitahs*; a kesitah was a unit of money of unknown weight and value.
[e]20 *El Elohe Israel* can mean *God, the God of Israel* or *mighty is the God of Israel.*
[a]7 Or *against*   [b]10 Or *move about freely*; also in verse 21

pay whatever you ask me. Only give me the girl as my wife."

13Because their sister Dinah had been defiled, Jacob's sons replied deceitfully as they spoke to Shechem and his father Hamor. 14They said to them, "We can't do such a thing; we can't give our sister to a man who is not circumcised. That would be a disgrace to us. 15We will give our consent to you on one condition only: that you become like us by circumcising all your males. 16Then we will give you our daughters and take your daughters for ourselves. We'll settle among you and become one people with you. 17But if you will not agree to be circumcised, we'll take our sister*c* and go."

18Their proposal seemed good to Hamor and his son Shechem. 19The young man, who was the most honoured of all his father's household, lost no time in doing what they said, because he was delighted with Jacob's daughter. 20So Hamor and his son Shechem went to the gate of their city to speak to their fellow townsmen. 21"These men are friendly towards us," they said. "Let them live in our land and trade in it; the land has plenty of room for them. We can marry their daughters and they can marry ours. 22But the men will consent to live with us as one people only on the condition that our males be circumcised, as they themselves are. 23Won't their livestock, their property and all their other animals become ours? So let us give our consent to them, and they will settle among us."

24All the men who went out of the city gate agreed with Hamor and his son Shechem, and every male in the city was circumcised.

25Three days later, while all of them were still in pain, two of Jacob's sons, Simeon and Levi, Dinah's brothers, took their swords and attacked the unsuspecting city, killing every male. 26They put Hamor and his son Shechem to the sword and took Dinah from Shechem's house and left. 27The sons of Jacob came upon the dead bodies and looted the city where*d*

their sister had been defiled. 28They seized their flocks and herds and donkeys and everything else of theirs in the city and out in the fields. 29They carried off all their wealth and all their women and children, taking as plunder everything in the houses.

30Then Jacob said to Simeon and Levi, "You have brought trouble on me by making me a stench to the Canaanites and Perizzites, the people living in this land. We are few in number, and if they join forces against me and attack me, I and my household will be destroyed."

31But they replied, "Should he have treated our sister like a prostitute?"

Jacob Returns to Bethel

35 Then God said to Jacob, "Go up to Bethel and settle there, and build an altar there to God, who appeared to you when you were fleeing from your brother Esau."

2So Jacob said to his household and to all who were with him, "Get rid of the foreign gods you have with you, and purify yourselves and change your clothes. 3Then come, let us go up to Bethel, where I will build an altar to God, who answered me in the day of my distress and who has been with me wherever I have gone." 4So they gave Jacob all the foreign gods they had and the rings in their ears, and Jacob buried them under the oak at Shechem. 5Then they set out, and the terror of God fell upon the towns all around them so that no-one pursued them.

6Jacob and all the people with him came to Luz (that is, Bethel) in the land of Canaan. 7There he built an altar, and he called the place El Bethel,*a* because it was there that God revealed himself to him when he was fleeing from his brother.

8Now Deborah, Rebekah's nurse, died and was buried under the oak below Bethel. So it was named Allon Bacuth.*b*

9After Jacob returned from Paddan

---

*c*17 Hebrew *daughter*　　*d*27 Or *because*
*a*7 *El Bethel* means *God of Bethel*.　　*b*8 *Allon Bacuth* means *oak of weeping*.

Aram,*c* God appeared to him again and blessed him. [10]God said to him, "Your name is Jacob,*d* but you will no longer be called Jacob; your name will be Israel."*e* So he named him Israel.

[11]And God said to him, "I am God Almighty;*f* be fruitful and increase in number. A nation and a community of nations will come from you, and kings will come from your body. [12]The land I gave to Abraham and Isaac I also give to you, and I will give this land to your descendants after you." [13]Then God went up from him at the place where he had talked with him.

[14]Jacob set up a stone pillar at the place where God had talked with him, and he poured out a drink offering on it; he also poured oil on it. [15]Jacob called the place where God had talked with him Bethel.*g*

The Deaths of Rachel and Isaac

[16]Then they moved on from Bethel. While they were still some distance from Ephrath, Rachel began to give birth and had great difficulty. [17]And as she was having great difficulty in childbirth, the midwife said to her, "Don't be afraid, for you have another son." [18]As she breathed her last—for she was dying—she named her son Ben-Oni.*h* But his father named him Benjamin.*i*

[19]So Rachel died and was buried on the way to Ephrath (that is, Bethlehem). [20]Over her tomb Jacob set up a pillar, and to this day that pillar marks Rachel's tomb.

[21]Israel moved on again and pitched his tent beyond Migdal Eder. [22]While Israel was living in that region, Reuben went in and slept with his father's concubine Bilhah, and Israel heard of it.

Jacob had twelve sons:
[23]The sons of Leah:
Reuben the firstborn of Jacob,
Simeon, Levi, Judah, Issachar and Zebulun.

[24]The sons of Rachel:
Joseph and Benjamin.
[25]The sons of Rachel's maidservant Bilhah:
Dan and Naphtali.
[26]The sons of Leah's maidservant Zilpah:
Gad and Asher.

These were the sons of Jacob, who were born to him in Paddan Aram.

[27]Jacob came home to his father Isaac in Mamre, near Kiriath Arba (that is, Hebron), where Abraham and Isaac had stayed. [28]Isaac lived a hundred and eighty years. [29]Then he breathed his last and died and was gathered to his people, old and full of years. And his sons Esau and Jacob buried him.

Esau's Descendants

36

This is the account of Esau (that is, Edom).

[2]Esau took his wives from the women of Canaan: Adah daughter of Elon the Hittite, and Oholibamah daughter of Anah and granddaughter of Zibeon the Hivite—[3]also Basemath daughter of Ishmael and sister of Nebaioth.

[4]Adah bore Eliphaz to Esau, Basemath bore Reuel, [5]and Oholibamah bore Jeush, Jalam and Korah. These were the sons of Esau, who were born to him in Canaan.

[6]Esau took his wives and sons and daughters and all the members of his household, as well as his livestock and all his other animals and all the goods he had acquired in Canaan, and moved to a land some distance from his brother Jacob. [7]Their possessions were too great for them to remain together; the land where they were staying could not support them both because of their livestock. [8]So Esau (that is, Edom) settled in the hill country of Seir.

---

c9 That is, North-west Mesopotamia; also in verse 26   *d10* Jacob means *he grasps the heel* (figuratively, *he deceives*).
e10 Israel means *he struggles with God.*   *f11* Hebrew *El-Shaddai*   *g15* Bethel means *house of God.*
h18 Ben-Oni means *son of my trouble.*   *i18* Benjamin means *son of my right hand.*

9This is the account of Esau the father of the Edomites in the hill country of Seir.

10These are the names of Esau's sons:
Eliphaz, the son of Esau's wife Adah, and Reuel, the son of Esau's wife Basemath.
11The sons of Eliphaz:
Teman, Omar, Zepho, Gatam and Kenaz.
12Esau's son Eliphaz also had a concubine named Timna, who bore him Amalek. These were grandsons of Esau's wife Adah.
13The sons of Reuel:
Nahath, Zerah, Shammah and Mizzah. These were grandsons of Esau's wife Basemath.
14The sons of Esau's wife Oholibamah daughter of Anah and granddaughter of Zibeon, whom she bore to Esau:
Jeush, Jalam and Korah.

15These were the chiefs among Esau's descendants:
The sons of Eliphaz the firstborn of Esau:
Chiefs Teman, Omar, Zepho, Kenaz, 16Korah,*a* Gatam and Amalek. These were the chiefs descended from Eliphaz in Edom; they were grandsons of Adah.
17The sons of Esau's son Reuel:
Chiefs Nahath, Zerah, Shammah and Mizzah. These were the chiefs descended from Reuel in Edom; they were grandsons of Esau's wife Basemath.
18The sons of Esau's wife Oholibamah:
Chiefs Jeush, Jalam and Korah. These were the chiefs descended from Esau's wife Oholibamah daughter of Anah.
19These were the sons of Esau (that is, Edom), and these were their chiefs.

20These were the sons of Seir the Horite, who were living in the region:
Lotan, Shobal, Zibeon, Anah, 21Dishon, Ezer and Dishan. These sons of Seir in Edom were Horite chiefs.
22The sons of Lotan:
Hori and Homam.*b* Timna was Lotan's sister.
23The sons of Shobal:
Alvan, Manahath, Ebal, Shepho and Onam.
24The sons of Zibeon:
Aiah and Anah. This is the Anah who discovered the hot springs*c* in the desert while he was grazing the donkeys of his father Zibeon.
25The children of Anah:
Dishon and Oholibamah daughter of Anah.
26The sons of Dishon:*d*
Hemdan, Eshban, Ithran and Keran.
27The sons of Ezer:
Bilhan, Zaavan and Akan.
28The sons of Dishan:
Uz and Aran.
29These were the Horite chiefs:
Lotan, Shobal, Zibeon, Anah, 30Dishon, Ezer and Dishan. These were the Horite chiefs, according to their divisions, in the land of Seir.

The Rulers of Edom

31These were the kings who reigned in Edom before any Israelite king reigned:*e*
32Bela son of Beor became king of Edom. His city was named Dinhabah.
33When Bela died, Jobab son of Zerah from Bozrah succeeded him as king.
34When Jobab died, Husham from the land of the Temanites succeeded him as king.
35When Husham died, Hadad son of Bedad, who defeated Midian in the country of Moab, succeeded him as king. His city was named Avith.
36When Hadad died, Samlah from

---

a16 Masoretic Text; Samaritan Pentateuch (see also Gen. 36:11 and 1 Chron. 1:36) does not have *Korah.*
b22 Hebrew *Hemam,* a variant of *Homam* (see 1 Chron. 1:39)
c24 Vulgate; Syriac *discovered water*; the meaning of the Hebrew for this word is uncertain.
d26 Hebrew *Dishan,* a variant of *Dishon*   *e31* Or *before an Israelite king reigned over them*

Masrekah succeeded him as king. [37]When Samlah died, Shaul from Rehoboth on the river*f* succeeded him as king. [38]When Shaul died, Baal-Hanan son of Acbor succeeded him as king. [39]When Baal-Hanan son of Acbor died, Hadad*g* succeeded him as king. His city was named Pau, and his wife's name was Mehetabel daughter of Matred, the daughter of Me-Zahab.

[40]These were the chiefs descended from Esau, by name, according to their clans and regions:

Timna, Alvah, Jetheth, [41]Oholibamah, Elah, Pinon, [42]Kenaz, Teman, Mibzar, [43]Magdiel and Iram. These were the chiefs of Edom, according to their settlements in the land they occupied.

This was Esau the father of the Edomites.

Joseph's Dreams

37 Jacob lived in the land where his father had stayed, the land of Canaan.

[2]This is the account of Jacob.

Joseph, a young man of seventeen, was tending the flocks with his brothers, the sons of Bilhah and the sons of Zilpah, his father's wives, and he brought their father a bad report about them.

[3]Now Israel loved Joseph more than any of his other sons, because he had been born to him in his old age; and he made a richly ornamented*a* robe for him. [4]When his brothers saw that their father loved him more than any of them, they hated him and could not speak a kind word to him.

[5]Joseph had a dream, and when he told it to his brothers, they hated him all the more. [6]He said to them, "Listen to this dream I had: [7]We were binding sheaves of corn out in the field when suddenly my sheaf rose and stood upright, while your sheaves gathered round mine and bowed down to it."

[8]His brothers said to him, "Do you intend to reign over us? Will you actually rule us?" And they hated him all the more because of his dream and what he had said.

[9]Then he had another dream, and he told it to his brothers. "Listen," he said, "I had another dream, and this time the sun and moon and eleven stars were bowing down to me."

[10]When he told his father as well as his brothers, his father rebuked him and said, "What is this dream you had? Will your mother and I and your brothers actually come and bow down to the ground before you?" [11]His brothers were jealous of him, but his father kept the matter in mind.

Joseph Sold by His Brothers

[12]Now his brothers had gone to graze their father's flocks near Shechem, [13]and Israel said to Joseph, "As you know, your brothers are grazing the flocks near Shechem. Come, I am going to send you to them."

"Very well," he replied.

[14]So he said to him, "Go and see if all is well with your brothers and with the flocks, and bring word back to me." Then he sent him off from the Valley of Hebron.

When Joseph arrived at Shechem, [15]a man found him wandering around in the fields and asked him, "What are you looking for?"

[16]He replied, "I'm looking for my brothers. Can you tell me where they are grazing their flocks?"

[17]"They have moved on from here," the man answered. "I heard them say, 'Let's go to Dothan.'"

f37 Possibly the Euphrates
g39 Many manuscripts of the Masoretic Text, Samaritan Pentateuch and Syriac (see also 1 Chron. 1:50); most manuscripts of the Masoretic Text *Hadar*
a3 The meaning of the Hebrew for *richly ornamented* is uncertain; also in verses 23 and 32.

So Joseph went after his brothers and found them near Dothan. [18]But they saw him in the distance, and before he reached them, they plotted to kill him.

[19]"Here comes that dreamer!" they said to each other. [20]"Come now, let's kill him and throw him into one of these cisterns and say that a ferocious animal devoured him. Then we'll see what comes of his dreams."

[21]When Reuben heard this, he tried to rescue him from their hands. "Let's not take his life," he said. [22]"Don't shed any blood. Throw him into this cistern here in the desert, but don't lay a hand on him." Reuben said this to rescue him from them and take him back to his father.

[23]So when Joseph came to his brothers, they stripped him of his robe—the richly ornamented robe he was wearing—[24]and they took him and threw him into the cistern. Now the cistern was empty; there was no water in it.

[25]As they sat down to eat their meal, they looked up and saw a caravan of Ishmaelites coming from Gilead. Their camels were loaded with spices, balm and myrrh, and they were on their way to take them down to Egypt.

[26]Judah said to his brothers, "What will we gain if we kill our brother and cover up his blood? [27]Come, let's sell him to the Ishmaelites and not lay our hands on him; after all, he is our brother, our own flesh and blood." His brothers agreed.

[28]So when the Midianite merchants came by, his brothers pulled Joseph up out of the cistern and sold him for twenty shekels[b] of silver to the Ishmaelites, who took him to Egypt.

[29]When Reuben returned to the cistern and saw that Joseph was not there, he tore his clothes. [30]He went back to his brothers and said, "The boy isn't there! Where can I turn now?"

[31]Then they got Joseph's robe, slaughtered a goat and dipped the robe in the blood. [32]They took the ornamented robe back to their father and said, "We found this. Examine it to see whether it is your son's robe."

[33]He recognised it and said, "It is my son's robe! Some ferocious animal has devoured him. Joseph has surely been torn to pieces."

[34]Then Jacob tore his clothes, put on sackcloth and mourned for his son many days. [35]All his sons and daughters came to comfort him, but he refused to be comforted. "No," he said, "in mourning will I go down to the grave[c] to my son." So his father wept for him.

[36]Meanwhile, the Midianites[d] sold Joseph in Egypt to Potiphar, one of Pharaoh's officials, the captain of the guard.

Judah and Tamar

38 At that time, Judah left his brothers and went down to stay with a man of Adullam named Hirah. [2]There Judah met the daughter of a Canaanite man named Shua. He married her and lay with her; [3]she became pregnant and gave birth to a son, who was named Er. [4]She conceived again and gave birth to a son and named him Onan. [5]She gave birth to still another son and named him Shelah. It was at Kezib that she gave birth to him.

[6]Judah got a wife for Er, his firstborn, and her name was Tamar. [7]But Er, Judah's firstborn, was wicked in the LORD's sight; so the LORD put him to death.

[8]Then Judah said to Onan, "Lie with your brother's wife and fulfil your duty to her as a brother-in-law to produce offspring for your brother." [9]But Onan knew that the offspring would not be his; so whenever he lay with his brother's wife, he spilled his semen on the ground to keep from producing offspring for his brother. [10]What he did was wicked in the LORD's sight; so he put him to death also.

[11]Judah then said to his daughter-in-law Tamar, "Live as a widow in your father's house until my son Shelah grows up." For he thought, "He may die too, just like his brothers." So Tamar went to live in her father's house.

b28 That is, about 8 ounces (about 0.2 kilogram)   c35 Hebrew Sheol
d36 Samaritan Pentateuch, Septuagint, Vulgate and Syriac (see also verse 28); Masoretic Text Medanites

¹²After a long time Judah's wife, the daughter of Shua, died. When Judah had recovered from his grief, he went up to Timnah, to the men who were shearing his sheep, and his friend Hirah the Adullamite went with him.

¹³When Tamar was told, "Your father-in-law is on his way to Timnah to shear his sheep," ¹⁴she took off her widow's clothes, covered herself with a veil to disguise herself, and then sat down at the entrance to Enaim, which is on the road to Timnah. For she saw that, though Shelah had now grown up, she had not been given to him as his wife.

¹⁵When Judah saw her, he thought she was a prostitute, for she had covered her face. ¹⁶Not realising that she was his daughter-in-law, he went over to her by the roadside and said, "Come now, let me sleep with you."

"And what will you give me to sleep with you?" she asked.

¹⁷"I'll send you a young goat from my flock," he said.

"Will you give me something as a pledge until you send it?" she asked.

¹⁸He said, "What pledge should I give you?"

"Your seal and its cord, and the staff in your hand," she answered. So he gave them to her and slept with her, and she became pregnant by him. ¹⁹After she left, she took off her veil and put on her widow's clothes again.

²⁰Meanwhile Judah sent the young goat by his friend the Adullamite in order to get his pledge back from the woman, but he did not find her. ²¹He asked the men who lived there, "Where is the shrine-prostitute who was beside the road at Enaim?"

"There hasn't been any shrine-prostitute here," they said.

²²So he went back to Judah and said, "I didn't find her. Besides, the men who lived there said, 'There hasn't been any shrine-prostitute here.'"

²³Then Judah said, "Let her keep what she has, or we will become a laughing-stock. After all, I did send her this young goat, but you didn't find her."

²⁴About three months later Judah was told, "Your daughter-in-law Tamar is guilty of prostitution, and as a result she is now pregnant."

Judah said, "Bring her out and have her burned to death!"

²⁵As she was being brought out, she sent a message to her father-in-law. "I am pregnant by the man who owns these," she said. And she added, "See if you recognise whose seal and cord and staff these are."

²⁶Judah recognised them and said, "She is more righteous than I, since I wouldn't give her to my son Shelah." And he did not sleep with her again.

²⁷When the time came for her to give birth, there were twin boys in her womb. ²⁸As she was giving birth, one of them put out his hand; so the midwife took a scarlet thread and tied it on his wrist and said, "This one came out first." ²⁹But when he drew back his hand, his brother came out, and she said, "So this is how you have broken out!" And he was named Perez.ᵃ ³⁰Then his brother, who had the scarlet thread on his wrist, came out and he was given the name Zerah.ᵇ

Joseph and Potiphar's Wife

39 Now Joseph had been taken down to Egypt. Potiphar, an Egyptian who was one of Pharaoh's officials, the captain of the guard, bought him from the Ishmaelites who had taken him there.

²The LORD was with Joseph and he prospered, and he lived in the house of his Egyptian master. ³When his master saw that the LORD was with him and that the LORD gave him success in everything he did, ⁴Joseph found favour in his eyes and became his attendant. Potiphar put him in charge of his household, and he entrusted to his care everything he owned. ⁵From the time he put him in charge of his household and of all that he owned, the LORD blessed the household of the Egyptian because of Joseph. The blessing of the LORD was on everything Potiphar had, both in the house and in the field. ⁶So he left in Joseph's care everything he had;

ᵃ29 Perez means breaking out.   ᵇ30 Zerah can mean scarlet or brightness.

with Joseph in charge, he did not concern himself with anything except the food he ate.

Now Joseph was well-built and handsome, 7and after a while his master's wife took notice of Joseph and said, "Come to bed with me!"

8But he refused. "With me in charge," he told her, "my master does not concern himself with anything in the house; everything he owns he has entrusted to my care. 9No-one is greater in this house than I am. My master has withheld nothing from me except you, because you are his wife. How then could I do such a wicked thing and sin against God?" 10And though she spoke to Joseph day after day, he refused to go to bed with her or even to be with her.

11One day he went into the house to attend to his duties, and none of the household servants was inside. 12She caught him by his cloak and said, "Come to bed with me!" But he left his cloak in her hand and ran out of the house.

13When she saw that he had left his cloak in her hand and had run out of the house, 14she called her household servants. "Look," she said to them, "this Hebrew has been brought to us to make sport of us! He came in here to sleep with me, but I screamed. 15When he heard me scream for help, he left his cloak beside me and ran out of the house."

16She kept his cloak beside her until his master came home. 17Then she told him this story: "That Hebrew slave you brought us came to me to make sport of me. 18But as soon as I screamed for help, he left his cloak beside me and ran out of the house."

19When his master heard the story his wife told him, saying, "This is how your slave treated me," he burned with anger. 20Joseph's master took him and put him in prison, the place where the king's prisoners were confined.

But while Joseph was there in the prison, 21the LORD was with him; he showed him kindness and granted him favour in the eyes of the prison warder. 22So the warder put Joseph in charge of all those held in the prison, and he was made responsible for all that was done there.

23The warder paid no attention to anything under Joseph's care, because the LORD was with Joseph and gave him success in whatever he did.

The Cupbearer and the Baker

40 Some time later, the cupbearer and the baker of the king of Egypt offended their master, the king of Egypt. 2Pharaoh was angry with his two officials, the chief cupbearer and the chief baker, 3and put them in custody in the house of the captain of the guard, in the same prison where Joseph was confined. 4The captain of the guard assigned them to Joseph, and he attended them.

After they had been in custody for some time, 5each of the two men—the cupbearer and the baker of the king of Egypt, who were being held in prison—had a dream the same night, and each dream had a meaning of its own.

6When Joseph came to them the next morning, he saw that they were dejected. 7So he asked Pharaoh's officials who were in custody with him in his master's house, "Why are your faces so sad today?"

8"We both had dreams," they answered, "but there is no-one to interpret them."

Then Joseph said to them, "Do not interpretations belong to God? Tell me your dreams."

9So the chief cupbearer told Joseph his dream. He said to him, "In my dream I saw a vine in front of me, 10and on the vine were three branches. As soon as it budded, it blossomed, and its clusters ripened into grapes. 11Pharaoh's cup was in my hand, and I took the grapes, squeezed them into Pharaoh's cup and put the cup in his hand."

12"This is what it means," Joseph said to him. "The three branches are three days. 13Within three days Pharaoh will lift up your head and restore you to your position, and you will put Pharaoh's cup in his hand, just as you used to do when you were his cupbearer. 14But when all goes well with you, remember me and show me kindness; mention me to Pharaoh and get me out of this prison. 15For I was forcibly carried off from the land of the Hebrews, and even here I have done nothing to deserve being put in a dungeon."

[16]When the chief baker saw that Joseph had given a favourable interpretation, he said to Joseph, "I too had a dream: On my head were three baskets of bread.[a] [17]In the top basket were all kinds of baked goods for Pharaoh, but the birds were eating them out of the basket on my head."

[18]"This is what it means," Joseph said. "The three baskets are three days. [19]Within three days Pharaoh will lift off your head and hang you on a tree.[b] And the birds will eat away your flesh."

[20]Now the third day was Pharaoh's birthday, and he gave a feast for all his officials. He lifted up the heads of the chief cupbearer and the chief baker in the presence of his officials: [21]He restored the chief cupbearer to his position, so that he once again put the cup into Pharaoh's hand, [22]but he hanged[c] the chief baker, just as Joseph had said to them in his interpretation.

[23]The chief cupbearer, however, did not remember Joseph; he forgot him.

Pharaoh's Dreams

41 When two full years had passed, Pharaoh had a dream: He was standing by the Nile, [2]when out of the river there came up seven cows, sleek and fat, and they grazed among the reeds. [3]After them, seven other cows, ugly and gaunt, came up out of the Nile and stood beside those on the riverbank. [4]And the cows that were ugly and gaunt ate up the seven sleek, fat cows. Then Pharaoh woke up.

[5]He fell asleep again and had a second dream: Seven ears of corn, healthy and good, were growing on a single stalk. [6]After them, seven other ears of corn sprouted—thin and scorched by the east wind. [7]The thin ears of corn swallowed up the seven healthy, full ears. Then Pharaoh woke up; it had been a dream.

[8]In the morning his mind was troubled, so he sent for all the magicians and wise men of Egypt. Pharaoh told them his dreams, but no-one could interpret them for him.

[9]Then the chief cupbearer said to Pharaoh, "Today I am reminded of my shortcomings. [10]Pharaoh was once angry with his servants, and he imprisoned me and the chief baker in the house of the captain of the guard. [11]Each of us had a dream the same night, and each dream had a meaning of its own. [12]Now a young Hebrew was there with us, a servant of the captain of the guard. We told him our dreams, and he interpreted them for us, giving each man the interpretation of his dream. [13]And things turned out exactly as he interpreted them to us: I was restored to my position, and the other man was hanged."[a]

[14]So Pharaoh sent for Joseph, and he was quickly brought from the dungeon. When he had shaved and changed his clothes, he came before Pharaoh.

[15]Pharaoh said to Joseph, "I had a dream, and no-one can interpret it. But I have heard it said of you that when you hear a dream you can interpret it."

[16]"I cannot do it," Joseph replied to Pharaoh, "but God will give Pharaoh the answer he desires."

[17]Then Pharaoh said to Joseph, "In my dream I was standing on the bank of the Nile, [18]when out of the river there came up seven cows, fat and sleek, and they grazed among the reeds. [19]After them, seven other cows came up—scrawny and very ugly and lean. I had never seen such ugly cows in all the land of Egypt. [20]The lean, ugly cows ate up the seven fat cows that came up first. [21]But even after they ate them, no-one could tell that they had done so; they looked just as ugly as before. Then I woke up.

[22]"In my dreams I also saw seven ears of corn, full and good, growing on a single stalk. [23]After them, seven other ears sprouted—withered and thin and scorched by the east wind. [24]The thin ears of corn swallowed up the seven good ears. I told this to the magicians, but none could explain it to me."

[25]Then Joseph said to Pharaoh, "The

---

[a]16 Or *three wicker baskets*   [b]19 Or *and impale you on a pole*   [c]22 Or *impaled*
[a]13 Or *impaled*

dreams of Pharaoh are one and the same. God has revealed to Pharaoh what he is about to do. 26The seven good cows are seven years, and the seven good ears of corn are seven years; it is one and the same dream. 27The seven lean, ugly cows that came up afterwards are seven years, and so are the seven worthless ears of corn scorched by the east wind: They are seven years of famine.

28"It is just as I said to Pharaoh: God has shown Pharaoh what he is about to do. 29Seven years of great abundance are coming throughout the land of Egypt, 30but seven years of famine will follow them. Then all the abundance in Egypt will be forgotten, and the famine will ravage the land. 31The abundance in the land will not be remembered, because the famine that follows it will be so severe. 32The reason the dream was given to Pharaoh in two forms is that the matter has been firmly decided by God, and God will do it soon.

33"And now let Pharaoh look for a discerning and wise man and put him in charge of the land of Egypt. 34Let Pharaoh appoint commissioners over the land to take a fifth of the harvest of Egypt during the seven years of abundance. 35They should collect all the food of these good years that are coming and store up the grain under the authority of Pharaoh, to be kept in the cities for food. 36This food should be held in reserve for the country, to be used during the seven years of famine that will come upon Egypt, so that the country may not be ruined by the famine."

37The plan seemed good to Pharaoh and to all his officials. 38So Pharaoh asked them, "Can we find anyone like this man, one in whom is the spirit of God?"[b]

39Then Pharaoh said to Joseph, "Since God has made all this known to you, there is no-one so discerning and wise as you. 40You shall be in charge of my palace, and all my people are to submit to your orders. Only with respect to the throne will I be greater than you."

Joseph in Charge of Egypt

41So Pharaoh said to Joseph, "I hereby put you in charge of the whole land of Egypt." 42Then Pharaoh took his signet ring from his finger and put it on Joseph's finger. He dressed him in robes of fine linen and put a gold chain around his neck. 43He had him ride in a chariot as his second-in-command,[c] and men shouted before him, "Make way!"[d] Thus he put him in charge of the whole land of Egypt.

44Then Pharaoh said to Joseph, "I am Pharaoh, but without your word no-one will lift hand or foot in all Egypt." 45Pharaoh gave Joseph the name Zaphenath-Paneah and gave him Asenath daughter of Potiphera, priest of On,[e] to be his wife. And Joseph went throughout the land of Egypt.

46Joseph was thirty years old when he entered the service of Pharaoh king of Egypt. And Joseph went out from Pharaoh's presence and travelled throughout Egypt. 47During the seven years of abundance the land produced plentifully. 48Joseph collected all the food produced in those seven years of abundance in Egypt and stored it in the cities. In each city he put the food grown in the fields surrounding it. 49Joseph stored up huge quantities of grain, like the sand of the sea; it was so much that he stopped keeping records because it was beyond measure.

50Before the years of famine came, two sons were born to Joseph by Asenath daughter of Potiphera, priest of On. 51Joseph named his firstborn Manasseh[f] and said, "It is because God has made me forget all my trouble and all my father's household." 52The second son he named Ephraim[g] and said, "It is because God has made me fruitful in the land of my suffering."

53The seven years of abundance in Egypt came to an end, 54and the seven years of famine began, just as Joseph had said. There was famine in all the other lands, but in the whole land of Egypt there

---

b38 Or of the gods   c43 Or in the chariot of his second-in-command; or in his second chariot
d43 Or Bow down   e45 That is, Heliopolis; also in verse 50
f51 Manasseh sounds like and may be derived from the Hebrew for forget.
g52 Ephraim sounds like the Hebrew for twice fruitful.

was food. [55]When all Egypt began to feel the famine, the people cried to Pharaoh for food. Then Pharaoh told all the Egyptians, "Go to Joseph and do what he tells you."

[56]When the famine had spread over the whole country, Joseph opened the storehouses and sold grain to the Egyptians, for the famine was severe throughout Egypt. [57]And all the countries came to Egypt to buy grain from Joseph, because the famine was severe in all the world.

Joseph's Brothers Go to Egypt

42 When Jacob learned that there was grain in Egypt, he said to his sons, "Why do you just keep looking at each other?" [2]He continued, "I have heard that there is grain in Egypt. Go down there and buy some for us, so that we may live and not die."

[3]Then ten of Joseph's brothers went down to buy grain from Egypt. [4]But Jacob did not send Benjamin, Joseph's brother, with the others, because he was afraid that harm might come to him. [5]So Israel's sons were among those who went to buy grain, for the famine was in the land of Canaan also.

[6]Now Joseph was the governor of the land, the one who sold grain to all its people. So when Joseph's brothers arrived, they bowed down to him with their faces to the ground. [7]As soon as Joseph saw his brothers, he recognised them, but he pretended to be a stranger and spoke harshly to them. "Where do you come from?" he asked.

"From the land of Canaan," they replied, "to buy food."

[8]Although Joseph recognised his brothers, they did not recognise him. [9]Then he remembered his dreams about them and said to them, "You are spies! You have come to see where our land is unprotected."

[10]"No, my lord," they answered. "Your servants have come to buy food. [11]We are all the sons of one man. Your servants are honest men, not spies."

[12]"No!" he said to them. "You have come to see where our land is unprotected."

[13]But they replied, "Your servants were twelve brothers, the sons of one man, who lives in the land of Canaan. The youngest is now with our father, and one is no more."

[14]Joseph said to them, "It is just as I told you: You are spies! [15]And this is how you will be tested: As surely as Pharaoh lives, you will not leave this place unless your youngest brother comes here. [16]Send one of your number to get your brother; the rest of you will be kept in prison, so that your words may be tested to see if you are telling the truth. If you are not, then as surely as Pharaoh lives, you are spies!" [17]And he put them all in custody for three days.

[18]On the third day, Joseph said to them, "Do this and you will live, for I fear God: [19]If you are honest men, let one of your brothers stay here in prison, while the rest of you go and take grain back for your starving households. [20]But you must bring your youngest brother to me, so that your words may be verified and that you may not die." This they proceeded to do.

[21]They said to one another, "Surely we are being punished because of our brother. We saw how distressed he was when he pleaded with us for his life, but we would not listen; that's why this distress has come upon us."

[22]Reuben replied, "Didn't I tell you not to sin against the boy? But you wouldn't listen! Now we must give an accounting for his blood." [23]They did not realise that Joseph could understand them, since he was using an interpreter.

[24]He turned away from them and began to weep, but then turned back and spoke to them again. He had Simeon taken from them and bound before their eyes.

[25]Joseph gave orders to fill their bags with grain, to put each man's silver back in his sack, and to give them provisions for their journey. After this was done for them, [26]they loaded their grain on their donkeys and left.

[27]At the place where they stopped for the night one of them opened his sack to get feed for his donkey, and he saw his

silver in the mouth of his sack. ²⁸"My silver has been returned," he said to his brothers. "Here it is in my sack."

Their hearts sank and they turned to each other trembling and said, "What is this that God has done to us?"

²⁹When they came to their father Jacob in the land of Canaan, they told him all that had happened to them. They said, ³⁰"The man who is lord over the land spoke harshly to us and treated us as though we were spying on the land. ³¹But we said to him, 'We are honest men; we are not spies. ³²We were twelve brothers, sons of one father. One is no more, and the youngest is now with our father in Canaan.'

³³"Then the man who is lord over the land said to us, 'This is how I will know whether you are honest men: Leave one of your brothers here with me, and take food for your starving households and go. ³⁴But bring your youngest brother to me so I will know that you are not spies but honest men. Then I will give your brother back to you, and you can trade*a* in the land.'"

³⁵As they were emptying their sacks, there in each man's sack was his pouch of silver! When they and their father saw the money pouches, they were frightened. ³⁶Their father Jacob said to them, "You have deprived me of my children. Joseph is no more and Simeon is no more, and now you want to take Benjamin. Everything is against me!"

³⁷Then Reuben said to his father, "You may put both of my sons to death if I do not bring him back to you. Entrust him to my care, and I will bring him back."

³⁸But Jacob said, "My son will not go down there with you; his brother is dead and he is the only one left. If harm comes to him on the journey you are taking, you will bring my grey head down to the grave*b* in sorrow."

The Second Journey to Egypt

43 Now the famine was still severe in the land. ²So when they had eaten all the grain they had brought from Egypt,

their father said to them, "Go back and buy us a little more food."

³But Judah said to him, "The man warned us solemnly, 'You will not see my face again unless your brother is with you.' ⁴If you will send our brother along with us, we will go down and buy food for you. ⁵But if you will not send him, we will not go down, because the man said to us, 'You will not see my face again unless your brother is with you.'"

⁶Israel asked, "Why did you bring this trouble on me by telling the man you had another brother?"

⁷They replied, "The man questioned us closely about ourselves and our family. 'Is your father still living?' he asked us. 'Do you have another brother?' We simply answered his questions. How were we to know he would say, 'Bring your brother down here'?"

⁸Then Judah said to Israel his father, "Send the boy along with me and we will go at once, so that we and you and our children may live and not die. ⁹I myself will guarantee his safety; you can hold me personally responsible for him. If I do not bring him back to you and set him here before you, I will bear the blame before you all my life. ¹⁰As it is, if we had not delayed, we could have gone and returned twice."

¹¹Then their father Israel said to them, "If it must be, then do this: Put some of the best products of the land in your bags and take them down to the man as a gift—a little balm and a little honey, some spices and myrrh, some pistachio nuts and almonds. ¹²Take double the amount of silver with you, for you must return the silver that was put back into the mouths of your sacks. Perhaps it was a mistake. ¹³Take your brother also and go back to the man at once. ¹⁴And may God Almighty*a* grant you mercy before the man so that he will let your other brother and Benjamin come back with you. As for me, if I am bereaved, I am bereaved."

¹⁵So the men took the gifts and double the amount of silver, and Benjamin also. They hurried down to Egypt and presented themselves to Joseph. ¹⁶When Joseph

---

a34 Or move about freely   *b38 Hebrew Sheol*
a14 Hebrew El-Shaddai

saw Benjamin with them, he said to the steward of his house, "Take these men to my house, slaughter an animal and prepare dinner; they are to eat with me at noon."

17The man did as Joseph told him and took the men to Joseph's house. 18Now the men were frightened when they were taken to his house. They thought, "We were brought here because of the silver that was put back into our sacks the first time. He wants to attack us and overpower us and seize us as slaves and take our donkeys."

19So they went up to Joseph's steward and spoke to him at the entrance to the house. 20"Please, sir," they said, "we came down here the first time to buy food. 21But at the place where we stopped for the night we opened our sacks and each of us found his silver—the exact weight—in the mouth of his sack. So we have brought it back with us. 22We have also brought additional silver with us to buy food. We don't know who put our silver in our sacks."

23"It's all right," he said. "Don't be afraid. Your God, the God of your father, has given you treasure in your sacks; I received your silver." Then he brought Simeon out to them.

24The steward took the men into Joseph's house, gave them water to wash their feet and provided fodder for their donkeys. 25They prepared their gifts for Joseph's arrival at noon, because they had heard that they were to eat there.

26When Joseph came home, they presented to him the gifts they had brought into the house, and they bowed down before him to the ground. 27He asked them how they were, and then he said, "How is your aged father you told me about? Is he still living?"

28They replied, "Your servant our father is still alive and well." And they bowed low to pay him honour.

29As he looked about and saw his brother Benjamin, his own mother's son, he asked, "Is this your youngest brother, the one you told me about?" And he said, "God be gracious to you, my son." 30Deeply moved at the sight of his brother, Joseph hurried out and looked for a place to weep. He went into his private room and wept there.

31After he had washed his face, he came out and, controlling himself, said, "Serve the food."

32They served him by himself, the brothers by themselves, and the Egyptians who ate with him by themselves, because Egyptians could not eat with Hebrews, for that is detestable to Egyptians. 33The men had been seated before him in the order of their ages, from the firstborn to the youngest; and they looked at each other in astonishment. 34When portions were served to them from Joseph's table, Benjamin's portion was five times as much as anyone else's. So they feasted and drank freely with him.

A Silver Cup in a Sack

44 Now Joseph gave these instructions to the steward of his house: "Fill the men's sacks with as much food as they can carry, and put each man's silver in the mouth of his sack. 2Then put my cup, the silver one, in the mouth of the youngest one's sack, along with the silver for his grain." And he did as Joseph said.

3As morning dawned, the men were sent on their way with their donkeys. 4They had not gone far from the city when Joseph said to his steward, "Go after those men at once, and when you catch up with them, say to them, 'Why have you repaid good with evil? 5Isn't this the cup my master drinks from and also uses for divination? This is a wicked thing you have done.'"

6When he caught up with them, he repeated these words to them. 7But they said to him, "Why does my lord say such things? Far be it from your servants to do anything like that! 8We even brought back to you from the land of Canaan the silver we found inside the mouths of our sacks. So why would we steal silver or gold from your master's house? 9If any of your servants is found to have it, he will die; and the rest of us will become my lord's slaves."

10"Very well, then," he said, "let it be as you say. Whoever is found to have it will become my slave; the rest of you will be free from blame."

¹¹Each of them quickly lowered his sack to the ground and opened it. ¹²Then the steward proceeded to search, beginning with the oldest and ending with the youngest. And the cup was found in Benjamin's sack. ¹³At this, they tore their clothes. Then they all loaded their donkeys and returned to the city.

¹⁴Joseph was still in the house when Judah and his brothers came in, and they threw themselves to the ground before him. ¹⁵Joseph said to them, "What is this you have done? Don't you know that a man like me can find things out by divination?"

¹⁶"What can we say to my lord?" Judah replied. "What can we say? How can we prove our innocence? God has uncovered your servants' guilt. We are now my lord's slaves—we ourselves and the one who was found to have the cup."

¹⁷But Joseph said, "Far be it from me to do such a thing! Only the man who was found to have the cup will become my slave. The rest of you, go back to your father in peace."

¹⁸Then Judah went up to him and said: "Please, my lord, let your servant speak a word to my lord. Do not be angry with your servant, though you are equal to Pharaoh himself. ¹⁹My lord asked his servants, 'Do you have a father or a brother?' ²⁰And we answered, 'We have an aged father, and there is a young son born to him in his old age. His brother is dead, and he is the only one of his mother's sons left, and his father loves him.'

²¹"Then you said to your servants, 'Bring him down to me so I can see him for myself.' ²²And we said to my lord, 'The boy cannot leave his father; if he leaves him, his father will die.' ²³But you told your servants, 'Unless your youngest brother comes down with you, you will not see my face again.' ²⁴When we went back to your servant my father, we told him what my lord had said.

²⁵"Then our father said, 'Go back and buy a little more food.' ²⁶But we said, 'We cannot go down. Only if our youngest brother is with us will we go. We cannot see the man's face unless our youngest brother is with us.'

²⁷"Your servant my father said to us, 'You know that my wife bore me two sons. ²⁸One of them went away from me, and I said, "He has surely been torn to pieces." And I have not seen him since. ²⁹If you take this one from me too and harm comes to him, you will bring my grey head down to the grave^a in misery.'

³⁰"So now, if the boy is not with us when I go back to your servant my father and if my father, whose life is closely bound up with the boy's life, ³¹sees that the boy isn't there, he will die. Your servants will bring the grey head of our father down to the grave in sorrow. ³²Your servant guaranteed the boy's safety to my father. I said, 'If I do not bring him back to you, I will bear the blame before you, my father, all my life!'

³³"Now then, please let your servant remain here as my lord's slave in place of the boy, and let the boy return with his brothers. ³⁴How can I go back to my father if the boy is not with me? No! Do not let me see the misery that would come upon my father."

Joseph Makes Himself Known

45 Then Joseph could no longer control himself before all his attendants, and he cried out, "Make everyone leave my presence!" So there was no-one with Joseph when he made himself known to his brothers. ²And he wept so loudly that the Egyptians heard him, and Pharaoh's household heard about it.

³Joseph said to his brothers, "I am Joseph! Is my father still living?" But his brothers were not able to answer him, because they were terrified at his presence.

⁴Then Joseph said to his brothers, "Come close to me." When they had done so, he said, "I am your brother Joseph, the one you sold into Egypt! ⁵And now, do not be distressed and do not be angry with

---

^{a}29 Hebrew *Sheol*; also in verse 31

yourselves for selling me here, because it was to save lives that God sent me ahead of you. 6For two years now there has been famine in the land, and for the next five years there will not be ploughing and reaping. 7But God sent me ahead of you to preserve for you a remnant on earth and to save your lives by a great deliverance.*a*

8"So then, it was not you who sent me here, but God. He made me father to Pharaoh, lord of his entire household and ruler of all Egypt. 9Now hurry back to my father and say to him, 'This is what your son Joseph says: God has made me lord of all Egypt. Come down to me; don't delay. 10You shall live in the region of Goshen and be near me—you, your children and grandchildren, your flocks and herds, and all you have. 11I will provide for you there, because five years of famine are still to come. Otherwise you and your household and all who belong to you will become destitute.'

12"You can see for yourselves, and so can my brother Benjamin, that it is really I who am speaking to you. 13Tell my father about all the honour accorded me in Egypt and about everything you have seen. And bring my father down here quickly."

14Then he threw his arms around his brother Benjamin and wept, and Benjamin embraced him, weeping. 15And he kissed all his brothers and wept over them. Afterwards his brothers talked with him.

16When the news reached Pharaoh's palace that Joseph's brothers had come, Pharaoh and all his officials were pleased. 17Pharaoh said to Joseph, "Tell your brothers, 'Do this: Load your animals and return to the land of Canaan, 18and bring your father and your families back to me. I will give you the best of the land of Egypt and you can enjoy the fat of the land.'

19"You are also directed to tell them, 'Do this: Take some carts from Egypt for your children and your wives, and get your father and come. 20Never mind about your belongings, because the best of all Egypt will be yours.'"

21So the sons of Israel did this. Joseph gave them carts, as Pharaoh had commanded, and he also gave them provisions for their journey. 22To each of them he gave new clothing, but to Benjamin he gave three hundred shekels*b* of silver and five sets of clothes. 23And this is what he sent to his father: ten donkeys loaded with the best things of Egypt, and ten female donkeys loaded with grain and bread and other provisions for his journey. 24Then he sent his brothers away, and as they were leaving he said to them, "Don't quarrel on the way!"

25So they went up out of Egypt and came to their father Jacob in the land of Canaan. 26They told him, "Joseph is still alive! In fact, he is ruler of all Egypt." Jacob was stunned; he did not believe them. 27But when they told him everything Joseph had said to them, and when he saw the carts Joseph had sent to carry him back, the spirit of their father Jacob revived. 28And Israel said, "I'm convinced! My son Joseph is still alive. I will go and see him before I die."

Jacob Goes to Egypt

46 So Israel set out with all that was his, and when he reached Beersheba, he offered sacrifices to the God of his father Isaac.

2And God spoke to Israel in a vision at night and said, "Jacob! Jacob!"

"Here I am," he replied.

3"I am God, the God of your father," he said. "Do not be afraid to go down to Egypt, for I will make you into a great nation there. 4I will go down to Egypt with you, and I will surely bring you back again. And Joseph's own hand will close your eyes."

5Then Jacob left Beersheba, and Israel's sons took their father Jacob and their children and their wives in the carts that Pharaoh had sent to transport him. 6They also took with them their livestock and the possessions they had acquired in Canaan, and Jacob and all his offspring went to Egypt. 7He took with him to Egypt his sons and grandsons and his daughters and granddaughters—all his offspring.

---

a7 Or *save you as a great band of survivors*   *b22* That is, about 7½ pounds (about 3.5 kilograms)

⁸These are the names of the sons of Israel (Jacob and his descendants) who went to Egypt:

Reuben the firstborn of Jacob.
⁹The sons of Reuben:
Hanoch, Pallu, Hezron and Carmi.
¹⁰The sons of Simeon:
Jemuel, Jamin, Ohad, Jakin, Zohar and Shaul the son of a Canaanite woman.
¹¹The sons of Levi:
Gershon, Kohath and Merari.
¹²The sons of Judah:
Er, Onan, Shelah, Perez and Zerah (but Er and Onan had died in the land of Canaan).
The sons of Perez:
Hezron and Hamul.
¹³The sons of Issachar:
Tola, Puah,ᵃ Jashubᵇ and Shimron.
¹⁴The sons of Zebulun:
Sered, Elon and Jahleel.

¹⁵These were the sons Leah bore to Jacob in Paddan Aram,ᶜ besides his daughter Dinah. These sons and daughters of his were thirty-three in all.

¹⁶The sons of Gad:
Zephon,ᵈ Haggi, Shuni, Ezbon, Eri, Arodi and Areli.
¹⁷The sons of Asher:
Imnah, Ishvah, Ishvi and Beriah.
Their sister was Serah.
The sons of Beriah:
Heber and Malkiel.
¹⁸These were the children born to Jacob by Zilpah, whom Laban had given to his daughter Leah—sixteen in all.

¹⁹The sons of Jacob's wife Rachel:
Joseph and Benjamin. ²⁰In Egypt, Manasseh and Ephraim were born to Joseph by Asenath daughter of Potiphera, priest of On.ᵉ
²¹The sons of Benjamin:
Bela, Beker, Ashbel, Gera, Naaman, Ehi, Rosh, Muppim, Huppim and Ard.
²²These were the sons of Rachel who were born to Jacob—fourteen in all.

²³The son of Dan:
Hushim.
²⁴The sons of Naphtali:
Jahziel, Guni, Jezer and Shillem.
²⁵These were the sons born to Jacob by Bilhah, whom Laban had given to his daughter Rachel—seven in all.

²⁶All those who went to Egypt with Jacob—those who were his direct descendants, not counting his sons' wives—numbered sixty-six persons. ²⁷With the two sonsᶠ who had been born to Joseph in Egypt, the members of Jacob's family, which went to Egypt, were seventyᵍ in all.

²⁸Now Jacob sent Judah ahead of him to Joseph to get directions to Goshen. When they arrived in the region of Goshen, ²⁹Joseph had his chariot made ready and went to Goshen to meet his father Israel. As soon as Joseph appeared before him, he threw his arms around his fatherʰ and wept for a long time.

³⁰Israel said to Joseph, "Now I am ready to die, since I have seen for myself that you are still alive."

³¹Then Joseph said to his brothers and to his father's household, "I will go up and speak to Pharaoh and will say to him, 'My brothers and my father's household, who were living in the land of Canaan, have come to me. ³²The men are shepherds; they tend livestock, and they have brought along their flocks and herds and everything they own.' ³³When Pharaoh calls you in and asks, 'What is your occupation?' ³⁴you should answer, 'Your servants have tended livestock from our boyhood on, just as our fathers did.' Then you

---

ᵃ13 Samaritan Pentateuch and Syriac (see also 1 Chron. 7:1); Masoretic Text *Puvah*
ᵇ13 Samaritan Pentateuch and some Septuagint manuscripts (see also Num. 26:24 and 1 Chron. 7:1); Masoretic Text *Job*
ᶜ15 That is, North-west Mesopotamia
ᵈ16 Samaritan Pentateuch and Septuagint (see also Num. 26:15); Masoretic Text *Ziphion*
ᵉ20 That is, Heliopolis   ᶠ27 Hebrew; Septuagint *the nine children*
ᵍ27 Hebrew (see also Exodus 1:5 and footnote); Septuagint (see also Acts 7:14) *seventy-five*
ʰ29 Hebrew *around him*

will be allowed to settle in the region of Goshen, for all shepherds are detestable to the Egyptians."

47 Joseph went and told Pharaoh, "My father and brothers, with their flocks and herds and everything they own, have come from the land of Canaan and are now in Goshen." ²He chose five of his brothers and presented them before Pharaoh.

³Pharaoh asked the brothers, "What is your occupation?"

"Your servants are shepherds," they replied to Pharaoh, "just as our fathers were." ⁴They also said to him, "We have come to live here awhile, because the famine is severe in Canaan and your servants' flocks have no pasture. So now, please let your servants settle in Goshen."

⁵Pharaoh said to Joseph, "Your father and your brothers have come to you, ⁶and the land of Egypt is before you; settle your father and your brothers in the best part of the land. Let them live in Goshen. And if you know of any among them with special ability, put them in charge of my own livestock."

⁷Then Joseph brought his father Jacob in and presented him before Pharaoh. After Jacob blessed*ᵃ* Pharaoh, ⁸Pharaoh asked him, "How old are you?"

⁹And Jacob said to Pharaoh, "The years of my pilgrimage are a hundred and thirty. My years have been few and difficult, and they do not equal the years of the pilgrimage of my fathers." ¹⁰Then Jacob blessed*ᵇ* Pharaoh and went out from his presence.

¹¹So Joseph settled his father and his brothers in Egypt and gave them property in the best part of the land, the district of Rameses, as Pharaoh directed. ¹²Joseph also provided his father and his brothers and all his father's household with food, according to the number of their children.

Joseph and the Famine

¹³There was no food, however, in the whole region because the famine was severe; both Egypt and Canaan wasted away because of the famine. ¹⁴Joseph collected all the money that was to be found in Egypt and Canaan in payment for the grain they were buying, and he brought it to Pharaoh's palace. ¹⁵When the money of the people of Egypt and Canaan was gone, all Egypt came to Joseph and said, "Give us food. Why should we die before your eyes? Our money is used up."

¹⁶"Then bring your livestock," said Joseph. "I will sell you food in exchange for your livestock, since your money is gone." ¹⁷So they brought their livestock to Joseph, and he gave them food in exchange for their horses, their sheep and goats, their cattle and donkeys. And he brought them through that year with food in exchange for all their livestock.

¹⁸When that year was over, they came to him the following year and said, "We cannot hide from our lord the fact that since our money is gone and our livestock belongs to you, there is nothing left for our lord except our bodies and our land. ¹⁹Why should we perish before your eyes—we and our land as well? Buy us and our land in exchange for food, and we with our land will be in bondage to Pharaoh. Give us seed so that we may live and not die, and that the land may not become desolate."

²⁰So Joseph bought all the land in Egypt for Pharaoh. The Egyptians, one and all, sold their fields, because the famine was too severe for them. The land became Pharaoh's, ²¹and Joseph reduced the people to servitude,*ᶜ* from one end of Egypt to the other. ²²However, he did not buy the land of the priests, because they received a regular allotment from Pharaoh and had food enough from the allotment Pharaoh gave them. That is why they did not sell their land.

²³Joseph said to the people, "Now that I have bought you and your land today for Pharaoh, here is seed for you so you can plant the ground. ²⁴But when the crop comes in, give a fifth of it to Pharaoh. The other four-fifths you may keep as seed for the fields and as food for yourselves and your households and your children."

²⁵"You have saved our lives," they said.

ᵃ7 Or *greeted*   *ᵇ10* Or *said farewell to*
ᶜ21 Samaritan Pentateuch and Septuagint (see also Vulgate); Masoretic Text *and he moved the people into the cities*

"May we find favour in the eyes of our lord; we will be in bondage to Pharaoh."

26So Joseph established it as a law concerning land in Egypt—still in force today—that a fifth of the produce belongs to Pharaoh. It was only the land of the priests that did not become Pharaoh's.

27Now the Israelites settled in Egypt in the region of Goshen. They acquired property there and were fruitful and increased greatly in number.

28Jacob lived in Egypt seventeen years, and the years of his life were a hundred and forty-seven. 29When the time drew near for Israel to die, he called for his son Joseph and said to him, "If I have found favour in your eyes, put your hand under my thigh and promise that you will show me kindness and faithfulness. Do not bury me in Egypt, 30but when I rest with my fathers, carry me out of Egypt and bury me where they are buried."

"I will do as you say," he said.

31"Swear to me," he said. Then Joseph swore to him, and Israel worshipped as he leaned on the top of his staff.d

Manasseh and Ephraim

48 Some time later Joseph was told, "Your father is ill." So he took his two sons Manasseh and Ephraim along with him. 2When Jacob was told, "Your son Joseph has come to you," Israel rallied his strength and sat up on the bed.

3Jacob said to Joseph, "God Almightya appeared to me at Luz in the land of Canaan, and there he blessed me 4and said to me, 'I am going to make you fruitful and will increase your numbers. I will make you a community of peoples, and I will give this land as an everlasting possession to your descendants after you.'

5"Now then, your two sons born to you in Egypt before I came to you here will be reckoned as mine; Ephraim and Manasseh will be mine, just as Reuben and Simeon are mine. 6Any children born to you after them will be yours; in the territory they inherit they will be reckoned under the names of their brothers. 7As I was returning from Paddan,b to my sorrow Rachel died in the land of Canaan while we were still on the way, a little distance from Ephrath. So I buried her there beside the road to Ephrath" (that is, Bethlehem).

8When Israel saw the sons of Joseph, he asked, "Who are these?"

9"They are the sons God has given me here," Joseph said to his father.

Then Israel said, "Bring them to me so that I may bless them."

10Now Israel's eyes were failing because of old age, and he could hardly see. So Joseph brought his sons close to him, and his father kissed them and embraced them.

11Israel said to Joseph, "I never expected to see your face again, and now God has allowed me to see your children too."

12Then Joseph removed them from Israel's knees and bowed down with his face to the ground. 13And Joseph took both of them, Ephraim on his right towards Israel's left hand and Manasseh on his left towards Israel's right hand, and brought them close to him. 14But Israel reached out his right hand and put it on Ephraim's head, though he was the younger, and crossing his arms, he put his left hand on Manasseh's head, even though Manasseh was the firstborn.

15Then he blessed Joseph and said,

"May the God before whom my
    fathers
  Abraham and Isaac walked,
the God who has been my shepherd
  all my life to this day,
16the Angel who has delivered me from
    all harm
  —may he bless these boys.
May they be called by my name
  and the names of my fathers
    Abraham and Isaac,
and may they increase greatly
  upon the earth."

---

d31 Or Israel bowed down at the head of his bed
a3 Hebrew El-Shaddai   b7 That is, North-west Mesopotamia

¹⁷When Joseph saw his father placing his right hand on Ephraim's head he was displeased; so he took hold of his father's hand to move it from Ephraim's head to Manasseh's head. ¹⁸Joseph said to him, "No, my father, this one is the firstborn; put your right hand on his head."

¹⁹But his father refused and said, "I know, my son, I know. He too will become a people, and he too will become great. Nevertheless, his younger brother will be greater than he, and his descendants will become a group of nations." ²⁰He blessed them that day and said,

> "In your*c* name will Israel pronounce
> this blessing:
>   'May God make you like Ephraim
> and Manasseh.'"

So he put Ephraim ahead of Manasseh.

²¹Then Israel said to Joseph, "I am about to die, but God will be with you*d* and take you*d* back to the land of your*d* fathers. ²²And to you, as one who is over your brothers, I give the ridge of land*e* I took from the Amorites with my sword and my bow."

Jacob Blesses His Sons

49 Then Jacob called for his sons and said: "Gather round so that I can tell you what will happen to you in days to come.

> ²"Assemble and listen, sons of Jacob;
> listen to your father Israel.

> ³"Reuben, you are my firstborn,
>   my might, the first sign of my
>   strength,
>   excelling in honour, excelling in
>   power.
> ⁴Turbulent as the waters, you will no
>   longer excel,

> for you went up onto your father's
>   bed,
> onto my couch and defiled it.

> ⁵"Simeon and Levi are brothers—
>   their swords*a* are weapons of
>   violence.
> ⁶Let me not enter their council,
>   let me not join their assembly,
> for they have killed men in their anger
>   and hamstrung oxen as they
>   pleased.
> ⁷Cursed be their anger, so fierce,
>   and their fury, so cruel!
> I will scatter them in Jacob
>   and disperse them in Israel.

> ⁸"Judah,*b* your brothers will praise you;
>   your hand will be on the neck of your
>   enemies;
>   your father's sons will bow down to
>   you.
> ⁹You are a lion's cub, O Judah;
>   you return from the prey, my son.
> Like a lion he crouches and lies down,
>   like a lioness—who dares to rouse
>   him?
> ¹⁰The sceptre will not depart from Judah,
>   nor the ruler's staff from between his
>   feet,
> until he comes to whom it belongs*c*
>   and the obedience of the nations is
>   his.
> ¹¹He will tether his donkey to a vine,
>   his colt to the choicest branch;
> he will wash his garments in wine,
>   his robes in the blood of grapes.
> ¹²His eyes will be darker than wine,
>   his teeth whiter than milk.*d*

> ¹³"Zebulun will live by the seashore
>   and become a haven for ships;
>   his border will extend towards
>   Sidon.

> ¹⁴"Issachar is a scrawny*e* donkey
>   lying down between two saddlebags.*f*

---

c20 The Hebrew is singular.   *d21* The Hebrew is plural.
e22 Or *And to you I give one portion more than to your brothers—the portion*
a5 The meaning of the Hebrew for this word is uncertain.
b8 *Judah* sounds like and may be derived from the Hebrew for *praise.*
c10 Or *until Shiloh comes*; or *until he comes to whom tribute belongs*
d12 Or *will be dull from wine, / his teeth white from milk*   *e14* Or *strong*   *f14* Or *campfires*

15When he sees how good is his resting
place
and how pleasant is his land,
he will bend his shoulder to the burden
and submit to forced labour.

16"Dan[g] will provide justice for his people
as one of the tribes of Israel.
17Dan will be a serpent by the roadside,
a viper along the path,
that bites the horse's heels
so that its rider tumbles backwards.

18"I look for your deliverance, O LORD.

19"Gad[h] will be attacked by a band of
raiders,
but he will attack them at their heels.

20"Asher's food will be rich;
he will provide delicacies fit for a
king.

21"Naphtali is a doe set free
that bears beautiful fawns.[i]

22"Joseph is a fruitful vine,
a fruitful vine near a spring,
whose branches climb over a wall.[j]
23With bitterness archers attacked him;
they shot at him with hostility.
24But his bow remained steady,
his strong arms stayed[k] supple,
because of the hand of the Mighty One
of Jacob,
because of the Shepherd, the Rock of
Israel,
25because of your father's God, who
helps you,
because of the Almighty,[l] who blesses
you
with blessings of the heavens above,
blessings of the deep that lies below,
blessings of the breast and womb.
26Your father's blessings are greater
than the blessings of the ancient
mountains,
than[m] the bounty of the age-old hills.

Let all these rest on the head of Joseph,
on the brow of the prince among[n] his
brothers.

27"Benjamin is a ravenous wolf;
in the morning he devours the prey,
in the evening he divides the
plunder."

28All these are the twelve tribes of
Israel, and this is what their father said to
them when he blessed them, giving each
the blessing appropriate to him.

The Death of Jacob

29Then he gave them these instructions:
"I am about to be gathered to my people.
Bury me with my fathers in the cave in the
field of Ephron the Hittite, 30the cave in
the field of Machpelah, near Mamre in
Canaan, which Abraham bought as a burial place from Ephron the Hittite, along
with the field. 31There Abraham and his
wife Sarah were buried, there Isaac and
his wife Rebekah were buried, and there I
buried Leah. 32The field and the cave in it
were bought from the Hittites."[o]

33When Jacob had finished giving instructions to his sons, he drew his feet up
into the bed, breathed his last and was
gathered to his people.

50 Joseph threw himself upon his
father and wept over him and
kissed him. 2Then Joseph directed the
physicians in his service to embalm his
father Israel. So the physicians embalmed
him, 3taking a full forty days, for that was
the time required for embalming. And the
Egyptians mourned for him seventy days.

4When the days of mourning had
passed, Joseph said to Pharaoh's court,
"If I have found favour in your eyes, speak
to Pharaoh for me. Tell him, 5'My father
made me swear an oath and said, "I am
about to die; bury me in the tomb I dug for
myself in the land of Canaan." Now let me
go up and bury my father; then I will
return.'"

---

g16 Dan here means *he provides justice.*   h19 Gad can mean *attack* and *band of raiders.*
i21 Or *free;* / *he utters beautiful words*
j22 Or *Joseph is a wild colt,* / *a wild colt near a spring,* / *a wild donkey on a terraced hill*
k23,24 Or *archers will attack . . . will shoot . . . will remain . . . will stay*   l25 Hebrew *Shaddai*
m26 Or *of my progenitors,* / *as great as*   n26 Or *the one separated from*   o32 Or *the sons of Heth*

[6]Pharaoh said, "Go up and bury your father, as he made you swear to do."

[7]So Joseph went up to bury his father. All Pharaoh's officials accompanied him—the dignitaries of his court and all the dignitaries of Egypt—[8]besides all the members of Joseph's household and his brothers and those belonging to his father's household. Only their children and their flocks and herds were left in Goshen. [9]Chariots and horsemen[a] also went up with him. It was a very large company.

[10]When they reached the threshing-floor of Atad, near the Jordan, they lamented loudly and bitterly; and there Joseph observed a seven-day period of mourning for his father. [11]When the Canaanites who lived there saw the mourning at the threshing-floor of Atad, they said, "The Egyptians are holding a solemn ceremony of mourning." That is why that place near the Jordan is called Abel Mizraim.[b]

[12]So Jacob's sons did as he had commanded them: [13]They carried him to the land of Canaan and buried him in the cave in the field of Machpelah, near Mamre, which Abraham had bought as a burial place from Ephron the Hittite, along with the field. [14]After burying his father, Joseph returned to Egypt, together with his brothers and all the others who had gone with him to bury his father.

Joseph Reassures His Brothers

[15]When Joseph's brothers saw that their father was dead, they said, "What if Joseph holds a grudge against us and pays us back for all the wrongs we did to him?"

[16]So they sent word to Joseph, saying, "Your father left these instructions before he died: [17]'This is what you are to say to Joseph: I ask you to forgive your brothers the sins and the wrongs they committed in treating you so badly.' Now please forgive the sins of the servants of the God of your father." When their message came to him, Joseph wept.

[18]His brothers then came and threw themselves down before him. "We are your slaves," they said.

[19]But Joseph said to them, "Don't be afraid. Am I in the place of God? [20]You intended to harm me, but God intended it for good to accomplish what is now being done, the saving of many lives. [21]So then, don't be afraid. I will provide for you and your children." And he reassured them and spoke kindly to them.

The Death of Joseph

[22]Joseph stayed in Egypt, along with all his father's family. He lived a hundred and ten years [23]and saw the third generation of Ephraim's children. Also the children of Makir son of Manasseh were placed at birth on Joseph's knees.[c]

[24]Then Joseph said to his brothers, "I am about to die. But God will surely come to your aid and take you up out of this land to the land he promised on oath to Abraham, Isaac and Jacob." [25]And Joseph made the sons of Israel swear an oath and said, "God will surely come to your aid, and then you must carry my bones up from this place."

[26]So Joseph died at the age of a hundred and ten. And after they embalmed him, he was placed in a coffin in Egypt.

---

[a]9 Or *charioteers*   [b]11 *Abel Mizraim* means *mourning of the Egyptians.*   [c]23 That is, were counted as his

Exodus

The Israelites Oppressed

1 These are the names of the sons of Israel who went to Egypt with Jacob, each with his family: ²Reuben, Simeon, Levi and Judah; ³Issachar, Zebulun and Benjamin; ⁴Dan and Naphtali; Gad and Asher. ⁵The descendants of Jacob numbered seventy[a] in all; Joseph was already in Egypt.

⁶Now Joseph and all his brothers and all that generation died, ⁷but the Israelites were fruitful and multiplied greatly and became exceedingly numerous, so that the land was filled with them.

⁸Then a new king, who did not know about Joseph, came to power in Egypt. ⁹"Look," he said to his people, "the Israelites have become much too numerous for us. ¹⁰Come, we must deal shrewdly with them or they will become even more numerous and, if war breaks out, will join our enemies, fight against us and leave the country."

¹¹So they put slave masters over them to oppress them with forced labour, and they built Pithom and Rameses as store cities for Pharaoh. ¹²But the more they were oppressed, the more they multiplied and spread; so the Egyptians came to dread the Israelites ¹³and worked them ruthlessly. ¹⁴They made their lives bitter with hard labour in brick and mortar and with all kinds of work in the fields; in all their hard labour the Egyptians used them ruthlessly.

¹⁵The king of Egypt said to the Hebrew midwives, whose names were Shiphrah and Puah, ¹⁶"When you help the Hebrew women in childbirth and observe them on the delivery stool, if it is a boy, kill him; but if it is a girl, let her live." ¹⁷The midwives, however, feared God and did not do what the king of Egypt had told them to do; they let the boys live. ¹⁸Then the king of Egypt summoned the midwives and asked them, "Why have you done this? Why have you let the boys live?"

¹⁹The midwives answered Pharaoh, "Hebrew women are not like Egyptian women; they are vigorous and give birth before the midwives arrive."

²⁰So God was kind to the midwives and the people increased and became even more numerous. ²¹And because the midwives feared God, he gave them families of their own.

²²Then Pharaoh gave this order to all his people: "Every boy that is born[b] you must throw into the Nile, but let every girl live."

The Birth of Moses

2 Now a man of the house of Levi married a Levite woman, ²and she became pregnant and gave birth to a son. When she saw that he was a fine child, she hid him for three months. ³But when she could hide him no longer, she got a papyrus basket for him and coated it with tar and pitch. Then she placed the child in it and put it among the reeds along the bank of the Nile. ⁴His sister stood at a distance to see what would happen to him.

---

[a]5 Masoretic Text (see also Gen. 46:27); Dead Sea Scrolls and Septuagint (see also Acts 7:14 and note at Gen. 46:27) *seventy-five*   [b]22 Masoretic Text; Samaritan Pentateuch, Septuagint and Targums *born to the Hebrews*

5Then Pharaoh's daughter went down to the Nile to bathe, and her attendants were walking along the river bank. She saw the basket among the reeds and sent her slave girl to get it. 6She opened it and saw the baby. He was crying, and she felt sorry for him. "This is one of the Hebrew babies," she said.

7Then his sister asked Pharaoh's daughter, "Shall I go and get one of the Hebrew women to nurse the baby for you?"

8"Yes, go," she answered. And the girl went and got the baby's mother. 9Pharaoh's daughter said to her, "Take this baby and nurse him for me, and I will pay you." So the woman took the baby and nursed him. 10When the child grew older, she took him to Pharaoh's daughter and he became her son. She named him Moses,a saying, "I drew him out of the water."

Moses Flees to Midian

11One day, after Moses had grown up, he went out to where his own people were and watched them at their hard labour. He saw an Egyptian beating a Hebrew, one of his own people. 12Glancing this way and that and seeing no-one, he killed the Egyptian and hid him in the sand. 13The next day he went out and saw two Hebrews fighting. He asked the one in the wrong, "Why are you hitting your fellow Hebrew?"

14The man said, "Who made you ruler and judge over us? Are you thinking of killing me as you killed the Egyptian?" Then Moses was afraid and thought, "What I did must have become known."

15When Pharaoh heard of this, he tried to kill Moses, but Moses fled from Pharaoh and went to live in Midian, where he sat down by a well. 16Now a priest of Midian had seven daughters, and they came to draw water and fill the troughs to water their father's flock. 17Some shepherds came along and drove them away, but Moses got up and came to their rescue and watered their flock.

18When the girls returned to Reuel their father, he asked them, "Why have you returned so early today?"

19They answered, "An Egyptian rescued us from the shepherds. He even drew water for us and watered the flock."

20"And where is he?" he asked his daughters. "Why did you leave him? Invite him to have something to eat."

21Moses agreed to stay with the man, who gave his daughter Zipporah to Moses in marriage. 22Zipporah gave birth to a son, and Moses named him Gershom,b saying, "I have become an alien in a foreign land."

23During that long period, the king of Egypt died. The Israelites groaned in their slavery and cried out, and their cry for help because of their slavery went up to God. 24God heard their groaning and he remembered his covenant with Abraham, with Isaac and with Jacob. 25So God looked on the Israelites and was concerned about them.

Moses and the Burning Bush

3 Now Moses was tending the flock of Jethro his father-in-law, the priest of Midian, and he led the flock to the far side of the desert and came to Horeb, the mountain of God. 2There the angel of the LORD appeared to him in flames of fire from within a bush. Moses saw that though the bush was on fire it did not burn up. 3So Moses thought, "I will go over and see this strange sight—why the bush does not burn up."

4When the LORD saw that he had gone over to look, God called to him from within the bush, "Moses! Moses!"

And Moses said, "Here I am."

5"Do not come any closer," God said. "Take off your sandals, for the place where you are standing is holy ground." 6Then he said, "I am the God of your father, the God of Abraham, the God of Isaac and the God of Jacob." At this, Moses hid his face, because he was afraid to look at God.

a10 *Moses* sounds like the Hebrew for *draw out.*   b22 *Gershom* sounds like the Hebrew for *an alien there.*

7The LORD said, "I have indeed seen the misery of my people in Egypt. I have heard them crying out because of their slave drivers, and I am concerned about their suffering. 8So I have come down to rescue them from the hand of the Egyptians and to bring them up out of that land into a good and spacious land, a land flowing with milk and honey—the home of the Canaanites, Hittites, Amorites, Perizzites, Hivites and Jebusites. 9And now the cry of the Israelites has reached me, and I have seen the way the Egyptians are oppressing them. 10So now, go. I am sending you to Pharaoh to bring my people the Israelites out of Egypt."

11But Moses said to God, "Who am I, that I should go to Pharaoh and bring the Israelites out of Egypt?"

12And God said, "I will be with you. And this will be the sign to you that it is I who have sent you: When you have brought the people out of Egypt, you*a* will worship God on this mountain."

13Moses said to God, "Suppose I go to the Israelites and say to them, 'The God of your fathers has sent me to you,' and they ask me, 'What is his name?' Then what shall I tell them?"

14God said to Moses, "I AM WHO I AM.*b* This is what you are to say to the Israelites: 'I AM has sent me to you.'"

15God also said to Moses, "Say to the Israelites, 'The LORD,*c* the God of your fathers—the God of Abraham, the God of Isaac and the God of Jacob—has sent me to you.' This is my name for ever, the name by which I am to be remembered from generation to generation.

16"Go, assemble the elders of Israel and say to them, 'The LORD, the God of your fathers—the God of Abraham, Isaac and Jacob—appeared to me and said: I have watched over you and have seen what has been done to you in Egypt. 17And I have promised to bring you up out of your misery in Egypt into the land of the Canaanites, Hittites, Amorites, Perizzites, Hivites and Jebusites—a land flowing with milk and honey.'

18"The elders of Israel will listen to you. Then you and the elders are to go to the king of Egypt and say to him, 'The LORD, the God of the Hebrews, has met with us. Let us take a three-day journey into the desert to offer sacrifices to the LORD our God.' 19But I know that the king of Egypt will not let you go unless a mighty hand compels him. 20So I will stretch out my hand and strike the Egyptians with all the wonders that I will perform among them. After that, he will let you go.

21"And I will make the Egyptians favourably disposed towards this people, so that when you leave you will not go empty-handed. 22Every woman is to ask her neighbour and any woman living in her house for articles of silver and gold and for clothing, which you will put on your sons and daughters. And so you will plunder the Egyptians."

Signs for Moses

4 Moses answered, "What if they do not believe me or listen to me and say, 'The LORD did not appear to you'?"

2Then the LORD said to him, "What is that in your hand?"

"A staff," he replied.

3The LORD said, "Throw it on the ground."

Moses threw it on the ground and it became a snake, and he ran from it. 4Then the LORD said to him, "Reach out your hand and take it by the tail." So Moses reached out and took hold of the snake and it turned back into a staff in his hand. 5"This," said the LORD, "is so that they may believe that the LORD, the God of their fathers—the God of Abraham, the God of Isaac and the God of Jacob—has appeared to you."

6Then the LORD said, "Put your hand inside your cloak." So Moses put his hand into his cloak, and when he took it out, it was leprous,*a* like snow.

---

a12 The Hebrew is plural.   *b14* Or *I WILL BE WHAT I WILL BE*
c15 The Hebrew for *LORD* sounds like and may be derived from the Hebrew for *I AM* in verse 14.
a6 The Hebrew word was used for various diseases affecting the skin—not necessarily leprosy.

7"Now put it back into your cloak," he said. So Moses put his hand back into his cloak, and when he took it out, it was restored, like the rest of his flesh.

8Then the LORD said, "If they do not believe you or pay attention to the first miraculous sign, they may believe the second. 9But if they do not believe these two signs or listen to you, take some water from the Nile and pour it on the dry ground. The water you take from the river will become blood on the ground."

10Moses said to the LORD, "O Lord, I have never been eloquent, neither in the past nor since you have spoken to your servant. I am slow of speech and tongue."

11The LORD said to him, "Who gave man his mouth? Who makes him deaf or mute? Who gives him sight or makes him blind? Is it not I, the LORD? 12Now go; I will help you speak and will teach you what to say."

13But Moses said, "O Lord, please send someone else to do it."

14Then the LORD's anger burned against Moses and he said, "What about your brother, Aaron the Levite? I know he can speak well. He is already on his way to meet you, and his heart will be glad when he sees you. 15You shall speak to him and put words in his mouth; I will help both of you speak and will teach you what to do. 16He will speak to the people for you, and it will be as if he were your mouth and as if you were God to him. 17But take this staff in your hand so that you can perform miraculous signs with it."

Moses Returns to Egypt

18Then Moses went back to Jethro his father-in-law and said to him, "Let me go back to my own people in Egypt to see if any of them are still alive."

Jethro said, "Go, and I wish you well."

19Now the LORD had said to Moses in Midian, "Go back to Egypt, for all the men who wanted to kill you are dead." 20So Moses took his wife and sons, put them on a donkey and started back to Egypt. And he took the staff of God in his hand.

21The LORD said to Moses, "When you return to Egypt, see that you perform before Pharaoh all the wonders I have given you the power to do. But I will harden his heart so that he will not let the people go. 22Then say to Pharaoh, 'This is what the LORD says: Israel is my firstborn son, 23and I told you, "Let my son go, so that he may worship me." But you refused to let him go; so I will kill your firstborn son.'"

24At a lodging place on the way, the LORD met ⌊Moses⌋*b* and was about to kill him. 25But Zipporah took a flint knife, cut off her son's foreskin and touched ⌊Moses'⌋ feet with it.*c* "Surely you are a bridegroom of blood to me," she said. 26So the LORD let him alone. (At that time she said "bridegroom of blood", referring to circumcision.)

27The LORD said to Aaron, "Go into the desert to meet Moses." So he met Moses at the mountain of God and kissed him. 28Then Moses told Aaron everything the LORD had sent him to say, and also about all the miraculous signs he had commanded him to perform.

29Moses and Aaron brought together all the elders of the Israelites, 30and Aaron told them everything the LORD had said to Moses. He also performed the signs before the people, 31and they believed. And when they heard that the LORD was concerned about them and had seen their misery, they bowed down and worshipped.

Bricks Without Straw

5 Afterwards Moses and Aaron went to Pharaoh and said, "This is what the LORD, the God of Israel, says: 'Let my people go, so that they may hold a festival to me in the desert.'"

2Pharaoh said, "Who is the LORD, that I should obey him and let Israel go? I do not know the LORD and I will not let Israel go."

b24 Or ⌊Moses' son⌋; Hebrew him   c25 Or and drew near ⌊Moses'⌋ feet

³Then they said, "The God of the Hebrews has met with us. Now let us take a three-day journey into the desert to offer sacrifices to the LORD our God, or he may strike us with plagues or with the sword."

⁴But the king of Egypt said, "Moses and Aaron, why are you taking the people away from their labour? Get back to your work!" ⁵Then Pharaoh said, "Look, the people of the land are now numerous, and you are stopping them from working."

⁶That same day Pharaoh gave this order to the slave drivers and foremen in charge of the people: ⁷"You are no longer to supply the people with straw for making bricks; let them go and gather their own straw. ⁸But require them to make the same number of bricks as before; don't reduce the quota. They are lazy; that is why they are crying out, 'Let us go and sacrifice to our God.' ⁹Make the work harder for the men so that they keep working and pay no attention to lies."

¹⁰Then the slave drivers and the foremen went out and said to the people, "This is what Pharaoh says: 'I will not give you any more straw. ¹¹Go and get your own straw wherever you can find it, but your work will not be reduced at all.'" ¹²So the people scattered all over Egypt to gather stubble to use for straw. ¹³The slave drivers kept pressing them, saying, "Complete the work required of you for each day, just as when you had straw." ¹⁴The Israelite foremen appointed by Pharaoh's slave drivers were beaten and were asked, "Why didn't you meet your quota of bricks yesterday or today, as before?"

¹⁵Then the Israelite foremen went and appealed to Pharaoh: "Why have you treated your servants this way? ¹⁶Your servants are given no straw, yet we are told, 'Make bricks!' Your servants are being beaten, but the fault is with your own people."

¹⁷Pharaoh said, "Lazy, that's what you are—lazy! That is why you keep saying, 'Let us go and sacrifice to the LORD.' ¹⁸Now get to work. You will not be given any straw, yet you must produce your full quota of bricks."

¹⁹The Israelite foremen realised they were in trouble when they were told, "You are not to reduce the number of bricks required of you for each day." ²⁰When they left Pharaoh, they found Moses and Aaron waiting to meet them, ²¹and they said, "May the LORD look upon you and judge you! You have made us a stench to Pharaoh and his officials and have put a sword in their hand to kill us."

God Promises Deliverance

²²Moses returned to the LORD and said, "O Lord, why have you brought trouble upon this people? Is this why you sent me? ²³Ever since I went to Pharaoh to speak in your name, he has brought trouble upon this people, and you have not rescued your people at all."

6 Then the LORD said to Moses, "Now you will see what I will do to Pharaoh: Because of my mighty hand he will let them go; because of my mighty hand he will drive them out of his country."

²God also said to Moses, "I am the LORD. ³I appeared to Abraham, to Isaac and to Jacob as God Almighty,ᵃ but by my name the LORDᵇ I did not make myself known to them.ᶜ ⁴I also established my covenant with them to give them the land of Canaan, where they lived as aliens. ⁵Moreover, I have heard the groaning of the Israelites, whom the Egyptians are enslaving, and I have remembered my covenant.

⁶"Therefore, say to the Israelites: 'I am the LORD, and I will bring you out from under the yoke of the Egyptians. I will free you from being slaves to them, and I will redeem you with an outstretched arm and with mighty acts of judgment. ⁷I will take you as my own people, and I will be your God. Then you will know that I am the LORD your God, who brought you out from under the yoke of the Egyptians. ⁸And I will bring you to the land I swore

---

ᵃ3 Hebrew *El-Shaddai*   ᵇ3 See note at Exodus 3:15.
ᶜ3 Or *Almighty, and by my name the* LORD *did I not let myself be known to them?*

with uplifted hand to give to Abraham, to Isaac and to Jacob. I will give it to you as a possession. I am the LORD.'"

⁹Moses reported this to the Israelites, but they did not listen to him because of their discouragement and cruel bondage.

¹⁰Then the LORD said to Moses, ¹¹"Go, tell Pharaoh king of Egypt to let the Israelites go out of his country."

¹²But Moses said to the LORD, "If the Israelites will not listen to me, why would Pharaoh listen to me, since I speak with faltering lips?"*d*

Family Record of Moses and Aaron

¹³Now the LORD spoke to Moses and Aaron about the Israelites and Pharaoh king of Egypt, and he commanded them to bring the Israelites out of Egypt.

¹⁴These were the heads of their families:*e*

The sons of Reuben the firstborn son of Israel were Hanoch and Pallu, Hezron and Carmi. These were the clans of Reuben.

¹⁵The sons of Simeon were Jemuel, Jamin, Ohad, Jakin, Zohar and Shaul the son of a Canaanite woman. These were the clans of Simeon.

¹⁶These were the names of the sons of Levi according to their records: Gershon, Kohath and Merari. Levi lived 137 years.

¹⁷The sons of Gershon, by clans, were Libni and Shimei.

¹⁸The sons of Kohath were Amram, Izhar, Hebron and Uzziel. Kohath lived 133 years.

¹⁹The sons of Merari were Mahli and Mushi.

These were the clans of Levi according to their records.

²⁰Amram married his father's sister Jochebed, who bore him Aaron and Moses. Amram lived 137 years.

²¹The sons of Izhar were Korah, Nepheg and Zicri.

²²The sons of Uzziel were Mishael, Elzaphan and Sithri.

²³Aaron married Elisheba, daughter of Amminadab and sister of Nahshon, and she bore him Nadab and Abihu, Eleazar and Ithamar.

²⁴The sons of Korah were Assir, Elkanah and Abiasaph. These were the Korahite clans.

²⁵Eleazar son of Aaron married one of the daughters of Putiel, and she bore him Phinehas.

These were the heads of the Levite families, clan by clan.

²⁶It was this same Aaron and Moses to whom the LORD said, "Bring the Israelites out of Egypt by their divisions." ²⁷They were the ones who spoke to Pharaoh king of Egypt about bringing the Israelites out of Egypt. It was the same Moses and Aaron.

Aaron to Speak for Moses

²⁸Now when the LORD spoke to Moses in Egypt, ²⁹he said to him, "I am the LORD. Tell Pharaoh king of Egypt everything I tell you."

³⁰But Moses said to the LORD, "Since I speak with faltering lips, why would Pharaoh listen to me?"

7 Then the LORD said to Moses, "See, I have made you like God to Pharaoh, and your brother Aaron will be your prophet. ²You are to say everything I command you, and your brother Aaron is to tell Pharaoh to let the Israelites go out of his country. ³But I will harden Pharaoh's heart, and though I multiply my miraculous signs and wonders in Egypt, ⁴he will not listen to you. Then I will lay my hand on Egypt and with mighty acts of judgment I will bring out my divisions, my people the Israelites. ⁵And the Egyptians will know that I am the LORD when I

---

*d12 Hebrew *I am uncircumcised of lips*; also in verse 30*
*e14 The Hebrew for *families* here and in verse 25 refers to units larger than clans.*

stretch out my hand against Egypt and bring the Israelites out of it.''

6Moses and Aaron did just as the LORD commanded them. 7Moses was eighty years old and Aaron eighty-three when they spoke to Pharaoh.

Aaron's Staff Becomes a Snake

8The LORD said to Moses and Aaron, 9''When Pharaoh says to you, 'Perform a miracle,' then say to Aaron, 'Take your staff and throw it down before Pharaoh,' and it will become a snake.''

10So Moses and Aaron went to Pharaoh and did just as the LORD commanded. Aaron threw his staff down in front of Pharaoh and his officials, and it became a snake. 11Pharaoh then summoned the wise men and sorcerers, and the Egyptian magicians also did the same things by their secret arts: 12Each one threw down his staff and it became a snake. But Aaron's staff swallowed up their staffs. 13Yet Pharaoh's heart became hard and he would not listen to them, just as the LORD had said.

The Plague of Blood

14Then the LORD said to Moses, ''Pharaoh's heart is unyielding; he refuses to let the people go. 15Go to Pharaoh in the morning as he goes out to the water. Wait on the bank of the Nile to meet him, and take in your hand the staff that was changed into a snake. 16Then say to him, 'The LORD, the God of the Hebrews, has sent me to say to you: Let my people go, so that they may worship me in the desert. But until now you have not listened. 17This is what the LORD says: By this you will know that I am the LORD: With the staff that is in my hand I will strike the water of the Nile, and it will be changed into blood. 18The fish in the Nile will die, and the river will stink; the Egyptians will not be able to drink its water.'''

19The LORD said to Moses, ''Tell Aaron, 'Take your staff and stretch out your hand over the waters of Egypt—over the streams and canals, over the ponds and all the reservoirs'—and they will turn to blood. Blood will be everywhere in Egypt, even in the wooden buckets and stone jars.''

20Moses and Aaron did just as the LORD had commanded. He raised his staff in the presence of Pharaoh and his officials and struck the water of the Nile, and all the water was changed into blood. 21The fish in the Nile died, and the river smelled so bad that the Egyptians could not drink its water. Blood was everywhere in Egypt.

22But the Egyptian magicians did the same things by their secret arts, and Pharaoh's heart became hard; he would not listen to Moses and Aaron, just as the LORD had said. 23Instead, he turned and went into his palace, and did not take even this to heart. 24And all the Egyptians dug along the Nile to get drinking water, because they could not drink the water of the river.

The Plague of Frogs

25Seven days passed after the LORD struck the Nile. 8 1Then the LORD said to Moses, ''Go to Pharaoh and say to him, 'This is what the LORD says: Let my people go, so that they may worship me. 2If you refuse to let them go, I will plague your whole country with frogs. 3The Nile will teem with frogs. They will come up into your palace and your bedroom and onto your bed, into the houses of your officials and on your people, and into your ovens and kneading troughs. 4The frogs will go up on you and your people and all your officials.'''

5Then the LORD said to Moses, ''Tell Aaron, 'Stretch out your hand with your staff over the streams and canals and ponds, and make frogs come up on the land of Egypt.'''

6So Aaron stretched out his hand over the waters of Egypt, and the frogs came up and covered the land. 7But the magicians did the same things by their secret arts; they also made frogs come up on the land of Egypt.

8Pharaoh summoned Moses and Aaron and said, ''Pray to the LORD to take the frogs away from me and my people, and I will let your people go to offer sacrifices to the LORD."

9Moses said to Pharaoh, "I leave to you the honour of setting the time for me to pray for you and your officials and your people that you and your houses may be rid of the frogs, except for those that remain in the Nile."

10"Tomorrow," Pharaoh said.

Moses replied, "It will be as you say, so that you may know there is no-one like the LORD our God. 11The frogs will leave you and your houses, your officials and your people; they will remain only in the Nile."

12After Moses and Aaron left Pharaoh, Moses cried out to the LORD about the frogs he had brought on Pharaoh. 13And the LORD did what Moses asked. The frogs died in the houses, in the courtyards and in the fields. 14They were piled into heaps, and the land reeked of them. 15But when Pharaoh saw that there was relief, he hardened his heart and would not listen to Moses and Aaron, just as the LORD had said.

The Plague of Gnats

16Then the LORD said to Moses, "Tell Aaron, 'Stretch out your staff and strike the dust of the ground,' and throughout the land of Egypt the dust will become gnats." 17They did this, and when Aaron stretched out his hand with the staff and struck the dust of the ground, gnats came upon men and animals. All the dust throughout the land of Egypt became gnats. 18But when the magicians tried to produce gnats by their secret arts, they could not. And the gnats were on men and animals.

19The magicians said to Pharaoh, "This is the finger of God." But Pharaoh's heart was hard and he would not listen, just as the LORD had said.

The Plague of Flies

20Then the LORD said to Moses, "Get up early in the morning and confront Pharaoh as he goes to the water and say to him, 'This is what the LORD says: Let my people go, so that they may worship me. 21If you do not let my people go, I will send swarms of flies on you and your officials, on your people and into your houses. The houses of the Egyptians will be full of flies, and even the ground where they are.

22"'But on that day I will deal differently with the land of Goshen, where my people live; no swarms of flies will be there, so that you will know that I, the LORD, am in this land. 23I will make a distinction*a* between my people and your people. This miraculous sign will occur tomorrow.'"

24And the LORD did this. Dense swarms of flies poured into Pharaoh's palace and into the houses of his officials, and throughout Egypt the land was ruined by the flies.

25Then Pharaoh summoned Moses and Aaron and said, "Go, sacrifice to your God here in the land."

26But Moses said, "That would not be right. The sacrifices we offer the LORD our God would be detestable to the Egyptians. And if we offer sacrifices that are detestable in their eyes, will they not stone us? 27We must take a three-day journey into the desert to offer sacrifices to the LORD our God, as he commands us."

28Pharaoh said, "I will let you go to offer sacrifices to the LORD your God in the desert, but you must not go very far. Now pray for me."

29Moses answered, "As soon as I leave you, I will pray to the LORD, and tomorrow the flies will leave Pharaoh and his officials and his people. Only be sure that Pharaoh does not act deceitfully again by not letting the people go to offer sacrifices to the LORD."

30Then Moses left Pharaoh and prayed to the LORD, 31and the LORD did what Moses asked: The flies left Pharaoh and his officials and his people; not a fly remained. 32But this time also Pharaoh hardened his heart and would not let the people go.

a23 Septuagint and Vulgate; Hebrew *will put a deliverance*

The Plague on Livestock

9 Then the LORD said to Moses, "Go to Pharaoh and say to him, 'This is what the LORD, the God of the Hebrews, says: "Let my people go, so that they may worship me."' ²If you refuse to let them go and continue to hold them back, ³the hand of the LORD will bring a terrible plague on your livestock in the field—on your horses and donkeys and camels and on your cattle and sheep and goats. ⁴But the LORD will make a distinction between the livestock of Israel and that of Egypt, so that no animal belonging to the Israelites will die.'"

⁵The LORD set a time and said, "Tomorrow the LORD will do this in the land." ⁶And the next day the LORD did it: All the livestock of the Egyptians died, but not one animal belonging to the Israelites died. ⁷Pharaoh sent men to investigate and found that not even one of the animals of the Israelites had died. Yet his heart was unyielding and he would not let the people go.

The Plague of Boils

⁸Then the LORD said to Moses and Aaron, "Take handfuls of soot from a furnace and have Moses toss it into the air in the presence of Pharaoh. ⁹It will become fine dust over the whole land of Egypt, and festering boils will break out on men and animals throughout the land."

¹⁰So they took soot from a furnace and stood before Pharaoh. Moses tossed it into the air, and festering boils broke out on men and animals. ¹¹The magicians could not stand before Moses because of the boils that were on them and on all the Egyptians. ¹²But the LORD hardened Pharaoh's heart and he would not listen to Moses and Aaron, just as the LORD had said to Moses.

The Plague of Hail

¹³Then the LORD said to Moses, "Get up early in the morning, confront Pharaoh and say to him, 'This is what the LORD, the God of the Hebrews, says: Let my people go, so that they may worship me, ¹⁴or this time I will send the full force of my plagues against you and against your officials and your people, so you may know that there is no-one like me in all the earth. ¹⁵For by now I could have stretched out my hand and struck you and your people with a plague that would have wiped you off the earth. ¹⁶But I have raised you up[a] for this very purpose, that I might show you my power and that my name might be proclaimed in all the earth. ¹⁷You still set yourself against my people and will not let them go. ¹⁸Therefore, at this time tomorrow I will send the worst hailstorm that has ever fallen on Egypt, from the day it was founded till now. ¹⁹Give an order now to bring your livestock and everything you have in the field to a place of shelter, because the hail will fall on every man and animal that has not been brought in and is still out in the field, and they will die.'"

²⁰Those officials of Pharaoh who feared the word of the LORD hurried to bring their slaves and their livestock inside. ²¹But those who ignored the word of the LORD left their slaves and livestock in the field.

²²Then the LORD said to Moses, "Stretch out your hand towards the sky so that hail will fall all over Egypt—on men and animals and on everything growing in the fields of Egypt." ²³When Moses stretched out his staff towards the sky, the LORD sent thunder and hail, and lightning flashed down to the ground. So the LORD rained hail on the land of Egypt; ²⁴hail fell and lightning flashed back and forth. It was the worst storm in all the land of Egypt since it had become a nation. ²⁵Throughout Egypt hail struck everything in the fields—both men and animals; it beat down everything growing in the fields and stripped every tree. ²⁶The only place it did not hail was the land of Goshen, where the Israelites were.

²⁷Then Pharaoh summoned Moses and Aaron. "This time I have sinned," he said

---

a16 Or have spared you

to them. "The LORD is in the right, and I and my people are in the wrong. ²⁸Pray to the LORD, for we have had enough thunder and hail. I will let you go; you don't have to stay any longer."

²⁹Moses replied, "When I have gone out of the city, I will spread out my hands in prayer to the LORD. The thunder will stop and there will be no more hail, so you may know that the earth is the LORD's. ³⁰But I know that you and your officials still do not fear the LORD God."

³¹(The flax and barley were destroyed, since the barley was in the ear and the flax was in bloom. ³²The wheat and spelt, however, were not destroyed, because they ripen later.)

³³Then Moses left Pharaoh and went out of the city. He spread out his hands towards the LORD; the thunder and hail stopped, and the rain no longer poured down on the land. ³⁴When Pharaoh saw that the rain and hail and thunder had stopped, he sinned again: He and his officials hardened their hearts. ³⁵So Pharaoh's heart was hard and he would not let the Israelites go, just as the LORD had said through Moses.

The Plague of Locusts

10 Then the LORD said to Moses, "Go to Pharaoh, for I have hardened his heart and the hearts of his officials so that I may perform these miraculous signs of mine among them, ²that you may tell your children and grandchildren how I dealt harshly with the Egyptians and how I performed my signs among them, and that you may know that I am the LORD."

³So Moses and Aaron went to Pharaoh and said to him, "This is what the LORD, the God of the Hebrews, says: 'How long will you refuse to humble yourself before me? Let my people go, so that they may worship me. ⁴If you refuse to let them go, I will bring locusts into your country tomorrow. ⁵They will cover the face of the ground so that it cannot be seen. They will devour what little you have left after the hail, including every tree that is growing in

your fields. ⁶They will fill your houses and those of all your officials and all the Egyptians—something neither your fathers nor your forefathers have ever seen from the day they settled in this land till now.'" Then Moses turned and left Pharaoh.

⁷Pharaoh's officials said to him, "How long will this man be a snare to us? Let the people go, so that they may worship the LORD their God. Do you not yet realise that Egypt is ruined?"

⁸Then Moses and Aaron were brought back to Pharaoh. "Go, worship the LORD your God," he said. "But just who will be going?"

⁹Moses answered, "We will go with our young and old, with our sons and daughters, and with our flocks and herds, because we are to celebrate a festival to the LORD."

¹⁰Pharaoh said, "The LORD be with you—if I let you go, along with your women and children! Clearly you are bent on evil.ᵃ ¹¹No! Let only the men go; and worship the LORD, since that's what you have been asking for." Then Moses and Aaron were driven out of Pharaoh's presence.

¹²And the LORD said to Moses, "Stretch out your hand over Egypt so that locusts will swarm over the land and devour everything growing in the fields, everything left by the hail."

¹³So Moses stretched out his staff over Egypt, and the LORD made an east wind blow across the land all that day and all that night. By morning the wind had brought the locusts; ¹⁴they invaded all Egypt and settled down in every area of the country in great numbers. Never before had there been such a plague of locusts, nor will there ever be again. ¹⁵They covered all the ground until it was black. They devoured all that was left after the hail—everything growing in the fields and the fruit on the trees. Nothing green remained on tree or plant in all the land of Egypt.

¹⁶Pharaoh quickly summoned Moses and Aaron and said, "I have sinned against the LORD your God and against

ᵃ10 Or *Be careful, trouble is in store for you!*

you. ¹⁷Now forgive my sin once more and pray to the LORD your God to take this deadly plague away from me."

¹⁸Moses then left Pharaoh and prayed to the LORD. ¹⁹And the LORD changed the wind to a very strong west wind, which caught up the locusts and carried them into the Red Sea.ᵇ Not a locust was left anywhere in Egypt. ²⁰But the LORD hardened Pharaoh's heart, and he would not let the Israelites go.

The Plague of Darkness

²¹Then the LORD said to Moses, "Stretch out your hand towards the sky so that darkness will spread over Egypt— darkness that can be felt." ²²So Moses stretched out his hand towards the sky, and total darkness covered all Egypt for three days. ²³No-one could see anyone else or leave his place for three days. Yet all the Israelites had light in the places where they lived.

²⁴Then Pharaoh summoned Moses and said, "Go, worship the LORD. Even your women and children may go with you; only leave your flocks and herds behind."

²⁵But Moses said, "You must allow us to have sacrifices and burnt offerings to present to the LORD our God. ²⁶Our livestock too must go with us; not a hoof is to be left behind. We have to use some of them in worshipping the LORD our God, and until we get there we will not know what we are to use to worship the LORD."

²⁷But the LORD hardened Pharaoh's heart, and he was not willing to let them go. ²⁸Pharaoh said to Moses, "Get out of my sight! Make sure you do not appear before me again! The day you see my face you will die."

²⁹"Just as you say," Moses replied, "I will never appear before you again."

The Plague on the Firstborn

11 Now the LORD said to Moses, "I will bring one more plague on Pharaoh and on Egypt. After that, he will

let you go from here, and when he does, he will drive you out completely. ²Tell the people that men and women alike are to ask their neighbours for articles of silver and gold." ³(The LORD made the Egyptians favourably disposed towards the people, and Moses himself was highly regarded in Egypt by Pharaoh's officials and by the people.)

⁴So Moses said, "This is what the LORD says: 'About midnight I will go throughout Egypt. ⁵Every firstborn son in Egypt will die, from the firstborn son of Pharaoh, who sits on the throne, to the firstborn son of the slave girl, who is at her hand mill, and all the firstborn of the cattle as well. ⁶There will be loud wailing throughout Egypt—worse than there has ever been or ever will be again. ⁷But among the Israelites not a dog will bark at any man or animal.' Then you will know that the LORD makes a distinction between Egypt and Israel. ⁸All these officials of yours will come to me, bowing down before me and saying, 'Go, you and all the people who follow you!' After that I will leave." Then Moses, hot with anger, left Pharaoh.

⁹The LORD had said to Moses, "Pharaoh will refuse to listen to you—so that my wonders may be multiplied in Egypt." ¹⁰Moses and Aaron performed all these wonders before Pharaoh, but the LORD hardened Pharaoh's heart, and he would not let the Israelites go out of his country.

The Passover

12 The LORD said to Moses and Aaron in Egypt, ²"This month is to be for you the first month, the first month of your year. ³Tell the whole community of Israel that on the tenth day of this month each man is to take a lambᵃ for his family, one for each household. ⁴If any household is too small for a whole lamb, they must share one with their nearest neighbour, having taken into account the number of people there are. You are to determine the amount of lamb needed in accordance with what each person will

---

ᵇ19 Hebrew *Yam Suph*; that is, Sea of Reeds
ᵃ3 The Hebrew word can mean *lamb* or *kid*; also in verse 4.

eat. [5]The animals you choose must be year-old males without defect, and you may take them from the sheep or the goats. [6]Take care of them until the fourteenth day of the month, when all the people of the community of Israel must slaughter them at twilight. [7]Then they are to take some of the blood and put it on the sides and tops of the door-frames of the houses where they eat the lambs. [8]That same night they are to eat the meat roasted over the fire, along with bitter herbs, and bread made without yeast. [9]Do not eat the meat raw or cooked in water, but roast it over the fire—head, legs and inner parts. [10]Do not leave any of it till morning; if some is left till morning, you must burn it. [11]This is how you are to eat it: with your cloak tucked into your belt, your sandals on your feet and your staff in your hand. Eat it in haste; it is the LORD's Passover.

[12]"On that same night I will pass through Egypt and strike down every firstborn—both men and animals—and I will bring judgment on all the gods of Egypt. I am the LORD. [13]The blood will be a sign for you on the houses where you are; and when I see the blood, I will pass over you. No destructive plague will touch you when I strike Egypt.

[14]"This is a day you are to commemorate; for the generations to come you shall celebrate it as a festival to the LORD—a lasting ordinance. [15]For seven days you are to eat bread made without yeast. On the first day remove the yeast from your houses, for whoever eats anything with yeast in it from the first day until the seventh must be cut off from Israel. [16]On the first day hold a sacred assembly, and another one on the seventh day. Do no work at all on these days, except to prepare food for everyone to eat—that is all you may do.

[17]"Celebrate the Feast of Unleavened Bread, because it was on this very day that I brought your divisions out of Egypt. Celebrate this day as a lasting ordinance for the generations to come. [18]In the first month you are to eat bread made without yeast, from the evening of the fourteenth day until the evening of the twenty-first

day. [19]For seven days no yeast is to be found in your houses. And whoever eats anything with yeast in it must be cut off from the community of Israel, whether he is an alien or native-born. [20]Eat nothing made with yeast. Wherever you live, you must eat unleavened bread."

[21]Then Moses summoned all the elders of Israel and said to them, "Go at once and select the animals for your families and slaughter the Passover lamb. [22]Take a bunch of hyssop, dip it into the blood in the basin and put some of the blood on the top and on both sides of the door-frame. Not one of you shall go out of the door of his house until morning. [23]When the LORD goes through the land to strike down the Egyptians, he will see the blood on the top and sides of the door-frame and will pass over that doorway, and he will not permit the destroyer to enter your houses and strike you down.

[24]"Obey these instructions as a lasting ordinance for you and your descendants. [25]When you enter the land that the LORD will give you as he promised, observe this ceremony. [26]And when your children ask you, 'What does this ceremony mean to you?' [27]then tell them, 'It is the Passover sacrifice to the LORD, who passed over the houses of the Israelites in Egypt and spared our homes when he struck down the Egyptians.'" Then the people bowed down and worshipped. [28]The Israelites did just what the LORD commanded Moses and Aaron.

[29]At midnight the LORD struck down all the firstborn in Egypt, from the firstborn of Pharaoh, who sat on the throne, to the firstborn of the prisoner, who was in the dungeon, and the firstborn of all the livestock as well. [30]Pharaoh and all his officials and all the Egyptians got up during the night, and there was loud wailing in Egypt, for there was not a house without someone dead.

The Exodus

[31]During the night Pharaoh summoned Moses and Aaron and said, "Up! Leave my people, you and the Israelites! Go, worship the LORD as you have requested.

³²Take your flocks and herds, as you have said, and go. And also bless me."

³³The Egyptians urged the people to hurry and leave the country. "For otherwise," they said, "we will all die!" ³⁴So the people took their dough before the yeast was added, and carried it on their shoulders in kneading troughs wrapped in clothing. ³⁵The Israelites did as Moses instructed and asked the Egyptians for articles of silver and gold and for clothing. ³⁶The LORD had made the Egyptians favourably disposed towards the people, and they gave them what they asked for; so they plundered the Egyptians.

³⁷The Israelites journeyed from Rameses to Succoth. There were about six hundred thousand men on foot, besides women and children. ³⁸Many other people went up with them, as well as large droves of livestock, both flocks and herds. ³⁹With the dough they had brought from Egypt, they baked cakes of unleavened bread. The dough was without yeast because they had been driven out of Egypt and did not have time to prepare food for themselves.

⁴⁰Now the length of time the Israelite people lived in Egypt*ᵇ* was 430 years. ⁴¹At the end of the 430 years, to the very day, all the LORD's divisions left Egypt. ⁴²Because the LORD kept vigil that night to bring them out of Egypt, on this night all the Israelites are to keep vigil to honour the LORD for the generations to come.

Passover Restrictions

⁴³The LORD said to Moses and Aaron, "These are the regulations for the Passover:

"No foreigner is to eat of it. ⁴⁴Any slave you have bought may eat of it after you have circumcised him, ⁴⁵but a temporary resident and a hired worker may not eat of it.

⁴⁶"It must be eaten inside one house; take none of the meat outside the house. Do not break any of the bones. ⁴⁷The whole community of Israel must celebrate it.

⁴⁸"An alien living among you who wants to celebrate the LORD's Passover must have all the males in his household circumcised; then he may take part like one born in the land. No uncircumcised male may eat of it. ⁴⁹The same law applies to the native-born and to the alien living among you."

⁵⁰All the Israelites did just what the LORD had commanded Moses and Aaron. ⁵¹And on that very day the LORD brought the Israelites out of Egypt by their divisions.

Consecration of the Firstborn

13 The LORD said to Moses, ²"Consecrate to me every firstborn male. The first offspring of every womb among the Israelites belongs to me, whether man or animal."

³Then Moses said to the people, "Commemorate this day, the day you came out of Egypt, out of the land of slavery, because the LORD brought you out of it with a mighty hand. Eat nothing containing yeast. ⁴Today, in the month of Abib, you are leaving. ⁵When the LORD brings you into the land of the Canaanites, Hittites, Amorites, Hivites and Jebusites—the land he swore to your forefathers to give you, a land flowing with milk and honey—you are to observe this ceremony in this month: ⁶For seven days eat bread made without yeast and on the seventh day hold a festival to the LORD. ⁷Eat unleavened bread during those seven days; nothing with yeast in it is to be seen among you, nor shall any yeast be seen anywhere within your borders. ⁸On that day tell your son, 'I do this because of what the LORD did for me when I came out of Egypt.' ⁹This observance will be for you like a sign on your hand and a reminder on your forehead that the law of the LORD is to be on your lips. For the LORD brought you out of Egypt with his mighty hand. ¹⁰You must keep this ordinance at the appointed time year after year.

¹¹"After the LORD brings you into the

land of the Canaanites and gives it to you, as he promised on oath to you and your forefathers, [12]you are to give over to the LORD the first offspring of every womb. All the firstborn males of your livestock belong to the LORD. [13]Redeem with a lamb every firstborn donkey, but if you do not redeem it, break its neck. Redeem every firstborn among your sons.

[14]"In days to come when your son asks you, 'What does this mean?' say to him, 'With a mighty hand the LORD brought us out of Egypt, out of the land of slavery. [15]When Pharaoh stubbornly refused to let us go, the LORD killed every firstborn in Egypt, both man and animal. This is why I sacrifice to the LORD the first male offspring of every womb and redeem each of my firstborn sons.' [16]And it will be like a sign on your hand and a symbol on your forehead that the LORD brought us out of Egypt with his mighty hand."

Crossing the Sea

[17]When Pharaoh let the people go, God did not lead them on the road through the Philistine country, though that was shorter. For God said, "If they face war, they might change their minds and return to Egypt." [18]So God led the people around by the desert road towards the Red Sea.[a] The Israelites went up out of Egypt armed for battle.

[19]Moses took the bones of Joseph with him because Joseph had made the sons of Israel swear an oath. He had said, "God will surely come to your aid, and then you must carry my bones up with you from this place."[b]

[20]After leaving Succoth they camped at Etham on the edge of the desert. [21]By day the LORD went ahead of them in a pillar of cloud to guide them on their way and by night in a pillar of fire to give them light, so that they could travel by day or night. [22]Neither the pillar of cloud by day nor the pillar of fire by night left its place in front of the people.

14 Then the LORD said to Moses, [2]"Tell the Israelites to turn back and camp near Pi Hahiroth, between Migdol and the sea. They are to camp by the sea, directly opposite Baal Zephon. [3]Pharaoh will think, 'The Israelites are wandering around the land in confusion, hemmed in by the desert.' [4]And I will harden Pharaoh's heart, and he will pursue them. But I will gain glory for myself through Pharaoh and all his army, and the Egyptians will know that I am the LORD." So the Israelites did this.

[5]When the king of Egypt was told that the people had fled, Pharaoh and his officials changed their minds about them and said, "What have we done? We have let the Israelites go and have lost their services!" [6]So he had his chariot made ready and took his army with him. [7]He took six hundred of the best chariots, along with all the other chariots of Egypt, with officers over all of them. [8]The LORD hardened the heart of Pharaoh king of Egypt, so that he pursued the Israelites, who were marching out boldly. [9]The Egyptians—all Pharaoh's horses and chariots, horsemen[a] and troops—pursued the Israelites and overtook them as they camped by the sea near Pi Hahiroth, opposite Baal Zephon.

[10]As Pharaoh approached, the Israelites looked up, and there were the Egyptians, marching after them. They were terrified and cried out to the LORD. [11]They said to Moses, "Was it because there were no graves in Egypt that you brought us to the desert to die? What have you done to us by bringing us out of Egypt? [12]Didn't we say to you in Egypt, 'Leave us alone; let us serve the Egyptians'? It would have been better for us to serve the Egyptians than to die in the desert!"

[13]Moses answered the people, "Do not be afraid. Stand firm and you will see the deliverance the LORD will bring you today. The Egyptians you see today you will never see again. [14]The LORD

---

a18 Hebrew *Yam Suph*; that is, Sea of Reeds   *b19* See Gen. 50:25.
a9 Or *charioteers*; also in verses 17, 18, 23, 26 and 28

will fight for you; you need only to be still."

¹⁵Then the LORD said to Moses, "Why are you crying out to me? Tell the Israelites to move on. ¹⁶Raise your staff and stretch out your hand over the sea to divide the water so that the Israelites can go through the sea on dry ground. ¹⁷I will harden the hearts of the Egyptians so that they will go in after them. And I will gain glory through Pharaoh and all his army, through his chariots and his horsemen. ¹⁸The Egyptians will know that I am the LORD when I gain glory through Pharaoh, his chariots and his horsemen."

¹⁹Then the angel of God, who had been travelling in front of Israel's army, withdrew and went behind them. The pillar of cloud also moved from in front and stood behind them, ²⁰coming between the armies of Egypt and Israel. Throughout the night the cloud brought darkness to the one side and light to the other; so neither went near the other all night long.

²¹Then Moses stretched out his hand over the sea, and all that night the LORD drove the sea back with a strong east wind and turned it into dry land. The waters were divided, ²²and the Israelites went through the sea on dry ground, with a wall of water on their right and on their left.

²³The Egyptians pursued them, and all Pharaoh's horses and chariots and horsemen followed them into the sea. ²⁴During the last watch of the night the LORD looked down from the pillar of fire and cloud at the Egyptian army and threw it into confusion. ²⁵He made the wheels of their chariots come off[b] so that they had difficulty driving. And the Egyptians said, "Let's get away from the Israelites! The LORD is fighting for them against Egypt."

²⁶Then the LORD said to Moses, "Stretch out your hand over the sea so that the waters may flow back over the Egyptians and their chariots and horsemen." ²⁷Moses stretched out his hand over the sea, and at daybreak the sea went back to its place. The Egyptians were fleeing towards[c] it, and the LORD swept them into the sea. ²⁸The water flowed back and

covered the chariots and horsemen—the entire army of Pharaoh that had followed the Israelites into the sea. Not one of them survived.

²⁹But the Israelites went through the sea on dry ground, with a wall of water on their right and on their left. ³⁰That day the LORD saved Israel from the hands of the Egyptians, and Israel saw the Egyptians lying dead on the shore. ³¹And when the Israelites saw the great power the LORD displayed against the Egyptians, the people feared the LORD and put their trust in him and in Moses his servant.

The Song of Moses and Miriam

15 Then Moses and the Israelites sang this song to the LORD:

"I will sing to the LORD,
　for he is highly exalted.
The horse and its rider
　he has hurled into the sea.
²The LORD is my strength and my song;
　he has become my salvation.
He is my God, and I will praise him,
　my father's God, and I will exalt
　him.
³The LORD is a warrior;
　the LORD is his name.
⁴Pharaoh's chariots and his army
　he has hurled into the sea.
The best of Pharaoh's officers
　are drowned in the Red Sea.[a]
⁵The deep waters have covered them;
　they sank to the depths like a stone.

⁶"Your right hand, O LORD,
　was majestic in power.
Your right hand, O LORD,
　shattered the enemy.
⁷In the greatness of your majesty
　you threw down those who opposed
　you.
You unleashed your burning anger;
　it consumed them like stubble.
⁸By the blast of your nostrils
　the waters piled up.
The surging waters stood firm like a
　wall;

---

b25 Or *He jammed the wheels of their chariots* (see Samaritan Pentateuch, Septuagint and Syriac)   *c27* Or *from*
a4 Hebrew *Yam Suph*; that is, Sea of Reeds; also in verse 22

the deep waters congealed in the
    heart of the sea.

9"The enemy boasted,
   'I will pursue, I will overtake them.
I will divide the spoils;
   I will gorge myself on them.
I will draw my sword
   and my hand will destroy them.'
10But you blew with your breath,
   and the sea covered them.
They sank like lead
   in the mighty waters.

11"Who among the gods is like you, O
   LORD?
   Who is like you—
      majestic in holiness,
      awesome in glory,
      working wonders?
12You stretched out your right hand
   and the earth swallowed them.

13"In your unfailing love you will lead
   the people you have redeemed.
In your strength you will guide them
   to your holy dwelling.
14The nations will hear and tremble;
   anguish will grip the people of
      Philistia.
15The chiefs of Edom will be terrified,
   the leaders of Moab will be seized
      with trembling,
the people*b* of Canaan will melt away;
16 terror and dread will fall upon them.
   By the power of your arm
      they will be as still as a stone—
until your people pass by, O LORD,
   until the people you bought*c* pass by.
17You will bring them in and plant them
   on the mountain of your
      inheritance—
the place, O LORD, you made for your
      dwelling,
   the sanctuary, O Lord, your hands
      established.
18The LORD will reign
   for ever and ever."

19When Pharaoh's horses, chariots and
horsemen*d* went into the sea, the LORD
brought the waters of the sea back over
them, but the Israelites walked through
the sea on dry ground. 20Then Miriam the
prophetess, Aaron's sister, took a tambourine in her hand, and all the women
followed her, with tambourines and dancing. 21Miriam sang to them:

  "Sing to the LORD,
   for he is highly exalted.
The horse and its rider
   he has hurled into the sea."

The Waters of Marah and Elim

22Then Moses led Israel from the Red
Sea and they went into the Desert of Shur.
For three days they travelled in the desert
without finding water. 23When they came
to Marah, they could not drink its water
because it was bitter. (That is why the
place is called Marah.*e*) 24So the people
grumbled against Moses, saying, "What
are we to drink?"

25Then Moses cried out to the LORD,
and the LORD showed him a piece of wood.
He threw it into the water, and the water
became sweet.

There the LORD made a decree and a law
for them, and there he tested them. 26He
said, "If you listen carefully to the voice of
the LORD your God and do what is right in
his eyes, if you pay attention to his commands and keep all his decrees, I will not
bring on you any of the diseases I brought
on the Egyptians, for I am the LORD, who
heals you."

27Then they came to Elim, where there
were twelve springs and seventy palm
trees, and they camped there near the
water.

Manna and Quail

16 The whole Israelite community set
out from Elim and came to the
Desert of Sin, which is between Elim and
Sinai, on the fifteenth day of the second
month after they had come out of Egypt.

---

b15 Or *rulers*   *c16* Or *created*   *d19* Or *charioteers*   *e23* *Marah* means *bitter.*

2In the desert the whole community grumbled against Moses and Aaron. 3The Israelites said to them, "If only we had died by the LORD's hand in Egypt! There we sat round pots of meat and ate all the food we wanted, but you have brought us out into this desert to starve this entire assembly to death."

4Then the LORD said to Moses, "I will rain down bread from heaven for you. The people are to go out each day and gather enough for that day. In this way I will test them and see whether they will follow my instructions. 5On the sixth day they are to prepare what they bring in, and that is to be twice as much as they gather on the other days."

6So Moses and Aaron said to all the Israelites, "In the evening you will know that it was the LORD who brought you out of Egypt, 7and in the morning you will see the glory of the LORD, because he has heard your grumbling against him. Who are we, that you should grumble against us?" 8Moses also said, "You will know that it was the LORD when he gives you meat to eat in the evening and all the bread you want in the morning, because he has heard your grumbling against him. Who are we? You are not grumbling against us, but against the LORD."

9Then Moses told Aaron, "Say to the entire Israelite community, 'Come before the LORD, for he has heard your grumbling.'"

10While Aaron was speaking to the whole Israelite community, they looked towards the desert, and there was the glory of the LORD appearing in the cloud.

11The LORD said to Moses, 12"I have heard the grumbling of the Israelites. Tell them, 'At twilight you will eat meat, and in the morning you will be filled with bread. Then you will know that I am the LORD your God.'"

13That evening quail came and covered the camp, and in the morning there was a layer of dew around the camp. 14When the dew was gone, thin flakes like frost on the ground appeared on the desert floor.

15When the Israelites saw it, they said to each other, "What is it?" For they did not know what it was.

Moses said to them, "It is the bread the LORD has given you to eat. 16This is what the LORD has commanded: 'Each one is to gather as much as he needs. Take an omer[a] for each person you have in your tent.'"

17The Israelites did as they were told; some gathered much, some little. 18And when they measured it by the omer, he who gathered much did not have too much, and he who gathered little did not have too little. Each one gathered as much as he needed.

19Then Moses said to them, "No-one is to keep any of it until morning."

20However, some of them paid no attention to Moses; they kept part of it until morning, but it was full of maggots and began to smell. So Moses was angry with them.

21Each morning everyone gathered as much as he needed, and when the sun grew hot, it melted away. 22On the sixth day, they gathered twice as much—two omers[b] for each person—and the leaders of the community came and reported this to Moses. 23He said to them, "This is what the LORD commanded: 'Tomorrow is to be a day of rest, a holy Sabbath to the LORD. So bake what you want to bake and boil what you want to boil. Save whatever is left and keep it until morning.'"

24So they saved it until morning, as Moses commanded, and it did not stink or get maggots in it. 25"Eat it today," Moses said, "because today is a Sabbath to the LORD. You will not find any of it on the ground today. 26Six days you are to gather it, but on the seventh day, the Sabbath, there will not be any."

27Nevertheless, some of the people went out on the seventh day to gather it, but they found none. 28Then the LORD said to Moses, "How long will you[c] refuse to keep my commands and my instructions? 29Bear in mind that the LORD has given you the Sabbath; that is why on the sixth day

---

a16 That is, probably about 4 pints (about 2 litres); also in verses 18, 32, 33 and 36
b22 That is, probably about 7½ pints (about 4.5 litres)   c28 The Hebrew is plural.

he gives you bread for two days. Everyone is to stay where he is on the seventh day; no-one is to go out." ³⁰So the people rested on the seventh day.

³¹The people of Israel called the bread manna.ᵈ It was white like coriander seed and tasted like wafers made with honey. ³²Moses said, "This is what the LORD has commanded: 'Take an omer of manna and keep it for the generations to come, so they can see the bread I gave you to eat in the desert when I brought you out of Egypt.'"

³³So Moses said to Aaron, "Take a jar and put an omer of manna in it. Then place it before the LORD to be kept for the generations to come."

³⁴As the LORD commanded Moses, Aaron put the manna in front of the Testimony, that it might be kept. ³⁵The Israelites ate manna for forty years, until they came to a land that was settled; they ate manna until they reached the border of Canaan.

³⁶(An omer is one tenth of an ephah.)

Water From the Rock

17 The whole Israelite community set out from the Desert of Sin, travelling from place to place as the LORD commanded. They camped at Rephidim, but there was no water for the people to drink. ²So they quarrelled with Moses and said, "Give us water to drink."

Moses replied, "Why do you quarrel with me? Why do you put the LORD to the test?"

³But the people were thirsty for water there, and they grumbled against Moses. They said, "Why did you bring us up out of Egypt to make us and our children and livestock die of thirst?"

⁴Then Moses cried out to the LORD, "What am I to do with these people? They are almost ready to stone me."

⁵The LORD answered Moses, "Walk on ahead of the people. Take with you some of the elders of Israel and take in your

hand the staff with which you struck the Nile, and go. ⁶I will stand there before you by the rock at Horeb. Strike the rock, and water will come out of it for the people to drink." So Moses did this in the sight of the elders of Israel. ⁷And he called the place Massahᵃ and Meribahᵇ because the Israelites quarrelled and because they tested the LORD saying, "Is the LORD among us or not?"

The Amalekites Defeated

⁸The Amalekites came and attacked the Israelites at Rephidim. ⁹Moses said to Joshua, "Choose some of our men and go out to fight the Amalekites. Tomorrow I will stand on top of the hill with the staff of God in my hands."

¹⁰So Joshua fought the Amalekites as Moses had ordered, and Moses, Aaron and Hur went to the top of the hill. ¹¹As long as Moses held up his hands, the Israelites were winning, but whenever he lowered his hands, the Amalekites were winning. ¹²When Moses' hands grew tired, they took a stone and put it under him and he sat on it. Aaron and Hur held his hands up—one on one side, one on the other—so that his hands remained steady till sunset. ¹³So Joshua overcame the Amalekite army with the sword.

¹⁴Then the LORD said to Moses, "Write this on a scroll as something to be remembered and make sure that Joshua hears it, because I will completely blot out the memory of Amalek from under heaven."

¹⁵Moses built an altar and called it The LORD is my Banner. ¹⁶He said, "For hands were lifted up to the throne of the LORD. Theᶜ LORD will be at war against the Amalekites from generation to generation."

Jethro Visits Moses

18 Now Jethro, the priest of Midian and father-in-law of Moses, heard of everything God had done for Moses

---

ᵈ31 Manna means *What is it?* (see verse 15).
ᵃ7 Massah means *testing.*   ᵇ7 Meribah means *quarrelling.*
ᶜ16 Or "Because a hand was against the throne of the LORD, the

and for his people Israel, and how the LORD had brought Israel out of Egypt.

²After Moses had sent away his wife Zipporah, his father-in-law Jethro received her ³and her two sons. One son was named Gershom,ᵃ for Moses said, "I have become an alien in a foreign land"; ⁴and the other was named Eliezer,ᵇ for he said, "My father's God was my helper; he saved me from the sword of Pharaoh."

⁵Jethro, Moses' father-in-law, together with Moses' sons and wife, came to him in the desert, where he was camped near the mountain of God. ⁶Jethro had sent word to him, "I, your father-in-law Jethro, am coming to you with your wife and her two sons."

⁷So Moses went out to meet his father-in-law and bowed down and kissed him. They greeted each other and then went into the tent. ⁸Moses told his father-in-law about everything the LORD had done to Pharaoh and the Egyptians for Israel's sake and about all the hardships they had met along the way and how the LORD had saved them.

⁹Jethro was delighted to hear about all the good things the LORD had done for Israel in rescuing them from the hand of the Egyptians. ¹⁰He said, "Praise be to the LORD, who rescued you from the hand of the Egyptians and of Pharaoh, and who rescued the people from the hand of the Egyptians. ¹¹Now I know that the LORD is greater than all other gods, for he did this to those who had treated Israel arrogantly." ¹²Then Jethro, Moses' father-in-law, brought a burnt offering and other sacrifices to God, and Aaron came with all the elders of Israel to eat bread with Moses' father-in-law in the presence of God.

¹³The next day Moses took his seat to serve as judge for the people, and they stood round him from morning till evening. ¹⁴When his father-in-law saw all that Moses was doing for the people, he said, "What is this you are doing for the people? Why do you alone sit as judge, while all these people stand round you from morning till evening?"

¹⁵Moses answered him, "Because the people come to me to seek God's will. ¹⁶Whenever they have a dispute, it is brought to me, and I decide between the parties and inform them of God's decrees and laws."

¹⁷Moses' father-in-law replied, "What you are doing is not good. ¹⁸You and these people who come to you will only wear yourselves out. The work is too heavy for you; you cannot handle it alone. ¹⁹Listen now to me and I will give you some advice, and may God be with you. You must be the people's representative before God and bring their disputes to him. ²⁰Teach them the decrees and laws, and show them the way to live and the duties they are to perform. ²¹But select capable men from all the people—men who fear God, trustworthy men who hate dishonest gain—and appoint them as officials over thousands, hundreds, fifties and tens. ²²Have them serve as judges for the people at all times, but have them bring every difficult case to you; the simple cases they can decide themselves. That will make your load lighter, because they will share it with you. ²³If you do this and God so commands, you will be able to stand the strain, and all these people will go home satisfied."

²⁴Moses listened to his father-in-law and did everything he said. ²⁵He chose capable men from all Israel and made them leaders of the people, officials over thousands, hundreds, fifties and tens. ²⁶They served as judges for the people at all times. The difficult cases they brought to Moses, but the simple ones they decided themselves.

²⁷Then Moses sent his father-in-law on his way, and Jethro returned to his own country.

At Mount Sinai

19 In the third month after the Israelites left Egypt—on the very day—they came to the Desert of Sinai. ²After they set out from Rephidim, they

---

ᵃ3 *Gershom* sounds like the Hebrew for *an alien there*.   ᵇ4 *Eliezer* means *my God is helper*.

entered the Desert of Sinai, and Israel camped there in the desert in front of the mountain.

³Then Moses went up to God, and the LORD called to him from the mountain and said, "This is what you are to say to the house of Jacob and what you are to tell the people of Israel: ⁴'You yourselves have seen what I did to Egypt, and how I carried you on eagles' wings and brought you to myself. ⁵Now if you obey me fully and keep my covenant, then out of all nations you will be my treasured possession. Although the whole earth is mine, ⁶you*a* will be for me a kingdom of priests and a holy nation.' These are the words you are to speak to the Israelites."

⁷So Moses went back and summoned the elders of the people and set before them all the words the LORD had commanded him to speak. ⁸The people all responded together, "We will do everything the LORD has said." So Moses brought their answer back to the LORD.

⁹The LORD said to Moses, "I am going to come to you in a dense cloud, so that people will hear me speaking with you and will always put their trust in you." Then Moses told the LORD what the people had said.

¹⁰And the LORD said to Moses, "Go to the people and consecrate them today and tomorrow. Make them wash their clothes ¹¹and be ready by the third day, because on that day the LORD will come down on Mount Sinai in the sight of all the people. ¹²Put limits for the people around the mountain and tell them, 'Be careful that you do not go up the mountain or touch the foot of it. Whoever touches the mountain shall surely be put to death. ¹³He shall surely be stoned or shot with arrows; not a hand is to be laid on him. Whether man or animal, he shall not be permitted to live.' Only when the ram's horn sounds a long blast may they go up to the mountain."

¹⁴After Moses had gone down the mountain to the people, he consecrated them, and they washed their clothes. ¹⁵Then he said to the people, "Prepare yourselves for the third day. Abstain from sexual relations."

¹⁶On the morning of the third day there was thunder and lightning, with a thick cloud over the mountain, and a very loud trumpet blast. Everyone in the camp trembled. ¹⁷Then Moses led the people out of the camp to meet with God, and they stood at the foot of the mountain. ¹⁸Mount Sinai was covered with smoke, because the LORD descended on it in fire. The smoke billowed up from it like smoke from a furnace, the whole mountain*b* trembled violently, ¹⁹and the sound of the trumpet grew louder and louder. Then Moses spoke and the voice of God answered him.*c*

²⁰The LORD descended to the top of Mount Sinai and called Moses to the top of the mountain. So Moses went up ²¹and the LORD said to him, "Go down and warn the people so they do not force their way through to see the LORD and many of them perish. ²²Even the priests, who approach the LORD, must consecrate themselves, or the LORD will break out against them."

²³Moses said to the LORD, "The people cannot come up Mount Sinai, because you yourself warned us, 'Put limits around the mountain and set it apart as holy.'"

²⁴The LORD replied, "Go down and bring Aaron up with you. But the priests and the people must not force their way through to come up to the LORD, or he will break out against them."

²⁵So Moses went down to the people and told them.

The Ten Commandments

20 And God spoke all these words:

²"I am the LORD your God, who brought you out of Egypt, out of the land of slavery.

---

a5,6 Or *possession, for the whole earth is mine.* ⁶*You*
b18 Most Hebrew manuscripts; a few Hebrew manuscripts and Septuagint *all the people*
c19 Or *and God answered him with thunder*

³"You shall have no other gods before[a] me.

⁴"You shall not make for yourself an idol in the form of anything in heaven above or on the earth beneath or in the waters below. ⁵You shall not bow down to them or worship them; for I, the LORD your God, am a jealous God, punishing the children for the sin of the fathers to the third and fourth generation of those who hate me, ⁶but showing love to a thousand ⌊generations⌋ of those who love me and keep my commandments.

⁷"You shall not misuse the name of the LORD your God, for the LORD will not hold anyone guiltless who misuses his name.

⁸"Remember the Sabbath day by keeping it holy. ⁹Six days you shall labour and do all your work, ¹⁰but the seventh day is a Sabbath to the LORD your God. On it you shall not do any work, neither you, nor your son or daughter, nor your manservant or maidservant, nor your animals, nor the alien within your gates. ¹¹For in six days the LORD made the heavens and the earth, the sea, and all that is in them, but he rested on the seventh day. Therefore the LORD blessed the Sabbath day and made it holy.

¹²"Honour your father and your mother, so that you may live long in the land the LORD your God is giving you.

¹³"You shall not murder.

¹⁴"You shall not commit adultery.

¹⁵"You shall not steal.

¹⁶"You shall not give false testimony against your neighbour.

¹⁷"You shall not covet your neighbour's house. You shall not covet your neighbour's wife, or his manservant or maidservant, his ox or donkey, or anything that belongs to your neighbour."

¹⁸When the people saw the thunder and lightning and heard the trumpet and saw the mountain in smoke, they trembled with fear. They stayed at a distance ¹⁹and said to Moses, "Speak to us yourself and we will listen. But do not have God speak to us or we will die."

²⁰Moses said to the people, "Do not be afraid. God has come to test you, so that the fear of God will be with you to keep you from sinning."

²¹The people remained at a distance, while Moses approached the thick darkness where God was.

Idols and Altars

²²Then the LORD said to Moses, "Tell the Israelites this: 'You have seen for yourselves that I have spoken to you from heaven: ²³Do not make any gods to be alongside me; do not make for yourselves gods of silver or gods of gold.

²⁴"Make an altar of earth for me and sacrifice on it your burnt offerings and fellowship offerings,[b] your sheep and goats and your cattle. Wherever I cause my name to be honoured, I will come to you and bless you. ²⁵If you make an altar of stones for me, do not build it with dressed stones, for you will defile it if you use a tool on it. ²⁶And do not go up to my altar on steps, lest your nakedness be exposed on it.'

21 "These are the laws you are to set before them:

Hebrew Servants

²"If you buy a Hebrew servant, he is to serve you for six years. But in the seventh year, he shall go free, without paying anything. ³If he comes alone, he is to go free alone; but if he has a wife when he comes, she is to go with him. ⁴If his master gives him a wife and she bears him sons or

---

*a*3 Or *besides*   *b*24 Traditionally *peace offerings*

daughters, the woman and her children shall belong to her master, and only the man shall go free.

5"But if the servant declares, 'I love my master and my wife and children and do not want to go free,' 6then his master must take him before the judges.*a* He shall take him to the door or the door-post and pierce his ear with an awl. Then he will be his servant for life.

7"If a man sells his daughter as a servant, she is not to go free as menservants do. 8If she does not please the master who has selected her for himself,*b* he must let her be redeemed. He has no right to sell her to foreigners, because he has broken faith with her. 9If he selects her for his son, he must grant her the rights of a daughter. 10If he marries another woman, he must not deprive the first one of her food, clothing and marital rights. 11If he does not provide her with these three things, she is to go free, without any payment of money.

Personal Injuries

12"Anyone who strikes a man and kills him shall surely be put to death. 13However, if he does not do it intentionally, but God lets it happen, he is to flee to a place I will designate. 14But if a man schemes and kills another man deliberately, take him away from my altar and put him to death.

15"Anyone who attacks*c* his father or his mother must be put to death.

16"Anyone who kidnaps another and either sells him or still has him when he is caught must be put to death.

17"Anyone who curses his father or mother must be put to death.

18"If men quarrel and one hits the other with a stone or with his fist*d* and he does not die but is confined to bed, 19the one who struck the blow will not be held responsible if the other gets up and walks around outside with his staff; however, he must pay the injured man for the loss of his time and see that he is completely healed.

20"If a man beats his male or female slave with a rod and the slave dies as a direct result, he must be punished, 21but he is not to be punished if the slave gets up after a day or two, since the slave is his property.

22"If men who are fighting hit a pregnant woman and she gives birth prematurely*e* but there is no serious injury, the offender must be fined whatever the woman's husband demands and the court allows. 23But if there is serious injury, you are to take life for life, 24eye for eye, tooth for tooth, hand for hand, foot for foot, 25burn for burn, wound for wound, bruise for bruise.

26"If a man hits a manservant or maidservant in the eye and destroys it, he must let the servant go free to compensate for the eye. 27And if he knocks out the tooth of a manservant or maidservant, he must let the servant go free to compensate for the tooth.

28"If a bull gores a man or a woman to death, the bull must be stoned to death, and its meat must not be eaten. But the owner of the bull will not be held responsible. 29If, however, the bull has had the habit of goring and the owner has been warned but has not kept it penned up and it kills a man or woman, the bull must be stoned and the owner also must be put to death. 30However, if payment is demanded of him, he may redeem his life by paying whatever is demanded. 31This law also applies if the bull gores a son or a daughter. 32If the bull gores a male or female slave, the owner must pay thirty shekels*f* of silver to the master of the slave, and the bull must be stoned.

33"If a man uncovers a pit or digs one and fails to cover it and an ox or a donkey falls into it, 34the owner of the pit must pay for the loss; he must pay its owner, and the dead animal will be his.

35"If a man's bull injures the bull of another and it dies, they are to sell the live one and divide both the money and the

---

*a*6 Or *before God*   *b*8 Or *master so that he does not choose her*   *c*15 Or *kills*
*d*18 Or *with a tool*   *e*22 Or *she has a miscarriage*   *f*32 That is, about 12 ounces (about 0.3 kilogram)

dead animal equally. [36]However, if it was known that the bull had the habit of goring, yet the owner did not keep it penned up, the owner must pay, animal for animal, and the dead animal will be his.

Protection of Property

22 "If a man steals an ox or a sheep and slaughters it or sells it, he must pay back five head of cattle for the ox and four sheep for the sheep.

[2]"If a thief is caught breaking in and is struck so that he dies, the defender is not guilty of bloodshed; [3]but if it happens[a] after sunrise, he is guilty of bloodshed.

"A thief must certainly make restitution, but if he has nothing, he must be sold to pay for his theft.

[4]"If the stolen animal is found alive in his possession—whether ox or donkey or sheep—he must pay back double.

[5]"If a man grazes his livestock in a field or vineyard and lets them stray and they graze in another man's field, he must make restitution from the best of his own field or vineyard.

[6]"If a fire breaks out and spreads into thornbushes so that it burns shocks of grain or standing corn or the whole field, the one who started the fire must make restitution.

[7]"If a man gives his neighbour silver or goods for safekeeping and they are stolen from the neighbour's house, the thief, if he is caught, must pay back double. [8]But if the thief is not found, the owner of the house must appear before the judges[b] to determine whether he has laid his hands on the other man's property. [9]In all cases of illegal possession of an ox, a donkey, a sheep, a garment, or any other lost property about which somebody says, 'This is mine,' both parties are to bring their cases before the judges. The one whom the judges declare[c] guilty must pay back double to his neighbour.

[10]"If a man gives a donkey, an ox, a sheep or any other animal to his neighbour for safekeeping and it dies or is injured or is taken away while no-one is looking, [11]the issue between them will be settled by the taking of an oath before the LORD that the neighbour did not lay hands on the other person's property. The owner is to accept this, and no restitution is required. [12]But if the animal was stolen from the neighbour, he must make restitution to the owner. [13]If it was torn to pieces by a wild animal, he shall bring in the remains as evidence and he will not be required to pay for the torn animal.

[14]"If a man borrows an animal from his neighbour and it is injured or dies while the owner is not present, he must make restitution. [15]But if the owner is with the animal, the borrower will not have to pay. If the animal was hired, the money paid for the hire covers the loss.

Social Responsibility

[16]"If a man seduces a virgin who is not pledged to be married and sleeps with her, he must pay the bride-price, and she shall be his wife. [17]If her father absolutely refuses to give her to him, he must still pay the bride-price for virgins.

[18]"Do not allow a sorceress to live.

[19]"Anyone who has sexual relations with an animal must be put to death.

[20]"Whoever sacrifices to any god other than the LORD must be destroyed.[d]

[21]"Do not ill-treat an alien or oppress him, for you were aliens in Egypt.

[22]"Do not take advantage of a widow or an orphan. [23]If you do and they cry out to me, I will certainly hear their cry. [24]My anger will be aroused, and I will kill you with the sword; your wives will become widows and your children fatherless.

[25]"If you lend money to one of my people among you who is needy, do not be like a money-lender; charge him no interest.[e] [26]If you take your neighbour's cloak as a pledge, return it to him by sunset, [27]because his cloak is the only covering he has for his body. What else

[a]3 Or *if he strikes him*   [b]8 Or *before God*; also in verse 9   [c]9 Or *whom God declares*
[d]20 The Hebrew term refers to the irrevocable giving over of things or persons to the LORD, often by totally destroying them.
[e]25 Or *excessive interest*

will he sleep in? When he cries out to me, I will hear, for I am compassionate.

²⁸"Do not blaspheme God*f* or curse the ruler of your people.

²⁹"Do not hold back offerings from your granaries or your vats.*g*

"You must give me the firstborn of your sons. ³⁰Do the same with your cattle and your sheep. Let them stay with their mothers for seven days, but give them to me on the eighth day.

³¹"You are to be my holy people. So do not eat the meat of an animal torn by wild beasts; throw it to the dogs.

Laws of Justice and Mercy

23 "Do not spread false reports. Do not help a wicked man by being a malicious witness.

²"Do not follow the crowd in doing wrong. When you give testimony in a lawsuit, do not pervert justice by siding with the crowd, ³and do not show favouritism to a poor man in his lawsuit.

⁴"If you come across your enemy's ox or donkey wandering off, be sure to take it back to him. ⁵If you see the donkey of someone who hates you fallen down under its load, do not leave it there; be sure you help him with it.

⁶"Do not deny justice to your poor people in their lawsuits. ⁷Have nothing to do with a false charge and do not put an innocent or honest person to death, for I will not acquit the guilty.

⁸"Do not accept a bribe, for a bribe blinds those who see and twists the words of the righteous.

⁹"Do not oppress an alien; you yourselves know how it feels to be aliens, because you were aliens in Egypt.

Sabbath Laws

¹⁰"For six years you are to sow your fields and harvest the crops, ¹¹but during the seventh year let the land lie unploughed and unused. Then the poor among your people may get food from it, and the wild animals may eat what they leave. Do the same with your vineyard and your olive grove.

¹²"Six days do your work, but on the seventh day do not work, so that your ox and your donkey may rest and the slave born in your household, and the alien as well, may be refreshed.

¹³"Be careful to do everything I have said to you. Do not invoke the names of other gods; do not let them be heard on your lips.

The Three Annual Festivals

¹⁴"Three times a year you are to celebrate a festival to me.

¹⁵"Celebrate the Feast of Unleavened Bread; for seven days eat bread made without yeast, as I commanded you. Do this at the appointed time in the month of Abib, for in that month you came out of Egypt.

"No-one is to appear before me empty-handed.

¹⁶"Celebrate the Feast of Harvest with the firstfruits of the crops you sow in your field.

"Celebrate the Feast of Ingathering at the end of the year, when you gather in your crops from the field.

¹⁷"Three times a year all the men are to appear before the Sovereign LORD.

¹⁸"Do not offer the blood of a sacrifice to me along with anything containing yeast.

"The fat of my festival offerings must not be kept until morning.

¹⁹"Bring the best of the firstfruits of your soil to the house of the LORD your God.

"Do not cook a young goat in its mother's milk.

God's Angel to Prepare the Way

²⁰"See, I am sending an angel ahead of you to guard you along the way and to bring you to the place I have prepared. ²¹Pay attention to him and listen to what he says. Do not rebel against him; he will not forgive your rebellion, since my Name

---

f28 Or *Do not revile the judges*   *g29* The meaning of the Hebrew for this phrase is uncertain.

is in him. ²²If you listen carefully to what he says and do all that I say, I will be an enemy to your enemies and will oppose those who oppose you. ²³My angel will go ahead of you and bring you into the land of the Amorites, Hittites, Perizzites, Canaanites, Hivites and Jebusites, and I will wipe them out. ²⁴Do not bow down before their gods or worship or follow their practices. You must demolish them and break their sacred stones to pieces. ²⁵Worship the LORD your God, and his blessing will be on your food and water. I will take away sickness from among you, ²⁶and none will miscarry or be barren in your land. I will give you a full life span.

²⁷"I will send my terror ahead of you and throw into confusion every nation you encounter. I will make all your enemies turn their backs and run. ²⁸I will send the hornet ahead of you to drive the Hivites, Canaanites and Hittites out of your way. ²⁹But I will not drive them out in a single year, because the land would become desolate and the wild animals too numerous for you. ³⁰Little by little I will drive them out before you, until you have increased enough to take possession of the land.

³¹"I will establish your borders from the Red Sea[a] to the Sea of the Philistines,[b] and from the desert to the River.[c] I will hand over to you the people who live in the land and you will drive them out before you. ³²Do not make a covenant with them or with their gods. ³³Do not let them live in your land, or they will cause you to sin against me, because the worship of their gods will certainly be a snare to you."

The Covenant Confirmed

24 Then he said to Moses, "Come up to the LORD, you and Aaron, Nadab and Abihu, and seventy of the elders of Israel. You are to worship at a distance, ²but Moses alone is to approach the LORD; the others must not come near. And the people may not come up with him."

³When Moses went and told the people all the LORD's words and laws, they responded with one voice, "Everything the LORD has said we will do." ⁴Moses then wrote down everything the LORD had said.

He got up early the next morning and built an altar at the foot of the mountain and set up twelve stone pillars representing the twelve tribes of Israel. ⁵Then he sent young Israelite men, and they offered burnt offerings and sacrificed young bulls as fellowship offerings[a] to the LORD. ⁶Moses took half of the blood and put it in bowls, and the other half he sprinkled on the altar. ⁷Then he took the Book of the Covenant and read it to the people. They responded, "We will do everything the LORD has said; we will obey."

⁸Moses then took the blood, sprinkled it on the people and said, "This is the blood of the covenant that the LORD has made with you in accordance with all these words."

⁹Moses and Aaron, Nadab and Abihu, and the seventy elders of Israel went up ¹⁰and saw the God of Israel. Under his feet was something like a pavement made of sapphire,[b] clear as the sky itself. ¹¹But God did not raise his hand against these leaders of the Israelites; they saw God, and they ate and drank.

¹²The LORD said to Moses, "Come up to me on the mountain and stay here, and I will give you the tablets of stone, with the law and commands I have written for their instruction."

¹³Then Moses set out with Joshua his assistant, and Moses went up on the mountain of God. ¹⁴He said to the elders, "Wait here for us until we come back to you. Aaron and Hur are with you, and anyone involved in a dispute can go to them."

¹⁵When Moses went up on the mountain, the cloud covered it, ¹⁶and the glory of the LORD settled on Mount Sinai. For six days the cloud covered the mountain, and on the seventh day the LORD called to Moses from within the cloud. ¹⁷To the Israelites the glory of the LORD looked like

---

^a31 Hebrew *Yam Suph*; that is, Sea of Reeds   ^b31 That is, the Mediterranean   ^c31 That is, the Euphrates
^a5 Traditionally *peace offerings*   ^b10 Or *lapis lazuli*

a consuming fire on top of the mountain. [18]Then Moses entered the cloud as he went on up the mountain. And he stayed on the mountain forty days and forty nights.

Offerings for the Tabernacle

25 The LORD said to Moses, [2]"Tell the Israelites to bring me an offering. You are to receive the offering for me from each man whose heart prompts him to give. [3]These are the offerings you are to receive from them: gold, silver and bronze; [4]blue, purple and scarlet yarn and fine linen; goat hair; [5]ram skins dyed red and hides of sea cows;[a] acacia wood; [6]olive oil for the light; spices for the anointing oil and for the fragrant incense; [7]and onyx stones and other gems to be mounted on the ephod and breastpiece.

[8]"Then have them make a sanctuary for me, and I will dwell among them. [9]Make this tabernacle and all its furnishings exactly like the pattern I will show you.

The Ark

[10]"Have them make a chest of acacia wood—two and a half cubits long, a cubit and a half wide, and a cubit and a half high.[b] [11]Overlay it with pure gold, both inside and out, and make a gold moulding around it. [12]Cast four gold rings for it and fasten them to its four feet, with two rings on one side and two rings on the other. [13]Then make poles of acacia wood and overlay them with gold. [14]Insert the poles into the rings on the sides of the chest to carry it. [15]The poles are to remain in the rings of this ark; they are not to be removed. [16]Then put in the ark the Testimony, which I will give you.

[17]"Make an atonement cover[c] of pure gold—two and a half cubits long and a cubit and a half wide.[d] [18]And make two cherubim out of hammered gold at the ends of the cover. [19]Make one cherub on one end and the second cherub on the other; make the cherubim of one piece with the cover, at the two ends. [20]The cherubim are to have their wings spread upwards, overshadowing the cover with them. The cherubim are to face each other, looking towards the cover. [21]Place the cover on top of the ark and put in the ark the Testimony, which I will give you. [22]There, above the cover between the two cherubim that are over the ark of the Testimony, I will meet with you and give you all my commands for the Israelites.

The Table

[23]"Make a table of acacia wood—two cubits long, a cubit wide and a cubit and a half high.[e] [24]Overlay it with pure gold and make a gold moulding around it. [25]Also make around it a rim a handbreadth[f] wide and put a gold moulding on the rim. [26]Make four gold rings for the table and fasten them to the four corners, where the four legs are. [27]The rings are to be close to the rim to hold the poles used in carrying the table. [28]Make the poles of acacia wood, overlay them with gold and carry the table with them. [29]And make its plates and dishes of pure gold, as well as its pitchers and bowls for the pouring out of offerings. [30]Put the bread of the Presence on this table to be before me at all times.

The Lampstand

[31]"Make a lampstand of pure gold and hammer it out, base and shaft; its flower-like cups, buds and blossoms shall be of one piece with it. [32]Six branches are to extend from the sides of the lampstand—three on one side and three on the other. [33]Three cups shaped like almond flowers with buds and blossoms are to be on one branch, three on the next branch, and the same for all six branches extending from the lampstand. [34]And on the lampstand there are to be four cups shaped like

[a]5 That is, large aquatic mammals
[b]10 That is, about 3¾ feet (about 1.1 metres) long and 2¼ feet (about 0.7 metre) wide and high
[c]17 Traditionally a mercy seat   [d]17 That is, about 3¾ feet (about 1.1 metres) long and 2¼ feet (about 0.7 metre) wide
[e]23 That is, about 3 feet (about 0.9 metre) long and 1½ feet (about 0.5 metre) wide and 2¼ feet (about 0.7 metre) high
[f]25 That is, about 3 inches (about 8 centimetres)

almond flowers with buds and blossoms. ³⁵One bud shall be under the first pair of branches extending from the lampstand, a second bud under the second pair, and a third bud under the third pair—six branches in all. ³⁶The buds and branches shall all be of one piece with the lampstand, hammered out of pure gold.

³⁷"Then make its seven lamps and set them up on it so that they light the space in front of it. ³⁸Its wick trimmers and trays are to be of pure gold. ³⁹A talent*g* of pure gold is to be used for the lampstand and all these accessories. ⁴⁰See that you make them according to the pattern shown you on the mountain.

The Tabernacle

26 "Make the tabernacle with ten curtains of finely twisted linen and blue, purple and scarlet yarn, with cherubim worked into them by a skilled craftsman. ²All the curtains are to be the same size—twenty-eight cubits long and four cubits wide.*a* ³Join five of the curtains together, and do the same with the other five. ⁴Make loops of blue material along the edge of the end curtain in one set, and do the same with the end curtain in the other set. ⁵Make fifty loops on one curtain and fifty loops on the end curtain of the other set, with the loops opposite each other. ⁶Then make fifty gold clasps and use them to fasten the curtains together so that the tabernacle is a unit.

⁷"Make curtains of goat hair for the tent over the tabernacle—eleven altogether. ⁸All eleven curtains are to be the same size—thirty cubits long and four cubits wide.*b* ⁹Join five of the curtains together into one set and the other six into another set. Fold the sixth curtain double at the front of the tent. ¹⁰Make fifty loops along the edge of the end curtain in one set and also along the edge of the end curtain in the other set. ¹¹Then make fifty bronze clasps and put them in the loops to fasten

the tent together as a unit. ¹²As for the additional length of the tent curtains, the half curtain that is left over is to hang down at the rear of the tabernacle. ¹³ The tent curtains will be a cubit*c* longer on both sides; what is left will hang over the sides of the tabernacle so as to cover it. ¹⁴Make for the tent a covering of ram skins dyed red, and over that a covering of hides of sea cows.*d*

¹⁵"Make upright frames of acacia wood for the tabernacle. ¹⁶Each frame is to be ten cubits long and a cubit and a half wide,*e* ¹⁷with two projections set parallel to each other. Make all the frames of the tabernacle in this way. ¹⁸Make twenty frames for the south side of the tabernacle ¹⁹and make forty silver bases to go under them—two bases for each frame, one under each projection. ²⁰For the other side, the north side of the tabernacle, make twenty frames ²¹and forty silver bases—two under each frame. ²²Make six frames for the far end, that is, the west end of the tabernacle, ²³and make two frames for the corners at the far end. ²⁴At these two corners they must be double from the bottom all the way to the top, and fitted into a single ring; both shall be like that. ²⁵So there will be eight frames and sixteen silver bases—two under each frame.

²⁶"Also make crossbars of acacia wood: five for the frames on one side of the tabernacle, ²⁷five for those on the other side, and five for the frames on the west, at the far end of the tabernacle. ²⁸The centre crossbar is to extend from end to end at the middle of the frames. ²⁹Overlay the frames with gold and make gold rings to hold the crossbars. Also overlay the crossbars with gold.

³⁰"Set up the tabernacle according to the plan shown you on the mountain.

³¹"Make a curtain of blue, purple and scarlet yarn and finely twisted linen, with cherubim worked into it by a skilled craftsman. ³²Hang it with gold hooks on four

---

g39 That is, about 75 pounds (about 34 kilograms)
a2 That is, about 42 feet (about 13 metres) long and 6 feet (about 1.8 metres) wide
b8 That is, about 45 feet (about 13.5 metres) long and 6 feet (about 1.8 metres) wide
c13 That is, about 1½ feet (about 0.5 metre)   *d14* That is, large aquatic mammals
e16 That is, about 15 feet (about 4.5 metres) long and 2¼ feet (about 0.7 metre) wide

posts of acacia wood overlaid with gold and standing on four silver bases. ³³Hang the curtain from the clasps and place the ark of the Testimony behind the curtain. The curtain will separate the Holy Place from the Most Holy Place. ³⁴Put the atonement cover on the ark of the Testimony in the Most Holy Place. ³⁵Place the table outside the curtain on the north side of the tabernacle and put the lampstand opposite it on the south side.

³⁶"For the entrance to the tent make a curtain of blue, purple and scarlet yarn and finely twisted linen—the work of an embroiderer. ³⁷Make gold hooks for this curtain and five posts of acacia wood overlaid with gold. And cast five bronze bases for them.

The Altar of Burnt Offering

27 "Build an altar of acacia wood, three cubits^a high; it is to be square, five cubits long and five cubits wide.^b ²Make a horn at each of the four corners, so that the horns and the altar are of one piece, and overlay the altar with bronze. ³Make all its utensils of bronze— its pots to remove the ashes, and its shovels, sprinkling bowls, meat forks and firepans. ⁴Make a grating for it, a bronze network, and make a bronze ring at each of the four corners of the network. ⁵Put it under the ledge of the altar so that it is halfway up the altar. ⁶Make poles of acacia wood for the altar and overlay them with bronze. ⁷The poles are to be inserted into the rings so they will be on two sides of the altar when it is carried. ⁸Make the altar hollow, out of boards. It is to be made just as you were shown on the mountain.

The Courtyard

⁹"Make a courtyard for the tabernacle. The south side shall be a hundred cubits^c long and is to have curtains of finely twisted linen, ¹⁰with twenty posts and twenty bronze bases and with silver hooks and bands on the posts. ¹¹The north side shall also be a hundred cubits long and is to have curtains, with twenty posts and twenty bronze bases and with silver hooks and bands on the posts.

¹²"The west end of the courtyard shall be fifty cubits^d wide and have curtains, with ten posts and ten bases. ¹³On the east end, towards the sunrise, the courtyard shall also be fifty cubits wide. ¹⁴Curtains fifteen cubits^e long are to be on one side of the entrance, with three posts and three bases, ¹⁵and curtains fifteen cubits long are to be on the other side, with three posts and three bases.

¹⁶"For the entrance to the courtyard, provide a curtain twenty cubits^f long, of blue, purple and scarlet yarn and finely twisted linen—the work of an embroiderer—with four posts and four bases. ¹⁷All the posts around the courtyard are to have silver bands and hooks, and bronze bases. ¹⁸The courtyard shall be a hundred cubits long and fifty cubits wide,^g with curtains of finely twisted linen five cubits^h high, and with bronze bases. ¹⁹All the other articles used in the service of the tabernacle, whatever their function, including all the tent pegs for it and those for the courtyard, are to be of bronze.

Oil for the Lampstand

²⁰"Command the Israelites to bring you clear oil of pressed olives for the light so that the lamps may be kept burning. ²¹In the Tent of Meeting, outside the curtain that is in front of the Testimony, Aaron and his sons are to keep the lamps burning before the LORD from evening till morning. This is to be a lasting ordinance among the Israelites for the generations to come.

---

^a1 That is, about 4½ feet (about 1.4 metres)   ^b1 That is, about 7½ feet (about 2.3 metres) long and wide
^c9 That is, about 150 feet (about 46 metres); also in verse 11
^d12 That is, about 75 feet (about 23 metres); also in verse 13
^e14 That is, about 22½ feet (about 6.9 metres); also in verse 15   ^f16 That is, about 30 feet (about 9 metres)
^g18 That is, about 150 feet (about 46 metres) long and 75 feet (about 23 metres) wide
^h18 That is, about 7½ feet (about 2.3 metres)

The Priestly Garments

28 "Have Aaron your brother brought to you from among the Israelites, with his sons Nadab and Abihu, Eleazar and Ithamar, so that they may serve me as priests. ²Make sacred garments for your brother Aaron, to give him dignity and honour. ³Tell all the skilled men to whom I have given wisdom in such matters that they are to make garments for Aaron, for his consecration, so that he may serve me as priest. ⁴These are the garments they are to make: a breastpiece, an ephod, a robe, a woven tunic, a turban and a sash. They are to make these sacred garments for your brother Aaron and his sons, so that they may serve me as priests. ⁵Make them use gold, and blue, purple and scarlet yarn, and fine linen.

The Ephod

⁶"Make the ephod of gold, and of blue, purple and scarlet yarn, and of finely twisted linen—the work of a skilled craftsman. ⁷It is to have two shoulder pieces attached to two of its corners, so that it can be fastened. ⁸Its skilfully woven waistband is to be like it—of one piece with the ephod and made with gold, and with blue, purple and scarlet yarn, and with finely twisted linen.

⁹"Take two onyx stones and engrave on them the names of the sons of Israel ¹⁰in the order of their birth—six names on one stone and the remaining six on the other. ¹¹Engrave the names of the sons of Israel on the two stones the way a gem cutter engraves a seal. Then mount the stones in gold filigree settings ¹²and fasten them on the shoulder pieces of the ephod as memorial stones for the sons of Israel. Aaron is to bear the names on his shoulders as a memorial before the Lord. ¹³Make gold filigree settings ¹⁴and two braided chains of pure gold, like a rope, and attach the chains to the settings.

The Breastpiece

¹⁵"Fashion a breastpiece for making decisions—the work of a skilled craftsman. Make it like the ephod: of gold, and of blue, purple and scarlet yarn, and of finely twisted linen. ¹⁶It is to be square—a span^a long and a span wide—and folded double. ¹⁷Then mount four rows of precious stones on it. In the first row there shall be a ruby, a topaz and a beryl; ¹⁸in the second row a turquoise, a sapphire^b and an emerald; ¹⁹in the third row a jacinth, an agate and an amethyst; ²⁰in the fourth row a chrysolite, an onyx and a jasper.^{c} Mount them in gold filigree settings. ²¹There are to be twelve stones, one for each of the names of the sons of Israel, each engraved like a seal with the name of one of the twelve tribes.

²²"For the breastpiece make braided chains of pure gold, like a rope. ²³Make two gold rings for it and fasten them to two corners of the breastpiece. ²⁴Fasten the two gold chains to the rings at the corners of the breastpiece, ²⁵and the other ends of the chains to the two settings, attaching them to the shoulder pieces of the ephod at the front. ²⁶Make two gold rings and attach them to the other two corners of the breastpiece on the inside edge next to the ephod. ²⁷Make two more gold rings and attach them to the bottom of the shoulder pieces on the front of the ephod, close to the seam just above the waistband of the ephod. ²⁸The rings of the breastpiece are to be tied to the rings of the ephod with blue cord, connecting it to the waistband, so that the breastpiece will not swing out from the ephod.

²⁹"Whenever Aaron enters the Holy Place, he will bear the names of the sons of Israel over his heart on the breastpiece of decision as a continuing memorial before the Lord. ³⁰Also put the Urim and the Thummim in the breastpiece, so they may be over Aaron's heart whenever he enters the presence of the Lord. Thus Aaron will

---

^{a}16 That is, about 9 inches (about 23 centimetres) ^{b}18 Or *lapis lazuli*
^{c}20 The precise identification of some of these precious stones is uncertain.

always bear the means of making decisions for the Israelites over his heart before the LORD.

Other Priestly Garments

[31]"Make the robe of the ephod entirely of blue cloth, [32]with an opening for the head in its centre. There shall be a woven edge like a collar[d] around this opening, so that it will not tear. [33]Make pomegranates of blue, purple and scarlet yarn around the hem of the robe, with gold bells between them. [34]The gold bells and the pomegranates are to alternate around the hem of the robe. [35]Aaron must wear it when he ministers. The sound of the bells will be heard when he enters the Holy Place before the LORD and when he comes out, so that he will not die.

[36]"Make a plate of pure gold and engrave on it as on a seal: HOLY TO THE LORD. [37]Fasten a blue cord to it to attach it to the turban; it is to be on the front of the turban. [38]It will be on Aaron's forehead, and he will bear the guilt involved in the sacred gifts the Israelites consecrate, whatever their gifts may be. It will be on Aaron's forehead continually so that they will be acceptable to the LORD.

[39]"Weave the tunic of fine linen and make the turban of fine linen. The sash is to be the work of an embroiderer. [40]Make tunics, sashes and headbands for Aaron's sons, to give them dignity and honour. [41]After you put these clothes on your brother Aaron and his sons, anoint and ordain them. Consecrate them so they may serve me as priests.

[42]"Make linen undergarments as a covering for the body, reaching from the waist to the thigh. [43]Aaron and his sons must wear them whenever they enter the Tent of Meeting or approach the altar to minister in the Holy Place, so that they will not incur guilt and die.

"This is to be a lasting ordinance for Aaron and his descendants.

Consecration of the Priests

29 "This is what you are to do to consecrate them, so that they may serve me as priests: Take a young bull and two rams without defect. [2]And from fine wheat flour, without yeast, make bread, and cakes mixed with oil, and wafers spread with oil. [3]Put them in a basket and present them in it—along with the bull and the two rams. [4]Then bring Aaron and his sons to the entrance to the Tent of Meeting and wash them with water. [5]Take the garments and dress Aaron with the tunic, the robe of the ephod, the ephod itself and the breastpiece. Fasten the ephod on him by its skilfully woven waistband. [6]Put the turban on his head and attach the sacred diadem to the turban. [7]Take the anointing oil and anoint him by pouring it on his head. [8]Bring his sons and dress them in tunics [9]and put headbands on them. Then tie sashes on Aaron and his sons.[a] The priesthood is theirs by a lasting ordinance. In this way you shall ordain Aaron and his sons.

[10]"Bring the bull to the front of the Tent of Meeting, and Aaron and his sons shall lay their hands on its head. [11]Slaughter it in the LORD's presence at the entrance to the Tent of Meeting. [12]Take some of the bull's blood and put it on the horns of the altar with your finger, and pour out the rest of it at the base of the altar. [13]Then take all the fat around the inner parts, the covering of the liver, and both kidneys with the fat on them, and burn them on the altar. [14]But burn the bull's flesh and its hide and its offal outside the camp. It is a sin offering.

[15]"Take one of the rams, and Aaron and his sons shall lay their hands on its head. [16]Slaughter it and take the blood and sprinkle it against the altar on all sides. [17]Cut the ram into pieces and wash the inner parts and the legs, putting them with the head and the other pieces. [18]Then burn the entire ram on the altar. It is a

---

d32 The meaning of the Hebrew for this word is uncertain.
a9 Hebrew; Septuagint *on them*

burnt offering to the LORD, a pleasing aroma, an offering made to the LORD by fire.

¹⁹"Take the other ram, and Aaron and his sons shall lay their hands on its head. ²⁰Slaughter it, take some of its blood and put it on the lobes of the right ears of Aaron and his sons, on the thumbs of their right hands, and on the big toes of their right feet. Then sprinkle blood against the altar on all sides. ²¹And take some of the blood on the altar and some of the anointing oil and sprinkle it on Aaron and his garments and on his sons and their garments. Then he and his sons and their garments will be consecrated.

²²"Take from this ram the fat, the fat tail, the fat around the inner parts, the covering of the liver, both kidneys with the fat on them, and the right thigh. (This is the ram for the ordination.) ²³From the basket of bread made without yeast, which is before the LORD, take a loaf, and a cake made with oil, and a wafer. ²⁴Put all these in the hands of Aaron and his sons and wave them before the LORD as a wave offering. ²⁵Then take them from their hands and burn them on the altar along with the burnt offering for a pleasing aroma to the LORD, an offering made to the LORD by fire. ²⁶After you take the breast of the ram for Aaron's ordination, wave it before the LORD as a wave offering, and it will be your share.

²⁷"Consecrate those parts of the ordination ram that belong to Aaron and his sons: the breast that was waved and the thigh that was presented. ²⁸This is always to be the regular share from the Israelites for Aaron and his sons. It is the contribution the Israelites are to make to the LORD from their fellowship offerings.*b*

²⁹"Aaron's sacred garments will belong to his descendants so that they can be anointed and ordained in them. ³⁰The son who succeeds him as priest and comes to the Tent of Meeting to minister in the Holy Place is to wear them seven days.

³¹"Take the ram for the ordination and cook the meat in a sacred place. ³²At the entrance to the Tent of Meeting, Aaron and his sons are to eat the meat of the ram and the bread that is in the basket. ³³They are to eat these offerings by which atonement was made for their ordination and consecration. But no-one else may eat them, because they are sacred. ³⁴And if any of the meat of the ordination ram or any bread is left over till morning, burn it up. It must not be eaten, because it is sacred.

³⁵"Do for Aaron and his sons everything I have commanded you, taking seven days to ordain them. ³⁶Sacrifice a bull each day as a sin offering to make atonement. Purify the altar by making atonement for it, and anoint it to consecrate it. ³⁷For seven days make atonement for the altar and consecrate it. Then the altar will be most holy, and whatever touches it will be holy.

³⁸"This is what you are to offer on the altar regularly each day: two lambs a year old. ³⁹Offer one in the morning and the other at twilight. ⁴⁰With the first lamb offer a tenth of an ephah*c* of fine flour mixed with a quarter of a hin*d* of oil from pressed olives, and a quarter of a hin of wine as a drink offering. ⁴¹Sacrifice the other lamb at twilight with the same grain offering and its drink offering as in the morning—a pleasing aroma, an offering made to the LORD by fire.

⁴²"For the generations to come this burnt offering is to be made regularly at the entrance to the Tent of Meeting before the LORD. There I will meet you and speak to you; ⁴³there also I will meet with the Israelites, and the place will be consecrated by my glory.

⁴⁴"So I will consecrate the Tent of Meeting and the altar and will consecrate Aaron and his sons to serve me as priests. ⁴⁵Then I will dwell among the Israelites and be their God. ⁴⁶They will know that I am the LORD their God, who brought them out of Egypt so that I might dwell among them. I am the LORD their God.

---

b28 Traditionally *peace offerings*   *c40* That is, probably about 4 pints (about 2 litres)
d40 That is, probably about 1½ pints (about 1 litre)

The Altar of Incense

30 "Make an altar of acacia wood for burning incense. ²It is to be square, a cubit long and a cubit wide, and two cubits high*a*—its horns of one piece with it. ³Overlay the top and all the sides and the horns with pure gold, and make a gold moulding around it. ⁴Make two gold rings for the altar below the moulding— two on opposite sides—to hold the poles used to carry it. ⁵Make the poles of acacia wood and overlay them with gold. ⁶Put the altar in front of the curtain that is before the ark of the Testimony—before the atonement cover that is over the Testimony—where I will meet with you.

⁷"Aaron must burn fragrant incense on the altar every morning when he tends the lamps. ⁸He must burn incense again when he lights the lamps at twilight so that incense will burn regularly before the LORD for the generations to come. ⁹Do not offer on this altar any other incense or any burnt offering or grain offering, and do not pour a drink offering on it. ¹⁰Once a year Aaron shall make atonement on its horns. This annual atonement must be made with the blood of the atoning sin offering for the generations to come. It is most holy to the LORD."

Atonement Money

¹¹Then the LORD said to Moses, ¹²"When you take a census of the Israelites to count them, each one must pay the LORD a ransom for his life at the time he is counted. Then no plague will come on them when you number them. ¹³Each one who crosses over to those already counted is to give a half shekel,*b* according to the sanctuary shekel, which weighs twenty gerahs. This half shekel is an offering to the LORD. ¹⁴All who cross over, those twenty years old or more, are to give an offering to the LORD. ¹⁵The rich are not to give more than a half shekel and the poor are not to give less when you make the offering to the LORD to atone for

your lives. ¹⁶Receive the atonement money from the Israelites and use it for the service of the Tent of Meeting. It will be a memorial for the Israelites before the LORD, making atonement for your lives."

Basin for Washing

¹⁷Then the LORD said to Moses, ¹⁸"Make a bronze basin, with its bronze stand, for washing. Place it between the Tent of Meeting and the altar, and put water in it. ¹⁹Aaron and his sons are to wash their hands and feet with water from it. ²⁰Whenever they enter the Tent of Meeting, they shall wash with water so that they will not die. Also, when they approach the altar to minister by presenting an offering made to the LORD by fire, ²¹they shall wash their hands and feet so that they will not die. This is to be a lasting ordinance for Aaron and his descendants for the generations to come."

Anointing Oil

²²Then the LORD said to Moses, ²³"Take the following fine spices: 500 shekels*c* of liquid myrrh, half as much (that is, 250 shekels) of fragrant cinnamon, 250 shekels of fragrant cane, ²⁴500 shekels of cassia—all according to the sanctuary shekel—and a hin*d* of olive oil. ²⁵Make these into a sacred anointing oil, a fragrant blend, the work of a perfumer. It will be the sacred anointing oil. ²⁶Then use it to anoint the Tent of Meeting, the ark of the Testimony, ²⁷the table and all its articles, the lampstand and its accessories, the altar of incense, ²⁸the altar of burnt offering and all its utensils, and the basin with its stand. ²⁹You shall consecrate them so they will be most holy, and whatever touches them will be holy.

³⁰"Anoint Aaron and his sons and consecrate them so they may serve me as priests. ³¹Say to the Israelites, 'This is to be my sacred anointing oil for the generations to come. ³²Do not pour it on men's

---

a2 That is, about 1½ feet (about 0.5 metre) long and wide and about 3 feet (about 0.9 metre) high
b13 That is, about ⅕ ounce (about 6 grams); also in verse 15   *c23* That is, about 12½ pounds (about 6 kilograms)
d24 That is, probably about 6½ pints (about 4 litres)

bodies and do not make any oil with the same formula. It is sacred, and you are to consider it sacred. 33Whoever makes perfume like it and whoever puts it on anyone other than a priest must be cut off from his people.'"

Incense

34Then the LORD said to Moses, "Take fragrant spices—gum resin, onycha and galbanum—and pure frankincense, all in equal amounts, 35and make a fragrant blend of incense, the work of a perfumer. It is to be salted and pure and sacred. 36Grind some of it to powder and place it in front of the Testimony in the Tent of Meeting, where I will meet with you. It shall be most holy to you. 37Do not make any incense with this formula for yourselves; consider it holy to the LORD. 38Whoever makes any like it to enjoy its fragrance must be cut off from his people."

Bezalel and Oholiab

31 Then the LORD said to Moses, 2"See I have chosen Bezalel son of Uri, the son of Hur, of the tribe of Judah, 3and I have filled him with the Spirit of God, with skill, ability and knowledge in all kinds of crafts—4to make artistic designs for work in gold, silver and bronze, 5to cut and set stones, to work in wood, and to engage in all kinds of craftsmanship. 6Moreover, I have appointed Oholiab son of Ahisamach, of the tribe of Dan, to help him. Also I have given skill to all the craftsmen to make everything I have commanded you: 7the Tent of Meeting, the ark of the Testimony with the atonement cover on it, and all the other furnishings of the tent—8the table and its articles, the pure gold lampstand and all its accessories, the altar of incense, 9the altar of burnt offering and all its utensils, the basin with its stand—10and also the woven garments, both the sacred

garments for Aaron the priest and the garments for his sons when they serve as priests, 11and the anointing oil and fragrant incense for the Holy Place. They are to make them just as I commanded you."

The Sabbath

12Then the LORD said to Moses, 13"Say to the Israelites, 'You must observe my Sabbaths. This will be a sign between me and you for the generations to come, so that you may know that I am the LORD, who makes you holy.[a]

14"'Observe the Sabbath, because it is holy to you. Anyone who desecrates it must be put to death; whoever does any work on that day must be cut off from his people. 15For six days, work is to be done, but the seventh day is a Sabbath of rest, holy to the LORD. Whoever does any work on the Sabbath day must be put to death. 16The Israelites are to observe the Sabbath, celebrating it for the generations to come as a lasting covenant. 17It will be a sign between me and the Israelites for ever, for in six days the LORD made the heavens and the earth, and on the seventh day he abstained from work and rested.'"

18When the LORD finished speaking to Moses on Mount Sinai, he gave him the two tablets of the Testimony, the tablets of stone inscribed by the finger of God.

The Golden Calf

32 When the people saw that Moses was so long in coming down from the mountain, they gathered round Aaron and said, "Come, make us gods[a] who will go before us. As for this fellow Moses who brought us up out of Egypt, we don't know what has happened to him."

2Aaron answered them, "Take off the gold ear-rings that your wives, your sons and your daughters are wearing, and bring them to me." 3So all the people took off their ear-rings and brought them to Aaron. 4He took what they handed him

---

[a]13 Or who sanctifies you; or who sets you apart as holy
[a]1 Or a god; also in verses 23 and 31

and made it into an idol cast in the shape of a calf, fashioning it with a tool. Then they said, "These are your gods,*b* O Israel, who brought you up out of Egypt."

⁵When Aaron saw this, he built an altar in front of the calf and announced, "Tomorrow there will be a festival to the LORD." ⁶So the next day the people rose early and sacrificed burnt offerings and presented fellowship offerings.*c* Afterwards they sat down to eat and drink and got up to indulge in revelry.

⁷Then the LORD said to Moses, "Go down, because your people, whom you brought up out of Egypt, have become corrupt. ⁸They have been quick to turn away from what I commanded them and have made themselves an idol cast in the shape of a calf. They have bowed down to it and sacrificed to it and have said, 'These are your gods, O Israel, who brought you up out of Egypt.'

⁹"I have seen these people," the LORD said to Moses, "and they are a stiff-necked people. ¹⁰Now leave me alone so that my anger may burn against them and that I may destroy them. Then I will make you into a great nation."

¹¹But Moses sought the favour of the LORD his God. "O LORD," he said, "why should your anger burn against your people, whom you brought out of Egypt with great power and a mighty hand? ¹²Why should the Egyptians say, 'It was with evil intent that he brought them out, to kill them in the mountains and to wipe them off the face of the earth'? Turn from your fierce anger; relent and do not bring disaster on your people. ¹³Remember your servants Abraham, Isaac and Israel, to whom you swore by your own self: 'I will make your descendants as numerous as the stars in the sky and I will give your descendants all this land I promised them, and it will be their inheritance for ever.'" ¹⁴Then the LORD relented and did not bring on his people the disaster he had threatened.

¹⁵Moses turned and went down the mountain with the two tablets of the Testimony in his hands. They were inscribed on both sides, front and back. ¹⁶The tablets were the work of God; the writing was the writing of God, engraved on the tablets.

¹⁷When Joshua heard the noise of the people shouting, he said to Moses, "There is the sound of war in the camp."

¹⁸Moses replied:

"It is not the sound of victory,
    it is not the sound of defeat;
    it is the sound of singing that I hear."

¹⁹When Moses approached the camp and saw the calf and the dancing, his anger burned and he threw the tablets out of his hands, breaking them to pieces at the foot of the mountain. ²⁰And he took the calf they had made and burned it in the fire; then he ground it to powder, scattered it on the water and made the Israelites drink it.

²¹He said to Aaron, "What did these people do to you, that you led them into such great sin?"

²²"Do not be angry, my lord," Aaron answered. "You know how prone these people are to evil. ²³They said to me, 'Make us gods who will go before us. As for this fellow Moses who brought us up out of Egypt, we don't know what has happened to him.' ²⁴So I told them, 'Whoever has any gold jewellery, take it off.' Then they gave me the gold, and I threw it into the fire, and out came this calf!"

²⁵Moses saw that the people were running wild and that Aaron had let them get out of control and so become a laughing-stock to their enemies. ²⁶So he stood at the entrance to the camp and said, "Whoever is for the LORD, come to me." And all the Levites rallied to him.

²⁷Then he said to them, "This is what the LORD, the God of Israel, says: 'Each man strap a sword to his side. Go back and forth through the camp from one end to the other, each killing his brother and friend and neighbour.'" ²⁸The Levites did as Moses commanded, and that day about three thousand of the people died. ²⁹Then Moses said, "You have been set apart to

---

*b*4 Or *This is your god*; also in verse 8   *c*6 Traditionally *peace offerings* the LORD today, for you were against your own sons and brothers, and he has blessed you this day."

30The next day Moses said to the people, "You have committed a great sin. But now I will go up to the LORD; perhaps I can make atonement for your sin."

31So Moses went back to the LORD and said, "Oh, what a great sin these people have committed! They have made themselves gods of gold. 32But now, please forgive their sin—but if not, then blot me out of the book you have written."

33The LORD replied to Moses, "Whoever has sinned against me I will blot out of my book. 34Now go, lead the people to the place I spoke of, and my angel will go before you. However, when the time comes for me to punish, I will punish them for their sin."

35And the LORD struck the people with a plague because of what they did with the calf Aaron had made.

33 Then the LORD said to Moses, "Leave this place, you and the people you brought up out of Egypt, and go up to the land I promised on oath to Abraham, Isaac and Jacob, saying, 'I will give it to your descendants.' 2I will send an angel before you and drive out the Canaanites, Amorites, Hittites, Perizzites, Hivites and Jebusites. 3Go up to the land flowing with milk and honey. But I will not go with you, because you are a stiff-necked people and I might destroy you on the way."

4When the people heard these distressing words, they began to mourn and no-one put on any ornaments. 5For the LORD had said to Moses, "Tell the Israelites, 'You are a stiff-necked people. If I were to go with you even for a moment, I might destroy you. Now take off your ornaments and I will decide what to do with you.'" 6So the Israelites stripped off their ornaments at Mount Horeb.

The Tent of Meeting

7Now Moses used to take a tent and pitch it outside the camp some distance away, calling it the "tent of meeting". Anyone enquiring of the LORD would go to the tent of meeting outside the camp. 8And whenever Moses went out to the tent, all the people rose and stood at the entrances to their tents, watching Moses until he entered the tent. 9As Moses went into the tent, the pillar of cloud would come down and stay at the entrance, while the LORD spoke with Moses. 10Whenever the people saw the pillar of cloud standing at the entrance to the tent, they all stood and worshipped, each at the entrance to his tent. 11The LORD would speak to Moses face to face, as a man speaks with his friend. Then Moses would return to the camp, but his young assistant Joshua son of Nun did not leave the tent.

Moses and the Glory of the LORD

12Moses said to the LORD, "You have been telling me, 'Lead these people,' but you have not let me know whom you will send with me. You have said, 'I know you by name and you have found favour with me.' 13If you are pleased with me, teach me your ways so I may know you and continue to find favour with you. Remember that this nation is your people."

14The LORD replied, "My Presence will go with you, and I will give you rest."

15Then Moses said to him, "If your Presence does not go with us, do not send us up from here. 16How will anyone know that you are pleased with me and with your people unless you go with us? What else will distinguish me and your people from all the other people on the face of the earth?"

17And the LORD said to Moses, "I will do the very thing you have asked, because I am pleased with you and I know you by name."

18Then Moses said, "Now show me your glory."

19And the LORD said, "I will cause all my goodness to pass in front of you, and I will proclaim my name, the LORD, in your presence. I will have mercy on whom I will have mercy, and I will have compassion on whom I will have compassion. 20But," he said, "you cannot see my face, for no-one may see me and live."

21Then the LORD said, "There is a place near me where you may stand on a rock. 22When my glory passes by, I will put you in a cleft in the rock and cover you with my hand until I have passed by. 23Then I will remove my hand and you will see my back; but my face must not be seen."

The New Stone Tablets

34 The LORD said to Moses, "Chisel out two stone tablets like the first ones, and I will write on them the words that were on the first tablets, which you broke. 2Be ready in the morning, and then come up on Mount Sinai. Present yourself to me there on top of the mountain. 3No-one is to come with you or be seen anywhere on the mountain; not even the flocks and herds may graze in front of the mountain."

4So Moses chiselled out two stone tablets like the first ones and went up Mount Sinai early in the morning, as the LORD had commanded him; and he carried the two stone tablets in his hands. 5Then the LORD came down in the cloud and stood there with him and proclaimed his name, the LORD. 6And he passed in front of Moses, proclaiming, "The LORD, the LORD, the compassionate and gracious God, slow to anger, abounding in love and faithfulness, 7maintaining love to thousands, and forgiving wickedness, rebellion and sin. Yet he does not leave the guilty unpunished; he punishes the children and their children for the sin of the fathers to the third and fourth generation."

8Moses bowed to the ground at once and worshipped. 9"O Lord, if I have found favour in your eyes," he said, "then let the Lord go with us. Although this is a stiff-necked people, forgive our wickedness and our sin, and take us as your inheritance."

10Then the LORD said: "I am making a covenant with you. Before all your people I will do wonders never before done in any nation in all the world. The people you live among will see how awesome is the work that I, the LORD, will do for you. 11Obey what I command you today. I will drive out before you the Amorites, Canaanites, Hittites, Perizzites, Hivites and Jebusites. 12Be careful not to make a treaty with those who live in the land where you are going, or they will be a snare among you. 13Break down their altars, smash their sacred stones and cut down their Asherah poles.[a] 14Do not worship any other god, for the LORD, whose name is Jealous, is a jealous God.

15"Be careful not to make a treaty with those who live in the land; for when they prostitute themselves to their gods and sacrifice to them, they will invite you and you will eat their sacrifices. 16And when you choose some of their daughters as wives for your sons and those daughters prostitute themselves to their gods, they will lead your sons to do the same.

17"Do not make cast idols.

18"Celebrate the Feast of Unleavened Bread. For seven days eat bread made without yeast, as I commanded you. Do this at the appointed time in the month of Abib, for in that month you came out of Egypt.

19"The first offspring of every womb belongs to me, including all the firstborn males of your livestock, whether from herd or flock. 20Redeem the firstborn donkey with a lamb, but if you do not redeem it, break its neck. Redeem all your firstborn sons.

"No-one is to appear before me empty-handed.

21"Six days you shall labour, but on the seventh day you shall rest; even during the ploughing season and harvest you must rest.

22"Celebrate the Feast of Weeks with the firstfruits of the wheat harvest, and the Feast of Ingathering at the turn of the year.[b] 23Three times a year all your men are to appear before the Sovereign LORD, the God of Israel. 24I will drive out nations before you and enlarge your territory, and

---

a13 That is, symbols of the goddess Asherah   *b22* That is, in the autumn no-one will covet your land when you go up three times each year to appear before the LORD your God.

25"Do not offer the blood of a sacrifice to me along with anything containing yeast, and do not let any of the sacrifice from the Passover Feast remain until morning.

26"Bring the best of the firstfruits of your soil to the house of the LORD your God.

"Do not cook a young goat in its mother's milk."

27Then the LORD said to Moses, "Write down these words, for in accordance with these words I have made a covenant with you and with Israel." 28Moses was there with the LORD forty days and forty nights without eating bread or drinking water. And he wrote on the tablets the words of the covenant—the Ten Commandments.

The Radiant Face of Moses

29When Moses came down from Mount Sinai with the two tablets of the Testimony in his hands, he was not aware that his face was radiant because he had spoken with the LORD. 30When Aaron and all the Israelites saw Moses, his face was radiant, and they were afraid to come near him. 31But Moses called to them; so Aaron and all the leaders of the community came back to him, and he spoke to them. 32Afterwards all the Israelites came near him, and he gave them all the commands the LORD had given him on Mount Sinai.

33When Moses finished speaking to them, he put a veil over his face. 34But whenever he entered the LORD's presence to speak with him, he removed the veil until he came out. And when he came out and told the Israelites what he had been commanded, 35they saw that his face was radiant. Then Moses would put the veil back over his face until he went in to speak with the LORD.

Sabbath Regulations

35 Moses assembled the whole Israelite community and said to them, "These are the things the LORD has commanded you to do: 2For six days, work is to be done, but the seventh day shall be your holy day, a Sabbath of rest to the LORD. Whoever does any work on it must be put to death. 3Do not light a fire in any of your dwellings on the Sabbath day."

Materials for the Tabernacle

4Moses said to the whole Israelite community, "This is what the LORD has commanded: 5From what you have, take an offering for the LORD. Everyone who is willing is to bring to the LORD an offering of gold, silver and bronze; 6blue, purple and scarlet yarn and fine linen; goat hair; 7ram skins dyed red and hides of sea cows;[a] acacia wood; 8olive oil for the light; spices for the anointing oil and for the fragrant incense; 9and onyx stones and other gems to be mounted on the ephod and breastpiece.

10"All who are skilled among you are to come and make everything the LORD has commanded: 11the tabernacle with its tent and its covering, clasps, frames, crossbars, posts and bases; 12the ark with its poles and the atonement cover and the curtain that shields it; 13the table with its poles and all its articles and the bread of the Presence; 14the lampstand that is for light with its accessories, lamps and oil for the light; 15the altar of incense with its poles, the anointing oil and the fragrant incense; the curtain for the doorway at the entrance to the tabernacle; 16the altar of burnt offering with its bronze grating, its poles and all its utensils; the bronze basin with its stand; 17the curtains of the courtyard with its posts and bases, and the curtain for the entrance to the courtyard; 18the tent pegs for the tabernacle and for the courtyard,

---

a7 That is, large aquatic mammals; also in verse 23

and their ropes; ¹⁹the woven garments worn for ministering in the sanctuary—both the sacred garments for Aaron the priest and the garments for his sons when they serve as priests."

²⁰Then the whole Israelite community withdrew from Moses' presence, ²¹and everyone who was willing and whose heart moved him came and brought an offering to the LORD for the work on the Tent of Meeting, for all its service, and for the sacred garments. ²²All who were willing, men and women alike, came and brought gold jewellery of all kinds: brooches, earrings, rings and ornaments. They all presented their gold as a wave offering to the LORD. ²³Everyone who had blue, purple or scarlet yarn or fine linen, or goat hair, ram skins dyed red or hides of sea cows brought them. ²⁴Those presenting an offering of silver or bronze brought it as an offering to the LORD, and everyone who had acacia wood for any part of the work brought it. ²⁵Every skilled woman spun with her hands and brought what she had spun—blue, purple or scarlet yarn or fine linen. ²⁶And all the women who were willing and had the skill spun the goat hair. ²⁷The leaders brought onyx stones and other gems to be mounted on the ephod and breastpiece. ²⁸They also brought spices and olive oil for the light and for the anointing oil and for the fragrant incense. ²⁹All the Israelite men and women who were willing brought to the LORD freewill offerings for all the work the LORD through Moses had commanded them to do.

Bezalel and Oholiab

³⁰Then Moses said to the Israelites, "See, the LORD has chosen Bezalel son of Uri, the son of Hur, of the tribe of Judah, ³¹and he has filled him with the Spirit of God, with skill, ability and knowledge in all kinds of crafts—³²to make artistic designs for work in gold, silver and bronze, ³³to cut and set stones, to work in wood and to engage in all kinds of artistic craftsmanship. ³⁴And

he has given both him and Oholiab son of Ahisamach, of the tribe of Dan, the ability to teach others. ³⁵He has filled them with skill to do all kinds of work as craftsmen, designers, embroiderers in blue, purple and scarlet yarn and fine linen, and weavers—all of them master craftsmen and designers.

36 ¹So Bezalel, Oholiab and every skilled person to whom the LORD has given skill and ability to know how to carry out all the work of constructing the sanctuary are to do the work just as the LORD has commanded."

²Then Moses summoned Bezalel and Oholiab and every skilled person to whom the LORD had given ability and who was willing to come and do the work. ³They received from Moses all the offerings the Israelites had brought to carry out the work of constructing the sanctuary. And the people continued to bring freewill offerings morning after morning. ⁴So all the skilled craftsmen who were doing all the work on the sanctuary left their work ⁵and said to Moses, "The people are bringing more than enough for doing the work the LORD commanded to be done."

⁶Then Moses gave an order and they sent this word throughout the camp: "No man or woman is to make anything else as an offering for the sanctuary." And so the people were restrained from bringing more, ⁷because what they already had was more than enough to do all the work.

The Tabernacle

⁸All the skilled men among the workmen made the tabernacle with ten curtains of finely twisted linen and blue, purple and scarlet yarn, with cherubim worked into them by a skilled craftsman. ⁹All the curtains were the same size—twenty-eight cubits long and four cubits wide.ᵃ ¹⁰They joined five of the curtains together and did the same with the other five. ¹¹Then they made loops of blue material along the edge of the end curtain in one set, and the same was done with the end curtain in the

ᵃ9 That is, about 42 feet (about 13 metres) long and 6 feet (about 1.8 metres) wide other set. [12]They also made fifty loops on one curtain and fifty loops on the end curtain of the other set, with the loops opposite each other. [13]Then they made fifty gold clasps and used them to fasten the two sets of curtains together so that the tabernacle was a unit.

[14]They made curtains of goat hair for the tent over the tabernacle—eleven altogether. [15]All eleven curtains were the same size—thirty cubits long and four cubits wide.[b] [16]They joined five of the curtains into one set and the other six into another set. [17]Then they made fifty loops along the edge of the end curtain in one set and also along the edge of the end curtain in the other set. [18]They made fifty bronze clasps to fasten the tent together as a unit. [19]Then they made for the tent a covering of ram skins dyed red, and over that a covering of hides of sea cows.[c]

[20]They made upright frames of acacia wood for the tabernacle. [21]Each frame was ten cubits long and a cubit and a half wide,[d] [22]with two projections set parallel to each other. They made all the frames of the tabernacle in this way. [23]They made twenty frames for the south side of the tabernacle [24]and made forty silver bases to go under them—two bases for each frame, one under each projection. [25]For the other side, the north side of the tabernacle, they made twenty frames [26]and forty silver bases—two under each frame. [27]They made six frames for the far end, that is, the west end of the tabernacle, [28]and two frames were made for the corners of the tabernacle at the far end. [29]At these two corners the frames were double from the bottom all the way to the top and fitted into a single ring; both were made alike. [30]So there were eight frames and sixteen silver bases—two under each frame.

[31]They also made crossbars of acacia wood: five for the frames on one side of the tabernacle, [32]five for those on the other side, and five for the frames on the

west, at the far end of the tabernacle. [33]They made the centre crossbar so that it extended from end to end at the middle of the frames. [34]They overlaid the frames with gold and made gold rings to hold the crossbars. They also overlaid the crossbars with gold.

[35]They made the curtain of blue, purple and scarlet yarn and finely twisted linen, with cherubim worked into it by a skilled craftsman. [36]They made four posts of acacia wood for it and overlaid them with gold. They made gold hooks for them and cast their four silver bases. [37]For the entrance to the tent they made a curtain of blue, purple and scarlet yarn and finely twisted linen—the work of an embroiderer; [38]and they made five posts with hooks for them. They overlaid the tops of the posts and their bands with gold and made their five bases of bronze.

The Ark

37 Bezalel made the ark of acacia wood—two and a half cubits long, a cubit and a half wide, and a cubit and a half high.[a] [2]He overlaid it with pure gold, both inside and out, and made a gold moulding around it. [3]He cast four gold rings for it and fastened them to its four feet, with two rings on one side and two rings on the other. [4]Then he made poles of acacia wood and overlaid them with gold. [5]And he inserted the poles into the rings on the sides of the ark to carry it.

[6]He made the atonement cover of pure gold—two and a half cubits long and a cubit and a half wide.[b] [7]Then he made two cherubim out of hammered gold at the ends of the cover. [8]He made one cherub on one end and the second cherub on the other; at the two ends he made them of one piece with the cover. [9]The cherubim had their wings spread upwards, overshadowing the cover with them. The cherubim faced each other, looking towards the cover.

---

[b]15 That is, about 45 feet (about 13.5 metres) long and 6 feet (about 1.8 metres) wide
[c]19 That is, large aquatic mammals
[d]21 That is, about 15 feet (about 4.5 metres) long and 2¼ feet (about 0.7 metre) wide
[a]1 That is, about 3¾ feet (about 1.1 metres) long and 2¼ feet (about 0.7 metre) wide and high
[b]6 That is, about 3¾ feet (about 1.1 metres) long and 2¼ feet (about 0.7 metre) wide

The Table

¹⁰They^c made the table of acacia wood—two cubits long, a cubit wide, and a cubit and a half high.^d ¹¹Then they overlaid it with pure gold and made a gold moulding around it. ¹²They also made around it a rim a handbreadth^e wide and put a gold moulding on the rim. ¹³They cast four gold rings for the table and fastened them to the four corners, where the four legs were. ¹⁴The rings were put close to the rim to hold the poles used in carrying the table. ¹⁵The poles for carrying the table were made of acacia wood and were overlaid with gold. ¹⁶And they made from pure gold the articles for the table—its plates and dishes and bowls and its pitchers for the pouring out of drink offerings.

The Lampstand

¹⁷They made the lampstand of pure gold and hammered it out, base and shaft; its flowerlike cups, buds and blossoms were of one piece with it. ¹⁸Six branches extended from the sides of the lampstand—three on one side and three on the other. ¹⁹Three cups shaped like almond flowers with buds and blossoms were on one branch, three on the next branch and the same for all six branches extending from the lampstand. ²⁰And on the lampstand were four cups shaped like almond flowers with buds and blossoms. ²¹One bud was under the first pair of branches extending from the lampstand, a second bud under the second pair, and a third bud under the third pair—six branches in all. ²²The buds and the branches were all of one piece with the lampstand, hammered out of pure gold.

²³They made its seven lamps, as well as its wick trimmers and trays, of pure gold. ²⁴They made the lampstand and all its accessories from one talent^f of pure gold.

The Altar of Incense

²⁵They made the altar of incense out of acacia wood. It was square, a cubit long and a cubit wide, and two cubits high^g—its horns of one piece with it. ²⁶They overlaid the top and all the sides and the horns with pure gold, and made a gold moulding around it. ²⁷They made two gold rings below the moulding—two on opposite sides—to hold the poles used to carry it. ²⁸They made the poles of acacia wood and overlaid them with gold.

²⁹They also made the sacred anointing oil and the pure, fragrant incense—the work of a perfumer.

The Altar of Burnt Offering

38 They^a built the altar of burnt offering of acacia wood, three cubits^b high; it was square, five cubits long and five cubits wide.^c ²They made a horn at each of the four corners, so that the horns and the altar were of one piece, and they overlaid the altar with bronze. ³They made all its utensils of bronze—its pots, shovels, sprinkling bowls, meat forks and firepans. ⁴They made a grating for the altar, a bronze network, to be under its ledge, halfway up the altar. ⁵They cast bronze rings to hold the poles for the four corners of the bronze grating. ⁶They made the poles of acacia wood and overlaid them with bronze. ⁷They inserted the poles into the rings so they would be on the sides of the altar for carrying it. They made it hollow, out of boards.

Basin for Washing

⁸They made the bronze basin and its bronze stand from the mirrors of the women who served at the entrance to the Tent of Meeting.

^c10 Or *He*; also in verses 11–29
^d10 That is, about 3 feet (about 0.9 metre) long, 1½ feet (about 0.5 metre) wide, and 2¼ feet (about 0.7 metre) high
^e12 That is, about 3 inches (about 8 centimetres)　　^f24 That is, about 75 pounds (about 34 kilograms)
^g25 That is, about 1½ feet (about 0.5 metre) long and wide, and about 3 feet (about 0.9 metre) high
^a1 Or *He*; also in verses 2–9　　^b1 That is, about 4½ feet (about 1.4 metres)
^c1 That is, about 7½ feet (about 2.3 metres) long and wide

The Courtyard

⁹Next they made the courtyard. The south side was a hundred cubits*d* long and had curtains of finely twisted linen, ¹⁰with twenty posts and twenty bronze bases, and with silver hooks and bands on the posts. ¹¹The north side was also a hundred cubits long and had twenty posts and twenty bronze bases, with silver hooks and bands on the posts.

¹²The west end was fifty cubits*e* wide and had curtains, with ten posts and ten bases, with silver hooks and bands on the posts. ¹³The east end, towards the sunrise, was also fifty cubits wide. ¹⁴Curtains fifteen cubits*f* long were on one side of the entrance, with three posts and three bases, ¹⁵and curtains fifteen cubits long were on the other side of the entrance to the courtyard, with three posts and three bases. ¹⁶All the curtains around the courtyard were of finely twisted linen. ¹⁷The bases for the posts were bronze. The hooks and bands on the posts were silver, and their tops were overlaid with silver; so all the posts of the courtyard had silver bands.

¹⁸The curtain for the entrance to the courtyard was of blue, purple and scarlet yarn and finely twisted linen—the work of an embroiderer. It was twenty cubits*g* long and, like the curtains of the courtyard, five cubits*h* high, ¹⁹with four posts and four bronze bases. Their hooks and bands were silver, and their tops were overlaid with silver. ²⁰All the tent pegs of the tabernacle and of the surrounding courtyard were bronze.

The Materials Used

²¹These are the amounts of the materials used for the tabernacle, the tabernacle of the Testimony, which were recorded at Moses' command by the Levites under the direction of Ithamar son of Aaron, the priest. ²²(Bezalel son of Uri, the son of Hur, of the tribe of Judah, made everything the LORD commanded Moses; ²³with him was Oholiab son of Ahisamach, of the tribe of Dan—a craftsman and designer, and an embroiderer in blue, purple and scarlet yarn and fine linen.) ²⁴The total amount of the gold from the wave offering used for all the work on the sanctuary was 29 talents and 730 shekels,*i* according to the sanctuary shekel.

²⁵The silver obtained from those of the community who were counted in the census was 100 talents and 1,775 shekels,*j* according to the sanctuary shekel—²⁶one beka per person, that is, half a shekel,*k* according to the sanctuary shekel, from everyone who had crossed over to those counted, twenty years old or more, a total of 603,550 men. ²⁷The 100 talents*l* of silver were used to cast the bases for the sanctuary and for the curtain—100 bases from the 100 talents, one talent for each base. ²⁸They used the 1,775 shekels*m* to make the hooks for the posts, to overlay the tops of the posts, and to make their bands.

²⁹The bronze from the wave offering was 70 talents and 2,400 shekels.*n* ³⁰They used it to make the bases for the entrance to the Tent of Meeting, the bronze altar with its bronze grating and all its utensils, ³¹the bases for the surrounding courtyard and those for its entrance and all the tent pegs for the tabernacle and those for the surrounding courtyard.

The Priestly Garments

39

From the blue, purple and scarlet yarn they made woven garments for ministering in the sanctuary. They also made sacred garments for Aaron, as the LORD commanded Moses.

The Ephod

²They*a* made the ephod of gold, and of blue, purple and scarlet yarn, and of finely

---

d9 That is, about 150 feet (about 46 metres)   *e12* That is, about 75 feet (about 23 metres)
f14 That is, about 22½ feet (about 6.9 metres)   *g18* That is, about 30 feet (about 9 metres)
h18 That is, about 7½ feet (about 2.3 metres)   *i24* The weight of the gold was about one ton (about 1 metric ton)
j25 The weight of the silver was about 3¾ tons (about 3.4 metric tons).
k26 That is, about ⅕ ounce (about 6 grams)   *l27* That is, about 3¾ tons (about 3.4 metric tons)
m28 That is, about 45 pounds (about 20 kilograms)
n29 The weight of the bronze was about 2⅓ tons (about 2.4 metric tons).
a2 Or *He*; also in verses 7, 8 and 22

twisted linen. [3]They hammered out thin sheets of gold and cut strands to be worked into the blue, purple and scarlet yarn and fine linen—the work of a skilled craftsman. [4]They made shoulder pieces for the ephod, which were attached to two of its corners, so that it could be fastened. [5]Its skilfully woven waistband was like it—of one piece with the ephod and made with gold, and with blue, purple and scarlet yarn, and with finely twisted linen, as the LORD commanded Moses.

[6]They mounted the onyx stones in gold filigree settings and engraved them like a seal with the names of the sons of Israel. [7]Then they fastened them on the shoulder pieces of the ephod as memorial stones for the sons of Israel, as the LORD commanded Moses.

The Breastpiece

[8]They fashioned the breastpiece—the work of a skilled craftsman. They made it like the ephod: of gold, and of blue, purple and scarlet yarn, and of finely twisted linen. [9]It was square—a span[b] long and a span wide—and folded double. [10]Then they mounted four rows of precious stones on it. In the first row there was a ruby, a topaz and a beryl; [11]in the second row a turquoise, a sapphire[c] and an emerald; [12]in the third row a jacinth, an agate and an amethyst; [13]in the fourth row a chrysolite, an onyx and a jasper.[d] They were mounted in gold filigree settings. [14]There were twelve stones, one for each of the names of the sons of Israel, each engraved like a seal with the name of one of the twelve tribes.

[15]For the breastpiece they made braided chains of pure gold, like a rope. [16]They made two gold filigree settings and two gold rings, and fastened the rings to two of the corners of the breastpiece. [17]They fastened the two gold chains to the rings at the corners of the breastpiece, [18]and the other ends of the chains to the two settings, attaching them to the shoulder pieces of the ephod at the front.

[19]They made two gold rings and attached them to the other two corners of the breastpiece on the inside edge next to the ephod. [20]Then they made two more gold rings and attached them to the bottom of the shoulder pieces on the front of the ephod, close to the seam just above the waistband of the ephod. [21]They tied the rings of the breastpiece to the rings of the ephod with blue cord, connecting it to the waistband so that the breastpiece would not swing out from the ephod—as the LORD commanded Moses.

Other Priestly Garments

[22]They made the robe of the ephod entirely of blue cloth—the work of a weaver—[23]with an opening in the centre of the robe like the opening of a collar,[e] and a band around this opening, so that it would not tear. [24]They made pomegranates of blue, purple and scarlet yarn and finely twisted linen around the hem of the robe. [25]And they made bells of pure gold and attached them around the hem between the pomegranates. [26]The bells and pomegranates alternated around the hem of the robe to be worn for ministering, as the LORD commanded Moses.

[27]For Aaron and his sons, they made tunics of fine linen—the work of a weaver—[28]and the turban of fine linen, the linen headbands and the undergarments of finely twisted linen. [29]The sash was of finely twisted linen and blue, purple and scarlet yarn—the work of an embroiderer—as the LORD commanded Moses.

[30]They made the plate, the sacred diadem, out of pure gold and engraved on it, like an inscription on a seal: HOLY TO THE LORD. [31]Then they fastened a blue cord to it to attach it to the turban, as the LORD commanded Moses.

Moses Inspects the Tabernacle

[32]So all the work on the tabernacle, the Tent of Meeting, was completed. The Israelites did everything just as the LORD

---

b9 That is, about 9 inches (about 23 centimetres)   c11 Or lapis lazuli
d13 The precise identification of some of these precious stones is uncertain.
e23 The meaning of the Hebrew for this word is uncertain.

commanded Moses. [33]Then they brought the tabernacle to Moses: the tent and all its furnishings, its clasps, frames, crossbars, posts and bases; [34]the covering of ram skins dyed red, the covering of hides of sea cows[f] and the shielding curtain; [35]the ark of the Testimony with its poles and the atonement cover; [36]the table with all its articles and the bread of the Presence; [37]the pure gold lampstand with its row of lamps and all its accessories, and the oil for the light; [38]the gold altar, the anointing oil, the fragrant incense, and the curtain for the entrance to the tent; [39]the bronze altar with its bronze grating, its poles and all its utensils; the basin with its stand; [40]the curtains of the courtyard with its posts and bases, and the curtain for the entrance to the courtyard; the ropes and tent pegs for the courtyard; all the furnishings for the tabernacle, the Tent of Meeting; [41]and the woven garments worn for ministering in the sanctuary, both the sacred garments for Aaron the priest and the garments for his sons when serving as priests.

[42]The Israelites had done all the work just as the LORD had commanded Moses. [43]Moses inspected the work and saw that they had done it just as the LORD had commanded. So Moses blessed them.

Setting Up the Tabernacle

40 Then the LORD said to Moses: [2]"Set up the tabernacle, the Tent of Meeting, on the first day of the first month. [3]Place the ark of the Testimony in it and shield the ark with the curtain. [4]Bring in the table and set out what belongs on it. Then bring in the lampstand and set up its lamps. [5]Place the gold altar of incense in front of the ark of the Testimony and put the curtain at the entrance to the tabernacle.

[6]"Place the altar of burnt offering in front of the entrance to the tabernacle, the Tent of Meeting; [7]place the basin between the Tent of Meeting and the altar and put water in it. [8]Set up the courtyard around it

and put the curtain at the entrance to the courtyard.

[9]"Take the anointing oil and anoint the tabernacle and everything in it; consecrate it and all its furnishings, and it will be holy. [10]Then anoint the altar of burnt offering and all its utensils; consecrate the altar, and it will be most holy. [11]Anoint the basin and its stand and consecrate them.

[12]"Bring Aaron and his sons to the entrance to the Tent of Meeting and wash them with water. [13]Then dress Aaron in the sacred garments, anoint him and consecrate him so that he may serve me as priest. [14]Bring his sons and dress them in tunics. [15]Anoint them just as you anointed their father, so that they may serve me as priests. Their anointing will be to a priesthood that will continue for all generations to come." [16]Moses did everything just as the LORD commanded him.

[17]So the tabernacle was set up on the first day of the first month in the second year. [18]When Moses set up the tabernacle, he put the bases in place, erected the frames, inserted the crossbars and set up the posts. [19]Then he spread the tent over the tabernacle and put the covering over the tent, as the LORD commanded him.

[20]He took the Testimony and placed it in the ark, attached the poles to the ark and put the atonement cover over it. [21]Then he brought the ark into the tabernacle and hung the shielding curtain and shielded the ark of the Testimony, as the LORD commanded him.

[22]Moses placed the table in the Tent of Meeting on the north side of the tabernacle outside the curtain [23]and set out the bread on it before the LORD, as the LORD commanded him.

[24]He placed the lampstand in the Tent of Meeting opposite the table on the south side of the tabernacle [25]and set up the lamps before the LORD, as the LORD commanded him.

[26]Moses placed the gold altar in the Tent of Meeting in front of the curtain [27]and burned fragrant incense on it, as the LORD commanded him. [28]Then he put up the

f34 That is, large aquatic mammals

curtain at the entrance to the tabernacle.

²⁹He set the altar of burnt offering near the entrance to the tabernacle, the Tent of Meeting, and offered on it burnt offerings and grain offerings, as the LORD commanded him.

³⁰He placed the basin between the Tent of Meeting and the altar and put water in it for washing, ³¹and Moses and Aaron and his sons used it to wash their hands and feet. ³²They washed whenever they entered the Tent of Meeting or approached the altar, as the LORD commanded Moses.

³³Then Moses set up the courtyard around the tabernacle and altar and put up the curtain at the entrance to the courtyard. And so Moses finished the work.

The Glory of the LORD

³⁴Then the cloud covered the Tent of Meeting, and the glory of the LORD filled the tabernacle. ³⁵Moses could not enter the Tent of Meeting because the cloud had settled upon it, and the glory of the LORD filled the tabernacle.

³⁶In all the travels of the Israelites, whenever the cloud lifted from above the tabernacle, they would set out; ³⁷but if the cloud did not lift, they did not set out—until the day it lifted. ³⁸So the cloud of the LORD was over the tabernacle by day, and fire was in the cloud by night, in the sight of all the house of Israel during all their travels.

Leviticus

The Burnt Offering

1 The LORD called to Moses and spoke to him from the Tent of Meeting. He said, [2]"Speak to the Israelites and say to them: 'When any of you brings an offering to the LORD, bring as your offering an animal from either the herd or the flock.

[3]"'If the offering is a burnt offering from the herd, he is to offer a male without defect. He must present it at the entrance to the Tent of Meeting so that it[a] will be acceptable to the LORD. [4]He is to lay his hand on the head of the burnt offering, and it will be accepted on his behalf to make atonement for him. [5]He is to slaughter the young bull before the LORD, and then Aaron's sons the priests shall bring the blood and sprinkle it against the altar on all sides at the entrance to the Tent of Meeting. [6]He is to skin the burnt offering and cut it into pieces. [7]The sons of Aaron the priest are to put fire on the altar and arrange wood on the fire. [8]Then Aaron's sons the priests shall arrange the pieces, including the head and the fat, on the burning wood that is on the altar. [9]He is to wash the inner parts and the legs with water, and the priest is to burn all of it on the altar. It is a burnt offering, an offering made by fire, an aroma pleasing to the LORD.

[10]"'If the offering is a burnt offering from the flock, from either the sheep or the goats, he is to offer a male without defect. [11]He is to slaughter it at the north side of the altar before the LORD, and Aaron's sons the priests shall sprinkle its blood against the altar on all sides. [12]He is to cut it into pieces, and the priest shall arrange them, including the head and the fat, on the burning wood that is on the altar. [13]He is to wash the inner parts and the legs with water, and the priest is to bring all of it and burn it on the altar. It is a burnt offering, an offering made by fire, an aroma pleasing to the LORD.

[14]"'If the offering to the LORD is a burnt offering of birds, he is to offer a dove or a young pigeon. [15]The priest shall bring it to the altar, wring off the head and burn it on the altar; its blood shall be drained out on the side of the altar. [16]He is to remove the crop with its contents[b] and throw it to the east side of the altar, where the ashes are. [17]He shall tear it open by the wings, not severing it completely, and then the priest shall burn it on the wood that is on the fire on the altar. It is a burnt offering, an offering made by fire, an aroma pleasing to the LORD.

The Grain Offering

2 "'When someone brings a grain offering to the LORD, his offering is to be of fine flour. He is to pour oil on it, put incense on it [2]and take it to Aaron's sons the priests. The priest shall take a handful of the fine flour and oil, together with all the incense, and burn this as a memorial portion on the altar, an offering made by fire, an aroma pleasing to the LORD. [3]The rest of the grain offering belongs to Aaron and his sons; it is a most holy part of the offerings made to the LORD by fire.

[a]3 Or he   [b]16 Or *crop and the feathers*; the meaning of the Hebrew for this word is uncertain.

[4] " 'If you bring a grain offering baked in an oven, it is to consist of fine flour: cakes made without yeast and mixed with oil, or[a] wafers made without yeast and spread with oil. [5]If your grain offering is prepared on a griddle, it is to be made of fine flour mixed with oil, and without yeast. [6]Crumble it and pour oil on it; it is a grain offering. [7]If your grain offering is cooked in a pan, it is to be made of fine flour and oil. [8]Bring the grain offering made of these things to the LORD; present it to the priest, who shall take it to the altar. [9]He shall take out the memorial portion from the grain offering and burn it on the altar as an offering made by fire, an aroma pleasing to the LORD. [10]The rest of the grain offering belongs to Aaron and his sons; it is a most holy part of the offerings made to the LORD by fire.

[11] " 'Every grain offering you bring to the LORD must be made without yeast, for you are not to burn any yeast or honey in an offering made to the LORD by fire. [12]You may bring them to the LORD as an offering of the firstfruits, but they are not to be offered on the altar as a pleasing aroma. [13]Season all your grain offerings with salt. Do not leave the salt of the covenant of your God out of your grain offerings; add salt to all your offerings.

[14] " 'If you bring a grain offering of firstfruits to the LORD, offer crushed heads of new grain roasted in the fire. [15]Put oil and incense on it; it is a grain offering. [16]The priest shall burn the memorial portion of the crushed grain and the oil, together with all the incense, as an offering made to the LORD by fire.

The Fellowship Offering

3 " 'If someone's offering is a fellowship offering,[a] and he offers an animal from the herd, whether male or female, he is to present before the LORD an animal without defect. [2]He is to lay his hand on the head of his offering and slaughter it at the entrance to the Tent of Meeting. Then Aaron's sons the priests shall sprinkle the blood against the altar on all sides. [3]From the fellowship offering he is to bring a sacrifice made to the LORD by fire: all the fat that covers the inner parts or is connected to them, [4]both kidneys with the fat on them near the loins, and the covering of the liver, which he will remove with the kidneys. [5]Then Aaron's sons are to burn it on the altar on top of the burnt offering that is on the burning wood, as an offering made by fire, an aroma pleasing to the LORD.

[6] " 'If he offers an animal from the flock as a fellowship offering to the LORD, he is to offer a male or female without defect. [7]If he offers a lamb, he is to present it before the LORD. [8]He is to lay his hand on the head of his offering and slaughter it in front of the Tent of Meeting. Then Aaron's sons shall sprinkle its blood against the altar on all sides. [9]From the fellowship offering he is to bring a sacrifice made to the LORD by fire: its fat, the entire fat tail cut off close to the backbone, all the fat that covers the inner parts or is connected to them, [10]both kidneys with the fat on them near the loins, and the covering of the liver, which he will remove with the kidneys. [11]The priest shall burn them on the altar as food, an offering made to the LORD by fire.

[12] " 'If his offering is a goat, he is to present it before the LORD. [13]He is to lay his hand on its head and slaughter it in front of the Tent of Meeting. Then Aaron's sons shall sprinkle its blood against the altar on all sides. [14]From what he offers he is to make this offering to the LORD by fire: all the fat that covers the inner parts or is connected to them, [15]both kidneys with the fat on them near the loins, and the covering of the liver, which he will remove with the kidneys. [16]The priest shall burn them on the altar as food, an offering made by fire, a pleasing aroma. All the fat is the LORD's.

[17] " 'This is a lasting ordinance for the generations to come, wherever you live: You must not eat any fat or any blood.' "

---

[a]4 Or *and*
[a]1 Traditionally *peace offering*; also in verses 3, 6 and 9

The Sin Offering

4 The LORD said to Moses, [2]"Say to the Israelites: 'When anyone sins unintentionally and does what is forbidden in any of the LORD's commands—

[3]"'If the anointed priest sins, bringing guilt on the people, he must bring to the LORD a young bull without defect as a sin offering for the sin he has committed. [4]He is to present the bull at the entrance to the Tent of Meeting before the LORD. He is to lay his hand on its head and slaughter it before the LORD. [5]Then the anointed priest shall take some of the bull's blood and carry it into the Tent of Meeting. [6]He is to dip his finger into the blood and sprinkle some of it seven times before the LORD, in front of the curtain of the sanctuary. [7]The priest shall then put some of the blood on the horns of the altar of fragrant incense that is before the LORD in the Tent of Meeting. The rest of the bull's blood he shall pour out at the base of the altar of burnt offering at the entrance to the Tent of Meeting. [8]He shall remove all the fat from the bull of the sin offering—the fat that covers the inner parts or is connected to them, [9]both kidneys with the fat on them near the loins, and the covering of the liver, which he will remove with the kidneys—[10]just as the fat is removed from the ox[a] sacrificed as a fellowship offering.[b] Then the priest shall burn them on the altar of burnt offering. [11]But the hide of the bull and all its flesh, as well as the head and legs, the inner parts and offal—[12]that is, all the rest of the bull—he must take outside the camp to a place ceremonially clean, where the ashes are thrown, and burn it in a wood fire on the ash heap.

[13]"'If the whole Israelite community sins unintentionally and does what is forbidden in any of the LORD's commands, even though the community is unaware of the matter, they are guilty. [14]When they become aware of the sin they committed, the assembly must bring a young bull as a sin offering and present it before the Tent of Meeting. [15]The elders of the community are to lay their hands on the bull's head before the LORD, and the bull shall be slaughtered before the LORD. [16]Then the anointed priest is to take some of the bull's blood into the Tent of Meeting. [17]He shall dip his finger into the blood and sprinkle it before the LORD seven times in front of the curtain. [18]He is to put some of the blood on the horns of the altar that is before the LORD in the Tent of Meeting. The rest of the blood he shall pour out at the base of the altar of burnt offering at the entrance to the Tent of Meeting. [19]He shall remove all the fat from it and burn it on the altar, [20]and do with this bull just as he did with the bull for the sin offering. In this way the priest will make atonement for them, and they will be forgiven. [21]Then he shall take the bull outside the camp and burn it as he burned the first bull. This is the sin offering for the community.

[22]"'When a leader sins unintentionally and does what is forbidden in any of the commands of the LORD his God, he is guilty. [23]When he is made aware of the sin he committed, he must bring as his offering a male goat without defect. [24]He is to lay his hand on the goat's head and slaughter it at the place where the burnt offering is slaughtered before the LORD. It is a sin offering. [25]Then the priest shall take some of the blood of the sin offering with his finger and put it on the horns of the altar of burnt offering and pour out the rest of the blood at the base of the altar. [26]He shall burn all the fat on the altar as he burned the fat of the fellowship offering. In this way the priest will make atonement for the man's sin, and he will be forgiven.

[27]"'If a member of the community sins unintentionally and does what is forbidden in any of the LORD's commands, he is guilty. [28]When he is made aware of the sin he committed, he must bring as his offering for the sin he committed a female goat without defect. [29]He is to lay his hand on

---

[a]10 The Hebrew word can include both male and female.
[b]10 Traditionally *peace offering*; also in verses 26, 31 and 35

the head of the sin offering and slaughter it at the place of the burnt offering. ³⁰Then the priest is to take some of the blood with his finger and put it on the horns of the altar of burnt offering and pour out the rest of the blood at the base of the altar. ³¹He shall remove all the fat, just as the fat is removed from the fellowship offering, and the priest shall burn it on the altar as an aroma pleasing to the LORD. In this way the priest will make atonement for him, and he will be forgiven.

³²"If he brings a lamb as his sin offering, he is to bring a female without defect. ³³He is to lay his hand on its head and slaughter it for a sin offering at the place where the burnt offering is slaughtered. ³⁴Then the priest shall take some of the blood of the sin offering with his finger and put it on the horns of the altar of burnt offering and pour out the rest of the blood at the base of the altar. ³⁵He shall remove all the fat, just as the fat is removed from the lamb of the fellowship offering, and the priest shall burn it on the altar on top of the offerings made to the LORD by fire. In this way the priest will make atonement for him for the sin he has committed, and he will be forgiven.

⁵ " 'If a person sins because he does not speak up when he hears a public charge to testify regarding something he has seen or learned about, he will be held responsible.

²" 'Or if a person touches anything ceremonially unclean—whether the carcasses of unclean wild animals or of unclean livestock or of unclean creatures that move along the ground—even though he is unaware of it, he has become unclean and is guilty.

³" 'Or if he touches human uncleanness—anything that would make him unclean—even though he is unaware of it, when he learns of it he will be guilty.

⁴" 'Or if a person thoughtlessly takes an oath to do anything, whether good or evil—in any matter one might carelessly swear about—even though he is unaware

of it, in any case when he learns of it he will be guilty.

⁵" 'When anyone is guilty in any of these ways, he must confess in what way he has sinned ⁶and, as a penalty for the sin he has committed, he must bring to the LORD a female lamb or goat from the flock as a sin offering; and the priest shall make atonement for him for his sin.

⁷" 'If he cannot afford a lamb, he is to bring two doves or two young pigeons to the LORD as a penalty for his sin—one for a sin offering and the other for a burnt offering. ⁸He is to bring them to the priest, who shall first offer the one for the sin offering. He is to wring its head from its neck, not severing it completely, ⁹and is to sprinkle some of the blood of the sin offering against the side of the altar; the rest of the blood must be drained out at the base of the altar. It is a sin offering. ¹⁰The priest shall then offer the other as a burnt offering in the prescribed way and make atonement for him for the sin he has committed, and he will be forgiven.

¹¹" 'If, however, he cannot afford two doves or two young pigeons, he is to bring as an offering for his sin a tenth of an ephah^a of fine flour for a sin offering. He must not put oil or incense on it, because it is a sin offering. ¹²He is to bring it to the priest, who shall take a handful of it as a memorial portion and burn it on the altar on top of the offerings made to the LORD by fire. It is a sin offering. ¹³In this way the priest will make atonement for him for any of these sins he has committed, and he will be forgiven. The rest of the offering will belong to the priest, as in the case of the grain offering.' "

The Guilt Offering

¹⁴The LORD said to Moses: ¹⁵"When a person commits a violation and sins unintentionally in regard to any of the LORD's holy things, he is to bring to the LORD as a penalty a ram from the flock, one without defect and of the proper value in silver, according to the sanctuary shekel.^b It is a

---

^a11 That is, probably about 4 pints (about 2 litres)   ^b15 That is, about ⅖ ounce (about 11.5 grams)

guilt offering. ¹⁶He must make restitution for what he has failed to do in regard to the holy things, add a fifth of the value to that and give it all to the priest, who will make atonement for him with the ram as a guilt offering, and he will be forgiven.

¹⁷"If a person sins and does what is forbidden in any of the LORD's commands, even though he does not know it, he is guilty and will be held responsible. ¹⁸He is to bring to the priest as a guilt offering a ram from the flock, one without defect and of the proper value. In this way the priest will make atonement for him for the wrong he has committed unintentionally, and he will be forgiven. ¹⁹It is a guilt offering; he has been guilty of*c* wrongdoing against the LORD."

6 The LORD said to Moses: ²"If anyone sins and is unfaithful to the LORD by deceiving his neighbour about something entrusted to him or left in his care or stolen, or if he cheats him, ³or if he finds lost property and lies about it, or if he swears falsely, or if he commits any such sin that people may do—⁴when he thus sins and becomes guilty, he must return what he has stolen or taken by extortion, or what was entrusted to him, or the lost property he found, ⁵or whatever it was he swore falsely about. He must make restitution in full, add a fifth of the value to it and give it all to the owner on the day he presents his guilt offering. ⁶And as a penalty he must bring to the priest, that is, to the LORD, his guilt offering, a ram from the flock, one without defect and of the proper value. ⁷In this way the priest will make atonement for him before the LORD, and he will be forgiven for any of these things he did that made him guilty."

The Burnt Offering

⁸The LORD said to Moses: ⁹"Give Aaron and his sons this command: 'These are the regulations for the burnt offering: The burnt offering is to remain on the altar hearth throughout the night, till morning, and the fire must be kept burning on the altar. ¹⁰The priest shall then put on his linen clothes, with linen undergarments next to his body, and shall remove the ashes of the burnt offering that the fire has consumed on the altar and place them beside the altar. ¹¹Then he is to take off these clothes and put on others, and carry the ashes outside the camp to a place that is ceremonially clean. ¹²The fire on the altar must be kept burning; it must not go out. Every morning the priest is to add firewood and arrange the burnt offering on the fire and burn the fat of the fellowship offerings*a* on it. ¹³The fire must be kept burning on the altar continuously; it must not go out.

The Grain Offering

¹⁴"'These are the regulations for the grain offering: Aaron's sons are to bring it before the LORD, in front of the altar. ¹⁵The priest is to take a handful of fine flour and oil, together with all the incense on the grain offering, and burn the memorial portion on the altar as an aroma pleasing to the LORD. ¹⁶Aaron and his sons shall eat the rest of it, but it is to be eaten without yeast in a holy place; they are to eat it in the courtyard of the Tent of Meeting. ¹⁷It must not be baked with yeast; I have given it as their share of the offerings made to me by fire. Like the sin offering and the guilt offering, it is most holy. ¹⁸Any male descendant of Aaron may eat it. It is his regular share of the offerings made to the LORD by fire for the generations to come. Whatever touches it will become holy.'"*b*

¹⁹The LORD also said to Moses, ²⁰"This is the offering Aaron and his sons are to bring to the LORD on the day he*c* is anointed: a tenth of an ephah*d* of fine flour as a regular grain offering, half of it in the morning and half in the evening. ²¹Prepare it with oil on a griddle; bring it

---

c19 Or *has made full expiation for his*
a12 Traditionally *peace offerings*   *b18* Or *Whoever touches them must be holy*; similarly in verse 27
c20 Or *each*   *d20* That is, probably about 4 pints (about 2 litres)

well-mixed and present the grain offering broken[e] in pieces as an aroma pleasing to the LORD. [22]The son who is to succeed him as anointed priest shall prepare it. It is the LORD's regular share and is to be burned completely. [23]Every grain offering of a priest shall be burned completely; it must not be eaten."

The Sin Offering

[24]The LORD said to Moses, [25]"Say to Aaron and his sons: 'These are the regulations for the sin offering: The sin offering is to be slaughtered before the LORD in the place where the burnt offering is slaughtered; it is most holy. [26]The priest who offers it shall eat it; it is to be eaten in a holy place, in the courtyard of the Tent of Meeting. [27]Whatever touches any of the flesh will become holy, and if any of the blood is spattered on a garment, you must wash it in a holy place. [28]The clay pot that the meat is cooked in must be broken; but if it is cooked in a bronze pot, the pot is to be scoured and rinsed with water. [29]Any male in a priest's family may eat it; it is most holy. [30]But any sin offering whose blood is brought into the Tent of Meeting to make atonement in the Holy Place must not be eaten; it must be burned.

The Guilt Offering

7 "'These are the regulations for the guilt offering, which is most holy: [2]The guilt offering is to be slaughtered in the place where the burnt offering is slaughtered, and its blood is to be sprinkled against the altar on all sides. [3]All its fat shall be offered: the fat tail and the fat that covers the inner parts, [4]both kidneys with the fat on them near the loins, and the covering of the liver, which is to be removed with the kidneys. [5]The priest shall burn them on the altar as an offering made to the LORD by fire. It is a guilt offering. [6]Any male in a priest's family

may eat it, but it must be eaten in a holy place; it is most holy.

[7]"'The same law applies to both the sin offering and the guilt offering: They belong to the priest who makes atonement with them. [8]The priest who offers a burnt offering for anyone may keep its hide for himself. [9]Every grain offering baked in an oven or cooked in a pan or on a griddle belongs to the priest who offers it, [10]and every grain offering, whether mixed with oil or dry, belongs equally to all the sons of Aaron.

The Fellowship Offering

[11]"'These are the regulations for the fellowship offering[a] a person may present to the LORD:

[12]"'If he offers it as an expression of thankfulness, then along with this thank-offering he is to offer cakes of bread made without yeast and mixed with oil, wafers made without yeast and spread with oil, and cakes of fine flour well-kneaded and mixed with oil. [13]Along with his fellowship offering of thanksgiving he is to present an offering with cakes of bread made with yeast. [14]He is to bring one of each kind as an offering, a contribution to the LORD; it belongs to the priest who sprinkles the blood of the fellowship offerings. [15]The meat of his fellowship offering of thanksgiving must be eaten on the day it is offered; he must leave none of it till morning.

[16]"'If, however, his offering is the result of a vow or is a freewill offering, the sacrifice shall be eaten on the day he offers it, but anything left over may be eaten on the next day. [17]Any meat of the sacrifice left over till the third day must be burned up. [18]If any meat of the fellowship offering is eaten on the third day, it will not be accepted. It will not be credited to the one who offered it, for it is impure; the person who eats any of it will be held responsible.

[19]"'Meat that touches anything ceremonially unclean must not be eaten; it

---

[e]21 The meaning of the Hebrew for this word is uncertain.
[a]11 Traditionally *peace offering*; also in verses 13–37

must be burned up. As for other meat, anyone ceremonially clean may eat it. [20]But if anyone who is unclean eats any meat of the fellowship offering belonging to the LORD, that person must be cut off from his people. [21]If anyone touches something unclean—whether human uncleanness or an unclean animal or any unclean, detestable thing—and then eats any of the meat of the fellowship offering belonging to the LORD, that person must be cut off from his people.' "

Eating Fat and Blood Forbidden

[22]The LORD said to Moses, [23]"Say to the Israelites: 'Do not eat any of the fat of cattle, sheep or goats. [24]The fat of an animal found dead or torn by wild animals may be used for any other purpose, but you must not eat it. [25]Anyone who eats the fat of an animal from which an offering by fire may be[b] made to the LORD must be cut off from his people. [26]And wherever you live, you must not eat the blood of any bird or animal. [27]If anyone eats blood, that person must be cut off from his people.' "

The Priests' Share

[28]The LORD said to Moses, [29]"Say to the Israelites: 'Anyone who brings a fellowship offering to the LORD is to bring part of it as his sacrifice to the LORD. [30]With his own hands he is to bring the offering made to the LORD by fire; he is to bring the fat, together with the breast, and wave the breast before the LORD as a wave offering. [31]The priest shall burn the fat on the altar, but the breast belongs to Aaron and his sons. [32]You are to give the right thigh of your fellowship offerings to the priest as a contribution. [33]The son of Aaron who offers the blood and the fat of the fellowship offering shall have the right thigh as his share. [34]From the fellowship offerings of the Israelites, I have taken the breast that is waved and the thigh that is presented and have given them to Aaron the priest and his sons as their regular share from the Israelites.' "

[35]This is the portion of the offerings made to the LORD by fire that were allotted to Aaron and his sons on the day they were presented to serve the LORD as priests. [36]On the day they were anointed, the LORD commanded that the Israelites give this to them as their regular share for the generations to come.

[37]These, then, are the regulations for the burnt offering, the grain offering, the sin offering, the guilt offering, the ordination offering and the fellowship offering, [38]which the LORD gave Moses on Mount Sinai on the day he commanded the Israelites to bring their offerings to the LORD, in the Desert of Sinai.

The Ordination of Aaron and His Sons

8 The LORD said to Moses, [2]"Bring Aaron and his sons, their garments, the anointing oil, the bull for the sin offering, the two rams and the basket containing bread made without yeast, [3]and gather the entire assembly at the entrance to the Tent of Meeting." [4]Moses did as the LORD commanded him, and the assembly gathered at the entrance to the Tent of Meeting.

[5]Moses said to the assembly, "This is what the LORD has commanded to be done." [6]Then Moses brought Aaron and his sons forward and washed them with water. [7]He put the tunic on Aaron, tied the sash around him, clothed him with the robe and put the ephod on him. He also tied the ephod to him by its skilfully woven waistband; so it was fastened on him. [8]He placed the breastpiece on him and put the Urim and Thummim in the breastpiece. [9]Then he placed the turban on Aaron's head and set the gold plate, the sacred diadem, on the front of it, as the LORD commanded Moses.

[10]Then Moses took the anointing oil and anointed the tabernacle and everything in it, and so consecrated them. [11]He sprinkled some of the oil on the altar seven times, anointing the altar and all its utensils and the basin with its stand, to

consecrate them. [12]He poured some of the anointing oil on Aaron's head and anointed him to consecrate him. [13]Then he brought Aaron's sons forward, put tunics on them, tied sashes around them and put headbands on them, as the LORD commanded Moses.

[14]He then presented the bull for the sin offering, and Aaron and his sons laid their hands on its head. [15]Moses slaughtered the bull and took some of the blood, and with his finger he put it on all the horns of the altar to purify the altar. He poured out the rest of the blood at the base of the altar. So he consecrated it to make atonement for it. [16]Moses also took all the fat around the inner parts, the covering of the liver, and both kidneys and their fat, and burned it on the altar. [17]But the bull with its hide and its flesh and its offal he burned up outside the camp, as the LORD commanded Moses.

[18]He then presented the ram for the burnt offering, and Aaron and his sons laid their hands on its head. [19]Then Moses slaughtered the ram and sprinkled the blood against the altar on all sides. [20]He cut the ram into pieces and burned the head, the pieces and the fat. [21]He washed the inner parts and the legs with water and burned the whole ram on the altar as a burnt offering, a pleasing aroma, an offering made to the LORD by fire, as the LORD commanded Moses.

[22]He then presented the other ram, the ram for the ordination, and Aaron and his sons laid their hands on its head. [23]Moses slaughtered the ram and took some of its blood and put it on the lobe of Aaron's right ear, on the thumb of his right hand and on the big toe of his right foot. [24]Moses also brought Aaron's sons forward and put some of the blood on the lobes of their right ears, on the thumbs of their right hands and on the big toes of their right feet. Then he sprinkled blood against the altar on all sides. [25]He took the fat, the fat tail, all the fat around the inner parts, the covering of the liver, both kidneys and their fat and the right thigh. [26]Then from the basket of bread made

without yeast, which was before the LORD, he took a cake of bread, and one made with oil, and a wafer; he put these on the fat portions and on the right thigh. [27]He put all these in the hands of Aaron and his sons and waved them before the LORD as a wave offering. [28]Then Moses took them from their hands and burned them on the altar on top of the burnt offering as an ordination offering, a pleasing aroma, an offering made to the LORD by fire. [29]He also took the breast—Moses' share of the ordination ram—and waved it before the LORD as a wave offering, as the LORD commanded Moses.

[30]Then Moses took some of the anointing oil and some of the blood from the altar and sprinkled them on Aaron and his garments and on his sons and their garments. So he consecrated Aaron and his garments and his sons and their garments.

[31]Moses then said to Aaron and his sons, "Cook the meat at the entrance to the Tent of Meeting and eat it there with the bread from the basket of ordination offerings, as I commanded, saying,[a] 'Aaron and his sons are to eat it.' [32]Then burn up the rest of the meat and the bread. [33]Do not leave the entrance to the Tent of Meeting for seven days, until the days of your ordination are completed, for your ordination will last seven days. [34]What has been done today was commanded by the LORD to make atonement for you. [35]You must stay at the entrance to the Tent of Meeting day and night for seven days and do what the LORD requires, so that you will not die; for that is what I have been commanded." [36]So Aaron and his sons did everything the LORD commanded through Moses.

The Priests Begin Their Ministry

9 On the eighth day Moses summoned Aaron and his sons and the elders of Israel. [2]He said to Aaron, "Take a bull calf for your sin offering and a ram for your burnt offering, both without defect, and present them before the LORD. [3]Then say to the Israelites: 'Take a male goat for

---

[a]31 Or *I was commanded:*

a sin offering, a calf and a lamb—both a year old and without defect—for a burnt offering, ⁴and an ox[a] and a ram for a fellowship offering[b] to sacrifice before the LORD, together with a grain offering mixed with oil. For today the LORD will appear to you.'"

⁵They took the things Moses commanded to the front of the Tent of Meeting, and the entire assembly came near and stood before the LORD. ⁶Then Moses said, "This is what the LORD has commanded you to do, so that the glory of the LORD may appear to you."

⁷Moses said to Aaron, "Come to the altar and sacrifice your sin offering and your burnt offering and make atonement for yourself and the people; sacrifice the offering that is for the people and make atonement for them, as the LORD has commanded."

⁸So Aaron came to the altar and slaughtered the calf as a sin offering for himself. ⁹His sons brought the blood to him, and he dipped his finger into the blood and put it on the horns of the altar; the rest of the blood he poured out at the base of the altar. ¹⁰On the altar he burned the fat, the kidneys and the covering of the liver from the sin offering, as the LORD commanded Moses; ¹¹the flesh and the hide he burned up outside the camp.

¹²Then he slaughtered the burnt offering. His sons handed him the blood, and he sprinkled it against the altar on all sides. ¹³They handed him the burnt offering piece by piece, including the head, and he burned them on the altar. ¹⁴He washed the inner parts and the legs and burned them on top of the burnt offering on the altar.

¹⁵Aaron then brought the offering that was for the people. He took the goat for the people's sin offering and slaughtered it and offered it for a sin offering as he did with the first one.

¹⁶He brought the burnt offering and offered it in the prescribed way. ¹⁷He also brought the grain offering, took a handful of it and burned it on the altar in addition to the morning's burnt offering.

¹⁸He slaughtered the ox and the ram as the fellowship offering for the people. His sons handed him the blood, and he sprinkled it against the altar on all sides. ¹⁹But the fat portions of the ox and the ram—the fat tail, the layer of fat, the kidneys and the covering of the liver—²⁰these they laid on the breasts, and then Aaron burned the fat on the altar. ²¹Aaron waved the breasts and the right thigh before the LORD as a wave offering, as Moses commanded.

²²Then Aaron lifted his hands towards the people and blessed them. And having sacrificed the sin offering, the burnt offering and the fellowship offering, he stepped down.

²³Moses and Aaron then went into the Tent of Meeting. When they came out, they blessed the people; and the glory of the LORD appeared to all the people. ²⁴Fire came out from the presence of the LORD and consumed the burnt offering and the fat portions on the altar. And when all the people saw it, they shouted for joy and fell face down.

The Death of Nadab and Abihu

10 Aaron's sons Nadab and Abihu took their censers, put fire in them and added incense; and they offered unauthorised fire before the LORD, contrary to his command. ²So fire came out from the presence of the LORD and consumed them, and they died before the LORD. ³Moses then said to Aaron, "This is what the LORD spoke of when he said:

"'Among those who approach me
I will show myself holy;
in the sight of all the people
I will be honoured.'"

Aaron remained silent.

⁴Moses summoned Mishael and Elzaphan, sons of Aaron's uncle Uzziel,

---

a4 The Hebrew word can include both male and female; also in verses 18 and 19.
b4 Traditionally *peace offering*; also in verses 18 and 22

and said to them, "Come here; carry your cousins outside the camp, away from the front of the sanctuary." 5So they came and carried them, still in their tunics, outside the camp, as Moses ordered.

6Then Moses said to Aaron and his sons Eleazar and Ithamar, "Do not let your hair become unkempt,*a* and do not tear your clothes, or you will die and the LORD will be angry with the whole community. But your relatives, all the house of Israel, may mourn for those the LORD has destroyed by fire. 7Do not leave the entrance to the Tent of Meeting or you will die, because the LORD's anointing oil is on you." So they did as Moses said.

8Then the LORD said to Aaron, 9"You and your sons are not to drink wine or other fermented drink whenever you go into the Tent of Meeting, or you will die. This is a lasting ordinance for the generations to come. 10You must distinguish between the holy and the common, between the unclean and the clean, 11and you must teach the Israelites all the decrees the LORD has given them through Moses."

12Moses said to Aaron and his remaining sons, Eleazar and Ithamar, "Take the grain offering left over from the offerings made to the LORD by fire and eat it prepared without yeast beside the altar, for it is most holy. 13Eat it in a holy place, because it is your share and your sons' share of the offerings made to the LORD by fire; for so I have been commanded. 14But you and your sons and your daughters may eat the breast that was waved and the thigh that was presented. Eat them in a ceremonially clean place; they have been given to you and your children as your share of the Israelites' fellowship offerings.*b* 15The thigh that was presented and the breast that was waved must be brought with the fat portions of the offerings made by fire, to be waved before the LORD as a wave offering. This will be the regular share for you and your children, as the LORD has commanded."

16When Moses enquired about the goat of the sin offering and found that it had been burned up, he was angry with Eleazar and Ithamar, Aaron's remaining sons, and asked, 17"Why didn't you eat the sin offering in the sanctuary area? It is most holy; it was given to you to take away the guilt of the community by making atonement for them before the LORD. 18Since its blood was not taken into the Holy Place, you should have eaten the goat in the sanctuary area, as I commanded."

19Aaron replied to Moses, "Today they sacrificed their sin offering and their burnt offering before the LORD, but such things as this have happened to me. Would the LORD have been pleased if I had eaten the sin offering today?" 20When Moses heard this, he was satisfied.

Clean and Unclean Food

11 The LORD said to Moses and Aaron, 2"Say to the Israelites: 'Of all the animals that live on land, these are the ones you may eat: 3You may eat any animal that has a split hoof completely divided and that chews the cud.

4"'There are some that only chew the cud or only have a split hoof, but you must not eat them. The camel, though it chews the cud, does not have a split hoof; it is ceremonially unclean for you. 5The coney,*a* though it chews the cud, does not have a split hoof; it is unclean for you. 6The rabbit, though it chews the cud, does not have a split hoof; it is unclean for you. 7And the pig, though it has a split hoof completely divided, does not chew the cud; it is unclean for you. 8You must not eat their meat or touch their carcasses; they are unclean for you.

9"'Of all the creatures living in the water of the seas and the streams, you may eat any that have fins and scales. 10But all creatures in the seas or streams that do not have fins and scales—whether among all the swarming things or among all the other living creatures in the water—you are to

---

a6 Or *Do not uncover your heads*   *b14* Traditionally *peace offerings*
a5 That is, the hyrax or rock badger

detest. ¹¹And since you are to detest them, you must not eat their meat and you must detest their carcasses. ¹²Anything living in the water that does not have fins and scales is to be detestable to you.

¹³" 'These are the birds you are to detest and not eat because they are detestable: the eagle, the vulture, the black vulture, ¹⁴the red kite, any kind of black kite, ¹⁵any kind of raven, ¹⁶the horned owl, the screech owl, the gull, any kind of hawk, ¹⁷the little owl, the cormorant, the great owl, ¹⁸the white owl, the desert owl, the osprey, ¹⁹the stork, any kind of heron, the hoopoe and the bat.ᵇ

²⁰" 'All flying insects that walk on all fours are to be detestable to you. ²¹There are, however, some winged creatures that walk on all fours that you may eat: those that have jointed legs for hopping on the ground. ²²Of these you may eat any kind of locust, katydid, cricket or grasshopper. ²³But all other winged creatures that have four legs you are to detest.

²⁴" 'You will make yourselves unclean by these; whoever touches their carcasses will be unclean till evening. ²⁵Whoever picks up one of their carcasses must wash his clothes, and he will be unclean till evening.

²⁶" 'Every animal that has a split hoof not completely divided or that does not chew the cud is unclean for you; whoever touches ˻the carcass of˼ any of them will be unclean. ²⁷Of all the animals that walk on all fours, those that walk on their paws are unclean for you; whoever touches their carcasses will be unclean till evening. ²⁸Anyone who picks up their carcasses must wash his clothes, and he will be unclean till evening. They are unclean for you.

²⁹" 'Of the animals that move about on the ground, these are unclean for you: the weasel, the rat, any kind of great lizard, ³⁰the gecko, the monitor lizard, the wall lizard, the skink and the chameleon. ³¹Of all those that move along the ground, these are unclean for you. Whoever touches them when they are dead will be unclean till evening. ³²When one of them

dies and falls on something, that article, whatever its use, will be unclean, whether it is made of wood, cloth, hide or sackcloth. Put it in water; it will be unclean till evening, and then it will be clean. ³³If one of them falls into a clay pot, everything in it will be unclean, and you must break the pot. ³⁴Any food that could be eaten but has water on it from such a pot is unclean, and any liquid that could be drunk from it is unclean. ³⁵Anything that one of their carcasses falls on becomes unclean; an oven or cooking pot must be broken up. They are unclean, and you are to regard them as unclean. ³⁶A spring, however, or a cistern for collecting water remains clean, but anyone who touches one of these carcasses is unclean. ³⁷If a carcass falls on any seeds that are to be planted, they remain clean. ³⁸But if water has been put on the seed and a carcass falls on it, it is unclean for you.

³⁹" 'If an animal that you are allowed to eat dies, anyone who touches the carcass will be unclean till evening. ⁴⁰Anyone who eats some of the carcass must wash his clothes, and he will be unclean till evening. Anyone who picks up the carcass must wash his clothes, and he will be unclean till evening.

⁴¹" 'Every creature that moves about on the ground is detestable; it is not to be eaten. ⁴²You are not to eat any creature that moves about on the ground, whether it moves on its belly or walks on all fours or on many feet; it is detestable. ⁴³Do not defile yourselves by any of these creatures. Do not make yourselves unclean by means of them or be made unclean by them. ⁴⁴I am the LORD your God; consecrate yourselves and be holy, because I am holy. Do not make yourselves unclean by any creature that moves about on the ground. ⁴⁵I am the LORD who brought you up out of Egypt to be your God; therefore be holy, because I am holy.

⁴⁶" 'These are the regulations concerning animals, birds, every living thing that moves in the water and every creature that moves about on the ground. ⁴⁷You must distinguish between the unclean and the

---

ᵇ19 The precise identification of some of the birds, insects and animals in this chapter is uncertain.

clean, between living creatures that may be eaten and those that may not be eaten.'"

Purification After Childbirth

12 The LORD said to Moses, 2"Say to the Israelites: 'A woman who becomes pregnant and gives birth to a son will be ceremonially unclean for seven days, just as she is unclean during her monthly period. 3On the eighth day the boy is to be circumcised. 4Then the woman must wait thirty-three days to be purified from her bleeding. She must not touch anything sacred or go to the sanctuary until the days of her purification are over. 5If she gives birth to a daughter, for two weeks the woman will be unclean, as during her period. Then she must wait sixty-six days to be purified from her bleeding.

6"'When the days of her purification for a son or daughter are over, she is to bring to the priest at the entrance to the Tent of Meeting a year-old lamb for a burnt offering and a young pigeon or a dove for a sin offering. 7He shall offer them before the LORD to make atonement for her, and then she will be ceremonially clean from her flow of blood.

"'These are the regulations for the woman who gives birth to a boy or a girl. 8If she cannot afford a lamb, she is to bring two doves or two young pigeons, one for a burnt offering and the other for a sin offering. In this way the priest will make atonement for her, and she will be clean.'"

Regulations About Infectious Skin Diseases

13 The LORD said to Moses and Aaron, 2"When anyone has a swelling or a rash or a bright spot on his skin that may become an infectious skin disease,[a] he must be brought to Aaron the priest or to one of his sons[b] who is a priest. 3The priest is to examine the sore on his skin, and if the hair in the sore has turned white and the sore appears to be more than skin deep,[c] it is an infectious skin disease. When the priest examines him, he shall pronounce him ceremonially unclean. 4If the spot on his skin is white but does not appear to be more than skin deep and the hair in it has not turned white, the priest is to put the infected person in isolation for seven days. 5On the seventh day the priest is to examine him, and if he sees that the sore is unchanged and has not spread in the skin, he is to keep him in isolation another seven days. 6On the seventh day the priest is to examine him again, and if the sore has faded and has not spread in the skin, the priest shall pronounce him clean; it is only a rash. The man must wash his clothes, and he will be clean. 7But if the rash does spread in his skin after he has shown himself to the priest to be pronounced clean, he must appear before the priest again. 8The priest is to examine him, and if the rash has spread in the skin, he shall pronounce him unclean; it is an infectious disease.

9"When anyone has an infectious skin disease, he must be brought to the priest. 10The priest is to examine him, and if there is a white swelling in the skin that has turned the hair white and if there is raw flesh in the swelling, 11it is a chronic skin disease and the priest shall pronounce him unclean. He is not to put him in isolation, because he is already unclean.

12"If the disease breaks out all over his skin and, so far as the priest can see, it covers all the skin of the infected person from head to foot, 13the priest is to examine him, and if the disease has covered his whole body, he shall pronounce that person clean. Since it has all turned white, he is clean. 14But whenever raw flesh appears on him, he will be unclean. 15When the priest sees the raw flesh, he shall pronounce him unclean. The raw flesh is unclean; he has an infectious

---

a2 Traditionally *leprosy*; the Hebrew word was used for various diseases affecting the skin—not necessarily leprosy; also elsewhere in this chapter.   *b2* Or *descendants*
c3 Or *be lower than the rest of the skin*; also elsewhere in this chapter

disease. ¹⁶Should the raw flesh change and turn white, he must go to the priest. ¹⁷The priest is to examine him, and if the sores have turned white, the priest shall pronounce the infected person clean; then he will be clean.

¹⁸"When someone has a boil on his skin and it heals, ¹⁹and in the place where the boil was, a white swelling or reddish-white spot appears, he must present himself to the priest. ²⁰The priest is to examine it, and if it appears to be more than skin deep and the hair in it has turned white, the priest shall pronounce him unclean. It is an infectious skin disease that has broken out where the boil was. ²¹But if, when the priest examines it, there is no white hair in it and it is not more than skin deep and has faded, then the priest is to put him in isolation for seven days. ²²If it is spreading in the skin, the priest shall pronounce him unclean; it is infectious. ²³But if the spot is unchanged and has not spread, it is only a scar from the boil, and the priest shall pronounce him clean.

²⁴"When someone has a burn on his skin and a reddish-white or white spot appears in the raw flesh of the burn, ²⁵the priest is to examine the spot, and if the hair in it has turned white, and it appears to be more than skin deep, it is an infectious disease that has broken out in the burn. The priest shall pronounce him unclean; it is an infectious skin disease. ²⁶But if the priest examines it and there is no white hair in the spot and if it is not more than skin deep and has faded, then the priest is to put him in isolation for seven days. ²⁷On the seventh day the priest is to examine him, and if it is spreading in the skin, the priest shall pronounce him unclean; it is an infectious skin disease. ²⁸If, however, the spot is unchanged and has not spread in the skin but has faded, it is a swelling from the burn, and the priest shall pronounce him clean; it is only a scar from the burn.

²⁹"If a man or woman has a sore on the head or on the chin, ³⁰the priest is to examine the sore, and if it appears to be more than skin deep and the hair in it is yellow and thin, the priest shall pronounce that person unclean; it is an itch, an infectious disease of the head or chin. ³¹But if, when the priest examines this kind of sore, it does not seem to be more than skin deep and there is no black hair in it, then the priest is to put the infected person in isolation for seven days. ³²On the seventh day the priest is to examine the sore, and if the itch has not spread and there is no yellow hair in it and it does not appear to be more than skin deep, ³³he must be shaved except for the diseased area, and the priest is to keep him in isolation another seven days. ³⁴On the seventh day the priest is to examine the itch, and if it has not spread in the skin and appears to be no more than skin deep, the priest shall pronounce him clean. He must wash his clothes, and he will be clean. ³⁵But if the itch does spread in the skin after he is pronounced clean, ³⁶the priest is to examine him, and if the itch has spread in the skin, the priest does not need to look for yellow hair; the person is unclean. ³⁷If, however, in his judgment it is unchanged and black hair has grown in it, the itch is healed. He is clean, and the priest shall pronounce him clean.

³⁸"When a man or woman has white spots on the skin, ³⁹the priest is to examine them, and if the spots are dull white, it is a harmless rash that has broken out on the skin; that person is clean.

⁴⁰"When a man has lost his hair and is bald, he is clean. ⁴¹If he has lost his hair from the front of his scalp and has a bald forehead, he is clean. ⁴²But if he has a reddish-white sore on his bald head or forehead, it is an infectious disease breaking out on his head or forehead. ⁴³The priest is to examine him, and if the swollen sore on his head or forehead is reddish-white like an infectious skin disease, ⁴⁴the man is diseased and is unclean. The priest shall pronounce him unclean because of the sore on his head.

⁴⁵"The person with such an infectious disease must wear torn clothes, let his hair be unkempt,ᵈ cover the lower part of his face and cry out, 'Unclean! Unclean!' ⁴⁶As

ᵈ45 Or *clothes, uncover his head*

long as he has the infection he remains unclean. He must live alone; he must live outside the camp.

Regulations About Mildew

[47]"If any clothing is contaminated with mildew—any woollen or linen clothing, [48]any woven or knitted material of linen or wool, any leather or anything made of leather—[49]and if the contamination in the clothing, or leather, or woven or knitted material, or any leather article, is greenish or reddish, it is a spreading mildew and must be shown to the priest. [50]The priest is to examine the mildew and isolate the affected article for seven days. [51]On the seventh day he is to examine it, and if the mildew has spread in the clothing, or the woven or knitted material, or the leather, whatever its use, it is a destructive mildew; the article is unclean. [52]He must burn up the clothing, or the woven or knitted material of wool or linen, or any leather article that has the contamination in it, because the mildew is destructive; the article must be burned up.

[53]"But if, when the priest examines it, the mildew has not spread in the clothing, or the woven or knitted material, or the leather article, [54]he shall order that the contaminated article be washed. Then he is to isolate it for another seven days. [55]After the affected article has been washed, the priest is to examine it, and if the mildew has not changed its appearance, even though it has not spread, it is unclean. Burn it with fire, whether the mildew has affected one side or the other. [56]If, when the priest examines it, the mildew has faded after the article has been washed, he is to tear the contaminated part out of the clothing, or the leather, or the woven or knitted material. [57]But if it reappears in the clothing, or in the woven or knitted material, or in the leather article, it is spreading, and whatever has the mildew must be burned with fire. [58]The clothing, or the woven or knitted material,

or any leather article that has been washed and is rid of the mildew, must be washed again, and it will be clean."

[59]These are the regulations concerning contamination by mildew in woollen or linen clothing, woven or knitted material, or any leather article, for pronouncing them clean or unclean.

Cleansing From Infectious Skin Diseases

14 The LORD said to Moses, [2]"These are the regulations for the diseased person at the time of his ceremonial cleansing, when he is brought to the priest: [3]The priest is to go outside the camp and examine him. If the person has been healed of his infectious skin disease,*a* [4]the priest shall order that two live clean birds and some cedar wood, scarlet yarn and hyssop be brought for the one to be cleansed. [5]Then the priest shall order that one of the birds be killed over fresh water in a clay pot. [6]He is then to take the live bird and dip it, together with the cedar wood, the scarlet yarn and the hyssop, into the blood of the bird that was killed over the fresh water. [7]Seven times he shall sprinkle the one to be cleansed of the infectious disease and pronounce him clean. Then he is to release the live bird in the open fields.

[8]"The person to be cleansed must wash his clothes, shave off all his hair and bathe with water; then he will be ceremonially clean. After this he may come into the camp, but he must stay outside his tent for seven days. [9]On the seventh day he must shave off all his hair; he must shave his head, his beard, his eyebrows and the rest of his hair. He must wash his clothes and bathe himself with water, and he will be clean.

[10]"On the eighth day he must bring two male lambs and one ewe lamb a year old, each without defect, along with three-tenths of an ephah*b* of fine flour mixed with oil for a grain offering, and one log*c* of

---

a3 Traditionally *leprosy*; the Hebrew word was used for various diseases affecting the skin—not necessarily leprosy; also elsewhere in this chapter.   *b10* That is, probably about 11½ pints (about 6.5 litres)
c10 That is, probably about ½ pint (about 0.3 litre); also in verses 12, 15, 21 and 24

oil. ¹¹The priest who pronounces him clean shall present both the one to be cleansed and his offerings before the Lord at the entrance to the Tent of Meeting.

¹²"Then the priest is to take one of the male lambs and offer it as a guilt offering, along with the log of oil; he shall wave them before the Lord as a wave offering. ¹³He is to slaughter the lamb in the holy place where the sin offering and the burnt offering are slaughtered. Like the sin offering, the guilt offering belongs to the priest; it is most holy. ¹⁴The priest is to take some of the blood of the guilt offering and put it on the lobe of the right ear of the one to be cleansed, on the thumb of his right hand and on the big toe of his right foot. ¹⁵The priest shall then take some of the log of oil, pour it in the palm of his own left hand, ¹⁶dip his right forefinger into the oil in his palm, and with his finger sprinkle some of it before the Lord seven times. ¹⁷The priest is to put some of the oil remaining in his palm on the lobe of the right ear of the one to be cleansed, on the thumb of his right hand and on the big toe of his right foot, on top of the blood of the guilt offering. ¹⁸The rest of the oil in his palm the priest shall put on the head of the one to be cleansed and make atonement for him before the Lord.

¹⁹"Then the priest is to sacrifice the sin offering and make atonement for the one to be cleansed from his uncleanness. After that, the priest shall slaughter the burnt offering ²⁰and offer it on the altar, together with the grain offering, and make atonement for him, and he will be clean.

²¹"If, however, he is poor and cannot afford these, he must take one male lamb as a guilt offering to be waved to make atonement for him, together with a tenth of an ephah*d* of fine flour mixed with oil for a grain offering, a log of oil, ²²and two doves or two young pigeons, which he can afford, one for a sin offering and the other for a burnt offering.

²³"On the eighth day he must bring them for his cleansing to the priest at the entrance to the Tent of Meeting, before the Lord. ²⁴The priest is to take the lamb for the guilt offering, together with the log of oil, and wave them before the Lord as a wave offering. ²⁵He shall slaughter the lamb for the guilt offering and take some of its blood and put it on the lobe of the right ear of the one to be cleansed, on the thumb of his right hand and on the big toe of his right foot. ²⁶The priest is to pour some of the oil into the palm of his own left hand, ²⁷and with his right forefinger sprinkle some of the oil from his palm seven times before the Lord. ²⁸Some of the oil in his palm he is to put on the same places he put the blood of the guilt offering—on the lobe of the right ear of the one to be cleansed, on the thumb of his right hand and on the big toe of his right foot. ²⁹The rest of the oil in his palm the priest shall put on the head of the one to be cleansed, to make atonement for him before the Lord. ³⁰Then he shall sacrifice the doves or the young pigeons, which the person can afford, ³¹one*e* as a sin offering and the other as a burnt offering, together with the grain offering. In this way the priest will make atonement before the Lord on behalf of the one to be cleansed."

³²These are the regulations for anyone who has an infectious skin disease and who cannot afford the regular offerings for his cleansing.

Cleansing From Mildew

³³The Lord said to Moses and Aaron, ³⁴"When you enter the land of Canaan, which I am giving you as your possession, and I put a spreading mildew in a house in that land, ³⁵the owner of the house must go and tell the priest, 'I have seen something that looks like mildew in my house.' ³⁶The priest is to order the house to be emptied before he goes in to examine the mildew, so that nothing in the house will be pronounced unclean. After this the priest is to go in and inspect the house.

d21 That is, probably about 4 pints (about 2 litres)
e31 Septuagint and Syriac; Hebrew ³¹*such as the person can afford, one*

37He is to examine the mildew on the walls, and if it has greenish or reddish depressions that appear to be deeper than the surface of the wall, 38the priest shall go out of the doorway of the house and close it up for seven days. 39On the seventh day the priest shall return to inspect the house. If the mildew has spread on the walls, 40he is to order that the contaminated stones be torn out and thrown into an unclean place outside the town. 41He must have all the inside walls of the house scraped and the material that is scraped off dumped into an unclean place outside the town. 42Then they are to take other stones to replace these and take new clay and plaster the house.

43"If the mildew reappears in the house after the stones have been torn out and the house scraped and plastered, 44the priest is to go and examine it and, if the mildew has spread in the house, it is a destructive mildew; the house is unclean. 45It must be torn down—its stones, timbers and all the plaster—and taken out of the town to an unclean place.

46"Anyone who goes into the house while it is closed up will be unclean till evening. 47Anyone who sleeps or eats in the house must wash his clothes.

48"But if the priest comes to examine it and the mildew has not spread after the house has been plastered, he shall pronounce the house clean, because the mildew is gone. 49To purify the house he is to take two birds and some cedar wood, scarlet yarn and hyssop. 50He shall kill one of the birds over fresh water in a clay pot. 51Then he is to take the cedar wood, the hyssop, the scarlet yarn and the live bird, dip them into the blood of the dead bird and the fresh water, and sprinkle the house seven times. 52He shall purify the house with the bird's blood, the fresh water, the live bird, the cedar wood, the hyssop and the scarlet yarn. 53Then he is to release the live bird in the open fields outside the town. In this way he will make atonement for the house, and it will be clean."

54These are the regulations for any infectious skin disease, for an itch, 55for mildew in clothing or in a house, 56and for a swelling, a rash or a bright spot, 57to determine when something is clean or unclean.

These are the regulations for infectious skin diseases and mildew.

Discharges Causing Uncleanness

15 The LORD said to Moses and Aaron, 2"Speak to the Israelites and say to them: 'When any man has a bodily discharge, the discharge is unclean. 3Whether it continues flowing from his body or is blocked, it will make him unclean. This is how his discharge will bring about uncleanness:

4"'Any bed the man with a discharge lies on will be unclean, and anything he sits on will be unclean. 5Anyone who touches his bed must wash his clothes and bathe with water, and he will be unclean till evening. 6Whoever sits on anything that the man with a discharge sat on must wash his clothes and bathe with water, and he will be unclean till evening.

7"'Whoever touches the man who has a discharge must wash his clothes and bathe with water, and he will be unclean till evening.

8"'If the man with the discharge spits on someone who is clean, that person must wash his clothes and bathe with water, and he will be unclean till evening.

9"'Everything the man sits on when riding will be unclean, 10and whoever touches any of the things that were under him will be unclean till evening; whoever picks up those things must wash his clothes and bathe with water, and he will be unclean till evening.

11"'Anyone the man with a discharge touches without rinsing his hands with water must wash his clothes and bathe with water, and he will be unclean till evening.

12"'A clay pot that the man touches must be broken, and any wooden article is to be rinsed with water.

13"'When a man is cleansed from his discharge, he is to count off seven days for his ceremonial cleansing; he must wash his clothes and bathe himself with fresh water, and he will be clean. ¹⁴On the eighth day he must take two doves or two young pigeons and come before the LORD to the entrance to the Tent of Meeting and give them to the priest. ¹⁵The priest is to sacrifice them, the one for a sin offering and the other for a burnt offering. In this way he will make atonement before the LORD for the man because of his discharge.

¹⁶"When a man has an emission of semen, he must bathe his whole body with water, and he will be unclean till evening. ¹⁷Any clothing or leather that has semen on it must be washed with water, and it will be unclean till evening. ¹⁸When a man lies with a woman and there is an emission of semen, both must bathe with water, and they will be unclean till evening.

¹⁹"When a woman has her regular flow of blood, the impurity of her monthly period will last seven days, and anyone who touches her will be unclean till evening.

²⁰"Anything she lies on during her period will be unclean, and anything she sits on will be unclean. ²¹Whoever touches her bed must wash his clothes and bathe with water, and he will be unclean till evening. ²²Whoever touches anything she sits on must wash his clothes and bathe with water, and he will be unclean till evening. ²³Whether it is the bed or anything she was sitting on, when anyone touches it, he will be unclean till evening.

²⁴"If a man lies with her and her monthly flow touches him, he will be unclean for seven days; any bed he lies on will be unclean.

²⁵"When a woman has a discharge of blood for many days at a time other than her monthly period or has a discharge that continues beyond her period, she will be unclean as long as she has the discharge, just as in the days of her period. ²⁶Any bed she lies on while her discharge continues will be unclean, as is her bed during her monthly period, and anything she sits on will be unclean, as during her period. ²⁷Whoever touches them will be unclean; he must wash his clothes and bathe with

water, and he will be unclean till evening.

²⁸"When she is cleansed from her discharge, she must count off seven days, and after that she will be ceremonially clean. ²⁹On the eighth day she must take two doves or two young pigeons and bring them to the priest at the entrance to the Tent of Meeting. ³⁰The priest is to sacrifice one for a sin offering and the other for a burnt offering. In this way he will make atonement for her before the LORD for the uncleanness of her discharge.

³¹"You must keep the Israelites separate from things that make them unclean, so they will not die in their uncleanness for defiling my dwelling-place,ᵃ which is among them.'"

³²These are the regulations for a man with a discharge, for anyone made unclean by an emission of semen, ³³for a woman in her monthly period, for a man or a woman with a discharge, and for a man who lies with a woman who is ceremonially unclean.

The Day of Atonement

16 The LORD spoke to Moses after the death of the two sons of Aaron who died when they approached the LORD. ²The LORD said to Moses: "Tell your brother Aaron not to come whenever he chooses into the Most Holy Place behind the curtain in front of the atonement cover on the ark, or else he will die, because I appear in the cloud over the atonement cover.

³"This is how Aaron is to enter the sanctuary area: with a young bull for a sin offering and a ram for a burnt offering. ⁴He is to put on the sacred linen tunic, with linen undergarments next to his body; he is to tie the linen sash around him and put on the linen turban. These are sacred garments; so he must bathe himself with water before he puts them on. ⁵From the Israelite community he is to take two male goats for a sin offering and a ram for a burnt offering.

⁶"Aaron is to offer the bull for his own

ᵃ31 Or *my tabernacle*

Simon Hall, *writer*
Having read Philosophy and Theology at University, Simon is currently a part-time pastor of a new church in Leeds, **revive**. He has worked as a community worker, youth pastor, youthwork teacher and has helped to establish a number of young people's churches. He writes regularly for the magazine YOUTHWORK and is married to Anna and they live in Leeds.

Andrew Darmanin, *designer*. Andrew Darmanin has his own design company, well out-poured design and also works as a worship-youth-schools worker for New Covenant Church, Weymouth. Married to Wendy with a little girl, Grace, Andrew's favourite Bible passage at present is Galatians 6:9. Andrew and his buddy Paul White designed *Read This: John's Gospel* for young people.

Emma Sealey,
editorial director
Has been working in Bible publishing at Hodder & Stoughton for nearly ten years and is a big Bible fan (especially John 11:25-26; Isaiah 43 and Deuteronomy).

Ann from New Zealand works in Information Technology for a major finance institution in the City. She attends St Helen's Church, Bishopsgate. Ann became a Christian at 16. Her favourite Bible passage is Matthew 10:32.

Jonathan is studying Mathematical Physics at Nottingham University where he attends Trent Vineyard. His favourite Bible passage is Ezekiel 1-3. A trekkie, Jonathan likes Radiohead and the Stephen Lawhead books about King Arthur. Into individual expression in worship, he still believes in Father Christmas and loves his mum (and her cooking)!

Our anonymous contributor is happily married with two boys. Currently working in Christian ministry, Anon has more than one favourite Bible passage: Matthew 22:37-39 and Philippians 1:6; 3:7-16 and says that the Bible is 'my favourite book by far.'

Pat attends Brixton Baptist (Kenyon) Church and works for a local authority as a youth officer. Her favourite passage is the whole of Romans 8. Pat's job is very demanding but she makes sure she has some good holidays away and she and her mother foster children.

Paul works as a nurse in Intensive Care. Paul's favourite Bible passages are Colossians 3:15 and Psalm 23. He's into the Teenage Fan Club, Match of the Day and playing his guitar. He is currently questioning a number of issues relating to his faith. His answer so far is 'be yourself'.

Penny teaches the piano in Southampton. She attends Bridge Christian Fellowship. Her favourite Bible passage is Jeremiah 17:5-8. A fan of classical music, jazz and Calvin & Hobbs, Penny has an aversion to having her photo taken but likes hockey and horse riding.

FRIENDS

Anon For me the whole concept of the creator of absolutely everything getting involved in our lives and just touching the most intimate parts is nothing short of amazing.

What do we mean when we say we have a relationship with God? And how do we keep that going?

Ann We can have a relationship with God, but we're having a relationship now because we're talking to each other. It can be difficult to work out how to talk to God. It's just great to know that when you do talk to him he is just the same, it's like a friendship, you don't spend time with someone for over a year, and then you're on the phone and your friend is just the same, she's not angry with you, she's just herself. I think that's what God is like.

Penny I like spending time with God, just on my own.

Ann It's letting God come into my other relationships instead of just leaving him at home with my Bible and my bedroom, to actually take him with me and remember that he is with me always.

Pat To stay friends with God, I maintain my relationships with friends: worshipping, going to church is extremely important for me. So is prayer, I pray when I'm driving, when I'm at work sitting at my desk, wherever the opportunity arises.

d you must deny
ng ordinance. ³²The
ed and ordained to
igh priest is to make
put on the sacred
make atonement for
or the Tent of Meet-
for the priests and all
munity.
asting ordinance for
be made once a year
sraelites.''
s the LORD comman-

den

d to Moses, ²"Speak
his sons and to all the
them: 'This is what
nded: ³Any Israelite
a a lamb or a goat in
of it ⁴instead of bring-
to the Tent of Meet-
offering to the LORD
nacle of the LORD—
considered guilty of
ed blood and must be
le. ⁵This is so that the
to the LORD the sac-
making in the open
ng them to the priest,
at the entrance to the
nd sacrifice them as
s.*b* ⁶The priest is to
gainst the altar of the
e to the Tent of Meet-
as an aroma pleasing
must no longer offer
es to the goat idols*c* to
te themselves. This is
ance for them and for
ome.'
'Any Israelite or any
them who offers a
acrifice ⁹and must not
rance to the Tent of
e it to the LORD—that
f from his people.
e or any alien living

among them who eats any blood—
set my face against that person wh
blood and will cut him off from his p
¹¹For the life of a creature is in the
and I have given it to you to make
ment for yourselves on the altar; it
blood that makes atonement for one
¹²Therefore I say to the Israelites, '
of you may eat blood, nor may an
living among you eat blood.'
¹³"'Any Israelite or any alien
among you who hunts any animal o
that may be eaten must drain ou
blood and cover it with earth, ¹⁴be
the life of every creature is its blood
is why I have said to the Israelites,
must not eat the blood of any crea
because the life of every creature
blood; anyone who eats it must b
off.'
¹⁵"'Anyone, whether native-bo
alien, who eats anything found de
torn by wild animals must wash his cl
and bathe with water, and he will be
monially unclean till evening; then h
be clean. ¹⁶But if he does not was
clothes and bathe himself, he will be
responsible.'"

Unlawful Sexual Relations

18 The LORD said to Moses, ²"S
to the Israelites and say to the
am the LORD your God. ³You must n
as they do in Egypt, where you us
live, and you must not do as they do i
land of Canaan, where I am bringing
Do not follow their practices. ⁴You
obey my laws and be careful to follo
decrees. I am the LORD your God. ⁵
my decrees and laws, for the man
obeys them will live by them. I an
LORD.
⁶"'No-one is to approach any close
tive to have sexual relations. I an
LORD.
⁷"'Do not dishonour your fathe
having sexual relations with your mo
She is your mother; do not have rela
with her.

nclude both male and female.   *b5* Traditionally *peace offerings*   *c7* Or *demo*

with
GOD

What is prayer?

Ann Sometimes I pray
with my eyes open and look all around
at creation because that's inspiring me
just to talk to God. You don't need to use
long words, you don't need to use the Lord's
Prayer although you can, you can call him whatever
you like, because he knows your heart and can tell what
you want to say even though you're not
performing correctly.

Paul I'd been going through a period of
nearly a year when I prayed for an hour
every morning and now I'm going through
period when I hardly pray and I think
that's normal. In a real relationship, there
are periods when you just don't talk . . .

Jonathan I always tend to stick some
music on because it just helps me,
stops me drifting. I tend to pray very
physically, it's the way I like to express
myself, dancing or whatever. I'm a useless
dancer, but, you know, I like jumping
around my room, because it just helps me
focus on God. I think it's really key that
you do listen as much as you talk.

What is prayer?
....
Just gassing with God

It's asking for things

It's thanks as well

Talking with God

Being myself

Including God, a partnership

③

Responding to change and Moving Forward

Once you have read these passages, reflect on these questions, and any others which come to mind:

Imagine how Abraham, Matthew and Paul (ordinary people, not perfect) felt.

➤What adjustments would they have to have made as they each obeyed God?

➤Have your parents or have you ever moved house? Consider the stress and activity of this event. What feelings and emotions did the event set in motion?

➤ How did pulling up roots and leaving friends feel?

➤ Would Matthew have lost status when he left his job? How much status and power do we associate with a person's job?

➤ People often say that they have sacrificed this or that, what do they mean? What would you mean if you used that phrase? Have you ever made any sacrifices?

➤ Paul had what some would claim was a conversion experience. What does this mean? Is it a once and for all experience? Should all Christians be able to name a day and time when such an experience happened to them? What has been converted or changed in your life? Are

WHERE were Abraham's roots and home?

HOW did Abraham respond to God's call and promise?

WHAT effect did Abraham's response have on him and others? (See Hebrews 11: 8-19 p1209 for a helpful summary)

HOW did Matthew respond to Jesus?

WHAT had Paul been doing before the events on the road to Damascus?

HOW did this event impact on Paul's whole life?

you still being changed?

➤ What do the lives of these three Bible characters suggest to you regarding obedience, responding to change and dealing with the consequences? How do the changes in their lives link into your life and experience to date?

➤ Do you know anyone who has given up a good job and salary in order to take up Christian service? Why not talk to them about their experiences?

✔ *Think about any changes you know you need to make in your life at school, at work, at home, in relationships and lifestyle. What will it take to get you started? What help do you need in order to make that change?*

✔ *Ask yourself: Do you need to set fresh goals for your life?*

✔ *Pray and thank God for the way he has led you so far and ask for the help and power of the Holy Spirit as you seek to discern and identify possible changes of direction in your life. As you trust God and seek to be obedient to him, the way will become clear.*

(4)

---

in offering to make atonement fo elf and his household. 7Then he is t he two goats and present them befo LORD at the entrance to the Tent of ng. 8He is to cast lots for the two g one lot for the LORD and the other scapegoat.*a* 9Aaron shall bring the whose lot falls to the LORD and sacri for a sin offering. 10But the goat chos ot as the scapegoat shall be prese live before the LORD to be used for ng atonement by sending it into the d s a scapegoat.

11"Aaron shall bring the bull for his in offering to make atonement for elf and his household, and he is to sla er the bull for his own sin offering. 12 to take a censer full of burning coals f he altar before the LORD and two hand of finely ground fragrant incense and them behind the curtain. 13He is to put ncense on the fire before the LORD, he smoke of the incense will conceal atonement cover above the Testimony hat he will not die. 14He is to take som he bull's blood and with his finger spr kle it on the front of the atonement cov hen he shall sprinkle some of it with inger seven times before the atoneme cover.

15"He shall then slaughter the goat f he sin offering for the people and take blood behind the curtain and do with it he did with the bull's blood: He sha sprinkle it on the atonement cover and ront of it. 16In this way he will mak atonement for the Most Holy Place be ause of the uncleanness and rebellion c he Israelites, whatever their sins hav been. He is to do the same for the Tent c Meeting, which is among them in th nidst of their uncleanness. 17No-one is t be in the Tent of Meeting from the time Aaron goes in to make atonement in th Most Holy Place until he comes out, hav ng made atonement for himself, his ousehold and the whole community of srael. 18"Then he shall come out to the altar hat is before the LORD and make atone nent for it. He shall take some of the

8 That is, the goat of removal; Hebrew azazel; *also in ver*

---

sabbath of rest, a yourselves; it is a las priest who is anoin succeed his father as atonement. He is t linen garments 33and the Most Holy Place ing and the altar, and the people of the co

34"This is to be a you: Atonement is t for all the sins of the

And it was done, ded Moses.

Eating Blood Forbi

17 The LORD s to Aaron an Israelites and say t the LORD has comm who sacrifices an o the camp or outside ing it to the entranc ing to present it as a in front of the tab that man shall be bloodshed; he has s cut off from his peo Israelites will bring rifices they are no fields. They must b that is, to the LORD Tent of Meeting fellowship offering sprinkle the blood LORD at the entran ing and burn the fa to the LORD. 7The any of their sacrifi whom they prostit to be a lasting ordi the generations to

8"Say to them: alien living amon burnt offering or bring it to the er Meeting to sacrifi man must be cut o

10"Any Israeli

a3 The Hebrew word car

8"'Do not have sexual relations with your father's wife; that would dishonour your father.

9"'Do not have sexual relations with your sister, either your father's daughter or your mother's daughter, whether she was born in the same home or elsewhere.

10"'Do not have sexual relations with your son's daughter or your daughter's daughter; that would dishonour you.

11"'Do not have sexual relations with the daughter of your father's wife, born to your father; she is your sister.

12"'Do not have sexual relations with your father's sister; she is your father's close relative.

13"'Do not have sexual relations with your mother's sister, because she is your mother's close relative.

14"'Do not dishonour your father's brother by approaching his wife to have sexual relations; she is your aunt.

15"'Do not have sexual relations with your daughter-in-law. She is your son's wife; do not have relations with her.

16"'Do not have sexual relations with your brother's wife; that would dishonour your brother.

17"'Do not have sexual relations with both a woman and her daughter. Do not have sexual relations with either her son's daughter or her daughter's daughter; they are her close relatives. That is wickedness.

18"'Do not take your wife's sister as a rival wife and have sexual relations with her while your wife is living.

19"'Do not approach a woman to have sexual relations during the uncleanness of her monthly period.

20"'Do not have sexual relations with your neighbour's wife and defile yourself with her.

21"'Do not give any of your children to be sacrificed[a] to Molech, for you must not profane the name of your God. I am the LORD.

22"'Do not lie with a man as one lies with a woman; that is detestable.

23"'Do not have sexual relations with an animal and defile yourself with it. A woman must not present herself to an animal to have sexual relations with it; that is a perversion.

24"'Do not defile yourselves in any of these ways, because this is how the nations that I am going to drive out before you became defiled. 25Even the land was defiled; so I punished it for its sin, and the land vomited out its inhabitants. 26But you must keep my decrees and my laws. The native-born and the aliens living among you must not do any of these detestable things, 27for all these things were done by the people who lived in the land before you, and the land became defiled. 28And if you defile the land, it will vomit you out as it vomited out the nations that were before you.

29"'Everyone who does any of these detestable things—such persons must be cut off from their people. 30Keep my requirements and do not follow any of the detestable customs that were practised before you came and do not defile yourselves with them. I am the LORD your God.'"

Various Laws

19 The LORD said to Moses, 2"Speak to the entire assembly of Israel and say to them: 'Be holy because I, the LORD your God, am holy.

3"'Each of you must respect his mother and father, and you must observe my Sabbaths. I am the LORD your God.

4"'Do not turn to idols or make gods of cast metal for yourselves. I am the LORD your God.

5"'When you sacrifice a fellowship offering[a] to the LORD, sacrifice it in such a way that it will be accepted on your behalf. 6It shall be eaten on the day you sacrifice it or on the next day; anything left over until the third day must be burned up. 7If any of it is eaten on the third day, it is impure and will not be accepted. 8Whoever eats it will be held responsible because he has desecrated what is holy to the LORD; that person must be cut off from his people.

9"'When you reap the harvest of your

---

a21 Or *to be passed through* ⌊*the fire*⌋
a5 Traditionally *peace offering*

land, do not reap to the very edges of your field or gather the gleanings of your harvest. [10]Do not go over your vineyard a second time or pick up the grapes that have fallen. Leave them for the poor and the alien. I am the LORD your God.

[11]" 'Do not steal.

" 'Do not lie.

" 'Do not deceive one another.

[12]" 'Do not swear falsely by my name and so profane the name of your God. I am the LORD.

[13]" 'Do not defraud your neighbour or rob him.

" 'Do not hold back the wages of a hired man overnight.

[14]" 'Do not curse the deaf or put a stumbling-block in front of the blind, but fear your God. I am the LORD.

[15]" 'Do not pervert justice; do not show partiality to the poor or favouritism to the great, but judge your neighbour fairly.

[16]" 'Do not go about spreading slander among your people.

" 'Do not do anything that endangers your neighbour's life. I am the LORD.

[17]" 'Do not hate your brother in your heart. Rebuke your neighbour frankly so that you will not share in his guilt.

[18]" 'Do not seek revenge or bear a grudge against one of your people, but love your neighbour as yourself. I am the LORD.

[19]" 'Keep my decrees.

" 'Do not mate different kinds of animals.

" 'Do not plant your field with two kinds of seed.

" 'Do not wear clothing woven of two kinds of material.

[20]" 'If a man sleeps with a woman who is a slave girl promised to another man but who has not been ransomed or given her freedom, there must be due punishment. Yet they are not to be put to death, because she had not been freed. [21]The man, however, must bring a ram to the entrance to the Tent of Meeting for a guilt offering to the LORD. [22]With the ram of the guilt offering the priest is to make atonement for him before the LORD for the sin he has committed, and his sin will be forgiven.

[23]" 'When you enter the land and plant any kind of fruit tree, regard its fruit as forbidden.[b] For three years you are to consider it forbidden;[b] it must not be eaten. [24]In the fourth year all its fruit will be holy, an offering of praise to the LORD. [25]But in the fifth year you may eat its fruit. In this way your harvest will be increased. I am the LORD your God.

[26]" 'Do not eat any meat with the blood still in it.

" 'Do not practise divination or sorcery.

[27]" 'Do not cut the hair at the sides of your head or clip off the edges of your beard.

[28]" 'Do not cut your bodies for the dead or put tattoo marks on yourselves. I am the LORD.

[29]" 'Do not degrade your daughter by making her a prostitute, or the land will turn to prostitution and be filled with wickedness.

[30]" 'Observe my Sabbaths and have reverence for my sanctuary. I am the LORD.

[31]" 'Do not turn to mediums or seek out spiritists, for you will be defiled by them. I am the LORD your God.

[32]" 'Rise in the presence of the aged, show respect for the elderly and revere your God. I am the LORD.

[33]" 'When an alien lives with you in your land, do not ill-treat him. [34]The alien living with you must be treated as one of your native-born. Love him as yourself, for you were aliens in Egypt. I am the LORD your God.

[35]" 'Do not use dishonest standards when measuring length, weight or quantity. [36]Use honest scales and honest weights, an honest ephah[c] and an honest hin.[d] I am the LORD your God, who brought you out of Egypt.

[37]" 'Keep all my decrees and all my laws and follow them. I am the LORD.' "

---

b23 Hebrew *uncircumcised*   *c36* An ephah was a dry measure.   *d36* A hin was a liquid measure.

Punishments for Sin

20 The LORD said to Moses, ²"Say to the Israelites: 'Any Israelite or any alien living in Israel who gives*ᵃ* any of his children to Molech must be put to death. The people of the community are to stone him. ³I will set my face against that man and I will cut him off from his people; for by giving his children to Molech, he has defiled my sanctuary and profaned my holy name. ⁴If the people of the community close their eyes when that man gives one of his children to Molech and they fail to put him to death, ⁵I will set my face against that man and his family and will cut off from their people both him and all who follow him in prostituting themselves to Molech.

⁶"'I will set my face against the person who turns to mediums and spiritists to prostitute himself by following them, and I will cut him off from his people.

⁷"'Consecrate yourselves and be holy, because I am the LORD your God. ⁸Keep my decrees and follow them. I am the LORD, who makes you holy.*ᵇ*

⁹"'If anyone curses his father or mother, he must be put to death. He has cursed his father or his mother, and his blood will be on his own head.

¹⁰"'If a man commits adultery with another man's wife—with the wife of his neighbour—both the adulterer and the adulteress must be put to death.

¹¹"'If a man sleeps with his father's wife, he has dishonoured his father. Both the man and the woman must be put to death; their blood will be on their own heads.

¹²"'If a man sleeps with his daughter-in-law, both of them must be put to death. What they have done is a perversion; their blood will be on their own heads.

¹³"'If a man lies with a man as one lies with a woman, both of them have done what is detestable. They must be put to death; their blood will be on their own heads.

¹⁴"'If a man marries both a woman and her mother, it is wicked. Both he and they must be burned in the fire, so that no wickedness will be among you.

¹⁵"'If a man has sexual relations with an animal, he must be put to death, and you must kill the animal.

¹⁶"'If a woman approaches an animal to have sexual relations with it, kill both the woman and the animal. They must be put to death; their blood will be on their own heads.

¹⁷"'If a man marries his sister, the daughter of either his father or his mother, and they have sexual relations, it is a disgrace. They must be cut off before the eyes of their people. He has dishonoured his sister and will be held responsible.

¹⁸"'If a man lies with a woman during her monthly period and has sexual relations with her, he has exposed the source of her flow, and she has also uncovered it. Both of them must be cut off from their people.

¹⁹"'Do not have sexual relations with the sister of either your mother or your father, for that would dishonour a close relative; both of you would be held responsible.

²⁰"'If a man sleeps with his aunt, he has dishonoured his uncle. They will be held responsible; they will die childless.

²¹"'If a man marries his brother's wife, it is an act of impurity; he has dishonoured his brother. They will be childless.

²²"'Keep all my decrees and laws and follow them, so that the land where I am bringing you to live may not vomit you out. ²³You must not live according to the customs of the nations I am going to drive out before you. Because they did all these things, I abhorred them. ²⁴But I said to you, "You will possess their land; I will give it to you as an inheritance, a land flowing with milk and honey." I am the LORD your God, who has set you apart from the nations.

²⁵"'You must therefore make a distinction between clean and unclean animals and between unclean and clean birds. Do not defile yourselves by any animal or bird or anything that moves along the ground—those which I have set apart as

---

*ᵃ*2 Or *sacrifices*; also in verses 3 and 4   *ᵇ*8 Or *who sanctifies you*; or *who sets you apart as holy* unclean for you. [26]You are to be holy to me[c] because I, the LORD, am holy, and I have set you apart from the nations to be my own.

[27]"'A man or woman who is a medium or spiritist among you must be put to death. You are to stone them; their blood will be on their own heads.'"

Rules for Priests

21 The LORD said to Moses, "Speak to the priests, the sons of Aaron, and say to them: 'A priest must not make himself ceremonially unclean for any of his people who die, [2]except for a close relative, such as his mother or father, his son or daughter, his brother, [3]or an unmarried sister who is dependent on him since she has no husband—for her he may make himself unclean. [4]He must not make himself unclean for people related to him by marriage,[a] and so defile himself.

[5]"'Priests must not shave their heads or shave off the edges of their beards or cut their bodies. [6]They must be holy to their God and must not profane the name of their God. Because they present the offerings made to the LORD by fire, the food of their God, they are to be holy.

[7]"'They must not marry women defiled by prostitution or divorced from their husbands, because priests are holy to their God. [8]Regard them as holy, because they offer up the food of your God. Consider them holy, because I the LORD am holy—I who make you holy.[b]

[9]"'If a priest's daughter defiles herself by becoming a prostitute, she disgraces her father; she must be burned in the fire.

[10]"'The high priest, the one among his brothers who has had the anointing oil poured on his head and who has been ordained to wear the priestly garments, must not let his hair become unkempt[c] or tear his clothes. [11]He must not enter a place where there is a dead body. He must not make himself unclean, even for his father or mother, [12]nor leave the sanctuary of his God or desecrate it, because he has been dedicated by the anointing oil of his God. I am the LORD.

[13]"'The woman he marries must be a virgin. [14]He must not marry a widow, a divorced woman, or a woman defiled by prostitution, but only a virgin from his own people, [15]so that he will not defile his offspring among his people. I am the LORD, who makes him holy.'"[d]

[16]The LORD said to Moses, [17]"Say to Aaron: 'For the generations to come none of your descendants who has a defect may come near to offer the food of his God. [18]No man who has any defect may come near: no man who is blind or lame, disfigured or deformed; [19]no man with a crippled foot or hand, [20]or who is hunchbacked or dwarfed, or who has any eye defect, or who has festering or running sores or damaged testicles. [21]No descendant of Aaron the priest who has any defect is to come near to present the offerings made to the LORD by fire. He has a defect; he must not come near to offer the food of his God. [22]He may eat the most holy food of his God, as well as the holy food; [23]yet because of his defect, he must not go near the curtain or approach the altar, and so desecrate my sanctuary. I am the LORD, who makes them holy.'"[e]

[24]So Moses told this to Aaron and his sons and to all the Israelites.

22 The LORD said to Moses, [2]"Tell Aaron and his sons to treat with respect the sacred offerings the Israelites consecrate to me, so that they will not profane my holy name. I am the LORD.

[3]"Say to them: 'For the generations to come, if any of your descendants is ceremonially unclean and yet comes near the sacred offerings that the Israelites consecrate to the LORD, that person must be cut off from my presence. I am the LORD.

[4]"'If a descendant of Aaron has an infectious skin disease[a] or a bodily

---

[c]26 Or *be my holy ones*
[a]4 Or *unclean as a leader among his people*   [b]8 Or *who sanctify you*; or *who set you apart as holy*
[c]10 Or *not uncover his head*   [d]15 Or *who sanctifies him*; or *who sets him apart as holy*
[e]23 Or *who sanctifies them*; or *who sets them apart as holy*
[a]4 Traditionally *leprosy*; the Hebrew word was used for various diseases affecting the skin—not necessarily leprosy.

discharge, he may not eat the sacred offerings until he is cleansed. He will also be unclean if he touches something defiled by a corpse or by anyone who has an emission of semen, [5]or if he touches any crawling thing that makes him unclean, or any person who makes him unclean, whatever the uncleanness may be. [6]The one who touches any such thing will be unclean till evening. He must not eat any of the sacred offerings unless he has bathed himself with water. [7]When the sun goes down, he will be clean, and after that he may eat the sacred offerings, for they are his food. [8]He must not eat anything found dead or torn by wild animals, and so become unclean through it. I am the LORD.

[9]"'The priests are to keep my requirements so that they do not become guilty and die for treating them with contempt. I am the LORD, who makes them holy.[b]

[10]"'No-one outside a priest's family may eat the sacred offering, nor may the guest of a priest or his hired worker eat it. [11]But if a priest buys a slave with money, or if a slave is born in his household, that slave may eat his food. [12]If a priest's daughter marries anyone other than a priest, she may not eat any of the sacred contributions. [13]But if a priest's daughter becomes a widow or is divorced, yet has no children, and she returns to live in her father's house as in her youth, she may eat of her father's food. No unauthorised person, however, may eat any of it.

[14]"'If anyone eats a sacred offering by mistake, he must make restitution to the priest for the offering and add a fifth of the value to it. [15]The priests must not desecrate the sacred offerings the Israelites present to the LORD [16]by allowing them to eat the sacred offerings and so bring upon them guilt requiring payment. I am the LORD, who makes them holy.'"

Unacceptable Sacrifices

[17]The LORD said to Moses, [18]"Speak to Aaron and his sons and to all the Israelites and say to them: 'If any of you—either an Israelite or an alien living in Israel—presents a gift for a burnt offering to the LORD, either to fulfil a vow or as a freewill offering, [19]you must present a male without defect from the cattle, sheep or goats in order that it may be accepted on your behalf. [20]Do not bring anything with a defect, because it will not be accepted on your behalf. [21]When anyone brings from the herd or flock a fellowship offering[c] to the LORD to fulfil a special vow or as a freewill offering, it must be without defect or blemish to be acceptable. [22]Do not offer to the LORD the blind, the injured or the maimed, or anything with warts or festering or running sores. Do not place any of these on the altar as an offering made to the LORD by fire. [23]You may, however, present as a freewill offering an ox[d] or a sheep that is deformed or stunted, but it will not be accepted in fulfilment of a vow. [24]You must not offer to the LORD an animal whose testicles are bruised, crushed, torn or cut. You must not do this in your own land, [25]and you must not accept such animals from the hand of a foreigner and offer them as the food of your God. They will not be accepted on your behalf, because they are deformed and have defects.'"

[26]The LORD said to Moses, [27]"When a calf, a lamb or a goat is born, it is to remain with its mother for seven days. From the eighth day on, it will be acceptable as an offering made to the LORD by fire. [28]Do not slaughter a cow or a sheep and its young on the same day.

[29]"When you sacrifice a thank-offering to the LORD, sacrifice it in such a way that it will be accepted on your behalf. [30]It must be eaten that same day; leave none of it till morning. I am the LORD.

[31]"Keep my commands and follow them. I am the LORD. [32]Do not profane my holy name. I must be acknowledged as holy by the Israelites. I am the LORD, who makes[e] you holy[f] [33]and who brought you out of Egypt to be your God. I am the LORD."

---

[b]9 Or *who sanctifies them*; or *who sets them apart as holy*; also in verse 16   [c]21 Traditionally *peace offering*
[d]23 The Hebrew word can include both male and female.   [e]32 Or *made*
[f]32 Or *who sanctifies you*; or *who sets you apart as holy*

23
The LORD said to Moses, ²"Speak to the Israelites and say to them: 'These are my appointed feasts, the appointed feasts of the LORD, which you are to proclaim as sacred assemblies.

The Sabbath

³"'There are six days when you may work, but the seventh day is a Sabbath of rest, a day of sacred assembly. You are not to do any work; wherever you live, it is a Sabbath to the LORD.

The Passover and Unleavened Bread

⁴"'These are the LORD's appointed feasts, the sacred assemblies you are to proclaim at their appointed times: ⁵The LORD's Passover begins at twilight on the fourteenth day of the first month. ⁶On the fifteenth day of that month the LORD's Feast of Unleavened Bread begins; for seven days you must eat bread made without yeast. ⁷On the first day hold a sacred assembly and do no regular work. ⁸For seven days present an offering made to the LORD by fire. And on the seventh day hold a sacred assembly and do no regular work.'"

Firstfruits

⁹The LORD said to Moses, ¹⁰"Speak to the Israelites and say to them: 'When you enter the land I am going to give you and you reap its harvest, bring to the priest a sheaf of the first grain you harvest. ¹¹He is to wave the sheaf before the LORD so that it will be accepted on your behalf; the priest is to wave it on the day after the Sabbath. ¹²On the day you wave the sheaf, you must sacrifice as a burnt offering to the LORD a lamb a year old without defect, ¹³together with its grain offering of two-tenths of an ephah^a of fine flour mixed with oil—an offering made to the LORD by fire, a pleasing aroma—and its drink offering of a quarter of a hin^b of wine. ¹⁴You must not eat any bread, or roasted or new grain, until the very day you bring this offering to your God. This is to be a lasting ordinance for the generations to come, wherever you live.

Feast of Weeks

¹⁵"'From the day after the Sabbath, the day you brought the sheaf of the wave offering, count off seven full weeks. ¹⁶Count off fifty days up to the day after the seventh Sabbath, and then present an offering of new grain to the LORD. ¹⁷From wherever you live, bring two loaves made of two-tenths of an ephah of fine flour, baked with yeast, as a wave offering of firstfruits to the LORD. ¹⁸Present with this bread seven male lambs, each a year old and without defect, one young bull and two rams. They will be a burnt offering to the LORD, together with their grain offerings and drink offerings—an offering made by fire, an aroma pleasing to the LORD. ¹⁹Then sacrifice one male goat for a sin offering and two lambs, each a year old, for a fellowship offering.^{c} ²⁰The priest is to wave the two lambs before the LORD as a wave offering, together with the bread of the firstfruits. They are a sacred offering to the LORD for the priest. ²¹On that same day you are to proclaim a sacred assembly and do no regular work. This is to be a lasting ordinance for the generations to come, wherever you live.

²²"'When you reap the harvest of your land, do not reap to the very edges of your field or gather the gleanings of your harvest. Leave them for the poor and the alien. I am the LORD your God.'"

Feast of Trumpets

²³The LORD said to Moses, ²⁴"Say to the Israelites: 'On the first day of the seventh month you are to have a day of rest, a sacred assembly commemorated with trumpet blasts. ²⁵Do no regular work, but present an offering made to the LORD by fire.'"

---

^{a}13 That is, probably about 7½ pints (about 4.5 litres); also in verse 17
^{b}13 That is, probably about 1½ pints (about 1 litre) ^{c}19 Traditionally *peace offering*

Day of Atonement

26The LORD said to Moses, 27"The tenth day of this seventh month is the Day of Atonement. Hold a sacred assembly and deny yourselves,d and present an offering made to the LORD by fire. 28Do no work on that day, because it is the Day of Atonement, when atonement is made for you before the LORD your God. 29Anyone who does not deny himself on that day must be cut off from his people. 30I will destroy from among his people anyone who does any work on that day. 31You shall do no work at all. This is to be a lasting ordinance for the generations to come, wherever you live. 32It is a sabbath of rest for you, and you must deny yourselves. From the evening of the ninth day of the month until the following evening you are to observe your sabbath."

Feast of Tabernacles

33The LORD said to Moses, 34"Say to the Israelites: 'On the fifteenth day of the seventh month the LORD's Feast of Tabernacles begins, and it lasts for seven days. 35The first day is a sacred assembly; do no regular work. 36For seven days present offerings made to the LORD by fire, and on the eighth day hold a sacred assembly and present an offering made to the LORD by fire. It is the closing assembly; do no regular work.

37("'These are the LORD's appointed feasts, which you are to proclaim as sacred assemblies for bringing offerings made to the LORD by fire—the burnt offerings and grain offerings, sacrifices and drink offerings required for each day. 38These offerings are in addition to those for the LORD's Sabbaths ande in addition to your gifts and whatever you have vowed and all the freewill offerings you give to the LORD.)

39"'So beginning with the fifteenth day of the seventh month, after you have gathered the crops of the land, celebrate the festival to the LORD for seven days; the first day is a day of rest, and the eighth day also is a day of rest. 40On the first day you are to take choice fruit from the trees, and palm fronds, leafy branches and poplars, and rejoice before the LORD your God for seven days. 41Celebrate this as a festival to the LORD for seven days each year. This is to be a lasting ordinance for the generations to come; celebrate it in the seventh month. 42Live in booths for seven days: All native-born Israelites are to live in booths 43so that your descendants will know that I made the Israelites live in booths when I brought them out of Egypt. I am the LORD your God.'"

44So Moses announced to the Israelites the appointed feasts of the LORD.

Oil and Bread Set Before the LORD

24 The LORD said to Moses, 2"Command the Israelites to bring you clear oil of pressed olives for the light so that the lamps may be kept burning continually. 3Outside the curtain of the Testimony in the Tent of Meeting, Aaron is to tend the lamps before the LORD from evening till morning, continually. This is to be a lasting ordinance for the generations to come. 4The lamps on the pure gold lampstand before the LORD must be tended continually.

5"Take fine flour and bake twelve loaves of bread, using two-tenths of an ephaha for each loaf. 6Set them in two rows, six in each row, on the table of pure gold before the LORD. 7Along each row put some pure incense as a memorial portion to represent the bread and to be an offering made to the LORD by fire. 8This bread is to be set out before the LORD regularly, Sabbath after Sabbath, on behalf of the Israelites, as a lasting covenant. 9It belongs to Aaron and his sons, who are to eat it in a holy place, because it is a most holy part of their regular share of the offerings made to the LORD by fire."

---

d27 Or *and fast*; also in verses 29 and 32
e38 Or *These feasts are in addition to the LORD's Sabbaths, and these offerings are*
a5 That is, probably about 7½ pints (about 4.5 litres)

A Blasphemer Stoned

¹⁰Now the son of an Israelite mother and an Egyptian father went out among the Israelites, and a fight broke out in the camp between him and an Israelite. ¹¹The son of the Israelite woman blasphemed the Name with a curse; so they brought him to Moses. (His mother's name was Shelomith, the daughter of Dibri the Danite.) ¹²They put him in custody until the will of the LORD should be made clear to them.

¹³Then the LORD said to Moses: ¹⁴"Take the blasphemer outside the camp. All those who heard him are to lay their hands on his head, and the entire assembly is to stone him. ¹⁵Say to the Israelites: 'If anyone curses his God, he will be held responsible; ¹⁶anyone who blasphemes the name of the LORD must be put to death. The entire assembly must stone him. Whether an alien or native-born, when he blasphemes the Name, he must be put to death.

¹⁷"'If anyone takes the life of a human being, he must be put to death. ¹⁸Anyone who takes the life of someone's animal must make restitution—life for life. ¹⁹If anyone injures his neighbour, whatever he has done must be done to him: ²⁰fracture for fracture, eye for eye, tooth for tooth. As he has injured the other, so he is to be injured. ²¹Whoever kills an animal must make restitution, but whoever kills a man must be put to death. ²²You are to have the same law for the alien and the native-born. I am the LORD your God.'"

²³Then Moses spoke to the Israelites, and they took the blasphemer outside the camp and stoned him. The Israelites did as the LORD commanded Moses.

The Sabbath Year

25 The LORD said to Moses on Mount Sinai, ²"Speak to the Israelites and say to them: 'When you enter the land I am going to give you, the land itself must observe a sabbath to the LORD. ³For six years sow your fields, and for six years prune your vineyards and gather their crops. ⁴But in the seventh year the land is to have a sabbath of rest, a sabbath to the LORD. Do not sow your fields or prune your vineyards. ⁵Do not reap what grows of itself or harvest the grapes of your untended vines. The land is to have a year of rest. ⁶Whatever the land yields during the sabbath year will be food for you—for yourself, your manservant and maidservant, and the hired worker and temporary resident who live among you, ⁷as well as for your livestock and the wild animals in your land. Whatever the land produces may be eaten.

The Year of Jubilee

⁸"'Count off seven sabbaths of years— seven times seven years—so that the seven sabbaths of years amount to a period of forty-nine years. ⁹Then have the trumpet sounded everywhere on the tenth day of the seventh month; on the Day of Atonement sound the trumpet throughout your land. ¹⁰Consecrate the fiftieth year and proclaim liberty throughout the land to all its inhabitants. It shall be a jubilee for you; each one of you is to return to his family property and each to his own clan. ¹¹The fiftieth year shall be a jubilee for you; do not sow and do not reap what grows of itself or harvest the untended vines. ¹²For it is a jubilee and is to be holy for you; eat only what is taken directly from the fields.

¹³"'In this Year of Jubilee everyone is to return to his own property.

¹⁴"'If you sell land to one of your countrymen or buy any from him, do not take advantage of each other. ¹⁵You are to buy from your countryman on the basis of the number of years since the Jubilee. And he is to sell to you on the basis of the number of years left for harvesting crops. ¹⁶When the years are many, you are to increase the price, and when the years are few, you are to decrease the price, because what he is really selling you is the number of crops. ¹⁷Do not take advantage of each other, but fear your God. I am the LORD your God.

¹⁸"'Follow my decrees and be careful to obey my laws, and you will live safely in the land. ¹⁹Then the land will yield its

fruit, and you will eat your fill and live there in safety. ²⁰You may ask, "What will we eat in the seventh year if we do not plant or harvest our crops?" ²¹I will send you such a blessing in the sixth year that the land will yield enough for three years. ²²While you plant during the eighth year, you will eat from the old crop and will continue to eat from it until the harvest of the ninth year comes in.

²³"'The land must not be sold permanently, because the land is mine and you are but aliens and my tenants. ²⁴Throughout the country that you hold as a possession, you must provide for the redemption of the land.

²⁵"'If one of your countrymen becomes poor and sells some of his property, his nearest relative is to come and redeem what his countryman has sold. ²⁶If, however, a man has no-one to redeem it for him but he himself prospers and acquires sufficient means to redeem it, ²⁷he is to determine the value for the years since he sold it and refund the balance to the man to whom he sold it; he can then go back to his own property. ²⁸But if he does not acquire the means to repay him, what he sold will remain in the possession of the buyer until the Year of Jubilee. It will be returned in the Jubilee, and he can then go back to his property.

²⁹"'If a man sells a house in a walled city, he retains the right of redemption a full year after its sale. During that time he may redeem it. ³⁰If it is not redeemed before a full year has passed, the house in the walled city shall belong permanently to the buyer and his descendants. It is not to be returned in the Jubilee. ³¹But houses in villages without walls round them are to be considered as open country. They can be redeemed, and they are to be returned in the Jubilee.

³²"'The Levites always have the right to redeem their houses in the Levitical towns, which they possess. ³³So the property of the Levites is redeemable—that is, a house sold in any town they hold—and is to be returned in the Jubilee, because the houses in the towns of the Levites are their property among the Israelites. ³⁴But the pasture-land belonging to their towns must not be sold; it is their permanent possession.

³⁵"'If one of your countrymen becomes poor and is unable to support himself among you, help him as you would an alien or a temporary resident, so that he can continue to live among you. ³⁶Do not take interest of any kind^a from him, but fear your God, so that your countryman may continue to live among you. ³⁷You must not lend him money at interest or sell him food at a profit. ³⁸I am the LORD your God, who brought you out of Egypt to give you the land of Canaan and to be your God.

³⁹"'If one of your countrymen becomes poor among you and sells himself to you, do not make him work as a slave. ⁴⁰He is to be treated as a hired worker or a temporary resident among you; he is to work for you until the Year of Jubilee. ⁴¹Then he and his children are to be released, and he will go back to his own clan and to the property of his forefathers. ⁴²Because the Israelites are my servants, whom I brought out of Egypt, they must not be sold as slaves. ⁴³Do not rule over them ruthlessly, but fear your God.

⁴⁴"'Your male and female slaves are to come from the nations around you; from them you may buy slaves. ⁴⁵You may also buy some of the temporary residents living among you and members of their clans born in your country, and they will become your property. ⁴⁶You can will them to your children as inherited property and can make them slaves for life, but you must not rule over your fellow Israelites ruthlessly.

⁴⁷"'If an alien or a temporary resident among you becomes rich and one of your countrymen becomes poor and sells himself to the alien living among you or to a member of the alien's clan, ⁴⁸he retains the right of redemption after he has sold himself. One of his relatives may redeem him: ⁴⁹An uncle or a cousin or any blood-relative in his clan may redeem him. Or if he prospers, he may redeem himself. ⁵⁰He

---

^a36 Or *take excessive interest*; similarly in verse 37

and his buyer are to count the time from the year he sold himself up to the Year of Jubilee. The price for his release is to be based on the rate paid to a hired man for that number of years. [51]If many years remain, he must pay for his redemption a larger share of the price paid for him. [52]If only a few years remain until the Year of Jubilee, he is to compute that and pay for his redemption accordingly. [53]He is to be treated as a man hired from year to year; you must see to it that his owner does not rule over him ruthlessly.

[54]"Even if he is not redeemed in any of these ways, he and his children are to be released in the Year of Jubilee, [55]for the Israelites belong to me as servants. They are my servants, whom I brought out of Egypt. I am the LORD your God.

Reward for Obedience

26 "'Do not make idols or set up an image or a sacred stone for yourselves, and do not place a carved stone in your land to bow down before it. I am the LORD your God.

[2]"'Observe my Sabbaths and have reverence for my sanctuary. I am the LORD.

[3]"'If you follow my decrees and are careful to obey my commands, [4]I will send you rain in its season, and the ground will yield its crops and the trees of the field their fruit. [5]Your threshing will continue until grape harvest and the grape harvest will continue until planting, and you will eat all the food you want and live in safety in your land.

[6]"'I will grant peace in the land, and you will lie down and no-one will make you afraid. I will remove savage beasts from the land, and the sword will not pass through your country. [7]You will pursue your enemies, and they will fall by the sword before you. [8]Five of you will chase a hundred, and a hundred of you will chase ten thousand, and your enemies will fall by the sword before you.

[9]"'I will look on you with favour and make you fruitful and increase your numbers, and I will keep my covenant with you. [10]You will still be eating last year's harvest when you will have to move it out to make room for the new. [11]I will put my dwelling-place[a] among you, and I will not abhor you. [12]I will walk among you and be your God, and you will be my people. [13]I am the LORD your God, who brought you out of Egypt so that you would no longer be slaves to the Egyptians; I broke the bars of your yoke and enabled you to walk with heads held high.

Punishment for Disobedience

[14]"'But if you will not listen to me and carry out all these commands, [15]and if you reject my decrees and abhor my laws and fail to carry out all my commands and so violate my covenant, [16]then I will do this to you: I will bring upon you sudden terror, wasting diseases and fever that will destroy your sight and drain away your life. You will plant seed in vain, because your enemies will eat it. [17]I will set my face against you so that you will be defeated by your enemies; those who hate you will rule over you, and you will flee even when no-one is pursuing you.

[18]"'If after all this you will not listen to me, I will punish you for your sins seven times over. [19]I will break down your stubborn pride and make the sky above you like iron and the ground beneath you like bronze. [20]Your strength will be spent in vain, because your soil will not yield its crops, nor will the trees of the land yield their fruit.

[21]"'If you remain hostile towards me and refuse to listen to me, I will multiply your afflictions seven times over, as your sins deserve. [22]I will send wild animals against you, and they will rob you of your children, destroy your cattle and make you so few in number that your roads will be deserted.

[23]"'If in spite of these things you do not accept my correction but continue to be hostile towards me, [24]I myself will be hostile towards you and will afflict you for your sins seven times over. [25]And I will bring the sword upon you to avenge the

---

[a]11 Or *my tabernacle*

breaking of the covenant. When you withdraw into your cities, I will send a plague among you, and you will be given into enemy hands. 26When I cut off your supply of bread, ten women will be able to bake your bread in one oven, and they will dole out the bread by weight. You will eat, but you will not be satisfied.

27"If in spite of this you still do not listen to me but continue to be hostile towards me, 28then in my anger I will be hostile towards you, and I myself will punish you for your sins seven times over. 29You will eat the flesh of your sons and the flesh of your daughters. 30I will destroy your high places, cut down your incense altars and pile your dead bodies on the lifeless forms of your idols, and I will abhor you. 31I will turn your cities into ruins and lay waste your sanctuaries, and I will take no delight in the pleasing aroma of your offerings. 32I will lay waste the land, so that your enemies who live there will be appalled. 33I will scatter you among the nations and will draw out my sword and pursue you. Your land will be laid waste, and your cities will lie in ruins. 34Then the land will enjoy its sabbath years all the time that it lies desolate and you are in the country of your enemies; then the land will rest and enjoy its sabbaths. 35All the time that it lies desolate, the land will have the rest it did not have during the sabbaths you lived in it.

36"As for those of you who are left, I will make their hearts so fearful in the lands of their enemies that the sound of a wind-blown leaf will put them to flight. They will run as though fleeing from the sword, and they will fall, even though no-one is pursuing them. 37They will stumble over one another as though fleeing from the sword, even though no-one is pursuing them. So you will not be able to stand before your enemies. 38You will perish among the nations; the land of your enemies will devour you. 39Those of you who are left will waste away in the lands of their enemies because of their sins; also

because of their fathers' sins they will waste away.

40"But if they will confess their sins and the sins of their fathers—their treachery against me and their hostility towards me, 41which made me hostile towards them so that I sent them into the land of their enemies—then when their uncircumcised hearts are humbled and they pay for their sin, 42I will remember my covenant with Jacob and my covenant with Isaac and my covenant with Abraham, and I will remember the land. 43For the land will be deserted by them and will enjoy its sabbaths while it lies desolate without them. They will pay for their sins because they rejected my laws and abhorred my decrees. 44Yet in spite of this, when they are in the land of their enemies, I will not reject them or abhor them so as to destroy them completely, breaking my covenant with them. I am the LORD their God. 45But for their sake I will remember the covenant with their ancestors whom I brought out of Egypt in the sight of the nations to be their God. I am the LORD.'"

46These are the decrees, the laws and the regulations that the LORD established on Mount Sinai between himself and the Israelites through Moses.

Redeeming What Is the LORD's

27 The LORD said to Moses, 2"Speak to the Israelites and say to them: 'If anyone makes a special vow to dedicate persons to the LORD by giving equivalent values, 3set the value of a male between the ages of twenty and sixty at fifty shekels*a* of silver, according to the sanctuary shekel;*b* 4and if it is a female, set her value at thirty shekels.*c* 5If it is a person between the ages of five and twenty, set the value of a male at twenty shekels*d* and of a female at ten shekels.*e* 6If it is a person between one month and five years, set the value of a male at five shekels*f* of silver and that of a female at three shekels*g* of

a3 That is, about 1¼ pounds (about 0.6 kilogram); also in verse 16
b3 That is, about ⅖ ounce (about 11.5 grams); also in verse 25   *c4* That is, about 12 ounces (about 0.3 kilogram)
d5 That is, about 8 ounces (about 0.2 kilogram)   *e5* That is, about 4 ounces (about 115 grams); also in verse 7
f6 That is, about 2 ounces (about 55 grams)   *g6* That is, about 1¼ ounces (about 35 grams)

silver. [7]If it is a person sixty years old or more, set the value of a male at fifteen shekels[h] and of a female at ten shekels. [8]If anyone making the vow is too poor to pay the specified amount, he is to present the person to the priest, who will set the value for him according to what the man making the vow can afford.

[9]"If what he vowed is an animal that is acceptable as an offering to the LORD, such an animal given to the LORD becomes holy. [10]He must not exchange it or substitute a good one for a bad one, or a bad one for a good one; if he should substitute one animal for another, both it and the substitute become holy. [11]If what he vowed is a ceremonially unclean animal—one that is not acceptable as an offering to the LORD—the animal must be presented to the priest, [12]who will judge its quality as good or bad. Whatever value the priest then sets, that is what it will be. [13]If the owner wishes to redeem the animal, he must add a fifth to its value.

[14]"If a man dedicates his house as something holy to the LORD, the priest will judge its quality as good or bad. Whatever value the priest then sets, so it will remain. [15]If the man who dedicates his house redeems it, he must add a fifth to its value, and the house will again become his.

[16]"If a man dedicates to the LORD part of his family land, its value is to be set according to the amount of seed required for it—fifty shekels of silver to a homer[i] of barley seed. [17]If he dedicates his field during the Year of Jubilee, the value that has been set remains. [18]But if he dedicates his field after the Jubilee, the priest will determine the value according to the number of years that remain until the next Year of Jubilee, and its set value will be reduced. [19]If the man who dedicates the field wishes to redeem it, he must add a fifth to its value, and the field will again become his. [20]If, however, he does not redeem the field, or if he has sold it to someone else, it can never be redeemed. [21]When the field is released in the Jubilee, it will become holy, like a field devoted to the LORD; it will become the property of the priests.[j]

[22]"If a man dedicates to the LORD a field he has bought, which is not part of his family land, [23]the priest will determine its value up to the Year of Jubilee, and the man must pay its value on that day as something holy to the LORD. [24]In the Year of Jubilee the field will revert to the person from whom he bought it, the one whose land it was. [25]Every value is to be set according to the sanctuary shekel, twenty gerahs to the shekel.

[26]"No-one, however, may dedicate the firstborn of an animal, since the firstborn already belongs to the LORD; whether an ox[k] or a sheep, it is the LORD's. [27]If it is one of the unclean animals, he may buy it back at its set value, adding a fifth of the value to it. If he does not redeem it, it is to be sold at its set value.

[28]"But nothing that a man owns and devotes[l] to the LORD—whether man or animal or family land—may be sold or redeemed; everything so devoted is most holy to the LORD.

[29]"No person devoted to destruction[m] may be ransomed; he must be put to death.

[30]"A tithe of everything from the land, whether grain from the soil or fruit from the trees, belongs to the LORD; it is holy to the LORD. [31]If a man redeems any of his tithe, he must add a fifth of the value to it. [32]The entire tithe of the herd and flock—every tenth animal that passes under the shepherd's rod—will be holy to the LORD. [33]He must not pick out the good from the bad or make any substitution. If he does make a substitution, both the animal and its substitute become holy and cannot be redeemed.'"

[34]These are the commands the LORD gave Moses on Mount Sinai for the Israelites.

---

[h]7 That is, about 6 ounces (about 170 grams)   [i]16 That is, probably about 6 bushels (about 220 litres)
[j]21 Or *priest*   [k]26 The Hebrew word can include both male and female.
[l]28 The Hebrew term refers to the irrevocable giving over of things or persons to the LORD.
[m]29 The Hebrew term refers to the irrevocable giving over of things or persons to the LORD, often by totally destroying them.

Numbers

The Census

1 The LORD spoke to Moses in the Tent of Meeting in the Desert of Sinai on the first day of the second month of the second year after the Israelites came out of Egypt. He said: 2"Take a census of the whole Israelite community by their clans and families, listing every man by name, one by one. 3You and Aaron are to number by their divisions all the men in Israel twenty years old or more who are able to serve in the army. 4One man from each tribe, each the head of his family, is to help you. 5These are the names of the men who are to assist you:

from Reuben, Elizur son of Shedeur;
6from Simeon, Shelumiel son of Zurishaddai;
7from Judah, Nahshon son of Amminadab;
8from Issachar, Nethanel son of Zuar;
9from Zebulun, Eliab son of Helon;
10from the sons of Joseph:
from Ephraim, Elishama son of Ammihud;
from Manasseh, Gamaliel son of Pedahzur;
11from Benjamin, Abidan son of Gideoni;
12from Dan, Ahiezer son of Ammishaddai;
13from Asher, Pagiel son of Ocran;
14from Gad, Eliasaph son of Deuel;
15from Naphtali, Ahira son of Enan."

16These were the men appointed from the community, the leaders of their ancestral tribes. They were the heads of the clans of Israel.

17Moses and Aaron took these men whose names had been given, 18and they called the whole community together on the first day of the second month. The people indicated their ancestry by their clans and families, and the men twenty years old or more were listed by name, one by one, 19as the LORD commanded Moses. And so he counted them in the Desert of Sinai:

20From the descendants of Reuben the firstborn son of Israel:
All the men twenty years old or more who were able to serve in the army were listed by name, one by one, according to the records of their clans and families. 21The number from the tribe of Reuben was 46,500.

22From the descendants of Simeon:
All the men twenty years old or more who were able to serve in the army were counted and listed by name, one by one, according to the records of their clans and families. 23The number from the tribe of Simeon was 59,300.

24From the descendants of Gad:
All the men twenty years old or more who were able to serve in the army were listed by name, according to the records of their clans and families. 25The number from the tribe of Gad was 45,650.

²⁶From the descendants of Judah:

All the men twenty years old or more who were able to serve in the army were listed by name, according to the records of their clans and families. ²⁷The number from the tribe of Judah was 74,600.

²⁸From the descendants of Issachar:

All the men twenty years old or more who were able to serve in the army were listed by name, according to the records of their clans and families. ²⁹The number from the tribe of Issachar was 54,400.

³⁰From the descendants of Zebulun:

All the men twenty years old or more who were able to serve in the army were listed by name, according to the records of their clans and families. ³¹The number from the tribe of Zebulun was 57,400.

³²From the sons of Joseph:

From the descendants of Ephraim:

All the men twenty years old or more who were able to serve in the army were listed by name, according to the records of their clans and families. ³³The number from the tribe of Ephraim was 40,500.

³⁴From the descendants of Manasseh:

All the men twenty years old or more who were able to serve in the army were listed by name, according to the records of their clans and families. ³⁵The number from the tribe of Manasseh was 32,200.

³⁶From the descendants of Benjamin:

All the men twenty years old or more who were able to serve in the army were listed by name, according to the records of their clans and families. ³⁷The number from the tribe of Benjamin was 35,400.

³⁸From the descendants of Dan:

All the men twenty years old or more who were able to serve in the army were listed by name, according to the records of their clans and families. ³⁹The number from the tribe of Dan was 62,700.

⁴⁰From the descendants of Asher:

All the men twenty years old or more who were able to serve in the army were listed by name, according to the records of their clans and families. ⁴¹The number from the tribe of Asher was 41,500.

⁴²From the descendants of Naphtali:

All the men twenty years old or more who were able to serve in the army were listed by name, according to the records of their clans and families. ⁴³The number from the tribe of Naphtali was 53,400.

⁴⁴These were the men counted by Moses and Aaron and the twelve leaders of Israel, each one representing his family. ⁴⁵All the Israelites twenty years old or more who were able to serve in Israel's army were counted according to their families. ⁴⁶The total number was 603,550.

⁴⁷The families of the tribe of Levi, however, were not counted along with the others. ⁴⁸The LORD had said to Moses: ⁴⁹"You must not count the tribe of Levi or include them in the census of the other Israelites. ⁵⁰Instead, appoint the Levites to be in charge of the tabernacle of the Testimony—over all its furnishings and everything belonging to it. They are to carry the tabernacle and all its furnishings; they are to take care of it and encamp round it. ⁵¹Whenever the tabernacle is to move, the Levites are to take it down, and whenever the tabernacle is to be set up, the Levites shall do it. Anyone else who goes near it shall be put to death. ⁵²The Israelites are to set up their tents by divisions, each man in his own camp under his own standard. ⁵³The Levites, however, are to set up their tents round the tabernacle of the Testimony so that wrath will not fall on the Israelite community. The Levites are to be responsible for the care of the tabernacle of the Testimony."

⁵⁴The Israelites did all this just as the LORD commanded Moses.

The Arrangement of the Tribal Camps

2 The LORD said to Moses and Aaron: ²"The Israelites are to camp round the Tent of Meeting some distance from it, each man under his standard with the banners of his family."

³On the east, towards the sunrise, the divisions of the camp of Judah are to encamp under their standard. The leader of the people of Judah is Nahshon son of Amminadab. ⁴His division numbers 74,600.

⁵The tribe of Issachar will camp next to them. The leader of the people of Issachar is Nethanel son of Zuar. ⁶His division numbers 54,400.

⁷The tribe of Zebulun will be next. The leader of the people of Zebulun is Eliab son of Helon. ⁸His division numbers 57,400.

⁹All the men assigned to the camp of Judah, according to their divisions, number 186,400. They will set out first.

¹⁰On the south will be the divisions of the camp of Reuben under their standard. The leader of the people of Reuben is Elizur son of Shedeur. ¹¹His division numbers 46,500.

¹²The tribe of Simeon will camp next to them. The leader of the people of Simeon is Shelumiel son of Zurishaddai. ¹³His division numbers 59,300.

¹⁴The tribe of Gad will be next. The leader of the people of Gad is Eliasaph son of Deuel.*ᵃ* ¹⁵His division numbers 45,650.

¹⁶All the men assigned to the camp of Reuben, according to their divisions, number 151,450. They will set out second.

¹⁷Then the Tent of Meeting and the camp of the Levites will set out in the middle of the camps. They will set out in the same order as they encamp, each in his own place under his standard.

¹⁸On the west will be the divisions of the camp of Ephraim under their standard. The leader of the people of Ephraim is Elishama son of Ammihud. ¹⁹His division numbers 40,500.

²⁰The tribe of Manasseh will be next to them. The leader of the people of Manasseh is Gamaliel son of Pedahzur. ²¹His division numbers 32,200.

²²The tribe of Benjamin will be next. The leader of the people of Benjamin is Abidan son of Gideoni. ²³His division numbers 35,400.

²⁴All the men assigned to the camp of Ephraim, according to their divisions, number 108,100. They will set out third.

²⁵On the north will be the divisions of the camp of Dan, under their standard. The leader of the people of Dan is Ahiezer son of Ammishaddai. ²⁶His division numbers 62,700.

²⁷The tribe of Asher will camp next to them. The leader of the people of Asher is Pagiel son of Ocran. ²⁸His division numbers 41,500.

²⁹The tribe of Naphtali will be next. The leader of the people of Naphtali is Ahira son of Enan. ³⁰His division numbers 53,400.

³¹All the men assigned to the camp of Dan number 157,600. They will set out last, under their standards.

³²These are the Israelites, counted according to their families. All those in the camps, by their divisions, number 603,550. ³³The Levites, however, were not counted along with the other

ᵃ14 Many manuscripts of the Masoretic Text, Samaritan Pentateuch and Vulgate (see also Num. 1:14); most manuscripts of the Masoretic Text *Reuel*

Israelites, as the LORD commanded Moses.

³⁴So the Israelites did everything the LORD commanded Moses; that is the way they encamped under their standards, and that is the way they set out, each with his clan and family.

The Levites

3 This is the account of the family of Aaron and Moses at the time the LORD talked with Moses on Mount Sinai.

²The names of the sons of Aaron were Nadab the firstborn and Abihu, Eleazar and Ithamar. ³Those were the names of Aaron's sons, the anointed priests, who were ordained to serve as priests. ⁴Nadab and Abihu, however, fell dead before the LORD when they made an offering with unauthorised fire before him in the Desert of Sinai. They had no sons; so only Eleazar and Ithamar served as priests during the lifetime of their father Aaron.

⁵The LORD said to Moses, ⁶"Bring the tribe of Levi and present them to Aaron the priest to assist him. ⁷They are to perform duties for him and for the whole community at the Tent of Meeting by doing the work of the tabernacle. ⁸They are to take care of all the furnishings of the Tent of Meeting, fulfilling the obligations of the Israelites by doing the work of the tabernacle. ⁹Give the Levites to Aaron and his sons; they are the Israelites who are to be given wholly to him.ᵃ ¹⁰Appoint Aaron and his sons to serve as priests; anyone else who approaches the sanctuary must be put to death."

¹¹The LORD also said to Moses, ¹²"I have taken the Levites from among the Israelites in place of the first male offspring of every Israelite woman. The Levites are mine, ¹³for all the firstborn are mine. When I struck down all the firstborn in Egypt, I set apart for myself every firstborn in Israel, whether man or animal. They are to be mine. I am the LORD."

¹⁴The LORD said to Moses in the Desert of Sinai, ¹⁵"Count the Levites by their families and clans. Count every male a month old or more." ¹⁶So Moses counted them, as he was commanded by the word of the LORD.

¹⁷These were the names of the sons of Levi:

Gershon, Kohath and Merari.

¹⁸These were the names of the Gershonite clans:

Libni and Shimei.

¹⁹The Kohathite clans:

Amram, Izhar, Hebron and Uzziel.

²⁰The Merarite clans:

Mahli and Mushi.

These were the Levite clans, according to their families.

²¹To Gershon belonged the clans of the Libnites and Shimeites; these were the Gershonite clans. ²²The number of all the males a month old or more who were counted was 7,500. ²³The Gershonite clans were to camp on the west, behind the tabernacle. ²⁴The leader of the families of the Gershonites was Eliasaph son of Lael. ²⁵At the Tent of Meeting the Gershonites were responsible for the care of the tabernacle and tent, its coverings, the curtain at the entrance to the Tent of Meeting, ²⁶the curtains of the courtyard, the curtain at the entrance to the courtyard surrounding the tabernacle and altar, and the ropes—and everything related to their use.

²⁷To Kohath belonged the clans of the Amramites, Izharites, Hebronites and Uzzielites; these were the Kohathite clans. ²⁸The number of all the males a month old or more was 8,600.ᵇ The Kohathites were responsible for the care of the sanctuary. ²⁹The Kohathite clans were to camp on the south side of the tabernacle. ³⁰The leader of the families of the Kohathite clans was Elizaphan son of Uzziel. ³¹They were responsible for the

---

ᵃ9 Most manuscripts of the Masoretic Text; some manuscripts of the Masoretic Text, Samaritan Pentateuch and Septuagint (see also Num. 8:16) *to me*   ᵇ28 Hebrew; some Septuagint manuscripts *8,300* care of the ark, the table, the lampstand, the altars, the articles of the sanctuary used in ministering, the curtain, and everything related to their use. [32]The chief leader of the Levites was Eleazar son of Aaron, the priest. He was appointed over those who were responsible for the care of the sanctuary.

[33]To Merari belonged the clans of the Mahlites and the Mushites; these were the Merarite clans. [34]The number of all the males a month old or more who were counted was 6,200. [35]The leader of the families of the Merarite clans was Zuriel son of Abihail; they were to camp on the north side of the tabernacle. [36]The Merarites were appointed to take care of the frames of the tabernacle, its crossbars, posts, bases, all its equipment, and everything related to their use, [37]as well as the posts of the surrounding courtyard with their bases, tent pegs and ropes.

[38]Moses and Aaron and his sons were to camp to the east of the tabernacle, towards the sunrise, in front of the Tent of Meeting. They were responsible for the care of the sanctuary on behalf of the Israelites. Anyone else who approached the sanctuary was to be put to death.

[39]The total number of Levites counted at the LORD's command by Moses and Aaron according to their clans, including every male a month old or more, was 22,000.

[40]The LORD said to Moses, "Count all the firstborn Israelite males who are a month old or more and make a list of their names. [41]Take the Levites for me in place of all the firstborn of the Israelites, and the livestock of the Levites in place of all the firstborn of the livestock of the Israelites. I am the LORD." [42]So Moses counted all the firstborn of the Israelites, as the LORD commanded him. [43]The total number of firstborn males

a month old or more, listed by name, was 22,273.

[44]The LORD also said to Moses, [45]"Take the Levites in place of all the firstborn of Israel, and the livestock of the Levites in place of their livestock. The Levites are to be mine. I am the LORD. [46]To redeem the 273 firstborn Israelites who exceed the number of the Levites, [47]collect five shekels[c] for each one, according to the sanctuary shekel, which weighs twenty gerahs. [48]Give the money for the redemption of the additional Israelites to Aaron and his sons."

[49]So Moses collected the redemption money from those who exceeded the number redeemed by the Levites. [50]From the firstborn of the Israelites he collected silver weighing 1,365 shekels,[d] according to the sanctuary shekel. [51]Moses gave the redemption money to Aaron and his sons, as he was commanded by the word of the LORD.

The Kohathites

4 The LORD said to Moses and Aaron: [2]"Take a census of the Kohathite branch of the Levites by their clans and families. [3]Count all the men from thirty to fifty years of age who come to serve in the work in the Tent of Meeting.

[4]"This is the work of the Kohathites in the Tent of Meeting: the care of the most holy things. [5]When the camp is to move, Aaron and his sons are to go in and take down the shielding curtain and cover the ark of the Testimony with it. [6]Then they are to cover this with hides of sea cows,[a] spread a cloth of solid blue over that and put the poles in place.

[7]"Over the table of the Presence they are to spread a blue cloth and put on it the plates, dishes and bowls, and the jars for drink offerings; the bread that is continually there is to remain on it. [8]Over these they are to spread a scarlet cloth, cover that with hides of sea cows and put its poles in place.

[9]"They are to take a blue cloth and

---

[c]47 That is, about 2 ounces (about 55 grams)   [d]50 That is, about 35 pounds (about 15.5 kilograms)
[a]6 That is, large aquatic mammals; also elsewhere in this chapter

cover the lampstand that is for light, together with its lamps, its wick trimmers and trays, and all its jars for the oil used to supply it. [10]Then they are to wrap it and all its accessories in a covering of hides of sea cows and put it on a carrying frame.

[11]"Over the gold altar they are to spread a blue cloth and cover that with hides of sea cows and put its poles in place.

[12]"They are to take all the articles used for ministering in the sanctuary, wrap them in a blue cloth, cover that with hides of sea cows and put them on a carrying frame.

[13]"They are to remove the ashes from the bronze altar and spread a purple cloth over it. [14]Then they are to place on it all the utensils used for ministering at the altar, including the firepans, meat forks, shovels and sprinkling bowls. Over it they are to spread a covering of hides of sea cows and put its poles in place.

[15]"After Aaron and his sons have finished covering the holy furnishings and all the holy articles, and when the camp is ready to move, the Kohathites are to come to do the carrying. But they must not touch the holy things or they will die. The Kohathites are to carry those things that are in the Tent of Meeting.

[16]"Eleazar son of Aaron, the priest, is to have charge of the oil for the light, the fragrant incense, the regular grain offering and the anointing oil. He is to be in charge of the entire tabernacle and everything in it, including its holy furnishings and articles."

[17]The LORD said to Moses and Aaron, [18]"See that the Kohathite tribal clans are not cut off from the Levites. [19]So that they may live and not die when they come near the most holy things, do this for them: Aaron and his sons are to go into the sanctuary and assign to each man his work and what he is to carry. [20]But the Kohathites must not go in to look at the holy things, even for a moment, or they will die."

The Gershonites

[21]The LORD said to Moses, [22]"Take a census also of the Gershonites by their families and clans. [23]Count all the men from thirty to fifty years of age who come to serve in the work at the Tent of Meeting.

[24]"This is the service of the Gershonite clans as they work and carry burdens: [25]They are to carry the curtains of the tabernacle, the Tent of Meeting, its covering and the outer covering of hides of sea cows, the curtains for the entrance to the Tent of Meeting, [26]the curtains of the courtyard surrounding the tabernacle and altar, the curtain for the entrance, the ropes and all the equipment used in its service. The Gershonites are to do all that needs to be done with these things. [27]All their service, whether carrying or doing other work, is to be done under the direction of Aaron and his sons. You shall assign to them as their responsibility all they are to carry. [28]This is the service of the Gershonite clans at the Tent of Meeting. Their duties are to be under the direction of Ithamar son of Aaron, the priest.

The Merarites

[29]"Count the Merarites by their clans and families. [30]Count all the men from thirty to fifty years of age who come to serve in the work at the Tent of Meeting. [31]This is their duty as they perform service at the Tent of Meeting: to carry the frames of the tabernacle, its crossbars, posts and bases, [32]as well as the posts of the surrounding courtyard with their bases, tent pegs, ropes, all their equipment and everything related to their use. Assign to each man the specific things he is to carry. [33]This is the service of the Merarite clans as they work at the Tent of Meeting under the direction of Ithamar son of Aaron, the priest."

The Numbering of the Levite Clans

[34]Moses, Aaron and the leaders of the community counted the Kohathites by their clans and families. [35]All the men from thirty to fifty years of age who came to serve in the work in the Tent of

Meeting, [36]counted by clans, were 2,750. [37]This was the total of all those in the Kohathite clans who served in the Tent of Meeting. Moses and Aaron counted them according to the LORD's command through Moses.

[38]The Gershonites were counted by their clans and families. [39]All the men from thirty to fifty years of age who came to serve in the work at the Tent of Meeting, [40]counted by their clans and families, were 2,630. [41]This was the total of those in the Gershonite clans who served at the Tent of Meeting. Moses and Aaron counted them according to the LORD's command.

[42]The Merarites were counted by their clans and families. [43]All the men from thirty to fifty years of age who came to serve in the work at the Tent of Meeting, [44]counted by their clans, were 3,200. [45]This was the total of those in the Merarite clans. Moses and Aaron counted them according to the LORD's command through Moses.

[46]So Moses, Aaron and the leaders of Israel counted all the Levites by their clans and families. [47]All the men from thirty to fifty years of age who came to do the work of serving and carrying the Tent of Meeting [48]numbered 8,580. [49]At the LORD's command through Moses, each was assigned his work and told what to carry.

Thus they were counted, as the LORD commanded Moses.

The Purity of the Camp

5 The LORD said to Moses, [2]"Command the Israelites to send away from the camp anyone who has an infectious skin disease[a] or a discharge of any kind, or who is ceremonially unclean because of a dead body. [3]Send away male and female alike; send them outside the camp so that they will not defile their camp, where I dwell among them." [4]The Israelites did this; they sent them outside the camp. They did just as the LORD had instructed Moses.

Restitution for Wrongs

[5]The LORD said to Moses, [6]"Say to the Israelites: 'When a man or woman wrongs another in any way[b] and so is unfaithful to the LORD, that person is guilty [7]and must confess the sin he has committed. He must make full restitution for his wrong, add one fifth to it and give it all to the person he has wronged. [8]But if that person has no close relative to whom restitution can be made for the wrong, the restitution belongs to the LORD and must be given to the priest, along with the ram with which atonement is made for him. [9]All the sacred contributions the Israelites bring to a priest will belong to him. [10]Each man's sacred gifts are his own, but what he gives to the priest will belong to the priest.'"

The Test for an Unfaithful Wife

[11]Then the LORD said to Moses, [12]"Speak to the Israelites and say to them: 'If a man's wife goes astray and is unfaithful to him [13]by sleeping with another man, and this is hidden from her husband and her impurity is undetected (since there is no witness against her and she has not been caught in the act), [14]and if feelings of jealousy come over her husband and he suspects his wife and she is impure—or if he is jealous and suspects her even though she is not impure— [15]then he is to take his wife to the priest. He must also take an offering of a tenth of an ephah[c] of barley flour on her behalf. He must not pour oil on it or put incense on it, because it is a grain offering for jealousy, a reminder offering to draw attention to guilt.

[16]" 'The priest shall bring her and make her stand before the LORD. [17]Then he shall take some holy water in a clay jar and put some dust from the tabernacle floor into the water. [18]After the priest has made the woman stand before the LORD, he shall loosen her hair and place in her hands the reminder offering, the grain offering for jealousy, while he himself holds the bitter water that brings a curse. [19]Then the priest

---

a2 Traditionally *leprosy*; the Hebrew word was used for various diseases affecting the skin—not necessarily leprosy.
b6 Or *woman commits any wrong common to mankind*   *c15* That is, probably about 4 pints (about 2 litres)

shall put the woman under oath and say to her, "If no other man has slept with you and you have not gone astray and become impure while married to your husband, may this bitter water that brings a curse not harm you. 20But if you have gone astray while married to your husband and you have defiled yourself by sleeping with a man other than your husband" —21here the priest is to put the woman under this curse of the oath—"may the LORD cause your people to curse and denounce you when he causes your thigh to waste away and your abdomen to swell.*d* 22May this water that brings a curse enter your body so that your abdomen swells and your thigh wastes away."*e*

" 'Then the woman is to say, "Amen. So be it."

23" 'The priest is to write these curses on a scroll and then wash them off into the bitter water. 24He shall make the woman drink the bitter water that brings a curse, and this water will enter her and cause bitter suffering. 25The priest is to take from her hands the grain offering for jealousy, wave it before the LORD and bring it to the altar. 26The priest is then to take a handful of the grain offering as a memorial offering and burn it on the altar; after that, he is to make the woman drink the water. 27If she has defiled herself and been unfaithful to her husband, then when she is made to drink the water that brings a curse, it will go into her and cause bitter suffering; her abdomen will swell and her thigh waste away,*f* and she will become accursed among her people. 28If, however, the woman has not defiled herself and is free from impurity, she will be cleared of guilt and will be able to have children.

29" 'This, then, is the law of jealousy when a woman goes astray and defiles herself while married to her husband, 30or when feelings of jealousy come over a man because he suspects his wife. The priest is to make her stand before the LORD and is to apply this entire law to her. 31The

husband will be innocent of any wrong-doing, but the woman will bear the consequences of her sin.' "

The Nazirite

6 The LORD said to Moses, 2"Speak to the Israelites and say to them: 'If a man or woman wants to make a special vow, a vow of separation to the LORD as a Nazirite, 3he must abstain from wine and other fermented drink and must not drink vinegar made from wine or from other fermented drink. He must not drink grape juice or eat grapes or raisins. 4As long as he is a Nazirite, he must not eat anything that comes from the grapevine, not even the seeds or skins.

5" 'During the entire period of his vow of separation no razor may be used on his head. He must be holy until the period of his separation to the LORD is over; he must let the hair of his head grow long. 6Throughout the period of his separation to the LORD he must not go near a dead body. 7Even if his own father or mother or brother or sister dies, he must not make himself ceremonially unclean on account of them, because the symbol of his separation to God is on his head. 8Throughout the period of his separation he is consecrated to the LORD.

9" 'If someone dies suddenly in his presence, thus defiling the hair he has dedicated, he must shave his head on the day of his cleansing—the seventh day. 10Then on the eighth day he must bring two doves or two young pigeons to the priest at the entrance to the Tent of Meeting. 11The priest is to offer one as a sin offering and the other as a burnt offering to make atonement for him because he sinned by being in the presence of the dead body. That same day he is to consecrate his head. 12He must dedicate himself to the LORD for the period of his separation and must bring a year-old male lamb as a guilt offering. The previous days do not count,

---

d21 Or causes you to have a miscarrying womb and barrenness
e22 Or body and cause you to be barren and have a miscarrying womb
f27 Or suffering; she will have barrenness and a miscarrying womb

because he became defiled during his separation.

13" 'Now this is the law for the Nazirite when the period of his separation is over. He is to be brought to the entrance to the Tent of Meeting. 14There he is to present his offerings to the LORD: a year-old male lamb without defect for a burnt offering, a year-old ewe lamb without defect for a sin offering, a ram without defect for a fellowship offering,*a* 15together with their grain offerings and drink offerings, and a basket of bread made without yeast—cakes made of fine flour mixed with oil, and wafers spread with oil.

16" 'The priest is to present them before the LORD and make the sin offering and the burnt offering. 17He is to present the basket of unleavened bread and is to sacrifice the ram as a fellowship offering to the LORD, together with its grain offering and drink offering.

18" 'Then at the entrance to the Tent of Meeting, the Nazirite must shave off the hair that he dedicated. He is to take the hair and put it in the fire that is under the sacrifice of the fellowship offering.

19" 'After the Nazirite has shaved off the hair of his dedication, the priest is to place in his hands a boiled shoulder of the ram, and a cake and a wafer from the basket, both made without yeast. 20The priest shall then wave them before the LORD as a wave offering; they are holy and belong to the priest, together with the breast that was waved and the thigh that was presented. After that, the Nazirite may drink wine.

21" 'This is the law of the Nazirite who vows his offering to the LORD in accordance with his separation, in addition to whatever else he can afford. He must fulfil the vow he has made, according to the law of the Nazirite.' "

The Priestly Blessing

22The LORD said to Moses, 23"Tell Aaron and his sons, 'This is how you are to bless the Israelites. Say to them:

24" ' "The LORD bless you
　　and keep you;
25the LORD make his face shine upon you
　　and be gracious to you;
26the LORD turn his face towards you
　　and give you peace." '

27"So they will put my name on the Israelites, and I will bless them."

Offerings at the Dedication of the Tabernacle

7 When Moses finished setting up the tabernacle, he anointed it and consecrated it and all its furnishings. He also anointed and consecrated the altar and all its utensils. 2Then the leaders of Israel, the heads of families who were the tribal leaders in charge of those who were counted, made offerings. 3They brought as their gifts before the LORD six covered carts and twelve oxen—an ox from each leader and a cart from every two. These they presented before the tabernacle.

4The LORD said to Moses, 5"Accept these from them, that they may be used in the work at the Tent of Meeting. Give them to the Levites as each man's work requires."

6So Moses took the carts and oxen and gave them to the Levites. 7He gave two carts and four oxen to the Gershonites, as their work required, 8and he gave four carts and eight oxen to the Merarites, as their work required. They were all under the direction of Ithamar son of Aaron, the priest. 9But Moses did not give any to the Kohathites, because they were to carry on their shoulders the holy things, for which they were responsible.

10When the altar was anointed, the leaders brought their offerings for its dedication and presented them before the altar. 11For the LORD had said to Moses, "Each day one leader is to bring his offering for the dedication of the altar."

12The one who brought his offering on the first day was Nahshon son of Amminadab of the tribe of Judah.

---

a14 Traditionally *peace offering*; also in verses 17 and 18

[13]His offering was one silver plate weighing a hundred and thirty shekels,[a] and one silver sprinkling bowl weighing seventy shekels,[b] both according to the sanctuary shekel, each filled with fine flour mixed with oil as a grain offering; [14]one gold dish weighing ten shekels,[c] filled with incense; [15]one young bull, one ram and one male lamb a year old, for a burnt offering; [16]one male goat for a sin offering; [17]and two oxen, five rams, five male goats and five male lambs a year old, to be sacrificed as a fellowship offering.[d] This was the offering of Nahshon son of Amminadab.

[18]On the second day Nethanel son of Zuar, the leader of Issachar, brought his offering.

[19]The offering he brought was one silver plate weighing a hundred and thirty shekels, and one silver sprinkling bowl weighing seventy shekels, both according to the sanctuary shekel, each filled with fine flour mixed with oil as a grain offering; [20]one gold dish weighing ten shekels, filled with incense; [21]one young bull, one ram and one male lamb a year old, for a burnt offering; [22]one male goat for a sin offering; [23]and two oxen, five rams, five male goats and five male lambs a year old, to be sacrificed as a fellowship offering. This was the offering of Nethanel son of Zuar.

[24]On the third day, Eliab son of Helon, the leader of the people of Zebulun, brought his offering.

[25]His offering was one silver plate weighing a hundred and thirty shekels, and one silver sprinkling bowl weighing seventy shekels, both according to the sanctuary shekel, each filled with fine flour mixed with oil as a grain offering; [26]one gold dish weighing ten shekels, filled with incense; [27]one young bull, one ram and one male lamb a year old, for a burnt offering; [28]one male goat for a sin offering; [29]and two oxen, five rams, five male goats and five male lambs a year old, to be sacrificed as a fellowship offering. This was the offering of Eliab son of Helon.

[30]On the fourth day Elizur son of Shedeur, the leader of the people of Reuben, brought his offering.

[31]His offering was one silver plate weighing a hundred and thirty shekels, and one silver sprinkling bowl weighing seventy shekels, both according to the sanctuary shekel, each filled with fine flour mixed with oil as a grain offering; [32]one gold dish weighing ten shekels, filled with incense; [33]one young bull, one ram and one male lamb a year old, for a burnt offering; [34]one male goat for a sin offering; [35]and two oxen, five rams, five male goats and five male lambs a year old, to be sacrificed as a fellowship offering. This was the offering of Elizur son of Shedeur.

[36]On the fifth day Shelumiel son of Zurishaddai, the leader of the people of Simeon, brought his offering.

[37]His offering was one silver plate weighing a hundred and thirty shekels, and one silver sprinkling bowl weighing seventy shekels, both according to the sanctuary shekel, each filled with fine flour mixed with oil as a grain offering; [38]one gold dish weighing ten shekels, filled with incense; [39]one young bull, one ram and one male lamb a year old, for a burnt offering; [40]one male goat for a sin offering; [41]and two oxen, five rams, five male goats and five male lambs a year old, to be sacrificed as a fellowship offering. This was the offering of Shelumiel son of Zurishaddai.

---

[a]13 That is, about 3¼ pounds (about 1.5 kilograms); also elsewhere in this chapter
[b]13 That is, about 1¾ pounds (about 0.8 kilogram); also elsewhere in this chapter
[c]14 That is, about 4 ounces (about 115 grams); also elsewhere in this chapter
[d]17 Traditionally *peace offering*; also elsewhere in this chapter

[42]On the sixth day Eliasaph son of Deuel, the leader of the people of Gad, brought his offering.

[43]His offering was one silver plate weighing a hundred and thirty shekels, and one silver sprinkling bowl weighing seventy shekels, both according to the sanctuary shekel, each filled with fine flour mixed with oil as a grain offering; [44]one gold dish weighing ten shekels, filled with incense; [45]one young bull, one ram and one male lamb a year old, for a burnt offering; [46]one male goat for a sin offering; [47]and two oxen, five rams, five male goats and five male lambs a year old, to be sacrificed as a fellowship offering. This was the offering of Eliasaph son of Deuel.

[48]On the seventh day Elishama son of Ammihud, the leader of the people of Ephraim, brought his offering.

[49]His offering was one silver plate weighing a hundred and thirty shekels, and one silver sprinkling bowl weighing seventy shekels, both according to the sanctuary shekel, each filled with fine flour mixed with oil as a grain offering; [50]one gold dish weighing ten shekels, filled with incense; [51]one young bull, one ram and one male lamb a year old, for a burnt offering; [52]one male goat for a sin offering; [53]and two oxen, five rams, five male goats and five male lambs a year old, to be sacrificed as a fellowship offering. This was the offering of Elishama son of Ammihud.

[54]On the eighth day Gamaliel son of Pedahzur, the leader of the people of Manasseh, brought his offering.

[55]His offering was one silver plate weighing a hundred and thirty shekels, and one silver sprinkling bowl weighing seventy shekels, both according to the sanctuary shekel, each filled with fine flour mixed with oil as a grain offering; [56]one gold dish weighing ten shekels, filled with incense; [57]one young bull, one ram and one male lamb a year old, for a burnt

offering; [58]one male goat for a sin offering; [59]and two oxen, five rams, five male goats and five male lambs a year old, to be sacrificed as a fellowship offering. This was the offering of Gamaliel son of Pedahzur.

[60]On the ninth day Abidan son of Gideoni, the leader of the people of Benjamin, brought his offering.

[61]His offering was one silver plate weighing a hundred and thirty shekels, and one silver sprinkling bowl weighing seventy shekels, both according to the sanctuary shekel, each filled with fine flour mixed with oil as a grain offering; [62]one gold dish weighing ten shekels, filled with incense; [63]one young bull, one ram and one male lamb a year old, for a burnt offering; [64]one male goat for a sin offering; [65]and two oxen, five rams, five male goats and five male lambs a year old, to be sacrificed as a fellowship offering. This was the offering of Abidan son of Gideoni.

[66]On the tenth day Ahiezer son of Ammishaddai, the leader of the people of Dan, brought his offering.

[67]His offering was one silver plate weighing a hundred and thirty shekels, and one silver sprinkling bowl weighing seventy shekels, both according to the sanctuary shekel, each filled with fine flour mixed with oil as a grain offering; [68]one gold dish weighing ten shekels, filled with incense; [69]one young bull, one ram and one male lamb a year old, for a burnt offering; [70]one male goat for a sin offering; [71]and two oxen, five rams, five male goats and five male lambs a year old, to be sacrificed as a fellowship offering. This was the offering of Ahiezer son of Ammishaddai.

[72]On the eleventh day Pagiel son of Ocran, the leader of the people of Asher, brought his offering.

[73]His offering was one silver plate weighing a hundred and thirty shekels, and one silver sprinkling

bowl weighing seventy shekels, both according to the sanctuary shekel, each filled with fine flour mixed with oil as a grain offering; 74one gold dish weighing ten shekels, filled with incense; 75one young bull, one ram and one male lamb a year old, for a burnt offering; 76one male goat for a sin offering; 77and two oxen, five rams, five male goats and five male lambs a year old, to be sacrificed as a fellowship offering. This was the offering of Pagiel son of Ocran.

78On the twelfth day Ahira son of Enan, the leader of the people of Naphtali, brought his offering.

79His offering was one silver plate weighing a hundred and thirty shekels, and one silver sprinkling bowl weighing seventy shekels, both according to the sanctuary shekel, each filled with fine flour mixed with oil as a grain offering; 80one gold dish weighing ten shekels, filled with incense; 81one young bull, one ram and one male lamb a year old, for a burnt offering; 82one male goat for a sin offering; 83and two oxen, five rams, five male goats and five male lambs a year old, to be sacrificed as a fellowship offering. This was the offering of Ahira son of Enan.

84These were the offerings of the Israelite leaders for the dedication of the altar when it was anointed: twelve silver plates, twelve silver sprinkling bowls and twelve gold dishes. 85Each silver plate weighed a hundred and thirty shekels, and each sprinkling bowl seventy shekels. Altogether, the silver dishes weighed two thousand four hundred shekels,e according to the sanctuary shekel. 86The twelve gold dishes filled with incense weighed ten shekels each, according to the sanctuary shekel. Altogether, the gold dishes weighed a hundred and twenty shekels.f 87The total number of animals for the burnt offering came to twelve young bulls,

twelve rams and twelve male lambs a year old, together with their grain offering. Twelve male goats were used for the sin offering. 88The total number of animals for the sacrifice of the fellowship offering came to twenty-four oxen, sixty rams, sixty male goats and sixty male lambs a year old. These were the offerings for the dedication of the altar after it was anointed.

89When Moses entered the Tent of Meeting to speak with the LORD, he heard the voice speaking to him from between the two cherubim above the atonement cover on the ark of the Testimony. And he spoke with him.

Setting Up the Lamps

8 The LORD said to Moses, 2"Speak to Aaron and say to him, 'When you set up the seven lamps, they are to light the area in front of the lampstand.'"

3Aaron did so; he set up the lamps so that they faced forward on the lampstand, just as the LORD commanded Moses. 4This is how the lampstand was made: It was made of hammered gold—from its base to its blossoms. The lampstand was made exactly like the pattern the LORD had shown Moses.

The Setting Apart of the Levites

5The LORD said to Moses: 6"Take the Levites from among the other Israelites and make them ceremonially clean. 7To purify them, do this: Sprinkle the water of cleansing on them; then make them shave their whole bodies and wash their clothes, and so purify themselves. 8Make them take a young bull with its grain offering of fine flour mixed with oil; then you are to take a second young bull for a sin offering. 9Bring the Levites to the front of the Tent of Meeting and assemble the whole Israelite community. 10You are to bring the Levites before the LORD, and the Israelites are to lay their hands on them. 11Aaron is to present the Levites before

e85 That is, about 61 pounds (about 28 kilograms)
f86 That is, about 3 pounds (about 1.4 kilograms)

the LORD as a wave offering from the Israelites, so that they may be ready to do the work of the LORD.

¹²"After the Levites lay their hands on the heads of the bulls, use the one for a sin offering to the LORD and the other for a burnt offering, to make atonement for the Levites. ¹³Make the Levites stand in front of Aaron and his sons and then present them as a wave offering to the LORD. ¹⁴In this way you are to set the Levites apart from the other Israelites, and the Levites will be mine.

¹⁵"After you have purified the Levites and presented them as a wave offering, they are to come to do their work at the Tent of Meeting. ¹⁶They are the Israelites who are to be given wholly to me. I have taken them as my own in place of the firstborn, the first male offspring from every Israelite woman. ¹⁷Every firstborn male in Israel, whether man or animal, is mine. When I struck down all the firstborn in Egypt, I set them apart for myself. ¹⁸And I have taken the Levites in place of all the firstborn sons in Israel. ¹⁹Of all the Israelites, I have given the Levites as gifts to Aaron and his sons to do the work at the Tent of Meeting on behalf of the Israelites and to make atonement for them so that no plague will strike the Israelites when they go near the sanctuary."

²⁰Moses, Aaron and the whole Israelite community did with the Levites just as the LORD commanded Moses. ²¹The Levites purified themselves and washed their clothes. Then Aaron presented them as a wave offering before the LORD and made atonement for them to purify them. ²²After that, the Levites came to do their work at the Tent of Meeting under the supervision of Aaron and his sons. They did with the Levites just as the LORD commanded Moses.

²³The LORD said to Moses, ²⁴"This applies to the Levites: Men twenty-five years old or more shall come to take part in the work at the Tent of Meeting, ²⁵but at the age of fifty, they must retire from their regular service and work no longer. ²⁶They may assist their brothers in performing their duties at the Tent of Meeting, but they themselves must not do the work. This, then, is how you are to assign the responsibilities of the Levites."

The Passover

9 The LORD spoke to Moses in the Desert of Sinai in the first month of the second year after they came out of Egypt. He said, ²"Make the Israelites celebrate the Passover at the appointed time. ³Celebrate it at the appointed time, at twilight on the fourteenth day of this month, in accordance with all its rules and regulations."

⁴So Moses told the Israelites to celebrate the Passover, ⁵and they did so in the Desert of Sinai at twilight on the fourteenth day of the first month. The Israelites did everything just as the LORD commanded Moses.

⁶But some of them could not celebrate the Passover on that day because they were ceremonially unclean on account of a dead body. So they came to Moses and Aaron that same day ⁷and said to Moses, "We have become unclean because of a dead body, but why should we be kept from presenting the LORD's offering with the other Israelites at the appointed time?"

⁸Moses answered them, "Wait until I find out what the LORD commands concerning you."

⁹Then the LORD said to Moses, ¹⁰"Tell the Israelites: 'When any of you or your descendants are unclean because of a dead body or are away on a journey, they may still celebrate the LORD's Passover. ¹¹They are to celebrate it on the fourteenth day of the second month at twilight. They are to eat the lamb, together with unleavened bread and bitter herbs. ¹²They must not leave any of it till morning or break any of its bones. When they celebrate the Passover, they must follow all the regulations. ¹³But if a man who is ceremonially clean and not on a journey fails to celebrate the Passover, that person must be cut off from his people because he did not present the LORD's offering at the appointed time. That man will bear the consequences of his sin.

¹⁴"'An alien living among you who

wants to celebrate the LORD's Passover must do so in accordance with its rules and regulations. You must have the same regulations for the alien and the native-born.'"

The Cloud Above the Tabernacle

15On the day the tabernacle, the Tent of the Testimony, was set up, the cloud covered it. From evening till morning the cloud above the tabernacle looked like fire. 16That is how it continued to be; the cloud covered it, and at night it looked like fire. 17Whenever the cloud lifted from above the Tent, the Israelites set out; wherever the cloud settled, the Israelites encamped. 18At the LORD's command the Israelites set out, and at his command they encamped. As long as the cloud stayed over the tabernacle, they remained in camp. 19When the cloud remained over the tabernacle a long time, the Israelites obeyed the LORD's order and did not set out. 20Sometimes the cloud was over the tabernacle only a few days; at the LORD's command they would encamp, and then at his command they would set out. 21Sometimes the cloud stayed only from evening till morning, and when it lifted in the morning, they set out. Whether by day or by night, whenever the cloud lifted, they set out. 22Whether the cloud stayed over the tabernacle for two days or a month or a year, the Israelites would remain in camp and not set out; but when it lifted, they would set out. 23At the LORD's command they encamped, and at the LORD's command they set out. They obeyed the LORD's order, in accordance with his command through Moses.

The Silver Trumpets

10 The LORD said to Moses: 2"Make two trumpets of hammered silver, and use them for calling the community together and for having the camps set out. 3When both are sounded, the whole community is to assemble before you at the entrance to the Tent of Meeting. 4If only one is sounded, the leaders—the heads of the clans of Israel—are to assemble before you. 5When a trumpet blast is sounded, the tribes camping on the east are to set out. 6At the sounding of a second blast, the camps on the south are to set out. The blast will be the signal for setting out. 7To gather the assembly, blow the trumpets, but not with the same signal.

8"The sons of Aaron, the priests, are to blow the trumpets. This is to be a lasting ordinance for you and the generations to come. 9When you go into battle in your own land against an enemy who is oppressing you, sound a blast on the trumpets. Then you will be remembered by the LORD your God and rescued from your enemies. 10Also at your times of rejoicing—your appointed feasts and New Moon festivals—you are to sound the trumpets over your burnt offerings and fellowship offerings,[a] and they will be a memorial for you before your God. I am the LORD your God."

The Israelites Leave Sinai

11On the twentieth day of the second month of the second year, the cloud lifted from above the tabernacle of the Testimony. 12Then the Israelites set out from the Desert of Sinai and travelled from place to place until the cloud came to rest in the Desert of Paran. 13They set out, this first time, at the LORD's command through Moses.

14The divisions of the camp of Judah went first, under their standard. Nahshon son of Amminadab was in command. 15Nethanel son of Zuar was over the division of the tribe of Issachar, 16and Eliab son of Helon was over the division of the tribe of Zebulun. 17Then the tabernacle was taken down, and the Gershonites and Merarites, who carried it, set out.

18The divisions of the camp of Reuben went next, under their standard. Elizur son of Shedeur was in command. 19Shelumiel son of Zurishaddai was over the division of the tribe of Simeon, 20and Eliasaph son of Deuel was over the

a10 Traditionally peace offerings

division of the tribe of Gad. [21]Then the Kohathites set out, carrying the holy things. The tabernacle was to be set up before they arrived.

[22]The divisions of the camp of Ephraim went next, under their standard. Elishama son of Ammihud was in command. [23]Gamaliel son of Pedahzur was over the division of the tribe of Manasseh, [24]and Abidan son of Gideoni was over the division of the tribe of Benjamin.

[25]Finally, as the rear guard for all the units, the divisions of the camp of Dan set out, under their standard. Ahiezer son of Ammishaddai was in command. [26]Pagiel son of Ocran was over the division of the tribe of Asher, [27]and Ahira son of Enan was over the division of the tribe of Naphtali. [28]This was the order of march for the Israelite divisions as they set out.

[29]Now Moses said to Hobab son of Reuel the Midianite, Moses' father-in-law, "We are setting out for the place about which the LORD said, 'I will give it to you.' Come with us and we will treat you well, for the LORD has promised good things to Israel."

[30]He answered, "No, I will not go; I am going back to my own land and my own people."

[31]But Moses said, "Please do not leave us. You know where we should camp in the desert, and you can be our eyes. [32]If you come with us, we will share with you whatever good things the LORD gives us."

[33]So they set out from the mountain of the LORD and travelled for three days. The ark of the covenant of the LORD went before them during those three days to find them a place to rest. [34]The cloud of the LORD was over them by day when they set out from the camp.

[35]Whenever the ark set out, Moses said,

"Rise up, O LORD!
    May your enemies be scattered;
    may your foes flee before you."

[36]Whenever it came to rest, he said,

"Return, O LORD,
    to the countless thousands of Israel."

Fire From the LORD

11

Now the people complained about their hardships in the hearing of the LORD, and when he heard them his anger was aroused. Then fire from the LORD burned among them and consumed some of the outskirts of the camp. [2]When the people cried out to Moses, he prayed to the LORD and the fire died down. [3]So that place was called Taberah,[a] because fire from the LORD had burned among them.

Quail From the LORD

[4]The rabble with them began to crave other food, and again the Israelites started wailing and said, "If only we had meat to eat! [5]We remember the fish we ate in Egypt at no cost—also the cucumbers, melons, leeks, onions and garlic. [6]But now we have lost our appetite; we never see anything but this manna!"

[7]The manna was like coriander seed and looked like resin. [8]The people went around gathering it, and then ground it in a hand mill or crushed it in a mortar. They cooked it in a pot or made it into cakes. And it tasted like something made with olive oil. [9]When the dew settled on the camp at night, the manna also came down.

[10]Moses heard the people of every family wailing, each at the entrance to his tent. The LORD became exceedingly angry, and Moses was troubled. [11]He asked the LORD, "Why have you brought this trouble on your servant? What have I done to displease you that you put the burden of all these people on me? [12]Did I conceive all these people? Did I give them birth? Why do you tell me to carry them in my arms, as a nurse carries an infant, to the land you promised on oath to their forefathers? [13]Where can I get meat for all these people? They keep wailing to me, 'Give us meat to eat!' [14]I cannot carry all these people by myself; the burden is too heavy for me. [15]If this is how you are going to treat me, put me to death right now—if I have found favour in your eyes—and do not let me face my own ruin."

---

[a]3 *Taberah* means *burning.*

[16]The LORD said to Moses: "Bring me seventy of Israel's elders who are known to you as leaders and officials among the people. Make them come to the Tent of Meeting, that they may stand there with you. [17]I will come down and speak with you there, and I will take of the Spirit that is on you and put the Spirit on them. They will help you carry the burden of the people so that you will not have to carry it alone.

[18]"Tell the people: 'Consecrate yourselves in preparation for tomorrow, when you will eat meat. The LORD heard you when you wailed, "If only we had meat to eat! We were better off in Egypt!" Now the LORD will give you meat, and you will eat it. [19]You will not eat it for just one day, or two days, or five, ten or twenty days, [20]but for a whole month—until it comes out of your nostrils and you loathe it—because you have rejected the LORD, who is among you, and have wailed before him, saying, "Why did we ever leave Egypt?"'"

[21]But Moses said, "Here I am among six hundred thousand men on foot, and you say, 'I will give them meat to eat for a whole month!' [22]Would they have enough if flocks and herds were slaughtered for them? Would they have enough if all the fish in the sea were caught for them?"

[23]The LORD answered Moses, "Is the LORD's arm too short? You will now see whether or not what I say will come true for you."

[24]So Moses went out and told the people what the LORD had said. He brought together seventy of their elders and made them stand round the Tent. [25]Then the LORD came down in the cloud and spoke with him, and he took of the Spirit that was on him and put the Spirit on the seventy elders. When the Spirit rested on them, they prophesied, but they did not do so again.[b]

[26]However, two men, whose names were Eldad and Medad, had remained in the camp. They were listed among the elders, but did not go out to the Tent. Yet the Spirit also rested on them, and they prophesied in the camp. [27]A young man ran and told Moses, "Eldad and Medad are prophesying in the camp."

[28]Joshua son of Nun, who had been Moses' assistant since youth, spoke up and said, "Moses, my lord, stop them!"

[29]But Moses replied, "Are you jealous for my sake? I wish that all the LORD's people were prophets and that the LORD would put his Spirit on them!" [30]Then Moses and the elders of Israel returned to the camp.

[31]Now a wind went out from the LORD and drove quail in from the sea. It brought them[c] down all around the camp to about three feet[d] above the ground, as far as a day's walk in any direction. [32]All that day and night and all the next day the people went out and gathered quail. No-one gathered less than ten homers.[e] Then they spread them out all around the camp. [33]But while the meat was still between their teeth and before it could be consumed, the anger of the LORD burned against the people, and he struck them with a severe plague. [34]Therefore the place was named Kibroth Hattaavah,[f] because there they buried the people who had craved other food.

[35]From Kibroth Hattaavah the people travelled to Hazeroth and stayed there.

Miriam and Aaron Oppose Moses

12 Miriam and Aaron began to talk against Moses because of his Cushite wife, for he had married a Cushite. [2]"Has the LORD spoken only through Moses?" they asked. "Hasn't he also spoken through us?" And the LORD heard this.

[3](Now Moses was a very humble man, more humble than anyone else on the face of the earth.)

[4]At once the LORD said to Moses, Aaron and Miriam, "Come out to the Tent of Meeting, all three of you." So the three of them came out. [5]Then the LORD came

---

b25 Or prophesied and continued to do so   c31 Or They flew   d31 Hebrew two cubits (about 0.9 metre)
e32 That is, probably about 60 bushels (about 2.2 kilolitres)   f34 Kibroth Hattaavah means graves of craving.

down in a pillar of cloud; he stood at the entrance to the Tent and summoned Aaron and Miriam. When both of them stepped forward, [6]he said, "Listen to my words:

"When a prophet of the LORD is among you,
   I reveal myself to him in visions,
   I speak to him in dreams.
[7]But this is not true of my servant Moses;
   he is faithful in all my house.
[8]With him I speak face to face,
   clearly and not in riddles;
   he sees the form of the LORD.
Why then were you not afraid
   to speak against my servant Moses?"

[9]The anger of the LORD burned against them, and he left them.

[10]When the cloud lifted from above the Tent, there stood Miriam—leprous,[a] like snow. Aaron turned towards her and saw that she had leprosy; [11]and he said to Moses, "Please, my lord, do not hold against us the sin we have so foolishly committed. [12]Do not let her be like a stillborn infant coming from its mother's womb with its flesh half eaten away."

[13]So Moses cried out to the LORD, "O God, please heal her!"

[14]The LORD replied to Moses, "If her father had spat in her face, would she not have been in disgrace for seven days? Confine her outside the camp for seven days; after that she can be brought back." [15]So Miriam was confined outside the camp for seven days, and the people did not move on till she was brought back.

[16]After that, the people left Hazeroth and encamped in the Desert of Paran.

Exploring Canaan

13 The LORD said to Moses, [2]"Send some men to explore the land of Canaan, which I am giving to the Israelites. From each ancestral tribe send one of its leaders."

[3]So at the LORD's command Moses sent them out from the Desert of Paran. All of them were leaders of the Israelites. [4]These are their names:

   from the tribe of Reuben, Shammua son of Zaccur;
[5]from the tribe of Simeon, Shaphat son of Hori;
[6]from the tribe of Judah, Caleb son of Jephunneh;
[7]from the tribe of Issachar, Igal son of Joseph;
[8]from the tribe of Ephraim, Hoshea son of Nun;
[9]from the tribe of Benjamin, Palti son of Raphu;
[10]from the tribe of Zebulun, Gaddiel son of Sodi;
[11]from the tribe of Manasseh (a tribe of Joseph), Gaddi son of Susi;
[12]from the tribe of Dan, Ammiel son of Gemalli;
[13]from the tribe of Asher, Sethur son of Michael;
[14]from the tribe of Naphtali, Nahbi son of Vophsi;
[15]from the tribe of Gad, Geuel son of Maki.

[16]These are the names of the men Moses sent to explore the land. (Moses gave Hoshea son of Nun the name Joshua.)

[17]When Moses sent them to explore Canaan, he said, "Go up through the Negev and on into the hill country. [18]See what the land is like and whether the people who live there are strong or weak, few or many. [19]What kind of land do they live in? Is it good or bad? What kind of towns do they live in? Are they unwalled or fortified? [20]How is the soil? Is it fertile or poor? Are there trees on it or not? Do your best to bring back some of the fruit of the land." (It was the season for the first ripe grapes.)

[21]So they went up and explored the land from the Desert of Zin as far as Rehob, towards Lebo[a] Hamath. [22]They went up through the Negev and came to Hebron, where Ahiman, Sheshai and Talmai, the

---

[a]10 The Hebrew word was used for various diseases affecting the skin—not necessarily leprosy.
[a]21 Or towards the entrance to

descendants of Anak, lived. (Hebron had been built seven years before Zoan in Egypt.) 23When they reached the Valley of Eshcol,*b* they cut off a branch bearing a single cluster of grapes. Two of them carried it on a pole between them, along with some pomegranates and figs. 24That place was called the Valley of Eshcol because of the cluster of grapes the Israelites cut off there. 25At the end of forty days they returned from exploring the land.

Report on the Exploration

26They came back to Moses and Aaron and the whole Israelite community at Kadesh in the Desert of Paran. There they reported to them and to the whole assembly and showed them the fruit of the land. 27They gave Moses this account: "We went into the land to which you sent us, and it does flow with milk and honey! Here is its fruit. 28But the people who live there are powerful, and the cities are fortified and very large. We even saw descendants of Anak there. 29The Amalekites live in the Negev; the Hittites, Jebusites and Amorites live in the hill country; and the Canaanites live near the sea and along the Jordan."

30Then Caleb silenced the people before Moses and said, "We should go up and take possession of the land, for we can certainly do it."

31But the men who had gone up with him said, "We can't attack those people; they are stronger than we are." 32And they spread among the Israelites a bad report about the land they had explored. They said, "The land we explored devours those living in it. All the people we saw there are of great size. 33We saw the Nephilim there (the descendants of Anak come from the Nephilim). We seemed like grasshoppers in our own eyes, and we looked the same to them."

The People Rebel

14 That night all the people of the community raised their voices and wept aloud. 2All the Israelites grumbled against Moses and Aaron, and the whole assembly said to them, "If only we had died in Egypt! Or in this desert! 3Why is the LORD bringing us to this land only to let us fall by the sword? Our wives and children will be taken as plunder. Wouldn't it be better for us to go back to Egypt?" 4And they said to each other, "We should choose a leader and go back to Egypt."

5Then Moses and Aaron fell face down in front of the whole Israelite assembly gathered there. 6Joshua son of Nun and Caleb son of Jephunneh, who were among those who had explored the land, tore their clothes 7and said to the entire Israelite assembly, "The land we passed through and explored is exceedingly good. 8If the LORD is pleased with us, he will lead us into that land, a land flowing with milk and honey, and will give it to us. 9Only do not rebel against the LORD. And do not be afraid of the people of the land, because we will swallow them up. Their protection is gone, but the LORD is with us. Do not be afraid of them."

10But the whole assembly talked about stoning them. Then the glory of the LORD appeared at the Tent of Meeting to all the Israelites. 11The LORD said to Moses, "How long will these people treat me with contempt? How long will they refuse to believe in me, in spite of all the miraculous signs I have performed among them? 12I will strike them down with a plague and destroy them, but I will make you into a nation greater and stronger than they."

13Moses said to the LORD, "Then the Egyptians will hear about it! By your power you brought these people up from among them. 14And they will tell the inhabitants of this land about it. They have already heard that you, O LORD, are with these people and that you, O LORD, have been seen face to face, that your cloud stays over them, and that you go before them in a pillar of cloud by day and a pillar of fire by night. 15If you put these people to death all at one time, the nations who have heard this report about you will say, 16'The LORD was not able to bring these people into the land he promised them on

b23 Eshcol means cluster; also in verse 24.

oath; so he slaughtered them in the desert.'

17"Now may the Lord's strength be displayed, just as you have declared: 18'The LORD is slow to anger, abounding in love and forgiving sin and rebellion. Yet he does not leave the guilty unpunished; he punishes the children for the sin of the fathers to the third and fourth generation.' 19In accordance with your great love, forgive the sin of these people, just as you have pardoned them from the time they left Egypt until now."

20The LORD replied, "I have forgiven them, as you asked. 21Nevertheless, as surely as I live and as surely as the glory of the LORD fills the whole earth, 22not one of the men who saw my glory and the miraculous signs I performed in Egypt and in the desert but who disobeyed me and tested me ten times—23not one of them will ever see the land I promised on oath to their forefathers. No-one who has treated me with contempt will ever see it. 24But because my servant Caleb has a different spirit and follows me wholeheartedly, I will bring him into the land he went to, and his descendants will inherit it. 25Since the Amalekites and Canaanites are living in the valleys, turn back tomorrow and set out towards the desert along the route to the Red Sea."*a*

26The LORD said to Moses and Aaron: 27"How long will this wicked community grumble against me? I have heard the complaints of these grumbling Israelites. 28So tell them, 'As surely as I live, declares the LORD, I will do to you the very things I heard you say: 29In this desert your bodies will fall—every one of you twenty years old or more who was counted in the census and who has grumbled against me. 30Not one of you will enter the land I swore with uplifted hand to make your home, except Caleb son of Jephunneh and Joshua son of Nun. 31As for your children that you said would be taken as plunder, I will bring them in to enjoy the land you have rejected. 32But you—your bodies will fall in this desert. 33Your children will be shepherds here for forty years, suffering

for your unfaithfulness, until the last of your bodies lies in the desert. 34For forty years—one year for each of the forty days you explored the land—you will suffer for your sins and know what it is like to have me against you.' 35I, the LORD, have spoken, and I will surely do these things to this whole wicked community, which has banded together against me. They will meet their end in this desert; here they will die."

36So the men Moses had sent to explore the land, who returned and made the whole community grumble against him by spreading a bad report about it—37these men responsible for spreading the bad report about the land were struck down and died of a plague before the LORD. 38Of the men who went to explore the land, only Joshua son of Nun and Caleb son of Jephunneh survived.

39When Moses reported this to all the Israelites, they mourned bitterly. 40Early the next morning they went up towards the high hill country. "We have sinned," they said. "We will go up to the place the LORD promised."

41But Moses said, "Why are you disobeying the LORD's command? This will not succeed! 42Do not go up, because the LORD is not with you. You will be defeated by your enemies, 43for the Amalekites and Canaanites will face you there. Because you have turned away from the LORD, he will not be with you and you will fall by the sword."

44Nevertheless, in their presumption they went up towards the high hill country, though neither Moses nor the ark of the LORD's covenant moved from the camp. 45Then the Amalekites and Canaanites who lived in that hill country came down and attacked them and beat them down all the way to Hormah.

Supplementary Offerings

15 The LORD said to Moses, 2"Speak to the Israelites and say to them: 'After you enter the land I am giving you as a home 3and you present to the LORD

a25 Hebrew Yam Suph; that is, Sea of Reeds

offerings made by fire, from the herd or the flock, as an aroma pleasing to the LORD—whether burnt offerings or sacrifices, for special vows or freewill offerings or festival offerings—⁴then the one who brings his offering shall present to the LORD a grain offering of a tenth of an ephah*a* of fine flour mixed with a quarter of a hin*b* of oil. ⁵With each lamb for the burnt offering or the sacrifice, prepare a quarter of a hin of wine as a drink offering.

⁶"'With a ram prepare a grain offering of two-tenths of an ephah*c* of fine flour mixed with a third of a hin*d* of oil, ⁷and a third of a hin of wine as a drink offering. Offer it as an aroma pleasing to the LORD.

⁸"'When you prepare a young bull as a burnt offering or sacrifice, for a special vow or a fellowship offering*e* to the LORD, ⁹bring with the bull a grain offering of three-tenths of an ephah*f* of fine flour mixed with half a hin*g* of oil. ¹⁰Also bring half a hin of wine as a drink offering. It will be an offering made by fire, an aroma pleasing to the LORD. ¹¹Each bull or ram, each lamb or young goat, is to be prepared in this manner. ¹²Do this for each one, for as many as you prepare.

¹³"'Everyone who is native-born must do these things in this way when he brings an offering made by fire as an aroma pleasing to the LORD. ¹⁴For the generations to come, whenever an alien or anyone else living among you presents an offering made by fire as an aroma pleasing to the LORD, he must do exactly as you do. ¹⁵The community is to have the same rules for you and for the alien living among you; this is a lasting ordinance for the generations to come. You and the alien shall be the same before the LORD: ¹⁶The same laws and regulations will apply both to you and to the alien living among you.'"

¹⁷The LORD said to Moses, ¹⁸"Speak to the Israelites and say to them: 'When you enter the land to which I am taking you ¹⁹and you eat the food of the land, present a portion as an offering to the LORD.

²⁰Present a cake from the first of your ground meal and present it as an offering from the threshing-floor. ²¹Throughout the generations to come you are to give this offering to the LORD from the first of your ground meal.

Offerings for Unintentional Sins

²²"'Now if you unintentionally fail to keep any of these commands the LORD gave Moses—²³any of the LORD's commands to you through him, from the day the LORD gave them and continuing through the generations to come—²⁴and if this is done unintentionally without the community being aware of it, then the whole community is to offer a young bull for a burnt offering as an aroma pleasing to the LORD, along with its prescribed grain offering and drink offering, and a male goat for a sin offering. ²⁵The priest is to make atonement for the whole Israelite community, and they will be forgiven, for it was not intentional and they have brought to the LORD for their wrong an offering made by fire and a sin offering. ²⁶The whole Israelite community and the aliens living among them will be forgiven, because all the people were involved in the unintentional wrong.

²⁷"'But if just one person sins unintentionally, he must bring a year-old female goat for a sin offering. ²⁸The priest is to make atonement before the LORD for the one who erred by sinning unintentionally, and when atonement has been made for him, he will be forgiven. ²⁹One and the same law applies to everyone who sins unintentionally, whether he is a native-born Israelite or an alien.

³⁰"'But anyone who sins defiantly, whether native-born or alien, blasphemes the LORD, and that person must be cut off from his people. ³¹Because he has despised the LORD's word and broken his commands, that person must surely be cut off; his guilt remains on him.'"

---

a4 That is, probably about 4 pints (about 2 litres)   *b4* That is, probably about 1½ pints (about 1 litre); also in verse 5
c6 That is, probably about 7½ pints (about 4.5 litres)
d6 That is, probably about 2¼ pints (about 1.2 litres); also in verse 7   *e8* Traditionally *peace offering*
f9 That is, probably about 11½ pints (about 6.5 litres)
g10 That is, probably about 3 pints (about 2 litres); also in verse 10

The Sabbath-Breaker Put to Death

[32]While the Israelites were in the desert, a man was found gathering wood on the Sabbath day. [33]Those who found him gathering wood brought him to Moses and Aaron and the whole assembly, [34]and they kept him in custody, because it was not clear what should be done to him. [35]Then the LORD said to Moses, "The man must die. The whole assembly must stone him outside the camp." [36]So the assembly took him outside the camp and stoned him to death, as the LORD commanded Moses.

Tassels on Garments

[37]The LORD said to Moses, [38]"Speak to the Israelites and say to them: 'Throughout the generations to come you are to make tassels on the corners of your garments, with a blue cord on each tassel. [39]You will have these tassels to look at and so you will remember all the commands of the LORD, that you may obey them and not prostitute yourselves by going after the lusts of your own hearts and eyes. [40]Then you will remember to obey all my commands and will be consecrated to your God. [41]I am the LORD your God, who brought you out of Egypt to be your God. I am the LORD your God.'"

Korah, Dathan and Abiram

16 Korah son of Izhar, the son of Kohath, the son of Levi, and certain Reubenites—Dathan and Abiram, sons of Eliab, and On son of Peleth—became insolent[a] [2]and rose up against Moses. With them were 250 Israelite men, well-known community leaders who had been appointed members of the council. [3]They came as a group to oppose Moses and Aaron and said to them, "You have gone too far! The whole community is holy, every one of them, and the LORD is with them. Why then do you set yourselves above the LORD's assembly?"

[4]When Moses heard this, he fell face down. [5]Then he said to Korah and all his followers: "In the morning the LORD will show who belongs to him and who is holy, and he will make that person come near him. The man he chooses he will cause to come near him. [6]You, Korah, and all your followers are to do this: Take censers [7]and tomorrow put fire and incense in them before the LORD. The man the LORD chooses will be the one who is holy. You Levites have gone too far!"

[8]Moses also said to Korah, "Now listen, you Levites! [9]Isn't it enough for you that the God of Israel has separated you from the rest of the Israelite community and brought you near himself to do the work at the LORD's tabernacle and to stand before the community and minister to them? [10]He has brought you and all your fellow Levites near himself, but now you are trying to get the priesthood too. [11]It is against the LORD that you and all your followers have banded together. Who is Aaron that you should grumble against him?"

[12]Then Moses summoned Dathan and Abiram, the sons of Eliab. But they said, "We will not come! [13]Isn't it enough that you have brought us up out of a land flowing with milk and honey to kill us in the desert? And now you also want to lord it over us? [14]Moreover, you haven't brought us into a land flowing with milk and honey or given us an inheritance of fields and vineyards. Will you gouge out the eyes of[b] these men? No, we will not come!"

[15]Then Moses became very angry and said to the LORD, "Do not accept their offering. I have not taken so much as a donkey from them, nor have I wronged any of them."

[16]Moses said to Korah, "You and all your followers are to appear before the LORD tomorrow—you and they and Aaron. [17]Each man is to take his censer and put incense in it—250 censers in all—and present it before the LORD. You and Aaron are to present your censers also." [18]So each man took his censer, put fire and incense in it, and stood with Moses and Aaron at the entrance to the Tent of

---

[a]1 Or Peleth—took ⌊men⌋
[b]14 Or you make slaves of; or you deceive

Meeting. ¹⁹When Korah had gathered all his followers in opposition to them at the entrance to the Tent of Meeting, the glory of the LORD appeared to the entire assembly. ²⁰The LORD said to Moses and Aaron, ²¹"Separate yourselves from this assembly so that I can put an end to them at once."

²²But Moses and Aaron fell face down and cried out, "O God, God of the spirits of all mankind, will you be angry with the entire assembly when only one man sins?"

²³Then the LORD said to Moses, ²⁴"Say to the assembly, 'Move away from the tents of Korah, Dathan and Abiram.'"

²⁵Moses got up and went to Dathan and Abiram, and the elders of Israel followed him. ²⁶He warned the assembly, "Move back from the tents of these wicked men! Do not touch anything belonging to them, or you will be swept away because of all their sins." ²⁷So they moved away from the tents of Korah, Dathan and Abiram. Dathan and Abiram had come out and were standing with their wives, children and little ones at the entrances to their tents.

²⁸Then Moses said, "This is how you will know that the LORD has sent me to do all these things and that it was not my idea: ²⁹If these men die a natural death and experience only what usually happens to men, then the LORD has not sent me. ³⁰But if the LORD brings about something totally new, and the earth opens its mouth and swallows them, with everything that belongs to them, and they go down alive into the grave,ᶜ then you will know that these men have treated the LORD with contempt."

³¹As soon as he finished saying all this, the ground under them split apart ³²and the earth opened its mouth and swallowed them, with their households and all Korah's men and all their possessions. ³³They went down alive into the grave, with everything they owned; the earth closed over them, and they perished and were gone from the community. ³⁴At their cries, all the Israelites around them fled, shouting, "The earth is going to swallow us too!"

³⁵And fire came out from the LORD and consumed the 250 men who were offering the incense.

³⁶The LORD said to Moses, ³⁷"Tell Eleazar son of Aaron, the priest, to take the censers out of the smouldering remains and scatter the coals some distance away, for the censers are holy— ³⁸the censers of the men who sinned at the cost of their lives. Hammer the censers into sheets to overlay the altar, for they were presented before the LORD and have become holy. Let them be a sign to the Israelites."

³⁹So Eleazar the priest collected the bronze censers brought by those who had been burned up, and he had them hammered out to overlay the altar, ⁴⁰as the LORD directed him through Moses. This was to remind the Israelites that no-one except a descendant of Aaron should come to burn incense before the LORD, or he would become like Korah and his followers.

⁴¹The next day the whole Israelite community grumbled against Moses and Aaron. "You have killed the LORD's people," they said.

⁴²But when the assembly gathered in opposition to Moses and Aaron and turned towards the Tent of Meeting, suddenly the cloud covered it and the glory of the LORD appeared. ⁴³Then Moses and Aaron went to the front of the Tent of Meeting, ⁴⁴and the LORD said to Moses, ⁴⁵"Get away from this assembly so that I can put an end to them at once." And they fell face down.

⁴⁶Then Moses said to Aaron, "Take your censer and put incense in it, along with fire from the altar, and hurry to the assembly to make atonement for them. Wrath has come out from the LORD; the plague has started." ⁴⁷So Aaron did as Moses said, and ran into the midst of the assembly. The plague had already started among the people, but Aaron offered the incense and made atonement for them. ⁴⁸He stood between the living and the dead, and the plague stopped. ⁴⁹But 14,700 people died from the plague, in

---

ᶜ30 Hebrew *Sheol*; also in verse 33

addition to those who had died because of Korah. 50Then Aaron returned to Moses at the entrance to the Tent of Meeting, for the plague had stopped.

The Budding of Aaron's Staff

17 The LORD said to Moses, 2"Speak to the Israelites and get twelve staffs from them, one from the leader of each of their ancestral tribes. Write the name of each man on his staff. 3On the staff of Levi write Aaron's name, for there must be one staff for the head of each ancestral tribe. 4Place them in the Tent of Meeting in front of the Testimony, where I meet with you. 5The staff belonging to the man I choose will sprout, and I will rid myself of this constant grumbling against you by the Israelites."

6So Moses spoke to the Israelites, and their leaders gave him twelve staffs, one for the leader of each of their ancestral tribes, and Aaron's staff was among them. 7Moses placed the staffs before the LORD in the Tent of the Testimony.

8The next day Moses entered the Tent of the Testimony and saw that Aaron's staff, which represented the house of Levi, had not only sprouted but had budded, blossomed and produced almonds. 9Then Moses brought out all the staffs from the LORD's presence to all the Israelites. They looked at them, and each man took his own staff.

10The LORD said to Moses, "Put back Aaron's staff in front of the Testimony, to be kept as a sign to the rebellious. This will put an end to their grumbling against me, so that they will not die." 11Moses did just as the LORD commanded him.

12The Israelites said to Moses, "We shall die! We are lost, we are all lost! 13Anyone who even comes near the tabernacle of the LORD will die. Are we all going to die?"

Duties of Priests and Levites

18 The LORD said to Aaron, "You, your sons and your father's family are to bear the responsibility for offences against the sanctuary, and you and your sons alone are to bear the responsibility for offences against the priesthood. 2Bring your fellow Levites from your ancestral tribe to join you and assist you when you and your sons minister before the Tent of the Testimony. 3They are to be responsible to you and are to perform all the duties of the Tent, but they must not go near the furnishings of the sanctuary or the altar, or both they and you will die. 4They are to join you and be responsible for the care of the Tent of Meeting—all the work at the Tent—and no-one else may come near where you are.

5"You are to be responsible for the care of the sanctuary and the altar, so that wrath will not fall on the Israelites again. 6I myself have selected your fellow Levites from among the Israelites as a gift to you, dedicated to the LORD to do the work at the Tent of Meeting. 7But only you and your sons may serve as priests in connection with everything at the altar and inside the curtain. I am giving you the service of the priesthood as a gift. Anyone else who comes near the sanctuary must be put to death."

Offerings for Priests and Levites

8Then the LORD said to Aaron, "I myself have put you in charge of the offerings presented to me; all the holy offerings the Israelites give me I give to you and your sons as your portion and regular share. 9You are to have the part of the most holy offerings that is kept from the fire. From all the gifts they bring me as most holy offerings, whether grain or sin or guilt offerings, that part belongs to you and your sons. 10Eat it as something most holy; every male shall eat it. You must regard it as holy.

11"This also is yours: whatever is set aside from the gifts of all the wave offerings of the Israelites. I give this to you and your sons and daughters as your regular share. Everyone in your household who is ceremonially clean may eat it.

12"I give you all the finest olive oil and all the finest new wine and grain they give to the LORD as the firstfruits of their harvest. 13All the land's firstfruits that they bring to the LORD will be yours. Everyone in your household who is ceremonially clean may eat it.

[14]"Everything in Israel that is devoted[a] to the LORD is yours. [15]The first offspring of every womb, both man and animal, that is offered to the LORD is yours. But you must redeem every firstborn son and every firstborn male of unclean animals. [16]When they are a month old, you must redeem them at the redemption price set at five shekels[b] of silver, according to the sanctuary shekel, which weighs twenty gerahs.

[17]"But you must not redeem the firstborn of an ox, a sheep or a goat; they are holy. Sprinkle their blood on the altar and burn their fat as an offering made by fire, an aroma pleasing to the LORD. [18]Their meat is to be yours, just as the breast of the wave offering and the right thigh are yours. [19]Whatever is set aside from the holy offerings the Israelites present to the LORD I give to you and your sons and daughters as your regular share. It is an everlasting covenant of salt before the LORD for both you and your offspring."

[20]The LORD said to Aaron, "You will have no inheritance in their land, nor will you have any share among them; I am your share and your inheritance among the Israelites.

[21]"I give to the Levites all the tithes in Israel as their inheritance in return for the work they do while serving at the Tent of Meeting. [22]From now on the Israelites must not go near the Tent of Meeting, or they will bear the consequences of their sin and will die. [23]It is the Levites who are to do the work at the Tent of Meeting and bear the responsibility for offences against it. This is a lasting ordinance for the generations to come. They will receive no inheritance among the Israelites. [24]Instead, I give to the Levites as their inheritance the tithes that the Israelites present as an offering to the LORD. That is why I said concerning them: 'They will have no inheritance among the Israelites.'"

[25]The LORD said to Moses, [26]"Speak to the Levites and say to them: 'When you receive from the Israelites the tithe I give you as your inheritance, you must present a tenth of that tithe as the LORD's offering. [27]Your offering will be reckoned to you as grain from the threshing-floor or juice from the winepress. [28]In this way you also will present an offering to the LORD from all the tithes you receive from the Israelites. From these tithes you must give the LORD's portion to Aaron the priest. [29]You must present as the LORD's portion the best and holiest part of everything given to you.'

[30]"Say to the Levites: 'When you present the best part, it will be reckoned to you as the product of the threshing-floor or the winepress. [31]You and your households may eat the rest of it anywhere, for it is your wages for your work at the Tent of Meeting. [32]By presenting the best part of it you will not be guilty in this matter; then you will not defile the holy offerings of the Israelites, and you will not die.'"

The Water of Cleansing

19 The LORD said to Moses and Aaron: [2]"This is a requirement of the law that the LORD has commanded: Tell the Israelites to bring you a red heifer without defect or blemish and that has never been under a yoke. [3]Give it to Eleazar the priest; it is to be taken outside the camp and slaughtered in his presence. [4]Then Eleazar the priest is to take some of its blood on his finger and sprinkle it seven times towards the front of the Tent of Meeting. [5]While he watches, the heifer is to be burned—its hide, flesh, blood and offal. [6]The priest is to take some cedar wood, hyssop and scarlet wool and throw them onto the burning heifer. [7]After that, the priest must wash his clothes and bathe himself with water. He may then come into the camp, but he will be ceremonially unclean till evening. [8]The man who burns it must also wash his clothes and bathe with water, and he too will be unclean till evening.

---

[a]14 The Hebrew term refers to the irrevocable giving over of things or persons to the LORD.
[b]16 That is, about 2 ounces (about 55 grams)

⁹"A man who is clean shall gather up the ashes of the heifer and put them in a ceremonially clean place outside the camp. They shall be kept by the Israelite community for use in the water of cleansing; it is for purification from sin. ¹⁰The man who gathers up the ashes of the heifer must also wash his clothes, and he too will be unclean till evening. This will be a lasting ordinance both for the Israelites and for the aliens living among them.

¹¹"Whoever touches the dead body of anyone will be unclean for seven days. ¹²He must purify himself with the water on the third day and on the seventh day; then he will be clean. But if he does not purify himself on the third and seventh days, he will not be clean. ¹³Whoever touches the dead body of anyone and fails to purify himself defiles the LORD's tabernacle. That person must be cut off from Israel. Because the water of cleansing has not been sprinkled on him, he is unclean; his uncleanness remains on him.

¹⁴"This is the law that applies when a person dies in a tent: Anyone who enters the tent and anyone who is in it will be unclean for seven days, ¹⁵and every open container without a lid fastened on it will be unclean.

¹⁶"Anyone out in the open who touches someone who has been killed with a sword or someone who has died a natural death, or anyone who touches a human bone or a grave, will be unclean for seven days.

¹⁷"For the unclean person, put some ashes from the burned purification offering into a jar and pour fresh water over them. ¹⁸Then a man who is ceremonially clean is to take some hyssop, dip it in the water and sprinkle the tent and all the furnishings and the people who were there. He must also sprinkle anyone who has touched a human bone or a grave or someone who has been killed or someone who has died a natural death. ¹⁹The man who is clean is to sprinkle the unclean person on the third and seventh days, and on the seventh day he is to purify him. The person being cleansed must wash his clothes and bathe with water, and that evening he will be clean. ²⁰But if a person

who is unclean does not purify himself, he must be cut off from the community, because he has defiled the sanctuary of the LORD. The water of cleansing has not been sprinkled on him, and he is unclean. ²¹This is a lasting ordinance for them.

"The man who sprinkles the water of cleansing must also wash his clothes, and anyone who touches the water of cleansing will be unclean till evening. ²²Anything that an unclean person touches becomes unclean, and anyone who touches it becomes unclean till evening."

Water From the Rock

20 In the first month the whole Israelite community arrived at the Desert of Zin, and they stayed at Kadesh. There Miriam died and was buried.

²Now there was no water for the community, and the people gathered in opposition to Moses and Aaron. ³They quarrelled with Moses and said, "If only we had died when our brothers fell dead before the LORD! ⁴Why did you bring the LORD's community into this desert, that we and our livestock should die here? ⁵Why did you bring us up out of Egypt to this terrible place? It has no grain or figs, grapevines or pomegranates. And there is no water to drink!"

⁶Moses and Aaron went from the assembly to the entrance to the Tent of Meeting and fell face down, and the glory of the LORD appeared to them. ⁷The LORD said to Moses, ⁸"Take the staff, and you and your brother Aaron gather the assembly together. Speak to that rock before their eyes and it will pour out its water. You will bring water out of the rock for the community so that they and their livestock can drink."

⁹So Moses took the staff from the LORD's presence, just as he commanded him. ¹⁰He and Aaron gathered the assembly together in front of the rock and Moses said to them, "Listen, you rebels, must we bring you water out of this rock?" ¹¹Then Moses raised his arm and struck the rock twice with his staff. Water gushed out, and the community and their livestock drank.

¹²But the LORD said to Moses and

Aaron, "Because you did not trust in me enough to honour me as holy in the sight of the Israelites, you will not bring this community into the land I give them."

¹³These were the waters of Meribah,ᵃ where the Israelites quarrelled with the LORD and where he showed himself holy among them.

Edom Denies Israel Passage

¹⁴Moses sent messengers from Kadesh to the king of Edom, saying:

"This is what your brother Israel says: You know about all the hardships that have come upon us. ¹⁵Our forefathers went down into Egypt, and we lived there many years. The Egyptians ill-treated us and our fathers, ¹⁶but when we cried out to the LORD, he heard our cry and sent an angel and brought us out of Egypt.

"Now we are here at Kadesh, a town on the edge of your territory. ¹⁷Please let us pass through your country. We will not go through any field or vineyard, or drink water from any well. We will travel along the king's highway and not turn to the right or to the left until we have passed through your territory."

¹⁸But Edom answered:

"You may not pass through here; if you try, we will march out and attack you with the sword."

¹⁹The Israelites replied:

"We will go along the main road, and if we or our livestock drink any of your water, we will pay for it. We only want to pass through on foot—nothing else."

²⁰Again they answered:

"You may not pass through."

Then Edom came out against them with a large and powerful army. ²¹Since Edom refused to let them go through their territory, Israel turned away from them.

The Death of Aaron

²²The whole Israelite community set out from Kadesh and came to Mount Hor. ²³At Mount Hor, near the border of Edom, the LORD said to Moses and Aaron, ²⁴"Aaron will be gathered to his people. He will not enter the land I give the Israelites, because both of you rebelled against my command at the waters of Meribah. ²⁵Call Aaron and his son Eleazar and take them up Mount Hor. ²⁶Remove Aaron's garments and put them on his son Eleazar, for Aaron will be gathered to his people; he will die there."

²⁷Moses did as the LORD commanded: They went up Mount Hor in the sight of the whole community. ²⁸Moses removed Aaron's garments and put them on his son Eleazar. And Aaron died there on top of the mountain. Then Moses and Eleazar came down from the mountain, ²⁹and when the whole community learned that Aaron had died, the entire house of Israel mourned for him thirty days.

Arad Destroyed

21 When the Canaanite king of Arad, who lived in the Negev, heard that Israel was coming along the road to Atharim, he attacked the Israelites and captured some of them. ²Then Israel made this vow to the LORD: "If you will deliver these people into our hands, we will totally destroyᵃ their cities." ³The LORD listened to Israel's plea and gave the Canaanites over to them. They completely destroyed them and their towns; so the place was named Hormah.ᵇ

The Bronze Snake

⁴They travelled from Mount Hor along the route to the Red Sea,ᶜ to go round

---

ᵃ13 *Meribah* means *quarrelling.*
ᵃ2 The Hebrew term refers to the irrevocable giving over of things or persons to the LORD, often by totally destroying them; also in verse 3.   ᵇ3 *Hormah* means *destruction.*   ᶜ4 Hebrew *Yam Suph;* that is, Sea of Reeds

Edom. But the people grew impatient on the way; [5]they spoke against God and against Moses, and said, "Why have you brought us up out of Egypt to die in the desert? There is no bread! There is no water! And we detest this miserable food!"

[6]Then the LORD sent venomous snakes among them; they bit the people and many Israelites died. [7]The people came to Moses and said, "We sinned when we spoke against the LORD and against you. Pray that the LORD will take the snakes away from us." So Moses prayed for the people.

[8]The LORD said to Moses, "Make a snake and put it up on a pole; anyone who is bitten can look at it and live." [9]So Moses made a bronze snake and put it up on a pole. Then when anyone was bitten by a snake and looked at the bronze snake, he lived.

The Journey to Moab

[10]The Israelites moved on and camped at Oboth. [11]Then they set out from Oboth and camped in Iye Abarim, in the desert that faces Moab towards the sunrise. [12]From there they moved on and camped in the Zered Valley. [13]They set out from there and camped alongside the Arnon, which is in the desert extending into Amorite territory. The Arnon is the border of Moab, between Moab and the Amorites. [14]That is why the Book of the Wars of the LORD says:

". . . Waheb in Suphah[d] and the
      ravines,
  the Arnon [15]and[e] the slopes of the
      ravines
that lead to the site of Ar
  and lie along the border of Moab."

[16]From there they continued on to Beer, the well where the LORD said to Moses, "Gather the people together and I will give them water."

[17]Then Israel sang this song:

"Spring up, O well!
  Sing about it,
[18]about the well that the princes dug,
  that the nobles of the people sank—
  the nobles with sceptres and staffs."

Then they went from the desert to Mattanah, [19]from Mattanah to Nahaliel, from Nahaliel to Bamoth, [20]and from Bamoth to the valley in Moab where the top of Pisgah overlooks the wasteland.

Defeat of Sihon and Og

[21]Israel sent messengers to say to Sihon king of the Amorites:

[22]"Let us pass through your country. We will not turn aside into any field or vineyard, or drink water from any well. We will travel along the king's highway until we have passed through your territory."

[23]But Sihon would not let Israel pass through his territory. He mustered his entire army and marched out into the desert against Israel. When he reached Jahaz, he fought with Israel. [24]Israel, however, put him to the sword and took over his land from the Arnon to the Jabbok, but only as far as the Ammonites, because their border was fortified. [25]Israel captured all the cities of the Amorites and occupied them, including Heshbon and all its surrounding settlements. [26]Heshbon was the city of Sihon king of the Amorites, who had fought against the former king of Moab and had taken from him all his land as far as the Arnon.

[27]That is why the poets say:

"Come to Heshbon and let it be rebuilt;
  let Sihon's city be restored.

[28]"Fire went out from Heshbon,
  a blaze from the city of Sihon.
It consumed Ar of Moab,
  the citizens of Arnon's heights.

---

[d]14 The meaning of the Hebrew for this phrase is uncertain.
[e]14,15 Or "I have been given from Suphah and the ravines / of the Arnon[15] to

29Woe to you, O Moab!
　You are destroyed, O people of
　　Chemosh!
He has given up his sons as fugitives
　and his daughters as captives
　to Sihon king of the Amorites.

30"But we have overthrown them;
　Heshbon is destroyed all the way to
　　Dibon.
We have demolished them as far as
　　Nophah,
which extends to Medeba."

31So Israel settled in the land of the Amorites.

32After Moses had sent spies to Jazer, the Israelites captured its surrounding settlements and drove out the Amorites who were there. 33Then they turned and went up along the road towards Bashan, and Og king of Bashan and his whole army marched out to meet them in battle at Edrei.

34The LORD said to Moses, "Do not be afraid of him, for I have handed him over to you, with his whole army and his land. Do to him what you did to Sihon king of the Amorites, who reigned in Heshbon."

35So they struck him down, together with his sons and his whole army, leaving them no survivors. And they took possession of his land.

Balak Summons Balaam

22 Then the Israelites travelled to the plains of Moab and camped along the Jordan across from Jericho.*a*

2Now Balak son of Zippor saw all that Israel had done to the Amorites, 3and Moab was terrified because there were so many people. Indeed, Moab was filled with dread because of the Israelites.

4The Moabites said to the elders of Midian, "This horde is going to lick up everything around us, as an ox licks up the grass of the field."

So Balak son of Zippor, who was king of Moab at that time, 5sent messengers to summon Balaam son of Beor, who was at Pethor, near the River,*b* in his native land. Balak said:

"A people has come out of Egypt; they cover the face of the land and have settled next to me. 6Now come and put a curse on these people, because they are too powerful for me. Perhaps then I will be able to defeat them and drive them out of the country. For I know that those you bless are blessed, and those you curse are cursed."

7The elders of Moab and Midian left, taking with them the fee for divination. When they came to Balaam, they told him what Balak had said.

8"Spend the night here," Balaam said to them, "and I will bring you back the answer the LORD gives me." So the Moabite princes stayed with him.

9God came to Balaam and asked, "Who are these men with you?"

10Balaam said to God, "Balak son of Zippor, king of Moab, sent me this message: 11'A people that has come out of Egypt covers the face of the land. Now come and put a curse on them for me. Perhaps then I will be able to fight them and drive them away.'"

12But God said to Balaam, "Do not go with them. You must not put a curse on those people, because they are blessed."

13The next morning Balaam got up and said to Balak's princes, "Go back to your own country, for the LORD has refused to let me go with you."

14So the Moabite princes returned to Balak and said, "Balaam refused to come with us."

15Then Balak sent other princes, more numerous and more distinguished than the first. 16They came to Balaam and said:

"This is what Balak son of Zippor says: Do not let anything keep you from coming to me, 17because I will reward you handsomely and do whatever you say. Come and put a curse on these people for me."

a1 Hebrew *Jordan of Jericho*; possibly an ancient name for the Jordan River　　*b5* That is, the Euphrates

[18]But Balaam answered them, "Even if Balak gave me his palace filled with silver and gold, I could not do anything great or small to go beyond the command of the LORD my God. [19]Now stay here tonight as the others did, and I will find out what else the LORD will tell me."

[20]That night God came to Balaam and said, "Since these men have come to summon you, go with them, but do only what I tell you."

Balaam's Donkey

[21]Balaam got up in the morning, saddled his donkey and went with the princes of Moab. [22]But God was very angry when he went, and the angel of the LORD stood in the road to oppose him. Balaam was riding on his donkey, and his two servants were with him. [23]When the donkey saw the angel of the LORD standing in the road with a drawn sword in his hand, she turned off the road into a field. Balaam beat her to get her back on the road.

[24]Then the angel of the LORD stood in a narrow path between two vineyards, with walls on both sides. [25]When the donkey saw the angel of the LORD, she pressed close to the wall, crushing Balaam's foot against it. So he beat her again.

[26]Then the angel of the LORD moved on ahead and stood in a narrow place where there was no room to turn, either to the right or to the left. [27]When the donkey saw the angel of the LORD, she lay down under Balaam, and he was angry and beat her with his staff. [28]Then the LORD opened the donkey's mouth, and she said to Balaam, "What have I done to you to make you beat me these three times?"

[29]Balaam answered the donkey, "You have made a fool of me! If I had a sword in my hand, I would kill you right now."

[30]The donkey said to Balaam, "Am I not your own donkey, which you have always ridden, to this day? Have I been in the habit of doing this to you?"

"No," he said.

[31]Then the LORD opened Balaam's eyes, and he saw the angel of the LORD standing in the road with his sword drawn. So he bowed low and fell face down.

[32]The angel of the LORD asked him, "Why have you beaten your donkey these three times? I have come here to oppose you because your path is a reckless one before me.[c] [33]The donkey saw me and turned away from me these three times. If she had not turned away, I would certainly have killed you by now, but I would have spared her."

[34]Balaam said to the angel of the LORD, "I have sinned. I did not realise you were standing in the road to oppose me. Now if you are displeased, I will go back."

[35]The angel of the LORD said to Balaam, "Go with the men, but speak only what I tell you." So Balaam went with the princes of Balak.

[36]When Balak heard that Balaam was coming, he went out to meet him at the Moabite town on the Arnon border, at the edge of his territory. [37]Balak said to Balaam, "Did I not send you an urgent summons? Why didn't you come to me? Am I really not able to reward you?"

[38]"Well, I have come to you now," Balaam replied. "But can I say just anything? I must speak only what God puts in my mouth."

[39]Then Balaam went with Balak to Kiriath Huzoth. [40]Balak sacrificed cattle and sheep, and gave some to Balaam and the princes who were with him. [41]The next morning Balak took Balaam up to Bamoth Baal, and from there he saw part of the people.

Balaam's First Oracle

23 Balaam said, "Build me seven altars here, and prepare seven bulls and seven rams for me." [2]Balak did as Balaam said, and the two of them offered a bull and a ram on each altar.

[3]Then Balaam said to Balak, "Stay here beside your offering while I go aside. Perhaps the LORD will come to meet with me. Whatever he reveals to me I will tell you." Then he went off to a barren height.

[4]God met with him, and Balaam said, "I

---

[c]32 The meaning of the Hebrew for this clause is uncertain.

have prepared seven altars, and on each altar I have offered a bull and a ram."

⁵The LORD put a message in Balaam's mouth and said, "Go back to Balak and give him this message."

⁶So he went back to him and found him standing beside his offering, with all the princes of Moab. ⁷Then Balaam uttered his oracle:

"Balak brought me from Aram,
the king of Moab from the eastern
mountains.
'Come,' he said, 'curse Jacob for me;
come, denounce Israel.'
⁸How can I curse
those whom God has not cursed?
How can I denounce
those whom the LORD has not
denounced?
⁹From the rocky peaks I see them,
from the heights I view them.
I see people who live apart
and do not consider themselves one
of the nations.
¹⁰Who can count the dust of Jacob
or number the fourth part of Israel?
Let me die the death of the righteous,
and may my end be like theirs!"

¹¹Balak said to Balaam, "What have you done to me? I brought you to curse my enemies, but you have done nothing but bless them!"

¹²He answered, "Must I not speak what the LORD puts in my mouth?"

Balaam's Second Oracle

¹³Then Balak said to him, "Come with me to another place where you can see them; you will see only a part but not all of them. And from there, curse them for me." ¹⁴So he took him to the field of Zophim on the top of Pisgah, and there he built seven altars and offered a bull and a ram on each altar.

¹⁵Balaam said to Balak, "Stay here beside your offering while I meet with him over there."

¹⁶The LORD met with Balaam and put a message in his mouth and said, "Go back to Balak and give him this message."

¹⁷So he went to him and found him standing beside his offering, with the princes of Moab. Balak asked him, "What did the LORD say?"

¹⁸Then he uttered his oracle:

"Arise, Balak, and listen;
hear me, son of Zippor.
¹⁹God is not a man, that he should lie,
nor a son of man, that he should
change his mind.
Does he speak and then not act?
Does he promise and not fulfil?
²⁰I have received a command to bless;
he has blessed, and I cannot change
it.

²¹"No misfortune is seen in Jacob,
no misery observed in Israel.ᵃ
The LORD their God is with them;
the shout of the King is among them.
²²God brought them out of Egypt;
they have the strength of a wild ox.
²³There is no sorcery against Jacob,
no divination against Israel.
It will now be said of Jacob
and of Israel, 'See what God has
done!'
²⁴The people rise like a lioness;
they rouse themselves like a lion
that does not rest till he devours his
prey
and drinks the blood of his victims."

²⁵Then Balak said to Balaam, "Neither curse them at all nor bless them at all!"

²⁶Balaam answered, "Did I not tell you I must do whatever the LORD says?"

Balaam's Third Oracle

²⁷Then Balak said to Balaam, "Come, let me take you to another place. Perhaps it will please God to let you curse them for me from there." ²⁸And Balak took Balaam to the top of Peor, overlooking the wasteland.

²⁹Balaam said, "Build me seven altars here, and prepare seven bulls and seven

---

ᵃ21 Or *He has not looked on Jacob's offences* / *or on the wrongs found in Israel.*

rams for me.'' ³⁰Balak did as Balaam had said, and offered a bull and a ram on each altar.

24 Now when Balaam saw that it pleased the LORD to bless Israel, he did not resort to sorcery as at other times, but turned his face towards the desert. ²When Balaam looked out and saw Israel encamped tribe by tribe, the Spirit of God came upon him ³and he uttered his oracle:

"The oracle of Balaam son of Beor,
  the oracle of one whose eye sees
    clearly,
⁴the oracle of one who hears the words
    of God,
  who sees a vision from the
    Almighty,*a*
  who falls prostrate, and whose eyes
    are opened:

⁵"How beautiful are your tents, O
    Jacob,
  your dwelling-places, O Israel!

⁶"Like valleys they spread out,
  like gardens beside a river,
 like aloes planted by the LORD,
  like cedars beside the waters.
⁷Water will flow from their buckets;
  their seed will have abundant water.

"Their king will be greater than Agag;
  their kingdom will be exalted.

⁸"God brought them out of Egypt;
  they have the strength of a wild ox.
 They devour hostile nations
  and break their bones in pieces;
  with their arrows they pierce them.
⁹Like a lion they crouch and lie down,
  like a lioness—who dares to rouse
    them?

"May those who bless you be blessed
  and those who curse you be cursed!"

¹⁰Then Balak's anger burned against Balaam. He struck his hands together and said to him, "I summoned you to curse my enemies, but you have blessed them these three times. ¹¹Now leave at once and go home! I said I would reward you handsomely, but the LORD has kept you from being rewarded.''

¹²Balaam answered Balak, "Did I not tell the messengers you sent me, ¹³'Even if Balak gave me his palace filled with silver and gold, I could not do anything of my own accord, good or bad, to go beyond the command of the LORD—and I must say only what the LORD says'? ¹⁴Now I am going back to my people, but come, let me warn you of what this people will do to your people in days to come.''

Balaam's Fourth Oracle

¹⁵Then he uttered his oracle:

"The oracle of Balaam son of Beor,
  the oracle of one whose eye sees
    clearly,
¹⁶the oracle of one who hears the words
    of God,
  who has knowledge from the Most
    High,
 who sees a vision from the Almighty,
  who falls prostrate, and whose eyes
    are opened:

¹⁷"I see him, but not now;
  I behold him, but not near.
 A star will come out of Jacob;
  a sceptre will rise out of Israel.
 He will crush the foreheads of Moab,
  the skulls*b* of*c* all the sons of Sheth.*d*
¹⁸Edom will be conquered;
  Seir, his enemy, will be conquered,
  but Israel will grow strong.
¹⁹A ruler will come out of Jacob
  and destroy the survivors of the city.''

Balaam's Final Oracles

²⁰Then Balaam saw Amalek and uttered his oracle:

"Amalek was first among the nations,
  but he will come to ruin at last.''

---

a4 Hebrew *Shaddai*; also in verse 16
b17 Samaritan Pentateuch (see also Jer. 48:45); the meaning of the word in the Masoretic Text is uncertain.
c17 Or possibly *Moab, / batter*   *d17* Or *all the noisy boasters*

²¹Then he saw the Kenites and uttered his oracle:

"Your dwelling-place is secure,
    your nest is set in a rock;
²²yet you Kenites will be destroyed
    when Asshur takes you captive."

²³Then he uttered his oracle:

"Ah, who can live when God does this?[e]
²⁴   Ships will come from the shores of
        Kittim;
    they will subdue Asshur and Eber,
        but they too will come to ruin."

²⁵Then Balaam got up and returned home and Balak went his own way.

Moab Seduces Israel

25 While Israel was staying in Shittim, the men began to indulge in sexual immorality with Moabite women, ²who invited them to the sacrifices to their gods. The people ate and bowed down before these gods. ³So Israel joined in worshipping the Baal of Peor. And the LORD's anger burned against them.

⁴The LORD said to Moses, "Take all the leaders of these people, kill them and expose them in broad daylight before the LORD, so that the LORD's fierce anger may turn away from Israel."

⁵So Moses said to Israel's judges, "Each of you must put to death those of your men who have joined in worshipping the Baal of Peor."

⁶Then an Israelite man brought to his family a Midianite woman right before the eyes of Moses and the whole assembly of Israel while they were weeping at the entrance to the Tent of Meeting. ⁷When Phinehas son of Eleazar, the son of Aaron, the priest, saw this, he left the assembly, took a spear in his hand ⁸and followed the Israelite into the tent. He drove the spear through both of them— through the Israelite and into the woman's body. Then the plague against the Israelites was stopped; ⁹but those who died in the plague numbered 24,000.

¹⁰The LORD said to Moses, ¹¹"Phinehas son of Eleazar, the son of Aaron, the priest, has turned my anger away from the Israelites; for he was as zealous as I am for my honour among them, so that in my zeal I did not put an end to them. ¹²Therefore tell him I am making my covenant of peace with him. ¹³He and his descendants will have a covenant of a lasting priesthood, because he was zealous for the honour of his God and made atonement for the Israelites."

¹⁴The name of the Israelite who was killed with the Midianite woman was Zimri son of Salu, the leader of a Simeonite family. ¹⁵And the name of the Midianite woman who was put to death was Cozbi daughter of Zur, a tribal chief of a Midianite family.

¹⁶The LORD said to Moses, ¹⁷"Treat the Midianites as enemies and kill them, ¹⁸because they treated you as enemies when they deceived you in the affair of Peor and their sister Cozbi, the daughter of a Midianite leader, the woman who was killed when the plague came as a result of Peor."

The Second Census

26 After the plague the LORD said to Moses and Eleazar son of Aaron, the priest, ²"Take a census of the whole Israelite community by families—all those twenty years old or more who are able to serve in the army of Israel." ³So on the plains of Moab by the Jordan across from Jericho,[a] Moses and Eleazar the priest spoke with them and said, ⁴"Take a census of men twenty years old or more, as the LORD commanded Moses."

These were the Israelites who came out of Egypt:

⁵The descendants of Reuben, the firstborn son of Israel, were:
    through Hanoch, the Hanochite clan;

---

[e]23 Masoretic Text; with a different word division of the Hebrew *A people will gather from the north.*
[a]3 Hebrew *Jordan of Jericho*; possibly an ancient name for the Jordan River; also in verse 63

through Pallu, the Palluite clan;
⁶through Hezron, the Hezronite clan;
through Carmi, the Carmite clan.
⁷These were the clans of Reuben; those numbered were 43,730.

⁸The son of Pallu was Eliab, ⁹and the sons of Eliab were Nemuel, Dathan and Abiram. The same Dathan and Abiram were the community officials who rebelled against Moses and Aaron and were among Korah's followers when they rebelled against the LORD. ¹⁰The earth opened its mouth and swallowed them along with Korah, whose followers died when the fire devoured the 250 men. And they served as a warning sign. ¹¹The line of Korah, however, did not die out.

¹²The descendants of Simeon by their clans were:
    through Nemuel, the Nemuelite clan;
    through Jamin, the Jaminite clan;
    through Jakin, the Jakinite clan;
    ¹³through Zerah, the Zerahite clan;
    through Shaul, the Shaulite clan.
¹⁴These were the clans of Simeon; there were 22,200 men.

¹⁵The descendants of Gad by their clans were:
    through Zephon, the Zephonite clan;
    through Haggi, the Haggite clan;
    through Shuni, the Shunite clan;
    ¹⁶through Ozni, the Oznite clan;
    through Eri, the Erite clan;
    ¹⁷through Arodi,ᵇ the Arodite clan;
    through Areli, the Arelite clan.
¹⁸These were the clans of Gad; those numbered were 40,500.

¹⁹Er and Onan were sons of Judah, but they died in Canaan.
²⁰The descendants of Judah by their clans were:
    through Shelah, the Shelanite clan;
    through Perez, the Perezite clan;
    through Zerah, the Zerahite clan.
²¹The descendants of Perez were:
    through Hezron, the Hezronite clan;
    through Hamul, the Hamulite clan.

²²These were the clans of Judah; those numbered were 76,500.

²³The descendants of Issachar by their clans were:
    through Tola, the Tolaite clan;
    through Puah, the Puiteᶜ clan;
    ²⁴through Jashub, the Jashubite clan;
    through Shimron, the Shimronite clan.
²⁵These were the clans of Issachar; those numbered were 64,300.

²⁶The descendants of Zebulun by their clans were:
    through Sered, the Seredite clan;
    through Elon, the Elonite clan;
    through Jahleel, the Jahleelite clan.
²⁷These were the clans of Zebulun; those numbered were 60,500.

²⁸The descendants of Joseph by their clans through Manasseh and Ephraim were:

²⁹The descendants of Manasseh:
    through Makir, the Makirite clan (Makir was the father of Gilead);
    through Gilead, the Gileadite clan.
³⁰These were the descendants of Gilead:
    through Iezer, the Iezerite clan;
    through Helek, the Helekite clan;
    ³¹through Asriel, the Asrielite clan;
    through Shechem, the Shechemite clan;
    ³²through Shemida, the Shemidaite clan;
    through Hepher, the Hepherite clan.
    ³³(Zelophehad son of Hepher had no sons; he had only daughters, whose names were Mahlah, Noah, Hoglah, Milcah and Tirzah.)
³⁴These were the clans of Manasseh; those numbered were 52,700.

³⁵These were the descendants of Ephraim by their clans:
    through Shuthelah, the Shuthelahite clan;
    through Beker, the Bekerite clan;
    through Tahan, the Tahanite clan.
³⁶These were the descendants of Shuthelah:

ᵇ17 Samaritan Pentateuch and Syriac (see also Gen. 46:16); Masoretic Text *Arod*
ᶜ23 Samaritan Pentateuch, Septuagint, Vulgate and Syriac (see also 1 Chron. 7:1); Masoretic Text *through Puvah, the Punite*

through Eran, the Eranite clan.
37These were the clans of Ephraim; those numbered were 32,500.

These were the descendants of Joseph by their clans.

38The descendants of Benjamin by their clans were:
    through Bela, the Belaite clan;
    through Ashbel, the Ashbelite clan;
    through Ahiram, the Ahiramite clan;
39through Shupham,d the Shuphamite clan;
    through Hupham, the Huphamite clan.
40The descendants of Bela through Ard and Naaman were:
    through Ard,e the Ardite clan;
    through Naaman, the Naamite clan.
41These were the clans of Benjamin; those numbered were 45,600.

42These were the descendants of Dan by their clans:
    through Shuham, the Shuhamite clan.
These were the clans of Dan: 43All of them were Shuhamite clans; and those numbered were 64,400.

44The descendants of Asher by their clans were:
    through Imnah, the Imnite clan;
    through Ishvi, the Ishvite clan;
    through Beriah, the Beriite clan;
45and through the descendants of Beriah:
    through Heber, the Heberite clan;
    through Malkiel, the Malkielite clan.
46(Asher had a daughter named Serah.)
47These were the clans of Asher; those numbered were 53,400.

48The descendants of Naphtali by their clans were:
    through Jahzeel, the Jahzeelite clan;
    through Guni, the Gunite clan;
49through Jezer, the Jezerite clan;
    through Shillem, the Shillemite clan.
50These were the clans of Naphtali; those numbered were 45,400.

51The total number of the men of Israel was 601,730.

52The LORD said to Moses, 53"The land is to be allotted to them as an inheritance based on the number of names. 54To a larger group give a larger inheritance, and to a smaller group a smaller one; each is to receive its inheritance according to the number of those listed. 55Be sure that the land is distributed by lot. What each group inherits will be according to the names for its ancestral tribe. 56Each inheritance is to be distributed by lot among the larger and smaller groups."

57These were the Levites who were counted by their clans:
    through Gershon, the Gershonite clan;
    through Kohath, the Kohathite clan;
    through Merari, the Merarite clan.
58These also were Levite clans:
    the Libnite clan,
    the Hebronite clan,
    the Mahlite clan,
    the Mushite clan,
    the Korahite clan.
    (Kohath was the forefather of Amram; 59the name of Amram's wife was Jochebed, a descendant of Levi, who was born to the Levitesf in Egypt. To Amram she bore Aaron, Moses and their sister Miriam. 60Aaron was the father of Nadab and Abihu, Eleazar and Ithamar. 61But Nadab and Abihu died when they made an offering before the LORD with unauthorised fire.)

62All the male Levites a month old or more numbered 23,000. They were not counted along with the other Israelites because they received no inheritance among them.

63These are the ones counted by Moses and Eleazar the priest when they counted the Israelites on the plains of Moab by the Jordan across from Jericho. 64Not one of

d39 A few manuscripts of the Masoretic Text, Samaritan Pentateuch, Vulgate and Syriac (see also Septuagint); most manuscripts of the Masoretic Text *Shephupham*
e40 Samaritan Pentateuch and Vulgate (see also Septuagint); Masoretic Text does not have *through Ard,*
f59 Or *Jochebed, a daughter of Levi, who was born to Levi*

them was among those counted by Moses and Aaron the priest when they counted the Israelites in the Desert of Sinai. ⁶⁵For the LORD had told those Israelites they would surely die in the desert, and not one of them was left except Caleb son of Jephunneh and Joshua son of Nun.

Zelophehad's Daughters

27 The daughters of Zelophehad son of Hepher, the son of Gilead, the son of Makir, the son of Manasseh, belonged to the clans of Manasseh son of Joseph. The names of the daughters were Mahlah, Noah, Hoglah, Milcah and Tirzah. They approached ²the entrance to the Tent of Meeting and stood before Moses, Eleazar the priest, the leaders and the whole assembly, and said, ³"Our father died in the desert. He was not among Korah's followers, who banded together against the LORD, but he died for his own sin and left no sons. ⁴Why should our father's name disappear from his clan because he had no son? Give us property among our father's relatives."

⁵So Moses brought their case before the LORD ⁶and the LORD said to him, ⁷"What Zelophehad's daughters are saying is right. You must certainly give them property as an inheritance among their father's relatives and give their father's inheritance over to them.

⁸"Say to the Israelites, 'If a man dies and leaves no son, give his inheritance over to his daughter. ⁹If he has no daughter, give his inheritance to his brothers. ¹⁰If he has no brothers, give his inheritance to his father's brothers. ¹¹If his father had no brothers, give his inheritance to the nearest relative in his clan, that he may possess it. This is to be a legal requirement for the Israelites, as the LORD commanded Moses.'"

Joshua to Succeed Moses

¹²Then the LORD said to Moses, "Go up this mountain in the Abarim Range and see the land I have given the Israelites. ¹³After you have seen it, you too will be gathered to your people, as your brother Aaron was, ¹⁴for when the community rebelled at the waters in the Desert of Zin, both of you disobeyed my command to honour me as holy before their eyes." (These were the waters of Meribah Kadesh, in the Desert of Zin.)

¹⁵Moses said to the LORD, ¹⁶"May the LORD, the God of the spirits of all mankind, appoint a man over this community ¹⁷to go out and come in before them, one who will lead them out and bring them in, so that the LORD's people will not be like sheep without a shepherd."

¹⁸So the LORD said to Moses, "Take Joshua son of Nun, a man in whom is the spirit,ᵃ and lay your hand on him. ¹⁹Make him stand before Eleazar the priest and the entire assembly and commission him in their presence. ²⁰Give him some of your authority so that the whole Israelite community will obey him. ²¹He is to stand before Eleazar the priest, who will obtain decisions for him by enquiring of the Urim before the LORD. At his command he and the entire community of the Israelites will go out, and at his command they will come in."

²²Moses did as the LORD commanded him. He took Joshua and made him stand before Eleazar the priest and the whole assembly. ²³Then he laid his hands on him and commissioned him, as the LORD instructed through Moses.

Daily Offerings

28 The LORD said to Moses, ²"Give this command to the Israelites and say to them: 'See that you present to me at the appointed time the food for my offerings made by fire, as an aroma pleasing to me.' ³Say to them: 'This is the offering made by fire that you are to present to the LORD: two lambs a year old without defect, as a regular burnt offering each day. ⁴Prepare one lamb in the morning and the other at twilight, ⁵together with a grain

---

ᵃ *Or Spirit*

offering of a tenth of an ephah*a* of fine flour mixed with a quarter of a hin*b* of oil from pressed olives. 6This is the regular burnt offering instituted at Mount Sinai as a pleasing aroma, an offering made to the LORD by fire. 7The accompanying drink offering is to be a quarter of a hin of fermented drink with each lamb. Pour out the drink offering to the LORD at the sanctuary. 8Prepare the second lamb at twilight, along with the same kind of grain offering and drink offering that you prepare in the morning. This is an offering made by fire, an aroma pleasing to the LORD.

Sabbath Offerings

9"'On the Sabbath day, make an offering of two lambs a year old without defect, together with its drink offering and a grain offering of two-tenths of an ephah*c* of fine flour mixed with oil. 10This is the burnt offering for every Sabbath, in addition to the regular burnt offering and its drink offering.

Monthly Offerings

11"'On the first of every month, present to the LORD a burnt offering of two young bulls, one ram and seven male lambs a year old, all without defect. 12With each bull there is to be a grain offering of three-tenths of an ephah*d* of fine flour mixed with oil; with the ram, a grain offering of two-tenths of an ephah of fine flour mixed with oil; 13and with each lamb, a grain offering of a tenth of an ephah of fine flour mixed with oil. This is for a burnt offering, a pleasing aroma, an offering made to the LORD by fire. 14With each bull there is to be a drink offering of half a hin*e* of wine; with the ram, a third of a hin;*f* and with each lamb, a quarter of a hin. This is the monthly burnt offering to be made at each new moon during the year. 15Besides the regular burnt offering with its drink

offering, one male goat is to be presented to the LORD as a sin offering.

The Passover

16"'On the fourteenth day of the first month the LORD's Passover is to be held. 17On the fifteenth day of this month there is to be a festival; for seven days eat bread made without yeast. 18On the first day hold a sacred assembly and do no regular work. 19Present to the LORD an offering made by fire, a burnt offering of two young bulls, one ram and seven male lambs a year old, all without defect. 20With each bull prepare a grain offering of three-tenths of an ephah of fine flour mixed with oil; with the ram, two-tenths, 21and with each of the seven lambs, one tenth. 22Include one male goat as a sin offering to make atonement for you. 23Prepare these in addition to the regular morning burnt offering. 24In this way prepare the food for the offering made by fire every day for seven days as an aroma pleasing to the LORD; it is to be prepared in addition to the regular burnt offering and its drink offering. 25On the seventh day hold a sacred assembly and do no regular work.

Feast of Weeks

26"'On the day of firstfruits, when you present to the LORD an offering of new grain during the Feast of Weeks, hold a sacred assembly and do no regular work. 27Present a burnt offering of two young bulls, one ram and seven male lambs a year old as an aroma pleasing to the LORD. 28With each bull there is to be a grain offering of three-tenths of an ephah of fine flour mixed with oil; with the ram, two-tenths; 29and with each of the seven lambs, one-tenth. 30Include one male goat to make atonement for you. 31Prepare these together with their drink offerings, in addition to the regular burnt offering and

---

a5 That is, probably about 4 pints (about 2 litres); also in verses 13, 21 and 29
b5 That is, probably about 1½ pints (about 1 litre); also in verses 7 and 14
c9 That is, probably about 7½ pints (about 4.5 litres); also in verses 12, 20 and 28
d12 That is, probably about 11½ pints (about 6.5 litres); also in verses 20 and 28
e14 That is, probably about 3 pints (about 2 litres)   *f14* That is, probably about 2¼ pints (about 1.2 litres)

its grain offering. Be sure the animals are without defect.

Feast of Trumpets

29 "'On the first day of the seventh month hold a sacred assembly and do no regular work. It is a day for you to sound the trumpets. ²As an aroma pleasing to the Lord, prepare a burnt offering of one young bull, one ram and seven male lambs a year old, all without defect. ³With the bull prepare a grain offering of three-tenths of an ephah*a* of fine flour mixed with oil; with the ram, two-tenths;*b* ⁴and with each of the seven lambs, one-tenth.*c* ⁵Include one male goat as a sin offering to make atonement for you. ⁶These are in addition to the monthly and daily burnt offerings with their grain offerings and drink offerings as specified. They are offerings made to the Lord by fire—a pleasing aroma.

Day of Atonement

⁷"'On the tenth day of this seventh month hold a sacred assembly. You must deny yourselves*d* and do no work. ⁸Present as an aroma pleasing to the Lord a burnt offering of one young bull, one ram and seven male lambs a year old, all without defect. ⁹With the bull prepare a grain offering of three-tenths of an ephah of fine flour mixed with oil; with the ram, two-tenths; ¹⁰and with each of the seven lambs, one-tenth. ¹¹Include one male goat as a sin offering, in addition to the sin offering for atonement and the regular burnt offering with its grain offering, and their drink offerings.

Feast of Tabernacles

¹²"'On the fifteenth day of the seventh month, hold a sacred assembly and do no regular work. Celebrate a festival to the Lord for seven days. ¹³Present an offering made by fire as an aroma pleasing to the Lord, a burnt offering of thirteen young bulls, two rams and fourteen male lambs a year old, all without defect. ¹⁴With each of the thirteen bulls prepare a grain offering of three-tenths of an ephah of fine flour mixed with oil; with each of the two rams, two-tenths; ¹⁵and with each of the fourteen lambs, one-tenth. ¹⁶Include one male goat as a sin offering, in addition to the regular burnt offering with its grain offering and drink offering.

¹⁷"'On the second day prepare twelve young bulls, two rams and fourteen male lambs a year old, all without defect. ¹⁸With the bulls, rams and lambs, prepare their grain offerings and drink offerings according to the number specified. ¹⁹Include one male goat as a sin offering, in addition to the regular burnt offering with its grain offering, and their drink offerings.

²⁰"'On the third day prepare eleven bulls, two rams and fourteen male lambs a year old, all without defect. ²¹With the bulls, rams and lambs, prepare their grain offerings and drink offerings according to the number specified. ²²Include one male goat as a sin offering, in addition to the regular burnt offering with its grain offering and drink offering.

²³"'On the fourth day prepare ten bulls, two rams and fourteen male lambs a year old, all without defect. ²⁴With the bulls, rams and lambs, prepare their grain offerings and drink offerings according to the number specified. ²⁵Include one male goat as a sin offering, in addition to the regular burnt offering with its grain offering and drink offering.

²⁶"'On the fifth day prepare nine bulls, two rams and fourteen male lambs a year old, all without defect. ²⁷With the bulls, rams and lambs, prepare their grain offerings and drink offerings according to the number specified. ²⁸Include one male goat as a sin offering, in addition to the regular burnt offering with its grain offering and drink offering.

²⁹"'On the sixth day prepare eight bulls, two rams and fourteen male lambs a year old, all without defect. ³⁰With the bulls,

---

a3 That is, probably about 11½ pints (about 6·5 litres); also in verses 9 and 14
b3 That is, probably about 7½ pints (about 4.5 litres); also in verses 9 and 14
c4 That is, probably about 4 pints (about 2 litres); also in verses 10 and 15   *d7* Or *must fast*

rams and lambs, prepare their grain offerings and drink offerings according to the number specified. [31]Include one male goat as a sin offering, in addition to the regular burnt offering with its grain offering and drink offering.

[32]"On the seventh day prepare seven bulls, two rams and fourteen male lambs a year old, all without defect. [33]With the bulls, rams and lambs, prepare their grain offerings and drink offerings according to the number specified. [34]Include one male goat as a sin offering, in addition to the regular burnt offering with its grain offering and drink offering.

[35]"On the eighth day hold an assembly and do no regular work. [36]Present an offering made by fire as an aroma pleasing to the LORD, a burnt offering of one bull, one ram and seven male lambs a year old, all without defect. [37]With the bull, the ram and the lambs, prepare their grain offerings and drink offerings according to the number specified. [38]Include one male goat as a sin offering, in addition to the regular burnt offering with its grain offering and drink offering.

[39]"In addition to what you vow and your freewill offerings, prepare these for the LORD at your appointed feasts: your burnt offerings, grain offerings, drink offerings and fellowship offerings.'"[e]

[40]Moses told the Israelites all that the LORD commanded him.

Vows

30 Moses said to the heads of the tribes of Israel: "This is what the LORD commands: [2]When a man makes a vow to the LORD or takes an oath to bind himself by a pledge, he must not break his word but must do everything he said.

[3]"When a young woman still living in her father's house makes a vow to the LORD or binds herself by a pledge [4]and her father hears about her vow or pledge but says nothing to her, then all her vows and every pledge by which she bound herself will stand. [5]But if her father forbids her when he hears about it, none of her vows

or the pledges by which she bound herself will stand; the LORD will release her because her father has forbidden her.

[6]"If she marries after she makes a vow or after her lips utter a rash promise by which she binds herself [7]and her husband hears about it but says nothing to her, then her vows or the pledges by which she bound herself will stand. [8]But if her husband forbids her when he hears about it, he nullifies the vow that binds her or the rash promise by which she binds herself, and the LORD will release her.

[9]"Any vow or obligation taken by a widow or divorced woman will be binding on her.

[10]"If a woman living with her husband makes a vow or binds herself by a pledge under oath [11]and her husband hears about it but says nothing to her and does not forbid her, then all her vows or the pledges by which she bound herself will stand. [12]But if her husband nullifies them when he hears about them, then none of the vows or pledges that came from her lips will stand. Her husband has nullified them, and the LORD will release her. [13]Her husband may confirm or nullify any vow she makes or any sworn pledge to deny herself. [14]But if her husband says nothing to her about it from day to day, then he confirms all her vows or the pledges binding on her. He confirms them by saying nothing to her when he hears about them. [15]If, however, he nullifies them some time after he hears about them, then he is responsible for her guilt."

[16]These are the regulations the LORD gave Moses concerning relationships between a man and his wife, and between a father and his young daughter still living in his house.

Vengeance on the Midianites

31 The LORD said to Moses, [2]"Take vengeance on the Midianites for the Israelites. After that, you will be gathered to your people."

[3]So Moses said to the people, "Arm some of your men to go to war against the

e39 Traditionally peace offerings

Midianites and to carry out the LORD's vengeance on them. ⁴Send into battle a thousand men from each of the tribes of Israel." ⁵So twelve thousand men armed for battle, a thousand from each tribe, were supplied from the clans of Israel. ⁶Moses sent them into battle, a thousand from each tribe, along with Phinehas son of Eleazar, the priest, who took with him articles from the sanctuary and the trumpets for signalling.

⁷They fought against Midian, as the LORD commanded Moses, and killed every man. ⁸Among their victims were Evi, Rekem, Zur, Hur and Reba—the five kings of Midian. They also killed Balaam son of Beor with the sword. ⁹The Israelites captured the Midianite women and children and took all the Midianite herds, flocks and goods as plunder. ¹⁰They burned all the towns where the Midianites had settled, as well as all their camps. ¹¹They took all the plunder and spoils, including the people and animals, ¹²and brought the captives, spoils and plunder to Moses and Eleazar the priest and the Israelite assembly at their camp on the plains of Moab, by the Jordan across from Jericho.ᵃ

¹³Moses, Eleazar the priest and all the leaders of the community went to meet them outside the camp. ¹⁴Moses was angry with the officers of the army—the commanders of thousands and commanders of hundreds—who returned from the battle.

¹⁵"Have you allowed all the women to live?" he asked them. ¹⁶"They were the ones who followed Balaam's advice and were the means of turning the Israelites away from the LORD in what happened at Peor, so that a plague struck the LORD's people. ¹⁷Now kill all the boys. And kill every woman who has slept with a man, ¹⁸but save for yourselves every girl who has never slept with a man.

¹⁹"All of you who have killed anyone or touched anyone who was killed must stay outside the camp seven days. On the third and seventh days you must purify yourselves and your captives. ²⁰Purify every

garment as well as everything made of leather, goat hair or wood."

²¹Then Eleazar the priest said to the soldiers who had gone into battle, "This is the requirement of the law that the LORD gave Moses: ²²Gold, silver, bronze, iron, tin, lead ²³and anything else that can withstand fire must be put through the fire, and then it will be clean. But it must also be purified with the water of cleansing. And whatever cannot withstand fire must be put through that water. ²⁴On the seventh day wash your clothes and you will be clean. Then you may come into the camp."

Dividing the Spoils

²⁵The LORD said to Moses, ²⁶"You and Eleazar the priest and the family heads of the community are to count all the people and animals that were captured. ²⁷Divide the spoils between the soldiers who took part in the battle and the rest of the community. ²⁸From the soldiers who fought in the battle, set apart as tribute for the LORD one out of every five hundred, whether persons, cattle, donkeys, sheep or goats. ²⁹Take this tribute from their half share and give it to Eleazar the priest as the LORD's part. ³⁰From the Israelites' half, select one out of every fifty, whether persons, cattle, donkeys, sheep, goats or other animals. Give them to the Levites, who are responsible for the care of the LORD's tabernacle." ³¹So Moses and Eleazar the priest did as the LORD commanded Moses.

³²The plunder remaining from the spoils that the soldiers took was 675,000 sheep, ³³72,000 cattle, ³⁴61,000 donkeys ³⁵and 32,000 women who had never slept with a man.

³⁶The half share of those who fought in the battle was:

337,500 sheep, ³⁷of which the tribute for the LORD was 675;
³⁸36,000 cattle, of which the tribute for the LORD was 72;

ᵃ12 Hebrew *Jordan of Jericho*; possibly an ancient name for the Jordan River

[39] 30,500 donkeys, of which the tribute for the LORD was 61; [40] 16,000 people, of which the tribute for the LORD was 32.

[41] Moses gave the tribute to Eleazar the priest as the LORD's part, as the LORD commanded Moses.

[42] The half belonging to the Israelites, which Moses set apart from that of the fighting men— [43] the community's half— was 337,500 sheep, [44] 36,000 cattle, [45] 30,500 donkeys [46] and 16,000 people. [47] From the Israelites' half, Moses selected one out of every fifty persons and animals, as the LORD commanded him, and gave them to the Levites, who were responsible for the care of the LORD's tabernacle.

[48] Then the officers who were over the units of the army—the commanders of thousands and commanders of hundreds—went to Moses [49] and said to him, "Your servants have counted the soldiers under our command, and not one is missing. [50] So we have brought as an offering to the LORD the gold articles each of us acquired—armlets, bracelets, signet rings, ear-rings and necklaces—to make atonement for ourselves before the LORD."

[51] Moses and Eleazar the priest accepted from them the gold—all the handcrafted articles. [52] All the gold from the commanders of thousands and commanders of hundreds that Moses and Eleazar presented as a gift to the LORD weighed 16,750 shekels.[b] [53] Each soldier had taken plunder for himself. [54] Moses and Eleazar the priest accepted the gold from the commanders of thousands and commanders of hundreds and brought it into the Tent of Meeting as a memorial for the Israelites before the LORD.

The Transjordan Tribes

32 The Reubenites and Gadites, who had very large herds and flocks, saw that the lands of Jazer and Gilead were suitable for livestock. [2] So they came to Moses and Eleazar the priest and to the leaders of the community, and said, [3] "Ataroth, Dibon, Jazer, Nimrah, Heshbon, Elealeh, Sebam, Nebo and Beon— [4] the land the LORD subdued before the people of Israel—are suitable for livestock, and your servants have livestock. [5] If we have found favour in your eyes," they said, "let this land be given to your servants as our possession. Do not make us cross the Jordan."

[6] Moses said to the Gadites and Reubenites, "Shall your countrymen go to war while you sit here? [7] Why do you discourage the Israelites from going over into the land the LORD has given them? [8] This is what your fathers did when I sent them from Kadesh Barnea to look over the land. [9] After they went up to the Valley of Eshcol and viewed the land, they discouraged the Israelites from entering the land the LORD had given them. [10] The LORD's anger was aroused that day and he swore this oath: [11] 'Because they have not followed me wholeheartedly, not one of the men twenty years old or more who came up out of Egypt will see the land I promised on oath to Abraham, Isaac and Jacob— [12] not one except Caleb son of Jephunneh the Kenizzite and Joshua son of Nun, for they followed the LORD wholeheartedly.' [13] The LORD's anger burned against Israel and he made them wander in the desert for forty years, until the whole generation of those who had done evil in his sight was gone.

[14] "And here you are, a brood of sinners, standing in the place of your fathers and making the LORD even more angry with Israel. [15] If you turn away from following him, he will again leave all this people in the desert, and you will be the cause of their destruction."

[16] Then they came up to him and said, "We would like to build pens here for our livestock and cities for our women and children. [17] But we are ready to arm ourselves and go ahead of the Israelites until we have brought them to their place. Meanwhile our women and children will live in fortified cities, for protection from the inhabitants of the land. [18] We will not

[b]52 That is, about 420 pounds (about 190 kilograms)

return to our homes until every Israelite has received his inheritance. [19]We will not receive any inheritance with them on the other side of the Jordan, because our inheritance has come to us on the east side of the Jordan."

[20]Then Moses said to them, "If you will do this—if you will arm yourselves before the LORD for battle, [21]and if all of you will go armed over the Jordan before the LORD until he has driven his enemies out before him—[22]then when the land is subdued before the LORD, you may return and be free from your obligation to the LORD and to Israel. And this land will be your possession before the LORD.

[23]"But if you fail to do this, you will be sinning against the LORD; and you may be sure that your sin will find you out. [24]Build cities for your women and children, and pens for your flocks, but do what you have promised."

[25]The Gadites and Reubenites said to Moses, "We your servants will do as our lord commands. [26]Our children and wives, our flocks and herds will remain here in the cities of Gilead. [27]But your servants, every man armed for battle, will cross over to fight before the LORD, just as our lord says."

[28]Then Moses gave orders about them to Eleazar the priest and Joshua son of Nun and to the family heads of the Israelite tribes. [29]He said to them, "If the Gadites and Reubenites, every man armed for battle, cross over the Jordan with you before the LORD, then when the land is subdued before you, give them the land of Gilead as their possession. [30]But if they do not cross over with you armed, they must accept their possession with you in Canaan."

[31]The Gadites and Reubenites answered, "Your servants will do what the LORD has said. [32]We will cross over before the LORD into Canaan armed, but the property we inherit will be on this side of the Jordan."

[33]Then Moses gave to the Gadites, the Reubenites and the half-tribe of Manasseh son of Joseph the kingdom of Sihon king of the Amorites and the kingdom of Og king of Bashan—the whole land with its cities and the territory around them.

[34]The Gadites built up Dibon, Ataroth, Aroer, [35]Atroth Shophan, Jazer, Jogbehah, [36]Beth Nimrah and Beth Haran as fortified cities, and built pens for their flocks. [37]And the Reubenites rebuilt Heshbon, Elealeh and Kiriathaim, [38]as well as Nebo and Baal Meon (these names were changed) and Sibmah. They gave names to the cities they rebuilt.

[39]The descendants of Makir son of Manasseh went to Gilead, captured it and drove out the Amorites who were there. [40]So Moses gave Gilead to the Makirites, the descendants of Manasseh, and they settled there. [41]Jair, a descendant of Manasseh, captured their settlements and called them Havvoth Jair.[a] [42]And Nobah captured Kenath and its surrounding settlements and called it Nobah after himself.

Stages in Israel's Journey

33 Here are the stages in the journey of the Israelites when they came out of Egypt by divisions under the leadership of Moses and Aaron. [2]At the LORD's command Moses recorded the stages in their journey. This is their journey by stages:

[3]The Israelites set out from Rameses on the fifteenth day of the first month, the day after the Passover. They marched out boldly in full view of all the Egyptians, [4]who were burying all their firstborn, whom the LORD had struck down among them; for the LORD had brought judgment on their gods.

[5]The Israelites left Rameses and camped at Succoth.

[6]They left Succoth and camped at Etham, on the edge of the desert.

[7]They left Etham, turned back to Pi Hahiroth, to the east of Baal Zephon, and camped near Migdol.

[a]41 Or *them the settlements of Jair*

8They left Pi Hahiroth[a] and passed through the sea into the desert, and when they had travelled for three days in the Desert of Etham, they camped at Marah.

9They left Marah and went to Elim, where there were twelve springs and seventy palm trees, and they camped there.

10They left Elim and camped by the Red Sea.[b]

11They left the Red Sea and camped in the Desert of Sin.

12They left the Desert of Sin and camped at Dophkah.

13They left Dophkah and camped at Alush.

14They left Alush and camped at Rephidim, where there was no water for the people to drink.

15They left Rephidim and camped in the Desert of Sinai.

16They left the Desert of Sinai and camped at Kibroth Hattaavah.

17They left Kibroth Hattaavah and camped at Hazeroth.

18They left Hazeroth and camped at Rithmah.

19They left Rithmah and camped at Rimmon Perez.

20They left Rimmon Perez and camped at Libnah.

21They left Libnah and camped at Rissah.

22They left Rissah and camped at Kehelathah.

23They left Kehelathah and camped at Mount Shepher.

24They left Mount Shepher and camped at Haradah.

25They left Haradah and camped at Makheloth.

26They left Makheloth and camped at Tahath.

27They left Tahath and camped at Terah.

28They left Terah and camped at Mithcah.

29They left Mithcah and camped at Hashmonah.

30They left Hashmonah and camped at Moseroth.

31They left Moseroth and camped at Bene Jaakan.

32They left Bene Jaakan and camped at Hor Haggidgad.

33They left Hor Haggidgad and camped at Jotbathah.

34They left Jotbathah and camped at Abronah.

35They left Abronah and camped at Ezion Geber.

36They left Ezion Geber and camped at Kadesh, in the Desert of Zin.

37They left Kadesh and camped at Mount Hor, on the border of Edom. 38At the LORD's command Aaron the priest went up Mount Hor, where he died on the first day of the fifth month of the fortieth year after the Israelites came out of Egypt. 39Aaron was a hundred and twenty-three years old when he died on Mount Hor.

40The Canaanite king of Arad, who lived in the Negev of Canaan, heard that the Israelites were coming.

41They left Mount Hor and camped at Zalmonah.

42They left Zalmonah and camped at Punon.

43They left Punon and camped at Oboth.

44They left Oboth and camped at Iye Abarim, on the border of Moab.

45They left Iyim[c] and camped at Dibon Gad.

46They left Dibon Gad and camped at Almon Diblathaim.

47They left Almon Diblathaim and camped in the mountains of Abarim, near Nebo.

48They left the mountains of Abarim and camped on the plains of Moab by the Jordan across from Jericho.[d] 49There on the plains of Moab they camped along the Jordan from Beth Jeshimoth to Abel Shittim.

---

[a]8 Many manuscripts of the Masoretic Text, Samaritan Pentateuch and Vulgate; most manuscripts of the Masoretic Text *left from before Hahiroth*   [b]10 Hebrew *Yam Suph*; that is, Sea of Reeds; also in verse 11   [c]45 That is, Iye Abarim   [d]48 Hebrew *Jordan of Jericho*; possibly an ancient name for the Jordan River; also in verse 50

⁵⁰On the plains of Moab by the Jordan across from Jericho the LORD said to Moses, ⁵¹"Speak to the Israelites and say to them: 'When you cross the Jordan into Canaan, ⁵²drive out all the inhabitants of the land before you. Destroy all their carved images and their cast idols, and demolish all their high places. ⁵³Take possession of the land and settle in it, for I have given you the land to possess. ⁵⁴Distribute the land by lot, according to your clans. To a larger group give a larger inheritance, and to a smaller group a smaller one. Whatever falls to them by lot will be theirs. Distribute it according to your ancestral tribes.

⁵⁵"'But if you do not drive out the inhabitants of the land, those you allow to remain will become barbs in your eyes and thorns in your sides. They will give you trouble in the land where you will live. ⁵⁶And then I will do to you what I plan to do to them.'"

Boundaries of Canaan

34 The LORD said to Moses, ²"Command the Israelites and say to them: 'When you enter Canaan, the land that will be allotted to you as an inheritance will have these boundaries:

³"'Your southern side will include some of the Desert of Zin along the border of Edom. On the east, your southern boundary will start from the end of the Salt Sea,ᵃ ⁴cross south of Scorpionᵇ Pass, continue on to Zin and go south of Kadesh Barnea. Then it will go to Hazar Addar and over to Azmon, ⁵where it will turn, join the Wadi of Egypt and end at the Sea.ᶜ

⁶"'Your western boundary will be the coast of the Great Sea. This will be your boundary on the west.

⁷"'For your northern boundary, run a line from the Great Sea to Mount Hor ⁸and from Mount Hor to Leboᵈ Hamath. Then the boundary will go to Zedad, ⁹continue to Ziphron and end at Hazar Enan. This will be your boundary on the north.

¹⁰"'For your eastern boundary, run a line from Hazar Enan to Shepham. ¹¹The boundary will go down from Shepham to Riblah on the east side of Ain and continue along the slopes east of the Sea of Kinnereth.ᵉ ¹²Then the boundary will go down along the Jordan and end at the Salt Sea.

"'This will be your land, with its boundaries on every side.'"

¹³Moses commanded the Israelites: "Assign this land by lot as an inheritance. The LORD has ordered that it be given to the nine and a half tribes, ¹⁴because the families of the tribe of Reuben, the tribe of Gad and the half-tribe of Manasseh have received their inheritance. ¹⁵These two and a half tribes have received their inheritance on the east side of the Jordan of Jericho,ᶠ towards the sunrise."

¹⁶The LORD said to Moses, ¹⁷"These are the names of the men who are to assign the land for you as an inheritance: Eleazar the priest and Joshua son of Nun. ¹⁸And appoint one leader from each tribe to help assign the land. ¹⁹These are their names:

Caleb son of Jephunneh,
    from the tribe of Judah;
²⁰Shemuel son of Ammihud,
    from the tribe of Simeon;
²¹Elidad son of Kislon,
    from the tribe of Benjamin;
²²Bukki son of Jogli,
    the leader from the tribe of Dan;
²³Hanniel son of Ephod,
    the leader from the tribe of
    Manasseh son of Joseph;
²⁴Kemuel son of Shiphtan,
    the leader from the tribe of Ephraim
    son of Joseph;
²⁵Elizaphan son of Parnach,
    the leader from the tribe of
    Zebulun;
²⁶Paltiel son of Azzan,
    the leader from the tribe of Issachar;
²⁷Ahihud son of Shelomi,
    the leader from the tribe of Asher;

ᵃ3 That is, the Dead Sea; also in verse 12   ᵇ4 Hebrew *Akrabbim*
ᶜ5 That is, the Mediterranean; also in verses 6 and 7   ᵈ8 Or *to the entrance to*
ᵉ11 That is, Galilee   ᶠ15 *Jordan of Jericho* was possibly an ancient name for the Jordan River.

²⁸Pedahel son of Ammihud,
    the leader from the tribe of
    Naphtali."

²⁹These are the men the LORD commanded to assign the inheritance to the Israelites in the land of Canaan.

Towns for the Levites

35 On the plains of Moab by the Jordan across from Jericho,^a the LORD said to Moses, ²"Command the Israelites to give the Levites towns to live in from the inheritance the Israelites will possess. And give them pasture-lands around the towns. ³Then they will have towns to live in and pasture-lands for their cattle, flocks and all their other livestock.

⁴"The pasture-lands around the towns that you give the Levites will extend out fifteen hundred feet^b from the town wall. ⁵Outside the town, measure three thousand feet^c on the east side, three thousand on the south side, three thousand on the west and three thousand on the north, with the town in the centre. They will have this area as pasture-land for the towns.

Cities of Refuge

⁶"Six of the towns you give the Levites will be cities of refuge, to which a person who has killed someone may flee. In addition, give them forty-two other towns. ⁷In all you must give the Levites forty-eight towns, together with their pasture-lands. ⁸The towns you give the Levites from the land the Israelites possess are to be given in proportion to the inheritance of each tribe: Take many towns from a tribe that has many, but few from one that has few."

⁹Then the LORD said to Moses: ¹⁰"Speak to the Israelites and say to them: 'When you cross the Jordan into Canaan, ¹¹select some towns to be your cities of refuge, to which a person who has killed someone accidentally may flee. ¹²They will be places of refuge from the avenger, so that a person accused of murder may not die

before he stands trial before the assembly. ¹³These six towns you give will be your cities of refuge. ¹⁴Give three on this side of the Jordan and three in Canaan as cities of refuge. ¹⁵These six towns will be a place of refuge for Israelites, aliens and any other people living among them, so that anyone who has killed another accidentally can flee there.

¹⁶"'If a man strikes someone with an iron object so that he dies, he is a murderer; the murderer shall be put to death. ¹⁷Or if anyone has a stone in his hand that could kill, and he strikes someone so that he dies, he is a murderer; the murderer shall be put to death. ¹⁸Or if anyone has a wooden object in his hand that could kill, and he hits someone so that he dies, he is a murderer; the murderer shall be put to death. ¹⁹The avenger of blood shall put the murderer to death; when he meets him, he shall put him to death. ²⁰If anyone with malice aforethought pushes another or throws something at him intentionally so that he dies ²¹or if in hostility he hits him with his fist so that he dies, that person shall be put to death; he is a murderer. The avenger of blood shall put the murderer to death when he meets him.

²²"'But if without hostility someone suddenly pushes another or throws something at him unintentionally ²³or, without seeing him, drops a stone on him that could kill him, and he dies, then since he was not his enemy and he did not intend to harm him, ²⁴the assembly must judge between him and the avenger of blood according to these regulations. ²⁵The assembly must protect the one accused of murder from the avenger of blood and send him back to the city of refuge to which he fled. He must stay there until the death of the high priest, who was anointed with holy oil.

²⁶"'But if the accused ever goes outside the limits of the city of refuge to which he has fled ²⁷and the avenger of blood finds him outside the city, the avenger of blood may kill the accused without being guilty of murder. ²⁸The accused must stay in hi

^a1 Hebrew *Jordan of Jericho*; possibly an ancient name for the Jordan River
^b4 Hebrew *a thousand cubits* (about 450 metres)   ^c5 Hebrew *two thousand cubits* (about 900 metres)

city of refuge until the death of the high priest; only after the death of the high priest may he return to his own property.

29" 'These are to be legal requirements for you throughout the generations to come, wherever you live.

30" 'Anyone who kills a person is to be put to death as a murderer only on the testimony of witnesses. But no-one is to be put to death on the testimony of only one witness.

31" 'Do not accept a ransom for the life of a murderer, who deserves to die. He must surely be put to death.

32" 'Do not accept a ransom for anyone who has fled to a city of refuge and so allow him to go back and live on his own land before the death of the high priest.

33" 'Do not pollute the land where you are. Bloodshed pollutes the land, and atonement cannot be made for the land on which blood has been shed, except by the blood of the one who shed it. 34Do not defile the land where you live and where I dwell, for I, the LORD, dwell among the Israelites.' "

Inheritance of Zelophehad's Daughters

36 The family heads of the clan of Gilead son of Makir, the son of Manasseh, who were from the clans of the descendants of Joseph, came and spoke before Moses and the leaders, the heads of the Israelite families. 2They said, "When the LORD commanded my lord to give the land as an inheritance to the Israelites by lot, he ordered you to give the inheritance of our brother Zelophehad to his daughters. 3Now suppose they marry men from other Israelite tribes; then their inheritance will be taken from our ancestral inheritance and added to that of the tribe they marry into. And so part of the inheritance allotted to us will be taken away. 4When the Year of Jubilee for the Israelites comes, their inheritance will be added to that of the tribe into which they marry, and their property will be taken from the tribal inheritance of our forefathers."

5Then at the LORD's command Moses gave this order to the Israelites: "What the tribe of the descendants of Joseph is saying is right. 6This is what the LORD commands for Zelophehad's daughters: They may marry anyone they please as long as they marry within the tribal clan of their father. 7No inheritance in Israel is to pass from tribe to tribe, for every Israelite shall keep the tribal land inherited from his forefathers. 8Every daughter who inherits land in any Israelite tribe must marry someone in her father's tribal clan, so that every Israelite will possess the inheritance of his fathers. 9No inheritance may pass from tribe to tribe, for each Israelite tribe is to keep the land it inherits."

10So Zelophehad's daughters did as the LORD commanded Moses. 11Zelophehad's daughters—Mahlah, Tirzah, Hoglah, Milcah and Noah—married their cousins on their father's side. 12They married within the clans of the descendants of Manasseh son of Joseph, and their inheritance remained in their father's clan and tribe.

13These are the commands and regulations the LORD gave through Moses to the Israelites on the plains of Moab by the Jordan across from Jericho.[a]

---

[a]13 Hebrew *Jordan of Jericho*; possibly an ancient name for the Jordan River

Deuteronomy

The Command to Leave Horeb

1 These are the words Moses spoke to all Israel in the desert east of the Jordan—that is, in the Arabah—opposite Suph, between Paran and Tophel, Laban, Hazeroth and Dizahab. ²(It takes eleven days to go from Horeb to Kadesh Barnea by the Mount Seir road.)

³In the fortieth year, on the first day of the eleventh month, Moses proclaimed to the Israelites all that the LORD had commanded him concerning them. ⁴This was after he had defeated Sihon king of the Amorites, who reigned in Heshbon, and at Edrei had defeated Og king of Bashan, who reigned in Ashtaroth.

⁵East of the Jordan in the territory of Moab, Moses began to expound this law, saying:

⁶The LORD our God said to us at Horeb, "You have stayed long enough at this mountain. ⁷Break camp and advance into the hill country of the Amorites; go to all the neighbouring peoples in the Arabah, in the mountains, in the western foothills, in the Negev and along the coast, to the land of the Canaanites and to Lebanon, as far as the great river, the Euphrates. ⁸See, I have given you this land. Go in and take possession of the land that the LORD swore he would give to your fathers—to Abraham, Isaac and Jacob—and to their descendants after them."

The Appointment of Leaders

⁹At that time I said to you, "You are too heavy a burden for me to carry alone. ¹⁰The LORD your God has increased your numbers so that today you are as many as the stars in the sky. ¹¹May the LORD, the God of your fathers, increase you a thousand times and bless you as he has promised! ¹²But how can I bear your problems and your burdens and your disputes all by myself? ¹³Choose some wise, understanding and respected men from each of your tribes, and I will set them over you."

¹⁴You answered me, "What you propose to do is good."

¹⁵So I took the leading men of your tribes, wise and respected men, and appointed them to have authority over you—as commanders of thousands, of hundreds, of fifties and of tens and as tribal officials. ¹⁶And I charged your judges at that time: Hear the disputes between your brothers and judge fairly, whether the case is between brother Israelites or between one of them and an alien. ¹⁷Do not show partiality in judging; hear both small and great alike. Do not be afraid of any man, for judgment belongs to God. Bring me any case too hard for you, and I will hear it. ¹⁸And at that time I told you everything you were to do.

Spies Sent Out

¹⁹Then, as the LORD our God commanded us, we set out from Horeb and went towards the hill country of the Amorites through all that vast and dreadful desert that you have seen, and so we reached Kadesh Barnea. ²⁰Then I said to you, "You have reached the hill country of the Amorites, which the LORD our God is

giving us. ²¹See, the LORD your God has given you the land. Go up and take possession of it as the LORD, the God of your fathers, told you. Do not be afraid; do not be discouraged."

²²Then all of you came to me and said, "Let us send men ahead to spy out the land for us and bring back a report about the route we are to take and the towns we will come to."

²³The idea seemed good to me; so I selected twelve of you, one man from each tribe. ²⁴They left and went up into the hill country, and came to the Valley of Eshcol and explored it. ²⁵Taking with them some of the fruit of the land, they brought it down to us and reported, "It is a good land that the LORD our God is giving us."

Rebellion Against the LORD

²⁶But you were unwilling to go up; you rebelled against the command of the LORD your God. ²⁷You grumbled in your tents and said, "The LORD hates us; so he brought us out of Egypt to deliver us into the hands of the Amorites to destroy us. ²⁸Where can we go? Our brothers have made us lose heart. They say, 'The people are stronger and taller than we are; the cities are large, with walls up to the sky. We even saw the Anakites there.'"

²⁹Then I said to you, "Do not be terrified; do not be afraid of them. ³⁰The LORD your God, who is going before you, will fight for you, as he did for you in Egypt, before your very eyes, ³¹and in the desert. There you saw how the LORD your God carried you, as a father carries his son, all the way you went until you reached this place."

³²In spite of this, you did not trust in the LORD your God, ³³who went ahead of you on your journey, in fire by night and in a cloud by day, to search out places for you to camp and to show you the way you should go.

³⁴When the LORD heard what you said, he was angry and solemnly swore: ³⁵"Not a man of this evil generation shall see the good land I swore to give your forefathers, ³⁶except Caleb son of Jephunneh. He will see it, and I will give him and his descendants the land he set his feet on, because he followed the LORD wholeheartedly."

³⁷Because of you the LORD became angry with me also and said, "You shall not enter it, either. ³⁸But your assistant, Joshua son of Nun, will enter it. Encourage him, because he will lead Israel to inherit it. ³⁹And the little ones that you said would be taken captive, your children who do not yet know good from bad—they will enter the land. I will give it to them and they will take possession of it. ⁴⁰But as for you, turn round and set out towards the desert along the route to the Red Sea."^a

⁴¹Then you replied, "We have sinned against the LORD. We will go up and fight, as the LORD our God commanded us." So every one of you put on his weapons, thinking it easy to go up into the hill country.

⁴²But the LORD said to me, "Tell them, 'Do not go up and fight, because I will not be with you. You will be defeated by your enemies.'"

⁴³So I told you, but you would not listen. You rebelled against the LORD's command and in your arrogance you marched up into the hill country. ⁴⁴The Amorites who lived in those hills came out against you; they chased you like a swarm of bees and beat you down from Seir all the way to Hormah. ⁴⁵You came back and wept before the LORD, but he paid no attention to your weeping and turned a deaf ear to you. ⁴⁶And so you stayed in Kadesh many days—all the time you spent there.

Wanderings in the Desert

2 Then we turned back and set out towards the desert along the route to the Red Sea,^a as the LORD had directed me. For a long time we made our way around the hill country of Seir.

---

^a40 Hebrew *Yam Suph*; that is, Sea of Reeds
^a1 Hebrew *Yam Suph*; that is, Sea of Reeds

²Then the LORD said to me, ³"You have made your way around this hill country long enough; now turn north. ⁴Give the people these orders: 'You are about to pass through the territory of your brothers the descendants of Esau, who live in Seir. They will be afraid of you, but be very careful. ⁵Do not provoke them to war, for I will not give you any of their land, not even enough to put your foot on. I have given Esau the hill country of Seir as his own. ⁶You are to pay them in silver for the food you eat and the water you drink.'"

⁷The LORD your God has blessed you in all the work of your hands. He has watched over your journey through this vast desert. These forty years the LORD your God has been with you, and you have not lacked anything.

⁸So we went on past our brothers the descendants of Esau, who live in Seir. We turned from the Arabah road, which comes up from Elath and Ezion Geber, and travelled along the desert road of Moab.

⁹Then the LORD said to me, "Do not harass the Moabites or provoke them to war, for I will not give you any part of their land. I have given Ar to the descendants of Lot as a possession."

¹⁰(The Emites used to live there—a people strong and numerous, and as tall as the Anakites. ¹¹Like the Anakites, they too were considered Rephaites, but the Moabites called them Emites. ¹²Horites used to live in Seir, but the descendants of Esau drove them out. They destroyed the Horites from before them and settled in their place, just as Israel did in the land the LORD gave them as their possession.)

¹³And the LORD said, "Now get up and cross the Zered Valley." So we crossed the valley.

¹⁴Thirty-eight years passed from the time we left Kadesh Barnea until we crossed the Zered Valley. By then, that entire generation of fighting men had perished from the camp, as the LORD had sworn to them. ¹⁵The LORD's hand was against them until he had completely eliminated them from the camp.

¹⁶Now when the last of these fighting men among the people had died, ¹⁷the LORD said to me, ¹⁸"Today you are to pass by the region of Moab at Ar. ¹⁹When you come to the Ammonites, do not harass them or provoke them to war, for I will not give you possession of any land belonging to the Ammonites. I have given it as a possession to the descendants of Lot."

²⁰(That too was considered a land of the Rephaites, who used to live there; but the Ammonites called them Zamzummites. ²¹They were a people strong and numerous, and as tall as the Anakites. The LORD destroyed them from before the Ammonites, who drove them out and settled in their place. ²²The LORD had done the same for the descendants of Esau, who lived in Seir, when he destroyed the Horites from before them. They drove them out and have lived in their place to this day. ²³And as for the Avvites who lived in villages as far as Gaza, the Caphtorites coming out from Caphtor*ᵇ* destroyed them and settled in their place.)

Defeat of Sihon King of Heshbon

²⁴"Set out now and cross the Arnon Gorge. See, I have given into your hand Sihon the Amorite, king of Heshbon, and his country. Begin to take possession of it and engage him in battle. ²⁵This very day I will begin to put the terror and fear of you on all the nations under heaven. They will hear reports of you and will tremble and be in anguish because of you."

²⁶From the desert of Kedemoth I sent messengers to Sihon king of Heshbon offering peace and saying, ²⁷"Let us pass through your country. We will stay on the main road; we will not turn aside to the right or to the left. ²⁸Sell us food to eat and water to drink for their price in silver. Only let us pass through on foot—²⁹as the descendants of Esau, who live in Seir, and the Moabites, who live in Ar, did for us—until we cross the Jordan into the land the LORD our God is giving us." ³⁰But Sihon king of Heshbon refused to let us pass through. For the LORD your God had made his spirit stubborn and his heart

ᵇ23 That is, Crete

obstinate in order to give him into your hands, as he has now done.

³¹The LORD said to me, "See, I have begun to deliver Sihon and his country over to you. Now begin to conquer and possess his land."

³²When Sihon and all his army came out to meet us in battle at Jahaz, ³³the LORD our God delivered him over to us and we struck him down, together with his sons and his whole army. ³⁴At that time we took all his towns and completely destroyed[c] them—men, women and children. We left no survivors. ³⁵But the livestock and the plunder from the towns we had captured we carried off for ourselves. ³⁶From Aroer on the rim of the Arnon Gorge, and from the town in the gorge, even as far as Gilead, not one town was too strong for us. The LORD our God gave us all of them. ³⁷But in accordance with the command of the LORD our God, you did not encroach on any of the land of the Ammonites, neither the land along the course of the Jabbok nor that around the towns in the hills.

Defeat of Og King of Bashan

3 Next we turned and went up along the road towards Bashan, and Og king of Bashan with his whole army marched out to meet us in battle at Edrei. ²The LORD said to me, "Do not be afraid of him, for I have handed him over to you with his whole army and his land. Do to him what you did to Sihon king of the Amorites, who reigned in Heshbon."

³So the LORD our God also gave into our hands Og king of Bashan and all his army. We struck them down, leaving no survivors. ⁴At that time we took all his cities. There was not one of the sixty cities that we did not take from them—the whole region of Argob, Og's kingdom in Bashan. ⁵All these cities were fortified with high walls and with gates and bars, and there were also a great many unwalled

villages. ⁶We completely destroyed[a] them, as we had done with Sihon king of Heshbon, destroying[a] every city—men, women and children. ⁷But all the livestock and the plunder from their cities we carried off for ourselves.

⁸So at that time we took from these two kings of the Amorites the territory east of the Jordan, from the Arnon Gorge as far as Mount Hermon. ⁹(Hermon is called Sirion by the Sidonians; the Amorites call it Senir.) ¹⁰We took all the towns on the plateau, and all Gilead, and all Bashan as far as Salecah and Edrei, towns of Og's kingdom in Bashan. ¹¹(Only Og king of Bashan was left of the remnant of the Rephaites. His bed[b] was made of iron and was more than thirteen feet long and six feet wide.[c] It is still in Rabbah of the Ammonites.)

Division of the Land

¹²Of the land that we took over at that time, I gave the Reubenites and the Gadites the territory north of Aroer by the Arnon Gorge, including half the hill country of Gilead, together with its towns. ¹³The rest of Gilead and also all of Bashan, the kingdom of Og, I gave to the half-tribe of Manasseh. (The whole region of Argob in Bashan used to be known as a land of the Rephaites. ¹⁴Jair, a descendant of Manasseh, took the whole region of Argob as far as the border of the Geshurites and the Maacathites; it was named after him, so that to this day Bashan is called Havvoth Jair.[d]) ¹⁵And I gave Gilead to Makir. ¹⁶But to the Reubenites and the Gadites I gave the territory extending from Gilead down to the Arnon Gorge (the middle of the gorge being the border) and out to the Jabbok River, which is the border of the Ammonites. ¹⁷Its western border was the Jordan in the Arabah, from Kinnereth to the Sea of the Arabah (the Salt Sea[e]), below the slopes of Pisgah.

---

[c]34 The Hebrew term refers to the irrevocable giving over of things or persons to the LORD, often by totally destroying them.

[a]6 The Hebrew term refers to the irrevocable giving over of things or persons to the LORD, often by totally destroying them.   [b]11 Or *sarcophagus*

[c]11 Hebrew *nine cubits long and four cubits wide* (about 4 metres long and 1.8 metres wide)

[d]14 Or *called the settlements of Jair*   [e]17 That is, the Dead Sea

18I commanded you at that time: "The LORD your God has given you this land to take possession of it. But all your able-bodied men, armed for battle, must cross over ahead of your brother Israelites. 19However, your wives, your children and your livestock (I know you have much livestock) may stay in the towns I have given you, 20until the LORD gives rest to your brothers as he has to you, and they too have taken over the land that the LORD your God is giving them, across the Jordan. After that, each of you may go back to the possession I have given you."

Moses Forbidden to Cross the Jordan

21At that time I commanded Joshua: "You have seen with your own eyes all that the LORD your God has done to these two kings. The LORD will do the same to all the kingdoms over there where you are going. 22Do not be afraid of them; the LORD your God himself will fight for you."

23At that time I pleaded with the LORD: 24"O Sovereign LORD, you have begun to show to your servant your greatness and your strong hand. For what god is there in heaven or on earth who can do the deeds and mighty works you do? 25Let me go over and see the good land beyond the Jordan—that fine hill country and Lebanon."

26But because of you the LORD was angry with me and would not listen to me. "That is enough," the LORD said. "Do not speak to me any more about this matter. 27Go up to the top of Pisgah and look west and north and south and east. Look at the land with your own eyes, since you are not going to cross this Jordan. 28But commission Joshua, and encourage and strengthen him, for he will lead this people across and will cause them to inherit the land that you will see." 29So we stayed in the valley near Beth Peor.

Obedience Commanded

4 Hear now, O Israel, the decrees and laws I am about to teach you. Follow them so that you may live and may go in and take possession of the land that the LORD, the God of your fathers, is giving you. 2Do not add to what I command you and do not subtract from it, but keep the commands of the LORD your God that I give you.

3You saw with your own eyes what the LORD did at Baal Peor. The LORD your God destroyed from among you everyone who followed the Baal of Peor, 4but all of you who held fast to the LORD your God are still alive today.

5See, I have taught you decrees and laws as the LORD my God commanded me, so that you may follow them in the land you are entering to take possession of it. 6Observe them carefully, for this will show your wisdom and understanding to the nations, who will hear about all these decrees and say, "Surely this great nation is a wise and understanding people." 7What other nation is so great as to have their gods near them the way the LORD our God is near us whenever we pray to him? 8And what other nation is so great as to have such righteous decrees and laws as this body of laws I am setting before you today?

9Only be careful, and watch yourselves closely so that you do not forget the things your eyes have seen or let them slip from your heart as long as you live. Teach them to your children and to their children after them. 10Remember the day you stood before the LORD your God at Horeb, when he said to me, "Assemble the people before me to hear my words so that they may learn to revere me as long as they live in the land and may teach them to their children." 11You came near and stood at the foot of the mountain while it blazed with fire to the very heavens, with black clouds and deep darkness. 12Then the LORD spoke to you out of the fire. You heard the sound of words but saw no form; there was only a voice. 13He declared to you his covenant, the Ten Commandments, which he commanded you to follow and then wrote them on two stone tablets. 14And the LORD directed me at that time to teach you the decrees and laws you are to follow in the land that you are crossing the Jordan to possess.

Idolatry Forbidden

¹⁵You saw no form of any kind the day the LORD spoke to you at Horeb out of the fire. Therefore watch yourselves very carefully, ¹⁶so that you do not become corrupt and make for yourselves an idol, an image of any shape, whether formed like a man or a woman, ¹⁷or like any animal on earth or any bird that flies in the air, ¹⁸or like any creature that moves along the ground or any fish in the waters below. ¹⁹And when you look up to the sky and see the sun, the moon and the stars—all the heavenly array—do not be enticed into bowing down to them and worshipping things the LORD your God has apportioned to all the nations under heaven. ²⁰But as for you, the LORD took you and brought you out of the iron-smelting furnace, out of Egypt, to be the people of his inheritance, as you now are.

²¹The LORD was angry with me because of you, and he solemnly swore that I would not cross the Jordan and enter the good land the LORD your God is giving you as your inheritance. ²²I will die in this land; I will not cross the Jordan; but you are about to cross over and take possession of that good land. ²³Be careful not to forget the covenant of the LORD your God that he made with you; do not make for yourselves an idol in the form of anything the LORD your God has forbidden. ²⁴For the LORD your God is a consuming fire, a jealous God.

²⁵After you have had children and grandchildren and have lived in the land a long time—if you then become corrupt and make any kind of idol, doing evil in the eyes of the LORD your God and provoking him to anger, ²⁶I call heaven and earth as witnesses against you this day that you will quickly perish from the land that you are crossing the Jordan to possess. You will not live there long but will certainly be destroyed. ²⁷The LORD will scatter you among the peoples, and only a few of you will survive among the nations to which the LORD will drive you. ²⁸There you will worship man-made gods of wood and stone, which cannot see or hear or eat or smell. ²⁹But if from there you seek the LORD your God, you will find him if you look for him with all your heart and with all your soul. ³⁰When you are in distress and all these things have happened to you, then in later days you will return to the LORD your God and obey him. ³¹For the LORD your God is a merciful God; he will not abandon or destroy you or forget the covenant with your forefathers, which he confirmed to them by oath.

The LORD Is God

³²Ask now about the former days, long before your time, from the day God created man on the earth; ask from one end of the heavens to the other. Has anything so great as this ever happened, or has anything like it ever been heard of? ³³Has any other people heard the voice of God[a] speaking out of fire, as you have, and lived? ³⁴Has any god ever tried to take for himself one nation out of another nation, by testings, by miraculous signs and wonders, by war, by a mighty hand and an outstretched arm, or by great and awesome deeds, like all the things the LORD your God did for you in Egypt before your very eyes?

³⁵You were shown these things so that you might know that the LORD is God; besides him there is no other. ³⁶From heaven he made you hear his voice to discipline you. On earth he showed you his great fire, and you heard his words from out of the fire. ³⁷Because he loved your forefathers and chose their descendants after them, he brought you out of Egypt by his Presence and his great strength, ³⁸to drive out before you nations greater and stronger than you and to bring you into their land to give it to you for your inheritance, as it is today.

³⁹Acknowledge and take to heart this day that the LORD is God in heaven above and on the earth below. There is no other. ⁴⁰Keep his decrees and commands, which I am giving you today, so that it may go

a33 Or *of a god*

well with you and your children after you and that you may live long in the land the LORD your God gives you for all time.

Cities of Refuge

41Then Moses set aside three cities east of the Jordan, 42to which anyone who had killed a person could flee if he had unintentionally killed his neighbour without malice aforethought. He could flee into one of these cities and save his life. 43The cities were these: Bezer in the desert plateau, for the Reubenites; Ramoth in Gilead, for the Gadites; and Golan in Bashan, for the Manassites.

Introduction to the Law

44This is the law Moses set before the Israelites. 45These are the stipulations, decrees and laws Moses gave them when they came out of Egypt 46and were in the valley near Beth Peor east of the Jordan, in the land of Sihon king of the Amorites, who reigned in Heshbon and was defeated by Moses and the Israelites as they came out of Egypt. 47They took possession of his land and the land of Og king of Bashan, the two Amorite kings east of the Jordan. 48This land extended from Aroer on the rim of the Arnon Gorge to Mount Siyonb (that is, Hermon), 49and included all the Arabah east of the Jordan, as far as the Sea of the Arabah,c below the slopes of Pisgah.

The Ten Commandments

5 Moses summoned all Israel and said: Hear, O Israel, the decrees and the laws I declare in your hearing today. Learn them and be sure to follow them. 2The LORD our God made a covenant with us at Horeb. 3It was not with our fathers that the LORD made this covenant, but with us, with all of us who are alive here today. 4The LORD spoke to you face to face out of the fire on the mountain. 5(At that time I stood between the LORD and you to

declare to you the word of the LORD, because you were afraid of the fire and did not go up the mountain.) And he said:

6"I am the LORD your God, who brought you out of Egypt, out of the land of slavery.

7"You shall have no other gods before[a] me.

8"You shall not make for yourself an idol in the form of anything in heaven above or on the earth beneath or in the waters below. 9You shall not bow down to them or worship them; for I, the LORD your God, am a jealous God, punishing the children for the sin of the fathers to the third and fourth generation of those who hate me, 10but showing love to a thousand ⌊generations⌋ of those who love me and keep my commandments.

11"You shall not misuse the name of the LORD your God, for the LORD will not hold anyone guiltless who misuses his name.

12"Observe the Sabbath day by keeping it holy, as the LORD your God has commanded you. 13Six days you shall labour and do all your work, 14but the seventh day is a Sabbath to the LORD your God. On it you shall not do any work, neither you, nor your son or daughter, nor your manservant or maidservant, nor your ox, your donkey or any of your animals, nor the alien within your gates, so that your manservant and maidservant may rest, as you do. 15Remember that you were slaves in Egypt and that the LORD your God brought you out of there with a mighty hand and an outstretched arm. Therefore the LORD your God has commanded you to observe the Sabbath day.

b48 Hebrew; Syriac (see also Deut. 3:9) Sirion   c49 That is, the Dead Sea
a7 Or besides

[16]"Honour your father and your mother, as the LORD your God has commanded you, so that you may live long and that it may go well with you in the land the LORD your God is giving you.

[17]"You shall not murder.

[18]"You shall not commit adultery.

[19]"You shall not steal.

[20]"You shall not give false testimony against your neighbour.

[21]"You shall not covet your neighbour's wife. You shall not set your desire on your neighbour's house or land, his manservant or maidservant, his ox or donkey, or anything that belongs to your neighbour."

[22]These are the commandments the LORD proclaimed in a loud voice to your whole assembly there on the mountain from out of the fire, the cloud and the deep darkness; and he added nothing more. Then he wrote them on two stone tablets and gave them to me.

[23]When you heard the voice out of the darkness, while the mountain was ablaze with fire, all the leading men of your tribes and your elders came to me. [24]And you said, "The LORD our God has shown us his glory and his majesty, and we have heard his voice from the fire. Today we have seen that a man can live even if God speaks with him. [25]But now, why should we die? This great fire will consume us, and we will die if we hear the voice of the LORD our God any longer. [26]For what mortal man has ever heard the voice of the living God speaking out of fire, as we have, and survived? [27]Go near and listen to all that the LORD our God says. Then tell us whatever the LORD our God tells you. We will listen and obey."

[28]The LORD heard you when you spoke to me and the LORD said to me, "I have heard what this people said to you. Everything they said was good. [29]Oh, that their hearts would be inclined to fear me and keep all my commands always, so that it might go well with them and their children for ever!

[30]"Go, tell them to return to their tents. [31]But you stay here with me so that I may give you all the commands, decrees and laws that you are to teach them to follow in the land I am giving them to possess."

[32]So be careful to do what the LORD your God has commanded you; do not turn aside to the right or to the left. [33]Walk in all the way that the LORD your God has commanded you, so that you may live and prosper and prolong your days in the land that you will possess.

Love the LORD Your God

6 These are the commands, decrees and laws the LORD your God directed me to teach you to observe in the land that you are crossing the Jordan to possess, [2]so that you, your children and their children after them may fear the LORD your God as long as you live by keeping all his decrees and commands that I give you, and so that you may enjoy long life. [3]Hear, O Israel, and be careful to obey so that it may go well with you and that you may increase greatly in a land flowing with milk and honey, just as the LORD, the God of your fathers, promised you.

[4]Hear, O Israel: The LORD our God, the LORD is one.[a] [5]Love the LORD your God with all your heart and with all your soul and with all your strength. [6]These commandments that I give you today are to be upon your hearts. [7]Impress them on your children. Talk about them when you sit at home and when you walk along the road, when you lie down and when you get up. [8]Tie them as symbols on your hands and bind them on your foreheads. [9]Write them on the door-frames of your houses and on your gates.

[10]When the LORD your God brings you into the land he swore to your fathers, to Abraham, Isaac and Jacob, to give you—a land with large, flourishing cities you did

---

[a]4 Or *The LORD our God is one LORD*; or *The LORD is our God, the LORD is one*; or *The LORD is our God, the LORD alone*

not build, ¹¹houses filled with all kinds of good things you did not provide, wells you did not dig, and vineyards and olive groves you did not plant—then when you eat and are satisfied, ¹²be careful that you do not forget the LORD, who brought you out of Egypt, out of the land of slavery.

¹³Fear the LORD your God, serve him only and take your oaths in his name. ¹⁴Do not follow other gods, the gods of the peoples around you; ¹⁵for the LORD your God, who is among you, is a jealous God and his anger will burn against you, and he will destroy you from the face of the land. ¹⁶Do not test the LORD your God as you did at Massah. ¹⁷Be sure to keep the commands of the LORD your God and the stipulations and decrees he has given you. ¹⁸Do what is right and good in the LORD's sight, so that it may go well with you and you may go in and take over the good land that the LORD promised on oath to your forefathers, ¹⁹thrusting out all your enemies before you, as the LORD said.

²⁰In the future, when your son asks you, "What is the meaning of the stipulations, decrees and laws the LORD our God has commanded you?" ²¹tell him: "We were slaves of Pharaoh in Egypt, but the LORD brought us out of Egypt with a mighty hand. ²²Before our eyes the LORD sent miraculous signs and wonders—great and terrible—upon Egypt and Pharaoh and his whole household. ²³But he brought us out from there to bring us in and give us the land that he promised on oath to our forefathers. ²⁴The LORD commanded us to obey all these decrees and to fear the LORD our God, so that we might always prosper and be kept alive, as is the case today. ²⁵And if we are careful to obey all this law before the LORD our God, as he has commanded us, that will be our righteousness."

Driving Out the Nations

7 When the LORD your God brings you into the land you are entering to possess and drives out before you many nations—the Hittites, Girgashites, Amorites, Canaanites, Perizzites, Hivites and Jebusites, seven nations larger and stronger than you—²and when the LORD your God has delivered them over to you and you have defeated them, then you must destroy them totally.ᵃ Make no treaty with them, and show them no mercy. ³Do not intermarry with them. Do not give your daughters to their sons or take their daughters for your sons, ⁴for they will turn your sons away from following me to serve other gods, and the LORD's anger will burn against you and will quickly destroy you. ⁵This is what you are to do to them: Break down their altars, smash their sacred stones, cut down their Asherah polesᵇ and burn their idols in the fire. ⁶For you are a people holy to the LORD your God. The LORD your God has chosen you out of all the peoples on the face of the earth to be his people, his treasured possession.

⁷The LORD did not set his affection on you and choose you because you were more numerous than other peoples, for you were the fewest of all peoples. ⁸But it was because the LORD loved you and kept the oath he swore to your forefathers that he brought you out with a mighty hand and redeemed you from the land of slavery, from the power of Pharaoh king of Egypt. ⁹Know therefore that the LORD your God is God; he is the faithful God, keeping his covenant of love to a thousand generations of those who love him and keep his commands. ¹⁰But

those who hate him he will repay to their
face by destruction;
he will not be slow to repay to their
face those who hate him.

¹¹Therefore, take care to follow the commands, decrees and laws I give you today.

¹²If you pay attention to these laws and are careful to follow them, then the LORD your God will keep his covenant of love with you, as he swore to your forefathers.

ᵃ2 The Hebrew term refers to the irrevocable giving over of things or persons to the LORD, often by totally destroying them; also in verse 26.   ᵇ5 That is, symbols of the goddess Asherah; here and elsewhere in Deuteronomy

[13]He will love you and bless you and increase your numbers. He will bless the fruit of your womb, the crops of your land—your grain, new wine and oil—the calves of your herds and the lambs of your flocks in the land that he swore to your forefathers to give you. [14]You will be blessed more than any other people; none of your men or women will be childless, nor any of your livestock without young. [15]The LORD will keep you free from every disease. He will not inflict on you the horrible diseases you knew in Egypt, but he will inflict them on all who hate you. [16]You must destroy all the peoples the LORD your God gives over to you. Do not look on them with pity and do not serve their gods, for that will be a snare to you.

[17]You may say to yourselves, "These nations are stronger than we are. How can we drive them out?" [18]But do not be afraid of them; remember well what the LORD your God did to Pharaoh and to all Egypt. [19]You saw with your own eyes the great trials, the miraculous signs and wonders, the mighty hand and outstretched arm, with which the LORD your God brought you out. The LORD your God will do the same to all the peoples you now fear. [20]Moreover, the LORD your God will send the hornet among them until even the survivors who hide from you have perished. [21]Do not be terrified by them, for the LORD your God, who is among you, is a great and awesome God. [22]The LORD your God will drive out those nations before you, little by little. You will not be allowed to eliminate them all at once, or the wild animals will multiply around you. [23]But the LORD your God will deliver them over to you, throwing them into great confusion until they are destroyed. [24]He will give their kings into your hand, and you will wipe out their names from under heaven. No-one will be able to stand up against you; you will destroy them. [25]The images of their gods you are to burn in the fire. Do not covet the silver and gold on them, and do not take it for yourselves, or you will be ensnared by it, for it is detestable to the LORD your God. [26]Do not bring a detestable thing into your house or you,

like it, will be set apart for destruction. Utterly abhor and detest it, for it is set apart for destruction.

Do Not Forget the LORD

8 Be careful to follow every command I am giving you today, so that you may live and increase and may enter and possess the land that the LORD promised on oath to your forefathers. [2]Remember how the LORD your God led you all the way in the desert these forty years, to humble you and to test you in order to know what was in your heart, whether or not you would keep his commands. [3]He humbled you, causing you to hunger and then feeding you with manna, which neither you nor your fathers had known, to teach you that man does not live on bread alone but on every word that comes from the mouth of the LORD. [4]Your clothes did not wear out and your feet did not swell during these forty years. [5]Know then in your heart that as a man disciplines his son, so the LORD your God disciplines you.

[6]Observe the commands of the LORD your God, walking in his ways and revering him. [7]For the LORD your God is bringing you into a good land—a land with streams and pools of water, with springs flowing in the valleys and hills; [8]a land with wheat and barley, vines and fig-trees, pomegranates, olive oil and honey; [9]a land where bread will not be scarce and you will lack nothing; a land where the rocks are iron and you can dig copper out of the hills.

[10]When you have eaten and are satisfied, praise the LORD your God for the good land he has given you. [11]Be careful that you do not forget the LORD your God, failing to observe his commands, his laws and his decrees that I am giving you this day. [12]Otherwise, when you eat and are satisfied, when you build fine houses and settle down, [13]and when your herds and flocks grow large and your silver and gold increase and all you have is multiplied, [14]then your heart will become proud and you will forget the LORD your God, who brought you out of Egypt, out of the land

of slavery. ¹⁵He led you through the vast and dreadful desert, that thirsty and waterless land, with its venomous snakes and scorpions. He brought you water out of hard rock. ¹⁶He gave you manna to eat in the desert, something your fathers had never known, to humble and to test you so that in the end it might go well with you. ¹⁷You may say to yourself, "My power and the strength of my hands have produced this wealth for me." ¹⁸But remember the LORD your God, for it is he who gives you the ability to produce wealth, and so confirms his covenant, which he swore to your forefathers, as it is today.

¹⁹If you ever forget the LORD your God and follow other gods and worship and bow down to them, I testify against you today that you will surely be destroyed. ²⁰Like the nations the LORD destroyed before you, so you will be destroyed for not obeying the LORD your God.

Not Because of Israel's Righteousness

9 Hear, O Israel. You are now about to cross the Jordan to go in and dispossess nations greater and stronger than you, with large cities that have walls up to the sky. ²The people are strong and tall—Anakites! You know about them and have heard it said: "Who can stand up against the Anakites?" ³But be assured today that the LORD your God is the one who goes across ahead of you like a devouring fire. He will destroy them; he will subdue them before you. And you will drive them out and annihilate them quickly, as the LORD has promised you.

⁴After the LORD your God has driven them out before you, do not say to yourself, "The LORD has brought me here to take possession of this land because of my righteousness." No, it is on account of the wickedness of these nations that the LORD is going to drive them out before you. ⁵It is not because of your righteousness or your integrity that you are going in to take possession of their land; but on account of the wickedness of these nations, the LORD your God will drive them out before you, to accomplish what he swore to your fathers, to Abraham, Isaac and Jacob. ⁶Understand, then, that it is not because of your righteousness that the LORD your God is giving you this good land to possess, for you are a stiff-necked people.

The Golden Calf

⁷Remember this and never forget how you provoked the LORD your God to anger in the desert. From the day you left Egypt until you arrived here, you have been rebellious against the LORD. ⁸At Horeb you aroused the LORD's wrath so that he was angry enough to destroy you. ⁹When I went up on the mountain to receive the tablets of stone, the tablets of the covenant that the LORD had made with you, I stayed on the mountain forty days and forty nights; I ate no bread and drank no water. ¹⁰The LORD gave me two stone tablets inscribed by the finger of God. On them were all the commandments the LORD proclaimed to you on the mountain out of the fire, on the day of the assembly.

¹¹At the end of the forty days and forty nights, the LORD gave me the two stone tablets, the tablets of the covenant. ¹²Then the LORD told me, "Go down from here at once, because your people whom you brought out of Egypt have become corrupt. They have turned away quickly from what I commanded them and have made a cast idol for themselves."

¹³And the LORD said to me, "I have seen this people, and they are a stiff-necked people indeed! ¹⁴Let me alone, so that I may destroy them and blot out their name from under heaven. And I will make you into a nation stronger and more numerous than they."

¹⁵So I turned and went down from the mountain while it was ablaze with fire. And the two tablets of the covenant were in my hands.ᵃ ¹⁶When I looked, I saw that you had sinned against the LORD your God; you had made for yourselves an idol cast in the shape of a calf. You had turned

---

ᵃ15 Or And I had the two tablets of the covenant with me, one in each hand aside quickly from the way that the LORD had commanded you. ¹⁷So I took the two tablets and threw them out of my hands, breaking them to pieces before your eyes.

¹⁸Then once again I fell prostrate before the LORD for forty days and forty nights; I ate no bread and drank no water, because of all the sin you had committed, doing what was evil in the LORD's sight and so provoking him to anger. ¹⁹I feared the anger and wrath of the LORD, for he was angry enough with you to destroy you. But again the LORD listened to me. ²⁰And the LORD was angry enough with Aaron to destroy him, but at that time I prayed for Aaron too. ²¹Also I took that sinful thing of yours, the calf you had made, and burned it in the fire. Then I crushed it and ground it to powder as fine as dust and threw the dust into a stream that flowed down the mountain.

²²You also made the LORD angry at Taberah, at Massah and at Kibroth Hattaavah.

²³And when the LORD sent you out from Kadesh Barnea, he said, "Go up and take possession of the land I have given you." But you rebelled against the command of the LORD your God. You did not trust him or obey him. ²⁴You have been rebellious against the LORD ever since I have known you.

²⁵I lay prostrate before the LORD those forty days and forty nights because the LORD had said he would destroy you. ²⁶I prayed to the LORD and said, "O Sovereign LORD, do not destroy your people, your own inheritance that you redeemed by your great power and brought out of Egypt with a mighty hand. ²⁷Remember your servants Abraham, Isaac and Jacob. Overlook the stubbornness of this people, their wickedness and their sin. ²⁸Otherwise, the country from which you brought us will say, 'Because the LORD was not able to take them into the land he had promised them, and because he hated them, he brought them out to put them to death in the desert.' ²⁹But they are your people, your inheritance

that you brought out by your great power and your outstretched arm."

Tablets Like the First Ones

10 At that time the LORD said to me, "Chisel out two stone tablets like the first ones and come up to me on the mountain. Also make a wooden chest.^a ²I will write on the tablets the words that were on the first tablets, which you broke. Then you are to put them in the chest."

³So I made the ark out of acacia wood and chiselled out two stone tablets like the first ones, and I went up on the mountain with the two tablets in my hands. ⁴The LORD wrote on these tablets what he had written before, the Ten Commandments he had proclaimed to you on the mountain, out of the fire, on the day of the assembly. And the LORD gave them to me. ⁵Then I came back down the mountain and put the tablets in the ark I had made, as the LORD commanded me, and they are there now.

⁶(The Israelites travelled from the wells of the Jaakanites to Moserah. There Aaron died and was buried, and Eleazar his son succeeded him as priest. ⁷From there they travelled to Gudgodah and on to Jotbathah, a land with streams of water. ⁸At that time the LORD set apart the tribe of Levi to carry the ark of the covenant of the LORD, to stand before the LORD to minister and to pronounce blessings in his name, as they still do today. ⁹That is why the Levites have no share or inheritance among their brothers; the LORD is their inheritance, as the LORD your God told them.)

¹⁰Now I had stayed on the mountain forty days and nights, as I did the first time, and the LORD listened to me at this time also. It was not his will to destroy you. ¹¹"Go," the LORD said to me, "and lead the people on their way, so that they may enter and possess the land that I swore to their fathers to give them."

^a1 That is, an ark

Fear the LORD

¹²And now, O Israel, what does the LORD your God ask of you but to fear the LORD your God, to walk in all his ways, to love him, to serve the LORD your God with all your heart and with all your soul, ¹³and to observe the LORD's commands and decrees that I am giving you today for your own good?

¹⁴To the LORD your God belong the heavens, even the highest heavens, the earth and everything in it. ¹⁵Yet the LORD set his affection on your forefathers and loved them, and he chose you, their descendants, above all the nations, as it is today. ¹⁶Circumcise your hearts, therefore, and do not be stiff-necked any longer. ¹⁷For the LORD your God is God of gods and Lord of lords, the great God, mighty and awesome, who shows no partiality and accepts no bribes. ¹⁸He defends the cause of the fatherless and the widow, and loves the alien, giving him food and clothing. ¹⁹And you are to love those who are aliens, for you yourselves were aliens in Egypt. ²⁰Fear the LORD your God and serve him. Hold fast to him and take your oaths in his name. ²¹He is your praise; he is your God, who performed for you those great and awesome wonders you saw with your own eyes. ²²Your forefathers who went down into Egypt were seventy in all, and now the LORD your God has made you as numerous as the stars in the sky.

Love and Obey the LORD

11 Love the LORD your God and keep his requirements, his decrees, his laws and his commands always. ²Remember today that your children were not the ones who saw and experienced the discipline of the LORD your God: his majesty, his mighty hand, his outstretched arm; ³the signs he performed and the things he did in the heart of Egypt, both to Pharaoh king of Egypt and to his whole country; ⁴what he did to the Egyptian army, to its horses and chariots, how he overwhelmed them with the waters of the Red Sea[a] as they were pursuing you, and how the LORD brought lasting ruin on them. ⁵It was not your children who saw what he did for you in the desert until you arrived at this place, ⁶and what he did to Dathan and Abiram, sons of Eliab the Reubenite, when the earth opened its mouth right in the middle of all Israel and swallowed them up with their households, their tents and every living thing that belonged to them. ⁷But it was your own eyes that saw all these great things the LORD has done.

⁸Observe therefore all the commands I am giving you today, so that you may have the strength to go in and take over the land that you are crossing the Jordan to possess, ⁹and so that you may live long in the land that the LORD swore to your forefathers to give to them and their descendants, a land flowing with milk and honey. ¹⁰The land you are entering to take over is not like the land of Egypt, from which you have come, where you planted your seed and irrigated it by foot as in a vegetable garden. ¹¹But the land you are crossing the Jordan to take possession of is a land of mountains and valleys that drinks rain from heaven. ¹²It is a land the LORD your God cares for; the eyes of the LORD your God are continually on it from the beginning of the year to its end.

¹³So if you faithfully obey the commands I am giving you today—to love the LORD your God and to serve him with all your heart and with all your soul—¹⁴then I will send rain on your land in its season, both autumn and spring rains, so that you may gather in your grain, new wine and oil. ¹⁵I will provide grass in the fields for your cattle, and you will eat and be satisfied.

¹⁶Be careful, or you will be enticed to turn away and worship other gods and bow down to them. ¹⁷Then the LORD's anger will burn against you, and he will shut the heavens so that it will not rain and the ground will yield no produce, and you will soon perish from the good land the LORD is giving you. ¹⁸Fix these words of

_____
a4 Hebrew Yam Suph; that is, Sea of Reeds

mine in your hearts and minds; tie them as symbols on your hands and bind them on your foreheads. [19]Teach them to your children, talking about them when you sit at home and when you walk along the road, when you lie down and when you get up. [20]Write them on the door-frames of your houses and on your gates, [21]so that your days and the days of your children may be many in the land that the LORD swore to give your forefathers, as many as the days that the heavens are above the earth.

[22]If you carefully observe all these commands I am giving you to follow—to love the LORD your God, to walk in all his ways and to hold fast to him—[23]then the LORD will drive out all these nations before you, and you will dispossess nations larger and stronger than you. [24]Every place where you set your foot will be yours: Your territory will extend from the desert to Lebanon, and from the Euphrates River to the western sea.[b] [25]No man will be able to stand against you. The LORD your God, as he promised you, will put the terror and fear of you on the whole land, wherever you go.

[26]See, I am setting before you today a blessing and a curse—[27]the blessing if you obey the commands of the LORD your God that I am giving you today; [28]the curse if you disobey the commands of the LORD your God and turn from the way that I command you today by following other gods, which you have not known. [29]When the LORD your God has brought you into the land you are entering to possess, you are to proclaim on Mount Gerizim the blessings, and on Mount Ebal the curses. [30]As you know, these mountains are across the Jordan, west of the road,[c] towards the setting sun, near the great trees of Moreh, in the territory of those Canaanites living in the Arabah in the vicinity of Gilgal. [31]You are about to cross the Jordan to enter and take possession of the land the LORD your God is giving you. When you have taken it over and are living there, [32]be sure that you obey all the decrees and laws I am setting before you today.

The One Place of Worship

12 These are the decrees and laws you must be careful to follow in the land that the LORD, the God of your fathers, has given you to possess—as long as you live in the land. [2]Destroy completely all the places on the high mountains and on the hills and under every spreading tree where the nations you are dispossessing worship their gods. [3]Break down their altars, smash their sacred stones and burn their Asherah poles in the fire; cut down the idols of their gods and wipe out their names from those places.

[4]You must not worship the LORD your God in their way. [5]But you are to seek the place the LORD your God will choose from among all your tribes to put his Name there for his dwelling. To that place you must go; [6]there bring your burnt offerings and sacrifices, your tithes and special gifts, what you have vowed to give and your freewill offerings, and the firstborn of your herds and flocks. [7]There, in the presence of the LORD your God, you and your families shall eat and shall rejoice in everything you have put your hand to, because the LORD your God has blessed you.

[8]You are not to do as we do here today, everyone as he sees fit, [9]since you have not yet reached the resting place and the inheritance the LORD your God is giving you. [10]But you will cross the Jordan and settle in the land the LORD your God is giving you as an inheritance, and he will give you rest from all your enemies around you so that you will live in safety. [11]Then to the place the LORD your God will choose as a dwelling for his Name—there you are to bring everything I command you: your burnt offerings and sacrifices, your tithes and special gifts, and all the choice possessions you have vowed to the LORD. [12]And there rejoice before the LORD your God, you, your sons and daughters, your menservants and maidservants, and the Levites from your towns, who have no allotment or inheritance of their own. [13]Be careful not to

---

b24 That is, the Mediterranean   *c30* Or *Jordan, westward* sacrifice your burnt offerings anywhere you please. ¹⁴Offer them only at the place the LORD will choose in one of your tribes, and there observe everything I command you.

¹⁵Nevertheless, you may slaughter your animals in any of your towns and eat as much of the meat as you want, as if it were gazelle or deer, according to the blessing the LORD your God gives you. Both the ceremonially unclean and the clean may eat it. ¹⁶But you must not eat the blood; pour it out on the ground like water. ¹⁷You must not eat in your own towns the tithe of your grain and new wine and oil, or the firstborn of your herds and flocks, or whatever you have vowed to give, or your freewill offerings or special gifts. ¹⁸Instead, you are to eat them in the presence of the LORD your God at the place the LORD your God will choose—you, your sons and daughters, your menservants and maidservants, and the Levites from your towns—and you are to rejoice before the LORD your God in everything you put your hand to. ¹⁹Be careful not to neglect the Levites as long as you live in your land.

²⁰When the LORD your God has enlarged your territory as he promised you, and you crave meat and say, "I would like some meat," then you may eat as much of it as you want. ²¹If the place where the LORD your God chooses to put his Name is too far away from you, you may slaughter animals from the herds and flocks the LORD has given you, as I have commanded you, and in your own towns you may eat as much of them as you want. ²²Eat them as you would gazelle or deer. Both the ceremonially unclean and the clean may eat. ²³But be sure you do not eat the blood, because the blood is the life, and you must not eat the life with the meat. ²⁴You must not eat the blood; pour it out on the ground like water. ²⁵Do not eat it, so that it may go well with you and your children after you, because you will be doing what is right in the eyes of the LORD.

²⁶But take your consecrated things and whatever you have vowed to give, and go to the place the LORD will choose. ²⁷Present your burnt offerings on the altar of the LORD your God, both the meat and the blood. The blood of your sacrifices must be poured beside the altar of the LORD your God, but you may eat the meat. ²⁸Be careful to obey all these regulations I am giving you, so that it may always go well with you and your children after you, because you will be doing what is good and right in the eyes of the LORD your God.

²⁹The LORD your God will cut off before you the nations you are about to invade and dispossess. But when you have driven them out and settled in their land, ³⁰and after they have been destroyed before you, be careful not to be ensnared by enquiring about their gods, saying, "How do these nations serve their gods? We will do the same." ³¹You must not worship the LORD your God in their way, because in worshipping their gods, they do all kinds of detestable things the LORD hates. They even burn their sons and daughters in the fire as sacrifices to their gods.

³²See that you do all I command you; do not add to it or take away from it.

Worshipping Other Gods

13 If a prophet, or one who foretells by dreams, appears among you and announces to you a miraculous sign or wonder, ²and if the sign or wonder of which he has spoken takes place, and he says, "Let us follow other gods" (gods you have not known) "and let us worship them," ³you must not listen to the words of that prophet or dreamer. The LORD your God is testing you to find out whether you love him with all your heart and with all your soul. ⁴It is the LORD your God you must follow, and him you must revere. Keep his commands and obey him; serve him and hold fast to him. ⁵That prophet or dreamer must be put to death, because he preached rebellion against the LORD your God, who brought you out of Egypt and redeemed you from the land of slavery; he has tried to turn you from the way the LORD your God commanded you to follow. You must purge the evil from among you.

⁶If your very own brother, or your son or daughter, or the wife you love, or your closest friend secretly entices you, saying,

"Let us go and worship other gods" (gods that neither you nor your fathers have known, [7]gods of the peoples around you, whether near or far, from one end of the land to the other), [8]do not yield to him or listen to him. Show him no pity. Do not spare him or shield him. [9]You must certainly put him to death. Your hand must be the first in putting him to death, and then the hands of all the people. [10]Stone him to death, because he tried to turn you away from the LORD your God, who brought you out of Egypt, out of the land of slavery. [11]Then all Israel will hear and be afraid, and no-one among you will do such an evil thing again.

[12]If you hear it said about one of the towns the LORD your God is giving you to live in [13]that wicked men have arisen among you and have led the people of their town astray, saying, "Let us go and worship other gods" (gods you have not known), [14]then you must enquire, probe and investigate it thoroughly. And if it is true and it has been proved that this detestable thing has been done among you, [15]you must certainly put to the sword all who live in that town. Destroy it completely,[a] both its people and its livestock. [16]Gather all the plunder of the town into the middle of the public square and completely burn the town and all its plunder as a whole burnt offering to the LORD your God. It is to remain a ruin for ever, never to be rebuilt. [17]None of those condemned things[a] shall be found in your hands, so that the LORD will turn from his fierce anger; he will show you mercy, have compassion on you, and increase your numbers, as he promised on oath to your forefathers, [18]because you obey the LORD your God, keeping all his commands that I am giving you today and doing what is right in his eyes.

Clean and Unclean Food

14 You are the children of the LORD your God. Do not cut yourselves or shave the front of your heads for the dead, [2]for you are a people holy to the LORD your God. Out of all the peoples on the face of the earth, the LORD has chosen you to be his treasured possession.

[3]Do not eat any detestable thing. [4]These are the animals you may eat: the ox, the sheep, the goat, [5]the deer, the gazelle, the roe deer, the wild goat, the ibex, the antelope and the mountain sheep.[a] [6]You may eat any animal that has a split hoof divided in two and that chews the cud. [7]However, of those that chew the cud or that have a split hoof completely divided you may not eat the camel, the rabbit or the coney.[b] Although they chew the cud, they do not have a split hoof; they are ceremonially unclean for you. [8]The pig is also unclean; although it has a split hoof, it does not chew the cud. You are not to eat their meat or touch their carcasses.

[9]Of all the creatures living in the water, you may eat any that has fins and scales. [10]But anything that does not have fins and scales you may not eat; for you it is unclean.

[11]You may eat any clean bird. [12]But these you may not eat: the eagle, the vulture, the black vulture, [13]the red kite, the black kite, any kind of falcon, [14]any kind of raven, [15]the horned owl, the screech owl, the gull, any kind of hawk, [16]the little owl, the great owl, the white owl, [17]the desert owl, the osprey, the cormorant, [18]the stork, any kind of heron, the hoopoe and the bat.

[19]All flying insects that swarm are unclean to you; do not eat them. [20]But any winged creature that is clean you may eat.

[21]Do not eat anything you find already dead. You may give it to an alien living in any of your towns, and he may eat it, or you may sell it to a foreigner. But you are a people holy to the LORD your God.

Do not cook a young goat in its mother's milk.

---

[a]15,17 The Hebrew term refers to the irrevocable giving over of things or persons to the LORD, often by totally destroying them.
[a]5 The precise identification of some of the birds and animals in this chapter is uncertain.
[b]7 That is, the hyrax or rock badger

Tithes

22Be sure to set aside a tenth of all that your fields produce each year. 23Eat the tithe of your grain, new wine and oil, and the firstborn of your herds and flocks in the presence of the LORD your God at the place he will choose as a dwelling for his Name, so that you may learn to revere the LORD your God always. 24But if that place is too distant and you have been blessed by the LORD your God and cannot carry your tithe (because the place where the LORD will choose to put his Name is so far away), 25then exchange your tithe for silver, and take the silver with you and go to the place the LORD your God will choose. 26Use the silver to buy whatever you like: cattle, sheep, wine or other fermented drink, or anything you wish. Then you and your household shall eat there in the presence of the LORD your God and rejoice. 27And do not neglect the Levites living in your towns, for they have no allotment or inheritance of their own.

28At the end of every three years, bring all the tithes of that year's produce and store it in your towns, 29so that the Levites (who have no allotment or inheritance of their own) and the aliens, the fatherless and the widows who live in your towns may come and eat and be satisfied, and so that the LORD your God may bless you in all the work of your hands.

The Year for Cancelling Debts

15 At the end of every seven years you must cancel debts. 2This is how it is to be done: Every creditor shall cancel the loan he has made to his fellow Israelite. He shall not require payment from his fellow Israelite or brother, because the LORD's time for cancelling debts has been proclaimed. 3You may require payment from a foreigner, but you must cancel any debt your brother owes you. 4However, there should be no poor among you, for in the land the LORD your God is giving you to possess as your inheritance, he will richly bless you, 5if only you fully obey the LORD your God and are careful to follow all these commands I am giving you

today. 6For the LORD your God will bless you as he has promised, and you will lend to many nations but will borrow from none. You will rule over many nations but none will rule over you.

7If there is a poor man among your brothers in any of the towns of the land that the LORD your God is giving you, do not be hard-hearted or tight-fisted towards your poor brother. 8Rather be open-handed and freely lend him whatever he needs. 9Be careful not to harbour this wicked thought: "The seventh year, the year for cancelling debts, is near," so that you do not show ill will towards your needy brother and give him nothing. He may then appeal to the LORD against you, and you will be found guilty of sin. 10Give generously to him and do so without a grudging heart; then because of this the LORD your God will bless you in all your work and in everything you put your hand to. 11There will always be poor people in the land. Therefore I command you to be open-handed towards your brothers and towards the poor and needy in your land.

Freeing Servants

12If a fellow Hebrew, a man or woman, sells himself to you and serves you six years, in the seventh year you must let him go free. 13And when you release him, do not send him away empty-handed. 14Supply him liberally from your flock, your threshing-floor and your winepress. Give to him as the LORD your God has blessed you. 15Remember that you were slaves in Egypt and the LORD your God redeemed you. That is why I give you this command today.

16But if your servant says to you, "I do not want to leave you," because he loves you and your family and is well off with you, 17then take an awl and push it through his ear lobe into the door, and he will become your servant for life. Do the same for your maidservant.

18Do not consider it a hardship to set your servant free, because his service to you these six years has been worth twice as much as that of a hired hand. And the

LORD your God will bless you in everything you do.

The Firstborn Animals

[19]Set apart for the LORD your God every firstborn male of your herds and flocks. Do not put the firstborn of your oxen to work, and do not shear the firstborn of your sheep. [20]Each year you and your family are to eat them in the presence of the LORD your God at the place he will choose. [21]If an animal has a defect, is lame or blind, or has any serious flaw, you must not sacrifice it to the LORD your God. [22]You are to eat it in your own towns. Both the ceremonially unclean and the clean may eat it, as if it were gazelle or deer. [23]But you must not eat the blood; pour it out on the ground like water.

Passover

16 Observe the month of Abib and celebrate the Passover of the LORD your God, because in the month of Abib he brought you out of Egypt by night. [2]Sacrifice as the Passover to the LORD your God an animal from your flock or herd at the place the LORD will choose as a dwelling for his Name. [3]Do not eat it with bread made with yeast, but for seven days eat unleavened bread, the bread of affliction, because you left Egypt in haste—so that all the days of your life you may remember the time of your departure from Egypt. [4]Let no yeast be found in your possession in all your land for seven days. Do not let any of the meat you sacrifice on the evening of the first day remain until morning.

[5]You must not sacrifice the Passover in any town the LORD your God gives you, [6]except in the place he will choose as a dwelling for his Name. There you must sacrifice the Passover in the evening, when the sun goes down, on the anniversary[a] of your departure from Egypt. [7]Roast it and eat it at the place the LORD your God will choose. Then in the morning return to your tents. [8]For six days eat unleavened bread and on the seventh day hold an

assembly to the LORD your God and do no work.

Feast of Weeks

[9]Count off seven weeks from the time you begin to put the sickle to the standing corn. [10]Then celebrate the Feast of Weeks to the LORD your God by giving a freewill offering in proportion to the blessings the LORD your God has given you. [11]And rejoice before the LORD your God at the place he will choose as a dwelling for his Name—you, your sons and daughters, your menservants and maidservants, the Levites in your towns, and the aliens, the fatherless and the widows living among you. [12]Remember that you were slaves in Egypt, and follow carefully these decrees.

Feast of Tabernacles

[13]Celebrate the Feast of Tabernacles for seven days after you have gathered the produce of your threshing-floor and your winepress. [14]Be joyful at your Feast—you, your sons and daughters, your menservants and maidservants, and the Levites, the aliens, the fatherless and the widows who live in your towns. [15]For seven days celebrate the Feast to the LORD your God at the place the LORD will choose. For the LORD your God will bless you in all your harvest and in all the work of your hands, and your joy will be complete.

[16]Three times a year all your men must appear before the LORD your God at the place he will choose: at the Feast of Unleavened Bread, the Feast of Weeks and the Feast of Tabernacles. No man should appear before the LORD empty-handed: [17]Each of you must bring a gift in proportion to the way the LORD your God has blessed you.

Judges

[18]Appoint judges and officials for each of your tribes in every town the LORD your God is giving you, and they shall judge the

---

[a]6 Or *down, at the time of day*

people fairly. ¹⁹Do not pervert justice or show partiality. Do not accept a bribe, for a bribe blinds the eyes of the wise and twists the words of the righteous. ²⁰Follow justice and justice alone, so that you may live and possess the land the LORD your God is giving you.

Worshipping Other Gods

²¹Do not set up any wooden Asherah pole*b* beside the altar you build to the LORD your God, ²²and do not erect a sacred stone, for these the LORD your God hates.

17 Do not sacrifice to the LORD your God an ox or a sheep that has any defect or flaw in it, for that would be detestable to him.

²If a man or woman living among you in one of the towns the LORD gives you is found doing evil in the eyes of the LORD your God in violation of his covenant, ³and contrary to my command has worshipped other gods, bowing down to them or to the sun or the moon or the stars of the sky, ⁴and this has been brought to your attention, then you must investigate it thoroughly. If it is true and it has been proved that this detestable thing has been done in Israel, ⁵take the man or woman who has done this evil deed to your city gate and stone that person to death. ⁶On the testimony of two or three witnesses a man shall be put to death, but no-one shall be put to death on the testimony of only one witness. ⁷The hands of the witnesses must be the first in putting him to death, and then the hands of all the people. You must purge the evil from among you.

Law Courts

⁸If cases come before your courts that are too difficult for you to judge—whether bloodshed, lawsuits or assaults—take them to the place the LORD your God will choose. ⁹Go to the priests, who are Levites, and to the judge who is in office at that time. Enquire of them and they will give you the verdict. ¹⁰You must act according to the decisions they give you at the place the LORD will choose. Be careful to do everything they direct you to do. ¹¹Act according to the law they teach you and the decisions they give you. Do not turn aside from what they tell you, to the right or to the left. ¹²The man who shows contempt for the judge or for the priest who stands ministering there to the LORD your God must be put to death. You must purge the evil from Israel. ¹³All the people will hear and be afraid, and will not be contemptuous again.

The King

¹⁴When you enter the land the LORD your God is giving you and have taken possession of it and settled in it, and you say, "Let us set a king over us like all the nations around us," ¹⁵be sure to appoint over you the king the LORD your God chooses. He must be from among your own brothers. Do not place a foreigner over you, one who is not a brother Israelite. ¹⁶The king, moreover, must not acquire great numbers of horses for himself or make the people return to Egypt to get more of them, for the LORD has told you, "You are not to go back that way again." ¹⁷He must not take many wives, or his heart will be led astray. He must not accumulate large amounts of silver and gold.

¹⁸When he takes the throne of his kingdom, he is to write for himself on a scroll a copy of this law, taken from that of the priests, who are Levites. ¹⁹It is to be with him, and he is to read it all the days of his life so that he may learn to revere the LORD his God and follow carefully all the words of this law and these decrees ²⁰and not consider himself better than his brothers and turn from the law to the right or to the left. Then he and his descendants will reign a long time over his kingdom in Israel.

b21 Or Do not plant any tree dedicated to Asherah

Offerings for Priests and Levites

18 The priests, who are Levites—indeed the whole tribe of Levi—are to have no allotment or inheritance with Israel. They shall live on the offerings made to the LORD by fire, for that is their inheritance. ²They shall have no inheritance among their brothers; the LORD is their inheritance, as he promised them.

³This is the share due to the priests from the people who sacrifice a bull or a sheep: the shoulder, the jowls and the inner parts. ⁴You are to give them the firstfruits of your grain, new wine and oil, and the first wool from the shearing of your sheep, ⁵for the LORD your God has chosen them and their descendants out of all your tribes to stand and minister in the LORD's name always.

⁶If a Levite moves from one of your towns anywhere in Israel where he is living, and comes in all earnestness to the place the LORD will choose, ⁷he may minister in the name of the LORD his God like all his fellow Levites who serve there in the presence of the LORD. ⁸He is to share equally in their benefits even though he has received money from the sale of family possessions.

Detestable Practices

⁹When you enter the land the LORD your God is giving you, do not learn to imitate the detestable ways of the nations there. ¹⁰Let no-one be found among you who sacrifices his son or daughter in*ᵃ* the fire, who practises divination or sorcery, interprets omens, engages in witchcraft, ¹¹or casts spells, or who is a medium or spiritist or who consults the dead. ¹²Anyone who does these things is detestable to the LORD, and because of these detestable practices the LORD your God will drive out those nations before you. ¹³You must be blameless before the LORD your God.

The Prophet

¹⁴The nations you will dispossess listen to those who practise sorcery or divination. But as for you, the LORD your God has not permitted you to do so. ¹⁵The LORD your God will raise up for you a prophet like me from among your own brothers. You must listen to him. ¹⁶For this is what you asked of the LORD your God at Horeb on the day of the assembly when you said, "Let us not hear the voice of the LORD our God nor see this great fire any more, or we will die."

¹⁷The LORD said to me: "What they say is good. ¹⁸I will raise up for them a prophet like you from among their brothers; I will put my words in his mouth, and he will tell them everything I command him. ¹⁹If anyone does not listen to my words that the prophet speaks in my name, I myself will call him to account. ²⁰But a prophet who presumes to speak in my name anything I have not commanded him to say, or a prophet who speaks in the name of other gods, must be put to death."

²¹You may say to yourselves, "How can we know when a message has not been spoken by the LORD?" ²²If what a prophet proclaims in the name of the LORD does not take place or come true, that is a message the LORD has not spoken. That prophet has spoken presumptuously. Do not be afraid of him.

Cities of Refuge

19 When the LORD your God has destroyed the nations whose land he is giving you, and when you have driven them out and settled in their towns and houses, ²then set aside for yourselves three cities centrally located in the land the LORD your God is giving you to possess. ³Build roads to them and divide into three parts the land the LORD your God is giving you as an inheritance, so that anyone who kills a man may flee there.

⁴This is the rule concerning the man who kills another and flees there to save his life—one who kills his neighbour unintentionally, without malice aforethought. ⁵For instance, a man may go into the forest with his neighbour to cut wood, and as he swings his axe to fell a tree, the head may

ᵃ10 Or who makes his son or daughter pass through

fly off and hit his neighbour and kill him. That man may flee to one of these cities and save his life. 6Otherwise, the avenger of blood might pursue him in a rage, overtake him if the distance is too great, and kill him even though he is not deserving of death, since he did it to his neighbour without malice aforethought. 7This is why I command you to set aside for yourselves three cities.

8If the LORD your God enlarges your territory, as he promised on oath to your forefathers, and gives you the whole land he promised them, 9because you carefully follow all these laws I command you today—to love the LORD your God and to walk always in his ways—then you are to set aside three more cities. 10Do this so that innocent blood will not be shed in your land, which the LORD your God is giving you as your inheritance, and so that you will not be guilty of bloodshed.

11But if a man hates his neighbour and lies in wait for him, assaults and kills him, and then flees to one of these cities, 12the elders of his town shall send for him, bring him back from the city, and hand him over to the avenger of blood to die. 13Show him no pity. You must purge from Israel the guilt of shedding innocent blood, so that it may go well with you.

14Do not move your neighbour's boundary stone set up by your predecessors in the inheritance you receive in the land the LORD your God is giving you to possess.

Witnesses

15One witness is not enough to convict a man accused of any crime or offence he may have committed. A matter must be established by the testimony of two or three witnesses.

16If a malicious witness takes the stand to accuse a man of a crime, 17the two men involved in the dispute must stand in the presence of the LORD before the priests and the judges who are in office at the time. 18The judges must make a thorough investigation, and if the witness proves to be a liar, giving false testimony against his brother, 19then do to him as he intended to do to his brother. You must purge the evil from among you. 20The rest of the people will hear of this and be afraid, and never again will such an evil thing be done among you. 21Show no pity: life for life, eye for eye, tooth for tooth, hand for hand, foot for foot.

Going to War

20 When you go to war against your enemies and see horses and chariots and an army greater than yours, do not be afraid of them, because the LORD your God, who brought you up out of Egypt, will be with you. 2When you are about to go into battle, the priest shall come forward and address the army. 3He shall say: "Hear, O Israel, today you are going into battle against your enemies. Do not be faint-hearted or afraid; do not be terrified or give way to panic before them. 4For the LORD your God is the one who goes with you to fight for you against your enemies to give you victory."

5The officers shall say to the army: "Has anyone built a new house and not dedicated it? Let him go home, or he may die in battle and someone else may dedicate it. 6Has anyone planted a vineyard and not begun to enjoy it? Let him go home, or he may die in battle and someone else enjoy it. 7Has anyone become pledged to a woman and not married her? Let him go home, or he may die in battle and someone else marry her." 8Then the officers shall add, "Is any man afraid or faint-hearted? Let him go home so that his brothers will not become disheartened too." 9When the officers have finished speaking to the army, they shall appoint commanders over it.

10When you march up to attack a city, make its people an offer of peace. 11If they accept and open their gates, all the people in it shall be subject to forced labour and shall work for you. 12If they refuse to make peace and they engage you in battle, lay siege to that city. 13When the LORD your God delivers it into your hand, put to the sword all the men in it. 14As for the women, the children, the livestock and everything else in the city, you may take these as plunder for yourselves. And you may use the plunder the LORD your God gives you from your enemies. 15This is how you are to treat all the cities that are at a distance from you and do not belong to the nations nearby.

16However, in the cities of the nations the LORD your God is giving you as an inheritance, do not leave alive anything that breathes. 17Completely destroy*a* them —the Hittites, Amorites, Canaanites, Perizzites, Hivites and Jebusites—as the LORD your God has commanded you. 18Otherwise, they will teach you to follow all the detestable things they do in worshipping their gods, and you will sin against the LORD your God.

19When you lay siege to a city for a long time, fighting against it to capture it, do not destroy its trees by putting an axe to them, because you can eat their fruit. Do not cut them down. Are the trees of the field people, that you should besiege them?*b* 20However, you may cut down trees that you know are not fruit trees and use them to build siege works until the city at war with you falls.

Atonement for an Unsolved Murder

21 If a man is found slain, lying in a field in the land the LORD your God is giving you to possess, and it is not known who killed him, 2your elders and judges shall go out and measure the distance from the body to the neighbouring towns. 3Then the elders of the town nearest the body shall take a heifer that has never been worked and has never worn a yoke 4and lead her down to a valley that has not been ploughed or planted and where there is a flowing stream. There in the valley they are to break the heifer's neck. 5The priests, the sons of Levi, shall step forward, for the LORD your God has chosen them to minister and to pronounce blessings in the name of the LORD and to decide all cases of dispute and assault. 6Then all the elders of the town nearest the body shall wash their hands over the heifer

whose neck was broken in the valley, 7and they shall declare: "Our hands did not shed this blood, nor did our eyes see it done. 8Accept this atonement for your people Israel, whom you have redeemed, O LORD, and do not hold your people guilty of the blood of an innocent man." And the bloodshed will be atoned for. 9So you will purge from yourselves the guilt of shedding innocent blood, since you have done what is right in the eyes of the LORD.

Marrying a Captive Woman

10When you go to war against your enemies and the LORD your God delivers them into your hands and you take captives, 11if you notice among the captives a beautiful woman and are attracted to her, you may take her as your wife. 12Bring her into your home and make her shave her head, trim her nails 13and put aside the clothes she was wearing when captured. After she has lived in your house and mourned her father and mother for a full month, then you may go to her and be her husband and she shall be your wife. 14If you are not pleased with her, let her go wherever she wishes. You must not sell her or treat her as a slave, since you have dishonoured her.

The Right of the Firstborn

15If a man has two wives, and he loves one but not the other, and both bear him sons but the firstborn is the son of the wife he does not love, 16when he wills his property to his sons, he must not give the rights of the firstborn to the son of the wife he loves in preference to his actual firstborn, the son of the wife he does not love. 17He must acknowledge the son of his unloved wife as the firstborn by giving him a double share of all he has. That son is the first sign of his father's strength. The right of the firstborn belongs to him.

---

a17 The Hebrew term refers to the irrevocable giving over of things or persons to the LORD, often by totally destroying them.
b19 Or *down to use in the siege, for the fruit trees are for the benefit of man.*

A Rebellious Son

[18]If a man has a stubborn and rebellious son who does not obey his father and mother and will not listen to them when they discipline him, [19]his father and mother shall take hold of him and bring him to the elders at the gate of his town. [20]They shall say to the elders, "This son of ours is stubborn and rebellious. He will not obey us. He is a profligate and a drunkard." [21]Then all the men of his town shall stone him to death. You must purge the evil from among you. All Israel will hear of it and be afraid.

Various Laws

[22]If a man guilty of a capital offence is put to death and his body is hung on a tree, [23]you must not leave his body on the tree overnight. Be sure to bury him that same day, because anyone who is hung on a tree is under God's curse. You must not desecrate the land the LORD your God is giving you as an inheritance.

22 If you see your brother's ox or sheep straying, do not ignore it but be sure to take it back to him. [2]If the brother does not live near you or if you do not know who he is, take it home with you and keep it until he comes looking for it. Then give it back to him. [3]Do the same if you find your brother's donkey or his cloak or anything he loses. Do not ignore it.

[4]If you see your brother's donkey or his ox fallen on the road, do not ignore it. Help him to get it to its feet.

[5]A woman must not wear men's clothing, nor a man wear women's clothing, for the LORD your God detests anyone who does this.

[6]If you come across a bird's nest beside the road, either in a tree or on the ground, and the mother is sitting on the young or on the eggs, do not take the mother with the young. [7]You may take the young, but be sure to let the mother go, so that it may go well with you and you may have a long life.

[8]When you build a new house, make a parapet around your roof so that you may not bring the guilt of bloodshed on your house if someone falls from the roof.

[9]Do not plant two kinds of seed in your vineyard; if you do, not only the crops you plant but also the fruit of the vineyard will be defiled.[a]

[10]Do not plough with an ox and a donkey yoked together.

[11]Do not wear clothes of wool and linen woven together.

[12]Make tassels on the four corners of the cloak you wear.

Marriage Violations

[13]If a man takes a wife and, after lying with her, dislikes her [14]and slanders her and gives her a bad name, saying, "I married this woman, but when I approached her, I did not find proof of her virginity," [15]then the girl's father and mother shall bring proof that she was a virgin to the town elders at the gate. [16]The girl's father will say to the elders, "I gave my daughter in marriage to this man, but he dislikes her. [17]Now he has slandered her and said, 'I did not find your daughter to be a virgin.' But here is the proof of my daughter's virginity." Then her parents shall display the cloth before the elders of the town, [18]and the elders shall take the man and punish him. [19]They shall fine him a hundred shekels of silver[b] and give them to the girl's father, because this man has given an Israelite virgin a bad name. She shall continue to be his wife; he must not divorce her as long as he lives.

[20]If, however, the charge is true and no proof of the girl's virginity can be found, [21]she shall be brought to the door of her father's house and there the men of her town shall stone her to death. She has done a disgraceful thing in Israel by being promiscuous while still in her father's house. You must purge the evil from among you.

[22]If a man is found sleeping with another man's wife, both the man who slept with her and the woman must die. You must purge the evil from Israel.

---

[a]9 Or be forfeited to the sanctuary   [b]19 That is, about 2½ pounds (about 1 kilogram)

²³If a man happens to meet in a town a virgin pledged to be married and he sleeps with her, ²⁴you shall take both of them to the gate of that town and stone them to death—the girl because she was in a town and did not scream for help, and the man because he violated another man's wife. You must purge the evil from among you.

²⁵But if out in the country a man happens to meet a girl pledged to be married and rapes her, only the man who has done this shall die. ²⁶Do nothing to the girl; she has committed no sin deserving death. This case is like that of someone who attacks and murders his neighbour, ²⁷for the man found the girl out in the country, and though the betrothed girl screamed, there was no-one to rescue her.

²⁸If a man happens to meet a virgin who is not pledged to be married and rapes her and they are discovered, ²⁹he shall pay the girl's father fifty shekels of silver.ᶜ He must marry the girl, for he has violated her. He can never divorce her as long as he lives.

³⁰A man is not to marry his father's wife; he must not dishonour his father's bed.

Exclusion From the Assembly

23 No-one who has been emasculated by crushing or cutting may enter the assembly of the LORD.

²No-one born of a forbidden marriageᵃ nor any of his descendants may enter the assembly of the LORD, even down to the tenth generation.

³No Ammonite or Moabite or any of his descendants may enter the assembly of the LORD, even down to the tenth generation. ⁴For they did not come to meet you with bread and water on your way when you came out of Egypt, and they hired Balaam son of Beor from Pethor in Aram Naharaimᵇ to pronounce a curse on you. ⁵However, the LORD your God would not listen to Balaam but turned the curse into a blessing for you, because the LORD your God loves you. ⁶Do not seek a treaty of friendship with them as long as you live.

⁷Do not abhor an Edomite, for he is your brother. Do not abhor an Egyptian, because you lived as an alien in his country. ⁸The third generation of children born to them may enter the assembly of the LORD.

Uncleanness in the Camp

⁹When you are encamped against your enemies, keep away from everything impure. ¹⁰If one of your men is unclean because of a nocturnal emission, he is to go outside the camp and stay there. ¹¹But as evening approaches he is to wash himself, and at sunset he may return to the camp.

¹²Designate a place outside the camp where you can go to relieve yourself. ¹³As part of your equipment have something to dig with, and when you relieve yourself, dig a hole and cover up your excrement. ¹⁴For the LORD your God moves about in your camp to protect you and to deliver your enemies to you. Your camp must be holy, so that he will not see among you anything indecent and turn away from you.

Miscellaneous Laws

¹⁵If a slave has taken refuge with you, do not hand him over to his master. ¹⁶Let him live among you wherever he likes and in whatever town he chooses. Do not oppress him.

¹⁷No Israelite man or woman is to become a shrine-prostitute. ¹⁸You must not bring the earnings of a female prostitute or of a male prostituteᶜ into the house of the LORD your God to pay any vow, because the LORD your God detests them both.

¹⁹Do not charge your brother interest, whether on money or food or anything else that may earn interest. ²⁰You may charge a foreigner interest, but not a brother Israelite, so that the LORD your God may bless you in everything you put your hand to in the land you are entering to possess.

²¹If you make a vow to the LORD your

ᶜ29 That is, about 1¼ pounds (about 0.6 kilogram)
ᵃ2 Or *one of illegitimate birth*   ᵇ4 That is, North-west Mesopotamia   ᶜ18 Hebrew *of a dog*

God, do not be slow to pay it, for the LORD your God will certainly demand it of you and you will be guilty of sin. [22]But if you refrain from making a vow, you will not be guilty. [23]Whatever your lips utter you must be sure to do, because you made your vow freely to the LORD your God with your own mouth.

[24]If you enter your neighbour's vineyard, you may eat all the grapes you want, but do not put any in your basket. [25]If you enter your neighbour's cornfield, you may pick the ears with your hands, but you must not put a sickle to his standing corn.

24 If a man marries a woman who becomes displeasing to him because he finds something indecent about her, and he writes her a certificate of divorce, gives it to her and sends her from his house, [2]and if after she leaves his house she becomes the wife of another man, [3]and her second husband dislikes her and writes her a certificate of divorce, gives it to her and sends her from his house, or if he dies, [4]then her first husband, who divorced her, is not allowed to marry her again after she has been defiled. That would be detestable in the eyes of the LORD. Do not bring sin upon the land the LORD your God is giving you as an inheritance.

[5]If a man has recently married, he must not be sent to war or have any other duty laid on him. For one year he is to be free to stay at home and bring happiness to the wife he has married.

[6]Do not take a pair of millstones—not even the upper one—as security for a debt, because that would be taking a man's livelihood as security.

[7]If a man is caught kidnapping one of his brother Israelites and treats him as a slave or sells him, the kidnapper must die. You must purge the evil from among you.

[8]In cases of leprous[a] diseases be very careful to do exactly as the priests, who are Levites, instruct you. You must follow carefully what I have commanded them. [9]Remember what the LORD your God did to Miriam along the way after you came out of Egypt.

[10]When you make a loan of any kind to your neighbour, do not go into his house to get what he is offering as a pledge. [11]Stay outside and let the man to whom you are making the loan bring the pledge out to you. [12]If the man is poor, do not go to sleep with his pledge in your possession. [13]Return his cloak to him by sunset so that he may sleep in it. Then he will thank you, and it will be regarded as a righteous act in the sight of the LORD your God.

[14]Do not take advantage of a hired man who is poor and needy, whether he is a brother Israelite or an alien living in one of your towns. [15]Pay him his wages each day before sunset, because he is poor and is counting on it. Otherwise he may cry to the LORD against you, and you will be guilty of sin.

[16]Fathers shall not be put to death for their children, nor children put to death for their fathers; each is to die for his own sin.

[17]Do not deprive the alien or the fatherless of justice, or take the cloak of the widow as a pledge. [18]Remember that you were slaves in Egypt and the LORD your God redeemed you from there. That is why I command you to do this.

[19]When you are harvesting in your field and you overlook a sheaf, do not go back to get it. Leave it for the alien, the fatherless and the widow, so that the LORD your God may bless you in all the work of your hands. [20]When you beat the olives from your trees, do not go over the branches a second time. Leave what remains for the alien, the fatherless and the widow. [21]When you harvest the grapes in your vineyard, do not go over the vines again. Leave what remains for the alien, the fatherless and the widow. [22]Remember that you were slaves in Egypt. That is why I command you to do this.

25 When men have a dispute, they are to take it to court and the judges will decide the case, acquitting the innocent and condemning the guilty. [2]If the guilty man deserves to be beaten, the judge shall make him lie down and have him flogged in his presence with the

---

a8 The Hebrew word was used for various diseases affecting the skin—not necessarily leprosy.

number of lashes his crime deserves, [3]but he must not give him more than forty lashes. If he is flogged more than that, your brother will be degraded in your eyes.

[4]Do not muzzle an ox while it is treading out the grain.

[5]If brothers are living together and one of them dies without a son, his widow must not marry outside the family. Her husband's brother shall take her and marry her and fulfil the duty of a brother-in-law to her. [6]The first son she bears shall carry on the name of the dead brother so that his name will not be blotted out from Israel.

[7]However, if a man does not want to marry his brother's wife, she shall go to the elders at the town gate and say, "My husband's brother refuses to carry on his brother's name in Israel. He will not fulfil the duty of a brother-in-law to me." [8]Then the elders of his town shall summon him and talk to him. If he persists in saying, "I do not want to marry her," [9]his brother's widow shall go up to him in the presence of the elders, take off one of his sandals, spit in his face and say, "This is what is done to the man who will not build up his brother's family line." [10]That man's line shall be known in Israel as The Family of the Unsandalled.

[11]If two men are fighting and the wife of one of them comes to rescue her husband from his assailant, and she reaches out and seizes him by his private parts, [12]you shall cut off her hand. Show her no pity.

[13]Do not have two differing weights in your bag—one heavy, one light. [14]Do not have two differing measures in your house—one large, one small. [15]You must have accurate and honest weights and measures, so that you may live long in the land the LORD your God is giving you. [16]For the LORD your God detests anyone who does these things, anyone who deals dishonestly.

[17]Remember what the Amalekites did to you along the way when you came out of Egypt. [18]When you were weary and worn out, they met you on your journey and cut off all who were lagging behind; they had no fear of God. [19]When the LORD your God gives you rest from all the enemies around you in the land he is giving you to possess as an inheritance, you shall blot out the memory of Amalek from under heaven. Do not forget!

Firstfruits and Tithes

26 When you have entered the land that the LORD your God is giving you as an inheritance and have taken possession of it and settled in it, [2]take some of the firstfruits of all that you produce from the soil of the land that the LORD your God is giving you and put them in a basket. Then go to the place that the LORD your God will choose as a dwelling for his Name [3]and say to the priest in office at the time, "I declare today to the LORD your God that I have come to the land that the LORD swore to our forefathers to give us." [4]The priest shall take the basket from your hands and set it down in front of the altar of the LORD your God. [5]Then you shall declare before the LORD your God: "My father was a wandering Aramean, and he went down into Egypt with a few people and lived there and became a great nation, powerful and numerous. [6]But the Egyptians ill-treated us and made us suffer, putting us to hard labour. [7]Then we cried out to the LORD, the God of our fathers, and the LORD heard our voice and saw our misery, toil and oppression. [8]So the LORD brought us out of Egypt with a mighty hand and an outstretched arm, with great terror and with miraculous signs and wonders. [9]He brought us to this place and gave us this land, a land flowing with milk and honey; [10]and now I bring the firstfruits of the soil that you, O LORD, have given me." Place the basket before the LORD your God and bow down before him. [11]And you and the Levites and the aliens among you shall rejoice in all the good things the LORD your God has given to you and your household.

[12]When you have finished setting aside a tenth of all your produce in the third year, the year of the tithe, you shall give it to the Levite, the alien, the fatherless and the widow, so that they may eat in your towns and be satisfied. [13]Then say to the LORD your God: "I have removed from my house the sacred portion and have given it

to the Levite, the alien, the fatherless and the widow, according to all you commanded. I have not turned aside from your commands nor have I forgotten any of them. [14]I have not eaten any of the sacred portion while I was in mourning, nor have I removed any of it while I was unclean, nor have I offered any of it to the dead. I have obeyed the LORD my God; I have done everything you commanded me. [15]Look down from heaven, your holy dwelling-place, and bless your people Israel and the land you have given us as you promised on oath to our forefathers, a land flowing with milk and honey."

Follow the LORD's Commands

[16]The LORD your God commands you this day to follow these decrees and laws; carefully observe them with all your heart and with all your soul. [17]You have declared this day that the LORD is your God and that you will walk in his ways, that you will keep his decrees, commands and laws, and that you will obey him. [18]And the LORD has declared this day that you are his people, his treasured possession as he promised, and that you are to keep all his commands. [19]He has declared that he will set you in praise, fame and honour high above all the nations he has made and that you will be a people holy to the LORD your God, as he promised.

The Altar on Mount Ebal

27 Moses and the elders of Israel commanded the people: "Keep all these commands that I give you today. [2]When you have crossed the Jordan into the land the LORD your God is giving you, set up some large stones and coat them with plaster. [3]Write on them all the words of this law when you have crossed over to enter the land the LORD your God is giving you, a land flowing with milk and honey, just as the LORD, the God of your fathers, promised you. [4]And when you have crossed the Jordan, set up these stones on Mount Ebal, as I command you today,

and coat them with plaster. [5]Build there an altar to the LORD your God, an altar of stones. Do not use any iron tool upon them. [6]Build the altar of the LORD your God with stones from the field and offer burnt offerings on it to the LORD your God. [7]Sacrifice fellowship offerings[a] there, eating them and rejoicing in the presence of the LORD your God. [8]And you shall write very clearly all the words of this law on these stones you have set up."

Curses From Mount Ebal

[9]Then Moses and the priests, who are Levites, said to all Israel, "Be silent, O Israel, and listen! You have now become the people of the LORD your God. [10]Obey the LORD your God and follow his commands and decrees that I give you today."

[11]On the same day Moses commanded the people:

[12]When you have crossed the Jordan, these tribes shall stand on Mount Gerizim to bless the people: Simeon, Levi, Judah, Issachar, Joseph and Benjamin. [13]And these tribes shall stand on Mount Ebal to pronounce curses: Reuben, Gad, Asher, Zebulun, Dan and Naphtali.

[14]The Levites shall recite to all the people of Israel in a loud voice:

[15]"Cursed is the man who carves an image or casts an idol—a thing detestable to the LORD, the work of the craftsman's hands—and sets it up in secret."

Then all the people shall say,
"Amen!"

[16]"Cursed is the man who dishonours his father or his mother."

Then all the people shall say,
"Amen!"

[17]"Cursed is the man who moves his neighbour's boundary stone."

Then all the people shall say,
"Amen!"

[18]"Cursed is the man who leads the blind astray on the road."

Then all the people shall say,
"Amen!"

---

*a*7 Traditionally *peace offerings*

[19]"Cursed is the man who withholds justice from the alien, the fatherless or the widow."

Then all the people shall say,

"Amen!"

[20]"Cursed is the man who sleeps with his father's wife, for he dishonours his father's bed."

Then all the people shall say,

"Amen!"

[21]"Cursed is the man who has sexual relations with any animal."

Then all the people shall say,

"Amen!"

[22]"Cursed is the man who sleeps with his sister, the daughter of his father or the daughter of his mother."

Then all the people shall say,

"Amen!"

[23]"Cursed is the man who sleeps with his mother-in-law."

Then all the people shall say,

"Amen!"

[24]"Cursed is the man who kills his neighbour secretly."

Then all the people shall say,

"Amen!"

[25]"Cursed is the man who accepts a bribe to kill an innocent person."

Then all the people shall say,

"Amen!"

[26]"Cursed is the man who does not uphold the words of this law by carrying them out."

Then all the people shall say,

"Amen!"

Blessings for Obedience

28 If you fully obey the LORD your God and carefully follow all his commands that I give you today, the LORD your God will set you high above all the nations on earth. [2]All these blessings will come upon you and accompany you if you obey the LORD your God:

[3]You will be blessed in the city and blessed in the country.

[4]The fruit of your womb will be blessed, and the crops of your land and the young of your livestock—the calves of your herds and the lambs of your flocks.

[5]Your basket and your kneading trough will be blessed.

[6]You will be blessed when you come in and blessed when you go out.

[7]The LORD will grant that the enemies who rise up against you will be defeated before you. They will come at you from one direction but flee from you in seven.

[8]The LORD will send a blessing on your barns and on everything you put your hand to. The LORD your God will bless you in the land he is giving you.

[9]The LORD will establish you as his holy people, as he promised you on oath, if you keep the commands of the LORD your God and walk in his ways. [10]Then all the peoples on earth will see that you are called by the name of the LORD, and they will fear you. [11]The LORD will grant you abundant prosperity—in the fruit of your womb, the young of your livestock and the crops of your ground—in the land he swore to your forefathers to give you.

[12]The LORD will open the heavens, the storehouse of his bounty, to send rain on your land in season and to bless all the work of your hands. You will lend to many nations but will borrow from none. [13]The LORD will make you the head, not the tail. If you pay attention to the commands of the LORD your God that I give you this day and carefully follow them, you will always be at the top, never at the bottom. [14]Do not turn aside from any of the commands I give you today, to the right or to the left, following other gods and serving them.

Curses for Disobedience

[15]However, if you do not obey the LORD your God and do not carefully follow all his commands and decrees I am giving you today, all these curses will come upon you and overtake you:

[16]You will be cursed in the city and cursed in the country.

[17]Your basket and your kneading trough will be cursed.

[18]The fruit of your womb will be

cursed, and the crops of your land, and the calves of your herds and the lambs of your flocks.

19You will be cursed when you come in and cursed when you go out.

20The LORD will send on you curses, confusion and rebuke in everything you put your hand to, until you are destroyed and come to sudden ruin because of the evil you have done in forsaking him.*a*
21The LORD will plague you with diseases until he has destroyed you from the land you are entering to possess. 22The LORD will strike you with wasting disease, with fever and inflammation, with scorching heat and drought, with blight and mildew, which will plague you until you perish. 23The sky over your head will be bronze, the ground beneath you iron. 24The LORD will turn the rain of your country into dust and powder; it will come down from the skies until you are destroyed.

25The LORD will cause you to be defeated before your enemies. You will come at them from one direction but flee from them in seven, and you will become a thing of horror to all the kingdoms on earth. 26Your carcasses will be food for all the birds of the air and the beasts of the earth, and there will be no-one to frighten them away. 27The LORD will afflict you with the boils of Egypt and with tumours, festering sores and the itch, from which you cannot be cured. 28The LORD will afflict you with madness, blindness and confusion of mind. 29At midday you will grope about like a blind man in the dark. You will be unsuccessful in everything you do; day after day you will be oppressed and robbed, with no-one to rescue you.

30You will be pledged to be married to a woman, but another will take her and ravish her. You will build a house, but you will not live in it. You will plant a vineyard, but you will not even begin to enjoy its fruit. 31Your ox will be slaughtered before your eyes, but you will eat none of it. Your donkey will be forcibly taken from you and will not be returned. Your sheep will be given to your enemies,

and no-one will rescue them. 32Your sons and daughters will be given to another nation, and you will wear out your eyes watching for them day after day, powerless to lift a hand. 33A people that you do not know will eat what your land and labour produce, and you will have nothing but cruel oppression all your days. 34The sights you see will drive you mad. 35The LORD will afflict your knees and legs with painful boils that cannot be cured, spreading from the soles of your feet to the top of your head.

36The LORD will drive you and the king you set over you to a nation unknown to you or your fathers. There you will worship other gods, gods of wood and stone. 37You will become a thing of horror and an object of scorn and ridicule to all the nations where the LORD will drive you.

38You will sow much seed in the field but you will harvest little, because locusts will devour it. 39You will plant vineyards and cultivate them but you will not drink the wine or gather the grapes, because worms will eat them. 40You will have olive trees throughout your country but you will not use the oil, because the olives will drop off. 41You will have sons and daughters but you will not keep them, because they will go into captivity. 42Swarms of locusts will take over all your trees and the crops of your land.

43The alien who lives among you will rise above you higher and higher, but you will sink lower and lower. 44He will lend to you, but you will not lend to him. He will be the head, but you will be the tail.

45All these curses will come upon you. They will pursue you and overtake you until you are destroyed, because you did not obey the LORD your God and observe the commands and decrees he gave you. 46They will be a sign and a wonder to you and your descendants for ever. 47Because you did not serve the LORD your God joyfully and gladly in the time of prosperity, 48therefore in hunger and thirst, in nakedness and dire poverty, you will serve the enemies the LORD sends against you.

a20 Hebrew me

He will put an iron yoke on your neck until he has destroyed you.

⁴⁹The LORD will bring a nation against you from far away, from the ends of the earth, like an eagle swooping down, a nation whose language you will not understand, ⁵⁰a fierce-looking nation without respect for the old or pity for the young. ⁵¹They will devour the young of your livestock and the crops of your land until you are destroyed. They will leave you no grain, new wine or oil, nor any calves of your herds or lambs of your flocks until you are ruined. ⁵²They will lay siege to all the cities throughout your land until the high fortified walls in which you trust fall down. They will besiege all the cities throughout the land the LORD your God is giving you.

⁵³Because of the suffering that your enemy will inflict on you during the siege, you will eat the fruit of the womb, the flesh of the sons and daughters the LORD your God has given you. ⁵⁴Even the most gentle and sensitive man among you will have no compassion on his own brother or the wife he loves or his surviving children, ⁵⁵and he will not give to one of them any of the flesh of his children that he is eating. It will be all he has left because of the suffering that your enemy will inflict on you during the siege of all your cities. ⁵⁶The most gentle and sensitive woman among you—so sensitive and gentle that she would not venture to touch the ground with the sole of her foot—will begrudge the husband she loves and her own son or daughter ⁵⁷the afterbirth from her womb and the children she bears. For she intends to eat them secretly during the siege and in the distress that your enemy will inflict on you in your cities.

⁵⁸If you do not carefully follow all the words of this law, which are written in this book, and do not revere this glorious and awesome name—the LORD your God— ⁵⁹the LORD will send fearful plagues on you and your descendants, harsh and prolonged disasters, and severe and lingering illnesses. ⁶⁰He will bring upon you all the diseases of Egypt that you dreaded, and they will cling to you. ⁶¹The LORD will also bring on you every kind of sickness and disaster not recorded in this Book of the Law, until you are destroyed. ⁶²You who were as numerous as the stars in the sky will be left but few in number, because you did not obey the LORD your God. ⁶³Just as it pleased the LORD to make you prosper and increase in number, so it will please him to ruin and destroy you. You will be uprooted from the land you are entering to possess.

⁶⁴Then the LORD will scatter you among all nations, from one end of the earth to the other. There you will worship other gods—gods of wood and stone, which neither you nor your fathers have known. ⁶⁵Among those nations you will find no repose, no resting place for the sole of your foot. There the LORD will give you an anxious mind, eyes weary with longing, and a despairing heart. ⁶⁶You will live in constant suspense, filled with dread both night and day, never sure of your life. ⁶⁷In the morning you will say, "If only it were evening!" and in the evening, "If only it were morning!"—because of the terror that will fill your hearts and the sights that your eyes will see. ⁶⁸The LORD will send you back in ships to Egypt on a journey I said you should never make again. There you will offer yourselves for sale to your enemies as male and female slaves, but no-one will buy you.

Renewal of the Covenant

29 These are the terms of the covenant the LORD commanded Moses to make with the Israelites in Moab, in addition to the covenant he had made with them at Horeb.

²Moses summoned all the Israelites and said to them:

Your eyes have seen all that the LORD did in Egypt to Pharaoh, to all his officials and to all his land. ³With your own eyes you saw those great trials, those miraculous signs and great wonders. ⁴But to this day the LORD has not given you a mind that understands or eyes that see or ears that hear. ⁵During the forty years that I led you through the desert, your clothes did not wear out, nor did the sandals on your feet.

⁶You ate no bread and drank no wine or other fermented drink. I did this so that you might know that I am the LORD your God.

⁷When you reached this place, Sihon king of Heshbon and Og king of Bashan came out to fight against us, but we defeated them. ⁸We took their land and gave it as an inheritance to the Reubenites, the Gadites and the half-tribe of Manasseh.

⁹Carefully follow the terms of this covenant, so that you may prosper in everything you do. ¹⁰All of you are standing today in the presence of the LORD your God—your leaders and chief men, your elders and officials, and all the other men of Israel, ¹¹together with your children and your wives, and the aliens living in your camps who chop your wood and carry your water. ¹²You are standing here in order to enter into a covenant with the LORD your God, a covenant the LORD is making with you this day and sealing with an oath, ¹³to confirm you this day as his people, that he may be your God as he promised you and as he swore to your fathers, Abraham, Isaac and Jacob. ¹⁴I am making this covenant, with its oath, not only with you ¹⁵who are standing here with us today in the presence of the LORD our God but also with those who are not here today.

¹⁶You yourselves know how we lived in Egypt and how we passed through the countries on the way here. ¹⁷You saw among them their detestable images and idols of wood and stone, of silver and gold. ¹⁸Make sure there is no man or woman, clan or tribe among you today whose heart turns away from the LORD our God to go and worship the gods of those nations; make sure there is no root among you that produces such bitter poison.

¹⁹When such a person hears the words of this oath, he invokes a blessing on himself and therefore thinks, "I will be safe, even though I persist in going my own way." This will bring disaster on the watered land as well as the dry.ᵃ ²⁰The LORD will never be willing to forgive him; his wrath and zeal will burn against that

man. All the curses written in this book will fall upon him, and the LORD will blot out his name from under heaven. ²¹The LORD will single him out from all the tribes of Israel for disaster, according to all the curses of the covenant written in this Book of the Law.

²²Your children who follow you in later generations and foreigners who come from distant lands will see the calamities that have fallen on the land and the diseases with which the LORD has afflicted it. ²³The whole land will be a burning waste of salt and sulphur—nothing planted, nothing sprouting, no vegetation growing on it. It will be like the destruction of Sodom and Gomorrah, Admah and Zeboiim, which the LORD overthrew in fierce anger. ²⁴All the nations will ask: "Why has the LORD done this to this land? Why this fierce, burning anger?"

²⁵And the answer will be: "It is because this people abandoned the covenant of the LORD, the God of their fathers, the covenant he made with them when he brought them out of Egypt. ²⁶They went off and worshipped other gods and bowed down to them, gods they did not know, gods he had not given them. ²⁷Therefore the LORD's anger burned against this land, so that he brought on it all the curses written in this book. ²⁸In furious anger and in great wrath the LORD uprooted them from their land and thrust them into another land, as it is now."

²⁹The secret things belong to the LORD our God, but the things revealed belong to us and to our children for ever, that we may follow all the words of this law.

Prosperity After Turning to the LORD

30 When all these blessings and curses I have set before you come upon you and you take them to heart wherever the LORD your God disperses you among the nations, ²and when you and your children return to the LORD your God and obey him with all your heart and with all your soul according to everything I command you today, ³then the LORD your

ᵃ19 *Or way, in order to add drunkenness to thirst.*

God will restore your fortunes*a* and have compassion on you and gather you again from all the nations where he scattered you. 4Even if you have been banished to the most distant land under the heavens, from there the LORD your God will gather you and bring you back. 5He will bring you to the land that belonged to your fathers, and you will take possession of it. He will make you more prosperous and numerous than your fathers. 6The LORD your God will circumcise your hearts and the hearts of your descendants, so that you may love him with all your heart and with all your soul, and live. 7The LORD your God will put all these curses on your enemies who hate and persecute you. 8You will again obey the LORD and follow all his commands I am giving you today. 9Then the LORD your God will make you most prosperous in all the work of your hands and in the fruit of your womb, the young of your livestock and the crops of your land. The LORD will again delight in you and make you prosperous, just as he delighted in your fathers, 10if you obey the LORD your God and keep his commands and decrees that are written in this Book of the Law and turn to the LORD your God with all your heart and with all your soul.

The Offer of Life or Death

11Now what I am commanding you today is not too difficult for you or beyond your reach. 12It is not up in heaven, so that you have to ask, "Who will ascend into heaven to get it and proclaim it to us so that we may obey it?" 13Nor is it beyond the sea, so that you have to ask, "Who will cross the sea to get it and proclaim it to us so that we may obey it?" 14No, the word is very near you; it is in your mouth and in your heart so that you may obey it.

15See, I set before you today life and prosperity, death and destruction. 16For I command you today to love the LORD your God, to walk in his ways, and to keep his commands, decrees and laws; then you will live and increase, and the LORD your

God will bless you in the land you are entering to possess.

17But if your heart turns away and you are not obedient, and if you are drawn away to bow down to other gods and worship them, 18I declare to you this day that you will certainly be destroyed. You will not live long in the land you are crossing the Jordan to enter and possess.

19This day I call heaven and earth as witnesses against you that I have set before you life and death, blessings and curses. Now choose life, so that you and your children may live 20and that you may love the LORD your God, listen to his voice, and hold fast to him. For the LORD is your life, and he will give you many years in the land he swore to give to your fathers, Abraham, Isaac and Jacob.

Joshua to Succeed Moses

31 Then Moses went out and spoke these words to all Israel: 2"I am now a hundred and twenty years old and I am no longer able to lead you. The LORD has said to me, 'You shall not cross the Jordan.' 3The LORD your God himself will cross over ahead of you. He will destroy these nations before you, and you will take possession of their land. Joshua also will cross over ahead of you, as the LORD said. 4And the LORD will do to them what he did to Sihon and Og, the kings of the Amorites, whom he destroyed along with their land. 5The LORD will deliver them to you, and you must do to them all that I have commanded you. 6Be strong and courageous. Do not be afraid or terrified because of them, for the LORD your God goes with you; he will never leave you nor forsake you."

7Then Moses summoned Joshua and said to him in the presence of all Israel, "Be strong and courageous, for you must go with this people into the land that the LORD swore to their forefathers to give them, and you must divide it among them as their inheritance. 8The LORD himself goes before you and will be with you; he

---

a3 Or *will bring you back from captivity*

will never leave you nor forsake you. Do not be afraid; do not be discouraged."

The Reading of the Law

9So Moses wrote down this law and gave it to the priests, the sons of Levi, who carried the ark of the covenant of the LORD, and to all the elders of Israel. 10Then Moses commanded them: "At the end of every seven years, in the year for cancelling debts, during the Feast of Tabernacles, 11when all Israel comes to appear before the LORD your God at the place he will choose, you shall read this law before them in their hearing. 12Assemble the people—men, women and children, and the aliens living in your towns—so that they can listen and learn to fear the LORD your God and follow carefully all the words of this law. 13Their children, who do not know this law, must hear it and learn to fear the LORD your God as long as you live in the land you are crossing the Jordan to possess."

Israel's Rebellion Predicted

14The LORD said to Moses, "Now the day of your death is near. Call Joshua and present yourselves at the Tent of Meeting, where I will commission him." So Moses and Joshua came and presented themselves at the Tent of Meeting.

15Then the LORD appeared at the Tent in a pillar of cloud, and the cloud stood over the entrance to the Tent. 16And the LORD said to Moses: "You are going to rest with your fathers, and these people will soon prostitute themselves to the foreign gods of the land they are entering. They will forsake me and break the covenant I made with them. 17On that day I will become angry with them and forsake them; I will hide my face from them, and they will be destroyed. Many disasters and difficulties will come upon them, and on that day they will ask, 'Have not these disasters come upon us because our God is not with us?' 18And I will certainly hide my face on that day because of all their wickedness in turning to other gods.

19"Now write down for yourselves this song and teach it to the Israelites and make them sing it, so that it may be a witness for me against them. 20When I have brought them into the land flowing with milk and honey, the land I promised on oath to their forefathers, and when they eat their fill and thrive, they will turn to other gods and worship them, rejecting me and breaking my covenant. 21And when many disasters and difficulties come upon them, this song will testify against them, because it will not be forgotten by their descendants. I know what they are disposed to do, even before I bring them into the land I promised them on oath." 22So Moses wrote down this song that day and taught it to the Israelites.

23The LORD gave this command to Joshua son of Nun: "Be strong and courageous, for you will bring the Israelites into the land I promised them on oath, and I myself will be with you."

24After Moses finished writing in a book the words of this law from beginning to end, 25he gave this command to the Levites who carried the ark of the covenant of the LORD: 26"Take this Book of the Law and place it beside the ark of the covenant of the LORD your God. There it will remain as a witness against you. 27For I know how rebellious and stiff-necked you are. If you have been rebellious against the LORD while I am still alive and with you, how much more will you rebel after I die! 28Assemble before me all the elders of your tribes and all your officials, so that I can speak these words in their hearing and call heaven and earth to testify against them. 29For I know that after my death you are sure to become utterly corrupt and to turn from the way I have commanded you. In days to come, disaster will fall upon you because you will do evil in the sight of the LORD and provoke him to anger by what your hands have made."

The Song of Moses

30And Moses recited the words of this song from beginning to end in the hearing of the whole assembly of Israel:

32 Listen, O heavens, and I will speak;
    hear, O earth, the words of my mouth.
2Let my teaching fall like rain
    and my words descend like dew,
like showers on new grass,
    like abundant rain on tender plants.

3I will proclaim the name of the LORD.
    Oh, praise the greatness of our God!
4He is the Rock, his works are perfect,
    and all his ways are just.
A faithful God who does no wrong,
    upright and just is he.

5They have acted corruptly towards him;
    to their shame they are no longer his
    children,
    but a warped and crooked
    generation.*a*
6Is this the way you repay the LORD,
    O foolish and unwise people?
Is he not your Father, your Creator,*b*
    who made you and formed you?

7Remember the days of old;
    consider the generations long past.
Ask your father and he will tell you,
    your elders, and they will explain to
    you.
8When the Most High gave the nations
    their inheritance,
    when he divided all mankind,
he set up boundaries for the peoples
    according to the number of the sons
    of Israel.*c*
9For the LORD's portion is his people,
    Jacob his allotted inheritance.

10In a desert land he found him,
    in a barren and howling waste.
He shielded him and cared for him;
    he guarded him as the apple of his
    eye,
11like an eagle that stirs up its nest
    and hovers over its young,
that spreads its wings to catch them
    and carries them on its pinions.
12The LORD alone led him;
    no foreign god was with him.

13He made him ride on the heights of the
    land
    and fed him with the fruit of the
    fields.
He nourished him with honey from the
    rock,
    and with oil from the flinty crag,
14with curds and milk from herd and flock
    and with fattened lambs and goats,
with choice rams of Bashan
    and the finest grains of wheat.
You drank the foaming blood of the
    grape.

15Jeshurun*d* grew fat and kicked;
    filled with food, he became heavy and
    sleek.
He abandoned the God who made him
    and rejected the Rock his Saviour.
16They made him jealous with their
    foreign gods
    and angered him with their detestable
    idols.
17They sacrificed to demons, which are
    not God—
    gods they had not known,
    gods that recently appeared,
    gods your fathers did not fear.
18You deserted the Rock, who fathered
    you;
    you forgot the God who gave you
    birth.

19The LORD saw this and rejected them
    because he was angered by his sons
    and daughters.
20"I will hide my face from them," he
    said,
    "and see what their end will be;
for they are a perverse generation,
    children who are unfaithful.
21They made me jealous by what is no
    god
    and angered me with their worthless
    idols.
I will make them envious by those who
    are not a people;
    I will make them angry by a nation
    that has no understanding.

a5 Or *Corrupt are they and not his children, / a generation warped and twisted to their shame*
b6 Or *Father, who bought you*   *c8* Masoretic Text; Dead Sea Scrolls (see also Septuagint) *sons of God*
d15 *Jeshurun* means *the upright one,* that is, Israel.

22For a fire has been kindled by my
wrath,
one that burns to the realm of death[e]
below.
It will devour the earth and its harvests
and set on fire the foundations of the
mountains.

23"I will heap calamities upon them
and expend my arrows against them.
24I will send wasting famine against them,
consuming pestilence and deadly
plague;
I will send against them the fangs of
wild beasts,
the venom of vipers that glide in the
dust.
25In the street the sword will make them
childless;
in their homes terror will reign.
Young men and young women will
perish,
infants and grey-haired men.
26I said I would scatter them
and blot out their memory from
mankind,
27but I dreaded the taunt of the enemy,
lest the adversary misunderstand
and say, 'Our hand has triumphed;
the LORD has not done all this.'"

28They are a nation without sense,
there is no discernment in them.
29If only they were wise and would
understand this
and discern what their end will be!
30How could one man chase a thousand,
or two put ten thousand to flight,
unless their Rock had sold them,
unless the LORD had given them up?
31For their rock is not like our Rock,
as even our enemies concede.
32Their vine comes from the vine of
Sodom
and from the fields of Gomorrah.
Their grapes are filled with poison,
and their clusters with bitterness.
33Their wine is the venom of serpents,
the deadly poison of cobras.

34"Have I not kept this in reserve
and sealed it in my vaults?
35It is mine to avenge; I will repay.
In due time their foot will slip;
their day of disaster is near
and their doom rushes upon them."

36The LORD will judge his people
and have compassion on his servants
when he sees their strength is gone
and no-one is left, slave or free.
37He will say: "Now where are their gods,
the rock they took refuge in,
38the gods who ate the fat of their
sacrifices
and drank the wine of their drink
offerings?
Let them rise up to help you!
Let them give you shelter!

39"See now that I myself am He!
There is no god besides me.
I put to death and I bring to life,
I have wounded and I will heal,
and no-one can deliver out of my
hand.
40I lift my hand to heaven and declare:
As surely as I live for ever,
41when I sharpen my flashing sword
and my hand grasps it in judgment,
I will take vengeance on my adversaries
and repay those who hate me.
42I will make my arrows drunk with
blood,
while my sword devours flesh:
the blood of the slain and the captives,
the heads of the enemy leaders."

43Rejoice, O nations, with his people,[f,g]
for he will avenge the blood of his
servants;
he will take vengeance on his enemies
and make atonement for his land and
people.

44Moses came with Joshua[h] son of Nun
and spoke all the words of this song in the
hearing of the people. 45When Moses
finished reciting all these words to all

---

e22 Hebrew *to Sheol*   f43 Or *Make his people rejoice, O nations*
g43 Masoretic Text; Dead Sea Scrolls (see also Septuagint) *people, / and let all the angels worship him /*
h44 Hebrew *Hoshea*, a variant of *Joshua*

Israel, [46]he said to them, "Take to heart all the words I have solemnly declared to you this day, so that you may command your children to obey carefully all the words of this law. [47]They are not just idle words for you—they are your life. By them you will live long in the land you are crossing the Jordan to possess."

Moses to Die on Mount Nebo

[48]On that same day the LORD told Moses, [49]"Go up into the Abarim Range to Mount Nebo in Moab, across from Jericho, and view Canaan, the land I am giving the Israelites as their own possession. [50]There on the mountain that you have climbed you will die and be gathered to your people, just as your brother Aaron died on Mount Hor and was gathered to his people. [51]This is because both of you broke faith with me in the presence of the Israelites at the waters of Meribah Kadesh in the Desert of Zin and because you did not uphold my holiness among the Israelites. [52]Therefore, you will see the land only from a distance; you will not enter the land I am giving to the people of Israel."

Moses Blesses the Tribes

33 This is the blessing that Moses the man of God pronounced on the Israelites before his death. [2]He said:

"The LORD came from Sinai
and dawned over them from Seir;
he shone forth from Mount Paran.
He came with[a] myriads of holy ones
from the south, from his mountain
slopes.[b]
[3]Surely it is you who love the people;
all the holy ones are in your hand.
At your feet they all bow down,
and from you receive instruction,
[4]the law that Moses gave us,
the possession of the assembly of
Jacob.

[5]He was king over Jeshurun[c]
when the leaders of the people
assembled,
along with the tribes of Israel.

[6]"Let Reuben live and not die,
nor[d] his men be few."

[7]And this he said about Judah:

"Hear, O LORD, the cry of Judah;
bring him to his people.
With his own hands he defends his
cause.
Oh, be his help against his foes!"

[8]About Levi he said:

"Your Thummim and Urim belong
to the man you favoured.
You tested him at Massah;
you contended with him at the waters
of Meribah.
[9]He said of his father and mother,
'I have no regard for them.'
He did not recognise his brothers
or acknowledge his own children,
but he watched over your word
and guarded your covenant.
[10]He teaches your precepts to Jacob
and your law to Israel.
He offers incense before you
and whole burnt offerings on your
altar.
[11]Bless all his skills, O LORD,
and be pleased with the work of his
hands.
Smite the loins of those who rise up
against him;
strike his foes till they rise no more."

[12]About Benjamin he said:

"Let the beloved of the LORD rest
secure in him,
for he shields him all day long,
and the one the LORD loves rests
between his shoulders."

[13]About Joseph he said:

---

[a]2 Or *from*　　[b]2 The meaning of the Hebrew for this phrase is uncertain.
[c]5 *Jeshurun* means *the upright one*, that is, Israel; also in verse 26.　　[d]6 Or *but let*

"May the LORD bless his land
　with the precious dew from heaven
　　above
　and with the deep waters that lie
　　below;
14with the best the sun brings forth
　and the finest the moon can yield;
15with the choicest gifts of the ancient
　　mountains
　and the fruitfulness of the everlasting
　　hills;
16with the best gifts of the earth and its
　　fulness
　and the favour of him who dwelt in
　　the burning bush.
Let all these rest on the head of Joseph,
　on the brow of the prince among*e* his
　　brothers.
17In majesty he is like a firstborn bull;
　his horns are the horns of a wild ox.
With them he will gore the nations,
　even those at the ends of the earth.
Such are the ten thousands of Ephraim;
　such are the thousands of
　　Manasseh."

18About Zebulun he said:

"Rejoice, Zebulun, in your going out,
　and you, Issachar, in your tents.
19They will summon peoples to the
　　mountain
　and there offer sacrifices of
　　righteousness;
they will feast on the abundance of the
　　seas,
　on the treasures hidden in the sand."

20About Gad he said:

"Blessed is he who enlarges Gad's
　　domain!
　Gad lives there like a lion,
　　tearing at arm or head.
21He chose the best land for himself;
　the leader's portion was kept for him.
When the heads of the people
　　assembled,
　he carried out the LORD's righteous
　　will,
　and his judgments concerning
　　Israel."

22About Dan he said:

"Dan is a lion's cub,
　springing out of Bashan."

23About Naphtali he said:

"Naphtali is abounding with the
　　favour of the LORD
　and is full of his blessing;
　he will inherit southward to the
　　lake."

24About Asher he said:

"Most blessed of sons is Asher;
　let him be favoured by his brothers,
　and let him bathe his feet in oil.
25The bolts of your gates will be iron and
　　bronze,
　and your strength will equal your
　　days.

26"There is no-one like the God of
　　Jeshurun,
　who rides on the heavens to help you
　and on the clouds in his majesty.
27The eternal God is your refuge,
　and underneath are the everlasting
　　arms.
He will drive out your enemy before
　　you,
　saying, 'Destroy him!'
28So Israel will live in safety alone;
　Jacob's spring is secure
in a land of grain and new wine,
　where the heavens drop
　　dew.
29Blessed are you, O Israel!
　Who is like you,
　a people saved by the LORD?
He is your shield and helper
　and your glorious sword.
Your enemies will cower before you,
　and you will trample down their high
　　places."*f*

The Death of Moses

34　Then Moses climbed Mount Nebo
　　from the plains of Moab to the top
of Pisgah, across from Jericho. There the

*e*16 Or *of the one separated from*　　*f*29 Or *will tread upon their bodies*

LORD showed him the whole land—from Gilead to Dan, [2]all of Naphtali, the territory of Ephraim and Manasseh, all the land of Judah as far as the western sea,[a] [3]the Negev and the whole region from the Valley of Jericho, the City of Palms, as far as Zoar. [4]Then the LORD said to him, "This is the land I promised on oath to Abraham, Isaac and Jacob when I said, 'I will give it to your descendants.' I have let you see it with your eyes, but you will not cross over into it."

[5]And Moses the servant of the LORD died there in Moab, as the LORD had said. [6]He buried him[b] in Moab, in the valley opposite Beth Peor, but to this day no-one knows where his grave is. [7]Moses was a hundred and twenty years old when he died, yet his eyes were not weak nor his strength gone. [8]The Israelites grieved for Moses in the plains of Moab thirty days, until the time of weeping and mourning was over.

[9]Now Joshua son of Nun was filled with the spirit[c] of wisdom because Moses had laid his hands on him. So the Israelites listened to him and did what the LORD had commanded Moses.

[10]Since then, no prophet has risen in Israel like Moses, whom the LORD knew face to face, [11]who did all those miraculous signs and wonders the LORD sent him to do in Egypt—to Pharaoh and to all his officials and to his whole land. [12]For no-one has ever shown the mighty power or performed the awesome deeds that Moses did in the sight of all Israel.

---

[a]2 That is, the Mediterranean   [b]6 Or He was buried   [c]9 Or Spirit

Joshua

The LORD Commands Joshua

1 After the death of Moses the servant of the LORD, the LORD said to Joshua son of Nun, Moses' assistant: [2]"Moses my servant is dead. Now then, you and all these people, get ready to cross the Jordan River into the land I am about to give to them—to the Israelites. [3]I will give you every place where you set your foot, as I promised Moses. [4]Your territory will extend from the desert to Lebanon, and from the great river, the Euphrates—all the Hittite country—to the Great Sea[a] on the west. [5]No-one will be able to stand up against you all the days of your life. As I was with Moses, so I will be with you; I will never leave you nor forsake you.

[6]"Be strong and courageous, because you will lead these people to inherit the land I swore to their forefathers to give them. [7]Be strong and very courageous. Be careful to obey all the law my servant Moses gave you; do not turn from it to the right or to the left, that you may be successful wherever you go. [8]Do not let this Book of the Law depart from your mouth; meditate on it day and night, so that you may be careful to do everything written in it. Then you will be prosperous and successful. [9]Have I not commanded you? Be strong and courageous. Do not be terrified; do not be discouraged, for the LORD your God will be with you wherever you go."

[10]So Joshua ordered the officers of the people: [11]"Go through the camp and tell the people, 'Get your supplies ready. Three days from now you will cross the Jordan here to go in and take possession of the land the LORD your God is giving you for your own.'"

[12]But to the Reubenites, the Gadites and the half-tribe of Manasseh, Joshua said, [13]"Remember the command that Moses the servant of the LORD gave you: 'The LORD your God is giving you rest and has granted you this land.' [14]Your wives, your children and your livestock may stay in the land that Moses gave you east of the Jordan, but all your fighting men, fully armed, must cross over ahead of your brothers. You are to help your brothers [15]until the LORD gives them rest, as he has done for you, and until they too have taken possession of the land that the LORD your God is giving them. After that, you may go back and occupy your own land, which Moses the servant of the LORD gave you east of the Jordan towards the sunrise."

[16]Then they answered Joshua, "Whatever you have commanded us we will do, and wherever you send us we will go. [17]Just as we fully obeyed Moses, so we will obey you. Only may the LORD your God be with you as he was with Moses. [18]Whoever rebels against your word and does not obey your words, whatever you may command them, will be put to death. Only be strong and courageous!"

Rahab and the Spies

2 Then Joshua son of Nun secretly sent two spies from Shittim. "Go, look over the land," he said, "especially

[a]4 That is, the Mediterranean

Jericho." So they went and entered the house of a prostitute[a] named Rahab and stayed there.

²The king of Jericho was told, "Look! Some of the Israelites have come here tonight to spy out the land." ³So the king of Jericho sent this message to Rahab: "Bring out the men who came to you and entered your house, because they have come to spy out the whole land."

⁴But the woman had taken the two men and hidden them. She said, "Yes, the men came to me, but I did not know where they had come from. ⁵At dusk, when it was time to close the city gate, the men left. I don't know which way they went. Go after them quickly. You may catch up with them." ⁶(But she had taken them up to the roof and hidden them under the stalks of flax she had laid out on the roof.) ⁷So the men set out in pursuit of the spies on the road that leads to the fords of the Jordan, and as soon as the pursuers had gone out, the gate was shut.

⁸Before the spies lay down for the night, she went up on the roof ⁹and said to them, "I know that the LORD has given this land to you and that a great fear of you has fallen on us, so that all who live in this country are melting in fear because of you. ¹⁰We have heard how the LORD dried up the water of the Red Sea[b] for you when you came out of Egypt, and what you did to Sihon and Og, the two kings of the Amorites east of the Jordan, whom you completely destroyed.[c] ¹¹When we heard of it, our hearts sank[d] and everyone's courage failed because of you, for the LORD your God is God in heaven above and on the earth below. ¹²Now then, please swear to me by the LORD that you will show kindness to my family, because I have shown kindness to you. Give me a sure sign ¹³that you will spare the lives of my father and mother, my brothers and sisters, and all who belong to them, and that you will save us from death."

¹⁴"Our lives for your lives!" the men assured her. "If you don't tell what we are doing, we will treat you kindly and faith-fully when the LORD gives us the land."

¹⁵So she let them down by a rope through the window, for the house she lived in was part of the city wall. ¹⁶Now she had said to them, "Go to the hills so that the pursuers will not find you. Hide yourselves there three days until they return, and then go on your way."

¹⁷The men said to her, "This oath you made us swear will not be binding on us ¹⁸unless, when we enter the land, you have tied this scarlet cord in the window through which you let us down, and unless you have brought your father and mother, your brothers and all your family into your house. ¹⁹If anyone goes outside your house into the street, his blood will be on his own head; we will not be responsible. As for anyone who is in the house with you, his blood will be on our head if a hand is laid on him. ²⁰But if you tell what we are doing, we will be released from the oath you made us swear."

²¹"Agreed," she replied. "Let it be as you say." So she sent them away and they departed. And she tied the scarlet cord in the window.

²²When they left, they went into the hills and stayed there three days, until the pursuers had searched all along the road and returned without finding them. ²³Then the two men started back. They went down out of the hills, forded the river and came to Joshua son of Nun and told him everything that had happened to them. ²⁴They said to Joshua, "The LORD has surely given the whole land into our hands; all the people are melting in fear because of us."

Crossing the Jordan

3 Early in the morning Joshua and all the Israelites set out from Shittim and went to the Jordan, where they camped before crossing over. ²After three days the officers went throughout the camp, ³giving orders to the people: "When you see the ark of the covenant of the LORD your God, and the priests, who are Levites, carrying

---

[a]1 Or possibly *an innkeeper*   [b]10 Hebrew *Yam Suph*; that is, Sea of Reeds
[c]10 The Hebrew term refers to the irrevocable giving over of things or persons to the LORD, often by totally destroying them.   [d]11 Hebrew *melted*

it, you are to move out from your positions and follow it. ⁴Then you will know which way to go, since you have never been this way before. But keep a distance of about a thousand yards[a] between you and the ark; do not go near it."

⁵Joshua told the people, "Consecrate yourselves, for tomorrow the LORD will do amazing things among you."

⁶Joshua said to the priests, "Take up the ark of the covenant and pass on ahead of the people." So they took it up and went ahead of them.

⁷And the LORD said to Joshua, "Today I will begin to exalt you in the eyes of all Israel, so that they may know that I am with you as I was with Moses. ⁸Tell the priests who carry the ark of the covenant: 'When you reach the edge of the Jordan's waters, go and stand in the river.'"

⁹Joshua said to the Israelites, "Come here and listen to the words of the LORD your God. ¹⁰This is how you will know that the living God is among you and that he will certainly drive out before you the Canaanites, Hittites, Hivites, Perizzites, Girgashites, Amorites and Jebusites. ¹¹See, the ark of the covenant of the Lord of all the earth will go into the Jordan ahead of you. ¹²Now then, choose twelve men from the tribes of Israel, one from each tribe. ¹³And as soon as the priests who carry the ark of the LORD—the Lord of all the earth—set foot in the Jordan, its waters flowing downstream will be cut off and stand up in a heap."

¹⁴So when the people broke camp to cross the Jordan, the priests carrying the ark of the covenant went ahead of them. ¹⁵Now the Jordan is in flood all during harvest. Yet as soon as the priests who carried the ark reached the Jordan and their feet touched the water's edge, ¹⁶the water from upstream stopped flowing. It piled up in a heap a great distance away, at a town called Adam in the vicinity of Zarethan, while the water flowing down to the Sea of the Arabah (the Salt Sea[b]) was completely cut off. So the people crossed over opposite Jericho. ¹⁷The priests who

carried the ark of the covenant of the LORD stood firm on dry ground in the middle of the Jordan, while all Israel passed by until the whole nation had completed the crossing on dry ground.

4 When the whole nation had finished crossing the Jordan, the LORD said to Joshua, ²"Choose twelve men from among the people, one from each tribe, ³and tell them to take up twelve stones from the middle of the Jordan from right where the priests stood and to carry them over with you and put them down at the place where you stay tonight."

⁴So Joshua called together the twelve men he had appointed from the Israelites, one from each tribe, ⁵and said to them, "Go over before the ark of the LORD your God into the middle of the Jordan. Each of you is to take up a stone on his shoulder, according to the number of the tribes of the Israelites, ⁶to serve as a sign among you. In the future, when your children ask you, 'What do these stones mean?' ⁷tell them that the flow of the Jordan was cut off before the ark of the covenant of the LORD. When it crossed the Jordan, the waters of the Jordan were cut off. These stones are to be a memorial to the people of Israel for ever."

⁸So the Israelites did as Joshua commanded them. They took twelve stones from the middle of the Jordan, according to the number of the tribes of the Israelites, as the LORD had told Joshua; and they carried them over with them to their camp, where they put them down. ⁹Joshua set up the twelve stones that had been[a] in the middle of the Jordan at the spot where the priests who carried the ark of the covenant had stood. And they are there to this day.

¹⁰Now the priests who carried the ark remained standing in the middle of the Jordan until everything the LORD had commanded Joshua was done by the people, just as Moses had directed Joshua. The people hurried over, ¹¹and as soon as all of them had crossed, the ark of the LORD and the priests came to the other

---

a4 Hebrew *about two thousand cubits* (about 900 metres)   b16 That is, the Dead Sea
a9 Or *Joshua also set up twelve stones*

side while the people watched. [12]The men of Reuben, Gad and the half-tribe of Manasseh crossed over, armed, in front of the Israelites, as Moses had directed them. [13]About forty thousand armed for battle crossed over before the LORD to the plains of Jericho for war.

[14]That day the LORD exalted Joshua in the sight of all Israel; and they revered him all the days of his life, just as they had revered Moses.

[15]Then the LORD said to Joshua, [16]"Command the priests carrying the ark of the Testimony to come up out of the Jordan."

[17]So Joshua commanded the priests, "Come up out of the Jordan."

[18]And the priests came up out of the river carrying the ark of the covenant of the LORD. No sooner had they set their feet on the dry ground than the waters of the Jordan returned to their place and ran in flood as before.

[19]On the tenth day of the first month the people went up from the Jordan and camped at Gilgal on the eastern border of Jericho. [20]And Joshua set up at Gilgal the twelve stones they had taken out of the Jordan. [21]He said to the Israelites, "In the future when your descendants ask their fathers, 'What do these stones mean?' [22]tell them, 'Israel crossed the Jordan on dry ground.' [23]For the LORD your God dried up the Jordan before you until you had crossed over. The LORD your God did to the Jordan just what he had done to the Red Sea[b] when he dried it up before us until we had crossed over. [24]He did this so that all the peoples of the earth might know that the hand of the LORD is powerful and so that you might always fear the LORD your God."

Circumcision at Gilgal

5 Now when all the Amorite kings west of the Jordan and all the Canaanite kings along the coast heard how the LORD had dried up the Jordan before the Israelites until we had crossed over, their hearts sank[a] and they no longer had the courage to face the Israelites.

[2]At that time the LORD said to Joshua, "Make flint knives and circumcise the Israelites again." [3]So Joshua made flint knives and circumcised the Israelites at Gibeath Haaraloth.[b]

[4]Now this is why he did so: All those who came out of Egypt—all the men of military age—died in the desert on the way after leaving Egypt. [5]All the people that came out had been circumcised, but all the people born in the desert during the journey from Egypt had not. [6]The Israelites had moved about in the desert forty years until all the men who were of military age when they left Egypt had died, since they had not obeyed the LORD. For the LORD had sworn to them that they would not see the land that he had solemnly promised their fathers to give us, a land flowing with milk and honey. [7]So he raised up their sons in their place, and these were the ones Joshua circumcised. They were still uncircumcised because they had not been circumcised on the way. [8]And after the whole nation had been circumcised, they remained where they were in camp until they were healed.

[9]Then the LORD said to Joshua, "Today I have rolled away the reproach of Egypt from you." So the place has been called Gilgal[c] to this day.

[10]On the evening of the fourteenth day of the month, while camped at Gilgal on the plains of Jericho, the Israelites celebrated the Passover. [11]The day after the Passover, that very day, they ate some of the produce of the land: unleavened bread and roasted grain. [12]The manna stopped the day after[d] they ate this food from the land; there was no longer any manna for the Israelites, but that year they ate of the produce of Canaan.

The Fall of Jericho

[13]Now when Joshua was near Jericho, he looked up and saw a man standing in front of him with a drawn sword in his

---

b23 Hebrew *Yam Suph*; that is, Sea of Reeds
b3 *Gibeath Haaraloth* means *hill of foreskins*.
a1 Hebrew *melted*
c9 *Gilgal* sounds like the Hebrew for *roll.*   d12 Or *the day*

hand. Joshua went up to him and asked, "Are you for us or for our enemies?"

14"Neither," he replied, "but as commander of the army of the LORD I have now come." Then Joshua fell face down to the ground in reverence, and asked him, "What message does my Lord^e have for his servant?"

15The commander of the LORD's army replied, "Take off your sandals, for the place where you are standing is holy." And Joshua did so.

6 Now Jericho was tightly shut up because of the Israelites. No-one went out and no-one came in.

2Then the LORD said to Joshua, "See, I have delivered Jericho into your hands, along with its king and its fighting men. 3March around the city once with all the armed men. Do this for six days. 4Make seven priests carry trumpets of rams' horns in front of the ark. On the seventh day, march around the city seven times, with the priests blowing the trumpets. 5When you hear them sound a long blast on the trumpets, make all the people give a loud shout; then the wall of the city will collapse and the people will go up, every man straight in."

6So Joshua son of Nun called the priests and said to them, "Take up the ark of the covenant of the LORD and make seven priests carry trumpets in front of it." 7And he ordered the people, "Advance! March around the city, with the armed guard going ahead of the ark of the LORD."

8When Joshua had spoken to the people, the seven priests carrying the seven trumpets before the LORD went forward, blowing their trumpets, and the ark of the LORD's covenant followed them. 9The armed guard marched ahead of the priests who blew the trumpets, and the rear guard followed the ark. All this time the trumpets were sounding. 10But Joshua had commanded the people, "Do not give a war cry, do not raise your voices, do not say a word until the day I tell you to shout. Then shout!" 11So he had the ark of the LORD carried around the city, circling it

once. Then the people returned to camp and spent the night there.

12Joshua got up early the next morning and the priests took up the ark of the LORD. 13The seven priests carrying the seven trumpets went forward, marching before the ark of the LORD and blowing the trumpets. The armed men went ahead of them and the rear guard followed the ark of the LORD, while the trumpets kept sounding. 14So on the second day they marched around the city once and returned to the camp. They did this for six days.

15On the seventh day, they got up at daybreak and marched around the city seven times in the same manner, except that on that day they circled the city seven times. 16The seventh time around, when the priests sounded the trumpet blast, Joshua commanded the people, "Shout! For the LORD has given you the city! 17The city and all that is in it are to be devoted^a to the LORD. Only Rahab the prostitute^b and all who are with her in her house shall be spared, because she hid the spies we sent. 18But keep away from the devoted things, so that you will not bring about your own destruction by taking any of them. Otherwise you will make the camp of Israel liable to destruction and bring trouble on it. 19All the silver and gold and the articles of bronze and iron are sacred to the LORD and must go into his treasury."

20When the trumpets sounded, the people shouted, and at the sound of the trumpet, when the people gave a loud shout, the wall collapsed; so every man charged straight in, and they took the city. 21They devoted the city to the LORD and destroyed with the sword every living thing in it—men and women, young and old, cattle, sheep and donkeys.

22Joshua said to the two men who had spied out the land, "Go into the prostitute's house and bring her out and all who belong to her, in accordance with your oath to her." 23So the young men who had done the spying went in and brought out Rahab, her father and mother and

---

^{e}14 Or lord
^{a}17 The Hebrew term refers to the irrevocable giving over of things or persons to the LORD, often by totally destroying them; also in verses 18 and 21. ^{b}17 Or possibly innkeeper; also in verses 22 and 25

brothers and all who belonged to her. They brought out her entire family and put them in a place outside the camp of Israel.

24Then they burned the whole city and everything in it, but they put the silver and gold and the articles of bronze and iron into the treasury of the LORD's house. 25But Joshua spared Rahab the prostitute, with her family and all who belonged to her, because she hid the men Joshua had sent as spies to Jericho—and she lives among the Israelites to this day.

26At that time Joshua pronounced this solemn oath: "Cursed before the LORD is the man who undertakes to rebuild this city, Jericho:

"At the cost of his firstborn son
  will he lay its foundations;
at the cost of his youngest
  will he set up its gates."

27So the LORD was with Joshua, and his fame spread throughout the land.

Achan's Sin

7 But the Israelites acted unfaithfully in regard to the devoted things:[a] Achan son of Carmi, the son of Zimri,[b] the son of Zerah, of the tribe of Judah, took some of them. So the LORD's anger burned against Israel.

2Now Joshua sent men from Jericho to Ai, which is near Beth Aven to the east of Bethel, and told them, "Go up and spy out the region." So the men went up and spied out Ai.

3When they returned to Joshua, they said, "Not all the people will have to go up against Ai. Send two or three thousand men to take it and do not weary all the people, for only a few men are there." 4So about three thousand men went up; but they were routed by the men of Ai, 5who killed about thirty-six of them. They chased the Israelites from the city gate as far as the stone quarries[c] and struck them down on the slopes. At this the hearts of the people melted and became like water.

6Then Joshua tore his clothes and fell face down to the ground before the ark of the LORD, remaining there till evening. The elders of Israel did the same, and sprinkled dust on their heads. 7And Joshua said, "Ah, Sovereign LORD, why did you ever bring this people across the Jordan to deliver us into the hands of the Amorites to destroy us? If only we had been content to stay on the other side of the Jordan! 8O Lord, what can I say, now that Israel has been routed by its enemies? 9The Canaanites and the other people of the country will hear about this and they will surround us and wipe out our name from the earth. What then will you do for your own great name?"

10The LORD said to Joshua, "Stand up! What are you doing down on your face? 11Israel has sinned; they have violated my covenant, which I commanded them to keep. They have taken some of the devoted things; they have stolen, they have lied, they have put them with their own possessions. 12That is why the Israelites cannot stand against their enemies; they turn their backs and run because they have been made liable to destruction. I will not be with you any more unless you destroy whatever among you is devoted to destruction.

13"Go, consecrate the people. Tell them, 'Consecrate yourselves in preparation for tomorrow; for this is what the LORD, the God of Israel, says: That which is devoted is among you, O Israel. You cannot stand against your enemies until you remove it.

14"'In the morning, present yourselves tribe by tribe. The tribe that the LORD takes shall come forward clan by clan; the clan that the LORD takes shall come forward family by family; and the family that the LORD takes shall come forward man by man. 15He who is caught with the devoted things shall be destroyed by fire, along with all that belongs to him. He has violated the covenant of the LORD and has done a disgraceful thing in Israel!'"

---

a1 The Hebrew term refers to the irrevocable giving over of things or persons to the LORD, often by totally destroying them; also in verses 11, 12, 13 and 15.   b1 See Septuagint and 1 Chron. 2:6; Hebrew Zabdi; also in verses 17 and 18.
c5 Or as far as Shebarim

¹⁶Early the next morning Joshua had Israel come forward by tribes, and Judah was taken. ¹⁷The clans of Judah came forward, and he took the Zerahites. He had the clan of the Zerahites come forward by families, and Zimri was taken. ¹⁸Joshua had his family come forward man by man, and Achan son of Carmi, the son of Zimri, the son of Zerah, of the tribe of Judah, was taken.

¹⁹Then Joshua said to Achan, "My son, give glory to the LORD,*d* the God of Israel, and give him the praise.*e* Tell me what you have done; do not hide it from me."

²⁰Achan replied, "It is true! I have sinned against the LORD, the God of Israel. This is what I have done: ²¹When I saw in the plunder a beautiful robe from Babylonia,*f* two hundred shekels*g* of silver and a wedge of gold weighing fifty shekels,*h* I coveted them and took them. They are hidden in the ground inside my tent, with the silver underneath."

²²So Joshua sent messengers, and they ran to the tent, and there it was, hidden in his tent, with the silver underneath. ²³They took the things from the tent, brought them to Joshua and all the Israelites and spread them out before the LORD.

²⁴Then Joshua, together with all Israel, took Achan son of Zerah, the silver, the robe, the gold wedge, his sons and daughters, his cattle, donkeys and sheep, his tent and all that he had, to the Valley of Achor. ²⁵Joshua said, "Why have you brought this trouble on us? The LORD will bring trouble on you today."

Then all Israel stoned him, and after they had stoned the rest, they burned them. ²⁶Over Achan they heaped up a large pile of rocks, which remains to this day. Then the LORD turned from his fierce anger. Therefore that place has been called the Valley of Achor*i* ever since.

Ai Destroyed

8 Then the LORD said to Joshua, "Do not be afraid; do not be discouraged. Take the whole army with you, and go up and attack Ai. For I have delivered into your hands the king of Ai, his people, his city and his land. ²You shall do to Ai and its king as you did to Jericho and its king, except that you may carry off their plunder and livestock for yourselves. Set an ambush behind the city."

³So Joshua and the whole army moved out to attack Ai. He chose thirty thousand of his best fighting men and sent them out at night ⁴with these orders: "Listen carefully. You are to set an ambush behind the city. Don't go very far from it. All of you be on the alert. ⁵I and all those with me will advance on the city, and when the men come out against us, as they did before, we will flee from them. ⁶They will pursue us until we have lured them away from the city, for they will say, 'They are running away from us as they did before.' So when we flee from them, ⁷you are to rise up from ambush and take the city. The LORD your God will give it into your hand. ⁸When you have taken the city, set it on fire. Do what the LORD has commanded. See to it; you have my orders."

⁹Then Joshua sent them off, and they went to the place of ambush and lay in wait between Bethel and Ai, to the west of Ai—but Joshua spent that night with the people.

¹⁰Early the next morning Joshua mustered his men, and he and the leaders of Israel marched before them to Ai. ¹¹The entire force that was with him marched up and approached the city and arrived in front of it. They set up camp north of Ai, with the valley between them and the city. ¹²Joshua had taken about five thousand men and set them in ambush between Bethel and Ai, to the west of the city. ¹³They had the soldiers take up their positions—all those in the camp to the north of the city and the ambush to the west of it. That night Joshua went into the valley.

¹⁴When the king of Ai saw this, he and all the men of the city hurried out early in the morning to meet Israel in battle at a certain place overlooking the Arabah. But he did not know that an ambush had been

---

d19 A solemn charge to tell the truth   *e19* Or *and confess to him*   *f21* Hebrew *Shinar*
g21 That is, about 5 pounds (about 2.3 kilograms)   *h21* That is, about 1¼ pounds (about 0.6 kilogram)
i26 *Achor* means *trouble.*

set against him behind the city. [15]Joshua and all Israel let themselves be driven back before them, and they fled towards the desert. [16]All the men of Ai were called to pursue them, and they pursued Joshua and were lured away from the city. [17]Not a man remained in Ai or Bethel who did not go after Israel. They left the city open and went in pursuit of Israel.

[18]Then the LORD said to Joshua, "Hold out towards Ai the javelin that is in your hand, for into your hand I will deliver the city." So Joshua held out his javelin towards Ai. [19]As soon as he did this, the men in the ambush rose quickly from their position and rushed forward. They entered the city and captured it and quickly set it on fire.

[20]The men of Ai looked back and saw the smoke of the city rising against the sky, but they had no chance to escape in any direction, for the Israelites who had been fleeing towards the desert had turned back against their pursuers. [21]For when Joshua and all Israel saw that the ambush had taken the city and that smoke was going up from the city, they turned round and attacked the men of Ai. [22]The men of the ambush also came out of the city against them, so that they were caught in the middle, with Israelites on both sides. Israel cut them down, leaving them neither survivors nor fugitives. [23]But they took the king of Ai alive and brought him to Joshua.

[24]When Israel had finished killing all the men of Ai in the fields and in the desert where they had chased them, and when every one of them had been put to the sword, all the Israelites returned to Ai and killed those who were in it. [25]Twelve thousand men and women fell that day—all the people of Ai. [26]For Joshua did not draw back the hand that held out his javelin until he had destroyed[a] all who lived in Ai. [27]But Israel did carry off for themselves the livestock and plunder of this city, as the LORD had instructed Joshua.

[28]So Joshua burned Ai and made it a permanent heap of ruins, a desolate place to this day. [29]He hung the king of Ai on a

tree and left him there until evening. At sunset, Joshua ordered them to take his body from the tree and throw it down at the entrance of the city gate. And they raised a large pile of rocks over it, which remains to this day.

The Covenant Renewed at Mount Ebal

[30]Then Joshua built on Mount Ebal an altar to the LORD, the God of Israel, [31]as Moses the servant of the LORD had commanded the Israelites. He built it according to what is written in the Book of the Law of Moses—an altar of uncut stones, on which no iron tool had been used. On it they offered to the LORD burnt offerings and sacrificed fellowship offerings.[b] [32]There, in the presence of the Israelites, Joshua copied on stones the law of Moses, which he had written. [33]All Israel, aliens and citizens alike, with their elders, officials and judges, were standing on both sides of the ark of the covenant of the LORD, facing those who carried it—the priests, who were Levites. Half of the people stood in front of Mount Gerizim and half of them in front of Mount Ebal, as Moses the servant of the LORD had formerly commanded when he gave instructions to bless the people of Israel.

[34]Afterwards, Joshua read all the words of the law—the blessings and the curses—just as it is written in the Book of the Law. [35]There was not a word of all that Moses had commanded that Joshua did not read to the whole assembly of Israel, including the women and children, and the aliens who lived among them.

The Gibeonite Deception

9 Now when all the kings west of the Jordan heard about these things—those in the hill country, in the western foothills, and along the entire coast of the Great Sea[a] as far as Lebanon (the kings of the Hittites, Amorites, Canaanites, Perizzites, Hivites and Jebusites)—[2]they came together to make war against Joshua and Israel.

---

[a]26 The Hebrew term refers to the irrevocable giving over of things or persons to the LORD, often by totally destroying them.   [b]31 Traditionally *peace offerings*   [a]1 That is, the Mediterranean

³However, when the people of Gibeon heard what Joshua had done to Jericho and Ai, ⁴they resorted to a ruse: They went as a delegation whose donkeys were loaded*b* with worn-out sacks and old wineskins, cracked and mended. ⁵The men put worn and patched sandals on their feet and wore old clothes. All the bread of their food supply was dry and mouldy. ⁶Then they went to Joshua in the camp at Gilgal and said to him and the men of Israel, "We have come from a distant country; make a treaty with us."

⁷The men of Israel said to the Hivites, "But perhaps you live near us. How then can we make a treaty with you?"

⁸"We are your servants," they said to Joshua.

But Joshua asked, "Who are you and where do you come from?"

⁹They answered: "Your servants have come from a very distant country because of the fame of the LORD your God. For we have heard reports of him: all that he did in Egypt, ¹⁰and all that he did to the two kings of the Amorites east of the Jordan— Sihon king of Heshbon, and Og king of Bashan, who reigned in Ashtaroth. ¹¹And our elders and all those living in our country said to us, 'Take provisions for your journey; go and meet them and say to them, "We are your servants; make a treaty with us."' ¹²This bread of ours was warm when we packed it at home on the day we left to come to you. But now see how dry and mouldy it is. ¹³And these wineskins that we filled were new, but see how cracked they are. And our clothes and sandals are worn out by the very long journey."

¹⁴The men of Israel sampled their provisions but did not enquire of the LORD. ¹⁵Then Joshua made a treaty of peace with them to let them live, and the leaders of the assembly ratified it by oath.

¹⁶Three days after they made the treaty with the Gibeonites, the Israelites heard that they were neighbours, living near them. ¹⁷So the Israelites set out and on the third day came to their cities: Gibeon, Kephirah, Beeroth and Kiriath Jearim. ¹⁸But the Israelites did not attack them, because the leaders of the assembly had sworn an oath to them by the LORD, the God of Israel.

The whole assembly grumbled against the leaders, ¹⁹but all the leaders answered, "We have given them our oath by the LORD, the God of Israel, and we cannot touch them now. ²⁰This is what we will do to them: We will let them live, so that wrath will not fall on us for breaking the oath we swore to them." ²¹They continued, "Let them live, but let them be woodcutters and water-carriers for the entire community." So the leaders' promise to them was kept.

²²Then Joshua summoned the Gibeonites and said, "Why did you deceive us by saying, 'We live a long way from you,' while actually you live near us? ²³You are now under a curse: You will never cease to serve as woodcutters and water-carriers for the house of my God."

²⁴They answered Joshua, "Your servants were clearly told how the LORD your God had commanded his servant Moses to give you the whole land and to wipe out all its inhabitants from before you. So we feared for our lives because of you, and that is why we did this. ²⁵We are now in your hands. Do to us whatever seems good and right to you."

²⁶So Joshua saved them from the Israelites, and they did not kill them. ²⁷That day he made the Gibeonites woodcutters and water-carriers for the community and for the altar of the LORD at the place the LORD would choose. And that is what they are to this day.

The Sun Stands Still

10 Now Adoni-Zedek king of Jerusalem heard that Joshua had taken Ai and totally destroyed*a* it, doing to Ai and its king as he had done to Jericho and its king, and that the people of Gibeon had

---

*b*4 Most Hebrew manuscripts; some Hebrew manuscripts, Vulgate and Syriac (see also Septuagint) *They prepared provisions and loaded their donkeys*
*a*1 The Hebrew term refers to the irrevocable giving over of things or persons to the LORD, often by totally destroying them; also in verses 28, 35, 37, 39 and 40.

made a treaty of peace with Israel and were living near them. ²He and his people were very much alarmed at this, because Gibeon was an important city, like one of the royal cities; it was larger than Ai, and all its men were good fighters. ³So Adoni-Zedek king of Jerusalem appealed to Hoham king of Hebron, Piram king of Jarmuth, Japhia king of Lachish and Debir king of Eglon. ⁴"Come up and help me attack Gibeon," he said, "because it has made peace with Joshua and the Israelites."

⁵Then the five kings of the Amorites—the kings of Jerusalem, Hebron, Jarmuth, Lachish and Eglon—joined forces. They moved up with all their troops and took up positions against Gibeon and attacked it.

⁶The Gibeonites then sent word to Joshua in the camp at Gilgal: "Do not abandon your servants. Come up to us quickly and save us! Help us, because all the Amorite kings from the hill country have joined forces against us."

⁷So Joshua marched up from Gilgal with his entire army, including all the best fighting men. ⁸The LORD said to Joshua, "Do not be afraid of them; I have given them into your hand. Not one of them will be able to withstand you."

⁹After an all-night march from Gilgal, Joshua took them by surprise. ¹⁰The LORD threw them into confusion before Israel, who defeated them in a great victory at Gibeon. Israel pursued them along the road going up to Beth Horon and cut them down all the way to Azekah and Makkedah. ¹¹As they fled before Israel on the road down from Beth Horon to Azekah, the LORD hurled large hailstones down on them from the sky, and more of them died from the hailstones than were killed by the swords of the Israelites.

¹²On the day the LORD gave the Amorites over to Israel, Joshua said to the LORD in the presence of Israel:

"O sun, stand still over Gibeon,
    O moon, over the Valley of Aijalon."
¹³So the sun stood still,
    and the moon stopped,

till the nation avenged itself on*ᵇ* its
    enemies,

as it is written in the Book of Jashar.

The sun stopped in the middle of the sky and delayed going down about a full day. ¹⁴There has never been a day like it before or since, a day when the LORD listened to a man. Surely the LORD was fighting for Israel!

¹⁵Then Joshua returned with all Israel to the camp at Gilgal.

Five Amorite Kings Killed

¹⁶Now the five kings had fled and hidden in the cave at Makkedah. ¹⁷When Joshua was told that the five kings had been found hiding in the cave at Makkedah, ¹⁸he said, "Roll large rocks up to the mouth of the cave, and post some men there to guard it. ¹⁹But don't stop! Pursue your enemies, attack them from the rear and don't let them reach their cities, for the LORD your God has given them into your hand."

²⁰So Joshua and the Israelites destroyed them completely—almost to a man—but the few who were left reached their fortified cities. ²¹The whole army then returned safely to Joshua in the camp at Makkedah, and no-one uttered a word against the Israelites.

²²Joshua said, "Open the mouth of the cave and bring those five kings out to me." ²³So they brought the five kings out of the cave—the kings of Jerusalem, Hebron, Jarmuth, Lachish and Eglon. ²⁴When they had brought these kings to Joshua, he summoned all the men of Israel and said to the army commanders who had come with him, "Come here and put your feet on the necks of these kings." So they came forward and placed their feet on their necks.

²⁵Joshua said to them, "Do not be afraid; do not be discouraged. Be strong and courageous. This is what the LORD will do to all the enemies you are going to fight." ²⁶Then Joshua struck and killed the kings and hung them on five trees, and they were left hanging on the trees until evening.

²⁷At sunset Joshua gave the order and

ᵇ13 Or nation triumphed over

they took them down from the trees and threw them into the cave where they had been hiding. At the mouth of the cave they placed large rocks, which are there to this day.

28That day Joshua took Makkedah. He put the city and its king to the sword and totally destroyed everyone in it. He left no survivors. And he did to the king of Makkedah as he had done to the king of Jericho.

Southern Cities Conquered

29Then Joshua and all Israel with him moved on from Makkedah to Libnah and attacked it. 30The LORD also gave that city and its king into Israel's hand. The city and everyone in it Joshua put to the sword. He left no survivors there. And he did to its king as he had done to the king of Jericho.

31Then Joshua and all Israel with him moved on from Libnah to Lachish; he took up positions against it and attacked it. 32The LORD handed Lachish over to Israel, and Joshua took it on the second day. The city and everyone in it he put to the sword, just as he had done to Libnah. 33Meanwhile, Horam king of Gezer had come up to help Lachish, but Joshua defeated him and his army—until no survivors were left.

34Then Joshua and all Israel with him moved on from Lachish to Eglon; they took up positions against it and attacked it. 35They captured it that same day and put it to the sword and totally destroyed everyone in it, just as they had done to Lachish.

36Then Joshua and all Israel with him went up from Eglon to Hebron and attacked it. 37They took the city and put it to the sword, together with its king, its villages and everyone in it. They left no survivors. Just as at Eglon, they totally destroyed it and everyone in it.

38Then Joshua and all Israel with him turned round and attacked Debir. 39They took the city, its king and its villages, and put them to the sword. Everyone in it they

totally destroyed. They left no survivors. They did to Debir and its king as they had done to Libnah and its king and to Hebron.

40So Joshua subdued the whole region, including the hill country, the Negev, the western foothills and the mountain slopes, together with all their kings. He left no survivors. He totally destroyed all who breathed, just as the LORD, the God of Israel, had commanded. 41Joshua subdued them from Kadesh Barnea to Gaza and from the whole region of Goshen to Gibeon. 42All these kings and their lands Joshua conquered in one campaign, because the LORD, the God of Israel, fought for Israel.

43Then Joshua returned with all Israel to the camp at Gilgal.

Northern Kings Defeated

11 When Jabin king of Hazor heard of this, he sent word to Jobab king of Madon, to the kings of Shimron and Acshaph, 2and to the northern kings who were in the mountains, in the Arabah south of Kinnereth, in the western foothills and in Naphoth Dor*a* on the west; 3to the Canaanites in the east and west; to the Amorites, Hittites, Perizzites and Jebusites in the hill country; and to the Hivites below Hermon in the region of Mizpah. 4They came out with all their troops and a large number of horses and chariots—a huge army, as numerous as the sand on the seashore. 5All these kings joined forces and made camp together at the Waters of Merom, to fight against Israel.

6The LORD said to Joshua, "Do not be afraid of them, because by this time tomorrow I will hand all of them over to Israel, slain. You are to hamstring their horses and burn their chariots."

7So Joshua and his whole army came against them suddenly at the Waters of Merom and attacked them, 8and the LORD gave them into the hand of Israel. They defeated them and pursued them all the way to Greater Sidon, to Misrephoth Maim, and to the Valley of Mizpah on the

a2 Or in the heights of Dor

east, until no survivors were left. ⁹Joshua did to them as the LORD had directed: He hamstrung their horses and burned their chariots.

¹⁰At that time Joshua turned back and captured Hazor and put its king to the sword. (Hazor had been the head of all these kingdoms.) ¹¹Everyone in it they put to the sword. They totally destroyed*ᵇ* them, not sparing anything that breathed, and he burned up Hazor itself.

¹²Joshua took all these royal cities and their kings and put them to the sword. He totally destroyed them, as Moses the servant of the LORD had commanded. ¹³Yet Israel did not burn any of the cities built on their mounds—except Hazor, which Joshua burned. ¹⁴The Israelites carried off for themselves all the plunder and livestock of these cities, but all the people they put to the sword until they completely destroyed them, not sparing anyone that breathed. ¹⁵As the LORD commanded his servant Moses, so Moses commanded Joshua, and Joshua did it; he left nothing undone of all that the LORD commanded Moses.

¹⁶So Joshua took this entire land: the hill country, all the Negev, the whole region of Goshen, the western foothills, the Arabah and the mountains of Israel with their foothills, ¹⁷from Mount Halak, which rises towards Seir, to Baal Gad in the Valley of Lebanon below Mount Hermon. He captured all their kings and struck them down, putting them to death. ¹⁸Joshua waged war against all these kings for a long time. ¹⁹Except for the Hivites living in Gibeon, not one city made a treaty of peace with the Israelites, who took them all in battle. ²⁰For it was the LORD himself who hardened their hearts to wage war against Israel, so that he might destroy them totally, exterminating them without mercy, as the LORD had commanded Moses.

²¹At that time Joshua went and destroyed the Anakites from the hill country: from Hebron, Debir and Anab, from all the hill country of Judah,and from all the

hill country of Israel. Joshua totally destroyed them and their towns. ²²No Anakites were left in Israelite territory; only in Gaza, Gath and Ashdod did any survive. ²³So Joshua took the entire land, just as the LORD had directed Moses, and he gave it as an inheritance to Israel according to their tribal divisions.

Then the land had rest from war.

List of Defeated Kings

12 These are the kings of the land whom the Israelites had defeated and whose territory they took over east of the Jordan, from the Arnon Gorge to Mount Hermon, including all the eastern side of the Arabah:

²Sihon king of the Amorites,
who reigned in Heshbon. He ruled from Aroer on the rim of the Arnon Gorge—from the middle of the gorge—to the Jabbok River, which is the border of the Ammonites. This included half of Gilead. ³He also ruled over the eastern Arabah from the Sea of Kinnereth*ᵃ* to the Sea of the Arabah (the Salt Sea*ᵇ*), to Beth Jeshimoth, and then southward below the slopes of Pisgah.

⁴And the territory of Og king of Bashan, one of the last of the Rephaites, who reigned in Ashtaroth and Edrei. ⁵He ruled over Mount Hermon, Salecah, all of Bashan to the border of the people of Geshur and Maacah, and half of Gilead to the border of Sihon king of Heshbon.

⁶Moses, the servant of the LORD, and the Israelites conquered them. And Moses the servant of the LORD gave their land to the Reubenites, the Gadites and the half-tribe of Manasseh to be their possession.

⁷These are the kings of the land that

ᵇ11 The Hebrew term refers to the irrevocable giving over of things or persons to the LORD, often by totally destroying them; also in verses 12, 20 and 21.   *ᵃ3* That is, Galilee   *ᵇ3* That is, the Dead Sea

Joshua and the Israelites conquered on the west side of the Jordan, from Baal Gad in the Valley of Lebanon to Mount Halak, which rises towards Seir (their lands Joshua gave as an inheritance to the tribes of Israel according to their tribal divisions—⁸the hill country, the western foothills, the Arabah, the mountain slopes, the desert and the Negev—the lands of the Hittites, Amorites, Canaanites, Perizzites, Hivites and Jebusites):

⁹the king of Jericho	one
the king of Ai (near Bethel)	one
¹⁰the king of Jerusalem	one
the king of Hebron	one
¹¹the king of Jarmuth	one
the king of Lachish	one
¹²the king of Eglon	one
the king of Gezer	one
¹³the king of Debir	one
the king of Geder	one
¹⁴the king of Hormah	one
the king of Arad	one
¹⁵the king of Libnah	one
the king of Adullam	one
¹⁶the king of Makkedah	one
the king of Bethel	one
¹⁷the king of Tappuah	one
the king of Hepher	one
¹⁸the king of Aphek	one
the king of Lasharon	one
¹⁹the king of Madon	one
the king of Hazor	one
²⁰the king of Shimron Meron	one
the king of Acshaph	one
²¹the king of Taanach	one
the king of Megiddo	one
²²the king of Kedesh	one
the king of Jokneam in Carmel	one
²³the king of Dor (in Naphoth Dorᶜ)	one
the king of Goyim in Gilgal	one
²⁴the king of Tirzah	one

thirty-one kings in all.

Land Still to Be Taken

13 When Joshua was old and well advanced in years, the Lord said to him, "You are very old, and there are still very large areas of land to be taken over.

²"This is the land that remains: all the regions of the Philistines and Geshurites: ³from the Shihor River on the east of Egypt to the territory of Ekron on the north, all of it counted as Canaanite (the territory of the five Philistine rulers in Gaza, Ashdod, Ashkelon, Gath and Ekron—that of the Avvites); ⁴from the south, all the land of the Canaanites, from Arah of the Sidonians as far as Aphek, the region of the Amorites, ⁵the area of the Gebalites;ᵃ and all Lebanon to the east, from Baal Gad below Mount Hermon to Leboᵇ Hamath.

⁶"As for all the inhabitants of the mountain regions from Lebanon to Misrephoth Maim, that is, all the Sidonians, I myself will drive them out before the Israelites. Be sure to allocate this land to Israel for an inheritance, as I have instructed you, ⁷and divide it as an inheritance among the nine tribes and half of the tribe of Manasseh."

Division of the Land East of the Jordan

⁸The other half of Manasseh,ᶜ the Reubenites and the Gadites had received the inheritance that Moses had given them east of the Jordan, as he, the servant of the Lord, had assigned it to them.

⁹It extended from Aroer on the rim of the Arnon Gorge, and from the town in the middle of the gorge, and included the whole plateau of Medeba as far as Dibon, ¹⁰and all the towns of Sihon king of the Amorites, who ruled in Heshbon, out to the border of the Ammonites. ¹¹It also included Gilead, the territory of the people of Geshur and Maacah, all of Mount Hermon and all Bashan as far as Salecah

---

ᶜ23 Or *in the heights of Dor*   ᵃ5 That is, the area of Byblos   ᵇ5 Or *to the entrance to*
ᶜ8 Hebrew *With it* (that is, with the other half of Manasseh)

—[12]that is, the whole kingdom of Og in Bashan, who had reigned in Ashtaroth and Edrei and had survived as one of the last of the Rephaites. Moses had defeated them and taken over their land. [13]But the Israelites did not drive out the people of Geshur and Maacah, so they continue to live among the Israelites to this day.

[14]But to the tribe of Levi he gave no inheritance, since the offerings made by fire to the LORD, the God of Israel, are their inheritance, as he promised them.

[15]This is what Moses had given to the tribe of Reuben, clan by clan:

[16]The territory from Aroer on the rim of the Arnon Gorge, and from the town in the middle of the gorge, and the whole plateau past Medeba [17]to Heshbon and all its towns on the plateau, including Dibon, Bamoth Baal, Beth Baal Meon, [18]Jahaz, Kedemoth, Mephaath, [19]Kiriathaim, Sibmah, Zereth Shahar on the hill in the valley, [20]Beth Peor, the slopes of Pisgah, and Beth Jeshimoth [21]—all the towns on the plateau and the entire realm of Sihon king of the Amorites, who ruled at Heshbon. Moses had defeated him and the Midianite chiefs, Evi, Rekem, Zur, Hur and Reba—princes allied with Sihon—who lived in that country. [22]In addition to those slain in battle, the Israelites had put to the sword Balaam son of Beor, who practised divination. [23]The boundary of the Reubenites was the bank of the Jordan. These towns and their villages were the inheritance of the Reubenites, clan by clan.

[24]This is what Moses had given to the tribe of Gad, clan by clan:

[25]The territory of Jazer, all the towns of Gilead and half the Ammonite country as far as Aroer, near Rabbah; [26]and from Heshbon to Ramath Mizpah and Betonim, and from Mahanaim to the territory of Debir; [27]and in the valley, Beth Haram, Beth Nimrah, Succoth and Zaphon with the rest of the realm of Sihon king of Heshbon (the east side of the Jordan, the territory up to the end of the Sea of Kinnereth[d]). [28]These towns and their villages were the inheritance of the Gadites, clan by clan.

[29]This is what Moses had given to the half-tribe of Manasseh, that is, to half the family of the descendants of Manasseh, clan by clan:

[30]The territory extending from Mahanaim and including all of Bashan, the entire realm of Og king of Bashan—all the settlements of Jair in Bashan, sixty towns, [31]half of Gilead, and Ashtaroth and Edrei (the royal cities of Og in Bashan). This was for the descendants of Makir son of Manasseh—for half of the sons of Makir, clan by clan.

[32]This is the inheritance Moses had given when he was in the plains of Moab across the Jordan east of Jericho. [33]But to the tribe of Levi, Moses had given no inheritance; the LORD, the God of Israel, is their inheritance, as he promised them.

Division of the Land West of the Jordan

14 Now these are the areas the Israelites received as an inheritance in the land of Canaan, which Eleazar the priest, Joshua son of Nun and the heads of the tribal clans of Israel allotted to them. [2]Their inheritances were assigned by lot to the nine-and-a-half tribes, as the LORD had commanded through Moses. [3]Moses had granted the two-and-a-half tribes their inheritance east of the Jordan but had not granted the Levites an inheritance among the rest, [4]for the sons of Joseph had become two tribes

—Manasseh and Ephraim. The Levites received no share of the land but only towns to live in, with pasture-lands for their flocks and herds. ⁵So the Israelites divided the land, just as the LORD had commanded Moses.

Hèbron Given to Caleb

⁶Now the men of Judah approached Joshua at Gilgal, and Caleb son of Jephunneh the Kenizzite said to him, "You know what the LORD said to Moses the man of God at Kadesh Barnea about you and me. ⁷I was forty years old when Moses the servant of the LORD sent me from Kadesh Barnea to explore the land. And I brought him back a report according to my convictions, ⁸but my brothers who went up with me made the hearts of the people sink.ᵃ I, however, followed the LORD my God wholeheartedly. ⁹So on that day Moses swore to me, 'The land on which your feet have walked will be your inheritance and that of your children for ever, because you have followed the LORD my God wholeheartedly.'ᵇ

¹⁰"Now then, just as the LORD promised, he has kept me alive for forty-five years since the time he said this to Moses, while Israel moved about in the desert. So here I am today, eighty-five years old! ¹¹I am still as strong today as the day Moses sent me out; I'm just as vigorous to go out to battle now as I was then. ¹²Now give me this hill country that the LORD promised me that day. You yourself heard then that the Anakites were there and their cities were large and fortified, but, the LORD helping me, I will drive them out just as he said."

¹³Then Joshua blessed Caleb son of Jephunneh and gave him Hebron as his inheritance. ¹⁴So Hebron has belonged to Caleb son of Jephunneh the Kenizzite ever since, because he followed the LORD, the God of Israel, wholeheartedly. ¹⁵(Hebron used to be called Kiriath Arba after Arba, who was the greatest man among the Anakites.)

Then the land had rest from war.

Allotment for Judah

15 The allotment for the tribe of Judah, clan by clan, extended down to the territory of Edom, to the Desert of Zin in the extreme south.

²Their southern boundary started from the bay at the southern end of the Salt Sea,ᵃ ³crossed south of Scorpionᵇ Pass, continued on to Zin and went over to the south of Kadesh Barnea. Then it ran past Hezron up to Addar and curved around to Karka. ⁴It then passed along to Azmon and joined the Wadi of Egypt, ending at the sea. This is theirᶜ southern boundary.

⁵The eastern boundary is the Salt Sea as far as the mouth of the Jordan.

The northern boundary started from the bay of the sea at the mouth of the Jordan, ⁶went up to Beth Hoglah and continued north of Beth Arabah to the Stone of Bohan son of Reuben. ⁷The boundary then went up to Debir from the Valley of Achor and turned north to Gilgal, which faces the Pass of Adummim south of the gorge. It continued along to the waters of En Shemesh and came out at En Rogel. ⁸Then it ran up the Valley of Ben Hinnom along the southern slope of the Jebusite city (that is, Jerusalem). From there it climbed to the top of the hill west of the Hinnom Valley at the northern end of the Valley of Rephaim. ⁹From the hilltop the boundary headed towards the spring of the waters of Nephtoah, came out at the towns of Mount Ephron and went down towards Baalah (that is, Kiriath Jearim). ¹⁰Then it curved westward from Baalah to Mount Seir, ran along the northern slope of Mount Jearim (that is, Kesalon), continued down to Beth Shemesh and crossed to Timnah. ¹¹It went to the northern slope of Ekron, turned towards Shikkeron, passed along to Mount Baalah and

---

reached Jabneel. The boundary ended at the sea.

¹²The western boundary is the coastline of the Great Sea.*d*

These are the boundaries around the people of Judah by their clans.

¹³In accordance with the LORD's command to him, Joshua gave to Caleb son of Jephunneh a portion in Judah—Kiriath Arba, that is, Hebron. (Arba was the forefather of Anak.) ¹⁴From Hebron Caleb drove out the three Anakites—Sheshai, Ahiman and Talmai—descendants of Anak. ¹⁵From there he marched against the people living in Debir (formerly called Kiriath Sepher). ¹⁶And Caleb said, "I will give my daughter Acsah in marriage to the man who attacks and captures Kiriath Sepher." ¹⁷Othniel son of Kenaz, Caleb's brother, took it; so Caleb gave his daughter Acsah to him in marriage.

¹⁸One day when she came to Othniel, she urged him*e* to ask her father for a field. When she got off her donkey, Caleb asked her, "What can I do for you?"

¹⁹She replied, "Do me a special favour. Since you have given me land in the Negev, give me also springs of water." So Caleb gave her the upper and lower springs.

²⁰This is the inheritance of the tribe of Judah, clan by clan:

²¹The southernmost towns of the tribe of Judah in the Negev towards the boundary of Edom were:

Kabzeel, Eder, Jagur,· ²²Kinah, Dimonah, Adadah, ²³Kedesh, Hazor, Ithnan, ²⁴Ziph, Telem, Bealoth, ²⁵Hazor Hadattah, Kerioth Hezron (that is, Hazor), ²⁶Amam, Shema, Moladah, ²⁷Hazar Gaddah, Heshmon, Beth Pelet, ²⁸Hazar Shual, Beersheba, Biziothiah, ²⁹Baalah, Iim, Ezem, ³⁰Eltolad, Kesil, Hormah, ³¹Ziklag, Madmannah, Sansannah, ³²Lebaoth, Shilhim, Ain and

Rimmon—a total of twenty-nine towns and their villages.

³³In the western foothills:

Eshtaol, Zorah, Ashnah, ³⁴Zanoah, En Gannim, Tappuah, Enam, ³⁵Jarmuth, Adullam, Socoh, Azekah, ³⁶Shaaraim, Adithaim and Gederah (or Gederothaim)*f*—fourteen towns and their villages.

³⁷Zenan, Hadashah, Migdal Gad, ³⁸Dilean, Mizpah, Joktheel, ³⁹Lachish, Bozkath, Eglon, ⁴⁰Cabbon, Lahmas, Kitlish, ⁴¹Gederoth, Beth Dagon, Naamah and Makkedah—sixteen towns and their villages.

⁴²Libnah, Ether, Ashan, ⁴³Iphtah, Ashnah, Nezib, ⁴⁴Keilah, Aczib and Mareshah—nine towns and their villages.

⁴⁵Ekron, with its surrounding settlements and villages; ⁴⁶west of Ekron, all that were in the vicinity of Ashdod, together with their villages; ⁴⁷Ashdod, its surrounding settlements and villages; and Gaza, its settlements and villages, as far as the Wadi of Egypt and the coastline of the Great Sea.

⁴⁸In the hill country:

Shamir, Jattir, Socoh, ⁴⁹Dannah, Kiriath Sannah (that is, Debir), ⁵⁰Anab, Eshtemoh, Anim, ⁵¹Goshen, Holon and Giloh—eleven towns and their villages.

⁵²Arab, Dumah, Eshan, ⁵³Janim, Beth Tappuah, Aphekah, ⁵⁴Humtah, Kiriath Arba (that is, Hebron) and Zior—nine towns and their villages.

⁵⁵Maon, Carmel, Ziph, Juttah, ⁵⁶Jezreel, Jokdeam, Zanoah, ⁵⁷Kain, Gibeah and Timnah—ten towns and their villages.

⁵⁸Halhul, Beth Zur, Gedor, ⁵⁹Maarath, Beth Anoth and Eltekon—six towns and their villages.

⁶⁰Kiriath Baal (that is, Kiriath Jearim) and Rabbah—two towns and their villages.

---

d12 That is, the Mediterranean; also in verse 47
e18 Hebrew and some Septuagint manuscripts; other Septuagint manuscripts (see also note at Judges 1:14) *Othniel, he urged her*   *f36* Or *Gederah and Gederothaim*

⁶¹In the desert:

Beth Arabah, Middin, Secacah, ⁶²Nibshan, the City of Salt and En Gedi—six towns and their villages.

⁶³Judah could not dislodge the Jebusites, who were living in Jerusalem; to this day the Jebusites live there with the people of Judah.

Allotment for Ephraim and Manasseh

16 The allotment for Joseph began at the Jordan of Jericho,ᵃ east of the waters of Jericho, and went up from there through the desert into the hill country of Bethel. ²It went on from Bethel (that is, Luz),ᵇ crossed over to the territory of the Arkites in Ataroth, ³descended westward to the territory of the Japhletites as far as the region of Lower Beth Horon and on to Gezer, ending at the sea.

⁴So Manasseh and Ephraim, the descendants of Joseph, received their inheritance.

⁵This was the territory of Ephraim, clan by clan:

The boundary of their inheritance went from Ataroth Addar in the east to Upper Beth Horon ⁶and continued to the sea. From Micmethath on the north it curved eastward to Taanath Shiloh, passing by it to Janoah on the east. ⁷Then it went down from Janoah to Ataroth and Naarah, touched Jericho and came out at the Jordan. ⁸From Tappuah the border went west to the Kanah Ravine and ended at the sea. This was the inheritance of the tribe of the Ephraimites, clan by clan. ⁹It also included all the towns and their villages that were set aside for the Ephraimites within the inheritance of the Manassites.

¹⁰They did not dislodge the Canaanites living in Gezer; to this day the Canaanites live among the people of Ephraim but are required to do forced labour.

17 This was the allotment for the tribe of Manasseh as Joseph's firstborn, that is, for Makir, Manasseh's firstborn. Makir was the ancestor of the Gileadites, who had received Gilead and Bashan because the Makirites were great soldiers. ²So this allotment was for the rest of the people of Manasseh—the clans of Abiezer, Helek, Asriel, Shechem, Hepher and Shemida. These are the other male descendants of Manasseh son of Joseph by their clans.

³Now Zelophehad son of Hepher, the son of Gilead, the son of Makir, the son of Manasseh, had no sons but only daughters, whose names were Mahlah, Noah, Hoglah, Milcah and Tirzah. ⁴They went to Eleazar the priest, Joshua son of Nun, and the leaders and said, "The LORD commanded Moses to give us an inheritance among our brothers." So Joshua gave them an inheritance along with the brothers of their father, according to the LORD's command. ⁵Manasseh's share consisted of ten tracts of land besides Gilead and Bashan east of the Jordan, ⁶because the daughters of the tribe of Manasseh received an inheritance among the sons. The land of Gilead belonged to the rest of the descendants of Manasseh.

⁷The territory of Manasseh extended from Asher to Micmethath east of Shechem. The boundary ran southward from there to include the people living at En Tappuah. ⁸(Manasseh had the land of Tappuah, but Tappuah itself, on the boundary of Manasseh, belonged to the Ephraimites.) ⁹Then the boundary continued south to the Kanah Ravine. There were towns belonging to Ephraim lying among the towns of Manasseh, but the boundary of Manasseh was the northern side of the ravine and ended at the sea. ¹⁰On the south the land belonged to Ephraim, on the north to Manasseh. The territory of Manasseh reached the sea and bordered Asher on the north and Issachar on the east.

¹¹Within Issachar and Asher, Manasseh also had Beth Shan, Ibleam and the people of Dor, Endor, Taanach and Megiddo, together with their

---

ᵃ1 *Jordan of Jericho* was possibly an ancient name for the Jordan River.   ᵇ2 Septuagint; Hebrew *Bethel to Luz* surrounding settlements (the third in the list is Naphoth[a]).

[12] Yet the Manassites were not able to occupy these towns, for the Canaanites were determined to live in that region. [13] However, when the Israelites grew stronger, they subjected the Canaanites to forced labour but did not drive them out completely.

[14] The people of Joseph said to Joshua, "Why have you given us only one allotment and one portion for an inheritance? We are a numerous people and the LORD has blessed us abundantly."

[15] "If you are so numerous," Joshua answered, "and if the hill country of Ephraim is too small for you, go up into the forest and clear land for yourselves there in the land of the Perizzites and Rephaites."

[16] The people of Joseph replied, "The hill country is not enough for us, and all the Canaanites who live in the plain have iron chariots, both those in Beth Shan and its settlements and those in the Valley of Jezreel."

[17] But Joshua said to the house of Joseph—to Ephraim and Manasseh— "You are numerous and very powerful. You will have not only one allotment [18] but the forested hill country as well. Clear it, and its farthest limits will be yours; though the Canaanites have iron chariots and though they are strong, you can drive them out."

Division of the Rest of the Land

18 The whole assembly of the Israelites gathered at Shiloh and set up the Tent of Meeting there. The country was brought under their control, [2] but there were still seven Israelite tribes who had not yet received their inheritance.

[3] So Joshua said to the Israelites: "How long will you wait before you begin to take possession of the land that the LORD, the God of your fathers, has given you? [4] Appoint three men from each tribe. I will send them out to make a survey of the land and to write a description of it, according to the inheritance of each. Then they will return to me. [5] You are to divide the land into seven parts. Judah is to remain in its territory on the south and the house of Joseph in its territory on the north. [6] After you have written descriptions of the seven parts of the land, bring them here to me and I will cast lots for you in the presence of the LORD our God. [7] The Levites, however, do not get a portion among you, because the priestly service of the LORD is their inheritance. And Gad, Reuben and the half-tribe of Manasseh have already received their inheritance on the east side of the Jordan. Moses the servant of the LORD gave it to them."

[8] As the men started on their way to map out the land, Joshua instructed them, "Go and make a survey of the land and write a description of it. Then return to me, and I will cast lots for you here at Shiloh in the presence of the LORD." [9] So the men left and went through the land. They wrote its description on a scroll, town by town, in seven parts, and returned to Joshua in the camp at Shiloh. [10] Joshua then cast lots for them in Shiloh in the presence of the LORD, and there he distributed the land to the Israelites according to their tribal divisions.

Allotment for Benjamin

[11] The lot came up for the tribe of Benjamin, clan by clan. Their allotted territory lay between the tribes of Judah and Joseph:

[12] On the north side their boundary began at the Jordan, passed the northern slope of Jericho and headed west into the hill country, coming out at the desert of Beth Aven. [13] From there it crossed to the south slope of Luz (that is, Bethel) and went down to Ataroth Addar on the hill south of Lower Beth Horon.

[14] From the hill facing Beth Horon on the south the boundary turned

south along the western side and came out at Kiriath Baal (that is, Kiriath Jearim), a town of the people of Judah. This was the western side.

15The southern side began at the outskirts of Kiriath Jearim on the west, and the boundary came out at the spring of the waters of Nephtoah. 16The boundary went down to the foot of the hill facing the Valley of Ben Hinnom, north of the Valley of Rephaim. It continued down the Hinnom Valley along the southern slope of the Jebusite city and so to En Rogel. 17It then curved north, went to En Shemesh, continued to Geliloth, which faces the Pass of Adummim, and ran down to the Stone of Bohan son of Reuben. 18It continued to the northern slope of Beth Arabah*a* and on down into the Arabah. 19It then went to the northern slope of Beth Hoglah and came out at the northern bay of the Salt Sea,*b* at the mouth of the Jordan in the south. This was the southern boundary.

20The Jordan formed the boundary on the eastern side.

These were the boundaries that marked out the inheritance of the clans of Benjamin on all sides.

21The tribe of Benjamin, clan by clan, had the following cities:

Jericho, Beth Hoglah, Emek Keziz, 22Beth Arabah, Zemaraim, Bethel, 23Avvim, Parah, Ophrah, 24Kephar Ammoni, Ophni and Geba—twelve towns and their villages.

25Gibeon, Ramah, Beeroth, 26Mizpah, Kephirah, Mozah, 27Rekem, Irpeel, Taralah, 28Zelah, Haeleph, the Jebusite city (that is, Jerusalem), Gibeah and Kiriath—fourteen towns and their villages.

This was the inheritance of Benjamin for its clans.

Allotment for Simeon

19 The second lot came out for the tribe of Simeon, clan by clan. Their inheritance lay within the territory of Judah. 2It included:

Beersheba (or Sheba),*a* Moladah, 3Hazar Shual, Balah, Ezem, 4Eltolad, Bethul, Hormah, 5Ziklag, Beth Marcaboth, Hazar Susah, 6Beth Lebaoth and Sharuhen—thirteen towns and their villages;

7Ain, Rimmon, Ether and Ashan—four towns and their villages—8and all the villages around these towns as far as Baalath Beer (Ramah in the Negev).

This was the inheritance of the tribe of the Simeonites, clan by clan. 9The inheritance of the Simeonites was taken from the share of Judah, because Judah's portion was more than they needed. So the Simeonites received their inheritance within the territory of Judah.

Allotment for Zebulun

10The third lot came up for Zebulun, clan by clan:

The boundary of their inheritance went as far as Sarid. 11Going west it ran to Maralah, touched Dabbesheth, and extended to the ravine near Jokneam. 12It turned east from Sarid towards the sunrise to the territory of Kisloth Tabor and went on to Daberath and up to Japhia. 13Then it continued eastward to Gath Hepher and Eth Kazin; it came out at Rimmon and turned towards Neah. 14There the boundary went round on the north to Hannathon and ended at the Valley of Iphtah El. 15Included were Kattath, Nahalal, Shimron, Idalah and Bethlehem. There were twelve towns and their villages.

16These towns and their villages were the inheritance of Zebulun, clan by clan.

---

a18 Septuagint; Hebrew *slope facing the Arabah*   *b19* That is, the Dead Sea
a2 Or *Beersheba, Sheba*; 1 Chron. 4:28 does not have *Sheba.*

Allotment for Issachar

[17]The fourth lot came out for Issachar, clan by clan. [18]Their territory included:

Jezreel, Kesulloth, Shunem, [19]Hapharaim, Shion, Anaharath, [20]Rabbith, Kishion, Ebez, [21]Remeth, En Gannim, En Haddah and Beth Pazzez. [22]The boundary touched Tabor, Shahazumah and Beth Shemesh, and ended at the Jordan. There were sixteen towns and their villages.

[23]These towns and their villages were the inheritance of the tribe of Issachar, clan by clan.

Allotment for Asher

[24]The fifth lot came out for the tribe of Asher, clan by clan. [25]Their territory included:

Helkath, Hali, Beten, Acshaph, [26]Allammelech, Amad and Mishal. On the west the boundary touched Carmel and Shihor Libnath. [27]It then turned east towards Beth Dagon, touched Zebulun and the Valley of Iphtah El, and went north to Beth Emek and Neiel, passing Cabul on the left. [28]It went to Abdon,[b] Rehob, Hammon and Kanah, as far as Greater Sidon. [29]The boundary then turned back towards Ramah and went to the fortified city of Tyre, turned towards Hosah and came out at the sea in the region of Aczib, [30]Ummah, Aphek and Rehob. There were twenty-two towns and their villages.

[31]These towns and their villages were the inheritance of the tribe of Asher, clan by clan.

Allotment for Naphtali

[32]The sixth lot came out for Naphtali, clan by clan:

[33]Their boundary went from Heleph and the large tree in Zaanannim, passing Adami Nekeb and Jabneel to Lakkum and ending at the Jordan. [34]The boundary ran west through Aznoth Tabor and came out at Hukkok. It touched Zebulun on the south, Asher on the west and the Jordan[c] on the east. [35]The fortified cities were Ziddim, Zer, Hammath, Rakkath, Kinnereth, [36]Adamah, Ramah, Hazor, [37]Kedesh, Edrei, En Hazor, [38]Iron, Migdal El, Horem, Beth Anath and Beth Shemesh. There were nineteen towns and their villages.

[39]These towns and their villages were the inheritance of the tribe of Naphtali, clan by clan.

Allotment for Dan

[40]The seventh lot came out for the tribe of Dan, clan by clan. [41]The territory of their inheritance included:

Zorah, Eshtaol, Ir Shemesh, [42]Shaalabbin, Aijalon, Ithlah, [43]Elon, Timnah, Ekron, [44]Eltekeh, Gibbethon, Baalath, [45]Jehud, Bene Berak, Gath Rimmon, [46]Me Jarkon and Rakkon, with the area facing Joppa.

[47](But the Danites had difficulty taking possession of their territory, so they went up and attacked Leshem, took it, put it to the sword and occupied it. They settled in Leshem and named it Dan after their forefather.)

[48]These towns and their villages were the inheritance of the tribe of Dan, clan by clan.

Allotment for Joshua

[49]When they had finished dividing the land into its allotted portions, the Israelites gave Joshua son of Nun an inheritance among them, [50]as the LORD had commanded. They gave him the town he asked for—Timnath Serah[d] in the hill country of Ephraim. And he built up the town and settled there.

[51]These are the territories that Eleazar

---

[b]28 Some Hebrew manuscripts (see also Joshua 21:30); most Hebrew manuscripts *Ebron*   [c]34 Septuagint; Hebrew *west, and Judah, the Jordan,*   [d]50 Also known as *Timnath Heres* (see Judges 2:9)

the priest, Joshua son of Nun and the heads of the tribal clans of Israel assigned by lot at Shiloh in the presence of the LORD at the entrance to the Tent of Meeting. And so they finished dividing the land.

Cities of Refuge

20 Then the LORD said to Joshua: 2"Tell the Israelites to designate the cities of refuge, as I instructed you through Moses, 3so that anyone who kills a person accidentally and unintentionally may flee there and find protection from the avenger of blood.

4"When he flees to one of these cities, he is to stand in the entrance of the city gate and state his case before the elders of that city. Then they are to admit him into their city and give him a place to live with them. 5If the avenger of blood pursues him, they must not surrender the one accused, because he killed his neighbour unintentionally and without malice aforethought. 6He is to stay in that city until he has stood trial before the assembly and until the death of the high priest who is serving at that time. Then he may go back to his own home in the town from which he fled."

7So they set apart Kedesh in Galilee in the hill country of Naphtali, Shechem in the hill country of Ephraim, and Kiriath Arba (that is, Hebron) in the hill country of Judah. 8On the east side of the Jordan of Jericho[a] they designated Bezer in the desert on the plateau in the tribe of Reuben, Ramoth in Gilead in the tribe of Gad, and Golan in Bashan in the tribe of Manasseh. 9Any of the Israelites or any alien living among them who killed someone accidentally could flee to these designated cities and not be killed by the avenger of blood prior to standing trial before the assembly.

Towns for the Levites

21 Now the family heads of the Levites approached Eleazar the priest, Joshua son of Nun, and the heads of the other tribal families of Israel 2at Shiloh in Canaan and said to them, "The LORD commanded through Moses that you give us towns to live in, with pasture-lands for our livestock." 3So, as the LORD had commanded, the Israelites gave the Levites the following towns and pasture-lands out of their own inheritance:

4The first lot came out for the Kohathites, clan by clan. The Levites who were descendants of Aaron the priest were allotted thirteen towns from the tribes of Judah, Simeon and Benjamin. 5The rest of Kohath's descendants were allotted ten towns from the clans of the tribes of Ephraim, Dan and half of Manasseh.

6The descendants of Gershon were allotted thirteen towns from the clans of the tribes of Issachar, Asher, Naphtali and the half-tribe of Manasseh in Bashan.

7The descendants of Merari, clan by clan, received twelve towns from the tribes of Reuben, Gad and Zebulun.

8So the Israelites allotted to the Levites these towns and their pasture-lands, as the LORD had commanded through Moses.

9From the tribes of Judah and Simeon they allotted the following towns by name 10(these towns were assigned to the descendants of Aaron who were from the Kohathite clans of the Levites, because the first lot fell to them):

11They gave them Kiriath Arba (that is, Hebron), with its surrounding pasture-land, in the hill country of Judah. (Arba was the forefather of Anak.) 12But the fields and villages around the city they had given to Caleb son of Jephunneh as his possession.

13So to the descendants of Aaron the priest they gave Hebron (a city of refuge for one accused of murder), Libnah, 14Jattir, Eshtemoa, 15Holon, Debir, 16Ain, Juttah and Beth Shemesh, together with their pasture-lands—nine towns from these two tribes.

17And from the tribe of Benjamin

---

a8 *Jordan of Jericho* was possibly an ancient name for the Jordan River.

they gave them Gibeon, Geba, [18]Anathoth and Almon, together with their pasture-lands—four towns. [19]All the towns for the priests, the descendants of Aaron, were thirteen, together with their pasture-lands.

[20]The rest of the Kohathite clans of the Levites were allotted towns from the tribe of Ephraim:

[21]In the hill country of Ephraim they were given Shechem (a city of refuge for one accused of murder) and Gezer, [22]Kibzaim and Beth Horon, together with their pasture-lands—four towns.

[23]Also from the tribe of Dan they received Eltekeh, Gibbethon, [24]Aijalon and Gath Rimmon, together with their pasture-lands—four towns.

[25]From half the tribe of Manasseh they received Taanach and Gath Rimmon, together with their pasture-lands—two towns.

[26]All these ten towns and their pasture-lands were given to the rest of the Kohathite clans.

[27]The Levite clans of the Gershonites were given:

from the half-tribe of Manasseh,

Golan in Bashan (a city of refuge for one accused of murder) and Be Eshtarah, together with their pasture-lands—two towns;

[28]from the tribe of Issachar,

Kishion, Daberath, [29]Jarmuth and En Gannim, together with their pasture-lands—four towns;

[30]from the tribe of Asher,

Mishal, Abdon, [31]Helkath and Rehob, together with their pasture-lands—four towns;

[32]from the tribe of Naphtali,

Kedesh in Galilee (a city of refuge for one accused of murder), Hammoth Dor and Kartan, together with their pasture-lands—three towns.

[33]All the towns of the Gershonite clans were thirteen, together with their pasture-lands.

[34]The Merarite clans (the rest of the Levites) were given:

from the tribe of Zebulun,

Jokneam, Kartah, [35]Dimnah and Nahalal, together with their pasture-lands—four towns;

[36]from the tribe of Reuben,

Bezer, Jahaz, [37]Kedemoth and Mephaath, together with their pasture-lands—four towns;

[38]from the tribe of Gad,

Ramoth in Gilead (a city of refuge for one accused of murder), Mahanaim, [39]Heshbon and Jazer, together with their pasture-lands—four towns in all.

[40]All the towns allotted to the Merarite clans, who were the rest of the Levites, were twelve.

[41]The towns of the Levites in the territory held by the Israelites were forty-eight in all, together with their pasture-lands. [42]Each of these towns had pasture-lands surrounding it; this was true for all these towns.

[43]So the LORD gave Israel all the land he had sworn to give their forefathers, and they took possession of it and settled there. [44]The LORD gave them rest on every side, just as he had sworn to their forefathers. Not one of their enemies withstood them; the LORD handed all their enemies over to them. [45]Not one of all the LORD's good promises to the house of Israel failed; every one was fulfilled.

Eastern Tribes Return Home

22 Then Joshua summoned the Reubenites, the Gadites and the half-tribe of Manasseh [2]and said to them, "You have done all that Moses the servant of the LORD commanded, and you have obeyed me in everything I commanded. [3]For a long time now—to this very day—you have not deserted your brothers but have carried out the mission the LORD your God gave you. [4]Now that the LORD your God has given your brothers rest as he promised, return to your homes in the land that Moses the servant of the LORD gave you on the other side of the Jordan.

⁵But be very careful to keep the commandment and the law that Moses the servant of the LORD gave you: to love the LORD your God, to walk in all his ways, to obey his commands, to hold fast to him and to serve him with all your heart and all your soul."

⁶Then Joshua blessed them and sent them away, and they went to their homes. ⁷(To the half-tribe of Manasseh Moses had given land in Bashan, and to the other half of the tribe Joshua gave land on the west side of the Jordan with their brothers.) When Joshua sent them home, he blessed them, ⁸saying, "Return to your homes with your great wealth—with large herds of livestock, with silver, gold, bronze and iron, and a great quantity of clothing—and divide with your brothers the plunder from your enemies."

⁹So the Reubenites, the Gadites and the half-tribe of Manasseh left the Israelites at Shiloh in Canaan to return to Gilead, their own land, which they had acquired in accordance with the command of the LORD through Moses.

¹⁰When they came to Geliloth near the Jordan in the land of Canaan, the Reubenites, the Gadites and the half-tribe of Manasseh built an imposing altar there by the Jordan. ¹¹And when the Israelites heard that they had built the altar on the border of Canaan at Geliloth near the Jordan on the Israelite side, ¹²the whole assembly of Israel gathered at Shiloh to go to war against them.

¹³So the Israelites sent Phinehas son of Eleazar, the priest, to the land of Gilead—to Reuben, Gad and the half-tribe of Manasseh. ¹⁴With him they sent ten of the chief men, one for each of the tribes of Israel, each the head of a family division among the Israelite clans.

¹⁵When they went to Gilead—to Reuben, Gad and the half-tribe of Manasseh—they said to them: ¹⁶"The whole assembly of the LORD says: 'How could you break faith with the God of Israel like this? How could you turn away from the LORD and build yourselves an altar in rebellion against him now? ¹⁷Was not the sin of Peor enough for us? Up to this very day we have not cleansed ourselves from that sin, even though a plague fell on the community of the LORD! ¹⁸And are you now turning away from the LORD?

"'If you rebel against the LORD today, tomorrow he will be angry with the whole community of Israel. ¹⁹If the land you possess is defiled, come over to the LORD's land, where the LORD's tabernacle stands, and share the land with us. But do not rebel against the LORD or against us by building an altar for yourselves, other than the altar of the LORD our God. ²⁰When Achan son of Zerah acted unfaithfully regarding the devoted things,ᵃ did not wrath come upon the whole community of Israel? He was not the only one who died for his sin.'"

²¹Then Reuben, Gad and the half-tribe of Manasseh replied to the heads of the clans of Israel: ²²"The Mighty One, God, the LORD! The Mighty One, God, the LORD! He knows! And let Israel know! If this has been in rebellion or disobedience to the LORD, do not spare us this day. ²³If we have built our own altar to turn away from the LORD and to offer burnt offerings and grain offerings, or to sacrifice fellowship offeringsᵇ on it, may the LORD himself call us to account.

²⁴"No! We did it for fear that some day your descendants might say to ours, 'What do you have to do with the LORD, the God of Israel? ²⁵The LORD has made the Jordan a boundary between us and you—you Reubenites and Gadites! You have no share in the LORD.' So your descendants might cause ours to stop fearing the LORD.

²⁶"That is why we said, 'Let us get ready and build an altar—but not for burnt offerings or sacrifices.' ²⁷On the contrary, it is to be a witness between us and you and the generations that follow, that we will worship the LORD at his sanctuary with our burnt offerings, sacrifices and fellowship offerings. Then in the future your descendants will not be able to say to ours, 'You have no share in the LORD.'

ᵃ20 The Hebrew term refers to the irrevocable giving over of things or persons to the LORD, often by totally destroying them.   ᵇ23 Traditionally *peace offerings*; also in verse 27

28"And we said, 'If they ever say this to us, or to our descendants, we will answer: Look at the replica of the LORD's altar, which our fathers built, not for burnt offerings and sacrifices, but as a witness between us and you.'

29"Far be it from us to rebel against the LORD and turn away from him today by building an altar for burnt offerings, grain offerings and sacrifices, other than the altar of the LORD our God that stands before his tabernacle."

30When Phinehas the priest and the leaders of the community—the heads of the clans of the Israelites—heard what Reuben, Gad and Manasseh had to say, they were pleased. 31And Phinehas son of Eleazar, the priest, said to Reuben, Gad and Manasseh, "Today we know that the LORD is with us, because you have not acted unfaithfully towards the LORD in this matter. Now you have rescued the Israelites from the LORD's hand."

32Then Phinehas son of Eleazar, the priest, and the leaders returned to Canaan from their meeting with the Reubenites and Gadites in Gilead and reported to the Israelites. 33They were glad to hear the report and praised God. And they talked no more about going to war against them to devastate the country where the Reubenites and the Gadites lived.

34And the Reubenites and the Gadites gave the altar this name: A Witness Between Us that the LORD is God.

Joshua's Farewell to the Leaders

23 After a long time had passed and the LORD had given Israel rest from all their enemies around them, Joshua, by then old and well advanced in years, 2summoned all Israel—their elders, leaders, judges and officials—and said to them: "I am old and well advanced in years. 3You yourselves have seen everything the LORD your God has done to all these nations for your sake; it was the LORD your God who fought for you. 4Remember how I have allotted as an inheritance for your tribes all the land of the nations that remain—the nations I conquered—between the Jordan and the Great Sea*a* in the west. 5The LORD your God himself will drive them out of your way. He will push them out before you, and you will take possession of their land, as the LORD your God promised you.

6"Be very strong; be careful to obey all that is written in the Book of the Law of Moses, without turning aside to the right or to the left. 7Do not associate with these nations that remain among you; do not invoke the names of their gods or swear by them. You must not serve them or bow down to them. 8But you are to hold fast to the LORD your God, as you have until now.

9"The LORD has driven out before you great and powerful nations; to this day no-one has been able to withstand you. 10One of you routs a thousand, because the LORD your God fights for you, just as he promised. 11So be very careful to love the LORD your God.

12"But if you turn away and ally yourselves with the survivors of these nations that remain among you and if you intermarry with them and associate with them, 13then you may be sure that the LORD your God will no longer drive out these nations before you. Instead, they will become snares and traps for you, whips on your backs and thorns in your eyes, until you perish from this good land, which the LORD your God has given you.

14"Now I am about to go the way of all the earth. You know with all your heart and soul that not one of all the good promises the LORD your God gave you has failed. Every promise has been fulfilled; not one has failed. 15But just as every good promise of the LORD your God has come true, so the LORD will bring on you all the evil he has threatened, until he has destroyed you from this good land he has given you. 16If you violate the covenant of the LORD your God, which he commanded you, and go and serve other gods and bow down to them, the LORD's anger will burn against you, and you will quickly perish from the good land he has given you."

*a*4 That is, the Mediterranean

The Covenant Renewed at Shechem

24 Then Joshua assembled all the tribes of Israel at Shechem. He summoned the elders, leaders, judges and officials of Israel, and they presented themselves before God.

²Joshua said to all the people, "This is what the LORD, the God of Israel, says: 'Long ago your forefathers, including Terah the father of Abraham and Nahor, lived beyond the River[a] and worshipped other gods. ³But I took your father Abraham from the land beyond the River and led him throughout Canaan and gave him many descendants. I gave him Isaac, ⁴and to Isaac I gave Jacob and Esau. I assigned the hill country of Seir to Esau, but Jacob and his sons went down to Egypt.

⁵"'Then I sent Moses and Aaron, and I afflicted the Egyptians by what I did there, and I brought you out. ⁶When I brought your fathers out of Egypt, you came to the sea, and the Egyptians pursued them with chariots and horsemen[b] as far as the Red Sea.[c] ⁷But they cried to the LORD for help, and he put darkness between you and the Egyptians; he brought the sea over them and covered them. You saw with your own eyes what I did to the Egyptians. Then you lived in the desert for a long time.

⁸"'I brought you to the land of the Amorites who lived east of the Jordan. They fought against you, but I gave them into your hands. I destroyed them from before you, and you took possession of their land. ⁹When Balak son of Zippor, the king of Moab, prepared to fight against Israel, he sent for Balaam son of Beor to put a curse on you. ¹⁰But I would not listen to Balaam, so he blessed you again and again, and I delivered you out of his hand.

¹¹"'Then you crossed the Jordan and came to Jericho. The citizens of Jericho fought against you, as did also the Amorites, Perizzites, Canaanites, Hittites, Girgashites, Hivites and Jebusites, but I gave them into your hands. ¹²I sent the hornet ahead of you, which drove them out

before you—also the two Amorite kings. You did not do it with your own sword and bow. ¹³So I gave you a land on which you did not toil and cities you did not build; and you live in them and eat from vineyards and olive groves that you did not plant.'

¹⁴"Now fear the LORD and serve him with all faithfulness. Throw away the gods your forefathers worshipped beyond the River and in Egypt, and serve the LORD. ¹⁵But if serving the LORD seems undesirable to you, then choose for yourselves this day whom you will serve, whether the gods your forefathers served beyond the River, or the gods of the Amorites, in whose land you are living. But as for me and my household, we will serve the LORD."

¹⁶Then the people answered, "Far be it from us to forsake the LORD to serve other gods! ¹⁷It was the LORD our God himself who brought us and our fathers up out of Egypt, from that land of slavery, and performed those great signs before our eyes. He protected us on our entire journey and among all the nations through which we travelled. ¹⁸And the LORD drove out before us all the nations, including the Amorites, who lived in the land. We too will serve the LORD, because he is our God."

¹⁹Joshua said to the people, "You are not able to serve the LORD. He is a holy God; he is a jealous God. He will not forgive your rebellion and your sins. ²⁰If you forsake the LORD and serve foreign gods, he will turn and bring disaster on you and make an end of you, after he has been good to you."

²¹But the people said to Joshua, "No! We will serve the LORD."

²²Then Joshua said, "You are witnesses against yourselves that you have chosen to serve the LORD."

"Yes, we are witnesses," they replied.

²³"Now then," said Joshua, "throw away the foreign gods that are among you and yield your hearts to the LORD, the God of Israel."

---

[a]2 That is, the Euphrates; also in verses 3, 14 and 15
[c]6 Hebrew *Yam Suph*; that is, Sea of Reeds
[b]6 Or *charioteers*

24And the people said to Joshua, "We will serve the LORD our God and obey him."

25On that day Joshua made a covenant for the people, and there at Shechem he drew up for them decrees and laws. 26And Joshua recorded these things in the Book of the Law of God. Then he took a large stone and set it up there under the oak near the holy place of the LORD.

27"See!" he said to all the people. "This stone will be a witness against us. It has heard all the words the LORD has said to us. It will be a witness against you if you are untrue to your God."

Buried in the Promised Land

28Then Joshua sent the people away, each to his own inheritance.

29After these things, Joshua son of Nun, the servant of the LORD, died at the age of a hundred and ten. 30And they buried him in the land of his inheritance, at Timnath Serah*d* in the hill country of Ephraim, north of Mount Gaash.

31Israel served the LORD throughout the lifetime of Joshua and of the elders who outlived him and who had experienced everything the LORD had done for Israel.

32And Joseph's bones, which the Israelites had brought up from Egypt, were buried at Shechem in the tract of land that Jacob bought for a hundred pieces of silver*e* from the sons of Hamor, the father of Shechem. This became the inheritance of Joseph's descendants.

33And Eleazar son of Aaron died and was buried at Gibeah, which had been allotted to his son Phinehas in the hill country of Ephraim.

d30 Also known as *Timnath Heres* (see Judges 2:9)
e32 Hebrew *hundred kesitahs*; a kesitah was a unit of money of unknown weight and value.

Judges

Israel Fights the Remaining Canaanites

1 After the death of Joshua, the Israelites asked the LORD, "Who will be the first to go up and fight for us against the Canaanites?"

²The LORD answered, "Judah is to go; I have given the land into their hands."

³Then the men of Judah said to the Simeonites their brothers, "Come up with us into the territory allotted to us, to fight against the Canaanites. We in turn will go with you into yours." So the Simeonites went with them.

⁴When Judah attacked, the LORD gave the Canaanites and Perizzites into their hands and they struck down ten thousand men at Bezek. ⁵It was there that they found Adoni-Bezek and fought against him, putting to rout the Canaanites and Perizzites. ⁶Adoni-Bezek fled, but they chased him and caught him, and cut off his thumbs and big toes.

⁷Then Adoni-Bezek said, "Seventy kings with their thumbs and big toes cut off have picked up scraps under my table. Now God has paid me back for what I did to them." They brought him to Jerusalem, and he died there.

⁸The men of Judah attacked Jerusalem also and took it. They put the city to the sword and set it on fire.

⁹After that, the men of Judah went down to fight against the Canaanites living in the hill country, the Negev and the western foothills. ¹⁰They advanced against the Canaanites living in Hebron (formerly called Kiriath Arba) and defeated Sheshai, Ahiman and Talmai.

¹¹From there they advanced against the people living in Debir (formerly called Kiriath Sepher). ¹²And Caleb said, "I will give my daughter Acsah in marriage to the man who attacks and captures Kiriath Sepher." ¹³Othniel son of Kenaz, Caleb's younger brother, took it; so Caleb gave his daughter Acsah to him in marriage.

¹⁴One day when she came to Othniel, she urged him*ᵃ* to ask her father for a field. When she got off her donkey, Caleb asked her, "What can I do for you?"

¹⁵She replied, "Do me a special favour. Since you have given me land in the Negev, give me also springs of water." Then Caleb gave her the upper and lower springs.

¹⁶The descendants of Moses' father-in-law, the Kenite, went up from the City of Palms*ᵇ* with the men of Judah to live among the people of the Desert of Judah in the Negev near Arad.

¹⁷Then the men of Judah went with the Simeonites their brothers and attacked the Canaanites living in Zephath, and they totally destroyed*ᶜ* the city. Therefore it was called Hormah.*ᵈ* ¹⁸The men of Judah also took*ᵉ* Gaza, Ashkelon and Ekron—each city with its territory.

¹⁹The LORD was with the men of Judah. They took possession of the hill country, but they were unable to drive the people from the plains, because they had iron

---

ᵃ14 Hebrew; Septuagint and Vulgate *Othniel, he urged her*   *ᵇ16* That is, Jericho
ᶜ17 The Hebrew term refers to the irrevocable giving over of things or persons to the LORD, often by totally destroying them.   *ᵈ17 Hormah* means *destruction.*   *ᵉ18* Hebrew; Septuagint *Judah did not take*

chariots. 20As Moses had promised, Hebron was given to Caleb, who drove from it the three sons of Anak. 21The Benjamites, however, failed to dislodge the Jebusites, who were living in Jerusalem; to this day the Jebusites live there with the Benjamites.

22Now the house of Joseph attacked Bethel, and the LORD was with them. 23When they sent men to spy out Bethel (formerly called Luz), 24the spies saw a man coming out of the city and they said to him, "Show us how to get into the city and we will see that you are treated well." 25So he showed them, and they put the city to the sword but spared the man and his whole family. 26He then went to the land of the Hittites, where he built a city and called it Luz, which is its name to this day.

27But Manasseh did not drive out the people of Beth Shan or Taanach or Dor or Ibleam or Megiddo and their surrounding settlements, for the Canaanites were determined to live in that land. 28When Israel became strong, they pressed the Canaanites into forced labour but never drove them out completely. 29Nor did Ephraim drive out the Canaanites living in Gezer, but the Canaanites continued to live there among them. 30Neither did Zebulun drive out the Canaanites living in Kitron or Nahalol, who remained among them; but they did subject them to forced labour. 31Nor did Asher drive out those living in Acco or Sidon or Ahlab or Aczib or Helbah or Aphek or Rehob, 32and because of this the people of Asher lived among the Canaanite inhabitants of the land. 33Neither did Naphtali drive out those living in Beth Shemesh or Beth Anath; but the Naphtalites too lived among the Canaanite inhabitants of the land, and those living in Beth Shemesh and Beth Anath became forced labourers for them. 34The Amorites confined the Danites to the hill country, not allowing them to come down into the plain. 35And the Amorites were determined also to hold out in Mount Heres, Aijalon and Shaalbim, but when the power of the house of Joseph increased, they too were pressed into forced labour. 36The boundary of the Amorites was from Scorpion*f* Pass to Sela and beyond.

The Angel of the LORD at Bokim

2 The angel of the LORD went up from Gilgal to Bokim and said, "I brought you up out of Egypt and led you into the land that I swore to give to your forefathers. I said, 'I will never break my covenant with you, 2and you shall not make a covenant with the people of this land, but you shall break down their altars.' Yet you have disobeyed me. Why have you done this? 3Now therefore I tell you that I will not drive them out before you; they will be ⌊thorns⌋ in your sides and their gods will be a snare to you."

4When the angel of the LORD had spoken these things to all the Israelites, the people wept aloud, 5and they called that place Bokim.*a* There they offered sacrifices to the LORD.

Disobedience and Defeat

6After Joshua had dismissed the Israelites, they went to take possession of the land, each to his own inheritance. 7The people served the LORD throughout the lifetime of Joshua and of the elders who outlived him and who had seen all the great things the LORD had done for Israel.

8Joshua son of Nun, the servant of the LORD, died at the age of a hundred and ten. 9And they buried him in the land of his inheritance, at Timnath Heres*b* in the hill country of Ephraim, north of Mount Gaash.

10After that whole generation had been gathered to their fathers, another generation grew up, who knew neither the LORD nor what he had done for Israel. 11Then the Israelites did evil in the eyes of the LORD and served the Baals. 12They forsook the LORD, the God of their fathers, who had brought them out of Egypt. They followed and worshipped various gods of the peoples around them. They provoked the LORD to anger 13because they forsook

---

f36 Hebrew *Akrabbim*   *a5 Bokim* means *weepers.*
b9 Also known as *Timnath Serah* (see Joshua 19:50 and 24:30)

him and served Baal and the Ashtoreths. [14]In his anger against Israel the LORD handed them over to raiders who plundered them. He sold them to their enemies all around, whom they were no longer able to resist. [15]Whenever Israel went out to fight, the hand of the LORD was against them to defeat them, just as he had sworn to them. They were in great distress.

[16]Then the LORD raised up judges,[c] who saved them out of the hands of these raiders. [17]Yet they would not listen to their judges but prostituted themselves to other gods and worshiped them. Unlike their fathers, they quickly turned from the way in which their fathers had walked, the way of obedience to the LORD's commands. [18]Whenever the LORD raised up a judge for them, he was with the judge and saved them out of the hands of their enemies as long as the judge lived; for the LORD had compassion on them as they groaned under those who oppressed and afflicted them. [19]But when the judge died, the people returned to ways even more corrupt than those of their fathers, following other gods and serving and worshiping them. They refused to give up their evil practices and stubborn ways.

[20]Therefore the LORD was very angry with Israel and said, "Because this nation has violated the covenant that I laid down for their forefathers and has not listened to me, [21]I will no longer drive out before them any of the nations Joshua left when he died. [22]I will use them to test Israel and see whether they will keep the way of the LORD and walk in it as their forefathers did." [23]The LORD had allowed those nations to remain; he did not drive them out at once by giving them into the hands of Joshua.

3 These are the nations the LORD left to test all those Israelites who had not experienced any of the wars in Canaan [2](he did this only to teach warfare to the descendants of the Israelites who had not had previous battle experience): [3]the five rulers of the Philistines, all the Canaanites, the Sidonians, and the Hivites living in the Lebanon mountains from Mount Baal Hermon to Lebo[a] Hamath. [4]They were left to test the Israelites to see whether they would obey the LORD's commands, which he had given their forefathers through Moses.

[5]The Israelites lived among the Canaanites, Hittites, Amorites, Perizzites, Hivites and Jebusites. [6]They took their daughters in marriage and gave their own daughters to their sons, and served their gods.

Othniel

[7]The Israelites did evil in the eyes of the LORD; they forgot the LORD their God and served the Baals and the Asherahs. [8]The anger of the LORD burned against Israel so that he sold them into the hands of Cushan-Rishathaim king of Aram Naharaim,[b] to whom the Israelites were subject for eight years. [9]But when they cried out to the LORD, he raised up for them a deliverer, Othniel son of Kenaz, Caleb's younger brother, who saved them. [10]The Spirit of the LORD came upon him, so that he became Israel's judge[c] and went to war. The LORD gave Cushan-Rishathaim king of Aram into the hands of Othniel, who overpowered him. [11]So the land had peace for forty years, until Othniel son of Kenaz died.

Ehud

[12]Once again the Israelites did evil in the eyes of the LORD, and because they did this evil the LORD gave Eglon king of Moab power over Israel. [13]Getting the Ammonites and Amalekites to join him, Eglon came and attacked Israel, and they took possession of the City of Palms.[d] [14]The Israelites were subject to Eglon king of Moab for eighteen years.

[15]Again the Israelites cried out to the LORD, and he gave them a deliverer—Ehud, a left-handed man, the son of Gera the Benjamite. The Israelites sent him

---

[c]16 Or leaders; similarly in verses 17–19   [a]3 Or to the entrance to   [b]8 That is, North-west Mesopotamia
[c]10 Or leader   [d]13 That is, Jericho

with tribute to Eglon king of Moab. ¹⁶Now Ehud had made a double-edged sword about a foot and a half*e* long, which he strapped to his right thigh under his clothing. ¹⁷He presented the tribute to Eglon king of Moab, who was a very fat man. ¹⁸After Ehud had presented the tribute, he sent on their way the men who had carried it. ¹⁹At the idols*f* near Gilgal he himself turned back and said, "I have a secret message for you, O king."

The king said, "Quiet!" And all his attendants left him.

²⁰Ehud then approached him while he was sitting alone in the upper room of his summer palace*g* and said, "I have a message from God for you." As the king rose from his seat, ²¹Ehud reached with his left hand, drew the sword from his right thigh and plunged it into the king's belly. ²²Even the handle sank in after the blade, which came out of his back. Ehud did not pull the sword out, and the fat closed in over it. ²³Then Ehud went out to the porch;*h* he shut the doors of the upper room behind him and locked them.

²⁴After he had gone, the servants came and found the doors of the upper room locked. They said, "He must be relieving himself in the inner room of the house." ²⁵They waited to the point of embarrassment, but when he did not open the doors of the room, they took a key and unlocked them. There they saw their lord fallen to the floor, dead.

²⁶While they waited, Ehud got away. He passed by the idols and escaped to Seirah. ²⁷When he arrived there, he blew a trumpet in the hill country of Ephraim, and the Israelites went down with him from the hills, with him leading them.

²⁸"Follow me," he ordered, "for the LORD has given Moab, your enemy, into your hands." So they followed him down and, taking possession of the fords of the Jordan that led to Moab, they allowed no-one to cross over. ²⁹At that time they struck down about ten thousand Moabites, all vigorous and strong; not a man

escaped. ³⁰That day Moab was made subject to Israel, and the land had peace for eighty years.

Shamgar

³¹After Ehud came Shamgar son of Anath, who struck down six hundred Philistines with an ox-goad. He too saved Israel.

Deborah

4   After Ehud died, the Israelites once again did evil in the eyes of the LORD. ²So the LORD sold them into the hands of Jabin, a king of Canaan, who reigned in Hazor. The commander of his army was Sisera, who lived in Harosheth Haggoyim. ³Because he had nine hundred iron chariots and had cruelly oppressed the Israelites for twenty years, they cried to the LORD for help.

⁴Deborah, a prophetess, the wife of Lappidoth, was leading*a* Israel at that time. ⁵She held court under the Palm of Deborah between Ramah and Bethel in the hill country of Ephraim, and the Israelites came to her to have their disputes decided. ⁶She sent for Barak son of Abinoam from Kedesh in Naphtali and said to him, "The LORD, the God of Israel, commands you: 'Go, take with you ten thousand men of Naphtali and Zebulun and lead the way to Mount Tabor. ⁷I will lure Sisera, the commander of Jabin's army, with his chariots and his troops to the Kishon River and give him into your hands.'"

⁸Barak said to her, "If you go with me, I will go; but if you don't go with me, I won't go."

⁹"Very well," Deborah said, "I will go with you. But because of the way you are going about this,*b* the honour will not be yours, for the LORD will hand Sisera over to a woman." So Deborah went with Barak to Kedesh, ¹⁰where he summoned Zebulun and Naphtali. Ten thousand men

---

e16 Hebrew *a cubit* (about 0.5 metre)   *f19* Or *the stone quarries*; also in verse 26
g20 The meaning of the Hebrew for this phrase is uncertain.
h23 The meaning of the Hebrew for this word is uncertain.   *a4* Traditionally *judging*
b9 Or *But on the expedition you are undertaking*

followed him, and Deborah also went with him.

11Now Heber the Kenite had left the other Kenites, the descendants of Hobab, Moses' brother-in-law,*c* and pitched his tent by the great tree in Zaanannim near Kedesh.

12When they told Sisera that Barak son of Abinoam had gone up to Mount Tabor, 13Sisera gathered together his nine hundred iron chariots and all the men with him, from Harosheth Haggoyim to the Kishon River.

14Then Deborah said to Barak, "Go! This is the day the LORD has given Sisera into your hands. Has not the LORD gone ahead of you?" So Barak went down Mount Tabor, followed by ten thousand men. 15At Barak's advance, the LORD routed Sisera and all his chariots and army by the sword, and Sisera abandoned his chariot and fled on foot. 16But Barak pursued the chariots and army as far as Harosheth Haggoyim. All the troops of Sisera fell by the sword; not a man was left.

17Sisera, however, fled on foot to the tent of Jael, the wife of Heber the Kenite, because there were friendly relations between Jabin king of Hazor and the clan of Heber the Kenite.

18Jael went out to meet Sisera and said to him, "Come, my lord, come right in. Don't be afraid." So he entered her tent, and she put a covering over him.

19"I'm thirsty," he said. "Please give me some water." She opened a skin of milk, gave him a drink, and covered him up.

20"Stand in the doorway of the tent," he told her. "If someone comes by and asks you, 'Is anyone here?' say 'No.'"

21But Jael, Heber's wife, picked up a tent peg and a hammer and went quietly to him while he lay fast asleep, exhausted. She drove the peg through his temple into the ground, and he died.

22Barak came by in pursuit of Sisera, and Jael went out to meet him. "Come," she said, "I will show you the man you're looking for." So he went in with her, and there lay Sisera with the tent peg through his temple—dead.

23On that day God subdued Jabin, the Canaanite king, before the Israelites. 24And the hand of the Israelites grew stronger and stronger against Jabin, the Canaanite king, until they destroyed him.

The Song of Deborah

5 On that day Deborah and Barak son of Abinoam sang this song:

2"When the princes in Israel take the
        lead,
    when the people willingly offer
        themselves—
    praise the LORD!

3"Hear this, you kings! Listen, you
        rulers!
    I will sing to*a* the LORD, I will sing;
    I will make music to*b* the LORD, the
        God of Israel.

4"O LORD, when you went out from Seir,
    when you marched from the land of
        Edom,
    the earth shook, the heavens poured,
        the clouds poured down water.
5The mountains quaked before the
        LORD, the One of Sinai,
    before the LORD, the God of Israel.

6"In the days of Shamgar son of Anath,
    in the days of Jael, the roads were
        abandoned;
    travellers took to winding paths.
7Village life*c* in Israel ceased,
    ceased until I,*d* Deborah, arose,
    arose a mother in Israel.
8When they chose new gods,
    war came to the city gates,
    and not a shield or spear was seen
        among forty thousand in Israel.
9My heart is with Israel's princes,
    with the willing volunteers among the
        people.
    Praise the LORD!

10"You who ride on white donkeys,

---

c11 Or *father-in-law*   *a3* Or *of*   *b3* Or *I with song I will praise*   *c7* Or *Warriors*   *d7* Or *you*

DoiNg God's Will

[Joshua 1 (p. 216)]

Bible background

The book of Joshua tells the story of the Israelite invasion of Canaan under the leadership of Joshua, following the death of Moses. The nation had spent many years wandering in the desert and none of the generation who had left slavery in Egypt were to enter the promised land. Look back to Numbers 13 (p. 149) and to the story of the spies sent to Canaan, the decision not to enter the country and its consequences. The people had lost their nerve and they, including Moses himself, did not get a second chance to enter Canaan until forty years later when God tells Joshua to cross the Jordan River. Joshua was reminded that God was with him and of the need to keep God's word in its central place and to be 'strong and courageous'.

Trust in God

These are powerful verses of encouragement for those who are serious about serving God in the world. Perhaps these verses are for you right now! What new thing might God be calling you to? What factors might influence your response? What fears and unknowns will you need to face? Where do you need encouragement? Look at verses 2 and 6, which are commands from God (commands are not invitations!). How might these apply to you today? In verses 7 and 8 God sets out some conditions for his provision and care.

A presumption that God will take care of everybody and everything regardless, is not the right attitude. Joshua had to wait for the right moment to act, so do we and there will be conditions which we will need to heed and obey. The Christian experience is rooted in God's unconditional love but do not forget the conditions which need to be met in order to nurture and maintain a lively and on going relationship with God in Jesus. It is easy to leave God out. Allowing God, through Scripture, to affect and shape your life is more difficult.

The risk factor

God expects you to do your 'homework' if you sense that he is calling you into new experiences of him or into fresh fields of service. Obedience and faith (spelt R-I-S-K) are vital, for there is no 'magic wand' to sort things out if things go wrong. If you act solely on your own, following your emotions there will be consequences. Yes, God will still be there and you will learn from the experience, but you may make it harder than necessary for yourself.

9.00AM	10.00AM	11.00AM	12.00NOON

meeting...   job interview...   do NOT forget post...   call the MD by noon...   on call...

Penny Paul when he was going round the churches worked, so it is important to work to keep ourselves.

Jonathan I was talking with someone the other day and I tried to explain that with God it gives you a different perspective on life and your priorities. We had a particularly difficult maths assignment due in the following day and none of us could do it. This guy was getting really stressed about it and asked me what I was doing afterwards. That was the time I'd set aside to spend with God. I told him that and he said 'aren't you going to get really stressed about the work and everything?' See Matthew 6:33-34.

Pat It's difficult to say that God ordained paid work (Genesis 3:17-19), because where does that place the individuals who haven't got a job, those who are Christians who are cracking up?

Ann Society says, 'You've got to perform to this standard or else you're useless.' But God is saying to Jonathan, that he is worth his son dying for him (John 3:16) whether the assignment is done in time or not.

2.00PM	3.00PM	4.00PM	5.00PM

appointment with Mr & Mrs Willson... signing on time... job training... overtime...

Pat We need to highlight that it is important for us as Christians not to worry. Equally, we need to accept that at the end of the day Christians are going to be stressed about things because it is the nature of the society we are in. But it doesn't mean they have failed.

Emma Ecclesiastes is good isn't it, 1:3-11 and verse 3, 'What does man gain from all his labour?' Then it goes on about how God's in charge and we have eternity to aim for and that everything God does will endure for ever. Jonathan is right, why worry? (Luke 12:22-34)

Jonathan How much do you give to it? If you are doing it for God (Colossians 3:23-24), then it makes it really important, but it's God, not work, that's really important (Matthew 6:19-24).

Ann It's what's driving you that's important. God should be the centre of your life, not your work. As a single person working in a very high powered environment, I find that I easily fall into the trap of focusing solely on my job.

⑦

DOING GOD'S WILL

[part 2]

Life's rich tapestry

No matter how long or short your Christian journey has been or even if you've hardly begun, you are weaving a tapestry in your life. Looking at the underside of a tapestry reveals many loose ends and a very blurred image of what the real picture is. That's how life might seem to you but remember that God is looking at the design from the other side and can clearly see the full picture and how the different strands weave together in the uniqueness of your life. Reflect on your tapestry for a moment:

> ## What are the strands being woven together at this stage in your life? Name them!

people   events   HappeNiNgs

PLaceS   eXPerieNceS

ideaS   thoughts

dreaMS

poSSibiLitieS

On a separate piece of paper, or in a diary, use this information to draw a simple pattern of threads, in the spaces weave in some of the names from your lists. Use this as a resource for praise, thanksgiving and prayer.

sitting on your saddle blankets,
and you who walk along the road,
consider ¹¹the voice of the singers*e* at
the watering places.
They recite the righteous acts of the
LORD,
the righteous acts of his warriors*f* in
Israel.

"Then the people of the LORD
went down to the city gates.
¹²'Wake up, wake up, Deborah!
Wake up, wake up, break out in
song!
Arise, O Barak!
Take captive your captives, O son of
Abinoam.'

¹³"Then the men who were left
came down to the nobles;
the people of the LORD
came to me with the mighty.
¹⁴Some came from Ephraim, whose roots
were in Amalek;
Benjamin was with the people who
followed you.
From Makir captains came down,
from Zebulun those who bear a
commander's staff.
¹⁵The princes of Issachar were with
Deborah;
yes, Issachar was with Barak,
rushing after him into the valley.
In the districts of Reuben
there was much searching of heart.
¹⁶Why did you stay among the campfires*g*
to hear the whistling for the flocks?
In the districts of Reuben
there was much searching of heart.
¹⁷Gilead stayed beyond the Jordan.
And Dan, why did he linger by the
ships?
Asher remained on the coast
and stayed in his coves.
¹⁸The people of Zebulun risked their very
lives;
so did Naphtali on the heights of the
field.

¹⁹"Kings came, they fought;
the kings of Canaan fought

at Taanach by the waters of Megiddo,
but they carried off no silver, no
plunder.
²⁰From the heavens the stars fought,
from their courses they fought against
Sisera.
²¹The river Kishon swept them away,
the age-old river, the river Kishon.
March on, my soul; be strong!
²²Then thundered the horses' hoofs—
galloping, galloping go his mighty
steeds.
²³'Curse Meroz,' said the angel of the
LORD.
'Curse its people bitterly,
because they did not come to help the
LORD,
to help the LORD against the mighty.'

²⁴"Most blessed of women be Jael,
the wife of Heber the Kenite,
most blessed of tent-dwelling
women.
²⁵He asked for water, and she gave him
milk;
in a bowl fit for nobles she brought
him curdled milk.
²⁶Her hand reached for the tent peg,
her right hand for the workman's
hammer.
She struck Sisera, she crushed his head,
she shattered and pierced his
temple.
²⁷At her feet he sank,
he fell; there he lay.
At her feet he sank, he fell;
where he sank, there he fell—dead.

²⁸"Through the window peered Sisera's
mother;
behind the lattice she cried out,
'Why is his chariot so long in coming?
Why is the clatter of his chariots
delayed?'
²⁹The wisest of her ladies answer her;
indeed, she keeps saying to herself,
³⁰'Are they not finding and dividing the
spoils:
a girl or two for each man,
colourful garments as plunder for
Sisera,

---

e11 Or *archers*; the meaning of the Hebrew for this word is uncertain.   *f11* Or *villagers*   *g16* Or *saddlebags*

colourful garments embroidered,
highly embroidered garments for my
   neck—
all this as plunder?'

31"So may all your enemies perish, O
   LORD!
But may they who love you be like
   the sun
when it rises in its strength."

Then the land had peace for forty years.

Gideon

6 Again the Israelites did evil in the
   eyes of the LORD, and for seven years
he gave them into the hands of the
Midianites. 2Because the power of Midian
was so oppressive, the Israelites prepared
shelters for themselves in mountain clefts,
caves and strongholds. 3Whenever the
Israelites planted their crops, the
Midianites, Amalekites and other eastern
peoples invaded the country. 4They
camped on the land and ruined the crops
all the way to Gaza and did not spare a
living thing for Israel, neither sheep nor
cattle nor donkeys. 5They came up with
their livestock and their tents like swarms
of locusts. It was impossible to count the
men and their camels; they invaded the
land to ravage it. 6Midian so impoverished
the Israelites that they cried out to the
LORD for help.

7When the Israelites cried to the LORD
because of Midian, 8he sent them a
prophet, who said, "This is what the
LORD, the God of Israel, says: I brought
you up out of Egypt, out of the land of
slavery. 9I snatched you from the power of
Egypt and from the hand of all your
oppressors. I drove them from before you
and gave you their land. 10I said to you, 'I
am the LORD your God; do not worship the
gods of the Amorites, in whose land you
live.' But you have not listened to me."

11The angel of the LORD came and sat
down under the oak in Ophrah that belonged to Joash the Abiezrite, where his
son Gideon was threshing wheat in a
winepress to keep it from the Midianites.

12When the angel of the LORD appeared to
Gideon, he said, "The LORD is with you,
mighty warrior."

13"But sir," Gideon replied, "if the
LORD is with us, why has all this happened
to us? Where are all his wonders that our
fathers told us about when they said, 'Did
not the LORD bring us up out of Egypt?'
But now the LORD has abandoned us and
put us into the hand of Midian."

14The LORD turned to him and said, "Go
in the strength you have and save Israel
out of Midian's hand. Am I not sending
you?"

15"But Lord,"*a* Gideon asked, "how
can I save Israel? My clan is the weakest
in Manasseh, and I am the least in my
family."

16The LORD answered, "I will be with
you, and you will strike down all the
Midianites together."

17Gideon replied, "If now I have found
favour in your eyes, give me a sign that it is
really you talking to me. 18Please do not
go away until I come back and bring my
offering and set it before you."

And the LORD said, "I will wait until you
return."

19Gideon went in, prepared a young
goat, and from an ephah*b* of flour he made
bread without yeast. Putting the meat in a
basket and its broth in a pot, he brought
them out and offered them to him under
the oak.

20The angel of God said to him, "Take
the meat and the unleavened bread, place
them on this rock, and pour out the
broth." And Gideon did so. 21With the tip
of the staff that was in his hand, the angel
of the LORD touched the meat and the
unleavened bread. Fire flared from the
rock, consuming the meat and the bread.
And the angel of the LORD disappeared.
22When Gideon realised that it was the
angel of the LORD, he exclaimed, "Ah,
Sovereign LORD! I have seen the angel of
the LORD face to face!"

23But the LORD said to him, "Peace! Do
not be afraid. You are not going to die."

24So Gideon built an altar to the LORD
there and called it The LORD is Peace.

a15 Or *sir*   *b19* That is, probably about ⅗ bushel (about 22 litres)

To this day it stands in Ophrah of the Abiezrites.

²⁵That same night the LORD said to him, "Take the second bull from your father's herd, the one seven years old.ᶜ Tear down your father's altar to Baal and cut down the Asherah poleᵈ beside it. ²⁶Then build a proper kind ofᵉ altar to the LORD your God on the top of this height. Using the wood of the Asherah pole that you cut down, offer the secondᶠ bull as a burnt offering."

²⁷So Gideon took ten of his servants and did as the LORD told him. But because he was afraid of his family and the men of the town, he did it at night rather than in the daytime.

²⁸In the morning when the men of the town got up, there was Baal's altar, demolished, with the Asherah pole beside it cut down and the second bull sacrificed on the newly-built altar!

²⁹They asked each other, "Who did this?"

When they carefully investigated, they were told, "Gideon son of Joash did it."

³⁰The men of the town demanded of Joash, "Bring out your son. He must die, because he has broken down Baal's altar and cut down the Asherah pole beside it."

³¹But Joash replied to the hostile crowd around him, "Are you going to plead Baal's cause? Are you trying to save him? Whoever fights for him shall be put to death by morning! If Baal really is a god, he can defend himself when someone breaks down his altar." ³²So that day they called Gideon "Jerub-Baal",ᵍ saying, "Let Baal contend with him," because he broke down Baal's altar.

³³Now all the Midianites, Amalekites and other eastern peoples joined forces and crossed over the Jordan and camped in the Valley of Jezreel. ³⁴Then the Spirit of the LORD came upon Gideon, and he blew a trumpet, summoning the Abiezrites to follow him. ³⁵He sent messengers throughout Manasseh, calling them to arms, and also into Asher, Zebulun and Naphtali, so that they too went up to meet them.

³⁶Gideon said to God, "If you will save Israel by my hand as you have promised— ³⁷look, I will place a wool fleece on the threshing-floor. If there is dew only on the fleece and all the ground is dry, then I will know that you will save Israel by my hand, as you said." ³⁸And that is what happened. Gideon rose early the next day; he squeezed the fleece and wrung out the dew—a bowlful of water.

³⁹Then Gideon said to God, "Do not be angry with me. Let me make just one more request. Allow me one more test with the fleece. This time make the fleece dry and the ground covered with dew." ⁴⁰That night God did so. Only the fleece was dry; all the ground was covered with dew.

Gideon Defeats the Midianites

7 Early in the morning, Jerub-Baal (that is, Gideon) and all his men camped at the spring of Harod. The camp of Midian was north of them in the valley near the hill of Moreh. ²The LORD said to Gideon, "You have too many men for me to deliver Midian into their hands. In order that Israel may not boast against me that her own strength has saved her, ³announce now to the people, 'Anyone who trembles with fear may turn back and leave Mount Gilead.'" So twenty-two thousand men left, while ten thousand remained.

⁴But the LORD said to Gideon, "There are still too many men. Take them down to the water, and I will sift them out for you there. If I say, 'This one shall go with you,' he shall go; but if I say, 'This one shall not go with you,' he shall not go."

⁵So Gideon took the men down to the water. There the LORD told him, "Separate those who lap the water with their tongues like a dog from those who kneel down to drink." ⁶Three hundred men lapped with their hands to their mouths. All the rest got down on their knees to drink.

⁷The LORD said to Gideon, "With the

ᶜ25 Or *Take a full-grown, mature bull from your father's herd*
ᵈ25 That is, a symbol of the goddess Asherah; here and elsewhere in Judges　　ᵉ26 Or *build with layers of stone an*
ᶠ26 Or *full-grown*; also in verse 28　　ᵍ32 *Jerub-Baal* means *let Baal contend.*

three hundred men that lapped I will save you and give the Midianites into your hands. Let all the other men go, each to his own place." [8]So Gideon sent the rest of the Israelites to their tents but kept the three hundred, who took over the provisions and trumpets of the others.

Now the camp of Midian lay below him in the valley. [9]During that night the LORD said to Gideon, "Get up, go down against the camp, because I am going to give it into your hands. [10]If you are afraid to attack, go down to the camp with your servant Purah [11]and listen to what they are saying. Afterwards, you will be encouraged to attack the camp." So he and Purah his servant went down to the outposts of the camp. [12]The Midianites, the Amalekites and all the other eastern peoples had settled in the valley, thick as locusts. Their camels could no more be counted than the sand on the seashore.

[13]Gideon arrived just as a man was telling a friend his dream. "I had a dream," he was saying. "A round loaf of barley bread came tumbling into the Midianite camp. It struck the tent with such force that the tent overturned and collapsed."

[14]His friend responded, "This can be nothing other than the sword of Gideon son of Joash, the Israelite. God has given the Midianites and the whole camp into his hands."

[15]When Gideon heard the dream and its interpretation, he worshipped God. He returned to the camp of Israel and called out, "Get up! The LORD has given the Midianite camp into your hands." [16]Dividing the three hundred men into three companies, he placed trumpets and empty jars in the hands of all of them, with torches inside.

[17]"Watch me," he told them. "Follow my lead. When I get to the edge of the camp, do exactly as I do. [18]When I and all who are with me blow our trumpets, then from all around the camp blow yours and shout, 'For the LORD and for Gideon.'"

[19]Gideon and the hundred men with him reached the edge of the camp at the beginning of the middle watch, just after they had changed the guard. They blew their trumpets and broke the jars that were in their hands. [20]The three companies blew the trumpets and smashed the jars. Grasping the torches in their left hands and holding in their right hands the trumpets they were to blow, they shouted, "A sword for the LORD and for Gideon!" [21]While each man held his position around the camp, all the Midianites ran, crying out as they fled.

[22]When the three hundred trumpets sounded, the LORD caused the men throughout the camp to turn on each other with their swords. The army fled to Beth Shittah towards Zererah as far as the border of Abel Meholah near Tabbath. [23]Israelites from Naphtali, Asher and all Manasseh were called out, and they pursued the Midianites. [24]Gideon sent messengers throughout the hill country of Ephraim, saying, "Come down against the Midianites and seize the waters of the Jordan ahead of them as far as Beth Barah."

So all the men of Ephraim were called out and they took the waters of the Jordan as far as Beth Barah. [25]They also captured two of the Midianite leaders, Oreb and Zeeb. They killed Oreb at the rock of Oreb, and Zeeb at the winepress of Zeeb. They pursued the Midianites and brought the heads of Oreb and Zeeb to Gideon, who was by the Jordan.

Zebah and Zalmunna

8 Now the Ephraimites asked Gideon, "Why have you treated us like this? Why didn't you call us when you went to fight Midian?" And they criticised him sharply.

[2]But he answered them, "What have I accomplished compared to you? Aren't the gleanings of Ephraim's grapes better than the full grape harvest of Abiezer? [3]God gave Oreb and Zeeb, the Midianite leaders, into your hands. What was I able to do compared to you?" At this, their resentment against him subsided.

[4]Gideon and his three hundred men, exhausted yet keeping up the pursuit, came to the Jordan and crossed it. [5]He said to the men of Succoth, "Give my

troops some bread; they are worn out, and I am still pursuing Zebah and Zalmunna, the kings of Midian."

6But the officials of Succoth said, "Do you already have the hands of Zebah and Zalmunna in your possession? Why should we give bread to your troops?"

7Then Gideon replied, "Just for that, when the LORD has given Zebah and Zalmunna into my hand, I will tear your flesh with desert thorns and briers."

8From there he went up to Peniel[a] and made the same request of them, but they answered as the men of Succoth had. 9So he said to the men of Peniel, "When I return in triumph, I will tear down this tower."

10Now Zebah and Zalmunna were in Karkor with a force of about fifteen thousand men, all that were left of the armies of the eastern peoples; a hundred and twenty thousand swordsmen had fallen. 11Gideon went up by the route of the nomads east of Nobah and Jogbehah and fell upon the unsuspecting army. 12Zebah and Zalmunna, the two kings of Midian, fled, but he pursued them and captured them, routing their entire army.

13Gideon son of Joash then returned from the battle by the Pass of Heres. 14He caught a young man of Succoth and questioned him, and the young man wrote down for him the names of the seventy-seven officials of Succoth, the elders of the town. 15Then Gideon came and said to the men of Succoth, "Here are Zebah and Zalmunna, about whom you taunted me by saying, 'Do you already have the hands of Zebah and Zalmunna in your possession? Why should we give bread to your exhausted men?'" 16He took the elders of the town and taught the men of Succoth a lesson by punishing them with desert thorns and briers. 17He also pulled down the tower of Peniel and killed the men of the town.

18Then he asked Zebah and Zalmunna, "What kind of men did you kill at Tabor?"

"Men like you," they answered, "each one with the bearing of a prince."

19Gideon replied, "Those were my brothers, the sons of my own mother. As surely as the LORD lives, if you had spared their lives, I would not kill you." 20Turning to Jether, his oldest son, he said, "Kill them!" But Jether did not draw his sword, because he was only a boy and was afraid.

21Zebah and Zalmunna said, "Come, do it yourself. 'As is the man, so is his strength.'" So Gideon stepped forward and killed them, and took the ornaments off their camels' necks.

Gideon's Ephod

22The Israelites said to Gideon, "Rule over us—you, your son and your grandson—because you have saved us out of the hand of Midian."

23But Gideon told them, "I will not rule over you, nor will my son rule over you. The LORD will rule over you." 24And he said, "I do have one request, that each of you give me an ear-ring from your share of the plunder." (It was the custom of the Ishmaelites to wear gold ear-rings.)

25They answered, "We'll be glad to give them." So they spread out a garment, and each man threw a ring from his plunder onto it. 26The weight of the gold rings he asked for came to seventeen hundred shekels,[b] not counting the ornaments, the pendants and the purple garments worn by the kings of Midian or the chains that were on their camels' necks. 27Gideon made the gold into an ephod, which he placed in Ophrah, his town. All Israel prostituted themselves by worshipping it there, and it became a snare to Gideon and his family.

Gideon's Death

28Thus Midian was subdued before the Israelites and did not raise its head again. During Gideon's lifetime, the land enjoyed peace for forty years.

29Jerub-Baal son of Joash went back home to live. 30He had seventy sons of his own, for he had many wives. 31His concubine, who lived in Shechem, also bore

---

*a*8 Hebrew *Penuel*, a variant of *Peniel*; also in verses 9 and 17   *b*26 That is, about 43 pounds (about 19.5 kilograms)

him a son, whom he named Abimelech.
32Gideon son of Joash died at a good old age and was buried in the tomb of his father Joash in Ophrah of the Abiezrites.

33No sooner had Gideon died than the Israelites again prostituted themselves to the Baals. They set up Baal-Berith as their god and 34did not remember the LORD their God, who had rescued them from the hands of all their enemies on every side. 35They also failed to show kindness to the family of Jerub-Baal (that is, Gideon) for all the good things he had done for them.

Abimelech

9 Abimelech son of Jerub-Baal went to his mother's brothers in Shechem and said to them and to all his mother's clan, 2"Ask all the citizens of Shechem, 'Which is better for you: to have all seventy of Jerub-Baal's sons rule over you, or just one man?' Remember, I am your flesh and blood."

3When the brothers repeated all this to the citizens of Shechem, they were inclined to follow Abimelech, for they said, "He is our brother." 4They gave him seventy shekels*a* of silver from the temple of Baal-Berith, and Abimelech used it to hire reckless adventurers, who became his followers. 5He went to his father's home in Ophrah and on one stone murdered his seventy brothers, the sons of Jerub-Baal. But Jotham, the youngest son of Jerub-Baal, escaped by hiding. 6Then all the citizens of Shechem and Beth Millo gathered beside the great tree at the pillar in Shechem to crown Abimelech king.

7When Jotham was told about this, he climbed up on the top of Mount Gerizim and shouted to them, "Listen to me, citizens of Shechem, so that God may listen to you. 8One day the trees went out to anoint a king for themselves. They said to the olive tree, 'Be our king.'

9"But the olive tree answered, 'Should I give up my oil, by which both gods and men are honoured, to hold sway over the trees?'

10"Next, the trees said to the fig-tree, 'Come and be our king.'

11"But the fig-tree replied, 'Should I give up my fruit, so good and sweet, to hold sway over the trees?'

12"Then the trees said to the vine, 'Come and be our king.'

13"But the vine answered, 'Should I give up my wine, which cheers both gods and men, to hold sway over the trees?'

14"Finally all the trees said to the thornbush, 'Come and be our king.'

15"The thornbush said to the trees, 'If you really want to anoint me king over you, come and take refuge in my shade; but if not, then let fire come out of the thornbush and consume the cedars of Lebanon!'

16"Now if you have acted honourably and in good faith when you made Abimelech king, and if you have been fair to Jerub-Baal and his family, and if you have treated him as he deserves—17and to think that my father fought for you, risked his life to rescue you from the hand of Midian 18(but today you have revolted against my father's family, murdered his seventy sons on a single stone, and made Abimelech, the son of his slave girl, king over the citizens of Shechem because he is your brother)—19if then you have acted honourably and in good faith towards Jerub-Baal and his family today, may Abimelech be your joy, and may you be his, too! 20But if you have not, let fire come out from Abimelech and consume you, citizens of Shechem and Beth Millo, and let fire come out from you, citizens of Shechem and Beth Millo, and consume Abimelech!"

21Then Jotham fled, escaping to Beer, and he lived there because he was afraid of his brother Abimelech.

22After Abimelech had governed Israel for three years, 23God sent an evil spirit between Abimelech and the citizens of Shechem, who acted treacherously against Abimelech. 24God did this in order that the crime against Jerub-Baal's seventy sons, the shedding of their blood, might be avenged on their brother

---

*a*4 That is, about 1¾ pounds (about 0.8 kilogram)

Abimelech and on the citizens of Shechem, who had helped him murder his brothers. [25]In opposition to him these citizens of Shechem set men on the hilltops to ambush and rob everyone who passed by, and this was reported to Abimelech.

[26]Now Gaal son of Ebed moved with his brothers into Shechem, and its citizens put their confidence in him. [27]After they had gone out into the fields and gathered the grapes and trodden them, they held a festival in the temple of their god. While they were eating and drinking, they cursed Abimelech. [28]Then Gaal son of Ebed said, "Who is Abimelech, and who is Shechem, that we should be subject to him? Isn't he Jerub-Baal's son, and isn't Zebul his deputy? Serve the men of Hamor, Shechem's father! Why should we serve Abimelech? [29]If only this people were under my command! Then I would get rid of him. I would say to Abimelech, 'Call out your whole army!'"[b]

[30]When Zebul the governor of the city heard what Gaal son of Ebed said, he was very angry. [31]Under cover he sent messengers to Abimelech, saying, "Gaal son of Ebed and his brothers have come to Shechem and are stirring up the city against you. [32]Now then, during the night you and your men should come and lie in wait in the fields. [33]In the morning at sunrise, advance against the city. When Gaal and his men come out against you, do whatever your hand finds to do."

[34]So Abimelech and all his troops set out by night and took up concealed positions near Shechem in four companies. [35]Now Gaal son of Ebed had gone out and was standing at the entrance to the city gate just as Abimelech and his soldiers came out from their hiding-place.

[36]When Gaal saw them, he said to Zebul, "Look, people are coming down from the tops of the mountains!"

Zebul replied, "You mistake the shadows of the mountains for men."

[37]But Gaal spoke up again: "Look, people are coming down from the centre of the land, and a company is coming from the direction of the soothsayers' tree."

[38]Then Zebul said to him, "Where is your big talk now, you who said, 'Who is Abimelech that we should be subject to him?' Aren't these the men you ridiculed? Go out and fight them!"

[39]So Gaal led out[c] the citizens of Shechem and fought Abimelech. [40]Abimelech chased him, and many fell wounded in the flight—all the way to the entrance to the gate. [41]Abimelech stayed in Arumah, and Zebul drove Gaal and his brothers out of Shechem.

[42]The next day the people of Shechem went out to the fields, and this was reported to Abimelech. [43]So he took his men, divided them into three companies and set an ambush in the fields. When he saw the people coming out of the city, he rose to attack them. [44]Abimelech and the companies with him rushed forward to a position at the entrance to the city gate. Then two companies rushed upon those in the fields and struck them down. [45]All that day Abimelech pressed his attack against the city until he had captured it and killed its people. Then he destroyed the city and scattered salt over it.

[46]On hearing this, the citizens in the tower of Shechem went into the stronghold of the temple of El-Berith. [47]When Abimelech heard that they had assembled there, [48]he and all his men went up Mount Zalmon. He took an axe and cut off some branches, which he lifted to his shoulders. He ordered the men with him, "Quick! Do what you have seen me do!" [49]So all the men cut branches and followed Abimelech. They piled them against the stronghold and set it on fire over the people inside. So all the people in the tower of Shechem, about a thousand men and women, also died.

[50]Next Abimelech went to Thebez and besieged it and captured it. [51]Inside the city, however, was a strong tower, to which all the men and women—all the people of the city—fled. They locked themselves in and climbed up on the tower roof. [52]Abimelech went to the tower and stormed it. But as he approached the

[b]29 Septuagint; Hebrew *him." Then he said to Abimelech, "Call out your whole army!"*
[c]39 Or *Gaal went out in the sight of*

entrance to the tower to set it on fire, [53]a woman dropped an upper millstone on his head and cracked his skull.

[54]Hurriedly he called to his armour-bearer, "Draw your sword and kill me, so that they can't say, 'A woman killed him.'" So his servant ran him through, and he died. [55]When the Israelites saw that Abimelech was dead, they went home.

[56]Thus God repaid the wickedness that Abimelech had done to his father by murdering his seventy brothers. [57]God also made the men of Shechem pay for all their wickedness. The curse of Jotham son of Jerub-Baal came on them.

Tola

10 After the time of Abimelech a man of Issachar, Tola son of Puah, the son of Dodo, rose to save Israel. He lived in Shamir, in the hill country of Ephraim. [2]He led[a] Israel for twenty-three years; then he died, and was buried in Shamir.

Jair

[3]He was followed by Jair of Gilead, who led Israel for twenty-two years. [4]He had thirty sons, who rode thirty donkeys. They controlled thirty towns in Gilead, which to this day are called Havvoth Jair.[b] [5]When Jair died, he was buried in Kamon.

Jephthah

[6]Again the Israelites did evil in the eyes of the LORD. They served the Baals and the Ashtoreths, and the gods of Aram, the gods of Sidon, the gods of Moab, the gods of the Ammonites and the gods of the Philistines. And because the Israelites forsook the LORD and no longer served him, [7]he became angry with them. He sold them into the hands of the Philistines and the Ammonites, [8]who that year shattered and crushed them. For eighteen years they oppressed all the Israelites on the east side of the Jordan in Gilead, the land of the Amorites. [9]The Ammonites also crossed the Jordan to fight against Judah, Benjamin and the house of Ephraim; and Israel was in great distress. [10]Then the Israelites cried out to the LORD, "We have sinned against you, forsaking our God and serving the Baals."

[11]The LORD replied, "When the Egyptians, the Amorites, the Ammonites, the Philistines, [12]the Sidonians, the Amalekites and the Maonites[c] oppressed you and you cried to me for help, did I not save you from their hands? [13]But you have forsaken me and served other gods, so I will no longer save you. [14]Go and cry out to the gods you have chosen. Let them save you when you are in trouble!"

[15]But the Israelites said to the LORD, "We have sinned. Do with us whatever you think best, but please rescue us now." [16]Then they got rid of the foreign gods among them and served the LORD. And he could bear Israel's misery no longer.

[17]When the Ammonites were called to arms and camped in Gilead, the Israelites assembled and camped at Mizpah. [18]The leaders of the people of Gilead said to each other, "Whoever will launch the attack against the Ammonites will be the head of all those living in Gilead."

11 Jephthah the Gileadite was a mighty warrior. His father was Gilead; his mother was a prostitute. [2]Gilead's wife also bore him sons, and when they were grown up, they drove Jephthah away. "You are not going to get any inheritance in our family," they said, "because you are the son of another woman." [3]So Jephthah fled from his brothers and settled in the land of Tob, where a group of adventurers gathered around him and followed him.

[4]Some time later, when the Ammonites made war on Israel, [5]the elders of Gilead went to get Jephthah from the land of Tob. [6]"Come," they said, "be our commander, so we can fight the Ammonites."

[7]Jephthah said to them, "Didn't you hate me and drive me from my father's house? Why do you come to me now, when you're in trouble?"

[8]The elders of Gilead said to him,

---

[a]2 Traditionally *judged*; also in verse 3   [b]4 Or *called the settlements of Jair*
[c]12 Hebrew; some Septuagint manuscripts *Midianites*

"Nevertheless, we are turning to you now; come with us to fight the Ammonites, and you will be our head over all who live in Gilead."

⁹Jephthah answered, "Suppose you take me back to fight the Ammonites and the LORD gives them to me—will I really be your head?"

¹⁰The elders of Gilead replied, "The LORD is our witness; we will certainly do as you say." ¹¹So Jephthah went with the elders of Gilead, and the people made him head and commander over them. And he repeated all his words before the LORD in Mizpah.

¹²Then Jephthah sent messengers to the Ammonite king with the question: "What do you have against us that you have attacked our country?"

¹³The king of the Ammonites answered Jephthah's messengers, "When Israel came up out of Egypt, they took away my land from the Arnon to the Jabbok, all the way to the Jordan. Now give it back peaceably."

¹⁴Jephthah sent back messengers to the Ammonite king, ¹⁵saying:

"This is what Jephthah says: Israel did not take the land of Moab or the land of the Ammonites. ¹⁶But when they came up out of Egypt, Israel went through the desert to the Red Sea*a* and on to Kadesh. ¹⁷Then Israel sent messengers to the king of Edom, saying, 'Give us permission to go through your country,' but the king of Edom would not listen. They sent also to the king of Moab, and he refused. So Israel stayed at Kadesh.

¹⁸"Next they travelled through the desert, skirted the lands of Edom and Moab, passed along the eastern side of the country of Moab, and camped on the other side of the Arnon. They did not enter the territory of Moab, for the Arnon was its border.

¹⁹"Then Israel sent messengers to Sihon king of the Amorites, who ruled in Heshbon, and said to him,

'Let us pass through your country to our own place.' ²⁰Sihon, however, did not trust Israel*b* to pass through his territory. He mustered all his men and encamped at Jahaz and fought with Israel.

²¹"Then the LORD, the God of Israel, gave Sihon and all his men into Israel's hands, and they defeated them. Israel took over all the land of the Amorites who lived in that country, ²²capturing all of it from the Arnon to the Jabbok and from the desert to the Jordan.

²³"Now since the LORD, the God of Israel, has driven the Amorites out before his people Israel, what right have you to take it over? ²⁴Will you not take what your god Chemosh gives you? Likewise, whatever the LORD our God has given us, we will possess. ²⁵Are you better than Balak son of Zippor, king of Moab? Did he ever quarrel with Israel or fight with them? ²⁶For three hundred years Israel occupied Heshbon, Aroer, the surrounding settlements and all the towns along the Arnon. Why didn't you retake them during that time? ²⁷I have not wronged you, but you are doing me wrong by waging war against me. Let the LORD, the Judge,*c* decide the dispute this day between the Israelites and the Ammonites."

²⁸The king of Ammon, however, paid no attention to the message Jephthah sent him.

²⁹Then the Spirit of the LORD came upon Jephthah. He crossed Gilead and Manasseh, passed through Mizpah of Gilead, and from there he advanced against the Ammonites. ³⁰And Jephthah made a vow to the LORD: "If you give the Ammonites into my hands, ³¹whatever comes out of the door of my house to meet me when I return in triumph from the Ammonites will be the LORD's, and I will sacrifice it as a burnt offering."

³²Then Jephthah went over to fight the Ammonites, and the LORD gave them into

a16 Hebrew *Yam Suph*; that is, Sea of Reeds   *b20* Or *however, would not make an agreement for Israel*
c27 Or *Ruler*

his hands. ³³He devastated twenty towns from Aroer to the vicinity of Minnith, as far as Abel Keramim. Thus Israel subdued Ammon.

³⁴When Jephthah returned to his home in Mizpah, who should come out to meet him but his daughter, dancing to the sound of tambourines! She was an only child. Except for her he had neither son nor daughter. ³⁵When he saw her, he tore his clothes and cried, "Oh! My daughter! You have made me miserable and wretched, because I have made a vow to the LORD that I cannot break."

³⁶"My father," she replied, "you have given your word to the LORD. Do to me just as you promised, now that the LORD has avenged you of your enemies, the Ammonites. ³⁷But grant me this one request," she said. "Give me two months to roam the hills and weep with my friends, because I will never marry."

³⁸"You may go," he said. And he let her go for two months. She and the girls went into the hills and wept because she would never marry. ³⁹After the two months, she returned to her father and he did to her as he had vowed. And she was a virgin.

From this comes the Israelite custom ⁴⁰that each year the young women of Israel go out for four days to commemorate the daughter of Jephthah the Gileadite.

Jephthah and Ephraim

12 The men of Ephraim called out their forces, crossed over to Zaphon and said to Jephthah, "Why did you go to fight the Ammonites without calling us to go with you? We're going to burn down your house over your head."

²Jephthah answered, "I and my people were engaged in a great struggle with the Ammonites, and although I called, you didn't save me out of their hands. ³When I saw that you wouldn't help, I took my life in my hands and crossed over to fight the Ammonites, and the LORD gave me the victory over them. Now why have you come up today to fight me?"

⁴Jephthah then called together the men of Gilead and fought against Ephraim. The Gileadites struck them down because the Ephraimites had said, "You Gileadites are renegades from Ephraim and Manasseh." ⁵The Gileadites captured the fords of the Jordan leading to Ephraim, and whenever a survivor of Ephraim said, "Let me cross over," the men of Gilead asked him, "Are you an Ephraimite?" If he replied, "No," ⁶they said, "All right, say 'Shibboleth'." If he said, "Sibboleth", because he could not pronounce the word correctly, they seized him and killed him at the fords of the Jordan. Forty-two thousand Ephraimites were killed at that time.

⁷Jephthah led*ᵃ* Israel for six years. Then Jephthah the Gileadite died, and was buried in a town in Gilead.

Ibzan, Elon and Abdon

⁸After him, Ibzan of Bethlehem led Israel. ⁹He had thirty sons and thirty daughters. He gave his daughters away in marriage to those outside his clan, and for his sons he brought in thirty young women as wives from outside his clan. Ibzan led Israel for seven years. ¹⁰Then Ibzan died, and was buried in Bethlehem.

¹¹After him, Elon the Zebulunite led Israel for ten years. ¹²Then Elon died, and was buried in Aijalon in the land of Zebulun.

¹³After him, Abdon son of Hillel, from Pirathon, led Israel. ¹⁴He had forty sons and thirty grandsons, who rode on seventy donkeys. He led Israel for eight years. ¹⁵Then Abdon son of Hillel died, and was buried at Pirathon in Ephraim, in the hill country of the Amalekites.

The Birth of Samson

13 Again the Israelites did evil in the eyes of the LORD, so the LORD delivered them into the hands of the Philistines for forty years.

²A certain man of Zorah, named Manoah, from the clan of the Danites, had a

*ᵃ*7 Traditionally *judged*; also in verses 8–14

wife who was sterile and remained childless. ³The angel of the LORD appeared to her and said, "You are sterile and childless, but you are going to conceive and have a son. ⁴Now see to it that you drink no wine or other fermented drink and that you do not eat anything unclean, ⁵because you will conceive and give birth to a son. No razor may be used on his head, because the boy is to be a Nazirite, set apart to God from birth, and he will begin the deliverance of Israel from the hands of the Philistines."

⁶Then the woman went to her husband and told him, "A man of God came to me. He looked like an angel of God, very awesome. I didn't ask him where he came from, and he didn't tell me his name. ⁷But he said to me, 'You will conceive and give birth to a son. Now then, drink no wine or other fermented drink and do not eat anything unclean, because the boy will be a Nazirite of God from birth until the day of his death.'"

⁸Then Manoah prayed to the LORD: "O Lord, I beg you, let the man of God you sent to us come again to teach us how to bring up the boy who is to be born."

⁹God heard Manoah, and the angel of God came again to the woman while she was out in the field; but her husband Manoah was not with her. ¹⁰The woman hurried to tell her husband, "He's here! The man who appeared to me the other day!"

¹¹Manoah got up and followed his wife. When he came to the man, he said, "Are you the one who talked to my wife?"

"I am," he said.

¹²So Manoah asked him, "When your words are fulfilled, what is to be the rule for the boy's life and work?"

¹³The angel of the LORD answered, "Your wife must do all that I have told her. ¹⁴She must not eat anything that comes from the grapevine, nor drink any wine or other fermented drink nor eat anything unclean. She must do everything I have commanded her."

¹⁵Manoah said to the angel of the LORD, "We would like you to stay until we prepare a young goat for you."

¹⁶The angel of the LORD replied, "Even though you detain me, I will not eat any of your food. But if you prepare a burnt offering, offer it to the LORD." (Manoah did not realise that it was the angel of the LORD.)

¹⁷Then Manoah enquired of the angel of the LORD, "What is your name, so that we may honour you when your word comes true?"

¹⁸He replied, "Why do you ask my name? It is beyond understanding."ᵃ

¹⁹Then Manoah took a young goat, together with the grain offering, and sacrificed it on a rock to the LORD. And the LORD did an amazing thing while Manoah and his wife watched: ²⁰As the flame blazed up from the altar towards heaven, the angel of the LORD ascended in the flame. Seeing this, Manoah and his wife fell with their faces to the ground. ²¹When the angel of the LORD did not show himself again to Manoah and his wife, Manoah realised that it was the angel of the LORD.

²²"We are doomed to die!" he said to his wife. "We have seen God!"

²³But his wife answered, "If the LORD had meant to kill us, he would not have accepted a burnt offering and grain offering from our hands, nor shown us all these things or now told us this."

²⁴The woman gave birth to a boy and named him Samson. He grew and the LORD blessed him, ²⁵and the Spirit of the LORD began to stir him while he was in Mahaneh Dan, between Zorah and Eshtaol.

Samson's Marriage

14 Samson went down to Timnah and saw there a young Philistine woman. ²When he returned, he said to his father and mother, "I have seen a Philistine woman in Timnah; now get her for me as my wife."

³His father and mother replied, "Isn't there an acceptable woman among your relatives or among all our people? Must you go to the uncircumcised Philistines to get a wife?"

ᵃ18 Or is wonderful

But Samson said to his father, "Get her for me. She's the right one for me." 4(His parents did not know that this was from the LORD, who was seeking an occasion to confront the Philistines; for at that time they were ruling over Israel.) 5Samson went down to Timnah together with his father and mother. As they approached the vineyards of Timnah, suddenly a young lion came roaring towards him. 6The Spirit of the LORD came upon him in power so that he tore the lion apart with his bare hands as he might have torn a young goat. But he told neither his father nor his mother what he had done. 7Then he went down and talked with the woman, and he liked her.

8Some time later, when he went back to marry her, he turned aside to look at the lion's carcass. In it was a swarm of bees and some honey, 9which he scooped out with his hands and ate as he went along. When he rejoined his parents, he gave them some, and they too ate it. But he did not tell them that he had taken the honey from the lion's carcass.

10Now his father went down to see the woman. And Samson made a feast there, as was customary for bridegrooms. 11When he appeared, he was given thirty companions.

12"Let me tell you a riddle," Samson said to them. "If you can give me the answer within the seven days of the feast, I will give you thirty linen garments and thirty sets of clothes. 13If you can't tell me the answer, you must give me thirty linen garments and thirty sets of clothes."

"Tell us your riddle," they said. "Let's hear it."

14He replied,

"Out of the eater, something to eat;
    out of the strong, something sweet."

For three days they could not give the answer.

15On the fourth*a* day, they said to Samson's wife, "Coax your husband into explaining the riddle for us, or we will burn you and your father's household to death. Did you invite us here to rob us?"

16Then Samson's wife threw herself on him, sobbing, "You hate me! You don't really love me. You've given my people a riddle, but you haven't told me the answer."

"I haven't even explained it to my father or mother," he replied, "so why should I explain it to you?" 17She cried the whole seven days of the feast. So on the seventh day he finally told her, because she continued to press him. She in turn explained the riddle to her people.

18Before sunset on the seventh day the men of the town said to him,

"What is sweeter than honey?
    What is stronger than a lion?"

Samson said to them,

"If you had not ploughed with my
    heifer,
    you would not have solved my
    riddle."

19Then the Spirit of the LORD came upon him in power. He went down to Ashkelon, struck down thirty of their men, stripped them of their belongings and gave their clothes to those who had explained the riddle. Burning with anger, he went up to his father's house. 20And Samson's wife was given to the friend who had attended him at his wedding.

Samson's Vengeance on the Philistines

15 Later on, at the time of wheat harvest, Samson took a young goat and went to visit his wife. He said, "I'm going to my wife's room." But her father would not let him go in.

2"I was so sure you thoroughly hated her," he said, "that I gave her to your friend. Isn't her younger sister more attractive? Take her instead."

3Samson said to them, "This time I have a right to get even with the Philistines; I will really harm them." 4So he went out and caught three hundred foxes and tied them tail to tail in pairs. He then fastened a torch to every pair of tails, 5lit the torches and let the foxes loose in the

---

*a*15 Some Septuagint manuscripts and Syriac; Hebrew *seventh* standing corn of the Philistines. He burned up the shocks and standing corn, together with the vineyards and olive groves.

⁶When the Philistines asked, "Who did this?" they were told, "Samson, the Timnite's son-in-law, because his wife was given to his friend."

So the Philistines went up and burned her and her father to death. ⁷Samson said to them, "Since you've acted like this, I won't stop until I get my revenge on you." ⁸He attacked them viciously and slaughtered many of them. Then he went down and stayed in a cave in the rock of Etam.

⁹The Philistines went up and camped in Judah, spreading out near Lehi. ¹⁰The men of Judah asked, "Why have you come to fight us?"

"We have come to take Samson prisoner," they answered, "to do to him as he did to us."

¹¹Then three thousand men from Judah went down to the cave in the rock of Etam and said to Samson, "Don't you realise that the Philistines are rulers over us? What have you done to us?"

He answered, "I merely did to them what they did to me."

¹²They said to him, "We've come to tie you up and hand you over to the Philistines."

Samson said, "Swear to me that you won't kill me yourselves."

¹³"Agreed," they answered. "We will only tie you up and hand you over to them. We will not kill you." So they bound him with two new ropes and led him up from the rock. ¹⁴As he approached Lehi, the Philistines came towards him shouting. The Spirit of the LORD came upon him in power. The ropes on his arms became like charred flax, and the bindings dropped from his hands. ¹⁵Finding a fresh jaw-bone of a donkey, he grabbed it and struck down a thousand men.

¹⁶Then Samson said,

"With a donkey's jaw-bone
  I have made donkeys of them.ᵃ

"With a donkey's jaw-bone
  I have killed a thousand men."

¹⁷When he finished speaking, he threw away the jaw-bone; and the place was called Ramath Lehi.ᵇ

¹⁸Because he was very thirsty, he cried out to the LORD, "You have given your servant this great victory. Must I now die of thirst and fall into the hands of the uncircumcised?" ¹⁹Then God opened up the hollow place in Lehi, and water came out of it. When Samson drank, his strength returned and he revived. So the spring was called En Hakkore,ᶜ and it is still there in Lehi.

²⁰Samson ledᵈ Israel for twenty years in the days of the Philistines.

Samson and Delilah

16 One day Samson went to Gaza, where he saw a prostitute. He went in to spend the night with her. ²The people of Gaza were told, "Samson is here!" So they surrounded the place and lay in wait for him all night at the city gate. They made no move during the night, saying, "At dawn we'll kill him."

³But Samson lay there only until the middle of the night. Then he got up and took hold of the doors of the city gate, together with the two posts, and tore them loose, bar and all. He lifted them to his shoulders and carried them to the top of the hill that faces Hebron.

⁴Some time later, he fell in love with a woman in the Valley of Sorek whose name was Delilah. ⁵The rulers of the Philistines went to her and said, "See if you can lure him into showing you the secret of his great strength and how we can overpower him so that we may tie him up and subdue him. Each one of us will give you eleven hundred shekelsᵃ of silver."

⁶So Delilah said to Samson, "Tell me the secret of your great strength and how you can be tied up and subdued."

⁷Samson answered her, "If anyone ties me with seven fresh thongsᵇ that have not

---

ᵃ16 Or *made a heap or two*; the Hebrew for *donkey* sounds like the Hebrew for *heap*.
ᵇ17 *Ramath Lehi* means *jaw-bone hill*.   ᶜ19 *En Hakkore* means *caller's spring*.   ᵈ20 Traditionally *judged*
ᵃ5 That is, about 28 pounds (about 13 kilograms)   ᵇ7 Or *bow-strings*; also in verses 8 and 9

been dried, I'll become as weak as any other man.''

8Then the rulers of the Philistines brought her seven fresh thongs that had not been dried, and she tied him with them. 9With men hidden in the room, she called to him, "Samson, the Philistines are upon you!'' But he snapped the thongs as easily as a piece of string snaps when it comes close to a flame. So the secret of his strength was not discovered.

10Then Delilah said to Samson, "You have made a fool of me; you lied to me. Come now, tell me how you can be tied.''

11He said, "If anyone ties me securely with new ropes that have never been used, I'll become as weak as any other man.''

12So Delilah took new ropes and tied him with them. Then, with men hidden in the room, she called to him, "Samson, the Philistines are upon you!'' But he snapped the ropes off his arms as if they were threads.

13Delilah then said to Samson, "Until now, you have been making a fool of me and lying to me. Tell me how you can be tied.''

He replied, "If you weave the seven braids of my head into the fabric ⌊on the loom⌋ and tighten it with the pin, I'll become as weak as any other man.'' So while he was sleeping, Delilah took the seven braids of his head, wove them into the fabric 14and*c* tightened it with the pin.

Again she called to him, "Samson, the Philistines are upon you!'' He awoke from his sleep and pulled up the pin and the loom, with the fabric.

15Then she said to him, "How can you say, 'I love you,' when you won't confide in me? This is the third time you have made a fool of me and haven't told me the secret of your great strength.'' 16With such nagging she prodded him day after day until he was tired to death.

17So he told her everything. "No razor has ever been used on my head,'' he said, "because I have been a Nazirite set apart to God since birth. If my head were shaved, my strength would leave me, and

I would become as weak as any other man.''

18When Delilah saw that he had told her everything, she sent word to the rulers of the Philistines, "Come back once more; he has told me everything.'' So the rulers of the Philistines returned with the silver in their hands. 19Having put him to sleep on her lap, she called a man to shave off the seven braids of his hair, and so began to subdue him.*d* And his strength left him.

20Then she called, "Samson, the Philistines are upon you!''

He awoke from his sleep and thought, "I'll go out as before and shake myself free.'' But he did not know that the LORD had left him.

21Then the Philistines seized him, gouged out his eyes and took him down to Gaza. Binding him with bronze shackles, they set him to grinding in the prison. 22But the hair on his head began to grow again after it had been shaved.

The Death of Samson

23Now the rulers of the Philistines assembled to offer a great sacrifice to Dagon their god and to celebrate, saying, "Our god has delivered Samson, our enemy, into our hands.''

24When the people saw him, they praised their god, saying,

"Our god has delivered our enemy
　into our hands,
the one who laid waste our land
　and multiplied our slain.''

25While they were in high spirits, they shouted, "Bring out Samson to entertain us.'' So they called Samson out of the prison, and he performed for them.

When they stood him among the pillars, 26Samson said to the servant who held his hand, "Put me where I can feel the pillars that support the temple, so that I may lean against them.'' 27Now the temple was crowded with men and women; all the rulers of the Philistines were there, and on

---

c13, 14 Some Septuagint manuscripts; Hebrew "⌊I can⌋ if you weave the seven braids of my head into the fabric ⌊on the loom⌋." 14*So she*　*d19* Hebrew; some Septuagint manuscripts *and he began to weaken* the roof were about three thousand men and women watching Samson perform. [28]Then Samson prayed to the LORD, "O Sovereign LORD, remember me. O God, please strengthen me just once more, and let me with one blow get revenge on the Philistines for my two eyes." [29]Then Samson reached towards the two central pillars on which the temple stood. Bracing himself against them, his right hand on the one and his left hand on the other, [30]Samson said, "Let me die with the Philistines!" Then he pushed with all his might, and down came the temple on the rulers and all the people in it. Thus he killed many more when he died than while he lived.

[31]Then his brothers and his father's whole family went down to get him. They brought him back and buried him between Zorah and Eshtaol in the tomb of Manoah his father. He had led[e] Israel for twenty years

Micah's Idols

17 Now a man named Micah from the hill country of Ephraim [2]said to his mother, "The eleven hundred shekels[a] of silver that were taken from you and about which I heard you utter a curse—I have that silver with me; I took it."

Then his mother said, "The LORD bless you, my son!"

[3]When he returned the eleven hundred shekels of silver to his mother, she said, "I solemnly consecrate my silver to the LORD for my son to make a carved image and a cast idol. I will give it back to you."

[4]So he returned the silver to his mother, and she took two hundred shekels[b] of silver and gave them to a silversmith, who made them into the image and the idol. And they were put in Micah's house.

[5]Now this man Micah had a shrine, and he made an ephod and some idols and installed one of his sons as his priest. [6]In those days Israel had no king; everyone did as he saw fit.

[7]A young Levite from Bethlehem in Judah, who had been living within the clan of Judah, [8]left that town in search of some other place to stay. On his way[c] he came to Micah's house in the hill country of Ephraim.

[9]Micah asked him, "Where are you from?"

"I'm a Levite from Bethlehem in Judah," he said, "and I'm looking for a place to stay."

[10]Then Micah said to him, "Live with me and be my father and priest, and I'll give you ten shekels[d] of silver a year, your clothes and your food." [11]So the Levite agreed to live with him, and the young man was to him like one of his sons. [12]Then Micah installed the Levite, and the young man became his priest and lived in his house. [13]And Micah said, "Now I know that the LORD will be good to me, since this Levite has become my priest."

Danites Settle in Laish

18 In those days Israel had no king. And in those days the tribe of the Danites was seeking a place of their own where they might settle, because they had not yet come into an inheritance among the tribes of Israel. [2]So the Danites sent five warriors from Zorah and Eshtaol to spy out the land and explore it. These men represented all their clans. They told them, "Go, explore the land."

The men entered the hill country of Ephraim and came to the house of Micah, where they spent the night. [3]When they were near Micah's house, they recognised the voice of the young Levite; so they turned in there and asked him, "Who brought you here? What are you doing in this place? Why are you here?"

[4]He told them what Micah had done for him, and said, "He has hired me and I am his priest."

[5]Then they said to him, "Please enquire of God to learn whether our journey will be successful."

---

[e]31 Traditionally *judged*   [a]2 That is, about 28 pounds (about 13 kilograms)
[b]4 That is, about 5 pounds (about 2.3 kilograms)   [c]8 Or *To carry on his profession*
[d]10 That is, about 4 ounces (about 115 grams)

⁶The priest answered them, "Go in peace. Your journey has the LORD's approval."

⁷So the five men left and came to Laish, where they saw that the people were living in safety, like the Sidonians, unsuspecting and secure. And since their land lacked nothing, they were prosperous.ᵃ Also, they lived a long way from the Sidonians and had no relationship with anyone else.ᵇ

⁸When they returned to Zorah and Eshtaol, their brothers asked them, "How did you find things?"

⁹They answered, "Come on, let's attack them! We have seen that the land is very good. Aren't you going to do something? Don't hesitate to go there and take it over. ¹⁰When you get there, you will find an unsuspecting people and a spacious land that God has put into your hands, a land that lacks nothing whatever."

¹¹Then six hundred men from the clan of the Danites, armed for battle, set out from Zorah and Eshtaol. ¹²On their way they set up camp near Kiriath Jearim in Judah. This is why the place west of Kiriath Jearim is called Mahaneh Danᶜ to this day. ¹³From there they went on to the hill country of Ephraim and came to Micah's house.

¹⁴Then the five men who had spied out the land of Laish said to their brothers, "Do you know that one of these houses has an ephod, other household gods, a carved image and a cast idol? Now you know what to do." ¹⁵So they turned in there and went to the house of the young Levite at Micah's place and greeted him. ¹⁶The six hundred Danites, armed for battle, stood at the entrance to the gate. ¹⁷The five men who had spied out the land went inside and took the carved image, the ephod, the other household gods and the cast idol while the priest and the six hundred armed men stood at the entrance to the gate.

¹⁸When these men went into Micah's house and took the carved image, the ephod, the other household gods and the cast idol, the priest said to them, "What are you doing?"

¹⁹They answered him, "Be quiet! Don't say a word. Come with us, and be our father and priest. Isn't it better that you serve a tribe and clan in Israel as priest rather than just one man's household?" ²⁰Then the priest was glad. He took the ephod, the other household gods and the carved image and went along with the people. ²¹Putting their little children, their livestock and their possessions in front of them, they turned away and left.

²²When they had gone some distance from Micah's house, the men who lived near Micah were called together and overtook the Danites. ²³As they shouted after them, the Danites turned and said to Micah, "What's the matter with you that you called out your men to fight?"

²⁴He replied, "You took the gods I made, and my priest, and went away. What else do I have? How can you ask, 'What's the matter with you?'"

²⁵The Danites answered, "Don't argue with us, or some hot-tempered men will attack you, and you and your family will lose your lives." ²⁶So the Danites went their way, and Micah, seeing that they were too strong for him, turned round and went back home.

²⁷Then they took what Micah had made, and his priest, and went on to Laish, against a peaceful and unsuspecting people. They attacked them with the sword and burned down their city. ²⁸There was no-one to rescue them because they lived a long way from Sidon and had no relationship with anyone else. The city was in a valley near Beth Rehob.

The Danites rebuilt the city and settled there. ²⁹They named it Dan after their forefather Dan, who was born to Israel— though the city used to be called Laish. ³⁰There the Danites set up for themselves the idols, and Jonathan son of Gershom, the son of Moses,ᵈ and his sons were priests for the tribe of Dan until the time of the captivity of the land. ³¹They continued

---

ᵃ7 The meaning of the Hebrew for this clause is uncertain.
ᵇ7 Hebrew; some Septuagint manuscripts *with the Arameans*   ᶜ12 *Mahaneh Dan* means *Dan's camp.*
ᵈ30 An ancient Hebrew scribal tradition, some Septuagint manuscripts and Vulgate: Masoretic Text *Manasseh*

to use the idols Micah had made, all the time the house of God was in Shiloh.

A Levite and His Concubine

19 In those days Israel had no king. Now a Levite who lived in a remote area in the hill country of Ephraim took a concubine from Bethlehem in Judah. ²But she was unfaithful to him. She left him and went back to her father's house in Bethlehem, Judah. After she had been there for four months, ³her husband went to her to persuade her to return. He had with him his servant and two donkeys. She took him into her father's house, and when her father saw him, he gladly welcomed him. ⁴His father-in-law, the girl's father, prevailed upon him to stay; so he remained with him three days, eating and drinking, and sleeping there.

⁵On the fourth day they got up early and he prepared to leave, but the girl's father said to his son-in-law, "Refresh yourself with something to eat; then you can go." ⁶So the two of them sat down to eat and drink together. Afterwards the girl's father said, "Please stay tonight and enjoy yourself." ⁷And when the man got up to go, his father-in-law persuaded him, so he stayed there that night. ⁸On the morning of the fifth day, when he rose to go, the girl's father said, "Refresh yourself. Wait till afternoon!" So the two of them ate together.

⁹Then when the man, with his concubine and his servant, got up to leave, his father-in-law, the girl's father, said, "Now look, it's almost evening. Spend the night here; the day is nearly over. Stay and enjoy yourself. Early tomorrow morning you can get up and be on your way home." ¹⁰But, unwilling to stay another night, the man left and went towards Jebus (that is, Jerusalem), with his two saddled donkeys and his concubine.

¹¹When they were near Jebus and the day was almost gone, the servant said to his master, "Come, let's stop at this city of the Jebusites and spend the night."

¹²His master replied, "No. We won't go into an alien city, whose people are not Israelites. We will go on to Gibeah." ¹³He added, "Come, let's try to reach Gibeah or Ramah and spend the night in one of those places." ¹⁴So they went on, and the sun set as they neared Gibeah in Benjamin. ¹⁵There they stopped to spend the night. They went and sat in the city square, but no-one took them into his home for the night.

¹⁶That evening an old man from the hill country of Ephraim, who was living in Gibeah (the men of the place were Benjamites), came in from his work in the fields. ¹⁷When he looked and saw the traveller in the city square, the old man asked, "Where are you going? Where did you come from?"

¹⁸He answered, "We are on our way from Bethlehem in Judah to a remote area in the hill country of Ephraim where I live. I have been to Bethlehem in Judah and now I am going to the house of the LORD. No-one has taken me into his house. ¹⁹We have both straw and fodder for our donkeys and bread and wine for ourselves your servants—me, your maidservant, and the young man with us. We don't need anything."

²⁰"You are welcome at my house," the old man said. "Let me supply whatever you need. Only don't spend the night in the square." ²¹So he took him into his house and fed his donkeys. After they had washed their feet, they had something to eat and drink.

²²While they were enjoying themselves, some of the wicked men of the city surrounded the house. Pounding on the door, they shouted to the old man who owned the house, "Bring out the man who came to your house so we can have sex with him."

²³The owner of the house went outside and said to them, "No, my friends, don't be so vile. Since this man is my guest, don't do this disgraceful thing. ²⁴Look, here is my virgin daughter, and his concubine. I will bring them out to you now, and you can use them and do to them whatever you wish. But to this man, don't do such a disgraceful thing."

²⁵But the men would not listen to him. So the man took his concubine and sent her outside to them, and they raped her

and abused her throughout the night, and at dawn they let her go. 26At daybreak the woman went back to the house where her master was staying, fell down at the door and lay there until daylight.

27When her master got up in the morning and opened the door of the house and stepped out to continue on his way, there lay his concubine, fallen in the doorway of the house, with her hands on the threshold. 28He said to her, "Get up; let's go." But there was no answer. Then the man put her on his donkey and set out for home.

29When he reached home, he took a knife and cut up his concubine, limb by limb, into twelve parts and sent them into all the areas of Israel. 30Everyone who saw it said, "Such a thing has never been seen or done, not since the day the Israelites came up out of Egypt. Think about it! Consider it! Tell us what to do!"

Israelites Fight the Benjamites

20 Then all the Israelites from Dan to Beersheba and from the land of Gilead came out as one man and assembled before the LORD in Mizpah. 2The leaders of all the people of the tribes of Israel took their places in the assembly of the people of God, four hundred thousand soldiers armed with swords. 3(The Benjamites heard that the Israelites had gone up to Mizpah.) Then the Israelites said, "Tell us how this awful thing happened."

4So the Levite, the husband of the murdered woman, said, "I and my concubine came to Gibeah in Benjamin to spend the night. 5During the night the men of Gibeah came after me and surrounded the house, intending to kill me. They raped my concubine, and she died. 6I took my concubine, cut her into pieces and sent one piece to each region of Israel's inheritance, because they committed this lewd and disgraceful act in Israel. 7Now, all you Israelites, speak up and give your verdict."

8All the people rose as one man, saying,

"None of us will go home. No, not one of us will return to his house. 9But now this is what we'll do to Gibeah: We'll go up against it as the lot directs. 10We'll take ten men out of every hundred from all the tribes of Israel, and a hundred from a thousand, and a thousand from ten thousand, to get provisions for the army. Then, when the army arrives at Gibeah*a* in Benjamin, it can give them what they deserve for all this vileness done in Israel." 11So all the men of Israel got together and united as one man against the city.

12The tribes of Israel sent men throughout the tribe of Benjamin, saying, "What about this awful crime that was committed among you? 13Now surrender those wicked men of Gibeah so that we may put them to death and purge the evil from Israel."

But the Benjamites would not listen to their fellow Israelites. 14From their towns they came together at Gibeah to fight against the Israelites. 15At once the Benjamites mobilised twenty-six thousand swordsmen from their towns, in addition to seven hundred chosen men from those living in Gibeah. 16Among all these soldiers there were seven hundred chosen men who were left-handed, each of whom could sling a stone at a hair and not miss.

17Israel, apart from Benjamin, mustered four hundred thousand swordsmen, all of them fighting men.

18The Israelites went up to Bethel*b* and enquired of God. They said, "Who of us shall go first to fight against the Benjamites?"

The LORD replied, "Judah shall go first."

19The next morning the Israelites got up and pitched camp near Gibeah. 20The men of Israel went out to fight the Benjamites and took up battle positions against them at Gibeah. 21The Benjamites came out of Gibeah and cut down twenty-two thousand Israelites on the battlefield that day. 22But the men of Israel encouraged one another and again took up their

---

*a*10 One Hebrew manuscript; most Hebrew manuscripts *Geba*, a variant of *Gibeah*
*b*18 Or *to the house of God*; also in verse 26

positions where they had stationed themselves the first day. ²³The Israelites went up and wept before the LORD until evening, and they enquired of the LORD. They said, "Shall we go up again to battle against the Benjamites, our brothers?"

The LORD answered, "Go up against them."

²⁴Then the Israelites drew near to Benjamin the second day. ²⁵This time, when the Benjamites came out from Gibeah to oppose them, they cut down another eighteen thousand Israelites, all of them armed with swords.

²⁶Then the Israelites, all the people, went up to Bethel, and there they sat weeping before the LORD. They fasted that day until evening and presented burnt offerings and fellowship offerings^c to the LORD. ²⁷And the Israelites enquired of the LORD. (In those days the ark of the covenant of God was there, ²⁸with Phinehas son of Eleazar, the son of Aaron, ministering before it.) They asked, "Shall we go up again to battle with Benjamin our brother, or not?"

The LORD responded, "Go, for tomorrow I will give them into your hands."

²⁹Then Israel set an ambush around Gibeah. ³⁰They went up against the Benjamites on the third day and took up positions against Gibeah as they had done before. ³¹The Benjamites came out to meet them and were drawn away from the city. They began to inflict casualties on the Israelites as before, so that about thirty men fell in the open field and on the roads—the one leading to Bethel and the other to Gibeah.

³²While the Benjamites were saying, "We are defeating them as before," the Israelites were saying, "Let's retreat and draw them away from the city to the roads."

³³All the men of Israel moved from their places and took up positions at Baal Tamar, and the Israelite ambush charged out of its place on the west^d of Gibeah.^e ³⁴Then ten thousand of Israel's finest men made a frontal attack on Gibeah. The fighting was so heavy that the Benjamites did not realise how near disaster was. ³⁵The LORD defeated Benjamin before Israel, and on that day the Israelites struck down 25,100 Benjamites, all armed with swords. ³⁶Then the Benjamites saw that they were beaten.

Now the men of Israel had given way before Benjamin, because they relied on the ambush they had set near Gibeah. ³⁷The men who had been in ambush made a sudden dash into Gibeah, spread out and put the whole city to the sword. ³⁸The men of Israel had arranged with the ambush that they should send up a great cloud of smoke from the city, ³⁹and then the men of Israel would turn in the battle.

The Benjamites had begun to inflict casualties on the men of Israel (about thirty), and they said, "We are defeating them as in the first battle." ⁴⁰But when the column of smoke began to rise from the city, the Benjamites turned and saw the smoke of the whole city going up into the sky. ⁴¹Then the men of Israel turned on them, and the men of Benjamin were terrified, because they realised that disaster had come upon them. ⁴²So they fled before the Israelites in the direction of the desert, but they could not escape the battle. And the men of Israel who came out of the towns cut them down there. ⁴³They surrounded the Benjamites, chased them and easily^f overran them in the vicinity of Gibeah on the east. ⁴⁴Eighteen thousand Benjamites fell, all of them valiant fighters. ⁴⁵As they turned and fled towards the desert to the rock of Rimmon, the Israelites cut down five thousand men along the roads. They kept pressing after the Benjamites as far as Gidom and struck down two thousand more.

⁴⁶On that day twenty-five thousand Benjamite swordsmen fell, all of them valiant fighters. ⁴⁷But six hundred men turned and fled into the desert to the rock of Rimmon, where they stayed for four months. ⁴⁸The men of Israel went back to Benjamin and put all the towns to the

^c26 Traditionally peace offerings
^d33 Some Septuagint manuscripts and Vulgate; the meaning of the Hebrew for this word is uncertain.
^e33 Hebrew Geba, a variant of Gibeah   ^f43 The meaning of the Hebrew for this word is uncertain.

sword, including the animals and everything else they found. All the towns they came across they set on fire.

Wives for the Benjamites

21 The men of Israel had taken an oath at Mizpah: "Not one of us will give his daughter in marriage to a Benjamite."

[2] The people went to Bethel,[a] where they sat before God until evening, raising their voices and weeping bitterly. [3] "O LORD, the God of Israel," they cried, "why has this happened to Israel? Why should one tribe be missing from Israel today?"

[4] Early the next day the people built an altar and presented burnt offerings and fellowship offerings.[b]

[5] Then the Israelites asked, "Who from all the tribes of Israel has failed to assemble before the LORD?" For they had taken a solemn oath that anyone who failed to assemble before the LORD at Mizpah should certainly be put to death.

[6] Now the Israelites grieved for their brothers, the Benjamites. "Today one tribe is cut off from Israel," they said. [7] "How can we provide wives for those who are left, since we have taken an oath by the LORD not to give them any of our daughters in marriage?" [8] Then they asked, "Which one of the tribes of Israel failed to assemble before the LORD at Mizpah?" They discovered that no-one from Jabesh Gilead had come to the camp for the assembly. [9] For when they counted the people, they found that none of the people of Jabesh Gilead were there.

[10] So the assembly sent twelve thousand fighting men with instructions to go to Jabesh Gilead and put to the sword those living there, including the women and children. [11] "This is what you are to do," they said. "Kill every male and every woman who is not a virgin." [12] They found among the people living in Jabesh Gilead

four hundred young women who had never slept with a man, and they took them to the camp at Shiloh in Canaan.

[13] Then the whole assembly sent an offer of peace to the Benjamites at the rock of Rimmon. [14] So the Benjamites returned at that time and were given the women of Jabesh Gilead who had been spared. But there were not enough for all of them.

[15] The people grieved for Benjamin, because the LORD had made a gap in the tribes of Israel. [16] And the elders of the assembly said, "With the women of Benjamin destroyed, how shall we provide wives for the men who are left? [17] The Benjamite survivors must have heirs," they said, "so that a tribe of Israel will not be wiped out. [18] We can't give them our daughters as wives, since we Israelites have taken this oath: 'Cursed be anyone who gives a wife to a Benjamite.' [19] But look, there is the annual festival of the LORD in Shiloh, to the north of Bethel, and east of the road that goes from Bethel to Shechem, and to the south of Lebonah."

[20] So they instructed the Benjamites, saying, "Go and hide in the vineyards [21] and watch. When the girls of Shiloh come out to join in the dancing, then rush from the vineyards and each of you seize a wife from the girls of Shiloh and go to the land of Benjamin. [22] When their fathers or brothers complain to us, we will say to them, 'Do us a kindness by helping them, because we did not get wives for them during the war, and you are innocent, since you did not give your daughters to them.'"

[23] So that is what the Benjamites did. While the girls were dancing, each man caught one and carried her off to be his wife. Then they returned to their inheritance and rebuilt the towns and settled in them.

[24] At that time the Israelites left that place and went home to their tribes and clans, each to his own inheritance.

[25] In those days Israel had no king; everyone did as he saw fit.

---

a2 Or *to the house of God*   *b4* Traditionally *peace offerings*

Ruth

Naomi and Ruth

1 In the days when the judges ruled,[a] there was a famine in the land, and a man from Bethlehem in Judah, together with his wife and two sons, went to live for a while in the country of Moab. ²The man's name was Elimelech, his wife's name Naomi, and the names of his two sons were Mahlon and Kilion. They were Ephrathites from Bethlehem, Judah. And they went to Moab and lived there.

³Now Elimelech, Naomi's husband, died, and she was left with her two sons. ⁴They married Moabite women, one named Orpah and the other Ruth. After they had lived there about ten years, ⁵both Mahlon and Kilion also died, and Naomi was left without her two sons and her husband.

⁶When she heard in Moab that the LORD had come to the aid of his people by providing food for them, Naomi and her daughters-in-law prepared to return home from there. ⁷With her two daughters-in-law she left the place where she had been living and set out on the road that would take them back to the land of Judah.

⁸Then Naomi said to her two daughters-in-law, "Go back, each of you, to your mother's home. May the LORD show kindness to you, as you have shown to your dead and to me. ⁹May the LORD grant that each of you will find rest in the home of another husband."

Then she kissed them and they wept aloud ¹⁰and said to her, "We will go back with you to your people."

¹¹But Naomi said, "Return home, my daughters. Why would you come with me? Am I going to have any more sons, who could become your husbands? ¹²Return home, my daughters; I am too old to have another husband. Even if I thought there was still hope for me—even if I had a husband tonight and then gave birth to sons—¹³would you wait until they grew up? Would you remain unmarried for them? No, my daughters. It is more bitter for me than for you, because the LORD's hand has gone out against me!"

¹⁴At this they wept again. Then Orpah kissed her mother-in-law good-bye, but Ruth clung to her.

¹⁵"Look," said Naomi, "your sister-in-law is going back to her people and her gods. Go back with her."

¹⁶But Ruth replied, "Don't urge me to leave you or to turn back from you. Where you go I will go, and where you stay I will stay. Your people will be my people and your God my God. ¹⁷Where you die I will die, and there I will be buried. May the LORD deal with me, be it ever so severely, if anything but death separates you and me." ¹⁸When Naomi realised that Ruth was determined to go with her, she stopped urging her.

¹⁹So the two women went on until they came to Bethlehem. When they arrived in Bethlehem, the whole town was stirred because of them, and the women exclaimed, "Can this be Naomi?"

²⁰"Don't call me Naomi,"[b] she told them. "Call me Mara,[c] because the

---

[a]1 Traditionally *judged*   [b]20 *Naomi* means *pleasant*; also in verse 21.   [c]20 *Mara* means *bitter*.

Almighty*d* has made my life very bitter. ²¹I went away full, but the LORD has brought me back empty. Why call me Naomi? The LORD has afflicted*e* me; the Almighty has brought misfortune upon me.''

²²So Naomi returned from Moab accompanied by Ruth the Moabitess, her daughter-in-law, arriving in Bethlehem as the barley harvest was beginning.

Ruth Meets Boaz

2 Now Naomi had a relative on her husband's side from the clan of Elimelech, a man of standing, whose name was Boaz.

²And Ruth the Moabitess said to Naomi, ''Let me go to the fields and pick up the leftover grain behind anyone in whose eyes I find favour.''

Naomi said to her, ''Go ahead, my daughter.'' ³So she went out and began to glean in the fields behind the harvesters. As it turned out, she found herself working in a field belonging to Boaz, who was from the clan of Elimelech.

⁴Just then Boaz arrived from Bethlehem and greeted the harvesters, ''The LORD be with you!''

''The LORD bless you!'' they called back.

⁵Boaz asked the foreman of his harvesters, ''Whose young woman is that?''

⁶The foreman replied, ''She is the Moabitess who came back from Moab with Naomi. ⁷She said, 'Please let me glean and gather among the sheaves behind the harvesters.' She went into the field and has worked steadily from morning till now, except for a short rest in the shelter.''

⁸So Boaz said to Ruth, ''My daughter, listen to me. Don't go and glean in another field and don't go away from here. Stay here with my servant girls. ⁹Watch the field where the men are harvesting, and follow along after the girls. I have told the men not to touch you. And whenever you are thirsty, go and get a drink from the water jars the men have filled.''

¹⁰At this, she bowed down with her face to the ground. She exclaimed, ''Why have I found such favour in your eyes that you notice me—a foreigner?''

¹¹Boaz replied, ''I've been told all about what you have done for your mother-in-law since the death of your husband—how you left your father and mother and your homeland and came to live with a people you did not know before. ¹²May the LORD repay you for what you have done. May you be richly rewarded by the LORD, the God of Israel, under whose wings you have come to take refuge.''

¹³''May I continue to find favour in your eyes, my lord,'' she said. ''You have given me comfort and have spoken kindly to your servant—though I do not have the standing of one of your servant girls.''

¹⁴At mealtime Boaz said to her, ''Come over here. Have some bread and dip it in the wine vinegar.''

When she sat down with the harvesters, he offered her some roasted grain. She ate all she wanted and had some left over. ¹⁵As she got up to glean, Boaz gave orders to his men, ''Even if she gathers among the sheaves, don't embarrass her. ¹⁶Rather, pull out some stalks for her from the bundles and leave them for her to pick up, and don't rebuke her.''

¹⁷So Ruth gleaned in the field until evening. Then she threshed the barley she had gathered, and it amounted to about an ephah.*a* ¹⁸She carried it back to town, and her mother-in-law saw how much she had gathered. Ruth also brought out and gave her what she had left over after she had eaten enough.

¹⁹Her mother-in-law asked her, ''Where did you glean today? Where did you work? Blessed be the man who took notice of you!''

Then Ruth told her mother-in-law about the one at whose place she had been working. ''The name of the man I worked with today is Boaz,'' she said.

²⁰''The LORD bless him!'' Naomi said to her daughter-in-law. ''He has not stopped showing his kindness to the living and the dead.'' She added, ''That man is our

---

d20 Hebrew *Shaddai*; also in verse 21   *e21* Or *has testified against*
a17 That is, probably about ⅗ bushel (about 22 litres)

close relative; he is one of our kinsman-redeemers.''

²¹Then Ruth the Moabitess said, "He even said to me, 'Stay with my workers until they finish harvesting all my grain.'''

²²Naomi said to Ruth her daughter-in-law, "It will be good for you, my daughter, to go with his girls, because in someone else's field you might be harmed.''

²³So Ruth stayed close to the servant girls of Boaz to glean until the barley and wheat harvests were finished. And she lived with her mother-in-law.

Ruth and Boaz at the Threshing-Floor

3 One day Naomi her mother-in-law said to her, "My daughter, should I not try to find a home*a* for you, where you will be well provided for? ²Is not Boaz, with whose servant girls you have been, a kinsman of ours? Tonight he will be winnowing barley on the threshing-floor. ³Wash and perfume yourself, and put on your best clothes. Then go down to the threshing-floor, but don't let him know you are there until he has finished eating and drinking. ⁴When he lies down, note the place where he is lying. Then go and uncover his feet and lie down. He will tell you what to do.''

⁵"I will do whatever you say," Ruth answered. ⁶So she went down to the threshing-floor and did everything her mother-in-law told her to do.

⁷When Boaz had finished eating and drinking and was in good spirits, he went over to lie down at the far end of the grain pile. Ruth approached quietly, uncovered his feet and lay down. ⁸In the middle of the night something startled the man, and he turned and discovered a woman lying at his feet.

⁹"Who are you?" he asked.

"I am your servant Ruth," she said. "Spread the corner of your garment over me, since you are a kinsman-redeemer.''

¹⁰"The LORD bless you, my daughter," he replied. "This kindness is greater than that which you showed earlier: You have

not run after the younger men, whether rich or poor. ¹¹And now, my daughter, don't be afraid. I will do for you all you ask. All my fellow townsmen know that you are a woman of noble character. ¹²Although it is true that I am near of kin, there is a kinsman-redeemer nearer than I. ¹³Stay here for the night, and in the morning if he wants to redeem, good; let him redeem. But if he is not willing, as surely as the LORD lives I will do it. Lie here until morning.''

¹⁴So she lay at his feet until morning, but got up before anyone could be recognised; and he said, "Don't let it be known that a woman came to the threshing-floor.''

¹⁵He also said, "Bring me the shawl you are wearing and hold it out." When she did so, he poured into it six measures of barley and put it on her. Then he*b* went back to town.

¹⁶When Ruth came to her mother-in-law, Naomi asked, "How did it go, my daughter?''

Then she told her everything Boaz had done for her ¹⁷and added, "He gave me these six measures of barley, saying, 'Don't go back to your mother-in-law empty-handed.'''

¹⁸Then Naomi said, "Wait, my daughter, until you find out what happens. For the man will not rest until the matter is settled today.''

Boaz Marries Ruth

4 Meanwhile Boaz went up to the town gate and sat there. When the kinsman-redeemer he had mentioned came along, Boaz said, "Come over here, my friend, and sit down." So he went over and sat down.

²Boaz took ten of the elders of the town and said, "Sit here," and they did so. ³Then he said to the kinsman-redeemer, "Naomi, who has come back from Moab, is selling the piece of land that belonged to our brother Elimelech. ⁴I thought I should bring the matter to your attention and

---

a1 Hebrew *find rest* (see Ruth 1:9)
b15 Most Hebrew manuscripts; many Hebrew manuscripts, Vulgate and Syriac *she*

suggest that you buy it in the presence of these seated here and in the presence of the elders of my people. If you will redeem it, do so. But if you[a] will not, tell me, so that I will know. For no-one has the right to do it except you, and I am next in line.'

"I will redeem it," he said.

5Then Boaz said, "On the day you buy the land from Naomi and from Ruth the Moabitess, you acquire[b] the dead man's widow, in order to maintain the name of the dead with his property."

6At this, the kinsman-redeemer said, "Then I cannot redeem it because I might endanger my own estate. You redeem it yourself. I cannot do it."

7(Now in earlier times in Israel, for the redemption and transfer of property to become final, one party took off his sandal and gave it to the other. This was the method of legalising transactions in Israel.)

8So the kinsman-redeemer said to Boaz, "Buy it yourself." And he removed his sandal.

9Then Boaz announced to the elders and all the people, "Today you are witnesses that I have bought from Naomi all the property of Elimelech, Kilion and Mahlon. 10I have also acquired Ruth the Moabitess, Mahlon's widow, as my wife, in order to maintain the name of the dead with his property, so that his name will not disappear from among his family or from the town records. Today you are witnesses!"

11Then the elders and all those at the gate said, "We are witnesses. May the LORD make the woman who is coming into your home like Rachel and Leah, who together built up the house of Israel. May you have standing in Ephrathah and be famous in Bethlehem. 12Through the offspring the LORD gives you by this young woman, may your family be like that of Perez, whom Tamar bore to Judah."

The Genealogy of David

13So Boaz took Ruth and she became his wife. Then he went to her, and the LORD enabled her to conceive, and she gave birth to a son. 14The women said to Naomi: "Praise be to the LORD, who this day has not left you without a kinsman-redeemer. May he become famous throughout Israel! 15He will renew your life and sustain you in your old age. For your daughter-in-law, who loves you and who is better to you than seven sons, has given him birth."

16Then Naomi took the child, laid him in her lap and cared for him. 17The women living there said, "Naomi has a son." And they named him Obed. He was the father of Jesse, the father of David.

18This, then, is the family line of Perez:

Perez was the father of Hezron,
19Hezron the father of Ram,
Ram the father of Amminadab,
20Amminadab the father of Nahshon,
Nahshon the father of Salmon,[c]
21Salmon the father of Boaz,
Boaz the father of Obed,
22Obed the father of Jesse,
and Jesse the father of David.

---

a4 Many Hebrew manuscripts, Septuagint, Vulgate and Syriac; most Hebrew manuscripts he
b5 Hebrew; Vulgate and Syriac Naomi, you acquire Ruth the Moabitess,
c20 A few Hebrew manuscripts, some Septuagint manuscripts and Vulgate (see also verse 21 and Septuagint of 1 Chron. 2:11); most Hebrew manuscripts Salma

1 Samuel

The Birth of Samuel

1 There was a certain man from Ramathaim, a Zuphite[a] from the hill country of Ephraim, whose name was Elkanah son of Jeroham, the son of Elihu, the son of Tohu, the son of Zuph, an Ephraimite. [2]He had two wives; one was called Hannah and the other Peninnah. Peninnah had children, but Hannah had none.

[3]Year after year this man went up from his town to worship and sacrifice to the LORD Almighty at Shiloh, where Hophni and Phinehas, the two sons of Eli, were priests of the LORD. [4]Whenever the day came for Elkanah to sacrifice, he would give portions of the meat to his wife Peninnah and to all her sons and daughters. [5]But to Hannah he gave a double portion because he loved her, and the LORD had closed her womb. [6]And because the LORD had closed her womb, her rival kept provoking her in order to irritate her. [7]This went on year after year. Whenever Hannah went up to the house of the LORD, her rival provoked her till she wept and would not eat. [8]Elkanah her husband would say to her, "Hannah, why are you weeping? Why don't you eat? Why are you downhearted? Don't I mean more to you than ten sons?"

[9]Once when they had finished eating and drinking in Shiloh, Hannah stood up. Now Eli the priest was sitting on a chair by the doorpost of the LORD's temple.[b] [10]In bitterness of soul Hannah wept much and prayed to the LORD. [11]And she made a vow, saying, "O LORD Almighty, if you will only look upon your servant's misery and remember me, and not forget your servant but give her a son, then I will give him to the LORD for all the days of his life, and no razor will ever be used on his head."

[12]As she kept on praying to the LORD, Eli observed her mouth. [13]Hannah was praying in her heart, and her lips were moving but her voice was not heard. Eli thought she was drunk [14]and said to her, "How long will you keep on getting drunk? Get rid of your wine."

[15]"Not so, my lord," Hannah replied, "I am a woman who is deeply troubled. I have not been drinking wine or beer; I was pouring out my soul to the LORD. [16]Do not take your servant for a wicked woman; I have been praying here out of my great anguish and grief."

[17]Eli answered, "Go in peace, and may the God of Israel grant you what you have asked of him."

[18]She said, "May your servant find favour in your eyes." Then she went her way and ate something, and her face was no longer downcast.

[19]Early the next morning they arose and worshipped before the LORD and then went back to their home at Ramah. Elkanah lay with Hannah his wife, and the LORD remembered her. [20]So in the course of time Hannah conceived and gave birth to a son. She named him Samuel,[c] saying, "Because I asked the LORD for him."

[a]1 Or *from Ramathaim Zuphim*   [b]9 That is, tabernacle   [c]20 *Samuel* sounds like the Hebrew for *heard of God*.

Hannah Dedicates Samuel

²¹When the man Elkanah went up with all his family to offer the annual sacrifice to the LORD and to fulfil his vow, ²²Hannah did not go. She said to her husband, "After the boy is weaned, I will take him and present him before the LORD, and he will live there always."

²³"Do what seems best to you," Elkanah her husband told her. "Stay here until you have weaned him; only may the LORD make good his*d* word." So the woman stayed at home and nursed her son until she had weaned him.

²⁴After he was weaned, she took the boy with her, young as he was, along with a three-year-old bull,*e* an ephah*f* of flour and a skin of wine, and brought him to the house of the LORD at Shiloh. ²⁵When they had slaughtered the bull, they brought the boy to Eli, ²⁶and she said to him, "As surely as you live, my lord, I am the woman who stood here beside you praying to the LORD. ²⁷I prayed for this child, and the LORD has granted me what I asked of him. ²⁸So now I give him to the LORD. For his whole life he shall be given over to the LORD." And he worshipped the LORD there.

Hannah's Prayer

2 Then Hannah prayed and said:

"My heart rejoices in the LORD;
    in the LORD my horn*a* is lifted high.
My mouth boasts over my enemies,
    for I delight in your deliverance.

²"There is no-one holy*b* like the LORD;
    there is no-one besides you;
    there is no Rock like our God.

³"Do not keep talking so proudly
    or let your mouth speak such arrogance,
for the LORD is a God who knows,
    and by him deeds are weighed.

⁴"The bows of the warriors are broken,
    but those who stumbled are armed with strength.
⁵Those who were full hire themselves out for food,
    but those who were hungry hunger no more.
She who was barren has borne seven children,
    but she who has had many sons pines away.

⁶"The LORD brings death and makes alive;
    he brings down to the grave*c* and raises up.
⁷The LORD sends poverty and wealth;
    he humbles and he exalts.
⁸He raises the poor from the dust
    and lifts the needy from the ash heap;
he seats them with princes
    and has them inherit a throne of honour.

"For the foundations of the earth are the LORD's;
    upon them he has set the world.
⁹He will guard the feet of his saints,
    but the wicked will be silenced in darkness.

"It is not by strength that one prevails;
10   those who oppose the LORD will be shattered.
He will thunder against them from heaven;
    the LORD will judge the ends of the earth.

"He will give strength to his king
    and exalt the horn of his anointed."

¹¹Then Elkanah went home to Ramah, but the boy ministered before the LORD under Eli the priest.

Eli's Wicked Sons

¹²Eli's sons were wicked men; they had no regard for the LORD. ¹³Now it was the

---

d23 Masoretic Text; Dead Sea Scrolls, Septuagint and Syriac *your*
e24 Dead Sea Scrolls, Septuagint and Syriac; Masoretic Text *with three bulls*
f24 That is, probably about ⅗ bushel (about 22 litres)   *a1* *Horn* here symbolises strength; also in verse 10.
b2 Or *no Holy One*   *c6* Hebrew *Sheol*

practice of the priests with the people that whenever anyone offered a sacrifice and while the meat was being boiled, the servant of the priest would come with a three-pronged fork in his hand. ¹⁴He would plunge it into the pan or kettle or cauldron or pot, and the priest would take for himself whatever the fork brought up. This is how they treated all the Israelites who came to Shiloh. ¹⁵But even before the fat was burned, the servant of the priest would come and say to the man who was sacrificing, "Give the priest some meat to roast; he won't accept boiled meat from you, but only raw."

¹⁶If the man said to him, "Let the fat be burned up first, and then take whatever you want," the servant would then answer, "No, hand it over now; if you don't, I'll take it by force."

¹⁷This sin of the young men was very great in the LORD's sight, for they*d* were treating the LORD's offering with contempt.

¹⁸But Samuel was ministering before the LORD—a boy wearing a linen ephod. ¹⁹Each year his mother made him a little robe and took it to him when she went up with her husband to offer the annual sacrifice. ²⁰Eli would bless Elkanah and his wife, saying, "May the LORD give you children by this woman to take the place of the one she prayed for and gave to the LORD." Then they would go home. ²¹And the LORD was gracious to Hannah; she conceived and gave birth to three sons and two daughters. Meanwhile, the boy Samuel grew up in the presence of the LORD.

²²Now Eli, who was very old, heard about everything his sons were doing to all Israel and how they slept with the women who served at the entrance to the Tent of Meeting. ²³So he said to them, "Why do you do such things? I hear from all the people about these wicked deeds of yours. ²⁴No, my sons; it is not a good report that I hear spreading among the LORD's people. ²⁵If a man sins against another man, God*e* may mediate for him; but if a man sins against the LORD, who will intercede for

him?" His sons, however, did not listen to their father's rebuke, for it was the LORD's will to put them to death.

²⁶And the boy Samuel continued to grow in stature and in favour with the LORD and with men.

Prophecy Against the House of Eli

²⁷Now a man of God came to Eli and said to him, "This is what the LORD says: 'Did I not clearly reveal myself to your father's house when they were in Egypt under Pharaoh? ²⁸I chose your father out of all the tribes of Israel to be my priest, to go up to my altar, to burn incense, and to wear an ephod in my presence. I also gave your father's house all the offerings made with fire by the Israelites. ²⁹Why do you*f* scorn my sacrifice and offering that I prescribed for my dwelling? Why do you honour your sons more than me by fattening yourselves on the choice parts of every offering made by my people Israel?'

³⁰"Therefore the LORD, the God of Israel, declares: 'I promised that your house and your father's house would minister before me for ever.' But now the LORD declares: 'Far be it from me! Those who honour me I will honour, but those who despise me will be disdained. ³¹The time is coming when I will cut short your strength and the strength of your father's house, so that there will not be an old man in your family line ³²and you will see distress in my dwelling. Although good will be done to Israel, in your family line there will never be an old man. ³³Every one of you that I do not cut off from my altar will be spared only to blind your eyes with tears and to grieve your heart, and all your descendants will die in the prime of life.

³⁴"'And what happens to your two sons, Hophni and Phinehas, will be a sign to you—they will both die on the same day. ³⁵I will raise up for myself a faithful priest, who will do according to what is in my heart and mind. I will firmly establish his house, and he will minister before my anointed one always. ³⁶Then everyone left in your family line will come and bow

---

d17 Or men   e25 Or the judges   f29 The Hebrew is plural.

down before him for a piece of silver and a crust of bread and plead, "Appoint me to some priestly office so that I can have food to eat.""'

The LORD Calls Samuel

3 The boy Samuel ministered before the LORD under Eli. In those days the word of the LORD was rare; there were not many visions.

2One night Eli, whose eyes were becoming so weak that he could barely see, was lying down in his usual place. 3The lamp of God had not yet gone out, and Samuel was lying down in the temple*a* of the LORD, where the ark of God was. 4Then the LORD called Samuel.

Samuel answered, "Here I am." 5And he ran to Eli and said, "Here I am; you called me."

But Eli said, "I did not call; go back and lie down." So he went and lay down.

6Again the LORD called, "Samuel!" And Samuel got up and went to Eli and said, "Here I am; you called me."

"My son," Eli said, "I did not call; go back and lie down."

7Now Samuel did not yet know the LORD: The word of the LORD had not yet been revealed to him.

8The LORD called Samuel a third time, and Samuel got up and went to Eli and said, "Here I am; you called me."

Then Eli realised that the LORD was calling the boy. 9So Eli told Samuel, "Go and lie down, and if he calls you, say, 'Speak, LORD, for your servant is listening.'" So Samuel went and lay down in his place.

10The LORD came and stood there, calling as at the other times, "Samuel! Samuel!"

Then Samuel said, "Speak, for your servant is listening."

11And the LORD said to Samuel: "See, I am about to do something in Israel that will make the ears of everyone who hears of it tingle. 12At that time I will carry out against Eli everything I spoke against his

family—from beginning to end. 13For I told him that I would judge his family for ever because of the sin he knew about; his sons made themselves contemptible,*b* and he failed to restrain them. 14Therefore, I swore to the house of Eli, 'The guilt of Eli's house will never be atoned for by sacrifice or offering.'"

15Samuel lay down until morning and then opened the doors of the house of the LORD. He was afraid to tell Eli the vision, 16but Eli called him and said, "Samuel, my son."

Samuel answered, "Here I am."

17"What was it he said to you?" Eli asked. "Do not hide it from me. May God deal with you, be it ever so severely, if you hide from me anything he told you." 18So Samuel told him everything, hiding nothing from him. Then Eli said, "He is the LORD; let him do what is good in his eyes."

19The LORD was with Samuel as he grew up, and he let none of his words fall to the ground. 20And all Israel from Dan to Beersheba recognised that Samuel was attested as a prophet of the LORD. 21The LORD continued to appear at Shiloh, and there he revealed himself to Samuel through his word.

4 And Samuel's word came to all Israel.

The Philistines Capture the Ark

Now the Israelites went out to fight against the Philistines. The Israelites camped at Ebenezer, and the Philistines at Aphek. 2The Philistines deployed their forces to meet Israel, and as the battle spread, Israel was defeated by the Philistines, who killed about four thousand of them on the battlefield. 3When the soldiers returned to camp, the elders of Israel asked, "Why did the LORD bring defeat upon us today before the Philistines? Let us bring the ark of the LORD's covenant from Shiloh, so that it*a* may go with us and save us from the hand of our enemies."

4So the people sent men to Shiloh, and they brought back the ark of the covenant

---

*a*3 That is, tabernacle
*b*13 Masoretic Text; an ancient Hebrew scribal tradition and Septuagint *sons blasphemed God*　　*a*3 Or he

of the Lord Almighty, who is enthroned between the cherubim. And Eli's two sons, Hophni and Phinehas, were there with the ark of the covenant of God.

[5]When the ark of the Lord's covenant came into the camp, all Israel raised such a great shout that the ground shook. [6]Hearing the uproar, the Philistines asked, "What's all this shouting in the Hebrew camp?"

When they learned that the ark of the Lord had come into the camp, [7]the Philistines were afraid. "A god has come into the camp," they said. "We're in trouble! Nothing like this has happened before. [8]Woe to us! Who will deliver us from the hand of these mighty gods? They are the gods who struck the Egyptians with all kinds of plagues in the desert. [9]Be strong, Philistines! Be men, or you will be subject to the Hebrews, as they have been to you. Be men, and fight!"

[10]So the Philistines fought, and the Israelites were defeated and every man fled to his tent. The slaughter was very great; Israel lost thirty thousand foot soldiers. [11]The ark of God was captured, and Eli's two sons, Hophni and Phinehas, died.

Death of Eli

[12]That same day a Benjamite ran from the battle line and went to Shiloh, his clothes torn and dust on his head. [13]When he arrived, there was Eli sitting on his chair by the side of the road, watching, because his heart feared for the ark of God. When the man entered the town and told what had happened, the whole town sent up a cry.

[14]Eli heard the outcry and asked, "What is the meaning of this uproar?"

The man hurried over to Eli, [15]who was ninety-eight years old and whose eyes were set so that he could not see. [16]He told Eli, "I have just come from the battle line; I fled from it this very day."

Eli asked, "What happened, my son?"

[17]The man who brought the news replied, "Israel fled before the Philistines,

and the army has suffered heavy losses. Also your two sons, Hophni and Phinehas, are dead, and the ark of God has been captured."

[18]When he mentioned the ark of God, Eli fell backwards off his chair by the side of the gate. His neck was broken and he died, for he was an old man and heavy. He had led[b] Israel for forty years.

[19]His daughter-in-law, the wife of Phinehas, was pregnant and near the time of delivery. When she heard the news that the ark of God had been captured and that her father-in-law and her husband were dead, she went into labour and gave birth, but was overcome by her labour pains. [20]As she was dying, the women attending her said, "Don't despair; you have given birth to a son." But she did not respond or pay any attention.

[21]She named the boy Ichabod,[c] saying, "The glory has departed from Israel"— because of the capture of the ark of God and the deaths of her father-in-law and her husband. [22]She said, "The glory has departed from Israel, for the ark of God has been captured."

The Ark in Ashdod and Ekron

5 After the Philistines had captured the ark of God, they took it from Ebenezer to Ashdod. [2]Then they carried the ark into Dagon's temple and set it beside Dagon. [3]When the people of Ashdod rose early the next day, there was Dagon, fallen on his face on the ground before the ark of the Lord! They took Dagon and put him back in his place. [4]But the following morning when they rose, there was Dagon, fallen on his face on the ground before the ark of the Lord! His head and hands had been broken off and were lying on the threshold; only his body remained. [5]That is why to this day neither the priests of Dagon nor any others who enter Dagon's temple at Ashdod step on the threshold.

[6]The Lord's hand was heavy upon the people of Ashdod and its vicinity; he brought devastation upon them and

---

b18 Traditionally judged   *c21 Ichabod means no glory.*

afflicted them with tumours.[a] [7]When the men of Ashdod saw what was happening, they said, "The ark of the god of Israel must not stay here with us, because his hand is heavy upon us and upon Dagon our god." [8]So they called together all the rulers of the Philistines and asked them, "What shall we do with the ark of the god of Israel?"

They answered, "Have the ark of the god of Israel moved to Gath." So they moved the ark of the God of Israel.

[9]But after they had moved it, the Lord's hand was against that city, throwing it into a great panic. He afflicted the people of the city, both young and old, with an outbreak of tumours.[b] [10]So they sent the ark of God to Ekron.

As the ark of God was entering Ekron, the people of Ekron cried out, "They have brought the ark of the god of Israel round to us to kill us and our people." [11]So they called together all the rulers of the Philistines and said, "Send the ark of the god of Israel away; let it go back to its own place, or it[c] will kill us and our people." For death had filled the city with panic; God's hand was very heavy upon it. [12]Those who did not die were afflicted with tumours, and the outcry of the city went up to heaven.

The Ark Returned to Israel

6 When the ark of the Lord had been in Philistine territory for seven months, [2]the Philistines called for the priests and the diviners and said, "What shall we do with the ark of the Lord? Tell us how we should send it back to its place."

[3]They answered, "If you return the ark of the god of Israel, do not send it away empty, but by all means send a guilt offering to him. Then you will be healed, and you will know why his hand has not been lifted from you."

[4]The Philistines asked, "What guilt offering should we send to him?"

They replied, "Five gold tumours and five gold rats, according to the number of the Philistine rulers, because the same plague has struck both you and your rulers. [5]Make models of the tumours and of the rats that are destroying the country, and pay honour to Israel's god. Perhaps he will lift his hand from you and your gods and your land. [6]Why do you harden your hearts as the Egyptians and Pharaoh did? When he[a] treated them harshly, did they not send the Israelites out so that they could go on their way?

[7]"Now then, get a new cart ready, with two cows that have calved and have never been yoked. Hitch the cows to the cart, but take their calves away and pen them up. [8]Take the ark of the Lord and put it on the cart, and in a chest beside it put the gold objects you are sending back to him as a guilt offering. Send it on its way, [9]but keep watching it. If it goes up to its own territory, towards Beth Shemesh, then the Lord has brought this great disaster on us. But if it does not, then we shall know that it was not his hand that struck us and that it happened to us by chance."

[10]So they did this. They took two such cows and hitched them to the cart and penned up their calves. [11]They placed the ark of the Lord on the cart and along with it the chest containing the gold rats and the models of the tumours. [12]Then the cows went straight up towards Beth Shemesh, keeping on the road and lowing all the way; they did not turn to the right or to the left. The rulers of the Philistines followed them as far as the border of Beth Shemesh.

[13]Now the people of Beth Shemesh were harvesting their wheat in the valley, and when they looked up and saw the ark, they rejoiced at the sight. [14]The cart came to the field of Joshua of Beth Shemesh, and there it stopped beside a large rock. The people chopped up the wood of the cart and sacrificed the cows as a burnt offering to the Lord. [15]The Levites took down the ark of the Lord, together with the chest containing the gold objects, and placed them on the large rock. On that day the people of Beth Shemesh offered burnt offerings and made sacrifices to the Lord. [16]The five rulers of the Philistines saw all

---

[a]6 Hebrew; Septuagint and Vulgate *tumours. And rats appeared in their land, and death and destruction were throughout the city*   [b]9 Or *with tumours in the groin* (see Septuagint)   [c]11 Or *he*   [a]6 That is, God

this and then returned that same day to Ekron.

[17]These are the gold tumours the Philistines sent as a guilt offering to the LORD—one each for Ashdod, Gaza, Ashkelon, Gath and Ekron. [18]And the number of the gold rats was according to the number of Philistine towns belonging to the five rulers—the fortified towns with their country villages. The large rock, on which[b] they set the ark of the LORD, is a witness to this day in the field of Joshua of Beth Shemesh.

[19]But God struck down some of the men of Beth Shemesh, putting seventy[c] of them to death because they had looked into the ark of the LORD. The people mourned because of the heavy blow the LORD had dealt them, [20]and the men of Beth Shemesh asked, "Who can stand in the presence of the LORD, this holy God? To whom will the ark go up from here?"

[21]Then they sent messengers to the people of Kiriath Jearim, saying, "The Philistines have returned the ark of the LORD. Come down and take it up to your place." [1]So the men of Kiriath Jearim came and took up the ark of the LORD. They took it to Abinadab's house on the hill and consecrated Eleazar his son to guard the ark of the LORD.

Samuel Subdues the Philistines at Mizpah

[2]It was a long time, twenty years in all, that the ark remained at Kiriath Jearim, and all the people of Israel mourned and sought after the LORD. [3]And Samuel said to the whole house of Israel, "If you are returning to the LORD with all your hearts, then rid yourselves of the foreign gods and the Ashtoreths and commit yourselves to the LORD and serve him only, and he will deliver you out of the hand of the Philistines." [4]So the Israelites put away their Baals and Ashtoreths, and served the LORD only.

[5]Then Samuel said, "Assemble all Israel at Mizpah and I will intercede with the LORD for you." [6]When they had assembled at Mizpah, they drew water and poured it out before the LORD. On that day they fasted and there they confessed, "We have sinned against the LORD." And Samuel was leader[a] of Israel at Mizpah.

[7]When the Philistines heard that Israel had assembled at Mizpah, the rulers of the Philistines came up to attack them. And when the Israelites heard of it, they were afraid because of the Philistines. [8]They said to Samuel, "Do not stop crying out to the LORD our God for us, that he may rescue us from the hand of the Philistines." [9]Then Samuel took a suckling lamb and offered it up as a whole burnt offering to the LORD. He cried out to the LORD on Israel's behalf, and the LORD answered him.

[10]While Samuel was sacrificing the burnt offering, the Philistines drew near to engage Israel in battle. But that day the LORD thundered with loud thunder against the Philistines and threw them into such a panic that they were routed before the Israelites. [11]The men of Israel rushed out of Mizpah and pursued the Philistines, slaughtering them along the way to a point below Beth Car.

[12]Then Samuel took a stone and set it up between Mizpah and Shen. He named it Ebenezer,[b] saying, "Thus far has the LORD helped us." [13]So the Philistines were subdued and did not invade Israelite territory again.

Throughout Samuel's lifetime, the hand of the LORD was against the Philistines. [14]The towns from Ekron to Gath that the Philistines had captured from Israel were restored to her, and Israel delivered the neighbouring territory from the power of the Philistines. And there was peace between Israel and the Amorites.

[15]Samuel continued as judge over Israel all the days of his life. [16]From year to year he went on a circuit from Bethel to Gilgal to Mizpah, judging Israel in all those places. [17]But he always went back to Ramah, where his home was, and there he also judged Israel. And he built an altar there to the LORD.

---

[b]18 A few Hebrew manuscripts (see also Septuagint); most Hebrew manuscripts *villages as far as Greater Abel, where*
[c]19 A few Hebrew manuscripts; most Hebrew manuscripts and Septuagint *50,070*   [a]6 Traditionally *judge*
[b]12 *Ebenezer* means *stone of help.*

Israel Asks for a King

8 When Samuel grew old, he appointed his sons as judges for Israel. ²The name of his firstborn was Joel and the name of his second was Abijah, and they served at Beersheba. ³But his sons did not walk in his ways. They turned aside after dishonest gain and accepted bribes and perverted justice.

⁴So all the elders of Israel gathered together and came to Samuel at Ramah. ⁵They said to him, "You are old, and your sons do not walk in your ways; now appoint a king to lead*a* us, such as all the other nations have."

⁶But when they said, "Give us a king to lead us," this displeased Samuel; so he prayed to the LORD. ⁷And the LORD told him: "Listen to all that the people are saying to you; it is not you they have rejected, but they have rejected me as their king. ⁸As they have done from the day I brought them up out of Egypt until this day, forsaking me and serving other gods, so they are doing to you. ⁹Now listen to them; but warn them solemnly and let them know what the king who will reign over them will do."

¹⁰Samuel told all the words of the LORD to the people who were asking him for a king. ¹¹He said, "This is what the king who will reign over you will do: He will take your sons and make them serve with his chariots and horses, and they will run in front of his chariots. ¹²Some he will assign to be commanders of thousands and commanders of fifties, and others to plough his ground and reap his harvest, and still others to make weapons of war and equipment for his chariots. ¹³He will take your daughters to be perfumers and cooks and bakers. ¹⁴He will take the best of your fields and vineyards and olive groves and give them to his attendants. ¹⁵He will take a tenth of your grain and of your vintage and give it to his officials and attendants. ¹⁶Your menservants and maidservants and the best of your cattle*b* and donkeys he will take for his own use. ¹⁷He will take a tenth of your flocks, and you yourselves

will become his slaves. ¹⁸When that day comes, you will cry out for relief from the king you have chosen, and the LORD will not answer you in that day."

¹⁹But the people refused to listen to Samuel. "No!" they said. "We want a king over us. ²⁰Then we shall be like all the other nations, with a king to lead us and to go out before us and fight our battles."

²¹When Samuel heard all that the people said, he repeated it before the LORD. ²²The LORD answered, "Listen to them and give them a king."

Then Samuel said to the men of Israel, "Everyone is to go back to his town."

Samuel Anoints Saul

9 There was a Benjamite, a man of standing, whose name was Kish son of Abiel, the son of Zeror, the son of Becorath, the son of Aphiah of Benjamin. ²He had a son named Saul, an impressive young man without equal among the Israelites—a head taller than any of the others.

³Now the donkeys belonging to Saul's father Kish were lost, and Kish said to his son Saul, "Take one of the servants with you and go and look for the donkeys." ⁴So he passed through the hill country of Ephraim and through the area around Shalisha, but they did not find them. They went on into the district of Shaalim, but the donkeys were not there. Then he passed through the territory of Benjamin, but they did not find them.

⁵When they reached the district of Zuph, Saul said to the servant who was with him, "Come, let's go back, or my father will stop thinking about the donkeys and start worrying about us."

⁶But the servant replied, "Look, in this town there is a man of God; he is highly respected, and everything he says comes true. Let's go there now. Perhaps he will tell us what way to take."

⁷Saul said to his servant, "If we go, what can we give the man? The food in our sacks is gone. We have no gift to take to the man of God. What do we have?"

---

a5 Traditionally *judge*; also in verses 6 and 20   *b16* Septuagint; Hebrew *young men*

[8]The servant answered him again. "Look," he said, "I have a quarter of a shekel[a] of silver. I will give it to the man of God so that he will tell us what way to take." [9](Formerly in Israel, if a man went to enquire of God, he would say, "Come, let us go to the seer," because the prophet of today used to be called a seer.)

[10]"Good," Saul said to his servant. "Come, let's go." So they set out for the town where the man of God was.

[11]As they were going up the hill to the town, they met some girls coming out to draw water, and they asked them, "Is the seer here?"

[12]"He is," they answered. "He's ahead of you. Hurry now; he has just come to our town today, for the people have a sacrifice at the high place. [13]As soon as you enter the town, you will find him before he goes up to the high place to eat. The people will not begin eating until he comes, because he must bless the sacrifice; afterwards, those who are invited will eat. Go up now; you should find him about this time."

[14]They went up to the town, and as they were entering it, there was Samuel, coming towards them on his way up to the high place.

[15]Now the day before Saul came, the LORD had revealed this to Samuel: [16]"About this time tomorrow I will send you a man from the land of Benjamin. Anoint him leader over my people Israel; he will deliver my people from the hand of the Philistines. I have looked upon my people, for their cry has reached me."

[17]When Samuel caught sight of Saul, the LORD said to him, "This is the man I spoke to you about; he will govern my people."

[18]Saul approached Samuel in the gateway and asked, "Would you please tell me where the seer's house is?"

[19]"I am the seer," Samuel replied. "Go up ahead of me to the high place, for today you are to eat with me, and in the morning I will let you go and will tell you all that is in your heart. [20]As for the donkeys you lost three days ago, do not worry about them; they have been found. And to whom is all the desire of Israel turned, if not to you and all your father's family?"

[21]Saul answered, "But am I not a Benjamite, from the smallest tribe of Israel, and is not my clan the least of all the clans of the tribe of Benjamin? Why do you say such a thing to me?"

[22]Then Samuel brought Saul and his servant into the hall and seated them at the head of those who were invited—about thirty in number. [23]Samuel said to the cook, "Bring the piece of meat I gave you, the one I told you to lay aside."

[24]So the cook took up the leg with what was on it and set it in front of Saul. Samuel said, "Here is what has been kept for you. Eat, because it was set aside for you for this occasion, from the time I said, 'I have invited guests.'" And Saul dined with Samuel that day.

[25]After they came down from the high place to the town, Samuel talked with Saul on the roof of his house. [26]They rose about daybreak and Samuel called to Saul on the roof, "Get ready, and I will send you on your way." When Saul got ready, he and Samuel went outside together. [27]As they were going down to the edge of the town, Samuel said to Saul, "Tell the servant to go on ahead of us"—and the servant did so—"but you stay here awhile, so that I may give you a message from God."

10 Then Samuel took a flask of oil and poured it on Saul's head and kissed him, saying, "Has not the LORD anointed you leader over his inheritance?[a] [2]When you leave me today, you will meet two men near Rachel's tomb, at Zelzah on the border of Benjamin. They will say to you, 'The donkeys you set out to look for have been found. And now your father has stopped thinking about them and is worried about you. He is asking, "What shall I do about my son?"'

[3]"Then you will go on from there until you reach the great tree of Tabor. Three men going up to God at Bethel will meet you there. One will be carrying three young goats, another three loaves of bread, and another a skin of wine. [4]They

---

[a]8 That is, about ¹⁄₁₀ ounce (about 3 grams)
[a]1 Hebrew; Septuagint and Vulgate *over his people Israel? You will reign over the LORD's people and save them from the power of their enemies round about. And this will be a sign to you that the LORD has anointed you leader over his inheritance:*

will greet you and offer you two loaves of bread, which you will accept from them.

5"After that you will go to Gibeah of God, where there is a Philistine outpost. As you approach the town, you will meet a procession of prophets coming down from the high place with lyres, tambourines, flutes and harps being played before them, and they will be prophesying. 6The Spirit of the LORD will come upon you in power, and you will prophesy with them; and you will be changed into a different person. 7Once these signs are fulfilled, do whatever your hand finds to do, for God is with you.

8"Go down ahead of me to Gilgal. I will surely come down to you to sacrifice burnt offerings and fellowship offerings,b but you must wait seven days until I come to you and tell you what you are to do."

Saul Made King

9As Saul turned to leave Samuel, God changed Saul's heart, and all these signs were fulfilled that day. 10When they arrived at Gibeah, a procession of prophets met him; the Spirit of God came upon him in power, and he joined in their prophesying. 11When all those who had formerly known him saw him prophesying with the prophets, they asked each other, "What is this that has happened to the son of Kish? Is Saul also among the prophets?"

12A man who lived there answered, "And who is their father?" So it became a saying: "Is Saul also among the prophets?" 13After Saul stopped prophesying, he went to the high place.

14Now Saul's uncle asked him and his servant, "Where have you been?"

"Looking for the donkeys," he said. "But when we saw they were not to be found, we went to Samuel."

15Saul's uncle said, "Tell me what Samuel said to you."

16Saul replied, "He assured us that the donkeys had been found." But he did not tell his uncle what Samuel had said about the kingship.

17Samuel summoned the people of Israel to the LORD at Mizpah 18and said to them, "This is what the LORD, the God of Israel, says: 'I brought Israel up out of Egypt, and I delivered you from the power of Egypt and all the kingdoms that oppressed you.' 19But you have now rejected your God, who saves you out of all your calamities and distresses. And you have said, 'No, set a king over us.' So now present yourselves before the LORD by your tribes and clans."

20When Samuel brought all the tribes of Israel near, the tribe of Benjamin was chosen. 21Then he brought forward the tribe of Benjamin, clan by clan, and Matri's clan was chosen. Finally Saul son of Kish was chosen. But when they looked for him, he was not to be found. 22So they enquired further of the LORD, "Has the man come here yet?"

And the LORD said, "Yes, he has hidden himself among the baggage."

23They ran and brought him out, and as he stood among the people he was a head taller than any of the others. 24Samuel said to all the people, "Do you see the man the LORD has chosen? There is no-one like him among all the people."

Then the people shouted, "Long live the king!"

25Samuel explained to the people the regulations of the kingship. He wrote them down on a scroll and deposited it before the LORD. Then Samuel dismissed the people, each to his own home.

26Saul also went to his home in Gibeah, accompanied by valiant men whose hearts God had touched. 27But some troublemakers said, "How can this fellow save us?" They despised him and brought him no gifts. But Saul kept silent.

Saul Rescues the City of Jabesh

11 Nahash the Ammonite went up and besieged Jabesh Gilead. And all the men of Jabesh said to him, "Make a treaty with us, and we will be subject to you."

2But Nahash the Ammonite replied, "I will make a treaty with you only on the condition that I gouge out the right eye of

b8 Traditionally *peace offerings*

every one of you and so bring disgrace on all Israel."

³The elders of Jabesh said to him, "Give us seven days so that we can send messengers throughout Israel; if no-one comes to rescue us, we will surrender to you."

⁴When the messengers came to Gibeah of Saul and reported these terms to the people, they all wept aloud. ⁵Just then Saul was returning from the fields, behind his oxen, and he asked, "What is wrong with the people? Why are they weeping?" Then they repeated to him what the men of Jabesh had said.

⁶When Saul heard their words, the Spirit of God came upon him in power, and he burned with anger. ⁷He took a pair of oxen, cut them into pieces, and sent the pieces by messengers throughout Israel, proclaiming, "This is what will be done to the oxen of anyone who does not follow Saul and Samuel." Then the terror of the LORD fell on the people, and they turned out as one man. ⁸When Saul mustered them at Bezek, the men of Israel numbered three hundred thousand and the men of Judah thirty thousand.

⁹They told the messengers who had come, "Say to the men of Jabesh Gilead, 'By the time the sun is hot tomorrow, you will be delivered.'" When the messengers went and reported this to the men of Jabesh, they were elated. ¹⁰They said to the Ammonites, "Tomorrow we will surrender to you, and you can do to us whatever seems good to you."

¹¹The next day Saul separated his men into three divisions; during the last watch of the night they broke into the camp of the Ammonites and slaughtered them until the heat of the day. Those who survived were scattered, so that no two of them were left together.

Saul Confirmed as King

¹²The people then said to Samuel, "Who was it that asked, 'Shall Saul reign over us?' Bring these men to us and we will put them to death."

¹³But Saul said, "No-one shall be put to death today, for this day the LORD has rescued Israel."

¹⁴Then Samuel said to the people, "Come, let us go to Gilgal and there reaffirm the kingship." ¹⁵So all the people went to Gilgal and confirmed Saul as king in the presence of the LORD. There they sacrificed fellowship offerings*ᵃ* before the LORD, and Saul and all the Israelites held a great celebration.

Samuel's Farewell Speech

12 Samuel said to all Israel, "I have listened to everything you said to me and have set a king over you. ²Now you have a king as your leader. As for me, I am old and grey, and my sons are here with you. I have been your leader from my youth until this day. ³Here I stand. Testify against me in the presence of the LORD and his anointed. Whose ox have I taken? Whose donkey have I taken? Whom have I cheated? Whom have I oppressed? From whose hand have I accepted a bribe to make me shut my eyes? If I have done any of these, I will make it right."

⁴"You have not cheated or oppressed us," they replied. "You have not taken anything from anyone's hand."

⁵Samuel said to them, "The LORD is witness against you, and also his anointed is witness this day, that you have not found anything in my hand."

"He is witness," they said.

⁶Then Samuel said to the people, "It is the LORD who appointed Moses and Aaron and brought your forefathers up out of Egypt. ⁷Now then, stand here, because I am going to confront you with evidence before the LORD as to all the righteous acts performed by the LORD for you and your fathers.

⁸"After Jacob entered Egypt, they cried to the LORD for help, and the LORD sent Moses and Aaron, who brought your forefathers out of Egypt and settled them in this place.

⁹"But they forgot the LORD their God; so he sold them into the hands of Sisera, the commander of the army of Hazor, and into the hands of the Philistines and the

ᵃ*15* Traditionally *peace offerings*

king of Moab, who fought against them. [10]They cried out to the LORD and said, 'We have sinned; we have forsaken the LORD and served the Baals and the Ashtoreths. But now deliver us from the hands of our enemies, and we will serve you.' [11]Then the LORD sent Jerub-Baal,[a] Barak,[b] Jephthah and Samuel,[c] and he delivered you from the hands of your enemies on every side, so that you lived securely.

[12]"But when you saw that Nahash king of the Ammonites was moving against you, you said to me, 'No, we want a king to rule over us'—even though the LORD your God was your king. [13]Now here is the king you have chosen, the one you asked for; see, the LORD has set a king over you. [14]If you fear the LORD and serve and obey him and do not rebel against his commands, and if both you and the king who reigns over you follow the LORD your God—good! [15]But if you do not obey the LORD, and if you rebel against his commands, his hand will be against you, as it was against your fathers.

[16]"Now then, stand still and see this great thing the LORD is about to do before your eyes! [17]Is it not wheat harvest now? I will call upon the LORD to send thunder and rain. And you will realise what an evil thing you did in the eyes of the LORD when you asked for a king."

[18]Then Samuel called upon the LORD, and that same day the LORD sent thunder and rain. So all the people stood in awe of the LORD and of Samuel.

[19]The people all said to Samuel, "Pray to the LORD your God for your servants so that we will not die, for we have added to all our other sins the evil of asking for a king."

[20]"Do not be afraid," Samuel replied. "You have done all this evil; yet do not turn away from the LORD, but serve the LORD with all your heart. [21]Do not turn away after useless idols. They can do you no good, nor can they rescue you, because

they are useless. [22]For the sake of his great name the LORD will not reject his people, because the LORD was pleased to make you his own. [23]As for me, far be it from me that I should sin against the LORD by failing to pray for you. And I will teach you the way that is good and right. [24]But be sure to fear the LORD and serve him faithfully with all your heart; consider what great things he has done for you. [25]Yet if you persist in doing evil, both you and your king will be swept away."

Samuel Rebukes Saul

13 Saul was ⌞thirty⌟[a] years old when he became king, and he reigned over Israel for ⌞forty-⌟[b] two years.

[2]Saul[c] chose three thousand men from Israel; two thousand were with him at Michmash and in the hill country of Bethel, and a thousand were with Jonathan at Gibeah in Benjamin. The rest of the men he sent back to their homes.

[3]Jonathan attacked the Philistine outpost at Geba, and the Philistines heard about it. Then Saul had the trumpet blown throughout the land and said, "Let the Hebrews hear!" [4]So all Israel heard the news: "Saul has attacked the Philistine outpost, and now Israel has become an offence to the Philistines." And the people were summoned to join Saul at Gilgal.

[5]The Philistines assembled to fight Israel, with three thousand[d] chariots, six thousand charioteers, and soldiers as numerous as the sand on the seashore. They went up and camped at Michmash, east of Beth Aven. [6]When the men of Israel saw that their situation was critical and that their army was hard pressed, they hid in caves and thickets, among the rocks, and in pits and cisterns. [7]Some Hebrews even crossed the Jordan to the land of Gad and Gilead.

Saul remained at Gilgal, and all the troops with him were quaking with fear.

---

[a]11 Also called *Gideon*   [b]11 Some Septuagint manuscripts and Syriac; Hebrew *Bedan*
[c]11 Hebrew; some Septuagint manuscripts and Syriac *Samson*
[a]1 A few late manuscripts of the Septuagint; Hebrew does not have *thirty*.
[b]1 See the round number in Acts 13:21; Hebrew does not have *forty-*.
[c]1, 2 Or *and when he had reigned over Israel for two years*, [2]*he*
[d]5 Some Septuagint manuscripts and Syriac; Hebrew *thirty thousand*

⁸He waited for seven days, the time set by Samuel; but Samuel did not come to Gilgal, and Saul's men began to scatter. ⁹So he said, "Bring me the burnt offering and the fellowship offerings."*e* And Saul offered up the burnt offering. ¹⁰Just as he finished making the offering, Samuel arrived, and Saul went out to greet him.

¹¹"What have you done?" asked Samuel.

Saul replied, "When I saw that the men were scattering, and that you did not come at the set time, and that the Philistines were assembling at Michmash, ¹²I thought, 'Now the Philistines will come down against me at Gilgal, and I have not sought the LORD's favour.' So I felt compelled to offer the burnt offering."

¹³"You acted foolishly," Samuel said. "You have not kept the command the LORD your God gave you; if you had, he would have established your kingdom over Israel for all time. ¹⁴But now your kingdom will not endure; the LORD has sought out a man after his own heart and appointed him leader of his people, because you have not kept the LORD's command."

¹⁵Then Samuel left Gilgal*f* and went up to Gibeah in Benjamin, and Saul counted the men who were with him. They numbered about six hundred.

Israel Without Weapons

¹⁶Saul and his son Jonathan and the men with them were staying in Gibeah*g* of Benjamin, while the Philistines camped at Michmash. ¹⁷Raiding parties went out from the Philistine camp in three detachments. One turned towards Ophrah in the vicinity of Shual, ¹⁸another towards Beth Horon, and the third towards the borderland overlooking the Valley of Zeboim facing the desert.

¹⁹Not a blacksmith could be found in the whole land of Israel, because the Philistines had said, "Otherwise the Hebrews will make swords or spears!" ²⁰So all Israel went down to the Philistines to have their ploughshares, mattocks, axes and sickles*h* sharpened. ²¹The price was two thirds of a shekel*i* for sharpening ploughshares and mattocks, and a third of a shekel*j* for sharpening forks and axes and for repointing goads.

²²So on the day of the battle not a soldier with Saul and Jonathan had a sword or spear in his hand; only Saul and his son Jonathan had them.

Jonathan Attacks the Philistines

²³Now a detachment of Philistines had gone out to the pass at Michmash.

14 ¹One day Jonathan son of Saul said to the young man bearing his armour, "Come, let's go over to the Philistine outpost on the other side." But he did not tell his father.

²Saul was staying on the outskirts of Gibeah under a pomegranate tree in Migron. With him were about six hundred men, ³among whom was Ahijah, who was wearing an ephod. He was a son of Ichabod's brother Ahitub son of Phinehas, the son of Eli, the LORD's priest in Shiloh. No-one was aware that Jonathan had left.

⁴On each side of the pass that Jonathan intended to cross to reach the Philistine outpost was a cliff; one was called Bozez, and the other Seneh. ⁵One cliff stood to the north towards Michmash, the other to the south towards Geba.

⁶Jonathan said to his young armour-bearer, "Come, let's go over to the outpost of those uncircumcised fellows. Perhaps the LORD will act on our behalf. Nothing can hinder the LORD from saving, whether by many or by few."

⁷"Do all that you have in mind," his armour-bearer said. "Go ahead; I am with you heart and soul."

⁸Jonathan said, "Come, then; we will

e9 Traditionally *peace offerings*
f15 Hebrew; Septuagint *Gilgal and went his way; the rest of the people went after Saul to meet the army, and they went out of Gilgal*   *g16* Two Hebrew manuscripts; most Hebrew manuscripts *Geba,* a variant of *Gibeah*
h20 Septuagint; Hebrew *ploughshares*   *i21* Hebrew *pim;* that is, about ¼ ounce (about 8 grams)
j21 That is, about ⅛ ounce (about 4 grams)

cross over towards the men and let them see us. ⁹If they say to us, 'Wait there until we come to you,' we will stay where we are and not go up to them. ¹⁰But if they say, 'Come up to us,' we will climb up, because that will be our sign that the LORD has given them into our hands."

¹¹So both of them showed themselves to the Philistine outpost. "Look!" said the Philistines. "The Hebrews are crawling out of the holes they were hiding in." ¹²The men of the outpost shouted to Jonathan and his armour-bearer, "Come up to us and we'll teach you a lesson."

So Jonathan said to his armour-bearer, "Climb up after me; the LORD has given them into the hand of Israel."

¹³Jonathan climbed up, using his hands and feet, with his armour-bearer right behind him. The Philistines fell before Jonathan, and his armour-bearer followed and killed behind him. ¹⁴In that first attack Jonathan and his armour-bearer killed some twenty men in an area of about half an acre.ᵃ

Israel Routs the Philistines

¹⁵Then panic struck the whole army— those in the camp and field, and those in the outposts and raiding parties—and the ground shook. It was a panic sent by God.ᵇ

¹⁶Saul's lookouts at Gibeah in Benjamin saw the army melting away in all directions. ¹⁷Then Saul said to the men who were with him, "Muster the forces and see who has left us." When they did, it was Jonathan and his armour-bearer who were not there.

¹⁸Saul said to Ahijah, "Bring the ark of God." (At that time it was with the Israelites.)ᶜ ¹⁹While Saul was talking to the priest, the tumult in the Philistine camp increased more and more. So Saul said to the priest, "Withdraw your hand."

²⁰Then Saul and all his men assembled and went to the battle. They found the Philistines in total confusion, striking each other with their swords. ²¹Those Hebrews who had previously been with the Philistines and had gone up with them to their camp went over to the Israelites who were with Saul and Jonathan. ²²When all the Israelites who had hidden in the hill country of Ephraim heard that the Philistines were on the run, they joined the battle in hot pursuit. ²³So the LORD rescued Israel that day, and the battle moved on beyond Beth Aven.

Jonathan Eats Honey

²⁴Now the men of Israel were in distress that day, because Saul had bound the people under an oath, saying, "Cursed be any man who eats food before evening comes, before I have avenged myself on my enemies!" So none of the troops tasted food.

²⁵The entire armyᵈ entered the woods, and there was honey on the ground. ²⁶When they went into the woods, they saw the honey oozing out, yet no-one put his hand to his mouth, because they feared the oath. ²⁷But Jonathan had not heard that his father had bound the people with the oath, so he reached out the end of the staff that was in his hand and dipped it into the honeycomb. He raised his hand to his mouth, and his eyes brightened.ᵉ ²⁸Then one of the soldiers told him, "Your father bound the army under a strict oath, saying, 'Cursed be any man who eats food today!' That is why the men are faint."

²⁹Jonathan said, "My father has made trouble for the country. See how my eyes brightenedᶠ when I tasted a little of this honey. ³⁰How much better it would have been if the men had eaten today some of the plunder they took from their enemies. Would not the slaughter of the Philistines have been even greater?"

³¹That day, after the Israelites had struck down the Philistines from Michmash to Aijalon, they were exhausted. ³²They pounced on the plunder and, taking sheep, cattle and calves, they butchered them on the ground and ate them, together with the blood. ³³Then someone

---

ᵃ14 Hebrew *half a yoke;* a "yoke" was the land ploughed by a yoke of oxen in one day.   ᵇ15 Or *a terrible panic*
ᶜ18 Hebrew; Septuagint *"Bring the ephod." (At that time he wore the ephod before the Israelites.)*
ᵈ25 Or *Now all the people of the land*   ᵉ27 Or *his strength was renewed*   ᶠ29 Or *my strength was renewed*

said to Saul, "Look, the men are sinning against the LORD by eating meat that has blood in it."

"You have broken faith," he said. "Roll a large stone over here at once." ³⁴Then he said, "Go out among the men and tell them, 'Each of you bring me your cattle and sheep, and slaughter them here and eat them. Do not sin against the LORD by eating meat with blood still in it.'"

So everyone brought his ox that night and slaughtered it there. ³⁵Then Saul built an altar to the LORD; it was the first time he had done this.

³⁶Saul said, "Let us go down after the Philistines by night and plunder them till dawn, and let us not leave one of them alive."

"Do whatever seems best to you," they replied.

But the priest said, "Let us enquire of God here."

³⁷So Saul asked God, "Shall I go down after the Philistines? Will you give them into Israel's hand?" But God did not answer him that day.

³⁸Saul therefore said, "Come here, all you who are leaders of the army, and let us find out what sin has been committed today. ³⁹As surely as the LORD who rescues Israel lives, even if it lies with my son Jonathan, he must die." But not one of the men said a word.

⁴⁰Saul then said to all the Israelites, "You stand over there; I and Jonathan my son will stand over here."

"Do what seems best to you," the men replied.

⁴¹Then Saul prayed to the LORD, the God of Israel, "Give me the right answer."^g And Jonathan and Saul were taken by lot, and the men were cleared. ⁴²Saul said, "Cast the lot between me and Jonathan my son." And Jonathan was taken.

⁴³Then Saul said to Jonathan, "Tell me what you have done."

So Jonathan told him, "I merely tasted a little honey with the end of my staff. And now must I die?"

⁴⁴Saul said, "May God deal with me, be it ever so severely, if you do not die, Jonathan."

⁴⁵But the men said to Saul, "Should Jonathan die—he who has brought about this great deliverance in Israel? Never! As surely as the LORD lives, not a hair of his head shall fall to the ground, for he did this today with God's help." So the men rescued Jonathan, and he was not put to death.

⁴⁶Then Saul stopped pursuing the Philistines, and they withdrew to their own land.

⁴⁷After Saul had assumed rule over Israel, he fought against their enemies on every side: Moab, the Ammonites, Edom, the kings^h of Zobah, and the Philistines. Wherever he turned, he inflicted punishment on them.ⁱ ⁴⁸He fought valiantly and defeated the Amalekites, delivering Israel from the hands of those who had plundered them.

Saul's Family

⁴⁹Saul's sons were Jonathan, Ishvi and Malki-Shua. The name of his older daughter was Merab, and that of the younger was Michal. ⁵⁰His wife's name was Ahinoam daughter of Ahimaaz. The name of the commander of Saul's army was Abner son of Ner, and Ner was Saul's uncle. ⁵¹Saul's father Kish and Abner's father Ner were sons of Abiel.

⁵²All the days of Saul there was bitter war with the Philistines, and whenever Saul saw a mighty or brave man, he took him into his service.

The LORD Rejects Saul as King

15 Samuel said to Saul, "I am the one the LORD sent to anoint you king over his people Israel; so listen now to the message from the LORD. ²This is what the LORD Almighty says: 'I will punish the Amalekites for what they did to Israel when they waylaid them as they came up from Egypt. ³Now go, attack the

---

^g41 Hebrew; Septuagint "Why have you not answered your servant today? If the fault is in me or my son Jonathan, respond with Urim, but if the men of Israel are at fault, respond with Thummim."
^h47 Masoretic Text; Dead Sea Scrolls and Septuagint king   ⁱ47 Hebrew; Septuagint he was victorious

Amalekites and totally destroy[a] everything that belongs to them. Do not spare them; put to death men and women, children and infants, cattle and sheep, camels and donkeys.'"

[4]So Saul summoned the men and mustered them at Telaim—two hundred thousand foot soldiers and ten thousand men from Judah. [5]Saul went to the city of Amalek and set an ambush in the ravine. [6]Then he said to the Kenites, "Go away, leave the Amalekites so that I do not destroy you along with them; for you showed kindness to all the Israelites when they came up out of Egypt." So the Kenites moved away from the Amalekites.

[7]Then Saul attacked the Amalekites all the way from Havilah to Shur, to the east of Egypt. [8]He took Agag king of the Amalekites alive, and all his people he totally destroyed with the sword. [9]But Saul and the army spared Agag and the best of the sheep and cattle, the fat calves[b] and lambs—everything that was good. These they were unwilling to destroy completely, but everything that was despised and weak they totally destroyed.

[10]Then the word of the LORD came to Samuel: [11]"I am grieved that I have made Saul king, because he has turned away from me and has not carried out my instructions." Samuel was troubled, and he cried out to the LORD all that night.

[12]Early in the morning Samuel got up and went to meet Saul, but he was told, "Saul has gone to Carmel. There he has set up a monument in his own honour and has turned and gone on down to Gilgal."

[13]When Samuel reached him, Saul said, "The LORD bless you! I have carried out the LORD's instructions."

[14]But Samuel said, "What then is this bleating of sheep in my ears? What is this lowing of cattle that I hear?"

[15]Saul answered, "The soldiers brought them from the Amalekites; they spared the best of the sheep and cattle to sacrifice to the LORD your God, but we totally destroyed the rest."

[16]"Stop!" Samuel said to Saul. "Let me tell you what the LORD said to me last night."

"Tell me," Saul replied.

[17]Samuel said, "Although you were once small in your own eyes, did you not become the head of the tribes of Israel? The LORD anointed you king over Israel. [18]And he sent you on a mission, saying, 'Go and completely destroy those wicked people, the Amalekites; make war on them until you have wiped them out.' [19]Why did you not obey the LORD? Why did you pounce on the plunder and do evil in the eyes of the LORD?"

[20]"But I did obey the LORD," Saul said. "I went on the mission the LORD assigned me. I completely destroyed the Amalekites and brought back Agag their king. [21]The soldiers took sheep and cattle from the plunder, the best of what was devoted to God, in order to sacrifice them to the LORD your God at Gilgal."

[22]But Samuel replied:

"Does the LORD delight in burnt
　　offerings and sacrifices
　as much as in obeying the voice of the
　　LORD?
To obey is better than sacrifice,
　and to heed is better than the fat of
　　rams.
[23]For rebellion is like the sin of
　　divination,
　and arrogance like the evil of
　　idolatry.
Because you have rejected the word of
　　the LORD,
　he has rejected you as king."

[24]Then Saul said to Samuel, "I have sinned. I violated the LORD's command and your instructions. I was afraid of the people and so I gave in to them. [25]Now I beg you, forgive my sin and come back with me, so that I may worship the LORD."

[26]But Samuel said to him, "I will not go back with you. You have rejected the word of the LORD, and the LORD has rejected you as king over Israel!"

[27]As Samuel turned to leave, Saul

a3 The Hebrew term refers to the irrevocable giving of things or persons to the LORD, often by totally destroying them; also in verses 8, 9, 15, 18, 20 and 21.　　*b9* Or *the grown bulls*; the meaning of the Hebrew for this phrase is uncertain.

caught hold of the hem of his robe, and it tore. ²⁸Samuel said to him, "The LORD has torn the kingdom of Israel from you today and has given it to one of your neighbours—to one better than you. ²⁹He who is the Glory of Israel does not lie or change his mind; for he is not a man, that he should change his mind."

³⁰Saul replied, "I have sinned. But please honour me before the elders of my people and before Israel; come back with me, so that I may worship the LORD your God." ³¹So Samuel went back with Saul, and Saul worshipped the LORD.

³²Then Samuel said, "Bring me Agag king of the Amalekites."

Agag came to him confidently,^c thinking, "Surely the bitterness of death is past."

³³But Samuel said,

"As your sword has made women
      childless,
   so will your mother be childless
      among women."

And Samuel put Agag to death before the LORD at Gilgal.

³⁴Then Samuel left for Ramah, but Saul went up to his home in Gibeah of Saul. ³⁵Until the day Samuel died, he did not go to see Saul again, though Samuel mourned for him. And the LORD was grieved that he had made Saul king over Israel.

Samuel Anoints David

16 The LORD said to Samuel, "How long will you mourn for Saul, since I have rejected him as king over Israel? Fill your horn with oil and be on your way; I am sending you to Jesse of Bethlehem. I have chosen one of his sons to be king."

²But Samuel said, "How can I go? Saul will hear about it and kill me."

The LORD said, "Take a heifer with you and say, 'I have come to sacrifice to the LORD.' ³Invite Jesse to the sacrifice, and I will show you what to do. You are to anoint for me the one I indicate."

⁴Samuel did what the LORD said. When he arrived at Bethlehem, the elders of the town trembled when they met him. They asked, "Do you come in peace?"

⁵Samuel replied, "Yes, in peace; I have come to sacrifice to the LORD. Consecrate yourselves and come to the sacrifice with me." Then he consecrated Jesse and his sons and invited them to the sacrifice.

⁶When they arrived, Samuel saw Eliab and thought, "Surely the LORD's anointed stands here before the LORD."

⁷But the LORD said to Samuel, "Do not consider his appearance or his height, for I have rejected him. The LORD does not look at the things man looks at. Man looks at the outward appearance, but the LORD looks at the heart."

⁸Then Jesse called Abinadab and made him pass in front of Samuel. But Samuel said, "The LORD has not chosen this one either." ⁹Jesse then made Shammah pass by, but Samuel said, "Nor has the LORD chosen this one." ¹⁰Jesse made seven of his sons pass before Samuel, but Samuel said to him, "The LORD has not chosen these." ¹¹So he asked Jesse, "Are these all the sons you have?"

"There is still the youngest," Jesse answered, "but he is tending the sheep."

Samuel said, "Send for him; we will not sit down^a until he arrives."

¹²So he sent and had him brought in. He was ruddy, with a fine appearance and handsome features.

Then the LORD said, "Rise and anoint him; he is the one."

¹³So Samuel took the horn of oil and anointed him in the presence of his brothers, and from that day on the Spirit of the LORD came upon David in power. Samuel then went to Ramah.

David in Saul's Service

¹⁴Now the Spirit of the LORD had departed from Saul, and an evil^b spirit from the LORD tormented him.

---

^c32 Or *him trembling, yet*   ^a11 Some Septuagint manuscripts; Hebrew *not gather round*
^b14 Or *injurious*; also in verses 15, 16 and 23

15Saul's attendants said to him, "See, an evil spirit from God is tormenting you. 16Let our lord command his servants here to search for someone who can play the harp. He will play when the evil spirit from God comes upon you, and you will feel better."

17So Saul said to his attendants, "Find someone who plays well and bring him to me."

18One of the servants answered, "I have seen a son of Jesse of Bethlehem who knows how to play the harp. He is a brave man and a warrior. He speaks well and is a fine-looking man. And the LORD is with him."

19Then Saul sent messengers to Jesse and said, "Send me your son David, who is with the sheep." 20So Jesse took a donkey loaded with bread, a skin of wine and a young goat and sent them with his son David to Saul.

21David came to Saul and entered his service. Saul liked him very much, and David became one of his armour-bearers. 22Then Saul sent word to Jesse, saying, "Allow David to remain in my service, for I am pleased with him."

23Whenever the spirit from God came upon Saul, David would take his harp and play. Then relief would come to Saul; he would feel better, and the evil spirit would leave him.

David and Goliath

17 Now the Philistines gathered their forces for war and assembled at Socoh in Judah. They pitched camp at Ephes Dammim, between Socoh and Azekah. 2Saul and the Israelites assembled and camped in the Valley of Elah and drew up their battle line to meet the Philistines. 3The Philistines occupied one hill and the Israelites another, with the valley between them.

4A champion named Goliath, who was from Gath, came out of the Philistine camp. He was over nine feet*a* tall. 5He had a bronze helmet on his head and wore a coat of scale armour of bronze weighing five thousand shekels;*b* 6on his legs he wore bronze greaves, and a bronze javelin was slung on his back. 7His spear shaft was like a weaver's rod, and its iron point weighed six hundred shekels.*c* His shield-bearer went ahead of him.

8Goliath stood and shouted to the ranks of Israel, "Why do you come out and line up for battle? Am I not a Philistine, and are you not the servants of Saul? Choose a man and have him come down to me. 9If he is able to fight and kill me, we will become your subjects; but if I overcome him and kill him, you will become our subjects and serve us." 10Then the Philistine said, "This day I defy the ranks of Israel! Give me a man and let us fight each other." 11On hearing the Philistine's words, Saul and all the Israelites were dismayed and terrified.

12Now David was the son of an Ephrathite named Jesse, who was from Bethlehem in Judah. Jesse had eight sons, and in Saul's time he was old and well advanced in years. 13Jesse's three oldest sons had followed Saul to the war: The firstborn was Eliab; the second, Abinadab; and the third, Shammah. 14David was the youngest. The three oldest followed Saul, 15but David went back and forth from Saul to tend his father's sheep at Bethlehem.

16For forty days the Philistine came forward every morning and evening and took his stand.

17Now Jesse said to his son David, "Take this ephah*d* of roasted grain and these ten loaves of bread for your brothers and hurry to their camp. 18Take along these ten cheeses to the commander of their unit.*e* See how your brothers are and bring back some assurance*f* from them. 19They are with Saul and all the men of Israel in the Valley of Elah, fighting against the Philistines."

20Early in the morning David left the flock with a shepherd, loaded up and set out, as Jesse had directed. He reached the camp as the army was going out to its

---

a4 Hebrew *was six cubits and a span* (about 3 metres)   *b5* That is, about 125 pounds (about 57 kilograms)
c7 That is, about 15 pounds (about 7 kilograms)   *d17* That is, probably about ⅗ bushel (about 22 litres)
e18 Hebrew *thousand*   *f18* Or *some token*; or *some pledge of spoils*

battle positions, shouting the war cry.
21Israel and the Philistines were drawing
up their lines facing each other. 22David
left his things with the keeper of supplies,
ran to the battle lines and greeted his
brothers. 23As he was talking with them,
Goliath, the Philistine champion from
Gath, stepped out from his lines and
shouted his usual defiance, and David
heard it. 24When the Israelites saw the
man, they all ran from him in great fear.

25Now the Israelites had been saying,
"Do you see how this man keeps coming
out? He comes out to defy Israel. The king
will give great wealth to the man who kills
him. He will also give him his daughter in
marriage and will exempt his father's
family from taxes in Israel."

26David asked the men standing near
him, "What will be done for the man who
kills this Philistine and removes this disgrace from Israel? Who is this uncircumcised Philistine that he should defy the
armies of the living God?"

27They repeated to him what they had
been saying and told him, "This is what
will be done for the man who kills him."

28When Eliab, David's oldest brother,
heard him speaking with the men, he
burned with anger at him and asked,
"Why have you come down here? And
with whom did you leave those few sheep
in the desert? I know how conceited you
are and how wicked your heart is; you
came down only to watch the battle."

29"Now what have I done?" said David.
"Can't I even speak?" 30He then turned
away to someone else and brought up the
same matter, and the men answered him
as before. 31What David said was overheard and reported to Saul, and Saul sent
for him.

32David said to Saul, "Let no-one lose
heart on account of this Philistine; your
servant will go and fight him."

33Saul replied, "You are not able to go
out against this Philistine and fight him;
you are only a boy, and he has been a
fighting man from his youth."

34But David said to Saul, "Your servant
has been keeping his father's sheep. When
a lion or a bear came and carried off a
sheep from the flock, 35I went after it,

struck it and rescued the sheep from its
mouth. When it turned on me, I seized it
by its hair, struck it and killed it. 36Your
servant has killed both the lion and the
bear; this uncircumcised Philistine will be
like one of them, because he has defied the
armies of the living God. 37The LORD who
delivered me from the paw of the lion and
the paw of the bear will deliver me from
the hand of this Philistine."

Saul said to David, "Go, and the LORD
be with you."

38Then Saul dressed David in his own
tunic. He put a coat of armour on him and
a bronze helmet on his head. 39David
fastened on his sword over the tunic and
tried walking around, because he was not
used to them.

"I cannot go in these," he said to Saul,
"because I am not used to them." So he
took them off. 40Then he took his staff in
his hand, chose five smooth stones from
the stream, put them in the pouch of his
shepherd's bag and, with his sling in his
hand, approached the Philistine.

41Meanwhile, the Philistine, with his
shield-bearer in front of him, kept coming
closer to David. 42He looked David over
and saw that he was only a boy, ruddy and
handsome, and he despised him. 43He said
to David, "Am I a dog, that you come at
me with sticks?" And the Philistine cursed
David by his gods. 44"Come here," he
said, "and I'll give your flesh to the birds
of the air and the beasts of the field!"

45David said to the Philistine, "You
come against me with sword and spear and
javelin, but I come against you in the
name of the LORD Almighty, the God of
the armies of Israel, whom you have
defied. 46This day the LORD will hand you
over to me, and I'll strike you down and
cut off your head. Today I will give the
carcasses of the Philistine army to the
birds of the air and the beasts of the earth,
and the whole world will know that there
is a God in Israel. 47All those gathered
here will know that it is not by sword or
spear that the LORD saves; for the battle is
the LORD's, and he will give all of you into
our hands."

48As the Philistine moved closer to
attack him, David ran quickly towards the

battle line to meet him. ⁴⁹Reaching into his bag and taking out a stone, he slung it and struck the Philistine on the forehead. The stone sank into his forehead, and he fell face down on the ground.

⁵⁰So David triumphed over the Philistine with a sling and a stone; without a sword in his hand he struck down the Philistine and killed him.

⁵¹David ran and stood over him. He took hold of the Philistine's sword and drew it from the scabbard. After he killed him, he cut off his head with the sword.

When the Philistines saw that their hero was dead, they turned and ran. ⁵²Then the men of Israel and Judah surged forward with a shout and pursued the Philistines to the entrance of Gathᵍ and to the gates of Ekron. Their dead were strewn along the Shaaraim road to Gath and Ekron. ⁵³When the Israelites returned from chasing the Philistines, they plundered their camp. ⁵⁴David took the Philistine's head and brought it to Jerusalem, and he put the Philistine's weapons in his own tent.

⁵⁵As Saul watched David going out to meet the Philistine, he said to Abner, commander of the army, "Abner, whose son is that young man?"

Abner replied, "As surely as you live, O king, I don't know."

⁵⁶The king said, "Find out whose son this young man is."

⁵⁷As soon as David returned from killing the Philistine, Abner took him and brought him before Saul, with David still holding the Philistine's head.

⁵⁸"Whose son are you, young man?" Saul asked him.

David said, "I am the son of your servant Jesse of Bethlehem."

Saul's Jealousy of David

18 After David had finished talking with Saul, Jonathan became one in spirit with David, and he loved him as himself. ²From that day Saul kept David with him and did not let him return to his father's house. ³And Jonathan made a covenant with David because he loved him as himself. ⁴Jonathan took off the robe he was wearing and gave it to David, along with his tunic, and even his sword, his bow and his belt.

⁵Whatever Saul sent him to do, David did it so successfullyᵃ that Saul gave him a high rank in the army. This pleased all the people, and Saul's officers as well.

⁶When the men were returning home after David had killed the Philistine, the women came out from all the towns of Israel to meet King Saul with singing and dancing, with joyful songs and with tambourines and lutes. ⁷As they danced, they sang:

"Saul has slain his thousands,
    and David his tens of thousands."

⁸Saul was very angry; this refrain galled him. "They have credited David with tens of thousands," he thought, "but me with only thousands. What more can he get but the kingdom?" ⁹And from that time on Saul kept a jealous eye on David.

¹⁰The next day an evilᵇ spirit from God came forcefully upon Saul. He was prophesying in his house, while David was playing the harp, as he usually did. Saul had a spear in his hand ¹¹and he hurled it, saying to himself, "I'll pin David to the wall." But David eluded him twice.

¹²Saul was afraid of David, because the LORD was with David but had left Saul. ¹³So he sent David away from him and gave him command over a thousand men, and David led the troops in their campaigns. ¹⁴In everything he did he had great success,ᶜ because the LORD was with him. ¹⁵When Saul saw how successfulᵈ he was, he was afraid of him. ¹⁶But all Israel and Judah loved David, because he led them in their campaigns.

¹⁷Saul said to David, "Here is my older daughter Merab. I will give her to you in marriage; only serve me bravely and fight the battles of the LORD." For Saul said to himself, "I will not raise a hand against him. Let the Philistines do that!"

¹⁸But David said to Saul, "Who am I,

g52 Some Septuagint manuscripts; Hebrew a valley   a5 Or wisely   b10 Or injurious
c14 Or he was very wise   d15 Or wise

and what is my family or my father's clan in Israel, that I should become the king's son-in-law?" ¹⁹So^e when the time came for Merab, Saul's daughter, to be given to David, she was given in marriage to Adriel of Meholah.

²⁰Now Saul's daughter Michal was in love with David, and when they told Saul about it, he was pleased. ²¹"I will give her to him," he thought, "so that she may be a snare to him and so that the hand of the Philistines may be against him." So Saul said to David, "Now you have a second opportunity to become my son-in-law."

²²Then Saul ordered his attendants: "Speak to David privately and say, 'Look, the king is pleased with you, and his attendants all like you; now become his son-in-law.'"

²³They repeated these words to David. But David said, "Do you think it is a small matter to become the king's son-in-law? I'm only a poor man and little known."

²⁴When Saul's servants told him what David had said, ²⁵Saul replied, "Say to David, 'The king wants no other price for the bride than a hundred Philistine foreskins, to take revenge on his enemies.'" Saul's plan was to have David fall by the hands of the Philistines.

²⁶When the attendants told David these things, he was pleased to become the king's son-in-law. So before the allotted time elapsed, ²⁷David and his men went out and killed two hundred Philistines. He brought their foreskins and presented the full number to the king so that he might become the king's son-in-law. Then Saul gave him his daughter Michal in marriage.

²⁸When Saul realised that the LORD was with David and that his daughter Michal loved David, ²⁹Saul became still more afraid of him, and he remained his enemy for the rest of his days.

³⁰The Philistine commanders continued to go out to battle, and as often as they did, David met with more success^f than the rest of Saul's officers, and his name became well known.

Saul Tries to Kill David

19 Saul told his son Jonathan and all the attendants to kill David. But Jonathan was very fond of David ²and warned him, "My father Saul is looking for a chance to kill you. Be on your guard tomorrow morning; go into hiding and stay there. ³I will go out and stand with my father in the field where you are. I'll speak to him about you and will tell you what I find out."

⁴Jonathan spoke well of David to Saul his father and said to him, "Let not the king do wrong to his servant David; he has not wronged you, and what he has done has benefited you greatly. ⁵He took his life in his hands when he killed the Philistine. The LORD won a great victory for all Israel, and you saw it and were glad. Why then would you do wrong to an innocent man like David by killing him for no reason?"

⁶Saul listened to Jonathan and took this oath: "As surely as the LORD lives, David will not be put to death."

⁷So Jonathan called David and told him the whole conversation. He brought him to Saul, and David was with Saul as before.

⁸Once more war broke out, and David went out and fought the Philistines. He struck them with such force that they fled before him.

⁹But an evil^a spirit from the LORD came upon Saul as he was sitting in his house with his spear in his hand. While David was playing the harp, ¹⁰Saul tried to pin him to the wall with his spear, but David eluded him as Saul drove the spear into the wall. That night David made good his escape.

¹¹Saul sent men to David's house to watch it and to kill him in the morning. But Michal, David's wife, warned him, "If you don't run for your life tonight, tomorrow you'll be killed." ¹²So Michal let David down through a window, and he fled and escaped. ¹³Then Michal took an idol^b and laid it on the bed, covering it

---

with a garment and putting some goats' hair at the head.

¹⁴When Saul sent the men to capture David, Michal said, "He is ill."

¹⁵Then Saul sent the men back to see David and told them, "Bring him up to me in his bed so that I may kill him." ¹⁶But when the men entered, there was the idol in the bed, and at the head was some goats' hair.

¹⁷Saul said to Michal, "Why did you deceive me like this and send my enemy away so that he escaped?"

Michal told him, "He said to me, 'Let me get away. Why should I kill you?'"

¹⁸When David had fled and made his escape, he went to Samuel at Ramah and told him all that Saul had done to him. Then he and Samuel went to Naioth and stayed there. ¹⁹Word came to Saul: "David is in Naioth at Ramah"; ²⁰so he sent men to capture him. But when they saw a group of prophets prophesying, with Samuel standing there as their leader, the Spirit of God came upon Saul's men and they also prophesied. ²¹Saul was told about it, and he sent more men, and they prophesied too. Saul sent men a third time, and they also prophesied. ²²Finally, he himself left for Ramah and went to the great cistern at Secu. And he asked, "Where are Samuel and David?"

"Over in Naioth at Ramah," they said.

²³So Saul went to Naioth at Ramah. But the Spirit of God came even upon him, and he walked along prophesying until he came to Naioth. ²⁴He stripped off his robes and also prophesied in Samuel's presence. He lay that way all that day and night. This is why people say, "Is Saul also among the prophets?"

David and Jonathan

20 Then David fled from Naioth at Ramah and went to Jonathan and asked, "What have I done? What is my crime? How have I wronged your father, that he is trying to take my life?"

²"Never!" Jonathan replied. "You are not going to die! Look, my father doesn't do anything, great or small, without confiding in me. Why should he hide this from me? It's not so!"

³But David took an oath and said, "Your father knows very well that I have found favour in your eyes, and he has said to himself, 'Jonathan must not know this or he will be grieved.' Yet as surely as the LORD lives and as you live, there is only a step between me and death."

⁴Jonathan said to David, "Whatever you want me to do, I'll do for you."

⁵So David said, "Look, tomorrow is the New Moon festival, and I am supposed to dine with the king; but let me go and hide in the field until the evening of the day after tomorrow. ⁶If your father misses me at all, tell him, 'David earnestly asked my permission to hurry to Bethlehem, his home town, because an annual sacrifice is being made there for his whole clan.' ⁷If he says, 'Very well,' then your servant is safe. But if he loses his temper, you can be sure that he is determined to harm me. ⁸As for you, show kindness to your servant, for you have brought him into a covenant with you before the LORD. If I am guilty, then kill me yourself! Why hand me over to your father?"

⁹"Never!" Jonathan said. "If I had the least inkling that my father was determined to harm you, wouldn't I tell you?"

¹⁰David asked, "Who will tell me if your father answers you harshly?"

¹¹"Come," Jonathan said, "let's go out into the field." So they went there together.

¹²Then Jonathan said to David: "By the LORD, the God of Israel, I will surely sound out my father by this time the day after tomorrow! If he is favourably disposed towards you, will I not send you word and let you know? ¹³But if my father is inclined to harm you, may the LORD deal with me, be it ever so severely, if I do not let you know and send you away safely. May the LORD be with you as he has been with my father. ¹⁴But show me unfailing kindness like that of the LORD as long as I live, so that I may not be killed, ¹⁵and do not ever cut off your kindness from my family—not even when the LORD has cut off every one of David's enemies from the face of the earth."

¹⁶So Jonathan made a covenant with the house of David, saying, "May the LORD

call David's enemies to account." [17]And Jonathan made David reaffirm his oath out of love for him, because he loved him as he loved himself.

[18]Then Jonathan said to David: "Tomorrow is the New Moon festival. You will be missed, because your seat will be empty. [19]The day after tomorrow, towards evening, go to the place where you hid when this trouble began, and wait by the stone Ezel. [20]I will shoot three arrows to the side of it, as though I were shooting at a target. [21]Then I will send a boy and say, 'Go, find the arrows.' If I say to him, 'Look, the arrows are on this side of you; bring them here,' then come, because, as surely as the LORD lives, you are safe; there is no danger. [22]But if I say to the boy, 'Look, the arrows are beyond you,' then you must go, because the LORD has sent you away. [23]And about the matter you and I discussed—remember, the LORD is witness between you and me for ever."

[24]So David hid in the field, and when the New Moon festival came, the king sat down to eat. [25]He sat in his customary place by the wall, opposite Jonathan,[a] and Abner sat next to Saul, but David's place was empty. [26]Saul said nothing that day, for he thought, "Something must have happened to David to make him ceremonially unclean—surely he is unclean." [27]But the next day, the second day of the month, David's place was empty again. Then Saul said to his son Jonathan, "Why hasn't the son of Jesse come to the meal, either yesterday or today?"

[28]Jonathan answered, "David earnestly asked me for permission to go to Bethlehem. [29]He said, 'Let me go, because our family is observing a sacrifice in the town and my brother has ordered me to be there. If I have found favour in your eyes, let me go to see my brothers.' That is why he has not come to the king's table."

[30]Saul's anger flared up at Jonathan and he said to him, "You son of a perverse and rebellious woman! Don't I know that you have sided with the son of Jesse to your own shame and to the shame of the mother who bore you? [31]As long as the son of Jesse lives on this earth, neither you nor your kingdom will be established. Now send and bring him to me, for he must die!"

[32]"Why should he be put to death? What has he done?" Jonathan asked his father. [33]But Saul hurled his spear at him to kill him. Then Jonathan knew that his father intended to kill David.

[34]Jonathan got up from the table in fierce anger; on that second day of the month he did not eat, because he was grieved at his father's shameful treatment of David.

[35]In the morning Jonathan went out to the field for his meeting with David. He had a small boy with him, [36]and he said to the boy, "Run and find the arrows I shoot." As the boy ran, he shot an arrow beyond him. [37]When the boy came to the place where Jonathan's arrow had fallen, Jonathan called out after him, "Isn't the arrow beyond you?" [38]Then he shouted, "Hurry! Go quickly! Don't stop!" The boy picked up the arrow and returned to his master. [39](The boy knew nothing of all this; only Jonathan and David knew.) [40]Then Jonathan gave his weapons to the boy and said, "Go, carry them back to town."

[41]After the boy had gone, David got up from the south side ⌊of the stone⌋ and bowed down before Jonathan three times, with his face to the ground. Then they kissed each other and wept together—but David wept the most.

[42]Jonathan said to David, "Go in peace, for we have sworn friendship with each other in the name of the LORD, saying, 'The LORD is witness between you and me, and between your descendants and my descendants for ever.'" Then David left, and Jonathan went back to the town.

David at Nob

21 David went to Nob, to Ahimelech the priest. Ahimelech trembled when he met him, and asked, "Why are you alone? Why is no-one with you?"

[2]David answered Ahimelech the priest,

---

a25 Septuagint; Hebrew wall. Jonathan arose

"The king charged me with a certain matter and said to me, 'No-one is to know anything about your mission and your instructions.' As for my men, I have told them to meet me at a certain place. [3]Now then, what have you to hand? Give me five loaves of bread, or whatever you can find."

[4]But the priest answered David, "I don't have any ordinary bread to hand; however, there is some consecrated bread here—provided the men have kept themselves from women."

[5]David replied, "Indeed women have been kept from us, as usual whenever[a] I set out. The men's things[b] are holy even on missions that are not holy. How much more so today!" [6]So the priest gave him the consecrated bread, since there was no bread there except the bread of the Presence that had been removed from before the LORD and replaced by hot bread on the day it was taken away.

[7]Now one of Saul's servants was there that day, detained before the LORD; he was Doeg the Edomite, Saul's head shepherd.

[8]David asked Ahimelech, "Don't you have a spear or sword here? I haven't brought my sword or any other weapon, because the king's business was urgent."

[9]The priest replied, "The sword of Goliath the Philistine, whom you killed in the Valley of Elah, is here; it is wrapped in a cloth behind the ephod. If you want it, take it; there is no sword here but that one."

David said, "There is none like it; give it to me."

David at Gath

[10]That day David fled from Saul and went to Achish king of Gath. [11]But the servants of Achish said to him, "Isn't this David, the king of the land? Isn't he the one they sing about in their dances:

"'Saul has slain his thousands,
and David his tens of thousands'?"

[12]David took these words to heart and was very much afraid of Achish king of Gath. [13]So he feigned insanity in their presence; and while he was in their hands he acted like a madman, making marks on the doors of the gate and letting saliva run down his beard.

[14]Achish said to his servants, "Look at the man! He is insane! Why bring him to me? [15]Am I so short of madmen that you have to bring this fellow here to carry on like this in front of me? Must this man come into my house?"

David at Adullam and Mizpah

22 David left Gath and escaped to the cave of Adullam. When his brothers and his father's household heard about it, they went down to him there. [2]All those who were in distress or in debt or discontented gathered round him, and he became their leader. About four hundred men were with him.

[3]From there David went to Mizpah in Moab and said to the king of Moab, "Would you let my father and mother come and stay with you until I learn what God will do for me?" [4]So he left them with the king of Moab, and they stayed with him as long as David was in the stronghold.

[5]But the prophet Gad said to David, "Do not stay in the stronghold. Go into the land of Judah." So David left and went to the forest of Hereth.

Saul Kills the Priests of Nob

[6]Now Saul heard that David and his men had been discovered. And Saul, spear in hand, was seated under the tamarisk tree on the hill at Gibeah, with all his officials standing round him. [7]Saul said to them, "Listen, men of Benjamin! Will the son of Jesse give all of you fields and vineyards? Will he make all of you commanders of thousands and commanders of hundreds? [8]Is that why you have all conspired against me? No-one tells me when my son makes a covenant with the

---

a5 Or from us in the past few days since   *b5 Or bodies* son of Jesse. None of you is concerned about me or tells me that my son has incited my servant to lie in wait for me, as he does today."

9But Doeg the Edomite, who was standing with Saul's officials, said, "I saw the son of Jesse come to Ahimelech son of Ahitub at Nob. 10Ahimelech enquired of the LORD for him; he also gave him provisions and the sword of Goliath the Philistine."

11Then the king sent for the priest Ahimelech son of Ahitub and his father's whole family, who were the priests at Nob, and they all came to the king. 12Saul said, "Listen now, son of Ahitub."

"Yes, my lord," he answered.

13Saul said to him, "Why have you conspired against me, you and the son of Jesse, giving him bread and a sword and enquiring of God for him, so that he has rebelled against me and lies in wait for me, as he does today?"

14Ahimelech answered the king, "Who of all your servants is as loyal as David, the king's son-in-law, captain of your bodyguard and highly respected in your household? 15Was that day the first time I enquired of God for him? Of course not! Let not the king accuse your servant or any of his father's family, for your servant knows nothing at all about this whole affair."

16But the king said, "You shall surely die, Ahimelech, you and your father's whole family."

17Then the king ordered the guards at his side: "Turn and kill the priests of the LORD, because they too have sided with David. They knew he was fleeing, yet they did not tell me."

But the king's officials were not willing to raise a hand to strike the priests of the LORD.

18The king then ordered Doeg, "You turn and strike down the priests." So Doeg the Edomite turned and struck them down. That day he killed eighty-five men who wore the linen ephod. 19He also put to the sword Nob, the town of the priests, with its men and women, its children and infants, and its cattle, donkeys and sheep. 20But Abiathar, son of Ahimelech son of Ahitub, escaped and fled to join David.

21He told David that Saul had killed the priests of the LORD. 22Then David said to Abiathar: "That day, when Doeg the Edomite was there, I knew he would be sure to tell Saul. I am responsible for the death of your father's whole family. 23Stay with me; don't be afraid; the man who is seeking your life is seeking mine also. You will be safe with me."

David Saves Keilah

23 When David was told, "Look, the Philistines are fighting against Keilah and are looting the threshing-floors," 2he enquired of the LORD, saying, "Shall I go and attack these Philistines?"

The LORD answered him, "Go, attack the Philistines and save Keilah."

3But David's men said to him, "Here in Judah we are afraid. How much more, then, if we go to Keilah against the Philistine forces!"

4Once again David enquired of the LORD, and the LORD answered him, "Go down to Keilah, for I am going to give the Philistines into your hand." 5So David and his men went to Keilah, fought the Philistines and carried off their livestock. He inflicted heavy losses on the Philistines and saved the people of Keilah. 6(Now Abiathar son of Ahimelech had brought the ephod down with him when he fled to David at Keilah.)

Saul Pursues David

7Saul was told that David had gone to Keilah, and he said, "God has handed him over to me, for David has imprisoned himself by entering a town with gates and bars." 8And Saul called up all his forces for battle, to go down to Keilah to besiege David and his men.

9When David learned that Saul was plotting against him, he said to Abiathar the priest, "Bring the ephod." 10David said, "O LORD, God of Israel, your servant has heard definitely that Saul plans to come to Keilah and destroy the town on account of me. 11Will the citizens of Keilah surrender me to him? Will Saul come down, as your servant has heard? O

LORD, God of Israel, tell your servant."

And the LORD said, "He will."

¹²Again David asked, "Will the citizens of Keilah surrender me and my men to Saul?"

And the LORD said, "They will."

¹³So David and his men, about six hundred in number, left Keilah and kept moving from place to place. When Saul was told that David had escaped from Keilah, he did not go there.

¹⁴David stayed in the desert strongholds and in the hills of the Desert of Ziph. Day after day Saul searched for him, but God did not give David into his hands.

¹⁵While David was at Horesh in the Desert of Ziph, he learned that Saul had come out to take his life. ¹⁶And Saul's son Jonathan went to David at Horesh and helped him to find strength in God. ¹⁷"Don't be afraid," he said. "My father Saul will not lay a hand on you. You shall be king over Israel, and I will be second to you. Even my father Saul knows this." ¹⁸The two of them made a covenant before the LORD. Then Jonathan went home, but David remained at Horesh.

¹⁹The Ziphites went up to Saul at Gibeah and said, "Is not David hiding among us in the strongholds at Horesh, on the hill of Hakilah, south of Jeshimon? ²⁰Now, O king, come down whenever it pleases you to do so, and we will be responsible for handing him over to the king."

²¹Saul replied, "The LORD bless you for your concern for me. ²²Go and make further preparation. Find out where David usually goes and who has seen him there. They tell me he is very crafty. ²³Find out about all the hiding-places he uses and come back to me with definite information.*ᵃ* Then I will go with you; if he is in the area, I will track him down among all the clans of Judah."

²⁴So they set out and went to Ziph ahead of Saul. Now David and his men were in the Desert of Maon, in the Arabah south of Jeshimon. ²⁵Saul and his men began the search, and when David was told about it, he went down to the rock and stayed in the Desert of Maon. When Saul heard this, he went into the Desert of Maon in pursuit of David.

²⁶Saul was going along one side of the mountain, and David and his men were on the other side, hurrying to get away from Saul. As Saul and his forces were closing in on David and his men to capture them, ²⁷a messenger came to Saul, saying, "Come quickly! The Philistines are raiding the land." ²⁸Then Saul broke off his pursuit of David and went to meet the Philistines. That is why they call this place Sela Hammahlekoth.*ᵇ* ²⁹And David went up from there and lived in the strongholds of En Gedi.

David Spares Saul's Life

24 After Saul returned from pursuing the Philistines, he was told, "David is in the Desert of En Gedi." ²So Saul took three thousand chosen men from all Israel and set out to look for David and his men near the Crags of the Wild Goats.

³He came to the sheep pens along the way; a cave was there, and Saul went in to relieve himself. David and his men were far back in the cave. ⁴The men said, "This is the day the LORD spoke of when he said*ᵃ* to you, 'I will give your enemy into your hands for you to deal with as you wish.'" Then David crept up unnoticed and cut off a corner of Saul's robe.

⁵Afterwards, David was conscience-stricken for having cut off a corner of his robe. ⁶He said to his men, "The LORD forbid that I should do such a thing to my master, the LORD's anointed, or lift my hand against him; for he is the anointed of the LORD." ⁷With these words David rebuked his men and did not allow them to attack Saul. And Saul left the cave and went his way.

⁸Then David went out of the cave and called out to Saul, "My lord the king!" When Saul looked behind him, David bowed down and prostrated himself with his face to the ground. ⁹He said to Saul, "Why do you listen when men say, 'David is bent on harming you'? ¹⁰This day you

have seen with your own eyes how the LORD gave you into my hands in the cave. Some urged me to kill you, but I spared you; I said, 'I will not lift my hand against my master, because he is the LORD's anointed.' [11]See, my father, look at this piece of your robe in my hand! I cut off the corner of your robe but did not kill you. Now understand and recognise that I am not guilty of wrongdoing or rebellion. I have not wronged you, but you are hunting me down to take my life. [12]May the LORD judge between you and me. And may the LORD avenge the wrongs you have done to me, but my hand will not touch you. [13]As the old saying goes, 'From evildoers come evil deeds,' so my hand will not touch you.

[14]"Against whom has the king of Israel come out? Whom are you pursuing? A dead dog? A flea? [15]May the LORD be our judge and decide between us. May he consider my cause and uphold it; may he vindicate me by delivering me from your hand."

[16]When David finished saying this, Saul asked, "Is that your voice, David my son?" And he wept aloud. [17]"You are more righteous than I," he said. "You have treated me well, but I have treated you badly. [18]You have just now told me of the good you did to me; the LORD gave me into your hands, but you did not kill me. [19]When a man finds his enemy, does he let him get away unharmed? May the LORD reward you well for the way you treated me today. [20]I know that you will surely be king and that the kingdom of Israel will be established in your hands. [21]Now swear to me by the LORD that you will not cut off my descendants or wipe out my name from my father's family."

[22]So David gave his oath to Saul. Then Saul returned home, but David and his men went up to the stronghold.

David, Nabal and Abigail

25 Now Samuel died, and all Israel assembled and mourned for him; and they buried him at his home in Ramah.

Then David moved down into the Desert of Maon.[a] [2]A certain man in Maon, who had property there at Carmel, was very wealthy. He had a thousand goats and three thousand sheep, which he was shearing in Carmel. [3]His name was Nabal and his wife's name was Abigail. She was an intelligent and beautiful woman, but her husband, a Calebite, was surly and mean in his dealings.

[4]While David was in the desert, he heard that Nabal was shearing sheep. [5]So he sent ten young men and said to them, "Go up to Nabal at Carmel and greet him in my name. [6]Say to him: 'Long life to you! Good health to you and your household! And good health to all that is yours!

[7]"'Now I hear that it is sheep-shearing time. When your shepherds were with us, we did not ill-treat them, and the whole time they were at Carmel nothing of theirs was missing. [8]Ask your own servants and they will tell you. Therefore be favourable towards my young men, since we come at a festive time. Please give your servants and your son David whatever you can find for them.'"

[9]When David's men arrived, they gave Nabal this message in David's name. Then they waited.

[10]Nabal answered David's servants, "Who is this David? Who is this son of Jesse? Many servants are breaking away from their masters these days. [11]Why should I take my bread and water, and the meat I have slaughtered for my shearers, and give it to men coming from who knows where?"

[12]David's men turned round and went back. When they arrived, they reported every word. [13]David said to his men, "Put on your swords!" So they put on their swords, and David put on his. About four hundred men went up with David, while two hundred stayed with the supplies.

[14]One of the servants told Nabal's wife Abigail: "David sent messengers from the desert to give our master his greetings, but he hurled insults at them. [15]Yet these men were very good to us. They did not ill-treat us, and the whole time we were out in the

---

[a]1 Some Septuagint manuscripts; Hebrew *Paran*

fields near them nothing was missing. [16]Night and day they were a wall around us all the time we were herding our sheep near them. [17]Now think it over and see what you can do, because disaster is hanging over our master and his whole household. He is such a wicked man that no-one can talk to him."

[18]Abigail lost no time. She took two hundred loaves of bread, two skins of wine, five dressed sheep, five seahs[b] of roasted grain, a hundred cakes of raisins and two hundred cakes of pressed figs, and loaded them on donkeys. [19]Then she told her servants, "Go on ahead; I'll follow you." But she did not tell her husband Nabal.

[20]As she came riding her donkey into a mountain ravine, there were David and his men descending towards her, and she met them. [21]David had just said, "It's been useless—all my watching over this fellow's property in the desert so that nothing of his was missing. He has paid me back evil for good. [22]May God deal with David,[c] be it ever so severely, if by morning I leave alive one male of all who belong to him!"

[23]When Abigail saw David, she quickly got off her donkey and bowed down before David with her face to the ground. [24]She fell at his feet and said: "My lord, let the blame be on me alone. Please let your servant speak to you; hear what your servant has to say. [25]May my lord pay no attention to that wicked man Nabal. He is just like his name—his name is Fool, and folly goes with him. But as for me, your servant, I did not see the men my master sent.

[26]"Now since the LORD has kept you, my master, from bloodshed and from avenging yourself with your own hands, as surely as the LORD lives and as you live, may your enemies and all who intend to harm my master be like Nabal. [27]And let this gift, which your servant has brought to my master, be given to the men who follow you. [28]Please forgive your servant's offence, for the LORD will certainly make a

lasting dynasty for my master, because he fights the LORD's battles. Let no wrongdoing be found in you as long as you live. [29]Even though someone is pursuing you to take your life, the life of my master will be bound securely in the bundle of the living by the LORD your God. But the lives of your enemies he will hurl away as from the pocket of a sling. [30]When the LORD has done for my master every good thing he promised concerning him and has appointed him leader over Israel, [31]my master will not have on his conscience the staggering burden of needless bloodshed or of having avenged himself. And when the LORD has brought my master success, remember your servant."

[32]David said to Abigail, "Praise be to the LORD, the God of Israel, who has sent you today to meet me. [33]May you be blessed for your good judgment and for keeping me from bloodshed this day and from avenging myself with my own hands. [34]Otherwise, as surely as the LORD, the God of Israel, lives, who has kept me from harming you, if you had not come quickly to meet me, not one male belonging to Nabal would have been left alive by daybreak."

[35]Then David accepted from her hand what she had brought to him and said, "Go home in peace. I have heard your words and granted your request."

[36]When Abigail went to Nabal, he was in the house holding a banquet like that of a king. He was in high spirits and very drunk. So she told him nothing until daybreak. [37]Then in the morning, when Nabal was sober, his wife told him all these things, and his heart failed him and he became like a stone. [38]About ten days later, the LORD struck Nabal and he died.

[39]When David heard that Nabal was dead, he said, "Praise be to the LORD, who has upheld my cause against Nabal for treating me with contempt. He has kept his servant from doing wrong and has brought Nabal's wrongdoing down on his own head."

Then David sent word to Abigail,

---

b18 That is, probably about a bushel (about 37 litres)
c22 Some Septuagint manuscripts; Hebrew *with David's enemies*

asking her to become his wife. [40]His servants went to Carmel and said to Abigail, "David has sent us to you to take you to become his wife."

[41]She bowed down with her face to the ground and said, "Here is your maidservant, ready to serve you and wash the feet of my master's servants." [42]Abigail quickly got on a donkey and, attended by her five maids, went with David's messengers and became his wife. [43]David had also married Ahinoam of Jezreel, and they both were his wives. [44]But Saul had given his daughter Michal, David's wife, to Paltiel[d] son of Laish, who was from Gallim.

David Again Spares Saul's Life

26 The Ziphites went to Saul at Gibeah and said, "Is not David hiding on the hill of Hakilah, which faces Jeshimon?"

[2]So Saul went down to the Desert of Ziph, with his three thousand chosen men of Israel, to search there for David. [3]Saul made his camp beside the road on the hill of Hakilah facing Jeshimon, but David stayed in the desert. When he saw that Saul had followed him there, [4]he sent out scouts and learned that Saul had definitely arrived.[a]

[5]Then David set out and went to the place where Saul had camped. He saw where Saul and Abner son of Ner, the commander of the army, had lain down. Saul was lying inside the camp, with the army encamped around him.

[6]David then asked Ahimelech the Hittite and Abishai son of Zeruiah, Joab's brother, "Who will go down into the camp with me to Saul?"

"I'll go with you," said Abishai.

[7]So David and Abishai went to the army by night, and there was Saul, lying asleep inside the camp with his spear stuck in the ground near his head. Abner and the soldiers were lying round him.

[8]Abishai said to David, "Today God has given your enemy into your hands. Now let me pin him to the ground with one thrust of my spear; I won't strike him twice."

[9]But David said to Abishai, "Don't destroy him! Who can lay a hand on the LORD's anointed and be guiltless? [10]As surely as the LORD lives," he said, "the LORD himself will strike him; either his time will come and he will die, or he will go into battle and perish. [11]But the LORD forbid that I should lay a hand on the LORD's anointed. Now get the spear and water jug that are near his head, and let's go."

[12]So David took the spear and water jug near Saul's head, and they left. No-one saw or knew about it, nor did anyone wake up. They were all sleeping, because the LORD had put them into a deep sleep.

[13]Then David crossed over to the other side and stood on top of the hill some distance away; there was a wide space between them. [14]He called out to the army and to Abner son of Ner, "Aren't you going to answer me, Abner?"

Abner replied, "Who are you who calls to the king?"

[15]David said, "You're a man, aren't you? And who is like you in Israel? Why didn't you guard your lord the king? Someone came to destroy your lord the king. [16]What you have done is not good. As surely as the LORD lives, you and your men deserve to die, because you did not guard your master, the LORD's anointed. Look around you. Where are the king's spear and water jug that were near his head?"

[17]Saul recognised David's voice and said, "Is that your voice, David my son?"

David replied, "Yes it is, my lord the king." [18]And he added, "Why is my lord pursuing his servant? What have I done, and what wrong am I guilty of? [19]Now let my lord the king listen to his servant's words. If the LORD has incited you against me, then may he accept an offering. If, however, men have done it, may they be cursed before the LORD! They have now driven me from my share in the LORD's inheritance and have said, 'Go, serve other gods.' [20]Now do not let my blood fall

---

_d44_ Hebrew _Palti,_ a variant of _Paltiel_　　_a4_ Or _had come to Nacon_ to the ground far from the presence of the LORD. The king of Israel has come out to look for a flea—as one hunts a partridge in the mountains."

21Then Saul said, "I have sinned. Come back, David my son. Because you considered my life precious today, I will not try to harm you again. Surely I have acted like a fool and have erred greatly."

22"Here is the king's spear," David answered. "Let one of your young men come over and get it. 23The LORD rewards every man for his righteousness and faithfulness. The LORD gave you into my hands today, but I would not lay a hand on the LORD's anointed. 24As surely as I valued your life today, so may the LORD value my life and deliver me from all trouble."

25Then Saul said to David, "May you be blessed, my son David; you will do great things and surely triumph."

So David went on his way, and Saul returned home.

David Among the Philistines

27 But David thought to himself, "One of these days I shall be destroyed by the hand of Saul. The best thing I can do is to escape to the land of the Philistines. Then Saul will give up searching for me anywhere in Israel, and I will slip out of his hand."

2So David and the six hundred men with him left and went over to Achish son of Maoch king of Gath. 3David and his men settled in Gath with Achish. Each man had his family with him, and David had his two wives: Ahinoam of Jezreel and Abigail of Carmel, the widow of Nabal. 4When Saul was told that David had fled to Gath, he no longer searched for him.

5Then David said to Achish, "If I have found favour in your eyes, let a place be assigned to me in one of the country towns, that I may live there. Why should your servant live in the royal city with you?"

6So on that day Achish gave him Ziklag, and it has belonged to the kings of Judah ever since. 7David lived in Philistine territory for a year and four months.

8Now David and his men went up and raided the Geshurites, the Girzites and the Amalekites. (From ancient times these peoples had lived in the land extending to Shur and Egypt.) 9Whenever David attacked an area, he did not leave a man or woman alive, but took sheep and cattle, donkeys and camels, and clothes. Then he returned to Achish.

10When Achish asked, "Where did you go raiding today?" David would say, "Against the Negev of Judah" or "Against the Negev of Jerahmeel" or "Against the Negev of the Kenites." 11He did not leave a man or woman alive to be brought to Gath, for he thought, "They might inform on us and say, 'This is what David did.'" And such was his practice as long as he lived in Philistine territory. 12Achish trusted David and said to himself, "He has become so odious to his people, the Israelites, that he will be my servant for ever."

Saul and the Witch of Endor

28 In those days the Philistines gathered their forces to fight against Israel. Achish said to David, "You must understand that you and your men will accompany me in the army."

2David said, "Then you will see for yourself what your servant can do."

Achish replied, "Very well, I will make you my bodyguard for life."

3Now Samuel was dead, and all Israel had mourned for him and buried him in his own town of Ramah. Saul had expelled the mediums and spiritists from the land.

4The Philistines assembled and came and set up camp at Shunem, while Saul gathered all the Israelites and set up camp at Gilboa. 5When Saul saw the Philistine army, he was afraid; terror filled his heart. 6He enquired of the LORD, but the LORD did not answer him by dreams or Urim or prophets. 7Saul then said to his attendants, "Find me a woman who is a medium, so that I may go and enquire of her."

"There is one in Endor," they said.

8So Saul disguised himself, putting on other clothes, and at night he and two men went to the woman. "Consult a spirit for

me," he said, "and bring up for me the one
I name."

⁹But the woman said to him, "Surely
you know what Saul has done. He has cut
off the mediums and spiritists from the
land. Why have you set a trap for my life to
bring about my death?"

¹⁰Saul swore to her by the LORD, "As
surely as the LORD lives, you will not be
punished for this."

¹¹Then the woman asked, "Whom shall
I bring up for you?"

"Bring up Samuel," he said.

¹²When the woman saw Samuel, she
cried out at the top of her voice and said to
Saul, "Why have you deceived me? You
are Saul!"

¹³The king said to her, "Don't be afraid.
What do you see?"

The woman said, "I see a spirit*ᵃ* coming
up out of the ground."

¹⁴"What does he look like?" he asked.

"An old man wearing a robe is coming
up," she said.

Then Saul knew it was Samuel, and he
bowed down and prostrated himself with
his face to the ground.

¹⁵Samuel said to Saul, "Why have you
disturbed me by bringing me up?"

"I am in great distress," Saul said. "The
Philistines are fighting against me, and
God has turned away from me. He no
longer answers me, either by prophets or
by dreams. So I have called on you to tell
me what to do."

¹⁶Samuel said, "Why do you consult
me, now that the LORD has turned away
from you and become your enemy? ¹⁷The
LORD has done what he predicted through
me. The LORD has torn the kingdom out of
your hands and given it to one of your
neighbours—to David. ¹⁸Because you did
not obey the LORD or carry out his fierce
wrath against the Amalekites, the LORD
has done this to you today. ¹⁹The LORD
will hand over both Israel and you to the
Philistines, and tomorrow you and your
sons will be with me. The LORD will also
hand over the army of Israel to the Philistines."

²⁰Immediately Saul fell full length on

the ground, filled with fear because of
Samuel's words. His strength was gone,
for he had eaten nothing all that day and
night.

²¹When the woman came to Saul and
saw that he was greatly shaken, she said,
"Look, your maidservant has obeyed you.
I took my life in my hands and did what
you told me to do. ²²Now please listen to
your servant and let me give you some
food so that you may eat and have the
strength to go on your way."

²³He refused and said, "I will not eat."

But his men joined the woman in urging
him, and he listened to them. He got up
from the ground and sat on the couch.

²⁴The woman had a fattened calf at the
house, which she slaughtered at once. She
took some flour, kneaded it and baked
bread without yeast. ²⁵Then she set it before Saul and his men, and they ate. That
same night they got up and left.

Achish Sends David Back to Ziklag

29 The Philistines gathered all their
forces at Aphek, and Israel
camped by the spring in Jezreel. ²As the
Philistine rulers marched with their units
of hundreds and thousands, David and
his men were marching at the rear
with Achish. ³The commanders of the
Philistines asked, "What about these
Hebrews?"

Achish replied, "Is this not David, who
was an officer of Saul king of Israel? He
has already been with me for over a year,
and from the day he left Saul until now, I
have found no fault in him."

⁴But the Philistine commanders were
angry with him and said, "Send the man
back, that he may return to the place you
assigned him. He must not go with us into
battle, or he will turn against us during the
fighting. How better could he regain his
master's favour than by taking the heads
of our own men? ⁵Isn't this the David they
sang about in their dances:

" 'Saul has slain his thousands,
and David his tens of thousands'?"

ᵃ13 Or see spirits; or see gods

⁶So Achish called David and said to him, "As surely as the LORD lives, you have been reliable, and I would be pleased to have you serve with me in the army. From the day you came to me until now, I have found no fault in you, but the rulers don't approve of you. ⁷Turn back and go in peace; do nothing to displease the Philistine rulers."

⁸"But what have I done?" asked David. "What have you found against your servant from the day I came to you until now? Why can't I go and fight against the enemies of my lord the king?"

⁹Achish answered, "I know that you have been as pleasing in my eyes as an angel of God; nevertheless, the Philistine commanders have said, 'He must not go up with us into battle.' ¹⁰Now get up early, along with your master's servants who have come with you, and leave in the morning as soon as it is light."

¹¹So David and his men got up early in the morning to go back to the land of the Philistines, and the Philistines went up to Jezreel.

David Destroys the Amalekites

30 David and his men reached Ziklag on the third day. Now the Amalekites had raided the Negev and Ziklag. They had attacked Ziklag and burned it, ²and had taken captive the women and all who were in it, both young and old. They killed none of them, but carried them off as they went on their way.

³When David and his men came to Ziklag, they found it destroyed by fire and their wives and sons and daughters taken captive. ⁴So David and his men wept aloud until they had no strength left to weep. ⁵David's two wives had been captured— Ahinoam of Jezreel and Abigail, the widow of Nabal of Carmel. ⁶David was greatly distressed because the men were talking of stoning him; each one was bitter in spirit because of his sons and daughters. But David found strength in the LORD his God.

⁷Then David said to Abiathar the priest, the son of Ahimelech, "Bring me the ephod." Abiathar brought it to him, ⁸and

David enquired of the LORD, "Shall I pursue this raiding party? Will I overtake them?"

"Pursue them," he answered. "You will certainly overtake them and succeed in the rescue."

⁹David and the six hundred men with him came to the Besor Ravine, where some stayed behind, ¹⁰for two hundred men were too exhausted to cross the ravine. But David and four hundred men continued the pursuit.

¹¹They found an Egyptian in a field and brought him to David. They gave him water to drink and food to eat—¹²part of a cake of pressed figs and two cakes of raisins. He ate and was revived, for he had not eaten any food or drunk any water for three days and three nights.

¹³David asked him, "To whom do you belong, and where do you come from?"

He said, "I am an Egyptian, the slave of an Amalekite. My master abandoned me when I became ill three days ago. ¹⁴We raided the Negev of the Kerethites and the territory belonging to Judah and the Negev of Caleb. And we burned Ziklag."

¹⁵David asked him, "Can you lead me down to this raiding party?"

He answered, "Swear to me before God that you will not kill me or hand me over to my master, and I will take you down to them."

¹⁶He led David down, and there they were, scattered over the countryside, eating, drinking and revelling because of the great amount of plunder they had taken from the land of the Philistines and from Judah. ¹⁷David fought them from dusk until the evening of the next day, and none of them got away, except four hundred young men who rode off on camels and fled. ¹⁸David recovered everything the Amalekites had taken, including his two wives. ¹⁹Nothing was missing: young or old, boy or girl, plunder or anything else they had taken. David brought everything back. ²⁰He took all the flocks and herds, and his men drove them ahead of the other livestock, saying, "This is David's plunder."

²¹Then David came to the two hundred men who had been too exhausted to follow him and who were left behind at the

Besor Ravine. They came out to meet David and the people with him. As David and his men approached, he greeted them. 22But all the evil men and troublemakers among David's followers said, "Because they did not go out with us, we will not share with them the plunder we recovered. However, each man may take his wife and children and go."

23David replied, "No, my brothers, you must not do that with what the LORD has given us. He has protected us and handed over to us the forces that came against us. 24Who will listen to what you say? The share of the man who stayed with the supplies is to be the same as that of him who went down to the battle. All shall share alike." 25David made this a statute and ordinance for Israel from that day to this.

26When David arrived in Ziklag, he sent some of the plunder to the elders of Judah, who were his friends, saying, "Here is a present for you from the plunder of the LORD's enemies."

27He sent it to those who were in Bethel, Ramoth Negev and Jattir; 28to those in Aroer, Siphmoth, Eshtemoa 29and Racal; to those in the towns of the Jerahmeelites and the Kenites; 30to those in Hormah, Bor Ashan, Athach 31and Hebron; and to those in all the other places where David and his men had roamed.

Saul Takes His Life

31 Now the Philistines fought against Israel; the Israelites fled before them, and many fell slain on Mount Gilboa. 2The Philistines pressed hard after Saul and his sons, and they killed his sons Jonathan, Abinadab and Malki-Shua.

3The fighting grew fierce around Saul, and when the archers overtook him, they wounded him critically.

4Saul said to his armour-bearer, "Draw your sword and run me through, or these uncircumcised fellows will come and run me through and abuse me."

But the armour-bearer was terrified and would not do it; so Saul took his own sword and fell on it. 5When the armour-bearer saw that Saul was dead, he too fell on his sword and died with him. 6So Saul and his three sons and his armour-bearer and all his men died together that same day.

7When the Israelites along the valley and those across the Jordan saw that the Israelite army had fled and that Saul and his sons had died, they abandoned their towns and fled. And the Philistines came and occupied them.

8The next day, when the Philistines came to strip the dead, they found Saul and his three sons fallen on Mount Gilboa. 9They cut off his head and stripped off his armour, and they sent messengers throughout the land of the Philistines to proclaim the news in the temple of their idols and among their people. 10They put his armour in the temple of the Ashtoreths and fastened his body to the wall of Beth Shan.

11When the people of Jabesh Gilead heard of what the Philistines had done to Saul, 12all their valiant men journeyed through the night to Beth Shan. They took down the bodies of Saul and his sons from the wall of Beth Shan and went to Jabesh, where they burned them. 13Then they took their bones and buried them under a tamarisk tree at Jabesh, and they fasted seven days.

2 Samuel

David Hears of Saul's Death

1 After the death of Saul, David returned from defeating the Amalekites and stayed in Ziklag two days. ²On the third day a man arrived from Saul's camp, with his clothes torn and with dust on his head. When he came to David, he fell to the ground to pay him honour.

³"Where have you come from?" David asked him.

He answered, "I have escaped from the Israelite camp."

⁴"What happened?" David asked. "Tell me."

He said, "The men fled from the battle. Many of them fell and died. And Saul and his son Jonathan are dead."

⁵Then David said to the young man who brought him the report, "How do you know that Saul and his son Jonathan are dead?"

⁶"I happened to be on Mount Gilboa," the young man said, "and there was Saul, leaning on his spear, with the chariots and riders almost upon him. ⁷When he turned round and saw me, he called out to me, and I said, 'What can I do?'

⁸"He asked me, 'Who are you?'

"'An Amalekite,' I answered.

⁹"Then he said to me, 'Stand over me and kill me! I am in the throes of death, but I'm still alive.'

¹⁰"So I stood over him and killed him, because I knew that after he had fallen he could not survive. And I took the crown that was on his head and the band on his arm and have brought them here to my lord."

¹¹Then David and all the men with him took hold of their clothes and tore them. ¹²They mourned and wept and fasted till evening for Saul and his son Jonathan, and for the army of the LORD and the house of Israel, because they had fallen by the sword.

¹³David said to the young man who brought him the report, "Where are you from?"

"I am the son of an alien, an Amalekite," he answered.

¹⁴David asked him, "Why were you not afraid to lift your hand to destroy the LORD's anointed?"

¹⁵Then David called one of his men and said, "Go, strike him down!" So he struck him down, and he died. ¹⁶For David had said to him, "Your blood be on your own head. Your own mouth testified against you when you said, 'I killed the LORD's anointed.'"

David's Lament for Saul and Jonathan

¹⁷David took up this lament concerning Saul and his son Jonathan, ¹⁸and ordered that the men of Judah be taught this lament of the bow (it is written in the Book of Jashar):

¹⁹"Your glory, O Israel, lies slain on
      your heights.
   How the mighty have fallen!

²⁰"Tell it not in Gath,
      proclaim it not in the streets of
         Ashkelon,

lest the daughters of the Philistines be
    glad,
  lest the daughters of the
    uncircumcised rejoice.

21"O mountains of Gilboa,
  may you have neither dew nor rain,
  nor fields that yield offerings ⌊of
    grain⌋.
For there the shield of the mighty was
    defiled,
  the shield of Saul—no longer rubbed
    with oil.
22From the blood of the slain,
  from the flesh of the mighty,
the bow of Jonathan did not turn back,
  the sword of Saul did not return
    unsatisfied.

23"Saul and Jonathan—
  in life they were loved and gracious,
  and in death they were not parted.
They were swifter than eagles,
  they were stronger than lions.

24"O daughters of Israel,
  weep for Saul,
who clothed you in scarlet and finery,
  who adorned your garments with
    ornaments of gold.

25"How the mighty have fallen in battle!
  Jonathan lies slain on your heights.
26I grieve for you, Jonathan my brother;
  you were very dear to me.
Your love for me was wonderful,
  more wonderful than that of women.

27"How the mighty have fallen!
  The weapons of war have perished!"

David Anointed King Over Judah

2 In the course of time, David enquired
of the LORD. "Shall I go up to one of
the towns of Judah?" he asked.
  The LORD said, "Go up."
  David asked, "Where shall I go?"
  "To Hebron," the LORD answered.
2So David went up there with his two
wives, Ahinoam of Jezreel and Abigail,

the widow of Nabal of Carmel. 3David
also took the men who were with him,
each with his family, and they settled in
Hebron and its towns. 4Then the men of
Judah came to Hebron and there they
anointed David king over the house of
Judah.

When David was told that it was the
men of Jabesh Gilead who had buried
Saul, 5he sent messengers to the men of
Jabesh Gilead to say to them, "The LORD
bless you for showing this kindness to Saul
your master by burying him. 6May the
LORD now show you kindness and faithfulness, and I too will show you the same
favour because you have done this. 7Now
then, be strong and brave, for Saul your
master is dead, and the house of Judah has
anointed me king over them."

War Between the Houses of David and Saul

8Meanwhile, Abner son of Ner, the
commander of Saul's army, had taken Ish-
Bosheth son of Saul and brought him over
to Mahanaim. 9He made him king over
Gilead, Ashuri[a] and Jezreel, and also over
Ephraim, Benjamin and all Israel.

10Ish-Bosheth son of Saul was forty
years old when he became king over
Israel, and he reigned two years. The
house of Judah, however, followed
David. 11The length of time David was
king in Hebron over the house of Judah
was seven years and six months.

12Abner son of Ner, together with the
men of Ish-Bosheth son of Saul, left
Mahanaim and went to Gibeon. 13Joab
son of Zeruiah and David's men went out
and met them at the pool of Gibeon. One
group sat down on one side of the pool and
one group on the other side.

14Then Abner said to Joab, "Let's have
some of the young men get up and fight
hand to hand in front of us."

"All right, let them do it," Joab said.
15So they stood up and were counted
off—twelve men for Benjamin and Ish-
Bosheth son of Saul, and twelve for
David. 16Then each man grabbed his

opponent by the head and thrust his dagger into his opponent's side, and they fell down together. So that place in Gibeon was called Helkath Hazzurim.*b*

17The battle that day was very fierce, and Abner and the men of Israel were defeated by David's men.

18The three sons of Zeruiah were there: Joab, Abishai and Asahel. Now Asahel was as fleet-footed as a wild gazelle. 19He chased Abner, turning neither to the right nor to the left as he pursued him. 20Abner looked behind him and asked, "Is that you, Asahel?"

"It is," he answered.

21Then Abner said to him, "Turn aside to the right or to the left; take on one of the young men and strip him of his weapons." But Asahel would not stop chasing him.

22Again Abner warned Asahel, "Stop chasing me! Why should I strike you down? How could I look your brother Joab in the face?"

23But Asahel refused to give up the pursuit; so Abner thrust the butt of his spear into Asahel's stomach, and the spear came out through his back. He fell there and died on the spot. And every man stopped when he came to the place where Asahel had fallen and died.

24But Joab and Abishai pursued Abner, and as the sun was setting, they came to the hill of Ammah, near Giah on the way to the wasteland of Gibeon. 25Then the men of Benjamin rallied behind Abner. They formed themselves into a group and took their stand on top of a hill.

26Abner called out to Joab, "Must the sword devour for ever? Don't you realise that this will end in bitterness? How long before you order your men to stop pursuing their brothers?"

27Joab answered, "As surely as God lives, if you had not spoken, the men would have continued the pursuit of their brothers until morning."*c*

28So Joab blew the trumpet, and all the men came to a halt; they no longer pursued Israel, nor did they fight any more.

29All that night Abner and his men marched through the Arabah. They crossed the Jordan, continued through the whole Bithron*d* and came to Mahanaim.

30Then Joab returned from pursuing Abner and assembled all his men. Besides Asahel, nineteen of David's men were found missing. 31But David's men had killed 360 Benjamites who were with Abner. 32They took Asahel and buried him in his father's tomb at Bethlehem. Then Joab and his men marched all night and arrived at Hebron by daybreak.

3 The war between the house of Saul and the house of David lasted a long time. David grew stronger and stronger, while the house of Saul grew weaker and weaker.

2Sons were born to David in Hebron:

His firstborn was Amnon the son of Ahinoam of Jezreel;

3his second, Kileab the son of Abigail the widow of Nabal of Carmel;

the third, Absalom the son of Maacah daughter of Talmai king of Geshur;

4the fourth, Adonijah the son of Haggith;

the fifth, Shephatiah the son of Abital;

5and the sixth, Ithream the son of David's wife Eglah.

These were born to David in Hebron.

Abner Goes Over to David

6During the war between the house of Saul and the house of David, Abner had been strengthening his own position in the house of Saul. 7Now Saul had had a concubine named Rizpah daughter of Aiah. And Ish-Bosheth said to Abner, "Why did you sleep with my father's concubine?"

8Abner was very angry because of what Ish-Bosheth said and he answered, "Am I a dog's head—on Judah's side? This very day I am loyal to the house of your father

---

b16   *Helkath Hazzurim* means *field of daggers* or *field of hostilities.*
c27   Or *spoken this morning, the men would not have taken up the pursuit of their brothers*; or *spoken, the men would have given up the pursuit of their brothers by morning*
d29   Or *morning*; or *ravine*; the meaning of the Hebrew for this word is uncertain.

Saul and to his family and friends. I haven't handed you over to David. Yet now you accuse me of an offence involving this woman! ⁹May God deal with Abner, be it ever so severely, if I do not do for David what the LORD promised him on oath ¹⁰and transfer the kingdom from the house of Saul and establish David's throne over Israel and Judah from Dan to Beersheba." ¹¹Ish-Bosheth did not dare to say another word to Abner, because he was afraid of him.

¹²Then Abner sent messengers on his behalf to say to David, "Whose land is it? Make an agreement with me, and I will help you bring all Israel over to you."

¹³"Good," said David. "I will make an agreement with you. But I demand one thing of you: Do not come into my presence unless you bring Michal daughter of Saul when you come to see me." ¹⁴Then David sent messengers to Ish-Bosheth son of Saul, demanding, "Give me my wife Michal, whom I betrothed to myself for the price of a hundred Philistine foreskins."

¹⁵So Ish-Bosheth gave orders and had her taken away from her husband Paltiel son of Laish. ¹⁶Her husband, however, went with her, weeping behind her all the way to Bahurim. Then Abner said to him, "Go back home!" So he went back.

¹⁷Abner conferred with the elders of Israel and said, "For some time you have wanted to make David your king. ¹⁸Now do it! For the LORD promised David, 'By my servant David I will rescue my people Israel from the hand of the Philistines and from the hand of all their enemies.'"

¹⁹Abner also spoke to the Benjamites in person. Then he went to Hebron to tell David everything that Israel and the whole house of Benjamin wanted to do. ²⁰When Abner, who had twenty men with him, came to David at Hebron, David prepared a feast for him and his men. ²¹Then Abner said to David, "Let me go at once and assemble all Israel for my lord the king, so that they may make a compact with you, and that you may rule over all

that your heart desires." So David sent Abner away, and he went in peace.

Joab Murders Abner

²²Just then David's men and Joab returned from a raid and brought with them a great deal of plunder. But Abner was no longer with David in Hebron, because David had sent him away, and he had gone in peace. ²³When Joab and all the soldiers with him arrived, he was told that Abner son of Ner had come to the king and that the king had sent him away and that he had gone in peace.

²⁴So Joab went to the king and said, "What have you done? Look, Abner came to you. Why did you let him go? Now he is gone! ²⁵You know Abner son of Ner; he came to deceive you and observe your movements and find out everything you are doing."

²⁶Joab then left David and sent messengers after Abner, and they brought him back from the well of Sirah. But David did not know it. ²⁷Now when Abner returned to Hebron, Joab took him aside into the gateway, as though to speak with him privately. And there, to avenge the blood of his brother Asahel, Joab stabbed him in the stomach, and he died.

²⁸Later, when David heard about this, he said, "I and my kingdom are for ever innocent before the LORD concerning the blood of Abner son of Ner. ²⁹May his blood fall upon the head of Joab and upon all his father's house! May Joab's house never be without someone who has a running sore or leprosy[a] or who leans on a crutch or who falls by the sword or who lacks food."

³⁰(Joab and his brother Abishai murdered Abner because he had killed their brother Asahel in the battle of Gibeon.)

³¹Then David said to Joab and all the people with him, "Tear your clothes and put on sackcloth and walk in mourning in front of Abner." King David himself walked behind the bier. ³²They buried Abner in Hebron, and the king wept aloud at Abner's tomb. All the people wept also.

---

a29 The Hebrew word was used for various diseases affecting the skin—not necessarily leprosy.

33The king sang this lament for Abner:

"Should Abner have died as the lawless
      die?
34   Your hands were not bound,
      your feet were not fettered.
You fell as one falls before wicked
      men."

And all the people wept over him again.
35Then they all came and urged David
to eat something while it was still day; but
David took an oath, saying, "May God
deal with me, be it ever so severely, if I
taste bread or anything else before the sun
sets!"
36All the people took note and were
pleased; indeed, everything the king did
pleased them. 37So on that day all the
people and all Israel knew that the king
had no part in the murder of Abner son of
Ner.
38Then the king said to his men, "Do
you not realise that a prince and a great
man has fallen in Israel this day? 39And
today, though I am the anointed king, I
am weak, and these sons of Zeruiah are
too strong for me. May the LORD repay the
evildoer according to his evil deeds!"

Ish-Bosheth Murdered

4 When Ish-Bosheth son of Saul heard
that Abner had died in Hebron,
he lost courage, and all Israel became
alarmed. 2Now Saul's son had two men
who were leaders of raiding bands. One
was named Baanah and the other Recab;
they were sons of Rimmon the Beerothite
from the tribe of Benjamin—Beeroth is
considered part of Benjamin, 3because the
people of Beeroth fled to Gittaim and
have lived there as aliens to this day.
4(Jonathan son of Saul had a son who
was lame in both feet. He was five years
old when the news about Saul and
Jonathan came from Jezreel. His nurse
picked him up and fled, but as she hurried
to leave, he fell and became crippled. His
name was Mephibosheth.)
5Now Recab and Baanah, the sons of
Rimmon the Beerothite, set out for the
house of Ish-Bosheth, and they arrived

there in the heat of the day while he was
taking his noonday rest. 6They went into
the inner part of the house as if to get some
wheat, and they stabbed him in the
stomach. Then Recab and his brother
Baanah slipped away.
7They had gone into the house while he
was lying on the bed in his bedroom. After
they stabbed and killed him, they cut off
his head. Taking it with them, they
travelled all night by way of the Arabah.
8They brought the head of Ish-Bosheth to
David at Hebron and said to the king,
"Here is the head of Ish-Bosheth son of
Saul, your enemy, who tried to take your
life. This day the LORD has avenged my
lord the king against Saul and his
offspring."
9David answered Recab and his brother
Baanah, the sons of Rimmon the
Beerothite, "As surely as the LORD lives,
who has delivered me out of all trouble,
10when a man told me, 'Saul is dead,' and
thought he was bringing good news, I
seized him and put him to death in Ziklag.
That was the reward I gave him for his
news! 11How much more—when wicked
men have killed an innocent man in his
own house and on his own bed—should I
not now demand his blood from your hand
and rid the earth of you!"
12So David gave an order to his men,
and they killed them. They cut off their
hands and feet and hung the bodies by the
pool in Hebron. But they took the head of
Ish-Bosheth and buried it in Abner's tomb
at Hebron.

David Becomes King Over Israel

5 All the tribes of Israel came to David
at Hebron and said, "We are your
own flesh and blood. 2In the past, while
Saul was king over us, you were the one
who led Israel on their military campaigns. And the LORD said to you, 'You
shall shepherd my people Israel, and you
shall become their ruler.'"
3When all the elders of Israel had come
to King David at Hebron, the king made a
compact with them at Hebron before the
LORD, and they anointed David king over
Israel.

[4]David was thirty years old when he became king, and he reigned for forty years. [5]In Hebron he reigned over Judah for seven years and six months, and in Jerusalem he reigned over all Israel and Judah for thirty-three years.

David Conquers Jerusalem

[6]The king and his men marched to Jerusalem to attack the Jebusites, who lived there. The Jebusites said to David, "You will not get in here; even the blind and the lame can ward you off." They thought, "David cannot get in here." [7]Nevertheless, David captured the fortress of Zion, the City of David.

[8]On that day, David said, "Anyone who conquers the Jebusites will have to use the water shaft[a] to reach those 'lame and blind' who are David's enemies."[b] That is why they say, "The 'blind and lame' will not enter the palace."

[9]David then took up residence in the fortress and called it the City of David. He built up the area around it, from the supporting terraces[c] inward. [10]And he became more and more powerful, because the LORD God Almighty was with him.

[11]Now Hiram king of Tyre sent messengers to David, along with cedar logs and carpenters and stonemasons, and they built a palace for David. [12]And David knew that the LORD had established him as king over Israel and had exalted his kingdom for the sake of his people Israel.

[13]After he left Hebron, David took more concubines and wives in Jerusalem, and more sons and daughters were born to him. [14]These are the names of the children born to him there: Shammua, Shobab, Nathan, Solomon, [15]Ibhar, Elishua, Nepheg, Japhia, [16]Elishama, Eliada and Eliphelet.

David Defeats the Philistines

[17]When the Philistines heard that David had been anointed king over Israel, they went up in full force to search for him, but David heard about it and went down to the stronghold. [18]Now the Philistines had come and spread out in the Valley of Rephaim; [19]so David enquired of the LORD, "Shall I go and attack the Philistines? Will you hand them over to me?"

The LORD answered him, "Go, for I will surely hand the Philistines over to you."

[20]So David went to Baal Perazim, and there he defeated them. He said, "As waters break out, the LORD has broken out against my enemies before me." So that place was called Baal Perazim.[d] [21]The Philistines abandoned their idols there, and David and his men carried them off.

[22]Once more the Philistines came up and spread out in the Valley of Rephaim; [23]so David enquired of the LORD, and he answered, "Do not go straight up, but circle round behind them and attack them in front of the balsam trees. [24]As soon as you hear the sound of marching in the tops of the balsam trees, move quickly, because that will mean the LORD has gone out in front of you to strike the Philistine army." [25]So David did as the LORD commanded him, and he struck down the Philistines all the way from Gibeon[e] to Gezer.

The Ark Brought to Jerusalem

6 David again brought together out of Israel chosen men, thirty thousand in all. [2]He and all his men set out from Baalah of Judah[a] to bring up from there the ark of God, which is called by the Name,[b] the name of the LORD Almighty, who is enthroned between the cherubim that are on the ark. [3]They set the ark of God on a new cart and brought it from the house of Abinadab, which was on the hill. Uzzah and Ahio, sons of Abinadab, were guiding the new cart [4]with the ark of God on it,[c] and Ahio was walking in front of it. [5]David and the whole house of Israel were celebrating with all their might before the

---

[a]8 Or *use scaling hooks*   [b]8 Or *are hated by David*   [c]9 Or *the Millo*
[d]20 *Baal Perazim* means *the lord who breaks out*.   [e]25 Septuagint (see also 1 Chron. 14:16); Hebrew *Geba*
[a]2 That is, Kiriath Jearim; Hebrew *Baale Judah*, a variant of *Baalah of Judah*
[b]2 Hebrew; Septuagint and Vulgate do not have *the Name*.
[c]3, 4 Dead Sea Scrolls and some Septuagint manuscripts; Masoretic Text *cart* [4]*and they brought it with the ark of God from the house of Abinadab, which was on the hill*

LORD, with songs[d] and with harps, lyres, tambourines, sistrums and cymbals.

6When they came to the threshing-floor of Nacon, Uzzah reached out and took hold of the ark of God, because the oxen stumbled. 7The LORD's anger burned against Uzzah because of his irreverent act; therefore God struck him down and he died there beside the ark of God.

8Then David was angry because the LORD's wrath had broken out against Uzzah, and to this day that place is called Perez Uzzah.[e]

9David was afraid of the LORD that day and said, "How can the ark of the LORD ever come to me?" 10He was not willing to take the ark of the LORD to be with him in the City of David. Instead, he took it aside to the house of Obed-Edom the Gittite. 11The ark of the LORD remained in the house of Obed-Edom the Gittite for three months, and the LORD blessed him and his entire household.

12Now King David was told, "The LORD has blessed the household of Obed-Edom and everything he has, because of the ark of God." So David went down and brought up the ark of God from the house of Obed-Edom to the City of David with rejoicing. 13When those who were carrying the ark of the LORD had taken six steps, he sacrificed a bull and a fattened calf. 14David, wearing a linen ephod, danced before the LORD with all his might, 15while he and the entire house of Israel brought up the ark of the LORD with shouts and the sound of trumpets.

16As the ark of the LORD was entering the City of David, Michal daughter of Saul watched from a window. And when she saw King David leaping and dancing before the LORD, she despised him in her heart.

17They brought the ark of the LORD and set it in its place inside the tent that David had pitched for it, and David sacrificed burnt offerings and fellowship offerings[f] before the LORD. 18After he had finished sacrificing the burnt offerings and fellowship offerings, he blessed the people in the name of the LORD Almighty. 19Then he gave a loaf of bread, a cake of dates and a cake of raisins to each person in the whole crowd of Israelites, both men and women. And all the people went to their homes.

20When David returned home to bless his household, Michal daughter of Saul came out to meet him and said, "How the king of Israel has distinguished himself today, disrobing in the sight of the slave girls of his servants as any vulgar fellow would."

21David said to Michal, "It was before the LORD, who chose me rather than your father or anyone from his house when he appointed me ruler over the LORD's people Israel—I will celebrate before the LORD. 22I will become even more undignified than this, and I will be humiliated in my own eyes. But by these slave girls you spoke of, I will be held in honour."

23And Michal daughter of Saul had no children to the day of her death.

God's Promise to David

7 After the king was settled in his palace and the LORD had given him rest from all his enemies around him, 2he said to Nathan the prophet, "Here I am, living in a palace of cedar, while the ark of God remains in a tent."

3Nathan replied to the king, "Whatever you have in mind, go ahead and do it, for the LORD is with you."

4That night the word of the LORD came to Nathan, saying:

5"Go and tell my servant David, 'This is what the LORD says: Are you the one to build me a house to dwell in? 6I have not dwelt in a house from the day I brought the Israelites up out of Egypt to this day. I have been moving from place to place with a tent as my dwelling. 7Wherever I have moved with all the Israelites, did I ever say to any of their rulers whom I commanded to shepherd my people

---

d5 See Dead Sea Scrolls, Septuagint and 1 Chron. 13:8; Masoretic Text *celebrating before the LORD with all kinds of instruments made of pine.*   e8 *Perez Uzzah* means *the outbreak against Uzzah.*
f17 Traditionally *peace offerings*; also in verse 18

Listening to God

[1 Kings 19:1-18 (p. 361)]

Read the passage through
Read it again in the context of chapters 17 and 18 (pp. 358-361) to appreciate the broader picture and to understand why Elijah is feeling as he is.

Identify the facts
➤ Make a list of what has happened in each chapter.
➤ Who is involved, their attitudes, behaviour, emotions?
➤ Focus on Elijah. What strikes you about his attitude and behaviour over the 3 chapters? Are there any changes? Why had Elijah 'had enough' (19:2-3,10,14)
➤ Focus on God's interaction with Elijah over the 3 chapters. What is his response to Elijah in chapter 19, what does he ask him twice? (19:9,13)

Reflect on God's question to Elijah at v9: 'What are you doing here…?'
➤ Focus on what 'here' means for you just now - emotionally, physically, spiritually?
➤ Elijah was afraid, think about what you are afraid of. What disturbs you most?
Why those particular people, things or events?
How might you overcome these fears?

> Elijah was commissioned for further service and given fresh tasks to undertake. Is God calling you to° fresh tasks in mission or service?
>
> **Spend some time in quiet and reflective prayer just listening to God.**

➤ Now focus on the 'you' of the question. What drives you as a Christian and as a person? Ambition, pressure, expectations, a desire to please God?

Read the passage through again and then read Psalms 38 & 39 (pp. 565-6)

Try and sum up.
➤ You have interacted with and reflected on this passage, so what is God saying to you? Fear is the enemy of faith. Facing and naming your fears will, with the help of the Holy Spirit, enable you not only to face them but to 'walk' through them and into the freedom God intends you to enjoy.

➤ Have you ever come to that place where, feeling so exhausted and drained, you've said 'I've had enough' or 'I'm giving up'? Recall that situation in the light of this passage and what God might be wanting to say. What might you have done differently? How could you have changed the feelings and emotions you felt at the time?

friends *family* + faith

Penny I'm from a Christian family and it's good because your family understand your values. It's also bad because you take your faith for granted and then you get to a point, suddenly, where you have to question, or I did, and that's quite hard.

Jonathan I've come from a Christian family as well and I don't think I ever really appreciated it until more recently. Thinking about it now I'm extremely grateful.

Pat My mother used to go to church only at Christmas and Easter to keep me quiet. It's really hard for me as a Christian knowing that the person I'm really close to and love dearly is not a Christian and it has a dilemma for me later on, meaning, eternity. It is something I pray for: that Jesus will actually come into her life and get her to change and become a Christian but it has not happened and I've been a Christian since I was sixteen.

Ann I became a Christian on a Christian holiday. I always remember getting back home and getting off the train and going to tell my mum and dad 'I'm a Christian, isn't it great' and my dad, he's so funny, he just rolled his eyes into the back of his head and said to my mum, 'Don't worry it's just a phase, she'll grow out of it'. In our church, other people socialised with my mum and dad so that they came to things and those people shared their faith with them not me. They wouldn't listen to me, I was their daughter. My parents did become Christians eventually.

Penny We put too much emphasis on whether our friends are Christians or non-Christians. If we are building friendships then a lot of being a friend to a Christian is the same as being a friend to a non-Christian. You like each other and something between you clicks.

r servant will be blessed

ctories

he course of time, David defeated e Philistines and subdued them, he took Metheg Ammah from the trol of the Philistines.

-David also defeated the Moabites. He made them lie down on the ground and measured them off with a length of cord. Every two lengths of them were put to death, and the third length was allowed to live. So the Moabites became subject to David and brought tribute.

³Moreover, David fought Hadadezer son of Rehob, king of Zobah, when he went to restore his control along the Euphrates River. ⁴David captured a thousand of his chariots, seven thousand charioteers[a] and twenty thousand foot soldiers. He hamstrung all but a hundred of the chariot horses.

⁵When the Arameans of Damascus came to help Hadadezer king of Zobah, David struck down twenty-two thousand of them. ⁶He put garrisons in the Aramean kingdom of Damascus, and the Arameans became subject to him and brought tribute. The LORD gave David victory wherever he went.

⁷David took the gold shields that be-nged to the officers of Hadadezer and ught them to Jerusalem. ⁸From b and Berothai, towns that be-to Hadadezer, King David took a antity of bronze.

Tou[c] king of Hamath heard that defeated the entire army of ¹⁰he sent his son Joram[d] to greet him and congratulate tory in battle over Hadad-been at war with Tou. ith him articles of silver e.

cated these articles to done with the silver

and gold from all the nations he ha dued: ¹²Edom[e] and Moab, the A nites and the Philistines, and Amale also dedicated the plunder taken Hadadezer son of Rehob, king of Z

¹³And David became famous aft returned from striking down eig thousand Edomites[f] in the Valley of

¹⁴He put garrisons throughout E and all the Edomites became subje David. The LORD gave David vi wherever he went.

David's Officials

¹⁵David reigned over all Israel, what was just and right for all his pe ¹⁶Joab son of Zeruiah was over the a Jehoshaphat son of Ahilud was reco ¹⁷Zadok son of Ahitub and Ahimelec of Abiathar were priests; Seraiah secretary; ¹⁸Benaiah son of Jehoiada over the Kerethites and Pelethites; David's sons were royal advisers.[g]

David and Mephibosheth

9 David asked, "Is there anyone left of the house of Saul to who can show kindness for Jonathan's sak

²Now there was a servant of S household named Ziba. They called to appear before David, and the king to him, "Are you Ziba?"

"Your servant," he replied.

³The king asked, "Is there no-one left of the house of Saul to whom I show God's kindness?"

Ziba answered the king, "There is s son of Jonathan; he is crippled in t feet."

⁴"Where is he?" the king asked.

Ziba answered, "He is at the hous Makir son of Ammiel in Lo Debar."

⁵So King David had him brought f Lo Debar, from the house of Makir so Ammiel.

⁶When Mephibosheth son of Jonath

Scrolls and 1 Chron. 18:4); Masoretic Text *captured seventeen hundred of his chario* ts (see also 1 Chron. 18:8); Hebrew *Betah.*
o in verse 10   d10 A variant of *Hadoram*
uagint and Syriac (see also 1 Chron. 18:11); most Hebrew manuscripts *Aram* gint and Syriac (see also 1 Chron. 18:12); most Hebrew manuscripts *Aram* (th

Paul If you are only friends with someone to get them to become a Christian that's the worst thing you can do. That's not mutual friendship.

What is the message?

Ann That Jesus is between you and the cross. You could even go back to Adam and Eve (Genesis) and say that sin came into a perfect world and put a massive wedge between us and God. The people tried all these different ways to atone or make things right by sacrifices and everything (Exodus and Deuteronomy) but nothing could actually make a bridge back to God. Then Christ came and died on the cross and the cross is the bridge but Jesus didn't stay dead, on the third day he rose again. Repenting and accepting God's forgiveness through Christ's death on the cross is what makes someone a Christian.

Emma But that is just the beginning of a journey from now into eternity, a process of learning and growing.

The cost

Paul I think we need to tell people interested in becoming a Christian that it is going to be costly, they are opting for a hard road not the cushy 'come to God and everything's sorted' kind of life, they might expect or hope for.

WHAT IS EVANGELISM?

Sharing your faith

Telling people about the brilliant stuff Jesus can do for them

Telling people how Jesus can change their life

Sharing something you are passionate about

Kevin Ford writes in his book *Jesus for a New Generation,* 1996, Hodder & Stoughton
I'm convinced that if we would think of all the non-believing people we meet [including family] as *pre–* Christian rather than *non*–Christian, we would be more conscious of how we can be a part of helping those people to find their destiny in Jesus Christ . . . So why not just think of them all as *pre–*Christians, then do everything we can to love them into the kingdom of God - with the actual work of redemption left up to God?'

On the spot with **Martin Smith**

MARTIN James Smith, 28, musician.

AMBITIONS To make better music, influence culture and have more children!

SCARIEST FAIRGROUND RIDE? The Haunted House when I was six.

HOW OLD WERE YOU WHEN YOU MET GOD? I've known God since I was eight, my mum and dad gave me my first Bible,

DO OTHERS IN YOUR FAMILY READ THE BIBLE? All my family read the Bible.

WHAT IS YOUR FAVOURITE PLACE TO READ THE BIBLE? I particularly like reading the Bible on the plane and praying but I also like to pray in the kitchen.

WHICH BIBLICAL STORY OR TRUTH DO YOU IDENTIFY WITH MOST? The biblical character I most identify with is Daniel because he was able, in his own way, to have an influence on the movers and shakers in the nation in which he lived.

WHAT DO YOU MOST LIKE ABOUT CHURCH? I like the sense of belonging, of community about going to church. I like it that my friends and family are there.

MOST IMPORTANT PERSON Next to God, the most important people in my life are Anna, my wife, and Elle-Anna, my daughter.

IF YOUR HOUSE WAS ON FIRE, WHICH TWO ITEMS WOULD YOU SAVE? In fact, one of my most precious possessions is our collection of photographs, and my Gibson J45 acoustic guitar made in 1957.

FUNNIEST MOMENT The speech at my wedding, cutting my chin open on my honeymoon and spending the week with a big bandage on it - very romantic!

BIGGEST ACHIEVEMENT Becoming a dad, being in Delirious?, playing at Brixton Academy in London.

WHAT SADDENS ME MOST ABOUT THE WORLD? The breakdown of marriage and family; that people die of starvation because their government has spent all its money on getting one person to the moon.

MY HEART'S DESIRE? To get to heaven knowing that I did my best.

Israel, "Why have you not built me a house of cedar?"'

8"Now then, tell my servant David, 'This is what the LORD Almighty says: I took you from the pasture and from following the flock to be ruler over my people Israel. 9I have been with you wherever you have gone, and I have cut off all your enemies from before you. Now I will make your name great, like the names of the greatest men of the earth. 10And I will provide a place for my people Israel and will plant them so that they can have a home of their own and no longer be disturbed. Wicked people shall not oppress them any more, as they did at the beginning 11and have done ever since the time I appointed leaders*a* over my people Israel. I will also give you rest from all your enemies.

"'The LORD declares to you that the LORD himself will establish a house for you: 12When your days are over and you rest with your fathers, I will raise up your offspring to succeed you, who will come from your own body, and I will establish his kingdom. 13He is the one who will build a house for my Name, and I will establish the throne of his kingdom for ever. 14I will be his father, and he shall be my son. When he does wrong, I will punish him with the rod of men, with floggings inflicted by men. 15But my love will never be taken away from him, as I took it away from Saul, whom I removed from before you. 16Your house and your kingdom shall endure for ever before me;*b* your throne shall be established for ev

17Nathan reported to Davi words of this entire revelation.

David's Prayer

18Then King David went in and sa fore the LORD, and he said:

"Who am I, O Sovereign LORD, and what is my family, that you have

*a*11 Traditionally *judges*   *b*16 Some Hebrew manuscripts
*c*23 See Septuagint and 1 Chron. 17:21; Hebrew *wonders for you*
Egypt, from the nations and their gods.

---

brought m
were no
Sovereig
spoke
of y
of
LORD?

20"What
you? For you k
Sovereign LORD.
your word and according
you have done this great thi
made it known to your servant.

22"How great you are, O Sovereign LORD! There is no-one like you, and there is no God but you, as we have heard with our own ears. 23And who is like your people Israel—the one nation on earth that God went out to redeem as a people for himself, and to make a name for himself, and to perform great and awesome wonders by driving out nations and their gods from before your people, whom you redeemed from Egypt?*c* 24You have established your people Israel as your very own for ever, and you, O LORD, have become their God.

25"And now, LORD God, keep for ever the promise you have made con cerning your servant and his h Do as you promised, 26so name will be great for ev will say, 'The LORD over Israel!' An servant Davi fore yo the son of Saul, came to David, he bowed down to pay him honour.

David said, "Mephibosheth!"

"Your servant," he replied.

7"Don't be afraid," David said to him, "for I will surely show you kindness for the sake of your father Jonathan. I will restore to you all the land that belonged to your grandfather Saul, and you will always eat at my table."

8Mephibosheth bowed down and said, "What is your servant, that you should notice a dead dog like me?"

9Then the king summoned Ziba, Saul's servant, and said to him, "I have given your master's grandson everything that belonged to Saul and his family. 10You and your sons and your servants are to farm the land for him and bring in the crops, so that your master's grandson may be provided for. And Mephibosheth, grandson of your master, will always eat at my table." (Now Ziba had fifteen sons and twenty servants.)

11Then Ziba said to the king, "Your servant will do whatever my lord the king commands his servant to do." So Mephibosheth ate at David's*a* table like one of the king's sons.

12Mephibosheth had a young son named Mica, and all the members of Ziba's household were servants of Mephibosheth. 13And Mephibosheth lived in Jerusalem, because he always ate at the king's table, and he was crippled in both feet.

David Defeats the Ammonites

10 In the course of time, the king of the Ammonites died, and his son Hanun succeeded him as king. 2David thought, "I will show kindness to Hanun son of Nahash, just as his father showed kindness to me." So David sent a delegation to express his sympathy to Hanun concerning his father.

When David's men came to the land of the Ammonites, 3the Ammonite nobles said to Hanun their lord, "Do you think David is honouring your father by sending

men to you to express sympathy? Hasn't David sent them to you to explore the city and spy it out and overthrow it?" 4So Hanun seized David's men, shaved off half of each man's beard, cut off their garments in the middle at the buttocks, and sent them away.

5When David was told about this, he sent messengers to meet the men, for they were greatly humiliated. The king said, "Stay at Jericho till your beards have grown, and then come back."

6When the Ammonites realised that they had become an offence to David's nostrils, they hired twenty thousand Aramean foot soldiers from Beth Rehob and Zobah, as well as the king of Maacah with a thousand men, and also twelve thousand men from Tob.

7On hearing this, David sent Joab out with the entire army of fighting men. 8The Ammonites came out and drew up in battle formation at the entrance to their city gate, while the Arameans of Zobah and Rehob and the men of Tob and Maacah were by themselves in the open country.

9Joab saw that there were battle lines in front of him and behind him; so he selected some of the best troops in Israel and deployed them against the Arameans. 10He put the rest of the men under the command of Abishai his brother and deployed them against the Ammonites. 11Joab said, "If the Arameans are too strong for me, then you are to come to my rescue; but if the Ammonites are too strong for you, then I will come to rescue you. 12Be strong and let us fight bravely for our people and the cities of our God. The LORD will do what is good in his sight."

13Then Joab and the troops with him advanced to fight the Arameans, and they fled before him. 14When the Ammonites saw that the Arameans were fleeing, they fled before Abishai and went inside the city. So Joab returned from fighting the Ammonites and came to Jerusalem.

15After the Arameans saw that they had been routed by Israel, they regrouped.

a11 Septuagint; Hebrew my

[16]Hadadezer had Arameans brought from beyond the River;[a] they went to Helam, with Shobach the commander of Hadadezer's army leading them.

[17]When David was told of this, he gathered all Israel, crossed the Jordan and went to Helam. The Arameans formed their battle lines to meet David and fought against him. [18]But they fled before Israel, and David killed seven hundred of their charioteers and forty thousand of their foot soldiers.[b] He also struck down Shobach the commander of their army, and he died there. [19]When all the kings who were vassals of Hadadezer saw that they had been defeated by Israel, they made peace with the Israelites and became subject to them.

So the Arameans were afraid to help the Ammonites any more.

David and Bathsheba

11 In the spring, at the time when kings go off to war, David sent Joab out with the king's men and the whole Israelite army. They destroyed the Ammonites and besieged Rabbah. But David remained in Jerusalem.

[2]One evening David got up from his bed and walked around on the roof of the palace. From the roof he saw a woman bathing. The woman was very beautiful, [3]and David sent someone to find out about her. The man said, "Isn't this Bathsheba, the daughter of Eliam and the wife of Uriah the Hittite?" [4]Then David sent messengers to get her. She came to him, and he slept with her. (She had purified herself from her uncleanness.) Then[a] she went back home. [5]The woman conceived and sent word to David, saying, "I am pregnant."

[6]So David sent this word to Joab: "Send me Uriah the Hittite." And Joab sent him to David. [7]When Uriah came to him, David asked him how Joab was, how the soldiers were and how the war was going. [8]Then David said to Uriah, "Go down to your house and wash your feet." So Uriah

left the palace, and a gift from the king was sent after him. [9]But Uriah slept at the entrance to the palace with all his master's servants and did not go down to his house.

[10]When David was told, "Uriah did not go home," he asked him, "Haven't you just come from a distance? Why didn't you go home?"

[11]Uriah said to David, "The ark and Israel and Judah are staying in tents, and my master Joab and my lord's men are camped in the open fields. How could I go to my house to eat and drink and lie with my wife? As surely as you live, I will not do such a thing!"

[12]Then David said to him, "Stay here one more day, and tomorrow I will send you back." So Uriah remained in Jerusalem that day and the next. [13]At David's invitation, he ate and drank with him, and David made him drunk. But in the evening Uriah went out to sleep on his mat among his master's servants; he did not go home.

[14]In the morning David wrote a letter to Joab and sent it with Uriah. [15]In it he wrote, "Put Uriah in the front line where the fighting is fiercest. Then withdraw from him so that he will be struck down and die."

[16]So while Joab had the city under siege, he put Uriah at a place where he knew the strongest defenders were. [17]When the men of the city came out and fought against Joab, some of the men in David's army fell; moreover, Uriah the Hittite died.

[18]Joab sent David a full account of the battle. [19]He instructed the messenger: "When you have finished giving the king this account of the battle, [20]the king's anger may flare up, and he may ask you, 'Why did you get so close to the city to fight? Didn't you know they would shoot arrows from the wall? [21]Who killed Abimelech son of Jerub-Besheth?[b] Didn't a woman throw an upper millstone on him from the wall, so that he died in Thebez? Why did you get so close to the wall?' If he asks you this, then say to him, 'Also, your

---

[a]16 That is, the Euphrates   [b]18 Some Septuagint manuscripts (see also 1 Chron. 19:18); Hebrew *horsemen*
[a]4 Or *with her. When she purified herself from her uncleanness,*   [b]21 Also known as *Jerub-Baal* (that is, Gideon)

servant Uriah the Hittite is dead.'"

22The messenger set out, and when he arrived he told David everything Joab had sent him to say. 23The messenger said to David, "The men overpowered us and came out against us in the open, but we drove them back to the entrance to the city gate. 24Then the archers shot arrows at your servants from the wall, and some of the king's men died. Moreover, your servant Uriah the Hittite is dead."

25David told the messenger, "Say this to Joab: 'Don't let this upset you; the sword devours one as well as another. Press the attack against the city and destroy it.' Say this to encourage Joab."

26When Uriah's wife heard that her husband was dead, she mourned for him. 27After the time of mourning was over, David had her brought to his house, and she became his wife and bore him a son. But the thing David had done displeased the LORD.

Nathan Rebukes David

12 The LORD sent Nathan to David. When he came to him, he said, "There were two men in a certain town, one rich and the other poor. 2The rich man had a very large number of sheep and cattle, 3but the poor man had nothing except one little ewe lamb that he had bought. He raised it, and it grew up with him and his children. It shared his food, drank from his cup and even slept in his arms. It was like a daughter to him.

4"Now a traveller came to the rich man, but the rich man refrained from taking one of his own sheep or cattle to prepare a meal for the traveller who had come to him. Instead, he took the ewe lamb that belonged to the poor man and prepared it for the one who had come to him."

5David burned with anger against the man and said to Nathan, "As surely as the LORD lives, the man who did this deserves to die! 6He must pay for that lamb four times over, because he did such a thing and had no pity."

7Then Nathan said to David, "You are

the man! This is what the LORD, the God of Israel, says: 'I anointed you king over Israel, and I delivered you from the hand of Saul. 8I gave your master's house to you, and your master's wives into your arms. I gave you the house of Israel and Judah. And if all this had been too little, I would have given you even more. 9Why did you despise the word of the LORD by doing what is evil in his eyes? You struck down Uriah the Hittite with the sword and took his wife to be your own. You killed him with the sword of the Ammonites. 10Now, therefore, the sword shall never depart from your house, because you despised me and took the wife of Uriah the Hittite to be your own.'

11"This is what the LORD says: 'Out of your own household I am going to bring calamity upon you. Before your very eyes I will take your wives and give them to one who is close to you, and he will lie with your wives in broad daylight. 12You did it in secret, but I will do this thing in broad daylight before all Israel.'"

13Then David said to Nathan, "I have sinned against the LORD."

Nathan replied, "The LORD has taken away your sin. You are not going to die. 14But because by doing this you have made the enemies of the LORD show utter contempt,a the son born to you will die."

15After Nathan had gone home, the LORD struck the child that Uriah's wife had borne to David, and he became ill. 16David pleaded with God for the child. He fasted and went into his house and spent the nights lying on the ground. 17The elders of his household stood beside him to get him up from the ground, but he refused, and he would not eat any food with them.

18On the seventh day the child died. David's servants were afraid to tell him that the child was dead, for they thought, "While the child was still living, we spoke to David but he would not listen to us. How can we tell him the child is dead? He may do something desperate."

19David noticed that his servants were whispering among themselves and he

---

a14 Masoretic Text; an ancient Hebrew scribal tradition *this you have shown utter contempt for the LORD* realised that the child was dead. "Is the child dead?" he asked.

"Yes," they replied, "he is dead."

20Then David got up from the ground. After he had washed, put on lotions and changed his clothes, he went into the house of the LORD and worshipped. Then he went to his own house, and at his request they served him food, and he ate.

21His servants asked him, "Why are you acting in this way? While the child was alive, you fasted and wept, but now that the child is dead, you get up and eat!"

22He answered, "While the child was still alive, I fasted and wept. I thought, 'Who knows? The LORD may be gracious to me and let the child live.' 23But now that he is dead, why should I fast? Can I bring him back again? I will go to him, but he will not return to me."

24Then David comforted his wife Bathsheba, and he went to her and lay with her. She gave birth to a son, and they named him Solomon. The LORD loved him; 25and because the LORD loved him, he sent word through Nathan the prophet to name him Jedidiah.b

26Meanwhile Joab fought against Rabbah of the Ammonites and captured the royal citadel. 27Joab then sent messengers to David, saying, "I have fought against Rabbah and taken its water supply. 28Now muster the rest of the troops and besiege the city and capture it. Otherwise I shall take the city, and it will be named after me."

29So David mustered the entire army and went to Rabbah, and attacked and captured it. 30He took the crown from the head of their kingc—its weight was a talentd of gold, and it was set with precious stones—and it was placed on David's head. He took a great quantity of plunder from the city 31and brought out the people who were there, consigning them to labour with saws and with iron picks and axes, and he made them work at brickmaking.e He did this to all the Ammonite towns. Then David and his entire army returned to Jerusalem.

Amnon and Tamar

13 In the course of time, Amnon son of David fell in love with Tamar, the beautiful sister of Absalom son of David.

2Amnon became frustrated to the point of illness on account of his sister Tamar, for she was a virgin, and it seemed impossible for him to do anything to her.

3Now Amnon had a friend named Jonadab son of Shimeah, David's brother. Jonadab was a very shrewd man. 4He asked Amnon, "Why do you, the king's son, look so haggard morning after morning? Won't you tell me?"

Amnon said to him, "I'm in love with Tamar, my brother Absalom's sister."

5"Go to bed and pretend to be ill," Jonadab said. "When your father comes to see you, say to him, 'I would like my sister Tamar to come and give me something to eat. Let her prepare the food in my sight so that I may watch her and then eat it from her hand.'"

6So Amnon lay down and pretended to be ill. When the king came to see him, Amnon said to him, "I would like my sister Tamar to come and make some special bread in my sight, so that I may eat from her hand."

7David sent word to Tamar at the palace: "Go to the house of your brother Amnon and prepare some food for him." 8So Tamar went to the house of her brother Amnon, who was lying down. She took some dough, kneaded it, made the bread in his sight and baked it. 9Then she took the pan and served him the bread, but he refused to eat.

"Send everyone out of here," Amnon said. So everyone left him. 10Then Amnon said to Tamar, "Bring the food here into my bedroom so that I may eat from your hand." And Tamar took the bread she had prepared and brought it to her brother Amnon in his bedroom. 11But when she took it to him to eat, he grabbed her and said, "Come to bed with me, my sister."

12"Don't, my brother!" she said to him.

---

b25 Jedidiah means loved by the LORD.   c30 Or of Milcom (that is, Molech)
d30 That is, about 75 pounds (about 34 kilograms)   e31 The meaning of the Hebrew for this clause is uncertain.

"Don't force me. Such a thing should not be done in Israel! Don't do this wicked thing. ¹³What about me? Where could I get rid of my disgrace? And what about you? You would be like one of the wicked fools in Israel. Please speak to the king; he will not keep me from being married to you." ¹⁴But he refused to listen to her, and since he was stronger than she, he raped her.

¹⁵Then Amnon hated her with intense hatred. In fact, he hated her more than he had loved her. Amnon said to her, "Get up and get out!"

¹⁶"No!" she said to him. "Sending me away would be a greater wrong than what you have already done to me."

But he refused to listen to her. ¹⁷He called his personal servant and said, "Get this woman out of here and bolt the door after her." ¹⁸So his servant put her out and bolted the door after her. She was wearing a richly ornamented[a] robe, for this was the kind of garment the virgin daughters of the king wore. ¹⁹Tamar put ashes on her head and tore the ornamented robe she was wearing. She put her hand on her head and went away, weeping aloud as she went.

²⁰Her brother Absalom said to her, "Has that Amnon, your brother, been with you? Be quiet now, my sister; he is your brother. Don't take this thing to heart." And Tamar lived in her brother Absalom's house, a desolate woman.

²¹When King David heard all this, he was furious. ²²Absalom never said a word to Amnon, either good or bad; he hated Amnon because he had disgraced his sister Tamar.

Absalom Kills Amnon

²³Two years later, when Absalom's sheep-shearers were at Baal Hazor near the border of Ephraim, he invited all the king's sons to come there. ²⁴Absalom went to the king and said, "Your servant has had shearers come. Will the king and his officials please join me?"

²⁵"No, my son," the king replied. "All

of us should not go; we would only be a burden to you." Although Absalom urged him, he still refused to go, but gave him his blessing.

²⁶Then Absalom said, "If not, please let my brother Amnon come with us."

The king asked him, "Why should he go with you?" ²⁷But Absalom urged him, so he sent with him Amnon and the rest of the king's sons.

²⁸Absalom ordered his men, "Listen! When Amnon is in high spirits from drinking wine and I say to you, 'Strike Amnon down,' then kill him. Don't be afraid. Have not I given you this order? Be strong and brave." ²⁹So Absalom's men did to Amnon what Absalom had ordered. Then all the king's sons got up, mounted their mules and fled.

³⁰While they were on their way, the report came to David: "Absalom has struck down all the king's sons; not one of them is left." ³¹The king stood up, tore his clothes and lay down on the ground; and all his servants stood by with their clothes torn.

³²But Jonadab son of Shimeah, David's brother, said, "My lord should not think that they killed all the princes; only Amnon is dead. This has been Absalom's expressed intention ever since the day that Amnon raped his sister Tamar. ³³My lord the king should not be concerned about the report that all the king's sons are dead. Only Amnon is dead."

³⁴Meanwhile, Absalom had fled.

Now the man standing watch looked up and saw many people on the road west of him, coming down the side of the hill. The watchman went and told the king, "I see men in the direction of Horonaim, on the side of the hill."[b]

³⁵Jonadab said to the king, "See, the king's sons are here; it has happened just as your servant said."

³⁶As he finished speaking, the king's sons came in, wailing loudly. The king, too, and all his servants wept very bitterly.

³⁷Absalom fled and went to Talmai son of Ammihud, the king of Geshur. But King David mourned for his son every day.

---

a18 The meaning of the Hebrew for this phrase is uncertain; also in verse 19.
b34 Septuagint; Hebrew does not have this sentence.

³⁸After Absalom fled and went to Geshur, he stayed there for three years. ³⁹And the spirit of the king[c] longed to go to Absalom, for he was consoled concerning Amnon's death.

Absalom Returns to Jerusalem

14 Joab son of Zeruiah knew that the king's heart longed for Absalom. ²So Joab sent someone to Tekoa and had a wise woman brought from there. He said to her, "Pretend you are in mourning. Dress in mourning clothes, and don't use any cosmetic lotions. Act like a woman who has spent many days grieving for the dead. ³Then go to the king and speak these words to him." And Joab put the words in her mouth.

⁴When the woman from Tekoa went[a] to the king, she fell with her face to the ground to pay him honour, and she said, "Help me, O king!"

⁵The king asked her, "What is troubling you?"

She said, "I am indeed a widow; my husband is dead. ⁶I your servant had two sons. They got into a fight with each other in the field, and no-one was there to separate them. One struck the other and killed him. ⁷Now the whole clan has risen up against your servant; they say, 'Hand over the one who struck his brother down, so that we may put him to death for the life of his brother whom he killed; then we will get rid of the heir as well.' They would put out the only burning coal I have left, leaving my husband neither name nor descendant on the face of the earth."

⁸The king said to the woman, "Go home, and I will issue an order on your behalf."

⁹But the woman from Tekoa said to him, "My lord the king, let the blame rest on me and on my father's family, and let the king and his throne be without guilt."

¹⁰The king replied, "If anyone says anything to you, bring him to me, and he will not bother you again."

¹¹She said, "Then let the king invoke the LORD his God to prevent the avenger of blood from adding to the destruction, so that my son shall not be destroyed."

"As surely as the LORD lives," he said, "not one hair of your son's head will fall to the ground."

¹²Then the woman said, "Let your servant speak a word to my lord the king."

"Speak," he replied.

¹³The woman said, "Why then have you devised a thing like this against the people of God? When the king says this, does he not convict himself, for the king has not brought back his banished son? ¹⁴Like water spilled on the ground, which cannot be recovered, so we must die. But God does not take away life; instead, he devises ways so that a banished person may not remain estranged from him.

¹⁵"And now I have come to say this to my lord the king because the people have made me afraid. Your servant thought, 'I will speak to the king; perhaps he will do what his servant asks. ¹⁶Perhaps the king will agree to deliver his servant from the hand of the man who is trying to cut off both me and my son from the inheritance God gave us.'

¹⁷"And now your servant says, 'May the word of my lord the king bring me rest, for my lord the king is like an angel of God in discerning good and evil. May the LORD your God be with you.'"

¹⁸Then the king said to the woman, "Do not keep from me the answer to what I am going to ask you."

"Let my lord the king speak," the woman said.

¹⁹The king asked, "Isn't the hand of Joab with you in all this?"

The woman answered, "As surely as you live, my lord the king, no-one can turn to the right or to the left from anything my lord the king says. Yes, it was your servant Joab who instructed me to do this and who put all these words into the mouth of your servant. ²⁰Your servant Joab did this to change the present situation. My lord has wisdom like that of an angel of God—he knows everything that happens in the land."

²¹The king said to Joab, "Very well, I

---

[c]39 Dead Sea Scrolls and some Septuagint manuscripts; Masoretic Text *But ⌞the spirit of⌟ David the king*
[a]4 Many Hebrew manuscripts, Septuagint, Vulgate and Syriac; most Hebrew manuscripts *spoke*

will do it. Go, bring back the young man Absalom."

22Joab fell with his face to the ground to pay him honour, and he blessed the king. Joab said, "Today your servant knows that he has found favour in your eyes, my lord the king, because the king has granted his servant's request."

23Then Joab went to Geshur and brought Absalom back to Jerusalem. 24But the king said, "He must go to his own house; he must not see my face." So Absalom went to his own house and did not see the face of the king.

25In all Israel there was not a man so highly praised for his handsome appearance as Absalom. From the top of his head to the sole of his foot there was no blemish in him. 26Whenever he cut the hair of his head—he used to cut his hair from time to time when it became too heavy for him— he would weigh it, and its weight was two hundred shekels*b* by the royal standard.

27Three sons and a daughter were born to Absalom. The daughter's name was Tamar, and she became a beautiful woman.

28Absalom lived for two years in Jerusalem without seeing the king's face. 29Then Absalom sent for Joab in order to send him to the king, but Joab refused to come to him. So he sent a second time, but he refused to come. 30Then he said to his servants, "Look, Joab's field is next to mine, and he has barley there. Go and set it on fire." So Absalom's servants set the field on fire.

31Then Joab did go to Absalom's house and he said to him, "Why have your servants set my field on fire?"

32Absalom said to Joab, "Look, I sent word to you and said, 'Come here so that I can send you to the king to ask, "Why have I come from Geshur? It would be better for me if I were still there!"' Now then, I want to see the king's face, and if I am guilty of anything, let him put me to death."

33So Joab went to the king and told him this. Then the king summoned Absalom, and he came in and bowed down with his face to the ground before the king. And the king kissed Absalom.

Absalom's Conspiracy

15 In the course of time, Absalom provided himself with a chariot and horses and with fifty men to run ahead of him. 2He would get up early and stand by the side of the road leading to the city gate. Whenever anyone came with a complaint to be placed before the king for a decision, Absalom would call out to him, "What town are you from?" He would answer, "Your servant is from one of the tribes of Israel." 3Then Absalom would say to him, "Look, your claims are valid and proper, but there is no representative of the king to hear you." 4And Absalom would add, "If only I were appointed judge in the land! Then everyone who has a complaint or case could come to me and I would see that he receives justice."

5Also, whenever anyone approached him to bow down before him, Absalom would reach out his hand, take hold of him and kiss him. 6Absalom behaved in this way towards all the Israelites who came to the king asking for justice, and so he stole the hearts of the men of Israel.

7At the end of four*a* years, Absalom said to the king, "Let me go to Hebron and fulfil a vow I made to the LORD. 8While your servant was living at Geshur in Aram, I made this vow: 'If the LORD takes me back to Jerusalem, I will worship the LORD in Hebron.'"*b*

9The king said to him, "Go in peace." So he went to Hebron.

10Then Absalom sent secret messengers throughout the tribes of Israel to say, "As soon as you hear the sound of the trumpets, then say, 'Absalom is king in Hebron.'" 11Two hundred men from Jerusalem had accompanied Absalom. They had been invited as guests and went quite innocently, knowing nothing about the matter. 12While Absalom was offering sacrifices, he also sent for Ahithophel the

---

b26 That is, about 5 pounds (about 2.3 kilograms)
a7 Some Septuagint manuscripts, Syriac and Josephus; Hebrew *forty*
b8 Some Septuagint manuscripts; Hebrew does not have *in Hebron.*

Gilonite, David's counsellor, to come from Giloh, his home town. And so the conspiracy gained strength, and Absalom's following kept on increasing.

David Flees

¹³A messenger came and told David, "The hearts of the men of Israel are with Absalom."

¹⁴Then David said to all his officials who were with him in Jerusalem, "Come! We must flee, or none of us will escape from Absalom. We must leave immediately, or he will move quickly to overtake us and bring ruin upon us and put the city to the sword."

¹⁵The king's officials answered him, "Your servants are ready to do whatever our lord the king chooses."

¹⁶The king set out, with his entire household following him; but he left ten concubines to take care of the palace. ¹⁷So the king set out, with all the people following him, and they halted at a place some distance away. ¹⁸All his men marched past him, along with all the Kerethites and Pelethites; and all the six hundred Gittites who had accompanied him from Gath marched before the king.

¹⁹The king said to Ittai the Gittite, "Why should you come along with us? Go back and stay with King Absalom. You are a foreigner, an exile from your homeland. ²⁰You came only yesterday. And today shall I make you wander about with us, when I do not know where I am going? Go back, and take your countrymen. May kindness and faithfulness be with you."

²¹But Ittai replied to the king, "As surely as the LORD lives, and as my lord the king lives, wherever my lord the king may be, whether it means life or death, there will your servant be."

²²David said to Ittai, "Go ahead, march on." So Ittai the Gittite marched on with all his men and the families that were with him.

²³The whole countryside wept aloud as all the people passed by. The king also crossed the Kidron Valley, and all the people moved on towards the desert.

²⁴Zadok was there, too, and all the Levites who were with him were carrying the ark of the covenant of God. They set down the ark of God, and Abiathar offered sacrifices[c] until all the people had finished leaving the city.

²⁵Then the king said to Zadok, "Take the ark of God back into the city. If I find favour in the LORD's eyes, he will bring me back and let me see it and his dwelling-place again. ²⁶But if he says, 'I am not pleased with you,' then I am ready; let him do to me whatever seems good to him."

²⁷The king also said to Zadok the priest, "Aren't you a seer? Go back to the city in peace, with your son Ahimaaz and Jonathan son of Abiathar. You and Abiathar take your two sons with you. ²⁸I will wait at the fords in the desert until word comes from you to inform me." ²⁹So Zadok and Abiathar took the ark of God back to Jerusalem and stayed there.

³⁰But David continued up the Mount of Olives, weeping as he went; his head was covered and he was barefoot. All the people with him covered their heads too and were weeping as they went up. ³¹Now David had been told, "Ahithophel is among the conspirators with Absalom." So David prayed, "O LORD, turn Ahithophel's counsel into foolishness."

³²When David arrived at the summit, where people used to worship God, Hushai the Arkite was there to meet him, his robe torn and dust on his head. ³³David said to him, "If you go with me, you will be a burden to me. ³⁴But if you return to the city and say to Absalom, 'I will be your servant, O king; I was your father's servant in the past, but now I will be your servant,' then you can help me by frustrating Ahithophel's advice. ³⁵Won't the priests Zadok and Abiathar be there with you? Tell them anything you hear in the king's palace. ³⁶Their two sons, Ahimaaz son of Zadok and Jonathan son of Abiathar, are there with them. Send them to me with anything you hear."

³⁷So David's friend Hushai arrived at

c24 Or *Abiathar went up*

Jerusalem as Absalom was entering the city.

David and Ziba

16 When David had gone a short distance beyond the summit, there was Ziba, the steward of Mephibosheth, waiting to meet him. He had a string of donkeys saddled and loaded with two hundred loaves of bread, a hundred cakes of raisins, a hundred cakes of figs and a skin of wine.

2The king asked Ziba, "Why have you brought these?"

Ziba answered, "The donkeys are for the king's household to ride on, the bread and fruit are for the men to eat, and the wine is to refresh those who become exhausted in the desert."

3The king then asked, "Where is your master's grandson?"

Ziba said to him, "He is staying in Jerusalem, because he thinks, 'Today the house of Israel will give me back my grandfather's kingdom.'"

4Then the king said to Ziba, "All that belonged to Mephibosheth is now yours."

"I humbly bow," Ziba said. "May I find favour in your eyes, my lord the king."

Shimei Curses David

5As King David approached Bahurim, a man from the same clan as Saul's family came out from there. His name was Shimei son of Gera, and he cursed as he came out. 6He pelted David and all the king's officials with stones, though all the troops and the special guard were on David's right and left. 7As he cursed, Shimei said, "Get out, get out, you man of blood, you scoundrel! 8The LORD has repaid you for all the blood you shed in the household of Saul, in whose place you have reigned. The LORD has handed the kingdom over to your son Absalom. You have come to ruin because you are a man of blood!"

9Then Abishai son of Zeruiah said to the king, "Why should this dead dog curse my lord the king? Let me go over and cut off his head."

10But the king said, "What do you and I have in common, you sons of Zeruiah? If he is cursing because the LORD said to him, 'Curse David,' who can ask, 'Why do you do this?'"

11David then said to Abishai and all his officials, "My son, who is of my own flesh, is trying to take my life. How much more, then, this Benjamite! Leave him alone; let him curse, for the LORD has told him to. 12It may be that the LORD will see my distress and repay me with good for the cursing I am receiving today."

13So David and his men continued along the road while Shimei was going along the hillside opposite him, cursing as he went and throwing stones at him and showering him with dirt. 14The king and all the people with him arrived at their destination exhausted. And there he refreshed himself.

The Advice of Hushai and Ahithophel

15Meanwhile, Absalom and all the men of Israel came to Jerusalem, and Ahithophel was with him. 16Then Hushai the Arkite, David's friend, went to Absalom and said to him, "Long live the king! Long live the king!"

17Absalom asked Hushai, "Is this the love you show your friend? Why didn't you go with your friend?"

18Hushai said to Absalom, "No, the one chosen by the LORD, by these people and by all the men of Israel—his I will be, and I will remain with him. 19Furthermore, whom should I serve? Should I not serve the son? Just as I served your father, so I will serve you."

20Absalom said to Ahithophel, "Give us your advice. What should we do?"

21Ahithophel answered, "Lie with your father's concubines whom he left to take care of the palace. Then all Israel will hear that you have made yourself an offence to your father's nostrils, and the hands of everyone with you will be strengthened." 22So they pitched a tent for Absalom on the roof, and he lay with his father's concubines in the sight of all Israel.

23Now in those days the advice Ahithophel gave was like that of one who enquires of God. That was how both

David and Absalom regarded all of Ahithophel's advice.

17 Ahithophel said to Absalom, "I would[a] choose twelve thousand men and set out tonight in pursuit of David. [2]I would[b] attack him while he is weary and weak. I would[b] strike him with terror, and then all the people with him will flee. I would[b] strike down only the king [3]and bring all the people back to you. The death of the man you seek will mean the return of all; all the people will be unharmed." [4]This plan seemed good to Absalom and to all the elders of Israel.

[5]But Absalom said, "Summon also Hushai the Arkite, so that we can hear what he has to say." [6]When Hushai came to him, Absalom said, "Ahithophel has given this advice. Should we do what he says? If not, give us your opinion."

[7]Hushai replied to Absalom, "The advice Ahithophel has given is not good this time. [8]You know your father and his men; they are fighters, and as fierce as a wild bear robbed of her cubs. Besides, your father is an experienced fighter; he will not spend the night with the troops. [9]Even now, he is hidden in a cave or some other place. If he should attack your troops first,[c] whoever hears about it will say, 'There has been a slaughter among the troops who follow Absalom.' [10]Then even the bravest soldier, whose heart is like the heart of a lion, will melt with fear, for all Israel knows that your father is a fighter and that those with him are brave.

[11]"So I advise you: Let all Israel, from Dan to Beersheba—as numerous as the sand on the seashore—be gathered to you, with you yourself leading them into battle. [12]Then we will attack him wherever he may be found, and we will fall on him as dew settles on the ground. Neither he nor any of his men will be left alive. [13]If he withdraws into a city, then all Israel will bring ropes to that city, and we will drag it down to the valley until not even a piece of it can be found."

[14]Absalom and all the men of Israel said, "The advice of Hushai the Arkite is better than that of Ahithophel." For the LORD had determined to frustrate the good advice of Ahithophel in order to bring disaster on Absalom.

[15]Hushai told Zadok and Abiathar, the priests, "Ahithophel has advised Absalom and the elders of Israel to do such and such, but I have advised them to do so and so. [16]Now send a message immediately and tell David, 'Do not spend the night at the fords in the desert; cross over without fail, or the king and all the people with him will be swallowed up.'"

[17]Jonathan and Ahimaaz were staying at En Rogel. A servant girl was to go and inform them, and they were to go and tell King David, for they could not risk being seen entering the city. [18]But a young man saw them and told Absalom. So the two of them left quickly and went to the house of a man in Bahurim. He had a well in his courtyard, and they climbed down into it. [19]His wife took a covering and spread it out over the opening of the well and scattered grain over it. No-one knew anything about it.

[20]When Absalom's men came to the woman at the house, they asked, "Where are Ahimaaz and Jonathan?"

The woman answered them, "They crossed over the brook."[d] The men searched but found no-one, so they returned to Jerusalem.

[21]After the men had gone, the two climbed out of the well and went to inform King David. They said to him, "Set out and cross the river at once; Ahithophel has advised such and such against you." [22]So David and all the people with him set out and crossed the Jordan. By daybreak, no-one was left who had not crossed the Jordan.

[23]When Ahithophel saw that his advice had not been followed, he saddled his donkey and set out for his house in his home town. He put his house in order and then hanged himself. So he died and was buried in his father's tomb.

[24]David went to Mahanaim, and Absalom crossed the Jordan with all the men of

---

a1 Or *Let me*   *b2* Or *will*   *c9* Or *When some of the men fall at the first attack*
d20 Or *"They passed by the sheep pen towards the water."*

Israel. 25Absalom had appointed Amasa over the army in place of Joab. Amasa was the son of a man named Jether,*e* an Israelite*f* who had married Abigail,*g* the daughter of Nahash and sister of Zeruiah the mother of Joab. 26The Israelites and Absalom camped in the land of Gilead.

27When David came to Mahanaim, Shobi son of Nahash from Rabbah of the Ammonites, and Makir son of Ammiel from Lo Debar, and Barzillai the Gileadite from Rogelim 28brought bedding and bowls and articles of pottery. They also brought wheat and barley, flour and roasted grain, beans and lentils,*h* 29honey and curds, sheep, and cheese from cows' milk for David and his people to eat. For they said, "The people have become hungry and tired and thirsty in the desert."

Absalom's Death

18 David mustered the men who were with him and appointed over them commanders of thousands and commanders of hundreds. 2David sent the troops out—a third under the command of Joab, a third under Joab's brother Abishai son of Zeruiah, and a third under Ittai the Gittite. The king told the troops, "I myself will surely march out with you."

3But the men said, "You must not go out; if we are forced to flee, they won't care about us. Even if half of us die, they won't care; but you are worth ten thousand of us.*a* It would be better now for you to give us support from the city."

4The king answered, "I will do whatever seems best to you."

So the king stood beside the gate while all the men marched out in units of hundreds and of thousands. 5The king commanded Joab, Abishai and Ittai, "Be gentle with the young man Absalom for my sake." And all the troops heard the king giving orders concerning Absalom to each of the commanders.

6The army marched into the field to fight Israel, and the battle took place in the forest of Ephraim. 7There the army of Israel was defeated by David's men, and the casualties that day were great—twenty thousand men. 8The battle spread out over the whole countryside, and the forest claimed more lives that day than the sword.

9Now Absalom happened to meet David's men. He was riding his mule, and as the mule went under the thick branches of a large oak, Absalom's head got caught in the tree. He was left hanging in mid-air, while the mule he was riding kept on going.

10When one of the men saw this, he told Joab, "I have just seen Absalom hanging in an oak tree."

11Joab said to the man who had told him this, "What! You saw him? Why didn't you strike him to the ground right there? Then I would have had to give you ten shekels*b* of silver and a warrior's belt."

12But the man replied, "Even if a thousand shekels*c* were weighed out into my hands, I would not lift my hand against the king's son. In our hearing the king commanded you and Abishai and Ittai, 'Protect the young man Absalom for my sake.'*d* 13And if I had put my life in jeopardy*e*—and nothing is hidden from the king—you would have kept your distance from me."

14Joab said, "I am not going to wait like this for you." So he took three javelins in his hand and plunged them into Absalom's heart while Absalom was still alive in the oak tree. 15And ten of Joab's armour-bearers surrounded Absalom, struck him and killed him.

16Then Joab sounded the trumpet, and the troops stopped pursuing Israel, for Joab halted them. 17They took Absalom,

---

e25 Hebrew *Ithra*, a variant of *Jether*   *f25* Hebrew and some Septuagint manuscripts; other Septuagint manuscripts (see also 1 Chron. 2:17) *Ishmaelite* or *Jezreelite*   *g25* Hebrew *Abigal*, a variant of *Abigail*
h28 Most Septuagint manuscripts and Syriac; Hebrew *lentils, and roasted grain*
a3 Two Hebrew manuscripts, some Septuagint manuscripts and Vulgate; most Hebrew manuscripts *care; for now there are ten thousand like us*   *b11* That is, about 4 ounces (about 115 grams)
c12 That is, about 25 pounds (about 11 kilograms)
d12 A few Hebrew manuscripts, Septuagint, Vulgate and Syriac; most Hebrew manuscripts may be translated *Absalom, whoever you may be.*   *e13* Or *Otherwise, if I had acted treacherously towards him*

threw him into a big pit in the forest and piled up a large heap of rocks over him. Meanwhile, all the Israelites fled to their homes.

18During his life-time Absalom had taken a pillar and erected it in the King's Valley as a monument to himself, for he thought, "I have no son to carry on the memory of my name." He named the pillar after himself, and it is called Absalom's Monument to this day.

David Mourns

19Now Ahimaaz son of Zadok said, "Let me run and take the news to the king that the LORD has delivered him from the hand of his enemies."

20"You are not the one to take the news today," Joab told him. "You may take the news another time, but you must not do so today, because the king's son is dead."

21Then Joab said to a Cushite, "Go, tell the king what you have seen." The Cushite bowed down before Joab and ran off.

22Ahimaaz son of Zadok again said to Joab, "Come what may, please let me run behind the Cushite."

But Joab replied, "My son, why do you want to go? You don't have any news that will bring you a reward."

23He said, "Come what may, I want to run."

So Joab said, "Run!" Then Ahimaaz ran by way of the plainf and outran the Cushite.

24While David was sitting between the inner and outer gates, the watchman went up to the roof of the gateway by the wall. As he looked out, he saw a man running alone. 25The watchman called out to the king and reported it.

The king said, "If he is alone, he must have good news." And the man came closer and closer.

26Then the watchman saw another man running, and he called down to the gatekeeper, "Look, another man running alone!"

The king said, "He must be bringing good news, too."

27The watchman said, "It seems to me that the first one runs like Ahimaaz son of Zadok."

"He's a good man," the king said. "He comes with good news."

28Then Ahimaaz called out to the king, "All is well!" He bowed down before the king with his face to the ground and said, "Praise be to the LORD your God! He has delivered up the men who lifted their hands against my lord the king."

29The king asked, "Is the young man Absalom safe?"

Ahimaaz answered, "I saw great confusion just as Joab was about to send the king's servant and me, your servant, but I don't know what it was."

30The king said, "Stand aside and wait here." So he stepped aside and stood there.

31Then the Cushite arrived and said, "My lord the king, hear the good news! The LORD has delivered you today from all who rose up against you."

32The king asked the Cushite, "Is the young man Absalom safe?"

The Cushite replied, "May the enemies of my lord the king and all who rise up to harm you be like that young man."

33The king was shaken. He went up to the room over the gateway and wept. As he went, he said: "O my son Absalom! My son, my son Absalom! If only I had died instead of you—O Absalom, my son, my son!"

19 Joab was told, "The king is weeping and mourning for Absalom." 2And for the whole army the victory that day was turned into mourning, because on that day the troops heard it said, "The king is grieving for his son." 3The men stole into the city that day as men steal in who are ashamed when they flee from battle. 4The king covered his face and cried aloud, "O my son Absalom! O Absalom, my son, my son!"

5Then Joab went into the house to the king and said, "Today you have humiliated all your men, who have just saved

f23 That is, the plain of the Jordan

your life and the lives of your sons and daughters and the lives of your wives and concubines. 6You love those who hate you and hate those who love you. You have made it clear today that the commanders and their men mean nothing to you. I see that you would be pleased if Absalom were alive today and all of us were dead. 7Now go out and encourage your men. I swear by the LORD that if you don't go out, not a man will be left with you by nightfall. This will be worse for you than all the calamities that have come upon you from your youth till now."

8So the king got up and took his seat in the gateway. When the men were told, "The king is sitting in the gateway," they all came before him.

David Returns to Jerusalem

Meanwhile, the Israelites had fled to their homes. 9Throughout the tribes of Israel, the people were all arguing with each other, saying, "The king delivered us from the hand of our enemies; he is the one who rescued us from the hand of the Philistines. But now he has fled the country because of Absalom; 10and Absalom, whom we anointed to rule over us, has died in battle. So why do you say nothing about bringing the king back?"

11King David sent this message to Zadok and Abiathar, the priests: "Ask the elders of Judah, 'Why should you be the last to bring the king back to his palace, since what is being said throughout Israel has reached the king at his quarters? 12You are my brothers, my own flesh and blood. So why should you be the last to bring back the king?' 13And say to Amasa, 'Are you not my own flesh and blood? May God deal with me, be it ever so severely, if from now on you are not the commander of my army in place of Joab.'"

14He won over the hearts of all the men of Judah as though they were one man. They sent word to the king, "Return, you and all your men." 15Then the king returned and went as far as the Jordan.

Now the men of Judah had come to Gilgal to go out and meet the king and bring him across the Jordan. 16Shimei son of Gera, the Benjamite from Bahurim, hurried down with the men of Judah to meet King David. 17With him were a thousand Benjamites, along with Ziba, the steward of Saul's household, and his fifteen sons and twenty servants. They rushed to the Jordan, where the king was. 18They crossed at the ford to take the king's household over and to do whatever he wished.

When Shimei son of Gera crossed the Jordan, he fell prostrate before the king 19and said to him, "May my lord not hold me guilty. Do not remember how your servant did wrong on the day my lord the king left Jerusalem. May the king put it out of his mind. 20For I your servant know that I have sinned, but today I have come here as the first of the whole house of Joseph to come down and meet my lord the king."

21Then Abishai son of Zeruiah said, "Shouldn't Shimei be put to death for this? He cursed the LORD's anointed."

22David replied, "What do you and I have in common, you sons of Zeruiah? This day you have become my adversaries! Should anyone be put to death in Israel today? Do I not know that today I am king over Israel?" 23So the king said to Shimei, "You shall not die." And the king promised him on oath.

24Mephibosheth, Saul's grandson, also went down to meet the king. He had not taken care of his feet or trimmed his moustache or washed his clothes from the day the king left until the day he returned safely. 25When he came from Jerusalem to meet the king, the king asked him, "Why didn't you go with me, Mephibosheth?"

26He said, "My lord the king, since I your servant am lame, I said, 'I will have my donkey saddled and will ride on it, so that I can go with the king.' But Ziba my servant betrayed me. 27And he has slandered your servant to my lord the king. My lord the king is like an angel of God; so do whatever pleases you. 28All my grandfather's descendants deserved nothing but death from my lord the king, but you gave your servant a place among those who eat at your table. So what right do I have to make any more appeals to the king?"

²⁹The king said to him, "Why say more? I order you and Ziba to divide the fields."

³⁰Mephibosheth said to the king, "Let him take everything, now that my lord the king has arrived home safely."

³¹Barzillai the Gileadite also came down from Rogelim to cross the Jordan with the king and to send him on his way from there. ³²Now Barzillai was a very old man, eighty years of age. He had provided for the king during his stay in Mahanaim, for he was a very wealthy man. ³³The king said to Barzillai, "Cross over with me and stay with me in Jerusalem, and I will provide for you."

³⁴But Barzillai answered the king, "How many more years shall I live, that I should go up to Jerusalem with the king? ³⁵I am now eighty years old. Can I tell the difference between what is good and what is not? Can your servant taste what he eats and drinks? Can I still hear the voices of men and women singers? Why should your servant be an added burden to my lord the king? ³⁶Your servant will cross over the Jordan with the king for a short distance, but why should the king reward me in this way? ³⁷Let your servant return, that I may die in my own town near the tomb of my father and mother. But here is your servant Kimham. Let him cross over with my lord the king. Do for him whatever pleases you."

³⁸The king said, "Kimham shall cross over with me, and I will do for him whatever pleases you. And anything you desire from me I will do for you."

³⁹So all the people crossed the Jordan, and then the king crossed over. The king kissed Barzillai and gave him his blessing, and Barzillai returned to his home.

⁴⁰When the king crossed over to Gilgal, Kimham crossed with him. All the troops of Judah and half the troops of Israel had taken the king over.

⁴¹Soon all the men of Israel were coming to the king and saying to him, "Why did our brothers, the men of Judah, steal the king away and bring him and his household across the Jordan, together with all his men?"

⁴²All the men of Judah answered the men of Israel, "We did this because the king is closely related to us. Why are you angry about it? Have we eaten any of the king's provisions? Have we taken anything for ourselves?"

⁴³Then the men of Israel answered the men of Judah, "We have ten shares in the king; and besides, we have a greater claim on David than you have. So why do you treat us with contempt? Were we not the first to speak of bringing back our king?"

But the men of Judah responded even more harshly than the men of Israel.

Sheba Rebels Against David

20 Now a troublemaker named Sheba son of Bicri, a Benjamite, happened to be there. He sounded the trumpet and shouted,

"We have no share in David,
  no part in Jesse's son!
Every man to his tent, O Israel!"

²So all the men of Israel deserted David to follow Sheba son of Bicri. But the men of Judah stayed by their king all the way from the Jordan to Jerusalem.

³When David returned to his palace in Jerusalem, he took the ten concubines he had left to take care of the palace and put them in a house under guard. He provided for them, but did not lie with them. They were kept in confinement till the day of their death, living as widows.

⁴Then the king said to Amasa, "Summon the men of Judah to come to me within three days, and be here yourself." ⁵But when Amasa went to summon Judah, he took longer than the time the king had set for him.

⁶David said to Abishai, "Now Sheba son of Bicri will do us more harm than Absalom did. Take your master's men and pursue him, or he will find fortified cities and escape from us." ⁷So Joab's men and the Kerethites and Pelethites and all the mighty warriors went out under the command of Abishai. They marched out from Jerusalem to pursue Sheba son of Bicri.

⁸While they were at the great rock in Gibeon, Amasa came to meet them. Joab

was wearing his military tunic, and strapped over it at his waist was a belt with a dagger in its sheath. As he stepped forward, it dropped out of its sheath.

9Joab said to Amasa, "How are you, my brother?" Then Joab took Amasa by the beard with his right hand to kiss him. 10Amasa was not on his guard against the dagger in Joab's hand, and Joab plunged it into his belly, and his intestines spilled out on the ground. Without being stabbed again, Amasa died. Then Joab and his brother Abishai pursued Sheba son of Bicri.

11One of Joab's men stood beside Amasa and said, "Whoever favours Joab, and whoever is for David, let him follow Joab!" 12Amasa lay wallowing in his blood in the middle of the road, and the man saw that all the troops came to a halt there. When he realised that everyone who came up to Amasa stopped, he dragged him from the road into a field and threw a garment over him. 13After Amasa had been removed from the road, all the men went on with Joab to pursue Sheba son of Bicri.

14Sheba passed through all the tribes of Israel to Abel Beth Maacah[a] and through the entire region of the Berites, who gathered together and followed him. 15All the troops with Joab came and besieged Sheba in Abel Beth Maacah. They built a siege ramp up to the city, and it stood against the outer fortifications. While they were battering the wall to bring it down, 16a wise woman called from the city, "Listen! Listen! Tell Joab to come here so that I can speak to him." 17He went towards her, and she asked, "Are you Joab?"

"I am," he answered.

She said, "Listen to what your servant has to say."

"I'm listening," he said.

18She continued, "Long ago they used to say, 'Get your answer at Abel,' and that settled it. 19We are the peaceful and faithful in Israel. You are trying to destroy a city that is a mother in Israel. Why do you want to swallow up the LORD's inheritance?"

20"Far be it from me!" Joab replied, "Far be it from me to swallow up or destroy! 21That is not the case. A man named Sheba son of Bicri, from the hill country of Ephraim, has lifted up his hand against the king, against David. Hand over this one man, and I'll withdraw from the city."

The woman said to Joab, "His head will be thrown to you from the wall."

22Then the woman went to all the people with her wise advice, and they cut off the head of Sheba son of Bicri and threw it to Joab. So he sounded the trumpet, and his men dispersed from the city, each returning to his home. And Joab went back to the king in Jerusalem.

23Joab was over Israel's entire army; Benaiah son of Jehoiada was over the Kerethites and Pelethites; 24Adoniram[b] was in charge of forced labour; Jehoshaphat son of Ahilud was recorder; 25Sheva was secretary; Zadok and Abiathar were priests; 26and Ira the Jairite was David's priest.

The Gibeonites Avenged

21 During the reign of David, there was a famine for three successive years; so David sought the face of the LORD. The LORD said, "It is on account of Saul and his blood-stained house; it is because he put the Gibeonites to death."

2The king summoned the Gibeonites and spoke to them. (Now the Gibeonites were not a part of Israel but were survivors of the Amorites; the Israelites had sworn to ˌspareˌ them, but Saul in his zeal for Israel and Judah had tried to annihilate them.) 3David asked the Gibeonites, "What shall I do for you? How shall I make amends so that you will bless the LORD's inheritance?"

4The Gibeonites answered him, "We have no right to demand silver or gold from Saul or his family, nor do we have the right to put anyone in Israel to death."

"What do you want me to do for you?" David asked.

5They answered the king, "As for the

---

a14 Or Abel, even Beth Maacah; also in verse 15
b24 Some Septuagint manuscripts (see also 1 Kings 4:6 and 5:14); Hebrew Adoram

man who destroyed us and plotted against us so that we have been decimated and have no place anywhere in Israel, ⁶let seven of his male descendants be given to us to be killed and exposed before the LORD at Gibeah of Saul—the LORD's chosen one."

So the king said, "I will give them to you."

⁷The king spared Mephibosheth son of Jonathan, the son of Saul, because of the oath before the LORD between David and Jonathan son of Saul. ⁸But the king took Armoni and Mephibosheth, the two sons of Aiah's daughter Rizpah, whom she had borne to Saul, together with the five sons of Saul's daughter Merab,ᵃ whom she had borne to Adriel son of Barzillai the Meholathite. ⁹He handed them over to the Gibeonites, who killed and exposed them on a hill before the LORD. All seven of them fell together; they were put to death during the first days of harvest, just as the barley harvest was beginning.

¹⁰Rizpah daughter of Aiah took sackcloth and spread it out for herself on a rock. From the beginning of the harvest till the rain poured down from the heavens on the bodies, she did not let the birds of the air touch them by day or the wild animals by night. ¹¹When David was told what Aiah's daughter Rizpah, Saul's concubine, had done, ¹²he went and took the bones of Saul and his son Jonathan from the citizens of Jabesh Gilead. (They had taken them secretly from the public square at Beth Shan, where the Philistines had hung them after they struck Saul down on Gilboa.) ¹³David brought the bones of Saul and his son Jonathan from there, and the bones of those who had been killed and exposed were gathered up.

¹⁴They buried the bones of Saul and his son Jonathan in the tomb of Saul's father Kish, at Zela in Benjamin, and did everything the king commanded. After that, God answered prayer on behalf of the land.

Wars Against the Philistines

¹⁵Once again there was a battle between the Philistines and Israel. David went down with his men to fight against the Philistines, and he became exhausted. ¹⁶And Ishbi-Benob, one of the descendants of Rapha, whose bronze spearhead weighed three hundred shekelsᵇ and who was armed with a new ˌswordˌ, said he would kill David. ¹⁷But Abishai son of Zeruiah came to David's rescue; he struck the Philistine down and killed him. Then David's men swore to him, saying, "Never again will you go out with us to battle, so that the lamp of Israel will not be extinguished."

¹⁸In the course of time, there was another battle with the Philistines, at Gob. At that time Sibbecai the Hushathite killed Saph, one of the descendants of Rapha.

¹⁹In another battle with the Philistines at Gob, Elhanan son of Jaare-Oregimᶜ the Bethlehemite killed Goliathᵈ the Gittite, who had a spear with a shaft like a weaver's rod.

²⁰In still another battle, which took place at Gath, there was a huge man with six fingers on each hand and six toes on each foot—twenty-four in all. He also was descended from Rapha. ²¹When he taunted Israel, Jonathan son of Shimeah, David's brother, killed him.

²²These four were descendants of Rapha in Gath, and they fell at the hands of David and his men.

David's Song of Praise

22 David sang to the LORD the words of this song when the LORD delivered him from the hand of all his enemies and from the hand of Saul. ²He said:

"The LORD is my rock, my fortress and my deliverer;
³ my God is my rock, in whom I take refuge,

ᵃ8 Two Hebrew manuscripts, some Septuagint manuscripts and Syriac (see also 1 Samuel 18:19); most Hebrew and Septuagint manuscripts *Michal*   ᵇ16 That is, about 7½ pounds (about 3.5 kilograms)
ᶜ19 Or *son of Jair the weaver*
ᵈ19 Hebrew and Septuagint; 1 Chron. 20:5 *son of Jair killed Lahmi the brother of Goliath*

my shield and the horn[a] of my
    salvation.
He is my stronghold, my refuge and my
    saviour—
    from violent men you save me.
⁴I call to the LORD, who is worthy of
    praise,
    and I am saved from my enemies.

⁵"The waves of death swirled about me;
    the torrents of destruction
      overwhelmed me.
⁶The cords of the grave[b] coiled around
    me;
    the snares of death confronted me.
⁷In my distress I called to the LORD;
    I called out to my God.
From his temple he heard my voice;
    my cry came to his ears.

⁸"The earth trembled and quaked,
    the foundations of the heavens[c]
      shook;
    they trembled because he was angry.
⁹Smoke rose from his nostrils;
    consuming fire came from his mouth,
    burning coals blazed out of it.
¹⁰He parted the heavens and came down;
    dark clouds were under his feet.
¹¹He mounted the cherubim and flew;
    he soared[d] on the wings of the wind.
¹²He made darkness his canopy around
    him—
    the dark[e] rain clouds of the sky.
¹³Out of the brightness of his presence
    bolts of lightning blazed forth.
¹⁴The LORD thundered from heaven;
    the voice of the Most High
      resounded.
¹⁵He shot arrows and scattered ⌊the
    enemies⌋,
    bolts of lightning and routed them.
¹⁶The valleys of the sea were exposed
    and the foundations of the earth laid
      bare
  at the rebuke of the LORD,
    at the blast of breath from his
      nostrils.

¹⁷"He reached down from on high and
    took hold of me;
    he drew me out of deep waters.
¹⁸He rescued me from my powerful
    enemy,
    from my foes, who were too strong
      for me.
¹⁹They confronted me in the day of my
    disaster,
    but the LORD was my support.
²⁰He brought me out into a spacious
    place;
    he rescued me because he delighted
      in me.

²¹"The LORD has dealt with me according
    to my righteousness;
    according to the cleanness of my
      hands he has rewarded me.
²²For I have kept the ways of the LORD;
    I have not done evil by turning from
      my God.
²³All his laws are before me;
    I have not turned away from his
      decrees.
²⁴I have been blameless before him
    and have kept myself from sin.
²⁵The LORD has rewarded me according
    to my righteousness,
    according to my cleanness[f] in his
      sight.

²⁶"To the faithful you show yourself
    faithful,
    to the blameless you show yourself
      blameless,
²⁷to the pure you show yourself pure,
    but to the crooked you show yourself
      shrewd.
²⁸You save the humble,
    but your eyes are on the haughty to
      bring them low.
²⁹You are my lamp, O LORD;
    the LORD turns my darkness into
      light.
³⁰With your help I can advance against a
    troop;[g]
    with my God I can scale a wall.

a3 Horn here symbolises strength.   *b6 Hebrew Sheol*
c8 Hebrew; Vulgate and Syriac (see also Psalm 18:7) mountains
d11 Many Hebrew manuscripts (see also Psalm 18:10); most Hebrew manuscripts appeared
e12 Septuagint and Vulgate (see also Psalm 18:11); Hebrew massed
f25 Hebrew; Septuagint and Vulgate (see also Psalm 18:24) to the cleanness of my hands
g30 Or can run through a barricade

³¹"As for God, his way is perfect;
 the word of the LORD is flawless.
He is a shield
 for all who take refuge in him.
³²For who is God besides the LORD?
 And who is the Rock except our
 God?
³³It is God who arms me with strength[h]
 and makes my way perfect.
³⁴He makes my feet like the feet of a
 deer;
 he enables me to stand on the
 heights.
³⁵He trains my hands for battle;
 my arms can bend a bow of bronze.
³⁶You give me your shield of victory;
 you stoop down to make me great.
³⁷You broaden the path beneath me,
 so that my ankles do not turn over.

³⁸"I pursued my enemies and crushed
 them;
 I did not turn back till they were
 destroyed.
³⁹I crushed them completely, and they
 could not rise;
 they fell beneath my feet.
⁴⁰You armed me with strength for battle;
 you made my adversaries bow at my
 feet.
⁴¹You made my enemies turn their backs
 in flight,
 and I destroyed my foes.
⁴²They cried for help, but there was
 no-one to save them—
 to the LORD, but he did not answer.
⁴³I beat them as fine as the dust of the
 earth;
 I pounded and trampled them like
 mud in the streets.

⁴⁴"You have delivered me from the
 attacks of my people;
 you have preserved me as the head of
 nations.
People I did not know are subject to
 me,
⁴⁵ and foreigners come cringing to me;
 as soon as they hear me, they obey
 me.

⁴⁶They all lose heart;
 they come trembling[i] from their
 strongholds.

⁴⁷"The LORD lives! Praise be to my Rock!
 Exalted be God, the Rock, my
 Saviour!
⁴⁸He is the God who avenges me,
 who puts the nations under me,
⁴⁹ who sets me free from my enemies.
You exalted me above my foes;
 from violent men you rescued me.
⁵⁰Therefore I will praise you, O LORD,
 among the nations;
 I will sing praises to your name.
⁵¹He gives his king great victories;
 he shows unfailing kindness to his
 anointed,
 to David and his descendants for
 ever."

The Last Words of David

23 These are the last words of
David:

"The oracle of David son of Jesse,
 the oracle of the man exalted by the
 Most High,
the man anointed by the God of Jacob,
 Israel's singer of songs:[a]

²"The Spirit of the LORD spoke through
 me;
 his word was on my tongue.
³The God of Israel spoke,
 the Rock of Israel said to me:
'When one rules over men in
 righteousness,
 when he rules in the fear of God,
⁴he is like the light of morning at sunrise
 on a cloudless morning,
like the brightness after rain
 that brings the grass from the earth.'

⁵"Is not my house right with God?
 Has he not made with me an
 everlasting covenant,
 arranged and secured in every part?

---

h33 Dead Sea Scrolls, some Septuagint manuscripts, Vulgate and Syriac (see also Psalm 18:32); Masoretic Text *who is my strong refuge*
i46 Some Septuagint manuscripts and Vulgate (see also Psalm 18:45); Masoretic Text *they arm themselves.*
a1 Or *Israel's beloved singer*

Will he not bring to fruition my
  salvation
and grant me my every desire?
6But evil men are all to be cast aside like
  thorns,
  which are not gathered with the
    hand.
7Whoever touches thorns
  uses a tool of iron or the shaft of a
    spear;
  they are burned up where they lie."

David's Mighty Men

8These are the names of David's mighty
men:
  Josheb-Basshebeth,*b* a Tahkemonite,*c*
was chief of the Three; he raised his
spear against eight hundred men, whom
he killed*d* in one encounter.
  9Next to him was Eleazar son of Dodai
the Ahohite. As one of the three mighty
men, he was with David when they
taunted the Philistines gathered ⌐at Pas
Dammim⌐*e* for battle. Then the men of
Israel retreated, 10but he stood his ground
and struck down the Philistines till his
hand grew tired and froze to the sword.
The LORD brought about a great victory
that day. The troops returned to Eleazar,
but only to strip the dead.
  11Next to him was Shammah son of
Agee the Hararite. When the Philistines
banded together at a place where there
was a field full of lentils, Israel's troops
fled from them. 12But Shammah took his
stand in the middle of the field. He defended it and struck the Philistines down,
and the LORD brought about a great victory.
  13During harvest time, three of the
thirty chief men came down to David at
the cave of Adullam, while a band of
Philistines was encamped in the Valley of
Rephaim. 14At that time David was in the
stronghold, and the Philistine garrison was
at Bethlehem. 15David longed for water

and said, "Oh, that someone would get
me a drink of water from the well near the
gate of Bethlehem!" 16So the three mighty
men broke through the Philistine lines,
drew water from the well near the gate of
Bethlehem and carried it back to David.
But he refused to drink it; instead, he
poured it out before the LORD. 17"Far be it
from me, O LORD, to do this!" he said. "Is
it not the blood of men who went at the
risk of their lives?" And David would not
drink it.
  Such were the exploits of the three
mighty men.
  18Abishai the brother of Joab son of
Zeruiah was chief of the Three.*f* He raised
his spear against three hundred men,
whom he killed, and so he became as
famous as the Three. 19Was he not held in
greater honour than the Three? He became their commander, even though he
was not included among them.
  20Benaiah son of Jehoiada was a valiant
fighter from Kabzeel, who performed
great exploits. He struck down two of
Moab's best men. He also went down into
a pit on a snowy day and killed a lion.
21And he struck down a huge Egyptian.
Although the Egyptian had a spear in his
hand, Benaiah went against him with a
club. He snatched the spear from the
Egyptian's hand and killed him with his
own spear. 22Such were the exploits of
Benaiah son of Jehoiada; he too was as
famous as the three mighty men. 23He was
held in greater honour than any of the
Thirty, but he was not included among the
Three. And David put him in charge of his
bodyguard.

  24Among the Thirty were:
    Asahel the brother of Joab,
    Elhanan son of Dodo from Beth-
      lehem,
  25Shammah the Harodite,
    Elika the Harodite,
  26Helez the Paltite,
    Ira son of Ikkesh from Tekoa,

---

b8 Hebrew; some Septuagint manuscripts suggest *Ish-Bosheth*, that is, *Esh-Baal* (see also 1 Chron. 11:11 *Jashobeam*).
c8 Probably a variant of *Hacmonite* (see 1 Chron. 11:11)
d8 Some Septuagint manuscripts (see also 1 Chron. 11:11); Hebrew and other Septuagint manuscripts *Three; it was Adino the Eznite who killed eight hundred men*   *e9* See 1 Chron. 11:13; Hebrew *gathered there*.
f18 Most Hebrew manuscripts (see also 1 Chron. 11:20); two Hebrew manuscripts and Syriac *Thirty*

[27]Abiezer from Anathoth,
Mebunnai[g] the Hushathite,
[28]Zalmon the Ahohite,
Maharai the Netophathite,
[29]Heled[h] son of Baanah the Netophathite,
Ithai son of Ribai from Gibeah in Benjamin,
[30]Benaiah the Pirathonite,
Hiddai[i] from the ravines of Gaash,
[31]Abi-Albon the Arbathite,
Azmaveth the Barhumite,
[32]Eliahba the Shaalbonite,
the sons of Jashen,
Jonathan [33]son of[j] Shammah the Hararite,
Ahiam son of Sharar[k] the Hararite,
[34]Eliphelet son of Ahasbai the Maacathite,
Eliam son of Ahithophel the Gilonite,
[35]Hezro the Carmelite,
Paarai the Arbite,
[36]Igal son of Nathan from Zobah,
the son of Hagri,[l]
[37]Zelek the Ammonite,
Naharai the Beerothite, the armour-bearer of Joab son of Zeruiah,
[38]Ira the Ithrite,
Gareb the Ithrite
[39]and Uriah the Hittite.
There were thirty-seven in all.

David Counts the Fighting Men

24 Again the anger of the LORD burned against Israel, and he incited David against them, saying, "Go and take a census of Israel and Judah."

[2]So the king said to Joab and the army commanders[a] with him, "Go throughout the tribes of Israel from Dan to Beersheba and enrol the fighting men, so that I may know how many there are."

[3]But Joab replied to the king, "May the LORD your God multiply the troops a hundred times over, and may the eyes of my lord the king see it. But why does my lord the king want to do such a thing?"

[4]The king's word, however, overruled Joab and the army commanders; so they left the presence of the king to enrol the fighting men of Israel.

[5]After crossing the Jordan, they camped near Aroer, south of the town in the gorge, and then went through Gad and on to Jazer. [6]They went to Gilead and the region of Tahtim Hodshi, and on to Dan Jaan and around towards Sidon. [7]Then they went towards the fortress of Tyre and all the towns of the Hivites and Canaanites. Finally, they went on to Beersheba in the Negev of Judah.

[8]After they had gone through the entire land, they came back to Jerusalem at the end of nine months and twenty days.

[9]Joab reported the number of the fighting men to the king: In Israel there were eight hundred thousand able-bodied men who could handle a sword, and in Judah five hundred thousand.

[10]David was conscience-stricken after he had counted the fighting men, and he said to the LORD, "I have sinned greatly in what I have done. Now, O LORD, I beg you, take away the guilt of your servant. I have done a very foolish thing."

[11]Before David got up the next morning, the word of the LORD had come to Gad the prophet, David's seer: [12]"Go and tell David, 'This is what the LORD says: I am giving you three options. Choose one of them for me to carry out against you.'"

[13]So Gad went to David and said to him, "Shall there come upon you three[b] years of famine in your land? Or three months of fleeing from your enemies while they pursue you? Or three days of plague in your land? Now then, think it over and decide how I should answer the one who sent me."

[g]27 Hebrew; some Septuagint manuscripts (see also 1 Chron. 11:29) *Sibbecai*
[h]29 Some Hebrew manuscripts and Vulgate (see also 1 Chron. 11:30); most Hebrew manuscripts *Heleb*
[i]30 Hebrew; some Septuagint manuscripts (see also 1 Chron. 11:32) *Hurai*
[j]33 Some Septuagint manuscripts (see also 1 Chron. 11:34); Hebrew does not have *son of*.
[k]33 Hebrew; some Septuagint manuscripts (see also 1 Chron. 11:35) *Sacar*
[l]36 Some Septuagint manuscripts (see also 1 Chron. 11:38); Hebrew *Haggadi*
[a]2 Septuagint (see also verse 4 and 1 Chron. 21:2); Hebrew *Joab the army commander*
[b]13 Septuagint (see also 1 Chron. 21:12); Hebrew *seven*

[14]David said to Gad, "I am in deep distress. Let us fall into the hands of the LORD, for his mercy is great; but do not let me fall into the hands of men."

[15]So the LORD sent a plague on Israel from that morning until the end of the time designated, and seventy thousand of the people from Dan to Beersheba died. [16]When the angel stretched out his hand to destroy Jerusalem, the LORD was grieved because of the calamity and said to the angel who was afflicting the people, "Enough! Withdraw your hand." The angel of the LORD was then at the threshing-floor of Araunah the Jebusite.

[17]When David saw the angel who was striking down the people, he said to the LORD, "I am the one who has sinned and done wrong. These are but sheep. What have they done? Let your hand fall upon me and my family."

David Builds an Altar

[18]On that day Gad went to David and said to him, "Go up and build an altar to the LORD on the threshing-floor of Araunah the Jebusite." [19]So David went up, as the LORD had commanded through

Gad. [20]When Araunah looked and saw the king and his men coming towards him, he went out and bowed down before the king with his face to the ground.

[21]Araunah said, "Why has my lord the king come to his servant?"

"To buy your threshing-floor," David answered, "so that I can build an altar to the LORD, that the plague on the people may be stopped."

[22]Araunah said to David, "Let my lord the king take whatever pleases him and offer it up. Here are oxen for the burnt offering, and here are threshing-sledges and ox yokes for the wood. [23]O king, Araunah gives all this to the king." Araunah also said to him, "May the LORD your God accept you."

[24]But the king replied to Araunah, "No, I insist on paying you for it. I will not sacrifice to the LORD my God burnt offerings that cost me nothing."

So David bought the threshing-floor and the oxen and paid fifty shekels[c] of silver for them. [25]David built an altar to the LORD there and sacrificed burnt offerings and fellowship offerings.[d] Then the LORD answered prayer on behalf of the land, and the plague on Israel was stopped.

[c]24 That is, about 1¼ pounds (about 0.6 kilogram)   [d]25 Traditionally *peace offerings*

1 Kings

Adonijah Sets Himself Up as King

1 When King David was old and well advanced in years, he could not keep warm even when they put covers over him. ²So his servants said to him, "Let us look for a young virgin to attend the king and take care of him. She can lie beside him so that our lord the king may keep warm."

³Then they searched throughout Israel for a beautiful girl and found Abishag, a Shunammite, and brought her to the king. ⁴The girl was very beautiful; she took care of the king and waited on him, but the king had no intimate relations with her.

⁵Now Adonijah, whose mother was Haggith, put himself forward and said, "I will be king." So he got chariots and horses[a] ready, with fifty men to run ahead of him. ⁶(His father had never interfered with him by asking, "Why do you behave as you do?" He was also very handsome and was born next after Absalom.)

⁷Adonijah conferred with Joab son of Zeruiah and with Abiathar the priest, and they gave him their support. ⁸But Zadok the priest, Benaiah son of Jehoiada, Nathan the prophet, Shimei and Rei[b] and David's special guard did not join Adonijah.

⁹Adonijah then sacrificed sheep, cattle and fattened calves at the Stone of Zoheleth near En Rogel. He invited all his brothers, the king's sons, and all the men of Judah who were royal officials, ¹⁰but he did not invite Nathan the prophet or

Benaiah or the special guard or his brother Solomon.

¹¹Then Nathan asked Bathsheba, Solomon's mother, "Have you not heard that Adonijah, the son of Haggith, has become king without our lord David's knowing it? ¹²Now then, let me advise you how you can save your own life and the life of your son Solomon. ¹³Go in to King David and say to him, 'My lord the king, did you not swear to me your servant: "Surely Solomon your son shall be king after me, and he will sit on my throne"? Why then has Adonijah become king?' ¹⁴While you are still there talking to the king, I will come in and confirm what you have said."

¹⁵So Bathsheba went to see the aged king in his room, where Abishag the Shunammite was attending him. ¹⁶Bathsheba bowed low and knelt before the king.

"What is it you want?" the king asked.

¹⁷She said to him, "My lord, you yourself swore to me your servant by the LORD your God: 'Solomon your son shall become king after me, and he will sit on my throne.' ¹⁸But now Adonijah has become king, and you, my lord the king, do not know about it. ¹⁹He has sacrificed great numbers of cattle, fattened calves, and sheep, and has invited all the king's sons, Abiathar the priest and Joab the commander of the army, but he has not invited Solomon your servant. ²⁰My lord the king, the eyes of all Israel are on you, to learn from you who will sit on the throne of my lord the king after him. ²¹Otherwise, as soon as my lord the king is laid to rest with

---

a5 Or *charioteers*　　*b8* Or *and his friends*

his fathers, I and my son Solomon will be treated as criminals."

²²While she was still speaking with the king, Nathan the prophet arrived. ²³And they told the king, "Nathan the prophet is here." So he went before the king and bowed with his face to the ground.

²⁴Nathan said, "Have you, my lord the king, declared that Adonijah shall be king after you, and that he will sit on your throne? ²⁵Today he has gone down and sacrificed great numbers of cattle, fattened calves, and sheep. He has invited all the king's sons, the commanders of the army and Abiathar the priest. At this very moment they are eating and drinking with him and saying, 'Long live King Adonijah!' ²⁶But me your servant, and Zadok the priest, and Benaiah son of Jehoiada, and your servant Solomon he did not invite. ²⁷Is this something my lord the king has done without letting his servants know who should sit on the throne of my lord the king after him?"

David Makes Solomon King

²⁸Then King David said, "Call in Bathsheba." So she came into the king's presence and stood before him.

²⁹The king then took an oath: "As surely as the LORD lives, who has delivered me out of every trouble, ³⁰I will surely carry out today what I swore to you by the LORD, the God of Israel: Solomon your son shall be king after me, and he will sit on my throne in my place."

³¹Then Bathsheba bowed low with her face to the ground and, kneeling before the king, said, "May my lord King David live for ever!"

³²King David said, "Call in Zadok the priest, Nathan the prophet and Benaiah son of Jehoiada." When they came before the king, ³³he said to them: "Take your lord's servants with you and set Solomon my son on my own mule and take him down to Gihon. ³⁴There shall Zadok the priest and Nathan the prophet anoint him king over Israel. Blow the trumpet and shout, 'Long live King Solomon!' ³⁵Then you are to go up with him, and he is to come and sit on my throne and reign in my

place. I have appointed him ruler over Israel and Judah."

³⁶Benaiah son of Jehoiada answered the king, "Amen! May the LORD, the God of my lord the king, so declare it. ³⁷As the LORD was with my lord the king, so may he be with Solomon to make his throne even greater than the throne of my lord King David!"

³⁸So Zadok the priest, Nathan the prophet, Benaiah son of Jehoiada, the Kerethites and the Pelethites went down and put Solomon on King David's mule and escorted him to Gihon. ³⁹Zadok the priest took the horn of oil from the sacred tent and anointed Solomon. Then they sounded the trumpet and all the people shouted, "Long live King Solomon!" ⁴⁰And all the people went up after him, playing flutes and rejoicing greatly, so that the ground shook with the sound.

⁴¹Adonijah and all the guests who were with him heard it as they were finishing their feast. On hearing the sound of the trumpet, Joab asked, "What's the meaning of all the noise in the city?"

⁴²Even as he was speaking, Jonathan son of Abiathar the priest arrived. Adonijah said, "Come in. A worthy man like you must be bringing good news."

⁴³"Not at all!" Jonathan answered. "Our lord King David has made Solomon king. ⁴⁴The king has sent with him Zadok the priest, Nathan the prophet, Benaiah son of Jehoiada, the Kerethites and the Pelethites, and they have put him on the king's mule, ⁴⁵and Zadok the priest and Nathan the prophet have anointed him king at Gihon. From there they have gone up cheering, and the city resounds with it. That's the noise you hear. ⁴⁶Moreover, Solomon has taken his seat on the royal throne. ⁴⁷Also, the royal officials have come to congratulate our lord King David, saying, 'May your God make Solomon's name more famous than yours and his throne greater than yours!' And the king bowed in worship on his bed ⁴⁸and said, 'Praise be to the LORD, the God of Israel, who has allowed my eyes to see a successor on my throne today.'"

⁴⁹At this, all Adonijah's guests rose in alarm and dispersed. ⁵⁰But Adonijah, in

fear of Solomon, went and took hold of the horns of the altar. ⁵¹Then Solomon was told, "Adonijah is afraid of King Solomon and is clinging to the horns of the altar. He says, 'Let King Solomon swear to me today that he will not put his servant to death with the sword.'"

⁵²Solomon replied, "If he shows himself to be a worthy man, not a hair of his head will fall to the ground; but if evil is found in him, he will die." ⁵³Then King Solomon sent men, and they brought him down from the altar. And Adonijah came and bowed down to King Solomon, and Solomon said, "Go to your home."

David's Charge to Solomon

2 When the time drew near for David to die, he gave a charge to Solomon his son.

²"I am about to go the way of all the earth," he said. "So be strong, show yourself a man, ³and observe what the LORD your God requires: Walk in his ways, and keep his decrees and commands, his laws and requirements, as written in the Law of Moses, so that you may prosper in all you do and wherever you go, ⁴and that the LORD may keep his promise to me: 'If your descendants watch how they live, and if they walk faithfully before me with all their heart and soul, you will never fail to have a man on the throne of Israel.'

⁵"Now you yourself know what Joab son of Zeruiah did to me—what he did to the two commanders of Israel's armies, Abner son of Ner and Amasa son of Jether. He killed them, shedding their blood in peacetime as if in battle, and with that blood stained the belt round his waist and the sandals on his feet. ⁶Deal with him according to your wisdom, but do not let his grey head go down to the grave[a] in peace.

⁷"But show kindness to the sons of Barzillai of Gilead and let them be among those who eat at your table. They stood by me when I fled from your brother Absalom.

⁸"And remember, you have with you Shimei son of Gera, the Benjamite from Bahurim, who called down bitter curses on me the day I went to Mahanaim. When he came down to meet me at the Jordan, I swore to him by the LORD: 'I will not put you to death by the sword.' ⁹But now, do not consider him innocent. You are a man of wisdom; you will know what to do to him. Bring his grey head down to the grave in blood."

¹⁰Then David rested with his fathers and was buried in the City of David. ¹¹He had reigned for forty years over Israel—seven years in Hebron and thirty-three in Jerusalem. ¹²So Solomon sat on the throne of his father David, and his rule was firmly established.

Solomon's Throne Established

¹³Now Adonijah, the son of Haggith, went to Bathsheba, Solomon's mother. Bathsheba asked him, "Do you come peacefully?"

He answered, "Yes, peacefully." ¹⁴Then he added, "I have something to say to you."

"You may say it," she replied.

¹⁵"As you know," he said, "the kingdom was mine. All Israel looked to me as their king. But things changed, and the kingdom has gone to my brother; for it has come to him from the LORD. ¹⁶Now I have one request to make of you. Do not refuse me."

"You may make it," she said.

¹⁷So he continued, "Please ask King Solomon—he will not refuse you—to give me Abishag the Shunammite as my wife."

¹⁸"Very well," Bathsheba replied, "I will speak to the king for you."

¹⁹When Bathsheba went to King Solomon to speak to him for Adonijah, the king stood up to meet her, bowed down to her and sat down on his throne. He had a throne brought for the king's mother, and she sat down at his right hand.

²⁰"I have one small request to make of you," she said. "Do not refuse me."

The king replied, "Make it, my mother; I will not refuse you."

---

[a]6 Hebrew *Sheol*; also in verse 9

²¹So she said, "Let Abishag the Shunammite be given in marriage to your brother Adonijah."

²²King Solomon answered his mother, "Why do you request Abishag the Shunammite for Adonijah? You might as well request the kingdom for him—after all, he is my older brother—yes, for him and for Abiathar the priest and Joab son of Zeruiah!"

²³Then King Solomon swore by the LORD: "May God deal with me, be it ever so severely, if Adonijah does not pay with his life for this request! ²⁴And now, as surely as the LORD lives—he who has established me securely on the throne of my father David and has founded a dynasty for me as he promised—Adonijah shall be put to death today!" ²⁵So King Solomon gave orders to Benaiah son of Jehoiada, and he struck down Adonijah and he died.

²⁶To Abiathar the priest the king said, "Go back to your fields in Anathoth. You deserve to die, but I will not put you to death now, because you carried the ark of the Sovereign LORD before my father David and shared all my father's hardships." ²⁷So Solomon removed Abiathar from the priesthood of the LORD, fulfilling the word the LORD had spoken at Shiloh about the house of Eli.

²⁸When the news reached Joab, who had conspired with Adonijah though not with Absalom, he fled to the tent of the LORD and took hold of the horns of the altar. ²⁹King Solomon was told that Joab had fled to the tent of the LORD and was beside the altar. Then Solomon ordered Benaiah son of Jehoiada, "Go, strike him down!"

³⁰So Benaiah entered the tent of the LORD and said to Joab, "The king says, 'Come out!'"

But he answered, "No, I will die here."

Benaiah reported to the king, "This is how Joab answered me."

³¹Then the king commanded Benaiah, "Do as he says. Strike him down and bury him, and so clear me and my father's house of the guilt of the innocent blood that Joab shed. ³²The LORD will repay him for the blood he shed, because without the knowledge of my father David he attacked two men and killed them with the sword. Both of them—Abner son of Ner, commander of Israel's army, and Amasa son of Jether, commander of Judah's army—were better men and more upright than he. ³³May the guilt of their blood rest on the head of Joab and his descendants for ever. But on David and his descendants, his house and his throne, may there be the LORD's peace for ever."

³⁴So Benaiah son of Jehoiada went up and struck down Joab and killed him, and he was buried on his own land[b] in the desert. ³⁵The king put Benaiah son of Jehoiada over the army in Joab's position and replaced Abiathar with Zadok the priest.

³⁶Then the king sent for Shimei and said to him, "Build yourself a house in Jerusalem and live there, but do not go anywhere else. ³⁷The day you leave and cross the Kidron Valley, you can be sure you will die; your blood will be on your own head."

³⁸Shimei answered the king, "What you say is good. Your servant will do as my lord the king has said." And Shimei stayed in Jerusalem for a long time.

³⁹But three years later, two of Shimei's slaves ran off to Achish son of Maacah, king of Gath, and Shimei was told, "Your slaves are in Gath." ⁴⁰At this, he saddled his donkey and went to Achish at Gath in search of his slaves. So Shimei went away and brought the slaves back from Gath.

⁴¹When Solomon was told that Shimei had gone from Jerusalem to Gath and had returned, ⁴²the king summoned Shimei and said to him, "Did I not make you swear by the LORD and warn you, 'On the day you leave to go anywhere else, you can be sure you will die'? At that time you said to me, 'What you say is good. I will obey.' ⁴³Why then did you not keep your oath to the LORD and obey the command I gave you?"

⁴⁴The king also said to Shimei, "You know in your heart all the wrong you did

---

b34 Or *buried in his tomb*

to my father David. Now the LORD will repay you for your wrongdoing. ⁴⁵But King Solomon will be blessed, and David's throne will remain secure before the LORD for ever."

⁴⁶Then the king gave the order to Benaiah son of Jehoiada, and he went out and struck Shimei down and killed him.

The kingdom was now firmly established in Solomon's hands.

Solomon Asks for Wisdom

3 Solomon made an alliance with Pharaoh king of Egypt and married his daughter. He brought her to the City of David until he finished building his palace and the temple of the LORD, and the wall around Jerusalem. ²The people, however, were still sacrificing at the high places, because a temple had not yet been built for the Name of the LORD. ³Solomon showed his love for the LORD by walking according to the statutes of his father David, except that he offered sacrifices and burned incense on the high places.

⁴The king went to Gibeon to offer sacrifices, for that was the most important high place, and Solomon offered a thousand burnt offerings on that altar. ⁵At Gibeon the LORD appeared to Solomon during the night in a dream, and God said, "Ask for whatever you want me to give you."

⁶Solomon answered, "You have shown great kindness to your servant, my father David, because he was faithful to you and righteous and upright in heart. You have continued this great kindness to him and have given him a son to sit on his throne this very day.

⁷"Now, O LORD my God, you have made your servant king in place of my father David. But I am only a little child and do not know how to carry out my duties. ⁸Your servant is here among the people you have chosen, a great people, too numerous to count or number. ⁹So give your servant a discerning heart to govern your people and to distinguish between right and wrong. For who is able to

govern this great people of yours?"

¹⁰The Lord was pleased that Solomon had asked for this. ¹¹So God said to him, "Since you have asked for this and not for long life or wealth for yourself, nor have asked for the death of your enemies but for discernment in administering justice, ¹²I will do what you have asked. I will give you a wise and discerning heart, so that there will never have been anyone like you, nor will there ever be. ¹³Moreover, I will give you what you have not asked for—both riches and honour—so that in your lifetime you will have no equal among kings. ¹⁴And if you walk in my ways and obey my statutes and commands as David your father did, I will give you a long life." ¹⁵Then Solomon awoke—and he realised it had been a dream.

He returned to Jerusalem, stood before the ark of the Lord's covenant and sacrificed burnt offerings and fellowship offerings.ᵃ Then he gave a feast for all his court.

A Wise Ruling

¹⁶Now two prostitutes came to the king and stood before him. ¹⁷One of them said, "My lord, this woman and I live in the same house. I had a baby while she was there with me. ¹⁸The third day after my child was born, this woman also had a baby. We were alone; there was no-one in the house but the two of us.

¹⁹"During the night this woman's son died because she lay on him. ²⁰So she got up in the middle of the night and took my son from my side while I your servant was asleep. She put him by her breast and put her dead son by my breast. ²¹The next morning, I got up to nurse my son—and he was dead! But when I looked at him closely in the morning light, I saw that it wasn't the son I had borne."

²²The other woman said, "No! The living one is my son; the dead one is yours."

But the first one insisted, "No! The dead one is yours; the living one is mine." And so they argued before the king.

²³The king said, "This one says, 'My son

ᵃ15 Traditionally *peace offerings*

is alive and your son is dead,' while that one says, 'No! Your son is dead and mine is alive.'"

²⁴Then the king said, "Bring me a sword." So they brought a sword for the king. ²⁵He then gave an order: "Cut the living child in two and give half to one and half to the other."

²⁶The woman whose son was alive was filled with compassion for her son and said to the king, "Please, my lord, give her the living baby! Don't kill him!"

But the other said, "Neither I nor you shall have him. Cut him in two!"

²⁷Then the king gave his ruling: "Give the living baby to the first woman. Do not kill him; she is his mother."

²⁸When all Israel heard the verdict the king had given, they held the king in awe, because they saw that he had wisdom from God to administer justice.

Solomon's Officials and Governors

4 So King Solomon ruled over all Israel. ²And these were his chief officials:

Azariah son of Zadok—the priest;
³Elihoreph and Ahijah, sons of Shisha—secretaries;
Jehoshaphat son of Ahilud—recorder;
⁴Benaiah son of Jehoiada—commander-in-chief;
Zadok and Abiathar—priests;
⁵Azariah son of Nathan—in charge of the district officers;
Zabud son of Nathan—a priest and personal adviser to the king;
⁶Ahishar—in charge of the palace;
Adoniram son of Abda—in charge of forced labour.

⁷Solomon also had twelve district governors over all Israel, who supplied provisions for the king and the royal household. Each one had to provide supplies for one month in the year. ⁸These are their names:

Ben-Hur—in the hill country of Ephraim;
⁹Ben-Deker—in Makaz, Shaalbim, Beth Shemesh and Elon Bethhanan;
¹⁰Ben-Hesed—in Arubboth (Socoh and all the land of Hepher were his);
¹¹Ben-Abinadab—in Naphoth Dorᵃ (he was married to Taphath daughter of Solomon);
¹²Baana son of Ahilud—in Taanach and Megiddo, and in all of Beth Shan next to Zarethan below Jezreel, from Beth Shan to Abel Meholah across to Jokmeam;
¹³Ben-Geber—in Ramoth Gilead (the settlements of Jair son of Manasseh in Gilead were his, as well as the district of Argob in Bashan and its sixty large walled cities with bronze gate bars);
¹⁴Ahinadab son of Iddo—in Mahanaim;
¹⁵Ahimaaz—in Naphtali (he had married Basemath daughter of Solomon);
¹⁶Baana son of Hushai—in Asher and in Aloth;
¹⁷Jehoshaphat son of Paruah—in Issachar;
¹⁸Shimei son of Ela—in Benjamin;
¹⁹Geber son of Uri—in Gilead (the country of Sihon king of the Amorites and the country of Og king of Bashan). He was the only governor over the district.

Solomon's Daily Provisions

²⁰The people of Judah and Israel were as numerous as the sand on the seashore; they ate, they drank and they were happy. ²¹And Solomon ruled over all the kingdoms from the Riverᵇ to the land of the Philistines, as far as the border of Egypt. These countries brought tribute and were Solomon's subjects all his life. ²²Solomon's daily provisions were thirty corsᶜ of fine flour and sixty corsᵈ of meal,

ᵃ11 Or *in the heights of Dor*   ᵇ21 That is, the Euphrates; also in verse 24
ᶜ22 That is, probably about 180 bushels (about 6.6 kilolitres)
ᵈ22 That is, probably about 365 bushels (about 13.2 kilolitres)

23ten head of stall-fed cattle, twenty of pasture-fed cattle and a hundred sheep and goats, as well as deer, gazelles, roebucks and choice fowl. 24For he ruled over all the kingdoms west of the River, from Tiphsah to Gaza, and had peace on all sides. 25During Solomon's lifetime Judah and Israel, from Dan to Beersheba, lived in safety, each man under his own vine and fig-tree.

26Solomon had four*e* thousand stalls for chariot horses, and twelve thousand horses.*f*

27The district officers, each in his month, supplied provisions for King Solomon and all who came to the king's table. They saw to it that nothing was lacking. 28They also brought to the proper place their quotas of barley and straw for the chariot horses and the other horses.

Solomon's Wisdom

29God gave Solomon wisdom and very great insight, and a breadth of understanding as measureless as the sand on the seashore. 30Solomon's wisdom was greater than the wisdom of all the men of the East, and greater than all the wisdom of Egypt. 31He was wiser than any other man, including Ethan the Ezrahite—wiser than Heman, Calcol and Darda, the sons of Mahol. And his fame spread to all the surrounding nations. 32He spoke three thousand proverbs and his songs numbered a thousand and five. 33He described plant life, from the cedar of Lebanon to the hyssop that grows out of walls. He also taught about animals and birds, reptiles and fish. 34Men of all nations came to listen to Solomon's wisdom, sent by all the kings of the world, who had heard of his wisdom.

Preparations for Building the Temple

5 When Hiram king of Tyre heard that Solomon had been anointed king to succeed his father David, he sent his envoys to Solomon, because he had always

been on friendly terms with David. 2Solomon sent back this message to Hiram:

3"You know that because of the wars waged against my father David from all sides, he could not build a temple for the Name of the LORD his God until the LORD put his enemies under his feet. 4But now the LORD my God has given me rest on every side, and there is no adversary or disaster. 5I intend, therefore, to build a temple for the Name of the LORD my God, as the LORD told my father David, when he said, 'Your son whom I will put on the throne in your place will build the temple for my Name.'

6"So give orders that cedars of Lebanon be cut for me. My men will work with yours, and I will pay you for your men whatever wages you set. You know that we have no-one so skilled in felling timber as the Sidonians."

7When Hiram heard Solomon's message, he was greatly pleased and said, "Praise be to the LORD today, for he has given David a wise son to rule over this great nation."

8So Hiram sent word to Solomon:

"I have received the message you sent me and will do all you want in providing the cedar and pine logs. 9My men will haul them down from Lebanon to the sea, and I will float them in rafts by sea to the place you specify. There I will separate them and you can take them away. And you are to grant my wish by providing food for my royal household."

10In this way Hiram kept Solomon supplied with all the cedar and pine logs he wanted, 11and Solomon gave Hiram twenty thousand cors*a* of wheat as food for his household, in addition to twenty thousand baths*b,c* of pressed olive oil. Solomon continued to do this for Hiram

---

e26 Some Septuagint manuscripts (see also 2 Chron. 9:25); Hebrew *forty*   *f26* Or *charioteers*
a11 That is, probably about 121,000 bushels (about 4,400 kilolitres)
b11 Septuagint (see also 2 Chron. 2:10); Hebrew *twenty cors*   *c11* That is, about 97,000 gallons (about 440 kilolitres)

year after year. [12]The LORD gave Solomon wisdom, just as he had promised him. There were peaceful relations between Hiram and Solomon, and the two of them made a treaty.

[13]King Solomon conscripted labourers from all Israel—thirty thousand men. [14]He sent them off to Lebanon in shifts of ten thousand a month, so that they spent one month in Lebanon and two months at home. Adoniram was in charge of the forced labour. [15]Solomon had seventy thousand carriers and eighty thousand stonecutters in the hills, [16]as well as thirty-three hundred[d] foremen who supervised the project and directed the workmen. [17]At the king's command they removed from the quarry large blocks of quality stone to provide a foundation of dressed stone for the temple. [18]The craftsmen of Solomon and Hiram and the men of Gebal[e] cut and prepared the timber and stone for the building of the temple.

Solomon Builds the Temple

6 In the four hundred and eightieth[a] year after the Israelites had come out of Egypt, in the fourth year of Solomon's reign over Israel, in the month of Ziv, the second month, he began to build the temple of the LORD.

[2]The temple that King Solomon built for the LORD was sixty cubits long, twenty wide and thirty high.[b] [3]The portico at the front of the main hall of the temple extended the width of the temple, that is twenty cubits,[c] and projected ten cubits[d] from the front of the temple. [4]He made narrow clerestory windows in the temple. [5]Against the walls of the main hall and inner sanctuary he built a structure around the building, in which there were side rooms. [6]The lowest floor was five cubits[e] wide, the middle floor six cubits[f] and the third floor seven.[g] He made offset ledges

around the outside of the temple so that nothing would be inserted into the temple walls.

[7]In building the temple, only blocks dressed at the quarry were used, and no hammer, chisel or any other iron tool was heard at the temple site while it was being built.

[8]The entrance to the lowest[h] floor was on the south side of the temple; a stairway led up to the middle level and from there to the third. [9]So he built the temple and completed it, roofing it with beams and cedar planks. [10]And he built the side rooms all along the temple. The height of each was five cubits, and they were attached to the temple by beams of cedar.

[11]The word of the LORD came to Solomon: [12]"As for this temple you are building, if you follow my decrees, carry out my regulations and keep all my commands and obey them, I will fulfil through you the promise I gave to David your father. [13]And I will live among the Israelites and will not abandon my people Israel."

[14]So Solomon built the temple and completed it. [15]He lined its interior walls with cedar boards, panelling them from the floor of the temple to the ceiling, and covered the floor of the temple with planks of pine. [16]He partitioned off twenty cubits[i] at the rear of the temple with cedar boards from floor to ceiling to form within the temple an inner sanctuary, the Most Holy Place. [17]The main hall in front of this room was forty cubits[j] long. [18]The inside of the temple was cedar, carved with gourds and open flowers. Everything was cedar; no stone was to be seen.

[19]He prepared the inner sanctuary within the temple to set the ark of the covenant of the LORD there. [20]The inner sanctuary was twenty cubits long, twenty wide and twenty high.[k] He overlaid the inside with pure gold, and he also overlaid the altar of cedar. [21]Solomon covered the inside of the

---

[d]16 Hebrew; some Septuagint manuscripts (see also 2 Chron. 2:2, 18) *thirty-six hundred*   [e]18 That is, Byblos
[a]1 Hebrew; Septuagint *four hundred and fortieth*
[b]2 That is, about 90 feet (about 27 metres) long and 30 feet (about 9 metres) wide and 45 feet (about 13.5 metres) high
[c]3 That is, about 30 feet (about 9 metres)   [d]3 That is, about 15 feet (about 4.5 metres)
[e]6 That is, about 7½ feet (about 2.3 metres); also in verses 10 and 24   [f]6 That is, about 9 feet (about 2.7 metres)
[g]6 That is, about 10½ feet (about 3.2 metres)   [h]8 Septuagint; Hebrew *middle*
[i]16 That is, about 30 feet (about 9 metres)   [j]17 That is, about 60 feet (about 18 metres)
[k]20 That is, about 30 feet (about 9 metres) long, wide and high

temple with pure gold, and he extended gold chains across the front of the inner sanctuary, which was overlaid with gold. ²²So he overlaid the whole interior with gold. He also overlaid with gold the altar that belonged to the inner sanctuary.

²³In the inner sanctuary he made a pair of cherubim of olive wood, each ten cubits*l* high. ²⁴One wing of the first cherub was five cubits long, and the other wing five cubits—ten cubits from wing tip to wing tip. ²⁵The second cherub also measured ten cubits, for the two cherubim were identical in size and shape. ²⁶The height of each cherub was ten cubits. ²⁷He placed the cherubim inside the innermost room of the temple, with their wings spread out. The wing of one cherub touched one wall, while the wing of the other touched the other wall, and their wings touched each other in the middle of the room. ²⁸He overlaid the cherubim with gold.

²⁹On the walls all round the temple, in both the inner and outer rooms, he carved cherubim, palm trees and open flowers. ³⁰He also covered the floors of both the inner and outer rooms of the temple with gold.

³¹For the entrance of the inner sanctuary he made doors of olive wood with five-sided jambs. ³²And on the two olive wood doors he carved cherubim, palm trees and open flowers, and overlaid the cherubim and palm trees with beaten gold. ³³In the same way he made four-sided jambs of olive wood for the entrance to the main hall. ³⁴He also made two pine doors, each having two leaves that turned in sockets. ³⁵He carved cherubim, palm trees and open flowers on them and overlaid them with gold hammered evenly over the carvings.

³⁶And he built the inner courtyard of three courses of dressed stone and one course of trimmed cedar beams.

³⁷The foundation of the temple of the LORD was laid in the fourth year, in the month of Ziv. ³⁸In the eleventh year in the month of Bul, the eighth month, the temple was finished in all its details according to its specifications. He had spent seven years building it.

Solomon Builds His Palace

7 It took Solomon thirteen years, however, to complete the construction of his palace. ²He built the Palace of the Forest of Lebanon a hundred cubits long, fifty wide and thirty high,*a* with four rows of cedar columns supporting trimmed cedar beams. ³It was roofed with cedar above the beams that rested on the columns—forty-five beams, fifteen to a row. ⁴Its windows were placed high in sets of three, facing each other. ⁵All the doorways had rectangular frames; they were in the front part in sets of three, facing each other.*b*

⁶He made a colonnade fifty cubits long and thirty wide.*c* In front of it was a portico, and in front of that were pillars and an overhanging roof.

⁷He built the throne hall, the Hall of Justice, where he was to judge, and he covered it with cedar from floor to ceiling.*d* ⁸And the palace in which he was to live, set farther back, was similar in design. Solomon also made a palace like this hall for Pharaoh's daughter, whom he had married.

⁹All these structures, from the outside to the great courtyard and from foundation to eaves, were made of blocks of high-grade stone cut to size and trimmed with a saw on their inner and outer faces. ¹⁰The foundations were laid with large stones of good quality, some measuring ten cubits*e* and some eight.*f* ¹¹Above were high-grade stones, cut to size, and cedar beams. ¹²The great courtyard was surrounded by a wall of three courses of dressed stone and one course of trimmed cedar beams, as was the inner courtyard of the temple of the LORD with its portico.

l23 That is, about 15 feet (about 4.5 metres)
a2 That is, about 150 feet (about 46 metres) long, 75 feet (about 23 metres) wide and 45 feet (about 13.5 metres) high
b5 The meaning of the Hebrew for this verse is uncertain.
c6 That is, about 75 feet (about 23 metres) long and 45 feet (about 13.5 metres) wide
d7 Vulgate and Syriac; Hebrew *floor*   *e10* That is, about 15 feet (about 4.5 metres)
f10 That is, about 12 feet (about 3.7 metres)

The Temple's Furnishings

[13] King Solomon sent to Tyre and brought Huram,[g] [14] whose mother was a widow from the tribe of Naphtali and whose father was a man of Tyre and a craftsman in bronze. Huram was highly skilled and experienced in all kinds of bronze work. He came to King Solomon and did all the work assigned to him.

[15] He cast two bronze pillars, each eighteen cubits high and twelve cubits round,[h] by line. [16] He also made two capitals of cast bronze to set on the tops of the pillars; each capital was five cubits[i] high. [17] A network of interwoven chains festooned the capitals on top of the pillars, seven for each capital. [18] He made pomegranates in two rows[j] encircling each network to decorate the capitals on top of the pillars.[k] He did the same for each capital. [19] The capitals on top of the pillars in the portico were in the shape of lilies, four cubits[l] high. [20] On the capitals of both pillars, above the bowl-shaped part next to the network, were the two hundred pomegranates in rows all around. [21] He erected the pillars at the portico of the temple. The pillar to the south he named Jakin[m] and the one to the north Boaz.[n] [22] The capitals on top were in the shape of lilies. And so the work on the pillars was completed.

[23] He made the Sea of cast metal, circular in shape, measuring ten cubits[o] from rim to rim and five cubits high. It took a line of thirty cubits[p] to measure round it. [24] Below the rim, gourds encircled it—ten to a cubit. The gourds were cast in two rows in one piece with the Sea.

[25] The Sea stood on twelve bulls, three facing north, three facing west, three facing south and three facing east. The Sea rested on top of them, and their hindquarters were towards the centre. [26] It was a handbreadth[q] in thickness, and its rim was like the rim of a cup, like a lily blossom. It held two thousand baths.[r]

[27] He also made ten movable stands of bronze; each was four cubits long, four wide and three high.[s] [28] This is how the stands were made: They had side panels attached to uprights. [29] On the panels between the uprights were lions, bulls and cherubim—and on the uprights as well. Above and below the lions and bulls were wreaths of hammered work. [30] Each stand had four bronze wheels with bronze axles, and each had a basin resting on four supports, cast with wreaths on each side. [31] On the inside of the stand there was an opening that had a circular frame one cubit[t] deep. This opening was round, and with its basework it measured a cubit and a half.[u] Around its opening there was engraving. The panels of the stands were square, not round. [32] The four wheels were under the panels, and the axles of the wheels were attached to the stand. The diameter of each wheel was a cubit and a half. [33] The wheels were made like chariot wheels; the axles, rims, spokes and hubs were all of cast metal.

[34] Each stand had four handles, one on each corner, projecting from the stand. [35] At the top of the stand there was a circular band half a cubit[v] deep. The supports and panels were attached to the top of the stand. [36] He engraved cherubim, lions and palm trees on the surfaces of the supports and on the panels, in every available space, with wreaths all around. [37] This is the way he made the ten stands. They

---

g13 Hebrew *Hiram*, a variant of *Huram*; also in verses 40 and 45
h15 That is, about 27 feet (about 8.2 metres) high and 18 feet (about 5.5 metres) round
i16 That is, about 7½ feet (about 2.3 metres); also in verse 23
j18 Two Hebrew manuscripts and Septuagint; most Hebrew manuscripts *made the pillars, and there were two rows*
k18 Many Hebrew manuscripts and Syriac; most Hebrew manuscripts *pomegranates*
l19 That is, about 6 feet (about 1.8 metres); also in verse 38
m21 *Jakin* probably means *he establishes.*   *n21* *Boaz* probably means *in him is strength.*
o23 That is, about 15 feet (about 4.5 metres)   *p23* That is, about 45 feet (about 13.7 metres)
q26 That is, about 3 inches (about 8 centimetres)
r26 That is, probably about 9,700 gallons (about 44 kilolitres); the Septuagint does not have this sentence.
s27 That is, about 6 feet (about 1.8 metres) long and wide and about 4½ feet (about 1.4 metres) high
t31 That is, about 1½ feet (about 0.5 metre)   *u31* That is, about 2¼ feet (about 0.7 metre); also in verse 32
v35 That is, about ¾ foot (about 0.2 metre)

were all cast in the same moulds and were identical in size and shape.

38He then made ten bronze basins, each holding forty baths[w] and measuring four cubits across, one basin to go on each of the ten stands. 39He placed five of the stands on the south side of the temple and five on the north. He placed the Sea on the south side, at the south-east corner of the temple. 40He also made the basins and shovels and sprinkling bowls.

So Huram finished all the work he had undertaken for King Solomon in the temple of the LORD:

41the two pillars;

the two bowl-shaped capitals on top of the pillars;

the two sets of network decorating the two bowl-shaped capitals on top of the pillars;

42the four hundred pomegranates for the two sets of network (two rows of pomegranates for each network, decorating the bowl-shaped capitals on top of the pillars);

43the ten stands with their ten basins;

44the Sea and the twelve bulls under it;

45the pots, shovels and sprinkling bowls.

All these objects that Huram made for King Solomon for the temple of the LORD were of burnished bronze. 46The king had them cast in clay moulds in the plain of the Jordan between Succoth and Zarethan. 47Solomon left all these things unweighed, because there were so many; the weight of the bronze was not determined.

48Solomon also made all the furnishings that were in the LORD's temple:

the golden altar;

the golden table on which was the bread of the Presence;

49the lampstands of pure gold (five on the right and five on the left, in front of the inner sanctuary);

the gold floral work and lamps and tongs;

50the pure gold dishes, wick trimmers, sprinkling bowls, dishes and censers;

and the gold sockets for the doors of the innermost room, the Most Holy Place, and also for the doors of the main hall of the temple.

51When all the work King Solomon had done for the temple of the LORD was finished, he brought in the things his father David had dedicated—the silver and gold and the furnishings—and he placed them in the treasuries of the LORD's temple.

The Ark Brought to the Temple

8 Then King Solomon summoned into his presence at Jerusalem the elders of Israel, all the heads of the tribes and the chiefs of the Israelite families, to bring up the ark of the LORD's covenant from Zion, the City of David. 2All the men of Israel came together to King Solomon at the time of the festival in the month of Ethanim, the seventh month.

3When all the elders of Israel had arrived, the priests took up the ark, 4and they brought up the ark of the LORD and the Tent of Meeting and all the sacred furnishings in it. The priests and Levites carried them up, 5and King Solomon and the entire assembly of Israel that had gathered about him were before the ark, sacrificing so many sheep and cattle that they could not be recorded or counted.

6The priests then brought the ark of the LORD's covenant to its place in the inner sanctuary of the temple, the Most Holy Place, and put it beneath the wings of the cherubim. 7The cherubim spread their wings over the place of the ark and overshadowed the ark and its carrying poles. 8These poles were so long that their ends could be seen from the Holy Place in front of the inner sanctuary, but not from outside the Holy Place; and they are still there today. 9There was nothing in the ark except the two stone tablets that Moses had placed in it at Horeb, where the LORD

w38 That is, about 195 gallons (about 880 litres)

made a covenant with the Israelites after they came out of Egypt.

[10]When the priests withdrew from the Holy Place, the cloud filled the temple of the LORD. [11]And the priests could not perform their service because of the cloud, for the glory of the LORD filled his temple.

[12]Then Solomon said, "The LORD has said that he would dwell in a dark cloud; [13]I have indeed built a magnificent temple for you, a place for you to dwell for ever."

[14]While the whole assembly of Israel was standing there, the king turned round and blessed them. [15]Then he said:

"Praise be to the LORD, the God of Israel, who with his own hand has fulfilled what he promised with his own mouth to my father David. For he said, [16]'Since the day I brought my people Israel out of Egypt, I have not chosen a city in any tribe of Israel to have a temple built for my Name to be there, but I have chosen David to rule my people Israel.'

[17]"My father David had it in his heart to build a temple for the Name of the LORD, the God of Israel. [18]But the LORD said to my father David, 'Because it was in your heart to build a temple for my Name, you did well to have this in your heart. [19]Nevertheless, you are not the one to build the temple, but your son, who is your own flesh and blood—he is the one who will build the temple for my Name.'

[20]"The LORD has kept the promise he made: I have succeeded David my father and now I sit on the throne of Israel, just as the LORD promised, and I have built the temple for the Name of the LORD, the God of Israel. [21]I have provided a place there for the ark, in which is the covenant of the LORD that he made with our fathers when he brought them out of Egypt."

Solomon's Prayer of Dedication

[22]Then Solomon stood before the altar of the LORD in front of the whole assembly of Israel, spread out his hands towards heaven [23]and said:

"O LORD, God of Israel, there is no God like you in heaven above or on earth below—you who keep your covenant of love with your servants who continue wholeheartedly in your way. [24]You have kept your promise to your servant David my father; with your mouth you have promised and with your hand you have fulfilled it— as it is today.

[25]"Now LORD, God of Israel, keep for your servant David my father the promises you made to him when you said, 'You shall never fail to have a man to sit before me on the throne of Israel, if only your sons are careful in all they do to walk before me as you have done.' [26]And now, O God of Israel, let your word that you promised your servant David my father come true.

[27]"But will God really dwell on earth? The heavens, even the highest heaven, cannot contain you. How much less this temple I have built! [28]Yet give attention to your servant's prayer and his plea for mercy, O LORD my God. Hear the cry and the prayer that your servant is praying in your presence this day. [29]May your eyes be open towards this temple night and day, this place of which you said, 'My Name shall be there,' so that you will hear the prayer your servant prays towards this place. [30]Hear the supplication of your servant and of your people Israel when they pray towards this place. Hear from heaven, your dwelling-place, and when you hear, forgive.

[31]"When a man wrongs his neighbour and is required to take an oath and he comes and swears the oath before your altar in this temple, [32]then hear from heaven and act. Judge between your servants, condemning the guilty and bringing down on his own head what he has done. Declare the innocent not guilty, and so establish his innocence.

33"When your people Israel have been defeated by an enemy because they have sinned against you, and when they turn back to you and confess your name, praying and making supplication to you in this temple, 34then hear from heaven and forgive the sin of your people Israel and bring them back to the land you gave to their fathers.

35"When the heavens are shut up and there is no rain because your people have sinned against you, and when they pray towards this place and confess your name and turn from their sin because you have afflicted them, 36then hear from heaven and forgive the sin of your servants, your people Israel. Teach them the right way to live, and send rain on the land you gave your people for an inheritance.

37"When famine or plague comes to the land, or blight or mildew, locusts or grasshoppers, or when an enemy besieges them in any of their cities, whatever disaster or disease may come, 38and when a prayer or plea is made by any of your people Israel—each one aware of the afflictions of his own heart, and spreading out his hands towards this temple —39then hear from heaven, your dwelling-place. Forgive and act; deal with each man according to all he does, since you know his heart (for you alone know the hearts of all men), 40so that they will fear you all the time they live in the land you gave our fathers.

41"As for the foreigner who does not belong to your people Israel but has come from a distant land because of your name—42for men will hear of your great name and your mighty hand and your outstretched arm— when he comes and prays towards this temple, 43then hear from heaven, your dwelling-place, and do whatever the foreigner asks of you, so that all the peoples of the earth may know your name and fear you, as do your own people Israel, and may know that this house I have built bears your Name.

44"When your people go to war against their enemies, wherever you send them, and when they pray to the LORD towards the city you have chosen and the temple I have built for your Name, 45then hear from heaven their prayer and their plea, and uphold their cause.

46"When they sin against you—for there is no-one who does not sin—and you become angry with them and give them over to the enemy, who takes them captive to his own land, far away or near; 47and if they have a change of heart in the land where they are held captive, and repent and plead with you in the land of their conquerors and say, 'We have sinned, we have done wrong, we have acted wickedly'; 48and if they turn back to you with all their heart and soul in the land of their enemies who took them captive, and pray to you towards the land you gave their fathers, towards the city you have chosen and the temple I have built for your Name; 49then from heaven, your dwelling-place, hear their prayer and their plea, and uphold their cause. 50And forgive your people, who have sinned against you; forgive all the offences they have committed against you, and cause their conquerors to show them mercy; 51for they are your people and your inheritance, whom you brought out of Egypt, out of that iron-smelting furnace.

52"May your eyes be open to your servant's plea and to the plea of your people Israel, and may you listen to them whenever they cry out to you. 53For you singled them out from all the nations of the world to be your own inheritance, just as you declared through your servant Moses when you, O Sovereign LORD, brought our fathers out of Egypt."

54When Solomon had finished all these prayers and supplications to the LORD, he rose from before the altar of the LORD, where he had been kneeling with his hands spread out towards heaven. ⁵⁵He stood and blessed the whole assembly of Israel in a loud voice, saying:

⁵⁶"Praise be to the LORD, who has given rest to his people Israel just as he promised. Not one word has failed of all the good promises he gave through his servant Moses. ⁵⁷May the LORD our God be with us as he was with our fathers; may he never leave us nor forsake us. ⁵⁸May he turn our hearts to him, to walk in all his ways and to keep the commands, decrees and regulations he gave our fathers. ⁵⁹And may these words of mine, which I have prayed before the LORD, be near to the LORD our God day and night, that he may uphold the cause of his servant and the cause of his people Israel according to each day's need, ⁶⁰so that all the peoples of the earth may know that the LORD is God and that there is no other. ⁶¹But your hearts must be fully committed to the LORD our God, to live by his decrees and obey his commands, as at this time."

The Dedication of the Temple

⁶²Then the king and all Israel with him offered sacrifices before the LORD. ⁶³Solomon offered a sacrifice of fellowship offerings*a* to the LORD: twenty-two thousand cattle and a hundred and twenty thousand sheep and goats. So the king and all the Israelites dedicated the temple of the LORD.

⁶⁴On that same day the king consecrated the middle part of the courtyard in front of the temple of the LORD, and there he offered burnt offerings, grain offerings and the fat of the fellowship offerings, because the bronze altar before the LORD was too small to hold the burnt offerings, the grain offerings and the fat of the fellowship offerings.

⁶⁵So Solomon observed the festival at that time, and all Israel with him—a vast assembly, people from Lebo*b* Hamath to the Wadi of Egypt. They celebrated it before the LORD our God for seven days and seven days more, fourteen days in all. ⁶⁶On the following day he sent the people away. They blessed the king and then went home, joyful and glad in heart for all the good things the LORD had done for his servant David and his people Israel.

The LORD Appears to Solomon

9 When Solomon had finished building the temple of the LORD and the royal palace, and had achieved all he had desired to do, ²the LORD appeared to him a second time, as he had appeared to him at Gibeon. ³The LORD said to him:

"I have heard the prayer and plea you have made before me; I have consecrated this temple, which you have built, by putting my Name there for ever. My eyes and my heart will always be there.

⁴"As for you, if you walk before me in integrity of heart and uprightness, as David your father did, and do all I command and observe my decrees and laws, ⁵I will establish your royal throne over Israel for ever, as I promised David your father when I said, 'You shall never fail to have a man on the throne of Israel.'

⁶"But if you*a* or your sons turn away from me and do not observe the commands and decrees I have given you*a* and go off to serve other gods and worship them, ⁷then I will cut off Israel from the land I have given them and will reject this temple I have consecrated for my Name. Israel will then become a byword and an object of ridicule among all peoples. ⁸And though this temple is now imposing, all who pass by will be appalled and will scoff and say, 'Why has the LORD done such a thing to this land and to

---

*a*63 Traditionally *peace offerings*; also in verse 64   *b*65 Or *from the entrance to*
*a*6 The Hebrew is plural.

this temple?' [9]People will answer, 'Because they have forsaken the LORD their God, who brought their fathers out of Egypt, and have embraced other gods, worshipping and serving them—that is why the LORD brought all this disaster on them.'"

Solomon's Other Activities

[10]At the end of twenty years, during which Solomon built these two buildings—the temple of the LORD and the royal palace—[11]King Solomon gave twenty towns in Galilee to Hiram king of Tyre, because Hiram had supplied him with all the cedar and pine and gold he wanted. [12]But when Hiram went from Tyre to see the towns that Solomon had given him, he was not pleased with them. [13]"What kind of towns are these you have given me, my brother?" he asked. And he called them the Land of Cabul,[b] a name they have to this day. [14]Now Hiram had sent to the king 120 talents[c] of gold.

[15]Here is the account of the forced labour King Solomon conscripted to build the LORD's temple, his own palace, the supporting terraces,[d] the wall of Jerusalem, and Hazor, Megiddo and Gezer. [16](Pharaoh king of Egypt had attacked and captured Gezer. He had set it on fire. He killed its Canaanite inhabitants, and then gave it as a wedding gift to his daughter, Solomon's wife. [17]And Solomon rebuilt Gezer.) He built up Lower Beth Horon, [18]Baalath, and Tadmor[e] in the desert, within his land, [19]as well as all his store cities and the towns for his chariots and for his horses[f]—whatever he desired to build in Jerusalem, in Lebanon and throughout all the territory he ruled.

[20]All the people left from the Amorites, Hittites, Perizzites, Hivites and Jebusites (these peoples were not Israelites), [21]that is, their descendants remaining in the land, whom the Israelites could not exterminate[g]—these Solomon conscripted for his slave labour force, as it is to this day. [22]But Solomon did not make slaves of any of the Israelites; they were his fighting men, his government officials, his officers, his captains, and the commanders of his chariots and charioteers. [23]They were also the chief officials in charge of Solomon's projects—550 officials supervising the men who did the work.

[24]After Pharaoh's daughter had come up from the City of David to the palace Solomon had built for her, he constructed the supporting terraces.

[25]Three times a year Solomon sacrificed burnt offerings and fellowship offerings[h] on the altar he had built for the LORD, burning incense before the LORD along with them, and so fulfilled the temple obligations.

[26]King Solomon also built ships at Ezion Geber, which is near Elath in Edom, on the shore of the Red Sea.[i] [27]And Hiram sent his men—sailors who knew the sea—to serve in the fleet with Solomon's men. [28]They sailed to Ophir and brought back 420 talents[j] of gold, which they delivered to King Solomon.

The Queen of Sheba Visits Solomon

10 When the queen of Sheba heard about the fame of Solomon and his relation to the name of the LORD, she came to test him with hard questions. [2]Arriving at Jerusalem with a very great caravan—with camels carrying spices, large quantities of gold, and precious stones—she came to Solomon and talked with him about all that she had on her mind. [3]Solomon answered all her questions; nothing was too hard for the king to explain to her. [4]When the queen of Sheba saw all the wisdom of Solomon and the palace he had built, [5]the food on his table, the seating of his officials, the attending servants in their robes, his cupbearers, and the burnt offerings he made at[a] the

---

b13   *Cabul* sounds like the Hebrew for *good-for-nothing.*   *c14*   That is, about 4 tons (about 4 metric tons)
d15   Or *the Millo;* also in verse 24   *e18*   The Hebrew may also be read *Tamar.*   *f19*   Or *charioteers*
g21   The Hebrew term refers to the irrevocable giving over of things or persons to the LORD, often by totally destroying them.   *h25*   Traditionally *peace offerings*   *i26*   Hebrew *Yam Suph;* that is, Sea of Reeds
j28   That is, about 14 tons (about 14.5 metric tons)   *a5*   Or *the ascent by which he went up to*

temple of the LORD, she was overwhelmed.

⁶She said to the king, "The report I heard in my own country about your achievements and your wisdom is true. ⁷But I did not believe these things until I came and saw with my own eyes. Indeed, not even half was told me; in wisdom and wealth you have far exceeded the report I heard. ⁸How happy your men must be! How happy your officials, who continually stand before you and hear your wisdom! ⁹Praise be to the LORD your God, who has delighted in you and placed you on the throne of Israel. Because of the LORD's eternal love for Israel, he has made you king, to maintain justice and righteousness."

¹⁰And she gave the king 120 talents*b* of gold, large quantities of spices, and precious stones. Never again were so many spices brought in as those the queen of Sheba gave to King Solomon.

¹¹(Hiram's ships brought gold from Ophir; and from there they brought great cargoes of almug-wood*c* and precious stones. ¹²The king used the almug-wood to make supports for the temple of the LORD and for the royal palace, and to make harps and lyres for the musicians. So much almug-wood has never been imported or seen since that day.)

¹³King Solomon gave the queen of Sheba all she desired and asked for, besides what he had given her out of his royal bounty. Then she left and returned to her own country.

Solomon's Splendour

¹⁴The weight of the gold that Solomon received yearly was 666 talents,*d* ¹⁵not including the revenues from merchants and traders and from all the Arabian kings and the governors of the land.

¹⁶King Solomon made two hundred large shields of hammered gold; six hundred bekas*e* of gold went into each shield. ¹⁷He also made three hundred small shields of hammered gold, with three minas*f* of gold in each shield. The king put them in the Palace of the Forest of Lebanon.

¹⁸Then the king made a great throne inlaid with ivory and overlaid with fine gold. ¹⁹The throne had six steps, and its back had a rounded top. On both sides of the seat were armrests, with a lion standing beside each of them. ²⁰Twelve lions stood on the six steps, one at either end of each step. Nothing like it had ever been made for any other kingdom. ²¹All King Solomon's goblets were gold, and all the household articles in the Palace of the Forest of Lebanon were pure gold. Nothing was made of silver, because silver was considered of little value in Solomon's days. ²²The king had a fleet of trading ships*g* at sea along with the ships of Hiram. Once every three years it returned carrying gold, silver and ivory, and apes and baboons.

²³King Solomon was greater in riches and wisdom than all the other kings of the earth. ²⁴The whole world sought audience with Solomon to hear the wisdom God had put in his heart. ²⁵Year after year, everyone who came brought a gift—articles of silver and gold, robes, weapons and spices, and horses and mules.

²⁶Solomon accumulated chariots and horses; he had fourteen hundred chariots and twelve thousand horses,*h* which he kept in the chariot cities and also with him in Jerusalem. ²⁷The king made silver as common in Jerusalem as stones, and cedar as plentiful as sycamore-fig trees in the foothills. ²⁸Solomon's horses were imported from Egypt*i* and from Kue*j*—the royal merchants purchased them from Kue.*j* ²⁹They imported a chariot from Egypt for six hundred shekels*k* of silver, and a horse for a hundred and fifty.*l* They also exported them to all the kings of the Hittites and of the Arameans.

---

b10 That is, about 4 tons (about 4 metric tons)   *c11* Probably a variant of *algum-wood*; also in verse 12
d14 That is, about 22½ tons (about 23 metric tons)   *e16* That is, about 7½ pounds (about 3.5 kilograms)
f17 That is, about 3¾ pounds (about 1.7 kilograms)   *g22* Hebrew *of ships of Tarshish*   *h26* Or *charioteers*
i28 Or possibly *Muzur*, a region in Cilicia; also in verse 29   *j28* Probably *Cilicia*
k29 That is, about 15 pounds (about 7 kilograms)   *l29* That is, about 3¾ pounds (about 1.7 kilograms)

Solomon's Wives

11 King Solomon, however, loved many foreign women besides Pharaoh's daughter—Moabites, Ammonites, Edomites, Sidonians and Hittites. ²They were from nations about which the LORD had told the Israelites, "You must not intermarry with them, because they will surely turn your hearts after their gods." Nevertheless, Solomon held fast to them in love. ³He had seven hundred wives of royal birth and three hundred concubines, and his wives led him astray. ⁴As Solomon grew old, his wives turned his heart after other gods, and his heart was not fully devoted to the LORD his God, as the heart of David his father had been. ⁵He followed Ashtoreth the goddess of the Sidonians, and Molech*ᵃ* the detestable god of the Ammonites. ⁶So Solomon did evil in the eyes of the LORD; he did not follow the LORD completely, as David his father had done.

⁷On a hill east of Jerusalem, Solomon built a high place for Chemosh the detestable god of Moab, and for Molech the detestable god of the Ammonites. ⁸He did the same for all his foreign wives, who burned incense and offered sacrifices to their gods.

⁹The LORD became angry with Solomon because his heart had turned away from the LORD, the God of Israel, who had appeared to him twice. ¹⁰Although he had forbidden Solomon to follow other gods, Solomon did not keep the LORD's command. ¹¹So the LORD said to Solomon, "Since this is your attitude and you have not kept my covenant and my decrees, which I commanded you, I will most certainly tear the kingdom away from you and give it to one of your subordinates. ¹²Nevertheless, for the sake of David your father, I will not do it during your lifetime. I will tear it out of the hand of your son. ¹³Yet I will not tear the whole kingdom from him, but will give him one tribe for the sake of David my servant and for the sake of Jerusalem, which I have chosen."

Solomon's Adversaries

¹⁴Then the LORD raised up against Solomon an adversary, Hadad the Edomite, from the royal line of Edom. ¹⁵Earlier when David was fighting with Edom, Joab the commander of the army, who had gone up to bury the dead, had struck down all the men in Edom. ¹⁶Joab and all the Israelites stayed there for six months, until they had destroyed all the men in Edom. ¹⁷But Hadad, still only a boy, fled to Egypt with some Edomite officials who had served his father. ¹⁸They set out from Midian and went to Paran. Then taking men from Paran with them, they went to Egypt, to Pharaoh king of Egypt, who gave Hadad a house and land and provided him with food.

¹⁹Pharaoh was so pleased with Hadad that he gave him a sister of his own wife, Queen Tahpenes, in marriage. ²⁰The sister of Tahpenes bore him a son named Genubath, whom Tahpenes brought up in the royal palace. There Genubath lived with Pharaoh's own children.

²¹While he was in Egypt, Hadad heard that David rested with his fathers and that Joab the commander of the army was also dead. Then Hadad said to Pharaoh, "Let me go, so that I may return to my own country."

²²"What have you lacked here that you want to go back to your own country?" Pharaoh asked.

"Nothing," Hadad replied, "but do let me go!"

²³And God raised up against Solomon another adversary, Rezon son of Eliada, who had fled from his master, Hadadezer king of Zobah. ²⁴He gathered men around him and became the leader of a band of rebels when David destroyed the forces*ᵇ* ⌞of Zobah⌟; the rebels went to Damascus, where they settled and took control. ²⁵Rezon was Israel's adversary as long as Solomon lived, adding to the trouble caused by Hadad. So Rezon ruled in Aram and was hostile towards Israel.

---

*ᵃ*5 Hebrew *Milcom*; also in verse 33   *ᵇ*24 Hebrew *destroyed them*

Jeroboam Rebels Against Solomon

26Also, Jeroboam son of Nebat rebelled against the king. He was one of Solomon's officials, an Ephraimite from Zeredah, and his mother was a widow named Zeruah.

27Here is the account of how he rebelled against the king: Solomon had built the supporting terraces[c] and had filled in the gap in the wall of the city of David his father. 28Now Jeroboam was a man of standing, and when Solomon saw how well the young man did his work, he put him in charge of the whole labour force of the house of Joseph.

29About that time Jeroboam was going out of Jerusalem, and Ahijah the prophet of Shiloh met him on the way, wearing a new cloak. The two of them were alone out in the country, 30and Ahijah took hold of the new cloak he was wearing and tore it into twelve pieces. 31Then he said to Jeroboam, "Take ten pieces for yourself, for this is what the LORD, the God of Israel, says: 'See, I am going to tear the kingdom out of Solomon's hand and give you ten tribes. 32But for the sake of my servant David and the city of Jerusalem, which I have chosen out of all the tribes of Israel, he will have one tribe. 33I will do this because they have[d] forsaken me and worshipped Ashtoreth the goddess of the Sidonians, Chemosh the god of the Moabites, and Molech the god of the Ammonites, and have not walked in my ways, nor done what is right in my eyes, nor kept my statutes and laws as David, Solomon's father, did.

34"'But I will not take the whole kingdom out of Solomon's hand; I have made him ruler all the days of his life for the sake of David my servant, whom I chose and who observed my commands and statutes. 35I will take the kingdom from his son's hands and give you ten tribes. 36I will give one tribe to his son so that David my servant may always have a lamp before me in Jerusalem, the city where I chose to put my Name. 37However, as for you, I will take you, and you will rule over all that your heart desires; you will be king over

Israel. 38If you do whatever I command you and walk in my ways and do what is right in my eyes by keeping my statutes and commands, as David my servant did, I will be with you. I will build you a dynasty as enduring as the one I built for David and will give Israel to you. 39I will humble David's descendants because of this, but not for ever.'"

40Solomon tried to kill Jeroboam, but Jeroboam fled to Egypt, to Shishak the king, and stayed there until Solomon's death.

Solomon's Death

41As for the other events of Solomon's reign—all he did and the wisdom he displayed—are they not written in the book of the annals of Solomon? 42Solomon reigned in Jerusalem over all Israel for forty years. 43Then he rested with his fathers and was buried in the city of David his father. And Rehoboam his son succeeded him as king.

Israel Rebels Against Rehoboam

12 Rehoboam went to Shechem, for all the Israelites had gone there to make him king. 2When Jeroboam son of Nebat heard this (he was still in Egypt, where he had fled from King Solomon), he returned from[a] Egypt. 3So they sent for Jeroboam, and he and the whole assembly of Israel went to Rehoboam and said to him: 4"Your father put a heavy yoke on us, but now lighten the harsh labour and the heavy yoke he put on us, and we will serve you."

5Rehoboam answered, "Go away for three days and then come back to me." So the people went away.

6Then King Rehoboam consulted the elders who had served his father Solomon during his lifetime. "How would you advise me to answer these people?" he asked.

7They replied, "If today you will be a servant to these people and serve them and give them a favourable answer, they will always be your servants."

---

c37 Or the Millo   d33 Hebrew; Septuagint, Vulgate and Syriac because he has   a2 Or he remained in

⁸But Rehoboam rejected the advice the elders gave him and consulted the young men who had grown up with him and were serving him. ⁹He asked them, "What is your advice? How should we answer these people who say to me, 'Lighten the yoke your father put on us'?"

¹⁰The young men who had grown up with him replied, "Tell these people who have said to you, 'Your father put a heavy yoke on us, but make our yoke lighter'—tell them, 'My little finger is thicker than my father's waist. ¹¹My father laid on you a heavy yoke; I will make it even heavier. My father scourged you with whips; I will scourge you with scorpions.'"

¹²Three days later Jeroboam and all the people returned to Rehoboam, as the king had said, "Come back to me in three days." ¹³The king answered the people harshly. Rejecting the advice given him by the elders, ¹⁴he followed the advice of the young men and said, "My father made your yoke heavy; I will make it even heavier. My father scourged you with whips; I will scourge you with scorpions." ¹⁵So the king did not listen to the people, for this turn of events was from the LORD, to fulfil the word the LORD had spoken to Jeroboam son of Nebat through Ahijah the Shilonite.

¹⁶When all Israel saw that the king refused to listen to them, they answered the king:

"What share do we have in David,
    what part in Jesse's son?
To your tents, O Israel!
    Look after your own house, O
        David!"

So the Israelites went home. ¹⁷But as for the Israelites who were living in the towns of Judah, Rehoboam still ruled over them.

¹⁸King Rehoboam sent out Adoniram,*b* who was in charge of forced labour, but all Israel stoned him to death. King Rehoboam, however, managed to get into his chariot and escape to Jerusalem. ¹⁹So

Israel has been in rebellion against the house of David to this day.

²⁰When all the Israelites heard that Jeroboam had returned, they sent and called him to the assembly and made him king over all Israel. Only the tribe of Judah remained loyal to the house of David.

²¹When Rehoboam arrived in Jerusalem, he mustered the whole house of Judah and the tribe of Benjamin—a hundred and eighty thousand fighting men— to make war against the house of Israel and to regain the kingdom for Rehoboam son of Solomon.

²²But this word of God came to Shemaiah the man of God: ²³"Say to Rehoboam son of Solomon king of Judah, to the whole house of Judah and Benjamin, and to the rest of the people, ²⁴'This is what the LORD says: Do not go up to fight against your brothers, the Israelites. Go home, every one of you, for this is my doing.'" So they obeyed the word of the LORD and went home again, as the LORD had ordered.

Golden Calves at Bethel and Dan

²⁵Then Jeroboam fortified Shechem in the hill country of Ephraim and lived there. From there he went out and built up Peniel.*c*

²⁶Jeroboam thought to himself, "The kingdom is now likely to revert to the house of David. ²⁷If these people go up to offer sacrifices at the temple of the LORD in Jerusalem, they will again give their allegiance to their lord, Rehoboam king of Judah. They will kill me and return to King Rehoboam."

²⁸After seeking advice, the king made two golden calves. He said to the people, "It is too much for you to go up to Jerusalem. Here are your gods, O Israel, who brought you up out of Egypt." ²⁹One he set up in Bethel, and the other in Dan. ³⁰And this thing became a sin; the people went even as far as Dan to worship the one there.

b18 Some Septuagint manuscripts and Syriac (see also 1 Kings 4:6 and 5:14); Hebrew *Adoram*
c25 Hebrew *Penuel*, a variant of *Peniel*

[31]Jeroboam built shrines on high places and appointed priests from all sorts of people, even though they were not Levites. [32]He instituted a festival on the fifteenth day of the eighth month, like the festival held in Judah, and offered sacrifices on the altar. This he did in Bethel, sacrificing to the calves he had made. And at Bethel he also installed priests at the high places he had made. [33]On the fifteenth day of the eighth month, a month of his own choosing, he offered sacrifices on the altar he had built at Bethel. So he instituted the festival for the Israelites and went up to the altar to make offerings.

The Man of God From Judah

13 By the word of the LORD a man of God came from Judah to Bethel, as Jeroboam was standing by the altar to make an offering. [2]He cried out against the altar by the word of the LORD: "O altar, altar! This is what the LORD says: 'A son named Josiah will be born to the house of David. On you he will sacrifice the priests of the high places who now make offerings here, and human bones will be burned on you.'" [3]That same day the man of God gave a sign: "This is the sign the LORD has declared: The altar will be split apart and the ashes on it will be poured out."

[4]When King Jeroboam heard what the man of God cried out against the altar at Bethel, he stretched out his hand from the altar and said, "Seize him!" But the hand he stretched out towards the man shrivelled up, so that he could not pull it back. [5]Also, the altar was split apart and its ashes poured out according to the sign given by the man of God by the word of the LORD.

[6]Then the king said to the man of God, "Intercede with the LORD your God and pray for me that my hand may be restored." So the man of God interceded with the LORD, and the king's hand was restored and became as it was before.

[7]The king said to the man of God, "Come home with me and have something to eat, and I will give you a gift."

[8]But the man of God answered the king, "Even if you were to give me half your possessions, I would not go with you, nor would I eat bread or drink water here. [9]For I was commanded by the word of the LORD: 'You must not eat bread or drink water or return by the way you came.'" [10]So he took another road and did not return by the way he had come to Bethel.

[11]Now there was a certain old prophet living in Bethel, whose sons came and told him all that the man of God had done there that day. They also told their father what he had said to the king. [12]Their father asked them, "Which way did he go?" And his sons showed him which road the man of God from Judah had taken. [13]So he said to his sons, "Saddle the donkey for me." And when they had saddled the donkey for him, he mounted it [14]and rode after the man of God. He found him sitting under an oak tree and asked, "Are you the man of God who came from Judah?"

"I am," he replied.

[15]So the prophet said to him, "Come home with me and eat."

[16]The man of God said, "I cannot turn back and go with you, nor can I eat bread or drink water with you in this place. [17]I have been told by the word of the LORD: 'You must not eat bread or drink water there or return by the way you came.'"

[18]The old prophet answered, "I too am a prophet, as you are. And an angel said to me by the word of the LORD: 'Bring him back with you to your house so that he may eat bread and drink water.'" (But he was lying to him.) [19]So the man of God returned with him and ate and drank in his house.

[20]While they were sitting at the table, the word of the LORD came to the old prophet who had brought him back. [21]He cried out to the man of God who had come from Judah, "This is what the LORD says: 'You have defied the word of the LORD and have not kept the command the LORD your God gave you. [22]You came back and ate bread and drank water in the place where he told you not to eat or drink. Therefore your body will not be buried in the tomb of your fathers.'"

²³When the man of God had finished eating and drinking, the prophet who had brought him back saddled his donkey for him. ²⁴As he went on his way, a lion met him on the road and killed him, and his body was thrown down on the road, with both the donkey and the lion standing beside it. ²⁵Some people who passed by saw the body thrown down there, with the lion standing beside the body, and they went and reported it in the city where the old prophet lived.

²⁶When the prophet who had brought him back from his journey heard of it, he said, "It is the man of God who defied the word of the LORD. The LORD has given him over to the lion, which has mauled him and killed him, as the word of the LORD had warned him."

²⁷The prophet said to his sons, "Saddle the donkey for me," and they did so. ²⁸Then he went out and found the body thrown down on the road, with the donkey and the lion standing beside it. The lion had neither eaten the body nor mauled the donkey. ²⁹So the prophet picked up the body of the man of God, laid it on the donkey, and brought it back to his own city to mourn for him and bury him. ³⁰Then he laid the body in his own tomb, and they mourned over him and said, "Oh, my brother!"

³¹After burying him, he said to his sons, "When I die, bury me in the grave where the man of God is buried; lay my bones beside his bones. ³²For the message he declared by the word of the LORD against the altar in Bethel and against all the shrines on the high places in the towns of Samaria will certainly come true."

³³Even after this, Jeroboam did not change his evil ways, but once more appointed priests for the high places from all sorts of people. Anyone who wanted to become a priest he consecrated for the high places. ³⁴This was the sin of the house of Jeroboam that led to its downfall and to its destruction from the face of the earth.

Ahijah's Prophecy Against Jeroboam

14 At that time Abijah son of Jeroboam became ill, ²and Jeroboam said to his wife, "Go, disguise yourself, so that you won't be recognised as the wife of Jeroboam. Then go to Shiloh. Ahijah the prophet is there—the one who told me I would be king over this people. ³Take ten loaves of bread with you, some cakes and a jar of honey, and go to him. He will tell you what will happen to the boy." ⁴So Jeroboam's wife did what he said and went to Ahijah's house in Shiloh.

Now Ahijah could not see; his sight was gone because of his age. ⁵But the LORD had told Ahijah, "Jeroboam's wife is coming to ask you about her son, for he is ill, and you are to give her such and such an answer. When she arrives, she will pretend to be someone else."

⁶So when Ahijah heard the sound of her footsteps at the door, he said, "Come in, wife of Jeroboam. Why this pretence? I have been sent to you with bad news. ⁷Go, tell Jeroboam that this is what the LORD, the God of Israel, says: 'I raised you up from among the people and made you a leader over my people Israel. ⁸I tore the kingdom away from the house of David and gave it to you, but you have not been like my servant David, who kept my commands and followed me with all his heart, doing only what was right in my eyes. ⁹You have done more evil than all who lived before you. You have made for yourself other gods, idols made of metal; you have provoked me to anger and thrust me behind your back.

¹⁰"'Because of this, I am going to bring disaster on the house of Jeroboam. I will cut off from Jeroboam every last male in Israel—slave or free. I will burn up the house of Jeroboam as one burns dung, until it is all gone. ¹¹Dogs will eat those belonging to Jeroboam who die in the city, and the birds of the air will feed on those who die in the country. The LORD has spoken!'

¹²"As for you, go back home. When you set foot in your city, the boy will die. ¹³All Israel will mourn for him and bury him. He is the only one belonging to Jeroboam who will be buried, because he is the only one in the house of Jeroboam in whom the LORD, the God of Israel, has found anything good.

¹⁴"The LORD will raise up for himself a

king over Israel who will cut off the family of Jeroboam. This is the day! What? Yes, even now.[a] ¹⁵And the LORD will strike Israel, so that it will be like a reed swaying in the water. He will uproot Israel from this good land that he gave to their forefathers and scatter them beyond the River,[b] because they provoked the LORD to anger by making Asherah poles.[c] ¹⁶And he will give Israel up because of the sins Jeroboam has committed and has caused Israel to commit."

¹⁷Then Jeroboam's wife got up and left and went to Tirzah. As soon as she stepped over the threshold of the house, the boy died. ¹⁸They buried him, and all Israel mourned for him, as the LORD had said through his servant the prophet Ahijah.

¹⁹The other events of Jeroboam's reign, his wars and how he ruled, are written in the book of the annals of the kings of Israel. ²⁰He reigned for twenty-two years and then rested with his fathers. And Nadab his son succeeded him as king.

Rehoboam King of Judah

²¹Rehoboam son of Solomon was king in Judah. He was forty-one years old when he became king, and he reigned for seventeen years in Jerusalem, the city the LORD had chosen out of all the tribes of Israel in which to put his Name. His mother's name was Naamah; she was an Ammonite.

²²Judah did evil in the eyes of the LORD. By the sins they committed they stirred up his jealous anger more than their fathers had done. ²³They also set up for themselves high places, sacred stones and Asherah poles on every high hill and under every spreading tree. ²⁴There were even male shrine-prostitutes in the land; the people engaged in all the detestable practices of the nations the LORD had driven out before the Israelites.

²⁵In the fifth year of King Rehoboam, Shishak king of Egypt attacked Jerusalem. ²⁶He carried off the treasures of the temple of the LORD and the treasures of the royal palace. He took everything, including all the gold shields Solomon had made. ²⁷So King Rehoboam made bronze shields to replace them and assigned these to the commanders of the guard on duty at the entrance to the royal palace. ²⁸Whenever the king went to the LORD's temple, the guards bore the shields, and afterwards they returned them to the guardroom.

²⁹As for the other events of Rehoboam's reign, and all he did, are they not written in the book of the annals of the kings of Judah? ³⁰There was continual warfare between Rehoboam and Jeroboam. ³¹And Rehoboam rested with his fathers and was buried with them in the City of David. His mother's name was Naamah; she was an Ammonite. And Abijah[d] his son succeeded him as king.

Abijah King of Judah

15 In the eighteenth year of the reign of Jeroboam son of Nebat, Abijah[a] became king of Judah, ²and he reigned in Jerusalem for three years. His mother's name was Maacah daughter of Abishalom.[b]

³He committed all the sins his father had done before him; his heart was not fully devoted to the LORD his God, as the heart of David his forefather had been. ⁴Nevertheless, for David's sake the LORD his God gave him a lamp in Jerusalem by raising up a son to succeed him and by making Jerusalem strong. ⁵For David had done what was right in the eyes of the LORD and had not failed to keep any of the LORD's commands all the days of his life— except in the case of Uriah the Hittite.

⁶There was war between Rehoboam[c] and Jeroboam throughout ⌐Abijah's⌐ lifetime. ⁷As for the other events of Abijah's reign, and all he did, are they not written in the book of the annals of the kings of Judah? There was war between Abijah

---

[a]14 The meaning of the Hebrew for this sentence is uncertain.   [b]15 That is, the Euphrates
[c]15 That is, symbols of the goddess Asherah; here and elsewhere in 1 Kings
[d]31 Some Hebrew manuscripts and Septuagint (see also 2 Chron. 12:16); most Hebrew manuscripts *Abijam*
[a]1 Some Hebrew manuscripts and Septuagint (see also 2 Chron. 12:16); most Hebrew manuscripts *Abijam*; also in verses 7 and 8   [b]2 A variant of *Absalom*; also in verse 10
[c]6 Most Hebrew manuscripts; some Hebrew manuscripts and Syriac *Abijam* (that is, Abijah)

and Jeroboam. [8]And Abijah rested with his fathers and was buried in the City of David. And Asa his son succeeded him as king.

Asa King of Judah

[9]In the twentieth year of Jeroboam king of Israel, Asa became king of Judah, [10]and he reigned in Jerusalem for forty-one years. His grandmother's name was Maacah daughter of Abishalom.

[11]Asa did what was right in the eyes of the LORD, as his father David had done. [12]He expelled the male shrine-prostitutes from the land and got rid of all the idols his fathers had made. [13]He even deposed his grandmother Maacah from her position as queen mother, because she had made a repulsive Asherah pole. Asa cut the pole down and burned it in the Kidron Valley. [14]Although he did not remove the high places, Asa's heart was fully committed to the LORD all his life. [15]He brought into the temple of the LORD the silver and gold and the articles that he and his father had dedicated.

[16]There was war between Asa and Baasha king of Israel throughout their reigns. [17]Baasha king of Israel went up against Judah and fortified Ramah to prevent anyone from leaving or entering the territory of Asa king of Judah.

[18]Asa then took all the silver and gold that was left in the treasuries of the LORD's temple and of his own palace. He entrusted it to his officials and sent them to Ben-Hadad son of Tabrimmon, the son of Hezion, the king of Aram, who was ruling in Damascus. [19]"Let there be a treaty between me and you," he said, "as there was between my father and your father. See, I am sending you a gift of silver and gold. Now break your treaty with Baasha king of Israel so that he will withdraw from me."

[20]Ben-Hadad agreed with King Asa and sent the commanders of his forces against the towns of Israel. He conquered Ijon, Dan, Abel Beth Maacah and all Kinnereth in addition to Naphtali. [21]When Baasha heard this, he stopped building Ramah and withdrew to Tirzah. [22]Then King Asa issued an order to all Judah—no-one was exempt—and they carried away from Ramah the stones and timber Baasha had been using there. With them King Asa built up Geba in Benjamin, and also Mizpah.

[23]As for all the other events of Asa's reign, all his achievements, all he did and the cities he built, are they not written in the book of the annals of the kings of Judah? In his old age, however, his feet became diseased. [24]Then Asa rested with his fathers and was buried with them in the city of his father David. And Jehoshaphat his son succeeded him as king.

Nadab King of Israel

[25]Nadab son of Jeroboam became king of Israel in the second year of Asa king of Judah, and he reigned over Israel for two years. [26]He did evil in the eyes of the LORD, walking in the ways of his father and in his sin, which he had caused Israel to commit.

[27]Baasha son of Ahijah of the house of Issachar plotted against him, and he struck him down at Gibbethon, a Philistine town, while Nadab and all Israel were besieging it. [28]Baasha killed Nadab in the third year of Asa king of Judah and succeeded him as king.

[29]As soon as he began to reign, he killed Jeroboam's whole family. He did not leave Jeroboam anyone that breathed, but destroyed them all, according to the word of the LORD given through his servant Ahijah the Shilonite—[30]because of the sins Jeroboam had committed and had caused Israel to commit, and because he provoked the LORD, the God of Israel, to anger.

[31]As for the other events of Nadab's reign, and all he did, are they not written in the book of the annals of the kings of Israel? [32]There was war between Asa and Baasha king of Israel throughout their reigns.

Baasha King of Israel

[33]In the third year of Asa king of Judah, Baasha son of Ahijah became king of all Israel in Tirzah, and he reigned for

twenty-four years. ³⁴He did evil in the eyes of the LORD, walking in the ways of Jeroboam and in his sin, which he had caused Israel to commit.

16 Then the word of the LORD came to Jehu son of Hanani against Baasha: ²"I lifted you up from the dust and made you leader of my people Israel, but you walked in the ways of Jeroboam and caused my people Israel to sin and to provoke me to anger by their sins. ³So I am about to consume Baasha and his house, and I will make your house like that of Jeroboam son of Nebat. ⁴Dogs will eat those belonging to Baasha who die in the city, and the birds of the air will feed on those who die in the country."

⁵As for the other events of Baasha's reign, what he did and his achievements, are they not written in the book of the annals of the kings of Israel? ⁶Baasha rested with his fathers and was buried in Tirzah. And Elah his son succeeded him as king.

⁷Moreover, the word of the LORD came through the prophet Jehu son of Hanani to Baasha and his house, because of all the evil he had done in the eyes of the LORD, provoking him to anger by the things he did, and becoming like the house of Jeroboam—and also because he destroyed it.

Elah King of Israel

⁸In the twenty-sixth year of Asa king of Judah, Elah son of Baasha became king of Israel, and he reigned in Tirzah for two years.

⁹Zimri, one of his officials, who had command of half his chariots, plotted against him. Elah was in Tirzah at the time, getting drunk in the home of Arza, the man in charge of the palace at Tirzah. ¹⁰Zimri came in, struck him down and killed him in the twenty-seventh year of Asa king of Judah. Then he succeeded him as king.

¹¹As soon as he began to reign and was seated on the throne, he killed off Baasha's whole family. He did not spare a single male, whether relative or friend. ¹²So Zimri destroyed the whole family of Baasha, in accordance with the word of the LORD spoken against Baasha through the prophet Jehu—¹³because of all the sins Baasha and his son Elah had committed and had caused Israel to commit, so that they provoked the LORD, the God of Israel, to anger by their worthless idols.

¹⁴As for the other events of Elah's reign, and all he did, are they not written in the book of the annals of the kings of Israel?

Zimri King of Israel

¹⁵In the twenty-seventh year of Asa king of Judah, Zimri reigned in Tirzah for seven days. The army was encamped near Gibbethon, a Philistine town. ¹⁶When the Israelites in the camp heard that Zimri had plotted against the king and murdered him, they proclaimed Omri, the commander of the army, king over Israel that very day there in the camp. ¹⁷Then Omri and all the Israelites with him withdrew from Gibbethon and laid siege to Tirzah. ¹⁸When Zimri saw that the city was taken, he went into the citadel of the royal palace and set the palace on fire around him. So he died, ¹⁹because of the sins he had committed, doing evil in the eyes of the LORD and walking in the ways of Jeroboam and in the sin he had committed and had caused Israel to commit.

²⁰As for the other events of Zimri's reign, and the rebellion he carried out, are they not written in the book of the annals of the kings of Israel?

Omri King of Israel

²¹Then the people of Israel were split into two factions; half supported Tibni son of Ginath for king, and the other half supported Omri. ²²But Omri's followers proved stronger than those of Tibni son of Ginath. So Tibni died and Omri became king.

²³In the thirty-first year of Asa king of Judah, Omri became king of Israel, and he reigned for twelve years, six of them in Tirzah. ²⁴He bought the hill of Samaria from Shemer for two talents*ᵃ* of silver and

---

ᵃ24 That is, about 150 pounds (about 70 kilograms)

built a city on the hill, calling it Samaria, after Shemer, the name of the former owner of the hill.

25But Omri did evil in the eyes of the LORD and sinned more than all those before him. 26He walked in all the ways of Jeroboam son of Nebat and in his sin, which he had caused Israel to commit, so that they provoked the LORD, the God of Israel, to anger by their worthless idols.

27As for the other events of Omri's reign, what he did and the things he achieved, are they not written in the book of the annals of the kings of Israel? 28Omri rested with his fathers and was buried in Samaria. And Ahab his son succeeded him as king.

Ahab Becomes King of Israel

29In the thirty-eighth year of Asa king of Judah, Ahab son of Omri became king of Israel, and he reigned in Samaria over Israel for twenty-two years. 30Ahab son of Omri did more evil in the eyes of the LORD than any of those before him. 31He not only considered it trivial to commit the sins of Jeroboam son of Nebat, but he also married Jezebel daughter of Ethbaal king of the Sidonians, and began to serve Baal and worship him. 32He set up an altar for Baal in the temple of Baal that he built in Samaria. 33Ahab also made an Asherah pole and did more to provoke the LORD, the God of Israel, to anger than did all the kings of Israel before him.

34In Ahab's time, Hiel of Bethel rebuilt Jericho. He laid its foundations at the cost of his firstborn son Abiram, and he set up its gates at the cost of his youngest son Segub, in accordance with the word of the LORD spoken by Joshua son of Nun.

Elijah Fed by Ravens

17 Now Elijah the Tishbite, from Tishbe*a* in Gilead, said to Ahab, "As the LORD, the God of Israel, lives, whom I serve, there will be neither dew nor rain in the next few years except at my word."

2Then the word of the LORD came to Elijah: 3"Leave here, turn eastward and hide in the Kerith Ravine, east of the Jordan. 4You will drink from the brook, and I have ordered the ravens to feed you there."

5So he did what the LORD had told him. He went to the Kerith Ravine, east of the Jordan, and stayed there. 6The ravens brought him bread and meat in the morning and bread and meat in the evening, and he drank from the brook.

The Widow at Zarephath

7Some time later the brook dried up because there had been no rain in the land. 8Then the word of the LORD came to him: 9"Go at once to Zarephath of Sidon and stay there. I have commanded a widow in that place to supply you with food." 10So he went to Zarephath. When he came to the town gate, a widow was there gathering sticks. He called to her and asked, "Would you bring me a little water in a jar so I may have a drink?" 11As she was going to get it, he called, "And bring me, please, a piece of bread."

12"As surely as the LORD your God lives," she replied, "I don't have any bread—only a handful of flour in a jar and a little oil in a jug. I am gathering a few sticks to take home and make a meal for myself and my son, that we may eat it—and die."

13Elijah said to her, "Don't be afraid. Go home and do as you have said. But first make a small cake of bread for me from what you have and bring it to me, and then make something for yourself and your son. 14For this is what the LORD, the God of Israel, says: 'The jar of flour will not be used up and the jug of oil will not run dry until the day the LORD gives rain on the land.'"

15She went away and did as Elijah had told her. So there was food every day for Elijah and for the woman and her family. 16For the jar of flour was not used up and the jug of oil did not run dry, in keeping with the word of the LORD spoken by Elijah.

a1 Or *Tishbite, of the settlers*

¹⁷Some time later the son of the woman who owned the house became ill. He grew worse and worse, and finally stopped breathing. ¹⁸She said to Elijah, "What do you have against me, man of God? Did you come to remind me of my sin and kill my son?"

¹⁹"Give me your son," Elijah replied. He took him from her arms, carried him to the upper room where he was staying, and laid him on his bed. ²⁰Then he cried out to the LORD, "O LORD my God, have you brought tragedy also upon this widow I am staying with, by causing her son to die?" ²¹Then he stretched himself out on the boy three times and cried to the LORD, "O LORD my God, let this boy's life return to him!"

²²The LORD heard Elijah's cry, and the boy's life returned to him, and he lived. ²³Elijah picked up the child and carried him down from the room into the house. He gave him to his mother and said, "Look, your son is alive!"

²⁴Then the woman said to Elijah, "Now I know that you are a man of God and that the word of the LORD from your mouth is the truth."

Elijah and Obadiah

18 After a long time, in the third year, the word of the LORD came to Elijah: "Go and present yourself to Ahab, and I will send rain on the land." ²So Elijah went to present himself to Ahab.

Now the famine was severe in Samaria, ³and Ahab had summoned Obadiah, who was in charge of his palace. (Obadiah was a devout believer in the LORD. ⁴While Jezebel was killing off the LORD's prophets, Obadiah had taken a hundred prophets and hidden them in two caves, fifty in each, and had supplied them with food and water.) ⁵Ahab had said to Obadiah, "Go through the land to all the springs and valleys. Maybe we can find some grass to keep the horses and mules alive so we will not have to kill any of our animals." ⁶So they divided the land they were to cover, Ahab going in one direction and Obadiah in another.

⁷As Obadiah was walking along, Elijah met him. Obadiah recognised him, bowed down to the ground, and said, "Is it really you, my lord Elijah?"

⁸"Yes," he replied. "Go tell your master, 'Elijah is here.'"

⁹"What have I done wrong," asked Obadiah, "that you are handing your servant over to Ahab to be put to death? ¹⁰As surely as the LORD your God lives, there is not a nation or kingdom where my master has not sent someone to look for you. And whenever a nation or kingdom claimed you were not there, he made them swear they could not find you. ¹¹But now you tell me to go to my master and say, 'Elijah is here.' ¹²I don't know where the Spirit of the LORD may carry you when I leave you. If I go and tell Ahab and he doesn't find you, he will kill me. Yet I your servant have worshipped the LORD since my youth. ¹³Haven't you heard, my lord, what I did while Jezebel was killing the prophets of the LORD? I hid a hundred of the LORD's prophets in two caves, fifty in each, and supplied them with food and water. ¹⁴And now you tell me to go to my master and say, 'Elijah is here.' He will kill me!"

¹⁵Elijah said, "As the LORD Almighty lives, whom I serve, I will surely present myself to Ahab today."

Elijah on Mount Carmel

¹⁶So Obadiah went to meet Ahab and told him, and Ahab went to meet Elijah. ¹⁷When he saw Elijah, he said to him, "Is that you, you troubler of Israel?"

¹⁸"I have not made trouble for Israel," Elijah replied. "But you and your father's family have. You have abandoned the LORD's commands and have followed the Baals. ¹⁹Now summon the people from all over Israel to meet me on Mount Carmel. And bring the four hundred and fifty prophets of Baal and the four hundred prophets of Asherah, who eat at Jezebel's table."

²⁰So Ahab sent word throughout all Israel and assembled the prophets on Mount Carmel. ²¹Elijah went before the people and said, "How long will you

waver between two opinions? If the LORD is God, follow him; but if Baal is God, follow him."

But the people said nothing.

²²Then Elijah said to them, "I am the only one of the LORD's prophets left, but Baal has four hundred and fifty prophets. ²³Get two bulls for us. Let them choose one for themselves, and let them cut it into pieces and put it on the wood but not set fire to it. I will prepare the other bull and put it on the wood but not set fire to it. ²⁴Then you call on the name of your god, and I will call on the name of the LORD. The god who answers by fire—he is God."

Then all the people said, "What you say is good."

²⁵Elijah said to the prophets of Baal, "Choose one of the bulls and prepare it first, since there are so many of you. Call on the name of your god, but do not light the fire." ²⁶So they took the bull given them and prepared it.

Then they called on the name of Baal from morning till noon. "O Baal, answer us!" they shouted. But there was no response; no-one answered. And they danced around the altar they had made.

²⁷At noon Elijah began to taunt them. "Shout louder!" he said. "Surely he is a god! Perhaps he is deep in thought, or busy, or travelling. Maybe he is sleeping and must be awakened." ²⁸So they shouted louder and slashed themselves with swords and spears, as was their custom, until their blood flowed. ²⁹Midday passed, and they continued their frantic prophesying until the time for the evening sacrifice. But there was no response, no-one answered, no-one paid attention.

³⁰Then Elijah said to all the people, "Come here to me." They came to him, and he repaired the altar of the LORD, which was in ruins. ³¹Elijah took twelve stones, one for each of the tribes descended from Jacob, to whom the word of the LORD had come, saying, "Your name shall be Israel." ³²With the stones he built an altar in the name of the LORD, and he dug a trench round it large enough to hold

two seahs*ᵃ* of seed. ³³He arranged the wood, cut the bull into pieces and laid it on the wood. Then he said to them, "Fill four large jars with water and pour it on the offering and on the wood."

³⁴"Do it again," he said, and they did it again.

"Do it a third time," he ordered, and they did it the third time. ³⁵The water ran down around the altar and even filled the trench.

³⁶At the time of sacrifice, the prophet Elijah stepped forward and prayed: "O LORD, God of Abraham, Isaac and Israel, let it be known today that you are God in Israel and that I am your servant and have done all these things at your command. ³⁷Answer me, O LORD, answer me, so these people will know that you, O LORD, are God, and that you are turning their hearts back again."

³⁸Then the fire of the LORD fell and burned up the sacrifice, the wood, the stones and the soil, and also licked up the water in the trench.

³⁹When all the people saw this, they fell prostrate and cried, "The LORD—he is God! The LORD—he is God!"

⁴⁰Then Elijah commanded them, "Seize the prophets of Baal. Don't let anyone get away!" They seized them, and Elijah had them brought down to the Kishon Valley and slaughtered there.

⁴¹And Elijah said to Ahab, "Go, eat and drink, for there is the sound of a heavy rain." ⁴²So Ahab went off to eat and drink, but Elijah climbed to the top of Carmel, bent down to the ground and put his face between his knees.

⁴³"Go and look towards the sea," he told his servant. And he went up and looked.

"There is nothing there," he said.

Seven times Elijah said, "Go back."

⁴⁴The seventh time the servant reported, "A cloud as small as a man's hand is rising from the sea."

So Elijah said, "Go and tell Ahab, 'Hitch up your chariot and go down before the rain stops you.'"

⁴⁵Meanwhile, the sky grew black with

ᵃ32 That is, probably about 26 pints (about 15 litres)

clouds, the wind rose, a heavy rain came on and Ahab rode off to Jezreel. ⁴⁶The power of the LORD came upon Elijah and, tucking his cloak into his belt, he ran ahead of Ahab all the way to Jezreel.

Elijah Flees to Horeb

19 Now Ahab told Jezebel everything Elijah had done and how he had killed all the prophets with the sword. ²So Jezebel sent a messenger to Elijah to say, "May the gods deal with me, be it ever so severely, if by this time tomorrow I do not make your life like that of one of them."

³Elijah was afraid[a] and ran for his life. When he came to Beersheba in Judah, he left his servant there, ⁴while he himself went a day's journey into the desert. He came to a broom tree, sat down under it and prayed that he might die. "I have had enough, LORD," he said. "Take my life; I am no better than my ancestors." ⁵Then he lay down under the tree and fell asleep.

All at once an angel touched him and said, "Get up and eat." ⁶He looked around, and there by his head was a cake of bread baked over hot coals, and a jar of water. He ate and drank and then lay down again.

⁷The angel of the LORD came back a second time and touched him and said, "Get up and eat, for the journey is too much for you." ⁸So he got up and ate and drank. Strengthened by that food, he travelled for forty days and forty nights until he reached Horeb, the mountain of God. ⁹There he went into a cave and spent the night.

The LORD Appears to Elijah

And the word of the LORD came to him: "What are you doing here, Elijah?"

¹⁰He replied, "I have been very zealous for the LORD God Almighty. The Israelites have rejected your covenant, broken down your altars, and put your prophets to death with the sword. I am the only one left, and now they are trying to kill me too."

¹¹The LORD said, "Go out and stand on the mountain in the presence of the LORD, for the LORD is about to pass by."

Then a great and powerful wind tore the mountains apart and shattered the rocks before the LORD, but the LORD was not in the wind. After the wind there was an earthquake, but the LORD was not in the earthquake. ¹²After the earthquake came a fire, but the LORD was not in the fire. And after the fire came a gentle whisper. ¹³When Elijah heard it, he pulled his cloak over his face and went out and stood at the mouth of the cave.

Then a voice said to him, "What are you doing here, Elijah?"

¹⁴He replied, "I have been very zealous for the LORD God Almighty. The Israelites have rejected your covenant, broken down your altars, and put your prophets to death with the sword. I am the only one left, and now they are trying to kill me too."

¹⁵The LORD said to him, "Go back the way you came, and go to the Desert of Damascus. When you get there, anoint Hazael king over Aram. ¹⁶Also, anoint Jehu son of Nimshi king over Israel, and anoint Elisha son of Shaphat from Abel Meholah to succeed you as prophet. ¹⁷Jehu will put to death any who escape the sword of Hazael, and Elisha will put to death any who escape the sword of Jehu. ¹⁸Yet I reserve seven thousand in Israel— all whose knees have not bowed down to Baal and all whose mouths have not kissed him."

The Call of Elisha

¹⁹So Elijah went from there and found Elisha son of Shaphat. He was ploughing with twelve yoke of oxen, and he himself was driving the twelfth pair. Elijah went up to him and threw his cloak around him. ²⁰Elisha then left his oxen and ran after Elijah. "Let me kiss my father and mother good-bye," he said, "and then I will come with you."

"Go back," Elijah replied. "What have I done to you?"

---

a3 Or *Elijah saw*

²¹So Elisha left him and went back. He took his yoke of oxen and slaughtered them. He burned the ploughing equipment to cook the meat and gave it to the people, and they ate. Then he set out to follow Elijah and became his attendant.

Ben-Hadad Attacks Samaria

20 Now Ben-Hadad king of Aram mustered his entire army. Accompanied by thirty-two kings with their horses and chariots, he went up and besieged Samaria and attacked it. ²He sent messengers into the city to Ahab king of Israel, saying, "This is what Ben-Hadad says: ³'Your silver and gold are mine, and the best of your wives and children are mine.'"

⁴The king of Israel answered, "Just as you say, my lord the king. I and all I have are yours."

⁵The messengers came again and said, "This is what Ben-Hadad says: 'I sent to demand your silver and gold, your wives and your children. ⁶But about this time tomorrow I am going to send my officials to search your palace and the houses of your officials. They will seize everything you value and carry it away.'"

⁷The king of Israel summoned all the elders of the land and said to them, "See how this man is looking for trouble! When he sent for my wives and my children, my silver and my gold, I did not refuse him."

⁸The elders and the people all answered, "Don't listen to him or agree to his demands."

⁹So he replied to Ben-Hadad's messengers, "Tell my lord the king, 'Your servant will do all you demanded the first time, but this demand I cannot meet.'" They left and took the answer back to Ben-Hadad.

¹⁰Then Ben-Hadad sent another message to Ahab: "May the gods deal with me, be it ever so severely, if enough dust remains in Samaria to give each of my men a handful."

¹¹The king of Israel answered, "Tell him: 'One who puts on his armour should not boast like one who takes it off.'"

¹²Ben-Hadad heard this message while he and the kings were drinking in their tents,ᵃ and he ordered his men: "Prepare to attack." So they prepared to attack the city.

Ahab Defeats Ben-Hadad

¹³Meanwhile a prophet came to Ahab king of Israel and announced, "This is what the LORD says: 'Do you see this vast army? I will give it into your hand today, and then you will know that I am the LORD.'"

¹⁴"But who will do this?" asked Ahab.

The prophet replied, "This is what the LORD says: 'The young officers of the provincial commanders will do it.'"

"And who will start the battle?" he asked.

The prophet answered, "You will."

¹⁵So Ahab summoned the young officers of the provincial commanders, 232 men. Then he assembled the rest of the Israelites, 7,000 in all. ¹⁶They set out at noon while Ben-Hadad and the 32 kings allied with him were in their tents getting drunk. ¹⁷The young officers of the provincial commanders went out first.

Now Ben-Hadad had dispatched scouts, who reported, "Men are advancing from Samaria."

¹⁸He said, "If they have come out for peace, take them alive; if they have come out for war, take them alive."

¹⁹The young officers of the provincial commanders marched out of the city with the army behind them ²⁰and each one struck down his opponent. At that, the Arameans fled, with the Israelites in pursuit. But Ben-Hadad king of Aram escaped on horseback with some of his horsemen. ²¹The king of Israel advanced and overpowered the horses and chariots and inflicted heavy losses on the Arameans.

²²Afterwards, the prophet came to the king of Israel and said, "Strengthen your position and see what must be done, because next spring the king of Aram will attack you again."

ᵃ12 Or *in Succoth*; also in verse 16

²³Meanwhile, the officials of the king of Aram advised him, "Their gods are gods of the hills. That is why they were too strong for us. But if we fight them on the plains, surely we will be stronger than they. ²⁴Do this: Remove all the kings from their commands and replace them with other officers. ²⁵You must also raise an army like the one you lost—horse for horse and chariot for chariot—so we can fight Israel on the plains. Then surely we will be stronger than they." He agreed with them and acted accordingly.

²⁶The next spring Ben-Hadad mustered the Arameans and went up to Aphek to fight against Israel. ²⁷When the Israelites were also mustered and given provisions, they marched out to meet them. The Israelites camped opposite them like two small flocks of goats, while the Arameans covered the countryside.

²⁸The man of God came up and told the king of Israel, "This is what the LORD says: 'Because the Arameans think the LORD is a god of the hills and not a god of the valleys, I will deliver this vast army into your hands, and you will know that I am the LORD.'"

²⁹For seven days they camped opposite each other, and on the seventh day the battle was joined. The Israelites inflicted a hundred thousand casualties on the Aramean foot soldiers in one day. ³⁰The rest of them escaped to the city of Aphek, where the wall collapsed on twenty-seven thousand of them. And Ben-Hadad fled to the city and hid in an inner room.

³¹His officials said to him, "Look, we have heard that the kings of the house of Israel are merciful. Let us go to the king of Israel with sackcloth round our waists and ropes round our heads. Perhaps he will spare your life."

³²Wearing sackcloth round their waists and ropes round their heads, they went to the king of Israel and said, "Your servant Ben-Hadad says: 'Please let me live.'"

The king answered, "Is he still alive? He is my brother."

³³The men took this as a good sign and were quick to pick up his word. "Yes, your brother Ben-Hadad!" they said.

"Go and get him," the king said. When Ben-Hadad came out, Ahab had him come up into his chariot.

³⁴"I will return the cities my father took from your father," Ben-Hadad offered. "You may set up your own market areas in Damascus, as my father did in Samaria."

⌐Ahab said,⌐ "On the basis of a treaty I will set you free." So he made a treaty with him, and let him go.

A Prophet Condemns Ahab

³⁵By the word of the LORD one of the sons of the prophets said to his companion, "Strike me with your weapon," but the man refused.

³⁶So the prophet said, "Because you have not obeyed the LORD, as soon as you leave me a lion will kill you." And after the man went away, a lion found him and killed him.

³⁷The prophet found another man and said, "Strike me, please." So the man struck him and wounded him. ³⁸Then the prophet went and stood by the road waiting for the king. He disguised himself with his headband down over his eyes. ³⁹As the king passed by, the prophet called out to him, "Your servant went into the thick of the battle, and someone came to me with a captive and said, 'Guard this man. If he is missing, it will be your life for his life, or you must pay a talent*b* of silver.' ⁴⁰While your servant was busy here and there, the man disappeared."

"That is your sentence," the king of Israel said. "You have pronounced it yourself."

⁴¹Then the prophet quickly removed the headband from his eyes, and the king of Israel recognised him as one of the prophets. ⁴²He said to the king, "This is what the LORD says: 'You have set free a man I had determined should die.*c* Therefore it is your life for his life, your people

---

b39 That is, about 75 pounds (about 34 kilograms)
c42 The Hebrew term refers to the irrevocable giving over of things or persons to the LORD, often by totally destroying them.

for his people.'" [43]Sullen and angry, the king of Israel went to his palace in Samaria.

Naboth's Vineyard

21 Some time later there was an incident involving a vineyard belonging to Naboth the Jezreelite. The vineyard was in Jezreel, close to the palace of Ahab king of Samaria. [2]Ahab said to Naboth, "Let me have your vineyard to use for a vegetable garden, since it is close to my palace. In exchange I will give you a better vineyard or, if you prefer, I will pay you whatever it is worth."

[3]But Naboth replied, "The LORD forbid that I should give you the inheritance of my fathers."

[4]So Ahab went home, sullen and angry because Naboth the Jezreelite had said, "I will not give you the inheritance of my fathers." He lay on his bed sulking and refused to eat.

[5]His wife Jezebel came in and asked him, "Why are you so sullen? Why won't you eat?"

[6]He answered her, "Because I said to Naboth the Jezreelite, 'Sell me your vineyard; or if you prefer, I will give you another vineyard in its place.' But he said, 'I will not give you my vineyard.'"

[7]Jezebel his wife said, "Is this how you act as king over Israel? Get up and eat! Cheer up. I'll get you the vineyard of Naboth the Jezreelite."

[8]So she wrote letters in Ahab's name, placed his seal on them, and sent them to the elders and nobles who lived in Naboth's city with him. [9]In those letters she wrote:

"Proclaim a day of fasting and seat Naboth in a prominent place among the people. [10]But seat two scoundrels opposite him and have them testify that he has cursed both God and the king. Then take him out and stone him to death."

[11]So the elders and nobles who lived in Naboth's city did as Jezebel directed in the letters she had written to them. [12]They proclaimed a fast and seated Naboth in a prominent place among the people. [13]Then two scoundrels came and sat opposite him and brought charges against Naboth before the people, saying, "Naboth has cursed both God and the king." So they took him outside the city and stoned him to death. [14]Then they sent word to Jezebel: "Naboth has been stoned and is dead."

[15]As soon as Jezebel heard that Naboth had been stoned to death, she said to Ahab, "Get up and take possession of the vineyard of Naboth the Jezreelite that he refused to sell you. He is no longer alive, but dead." [16]When Ahab heard that Naboth was dead, he got up and went down to take possession of Naboth's vineyard.

[17]Then the word of the LORD came to Elijah the Tishbite: [18]"Go down to meet Ahab king of Israel, who rules in Samaria. He is now in Naboth's vineyard, where he has gone to take possession of it. [19]Say to him, 'This is what the LORD says: Have you not murdered a man and seized his property?' Then say to him, 'This is what the LORD says: In the place where dogs licked up Naboth's blood, dogs will lick up your blood—yes, yours!'"

[20]Ahab said to Elijah, "So you have found me, my enemy!"

"I have found you," he answered, "because you have sold yourself to do evil in the eyes of the LORD. [21]I am going to bring disaster on you. I will consume your descendants and cut off from Ahab every last male in Israel—slave or free. [22]I will make your house like that of Jeroboam son of Nebat and that of Baasha son of Ahijah, because you have provoked me to anger and have caused Israel to sin.'

[23]"And also concerning Jezebel the LORD says: 'Dogs will devour Jezebel by the wall of[a] Jezreel.'

[24]"Dogs will eat those belonging to Ahab who die in the city, and the birds of the air will feed on those who die in the country."

---

[a]23 Most Hebrew manuscripts; a few Hebrew manuscripts, Vulgate and Syriac (see also 2 Kings 9:26) *the plot of ground at*

25(There was never a man like Ahab, who sold himself to do evil in the eyes of the LORD, urged on by Jezebel his wife. 26He behaved in the vilest manner by going after idols, like the Amorites the LORD drove out before Israel.) 27When Ahab heard these words, he tore his clothes, put on sackcloth and fasted. He lay in sackcloth and went around meekly.

28Then the word of the LORD came to Elijah the Tishbite: 29"Have you noticed how Ahab has humbled himself before me? Because he has humbled himself, I will not bring this disaster in his day, but I will bring it on his house in the days of his son."

Micaiah Prophesies Against Ahab

22 For three years there was no war between Aram and Israel. 2But in the third year Jehoshaphat king of Judah went down to see the king of Israel. 3The king of Israel had said to his officials, "Don't you know that Ramoth Gilead belongs to us and yet we are doing nothing to retake it from the king of Aram?"

4So he asked Jehoshaphat, "Will you go with me to fight against Ramoth Gilead?"

Jehoshaphat replied to the king of Israel, "I am as you are, my people as your people, my horses as your horses." 5But Jehoshaphat also said to the king of Israel, "First seek the counsel of the LORD."

6So the king of Israel brought together the prophets—about four hundred men—and asked them, "Shall I go to war against Ramoth Gilead, or shall I refrain?"

"Go," they answered, "for the Lord will give it into the king's hand."

7But Jehoshaphat asked, "Is there not a prophet of the LORD here whom we can enquire of?"

8The king of Israel answered Jehoshaphat, "There is still one man through whom we can enquire of the LORD, but I hate him because he never prophesies anything good about me, but always bad. He is Micaiah son of Imlah."

"The king should not say that," Jehoshaphat replied.

9So the king of Israel called one of his officials and said, "Bring Micaiah son of Imlah at once."

10Dressed in their royal robes, the king of Israel and Jehoshaphat king of Judah were sitting on their thrones at the threshing-floor by the entrance of the gate of Samaria, with all the prophets prophesying before them. 11Now Zedekiah son of Kenaanah had made iron horns and he declared, "This is what the LORD says: 'With these you will gore the Arameans until they are destroyed.'"

12All the other prophets were prophesying the same thing. "Attack Ramoth Gilead and be victorious," they said, "for the LORD will give it into the king's hand."

13The messenger who had gone to summon Micaiah said to him, "Look, as one man the other prophets are predicting success for the king. Let your word agree with theirs, and speak favourably."

14But Micaiah said, "As surely as the LORD lives, I can tell him only what the LORD tells me."

15When he arrived, the king asked him, "Micaiah, shall we go to war against Ramoth Gilead, or shall I refrain?"

"Attack and be victorious," he answered, "for the LORD will give it into the king's hand."

16The king said to him, "How many times must I make you swear to tell me nothing but the truth in the name of the LORD?"

17Then Micaiah answered, "I saw all Israel scattered on the hills like sheep without a shepherd, and the LORD said, 'These people have no master. Let each one go home in peace.'"

18The king of Israel said to Jehoshaphat, "Didn't I tell you that he never prophesies anything good about me, but only bad?"

19Micaiah continued, "Therefore hear the word of the LORD: I saw the LORD sitting on his throne with all the host of heaven standing round him on his right and on his left. 20And the LORD said, 'Who will entice Ahab into attacking Ramoth Gilead and going to his death there?'

"One suggested this, and another that. 21Finally, a spirit came forward, stood before the LORD and said, 'I will entice him.'

22"'By what means?' the LORD asked.

" 'I will go out and be a lying spirit in the mouths of all his prophets,' he said.

" 'You will succeed in enticing him,' said the LORD. 'Go and do it.'

23"So now the LORD has put a lying spirit in the mouths of all these prophets of yours. The LORD has decreed disaster for you."

24Then Zedekiah son of Kenaanah went up and slapped Micaiah in the face. "Which way did the spirit from*a* the LORD go when he went from me to speak to you?" he asked.

25Micaiah replied, "You will find out on the day you go to hide in an inner room."

26The king of Israel then ordered, "Take Micaiah and send him back to Amon the ruler of the city and to Joash the king's son 27and say, 'This is what the king says: Put this fellow in prison and give him nothing but bread and water until I return safely.' "

28Micaiah declared, "If you ever return safely, the LORD has not spoken through me." Then he added, "Mark my words, all you people!"

Ahab Killed at Ramoth Gilead

29So the king of Israel and Jehoshaphat king of Judah went up to Ramoth Gilead. 30The king of Israel said to Jehoshaphat, "I will enter the battle in disguise, but you wear your royal robes." So the king of Israel disguised himself and went into battle.

31Now the king of Aram had ordered his thirty-two chariot commanders, "Do not fight with anyone, small or great, except the king of Israel." 32When the chariot commanders saw Jehoshaphat, they thought, "Surely this is the king of Israel." So they turned to attack him, but when Jehoshaphat cried out, 33the chariot commanders saw that he was not the king of Israel and stopped pursuing him.

34But someone drew his bow at random and hit the king of Israel between the sections of his armour. The king told his chariot driver, "Wheel round and get me out of the fighting. I've been wounded."

35All day long the battle raged, and the king was propped up in his chariot facing the Arameans. The blood from his wound ran onto the floor of the chariot, and that evening he died. 36As the sun was setting, a cry spread through the army: "Every man to his town; everyone to his land!"

37So the king died and was brought to Samaria, and they buried him there. 38They washed the chariot at a pool in Samaria (where the prostitutes bathed),*b* and the dogs licked up his blood, as the word of the LORD had declared.

39As for the other events of Ahab's reign, including all he did, the palace he built and inlaid with ivory, and the cities he fortified, are they not written in the book of the annals of the kings of Israel? 40Ahab rested with his fathers. And Ahaziah his son succeeded him as king.

Jehoshaphat King of Judah

41Jehoshaphat son of Asa became king of Judah in the fourth year of Ahab king of Israel. 42Jehoshaphat was thirty-five years old when he became king, and he reigned in Jerusalem for twenty-five years. His mother's name was Azubah daughter of Shilhi. 43In everything he walked in the ways of his father Asa and did not stray from them; he did what was right in the eyes of the LORD. The high places, however, were not removed, and the people continued to offer sacrifices and burn incense there. 44Jehoshaphat was also at peace with the king of Israel.

45As for the other events of Jehoshaphat's reign, the things he achieved and his military exploits, are they not written in the book of the annals of the kings of Judah? 46He rid the land of the rest of the male shrine-prostitutes who remained there even after the reign of his father Asa. 47There was then no king in Edom; a deputy ruled.

48Now Jehoshaphat built a fleet of trading ships*c* to go to Ophir for gold, but they never set sail—they were wrecked at Ezion Geber. 49At that time Ahaziah son of Ahab said to Jehoshaphat, "Let my

---

a24 Or *Spirit of*   *b38* Or *Samaria and cleaned the weapons*   *c48* Hebrew *of ships of Tarshish* men sail with your men," but Jehoshaphat refused.

⁵⁰Then Jehoshaphat rested with his fathers and was buried with them in the city of David his father. And Jehoram his son succeeded him.

Ahaziah King of Israel

⁵¹Ahaziah son of Ahab became king of Israel in Samaria in the seventeenth year of Jehoshaphat king of Judah, and he reigned over Israel for two years. ⁵²He did evil in the eyes of the LORD, because he walked in the ways of his father and mother and in the ways of Jeroboam son of Nebat, who caused Israel to sin. ⁵³He served and worshipped Baal and provoked the LORD, the God of Israel, to anger, just as his father had done.

2 Kings

The LORD's Judgment on Ahaziah

1 After Ahab's death, Moab rebelled against Israel. ²Now Ahaziah had fallen through the lattice of his upper room in Samaria and injured himself. So he sent messengers, saying to them, "Go and consult Baal-Zebub, the god of Ekron, to see if I will recover from this injury."

³But the angel of the LORD said to Elijah the Tishbite, "Go up and meet the messengers of the king of Samaria and ask them, 'Is it because there is no God in Israel that you are going off to consult Baal-Zebub, the god of Ekron?' ⁴Therefore this is what the LORD says: 'You will not leave the bed you are lying on. You will certainly die!'" So Elijah went.

⁵When the messengers returned to the king, he asked them, "Why have you come back?"

⁶"A man came to meet us," they replied. "And he said to us, 'Go back to the king who sent you and tell him, "This is what the LORD says: Is it because there is no God in Israel that you are sending men to consult Baal-Zebub, the god of Ekron? Therefore you will not leave the bed you are lying on. You will certainly die!"'"

⁷The king asked them, "What kind of man was it who came to meet you and told you this?"

⁸They replied, "He was a man with a garment of hair and with a leather belt round his waist."

The king said, "That was Elijah the Tishbite."

⁹Then he sent to Elijah a captain with his company of fifty men. The captain went up to Elijah, who was sitting on the top of a hill, and said to him, "Man of God, the king says, 'Come down!'"

¹⁰Elijah answered the captain, "If I am a man of God, may fire come down from heaven and consume you and your fifty men!" Then the fire fell from heaven and consumed the captain and his men.

¹¹At this the king sent to Elijah another captain with his fifty men. The captain said to him, "Man of God, this is what the king says, 'Come down at once!'"

¹²"If I am a man of God," Elijah replied, "may fire come down from heaven and consume you and your fifty men!" Then the fire of God fell from heaven and consumed him and his fifty men.

¹³So the king sent a third captain with his fifty men. This third captain went up and fell on his knees before Elijah. "Man of God," he begged, "please have respect for my life and the lives of these fifty men, your servants! ¹⁴See, fire has fallen from heaven and consumed the first two captains and all their men. But now have respect for my life!"

¹⁵The angel of the LORD said to Elijah, "Go down with him; do not be afraid of him." So Elijah got up and went down with him to the king.

¹⁶He told the king, "This is what the LORD says: Is it because there is no God in Israel for you to consult that you have sent messengers to consult Baal-Zebub, the god of Ekron? Because you have done this, you will never leave the bed you are lying on. You will certainly die!" ¹⁷So he died, according to the word of the LORD that Elijah had spoken.

Because Ahaziah had no son, Joram^a succeeded him as king in the second year of Jehoram son of Jehoshaphat king of Judah. ¹⁸As for all the other events of Ahaziah's reign, and what he did, are they not written in the book of the annals of the kings of Israel?

Elijah Taken Up to Heaven

2 When the LORD was about to take Elijah up to heaven in a whirlwind, Elijah and Elisha were on their way from Gilgal. ²Elijah said to Elisha, "Stay here; the LORD has sent me to Bethel."

But Elisha said, "As surely as the LORD lives and as you live, I will not leave you." So they went down to Bethel.

³The company of the prophets at Bethel came out to Elisha and asked, "Do you know that the LORD is going to take your master from you today?"

"Yes, I know," Elisha replied, "but do not speak of it."

⁴Then Elijah said to him, "Stay here, Elisha; the LORD has sent me to Jericho."

And he replied, "As surely as the LORD lives and as you live, I will not leave you." So they went to Jericho.

⁵The company of the prophets at Jericho went up to Elisha and asked him, "Do you know that the LORD is going to take your master from you today?"

"Yes, I know," he replied, "but do not speak of it."

⁶Then Elijah said to him, "Stay here; the LORD has sent me to the Jordan."

And he replied, "As surely as the LORD lives and as you live, I will not leave you." So the two of them walked on.

⁷Fifty men of the company of the prophets went and stood at a distance, facing the place where Elijah and Elisha had stopped at the Jordan. ⁸Elijah took his cloak, rolled it up and struck the water with it. The water divided to the right and to the left, and the two of them crossed over on dry ground.

⁹When they had crossed, Elijah said to Elisha, "Tell me, what can I do for you before I am taken from you?"

"Let me inherit a double portion of your spirit," Elisha replied.

¹⁰"You have asked a difficult thing," Elijah said, "yet if you see me when I am taken from you, it will be yours—otherwise not."

¹¹As they were walking along and talking together, suddenly a chariot of fire and horses of fire appeared and separated the two of them, and Elijah went up to heaven in a whirlwind. ¹²Elisha saw this and cried out, "My father! My father! The chariots and horsemen of Israel!" And Elisha saw him no more. Then he took hold of his own clothes and tore them apart.

¹³He picked up the cloak that had fallen from Elijah and went back and stood on the bank of the Jordan. ¹⁴Then he took the cloak that had fallen from him and struck the water with it. "Where now is the LORD, the God of Elijah?" he asked. When he struck the water, it divided to the right and to the left, and he crossed over.

¹⁵The company of the prophets from Jericho, who were watching, said, "The spirit of Elijah is resting on Elisha." And they went to meet him and bowed to the ground before him. ¹⁶"Look," they said, "we your servants have fifty able men. Let them go and look for your master. Perhaps the Spirit of the LORD has picked him up and set him down on some mountain or in some valley."

"No," Elisha replied, "do not send them."

¹⁷But they persisted until he was too ashamed to refuse. So he said, "Send them." And they sent fifty men, who searched for three days but did not find him. ¹⁸When they returned to Elisha, who was staying in Jericho, he said to them, "Didn't I tell you not to go?"

Healing of the Water

¹⁹The men of the city said to Elisha, "Look, our lord, this town is well situated, as you can see, but the water is bad and the land is unproductive."

²⁰"Bring me a new bowl," he said, "and put salt in it." So they brought it to him.

^a17 Hebrew *Jehoram*, a variant of *Joram*

²¹Then he went out to the spring and threw the salt into it, saying, "This is what the LORD says: 'I have healed this water. Never again will it cause death or make the land unproductive.'" ²²And the water has remained wholesome to this day, according to the word Elisha had spoken.

Elisha Is Jeered

²³From there Elisha went up to Bethel. As he was walking along the road, some youths came out of the town and jeered at him. "Go on up, you baldhead!" they said. "Go on up, you baldhead!" ²⁴He turned round, looked at them and called down a curse on them in the name of the LORD. Then two bears came out of the woods and mauled forty-two of the youths. ²⁵And he went on to Mount Carmel and from there returned to Samaria.

Moab Revolts

3 Joram*ᵃ* son of Ahab became king of Israel in Samaria in the eighteenth year of Jehoshaphat king of Judah, and he reigned for twelve years. ²He did evil in the eyes of the LORD, but not as his father and mother had done. He got rid of the sacred stone of Baal that his father had made. ³Nevertheless he clung to the sins of Jeroboam son of Nebat, which he had caused Israel to commit; he did not turn away from them.

⁴Now Mesha king of Moab raised sheep, and he had to supply the king of Israel with a hundred thousand lambs and with the wool of a hundred thousand rams. ⁵But after Ahab died, the king of Moab rebelled against the king of Israel. ⁶So at that time King Joram set out from Samaria and mobilised all Israel. ⁷He also sent this message to Jehoshaphat king of Judah: "The king of Moab has rebelled against me. Will you go with me to fight against Moab?"

"I will go with you," he replied. "I am as you are, my people as your people, my horses as your horses."

⁸"By what route shall we attack?" he asked.

"Through the Desert of Edom," he answered.

⁹So the king of Israel set out with the king of Judah and the king of Edom. After a roundabout march of seven days, the army had no more water for themselves or for the animals with them.

¹⁰"What!" exclaimed the king of Israel. "Has the LORD called us three kings together only to hand us over to Moab?"

¹¹But Jehoshaphat asked, "Is there no prophet of the LORD here, that we may enquire of the LORD through him?"

An officer of the king of Israel answered, "Elisha son of Shaphat is here. He used to pour water on the hands of Elijah."*ᵇ*

¹²Jehoshaphat said, "The word of the LORD is with him." So the king of Israel and Jehoshaphat and the king of Edom went down to him.

¹³Elisha said to the king of Israel, "What do we have to do with each other? Go to the prophets of your father and the prophets of your mother."

"No," the king of Israel answered, "because it was the LORD who called us three kings together to hand us over to Moab."

¹⁴Elisha said, "As surely as the LORD Almighty lives, whom I serve, if I did not have respect for the presence of Jehoshaphat king of Judah, I would not look at you or even notice you. ¹⁵But now bring me a harpist."

While the harpist was playing, the hand of the LORD came upon Elisha ¹⁶and he said, "This is what the LORD says: Make this valley full of ditches. ¹⁷For this is what the LORD says: You will see neither wind nor rain, yet this valley will be filled with water, and you, your cattle and your other animals will drink. ¹⁸This is an easy thing in the eyes of the LORD; he will also hand Moab over to you. ¹⁹You will overthrow every fortified city and every major town. You will cut down every good tree, stop up all the springs, and ruin every good field with stones."

ᵃ1 Hebrew *Jehoram*, a variant of *Joram*; also in verse 6   *ᵇ11* That is, he was Elijah's personal servant.

²⁰The next morning, about the time for offering the sacrifice, there it was—water flowing from the direction of Edom! And the land was filled with water.

²¹Now all the Moabites had heard that the kings had come to fight against them; so every man, young and old, who could bear arms was called up and stationed on the border. ²²When they got up early in the morning, the sun was shining on the water. To the Moabites across the way, the water looked red—like blood. ²³"That's blood!" they said. "Those kings must have fought and slaughtered each other. Now to the plunder, Moab!"

²⁴But when the Moabites came to the camp of Israel, the Israelites rose up and fought them until they fled. And the Israelites invaded the land and slaughtered the Moabites. ²⁵They destroyed the towns, and each man threw a stone on every good field until it was covered. They stopped up all the springs and cut down every good tree. Only Kir Hareseth was left with its stones in place, but men armed with slings surrounded it and attacked it as well.

²⁶When the king of Moab saw that the battle had gone against him, he took with him seven hundred swordsmen to break through to the king of Edom, but they failed. ²⁷Then he took his firstborn son, who was to succeed him as king, and offered him as a sacrifice on the city wall. The fury against Israel was great; they withdrew and returned to their own land.

The Widow's Oil

4 The wife of a man from the company of the prophets cried out to Elisha, "Your servant my husband is dead, and you know that he revered the LORD. But now his creditor is coming to take my two boys as his slaves."

²Elisha replied to her, "How can I help you? Tell me, what do you have in your house?"

"Your servant has nothing there at all," she said, "except a little oil."

³Elisha said, "Go round and ask all your neighbours for empty jars. Don't ask for just a few. ⁴Then go inside and shut the door behind you and your sons. Pour oil into all the jars, and as each is filled, put it to one side."

⁵She left him and afterwards shut the door behind her and her sons. They brought the jars to her and she kept pouring. ⁶When all the jars were full, she said to her son, "Bring me another one."

But he replied, "There is not a jar left." Then the oil stopped flowing.

⁷She went and told the man of God, and he said, "Go, sell the oil and pay your debts. You and your sons can live on what is left."

The Shunammite's Son Restored to Life

⁸One day Elisha went to Shunem. And a well-to-do woman was there, who urged him to stay for a meal. So whenever he came by, he stopped there to eat. ⁹She said to her husband, "I know that this man who often comes our way is a holy man of God. ¹⁰Let's make a small room on the roof and put in it a bed and a table, a chair and a lamp for him. Then he can stay there whenever he comes to us."

¹¹One day when Elisha came, he went up to his room and lay down there. ¹²He said to his servant Gehazi, "Call the Shunammite." So he called her, and she stood before him. ¹³Elisha said to him, "Tell her, 'You have gone to all this trouble for us. Now what can be done for you? Can we speak on your behalf to the king or the commander of the army?'"

She replied, "I have a home among my own people."

¹⁴"What can be done for her?" Elisha asked.

Gehazi said, "Well, she has no son and her husband is old."

¹⁵Then Elisha said, "Call her." So he called her, and she stood in the doorway. ¹⁶"About this time next year," Elisha said, "you will hold a son in your arms."

"No, my lord," she objected. "Don't mislead your servant, O man of God!"

¹⁷But the woman became pregnant, and the next year about that same time she gave birth to a son, just as Elisha had told her.

18The child grew, and one day he went out to his father, who was with the reapers. 19"My head! My head!" he said to his father.

His father told a servant, "Carry him to his mother." 20After the servant had lifted him up and carried him to his mother, the boy sat on her lap until noon, and then he died. 21She went up and laid him on the bed of the man of God, then shut the door and went out.

22She called her husband and said, "Please send me one of the servants and a donkey so I can go to the man of God quickly and return."

23"Why go to him today?" he asked. "It's not the New Moon or the Sabbath."

"It's all right," she said.

24She saddled the donkey and said to her servant, "Lead on; don't slow down for me unless I tell you." 25So she set out and came to the man of God at Mount Carmel.

When he saw her in the distance, the man of God said to his servant Gehazi, "Look! There's the Shunammite! 26Run to meet her and ask her, 'Are you all right? Is your husband all right? Is your child all right?'"

"Everything is all right," she said.

27When she reached the man of God at the mountain, she took hold of his feet. Gehazi came over to push her away, but the man of God said, "Leave her alone! She is in bitter distress, but the LORD has hidden it from me and has not told me why."

28"Did I ask you for a son, my lord?" she said. "Didn't I tell you, 'Don't raise my hopes'?"

29Elisha said to Gehazi, "Tuck your cloak into your belt, take my staff in your hand and run. If you meet anyone, do not greet him, and if anyone greets you, do not answer. Lay my staff on the boy's face."

30But the child's mother said, "As surely as the LORD lives and as you live, I will not leave you." So he got up and followed her.

31Gehazi went on ahead and laid the staff on the boy's face, but there was no sound or response. So Gehazi went back

to meet Elisha and told him, "The boy has not awakened."

32When Elisha reached the house, there was the boy lying dead on his couch. 33He went in, shut the door on the two of them and prayed to the LORD. 34Then he got on the bed and lay upon the boy, mouth to mouth, eyes to eyes, hands to hands. As he stretched himself out upon him, the boy's body grew warm. 35Elisha turned away and walked back and forth in the room and then got onto the bed and stretched out upon him once more. The boy sneezed seven times and opened his eyes.

36Elisha summoned Gehazi and said, "Call the Shunammite." And he did. When she came, he said, "Take your son." 37She came in, fell at his feet and bowed to the ground. Then she took her son and went out.

Death in the Pot

38Elisha returned to Gilgal and there was a famine in that region. While the company of the prophets was meeting with him, he said to his servant, "Put on the large pot and cook some stew for these men."

39One of them went out into the fields to gather herbs and found a wild vine. He gathered some of its gourds and filled the fold of his cloak. When he returned, he cut them up into the pot of stew, though no-one knew what they were. 40The stew was poured out for the men, but as they began to eat it, they cried out, "O man of God, there is death in the pot!" And they could not eat it.

41Elisha said, "Get some flour." He put it into the pot and said, "Serve it to the people to eat." And there was nothing harmful in the pot.

Feeding of a Hundred

42A man came from Baal Shalishah, bringing the man of God twenty loaves of barley bread baked from the first ripe corn, along with some ears of new corn. "Give it to the people to eat," Elisha said.

43"How can I set this before a hundred men?" his servant asked.

But Elisha answered, "Give it to the people to eat. For this is what the LORD says: 'They will eat and have some left over.'" 44Then he set it before them, and they ate and had some left over, according to the word of the LORD.

Naaman Healed of Leprosy

5 Now Naaman was commander of the army of the king of Aram. He was a great man in the sight of his master and highly regarded, because through him the LORD had given victory to Aram. He was a valiant soldier, but he had leprosy.[a]

2Now bands from Aram had gone out and had taken captive a young girl from Israel, and she served Naaman's wife. 3She said to her mistress, "If only my master would see the prophet who is in Samaria! He would cure him of his leprosy."

4Naaman went to his master and told him what the girl from Israel had said. 5"By all means, go," the king of Aram replied. "I will send a letter to the king of Israel." So Naaman left, taking with him ten talents[b] of silver, six thousand shekels[c] of gold and ten sets of clothing. 6The letter that he took to the king of Israel read: "With this letter I am sending my servant Naaman to you so that you may cure him of his leprosy."

7As soon as the king of Israel read the letter, he tore his robes and said, "Am I God? Can I kill and bring back to life? Why does this fellow send someone to me to be cured of his leprosy? See how he is trying to pick a quarrel with me!"

8When Elisha the man of God heard that the king of Israel had torn his robes, he sent him this message: "Why have you torn your robes? Make the man come to me and he will know that there is a prophet in Israel." 9So Naaman went with his horses and chariots and stopped at the door of Elisha's house. 10Elisha sent a messenger to say to him, "Go, wash yourself seven times in the Jordan, and your flesh will be restored and you will be cleansed."

11But Naaman went away angry and said, "I thought that he would surely come out to me and stand and call on the name of the LORD his God, wave his hand over the spot and cure me of my leprosy. 12Are not Abana and Pharpar, the rivers of Damascus, better than any of the waters of Israel? Couldn't I wash in them and be cleansed?" So he turned and went off in a rage.

13Naaman's servants went to him and said, "My father, if the prophet had told you to do some great thing, would you not have done it? How much more, then, when he tells you, 'Wash and be cleansed'?" 14So he went down and dipped himself in the Jordan seven times, as the man of God had told him, and his flesh was restored and became clean like that of a young boy.

15Then Naaman and all his attendants went back to the man of God. He stood before him and said, "Now I know that there is no God in all the world except in Israel. Please accept now a gift from your servant."

16The prophet answered, "As surely as the LORD lives, whom I serve, I will not accept a thing." And even though Naaman urged him, he refused.

17"If you will not," said Naaman, "please let me, your servant, be given as much earth as a pair of mules can carry, for your servant will never again make burnt offerings and sacrifices to any other god but the LORD. 18But may the LORD forgive your servant for this one thing: When my master enters the temple of Rimmon to bow down and he is leaning on my arm and I bow there also—when I bow down in the temple of Rimmon, may the LORD forgive your servant for this."

19"Go in peace," Elisha said.

After Naaman had travelled some distance, 20Gehazi, the servant of Elisha the man of God, said to himself, "My master was too easy on Naaman, this Aramean, by not accepting from him what he brought. As surely as the LORD lives, I will

---

a1 The Hebrew word was used for various diseases affecting the skin—not necessarily leprosy; also in verses 3, 6, 7, 11 and 27.   *b5* That is, about 750 pounds (about 340 kilograms)   *c5* That is, about 150 pounds (about 70 kilograms) run after him and get something from him."

21So Gehazi hurried after Naaman. When Naaman saw him running towards him, he got down from the chariot to meet him. "Is everything all right?" he asked.

22"Everything is all right," Gehazi answered. "My master sent me to say, 'Two young men from the company of the prophets have just come to me from the hill country of Ephraim. Please give them a talent*d* of silver and two sets of clothing.'"

23"By all means, take two talents," said Naaman. He urged Gehazi to accept them, and then tied up the two talents of silver in two bags, with two sets of clothing. He gave them to two of his servants, and they carried them ahead of Gehazi. 24When Gehazi came to the hill, he took the things from the servants and put them away in the house. He sent the men away and they left. 25Then he went in and stood before his master Elisha.

"Where have you been, Gehazi?" Elisha asked.

"Your servant didn't go anywhere," Gehazi answered.

26But Elisha said to him, "Was not my spirit with you when the man got down from his chariot to meet you? Is this the time to take money, or to accept clothes, olive groves, vineyards, flocks, herds, or menservants and maidservants? 27Naaman's leprosy will cling to you and to your descendants for ever." Then Gehazi went from Elisha's presence and he was leprous, as white as snow.

An Axe-Head Floats

6 The company of the prophets said to Elisha, "Look, the place where we meet with you is too small for us. 2Let us go to the Jordan, where each of us can get a pole; and let us build a place there for us to live."

And he said, "Go."

3Then one of them said, "Won't you please come with your servants?"

"I will," Elisha replied. 4And he went with them.

They went to the Jordan and began to cut down trees. 5As one of them was cutting down a tree, the iron axe-head fell into the water. "Oh, my lord," he cried out, "it was borrowed!"

6The man of God asked, "Where did it fall?" When he showed him the place, Elisha cut a stick and threw it there, and made the iron float. 7"Lift it out," he said. Then the man reached out his hand and took it.

Elisha Traps Blinded Arameans

8Now the king of Aram was at war with Israel. After conferring with his officers, he said, "I will set up my camp in such and such a place."

9The man of God sent word to the king of Israel: "Beware of passing that place, because the Arameans are going down there." 10So the king of Israel checked on the place indicated by the man of God. Time and again Elisha warned the king, so that he was on his guard in such places.

11This enraged the king of Aram. He summoned his officers and demanded of them, "Will you not tell me which of us is on the side of the king of Israel?"

12"None of us, my lord the king," said one of his officers, "but Elisha, the prophet who is in Israel, tells the king of Israel the very words you speak in your bedroom."

13"Go, find out where he is," the king ordered, "so that I can send men and capture him." The report came back: "He is in Dothan." 14Then he sent horses and chariots and a strong force there. They went by night and surrounded the city.

15When the servant of the man of God got up and went out early the next morning, an army with horses and chariots had surrounded the city. "Oh, my lord, what shall we do?" the servant asked.

16"Don't be afraid," the prophet answered. "Those who are with us are more than those who are with them."

17And Elisha prayed, "O LORD, open

d22 That is, about 75 pounds (about 34 kilograms)

his eyes so that he may see." Then the LORD opened the servant's eyes, and he looked and saw the hills full of horses and chariots of fire all round Elisha.

18As the enemy came down towards him, Elisha prayed to the LORD, "Strike these people with blindness." So he struck them with blindness, as Elisha had asked.

19Elisha told them, "This is not the road and this is not the city. Follow me, and I will lead you to the man you are looking for." And he led them to Samaria.

20After they entered the city, Elisha said, "LORD, open the eyes of these men so that they can see." Then the LORD opened their eyes and they looked, and there they were, inside Samaria.

21When the king of Israel saw them, he asked Elisha, "Shall I kill them, my father? Shall I kill them?"

22"Do not kill them," he answered. "Would you kill men you have captured with your own sword or bow? Set food and water before them so that they may eat and drink and then go back to their master." 23So he prepared a great feast for them, and after they had finished eating and drinking, he sent them away, and they returned to their master. So the bands from Aram stopped raiding Israel's territory.

Famine in Besieged Samaria

24Some time later, Ben-Hadad king of Aram mobilised his entire army and marched up and laid siege to Samaria. 25There was a great famine in the city; the siege lasted so long that a donkey's head sold for eighty shekels[a] of silver, and a quarter of a cab[b] of seed pods[c] for five shekels.[d]

26As the king of Israel was passing by on the wall, a woman cried to him, "Help me, my lord the king!"

27The king replied, "If the LORD does not help you, where can I get help for you? From the threshing-floor? From the winepress?" 28Then he asked her, "What's the matter?"

She answered, "This woman said to me, 'Give up your son so that we may eat him today, and tomorrow we'll eat my son.' 29So we cooked my son and ate him. The next day I said to her, 'Give up your son so that we may eat him,' but she had hidden him."

30When the king heard the woman's words, he tore his robes. As he went along the wall, the people looked, and there, underneath, he had sackcloth on his body. 31He said, "May God deal with me, be it ever so severely, if the head of Elisha son of Shaphat remains on his shoulders today!"

32Now Elisha was sitting in his house, and the elders were sitting with him. The king sent a messenger ahead, but before he arrived, Elisha said to the elders, "Don't you see how this murderer is sending someone to cut off my head? Look, when the messenger comes, shut the door and hold it shut against him. Is not the sound of his master's footsteps behind him?"

33While he was still talking to them, the messenger came down to him. And ⌐the king⌐ said, "This disaster is from the LORD. Why should I wait for the LORD any longer?"

7 Elisha said, "Hear the word of the LORD. This is what the LORD says: About this time tomorrow, a seah[a] of flour will sell for a shekel[b] and two seahs[c] of barley for a shekel at the gate of Samaria."

2The officer on whose arm the king was leaning said to the man of God, "Look, even if the LORD should open the floodgates of the heavens, could this happen?"

"You will see it with your own eyes," answered Elisha, "but you will not eat any of it!"

The Siege Lifted

3Now there were four men with leprosy[d] at the entrance of the city gate. They said

---

a25 That is, about 2 pounds (about 1 kilogram)   b25 That is, probably about ½ pint (about 0.3 litre)
c25 Or of dove's dung   d25 That is, about 2 ounces (about 55 grams)
a1 That is, probably about 13 pints (about 7.3 litres); also in verses 16 and 18
b1 That is, about ⅔ ounce (about 11 grams); also in verses 16 and 18
c1 That is, probably about 13 quarts (about 15 litres); also in verses 16 and 18
d3 The Hebrew word is used for various diseases affecting the skin—not necessarily leprosy; also in verse 8.

to each other, "Why stay here until we die? ⁴If we say, 'We'll go into the city'— the famine is there, and we will die. And if we stay here, we will die. So let's go over to the camp of the Arameans and surrender. If they spare us, we live; if they kill us, then we die."

⁵At dusk they got up and went to the camp of the Arameans. When they reached the edge of the camp, not a man was there, ⁶for the Lord had caused the Arameans to hear the sound of chariots and horses and a great army, so that they said to one another, "Look, the king of Israel has hired the Hittite and Egyptian kings to attack us!" ⁷So they got up and fled in the dusk and abandoned their tents and their horses and donkeys. They left the camp as it was and ran for their lives.

⁸The men who had leprosy reached the edge of the camp and entered one of the tents. They ate and drank, and carried away silver, gold and clothes, and went off and hid them. They returned and entered another tent and took some things from it and hid them also.

⁹Then they said to each other, "We're not doing right. This is a day of good news and we are keeping it to ourselves. If we wait until daylight, punishment will overtake us. Let's go at once and report this to the royal palace."

¹⁰So they went and called out to the city gatekeepers and told them, "We went into the Aramean camp and not a man was there—not a sound of anyone—only tethered horses and donkeys, and the tents left just as they were." ¹¹The gatekeepers shouted the news, and it was reported within the palace.

¹²The king got up in the night and said to his officers, "I will tell you what the Arameans have done to us. They know we are starving; so they have left the camp to hide in the countryside, thinking, 'They will surely come out, and then we will take them alive and get into the city.'"

¹³One of his officers answered, "Make some men take five of the horses that are left in the city. Their plight will be like that of all the Israelites left here—yes, they will only be like all these Israelites who are doomed. So let us send them to find out what happened."

¹⁴So they selected two chariots with their horses, and the king sent them after the Aramean army. He commanded the drivers, "Go and find out what has happened." ¹⁵They followed them as far as the Jordan, and they found the whole road strewn with the clothing and equipment the Arameans had thrown away in their headlong flight. So the messengers returned and reported to the king. ¹⁶Then the people went out and plundered the camp of the Arameans. So a seah of flour sold for a shekel, and two seahs of barley sold for a shekel, as the LORD had said.

¹⁷Now the king had put the officer on whose arm he leaned in charge of the gate, and the people trampled him in the gateway, and he died, just as the man of God had foretold when the king came down to his house. ¹⁸It happened as the man of God had said to the king: "About this time tomorrow, a seah of flour will sell for a shekel and two seahs of barley for a shekel at the gate of Samaria."

¹⁹The officer had said to the man of God, "Look, even if the LORD should open the floodgates of the heavens, could this happen?" The man of God had replied, "You will see it with your own eyes, but you will not eat any of it!" ²⁰And that is exactly what happened to him, for the people trampled him in the gateway, and he died.

The Shunammite's Land Restored

8 Now Elisha had said to the woman whose son he had restored to life, "Go away with your family and stay for a while wherever you can, because the LORD has decreed a famine in the land that will last seven years." ²The woman proceeded to do as the man of God said. She and her family went away and stayed in the land of the Philistines for seven years.

³At the end of the seven years she came back from the land of the Philistines and went to the king to beg for her house and land. ⁴The king was talking to Gehazi, the servant of the man of God, and had said, "Tell me about all the great things Elisha

has done." ⁵Just as Gehazi was telling the king how Elisha had restored the dead to life, the woman whose son Elisha had brought back to life came to beg the king for her house and land.

Gehazi said, "This is the woman, my lord the king, and this is her son whom Elisha restored to life." ⁶The king asked the woman about it, and she told him.

Then he assigned an official to her case and said to him, "Give back everything that belonged to her, including all the income from her land from the day she left the country until now."

Hazael Murders Ben-Hadad

⁷Elisha went to Damascus, and Ben-Hadad king of Aram was ill. When the king was told, "The man of God has come all the way up here," ⁸he said to Hazael, "Take a gift with you and go to meet the man of God. Consult the LORD through him; ask him, 'Will I recover from this illness?'"

⁹Hazael went to meet Elisha, taking with him as a gift forty camel-loads of all the finest wares of Damascus. He went in and stood before him, and said, "Your son Ben-Hadad king of Aram has sent me to ask, 'Will I recover from this illness?'"

¹⁰Elisha answered, "Go and say to him, 'You will certainly recover'; but* the LORD has revealed to me that he will in fact die." ¹¹He stared at him with a fixed gaze until Hazael felt ashamed. Then the man of God began to weep.

¹²"Why is my lord weeping?" asked Hazael.

"Because I know the harm you will do to the Israelites," he answered. "You will set fire to their fortified places, kill their young men with the sword, dash their little children to the ground, and rip open their pregnant women." ¹³Hazael said, "How could your servant, a mere dog, accomplish such a feat?"

"The LORD has shown me that you will become king of Aram," answered Elisha.

¹⁴Then Hazael left Elisha and returned to his master. When Ben-Hadad asked, "What did Elisha say to you?" Hazael replied, "He told me that you would certainly recover." ¹⁵But the next day he took a thick cloth, soaked it in water and spread it over the king's face, so that he died. Then Hazael succeeded him as king.

Jehoram King of Judah

¹⁶In the fifth year of Joram son of Ahab king of Israel, when Jehoshaphat was king of Judah, Jehoram son of Jehoshaphat began his reign as king of Judah. ¹⁷He was thirty-two years old when he became king, and he reigned in Jerusalem for eight years. ¹⁸He walked in the ways of the kings of Israel, as the house of Ahab had done, for he married a daughter of Ahab. He did evil in the eyes of the LORD. ¹⁹Nevertheless, for the sake of his servant David, the LORD was not willing to destroy Judah. He had promised to maintain a lamp for David and his descendants for ever.

²⁰In the time of Jehoram, Edom rebelled against Judah and set up its own king. ²¹So Jehoramᵇ went to Zair with all his chariots. The Edomites surrounded him and his chariot commanders, but he rose up and broke through by night; his army, however, fled back home. ²²To this day Edom has been in rebellion against Judah. Libnah revolted at the same time.

²³As for the other events of Jehoram's reign, and all he did, are they not written in the book of the annals of the kings of Judah? ²⁴Jehoram rested with his fathers and was buried with them in the City of David. And Ahaziah his son succeeded him as king.

Ahaziah King of Judah

²⁵In the twelfth year of Joram son of Ahab king of Israel, Ahaziah son of Jehoram king of Judah began to reign. ²⁶Ahaziah was twenty-two years old when he became king, and he reigned in Jerusalem for one year. His mother's name was Athaliah, a granddaughter of Omri king of Israel. ²⁷He walked in the ways of

---

ᵃ10 The Hebrew may also be read Go and say, 'You will certainly not recover,' for.
ᵇ21 Hebrew Joram, a variant of Jehoram; also in verses 23 and 24

the house of Ahab and did evil in the eyes of the LORD, as the house of Ahab had done, for he was related by marriage to Ahab's family.

28Ahaziah went with Joram son of Ahab to war against Hazael king of Aram at Ramoth Gilead. The Arameans wounded Joram; 29so King Joram returned to Jezreel to recover from the wounds the Arameans had inflicted on him at Ramoth*c* in his battle with Hazael king of Aram.

Then Ahaziah son of Jehoram king of Judah went down to Jezreel to see Joram son of Ahab, because he had been wounded.

Jehu Anointed King of Israel

9 The prophet Elisha summoned a man from the company of the prophets and said to him, "Tuck your cloak into your belt, take this flask of oil with you and go to Ramoth Gilead. 2When you get there, look for Jehu son of Jehoshaphat, the son of Nimshi. Go to him, get him away from his companions and take him into an inner room. 3Then take the flask and pour the oil on his head and declare, 'This is what the LORD says: I anoint you king over Israel.' Then open the door and run; don't delay!"

4So the young man, the prophet, went to Ramoth Gilead. 5When he arrived, he found the army officers sitting together. "I have a message for you, commander," he said.

"For which of us?" asked Jehu.

"For you, commander," he replied.

6Jehu got up and went into the house. Then the prophet poured the oil on Jehu's head and declared, "This is what the LORD, the God of Israel, says: 'I anoint you king over the LORD's people Israel. 7You are to destroy the house of Ahab your master, and I will avenge the blood of my servants the prophets and the blood of all the LORD's servants shed by Jezebel. 8The whole house of Ahab will perish. I will cut off from Ahab every last male in Israel—slave or free. 9I will make the house of Ahab like the house of Jeroboam

son of Nebat and like the house of Baasha son of Ahijah. 10As for Jezebel, dogs will devour her on the plot of ground at Jezreel, and no-one will bury her.'" Then he opened the door and ran.

11When Jehu went out to his fellow officers, one of them asked him, "Is everything all right? Why did this madman come to you?"

"You know the man and the sort of things he says," Jehu replied.

12"That's not true!" they said. "Tell us."

Jehu said, "Here is what he told me: 'This is what the LORD says: I anoint you king over Israel.'"

13They hurried and took their cloaks and spread them under him on the bare steps. Then they blew the trumpet and shouted, "Jehu is king!"

Jehu Kills Joram and Ahaziah

14So Jehu son of Jehoshaphat, the son of Nimshi, conspired against Joram. (Now Joram and all Israel had been defending Ramoth Gilead against Hazael king of Aram, 15but King Joram*a* had returned to Jezreel to recover from the wounds the Arameans had inflicted on him in the battle with Hazael king of Aram.) Jehu said, "If this is the way you feel, don't let anyone slip out of the city to go and tell the news in Jezreel." 16Then he got into his chariot and rode to Jezreel, because Joram was resting there and Ahaziah king of Judah had gone down to see him.

17When the lookout standing on the tower in Jezreel saw Jehu's troops approaching, he called out, "I see some troops coming."

"Get a horseman," Joram ordered. "Send him to meet them and ask, 'Do you come in peace?'"

18The horseman rode off to meet Jehu and said, "This is what the king says: 'Do you come in peace?'"

"What do you have to do with peace?" Jehu replied. "Fall in behind me."

The lookout reported, "The messenger

---

c29 Hebrew *Ramah*, a variant of *Ramoth*   *a15* Hebrew *Jehoram*, a variant of *Joram*; also in verses 17 and 21-24 has reached them, but he isn't coming back."

[19]So the king sent out a second horseman. When he came to them he said, "This is what the king says: 'Do you come in peace?'"

Jehu replied, "What do you have to do with peace? Fall in behind me."

[20]The lookout reported, "He has reached them, but he isn't coming back either. The driving is like that of Jehu son of Nimshi—he drives like a madman."

[21]"Hitch up my chariot," Joram ordered. And when it was hitched up, Joram king of Israel and Ahaziah king of Judah rode out, each in his own chariot, to meet Jehu. They met him at the plot of ground that had belonged to Naboth the Jezreelite. [22]When Joram saw Jehu he asked, "Have you come in peace, Jehu?"

"How can there be peace," Jehu replied, "as long as all the idolatry and witchcraft of your mother Jezebel abound?"

[23]Joram turned about and fled, calling out to Ahaziah, "Treachery, Ahaziah!"

[24]Then Jehu drew his bow and shot Joram between the shoulders. The arrow pierced his heart and he slumped down in his chariot. [25]Jehu said to Bidkar, his chariot officer, "Pick him up and throw him on the field that belonged to Naboth the Jezreelite. Remember how you and I were riding together in chariots behind Ahab his father when the LORD made this prophecy about him: [26]'Yesterday I saw the blood of Naboth and the blood of his sons, declares the LORD, and I will surely make you pay for it on this plot of ground, declares the LORD.'[b] Now then, pick him up and throw him on that plot, in accordance with the word of the LORD."

[27]When Ahaziah king of Judah saw what had happened, he fled up the road to Beth Haggan.[c] Jehu chased him, shouting, "Kill him too!" They wounded him in his chariot on the way up to Gur near Ibleam, but he escaped to Megiddo and died there. [28]His servants took him by chariot to Jerusalem and buried him with

his fathers in his tomb in the City of David. [29](In the eleventh year of Joram son of Ahab, Ahaziah had become king of Judah.)

Jezebel Killed

[30]Then Jehu went to Jezreel. When Jezebel heard about it, she painted her eyes, arranged her hair and looked out of a window. [31]As Jehu entered the gate, she asked, "Have you come in peace, Zimri, you murderer of your master?"[d]

[32]He looked up at the window and called out, "Who is on my side? Who?" Two or three eunuchs looked down at him. [33]"Throw her down!" Jehu said. So they threw her down, and some of her blood spattered the wall and the horses as they trampled her underfoot.

[34]Jehu went in and ate and drank. "Take care of that cursed woman," he said, "and bury her, for she was a king's daughter." [35]But when they went out to bury her, they found nothing except her skull, her feet and her hands. [36]They went back and told Jehu, who said, "This is the word of the LORD that he spoke through his servant Elijah the Tishbite: On the plot of ground at Jezreel dogs will devour Jezebel's flesh.[e] [37]Jezebel's body will be like refuse on the ground in the plot at Jezreel, so that no-one will be able to say, 'This is Jezebel.'"

Ahab's Family Killed

10 Now there were in Samaria seventy sons of the house of Ahab. So Jehu wrote letters and sent them to Samaria: to the officials of Jezreel,[a] to the elders and to the guardians of Ahab's children. He said, [2]"As soon as this letter reaches you, since your master's sons are with you and you have chariots and horses, a fortified city and weapons, [3]choose the best and most worthy of your master's sons and set him on his father's throne. Then fight for your master's house."

b26 See 1 Kings 21:19.   c27 Or fled by way of the garden house
d31 Or "Did Zimri have peace, who murdered his master?"   e36 See 1 Kings 21:23.
a1 Hebrew; some Septuagint manuscripts and Vulgate of the city

⁴But they were terrified and said, "If two kings could not resist him, how can we?"

⁵So the palace administrator, the city governor, the elders and the guardians sent this message to Jehu: "We are your servants and we will do anything you say. We will not appoint anyone as king; you do whatever you think best."

⁶Then Jehu wrote them a second letter, saying, "If you are on my side and will obey me, take the heads of your master's sons and come to me in Jezreel by this time tomorrow."

Now the royal princes, seventy of them, were with the leading men of the city, who were bringing them up. ⁷When the letter arrived, these men took the princes and slaughtered all seventy of them. They put their heads in baskets and sent them to Jehu in Jezreel. ⁸When the messenger arrived, he told Jehu, "They have brought the heads of the princes."

Then Jehu ordered, "Put them in two piles at the entrance of the city gate until morning."

⁹The next morning Jehu went out. He stood before all the people and said, "You are innocent. It was I who conspired against my master and killed him, but who killed all these? ¹⁰Know then, that not a word the LORD has spoken against the house of Ahab will fail. The LORD has done what he promised through his servant Elijah." ¹¹So Jehu killed everyone in Jezreel who remained of the house of Ahab, as well as all his chief men, his close friends and his priests, leaving him no survivor.

¹²Jehu then set out and went towards Samaria. At Beth Eked of the Shepherds, ¹³he met some relatives of Ahaziah king of Judah and asked, "Who are you?"

They said, "We are relatives of Ahaziah, and we have come down to greet the families of the king and of the queen mother."

¹⁴"Take them alive!" he ordered. So they took them alive and slaughtered them by the well of Beth Eked—forty-two men. He left no survivor.

¹⁵After he left there, he came upon Jehonadab son of Recab, who was on his way to meet him. Jehu greeted him and said, "Are you in accord with me, as I am with you?"

"I am," Jehonadab answered.

"If so," said Jehu, "give me your hand." So he did, and Jehu helped him up into the chariot. ¹⁶Jehu said, "Come with me and see my zeal for the LORD." Then he made him ride in his chariot.

¹⁷When Jehu came to Samaria, he killed all who were left there of Ahab's family; he destroyed them, according to the word of the LORD spoken to Elijah.

Ministers of Baal Killed

¹⁸Then Jehu brought all the people together and said to them, "Ahab served Baal a little; Jehu will serve him much. ¹⁹Now summon all the prophets of Baal, all his ministers and all his priests. See that no-one is missing, because I am going to hold a great sacrifice for Baal. Anyone who fails to come will no longer live." But Jehu was acting deceptively in order to destroy the ministers of Baal.

²⁰Jehu said, "Call an assembly in honour of Baal." So they proclaimed it. ²¹Then he sent word throughout Israel, and all the ministers of Baal came; not one stayed away. They crowded into the temple of Baal until it was full from one end to the other. ²²And Jehu said to the keeper of the wardrobe, "Bring robes for all the ministers of Baal." So he brought out robes for them.

²³Then Jehu and Jehonadab son of Recab went into the temple of Baal. Jehu said to the ministers of Baal, "Look around and see that no servants of the LORD are here with you—only ministers of Baal." ²⁴So they went in to make sacrifices and burnt offerings. Now Jehu had posted eighty men outside with this warning: "If one of you lets any of the men I am placing in your hands escape, it will be your life for his life."

²⁵As soon as Jehu had finished making the burnt offering, he ordered the guards and officers: "Go in and kill them; let no-one escape." So they cut them down with the sword. The guards and officers threw the bodies out and then entered the

inner shrine of the temple of Baal. ²⁶They brought the sacred stone out of the temple of Baal and burned it. ²⁷They demolished the sacred stone of Baal and tore down the temple of Baal, and people have used it for a latrine to this day.

²⁸So Jehu destroyed Baal worship in Israel. ²⁹However, he did not turn away from the sins of Jeroboam son of Nebat, which he had caused Israel to commit— the worship of the golden calves at Bethel and Dan.

³⁰The LORD said to Jehu, "Because you have done well in accomplishing what is right in my eyes and have done to the house of Ahab all I had in mind to do, your descendants will sit on the throne of Israel to the fourth generation." ³¹Yet Jehu was not careful to keep the law of the LORD, the God of Israel, with all his heart. He did not turn away from the sins of Jeroboam, which he had caused Israel to commit.

³²In those days the LORD began to reduce the size of Israel. Hazael overpowered the Israelites throughout their territory ³³east of the Jordan in all the land of Gilead (the region of Gad, Reuben and Manasseh), from Aroer by the Arnon Gorge through Gilead to Bashan.

³⁴As for the other events of Jehu's reign, all he did, and all his achievements, are they not written in the book of the annals of the kings of Israel?

³⁵Jehu rested with his fathers and was buried in Samaria. And Jehoahaz his son succeeded him as king. ³⁶The time that Jehu reigned over Israel in Samaria was twenty-eight years.

Athaliah and Joash

11 When Athaliah the mother of Ahaziah saw that her son was dead, she proceeded to destroy the whole royal family. ²But Jehosheba, the daughter of King Jehoram*ᵃ* and sister of Ahaziah, took Joash son of Ahaziah and stole him away from among the royal princes, who were about to be murdered. She put him and his nurse in a bedroom to hide him from Athaliah; so he was not killed.

³He remained hidden with his nurse at the temple of the LORD for six years while Athaliah ruled the land.

⁴In the seventh year Jehoiada sent for the commanders of units of a hundred, the Carites and the guards and had them brought to him at the temple of the LORD. He made a covenant with them and put them under oath at the temple of the LORD. Then he showed them the king's son. ⁵He commanded them, saying, "This is what you are to do: You who are in the three companies that are going on duty on the Sabbath—a third of you guarding the royal palace, ⁶a third at the Sur Gate, and a third at the gate behind the guard, who take turns guarding the temple—⁷and you who are in the other two companies that normally go off Sabbath duty are all to guard the temple for the king. ⁸Station yourselves round the king, each man with his weapon in his hand. Anyone who approaches your ranks*ᵇ* must be put to death. Stay close to the king wherever he goes."

⁹The commanders of units of a hundred did just as Jehoiada the priest ordered. Each one took his men—those who were going on duty on the Sabbath and those who were going off duty—and came to Jehoiada the priest. ¹⁰Then he gave the commanders the spears and shields that had belonged to King David and that were in the temple of the LORD. ¹¹The guards, each with his weapon in his hand, stationed themselves round the king—near the altar and the temple, from the south side to the north side of the temple.

¹²Jehoiada brought out the king's son and put the crown on him; he presented him with a copy of the covenant and proclaimed him king. They anointed him, and the people clapped their hands and shouted, "Long live the king!"

¹³When Athaliah heard the noise made by the guards and the people, she went to the people at the temple of the LORD. ¹⁴She looked and there was the king, standing by the pillar, as the custom was. The officers and the trumpeters were beside the king, and all the people of the land

---

ᵃ2 Hebrew *Joram*, a variant of *Jehoram*   *ᵇ8* Or *approaches the precincts* were rejoicing and blowing trumpets. Then Athaliah tore her robes and called out, "Treason! Treason!"

15Jehoiada the priest ordered the commanders of units of a hundred, who were in charge of the troops: "Bring her out between the ranks[c] and put to the sword anyone who follows her." For the priest had said, "She must not be put to death in the temple of the LORD." 16So they seized her as she reached the place where the horses enter the palace grounds, and there she was put to death.

17Jehoiada then made a covenant between the LORD and the king and people that they would be the LORD's people. He also made a covenant between the king and the people. 18All the people of the land went to the temple of Baal and tore it down. They smashed the altars and idols to pieces and killed Mattan the priest of Baal in front of the altars.

Then Jehoiada the priest posted guards at the temple of the LORD. 19He took with him the commanders of hundreds, the Carites, the guards and all the people of the land, and together they brought the king down from the temple of the LORD and went into the palace, entering by way of the gate of the guards. The king then took his place on the royal throne, 20and all the people of the land rejoiced. And the city was quiet, because Athaliah had been slain with the sword at the palace.

21Joash[d] was seven years old when he began his reign.

Joash Repairs the Temple

12 In the seventh year of Jehu, Joash[a] became king, and he reigned in Jerusalem for forty years. His mother's name was Zibiah; she was from Beersheba. 2Joash did what was right in the eyes of the LORD all the years Jehoiada the priest instructed him. 3The high places, however, were not removed; the people continued to offer sacrifices and burn incense there.

4Joash said to the priests, "Collect all the money that is brought as sacred offerings to the temple of the LORD—the money collected in the census, the money received from personal vows and the money brought voluntarily to the temple. 5Let every priest receive the money from one of the treasurers, and let it be used to repair whatever damage is found in the temple."

6But by the twenty-third year of King Joash the priests still had not repaired the temple. 7Therefore King Joash summoned Jehoiada the priest and the other priests and asked them, "Why aren't you repairing the damage done to the temple? Take no more money from your treasurers, but hand it over for repairing the temple." 8The priests agreed that they would not collect any more money from the people and that they would not repair the temple themselves.

9Jehoiada the priest took a chest and bored a hole in its lid. He placed it beside the altar, on the right side as one enters the temple of the LORD. The priests who guarded the entrance put into the chest all the money that was brought to the temple of the LORD. 10Whenever they saw that there was a large amount of money in the chest, the royal secretary and the high priest came, counted the money that had been brought into the temple of the LORD and put it into bags. 11When the amount had been determined, they gave the money to the men appointed to supervise the work on the temple. With it they paid those who worked on the temple of the LORD—the carpenters and builders, 12the masons and stonecutters. They purchased timber and dressed stone for the repair of the temple of the LORD, and met all the other expenses of restoring the temple.

13The money brought into the temple was not spent for making silver basins, wick trimmers, sprinkling bowls, trumpets or any other articles of gold or silver for the temple of the LORD; 14it was paid to the workmen, who used it to repair the temple. 15They did not require an accounting from those to whom they gave the money to pay the workers, because they acted with complete honesty. 16The

c15 Or out from the precincts   d21 Hebrew Jehoash, a variant of Joash
a1 Hebrew Jehoash, a variant of Joash; also in verses 2, 4, 6, 7 and 18

money from the guilt offerings and sin offerings was not brought into the temple of the LORD; it belonged to the priests.

¹⁷About this time Hazael king of Aram went up and attacked Gath and captured it. Then he turned to attack Jerusalem. ¹⁸But Joash king of Judah took all the sacred objects dedicated by his fathers— Jehoshaphat, Jehoram and Ahaziah, the kings of Judah—and the gifts he himself had dedicated and all the gold found in the treasuries of the temple of the LORD and of the royal palace, and he sent them to Hazael king of Aram, who then withdrew from Jerusalem.

¹⁹As for the other events of the reign of Joash, and all he did, are they not written in the book of the annals of the kings of Judah? ²⁰His officials conspired against him and assassinated him at Beth Millo, on the road down to Silla. ²¹The officials who murdered him were Jozabad son of Shimeath and Jehozabad son of Shomer. He died and was buried with his fathers in the City of David. And Amaziah his son succeeded him as king.

Jehoahaz King of Israel

13 In the twenty-third year of Joash son of Ahaziah king of Judah, Jehoahaz son of Jehu became king of Israel in Samaria, and he reigned for seventeen years. ²He did evil in the eyes of the LORD by following the sins of Jeroboam son of Nebat, which he had caused Israel to commit, and he did not turn away from them. ³So the LORD's anger burned against Israel, and for a long time he kept them under the power of Hazael king of Aram and Ben-Hadad his son.

⁴Then Jehoahaz sought the LORD's favour, and the LORD listened to him, for he saw how severely the king of Aram was oppressing Israel. ⁵The LORD provided a deliverer for Israel, and they escaped from the power of Aram. So the Israelites lived in their own homes as they had before. ⁶But they did not turn away from the sins of the house of Jeroboam, which he had caused Israel to commit; they continued in

them. Also, the Asherah pole^a remained standing in Samaria.

⁷Nothing had been left of the army of Jehoahaz except fifty horsemen, ten chariots and ten thousand foot soldiers, for the king of Aram had destroyed the rest and made them like the dust at threshing time.

⁸As for the other events of the reign of Jehoahaz, all he did and his achievements, are they not written in the book of the annals of the kings of Israel? ⁹Jehoahaz rested with his fathers and was buried in Samaria. And Jehoash^b his son succeeded him as king.

Jehoash King of Israel

¹⁰In the thirty-seventh year of Joash king of Judah, Jehoash son of Jehoahaz became king of Israel in Samaria, and he reigned for sixteen years. ¹¹He did evil in the eyes of the LORD and did not turn away from any of the sins of Jeroboam son of Nebat, which he had caused Israel to commit; he continued in them.

¹²As for the other events of the reign of Jehoash, all he did and his achievements, including his war against Amaziah king of Judah, are they not written in the book of the annals of the kings of Israel? ¹³Jehoash rested with his fathers, and Jeroboam succeeded him on the throne. Jehoash was buried in Samaria with the kings of Israel.

¹⁴Now Elisha was suffering from the illness from which he died. Jehoash king of Israel went down to see him and wept over him. "My father! My father!" he cried. "The chariots and horsemen of Israel!"

¹⁵Elisha said, "Get a bow and some arrows," and he did so. ¹⁶"Take the bow in your hands," he said to the king of Israel. When he had taken it, Elisha put his hands on the king's hands.

¹⁷"Open the east window," he said, and he opened it. "Shoot!" Elisha said, and he shot. "The LORD's arrow of victory, the arrow of victory over Aram!" Elisha declared. "You will completely destroy the Arameans at Aphek."

^a6 That is, a symbol of the goddess Asherah; here and elsewhere in 2 Kings
^b9 Hebrew *Joash*, a variant of *Jehoash*; also in verses 12–14 and 25

18Then he said, "Take the arrows," and the king took them. Elisha told him, "Strike the ground." He struck it three times and stopped. 19The man of God was angry with him and said, "You should have struck the ground five or six times; then you would have defeated Aram and completely destroyed it. But now you will defeat it only three times."

20Elisha died and was buried.

Now Moabite raiders used to enter the country every spring. 21Once while some Israelites were burying a man, suddenly they saw a band of raiders; so they threw the man's body into Elisha's tomb. When the body touched Elisha's bones, the man came to life and stood up on his feet.

22Hazael king of Aram oppressed Israel throughout the reign of Jehoahaz. 23But the LORD was gracious to them and had compassion and showed concern for them because of his covenant with Abraham, Isaac and Jacob. To this day he has been unwilling to destroy them or banish them from his presence.

24Hazael king of Aram died, and Ben-Hadad his son succeeded him as king. 25Then Jehoash son of Jehoahaz recaptured from Ben-Hadad son of Hazael the towns he had taken in battle from his father Jehoahaz. Three times Jehoash defeated him, and so he recovered the Israelite towns.

Amaziah King of Judah

14 In the second year of Jehoash[a] son of Jehoahaz king of Israel, Amaziah son of Joash king of Judah began to reign. 2He was twenty-five years old when he became king, and he reigned in Jerusalem for twenty-nine years. His mother's name was Jehoaddin; she was from Jerusalem. 3He did what was right in the eyes of the LORD, but not as his father David had done. In everything he followed the example of his father Joash. 4The high places, however, were not removed; the people continued to offer sacrifices and burn incense there.

5After the kingdom was firmly in his grasp, he executed the officials who had murdered his father the king. 6Yet he did not put the sons of the assassins to death, in accordance with what is written in the Book of the Law of Moses where the LORD commanded: "Fathers shall not be put to death for their children, nor children put to death for their fathers; each is to die for his own sins."[b]

7He was the one who defeated ten thousand Edomites in the Valley of Salt and captured Sela in battle, calling it Joktheel, the name it has to this day.

8Then Amaziah sent messengers to Jehoash son of Jehoahaz, the son of Jehu, king of Israel, with the challenge: "Come, meet me face to face."

9But Jehoash king of Israel replied to Amaziah king of Judah: "A thistle in Lebanon sent a message to a cedar in Lebanon, 'Give your daughter to my son in marriage.' Then a wild beast in Lebanon came along and trampled the thistle underfoot. 10You have indeed defeated Edom and now you are arrogant. Glory in your victory, but stay at home! Why ask for trouble and cause your own downfall and that of Judah also?"

11Amaziah, however, would not listen, so Jehoash king of Israel attacked. He and Amaziah king of Judah faced each other at Beth Shemesh in Judah. 12Judah was routed by Israel, and every man fled to his home. 13Jehoash king of Israel captured Amaziah king of Judah, the son of Joash, the son of Ahaziah, at Beth Shemesh. Then Jehoash went to Jerusalem and broke down the wall of Jerusalem from the Ephraim Gate to the Corner Gate—a section about six hundred feet long.[c] 14He took all the gold and silver and all the articles found in the temple of the LORD and in the treasuries of the royal palace. He also took hostages and returned to Samaria.

15As for the other events of the reign of Jehoash, what he did and his achievements, including his war against Amaziah king of Judah, are they not written in the book of the annals of the kings of Israel? 16Jehoash rested with his fathers and was

a1 Hebrew Joash, a variant of Jehoash; also in verses 13, 23 and 27   b6 Deut. 24:16
c13 Hebrew four hundred cubits (about 180 metres)

buried in Samaria with the kings of Israel. And Jeroboam his son succeeded him as king.

¹⁷Amaziah son of Joash king of Judah lived for fifteen years after the death of Jehoash son of Jehoahaz king of Israel. ¹⁸As for the other events of Amaziah's reign, are they not written in the book of the annals of the kings of Judah?

¹⁹They conspired against him in Jerusalem, and he fled to Lachish, but they sent men after him to Lachish and killed him there. ²⁰He was brought back by horse and was buried in Jerusalem with his fathers, in the City of David.

²¹Then all the people of Judah took Azariah,*d* who was sixteen years old, and made him king in place of his father Amaziah. ²²He was the one who rebuilt Elath and restored it to Judah after Amaziah rested with his fathers.

Jeroboam II King of Israel

²³In the fifteenth year of Amaziah son of Joash king of Judah, Jeroboam son of Jehoash king of Israel became king in Samaria, and he reigned for forty-one years. ²⁴He did evil in the eyes of the LORD and did not turn away from any of the sins of Jeroboam son of Nebat, which he had caused Israel to commit. ²⁵He was the one who restored the boundaries of Israel from Lebo*e* Hamath to the Sea of the Arabah,*f* in accordance with the word of the LORD, the God of Israel, spoken through his servant Jonah son of Amittai, the prophet from Gath Hepher.

²⁶The LORD had seen how bitterly everyone in Israel, whether slave or free, was suffering; there was no-one to help them. ²⁷And since the LORD had not said he would blot out the name of Israel from under heaven, he saved them by the hand of Jeroboam son of Jehoash.

²⁸As for the other events of Jeroboam's reign, all he did, and his military achievements, including how he recovered for Israel both Damascus and Hamath, which

had belonged to Yaudi,*g* are they not written in the book of the annals of the kings of Israel? ²⁹Jeroboam rested with his fathers, the kings of Israel. And Zechariah his son succeeded him as king.

Azariah King of Judah

15 In the twenty-seventh year of Jeroboam king of Israel, Azariah son of Amaziah king of Judah began to reign. ²He was sixteen years old when he became king, and he reigned in Jerusalem for fifty-two years. His mother's name was Jecoliah; she was from Jerusalem. ³He did what was right in the eyes of the LORD, just as his father Amaziah had done. ⁴The high places, however, were not removed; the people continued to offer sacrifices and burn incense there.

⁵The LORD afflicted the king with leprosy*a* until the day he died, and he lived in a separate house.*b* Jotham the king's son had charge of the palace and governed the people of the land.

⁶As for the other events of Azariah's reign, and all he did, are they not written in the book of the annals of the kings of Judah? ⁷Azariah rested with his fathers and was buried near them in the City of David. And Jotham his son succeeded him as king.

Zechariah King of Israel

⁸In the thirty-eighth year of Azariah king of Judah, Zechariah son of Jeroboam became king of Israel in Samaria, and he reigned for six months. ⁹He did evil in the eyes of the LORD, as his fathers had done. He did not turn away from the sins of Jeroboam son of Nebat, which he had caused Israel to commit.

¹⁰Shallum son of Jabesh conspired against Zechariah. He attacked him in front of the people,*c* assassinated him and succeeded him as king. ¹¹The other events of Zechariah's reign are written in the book of the annals of the kings of Israel.

---

d21 Also called *Uzziah*   *e25* Or *from the entrance to*   *f25* That is, the Dead Sea   *g28* Or *Judah*
a5 The Hebrew word was used for various diseases affecting the skin—not necessarily leprosy.
b5 Or *in a house where he was relieved of responsibility*
c10 Hebrew; some Septuagint manuscripts *in Ibleam*

[12]So the word of the LORD spoken to Jehu was fulfilled: "Your descendants will sit on the throne of Israel to the fourth generation."[d]

Shallum King of Israel

[13]Shallum son of Jabesh became king in the thirty-ninth year of Uzziah king of Judah, and he reigned in Samaria for one month. [14]Then Menahem son of Gadi went from Tirzah up to Samaria. He attacked Shallum son of Jabesh in Samaria, assassinated him and succeeded him as king.

[15]The other events of Shallum's reign, and the conspiracy he led, are written in the book of the annals of the kings of Israel.

[16]At that time Menahem, starting out from Tirzah, attacked Tiphsah and everyone in the city and its vicinity, because they refused to open their gates. He sacked Tiphsah and ripped open all the pregnant women.

Menahem King of Israel

[17]In the thirty-ninth year of Azariah king of Judah, Menahem son of Gadi became king of Israel, and he reigned in Samaria for ten years. [18]He did evil in the eyes of the LORD. During his entire reign he did not turn away from the sins of Jeroboam son of Nebat, which he had caused Israel to commit.

[19]Then Pul[e] king of Assyria invaded the land, and Menahem gave him a thousand talents[f] of silver to gain his support and strengthen his own hold on the kingdom. [20]Menahem exacted this money from Israel. Every wealthy man had to contribute fifty shekels[g] of silver to be given to the king of Assyria. So the king of Assyria withdrew and stayed in the land no longer.

[21]As for the other events of Menahem's reign, and all he did, are they not written in the book of the annals of the kings of Israel? [22]Menahem rested with his fathers. And Pekahiah his son succeeded him as king.

Pekahiah King of Israel

[23]In the fiftieth year of Azariah king of Judah, Pekahiah son of Menahem became king of Israel in Samaria, and he reigned for two years. [24]Pekahiah did evil in the eyes of the LORD. He did not turn away from the sins of Jeroboam son of Nebat, which he had caused Israel to commit. [25]One of his chief officers, Pekah son of Remaliah, conspired against him. Taking fifty men of Gilead with him, he assassinated Pekahiah, along with Argob and Arieh, in the citadel of the royal palace at Samaria. So Pekah killed Pekahiah and succeeded him as king.

[26]The other events of Pekahiah's reign, and all he did, are written in the book of the annals of the kings of Israel.

Pekah King of Israel

[27]In the fifty-second year of Azariah king of Judah, Pekah son of Remaliah became king of Israel in Samaria, and he reigned for twenty years. [28]He did evil in the eyes of the LORD. He did not turn away from the sins of Jeroboam son of Nebat, which he had caused Israel to commit.

[29]In the time of Pekah king of Israel, Tiglath-Pileser king of Assyria came and took Ijon, Abel Beth Maacah, Janoah, Kedesh and Hazor. He took Gilead and Galilee, including all the land of Naphtali, and deported the people to Assyria. [30]Then Hoshea son of Elah conspired against Pekah son of Remaliah. He attacked and assassinated him, and then succeeded him as king in the twentieth year of Jotham son of Uzziah.

[31]As for the other events of Pekah's reign, and all he did, are they not written in the book of the annals of the kings of Israel?

Jotham King of Judah

[32]In the second year of Pekah son of Remaliah king of Israel, Jotham son of Uzziah king of Judah began to reign. [33]He was twenty-five years old when he became king, and he reigned in Jerusalem

d12 2 Kings 10:30   e19 Also called Tiglath-Pileser
820 That is, about 1¼ pounds (about 0.6 kilogram)   f19 That is, about 34 tons (about 34 metric tons)

for sixteen years. His mother's name was Jerusha daughter of Zadok. ³⁴He did what was right in the eyes of the LORD, just as his father Uzziah had done. ³⁵The high places, however, were not removed; the people continued to offer sacrifices and burn incense there. Jotham rebuilt the Upper Gate of the temple of the LORD.

³⁶As for the other events of Jotham's reign, and what he did, are they not written in the book of the annals of the kings of Judah? ³⁷(In those days the LORD began to send Rezin king of Aram and Pekah son of Remaliah against Judah.) ³⁸Jotham rested with his fathers and was buried with them in the City of David, the city of his father. And Ahaz his son succeeded him as king.

Ahaz King of Judah

16 In the seventeenth year of Pekah son of Remaliah, Ahaz son of Jotham king of Judah began to reign. ²Ahaz was twenty years old when he became king, and he reigned in Jerusalem for sixteen years. Unlike David his father, he did not do what was right in the eyes of the LORD his God. ³He walked in the ways of the kings of Israel and even sacrificed his son in*ᵃ* the fire, following the detestable ways of the nations the LORD had driven out before the Israelites. ⁴He offered sacrifices and burned incense at the high places, on the hilltops and under every spreading tree.

⁵Then Rezin king of Aram and Pekah son of Remaliah king of Israel marched up to fight against Jerusalem and besieged Ahaz, but they could not overpower him. ⁶At that time, Rezin king of Aram recovered Elath for Aram by driving out the men of Judah. Edomites then moved into Elath and have lived there to this day.

⁷Ahaz sent messengers to say to Tiglath-Pileser king of Assyria, "I am your servant and vassal. Come up and save me out of the hand of the king of Aram and of the king of Israel who are attacking me." ⁸And Ahaz took the silver and gold found in the temple of the LORD and in the treasuries of the royal palace and sent it as a gift to the king of Assyria. ⁹The king of

Assyria complied by attacking Damascus and capturing it. He deported its inhabitants to Kir and put Rezin to death.

¹⁰Then King Ahaz went to Damascus to meet Tiglath-Pileser king of Assyria. He saw an altar in Damascus and sent to Uriah the priest a sketch of the altar, with detailed plans for its construction. ¹¹So Uriah the priest built an altar in accordance with all the plans that King Ahaz had sent from Damascus and finished it before King Ahaz returned. ¹²When the king came back from Damascus and saw the altar, he approached it and presented offerings*ᵇ* on it. ¹³He offered up his burnt offering and grain offering, poured out his drink offering, and sprinkled the blood of his fellowship offerings*ᶜ* on the altar. ¹⁴The bronze altar that stood before the LORD he brought from the front of the temple—from between the new altar and the temple of the LORD—and put it on the north side of the new altar.

¹⁵King Ahaz then gave these orders to Uriah the priest: "On the large new altar, offer the morning burnt offering and the evening grain offering, the king's burnt offering and his grain offering, and the burnt offering of all the people of the land, and their grain offering and their drink offering. Sprinkle on the altar all the blood of the burnt offerings and sacrifices. But I will use the bronze altar for seeking guidance." ¹⁶And Uriah the priest did just as King Ahaz had ordered.

¹⁷King Ahaz took away the side panels and removed the basins from the movable stands. He removed the Sea from the bronze bulls that supported it and set it on a stone base. ¹⁸He took away the Sabbath canopy*ᵈ* that had been built at the temple and removed the royal entrance outside the temple of the LORD, in deference to the king of Assyria.

¹⁹As for the other events of the reign of Ahaz, and what he did, are they not written in the book of the annals of the kings of Judah? ²⁰Ahaz rested with his fathers and was buried with them in the City of David. And Hezekiah his son succeeded him as king.

ᵃ3 Or *even made his son pass through*   ᵇ12 Or *and went up*   ᶜ13 Traditionally *peace offerings*
ᵈ18 Or *the dais of his throne* (see Septuagint)

Hoshea Last King of Israel

17 In the twelfth year of Ahaz king of Judah, Hoshea son of Elah became king of Israel in Samaria, and he reigned for nine years. ²He did evil in the eyes of the LORD, but not like the kings of Israel who preceded him.

³Shalmaneser king of Assyria came up to attack Hoshea, who had been Shalmaneser's vassal and had paid him tribute. ⁴But the king of Assyria discovered that Hoshea was a traitor, for he had sent envoys to So*ᵃ* king of Egypt, and he no longer paid tribute to the king of Assyria, as he had done year by year. Therefore Shalmaneser seized him and put him in prison. ⁵The king of Assyria invaded the entire land, marched against Samaria and laid siege to it for three years. ⁶In the ninth year of Hoshea, the king of Assyria captured Samaria and deported the Israelites to Assyria. He settled them in Halah, in Gozan on the Habor River and in the towns of the Medes.

Israel Exiled Because of Sin

⁷All this took place because the Israelites had sinned against the LORD their God, who had brought them out of Egypt from under the power of Pharaoh king of Egypt. They worshipped other gods ⁸and followed the practices of the nations the LORD had driven out before them, as well as the practices that the kings of Israel had introduced. ⁹The Israelites secretly did things against the LORD their God that were not right. From watchtower to fortified city they built themselves high places in all their towns. ¹⁰They set up sacred stones and Asherah poles on every high hill and under every spreading tree. ¹¹At every high place they burned incense, as the nations whom the LORD had driven out before them had done. They did wicked things that provoked the LORD to anger. ¹²They worshipped idols, though the LORD had said, "You shall not do this."*ᵇ* ¹³The LORD warned Israel and Judah through all his prophets

and seers: "Turn from your evil ways. Observe my commands and decrees, in accordance with the entire Law that I commanded your fathers to obey and that I delivered to you through my servants the prophets."

¹⁴But they would not listen and were as stiff-necked as their fathers, who did not trust in the LORD their God. ¹⁵They rejected his decrees and the covenant he had made with their fathers and the warnings he had given them. They followed worthless idols and themselves became worthless. They imitated the nations around them although the LORD had ordered them, "Do not do as they do," and they did the things the LORD had forbidden them to do.

¹⁶They forsook all the commands of the LORD their God and made for themselves two idols cast in the shape of calves, and an Asherah pole. They bowed down to all the starry hosts, and they worshipped Baal. ¹⁷They sacrificed their sons and daughters in*ᶜ* the fire. They practised divination and sorcery and sold themselves to do evil in the eyes of the LORD, provoking him to anger.

¹⁸So the LORD was very angry with Israel and removed them from his presence. Only the tribe of Judah was left, ¹⁹and even Judah did not keep the commands of the LORD their God. They followed the practices Israel had introduced. ²⁰Therefore the LORD rejected all the people of Israel; he afflicted them and gave them into the hands of plunderers, until he thrust them from his presence.

²¹When he tore Israel away from the house of David, they made Jeroboam son of Nebat their king. Jeroboam enticed Israel away from following the LORD and caused them to commit a great sin. ²²The Israelites persisted in all the sins of Jeroboam and did not turn away from them ²³until the LORD removed them from his presence, as he had warned through all his servants the prophets. So the people of Israel were taken from their homeland into exile in Assyria, and they are still there.

ᵃ4 Or to Sais, to the; So is possibly an abbreviation for Osorkon.   *ᵇ12 Exodus 20:4, 5*
ᶜ17 Or They made their sons and daughters pass through

Samaria Resettled

24The king of Assyria brought people from Babylon, Cuthah, Avva, Hamath and Sepharvaim and settled them in the towns of Samaria to replace the Israelites. They took over Samaria and lived in its towns. 25When they first lived there, they did not worship the LORD; so he sent lions among them and they killed some of the people. 26It was reported to the king of Assyria: "The people you deported and resettled in the towns of Samaria do not know what the god of that country requires. He has sent lions among them, which are killing them off, because the people do not know what he requires."

27Then the king of Assyria gave this order: "Make one of the priests you took captive from Samaria go back to live there and teach the people what the god of the land requires." 28So one of the priests who had been exiled from Samaria came to live in Bethel and taught them how to worship the LORD.

29Nevertheless, each national group made its own gods in the several towns where they settled, and set them up in the shrines the people of Samaria had made at the high places. 30The men from Babylon made Succoth Benoth, the men from Cuthah made Nergal, and the men from Hamath made Ashima; 31the Avvites made Nibhaz and Tartak, and the Sepharvites burned their children in the fire as sacrifices to Adrammelech and Anammelech, the gods of Sepharvaim. 32They worshipped the LORD, but they also appointed all sorts of their own people to officiate for them as priests in the shrines at the high places. 33They worshipped the LORD, but they also served their own gods in accordance with the customs of the nations from which they had been brought.

34To this day they persist in their former practices. They neither worship the LORD nor adhere to the decrees and ordinances, the laws and commands that the LORD gave the descendants of Jacob, whom he named Israel. 35When the LORD made a covenant with the Israelites, he commanded them: "Do not worship any other gods or bow down to them, serve them or sacrifice to them. 36But the LORD, who brought you up out of Egypt with mighty power and outstretched arm, is the one you must worship. To him you shall bow down and to him offer sacrifices. 37You must always be careful to keep the decrees and ordinances, the laws and commands he wrote for you. Do not worship other gods. 38Do not forget the covenant I have made with you, and do not worship other gods. 39Rather, worship the LORD your God; it is he who will deliver you from the hand of all your enemies."

40They would not listen, however, but persisted in their former practices. 41Even while these people were worshipping the LORD, they were serving their idols. To this day their children and grandchildren continue to do as their fathers did.

Hezekiah King of Judah

18 In the third year of Hoshea son of Elah king of Israel, Hezekiah son of Ahaz king of Judah began to reign. 2He was twenty-five years old when he became king, and he reigned in Jerusalem for twenty-nine years. His mother's name was Abijah[a] daughter of Zechariah. 3He did what was right in the eyes of the LORD, just as his father David had done. 4He removed the high places, smashed the sacred stones and cut down the Asherah poles. He broke into pieces the bronze snake Moses had made, for up to that time the Israelites had been burning incense to it. (It was called[b] Nehushtan.[c])

5Hezekiah trusted in the LORD, the God of Israel. There was no-one like him among all the kings of Judah, either before him or after him. 6He held fast to the LORD and did not cease to follow him; he kept the commands the LORD had given Moses. 7And the LORD was with him; he was successful in whatever he undertook. He rebelled against the king of Assyria and did not serve him. 8From watchtower to fortified city, he defeated the Philistines,

---

a2 Hebrew *Abi*, a variant of *Abijah*   *b4* Or *He called it*
c4 Nehushtan sounds like the Hebrew for *bronze* and *snake* and *unclean thing.*

as far as Gaza and its territory.

⁹In King Hezekiah's fourth year, which was the seventh year of Hoshea son of Elah king of Israel, Shalmaneser king of Assyria marched against Samaria and laid siege to it. ¹⁰At the end of three years the Assyrians took it. So Samaria was captured in Hezekiah's sixth year, which was the ninth year of Hoshea king of Israel. ¹¹The king of Assyria deported Israel to Assyria and settled them in Halah, in Gozan on the Habor River, and in towns of the Medes. ¹²This happened because they had not obeyed the LORD their God, but had violated his covenant—all that Moses the servant of the LORD commanded. They neither listened to the commands nor carried them out.

¹³In the fourteenth year of King Hezekiah's reign, Sennacherib king of Assyria attacked all the fortified cities of Judah and captured them. ¹⁴So Hezekiah king of Judah sent this message to the king of Assyria at Lachish: "I have done wrong. Withdraw from me, and I will pay whatever you demand of me." The king of Assyria exacted from Hezekiah king of Judah three hundred talents*ᵈ* of silver and thirty talents*ᵉ* of gold. ¹⁵So Hezekiah gave him all the silver that was found in the temple of the LORD and in the treasuries of the royal palace.

¹⁶At this time Hezekiah king of Judah stripped off the gold with which he had covered the doors and doorposts of the temple of the LORD, and gave it to the king of Assyria.

Sennacherib Threatens Jerusalem

¹⁷The king of Assyria sent his supreme commander, his chief officer and his field commander with a large army, from Lachish to King Hezekiah at Jerusalem. They came up to Jerusalem and stopped at the aqueduct of the Upper Pool, on the road to the Washerman's Field. ¹⁸They called for the king; and Eliakim son of Hilkiah the palace administrator, Shebna the secretary, and Joah son of Asaph the recorder went out to them.

¹⁹The field commander said to them, "Tell Hezekiah:

"'This is what the great king, the king of Assyria, says: On what are you basing this confidence of yours? ²⁰You say you have strategy and military strength—but you speak only empty words. On whom are you depending, that you rebel against me? ²¹Look now, you are depending on Egypt, that splintered reed of a staff, which pierces a man's hand and wounds him if he leans on it! Such is Pharaoh king of Egypt to all who depend on him. ²²And if you say to me, "We are depending on the LORD our God"—isn't he the one whose high places and altars Hezekiah removed, saying to Judah and Jerusalem, "You must worship before this altar in Jerusalem"?

²³"'Come now, make a bargain with my master, the king of Assyria: I will give you two thousand horses—if you can put riders on them! ²⁴How can you repulse one officer of the least of my master's officials, even though you are depending on Egypt for chariots and horsemen?*ᶠ* ²⁵Furthermore, have I come to attack and destroy this place without word from the LORD? The LORD himself told me to march against this country and destroy it.'"

²⁶Then Eliakim son of Hilkiah, and Shebna and Joah said to the field commander, "Please speak to your servants in Aramaic, since we understand it. Don't speak to us in Hebrew in the hearing of the people on the wall."

²⁷But the commander replied, "Was it only to your master and you that my master sent me to say these things, and not to the men sitting on the wall—who, like you, will have to eat their own filth and drink their own urine?"

²⁸Then the commander stood and called out in Hebrew: "Hear the word of the great king, the king of Assyria! ²⁹This is what the king says: Do not let Hezekiah deceive you. He cannot deliver you from

---

d14 That is, about 10 tons (about 10 metric tons)   *e14* That is, about 1 ton (about 1 metric ton)
f24 Or *charioteers*

my hand. ³⁰Do not let Hezekiah persuade you to trust in the LORD when he says, 'The LORD will surely deliver us; this city will not be given into the hand of the king of Assyria.'

³¹"Do not listen to Hezekiah. This is what the king of Assyria says: Make peace with me and come out to me. Then every one of you will eat from his own vine and fig-tree and drink water from his own cistern, ³²until I come and take you to a land like your own, a land of grain and new wine, a land of bread and vineyards, a land of olive trees and honey. Choose life and not death!

"Do not listen to Hezekiah, for he is misleading you when he says, 'The LORD will deliver us.' ³³Has the god of any nation ever delivered his land from the hand of the king of Assyria? ³⁴Where are the gods of Hamath and Arpad? Where are the gods of Sepharvaim, Hena and Ivvah? Have they rescued Samaria from my hand? ³⁵Who of all the gods of these countries has been able to save his land from me? How then can the LORD deliver Jerusalem from my hand?"

³⁶But the people remained silent and said nothing in reply, because the king had commanded, "Do not answer him."

³⁷Then Eliakim son of Hilkiah the palace administrator, Shebna the secretary and Joah son of Asaph the recorder went to Hezekiah, with their clothes torn, and told him what the field commander had said.

Jerusalem's Deliverance Foretold

19 When King Hezekiah heard this, he tore his clothes and put on sackcloth and went into the temple of the LORD. ²He sent Eliakim the palace administrator, Shebna the secretary and the leading priests, all wearing sackcloth, to the prophet Isaiah son of Amoz. ³They told him, "This is what Hezekiah says: This day is a day of distress and rebuke and disgrace, as when children come to the point of birth and there is no strength to deliver them. ⁴It may be that the LORD

your God will hear all the words of the field commander, whom his master, the king of Assyria, has sent to ridicule the living God, and that he will rebuke him for the words the LORD your God has heard. Therefore pray for the remnant that still survives."

⁵When King Hezekiah's officials came to Isaiah, ⁶Isaiah said to them, "Tell your master, 'This is what the LORD says: Do not be afraid of what you have heard—those words with which the underlings of the king of Assyria have blasphemed me. ⁷Listen! I am going to put such a spirit in him that when he hears a certain report, he will return to his own country, and there I will have him cut down with the sword.'"

⁸When the field commander heard that the king of Assyria had left Lachish, he withdrew and found the king fighting against Libnah.

⁹Now Sennacherib received a report that Tirhakah, the Cushite[a] king ⌊of Egypt⌋, was marching out to fight against him. So he again sent messengers to Hezekiah with this word: ¹⁰"Say to Hezekiah king of Judah: Do not let the god you depend on deceive you when he says, 'Jerusalem will not be handed over to the king of Assyria.' ¹¹Surely you have heard what the kings of Assyria have done to all the countries, destroying them completely. And will you be delivered? ¹²Did the gods of the nations that were destroyed by my forefathers deliver them: the gods of Gozan, Haran, Rezeph and the people of Eden who were in Tel Assar? ¹³Where is the king of Hamath, the king of Arpad, the king of the city of Sepharvaim, or of Hena or Ivvah?"

Hezekiah's Prayer

¹⁴Hezekiah received the letter from the messengers and read it. Then he went up to the temple of the LORD and spread it out before the LORD. ¹⁵And Hezekiah prayed to the LORD: "O LORD, God of Israel, enthroned between the cherubim, you alone are God over all the kingdoms of the

earth. You have made heaven and earth.
¹⁶Give ear, O LORD, and hear; open your
eyes, O LORD, and see; listen to the words
Sennacherib has sent to insult the living
God.

¹⁷"It is true, O LORD, that the Assyrian
kings have laid waste these nations and
their lands. ¹⁸They have thrown their gods
into the fire and destroyed them, for they
were not gods but only wood and stone,
fashioned by men's hands. ¹⁹Now, O LORD
our God, deliver us from his hand, so that
all kingdoms on earth may know that you
alone, O LORD, are God."

Isaiah Prophesies Sennacherib's Fall

²⁰Then Isaiah son of Amoz sent a message to Hezekiah: "This is what the LORD,
the God of Israel, says: I have heard your
prayer concerning Sennacherib king of
Assyria. ²¹This is the word that the LORD
has spoken against him:

" 'The Virgin Daughter of Zion
    despises you and mocks you.
The Daughter of Jerusalem
    tosses her head as you flee.
²²Who is it you have insulted and
    blasphemed?
    Against whom have you raised your
      voice
and lifted your eyes in pride?
    Against the Holy One of Israel!
²³By your messengers
    you have heaped insults on the Lord.
And you have said,
    "With my many chariots
I have ascended the heights of the
    mountains,
    the utmost heights of Lebanon.
I have cut down its tallest cedars,
    the choicest of its pines.
I have reached its remotest parts,
    the finest of its forests.
²⁴I have dug wells in foreign lands
    and drunk the water there.
With the soles of my feet
    I have dried up all the streams of
      Egypt."

²⁵"'Have you not heard?
    Long ago I ordained it.

In days of old I planned it;
    now I have brought it to pass,
that you have turned fortified cities
    into piles of stone.
²⁶Their people, drained of power,
    are dismayed and put to shame.
They are like plants in the field,
    like tender green shoots,
like grass sprouting on the roof,
    scorched before it grows up.

²⁷"'But I know where you stay
    and when you come and go
    and how you rage against me.
²⁸Because you rage against me
    and your insolence has reached my
      ears,
I will put my hook in your nose
    and my bit in your mouth,
and I will make you return
    by the way you came.'

²⁹"This will be the sign for you, O Hezekiah:

This year you will eat what grows by
      itself,
    and the second year what springs
      from that.
But in the third year sow and reap,
    plant vineyards and eat their fruit.
³⁰Once more a remnant of the house of
      Judah
    will take root below and bear fruit
      above.
³¹For out of Jerusalem will come a
      remnant,
    and out of Mount Zion a band of
      survivors.

The zeal of the LORD Almighty will accomplish this.

³²"Therefore this is what the LORD says
concerning the king of Assyria:

"He will not enter this city
    or shoot an arrow here.
He will not come before it with shield
    or build a siege ramp against it.
³³By the way that he came he will return;
    he will not enter this city,
             declares the LORD.

³⁴I will defend this city and save it,
   for my sake and for the sake of David
   my servant."

³⁵That night the angel of the LORD went
out and put to death a hundred and eighty-
five thousand men in the Assyrian camp.
When the people got up the next morn-
ing—there were all the dead bodies! ³⁶So
Sennacherib king of Assyria broke camp
and withdrew. He returned to Nineveh
and stayed there.

³⁷One day, while he was worshipping in
the temple of his god Nisroch, his sons
Adrammelech and Sharezer cut him down
with the sword, and they escaped to the
land of Ararat. And Esarhaddon his son
succeeded him as king.

Hezekiah's Illness

20 In those days Hezekiah became ill
and was at the point of death. The
prophet Isaiah son of Amoz went to him
and said, "This is what the LORD says: Put
your house in order, because you are
going to die; you will not recover."

²Hezekiah turned his face to the wall
and prayed to the LORD, ³"Remember, O
LORD, how I have walked before you faithfully and with wholehearted devotion and
have done what is good in your eyes."
And Hezekiah wept bitterly.

⁴Before Isaiah had left the middle court,
the word of the LORD came to him: ⁵"Go
back and tell Hezekiah, the leader of my
people, 'This is what the LORD, the God of
your father David, says: I have heard your
prayer and seen your tears; I will heal you.
On the third day from now you will go up
to the temple of the LORD. ⁶I will add
fifteen years to your life. And I will deliver
you and this city from the hand of the king
of Assyria. I will defend this city for my
sake and for the sake of my servant
David.'"

⁷Then Isaiah said, "Prepare a poultice
of figs." They did so and applied it to the
boil, and he recovered.

⁸Hezekiah had asked Isaiah, "What will
be the sign that the LORD will heal me and
that I will go up to the temple of the LORD
on the third day from now?"

⁹Isaiah answered, "This is the LORD's
sign to you that the LORD will do what he
has promised: Shall the shadow go forward ten steps, or shall it go back ten
steps?"

¹⁰"It is a simple matter for the shadow
to go forward ten steps," said Hezekiah.
"Rather, have it go back ten steps."

¹¹Then the prophet Isaiah called upon
the LORD, and the LORD made the shadow
go back the ten steps it had gone down on
the stairway of Ahaz.

Envoys From Babylon

¹²At that time Merodach-Baladan son
of Baladan king of Babylon sent Hezekiah
letters and a gift, because he had heard of
Hezekiah's illness. ¹³Hezekiah received
the messengers and showed them all that
was in his storehouses—the silver, the
gold, the spices and the fine oil—his
armoury and everything found among his
treasures. There was nothing in his palace
or in all his kingdom that Hezekiah did not
show them.

¹⁴Then Isaiah the prophet went to King
Hezekiah and asked, "What did those
men say, and where did they come from?"

"From a distant land," Hezekiah replied. "They came from Babylon."

¹⁵The prophet asked, "What did they
see in your palace?"

"They saw everything in my palace,"
Hezekiah said. "There is nothing among
my treasures that I did not show them."

¹⁶Then Isaiah said to Hezekiah, "Hear
the word of the LORD: ¹⁷The time will
surely come when everything in your
palace, and all that your fathers have
stored up until this day, will be carried off
to Babylon. Nothing will be left, says the
LORD. ¹⁸And some of your descendants,
your own flesh and blood, that will be born
to you, will be taken away, and they will
become eunuchs in the palace of the king
of Babylon."

¹⁹"The word of the LORD you have
spoken is good," Hezekiah replied. For he
thought, "Will there not be peace and
security in my lifetime?"

²⁰As for the other events of Hezekiah's
reign, all his achievements and how he

made the pool and the tunnel by which he brought water into the city, are they not written in the book of the annals of the kings of Judah? [21]Hezekiah rested with his fathers. And Manasseh his son succeeded him as king.

Manasseh King of Judah

21 Manasseh was twelve years old when he became king, and he reigned in Jerusalem for fifty-five years. His mother's name was Hephzibah. [2]He did evil in the eyes of the LORD, following the detestable practices of the nations the LORD had driven out before the Israelites. [3]He rebuilt the high places his father Hezekiah had destroyed; he also erected altars to Baal and made an Asherah pole, as Ahab king of Israel had done. He bowed down to all the starry hosts and worshipped them. [4]He built altars in the temple of the LORD, of which the LORD had said, "In Jerusalem I will put my Name." [5]In both courts of the temple of the LORD, he built altars to all the starry hosts. [6]He sacrificed his own son in[a] the fire, practised sorcery and divination, and consulted mediums and spiritists. He did much evil in the eyes of the LORD, provoking him to anger.

[7]He took the carved Asherah pole he had made and put it in the temple, of which the LORD had said to David and to his son Solomon, "In this temple and in Jerusalem, which I have chosen out of all the tribes of Israel, I will put my Name for ever. [8]I will not again make the feet of the Israelites wander from the land I gave their forefathers, if only they will be careful to do everything I commanded them and will keep the whole Law that my servant Moses gave them." [9]But the people did not listen. Manasseh led them astray, so that they did more evil than the nations the LORD had destroyed before the Israelites.

[10]The LORD said through his servants the prophets: [11]"Manasseh king of Judah has committed these detestable sins. He has done more evil than the Amorites who preceded him and has led Judah into sin with his idols. [12]Therefore this is what the LORD, the God of Israel, says: I am going to bring such disaster on Jerusalem and Judah that the ears of everyone who hears of it will tingle. [13]I will stretch out over Jerusalem the measuring line used against Samaria and the plumb-line used against the house of Ahab. I will wipe out Jerusalem as one wipes out a dish, wiping it and turning it upside-down. [14]I will forsake the remnant of my inheritance and hand them over to their enemies. They will be looted and plundered by all their foes, [15]because they have done evil in my eyes and have provoked me to anger from the day their forefathers came out of Egypt until this day."

[16]Moreover, Manasseh also shed so much innocent blood that he filled Jerusalem from end to end—besides the sin that he had caused Judah to commit, so that they did evil in the eyes of the LORD.

[17]As for the other events of Manasseh's reign, and all he did, including the sin he committed, are they not written in the book of the annals of the kings of Judah? [18]Manasseh rested with his fathers and was buried in his palace garden, the garden of Uzza. And Amon his son succeeded him as king.

Amon King of Judah

[19]Amon was twenty-two years old when he became king, and he reigned in Jerusalem for two years. His mother's name was Meshullemeth daughter of Haruz; she was from Jotbah. [20]He did evil in the eyes of the LORD, as his father Manasseh had done. [21]He walked in all the ways of his father; he worshipped the idols his father had worshipped, and bowed down to them. [22]He forsook the LORD, the God of his fathers, and did not walk in the way of the LORD.

[23]Amon's officials conspired against him and assassinated the king in his palace. [24]Then the people of the land killed all who had plotted against King

_____
[a]6 Or He made his own son pass through

Amon, and they made Josiah his son king in his place.

^{25}As for the other events of Amon's reign, and what he did, are they not written in the book of the annals of the kings of Judah? ^{26}He was buried in his grave in the garden of Uzza. And Josiah his son succeeded him as king.

The Book of the Law Found

22 Josiah was eight years old when he became king, and he reigned in Jerusalem for thirty-one years. His mother's name was Jedidah daughter of Adaiah; she was from Bozkath. ^{2}He did what was right in the eyes of the LORD and walked in all the ways of his father David, not turning aside to the right or to the left.

^{3}In the eighteenth year of his reign, King Josiah sent the secretary, Shaphan son of Azaliah, the son of Meshullam, to the temple of the LORD. He said: ^{4}"Go up to Hilkiah the high priest and make him get ready the money that has been brought into the temple of the LORD, which the doorkeepers have collected from the people. ^{5}Make them entrust it to the men appointed to supervise the work on the temple. And make these men pay the workers who repair the temple of the LORD—^{6}the carpenters, the builders and the masons. Also make them purchase timber and dressed stone to repair the temple. ^{7}But they need not account for the money entrusted to them, because they are acting faithfully."

^{8}Hilkiah the high priest said to Shaphan the secretary, "I have found the Book of the Law in the temple of the LORD." He gave it to Shaphan, who read it. ^{9}Then Shaphan the secretary went to the king and reported to him: "Your officials have paid out the money that was in the temple of the LORD and have entrusted it to the workers and supervisors at the temple." ^{10}Then Shaphan the secretary informed the king, "Hilkiah the priest has given me a book." And Shaphan read from it in the presence of the king.

^{11}When the king heard the words of the Book of the Law, he tore his robes. ^{12}He gave these orders to Hilkiah the priest, Ahikam son of Shaphan, Acbor son of Micaiah, Shaphan the secretary and Asaiah the king's attendant: ^{13}"Go and enquire of the LORD for me and for the people and for all Judah about what is written in this book that has been found. Great is the LORD's anger that burns against us because our fathers have not obeyed the words of this book; they have not acted in accordance with all that is written there concerning us."

^{14}Hilkiah the priest, Ahikam, Acbor, Shaphan and Asaiah went to speak to the prophetess Huldah, who was the wife of Shallum son of Tikvah, the son of Harhas, keeper of the wardrobe. She lived in Jerusalem, in the Second District.

^{15}She said to them, "This is what the LORD, the God of Israel, says: Tell the man who sent you to me, ^{16}'This is what the LORD says: I am going to bring disaster on this place and its people, according to everything written in the book the king of Judah has read. ^{17}Because they have forsaken me and burned incense to other gods and provoked me to anger by all the idols their hands have made,^{a} my anger will burn against this place and will not be quenched.' ^{18}Tell the king of Judah, who sent you to enquire of the LORD, 'This is what the LORD, the God of Israel, says concerning the words you heard: ^{19}Because your heart was responsive and you humbled yourself before the LORD when you heard what I have spoken against this place and its people, that they would become accursed and laid waste, and because you tore your robes and wept in my presence, I have heard you, declares the LORD. ^{20}Therefore I will gather you to your fathers, and you will be buried in peace. Your eyes will not see all the disaster I am going to bring on this place.'"

So they took her answer back to the king.

Josiah Renews the Covenant

23 Then the king called together all the elders of Judah and Jerusalem. ^{2}He went up to the temple of the LORD

^{a}17 Or by everything they have done

with the men of Judah, the people of Jerusalem, the priests and the prophets—all the people from the least to the greatest. He read in their hearing all the words of the Book of the Covenant, which had been found in the temple of the LORD. 3The king stood by the pillar and renewed the covenant in the presence of the LORD—to follow the LORD and keep his commands, regulations and decrees with all his heart and all his soul, thus confirming the words of the covenant written in this book. Then all the people pledged themselves to the covenant.

4The king ordered Hilkiah the high priest, the priests next in rank and the doorkeepers to remove from the temple of the LORD all the articles made for Baal and Asherah and all the starry hosts. He burned them outside Jerusalem in the fields of the Kidron Valley and took the ashes to Bethel. 5He did away with the pagan priests appointed by the kings of Judah to burn incense on the high places of the towns of Judah and on those around Jerusalem—those who burned incense to Baal, to the sun and moon, to the constellations and to all the starry hosts. 6He took the Asherah pole from the temple of the LORD to the Kidron Valley outside Jerusalem and burned it there. He ground it to powder and scattered the dust over the graves of the common people. 7He also tore down the quarters of the male shrine-prostitutes, which were in the temple of the LORD and where women did weaving for Asherah.

8Josiah brought all the priests from the towns of Judah and desecrated the high places, from Geba to Beersheba, where the priests had burned incense. He broke down the shrines*a* at the gates—at the entrance to the Gate of Joshua, the city governor, which is on the left of the city gate. 9Although the priests of the high places did not serve at the altar of the LORD in Jerusalem, they ate unleavened bread with their fellow priests.

10He desecrated Topheth, which was in the Valley of Ben Hinnom, so no-one could use it to sacrifice his son or daughter in*b* the fire to Molech. 11He removed from the entrance to the temple of the LORD the horses that the kings of Judah had dedicated to the sun. They were in the court near the room of an official named Nathan-Melech. Josiah then burned the chariots dedicated to the sun.

12He pulled down the altars the kings of Judah had erected on the roof near the upper room of Ahaz, and the altars Manasseh had built in the two courts of the temple of the LORD. He removed them from there, smashed them to pieces and threw the rubble into the Kidron Valley. 13The king also desecrated the high places that were east of Jerusalem on the south of the Hill of Corruption—the ones Solomon king of Israel had built for Ashtoreth the vile goddess of the Sidonians, for Chemosh the vile god of Moab, and for Molech*c* the detestable god of the people of Ammon. 14Josiah smashed the sacred stones and cut down the Asherah poles and covered the sites with human bones.

15Even the altar at Bethel, the high place made by Jeroboam son of Nebat, who had caused Israel to sin—even that altar and high place he demolished. He burned the high place and ground it to powder, and burned the Asherah pole also. 16Then Josiah looked around, and when he saw the tombs that were there on the hillside, he had the bones removed from them and burned on the altar to defile it, in accordance with the word of the LORD proclaimed by the man of God who foretold these things.

17The king asked, "What is that tombstone I see?"

The men of the city said, "It marks the tomb of the man of God who came from Judah and pronounced against the altar of Bethel the very things you have done to it."

18"Leave it alone," he said. "Don't let anyone disturb his bones." So they spared his bones and those of the prophet who had come from Samaria.

19Just as he had done at Bethel, Josiah removed and defiled all the shrines at the high places that the kings of Israel had

---

a8 Or *high places*   *b10* Or *to make his son or daughter pass through*   *c13* Hebrew *Milcom* built in the towns of Samaria that had provoked the LORD to anger. [20]Josiah slaughtered all the priests of those high places on the altars and burned human bones on them. Then he went back to Jerusalem.

[21]The king gave this order to all the people: "Celebrate the Passover to the LORD your God, as it is written in this Book of the Covenant." [22]Not since the days of the judges who led Israel, nor throughout the days of the kings of Israel and the kings of Judah, had any such Passover been observed. [23]But in the eighteenth year of King Josiah, this Passover was celebrated to the LORD in Jerusalem.

[24]Furthermore, Josiah got rid of the mediums and spiritists, the household gods, the idols and all the other detestable things seen in Judah and Jerusalem. This he did to fulfil the requirements of the law written in the book that Hilkiah the priest had discovered in the temple of the LORD. [25]Neither before nor after Josiah was there a king like him who turned to the LORD as he did—with all his heart and with all his soul and with all his strength, in accordance with all the Law of Moses.

[26]Nevertheless, the LORD did not turn away from the heat of his fierce anger, which burned against Judah because of all that Manasseh had done to provoke him to anger. [27]So the LORD said, "I will remove Judah also from my presence as I removed Israel, and I will reject Jerusalem, the city I chose, and this temple, about which I said, 'There shall my Name be.'[d]"

[28]As for the other events of Josiah's reign, and all he did, are they not written in the book of the annals of the kings of Judah?

[29]While Josiah was king, Pharaoh Neco king of Egypt went up to the Euphrates River to help the king of Assyria. King Josiah marched out to meet him in battle, but Neco faced him and killed him at Megiddo. [30]Josiah's servants brought his body in a chariot from Megiddo to Jerusalem and buried him in his own tomb. And the people of the land took Jehoahaz son of Josiah and anointed him and made him king in place of his father.

Jehoahaz King of Judah

[31]Jehoahaz was twenty-three years old when he became king, and he reigned in Jerusalem for three months. His mother's name was Hamutal daughter of Jeremiah; she was from Libnah. [32]He did evil in the eyes of the LORD, just as his fathers had done. [33]Pharaoh Neco put him in chains at Riblah in the land of Hamath[e] so that he might not reign in Jerusalem, and he imposed on Judah a levy of a hundred talents[f] of silver and a talent[g] of gold. [34]Pharaoh Neco made Eliakim son of Josiah king in place of his father Josiah and changed Eliakim's name to Jehoiakim. But he took Jehoahaz and carried him off to Egypt, and there he died. [35]Jehoiakim paid Pharaoh Neco the silver and gold he demanded. In order to do so, he taxed the land and exacted the silver and gold from the people of the land according to their assessments.

Jehoiakim King of Judah

[36]Jehoiakim was twenty-five years old when he became king, and he reigned in Jerusalem for eleven years. His mother's name was Zebidah daughter of Pedaiah; she was from Rumah. [37]And he did evil in the eyes of the LORD, just as his fathers had done.

24 During Jehoiakim's reign, Nebuchadnezzar king of Babylon invaded the land, and Jehoiakim became his vassal for three years. But then he changed his mind and rebelled against Nebuchadnezzar. [2]The LORD sent Babylonian,[a] Aramean, Moabite and Ammonite raiders against him. He sent them to destroy Judah, in accordance with the word of the LORD proclaimed by his servants the prophets. [3]Surely these things happened to Judah according to the LORD's

---

[d]27 1 Kings 8:29　　[e]33 Hebrew; Septuagint (see also 2 Chron. 36:3) *Neco at Riblah in Hamath removed him*
[f]33 That is, about 3½ tons (about 3.4 metric tons)　　[g]33 That is, about 75 pounds (about 34 kilograms)
[a]2 Or *Chaldean*

command, in order to remove them from his presence because of the sins of Manasseh and all he had done, [4]including the shedding of innocent blood. For he had filled Jerusalem with innocent blood, and the LORD was not willing to forgive.

[5]As for the other events of Jehoiakim's reign, and all he did, are they not written in the book of the annals of the kings of Judah? [6]Jehoiakim rested with his fathers. And Jehoiachin his son succeeded him as king.

[7]The king of Egypt did not march out from his own country again, because the king of Babylon had taken all his territory, from the Wadi of Egypt to the Euphrates River.

Jehoiachin King of Judah

[8]Jehoiachin was eighteen years old when he became king, and he reigned in Jerusalem for three months. His mother's name was Nehushta daughter of Elnathan; she was from Jerusalem. [9]He did evil in the eyes of the LORD, just as his father had done.

[10]At that time the officers of Nebuchadnezzar king of Babylon advanced on Jerusalem and laid siege to it, [11]and Nebuchadnezzar himself came up to the city while his officers were besieging it. [12]Jehoiachin king of Judah, his mother, his attendants, his nobles and his officials all surrendered to him.

In the eighth year of the reign of the king of Babylon, he took Jehoiachin prisoner. [13]As the LORD had declared, Nebuchadnezzar removed all the treasures from the temple of the LORD and from the royal palace, and took away all the gold articles that Solomon king of Israel had made for the temple of the LORD. [14]He carried into exile all Jerusalem: all the officers and fighting men, and all the craftsmen and artisans—a total of ten thousand. Only the poorest people of the land were left.

[15]Nebuchadnezzar took Jehoiachin captive to Babylon. He also took from Jerusalem to Babylon the king's mother, his wives, his officials and the leading men of the land. [16]The king of Babylon also deported to Babylon the entire force of seven thousand fighting men, strong and fit for war, and a thousand craftsmen and artisans. [17]He made Mattaniah, Jehoiachin's uncle, king in his place and changed his name to Zedekiah.

Zedekiah King of Judah

[18]Zedekiah was twenty-one years old when he became king, and he reigned in Jerusalem for eleven years. His mother's name was Hamutal daughter of Jeremiah; she was from Libnah. [19]He did evil in the eyes of the LORD, just as Jehoiakim had done. [20]It was because of the LORD's anger that all this happened to Jerusalem and Judah, and in the end he thrust them from his presence.

The Fall of Jerusalem

Now Zedekiah rebelled against the king of Babylon.

25 So in the ninth year of Zedekiah's reign, on the tenth day of the tenth month, Nebuchadnezzar king of Babylon marched against Jerusalem with his whole army. He encamped outside the city and built siege works all around it. [2]The city was kept under siege until the eleventh year of King Zedekiah. [3]By the ninth day of the ⌊fourth⌋[a] month the famine in the city had become so severe that there was no food for the people to eat. [4]Then the city wall was broken through, and the whole army fled at night through the gate between the two walls near the king's garden, though the Babylonians[b] were surrounding the city. They fled towards the Arabah,[c] [5]but the Babylonian[d] army pursued the king and overtook him in the plains of Jericho. All his soldiers were separated from him and scattered, [6]and he was captured. He was taken to the king of Babylon at Riblah, where sentence was pronounced on him. [7]They killed the sons of Zedekiah before his eyes. Then they put out his eyes, bound him with bronze shackles and took him to Babylon.

---

*a*3 See Jer. 52:6.   *b*4 Or *Chaldeans*; also in verses 13, 25 and 26   *c*4 Or *the Jordan Valley*
*d*5 Or *Chaldean*; also in verses 10 and 24

⁸On the seventh day of the fifth month, in the nineteenth year of Nebuchadnezzar king of Babylon, Nebuzaradan commander of the imperial guard, an official of the king of Babylon, came to Jerusalem. ⁹He set fire to the temple of the LORD, the royal palace and all the houses of Jerusalem. Every important building he burned down. ¹⁰The whole Babylonian army, under the commander of the imperial guard, broke down the walls around Jerusalem. ¹¹Nebuzaradan the commander of the guard carried into exile the people who remained in the city, along with the rest of the populace and those who had gone over to the king of Babylon. ¹²But the commander left behind some of the poorest people of the land to work the vineyards and fields.

¹³The Babylonians broke up the bronze pillars, the movable stands and the bronze Sea that were at the temple of the LORD and they carried the bronze to Babylon. ¹⁴They also took away the pots, shovels, wick trimmers, dishes and all the bronze articles used in the temple service. ¹⁵The commander of the imperial guard took away the censers and sprinkling bowls— all that were made of pure gold or silver.

¹⁶The bronze from the two pillars, the Sea and the movable stands, which Solomon had made for the temple of the LORD, was more than could be weighed. ¹⁷Each pillar was twenty-seven feet^e high. The bronze capital on top of one pillar was four and a half feet^f high and was decorated with a network and pomegranates of bronze all around. The other pillar, with its network, was similar.

¹⁸The commander of the guard took as prisoners Seraiah the chief priest, Zephaniah the priest next in rank and the three doorkeepers. ¹⁹Of those still in the city, he took the officer in charge of the fighting men and five royal advisers. He also took the secretary who was chief officer in charge of conscripting the people of the land and sixty of his men who were found

in the city. ²⁰Nebuzaradan the commander took them all and brought them to the king of Babylon at Riblah. ²¹There at Riblah, in the land of Hamath, the king had them executed.

So Judah went into captivity, away from her land.

²²Nebuchadnezzar king of Babylon appointed Gedaliah son of Ahikam, the son of Shaphan, to be over the people he had left behind in Judah. ²³When all the army officers and their men heard that the king of Babylon had appointed Gedaliah as governor, they came to Gedaliah at Mizpah—Ishmael son of Nethaniah, Johanan son of Kareah, Seraiah son of Tanhumeth the Netophathite, Jaazaniah the son of the Maacathite, and their men. ²⁴Gedaliah took an oath to reassure them and their men. "Do not be afraid of the Babylonian officials," he said. "Settle down in the land and serve the king of Babylon, and it will go well with you."

²⁵In the seventh month, however, Ishmael son of Nethaniah, the son of Elishama, who was of royal blood, came with ten men and assassinated Gedaliah and also the men of Judah and the Babylonians who were with him at Mizpah. ²⁶At this, all the people from the least to the greatest, together with the army officers, fled to Egypt for fear of the Babylonians.

Jehoiachin Released

²⁷In the thirty-seventh year of the exile of Jehoiachin king of Judah, in the year Evil-Merodach^g became king of Babylon, he released Jehoiachin from prison on the twenty-seventh day of the twelfth month. ²⁸He spoke kindly to him and gave him a seat of honour higher than those of the other kings who were with him in Babylon. ²⁹So Jehoiachin put aside his prison clothes and for the rest of his life ate regularly at the king's table. ³⁰Day by day the king gave Jehoiachin a regular allowance as long as he lived.

---

^{e}17 Hebrew *eighteen cubits* (about 8.2 metres) ^{f}17 Hebrew *three cubits* (about 1.4 metres)
^{g}27 Also called *Amel-Marduk*

1 Chronicles

Historical Records From Adam to Abraham

To Noah's Sons

1 Adam, Seth, Enosh, ²Kenan, Mahalalel, Jared, ³Enoch, Methuselah,
Lamech, Noah.

⁴The sons of Noah:ᵃ
Shem, Ham and Japheth.

The Japhethites

⁵The sonsᵇ of Japheth:
Gomer, Magog, Madai, Javan,
Tubal, Meshech and Tiras.

⁶The sons of Gomer:
Ashkenaz, Riphathᶜ and Togarmah.

⁷The sons of Javan:
Elishah, Tarshish, the Kittim and
the Rodanim.

The Hamites

⁸The sons of Ham:
Cush, Mizraim,ᵈ Put and Canaan.

⁹The sons of Cush:
Seba, Havilah, Sabta, Raamah and
Sabteca.

The sons of Raamah:
Sheba and Dedan.

¹⁰Cush was the fatherᵉ of
Nimrod, who grew to be a mighty
warrior on earth.

¹¹Mizraim was the father of
the Ludites, Anamites, Lehabites,
Naphtuhites, ¹²Pathrusites, Caslu-
hites (from whom the Philistines
came) and Caphtorites.

¹³Canaan was the father of
Sidon his firstborn,ᶠ and of the
Hittites, ¹⁴Jebusites, Amorites,
Girgashites, ¹⁵Hivites, Arkites,
Sinites, ¹⁶Arvadites, Zemarites
and Hamathites.

The Semites

¹⁷The sons of Shem:
Elam, Asshur, Arphaxad, Lud and
Aram.

The sons of Aram:ᵍ
Uz, Hul, Gether and Meshech.

¹⁸Arphaxad was the father of Shelah,
and Shelah the father of Eber.

¹⁹Two sons were born to Eber:
One was named Peleg,ʰ because in
his time the earth was divided; his
brother was named Joktan.

²⁰Joktan was the father of
Almodad, Sheleph, Hazarmaveth,
Jerah, ²¹Hadoram, Uzal, Diklah,
²²Obal,ⁱ Abimael, Sheba, ²³Ophir,

ᵃ4 Septuagint; Hebrew does not have The sons of Noah:
ᵇ5 Sons may mean descendants or successors or nations; also in verses 6–10, 17 and 20.
ᶜ6 Many Hebrew manuscripts and Vulgate (see also Septuagint and Gen. 10:3); most Hebrew manuscripts Diphath
ᵈ8 That is, Egypt; also in verse 11
ᵉ10 Father may mean ancestor or predecessor or founder; also in verses 11, 13, 18 and 20.
ᶠ13 Or of the Sidonians, the foremost
ᵍ17 One Hebrew manuscript and some Septuagint manuscripts (see also Gen. 10:23); most Hebrew manuscripts do not
have this line.   ʰ19 Peleg means division.
ⁱ22 Some Hebrew manuscripts and Syriac (see also Gen. 10:28); most Hebrew manuscripts Ebal

Havilah and Jobab. All these were sons of Joktan.

²⁴Shem, Arphaxad,ʲ Shelah,
²⁵Eber, Peleg, Reu,
²⁶Serug, Nahor, Terah
²⁷and Abram (that is, Abraham).

The Family of Abraham

²⁸The sons of Abraham:
Isaac and Ishmael.

Descendants of Hagar

²⁹These were their descendants:
Nebaioth the firstborn of Ishmael, Kedar, Adbeel, Mibsam, ³⁰Mishma, Dumah, Massa, Hadad, Tema, ³¹Jetur, Naphish and Kedemah. These were the sons of Ishmael.

Descendants of Keturah

³²The sons born to Keturah,
Abraham's concubine:
Zimran, Jokshan, Medan, Midian, Ishbak and Shuah.
The sons of Jokshan:
Sheba and Dedan.
³³The sons of Midian:
Ephah, Epher, Hanoch, Abida and Eldaah.
All these were descendants of Keturah.

Descendants of Sarah

³⁴Abraham was the father of Isaac.
The sons of Isaac:
Esau and Israel.

Esau's Sons

³⁵The sons of Esau:
Eliphaz, Reuel, Jeush, Jalam and Korah.
³⁶The sons of Eliphaz:

Teman, Omar, Zepho,ᵏ Gatam and Kenaz;
by Timna: Amalek.ˡ
³⁷The sons of Reuel:
Nahath, Zerah, Shammah and Mizzah.

The People of Seir in Edom

³⁸The sons of Seir:
Lotan, Shobal, Zibeon, Anah, Dishon, Ezer and Dishan.
³⁹The sons of Lotan:
Hori and Homam. Timna was Lotan's sister.
⁴⁰The sons of Shobal:
Alvan,ᵐ Manahath, Ebal, Shepho and Onam.
The sons of Zibeon:
Aiah and Anah.
⁴¹The son of Anah:
Dishon.
The sons of Dishon:
Hemdan,ⁿ Eshban, Ithran and Keran.
⁴²The sons of Ezer:
Bilhan, Zaavan and Akan.ᵒ
The sons of Dishan:ᵖ
Uz and Aran.

The Rulers of Edom

⁴³These were the kings who reigned in Edom before any Israelite king reigned:�q
Bela son of Beor, whose city was named Dinhabah.
⁴⁴When Bela died, Jobab son of Zerah from Bozrah succeeded him as king.
⁴⁵When Jobab died, Husham from the land of the Temanites succeeded him as king.
⁴⁶When Husham died, Hadad son of Bedad, who defeated Midian in the

---

ʲ24 Hebrew; some Septuagint manuscripts *Arphaxad, Cainan* (see also note at Gen. 11:10)
ᵏ36 Many Hebrew manuscripts, some Septuagint manuscripts and Syriac (see also Gen. 36:11); most Hebrew manuscripts *Zephi*
ˡ36 Some Septuagint manuscripts (see also Gen. 36:12); Hebrew *Gatam, Kenaz, Timna and Amalek*
ᵐ40 Many Hebrew manuscripts and some Septuagint manuscripts (see also Gen. 36:23); most Hebrew manuscripts *Alian*
ⁿ41 Many Hebrew manuscripts and some Septuagint manuscripts (see also Gen. 36:26); most Hebrew manuscripts *Hamran*
ᵒ42 Many Hebrew and Septuagint manuscripts (see also Gen. 36:27); most Hebrew manuscripts *Zaavan, Jaakan*
ᵖ42 Hebrew *Dishon*, a variant of *Dishan*   q43 Or *before an Israelite king reigned over them*

country of Moab, succeeded him as king. His city was named Avith. ⁴⁷When Hadad died, Samlah from Masrekah succeeded him as king. ⁴⁸When Samlah died, Shaul from Rehoboth on the river^r succeeded him as king. ⁴⁹When Shaul died, Baal-Hanan son of Acbor succeeded him as king. ⁵⁰When Baal-Hanan died, Hadad succeeded him as king. His city was named Pau,^{s} and his wife's name was Mehetabel daughter of Matred, the daughter of Me-Zahab. ⁵¹Hadad also died.

The chiefs of Edom were:

Timna, Alvah, Jetheth, ⁵²Oholibamah, Elah, Pinon, ⁵³Kenaz, Teman, Mibzar, ⁵⁴Magdiel and Iram. These were the chiefs of Edom.

Israel's Sons

2 These were the sons of Israel: Reuben, Simeon, Levi, Judah, Issachar, Zebulun, ²Dan, Joseph, Benjamin, Napthali, Gad and Asher.

Judah

To Hezron's Sons

³The sons of Judah:

Er, Onan and Shelah. These three were born to him by a Canaanite woman, the daughter of Shua. Er, Judah's firstborn, was wicked in the LORD's sight; so the LORD put him to death. ⁴Tamar, Judah's daughter-in-law, bore him Perez and Zerah. Judah had five sons in all.

⁵The sons of Perez:

Hezron and Hamul.

⁶The sons of Zerah:

Zimri, Ethan, Heman, Calcol and Darda^a—five in all.

⁷The son of Carmi:

Achar,^{b} who brought trouble on Israel by violating the ban on taking devoted things.^{c}

⁸The son of Ethan:

Azariah.

⁹The sons born to Hezron were:

Jerahmeel, Ram and Caleb.^{d}

From Ram Son of Hezron

¹⁰Ram was the father of

Amminadab, and Amminadab the father of Nahshon, the leader of the people of Judah. ¹¹Nahshon was the father of Salmon,^{e} Salmon the father of Boaz, ¹²Boaz the father of Obed and Obed the father of Jesse.

¹³Jesse was the father of

Eliab his firstborn; the second son was Abinadab, the third Shimea, ¹⁴the fourth Nethanel, the fifth Raddai, ¹⁵the sixth Ozem and the seventh David. ¹⁶Their sisters were Zeruiah and Abigail. Zeruiah's three sons were Abishai, Joab and Asahel. ¹⁷Abigail was the mother of Amasa, whose father was Jether the Ishmaelite.

Caleb Son of Hezron

¹⁸Caleb son of Hezron had children by his wife Azubah (and by Jerioth). These were her sons: Jesher, Shobab and Ardon. ¹⁹When Azubah died, Caleb married Ephrath, who bore him Hur. ²⁰Hur was the father of Uri, and Uri the father of Bezalel.

²¹Later, Hezron lay with the daughter of Makir the father of Gilead (he had married her when he was sixty years old), and she bore him Segub. ²²Segub was the father of Jair, who controlled twenty-three

---

^{r}48 Possibly the Euphrates
^{s}50 Many Hebrew manuscripts, some Septuagint manuscripts, Vulgate and Syriac (see also Gen. 36:39); most Hebrew manuscripts *Pai*
^{a}6 Many Hebrew manuscripts, some Septuagint manuscripts and Syriac (see also 1 Kings 4:31); most Hebrew manuscripts *Dara* ^{b}7 *Achar* means *trouble*; *Achar* is called *Achan* in Joshua.
^{c}7 The Hebrew term refers to the irrevocable giving over of things or persons to the LORD, often by totally destroying them. ^{d}9 Hebrew *Kelubai*, a variant of *Caleb* ^{e}11 Septuagint (see also Ruth 4:21); Hebrew *Salma*

towns in Gilead. ²³(But Geshur and Aram captured Havvoth Jair,*f* as well as Kenath with its surrounding settlements—sixty towns.) All these were descendants of Makir the father of Gilead.

²⁴After Hezron died in Caleb Ephrathah, Abijah the wife of Hezron bore him Ashhur the father*g* of Tekoa.

Jerahmeel Son of Hezron

²⁵The sons of Jerahmeel the firstborn of Hezron:
Ram his firstborn, Bunah, Oren, Ozem and*h* Ahijah. ²⁶Jerahmeel had another wife, whose name was Atarah; she was the mother of Onam.

²⁷The sons of Ram the firstborn of Jerahmeel:
Maaz, Jamin and Eker.

²⁸The sons of Onam:
Shammai and Jada.
The sons of Shammai:
Nadab and Abishur.

²⁹Abishur's wife was named Abihail, who bore him Ahban and Molid.

³⁰The sons of Nadab:
Seled and Appaim. Seled died without children.

³¹The son of Appaim:
Ishi, who was the father of Sheshan.
Sheshan was the father of Ahlai.

³²The sons of Jada, Shammai's brother:
Jether and Jonathan. Jether died without children.

³³The sons of Jonathan:
Peleth and Zaza.
These were the descendants of Jerahmeel.

³⁴Sheshan had no sons—only daughters.
He had an Egyptian servant named Jarha. ³⁵Sheshan gave his daughter in marriage to his servant Jarha, and she bore him Attai.

³⁶Attai was the father of Nathan, Nathan the father of Zabad,

³⁷Zabad the father of Ephlal, Ephlal the father of Obed,

³⁸Obed the father of Jehu, Jehu the father of Azariah,

³⁹Azariah the father of Helez, Helez the father of Eleasah,

⁴⁰Eleasah the father of Sismai, Sismai the father of Shallum,

⁴¹Shallum the father of Jekamiah, and Jekamiah the father of Elishama.

The Clans of Caleb

⁴²The sons of Caleb the brother of Jerahmeel:
Mesha his firstborn, who was the father of Ziph, and his son Mareshah,*i* who was the father of Hebron.

⁴³The sons of Hebron:
Korah, Tappuah, Rekem and Shema. ⁴⁴Shema was the father of Raham, and Raham the father of Jorkeam. Rekem was the father of Shammai. ⁴⁵The son of Shammai was Maon, and Maon was the father of Beth Zur.

⁴⁶Caleb's concubine Ephah was the mother of Haran, Moza and Gazez. Haran was the father of Gazez.

⁴⁷The sons of Jahdai:
Regem, Jotham, Geshan, Pelet, Ephah and Shaaph.

⁴⁸Caleb's concubine Maacah was the mother of Sheber and Tirhanah. ⁴⁹She also gave birth to Shaaph the father of Madmannah and to Sheva the father of Macbenah and Gibea. Caleb's daughter was Acsah. ⁵⁰These were the descendants of Caleb.

The sons of Hur the firstborn of Ephrathah:
Shobal the father of Kiriath Jearim, ⁵¹Salma the father of Bethlehem, and Hareph the father of Beth Gader.

⁵²The descendants of Shobal the father of Kiriath Jearim were:

f23 Or *captured the settlements of Jair*
g24 *Father* may mean *civic leader* or *military leader*; also in verses 42, 45, 49–52 and possibly elsewhere.
h25 Or *Oren and Ozem, by*   *i42* The meaning of the Hebrew for this phrase is uncertain.

Haroeh, half the Manahathites,
⁵³and the clans of Kiriath Jearim:
the Ithrites, Puthites, Shumathites
and Mishraites. From these descended the Zorathites and Eshtaolites.

⁵⁴The descendants of Salma:
Bethlehem, the Netophathites,
Atroth Beth Joab, half the Manahathites, the Zorites, ⁵⁵and the
clans of scribes*j* who lived at Jabez:
the Tirathites, Shimeathites and
Sucathites. These are the Kenites
who came from Hammath, the
father of the house of Recab.*k*

The Sons of David

3 These were the sons of David born to
him in Hebron:
The firstborn was Amnon the son
of Ahinoam of Jezreel;
the second, Daniel the son of Abigail of Carmel;
²the third, Absalom the son of
Maacah daughter of Talmai king of
Geshur;
the fourth, Adonijah the son of
Haggith;
³the fifth, Shephatiah the son of
Abital;
and the sixth, Ithream, by his wife
Eglah.
⁴These six were born to David in
Hebron, where he reigned for
seven years and six months.
David reigned in Jerusalem for thirty-three years, ⁵and these were the children
born to him there:
Shammua,*a* Shobab, Nathan and
Solomon. These four were by
Bathsheba*b* daughter of Ammiel.
⁶There were also Ibhar, Elishua,*c*
Eliphelet, ⁷Nogah, Nepheg,
Japhia, ⁸Elishama, Eliada and
Eliphelet—nine in all. ⁹All these
were the sons of David, besides his
sons by his concubines. And Tamar
was their sister.

The Kings of Judah

¹⁰Solomon's son was Rehoboam,
Abijah his son,
Asa his son,
Jehoshaphat his son,
¹¹Jehoram*d* his son,
Ahaziah his son,
Joash his son,
¹²Amaziah his son,
Azariah his son,
Jotham his son,
¹³Ahaz his son,
Hezekiah his son,
Manasseh his son,
¹⁴Amon his son,
Josiah his son.
¹⁵The sons of Josiah:
Johanan the firstborn,
Jehoiakim the second son,
Zedekiah the third,
Shallum the fourth.
¹⁶The successors of Jehoiakim:
Jehoiachin*e* his son,
and Zedekiah.

The Royal Line After the Exile

¹⁷The descendants of Jehoiachin the
captive:
Shealtiel his son, ¹⁸Malkiram,
Pedaiah, Shenazzar, Jekamiah,
Hoshama and Nedabiah.
¹⁹The sons of Pedaiah:
Zerubbabel and Shimei.
The sons of Zerubbabel:
Meshullam and Hananiah.
Shelomith was their sister.
²⁰There were also five others:
Hashubah, Ohel, Berekiah, Hasadiah and Jushab-Hesed.
²¹The descendants of Hananiah:
Pelatiah and Jeshaiah, and the sons
of Rephaiah, of Arnan, of Obadiah
and of Shecaniah.
²²The descendants of Shecaniah:
Shemaiah and his sons:
Hattush, Igal, Bariah, Neariah and
Shaphat—six in all.
²³The sons of Neariah:

---

j55 Or *of the Sopherites*   *k55* Or *father of Beth Recab*
a5 Hebrew *Shimea*, a variant of *Shammua*
b5 One Hebrew manuscript and Vulgate (see also Septuagint and 2 Sam. 11:3); most Hebrew manuscripts *Bathshua*
c6 Two Hebrew manuscripts (see also 2 Sam. 5:15 and 1 Chron. 14:5); most Hebrew manuscripts *Elishama*
d11 Hebrew *Joram*, a variant of *Jehoram*   *e16* Hebrew *Jeconiah*, a variant of *Jehoiachin*; also in verse 17

Elioenai, Hizkiah and Azrikam—
three in all.

²⁴The sons of Elioenai:

Hodaviah, Eliashib, Pelaiah,
Akkub, Johanan, Delaiah and
Anani—seven in all.

Other Clans of Judah

4 The descendants of Judah:
Perez, Hezron, Carmi, Hur and
Shobal.

²Reaiah son of Shobal was the father
of Jahath, and Jahath the father of
Ahumai and Lahad. These were
the clans of the Zorathites.

³These were the sons*a* of Etam:

Jezreel, Ishma and Idbash. Their
sister was named Hazzelelponi.
⁴Penuel was the father of Gedor,
and Ezer the father of Hushah.

These were the descendants of Hur,
the firstborn of Ephrathah and
father*b* of Bethlehem.

⁵Ashhur the father of Tekoa had two
wives, Helah and Naarah.

⁶Naarah bore him Ahuzzam, Hepher,
Temeni and Haahashtari. These
were the descendants of Naarah.

⁷The sons of Helah:

Zereth, Zohar, Ethnan, ⁸and Koz,
who was the father of Anub and
Hazzobebah and of the clans of
Aharhel son of Harum.

⁹Jabez was more honourable than his
brothers. His mother had named him
Jabez,*c* saying, "I gave birth to him in
pain." ¹⁰Jabez cried out to the God of
Israel, "Oh, that you would bless me and
enlarge my territory! Let your hand be
with me, and keep me from harm so that I
will be free from pain." And God granted
his request.

¹¹Kelub, Shuhah's brother, was the
father of Mehir, who was the father
of Eshton. ¹²Eshton was the father
of Beth Rapha, Paseah and

Tehinnah the father of Ir Nahash.*d*
These were the men of Recah.

¹³The sons of Kenaz:

Othniel and Seraiah.

The sons of Othniel:

Hathath and Meonothai.*e* ¹⁴Meo-
nothai was the father of Ophrah.

Seraiah was the father of Joab, the
father of Ge Harashim.*f*
It was called this because its people
were craftsmen.

¹⁵The sons of Caleb son of Jephunneh:

Iru, Elah and Naam.

The son of Elah:

Kenaz.

¹⁶The sons of Jehallelel:

Ziph, Ziphah, Tiria and Asarel.

¹⁷The sons of Ezrah:

Jether, Mered, Epher and Jalon.
One of Mered's wives gave birth to
Miriam, Shammai and Ishbah the
father of Eshtemoa. ¹⁸(His Judean
wife gave birth to Jered the father
of Gedor, Heber the father of
Soco, and Jekuthiel the father of
Zanoah.) These were the children
of Pharaoh's daughter Bithiah,
whom Mered had married.

¹⁹The sons of Hodiah's wife, the sister
of Naham:

the father of Keilah the Garmite,
and Eshtemoa the Maacathite.

²⁰The sons of Shimon:

Amnon, Rinnah, Ben-Hanan and
Tilon.

The descendants of Ishi:

Zoheth and Ben-Zoheth.

²¹The sons of Shelah son of Judah:

Er the father of Lecah, Laadah the
father of Mareshah and the clans of
the linen workers at Beth Ashbea,
²²Jokim, the men of Cozeba, and
Joash and Saraph, who ruled in
Moab and Jashubi Lehem. (These
records are from ancient times.)
²³They were the potters who lived
at Netaim and Gederah; they

---

a3 Some Septuagint manuscripts (see also Vulgate); Hebrew *father*
b4 Father may mean *civic leader* or *military leader*; also in verses 12, 14, 17, 18 and possibly elsewhere.
c9 Jabez sounds like the Hebrew for *pain*.   *d12* Or *of the city of Nahash*
e13 Some Septuagint manuscripts and Vulgate; Hebrew does not have *and Meonothai.*
f14 Ge Harashim means *valley of craftsmen.*

stayed there and worked for the king.

Simeon

²⁴The descendants of Simeon:

Nemuel, Jamin, Jarib, Zerah and Shaul;
²⁵Shallum was Shaul's son, Mibsam his son and Mishma his son.
²⁶The descendants of Mishma:
Hammuel his son, Zaccur his son and Shimei his son.

²⁷Shimei had sixteen sons and six daughters, but his brothers did not have many children; so their entire clan did not become as numerous as the people of Judah. ²⁸They lived in Beersheba, Moladah, Hazar Shual, ²⁹Bilhah, Ezem, Tolad, ³⁰Bethuel, Hormah, Ziklag, ³¹Beth Marcaboth, Hazar Susim, Beth Biri and Shaaraim. These were their towns until the reign of David. ³²Their surrounding villages were Etam, Ain, Rimmon, Token and Ashan—five towns—³³and all the villages around these towns as far as Baalath.ᵍ These were their settlements. And they kept a genealogical record.

³⁴Meshobab, Jamlech, Joshah son of Amaziah, ³⁵Joel, Jehu son of Joshibiah, the son of Seraiah, the son of Asiel, ³⁶also Elioenai, Jaakobah, Jeshohaiah, Asaiah, Adiel, Jesimiel, Benaiah, ³⁷and Ziza son of Shiphi, the son of Allon, the son of Jedaiah, the son of Shimri, the son of Shemaiah.

³⁸The men listed above by name were leaders of their clans. Their families increased greatly, ³⁹and they went to the outskirts of Gedor to the east of the valley in search of pasture for their flocks. ⁴⁰They found rich, good pasture, and the land was spacious, peaceful and quiet. Some Hamites had lived there formerly.

⁴¹The men whose names were listed came in the days of Hezekiah king of Judah. They attacked the Hamites in their dwellings and also the Meunites who were there and completely destroyedʰ them, as is evident to this day. Then they settled in their place, because there was pasture for their flocks. ⁴²And five hundred of these Simeonites, led by Pelatiah, Neariah, Rephaiah and Uzziel, the sons of Ishi, invaded the hill country of Seir. ⁴³They killed the remaining Amalekites who had escaped, and they have lived there to this day.

Reuben

5 The sons of Reuben the firstborn of Israel (he was the firstborn, but when he defiled his father's marriage bed, his rights as firstborn were given to the sons of Joseph son of Israel; so he could not be listed in the genealogical record in accordance with his birthright, ²and though Judah was the strongest of his brothers and a ruler came from him, the rights of the firstborn belonged to Joseph)—³the sons of Reuben the firstborn of Israel:

Hanoch, Pallu, Hezron and Carmi.
⁴The descendants of Joel:
Shemaiah his son, Gog his son, Shimei his son, ⁵Micah his son, Reaiah his son, Baal his son,
⁶and Beerah his son, whom Tiglath-Pileserᵃ king of Assyria took into exile. Beerah was a leader of the Reubenites.

⁷Their relatives by clans, listed according to their genealogical records:

Jeiel the chief, Zechariah, ⁸and Bela son of Azaz, the son of Shema, the son of Joel. They settled in the area from Aroer to Nebo and Baal Meon. ⁹To the east they occupied the land up to the edge of the desert that extends to the Euphrates River, because their livestock had increased in Gilead.

¹⁰During Saul's reign they waged war against the Hagrites, who were defeated at their hands; they occupied the dwellings of the Hagrites

---

ᵍ33 Some Septuagint manuscripts (see also Joshua 19:8); Hebrew *Baal*
ʰ41 The Hebrew term refers to the irrevocable giving over of things or persons to the LORD, often by totally destroying them.   ᵃ6 Hebrew *Tilgath-Pilneser*, a variant of *Tiglath-Pileser*; also in verse 26

throughout the entire region east of Gilead.

Gad

11The Gadites lived next to them in Bashan, as far as Salecah:
12Joel was the chief, Shapham the second, then Janai and Shaphat, in Bashan.
13Their relatives, by families, were:
Michael, Meshullam, Sheba, Jorai, Jacan, Zia and Eber—seven in all.
14These were the sons of Abihail son of Huri, the son of Jaroah, the son of Gilead, the son of Michael, the son of Jeshishai, the son of Jahdo, the son of Buz.
15Ahi son of Abdiel, the son of Guni, was head of their family.
16The Gadites lived in Gilead, in Bashan and its outlying villages, and on all the pasturelands of Sharon as far as they extended.
17All these were entered in the genealogical records during the reigns of Jotham king of Judah and Jeroboam king of Israel.

18The Reubenites, the Gadites and the half-tribe of Manasseh had 44,760 men ready for military service—able-bodied men who could handle shield and sword, who could use a bow, and who were trained for battle. 19They waged war against the Hagrites, Jetur, Naphish and Nodab. 20They were helped in fighting them, and God handed the Hagrites and all their allies over to them, because they cried out to him during the battle. He answered their prayers, because they trusted in him. 21They seized the livestock of the Hagrites—fifty thousand camels, two hundred and fifty thousand sheep and two thousand donkeys. They also took one hundred thousand people captive, 22and many others fell slain, because the battle was God's. And they occupied the land until the exile.

The Half-Tribe of Manasseh

23The people of the half-tribe of Manasseh were numerous; they settled in the land from Bashan to Baal Hermon, that is, to Senir (Mount Hermon).

24These were the heads of their families: Epher, Ishi, Eliel, Azriel, Jeremiah, Hodaviah and Jahdiel. They were brave warriors, famous men, and heads of their families. 25But they were unfaithful to the God of their fathers and prostituted themselves to the gods of the peoples of the land, whom God had destroyed before them. 26So the God of Israel stirred up the spirit of Pul king of Assyria (that is, Tiglath-Pileser king of Assyria), who took the Reubenites, the Gadites and the half-tribe of Manasseh into exile. He took them to Halah, Habor, Hara and the river of Gozan, where they are to this day.

Levi

6 The sons of Levi:
Gershon, Kohath and Merari.
2The sons of Kohath:
Amram, Izhar, Hebron and Uzziel.
3The children of Amram:
Aaron, Moses and Miriam.
The sons of Aaron:
Nadab, Abihu, Eleazar and Ithamar.
4Eleazar was the father of Phinehas, Phinehas the father of Abishua,
5Abishua the father of Bukki, Bukki the father of Uzzi,
6Uzzi the father of Zerahiah, Zerahiah the father of Meraioth,
7Meraioth the father of Amariah, Amariah the father of Ahitub,
8Ahitub the father of Zadok, Zadok the father of Ahimaaz,
9Ahimaaz the father of Azariah, Azariah the father of Johanan,
10Johanan the father of Azariah (it was he who served as priest in the temple Solomon built in Jerusalem),
11Azariah the father of Amariah, Amariah the father of Ahitub,
12Ahitub the father of Zadok, Zadok the father of Shallum,
13Shallum the father of Hilkiah, Hilkiah the father of Azariah,
14Azariah the father of Seraiah, and

Seraiah the father of Jehozadak.

¹⁵Jehozadak was deported when the LORD sent Judah and Jerusalem into exile by the hand of Nebuchadnezzar.

¹⁶The sons of Levi:
Gershon,ᵃ Kohath and Merari.

¹⁷These are the names of the sons of Gershon:
Libni and Shimei.

¹⁸The sons of Kohath:
Amram, Izhar, Hebron and Uzziel.

¹⁹The sons of Merari:
Mahli and Mushi.

These are the clans of the Levites listed according to their fathers:

²⁰Of Gershon:
Libni his son, Jehath his son, Zimmah his son, ²¹Joah his son, Iddo his son, Zerah his son and Jeatherai his son.

²²The descendants of Kohath:
Amminadab his son, Korah his son, Assir his son, ²³Elkanah his son, Ebiasaph his son, Assir his son, ²⁴Tahath his son, Uriel his son, Uzziah his son and Shaul his son.

²⁵The descendants of Elkanah:
Amasai, Ahimoth, ²⁶Elkanah his son,ᵇ Zophai his son, Nahath his son, ²⁷Eliab his son, Jeroham his son, Elkanah his son and Samuel his son.ᶜ

²⁸The sons of Samuel:
Joelᵈ the firstborn and Abijah the second son.

²⁹The descendants of Merari:
Mahli, Libni his son, Shimei his son, Uzzah his son, ³⁰Shimea his son, Haggiah his son and Asaiah his son.

The Temple Musicians

³¹These are the men David put in charge of the music in the house of the LORD after the ark came to rest there. ³²They ministered with music before the tabernacle, the Tent of Meeting, until Solomon built the temple of the LORD in Jerusalem. They performed their duties according to the regulations laid down for them.

³³Here are the men who served, together with their sons:

From the Kohathites:
Heman, the musician, the son of Joel, the son of Samuel, ³⁴the son of Elkanah, the son of Jeroham, the son of Eliel, the son of Toah, ³⁵the son of Zuph, the son of Elkanah, the son of Mahath, the son of Amasai, ³⁶the son of Elkanah, the son of Joel, the son of Azariah, the son of Zephaniah, ³⁷the son of Tahath, the son of Assir, the son of Ebiasaph, the son of Korah, ³⁸the son of Izhar, the son of Kohath, the son of Levi, the son of Israel;

³⁹and Heman's associate Asaph, who served at his right hand:
Asaph son of Berekiah, the son of Shimea, ⁴⁰the son of Michael, the son of Baaseiah,ᵉ the son of Malkijah, ⁴¹the son of Ethni, the son of Zerah, the son of Adaiah, ⁴²the son of Ethan, the son of Zimmah, the son of Shimei, ⁴³the son of Jahath, the son of Gershon, the son of Levi;

⁴⁴and from their associates, the Merarites, at his left hand:
Ethan son of Kishi, the son of Abdi, the son of Malluch, ⁴⁵the son of Hashabiah, the son of Amaziah, the son of Hilkiah,

---

ᵃ16 Hebrew *Gershom*, a variant of *Gershon*; also in verses 17, 20, 43, 62 and 71
ᵇ26 Some Hebrew manuscripts, Septuagint and Syriac; most Hebrew manuscripts *Ahimoth* ²⁶ and *Elkanah. The sons of Elkanah:* ᶜ27 Some Septuagint manuscripts (see also 1 Sam. 1:19, 20 and 1 Chron. 6:33, 34); Hebrew does not have *and Samuel his son.*
ᵈ28 Some Septuagint manuscripts and Syriac (see also 1 Sam. 8:2 and 1 Chron. 6:33); Hebrew does not have *Joel.*
ᵉ40 Most Hebrew manuscripts; some Hebrew manuscripts, one Septuagint manuscript and Syriac *Maaseiah*

46the son of Amzi, the son of Bani,
the son of Shemer, 47the son of Mahli,
the son of Mushi, the son of Merari,
the son of Levi.

48Their fellow Levites were assigned to all the other duties of the tabernacle, the house of God. 49But Aaron and his descendants were the ones who presented offerings on the altar of burnt offering and on the altar of incense in connection with all that was done in the Most Holy Place, making atonement for Israel, in accordance with all that Moses the servant of God had commanded.

50These were the descendants of Aaron:
Eleazar his son, Phinehas his son,
Abishua his son, 51Bukki his son,
Uzzi his son, Zerahiah his son,
52Meraioth his son, Amariah his son,
Ahitub his son, 53Zadok his son
and Ahimaaz his son.

54These were the locations of their settlements allotted as their territory (they were assigned to the descendants of Aaron who were from the Kohathite clan, because the first lot was for them):
55They were given Hebron in Judah with its surrounding pasture-lands. 56But the fields and villages around the city were given to Caleb son of Jephunneh.
57So the descendants of Aaron were given Hebron (a city of refuge), and Libnah,f Jattir, Eshtemoa, 58Hilen, Debir, 59Ashan, Juttahg and Beth Shemesh, together with their pasture-lands. 60And from the tribe of Benjamin they were given Gibeon,h Geba, Alemeth and Anathoth, together with their pasture-lands.
These towns, which were distributed among the Kohathite clans, were thirteen in all.

61The rest of Kohath's descendants were allotted ten towns from the clans of half the tribe of Manasseh.
62The descendants of Gershon, clan by clan, were allotted thirteen towns from the tribes of Issachar, Asher and Naphtali, and from the part of the tribe of Manasseh that is in Bashan.
63The descendants of Merari, clan by clan, were allotted twelve towns from the tribes of Reuben, Gad and Zebulun.
64So the Israelites gave the Levites these towns and their pasture-lands. 65From the tribes of Judah, Simeon and Benjamin they allotted the previously named towns.
66Some of the Kohathite clans were given as their territory towns from the tribe of Ephraim.
67In the hill country of Ephraim they were given Shechem (a city of refuge), and Gezer,i 68Jokmeam, Beth Horon, 69Aijalon and Gath Rimmon, together with their pasture-lands.
70And from half the tribe of Manasseh the Israelites gave Aner and Bileam, together with their pasture-lands, to the rest of the Kohathite clans.

71The Gershonites received the following:
From the clan of the half-tribe of Manasseh
they received Golan in Bashan and also Ashtaroth, together with their pasture-lands:
72from the tribe of Issachar
they received Kedesh, Daberath, 73Ramoth and Anem, together with their pasture-lands;
74from the tribe of Asher
they received Mashal, Abdon, 75Hukok and Rehob, together with their pasture-lands;
76and from the tribe of Naphtali
they received Kedesh in Galilee, Hammon and Kiriathaim, together with their pasture-lands.

f57 See Joshua 21:13; Hebrew *given the cities of refuge: Hebron, Libnah.*
g59 Syriac (see also Septuagint and Joshua 21:16); Hebrew does not have *Juttah.*
h60 See Joshua 21:17; Hebrew does not have *Gibeon.*
i67 See Joshua 21:21; Hebrew *given the cities of refuge: Shechem, Gezer.*

77The Merarites (the rest of the Levites) received the following:

From the tribe of Zebulun they received Jokneam, Kartah,[j] Rimmono and Tabor, together with their pasture-lands;

78from the tribe of Reuben across the Jordan east of Jericho they received Bezer in the desert, Jahzah, 79Kedemoth and Mephaath, together with their pasture-lands;

80and from the tribe of Gad they received Ramoth in Gilead, Mahanaim, 81Heshbon and Jazer, together with their pasture-lands.

Issachar

7 The sons of Issachar:
Tola, Puah, Jashub and Shimron—four in all.

2The sons of Tola:
Uzzi, Rephaiah, Jeriel, Jahmai, Ibsam and Samuel—heads of their families. During the reign of David, the descendants of Tola listed as fighting men in their genealogy numbered 22,600.

3The son of Uzzi:
Izrahiah.

The sons of Izrahiah:
Michael, Obadiah, Joel and Isshiah. All five of them were chiefs. 4According to their family genealogy, they had 36,000 men ready for battle, for they had many wives and children.

5The relatives who were fighting men belonging to all the clans of Issachar, as listed in their genealogy, were 87,000 in all.

Benjamin

6Three sons of Benjamin:
Bela, Beker and Jediael.

7The sons of Bela:
Ezbon, Uzzi, Uzziel, Jerimoth and Iri, heads of families—five in all.

Their genealogical record listed 22,034 fighting men.

8The sons of Beker:
Zemirah, Joash, Eliezer, Elioenai, Omri, Jeremoth, Abijah, Anathoth and Alemeth. All these were the sons of Beker. 9Their genealogical record listed the heads of families and 20,200 fighting men.

10The son of Jediael:
Bilhan.

The sons of Bilhan:
Jeush, Benjamin, Ehud, Kenaanah, Zethan, Tarshish and Ahishahar. 11All these sons of Jediael were heads of families. There were 17,200 fighting men ready to go out to war.

12The Shuppites and Huppites were the descendants of Ir, and the Hushites the descendants of Aher.

Naphtali

13The sons of Naphtali:
Jahziel, Guni, Jezer and Shillem[a]—the descendants of Bilhah.

Manasseh

14The descendants of Manasseh:
Asriel was his descendant through his Aramean concubine. She gave birth to Makir the father of Gilead. 15Makir took a wife from among the Huppites and Shuppites. His sister's name was Maacah.

Another descendant was named Zelophehad, who had only daughters.

16Makir's wife Maacah gave birth to a son and named him Peresh. His brother was named Sheresh, and his sons were Ulam and Rakem.

17The son of Ulam:
Bedan.

These were the sons of Gilead son of Makir, the son of Manasseh.

j77 See Septuagint and Joshua 21:34; Hebrew does not have Jokneam, Kartah.
a13 Some Hebrew and Septuagint manuscripts (see also Gen. 46:24 and Num. 26:49); most Hebrew manuscripts Shallum

[18]His sister Hammoleketh gave birth to Ishhod, Abiezer and Mahlah.

[19]The sons of Shemida were:

Ahian, Shechem, Likhi and Aniam.

Ephraim

[20]The descendants of Ephraim:

Shuthelah, Bered his son,
Tahath his son, Eleadah his son,
Tahath his son, [21]Zabad his son
and Shuthelah his son.

Ezer and Elead were killed by the native-born men of Gath, when they went down to seize their livestock. [22]Their father Ephraim mourned for them many days, and his relatives came to comfort him. [23]Then he lay with his wife again, and she became pregnant and gave birth to a son. He named him Beriah,[b] because there had been misfortune in his family. [24]His daughter was Sheerah, who built Lower and Upper Beth Horon as well as Uzzen Sheerah.

[25]Rephah was his son, Resheph his son,[c]

Telah his son, Tahan his son,
[26]Ladan his son, Ammihud his son,
Elishama his son, [27]Nun his son
and Joshua his son.

[28]Their lands and settlements included Bethel and its surrounding villages, Naaran to the east, Gezer and its villages to the west, and Shechem and its villages all the way to Ayyah and its villages. [29]Along the borders of Manasseh were Beth Shan, Taanach, Megiddo and Dor, together with their villages. The descendants of Joseph son of Israel lived in these towns.

Asher

[30]The sons of Asher:

Imnah, Ishvah, Ishvi and Beriah.
Their sister was Serah.

[31]The sons of Beriah:

Heber and Malkiel, who was the father of Birzaith.

[32]Heber was the father of Japhlet, Shomer and Hotham and of their sister Shua.

[33]The sons of Japhlet:

Pasach, Bimhal and Ashvath.
These were Japhlet's sons.

[34]The sons of Shomer:

Ahi, Rohgah,[d] Hubbah and Aram.

[35]The sons of his brother Helem:

Zophah, Imna, Shelesh and Amal.

[36]The sons of Zophah:

Suah, Harnepher, Shual, Beri, Imrah, [37]Bezer, Hod, Shamma, Shilshah, Ithran[e] and Beera.

[38]The sons of Jether:

Jephunneh, Pispah and Ara.

[39]The sons of Ulla:

Arah, Hanniel and Rizia.

[40]All these were descendants of Asher—heads of families, choice men, brave warriors and outstanding leaders. The number of men ready for battle, as listed in their genealogy, was 26,000.

The Genealogy of Saul the Benjamite

8 Benjamin was the father of Bela his firstborn,

Ashbel the second son, Aharah the third,
[2]Nohah the fourth and Rapha the fifth.

[3]The sons of Bela were:

Addar, Gera, Abihud,[a] [4]Abishua, Naaman, Ahoah, [5]Gera, Shephuphan and Huram.

[6]These were the descendants of Ehud, who were heads of families of those living in Geba and were deported to Manahath:

[7]Naaman, Ahijah and Gera, who deported them and who was the father of Uzza and Ahihud.

[8]Sons were born to Shaharaim in Moab after he had divorced his wives Hushim and Baara. [9]By his wife Hodesh he had Jobab, Zibia, Mesha, Malcam, [10]Jeuz, Sakia and Mirmah. These were his sons, heads of families. [11]By Hushim he had Abitub and Elpaal.

---

[b]23 *Beriah* sounds like the Hebrew for *misfortune.*
[c]25 Some Septuagint manuscripts; Hebrew does not have *his son.*
[d]34 Or *of his brother Shomer: Rohgah*   [e]37 Possibly a variant of *Jether*   [a]3 Or *Gera the father of Ehud*

12The sons of Elpaal:

Eber, Misham, Shemed (who built Ono and Lod with its surrounding villages), 13and Beriah and Shema, who were heads of families of those living in Aijalon and who drove out the inhabitants of Gath.

14Ahio, Shashak, Jeremoth, 15Zebadiah, Arad, Eder, 16Michael, Ishpah and Joha were the sons of Beriah.

17Zebadiah, Meshullam, Hizki, Heber, 18Ishmerai, Izliah and Jobab were the sons of Elpaal.

19Jakim, Zicri, Zabdi, 20Elienai, Zillethai, Eliel, 21Adaiah, Beraiah and Shimrath were the sons of Shimei.

22Ishpan, Eber, Eliel, 23Abdon, Zicri, Hanan, 24Hananiah, Elam, Anthothijah, 25Iphdeiah and Penuel were the sons of Shashak.

26Shamsherai, Shehariah, Athaliah, 27Jaareshiah, Elijah and Zicri were the sons of Jeroham.

28All these were heads of families, chiefs as listed in their genealogy, and they lived in Jerusalem.

29Jeielb the fatherc of Gibeon lived in Gibeon.

His wife's name was Maacah, 30and his firstborn son was Abdon, followed by Zur, Kish, Baal, Ner,d Nadab, 31Gedor, Ahio, Zeker 32and Mikloth, who was the father of Shimeah. They too lived near their relatives in Jerusalem.

33Ner was the father of Kish, Kish the father of Saul, and Saul the father of Jonathan, Malki-Shua, Abinadab and Esh-Baal.e

34The son of Jonathan:

Merib-Baal,f who was the father of Micah.

35The sons of Micah:

Pithon, Melech, Tarea and Ahaz.

36Ahaz was the father of Jehoaddah, Jehoaddah was the father of Alemeth, Azmaveth and Zimri, and Zimri was the father of Moza.

37Moza was the father of Binea; Raphah was his son, Eleasah his son and Azel his son.

38Azel had six sons, and these were their names:

Azrikam, Bokeru, Ishmael, Sheariah, Obadiah and Hanan. All these were the sons of Azel.

39The sons of his brother Eshek:

Ulam his firstborn, Jeush the second son and Eliphelet the third. 40The sons of Ulam were brave warriors who could handle the bow. They had many sons and grandsons—150 in all.

All these were descendants of Benjamin.

9 All Israel was listed in the genealogies in the book of the kings of Israel.

The People in Jerusalem

The people of Judah were taken captive to Babylon because of their unfaithfulness. 2Now the first to resettle on their own property in their own towns were some Israelites, priests, Levites and temple servants.

3Those from Judah, from Benjamin, and from Ephraim and Manasseh who lived in Jerusalem were:

4Uthai son of Ammihud, the son of Omri, the son of Imri, the son of Bani, a descendant of Perez son of Judah.

5Of the Shilonites:

Asaiah the firstborn and his sons.

6Of the Zerahites:

Jeuel.

The people from Judah numbered 690.

7Of the Benjamites:

Sallu son of Meshullam, the son of Hodaviah, the son of Hassenuah; 8Ibneiah son of Jeroham; Elah son of Uzzi, the son of Micri; and

---

b29 Some Septuagint manuscripts (see also 1 Chron. 9:35); Hebrew does not have *Jeiel*.
c29 *Father* may mean *civic leader* or *military leader*.
d30 Some Septuagint manuscripts (see also 1 Chron. 9:36); Hebrew does not have *Ner*.
e33 Also known as *Ish-Bosheth*   f34 Also known as *Mephibosheth*

Meshullam son of Shephatiah, the son of Reuel, the son of Ibnijah.

⁹The people from Benjamin, as listed in their genealogy, numbered 956. All these men were heads of their families.

¹⁰Of the priests:

Jedaiah; Jehoiarib; Jakin;

¹¹Azariah son of Hilkiah, the son of Meshullam, the son of Zadok, the son of Meraioth, the son of Ahitub, the official in charge of the house of God;

¹²Adaiah son of Jeroham, the son of Pashhur, the son of Malkijah; and Maasai son of Adiel, the son of Jahzerah, the son of Meshullam, the son of Meshillemith, the son of Immer.

¹³The priests, who were heads of families, numbered 1,760. They were able men, responsible for ministering in the house of God.

¹⁴Of the Levites:

Shemaiah son of Hasshub, the son of Azrikam, the son of Hashabiah, a Merarite; ¹⁵Bakbakkar, Heresh, Galal and Mattaniah son of Mica, the son of Zicri, the son of Asaph; ¹⁶Obadiah son of Shemaiah, the son of Galal, the son of Jeduthun; and Berekiah son of Asa, the son of Elkanah, who lived in the villages of the Netophathites.

¹⁷The gatekeepers:

Shallum, Akkub, Talmon, Ahiman and their brothers, Shallum their chief ¹⁸being stationed at the King's Gate on the east, up to the present time. These were the gatekeepers belonging to the camp of the Levites. ¹⁹Shallum son of Kore, the son of Ebiasaph, the son of Korah, and his fellow gatekeepers from his family (the Korahites) were responsible for guarding the thresholds of the Tent*a* just as their fathers had been responsible for guarding the entrance to the dwelling of the LORD. ²⁰In earlier times Phinehas son of Eleazar was in charge of the gatekeepers, and the LORD was with him.

²¹Zechariah son of Meshelemiah was the gatekeeper at the entrance to the Tent of Meeting.

²²Altogether, those chosen to be gatekeepers at the thresholds numbered 212. They were registered by genealogy in their villages. The gatekeepers had been assigned to their positions of trust by David and Samuel the seer. ²³They and their descendants were in charge of guarding the gates of the house of the LORD—the house called the Tent. ²⁴The gatekeepers were on the four sides: east, west, north and south. ²⁵Their brothers in their villages had to come from time to time and share their duties for seven-day periods. ²⁶But the four principal gatekeepers, who were Levites, were entrusted with the responsibility for the rooms and treasuries in the house of God. ²⁷They would spend the night stationed round the house of God, because they had to guard it; and they had charge of the key for opening it each morning.

²⁸Some of them were in charge of the articles used in the temple service; they counted them when they were brought in and when they were taken out. ²⁹Others were assigned to take care of the furnishings and all the other articles of the sanctuary, as well as the flour and wine, and the oil, incense and spices. ³⁰But some of the priests took care of mixing the spices. ³¹A Levite named Mattithiah, the firstborn son of Shallum the Korahite, was entrusted with the responsibility for baking the offering bread. ³²Some of their Kohathite brothers were in charge of preparing for every Sabbath the bread set out on the table.

³³Those who were musicians, heads of Levite families, stayed in the rooms of the temple and were exempt from other duties because they were responsible for the work day and night.

³⁴All these were heads of Levite families, chiefs as listed in their genealogy, and they lived in Jerusalem.

---

a19 That is, the temple; also in verses 21 and 23

The Genealogy of Saul

35Jeiel the father*b* of Gibeon lived in Gibeon.

His wife's name was Maacah, 36and his firstborn son was Abdon, followed by Zur, Kish, Baal, Ner, Nadab, 37Gedor, Ahio, Zechariah and Mikloth. 38Mikloth was the father of Shimeam. They too lived near their relatives in Jerusalem.

39Ner was the father of Kish, Kish the father of Saul, and Saul the father of Jonathan, Malki-Shua, Abinadab and Esh-Baal.*c*

40The son of Jonathan:

Merib-Baal,*d* who was the father of Micah.

41The sons of Micah:

Pithon, Melech, Tahrea and Ahaz.*e*

42Ahaz was the father of Jadah, Jadah*f* was the father of Alemeth, Azmaveth and Zimri, and Zimri was the father of Moza. 43Moza was the father of Binea; Rephaiah was his son, Eleasah his son and Azel his son.

44Azel had six sons, and these were their names:

Azrikam, Bokeru, Ishmael, Sheariah, Obadiah and Hanan. These were the sons of Azel.

Saul Takes His Life

10 Now the Philistines fought against Israel; the Israelites fled before them, and many fell slain on Mount Gilboa. 2The Philistines pressed hard after Saul and his sons, and they killed his sons Jonathan, Abinadab and Malki-Shua. 3The fighting grew fierce around Saul, and when the archers overtook him, they wounded him.

4Saul said to his armour-bearer, "Draw your sword and run me through, or these uncircumcised fellows will come and abuse me."

But his armour-bearer was terrified and would not do it; so Saul took his own sword and fell on it. 5When the armour-bearer saw that Saul was dead, he too fell on his sword and died. 6So Saul and his three sons died, and all his house died together.

7When all the Israelites in the valley saw that the army had fled and that Saul and his sons had died, they abandoned their towns and fled. And the Philistines came and occupied them.

8The next day, when the Philistines came to strip the dead, they found Saul and his sons fallen on Mount Gilboa. 9They stripped him and took his head and his armour, and sent messengers throughout the land of the Philistines to proclaim the news among their idols and their people. 10They put his armour in the temple of their gods and hung up his head in the temple of Dagon.

11When all the inhabitants of Jabesh Gilead heard of everything the Philistines had done to Saul, 12all their valiant men went and took the bodies of Saul and his sons and brought them to Jabesh. Then they buried their bones under the great tree in Jabesh, and they fasted seven days.

13Saul died because he was unfaithful to the LORD; he did not keep the word of the LORD, and even consulted a medium for guidance, 14and did not enquire of the LORD. So the LORD put him to death and turned the kingdom over to David son of Jesse.

David Becomes King Over Israel

11 All Israel came together to David at Hebron and said, "We are your own flesh and blood. 2In the past, even while Saul was king, you were the one who led Israel on their military campaigns. And the LORD your God said to you, 'You will shepherd my people Israel, and you will become their ruler.'"

3When all the elders of Israel had come

---

b35 *Father* may mean *civic leader* or *military leader.*   *c39* Also known as *Ish-Bosheth*
d40 Also known as *Mephibosheth*
e41 Vulgate and Syriac (see also Septuagint and 1 Chron. 8:35); Hebrew does not have *and Ahaz.*
f42 Some Hebrew manuscripts and Septuagint (see also 1 Chron. 8:36); most Hebrew manuscripts *Jarah, Jarah*

to King David at Hebron, he made a compact with them at Hebron before the LORD, and they anointed David king over Israel, as the LORD had promised through Samuel.

David Conquers Jerusalem

[4] David and all the Israelites marched to Jerusalem (that is, Jebus). The Jebusites who lived there [5] said to David, "You will not get in here." Nevertheless, David captured the fortress of Zion, the City of David.

[6] David had said, "Whoever leads the attack on the Jebusites will become commander-in-chief." Joab son of Zeruiah went up first, and so he received the command.

[7] David then took up residence in the fortress, and so it was called the City of David. [8] He built up the city around it, from the supporting terraces[a] to the surrounding wall, while Joab restored the rest of the city. [9] And David became more and more powerful, because the LORD Almighty was with him.

David's Mighty Men

[10] These were the chiefs of David's mighty men—they, together with all Israel, gave his kingship strong support to extend it over the whole land, as the LORD had promised—[11] this is the list of David's mighty men:

Jashobeam,[b] a Hacmonite, was chief of the officers;[c] he raised his spear against three hundred men, whom he killed in one encounter.

[12] Next to him was Eleazar son of Dodai the Ahohite, one of the three mighty men. [13] He was with David at Pas Dammim when the Philistines gathered there for battle. At a place where there was a field full of barley, the troops fled from the Philistines. [14] But they took their stand in the middle of the field. They defended it and struck the Philistines down, and the LORD brought about a great victory.

[15] Three of the thirty chiefs came down to David to the rock at the cave of Adullam, while a band of Philistines was encamped in the Valley of Rephaim. [16] At that time David was in the stronghold, and the Philistine garrison was at Bethlehem. [17] David longed for water and said, "Oh, that someone would get me a drink of water from the well near the gate of Bethlehem!" [18] So the Three broke through the Philistine lines, drew water from the well near the gate of Bethlehem and carried it back to David. But he refused to drink it; instead, he poured it out before the LORD. [19] "God forbid that I should do this!" he said. "Should I drink the blood of these men who went at the risk of their lives? Because they risked their lives to bring it back, David would not drink it.

Such were the exploits of the three mighty men.

[20] Abishai the brother of Joab was chief of the Three. He raised his spear against three hundred men, whom he killed, and so he became as famous as the Three. [21] He was doubly honoured above the Three and became their commander, even though he was not included among them.

[22] Benaiah son of Jehoiada was a valiant fighter from Kabzeel, who performed great exploits. He struck down two of Moab's best men. He also went down into a pit on a snowy day and killed a lion. [23] And he struck down an Egyptian who was seven and a half feet[d] tall. Although the Egyptian had a spear like a weaver's rod in his hand, Benaiah went against him with a club. He snatched the spear from the Egyptian's hand and killed him with his own spear. [24] Such were the exploits of Benaiah son of Jehoiada; he too was as famous as the three mighty men. [25] He was held in greater honour than any of the Thirty, but he was not included among the Three. And David put him in charge of his bodyguard.

[26] The mighty men were:

Asahel the brother of Joab,
Elhanan son of Dodo from Bethlehem,
[27] Shammoth the Harorite,
Helez the Pelonite,

---

[a] 8 Or the Millo   [b] 11 Possibly a variant of Jashob-Baal
[c] 11 Or Thirty; some Septuagint manuscripts Three (see also 2 Sam. 23:8)   [d] 23 Hebrew five cubits (about 2.3 metres)

28Ira son of Ikkesh from Tekoa,
   Abiezer from Anathoth,
29Sibbecai the Hushathite,
   Ilai the Ahohite,
30Maharai the Netophathite,
   Heled son of Baanah the
   Netophathite,
31Ithai son of Ribai from Gibeah in
   Benjamin,
   Benaiah the Pirathonite,
32Hurai from the ravines of Gaash,
   Abiel the Arbathite,
33Azmaveth the Baharumite,
   Eliahba the Shaalbonite,
34the sons of Hashem the Gizonite,
   Jonathan son of Shagee the Hararite,
35Ahiam son of Sacar the Hararite,
   Eliphal son of Ur,
36Hepher the Mekerathite,
   Ahijah the Pelonite,
37Hezro the Carmelite,
   Naarai son of Ezbai,
38Joel the brother of Nathan,
   Mibhar son of Hagri,
39Zelek the Ammonite,
   Naharai the Berothite, the armour-
   bearer of Joab son of Zeruiah,
40Ira the Ithrite,
   Gareb the Ithrite,
41Uriah the Hittite,
   Zabad son of Ahlai,
42Adina son of Shiza the Reubenite,
   who was chief of the Reubenites,
   and the thirty with him,
43Hanan son of Maacah,
   Joshaphat the Mithnite,
44Uzzia the Ashterathite,
   Shama and Jeiel the sons of
   Hotham the Aroerite,
45Jediael son of Shimri,
   his brother Joha the Tizite,
46Eliel the Mahavite,
   Jeribai and Joshaviah the sons of
   Elnaam,
   Ithmah the Moabite,
47Eliel, Obed and Jaasiel the
   Mezobaite.

Warriors Join David

12 These were the men who came to
David at Ziklag, while he was
banished from the presence of Saul son of

Kish (they were among the warriors who
helped him in battle; 2they were armed
with bows and were able to shoot arrows
or to sling stones right-handed or left-
handed; they were kinsmen of Saul from
the tribe of Benjamin):

3Ahiezer their chief and Joash the
sons of Shemaah the Gibeathite;
Jeziel and Pelet the sons of
Azmaveth; Beracah, Jehu the
Anathothite, 4and Ishmaiah the
Gibeonite, a mighty man among the
Thirty, who was a leader of the
Thirty; Jeremiah, Jahaziel, Johanan,
Jozabad the Gederathite, 5Eluzai,
Jerimoth, Bealiah, Shemariah and
Shephatiah the Haruphite; 6Elkanah,
Isshiah, Azarel, Joezer and
Jashobeam the Korahites; 7and
Joelah and Zebadiah the sons of Jero-
ham from Gedor.

8Some Gadites defected to David at his
stronghold in the desert. They were brave
warriors, ready for battle and able to
handle the shield and spear. Their faces
were the faces of lions, and they were as
swift as gazelles in the mountains.
9Ezer was the chief,
   Obadiah the second in command,
   Eliab the third,
10Mishmannah the fourth, Jeremiah
   the fifth,
11Attai the sixth, Eliel the seventh,
12Johanan the eighth, Elzabad the ninth,
13Jeremiah the tenth and Macbannai
   the eleventh.

14These Gadites were army commanders; the least was a match for a hundred,
and the greatest for a thousand. 15It was
they who crossed the Jordan in the first
month when it was overflowing all its banks,
and they put to flight everyone living in
the valleys, to the east and to the west.

16Other Benjamites and some men from
Judah also came to David in his stronghold. 17David went out to meet them and
said to them, "If you have come to me in
peace, to help me, I am ready to have you
unite with me. But if you have come to
betray me to my enemies when my hands
are free from violence, may the God of
our fathers see it and judge you."

¹⁸Then the Spirit came upon Amasai, chief of the Thirty, and he said:

"We are yours, O David!
  We are with you, O son of Jesse!
Success, success to you,
  and success to those who help you,
    for your God will help you."

So David received them and made them leaders of his raiding bands.

¹⁹Some of the men of Manasseh defected to David when he went with the Philistines to fight against Saul. (He and his men did not help the Philistines because, after consultation, their rulers sent him away. They said, "It will cost us our heads if he deserts to his master Saul.") ²⁰When David went to Ziklag, these were the men of Manasseh who defected to him: Adnah, Jozabad, Jediael, Michael, Jozabad, Elihu and Zillethai, leaders of units of a thousand in Manasseh. ²¹They helped David against raiding bands, for all of them were brave warriors, and they were commanders in his army. ²²Day after day men came to help David, until he had a great army, like the army of God.ᵃ

Others Join David at Hebron

²³These are the numbers of the men armed for battle who came to David at Hebron to turn Saul's kingdom over to him, as the LORD had said:

²⁴men of Judah, carrying shield and spear—6,800 armed for battle;
²⁵men of Simeon, warriors ready for battle—7,100;
²⁶men of Levi—4,600, ²⁷including Jehoiada, leader of the family of Aaron with 3,700 men, ²⁸and Zadok, a brave young warrior, with 22 officers from his family;
²⁹men of Benjamin, Saul's kinsmen—3,000, most of whom had remained loyal to Saul's house until then;
³⁰men of Ephraim, brave warriors, famous in their own clans—20,800;
³¹men of half the tribe of Manasseh, designated by name to come and make David king—18,000;
³²men of Issachar, who understood the times and knew what Israel should do—200 chiefs, with all their relatives under their command;
³³men of Zebulun, experienced soldiers prepared for battle with every type of weapon, to help David with undivided loyalty—50,000;
³⁴men of Naphtali—1,000 officers, together with 37,000 men carrying shields and spears;
³⁵men of Dan, ready for battle—28,600;
³⁶men of Asher, experienced soldiers prepared for battle—40,000;
³⁷and from east of the Jordan, men of Reuben, Gad, and the half-tribe of Manasseh, armed with every type of weapon—120,000.

³⁸All these were fighting men who volunteered to serve in the ranks. They came to Hebron fully determined to make David king over all Israel. All the rest of the Israelites were also of one mind to make David king. ³⁹The men spent three days there with David, eating and drinking, for their families had supplied provisions for them. ⁴⁰Also, their neighbours from as far away as Issachar, Zebulun and Naphtali came bringing food on donkeys, camels, mules and oxen. There were plentiful supplies of flour, fig cakes, raisin cakes, wine, oil, cattle and sheep, for there was joy in Israel.

Bringing Back the Ark

13 David conferred with each of his officers, the commanders of thousands and commanders of hundreds. ²He then said to the whole assembly of Israel, "If it seems good to you and if it is the will of the LORD our God, let us send word far and wide to the rest of our brothers throughout the territories of Israel, and also to the priests and Levites who are with them in their towns and pasture-lands, to come and join us. ³Let us bring the ark of our God back to us, for we did not enquire ofᵃ itᵇ during the reign of Saul." ⁴The whole assembly agreed to do

---

ᵃ22 Or *a great and mighty army.*   ᵃ3 Or *we neglected*   ᵇ3 Or *him* this, because it seemed right to all the people.

⁵So David assembled all the Israelites, from the Shihor River in Egypt to Lebo*ᶜ* Hamath, to bring the ark of God from Kiriath Jearim. ⁶David and all the Israelites then went to Baalah of Judah (Kiriath Jearim) to bring up from there the ark of God the LORD, who is enthroned between the cherubim—the ark that is called by the Name.

⁷They moved the ark of God from Abinadab's house on a new cart, with Uzzah and Ahio guiding it. ⁸David and all the Israelites were celebrating with all their might before God, with songs and with harps, lyres, tambourines, cymbals and trumpets.

⁹When they came to the threshing-floor of Kidon, Uzzah reached out his hand to steady the ark, because the oxen stumbled. ¹⁰The LORD's anger burned against Uzzah, and he struck him down because he had put his hand on the ark. So he died there before God.

¹¹Then David was angry because the LORD's wrath had broken out against Uzzah, and to this day that place is called Perez Uzzah.*ᵈ*

¹²David was afraid of God that day and asked, "How can I ever bring the ark of God to me?" ¹³He did not take the ark to be with him in the City of David. Instead, he took it aside to the house of Obed-Edom the Gittite. ¹⁴The ark of God remained with the family of Obed-Edom in his house for three months, and the LORD blessed his household and everything he had.

David's House and Family

14 Now Hiram king of Tyre sent messengers to David, along with cedar logs, stonemasons and carpenters to build a palace for him. ²And David knew that the LORD had established him as king over Israel and that his kingdom had been highly exalted for the sake of his people Israel.

³In Jerusalem David took more wives and became the father of more sons and daughters. ⁴These are the names of the children born to him there: Shammua, Shobab, Nathan, Solomon, ⁵Ibhar, Elishua, Elpelet, ⁶Nogah, Nepheg, Japhia, ⁷Elishama, Beeliada*ᵃ* and Eliphelet.

David Defeats the Philistines

⁸When the Philistines heard that David had been anointed king over all Israel, they went up in full force to search for him, but David heard about it and went out to meet them. ⁹Now the Philistines had come and raided the Valley of Rephaim; ¹⁰so David enquired of God: "Shall I go and attack the Philistines? Will you hand them over to me?"

The LORD answered him, "Go, I will hand them over to you."

¹¹So David and his men went up to Baal Perazim, and there he defeated them. He said, "As waters break out, God has broken out against my enemies by my hand." So that place was called Baal Perazim.*ᵇ* ¹²The Philistines had abandoned their gods there, and David gave orders to burn them in the fire.

¹³Once more the Philistines raided the valley; ¹⁴so David enquired of God again, and God answered him, "Do not go straight up, but circle round them and attack them in front of the balsam trees. ¹⁵As soon as you hear the sound of marching in the tops of the balsam trees, move out to battle, because that will mean God has gone out in front of you to strike the Philistine army." ¹⁶So David did as God commanded him, and they struck down the Philistine army, all the way from Gibeon to Gezer.

¹⁷So David's fame spread throughout every land, and the LORD made all the nations fear him.

The Ark Brought to Jerusalem

15 After David had constructed buildings for himself in the City of David, he prepared a place for the ark of

---

ᶜ5 Or *to the entrance to*   *ᵈ11 Perez Uzzah* means *outbreak against Uzzah.*
ᵃ7 A variant of *Eliada*   *ᵇ11 Baal Perazim* means *the lord who breaks out.*

God and pitched a tent for it. [2]Then David said, "No-one but the Levites may carry the ark of God, because the LORD chose them to carry the ark of the LORD and to minister before him for ever."

[3]David assembled all Israel in Jerusalem to bring up the ark of the LORD to the place he had prepared for it. [4]He called together the descendants of Aaron and the Levites:

[5]From the descendants of Kohath,
  Uriel the leader and 120 relatives;
[6]from the descendants of Merari,
  Asaiah the leader and 220 relatives;
[7]from the descendants of Gershon,[a]
  Joel the leader and 130 relatives;
[8]from the descendants of Elizaphan,
  Shemaiah the leader and 200 relatives;
[9]from the descendants of Hebron,
  Eliel the leader and 80 relatives;
[10]from the descendants of Uzziel,
  Amminadab the leader and 112 relatives.

[11]Then David summoned Zadok and Abiathar the priests, and Uriel, Asaiah, Joel, Shemaiah, Eliel and Amminadab the Levites. [12]He said to them, "You are the heads of the Levitical families; you and your fellow Levites are to consecrate yourselves and bring up the ark of the LORD, the God of Israel, to the place I have prepared for it. [13]It was because you, the Levites, did not bring it up the first time that the LORD our God broke out in anger against us. We did not enquire of him about how to do it in the prescribed way." [14]So the priests and Levites consecrated themselves in order to bring up the ark of the LORD, the God of Israel. [15]And the Levites carried the ark of God with the poles on their shoulders, as Moses had commanded in accordance with the word of the LORD.

[16]David told the leaders of the Levites to appoint their brothers as singers to sing joyful songs, accompanied by musical instruments: lyres, harps and cymbals.

[17]So the Levites appointed Heman son of Joel; from his brothers, Asaph son of Berekiah; and from their brothers the Merarites, Ethan son of Kushaiah; [18]and with them their brothers next in rank: Zechariah,[b] Jaaziel, Shemiramoth, Jehiel, Unni, Eliab, Benaiah, Maaseiah, Mattithiah, Eliphelehu, Mikneiah, Obed-Edom and Jeiel,[c] the gatekeepers.

[19]The musicians Heman, Asaph and Ethan were to sound the bronze cymbals; [20]Zechariah, Aziel, Shemiramoth, Jehiel, Unni, Eliab, Maaseiah and Benaiah were to play the lyres according to *alamoth*,[d] [21]and Mattithiah, Eliphelehu, Mikneiah, Obed-Edom, Jeiel and Azaziah were to play the harps, directing according to *sheminith*.[e] [22]Kenaniah the head Levite was in charge of the singing; that was his responsibility because he was skilful at it.

[23]Berekiah and Elkanah were to be doorkeepers for the ark. [24]Shebaniah, Joshaphat, Nethanel, Amasai, Zechariah, Benaiah and Eliezer the priests were to blow trumpets before the ark of God. Obed-Edom and Jehiah were also to be doorkeepers for the ark.

[25]So David and the elders of Israel and the commanders of units of a thousand went to bring up the ark of the covenant of the LORD from the house of Obed-Edom, with rejoicing. [26]Because God had helped the Levites who were carrying the ark of the covenant of the LORD, seven bulls and seven rams were sacrificed. [27]Now David was clothed in a robe of fine linen, as were all the Levites who were carrying the ark, and as were the singers, and Kenaniah, who was in charge of the singing of the choirs. David also wore a linen ephod. [28]So all Israel brought up the ark of the covenant of the LORD with shouts, with the sounding of rams' horns and trumpets, and of cymbals, and the playing of lyres and harps.

[29]As the ark of the covenant of the LORD was entering the City of David, Michal daughter of Saul watched from a window. And when she saw King David dancing

---

[a]7 Hebrew *Gershom*, a variant of *Gershon*
[b]18 Three Hebrew manuscripts and most Septuagint manuscripts (see also verse 20 and 1 Chron. 16:5); most Hebrew manuscripts *Zechariah son and* or *Zechariah, Ben and*
[c]18 Hebrew; Septuagint (see also verse 21) *Jeiel and Azaziah*
[d]20 Probably a musical term   [e]21 Probably a musical term

and celebrating, she despised him in her heart.

16 They brought the ark of God and set it inside the tent that David had pitched for it, and they presented burnt offerings and fellowship offerings[a] before God. [2]After David had finished sacrificing the burnt offerings and fellowship offerings, he blessed the people in the name of the LORD. [3]Then he gave a loaf of bread, a cake of dates and a cake of raisins to each Israelite man and woman.

[4]He appointed some of the Levites to minister before the ark of the LORD, to make petition, to give thanks, and to praise the LORD, the God of Israel: [5]Asaph was the chief, Zechariah second, then Jeiel, Shemiramoth, Jehiel, Mattithiah, Eliab, Benaiah, Obed-Edom and Jeiel. They were to play the lyres and harps, Asaph was to sound the cymbals, [6]and Benaiah and Jahaziel the priests were to blow the trumpets regularly before the ark of the covenant of God.

David's Psalm of Thanks

[7]That day David first committed to Asaph and his associates this psalm of thanks to the LORD:

[8]Give thanks to the LORD, call on his name;
　　make known among the nations what he has done.
[9]Sing to him, sing praise to him;
　　tell of all his wonderful acts.
[10]Glory in his holy name;
　　let the hearts of those who seek the LORD rejoice.
[11]Look to the LORD and his strength;
　　seek his face always.
[12]Remember the wonders he has done,
　　his miracles, and the judgments he pronounced,
[13]O descendants of Israel his servant,
　　O sons of Jacob, his chosen ones.

[14]He is the LORD our God;
　　his judgments are in all the earth.

[15]He remembers[b] his covenant for ever,
　　the word he commanded, for a thousand generations,
[16]the covenant he made with Abraham,
　　the oath he swore to Isaac.
[17]He confirmed it to Jacob as a decree,
　　to Israel as an everlasting covenant:
[18]"To you I will give the land of Canaan
　　as the portion you will inherit."

[19]When they were but few in number,
　　few indeed, and strangers in it,
[20]they[c] wandered from nation to nation,
　　from one kingdom to another.
[21]He allowed no man to oppress them;
　　for their sake he rebuked kings:
[22]"Do not touch my anointed ones;
　　do my prophets no harm."

[23]Sing to the LORD, all the earth;
　　proclaim his salvation day after day.
[24]Declare his glory among the nations,
　　his marvellous deeds among all peoples.
[25]For great is the LORD and most worthy of praise;
　　he is to be feared above all gods.
[26]For all the gods of the nations are idols,
　　but the LORD made the heavens.
[27]Splendour and majesty are before him;
　　strength and joy in his dwelling-place.
[28]Ascribe to the LORD, O families of nations,
　　ascribe to the LORD glory and strength,
[29]　ascribe to the LORD the glory due to his name.
　Bring an offering and come before him;
　　worship the LORD in the splendour of his[d] holiness.
[30]Tremble before him, all the earth!
　　The world is firmly established; it cannot be moved.
[31]Let the heavens rejoice, let the earth be glad;
　　let them say among the nations,
　　"The LORD reigns!"

---

[a]1 Traditionally peace offerings; also in verse 2
[b]15 Some Septuagint manuscripts (see also Psalm 105:8); Hebrew Remember
[c]18–20 One Hebrew manuscript, Septuagint and Vulgate (see also Psalm 105:12); most Hebrew manuscripts inherit, /
[19]though you are but few in number, / few indeed, and strangers in it." / [20]They　　[d]29 Or LORD with the splendour of

³²Let the sea resound, and all that is in it;
  let the fields be jubilant, and
    everything in them!
³³Then the trees of the forest will sing,
  they will sing for joy before the
    LORD,
  for he comes to judge the earth.

³⁴Give thanks to the LORD, for he is
    good;
  his love endures for ever.
³⁵Cry out, "Save us, O God our Saviour;
  gather us and deliver us from the
    nations,
  that we may give thanks to your holy
    name,
  that we may glory in your praise."
³⁶Praise be to the LORD, the God of
    Israel,
  from everlasting to everlasting.

Then all the people said "Amen" and
"Praise the LORD."

³⁷David left Asaph and his associates
before the ark of the covenant of the LORD
to minister there regularly, according to
each day's requirements. ³⁸He also left
Obed-Edom and his sixty-eight associates
to minister with them. Obed-Edom son of
Jeduthun, and also Hosah, were
gatekeepers.

³⁹David left Zadok the priest and his
fellow priests before the tabernacle of the
LORD at the high place in Gibeon ⁴⁰to
present burnt offerings to the LORD on the
altar of burnt offering regularly, morning
and evening, in accordance with everything written in the Law of the LORD,
which he had given Israel. ⁴¹With them
were Heman and Jeduthun and the rest of
those chosen and designated by name to
give thanks to the LORD, "for his love
endures for ever." ⁴²Heman and Jeduthun
were responsible for the sounding of the
trumpets and cymbals and for the playing
of the other instruments for sacred song.
The sons of Jeduthun were stationed at
the gate.

⁴³Then all the people left, each for his
own home, and David returned home to
bless his family.

God's Promise to David

17 After David was settled in his
palace, he said to Nathan the
prophet, "Here I am, living in a palace of
cedar, while the ark of the covenant of the
LORD is under a tent."

²Nathan replied to David, "Whatever
you have in mind, do it, for God is with
you."

³That night the word of God came to
Nathan, saying:

⁴"Go and tell my servant David,
'This is what the LORD says: You are
not the one to build me a house to
dwell in. ⁵I have not dwelt in a house
from the day I brought Israel up out of
Egypt to this day. I have moved from
one tent site to another, from one
dwelling-place to another. ⁶Wherever
I have moved with all the Israelites,
did I ever say to any of their leaders*ᵃ*
whom I commanded to shepherd my
people, "Why have you not built me a
house of cedar?"'

⁷"Now then, tell my servant David,
'This is what the LORD Almighty says:
I took you from the pasture and from
following the flock, to be ruler over
my people Israel. ⁸I have been with
you wherever you have gone, and I
have cut off all your enemies from
before you. Now I will make your
name like the names of the greatest
men of the earth. ⁹And I will provide
a place for my people Israel and will
plant them so that they can have a
home of their own and no longer be
disturbed. Wicked people will not
oppress them any more, as they did at
the beginning ¹⁰and have done ever
since the time I appointed leaders
over my people Israel. I will also subdue all your enemies.

"'I declare to you that the LORD will
build a house for you: ¹¹When your
days are over and you go to be with
your fathers, I will raise up your
offspring to succeed you, one of your
own sons, and I will establish his kingdom. ¹²He is the one who will build a

---

ᵃ6 Traditionally judges; also in verse 10

house for me, and I will establish his throne for ever. ¹³I will be his father, and he will be my son. I will never take my love away from him, as I took it away from your predecessor. ¹⁴I will set him over my house and my kingdom for ever; his throne will be established for ever.'"

¹⁵Nathan reported to David all the words of this entire revelation.

David's Prayer

¹⁶Then King David went in and sat before the LORD, and he said:

"Who am I, O LORD God, and what is my family, that you have brought me this far? ¹⁷And as if this were not enough in your sight, O God, you have spoken about the future of the house of your servant. You have looked on me as though I were the most exalted of men, O LORD God.

¹⁸"What more can David say to you for honouring your servant? For you know your servant, ¹⁹O LORD. For the sake of your servant and according to your will, you have done this great thing and made known all these great promises.

²⁰"There is no-one like you, O LORD, and there is no God but you, as we have heard with our own ears. ²¹And who is like your people Israel—the one nation on earth whose God went out to redeem a people for himself, and to make a name for yourself, and to perform great and awesome wonders by driving out nations from before your people, whom you redeemed from Egypt? ²²You made your people Israel your very own for ever, and you, O LORD, have become their God.

²³"And now, LORD, let the promise you have made concerning your servant and his house be established for ever. Do as you promised, ²⁴so that it

will be established and that your name will be great for ever. Then men will say, 'The LORD Almighty, the God over Israel, is Israel's God!' And the house of your servant David will be established before you.

²⁵"You, my God, have revealed to your servant that you will build a house for him. So your servant has found courage to pray to you. ²⁶O LORD, you are God! You have promised these good things to your servant. ²⁷Now you have been pleased to bless the house of your servant, that it may continue for ever in your sight; for you, O LORD, have blessed it, and it will be blessed for ever."

David's Victories

18 In the course of time, David defeated the Philistines and subdued them, and he took Gath and its surrounding villages from the control of the Philistines.

²David also defeated the Moabites, and they became subject to him and brought tribute.

³Moreover, David fought Hadadezer king of Zobah, as far as Hamath, when he went to establish his control along the Euphrates River. ⁴David captured a thousand of his chariots, seven thousand charioteers and twenty thousand foot soldiers. He hamstrung all but a hundred of the chariot horses.

⁵When the Arameans of Damascus came to help Hadadezer king of Zobah, David struck down twenty-two thousand of them. ⁶He put garrisons in the Aramean kingdom of Damascus, and the Arameans became subject to him and brought tribute. The LORD gave David victory everywhere he went.

⁷David took the gold shields carried by the officers of Hadadezer and brought them to Jerusalem. ⁸From Tebah*ᵃ* and Cun, towns that belonged to Hadadezer, David took a great quantity of bronze, which Solomon used to make the bronze Sea, the pillars and various bronze articles.

ᵃ8 Hebrew *Tibhath*, a variant of *Tebah*

⁹When Tou king of Hamath heard that David had defeated the entire army of Hadadezer king of Zobah, ¹⁰he sent his son Hadoram to King David to greet him and congratulate him on his victory in battle over Hadadezer, who had been at war with Tou. Hadoram brought all kinds of articles of gold and silver and bronze.

¹¹King David dedicated these articles to the LORD, as he had done with the silver and gold he had taken from all these nations: Edom and Moab, the Ammonites and the Philistines, and Amalek.

¹²Abishai son of Zeruiah struck down eighteen thousand Edomites in the Valley of Salt. ¹³He put garrisons in Edom, and all the Edomites became subject to David. The LORD gave David victory everywhere he went.

David's Officials

¹⁴David reigned over all Israel, doing what was just and right for all his people. ¹⁵Joab son of Zeruiah was over the army; Jehoshaphat son of Ahilud was recorder; ¹⁶Zadok son of Ahitub and Ahimelech[b] son of Abiathar were priests; Shavsha was secretary; ¹⁷Benaiah son of Jehoiada was over the Kerethites and Pelethites; and David's sons were chief officials at the king's side.

The Battle Against the Ammonites

19 In the course of time, Nahash king of the Ammonites died, and his son succeeded him as king. ²David thought, "I will show kindness to Hanun son of Nahash, because his father showed kindness to me." So David sent a delegation to express his sympathy to Hanun concerning his father.

When David's men came to Hanun in the land of the Ammonites to express sympathy to him, ³the Ammonite nobles said to Hanun, "Do you think David is honouring your father by sending men to you to express sympathy? Haven't his men come to you to explore and spy out the country and overthrow it?" ⁴So Hanun seized David's men, shaved them, cut off

their garments in the middle at the buttocks, and sent them away.

⁵When someone came and told David about the men, he sent messengers to meet them, for they were greatly humiliated. The king said, "Stay at Jericho till your beards have grown, and then come back."

⁶When the Ammonites realised that they had become an offence to David's nostrils, Hanun and the Ammonites sent a thousand talents[a] of silver to hire chariots and charioteers from Aram Naharaim,[b] Aram Maacah and Zobah. ⁷They hired thirty-two thousand chariots and charioteers, as well as the king of Maacah with his troops, who came and camped near Medeba, while the Ammonites were mustered from their towns and moved out for battle.

⁸On hearing this, David sent Joab out with the entire army of fighting men. ⁹The Ammonites came out and drew up in battle formation at the entrance to their city, while the kings who had come were by themselves in the open country.

¹⁰Joab saw that there were battle lines in front of him and behind him; so he selected some of the best troops in Israel and deployed them against the Arameans. ¹¹He put the rest of the men under the command of Abishai his brother, and they were deployed against the Ammonites. ¹²Joab said, "If the Arameans are too strong for me, then you are to rescue me; but if the Ammonites are too strong for you, then I will rescue you. ¹³Be strong and let us fight bravely for our people and the cities of our God. The LORD will do what is good in his sight."

¹⁴Then Joab and the troops with him advanced to fight the Arameans, and they fled before him. ¹⁵When the Ammonites saw that the Arameans were fleeing, they too fled before his brother Abishai and went inside the city. So Joab went back to Jerusalem.

¹⁶After the Arameans saw that they had been routed by Israel, they sent messengers and had Arameans brought from beyond the River,[c] with Shophach the

---

b16 Some Hebrew manuscripts, Vulgate and Syriac (see also 2 Sam. 8:17); most Hebrew manuscripts *Abimelech*
a6 That is, about 34 tons (about 34 metric tons)   *b6* That is, North-west Mesopotamia   *c16* That is, the Euphrates

commander of Hadadezer's army leading them.

17When David was told of this, he gathered all Israel and crossed the Jordan; he advanced against them and formed his battle lines opposite them. David formed his lines to meet the Arameans in battle, and they fought against him. 18But they fled before Israel, and David killed seven thousand of their charioteers and forty thousand of their foot soldiers. He also killed Shophach the commander of their army.

19When the vassals of Hadadezer saw that they had been defeated by Israel, they made peace with David and became subject to him.

So the Arameans were not willing to help the Ammonites any more.

The Capture of Rabbah

20 In the spring, at the time when kings go off to war, Joab led out the armed forces. He laid waste the land of the Ammonites and went to Rabbah and besieged it, but David remained in Jerusalem. Joab attacked Rabbah and left it in ruins. 2David took the crown from the head of their king*a*—its weight was found to be a talent*b* of gold, and it was set with precious stones—and it was placed on David's head. He took a great quantity of plunder from the city 3and brought out the people who were there, consigning them to labour with saws and with iron picks and axes. David did this to all the Ammonite towns. Then David and his entire army returned to Jerusalem.

War With the Philistines

4In the course of time, war broke out with the Philistines, at Gezer. At that time Sibbecai the Hushathite killed Sippai, one of the descendants of the Rephaites, and the Philistines were subjugated.

5In another battle with the Philistines, Elhanan son of Jair killed Lahmi the brother of Goliath the Gittite, who had a spear with a shaft like a weaver's rod.

6In still another battle, which took place at Gath, there was a huge man with six fingers on each hand and six toes on each foot—twenty-four in all. He also was descended from Rapha. 7When he taunted Israel, Jonathan son of Shimea, David's brother, killed him.

8These were descendants of Rapha in Gath, and they fell at the hands of David and his men.

David Numbers the Fighting Men

21 Satan rose up against Israel and incited David to take a census of Israel. 2So David said to Joab and the commanders of the troops, "Go and count the Israelites from Beersheba to Dan. Then report back to me so that I may know how many there are."

3But Joab replied, "May the LORD multiply his troops a hundred times over. My lord the king, are they not all my lord's subjects? Why does my lord want to do this? Why should he bring guilt on Israel?"

4The king's word, however, overruled Joab; so Joab left and went throughout Israel and then came back to Jerusalem. 5Joab reported the number of the fighting men to David: In all Israel there were one million one hundred thousand men who could handle a sword, including four hundred and seventy thousand in Judah.

6But Joab did not include Levi and Benjamin in the numbering, because the king's command was repulsive to him. 7This command was also evil in the sight of God; so he punished Israel.

8Then David said to God, "I have sinned greatly by doing this. Now, I beg you, take away the guilt of your servant. I have done a very foolish thing."

9The LORD said to Gad, David's seer, 10"Go and tell David, 'This is what the LORD says: I am giving you three options. Choose one of them for me to carry out against you.'"

11So Gad went to David and said to him, "This is what the LORD says: 'Take your choice: 12three years of famine, three months of being swept away*a* before your

---

a2 Or *of Milcom, that is, Molech*   *b2* That is, about 75 pounds (about 34 kilograms)
a12 Hebrew; Septuagint and Vulgate (see also 2 Sam. 24:13) *of fleeing*

enemies, with their swords overtaking you, or three days of the sword of the LORD—days of plague in the land with the angel of the LORD ravaging every part of Israel.' Now then, decide how I should answer the one who sent me."

¹³David said to Gad, "I am in deep distress. Let me fall into the hands of the LORD, for his mercy is very great; but do not let me fall into the hands of men."

¹⁴So the LORD sent a plague on Israel, and seventy thousand men of Israel fell dead. ¹⁵And God sent an angel to destroy Jerusalem. But as the angel was doing so, the LORD saw it and was grieved because of the calamity and said to the angel who was destroying the people, "Enough! Withdraw your hand." The angel of the LORD was then standing at the threshing-floor of Araunahᵇ the Jebusite.

¹⁶David looked up and saw the angel of the LORD standing between heaven and earth, with a drawn sword in his hand extended over Jerusalem. Then David and the elders, clothed in sackcloth, fell face down.

¹⁷David said to God, "Was it not I who ordered the fighting men to be counted? I am the one who has sinned and done wrong. These are but sheep. What have they done? O LORD my God, let your hand fall upon me and my family, but do not let this plague remain on your people."

¹⁸Then the angel of the LORD ordered Gad to tell David to go up and build an altar to the LORD on the threshing-floor of Araunah the Jebusite. ¹⁹So David went up in obedience to the word that Gad had spoken in the name of the LORD.

²⁰While Araunah was threshing wheat, he turned and saw the angel; his four sons who were with him hid themselves. ²¹Then David approached, and when Araunah looked and saw him, he left the threshing-floor and bowed down before David with his face to the ground.

²²David said to him, "Let me have the site of your threshing-floor so that I can build an altar to the LORD, that the plague on the people may be stopped. Sell it to me at the full price."

²³Araunah said to David, "Take it! Let my lord the king do whatever pleases him. Look, I will give the oxen for the burnt offerings, the threshing-sledges for the wood, and the wheat for the grain offering. I will give all this."

²⁴But King David replied to Araunah, "No, I insist on paying the full price. I will not take for the LORD what is yours, or sacrifice a burnt offering that costs me nothing."

²⁵So David paid Araunah six hundred shekelsᶜ of gold for the site. ²⁶David built an altar to the LORD there and sacrificed burnt offerings and fellowship offerings.ᵈ He called on the LORD, and the LORD answered him with fire from heaven on the altar of burnt offering.

²⁷Then the LORD spoke to the angel, and he put his sword back into its sheath. ²⁸At that time, when David saw that the LORD had answered him on the threshing-floor of Araunah the Jebusite, he offered sacrifices there. ²⁹The tabernacle of the LORD, which Moses had made in the desert, and the altar of burnt offering were at that time on the high place at Gibeon. ³⁰But David could not go before it to enquire of God, because he was afraid of the sword of the angel of the LORD.

22 Then David said, "The house of the LORD God is to be here, and also the altar of burnt offering for Israel."

Preparations for the Temple

²So David gave orders to assemble the aliens living in Israel, and from among them he appointed stonecutters to prepare dressed stone for building the house of God. ³He provided a large amount of iron to make nails for the doors of the gateways and for the fittings, and more bronze than could be weighed. ⁴He also provided more cedar logs than could be counted, for the Sidonians and Tyrians had brought large numbers of them to David.

⁵David said, "My son Solomon is young and inexperienced, and the house to be built for the LORD should be of great

---

ᵇ15 Hebrew *Ornan*, a variant of *Araunah*; also in verses 18–28   ᶜ25 That is, about 15 pounds (about 7 kilograms)
ᵈ26 Traditionally *peace offerings*

magnificence and fame and splendour in the sight of all the nations. Therefore I will make preparations for it." So David made extensive preparations before his death.

6Then he called for his son Solomon and charged him to build a house for the LORD, the God of Israel. 7David said to Solomon: "My son, I had it in my heart to build a house for the Name of the LORD my God. 8But this word of the LORD came to me: 'You have shed much blood and have fought many wars. You are not to build a house for my Name, because you have shed much blood on the earth in my sight. 9But you will have a son who will be a man of peace and rest, and I will give him rest from all his enemies on every side. His name will be Solomon,*a* and I will grant Israel peace and quiet during his reign. 10He is the one who will build a house for my Name. He will be my son, and I will be his father. And I will establish the throne of his kingdom over Israel for ever.'

11"Now, my son, the LORD be with you, and may you have success and build the house of the LORD your God, as he said you would. 12May the LORD give you discretion and understanding when he puts you in command over Israel, so that you may keep the law of the LORD your God. 13Then you will have success if you are careful to observe the decrees and laws that the LORD gave to Moses for Israel. Be strong and courageous. Do not be afraid or discouraged.

14"I have taken great pains to provide for the temple of the LORD a hundred thousand talents*b* of gold, a million talents*c* of silver, quantities of bronze and iron too great to be weighed, and wood and stone. And you may add to them. 15You have many workmen: stonecutters, masons and carpenters, as well as men skilled in every kind of work 16in gold and silver, bronze and iron—craftsmen beyond number. Now begin the work, and the LORD be with you."

17Then David ordered all the leaders of Israel to help his son Solomon. 18He said

to them, "Is not the LORD your God with you? And has he not granted you rest on every side? For he has handed the inhabitants of the land over to me, and the land is subject to the LORD and to his people. 19Now devote your heart and soul to seeking the LORD your God. Begin to build the sanctuary of the LORD God, so that you may bring the ark of the covenant of the LORD and the sacred articles belonging to God into the temple that will be built for the Name of the LORD."

The Levites

23 When David was old and full of years, he made his son Solomon king over Israel.

2He also gathered together all the leaders of Israel, as well as the priests and Levites. 3The Levites thirty years old or more were counted, and the total number of men was thirty-eight thousand. 4David said, "Of these, twenty-four thousand are to supervise the work of the temple of the LORD and six thousand are to be officials and judges. 5Four thousand are to be gatekeepers and four thousand are to praise the LORD with the musical instruments I have provided for that purpose."

6David divided the Levites into groups corresponding to the sons of Levi: Gershon, Kohath and Merari.

Gershonites

7Belonging to the Gershonites:
  Ladan and Shimei.

8The sons of Ladan:
  Jehiel the first, Zetham and Joel—
  three in all.

9The sons of Shimei:
  Shelomoth, Haziel and Haran—
  three in all.
  These were the heads of the families of Ladan.

10And the sons of Shimei:
  Jahath, Ziza,*a* Jeush and Beriah.
  These were the sons of Shimei—
  four in all.

---

a9 *Solomon* sounds like and may be derived from the Hebrew for *peace.*
b14 That is, about 3,395 tons (about 3,450 metric tons)   *c14* That is, about 33,950 tons (about 34,500 metric tons)
a10 One Hebrew manuscript, Septuagint and Vulgate (see also verse 11); most Hebrew manuscripts *Zina*

[11]Jahath was the first and Ziza the second, but Jeush and Beriah did not have many sons; so they were counted as one family with one assignment.

Kohathites

[12]The sons of Kohath:
Amram, Izhar, Hebron and Uzziel—four in all.
[13]The sons of Amram:
Aaron and Moses.

Aaron was set apart, he and his descendants for ever, to consecrate the most holy things, to offer sacrifices before the LORD, to minister before him and to pronounce blessings in his name for ever. [14]The sons of Moses the man of God were counted as part of the tribe of Levi.
[15]The sons of Moses:
Gershom and Eliezer.
[16]The descendants of Gershom:
Shubael was the first.
[17]The descendants of Eliezer:
Rehabiah was the first.

Eliezer had no other sons, but the sons of Rehabiah were very numerous.
[18]The sons of Izhar:
Shelomith was the first.
[19]The sons of Hebron:
Jeriah the first, Amariah the second, Jahaziel the third and Jekameam the fourth.
[20]The sons of Uzziel:
Micah the first and Isshiah the second.

Merarites

[21]The sons of Merari:
Mahli and Mushi.
The sons of Mahli:
Eleazar and Kish.
[22]Eleazar died without having sons: he had only daughters. Their cousins, the sons of Kish, married them.
[23]The sons of Mushi:
Mahli, Eder and Jerimoth—three in all.

[24]These were the descendants of Levi by their families—the heads of families as they were registered under their names and counted individually, that is, the workers twenty years old or more who served in the temple of the LORD. [25]For David had said, "Since the LORD, the God of Israel, has granted rest to his people and has come to dwell in Jerusalem for ever, [26]the Levites no longer need to carry the tabernacle or any of the articles used in its service." [27]According to the last instructions of David, the Levites were counted from those twenty years old or more.

[28]The duty of the Levites was to help Aaron's descendants in the service of the temple of the LORD: to be in charge of the courtyards, the side rooms, the purification of all sacred things and the performance of other duties at the house of God. [29]They were in charge of the bread set out on the table, the flour for the grain offerings, the unleavened wafers, the baking and the mixing, and all measurements of quantity and size. [30]They were also to stand every morning to thank and praise the LORD. They were to do the same in the evening [31]and whenever burnt offerings were presented to the LORD on Sabbaths and at New Moon festivals and at appointed feasts. They were to serve before the LORD regularly in the proper number and in the way prescribed for them.

[32]And so the Levites carried out their responsibilities for the Tent of Meeting, for the Holy Place and, under their brothers the descendants of Aaron, for the service of the temple of the LORD.

The Divisions of Priests

24 These were the divisions of the sons of Aaron:

The sons of Aaron were Nadab, Abihu, Eleazar and Ithamar. [2]But Nadab and Abihu died before their father did, and they had no sons; so Eleazar and Ithamar served as the priests. [3]With the help of Zadok a descendant of Eleazar and Ahimelech a descendant of Ithamar, David separated them into divisions for their appointed order of ministering. [4]A larger number of leaders were found among Eleazar's descendants than among Ithamar's, and they were divided accordingly: sixteen heads of families from Eleazar's descendants and eight heads of families from Ithamar's descendants. [5]They divided them impartially by drawing lots, for there were officials of the sanctuary and officials of God among the descendants of both Eleazar and Ithamar.

[6]The scribe Shemaiah son of Nethanel, a Levite, recorded their names in the presence of the king and of the officials: Zadok the priest, Ahimelech son of Abiathar and the heads of families of the priests and of the Levites—one family being taken from Eleazar and then one from Ithamar.

[7]The first lot fell to Jehoiarib,
   the second to Jedaiah,
[8]the third to Harim,
   the fourth to Seorim,
[9]the fifth to Malkijah,
   the sixth to Mijamin,
[10]the seventh to Hakkoz,
   the eighth to Abijah,
[11]the ninth to Jeshua,
   the tenth to Shecaniah,
[12]the eleventh to Eliashib,
   the twelfth to Jakim,
[13]the thirteenth to Huppah,
   the fourteenth to Jeshebeab,
[14]the fifteenth to Bilgah,
   the sixteenth to Immer,
[15]the seventeenth to Hezir,
   the eighteenth to Happizzez,
[16]the nineteenth to Pethahiah,
   the twentieth to Jehezkel,
[17]the twenty-first to Jakin,
   the twenty-second to Gamul,
[18]the twenty-third to Delaiah
   and the twenty-fourth to Maaziah.

[19]This was their appointed order of ministering when they entered the temple of the LORD, according to the regulations prescribed for them by their forefather Aaron, as the LORD, the God of Israel, had commanded him.

The Rest of the Levites

[20]As for the rest of the descendants of Levi:

   from the sons of Amram:
      Shubael;
   from the sons of Shubael:
      Jehdeiah.
   [21]As for Rehabiah, from his sons:
      Isshiah was the first.
[22]From the Izharites: Shelomoth; from the sons of Shelomoth: Jahath.
[23]The sons of Hebron: Jeriah the first,[a] Amariah the second, Jahaziel the third and Jekameam the fourth.
[24]The son of Uzziel: Micah;
   from the sons of Micah: Shamir.
   [25]The brother of Micah: Isshiah;
   from the sons of Isshiah: Zechariah.
[26]The sons of Merari: Mahli and Mushi. The son of Jaaziah: Beno.
[27]The sons of Merari:
   from Jaaziah: Beno, Shoham, Zaccur and Ibri.
[28]From Mahli: Eleazar, who had no sons.
[29]From Kish: the son of Kish: Jerahmeel.
[30]And the sons of Mushi: Mahli, Eder and Jerimoth.

These were the Levites, according to their families. [31]They also cast lots, just as their brothers the descendants of Aaron did, in the presence of King David and of Zadok, Ahimelech, and the heads of families of the priests and of the Levites. The families of the oldest brother were treated the same as those of the youngest.

The Singers

25 David, together with the commanders of the army, set apart some of the sons of Asaph, Heman and Jeduthun for the ministry of prophesying, accompanied by harps, lyres and cymbals. Here is the list of the men who performed this service:

---

[a]23 Two Hebrew manuscripts and some Septuagint manuscripts (see also 1 Chron. 23:19); most Hebrew manuscripts *The sons of Jeriah:*

²From the sons of Asaph:

Zaccur, Joseph, Nethaniah and Asarelah. The sons of Asaph were under the supervision of Asaph, who prophesied under the king's supervision.

³As for Jeduthun, from his sons:

Gedaliah, Zeri, Jeshaiah, Shimei,ᵃ Hashabiah and Mattithiah, six in all, under the supervision of their father Jeduthun, who prophesied, using the harp in thanking and praising the LORD.

⁴As for Heman, from his sons:

Bukkiah, Mattaniah, Uzziel, Shubael and Jerimoth; Hananiah, Hanani, Eliathah, Giddalti and Romamti-Ezer; Joshbekashah, Mallothi, Hothir and Mahazioth.

⁵All these were sons of Heman the king's seer. They were given to him through the promises of God to exalt him.ᵇ God gave Heman fourteen sons and three daughters.

⁶All these men were under the supervision of their fathers for the music of the temple of the LORD, with cymbals, lyres and harps, for the ministry at the house of God. Asaph, Jeduthun and Heman were under the supervision of the king. ⁷Along with their relatives—all of them trained and skilled in music for the LORD—they numbered 288. ⁸Young and old alike, teacher as well as student, cast lots for their duties.

⁹The first lot, which was for Asaph, fell to Joseph,

his sons and relatives,ᶜ	12ᵈ
the second to Gedaliah,	
he and his relatives	
and sons,	12
¹⁰the third to Zaccur,	
his sons and relatives,	12
¹¹the fourth to Izri,ᵉ	
his sons and relatives,	12
¹²the fifth to Nethaniah,	
his sons and relatives,	12
¹³the sixth to Bukkiah,	
his sons and relatives,	12
¹⁴the seventh to Jesarelah,ᶠ	
his sons and relatives,	12
¹⁵the eighth to Jeshaiah,	
his sons and relatives,	12
¹⁶the ninth to Mattaniah,	
his sons and relatives,	12
¹⁷the tenth to Shimei,	
his sons and relatives,	12
¹⁸the eleventh to Azarel,ᵍ	
his sons and relatives,	12
¹⁹the twelfth to Hashabiah,	
his sons and relatives,	12
²⁰the thirteenth to Shubael,	
his sons and relatives,	12
²¹the fourteenth to Mattithiah,	
his sons and relatives,	12
²²the fifteenth to Jerimoth,	
his sons and relatives,	12
²³the sixteenth to Hananiah,	
his sons and relatives,	12
²⁴the seventeenth to Joshbekashah,	
his sons and relatives,	12
²⁵the eighteenth to Hanani,	
his sons and relatives,	12
²⁶the nineteenth to Mallothi,	
his sons and relatives,	12
²⁷the twentieth to Eliathah,	
his sons and relatives,	12
²⁸the twenty-first to Hothir,	
his sons and relatives,	12
²⁹the twenty-second to Giddalti,	
his sons and relatives,	12
³⁰the twenty-third to Mahazioth,	
his sons and relatives,	12
³¹the twenty-fourth to Romamti-Ezer,	
his sons and relatives.	12

The Gatekeepers

26 The divisions of the gatekeepers:

From the Korahites: Meshelemiah son of Kore, one of the sons of Asaph.

²Meshelemiah had sons:

Zechariah the firstborn,

ᵃ3 One Hebrew manuscript and some Septuagint manuscripts (see also verse 17); most Hebrew manuscripts do not have *Shimei*.   ᵇ5 Hebrew *exalt the horn*   ᶜ9 See Septuagint; Hebrew does not have *his sons and relatives*.
ᵈ9 See the total in verse 7; Hebrew does not have *twelve*.   ᵉ11 A variant of *Zeri*   ᶠ14 A variant of *Asarelah*
ᵍ18 A variant of *Uzziel*

Jediael the second,
Zebadiah the third,
Jathniel the fourth,
3Elam the fifth,
Jehohanan the sixth
and Eliehoenai the seventh.

4Obed-Edom also had sons:
Shemaiah the firstborn,
Jehozabad the second,
Joah the third,
Sacar the fourth,
Nethanel the fifth,
5Ammiel the sixth,
Issachar the seventh
and Peullethai the eighth.
(For God had blessed Obed-
Edom.)

6His son Shemaiah also had sons, who
were leaders in their father's family
because they were very capable
men. 7The sons of Shemaiah:
Othni, Rephael, Obed and Elzabad; his relatives Elihu and Sema-
kiah were also able men. 8All these
were descendants of Obed-Edom;
they and their sons and their relatives were capable men with the
strength to do the work—descendants of Obed-Edom, 62 in all.

9Meshelemiah had sons and relatives,
who were able men—18 in all.

10Hosah the Merarite had sons: Shimri
the first (although he was not the
firstborn, his father had appointed
him the first), 11Hilkiah the second,
Tabaliah the third and Zechariah
the fourth. The sons and relatives
of Hosah were 13 in all.

12These divisions of the gatekeepers,
through their chief men, had duties for
ministering in the temple of the LORD, just
as their relatives had. 13Lots were cast for
each gate, according to their families,
young and old alike.

14The lot for the East Gate fell to
Shelemiah.*a* Then lots were cast for his son
Zechariah, a wise counsellor, and the lot
for the North Gate fell to him. 15The lot
for the South Gate fell to Obed-Edom,
and the lot for the storehouse fell to his
sons. 16The lots for the West Gate and the
Shalleketh Gate on the upper road fell to
Shuppim and Hosah.

Guard was alongside guard: 17There
were six Levites a day on the east, four a
day on the north, four a day on the south
and two at a time at the storehouse. 18As
for the court to the west, there were four
at the road and two at the court itself.

19These were the divisions of the
gatekeepers who were descendants of
Korah and Merari.

The Treasurers and Other Officials

20Their fellow Levites were*b* in charge
of the treasuries of the house of God and
the treasuries for the dedicated things.

21The descendants of Ladan, who were
Gershonites through Ladan and who were
heads of families belonging to Ladan the
Gershonite, were Jehieli, 22the sons of
Jehieli, Zetham and his brother Joel.
They were in charge of the treasuries of
the temple of the LORD.

23From the Amramites, the Izharites,
the Hebronites and the Uzzielites:

24Shubael, a descendant of Gershom
son of Moses, was the officer in
charge of the treasuries. 25His relatives through Eliezer: Rehabiah his
son, Jeshaiah his son, Joram his
son, Zicri his son and Shelomith his
son. 26Shelomith and his relatives
were in charge of all the treasuries
for the things dedicated by King
David, by the heads of families who
were the commanders of thousands
and commanders of hundreds, and
by the other army commanders.
27Some of the plunder taken in battle they dedicated for the repair of
the temple of the LORD. 28And
everything dedicated by Samuel
the seer and by Saul son of Kish,
Abner son of Ner and Joab son of
Zeruiah, and all the other dedicated things were in the care of
Shelomith and his relatives.

29From the Izharites: Kenaniah and his
sons were assigned duties away
from the temple, as officials and
judges over Israel.

---

a14 A variant of *Meshelemiah*   *b20* Septuagint; Hebrew *As for the Levites, Ahijah was*

[30]From the Hebronites: Hashabiah and his relatives—seventeen hundred able men—were responsible in Israel west of the Jordan for all the work of the LORD and for the king's service. [31]As for the Hebronites, Jeriah was their chief according to the genealogical records of their families. In the fortieth year of David's reign a search was made in the records, and capable men among the Hebronites were found at Jazer in Gilead. [32]Jeriah had two thousand seven hundred relatives, who were able men and heads of families, and King David put them in charge of the Reubenites, the Gadites and the half-tribe of Manasseh for every matter pertaining to God and for the affairs of the king.

Army Divisions

27 This is the list of the Israelites—heads of families, commanders of thousands and commanders of hundreds, and their officers, who served the king in all that concerned the army divisions that were on duty month by month throughout the year. Each division consisted of 24,000 men.

[2]In charge of the first division, for the first month, was Jashobeam son of Zabdiel. There were 24,000 men in his division. [3]He was a descendant of Perez and chief of all the army officers for the first month.

[4]In charge of the division for the second month was Dodai the Ahohite; Mikloth was the leader of his division. There were 24,000 men in his division.

[5]The third army commander, for the third month, was Benaiah son of Jehoiada the priest. He was chief and there were 24,000 men in his division. [6]This was the Benaiah who was a mighty man among the Thirty and was over the Thirty. His son Ammizabad was in charge of his division.

[7]The fourth, for the fourth month, was Asahel the brother of Joab; his son Zebadiah was his successor. There were 24,000 men in his division.

[8]The fifth, for the fifth month, was the commander Shamhuth the Izrahite. There were 24,000 men in his division.

[9]The sixth, for the sixth month, was Ira the son of Ikkesh the Tekoite. There were 24,000 men in his division.

[10]The seventh, for the seventh month, was Helez the Pelonite, an Ephraimite. There were 24,000 men in his division.

[11]The eighth, for the eighth month, was Sibbecai the Hushathite, a Zerahite. There were 24,000 men in his division.

[12]The ninth, for the ninth month, was Abiezer the Anathothite, a Benjamite. There were 24,000 men in his division.

[13]The tenth, for the tenth month, was Maharai the Netophathite, a Zerahite. There were 24,000 men in his division.

[14]The eleventh, for the eleventh month, was Benaiah the Pirathonite, an Ephraimite. There were 24,000 men in his division.

[15]The twelfth, for the twelfth month, was Heldai the Netophathite, from the family of Othniel. There were 24,000 men in his division.

Officers of the Tribes

[16]The officers over the tribes of Israel:

over the Reubenites: Eliezer son of Zicri;

over the Simeonites: Shephatiah son of Maacah;

[17]over Levi: Hashabiah son of Kemuel;

over Aaron: Zadok;

[18]over Judah: Elihu, a brother of David;

over Issachar: Omri son of Michael;

[19]over Zebulun: Ishmaiah son of Obadiah;

over Naphtali: Jerimoth son of Azriel;

[20]over the Ephraimites: Hoshea son of Azaziah;

over half the tribe of Manasseh: Joel son of Pedaiah;

²¹over the half-tribe of Manasseh in Gilead: Iddo son of Zechariah;

over Benjamin: Jaasiel son of Abner;

²²over Dan: Azarel son of Jeroham.

These were the officers over the tribes of Israel.

²³David did not take the number of the men twenty years old or less, because the LORD had promised to make Israel as numerous as the stars in the sky. ²⁴Joab son of Zeruiah began to count the men but did not finish. Wrath came on Israel on account of this numbering, and the number was not entered in the book*ᵃ* of the annals of King David.

The King's Overseers

²⁵Azmaveth son of Adiel was in charge of the royal storehouses.

Jonathan son of Uzziah was in charge of the storehouses in the outlying districts, in the towns, the villages and the watch-towers.

²⁶Ezri son of Kelub was in charge of the field workers who farmed the land.

²⁷Shimei the Ramathite was in charge of the vineyards.

Zabdi the Shiphmite was in charge of the produce of the vineyards for the wine vats.

²⁸Baal-Hanan the Gederite was in charge of the olive and sycamore-fig trees in the western foothills.

Joash was in charge of the supplies of olive oil.

²⁹Shitrai the Sharonite was in charge of the herds grazing in Sharon.

Shaphat son of Adlai was in charge of the herds in the valleys.

³⁰Obil the Ishmaelite was in charge of the camels.

Jehdeiah the Meronothite was in charge of the donkeys.

³¹Jaziz the Hagrite was in charge of the flocks.

All these were the officials in charge of King David's property.

³²Jonathan, David's uncle, was a counsellor, a man of insight and a scribe. Jehiel son of Hacmoni took care of the king's sons.

³³Ahithophel was the king's counsellor. Hushai the Arkite was the king's friend. ³⁴Ahithophel was succeeded by Jehoiada son of Benaiah and by Abiathar.

Joab was the commander of the royal army.

David's Plans for the Temple

28 David summoned all the officials of Israel to assemble at Jerusalem: the officers over the tribes, the commanders of the divisions in the service of the king, the commanders of thousands and commanders of hundreds, and the officials in charge of all the property and livestock belonging to the king and his sons, together with the palace officials, the mighty men and all the brave warriors.

²King David rose to his feet and said: "Listen to me, my brothers and my people. I had it in my heart to build a house as a place of rest for the ark of the covenant of the LORD, for the footstool of our God, and I made plans to build it. ³But God said to me, 'You are not to build a house for my Name, because you are a warrior and have shed blood.'

⁴"Yet the LORD, the God of Israel, chose me from my whole family to be king over Israel for ever. He chose Judah as leader, and from the house of Judah he chose my family, and from my father's sons he was pleased to make me king over all Israel. ⁵Of all my sons—and the LORD has given me many—he has chosen my son Solomon to sit on the throne of the kingdom of the LORD over Israel. ⁶He said to me, 'Solomon your son is the one who will build my house and my courts, for I have chosen him to be my son, and I will be his father. ⁷I will establish his kingdom for ever if he is unswerving in carrying out my commands and laws, as is being done at this time.'

⁸"So now I charge you in the sight of all Israel and of the assembly of the LORD,

---

ᵃ24 Septuagint; Hebrew *number*

and in the hearing of our God: Be careful to follow all the commands of the LORD your God, that you may possess this good land and pass it on as an inheritance to your descendants for ever.

9"And you, my son Solomon, acknowledge the God of your father, and serve him with wholehearted devotion and with a willing mind, for the LORD searches every heart and understands every motive behind the thoughts. If you seek him, he will be found by you; but if you forsake him, he will reject you for ever. 10Consider now, for the LORD has chosen you to build a temple as a sanctuary. Be strong and do the work."

11Then David gave his son Solomon the plans for the portico of the temple, its buildings, its storerooms, its upper parts, its inner rooms and the place of atonement. 12He gave him the plans of all that the Spirit had put in his mind for the courts of the temple of the LORD and all the surrounding rooms, for the treasuries of the temple of God and for the treasuries for the dedicated things. 13He gave him instructions for the divisions of the priests and Levites, and for all the work of serving in the temple of the LORD, as well as for all the articles to be used in its service. 14He designated the weight of gold for all the gold articles to be used in various kinds of service, and the weight of silver for all the silver articles to be used in various kinds of service: 15the weight of gold for the gold lampstands and their lamps, with the weight for each lampstand and its lamps; and the weight of silver for each silver lampstand and its lamps, according to the use of each lampstand; 16the weight of gold for each table for consecrated bread; the weight of silver for the silver tables; 17the weight of pure gold for the forks, sprinkling bowls and pitchers; the weight of gold for each gold dish; the weight of silver for each silver dish; 18and the weight of the refined gold for the altar of incense. He also gave him the plan for the chariot, that is, the cherubim of gold that spread their wings and shelter the ark of the covenant of the LORD.

19"All this," David said, "I have in writing from the hand of the LORD upon me, and he gave me understanding in all the details of the plan."

20David also said to Solomon his son, "Be strong and courageous, and do the work. Do not be afraid or discouraged, for the LORD God, my God, is with you. He will not fail you or forsake you until all the work for the service of the temple of the LORD is finished. 21The divisions of the priests and Levites are ready for all the work on the temple of God, and every willing man skilled in any craft will help you in all the work. The officials and all the people will obey your every command."

Gifts for Building the Temple

29 Then King David said to the whole assembly: "My son Solomon, the one whom God has chosen, is young and inexperienced. The task is great, because this palatial structure is not for man but for the LORD God. 2With all my resources I have provided for the temple of my God— gold for the gold work, silver for the silver, bronze for the bronze, iron for the iron and wood for the wood, as well as onyx for the settings, turquoise,*a* stones of various colours, and all kinds of fine stone and marble—all of these in large quantities. 3Besides, in my devotion to the temple of my God I now give my personal treasures of gold and silver for the temple of my God, over and above everything I have provided for this holy temple: 4three thousand talents*b* of gold (gold of Ophir) and seven thousand talents*c* of refined silver, for the overlaying of the walls of the buildings, 5for the gold work and the silver work, and for all the work to be done by the craftsmen. Now, who is willing to consecrate himself today to the LORD?"

6Then the leaders of families, the officers of the tribes of Israel, the commanders of thousands and commanders of hundreds, and the officials in charge of the

---

a2 The meaning of the Hebrew for this word is uncertain.
c4 That is, about 240 tons (about 240 metric tons)

b4 That is, about 100 tons (about 100 metric tons)

king's work gave willingly. ⁷They gave towards the work on the temple of God five thousand talents*d* and ten thousand darics*e* of gold, ten thousand talents*f* of silver, eighteen thousand talents*g* of bronze and a hundred thousand talents*h* of iron. ⁸Any who had precious stones gave them to the treasury of the temple of the LORD in the custody of Jehiel the Gershonite. ⁹The people rejoiced at the willing response of their leaders, for they had given freely and wholeheartedly to the LORD. David the king also rejoiced greatly.

David's Prayer

¹⁰David praised the LORD in the presence of the whole assembly, saying,

"Praise be to you, O LORD,
  God of our father Israel,
  from everlasting to everlasting.
¹¹Yours, O LORD, is the greatness and the power
  and the glory and the majesty and the splendour,
  for everything in heaven and earth is yours.
Yours, O LORD, is the kingdom;
  you are exalted as head over all.
¹²Wealth and honour come from you;
  you are the ruler of all things.
In your hands are strength and power
  to exalt and give strength to all.
¹³Now, our God, we give you thanks,
  and praise your glorious name.

¹⁴"But who am I, and who are my people, that we should be able to give as generously as this? Everything comes from you, and we have given you only what comes from your hand. ¹⁵We are aliens and strangers in your sight, as were all our forefathers. Our days on earth are like a shadow, without hope. ¹⁶O LORD our God, as for all this abundance that we have provided for building you a temple for your Holy Name, it comes from your hand, and all of it belongs to you. ¹⁷I

know, my God, that you test the heart and are pleased with integrity. All these things have I given willingly and with honest intent. And now I have seen with joy how willingly your people who are here have given to you. ¹⁸O LORD, God of our fathers Abraham, Isaac and Israel, keep this desire in the hearts of your people for ever, and keep their hearts loyal to you. ¹⁹And give my son Solomon the wholehearted devotion to keep your commands, requirements and decrees and to do everything to build the palatial structure for which I have provided."

²⁰Then David said to the whole assembly, "Praise the LORD your God." So they all praised the LORD, the God of their fathers; they bowed low and fell prostrate before the LORD and the king.

Solomon Acknowledged as King

²¹The next day they made sacrifices to the LORD and presented burnt offerings to him: a thousand bulls, a thousand rams and a thousand male lambs, together with their drink offerings, and other sacrifices in abundance for all Israel. ²²They ate and drank with great joy in the presence of the LORD that day.

Then they acknowledged Solomon son of David as king a second time, anointing him before the LORD to be ruler and Zadok to be priest. ²³So Solomon sat on the throne of the LORD as king in place of his father David. He prospered and all Israel obeyed him. ²⁴All the officers and mighty men, as well as all of King David's sons, pledged their submission to King Solomon.

²⁵The LORD highly exalted Solomon in the sight of all Israel and bestowed on him royal splendour such as no king over Israel ever had before.

The Death of David

²⁶David son of Jesse was king over all Israel. ²⁷He ruled over Israel for forty

---

d7 That is, about 170 tons (about 170 metric tons)
f7 That is, about 340 tons (about 345 metric tons)
h7 That is, about 3,400 tons (about 3,450 metric tons)

e7 That is, about 185 pounds (about 84 kilograms)
g7 That is, about 610 tons (about 620 metric tons)

years—seven in Hebron and thirty-three in Jerusalem. ²⁸He died at a good old age, having enjoyed long life, wealth and honour. His son Solomon succeeded him as king.

²⁹As for the events of King David's reign, from beginning to end, they are written in the records of Samuel the seer, the records of Nathan the prophet and the records of Gad the seer, ³⁰together with the details of his reign and power, and the circumstances that surrounded him and Israel and the kingdoms of all the other lands.

2 Chronicles

Solomon Asks for Wisdom

1 Solomon son of David established himself firmly over his kingdom, for the LORD his God was with him and made him exceedingly great.

²Then Solomon spoke to all Israel—to the commanders of thousands and commanders of hundreds, to the judges and to all the leaders in Israel, the heads of families—³and Solomon and the whole assembly went to the high place at Gibeon, for God's Tent of Meeting was there, which Moses the LORD's servant had made in the desert. ⁴Now David had brought up the ark of God from Kiriath Jearim to the place he had prepared for it, because he had pitched a tent for it in Jerusalem. ⁵But the bronze altar that Bezalel son of Uri, the son of Hur, had made was in Gibeon in front of the tabernacle of the LORD; so Solomon and the assembly enquired of him there. ⁶Solomon went up to the bronze altar before the LORD in the Tent of Meeting and offered a thousand burnt offerings on it.

⁷That night God appeared to Solomon and said to him, "Ask for whatever you want me to give you."

⁸Solomon answered God, "You have shown great kindness to David my father and have made me king in his place. ⁹Now, LORD God, let your promise to my father David be confirmed, for you have made me king over a people who are as numerous as the dust of the earth. ¹⁰Give me wisdom and knowledge, that I may lead this people, for who is able to govern this great people of yours?"

¹¹God said to Solomon, "Since this is your heart's desire and you have not asked for wealth, riches or honour, nor for the death of your enemies, and since you have not asked for a long life but for wisdom and knowledge to govern my people over whom I have made you king, ¹²therefore wisdom and knowledge will be given you. And I will also give you wealth, riches and honour, such as no king who was before you ever had and none after you will have."

¹³Then Solomon went to Jerusalem from the high place at Gibeon, from before the Tent of Meeting. And he reigned over Israel.

¹⁴Solomon accumulated chariots and horses; he had fourteen hundred chariots and twelve thousand horses,ᵃ which he kept in the chariot cities and also with him in Jerusalem. ¹⁵The king made silver and gold as common in Jerusalem as stones, and cedar as plentiful as sycamore-fig trees in the foothills. ¹⁶Solomon's horses were imported from Egyptᵇ and from Kueᶜ—the royal merchants purchased them from Kue. ¹⁷They imported a chariot from Egypt for six hundred shekelsᵈ of silver, and a horse for a hundred and fifty.ᵉ They also exported them to all the kings of the Hittites and of the Arameans.

ᵃ14 Or charioteers   ᵇ16 Or possibly Muzur, a region in Cilicia; also in verse 17   ᶜ16 Probably Cilicia
ᵈ17 That is, about 15 pounds (about 7 kilograms)   ᵉ17 That is, about 3¾ pounds (about 1.7 kilograms)

Preparations for Building the Temple

2 Solomon gave orders to build a temple for the Name of the LORD and a royal palace for himself. ²He conscripted seventy thousand men as carriers and eighty thousand as stonecutters in the hills and thirty-six hundred as foremen over them.

³Solomon sent this message to Hiram*ᵃ* king of Tyre:

"Send me cedar logs as you did for my father David when you sent him cedar to build a palace to live in. ⁴Now I am about to build a temple for the Name of the LORD my God and to dedicate it to him for burning fragrant incense before him, for setting out the consecrated bread regularly, and for making burnt offerings every morning and evening and on Sabbaths and New Moons and at the appointed feasts of the LORD our God. This is a lasting ordinance for Israel.

⁵"The temple I am going to build will be great, because our God is greater than all other gods. ⁶But who is able to build a temple for him, since the heavens, even the highest heavens, cannot contain him? Who then am I to build a temple for him, except as a place to burn sacrifices before him?

⁷"Send me, therefore, a man skilled to work in gold and silver, bronze and iron, and in purple, crimson and blue yarn, and experienced in the art of engraving, to work in Judah and Jerusalem with my skilled craftsmen, whom my father David provided.

⁸"Send me also cedar, pine and algum*ᵇ* logs from Lebanon, for I know that your men are skilled in cutting timber there. My men shall work with yours ⁹to provide me with plenty of timber, because the temple I build must be large and magnificent. ¹⁰I will give your servants, the woodsmen who cut the timber, twenty thousand cors*ᶜ* of ground wheat, twenty thousand cors of barley, twenty thousand baths*ᵈ* of wine and twenty thousand baths of olive oil."

¹¹Hiram king of Tyre replied by letter to Solomon:

"Because the LORD loves his people, he has made you their king."

¹²And Hiram added:

"Praise be to the LORD, the God of Israel, who made heaven and earth! He has given King David a wise son, endowed with intelligence and discernment, who will build a temple for the LORD and a palace for himself.

¹³"I am sending you Huram-Abi, a man of great skill, ¹⁴whose mother was from Dan and whose father was from Tyre. He is trained to work in gold and silver, bronze and iron, stone and wood, and with purple and blue and crimson yarn and fine linen. He is experienced in all kinds of engraving and can execute any design given to him. He will work with your craftsmen and with those of my lord, David your father.

¹⁵"Now let my lord send his servants the wheat and barley and the olive oil and wine he promised, ¹⁶and we will cut all the logs from Lebanon that you need and will float them in rafts by sea down to Joppa. You can then take them up to Jerusalem."

¹⁷Solomon took a census of all the aliens who were in Israel, after the census his father David had taken; and they were found to be 153,600. ¹⁸He assigned 70,000 of them to be carriers and 80,000 to be stonecutters in the hills, with 3,600 foremen over them to keep the people working.

Solomon Builds the Temple

3 Then Solomon began to build the temple of the LORD in Jerusalem on Mount Moriah, where the LORD had

---

ᵃ3 Hebrew *Huram*, a variant of *Hiram*; also in verses 11 and 12
ᶜ10 That is, probably about 120,000 bushels (about 4,400 kilolitres)
ᵈ10 That is, probably about 95,000 gallons (about 440 kilolitres)
ᵇ8 Probably a variant of *almug*; possibly juniper

appeared to his father David. It was on the threshing-floor of Araunah[a] the Jebusite, the place provided by David. [2]He began building on the second day of the second month in the fourth year of his reign.

[3]The foundation Solomon laid for building the temple of God was sixty cubits long and twenty cubits wide[b] (using the cubit of the old standard). [4]The portico at the front of the temple was twenty cubits[c] long across the width of the building and twenty cubits[d] high.

He overlaid the inside with pure gold. [5]He panelled the main hall with pine and covered it with fine gold and decorated it with palm tree and chain designs. [6]He adorned the temple with precious stones. And the gold he used was gold of Parvaim. [7]He overlaid the ceiling beams, doorframes, walls and doors of the temple with gold, and he carved cherubim on the walls.

[8]He built the Most Holy Place, its length corresponding to the width of the temple —twenty cubits long and twenty cubits wide. He overlaid the inside with six hundred talents[e] of fine gold. [9]The gold nails weighed fifty shekels.[f] He also overlaid the upper parts with gold.

[10]In the Most Holy Place he made a pair of sculptured cherubim and overlaid them with gold. [11]The total wing-span of the cherubim was twenty cubits. One wing of the first cherub was five cubits[g] long and touched the temple wall, while its other wing, also five cubits long, touched the wing of the other cherub. [12]Similarly one wing of the second cherub was five cubits long and touched the other temple wall, and its other wing, also five cubits long, touched the wing of the first cherub. [13]The wings of these cherubim extended twenty cubits. They stood on their feet, facing the main hall.[h]

[14]He made the curtain of blue, purple and crimson yarn and fine linen, with cherubim worked into it.

[15]In the front of the temple he made two pillars, which ⌊together⌋ were thirty-five cubits[i] long, each with a capital on top measuring five cubits. [16]He made interwoven chains[j] and put them on top of the pillars. He also made a hundred pomegranates and attached them to the chains. [17]He erected the pillars in the front of the temple, one to the south and one to the north. The one to the south he named Jakin[k] and the one to the north Boaz.[l]

The Temple's Furnishings

4 He made a bronze altar twenty cubits long, twenty cubits wide and ten cubits high.[a] [2]He made the Sea of cast metal, circular in shape, measuring ten cubits from rim to rim and five cubits[b] high. It took a line of thirty cubits[c] to measure round it. [3]Below the rim, figures of bulls encircled it—ten to a cubit.[d] The bulls were cast in two rows in one piece with the Sea.

[4]The Sea stood on twelve bulls, three facing north, three facing west, three facing south and three facing east. The Sea rested on top of them, and their hindquarters were towards the centre. [5]It was a handbreadth[e] in thickness, and its rim was like the rim of a cup, like a lily blossom. It held three thousand baths.[f]

[6]He then made ten basins for washing and placed five on the south side and five on the north. In them the things to be used for the burnt offerings were rinsed, but the Sea was to be used by the priests for washing.

---

[a]1 Hebrew *Ornan*, a variant of *Araunah*
[b]3 That is, about 90 feet (about 27 metres) long and 30 feet (about 9 metres) wide
[c]4 That is, about 30 feet (about 9 metres); also in verses 8, 11 and 13
[d]4 Some Septuagint and Syriac manuscripts; Hebrew *and a hundred and twenty*
[e]8 That is, about 20 tons (about 21 metric tons)   [f]9 That is, about 1¼ pounds (about 0.6 kilogram)
[g]11 That is, about 7½ feet (about 2.3 metres); also in verse 15   [h]13 Or *facing inward*
[i]15 That is, about 52 feet (about 16 metres)
[j]16 Or possibly *made chains in the inner sanctuary*; the meaning of the Hebrew for this phrase is uncertain.
[k]17 *Jakin* probably means *he establishes*.   [l]17 *Boaz* probably means *in him is strength*.
[a]1 That is, about 30 feet (about 9 metres) long and wide, and about 15 feet (about 4.5 metres) high
[b]2 That is, about 7½ feet (about 2.3 metres)   [c]2 That is, about 45 feet (about 13.5 metres)
[d]3 That is, about 1½ feet (about 0.5 metre)   [e]5 That is, about 3 inches (about 8 centimetres)
[f]5 That is, about 14,500 gallons (about 66 kilolitres)

[7]He made ten gold lampstands according to the specifications for them and placed them in the temple, five on the south side and five on the north.

[8]He made ten tables and placed them in the temple, five on the south side and five on the north. He also made a hundred gold sprinkling bowls.

[9]He made the courtyard of the priests, and the large court and the doors for the court, and overlaid the doors with bronze. [10]He placed the Sea on the south side, at the south-east corner.

[11]He also made the pots and shovels and sprinkling bowls.

So Huram finished the work he had undertaken for King Solomon in the temple of God:

[12]the two pillars;
the two bowl-shaped capitals on top of the pillars;
the two sets of network decorating the two bowl-shaped capitals on top of the pillars;
[13]the four hundred pomegranates for the two sets of network (two rows of pomegranates for each network, decorating the bowl-shaped capitals on top of the pillars);
[14]the stands with their basins;
[15]the Sea and the twelve bulls under it;
[16]the pots, shovels, meat forks and all related articles.

All the objects that Huram-Abi made for King Solomon for the temple of the LORD were of polished bronze. [17]The king had them cast in clay moulds in the plain of the Jordan between Succoth and Zarethan.[g] [18]All these things that Solomon made amounted to so much that the weight of the bronze was not determined.

[19]Solomon also made all the furnishings that were in God's temple:

the golden altar;
the tables on which was the bread of the Presence;
[20]the lampstands of pure gold with their lamps, to burn in front of the inner sanctuary as prescribed;

[21]the gold floral work and lamps and tongs (they were solid gold);
[22]the pure gold wick trimmers, sprinkling bowls, dishes and censers; and the gold doors of the temple: the inner doors to the Most Holy Place and the doors of the main hall.

5 When all the work Solomon had done for the temple of the LORD was finished, he brought in the things his father David had dedicated—the silver and gold and all the furnishings—and he placed them in the treasuries of God's temple.

The Ark Brought to the Temple

[2]Then Solomon summoned to Jerusalem the elders of Israel, all the heads of the tribes and the chiefs of the Israelite families, to bring up the ark of the LORD's covenant from Zion, the City of David. [3]And all the men of Israel came together to the king at the time of the festival in the seventh month.

[4]When all the elders of Israel had arrived, the Levites took up the ark, [5]and they brought up the ark and the Tent of Meeting and all the sacred furnishings in it. The priests, who were Levites, carried them up; [6]and King Solomon and the entire assembly of Israel that had gathered about him were before the ark, sacrificing so many sheep and cattle that they could not be recorded or counted.

[7]The priests then brought the ark of the LORD's covenant to its place in the inner sanctuary of the temple, the Most Holy Place, and put it beneath the wings of the cherubim. [8]The cherubim spread their wings over the place of the ark and covered the ark and its carrying poles. [9]These poles were so long that their ends, extending from the ark, could be seen from in front of the inner sanctuary, but not from outside the Holy Place; and they are still there today. [10]There was nothing in the ark except the two tablets that Moses had placed in it at Horeb, where the LORD made a covenant with the Israelites after they came out of Egypt.

g17 Hebrew Zeredatha, a variant of Zarethan

¹¹The priests then withdrew from the Holy Place. All the priests who were there had consecrated themselves, regardless of their divisions. ¹²All the Levites who were musicians—Asaph, Heman, Jeduthun and their sons and relatives—stood on the east side of the altar, dressed in fine linen and playing cymbals, harps and lyres. They were accompanied by 120 priests sounding trumpets. ¹³The trumpeters and singers joined in unison, as with one voice, to give praise and thanks to the LORD. Accompanied by trumpets, cymbals and other instruments, they raised their voices in praise to the LORD and sang:

"He is good;
   his love endures for ever."

Then the temple of the LORD was filled with a cloud, ¹⁴and the priests could not perform their service because of the cloud, for the glory of the LORD filled the temple of God.

6 Then Solomon said, "The LORD has said that he would dwell in a dark cloud; ²I have built a magnificent temple for you, a place for you to dwell for ever."

³While the whole assembly of Israel was standing there, the king turned round and blessed them. ⁴Then he said:

"Praise be to the LORD, the God of Israel, who with his hands has fulfilled what he promised with his mouth to my father David. For he said, ⁵'Since the day I brought my people out of Egypt, I have not chosen a city in any tribe of Israel to have a temple built for my Name to be there, nor have I chosen anyone to be the leader over my people Israel. ⁶But now I have chosen Jerusalem for my Name to be there, and I have chosen David to rule my people Israel.'

⁷"My father David had it in his heart to build a temple for the Name of the LORD, the God of Israel. ⁸But the LORD said to my father David, 'Because it was in your heart to build a temple for my Name, you did well to have this in your heart.

⁹Nevertheless, you are not the one to build the temple, but your son, who is your own flesh and blood—he is the one who will build the temple for my Name.'

¹⁰"The LORD has kept the promise he made. I have succeeded David my father and now I sit on the throne of Israel, just as the LORD promised, and I have built the temple for the Name of the LORD, the God of Israel. ¹¹There I have placed the ark, in which is the covenant of the LORD that he made with the people of Israel."

Solomon's Prayer of Dedication

¹²Then Solomon stood before the altar of the LORD in front of the whole assembly of Israel and spread out his hands. ¹³Now he had made a bronze platform, five cubits[a] long, five cubits wide and three cubits[b] high, and had placed it in the centre of the outer court. He stood on the platform and then knelt down before the whole assembly of Israel and spread out his hands towards heaven. ¹⁴He said:

"O LORD, God of Israel, there is no God like you in heaven or on earth—you who keep your covenant of love with your servants who continue wholeheartedly in your way. ¹⁵You have kept your promise to your servant David my father; with your mouth you have promised and with your hand you have fulfilled it—as it is today.

¹⁶"Now LORD, God of Israel, keep for your servant David my father the promises you made to him when you said, 'You shall never fail to have a man to sit before me on the throne of Israel, if only your sons are careful in all they do to walk before me according to my law, as you have done.' ¹⁷And now, O LORD, God of Israel, let your word that you promised your servant David come true.

¹⁸"But will God really dwell on earth with men? The heavens, even

---

a13 That is, about 7½ feet (about 2.3 metres)   *b13* That is, about 4½ feet (about 1.4 metres) the highest heavens, cannot contain you. How much less this temple that I have built! ¹⁹Yet give attention to your servant's prayer and his plea for mercy, O LORD my God. Hear the cry and the prayer that your servant is praying in your presence. ²⁰May your eyes be open towards this temple day and night, this place of which you said you would put your Name there. May you hear the prayer your servant prays towards this place. ²¹Hear the supplications of your servant and of your people Israel when they pray towards this place. Hear from heaven, your dwelling-place; and when you hear, forgive.

²²"When a man wrongs his neighbour and is required to take an oath and he comes and swears the oath before your altar in this temple, ²³then hear from heaven and act. Judge between your servants, repaying the guilty by bringing down on his own head what he has done. Declare the innocent not guilty and so establish his innocence.

²⁴"When your people Israel have been defeated by an enemy because they have sinned against you and when they turn back and confess your name, praying and making supplication before you in this temple, ²⁵then hear from heaven and forgive the sin of your people Israel and bring them back to the land you gave to them and their fathers.

²⁶"When the heavens are shut up and there is no rain because your people have sinned against you, and when they pray towards this place and confess your name and turn from their sin because you have afflicted them, ²⁷then hear from heaven and forgive the sin of your servants, your people Israel. Teach them the right way to live, and send rain on the land that you gave your people for an inheritance.

²⁸"When famine or plague comes to the land, or blight or mildew, locusts or grasshoppers, or when enemies besiege them in any of their cities, whatever disaster or disease may come, ²⁹and when a prayer or plea is made by any of your people Israel—each one aware of his afflictions and pains, and spreading out his hands towards this temple—³⁰then hear from heaven, your dwelling-place. Forgive, and deal with each man according to all he does, since you know his heart (for you alone know the hearts of men), ³¹so that they will fear you and walk in your ways all the time they live in the land that you gave our fathers.

³²"As for the foreigner who does not belong to your people Israel but has come from a distant land because of your great name and your mighty hand and your outstretched arm—when he comes and prays towards this temple, ³³then hear from heaven, your dwelling-place, and do whatever the foreigner asks of you, so that all the peoples of the earth may know your name and fear you, as do your own people Israel, and may know that this house that I have built bears your Name.

³⁴"When your people go to war against their enemies, wherever you send them, and when they pray to you towards this city you have chosen and the temple I have built for your Name, ³⁵then hear from heaven their prayer and their plea, and uphold their cause.

³⁶"When they sin against you—for there is no-one who does not sin—and you become angry with them and give them over to the enemy, who takes them captive to a land far away or near; ³⁷and if they have a change of heart in the land where they are held captive, and repent and plead with you in the land of their captivity and say, 'We have sinned, we have done wrong and acted wickedly'; ³⁸and if they turn back to you with all their heart and soul in the land of their captivity where they were taken, and pray towards the land that you gave their fathers, towards the city you

have chosen and towards the temple that I have built for your Name; ³⁹then from heaven, your dwelling-place, hear their prayer and their pleas, and uphold their cause. And forgive your people, who have sinned against you.

⁴⁰"Now, my God, may your eyes be open and your ears attentive to the prayers offered in this place.

⁴¹"Now arise, O LORD God, and
    come to your resting place,
  you and the ark of your might.
May your priests, O LORD God, be
    clothed with salvation,
  may your saints rejoice in your
    goodness.
⁴²O LORD God, do not reject your
    anointed one.
  Remember the great love
    promised to David your
    servant."

The Dedication of the Temple

7 When Solomon finished praying, fire came down from heaven and consumed the burnt offering and the sacrifices, and the glory of the LORD filled the temple. ²The priests could not enter the temple of the LORD because the glory of the LORD filled it. ³When all the Israelites saw the fire coming down and the glory of the LORD above the temple, they knelt on the pavement with their faces to the ground, and they worshipped and gave thanks to the LORD, saying,

"He is good;
  his love endures for ever."

⁴Then the king and all the people offered sacrifices before the LORD. ⁵And King Solomon offered a sacrifice of twenty-two thousand head of cattle and a hundred and twenty thousand sheep and goats. So the king and all the people dedicated the temple of God. ⁶The priests took their positions, as did the Levites with the LORD's musical instruments, which King David had made for praising the LORD and which were used when he gave thanks,

saying, "His love endures for ever." Opposite the Levites, the priests blew their trumpets, and all the Israelites were standing.

⁷Solomon consecrated the middle part of the courtyard in front of the temple of the LORD, and there he offered burnt offerings and the fat of the fellowship offerings,ᵃ because the bronze altar he had made could not hold the burnt offerings, the grain offerings and the fat portions.

⁸So Solomon observed the festival at that time for seven days, and all Israel with him—a vast assembly, people from Leboᵇ Hamath to the Wadi of Egypt. ⁹On the eighth day they held an assembly, for they had celebrated the dedication of the altar for seven days and the festival for seven days more. ¹⁰On the twenty-third day of the seventh month he sent the people to their homes, joyful and glad in heart for the good things the LORD had done for David and Solomon and for his people Israel.

The LORD Appears to Solomon

¹¹When Solomon had finished the temple of the LORD and the royal palace, and had succeeded in carrying out all he had in mind to do in the temple of the LORD and in his own palace, ¹²the LORD appeared to him at night and said:

"I have heard your prayer and have chosen this place for myself as a temple for sacrifices.

¹³"When I shut up the heavens so that there is no rain, or command locusts to devour the land or send a plague among my people, ¹⁴if my people, who are called by my name, will humble themselves and pray and seek my face and turn from their wicked ways, then will I hear from heaven and will forgive their sin and will heal their land. ¹⁵Now my eyes will be open and my ears attentive to the prayers offered in this place. ¹⁶I have chosen and consecrated this temple so that my Name may be there for ever. My eyes and my heart will always be there.

ᵃ7 Traditionally peace offerings   ᵇ8 Or from the entrance to

[17]"As for you, if you walk before me as David your father did, and do all I command, and observe my decrees and laws, [18]I will establish your royal throne, as I covenanted with David your father when I said, 'You shall never fail to have a man to rule over Israel.'

[19]"But if you[c] turn away and forsake the decrees and commands I have given you[c] and go off to serve other gods and worship them, [20]then I will uproot Israel from my land, which I have given them, and will reject this temple which I have consecrated for my Name. I will make it a byword and an object of ridicule among all peoples. [21]And though this temple is now so imposing, all who pass by will be appalled and say, 'Why has the LORD done such a thing to this land and to this temple?' [22]People will answer, 'Because they have forsaken the LORD, the God of their fathers, who brought them out of Egypt, and have embraced other gods, worshipping and serving them—that is why he brought all this disaster on them.'"

Solomon's Other Activities

8 At the end of twenty years, during which Solomon built the temple of the LORD and his own palace, [2]Solomon rebuilt the villages that Hiram[a] had given him, and settled Israelites in them. [3]Solomon then went to Hamath Zobah and captured it. [4]He also built up Tadmor in the desert and all the store cities he had built in Hamath. [5]He rebuilt Upper Beth Horon and Lower Beth Horon as fortified cities, with walls and with gates and bars, [6]as well as Baalath and all his store cities, and all the cities for his chariots and for his horses[b]—whatever he desired to build in Jerusalem, in Lebanon and throughout all the territory that he ruled.

[7]All the people left from the Hittites, Amorites, Perizzites, Hivites and Jebusites (these peoples were not Israelites), [8]that is, their descendants remaining in the land, whom the Israelites had not destroyed—these Solomon conscripted for his slave labour force, as it is to this day. [9]But Solomon did not make slaves of the Israelites for his work; they were his fighting men, commanders of his captains, and commanders of his chariots and charioteers. [10]They were also King Solomon's chief officials—two hundred and fifty officials supervising the men.

[11]Solomon brought Pharaoh's daughter up from the City of David to the palace he had built for her, for he said, "My wife must not live in the palace of David king of Israel, because the places the ark of the LORD has entered are holy."

[12]On the altar of the LORD that he had built in front of the portico, Solomon sacrificed burnt offerings to the LORD, [13]according to the daily requirement for offerings commanded by Moses for Sabbaths, New Moons and the three annual feasts—the Feast of Unleavened Bread, the Feast of Weeks and the Feast of Tabernacles. [14]In keeping with the ordinance of his father David, he appointed the divisions of the priests for their duties and the Levites to lead the praise and to assist the priests according to each day's requirement. He also appointed the gatekeepers by divisions for the various gates, because this was what David the man of God had ordered. [15]They did not deviate from the king's commands to the priests or to the Levites in any matter, including that of the treasuries.

[16]All Solomon's work was carried out, from the day the foundation of the temple of the LORD was laid until its completion. So the temple of the LORD was finished.

[17]Then Solomon went to Ezion Geber and Elath on the coast of Edom. [18]And Hiram sent him ships commanded by his own officers, men who knew the sea. These, with Solomon's men, sailed to Ophir and brought back four hundred and fifty talents[c] of gold, which they delivered to King Solomon.

---

[c]19 The Hebrew is plural.　　[a]2 Hebrew *Huram*, a variant of *Hiram*; also in verse 18
[b]6 Or *charioteers*　　[c]18 That is, about 17 tons (about 16 metric tons)

The Queen of Sheba Visits Solomon

9 When the queen of Sheba heard of Solomon's fame, she came to Jerusalem to test him with hard questions. Arriving with a very great caravan—with camels carrying spices, large quantities of gold, and precious stones—she came to Solomon and talked with him about all she had on her mind. ²Solomon answered all her questions; nothing was too hard for him to explain to her. ³When the queen of Sheba saw the wisdom of Solomon, as well as the palace he had built, ⁴the food on his table, the seating of his officials, the attending servants in their robes, the cup-bearers in their robes and the burnt offerings he made at*ᵃ* the temple of the LORD, she was overwhelmed.

⁵She said to the king, "The report I heard in my own country about your achievements and your wisdom is true. ⁶But I did not believe what they said until I came and saw with my own eyes. Indeed, not even half the greatness of your wisdom was told me; you have far exceeded the report I heard. ⁷How happy your men must be! How happy your officials, who continually stand before you and hear your wisdom! ⁸Praise be to the LORD your God, who has delighted in you and placed you on his throne as king to rule for the LORD your God. Because of the love of your God for Israel and his desire to uphold them for ever, he has made you king over them, to maintain justice and righteousness."

⁹Then she gave the king 120 talents*ᵇ* of gold, large quantities of spices, and precious stones. There had never been such spices as those the queen of Sheba gave to King Solomon.

¹⁰(The men of Hiram and the men of Solomon brought gold from Ophir; they also brought algum-wood*ᶜ* and precious stones. ¹¹The king used the algum-wood to make steps for the temple of the LORD and for the royal palace, and to make harps and lyres for the musicians. Nothing like them had ever been seen in Judah.)

¹²King Solomon gave the queen of Sheba all she desired and asked for; he gave her more than she had brought to him. Then she left and returned with her retinue to her own country.

Solomon's Splendour

¹³The weight of the gold that Solomon received yearly was 666 talents,*ᵈ* ¹⁴not including the revenues brought in by merchants and traders. Also all the kings of Arabia and the governors of the land brought gold and silver to Solomon.

¹⁵King Solomon made two hundred large shields of hammered gold; six hundred bekas*ᵉ* of hammered gold went into each shield. ¹⁶He also made three hundred small shields of hammered gold, with three hundred bekas*ᶠ* of gold in each shield. The king put them in the Palace of the Forest of Lebanon.

¹⁷Then the king made a great throne inlaid with ivory and overlaid with pure gold. ¹⁸The throne had six steps, and a footstool of gold was attached to it. On both sides of the seat were armrests, with a lion standing beside each of them. ¹⁹Twelve lions stood on the six steps, one at either end of each step. Nothing like it had ever been made for any other kingdom. ²⁰All King Solomon's goblets were gold, and all the household articles in the Palace of the Forest of Lebanon were pure gold. Nothing was made of silver, because silver was considered of little value in Solomon's day. ²¹The king had a fleet of trading ships*ᵍ* manned by Hiram's*ʰ* men. Once every three years it returned, carrying gold, silver and ivory, and apes and baboons.

²²King Solomon was greater in riches and wisdom than all the other kings of the earth. ²³All the kings of the earth sought audience with Solomon to hear the wisdom God had put in his heart. ²⁴Year after year, everyone who came brought a gift— articles of silver and gold, and robes,

---

ᵃ4 Or *the ascent by which he went up to*   *ᵇ9* That is, about 4 tons (about 4 metric tons)
ᶜ10 Probably a variant of *almug-wood*   *ᵈ13* That is, about 23 tons (about 23 metric tons)
ᵉ15 That is, about 7½ pounds (about 3.5 kilograms)   *ᶠ16* That is, about 3¾ pounds (about 1.7 kilograms)
ᵍ21 Hebrew *of ships that could go to Tarshish*   *ʰ21* Hebrew *Huram,* a variant of *Hiram*

weapons and spices, and horses and mules. [25]Solomon had four thousand stalls for horses and chariots, and twelve thousand horses,[i] which he kept in the chariot cities and also with him in Jerusalem. [26]He ruled over all the kings from the River[j] to the land of the Philistines, as far as the border of Egypt. [27]The king made silver as common in Jerusalem as stones, and cedar as plentiful as sycamore-fig trees in the foothills. [28]Solomon's horses were imported from Egypt[k] and from all other countries.

Solomon's Death

[29]As for the other events of Solomon's reign, from beginning to end, are they not written in the records of Nathan the prophet, in the prophecy of Ahijah the Shilonite and in the visions of Iddo the seer concerning Jeroboam son of Nebat? [30]Solomon reigned in Jerusalem over all Israel for forty years. [31]Then he rested with his fathers and was buried in the city of David his father. And Rehoboam his son succeeded him as king.

Israel Rebels Against Rehoboam

10 Rehoboam went to Shechem, for all the Israelites had gone there to make him king. [2]When Jeroboam son of Nebat heard this (he was in Egypt, where he had fled from King Solomon), he returned from Egypt. [3]So they sent for Jeroboam, and he and all Israel went to Rehoboam and said to him: [4]"Your father put a heavy yoke on us, but now lighten the harsh labour and the heavy yoke he put on us, and we will serve you."

[5]Rehoboam answered, "Come back to me in three days." So the people went away.

[6]Then King Rehoboam consulted the elders who had served his father Solomon during his lifetime. "How would you advise me to answer these people?" he asked.

[7]They replied, "If you will be kind to these people and please them and give them a favourable answer, they will always be your servants."

[8]But Rehoboam rejected the advice the elders gave him and consulted the young men who had grown up with him and were serving him. [9]He asked them, "What is your advice? How should we answer these people who say to me, 'Lighten the yoke your father put on us'?"

[10]The young men who had grown up with him replied, "Tell the people who have said to you, 'Your father put a heavy yoke on us, but make our yoke lighter'— tell them, 'My little finger is thicker than my father's waist. [11]My father laid on you a heavy yoke; I will make it even heavier. My father scourged you with whips; I will scourge you with scorpions.'"

[12]Three days later Jeroboam and all the people returned to Rehoboam, as the king had said, "Come back to me in three days." [13]The king answered them harshly. Rejecting the advice of the elders, [14]he followed the advice of the young men and said, "My father made your yoke heavy; I will make it even heavier. My father scourged you with whips; I will scourge you with scorpions." [15]So the king did not listen to the people, for this turn of events was from God, to fulfil the word that the LORD had spoken to Jeroboam son of Nebat through Ahijah the Shilonite.

[16]When all Israel saw that the king refused to listen to them, they answered the king:

"What share do we have in David,
    what part in Jesse's son?
To your tents, O Israel!
    Look after your own house, O
      David!"

So all the Israelites went home. [17]But as for the Israelites who were living in the towns of Judah, Rehoboam still ruled over them.

[18]King Rehoboam sent out Adoniram,[a] who was in charge of forced labour, but the Israelites stoned him to death. King Rehoboam, however, managed to get into his chariot and escape to Jerusalem. [19]So

---

i25 Or *charioteers*   *j26* That is, the Euphrates   *k28* Or possibly *Muzur*, a region in Cilicia
a18 Hebrew *Hadoram*, a variant of *Adoniram*

Israel has been in rebellion against the house of David to this day.

11 When Rehoboam arrived in Jerusalem, he mustered the house of Judah and Benjamin—a hundred and eighty thousand fighting men—to make war against Israel and to regain the kingdom for Rehoboam.

²But this word of the LORD came to Shemaiah the man of God: ³"Say to Rehoboam son of Solomon king of Judah and to all the Israelites in Judah and Benjamin, ⁴'This is what the LORD says: Do not go up to fight against your brothers. Go home, every one of you, for this is my doing.'" So they obeyed the words of the LORD and turned back from marching against Jeroboam.

Rehoboam Fortifies Judah

⁵Rehoboam lived in Jerusalem and built up towns for defence in Judah: ⁶Bethlehem, Etam, Tekoa, ⁷Beth Zur, Soco, Adullam, ⁸Gath, Mareshah, Ziph, ⁹Adoraim, Lachish, Azekah, ¹⁰Zorah, Aijalon and Hebron. These were fortified cities in Judah and Benjamin. ¹¹He strengthened their defences and put commanders in them, with supplies of food, olive oil and wine. ¹²He put shields and spears in all the cities, and made them very strong. So Judah and Benjamin were his.

¹³The priests and Levites from all their districts throughout Israel sided with him. ¹⁴The Levites even abandoned their pasture-lands and property, and came to Judah and Jerusalem because Jeroboam and his sons had rejected them as priests of the LORD. ¹⁵And he appointed his own priests for the high places and for the goat and calf idols he had made. ¹⁶Those from every tribe of Israel who set their hearts on seeking the LORD, the God of Israel, followed the Levites to Jerusalem to offer sacrifices to the LORD, the God of their fathers. ¹⁷They strengthened the kingdom of Judah and supported Rehoboam son of Solomon for three years, walking in the ways of David and Solomon during this time.

Rehoboam's Family

¹⁸Rehoboam married Mahalath, who was the daughter of David's son Jerimoth and of Abihail, the daughter of Jesse's son Eliab. ¹⁹She bore him sons: Jeush, Shemariah and Zaham. ²⁰Then he married Maacah daughter of Absalom, who bore him Abijah, Attai, Ziza and Shelomith. ²¹Rehoboam loved Maacah daughter of Absalom more than any of his other wives and concubines. In all he had eighteen wives and sixty concubines, twenty-eight sons and sixty daughters.

²²Rehoboam appointed Abijah son of Maacah to be the chief prince among his brothers, in order to make him king. ²³He acted wisely, dispersing some of his sons throughout the districts of Judah and Benjamin, and to all the fortified cities. He gave them abundant provisions and took many wives for them.

Shishak Attacks Jerusalem

12 After Rehoboam's position as king was established and he had become strong, he and all Israel*a* with him abandoned the law of the LORD. ²Because they had been unfaithful to the LORD, Shishak king of Egypt attacked Jerusalem in the fifth year of King Rehoboam. ³With twelve hundred chariots and sixty thousand horsemen and the innumerable troops of Libyans, Sukkites and Cushites*b* that came with him from Egypt, ⁴he captured the fortified cities of Judah and came as far as Jerusalem.

⁵Then the prophet Shemaiah came to Rehoboam and to the leaders of Judah who had assembled in Jerusalem for fear of Shishak, and he said to them, "This is what the LORD says: 'You have abandoned me; therefore I now abandon you to Shishak.'"

⁶The leaders of Israel and the king humbled themselves and said, "The LORD is just."

⁷When the LORD saw that they humbled themselves, this word of the LORD came to Shemaiah: "Since they have humbled themselves, I will not destroy them but

---

a1 That is, Judah, as frequently in 2 Chronicles   *b3* That is, people from the upper Nile region will soon give them deliverance. My wrath will not be poured out on Jerusalem through Shishak. ⁸They will, however, become subject to him, so that they may learn the difference between serving me and serving the kings of other lands."

⁹When Shishak king of Egypt attacked Jerusalem, he carried off the treasures of the temple of the Lord and the treasures of the royal palace. He took everything, including the gold shields that Solomon had made. ¹⁰So King Rehoboam made bronze shields to replace them and assigned these to the commanders of the guard on duty at the entrance to the royal palace. ¹¹Whenever the king went to the Lord's temple, the guards went with him, bearing the shields, and afterwards they returned them to the guardroom.

¹²Because Rehoboam humbled himself, the Lord's anger turned from him, and he was not totally destroyed. Indeed, there was some good in Judah.

¹³King Rehoboam established himself firmly in Jerusalem and continued as king. He was forty-one years old when he became king, and he reigned for seventeen years in Jerusalem, the city the Lord had chosen out of all the tribes of Israel in which to put his Name. His mother's name was Naamah; she was an Ammonite. ¹⁴He did evil because he had not set his heart on seeking the Lord.

¹⁵As for the events of Rehoboam's reign, from beginning to end, are they not written in the records of Shemaiah the prophet and of Iddo the seer that deal with genealogies? There was continual warfare between Rehoboam and Jeroboam. ¹⁶Rehoboam rested with his fathers and was buried in the City of David. And Abijah his son succeeded him as king.

Abijah King of Judah

13 In the eighteenth year of the reign of Jeroboam, Abijah became king of Judah, ²and he reigned in Jerusalem for three years. His mother's name was Maacah,ᵃ a daughterᵇ of Uriel of Gibeah.

There was war between Abijah and Jeroboam. ³Abijah went into battle with a force of four hundred thousand able fighting men, and Jeroboam drew up a battle line against him with eight hundred thousand able troops.

⁴Abijah stood on Mount Zemaraim, in the hill country of Ephraim, and said, "Jeroboam and all Israel, listen to me! ⁵Don't you know that the Lord, the God of Israel, has given the kingship of Israel to David and his descendants for ever by a covenant of salt? ⁶Yet Jeroboam son of Nebat, an official of Solomon son of David, rebelled against his master. ⁷Some worthless scoundrels gathered around him and opposed Rehoboam son of Solomon when he was young and indecisive and not strong enough to resist them.

⁸"And now you plan to resist the kingdom of the Lord, which is in the hands of David's descendants. You are indeed a vast army and have with you the golden calves that Jeroboam made to be your gods. ⁹But didn't you drive out the priests of the Lord, the sons of Aaron, and the Levites, and make priests of your own as the peoples of other lands do? Whoever comes to consecrate himself with a young bull and seven rams may become a priest of what are not gods.

¹⁰"As for us, the Lord is our God, and we have not forsaken him. The priests who serve the Lord are sons of Aaron, and the Levites assist them. ¹¹Every morning and evening they present burnt offerings and fragrant incense to the Lord. They set out the bread on the ceremonially clean table and light the lamps on the gold lampstand every evening. We are observing the requirements of the Lord our God. But you have forsaken him. ¹²God is with us; he is our leader. His priests with their trumpets will sound the battle cry against you. Men of Israel, do not fight against the Lord, the God of your fathers, for you will not succeed."

¹³Now Jeroboam had sent troops round to the rear, so that while he was in front of Judah the ambush was behind them. ¹⁴Judah turned and saw that they were being attacked at both front and rear.

ᵃ2 Most Septuagint manuscripts and Syriac (see also 2 Chron. 11:20 and 1 Kings 15:2); Hebrew *Micaiah*
ᵇ2 Or *granddaughter*

Then they cried out to the LORD. The priests blew their trumpets [15]and the men of Judah raised the battle cry. At the sound of their battle cry, God routed Jeroboam and all Israel before Abijah and Judah. [16]The Israelites fled before Judah, and God delivered them into their hands. [17]Abijah and his men inflicted heavy losses on them, so that there were five hundred thousand casualties among Israel's able men. [18]The men of Israel were subdued on that occasion, and the men of Judah were victorious because they relied on the LORD, the God of their fathers.

[19]Abijah pursued Jeroboam and took from him the towns of Bethel, Jeshanah and Ephron, with their surrounding villages. [20]Jeroboam did not regain power during the time of Abijah. And the LORD struck him down and he died.

[21]But Abijah grew in strength. He married fourteen wives and had twenty-two sons and sixteen daughters.

[22]The other events of Abijah's reign, what he did and what he said, are written in the annotations of the prophet Iddo.

14 And Abijah rested with his fathers and was buried in the City of David. Asa his son succeeded him as king, and in his days the country was at peace for ten years.

Asa King of Judah

[2]Asa did what was good and right in the eyes of the LORD his God. [3]He removed the foreign altars and the high places, smashed the sacred stones and cut down the Asherah poles.[a] [4]He commanded Judah to seek the LORD, the God of their fathers, and to obey his laws and commands. [5]He removed the high places and incense altars in every town in Judah, and the kingdom was at peace under him. [6]He built up the fortified cities of Judah, since the land was at peace. No-one was at war with him during those years, for the LORD gave him rest.

[7]"Let us build up these towns," he said to Judah, "and put walls round them, with

towers, gates and bars. The land is still ours, because we have sought the LORD our God; we sought him and he has given us rest on every side." So they built and prospered.

[8]Asa had an army of three hundred thousand men from Judah, equipped with large shields and with spears, and two hundred and eighty thousand from Benjamin, armed with small shields and with bows. All these were brave fighting men.

[9]Zerah the Cushite marched out against them with a vast army[b] and three hundred chariots, and came as far as Mareshah. [10]Asa went out to meet him, and they took up battle positions in the Valley of Zephathah near Mareshah.

[11]Then Asa called to the LORD his God and said, "LORD, there is no-one like you to help the powerless against the mighty. Help us, O LORD our God, for we rely on you, and in your name we have come against this vast army. O LORD, you are our God; do not let man prevail against you."

[12]The LORD struck down the Cushites before Asa and Judah. The Cushites fled, [13]and Asa and his army pursued them as far as Gerar. Such a great number of Cushites fell that they could not recover; they were crushed before the LORD and his forces. The men of Judah carried off a large amount of plunder. [14]They destroyed all the villages around Gerar, for the terror of the LORD had fallen upon them. They plundered all these villages, since there was much booty there. [15]They also attacked the camps of the herdsmen and carried off droves of sheep and goats and camels. Then they returned to Jerusalem.

Asa's Reform

15 The Spirit of God came upon Azariah son of Oded. [2]He went out to meet Asa and said to him, "Listen to me, Asa and all Judah and Benjamin. The LORD is with you when you are with him. If you seek him, he will be found by you, but if you forsake him, he will forsake

---

a3 That is, symbols of the goddess Asherah; here and elsewhere in 2 Chronicles
b9 Hebrew *with an army of a thousand thousands* or *with an army of thousands upon thousands*

you. ³For a long time Israel was without the true God, without a priest to teach and without the law. ⁴But in their distress they turned to the LORD, the God of Israel, and sought him, and he was found by them. ⁵In those days it was not safe to travel about, for all the inhabitants of the lands were in great turmoil. ⁶One nation was being crushed by another and one city by another, because God was troubling them with every kind of distress. ⁷But as for you, be strong and do not give up, for your work will be rewarded."

⁸When Asa heard these words and the prophecy of Azariah son of^a Oded the prophet, he took courage. He removed the detestable idols from the whole land of Judah and Benjamin and from the towns he had captured in the hills of Ephraim. He repaired the altar of the LORD that was in front of the portico of the LORD's temple.

⁹Then he assembled all Judah and Benjamin and the people from Ephraim, Manasseh and Simeon who had settled among them, for large numbers had come over to him from Israel when they saw that the LORD his God was with him.

¹⁰They assembled at Jerusalem in the third month of the fifteenth year of Asa's reign. ¹¹At that time they sacrificed to the LORD seven hundred head of cattle and seven thousand sheep and goats from the plunder they had brought back. ¹²They entered into a covenant to seek the LORD, the God of their fathers, with all their heart and soul. ¹³All who would not seek the LORD, the God of Israel, were to be put to death, whether small or great, man or woman. ¹⁴They took an oath to the LORD with loud acclamation, with shouting and with trumpets and horns. ¹⁵All Judah rejoiced about the oath because they had sworn it wholeheartedly. They sought God eagerly, and he was found by them. So the LORD gave them rest on every side.

¹⁶King Asa also deposed his grandmother Maacah from her position as queen mother, because she had made a repulsive Asherah pole. Asa cut the pole down, broke it up and burned it in the Kidron Valley. ¹⁷Although he did not remove the high places from Israel, Asa's heart was fully committed ⌊to the LORD⌋ all his life. ¹⁸He brought into the temple of God the silver and gold and the articles that he and his father had dedicated.

¹⁹There was no more war until the thirty-fifth year of Asa's reign.

Asa's Last Years

16 In the thirty-sixth year of Asa's reign Baasha king of Israel went up against Judah and fortified Ramah to prevent anyone from leaving or entering the territory of Asa king of Judah.

²Asa then took the silver and gold out of the treasuries of the LORD's temple and of his own palace and sent it to Ben-Hadad king of Aram, who was ruling in Damascus. ³"Let there be a treaty between me and you," he said, "as there was between my father and your father. See, I am sending you silver and gold. Now break your treaty with Baasha king of Israel so that he will withdraw from me."

⁴Ben-Hadad agreed with King Asa and sent the commanders of his forces against the towns of Israel. They conquered Ijon, Dan, Abel Maim^a and all the store cities of Naphtali. ⁵When Baasha heard this, he stopped building Ramah and abandoned his work. ⁶Then King Asa brought all the men of Judah, and they carried away from Ramah the stones and timber Baasha had been using. With them he built up Geba and Mizpah.

⁷At that time Hanani the seer came to Asa king of Judah and said to him: "Because you relied on the king of Aram and not on the LORD your God, the army of the king of Aram has escaped from your hand. ⁸Were not the Cushites^b and Libyans a mighty army with great numbers of chariots and horsemen^c? Yet when you relied on the LORD, he delivered them into your hand. ⁹For the eyes of the LORD range throughout the earth to strengthen those whose hearts are fully committed to him. You have done a foolish thing, and from now on you will be at war."

---

^{a}8 Vulgate and Syriac (see also Septuagint and verse 1); Hebrew does not have *Azariah son of.*
^{a}4 Also known as *Abel Beth Maacah* ^{b}8 That is, people from the upper Nile region ^{c}8 Or *charioteers*

10Asa was angry with the seer because of this; he was so enraged that he put him in prison. At the same time Asa brutally oppressed some of the people.

11The events of Asa's reign, from beginning to end, are written in the book of the kings of Judah and Israel. 12In the thirty-ninth year of his reign Asa was afflicted with a disease in his feet. Though his disease was severe, even in his illness he did not seek help from the LORD, but only from the physicians. 13Then in the forty-first year of his reign Asa died and rested with his fathers. 14They buried him in the tomb that he had cut out for himself in the City of David. They laid him on a bier covered with spices and various blended perfumes, and they made a huge fire in his honour.

Jehoshaphat King of Judah

17 Jehoshaphat his son succeeded him as king and strengthened himself against Israel. 2He stationed troops in all the fortified cities of Judah and put garrisons in Judah and in the towns of Ephraim that his father Asa had captured.

3The LORD was with Jehoshaphat because in his early years he walked in the ways that his father David had followed. He did not consult the Baals 4but sought the God of his father and followed his commands rather than the practices of Israel. 5The LORD established the kingdom under his control; and all Judah brought gifts to Jehoshaphat, so that he had great wealth and honour. 6His heart was devoted to the ways of the LORD; furthermore, he removed the high places and the Asherah poles from Judah.

7In the third year of his reign he sent his officials Ben-Hail, Obadiah, Zechariah, Nethanel and Micaiah to teach in the towns of Judah. 8With them were certain Levites—Shemaiah, Nethaniah, Zebadiah, Asahel, Shemiramoth, Jehonathan, Adonijah, Tobijah and Tob-Adonijah—and the priests Elishama and Jehoram. 9They taught throughout Judah, taking with them the Book of the Law of the LORD; they went round to all the towns of Judah and taught the people.

10The fear of the LORD fell on all the kingdoms of the lands surrounding Judah, so that they did not make war with Jehoshaphat. 11Some Philistines brought Jehoshaphat gifts and silver as tribute, and the Arabs brought him flocks: seven thousand seven hundred rams and seven thousand seven hundred goats.

12Jehoshaphat became more and more powerful; he built forts and store cities in Judah 13and had large supplies in the towns of Judah. He also kept experienced fighting men in Jerusalem. 14Their enrolment by families was as follows:

From Judah, commanders of units of 1,000:
　Adnah the commander, with 300,000 fighting men;
15next, Jehohanan the commander, with 280,000;
16next, Amasiah son of Zicri, who volunteered himself for the service of the LORD, with 200,000.
17From Benjamin:
　Eliada, a valiant soldier, with 200,000 men armed with bows and shields;
18next, Jehozabad, with 180,000 men armed for battle.

19These were the men who served the king, besides those he stationed in the fortified cities throughout Judah.

Micaiah Prophesies Against Ahab

18 Now Jehoshaphat had great wealth and honour, and he allied himself with Ahab by marriage. 2Some years later he went down to visit Ahab in Samaria. Ahab slaughtered many sheep and cattle for him and the people with him and urged him to attack Ramoth Gilead. 3Ahab king of Israel asked Jehoshaphat king of Judah, "Will you go with me against Ramoth Gilead?"

Jehoshaphat replied, "I am as you are, and my people as your people; we will join you in the war." 4But Jehoshaphat also said to the king of Israel, "First seek the counsel of the LORD."

5So the king of Israel brought together the prophets—four hundred men—and asked them, "Shall we go to war against Ramoth Gilead, or shall I refrain?"

"Go," they answered, "for God will give it into the king's hand."

⁶But Jehoshaphat asked, "Is there not a prophet of the LORD here whom we can enquire of?"

⁷The king of Israel answered Jehoshaphat, "There is still one man through whom we can enquire of the LORD, but I hate him because he never prophesies anything good about me, but always bad. He is Micaiah son of Imlah."

"The king should not say that," Jehoshaphat replied.

⁸So the king of Israel called one of his officials and said, "Bring Micaiah son of Imlah at once."

⁹Dressed in their royal robes, the king of Israel and Jehoshaphat king of Judah were sitting on their thrones at the threshing-floor by the entrance to the gate of Samaria, with all the prophets prophesying before them. ¹⁰Now Zedekiah son of Kenaanah had made iron horns, and he declared, "This is what the LORD says: 'With these you will gore the Arameans until they are destroyed.'"

¹¹All the other prophets were prophesying the same thing. "Attack Ramoth Gilead and be victorious," they said, "for the LORD will give it into the king's hand."

¹²The messenger who had gone to summon Micaiah said to him, "Look, as one man the other prophets are predicting success for the king. Let your word agree with theirs, and speak favourably."

¹³But Micaiah said, "As surely as the LORD lives, I can tell him only what my God says."

¹⁴When he arrived, the king asked him, "Micaiah, shall we go to war against Ramoth Gilead, or shall I refrain?"

"Attack and be victorious," he answered, "for they will be given into your hand."

¹⁵The king said to him, "How many times must I make you swear to tell me nothing but the truth in the name of the LORD?"

¹⁶Then Micaiah answered, "I saw all Israel scattered on the hills like sheep without a shepherd, and the LORD said, 'These people have no master. Let each one go home in peace.'"

¹⁷The king of Israel said to Jehoshaphat, "Didn't I tell you that he never prophesies anything good about me, but only bad?"

¹⁸Micaiah continued, "Therefore hear the word of the LORD: I saw the LORD sitting on his throne with all the host of heaven standing on his right and on his left. ¹⁹And the LORD said, 'Who will entice Ahab king of Israel into attacking Ramoth Gilead and going to his death there?'

"One suggested this, and another that. ²⁰Finally, a spirit came forward, stood before the LORD and said, 'I will entice him.'

"'By what means?' the LORD asked.

²¹"'I will go and be a lying spirit in the mouths of all his prophets,' he said.

"'You will succeed in enticing him,' said the LORD. 'Go and do it.'

²²"So now the LORD has put a lying spirit in the mouths of these prophets of yours. The LORD has decreed disaster for you."

²³Then Zedekiah son of Kenaanah went up and slapped Micaiah in the face. "Which way did the spirit from*ᵃ* the LORD go when he went from me to speak to you?" he asked.

²⁴Micaiah replied, "You will find out on the day you go to hide in an inner room."

²⁵The king of Israel then ordered, "Take Micaiah and send him back to Amon the ruler of the city and to Joash the king's son, ²⁶and say, 'This is what the king says: Put this fellow in prison and give him nothing but bread and water until I return safely.'"

²⁷Micaiah declared, "If you ever return safely, the LORD has not spoken through me." Then he added, "Mark my words, all you people!"

Ahab Killed at Ramoth Gilead

²⁸So the king of Israel and Jehoshaphat king of Judah went up to Ramoth Gilead. ²⁹The king of Israel said to Jehoshaphat, "I will enter the battle in disguise, but you wear your royal robes." So the king of

ᵃ23 Or Spirit of

Israel disguised himself and went into battle.

³⁰Now the king of Aram had ordered his chariot commanders, "Do not fight with anyone, small or great, except the king of Israel." ³¹When the chariot commanders saw Jehoshaphat, they thought, "This is the king of Israel." So they turned to attack him, but Jehoshaphat cried out, and the LORD helped him. God drew them away from him, ³²for when the chariot commanders saw that he was not the king of Israel, they stopped pursuing him.

³³But someone drew his bow at random and hit the king of Israel between the sections of his armour. The king told the chariot driver, "Wheel around and get me out of the fighting. I've been wounded." ³⁴All day long the battle raged, and the king of Israel propped himself up in his chariot facing the Arameans until evening. Then at sunset he died.

19 When Jehoshaphat king of Judah returned safely to his palace in Jerusalem, ²Jehu the seer, the son of Hanani, went out to meet him and said to the king, "Should you help the wicked and love*ᵃ* those who hate the LORD? Because of this, the wrath of the LORD is upon you. ³There is, however, some good in you, for you have rid the land of the Asherah poles and have set your heart on seeking God."

Jehoshaphat Appoints Judges

⁴Jehoshaphat lived in Jerusalem, and he went out again among the people from Beersheba to the hill country of Ephraim and turned them back to the LORD, the God of their fathers. ⁵He appointed judges in the land, in each of the fortified cities of Judah. ⁶He told them, "Consider carefully what you do, because you are not judging for man but for the LORD, who is with you whenever you give a verdict. ⁷Now let the fear of the LORD be upon you. Judge carefully, for with the LORD our God there is no injustice or partiality or bribery."

⁸In Jerusalem also, Jehoshaphat appointed some of the Levites, priests and heads of Israelite families to administer the law of the LORD and to settle disputes. And they lived in Jerusalem.⁹ He gave them these orders: "You must serve faithfully and wholeheartedly in the fear of the LORD. ¹⁰In every case that comes before you from your fellow countrymen who live in the cities—whether bloodshed or other concerns of the law, commands, decrees or ordinances—you are to warn them not to sin against the LORD; otherwise his wrath will come on you and your brothers. Do this, and you will not sin.

¹¹"Amariah the chief priest will be over you in any matter concerning the LORD, and Zebadiah son of Ishmael, the leader of the tribe of Judah, will be over you in any matter concerning the king, and the Levites will serve as officials before you. Act with courage, and may the LORD be with those who do well."

Jehoshaphat Defeats Moab and Ammon

20 After this, the Moabites and Ammonites with some of the Meunites*ᵃ* came to make war on Jehoshaphat.

²Some men came and told Jehoshaphat, "A vast army is coming against you from Edom,*ᵇ* from the other side of the Sea.*ᶜ* It is already in Hazezon Tamar" (that is, En Gedi). ³Alarmed, Jehoshaphat resolved to enquire of the LORD, and he proclaimed a fast for all Judah. ⁴The people of Judah came together to seek help from the LORD; indeed, they came from every town in Judah to seek him.

⁵Then Jehoshaphat stood up in the assembly of Judah and Jerusalem at the temple of the LORD in the front of the new courtyard ⁶and said:

"O LORD, God of our fathers, are you not the God who is in heaven? You rule over all the kingdoms of the nations. Power and might are in your hand, and no-one can withstand you. ⁷O our God, did you not drive out the

---

ᵃ2 Or *and make alliances with*   *ᵃ1* Some Septuagint manuscripts; Hebrew *Ammonites*
ᵇ2 One Hebrew manuscript; most Hebrew manuscripts, Septuagint and Vulgate *Aram*
ᶜ2 That is, the Dead Sea

inhabitants of this land before your people Israel and give it for ever to the descendants of Abraham your friend? 8They have lived in it and have built in it a sanctuary for your Name, saying, 9'If calamity comes upon us, whether the sword of judgment, or plague or famine, we will stand in your presence before this temple that bears your Name and will cry out to you in our distress, and you will hear us and save us.'

10'But now here are men from Ammon, Moab and Mount Seir, whose territory you would not allow Israel to invade when they came from Egypt; so they turned away from them and did not destroy them. 11See how they are repaying us by coming to drive us out of the possession you gave us as an inheritance. 12O our God, will you not judge them? For we have no power to face this vast army that is attacking us. We do not know what to do, but our eyes are upon you."

13All the men of Judah, with their wives and children and little ones, stood there before the LORD.

14Then the Spirit of the LORD came upon Jahaziel son of Zechariah, the son of Benaiah, the son of Jeiel, the son of Mattaniah, a Levite and descendant of Asaph, as he stood in the assembly.

15He said, "Listen, King Jehoshaphat and all who live in Judah and Jerusalem! This is what the LORD says to you: 'Do not be afraid or discouraged because of this vast army. For the battle is not yours, but God's. 16Tomorrow march down against them. They will be climbing up by the Pass of Ziz, and you will find them at the end of the gorge in the Desert of Jeruel. 17You will not have to fight this battle. Take up your positions; stand firm and see the deliverance the LORD will give you, O Judah and Jerusalem. Do not be afraid; do not be discouraged. Go out to face them tomorrow, and the LORD will be with you.'"

18Jehoshaphat bowed with his face to the ground, and all the people of Judah and Jerusalem fell down in worship before the LORD. 19Then some Levites from the Kohathites and Korahites stood up and praised the LORD, the God of Israel, with a very loud voice.

20Early in the morning they left for the Desert of Tekoa. As they set out, Jehoshaphat stood and said, "Listen to me, Judah and people of Jerusalem! Have faith in the LORD your God and you will be upheld; have faith in his prophets and you will be successful." 21After consulting the people, Jehoshaphat appointed men to sing to the LORD and to praise him for the splendour of his*d* holiness as they went out at the head of the army, saying:

"Give thanks to the LORD,
for his love endures for ever."

22As they began to sing and praise, the LORD set ambushes against the men of Ammon and Moab and Mount Seir who were invading Judah, and they were defeated. 23The men of Ammon and Moab rose up against the men from Mount Seir to destroy and annihilate them. After they finished slaughtering the men from Seir, they helped to destroy one another.

24When the men of Judah came to the place that overlooks the desert and looked towards the vast army, they saw only dead bodies lying on the ground; no-one had escaped. 25So Jehoshaphat and his men went to carry off their plunder, and they found among them a great amount of equipment and clothing*e* and also articles of value—more than they could take away. There was so much plunder that it took three days to collect it. 26On the fourth day they assembled in the Valley of Beracah, where they praised the LORD. This is why it is called the Valley of Beracah*f* to this day.

27Then, led by Jehoshaphat, all the men of Judah and Jerusalem returned joyfully to Jerusalem, for the LORD had given them cause to rejoice over their enemies. 28They entered Jerusalem and went to the

---

d21 Or *him with the splendour of*
f26 *Beracah* means *praise.*
e25 Some Hebrew manuscripts and Vulgate; most Hebrew manuscripts *corpses*

temple of the LORD with harps and lutes and trumpets.

²⁹The fear of God came upon all the kingdoms of the countries when they heard how the LORD had fought against the enemies of Israel. ³⁰And the kingdom of Jehoshaphat was at peace, for his God had given him rest on every side.

The End of Jehoshaphat's Reign

³¹So Jehoshaphat reigned over Judah. He was thirty-five years old when he became king of Judah, and he reigned in Jerusalem for twenty-five years. His mother's name was Azubah daughter of Shilhi. ³²He walked in the ways of his father Asa and did not stray from them; he did what was right in the eyes of the LORD. ³³The high places, however, were not removed, and the people still had not set their hearts on the God of their fathers.

³⁴The other events of Jehoshaphat's reign, from beginning to end, are written in the annals of Jehu son of Hanani, which are recorded in the book of the kings of Israel.

³⁵Later, Jehoshaphat king of Judah made an alliance with Ahaziah king of Israel, who was guilty of wickedness. ³⁶He agreed with him to construct a fleet of trading ships.ᵍ After these were built at Ezion Geber, ³⁷Eliezer son of Dodavahu of Mareshah prophesied against Jehoshaphat, saying, "Because you have made an alliance with Ahaziah, the LORD will destroy what you have made." The ships were wrecked and were not able to set sail to trade.ʰ

21 Then Jehoshaphat rested with his fathers and was buried with them in the City of David. And Jehoram his son succeeded him as king. ²Jehoram's brothers, the sons of Jehoshaphat, were Azariah, Jehiel, Zechariah, Azariahu, Michael and Shephatiah. All these were sons of Jehoshaphat king of Israel.ᵃ ³Their father had given them many gifts of silver and gold and articles of value, as well as fortified cities in Judah, but he had given the kingdom to Jehoram because he was his firstborn son.

Jehoram King of Judah

⁴When Jehoram established himself firmly over his father's kingdom, he put all his brothers to the sword along with some of the princes of Israel. ⁵Jehoram was thirty-two years old when he became king, and he reigned in Jerusalem for eight years. ⁶He walked in the ways of the kings of Israel, as the house of Ahab had done, for he married a daughter of Ahab. He did evil in the eyes of the LORD. ⁷Nevertheless, because of the covenant the LORD had made with David, the LORD was not willing to destroy the house of David. He had promised to maintain a lamp for him and his descendants for ever.

⁸In the time of Jehoram, Edom rebelled against Judah and set up its own king. ⁹So Jehoram went there with his officers and all his chariots. The Edomites surrounded him and his chariot commanders, but he rose up and broke through by night. ¹⁰To this day Edom has been in rebellion against Judah.

Libnah revolted at the same time, because Jehoram had forsaken the LORD, the God of his fathers. ¹¹He had also built high places on the hills of Judah and had caused the people of Jerusalem to prostitute themselves and had led Judah astray.

¹²Jehoram received a letter from Elijah the prophet, which said:

"This is what the LORD, the God of your father David, says: 'You have not walked in the ways of your father Jehoshaphat or of Asa king of Judah. ¹³But you have walked in the ways of the kings of Israel, and you have led Judah and the people of Jerusalem to prostitute themselves, just as the house of Ahab did. You have also murdered your own brothers, members of your father's house, men who were better than you. ¹⁴So now the LORD is about to strike your people, your sons, your wives and everything that is yours, with a heavy blow. ¹⁵You yourself will be very ill with a lingering disease of the bowels, until

---

ᵍ36 Hebrew *of ships that could go to Tarshish*   ʰ37 Hebrew *sail for Tarshish*
ᵃ2 That is, Judah, as frequently in 2 Chronicles

the disease causes your bowels to come out.'"

¹⁶The LORD aroused against Jehoram the hostility of the Philistines and of the Arabs who lived near the Cushites. ¹⁷They attacked Judah, invaded it and carried off all the goods found in the king's palace, together with his sons and wives. Not a son was left to him except Ahaziah,ᵇ the youngest.

¹⁸After all this, the LORD afflicted Jehoram with an incurable disease of the bowels. ¹⁹In the course of time, at the end of the second year, his bowels came out because of the disease, and he died in great pain. His people made no fire in his honour, as they had for his fathers.

²⁰Jehoram was thirty-two years old when he became king, and he reigned in Jerusalem for eight years. He passed away, to no-one's regret, and was buried in the City of David, but not in the tombs of the kings.

Ahaziah King of Judah

22 The people of Jerusalem made Ahaziah, Jehoram's youngest son, king in his place, since the raiders, who came with the Arabs into the camp, had killed all the older sons. So Ahaziah son of Jehoram king of Judah began to reign.

²Ahaziah was twenty-twoᵃ years old when he became king, and he reigned in Jerusalem for one year. His mother's name was Athaliah, a granddaughter of Omri.

³He too walked in the ways of the house of Ahab, for his mother encouraged him in doing wrong. ⁴He did evil in the eyes of the LORD, as the house of Ahab had done, for after his father's death they became his advisers, to his undoing. ⁵He also followed their counsel when he went with Joramᵇ son of Ahab king of Israel to war against Hazael king of Aram at Ramoth Gilead. The Arameans wounded Joram; ⁶so he

returned to Jezreel to recover from the wounds they had inflicted on him at Ramothᶜ in his battle with Hazael king of Aram.

Then Ahaziahᵈ son of Jehoram king of Judah went down to Jezreel to see Joram son of Ahab because he had been wounded.

⁷Through Ahaziah's visit to Joram, God brought about Ahaziah's downfall. When Ahaziah arrived, he went out with Joram to meet Jehu son of Nimshi, whom the LORD had anointed to destroy the house of Ahab. ⁸While Jehu was executing judgment on the house of Ahab, he found the princes of Judah and the sons of Ahaziah's relatives, who had been attending Ahaziah, and he killed them. ⁹He then went in search of Ahaziah, and his men captured him while he was hiding in Samaria. He was brought to Jehu and put to death. They buried him, for they said, "He was a son of Jehoshaphat, who sought the LORD with all his heart." So there was no-one in the house of Ahaziah powerful enough to retain the kingdom.

Athaliah and Joash

¹⁰When Athaliah the mother of Ahaziah saw that her son was dead, she proceeded to destroy the whole royal family of the house of Judah. ¹¹But Jehosheba,ᵉ the daughter of King Jehoram, took Joash son of Ahaziah and stole him away from among the royal princes who were about to be murdered and put him and his nurse in a bedroom. Because Jehosheba,ᵉ the daughter of King Jehoram and wife of the priest Jehoiada, was Ahaziah's sister, she hid the child from Athaliah so that she could not kill him. ¹²He remained hidden with them at the temple of God for six years while Athaliah ruled the land.

23 In the seventh year Jehoiada showed his strength. He made a covenant with the commanders of units of a hundred: Azariah son of Jeroham,

---

ᵇ17 Hebrew *Jehoahaz*, a variant of *Ahaziah*
ᵃ2 Some Septuagint manuscripts and Syriac (see also 2 Kings 8:26); Hebrew *forty-two*
ᵇ5 Hebrew *Jehoram*, a variant of *Joram*; also in verses 6 and 7
ᶜ6 Hebrew *Ramah*, a variant of *Ramoth*
ᵈ6 Some Hebrew manuscripts, Septuagint, Vulgate and Syriac (see also 2 Kings 8:29); most Hebrew manuscripts *Azariah*   ᵉ11 Hebrew *Jehoshabeath*, a variant of *Jehosheba*

Ishmael son of Jehohanan, Azariah son of Obed, Maaseiah son of Adaiah, and Elishaphat son of Zicri. ²They went throughout Judah and gathered the Levites and the heads of Israelite families from all the towns. When they came to Jerusalem, ³the whole assembly made a covenant with the king at the temple of God.

Jehoiada said to them, "The king's son shall reign, as the LORD promised concerning the descendants of David. ⁴Now this is what you are to do: A third of you priests and Levites who are going on duty on the Sabbath are to keep watch at the doors, ⁵a third of you at the royal palace and a third at the Foundation Gate, and all the other men are to be in the courtyards of the temple of the LORD. ⁶No-one is to enter the temple of the LORD except the priests and Levites on duty; they may enter because they are consecrated, but all the other men are to guard what the LORD has assigned to them.ᵃ ⁷The Levites are to station themselves round the king, each man with his weapons in his hand. Anyone who enters the temple must be put to death. Stay close to the king wherever he goes."

⁸The Levites and all the men of Judah did just as Jehoiada the priest ordered. Each one took his men—those who were going on duty on the Sabbath and those who were going off duty—for Jehoiada the priest had not released any of the divisions. ⁹Then he gave the commanders of units of a hundred the spears and the large and small shields that had belonged to King David and that were in the temple of God. ¹⁰He stationed all the men, each with his weapon in his hand, round the king—near the altar and the temple, from the south side to the north side of the temple.

¹¹Jehoiada and his sons brought out the king's son and put the crown on him; they presented him with a copy of the covenant and proclaimed him king. They anointed him and shouted, "Long live the king!"

¹²When Athaliah heard the noise of the people running and cheering the king, she went to them at the temple of the LORD. ¹³She looked, and there was the king, standing by his pillar at the entrance. The officers and the trumpeters were beside the king, and all the people of the land were rejoicing and blowing trumpets, and singers with musical instruments were leading the praises. Then Athaliah tore her robes and shouted, "Treason! Treason!"

¹⁴Jehoiada the priest sent out the commanders of units of a hundred, who were in charge of the troops, and said to them: "Bring her out between the ranksᵇ and put to the sword anyone who follows her." For the priest had said, "Do not put her to death at the temple of the LORD." ¹⁵So they seized her as she reached the entrance of the Horse Gate on the palace grounds, and there they put her to death.

¹⁶Jehoiada then made a covenant that he and the people and the kingᶜ would be the LORD's people. ¹⁷All the people went to the temple of Baal and tore it down. They smashed the altars and idols and killed Mattan the priest of Baal in front of the altars.

¹⁸Then Jehoiada placed the oversight of the temple of the LORD in the hands of the priests, who were Levites, to whom David had made assignments in the temple, to present the burnt offerings of the LORD as written in the Law of Moses, with rejoicing and singing, as David had ordered. ¹⁹He also stationed doorkeepers at the gates of the LORD's temple so that no-one who was in any way unclean might enter.

²⁰He took with him the commanders of hundreds, the nobles, the rulers of the people and all the people of the land and brought the king down from the temple of the LORD. They went into the palace through the Upper Gate and seated the king on the royal throne, ²¹and all the people of the land rejoiced. And the city was quiet, because Athaliah had been slain with the sword.

Joash Repairs the Temple

24 Joash was seven years old when he became king, and he reigned in Jerusalem for forty years. His mother's

---

ᵃ6 Or to observe the LORD's command ⌐not to enter⌐   ᵇ14 Or out from the precincts
ᶜ16 Or covenant between ⌐the LORD⌐ and the people and the king that they (see 2 Kings 11:17)

name was Zibiah; she was from Beersheba. ²Joash did what was right in the eyes of the LORD all the years of Jehoiada the priest. ³Jehoiada chose two wives for him, and he had sons and daughters.

⁴Some time later Joash decided to restore the temple of the LORD. ⁵He called together the priests and Levites and said to them, "Go to the towns of Judah and collect the money due annually from all Israel, to repair the temple of your God. Do it now." But the Levites did not act at once.

⁶Therefore the king summoned Jehoiada the chief priest and said to him, "Why haven't you required the Levites to bring in from Judah and Jerusalem the tax imposed by Moses the servant of the LORD and by the assembly of Israel for the Tent of the Testimony?"

⁷Now the sons of that wicked woman Athaliah had broken into the temple of God and had used even its sacred objects for the Baals.

⁸At the king's command, a chest was made and placed outside, at the gate of the temple of the LORD. ⁹A proclamation was then issued in Judah and Jerusalem that they should bring to the LORD the tax that Moses the servant of God had required of Israel in the desert. ¹⁰All the officials and all the people brought their contributions gladly, dropping them into the chest until it was full. ¹¹Whenever the chest was brought in by the Levites to the king's officials and they saw that there was a large amount of money, the royal secretary and the officer of the chief priest would come and empty the chest and carry it back to its place. They did this regularly and collected a great amount of money. ¹²The king and Jehoiada gave it to the men who carried out the work required for the temple of the LORD. They hired masons and carpenters to restore the LORD's temple, and also workers in iron and bronze to repair the temple.

¹³The men in charge of the work were diligent, and the repairs progressed under them. They rebuilt the temple of God according to its original design and reinforced it. ¹⁴When they had finished, they brought the rest of the money to the king and Jehoiada, and with it were made articles for the LORD's temple: articles for the service and for the burnt offerings, and also dishes and other objects of gold and silver. As long as Jehoiada lived, burnt offerings were presented continually in the temple of the LORD.

¹⁵Now Jehoiada was old and full of years, and he died at the age of a hundred and thirty. ¹⁶He was buried with the kings in the City of David, because of the good he had done in Israel for God and his temple.

The Wickedness of Joash

¹⁷After the death of Jehoiada, the officials of Judah came and paid homage to the king, and he listened to them. ¹⁸They abandoned the temple of the LORD, the God of their fathers, and worshipped Asherah poles and idols. Because of their guilt, God's anger came upon Judah and Jerusalem. ¹⁹Although the LORD sent prophets to the people to bring them back to him, and though they testified against them, they would not listen.

²⁰Then the Spirit of God came upon Zechariah son of Jehoiada the priest. He stood before the people and said, "This is what God says: 'Why do you disobey the LORD's commands? You will not prosper. Because you have forsaken the LORD, he has forsaken you.'"

²¹But they plotted against him, and by order of the king they stoned him to death in the courtyard of the LORD's temple. ²²King Joash did not remember the kindness Zechariah's father Jehoiada had shown him but killed his son, who said as he lay dying, "May the LORD see this and call you to account."

²³At the turn of the year,ᵃ the army of Aram marched against Joash; it invaded Judah and Jerusalem and killed all the leaders of the people. They sent all the plunder to their king in Damascus. ²⁴Although the Aramean army had come with only a few men, the LORD delivered

ᵃ23 Probably in the spring

into their hands a much larger army. Because Judah had forsaken the LORD, the God of their fathers, judgment was executed on Joash. ²⁵When the Arameans withdrew, they left Joash severely wounded. His officials conspired against him for murdering the son of Jehoiada the priest, and they killed him in his bed. So he died and was buried in the City of David, but not in the tombs of the kings.

²⁶Those who conspired against him were Zabad,[b] son of Shimeath an Ammonite woman, and Jehozabad, son of Shimrith[c] a Moabite woman. ²⁷The account of his sons, the many prophecies about him, and the record of the restoration of the temple of God are written in the annotations on the book of the kings. And Amaziah his son succeeded him as king.

Amaziah King of Judah

25 Amaziah was twenty-five years old when he became king, and he reigned in Jerusalem for twenty-nine years. His mother's name was Jehoaddin;[a] she was from Jerusalem. ²He did what was right in the eyes of the LORD, but not wholeheartedly. ³After the kingdom was firmly in his control, he executed the officials who had murdered his father the king. ⁴Yet he did not put their sons to death, but acted in accordance with what is written in the Law, in the Book of Moses, where the LORD commanded: "Fathers shall not be put to death for their children, nor children put to death for their fathers; each is to die for his own sins."[b]

⁵Amaziah called the people of Judah together and assigned them according to their families to commanders of thousands and commanders of hundreds for all Judah and Benjamin. He then mustered those twenty years old or more and found that there were three hundred thousand men ready for military service, able to handle the spear and shield. ⁶He also hired a hundred thousand fighting men from Israel for a hundred talents[c] of silver.

⁷But a man of God came to him and said, "O king, these troops from Israel must not march with you, for the LORD is not with Israel—not with any of the people of Ephraim. ⁸Even if you go and fight courageously in battle, God will overthrow you before the enemy, for God has the power to help or to overthrow."

⁹Amaziah asked the man of God, "But what about the hundred talents I paid for these Israelite troops?"

The man of God replied, "The LORD can give you much more than that."

¹⁰So Amaziah dismissed the troops who had come to him from Ephraim and sent them home. They were furious with Judah and left for home in a great rage.

¹¹Amaziah then marshalled his strength and led his army to the Valley of Salt, where he killed ten thousand men of Seir. ¹²The army of Judah also captured ten thousand men alive, took them to the top of a cliff and threw them down so that all were dashed to pieces.

¹³Meanwhile the troops that Amaziah had sent back and had not allowed to take part in the war raided Judean towns from Samaria to Beth Horon. They killed three thousand people and carried off great quantities of plunder.

¹⁴When Amaziah returned from slaughtering the Edomites, he brought back the gods of the people of Seir. He set them up as his own gods, bowed down to them and burned sacrifices to them. ¹⁵The anger of the LORD burned against Amaziah, and he sent a prophet to him, who said, "Why do you consult this people's gods, which could not save their own people from your hand?"

¹⁶While he was still speaking, the king said to him, "Have we appointed you an adviser to the king? Stop! Why be struck down?"

So the prophet stopped but said, "I know that God has determined to destroy you, because you have done this and have not listened to my counsel."

¹⁷After Amaziah king of Judah consulted his advisers, he sent this challenge to Jehoash[d] son of Jehoahaz, the son of

---

b26 A variant of *Jozabad*   *c26* A variant of *Shomer*   *a1* Hebrew *Jehoaddan,* a variant of *Jehoaddin*
b4 Deut. 24:16   *c6* That is, about 3½ tons (about 3.4 metric tons); also in verse 9
d17 Hebrew *Joash,* a variant of *Jehoash;* also in verses 18, 21, 23 and 25

Jehu, king of Israel: "Come, meet me face to face."

[18] But Jehoash king of Israel replied to Amaziah king of Judah, "A thistle in Lebanon sent a message to a cedar in Lebanon, 'Give your daughter to my son in marriage.' Then a wild beast in Lebanon came along and trampled the thistle underfoot. [19] You say to yourself that you have defeated Edom, and now you are arrogant and proud. But stay at home! Why ask for trouble and cause your own downfall and that of Judah also?"

[20] Amaziah, however, would not listen, for God so worked that he might hand them over to ⌊Jehoash⌋, because they sought the gods of Edom. [21] So Jehoash king of Israel attacked. He and Amaziah king of Judah faced each other at Beth Shemesh in Judah. [22] Judah was routed by Israel, and every man fled to his home. [23] Jehoash king of Israel captured Amaziah king of Judah, the son of Joash, the son of Ahaziah,[e] at Beth Shemesh. Then Jehoash brought him to Jerusalem and broke down the wall of Jerusalem from the Ephraim Gate to the Corner Gate—a section about six hundred feet[f] long. [24] He took all the gold and silver and all the articles found in the temple of God that had been in the care of Obed-Edom, together with the palace treasures and the hostages, and returned to Samaria.

[25] Amaziah son of Joash king of Judah lived for fifteen years after the death of Jehoash son of Jehoahaz king of Israel. [26] As for the other events of Amaziah's reign, from beginning to end, are they not written in the book of the kings of Judah and Israel? [27] From the time that Amaziah turned away from following the LORD, they conspired against him in Jerusalem and he fled to Lachish, but they sent men after him to Lachish and killed him there. [28] He was brought back by horse and was buried with his fathers in the City of Judah.

Uzziah King of Judah

26 Then all the people of Judah took Uzziah,[a] who was sixteen years old, and made him king in place of his father Amaziah. [2] He was the one who rebuilt Elath and restored it to Judah after Amaziah rested with his fathers.

[3] Uzziah was sixteen years old when he became king, and he reigned in Jerusalem for fifty-two years. His mother's name was Jecoliah; she was from Jerusalem. [4] He did what was right in the eyes of the LORD, just as his father Amaziah had done. [5] He sought God during the days of Zechariah, who instructed him in the fear[b] of God. As long as he sought the LORD, God gave him success.

[6] He went to war against the Philistines and broke down the walls of Gath, Jabneh and Ashdod. He then rebuilt towns near Ashdod and elsewhere among the Philistines. [7] God helped him against the Philistines and against the Arabs who lived in Gur Baal and against the Meunites. [8] The Ammonites brought tribute to Uzziah, and his fame spread as far as the border of Egypt, because he had become very powerful.

[9] Uzziah built towers in Jerusalem at the Corner Gate, at the Valley Gate and at the angle of the wall, and he fortified them. [10] He also built towers in the desert and dug many cisterns, because he had much livestock in the foothills and in the plain. He had people working his fields and vineyards in the hills and in the fertile lands, for he loved the soil.

[11] Uzziah had a well-trained army, ready to go out by divisions according to their numbers as mustered by Jeiel the secretary and Maaseiah the officer under the direction of Hananiah, one of the royal officials. [12] The total number of family leaders over the fighting men was 2,600. [13] Under their command was an army of 307,500 men trained for war, a powerful force to support the king against his enemies. [14] Uzziah provided shields, spears, helmets, coats of armour, bows and slingstones for the entire army. [15] In Jerusalem he made machines designed by skilful men for use on the towers and on the corner defences to shoot arrows and hurl large stones. His fame spread far and wide, for

---

e23 Hebrew *Jehoahaz*, a variant of *Ahaziah*   *f23* Hebrew *four hundred cubits* (about 180 metres)
a1 Also called *Azariah*   *b5* Many Hebrew manuscripts, Septuagint and Syriac; other Hebrew manuscripts *vision*

he was greatly helped until he became powerful.

¹⁶But after Uzziah became powerful, his pride led to his downfall. He was unfaithful to the Lord his God, and entered the temple of the Lord to burn incense on the altar of incense. ¹⁷Azariah the priest with eighty other courageous priests of the Lord followed him in. ¹⁸They confronted him and said, "It is not right for you, Uzziah, to burn incense to the Lord. That is for the priests, the descendants of Aaron, who have been consecrated to burn incense. Leave the sanctuary, for you have been unfaithful; and you will not be honoured by the Lord God."

¹⁹Uzziah, who had a censer in his hand ready to burn incense, became angry. While he was raging at the priests in their presence before the incense altar in the Lord's temple, leprosy[c] broke out on his forehead. ²⁰When Azariah the chief priest and all the other priests looked at him, they saw that he had leprosy on his forehead, so they hurried him out. Indeed, he himself was eager to leave, because the Lord had afflicted him.

²¹King Uzziah had leprosy until the day he died. He lived in a separate house[d]—leprous, and excluded from the temple of the Lord. Jotham his son had charge of the palace and governed the people of the land.

²²The other events of Uzziah's reign, from beginning to end, are recorded by the prophet Isaiah son of Amoz. ²³Uzziah rested with his fathers and was buried near them in a field for burial that belonged to the kings, for people said, "He had leprosy." And Jotham his son succeeded him as king.

Jotham King of Judah

27 Jotham was twenty-five years old when he became king, and he reigned in Jerusalem for sixteen years. His mother's name was Jerusha daughter of Zadok. ²He did what was right in the eyes of the Lord, just as his father Uzziah had

done, but unlike him he did not enter the temple of the Lord. The people, however, continued their corrupt practices. ³Jotham rebuilt the Upper Gate of the temple of the Lord and did extensive work on the wall at the hill of Ophel. ⁴He built towns in the Judean hills and forts and towers in the wooded areas.

⁵Jotham made war on the king of the Ammonites and conquered them. That year the Ammonites paid him a hundred talents[a] of silver, ten thousand cors[b] of wheat and ten thousand cors of barley. The Ammonites brought him the same amount also in the second and third years.

⁶Jotham grew powerful because he walked steadfastly before the Lord his God.

⁷The other events in Jotham's reign, including all his wars and the other things he did, are written in the book of the kings of Israel and Judah. ⁸He was twenty-five years old when he became king, and he reigned in Jerusalem for sixteen years. ⁹Jotham rested with his fathers and was buried in the City of David. And Ahaz his son succeeded him as king.

Ahaz King of Judah

28 Ahaz was twenty years old when he became king, and he reigned in Jerusalem for sixteen years. Unlike David his father, he did not do what was right in the eyes of the Lord. ²He walked in the ways of the kings of Israel and also made cast idols for worshipping the Baals. ³He burned sacrifices in the Valley of Ben Hinnom and sacrificed his sons in the fire, following the detestable ways of the nations that the Lord had driven out before the Israelites. ⁴He offered sacrifices and burned incense at the high places, on the hilltops and under every spreading tree.

⁵Therefore the Lord his God handed him over to the king of Aram. The Arameans defeated him and took many of his people as prisoners and brought them to Damascus.

He was also given into the hands of the

---

[c]19 The Hebrew word was used for various diseases affecting the skin—not necessarily leprosy; also in verses 20, 21 and 23.   [d]21 Or *in a house where he was relieved of responsibilities*
[a]5 That is, about 3⅓ tons (about 3.4 metric tons)   [b]5 That is, probably about 60,500 bushels (about 2,200 kilolitres)

king of Israel, who inflicted heavy casualties on him. ⁶In one day Pekah son of Remaliah killed a hundred and twenty thousand soldiers in Judah—because Judah had forsaken the LORD, the God of their fathers. ⁷Zicri, an Ephraimite warrior, killed Maaseiah the king's son, Azrikam the officer in charge of the palace, and Elkanah, second to the king. ⁸The Israelites took captive from their kinsmen two hundred thousand wives, sons and daughters. They also took a great deal of plunder, which they carried back to Samaria.

⁹But a prophet of the LORD named Oded was there, and he went out to meet the army when it returned to Samaria. He said to them, "Because the LORD, the God of your fathers, was angry with Judah, he gave them into your hand. But you have slaughtered them in a rage that reaches to heaven. ¹⁰And now you intend to make the men and women of Judah and Jerusalem your slaves. But aren't you also guilty of sins against the LORD your God? ¹¹Now listen to me! Send back your fellow countrymen that you have taken as prisoners, for the LORD's fierce anger rests on you."

¹²Then some of the leaders in Ephraim—Azariah son of Jehohanan, Berekiah son of Meshillemoth, Jehizkiah son of Shallum, and Amasa son of Hadlai—confronted those who were arriving from the war. ¹³"You must not bring those prisoners here," they said, "or we will be guilty before the LORD. Do you intend to add to our sin and guilt? For our guilt is already great, and his fierce anger rests on Israel."

¹⁴So the soldiers gave up the prisoners and plunder in the presence of the officials and all the assembly. ¹⁵The men designated by name took the prisoners, and from the plunder they clothed all who were naked. They provided them with clothes and sandals, food and drink, and healing balm. All those who were weak they put on donkeys. So they took them back to their fellow countrymen at Jericho, the City of Palms, and returned to Samaria.

¹⁶At that time King Ahaz sent to the king*ᵃ* of Assyria for help. ¹⁷The Edomites had again come and attacked Judah and carried away prisoners, ¹⁸while the Philistines had raided towns in the foothills and in the Negev of Judah. They captured and occupied Beth Shemesh, Aijalon and Gederoth, as well as Soco, Timnah and Gimzo, with their surrounding villages. ¹⁹The LORD had humbled Judah because of Ahaz king of Israel,*ᵇ* for he had promoted wickedness in Judah and had been most unfaithful to the LORD. ²⁰Tiglath-Pileser*ᶜ* king of Assyria came to him, but gave him trouble instead of help. ²¹Ahaz took some of the things from the temple of the LORD and from the royal palace and from the princes and presented them to the king of Assyria, but that did not help him.

²²In his time of trouble King Ahaz became even more unfaithful to the LORD. ²³He offered sacrifices to the gods of Damascus, who had defeated him; for he thought, "Since the gods of the kings of Aram have helped them, I will sacrifice to them so that they will help me." But they were his downfall and the downfall of all Israel.

²⁴Ahaz gathered together the furnishings from the temple of God and took them away.*ᵈ* He shut the doors of the LORD's temple and set up altars at every street corner in Jerusalem. ²⁵In every town in Judah he built high places to burn sacrifices to other gods and provoked the LORD, the God of his fathers, to anger.

²⁶The other events of his reign and all his ways, from beginning to end, are written in the book of the kings of Judah and Israel. ²⁷Ahaz rested with his fathers and was buried in the city of Jerusalem, but he was not placed in the tombs of the kings of Israel. And Hezekiah his son succeeded him as king.

Hezekiah Purifies the Temple

29 Hezekiah was twenty-five years old when he became king, and he reigned in Jerusalem for twenty-nine

---

ᵃ16 One Hebrew manuscript, Septuagint and Vulgate (see also 2 Kings 16:7); most Hebrew manuscripts *kings*
ᵇ19 That is, Judah, as frequently in 2 Chronicles   *ᶜ20* Hebrew *Tilgath-Pilneser*, a variant of *Tiglath-Pileser*
ᵈ24 Or *and cut them up*

years. His mother's name was Abijah daughter of Zechariah. ²He did what was right in the eyes of the LORD, just as his father David had done.

³In the first month of the first year of his reign, he opened the doors of the temple of the LORD and repaired them. ⁴He brought in the priests and the Levites, assembled them in the square on the east side ⁵and said, "Listen to me, Levites! Consecrate yourselves now and consecrate the temple of the LORD, the God of your fathers. Remove all defilement from the sanctuary. ⁶Our fathers were unfaithful; they did evil in the eyes of the LORD our God and forsook him. They turned their faces away from the LORD's dwelling-place and turned their backs on him. ⁷They also shut the doors of the portico and put out the lamps. They did not burn incense or present any burnt offerings at the sanctuary to the God of Israel. ⁸Therefore, the anger of the LORD has fallen on Judah and Jerusalem; he has made them an object of dread and horror and scorn, as you can see with your own eyes. ⁹This is why our fathers have fallen by the sword and why our sons and daughters and our wives are in captivity. ¹⁰Now I intend to make a covenant with the LORD, the God of Israel, so that his fierce anger will turn away from us. ¹¹My sons, do not be negligent now, for the LORD has chosen you to stand before him and serve him, to minister before him and to burn incense."

¹²Then these Levites set to work:
    from the Kohathites,
        Mahath son of Amasai and Joel son of Azariah;
    from the Merarites,
        Kish son of Abdi and Azariah son of Jehallelel;
    from the Gershonites,
        Joah son of Zimmah and Eden son of Joah;
¹³from the descendants of Elizaphan, Shimri and Jeiel;
    from the descendants of Asaph, Zechariah and Mattaniah;
¹⁴from the descendants of Heman, Jehiel and Shimei;
    from the descendants of Jeduthun, Shemaiah and Uzziel.

¹⁵When they had assembled their brothers and consecrated themselves, they went in to purify the temple of the LORD, as the king had ordered, following the word of the LORD. ¹⁶The priests went into the sanctuary of the LORD to purify it. They brought out to the courtyard of the LORD's temple everything unclean that they found in the temple of the LORD. The Levites took it and carried it out to the Kidron Valley. ¹⁷They began the consecration on the first day of the first month, and by the eighth day of the month they reached the portico of the LORD. For eight more days they consecrated the temple of the LORD itself, finishing in the sixteenth day of the first month.

¹⁸Then they went in to King Hezekiah and reported: "We have purified the entire temple of the LORD, the altar of burnt offering with all its utensils, and the table for setting out the consecrated bread, with all its articles. ¹⁹We have prepared and consecrated all the articles that King Ahaz removed in his unfaithfulness while he was king. They are now in front of the LORD's altar."

²⁰Early the next morning King Hezekiah gathered the city officials together and went up to the temple of the LORD. ²¹They brought seven bulls, seven rams, seven male lambs and seven male goats as a sin offering for the kingdom, for the sanctuary and for Judah. The king commanded the priests, the descendants of Aaron, to offer these on the altar of the LORD. ²²So they slaughtered the bulls, and the priests took the blood and sprinkled it on the altar; next they slaughtered the rams and sprinkled their blood on the altar; then they slaughtered the lambs and sprinkled their blood on the altar. ²³The goats for the sin offering were brought before the king and the assembly, and they laid their hands on them. ²⁴The priests then slaughtered the goats and presented their blood on the altar for a sin offering to atone for all Israel, because the king had ordered the burnt offering and the sin offering for all Israel.

²⁵He stationed the Levites in the temple of the LORD with cymbals, harps and lyres in the way prescribed by David and Gad

the king's seer and Nathan the prophet; this was commanded by the LORD through his prophets. ²⁶So the Levites stood ready with David's instruments, and the priests with their trumpets.

²⁷Hezekiah gave the order to sacrifice the burnt offering on the altar. As the offering began, singing to the LORD began also, accompanied by trumpets and the instruments of David king of Israel. ²⁸The whole assembly bowed in worship, while the singers sang and the trumpeters played. All this continued until the sacrifice of the burnt offering was completed.

²⁹When the offerings were finished, the king and everyone present with him knelt down and worshipped. ³⁰King Hezekiah and his officials ordered the Levites to praise the LORD with the words of David and of Asaph the seer. So they sang praises with gladness and bowed their heads and worshipped.

³¹Then Hezekiah said, "You have now dedicated yourselves to the LORD. Come and bring sacrifices and thank-offerings to the temple of the LORD." So the assembly brought sacrifices and thank-offerings, and all whose hearts were willing brought burnt offerings.

³²The number of burnt offerings the assembly brought was seventy bulls, a hundred rams and two hundred male lambs—all of them for burnt offerings to the LORD. ³³The animals consecrated as sacrifices amounted to six hundred bulls and three thousand sheep and goats. ³⁴The priests, however, were too few to skin all the burnt offerings; so their kinsmen the Levites helped them until the task was finished and until other priests had been consecrated, for the Levites had been more conscientious in consecrating themselves than the priests had been. ³⁵There were burnt offerings in abundance, together with the fat of the fellowship offerings*a* and the drink offerings that accompanied the burnt offerings.

So the service of the temple of the LORD was re-established. ³⁶Hezekiah and all the people rejoiced at what God had brought about for his people, because it was done so quickly.

---

a35 Traditionally peace offerings

Hezekiah Celebrates the Passover

30 Hezekiah sent word to all Israel and Judah and also wrote letters to Ephraim and Manasseh, inviting them to come to the temple of the LORD in Jerusalem and celebrate the Passover to the LORD, the God of Israel. ²The king and his officials and the whole assembly in Jerusalem decided to celebrate the Passover in the second month. ³They had not been able to celebrate it at the regular time because not enough priests had consecrated themselves and the people had not assembled in Jerusalem. ⁴The plan seemed right both to the king and to the whole assembly. ⁵They decided to send a proclamation throughout Israel, from Beersheba to Dan, calling the people to come to Jerusalem and celebrate the Passover to the LORD, the God of Israel. It had not been celebrated in large numbers according to what was written.

⁶At the king's command, couriers went throughout Israel and Judah with letters from the king and from his officials, which read:

"People of Israel, return to the LORD, the God of Abraham, Isaac and Israel, that he may return to you who are left, who have escaped from the hand of the kings of Assyria. ⁷Do not be like your fathers and brothers, who were unfaithful to the LORD, the God of their fathers, so that he made them an object of horror, as you see. ⁸Do not be stiff-necked, as your fathers were; submit to the LORD. Come to the sanctuary, which he has consecrated for ever. Serve the LORD your God, so that his fierce anger will turn away from you. ⁹If you return to the LORD, then your brothers and your children will be shown compassion by their captors and will come back to this land, for the LORD your God is gracious and compassionate. He will not turn his face from you if you return to him."

[10]The couriers went from town to town in Ephraim and Manasseh, as far as Zebulun, but the people scorned and ridiculed them. [11]Nevertheless, some men of Asher, Manasseh and Zebulun humbled themselves and went to Jerusalem. [12]Also in Judah the hand of God was on the people to give them unity of mind to carry out what the king and his officials had ordered, following the word of the LORD.

[13]A very large crowd of people assembled in Jerusalem to celebrate the Feast of Unleavened Bread in the second month. [14]They removed the altars in Jerusalem and cleared away the incense altars and threw them into the Kidron Valley.

[15]They slaughtered the Passover lamb on the fourteenth day of the second month. The priests and the Levites were ashamed and consecrated themselves and brought burnt offerings to the temple of the LORD. [16]Then they took up their regular positions as prescribed in the Law of Moses the man of God. The priests sprinkled the blood handed to them by the Levites. [17]Since many in the crowd had not consecrated themselves, the Levites had to kill the Passover lambs for all those who were not ceremonially clean and could not consecrate ⌊their lambs⌋ to the LORD. [18]Although most of the many people who came from Ephraim, Manasseh, Issachar and Zebulun had not purified themselves, yet they ate the Passover, contrary to what was written. But Hezekiah prayed for them, saying, "May the LORD, who is good, pardon everyone [19]who sets his heart on seeking God—the LORD, the God of his fathers—even if he is not clean according to the rules of the sanctuary." [20]And the LORD heard Hezekiah and healed the people.

[21]The Israelites who were present in Jerusalem celebrated the Feast of Unleavened Bread for seven days with great rejoicing, while the Levites and priests sang to the LORD every day, accompanied by the LORD's instruments of praise.[a] [22]Hezekiah spoke encouragingly to all the Levites, who showed good understanding of the service of the LORD. For the seven days they ate their assigned portion and offered fellowship offerings[b] and praised the LORD, the God of their fathers.

[23]The whole assembly then agreed to celebrate the festival seven more days; so for another seven days they celebrated joyfully. [24]Hezekiah king of Judah provided a thousand bulls and seven thousand sheep and goats for the assembly, and the officials provided them with a thousand bulls and ten thousand sheep and goats. A great number of priests consecrated themselves. [25]The entire assembly of Judah rejoiced, along with the priests and Levites and all who had assembled from Israel, including the aliens who had come from Israel and those who lived in Judah. [26]There was great joy in Jerusalem, for since the days of Solomon son of David king of Israel there had been nothing like this in Jerusalem. [27]The priests and the Levites stood to bless the people, and God heard them, for their prayer reached heaven, his holy dwelling-place.

31 When all this had ended, the Israelites who were there went out to the towns of Judah, smashed the sacred stones and cut down the Asherah poles. They destroyed the high places and the altars throughout Judah and Benjamin and in Ephraim and Manasseh. After they had destroyed all of them, the Israelites returned to their own towns and to their own property.

Contributions for Worship

[2]Hezekiah assigned the priests and Levites to divisions—each of them according to their duties as priests or Levites—to offer burnt offerings and fellowship offerings,[a] to minister, to give thanks and to sing praises at the gates of the LORD's dwelling. [3]The king contributed from his own possessions for the morning and evening burnt offerings and for the burnt offerings on the Sabbaths, New Moons and appointed feasts as written in the Law of the LORD. [4]He ordered the people living in Jerusalem to give the portion due to the

---

[a]21 Or *priests praised the* LORD *every day with resounding instruments belonging to the* LORD.
[b]22 Traditionally *peace offerings*   [a]2 Traditionally *peace offerings*

priests and Levites so that they could devote themselves to the Law of the LORD. [5]As soon as the order went out, the Israelites generously gave the firstfruits of their grain, new wine, oil and honey and all that the fields produced. They brought a great amount, a tithe of everything. [6]The men of Israel and Judah who lived in the towns of Judah also brought a tithe of their herds and flocks and a tithe of the holy things dedicated to the LORD their God, and they piled them in heaps. [7]They began doing this in the third month and finished in the seventh month. [8]When Hezekiah and his officials came and saw the heaps, they praised the LORD and blessed his people Israel.

[9]Hezekiah asked the priests and Levites about the heaps; [10]and Azariah the chief priest, from the family of Zadok, answered, "Since the people began to bring their contributions to the temple of the LORD, we have had enough to eat and plenty to spare, because the LORD has blessed his people, and this great amount is left over."

[11]Hezekiah gave orders to prepare storerooms in the temple of the LORD, and this was done. [12]Then they faithfully brought in the contributions, tithes and dedicated gifts. Conaniah, a Levite, was in charge of these things, and his brother Shimei was next in rank. [13]Jehiel, Azaziah, Nahath, Asahel, Jerimoth, Jozabad, Eliel, Ismakiah, Mahath and Benaiah were supervisors under Conaniah and Shimei his brother, by appointment of King Hezekiah and Azariah the official in charge of the temple of God.

[14]Kore son of Imnah the Levite, keeper of the East Gate, was in charge of the freewill offerings given to God, distributing the contributions made to the LORD and also the consecrated gifts. [15]Eden, Miniamin, Jeshua, Shemaiah, Amariah and Shecaniah assisted him faithfully in the towns of the priests, distributing to their fellow priests according to their divisions, old and young alike.

[16]In addition, they distributed to the males three years old or more whose names were in the genealogical records— all who would enter the temple of the LORD to perform the daily duties of their various tasks, according to their responsibilities and their divisions. [17]And they distributed to the priests enrolled by their families in the genealogical records and likewise to the Levites twenty years old or more, according to their responsibilities and their divisions. [18]They included all the little ones, the wives, and the sons and daughters of the whole community listed in these genealogical records. For they were faithful in consecrating themselves.

[19]As for the priests, the descendants of Aaron, who lived on the farm lands around their towns or in any other towns, men were designated by name to distribute portions to every male among them and to all who were recorded in the genealogies of the Levites.

[20]This is what Hezekiah did throughout Judah, doing what was good and right and faithful before the LORD his God. [21]In everything that he undertook in the service of God's temple and in obedience to the law and the commands, he sought his God and worked wholeheartedly. And so he prospered.

Sennacherib Threatens Jerusalem

32 After all that Hezekiah had so faithfully done, Sennacherib king of Assyria came and invaded Judah. He laid siege to the fortified cities, thinking to conquer them for himself. [2]When Hezekiah saw that Sennacherib had come and that he intended to make war on Jerusalem, [3]he consulted with his officials and military staff about blocking off the water from the springs outside the city, and they helped him. [4]A large force of men assembled, and they blocked all the springs and the stream that flowed through the land. "Why should the kings[a] of Assyria come and find plenty of water?" they said. [5]Then he worked hard repairing all the broken sections of the wall and building towers on it. He built another wall outside that one and reinforced the supporting terraces[b] of the City of David. He also

[a]4 Hebrew; Septuagint and Syriac *king*   [b]5 Or *the Millo*

made large numbers of weapons and shields.

6He appointed military officers over the people and assembled them before him in the square at the city gate and encouraged them with these words: 7"Be strong and courageous. Do not be afraid or discouraged because of the king of Assyria and the vast army with him, for there is a greater power with us than with him. 8With him is only the arm of flesh, but with us is the LORD our God to help us and to fight our battles." And the people gained confidence from what Hezekiah the king of Judah said.

9Later, when Sennacherib king of Assyria and all his forces were laying siege to Lachish, he sent his officers to Jerusalem with this message for Hezekiah king of Judah and for all the people of Judah who were there:

10"This is what Sennacherib king of Assyria says: On what are you basing your confidence, that you remain in Jerusalem under siege? 11When Hezekiah says, 'The LORD our God will save us from the hand of the king of Assyria,' he is misleading you, to let you die of hunger and thirst. 12Did not Hezekiah himself remove this god's high places and altars, saying to Judah and Jerusalem, 'You must worship before one altar and burn sacrifices on it'?

13"Do you not know what I and my fathers have done to all the peoples of the other lands? Were the gods of those nations ever able to deliver their land from my hand? 14Who of all the gods of these nations that my fathers destroyed has been able to save his people from me? How then can your god deliver you from my hand? 15Now do not let Hezekiah deceive you and mislead you like this. Do not believe him, for no god of any nation or kingdom has been able to deliver his people from my hand or the hand of my fathers. How much less will your god deliver you from my hand!"

16Sennacherib's officers spoke further against the LORD God and against his servant Hezekiah. 17The king also wrote letters insulting the LORD, the God of Israel, and saying this against him: "Just as the gods of the peoples of the other lands did not rescue their people from my hand, so the god of Hezekiah will not rescue his people from my hand." 18Then they called out in Hebrew to the people of Jerusalem who were on the wall, to terrify them and make them afraid in order to capture the city. 19They spoke about the God of Jerusalem as they did about the gods of the other peoples of the world—the work of men's hands.

20King Hezekiah and the prophet Isaiah son of Amoz cried out in prayer to heaven about this. 21And the LORD sent an angel, who annihilated all the fighting men and the leaders and officers in the camp of the Assyrian king. So he withdrew to his own land in disgrace. And when he went into the temple of his god, some of his sons cut him down with the sword.

22So the LORD saved Hezekiah and the people of Jerusalem from the hand of Sennacherib king of Assyria and from the hand of all others. He took care of themc on every side. 23Many brought offerings to Jerusalem for the LORD and valuable gifts for Hezekiah king of Judah. From then on he was highly regarded by all the nations.

Hezekiah's Pride, Success and Death

24In those days Hezekiah became ill and was at the point of death. He prayed to the LORD, who answered him and gave him a miraculous sign. 25But Hezekiah's heart was proud and he did not respond to the kindness shown him; therefore the LORD's wrath was on him and on Judah and Jerusalem. 26Then Hezekiah repented of the pride of his heart, as did the people of Jerusalem; therefore the LORD's wrath did not come upon them during the days of Hezekiah.

27Hezekiah had very great riches and honour, and he made treasuries for his

c22 Hebrew; Septuagint and Vulgate *He gave them rest*

silver and gold and for his precious stones, spices, shields and all kinds of valuables. [28]He also made buildings to store the harvest of grain, new wine and oil; and he made stalls for various kinds of cattle, and pens for the flocks. [29]He built villages and acquired great numbers of flocks and herds, for God had given him very great riches.

[30]It was Hezekiah who blocked the upper outlet of the Gihon spring and channelled the water down to the west side of the City of David. He succeeded in everything he undertook. [31]But when envoys were sent by the rulers of Babylon to ask him about the miraculous sign that had occurred in the land, God left him to test him and to know everything that was in his heart.

[32]The other events of Hezekiah's reign and his acts of devotion are written in the vision of the prophet Isaiah son of Amoz in the book of the kings of Judah and Israel. [33]Hezekiah rested with his fathers and was buried on the hill where the tombs of David's descendants are. All Judah and the people of Jerusalem honoured him when he died. And Manasseh his son succeeded him as king.

Manasseh King of Judah

33 Manasseh was twelve years old when he became king, and he reigned in Jerusalem for fifty-five years. [2]He did evil in the eyes of the LORD, following the detestable practices of the nations the LORD had driven out before the Israelites. [3]He rebuilt the high places his father Hezekiah had demolished; he also erected altars to the Baals and made Asherah poles. He bowed down to all the starry hosts and worshipped them. [4]He built altars in the temple of the LORD, of which the LORD had said, "My Name will remain in Jerusalem for ever." [5]In both courts of the temple of the LORD, he built altars to all the starry hosts. [6]He sacrificed his sons in[a] the fire in the Valley of Ben Hinnom, practised sorcery, divination and witchcraft, and consulted mediums and spiritists. He did much evil in the eyes of the LORD, provoking him to anger.

[7]He took the carved image he had made and put it in God's temple, of which God had said to David and to his son Solomon, "In this temple and in Jerusalem, which I have chosen out of all the tribes of Israel, I will put my Name for ever. [8]I will not again make the feet of the Israelites leave the land I assigned to your forefathers, if only they will be careful to do everything that I commanded them concerning all the laws, decrees and ordinances given through Moses." [9]But Manasseh led Judah and the people of Jerusalem astray, so that they did more evil than the nations the LORD had destroyed before the Israelites.

[10]The LORD spoke to Manasseh and his people, but they paid no attention. [11]So the LORD brought against them the army commanders of the king of Assyria, who took Manasseh prisoner, put a hook in his nose, bound him with bronze shackles and took him to Babylon. [12]In his distress he sought the favour of the LORD his God and humbled himself greatly before the God of his fathers. [13]And when he prayed to him, the LORD was moved by his entreaty and listened to his plea; so he brought him back to Jerusalem and to his kingdom. Then Manasseh knew that the LORD is God.

[14]Afterwards he rebuilt the outer wall of the City of David, west of the Gihon spring in the valley, as far as the entrance of the Fish Gate and encircling the hill of Ophel; he also made it much higher. He stationed military commanders in all the fortified cities in Judah.

[15]He got rid of the foreign gods and removed the image from the temple of the LORD, as well as all the altars he had built on the temple hill and in Jerusalem; and he threw them out of the city. [16]Then he restored the altar of the LORD and sacrificed fellowship offerings[b] and thank-offerings on it, and told Judah to serve the LORD, the God of Israel. [17]The people, however, continued to sacrifice at the high places, but only to the LORD their God.

---

[a]6 Or *He made his sons pass through*   [b]16 Traditionally *peace offerings*

18The other events of Manasseh's reign, including his prayer to his God and the words the seers spoke to him in the name of the LORD, the God of Israel, are written in the annals of the kings of Israel.c 19His prayer and how God was moved by his entreaty, as well as all his sins and unfaithfulness, and the sites where he built high places and set up Asherah poles and idols before he humbled himself—all are written in the records of the seers.d 20Manasseh rested with his fathers and was buried in his palace. And Amon his son succeeded him as king.

Amon King of Judah

21Amon was twenty-two years old when he became king, and he reigned in Jerusalem for two years. 22He did evil in the eyes of the LORD, as his father Manasseh had done. Amon worshipped and offered sacrifices to all the idols Manasseh had made. 23But unlike his father Manasseh, he did not humble himself before the LORD; Amon increased his guilt.

24Amon's officials conspired against him and assassinated him in his palace. 25Then the people of the land killed all who had plotted against King Amon, and they made Josiah his son king in his place.

Josiah's Reforms

34 Josiah was eight years old when he became king, and he reigned in Jerusalem for thirty-one years. 2He did what was right in the eyes of the LORD and walked in the ways of his father David, not turning aside to the right or to the left.

3In the eighth year of his reign, while he was still young, he began to seek the God of his father David. In his twelfth year he began to purge Judah and Jerusalem of high places, Asherah poles, carved idols and cast images. 4Under his direction the altars of the Baals were torn down; he cut to pieces the incense altars that were above them, and smashed the Asherah poles, the idols and the images. These he broke to pieces and scattered over the graves of those who had sacrificed to them. 5He burned the bones of the priests on their altars, and so he purged Judah and Jerusalem. 6In the towns of Manasseh, Ephraim and Simeon, as far as Naphtali, and in the ruins around them, 7he tore down the altars and the Asherah poles and crushed the idols to powder and cut to pieces all the incense altars throughout Israel. Then he went back to Jerusalem.

8In the eighteenth year of Josiah's reign, to purify the land and the temple, he sent Shaphan son of Azaliah and Maaseiah the ruler of the city, with Joah son of Joahaz, the recorder, to repair the temple of the LORD his God.

9They went to Hilkiah the high priest and gave him the money that had been brought into the temple of God, which the Levites who were the doorkeepers had collected from the people of Manasseh, Ephraim and the entire remnant of Israel and from all the people of Judah and Benjamin and the inhabitants of Jerusalem. 10Then they entrusted it to the men appointed to supervise the work on the LORD's temple. These men paid the workers who repaired and restored the temple. 11They also gave money to the carpenters and builders to purchase dressed stone, and timber for joists and beams for the buildings that the kings of Judah had allowed to fall into ruin.

12The men did the work faithfully. Over them to direct them were Jahath and Obadiah, Levites descended from Merari, and Zechariah and Meshullam, descended from Kohath. The Levites—all who were skilled in playing musical instruments— 13had charge of the labourers and supervised all the workers from job to job. Some of the Levites were secretaries, scribes and doorkeepers.

The Book of the Law Found

14While they were bringing out the money that had been taken into the temple of the LORD, Hilkiah the priest found the Book of the Law of the LORD that had

---

c18 That is, Judah, as frequently in 2 Chronicles
d19 One Hebrew manuscript and Septuagint; most Hebrew manuscripts of Hozai

been given through Moses. ¹⁵Hilkiah said to Shaphan the secretary, "I have found the Book of the Law in the temple of the Lord." He gave it to Shaphan.

¹⁶Then Shaphan took the book to the king and reported to him: "Your officials are doing everything that has been committed to them. ¹⁷They have paid out the money that was in the temple of the Lord and have entrusted it to the supervisors and workers." ¹⁸Then Shaphan the secretary informed the king, "Hilkiah the priest has given me a book." And Shaphan read from it in the presence of the king.

¹⁹When the king heard the words of the Law, he tore his robes. ²⁰He gave these orders to Hilkiah, Ahikam son of Shaphan, Abdon son of Micah,ᵃ Shaphan the secretary and Asaiah the king's attendant: ²¹"Go and enquire of the Lord for me and for the remnant in Israel and Judah about what is written in this book that has been found. Great is the Lord's anger that is poured out on us because our fathers have not kept the word of the Lord; they have not acted in accordance with all that is written in this book."

²²Hilkiah and those the king had sent with himᵇ went to speak to the prophetess Huldah, who was the wife of Shallum son of Tokhath,ᶜ the son of Hasrah,ᵈ keeper of the wardrobe. She lived in Jerusalem, in the Second District.

²³She said to them, "This is what the Lord, the God of Israel, says: Tell the man who sent you to me, ²⁴'This is what the Lord says: I am going to bring disaster on this place and its people—all the curses written in the book that has been read in the presence of the king of Judah. ²⁵Because they have forsaken me and burned incense to other gods and provoked me to anger by all that their hands have made,ᵉ my anger will be poured out on this place and will not be quenched.' ²⁶Tell the king of Judah, who sent you to enquire of the Lord, 'This is what the Lord, the God of Israel, says concerning the words you heard: ²⁷Because your heart was responsive and you humbled

yourself before God when you heard what he spoke against this place and its people, and because you humbled yourself before me and tore your robes and wept in my presence, I have heard you, declares the Lord. ²⁸Now I will gather you to your fathers, and you will be buried in peace. Your eyes will not see all the disaster I am going to bring on this place and on those who live here.' "

So they took her answer back to the king.

²⁹Then the king called together all the elders of Judah and Jerusalem. ³⁰He went up to the temple of the Lord with the men of Judah, the people of Jerusalem, the priests and the Levites—all the people from the least to the greatest. He read in their hearing all the words of the Book of the Covenant, which had been found in the temple of the Lord. ³¹The king stood by his pillar and renewed the covenant in the presence of the Lord—to follow the Lord and keep his commands, regulations and decrees with all his heart and all his soul, and to obey the words of the covenant written in this book.

³²Then he made everyone in Jerusalem and Benjamin pledge themselves to it; the people of Jerusalem did this in accordance with the covenant of God, the God of their fathers.

³³Josiah removed all the detestable idols from all the territory belonging to the Israelites, and he made all who were present in Israel serve the Lord their God. As long as he lived, they did not fail to follow the Lord, the God of their fathers.

Josiah Celebrates the Passover

35 Josiah celebrated the Passover to the Lord in Jerusalem, and the Passover lamb was slaughtered on the fourteenth day of the first month. ²He appointed the priests to their duties and encouraged them in the service of the Lord's temple. ³He said to the Levites, who instructed all Israel and who had been consecrated to the Lord: "Put the sacred

---

ᵃ20 Also called *Acbor son of Micaiah*
ᵇ22 One Hebrew manuscript, Vulgate and Syriac; most Hebrew manuscripts do not have *had sent with him*.
ᶜ22 Also called *Tikvah*   ᵈ22 Also called *Harhas*   ᵉ25 Or *by everything they have done*

ark in the temple that Solomon son of David king of Israel built. It is not to be carried about on your shoulders. Now serve the LORD your God and his people Israel. ⁴Prepare yourselves by families in your divisions, according to the directions written by David king of Israel and by his son Solomon.

⁵"Stand in the holy place with a group of Levites for each sub-division of the families of your fellow countrymen, the lay people. ⁶Slaughter the Passover lambs, consecrate yourselves and prepare ˌthe lambsˌ for your fellow countrymen, doing what the LORD commanded through Moses."

⁷Josiah provided for all the lay people who were there a total of thirty thousand sheep and goats for the Passover offerings, and also three thousand cattle—all from the king's own possessions.

⁸His officials also contributed voluntarily to the people and the priests and Levites. Hilkiah, Zechariah and Jehiel, the administrators of God's temple, gave the priests two thousand six hundred Passover offerings and three hundred cattle. ⁹Also Conaniah along with Shemaiah and Nethanel, his brothers, and Hashabiah, Jeiel and Jozabad, the leaders of the Levites, provided five thousand Passover offerings and five hundred head of cattle for the Levites.

¹⁰The service was arranged and the priests stood in their places with the Levites in their divisions as the king had ordered. ¹¹The Passover lambs were slaughtered, and the priests sprinkled the blood handed to them, while the Levites skinned the animals. ¹²They set aside the burnt offerings to give them to the sub-divisions of the families of the people to offer to the LORD, as is written in the Book of Moses. They did the same with the cattle. ¹³They roasted the Passover animals over the fire as prescribed, and boiled the holy offerings in pots, cauldrons and pans and served them quickly to all the people. ¹⁴After this, they made preparations for themselves and for the priests, because the priests, the descendants of Aaron, were sacrificing the burnt offerings and the fat portions until nightfall. So the Levites made preparations for themselves and for the Aaronic priests.

¹⁵The musicians, the descendants of Asaph, were in the places prescribed by David, Asaph, Heman and Jeduthun the king's seer. The gatekeepers at each gate did not need to leave their posts, because their fellow Levites made the preparations for them.

¹⁶So at that time the entire service of the LORD was carried out for the celebration of the Passover and the offering of burnt offerings on the altar of the LORD, as King Josiah had ordered. ¹⁷The Israelites who were present celebrated the Passover at that time and observed the Feast of Unleavened Bread for seven days. ¹⁸The Passover had not been observed like this in Israel since the days of the prophet Samuel; and none of the kings of Israel had ever celebrated such a Passover as did Josiah, with the priests, the Levites and all Judah and Israel who were there with the people of Jerusalem. ¹⁹This Passover was celebrated in the eighteenth year of Josiah's reign.

The Death of Josiah

²⁰After all this, when Josiah had set the temple in order, Neco king of Egypt went up to fight at Carchemish on the Euphrates, and Josiah marched out to meet him in battle. ²¹But Neco sent messengers to him saying, "What quarrel is there between you and me, O king of Judah? It is not you I am attacking at this time, but the house with which I am at war. God has told me to hurry; so stop opposing God, who is with me, or he will destroy you."

²²Josiah, however, would not turn away from him, but disguised himself to engage him in battle. He would not listen to what Neco had said at God's command but went to fight him on the plain of Megiddo.

²³Archers shot King Josiah, and he told his officers, "Take me away; I am badly wounded." ²⁴So they took him out of his chariot, put him in the other chariot he had and brought him to Jerusalem, where he died. He was buried in the tombs of his fathers, and all Judah and Jerusalem mourned for him.

²⁵Jeremiah composed laments for Josiah, and to this day all the men and women singers commemorate Josiah in the laments. These became a tradition in Israel and are written in the Laments.

²⁶The other events of Josiah's reign and his acts of devotion, according to what is written in the Law of the LORD—²⁷all the events, from beginning to end, are written in the book of the kings of Israel and **36** Judah. ¹And the people of the land took Jehoahaz son of Josiah and made him king in Jerusalem in place of his father.

Jehoahaz King of Judah

²Jehoahaz*ᵃ* was twenty-three years old when he became king, and he reigned in Jerusalem for three months. ³The king of Egypt dethroned him in Jerusalem and imposed on Judah a levy of a hundred talents*ᵇ* of silver and a talent*ᶜ* of gold. ⁴The king of Egypt made Eliakim, a brother of Jehoahaz, king over Judah and Jerusalem and changed Eliakim's name to Jehoiakim. But Neco took Eliakim's brother Jehoahaz and carried him off to Egypt.

Jehoiakim King of Judah

⁵Jehoiakim was twenty-five years old when he became king, and he reigned in Jerusalem for eleven years. He did evil in the eyes of the LORD his God. ⁶Nebuchadnezzar king of Babylon attacked him and bound him with bronze shackles to take him to Babylon. ⁷Nebuchadnezzar also took to Babylon articles from the temple of the LORD and put them in his temple*ᵈ* there.

⁸The other events of Jehoiakim's reign, the detestable things he did and all that was found against him, are written in the book of the kings of Israel and Judah. And Jehoiachin his son succeeded him as king.

Jehoiachin King of Judah

⁹Jehoiachin was eighteen*ᵉ* years old when he became king, and he reigned in Jerusalem for three months and ten days. He did evil in the eyes of the LORD. ¹⁰In the spring, King Nebuchadnezzar sent for him and brought him to Babylon, together with articles of value from the temple of the LORD, and he made Jehoiachin's uncle,*ᶠ* Zedekiah, king over Judah and Jerusalem.

Zedekiah King of Judah

¹¹Zedekiah was twenty-one years old when he became king, and he reigned in Jerusalem for eleven years. ¹²He did evil in the eyes of the LORD his God and did not humble himself before Jeremiah the prophet, who spoke the word of the LORD. ¹³He also rebelled against King Nebuchadnezzar, who had made him take an oath in God's name. He became stiff-necked and hardened his heart and would not turn to the LORD, the God of Israel. ¹⁴Furthermore, all the leaders of the priests and the people became more and more unfaithful, following all the detestable practices of the nations and defiling the temple of the LORD, which he had consecrated in Jerusalem.

The Fall of Jerusalem

¹⁵The LORD, the God of their fathers, sent word to them through his messengers again and again, because he had pity on his people and on his dwelling-place. ¹⁶But they mocked God's messengers, despised his words and scoffed at his prophets until the wrath of the LORD was aroused against his people and there was no remedy. ¹⁷He brought up against them the king of the Babylonians,*ᵍ* who killed their young men with the sword in the sanctuary, and spared neither young man nor young woman, old man or aged. God

---

ᵃ2 Hebrew *Joahaz*, a variant of *Jehoahaz*; also in verse 4   *ᵇ3* That is, about 3⅓ tons (about 3.4 metric tons)
ᶜ3 That is, about 75 pounds (about 34 kilograms)   *ᵈ7* Or *palace*
ᵉ9 One Hebrew manuscript, some Septuagint manuscripts and Syriac (see also 2 Kings 24:8); most Hebrew manuscripts *eight*   *ᶠ10* Hebrew *brother*, that is, relative (see 2 Kings 24:17)
ᵍ17 Or *Chaldeans*

handed all of them over to Nebuchadnez-zar. [18]He carried to Babylon all the articles from the temple of God, both large and small, and the treasures of the LORD's temple and the treasures of the king and his officials. [19]They set fire to God's temple and broke down the wall of Jerusalem; they burned all the palaces and destroyed everything of value there.

[20]He carried into exile to Babylon the remnant who escaped from the sword, and they became servants to him and his sons until the kingdom of Persia came to power. [21]The land enjoyed its sabbath rests; all the time of its desolation it rested, until the seventy years were completed in fulfilment of the word of the LORD spoken by Jeremiah.

[22]In the first year of Cyrus king of Persia, in order to fulfil the word of the LORD spoken by Jeremiah, the LORD moved the heart of Cyrus king of Persia to make a proclamation throughout his realm and to put it in writing:

[23]"This is what Cyrus king of Persia says:

"'The LORD, the God of heaven, has given me all the kingdoms of the earth and he has appointed me to build a temple for him at Jerusalem in Judah. Anyone of his people among you—may the LORD his God be with him, and let him go up.'"

Ezra

Cyrus Helps the Exiles to Return

1 In the first year of Cyrus king of Persia, in order to fulfil the word of the LORD spoken by Jeremiah, the LORD moved the heart of Cyrus king of Persia to make a proclamation throughout his realm and to put it in writing:

2"This is what Cyrus king of Persia says:

"'The LORD, the God of heaven, has given me all the kingdoms of the earth and he has appointed me to build a temple for him at Jerusalem in Judah. 3Anyone of his people among you—may his God be with him, and let him go up to Jerusalem in Judah and build the temple of the LORD, the God of Israel, the God who is in Jerusalem. 4And the people of any place where survivors may now be living are to provide him with silver and gold, with goods and livestock, and with freewill offerings for the temple of God in Jerusalem.'"

5Then the family heads of Judah and Benjamin, and the priests and Levites—everyone whose heart God had moved—prepared to go up and build the house of the LORD in Jerusalem. 6All their neighbours assisted them with articles of silver and gold, with goods and livestock, and with valuable gifts, in addition to all the freewill offerings. 7Moreover, King Cyrus brought out the articles belonging to the temple of the LORD, which Nebuchadnezzar had carried away from Jerusalem and had placed in the temple of his god.*a* 8Cyrus king of Persia had them brought by Mithredath the treasurer, who counted them out to Sheshbazzar the prince of Judah.

9This was the inventory:

gold dishes	30
silver dishes	1,000
silver pans*b*	29
10gold bowls	30
matching silver bowls	410
other articles	1,000

11In all, there were 5,400 articles of gold and of silver. Sheshbazzar brought all these along when the exiles came up from Babylon to Jerusalem.

The List of the Exiles Who Returned

2 Now these are the people of the province who came up from the captivity of the exiles, whom Nebuchadnezzar king of Babylon had taken captive to Babylon (they returned to Jerusalem and Judah, each to his own town, 2in company with Zerubbabel, Jeshua, Nehemiah, Seraiah, Reelaiah, Mordecai, Bilshan, Mispar, Bigvai, Rehum and Baanah):

The list of the men of the people of Israel:

3the descendants of Parosh	2,172
4of Shephatiah	372

⁵of Arah 775

⁶of Pahath-Moab (through the
line of Jeshua and Joab) 2,812

⁷of Elam 1,254

⁸of Zattu 945

⁹of Zaccai 760

¹⁰of Bani 642

¹¹of Bebai 623

¹²of Azgad 1,222

¹³of Adonikam 666

¹⁴of Bigvai 2,056

¹⁵of Adin 454

¹⁶of Ater (through Hezekiah) 98

¹⁷of Bezai 323

¹⁸of Jorah 112

¹⁹of Hashum 223

²⁰of Gibbar 95

²¹the men of Bethlehem 123

²²of Netophah 56

²³of Anathoth 128

²⁴of Azmaveth 42

²⁵of Kiriath Jearim,ᵃ
Kephirah and Beeroth 743

²⁶of Ramah and Geba 621

²⁷of Michmash 122

²⁸of Bethel and Ai 223

²⁹of Nebo 52

³⁰of Magbish 156

³¹of the other Elam 1,254

³²of Harim 320

³³of Lod, Hadid and Ono 725

³⁴of Jericho 345

³⁵of Senaah 3,630

³⁶The priests:

the descendants of Jedaiah
(through the family of Jeshua) 973

³⁷of Immer 1,052

³⁸of Pashhur 1,247

³⁹of Harim 1,017

⁴⁰The Levites:

the descendants of Jeshua
and Kadmiel (through
the line of Hodaviah) 74

⁴¹The singers:

the descendants of Asaph 128

⁴²The gatekeepers of the temple:

the descendants of
Shallum, Ater, Talmon,
Akkub, Hatita and
Shobai 139

⁴³The temple servants:

the descendants of
Ziha, Hasupha, Tabbaoth,
⁴⁴Keros, Siaha, Padon,
⁴⁵Lebanah, Hagabah, Akkub,
⁴⁶Hagab, Shalmai, Hanan,
⁴⁷Giddel, Gahar, Reaiah,
⁴⁸Rezin, Nekoda, Gazzam,
⁴⁹Uzza, Paseah, Besai,
⁵⁰Asnah, Meunim, Nephussim,
⁵¹Bakbuk, Hakupha, Harhur,
⁵²Bazluth, Mehida, Harsha,
⁵³Barkos, Sisera, Temah,
⁵⁴Neziah and Hatipha

⁵⁵The descendants of the servants of
Solomon:

the descendants of
Sotai, Hassophereth, Peruda,
⁵⁶Jaala, Darkon, Giddel,
⁵⁷Shephatiah, Hattil,
Pokereth-Hazzebaim and
Ami

⁵⁸The temple servants and
the descendants of the
servants of Solomon 392

⁵⁹The following came up from the
towns of Tel Melah, Tel Harsha,
Kerub, Addon and Immer, but they
could not show that their families
were descended from Israel:

⁶⁰The descendants of
Delaiah, Tobiah and
Nekoda 652

⁶¹And from among the priests:

The descendants of
Hobaiah, Hakkoz and
Barzillai (a man who had

ᵃ25 See Septuagint (see also Neh. 7:29); Hebrew *Kiriath Arim*.

married a daughter of Barzillai the Gileadite and was called by that name). [62]These searched for their family records, but they could not find them and so were excluded from the priesthood as unclean. [63]The governor ordered them not to eat any of the most sacred food until there was a priest ministering with the Urim and Thummim.

[64]The whole company numbered 42,360, [65]besides their 7,337 menservants and maidservants; and they also had 200 men and women singers. [66]They had 736 horses, 245 mules, [67]435 camels and 6,720 donkeys.

[68]When they arrived at the house of the LORD in Jerusalem, some of the heads of the families gave freewill offerings towards the rebuilding of the house of God on its site. [69]According to their ability they gave to the treasury for this work 61,000 drachmas[b] of gold, 5,000 minas[c] of silver and 100 priestly garments.

[70]The priests, the Levites, the singers, the gatekeepers and the temple servants settled in their own towns, along with some of the other people, and the rest of the Israelites settled in their towns.

Rebuilding the Altar

3 When the seventh month came and the Israelites had settled in their towns, the people assembled as one man in Jerusalem. [2]Then Jeshua son of Jozadak and his fellow priests and Zerubbabel son of Shealtiel and his associates began to build the altar of the God of Israel to sacrifice burnt offerings on it, in accordance with what is written in the Law of Moses the man of God. [3]Despite their fear of the peoples around them, they built the altar on its foundation and sacrificed burnt offerings on it to the LORD, both the morning and evening sacrifices. [4]Then in accordance with what is written, they celebrated the Feast of Tabernacles with the required number of burnt offerings prescribed for each day. [5]After that, they presented the regular burnt offerings, the New Moon sacrifices and the sacrifices for all the appointed sacred feasts of the LORD, as well as those brought as freewill offerings to the LORD. [6]On the first day of the seventh month they began to offer burnt offerings to the LORD, though the foundation of the LORD's temple had not yet been laid.

Rebuilding the Temple

[7]Then they gave money to the masons and carpenters, and gave food and drink and oil to the people of Sidon and Tyre, so that they would bring cedar logs by sea from Lebanon to Joppa, as authorised by Cyrus king of Persia.

[8]In the second month of the second year after their arrival at the house of God in Jerusalem, Zerubbabel son of Shealtiel, Jeshua son of Jozadak and the rest of their brothers (the priests and the Levites and all who had returned from the captivity to Jerusalem) began the work, appointing Levites twenty years of age and older to supervise the building of the house of the LORD. [9]Jeshua and his sons and brothers and Kadmiel and his sons (descendants of Hodaviah[a]) and the sons of Henadad and their sons and brothers—all Levites—joined together in supervising those working on the house of God.

[10]When the builders laid the foundation of the temple of the LORD, the priests in their vestments and with trumpets, and the Levites (the sons of Asaph) with cymbals, took their places to praise the LORD, as prescribed by David king of Israel. [11]With praise and thanksgiving they sang to the LORD:

"He is good;
  his love to Israel endures for ever."

And all the people gave a great shout of praise to the LORD, because the foundation of the house of the LORD was laid. [12]But many of the older priests and

---

[b]69 That is, about 1,100 pounds (about 500 kilograms)
[a]9 Hebrew Yehudah, probably a variant of Hodaviah

[c]69 That is, about 2⅖ tons (about 2.9 metric tons)

Levites and family heads, who had seen the former temple, wept aloud when they saw the foundation of this temple being laid, while many others shouted for joy. 13No-one could distinguish the sound of the shouts of joy from the sound of weeping, because the people made so much noise. And the sound was heard far away.

Opposition to the Rebuilding

4 When the enemies of Judah and Benjamin heard that the exiles were building a temple for the LORD, the God of Israel, 2they came to Zerubbabel and to the heads of the families and said, "Let us help you build because, like you, we seek your God and have been sacrificing to him since the time of Esarhaddon king of Assyria, who brought us here."

3But Zerubbabel, Jeshua and the rest of the heads of the families of Israel answered, "You have no part with us in building a temple to our God. We alone will build it for the LORD, the God of Israel, as King Cyrus, the king of Persia, commanded us."

4Then the peoples around them set out to discourage the people of Judah and make them afraid to go on building.*a*

5They hired counsellors to work against them and frustrate their plans during the entire reign of Cyrus king of Persia and down to the reign of Darius king of Persia.

Later Opposition Under Xerxes and Artaxerxes

6At the beginning of the reign of Xerxes,*b* they lodged an accusation against the people of Judah and Jerusalem.

7And in the days of Artaxerxes king of Persia, Bishlam, Mithredath, Tabeel and the rest of his associates wrote a letter to Artaxerxes. The letter was written in Aramaic script and in the Aramaic language.*c,d*

8Rehum the commanding officer and Shimshai the secretary wrote a letter against Jerusalem to Artaxerxes the king as follows:

9Rehum the commanding officer and Shimshai the secretary, together with the rest of their associates—the judges and officials over the men from Tripolis, Persia,*e* Erech and Babylon, the Elamites of Susa, 10and the other people whom the great and honourable Ashurbanipal*f* deported and settled in the city of Samaria and elsewhere in Trans-Euphrates.

11(This is a copy of the letter they sent him.)

To King Artaxerxes,

From your servants, the men of Trans-Euphrates:

12The king should know that the Jews who came up to us from you have gone to Jerusalem and are rebuilding that rebellious and wicked city. They are restoring the walls and repairing the foundations.

13Furthermore, the king should know that if this city is built and its walls are restored, no more taxes, tribute or duty will be paid, and the royal revenues will suffer. 14Now since we are under obligation to the palace and it is not proper for us to see the king dishonoured, we are sending this message to inform the king, 15so that a search may be made in the archives of your predecessors. In these records you will find that this city is a rebellious city, troublesome to kings and provinces, a place of rebellion from ancient times. That is why this city was destroyed. 16We inform the king that if this city is built and its walls are restored, you will be left with nothing in Trans-Euphrates.

17The king sent this reply:

---

a4 Or *and troubled them as they built*
c7 Or *written in Aramaic and translated*
e9 Or *officials, magistrates and governors over the men from*
b6 Hebrew *Ahasuerus,* a variant of Xerxes' Persian name
d7 The text of Ezra 4:8–6:18 is in Aramaic.
f10 Aramaic *Osnappar,* a variant of *Ashurbanipal*

To Rehum the commanding officer, Shimshai the secretary and the rest of their associates living in Samaria and elsewhere in Trans-Euphrates:

Greetings.

[18]The letter you sent us has been read and translated in my presence. [19]I issued an order and a search was made, and it was found that this city has a long history of revolt against kings and has been a place of rebellion and sedition. [20]Jerusalem has had powerful kings ruling over the whole of Trans-Euphrates, and taxes, tribute and duty were paid to them. [21]Now issue an order to these men to stop work, so that this city will not be rebuilt until I so order. [22]Be careful not to neglect this matter. Why let this threat grow, to the detriment of the royal interests?

[23]As soon as the copy of the letter of King Artaxerxes was read to Rehum and Shimshai the secretary and their associates, they went immediately to the Jews in Jerusalem and compelled them by force to stop.

[24]Thus the work on the house of God in Jerusalem came to a standstill until the second year of the reign of Darius king of Persia.

Tattenai's Letter to Darius

5 Now Haggai the prophet and Zechariah the prophet, a descendant of Iddo, prophesied to the Jews in Judah and Jerusalem in the name of the God of Israel, who was over them. [2]Then Zerubbabel son of Shealtiel and Jeshua son of Jozadak set to work to rebuild the house of God in Jerusalem. And the prophets of God were with them, helping them.

[3]At that time Tattenai, governor of Trans-Euphrates, and Shethar-Bozenai and their associates went to them and asked, "Who authorised you to rebuild this temple and restore this structure?" [4]They also asked, "What are the names of the men constructing this building?"[a] [5]But the eye of their God was watching over the elders of the Jews, and they were not stopped until a report could go to Darius and his written reply be received.

[6]This is a copy of the letter that Tattenai, governor of Trans-Euphrates, and Shethar-Bozenai and their associates, the officials of Trans-Euphrates, sent to King Darius. [7]The report they sent him read as follows:

To King Darius:

Cordial greetings.

[8]The king should know that we went to the district of Judah, to the temple of the great God. The people are building it with large stones and placing the timbers in the walls. The work is being carried on with diligence and is making rapid progress under their direction.

[9]We questioned the elders and asked them, "Who authorised you to rebuild this temple and restore this structure?" [10]We also asked them their names, so that we could write down the names of their leaders for your information.

[11]This is the answer they gave us:

"We are the servants of the God of heaven and earth, and we are rebuilding the temple that was built many years ago, one that a great king of Israel built and finished. [12]But because our fathers angered the God of heaven, he handed them over to Nebuchadnezzar the Chaldean, king of Babylon, who destroyed this temple and deported the people to Babylon.

[13]"However, in the first year of Cyrus king of Babylon, King Cyrus issued a decree to rebuild this house of God. [14]He even removed from the temple[b] of Babylon the gold and

---

[a]4 See Septuagint; Aramaic [4]We told them the names of the men constructing this building.
[b]14 Or palace

silver articles of the house of God, which Nebuchadnezzar had taken from the temple in Jerusalem and brought to the temple[b] in Babylon.

"Then King Cyrus gave them to a man named Sheshbazzar, whom he had appointed governor, [15]and he told him, 'Take these articles and go and deposit them in the temple in Jerusalem. And rebuild the house of God on its site.' [16]So this Sheshbazzar came and laid the foundations of the house of God in Jerusalem. From that day to the present it has been under construction but is not yet finished."

[17]Now if it pleases the king, let a search be made in the royal archives of Babylon to see if King Cyrus did in fact issue a decree to rebuild this house of God in Jerusalem. Then let the king send us his decision in this matter.

The Decree of Darius

6 King Darius then issued an order, and they searched in the archives stored in the treasury at Babylon. [2]A scroll was found in the citadel of Ecbatana in the province of Media, and this was written on it:

Memorandum:

[3]In the first year of King Cyrus, the king issued a decree concerning the temple of God in Jerusalem:

Let the temple be rebuilt as a place to present sacrifices, and let its foundations be laid. It is to be ninety feet[a] high and ninety feet wide, [4]with three courses of large stones and one of timbers. The costs are to be paid by the royal treasury. [5]Also, the gold and silver articles of the house of God, which Nebuchadnezzar took from the temple in Jerusalem and brought to Babylon, are to be returned to their places in the temple in

Jerusalem; they are to be deposited in the house of God.

[6]Now then, Tattenai, governor of Trans-Euphrates, and Shethar-Bozenai and you, their fellow officials of that province, stay away from there. [7]Do not interfere with the work on this temple of God. Let the governor of the Jews and the Jewish elders rebuild this house of God on its site.

[8]Moreover, I hereby decree what you are to do for these elders of the Jews in the construction of this house of God:

The expenses of these men are to be fully paid out of the royal treasury, from the revenues of Trans-Euphrates, so that the work will not stop. [9]Whatever is needed—young bulls, rams, male lambs for burnt offerings to the God of heaven, and wheat, salt, wine and oil, as requested by the priests in Jerusalem—must be given them daily without fail, [10]so that they may offer sacrifices pleasing to the God of heaven and pray for the well-being of the king and his sons.

[11]Furthermore, I decree that if anyone changes this edict, a beam is to be pulled from his house and he is to be lifted up and impaled on it. And for this crime his house is to be made a pile of rubble. [12]May God, who has caused his Name to dwell there, overthrow any king or people who lifts a hand to change this decree or to destroy this temple in Jerusalem.

I Darius have decreed it. Let it be carried out with diligence.

Completion and Dedication of the Temple

[13]Then, because of the decree King Darius had sent, Tattenai, governor of Trans-Euphrates, and Shethar-Bozenai and their associates carried it out with diligence. [14]So the elders of the Jews continued to build and prosper under the preaching of Haggai the prophet and

b14 Or palace   a3 Aramaic sixty cubits (about 27 metres)

Zechariah, a descendant of Iddo. They finished building the temple according to the command of the God of Israel and the decrees of Cyrus, Darius and Artaxerxes, kings of Persia. ¹⁵The temple was completed on the third day of the month Adar, in the sixth year of the reign of King Darius.

¹⁶Then the people of Israel—the priests, the Levites and the rest of the exiles—celebrated the dedication of the house of God with joy. ¹⁷For the dedication of this house of God they offered a hundred bulls, two hundred rams, four hundred male lambs and, as a sin offering for all Israel, twelve male goats, one for each of the tribes of Israel. ¹⁸And they installed the priests in their divisions and the Levites in their groups for the service of God at Jerusalem, according to what is written in the Book of Moses.

The Passover

¹⁹On the fourteenth day of the first month, the exiles celebrated the Passover. ²⁰The priests and Levites had purified themselves and were all ceremonially clean. The Levites slaughtered the Passover lamb for all the exiles, for their brothers the priests and for themselves. ²¹So the Israelites who had returned from the exile ate it, together with all who had separated themselves from the unclean practices of their Gentile neighbours in order to seek the LORD, the God of Israel. ²²For seven days they celebrated with joy the Feast of Unleavened Bread, because the LORD had filled them with joy by changing the attitude of the king of Assyria, so that he assisted them in the work on the house of God, the God of Israel.

Ezra Comes to Jerusalem

7 After these things, during the reign of Artaxerxes king of Persia, Ezra son of Seraiah, the son of Azariah, the son of Hilkiah, ²the son of Shallum, the son of Zadok, the son of Ahitub, ³the son of Amariah, the son of Azariah, the son of

Meraioth, ⁴the son of Zerahiah, the son of Uzzi, the son of Bukki, ⁵the son of Abishua, the son of Phinehas, the son of Eleazar, the son of Aaron the chief priest—⁶this Ezra came up from Babylon. He was a teacher well versed in the Law of Moses, which the LORD, the God of Israel, had given. The king had granted him everything he asked, for the hand of the LORD his God was on him. ⁷Some of the Israelites, including priests, Levites, singers, gatekeepers and temple servants, also came up to Jerusalem in the seventh year of King Artaxerxes.

⁸Ezra arrived in Jerusalem in the fifth month of the seventh year of the king. ⁹He had begun his journey from Babylon on the first day of the first month, and he arrived in Jerusalem on the first day of the fifth month, for the gracious hand of his God was on him. ¹⁰For Ezra had devoted himself to the study and observance of the Law of the LORD, and to teaching its decrees and laws in Israel.

King Artaxerxes' Letter to Ezra

¹¹This is a copy of the letter King Artaxerxes had given to Ezra the priest and teacher, a man learned in matters concerning the commands and decrees of the LORD for Israel:

¹²ᵃArtaxerxes, king of kings,

To Ezra the priest, a teacher of the Law of the God of heaven:

Greetings.

¹³Now I decree that any of the Israelites in my kingdom, including priests and Levites, who wish to go to Jerusalem with you, may go. ¹⁴You are sent by the king and his seven advisers to enquire about Judah and Jerusalem with regard to the Law of your God, which is in your hand. ¹⁵Moreover, you are to take with you the silver and gold that the king and his advisers have freely given to the

---

ᵃ12 The text of Ezra 7:12–26 is in Aramaic.

God of Israel, whose dwelling is in Jerusalem, [16]together with all the silver and gold you may obtain from the province of Babylon, as well as the freewill offerings of the people and priests for the temple of their God in Jerusalem. [17]With this money be sure to buy bulls, rams and male lambs, together with their grain offerings and drink offerings, and sacrifice them on the altar of the temple of your God in Jerusalem.

[18]You and your brother Jews may then do whatever seems best with the rest of the silver and gold, in accordance with the will of your God. [19]Deliver to the God of Jerusalem all the articles entrusted to you for worship in the temple of your God. [20]And anything else needed for the temple of your God that you may have occasion to supply, you may provide from the royal treasury.

[21]Now I, King Artaxerxes, order all the treasurers of Trans-Euphrates to provide with diligence whatever Ezra the priest, a teacher of the Law of the God of heaven, may ask of you—[22]up to a hundred talents[b] of silver, a hundred cors[c] of wheat, a hundred baths[d] of wine, a hundred baths[d] of olive oil, and salt without limit. [23]Whatever the God of heaven has prescribed, let it be done with diligence for the temple of the God of heaven. Why should there be wrath against the realm of the king and of his sons? [24]You are also to know that you have no authority to impose taxes, tribute or duty on any of the priests, Levites, singers, gatekeepers, temple servants or other workers at this house of God.

[25]And you, Ezra, in accordance with the wisdom of your God, which you possess, appoint magistrates and judges to administer justice to all the people of Trans-Euphrates—all who know the laws of your God. And you are to teach any who do not know them. [26]Whoever does not obey the law of your God and the law of the king must surely be punished by death, banishment, confiscation of property, or imprisonment.

[27]Praise be to the LORD, the God of our fathers, who has put it into the king's heart to bring honour to the house of the LORD in Jerusalem in this way [28]and who has extended his good favour to me before the king and his advisers and all the king's powerful officials. Because the hand of the LORD my God was on me, I took courage and gathered leading men from Israel to go up with me.

List of the Family Heads Returning With Ezra

8 These are the family heads and those registered with them who came up with me from Babylon during the reign of King Artaxerxes:

[2]of the descendants of Phinehas, Gershom;

of the descendants of Ithamar, Daniel;

of the descendants of David, Hattush [3]of the descendants of Shecaniah;

of the descendants of Parosh, Zechariah, and with him were registered 150 men;

[4]of the descendants of Pahath-Moab, Eliehoenai son of Zerahiah, and with him 200 men;

[5]of the descendants of Zattu,[a] Shecaniah son of Jahaziel, and with him 300 men;

[6]of the descendants of Adin, Ebed son of Jonathan, and with him 50 men;

[7]of the descendants of Elam, Jeshaiah son of Athaliah, and with him 70 men;

[8]of the descendants of Shephatiah, Zebadiah son of Michael, and with him 80 men;

[9]of the descendants of Joab, Obadiah

---

b22 That is, about 3⅓ tons (about 3.4 metric tons)
d22 That is, probably about 500 gallons (about 2.2 kilolitres)
a5 Some Septuagint manuscripts (also 1 Esdras 8:32); Hebrew does not have *Zattu*.
c22 That is, probably about 600 bushels (about 22 kilolitres)

son of Jehiel, and with him 218 men;

[10]of the descendants of Bani,[b] Shelomith son of Josiphiah, and with him 160 men;

[11]of the descendants of Bebai, Zechariah son of Bebai, and with him 28 men;

[12]of the descendants of Azgad, Johanan son of Hakkatan, and with him 110 men;

[13]of the descendants of Adonikam, the last ones, whose names were Eliphelet, Jeuel and Shemaiah, and with them 60 men;

[14]of the descendants of Bigvai, Uthai and Zaccur, and with them 70 men.

The Return to Jerusalem

[15]I assembled them at the canal that flows towards Ahava, and we camped there three days. When I checked among the people and the priests, I found no Levites there. [16]So I summoned Eliezer, Ariel, Shemaiah, Elnathan, Jarib, Elnathan, Nathan, Zechariah and Meshullam, who were leaders, and Joiarib and Elnathan, who were men of learning, [17]and I sent them to Iddo, the leader in Casiphia. I told them what to say to Iddo and his kinsmen, the temple servants in Casiphia, so that they might bring attendants to us for the house of our God. [18]Because the gracious hand of our God was on us, they brought us Sherebiah, a capable man, from the descendants of Mahli son of Levi, the son of Israel, and Sherebiah's sons and brothers, 18 men; [19]and Hashabiah, together with Jeshaiah from the descendants of Merari, and his brothers and nephews, 20 men. [20]They also brought 220 of the temple servants—a body that David and the officials had established to assist the Levites. All were registered by name.

[21]There, by the Ahava Canal, I proclaimed a fast, so that we might humble ourselves before our God and ask him for a safe journey for us and our children, with all our possessions. [22]I was ashamed to ask the king for soldiers and horsemen to protect us from enemies on the road, because we had told the king, "The gracious hand of our God is on everyone who looks to him, but his great anger is against all who forsake him." [23]So we fasted and petitioned our God about this, and he answered our prayer.

[24]Then I set apart twelve of the leading priests, together with Sherebiah, Hashabiah and ten of their brothers, [25]and I weighed out to them the offering of silver and gold and the articles that the king, his advisers, his officials and all Israel present there had donated for the house of our God. [26]I weighed out to them 650 talents[c] of silver, silver articles weighing 100 talents,[d] 100 talents[d] of gold, [27]20 bowls of gold valued at 1,000 darics,[e] and two fine articles of polished bronze, as precious as gold.

[28]I said to them, "You as well as these articles are consecrated to the LORD. The silver and gold are a freewill offering to the LORD, the God of your fathers. [29]Guard them carefully until you weigh them out in the chambers of the house of the LORD in Jerusalem before the leading priests and the Levites and the family heads of Israel." [30]Then the priests and Levites received the silver and gold and sacred articles that had been weighed out to be taken to the house of our God in Jerusalem.

[31]On the twelfth day of the first month we set out from the Ahava Canal to go to Jerusalem. The hand of our God was on us, and he protected us from enemies and bandits along the way. [32]So we arrived in Jerusalem, where we rested three days.

[33]On the fourth day, in the house of our God, we weighed out the silver and gold and the sacred articles into the hands of Meremoth son of Uriah, the priest. Eleazar son of Phinehas was with him, and so were the Levites Jozabad son of Jeshua and Noadiah son of Binnui. [34]Everything was accounted for by number and weight,

---

[b]10 Some Septuagint manuscripts (also 1 Esdras 8:36); Hebrew does not have *Bani*.
[c]26 That is, about 22 tons (about 22 metric tons)   [d]26 That is, about 3⅓ tons (about 3.4 metric tons)
[e]27 That is, about 19 pounds (about 8.5 kilograms)

and the entire weight was recorded at that time.

[35]Then the exiles who had returned from captivity sacrificed burnt offerings to the God of Israel: twelve bulls for all Israel, ninety-six rams, seventy-seven male lambs, and, as a sin offering, twelve male goats. All this was a burnt offering to the LORD. [36]They also delivered the king's orders to the royal satraps and to the governors of Trans-Euphrates who then gave assistance to the people and to the house of God.

Ezra's Prayer About Intermarriage

9 After these things had been done, the leaders came to me and said, "The people of Israel, including the priests and the Levites, have not kept themselves separate from the neighbouring peoples with their detestable practices, like those of the Canaanites, Hittites, Perizzites, Jebusites, Ammonites, Moabites, Egyptians and Amorites. [2]They have taken some of their daughters as wives for themselves and their sons, and have mingled the holy race with the peoples around them. And the leaders and officials have led the way in this unfaithfulness."

[3]When I heard this, I tore my tunic and cloak, pulled hair from my head and beard and sat down appalled. [4]Then everyone who trembled at the words of the God of Israel gathered round me because of this unfaithfulness of the exiles. And I sat there appalled until the evening sacrifice.

[5]Then, at the evening sacrifice, I rose from my self-abasement, with my tunic and cloak torn, and fell on my knees with my hands spread out to the LORD my God [6]and prayed:

"O my God, I am too ashamed and disgraced to lift up my face to you, my God, because our sins are higher than our heads and our guilt has reached to the heavens. [7]From the days of our forefathers until now, our guilt has been great. Because of our sins, we and our kings and our priests have been subjected to the sword and captivity, to pillage and humiliation at the hand of foreign kings, as it is today.

[8]"But now, for a brief moment, the LORD our God has been gracious in leaving us a remnant and giving us a firm place in his sanctuary, and so our God gives light to our eyes and a little relief in our bondage. [9]Though we are slaves, our God has not deserted us in our bondage. He has shown us kindness in the sight of the kings of Persia: He has granted us new life to rebuild the house of our God and repair its ruins, and he has given us a wall of protection in Judah and Jerusalem.

[10]"But now, O our God, what can we say after this? For we have disregarded the commands [11]you gave through your servants the prophets when you said: 'The land you are entering to possess is a land polluted by the corruption of its peoples. By their detestable practices they have filled it with their impurity from one end to the other. [12]Therefore, do not give your daughters in marriage to their sons or take their daughters for your sons. Do not seek a treaty of friendship with them at any time, that you may be strong and eat the good things of the land and leave it to your children as an everlasting inheritance.'

[13]"What has happened to us is a result of our evil deeds and our great guilt, and yet, our God, you have punished us less than our sins have deserved and have given us a remnant like this. [14]Shall we again break your commands and intermarry with the peoples who commit such detestable practices? Would you not be angry enough with us to destroy us, leaving us no remnant or survivor? [15]O LORD, God of Israel, you are righteous! We are left this day as a remnant. Here we are before you in our guilt, though because of it not one of us can stand in your presence."

The People's Confession of Sin

10 While Ezra was praying and confessing, weeping and throwing himself down before the house of God, a large crowd of Israelites—men, women and children—gathered round him. They too wept bitterly. ²Then Shecaniah son of Jehiel, one of the descendants of Elam, said to Ezra, "We have been unfaithful to our God by marrying foreign women from the peoples around us. But in spite of this, there is still hope for Israel. ³Now let us make a covenant before our God to send away all these women and their children, in accordance with the counsel of my lord and of those who fear the commands of our God. Let it be done according to the Law. ⁴Rise up; this matter is in your hands. We will support you, so take courage and do it."

⁵So Ezra rose up and put the leading priests and Levites and all Israel under oath to do what had been suggested. And they took the oath. ⁶Then Ezra withdrew from before the house of God and went to the room of Jehohanan son of Eliashib. While he was there, he ate no food and drank no water, because he continued to mourn over the unfaithfulness of the exiles.

⁷A proclamation was then issued throughout Judah and Jerusalem for all the exiles to assemble in Jerusalem. ⁸Anyone who failed to appear within three days would forfeit all his property, in accordance with the decision of the officials and elders, and would himself be expelled from the assembly of the exiles.

⁹Within the three days, all the men of Judah and Benjamin had gathered in Jerusalem. And on the twentieth day of the ninth month, all the people were sitting in the square before the house of God, greatly distressed by the occasion and because of the rain. ¹⁰Then Ezra the priest stood up and said to them, "You have been unfaithful; you have married foreign women, adding to Israel's guilt. ¹¹Now make confession to the Lord, the God of your fathers, and do his will. Separate yourselves from the peoples around you and from your foreign wives."

¹²The whole assembly responded with a loud voice: "You are right! We must do as you say. ¹³But there are many people here and it is the rainy season; so we cannot stand outside. Besides, this matter cannot be taken care of in a day or two, because we have sinned greatly in this thing. ¹⁴Let our officials act for the whole assembly. Then let everyone in our towns who has married a foreign woman come at a set time, along with the elders and judges of each town, until the fierce anger of our God in this matter is turned away from us." ¹⁵Only Jonathan son of Asahel and Jahzeiah son of Tikvah, supported by Meshullam and Shabbethai the Levite, opposed this.

¹⁶So the exiles did as was proposed. Ezra the priest selected men who were family heads, one from each family division, and all of them designated by name. On the first day of the tenth month they sat down to investigate the cases, ¹⁷and by the first day of the first month they finished dealing with all the men who had married foreign women.

Those Guilty of Intermarriage

¹⁸Among the descendants of the priests, the following had married foreign women:

From the descendants of Jeshua son of Jozadak, and his brothers: Maaseiah, Eliezer, Jarib and Gedaliah. ¹⁹(They all gave their hands in pledge to put away their wives, and for their guilt they each presented a ram from the flock as a guilt offering.)

²⁰From the descendants of Immer: Hanani and Zebadiah.

²¹From the descendants of Harim: Maaseiah, Elijah, Shemaiah, Jehiel and Uzziah.

²²From the descendants of Pashhur: Elioenai, Maaseiah, Ishmael, Nethanel, Jozabad and Elasah.

²³Among the Levites:

Jozabad, Shimei, Kelaiah (that is Kelita), Pethahiah, Judah and Eliezer.

[24]From the singers:

Eliashib.

From the gatekeepers:

Shallum, Telem and Uri.

[25]And among the other Israelites:

From the descendants of Parosh:

Ramiah, Izziah, Malkijah, Mijamin, Eleazar, Malkijah and Benaiah.

[26]From the descendants of Elam:

Mattaniah, Zechariah, Jehiel, Abdi, Jeremoth and Elijah.

[27]From the descendants of Zattu:

Elioenai, Eliashib, Mattaniah, Jeremoth, Zabad and Aziza.

[28]From the descendants of Bebai:

Jehohanan, Hananiah, Zabbai and Athlai.

[29]From the descendants of Bani:

Meshullam, Malluch, Adaiah, Jashub, Sheal and Jeremoth.

[30]From the descendants of Pahath-Moab:

Adna, Kelal, Benaiah, Maaseiah, Mattaniah, Bezalel, Binnui and Manasseh.

[31]From the descendants of Harim:

Eliezer, Ishijah, Malkijah, Shemaiah, Shimeon, [32]Benjamin, Malluch and Shemariah.

[33]From the descendants of Hashum:

Mattenai, Mattattah, Zabad, Eliphelet, Jeremai, Manasseh and Shimei.

[34]From the descendants of Bani:

Maadai, Amram, Uel, [35]Benaiah, Bedeiah, Keluhi, [36]Vaniah, Meremoth, Eliashib, [37]Mattaniah, Mattenai and Jaasu.

[38]From the descendants of Binnui:[a]

Shimei, [39]Shelemiah, Nathan, Adaiah, [40]Macnadebai, Shashai, Sharai, [41]Azarel, Shelemiah, Shemariah, [42]Shallum, Amariah and Joseph.

[43]From the descendants of Nebo:

Jeiel, Mattithiah, Zabad, Zebina, Jaddai, Joel and Benaiah.

[44]All these had married foreign women, and some of them had children by these wives.[b]

---

[a]37,38 See Septuagint (also 1 Esdras 9:34); Hebrew *Jaasu*[38] *and Bani and Binnui,*
[b]44 Or *and they sent them away with their children*

Nehemiah

Nehemiah's Prayer

1 The words of Nehemiah son of Hacaliah:

In the month of Kislev in the twentieth
year, while I was in the citadel of Susa,
²Hanani, one of my brothers, came from
Judah with some other men, and I questioned them about the Jewish remnant
that survived the exile, and also about
Jerusalem.

³They said to me, "Those who survived
the exile and are back in the province are
in great trouble and disgrace. The wall of
Jerusalem is broken down, and its gates
have been burned with fire."

⁴When I heard these things, I sat down
and wept. For some days I mourned and
fasted and prayed before the God of
heaven. ⁵Then I said:

"O LORD, God of heaven, the great
and awesome God, who keeps his
covenant of love with those who love
him and obey his commands, ⁶let your
ear be attentive and your eyes open to
hear the prayer your servant is
praying before you day and night for
your servants, the people of Israel. I
confess the sins we Israelites, including myself and my father's house,
have committed against you. ⁷We
have acted very wickedly towards
you. We have not obeyed the commands, decrees and laws you gave
your servant Moses.

⁸"Remember the instruction you
gave your servant Moses, saying, 'If

you are unfaithful, I will scatter you
among the nations, ⁹but if you return
to me and obey my commands, then
even if your exiled people are at the
farthest horizon, I will gather them
from there and bring them to the
place I have chosen as a dwelling for
my Name.'

¹⁰"They are your servants and your
people, whom you redeemed by your
great strength and your mighty hand.
¹¹O Lord, let your ear be attentive to
the prayer of this your servant and to
the prayer of your servants who delight in revering your name. Give
your servant success today by grant-
ing him favour in the presence of this
man."

I was cupbearer to the king.

Artaxerxes Sends Nehemiah to Jerusalem

2 In the month of Nisan in the twentieth year of King Artaxerxes, when
wine was brought for him, I took the wine
and gave it to the king. I had not been sad
in his presence before; ²so the king asked
me, "Why does your face look so sad
when you are not ill? This can be nothing
but sadness of heart."

I was very much afraid, ³but I said to the
king, "May the king live for ever! Why
should my face not look sad when the city
where my fathers are buried lies in ruins,
and its gates have been destroyed by fire?"

⁴The king said to me, "What is it you
want?"

Then I prayed to the God of heaven,

⁵and I answered the king, "If it pleases the king and if your servant has found favour in his sight, let him send me to the city in Judah where my fathers are buried so that I can rebuild it."

⁶Then the king, with the queen sitting beside him, asked me, "How long will your journey take, and when will you get back?" It pleased the king to send me; so I set a time.

⁷I also said to him, "If it pleases the king, may I have letters to the governors of Trans-Euphrates, so that they will provide me safe-conduct until I arrive in Judah? ⁸And may I have a letter to Asaph, keeper of the king's forest, so he will give me timber to make beams for the gates of the citadel by the temple and for the city wall and for the residence I will occupy?" And because the gracious hand of my God was upon me, the king granted my requests. ⁹So I went to the governors of Trans-Euphrates and gave them the king's letters. The king had also sent army officers and cavalry with me.

¹⁰When Sanballat the Horonite and Tobiah the Ammonite official heard about this, they were very much disturbed that someone had come to promote the welfare of the Israelites.

Nehemiah Inspects Jerusalem's Walls

¹¹I went to Jerusalem, and after staying there three days ¹²I set out during the night with a few men. I had not told anyone what my God had put in my heart to do for Jerusalem. There were no mounts with me except the one I was riding on. ¹³By night I went out through the Valley Gate towards the Jackal[a] Well and the Dung Gate, examining the walls of Jerusalem, which had been broken down, and its gates, which had been destroyed by fire. ¹⁴Then I moved on towards the Fountain Gate and the King's Pool, but there was not enough room for my mount to get through; ¹⁵so I went up the valley by night, examining the wall. Finally, I turned back and re-entered through the Valley Gate. ¹⁶The officials did not know where I had

gone or what I was doing, because as yet I had said nothing to the Jews or the priests or nobles or officials or any others who would be doing the work.

¹⁷Then I said to them, "You see the trouble we are in: Jerusalem lies in ruins, and its gates have been burned with fire. Come, let us rebuild the wall of Jerusalem, and we will no longer be in disgrace." ¹⁸I also told them about the gracious hand of my God upon me and what the king had said to me.

They replied, "Let us start rebuilding." So they began this good work.

¹⁹But when Sanballat the Horonite, Tobiah the Ammonite official and Geshem the Arab heard about it, they mocked and ridiculed us. "What is it you are doing?" they asked. "Are you rebelling against the king?"

²⁰I answered them by saying, "The God of heaven will give us success. We his servants will start rebuilding, but as for you, you have no share in Jerusalem or any claim or historic right to it."

Builders of the Wall

3 Eliashib the high priest and his fellow priests went to work and rebuilt the Sheep Gate. They dedicated it and set its doors in place, building as far as the Tower of the Hundred, which they dedicated, and as far as the Tower of Hananel. ²The men of Jericho built the adjoining section, and Zaccur son of Imri built next to them.

³The Fish Gate was rebuilt by the sons of Hassenaah. They laid its beams and put its doors and bolts and bars in place. ⁴Meremoth son of Uriah, the son of Hakkoz, repaired the next section. Next to him Meshullam son of Berekiah, the son of Meshezabel, made repairs, and next to him Zadok son of Baana also made repairs. ⁵The next section was repaired by the men of Tekoa, but their nobles would not put their shoulders to the work under their supervisors.[a]

---

[a]13 Or Serpent or Fig   [a]5 Or their Lord or the governor

[6]The Jeshanah[b] Gate was repaired by Joiada son of Paseah and Meshullam son of Besodeiah. They laid its beams and put its doors and bolts and bars in place. [7]Next to them, repairs were made by men from Gibeon and Mizpah—Melatiah of Gibeon and Jadon of Meronoth—places under the authority of the governor of Trans-Euphrates. [8]Uzziel son of Harhaiah, one of the goldsmiths, repaired the next section; and Hananiah, one of the perfume-makers, made repairs next to that. They restored[c] Jerusalem as far as the Broad Wall. [9]Rephaiah son of Hur, ruler of a half-district of Jerusalem, repaired the next section. [10]Adjoining this, Jedaiah son of Harumaph made repairs opposite his house, and Hattush son of Hashabneiah made repairs next to him. [11]Malkijah son of Harim and Hasshub son of Pahath-Moab repaired another section and the Tower of the Ovens. [12]Shallum son of Hallohesh, ruler of a half-district of Jerusalem, repaired the next section with the help of his daughters.

[13]The Valley Gate was repaired by Hanun and the residents of Zanoah. They rebuilt it and put its doors and bolts and bars in place. They also repaired five hundred yards[d] of the wall as far as the Dung Gate.

[14]The Dung Gate was repaired by Malkijah son of Recab, ruler of the district of Beth Hakkerem. He rebuilt it and put its doors and bolts and bars in place.

[15]The Fountain Gate was repaired by Shallun son of Col-Hozeh, ruler of the district of Mizpah. He rebuilt it, roofing it over and putting its doors and bolts and bars in place. He also repaired the wall of the Pool of Siloam,[e] by the King's Garden, as far as the steps going down from the City of David. [16]Beyond him, Nehemiah son of Azbuk, ruler of a half-district of Beth Zur, made repairs up to a point opposite the tombs[f] of David, as far as the artificial pool and the House of the Heroes.

[17]Next to him, the repairs were made by the Levites under Rehum son of Bani. Beside him, Hashabiah, ruler of half the district of Keilah, carried out repairs for his district. [18]Next to him, the repairs were made by their countrymen under Binnui[g] son of Henadad, ruler of the other half-district of Keilah. [19]Next to him, Ezer son of Jeshua, ruler of Mizpah, repaired another section, from a point facing the ascent to the armoury as far as the angle. [20]Next to him, Baruch son of Zabbai zealously repaired another section, from the angle to the entrance of the house of Eliashib the high priest. [21]Next to him, Meremoth son of Uriah, the son of Hak-koz, repaired another section, from the entrance of Eliashib's house to the end of it.

[22]The repairs next to him were made by the priests from the surrounding region. [23]Beyond them, Benjamin and Hasshub made repairs in front of their house; and next to them, Azariah son of Maaseiah, the son of Ananiah, made repairs beside his house. [24]Next to him, Binnui son of Henadad repaired another section, from Azariah's house to the angle and the corner, [25]and Palal son of Uzai worked opposite the angle and the tower projecting from the upper palace near the court of the guard. Next to him, Pedaiah son of Parosh [26]and the temple servants living on the hill of Ophel made repairs up to a point opposite the Water Gate towards the east and the projecting tower. [27]Next to them, the men of Tekoa repaired another section, from the great projecting tower to the wall of Ophel.

[28]Above the Horse Gate, the priests made repairs, each in front of his own house. [29]Next to them, Zadok son of Immer made repairs opposite his house. Next to him, Shemaiah son of Shecaniah, the guard at the East Gate, made repairs. [30]Next to him, Hananiah son of

---

[b]6 Or Old   [c]8 Or They left out part of   [d]13 Hebrew a thousand cubits (about 450 metres)
[e]15 Hebrew Shelah, a variant of Shiloah, that is, Siloam
[f]16 Hebrew; Septuagint, some Vulgate manuscripts and Syriac tomb
[g]18 Two Hebrew manuscripts and Syriac (see also Septuagint and verse 24); most Hebrew manuscripts Bavvai

Shelemiah, and Hanun, the sixth son of Zalaph, repaired another section. Next to them, Meshullam son of Berekiah made repairs opposite his living quarters. ³¹Next to him, Malkijah, one of the goldsmiths, made repairs as far as the house of the temple servants and the merchants, opposite the Inspection Gate, and as far as the room above the corner; ³²and between the room above the corner and the Sheep Gate the goldsmiths and merchants made repairs.

Opposition to the Rebuilding

4 When Sanballat heard that we were rebuilding the wall, he became angry and was greatly incensed. He ridiculed the Jews, ²and in the presence of his associates and the army of Samaria, he said, "What are those feeble Jews doing? Will they restore their wall? Will they offer sacrifices? Will they finish in a day? Can they bring the stones back to life from those heaps of rubble—burned as they are?"

³Tobiah the Ammonite, who was at his side, said, "What they are building—if even a fox climbed up on it, he would break down their wall of stones!"

⁴Hear us, O our God, for we are despised. Turn their insults back on their own heads. Give them over as plunder in a land of captivity. ⁵Do not cover up their guilt or blot out their sins from your sight, for they have thrown insults in the face of*ᵃ* the builders.

⁶So we rebuilt the wall till all of it reached half its height, for the people worked with all their heart.

⁷But when Sanballat, Tobiah, the Arabs, the Ammonites and the men of Ashdod heard that the repairs to Jerusalem's walls had gone ahead and that the gaps were being closed, they were very angry. ⁸They all plotted together to come and fight against Jerusalem and stir up trouble against it. ⁹But we prayed to our God and posted a guard day and night to meet this threat.

¹⁰Meanwhile, the people in Judah said, "The strength of the labourers is giving out, and there is so much rubble that we cannot rebuild the wall."

¹¹Also our enemies said, "Before they know it or see us, we will be right there among them and will kill them and put an end to the work."

¹²Then the Jews who lived near them came and told us ten times over, "Wherever you turn, they will attack us."

¹³Therefore I stationed some of the people behind the lowest points of the wall at the exposed places, posting them by families, with their swords, spears and bows. ¹⁴After I looked things over, I stood up and said to the nobles, the officials and the rest of the people, "Don't be afraid of them. Remember the Lord, who is great and awesome, and fight for your brothers, your sons and your daughters, your wives and your homes."

¹⁵When our enemies heard that we were aware of their plot and that God had frustrated it, we all returned to the wall, each to his own work.

¹⁶From that day on, half of my men did the work, while the other half were equipped with spears, shields, bows and armour. The officers posted themselves behind all the people of Judah ¹⁷who were building the wall. Those who carried materials did their work with one hand and held a weapon in the other, ¹⁸and each of the builders wore his sword at his side as he worked. But the man who sounded the trumpet stayed with me.

¹⁹Then I said to the nobles, the officials and the rest of the people, "The work is extensive and spread out, and we are widely separated from each other along the wall. ²⁰Wherever you hear the sound of the trumpet, join us there. Our God will fight for us!"

²¹So we continued the work with half the men holding spears, from the first light of dawn till the stars came out. ²²At that time I also said to the people, "Have every man and his helper stay inside Jerusalem at night, so that they can serve us as guards by night and workmen by day." ²³Neither

ᵃ5 Or have provoked you to anger before

I nor my brothers nor my men nor the guards with me took off our clothes; each had his weapon, even when he went for water.*b*

Nehemiah Helps the Poor

5 Now the men and their wives raised a great outcry against their Jewish brothers. [2]Some were saying, "We and our sons and daughters are numerous; in order for us to eat and stay alive, we must get grain."

[3]Others were saying, "We are mortgaging our fields, our vineyards and our homes to get grain during the famine."

[4]Still others were saying, "We have had to borrow money to pay the king's tax on our fields and vineyards. [5]Although we are of the same flesh and blood as our countrymen and though our sons are as good as theirs, yet we have to subject our sons and daughters to slavery. Some of our daughters have already been enslaved, but we are powerless, because our fields and our vineyards belong to others."

[6]When I heard their outcry and these charges, I was very angry. [7]I pondered them in my mind and then accused the nobles and officials. I told them, "You are exacting usury from your own countrymen!" So I called together a large meeting to deal with them [8]and said: "As far as possible, we have bought back our Jewish brothers who were sold to the Gentiles. Now you are selling your brothers, only for them to be sold back to us!" They kept quiet, because they could find nothing to say.

[9]So I continued, "What you are doing is not right. Shouldn't you walk in the fear of our God to avoid the reproach of our Gentile enemies? [10]I and my brothers and my men are also lending the people money and grain. But let the exacting of usury stop! [11]Give back to them immediately their fields, vineyards, olive groves and houses, and also the usury you are charging them—the hundredth part of the money, grain, new wine and oil."

[12]"We will give it back," they said. "And we will not demand anything more from them. We will do as you say."

Then I summoned the priests and made the nobles and officials take an oath to do what they had promised. [13]I also shook out the folds of my robe and said, "In this way may God shake out of his house and possessions every man who does not keep this promise. So may such a man be shaken out and emptied!"

At this the whole assembly said, "Amen," and praised the LORD. And the people did as they had promised.

[14]Moreover, from the twentieth year of King Artaxerxes, when I was appointed to be their governor in the land of Judah, until his thirty-second year—twelve years—neither I nor my brothers ate the food allotted to the governor. [15]But the earlier governors—those preceding me—placed a heavy burden on the people and took forty shekels*a* of silver from them in addition to food and wine. Their assistants also lorded it over the people. But out of reverence for God I did not act like that. [16]Instead, I devoted myself to the work on this wall. All my men were assembled there for the work; we*b* did not acquire any land.

[17]Furthermore, a hundred and fifty Jews and officials ate at my table, as well as those who came to us from the surrounding nations. [18]Each day one ox, six choice sheep and some poultry were prepared for me, and every ten days an abundant supply of wine of all kinds. In spite of all this, I never demanded the food allotted to the governor, because the demands were heavy on these people.

[19]Remember me with favour, O my God, for all I have done for these people.

Further Opposition to the Rebuilding

6 When word came to Sanballat, Tobiah, Geshem the Arab and the rest of our enemies that I had rebuilt the wall and not a gap was left in it—though up to that time I had not set the doors in

---

b23 The meaning of the Hebrew for this clause is uncertain.
a15 That is, about 1 pound (about 0.5 kilogram)
b16 Most Hebrew manuscripts; some Hebrew manuscripts, Septuagint, Vulgate and Syriac *I*

the gates—[2]Sanballat and Geshem sent me this message: "Come, let us meet together in one of the villages[a] on the plain of Ono."

But they were scheming to harm me; [3]so I sent messengers to them with this reply: "I am carrying on a great project and cannot go down. Why should the work stop while I leave it and go down to you?" [4]Four times they sent me the same message, and each time I gave them the same answer.

[5]Then, the fifth time, Sanballat sent his assistant to me with the same message, and in his hand was an unsealed letter [6]in which was written:

"It is reported among the nations—and Geshem[b] says it is true—that you and the Jews are plotting to revolt, and therefore you are building the wall. Moreover, according to these reports you are about to become their king [7]and have even appointed prophets to make this proclamation about you in Jerusalem: 'There is a king in Judah!' Now this report will get back to the king; so come, let us confer together."

[8]I sent him this reply: "Nothing like what you are saying is happening; you are just making it up out of your head."

[9]They were all trying to frighten us, thinking, "Their hands will get too weak for the work, and it will not be completed."

⌐But I prayed,⌐ "Now strengthen my hands."

[10]One day I went to the house of Shemaiah son of Delaiah, the son of Mehetabel, who was shut in at his home. He said, "Let us meet in the house of God, inside the temple, and let us close the temple doors, because men are coming to kill you—by night they are coming to kill you."

[11]But I said, "Should a man like me run away? Or should one like me go into the temple to save his life? I will not go!" [12]I realised that God had not sent him, but that he had prophesied against me because Tobiah and Sanballat had hired him. [13]He had been hired to intimidate me so that I would commit a sin by doing this, and then they would give me a bad name to discredit me.

[14]Remember Tobiah and Sanballat, O my God, because of what they have done; remember also the prophetess Noadiah and the rest of the prophets who have been trying to intimidate me.

The Completion of the Wall

[15]So the wall was completed on the twenty-fifth of Elul, in fifty-two days. [16]When all our enemies heard about this, all the surrounding nations were afraid and lost their self-confidence, because they realised that this work had been done with the help of our God.

[17]Also, in those days the nobles of Judah were sending many letters to Tobiah, and replies from Tobiah kept coming to them. [18]For many in Judah were under oath to him, since he was son-in-law to Shecaniah son of Arah, and his son Jehohanan had married the daughter of Meshullam son of Berekiah. [19]Moreover, they kept reporting to me his good deeds and then telling him what I said. And Tobiah sent letters to intimidate me.

7 After the wall had been rebuilt and I had set the doors in place, the gatekeepers and the singers and the Levites were appointed. [2]I put in charge of Jerusalem my brother Hanani, along with[a] Hananiah the commander of the citadel, because he was a man of integrity and feared God more than most men do. [3]I said to them, "The gates of Jerusalem are not to be opened until the sun is hot. While the gatekeepers are still on duty, make them shut the doors and bar them. Also appoint residents of Jerusalem as guards, some at their posts and some near their own houses."

---

[a]2 Or in Kephirim　　[b]6 Hebrew Gashmu, a variant of Geshem　　[a]2 Or Hanani, that is,

The List of the Exiles Who Returned

[4]Now the city was large and spacious, but there were few people in it, and the houses had not yet been rebuilt. [5]So my God put it into my heart to assemble the nobles, the officials and the common people for registration by families. I found the genealogical record of those who had been the first to return. This is what I found written there:

[6]These are the people of the province who came up from the captivity of the exiles whom Nebuchadnezzar king of Babylon had taken captive (they returned to Jerusalem and Judah, each to his own town, [7]in company with Zerubbabel, Jeshua, Nehemiah, Azariah, Raamiah, Nahamani, Mordecai, Bilshan, Mispereth, Bigvai, Nehum and Baanah):

The list of the men of Israel:

[8]the descendants of Parosh	2,172
[9]of Shephatiah	372
[10]of Arah	652
[11]of Pahath-Moab (through the line of Jeshua and Joab)	2,818
[12]of Elam	1,254
[13]of Zattu	845
[14]of Zaccai	760
[15]of Binnui	648
[16]of Bebai	628
[17]of Azgad	2,322
[18]of Adonikam	667
[19]of Bigvai	2,067
[20]of Adin	655
[21]of Ater (through Hezekiah)	98
[22]of Hashum	328
[23]of Bezai	324
[24]of Hariph	112
[25]of Gibeon	95
[26]the men of Bethlehem and Netophah	188
[27]of Anathoth	128
[28]of Beth Azmaveth	42
[29]of Kiriath Jearim, Kephirah and Beeroth	743
[30]of Ramah and Geba	621
[31]of Michmash	122
[32]of Bethel and Ai	123
[33]of the other Nebo	52
[34]of the other Elam	1,254
[35]of Harim	320
[36]of Jericho	345
[37]of Lod, Hadid and Ono	721
[38]of Senaah	3,930

[39]The priests:

the descendants of Jedaiah (through the family of Jeshua)	973
[40]of Immer	1,052
[41]of Pashhur	1,247
[42]of Harim	1,017

[43]The Levites:

the descendants of Jeshua (through Kadmiel through the line of Hodaviah)	74

[44]The singers:

the descendants of Asaph	148

[45]The gatekeepers:

the descendants of Shallum, Ater, Talmon, Akkub, Hatita and Shobai	138

[46]The temple servants:

the descendants of
Ziha, Hasupha, Tabbaoth,
[47]Keros, Sia, Padon,
[48]Lebana, Hagaba, Shalmai,
[49]Hanan, Giddel, Gahar,
[50]Reaiah, Rezin, Nekoda,
[51]Gazzam, Uzza, Paseah,
[52]Besai, Meunim, Nephussim,
[53]Bakbuk, Hakupha, Harhur,
[54]Bazluth, Mehida, Harsha,
[55]Barkos, Sisera, Temah,
[56]Neziah and Hatipha

[57]The descendants of the servants of Solomon:

the descendants of
Sotai, Sophereth, Perida,

⁵⁸Jaala, Darkon, Giddel,
⁵⁹Shephatiah, Hattil,
Pokereth-Hazzebaim and Amon

⁶⁰The temple servants and
the descendants of the
servants of Solomon   392

⁶¹The following came up from the
towns of Tel Melah, Tel Harsha,
Kerub, Addon and Immer, but they
could not show that their families
were descended from Israel:

⁶²the descendants of
Delaiah, Tobiah and Nekoda   642

⁶³And from among the priests:

the descendants of
Hobaiah, Hakkoz and Barzillai
(a man who had married a daughter
of Barzillai the Gileadite and
was called by that name).
⁶⁴These searched for their family
records, but they could not find them
and so were excluded from the priesthood as unclean. ⁶⁵The governor,
therefore, ordered them not to eat
any of the most sacred food until
there should be a priest ministering
with the Urim and Thummim.

⁶⁶The whole company numbered
42,360, ⁶⁷besides their 7,337 menservants and maidservants; and they also
had 245 men and women singers.
⁶⁸There were 736 horses, 245 mules,ᵇ
⁶⁹435 camels and 6,720 donkeys.

⁷⁰Some of the heads of the families
contributed to the work. The governor gave to the treasury 1,000
drachmasᶜ of gold, 50 bowls and 530
garments for priests. ⁷¹Some of the
heads of the families gave to the treasury for the work 20,000 drachmasᵈ of
gold and 2,200 minasᵉ of silver. ⁷²The
total given by the rest of the people
was 20,000 drachmas of gold, 2,000

minasᶠ of silver and 67 garments for
priests.
⁷³The priests, the Levites, the
gatekeepers, the singers and the temple servants, along with certain of the
people and the rest of the Israelites,
settled in their own towns.

Ezra Reads the Law

When the seventh month came and the
Israelites had settled in their towns,
8 ¹all the people assembled as one man
in the square before the Water Gate.
They told Ezra the scribe to bring out the
Book of the Law of Moses, which the
LORD had commanded for Israel.

²So on the first day of the seventh
month, Ezra the priest brought the Law
before the assembly, which was made up
of men and women and all who were able
to understand. ³He read it aloud from
daybreak till noon as he faced the square
before the Water Gate in the presence of
the men, women and others who could
understand. And all the people listened
attentively to the Book of the Law.

⁴Ezra the scribe stood on a high wooden
platform built for the occasion. Beside
him on his right stood Mattithiah, Shema,
Anaiah, Uriah, Hilkiah and Maaseiah;
and on his left were Pedaiah, Mishael,
Malkijah, Hashum, Hashbaddanah,
Zechariah and Meshullam.

⁵Ezra opened the book. All the people
could see him because he was standing
above them; and as he opened it, the
people all stood up. ⁶Ezra praised the
LORD, the great God; and all the people
lifted their hands and responded, "Amen!
Amen!" Then they bowed down and worshipped the LORD with their faces to the
ground.

⁷The Levites—Jeshua, Bani, Sherebiah, Jamin, Akkub, Shabbethai,
Hodiah, Maaseiah, Kelita, Azariah, Jozabad, Hanan and Pelaiah—instructed the
people in the Law while the people were
standing there. ⁸They read from the Book

ᵇ68 Some Hebrew manuscripts (see also Ezra 2:66); most Hebrew manuscripts do not have this verse.
ᶜ70 That is, about 19 pounds (about 8.5 kilograms)
ᵈ71 That is, about 375 pounds (about 170 kilograms); also in verse 72   ᵉ71 That is, about 1¼ tons (about 1.3 metric
tons)   ᶠ72 That is, about 1 ton (about 1.1 metric tons)

of the Law of God, making it clear[a] and giving the meaning so that the people could understand what was being read.

9Then Nehemiah the governor, Ezra the priest and scribe, and the Levites who were instructing the people said to them all, "This day is sacred to the LORD your God. Do not mourn or weep." For all the people had been weeping as they listened to the words of the Law.

10Nehemiah said, "Go and enjoy choice food and sweet drinks, and send some to those who have nothing prepared. This day is sacred to our Lord. Do not grieve, for the joy of the LORD is your strength."

11The Levites calmed all the people, saying, "Be still, for this is a sacred day. Do not grieve."

12Then all the people went away to eat and drink, to send portions of food and to celebrate with great joy, because they now understood the words that had been made known to them.

13On the second day of the month, the heads of all the families, along with the priests and the Levites, gathered round Ezra the scribe to give attention to the words of the Law. 14They found written in the Law, which the LORD had commanded through Moses, that the Israelites were to live in booths during the feast of the seventh month 15and that they should proclaim this word and spread it throughout their towns and in Jerusalem: "Go out into the hill country and bring back branches from olive and wild olive trees, and from myrtles, palms and shade trees, to make booths"—as it is written.[b]

16So the people went out and brought back branches and built themselves booths on their own roofs, in their courtyards, in the courts of the house of God and in the square by the Water Gate and the one by the Gate of Ephraim. 17The whole company that had returned from exile built booths and lived in them. From the days of Joshua son of Nun until that day, the Israelites had not celebrated it like this. And their joy was very great.

18Day after day, from the first day to the last, Ezra read from the Book of the Law

of God. They celebrated the feast for seven days, and on the eighth day, in accordance with the regulation, there was an assembly.

The Israelites Confess Their Sins

9 On the twenty-fourth day of the same month, the Israelites gathered together, fasting and wearing sackcloth and having dust on their heads. 2Those of Israelite descent had separated themselves from all foreigners. They stood in their places and confessed their sins and the wickedness of their fathers. 3They stood where they were and read from the Book of the Law of the LORD their God for a quarter of the day, and spent another quarter in confession and in worshipping the LORD their God. 4Standing on the stairs were the Levites—Jeshua, Bani, Kadmiel, Shebaniah, Bunni, Sherebiah, Bani and Kenani—who called with loud voices to the LORD their God. 5And the Levites—Jeshua, Kadmiel, Bani, Hashabneiah, Sherebiah, Hodiah, Shebaniah and Pethahiah—said: "Stand up and praise the LORD your God, who is from everlasting to everlasting."[a]

"Blessed be your glorious name, and may it be exalted above all blessing and praise. 6You alone are the LORD. You made the heavens, even the highest heavens, and all their starry host, the earth and all that is on it, the seas and all that is in them. You give life to everything, and the multitudes of heaven worship you.

7"You are the LORD God, who chose Abram and brought him out of Ur of the Chaldeans and named him Abraham. 8You found his heart faithful to you, and you made a covenant with him to give to his descendants the land of the Canaanites, Hittites, Amorites, Perizzites, Jebusites and Girgashites. You have kept your promise because you are righteous.

9"You saw the suffering of our forefathers in Egypt; you heard their cry at the Red Sea.*b* [10]You sent miraculous signs and wonders against Pharaoh, against all his officials and all the people of his land, for you knew how arrogantly the Egyptians treated them. You made a name for yourself, which remains to this day. [11]You divided the sea before them, so that they passed through it on dry ground, but you hurled their pursuers into the depths, like a stone into mighty waters. [12]By day you led them with a pillar of cloud, and by night with a pillar of fire to give them light on the way they were to take.

[13]"You came down on Mount Sinai; you spoke to them from heaven. You gave them regulations and laws that are just and right, and decrees and commands that are good. [14]You made known to them your holy Sabbath and gave them commands, decrees and laws through your servant Moses. [15]In their hunger you gave them bread from heaven and in their thirst you brought them water from the rock; you told them to go in and take possession of the land you had sworn with uplifted hand to give them.

[16]"But they, our forefathers, became arrogant and stiff-necked, and did not obey your commands. [17]They refused to listen and failed to remember the miracles you performed among them. They became stiff-necked and in their rebellion appointed a leader in order to return to their slavery. But you are a forgiving God, gracious and compassionate, slow to anger and abounding in love. Therefore you did not desert them, [18]even when they cast for themselves an image of a calf and said, 'This is your god, who brought you up out of Egypt,' or when they committed awful blasphemies.

[19]"Because of your great compassion you did not abandon them in the desert. By day the pillar of cloud did not cease to guide them on their path, nor the pillar of fire by night to shine on the way they were to take. [20]You gave your good Spirit to instruct them. You did not withhold your manna from their mouths, and you gave them water for their thirst. [21]For forty years you sustained them in the desert; they lacked nothing, their clothes did not wear out nor did their feet become swollen.

[22]"You gave them kingdoms and nations, allotting to them even the remotest frontiers. They took over the country of Sihon*c* king of Heshbon and the country of Og king of Bashan. [23]You made their sons as numerous as the stars in the sky, and you brought them into the land that you told their fathers to enter and possess. [24]Their sons went in and took possession of the land. You subdued before them the Canaanites, who lived in the land; you handed the Canaanites over to them, along with their kings and the peoples of the land, to deal with them as they pleased. [25]They captured fortified cities and fertile land; they took possession of houses filled with all kinds of good things, wells already dug, vineyards, olive groves and fruit trees in abundance. They ate to the full and were well-nourished; they revelled in your great goodness.

[26]"But they were disobedient and rebelled against you; they put your law behind their backs. They killed your prophets, who had admonished them in order to turn them back to you; they committed awful blasphemies. [27]So you handed them over to their enemies, who oppressed them. But when they were oppressed they cried out to you. From heaven you heard them, and in your great compassion you gave them deliverers, who rescued them from the hand of their enemies.

[28]"But as soon as they were at rest,

---

b9 Hebrew *Yam Suph;* that is, Sea of Reeds
c22 One Hebrew manuscript and Septuagint; most Hebrew manuscripts *Sihon, that is, the country of the*

they again did what was evil in your sight. Then you abandoned them to the hand of their enemies so that they ruled over them. And when they cried out to you again, you heard from heaven, and in your compassion you delivered them time after time.

29"You warned them to return to your law, but they became arrogant and disobeyed your commands. They sinned against your ordinances, by which a man will live if he obeys them. Stubbornly they turned their backs on you, became stiff-necked and refused to listen. 30For many years you were patient with them. By your Spirit you admonished them through your prophets. Yet they paid no attention, so you handed them over to the neighbouring peoples. 31But in your great mercy you did not put an end to them or abandon them, for you are a gracious and merciful God.

32"Now therefore, O our God, the great, mighty and awesome God, who keeps his covenant of love, do not let all this hardship seem trifling in your eyes—the hardship that has come upon us, upon our kings and leaders, upon our priests and prophets, upon our fathers and all your people, from the days of the kings of Assyria until today. 33In all that has happened to us, you have been just; you have acted faithfully, while we did wrong. 34Our kings, our leaders, our priests and our fathers did not follow your law; they did not pay attention to your commands or the warnings you gave them. 35Even while they were in their kingdom, enjoying your great goodness to them in the spacious and fertile land you gave them, they did not serve you or turn from their evil ways.

36"But see, we are slaves today, slaves in the land you gave our forefathers so that they could eat its fruit and the other good things it produces. 37Because of our sins, its abundant harvest goes to the kings you have placed over us. They rule over our bodies and our cattle as they please. We are in great distress.

The Agreement of the People

38"In view of all this, we are making a binding agreement, putting it in writing, and our leaders, our Levites and our priests are affixing their seals to it."

10 Those who sealed it were:

Nehemiah the governor, the son of Hacaliah.

Zedekiah, 2Seraiah, Azariah, Jeremiah,
3Pashhur, Amariah, Malkijah,
4Hattush, Shebaniah, Malluch,
5Harim, Meremoth, Obadiah,
6Daniel, Ginnethon, Baruch,
7Meshullam, Abijah, Mijamin,
8Maaziah, Bilgai and Shemaiah.
These were the priests.

9The Levites:

Jeshua son of Azaniah,
Binnui of the sons of Henadad,
Kadmiel,
10and their associates:
Shebaniah, Hodiah, Kelita,
Pelaiah, Hanan,
11Mica, Rehob, Hashabiah,
12Zaccur, Sherebiah, Shebaniah,
13Hodiah, Bani and Beninu.

14The leaders of the people:

Parosh, Pahath-Moab, Elam,
Zattu, Bani,
15Bunni, Azgad, Bebai,
16Adonijah, Bigvai, Adin,
17Ater, Hezekiah, Azzur,
18Hodiah, Hashum, Bezai,
19Hariph, Anathoth, Nebai,
20Magpiash, Meshullam, Hezir,
21Meshezabel, Zadok, Jaddua,
22Pelatiah, Hanan, Anaiah,
23Hoshea, Hananiah, Hasshub,
24Hallohesh, Pilha, Shobek,
25Rehum, Hashabnah, Maaseiah,
26Ahiah, Hanan, Anan,
27Malluch, Harim and Baanah.

28"The rest of the people—priests, Levites, gatekeepers, singers, temple servants and all who separated themselves from the neighbouring peoples for the sake of the Law of God, together with their wives and all their sons and daughters who are able to understand—[29]all these now join their brothers the nobles, and bind themselves with a curse and an oath to follow the Law of God given through Moses the servant of God and to obey carefully all the commands, regulations and decrees of the LORD our Lord.

[30]"We promise not to give our daughters in marriage to the peoples around us or take their daughters for our sons.

[31]"When the neighbouring peoples bring merchandise or grain to sell on the Sabbath, we will not buy from them on the Sabbath or on any holy day. Every seventh year we will forgo working the land and will cancel all debts.

[32]"We assume the responsibility for carrying out the commands to give a third of a shekel[a] each year for the service of the house of our God: [33]for the bread set out on the table; for the regular grain offerings and burnt offerings; for the offerings on the Sabbaths, New Moon festivals and appointed feasts; for the holy offerings; for sin offerings to make atonement for Israel; and for all the duties of the house of our God.

[34]"We—the priests, the Levites and the people—have cast lots to determine when each of our families is to bring to the house of our God at set times each year a contribution of wood to burn on the altar of the LORD our God, as it is written in the Law.

[35]"We also assume responsibility for bringing to the house of the LORD each year the firstfruits of our crops and of every fruit tree.

[36]"As it is also written in the Law, we will bring the firstborn of our sons and of our cattle, of our herds and of our flocks to the house of our

God, to the priests ministering there.

[37]"Moreover, we will bring to the storerooms of the house of our God, to the priests, the first of our ground meal, of our ˌgrainˌ offerings, of the fruit of all our trees and of our new wine and oil. And we will bring a tithe of our crops to the Levites, for it is the Levites who collect the tithes in all the towns where we work. [38]A priest descended from Aaron is to accompany the Levites when they receive the tithes, and the Levites are to bring a tenth of the tithes up to the house of our God, to the storerooms of the treasury. [39]The people of Israel, including the Levites, are to bring their contributions of grain, new wine and oil to the storerooms where the articles for the sanctuary are kept and where the ministering priests, the gatekeepers and the singers stay.

"We will not neglect the house of our God."

The New Residents of Jerusalem

11 Now the leaders of the people settled in Jerusalem, and the rest of the people cast lots to bring one out of every ten to live in Jerusalem, the holy city, while the remaining nine were to stay in their own towns. [2]The people commended all the men who volunteered to live in Jerusalem.

[3]These are the provincial leaders who settled in Jerusalem (now some Israelites, priests, Levites, temple servants and descendants of Solomon's servants lived in the towns of Judah, each on his own property in the various towns, [4]while other people from both Judah and Benjamin lived in Jerusalem):

From the descendants of Judah:

Athaiah son of Uzziah, the son of Zechariah, the son of Amariah, the son of Shephatiah, the son of Mahalalel, a descendant of Perez; [5]and Maaseiah son of Baruch, the son of

---

[a]32 That is, about ⅛ ounce (about 4 grams)

Col-Hozeh, the son of Hazaiah, the son of Adaiah, the son of Joiarib, the son of Zechariah, a descendant of Shelah. [6]The descendants of Perez who lived in Jerusalem totalled 468 able men.

[7]From the descendants of Benjamin:

Sallu son of Meshullam, the son of Joed, the son of Pedaiah, the son of Kolaiah, the son of Maaseiah, the son of Ithiel, the son of Jeshaiah, [8]and his followers, Gabbai and Sallai—928 men. [9]Joel son of Zicri was their chief officer, and Judah son of Hassenuah was over the Second District of the city.

[10]From the priests:

Jedaiah; the son of Joiarib; Jakin; [11]Seraiah son of Hilkiah, the son of Meshullam, the son of Zadok, the son of Meraioth, the son of Ahitub, supervisor in the house of God, [12]and their associates, who carried on work for the temple—822 men; Adaiah son of Jeroham, the son of Pelaliah, the son of Amzi, the son of Zechariah, the son of Pashhur, the son of Malkijah, [13]and his associates, who were heads of families—242 men; Amashsai son of Azarel, the son of Ahzai, the son of Meshillemoth, the son of Immer, [14]and his[a] associates, who were able men—128 men. Their chief officer was Zabdiel son of Haggedolim.

[15]From the Levites:

Shemaiah son of Hasshub, the son of Azrikam, the son of Hashabiah, the son of Bunni; [16]Shabbethai and Jozabad, two of the heads of the Levites, who had charge of the outside work of the house of God; [17]Mattaniah son of Mica, the son of Zabdi, the son of Asaph, the director who led in thanksgiving and prayer; Bakbukiah,

second among his associates; and Abda son of Shammua, the son of Galal, the son of Jeduthun. [18]The Levites in the holy city totalled 284.

[19]The gatekeepers:

Akkub, Talmon and their associates, who kept watch at the gates—172 men.

[20]The rest of the Israelites, with the priests and Levites, were in all the towns of Judah, each on his ancestral property.

[21]The temple servants lived on the hill of Ophel, and Ziha and Gishpa were in charge of them.

[22]The chief officer of the Levites in Jerusalem was Uzzi son of Bani, the son of Hashabiah, the son of Mattaniah, the son of Mica. Uzzi was one of Asaph's descendants, who were the singers responsible for the service of the house of God. [23]The singers were under the king's orders, which regulated their daily activity.

[24]Pethahiah son of Meshezabel, one of the descendants of Zerah son of Judah, was the king's agent in all affairs relating to the people.

[25]As for the villages with their fields, some of the people of Judah lived in Kiriath Arba and its surrounding settlements, in Dibon and its settlements, in Jekabzeel and its villages, [26]in Jeshua, in Moladah, in Beth Pelet, [27]in Hazar Shual, in Beersheba and its settlements, [28]in Ziklag, in Meconah and its settlements, [29]in En Rimmon, in Zorah, in Jarmuth, [30]Zanoah, Adullam and their villages, in Lachish and its fields, and in Azekah and its settlements. So they were living all the way from Beersheba to the Valley of Hinnom.

[31]The descendants of the Benjamites from Geba lived in Michmash, Aija, Bethel and its settlements, [32]in Anathoth, Nob and Ananiah, [33]in Hazor, Ramah and Gittaim, [34]in Hadid, Zeboim and Neballat, [35]in Lod and Ono, and in the Valley of the Craftsmen.

[a]14 Most Septuagint manuscripts; Hebrew *their*

36Some of the divisions of the Levites of Judah settled in Benjamin.

Priests and Levites

12 These were the priests and Levites who returned with Zerubbabel son of Shealtiel and with Jeshua:
Seraiah, Jeremiah, Ezra,
2Amariah, Malluch, Hattush,
3Shecaniah, Rehum, Meremoth,
4Iddo, Ginnethon,a Abijah,
5Mijamin,b Moadiah, Bilgah,
6Shemaiah, Joiarib, Jedaiah,
7Sallu, Amok, Hilkiah and Jedaiah.
These were the leaders of the priests and their associates in the days of Jeshua.

8The Levites were Jeshua, Binnui, Kadmiel, Sherebiah, Judah, and also Mattaniah, who, together with his associates, was in charge of the songs of thanksgiving. 9Bakbukiah and Unni, their associates, stood opposite them in the services.

10Jeshua was the father of Joiakim, Joiakim the father of Eliashib, Eliashib the father of Joiada, 11Joiada the father of Jonathan, and Jonathan the father of Jaddua.

12In the days of Joiakim, these were the heads of the priestly families:
of Seraiah's family, Meraiah;
of Jeremiah's, Hananiah;
13of Ezra's, Meshullam;
of Amariah's, Jehohanan;
14of Malluch's, Jonathan;
of Shecaniah's,c Joseph;
15of Harim's, Adna;
of Meremoth's,d Helkai;
16of Iddo's, Zechariah;
of Ginnethon's, Meshullam;
17of Abijah's, Zicri;
of Miniamin's and of Moadiah's, Piltai;
18of Bilgah's, Shammua;
of Shemaiah's, Jehonathan;
19of Joiarib's, Mattenai;
of Jedaiah's, Uzzi;
20of Sallu's, Kallai;
of Amok's, Eber;
21of Hilkiah's, Hashabiah;
of Jedaiah's, Nethanel.

22The family heads of the Levites in the days of Eliashib, Joiada, Johanan and Jaddua, as well as those of the priests, were recorded in the reign of Darius the Persian. 23The family heads among the descendants of Levi up to the time of Johanan son of Eliashib were recorded in the book of the annals. 24And the leaders of the Levites were Hashabiah, Sherebiah, Jeshua son of Kadmiel, and their associates, who stood opposite them to give praise and thanksgiving, one section responding to the other, as prescribed by David the man of God.

25Mattaniah, Bakbukiah, Obadiah, Meshullam, Talmon and Akkub were gatekeepers who guarded the storerooms at the gates. 26They served in the days of Joiakim son of Jeshua, the son of Jozadak, and in the days of Nehemiah the governor and of Ezra the priest and scribe.

Dedication of the Wall of Jerusalem

27At the dedication of the wall of Jerusalem, the Levites were sought out from where they lived and were brought to Jerusalem to celebrate joyfully the dedication with songs of thanksgiving and with the music of cymbals, harps and lyres. 28The singers also were brought together from the region around Jerusalem—from the villages of the Netophathites, 29from Beth Gilgal, and from the area of Geba and Azmaveth, for the singers had built villages for themselves around Jerusalem. 30When the priests and Levites had purified themselves ceremonially, they purified the people, the gates and the wall.

31I had the leaders of Judah go up on tope of the wall. I also assigned two large choirs to give thanks. One was to proceed on topf of the wall to the right, towards the Dung Gate. 32Hoshaiah and half the leaders of Judah followed them, 33along with Azariah, Ezra, Meshullam, 34Judah,

a4 Many Hebrew manuscripts and Vulgate (see also Neh. 12:16); most Hebrew manuscripts *Ginnethoi*
b5 A variant of *Miniamin*
c14 Very many Hebrew manuscripts, some Septuagint manuscripts and Syriac (see also Neh. 12:3); most Hebrew manuscripts *Shebaniah's*   d15 Some Septuagint manuscripts (see also Neh. 12:3); Hebrew *Meraioth's*
e31 Or *go alongside*   f31 Or *proceed alongside*

Benjamin, Shemaiah, Jeremiah, [35]as well as some priests with trumpets, and also Zechariah son of Jonathan, the son of Shemaiah, the son of Mattaniah, the son of Micaiah, the son of Zaccur, the son of Asaph, [36]and his associates—Shemaiah, Azarel, Milalai, Gilalai, Maai, Nethanel, Judah and Hanani—with musical instruments ⌐prescribed by⌐ David the man of God. Ezra the scribe led the procession. [37]At the Fountain Gate they continued directly up the steps of the City of David on the ascent to the wall and passed above the house of David to the Water Gate on the east.

[38]The second choir proceeded in the opposite direction. I followed them on top[g] of the wall, together with half the people—past the Tower of the Ovens to the Broad Wall, [39]over the Gate of Ephraim, the Jeshanah[h] Gate, the Fish Gate, the Tower of Hananel and the Tower of the Hundred, as far as the Sheep Gate. At the Gate of the Guard they stopped.

[40]The two choirs that gave thanks then took their places in the house of God; so did I, together with half the officials, [41]as well as the priests—Eliakim, Maaseiah, Miniamin, Micaiah, Elioenai, Zechariah and Hananiah with their trumpets—[42]and also Maaseiah, Shemaiah, Eleazar, Uzzi, Jehohanan, Malkijah, Elam and Ezer. The choirs sang under the direction of Jezrahiah. [43]And on that day they offered great sacrifices, rejoicing because God had given them great joy. The women and children also rejoiced. The sound of rejoicing in Jerusalem could be heard far away.

[44]At that time men were appointed to be in charge of the storerooms for the contributions, firstfruits and tithes. From the fields around the towns they were to bring into the storerooms the portions required by the Law for the priests and the Levites, for Judah was pleased with the ministering priests and Levites. [45]They performed the service of their God and the service of purification, as did also the singers and gatekeepers, according to the commands of David and his son Solomon. [46]For long ago, in the days of David and Asaph, there had been directors for the singers and for the songs of praise and thanksgiving to God. [47]So in the days of Zerubbabel and of Nehemiah, all Israel contributed the daily portions for the singers and gatekeepers. They also set aside the portion for the other Levites, and the Levites set aside the portion for the descendants of Aaron.

Nehemiah's Final Reforms

13 On that day the Book of Moses was read aloud in the hearing of the people and there it was found written that no Ammonite or Moabite should ever be admitted into the assembly of God, [2]because they had not met the Israelites with food and water but had hired Balaam to call a curse down on them. (Our God, however, turned the curse into a blessing.) [3]When the people heard this law, they excluded from Israel all who were of foreign descent.

[4]Before this, Eliashib the priest had been put in charge of the storerooms of the house of our God. He was closely associated with Tobiah, [5]and he had provided him with a large room formerly used to store the grain offerings and incense and temple articles, and also the tithes of grain, new wine and oil prescribed for the Levites, singers and gatekeepers, as well as the contributions for the priests.

[6]But while all this was going on, I was not in Jerusalem, for in the thirty-second year of Artaxerxes king of Babylon I had returned to the king. Some time later I asked his permission [7]and came back to Jerusalem. Here I learned about the evil thing Eliashib had done in providing Tobiah a room in the courts of the house of God. [8]I was greatly displeased and threw all Tobiah's household goods out of the room. [9]I gave orders to purify the rooms, and then I put back into them the equipment of the house of God, with the grain offerings and the incense.

[10]I also learned that the portions

assigned to the Levites had not been given to them, and that all the Levites and singers responsible for the service had gone back to their own fields. [11]So I rebuked the officials and asked them, "Why is the house of God neglected?" Then I called them together and stationed them at their posts.

[12]All Judah brought the tithes of grain, new wine and oil into the storerooms. [13]I put Shelemiah the priest, Zadok the scribe, and a Levite named Pedaiah in charge of the storerooms and made Hanan son of Zaccur, the son of Mattaniah, their assistant, because these men were considered trustworthy. They were made responsible for distributing the supplies to their brothers.

[14]Remember me for this, O my God, and do not blot out what I have so faithfully done for the house of my God and its services.

[15]In those days I saw men in Judah treading winepresses on the Sabbath and bringing in grain and loading it on donkeys, together with wine, grapes, figs and all other kinds of loads. And they were bringing all this into Jerusalem on the Sabbath. Therefore I warned them against selling food on that day. [16]Men from Tyre who lived in Jerusalem were bringing in fish and all kinds of merchandise and selling them in Jerusalem on the Sabbath to the people of Judah. [17]I rebuked the nobles of Judah and said to them, "What is this wicked thing you are doing—desecrating the Sabbath day? [18]Didn't your forefathers do the same things, so that our God brought all this calamity upon us and upon this city? Now you are stirring up more wrath against Israel by desecrating the Sabbath."

[19]When evening shadows fell on the gates of Jerusalem before the Sabbath, I ordered the doors to be shut and not opened until the Sabbath was over. I stationed some of my own men at the gates so that no load could be brought in on the Sabbath day. [20]Once or twice the merchants and sellers of all kinds of goods spent the night outside Jerusalem. [21]But I warned them and said, "Why do you spend the night by the wall? If you do this again, I will lay hands on you." From that time on they no longer came on the Sabbath. [22]Then I commanded the Levites to purify themselves and go and guard the gates in order to keep the Sabbath day holy.

Remember me for this also, O my God, and show mercy to me according to your great love.

[23]Moreover, in those days I saw men of Judah who had married women from Ashdod, Ammon and Moab. [24]Half of their children spoke the language of Ashdod or the language of one of the other peoples, and did not know how to speak the language of Judah. [25]I rebuked them and called curses down on them. I beat some of the men and pulled out their hair. I made them take an oath in God's name and said: "You are not to give your daughters in marriage to their sons, nor are you to take their daughters in marriage for your sons or for yourselves. [26]Was it not because of marriages like these that Solomon king of Israel sinned? Among the many nations there was no king like him. He was loved by his God, and God made him king over all Israel, but even he was led into sin by foreign women. [27]Must we hear now that you too are doing all this terrible wickedness and are being unfaithful to our God by marrying foreign women?"

[28]One of the sons of Joiada son of Eliashib the high priest was son-in-law to Sanballat the Horonite. And I drove him away from me.

[29]Remember them, O my God, because they defiled the priestly office and the covenant of the priesthood and of the Levites.

[30]So I purified the priests and the Levites of everything foreign, and assigned them duties, each to his own task. [31]I also made provision for contributions of wood at designated times, and for the firstfruits.

Remember me with favour, O my God.

Esther

Queen Vashti Deposed

1 This is what happened during the time of Xerxes,[a] the Xerxes who ruled over 127 provinces stretching from India to Cush:[b] ²At that time King Xerxes reigned from his royal throne in the citadel of Susa, ³and in the third year of his reign he gave a banquet for all his nobles and officials. The military leaders of Persia and Media, the princes, and the nobles of the provinces were present.

⁴For a full 180 days he displayed the vast wealth of his kingdom and the splendour and glory of his majesty. ⁵When these days were over, the king gave a banquet, lasting seven days, in the enclosed garden of the king's palace, for all the people from the least to the greatest, who were in the citadel of Susa. ⁶The garden had hangings of white and blue linen, fastened with cords of white linen and purple material to silver rings on marble pillars. There were couches of gold and silver on a mosaic pavement of porphyry, marble, mother-of-pearl and other costly stones. ⁷Wine was served in goblets of gold, each one different from the other, and the royal wine was abundant, in keeping with the king's liberality. ⁸By the king's command each guest was allowed to drink in his own way, for the king instructed all the wine stewards to serve each man what he wished.

⁹Queen Vashti also gave a banquet for the women in the royal palace of King Xerxes.

¹⁰On the seventh day, when King Xerxes was in high spirits from wine, he commanded the seven eunuchs who served him—Mehuman, Biztha, Harbona, Bigtha, Abagtha, Zethar and Carcas— ¹¹to bring before him Queen Vashti, wearing her royal crown, in order to display her beauty to the people and nobles, for she was lovely to look at. ¹²But when the attendants delivered the king's command, Queen Vashti refused to come. Then the king became furious and burned with anger.

¹³Since it was customary for the king to consult experts in matters of law and justice, he spoke with the wise men who understood the times ¹⁴and were closest to the king—Carshena, Shethar, Admatha, Tarshish, Meres, Marsena and Memucan, the seven nobles of Persia and Media who had special access to the king and were highest in the kingdom.

¹⁵"According to law, what must be done to Queen Vashti?" he asked. "She has not obeyed the command of King Xerxes that the eunuchs have taken to her."

¹⁶Then Memucan replied in the presence of the king and the nobles, "Queen Vashti has done wrong, not only against the king but also against all the nobles and the peoples of all the provinces of King Xerxes. ¹⁷For the queen's conduct will become known to all the women, and so they will despise their husbands and say, 'King Xerxes commanded Queen Vashti to be brought before him, but she would not come.' ¹⁸This very day the Persian and

---

*a*1 Hebrew *Ahasuerus*, a variant of Xerxes' Persian name; here and throughout Esther
*b*1 That is, the upper Nile region

Median women of the nobility who have heard about the queen's conduct will respond to all the king's nobles in the same way. There will be no end of disrespect and discord.

19"Therefore, if it pleases the king, let him issue a royal decree and let it be written in the laws of Persia and Media, which cannot be repealed, that Vashti is never again to enter the presence of King Xerxes. Also let the king give her royal position to someone else who is better than she. 20Then when the king's edict is proclaimed throughout all his vast realm, all the women will respect their husbands, from the least to the greatest."

21The king and his nobles were pleased with this advice, so the king did as Memucan proposed. 22He sent dispatches to all parts of the kingdom, to each province in its own script and to each people in its own language, proclaiming in each people's tongue that every man should be ruler over his own household.

Esther Made Queen

2 Later when the anger of King Xerxes had subsided, he remembered Vashti and what she had done and what he had decreed about her. 2Then the king's personal attendants proposed, "Let a search be made for beautiful young virgins for the king. 3Let the king appoint commissioners in every province of his realm to bring all these beautiful girls into the harem at the citadel of Susa. Let them be placed under the care of Hegai, the king's eunuch, who is in charge of the women; and let beauty treatments be given to them. 4Then let the girl who pleases the king be queen instead of Vashti." This advice appealed to the king, and he followed it.

5Now there was in the citadel of Susa a Jew of the tribe of Benjamin, named Mordecai son of Jair, the son of Shimei, the son of Kish, 6who had been carried into exile from Jerusalem by Nebuchadnezzar king of Babylon, among those taken captive with Jehoiachin[a] king of Judah. 7Mordecai had a cousin named Hadassah,

whom he had brought up because she had neither father nor mother. This girl, who was also known as Esther, was lovely in form and features, and Mordecai had taken her as his own daughter when her father and mother died.

8When the king's order and edict had been proclaimed, many girls were brought to the citadel of Susa and put under the care of Hegai. Esther also was taken to the king's palace and entrusted to Hegai, who had charge of the harem. 9The girl pleased him and won his favour. Immediately he provided her with her beauty treatments and special food. He assigned to her seven maids selected from the king's palace and moved her and her maids into the best place in the harem.

10Esther had not revealed her nationality and family background, because Mordecai had forbidden her to do so. 11Every day he walked to and fro near the courtyard of the harem to find out how Esther was and what was happening to her.

12Before a girl's turn came to go in to King Xerxes, she had to complete twelve months of beauty treatments prescribed for the women, six months with oil of myrrh and six with perfumes and cosmetics. 13And this is how she would go to the king: Anything she wanted was given to her to take with her from the harem to the king's palace. 14In the evening she would go there and in the morning return to another part of the harem to the care of Shaashgaz, the king's eunuch who was in charge of the concubines. She would not return to the king unless he was pleased with her and summoned her by name.

15When the turn came for Esther (the girl Mordecai had adopted, the daughter of his uncle Abihail) to go to the king, she asked for nothing other than what Hegai, the king's eunuch who was in charge of the harem, suggested. And Esther won the favour of everyone who saw her. 16She was taken to King Xerxes in the royal residence in the tenth month, the month of Tebeth, in the seventh year of his reign.

17Now the king was attracted to Esther more than to any of the other women, and

a6 Hebrew Jeconiah, a variant of Jehoiachin

she won his favour and approval more than any of the other virgins. So he set a royal crown on her head and made her queen instead of Vashti. ¹⁸And the king gave a great banquet, Esther's banquet, for all his nobles and officials. He proclaimed a holiday throughout the provinces and distributed gifts with royal liberality.

Mordecai Uncovers a Conspiracy

¹⁹When the virgins were assembled a second time, Mordecai was sitting at the king's gate. ²⁰But Esther had kept secret her family background and nationality just as Mordecai had told her to do, for she continued to follow Mordecai's instructions as she had done when he was bringing her up. ²¹During the time Mordecai was sitting at the king's gate, Bigthana[b] and Teresh, two of the king's officers who guarded the doorway, became angry and conspired to assassinate King Xerxes. ²²But Mordecai found out about the plot and told Queen Esther, who in turn reported it to the king, giving credit to Mordecai. ²³And when the report was investigated and found to be true, the two officials were hanged on a gallows.[c] All this was recorded in the book of the annals in the presence of the king.

Haman's Plot to Destroy the Jews

3 After these events, King Xerxes honoured Haman son of Hammedatha, the Agagite, elevating him and giving him a seat of honour higher than that of all the other nobles. ²All the royal officials at the king's gate knelt down and paid honour to Haman, for the king had commanded this concerning him. But Mordecai would not kneel down or pay him honour.

³Then the royal officials at the king's gate asked Mordecai, "Why do you disobey the king's command?" ⁴Day after day they spoke to him but he refused to comply. Therefore they told Haman about it to see whether Mordecai's behaviour would be tolerated, for he had told them he was a Jew.

⁵When Haman saw that Mordecai would not kneel down or pay him honour, he was enraged. ⁶Yet having learned who Mordecai's people were, he scorned the idea of killing only Mordecai. Instead Haman looked for a way to destroy all Mordecai's people, the Jews, throughout the whole kingdom of Xerxes.

⁷In the twelfth year of King Xerxes, in the first month, the month of Nisan, they cast the *pur* (that is, the lot) in the presence of Haman to select a day and month. And the lot fell on [a] the twelfth month, the month of Adar.

⁸Then Haman said to King Xerxes, "There is a certain people dispersed and scattered among the peoples in all the provinces of your kingdom whose customs are different from those of all other people and who do not obey the king's laws; it is not in the king's best interest to tolerate them. ⁹If it pleases the king, let a decree be issued to destroy them, and I will put ten thousand talents[b] of silver into the royal treasury for the men who carry out this business."

¹⁰So the king took his signet ring from his finger and gave it to Haman son of Hammedatha, the Agagite, the enemy of the Jews. ¹¹"Keep the money," the king said to Haman, "and do with the people as you please."

¹²Then on the thirteenth day of the first month the royal secretaries were summoned. They wrote out in the script of each province and in the language of each people all Haman's orders to the king's satraps, the governors of the various provinces and the nobles of the various peoples. These were written in the name of King Xerxes himself and sealed with his own ring. ¹³Dispatches were sent by couriers to all the king's provinces with the order to destroy, kill and annihilate all the Jews—young and old, women and little children—on a single day, the thirteenth day of the twelfth month, the month of Adar, and to plunder their goods. ¹⁴A

---

b21 Hebrew *Bigthan*, a variant of *Bigthana*   *c23* Or *were hung* (or *impaled*) *on poles*; similarly elsewhere in Esther
a7 Septuagint; Hebrew does not have *And the lot fell on*.   *b9* That is, about 340 tons (about 345 metric tons)

copy of the text of the edict was to be issued as law in every province and made known to the people of every nationality so that they would be ready for that day.

[15]Spurred on by the king's command, the couriers went out, and the edict was issued in the citadel of Susa. The king and Haman sat down to drink, but the city of Susa was bewildered.

Mordecai Persuades Esther to Help

4 When Mordecai learned of all that had been done, he tore his clothes, put on sackcloth and ashes, and went out into the city, wailing loudly and bitterly. [2]But he went only as far as the king's gate, because no-one clothed in sackcloth was allowed to enter it. [3]In every province to which the edict and order of the king came, there was great mourning among the Jews, with fasting, weeping and wailing. Many lay in sackcloth and ashes.

[4]When Esther's maids and eunuchs came and told her about Mordecai, she was in great distress. She sent clothes for him to put on instead of his sackcloth, but he would not accept them. [5]Then Esther summoned Hathach, one of the king's eunuchs assigned to attend her, and ordered him to find out what was troubling Mordecai and why.

[6]So Hathach went out to Mordecai in the open square of the city in front of the king's gate. [7]Mordecai told him everything that had happened to him, including the exact amount of money Haman had promised to pay into the royal treasury for the destruction of the Jews. [8]He also gave him a copy of the text of the edict for their annihilation, which had been published in Susa, to show to Esther and explain it to her, and he told him to urge her to go into the king's presence to beg for mercy and plead with him for her people.

[9]Hathach went back and reported to Esther what Mordecai had said. [10]Then she instructed him to say to Mordecai, [11]"All the king's officials and the people of the royal provinces know that for any man or woman who approaches the king in the inner court without being summoned the

king has but one law: that he be put to death. The only exception to this is for the king to extend the gold sceptre to him and spare his life. But thirty days have passed since I was called to go to the king."

[12]When Esther's words were reported to Mordecai, [13]he sent back this answer: "Do not think that because you are in the king's house you alone of all the Jews will escape. [14]For if you remain silent at this time, relief and deliverance for the Jews will arise from another place, but you and your father's family will perish. And who knows but that you have come to royal position for such a time as this?"

[15]Then Esther sent this reply to Mordecai: [16]"Go, gather together all the Jews who are in Susa, and fast for me. Do not eat or drink for three days, night or day. I and my maids will fast as you do. When this is done, I will go to the king, even though it is against the law. And if I perish, I perish."

[17]So Mordecai went away and carried out all of Esther's instructions.

Esther's Request to the King

5 On the third day Esther put on her royal robes and stood in the inner court of the palace, in front of the king's hall. The king was sitting on his royal throne in the hall, facing the entrance. [2]When he saw Queen Esther standing in the court, he was pleased with her and held out to her the gold sceptre that was in his hand. So Esther approached and touched the tip of the sceptre.

[3]Then the king asked, "What is it, Queen Esther? What is your request? Even up to half the kingdom, it will be given you."

[4]"If it pleases the king," replied Esther, "let the king, together with Haman, come today to a banquet I have prepared for him."

[5]"Bring Haman at once," the king said, "so that we may do what Esther asks."

So the king and Haman went to the banquet Esther had prepared. [6]As they were drinking wine, the king again asked Esther, "Now what is your petition? It will be given you. And what is your request?

Even up to half the kingdom, it will be granted."

[7]Esther replied, "My petition and my request is this: [8]If the king regards me with favour and if it pleases the king to grant my petition and fulfil my request, let the king and Haman come tomorrow to the banquet I will prepare for them. Then I will answer the king's question."

Haman's Rage Against Mordecai

[9]Haman went out that day happy and in high spirits. But when he saw Mordecai at the king's gate and observed that he neither rose nor showed fear in his presence, he was filled with rage against Mordecai. [10]Nevertheless, Haman restrained himself and went home.

Calling together his friends and Zeresh, his wife, [11]Haman boasted to them about his vast wealth, his many sons, and all the ways the king had honoured him and how he had elevated him above the other nobles and officials. [12]"And that's not all," Haman added. "I'm the only person Queen Esther invited to accompany the king to the banquet she gave. And she has invited me along with the king tomorrow. [13]But all this gives me no satisfaction as long as I see that Jew Mordecai sitting at the king's gate."

[14]His wife Zeresh and all his friends said to him, "Have a gallows built, seventy-five feet[a] high, and ask the king in the morning to have Mordecai hanged on it. Then go with the king to the dinner and be happy." This suggestion delighted Haman, and he had the gallows built.

Mordecai Honoured

6 That night the king could not sleep; so he ordered the book of the chronicles, the record of his reign, to be brought in and read to him. [2]It was found recorded there that Mordecai had exposed Bigthana and Teresh, two of the king's officers who guarded the doorway, who had conspired to assassinate King Xerxes.

[3]"What honour and recognition has Mordecai received for this?" the king asked.

"Nothing has been done for him," his attendants answered.

[4]The king said, "Who is in the court?" Now Haman had just entered the outer court of the palace to speak to the king about hanging Mordecai on the gallows he had erected for him.

[5]His attendants answered, "Haman is standing in the court."

"Bring him in," the king ordered.

[6]When Haman entered, the king asked him, "What should be done for the man the king delights to honour?"

Now Haman thought to himself, "Who is there that the king would rather honour than me?" [7]So he answered the king, "For the man the king delights to honour, [8]have them bring a royal robe the king has worn and a horse the king has ridden, one with a royal crest placed on its head. [9]Then let the robe and horse be entrusted to one of the king's most noble princes. Let them robe the man the king delights to honour, and lead him on the horse through the city streets, proclaiming before him, 'This is what is done for the man the king delights to honour!'"

[10]"Go at once," the king commanded Haman. "Get the robe and the horse and do just as you have suggested for Mordecai the Jew, who sits at the king's gate. Do not neglect anything you have recommended."

[11]So Haman got the robe and the horse. He robed Mordecai, and led him on horseback through the city streets, proclaiming before him, "This is what is done for the man the king delights to honour!"

[12]Afterwards Mordecai returned to the king's gate. But Haman rushed home, with his head covered, in grief, [13]and told Zeresh his wife and all his friends everything that had happened to him.

His advisers and his wife Zeresh said to him, "Since Mordecai, before whom your downfall has started, is of Jewish origin, you cannot stand against him—you will surely come to ruin!" [14]While they were still talking with him, the king's eunuchs

---

[a]14 Hebrew *fifty cubits* (about 23 metres)

arrived and hurried Haman away to the banquet Esther had prepared.

Haman Hanged

7 So the king and Haman went to dine with Queen Esther, [2]and as they were drinking wine on that second day, the king again asked, "Queen Esther, what is your petition? It will be given you. What is your request? Even up to half the kingdom, it will be granted."

[3]Then Queen Esther answered, "If I have found favour with you, O king, and if it pleases your majesty, grant me my life— this is my petition. And spare my people— this is my request. [4]For I and my people have been sold for destruction and slaughter and annihilation. If we had merely been sold as male and female slaves, I would have kept quiet, because no such distress would justify disturbing the king."[a]

[5]King Xerxes asked Queen Esther, "Who is he? Where is the man who has dared to do such a thing?"

[6]Esther said, "The adversary and enemy is this vile Haman."

Then Haman was terrified before the king and queen. [7]The king got up in a rage, left his wine and went out into the palace garden. But Haman, realising that the king had already decided his fate, stayed behind to beg Queen Esther for his life.

[8]Just as the king returned from the palace garden to the banquet hall, Haman was falling on the couch where Esther was reclining.

The king exclaimed, "Will he even molest the queen while she is with me in the house?"

As soon as the word left the king's mouth, they covered Haman's face. [9]Then Harbona, one of the eunuchs attending the king, said, "A gallows seventy-five feet[b] high stands by Haman's house. He had it made for Mordecai, who spoke up to help the king."

The king said, "Hang him on it!" [10]So they hanged Haman on the gallows he had prepared for Mordecai. Then the king's fury subsided.

The King's Edict on Behalf of the Jews

8 That same day King Xerxes gave Queen Esther the estate of Haman, the enemy of the Jews. And Mordecai came into the presence of the king, for Esther had told how he was related to her. [2]The king took off his signet ring, which he had reclaimed from Haman, and presented it to Mordecai. And Esther appointed him over Haman's estate.

[3]Esther again pleaded with the king, falling at his feet and weeping. She begged him to put an end to the evil plan of Haman the Agagite, which he had devised against the Jews. [4]Then the king extended the gold sceptre to Esther and she arose and stood before him.

[5]"If it pleases the king," she said, "and if he regards me with favour and thinks it the right thing to do, and if he is pleased with me, let an order be written overruling the dispatches that Haman son of Hammedatha, the Agagite, devised and wrote to destroy the Jews in all the king's provinces. [6]For how can I bear to see disaster fall on my people? How can I bear to see the destruction of my family?"

[7]King Xerxes replied to Queen Esther and to Mordecai the Jew, "Because Haman attacked the Jews, I have given his estate to Esther, and they have hanged him on the gallows. [8]Now write another decree in the king's name on behalf of the Jews as seems best to you, and seal it with the king's signet ring—for no document written in the king's name and sealed with his ring can be revoked."

[9]At once the royal secretaries were summoned—on the twenty-third day of the third month, the month of Sivan. They wrote out all Mordecai's orders to the Jews, and to the satraps, governors and nobles of the 127 provinces stretching from India to Cush.[a] These orders were written in the script of each province and the language of each people and also to the Jews in their own script and language.

---

[a]4 Or *quiet, but the compensation our adversary offers cannot be compared with the loss the king would suffer*
[b]9 Hebrew *fifty cubits* (about 23 metres)   [a]9 That is, the upper Nile region

10Mordecai wrote in the name of King Xerxes, sealed the dispatches with the king's signet ring, and sent them by mounted couriers, who rode fast horses especially bred for the king.

11The king's edict granted the Jews in every city the right to assemble and protect themselves; to destroy, kill and annihilate any armed force of any nationality or province that might attack them and their women and children; and to plunder the property of their enemies. 12The day appointed for the Jews to do this in all the provinces of King Xerxes was the thirteenth day of the twelfth month, the month of Adar. 13A copy of the text of the edict was to be issued as law in every province and made known to the people of every nationality so that the Jews would be ready on that day to avenge themselves on their enemies.

14The couriers, riding the royal horses, raced out, spurred on by the king's command. And the edict was also issued in the citadel of Susa.

15Mordecai left the king's presence wearing royal garments of blue and white, a large crown of gold and a purple robe of fine linen. And the city of Susa held a joyous celebration. 16For the Jews it was a time of happiness and joy, gladness and honour. 17In every province and in every city, wherever the edict of the king went, there was joy and gladness among the Jews, with feasting and celebrating. And many people of other nationalities became Jews because fear of the Jews had seized them.

Triumph of the Jews

9 On the thirteenth day of the twelfth month, the month of Adar, the edict commanded by the king was to be carried out. On this day the enemies of the Jews had hoped to overpower them, but now the tables were turned and the Jews got the upper hand over those who hated them. 2The Jews assembled in their cities in all the provinces of King Xerxes to attack those seeking their destruction. No-one could stand against them, because the people of all the other nationalities

were afraid of them. 3And all the nobles of the provinces, the satraps, the governors and the king's administrators helped the Jews, because fear of Mordecai had seized them. 4Mordecai was prominent in the palace; his reputation spread throughout the provinces, and he became more and more powerful.

5The Jews struck down all their enemies with the sword, killing and destroying them, and they did what they pleased to those who hated them. 6In the citadel of Susa, the Jews killed and destroyed five hundred men. 7They also killed Parshandatha, Dalphon, Aspatha, 8Poratha, Adalia, Aridatha, 9Parmashta, Arisai, Aridai and Vaizatha, 10the ten sons of Haman son of Hammedatha, the enemy of the Jews. But they did not lay their hands on the plunder.

11The number of those slain in the citadel of Susa was reported to the king that same day. 12The king said to Queen Esther, "The Jews have killed and destroyed five hundred men and the ten sons of Haman in the citadel of Susa. What have they done in the rest of the king's provinces? Now what is your petition? It will be given you. What is your request? It will also be granted."

13"If it pleases the king," Esther answered, "give the Jews in Susa permission to carry out this day's edict tomorrow also, and let Haman's ten sons be hanged on gallows."

14So the king commanded that this be done. An edict was issued in Susa, and they hanged the ten sons of Haman. 15The Jews in Susa came together on the fourteenth day of the month of Adar, and they put to death in Susa three hundred men, but they did not lay their hands on the plunder.

16Meanwhile, the remainder of the Jews who were in the king's provinces also assembled to protect themselves and get relief from their enemies. They killed seventy-five thousand of them but did not lay their hands on the plunder. 17This happened on the thirteenth day of the month of Adar, and on the fourteenth they rested and made it a day of feasting and joy.

Purim Celebrated

18The Jews in Susa, however, had assembled on the thirteenth and fourteenth, and then on the fifteenth they rested and made it a day of feasting and joy.

19That is why rural Jews—those living in villages—observe the fourteenth of the month of Adar as a day of joy and feasting, a day for giving presents to each other.

20Mordecai recorded these events, and he sent letters to all the Jews throughout the provinces of King Xerxes, near and far, 21to have them celebrate annually the fourteenth and fifteenth days of the month of Adar 22as the time when the Jews got relief from their enemies, and as the month when their sorrow was turned into joy and their mourning into a day of celebration. He wrote to them to observe the days as days of feasting and joy and giving presents of food to one another and gifts to the poor.

23So the Jews agreed to continue the celebration they had begun, doing what Mordecai had written to them. 24For Haman son of Hammedatha, the Agagite, the enemy of all the Jews, had plotted against the Jews to destroy them and had cast the *pur* (that is, the lot) for their ruin and destruction. 25But when the plot came to the king's attention,*a* he issued written orders that the evil scheme Haman had devised against the Jews should come back on to his own head, and that he and his sons should be hanged on the gallows. 26(Therefore these days were called Purim, from the word *pur*.) Because of everything written in this letter and because of what they had seen and what had happened to them, 27the Jews took it upon themselves to establish the custom that

they and their descendants and all who join them should without fail observe these two days every year, in the way prescribed and at the time appointed. 28These days should be remembered and observed in every generation by every family, and in every province and in every city. And these days of Purim should never cease to be celebrated by the Jews, nor should the memory of them die out among their descendants.

29So Queen Esther, daughter of Abihail, along with Mordecai the Jew, wrote with full authority to confirm this second letter concerning Purim. 30And Mordecai sent letters to all the Jews in the 127 provinces of the kingdom of Xerxes— words of goodwill and assurance—31to establish these days of Purim at their designated times, as Mordecai the Jew and Queen Esther had decreed for them, and as they had established for themselves and their descendants in regard to their times of fasting and lamentation. 32Esther's decree confirmed these regulations about Purim, and it was written down in the records.

The Greatness of Mordecai

10 King Xerxes imposed tribute throughout the empire, to its distant shores. 2And all his acts of power and might, together with a full account of the greatness of Mordecai to which the king had raised him, are they not written in the book of the annals of the kings of Media and Persia? 3Mordecai the Jew was second in rank to King Xerxes, pre-eminent among the Jews, and held in high esteem by his many fellow Jews, because he worked for the good of his people and spoke up for the welfare of all the Jews.

---

a25 Or when Esther came before the king

Job

Prologue

1 In the land of Uz there lived a man whose name was Job. This man was blameless and upright; he feared God and shunned evil. ²He had seven sons and three daughters, ³and he owned seven thousand sheep, three thousand camels, five hundred yoke of oxen and five hundred donkeys, and had a large number of servants. He was the greatest man among all the people of the East.

⁴His sons used to take turns holding feasts in their homes, and they would invite their three sisters to eat and drink with them. ⁵When a period of feasting had run its course, Job would send and have them purified. Early in the morning he would sacrifice a burnt offering for each of them, thinking, "Perhaps my children have sinned and cursed God in their hearts." This was Job's regular custom.

Job's First Test

⁶One day the angels[a] came to present themselves before the LORD, and Satan[b] also came with them. ⁷The LORD said to Satan, "Where have you come from?"

Satan answered the LORD, "From roaming through the earth and going to and fro in it."

⁸Then the LORD said to Satan, "Have you considered my servant Job? There is no-one on earth like him; he is blameless and upright, a man who fears God and shuns evil."

⁹"Does Job fear God for nothing?" Satan replied. ¹⁰"Have you not put a hedge around him and his household and everything he has? You have blessed the work of his hands, so that his flocks and herds are spread throughout the land. ¹¹But stretch out your hand and strike everything he has, and he will surely curse you to your face."

¹²The LORD said to Satan, "Very well, then, everything he has is in your hands, but on the man himself do not lay a finger."

Then Satan went out from the presence of the LORD.

¹³One day when Job's sons and daughters were feasting and drinking wine at the oldest brother's house, ¹⁴a messenger came to Job and said, "The oxen were ploughing and the donkeys were grazing nearby, ¹⁵and the Sabeans attacked and carried them off. They put the servants to the sword, and I am the only one who has escaped to tell you!"

¹⁶While he was still speaking, another messenger came and said, "The fire of God fell from the sky and burned up the sheep and the servants, and I am the only one who has escaped to tell you!"

¹⁷While he was still speaking, another messenger came and said, "The Chaldeans formed three raiding parties and swept down on your camels and carried them off. They put the servants to the sword, and I am the only one who has escaped to tell you!"

¹⁸While he was still speaking, yet

---

a6 Hebrew *the sons of God*   *b6* *Satan* means *accuser.*

another messenger came and said, "Your sons and daughters were feasting and drinking wine at the oldest brother's house, ¹⁹when suddenly a mighty wind swept in from the desert and struck the four corners of the house. It collapsed on them and they are dead, and I am the only one who has escaped to tell you!"

²⁰At this, Job got up and tore his robe and shaved his head. Then he fell to the ground in worship ²¹and said:

"Naked I came from my mother's
    womb,
  and naked I shall depart.ᶜ
The LORD gave and the LORD has taken
    away;
  may the name of the LORD be
    praised."

²²In all this, Job did not sin by charging God with wrongdoing.

Job's Second Test

2 On another day the angelsᵃ came to present themselves before the LORD, and Satan also came with them to present himself before him. ²And the LORD said to Satan, "Where have you come from?"

Satan answered the LORD, "From roaming through the earth and going to and fro in it."

³Then the LORD said to Satan, "Have you considered my servant Job? There is no-one on earth like him; he is blameless and upright, a man who fears God and shuns evil. And he still maintains his integrity, though you incited me against him to ruin him without any reason."

⁴"Skin for skin!" Satan replied. "A man will give all he has for his own life. ⁵But stretch out your hand and strike his flesh and bones, and he will surely curse you to your face."

⁶The LORD said to Satan, "Very well, then, he is in your hands; but you must spare his life."

⁷So Satan went out from the presence of the LORD and afflicted Job with painful sores from the soles of his feet to the top of his head. ⁸Then Job took a piece of broken pottery and scraped himself with it as he sat among the ashes.

⁹His wife said to him, "Are you still holding on to your integrity? Curse God and die!"

¹⁰He replied, "You are talking like a foolishᵇ woman. Shall we accept good from God, and not trouble?"

In all this, Job did not sin in what he said.

Job's Three Friends

¹¹When Job's three friends, Eliphaz the Temanite, Bildad the Shuhite and Zophar the Naamathite, heard about all the troubles that had come upon him, they set out from their homes and met together by agreement to go and sympathise with him and comfort him. ¹²When they saw him from a distance, they could hardly recognise him; they began to weep aloud, and they tore their robes and sprinkled dust on their heads. ¹³Then they sat on the ground with him for seven days and seven nights. No-one said a word to him, because they saw how great his suffering was.

Job Speaks

3 After this, Job opened his mouth and cursed the day of his birth. ²He said:

³"May the day of my birth perish,
    and the night it was said, 'A boy is
    born!'
⁴That day—may it turn to darkness;
    may God above not care about it;
    may no light shine upon it.
⁵May darkness and deep shadowᵃ claim
    it once more;
  may a cloud settle over it;
    may blackness overwhelm its light.
⁶That night—may thick darkness seize
    it;
  may it not be included among the
    days of the year
    nor be entered in any of the months.

ᶜ21 Or shall return there   ᵃ1 Hebrew the sons of God
ᵇ10 The Hebrew word rendered foolish denotes moral deficiency.   ᵃ5 Or and the shadow of death

7May that night be barren;
  may no shout of joy be heard in
    it.
8May those who curse days*b* curse that
    day,
  those who are ready to rouse
    Leviathan.
9May its morning stars become dark;
  may it wait for daylight in vain
  and not see the first rays of dawn,
10for it did not shut the doors of the
    womb on me
  to hide trouble from my eyes.

11"Why did I not perish at birth,
  and die as I came from the womb?
12Why were there knees to receive me
  and breasts that I might be nursed?
13For now I would be lying down in
    peace;
  I would be asleep and at rest
14with kings and counsellors of the earth,
  who built for themselves places now
    lying in ruins,
15with rulers who had gold,
  who filled their houses with silver.
16Or why was I not hidden in the ground
    like a stillborn child,
  like an infant who never saw the light
    of day?
17There the wicked cease from turmoil,
  and there the weary are at rest.
18Captives also enjoy their ease;
  they no longer hear the slave driver's
    shout.
19The small and the great are there,
  and the slave is freed from his
    master.

20"Why is light given to those in misery,
  and life to the bitter of soul,
21to those who long for death that does
    not come,
  who search for it more than for
    hidden treasure,
22who are filled with gladness
  and rejoice when they reach the
    grave?
23Why is life given to a man
  whose way is hidden,
  whom God has hedged in?

24For sighing comes to me instead of
    food;
  my groans pour out like water.
25What I feared has come upon me;
  what I dreaded has happened to me.
26I have no peace, no quietness;
  I have no rest, but only turmoil."

Eliphaz

4 Then Eliphaz the Temanite replied:

2"If someone ventures a word with you,
    will you be impatient?
  But who can keep from speaking?
3Think how you have instructed many,
  how you have strengthened feeble
    hands.
4Your words have supported those who
    stumbled;
  you have strengthened faltering
    knees.
5But now trouble comes to you, and you
    are discouraged;
  it strikes you, and you are dismayed.
6Should not your piety be your
    confidence
  and your blameless ways your
    hope?

7"Consider now: Who, being innocent,
    has ever perished?
  Where were the upright ever
    destroyed?
8As I have observed, those who plough
    evil
  and those who sow trouble reap it.
9At the breath of God they are
    destroyed;
  at the blast of his anger they perish.
10The lions may roar and growl,
  yet the teeth of the great lions are
    broken.
11The lion perishes for lack of prey,
  and the cubs of the lioness are
    scattered.

12"A word was secretly brought to me,
  my ears caught a whisper of it.
13Amid disquieting dreams in the night,
  when deep sleep falls on men,

b8 Or *the sea*

[14]fear and trembling seized me
and made all my bones shake.
[15]A spirit glided past my face,
and the hair on my body stood on
end.
[16]It stopped,
but I could not tell what it was.
A form stood before my eyes,
and I heard a hushed voice:
[17]'Can a mortal be more righteous than
God?
Can a man be more pure than his
Maker?
[18]If God places no trust in his servants,
if he charges his angels with error,
[19]how much more those who live in
houses of clay,
whose foundations are in the dust,
who are crushed more readily than a
moth!
[20]Between dawn and dusk they are
broken to pieces;
unnoticed, they perish for ever.
[21]Are not the cords of their tent pulled
up,
so that they die without wisdom?'[a]

5 "Call if you will, but who will answer
you?
To which of the holy ones will you
turn?
[2]Resentment kills a fool,
and envy slays the simple.
[3]I myself have seen a fool taking root,
but suddenly his house was cursed.
[4]His children are far from safety,
crushed in court without a defender.
[5]The hungry consume his harvest,
taking it even from among thorns,
and the thirsty pant after his wealth.
[6]For hardship does not spring from the
soil,
nor does trouble sprout from the
ground.
[7]Yet man is born to trouble
as surely as sparks fly upward.

[8]"But if it were I, I would appeal to
God;
I would lay my cause before him.

[9]He performs wonders that cannot be
fathomed,
miracles that cannot be counted.
[10]He bestows rain on the earth;
he sends water upon the countryside.
[11]The lowly he sets on high,
and those who mourn are lifted to
safety.
[12]He thwarts the plans of the crafty,
so that their hands achieve no
success.
[13]He catches the wise in their craftiness,
and the schemes of the wily are swept
away.
[14]Darkness comes upon them in the
daytime;
at noon they grope as in the night.
[15]He saves the needy from the sword in
their mouth;
he saves them from the clutches of
the powerful.
[16]So the poor have hope,
and injustice shuts its mouth.

[17]"Blessed is the man whom God
corrects;
so do not despise the discipline of the
Almighty.[a]
[18]For he wounds, but he also binds up;
he injures, but his hands also heal.
[19]From six calamities he will rescue you;
in seven no harm will befall you.
[20]In famine he will ransom you from
death,
and in battle from the stroke of the
sword.
[21]You will be protected from the lash of
the tongue,
and need not fear when destruction
comes.
[22]You will laugh at destruction and
famine,
and need not fear the beasts of the
earth.
[23]For you will have a covenant with the
stones of the field,
and the wild animals will be at peace
with you.
[24]You will know that your tent is secure;
you will take stock of your property
and find nothing missing.

---

[a]21 Some interpreters end the quotation after verse 17.   [a]17 Hebrew *Shaddai*; here and throughout Job

²⁵You will know that your children will be many,
  and your descendants like the grass of the earth.
²⁶You will come to the grave in full vigour,
  like sheaves gathered in season.

²⁷"We have examined this, and it is true. So hear it and apply it to yourself."

Job

6 Then Job replied:

²"If only my anguish could be weighed
  and all my misery be placed on the scales!
³It would surely outweigh the sand of the seas—
  no wonder my words have been impetuous.
⁴The arrows of the Almighty are in me,
  my spirit drinks in their poison;
  God's terrors are marshalled against me.
⁵Does a wild donkey bray when it has grass,
  or an ox bellow when it has fodder?
⁶Is tasteless food eaten without salt,
  or is there flavour in the white of an egg?^a
⁷I refuse to touch it;
  such food makes me ill.

⁸"Oh, that I might have my request,
  that God would grant what I hope for,
⁹that God would be willing to crush me,
  to let loose his hand and cut me off!
¹⁰Then I would still have this consolation—
  my joy in unrelenting pain—
  that I had not denied the words of the Holy One.

¹¹"What strength do I have, that I should still hope?
  What prospects, that I should be patient?
¹²Do I have the strength of stone?
  Is my flesh bronze?
¹³Do I have any power to help myself,
  now that success has been driven from me?

¹⁴"A despairing man should have the devotion of his friends,
  even though he forsakes the fear of the Almighty.
¹⁵But my brothers are as undependable as intermittent streams,
  as the streams that overflow
¹⁶when darkened by thawing ice
  and swollen with melting snow,
¹⁷but that cease to flow in the dry season,
  and in the heat vanish from their channels.
¹⁸Caravans turn aside from their routes;
  they go up into the wasteland and perish.
¹⁹The caravans of Tema look for water,
  the travelling merchants of Sheba look in hope.
²⁰They are distressed, because they had been confident;
  they arrive there, only to be disappointed.
²¹Now you too have proved to be of no help;
  you see something dreadful and are afraid.
²²Have I ever said, 'Give something on my behalf,
  pay a ransom for me from your wealth,
²³deliver me from the hand of the enemy,
  ransom me from the clutches of the ruthless'?

²⁴"Teach me, and I will be quiet;
  show me where I have been wrong.
²⁵How painful are honest words!
  But what do your arguments prove?
²⁶Do you mean to correct what I say,
  and treat the words of a despairing man as wind?
²⁷You would even cast lots for the fatherless
  and barter away your friend.

---

^a6 The meaning of the Hebrew for this phrase is uncertain.

²⁸"But now be so kind as to look at me.
   Would I lie to your face?
²⁹Relent, do not be unjust;
   reconsider, for my integrity is at
     stake.*b*
³⁰Is there any wickedness on my
   lips?
   Can my mouth not discern malice?

7   "Does not man have hard service on
   earth?
   Are not his days like those of a hired
     man?
²Like a slave longing for the evening
   shadows,
   or a hired man waiting eagerly for his
     wages,
³so I have been allotted months of
   futility,
   and nights of misery have been
     assigned to me.
⁴When I lie down I think, 'How long
   before I get up?'
   The night drags on, and I toss till
     dawn.
⁵My body is clothed with worms and
   scabs,
   my skin is broken and festering.

⁶"My days are swifter than a weaver's
   shuttle,
   and they come to an end without
     hope.
⁷Remember, O God, that my life is but a
   breath;
   my eyes will never see happiness
     again.
⁸The eye that now sees me will see me no
   longer;
   you will look for me, but I will be no
     more.
⁹As a cloud vanishes and is gone,
   so he who goes down to the grave*a*
     does not return.
¹⁰He will never come to his house again;
   his place will know him no more.

¹¹"Therefore I will not keep silent;
   I will speak out in the anguish of my
     spirit,

I will complain in the bitterness of my
   soul.
¹²Am I the sea, or the monster of the
   deep,
   that you put me under guard?
¹³When I think my bed will comfort me
   and my couch will ease my complaint,
¹⁴even then you frighten me with dreams
   and terrify me with visions,
¹⁵so that I prefer strangling and death,
   rather than this body of mine.
¹⁶I despise my life; I would not live for
   ever.
   Let me alone; my days have no
     meaning.

¹⁷"What is man that you make so much of
   him,
   that you give him so much atten-
     tion,
¹⁸that you examine him every morning
   and test him every moment?
¹⁹Will you never look away from me,
   or let me alone even for an instant?
²⁰If I have sinned, what have I done to
   you,
   O watcher of men?
   Why have you made me your target?
   Have I become a burden to you?*b*
²¹Why do you not pardon my offences
   and forgive my sins?
   For I shall soon lie down in the dust;
   you will search for me, but I shall be
     no more."

Bildad

8   Then Bildad the Shuhite replied:

²"How long will you say such things?
   Your words are a blustering wind.
³Does God pervert justice?
   Does the Almighty pervert what is
     right?
⁴When your children sinned against him,
   he gave them over to the penalty of
     their sin.
⁵But if you will look to God
   and plead with the Almighty,

---

b29 Or *my righteousness still stands*   *a9* Hebrew *Sheol*
b20 A few manuscripts of the Masoretic Text, an ancient Hebrew scribal tradition and Septuagint; most manuscripts of the
Masoretic Text *I have become a burden to myself.*

⁶if you are pure and upright,
even now he will rouse himself on
your behalf
and restore you to your rightful
place.
⁷Your beginnings will seem humble,
so prosperous will your future
be.

⁸"Ask the former generations
and find out what their fathers
learned,
⁹for we were born only yesterday and
know nothing,
and our days on earth are but a
shadow.
¹⁰Will they not instruct you and tell you?
Will they not bring forth words from
their understanding?
¹¹Can papyrus grow tall where there is no
marsh?
Can reeds thrive without water?
¹²While still growing and uncut,
they wither more quickly than grass.
¹³Such is the destiny of all who forget
God;
so perishes the hope of the godless.
¹⁴What he trusts in is fragile;*ᵃ*
what he relies on is a spider's web.
¹⁵He leans on his web, but it gives way;
he clings to it, but it does not hold.
¹⁶He is like a well-watered plant in the
sunshine,
spreading its shoots over the garden;
¹⁷it entwines its roots around a pile of
rocks
and looks for a place among the
stones.
¹⁸But when it is torn from its spot,
that place disowns it and says, 'I
never saw you.'
¹⁹Surely its life withers away,
and*ᵇ* from the soil other plants grow.

²⁰"Surely God does not reject a blameless
man
or strengthen the hands of evildoers.
²¹He will yet fill your mouth with laughter
and your lips with shouts of joy.
²²Your enemies will be clothed in shame,
and the tents of the wicked will be no
more."

Job

9

Then Job replied:

²"Indeed, I know that this is true.
But how can a mortal be righteous
before God?
³Though one wished to dispute with him,
he could not answer him one time out
of a thousand.
⁴His wisdom is profound, his power is
vast.
Who has resisted him and come out
unscathed?
⁵He moves mountains without their
knowing it
and overturns them in his anger.
⁶He shakes the earth from its place
and makes its pillars tremble.
⁷He speaks to the sun and it does not
shine;
he seals off the light of the stars.
⁸He alone stretches out the heavens
and treads on the waves of the sea.
⁹He is the Maker of the Bear and Orion,
the Pleiades and the constellations of
the south.
¹⁰He performs wonders that cannot be
fathomed,
miracles that cannot be counted.
¹¹When he passes me, I cannot see him;
when he goes by, I cannot perceive
him.
¹²If he snatches away, who can stop him?
Who can say to him, 'What are you
doing?'
¹³God does not restrain his anger;
even the cohorts of Rahab cowered at
his feet.

¹⁴"How then can I dispute with him?
How can I find words to argue with
him?
¹⁵Though I were innocent, I could not
answer him;
I could only plead with my Judge for
mercy.
¹⁶Even if I summoned him and he
responded,
I do not believe he would give me a
hearing.

ᵃ14 The meaning of the Hebrew for this word is uncertain.   *ᵇ19* Or *Surely all the joy it has / is that*

17He would crush me with a storm
and multiply my wounds for no
reason.
18He would not let me regain my breath
but would overwhelm me with
misery.
19If it is a matter of strength, he is mighty!
And if it is a matter of justice, who
will summon him?ª
20Even if I were innocent, my mouth
would condemn me;
if I were blameless, it would
pronounce me guilty.

21"Although I am blameless,
I have no concern for myself;
I despise my own life.
22It is all the same; that is why I say,
'He destroys both the blameless and
the wicked.'
23When a scourge brings sudden death,
he mocks the despair of the innocent.
24When a land falls into the hands of the
wicked,
he blindfolds its judges.
If it is not he, then who is it?

25"My days are swifter than a runner;
they fly away without a glimpse of
joy.
26They skim past like boats of papyrus,
like eagles swooping down on their
prey.
27If I say, 'I will forget my complaint,
I will change my expression, and
smile,'
28I still dread all my sufferings,
for I know you will not hold me
innocent.
29Since I am already found guilty,
why should I struggle in vain?
30Even if I washed myself with
soapᵇ
and my hands with washing soda,
31you would plunge me into a slime pit
so that even my clothes would detest
me.

32"He is not a man like me that I might
answer him,
that we might confront each other in
court.

33If only there were someone to arbitrate
between us,
to lay his hand upon us both,
34someone to remove God's rod from me,
so that his terror would frighten me
no more.
35Then I would speak up without fear of
him,
but as it now stands with me, I
cannot.

10 "I loathe my very life;
therefore I will give free rein to
my complaint
and speak out in the bitterness of my
soul.
2I will say to God: Do not condemn me,
but tell me what charges you have
against me.
3Does it please you to oppress me,
to spurn the work of your hands,
while you smile on the schemes of the
wicked?
4Do you have eyes of flesh?
Do you see as a mortal sees?
5Are your days like those of a mortal
or your years like those of a man,
6that you must search out my faults
and probe after my sin—
7though you know that I am not guilty
and that no-one can rescue me from
your hand?

8"Your hands shaped me and made me.
Will you now turn and destroy me?
9Remember that you moulded me like
clay.
Will you now turn me to dust again?
10Did you not pour me out like milk
and curdle me like cheese,
11clothe me with skin and flesh
and knit me together with bones and
sinews?
12You gave me life and showed me
kindness,
and in your providence watched over
my spirit.

13"But this is what you concealed in your
heart,
and I know that this was in your
mind:

ª19 See Septuagint; Hebrew me.   ᵇ30 Or snow

¹⁴If I sinned, you would be watching me
  and would not let my offence go
      unpunished.
¹⁵If I am guilty—woe to me!
  Even if I am innocent, I cannot lift
      my head,
  for I am full of shame
  and drowned in*a* my affliction.
¹⁶If I hold my head high, you stalk me
      like a lion
  and again display your awesome
      power against me.
¹⁷You bring new witnesses against me
  and increase your anger towards me;
  your forces come against me wave
      upon wave.

¹⁸"Why then did you bring me out of the
      womb?
  I wish I had died before any eye saw
      me.
¹⁹If only I had never come into being,
  or had been carried straight from the
      womb to the grave!
²⁰Are not my few days almost over?
  Turn away from me so that I can have
      a moment's joy
²¹before I go to the place of no return,
  to the land of gloom and deep
      shadow,*b*
²²to the land of deepest night,
  of deep shadow and disorder,
  where even the light is like
      darkness."

Zophar

11 Then Zophar the Naamathite re-
      plied:

²"Are all these words to go unanswered?
  Is this talker to be vindicated?
³Will your idle talk reduce men to
      silence?
  Will no-one rebuke you when you
      mock?
⁴You say to God, 'My beliefs are flawless
  and I am pure in your sight.'
⁵Oh, how I wish that God would speak,
  that he would open his lips against
      you

⁶and disclose to you the secrets of
      wisdom,
  for true wisdom has two sides.
  Know this: God has even forgotten
      some of your sin.

⁷"Can you fathom the mysteries of God?
  Can you probe the limits of the
      Almighty?
⁸They are higher than the
      heavens—what can you do?
  They are deeper than the depths of
      the grave*a*—what can you know?
⁹Their measure is longer than the earth
  and wider than the sea.

¹⁰"If he comes along and confines you in
      prison
  and convenes a court, who can
      oppose him?
¹¹Surely he recognises deceitful men;
  and when he sees evil, does he not
      take note?
¹²But a witless man can no more become
      wise
  than a wild donkey's colt can be born
      a man.*b*

¹³"Yet if you devote your heart to him
  and stretch out your hands to him,
¹⁴if you put away the sin that is in your
      hand
  and allow no evil to dwell in your
      tent,
¹⁵then you will lift up your face without
      shame;
  you will stand firm and without fear.
¹⁶You will surely forget your trouble,
  recalling it only as waters gone by.
¹⁷Life will be brighter than noonday,
  and darkness will become like
      morning.
¹⁸You will be secure, because there is
      hope;
  you will look about you and take your
      rest in safety.
¹⁹You will lie down, with no-one to make
      you afraid,
  and many will court your favour.

a15 Or *and aware of*   *b21* Or *and the shadow of death*; also in verse 22   *a8* Hebrew *than Sheol*
b12 Or *wild donkey can be born tame*

²⁰But the eyes of the wicked will fail,
  and escape will elude them;
  their hope will become a dying
      gasp.''

Job

12
Then Job replied:

²''Doubtless you are the people,
  and wisdom will die with you!
³But I have a mind as well as you;
  I am not inferior to you.
  Who does not know all these
      things?

⁴''I have become a laughing-stock to my
      friends,
  though I called upon God and he
      answered—
  a mere laughing-stock, though
      righteous and blameless!
⁵Men at ease have contempt for
      misfortune
  as the fate of those whose feet are
      slipping.
⁶The tents of marauders are
      undisturbed,
  and those who provoke God are
      secure—
  those who carry their god in their
      hands.*ᵃ*

⁷''But ask the animals, and they will
      teach you,
  or the birds of the air, and they will
      tell you;
⁸or speak to the earth, and it will teach
      you,
  or let the fish of the sea inform
      you.
⁹Which of all these does not know
  that the hand of the LORD has done
      this?
¹⁰In his hand is the life of every creature
  and the breath of all mankind.
¹¹Does not the ear test words
  as the tongue tastes food?
¹²Is not wisdom found among the aged?
  Does not long life bring
      understanding?

¹³''To God belong wisdom and power;
  counsel and understanding are his.
¹⁴What he tears down cannot be rebuilt;
  the man he imprisons cannot be
      released.
¹⁵If he holds back the waters, there is
      drought;
  if he lets them loose, they devastate
      the land.
¹⁶To him belong strength and victory;
  both deceived and deceiver are his.
¹⁷He leads counsellors away stripped
  and makes fools of judges.
¹⁸He takes off the shackles put on by
      kings
  and ties a loincloth*ᵇ* round their
      waist.
¹⁹He leads priests away stripped
  and overthrows men long
      established.
²⁰He silences the lips of trusted advisers
  and takes away the discernment of
      elders.
²¹He pours contempt on nobles
  and disarms the mighty.
²²He reveals the deep things of darkness
  and brings deep shadows into the
      light.
²³He makes nations great, and destroys
      them;
  he enlarges nations, and disperses
      them.
²⁴He deprives the leaders of the earth of
      their reason;
  he sends them wandering through a
      trackless waste.
²⁵They grope in darkness with no light;
  he makes them stagger like
      drunkards.

13
''My eyes have seen all this,
  my ears have heard and
      understood it.
²What you know, I also know;
  I am not inferior to you.
³But I desire to speak to the Almighty
  and to argue my case with God.
⁴You, however, smear me with lies;
  you are worthless physicians, all of
      you!

ᵃ6 Or *secure / in what God's hand brings them*   *ᵇ18* Or *shackles of kings / and ties a belt*

⁵If only you would be altogether silent!
  For you, that would be wisdom.
⁶Hear now my argument;
  listen to the plea of my lips.
⁷Will you speak wickedly on God's
    behalf?
  Will you speak deceitfully for him?
⁸Will you show him partiality?
  Will you argue the case for God?
⁹Would it turn out well if he examined
    you?
  Could you deceive him as you might
    deceive men?
¹⁰He would surely rebuke you
  if you secretly showed partiality.
¹¹Would not his splendour terrify you?
  Would not the dread of him fall on
    you?
¹²Your maxims are proverbs of ashes;
  your defences are defences of clay.

¹³"Keep silent and let me speak;
  then let come to me what may.
¹⁴Why do I put myself in jeopardy
  and take my life in my hands?
¹⁵Though he slay me, yet will I hope in
    him;
  I will surely*ᵃ* defend my ways to his
    face.
¹⁶Indeed, this will turn out for my
    deliverance,
  for no godless man would dare come
    before him!
¹⁷Listen carefully to my words;
  let your ears take in what I say.
¹⁸Now that I have prepared my case,
  I know I will be vindicated.
¹⁹Can anyone bring charges against me?
  If so, I will be silent and die.

²⁰"Only grant me these two things, O
    God,
  and then I will not hide from you:
²¹Withdraw your hand far from me,
  and stop frightening me with your
    terrors.
²²Then summon me and I will answer,
  or let me speak, and you reply.
²³How many wrongs and sins have I
    committed?
  Show me my offence and my sin.

²⁴Why do you hide your face
  and consider me your enemy?
²⁵Will you torment a wind-blown
    leaf?
  Will you chase after dry chaff?
²⁶For you write down bitter things against
    me
  and make me inherit the sins of my
    youth.
²⁷You fasten my feet in shackles;
  you keep close watch on all my paths
  by putting marks on the soles of my
    feet.

²⁸"So man wastes away like something
    rotten,
  like a garment eaten by moths.

14 "Man born of woman
      is of few days and full of trouble.
²He springs up like a flower and withers
    away;
  like a fleeting shadow, he does not
    endure.
³Do you fix your eye on such a one?
  Will you bring him*ᵃ* before you for
    judgment?
⁴Who can bring what is pure from the
    impure?
  No-one!
⁵Man's days are determined;
  you have decreed the number of his
    months
  and have set limits he cannot exceed.
⁶So look away from him and let him
    alone,
  till he has put in his time like a hired
    man.

⁷"At least there is hope for a tree:
  If it is cut down, it will sprout again,
  and its new shoots will not fail.
⁸Its roots may grow old in the ground
  and its stump die in the soil,
⁹yet at the scent of water it will bud
  and put forth shoots like a plant.
¹⁰But man dies and is laid low;
  he breathes his last and is no more.
¹¹As water disappears from the sea
  or a river bed becomes parched and
    dry,

ᵃ15 Or He will surely slay me; I have no hope— / yet I will   *ᵃ3 Septuagint, Vulgate and Syriac; Hebrew me*

¹²so man lies down and does not rise;
    till the heavens are no more, men will
       not awake
    or be roused from their sleep.

¹³"If only you would hide me in the
       grave*b*
    and conceal me till your anger has
       passed!
  If only you would set me a time
    and then remember me!
¹⁴If a man dies, will he live again?
    All the days of my hard service
    I will wait for my renewal*c* to come.
¹⁵You will call and I will answer you;
    you will long for the creature your
      hands have made.
¹⁶Surely then you will count my steps
    but not keep track of my sin.
¹⁷My offences will be sealed up in a bag;
    you will cover over my sin.

¹⁸"But as a mountain erodes and
       crumbles
    and as a rock is moved from its place,
¹⁹as water wears away stones
    and torrents wash away the soil,
    so you destroy man's hope.
²⁰You overpower him once for all, and he
      is gone;
    you change his countenance and send
      him away.
²¹If his sons are honoured, he does not
      know it;
    if they are brought low, he does not
      see it.
²²He feels but the pain of his own body
    and mourns only for himself."

Eliphaz

15 Then Eliphaz the Temanite replied:

²"Would a wise man answer with empty
      notions
    or fill his belly with the hot east wind?
³Would he argue with useless words,
    with speeches that have no
      value?
⁴But you even undermine piety
    and hinder devotion to God.

⁵Your sin prompts your mouth;
    you adopt the tongue of the crafty.
⁶Your own mouth condemns you, not
      mine;
    your own lips testify against you.

⁷"Are you the first man ever born?
    Were you brought forth before the
      hills?
⁸Do you listen in on God's council?
    Do you limit wisdom to yourself?
⁹What do you know that we do not
      know?
    What insights do you have that we do
      not have?
¹⁰The grey-haired and the aged are on
      our side,
    men even older than your father.
¹¹Are God's consolations not enough for
      you,
    words spoken gently to you?
¹²Why has your heart carried you away,
    and why do your eyes flash,
¹³so that you vent your rage against God
    and pour out such words from your
      mouth?

¹⁴"What is man, that he could be pure,
    or one born of woman, that he could
      be righteous?
¹⁵If God places no trust in his holy ones,
    if even the heavens are not pure in his
      eyes,
¹⁶how much less man, who is vile and
      corrupt,
    who drinks up evil like water!

¹⁷"Listen to me and I will explain to you;
    let me tell you what I have seen,
¹⁸what wise men have declared,
    hiding nothing received from their
      fathers
¹⁹(to whom alone the land was given
    when no alien passed among them):
²⁰All his days the wicked man suffers
      torment,
    the ruthless through all the years
      stored up for him.
²¹Terrifying sounds fill his ears;
    when all seems well, marauders
      attack him.

---

b13 Hebrew *Sheol*   *c14* Or *release*

22He despairs of escaping the darkness;
 he is marked for the sword.
23He wanders about—food for vultures;*a*
 he knows the day of darkness is at
 hand.
24Distress and anguish fill him with
 terror;
 they overwhelm him, like a king
 poised to attack,
25because he shakes his fist at God
 and vaunts himself against the
 Almighty,
26defiantly charging against him
 with a thick, strong shield.

27"Though his face is covered with fat
 and his waist bulges with flesh,
28he will inhabit ruined towns
 and houses where no-one lives,
 houses crumbling to rubble.
29He will no longer be rich and his wealth
 will not endure,
 nor will his possessions spread over
 the land.
30He will not escape the darkness;
 a flame will wither his shoots,
 and the breath of God's mouth will
 carry him away.
31Let him not deceive himself by trusting
 what is worthless,
 for he will get nothing in return.
32Before his time he will be paid in full,
 and his branches will not flourish.
33He will be like a vine stripped of its
 unripe grapes,
 like an olive tree shedding its
 blossoms.
34For the company of the godless will be
 barren,
 and fire will consume the tents of
 those who love bribes.
35They conceive trouble and give birth to
 evil;
 their womb fashions deceit.''

Job

16 Then Job replied:

2"I have heard many things like these;
 miserable comforters are you all!

3Will your long-winded speeches never
 end?
 What ails you that you keep on
 arguing?
4I also could speak like you,
 if you were in my place;
 I could make fine speeches against you
 and shake my head at you.
5But my mouth would encourage you;
 comfort from my lips would bring you
 relief.

6"Yet if I speak, my pain is not relieved;
 and if I refrain, it does not go away.
7Surely, O God, you have worn me out;
 you have devastated my entire
 household.
8You have bound me—and it has
 become a witness;
 my gauntness rises up and testifies
 against me.
9God assails me and tears me in his
 anger
 and gnashes his teeth at me;
 my opponent fastens on me his
 piercing eyes.
10Men open their mouths to jeer at me;
 they strike my cheek in scorn
 and unite together against me.
11God has turned me over to evil men
 and thrown me into the clutches of
 the wicked.
12All was well with me, but he shattered
 me;
 he seized me by the neck and crushed
 me.
 He has made me his target;
13 his archers surround me.
 Without pity, he pierces my kidneys
 and spills my gall on the ground.
14Again and again he bursts upon me;
 he rushes at me like a warrior.

15"I have sewed sackcloth over my skin
 and buried my brow in the dust.
16My face is red with weeping,
 deep shadows ring my eyes;
17yet my hands have been free of violence
 and my prayer is pure.

18"O earth, do not cover my blood;
 may my cry never be laid to rest!

a23 Or *about, looking for food*

¹⁹Even now my witness is in heaven;
  my advocate is on high.
²⁰My intercessor is my friend[a]
  as my eyes pour out tears to God;
²¹on behalf of a man he pleads with God
  as a man pleads for his friend.

²²"Only a few years will pass
  before I go on the journey of no
   return.

17 ¹My spirit is broken,
  my days are cut short,
  the grave awaits me.
²Surely mockers surround me;
  my eyes must dwell on their hostility.

³"Give me, O God, the pledge you
   demand.
  Who else will put up security for me?
⁴You have closed their minds to
   understanding;
  therefore you will not let them
   triumph.
⁵If a man denounces his friends for reward,
  the eyes of his children will fail.

⁶"God has made me a byword to
   everyone,
  a man in whose face people spit.
⁷My eyes have grown dim with grief;
  my whole frame is but a shadow.
⁸Upright men are appalled at this;
  the innocent are aroused against the
   ungodly.
⁹Nevertheless, the righteous will hold to
   their ways,
  and those with clean hands will grow
   stronger.

¹⁰"But come on, all of you, try again!
  I will not find a wise man among you.
¹¹My days have passed, my plans are
   shattered,
  and so are the desires of my heart.
¹²These men turn night into day;
  in the face of darkness they say,
   'Light is near.'
¹³If the only home I hope for is the
   grave,[a]
  if I spread out my bed in darkness,

¹⁴if I say to corruption, 'You are my
   father,'
  and to the worm, 'My mother' or 'My
   sister',
¹⁵where then is my hope?
  Who can see any hope for me?
¹⁶Will it go down to the gates of death?[b]
  Will we descend together into the
   dust?"

Bildad

18 Then Bildad the Shuhite replied:
²"When will you end these speeches?
  Be sensible, and then we can talk.
³Why are we regarded as cattle
  and considered stupid in your sight?
⁴You who tear yourself to pieces in your
   anger,
  is the earth to be abandoned for your
   sake?
  Or must the rocks be moved from
   their place?

⁵"The lamp of the wicked is snuffed out;
  the flame of his fire stops burning.
⁶The light in his tent becomes dark;
  the lamp beside him goes out.
⁷The vigour of his step is weakened;
  his own schemes throw him down.
⁸His feet thrust him into a net
  and he wanders into its mesh.
⁹A trap seizes him by the heel;
  a snare holds him fast.
¹⁰A noose is hidden for him on the
   ground;
  a trap lies in his path.
¹¹Terrors startle him on every side
  and dog his every step.
¹²Calamity is hungry for him;
  disaster is ready for him when he falls.
¹³It eats away parts of his skin;
  death's firstborn devours his limbs.
¹⁴He is torn from the security of his tent
  and marched off to the king of
   terrors.
¹⁵Fire resides[a] in his tent;
  burning sulphur is scattered over his
   dwelling.

a20 Or *My friends treat me with scorn*   a13 Hebrew *Sheol*   b16 Hebrew *to Sheol*
a15 Or *Nothing he had remains*

¹⁶His roots dry up below
  and his branches wither above.
¹⁷The memory of him perishes from the
    earth;
  he has no name in the land.
¹⁸He is driven from light into darkness
  and is banished from the world.
¹⁹He has no offspring or descendants
    among his people,
  no survivor where once he lived.
²⁰Men of the west are appalled at his fate;
  men of the east are seized with
    horror.
²¹Surely such is the dwelling of an evil
    man;
  such is the place of one who knows
    not God.''

Job

19
Then Job replied:

²''How long will you torment me
  and crush me with words?
³Ten times now you have reproached
    me;
  shamelessly you attack me.
⁴If it is true that I have gone astray,
  my error remains my concern alone.
⁵If indeed you would exalt yourselves
    above me
  and use my humiliation against me,
⁶then know that God has wronged me
  and drawn his net around me.

⁷''Though I cry, 'I've been wronged!' I
    get no response;
  though I call for help, there is no
    justice.
⁸He has blocked my way so that I cannot
    pass;
  he has shrouded my paths in
    darkness.
⁹He has stripped me of my honour
  and removed the crown from my head.
¹⁰He tears me down on every side till I am
    gone;
  he uproots my hope like a tree.
¹¹His anger burns against me;
  he counts me among his enemies.

¹²His troops advance in force;
  they build a siege ramp against me
  and encamp around my tent.

¹³''He has alienated my brothers from
    me;
  my acquaintances are completely
    estranged from me.
¹⁴My kinsmen have gone away;
  my friends have forgotten me.
¹⁵My guests and my maidservants count
    me a stranger;
  they look upon me as an alien.
¹⁶I summon my servant, but he does not
    answer,
  though I beg him with my own
    mouth.
¹⁷My breath is offensive to my wife;
  I am loathsome to my own brothers.
¹⁸Even the little boys scorn me;
  when I appear, they ridicule me.
¹⁹All my intimate friends detest me;
  those I love have turned against me.
²⁰I am nothing but skin and bones;
  I have escaped by only the skin of my
    teeth.*ᵃ*

²¹''Have pity on me, my friends, have
    pity,
  for the hand of God has struck me.
²²Why do you pursue me as God does?
  Will you never get enough of my
    flesh?

²³''Oh, that my words were recorded,
  that they were written on a
    scroll,
²⁴that they were inscribed with an iron
    tool on*ᵇ* lead,
  or engraved in rock for ever!
²⁵I know that my Redeemer*ᶜ* lives,
  and that in the end he will stand upon
    the earth.*ᵈ*
²⁶And after my skin has been destroyed,
  yet*ᵉ* in*ᶠ* my flesh I will see God;
²⁷I myself will see him
  with my own eyes—I, and not
    another.
  How my heart yearns within me!

ᵃ20 Or *only my gums*   *ᵇ24* Or *and*   *ᶜ25* Or *defender*   *ᵈ25* Or *upon my grave*
ᵉ26 Or *And after I awake, / though this ⌐body⌐ has been destroyed, / then*   *ᶠ26* Or / *apart from*

28"If you say, 'How we will hound him,
 since the root of the trouble lies in
 him,'^g
29you should fear the sword yourselves;
 for wrath will bring punishment by
 the sword,
 and then you will know that there is
 judgment.'^h

Zophar

20 Then Zophar the Naamathite replied:

2"My troubled thoughts prompt me to
 answer
 because I am greatly disturbed.
3I hear a rebuke that dishonours me,
 and my understanding inspires me to
 reply.

4"Surely you know how it has been from
 of old,
 ever since man^a was placed on the
 earth,
5that the mirth of the wicked is brief,
 the joy of the godless lasts but a
 moment.
6Though his pride reaches to the heavens
 and his head touches the clouds,
7he will perish for ever, like his own
 dung;
 those who have seen him will say,
 'Where is he?'
8Like a dream he flies away, no more to
 be found,
 banished like a vision of the night.
9The eye that saw him will not see him
 again;
 his place will look on him no more.
10His children must make amends to the
 poor;
 his own hands must give back his
 wealth.
11The youthful vigour that fills his bones
 will lie with him in the dust.

12"Though evil is sweet in his mouth
 and he hides it under his tongue,
13though he cannot bear to let it go
 and keeps it in his mouth,

14yet his food will turn sour in his stomach;
 it will become the venom of serpents
 within him.
15He will spit out the riches he swallowed;
 God will make his stomach vomit
 them up.
16He will suck the poison of serpents;
 the fangs of an adder will kill him.
17He will not enjoy the streams,
 the rivers flowing with honey and
 cream.
18What he toiled for he must give back
 uneaten;
 he will not enjoy the profit from his
 trading.
19For he has oppressed the poor and left
 them destitute;
 he has seized houses he did not build.

20"Surely he will have no respite from his
 craving;
 he cannot save himself by his
 treasure.
21Nothing is left for him to devour;
 his prosperity will not endure.
22In the midst of his plenty, distress will
 overtake him;
 the full force of misery will come
 upon him.
23When he has filled his belly,
 God will vent his burning anger
 against him
 and rain down his blows upon him.
24Though he flees from an iron weapon,
 a bronze-tipped arrow pierces him.
25He pulls it out of his back,
 the gleaming point out of his liver.
 Terrors will come over him;
26   total darkness lies in wait for his
 treasures.
 A fire unfanned will consume him
 and devour what is left in his tent.
27The heavens will expose his guilt;
 the earth will rise up against him.
28A flood will carry off his house,
 rushing waters^b on the day of God's
 wrath.
29Such is the fate God allots the wicked,
 the heritage appointed for them by
 God."

---

g28 Many Hebrew manuscripts, Septuagint and Vulgate; most Hebrew manuscripts *me*
h29 Or / *that you may come to know the Almighty*   *a4* Or *Adam*
b28 Or *The possessions in his house will be carried off,* / *washed away*

21 Then Job replied:

2"Listen carefully to my words;
    let this be the consolation you give
        me.
3Bear with me while I speak,
    and after I have spoken, mock on.

4"Is my complaint directed to man?
    Why should I not be impatient?
5Look at me and be astonished;
    clap your hand over your mouth.
6When I think about this, I am terrified;
    trembling seizes my body.
7Why do the wicked live on,
    growing old and increasing in power?
8They see their children established
        around them,
    their offspring before their eyes.
9Their homes are safe and free from
        fear;
    the rod of God is not upon them.
10Their bulls never fail to breed;
    their cows calve and do not miscarry.
11They send forth their children as a
        flock;
    their little ones dance about.
12They sing to the music of tambourine
        and harp;
    they make merry to the sound of the
        flute.
13They spend their years in prosperity
    and go down to the grave*a* in peace.*b*
14Yet they say to God, 'Leave us alone!
    We have no desire to know your
        ways.
15Who is the Almighty, that we should
        serve him?
    What would we gain by praying to
        him?'
16But their prosperity is not in their own
        hands,
    so I stand aloof from the counsel of
        the wicked.

17"Yet how often is the lamp of the
    wicked snuffed out?

How often does calamity come upon
        them,
    the fate God allots in his anger?
18How often are they like straw before
        the wind,
    like chaff swept away by a gale?
19⌊It is said,⌋ 'God stores up a man's
        punishment for his sons.'
    Let him repay the man himself, so
        that he will know it!
20Let his own eyes see his destruction;
    let him drink of the wrath of the
        Almighty.*c*
21For what does he care about the family
        he leaves behind
    when his allotted months come to an
        end?

22"Can anyone teach knowledge to God,
    since he judges even the highest?
23One man dies in full vigour,
    completely secure and at ease,
24his body*d* well nourished,
    his bones rich with marrow.
25Another man dies in bitterness of soul,
    never having enjoyed anything good.
26Side by side they lie in the dust,
    and worms cover them both.

27"I know full well what you are thinking,
    the schemes by which you would
        wrong me.
28You say, 'Where now is the great man's
        house,
    the tents where wicked men lived?'
29Have you never questioned those who
        travel?
    Have you paid no regard to their
        accounts—
30that the evil man is spared from the day
        of calamity,
    that he is delivered from*e* the day of
        wrath?
31Who denounces his conduct to his face?
    Who repays him for what he has
        done?
32He is carried to the grave,
    and watch is kept over his tomb.
33The soil in the valley is sweet to him;

---

a13 Hebrew *Sheol*   *b13* Or *in an instant*
c17–20 Verses 17 and 18 may be taken as exclamations and 19 and 20 as declarations.
d24 The meaning of the Hebrew for this word is uncertain.
e30 Or *man is reserved for the day of calamity, / that he is brought forth to*

all men follow after him,
and a countless throng goes/ before
him.

³⁴"So how can you console me with your
nonsense?
Nothing is left of your answers but
falsehood!"

Eliphaz

22 Then Eliphaz the Temanite replied:

²"Can a man be of benefit to God?
Can even a wise man benefit him?
³What pleasure would it give the
Almighty if you were righteous?
What would he gain if your ways
were blameless?

⁴"Is it for your piety that he rebukes you
and brings charges against you?
⁵Is not your wickedness great?
Are not your sins endless?
⁶You demanded security from your
brothers for no reason;
you stripped men of their clothing,
leaving them naked.
⁷You gave no water to the weary
and you withheld food from the
hungry,
⁸though you were a powerful man,
owning land—
an honoured man, living on it.
⁹And you sent widows away
empty-handed
and broke the strength of the
fatherless.
¹⁰That is why snares are all around you,
why sudden peril terrifies you,
¹¹why it is so dark that you cannot see,
and why a flood of water covers you.

¹²"Is not God in the heights of heaven?
And see how lofty are the highest
stars!
¹³Yet you say, 'What does God know?
Does he judge through such darkness?
¹⁴Thick clouds veil him, so he does not
see us

as he goes about in the vaulted
heavens.'
¹⁵Will you keep to the old path
that evil men have trod?
¹⁶They were carried off before their time,
their foundations washed away by a
flood.
¹⁷They said to God, 'Leave us alone!
What can the Almighty do to us?'
¹⁸Yet it was he who filled their houses
with good things,
so I stand aloof from the counsel of
the wicked.

¹⁹"The righteous see their ruin and
rejoice;
the innocent mock them, saying,
²⁰'Surely our foes are destroyed,
and fire devours their wealth.'

²¹"Submit to God and be at peace with
him;
in this way prosperity will come to
you.
²²Accept instruction from his mouth
and lay up his words in your heart.
²³If you return to the Almighty, you will
be restored:
If you remove wickedness far from
your tent
²⁴and assign your nuggets to the dust,
your gold of Ophir to the rocks in the
ravines,
²⁵then the Almighty will be your gold,
the choicest silver for you.
²⁶Surely then you will find delight in the
Almighty
and will lift up your face to God.
²⁷You will pray to him, and he will hear
you,
and you will fulfil your vows.
²⁸What you decide on will be done,
and light will shine on your ways.
²⁹When men are brought low and you
say, 'Lift them up!'
then he will save the downcast.
³⁰He will deliver even one who is not
innocent,
who will be delivered through the
cleanness of your hands."

f33 Or / as a countless throng went

Job

23

Then Job replied:

2 "Even today my complaint is bitter;
  his hand*a* is heavy in spite of*b* my
    groaning.
3 If only I knew where to find him;
  if only I could go to his dwelling!
4 I would state my case before him
  and fill my mouth with arguments.
5 I would find out what he would answer
    me,
  and consider what he would say.
6 Would he oppose me with great power?
  No, he would not press charges
    against me.
7 There an upright man could present his
    case before him,
  and I would be delivered for ever
    from my judge.

8 "But if I go to the east, he is not there;
  if I go to the west, I do not find
    him.
9 When he is at work in the north, I do
    not see him;
  when he turns to the south, I catch no
    glimpse of him.
10 But he knows the way that I take;
  when he has tested me, I shall come
    forth as gold.
11 My feet have closely followed his steps;
  I have kept to his way without turning
    aside.
12 I have not departed from the commands
    of his lips;
  I have treasured the words of his
    mouth more than my daily bread.

13 "But he stands alone, and who can
    oppose him?
  He does whatever he pleases.
14 He carries out his decree against me,
  and many such plans he still has in
    store.
15 That is why I am terrified before him;
  when I think of all this, I fear him
16 God has made my heart faint;
  the Almighty has terrified me.

17 Yet I am not silenced by the darkness,
  by the thick darkness that covers my
    face.

24

"Why does the Almighty not set
times for judgment?
  Why must those who know him look
    in vain for such days?
2 Men move boundary stones;
  they pasture flocks they have stolen.
3 They drive away the orphan's donkey
  and take the widow's ox in pledge.
4 They thrust the needy from the path
  and force all the poor of the land into
    hiding.
5 Like wild donkeys in the desert,
  the poor go about their labour of
    foraging food;
  the wasteland provides food for their
    children.
6 They gather fodder in the fields
  and glean in the vineyards of the wicked.
7 Lacking clothes, they spend the night
    naked;
  they have nothing to cover
    themselves in the cold.
8 They are drenched by mountain rains
  and hug the rocks for lack of shelter.
9 The fatherless child is snatched from
    the breast;
  the infant of the poor is seized for a
    debt.
10 Lacking clothes, they go about naked;
  they carry the sheaves, but still go
    hungry.
11 They crush olives among the terraces;*a*
  they tread the winepresses, yet suffer
    thirst.
12 The groans of the dying rise from the
    city,
  and the souls of the wounded cry out
    for help.
  But God charges no-one with
    wrongdoing.

13 "There are those who rebel against the
    light,
  who do not know its ways
  or stay in its paths.
14 When daylight is gone, the murderer
    rises up

---

a2 Septuagint and Syriac; Hebrew / *the hand on me*   *b2* Or *heavy on me in*
a11 Or *olives between the millstones*; the meaning of the Hebrew for this word is uncertain.

and kills the poor and needy;
in the night he steals forth like a thief.
¹⁵The eye of the adulterer watches for
dusk;
he thinks, 'No eye will see me,'
and he keeps his face concealed.
¹⁶In the dark, men break into houses,
but by day they shut themselves in;
they want nothing to do with the light.
¹⁷For all of them, deep darkness is their
morning;ᵇ
they make friends with the terrors of
darkness.ᶜ

¹⁸"Yet they are foam on the surface of
the water;
their portion of the land is cursed,
so that no-one goes to the vineyards.
¹⁹As heat and drought snatch away the
melted snow,
so the graveᵈ snatches away those
who have sinned.
²⁰The womb forgets them,
the worm feasts on them;
evil men are no longer remembered
but are broken like a tree.
²¹They prey on the barren and childless
woman,
and to the widow show no kindness.
²²But God drags away the mighty by his
power;
though they become established, they
have no assurance of life.
²³He may let them rest in a feeling of
security,
but his eyes are on their ways.
²⁴For a little while they are exalted, and
then they are gone;
they are brought low and gathered up
like all others;
they are cut off like ears of corn.

²⁵"If this is not so, who can prove me
false
and reduce my words to nothing?"

Bildad

25 Then Bildad the Shuhite replied:

²"Dominion and awe belong to God;

he establishes order in the heights of
heaven.
³Can his forces be numbered?
Upon whom does his light not rise?
⁴How then can a man be righteous
before God?
How can one born of woman be pure?
⁵If even the moon is not bright
and the stars are not pure in his eyes,
⁶how much less man, who is but a
maggot—
a son of man, who is only a worm!"

Job

26 Then Job replied:

²"How you have helped the powerless!
How you have saved the arm that is
feeble!
³What advice you have offered to one
without wisdom!
And what great insight you have
displayed!
⁴Who has helped you utter these words?
And whose spirit spoke from your
mouth?

⁵"The dead are in deep anguish,
those beneath the waters and all that
live in them.
⁶Deathᵃ is naked before God;
Destructionᵇ lies uncovered.
⁷He spreads out the northern ⌐skies¬
over empty space;
he suspends the earth over nothing.
⁸He wraps up the waters in his clouds,
yet the clouds do not burst under
their weight.
⁹He covers the face of the full moon,
spreading his clouds over it.
¹⁰He marks out the horizon on the face of
the waters
for a boundary between light and
darkness.
¹¹The pillars of the heavens quake,
aghast at his rebuke.
¹²By his power he churned up the sea;
by his wisdom he cut Rahab to
pieces.

ᵇ17 Or *them, their morning is like the shadow of death*   ᶜ17 Or *of the shadow of death*   ᵈ19 Hebrew *Sheol*
ᵃ6 Hebrew *Sheol*   ᵇ6 Hebrew *Abaddon*

¹³By his breath the skies became fair;
his hand pierced the gliding serpent.
¹⁴And these are but the outer fringe of his works;
how faint the whisper we hear of him!
Who then can understand the thunder of his power?''

27 And Job continued his discourse:

²''As surely as God lives, who has denied me justice,
the Almighty, who has made me taste bitterness of soul,
³as long as I have life within me,
the breath of God in my nostrils,
⁴my lips will not speak wickedness,
and my tongue will utter no deceit.
⁵I will never admit you are in the right;
till I die, I will not deny my integrity.
⁶I will maintain my righteousness and never let go of it;
my conscience will not reproach me as long as I live.

⁷''May my enemies be like the wicked,
my adversaries like the unjust!
⁸For what hope has the godless when he is cut off,
when God takes away his life?
⁹Does God listen to his cry
when distress comes upon him?
¹⁰Will he find delight in the Almighty?
Will he call upon God at all times?

¹¹''I will teach you about the power of God;
the ways of the Almighty I will not conceal.
¹²You have all seen this yourselves.
Why then this meaningless talk?

¹³''Here is the fate God allots to the wicked,
the heritage a ruthless man receives from the Almighty:
¹⁴However many his children, their fate is the sword;
his offspring will never have enough to eat.
¹⁵The plague will bury those who survive him,

and their widows will not weep for them.
¹⁶Though he heaps up silver like dust
and clothes like piles of clay,
¹⁷what he lays up the righteous will wear,
and the innocent will divide his silver.
¹⁸The house he builds is like a moth's cocoon,
like a hut made by a watchman.
¹⁹He lies down wealthy, but will do so no more;
when he opens his eyes, all is gone.
²⁰Terrors overtake him like a flood;
a tempest snatches him away in the night.
²¹The east wind carries him off, and he is gone;
it sweeps him out of his place.
²²It hurls itself against him without mercy
as he flees headlong from its power.
²³It claps its hands in derision
and hisses him out of his place.

28 ''There is a mine for silver
and a place where gold is refined.
²Iron is taken from the earth,
and copper is smelted from ore.
³Man puts an end to the darkness;
he searches the farthest recesses
for ore in the blackest darkness.
⁴Far from where people dwell he cuts a shaft,
in places forgotten by the foot of man;
far from men he dangles and sways.
⁵The earth, from which food comes,
is transformed below as by fire;
⁶sapphires[a] come from its rocks,
and its dust contains nuggets of gold.
⁷No bird of prey knows that hidden path,
no falcon's eye has seen it.
⁸Proud beasts do not set foot on it,
and no lion prowls there.
⁹Man's hand assaults the flinty rock
and lays bare the roots of the mountains.
¹⁰He tunnels through the rock;
his eyes see all its treasures.
¹¹He searches[b] the sources of the rivers
and brings hidden things to light.

---

[a]6 Or *lapis lazuli*; also in verse 16   [b]11 Septuagint, Aquila and Vulgate; Hebrew *He dams up*

12"But where can wisdom be found?
　　Where does understanding dwell?
13Man does not comprehend its worth;
　　it cannot be found in the land of the
　　　living.
14The deep says, 'It is not in me';
　　the sea says, 'It is not with me.'
15It cannot be bought with the finest gold,
　　nor can its price be weighed in silver.
16It cannot be bought with the gold of
　　Ophir,
　　with precious onyx or sapphires.
17Neither gold nor crystal can compare
　　with it,
　　nor can it be had for jewels of gold.
18Coral and jasper are not worthy of
　　mention;
　　the price of wisdom is beyond rubies.
19The topaz of Cush cannot compare with
　　it;
　　it cannot be bought with pure gold.

20"Where then does wisdom come from?
　　Where does understanding dwell?
21It is hidden from the eyes of every living
　　thing,
　　concealed even from the birds of the
　　　air.
22Destructionᶜ and Death say,
　　'Only a rumour of it has reached our
　　　ears.'
23God understands the way to it
　　and he alone knows where it dwells,
24for he views the ends of the earth
　　and sees everything under the
　　　heavens.
25When he established the force of the
　　wind
　　and measured out the waters,
26when he made a decree for the rain
　　and a path for the thunderstorm,
27then he looked at wisdom and
　　appraised it;
　　he confirmed it and tested it.
28And he said to man,
　　'The fear of the Lord—that is
　　　wisdom,
　　and to shun evil is understanding.'"

29
Job continued his discourse:
2"How I long for the months gone by,
for the days when God watched over
　　me,
3when his lamp shone upon my head
　　and by his light I walked through
　　　darkness!
4Oh, for the days when I was in my
　　prime,
　　when God's intimate friendship
　　　blessed my house,
5when the Almighty was still with me
　　and my children were around me,
6when my path was drenched with cream
　　and the rock poured out for me
　　　streams of olive oil.

7"When I went to the gate of the city
　　and took my seat in the public square,
8the young men saw me and stepped
　　aside
　　and the old men rose to their feet;
9the chief men refrained from speaking
　　and covered their mouths with their
　　　hands;
10the voices of the nobles were hushed,
　　and their tongues stuck to the roof of
　　　their mouths.
11Whoever heard me spoke well of me,
　　and those who saw me commended
　　　me,
12because I rescued the poor who cried
　　for help,
　　and the fatherless who had none to
　　　assist him.
13The man who was dying blessed me;
　　I made the widow's heart sing.
14I put on righteousness as my clothing;
　　justice was my robe and my turban.
15I was eyes to the blind
　　and feet to the lame.
16I was a father to the needy;
　　I took up the case of the stranger.
17I broke the fangs of the wicked
　　and snatched the victims from their
　　　teeth.

18"I thought, 'I shall die in my own house,
　　my days as numerous as the grains of
　　　sand.
19My roots will reach to the water,
　　and the dew will lie all night on my
　　　branches.

ᶜ22 Hebrew *Abaddon*

²⁰My glory will remain fresh in me,
　the bow ever new in my hand.'

²¹"Men listened to me expectantly,
　waiting in silence for my counsel.
²²After I had spoken, they spoke no
　　more;
　my words fell gently on their ears.
²³They waited for me as for showers
　and drank in my words as the spring
　　rain.
²⁴When I smiled at them, they scarcely
　　believed it;
　the light of my face was precious to
　　them.^a
²⁵I chose the way for them and sat as their
　　chief;
　I dwelt as a king among his troops;
　I was like one who comforts
　　mourners.

30 "But now they mock me,
　　men younger than I,
whose fathers I would have disdained
　to put with my sheep dogs.
²Of what use was the strength of their
　　hands to me,
　since their vigour had gone from
　　them?
³Haggard from want and hunger,
　they roamed^a the parched land
　in desolate wastelands at night.
⁴In the brush they gathered salt herbs,
　and their food^b was the root of the
　　broom tree.
⁵They were banished from their
　　fellow-men,
　shouted at as if they were thieves.
⁶They were forced to live in the dry
　　stream beds,
　among the rocks and in holes in the
　　ground.
⁷They brayed among the bushes
　and huddled in the undergrowth.
⁸A base and nameless brood,
　they were driven out of the land.

⁹"And now their sons mock me in song;
　I have become a byword among
　　them.
¹⁰They detest me and keep their distance;

they do not hesitate to spit in my
　　face.
¹¹Now that God has unstrung my bow
　　and afflicted me,
　they throw off restraint in my
　　presence.
¹²On my right the tribe^c attacks;
　they lay snares for my feet,
　they build their siege ramps against
　　me.
¹³They break up my road;
　they succeed in destroying me—
　without anyone's helping them.^d
¹⁴They advance as through a gaping
　　breach;
　amid the ruins they come rolling in.
¹⁵Terrors overwhelm me;
　my dignity is driven away as by the
　　wind,
　my safety vanishes like a cloud.

¹⁶"And now my life ebbs away;
　days of suffering grip me.
¹⁷Night pierces my bones;
　my gnawing pains never rest.
¹⁸In his great power ˻God˼ becomes like
　　clothing to me;^e
　he binds me like the neck of my
　　garment.
¹⁹He throws me into the mud,
　and I am reduced to dust and ashes.

²⁰"I cry out to you, O God, but you do
　　not answer;
　I stand up, but you merely look at
　　me.
²¹You turn on me ruthlessly;
　with the might of your hand you
　　attack me.
²²You snatch me up and drive me before
　　the wind;
　you toss me about in the storm.
²³I know you will bring me down to
　　death,
　to the place appointed for all the
　　living.

²⁴"Surely no-one lays a hand on a broken
　　man
　when he cries for help in his distress.
²⁵Have I not wept for those in trouble?

---

^a24 The meaning of the Hebrew for this clause is uncertain.
^a3 Or *gnawed*　　　^b4 Or *fuel*　　　^c12 The meaning of the Hebrew for this word is uncertain.
^d13 Or *me. / 'No-one can help him,' ˻they say˼*　　　^e18 Hebrew; Septuagint ˻God˼ *grasps my clothing*

Has not my soul grieved for the
  poor?

²⁶Yet when I hoped for good, evil came;
  when I looked for light, then came
    darkness.

²⁷The churning inside me never stops;
  days of suffering confront me.

²⁸I go about blackened, but not by the
    sun;
  I stand up in the assembly and cry for
    help.

²⁹I have become a brother of jackals,
  a companion of owls.

³⁰My skin grows black and peels;
  my body burns with fever.

³¹My harp is tuned to mourning,
  and my flute to the sound of wailing.

31 "I made a covenant with my eyes
  not to look lustfully at a girl.

²For what is man's lot from God above,
  his heritage from the Almighty on
    high?

³Is it not ruin for the wicked,
  disaster for those who do wrong?

⁴Does he not see my ways
  and count my every step?

⁵"If I have walked in falsehood
  or my foot has hurried after deceit—

⁶let God weigh me in honest scales
  and he will know that I am
    blameless—

⁷if my steps have turned from the path,
  if my heart has been led by my eyes,
  or if my hands have been defiled,

⁸then may others eat what I have sown,
  and may my crops be uprooted.

⁹"If my heart has been enticed by a
    woman,
  or if I have lurked at my neighbour's
    door,

¹⁰then may my wife grind another man's
    grain,
  and may other men sleep with her.

¹¹For that would have been shameful,
  a sin to be judged.

¹²It is a fire that burns to Destruction;ᵃ
  it would have uprooted my harvest.

¹³"If I have denied justice to my
    menservants and maidservants

when they had a grievance against me,

¹⁴what will I do when God confronts me?
  What will I answer when called to
    account?

¹⁵Did not he who made me in the womb
    make them?
  Did not the same one form us both
    within our mothers?

¹⁶"If I have denied the desires of the poor
  or let the eyes of the widow grow
    weary,

¹⁷if I have kept my bread to myself,
  not sharing it with the fatherless—

¹⁸but from my youth I reared him as
    would a father,
  and from my birth I guided the
    widow—

¹⁹if I have seen anyone perishing for lack
    of clothing,
  or a needy man without a garment,

²⁰and his heart did not bless me
  for warming him with the fleece from
    my sheep,

²¹if I have raised my hand against the
    fatherless,
  knowing that I had influence in court,

²²then let my arm fall from the shoulder,
  let it be broken off at the joint.

²³For I dreaded destruction from God,
  and for fear of his splendour I could
    not do such things.

²⁴"If I have put my trust in gold
  or said to pure gold, 'You are my
    security,'

²⁵if I have rejoiced over my great wealth,
  the fortune my hands had gained,

²⁶if I have regarded the sun in its radiance
  or the moon moving in splendour,

²⁷so that my heart was secretly enticed
  and my hand offered them a kiss of
    homage,

²⁸then these also would be sins to be
    judged,
  for I would have been unfaithful to
    God on high.

²⁹"If I have rejoiced at my enemy's
    misfortune
  or gloated over the trouble that came
    to him—

ᵃ12 Hebrew *Abaddon*

³⁰I have not allowed my mouth to sin
   by invoking a curse against his life—
³¹if the men of my household have never
       said,
   'Who has not had his fill of Job's
       meat?'—
³²but no stranger had to spend the night
       in the street,
   for my door was always open to the
       traveller—
³³if I have concealed my sin as men do,^b
   by hiding my guilt in my heart
³⁴because I so feared the crowd
   and so dreaded the contempt of the
       clans
   that I kept silent and would not go
       outside—

³⁵("Oh, that I had someone to hear me!
   I sign now my defence—let the
       Almighty answer me;
   let my accuser put his indictment in
       writing.
³⁶Surely I would wear it on my shoulder,
   I would put it on like a crown.
³⁷I would give him an account of my
       every step;
   like a prince I would approach
       him.)—

³⁸"if my land cries out against me
   and all its furrows are wet with tears,
³⁹if I have devoured its yield without
       payment
   or broken the spirit of its tenants,
⁴⁰then let briers come up instead of wheat
   and weeds instead of barley."

The words of Job are ended.

Elihu

32 So these three men stopped
       answering Job, because he was
righteous in his own eyes. ²But Elihu son
of Barakel the Buzite, of the family of
Ram, became very angry with Job for
justifying himself rather than God. ³He
was also angry with the three friends, because they had found no way to refute Job,
and yet had condemned him.^a ⁴Now Elihu

had waited before speaking to Job because they were older than he. ⁵But when
he saw that the three men had nothing
more to say, his anger was aroused.

⁶So Elihu son of Barakel the Buzite
said:

"I am young in years,
   and you are old;
that is why I was fearful,
   not daring to tell you what I
       know.
⁷I thought, 'Age should speak;
   advanced years should teach
       wisdom.'
⁸But it is the spirit^b in a man,
   the breath of the Almighty, that gives
       him understanding.
⁹It is not only the old^c who are wise,
   not only the aged who understand
       what is right.

¹⁰"Therefore I say: Listen to me;
   I too will tell you what I know.
¹¹I waited while you spoke,
   I listened to your reasoning;
while you were searching for words,
¹²   I gave you my full attention.
But not one of you has proved Job
       wrong;
   none of you has answered his
       arguments.
¹³Do not say, 'We have found wisdom;
   let God refute him, not man.'
¹⁴But Job has not marshalled his words
       against me,
   and I will not answer him with your
       arguments.

¹⁵"They are dismayed and have no more
       to say;
   words have failed them.
¹⁶Must I wait, now that they are silent,
   now that they stand there with no
       reply?
¹⁷I too will have my say;
   I too will tell what I know.
¹⁸For I am full of words,
   and the spirit within me compels me;
¹⁹inside I am like bottled-up wine,
   like new wineskins ready to burst.

---

^b33 Or *as Adam did*   ^a3 Masoretic Text; an ancient Hebrew scribal tradition *Job, and so had condemned God*
^b8 Or *Spirit*; also in verse 18   ^c9 Or *many*; or *great*

^{20}I must speak and find relief;
  I must open my lips and reply.
^{21}I will show partiality to no-one,
  nor will I flatter any man;
^{22}for if I were skilled in flattery,
  my Maker would soon take me away.

33

"But now, Job, listen to my words;
  pay attention to everything I say.
^{2}I am about to open my mouth;
  my words are on the tip of my
    tongue.
^{3}My words come from an upright heart;
  my lips sincerely speak what I know.
^{4}The Spirit of God has made me;
  the breath of the Almighty gives me
    life.
^{5}Answer me then, if you can;
  prepare yourself and confront me.
^{6}I am just like you before God;
  I too have been taken from clay.
^{7}No fear of me should alarm you,
  nor should my hand be heavy upon
    you.

^{8}"But you have said in my hearing—
  I heard the very words—
^{9}'I am pure and without sin;
  I am clean and free from guilt.
^{10}Yet God has found fault with me;
  he considers me his enemy.
^{11}He fastens my feet in shackles;
  he keeps close watch on all my paths.'

^{12}"But I tell you, in this you are not right,
  for God is greater than man.
^{13}Why do you complain to him
  that he answers none of man's
    words?^{a}
^{14}For God does speak—now one way,
    now another—
  though man may not perceive it.
^{15}In a dream, in a vision of the night,
  when deep sleep falls on men
    as they slumber in their beds,
^{16}he may speak in their ears
  and terrify them with warnings,
^{17}to turn man from wrongdoing
  and keep him from pride,
^{18}to preserve his soul from the pit,^{b}
  his life from perishing by the sword.^{c}

^{19}Or a man may be chastened on a bed of
    pain
  with constant distress in his bones,
^{20}so that his very being finds food
    repulsive
  and his soul loathes the choicest meal.
^{21}His flesh wastes away to nothing,
  and his bones, once hidden, now stick
    out.
^{22}His soul draws near to the pit,^{d}
  and his life to the messengers of
    death.^{e}

^{23}"Yet if there is an angel on his side
  as a mediator, one out of a thousand,
    to tell a man what is right for him,
^{24}to be gracious to him and say,
  'Spare him from going down to the
    pit;^{f}
  I have found a ransom for him'—
^{25}then his flesh is renewed like a child's;
  it is restored as in the days of his
    youth.
^{26}He prays to God and finds favour with
    him,
  he sees God's face and shouts for joy;
    he is restored by God to his righteous
      state.
^{27}Then he comes to men and says,
  'I have sinned, and perverted what
    was right,
  but I did not get what I deserved.
^{28}He redeemed my soul from going down
    to the pit,^{g}
  and I shall live to enjoy the light.'

^{29}"God does all these things to a man—
  twice, even three times—
^{30}to turn back his soul from the pit,^{h}
  that the light of life may shine on
    him.

^{31}"Pay attention, Job, and listen to me;
  be silent, and I will speak.
^{32}If you have anything to say, answer me;
  speak up, for I want you to be
    cleared.
^{33}But if not, then listen to me;
  be silent, and I will teach you
    wisdom."

^{a}13 Or *that he does not answer for any of his actions* ^{b}18 Or *preserve him from the grave*
^{c}18 Or *from crossing the River* ^{d}22 Or *He draws near to the grave* ^{e}22 Or *to the dead* ^{f}24 Or *grave*
^{g}28 Or *redeemed me from going down to the grave* ^{h}30 Or *turn him back from the grave*

34

Then Elihu said:

2"Hear my words, you wise men;
　　listen to me, you men of learning.
3For the ear tests words
　　as the tongue tastes food.
4Let us discern for ourselves what is
　　right;
　　let us learn together what is good.

5"Job says, 'I am innocent,
　　but God denies me justice.
6Although I am right,
　　I am considered a liar;
　although I am guiltless,
　　his arrow inflicts an incurable wound.'
7What man is like Job,
　　who drinks scorn like water?
8He keeps company with evildoers;
　　he associates with wicked men.
9For he says, 'It profits a man nothing
　　when he tries to please God.'

10"So listen to me, you men of
　　understanding.
　　Far be it from God to do evil,
　　from the Almighty to do wrong.
11He repays a man for what he has done;
　　he brings upon him what his conduct
　　deserves.
12It is unthinkable that God would do
　　wrong,
　　that the Almighty would pervert
　　justice.
13Who appointed him over the earth?
　　Who put him in charge of the whole
　　world?
14If it were his intention
　　and he withdrew his spirit[a] and
　　breath,
15all mankind would perish together
　　and man would return to the dust.

16"If you have understanding, hear this;
　　listen to what I say.
17Can he who hates justice govern?
　　Will you condemn the just and
　　mighty One?
18Is he not the One who says to kings,
　　'You are worthless,'
　　and to nobles, 'You are wicked,'

19who shows no partiality to princes
　　and does not favour the rich over the
　　poor,
　　for they are all the work of his hands?
20They die in an instant, in the middle of
　　the night;
　　the people are shaken and they pass
　　away;
　　the mighty are removed without
　　human hand.

21"His eyes are on the ways of men;
　　he sees their every step.
22There is no dark place, no deep
　　shadow,
　　where evildoers can hide.
23God has no need to examine men
　　further,
　　that they should come before him for
　　judgment.
24Without enquiry he shatters the mighty
　　and sets up others in their place.
25Because he takes note of their deeds,
　　he overthrows them in the night and
　　they are crushed.
26He punishes them for their wickedness
　　where everyone can see them,
27because they turned from following him
　　and had no regard for any of his
　　ways.
28They caused the cry of the poor to come
　　before him,
　　so that he heard the cry of the needy.
29But if he remains silent, who can
　　condemn him?
　　If he hides his face, who can see
　　him?
　Yet he is over man and nation alike,
30　to keep a godless man from ruling,
　　from laying snares for the people.

31"Suppose a man says to God,
　　'I am guilty but will offend no more.
32Teach me what I cannot see;
　　if I have done wrong, I will not do so
　　again.'
33Should God then reward you on your
　　terms,
　　when you refuse to repent?
　You must decide, not I;
　　so tell me what you know.

---

[a]14 Or Spirit

34"Men of understanding declare,
    wise men who hear me say to me,
35'Job speaks without knowledge;
    his words lack insight.'
36Oh, that Job might be tested to the
    utmost
    for answering like a wicked man!
37To his sin he adds rebellion;
    scornfully he claps his hands among
    us
    and multiplies his words against
    God."

35 Then Elihu said:

2"Do you think this is just?
    You say, 'I shall be cleared by God.'ᵃ
3Yet you ask him, 'What profit is it to
    me,ᵇ
    and what do I gain by not sinning?'

4"I would like to reply to you
    and to your friends with you.
5Look up at the heavens and see;
    gaze at the clouds so high above you.
6If you sin, how does that affect him?
    If your sins are many, what does that
    do to him?
7If you are righteous, what do you give
    to him,
    or what does he receive from your
    hand?
8Your wickedness affects only a man like
    yourself,
    and your righteousness only the sons
    of men.

9"Men cry out under a load of
    oppression;
    they plead for relief from the arm of
    the powerful.
10But no-one says, 'Where is God my
    Maker,
    who gives songs in the night,
11who teaches more to us than toᶜ the
    beasts of the earth
    and makes us wiser thanᵈ the birds of
    the air?'
12He does not answer when men cry out
    because of the arrogance of the
    wicked.

13Indeed, God does not listen to their
    empty plea;
    the Almighty pays no attention to it.
14How much less, then, will he listen
    when you say that you do not see him,
    that your case is before him
    and you must wait for him,
15and further, that his anger never
    punishes
    and he does not take the least notice
    of wickedness.ᵉ
16So Job opens his mouth with empty
    talk;
    without knowledge he multiplies
    words."

36 Elihu continued:

2"Bear with me a little longer and I will
    show you
    that there is more to be said on God's
    behalf.
3I get my knowledge from afar;
    I will ascribe justice to my Maker.
4Be assured that my words are not false;
    one perfect in knowledge is with you.

5"God is mighty, but does not despise
    men;
    he is mighty, and firm in his purpose.
6He does not keep the wicked alive
    but gives the afflicted their rights.
7He does not take his eyes off the
    righteous;
    he enthrones them with kings
    and exalts them for ever.
8But if men are bound in chains,
    held fast by cords of affliction,
9he tells them what they have done—
    that they have sinned arrogantly.
10He makes them listen to correction
    and commands them to repent of
    their evil.
11If they obey and serve him,
    they will spend the rest of their days
    in prosperity
    and their years in contentment.
12But if they do not listen,
    they will perish by the swordᵃ
    and die without knowledge.

ᵃ2 Or My righteousness is more than God's   ᵇ3 Or you   ᶜ11 Or teaches us by   ᵈ11 Or us wise by
ᵉ15 Symmachus, Theodotion and Vulgate; the meaning of the Hebrew for this word is uncertain.
ᵃ12 Or will cross the River

13"The godless in heart harbour
    resentment;
even when he fetters them, they do
    not cry for help.
14They die in their youth,
    among male prostitutes of the
        shrines.
15But those who suffer he delivers in their
        suffering;
    he speaks to them in their affliction.

16"He is wooing you from the jaws of
    distress
    to a spacious place free from
        restriction,
    to the comfort of your table laden
        with choice food.
17But now you are laden with the
        judgment due to the wicked;
    judgment and justice have taken hold
        of you.
18Be careful that no-one entices you by
        riches;
    do not let a large bribe turn you
        aside.
19Would your wealth
    or even all your mighty efforts
    sustain you so you would not be in
        distress?
20Do not long for the night,
    to drag people away from their
        homes.*b*
21Beware of turning to evil,
    which you seem to prefer to
        affliction.

22"God is exalted in his power.
    Who is a teacher like him?
23Who has prescribed his ways for him,
    or said to him, 'You have done
        wrong'?
24Remember to extol his work,
    which men have praised in song.
25All mankind has seen it;
    men gaze on it from afar.
26How great is God—beyond our
        understanding!
    The number of his years is past
        finding out.

27"He draws up the drops of water,
    which distil as rain to the streams;*c*
28the clouds pour down their moisture
    and abundant showers fall on
        mankind.
29Who can understand how he spreads
        out the clouds,
    how he thunders from his pavilion?
30See how he scatters his lightning about
        him,
    bathing the depths of the sea.
31This is the way he governs*d* the nations
    and provides food in abundance.
32He fills his hands with lightning
    and commands it to strike its mark.
33His thunder announces the coming
        storm;
    even the cattle make known its
        approach.*e*

37 "At this my heart pounds
        and leaps from its place.
2Listen! Listen to the roar of his voice,
    to the rumbling that comes from his
        mouth.
3He unleashes his lightning beneath the
        whole heaven
    and sends it to the ends of the earth.
4After that comes the sound of his roar;
    he thunders with his majestic
        voice.
When his voice resounds,
    he holds nothing back.
5God's voice thunders in marvellous
        ways;
    he does great things beyond our
        understanding.
6He says to the snow, 'Fall on the earth,'
    and to the rain shower, 'Be a mighty
        downpour.'
7So that all men he has made may know
        his work,
    he stops every man from his labour.*a*
8The animals take cover;
    they remain in their dens.
9The tempest comes out from its
        chamber,
    the cold from the driving winds.
10The breath of God produces ice,
    and the broad waters become frozen.

---

b20 The meaning of the Hebrew for verses 18–20 is uncertain.   *c27* Or *distil from the mist as rain*
d31 Or *nourishes*   *e33* Or *announces his coming—/ the One zealous against evil*
a7 Or / *he fills all men with fear by his power*

¹¹He loads the clouds with moisture;
   he scatters his lightning through them.
¹²At his direction they swirl around
   over the face of the whole earth
   to do whatever he commands
     them.
¹³He brings the clouds to punish men,
   or to water his earth*b* and show his
     love.

¹⁴"Listen to this, Job;
   stop and consider God's wonders.
¹⁵Do you know how God controls the
     clouds
   and makes his lightning flash?
¹⁶Do you know how the clouds hang
     poised,
   those wonders of him who is perfect
     in knowledge?
¹⁷You who swelter in your clothes
   when the land lies hushed under the
     south wind,
¹⁸can you join him in spreading out the
     skies,
   hard as a mirror of cast bronze?

¹⁹"Tell us what we should say to him;
   we cannot draw up our case because
     of our darkness.
²⁰Should he be told that I want to speak?
   Would any man ask to be swallowed
     up?
²¹Now no-one can look at the sun,
   bright as it is in the skies
   after the wind has swept them clean.
²²Out of the north he comes in golden
     splendour;
   God comes in awesome majesty.
²³The Almighty is beyond our reach and
     exalted in power;
   in his justice and great righteousness,
     he does not oppress.
²⁴Therefore, men revere him,
   for does he not have regard for all the
     wise in heart?"*c*

The LORD Speaks

38 Then the LORD answered Job out
of the storm. He said:

²"Who is this that darkens my counsel

with words without knowledge?
³Brace yourself like a man;
   I will question you,
   and you shall answer me.

⁴"Where were you when I laid the
     earth's foundation?
   Tell me, if you understand.
⁵Who marked off its dimensions? Surely
     you know!
   Who stretched a measuring line
     across it?
⁶On what were its footings set,
   or who laid its cornerstone—
⁷while the morning stars sang together
   and all the angels*a* shouted for
     joy?

⁸"Who shut up the sea behind doors
   when it burst forth from the
     womb,
⁹when I made the clouds its garment
   and wrapped it in thick darkness,
¹⁰when I fixed limits for it
   and set its doors and bars in place,
¹¹when I said, 'This far you may come
     and no farther;
   here is where your proud waves
     halt'?

¹²"Have you ever given orders to the
     morning,
   or shown the dawn its place,
¹³that it might take the earth by the
     edges
   and shake the wicked out of it?
¹⁴The earth takes shape like clay under a
     seal;
   its features stand out like those of a
     garment.
¹⁵The wicked are denied their light,
   and their upraised arm is broken.

¹⁶"Have you journeyed to the springs of
     the sea
   or walked in the recesses of the
     deep?
¹⁷Have the gates of death been shown to
     you?
   Have you seen the gates of the
     shadow of death?*b*

18Have you comprehended the vast
    expanses of the earth?
  Tell me, if you know all this.

19"What is the way to the abode of light?
  And where does darkness reside?
20Can you take them to their places?
  Do you know the paths to their
    dwellings?
21Surely you know, for you were already
    born!
  You have lived so many years!

22"Have you entered the storehouses of
    the snow
  or seen the storehouses of the hail,
23which I reserve for times of trouble,
  for days of war and battle?
24What is the way to the place where the
    lightning is dispersed,
  or the place where the east winds are
    scattered over the earth?
25Who cuts a channel for the torrents of
    rain,
  and a path for the thunderstorm,
26to water a land where no man lives,
  a desert with no-one in it,
27to satisfy a desolate wasteland
  and make it sprout with grass?
28Does the rain have a father?
  Who fathers the drops of dew?
29From whose womb comes the ice?
  Who gives birth to the frost from the
    heavens
30when the waters become hard as stone,
  when the surface of the deep is
    frozen?

31"Can you bind the beautiful^c Pleiades?
  Can you loose the cords of Orion?
32Can you bring forth the constellations
    in their seasons^d
  or lead out the Bear^e with its cubs?
33Do you know the laws of the heavens?
  Can you set up ˌGod's^{f}ˌ dominion
    over the earth?

34"Can you raise your voice to the clouds
  and cover yourself with a flood of
    water?

35Do you send the lightning bolts on their
    way?
  Do they report to you, 'Here we
    are'?
36Who endowed the heart^g with wisdom
  or gave understanding to the mind?^{h}
37Who has the wisdom to count the
    clouds?
  Who can tip over the water jars of the
    heavens
38when the dust becomes hard
  and the clods of earth stick together?

39"Do you hunt the prey for the lioness
  and satisfy the hunger of the lions
40when they crouch in their dens
  or lie in wait in a thicket?
41Who provides food for the raven
  when its young cry out to God
  and wander about for lack of
    food?

39 "Do you know when the mountain
    goats give birth?
  Do you watch when the doe bears her
    fawn?
2Do you count the months till they bear?
  Do you know the time they give
    birth?
3They crouch down and bring forth their
    young;
  their labour pains are ended.
4Their young thrive and grow strong in
    the wilds;
  they leave and do not return.

5"Who let the wild donkey go free?
  Who untied his ropes?
6I gave him the wasteland as his home,
  the salt flats as his habitat.
7He laughs at the commotion in the
    town;
  he does not hear a driver's shout.
8He ranges the hills for his pasture
  and searches for any green thing.

9"Will the wild ox consent to serve you?
  Will he stay by your manger at night?
10Can you hold him to the furrow with a
    harness?

---

^{c}31 Or *the twinkling*; or *the chains of the* ^{d}32 Or *the morning star in its season* ^{e}32 Or *out Leo*
^{f}33 Or *his*; or *their* ^{g}36 The meaning of the Hebrew for this word is uncertain.
^{h}36 The meaning of the Hebrew for this word is uncertain.

Will he till the valleys behind you?
11Will you rely on him for his great
    strength?
Will you leave your heavy work to
    him?
12Can you trust him to bring in your grain
    and gather it to your threshing-floor?

13"The wings of the ostrich flap joyfully,
    but they cannot compare with the
        pinions and feathers of the stork.
14She lays her eggs on the ground
    and lets them warm in the sand,
15unmindful that a foot may crush them,
    that some wild animal may trample
        them.
16She treats her young harshly, as if they
        were not hers;
    she cares not that her labour was in
        vain,
17for God did not endow her with wisdom
    or give her a share of good sense.
18Yet when she spreads her feathers to
        run,
    she laughs at horse and rider.

19"Do you give the horse his strength
    or clothe his neck with a flowing
        mane?
20Do you make him leap like a locust,
    striking terror with his proud
        snorting?
21He paws fiercely, rejoicing in his
        strength,
    and charges into the fray.
22He laughs at fear, afraid of nothing;
    he does not shy away from the sword.
23The quiver rattles against his side,
    along with the flashing spear and
        lance.
24In frenzied excitement he eats up the
        ground;
    he cannot stand still when the
        trumpet sounds.
25At the blast of the trumpet he snorts,
        'Aha!'
    He catches the scent of battle from
        afar,
    the shout of commanders and the
        battle cry.

26"Does the hawk take flight by your
        wisdom
and spread his wings towards the
        south?
27Does the eagle soar at your command
    and build his nest on high?
28He dwells on a cliff and stays there at
        night;
    a rocky crag is his stronghold.
29From there he seeks out his food;
    his eyes detect it from afar.
30His young ones feast on blood,
    and where the slain are, there is he."

40

The LORD said to Job:

2"Will the one who contends with the
        Almighty correct him?
    Let him who accuses God answer
        him!"

3Then Job answered the LORD:

4"I am unworthy—how can I reply to
        you?
    I put my hand over my mouth.
5I spoke once, but I have no answer—
    twice, but I will say no more."

6Then the LORD spoke to Job out of
the storm:

7"Brace yourself like a man;
    I will question you,
    and you shall answer me.

8"Would you discredit my justice?
    Would you condemn me to justify
        yourself?
9Do you have an arm like God's,
    and can your voice thunder like his?
10Then adorn yourself with glory and
        splendour,
    and clothe yourself in honour and
        majesty.
11Unleash the fury of your wrath,
    look at every proud man and bring
        him low,
12look at every proud man and humble
        him,
    crush the wicked where they stand.
13Bury them all in the dust together;
    shroud their faces in the grave.
14Then I myself will admit to you
    that your own right hand can save
        you.

¹⁵"Look at the behemoth,ᵃ
    which I made along with you
    and which feeds on grass like
        an ox.
¹⁶What strength he has in his loins,
    what power in the muscles of his
        belly!
¹⁷His tailᵇ sways like a cedar;
    the sinews of his thighs are close-knit.
¹⁸His bones are tubes of bronze,
    his limbs like rods of iron.
¹⁹He ranks first among the works of God,
    yet his Maker can approach him with
        his sword.
²⁰The hills bring him their produce,
    and all the wild animals play nearby.
²¹Under the lotus plant he lies,
    hidden among the reeds in the marsh.
²²The lotuses conceal him in their
        shadow;
    the poplars by the stream surround
        him.
²³When the river rages, he is not alarmed;
    he is secure, though the Jordan
        should surge against his mouth.
²⁴Can anyone capture him by the eyes,ᶜ
    or trap him and pierce his nose?

41 "Can you pull in the leviathanᵃ
    with a fishhook
    or tie down his tongue with a rope?
²Can you put a cord through his nose
    or pierce his jaw with a hook?
³Will he keep begging you for mercy?
    Will he speak to you with gentle
        words?
⁴Will he make an agreement with you
    for you to take him as your slave for
        life?
⁵Can you make a pet of him like a bird
    or put him on a leash for your girls?
⁶Will traders barter for him?
    Will they divide him up among the
        merchants?
⁷Can you fill his hide with harpoons
    or his head with fishing spears?
⁸If you lay a hand on him,
    you will remember the struggle and
        never do it again!
⁹Any hope of subduing him is false;

the mere sight of him is
    overpowering.
¹⁰No-one is fierce enough to rouse him.
    Who then is able to stand against me?
¹¹Who has a claim against me that I must
    pay?
    Everything under heaven belongs to
        me.

¹²"I will not fail to speak of his limbs,
    his strength and his graceful form.
¹³Who can strip off his outer coat?
    Who would approach him with a
        bridle?
¹⁴Who dares open the doors of his mouth,
    ringed about with his fearsome
        teeth?
¹⁵His back hasᵇ rows of shields
    tightly sealed together;
¹⁶each is so close to the next
    that no air can pass between.
¹⁷They are joined fast to one another;
    they cling together and cannot be
        parted.
¹⁸His snorting throws out flashes of light;
    his eyes are like the rays of dawn.
¹⁹Firebrands stream from his mouth;
    sparks of fire shoot out.
²⁰Smoke pours from his nostrils
    as from a boiling pot over a fire of
        reeds.
²¹His breath sets coals ablaze,
    and flames dart from his mouth.
²²Strength resides in his neck;
    dismay goes before him.
²³The folds of his flesh are tightly joined;
    they are firm and immovable.
²⁴His chest is hard as rock,
    hard as a lower millstone.
²⁵When he rises up, the mighty are
        terrified;
    they retreat before his thrashing.
²⁶The sword that reaches him has no
        effect,
    nor does the spear or the dart or the
        javelin.
²⁷Iron he treats like straw
    and bronze like rotten wood.
²⁸Arrows do not make him flee;
    slingstones are like chaff to him.

ᵃ15 Possibly the hippopotamus or the elephant   ᵇ17 Possibly trunk   ᶜ24 Or by a water hole
ᵃ1 Possibly the crocodile   ᵇ15 Or His pride is his

²⁹A club seems to him but a piece of straw;
  he laughs at the rattling of the lance.
³⁰His undersides are jagged potsherds,
  leaving a trail in the mud like a
    threshing-sledge.
³¹He makes the depths churn like a
    boiling cauldron
  and stirs up the sea like a pot of
    ointment.
³²Behind him he leaves a glistening wake;
  one would think the deep had white
    hair.
³³Nothing on earth is his equal—
  a creature without fear.
³⁴He looks down on all that are haughty;
  he is king over all that are proud."

Job

42

Then Job replied to the LORD:

²"I know that you can do all things;
  no plan of yours can be thwarted.
³⌊You asked,⌋ 'Who is this that obscures
  my counsel without knowledge?'
  Surely I spoke of things I did not
    understand,
  things too wonderful for me to know.

⁴⌊"You said,⌋ 'Listen now, and I will
    speak;
  I will question you,
  and you shall answer me.'
⁵My ears had heard of you
  but now my eyes have seen you.
⁶Therefore I despise myself
  and repent in dust and ashes."

Epilogue

⁷After the LORD had said these things to
Job, he said to Eliphaz the Temanite, "I
am angry with you and your two friends,
because you have not spoken of me what is
right, as my servant Job has. ⁸So now take
seven bulls and seven rams and go to my
servant Job and sacrifice a burnt offering
for yourselves. My servant Job will pray
for you, and I will accept his prayer and
not deal with you according to your folly.
You have not spoken of me what is right,
as my servant Job has." ⁹So Eliphaz the
Temanite, Bildad the Shuhite and Zophar
the Naamathite did what the LORD told
them; and the LORD accepted Job's
prayer.

¹⁰After Job had prayed for his friends,
the LORD made him prosperous again and
gave him twice as much as he had before.
¹¹All his brothers and sisters and everyone
who had known him before came and ate
with him in his house. They comforted
and consoled him over all the trouble the
LORD had brought upon him, and each
one gave him a piece of silver^a and a gold
ring.

¹²The LORD blessed the latter part of
Job's life more than the first. He had
fourteen thousand sheep, six thousand
camels, a thousand yoke of oxen and a
thousand donkeys. ¹³And he also had
seven sons and three daughters. ¹⁴The first
daughter he named Jemimah, the second
Keziah and the third Keren-Happuch.
¹⁵Nowhere in all the land were there found
women as beautiful as Job's daughters,
and their father granted them an inheritance along with their brothers.

¹⁶After this, Job lived a hundred and
forty years; he saw his children and their
children to the fourth generation. ¹⁷And
so he died, old and full of years.

---

^a11 Hebrew *him a kesitah*; a kesitah was a unit of money of unknown weight and value.

Psalms

BOOK I

Psalms 1–41

Psalm 1

¹Blessed is the man
　who does not walk in the counsel of
　　the wicked
　or stand in the way of sinners
　or sit in the seat of mockers.
²But his delight is in the law of the LORD,
　and on his law he meditates day and
　　night.
³He is like a tree planted by streams of
　　water,
　which yields its fruit in season
　and whose leaf does not wither.
　Whatever he does prospers.

⁴Not so the wicked!
　They are like chaff
　that the wind blows away.
⁵Therefore the wicked will not stand in
　　the judgment,
　nor sinners in the assembly of the
　　righteous.

⁶For the LORD watches over the way of
　　the righteous,
　but the way of the wicked will perish.

Psalm 2

¹Why do the nations conspire*ᵃ*
　and the peoples plot in vain?

²The kings of the earth take their stand
　and the rulers gather together against
　　the LORD
　and against his Anointed One.*ᵇ*
³"Let us break their chains," they say,
　"and throw off their fetters."

⁴The One enthroned in heaven laughs;
　the Lord scoffs at them.
⁵Then he rebukes them in his anger
　and terrifies them in his wrath,
　　saying,
⁶"I have installed my King*ᶜ*
　on Zion, my holy hill."

⁷I will proclaim the decree of the LORD:

　He said to me, "You are my Son;*ᵈ*
　today I have become your Father.*ᵉ*
⁸Ask of me,
　and I will make the nations your
　　inheritance,
　the ends of the earth your possession.
⁹You will rule them with an iron
　　sceptre;*ᶠ*
　you will dash them to pieces like
　　pottery."

¹⁰Therefore, you kings, be wise;
　be warned, you rulers of the earth.
¹¹Serve the LORD with fear
　and rejoice with trembling.
¹²Kiss the Son, lest he be angry
　and you be destroyed in your way,
　for his wrath can flare up in a moment.
　Blessed are all who take refuge in
　　him.

ᵃ1 Hebrew; Septuagint *rage*　　*ᵇ2* Or *anointed one*　　*ᶜ6* Or *king*　　*ᵈ7* Or *son*; also in verse 12
ᵉ7 Or *have begotten you*　　*ᶠ9* Or *will break them with a rod of iron*

Psalm 3

A psalm of David. When he fled from his son
Absalom.

[1]O LORD, how many are my foes!
  How many rise up against me!
[2]Many are saying of me,
  "God will not deliver him."   *Selah*[a]

[3]But you are a shield around me, O
    LORD;
  you bestow glory on me and lift[b] up
    my head.
[4]To the LORD I cry aloud,
  and he answers me from his holy hill.
                  Selah

[5]I lie down and sleep;
  I wake again, because the LORD
    sustains me.
[6]I will not fear the tens of thousands
  drawn up against me on every side.

[7]Arise, O LORD!
  Deliver me, O my God!
  Strike all my enemies on the jaw;
  break the teeth of the wicked.

[8]From the LORD comes deliverance.
  May your blessing be on your people.
                  Selah

Psalm 4

For the director of music. With stringed
instruments. A psalm of David.

[1]Answer me when I call to you,
  O my righteous God.
  Give me relief from my distress;
  be merciful to me and hear my
    prayer.

[2]How long, O men, will you turn my
  glory into shame?[a]
  How long will you love delusions and
    seek false gods?[b]   *Selah*
[3]Know that the LORD has set apart the
  godly for himself;

the LORD will hear when I call to him.

[4]In your anger do not sin;
  when you are on your beds,
  search your hearts and be silent.
                  Selah
[5]Offer right sacrifices
  and trust in the LORD.

[6]Many are asking, "Who can show us
    any good?"
  Let the light of your face shine upon
    us, O LORD.
[7]You have filled my heart with greater
    joy
  than when their grain and new wine
    abound.
[8]I will lie down and sleep in peace,
  for you alone, O LORD,
  make me dwell in safety.

Psalm 5

For the director of music. For flutes. A psalm
of David.

[1]Give ear to my words, O LORD,
  consider my sighing.
[2]Listen to my cry for help,
  my King and my God,
  for to you I pray.
[3]In the morning, O LORD, you hear my
    voice;
  in the morning I lay my requests
    before you
  and wait in expectation.

[4]You are not a God who takes pleasure
    in evil;
  with you the wicked cannot dwell.
[5]The arrogant cannot stand in your
    presence;
  you hate all who do wrong.
[6]You destroy those who tell lies;
  bloodthirsty and deceitful men
  the LORD abhors.

[7]But I, by your great mercy,
  will come into your house;
  in reverence will I bow down

---

[a]2 A word of uncertain meaning, occurring frequently in the Psalms; possibly a musical term
[b]3 Or LORD, / my Glorious One, who lifts   [a]2 Or you dishonour my Glorious One   [b]2 Or seek lies

towards your holy temple.
8Lead me, O Lord, in your
    righteousness
  because of my enemies—
  make straight your way before me.

9Not a word from their mouth can be
    trusted;
  their heart is filled with destruction.
  Their throat is an open grave;
  with their tongue they speak deceit.
10Declare them guilty, O God!
  Let their intrigues be their downfall.
  Banish them for their many sins,
  for they have rebelled against you.

11But let all who take refuge in you be
    glad;
  let them ever sing for joy.
  Spread your protection over them,
  that those who love your name may
    rejoice in you.
12For surely, O Lord, you bless the
    righteous;
  you surround them with your favour
  as with a shield.

Psalm 6

For the director of music. With stringed
instruments. According to *sheminith.*[a] A
psalm of David.

1O Lord, do not rebuke me in your
    anger
  or discipline me in your wrath.
2Be merciful to me, Lord, for I am faint;
  O Lord, heal me, for my bones are in
    agony.
3My soul is in anguish.
  How long, O Lord, how long?

4Turn, O Lord, and deliver me;
  save me because of your unfailing
    love.
5No-one remembers you when he is
    dead.
  Who praises you from his grave?[b]

6I am worn out from groaning;

all night long I flood my bed with
    weeping
  and drench my couch with tears.
7My eyes grow weak with sorrow;
  they fail because of all my foes.

8Away from me, all you who do evil,
  for the Lord has heard my weeping.
9The Lord has heard my cry for mercy;
  the Lord accepts my prayer.
10All my enemies will be ashamed and
    dismayed;
  they will turn back in sudden
    disgrace.

Psalm 7

A *shiggaion*[a] of David, which he sang to the
Lord concerning Cush, a Benjamite.

1O Lord my God, I take refuge in you;
  save and deliver me from all who
    pursue me,
2or they will tear me like a lion
  and rip me to pieces with no-one to
    rescue me.

3O Lord my God, if I have done this
  and there is guilt on my hands—
4if I have done evil to him who is at
    peace with me
  or without cause have robbed my
    foe—
5then let my enemy pursue and overtake
    me;
  let him trample my life to the ground
  and make me sleep in the dust.   *Selah*

6Arise, O Lord, in your anger;
  rise up against the rage of my
    enemies.
  Awake, my God; decree justice.
7Let the assembled peoples gather round
    you.
  Rule over them from on high;
8 let the Lord judge the peoples.
  Judge me, O Lord, according to my
    righteousness,
  according to my integrity, O Most
    High.
9O righteous God,

---

*a*Title: Probably a musical term   *b*5 Hebrew *Sheol*   *a*Title: Probably a literary or musical term

who searches minds and hearts,
bring to an end the violence of the
    wicked
and make the righteous secure.

[10]My shield[b] is God Most High,
    who saves the upright in heart.
[11]God is a righteous judge,
    a God who expresses his wrath every
    day.
[12]If he does not relent,
    he[c] will sharpen his sword;
    he will bend and string his bow.
[13]He has prepared his deadly weapons;
    he makes ready his flaming arrows.

[14]He who is pregnant with evil
    and conceives trouble gives birth to
    disillusionment.
[15]He who digs a hole and scoops it out
    falls into the pit he has made.
[16]The trouble he causes recoils on himself;
    his violence comes down on his own
    head.

[17]I will give thanks to the LORD because of
    his righteousness
and will sing praise to the name of the
    LORD Most High.

Psalm 8

For the director of music. According to
gittith.[a] A psalm of David.

[1]O LORD, our Lord,
    how majestic is your name in all the
    earth!

You have set your glory
    above the heavens.
[2]From the lips of children and infants
    you have ordained praise[b]
because of your enemies,
    to silence the foe and the avenger.

[3]When I consider your heavens,
    the work of your fingers,

the moon and the stars,
    which you have set in place,
[4]what is man that you are mindful of him,
    the son of man that you care for him?
[5]You made him a little lower than the
    heavenly beings[c]
and crowned him with glory and
    honour.

[6]You made him ruler over the works of
    your hands;
    you put everything under his feet:
[7]all flocks and herds,
    and the beasts of the field,
[8]the birds of the air,
    and the fish of the sea,
    all that swim the paths of the seas.

[9]O LORD, our Lord,
    how majestic is your name in all the
    earth!

Psalm 9[a]

For the director of music. To ⌊the tune of⌋
"The Death of the Son". A psalm of David.

[1]I will praise you, O LORD, with all my
    heart;
    I will tell of all your wonders.
[2]I will be glad and rejoice in you;
    I will sing praise to your name, O
    Most High.

[3]My enemies turn back;
    they stumble and perish before you.
[4]For you have upheld my right and my
    cause;
    you have sat on your throne, judging
    righteously.
[5]You have rebuked the nations and
    destroyed the wicked;
    you have blotted out their name for
    ever and ever.
[6]Endless ruin has overtaken the enemy,
    you have uprooted their cities;
    even the memory of them has
    perished.

---

*b*10 Or *sovereign*   *c*12 Or *If a man does not repent, / God*
*a*Title: Probably a musical term   *b*2 Or *strength*   *c*5 Or *than God*
*a*Psalms 9 and 10 may have been originally a single acrostic poem, the stanzas of which begin with the successive letters of
the Hebrew alphabet. In the Septuagint they constitute one psalm.

7The LORD reigns for ever;
   he has established his throne for
      judgment.
8He will judge the world in
   righteousness;
   he will govern the peoples with
      justice.
9The LORD is a refuge for the oppressed,
   a stronghold in times of trouble.
10Those who know your name will trust in
   you,
   for you, LORD, have never forsaken
   those who seek you.

11Sing praises to the LORD, enthroned in
   Zion;
   proclaim among the nations what he
   has done.
12For he who avenges blood remembers;
   he does not ignore the cry of the
   afflicted.

13O LORD, see how my enemies persecute
   me!
   Have mercy and lift me up from the
   gates of death,
14that I may declare your praises
   in the gates of the Daughter of Zion
   and there rejoice in your salvation.
15The nations have fallen into the pit they
   have dug;
   their feet are caught in the net they
   have hidden.
16The LORD is known by his justice;
   the wicked are ensnared by the work
   of their hands.   *Higgaion.b Selah*

17The wicked return to the grave,c
   all the nations that forget God.
18But the needy will not always be
   forgotten,
   nor the hope of the afflicted ever
   perish.

19Arise, O LORD, let not man triumph;
   let the nations be judged in your
   presence.
20Strike them with terror, O LORD;
   let the nations know they are but
   men.   *Selah*

Psalm 10a

1Why, O LORD, do you stand far off?
   Why do you hide yourself in times of
   trouble?

2In his arrogance the wicked man hunts
   down the weak,
   who are caught in the schemes he
   devises.
3He boasts of the cravings of his heart;
   he blesses the greedy and reviles the
   LORD.
4In his pride the wicked does not seek
   him;
   in all his thoughts there is no room
   for God.
5His ways are always prosperous;
   he is haughty and your laws are far
   from him;
   he sneers at all his enemies.
6He says to himself, "Nothing will shake
   me;
   I'll always be happy and never have
   trouble."
7His mouth is full of curses and lies and
   threats;
   trouble and evil are under his tongue.
8He lies in wait near the villages;
   from ambush he murders the
   innocent,
   watching in secret for his victims.
9He lies in wait like a lion in cover;
   he lies in wait to catch the helpless;
   he catches the helpless and drags
   them off in his net.
10His victims are crushed, they collapse;
   they fall under his strength.
11He says to himself, "God has forgotten;
   he covers his face and never sees."

12Arise, LORD! Lift up your hand, O God.
   Do not forget the helpless.
13Why does the wicked man revile God?
   Why does he say to himself,
   "He won't call me to account"?
14But you, O God, do see trouble and
   grief;
   you consider it to take it in hand.

---

b16 Or *Meditation*; possibly a musical notation   c17 Hebrew *Sheol*
aPsalms 9 and 10 may have been originally a single acrostic poem, the stanzas of which begin with the successive letters of
the Hebrew alphabet. In the Septuagint they constitute one psalm.

The victim commits himself to you;
    you are the helper of the fatherless.
15Break the arm of the wicked and evil
    man;
    call him to account for his wickedness
    that would not be found out.

16The LORD is King for ever and ever;
    the nations will perish from his land.
17You hear, O LORD, the desire of the
    afflicted;
    you encourage them, and you listen
    to their cry,
18defending the fatherless and the
    oppressed,
    in order that man, who is of the
    earth, may terrify no more.

Psalm 11

For the director of music. Of David.

1In the LORD I take refuge.
    How then can you say to me:
    "Flee like a bird to your mountain.
2For look, the wicked bend their bows;
    they set their arrows against the
    strings
to shoot from the shadows
    at the upright in heart.
3When the foundations are being
    destroyed,
    what can the righteous do?"[a]

4The LORD is in his holy temple;
    the LORD is on his heavenly throne.
He observes the sons of men;
    his eyes examine them.
5The LORD examines the righteous,
    but the wicked[b] and those who love
    violence
    his soul hates.
6On the wicked he will rain
    fiery coals and burning sulphur;
    a scorching wind will be their
    lot.

7For the LORD is righteous,
    he loves justice;

upright men will see his
    face.

Psalm 12

For the director of music. According to
sheminith.[a] A psalm of David.

1Help, LORD, for the godly are no more;
    the faithful have vanished from
    among men.
2Everyone lies to his neighbour;
    their flattering lips speak with
    deception.

3May the LORD cut off all flattering lips
    and every boastful tongue
4that says, "We will triumph with our
    tongues;
    we own our lips[b]—who is our
    master?"

5"Because of the oppression of the weak
    and the groaning of the needy,
I will now arise," says the LORD.
    "I will protect them from those who
    malign them."
6And the words of the LORD are flawless,
    like silver refined in a furnace of clay,
    purified seven times.

7O LORD, you will keep us safe
    and protect us from such people for
    ever.
8The wicked freely strut about
    when what is vile is honoured among
    men.

Psalm 13

For the director of music. A psalm of David.

1How long, O LORD? Will you forget me
    for ever?
    How long will you hide your face
    from me?
2How long must I wrestle with my
    thoughts

---

*a*3 Or *what is the Righteous One doing*   *b*5 Or *The LORD, the Righteous One, examines the wicked,/*
*a*Title: Probably a musical term   *b*4 Or */ our lips are our ploughshares*

and every day have sorrow in my
  heart?
How long will my enemy triumph
  over me?

³Look on me and answer, O LORD my
  God.
Give light to my eyes, or I will sleep
  in death;
⁴my enemy will say, "I have overcome
  him,"
and my foes will rejoice when I
  fall.

⁵But I trust in your unfailing love;
  my heart rejoices in your salvation.
⁶I will sing to the LORD,
  for he has been good to me.

Psalm 14

For the director of music. Of David.

¹The fool^a says in his heart,
  "There is no God."
They are corrupt, their deeds are vile;
  there is no-one who does good.

²The LORD looks down from heaven
  on the sons of men
to see if there are any who understand,
  any who seek God.
³All have turned aside,
  they have together become corrupt;
there is no-one who does good,
  not even one.

⁴Will evildoers never learn—
  those who devour my people as men
    eat bread
and who do not call on the LORD?
⁵There they are, overwhelmed with
    dread,
  for God is present in the company of
    the righteous.
⁶You evildoers frustrate the plans of the
    poor,
  but the LORD is their refuge.

⁷Oh, that salvation for Israel would
  come out of Zion!
When the LORD restores the fortunes
  of his people,
let Jacob rejoice and Israel be glad!

Psalm 15

A psalm of David.

¹LORD, who may dwell in your
  sanctuary?
Who may live on your holy hill?

²He whose walk is blameless
  and who does what is righteous,
who speaks the truth from his
    heart
³ and has no slander on his tongue,
who does his neighbour no wrong
  and casts no slur on his fellow-man,
⁴who despises a vile man
  but honours those who fear the
    LORD,
who keeps his oath
  even when it hurts,
⁵who lends his money without usury
  and does not accept a bribe against
    the innocent.

He who does these things
  will never be shaken.

Psalm 16

A *miktam*^a of David.

¹Keep me safe, O God,
  for in you I take refuge.

²I said to the LORD, "You are my Lord;
  apart from you I have no good
    thing."
³As for the saints who are in the land,
  they are the glorious ones in whom is
    all my delight.^b
⁴The sorrows of those will increase
  who run after other gods.

---

^a1 The Hebrew words rendered *fool* in Psalms denote one who is morally deficient.
^aTitle: Probably a literary or musical term
^b3 Or *As for the pagan priests who are in the land / and the nobles in whom all delight, I said:*

I will not pour out their libations of
    blood
  or take up their names on my lips.

5Lord, you have assigned me my portion
    and my cup;
  you have made my lot secure.
6The boundary lines have fallen for me
    in pleasant places;
  surely I have a delightful inheritance.

7I will praise the Lord, who counsels
    me;
  even at night my heart instructs
    me.
8I have set the Lord always before me.
  Because he is at my right hand,
  I shall not be shaken.

9Therefore my heart is glad and my
    tongue rejoices;
  my body also will rest secure,
10because you will not abandon me to the
    grave,*c*
  nor will you let your Holy One*d* see
    decay.
11You have made known*e* to me the path
    of life;
  you will fill me with joy in your
    presence,
  with eternal pleasures at your right
    hand.

Psalm 17

A prayer of David.

1Hear, O Lord, my righteous plea;
  listen to my cry.
Give ear to my prayer—
  it does not rise from deceitful lips.
2May my vindication come from you;
  may your eyes see what is right.

3Though you probe my heart and
    examine me at night,
  though you test me, you will find
    nothing;
  I have resolved that my mouth will
    not sin.

4As for the deeds of men—
  by the word of your lips
I have kept myself
  from the ways of the violent.
5My steps have held to your paths;
  my feet have not slipped.

6I call on you, O God, for you will
    answer me;
  give ear to me and hear my prayer.
7Show the wonder of your great love,
  you who save by your right hand
  those who take refuge in you from
    their foes.
8Keep me as the apple of your eye;
  hide me in the shadow of your
    wings
9from the wicked who assail me,
  from my mortal enemies who
    surround me.

10They close up their callous hearts,
  and their mouths speak with
    arrogance.
11They have tracked me down, they now
    surround me,
  with eyes alert, to throw me to the
    ground.
12They are like a lion hungry for prey,
  like a great lion crouching in cover.

13Rise up, O Lord, confront them, bring
    them down;
  rescue me from the wicked by your
    sword.
14O Lord, by your hand save me from
    such men,
  from men of this world whose reward
    is in this life.

You still the hunger of those you
    cherish;
  their sons have plenty,
  and they store up wealth for their
    children.
15And I—in righteousness I shall see your
    face;
  when I awake, I shall be satisfied with
    seeing your likeness.

---

c10 Hebrew *Sheol*   *d10* Or *your faithful one*   *e11* Or *You will make known*

Psalm 18

For the director of music. Of David the
servant of the LORD. He sang to the LORD the
words of this song when the LORD delivered
him from the hand of all his enemies and from
the hand of Saul. He said:

¹I love you, O LORD, my strength.

²The LORD is my rock, my fortress and
    my deliverer;
  my God is my rock, in whom I take
    refuge.
  He is my shield and the horn^a of my
    salvation, my stronghold.
³I call to the LORD, who is worthy of
    praise,
  and I am saved from my enemies.

⁴The cords of death entangled me;
  the torrents of destruction
    overwhelmed me.
⁵The cords of the grave^b coiled around
    me;
  the snares of death confronted me.
⁶In my distress I called to the LORD;
  I cried to my God for help.
 From his temple he heard my voice;
  my cry came before him, into his
    ears.

⁷The earth trembled and quaked,
  and the foundations of the mountains
    shook;
  they trembled because he was angry.
⁸Smoke rose from his nostrils;
  consuming fire came from his mouth,
  burning coals blazed out of it.
⁹He parted the heavens and came down;
  dark clouds were under his feet.
¹⁰He mounted the cherubim and flew;
  he soared on the wings of the wind.
¹¹He made darkness his covering, his
    canopy around him—
  the dark rain clouds of the sky.
¹²Out of the brightness of his presence
    clouds advanced,
  with hailstones and bolts of lightning.
¹³The LORD thundered from heaven;

the voice of the Most High
    resounded.^{c}
¹⁴He shot his arrows and scattered ˻the
    enemies˼,
  great bolts of lightning and routed
    them.
¹⁵The valleys of the sea were exposed
  and the foundations of the earth laid
    bare
 at your rebuke, O LORD,
  at the blast of breath from your
    nostrils.

¹⁶He reached down from on high and
    took hold of me;
  he drew me out of deep waters.
¹⁷He rescued me from my powerful
    enemy,
  from my foes, who were too strong
    for me.
¹⁸They confronted me in the day of my
    disaster,
  but the LORD was my support.
¹⁹He brought me out into a spacious
    place;
  he rescued me because he delighted
    in me.

²⁰The LORD has dealt with me according
    to my righteousness;
  according to the cleanness of my
    hands he has rewarded me.
²¹For I have kept the ways of the LORD;
  I have not done evil by turning from
    my God.
²²All his laws are before me;
  I have not turned away from his
    decrees.
²³I have been blameless before him
  and have kept myself from sin.
²⁴The LORD has rewarded me according
    to my righteousness,
  according to the cleanness of my
    hands in his sight.

²⁵To the faithful you show yourself
    faithful,
  to the blameless you show yourself
    blameless,

^{a}2 *Horn* here symbolises strength. ^{b}5 Hebrew *Sheol*
^{c}13 Some Hebrew manuscripts and Septuagint (see also 2 Samuel 22:14); most Hebrew manuscripts *resounded,/ amid
hailstones and bolts of lightning*

26to the pure you show yourself pure
   but to the crooked you show yourself
      shrewd.
27You save the humble
   but bring low those whose eyes are
      haughty.
28You, O LORD, keep my lamp burning;
   my God turns my darkness into light.
29With your help I can advance against a
      troop;[d]
   with my God I can scale a wall.

30As for God, his way is perfect;
   the word of the LORD is flawless.
He is a shield
   for all who take refuge in him.
31For who is God besides the LORD?
   And who is the Rock except our
      God?
32It is God who arms me with strength
   and makes my way perfect.
33He makes my feet like the feet of a
      deer;
   he enables me to stand on the heights.
34He trains my hands for battle;
   my arms can bend a bow of bronze.
35You give me your shield of victory,
   and your right hand sustains me;
   you stoop down to make me great.
36You broaden the path beneath me,
   so that my ankles do not turn over.

37I pursued my enemies and overtook
      them;
   I did not turn back till they were
      destroyed.
38I crushed them so that they could not
      rise;
   they fell beneath my feet.
39You armed me with strength for battle;
   you made my adversaries bow at my
      feet.
40You made my enemies turn their backs
      in flight,
   and I destroyed my foes.
41They cried for help, but there was
      no-one to save them—
   to the LORD, but he did not answer.
42I beat them as fine as dust borne on the
      wind;

I poured them out like mud in the
      streets.

43You have delivered me from the attacks
      of the people;
   you have made me the head of
      nations;
   people I did not know are subject to
      me.
44As soon as they hear me, they obey me;
   foreigners cringe before me.
45They all lose heart;
   they come trembling from their
      strongholds.

46The LORD lives! Praise be to my Rock!
   Exalted be God my Saviour!
47He is the God who avenges me,
   who subdues nations under me,
48   who saves me from my enemies.
You exalted me above my foes;
   from violent men you rescued me.
49Therefore I will praise you among the
      nations, O LORD;
   I will sing praises to your name.
50He gives his king great victories;
   he shows unfailing kindness to his
      anointed,
   to David and his descendants for
      ever.

Psalm 19

For the director of music. A psalm of David.

1The heavens declare the glory of God;
   the skies proclaim the work of his
      hands.
2Day after day they pour forth speech;
   night after night they display
      knowledge.
3There is no speech or language
   where their voice is not heard.[a]
4Their voice[b] goes out into all the earth,
   their words to the ends of the world.

In the heavens he has pitched a tent for
      the sun,
5   which is like a bridegroom coming
      forth from his pavilion,

---

d29 Or can run through a barricade   *a3 Or They have no speech, there are no words; / no sound is heard from them*
b4 Septuagint, Jerome and Syriac; Hebrew line

like a champion rejoicing to run his
course.
⁶It rises at one end of the heavens
and makes its circuit to the other;
nothing is hidden from its heat.

⁷The law of the LORD is perfect,
reviving the soul.
The statutes of the LORD are
trustworthy,
making wise the simple.
⁸The precepts of the LORD are right,
giving joy to the heart.
The commands of the LORD are radiant,
giving light to the eyes.
⁹The fear of the LORD is pure,
enduring for ever.
The ordinances of the LORD are sure
and altogether righteous.
¹⁰They are more precious than gold,
than much pure gold;
they are sweeter than honey,
than honey from the comb.
¹¹By them is your servant warned;
in keeping them there is great
reward.

¹²Who can discern his errors?
Forgive my hidden faults.
¹³Keep your servant also from wilful sins;
may they not rule over me.
Then will I be blameless,
innocent of great transgression.

¹⁴May the words of my mouth and the
meditation of my heart
be pleasing in your sight,
O LORD, my Rock and my Redeemer.

Psalm 20

For the director of music. A psalm of David.

¹May the LORD answer you when you are
in distress;
may the name of the God of Jacob
protect you.
²May he send you help from the
sanctuary
and grant you support from Zion.

³May he remember all your sacrifices
and accept your burnt offerings.
Selah
⁴May he give you the desire of your
heart
and make all your plans succeed.
⁵We will shout for joy when you are
victorious
and will lift up our banners in the
name of our God.
May the LORD grant all your requests.

⁶Now I know that the LORD saves his
anointed;
he answers him from his holy heaven
with the saving power of his right
hand.
⁷Some trust in chariots and some in
horses,
but we trust in the name of the LORD
our God.
⁸They are brought to their knees and
fall,
but we rise up and stand firm.

⁹O LORD, save the king!
Answer*ᵃ* us when we call!

Psalm 21

For the director of music. A psalm of David.

¹O LORD, the king rejoices in your
strength.
How great is his joy in the victories
you give!
²You have granted him the desire of his
heart
and have not withheld the request of
his lips.   *Selah*
³You welcomed him with rich blessings
and placed a crown of pure gold on
his head.
⁴He asked you for life, and you gave it to
him—
length of days, for ever and ever.
⁵Through the victories you gave, his
glory is great;
you have bestowed on him splendour
and majesty.

ᵃ9 Or *save! | O King, answer*

⁶Surely you have granted him eternal
      blessings
   and made him glad with the joy of
      your presence.
⁷For the king trusts in the LORD;
   through the unfailing love of the
      Most High
   he will not be shaken.

⁸Your hand will lay hold on all your
      enemies;
   your right hand will seize your foes.
⁹At the time of your appearing
   you will make them like a fiery
      furnace.
   In his wrath the LORD will swallow them
      up,
   and his fire will consume them.
¹⁰You will destroy their descendants from
      the earth,
   their posterity from mankind.
¹¹Though they plot evil against you
   and devise wicked schemes, they
      cannot succeed;
¹²for you will make them turn their backs
   when you aim at them with drawn
      bow.

¹³Be exalted, O LORD, in your strength;
   we will sing and praise your might.

Psalm 22

For the director of music. To ⌐the tune of⌐
"The Doe of the Morning". A psalm of
David.

¹My God, my God, why have you
      forsaken me?
   Why are you so far from saving me,
      so far from the words of my groaning?
²O my God, I cry out by day, but you do
      not answer,
   by night, and am not silent.

³Yet you are enthroned as the Holy
      One;
   you are the praise of Israel.ᵃ
⁴In you our fathers put their trust;
   they trusted and you delivered them.

⁵They cried to you and were saved;
   in you they trusted and were not
      disappointed.

⁶But I am a worm and not a man,
   scorned by men and despised by the
      people.
⁷All who see me mock me;
   they hurl insults, shaking their heads:
⁸"He trusts in the LORD;
   let the LORD rescue him.
   Let him deliver him,
   since he delights in him."

⁹Yet you brought me out of the womb;
   you made me trust in you
   even at my mother's breast.
¹⁰From birth I was cast upon you;
   from my mother's womb you have
      been my God.
¹¹Do not be far from me,
   for trouble is near
   and there is no-one to help.

¹²Many bulls surround me;
   strong bulls of Bashan encircle me.
¹³Roaring lions tearing their prey
   open their mouths wide against me.
¹⁴I am poured out like water,
   and all my bones are out of joint.
   My heart has turned to wax;
   it has melted away within me.
¹⁵My strength is dried up like a potsherd,
   and my tongue sticks to the roof of
      my mouth;
   you lay meᵇ in the dust of death.
¹⁶Dogs have surrounded me;
   a band of evil men has encircled me,
   they have piercedᶜ my hands and my
      feet.
¹⁷I can count all my bones;
   people stare and gloat over me.
¹⁸They divide my garments among them
   and cast lots for my clothing.

¹⁹But you, O LORD, be not far off;
   O my Strength, come quickly to help
      me.
²⁰Deliver my life from the sword,
   my precious life from the power of
      the dogs.

ᵃ3 Or Yet you are holy, / enthroned on the praises of Israel   ᵇ15 Or / I am laid
ᶜ16 Some Hebrew manuscripts, Septuagint and Syriac; most Hebrew manuscripts / like the lion,

[21]Rescue me from the mouth of the lions;
saved me from the horns of the wild
oxen.

[22]I will declare your name to my brothers;
in the congregation I will praise you.
[23]You who fear the LORD, praise him!
All you descendants of Jacob, honour
him!
Revere him, all you descendants of
Israel!
[24]For he has not despised or disdained
the suffering of the afflicted one;
he has not hidden his face from him
but has listened to his cry for help.

[25]From you comes the theme of my praise
in the great assembly;
before those who fear youe will I fulfil
my vows.
[26]The poor will eat and be satisfied;
they who seek the LORD will praise
him—
may your hearts live for ever!
[27]All the ends of the earth
will remember and turn to the LORD,
and all the families of the nations
will bow down before him,
[28]for dominion belongs to the LORD
and he rules over the nations.

[29]All the rich of the earth will feast and
worship;
all who go down to the dust will kneel
before him—
those who cannot keep themselves
alive.
[30]Posterity will serve him;
future generations will be told about
the Lord.
[31]They will proclaim his righteousness
to a people yet unborn—
for he has done it.

Psalm 23

A psalm of David.

[1]The LORD is my shepherd, I shall not be
in want.

[2] He makes me lie down in green
pastures,
he leads me beside quiet waters,
[3] he restores my soul.
He guides me in paths of righteousness
for his name's sake.
[4]Even though I walk
through the valley of the shadow of
death,a
I will fear no evil,
for you are with me;
your rod and your staff,
they comfort me.

[5]You prepare a table before me
in the presence of my enemies.
You anoint my head with oil;
my cup overflows.
[6]Surely goodness and love will follow me
all the days of my life,
and I will dwell in the house of the LORD
for ever.

Psalm 24

Of David. A psalm.

[1]The earth is the LORD's, and everything
in it,
the world, and all who live in it;
[2]for he founded it upon the seas
and established it upon the waters.

[3]Who may ascend the hill of the LORD?
Who may stand in his holy place?
[4]He who has clean hands and a pure
heart,
who does not lift up his soul to an idol
or swear by what is false.a
[5]He will receive blessing from the LORD
and vindication from God his
Saviour.
[6]Such is the generation of those who
seek him,
who seek your face, O God of
Jacob.b   Selah

[7]Lift up your heads, O you gates;
be lifted up, you ancient doors,
that the King of glory may come
in.

---

d21 Or / you have heard   e25 Hebrew him   a4 Or through the darkest valley   a4 Or swear falsely
b6 Two Hebrew manuscripts and Syriac (see also Septuagint); most Hebrew manuscripts face, Jacob

⁸Who is this King of glory?
  The LORD strong and mighty,
  the LORD mighty in battle.
⁹Lift up your heads, O you gates;
  lift them up, you ancient doors,
  that the King of glory may come in.
¹⁰Who is he, this King of glory?
  The LORD Almighty—
  he is the King of glory.   *Selah*

Psalm 25ᵃ

Of David.

¹To you, O LORD, I lift up my soul;
² in you I trust, O my God.
Do not let me be put to shame,
  nor let my enemies triumph over me.
³No-one whose hope is in you
  will ever be put to shame,
but they will be put to shame
  who are treacherous without excuse.

⁴Show me your ways, O LORD,
  teach me your paths;
⁵guide me in your truth and teach me,
  for you are God my Saviour,
  and my hope is in you all day long.
⁶Remember, O LORD, your great mercy
    and love,
  for they are from of old.
⁷Remember not the sins of my youth
    and my rebellious ways;
according to your love remember me,
  for you are good, O LORD.

⁸Good and upright is the LORD;
  therefore he instructs sinners in his
    ways.
⁹He guides the humble in what is right
  and teaches them his way.
¹⁰All the ways of the LORD are loving and
    faithful
  for those who keep the demands of
    his covenant.
¹¹For the sake of your name, O LORD,
  forgive my iniquity, though it is
    great.
¹²Who, then, is the man that fears the
    LORD?

He will instruct him in the way
  chosen for him.
¹³He will spend his days in prosperity,
  and his descendants will inherit the
    land.
¹⁴The LORD confides in those who fear
    him;
  he makes his covenant known to
    them.
¹⁵My eyes are ever on the LORD,
  for only he will release my feet from
    the snare.

¹⁶Turn to me and be gracious to me,
  for I am lonely and afflicted.
¹⁷The troubles of my heart have
    multiplied;
  free me from my anguish.
¹⁸Look upon my affliction and my distress
  and take away all my sins.
¹⁹See how my enemies have increased
  and how fiercely they hate me!
²⁰Guard my life and rescue me;
  let me not be put to shame,
  for I take refuge in you.
²¹May integrity and uprightness protect
    me,
  because my hope is in you.

²²Redeem Israel, O God,
  from all their troubles!

Psalm 26

Of David.

¹Vindicate me, O LORD,
  for I have led a blameless life;
I have trusted in the LORD
  without wavering.
²Test me, O LORD, and try me,
  examine my heart and my mind;
³for your love is ever before me,
  and I walk continually in your truth.
⁴I do not sit with deceitful men,
  nor do I consort with hypocrites;
⁵I abhor the assembly of evildoers
  and refuse to sit with the wicked.
⁶I wash my hands in innocence,
  and go about your altar, O LORD,

ᵃThis psalm is an acrostic poem, the verses of which begin with the successive letters of the Hebrew alphabet.

7proclaiming aloud your praise
  and telling of all your wonderful
    deeds.
8I love the house where you live, O
  LORD,
    the place where your glory dwells.

9Do not take away my soul along with
    sinners,
  my life with bloodthirsty men,
10in whose hands are wicked schemes,
  whose right hands are full of bribes.
11But I lead a blameless life;
  redeem me and be merciful to me.

12My feet stand on level ground;
  in the great assembly I will praise the
    LORD.

Psalm 27

Of David.

1The LORD is my light and my
    salvation—
  whom shall I fear?
The LORD is the stronghold of my life—
  of whom shall I be afraid?
2When evil men advance against me
  to devour my flesh,[a]
when my enemies and my foes attack me,
  they will stumble and fall.
3Though an army besiege me,
  my heart will not fear;
though war break out against me,
  even then will I be confident.

4One thing I ask of the LORD,
  this is what I seek:
that I may dwell in the house of the
    LORD
  all the days of my life,
to gaze upon the beauty of the LORD
  and to seek him in his temple.
5For in the day of trouble
  he will keep me safe in his dwelling;
he will hide me in the shelter of his
    tabernacle
  and set me high upon a rock.
6Then my head will be exalted

above the enemies who surround me;
at his tabernacle will I sacrifice with
    shouts of joy;
  I will sing and make music to the
    LORD.

7Hear my voice when I call, O LORD;
  be merciful to me and answer me.
8My heart says of you, "Seek his[b] face!"
  Your face, LORD, I will seek.
9Do not hide your face from me,
  do not turn your servant away in
    anger;
  you have been my helper.
Do not reject me or forsake me,
  O God my Saviour.
10Though my father and mother forsake
    me,
  the LORD will receive me.
11Teach me your way, O LORD;
  lead me in a straight path
  because of my oppressors.
12Do not hand me over to the desire of
    my foes,
  for false witnesses rise up against me,
  breathing out violence.

13I am still confident of this:
  I will see the goodness of the LORD
  in the land of the living.
14Wait for the LORD;
  be strong and take heart
  and wait for the LORD.

Psalm 28

Of David.

1To you I call, O LORD my Rock;
  do not turn a deaf ear to me.
For if you remain silent,
  I shall be like those who have gone
    down to the pit.
2Hear my cry for mercy
  as I call to you for help,
as I lift up my hands
  towards your Most Holy Place.

3Do not drag me away with the wicked,
  with those who do evil,

---

[a]2 Or *to slander me*   [b]8 Or *To you, O my heart, he has said, "Seek my*

who speak cordially with their
   neighbours
  but harbour malice in their hearts.
4Repay them for their deeds
  and for their evil work;
repay them for what their hands have
   done
  and bring back upon them what they
   deserve.
5Since they show no regard for the works
  of the LORD
  and what his hands have done,
he will tear them down
  and never build them up again.

6Praise be to the LORD,
  for he has heard my cry for mercy.
7The LORD is my strength and my shield;
  my heart trusts in him, and I am helped.
My heart leaps for joy
  and I will give thanks to him in song.

8The LORD is the strength of his people,
  a fortress of salvation for his anointed one.
9Save your people and bless your
   inheritance;
  be their shepherd and carry them for ever.

Psalm 29

A psalm of David.

1Ascribe to the LORD, O mighty ones,
  ascribe to the LORD glory and
   strength.
2Ascribe to the LORD the glory due to his
   name;
  worship the LORD in the splendour of
  his*a* holiness.

3The voice of the LORD is over the
   waters;
  the God of glory thunders,
  the LORD thunders over the mighty
   waters.
4The voice of the LORD is powerful;
  the voice of the LORD is majestic.
5The voice of the LORD breaks the
   cedars;

the LORD breaks in pieces the cedars
  of Lebanon.
6He makes Lebanon skip like a calf,
  Sirion*b* like a young wild ox.
7The voice of the LORD strikes
  with flashes of lightning.
8The voice of the LORD shakes the
   desert;
  the LORD shakes the Desert of
   Kadesh.
9The voice of the LORD twists the oaks*c*
  and strips the forests bare.
And in his temple all cry, "Glory!"

10The LORD sits*d* enthroned over the
   flood;
  the LORD is enthroned as King for
   ever.
11The LORD gives strength to his people;
  the LORD blesses his people with
   peace.

Psalm 30

A psalm. A song. For the dedication of the
temple.*a* Of David.

1I will exalt you, O LORD,
  for you lifted me out of the depths
  and did not let my enemies gloat over
   me.
2O LORD my God, I called to you for
   help
  and you healed me.
3O LORD, you brought me up from the
   grave;*b*
  you spared me from going down into
   the pit.

4Sing to the LORD, you saints of his;
  praise his holy name.
5For his anger lasts only a moment,
  but his favour lasts a lifetime;
weeping may remain for a night,
  but rejoicing comes in the morning.

6When I felt secure, I said,
  "I shall never be shaken."
7O LORD, when you favoured me,

---

a2 Or LORD with the splendour of
d10 Or sat   *aTitle: Or palace*
b6 That is, Mount Hermon
b3 Hebrew Sheol
c9 Or LORD makes the deer give birth

you made my mountain[c] stand firm;
but when you hid your face,
  I was dismayed.

[8]To you, O L ORD, I called;
  to the Lord I cried for mercy:
[9]"What gain is there in my destruction,[d]
  in my going down into the pit?
Will the dust praise you?
  Will it proclaim your faithfulness?
[10]Hear, O L ORD, and be merciful to me;
  O L ORD, be my help."

[11]You turned my wailing into dancing;
  you removed my sackcloth and
    clothed me with joy,
[12]that my heart may sing to you and not
    be silent.
  O L ORD my God, I will give you
    thanks for ever.

Psalm 31

For the director of music. A psalm of David.

[1]In you, O L ORD, I have taken refuge;
  let me never be put to shame;
  deliver me in your righteousness.
[2]Turn your ear to me,
  come quickly to my rescue;
 be my rock of refuge,
  a strong fortress to save me.
[3]Since you are my rock and my fortress,
  for the sake of your name lead and
    guide me.
[4]Free me from the trap that is set for me,
  for you are my refuge.
[5]Into your hands I commit my spirit;
  redeem me, O L ORD, the God of
    truth.

[6]I hate those who cling to worthless
    idols;
  I trust in the L ORD.
[7]I will be glad and rejoice in your love,
  for you saw my affliction
  and knew the anguish of my soul.
[8]You have not handed me over to the
    enemy

but have set my feet in a spacious
    place.

[9]Be merciful to me, O L ORD, for I am in
    distress;
  my eyes grow weak with sorrow,
  my soul and my body with grief.
[10]My life is consumed by anguish
  and my years by groaning;
 my strength fails because of my
    affliction,[a]
  and my bones grow weak.
[11]Because of all my enemies,
  I am the utter contempt of my
    neighbours;
 I am a dread to my friends—
  those who see me on the street flee
    from me.
[12]I am forgotten by them as though I were
    dead;
  I have become like broken pottery.
[13]For I hear the slander of many;
  there is terror on every side;
 they conspire against me
  and plot to take my life.

[14]But I trust in you, O L ORD;
  I say, "You are my God."
[15]My times are in your hands;
  deliver me from my enemies
  and from those who pursue me.
[16]Let your face shine on your servant;
  save me in your unfailing love.
[17]Let me not be put to shame, O L ORD,
  for I have cried out to you;
 but let the wicked be put to shame
  and lie silent in the grave.[b]
[18]Let their lying lips be silenced,
  for with pride and contempt
  they speak arrogantly against the
    righteous.

[19]How great is your goodness,
  which you have stored up for those
    who fear you,
 which you bestow in the sight of men
  on those who take refuge in you.
[20]In the shelter of your presence you hide
    them
  from the intrigues of men;

---

c7 Or *hill country*   *d9* Or *there if I am silenced*   *a10* Or *guilt*   *b17* Hebrew *Sheol*

in your dwelling you keep them safe
    from accusing tongues.

21Praise be to the LORD,
    for he showed his wonderful love to
        me
    when I was in a besieged city.
22In my alarm I said,
    "I am cut off from your sight!"
    Yet you heard my cry for mercy
        when I called to you for help.

23Love the LORD, all his saints!
    The LORD preserves the faithful,
        but the proud he pays back in full.
24Be strong and take heart,
    all you who hope in the LORD.

Psalm 32

Of David. A *maskil.*[a]

1Blessed is he
    whose transgressions are forgiven,
    whose sins are covered.
2Blessed is the man
    whose sin the LORD does not count
        against him
    and in whose spirit is no deceit.

3When I kept silent,
    my bones wasted away
    through my groaning all day long.
4For day and night
    your hand was heavy upon me;
    my strength was sapped
        as in the heat of summer.   *Selah*
5Then I acknowledged my sin to you
    and did not cover up my iniquity.
    I said, "I will confess
        my transgressions to the LORD"—
    and you forgave
        the guilt of my sin.   *Selah*

6Therefore let everyone who is godly
        pray to you
    while you may be found;
    surely when the mighty waters rise,
        they will not reach him.
7You are my hiding-place;

you will protect me from trouble
    and surround me with songs of
        deliverance.   *Selah*

8I will instruct you and teach you in the
        way you should go;
    I will counsel you and watch over
        you.
9Do not be like the horse or the mule,
    which have no understanding
    but must be controlled by bit and bridle
        or they will not come to you.
10Many are the woes of the wicked,
    but the LORD's unfailing love
        surrounds the man who trusts in him.

11Rejoice in the LORD and be glad, you
        righteous;
    sing, all you who are upright in
        heart!

Psalm 33

1Sing joyfully to the LORD, you
        righteous;
    it is fitting for the upright to praise
        him.
2Praise the LORD with the harp;
    make music to him on the
        ten-stringed lyre.
3Sing to him a new song;
    play skilfully, and shout for joy.

4For the word of the LORD is right and
        true;
    he is faithful in all he does.
5The LORD loves righteousness and
        justice;
    the earth is full of his unfailing love.

6By the word of the LORD were the
        heavens made,
    their starry host by the breath of his
        mouth.
7He gathers the waters of the sea into
        jars;[a]
    he puts the deep into storehouses.
8Let all the earth fear the LORD;
    let all the people of the world revere
        him.

---

*a*Title: Probably a literary or musical term   *a*7 Or *sea as into a heap*

⁹For he spoke, and it came to be;
  he commanded, and it stood firm.
¹⁰The LORD foils the plans of the nations;
  he thwarts the purposes of the
    peoples.
¹¹But the plans of the LORD stand firm for
    ever,
  the purposes of his heart through all
    generations.

¹²Blessed is the nation whose God is the
    LORD,
  the people he chose for his
    inheritance.
¹³From heaven the LORD looks down
  and sees all mankind;
¹⁴from his dwelling-place he watches
  all who live on earth—
¹⁵he who forms the hearts of all,
  who considers everything they do.
¹⁶No king is saved by the size of his army;
  no warrior escapes by his great
    strength.
¹⁷A horse is a vain hope for deliverance;
  despite all its great strength it cannot
    save.
¹⁸But the eyes of the LORD are on those
    who fear him,
  on those whose hope is in his
    unfailing love,
¹⁹to deliver them from death
  and keep them alive in famine.

²⁰We wait in hope for the LORD;
  he is our help and our shield.
²¹In him our hearts rejoice,
  for we trust in his holy name.
²²May your unfailing love rest upon us, O
    LORD,
  even as we put our hope in you.

Psalm 34[a]

Of David. When he pretended to be insane
before Abimelech, who drove him away, and
he left.

¹I will extol the LORD at all times;
  his praise will always be on my lips.
²My soul will boast in the LORD;
  let the afflicted hear and rejoice.

³Glorify the LORD with me:
  let us exalt his name together.

⁴I sought the LORD, and he answered me;
  he delivered me from all my fears.
⁵Those who look to him are radiant;
  their faces are never covered with
    shame.
⁶This poor man called, and the LORD
    heard him;
  he saved him out of all his troubles.
⁷The angel of the LORD encamps around
    those who fear him,
  and he delivers them.

⁸Taste and see that the LORD is good;
  blessed is the man who takes refuge
    in him.
⁹Fear the LORD, you his saints,
  for those who fear him lack nothing.
¹⁰The lions may grow weak and hungry,
  but those who seek the LORD lack no
    good thing.

¹¹Come, my children, listen to me;
  I will teach you the fear of the LORD.
¹²Whoever of you loves life
  and desires to see many good days,
¹³keep your tongue from evil
  and your lips from speaking lies.
¹⁴Turn from evil and do good;
  seek peace and pursue it.

¹⁵The eyes of the LORD are on the
    righteous
  and his ears are attentive to their cry;
¹⁶the face of the LORD is against those
    who do evil,
  to cut off the memory of them from
    the earth.

¹⁷The righteous cry out, and the LORD
    hears them;
  he delivers them from all their
    troubles.
¹⁸The LORD is close to the broken-hearted
  and saves those who are crushed in
    spirit.

¹⁹A righteous man may have many
    troubles,

---

[a]This psalm is an acrostic poem, the verses of which begin with the successive letters of the Hebrew alphabet.

but the LORD delivers him from them
  all;
²⁰he protects all his bones,
  not one of them will be broken.

²¹Evil will slay the wicked;
  the foes of the righteous will be
    condemned.
²²The LORD redeems his servants;
  no-one will be condemned who takes
    refuge in him.

Psalm 35

Of David.

¹Contend, O LORD, with those who
    contend with me;
  fight against those who fight against
    me.
²Take up shield and buckler;
  arise and come to my aid.
³Brandish spear and javelin[a]
  against those who pursue me.
  Say to my soul,
    "I am your salvation."

⁴May those who seek my life
  be disgraced and put to shame;
  may those who plot my ruin
  be turned back in dismay.
⁵May they be like chaff before the wind,
  with the angel of the LORD driving
    them away;
⁶may their path be dark and slippery,
  with the angel of the LORD pursuing
    them.
⁷Since they hid their net for me without
    cause
  and without cause dug a pit for me,
⁸may ruin overtake them by surprise—
  may the net they hid entangle them,
  may they fall into the pit, to their
    ruin.
⁹Then my soul will rejoice in the LORD
  and delight in his salvation.
¹⁰My whole being will exclaim,
  "Who is like you, O LORD?
  You rescue the poor from those too
    strong for them,

the poor and needy from those who
    rob them."
¹¹Ruthless witnesses come forward;
  they question me on things I know
    nothing about.
¹²They repay me evil for good
  and leave my soul forlorn.
¹³Yet when they were ill, I put on
    sackcloth
  and humbled myself with fasting.
  When my prayers returned to me
    unanswered,
¹⁴ I went about mourning
    as though for my friend or brother.
  I bowed my head in grief
    as though weeping for my mother.
¹⁵But when I stumbled, they gathered in
    glee;
  attackers gathered against me when I
    was unaware.
  They slandered me without ceasing.
¹⁶Like the ungodly they maliciously
    mocked;[b]
  they gnashed their teeth at me.
¹⁷O Lord, how long will you look on?
  Rescue my life from their ravages,
  my precious life from these lions.
¹⁸I will give you thanks in the great
    assembly;
  among throngs of people I will praise
    you.

¹⁹Let not those gloat over me
  who are my enemies without cause;
  let not those who hate me without
    reason
  maliciously wink the eye.
²⁰They do not speak peaceably,
  but devise false accusations
  against those who live quietly in the
    land.
²¹They gape at me and say, "Aha! Aha!
  With our own eyes we have seen it."

²²O LORD, you have seen this; be not
    silent.
  Do not be far from me, O Lord.
²³Awake, and rise to my defence!
  Contend for me, my God and
    Lord.

---

a3 Or *and block the way*   *b16* Septuagint; Hebrew may mean *ungodly circle of mockers.*

24Vindicate me in your righteousness, O
  LORD my God;
  do not let them gloat over me.
25Do not let them think, "Aha, just what
  we wanted!"
  or say, "We have swallowed him
  up."

26May all who gloat over my distress
  be put to shame and confusion;
  may all who exalt themselves over me
  be clothed with shame and disgrace.
27May those who delight in my
  vindication
  shout for joy and gladness;
  may they always say, "The LORD be
  exalted,
  who delights in the well-being of his
  servant."
28My tongue will speak of your
  righteousness
  and of your praises all day long.

Psalm 36

For the director of music. Of David the
  servant of the LORD.

1An oracle is within my heart
  concerning the sinfulness of the
  wicked:*a*
 There is no fear of God
  before his eyes.
2For in his own eyes he flatters himself
  too much to detect or hate his sin.
3The words of his mouth are wicked and
  deceitful;
  he has ceased to be wise and to do
  good.
4Even on his bed he plots evil;
  he commits himself to a sinful course
  and does not reject what is wrong.

5Your love, O LORD, reaches to the
  heavens,
  your faithfulness to the skies.
6Your righteousness is like the mighty
  mountains,
  your justice like the great deep.

O LORD, you preserve both man and
  beast.
7 How priceless is your unfailing love!
 Both high and low among men
  find*b* refuge in the shadow of your
  wings.
8They feast in the abundance of your
  house;
  you give them drink from your river
  of delights.
9For with you is the fountain of life;
  in your light we see light.

10Continue your love to those who know
  you,
  your righteousness to the upright in
  heart.
11May the foot of the proud not come
  against me,
  nor the hand of the wicked drive me
  away.
12See how the evildoers lie fallen—
  thrown down, not able to rise!

Psalm 37*a*

Of David.

1Do not fret because of evil men
  or be envious of those who do wrong;
2for like the grass they will soon wither,
  like green plants they will soon die
  away.

3Trust in the LORD and do good;
  dwell in the land and enjoy safe
  pasture.
4Delight yourself in the LORD
  and he will give you the desires of
  your heart.

5Commit your way to the LORD;
  trust in him and he will do this:
6He will make your righteousness shine
  like the dawn,
  the justice of your cause like the
  noonday sun.

7Be still before the LORD and wait

---

a1 Or *heart: / Sin proceeds from the wicked.*
b7 Or *love, O God! / Men find;* or *love! / Both heavenly beings and men / find*
*a*This psalm is an acrostic poem, the stanzas of which begin with the successive letters of the Hebrew alphabet.

patiently for him;
do not fret when men succeed in their
    ways,
when they carry out their wicked
    schemes.

8Refrain from anger and turn from
    wrath;
do not fret—it leads only to evil.
9For evil men will be cut off,
    but those who hope in the LORD will
        inherit the land.

10A little while, and the wicked will be no
    more;
    though you look for them, they will
        not be found.
11But the meek will inherit the land
    and enjoy great peace.

12The wicked plot against the righteous
    and gnash their teeth at them;
13but the Lord laughs at the wicked,
    for he knows their day is coming.

14The wicked draw the sword
    and bend the bow
to bring down the poor and needy,
    to slay those whose ways are
        upright.
15But their swords will pierce their own
    hearts,
    and their bows will be broken.

16Better the little that the righteous have
    than the wealth of many wicked;
17for the power of the wicked will be
    broken,
    but the LORD upholds the righteous.

18The days of the blameless are known to
    the LORD,
    and their inheritance will endure for
        ever.
19In times of disaster they will not wither;
    in days of famine they will enjoy
        plenty.

20But the wicked will perish:
    The LORD's enemies will be like the
        beauty of the fields,
    they will vanish—vanish like smoke.

21The wicked borrow and do not repay,
    but the righteous give generously;
22those the LORD blesses will inherit the
    land,
    but those he curses will be cut off.

23If the LORD delights in a man's way,
    he makes his steps firm;
24though he stumble, he will not fall,
    for the LORD upholds him with his
        hand.

25I was young and now I am old,
    yet I have never seen the righteous
        forsaken
    or their children begging bread.
26They are always generous and lend
    freely;
    their children will be blessed.

27Turn from evil and do good;
    then you will dwell in the land for
        ever.
28For the LORD loves the just
    and will not forsake his faithful ones.

They will be protected for ever,
    but the offspring of the wicked will be
        cut off;
29the righteous will inherit the land
    and dwell in it for ever.

30The mouth of the righteous man utters
    wisdom,
    and his tongue speaks what is
        just.
31The law of his God is in his heart;
    his feet do not slip.

32The wicked lie in wait for the righteous,
    seeking their very lives;
33but the LORD will not leave them in their
    power
    or let them be condemned when
        brought to trial.

34Wait for the LORD
    and keep his way.
He will exalt you to inherit the land;
    when the wicked are cut off, you will
        see it.

35I have seen a wicked and ruthless man

flourishing like a green tree in its
native soil,
[36]but he soon passed away and was no
more;
though I looked for him, he could not
be found.

[37]Consider the blameless, observe the
upright;
there is a future[b] for the man of peace.
[38]But all sinners will be destroyed;
the future[c] of the wicked will be cut off.

[39]The salvation of the righteous comes
from the LORD;
he is their stronghold in time of trouble.
[40]The LORD helps them and delivers them;
he delivers them from the wicked and
saves them,
because they take refuge in him.

Psalm 38

A psalm of David. A petition.

[1]O LORD, do not rebuke me in your
anger
or discipline me in your wrath.
[2]For your arrows have pierced me,
and your hand has come down upon
me.
[3]Because of your wrath there is no
health in my body;
my bones have no soundness because
of my sin.
[4]My guilt has overwhelmed me
like a burden too heavy to bear.

[5]My wounds fester and are loathsome
because of my sinful folly.
[6]I am bowed down and brought very
low;
all day long I go about mourning.
[7]My back is filled with searing pain;
there is no health in my body.
[8]I am feeble and utterly crushed;
I groan in anguish of heart.

[9]All my longings lie open before you, O
Lord:

my sighing is not hidden from you.
[10]My heart pounds, my strength fails me;
even the light has gone from my eyes.
[11]My friends and companions avoid me
because of my wounds;
my neighbours stay far away.
[12]Those who seek my life set their traps,
those who would harm me talk of my
ruin;
all day long they plot deception.

[13]I am like a deaf man, who cannot hear,
like a mute, who cannot open his
mouth;
[14]I have become like a man who does not
hear,
whose mouth can offer no reply.
[15]I wait for you, O LORD;
you will answer, O Lord my God.
[16]For I said, "Do not let them gloat
or exalt themselves over me
when my foot slips."

[17]For I am about to fall,
and my pain is ever with me.
[18]I confess my iniquity;
I am troubled by my sin.
[19]Many are those who are my vigorous
enemies;
those who hate me without reason
are numerous.
[20]Those who repay my good with evil
slander me when I pursue what is
good.

[21]O LORD, do not forsake me;
be not far from me, O my God.
[22]Come quickly to help me,
O Lord my Saviour.

Psalm 39

For the director of music. For Jeduthun. A
psalm of David.

[1]I said, "I will watch my ways
and keep my tongue from sin;
I will put a muzzle on my mouth

---

b37 Or *there will be posterity*   *c38* Or *posterity*

as long as the wicked are in my
presence."
2But when I was silent and still,
not even saying anything good,
my anguish increased.
3My heart grew hot within me,
and as I meditated, the fire burned;
then I spoke with my tongue:

4"Show me, O LORD, my life's end
and the number of my days;
let me know how fleeting is my life.
5You have made my days a mere
handbreadth;
the span of my years is as nothing
before you.
Each man's life is but a breath. *Selah*
6Man is a mere phantom as he goes to
and fro:
He bustles about, but only in vain;
he heaps up wealth, not knowing who
will get it.

7"But now, Lord, what do I look for?
My hope is in you.
8Save me from all my transgressions;
do not make me the scorn of fools.
9I was silent; I would not open my
mouth,
for you are the one who has done
this.
10Remove your scourge from me;
I am overcome by the blow of your
hand.
11You rebuke and discipline men for their
sin;
you consume their wealth like a
moth—
each man is but a breath. *Selah*

12"Hear my prayer, O LORD,
listen to my cry for help;
be not deaf to my weeping.
For I dwell with you as an alien,
a stranger, as all my fathers were.
13Look away from me, that I may rejoice
again
before I depart and am no more."

Psalm 40

For the director of music. Of David. A psalm.

1I waited patiently for the LORD;
he turned to me and heard my cry.
2He lifted me out of the slimy pit,
out of the mud and mire;
he set my feet on a rock
and gave me a firm place to stand.
3He put a new song in my mouth,
a hymn of praise to our God.
Many will see and fear
and put their trust in the LORD.

4Blessed is the man
who makes the LORD his trust,
who does not look to the proud,
to those who turn aside to false gods.*a*
5Many, O LORD my God,
are the wonders you have done.
The things you planned for us
no-one can recount to you;
were I to speak and tell of them,
they would be too many to declare.

6Sacrifice and offering you did not
desire,
but my ears you have pierced;*b,c*
burnt offerings and sin offerings
you did not require.
7Then I said, "Here I am, I have come—
it is written about me in the scroll.*d*
8I desire to do your will, O my God;
your law is within my heart."

9I proclaim righteousness in the great
assembly;
I do not seal my lips,
as you know, O LORD.
10I do not hide your righteousness in my
heart;
I speak of your faithfulness and
salvation.
I do not conceal your love and your
truth
from the great assembly.

11Do not withhold your mercy from me,
O LORD;

a4 Or to falsehood
b6 Hebrew; Septuagint but a body you have prepared for me (see also Symmachus and Theodotion)   *c6 Or opened*
d7 Or come / with the scroll written for me

Waiting on God

[Psalm 40 (p. 767)]

Background to the Psalms

➤ The Psalms, Israel's 'hymnbook' were composed over several centuries and arranged in their present order of five books probably in the fourth or third century B.C.

➤ Used widely in Israel's worship, some are clearly linked to certain feasts: Yom Kippur, Ps 130; the Passover, Ps 135; the Sabbath, Ps 92.

➤ Some Psalms (see 33, 98,150) mention the instruments used in worship: the ram's horn, the trumpet, the lyre, the cymbals. Some have a distinct theme of praise (Ps 146 to 150), others are royal psalms or instructional, for example.

➤ King David is usually associated with the Psalms but there were other authors including King Solomon (Ps 72), the Sons of Korah (Ps 42), Asaph (Ps 50), even Moses (Ps 90). This may help to explain why these 'hymns' cover the whole range of human experience and emotion.

➤ It is interesting that the New Testament quotes from Psalms more often than any other Old Testament book except Isaiah.

Psalm 40 is seen by some commentators to be linked to the events recorded in 1 Samuel 30 & 31 which provides helpful background.

Psalm 40 is a prayer by David for help in a time of desperate need.

Notes

➤ **v1 wait** means 'to stay in one place or remain inactive in expectation'. Waiting is not something that comes easily to the western culture at the end of the twentieth century with its emphasis on 'now' and 'fast'. Christians are called to a life long journey and recognise that no-one becomes perfect over night or understands everything immediately. Remember also that the process of conversion is not a once and for all experience. Each day you need to ask what has been converted in your life in the past 24 hours.

➤ **v2 rock** often used in the Bible to describe God, symbolising his unfailing strength as a refuge or deliverer.

➤ **v5 things planned for us** see 1 Corinthians 2:9

➤ **v6 pierced my ear** is a unique biblical expression which either relates to the custom of piercing the ear as consecration

what is
WORSHIP?

Emma   It's based on the word 'worth', when we worship we give God 'worth'.

Simon   One of the words translated as worship in the Bible means to kiss.

Andrew   Worship is also likened to a dog coming to lick its master's hand, affection given to the master.

Jonathan   That's what I think of when I think of worship: coming close to God.

Paul   I feel closest to God when I'm outside in nature, particularly when I'm by the sea, me, my thoughts, and God.

Penny   I'm exactly the same, because I'm from the coast as well so the sea has a special spiritual kind of oomph. It's the power of it I think. If something wows you then it reminds you of God (stars as well). See Psalm 8.

Andrew   Worship is costly. I see that in the Bible when I read about the lady with the alabaster jar (Matthew 26:6-13). Her love and devotion was a broken thing and costly.

worth   service   to kiss

Waiting on God

[part 2]

to service (Exodus 21:6) or to the idiom of opening the ear to God's word (Isaiah 50:5). In both cases, it is about obeying God after hearing his word.

➤ **v9-10 proclaim**
David does not keep his relationship with God secret, he joyfully makes it public knowledge.

➤ **v13 save** like all people, David recognises that he cannot put right his sins, he needs salvation from God.

➤ **v16 exalt** means 'to acknowledge something as great'. David longs that everyone should praise God.

➤ **v17 poor** refers to someone who is without resources to bring about their own deliverance or secure their own well-being, someone dependent on God.

APPLICATION
Now apply some or all of David's words to your own life:

wait

WAIT think back to when, as a child or adult, you have had to wait for things. Was it worthwhile? Have you learnt patience? When God has been slow to answer your prayers what has been your reaction? What alternatives have you tried and with what consequences? Be honest!

save

SAVE can you name a day and time or point to a period during which you became a Christian? (Don't worry if you can't.) How do you feel about the idea of life long change or conversion? What 'pits'(v2) have you been rescued from and when? What brought you to that situation? Was it your own fault? How did God enter the situation?

proclaim

PROCLAIM can you recall times when you have been open about your faith? What happened and how did you feel?

Spend some time in prayer allowing God to speak into your situation.

---

may your love and your truth always
    protect me.
[2]For troubles without number surround
    me;
    my sins have overtaken me, and I
        cannot see.
They are more than the hairs of my
        head,
    and my heart fails within me.

[3]Be pleased, O LORD, to save me;
    O LORD, come quickly to help me.
[4]May all who seek to take my life
    be put to shame and confusion;
may all who desire my ruin
    be turned back in disgrace.
[5]May those who say to me, "Aha! Aha!"
    be appalled at their own shame.
[6]But may all who seek you
    rejoice and be glad in you;
may those who love your salvation
        always say,
    "The LORD be exalted!"

[7]Yet I am poor and needy;
    may the Lord think of me.
You are my help and my deliverer;
    O my God, do not delay.

Psalm 41

For the director of music. A psalm of David.

[1]Blessed is he who has regard for the
        weak;
    the LORD delivers him in times of
        trouble.
[2]The LORD will protect him and preserve
        his life;
    he will bless him in the land
    and not surrender him to the desire of
        his foes.
[3]The LORD will sustain him on his
        sick-bed
    and restore him from his bed of
        illness.
[4]I said, "O LORD, have mercy on me;
    heal me, for I have sinned against
        you."

[a]In many Hebrew manuscripts Psalm 42 and 43 constitute one psalm.
[b]Title: Probably a literary or musical term

[5]My ene
    "Whe
            pe
[6]Whenev
    he spe
            ga
    then h
            ab

[7]All my e
            aga
    they in
            say
[8]"A vile d
    he will
            whe
[9]Even my
    he who
    has lift

[10]But you,
    raise m
[11]I know th
    for my
        me.
[12]In my inte
    and set

[13]Praise be t
        Israe
    from eve

Psalm

For the direc

[1]As the deer
    so my sou
[2]My soul thi
        God.
    When car
[3]My tears ha
        day and n

PSALM ·

while m
    "Whe
[4]These t
    as I p
how I u
    leadi
        G
    with sh
        amo

[5]Why ar
    Why
Put you
    for I
    my S

My[c] so
    there
from t
    the

[7]Deep
    in th
    all you
    have

[8]By da
    at n
    a pr

[9]I say
    "W
Why
    op
[10]My b
    as
sayin
    "V

[11]Why
    W
Put
    fo
        m

For the dire

[1]Vir
        a

[c]5, 6
    God,
[a]Title

y to me all day long,
your God?"
I remember
ut my soul:
go with the multitude,
procession to the house of

f joy and thanksgiving
festive throng.

downcast, O my soul?
turbed within me?
e in God,
t praise him,
r and ⁶my God.

owncast within me;
will remember you
l of the Jordan,
s of Hermon—from Mount

deep
of your waterfalls;
es and breakers
over me.

ORD directs his love,
song is with me—
the God of my life.

my Rock,
e you forgotten me?
o about mourning,
by the enemy?"
ffer mortal agony
taunt me,
all day long,
your God?"

downcast, O my soul?
turbed within me?
e in God,
t praise him,
r and my God.

Psalm 43ᵃ

, O God,
ny cause against an
nation;

---

rescue me from deceitful and w
men.
²You are God my stronghold.
Why have you rejected me?
Why must I go about mourning,
oppressed by the enemy?
³Send forth your light and your tru
let them guide me;
let them bring me to your holy
mountain,
to the place where you dwell.
⁴Then will I go to the altar of God,
to God, my joy and my delight.
I will praise you with the harp,
O God, my God.

⁵Why are you downcast, O my soul
Why so disturbed within me?
Put your hope in God,
for I will yet praise him,
my Saviour and my God.

Psalm 44

For the director of music. Of the Son
Korah. A *maskil.*ᵃ

¹We have heard with our ears, O G
our fathers have told us
what you did in their days,
in days long ago.
²With your hand you drove out the
nations
and planted our fathers;
you crushed the peoples
and made our fathers flourish.
³It was not by their sword that they
the land,
nor did their arm bring them vict
it was your right hand, your arm,
and the light of your face, for yo
loved them.

⁴You are my King and my God,
who decreesᵇ victories for Jacob.
⁵Through you we push back our
enemies;
through your name we trample o
foes.

---

manuscripts, Septuagint and Syriac; most Hebrew manuscripts *praise him for his saving help.*
any Hebrew manuscripts Psalms 42 and 43 constitute one psalm.
rary or musical term   b4 Septuagint, Aquila and Syriac; Hebrew *King, O God;* comm

---

Anon Devotion to him in all that you are, not just singing songs. It's everything, saying, 'God, I am yours.' Matthew 22:37: 'worship him with all your heart, mind, soul and strength'. It's living your life for God. Even if you never have a guitar, you never have anything valuable but say, 'I'm yours', that's true worship. It's being owned by God (Romans 12:1-2).

Penny It's offering your whole life and everything that you do back to God because of what he's done for you (John 3:16).

Paul God knows our hearts, that's the key, and he knows if we're just doing a load of show.

Anon It's showing God love in any way we can: 'I want to show you my token of love, God, I'm no good at preaching, Lord but I can't half dance.'

Pat Worship inspires me to continue the reltionship I have with God, which I feel I can't do on my own. I always think of worship as being with other people.

Ann It's not just about hymns, worship can be heavy metal music, Christian music, or you can have lots of different things. People tend to box things and you can't it's much bigger than that. Sometimes somebody else's form of worship won't be what you like or what you think it should be.

'love the Lord your God with all your heart, mind and strength'

It's showing God love

⁶I do not trust in my bow,
my sword does not bring me victory;
⁷but you give us victory over our
enemies,
you put our adversaries to shame.
⁸In God we make our boast all day long,
and we will praise your name for
ever.   *Selah*

⁹But now you have rejected and
humbled us;
you no longer go out with our armies.
¹⁰You made us retreat before the enemy,
and our adversaries have plundered
us.
¹¹You gave us up to be devoured like
sheep
and have scattered us among the
nations.
¹²You sold your people for a pittance,
gaining nothing from their sale.

¹³You have made us a reproach to our
neighbours,
the scorn and derision of those
around us.
¹⁴You have made us a byword among the
nations;
the peoples shake their heads at us.
¹⁵My disgrace is before me all day long,
and my face is covered with shame
¹⁶at the taunts of those who reproach and
revile me,
because of the enemy, who is bent on
revenge.

¹⁷All this happened to us,
though we had not forgotten you
or been false to your covenant.
¹⁸Our hearts had not turned back;
our feet had not strayed from your
path.
¹⁹But you crushed us and made us a haunt
for jackals
and covered us over with deep
darkness.

²⁰If we had forgotten the name of our
God
or spread out our hands to a foreign
god,

²¹would not God have discovered it,
since he knows the secrets of the
heart?
²²Yet for your sake we face death all day
long;
we are considered as sheep to be
slaughtered.

²³Awake, O Lord! Why do you sleep?
Rouse yourself! Do not reject us for
ever.
²⁴Why do you hide your face
and forget our misery and
oppression?

²⁵We are brought down to the dust;
our bodies cling to the ground.
²⁶Rise up and help us;
redeem us because of your unfailing
love.

Psalm 45

For the director of music. To ˻the tune of˼
"Lilies". Of the Sons of Korah. A *maskil.*[a] A
wedding song.

¹My heart is stirred by a noble theme
as I recite my verses for the king;
my tongue is the pen of a skilful
writer.

²You are the most excellent of men
and your lips have been anointed
with grace,
since God has blessed you for
ever.
³Gird your sword upon your side, O
mighty one;
clothe yourself with splendour and
majesty.
⁴In your majesty ride forth victoriously
on behalf of truth, humility and
righteousness;
let your right hand display awesome
deeds.
⁵Let your sharp arrows pierce the hearts
of the king's enemies;
let the nations fall beneath your
feet.

---

*a*Title: Probably a literary or musical term

6Your throne, O God, will last for ever
  and ever;
 a sceptre of justice will be the sceptre
  of your kingdom.
7You love righteousness and hate
  wickedness;
 therefore God, your God, has set you
  above your companions
 by anointing you with the oil of
  joy.
8All your robes are fragrant with myrrh
  and aloes and cassia;
 from palaces adorned with ivory
 the music of the strings makes you
  glad.
9Daughters of kings are among your
  honoured women;
 at your right hand is the royal bride in
  gold of Ophir.

10Listen, O daughter, consider and give
  ear:
 Forget your people and your father's
  house.
11The king is enthralled by your beauty;
 honour him, for he is your
  lord.
12The Daughter of Tyre will come with a
  gift,b
 men of wealth will seek your favour.

13All glorious is the princess within ⌜her
  chamber⌟;
 her gown is interwoven with
  gold.
14In embroidered garments she is led to
  the king;
 her virgin companions follow her
  and are brought to you.
15They are led in with joy and gladness;
 they enter the palace of the
  king.

16Your sons will take the place of your
  fathers;
 you will make them princes
  throughout the land.
17I will perpetuate your memory through
  all generations;
 therefore the nations will praise you
  for ever and ever.

Psalm 46

For the director of music. Of the Sons of
  Korah. According to *alamoth.*a A song.

1God is our refuge and strength,
 an ever-present help in trouble.
2Therefore we will not fear, though the
  earth give way
 and the mountains fall into the heart
  of the sea,
3though its waters roar and foam
 and the mountains quake with their
  surging.   *Selah*

4There is a river whose streams make
  glad the city of God,
 the holy place where the Most High
  dwells.
5God is within her, she will not fall;
 God will help her at break of day.
6Nations are in uproar, kingdoms fall;
 he lifts his voice, the earth melts.

7The LORD Almighty is with us;
 the God of Jacob is our fortress.
                  Selah

8Come and see the works of the LORD,
 the desolations he has brought on the
  earth.
9He makes wars cease to the ends of the
  earth;
 he breaks the bow and shatters the
  spear,
 he burns the shieldsb with fire.
10"Be still, and know that I am God;
 I will be exalted among the nations,
 I will be exalted in the earth."

11The LORD Almighty is with us;
 the God of Jacob is our fortress.
                  Selah

Psalm 47

For the director of music. Of the Sons of
  Korah. A psalm.

1Clap your hands, all you nations;
 shout to God with cries of joy.

---

b12 Or *A Tyrian robe is among the gifts*   *a*Title: Probably a musical term   *b9* Or *chariots*

2How awesome is the LORD Most High,
the great King over all the earth!
3He subdued nations under us,
peoples under our feet.
4He chose our inheritance for us,
the pride of Jacob, whom he loved.
Selah

5God has ascended amid shouts of joy,
the LORD amid the sounding of
trumpets.
6Sing praises to God, sing praises;
sing praises to our King, sing praises.

7For God is the King of all the earth;
sing to him a psalm*a* of praise.
8God reigns over the nations;
God is seated on his holy
throne.
9The nobles of the nations assemble
as the people of the God of
Abraham,
for the kings*b* of the earth belong to
God;
he is greatly exalted.

Psalm 48

A song. A psalm of the Sons of Korah.

1Great is the LORD, and most worthy of
praise,
in the city of our God, his holy
mountain.
2It is beautiful in its loftiness,
the joy of the whole earth.
Like the utmost heights of Zaphon*a* is
Mount Zion,
the*b* city of the Great King.
3God is in her citadels;
he has shown himself to be her
fortress.

4When the kings joined forces,
when they advanced together,
5they saw ⌊her⌋ and were astounded;
they fled in terror.
6Trembling seized them there,
pain like that of a woman in labour.

7You destroyed them like ships of
Tarshish
shattered by an east wind.

8As we have heard,
so have we seen
in the city of the LORD Almighty,
in the city of our God:
God makes her secure for ever. *Selah*

9Within your temple, O God,
we meditate on your unfailing
love.
10Like your name, O God,
your praise reaches to the ends of the
earth;
your right hand is filled with
righteousness.
11Mount Zion rejoices,
the villages of Judah are glad
because of your judgments.

12Walk about Zion, go round her,
count her towers,
13consider well her ramparts,
view her citadels,
that you may tell of them to the next
generation.
14For this God is our God for ever and
ever;
he will be our guide even to the
end.

Psalm 49

For the director of music. Of the Sons of
Korah. A psalm.

1Hear this, all you peoples;
listen, all who live in this world,
2both low and high,
rich and poor alike:
3My mouth will speak words of
wisdom;
the utterance from my heart will give
understanding.
4I will turn my ear to a proverb;
with the harp I will expound my
riddle:

*a*7 Or *a maskil* (probably a literary or musical term)   *b*9 Or *shields*
*a*2 *Zaphon* can refer to a sacred mountain or the direction north.
*b*2 Or *earth, | Mount Zion, on the northern side | of the*

⁵Why should I fear when evil days come,
    when wicked deceivers surround
        me—
⁶those who trust in their wealth
    and boast of their great riches?
⁷No man can redeem the life of another
    or give to God a ransom for him—
⁸the ransom for a life is costly,
    no payment is ever enough—
⁹that he should live on for ever
    and not see decay.

¹⁰For all can see that wise men die;
    the foolish and the senseless alike
        perish
    and leave their wealth to others.
¹¹Their tombs will remain their houses[a]
    for ever,
    their dwellings for endless
        generations,
    though they had[b] named lands after
        themselves.

¹²But man, despite his riches, does not
    endure;
    he is[c] like the beasts that perish.

¹³This is the fate of those who trust in
    themselves,
    and of their followers, who approve
    their sayings.   *Selah*
¹⁴Like sheep they are destined for the
    grave,[d]
    and death will feed on them.
The upright will rule over them in the
    morning;
    their forms will decay in the grave,[d]
    far from their princely mansions.
¹⁵But God will redeem my life[e] from the
    grave;
    he will surely take me to himself.
               Selah

¹⁶Do not be overawed when a man grows
    rich,
    when the splendour of his house
        increases;
¹⁷for he will take nothing with him when
    he dies,

his splendour will not descend with
    him.
¹⁸Though while he lived he counted
    himself blessed—
    and men praise you when you
        prosper—
¹⁹he will join the generation of his
    fathers,
    who will never see the light ⌊of life⌋.

²⁰A man who has riches without
    understanding
    is like the beasts that perish.

Psalm 50

A psalm of Asaph.

¹The Mighty One, God, the LORD,
    speaks and summons the earth
    from the rising of the sun to the place
        where it sets.
²From Zion, perfect in beauty,
    God shines forth.
³Our God comes and will not be silent;
    a fire devours before him,
    and around him a tempest rages.
⁴He summons the heavens above,
    and the earth, that he may judge his
        people:
⁵"Gather to me my consecrated ones,
    who made a covenant with me by
        sacrifice."
⁶And the heavens proclaim his
    righteousness,
    for God himself is judge.   *Selah*

⁷"Hear, O my people, and I will speak,
    O Israel, and I will testify against
        you:
    I am God, your God.
⁸I do not rebuke you for your sacrifices
    or your burnt offerings, which are
        ever before me.
⁹I have no need of a bull from your stall
    or of goats from your pens,
¹⁰for every animal of the forest is mine,
    and the cattle on a thousand hills.

---

a11 Septuagint and Syriac; Hebrew *In their thoughts their houses will remain*   *b11* Or / *for they have*
c12 Hebrew; Septuagint and Syriac read verse 12 the same as verse 20.   *d14* Hebrew *Sheol*; also in verse 15
e15 Or *soul*

11I know every bird in the mountains,
  and the creatures of the field are
    mine.
12If I were hungry I would not tell you,
  for the world is mine, and all that is in it.
13Do I eat the flesh of bulls
  or drink the blood of goats?
14Sacrifice thank-offerings to God,
  fulfil your vows to the Most High,
15and call upon me in the day of trouble;
  I will deliver you, and you will
    honour me."

16But to the wicked, God says:

"What right have you to recite my laws
  or take my covenant on your lips?
17You hate my instruction
  and cast my words behind you.
18When you see a thief, you join with him;
  you throw in your lot with adulterers.
19You use your mouth for evil
  and harness your tongue to deceit.
20You speak continually against your
    brother
  and slander your own mother's son.
21These things you have done and I kept
    silent;
  you thought I was altogether[a] like
    you.
But I will rebuke you
  and accuse you to your face.

22"Consider this, you who forget God,
  or I will tear you to pieces, with none
    to rescue:
23He who sacrifices thank-offerings
    honours me,
  and he prepares the way
  so that I may show him[b] the salvation
    of God."

Psalm 51

For the director of music. A psalm of David.
When the prophet Nathan came to him after
  David had committed adultery with
    Bathsheba.

1Have mercy on me, O God,
  according to your unfailing love;

according to your great compassion
  blot out my transgressions.
2Wash away all my iniquity
  and cleanse me from my sin.

3For I know my transgressions,
  and my sin is always before me.
4Against you, you only, have I sinned
  and done what is evil in your sight,
  so that you are proved right when you
    speak
  and justified when you judge.
5Surely I was sinful at birth,
  sinful from the time my mother
    conceived me.
6Surely you desire truth in the inner
    parts;[a]
  you teach[b] me wisdom in the inmost
    place.

7Cleanse me with hyssop, and I shall be
    clean;
  wash me, and I shall be whiter than
    snow.
8Let me hear joy and gladness;
  let the bones you have crushed
    rejoice.
9Hide your face from my sins
  and blot out all my iniquity.

10Create in me a pure heart, O God,
  and renew a steadfast spirit within
    me.
11Do not cast me from your presence
  or take your Holy Spirit from me.
12Restore to me the joy of your salvation
  and grant me a willing spirit, to
    sustain me.

13Then I will teach transgressors your
    ways,
  and sinners will turn back to you.
14Save me from bloodguilt, O God,
  the God who saves me,
  and my tongue will sing of your
    righteousness.
15O Lord, open my lips,
  and my mouth will declare your
    praise.
16You do not delight in sacrifice, or I
    would bring it;

---

a21 Or thought the 'I AM' was   b23 Or and to him who considers his way / I will show
a6 The meaning of the Hebrew for this phrase is uncertain.   b6 Or you desired . . . ; / you taught

you do not take pleasure in burnt
offerings.
[17]The sacrifices of God are[c] a broken
spirit;
a broken and contrite heart,
O God, you will not despise.

[18]In your good pleasure make Zion
prosper;
build up the walls of Jerusalem.
[19]Then there will be righteous sacrifices,
whole burnt offerings to delight you;
then bulls will be offered on your
altar.

Psalm 52

For the director of music. A *maskil*[a] of David.
When Doeg the Edomite had gone to Saul
and told him: "David has gone to the house of
Ahimelech."

[1]Why do you boast of evil, you mighty
man?
Why do you boast all day long,
you who are a disgrace in the eyes of
God?
[2]Your tongue plots destruction;
it is like a sharpened razor,
you who practise deceit.
[3]You love evil rather than good,
falsehood rather than speaking the
truth.   *Selah*
[4]You love every harmful word,
O you deceitful tongue!

[5]Surely God will bring you down to
everlasting ruin:
He will snatch you up and tear you
from your tent;
he will uproot you from the land of
the living.   *Selah*
[6]The righteous will see and fear;
they will laugh at him, saying,
[7]"Here now is the man
who did not make God his stronghold
but trusted in his great wealth
and grew strong by destroying
others!"

[8]But I am like an olive tree
flourishing in the house of God;
I trust in God's unfailing love
for ever and ever.
[9]I will praise you for ever for what you
have done;
in your name I will hope, for your
name is good.
I will praise you in the presence of
your saints.

Psalm 53

For the director of music. According to
mahalath.[a] A *maskil*[b] of David.

[1]The fool says in his heart,
"There is no God."
They are corrupt, and their ways are
vile;
there is no-one who does good.

[2]God looks down from heaven
on the sons of men
to see if there are any who understand,
any who seek God.
[3]Everyone has turned away,
they have together become corrupt;
there is no-one who does good,
not even one.

[4]Will the evildoers never learn—
those who devour my people as men
eat bread
and who do not call on God?
[5]There they were, overwhelmed with
dread,
where there was nothing to dread.
God scattered the bones of those who
attacked you;
you put them to shame, for God
despised them.

[6]Oh, that salvation for Israel would
come out of Zion!
When God restores the fortunes of
his people,
let Jacob rejoice and Israel be
glad!

[c]17 Or *My sacrifice, O God, is*   [a]Title: Probably a literary or musical term   [a]Title: Probably a musical term
[b]Title: Probably a literary or musical term

Psalm 54

For the director of music. With stringed instruments. A *maskil*[a] of David. When the Ziphites had gone to Saul and said, "Is not David hiding among us?"

[1]Save me, O God, by your name;
    vindicate me by your might.
[2]Hear my prayer, O God;
    listen to the words of my mouth.

[3]Strangers are attacking me;
    ruthless men seek my life—
    men without regard for God.   *Selah*

[4]Surely God is my help;
    the Lord is the one who sustains me.

[5]Let evil recoil on those who slander me;
    in your faithfulness destroy them.

[6]I will sacrifice a freewill offering to you;
    I will praise your name, O LORD,
    for it is good.
[7]For he has delivered me from all my troubles,
    and my eyes have looked in triumph on my foes.

Psalm 55

For the director of music. With stringed instruments. A *maskil*[a] of David.

[1]Listen to my prayer, O God,
    do not ignore my plea;
[2] hear me and answer me.
My thoughts trouble me and I am distraught
[3] at the voice of the enemy,
    at the stares of the wicked;
for they bring down suffering upon me
    and revile me in their anger.

[4]My heart is in anguish within me;
    the terrors of death assail me.
[5]Fear and trembling have beset me;
    horror has overwhelmed me.

[6]I said, "Oh, that I had the wings of a dove!
    I would fly away and be at rest—
[7]I would flee far away
    and stay in the desert;   *Selah*
[8]I would hurry to my place of shelter,
    far from the tempest and storm."

[9]Confuse the wicked, O Lord, confound their speech,
    for I see violence and strife in the city.
[10]Day and night they prowl about on its walls;
    malice and abuse are within it.
[11]Destructive forces are at work in the city;
    threats and lies never leave its streets.

[12]If an enemy were insulting me,
    I could endure it;
if a foe were raising himself against me,
    I could hide from him.
[13]But it is you, a man like myself,
    my companion, my close friend,
[14]with whom I once enjoyed sweet fellowship
    as we walked with the throng at the house of God.

[15]Let death take my enemies by surprise;
    let them go down alive to the grave,[b]
    for evil finds lodging among them.

[16]But I call to God,
    and the LORD saves me.
[17]Evening, morning and noon
    I cry out in distress,
    and he hears my voice.
[18]He ransoms me unharmed
    from the battle waged against me,
    even though many oppose me.
[19]God, who is enthroned for ever,
    will hear them and afflict them—
        Selah
men who never change their ways
    and have no fear of God.

[20]My companion attacks his friends;
    he violates his covenant.
[21]His speech is smooth as butter,
    yet war is in his heart;

his words are more soothing than oil,
yet they are drawn swords.

²²Cast your cares on the LORD
and he will sustain you;
he will never let the righteous fall.
²³But you, O God, will bring down the
wicked
into the pit of corruption;
bloodthirsty and deceitful men
will not live out half their days.

But as for me, I trust in you.

Psalm 56

For the director of music. To ⌜the tune of⌝ "A
Dove on Distant Oaks". Of David. A
*miktam.*ᵃ When the Philistines had seized him
in Gath.

¹Be merciful to me, O God, for men
hotly pursue me;
all day long they press their attack.
²My slanderers pursue me all day long;
many are attacking me in their pride.

³When I am afraid,
I will trust in you.
⁴In God, whose word I praise,
in God I trust; I will not be afraid.
What can mortal man do to me?

⁵All day long they twist my words;
they are always plotting to harm me.
⁶They conspire, they lurk,
they watch my steps,
eager to take my life.

⁷On no account let them escape;
in your anger, O God, bring down
the nations.
⁸Record my lament;
list my tears on your scrollᵇ—
are they not in your record?

⁹Then my enemies will turn back
when I call for help.
By this I will know that God is for
me.

¹⁰In God, whose word I praise,
in the LORD, whose word I praise—
¹¹in God I trust; I will not be afraid.
What can man do to me?

¹²I am under vows to you, O God;
I will present my thank-offerings to
you.
¹³For you have delivered meᶜ from death
and my feet from stumbling,
that I may walk before God
in the light of life.ᵈ

Psalm 57

For the director of music. ⌜To the tune of⌝
"Do Not Destroy". Of David. A *miktam.*ᵃ
When he had fled from Saul into the cave.

¹Have mercy on me, O God, have mercy
on me,
for in you my soul takes refuge.
I will take refuge in the shadow of your
wings
until the disaster has passed.

²I cry out to God Most High,
to God, who fulfils ⌜his purpose⌝ for
me.
³He sends from heaven and saves me,
rebuking those who hotly pursue me;
Selah
God sends his love and his
faithfulness.

⁴I am in the midst of lions;
I lie among ravenous beasts—
men whose teeth are spears and arrows,
whose tongues are sharp swords.

⁵Be exalted, O God, above the heavens;
let your glory be over all the earth.

⁶They spread a net for my feet—
I was bowed down in distress.
They dug a pit in my path—
but they have fallen into it
themselves.   *Selah*

⁷My heart is steadfast, O God,
my heart is steadfast;

ᵃTitle: Probably a literary or musical term   ᵇ8 Or / *put my tears in your wineskin*   ᶜ13 Or *my soul*
ᵈ13 Or *the land of the living*   ᵃTitle: Probably a literary or musical term

I will sing and make music.
[8]Awake, my soul!
   Awake, harp and lyre!
   I will awaken the dawn.

[9]I will praise you, O Lord, among the
   nations;
   I will sing of you among the peoples.
[10]For great is your love, reaching to the
   heavens;
   your faithfulness reaches to the skies.

[11]Be exalted, O God, above the heavens;
   let your glory be over all the earth.

Psalm 58

For the director of music. ⌐To the tune of⌐
"Do Not Destroy". Of David. A *miktam.*[a]

[1]Do you rulers indeed speak justly?
   Do you judge uprightly among
   men?
[2]No, in your heart you devise injustice,
   and your hands mete out violence on
   the earth.
[3]Even from birth the wicked go astray;
   from the womb they are wayward and
   speak lies.
[4]Their venom is like the venom of a
   snake,
   like that of a cobra that has stopped
   its ears,
[5]that will not heed the tune of the
   charmer,
   however skilful the enchanter may
   be.

[6]Break the teeth in their mouths, O
   God;
   tear out, O LORD, the fangs of the
   lions!
[7]Let them vanish like water that flows
   away;
   when they draw the bow, let their
   arrows be blunted.
[8]Like a slug melting away as it moves
   along,
   like a stillborn child, may they not see
   the sun.

[9]Before your pots can feel ⌐the heat of⌐
   the thorns—
   whether they be green or dry—the
   wicked will be swept away.[b]
[10]The righteous will be glad when they
   are avenged,
   when they bathe their feet in the
   blood of the wicked.
[11]Then men will say,
   "Surely the righteous still are
   rewarded;
   surely there is a God who judges the
   earth."

Psalm 59

For the director of music. ⌐To the tune of⌐
"Do Not Destroy". Of David. A *miktam.*[a]
When Saul had sent men to watch David's
house in order to kill him.

[1]Deliver me from my enemies, O God;
   protect me from those who rise up
   against me.
[2]Deliver me from evildoers
   and save me from bloodthirsty men.

[3]See how they lie in wait for me!
   Fierce men conspire against me
   for no offence or sin of mine, O
   LORD.
[4]I have done no wrong, yet they are
   ready to attack me.
   Arise to help me; look on my plight!
[5]O LORD God Almighty, the God of
   Israel,
   rouse yourself to punish all the
   nations;
   show no mercy to wicked traitors.
                   Selah

[6]They return at evening,
   snarling like dogs,
   and prowl about the city.
[7]See what they spew from their
   mouths—
   they spew out swords from their lips,
   and they say, "Who can hear us?"
[8]But you, O LORD, laugh at them;
   you scoff at all those nations.

---

[a]Title: Probably a literary or musical term   [b]9 The meaning of the Hebrew for this verse is uncertain.
[a]Title: Probably a literary or musical term

9 O my Strength, I watch for you;
   you, O God, are my fortress, 10 my
      loving God.

God will go before me
   and will let me gloat over those who
      slander me.
11 But do not kill them, O Lord our
      shield, *b*
   or my people will forget.
In your might make them wander about,
   and bring them down.
12 For the sins of their mouths,
   for the words of their lips,
   let them be caught in their pride.
For the curses and lies they utter,
13   consume them in wrath,
   consume them till they are no more.
Then it will be known to the ends of the
      earth
   that God rules over Jacob.   *Selah*

14 They return at evening,
   snarling like dogs,
   and prowl about the city.
15 They wander about for food
   and howl if not satisfied.
16 But I will sing of your strength,
   in the morning I will sing of your
      love;
for you are my fortress,
   my refuge in times of trouble.

17 O my Strength, I sing praise to you;
   you, O God, are my fortress, my
      loving God.

Psalm 60

For the director of music. To ˻the tune of˼
"The Lily of the Covenant". A *miktam*[a] of
David. For teaching. When he fought Aram
Naharaim[b] and Aram Zobah,[c] and when Joab
returned and struck down twelve thousand
Edomites in the Valley of Salt.

1 You have rejected us, O God, and burst
      forth upon us;
   you have been angry—now restore
      us!
2 You have shaken the land and torn it
      open;
   mend its fractures, for it is quaking.
3 You have shown your people desperate
      times;
   you have given us wine that makes us
      stagger.

4 But for those who fear you, you have
      raised a banner
   to be unfurled against the bow.
                              Selah

5 Save us and help us with your right
      hand,
   that those you love may be delivered.
6 God has spoken from his sanctuary:
   "In triumph I will parcel out
      Shechem
   and measure off the Valley of
      Succoth.
7 Gilead is mine, and Manasseh is mine;
   Ephraim is my helmet,
   Judah my sceptre.
8 Moab is my washbasin,
   upon Edom I toss my sandal;
   over Philistia I shout in triumph."

9 Who will bring me to the fortified city?
   Who will lead me to Edom?
10 Is it not you, O God, you who have
      rejected us
   and no longer go out with our
      armies?
11 Give us aid against the enemy,
   for the help of man is worthless.
12 With God we shall gain the victory,
   and he will trample down our
      enemies.

Psalm 61

For the director of music. With stringed
instruments. Of David.

1 Hear my cry, O God;
   listen to my prayer.

2 From the ends of the earth I call to you,
   I call as my heart grows faint;
   lead me to the rock that is higher than I.

*b*11 Or *sovereign*   *a*Title: Probably a literary or musical term
*b*Title: That is, Arameans of North-west Mesopotamia   *c*Title: That is, Arameans of central Syria

³For you have been my refuge,
    a strong tower against the foe.

⁴I long to dwell in your tent for ever
    and take refuge in the shelter of your
        wings.   *Selah*
⁵For you have heard my vows, O God;
    you have given me the heritage of
        those who fear your name.

⁶Increase the days of the king's life,
    his years for many generations.
⁷May he be enthroned in God's presence
        for ever;
    appoint your love and faithfulness to
        protect him.

⁸Then will I ever sing praise to your
        name
    and fulfil my vows day after day.

Psalm 62

For the director of music. For Jeduthun. A
    psalm of David.

¹My soul finds rest in God alone;
    my salvation comes from him.
²He alone is my rock and my salvation;
    he is my fortress, I shall never be
        shaken.

³How long will you assault a man?
    Would all of you throw him down—
    this leaning wall, this tottering
        fence?
⁴They fully intend to topple him
    from his lofty place;
    they take delight in lies.
With their mouths they bless,
    but in their hearts they curse.   *Selah*

⁵Find rest, O my soul, in God alone;
    my hope comes from him.
⁶He alone is my rock and my salvation;
    he is my fortress, I shall not be
        shaken.
⁷My salvation and my honour depend on
        God;*a*
    he is my mighty rock, my refuge.
⁸Trust in him at all times, O people;

pour out your hearts to him,
    for God is our refuge.   *Selah*

⁹Lowborn men are but a breath,
    the highborn are but a lie;
if weighed on a balance, they are
        nothing;
    together they are only a breath.
¹⁰Do not trust in extortion
    or take pride in stolen goods;
though your riches increase,
    do not set your heart on them.

¹¹One thing God has spoken,
    two things have I heard:
that you, O God, are strong,
¹²   and that you, O Lord, are loving.
Surely you will reward each person
    according to what he has done.

Psalm 63

A psalm of David. When he was in the Desert
    of Judah.

¹O God, you are my God,
    earnestly I seek you;
my soul thirsts for you,
    my body longs for you,
in a dry and weary land
    where there is no water.

²I have seen you in the sanctuary
    and beheld your power and your
        glory.
³Because your love is better than life,
    my lips will glorify you.
⁴I will praise you as long as I live,
    and in your name I will lift up my
        hands.
⁵My soul will be satisfied as with the
        richest of foods;
    with singing lips my mouth will praise
        you.

⁶On my bed I remember you;
    I think of you through the watches of
        the night.
⁷Because you are my help,
    I sing in the shadow of your wings.

---

a7 Or / God Most High is my salvation and my honour

8My soul clings to you;
  your right hand upholds me.

9They who seek my life will be
    destroyed;
  they will go down to the depths of the
    earth.
10They will be given over to the sword
  and become food for jackals.

11But the king will rejoice in God;
  all who swear by God's name will
    praise him,
  while the mouths of liars will be
    silenced.

Psalm 64

For the director of music. A psalm of David.

1Hear me, O God, as I voice my
    complaint;
  protect my life from the threat of the
    enemy.
2Hide me from the conspiracy of the
    wicked,
  from that noisy crowd of evildoers.

3They sharpen their tongues like swords
  and aim their words like deadly
    arrows.
4They shoot from ambush at the
    innocent man;
  they shoot at him suddenly, without
    fear.

5They encourage each other in evil
    plans,
  they talk about hiding their snares;
  they say, "Who will see them?"a
6They plot injustice and say,
  "We have devised a perfect plan!"
  Surely the mind and heart of man are
    cunning.

7But God will shoot them with arrows;
  suddenly they will be struck down.
8He will turn their own tongues against
    them
  and bring them to ruin;

all who see them will shake their
  heads in scorn.

9All mankind will fear;
  they will proclaim the works of God
  and ponder what he has done.
10Let the righteous rejoice in the LORD
  and take refuge in him;
  let all the upright in heart praise him!

Psalm 65

For the director of music. A psalm of David.
A song.

1Praise awaitsa you, O God, in Zion;
  to you our vows will be fulfilled.
2O you who hear prayer,
  to you all men will come.
3When we were overwhelmed by sins,
  you forgaveb our transgressions.
4Blessed are those you choose
  and bring near to live in your courts!
We are filled with the good things of
    your house,
  of your holy temple.

5You answer us with awesome deeds of
    righteousness,
  O God our Saviour,
the hope of all the ends of the earth
  and of the farthest seas,
6who formed the mountains by your
    power,
  having armed yourself with strength,
7who stilled the roaring of the seas,
  the roaring of their waves,
  and the turmoil of the nations.
8Those living far away fear your wonders;
  where morning dawns and evening
    fades
  you call forth songs of joy.

9You care for the land and water it;
  you enrich it abundantly.
The streams of God are filled with
    water
  to provide the people with corn,
  for so you have ordained it.c

---

a5 Or us   a1 Or befits; the meaning of the Hebrew for this word is uncertain.   b3 Or made atonement for
c9 Or for that is how you prepare the land

10You drench its furrows
    and level its ridges;
  you soften it with showers
    and bless its crops.
11You crown the year with your bounty,
    and your carts overflow with
      abundance.
12The grasslands of the desert overflow;
    the hills are clothed with gladness.
13The meadows are covered with flocks
    and the valleys are mantled with
      corn;
    they shout for joy and sing.

Psalm 66

For the director of music. A song. A psalm.

1Shout with joy to God, all the earth!
2   Sing the glory of his name;
    make his praise glorious!
3Say to God, "How awesome are your
      deeds!
  So great is your power
  that your enemies cringe before you.
4All the earth bows down to you;
    they sing praise to you,
    they sing praise to your name." *Selah*

5Come and see what God has done,
    how awesome his works on man's
      behalf!
6He turned the sea into dry land,
    they passed through the waters on
      foot—
    come, let us rejoice in him.
7He rules for ever by his power,
    his eyes watch the nations—
    let not the rebellious rise up against
      him.   *Selah*

8Praise our God, O peoples,
    let the sound of his praise be heard;
9he has preserved our lives
    and kept our feet from slipping.
10For you, O God, tested us;
    you refined us like silver.
11You brought us into prison
    and laid burdens on our backs.
12You let men ride over our heads;
    we went through fire and water,

but you brought us to a place of
    abundance.

13I will come to your temple with burnt
      offerings
    and fulfil my vows to you—
14vows my lips promised and my mouth
      spoke
    when I was in trouble.
15I will sacrifice fat animals to you
    and an offering of rams;
    I will offer bulls and goats.   *Selah*

16Come and listen, all you who fear God;
    let me tell you what he has done for
      me.
17I cried out to him with my mouth;
    his praise was on my tongue.
18If I had cherished sin in my heart,
    the Lord would not have listened;
19but God has surely listened
    and heard my voice in prayer.
20Praise be to God,
    who has not rejected my prayer
    or withheld his love from me!

Psalm 67

For the director of music. With stringed
    instruments. A psalm. A song.

1May God be gracious to us and bless us
    and make his face shine upon us,
                                    Selah
2that your ways may be known on earth,
    your salvation among all nations.

3May the peoples praise you, O God;
    may all the peoples praise you.
4May the nations be glad and sing for
      joy,
    for you rule the peoples justly
    and guide the nations of the earth.
                                    Selah
5May the peoples praise you, O God;
    may all the peoples praise you.

6Then the land will yield its harvest,
    and God, our God, will bless us.
7God will bless us,
    and all the ends of the earth will fear
      him.

Psalm 68

For the director of music. Of David. A psalm.
A song.

[1]May God arise, may his enemies be
    scattered;
    may his foes flee before him.
[2]As smoke is blown away by the wind,
    may you blow them away;
as wax melts before the fire,
    may the wicked perish before God.
[3]But may the righteous be glad
    and rejoice before God;
    may they be happy and joyful.

[4]Sing to God, sing praise to his name,
    extol him who rides on the clouds[a]—
his name is the LORD—
    and rejoice before him.
[5]A father to the fatherless, a defender of
    widows,
    is God in his holy dwelling.
[6]God sets the lonely in families,[b]
    he leads forth the prisoners with
        singing;
    but the rebellious live in a
        sun-scorched land.

[7]When you went out before your people,
    O God,
    when you marched through the
        wasteland,   Selah
[8]the earth shook,
    the heavens poured down rain,
before God, the One of Sinai,
    before God, the God of Israel.
[9]You gave abundant showers, O God;
    you refreshed your weary
        inheritance.
[10]Your people settled in it,
    and from your bounty, O God, you
        provided for the poor.

[11]The Lord announced the word,
    and great was the company of those
        who proclaimed it:
[12]"Kings and armies flee in haste;
    in the camps men divide the plunder.
[13]Even while you sleep among the
    campfires,[c]

the wings of ⌊my⌋ dove are sheathed
    with silver,
    its feathers with shining gold."
[14]When the Almighty[d] scattered the kings
    in the land,
    it was like snow fallen on Zalmon.

[15]The mountains of Bashan are majestic
    mountains;
    rugged are the mountains of Bashan.
[16]Why gaze in envy, O rugged mountains,
    at the mountain where God chooses
        to reign,
    where the LORD himself will dwell for
        ever?
[17]The chariots of God are tens of
    thousands
    and thousands of thousands;
    the Lord ⌊has come⌋ from Sinai into
        his sanctuary.
[18]When you ascended on high,
    you led captives in your train;
    you received gifts from men,
even from[e] the rebellious—
    that you,[f] O LORD God, might dwell
        there.

[19]Praise be to the Lord, to God our
    Saviour,
    who daily bears our burdens.   Selah
[20]Our God is a God who saves;
    from the Sovereign LORD comes
        escape from death.

[21]Surely God will crush the heads of his
    enemies,
    the hairy crowns of those who go on
        in their sins.
[22]The Lord says, "I will bring them from
    Bashan;
    I will bring them from the depths of
        the sea,
[23]that you may plunge your feet in the
    blood of your foes,
    while the tongues of your dogs have
        their share."

[24]Your procession has come into view, O
    God,
    the procession of my God and King
        into the sanctuary.

---

[a]4 Or / prepare the way for him who rides through the deserts   [b]6 Or the desolate in a homeland
[c]13 Or saddlebags   [d]14 Hebrew Shaddai   [e]18 Or gifts for men, / even
[f]18 Or they

25In front are the singers, after them the
musicians;
with them are the maidens playing
tambourines.
26Praise God in the great congregation;
praise the LORD in the assembly of
Israel.
27There is the little tribe of Benjamin,
leading them,
there the great throng of Judah's
princes,
and there the princes of Zebulun and
of Naphtali.

28Summon your power, O God;*g*
show us your strength, O God, as you
have done before.
29Because of your temple at Jerusalem
kings will bring you gifts.
30Rebuke the beast among the reeds,
the herd of bulls among the calves of
the nations.
Humbled, may it bring bars of silver.
Scatter the nations who delight in war.
31Envoys will come from Egypt;
Cush*h* will submit herself to God.

32Sing to God, O kingdoms of the earth,
sing praise to the Lord,   *Selah*
33to him who rides the ancient skies
above,
who thunders with mighty voice.
34Proclaim the power of God,
whose majesty is over Israel,
whose power is in the skies.
35You are awesome, O God, in your
sanctuary;
the God of Israel gives power and
strength to his people.

Praise be to God!

Psalm 69

For the director of music. To ⌐the tune of⌐
"Lilies". Of David.

1Save me, O God,
for the waters have come up to my
neck.

2I sink in the miry depths,
where there is no foothold.
I have come into the deep waters;
the floods engulf me.
3I am worn out calling for help;
my throat is parched.
My eyes fail,
looking for my God.
4Those who hate me without reason
outnumber the hairs of my head;
many are my enemies without cause,
those who seek to destroy me.
I am forced to restore
what I did not steal.

5You know my folly, O God;
my guilt is not hidden from you.

6May those who hope in you
not be disgraced because of me,
O Lord, the LORD Almighty;
may those who seek you
not be put to shame because of me,
O God of Israel.
7For I endure scorn for your sake,
and shame covers my face.
8I am a stranger to my brothers,
an alien to my own mother's
sons;
9for zeal for your house consumes me,
and the insults of those who insult
you fall on me.
10When I weep and fast,
I must endure scorn;
11when I put on sackcloth,
people make sport of me.
12Those who sit at the gate mock me,
and I am the song of the drunkards.

13But I pray to you, O LORD,
in the time of your favour;
in your great love, O God,
answer me with your sure salvation.
14Rescue me from the mire,
do not let me sink;
deliver me from those who hate me,
from the deep waters.
15Do not let the floodwaters engulf me
or the depths swallow me up
or the pit close its mouth over me.

*g28 Many Hebrew manuscripts, Septuagint and Syriac; most Hebrew manuscripts Your God has summoned power for
you   h31 That is, the upper Nile region*

16Answer me, O LORD, out of the
goodness of your love;
in your great mercy turn to me.
17Do not hide your face from your
servant;
answer me quickly, for I am in
trouble.
18Come near and rescue me;
redeem me because of my foes.

19You know how I am scorned, disgraced
and shamed;
all my enemies are before you.
20Scorn has broken my heart
and has left me helpless;
I looked for sympathy, but there was
none,
for comforters, but I found none.
21They put gall in my food
and gave me vinegar for my thirst.

22May the table set before them become a
snare;
may it become retribution and*a* a
trap.
23May their eyes be darkened so that they
cannot see,
and their backs be bent for ever.
24Pour out your wrath on them;
let your fierce anger overtake them.
25May their place be deserted;
let there be no-one to dwell in their
tents.
26For they persecute those you wound
and talk about the pain of those you
hurt.
27Charge them with crime upon crime;
do not let them share in your
salvation.
28May they be blotted out of the book of
life
and not be listed with the righteous.

29I am in pain and distress;
may your salvation, O God, protect
me.

30I will praise God's name in song
and glorify him with thanksgiving.
31This will please the LORD more than an
ox,

more than a bull with its horns and
hoofs.
32The poor will see and be glad—
you who seek God, may your hearts
live!
33The LORD hears the needy
and does not despise his captive
people.

34Let heaven and earth praise him,
the seas and all that move in them,
35for God will save Zion
and rebuild the cities of Judah.
Then people will settle there and
possess it;
36 the children of his servants will
inherit it,
and those who love his name will
dwell there.

Psalm 70

For the director of music. Of David. A
petition.

1Hasten, O God, to save me;
O LORD, come quickly to help me.
2May those who seek my life
be put to shame and confusion;
may all who desire my ruin
be turned back in disgrace.
3May those who say to me, "Aha! Aha!"
turn back because of their shame.
4But may all who seek you
rejoice and be glad in you;
may those who love your salvation
always say,
"Let God be exalted!"

5Yet I am poor and needy;
come quickly to me, O God.
You are my help and my deliverer;
O LORD, do not delay.

Psalm 71

1In you, O LORD, I have taken refuge;
let me never be put to shame.
2Rescue me and deliver me in your
righteousness;
turn your ear to me and save me.

---

*a*22 Or *snare / and their fellowship become*

3Be my rock of refuge,
  to which I can always go;
 give the command to save me,
  for you are my rock and my fortress.
4Deliver me, O my God, from the hand
  of the wicked,
  from the grasp of evil and cruel men.

5For you have been my hope, O
  Sovereign LORD,
  my confidence since my youth.
6From my birth I have relied on you;
  you brought me forth from my
  mother's womb.
  I will ever praise you.
7I have become like a portent to many,
  but you are my strong refuge.
8My mouth is filled with your praise,
  declaring your splendour all day long.

9Do not cast me away when I am old;
  do not forsake me when my strength
  is gone.
10For my enemies speak against me;
  those who wait to kill me conspire
  together.
11They say, "God has forsaken him;
  pursue him and seize him,
  for no-one will rescue him."
12Be not far from me, O God;
  come quickly, O my God, to help me.
13May my accusers perish in shame;
  may those who want to harm me
  be covered with scorn and disgrace.

14But as for me, I shall always have hope;
  I will praise you more and more.
15My mouth will tell of your
  righteousness,
  of your salvation all day long,
  though I know not its measure.
16I will come and proclaim your mighty
  acts, O Sovereign LORD;
  I will proclaim your righteousness,
  yours alone.
17Since my youth, O God, you have
  taught me,
  and to this day I declare your
  marvellous deeds.
18Even when I am old and grey,
  do not forsake me, O God,

till I declare your power to the next
  generation,
  your might to all who are to come.

19Your righteousness reaches to the skies,
  O God,
  you who have done great things.
  Who, O God, is like you?
20Though you have made me see
  troubles, many and bitter,
  you will restore my life again;
 from the depths of the earth
  you will again bring me up.
21You will increase my honour
  and comfort me once again.

22I will praise you with the harp
  for your faithfulness, O my God;
 I will sing praise to you with the lyre,
  O Holy One of Israel.
23My lips will shout for joy
  when I sing praise to you—
  I, whom you have redeemed.
24My tongue will tell of your righteous acts
  all day long,
 for those who wanted to harm me
  have been put to shame and
  confusion.

Psalm 72

Of Solomon.

1Endow the king with your justice, O
  God,
  the royal son with your
  righteousness.
2He will*a* judge your people in
  righteousness,
  your afflicted ones with justice.
3The mountains will bring prosperity to
  the people,
  the hills the fruit of righteousness.
4He will defend the afflicted among the
  people
  and save the children of the needy;
  he will crush the oppressor.

5He will endure*b* as long as the sun,
  as long as the moon, through all
  generations.

---

*a*2 Or *May he*; similarly in verses 3–11 and 17   *b*5 Septuagint; Hebrew *You will be feared*

⁶He will be like rain falling on a mown
  field,
  like showers watering the earth.
⁷In his days the righteous will flourish;
  prosperity will abound till the moon
    is no more.

⁸He will rule from sea to sea
  and from the River*c* to the ends of the
    earth.*d*
⁹The desert tribes will bow before him
  and his enemies will lick the dust.
¹⁰The kings of Tarshish and of distant
    shores
  will bring tribute to him;
  the kings of Sheba and Seba
  will present him gifts.
¹¹All kings will bow down to him
  and all nations will serve him.

¹²For he will deliver the needy who cry
    out,
  the afflicted who have no-one to help.
¹³He will take pity on the weak and the
    needy
  and save the needy from death.
¹⁴He will rescue them from oppression
    and violence,
  for precious is their blood in his sight.

¹⁵Long may he live!
  May gold from Sheba be given to him.
May people ever pray for him
  and bless him all day long.
¹⁶Let corn abound throughout the land;
  on the tops of the hills may it sway.
Let its fruit flourish like Lebanon;
  let it thrive like the grass of the field.
¹⁷May his name endure for ever;
  may it continue as long as the sun.

All nations will be blessed through him,
  and they will call him blessed.

¹⁸Praise be to the LORD God, the God of
    Israel,
  who alone does marvellous deeds.
¹⁹Praise be to his glorious name for ever;
  may the whole earth be filled with his
    glory.
          Amen and Amen.

²⁰This concludes the prayers of David son
    of Jesse.

BOOK III

Psalms 73–89

Psalm 73

A psalm of Asaph.

¹Surely God is good to Israel,
  to those who are pure in heart.

²But as for me, my feet had almost
    slipped;
  I had nearly lost my foothold.
³For I envied the arrogant
  when I saw the prosperity of the
    wicked.

⁴They have no struggles;
  their bodies are healthy and strong.*a*
⁵They are free from the burdens
    common to man;
  they are not plagued by human ills.
⁶Therefore pride is their necklace;
  they clothe themselves with violence.
⁷From their callous hearts comes
    iniquity;*b*
  the evil conceits of their minds know
    no limits.
⁸They scoff, and speak with malice;
  in their arrogance they threaten
    oppression.
⁹Their mouths lay claim to heaven,
  and their tongues take possession of
    the earth.
¹⁰Therefore their people turn to them
  and drink up waters in abundance.*c*
¹¹They say, "How can God know?
  Does the Most High have
    knowledge?"

¹²This is what the wicked are like—
  always carefree, they increase in
    wealth.

---

c8 That is, the Euphrates   *d8* Or *the end of the land*
a4 With a different word division of the Hebrew; Masoretic Text *struggles at their death; / their bodies are healthy*
b7 Syriac (see also Septuagint); Hebrew *Their eyes bulge with fat*
c10 The meaning of the Hebrew for this verse is uncertain.

13Surely in vain have I kept my heart
          pure;
     in vain have I washed my hands in
          innocence.
14All day long I have been plagued;
     I have been punished every morning.

15If I had said, "I will speak thus,"
     I would have betrayed your children.
16When I tried to understand all this,
     it was oppressive to me
17till I entered the sanctuary of God;
     then I understood their final destiny.

18Surely you place them on slippery
          ground;
     you cast them down to ruin.
19How suddenly are they destroyed,
     completely swept away by terrors!
20As a dream when one awakes,
     so when you arise, O Lord,
     you will despise them as fantasies.

21When my heart was grieved
     and my spirit embittered,
22I was senseless and ignorant;
     I was a brute beast before you.

23Yet I am always with you;
     you hold me by my right hand.
24You guide me with your counsel,
     and afterwards you will take me into
          glory.
25Whom have I in heaven but you?
     And earth has nothing I desire
          besides you.
26My flesh and my heart may fail,
     but God is the strength of my heart
     and my portion for ever.

27Those who are far from you will perish;
     you destroy all who are unfaithful to
          you.
28But as for me, it is good to be near God.
     I have made the Sovereign LORD my
          refuge;
     I will tell of all your deeds.

Psalm 74

A maskil[a] of Asaph.

1Why have you rejected us for ever, O
     God?

Why does your anger smoulder
     against the sheep of your pasture?
2Remember the people you purchased
     of old,
     the tribe of your inheritance, whom
          you redeemed—
Mount Zion, where you dwelt.
3Turn your steps towards these
          everlasting ruins,
     all this destruction the enemy has
          brought on the sanctuary.

4Your foes roared in the place where you
     met with us;
     they set up their standards as signs.
5They behaved like men wielding axes
     to cut through a thicket of trees.
6They smashed all the carved panelling
     with their axes and hatchets.
7They burned your sanctuary to the
          ground;
     they defiled the dwelling-place of
          your Name.
8They said in their hearts, "We will
          crush them completely!"
     They burned every place where God
          was worshipped in the land.
9We are given no miraculous signs;
     no prophets are left,
     and none of us knows how long this
          will be.

10How long will the enemy mock you, O
          God?
     Will the foe revile your name for
          ever?
11Why do you hold back your hand, your
          right hand?
     Take it from the folds of your
          garment and destroy them!

12But you, O God, are my king from of
          old;
     you bring salvation upon the earth.
13It was you who split open the sea by
          your power;
     you broke the heads of the monster in
          the waters.
14It was you who crushed the heads of
          Leviathan
     and gave him as food to the creatures
          of the desert.

aTitle: Probably a literary or musical term

¹⁵It was you who opened up springs and
    streams;
    you dried up the ever-flowing rivers.
¹⁶The day is yours, and yours also the
    night;
    you established the sun and moon.
¹⁷It was you who set all the boundaries of
    the earth;
    you made both summer and winter.

¹⁸Remember how the enemy has mocked
    you, O LORD,
    how foolish people have reviled your
    name.
¹⁹Do not hand over the life of your dove
    to wild beasts;
    do not forget the lives of your
    afflicted people for ever.
²⁰Have regard for your covenant,
    because haunts of violence fill the
    dark places of the land.
²¹Do not let the oppressed retreat in
    disgrace;
    may the poor and needy praise your
    name.

²²Rise up, O God, and defend your
    cause;
    remember how fools mock you all
    day long.
²³Do not ignore the clamour of your
    adversaries,
    the uproar of your enemies, which
    rises continually.

Psalm 75

For the director of music. ⌜To the tune of⌝
"Do Not Destroy". A psalm of Asaph. A
song.

¹We give thanks to you, O God,
    we give thanks, for your Name is
    near;
    men tell of your wonderful deeds.

²You say, "I choose the appointed time;
    it is I who judge uprightly.
³When the earth and all its people
    quake,
    it is I who hold its pillars firm.   *Selah*
⁴To the arrogant I say, 'Boast no more,'

and to the wicked, 'Do not lift up
    your horns.
⁵Do not lift your horns against heaven;
    do not speak with outstretched
    neck.'"

⁶No-one from the east or the west
    or from the desert can exalt a man.
⁷But it is God who judges:
    He brings one down, he exalts
    another.
⁸In the hand of the LORD is a cup
    full of foaming wine mixed with
    spices;
    he pours it out, and all the wicked of the
    earth
    drink it down to its very dregs.

⁹As for me, I will declare this for ever;
    I will sing praise to the God of Jacob.
¹⁰I will cut off the horns of all the wicked,
    but the horns of the righteous shall be
    lifted up.

Psalm 76

For the director of music. With stringed
instruments. A psalm of Asaph. A song.

¹In Judah God is known;
    his name is great in Israel.
²His tent is in Salem,
    his dwelling-place in Zion.
³There he broke the flashing arrows,
    the shields and the swords, the
    weapons of war.   *Selah*

⁴You are resplendent with light,
    more majestic than mountains rich
    with game.
⁵Valiant men lie plundered,
    they sleep their last sleep;
    not one of the warriors
    can lift his hands.
⁶At your rebuke, O God of Jacob,
    both horse and chariot lie still.
⁷You alone are to be feared.
    Who can stand before you when you
    are angry?
⁸From heaven you pronounced
    judgment,
    and the land feared and was quiet—
⁹when you, O God, rose up to judge,

to save all the afflicted of the land.
Selah

¹⁰Surely your wrath against men brings
you praise,
and the survivors of your wrath are
restrained.ᵃ

¹¹Make vows to the LORD your God and
fulfil them;
let all the neighbouring lands
bring gifts to the One to be feared.
¹²He breaks the spirit of rulers;
he is feared by the kings of the earth.

Psalm 77

For the director of music. For Jeduthun. Of
Asaph. A psalm.

¹I cried out to God for help;
I cried out to God to hear me.
²When I was in distress, I sought the Lord;
at night I stretched out untiring hands
and my soul refused to be comforted.

³I remembered you, O God, and I
groaned;
I mused, and my spirit grew faint.
Selah

⁴You kept my eyes from closing;
I was too troubled to speak.
⁵I thought about the former days,
the years of long ago;
⁶I remembered my songs in the night.
My heart mused and my spirit
enquired:

⁷"Will the Lord reject for ever?
Will he never show his favour again?
⁸Has his unfailing love vanished for
ever?
Has his promise failed for all time?
⁹Has God forgotten to be merciful?
Has he in anger withheld his
compassion?"   Selah

¹⁰Then I thought, "To this I will appeal:
the years of the right hand of the
Most High."
¹¹I will remember the deeds of the LORD;

yes, I will remember your miracles of
long ago.
¹²I will meditate on all your works
and consider all your mighty deeds.

¹³Your ways, O God, are holy.
What god is so great as our God?
¹⁴You are the God who performs
miracles;
you display your power among the
peoples.
¹⁵With your mighty arm you redeemed
your people,
the descendants of Jacob and Joseph.
Selah

¹⁶The waters saw you, O God,
the waters saw you and writhed;
the very depths were convulsed.
¹⁷The clouds poured down water,
the skies resounded with thunder;
your arrows flashed back and forth.
¹⁸Your thunder was heard in the
whirlwind,
your lightning lit up the world;
the earth trembled and quaked.
¹⁹Your path led through the sea,
your way through the mighty waters,
though your footprints were not seen.

²⁰You led your people like a flock
by the hand of Moses and Aaron.

Psalm 78

A maskilᵃ of Asaph.

¹O my people, hear my teaching;
listen to the words of my mouth.
²I will open my mouth in parables,
I will utter hidden things, things from
of old—
³what we have heard and known,
what our fathers have told us.
⁴We will not hide them from their
children;
we will tell the next generation
the praiseworthy deeds of the LORD,
his power, and the wonders he has
done.

ᵃ10 Or Surely the wrath of men brings you praise, / and with the remainder of wrath you arm yourself
ᵃTitle: Probably a literary or musical term

5He decreed statutes for Jacob
and established the law in Israel,
which he commanded our forefathers
to teach their children,
6so that the next generation would know
them,
even the children yet to be born,
and they in turn would tell their
children.
7Then they would put their trust in God
and would not forget his deeds
but would keep his commands.
8They would not be like their
forefathers—
a stubborn and rebellious generation,
whose hearts were not loyal to God,
whose spirits were not faithful to him.

9The men of Ephraim, though armed
with bows,
turned back on the day of battle;
10they did not keep God's covenant
and refused to live by his law.
11They forgot what he had done,
the wonders he had shown them.
12He did miracles in the sight of their
fathers
in the land of Egypt, in the region of
Zoan.
13He divided the sea and led them
through;
he made the water stand firm like a
wall.
14He guided them with the cloud by day
and with light from the fire all night.
15He split the rocks in the desert
and gave them water as abundant as
the seas;
16he brought streams out of a rocky crag
and made water flow down like rivers.

17But they continued to sin against him,
rebelling in the desert against the
Most High.
18They wilfully put God to the test
by demanding the food they craved.
19They spoke against God, saying,
"Can God spread a table in the
desert?
20When he struck the rock, water gushed
out,
and streams flowed abundantly.
But can he also give us food?

Can he supply meat for his people?"
21When the LORD heard them, he was
very angry;
his fire broke out against Jacob,
and his wrath rose against Israel,
22for they did not believe in God
or trust in his deliverance.
23Yet he gave a command to the skies
above
and opened the doors of the heavens;
24he rained down manna for the people to
eat,
he gave them the grain of heaven.
25Men ate the bread of angels;
he sent them all the food they could
eat.
26He let loose the east wind from the
heavens
and led forth the south wind by his
power.
27He rained meat down on them like
dust,
flying birds like sand on the seashore.
28He made them come down inside their
camp,
all around their tents.
29They ate till they had more than
enough,
for he had given them what they
craved.
30But before they turned from the food
they craved,
even while it was still in their mouths,
31God's anger rose against them;
he put to death the sturdiest among
them,
cutting down the young men of
Israel.

32In spite of all this, they kept on sinning;
in spite of his wonders, they did not
believe.
33So he ended their days in futility
and their years in terror.
34Whenever God slew them, they would
seek him;
they eagerly turned to him again.
35They remembered that God was their
Rock,
that God Most High was their
Redeemer.
36But then they would flatter him with
their mouths,

lying to him with their tongues;
³⁷their hearts were not loyal to him,
   they were not faithful to his
     covenant.
³⁸Yet he was merciful;
   he forgave their iniquities
    and did not destroy them.
  Time after time he restrained his anger
   and did not stir up his full wrath.
³⁹He remembered that they were but
   flesh,
   a passing breeze that does not
    return.

⁴⁰How often they rebelled against him in
   the desert
   and grieved him in the wasteland!
⁴¹Again and again they put God to the
   test;
   they vexed the Holy One of Israel.
⁴²They did not remember his power—
   the day he redeemed them from the
    oppressor,
⁴³the day he displayed his miraculous
   signs in Egypt,
   his wonders in the region of Zoan.
⁴⁴He turned their rivers to blood;
   they could not drink from their
    streams.
⁴⁵He sent swarms of flies that devoured
   them,
   and frogs that devastated them.
⁴⁶He gave their crops to the grasshopper,
   their produce to the locust.
⁴⁷He destroyed their vines with hail
   and their sycamore-figs with sleet.
⁴⁸He gave over their cattle to the hail,
   their livestock to bolts of lightning.
⁴⁹He unleashed against them his hot
   anger,
   his wrath, indignation and hostility—
   a band of destroying angels.
⁵⁰He prepared a path for his anger;
   he did not spare them from death
   but gave them over to the plague.
⁵¹He struck down all the firstborn of
   Egypt,
   the firstfruits of manhood in the tents
    of Ham.
⁵²But he brought his people out like a
   flock;
   he led them like sheep through the
    desert.

⁵³He guided them safely, so they were
   unafraid;
   but the sea engulfed their enemies.
⁵⁴Thus he brought them to the border of
   his holy land,
   to the hill country his right hand had
    taken.
⁵⁵He drove out nations before them
   and allotted their lands to them as an
    inheritance;
   he settled the tribes of Israel in their
    homes.

⁵⁶But they put God to the test
   and rebelled against the Most High;
   they did not keep his statutes.
⁵⁷Like their fathers they were disloyal
   and faithless,
   as unreliable as a faulty bow.
⁵⁸They angered him with their high
   places;
   they aroused his jealousy with their
    idols.
⁵⁹When God heard them, he was very
   angry;
   he rejected Israel completely.
⁶⁰He abandoned the tabernacle of Shiloh,
   the tent he had set up among men.
⁶¹He sent ⌊the ark of⌋ his might into
   captivity,
   his splendour into the hands of the
    enemy.
⁶²He gave his people over to the sword;
   he was very angry with his
    inheritance.
⁶³Fire consumed their young men,
   and their maidens had no wedding
    songs;
⁶⁴their priests were put to the sword,
   and their widows could not weep.

⁶⁵Then the Lord awoke as from sleep,
   as a man wakes from the stupor of
    wine.
⁶⁶He beat back his enemies;
   he put them to everlasting shame.
⁶⁷Then he rejected the tents of Joseph,
   he did not choose the tribe of
    Ephraim;
⁶⁸but he chose the tribe of Judah,
   Mount Zion, which he loved.
⁶⁹He built his sanctuary like the heights,

like the earth that he established for
ever.
⁷⁰He chose David his servant
and took him from the sheep pens;
⁷¹from tending the sheep he brought him
to be the shepherd of his people
Jacob,
of Israel his inheritance.
⁷²And David shepherded them with
integrity of heart;
with skilful hands he led them.

Psalm 79

A psalm of Asaph.

¹O God, the nations have invaded your
inheritance;
they have defiled your holy temple,
they have reduced Jerusalem to
rubble.
²They have given the dead bodies of
your servants
as food to the birds of the air,
the flesh of your saints to the beasts
of the earth.
³They have poured out blood like water
all around Jerusalem,
and there is no-one to bury the dead.
⁴We are objects of reproach to our
neighbours,
of scorn and derision to those around
us.

⁵How long, O LORD? Will you be angry
for ever?
How long will your jealousy burn like
fire?
⁶Pour out your wrath on the nations
that do not acknowledge you,
on the kingdoms
that do not call on your name;
⁷for they have devoured Jacob
and destroyed his homeland.
⁸Do not hold against us the sins of the
fathers;
may your mercy come quickly to
meet us,
for we are in desperate need.

⁹Help us, O God our Saviour,
for the glory of your name;

deliver us and forgive our sins
for your name's sake.
¹⁰Why should the nations say,
"Where is their God?"
Before our eyes, make known among
the nations
that you avenge the outpoured blood
of your servants.
¹¹May the groans of the prisoners come
before you;
by the strength of your arm
preserve those condemned to die.

¹²Pay back into the laps of our neighbours
seven times
the reproach they have hurled at you,
O Lord.
¹³Then we your people, the sheep of your
pasture,
will praise you for ever;
from generation to generation
we will recount your praise.

Psalm 80

For the director of music. To ⌐the tune of⌐
"The Lilies of the Covenant". Of Asaph. A
psalm.

¹Hear us, O Shepherd of Israel,
you who lead Joseph like a flock;
you who sit enthroned between the
cherubim, shine forth
²   before Ephraim, Benjamin and
Manasseh.
Awaken your might;
come and save us.

³Restore us, O God;
make your face shine upon us,
that we may be saved.

⁴O LORD God Almighty,
how long will your anger smoulder
against the prayers of your people?
⁵You have fed them with the bread of
tears;
you have made them drink tears by
the bowlful.
⁶You have made us a source of
contention to our neighbours,
and our enemies mock us.

⁷Restore us, O God Almighty;
　make your face shine upon us,
　that we may be saved.

⁸You brought a vine out of Egypt;
　you drove out the nations and
　　planted it.
⁹You cleared the ground for it,
　and it took root and filled the land.
¹⁰The mountains were covered with its
　　shade,
　the mighty cedars with its branches.
¹¹It sent out its boughs to the Sea,ᵃ
　its shoots as far as the River.ᵇ

¹²Why have you broken down its walls
　so that all who pass by pick its
　　grapes?
¹³Boars from the forest ravage it
　and the creatures of the field feed on it.
¹⁴Return to us, O God Almighty!
　Look down from heaven and see!
　Watch over this vine,
¹⁵　the root your right hand has planted,
　the sonᶜ you have raised up for
　　yourself.

¹⁶Your vine is cut down, it is burned with
　　fire;
　at your rebuke your people perish.
¹⁷Let your hand rest on the man at your
　　right hand,
　the son of man you have raised up for
　　yourself.
¹⁸Then we will not turn away from you;
　revive us, and we will call on your
　　name.

¹⁹Restore us, O LORD God Almighty;
　make your face shine upon us,
　that we may be saved.

Psalm 81

For the director of music. According to
　gittith.ᵃ Of Asaph.

¹Sing for joy to God our strength;
　shout aloud to the God of Jacob!

²Begin the music, strike the tambourine,
　play the melodious harp and lyre.

³Sound the ram's horn at the New
　　Moon,
　and when the moon is full, on the day
　of our Feast;
⁴this is a decree for Israel,
　an ordinance of the God of Jacob.
⁵He established it as a statute for Joseph
　when he went out against Egypt,
　where we heard a language we did
　not understand.ᵇ

⁶He says, "I removed the burden from
　their shoulders;
　their hands were set free from the
　　basket.
⁷In your distress you called and I rescued
　　you,
　I answered you out of a
　　thundercloud;
　I tested you at the waters of Meribah.
　　　　　　　　　　　　　　　Selah

⁸"Hear, O my people, and I will warn
　　you—
　if you would but listen to me, O
　　Israel!
⁹You shall have no foreign god among
　　you;
　you shall not bow down to an alien
　　god.
¹⁰I am the LORD your God,
　who brought you up out of Egypt.
　Open wide your mouth and I will fill
　　it.

¹¹"But my people would not listen to me;
　Israel would not submit to me.
¹²So I gave them over to their stubborn
　　hearts
　to follow their own devices.

¹³"If my people would but listen to me,
　if Israel would follow my ways,
¹⁴how quickly would I subdue their
　　enemies
　and turn my hand against their
　　foes!

ᵃ11 Probably the Mediterranean　　ᵇ11 That is, the Euphrates　　ᶜ15 Or branch
ᵃTitle: Probably a musical term　　ᵇ5 Or / and we heard a voice we had not known

¹⁵Those who hate the LORD would cringe
    before him,
  and their punishment would last for
    ever.
¹⁶But you would be fed with the finest of
    wheat;
  with honey from the rock I would
    satisfy you."

Psalm 82

A psalm of Asaph.

¹God presides in the great assembly;
  he gives judgment among the "gods":

²"How long will you*ᵃ* defend the unjust
  and show partiality to the wicked?
                                        Selah
³Defend the cause of the weak and
    fatherless;
  maintain the rights of the poor and
    oppressed.
⁴Rescue the weak and needy;
  deliver them from the hand of the
    wicked.

⁵"They know nothing, they understand
    nothing.
  They walk about in darkness;
  all the foundations of the earth are
    shaken.

⁶"I said, 'You are "gods";
  you are all sons of the Most High.'
⁷But you will die like mere men;
  you will fall like every other ruler."

⁸Rise up, O God, judge the earth,
  for all the nations are your
    inheritance.

Psalm 83

A song. A psalm of Asaph.

¹O God, do not keep silent;
  be not quiet, O God, be not still.

²See how your enemies are astir,
  how your foes rear their heads.
³With cunning they conspire against
    your people;
  they plot against those you cherish.
⁴"Come," they say, "let us destroy them
    as a nation,
  that the name of Israel be
    remembered no more."

⁵With one mind they plot together;
  they form an alliance against you—
⁶the tents of Edom and the Ishmaelites,
    of Moab and the Hagrites,
⁷Gebal,*ᵃ* Ammon and Amalek,
  Philistia, with the people of Tyre.
⁸Even Assyria has joined them
  to lend strength to the descendants of
    Lot.   *Selah*

⁹Do to them as you did to Midian,
  as you did to Sisera and Jabin at the
    river Kishon,
¹⁰who perished at Endor
  and became like refuse on the
    ground.
¹¹Make their nobles like Oreb and Zeeb,
  all their princes like Zebah and
    Zalmunna,
¹²who said, "Let us take possession
  of the pasture-lands of God."

¹³Make them like tumble-weed, O my
    God,
  like chaff before the wind.
¹⁴As fire consumes the forest
  or a flame sets the mountains ablaze,
¹⁵so pursue them with your tempest
  and terrify them with your storm.
¹⁶Cover their faces with shame
  so that men will seek your name, O
    LORD.

¹⁷May they ever be ashamed and
    dismayed;
  may they perish in disgrace.
¹⁸Let them know that you, whose name is
    the LORD—
  that you alone are the Most High over
    all the earth.

---

*ᵃ*2 The Hebrew is plural.   *ᵃ*7 That is, Byblos

Psalm 84

For the director of music. According to
gittith.[a] Of the Sons of Korah. A psalm.

[1]How lovely is your dwelling-place,
    O LORD Almighty!
[2]My soul yearns, even faints,
    for the courts of the LORD;
my heart and my flesh cry out
    for the living God.

[3]Even the sparrow has found a home,
    and the swallow a nest for herself,
    where she may have her young—
a place near your altar,
    O LORD Almighty, my King and my
        God.
[4]Blessed are those who dwell in your
        house;
    they are ever praising you.   *Selah*

[5]Blessed are those whose strength is in
        you,
    who have set their hearts on
        pilgrimage.
[6]As they pass through the Valley of
        Baca,
    they make it a place of springs;
    the autumn rains also cover it with
        pools.[b]
[7]They go from strength to strength,
    till each appears before God in
        Zion.

[8]Hear my prayer, O LORD God
        Almighty;
    listen to me, O God of Jacob.   *Selah*
[9]Look upon our shield,[c] O God;
    look with favour on your anointed
        one.

[10]Better is one day in your courts
    than a thousand elsewhere;
I would rather be a doorkeeper in the
        house of my God
    than dwell in the tents of the wicked.
[11]For the LORD God is a sun and shield;
    the LORD bestows favour and honour;
no good thing does he withhold
    from those whose walk is blameless.

[12]O LORD Almighty,
    blessed is the man who trusts in you.

Psalm 85

For the director of music. Of the Sons of
Korah. A psalm.

[1]You showed favour to your land, O
        LORD;
    you restored the fortunes of Jacob.
[2]You forgave the iniquity of your people
    and covered all their sins.   *Selah*
[3]You set aside all your wrath
    and turned from your fierce anger.

[4]Restore us again, O God our Saviour,
    and put away your displeasure
        towards us.
[5]Will you be angry with us for ever?
    Will you prolong your anger through
        all generations?
[6]Will you not revive us again,
    that your people may rejoice in
        you?
[7]Show us your unfailing love, O LORD,
    and grant us your salvation.

[8]I will listen to what God the LORD will
        say;
    he promises peace to his people, his
        saints—
    but let them not return to folly.
[9]Surely his salvation is near those who
        fear him,
    that his glory may dwell in our land.

[10]Love and faithfulness meet together;
    righteousness and peace kiss each
        other.
[11]Faithfulness springs forth from the
        earth,
    and righteousness looks down from
        heaven.
[12]The LORD will indeed give what is
        good,
    and our land will yield its harvest.
[13]Righteousness goes before him
    and prepares the way for his steps.

---

[a]Title: Probably a musical term   [b]6 Or *blessings*   [c]9 Or *sovereign*

Psalm 86

A prayer of David.

¹Hear, O LORD, and answer me,
  for I am poor and needy.
²Guard my life, for I am devoted to you.
  You are my God; save your servant
    who trusts in you.
³Have mercy on me, O Lord,
  for I call to you all day long.
⁴Bring joy to your servant,
  for to you, O Lord,
  I lift up my soul.

⁵You are forgiving and good, O Lord,
  abounding in love to all who call to
    you.
⁶Hear my prayer, O LORD;
  listen to my cry for mercy.
⁷In the day of my trouble I will call to
    you,
  for you will answer me.

⁸Among the gods there is none like you,
    O Lord;
  no deeds can compare with
    yours.
⁹All the nations you have made
  will come and worship before you, O
    Lord;
  they will bring glory to your
    name.
¹⁰For you are great and do marvellous
    deeds;
  you alone are God.

¹¹Teach me your way, O LORD,
  and I will walk in your truth;
  give me an undivided heart,
  that I may fear your name.
¹²I will praise you, O Lord my God, with
    all my heart;
  I will glorify your name for
    ever.
¹³For great is your love towards me;
  you have delivered me from the
    depths of the grave.*a*

¹⁴The arrogant are attacking me, O God;
  a band of ruthless men seeks my
    life—
  men without regard for you.
¹⁵But you, O Lord, are a compassionate
    and gracious God,
  slow to anger, abounding in love and
    faithfulness.
¹⁶Turn to me and have mercy on me;
  grant your strength to your servant
  and save the son of your
    maidservant.*b*
¹⁷Give me a sign of your goodness,
  that my enemies may see it and be
    put to shame,
  for you, O LORD, have helped me and
    comforted me.

Psalm 87

Of the Sons of Korah. A psalm. A song.

¹He has set his foundation on the holy
    mountain;
² the LORD loves the gates of Zion
  more than all the dwellings of Jacob.
³Glorious things are said of you,
  O city of God: *Selah*
⁴"I will record Rahab*a* and Babylon
  among those who acknowledge me—
  Philistia too, and Tyre, along with
    Cush*b*—
  and will say, 'This*c* one was born in
    Zion.'"

⁵Indeed, of Zion it will be said,
  "This one and that one were born in
    her,
  and the Most High himself will
    establish her."
⁶The LORD will write in the register of
    the peoples:
  "This one was born in Zion."
                               Selah
⁷As they make music they will sing,
  "All my fountains are in you."

---

a13 Hebrew *Sheol*   *b16* Or *save your faithful son*
a4 A poetic name for Egypt   *b4* That is, the upper Nile region
c4 Or *"O Rahab and Babylon, / Philistia, Tyre and Cush, / I will record concerning those who acknowledge me: / 'This*

Psalm 88

A song. A psalm of the Sons of Korah. For
the director of music. According to *mahalath
leannoth.*[a] A *maskil*[b] of Heman the Ezrahite.

¹O LORD, the God who saves me,
    day and night I cry out before you.
²May my prayer come before you;
    turn your ear to my cry.

³For my soul is full of trouble
    and my life draws near the grave.[c]
⁴I am counted among those who go
        down to the pit;
    I am like a man without strength.
⁵I am set apart with the dead,
    like the slain who lie in the grave,
whom you remember no more,
    who are cut off from your care.

⁶You have put me in the lowest pit,
    in the darkest depths.
⁷Your wrath lies heavily upon me;
    you have overwhelmed me with all
        your waves.   *Selah*
⁸You have taken from me my closest
        friends
    and have made me repulsive to them.
I am confined and cannot escape;
⁹   my eyes are dim with grief.

I call to you, O LORD, every day;
    I spread out my hands to you.
¹⁰Do you show your wonders to the
        dead?
    Do those who are dead rise up and
        praise you?   *Selah*
¹¹Is your love declared in the grave,
    your faithfulness in Destruction?[d]
¹²Are your wonders known in the place of
        darkness,
    or your righteous deeds in the land of
        oblivion?

¹³But I cry to you for help, O LORD;
    in the morning my prayer comes
        before you.
¹⁴Why, O LORD, do you reject me
    and hide your face from me?

¹⁵From my youth I have been afflicted
    and close to death;

I have suffered your terrors and am in
    despair.
¹⁶Your wrath has swept over me;
    your terrors have destroyed me.
¹⁷All day long they surround me like a
        flood;
    they have completely engulfed me.
¹⁸You have taken my companions and
        loved ones from me;
    the darkness is my closest friend.

Psalm 89

A *maskil*[a] of Ethan the Ezrahite.

¹I will sing of the LORD's great love for
        ever;
    with my mouth I will make your
        faithfulness known through all
        generations.
²I will declare that your love stands firm
        for ever,
    that you established your faithfulness
        in heaven itself.

³You said, "I have made a covenant with
        my chosen one,
    I have sworn to David my servant,
⁴'I will establish your line for ever
    and make your throne firm through
        all generations.' "   *Selah*

⁵The heavens praise your wonders, O
        LORD,
    your faithfulness too, in the assembly
        of the holy ones.
⁶For who in the skies above can compare
        with the LORD?
    Who is like the LORD among the
        heavenly beings?
⁷In the council of the holy ones God is
        greatly feared;
    he is more awesome than all who
        surround him.
⁸O LORD God Almighty, who is like you?
    You are mighty, O LORD, and your
        faithfulness surrounds you.

⁹You rule over the surging sea;
    when its waves mount up, you still
        them.

---

[a]Title: Possibly a tune, "The Suffering of Affliction"   [b]Title: Probably a literary or musical term
[c]3 Hebrew *Sheol*   [d]11 Hebrew *Abaddon*   [a]Title: Probably a literary or musical term

¹⁰You crushed Rahab like one of the
        slain;
    with your strong arm you scattered
        your enemies.
¹¹The heavens are yours, and yours also
        the earth;
    you founded the world and all that is
        in it.
¹²You created the north and the south;
    Tabor and Hermon sing for joy at
        your name.
¹³Your arm is endued with power;
    your hand is strong, your right hand
        exalted.

¹⁴Righteousness and justice are the
        foundation of your throne;
    love and faithfulness go before
        you.
¹⁵Blessed are those who have learned to
        acclaim you,
    who walk in the light of your
        presence, O Lᴏʀᴅ.
¹⁶They rejoice in your name all day long;
    they exult in your righteousness.
¹⁷For you are their glory and strength,
    and by your favour you exalt our
        horn.ᵇ
¹⁸Indeed, our shieldᶜ belongs to the
        Lᴏʀᴅ,
    our king to the Holy One of Israel.

¹⁹Once you spoke in a vision,
    to your faithful people you said:
"I have bestowed strength on a warrior;
    I have exalted a young man from
        among the people.
²⁰I have found David my servant;
    with my sacred oil I have anointed
        him.
²¹My hand will sustain him;
    surely my arm will strengthen him.
²²No enemy will subject him to tribute;
    no wicked man will oppress him.
²³I will crush his foes before him
    and strike down his adversaries.
²⁴My faithful love will be with him,
    and through my name his hornᵈ will
        be exalted.
²⁵I will set his hand over the sea,
    his right hand over the rivers.

²⁶He will call out to me, 'You are my
        Father,
    my God, the Rock my Saviour.'
²⁷I will also appoint him my firstborn,
    the most exalted of the kings of the
        earth.
²⁸I will maintain my love to him for ever,
    and my covenant with him will never
        fail.
²⁹I will establish his line for ever,
    his throne as long as the heavens
        endure.

³⁰"If his sons forsake my law
    and do not follow my statutes,
³¹if they violate my decrees
    and fail to keep my commands,
³²I will punish their sin with the rod,
    their iniquity with flogging;
³³but I will not take my love from him,
    nor will I ever betray my faithfulness.
³⁴I will not violate my covenant
    or alter what my lips have uttered.
³⁵Once for all, I have sworn by my
        holiness—
    and I will not lie to David—
³⁶that his line will continue for ever
    and his throne endure before me like
        the sun;
³⁷it will be established for ever like the
        moon,
    the faithful witness in the sky." Selah

³⁸But you have rejected, you have
        spurned,
    you have been very angry with your
        anointed one.
³⁹You have renounced the covenant with
        your servant
    and have defiled his crown in the
        dust.
⁴⁰You have broken through all his walls
    and reduced his strongholds to ruins.
⁴¹All who pass by have plundered him;
    he has become the scorn of his
        neighbours.
⁴²You have exalted the right hand of his
        foes;
    you have made all his enemies rejoice.
⁴³You have turned back the edge of his
        sword

ᵇ17 *Horn* here symbolises strong one.   ᶜ18 Or *sovereign*   ᵈ24 *Horn* here symbolises strength.

and have not supported him in battle.

⁴⁴You have put an end to his splendour
and cast his throne to the ground.
⁴⁵You have cut short the days of his
youth;
you have covered him with a mantle
of shame. *Selah*

⁴⁶How long, O LORD? Will you hide
yourself for ever?
How long will your wrath burn like
fire?
⁴⁷Remember how fleeting is my life.
For what futility you have created all
men!
⁴⁸What man can live and not see death,
or save himself from the power of the
grave?*ᵉ* *Selah*
⁴⁹O Lord, where is your former great
love,
which in your faithfulness you swore
to David?
⁵⁰Remember, Lord, how your servant
has*f* been mocked,
how I bear in my heart the taunts of
all the nations,
⁵¹the taunts with which your enemies
have mocked, O LORD,
with which they have mocked every
step of your anointed one.

⁵²Praise be to the LORD for ever!
Amen and Amen.

BOOK IV

Psalms 90–106

Psalm 90

A prayer of Moses the man of God.

¹Lord, you have been our dwelling-place
throughout all generations.
²Before the mountains were born
or you brought forth the earth and
the world,
from everlasting to everlasting you
are God.

³You turn men back to dust,
saying, "Return to dust, O sons of
men."
⁴For a thousand years in your sight
are like a day that has just gone by,
or like a watch in the night.
⁵You sweep men away in the sleep of
death;
they are like the new grass of the
morning—
⁶though in the morning it springs up
new,
by evening it is dry and withered.

⁷We are consumed by your anger
and terrified by your indignation.
⁸You have set our iniquities before
you,
our secret sins in the light of your
presence.
⁹All our days pass away under your
wrath;
we finish our years with a moan.
¹⁰The length of our days is seventy
years—
or eighty, if we have the strength;
yet their span*ᵃ* is but trouble and
sorrow,
for they quickly pass, and we fly
away.

¹¹Who knows the power of your anger?
For your wrath is as great as the fear
that is due to you.
¹²Teach us to number our days aright,
that we may gain a heart of wisdom.

¹³Relent, O LORD! How long will it be?
Have compassion on your
servants.
¹⁴Satisfy us in the morning with your
unfailing love,
that we may sing for joy and be glad
all our days.
¹⁵Make us glad for as many days as you
have afflicted us,
for as many years as we have seen
trouble.
¹⁶May your deeds be shown to your
servants,
your splendour to their children.

ᵉ48 Hebrew *Sheol*   *f50* Or *your servants have*   *ᵃ10* Or *yet the best of them*

¹⁷May the favour[b] of the Lord our God
    rest upon us;
  establish the work of our hands for
    us—
  yes, establish the work of our
    hands.

Psalm 91

¹He who dwells in the shelter of the
    Most High
  will rest in the shadow of the
    Almighty.[a]
²I will say[b] of the LORD, "He is my
    refuge and my fortress,
  my God, in whom I trust."

³Surely he will save you from the
    fowler's snare
  and from the deadly pestilence.
⁴He will cover you with his feathers,
    and under his wings you will find
    refuge;
  his faithfulness will be your shield
    and rampart.
⁵You will not fear the terror of night,
  nor the arrow that flies by day,
⁶nor the pestilence that stalks in the
    darkness,
  nor the plague that destroys at
    midday.
⁷A thousand may fall at your side,
  ten thousand at your right hand,
  but it will not come near you.
⁸You will only observe with your eyes
  and see the punishment of the
    wicked.

⁹If you make the Most High your
    dwelling—
  even the LORD, who is my refuge—
¹⁰then no harm will befall you,
  no disaster will come near your
    tent.
¹¹For he will command his angels
    concerning you
  to guard you in all your ways;
¹²they will lift you up in their hands,
  so that you will not strike your foot
    against a stone.

¹³You will tread upon the lion and the
    cobra;
  you will trample the great lion and
    the serpent.

¹⁴"Because he loves me," says the LORD,
    "I will rescue him;
  I will protect him, for he
    acknowledges my name.
¹⁵He will call upon me, and I will answer
    him;
  I will be with him in trouble,
  I will deliver him and honour
    him.
¹⁶With long life will I satisfy him
  and show him my salvation."

Psalm 92

A psalm. A song. For the Sabbath day.

¹It is good to praise the LORD
  and make music to your name, O
    Most High,
²to proclaim your love in the morning
  and your faithfulness at night,
³to the music of the ten-stringed lyre
  and the melody of the harp.

⁴For you make me glad by your deeds, O
    LORD;
  I sing for joy at the work of your
    hands.
⁵How great are your works, O LORD,
  how profound your thoughts!
⁶The senseless man does not know,
  fools do not understand,
⁷that though the wicked spring up like
    grass
  and all evildoers flourish,
  they will be for ever destroyed.

⁸But you, O LORD, are exalted for ever.

⁹For surely your enemies, O LORD,
  surely your enemies will perish;
  all evildoers will be scattered.
¹⁰You have exalted my horn[a] like that of
    a wild ox;
  fine oils have been poured upon me.

---

b17 Or *beauty*   *a1* Hebrew *Shaddai*   *b2* Or *He says*   *a10* *Horn* here symbolises strength.

¹¹My eyes have seen the defeat of my
adversaries;
my ears have heard the rout of my
wicked foes.

¹²The righteous will flourish like a palm
tree,
they will grow like a cedar of
Lebanon;
¹³planted in the house of the LORD,
they will flourish in the courts of our
God.
¹⁴They will still bear fruit in old age,
they will stay fresh and green,
¹⁵proclaiming, "The LORD is upright;
he is my Rock, and there is no
wickedness in him."

Psalm 93

¹The LORD reigns, he is robed in
majesty;
the LORD is robed in majesty
and is armed with strength.
The world is firmly established;
it cannot be moved.
²Your throne was established long ago;
you are from all eternity.

³The seas have lifted up, O LORD,
the seas have lifted up their voice;
the seas have lifted up their pounding
waves.
⁴Mightier than the thunder of the great
waters,
mightier than the breakers of the
sea—
the LORD on high is mighty.

⁵Your statutes stand firm;
holiness adorns your house
for endless days, O LORD.

Psalm 94

¹O LORD, the God who avenges,
O God who avenges, shine forth.
²Rise up, O Judge of the earth;
pay back to the proud what they
deserve.
³How long will the wicked, O LORD,
how long will the wicked be jubilant?

⁴They pour out arrogant words;
all the evildoers are full of boasting.
⁵They crush your people, O LORD;
they oppress your inheritance.
⁶They slay the widow and the alien;
they murder the fatherless.
⁷They say, "The LORD does not see;
the God of Jacob pays no heed."

⁸Take heed, you senseless ones among
the people;
you fools, when will you become
wise?
⁹Does he who implanted the ear not
hear?
Does he who formed the eye not see?
¹⁰Does he who disciplines nations not
punish?
Does he who teaches man lack
knowledge?
¹¹The LORD knows the thoughts of man;
he knows that they are futile.

¹²Blessed is the man you discipline, O
LORD,
the man you teach from your law;
¹³you grant him relief from days of
trouble,
till a pit is dug for the wicked.
¹⁴For the LORD will not reject his people;
he will never forsake his inheritance.
¹⁵Judgment will again be founded on
righteousness,
and all the upright in heart will follow
it.

¹⁶Who will rise up for me against the
wicked?
Who will take a stand for me against
evildoers?
¹⁷Unless the LORD had given me help,
I would soon have dwelt in the silence
of death.
¹⁸When I said, "My foot is slipping,"
your love, O LORD, supported me.
¹⁹When anxiety was great within me,
your consolation brought joy to my
soul.

²⁰Can a corrupt throne be allied with
you—
one that brings on misery by its
decrees?

21They band together against the
　　righteous
　　and condemn the innocent to
　　　death.
22But the LORD has become my fortress,
　　and my God the rock in whom I take
　　　refuge.
23He will repay them for their sins
　　and destroy them for their
　　　wickedness;
　　the LORD our God will destroy them.

Psalm 95

1Come, let us sing for joy to the LORD;
　　let us shout aloud to the Rock of our
　　　salvation.
2Let us come before him with
　　thanksgiving
　　and extol him with music and song.

3For the LORD is the great God,
　　the great King above all gods.
4In his hand are the depths of the earth,
　　and the mountain peaks belong to him.
5The sea is his, for he made it,
　　and his hands formed the dry land.

6Come, let us bow down in worship,
　　let us kneel before the LORD our
　　　Maker;
7for he is our God
　　and we are the people of his pasture,
　　the flock under his care.

　Today, if you hear his voice,
8　do not harden your hearts as you did
　　　at Meribah,*a*
　　as you did that day at Massah*b* in the
　　　desert,
9where your fathers tested and tried me,
　　though they had seen what I did.
10For forty years I was angry with that
　　generation;
　　I said, "They are a people whose
　　　hearts go astray,
　　and they have not known my ways."
11So I declared on oath in my anger,
　　"They shall never enter my rest."

Psalm 96

1Sing to the LORD a new song;
　　sing to the LORD, all the earth.
2Sing to the LORD, praise his name;
　　proclaim his salvation day after day.
3Declare his glory among the nations,
　　his marvellous deeds among all
　　　peoples.

4For great is the LORD and most worthy
　　of praise;
　　he is to be feared above all gods.
5For all the gods of the nations are idols,
　　but the LORD made the heavens.
6Splendour and majesty are before him;
　　strength and glory are in his
　　　sanctuary.

7Ascribe to the LORD, O families of
　　nations,
　　ascribe to the LORD glory and
　　　strength.
8Ascribe to the LORD the glory due to his
　　name;
　　bring an offering and come into his
　　　courts.
9Worship the LORD in the splendour of
　　his*a* holiness;
　　tremble before him, all the earth.

10Say among the nations, "The LORD
　　reigns."
　　The world is firmly established, it
　　　cannot be moved;
　　he will judge the peoples with equity.
11Let the heavens rejoice, let the earth be
　　glad;
　　let the sea resound, and all that is in
　　　it;
12　let the fields be jubilant, and
　　everything in them.
　Then all the trees of the forest will sing
　　for joy;
13　they will sing before the LORD, for he
　　comes,
　　he comes to judge the earth.
　He will judge the world in righteousness
　　and the peoples in his truth.

---

a8 Meribah means quarrelling.　　*b8 Massah means testing.*　　*a9 Or LORD with the splendour of*

Psalm 97

¹The LORD reigns, let the earth be glad;
  let the distant shores rejoice.

²Clouds and thick darkness surround
    him;
  righteousness and justice are the
    foundation of his throne.
³Fire goes before him
  and consumes his foes on every side.
⁴His lightning lights up the world;
  the earth sees and trembles.
⁵The mountains melt like wax before the
    LORD,
  before the Lord of all the earth.
⁶The heavens proclaim his
    righteousness,
  and all the peoples see his glory.

⁷All who worship images are put to
    shame,
  those who boast in idols—
  worship him, all you gods!

⁸Zion hears and rejoices
  and the villages of Judah are glad
  because of your judgments, O LORD.
⁹For you, O LORD, are the Most High
    over all the earth;
  you are exalted far above all gods.

¹⁰Let those who love the LORD hate evil,
  for he guards the lives of his faithful
    ones
  and delivers them from the hand of
    the wicked.
¹¹Light is shed upon the righteous
  and joy on the upright in
    heart.
¹²Rejoice in the LORD, you who are
    righteous,
  and praise his holy name.

Psalm 98

A psalm.

¹Sing to the LORD a new song,
  for he has done marvellous things;
his right hand and his holy arm
  have worked salvation for him.

²The LORD has made his salvation known
  and revealed his righteousness to the
    nations.
³He has remembered his love
  and his faithfulness to the house of
    Israel;
all the ends of the earth have seen
  the salvation of our God.

⁴Shout for joy to the LORD, all the earth,
  burst into jubilant song with music;
⁵make music to the LORD with the harp,
  with the harp and the sound of
    singing,
⁶with trumpets and the blast of the ram's
    horn—
  shout for joy before the LORD, the
    King.

⁷Let the sea resound, and everything in
    it,
  the world, and all who live in it.
⁸Let the rivers clap their hands,
  let the mountains sing together for
    joy;
⁹let them sing before the LORD,
  for he comes to judge the earth.
He will judge the world in righteousness
  and the peoples with equity.

Psalm 99

¹The LORD reigns,
  let the nations tremble;
he sits enthroned between the
    cherubim,
  let the earth shake.
²Great is the LORD in Zion;
  he is exalted over all the nations.
³Let them praise your great and
    awesome name—
  he is holy.

⁴The King is mighty, he loves justice—
  you have established equity;
in Jacob you have done
  what is just and right.
⁵Exalt the LORD our God
  and worship at his footstool;
  he is holy.

⁶Moses and Aaron were among his
    priests,

Samuel was among those who called
on his name;
they called on the LORD
and he answered them.
⁷He spoke to them from the pillar of cloud;
they kept his statutes and the decrees
he gave them.

⁸O LORD our God,
you answered them;
you were to Israel*a* a forgiving God,
though you punished their
misdeeds.*b*
⁹Exalt the LORD our God
and worship at his holy mountain,
for the LORD our God is holy.

Psalm 100

A psalm. For giving thanks.

¹Shout for joy to the LORD, all the earth.
² Worship the LORD with gladness;
come before him with joyful songs.
³Know that the LORD is God.
It is he who made us, and we are his;*a*
we are his people, the sheep of his
pasture.

⁴Enter his gates with thanksgiving
and his courts with praise;
give thanks to him and praise his
name.
⁵For the LORD is good and his love
endures for ever;
his faithfulness continues through all
generations.

Psalm 101

Of David. A psalm.

¹I will sing of your love and justice;
to you, O LORD, I will sing praise.
²I will be careful to lead a blameless
life—
when will you come to me?

I will walk in my house
with blameless heart.

³I will set before my eyes
no vile thing.

The deeds of faithless men I hate;
they shall not cling to me.
⁴Men of perverse heart shall be far from
me;
I will have nothing to do with evil.

⁵Whoever slanders his neighbour in
secret,
him will I put to silence;
whoever has haughty eyes and a proud
heart,
him will I not endure.

⁶My eyes will be on the faithful in the
land,
that they may dwell with me;
he whose walk is blameless
will minister to me.

⁷No-one who practises deceit
will dwell in my house;
no-one who speaks falsely
will stand in my presence.

⁸Every morning I will put to silence
all the wicked in the land;
I will cut off every evildoer
from the city of the LORD.

Psalm 102

A prayer of an afflicted man. When he is faint
and pours out his lament before the LORD.

¹Hear my prayer, O LORD;
let my cry for help come to you.
²Do not hide your face from me
when I am in distress.
Turn your ear to me;
when I call, answer me quickly.

³For my days vanish like smoke;
my bones burn like glowing embers.
⁴My heart is blighted and withered like
grass;
I forget to eat my food.
⁵Because of my loud groaning

---

a8 Hebrew *them*   *b8* Or / *an avenger of the wrongs done to them*   *a3* Or *and not we ourselves*

I am reduced to skin and bones.
⁶I am like a desert owl,
    like an owl among the ruins.
⁷I lie awake; I have become
    like a bird alone on a roof.
⁸All day long my enemies taunt me;
    those who rail against me use my
        name as a curse.
⁹For I eat ashes as my food
    and mingle my drink with tears
¹⁰because of your great wrath,
    for you have taken me up and thrown
        me aside.
¹¹My days are like the evening shadow;
    I wither away like grass.

¹²But you, O LORD, sit enthroned for
    ever;
    your renown endures through all
        generations.
¹³You will arise and have compassion on
    Zion,
    for it is time to show favour to her;
    the appointed time has come.
¹⁴For her stones are dear to your servants;
    her very dust moves them to pity.
¹⁵The nations will fear the name of the
    LORD,
    all the kings of the earth will revere
        your glory.
¹⁶For the LORD will rebuild Zion
    and appear in his glory.
¹⁷He will respond to the prayer of the
    destitute;
    he will not despise their plea.

¹⁸Let this be written for a future
    generation,
    that a people not yet created may
        praise the LORD:
¹⁹"The LORD looked down from his
    sanctuary on high,
    from heaven he viewed the earth,
²⁰to hear the groans of the prisoners
    and release those condemned to
        death."
²¹So the name of the LORD will be
    declared in Zion
    and his praise in Jerusalem
²²when the peoples and the kingdoms
    assemble to worship the LORD.

²³In the course of my life[a] he broke my
    strength;
    he cut short my days.
²⁴So I said:
    "Do not take me away, O my God, in
        the midst of my days;
    your years go on through all
        generations.
²⁵In the beginning you laid the
    foundations of the earth,
    and the heavens are the work of your
        hands.
²⁶They will perish, but you remain;
    they will all wear out like a garment.
    Like clothing you will change them
    and they will be discarded.
²⁷But you remain the same,
    and your years will never end.
²⁸The children of your servants will live in
    your presence;
    their descendants will be established
        before you."

Psalm 103

Of David.

¹Praise the LORD, O my soul;
    all my inmost being, praise his holy
        name.
²Praise the LORD, O my soul,
    and forget not all his benefits—
³who forgives all your sins
    and heals all your diseases,
⁴who redeems your life from the pit
    and crowns you with love and
        compassion,
⁵who satisfies your desires with good
    things
    so that your youth is renewed like the
        eagle's.

⁶The LORD works righteousness
    and justice for all the oppressed.

⁷He made known his ways to Moses,
    his deeds to the people of Israel:
⁸The LORD is compassionate and
    gracious,
    slow to anger, abounding in love.

---

[a]23 Or *By his power*

⁹He will not always accuse,
    nor will he harbour his anger for
        ever;
¹⁰he does not treat us as our sins deserve
    or repay us according to our
        iniquities.
¹¹For as high as the heavens are above the
        earth,
    so great is his love for those who fear
        him;
¹²as far as the east is from the west,
    so far has he removed our
        transgressions from us.
¹³As a father has compassion on his
        children,
    so the LORD has compassion on those
        who fear him;
¹⁴for he knows how we are formed,
    he remembers that we are dust.
¹⁵As for man, his days are like grass,
    he flourishes like a flower of the field;
¹⁶the wind blows over it and it is gone,
    and its place remembers it no more.
¹⁷But from everlasting to everlasting
    the LORD's love is with those who fear
        him,
    and his righteousness with their
        children's children—
¹⁸with those who keep his covenant
    and remember to obey his precepts.

¹⁹The LORD has established his throne in
        heaven,
    and his kingdom rules over all.

²⁰Praise the LORD, you his angels,
    you mighty ones who do his bidding,
    who obey his word.
²¹Praise the LORD, all his heavenly hosts,
    you his servants who do his will.
²²Praise the LORD, all his works
    everywhere in his dominion.

Praise the LORD, O my soul.

Psalm 104

¹Praise the LORD, O my soul.

O LORD my God, you are very great;
    you are clothed with splendour and
        majesty.

²He wraps himself in light as with a
        garment;
    he stretches out the heavens like a
        tent
3   and lays the beams of his upper
        chambers on their waters.
He makes the clouds his chariot
    and rides on the wings of the wind.
⁴He makes winds his messengers,ᵃ
    flames of fire his servants.

⁵He set the earth on its foundations;
    it can never be moved.
⁶You covered it with the deep as with a
        garment;
    the waters stood above the
        mountains.
⁷But at your rebuke the waters fled,
    at the sound of your thunder they
        took to flight;
⁸they flowed over the mountains,
    they went down into the valleys,
    to the place you assigned for them.
⁹You set a boundary they cannot cross;
    never again will they cover the earth.

¹⁰He makes springs pour water into the
        ravines;
    it flows between the mountains.
¹¹They give water to all the beasts of the
        field;
    the wild donkeys quench their
        thirst.
¹²The birds of the air nest by the waters;
    they sing among the branches.
¹³He waters the mountains from his
        upper chambers;
    the earth is satisfied by the fruit of his
        work.
¹⁴He makes grass grow for the cattle,
    and plants for man to cultivate—
    bringing forth food from the earth:
¹⁵wine that gladdens the heart of man,
    oil to make his face shine,
    and bread that sustains his heart.
¹⁶The trees of the LORD are well watered,
    the cedars of Lebanon that he
        planted.
¹⁷There the birds make their nests;
    the stork has its home in the pine
        trees.

ᵃ4 Or angels

¹⁸The high mountains belong to the wild
goats;
the crags are a refuge for the conies.ᵇ

¹⁹The moon marks off the seasons,
and the sun knows when to go down.
²⁰You bring darkness, it becomes night,
and all the beasts of the forest prowl.
²¹The lions roar for their prey
and seek their food from God.
²²The sun rises, and they steal away;
they return and lie down in their
dens.
²³Then man goes out to his work,
to his labour until evening.

²⁴How many are your works, O LORD!
In wisdom you made them all;
the earth is full of your creatures.
²⁵There is the sea, vast and spacious,
teeming with creatures beyond
number—
living things both large and small.
²⁶There the ships go to and fro,
and the leviathan, which you formed
to frolic there.

²⁷These all look to you
to give them their food at the proper
time.
²⁸When you give it to them,
they gather it up;
when you open your hand,
they are satisfied with good
things.
²⁹When you hide your face,
they are terrified;
when you take away their breath,
they die and return to the dust.
³⁰When you send your Spirit,
they are created,
and you renew the face of the earth.

³¹May the glory of the LORD endure for
ever;
may the LORD rejoice in his works—
³²he who looks at the earth, and it
trembles,
who touches the mountains, and they
smoke.

³³I will sing to the LORD all my life;
I will sing praise to my God as long as
I live.
³⁴May my meditation be pleasing to him,
as I rejoice in the LORD.
³⁵But may sinners vanish from the earth
and the wicked be no more.

Praise the LORD, O my soul.

Praise the LORD.ᶜ

Psalm 105

¹Give thanks to the LORD, call on his
name;
make known among the nations what
he has done.
²Sing to him, sing praise to him;
tell of all his wonderful acts.
³Glory in his holy name;
let the hearts of those who seek the
LORD rejoice.
⁴Look to the LORD and his strength;
seek his face always.

⁵Remember the wonders he has done,
his miracles, and the judgments he
pronounced,
⁶O descendants of Abraham his servant,
O sons of Jacob, his chosen ones.
⁷He is the LORD our God;
his judgments are in all the earth.

⁸He remembers his covenant for ever,
the word he commanded, for a
thousand generations,
⁹the covenant he made with Abraham,
the oath he swore to Isaac.
¹⁰He confirmed it to Jacob as a decree,
to Israel as an everlasting covenant:
¹¹"To you I will give the land of Canaan
as the portion you will inherit."

¹²When they were but few in number,
few indeed, and strangers in it,
¹³they wandered from nation to nation,
from one kingdom to another.
¹⁴He allowed no-one to oppress them;
for their sake he rebuked kings:

ᵇ18 That is, the hyrax or rock badger
ᶜ35 Hebrew *Hallelu Yah*; in the Septuagint this line stands at the beginning of Psalm 105.

15"Do not touch my anointed ones;
   do my prophets no harm."

16He called down famine on the land
   and destroyed all their supplies of
      food;
17and he sent a man before them—
   Joseph, sold as a slave.
18They bruised his feet with shackles,
   his neck was put in irons,
19till what he foretold came to pass,
   till the word of the LORD proved him
      true.
20The king sent and released him,
   the ruler of peoples set him free.
21He made him master of his household,
   ruler over all he possessed,
22to instruct his princes as he pleased
   and teach his elders wisdom.

23Then Israel entered Egypt;
   Jacob lived as an alien in the land of
      Ham.
24The LORD made his people very
      fruitful;
   he made them too numerous for their
      foes,
25whose hearts he turned to hate his
      people,
   to conspire against his servants.
26He sent Moses his servant,
   and Aaron, whom he had chosen.
27They performed his miraculous signs
      among them,
   his wonders in the land of Ham.
28He sent darkness and made the land
      dark—
   for had they not rebelled against his
      words?
29He turned their waters into blood,
   causing their fish to die.
30Their land teemed with frogs,
   which went up into the bedrooms of
      their rulers.
31He spoke, and there came swarms of
      flies,
   and gnats throughout their country.
32He turned their rain into hail,
   with lightning throughout their
      land;
33he struck down their vines and fig-trees

and shattered the trees of their
      country.
34He spoke, and the locusts came,
   grasshoppers without number;
35they ate up every green thing in their
      land,
   ate up the produce of their soil.
36Then he struck down all the firstborn in
      their land,
   the firstfruits of all their manhood.

37He brought out Israel, laden with silver
      and gold,
   and from among their tribes no-one
      faltered.
38Egypt was glad when they left,
   because dread of Israel had fallen on
      them.
39He spread out a cloud as a covering,
   and a fire to give light at night.
40They asked, and he brought them quail
   and satisfied them with the bread of
      heaven.
41He opened the rock, and water gushed
      out;
   like a river it flowed in the desert.

42For he remembered his holy promise
   given to his servant Abraham.
43He brought out his people with
      rejoicing,
   his chosen ones with shouts of joy;
44he gave them the lands of the nations,
   and they fell heir to what others had
      toiled for—
45that they might keep his precepts
   and observe his laws.

   Praise the LORD.*a*

Psalm 106

1Praise the LORD.*a*

   Give thanks to the LORD, for he is good;
      his love endures for ever.
2Who can proclaim the mighty acts of
      the LORD
   or fully declare his praise?
3Blessed are they who maintain justice,

a45 Hebrew *Hallelu Yah*   *a1* Hebrew *Hallelu Yah*; also in verse 48

who constantly do what is right.
⁴Remember me, O LORD, when you
show favour to your people,
come to my aid when you save them,
⁵that I may enjoy the prosperity of your
chosen ones,
that I may share in the joy of your
nation
and join your inheritance in giving
praise.

⁶We have sinned, even as our fathers
did;
we have done wrong and acted
wickedly.
⁷When our fathers were in Egypt,
they gave no thought to your
miracles;
they did not remember your many
kindnesses,
and they rebelled by the sea, the Red
Sea.*b*
⁸Yet he saved them for his name's sake,
to make his mighty power known.
⁹He rebuked the Red Sea, and it dried
up;
he led them through the depths as
through a desert.
¹⁰He saved them from the hand of the
foe;
from the hand of the enemy he
redeemed them.
¹¹The waters covered their adversaries;
not one of them survived.
¹²Then they believed his promises
and sang his praise.

¹³But they soon forgot what he had done
and did not wait for his counsel.
¹⁴In the desert they gave in to their
craving;
in the wasteland they put God to the
test.
¹⁵So he gave them what they asked for,
but sent a wasting disease upon them.

¹⁶In the camp they grew envious of Moses
and of Aaron, who was consecrated
to the LORD.
¹⁷The earth opened up and swallowed
Dathan;

it buried the company of Abiram.
¹⁸Fire blazed among their followers;
a flame consumed the wicked.

¹⁹At Horeb they made a calf
and worshipped an idol cast from
metal.
²⁰They exchanged their Glory
for an image of a bull, which eats
grass.
²¹They forgot the God who saved them,
who had done great things in Egypt,
²²miracles in the land of Ham
and awesome deeds by the Red Sea.
²³So he said he would destroy them—
had not Moses, his chosen one,
stood in the breach before him
to keep his wrath from destroying
them.

²⁴Then they despised the pleasant land;
they did not believe his promise.
²⁵They grumbled in their tents
and did not obey the LORD.
²⁶So he swore to them with uplifted hand
that he would make them fall in the
desert,
²⁷make their descendants fall among the
nations
and scatter them throughout the
lands.

²⁸They yoked themselves to the Baal of
Peor
and ate sacrifices offered to lifeless
gods;
²⁹they provoked the LORD to anger by
their wicked deeds,
and a plague broke out among them.
³⁰But Phinehas stood up and intervened,
and the plague was checked.
³¹This was credited to him as
righteousness
for endless generations to come.

³²By the waters of Meribah they angered
the LORD,
and trouble came to Moses because
of them;
³³for they rebelled against the Spirit of
God,

*b*7 Hebrew *Yam Suph*; that is, Sea of Reeds; also in verses 9 and 22

and rash words came from Moses'
lips.[c]

34They did not destroy the peoples
as the LORD had commanded them,
35but they mingled with the nations
and adopted their customs.
36They worshipped their idols,
which became a snare to them.
37They sacrificed their sons
and their daughters to demons.
38They shed innocent blood,
the blood of their sons and daughters,
whom they sacrificed to the idols of
Canaan,
and the land was desecrated by their
blood.
39They defiled themselves by what they
did;
by their deeds they prostituted
themselves.

40Therefore the LORD was angry with his
people
and abhorred his inheritance.
41He handed them over to the nations,
and their foes ruled over them.
42Their enemies oppressed them
and subjected them to their power.
43Many times he delivered them,
but they were bent on rebellion
and they wasted away in their sin.

44But he took note of their distress
when he heard their cry;
45for their sake he remembered his
covenant
and out of his great love he relented.
46He caused them to be pitied
by all who held them captive.

47Save us, O LORD our God,
and gather us from the nations,
that we may give thanks to your holy
name
and glory in your praise.

48Praise be to the LORD, the God of Israel,
from everlasting to everlasting.
Let all the people say, "Amen!"

Praise the LORD.

BOOK V

Psalms 107–150

Psalm 107

1Give thanks to the LORD, for he is good;
his love endures for ever.
2Let the redeemed of the LORD say
this—
those he redeemed from the hand of
the foe,
3those he gathered from the lands,
from east and west, from north and
south.[a]

4Some wandered in desert wastelands,
finding no way to a city where they
could settle.
5They were hungry and thirsty,
and their lives ebbed away.
6Then they cried out to the LORD in their
trouble,
and he delivered them from their
distress.
7He led them by a straight way
to a city where they could settle.
8Let them give thanks to the LORD for his
unfailing love
and his wonderful deeds for men,
9for he satisfies the thirsty
and fills the hungry with good
things.

10Some sat in darkness and the deepest
gloom,
prisoners suffering in iron chains,
11for they had rebelled against the words
of God
and despised the counsel of the Most
High.
12So he subjected them to bitter labour;
they stumbled, and there was no-one
to help.
13Then they cried to the LORD in their
trouble,
and he saved them from their
distress.
14He brought them out of darkness and
the deepest gloom

---

c33 Or against his spirit, / and rash words came from his lips *a3 Hebrew north and the sea*

and broke away their chains.
¹⁵Let them give thanks to the LORD for his
    unfailing love
  and his wonderful deeds for men,
¹⁶for he breaks down gates of bronze
  and cuts through bars of iron.

¹⁷Some became fools through their
    rebellious ways
  and suffered affliction because of
    their iniquities.
¹⁸They loathed all food
  and drew near the gates of death.
¹⁹Then they cried to the LORD in their
    trouble,
  and he saved them from their
    distress.
²⁰He sent forth his word and healed them;
  he rescued them from the grave.
²¹Let them give thanks to the LORD for his
    unfailing love
  and his wonderful deeds for men.
²²Let them sacrifice thank-offerings
  and tell of his works with songs of joy.

²³Others went out on the sea in ships;
  they were merchants on the mighty
    waters.
²⁴They saw the works of the LORD,
  his wonderful deeds in the deep.
²⁵For he spoke and stirred up a tempest
  that lifted high the waves.
²⁶They mounted up to the heavens and
    went down to the depths;
  in their peril their courage melted
    away.
²⁷They reeled and staggered like drunken
    men;
  they were at their wits' end.
²⁸Then they cried out to the LORD in their
    trouble,
  and he brought them out of their
    distress.
²⁹He stilled the storm to a whisper;
  the waves of the sea were hushed.
³⁰They were glad when it grew calm,
  and he guided them to their desired
    haven.
³¹Let them give thanks to the LORD for his
    unfailing love
  and his wonderful deeds for men.
³²Let them exalt him in the assembly of
  the people

and praise him in the council of the
    elders.

³³He turned rivers into a desert,
  flowing springs into thirsty ground,
³⁴and fruitful land into a salt waste,
  because of the wickedness of those
    who lived there.
³⁵He turned the desert into pools of water
  and the parched ground into flowing
    springs;
³⁶there he brought the hungry to live,
  and they founded a city where they
    could settle.
³⁷They sowed fields and planted
    vineyards
  that yielded a fruitful harvest;
³⁸he blessed them, and their numbers
    greatly increased,
  and he did not let their herds
    diminish.

³⁹Then their numbers decreased, and
    they were humbled
  by oppression, calamity and sorrow;
⁴⁰he who pours contempt on nobles
  made them wander in a trackless
    waste.
⁴¹But he lifted the needy out of their
    affliction
  and increased their families like
    flocks.
⁴²The upright see and rejoice,
  but all the wicked shut their mouths.

⁴³Whoever is wise, let him heed these
    things
  and consider the great love of the
    LORD.

Psalm 108

A song. A psalm of David.

¹My heart is steadfast, O God;
  I will sing and make music with all my
    soul.
²Awake, harp and lyre!
  I will awaken the dawn.
³I will praise you, O LORD, among the
    nations;
  I will sing of you among the peoples.

⁴For great is your love, higher than the
   heavens;
   your faithfulness reaches to the skies.
⁵Be exalted, O God, above the heavens,
   and let your glory be over all the
     earth.

⁶Save us and help us with your right
   hand,
   that those you love may be delivered.
⁷God has spoken from his sanctuary:
   "In triumph I will parcel out Shechem
   and measure off the Valley of
     Succoth.
⁸Gilead is mine, Manasseh is mine;
   Ephraim is my helmet,
   Judah my sceptre.
⁹Moab is my washbasin,
   upon Edom I toss my sandal;
   over Philistia I shout in triumph."

¹⁰Who will bring me to the fortified city?
   Who will lead me to Edom?
¹¹Is it not you, O God, you who have
   rejected us
   and no longer go out with our
     armies?
¹²Give us aid against the enemy,
   for the help of man is worthless.
¹³With God we shall gain the victory,
   and he will trample down our
     enemies.

Psalm 109

For the director of music. Of David. A psalm.

¹O God, whom I praise,
   do not remain silent,
²for wicked and deceitful men
   have opened their mouths against
     me;
   they have spoken against me with
     lying tongues.
³With words of hatred they surround
   me;
   they attack me without cause.
⁴In return for my friendship they accuse
   me,
   but I am a man of prayer.

⁵They repay me evil for good,
   and hatred for my friendship.

⁶Appoint^a an evil man^b to oppose him;
   let an accuser^c stand at his right hand.
⁷When he is tried, let him be found guilty,
   and may his prayers condemn him.
⁸May his days be few;
   may another take his place of
     leadership.
⁹May his children be fatherless
   and his wife a widow.
¹⁰May his children be wandering beggars;
   may they be driven^d from their ruined
     homes.
¹¹May a creditor seize all he has;
   may strangers plunder the fruits of his
     labour.
¹²May no-one extend kindness to him
   or take pity on his fatherless children.
¹³May his descendants be cut off,
   their names blotted out from the next
     generation.
¹⁴May the iniquity of his fathers be
   remembered before the LORD;
   may the sin of his mother never be
     blotted out.
¹⁵May their sins always remain before the
   LORD,
   that he may cut off the memory of
     them from the earth.

¹⁶For he never thought of doing a
   kindness,
   but hounded to death the poor
   and the needy and the
     broken-hearted.
¹⁷He loved to pronounce a curse—
   may it^e come on him;
   he found no pleasure in blessing—
   may it be^f far from him.
¹⁸He wore cursing as his garment;
   it entered into his body like water,
   into his bones like oil.
¹⁹May it be like a cloak wrapped about
   him,
   like a belt tied for ever round him.
²⁰May this be the LORD's payment to my
   accusers,
   to those who speak evil of me.

---

^{a}6 Or ⸢They say:⸥ "Appoint (with quotation marks at the end of verse 19) ^{b}6 Or the Evil One ^{c}6 Or let Satan
^{d}10 Septuagint; Hebrew sought ^{e}17 Or curse, / and it has ^{f}17 Or blessing, / and it is

21But you, O Sovereign LORD,
   deal well with me for your name's
      sake;
   out of the goodness of your love,
      deliver me.
22For I am poor and needy,
   and my heart is wounded within me.
23I fade away like an evening shadow;
   I am shaken off like a locust.
24My knees give way from fasting;
   my body is thin and gaunt.
25I am an object of scorn to my accusers;
   when they see me, they shake their
      heads.

26Help me, O LORD my God;
   save me in accordance with your
      love.
27Let them know that it is your hand,
   that you, O LORD, have done it.
28They may curse, but you will bless;
   when they attack they will be put to
      shame,
   but your servant will rejoice.
29My accusers will be clothed with
      disgrace
   and wrapped in shame as in a cloak.

30With my mouth I will greatly extol the
      LORD;
   in the great throng I will praise
      him.
31For he stands at the right hand of the
      needy one,
   to save his life from those who
      condemn him.

Psalm 110

Of David. A psalm.

1The LORD says to my Lord:
   "Sit at my right hand
until I make your enemies
   a footstool for your feet."

2The LORD will extend your mighty
   sceptre from Zion;

you will rule in the midst of your
      enemies.
3Your troops will be willing
   on your day of battle.
Arrayed in holy majesty,
   from the womb of the dawn
   you will receive the dew of your
      youth.*a*

4The LORD has sworn
   and will not change his mind:
"You are a priest for ever,
   in the order of Melchizedek."

5The Lord is at your right hand;
   he will crush kings on the day of his
      wrath.
6He will judge nations, heaping up the
      dead
   and crushing the rulers of the whole
      earth.
7He will drink from a brook beside the
      way;*b*
   therefore he will lift up his head.

Psalm 111*a*

1Praise the LORD.*b*

I will extol the LORD with all my heart
   in the council of the upright and in
      the assembly.

2Great are the works of the LORD;
   they are pondered by all who delight
      in them.
3Glorious and majestic are his deeds,
   and his righteousness endures for
      ever.
4He has caused his wonders to be
      remembered;
   the LORD is gracious and
      compassionate.
5He provides food for those who fear
      him;
   he remembers his covenant for
      ever.
6He has shown his people the power of
      his works,

---

a3 Or / *your young men will come to you like the dew*   *b7* Or / *The One who grants succession will set him in authority*
*a*This psalm is an acrostic poem, the lines of which begin with the successive letters of the Hebrew alphabet.
b1 Hebrew *Hallelu Yah*

giving them the lands of other
    nations.
7The works of his hands are faithful and
    just;
    all his precepts are trustworthy.
8They are steadfast for ever and ever,
    done in faithfulness and uprightness.
9He provided redemption for his people;
    he ordained his covenant for ever—
    holy and awesome is his name.

10The fear of the LORD is the beginning of
    wisdom;
    all who follow his precepts have good
    understanding.
    To him belongs eternal praise.

Psalm 112[a]

1Praise the LORD.[b]

Blessed is the man who fears the LORD,
    who finds great delight in his
    commands.

2His children will be mighty in the land;
    the generation of the upright will be
    blessed.
3Wealth and riches are in his house,
    and his righteousness endures for
    ever.
4Even in darkness light dawns for the
    upright,
    for the gracious and compassionate
    and righteous man.[c]
5Good will come to him who is generous
    and lends freely,
    who conducts his affairs with justice.
6Surely he will never be shaken;
    a righteous man will be remembered
    for ever.
7He will have no fear of bad news;
    his heart is steadfast, trusting in the
    LORD.
8His heart is secure, he will have no fear;
    in the end he will look in triumph on
    his foes.
9He has scattered abroad his gifts to the
    poor,

his righteousness endures for ever;
    his horn[d] will be lifted high in
    honour.

10The wicked man will see and be vexed,
    he will gnash his teeth and waste
    away;
    the longings of the wicked will come
    to nothing.

Psalm 113

1Praise the LORD.[a]

Praise, O servants of the LORD,
    praise the name of the LORD.
2Let the name of the LORD be praised,
    both now and for evermore.
3From the rising of the sun to the place
    where it sets,
    the name of the LORD is to be praised.

4The LORD is exalted over all the
    nations,
    his glory above the heavens.
5Who is like the LORD our God,
    the One who sits enthroned on high,
6who stoops down to look
    on the heavens and the earth?

7He raises the poor from the dust
    and lifts the needy from the ash heap;
8he seats them with princes,
    with the princes of their people.
9He settles the barren woman in her
    home
    as a happy mother of children.

Praise the LORD.

Psalm 114

1When Israel came out of Egypt,
    the house of Jacob from a people of
    foreign tongue,
2Judah became God's sanctuary,
    Israel his dominion.

---

[a]This psalm is an acrostic poem, the lines of which begin with the successive letters of the Hebrew alphabet.
[b]1 Hebrew *Hallelu Yah*   [c]4 Or / for ⌊the LORD⌋ is gracious and compassionate and righteous
[d]9 *Horn* here symbolises dignity.   [a]1 Hebrew *Hallelu Yah*; also in verse 9

³The sea looked and fled,
  the Jordan turned back;
⁴the mountains skipped like rams,
  the hills like lambs.

⁵Why was it, O sea, that you fled,
  O Jordan, that you turned back,
⁶you mountains, that you skipped like
    rams,
  you hills, like lambs?

⁷Tremble, O earth, at the presence of
    the Lord,
  at the presence of the God of Jacob,
⁸who turned the rock into a pool,
  the hard rock into springs of water.

Psalm 115

¹Not to us, O Lord, not to us
  but to your name be the glory,
  because of your love and faithfulness.

²Why do the nations say,
  "Where is their God?"
³Our God is in heaven;
  he does whatever pleases him.
⁴But their idols are silver and gold,
  made by the hands of men.
⁵They have mouths, but cannot speak,
  eyes, but they cannot see;
⁶they have ears, but cannot hear,
  noses, but they cannot smell;
⁷they have hands, but cannot feel,
  feet, but they cannot walk;
  nor can they utter a sound with their
    throats.
⁸Those who make them will be like
    them,
  and so will all who trust in them.

⁹O house of Israel, trust in the Lord—
  he is their help and shield.
¹⁰O house of Aaron, trust in the Lord—
  he is their help and shield.
¹¹You who fear him, trust in the Lord—
  he is their help and shield.

¹²The Lord remembers us and will bless
  us:

He will bless the house of Israel,
  he will bless the house of Aaron,
¹³he will bless those who fear the Lord—
  small and great alike.

¹⁴May the Lord make you increase,
  both you and your children.
¹⁵May you be blessed by the Lord,
  the Maker of heaven and earth.

¹⁶The highest heavens belong to the
    Lord,
  but the earth he has given to man.
¹⁷It is not the dead who praise the Lord,
  those who go down to silence;
¹⁸it is we who extol the Lord,
  both now and for evermore.

Praise the Lord.ᵃ

Psalm 116

¹I love the Lord, for he heard my voice;
  he heard my cry for mercy.
²Because he turned his ear to me,
  I will call on him as long as I live.

³The cords of death entangled me,
  the anguish of the graveᵃ came upon
    me;
  I was overcome by trouble and
    sorrow.
⁴Then I called on the name of the Lord:
  "O Lord, save me!"

⁵The Lord is gracious and righteous;
  our God is full of compassion.
⁶The Lord protects the simple-hearted;
  when I was in great need, he saved
    me.

⁷Be at rest once more, O my soul,
  for the Lord has been good to
    you.

⁸For you, O Lord, have delivered my
    soul from death,
  my eyes from tears,
  my feet from stumbling,
⁹that I may walk before the Lord
  in the land of the living.

¹⁰I believed; therefore[b] I said,
   "I am greatly afflicted."
¹¹And in my dismay I said,
   "All men are liars."

¹²How can I repay the LORD
   for all his goodness to me?
¹³I will lift up the cup of salvation
   and call on the name of the
   LORD.
¹⁴I will fulfil my vows to the LORD
   in the presence of all his people.

¹⁵Precious in the sight of the LORD
   is the death of his saints.
¹⁶O LORD, truly I am your servant;
   I am your servant, the son of your
   maidservant;[c]
   you have freed me from my chains.

¹⁷I will sacrifice a thank-offering to you
   and call on the name of the LORD.
¹⁸I will fulfil my vows to the LORD
   in the presence of all his people,
¹⁹in the courts of the house of the LORD—
   in your midst, O Jerusalem.

Praise the LORD.[d]

Psalm 117

¹Praise the LORD, all you nations;
   extol him, all you peoples.
²For great is his love towards us,
   and the faithfulness of the LORD
   endures for ever.

Praise the LORD.[d]

Psalm 118

¹Give thanks to the LORD, for he is good;
   his love endures for ever.

²Let Israel say:
   "His love endures for ever."
³Let the house of Aaron say:
   "His love endures for ever."
⁴Let those who fear the LORD say:
   "His love endures for ever."

⁵In my anguish I cried to the LORD,
   and he answered by setting me free.
⁶The LORD is with me; I will not be
   afraid.
   What can man do to me?
⁷The LORD is with me; he is my helper.
   I will look in triumph on my enemies.

⁸It is better to take refuge in the LORD
   than to trust in man.
⁹It is better to take refuge in the LORD
   than to trust in princes.

¹⁰All the nations surrounded me,
   but in the name of the LORD I cut
   them off.
¹¹They surrounded me on every side,
   but in the name of the LORD I cut
   them off.
¹²They swarmed around me like bees,
   but they died out as quickly as
   burning thorns;
   in the name of the LORD I cut them
   off.

¹³I was pushed back and about to fall,
   but the LORD helped me.
¹⁴The LORD is my strength and my song;
   he has become my salvation.

¹⁵Shouts of joy and victory
   resound in the tents of the righteous:
   "The LORD's right hand has done
   mighty things!
16   The LORD's right hand is lifted high;
   the LORD's right hand has done
   mighty things!"

¹⁷I will not die but live,
   and will proclaim what the LORD has
   done.
¹⁸The LORD has chastened me severely,
   but he has not given me over to
   death.

¹⁹Open for me the gates of righteousness;
   I will enter and give thanks to the
   LORD.
²⁰This is the gate of the LORD
   through which the righteous may
   enter.

---

b10 Or believed even when   c16 Or servant, your faithful son   d19, 2 Hebrew Hallelu Yah

²¹I will give you thanks, for you answered
me;
you have become my salvation.

²²The stone the builders rejected
has become the capstone;
²³the LORD has done this,
and it is marvellous in our
eyes.
²⁴This is the day the LORD has made;
let us rejoice and be glad in it.

²⁵O LORD, save us;
O LORD, grant us success.
²⁶Blessed is he who comes in the name of
the LORD.
From the house of the LORD we bless
you.*a*
²⁷The LORD is God,
and he has made his light shine upon
us.
With boughs in hand, join in the festal
procession
up*b* to the horns of the altar.

²⁸You are my God, and I will give thanks;
you are my God, and I will exalt you.

²⁹Give thanks to the LORD, for he is good;
his love endures for ever.

Psalm 119*a*

א Aleph

¹Blessed are they whose ways are
blameless,
who walk according to the law of the
LORD.
²Blessed are they who keep his statutes
and seek him with all their heart.
³They do nothing wrong;
they walk in his ways.
⁴You have laid down precepts
that are to be fully obeyed.
⁵Oh, that my ways were steadfast
in obeying your decrees!
⁶Then I would not be put to shame
when I consider all your commands.

⁷I will praise you with an upright heart
as I learn your righteous laws.
⁸I will obey your decrees;
do not utterly forsake me.

ב Beth

⁹How can a young man keep his way
pure?
By living according to your word.
¹⁰I seek you with all my heart;
do not let me stray from your
commands.
¹¹I have hidden your word in my heart
that I might not sin against you.
¹²Praise be to you, O LORD;
teach me your decrees.
¹³With my lips I recount
all the laws that come from your
mouth.
¹⁴I rejoice in following your statutes
as one rejoices in great riches.
¹⁵I meditate on your precepts
and consider your ways.
¹⁶I delight in your decrees;
I will not neglect your word.

ג Gimel

¹⁷Do good to your servant, and I will
live;
I will obey your word.
¹⁸Open my eyes that I may see
wonderful things in your law.
¹⁹I am a stranger on earth;
do not hide your commands from
me.
²⁰My soul is consumed with longing
for your laws at all times.
²¹You rebuke the arrogant, who are
cursed
and who stray from your commands.
²²Remove from me scorn and contempt,
for I keep your statutes.
²³Though rulers sit together and slander
me,
your servant will meditate on your
decrees.
²⁴Your statutes are my delight;
they are my counsellors.

---

*a*26 The Hebrew is plural.   *b*27 Or *Bind the festal sacrifice with ropes / and take it*
*a*This psalm is an acrostic poem; the verses of each stanza begin with the same letter of the Hebrew alphabet.

ד Daleth

25I am laid low in the dust;
  preserve my life according to your
    word.
26I recounted my ways and you answered
    me;
  teach me your decrees.
27Let me understand the teaching of your
    precepts;
  then I will meditate on your wonders.
28My soul is weary with sorrow;
  strengthen me according to your
    word.
29Keep me from deceitful ways;
  be gracious to me through your law.
30I have chosen the way of truth;
  I have set my heart on your laws.
31I hold fast to your statutes, O LORD;
  do not let me be put to shame.
32I run in the path of your commands,
  for you have set my heart free.

ה He

33Teach me, O LORD, to follow your
    decrees;
  then I will keep them to the end.
34Give me understanding, and I will keep
    your law
  and obey it with all my heart.
35Direct me in the path of your
    commands,
  for there I find delight.
36Turn my heart towards your statutes
  and not towards selfish gain.
37Turn my eyes away from worthless
    things;
  preserve my life according to your
    word.b
38Fulfil your promise to your servant,
  so that you may be feared.
39Take away the disgrace I dread,
  for your laws are good.
40How I long for your precepts!
  Preserve my life in your
    righteousness.

ו Waw

41May your unfailing love come to me, O
    LORD,

your salvation according to your
    promise;
42then I will answer the one who taunts
    me,
  for I trust in your word.
43Do not snatch the word of truth from
    my mouth,
  for I have put my hope in your laws.
44I will always obey your law,
  for ever and ever.
45I will walk about in freedom,
  for I have sought out your precepts.
46I will speak of your statutes before
    kings
  and will not be put to shame,
47for I delight in your commands
  because I love them.
48I lift up my hands toc your commands,
    which I love,
  and I meditate on your decrees.

ז Zayin

49Remember your word to your servant,
  for you have given me hope.
50My comfort in my suffering is this:
  Your promise preserves my life.
51The arrogant mock me without
    restraint,
  but I do not turn from your law.
52I remember your ancient laws, O LORD,
  and I find comfort in them.
53Indignation grips me because of the
    wicked,
  who have forsaken your law.
54Your decrees are the theme of my song
  wherever I lodge.
55In the night I remember your name, O
    LORD,
  and I will keep your law.
56This has been my practice:
  I obey your precepts.

ח Heth

57You are my portion, O LORD;
  I have promised to obey your words.
58I have sought your face with all my heart;
  be gracious to me according to your
    promise.

b37 Two manuscripts of the Masoretic Text and Dead Sea Scrolls; most manuscripts of the Masoretic Text life in your way
c48 Or for

⁵⁹I have considered my ways
    and have turned my steps to your
    statutes.
⁶⁰I will hasten and not delay
    to obey your commands.
⁶¹Though the wicked bind me with ropes,
    I will not forget your law.
⁶²At midnight I rise to give you thanks
    for your righteous laws.
⁶³I am a friend to all who fear you,
    to all who follow your precepts.
⁶⁴The earth is filled with your love, O
    LORD;
    teach me your decrees.

ט Teth

⁶⁵Do good to your servant
    according to your word, O LORD.
⁶⁶Teach me knowledge and good
    judgment,
    for I believe in your commands.
⁶⁷Before I was afflicted I went astray,
    but now I obey your word.
⁶⁸You are good, and what you do is good;
    teach me your decrees.
⁶⁹Though the arrogant have smeared me
    with lies,
    I keep your precepts with all my
    heart.
⁷⁰Their hearts are callous and unfeeling,
    but I delight in your law.
⁷¹It was good for me to be afflicted
    so that I might learn your decrees.
⁷²The law from your mouth is more
    precious to me
    than thousands of pieces of silver and
    gold.

י Yodh

⁷³Your hands made me and formed me;
    give me understanding to learn your
    commands.
⁷⁴May those who fear you rejoice when
    they see me,
    for I have put my hope in your word.
⁷⁵I know, O LORD, that your laws are
    righteous,
    and in faithfulness you have afflicted
    me.
⁷⁶May your unfailing love be my comfort,

according to your promise to your
    servant.
⁷⁷Let your compassion come to me that I
    may live,
    for your law is my delight.
⁷⁸May the arrogant be put to shame for
    wronging me without cause;
    but I will meditate on your precepts.
⁷⁹May those who fear you turn to me,
    those who understand your statutes.
⁸⁰May my heart be blameless towards
    your decrees,
    that I may not be put to shame.

כ Kaph

⁸¹My soul faints with longing for your
    salvation,
    but I have put my hope in your word.
⁸²My eyes fail, looking for your promise;
    I say, "When will you comfort me?"
⁸³Though I am like a wineskin in the
    smoke,
    I do not forget your decrees.
⁸⁴How long must your servant wait?
    When will you punish my
    persecutors?
⁸⁵The arrogant dig pitfalls for me,
    contrary to your law.
⁸⁶All your commands are trustworthy;
    help me, for men persecute me
    without cause.
⁸⁷They almost wiped me from the earth,
    but I have not forsaken your
    precepts.
⁸⁸Preserve my life according to your love,
    and I will obey the statutes of your
    mouth.

ל Lamedh

⁸⁹Your word, O LORD, is eternal;
    it stands firm in the heavens.
⁹⁰Your faithfulness continues through all
    generations;
    you established the earth, and it
    endures.
⁹¹Your laws endure to this day,
    for all things serve you.
⁹²If your law had not been my delight,
    I would have perished in my
    affliction.

93I will never forget your precepts,
  for by them you have preserved my
    life.
94Save me, for I am yours;
  I have sought out your precepts.
95The wicked are waiting to destroy me,
  but I will ponder your statutes.
96To all perfection I see a limit;
  but your commands are boundless.

מ Mem

97Oh, how I love your law!
  I meditate on it all day long.
98Your commands make me wiser than
    my enemies,
  for they are ever with me.
99I have more insight than all my
    teachers,
  for I meditate on your statutes.
100I have more understanding than the
    elders,
  for I obey your precepts.
101I have kept my feet from every evil
    path
  so that I might obey your word.
102I have not departed from your laws,
  for you yourself have taught me.
103How sweet are your words to my taste,
  sweeter than honey to my mouth!
104I gain understanding from your
    precepts;
  therefore I hate every wrong path.

נ Nun

105Your word is a lamp to my feet
  and a light for my path.
106I have taken an oath and confirmed it,
  that I will follow your righteous
    laws.
107I have suffered much;
  preserve my life, O LORD, according
    to your word.
108Accept, O LORD, the willing praise of
    my mouth,
  and teach me your laws.
109Though I constantly take my life in my
    hands,
  I will not forget your law.
110The wicked have set a snare for me,
  but I have not strayed from your
    precepts.

111Your statutes are my heritage for ever;
  they are the joy of my heart.
112My heart is set on keeping your
    decrees
  to the very end.

ס Samekh

113I hate double-minded men,
  but I love your law.
114You are my refuge and my shield;
  I have put my hope in your word.
115Away from me, you evildoers,
  that I may keep the commands of my
    God!
116Sustain me according to your promise,
    and I shall live;
  do not let my hopes be dashed.
117Uphold me, and I shall be delivered;
  I shall always have regard for your
    decrees.
118You reject all who stray from your
    decrees,
  for their deceitfulness is in vain.
119All the wicked of the earth you discard
    like dross;
  therefore I love your statutes.
120My flesh trembles in fear of you;
  I stand in awe of your laws.

ע Ayin

121I have done what is righteous and just;
  do not leave me to my oppressors.
122Ensure your servant's well-being;
  let not the arrogant oppress me.
123My eyes fail, looking for your
    salvation,
  looking for your righteous promise.
124Deal with your servant according to
    your love
  and teach me your decrees.
125I am your servant; give me
    discernment
  that I may understand your statutes.
126It is time for you to act, O LORD;
  your law is being broken.
127Because I love your commands
  more than gold, more than pure
    gold,
128and because I consider all your
    precepts right,
  I hate every wrong path.

�되 Pe

129Your statutes are wonderful;
    therefore I obey them.
130The unfolding of your words gives
    light;
    it gives understanding to the simple.
131I open my mouth and pant,
    longing for your commands.
132Turn to me and have mercy on me,
    as you always do to those who love
        your name.
133Direct my footsteps according to your
    word;
    let no sin rule over me.
134Redeem me from the oppression of
    men,
    that I may obey your precepts.
135Make your face shine upon your
    servant
    and teach me your decrees.
136Streams of tears flow from my eyes,
    for your law is not obeyed.

ㄈ Tsadhe

137Righteous are you, O Lord,
    and your laws are right.
138The statutes you have laid down are
    righteous;
    they are fully trustworthy.
139My zeal wears me out,
    for my enemies ignore your words.
140Your promises have been thoroughly
    tested,
    and your servant loves them.
141Though I am lowly and despised,
    I do not forget your precepts.
142Your righteousness is everlasting
    and your law is true.
143Trouble and distress have come upon
    me,
    but your commands are my delight.
144Your statutes are for ever right;
    give me understanding that I may
        live.

ㄆ Qoph

145I call with all my heart; answer me, O
    Lord,
    and I will obey your decrees.
146I call out to you; save me

and I will keep your statutes.
147I rise before dawn and cry for help;
    I have put my hope in your word.
148My eyes stay open through the watches
    of the night,
    that I may meditate on your
        promises.
149Hear my voice in accordance with your
    love;
    preserve my life, O Lord, according
        to your laws.
150Those who devise wicked schemes are
    near,
    but they are far from your law.
151Yet you are near, O Lord,
    and all your commands are true.
152Long ago I learned from your statutes
    that you established them to last for
        ever.

ㄱ Resh

153Look upon my suffering and deliver
    me,
    for I have not forgotten your law.
154Defend my cause and redeem me;
    preserve my life according to your
        promise.
155Salvation is far from the wicked,
    for they do not seek out your
        decrees.
156Your compassion is great, O Lord;
    preserve my life according to your
        laws.
157Many are the foes who persecute me,
    but I have not turned from your
        statutes.
158I look on the faithless with loathing,
    for they do not obey your word.
159See how I love your precepts;
    preserve my life, O Lord, according
        to your love.
160All your words are true;
    all your righteous laws are eternal.

ㄇ Sin and Shin

161Rulers persecute me without cause,
    but my heart trembles at your word.
162I rejoice in your promise
    like one who finds great spoil.
163I hate and abhor falsehood
    but I love your law.

¹⁶⁴Seven times a day I praise you
  for your righteous laws.
¹⁶⁵Great peace have they who love your
    law,
  and nothing can make them stumble.
¹⁶⁶I wait for your salvation, O LORD,
  and I follow your commands.
¹⁶⁷I obey your statutes,
  for I love them greatly.
¹⁶⁸I obey your precepts and your statutes,
  for all my ways are known to you.

ת Taw

¹⁶⁹May my cry come before you, O LORD;
  give me understanding according to
    your word.
¹⁷⁰May my supplication come before you;
  deliver me according to your
    promise.
¹⁷¹May my lips overflow with praise,
  for you teach me your decrees.
¹⁷²May my tongue sing of your word,
  for all your commands are righteous.
¹⁷³May your hand be ready to help me,
  for I have chosen your precepts.
¹⁷⁴I long for your salvation, O LORD,
  and your law is my delight.
¹⁷⁵Let me live that I may praise you,
  and may your laws sustain me.
¹⁷⁶I have strayed like a lost sheep.
  Seek your servant,
  for I have not forgotten your
    commands.

Psalm 120

A song of ascents.

¹I call on the LORD in my distress,
  and he answers me.
²Save me, O LORD, from lying lips
  and from deceitful tongues.

³What will he do to you,
  and what more besides, O deceitful
    tongue?
⁴He will punish you with a warrior's
    sharp arrows,
  with burning coals of the broom tree.

⁵Woe to me that I dwell in Meshech,
  that I live among the tents of Kedar!

⁶Too long have I lived
  among those who hate peace.
⁷I am a man of peace;
  but when I speak, they are for war.

Psalm 121

A song of ascents.

¹I lift up my eyes to the hills—
  where does my help come from?
²My help comes from the LORD,
  the Maker of heaven and earth.

³He will not let your foot slip—
  he who watches over you will not
    slumber;
⁴indeed, he who watches over Israel
  will neither slumber nor sleep.

⁵The LORD watches over you—
  the LORD is your shade at your right
    hand;
⁶the sun will not harm you by day,
  nor the moon by night.

⁷The LORD will keep you from all
    harm—
  he will watch over your life;
⁸the LORD will watch over your coming
    and going
  both now and for evermore.

Psalm 122

A song of ascents. Of David.

¹I rejoiced with those who said to me,
  "Let us go to the house of the LORD."
²Our feet are standing
  in your gates, O Jerusalem.

³Jerusalem is built like a city
  that is closely compacted together.
⁴That is where the tribes go up,
  the tribes of the LORD,
  to praise the name of the LORD
    according to the statute given to
      Israel.
⁵There the thrones for judgment stand,
  the thrones of the house of David.

⁶Pray for the peace of Jerusalem:
  "May those who love you be secure.
⁷May there be peace within your walls
  and security within your citadels."
⁸For the sake of my brothers and friends,
  I will say, "Peace be within you."
⁹For the sake of the house of the LORD
      our God,
  I will seek your prosperity.

Psalm 123

A song of ascents.

¹I lift up my eyes to you,
  to you whose throne is in heaven.
²As the eyes of slaves look to the hand of
      their master,
  as the eyes of a maid look to the hand
      of her mistress,
so our eyes look to the LORD our God,
  till he shows us his mercy.

³Have mercy on us, O LORD, have mercy
      on us,
  for we have endured much contempt.
⁴We have endured much ridicule from
      the proud,
  much contempt from the arrogant.

Psalm 124

A song of ascents. Of David.

¹If the LORD had not been on our side—
  let Israel say—
²if the LORD had not been on our side
  when men attacked us,
³when their anger flared against us,
  they would have swallowed us alive;
⁴the flood would have engulfed us,
  the torrent would have swept over us,
⁵the raging waters
  would have swept us away.

⁶Praise be to the LORD,
  who has not let us be torn by their
      teeth.
⁷We have escaped like a bird
  out of the fowler's snare;

the snare has been broken,
  and we have escaped.
⁸Our help is in the name of the LORD,
  the Maker of heaven and earth.

Psalm 125

A song of ascents.

¹Those who trust in the LORD are like
      Mount Zion,
  which cannot be shaken but endures
      for ever.
²As the mountains surround Jerusalem,
  so the LORD surrounds his people
  both now and for evermore.

³The sceptre of the wicked will not remain
      over the land allotted to the
          righteous,
  for then the righteous might use
      their hands to do evil.

⁴Do good, O LORD, to those who are
      good,
  to those who are upright in heart.
⁵But those who turn to crooked ways
  the LORD will banish with the
      evildoers.

Peace be upon Israel.

Psalm 126

A song of ascents.

¹When the LORD brought back the
      captives to^a Zion,
  we were like men who dreamed.^{b}
²Our mouths were filled with laughter,
  our tongues with songs of joy.
Then it was said among the nations,
  "The LORD has done great things for
      them."
³The LORD has done great things for us,
  and we are filled with joy.

⁴Restore our fortunes,^{c} O LORD,
  like streams in the Negev.

---

^{a}1 Or LORD *restored the fortunes of*   *^{b}1* Or *men restored to health*   *^{c}4* Or *Bring back our captives*

⁵Those who sow in tears
will reap with songs of joy.
⁶He who goes out weeping,
carrying seed to sow,
will return with songs of joy,
carrying sheaves with him.

Psalm 127

A song of ascents. Of Solomon.

¹Unless the LORD builds the house,
its builders labour in vain.
Unless the LORD watches over the city,
the watchmen stand guard in vain.
²In vain you rise early
and stay up late,
toiling for food to eat—
for he grants sleep to*ᵃ* those he loves.

³Sons are a heritage from the LORD,
children a reward from him.
⁴Like arrows in the hands of a warrior
are sons born in one's youth.
⁵Blessed is the man
whose quiver is full of them.
They will not be put to shame
when they contend with their
enemies in the gate.

Psalm 128

A song of ascents.

¹Blessed are all who fear the LORD,
who walk in his ways.
²You will eat the fruit of your labour;
blessings and prosperity will be
yours.
³Your wife will be like a fruitful vine
within your house;
your sons will be like olive shoots
round your table.
⁴Thus is the man blessed
who fears the LORD.

⁵May the LORD bless you from Zion
all the days of your life;

may you see the prosperity of
Jerusalem,
⁶ and may you live to see your
children's children.

Peace be upon Israel.

Psalm 129

A song of ascents.

¹They have greatly oppressed me from
my youth—
let Israel say—
²they have greatly oppressed me from
my youth,
but they have not gained the victory
over me.
³Ploughmen have ploughed my back
and made their furrows long.
⁴But the LORD is righteous;
he has cut me free from the cords of
the wicked.

⁵May all who hate Zion
be turned back in shame.
⁶May they be like grass on the roof,
which withers before it can grow;
⁷with it the reaper cannot fill his hands,
nor the one who gathers fill his arms.
⁸May those who pass by not say,
"The blessing of the LORD be upon
you;
we bless you in the name of the
LORD."

Psalm 130

A song of ascents.

¹Out of the depths I cry to you, O LORD;
² O Lord, hear my voice.
Let your ears be attentive
to my cry for mercy.

³If you, O LORD, kept a record of sins,
O Lord, who could stand?
⁴But with you there is forgiveness;
therefore you are feared.

ᵃ2 Or eat— / for while they sleep he provides for

⁵I wait for the LORD, my soul waits,
 and in his word I put my hope.
⁶My soul waits for the Lord
 more than watchmen wait for the
 morning,
 more than watchmen wait for the
 morning.

⁷O Israel, put your hope in the LORD,
 for with the LORD is unfailing love
 and with him is full redemption.
⁸He himself will redeem Israel
 from all their sins.

Psalm 131

A song of ascents. Of David.

¹My heart is not proud, O LORD,
 my eyes are not haughty;
 I do not concern myself with great
 matters
 or things too wonderful for me.
²But I have stilled and quietened my
 soul;
 like a weaned child with its mother,
 like a weaned child is my soul within
 me.

³O Israel, put your hope in the LORD
 both now and for evermore.

Psalm 132

A song of ascents.

¹O LORD, remember David
 and all the hardships he endured.

²He swore an oath to the LORD
 and made a vow to the Mighty One of
 Jacob:
³"I will not enter my house
 or go to my bed—
⁴I will allow no sleep to my eyes,
 no slumber to my eyelids,
⁵till I find a place for the LORD,
 a dwelling for the Mighty One of
 Jacob."

⁶We heard it in Ephrathah,
 we came upon it in the fields of
 Jaar: *a,b*
⁷"Let us go to his dwelling-place;
 let us worship at his footstool—
⁸arise, O LORD, and come to your resting
 place,
 you and the ark of your might.
⁹May your priests be clothed with
 righteousness;
 may your saints sing for joy."

¹⁰For the sake of David your servant,
 do not reject your anointed one.

¹¹The LORD swore an oath to David,
 a sure oath that he will not revoke:
 "One of your own descendants
 I will place on your throne—
¹²if your sons keep my covenant
 and the statutes I teach them,
 then their sons shall sit
 on your throne for ever and ever."

¹³For the LORD has chosen Zion,
 he has desired it for his dwelling:
¹⁴"This is my resting place for ever and
 ever;
 here I will sit enthroned, for I have
 desired it—
¹⁵I will bless her with abundant provisions;
 her poor will I satisfy with food.
¹⁶I will clothe her priests with salvation,
 and her saints shall ever sing for joy.

¹⁷"Here I will make a horn*c* grow for
 David
 and set up a lamp for my anointed
 one.
¹⁸I will clothe his enemies with shame,
 but the crown on his head shall be
 resplendent."

Psalm 133

A song of ascents. Of David.

¹How good and pleasant it is
 when brothers live together in unity!

a6 That is, Kiriath Jearim
b6 Or *heard of it in Ephrathah, / we found it in the fields of Jaar.* (and no quotation marks around verses 7–9)
c17 *Horn* here symbolises strong one, that is, king.

²It is like precious oil poured on the head,
    running down on the beard,
running down on Aaron's beard,
    down upon the collar of his robes.
³It is as if the dew of Hermon
    were falling on Mount Zion.
For there the LORD bestows his
        blessing,
    even life for evermore.

Psalm 134

A song of ascents.

¹Praise the LORD, all you servants of the
        LORD,
    who minister by night in the house of
        the LORD.
²Lift up your hands in the sanctuary
    and praise the LORD.

³May the LORD, the Maker of heaven
        and earth,
    bless you from Zion.

Psalm 135

¹Praise the LORD.ᵃ

Praise the name of the LORD;
    praise him, you servants of the LORD,
²you who minister in the house of the
        LORD,
    in the courts of the house of our
        God.

³Praise the LORD, for the LORD is good;
    sing praise to his name, for that is
        pleasant.
⁴For the LORD has chosen Jacob to be his
        own,
    Israel to be his treasured possession.

⁵I know that the LORD is great,
    that our Lord is greater than all
        gods.
⁶The LORD does whatever pleases him,
    in the heavens and on the earth,
    in the seas and all their depths.
⁷He makes clouds rise from the ends of
        the earth;

he sends lightning with the rain
    and brings out the wind from his
        storehouses.

⁸He struck down the firstborn of Egypt,
    the firstborn of men and animals.
⁹He sent his signs and wonders into your
        midst, O Egypt,
    against Pharaoh and all his servants.
¹⁰He struck down many nations
    and killed mighty kings—
¹¹Sihon king of the Amorites,
    Og king of Bashan
    and all the kings of Canaan—
¹²and he gave their land as an
        inheritance,
    an inheritance to his people Israel.

¹³Your name, O LORD, endures for ever,
    your renown, O LORD, through all
        generations.
¹⁴For the LORD will vindicate his people
    and have compassion on his servants.

¹⁵The idols of the nations are silver and
        gold,
    made by the hands of men.
¹⁶They have mouths, but cannot speak,
    eyes, but they cannot see;
¹⁷they have ears, but cannot hear,
    nor is there breath in their mouths.
¹⁸Those who make them will be like
        them,
    and so will all who trust in them.

¹⁹O house of Israel, praise the LORD;
    O house of Aaron, praise the LORD;
²⁰O house of Levi, praise the LORD;
    you who fear him, praise the LORD.
²¹Praise be to the LORD from Zion,
    to him who dwells in Jerusalem.

Praise the LORD.

Psalm 136

¹Give thanks to the LORD, for he is good.
    His love endures for ever.
²Give thanks to the God of gods.
    His love endures for ever.
³Give thanks to the Lord of lords:
    His love endures for ever.

ᵃ1 Hebrew *Hallelu Yah;* also in verses 3 and 21

⁴to him who alone does great wonders,
> *His love endures for ever.*

⁵who by his understanding made the
  heavens,
> *His love endures for ever.*

⁶who spread out the earth upon the
  waters,
> *His love endures for ever.*

⁷who made the great lights—
> *His love endures for ever.*

⁸the sun to govern the day,
> *His love endures for ever.*

⁹the moon and stars to govern the
  night;
> *His love endures for ever.*

¹⁰to him who struck down the firstborn of
  Egypt
> *His love endures for ever.*

¹¹and brought Israel out from among
  them
> *His love endures for ever.*

¹²with a mighty hand and outstretched
  arm;
> *His love endures for ever.*

¹³to him who divided the Red Sea[a]
  asunder
> *His love endures for ever.*

¹⁴and brought Israel through the midst of
  it,
> *His love endures for ever.*

¹⁵but swept Pharaoh and his army into
  the Red Sea;
> *His love endures for ever.*

¹⁶to him who led his people through the
  desert,
> *His love endures for ever.*

¹⁷who struck down great kings,
> *His love endures for ever.*

¹⁸and killed mighty kings—
> *His love endures for ever.*

¹⁹Sihon king of the Amorites
> *His love endures for ever.*

²⁰and Og king of Bashan—
> *His love endures for ever.*

²¹and gave their land as an
  inheritance,
> *His love endures for ever.*

²²an inheritance to his servant Israel;
> *His love endures for ever.*

²³to the One who remembered us in our
  low estate
> *His love endures for ever.*

²⁴and freed us from our enemies,
> *His love endures for ever.*

²⁵and who gives food to every creature.
> *His love endures for ever.*

²⁶Give thanks to the God of heaven.
> *His love endures for ever.*

Psalm 137

¹By the rivers of Babylon we sat and
  wept
  when we remembered Zion.
²There on the poplars
  we hung our harps,
³for there our captors asked us for
  songs,
  our tormentors demanded songs of
  joy;
  they said, "Sing us one of the songs of
  Zion!"

⁴How can we sing the songs of the LORD
  while in a foreign land?
⁵If I forget you, O Jerusalem,
  may my right hand forget ⌜its skill⌝.
⁶May my tongue cling to the roof of my
  mouth
  if I do not remember you,
  if I do not consider Jerusalem
  my highest joy.

⁷Remember, O LORD, what the
  Edomites did
  on the day Jerusalem fell.
"Tear it down," they cried,
  "tear it down to its foundations!"

⁸O Daughter of Babylon, doomed to
  destruction,
  happy is he who repays you
  for what you have done to us—
⁹he who seizes your infants
  and dashes them against the rocks.

[a]13 Hebrew *Yam Suph*; that is, Sea of Reeds; also in verse 15

Psalm 138

Of David.

¹I will praise you, O LORD, with all my
    heart;
    before the "gods" I will sing your
      praise.
²I will bow down towards your holy
    temple
    and will praise your name
    for your love and your faithfulness,
 for you have exalted above all things
    your name and your word.
³When I called, you answered me;
    you made me bold and stout-hearted.

⁴May all the kings of the earth praise
    you, O LORD,
    when they hear the words of your
      mouth.
⁵May they sing of the ways of the LORD,
    for the glory of the LORD is great.

⁶Though the LORD is on high, he looks
    upon the lowly,
    but the proud he knows from afar.
⁷Though I walk in the midst of trouble,
    you preserve my life;
 you stretch out your hand against the
    anger of my foes,
    with your right hand you save me.
⁸The LORD will fulfil ⌊his purpose⌋ for
    me;
    your love, O LORD, endures for
      ever—
    do not abandon the works of your
      hands.

Psalm 139

For the director of music. Of David. A psalm.

¹O LORD, you have searched me
    and you know me.
²You know when I sit and when I rise;
    you perceive my thoughts from afar.
³You discern my going out and my lying
    down;
    you are familiar with all my ways.

⁴Before a word is on my tongue
    you know it completely, O LORD.

⁵You hem me in—behind and before;
    you have laid your hand upon me.
⁶Such knowledge is too wonderful for
    me,
    too lofty for me to attain.

⁷Where can I go from your Spirit?
    Where can I flee from your presence?
⁸If I go up to the heavens, you are there;
    if I make my bed in the depths,ᵃ you
    are there.
⁹If I rise on the wings of the dawn,
    if I settle on the far side of the
      sea,
¹⁰even there your hand will guide me,
    your right hand will hold me fast.

¹¹If I say, "Surely the darkness will hide
    me
    and the light become night around
      me,"
¹²even the darkness will not be dark to
    you;
    the night will shine like the day,
    for darkness is as light to you.

¹³For you created my inmost being;
    you knit me together in my mother's
      womb.
¹⁴I praise you because I am fearfully and
    wonderfully made;
    your works are wonderful,
    I know that full well.
¹⁵My frame was not hidden from you
    when I was made in the secret place.
 When I was woven together in the
    depths of the earth,
¹⁶   your eyes saw my unformed body.
 All the days ordained for me
    were written in your book
    before one of them came to be.

¹⁷How precious toᵇ me are your thoughts,
    O God!
    How vast is the sum of them!
¹⁸Were I to count them,
    they would outnumber the grains of
      sand.

ᵃ8 Hebrew *Sheol*   ᵇ17 Or *concerning*

When I awake,
  I am still with you.

[19]If only you would slay the wicked, O
    God!
  Away from me, you bloodthirsty men!
[20]They speak of you with evil intent;
  your adversaries misuse your name.
[21]Do I not hate those who hate you, O
    LORD,
  and abhor those who rise up against
    you?
[22]I have nothing but hatred for them;
  I count them my enemies.

[23]Search me, O God, and know my heart;
  test me and know my anxious
    thoughts.
[24]See if there is any offensive way in me,
  and lead me in the way everlasting.

Psalm 140

For the director of music. A psalm of David.

[1]Rescue me, O LORD, from evil men;
  protect me from men of violence,
[2]who devise evil plans in their hearts
  and stir up war every day.
[3]They make their tongues as sharp as a
    serpent's;
  the poison of vipers is on their lips.
                                    Selah

[4]Keep me, O LORD, from the hands of
    the wicked;
  protect me from men of violence
  who plan to trip my feet.
[5]Proud men have hidden a snare for me;
  they have spread out the cords of
    their net
  and have set traps for me along my
    path.   *Selah*

[6]O LORD, I say to you, "You are my
    God."
  Hear, O LORD, my cry for mercy.
[7]O Sovereign LORD, my strong deliverer,
  who shields my head in the day of
    battle—

[8]do not grant the wicked their desires, O
    LORD;
  do not let their plans succeed,
  or they will become proud.   *Selah*

[9]Let the heads of those who surround me
  be covered with the trouble their lips
    have caused.
[10]Let burning coals fall upon them;
  may they be thrown into the fire,
  into miry pits, never to rise.
[11]Let slanderers not be established in the
    land;
  may disaster hunt down men of
    violence.

[12]I know that the LORD secures justice for
    the poor
  and upholds the cause of the needy.
[13]Surely the righteous will praise your
    name
  and the upright will live before you.

Psalm 141

A psalm of David.

[1]O LORD, I call to you; come quickly to me.
  Hear my voice when I call to you.
[2]May my prayer be set before you like
    incense;
  may the lifting up of my hands be like
    the evening sacrifice.

[3]Set a guard over my mouth, O LORD;
  keep watch over the door of my lips.
[4]Let not my heart be drawn to what is evil,
  to take part in wicked deeds
  with men who are evildoers;
    let me not eat of their delicacies.

[5]Let a righteous man[a] strike me—it is a
    kindness;
  let him rebuke me—it is oil on my head.
  My head will not refuse it.

  Yet my prayer is ever against the deeds
    of evildoers;
[6] their rulers will be thrown down from
      the cliffs,

*a*5 Or *Let the Righteous One*

and the wicked will learn that my
  words were well spoken.
7 ⌊They will say,⌋ "As one ploughs and
    breaks up the earth,
  so our bones have been scattered at
    the mouth of the grave."*b*

8But my eyes are fixed on you, O
    Sovereign LORD;
  in you I take refuge—do not give me
    over to death.
9Keep me from the snares they have laid
    for me,
  from the traps set by evildoers.
10Let the wicked fall into their own nets,
  while I pass by in safety.

Psalm 142

A *maskil*[a] of David. When he was in the cave.
A prayer.

1I cry aloud to the LORD;
  I lift up my voice to the LORD for
    mercy.
2I pour out my complaint before him;
  before him I tell my trouble.

3When my spirit grows faint within me,
  it is you who know my way.
  In the path where I walk
    men have hidden a snare for
      me.
4Look to my right and see;
  no-one is concerned for me.
  I have no refuge;
    no-one cares for my life.

5I cry to you, O LORD;
  I say, "You are my refuge,
    my portion in the land of the living."
6Listen to my cry,
  for I am in desperate need;
  rescue me from those who pursue me,
    for they are too strong for me.
7Set me free from my prison,
  that I may praise your name.

Then the righteous will gather about me
  because of your goodness to me.

Psalm 143

A psalm of David.

1O LORD, hear my prayer,
  listen to my cry for mercy;
  in your faithfulness and righteousness
    come to my relief.
2Do not bring your servant into
    judgment,
  for no-one living is righteous before
    you.

3The enemy pursues me,
  he crushes me to the ground;
  he makes me dwell in darkness
    like those long dead.
4So my spirit grows faint within me;
  my heart within me is dismayed.

5I remember the days of long ago;
  I meditate on all your works
    and consider what your hands have
      done.
6I spread out my hands to you;
  my soul thirsts for you like a parched
    land.   *Selah*

7Answer me quickly, O LORD;
  my spirit fails.
  Do not hide your face from me
    or I will be like those who go down to
      the pit.
8Let the morning bring me word of your
    unfailing love,
  for I have put my trust in you.
  Show me the way I should go,
    for to you I lift up my soul.
9Rescue me from my enemies, O LORD,
  for I hide myself in you.
10Teach me to do your will,
  for you are my God;
  may your good Spirit
    lead me on level ground.

11For your name's sake, O LORD,
    preserve my life;
  in your righteousness, bring me out
    of trouble.
12In your unfailing love, silence my
    enemies;

---

*b*7 Hebrew *Sheol*   *a*Title: Probably a literary or musical term

destroy all my foes,
for I am your servant.

Psalm 144

Of David.

¹Praise be to the LORD my Rock,
who trains my hands for war,
my fingers for battle.
²He is my loving God and my fortress,
my stronghold and my deliverer,
my shield, in whom I take refuge,
who subdues peoples*a* under me.

³O LORD, what is man that you care for
him,
the son of man that you think of him?
⁴Man is like a breath;
his days are like a fleeting shadow.

⁵Part your heavens, O LORD, and come
down;
touch the mountains, so that they
smoke.
⁶Send forth lightning and scatter ˪the
enemies˩;
shoot your arrows and rout them.
⁷Reach down your hand from on high;
deliver me and rescue me
from the mighty waters,
from the hands of foreigners
⁸whose mouths are full of lies,
whose right hands are deceitful.

⁹I will sing a new song to you, O God;
on the ten-stringed lyre I will make
music to you,
¹⁰to the One who gives victory to kings,
who delivers his servant David from
the deadly sword.

¹¹Deliver me and rescue me
from the hands of foreigners
whose mouths are full of lies,
whose right hands are deceitful.

¹²Then our sons in their youth
will be like well-nurtured plants,
and our daughters will be like pillars
carved to adorn a palace.
¹³Our barns will be filled
with every kind of provision.
Our sheep will increase by thousands,
by tens of thousands in our fields;
14   our oxen will draw heavy loads.*b*
There will be no breaching of walls,
no going into captivity,
no cry of distress in our streets.

¹⁵Blessed are the people of whom this is
true;
blessed are the people whose God is
the LORD.

Psalm 145*a*

A psalm of praise. Of David.

¹I will exalt you, my God the King;
I will praise your name for ever and
ever.
²Every day I will praise you
and extol your name for ever and
ever.

³Great is the LORD and most worthy of
praise;
his greatness no-one can fathom.
⁴One generation will commend your
works to another;
they will tell of your mighty acts.
⁵They will speak of the glorious
splendour of your majesty,
and I will meditate on your wonderful
works.*b*
⁶They will tell of the power of your
awesome works,
and I will proclaim your great deeds.
⁷They will celebrate your abundant
goodness
and joyfully sing of your
righteousness.

a2 Many manuscripts of the Masoretic Text, Dead Sea Scrolls, Aquila, Jerome and Syriac; most manuscripts of the
Masoretic Text *subdues my people*   *b14* Or *our chieftains will be firmly established*
*a*This psalm is an acrostic poem, the verses of which (including verse 13b) begin with the successive letters of the Hebrew
alphabet.
b5 Dead Sea Scrolls and Syriac (see also Septuagint); Masoretic Text *On the glorious splendour of your majesty / and on
your wonderful works I will meditate*

⁸The LORD is gracious and
  compassionate,
  slow to anger and rich in love.
⁹The LORD is good to all;
  he has compassion on all he has
    made.
¹⁰All you have made will praise you, O
    LORD;
  your saints will extol you.
¹¹They will tell of the glory of your
    kingdom
  and speak of your might,
¹²so that all men may know of your
    mighty acts
  and the glorious splendour of your
    kingdom.
¹³Your kingdom is an everlasting
    kingdom,
  and your dominion endures through
    all generations.

The LORD is faithful to all his promises
  and loving towards all he has made.ᶜ
¹⁴The LORD upholds all those who fall
  and lifts up all who are bowed down.
¹⁵The eyes of all look to you,
  and you give them their food at the
    proper time.
¹⁶You open your hand
  and satisfy the desires of every living
    thing.

¹⁷The LORD is righteous in all his ways
  and loving towards all he has made.
¹⁸The LORD is near to all who call on
    him,
  to all who call on him in truth.
¹⁹He fulfils the desires of those who fear
    him;
  he hears their cry and saves them.
²⁰The LORD watches over all who love
    him,
  but all the wicked he will destroy.

²¹My mouth will speak in praise of the
    LORD.
  Let every creature praise his holy
    name
  for ever and ever.

Psalm 146

¹Praise the LORD.ᵃ

Praise the LORD, O my soul.
² I will praise the LORD all my life;
  I will sing praise to my God as long as
    I live.

³Do not put your trust in princes,
  in mortal men, who cannot save.
⁴When their spirit departs, they return to
    the ground;
  on that very day their plans come to
    nothing.

⁵Blessed is he whose help is the God of
    Jacob,
  whose hope is in the LORD his God,
⁶the Maker of heaven and earth,
  the sea, and everything in them—
  the LORD, who remains faithful for
    ever.
⁷He upholds the cause of the oppressed
  and gives food to the hungry.
  The LORD sets prisoners free,
⁸ the LORD gives sight to the blind,
  the LORD lifts up those who are bowed
    down,
  the LORD loves the righteous.
⁹The LORD watches over the alien
  and sustains the fatherless and the
    widow,
  but he frustrates the ways of the
    wicked.

¹⁰The LORD reigns for ever,
  your God, O Zion, for all
    generations.

Praise the LORD.

Psalm 147

¹Praise the LORD.ᵃ

How good it is to sing praises to our
    God,

ᶜ13 One manuscript of the Masoretic Text, Dead Sea Scrolls and Syriac (see also Septuagint); most manuscripts of the Masoretic Text do not have the last two lines of verse 13.   ᵃ1 Hebrew *Hallelu Yah*; also in verse 10
ᵃ1 Hebrew *Hallelu Yah*; also in verse 20

how pleasant and fitting to praise
him!

²The LORD builds up Jerusalem;
he gathers the exiles of Israel.
³He heals the broken-hearted
and binds up their wounds.

⁴He determines the number of the stars
and calls them each by name.
⁵Great is our Lord and mighty in
power;
his understanding has no limit.
⁶The LORD sustains the humble
but casts the wicked to the ground.

⁷Sing to the LORD with thanksgiving;
make music to our God on the
harp.
⁸He covers the sky with clouds;
he supplies the earth with rain
and makes grass grow on the hills.
⁹He provides food for the cattle
and for the young ravens when they
call.

¹⁰His pleasure is not in the strength of the
horse,
nor his delight in the legs of a man;
¹¹the LORD delights in those who fear
him,
who put their hope in his unfailing
love.

¹²Extol the LORD, O Jerusalem;
praise your God, O Zion,
¹³for he strengthens the bars of your gates
and blesses your people within you.
¹⁴He grants peace to your borders
and satisfies you with the finest of
wheat.

¹⁵He sends his command to the earth;
his word runs swiftly.
¹⁶He spreads the snow like wool
and scatters the frost like ashes.
¹⁷He hurls down hail like pebbles.
Who can withstand his icy blast?
¹⁸He sends his word and melts them;
he stirs up his breezes, and the waters
flow.

¹⁹He has revealed his word to Jacob,
his laws and decrees to Israel.
²⁰He has done this for no other nation;
they do not know his laws.

Praise the LORD.

Psalm 148

¹Praise the LORD.ᵃ

Praise the LORD from the heavens,
praise him in the heights above.
²Praise him, all his angels,
praise him, all his heavenly hosts.
³Praise him, sun and moon,
praise him, all you shining stars.
⁴Praise him, you highest heavens
and you waters above the skies.
⁵Let them praise the name of the LORD,
for he commanded and they were
created.
⁶He set them in place for ever and ever;
he gave a decree that will never pass
away.

⁷Praise the LORD from the earth,
you great sea creatures and all ocean
depths,
⁸lightning and hail, snow and clouds,
stormy winds that do his bidding,
⁹you mountains and all hills,
fruit trees and all cedars,
¹⁰wild animals and all cattle,
small creatures and flying birds,
¹¹kings of the earth and all nations,
you princes and all rulers on earth,
¹²young men and maidens,
old men and children.

¹³Let them praise the name of the LORD,
for his name alone is exalted;
his splendour is above the earth and
the heavens.
¹⁴He has raised up for his people a horn,ᵇ
the praise of all his saints,
of Israel, the people close to his
heart.

Praise the LORD.

ᵃ1 Hebrew *Hallelu Yah*; also in verse 14   ᵇ14 *Horn* here symbolises strong one, that is, king.

Psalm 149

[1]Praise the LORD.[a]

Sing to the LORD a new song,
   his praise in the assembly of the
     saints.

[2]Let Israel rejoice in their Maker;
   let the people of Zion be glad in their
     King.
[3]Let them praise his name with dancing
   and make music to him with
     tambourine and harp.
[4]For the LORD takes delight in his
     people;
   he crowns the humble with
     salvation.
[5]Let the saints rejoice in this honour
   and sing for joy on their beds.

[6]May the praise of God be in their
     mouths
   and a double-edged sword in their
     hands,
[7]to inflict vengeance on the nations
   and punishment on the peoples,
[8]to bind their kings with fetters,
   their nobles with shackles of iron,

[9]to carry out the sentence written against
     them.
This is the glory of all his saints.

Praise the LORD.

Psalm 150

[1]Praise the LORD.[a]

Praise God in his sanctuary;
   praise him in his mighty heavens.
[2]Praise him for his acts of power;
   praise him for his surpassing
     greatness.
[3]Praise him with the sounding of the
     trumpet,
   praise him with the harp and lyre,
[4]praise him with tambourine and
     dancing,
   praise him with the strings and flute,
[5]praise him with the clash of cymbals,
   praise him with resounding cymbals.

[6]Let everything that has breath praise
     the LORD.

Praise the LORD.

---

[a]1 Hebrew *Hallelu Yah*; also in verse 9   [a]1 Hebrew *Hallelu Yah*; also in verse 6

Proverbs

Prologue: Purpose and Theme

1 The proverbs of Solomon son of David, king of Israel:

[2] for attaining wisdom and discipline;
   for understanding words of insight;
[3] for acquiring a disciplined and prudent life,
   doing what is right and just and fair;
[4] for giving prudence to the simple,
   knowledge and discretion to the young—
[5] let the wise listen and add to their learning,
   and let the discerning get guidance—
[6] for understanding proverbs and parables,
   the sayings and riddles of the wise.

[7] The fear of the LORD is the beginning of knowledge,
   but fools[a] despise wisdom and discipline.

Exhortations to Embrace Wisdom

Warning Against Enticement

[8] Listen, my son, to your father's instruction
   and do not forsake your mother's teaching.
[9] They will be a garland to grace your head
   and a chain to adorn your neck.

[10] My son, if sinners entice you,
   do not give in to them.
[11] If they say, "Come along with us;
   let's lie in wait for someone's blood,
   let's waylay some harmless soul;
[12] let's swallow them alive, like the grave,[b]
   and whole, like those who go down to the pit;
[13] we will get all sorts of valuable things
   and fill our houses with plunder;
[14] throw in your lot with us,
   and we will share a common purse"—
[15] my son, do not go along with them,
   do not set foot on their paths;
[16] for their feet rush into sin,
   they are swift to shed blood.
[17] How useless to spread a net
   in full view of all the birds!
[18] These men lie in wait for their own blood;
   they waylay only themselves!
[19] Such is the end of all who go after ill-gotten gain;
   it takes away the lives of those who get it.

Warning Against Rejecting Wisdom

[20] Wisdom calls aloud in the street,
   she raises her voice in the public squares;
[21] at the head of the noisy streets[c] she cries out,
   in the gateways of the city she makes her speech:

---

[a]7 The Hebrew words rendered *fool* in Proverbs, and often elsewhere in the Old Testament, denote one who is morally deficient.   [b]12 Hebrew *Sheol*   [c]21 Hebrew; Septuagint / *on the tops of the walls*

22"How long will you simple ones[d] love
        your simple ways?
    How long will mockers delight in
        mockery
    and fools hate knowledge?
23If you had responded to my rebuke,
    I would have poured out my heart to
        you
    and made my thoughts known to you.
24But since you rejected me when I called
    and no-one gave heed when I
        stretched out my hand,
25since you ignored all my advice
    and would not accept my rebuke,
26I in turn will laugh at your disaster;
    I will mock when calamity overtakes
        you—
27when calamity overtakes you like a
        storm,
    when disaster sweeps over you like a
        whirlwind,
    when distress and trouble overwhelm
        you.

28"Then they will call to me but I will not
        answer;
    they will look for me but will not find
        me.
29Since they hated knowledge
    and did not choose to fear the LORD,
30since they would not accept my advice
    and spurned my rebuke,
31they will eat the fruit of their ways
    and be filled with the fruit of their
        schemes.
32For the waywardness of the simple will
        kill them,
    and the complacency of fools will
        destroy them;
33but whoever listens to me will live in
        safety
    and be at ease, without fear of harm."

Moral Benefits of Wisdom

2 My son, if you accept my words
    and store up my commands within
        you,
2turning your ear to wisdom
    and applying your heart to
        understanding,

3and if you call out for insight
    and cry aloud for understanding,
4and if you look for it as for silver
    and search for it as for hidden
        treasure,
5then you will understand the fear of the
        LORD
    and find the knowledge of God.
6For the LORD gives wisdom,
    and from his mouth come knowledge
        and understanding.
7He holds victory in store for the
        upright,
    he is a shield to those whose walk is
        blameless,
8for he guards the course of the just
    and protects the way of his faithful
        ones.

9Then you will understand what is right
        and just
    and fair—every good path.
10For wisdom will enter your heart,
    and knowledge will be pleasant to
        your soul.
11Discretion will protect you,
    and understanding will guard
        you.

12Wisdom will save you from the ways of
        wicked men,
    from men whose words are perverse,
13who leave the straight paths
    to walk in dark ways,
14who delight in doing wrong
    and rejoice in the perverseness of
        evil,
15whose paths are crooked
    and who are devious in their ways.

16It will save you also from the adulteress,
    from the wayward wife with her
        seductive words,
17who has left the partner of her youth
    and ignored the covenant she made
        before God.[a]
18For her house leads down to death
    and her paths to the spirits of the
        dead.
19None who go to her return
    or attain the paths of life.

---

d22 The Hebrew word rendered *simple* in Proverbs generally denotes one without moral direction and inclined to evil.
a17 Or *covenant of her God*

²⁰Thus you will walk in the ways of good men
and keep to the paths of the righteous.
²¹For the upright will live in the land,
and the blameless will remain in it;
²²but the wicked will be cut off from the land,
and the unfaithful will be torn from it.

Further Benefits of Wisdom

3 My son, do not forget my teaching,
but keep my commands in your heart,
²for they will prolong your life many years
and bring you prosperity.

³Let love and faithfulness never leave you;
bind them around your neck,
write them on the tablet of your heart.
⁴Then you will win favour and a good name
in the sight of God and man.

⁵Trust in the LORD with all your heart
and lean not on your own understanding;
⁶in all your ways acknowledge him,
and he will make your paths straight.ᵃ

⁷Do not be wise in your own eyes;
fear the LORD and shun evil.
⁸This will bring health to your body
and nourishment to your bones.

⁹Honour the LORD with your wealth,
with the firstfruits of all your crops;
¹⁰then your barns will be filled to overflowing,
and your vats will brim over with new wine.

¹¹My son, do not despise the LORD's discipline
and do not resent his rebuke,
¹²because the LORD disciplines those he loves,

as a fatherᵇ the son he delights in.

¹³Blessed is the man who finds wisdom,
the man who gains understanding,
¹⁴for she is more profitable than silver
and yields better returns than gold.
¹⁵She is more precious than rubies;
nothing you desire can compare with her.
¹⁶Long life is in her right hand;
in her left hand are riches and honour.
¹⁷Her ways are pleasant ways,
and all her paths are peace.
¹⁸She is a tree of life to those who embrace her;
those who lay hold of her will be blessed.

¹⁹By wisdom the LORD laid the earth's foundations,
by understanding he set the heavens in place;
²⁰by his knowledge the deeps were divided,
and the clouds let drop the dew.

²¹My son, preserve sound judgment and discernment,
do not let them out of your sight;
²²they will be life for you,
an ornament to grace your neck.
²³Then you will go on your way in safety,
and your foot will not stumble;
²⁴when you lie down, you will not be afraid;
when you lie down, your sleep will be sweet.
²⁵Have no fear of sudden disaster
or of the ruin that overtakes the wicked,
²⁶for the LORD will be your confidence
and will keep your foot from being snared.

²⁷Do not withhold good from those who deserve it,
when it is in your power to act.
²⁸Do not say to your neighbour,
"Come back later; I'll give it tomorrow"—
when you now have it with you.

ᵃ6 Or *will direct your paths.*   ᵇ12 Hebrew; Septuagint / *and he punishes*

²⁹Do not plot harm against your
    neighbour,
    who lives trustfully near you.
³⁰Do not accuse a man for no reason—
    when he has done you no harm.

³¹Do not envy a violent man
    or choose any of his ways,
³²for the Lord detests a perverse man
    but takes the upright into his
      confidence.

³³The Lord's curse is on the house of the
    wicked,
    but he blesses the home of the
      righteous.
³⁴He mocks proud mockers
    but gives grace to the humble.
³⁵The wise inherit honour,
    but fools he holds up to shame.

Wisdom Is Supreme

4 Listen, my sons, to a father's
    instruction;
    pay attention and gain
      understanding.
²I give you sound learning,
    so do not forsake my teaching.
³When I was a boy in my father's house,
    still tender, and an only child of my
      mother,
⁴he taught me and said,
    "Lay hold of my words with all your
      heart;
    keep my commands and you will live.
⁵Get wisdom, get understanding;
    do not forget my words or swerve
      from them.
⁶Do not forsake wisdom, and she will
      protect you;
    love her, and she will watch over you.
⁷Wisdom is supreme; therefore get
    wisdom.
    Though it cost all you have,*ᵃ* get
      understanding.
⁸Esteem her, and she will exalt you;
    embrace her, and she will honour
      you.
⁹She will set a garland of grace on your
    head

and present you with a crown of
    splendour."

¹⁰Listen, my son, accept what I say,
    and the years of your life will be
      many.
¹¹I guide you in the way of wisdom
    and lead you along straight paths.
¹²When you walk, your steps will not be
      hampered;
    when you run, you will not stumble.
¹³Hold on to instruction, do not let it go;
    guard it well, for it is your life.
¹⁴Do not set foot on the path of the
    wicked
    or walk in the way of evil men.
¹⁵Avoid it, do not travel on it;
    turn from it and go on your way.
¹⁶For they cannot sleep till they do evil;
    they are robbed of slumber till
      they make someone fall.
¹⁷They eat the bread of wickedness
    and drink the wine of violence.

¹⁸The path of the righteous is like the first
    gleam of dawn,
    shining ever brighter till the full light
      of day.
¹⁹But the way of the wicked is like deep
    darkness;
    they do not know what makes them
      stumble.

²⁰My son, pay attention to what I say;
    listen closely to my words.
²¹Do not let them out of your sight,
    keep them within your heart;
²²for they are life to those who find them
    and health to a man's whole body.
²³Above all else, guard your heart,
    for it is the wellspring of life.
²⁴Put away perversity from your mouth;
    keep corrupt talk far from your
      lips.
²⁵Let your eyes look straight ahead,
    fix your gaze directly before
      you.
²⁶Make level*ᵇ* paths for your feet
    and take only ways that are firm.
²⁷Do not swerve to the right or the left;
    keep your foot from evil.

*ᵃ*7 Or *Whatever else you get*   *ᵇ*26 Or *Consider the*

Warning Against Adultery

5 My son, pay attention to my
wisdom,
    listen well to my words of insight,
2that you may maintain discretion
    and your lips may preserve
        knowledge.
3For the lips of an adulteress drip honey,
    and her speech is smoother than oil;
4but in the end she is bitter as gall,
    sharp as a double-edged sword.
5Her feet go down to death;
    her steps lead straight to the grave.*a*
6She gives no thought to the way of life;
    her paths are crooked, but she knows
        it not.

7Now then, my sons, listen to me;
    do not turn aside from what I say.
8Keep to a path far from her,
    do not go near the door of her house,
9lest you give your best strength to
        others
    and your years to one who is cruel,
10lest strangers feast on your wealth
    and your toil enrich another man's
        house.
11At the end of your life you will groan,
    when your flesh and body are spent.
12You will say, "How I hated discipline!
    How my heart spurned correction!
13I would not obey my teachers
    or listen to my instructors.
14I have come to the brink of utter ruin
    in the midst of the whole assembly."

15Drink water from your own cistern,
    running water from your own well.
16Should your springs overflow in the
        streets,
    your streams of water in the public
        squares?
17Let them be yours alone,
    never to be shared with strangers.
18May your fountain be blessed,
    and may you rejoice in the wife of
        your youth.
19A loving doe, a graceful deer—
    may her breasts satisfy you always,
    may you ever be captivated by her
        love.

20Why be captivated, my son, by an
        adulteress?
    Why embrace the bosom of another
        man's wife?

21For a man's ways are in full view of the
        LORD,
    and he examines all his paths.
22The evil deeds of a wicked man ensnare
        him;
    the cords of his sin hold him fast.
23He will die for lack of discipline,
    led astray by his own great folly.

Warnings Against Folly

6 My son, if you have put up security
for your neighbour,
    if you have struck hands in pledge for
        another,
2if you have been trapped by what you
        said,
    ensnared by the words of your
        mouth,
3then do this, my son, to free yourself,
    since you have fallen into your
        neighbour's hands:
Go and humble yourself;
    press your plea with your neighbour!
4Allow no sleep to your eyes,
    no slumber to your eyelids.
5Free yourself, like a gazelle from the
        hand of the hunter,
    like a bird from the snare of the
        fowler.

6Go to the ant, you sluggard;
    consider its ways and be wise!
7It has no commander,
    no overseer or ruler,
8yet it stores its provisions in summer
    and gathers its food at harvest.

9How long will you lie there, you
        sluggard?
    When will you get up from your
        sleep?
10A little sleep, a little slumber,
    a little folding of the hands to rest—
11and poverty will come on you like a
        bandit
    and scarcity like an armed man.*a*

a5 Hebrew *Sheol*   *a11* Or *like a vagrant / and scarcity like a beggar*

¹²A scoundrel and villain,
   who goes about with a corrupt
      mouth,
¹³ who winks with his eye,
   signals with his feet
   and motions with his fingers,
¹⁴ who plots evil with deceit in his
      heart—
   he always stirs up dissension.
¹⁵Therefore disaster will overtake him in
      an instant;
   he will suddenly be destroyed—
      without remedy.

¹⁶There are six things the LORD hates,
   seven that are detestable to him:
¹⁷   haughty eyes,
     a lying tongue,
     hands that shed innocent blood,
¹⁸   a heart that devises wicked
      schemes,
     feet that are quick to rush into evil,
¹⁹   a false witness who pours out lies
     and a man who stirs up dissension
      among brothers.

Warning Against Adultery

²⁰My son, keep your father's commands
   and do not forsake your mother's
      teaching.
²¹Bind them upon your heart for ever;
   fasten them around your neck.
²²When you walk, they will guide you;
   when you sleep, they will watch over
      you;
   when you awake, they will speak to
      you.
²³For these commands are a lamp,
   this teaching is a light,
 and the corrections of discipline
   are the way to life,
²⁴keeping you from the immoral woman,
   from the smooth tongue of the
      wayward wife.
²⁵Do not lust in your heart after her
      beauty
   or let her captivate you with her eyes,
²⁶for the prostitute reduces you to a loaf
      of bread,
   and the adulteress preys upon your
      very life.
²⁷Can a man scoop fire into his lap

without his clothes being burned?
²⁸Can a man walk on hot coals
   without his feet being scorched?
²⁹So is he who sleeps with another man's
      wife;
   no-one who touches her will go
      unpunished.

³⁰Men do not despise a thief if he steals
   to satisfy his hunger when he is
      starving.
³¹Yet if he is caught, he must pay
      sevenfold,
   though it costs him all the wealth of
      his house.
³²But a man who commits adultery lacks
      judgment;
   whoever does so destroys himself.
³³Blows and disgrace are his lot,
   and his shame will never be wiped
      away;
³⁴for jealousy arouses a husband's fury,
   and he will show no mercy when he
      takes revenge.
³⁵He will not accept any compensation;
   he will refuse the bribe, however
      great it is.

Warning Against the Adulteress

7 My son, keep my words
   and store up my commands
     within you.
²Keep my commands and you will live;
   guard my teachings as the apple of
      your eye.
³Bind them on your fingers;
   write them on the tablet of your
      heart.
⁴Say to wisdom, "You are my sister,"
   and call understanding your kinsman;
⁵they will keep you from the adulteress,
   from the wayward wife with her
      seductive words.

⁶At the window of my house
   I looked out through the lattice.
⁷I saw among the simple,
   I noticed among the young men,
   a youth who lacked judgment.
⁸He was going down the street near her
      corner,
   walking along in the direction of her
      house

[9] at twilight, as the day was fading,
as the dark of night set in.

[10] Then out came a woman to meet him,
dressed like a prostitute and with
crafty intent.
[11] (She is loud and defiant,
her feet never stay at home;
[12] now in the street, now in the squares,
at every corner she lurks.)
[13] She took hold of him and kissed him
and with a brazen face she said:

[14] "I have fellowship offerings[a] at home;
today I fulfilled my vows.
[15] So I came out to meet you;
I looked for you and have found you!
[16] I have covered my bed
with coloured linens from Egypt.
[17] I have perfumed my bed
with myrrh, aloes and cinnamon.
[18] Come, let's drink deep of love till
morning;
let's enjoy ourselves with love!
[19] My husband is not at home;
he has gone on a long journey.
[20] He took his purse filled with money
and will not be home till full moon."

[21] With persuasive words she led him
astray;
she seduced him with her smooth
talk.
[22] All at once he followed her
like an ox going to the slaughter,
like a deer[b] stepping into a noose[c]
[23]   till an arrow pierces his liver,
like a bird darting into a snare,
little knowing it will cost him his life.

[24] Now then, my sons, listen to me;
pay attention to what I say.
[25] Do not let your heart turn to her ways
or stray into her paths.
[26] Many are the victims she has brought
down;
her slain are a mighty throng.
[27] Her house is a highway to the grave,[d]
leading down to the chambers of
death.

Wisdom's Call

8 Does not wisdom call out?
Does not understanding raise her
voice?
[2] On the heights along the way,
where the paths meet, she takes her
stand;
[3] beside the gates leading into the city,
at the entrances, she cries aloud:
[4] "To you, O men, I call out;
I raise my voice to all mankind.
[5] You who are simple, gain prudence;
you who are foolish, gain
understanding.
[6] Listen, for I have worthy things to say;
I open my lips to speak what is right.
[7] My mouth speaks what is true,
for my lips detest wickedness.
[8] All the words of my mouth are just;
none of them is crooked or perverse.
[9] To the discerning all of them are right;
they are faultless to those who have
knowledge.
[10] Choose my instruction instead of silver,
knowledge rather than choice gold,
[11] for wisdom is more precious than rubies,
and nothing you desire can compare
with her.

[12] "I, wisdom, dwell together with
prudence;
I possess knowledge and discretion.
[13] To fear the LORD is to hate evil;
I hate pride and arrogance,
evil behaviour and perverse speech.
[14] Counsel and sound judgment are mine;
I have understanding and power.
[15] By me kings reign
and rulers make laws that are just;
[16] by me princes govern,
and all nobles who rule on earth.[a]
[17] I love those who love me,
and those who seek me find me.
[18] With me are riches and honour,
enduring wealth and prosperity.
[19] My fruit is better than fine gold;
what I yield surpasses choice silver.
[20] I walk in the way of righteousness,
along the paths of justice,

---

a14 Traditionally *peace offerings*   *b22* Syriac (see also Septuagint); Hebrew *fool*
c22 The meaning of the Hebrew for this line is uncertain.   *d27* Hebrew *Sheol*
a16 Many Hebrew manuscripts and Septuagint; most Hebrew manuscripts *and nobles—all righteous rulers*

21bestowing wealth on those who love me
and making their treasures full.

22"The LORD brought me forth as the
first of his works,b,c
before his deeds of old;
23I was appointedd from eternity,
from the beginning, before the world
began.
24When there were no oceans, I was given
birth,
when there were no springs
abounding with water;
25before the mountains were settled in
place,
before the hills, I was given birth,
26before he made the earth or its fields
or any of the dust of the world.
27I was there when he set the heavens in
place,
when he marked out the horizon on
the face of the deep,
28when he established the clouds above
and fixed securely the fountains of
the deep,
29when he gave the sea its boundary
so that the waters would not overstep
his command,
and when he marked out the
foundations of the earth.
30   Then I was the craftsman at his side.
I was filled with delight day after day,
rejoicing always in his presence,
31rejoicing in his whole world
and delighting in mankind.

32"Now then, my sons, listen to me;
blessed are those who keep my
ways.
33Listen to my instruction and be wise;
do not ignore it.
34Blessed is the man who listens to me,
watching daily at my doors,
waiting at my doorway.
35For whoever finds me finds life
and receives favour from the
LORD.
36But whoever fails to find me harms
himself;
all who hate me love death."

Invitations of Wisdom and of Folly

9 Wisdom has built her house;
she has hewn out its seven pillars.
2She has prepared her meat and mixed
her wine;
she has also set her table.
3She has sent out her maids, and she calls
from the highest point of the city.
4"Let all who are simple come in here!"
she says to those who lack judgment.
5"Come, eat my food
and drink the wine I have mixed.
6Leave your simple ways and you will
live;
walk in the way of understanding.

7"Whoever corrects a mocker invites
insult;
whoever rebukes a wicked man
incurs abuse.
8Do not rebuke a mocker or he will hate
you;
rebuke a wise man and he will love
you.
9Instruct a wise man and he will be wiser
still;
teach a righteous man and he will add
to his learning.

10"The fear of the LORD is the beginning
of wisdom,
and knowledge of the Holy One is
understanding.
11For through me your days will be many,
and years will be added to your life.
12If you are wise, your wisdom will
reward you;
if you are a mocker, you alone will
suffer."

13The woman Folly is loud;
she is undisciplined and without
knowledge.
14She sits at the door of her house,
on a seat at the highest point of the
city,
15calling out to those who pass by,
who go straight on their way.
16"Let all who are simple come in here!"
she says to those who lack judgment.

b22 Or way; or dominion
c22 Or The LORD possessed me at the beginning of his work; or The LORD brought me forth at the beginning of his
work   d23 Or fashioned

17"Stolen water is sweet;
  food eaten in secret is delicious!"
18But little do they know that the dead
    are there,
  that her guests are in the depths of
    the grave.[a]

Proverbs of Solomon

10 The proverbs of Solomon:

A wise son brings joy to his father,
  but a foolish son grief to his mother.

2Ill-gotten treasures are of no value,
  but righteousness delivers from
    death.

3The LORD does not let the righteous go
    hungry
  but he thwarts the craving of the
    wicked.

4Lazy hands make a man poor,
  but diligent hands bring wealth.

5He who gathers crops in summer is a
    wise son,
  but he who sleeps during harvest is a
    disgraceful son.

6Blessings crown the head of the
    righteous,
  but violence overwhelms the mouth
    of the wicked.[a]

7The memory of the righteous will be a
    blessing,
  but the name of the wicked will
    rot.

8The wise in heart accept commands,
  but a chattering fool comes to ruin.

9The man of integrity walks securely,
  but he who takes crooked paths will
    be found out.

10He who winks maliciously causes grief,
  and a chattering fool comes to
    ruin.

11The mouth of the righteous is a fountain
    of life,
  but violence overwhelms the mouth
    of the wicked.

12Hatred stirs up dissension,
  but love covers over all wrongs.

13Wisdom is found on the lips of the
    discerning,
  but a rod is for the back of him who
    lacks judgment.

14Wise men store up knowledge,
  but the mouth of a fool invites ruin.

15The wealth of the rich is their fortified
    city,
  but poverty is the ruin of the poor.

16The wages of the righteous bring them
    life,
  but the income of the wicked brings
    them punishment.

17He who heeds discipline shows the way
    to life,
  but whoever ignores correction leads
    others astray.

18He who conceals his hatred has lying
    lips,
  and whoever spreads slander is a
    fool.

19When words are many, sin is not
    absent,
  but he who holds his tongue is
    wise.

20The tongue of the righteous is choice
    silver,
  but the heart of the wicked is of little
    value.

21The lips of the righteous nourish many,
  but fools die for lack of judgment.

22The blessing of the LORD brings wealth,
  and he adds no trouble to it.

---

*a*18 Hebrew *Sheol*   *a*6 Or *but the mouth of the wicked conceals violence*; also in verse 11

23A fool finds pleasure in evil conduct,
   but a man of understanding delights
      in wisdom.

24What the wicked dreads will overtake
      him;
   what the righteous desire will be
      granted.

25When the storm has swept by, the
      wicked are gone,
   but the righteous stand firm for ever.

26As vinegar to the teeth and smoke to
      the eyes,
   so is a sluggard to those who send
      him.

27The fear of the LORD adds length to life,
   but the years of the wicked are cut
      short.

28The prospect of the righteous is joy,
   but the hopes of the wicked come to
      nothing.

29The way of the LORD is a refuge for the
      righteous,
   but it is the ruin of those who do evil.

30The righteous will never be uprooted,
   but the wicked will not remain in the
      land.

31The mouth of the righteous brings forth
      wisdom,
   but a perverse tongue will be cut out.

32The lips of the righteous know what is
      fitting,
   but the mouth of the wicked only
      what is perverse.

11 The LORD abhors dishonest
      scales,
   but accurate weights are his delight.

2When pride comes, then comes
      disgrace,
   but with humility comes wisdom.

3The integrity of the upright guides
      them,
   but the unfaithful are destroyed by
      their duplicity.

4Wealth is worthless in the day of wrath,
   but righteousness delivers from death.

5The righteousness of the blameless
      makes a straight way for them,
   but the wicked are brought down by
      their own wickedness.

6The righteousness of the upright
      delivers them,
   but the unfaithful are trapped by evil
      desires.

7When a wicked man dies, his hope
      perishes;
   all he expected from his power comes
      to nothing.

8The righteous man is rescued from
      trouble,
   and it comes on the wicked instead.

9With his mouth the godless destroys his
      neighbour,
   but through knowledge the righteous
      escape.

10When the righteous prosper, the city
      rejoices;
   when the wicked perish, there are
      shouts of joy.

11Through the blessing of the upright a
      city is exalted,
   but by the mouth of the wicked it is
      destroyed.

12A man who lacks judgment derides his
      neighbour,
   but a man of understanding holds his
      tongue.

13A gossip betrays a confidence,
   but a trustworthy man keeps a secret.

14For lack of guidance a nation falls,
   but many advisers make victory sure.

15He who puts up security for another will
      surely suffer,

but whoever refuses to strike hands in pledge is safe.

16A kind-hearted woman gains respect,
　but ruthless men gain only wealth.

17A kind man benefits himself,
　but a cruel man brings trouble on himself.

18The wicked man earns deceptive wages,
　but he who sows righteousness reaps a sure reward.

19The truly righteous man attains life,
　but he who pursues evil goes to his death.

20The LORD detests men of perverse heart
　but he delights in those whose ways are blameless.

21Be sure of this: The wicked will not go unpunished,
　but those who are righteous will go free.

22Like a gold ring in a pig's snout
　is a beautiful woman who shows no discretion.

23The desire of the righteous ends only in good,
　but the hope of the wicked only in wrath.

24One man gives freely, yet gains even more;
　another withholds unduly, but comes to poverty.

25A generous man will prosper;
　he who refreshes others will himself be refreshed.

26People curse the man who hoards grain,
　but blessing crowns him who is willing to sell.

27He who seeks good finds goodwill,
　but evil comes to him who searches for it.

28Whoever trusts in his riches will fall,
　but the righteous will thrive like a green leaf.

29He who brings trouble on his family will inherit only wind,
　and the fool will be servant to the wise.

30The fruit of the righteous is a tree of life,
　and he who wins souls is wise.

31If the righteous receive their due on earth,
　how much more the ungodly and the sinner!

12 Whoever loves discipline loves knowledge,
　but he who hates correction is stupid.

2A good man obtains favour from the LORD,
　but the LORD condemns a crafty man.

3A man cannot be established through wickedness,
　but the righteous cannot be uprooted.

4A wife of noble character is her husband's crown,
　but a disgraceful wife is like decay in his bones.

5The plans of the righteous are just,
　but the advice of the wicked is deceitful.

6The words of the wicked lie in wait for blood,
　but the speech of the upright rescues them.

7Wicked men are overthrown and are no more,
　but the house of the righteous stands firm.

8A man is praised according to his wisdom,
　but men with warped minds are despised.

⁹Better to be a nobody and yet have a
  servant
    than pretend to be somebody and
    have no food.

¹⁰A righteous man cares for the needs of
  his animal,
    but the kindest acts of the wicked are
    cruel.

¹¹He who works his land will have
  abundant food,
    but he who chases fantasies lacks
    judgment.

¹²The wicked desire the plunder of evil
  men,
    but the root of the righteous
    flourishes.

¹³An evil man is trapped by his sinful
  talk,
    but a righteous man escapes trouble.

¹⁴From the fruit of his lips a man is filled
  with good things
    as surely as the work of his hands
    rewards him.

¹⁵The way of a fool seems right to him,
    but a wise man listens to advice.

¹⁶A fool shows his annoyance at once,
    but a prudent man overlooks an
    insult.

¹⁷A truthful witness gives honest
  testimony,
    but a false witness tells lies.

¹⁸Reckless words pierce like a sword,
    but the tongue of the wise brings
    healing.

¹⁹Truthful lips endure for ever,
    but a lying tongue lasts only a
    moment.

²⁰There is deceit in the hearts of those
  who plot evil,
    but joy for those who promote peace.

²¹No harm befalls the righteous,
    but the wicked have their fill of
    trouble.

²²The LORD detests lying lips,
    but he delights in men who are
    truthful.

²³A prudent man keeps his knowledge to
  himself,
    but the heart of fools blurts out folly.

²⁴Diligent hands will rule,
    but laziness ends in slave labour.

²⁵An anxious heart weighs a man down,
    but a kind word cheers him up.

²⁶A righteous man is cautious in
  friendship,ᵃ
    but the way of the wicked leads them
    astray.

²⁷The lazy man does not roastᵇ his game,
    but the diligent man prizes his
    possessions.

²⁸In the way of righteousness there is life;
    along that path is immortality.

13 A wise son heeds his father's
    instruction,
    but a mocker does not listen to
    rebuke.

²From the fruit of his lips a man enjoys
  good things,
    but the unfaithful have a craving for
    violence.

³He who guards his lips guards his life,
    but he who speaks rashly will come to
    ruin.

⁴The sluggard craves and gets nothing,
    but the desires of the diligent are fully
    satisfied.

⁵The righteous hate what is false,
    but the wicked bring shame and
    disgrace.

ᵃ26 Or *man is a guide to his neighbour*   ᵇ27 The meaning of the Hebrew for this word is uncertain.

⁶Righteousness guards the man of
integrity,
but wickedness overthrows the
sinner.

⁷One man pretends to be rich, yet has
nothing;
another pretends to be poor, yet has
great wealth.

⁸A man's riches may ransom his life,
but a poor man hears no threat.

⁹The light of the righteous shines
brightly,
but the lamp of the wicked is snuffed
out.

¹⁰Pride only breeds quarrels,
but wisdom is found in those who
take advice.

¹¹Dishonest money dwindles away,
but he who gathers money little by
little makes it grow.

¹²Hope deferred makes the heart sick,
but a longing fulfilled is a tree of
life.

¹³He who scorns instruction will pay for
it,
but he who respects a command is
rewarded.

¹⁴The teaching of the wise is a fountain of
life,
turning a man from the snares of
death.

¹⁵Good understanding wins favour,
but the way of the unfaithful is
hard.ᵃ

¹⁶Every prudent man acts out of
knowledge,
but a fool exposes his folly.

¹⁷A wicked messenger falls into trouble,
but a trustworthy envoy brings
healing.

¹⁸He who ignores discipline comes to
poverty and shame,
but whoever heeds correction is
honoured.

¹⁹A longing fulfilled is sweet to the soul,
but fools detest turning from evil.

²⁰He who walks with the wise grows wise,
but a companion of fools suffers
harm.

²¹Misfortune pursues the sinner,
but prosperity is the reward of the
righteous.

²²A good man leaves an inheritance for
his children's children,
but a sinner's wealth is stored up for
the righteous.

²³A poor man's field may produce
abundant food,
but injustice sweeps it away.

²⁴He who spares the rod hates his son,
but he who loves him is careful to
discipline him.

²⁵The righteous eat to their hearts'
content,
but the stomach of the wicked goes
hungry.

14 The wise woman builds her
house,
but with her own hands the foolish
one tears hers down.

²He whose walk is upright fears the
Lord,
but he whose ways are devious
despises him.

³A fool's talk brings a rod to his back,
but the lips of the wise protect them.

⁴Where there are no oxen, the manger is
empty,
but from the strength of an ox comes
an abundant harvest.

ᵃ15 Or *unfaithful does not endure*

5 A truthful witness does not deceive,
　　but a false witness pours out lies.

6 The mocker seeks wisdom and finds
　　none,
　　but knowledge comes easily to the
　　discerning.

7 Stay away from a foolish man,
　　for you will not find knowledge on his
　　lips.

8 The wisdom of the prudent is to give
　　thought to their ways,
　　but the folly of fools is deception.

9 Fools mock at making amends for sin,
　　but goodwill is found among the
　　upright.

10 Each heart knows its own bitterness,
　　and no-one else can share its joy.

11 The house of the wicked will be
　　destroyed,
　　but the tent of the upright will
　　flourish.

12 There is a way that seems right to a
　　man,
　　but in the end it leads to death.

13 Even in laughter the heart may ache,
　　and joy may end in grief.

14 The faithless will be fully repaid for
　　their ways,
　　and the good man rewarded for his.

15 A simple man believes anything,
　　but a prudent man gives thought to
　　his steps.

16 A wise man fears the LORD and shuns
　　evil,
　　but a fool is hotheaded and
　　reckless.

17 A quick-tempered man does foolish
　　things,
　　and a crafty man is hated.

18 The simple inherit folly,
　　but the prudent are crowned with
　　knowledge.

19 Evil men will bow down in the presence
　　of the good,
　　and the wicked at the gates of the
　　righteous.

20 The poor are shunned even by their
　　neighbours,
　　but the rich have many friends.

21 He who despises his neighbour sins,
　　but blessed is he who is kind to the
　　needy.

22 Do not those who plot evil go astray?
　　But those who plan what is good find[a]
　　love and faithfulness.

23 All hard work brings a profit,
　　but mere talk leads only to poverty.

24 The wealth of the wise is their crown,
　　but the folly of fools yields folly.

25 A truthful witness saves lives,
　　but a false witness is deceitful.

26 He who fears the LORD has a secure
　　fortress,
　　and for his children it will be a refuge.

27 The fear of the LORD is a fountain of
　　life,
　　turning a man from the snares of
　　death.

28 A large population is a king's glory,
　　but without subjects a prince is ruined.

29 A patient man has great understanding,
　　but a quick-tempered man displays
　　folly.

30 A heart at peace gives life to the body,
　　but envy rots the bones.

31 He who oppresses the poor shows
　　contempt for their Maker,

a22 Or show

but whoever is kind to the needy
   honours God.

³²When calamity comes, the wicked are
   brought down,
   but even in death the righteous have
   a refuge.

³³Wisdom reposes in the heart of the
   discerning
   and even among fools she lets herself
   be known.*b*

³⁴Righteousness exalts a nation,
   but sin is a disgrace to any people.

³⁵A king delights in a wise servant,
   but a shameful servant incurs his
   wrath.

15 A gentle answer turns away
   wrath,
   but a harsh word stirs up anger.

²The tongue of the wise commends
   knowledge,
   but the mouth of the fool gushes folly.

³The eyes of the LORD are everywhere,
   keeping watch on the wicked and the
   good.

⁴The tongue that brings healing is a tree
   of life,
   but a deceitful tongue crushes the
   spirit.

⁵A fool spurns his father's discipline,
   but whoever heeds correction shows
   prudence.

⁶The house of the righteous contains
   great treasure,
   but the income of the wicked brings
   them trouble.

⁷The lips of the wise spread knowledge;
   not so the hearts of fools.

⁸The LORD detests the sacrifice of the
   wicked,

but the prayer of the upright pleases
   him.

⁹The LORD detests the way of the wicked
   but he loves those who pursue
   righteousness.

¹⁰Stern discipline awaits him who leaves
   the path;
   he who hates correction will die.

¹¹Death and Destruction*a* lie open before
   the LORD—
   how much more the hearts of men!

¹²A mocker resents correction;
   he will not consult the wise.

¹³A happy heart makes the face cheerful,
   but heartache crushes the spirit.

¹⁴The discerning heart seeks knowledge,
   but the mouth of a fool feeds on folly.

¹⁵All the days of the oppressed are
   wretched,
   but the cheerful heart has a continual
   feast.

¹⁶Better a little with the fear of the LORD
   than great wealth with turmoil.

¹⁷Better a meal of vegetables where there
   is love
   than a fattened calf with hatred.

¹⁸A hot-tempered man stirs up
   dissension,
   but a patient man calms a quarrel.

¹⁹The way of the sluggard is blocked with
   thorns,
   but the path of the upright is a
   highway.

²⁰A wise son brings joy to his father,
   but a foolish man despises his
   mother.

²¹Folly delights a man who lacks
   judgment,

---

b33 Hebrew; Septuagint and Syriac / *but in the heart of fools she is not known*   *a11* Hebrew *Sheol and Abaddon*

but a man of understanding keeps a
straight course.

22Plans fail for lack of counsel,
but with many advisers they succeed.

23A man finds joy in giving an apt reply—
and how good is a timely word!

24The path of life leads upward for the
wise
to keep him from going down to the
grave.*b*

25The LORD tears down the proud man's
house
but he keeps the widow's boundaries
intact.

26The LORD detests the thoughts of the
wicked,
but those of the pure are pleasing to
him.

27A greedy man brings trouble to his
family,
but he who hates bribes will live.

28The heart of the righteous weighs its
answers,
but the mouth of the wicked gushes
evil.

29The LORD is far from the wicked
but he hears the prayer of the
righteous.

30A cheerful look brings joy to the heart,
and good news gives health to the
bones.

31He who listens to a life-giving rebuke
will be at home among the wise.

32He who ignores discipline despises
himself,
but whoever heeds correction gains
understanding.

33The fear of the LORD teaches a man
wisdom,*c*
and humility comes before honour.

16 To man belong the plans of the
heart,
but from the LORD comes the reply of
the tongue.

2All a man's ways seem innocent to him,
but motives are weighed by the LORD.

3Commit to the LORD whatever you do,
and your plans will succeed.

4The LORD works out everything for his
own ends—
even the wicked for a day of disaster.

5The LORD detests all the proud of heart.
Be sure of this: They will not go
unpunished.

6Through love and faithfulness sin is
atoned for;
through the fear of the LORD a man
avoids evil.

7When a man's ways are pleasing to the
LORD,
he makes even his enemies live at
peace with him.

8Better a little with righteousness
than much gain with injustice.

9In his heart a man plans his course,
but the LORD determines his steps.

10The lips of a king speak as an oracle,
and his mouth should not betray
justice.

11Honest scales and balances are from the
LORD;
all the weights in the bag are of his
making.

12Kings detest wrongdoing,
for a throne is established through
righteousness.

13Kings take pleasure in honest lips;
they value a man who speaks the
truth.

b24 Hebrew *Sheol*   *c33* Or *Wisdom teaches the fear of the LORD*

¹⁴A king's wrath is a messenger of death,
   but a wise man will appease it.

¹⁵When a king's face brightens, it means
   life;
   his favour is like a rain cloud in
    spring.

¹⁶How much better to get wisdom than
   gold,
   to choose understanding rather than
    silver!

¹⁷The highway of the upright avoids evil;
   he who guards his way guards his life.

¹⁸Pride goes before destruction,
   a haughty spirit before a fall.

¹⁹Better to be lowly in spirit and among
   the oppressed
   than to share plunder with the proud.

²⁰Whoever gives heed to instruction
   prospers,
   and blessed is he who trusts in the
    LORD.

²¹The wise in heart are called discerning,
   and pleasant words promote
    instruction.^a

²²Understanding is a fountain of life to
   those who have it,
   but folly brings punishment to fools.

²³A wise man's heart guides his mouth,
   and his lips promote instruction.^b

²⁴Pleasant words are a honeycomb,
   sweet to the soul and healing to the
    bones.

²⁵There is a way that seems right to a man,
   but in the end it leads to death.

²⁶The labourer's appetite works for him;
   his hunger drives him on.

²⁷A scoundrel plots evil,
   and his speech is like a scorching fire.

²⁸A perverse man stirs up dissension,
   and a gossip separates close friends.

²⁹A violent man entices his neighbour
   and leads him down a path that is not
    good.

³⁰He who winks with his eye is plotting
   perversity;
   he who purses his lips is bent on evil.

³¹Grey hair is a crown of splendour;
   it is attained by a righteous life.

³²Better a patient man than a warrior,
   a man who controls his temper than
    one who takes a city.

³³The lot is cast into the lap,
   but its every decision is from the LORD.

17 Better a dry crust with peace and
   quiet
   than a house full of feasting,^a with
    strife.

²A wise servant will rule over a
   disgraceful son,
   and will share the inheritance as one
    of the brothers.

³The crucible for silver and the furnace
   for gold,
   but the LORD tests the heart.

⁴A wicked man listens to evil lips;
   a liar pays attention to a malicious
    tongue.

⁵He who mocks the poor shows
   contempt for their Maker;
   whoever gloats over disaster will not
    go unpunished.

⁶Children's children are a crown to the
   aged,
   and parents are the pride of their
    children.

⁷Arrogant^b lips are unsuited to a fool—
   how much worse lying lips to a ruler!

⁸A bribe is a charm to the one who gives
  it;
  wherever he turns, he succeeds.

⁹He who covers over an offence
  promotes love,
  but whoever repeats the matter
  separates close friends.

¹⁰A rebuke impresses a man of
  discernment
  more than a hundred lashes a fool.

¹¹An evil man is bent only on rebellion;
  a merciless official will be sent against
  him.

¹²Better to meet a bear robbed of her
  cubs
  than a fool in his folly.

¹³If a man pays back evil for good,
  evil will never leave his house.

¹⁴Starting a quarrel is like breaching a
  dam;
  so drop the matter before a dispute
  breaks out.

¹⁵Acquitting the guilty and condemning
  the innocent—
  the LORD detests them both.

¹⁶Of what use is money in the hand of a
  fool,
  since he has no desire to get
  wisdom?

¹⁷A friend loves at all times,
  and a brother is born for adversity.

¹⁸A man lacking in judgment strikes
  hands in pledge
  and puts up security for his
  neighbour.

¹⁹He who loves a quarrel loves sin;
  he who builds a high gate invites
  destruction.

²⁰A man of perverse heart does not
  prosper;
  he whose tongue is deceitful falls into
  trouble.

²¹To have a fool for a son brings grief;
  there is no joy for the father of a fool.

²²A cheerful heart is good medicine,
  but a crushed spirit dries up the
  bones.

²³A wicked man accepts a bribe in secret
  to pervert the course of justice.

²⁴A discerning man keeps wisdom in
  view,
  but a fool's eyes wander to the ends
  of the earth.

²⁵A foolish son brings grief to his father
  and bitterness to the one who bore
  him.

²⁶It is not good to punish an innocent
  man,
  or to flog officials for their integrity.

²⁷A man of knowledge uses words with
  restraint,
  and a man of understanding is
  even-tempered.

²⁸Even a fool is thought wise if he keeps
  silent,
  and discerning if he holds his tongue.

18 An unfriendly man pursues selfish
  ends;
  he defies all sound judgment.

²A fool finds no pleasure in understanding
  but delights in airing his own
  opinions.

³When wickedness comes, so does
  contempt,
  and with shame comes disgrace.

⁴The words of a man's mouth are deep
  waters,
  but the fountain of wisdom is a
  bubbling brook.

⁵It is not good to be partial to the wicked
  or to deprive the innocent of justice.

⁶A fool's lips bring him strife,
  and his mouth invites a beating.

7A fool's mouth is his undoing,
and his lips are a snare to his soul.

8The words of a gossip are like choice
morsels;
they go down to a man's inmost parts.

9One who is slack in his work
is brother to one who destroys.

10The name of the LORD is a strong tower;
the righteous run to it and are safe.

11The wealth of the rich is their fortified
city;
they imagine it an unscalable wall.

12Before his downfall a man's heart is
proud,
but humility comes before honour.

13He who answers before listening—
that is his folly and his shame.

14A man's spirit sustains him in sickness,
but a crushed spirit who can bear?

15The heart of the discerning acquires
knowledge;
the ears of the wise seek it out.

16A gift opens the way for the giver
and ushers him into the presence of
the great.

17The first to present his case seems right,
till another comes forward and
questions him.

18Casting the lot settles disputes
and keeps strong opponents apart.

19An offended brother is more unyielding
than a fortified city,
and disputes are like the barred gates
of a citadel.

20From the fruit of his mouth a man's
stomach is filled;
with the harvest from his lips he is
satisfied.

21The tongue has the power of life and
death,
and those who love it will eat its fruit.

22He who finds a wife finds what is good
and receives favour from the LORD.

23A poor man pleads for mercy,
but a rich man answers harshly.

24A man of many companions may come
to ruin,
but there is a friend who sticks closer
than a brother.

19 Better a poor man whose walk is
blameless
than a fool whose lips are perverse.

2It is not good to have zeal without
knowledge,
nor to be hasty and miss the way.

3A man's own folly ruins his life,
yet his heart rages against the LORD.

4Wealth brings many friends,
but a poor man's friend deserts him.

5A false witness will not go unpunished,
and he who pours out lies will not go
free.

6Many curry favour with a ruler,
and everyone is the friend of a man
who gives gifts.

7A poor man is shunned by all his
relatives—
how much more do his friends avoid
him!
Though he pursues them with pleading,
they are nowhere to be found.*a*

8He who gets wisdom loves his own soul;
he who cherishes understanding
prospers.

9A false witness will not go unpunished,
and he who pours out lies will
perish.

*a*7 The meaning of the Hebrew for this sentence is uncertain.

¹⁰It is not fitting for a fool to live in
luxury—
how much worse for a slave to rule
over princes!

¹¹A man's wisdom gives him patience;
it is to his glory to overlook an
offence.

¹²A king's rage is like the roar of a lion,
but his favour is like dew on the grass.

¹³A foolish son is his father's ruin,
and a quarrelsome wife is like a
constant dripping.

¹⁴Houses and wealth are inherited from
parents,
but a prudent wife is from the LORD.

¹⁵Laziness brings on deep sleep,
and the shiftless man goes hungry.

¹⁶He who obeys instructions guards his
life,
but he who is contemptuous of his
ways will die.

¹⁷He who is kind to the poor lends to the
LORD,
and he will reward him for what he
has done.

¹⁸Discipline your son, for in that there is
hope;
do not be a willing party to his death.

¹⁹A hot-tempered man must pay the
penalty;
if you rescue him, you will have to do
it again.

²⁰Listen to advice and accept instruction,
and in the end you will be wise.

²¹Many are the plans in a man's heart,
but it is the LORD's purpose that
prevails.

²²What a man desires is unfailing love;[b]
better to be poor than a liar.

²³The fear of the LORD leads to life:
Then one rests content, untouched by
trouble.

²⁴The sluggard buries his hand in the dish;
he will not even bring it back to his
mouth!

²⁵Flog a mocker, and the simple will learn
prudence;
rebuke a discerning man, and he will
gain knowledge.

²⁶He who robs his father and drives out
his mother
is a son who brings shame and
disgrace.

²⁷Stop listening to instruction, my son,
and you will stray from the words of
knowledge.

²⁸A corrupt witness mocks at justice,
and the mouth of the wicked gulps
down evil.

²⁹Penalties are prepared for mockers,
and beatings for the backs of fools.

20 Wine is a mocker and beer a
brawler;
whoever is led astray by them is not
wise.

²A king's wrath is like the roar of a lion;
he who angers him forfeits his life.

³It is to a man's honour to avoid strife,
but every fool is quick to quarrel.

⁴A sluggard does not plough in season;
so at harvest time he looks but finds
nothing.

⁵The purposes of a man's heart are deep
waters,
but a man of understanding draws
them out.

⁶Many a man claims to have unfailing
love,
but a faithful man who can find?

---

b22 Or A man's greed is his shame

7The righteous man leads a blameless
   life;
   blessed are his children after him.

8When a king sits on his throne to judge,
   he winnows out all evil with his eyes.

9Who can say, "I have kept my heart
   pure;
   I am clean and without sin"?

10Differing weights and differing
   measures—
   the LORD detests them both.

11Even a child is known by his actions,
   by whether his conduct is pure and
   right.

12Ears that hear and eyes that see—
   the LORD has made them both.

13Do not love sleep or you will grow
   poor;
   stay awake and you will have food to
   spare.

14"It's no good, it's no good!" says the
   buyer;
   then off he goes and boasts about his
   purchase.

15Gold there is, and rubies in abundance,
   but lips that speak knowledge are a
   rare jewel.

16Take the garment of one who puts up
   security for a stranger;
   hold it in pledge if he does it for a
   wayward woman.

17Food gained by fraud tastes sweet to a
   man,
   but he ends up with a mouth full of
   gravel.

18Make plans by seeking advice;
   if you wage war, obtain guidance.

19A gossip betrays a confidence;
   so avoid a man who talks too much.

20If a man curses his father or mother,
   his lamp will be snuffed out in pitch
   darkness.

21An inheritance quickly gained at the
   beginning
   will not be blessed at the end.

22Do not say, "I'll pay you back for this
   wrong!"
   Wait for the LORD, and he will deliver
   you.

23The LORD detests differing weights,
   and dishonest scales do not please
   him.

24A man's steps are directed by the LORD.
   How then can anyone understand his
   own way?

25It is a trap for a man to dedicate
   something rashly
   and only later to consider his vows.

26A wise king winnows out the wicked;
   he drives the threshing wheel over
   them.

27The lamp of the LORD searches the spirit
   of a man;[a]
   it searches out his inmost being.

28Love and faithfulness keep a king safe;
   through love his throne is made
   secure.

29The glory of young men is their
   strength,
   grey hair the splendour of the old.

30Blows and wounds cleanse away evil,
   and beatings purge the inmost being.

21 The king's heart is in the hand of
   the LORD;
   he directs it like a watercourse
   wherever he pleases.

2All a man's ways seem right to him,
   but the LORD weighs the heart.

a27 Or The spirit of man is the LORD's lamp

³To do what is right and just
　　is more acceptable to the LORD than
　　sacrifice.

⁴Haughty eyes and a proud heart,
　　the lamp of the wicked, are sin!

⁵The plans of the diligent lead to profit
　　as surely as haste leads to poverty.

⁶A fortune made by a lying tongue
　　is a fleeting vapour and a deadly
　　snare.ᵃ

⁷The violence of the wicked will drag
　　them away,
　　for they refuse to do what is right.

⁸The way of the guilty is devious,
　　but the conduct of the innocent is
　　upright.

⁹Better to live on a corner of the roof
　　than share a house with a
　　quarrelsome wife.

¹⁰The wicked man craves evil;
　　his neighbour gets no mercy from
　　him.

¹¹When a mocker is punished, the simple
　　gain wisdom;
　　when a wise man is instructed, he gets
　　knowledge.

¹²The Righteous Oneᵇ takes note of the
　　house of the wicked
　　and brings the wicked to ruin.

¹³If a man shuts his ears to the cry of the
　　poor,
　　he too will cry out and not be
　　answered.

¹⁴A gift given in secret soothes anger,
　　and a bribe concealed in the cloak
　　pacifies great wrath.

¹⁵When justice is done, it brings joy to
　　the righteous
　　but terror to evildoers.

¹⁶A man who strays from the path of
　　understanding
　　comes to rest in the company of the
　　dead.

¹⁷He who loves pleasure will become
　　poor;
　　whoever loves wine and oil will never
　　be rich.

¹⁸The wicked become a ransom for the
　　righteous,
　　and the unfaithful for the upright.

¹⁹Better to live in a desert
　　than with a quarrelsome and
　　ill-tempered wife.

²⁰In the house of the wise are stores of
　　choice food and oil,
　　but a foolish man devours all he has.

²¹He who pursues righteousness
　　and love
　　finds life, prosperityᶜ and honour.

²²A wise man attacks the city of the
　　mighty
　　and pulls down the stronghold in
　　which they trust.

²³He who guards his mouth and his
　　tongue
　　keeps himself from calamity.

²⁴The proud and arrogant man—
　　"Mocker" is his name;
　　he behaves with overweening
　　pride.

²⁵The sluggard's craving will be the death
　　of him,
　　because his hands refuse to work.

²⁶All day long he craves for more,
　　but the righteous give without
　　sparing.

²⁷The sacrifice of the wicked is
　　detestable—
　　how much more so when brought
　　with evil intent!

ᵃ6 Some Hebrew manuscripts, Septuagint and Vulgate; most Hebrew manuscripts *vapour for those who seek death*
ᵇ12 Or *The righteous man*　　ᶜ21 Or *righteousness*

28A false witness will perish,
  and whoever listens to him will be
    destroyed for ever.*d*

29A wicked man puts up a bold front,
  but an upright man gives thought to
    his ways.

30There is no wisdom, no insight, no plan
  that can succeed against the LORD.

31The horse is made ready for the day of
    battle,
  but victory rests with the LORD.

22 A good name is more desirable
    than great riches;
  to be esteemed is better than silver or
    gold.

2Rich and poor have this in common:
  The LORD is the Maker of them all.

3A prudent man sees danger and takes
    refuge,
  but the simple keep going and suffer
    for it.

4Humility and the fear of the LORD
  bring wealth and honour and life.

5In the paths of the wicked lie thorns and
    snares,
  but he who guards his soul stays far
    from them.

6Train*a* a child in the way he should go,
  and when he is old he will not turn
    from it.

7The rich rule over the poor,
  and the borrower is servant to the
    lender.

8He who sows wickedness reaps trouble,
  and the rod of his fury will be
    destroyed.

9A generous man will himself be blessed,
  for he shares his food with the poor.

10Drive out the mocker, and out goes
    strife;
  quarrels and insults are ended.

11He who loves a pure heart and whose
    speech is gracious
  will have the king for his friend.

12The eyes of the LORD keep watch over
    knowledge,
  but he frustrates the words of the
    unfaithful.

13The sluggard says, "There is a lion
    outside!"
  or, "I will be murdered in the
    streets!"

14The mouth of an adulteress is a deep
    pit;
  he who is under the LORD's wrath will
    fall into it.

15Folly is bound up in the heart of a child,
  but the rod of discipline will drive it
    far from him.

16He who oppresses the poor to increase
    his wealth
  and he who gives gifts to the rich—
    both come to poverty.

Sayings of the Wise

17Pay attention and listen to the sayings
    of the wise;
  apply your heart to what I teach,
18for it is pleasing when you keep them in
    your heart
  and have all of them ready on your
    lips.
19So that your trust may be in the LORD,
  I teach you today, even you.
20Have I not written thirty*b* sayings for
    you,
  sayings of counsel and knowledge,
21teaching you true and reliable words,
  so that you can give sound answers
    to him who sent you?

d28 Or / but the words of an obedient man will live on   *a6 Or Start*
b20 Or not formerly written; or not written excellent

²²Do not exploit the poor because they
are poor
and do not crush the needy in court,
²³for the LORD will take up their case
and will plunder those who plunder
them.

²⁴Do not make friends with a
hot-tempered man,
do not associate with one easily
angered,
²⁵or you may learn his ways
and get yourself ensnared.

²⁶Do not be a man who strikes hands in
pledge
or puts up security for debts;
²⁷if you lack the means to pay,
your very bed will be snatched from
under you.

²⁸Do not move an ancient boundary stone
set up by your forefathers.

²⁹Do you see a man skilled in his work?
He will serve before kings;
he will not serve before obscure men.

23 When you sit to dine with a ruler,
note well what*ᵃ* is before you,
²and put a knife to your throat
if you are given to gluttony.
³Do not crave his delicacies,
for that food is deceptive.

⁴Do not wear yourself out to get rich;
have the wisdom to show restraint.
⁵Cast but a glance at riches, and they are
gone,
for they will surely sprout wings
and fly off to the sky like an eagle.

⁶Do not eat the food of a stingy man,
do not crave his delicacies;
⁷for he is the kind of man
who is always thinking about the
cost.*ᵇ*
"Eat and drink," he says to you,
but his heart is not with you.
⁸You will vomit up the little you have
eaten

and will have wasted your
compliments.

⁹Do not speak to a fool,
for he will scorn the wisdom of your
words.

¹⁰Do not move an ancient boundary stone
or encroach on the fields of the
fatherless,
¹¹for their Defender is strong;
he will take up their case against you.

¹²Apply your heart to instruction
and your ears to words of knowledge.

¹³Do not withhold discipline from a child;
if you punish him with the rod, he will
not die.
¹⁴Punish him with the rod
and save his soul from death.*ᶜ*

¹⁵My son, if your heart is wise,
then my heart will be glad;
¹⁶my inmost being will rejoice
when your lips speak what is right.

¹⁷Do not let your heart envy sinners,
but always be zealous for the fear of
the LORD.
¹⁸There is surely a future hope for you,
and your hope will not be cut off.

¹⁹Listen, my son, and be wise,
and keep your heart on the right
path.
²⁰Do not join those who drink too much
wine
or gorge themselves on meat,
²¹for drunkards and gluttons become
poor,
and drowsiness clothes them in rags.

²²Listen to your father, who gave you life,
and do not despise your mother when
she is old.
²³Buy the truth and do not sell it;
get wisdom, discipline and
understanding.
²⁴The father of a righteous man has great
joy;

ᵃ1 Or *who*   *ᵇ7* Or *for as he thinks within himself, / so he is; or for as he puts on a feast, / so he is*
ᶜ14 Hebrew *Sheol*

he who has a wise son delights in him.
²⁵May your father and mother be glad;
　　may she who gave you birth rejoice!

²⁶My son, give me your heart
　　and let your eyes keep to my ways,
²⁷for a prostitute is a deep pit
　　and a wayward wife is a narrow well.
²⁸Like a bandit she lies in wait,
　　and multiplies the unfaithful among
　　　men.

²⁹Who has woe? Who has sorrow?
　　Who has strife? Who has complaints?
　　Who has needless bruises? Who has
　　　bloodshot eyes?
³⁰Those who linger over wine,
　　who go to sample bowls of mixed
　　　wine.
³¹Do not gaze at wine when it is red,
　　when it sparkles in the cup,
　　when it goes down smoothly!
³²In the end it bites like a snake
　　and poisons like a viper.
³³Your eyes will see strange sights
　　and your mind imagine confusing
　　　things.
³⁴You will be like one sleeping on the
　　high seas,
　　lying on top of the rigging.
³⁵"They hit me," you will say, "but I'm
　　not hurt!
　　They beat me, but I don't feel it!
　When will I wake up
　　so I can find another drink?"

24 Do not envy wicked men,
　　do not desire their company;
²for their hearts plot violence,
　　and their lips talk about making
　　　trouble.

³By wisdom a house is built,
　　and through understanding it is
　　　established;
⁴through knowledge its rooms are filled
　　with rare and beautiful treasures.

⁵A wise man has great power,
　　and a man of knowledge increases
　　　strength;
⁶for waging war you need guidance,
　　and for victory many advisers.

⁷Wisdom is too high for a fool;
　　in the assembly at the gate he has
　　　nothing to say.

⁸He who plots evil
　　will be known as a schemer.
⁹The schemes of folly are sin,
　　and men detest a mocker.

¹⁰If you falter in times of trouble,
　　how small is your strength!

¹¹Rescue those being led away to
　　death;
　　hold back those staggering towards
　　　slaughter.
¹²If you say, "But we knew nothing about
　　this,"
　　does not he who weighs the heart
　　　perceive it?
　Does not he who guards your life know
　　it?
　　Will he not repay each person
　　　according to what he has done?

¹³Eat honey, my son, for it is good;
　　honey from the comb is sweet to your
　　　taste.
¹⁴Know also that wisdom is sweet to your
　　soul;
　　if you find it, there is a future hope
　　　for you,
　　and your hope will not be cut off.

¹⁵Do not lie in wait like an outlaw against
　　a righteous man's house,
　　do not raid his dwelling-place;
¹⁶for though a righteous man falls seven
　　times, he rises again,
　　but the wicked are brought down by
　　　calamity.

¹⁷Do not gloat when your enemy falls;
　　when he stumbles, do not let your
　　　heart rejoice,
¹⁸or the LORD will see and disapprove
　　and turn his wrath away from him.

¹⁹Do not fret because of evil men
　　or be envious of the wicked,
²⁰for the evil man has no future hope,
　　and the lamp of the wicked will be
　　　snuffed out.

²¹Fear the LORD and the king, my son,
  and do not join with the rebellious,
²²for those two will send sudden
    destruction upon them,
  and who knows what calamities they
    can bring?

Further Sayings of the Wise

²³These also are sayings of the wise:

To show partiality in judging is not
    good:
²⁴Whoever says to the guilty, "You are
    innocent"—
  peoples will curse him and nations
    denounce him.
²⁵But it will go well with those who
    convict the guilty,
  and rich blessing will come upon
    them.

²⁶An honest answer
  is like a kiss on the lips.

²⁷Finish your outdoor work
  and get your fields ready;
  after that, build your house.

²⁸Do not testify against your neighbour
    without cause,
  or use your lips to deceive.
²⁹Do not say, "I'll do to him as he has
    done to me;
  I'll pay that man back for what he
    did."

³⁰I went past the field of the sluggard,
  past the vineyard of the man who
    lacks judgment;
³¹thorns had come up everywhere,
  the ground was covered with weeds,
  and the stone wall was in ruins.
³²I applied my heart to what I observed
  and learned a lesson from what I
    saw:
³³A little sleep, a little slumber,
  a little folding of the hands to rest—
³⁴and poverty will come on you like a
    bandit
  and scarcity like an armed man.[a]

More Proverbs of Solomon

25 These are more proverbs of Solomon, copied by the men of Hezekiah king of Judah:

²It is the glory of God to conceal a
    matter;
  to search out a matter is the glory of
    kings.

³As the heavens are high and the earth is
    deep,
  so the hearts of kings are
    unsearchable.

⁴Remove the dross from the silver,
  and out comes material for[a] the
    silversmith;
⁵remove the wicked from the king's
    presence,
  and his throne will be established
    through righteousness.

⁶Do not exalt yourself in the king's
    presence,
  and do not claim a place among great
    men;
⁷it is better for him to say to you, "Come
    up here,"
  than for him to humiliate you before
    a nobleman.

What you have seen with your eyes
8   do not bring[b] hastily to court,
for what will you do in the end
  if your neighbour puts you to shame?

⁹If you argue your case with a neighbour,
  do not betray another man's
    confidence,
¹⁰or he who hears it may shame you
  and you will never lose your bad
    reputation.

¹¹A word aptly spoken
  is like apples of gold in settings of
    silver.

¹²Like an ear-ring of gold or an ornament
    of fine gold

---

is a wise man's rebuke to a listening
     ear.

13Like the coolness of snow at harvest
     time
     is a trustworthy messenger to those
     who send him;
     he refreshes the spirit of his masters.

14Like clouds and wind without rain
     is a man who boasts of gifts he does
     not give.

15Through patience a ruler can be
     persuaded,
     and a gentle tongue can break a
     bone.

16If you find honey, eat just enough—
     too much of it, and you will vomit.
17Seldom set foot in your neighbour's
     house—
     too much of you, and he will hate
     you.

18Like a club or a sword or a sharp arrow
     is the man who gives false testimony
     against his neighbour.

19Like a bad tooth or a lame foot
     is reliance on the unfaithful in times
     of trouble.

20Like one who takes away a garment on
     a cold day,
     or like vinegar poured on soda,
     is one who sings songs to a heavy
     heart.

21If your enemy is hungry, give him food
     to eat;
     if he is thirsty, give him water to
     drink.
22In doing this, you will heap burning
     coals on his head,
     and the LORD will reward you.

23As a north wind brings rain,
     so a sly tongue brings angry looks.

24Better to live on a corner of the roof
     than share a house with a
     quarrelsome wife.

25Like cold water to a weary soul
     is good news from a distant land.

26Like a muddied spring or a polluted
     well
     is a righteous man who gives way to
     the wicked.

27It is not good to eat too much honey,
     nor is it honourable to seek one's own
     honour.

28Like a city whose walls are broken
     down
     is a man who lacks self-control.

26 Like snow in summer or rain in
     harvest,
     honour is not fitting for a fool.

2Like a fluttering sparrow or a darting
     swallow,
     an undeserved curse does not come
     to rest.

3A whip for the horse, a halter for the
     donkey,
     and a rod for the backs of fools!

4Do not answer a fool according to his
     folly,
     or you will be like him yourself.

5Answer a fool according to his folly,
     or he will be wise in his own eyes.

6Like cutting off one's feet or drinking
     violence
     is the sending of a message by the
     hand of a fool.

7Like a lame man's legs that hang limp
     is a proverb in the mouth of a fool.

8Like tying a stone in a sling
     is the giving of honour to a fool.

9Like a thornbush in a drunkard's hand
     is a proverb in the mouth of a fool.

10Like an archer who wounds at random
     is he who hires a fool or any
     passer-by.

¹¹As a dog returns to its vomit,
so a fool repeats his folly.

¹²Do you see a man wise in his own eyes?
There is more hope for a fool than for
him.

¹³The sluggard says, "There is a lion in
the road,
a fierce lion roaming the streets!"

¹⁴As a door turns on its hinges,
so a sluggard turns on his bed.

¹⁵The sluggard buries his hand in the
dish;
he is too lazy to bring it back to his
mouth.

¹⁶The sluggard is wiser in his own eyes
than seven men who answer
discreetly.

¹⁷Like one who seizes a dog by the ears
is a passer-by who meddles in a
quarrel not his own.

¹⁸Like a madman shooting
firebrands or deadly arrows
¹⁹is a man who deceives his neighbour
and says, "I was only joking!"

²⁰Without wood a fire goes out;
without gossip a quarrel dies down.

²¹As charcoal to embers and as wood to
fire,
so is a quarrelsome man for kindling
strife.

²²The words of a gossip are like choice
morsels;
they go down to a man's inmost parts.

²³Like a coating of glaze*ᵃ* over
earthenware
are fervent lips with an evil heart.

²⁴A malicious man disguises himself with
his lips,
but in his heart he harbours deceit.

²⁵Though his speech is charming, do not
believe him,
for seven abominations fill his
heart.
²⁶His malice may be concealed by
deception,
but his wickedness will be exposed in
the assembly.

²⁷If a man digs a pit, he will fall into it;
if a man rolls a stone, it will roll back
on him.

²⁸A lying tongue hates those it hurts,
and a flattering mouth works ruin.

27 Do not boast about tomorrow,
for you do not know what a day
may bring forth.

²Let another praise you, and not your
own mouth;
someone else, and not your own lips.

³Stone is heavy and sand a burden,
but provocation by a fool is heavier
than both.

⁴Anger is cruel and fury overwhelming,
but who can stand before jealousy?

⁵Better is open rebuke
than hidden love.

⁶Wounds from a friend can be trusted,
but an enemy multiplies kisses.

⁷He who is full loathes honey,
but to the hungry even what is bitter
tastes sweet.

⁸Like a bird that strays from its nest
is a man who strays from his home.

⁹Perfume and incense bring joy to the
heart,
and the pleasantness of one's friend
springs from his earnest counsel.

¹⁰Do not forsake your friend and the
friend of your father,

ᵃ23 With a different word division of the Hebrew; Masoretic Text *of silver dross*

and do not go to your brother's house
  when disaster strikes you—
better a neighbour nearby than a
  brother far away.

¹¹Be wise, my son, and bring joy to my
  heart;
  then I can answer anyone who treats
  me with contempt.

¹²The prudent see danger and take
  refuge,
  but the simple keep going and suffer
  for it.

¹³Take the garment of one who puts up
  security for a stranger;
  hold it in pledge if he does it for a
  wayward woman.

¹⁴If a man loudly blesses his neighbour
  early in the morning,
  it will be taken as a curse.

¹⁵A quarrelsome wife is like
  a constant dripping on a rainy day;
¹⁶restraining her is like restraining the
  wind
  or grasping oil with the hand.

¹⁷As iron sharpens iron,
  so one man sharpens another.

¹⁸He who tends a fig-tree will eat its fruit,
  and he who looks after his master will
  be honoured.

¹⁹As water reflects a face,
  so a man's heart reflects the man.

²⁰Death and Destruction[a] are never
  satisfied,
  and neither are the eyes of man.

²¹The crucible for silver and the furnace
  for gold,
  but man is tested by the praise he
  receives.

²²Though you grind a fool in a mortar,
  grinding him like grain with a pestle,

you will not remove his folly from
  him.

²³Be sure you know the condition of your
  flocks,
  give careful attention to your herds;
²⁴for riches do not endure for ever,
  and a crown is not secure for all
  generations.
²⁵When the hay is removed and new
  growth appears
  and the grass from the hills is
  gathered in,
²⁶the lambs will provide you with
  clothing,
  and the goats with the price of a field.
²⁷You will have plenty of goats' milk
  to feed you and your family
  and to nourish your servant girls.

28 The wicked man flees though
  no-one pursues,
  but the righteous are as bold as a lion.

²When a country is rebellious, it has
  many rulers,
  but a man of understanding and
  knowledge maintains order.

³A ruler[a] who oppresses the poor
  is like a driving rain that leaves no
  crops.

⁴Those who forsake the law praise the
  wicked,
  but those who keep the law resist
  them.

⁵Evil men do not understand justice,
  but those who seek the LORD
  understand it fully.

⁶Better a poor man whose walk is
  blameless
  than a rich man whose ways are
  perverse.

⁷He who keeps the law is a discerning
  son,
  but a companion of gluttons disgraces
  his father.

^a20 Hebrew *Sheol and Abaddon*   ^a3 Or *A poor man*

8He who increases his wealth by
 exorbitant interest
amasses it for another, who will be
 kind to the poor.

9If anyone turns a deaf ear to the law,
 even his prayers are detestable.

10He who leads the upright along an evil
 path
will fall into his own trap,
 but the blameless will receive a good
 inheritance.

11A rich man may be wise in his own eyes,
 but a poor man who has discernment
 sees through him.

12When the righteous triumph, there is
 great elation;
but when the wicked rise to power,
 men go into hiding.

13He who conceals his sins does not
 prosper,
but whoever confesses and renounces
 them finds mercy.

14Blessed is the man who always fears the
 LORD,
but he who hardens his heart falls
 into trouble.

15Like a roaring lion or a charging bear
 is a wicked man ruling over a helpless
 people.

16A tyrannical ruler lacks judgment,
 but he who hates ill-gotten gain will
 enjoy a long life.

17A man tormented by the guilt of murder
 will be a fugitive till death;
let no-one support him.

18He whose walk is blameless is kept safe,
 but he whose ways are perverse will
 suddenly fall.

19He who works his land will have
 abundant food,
but the one who chases fantasies will
 have his fill of poverty.

20A faithful man will be richly blessed,
 but one eager to get rich will not go
 unpunished.

21To show partiality is not good—
 yet a man will do wrong for a piece of
 bread.

22A stingy man is eager to get rich
 and is unaware that poverty awaits
 him.

23He who rebukes a man will in the end
 gain more favour
than he who has a flattering
 tongue.

24He who robs his father or mother
 and says, "It's not wrong"—
he is partner to him who destroys.

25A greedy man stirs up dissension,
 but he who trusts in the LORD will
 prosper.

26He who trusts in himself is a fool,
 but he who walks in wisdom is kept
 safe.

27He who gives to the poor will lack
 nothing,
but he who closes his eyes to them
 receives many curses.

28When the wicked rise to power, people
 go into hiding;
but when the wicked perish, the
 righteous thrive.

29 A man who remains stiff-necked
 after many rebukes
will suddenly be destroyed—without
 remedy.

2When the righteous thrive, the people
 rejoice;
when the wicked rule, the people
 groan.

3A man who loves wisdom brings joy to
 his father,
but a companion of prostitutes
 squanders his wealth.

⁴By justice a king gives a country
stability,
but one who is greedy for bribes tears
it down.

⁵Whoever flatters his neighbour
is spreading a net for his feet.

⁶An evil man is snared by his own sin,
but a righteous one can sing and be
glad.

⁷The righteous care about justice for the
poor,
but the wicked have no such concern.

⁸Mockers stir up a city,
but wise men turn away anger.

⁹If a wise man goes to court with a fool,
the fool rages and scoffs, and there is
no peace.

¹⁰Bloodthirsty men hate a man of integrity
and seek to kill the upright.

¹¹A fool gives full vent to his anger,
but a wise man keeps himself under
control.

¹²If a ruler listens to lies,
all his officials become wicked.

¹³The poor man and the oppressor have
this in common:
The LORD gives sight to the eyes of
both.

¹⁴If a king judges the poor with fairness,
his throne will always be secure.

¹⁵The rod of correction imparts wisdom,
but a child left to himself disgraces his
mother.

¹⁶When the wicked thrive, so does sin,
but the righteous will see their
downfall.

¹⁷Discipline your son, and he will give
you peace;
he will bring delight to your soul.

¹⁸Where there is no revelation, the
people cast off restraint;
but blessed is he who keeps the law.

¹⁹A servant cannot be corrected by mere
words;
though he understands, he will not
respond.

²⁰Do you see a man who speaks in haste?
There is more hope for a fool than for
him.

²¹If a man pampers his servant from youth,
he will bring grief[a] in the end.

²²An angry man stirs up dissension,
and a hot-tempered one commits
many sins.

²³A man's pride brings him low,
but a man of lowly spirit gains honour.

²⁴The accomplice of a thief is his own
enemy;
he is put under oath and dare not
testify.

²⁵Fear of man will prove to be a snare,
but whoever trusts in the LORD is kept
safe.

²⁶Many seek an audience with a ruler,
but it is from the LORD that man gets
justice.

²⁷The righteous detest the dishonest;
the wicked detest the upright.

Sayings of Agur

30 The sayings of Agur son of
Jakeh—an oracle:[a]

This man declared to Ithiel,
to Ithiel and to Ucal:[b]

²"I am the most ignorant of men;
I do not have a man's understanding.
³I have not learned wisdom,
nor have I knowledge of the Holy
One.

---

[a]21 The meaning of the Hebrew for this word is uncertain. [a]1 Or *Jakeh of Massa*
[b]1 Masoretic Text; with a different word division of the Hebrew *declared, "I am weary, O God; / I am weary, O God, and faint.*

4Who has gone up to heaven and come
    down?
  Who has gathered up the wind in the
    hollow of his hands?
  Who has wrapped up the waters in his
    cloak?
  Who has established all the ends of
    the earth?
  What is his name, and the name of his
    son?
    Tell me if you know!

5"Every word of God is flawless;
  he is a shield to those who take refuge
    in him.
6Do not add to his words,
  or he will rebuke you and prove you a
    liar.

7"Two things I ask of you, O Lord;
  do not refuse me before I die:
8Keep falsehood and lies far from me;
  give me neither poverty nor riches,
  but give me only my daily bread.
9Otherwise, I may have too much and
    disown you
  and say, 'Who is the Lord?'
  Or I may become poor and steal,
  and so dishonour the name of my God.

10"Do not slander a servant to his master,
  or he will curse you, and you will pay
    for it.

11"There are those who curse their
    fathers
  and do not bless their mothers;
12those who are pure in their own eyes
  and yet are not cleansed of their filth;
13those whose eyes are ever so haughty,
  whose glances are so disdainful;
14those whose teeth are swords
  and whose jaws are set with knives
to devour the poor from the earth,
  the needy from among mankind.

15"The leech has two daughters.
  'Give! Give!' they cry.

  "There are three things that are never
    satisfied,
  four that never say, 'Enough!':

16the grave,c the barren womb,
  land, which is never satisfied with
    water,
  and fire, which never says, 'Enough!'

17"The eye that mocks a father,
  that scorns obedience to a mother,
will be pecked out by the ravens of the
    valley,
  will be eaten by the vultures.

18"There are three things that are too
    amazing for me,
  four that I do not understand:
19the way of an eagle in the sky,
  the way of a snake on a rock,
the way of a ship on the high seas,
  and the way of a man with a maiden.

20"This is the way of an adulteress:
  She eats and wipes her mouth
  and says, 'I've done nothing wrong.'

21"Under three things the earth trembles,
  under four it cannot bear up:
22a servant who becomes king,
  a fool who is full of food,
23an unloved woman who is married,
  and a maidservant who displaces her
    mistress.

24"Four things on earth are small,
  yet they are extremely wise:
25Ants are creatures of little strength,
  yet they store up their food in the
    summer;
26coniesd are creatures of little power,
  yet they make their home in the
    crags;
27locusts have no king,
  yet they advance together in ranks;
28a lizard can be caught with the hand,
  yet it is found in kings' palaces.

29"There are three things that are stately
    in their stride,
  four that move with stately bearing:
30a lion, mighty among beasts,
  who retreats before nothing;
31a strutting cock, a he-goat,
  and a king with his army around him.e

---

c16 Hebrew *Sheol*   d26 That is, the hyrax or rock badger   e31 Or *king secure against revolt.*

³²"If you have played the fool and exalted
　　yourself,
　　or if you have planned evil,
　　clap your hand over your mouth!
³³For as churning the milk produces
　　butter,
　　and as twisting the nose produces
　　blood,
　　so stirring up anger produces strife."

Sayings of King Lemuel

31 The sayings of King Lemuel—an
oracle*ᵃ* his mother taught him:

²"O my son, O son of my womb,
　　O son of my vows,*ᵇ*
³do not spend your strength on women,
　　your vigour on those who ruin kings.

⁴"It is not for kings, O Lemuel—
　　not for kings to drink wine,
　　not for rulers to crave beer,
⁵lest they drink and forget what the law
　　decrees,
　　and deprive all the oppressed of their
　　rights.
⁶Give beer to those who are perishing,
　　wine to those who are in anguish;
⁷let them drink and forget their poverty
　　and remember their misery no more.

⁸"Speak up for those who cannot speak
　　for themselves,
　　for the rights of all who are destitute.
⁹Speak up and judge fairly;
　　defend the rights of the poor and
　　needy."

Epilogue: The Wife of Noble Character

¹⁰*ᶜ*A wife of noble character who can
　　find?
　　She is worth far more than rubies.
¹¹Her husband has full confidence in her
　　and lacks nothing of value.
¹²She brings him good, not harm,
　　all the days of her life.

¹³She selects wool and flax
　　and works with eager hands.
¹⁴She is like the merchant ships,
　　bringing her food from afar.
¹⁵She gets up while it is still dark;
　　she provides food for her family
　　and portions for her servant girls.
¹⁶She considers a field and buys it;
　　out of her earnings she plants a
　　vineyard.
¹⁷She sets about her work vigorously;
　　her arms are strong for her tasks.
¹⁸She sees that her trading is profitable,
　　and her lamp does not go out at night.
¹⁹In her hand she holds the distaff
　　and grasps the spindle with her
　　fingers.
²⁰She opens her arms to the poor
　　and extends her hands to the needy.
²¹When it snows, she has no fear for her
　　household;
　　for all of them are clothed in scarlet.
²²She makes coverings for her bed;
　　she is clothed in fine linen and purple.
²³Her husband is respected at the city
　　gate,
　　where he takes his seat among the
　　elders of the land.
²⁴She makes linen garments and sells
　　them,
　　and supplies the merchants with
　　sashes.
²⁵She is clothed with strength and dignity;
　　she can laugh at the days to come.
²⁶She speaks with wisdom,
　　and faithful instruction is on her
　　tongue.
²⁷She watches over the affairs of her
　　household
　　and does not eat the bread of idleness.
²⁸Her children arise and call her blessed;
　　her husband also, and he praises her:
²⁹"Many women do noble things,
　　but you surpass them all."
³⁰Charm is deceptive, and beauty is
　　fleeting;
　　but a woman who fears the Lᴏʀᴅ is to
　　be praised.
³¹Give her the reward she has earned,
　　and let her works bring her praise at
　　the city gate.

ᵃ1 Or *of Lemuel king of Massa, which*　　　*ᵇ2* Or / *the answer to my prayers*
ᶜ10 Verses 10–31 are an acrostic, each verse beginning with a successive letter of the Hebrew alphabet.

Ecclesiastes

1 The words of the Teacher,[a] son of
David, king of Jerusalem:

2"Meaningless! Meaningless!"
    says the Teacher.
  "Utterly meaningless!
    Everything is meaningless."

3What does man gain from all his labour
    at which he toils under the sun?
4Generations come and generations go,
    but the earth remains for ever.
5The sun rises and the sun sets,
    and hurries back to where it rises.
6The wind blows to the south
    and turns to the north;
  round and round it goes,
    ever returning on its course.
7All streams flow into the sea,
    yet the sea is never full.
  To the place the streams come from,
    there they return again.
8All things are wearisome,
    more than one can say.
  The eye never has enough of seeing,
    nor the ear its fill of hearing.
9What has been will be again,
    what has been done will be done
      again;
  there is nothing new under the sun.
10Is there anything of which one can say,
    "Look! This is something new"?
  It was here already, long ago;
    it was here before our time.
11There is no remembrance of men of
      old,

and even those who are yet to come
    will not be remembered
  by those who follow.

Wisdom Is Meaningless

12I, the Teacher, was king over Israel in
Jerusalem. 13I devoted myself to study and
to explore by wisdom all that is done
under heaven. What a heavy burden God
has laid on men! 14I have seen all the
things that are done under the sun; all of
them are meaningless, a chasing after the
wind.

15What is twisted cannot be straightened;
    what is lacking cannot be counted.

16I thought to myself, "Look, I have
grown and increased in wisdom more than
anyone who has ruled over Jerusalem before me; I have experienced much of wisdom and knowledge." 17Then I applied
myself to the understanding of wisdom,
and also of madness and folly, but I
learned that this, too, is a chasing after the
wind.

18For with much wisdom comes much
      sorrow;
    the more knowledge, the more grief.

Pleasures Are Meaningless

2 I thought in my heart, "Come now, I
will test you with pleasure to find
out what is good." But that also proved
to be meaningless. 2"Laughter," I said,

---

a1 Or leader of the assembly; also in verses 2 and 12

"is foolish. And what does pleasure accomplish?" [3]I tried cheering myself with wine, and embracing folly—my mind still guiding me with wisdom. I wanted to see what was worth while for men to do under heaven during the few days of their lives. [4]I undertook great projects: I built houses for myself and planted vineyards. [5]I made gardens and parks and planted all kinds of fruit trees in them. [6]I made reservoirs to water groves of flourishing trees. [7]I bought male and female slaves and had other slaves who were born in my house. I also owned more herds and flocks than anyone in Jerusalem before me. [8]I amassed silver and gold for myself, and the treasure of kings and provinces. I acquired men and women singers, and a harem[a] as well—the delights of the heart of man. [9]I became greater by far than anyone in Jerusalem before me. In all this my wisdom stayed with me.

[10]I denied myself nothing my eyes
    desired;
  I refused my heart no pleasure.
My heart took delight in all my work,
    and this was the reward for all my
    labour.
[11]Yet when I surveyed all that my hands
    had done
  and what I had toiled to achieve,
everything was meaningless, a chasing
    after the wind;
  nothing was gained under the sun.

Wisdom and Folly Are Meaningless

[12]Then I turned my thoughts to consider
    wisdom,
  and also madness and folly.
What more can the king's successor do
    than what has already been done?
[13]I saw that wisdom is better than folly,
    just as light is better than darkness.
[14]The wise man has eyes in his head,
    while the fool walks in the darkness;
  but I came to realise
    that the same fate overtakes them
    both.

[15]Then I thought in my heart,

"The fate of the fool will overtake me
    also.
  What then do I gain by being
    wise?"
I said in my heart,
  "This too is meaningless."
[16]For the wise man, like the fool, will not
    be long remembered;
  in days to come both will be
    forgotten.
Like the fool, the wise man too must
    die!

Toil Is Meaningless

[17]So I hated life, because the work that is done under the sun was grievous to me. All of it is meaningless, a chasing after the wind. [18]I hated all the things I had toiled for under the sun, because I must leave them to the one who comes after me. [19]And who knows whether he will be a wise man or a fool? Yet he will have control over all the work into which I have poured my effort and skill under the sun. This too is meaningless. [20]So my heart began to despair over all my toilsome labour under the sun. [21]For a man may do his work with wisdom, knowledge and skill, and then he must leave all he owns to someone who has not worked for it. This too is meaningless and a great misfortune. [22]What does a man get for all the toil and anxious striving with which he labours under the sun? [23]All his days his work is pain and grief; even at night his mind does not rest. This too is meaningless.

[24]A man can do nothing better than to eat and drink and find satisfaction in his work. This too, I see, is from the hand of God, [25]for without him, who can eat or find enjoyment? [26]To the man who pleases him, God gives wisdom, knowledge and happiness, but to the sinner he gives the task of gathering and storing up wealth to hand it over to the one who pleases God. This too is meaningless, a chasing after the wind.

---

[a]8 The meaning of the Hebrew for this phrase is uncertain.

A Time for Everything

3 There is a time for everything,
and a season for every activity under
heaven:

2 a time to be born and a time to die,
a time to plant and a time to uproot,
3 a time to kill and a time to heal,
a time to tear down and a time to
build,
4 a time to weep and a time to laugh,
a time to mourn and a time to dance,
5 a time to scatter stones and a time to
gather them,
a time to embrace and a time to
refrain,
6 a time to search and a time to give up,
a time to keep and a time to throw
away,
7 a time to tear and a time to mend,
a time to be silent and a time to
speak,
8 a time to love and a time to hate,
a time for war and a time for peace.

9What does the worker gain from his
toil? 10I have seen the burden God has laid
on men. 11He has made everything beautiful in its time. He has also set eternity in
the hearts of men; yet they cannot fathom
what God has done from beginning to
end. 12I know that there is nothing better
for men than to be happy and do good
while they live. 13That everyone may eat
and drink, and find satisfaction in all his
toil—this is the gift of God. 14I know that
everything God does will endure for ever;
nothing can be added to it and nothing
taken from it. God does it so that men will
revere him.

15Whatever is has already been,
and what will be has been before;
and God will call the past to account.*a*

16And I saw something else under the
sun:

In the place of judgment—wickedness
was there,

in the place of justice—wickedness
was there.

17I thought in my heart,

"God will bring to judgment
both the righteous and the wicked,
for there will be a time for every
activity,
a time for every deed."

18I also thought, "As for men, God tests
them so that they may see that they are
like the animals. 19Man's fate is like that of
the animals; the same fate awaits them
both: As one dies, so dies the other. All
have the same breath;*b* man has no advantage over the animal. Everything is
meaningless. 20All go to the same place;
all come from dust, and to dust all return.
21Who knows if the spirit of man rises
upward and if the spirit of the animal*c* goes
down into the earth?"

22So I saw that there is nothing better
for a man than to enjoy his work, because
that is his lot. For who can bring him to see
what will happen after him?

Oppression, Toil, Friendlessness

4 Again I looked and saw all the
oppression that was taking place
under the sun:

I saw the tears of the oppressed—
and they have no comforter;
power was on the side of their
oppressors—
and they have no comforter.
2And I declared that the dead,
who had already died,
are happier than the living,
who are still alive.
3But better than both
is he who has not yet been,
who has not seen the evil
that is done under the sun.

4And I saw that all labour and all
achievement spring from man's envy of his

---

*a*15 Or *God calls back the past*   *b*19 Or *spirit*
*c*21 Or *Who knows the spirit of man, which rises upward, or the spirit of the animal, which*

neighbour. This too is meaningless, a chasing after the wind.

⁵The fool folds his hands
　and ruins himself.
⁶Better one handful with tranquillity
　than two handfuls with toil
　and chasing after the wind.

⁷Again I saw something meaningless under the sun:

⁸There was a man all alone;
　he had neither son nor brother.
There was no end to his toil,
　yet his eyes were not content with his
　　wealth.
"For whom am I toiling," he asked,
　"and why am I depriving myself of
　　enjoyment?"
This too is meaningless—
　a miserable business!

⁹Two are better than one,
　because they have a good return for
　　their work:
¹⁰If one falls down,
　his friend can help him up.
But pity the man who falls
　and has no-one to help him up!
¹¹Also, if two lie down together, they will
　keep warm.
　But how can one keep warm alone?
¹²Though one may be overpowered,
　two can defend themselves.
A cord of three strands is not quickly
　broken.

Advancement Is Meaningless

¹³Better a poor but wise youth than an old but foolish king who no longer knows how to take warning. ¹⁴The youth may have come from prison to the kingship, or he may have been born in poverty within his kingdom. ¹⁵I saw that all who lived and walked under the sun followed the youth, the king's successor. ¹⁶There was no end to all the people who were before them. But those who came later were not pleased with the successor. This too is meaningless, a chasing after the wind.

Stand in Awe of God

5 Guard your steps when you go to the house of God. Go near to listen rather than to offer the sacrifice of fools, who do not know that they do wrong.

²Do not be quick with your mouth,
　do not be hasty in your heart
　to utter anything before God.
God is in heaven
　and you are on earth,
　so let your words be few.
³As a dream comes when there are many
　　cares,
　so the speech of a fool when there are
　　many words.

⁴When you make a vow to God, do not delay in fulfilling it. He has no pleasure in fools; fulfil your vow. ⁵It is better not to vow than to make a vow and not fulfil it. ⁶Do not let your mouth lead you into sin. And do not protest to the ⌐temple⌐ messenger, "My vow was a mistake." Why should God be angry at what you say and destroy the work of your hands? ⁷Much dreaming and many words are meaningless. Therefore stand in awe of God.

Riches Are Meaningless

⁸If you see the poor oppressed in a district, and justice and rights denied, do not be surprised at such things; for one official is eyed by a higher one, and over them both are others higher still. ⁹The increase from the land is taken by all; the king himself profits from the fields.

¹⁰Whoever loves money never has money
　　enough;
　whoever loves wealth is never
　　satisfied with his income.
　This too is meaningless.

¹¹As goods increase,
　so do those who consume them.
And what benefit are they to the owner
　except to feast his eyes on them?

¹²The sleep of a labourer is sweet,
　whether he eats little or much,

but the abundance of a rich man
   permits him no sleep.

¹³I have seen a grievous evil under the
sun:

wealth hoarded to the harm of its
   owner,
¹⁴ or wealth lost through some
      misfortune,
so that when he has a son
   there is nothing left for him.
¹⁵Naked a man comes from his mother's
   womb,
   and as he comes, so he departs.
He takes nothing from his labour
   that he can carry in his hand.

¹⁶This too is a grievous evil:

As a man comes, so he departs,
   and what does he gain,
   since he toils for the wind?
¹⁷All his days he eats in darkness,
   with great frustration, affliction and
      anger.

¹⁸Then I realised that it is good and
proper for a man to eat and drink, and to
find satisfaction in his toilsome labour
under the sun during the few days of life
God has given him—for this is his lot.
¹⁹Moreover, when God gives any man
wealth and possessions, and enables him
to enjoy them, to accept his lot and be
happy in his work—this is a gift of God.
²⁰He seldom reflects on the days of his life,
because God keeps him occupied with
gladness of heart.

6 I have seen another evil under the
   sun, and it weighs heavily on men:
²God gives a man wealth, possessions and
honour, so that he lacks nothing his heart
desires, but God does not enable him to
enjoy them, and a stranger enjoys them
instead. This is meaningless, a grievous
evil.

³A man may have a hundred children
and live many years; yet no matter how
long he lives, if he cannot enjoy his
prosperity and does not receive proper
burial, I say that a stillborn child is better
off than he. ⁴It comes without meaning, it

departs in darkness, and in darkness its
name is shrouded. ⁵Though it never saw
the sun or knew anything, it has more rest
than does that man—⁶even if he lives a
thousand years twice over but fails to enjoy his prosperity. Do not all go to the
same place?

⁷All man's efforts are for his mouth,
   yet his appetite is never satisfied.
⁸What advantage has a wise man
   over a fool?
What does a poor man gain
   by knowing how to conduct himself
      before others?
⁹Better what the eye sees
   than the roving of the appetite.
This too is meaningless,
   a chasing after the wind.

¹⁰Whatever exists has already been
   named,
   and what man is has been known;
no man can contend
   with one who is stronger than he.
¹¹The more the words,
   the less the meaning,
   and how does that profit anyone?

¹²For who knows what is good for a man
in life, during the few and meaningless
days he passes through like a shadow?
Who can tell him what will happen under
the sun after he is gone?

Wisdom

7 A good name is better than fine
   perfume,
   and the day of death better than the
      day of birth.
²It is better to go to a house of mourning
   than to go to a house of feasting,
for death is the destiny of every man;
   the living should take this to heart.
³Sorrow is better than laughter,
   because a sad face is good for the
      heart.
⁴The heart of the wise is in the house of
   mourning,
   but the heart of fools is in the house
      of pleasure.

⁵It is better to heed a wise man's rebuke
 than to listen to the song of fools.
⁶Like the crackling of thorns under the
  pot,
 so is the laughter of fools.
 This too is meaningless.

⁷Extortion turns a wise man into a fool,
 and a bribe corrupts the heart.

⁸The end of a matter is better than its
 beginning,
 and patience is better than pride.
⁹Do not be quickly provoked in your
 spirit,
 for anger resides in the lap of fools.

¹⁰Do not say, "Why were the old days
 better than these?"
 For it is not wise to ask such
  questions.

¹¹Wisdom, like an inheritance, is a good
 thing
 and benefits those who see the sun.
¹²Wisdom is a shelter
 as money is a shelter,
but the advantage of knowledge is this:
 that wisdom preserves the life of its
  possessor.

¹³Consider what God has done:

Who can straighten
 what he has made crooked?
¹⁴When times are good, be happy;
 but when times are bad, consider:
God has made the one
 as well as the other.
Therefore, a man cannot discover
 anything about his future.

¹⁵In this meaningless life of mine I have
seen both of these:

a righteous man perishing in his
 righteousness,
 and a wicked man living long in his
  wickedness.
¹⁶Do not be over-righteous,
 neither be overwise—

why destroy yourself?
¹⁷Do not be overwicked,
 and do not be a fool—
 why die before your time?
¹⁸It is good to grasp the one
 and not let go of the other.
 The man who fears God will avoid all
  ⌐extremes⌐.ᵃ

¹⁹Wisdom makes one wise man more
  powerful
 than ten rulers in a city.

²⁰There is not a righteous man on earth
 who does what is right and never sins.

²¹Do not pay attention to every word
  people say,
 or you may hear your servant cursing
  you—
²²for you know in your heart
 that many times you yourself have
  cursed others.

²³All this I tested by wisdom and I said,

"I am determined to be wise"—
 but this was beyond me.
²⁴Whatever wisdom may be,
 it is far off and most profound—
 who can discover it?
²⁵So I turned my mind to understand,
 to investigate and to search out
  wisdom and the scheme of things
and to understand the stupidity of
 wickedness
 and the madness of folly.

²⁶I find more bitter than death
 the woman who is a snare,
whose heart is a trap
 and whose hands are chains.
The man who pleases God will escape
  her,
 but the sinner she will ensnare.

²⁷"Look," says the Teacher,ᵇ "this is
what I have discovered:

"Adding one thing to another to
 discover the scheme of things—

ᵃ18 Or *will follow them both*   ᵇ27 Or *leader of the assembly*

28 while I was still searching
   but not finding—
I found one ⌐upright⌐ man among a
      thousand,
   but not one ⌐upright⌐ woman among
      them all.
29This only have I found:
   God made mankind upright,
   but men have gone in search of many
      schemes."

8 Who is like the wise man?
   Who knows the explanation of
      things?
   Wisdom brightens a man's face
   and changes its hard appearance.

Obey the King

2Obey the king's command, I say, because you took an oath before God. 3Do
not be in a hurry to leave the king's presence. Do not stand up for a bad cause, for
he will do whatever he pleases. 4Since a
king's word is supreme, who can say to
him, "What are you doing?"

5Whoever obeys his command will come
      to no harm,
   and the wise heart will know the
      proper time and procedure.
6For there is a proper time and
      procedure for every matter,
   though a man's misery weighs heavily
      upon him.

7Since no man knows the future,
   who can tell him what is to come?
8No man has power over the wind to
      contain it;*a*
   so no-one has power over the day of
      his death.
   As no-one is discharged in time of war,
      so wickedness will not release those
      who practise it.

9All this I saw, as I applied my mind to
everything done under the sun. There is a
time when a man lords it over others to his
own*b* hurt. 10Then too, I saw the wicked

buried—those who used to come and go
from the holy place and receive praise*c* in
the city where they did this. This too is
meaningless.
   11When the sentence for a crime is not
quickly carried out, the hearts of the people are filled with schemes to do wrong.
12Although a wicked man commits a hundred crimes and still lives a long time, I
know that it will go better with God-
fearing men, who are reverent before
God. 13Yet because the wicked do not fear
God, it will not go well with them, and
their days will not lengthen like a shadow.

14There is something else meaningless
that occurs on earth: righteous men who
get what the wicked deserve, and wicked
men who get what the righteous deserve.
This too, I say, is meaningless. 15So I
commend the enjoyment of life, because
nothing is better for a man under the sun
than to eat and drink and be glad. Then
joy will accompany him in his work all the
days of the life God has given him under
the sun.

16When I applied my mind to know
wisdom and to observe man's labour on
earth—his eyes not seeing sleep day or
night—17then I saw all that God has done.
No-one can comprehend what goes on
under the sun. Despite all his efforts to
search it out, man cannot discover its
meaning. Even if a wise man claims he
knows, he cannot really comprehend it.

A Common Destiny for All

9 So I reflected on all this and concluded that the righteous and the wise
and what they do are in God's hands, but
no man knows whether love or hate awaits
him. 2All share a common destiny—the
righteous and the wicked, the good and
the bad,*a* the clean and the unclean, those
who offer sacrifices and those who do not.

   As it is with the good man,
      so with the sinner;
   as it is with those who take oaths,
      so with those who are afraid to take
      them.

---

a8 Or *over his spirit to retain it*   *b9* Or *to their*
c10 Some Hebrew manuscripts and Septuagint (Aquila); most Hebrew manuscripts *and are forgotten*
a2 Septuagint (Aquila), Vulgate and Syriac; Hebrew does not have *and the bad.*

[3]This is the evil in everything that happens under the sun: The same destiny overtakes all. The hearts of men, moreover, are full of evil and there is madness in their hearts while they live, and afterwards they join the dead. [4]Anyone who is among the living has hope[b]—even a live dog is better off than a dead lion!

[5]For the living know that they will die,
  but the dead know nothing;
they have no further reward,
  and even the memory of them is
    forgotten.
[6]Their love, their hate
  and their jealousy have long since
    vanished;
never again will they have a part
  in anything that happens under the
    sun.

[7]Go, eat your food with gladness, and drink your wine with a joyful heart, for it is now that God favours what you do. [8]Always be clothed in white, and always anoint your head with oil. [9]Enjoy life with your wife, whom you love, all the days of this meaningless life that God has given you under the sun—all your meaningless days. For this is your lot in life and in your toilsome labour under the sun. [10]Whatever your hand finds to do, do it with all your might, for in the grave,[c] where you are going, there is neither working nor planning nor knowledge nor wisdom.

[11]I have seen something else under the sun:

The race is not to the swift
  or the battle to the strong,
nor does food come to the wise
  or wealth to the brilliant
  or favour to the learned;
but time and chance happen to them all.

[12]Moreover, no man knows when his hour will come:

As fish are caught in a cruel net,
  or birds are taken in a snare,

so men are trapped by evil times
  that fall unexpectedly upon them.

Wisdom Better Than Folly

[13]I also saw under the sun this example of wisdom that greatly impressed me: [14]There was once a small city with only a few people in it. And a powerful king came against it, surrounded it and built huge siegeworks against it. [15]Now there lived in that city a man poor but wise, and he saved the city by his wisdom. But nobody remembered that poor man. [16]So I said, "Wisdom is better than strength." But the poor man's wisdom is despised, and his words are no longer heeded.

[17]The quiet words of the wise are more to
    be heeded
  than the shouts of a ruler of fools.
[18]Wisdom is better than weapons of war,
  but one sinner destroys much good.

10 As dead flies give perfume a bad
    smell,
  so a little folly outweighs wisdom and
    honour.
[2]The heart of the wise inclines to the
    right,
  but the heart of the fool to the left.
[3]Even as he walks along the road,
    the fool lacks sense
  and shows everyone how stupid he is.
[4]If a ruler's anger rises against you,
    do not leave your post;
  calmness can lay great errors to rest.

[5]There is an evil I have seen under the
    sun,
  the sort of error that arises from a
    ruler:
[6]Fools are put in many high positions,
  while the rich occupy the low ones.
[7]I have seen slaves on horseback,
  while princes go on foot like slaves.

[8]Whoever digs a pit may fall into it;
  whoever breaks through a wall may
    be bitten by a snake.
[9]Whoever quarries stones may be
    injured by them;

---

b4 Or *What then is to be chosen? With all who live, there is hope*   *c10* Hebrew *Sheol*

whoever splits logs may be
endangered by them.

10If the axe is dull
and its edge unsharpened,
more strength is needed
but skill will bring success.

11If a snake bites before it is charmed,
there is no profit for the charmer.

12Words from a wise man's mouth are
gracious,
but a fool is consumed by his own
lips.
13At the beginning his words are folly;
at the end they are wicked madness—
14   and the fool multiplies words.

No-one knows what is coming—
who can tell him what will happen
after him?

15A fool's work wearies him;
he does not know the way to town.

16Woe to you, O land whose king was a
servant[a]
and whose princes feast in the
morning.
17Blessed are you, O land whose king is
of noble birth
and whose princes eat at a proper
time—
for strength and not for drunkenness.

18If a man is lazy, the rafters sag;
if his hands are idle, the house leaks.

19A feast is made for laughter,
and wine makes life merry,
but money is the answer for
everything.

20Do not revile the king even in your
thoughts,
or curse the rich in your bedroom,
because a bird of the air may carry
your words,
and a bird on the wing may report
what you say.

Bread Upon the Waters

11 Cast your bread upon the waters,
for after many days you will find it
again.
2Give portions to seven, yes to eight,
for you do not know what disaster
may come upon the land.

3If clouds are full of water,
they pour rain upon the earth.
Whether a tree falls to the south or to
the north,
in the place where it falls, there will it
lie.
4Whoever watches the wind will not
plant;
whoever looks at the clouds will not
reap.

5As you do not know the path of the
wind,
or how the body is formed[a] in a
mother's womb,
so you cannot understand the work of
God,
the Maker of all things.

6Sow your seed in the morning,
and at evening let not your hands be
idle,
for you do not know which will succeed,
whether this or that,
or whether both will do equally well.

Remember Your Creator While Young

7Light is sweet,
and it pleases the eyes to see the sun.
8However many years a man may live,
let him enjoy them all.
But let him remember the days of
darkness,
for they will be many.
Everything to come is meaningless.

9Be happy, young man, while you are
young,
and let your heart give you joy in the
days of your youth.

---

a16 Or *king is a child*   a5 Or *know how life* (or *the spirit*) / *enters the body being formed*

Follow the ways of your heart
and whatever your eyes see,
but know that for all these things
God will bring you to judgment.
[10]So then, banish anxiety from your heart
and cast off the troubles of your
body,
for youth and vigour are meaningless.

12 Remember your Creator
in the days of your youth,
before the days of trouble come
and the years approach when you will
say,
"I find no pleasure in them"—
[2]before the sun and the light
and the moon and the stars grow
dark,
and the clouds return after the rain;
[3]when the keepers of the house tremble,
and the strong men stoop,
when the grinders cease because they
are few,
and those looking through the
windows grow dim;
[4]when the doors to the street are closed
and the sound of grinding fades;
when men rise up at the sound of birds,
but all their songs grow faint;
[5]when men are afraid of heights
and of dangers in the streets;
when the almond tree blossoms
and the grasshopper drags himself
along
and desire no longer is stirred.
Then man goes to his eternal home
and mourners go about the streets.

[6]Remember him—before the silver cord
is severed,
or the golden bowl is broken;
before the pitcher is shattered at the
spring,
or the wheel broken at the well,
[7]and the dust returns to the ground it
came from,
and the spirit returns to God who
gave it.

[8]"Meaningless! Meaningless!" says the
Teacher.[a]
"Everything is meaningless!"

The Conclusion of the Matter

[9]Not only was the Teacher wise, but also
he imparted knowledge to the people. He
pondered and searched out and set in
order many proverbs. [10]The Teacher
searched to find just the right words, and
what he wrote was upright and true.

[11]The words of the wise are like goads,
their collected sayings like firmly em-
bedded nails—given by one Shepherd.
[12]Be warned, my son, of anything in addition to them.

Of making many books there is no end,
and much study wearies the body.

[13]Now all has been heard;
here is the conclusion of the matter:
Fear God and keep his commandments,
for this is the whole ⌞duty⌟ of man.
[14]For God will bring every deed into
judgment,
including every hidden thing,
whether it is good or evil.

[a]8 Or *the leader of the assembly*; also in verses 9 and 10

Song of Songs

1 Solomon's Song of Songs.

Beloved^a

²Let him kiss me with the kisses of his
mouth—
for your love is more delightful than
wine.
³Pleasing is the fragrance of your
perfumes;
your name is like perfume poured
out.
No wonder the maidens love you!
⁴Take me away with you—let us hurry!
Let the king bring me into his
chambers.

Friends

We rejoice and delight in you;^b
we will praise your love more than
wine.

Beloved

How right they are to adore you!

⁵Dark am I, yet lovely,
O daughters of Jerusalem,
dark like the tents of Kedar,
like the tent curtains of Solomon.^c
⁶Do not stare at me because I am dark,
because I am darkened by the sun.
My mother's sons were angry with me
and made me take care of the
vineyards;

my own vineyard I have neglected.
⁷Tell me, you whom I love, where you
graze your flock
and where you rest your sheep at
midday.
Why should I be like a veiled woman
beside the flocks of your friends?

Friends

⁸If you do not know, most beautiful of
women,
follow the tracks of the sheep
and graze your young goats
by the tents of the shepherds.

Lover

⁹I liken you, my darling, to a mare
harnessed to one of the chariots of
Pharaoh.
¹⁰Your cheeks are beautiful with
ear-rings,
your neck with strings of jewels.
¹¹We will make you ear-rings of gold,
studded with silver.

Beloved

¹²While the king was at his table,
my perfume spread its fragrance.
¹³My lover is to me a sachet of myrrh
resting between my breasts.
¹⁴My lover is to me a cluster of henna
blossoms
from the vineyards of En Gedi.

---

^a2 Primarily on the basis of the gender of the Hebrew pronouns used, male and female speakers are indicated in the
margins by the captions *Lover* and *Beloved* respectively. The words of others are marked *Friends*. In some instances the
divisions and their captions are debatable.   ^b4 The Hebrew is masculine singular.   ^c5 Or *Salma*

Lover

¹⁵How beautiful you are, my darling!
   Oh, how beautiful!
   Your eyes are doves.

Beloved

¹⁶How handsome you are, my lover!
   Oh, how charming!
   And our bed is verdant.

Lover

¹⁷The beams of our house are cedars;
   our rafters are firs.

Beloved[a]

2 I am a rose[b] of Sharon,
   a lily of the valleys.

Lover

²Like a lily among thorns
   is my darling among the maidens.

Beloved

³Like an apple tree among the trees of
      the forest
   is my lover among the young men.
I delight to sit in his shade,
   and his fruit is sweet to my taste.
⁴He has taken me to the banquet hall,
   and his banner over me is love.
⁵Strengthen me with raisins,
   refresh me with apples,
   for I am faint with love.
⁶His left arm is under my head,
   and his right arm embraces me.
⁷Daughters of Jerusalem, I charge you
   by the gazelles and by the does of the
      field:
Do not arouse or awaken love
   until it so desires.

⁸Listen! My lover!
   Look! Here he comes,
leaping across the mountains,
   bounding over the hills.

⁹My lover is like a gazelle or a young
      stag.
   Look! There he stands behind our
      wall,
gazing through the windows,
   peering through the lattice.
¹⁰My lover spoke and said to me,
   "Arise, my darling,
   my beautiful one, and come with me.
¹¹See! The winter is past;
   the rains are over and gone.
¹²Flowers appear on the earth;
   the season of singing has come,
   the cooing of doves
   is heard in our land.
¹³The fig-tree forms its early fruit;
   the blossoming vines spread their
      fragrance.
Arise, come, my darling;
   my beautiful one, come with me."

Lover

¹⁴My dove in the clefts of the rock,
   in the hiding-places on the
      mountainside,
show me your face,
   let me hear your voice;
for your voice is sweet,
   and your face is lovely.
¹⁵Catch for us the foxes,
   the little foxes
that ruin the vineyards,
   our vineyards that are in bloom.

Beloved

¹⁶My lover is mine and I am his;
   he browses among the lilies.
¹⁷Until the day breaks
   and the shadows flee,
turn, my lover,
   and be like a gazelle
or like a young stag
   on the rugged hills.[c]

3 All night long on my bed
   I looked for the one my heart loves;
   I looked for him but did not find him.
²I will get up now and go about the city,
   through its streets and squares;

---

[a]1 Or *Lover*   [b]1 Possibly a member of the crocus family   [c]17 Or *the hills of Bether*

I will search for the one my heart
     loves.
  So I looked for him but did not find
     him.
³The watchmen found me
     as they made their rounds in the city.
  "Have you seen the one my heart
     loves?"
⁴Scarcely had I passed them
     when I found the one my heart
     loves.
  I held him and would not let him go
     till I had brought him to my mother's
     house,
  to the room of the one who conceived
     me.
⁵Daughters of Jerusalem, I charge you
     by the gazelles and by the does of the
     field:
  Do not arouse or awaken love
     until it so desires.

⁶Who is this coming up from the desert
     like a column of smoke,
  perfumed with myrrh and incense
     made from all the spices of the
     merchant?
⁷Look! It is Solomon's carriage,
     escorted by sixty warriors,
     the noblest of Israel,
⁸all of them wearing the sword,
     all experienced in battle,
  each with his sword at his side,
     prepared for the terrors of the
     night.
⁹King Solomon made for himself the
     carriage;
  he made it of wood from Lebanon.
¹⁰Its posts he made of silver,
     its base of gold.
  Its seat was upholstered with purple,
     its interior lovingly inlaid
     byᵃ the daughters of Jerusalem.
¹¹Come out, you daughters of Zion,
     and look at King Solomon wearing
     the crown,
  the crown with which his mother
     crowned him
  on the day of his wedding,
     the day his heart rejoiced.

Lover

4 How beautiful you are, my darling!
     Oh, how beautiful!
  Your eyes behind your veil are doves.
  Your hair is like a flock of goats
     descending from Mount Gilead.
²Your teeth are like a flock of sheep just
     shorn,
     coming up from the washing.
  Each has its twin;
     not one of them is alone.
³Your lips are like a scarlet ribbon;
     your mouth is lovely.
  Your temples behind your veil
     are like the halves of a pomegranate.
⁴Your neck is like the tower of David,
     built with elegance;ᵃ
  on it hang a thousand shields,
     all of them shields of warriors.
⁵Your two breasts are like two fawns,
     like twin fawns of a gazelle
     that browse among the lilies.
⁶Until the day breaks
     and the shadows flee,
  I will go to the mountain of myrrh
     and to the hill of incense.
⁷All beautiful you are, my darling;
     there is no flaw in you.

⁸Come with me from Lebanon, my
     bride,
     come with me from Lebanon.
  Descend from the crest of Amana,
     from the top of Senir, the summit of
     Hermon,
  from the lions' dens
     and the mountain haunts of the
     leopards.
⁹You have stolen my heart, my sister,
     my bride;
  you have stolen my heart
  with one glance of your eyes,
     with one jewel of your necklace.
¹⁰How delightful is your love, my sister,
     my bride!
  How much more pleasing is your love
     than wine,
  and the fragrance of your perfume
     than any spice!

ᵃ10 Or *its inlaid interior a gift of love / from*
ᵃ4 The meaning of the Hebrew for this word is uncertain.

¹¹Your lips drop sweetness as the
    honeycomb, my bride;
  milk and honey are under your
    tongue.
  The fragrance of your garments is
    like that of Lebanon.
¹²You are a garden locked up, my sister,
    my bride;
  you are a spring enclosed, a sealed
    fountain.
¹³Your plants are an orchard of
    pomegranates
  with choice fruits,
  with henna and nard,
¹⁴ nard and saffron,
  calamus and cinnamon,
  with every kind of incense tree,
  with myrrh and aloes
  and all the finest spices.
¹⁵You are*b* a garden fountain,
  a well of flowing water
  streaming down from Lebanon.

Beloved

¹⁶Awake, north wind,
  and come, south wind!
Blow on my garden,
  that its fragrance may spread abroad.
Let my lover come into his garden
  and taste its choice fruits.

Lover

5 I have come into my garden, my
  sister, my bride;
  I have gathered my myrrh with my
    spice.
  I have eaten my honeycomb and my
    honey;
    I have drunk my wine and my milk.

Friends

  Eat, O friends, and drink;
    drink your fill, O lovers.

Beloved

²I slept but my heart was awake.
  Listen! My lover is knocking:

"Open to me, my sister, my darling,
  my dove, my flawless one.
My head is drenched with dew,
  my hair with the dampness of the
    night."
³I have taken off my robe—
  must I put it on again?
I have washed my feet—
  must I soil them again?
⁴My lover thrust his hand through the
    latch-opening;
  my heart began to pound for him.
⁵I arose to open for my lover,
  and my hands dripped with myrrh,
my fingers with flowing myrrh,
  on the handles of the lock.
⁶I opened for my lover,
  but my lover had left; he was gone.
  My heart sank at his departure.*a*
I looked for him but did not find him.
  I called him but he did not answer.
⁷The watchmen found me
  as they made their rounds in the city.
They beat me, they bruised me;
  they took away my cloak,
  those watchmen of the walls!
⁸O daughters of Jerusalem, I charge
    you—
  if you find my lover,
what will you tell him?
  Tell him I am faint with love.

Friends

⁹How is your beloved better than others,
  most beautiful of women?
How is your beloved better than others,
  that you charge us so?

Beloved

¹⁰My lover is radiant and ruddy,
  outstanding among ten thousand.
¹¹His head is purest gold;
  his hair is wavy
  and black as a raven.
¹²His eyes are like doves
  by the water streams,
washed in milk,
  mounted like jewels.

b15 Or *I am* (spoken by the *Beloved*)   *a6* Or *heart had gone out to him when he spoke*

13His cheeks are like beds of spice
  yielding perfume.
His lips are like lilies
  dripping with myrrh.
14His arms are rods of gold
  set with chrysolite.
His body is like polished ivory
  decorated with sapphires.b
15His legs are pillars of marble
  set on bases of pure gold.
His appearance is like Lebanon,
  choice as its cedars.
16His mouth is sweetness itself;
  he is altogether lovely.
This is my lover, this my friend,
  O daughters of Jerusalem.

Friends

6 Where has your lover gone,
  most beautiful of women?
Which way did your lover turn,
  that we may look for him with you?

Beloved

2My lover has gone down to his garden,
  to the beds of spices,
to browse in the gardens
  and to gather lilies.
3I am my lover's and my lover is mine;
  he browses among the lilies.

Lover

4You are beautiful, my darling, as
    Tirzah,
  lovely as Jerusalem,
  majestic as troops with banners.
5Turn your eyes from me;
  they overwhelm me.
Your hair is like a flock of goats
  descending from Gilead.
6Your teeth are like a flock of sheep
  coming up from the washing.
Each has its twin,
  not one of them is alone.
7Your temples behind your veil
  are like the halves of a pomegranate.
8Sixty queens there may be,
  and eighty concubines,
  and virgins beyond number;

9but my dove, my perfect one, is unique,
  the only daughter of her mother,
  the favourite of the one who bore
    her.
The maidens saw her and called her
    blessed;
  the queens and concubines praised
    her.

Friends

10Who is this that appears like the dawn,
  fair as the moon, bright as the sun,
  majestic as the stars in procession?

Lover

11I went down to the grove of nut trees
  to look at the new growth in the
    valley,
to see if the vines had budded
  or the pomegranates were in bloom.
12Before I realised it,
  my desire set me among the royal
    chariots of my people.a

Friends

13Come back, come back, O Shulammite;
  come back, come back, that we may
    gaze on you!

Lover

Why would you gaze on the
    Shulammite
  as on the dance of Mahanaim?

7 How beautiful your sandalled feet,
  O prince's daughter!
Your graceful legs are like jewels,
  the work of a craftsman's hands.
2Your navel is a rounded goblet
  that never lacks blended wine.
Your waist is a mound of wheat
  encircled by lilies.
3Your breasts are like two fawns,
  twins of a gazelle.
4Your neck is like an ivory tower.
Your eyes are the pools of Heshbon
  by the gate of Bath Rabbim.

b14 Or lapis lazuli   a12 Or among the chariots of Amminadab; or among the chariots of the people of the prince

Your nose is like the tower of Lebanon
　looking towards Damascus.
⁵Your head crowns you like Mount
　　Carmel.
Your hair is like royal tapestry;
　the king is held captive by its tresses.
⁶How beautiful you are and how
　　pleasing,
O love, with your delights!
⁷Your stature is like that of the palm,
　and your breasts like clusters of fruit.
⁸I said, "I will climb the palm tree;
　I will take hold of its fruit."
May your breasts be like the clusters of
　　the vine,
　the fragrance of your breath like
　　apples,
⁹　and your mouth like the best wine.

Beloved

May the wine go straight to my lover,
　flowing gently over lips and teeth.ᵃ
¹⁰I belong to my lover,
　and his desire is for me.
¹¹Come, my lover, let us go to the
　　countryside,
　let us spend the night in the villages.ᵇ
¹²Let us go early to the vineyards
　to see if the vines have budded,
if their blossoms have opened,
　and if the pomegranates are in
　　bloom—
　there I will give you my love.
¹³The mandrakes send out their
　　fragrance,
　and at our door is every delicacy,
both new and old,
　that I have stored up for you, my
　　lover.

8 If only you were to me like a
　brother,
　who was nursed at my mother's
　　breasts!
Then, if I found you outside,
　I would kiss you,
　and no-one would despise me.
²I would lead you
　and bring you to my mother's
　　house—

she who has taught me.
I would give you spiced wine to drink,
　the nectar of my pomegranates.
³His left arm is under my head
　and his right arm embraces me.
⁴Daughters of Jerusalem, I charge you:
　Do not arouse or awaken love
　until it so desires.

Friends

⁵Who is this coming up from the desert
　leaning on her lover?

Beloved

Under the apple tree I roused you;
　there your mother conceived you,
　there she who was in labour gave you
　　birth.
⁶Place me like a seal over your heart,
　like a seal on your arm;
for love is as strong as death,
　its jealousyᵃ unyielding as the grave.ᵇ
It burns like blazing fire,
　like a mighty flame.ᶜ
⁷Many waters cannot quench love;
　rivers cannot wash it away.
If one were to give
　all the wealth of his house for love,
　itᵈ would be utterly scorned.

Friends

⁸We have a young sister,
　and her breasts are not yet grown.
What shall we do for our sister
　for the day she is spoken for?
⁹If she is a wall,
　we will build towers of silver on her.
If she is a door,
　we will enclose her with panels of
　　cedar.

Beloved

¹⁰I am a wall,
　and my breasts are like towers.
Thus I have become in his eyes
　like one bringing contentment.

ᵃ9 Septuagint, Aquila, Vulgate and Syriac; Hebrew *lips of sleepers*   ᵇ11 Or *henna bushes*
ᵃ6 Or *ardour*   ᵇ6 Hebrew *Sheol*   ᶜ6 Or / *like the very flame of the* LORD   ᵈ7 Or *he*

11Solomon had a vineyard in Baal
    Hamon;
  he let out his vineyard to tenants.
Each was to bring for its fruit
  a thousand shekels*e* of silver.
12But my own vineyard is mine to
    give;
  the thousand shekels are for you, O
    Solomon,
and two hundred *f* are for those who
  tend its fruit.

Lover

13You who dwell in the gardens
  with friends in attendance,
  let me hear your voice!

Beloved

14Come away, my lover,
  and be like a gazelle
or like a young stag
  on the spice-laden mountains.

---

e11 That is, about 25 pounds (about 11.5 kilograms); also in verse 12
f12 That is, about 5 pounds (about 2.3 kilograms)

Isaiah

1 The vision concerning Judah and
Jerusalem that Isaiah son of Amoz
saw during the reigns of Uzziah, Jotham,
Ahaz and Hezekiah, kings of Judah.

A Rebellious Nation

²Hear, O heavens! Listen, O earth!
  For the LORD has spoken:
"I reared children and brought them
    up,
  but they have rebelled against me.
³The ox knows his master,
  the donkey his owner's manger,
but Israel does not know,
  my people do not understand."

⁴Ah, sinful nation,
  a people loaded with guilt,
a brood of evildoers,
  children given to corruption!
They have forsaken the LORD;
  they have spurned the Holy One of
    Israel
  and turned their backs on him.

⁵Why should you be beaten any more?
  Why do you persist in rebellion?
Your whole head is injured,
  your whole heart afflicted.
⁶From the sole of your foot to the top of
    your head
  there is no soundness—
only wounds and bruises
  and open sores,
not cleansed or bandaged
  or soothed with oil.

⁷Your country is desolate,
  your cities burned with fire;
your fields are being stripped by
    foreigners
  right before you,
  laid waste as when overthrown by
    strangers.
⁸The Daughter of Zion is left
  like a shelter in a vineyard,
like a hut in a field of melons,
  like a city under siege.
⁹Unless the LORD Almighty
  had left us some survivors,
we would have become like Sodom,
  we would have been like Gomorrah.

¹⁰Hear the word of the LORD,
  you rulers of Sodom;
listen to the law of our God,
  you people of Gomorrah!
¹¹"The multitude of your sacrifices—
  what are they to me?" says the LORD.
"I have more than enough of burnt
    offerings,
  of rams and the fat of fattened
    animals;
I have no pleasure
  in the blood of bulls and lambs and
    goats.
¹²When you come to appear before me,
  who has asked this of you,
  this trampling of my courts?
¹³Stop bringing meaningless offerings!
  Your incense is detestable to me.
New Moons, Sabbaths and
    convocations—
  I cannot bear your evil assemblies.

14Your New Moon festivals and your
    appointed feasts
  my soul hates.
They have become a burden to me;
  I am weary of bearing them.
15When you spread out your hands in
    prayer,
  I will hide my eyes from you;
even if you offer many prayers,
  I will not listen.
Your hands are full of blood;
16   wash and make yourselves clean.
Take your evil deeds
  out of my sight!
Stop doing wrong,
17   learn to do right!
Seek justice,
  encourage the oppressed.[a]
Defend the cause of the fatherless,
  plead the case of the widow.

18"Come now, let us reason together,"
  says the LORD.
"Though your sins are like scarlet,
  they shall be as white as snow;
though they are red as crimson,
  they shall be like wool.
19If you are willing and obedient,
  you will eat the best from the land;
20but if you resist and rebel,
  you will be devoured by the sword."
     For the mouth of the LORD has
          spoken.

21See how the faithful city
  has become a harlot!
She once was full of justice;
  righteousness used to dwell in her—
  but now murderers!
22Your silver has become dross,
  your choice wine is diluted with
    water.
23Your rulers are rebels,
  companions of thieves;
they all love bribes
  and chase after gifts.
They do not defend the cause of the
    fatherless;
  the widow's case does not come
    before them.
24Therefore the Lord, the LORD
  Almighty,

the Mighty One of Israel, declares:
"Ah, I will get relief from my foes
  and avenge myself on my enemies.
25I will turn my hand against you;
  I will thoroughly purge away your
    dross
  and remove all your impurities.
26I will restore your judges as in days of
    old,
  your counsellors as at the beginning.
Afterwards you will be called
  the City of Righteousness,
  the Faithful City."

27Zion will be redeemed with justice,
  her penitent ones with righteousness.
28But rebels and sinners will both be
    broken,
  and those who forsake the LORD will
    perish.

29"You will be ashamed because of the
    sacred oaks
  in which you have delighted;
you will be disgraced because of the
    gardens
  that you have chosen.
30You will be like an oak with fading
    leaves,
  like a garden without water.
31The mighty man will become tinder
  and his work a spark;
both will burn together,
  with no-one to quench the fire."

The Mountain of the LORD

2   This is what Isaiah son of Amoz saw
    concerning Judah and Jerusalem:

2In the last days

the mountain of the LORD's temple will
    be established
  as chief among the mountains;
it will be raised above the hills,
  and all nations will stream to it.

3Many peoples will come and say,

"Come, let us go up to the mountain of
    the LORD,
  to the house of the God of Jacob.

a17 Or / rebuke the oppressor

He will teach us his ways,
  so that we may walk in his paths.''
The law will go out from Zion,
  the word of the LORD from
    Jerusalem.
[4]He will judge between the nations
  and will settle disputes for many
    peoples.
They will beat their swords into
    ploughshares
  and their spears into pruning hooks.
Nation will not take up sword against
    nation,
  nor will they train for war any more.

[5]Come, O house of Jacob,
  let us walk in the light of the LORD.

The Day of the LORD

[6]You have abandoned your people,
  the house of Jacob.
They are full of superstitions from the
    East;
  they practise divination like the
    Philistines
  and clasp hands with pagans.
[7]Their land is full of silver and gold;
  there is no end to their treasures.
Their land is full of horses;
  there is no end to the chariots.
[8]Their land is full of idols;
  they bow down to the work of their
    hands,
  to what their fingers have made.
[9]So man will be brought low
  and mankind humbled—
  do not forgive them.[a]

[10]Go into the rocks,
  hide in the ground
from dread of the LORD
  and the splendour of his majesty!
[11]The eyes of the arrogant man will be
    humbled
  and the pride of men brought low;
the LORD alone will be exalted in that
    day.

[12]The LORD Almighty has a day in store
  for all the proud and lofty,

for all that is exalted
  (and they will be humbled),
[13]for all the cedars of Lebanon, tall and
    lofty,
  and all the oaks of Bashan,
[14]for all the towering mountains
  and all the high hills,
[15]for every lofty tower
  and every fortified wall,
[16]for every trading ship[b]
  and every stately vessel.
[17]The arrogance of man will be brought
    low
  and the pride of men humbled;
the LORD alone will be exalted in that
    day,
[18] and the idols will totally disappear.

[19]Men will flee to caves in the rocks
  and to holes in the ground
from the dread of the LORD
  and the splendour of his majesty,
  when he rises to shake the earth.
[20]In that day men will throw away
  to the rodents and bats
  their idols of silver and idols of gold,
  which they made to worship.
[21]They will flee to caverns in the rocks
  and to the overhanging crags
from dread of the LORD
  and the splendour of his majesty,
  when he rises to shake the earth.

[22]Stop trusting in man,
  who has but a breath in his nostrils.
  Of what account is he?

Judgment on Jerusalem and Judah

3 See now, the Lord,
  the LORD Almighty,
is about to take from Jerusalem and
    Judah
  both supply and support:
all supplies of food and all supplies of
    water,
[2] the hero and warrior,
  the judge and prophet,
  the soothsayer and elder,
[3]the captain of fifty and man of rank,

---

[a]9 Or *not raise them up*   [b]16 Hebrew *every ship of Tarshish*

the counsellor, skilled craftsman and
clever enchanter.

⁴I will make boys their officials;
mere children will govern them.
⁵People will oppress each other—
man against man, neighbour against
neighbour.
The young will rise up against the old,
the base against the honourable.

⁶A man will seize one of his brothers
at his father's home, and say,
"You have a cloak, you be our
leader;
take charge of this heap of ruins!"
⁷But in that day he will cry out,
"I have no remedy.
I have no food or clothing in my
house;
do not make me the leader of the
people."

⁸Jerusalem staggers,
Judah is falling;
their words and deeds are against the
LORD,
defying his glorious presence.
⁹The look on their faces testifies against
them;
they parade their sin like Sodom;
they do not hide it.
Woe to them!
They have brought disaster upon
themselves.

¹⁰Tell the righteous it will be well with
them,
for they will enjoy the fruit of their
deeds.
¹¹Woe to the wicked! Disaster is upon
them!
They will be paid back for what their
hands have done.

¹²Youths oppress my people,
women rule over them.
O my people, your guides lead you
astray;
they turn you from the path.

¹³The LORD takes his place in court;
he rises to judge the people.

¹⁴The LORD enters into judgment
against the elders and leaders of his
people:
"It is you who have ruined my vineyard;
the plunder from the poor is in your
houses.
¹⁵What do you mean by crushing my
people
and grinding the faces of the poor?"
declares the Lord, the LORD
Almighty.

¹⁶The LORD says,
"The women of Zion are haughty,
walking along with outstretched necks,
flirting with their eyes,
tripping along with mincing steps,
with ornaments jingling on their
ankles.
¹⁷Therefore the Lord will bring sores on
the heads of the women of Zion;
the LORD will make their scalps
bald."

¹⁸In that day the Lord will snatch away
their finery: the bangles and headbands
and crescent necklaces, ¹⁹the ear-rings
and bracelets and veils, ²⁰the head-dresses
and ankle chains and sashes, the perfume
bottles and charms, ²¹the signet rings and
nose rings, ²²the fine robes and the capes
and cloaks, the purses ²³and mirrors, and
the linen garments and tiaras and shawls.

²⁴Instead of fragrance there will be a
stench;
instead of a sash, a rope;
instead of well-dressed hair, baldness;
instead of fine clothing, sackcloth;
instead of beauty, branding.
²⁵Your men will fall by the sword,
your warriors in battle.
²⁶The gates of Zion will lament and
mourn;
destitute, she will sit on the ground.

4 In that day seven women
will take hold of one man
and say, "We will eat our own food
and provide our own clothes;
only let us be called by your name.
Take away our disgrace!"

The Branch of the LORD

²In that day the Branch of the LORD will be beautiful and glorious, and the fruit of the land will be the pride and glory of the survivors in Israel. ³Those who are left in Zion, who remain in Jerusalem, will be called holy, all who are recorded among the living in Jerusalem. ⁴The Lord will wash away the filth of the women of Zion; he will cleanse the bloodstains from Jerusalem by a spirit*ᵃ* of judgment and a spirit*ᵃ* of fire. ⁵Then the LORD will create over all of Mount Zion and over those who assemble there a cloud of smoke by day and a glow of flaming fire by night; over all the glory will be a canopy. ⁶It will be a shelter and shade from the heat of the day, and a refuge and hiding-place from the storm and rain.

The Song of the Vineyard

5 I will sing for the one I love
   a song about his vineyard:
My loved one had a vineyard
   on a fertile hillside.
²He dug it up and cleared it of stones
   and planted it with the choicest vines.
He built a watchtower in it
   and cut out a winepress as well.
Then he looked for a crop of good
      grapes,
   but it yielded only bad fruit.

³"Now you dwellers in Jerusalem and
      men of Judah,
   judge between me and my vineyard.
⁴What more could have been done for
      my vineyard
   than I have done for it?
When I looked for good grapes,
   why did it yield only bad?
⁵Now I will tell you
   what I am going to do to my
      vineyard:
I will take away its hedge,
   and it will be destroyed;
I will break down its wall,

and it will be trampled.
⁶I will make it a wasteland,
   neither pruned nor cultivated,
   and briers and thorns will grow there.
I will command the clouds
   not to rain on it."

⁷The vineyard of the LORD Almighty
   is the house of Israel,
and the men of Judah
   are the garden of his delight.
And he looked for justice, but saw
      bloodshed;
   for righteousness, but heard cries of
      distress.

Woes and Judgments

⁸Woe to you who add house to house
   and join field to field
till no space is left
   and you live alone in the land.

⁹The LORD Almighty has declared in my
hearing:

"Surely the great houses will become
      desolate,
   the fine mansions left without
      occupants.
¹⁰A ten-acre*ᵃ* vineyard will produce only
      a bath*ᵇ* of wine,
   a homer*ᶜ* of seed only an ephah*ᵈ* of
      grain."

¹¹Woe to those who rise early in the
      morning
   to run after their drinks,
who stay up late at night
   till they are inflamed with wine.
¹²They have harps and lyres at their
      banquets,
   tambourines and flutes and wine,
but they have no regard for the deeds of
      the LORD,
   no respect for the work of his hands.
¹³Therefore my people will go into exile
   for lack of understanding;
their men of rank will die of hunger
   and their masses will be parched with
      thirst.

ᵃ4 Or *the Spirit*
ᵃ10 Hebrew *ten-yoke*, that is, the land ploughed by 10 yoke of oxen in one day
ᵇ10 That is, probably about 5 gallons (about 22 litres)   *ᶜ10* That is, probably about 6 bushels (about 220 litres)
ᵈ10 That is, probably about ⅗ bushel (about 22 litres)

¹⁴Therefore the grave^e enlarges its
     appetite
  and opens its mouth without limit;
into it will descend their nobles and
     masses
  with all their brawlers and revellers.
¹⁵So man will be brought low
  and mankind humbled,
  the eyes of the arrogant humbled.
¹⁶But the LORD Almighty will be exalted
     by his justice,
  and the holy God will show himself
     holy by his righteousness.
¹⁷Then sheep will graze as in their own
     pasture;
  lambs will feed^f among the ruins of
     the rich.

¹⁸Woe to those who draw sin along with
     cords of deceit,
  and wickedness as with cart ropes,
¹⁹to those who say, "Let God hurry,
  let him hasten his work
  so that we may see it.
Let it approach,
  let the plan of the Holy One of Israel
     come,
  so that we may know it."

²⁰Woe to those who call evil good
  and good evil,
who put darkness for light
  and light for darkness,
who put bitter for sweet
  and sweet for bitter.

²¹Woe to those who are wise in their own
     eyes
  and clever in their own sight.

²²Woe to those who are heroes at
     drinking wine
  and champions at mixing drinks,
²³who acquit the guilty for a bribe,
  but deny justice to the innocent.
²⁴Therefore, as tongues of fire lick up
     straw
  and as dry grass sinks down in the
     flames,
  so their roots will decay
  and their flowers blow away like dust;

for they have rejected the law of the
     LORD Almighty
  and spurned the word of the Holy
     One of Israel.
²⁵Therefore the LORD's anger burns
     against his people;
  his hand is raised and he strikes them
     down.
The mountains shake,
  and the dead bodies are like refuse in
     the streets.

Yet for all this, his anger is not turned
     away,
  his hand is still upraised.

²⁶He lifts up a banner for the distant
     nations,
  he whistles for those at the ends of
     the earth.
Here they come,
  swiftly and speedily!
²⁷Not one of them grows tired or
     stumbles,
  not one slumbers or sleeps;
not a belt is loosened at the waist,
  not a sandal thong is broken.
²⁸Their arrows are sharp,
  all their bows are strung;
their horses' hoofs seem like flint,
  their chariot wheels like a whirlwind.
²⁹Their roar is like that of the lion,
  they roar like young lions;
they growl as they seize their prey
  and carry it off with no-one to rescue.
³⁰In that day they will roar over it
  like the roaring of the sea.
And if one looks at the land,
  he will see darkness and distress;
  even the light will be darkened by
     the clouds.

Isaiah's Commission

6 In the year that King Uzziah died, I saw the Lord seated on a throne, high and exalted, and the train of his robe filled the temple. ²Above him were seraphs, each with six wings: With two wings they covered their faces, with two they covered

---

^e14 Hebrew *Sheol*   ^f17 Septuagint; Hebrew / *strangers will eat*

their feet, and with two they were flying. ³And they were calling to one another:

> "Holy, holy, holy is the LORD Almighty;
> the whole earth is full of his glory."

⁴At the sound of their voices the doorposts and thresholds shook and the temple was filled with smoke. ⁵"Woe to me!" I cried. "I am ruined! For I am a man of unclean lips, and I live among a people of unclean lips, and my eyes have seen the King, the LORD Almighty."

⁶Then one of the seraphs flew to me with a live coal in his hand, which he had taken with tongs from the altar. ⁷With it he touched my mouth and said, "See, this has touched your lips; your guilt is taken away and your sin atoned for."

⁸Then I heard the voice of the Lord saying, "Whom shall I send? And who will go for us?"

And I said, "Here am I. Send me!"

⁹He said, "Go and tell this people:

> " 'Be ever hearing, but never
>   understanding;
> be ever seeing, but never perceiving.'
¹⁰Make the heart of this people calloused;
>   make their ears dull
>   and close their eyes.ᵃ
> Otherwise they might see with their
>   eyes,
>   hear with their ears,
>   understand with their hearts,
> and turn and be healed."

¹¹Then I said, "For how long, O Lord?" And he answered:

> "Until the cities lie ruined
>   and without inhabitant,
> until the houses are left deserted
>   and the fields ruined and ravaged,
¹²until the LORD has sent everyone far
>   away
>   and the land is utterly forsaken.
¹³And though a tenth remains in the land,
>   it will again be laid waste.

> But as the terebinth and oak
>   leave stumps when they are cut
>   down,
> so the holy seed will be the stump in
>   the land."

The Sign of Immanuel

7 When Ahaz son of Jotham, the son of Uzziah, was king of Judah, King Rezin of Aram and Pekah son of Remaliah king of Israel marched up to fight against Jerusalem, but they could not overpower it.

²Now the house of David was told, "Aram has allied itself withᵃ Ephraim"; so the hearts of Ahaz and his people were shaken, as the trees of the forest are shaken by the wind.

³Then the LORD said to Isaiah, "Go out, you and your son Shear-Jashub,ᵇ to meet Ahaz at the end of the aqueduct of the Upper Pool, on the road to the Washerman's Field. ⁴Say to him, 'Be careful, keep calm and don't be afraid. Do not lose heart because of these two smouldering stubs of firewood—because of the fierce anger of Rezin and Aram and of the son of Remaliah. ⁵Aram, Ephraim and Remaliah's son have plotted your ruin, saying, ⁶"Let us invade Judah; let us tear it apart and divide it among ourselves, and make the son of Tabeel king over it." ⁷Yet this is what the Sovereign LORD says:

> " 'It will not take place,
>   it will not happen,
⁸for the head of Aram is Damascus,
>   and the head of Damascus is only
>   Rezin.
> Within sixty-five years
>   Ephraim will be too shattered to be a
>   people.
⁹The head of Ephraim is Samaria,
>   and the head of Samaria is only
>   Remaliah's son.
> If you do not stand firm in your faith,
>   you will not stand at all.' "

ᵃ9, 10 Hebrew; Septuagint 'You will be ever hearing, but never understanding; / you will be ever seeing, but never perceiving.' / ¹⁰This people's heart has become calloused; / they hardly hear with their ears, / and they have closed their eyes   ᵃ2 Or has set up camp in   ᵇ3 Shear-Jashub means a remnant will return.

[10]Again the LORD spoke to Ahaz, [11]"Ask the LORD your God for a sign, whether in the deepest depths or in the highest heights."

[12]But Ahaz said, "I will not ask; I will not put the LORD to the test."

[13]Then Isaiah said, "Hear now, you house of David! Is it not enough to try the patience of men? Will you try the patience of my God also? [14]Therefore the Lord himself will give you[c] a sign: The virgin will be with child and will give birth to a son, and[d] will call him Immanuel.[e] [15]He will eat curds and honey when he knows enough to reject the wrong and choose the right. [16]But before the boy knows enough to reject the wrong and choose the right, the land of the two kings you dread will be laid waste. [17]The LORD will bring on you and on your people and on the house of your father a time unlike any since Ephraim broke away from Judah—he will bring the king of Assyria."

[18]In that day the LORD will whistle for flies from the distant streams of Egypt and for bees from the land of Assyria. [19]They will all come and settle in the steep ravines and in the crevices in the rocks, on all the thornbushes and at all the water holes. [20]In that day the Lord will use a razor hired from beyond the River[f]—the king of Assyria—to shave your head and the hair of your legs, and to take off your beards also. [21]In that day, a man will keep alive a young cow and two goats. [22]And because of the abundance of the milk they give, he will have curds to eat. All who remain in the land will eat curds and honey. [23]In that day, in every place where there were a thousand vines worth a thousand silver shekels,[g] there will be only briers and thorns. [24]Men will go there with bow and arrow, for the land will be covered with briers and thorns. [25]As for all the hills once cultivated by the hoe, you will no longer go there for fear of the briers and thorns; they will become places where cattle are turned loose and where sheep run.

Assyria, the LORD's Instrument

8 The LORD said to me, "Take a large scroll and write on it with an ordinary pen: Maher-Shalal-Hash-Baz.[a] [2]And I will call in Uriah the priest and Zechariah son of Jeberekiah as reliable witnesses for me."

[3]Then I went to the prophetess, and she conceived and gave birth to a son. And the LORD said to me, "Name him Maher-Shalal-Hash-Baz. [4]Before the boy knows how to say 'My father' or 'My mother', the wealth of Damascus and the plunder of Samaria will be carried off by the king of Assyria."

[5]The LORD spoke to me again:

[6]"Because this people has rejected
   the gently flowing waters of Shiloah
and rejoices over Rezin
   and the son of Remaliah,
[7]therefore the Lord is about to bring
      against them
   the mighty floodwaters of the
      River[b]—
   the king of Assyria with all his pomp.
It will overflow all its channels,
   run over all its banks
[8]and sweep on into Judah, swirling over
      it,
   passing through it and reaching up to
      the neck.
Its outspread wings will cover the
      breadth of your land,
   O Immanuel!"[c]

[9]Raise the war cry,[d] you nations, and be
      shattered!
   Listen, all you distant lands.
Prepare for battle, and be shattered!
   Prepare for battle, and be shattered!
[10]Devise your strategy, but it will be
      thwarted;
   propose your plan, but it will not
      stand,
   for God is with us.[e]

---

[c]14 The Hebrew is plural.   [d]14 Masoretic Text; Dead Sea Scrolls *and he* or *and they*
[e]14 *Immanuel* means *God with us*.   [f]20 That is, the Euphrates
[g]23 That is, about 25 pounds (about 11.5 kilograms)
[a]1 *Maher-Shalal-Hash-Baz* means *quick to the plunder, swift to the spoil*; also in verse 3.   [b]7 That is, the Euphrates
[c]8 *Immanuel* means *God with us*.   [d]9 Or *Do your worst*   [e]10 Hebrew *Immanuel*

Fear God

¹¹The LORD spoke to me with his strong hand upon me, warning me not to follow the way of this people. He said:

¹²"Do not call conspiracy
    everything that these people call
        conspiracy;*f*
 do not fear what they fear,
    and do not dread it.
¹³The LORD Almighty is the one you are
        to regard as holy,
    he is the one you are to fear,
    he is the one you are to dread,
¹⁴and he will be a sanctuary;
    but for both houses of Israel he
        will be
 a stone that causes men to stumble
    and a rock that makes them fall.
 And for the people of Jerusalem he
        will be
 a trap and a snare.
¹⁵Many of them will stumble;
    they will fall and be broken,
    they will be snared and captured."

¹⁶Bind up the testimony
    and seal up the law among my
        disciples.
¹⁷I will wait for the LORD,
    who is hiding his face from the house
        of Jacob.
 I will put my trust in him.

¹⁸Here am I, and the children the LORD has given me. We are signs and symbols in Israel from the LORD Almighty, who dwells on Mount Zion.
¹⁹When men tell you to consult mediums and spiritists, who whisper and mutter, should not a people enquire of their God? Why consult the dead on behalf of the living? ²⁰To the law and to the testimony! If they do not speak according to this word, they have no light of dawn. ²¹Distressed and hungry, they will roam through the land; when they are famished, they will become enraged and, looking upward, will curse their king and their God. ²²Then they will look towards the earth and see only distress and darkness and fearful gloom, and they will be thrust into utter darkness.

To Us a Child Is Born

9 Nevertheless, there will be no more gloom for those who were in distress. In the past he humbled the land of Zebulun and the land of Naphtali, but in the future he will honour Galilee of the Gentiles, by the way of the sea, along the Jordan—

²The people walking in darkness
    have seen a great light;
 on those living in the land of the shadow
        of death*a*
    a light has dawned.
³You have enlarged the nation
    and increased their joy;
 they rejoice before you
    as people rejoice at the harvest,
 as men rejoice
    when dividing the plunder.
⁴For as in the day of Midian's defeat,
    you have shattered
 the yoke that burdens them,
    the bar across their shoulders,
    the rod of their oppressor.
⁵Every warrior's boot used in battle
    and every garment rolled in blood
 will be destined for burning,
    will be fuel for the fire.
⁶For to us a child is born,
    to us a son is given,
    and the government will be on his
        shoulders.
 And he will be called
    Wonderful Counsellor,*b* Mighty
        God,
    Everlasting Father, Prince of Peace.
⁷Of the increase of his government and
        peace
    there will be no end.
 He will reign on David's throne
    and over his kingdom,
 establishing and upholding it
    with justice and righteousness
    from that time on and for ever.

---

f12 Or *Do not call for a treaty* / *every time these people call for a treaty*
a2 Or *land of darkness*   *b6* Or *Wonderful, Counsellor*

The zeal of the LORD Almighty
will accomplish this.

The LORD's Anger Against Israel

⁸The Lord has sent a message against
Jacob;
it will fall on Israel.
⁹All the people will know it—
Ephraim and the inhabitants of
Samaria—
who say with pride
and arrogance of heart,
¹⁰"The bricks have fallen down,
but we will rebuild with dressed
stone;
the fig-trees have been felled,
but we will replace them with cedars."
¹¹But the LORD has strengthened Rezin's
foes against them
and has spurred their enemies on.
¹²Arameans from the east and Philistines
from the west
have devoured Israel with open
mouth.

Yet for all this, his anger is not turned
away,
his hand is still upraised.

¹³But the people have not returned to
him who struck them,
nor have they sought the LORD
Almighty.
¹⁴So the LORD will cut off from Israel both
head and tail,
both palm branch and reed in a single
day;
¹⁵the elders and prominent men are the
head,
the prophets who teach lies are the
tail.
¹⁶Those who guide this people mislead
them,
and those who are guided are led
astray.
¹⁷Therefore the Lord will take no
pleasure in the young men,
nor will he pity the fatherless and
widows,
for everyone is ungodly and wicked,
every mouth speaks vileness.

Yet for all this, his anger is not turned
away,
his hand is still upraised.

¹⁸Surely wickedness burns like a fire;
it consumes briers and thorns,
it sets the forest thickets ablaze,
so that it rolls upward in a column of
smoke.
¹⁹By the wrath of the LORD Almighty
the land will be scorched
and the people will be fuel for the fire;
no-one will spare his brother.
²⁰On the right they will devour,
but still be hungry;
on the left they will eat,
but not be satisfied.
Each will feed on the flesh of his own
offspring:ᶜ
²¹ Manasseh will feed on Ephraim, and
Ephraim on Manasseh;
together they will turn against Judah.

Yet for all this, his anger is not turned
away,
his hand is still upraised.

10 Woe to those who make unjust
laws,
to those who issue oppressive
decrees,
²to deprive the poor of their rights
and withhold justice from the
oppressed of my people,
making widows their prey
and robbing the fatherless.
³What will you do on the day of
reckoning,
when disaster comes from afar?
To whom will you run for help?
Where will you leave your riches?
⁴Nothing will remain but to cringe
among the captives
or fall among the slain.

Yet for all this, his anger is not turned
away,
his hand is still upraised.

God's Judgment on Assyria

⁵"Woe to the Assyrian, the rod of my
anger,

ᶜ20 Or arm

JUStice

[Isaiah 58 and Amos 5:10-27]

In these Bible passages the issues are the focus. It is helpful to bear the following model in mind when reading this type of passage, it will help you make the connections between the 'then' of the Bible and the 'now' of today.

The
Bible
story

Issues in
the story

Issues
today

Feelings,
reactions

The issues: in the Bible

✳ Read through the passages a view times and make a note of:

a] the issues in each passage.

b] any feelings and reactions expressed or implicit within the text.

✳ Try and answer these questions:
Which words and phrases are most disturbing and challenging? Why?
What ideas and principles do you find it hard to understand? List them if it helps.
What else does the Bible have to say about the 'poor'?

The issues: today

✳ Find two or three recent newspapers - not all tabloids - and look through them. Circle any news items or reports which might have parallels with the Scripture passages.

★ What are the issues in the items you have circled? How do you react to these reports? Do you feel very concerned but powerless to do anything. Do you stay uninvolved because you are not really politically-minded? Do you feel angry about the injustice, exploitation, inequality and oppression in the world?

✳ Ask yourself how the Scripture passages (and other passages you may be familiar with) comment upon or relate to the issues you have found in the newspapers?

Taking Action!

✳ Ask yourself if there is anything you can do about these issues personally? Can you join a movement, pray, donate time or money to charity or write to your MP...? Do you need to be more informed and aware? If so how? In your neighbourhood and community are there similar situations? Is your school or church acting and if so, how?

Prayer and reflection.

✳ As you reflect on these passages spend some time praying about those places and people across the world who experience injustice, exploitation, inequality and oppression. As you bring these concerns to God, remember that he plans to rid the whole of his creation of all these things when he establishes his kingdom (Romans 8:18-39).

justice

social issues & politics

Emma The Israelites left part of the crop so that people could take the leftover grain, like Ruth did (Ruth 2). Our society seems to promote 'take', 'more', 'self', whereas the attitude of society in the Old Testament was 'we are in it together' and the emphasis is on 'us' which matched the religious beliefs of being a people of God.

Anon Isaiah 58 records God telling-off the people of Israel for fasting to impress and influence him, he didn't want all their rituals and fasting, what he wanted was that they be caring and compassionate. That's what I see in Jesus. He didn't live for himself, but for other people, by standing up for them, giving dignity and value to women and to lepers. He oozed care.

'We mustn't forget that when we help someone, we are doing it for Jesus.'

Is action possible?

Pat We can act politically by writing to our local politician about situations that concern us. We can act in our own community by caring for new neighbours, by not being xenophobic, by responding when people come to church on a Sunday morning saying 'I'm homeless', 'I'm hungry'. We mustn't forget that when we help someone, we are doing it for Jesus: (Matthew 25:34-46) 'I tell you the truth, whatever you did for one of the least of these brothers of mine, you did for me.'

Pat There is so much in the Bible that is relevant today to how people should be treated. To have any credibility in the eyes of those who are questioning the whole concept of Christianity, Christians need to be involved in social justice: faith with action.

Christians need to be involved in social justice: faith with action.

Secular society doesn't seem to care

Ann The way society is at the moment, a caring attitude is against the norm. Living in London it is very easy to walk past the homeless, not to know your neighbours, to go to church and be ignored and ignore other people. If as a Christian you do want to act it is important to know that you may be an exception by doing that.

Anon In my limited experience, loving your neighbour does make a difference, it changes you, softens your heart.

Ann God has provided for all of humanity's needs around the world but we need to remember that the world is not in God's direct control, he has given it over to us and we have made our choices.

Emma Ultimately, we will have to answer for our action or inaction (Matthew 25:31-46)

Anon I've found that being a Christian and living biblically is all about making choices. We need to choose life (Deuteronomy 30:15-20).

Emma A German theologian, Dietrich Bonhoeffer was hung by the Nazis because he stood up for Christ against what he saw as evil and there are other examples.

The Bible tells us 'If one of you says to him, "Go, I wish you well; keep warm and well fed," but does nothing about his physical needs, what good is it? In the same way, faith by itself, if it is not accompanied by action, is dead.'

Anon Political involvement may not be the only way. Gandhi is believed to have said 'if you want to know what I believe, look at my life'. I was impressed by Jimmy Carter, ex-US President, and Christian, who, after he had stepped down was on a building site voluntarily putting up homes for the homeless. I understood nothing about the politics at the time, but what he was doing told me an awful lot about what he actually believed.

Ann Christians can be involved in other ways, too. A church I used to attend always prayed for the Government and the local council, for those in authority that Christian ethics would come through their leadership (Romans 13:1-7).

Anon Our perspective needs to be more global - it's something I'm working on in my own life.

Penny It's up to every individual to decide how they are going to live biblically, act justly, love mercy and walk humbly with their God (Micah 6:6-8).

Emma The opportunities are bigger than ever to get involved globally and to give in time and energy not necessarily in money: there are holidays to Yugoslavia to give out aid; our designer at work went out to Brazil to work with street children there.

in whose hand is the club of my
    wrath!
⁶I send him against a godless nation,
    I dispatch him against a people who
        anger me,
to seize loot and snatch plunder,
    and to trample them down like mud
        in the streets.
⁷But this is not what he intends,
    this is not what he has in mind;
his purpose is to destroy,
    to put an end to many nations.
⁸'Are not my commanders all kings?' he
    says.
⁹   'Has not Calno fared like
        Carchemish?
Is not Hamath like Arpad,
    and Samaria like Damascus?
¹⁰As my hand seized the kingdoms of the
    idols,
    kingdoms whose images excelled
        those of Jerusalem and Samaria—
¹¹shall I not deal with Jerusalem and her
    images
    as I dealt with Samaria and her
        idols?' "

¹²When the Lord has finished all his
work against Mount Zion and Jerusalem,
he will say, "I will punish the king of
Assyria for the wilful pride of his heart and
the haughty look in his eyes. ¹³For he says:

" 'By the strength of my hand I have
    done this,
    and by my wisdom, because I have
        understanding.
I removed the boundaries of nations,
    I plundered their treasures;
    like a mighty one I subdued*a* their
        kings.
¹⁴As one reaches into a nest,
    so my hand reached for the wealth of
        the nations;
as men gather abandoned eggs,
    so I gathered all the countries;
not one flapped a wing,
    or opened its mouth to chirp.' "

¹⁵Does the axe raise itself above him who
    swings it,

or the saw boast against him who uses
    it?
As if a rod were to wield him who lifts it
    up,
    or a club brandish him who is not
        wood!
¹⁶Therefore, the Lord, the Lᴏʀᴅ
    Almighty,
    will send a wasting disease upon his
        sturdy warriors;
under his pomp a fire will be kindled
    like a blazing flame.
¹⁷The Light of Israel will become a fire,
    their Holy One a flame;
in a single day it will burn and consume
    his thorns and his briers.
¹⁸The splendour of his forests and fertile
    fields
    it will completely destroy,
    as when a sick man wastes away.
¹⁹And the remaining trees of his forests
    will be so few
    that a child could write them down.

The Remnant of Israel

²⁰In that day the remnant of Israel,
    the survivors of the house of Jacob,
will no longer rely on him
    who struck them down
but will truly rely on the Lᴏʀᴅ,
    the Holy One of Israel.
²¹A remnant will return,*b* a remnant of
    Jacob
    will return to the Mighty God.
²²Though your people, O Israel, be like
    the sand by the sea,
    only a remnant will return.
Destruction has been decreed,
    overwhelming and righteous.
²³The Lord, the Lᴏʀᴅ Almighty, will
    carry out
    the destruction decreed upon the
        whole land.

²⁴Therefore, this is what the Lord, the
Lᴏʀᴅ Almighty, says:

"O my people who live in Zion,
    do not be afraid of the Assyrians,
who beat you with a rod

---

a13 Or / *I subdued the mighty,*   *b21* Hebrew *shear-jashub*; also in verse 22

and lift up a club against you, as
    Egypt did.
25Very soon my anger against you will
    end
    and my wrath will be directed to their
        destruction.''

26The LORD Almighty will lash them with
    a whip,
    as when he struck down Midian at the
        rock of Oreb;
and he will raise his staff over the
    waters,
    as he did in Egypt.
27In that day their burden will be lifted
    from your shoulders,
    their yoke from your neck;
the yoke will be broken
    because you have grown so fat.c

28They enter Aiath;
    they pass through Migron;
    they store supplies at Michmash.
29They go over the pass, and say,
    "We will camp overnight at Geba."
Ramah trembles;
    Gibeah of Saul flees.
30Cry out, O Daughter of Gallim!
    Listen, O Laishah!
    Poor Anathoth!
31Madmenah is in flight;
    the people of Gebim take cover.
32This day they will halt at Nob;
    they will shake their fist
at the mount of the Daughter of Zion,
    at the hill of Jerusalem.

33See, the Lord, the LORD Almighty,
    will lop off the boughs with great
        power.
The lofty trees will be felled,
    the tall ones will be brought low.
34He will cut down the forest thickets
    with an axe;
    Lebanon will fall before the Mighty
        One.

The Branch From Jesse

11 A shoot will come up from the
    stump of Jesse;
    from his roots a Branch will bear
    fruit.

2The Spirit of the LORD will rest on
    him—
    the Spirit of wisdom and of
        understanding,
    the Spirit of counsel and of power,
    the Spirit of knowledge and of the
        fear of the LORD—
3and he will delight in the fear of the
    LORD.

He will not judge by what he sees with
    his eyes,
    or decide by what he hears with his
        ears;
4but with righteousness he will judge the
    needy,
    with justice he will give decisions for
        the poor of the earth.
He will strike the earth with the rod of
    his mouth;
    with the breath of his lips he will slay
        the wicked.
5Righteousness will be his belt
    and faithfulness the sash round his
        waist.

6The wolf will live with the lamb,
    the leopard will lie down with the
        goat,
the calf and the lion and the yearlinga
    together;
    and a little child will lead them.
7The cow will feed with the bear,
    their young will lie down together,
    and the lion will eat straw like the ox.
8The infant will play near the hole of the
    cobra,
    and the young child put his hand into
        the viper's nest.
9They will neither harm nor destroy
    on all my holy mountain,
for the earth will be full of the
        knowledge of the LORD
    as the waters cover the sea.

10In that day the Root of Jesse will stand
as a banner for the peoples; the nations
will rally to him, and his place of rest will
be glorious. 11In that day the Lord will
reach out his hand a second time to re-
claim the remnant that is left of his people
from Assyria, from Lower Egypt, from

---

c27 Hebrew; Septuagint *broken / from your shoulders*   a6 Hebrew; Septuagint *lion will feed*

Upper Egypt,*b* from Cush,*c* from Elam,
from Babylonia,*d* from Hamath and from
the islands of the sea.

¹²He will raise a banner for the nations
    and gather the exiles of Israel;
he will assemble the scattered people of
        Judah
    from the four quarters of the earth.
¹³Ephraim's jealousy will vanish,
    and Judah's enemies*e* will be cut off;
Ephraim will not be jealous of Judah,
    nor Judah hostile towards Ephraim.
¹⁴They will swoop down on the slopes of
        Philistia to the west;
    together they will plunder the people
        to the east.
They will lay hands on Edom and
        Moab,
    and the Ammonites will be subject to
        them.
¹⁵The LORD will dry up
    the gulf of the Egyptian sea;
with a scorching wind he will sweep his
        hand
    over the Euphrates River.*f*
He will break it up into seven streams
    so that men can cross over in sandals.
¹⁶There will be a highway for the remnant
        of his people
    that is left from Assyria,
as there was for Israel
    when they came up from Egypt.

Songs of Praise

12 In that day you will say:

"I will praise you, O LORD.
    Although you were angry with me,
your anger has turned away
    and you have comforted me.
²Surely God is my salvation;
    I will trust and not be afraid.
The LORD, the LORD, is my strength and
        my song;
    he has become my salvation."
³With joy you will draw water
    from the wells of salvation.

⁴In that day you will say:

"Give thanks to the LORD, call on his
        name;
    make known among the nations
        what he has done,
    and proclaim that his name is
        exalted.
⁵Sing to the LORD, for he has done
        glorious things;
    let this be known to all the world.
⁶Shout aloud and sing for joy, people of
        Zion,
    for great is the Holy One of Israel
        among you."

A Prophecy Against Babylon

13 An oracle concerning Babylon
that Isaiah son of Amoz saw:

²Raise a banner on a bare hilltop,
    shout to them;
beckon to them
    to enter the gates of the nobles.
³I have commanded my holy ones;
    I have summoned my warriors to
        carry out my wrath—
    those who rejoice in my triumph.

⁴Listen, a noise on the mountains,
    like that of a great multitude!
Listen, an uproar among the kingdoms,
    like nations massing together!
The LORD Almighty is mustering
    an army for war.
⁵They come from faraway lands,
    from the ends of the heavens—
the LORD and the weapons of his
        wrath—
    to destroy the whole country.

⁶Wail, for the day of the LORD is near;
    it will come like destruction from the
        Almighty.*a*
⁷Because of this, all hands will go limp,
    every man's heart will melt.
⁸Terror will seize them,
    pain and anguish will grip them;

b11 Hebrew *from Pathros*   *c11* That is, the upper Nile region   *d11* Hebrew *Shinar*   *e13* Or *hostility*
f15 Hebrew *the River*   *a6* Hebrew *Shaddai*

they will writhe like a woman in
labour.
They will look aghast at each other,
their faces aflame.

⁹See, the day of the LORD is coming—
a cruel day, with wrath and fierce
anger—
to make the land desolate
and destroy the sinners within it.
¹⁰The stars of heaven and their
constellations
will not show their light.
The rising sun will be darkened
and the moon will not give its light.
¹¹I will punish the world for its evil,
the wicked for their sins.
I will put an end to the arrogance of the
haughty
and will humble the pride of the
ruthless.
¹²I will make man scarcer than pure gold,
more rare than the gold of Ophir.
¹³Therefore I will make the heavens
tremble;
and the earth will shake from its place
at the wrath of the LORD Almighty,
in the day of his burning anger.

¹⁴Like a hunted gazelle,
like sheep without a shepherd,
each will return to his own people,
each will flee to his native land.
¹⁵Whoever is captured will be thrust
through;
all who are caught will fall by the
sword.
¹⁶Their infants will be dashed to pieces
before their eyes;
their houses will be looted and their
wives ravished.

¹⁷See, I will stir up against them the
Medes,
who do not care for silver
and have no delight in gold.
¹⁸Their bows will strike down the young
men;
they will have no mercy on infants
nor will they look with compassion on
children.

¹⁹Babylon, the jewel of kingdoms,
the glory of the Babylonians'ᵇ pride,
will be overthrown by God
like Sodom and Gomorrah.
²⁰She will never be inhabited
or lived in through all generations;
no Arab will pitch his tent there,
no shepherd will rest his flocks there.
²¹But desert creatures will lie there,
jackals will fill her houses;
there the owls will dwell,
and there the wild goats will leap
about.
²²Hyenas will howl in her strongholds,
jackals in her luxurious palaces.
Her time is at hand,
and her days will not be prolonged.

14 The LORD will have compassion
on Jacob;
once again he will choose Israel
and will settle them in their own land.
Aliens will join them
and unite with the house of Jacob.
²Nations will take them
and bring them to their own place.
And the house of Israel will possess the
nations
as menservants and maidservants in
the LORD's land.
They will make captives of their captors
and rule over their oppressors.

³On the day the LORD gives you relief
from suffering and turmoil and cruel
bondage, ⁴you will take up this taunt
against the king of Babylon:

How the oppressor has come to an end!
How his furyᵃ has ended!
⁵The LORD has broken the rod of the
wicked,
the sceptre of the rulers,
⁶which in anger struck down peoples
with unceasing blows,
and in fury subdued nations
with relentless aggression.
⁷All the lands are at rest and at peace;
they break into singing.

ᵇ19 Or Chaldeans'
ᵃ4 Dead Sea Scrolls, Septuagint and Syriac; the meaning of the word in the Masoretic Text is uncertain.

⁸Even the pine trees and the cedars of
Lebanon
exult over you and say,
"Now that you have been laid low,
no woodsman comes to cut us down."

⁹The grave*ᵇ* below is all astir
to meet you at your coming;
it rouses the spirits of the departed to
greet you—
all those who were leaders in the
world;
it makes them rise from their thrones—
all those who were kings over the
nations.
¹⁰They will all respond,
they will say to you,
"You also have become weak, as we are;
you have become like us."
¹¹All your pomp has been brought down
to the grave,
along with the noise of your harps;
maggots are spread out beneath you
and worms cover you.

¹²How you have fallen from heaven,
O morning star, son of the dawn!
You have been cast down to the earth,
you who once laid low the nations!
¹³You said in your heart,
"I will ascend to heaven;
I will raise my throne
above the stars of God;
I will sit enthroned on the mount of
assembly,
on the utmost heights of the sacred
mountain.*ᶜ*
¹⁴I will ascend above the tops of the
clouds;
I will make myself like the Most
High."
¹⁵But you are brought down to the grave,
to the depths of the pit.

¹⁶Those who see you stare at you,
they ponder your fate:
"Is this the man who shook the earth
and made kingdoms tremble,
¹⁷the man who made the world a desert,
who overthrew its cities
and would not let his captives go
home?"

¹⁸All the kings of the nations lie in state,
each in his own tomb.
¹⁹But you are cast out of your tomb
like a rejected branch;
you are covered with the slain,
with those pierced by the sword,
those who descend to the stones of
the pit.
Like a corpse trampled underfoot,
20   you will not join them in burial,
for you have destroyed your land
and killed your people.

The offspring of the wicked
will never be mentioned again.
²¹Prepare a place to slaughter his sons
for the sins of their forefathers;
they are not to rise to inherit the land
and cover the earth with their cities.

²²"I will rise up against them,"
declares the LORD Almighty.
"I will cut off from Babylon her name
and survivors,
her offspring and descendants,"
declares the LORD.
²³"I will turn her into a place for owls
and into swampland;
I will sweep her with the broom of
destruction,"
declares the LORD Almighty.

A Prophecy Against Assyria

²⁴The LORD Almighty has sworn,

"Surely, as I have planned, so it will be,
and as I have purposed, so it will
stand.
²⁵I will crush the Assyrian in my land;
on my mountains I will trample him
down.
His yoke will be taken from my people,
and his burden removed from their
shoulders."

²⁶This is the plan determined for the
whole world;
this is the hand stretched out over all
nations.
²⁷For the LORD Almighty has purposed,
and who can thwart him?

ᵇ9 Hebrew *Sheol*; also in verses 11 and 15   *ᶜ13* Or *the north*; Hebrew *Zaphon*

His hand is stretched out, and who
can turn it back?

A Prophecy Against the Philistines

²⁸This oracle came in the year King
Ahaz died:

²⁹Do not rejoice, all you Philistines,
that the rod that struck you is broken;
from the root of that snake will spring
up a viper,
its fruit will be a darting, venomous
serpent.
³⁰The poorest of the poor will find
pasture,
and the needy will lie down in safety.
But your root I will destroy by famine;
it will slay your survivors.

³¹Wail, O gate! Howl, O city!
Melt away, all you Philistines!
A cloud of smoke comes from the
north,
and there is not a straggler in its
ranks.
³²What answer shall be given
to the envoys of that nation?
"The Lᴏʀᴅ has established Zion,
and in her his afflicted people will
find refuge."

A Prophecy Against Moab

15

An oracle concerning Moab:

Ar in Moab is ruined,
destroyed in a night!
Kir in Moab is ruined,
destroyed in a night!
²Dibon goes up to its temple,
to its high places to weep;
Moab wails over Nebo and Medeba.
Every head is shaved
and every beard cut off.
³In the streets they wear sackcloth;
on the roofs and in the public squares
they all wail,
prostrate with weeping.
⁴Heshbon and Elealeh cry out,
their voices are heard all the way to
Jahaz.

Therefore the armed men of Moab cry
out,
and their hearts are faint.

⁵My heart cries out over Moab;
her fugitives flee as far as Zoar,
as far as Eglath Shelishiyah.
They go up the way to Luhith,
weeping as they go;
on the road to Horonaim
they lament their destruction.
⁶The waters of Nimrim are dried up
and the grass is withered;
the vegetation is gone
and nothing green is left.
⁷So the wealth they have acquired and
stored up
they carry away over the Ravine of
the Poplars.
⁸Their outcry echoes along the border of
Moab;
their wailing reaches as far as Eglaim,
their lamentation as far as Beer Elim.
⁹Dimon's*ᵃ* waters are full of blood,
but I will bring still more upon
Dimon*ᵃ*—
a lion upon the fugitives of Moab
and upon those who remain in the
land.

16

Send lambs as tribute
to the ruler of the land,
from Sela, across the desert,
to the mount of the Daughter of
Zion.
²Like fluttering birds
pushed from the nest,
so are the women of Moab
at the fords of the Arnon.

³"Give us counsel,
render a decision.
Make your shadow like night—
at high noon.
Hide the fugitives,
do not betray the refugees.
⁴Let the Moabite fugitives stay with you;
be their shelter from the destroyer."

The oppressor will come to an end,
and destruction will cease;

---

*ᵃ*9 Masoretic Text; Dead Sea Scrolls, some Septuagint manuscripts and Vulgate *Dibon*

the aggressor will vanish from the
    land.
⁵In love a throne will be established;
    in faithfulness a man will sit on it—
    one from the house*a* of David—
one who in judging seeks justice
    and speeds the cause of righteousness.

⁶We have heard of Moab's pride—
    her overweening pride and conceit,
her pride and her insolence—
    but her boasts are empty.
⁷Therefore the Moabites wail,
    they wail together for Moab.
Lament and grieve
    for the men*b* of Kir Hareseth.
⁸The fields of Heshbon wither,
    the vines of Sibmah also.
The rulers of the nations
    have trampled down the choicest
        vines,
which once reached Jazer
    and spread towards the desert.
Their shoots spread out
    and went as far as the sea.
⁹So I weep, as Jazer weeps,
    for the vines of Sibmah.
O Heshbon, O Elealeh,
    I drench you with tears!
The shouts of joy over your ripened
        fruit
    and over your harvests have been
        stilled.
¹⁰Joy and gladness are taken away from
        the orchards;
    no-one sings or shouts in the
        vineyards;
no-one treads out wine at the presses,
    for I have put an end to the shouting.
¹¹My heart laments for Moab like a harp,
    my inmost being for Kir Hareseth.
¹²When Moab appears at her high place,
    she only wears herself out;
when she goes to her shrine to pray,
    it is to no avail.

¹³This is the word the LORD has already
spoken concerning Moab. ¹⁴But now the
LORD says: "Within three years, as a servant bound by contract would count them,

Moab's splendour and all her many people
will be despised, and her survivors will be
very few and feeble."

An Oracle Against Damascus

17 An oracle concerning Damascus:

"See, Damascus will no longer be a city
    but will become a heap of ruins.
²The cities of Aroer will be deserted
    and left to flocks, which will lie down,
    with no-one to make them afraid.
³The fortified city will disappear from
        Ephraim,
    and royal power from Damascus;
the remnant of Aram will be
    like the glory of the Israelites,"
            declares the LORD Almighty.

⁴"In that day the glory of Jacob will
        fade;
    the fat of his body will waste away.
⁵It will be as when a reaper gathers the
        standing corn
    and harvests the corn with his arm—
as when a man gleans ears of corn
    in the Valley of Rephaim.
⁶Yet some gleanings will remain,
    as when an olive tree is beaten,
leaving two or three olives on the
        topmost branches,
    four or five on the fruitful boughs,"
            declares the LORD,
                the God of Israel.

⁷In that day men will look to their Maker
    and turn their eyes to the Holy One
        of Israel.
⁸They will not look to the altars,
    the work of their hands,
and they will have no regard for the
        Asherah poles*a*
    and the incense altars their fingers
        have made.

⁹In that day their strong cities, which
they left because of the Israelites, will be
like places abandoned to thickets and
undergrowth. And all will be desolation.

---

a5 Hebrew *tent*   *b7* Or *"raisin cakes,"* a word play
a8 That is, symbols of the goddess Asherah

[10]You have forgotten God your Saviour;
   you have not remembered the Rock,
      your fortress.
Therefore, though you set out the finest
      plants
   and plant imported vines,
[11]though on the day you set them out,
      you make them grow,
   and on the morning when you plant
      them, you bring them to bud,
yet the harvest will be as nothing
   in the day of disease and incurable
      pain.

[12]Oh, the raging of many nations—
   they rage like the raging sea!
Oh, the uproar of the peoples—
   they roar like the roaring of great
      waters!
[13]Although the peoples roar like the roar
      of surging waters,
   when he rebukes them they flee far
      away,
   driven before the wind like chaff on the
      hills,
   like tumble-weed before a gale.
[14]In the evening, sudden terror!
   Before the morning, they are gone!
This is the portion of those who loot us,
   the lot of those who plunder us.

A Prophecy Against Cush

18

Woe to the land of whirring
      wings[a]
   along the rivers of Cush,[b]
[2]which sends envoys by sea
   in papyrus boats over the water.

Go, swift messengers,
   to a people tall and smooth-skinned,
   to a people feared far and wide,
an aggressive nation of strange speech,
   whose land is divided by rivers.
[3]All you people of the world,
   you who live on the earth,
when a banner is raised on the
      mountains,
   you will see it,
and when a trumpet sounds,
   you will hear it.

[4]This is what the LORD says to me:
   "I will remain quiet and will look on
      from my dwelling-place,
like shimmering heat in the sunshine,
   like a cloud of dew in the heat of
      harvest."
[5]For, before the harvest, when the
      blossom is gone
   and the flower becomes a ripening
      grape,
he will cut off the shoots with pruning
      knives,
   and cut down and take away the
      spreading branches.
[6]They will all be left to the mountain
      birds of prey
   and to the wild animals;
the birds will feed on them all summer,
   the wild animals all winter.

[7]At that time gifts will be brought to the
LORD Almighty

from a people tall and smooth-skinned,
   from a people feared far and wide,
an aggressive nation of strange speech,
   whose land is divided by rivers—

the gifts will be brought to Mount Zion,
the place of the Name of the LORD
Almighty.

A Prophecy About Egypt

19

An oracle concerning Egypt:

See, the LORD rides on a swift cloud
   and is coming to Egypt.
The idols of Egypt tremble before him,
   and the hearts of the Egyptians melt
      within them.

[2]"I will stir up Egyptian against
      Egyptian—
brother will fight against brother,
   neighbour against neighbour,
city against city,
   kingdom against kingdom.
[3]The Egyptians will lose heart,
   and I will bring their plans to nothing;
they will consult the idols and the spirits
      of the dead,

---

a1 Or *of locusts*   *b1* That is, the upper Nile region

the mediums and the spiritists.
⁴I will hand the Egyptians over
    to the power of a cruel master,
and a fierce king will rule over them,"
    declares the Lord, the LORD
      Almighty.

⁵The waters of the river will dry up,
    and the river bed will be parched and
      dry.
⁶The canals will stink;
    the streams of Egypt will dwindle and
      dry up.
The reeds and rushes will wither,
⁷ also the plants along the Nile,
    at the mouth of the river.
Every sown field along the Nile
    will become parched, will blow away
      and be no more.
⁸The fishermen will groan and lament,
    all who cast hooks into the Nile;
those who throw nets on the water
    will pine away.
⁹Those who work with combed flax will
      despair,
    the weavers of fine linen will lose
      hope.
¹⁰The workers in cloth will be dejected,
    and all the wage earners will be sick
      at heart.

¹¹The officials of Zoan are nothing but
      fools;
    the wise counsellors of Pharaoh give
      senseless advice.
How can you say to Pharaoh,
    "I am one of the wise men,
    a disciple of the ancient kings"?

¹²Where are your wise men now?
    Let them show you and make known
what the LORD Almighty
    has planned against Egypt.
¹³The officials of Zoan have become
      fools,
    the leaders of Memphis*a* are
      deceived;
the cornerstones of her peoples
    have led Egypt astray.

¹⁴The LORD has poured into them
    a spirit of dizziness;
they make Egypt stagger in all that she
      does,
    as a drunkard staggers around in his
      vomit.
¹⁵There is nothing Egypt can do—
    head or tail, palm branch or reed.

¹⁶In that day the Egyptians will be like women. They will shudder with fear at the uplifted hand that the LORD Almighty raises against them. ¹⁷And the land of Judah will bring terror to the Egyptians; everyone to whom Judah is mentioned will be terrified, because of what the LORD Almighty is planning against them.

¹⁸In that day five cities in Egypt will speak the language of Canaan and swear allegiance to the LORD Almighty. One of them will be called the City of Destruction.*b*

¹⁹In that day there will be an altar to the LORD in the heart of Egypt, and a monument to the LORD at its border. ²⁰It will be a sign and witness to the LORD Almighty in the land of Egypt. When they cry out to the LORD because of their oppressors, he will send them a saviour and defender, and he will rescue them. ²¹So the LORD will make himself known to the Egyptians, and in that day they will acknowledge the LORD. They will worship with sacrifices and grain offerings; they will make vows to the LORD and keep them. ²²The LORD will strike Egypt with a plague; he will strike them and heal them. They will turn to the LORD, and he will respond to their pleas and heal them.

²³In that day there will be a highway from Egypt to Assyria. The Assyrians will go to Egypt and the Egyptians to Assyria. The Egyptians and Assyrians will worship together. ²⁴In that day Israel will be the third, along with Egypt and Assyria, a blessing on the earth. ²⁵The LORD Almighty will bless them, saying, "Blessed be Egypt my people, Assyria my handiwork, and Israel my inheritance."

---

a13 Hebrew *Noph*
b18 Most manuscripts of the Masoretic Text; some manuscripts of the Masoretic Text, Dead Sea Scrolls and Vulgate *City of the Sun* (that is, Heliopolis)

A Prophecy Against Egypt and Cush

20 In the year that the supreme commander, sent by Sargon king of Assyria, came to Ashdod and attacked and captured it—²at that time the LORD spoke through Isaiah son of Amoz. He said to him, "Take off the sackcloth from your body and the sandals from your feet." And he did so, going around stripped and barefoot.

³Then the LORD said, "Just as my servant Isaiah has gone stripped and barefoot for three years, as a sign and portent against Egypt and Cush,ᵃ ⁴so the king of Assyria will lead away stripped and barefoot the Egyptian captives and Cushite exiles, young and old, with buttocks bared—to Egypt's shame. ⁵Those who trusted in Cush and boasted in Egypt will be afraid and put to shame. ⁶In that day the people who live on this coast will say, 'See what has happened to those we relied on, those we fled to for help and deliverance from the king of Assyria! How then can we escape?'"

A Prophecy Against Babylon

21 An oracle concerning the Desert by the Sea:

Like whirlwinds sweeping through the
southland,
an invader comes from the desert,
from a land of terror.

²A dire vision has been shown to me:
The traitor betrays, the looter takes
loot.
Elam, attack! Media, lay siege!
I will bring to an end all the groaning
she caused.

³At this my body is racked with pain,
pangs seize me, like those of a
woman in labour;
I am staggered by what I hear,
I am bewildered by what I see.
⁴My heart falters,
fear makes me tremble;

the twilight I longed for
has become a horror to me.

⁵They set the tables,
they spread the rugs,
they eat, they drink!
Get up, you officers,
oil the shields!

⁶This is what the Lord says to me:

"Go, post a lookout
and have him report what he sees.
⁷When he sees chariots
with teams of horses,
riders on donkeys
or riders on camels,
let him be alert,
fully alert."

⁸And the lookoutᵃ shouted,

"Day after day, my lord, I stand on the
watchtower;
every night I stay at my post.
⁹Look, here comes a man in a chariot
with a team of horses.
And he gives back the answer:
'Babylon has fallen, has fallen!
All the images of its gods
lie shattered on the ground!'"

¹⁰O my people, crushed on the
threshing-floor,
I tell you what I have heard
from the LORD Almighty,
from the God of Israel.

A Prophecy Against Edom

¹¹An oracle concerning Dumah:ᵇ

Someone calls to me from Seir,
"Watchman, what is left of the night?
Watchman, what is left of the night?"
¹²The watchman replies,
"Morning is coming, but also the
night.
If you would ask, then ask;
and come back yet again."

ᵃ3 That is, the upper Nile region; also in verse 5   ᵃ8 Dead Sea Scrolls and Syriac; Masoretic Text A lion
ᵇ11 Dumah means silence or stillness, a word play on Edom.

A Prophecy Against Arabia

13An oracle concerning Arabia:

You caravans of Dedanites,
  who camp in the thickets of Arabia,
14 bring water for the thirsty;
you who live in Tema,
  bring food for the fugitives.
15They flee from the sword,
  from the drawn sword,
from the bent bow
  and from the heat of battle.

16This is what the Lord says to me:
"Within one year, as a servant bound by
contract would count it, all the pomp of
Kedar will come to an end. 17The survi-
vors of the bowmen, the warriors of
Kedar, will be few." The LORD, the God of
Israel, has spoken.

A Prophecy About Jerusalem

22 An oracle concerning the Valley
of Vision:

What troubles you now,
  that you have all gone up on the
    roofs,
2O town full of commotion,
  O city of tumult and revelry?
Your slain were not killed by the sword,
  nor did they die in battle.
3All your leaders have fled together;
  they have been captured without
    using the bow.
All you who were caught were taken
    prisoner together,
  having fled while the enemy was still
    far away.
4Therefore I said, "Turn away from me;
  let me weep bitterly.
Do not try to console me
  over the destruction of my people."

5The Lord, the LORD Almighty, has a
    day
  of tumult and trampling and terror
  in the Valley of Vision,
a day of battering down walls
  and of crying out to the mountains.
6Elam takes up the quiver,

with her charioteers and horses;
  Kir uncovers the shield.
7Your choicest valleys are full of
    chariots,
  and horsemen are posted at the city
    gates;
8 the defences of Judah are stripped
    away.

And you looked in that day
  to the weapons in the Palace of the
    Forest;
9you saw that the City of David
  had many breaches in its defences;
you stored up water
  in the Lower Pool.
10You counted the buildings in Jerusalem
  and tore down houses to strengthen
    the wall.
11You built a reservoir between the two
    walls
  for the water of the Old Pool,
but you did not look to the One who
    made it,
  or have regard for the One who
    planned it long ago.

12The Lord, the LORD Almighty,
  called you on that day
to weep and to wail,
  to tear out your hair and put on
    sackcloth.
13But see, there is joy and revelry,
  slaughtering of cattle and killing of
    sheep,
  eating of meat and drinking of wine!
"Let us eat and drink," you say,
  "for tomorrow we die!"

14The LORD Almighty has revealed this
in my hearing: "Till your dying day this sin
will not be atoned for," says the Lord, the
LORD Almighty.

15This is what the Lord, the LORD
Almighty, says:

"Go, say to this steward,
  to Shebna, who is in charge of the
    palace:
16What are you doing here and who gave
    you permission
  to cut out a grave for yourself here,

hewing your grave on the height
   and chiselling your resting place in
      the rock?

17"Beware, the LORD is about to take firm
    hold of you
   and hurl you away, O you mighty
     man.
18He will roll you up tightly like a ball
   and throw you into a large country.
There you will die
   and there your splendid chariots will
    remain—
   you disgrace to your master's house!
19I will depose you from your office,
   and you will be ousted from your
    position.

20"In that day I will summon my servant, Eliakim son of Hilkiah. 21I will clothe him with your robe and fasten your sash around him and hand your authority over to him. He will be a father to those who live in Jerusalem and to the house of Judah. 22I will place on his shoulder the key to the house of David; what he opens no-one can shut, and what he shuts no-one can open. 23I will drive him like a peg into a firm place; he will be a seat^a of honour for the house of his father. 24All the glory of his family will hang on him: its offspring and offshoots—all its lesser vessels, from the bowls to all the jars.

25"In that day," declares the LORD Almighty, "the peg driven into the firm place will give way; it will be sheared off and will fall, and the load hanging on it will be cut down." The LORD has spoken.

A Prophecy About Tyre

23 An oracle concerning Tyre:

Wail, O ships of Tarshish!
   For Tyre is destroyed
   and left without house or harbour.
From the land of Cyprus^a
   word has come to them.

2Be silent, you people of the island
   and you merchants of Sidon,
   whom the seafarers have enriched.
3On the great waters
   came the grain of the Shihor;
the harvest of the Nile^b was the revenue
    of Tyre,
   and she became the market-place of
    the nations.

4Be ashamed, O Sidon, and you, O
    fortress of the sea,
   for the sea has spoken:
"I have neither been in labour nor given
    birth;
I have neither reared sons nor
    brought up daughters."
5When word comes to Egypt,
   they will be in anguish at the report
    from Tyre.

6Cross over to Tarshish;
   wail, you people of the island.
7Is this your city of revelry,
   the old, old city,
whose feet have taken her
   to settle in far-off lands?
8Who planned this against Tyre,
   the bestower of crowns,
whose merchants are princes,
   whose traders are renowned in the
    earth?
9The LORD Almighty planned it,
   to bring low the pride of all glory
   and to humble all who are renowned
    on the earth.

10Till^c your land as along the Nile,
   O Daughter of Tarshish,
   for you no longer have a harbour.
11The LORD has stretched out his hand
    over the sea
   and made its kingdoms tremble.
He has given an order concerning
    Phoenicia^d
   that her fortresses be destroyed.
12He said, "No more of your revelling,
   O Virgin Daughter of Sidon, now
    crushed!

---

^{a}23 Or *throne* ^{a}1 Hebrew *Kittim*
^{b}2, 3 Masoretic Text; one Dead Sea Scroll *Sidon, / who cross over the sea; / your envoys* ^{3}*are on the great waters. / The grain of the Shihor, / the harvest of the Nile,*
^{c}10 Dead Sea Scrolls and some Septuagint manuscripts; Masoretic Text *Go through* ^{d}11 Hebrew *Canaan*

"Up, cross over to Cyprus;[e]
  even there you will find no rest."
[13]Look at the land of the Babylonians,[f]
  this people that is now of no account!
The Assyrians have made it
  a place for desert creatures;
they raised up their siege towers,
  they stripped its fortresses bare
  and turned it into a ruin.

[14]Wail, you ships of Tarshish;
  your fortress is destroyed!

[15]At that time Tyre will be forgotten for
seventy years, the span of a king's life. But
at the end of these seventy years, it will
happen to Tyre as in the song of the prostitute:

[16]"Take up a harp, walk through the city,
  O prostitute forgotten;
play the harp well, sing many a song,
  so that you will be remembered."

[17]At the end of seventy years, the LORD
will deal with Tyre. She will return to her
hire as a prostitute and will ply her trade
with all the kingdoms on the face of the
earth. [18]Yet her profit and her earnings
will be set apart for the LORD; they will not
be stored up or hoarded. Her profits will
go to those who live before the LORD, for
abundant food and fine clothes.

The LORD's Devastation of the Earth

24 See, the LORD is going to lay
  waste the earth
  and devastate it;
  he will ruin its face
  and scatter its inhabitants—
[2]it will be the same
  for priest as for people,
  for master as for servant,
  for mistress as for maid,
  for seller as for buyer,
  for borrower as for lender,
  for debtor as for creditor.
[3]The earth will be completely laid waste
  and totally plundered.
            The LORD has spoken
                this word.

[4]The earth dries up and withers,
  the world languishes and withers,
  the exalted of the earth languish.
[5]The earth is defiled by its people;
  they have disobeyed the laws,
violated the statutes
  and broken the everlasting covenant.
[6]Therefore a curse consumes the earth;
  its people must bear their guilt.
Therefore earth's inhabitants are
      burned up,
  and very few are left.
[7]The new wine dries up and the vine
      withers;
  all the merrymakers groan.
[8]The gaiety of the tambourines is stilled,
  the noise of the revellers has stopped,
  the joyful harp is silent.
[9]No longer do they drink wine with a
      song;
  the beer is bitter to its drinkers.
[10]The ruined city lies desolate;
  the entrance to every house is barred.
[11]In the streets they cry out for wine;
  all joy turns to gloom,
  all gaiety is banished from the earth.
[12]The city is left in ruins,
  its gate is battered to pieces.
[13]So will it be on the earth
  and among the nations,
as when an olive tree is beaten,
  or as when gleanings are left after the
      grape harvest.

[14]They raise their voices, they shout for
      joy;
  from the west they acclaim the LORD's
      majesty.
[15]Therefore in the east give glory to the
      LORD;
  exalt the name of the LORD, the God
      of Israel,
  in the islands of the sea.
[16]From the ends of the earth we hear
      singing:
  "Glory to the Righteous One."

But I said, "I waste away, I waste away!
  Woe to me!
The treacherous betray!
  With treachery the treacherous
      betray!"

---

[e]12 Hebrew *Kittim*   [f]13 Or *Chaldeans*

¹⁷Terror and pit and snare await you,
  O people of the earth.
¹⁸Whoever flees at the sound of terror
  will fall into a pit;
  whoever climbs out of the pit
  will be caught in a snare.

The floodgates of the heavens are
    opened,
  the foundations of the earth shake.
¹⁹The earth is broken up,
  the earth is split asunder,
  the earth is thoroughly shaken.
²⁰The earth reels like a drunkard,
  it sways like a hut in the wind;
so heavy upon it is the guilt of its
    rebellion
  that it falls—never to rise again.

²¹In that day the LORD will punish
  the powers in the heavens above
  and the kings on the earth below.
²²They will be herded together
  like prisoners bound in a dungeon;
they will be shut up in prison
  and be punished[a] after many days.
²³The moon will be abashed, the sun
    ashamed;
  for the LORD Almighty will reign
on Mount Zion and in Jerusalem,
  and before its elders, gloriously.

Praise to the LORD

25 O LORD, you are my God;
  I will exalt you and praise your
    name,
for in perfect faithfulness
  you have done marvellous things,
  things planned long ago.
²You have made the city a heap of
    rubble,
  the fortified town a ruin,
the foreigners' stronghold a city no
    more;
  it will never be rebuilt.
³Therefore strong peoples will honour
    you;
  cities of ruthless nations will revere
    you.
⁴You have been a refuge for the poor,

a refuge for the needy in his distress,
a shelter from the storm
  and a shade from the heat.
For the breath of the ruthless
  is like a storm driving against a wall
⁵ and like the heat of the desert.
You silence the uproar of foreigners;
  as heat is reduced by the shadow of a
    cloud,
so the song of the ruthless is stilled.

⁶On this mountain the LORD Almighty
    will prepare
  a feast of rich food for all peoples,
a banquet of aged wine—
  the best of meats and the finest of
    wines.
⁷On this mountain he will destroy
  the shroud that enfolds all peoples,
the sheet that covers all nations;
⁸ he will swallow up death for ever.
The Sovereign LORD will wipe away the
    tears
  from all faces;
he will remove the disgrace of his
    people
  from all the earth.
                    The LORD has spoken.

⁹In that day they will say,

"Surely this is our God;
  we trusted in him, and he saved us.
This is the LORD, we trusted in him;
  let us rejoice and be glad in his
    salvation."

¹⁰The hand of the LORD will rest on this
    mountain;
  but Moab will be trampled under him
as straw is trampled down in the
    manure.
¹¹They will spread out their hands in it,
  as a swimmer spreads out his hands to
    swim.
God will bring down their pride
  despite the cleverness[a] of their hands.
¹²He will bring down your high fortified
    walls
  and lay them low;

---

a22 Or released   *a11 The meaning of the Hebrew for this word is uncertain.*

he will bring them down to the ground,
   to the very dust.

A Song of Praise

26 In that day this song will be sung in the land of Judah:

We have a strong city;
   God makes salvation
   its walls and ramparts.
²Open the gates
   that the righteous nation may enter,
   the nation that keeps faith.
³You will keep in perfect peace
   him whose mind is steadfast,
   because he trusts in you.
⁴Trust in the LORD for ever,
   for the LORD, the LORD, is the Rock
    eternal.
⁵He humbles those who dwell on high,
   he lays the lofty city low;
 he levels it to the ground
   and casts it down to the dust.
⁶Feet trample it down—
   the feet of the oppressed,
   the footsteps of the poor.

⁷The path of the righteous is level;
   O upright One, you make the way of
    the righteous smooth.
⁸Yes, LORD, walking in the way of your
   laws,*ᵃ*
 we wait for you;
 your name and renown
   are the desire of our hearts.
⁹My soul yearns for you in the night;
   in the morning my spirit longs for
    you.
When your judgments come upon the
   earth,
   the people of the world learn
    righteousness.
¹⁰Though grace is shown to the wicked,
   they do not learn righteousness;
 even in a land of uprightness they go on
   doing evil
   and regard not the majesty of the
    LORD.
¹¹O LORD, your hand is lifted high,
   but they do not see it.

Let them see your zeal for your people
   and be put to shame;
 let the fire reserved for your enemies
   consume them.

¹²LORD, you establish peace for us;
   all that we have accomplished you
    have done for us.
¹³O LORD, our God, other lords besides
   you have ruled over us,
   but your name alone do we honour.
¹⁴They are now dead, they live no more;
   those departed spirits do not rise.
 You punished them and brought them
   to ruin;
   you wiped out all memory of them.
¹⁵You have enlarged the nation, O LORD;
   you have enlarged the nation.
 You have gained glory for yourself;
   you have extended all the borders of
    the land.

¹⁶LORD, they came to you in their distress;
   when you disciplined them,
   they could barely whisper a prayer.*ᵇ*
¹⁷As a woman with child and about to
   give birth
   writhes and cries out in her pain,
   so were we in your presence, O LORD.
¹⁸We were with child, we writhed in pain,
   but we gave birth to wind.
 We have not brought salvation to the
   earth;
   we have not given birth to people of
    the world.

¹⁹But your dead will live;
   their bodies will rise.
 You who dwell in the dust,
   wake up and shout for joy.
 Your dew is like the dew of the
   morning;
   the earth will give birth to her dead.

²⁰Go, my people, enter your rooms
   and shut the doors behind you;
 hide yourselves for a little while
   until his wrath has passed by.
²¹See, the LORD is coming out of his
   dwelling
   to punish the people of the earth for
    their sins.

ᵃ8 Or *judgments*   *ᵇ16* The meaning of the Hebrew for this clause is uncertain.

The earth will disclose the blood shed
    upon her;
  she will conceal her slain no longer.

Deliverance of Israel

27 In that day,

  the LORD will punish with his sword,
    his fierce, great and powerful sword,
Leviathan the gliding serpent,
  Leviathan the coiling serpent;
he will slay the monster of the sea.

[2]In that day—

"Sing about a fruitful vineyard:
[3] I, the LORD, watch over it;
  I water it continually.
I guard it day and night
  so that no-one may harm it.
[4] I am not angry.
If only there were briers and thorns
    confronting me!
  I would march against them in battle;
  I would set them all on fire.
[5]Or else let them come to me for refuge;
  let them make peace with me,
  yes, let them make peace with me."

[6]In days to come Jacob will take root,
  Israel will bud and blossom
  and fill all the world with fruit.

[7]Has ⌊the LORD⌋ struck her
  as he struck down those who struck
    her?
  Has she been killed
  as those were killed who killed her?
[8]By warfare[a] and exile you contend with
    her—
  with his fierce blast he drives her out,
  as on a day the east wind blows.
[9]By this, then, will Jacob's guilt be
    atoned for,
  and this will be the full fruitage of the
    removal of his sin:
When he makes all the altar stones
  to be like chalk stones crushed to
    pieces,

no Asherah poles[b] or incense altars
  will be left standing.
[10]The fortified city stands desolate,
  an abandoned settlement, forsaken
    like the desert;
there the calves graze,
  there they lie down;
  they strip its branches bare.
[11]When its twigs are dry, they are broken
    off
  and women come and make fires with
    them.
For this is a people without
    understanding;
  so their Maker has no compassion on
    them,
  and their Creator shows them no
    favour.

[12]In that day the LORD will thresh from
the flowing Euphrates[c] to the Wadi of
Egypt, and you, O Israelites, will be
gathered up one by one. [13]And in that day
a great trumpet will sound. Those who
were perishing in Assyria and those who
were exiled in Egypt will come and
worship the LORD on the holy mountain in
Jerusalem.

Woe to Ephraim

28 Woe to that wreath, the pride of
    Ephraim's drunkards,
  to the fading flower, his glorious
    beauty,
set on the head of a fertile valley—
  to that city, the pride of those laid
    low by wine!
[2]See, the Lord has one who is powerful
    and strong.
  Like a hailstorm and a destructive
    wind,
  like a driving rain and a flooding
    downpour,
  he will throw it forcefully to the
    ground.
[3]That wreath, the pride of Ephraim's
    drunkards,
  will be trampled underfoot.
[4]That fading flower, his glorious beauty,
  set on the head of a fertile valley,

---

a8 See Septuagint; the meaning of the Hebrew for this word is uncertain.
b9 That is, symbols of the goddess Asherah   *c12* Hebrew *River*

will be like a fig ripe before harvest—
  as soon as someone sees it and takes
    it in his hand,
  he swallows it.

[5]In that day the LORD Almighty
  will be a glorious crown,
a beautiful wreath
  for the remnant of his people.
[6]He will be a spirit of justice
  to him who sits in judgment,
a source of strength
  to those who turn back the battle at
    the gate.

[7]And these also stagger from wine
  and reel from beer:
Priests and prophets stagger from beer
  and are befuddled with wine;
they reel from beer,
  they stagger when seeing visions,
  they stumble when rendering
    decisions.
[8]All the tables are covered with vomit
  and there is not a spot without filth.

[9]"Who is it he is trying to teach?
  To whom is he explaining his
    message?
To children weaned from their milk,
  to those just taken from the breast?
[10]For it is:
  Do and do, do and do,
  rule on rule, rule on rule;[a]
  a little here, a little there."

[11]Very well then, with foreign lips and
    strange tongues
  God will speak to this people,
[12]to whom he said,
  "This is the resting-place, let the
    weary rest";
and, "This is the place of repose"—
  but they would not listen.
[13]So then, the word of the LORD to them
    will become:
  Do and do, do and do,
  rule on rule, rule on rule;
  a little here, a little there—

so that they will go and fall backwards,
  be injured and snared and captured.

[14]Therefore hear the word of the LORD,
    you scoffers
  who rule this people in Jerusalem.
[15]You boast, "We have entered into a
    covenant with death,
  with the grave[b] we have made an
    agreement.
When an overwhelming scourge sweeps
    by,
  it cannot touch us,
for we have made a lie our refuge
  and falsehood[c] our hiding-place."

[16]So this is what the Sovereign LORD
says:

"See, I lay a stone in Zion,
  a tested stone,
a precious cornerstone for a sure
    foundation;
  the one who trusts will never be
    dismayed.
[17]I will make justice the measuring line
  and righteousness the plumb-line;
hail will sweep away your refuge, the
    lie,
  and water will overflow your
    hiding-place.
[18]Your covenant with death will be
    annulled;
  your agreement with the grave will
    not stand.
When the overwhelming scourge
    sweeps by,
  you will be beaten down by it.
[19]As often as it comes it will carry you
    away;
  morning after morning, by day and
    by night,
  it will sweep through."

The understanding of this message
  will bring sheer terror.
[20]The bed is too short to stretch out on,
  the blanket too narrow to wrap
    around you.
[21]The LORD will rise up as he did at
    Mount Perazim,

---

[a]10 Hebrew / sav lasav sav lasav / kav lakav kav lakav (possibly meaningless sounds; perhaps a mimicking of the prophet's words); also in verse 13   [b]15 Hebrew Sheol; also in verse 18   [c]15 Or false gods

he will rouse himself as in the Valley
   of Gibeon—
to do his work, his strange work,
   and perform his task, his alien task.
²²Now stop your mocking,
   or your chains will become heavier;
the Lord, the LORD Almighty, has told
   me
of the destruction decreed against the
   whole land.

²³Listen and hear my voice;
   pay attention and hear what I say.
²⁴When a farmer ploughs for planting,
   does he plough continually?
Does he keep on breaking up and
   harrowing the soil?
²⁵When he has levelled the surface,
   does he not sow caraway and scatter
   cummin?
Does he not plant wheat in its place,[d]
   barley in its plot,[d]
   and spelt in its field?
²⁶His God instructs him
   and teaches him the right way.

²⁷Caraway is not threshed with a sledge,
   nor is a cartwheel rolled over
   cummin;
caraway is beaten out with a rod,
   and cummin with a stick.
²⁸Grain must be ground to make bread;
   so one does not go on threshing it for
   ever.
Though he drives the wheels of his
   threshing-cart over it,
   his horses do not grind it.
²⁹All this also comes from the LORD
   Almighty,
   wonderful in counsel and magnificent
   in wisdom.

Woe to David's City

29 Woe to you, Ariel, Ariel,
   the city where David settled!
Add year to year
   and let your cycle of festivals go on.
²Yet I will besiege Ariel;
   she will mourn and lament,

she will be to me like an altar hearth.[a]
³I will encamp against you all around;
   I will encircle you with towers
   and set up my siege works against
   you.
⁴Brought low, you will speak from the
   ground;
   your speech will mumble out of the
   dust.
Your voice will come ghostlike from the
   earth;
   out of the dust your speech will
   whisper.

⁵But your many enemies will become
   like fine dust,
   the ruthless hordes like blown chaff.
Suddenly, in an instant,
⁶ the LORD Almighty will come
with thunder and earthquake and great
   noise,
   with windstorm and tempest and
   flames of a devouring fire.
⁷Then the hordes of all the nations that
   fight against Ariel,
   that attack her and her fortress and
   besiege her,
will be as it is with a dream,
   with a vision in the night—
⁸as when a hungry man dreams that he is
   eating,
   but he awakens, and his hunger
   remains;
as when a thirsty man dreams that he is
   drinking,
   but he awakens faint, with his thirst
   unquenched.
So will it be with the hordes of all the
   nations
   that fight against Mount Zion.

⁹Be stunned and amazed,
   blind yourselves and be sightless;
be drunk, but not from wine,
   stagger, but not from beer.
¹⁰The LORD has brought over you a deep
   sleep:
He has sealed your eyes (the
   prophets);
he has covered your heads (the
   seers).

---

[d]25 The meaning of the Hebrew for this word is uncertain.
[a]2 The Hebrew for *altar hearth* sounds like the Hebrew for *Ariel*.

¹¹For you this whole vision is nothing but words sealed in a scroll. And if you give the scroll to someone who can read, and say to him, "Read this, please," he will answer, "I can't; it is sealed." ¹²Or if you give the scroll to someone who cannot read, and say, "Read this, please," he will answer, "I don't know how to read."

¹³The Lord says:

"These people come near to me with
their mouth
and honour me with their lips,
but their hearts are far from me.
Their worship of me
is made up only of rules taught by
men.^b
¹⁴Therefore once more I will astound
these people
with wonder upon wonder;
the wisdom of the wise will perish,
the intelligence of the intelligent will
vanish."
¹⁵Woe to those who go to great depths
to hide their plans from the LORD,
who do their work in darkness and
think,
"Who sees us? Who will know?"
¹⁶You turn things upside down,
as if the potter were thought to be
like the clay!
Shall what is formed say to him who
formed it,
"He did not make me"?
Can the pot say of the potter,
"He knows nothing"?

¹⁷In a very short time, will not Lebanon
be turned into a fertile field
and the fertile field seem like a
forest?
¹⁸In that day the deaf will hear the words
of the scroll,
and out of gloom and darkness
the eyes of the blind will see.
¹⁹Once more the humble will rejoice in
the LORD;
the needy will rejoice in the Holy
One of Israel.
²⁰The ruthless will vanish,

the mockers will disappear,
and all who have an eye for evil will
be cut down—
²¹those who with a word make a man out
to be guilty,
who ensnare the defender in court
and with false testimony deprive the
innocent of justice.

²²Therefore this is what the LORD, who redeemed Abraham, says to the house of Jacob:

"No longer will Jacob be ashamed;
no longer will their faces grow pale.
²³When they see among them their
children,
the work of my hands,
they will keep my name holy;
they will acknowledge the holiness of
the Holy One of Jacob,
and will stand in awe of the God of
Israel.
²⁴Those who are wayward in spirit will
gain understanding;
those who complain will accept
instruction."

Woe to the Obstinate Nation

30

"Woe to the obstinate children,"
declares the LORD,
"to those who carry out plans that are
not mine,
forming an alliance, but not by my
Spirit,
heaping sin upon sin;
²who go down to Egypt
without consulting me;
who look for help to Pharaoh's
protection,
to Egypt's shade for refuge.
³But Pharaoh's protection will be to your
shame,
Egypt's shade will bring you disgrace.
⁴Though they have officials in Zoan
and their envoys have arrived in
Hanes,
⁵everyone will be put to shame
because of a people useless to them,
who bring neither help nor advantage,
but only shame and disgrace."

---

b13 Hebrew; Septuagint *They worship me in vain; / their teachings are but rules taught by men.*

⁶An oracle concerning the animals of the Negev:

Through a land of hardship and
          distress,
     of lions and lionesses,
     of adders and darting snakes,
the envoys carry their riches on
          donkeys' backs,
     their treasures on the humps of
          camels,
to that unprofitable nation,
⁷   to Egypt, whose help is utterly
          useless.
Therefore I call her
     Rahab the Do-Nothing.

⁸Go now, write it on a tablet for them,
     inscribe it on a scroll,
that for the days to come
     it may be an everlasting witness.
⁹These are rebellious people, deceitful
          children,
     children unwilling to listen to the
          LORD's instruction.
¹⁰They say to the seers,
     "See no more visions!"
and to the prophets,
     "Give us no more visions of what is
          right!
Tell us pleasant things,
     prophesy illusions.
¹¹Leave this way,
     get off this path,
and stop confronting us
     with the Holy One of Israel!"

¹²Therefore, this is what the Holy One
of Israel says:

"Because you have rejected this
          message,
     relied on oppression
     and depended on deceit,
¹³this sin will become for you
     like a high wall, cracked and bulging,
     that collapses suddenly, in an instant.
¹⁴It will break in pieces like pottery,
     shattered so mercilessly
that among its pieces not a fragment
          will be found
     for taking coals from a hearth
     or scooping water out of a cistern."

¹⁵This is what the Sovereign LORD, the
Holy One of Israel, says:

"In repentance and rest is your
          salvation,
     in quietness and trust is your
          strength,
     but you would have none of it.
¹⁶You said, 'No, we will flee on horses.'
     Therefore you will flee!
You said, 'We will ride off on swift
          horses.'
     Therefore your pursuers will be swift!
¹⁷A thousand will flee
     at the threat of one;
at the threat of five
     you will all flee away,
till you are left
     like a flagstaff on a mountaintop,
     like a banner on a hill."

¹⁸Yet the LORD longs to be gracious to
          you;
     he rises to show you compassion.
For the LORD is a God of justice.
     Blessed are all who wait for him!

¹⁹O people of Zion, who live in Jerusalem, you will weep no more. How gracious he will be when you cry for help! As soon as he hears, he will answer you. ²⁰Although the Lord gives you the bread of adversity and the water of affliction, your teachers will be hidden no more; with your own eyes you will see them. ²¹Whether you turn to the right or to the left, your ears will hear a voice behind you, saying, "This is the way; walk in it." ²²Then you will defile your idols overlaid with silver and your images covered with gold; you will throw them away like a menstrual cloth and say to them, "Away with you!"

²³He will also send you rain for the seed you sow in the ground, and the food that comes from the land will be rich and plentiful. In that day your cattle will graze in broad meadows. ²⁴The oxen and donkeys that work the soil will eat fodder and mash, spread out with fork and shovel. ²⁵In the day of great slaughter, when the towers fall, streams of water will flow on

every high mountain and every lofty hill.
²⁶The moon will shine like the sun, and the
sunlight will be seven times brighter, like
the light of seven full days, when the LORD
binds up the bruises of his people and
heals the wounds he inflicted.

²⁷See, the Name of the LORD comes from
    afar,
      with burning anger and dense clouds
        of smoke;
his lips are full of wrath,
    and his tongue is a consuming fire.
²⁸His breath is like a rushing torrent,
    rising up to the neck.
He shakes the nations in the sieve of
    destruction;
    he places in the jaws of the peoples
      a bit that leads them astray.
²⁹And you will sing
    as on the night you celebrate a holy
      festival;
your hearts will rejoice
    as when people go up with flutes
to the mountain of the LORD,
    to the Rock of Israel.
³⁰The LORD will cause men to hear his
    majestic voice
    and will make them see his arm
      coming down
with raging anger and consuming fire,
    with cloudburst, thunderstorm and
      hail.
³¹The voice of the LORD will shatter
    Assyria;
    with his sceptre he will strike them
      down.
³²Every stroke the LORD lays on them
    with his punishing rod
will be to the music of tambourines and
    harps,
    as he fights them in battle with the
      blows of his arm.
³³Topheth has long been prepared;
    it has been made ready for the
      king.
Its fire pit has been made deep and
    wide,
    with an abundance of fire and
      wood;
the breath of the LORD,
    like a stream of burning sulphur,
    sets it ablaze.

Woe to Those Who Rely on Egypt

31 Woe to those who go down to
     Egypt for help,
who rely on horses,
who trust in the multitude of their
    chariots
    and in the great strength of their
      horsemen,
but do not look to the Holy One of
    Israel,
    or seek help from the LORD.
²Yet he too is wise and can bring
    disaster;
    he does not take back his words.
He will rise up against the house of the
    wicked,
    against those who help evildoers.
³But the Egyptians are men and not
    God;
    their horses are flesh and not spirit.
When the LORD stretches out his hand,
    he who helps will stumble,
    he who is helped will fall;
    both will perish together.

⁴This is what the LORD says to me:

"As a lion growls,
    a great lion over his prey—
and though a whole band of shepherds
    is called together against him,
he is not frightened by their shouts
    or disturbed by their clamour—
so the LORD Almighty will come down
    to do battle on Mount Zion and on its
      heights.
⁵Like birds hovering overhead,
    the LORD Almighty will shield
      Jerusalem;
he will shield it and deliver it,
    he will 'pass over' it and will
      rescue it."

⁶Return to him you have so greatly revolted against, O Israelites. ⁷For in that
day every one of you will reject the idols of
silver and gold your sinful hands have
made.

⁸"Assyria will fall by a sword that is not
    of man;

a sword, not of mortals, will devour
them.
They will flee before the sword
and their young men will be put to
forced labour.
⁹Their stronghold will fall because of
terror;
at sight of the battle standard their
commanders will panic,"
declares the LORD,
whose fire is in Zion,
whose furnace is in Jerusalem.

The Kingdom of Righteousness

32 See, a king will reign in
righteousness
and rulers will rule with justice.
²Each man will be like a shelter from the
wind
and a refuge from the storm,
like streams of water in the desert
and the shadow of a great rock in a
thirsty land.

³Then the eyes of those who see will no
longer be closed,
and the ears of those who hear will
listen.
⁴The mind of the rash will know and
understand,
and the stammering tongue will be
fluent and clear.
⁵No longer will the fool be called noble
nor the scoundrel be highly
respected.
⁶For the fool speaks folly,
his mind is busy with evil:
He practises ungodliness
and spreads error concerning the
LORD;
the hungry he leaves empty
and from the thirsty he withholds
water.
⁷The scoundrel's methods are wicked,
he makes up evil schemes
to destroy the poor with lies,
even when the plea of the needy is
just.
⁸But the noble man makes noble plans,
and by noble deeds he stands.

The Women of Jerusalem

⁹You women who are so complacent,
rise up and listen to me;
you daughters who feel secure,
hear what I have to say!
¹⁰In little more than a year
you who feel secure will tremble;
the grape harvest will fail,
and the harvest of fruit will not come.
¹¹Tremble, you complacent women;
shudder, you daughters who feel
secure!
Strip off your clothes,
put sackcloth round your waists.
¹²Beat your breasts for the pleasant
fields,
for the fruitful vines
¹³and for the land of my people,
a land overgrown with thorns and
briers—
yes, mourn for all houses of merriment
and for this city of revelry.
¹⁴The fortress will be abandoned,
the noisy city deserted;
citadel and watchtower will become a
wasteland for ever,
the delight of donkeys, a pasture for
flocks,
¹⁵till the Spirit is poured upon us from on
high,
and the desert becomes a fertile
field,
and the fertile field seems like a
forest.
¹⁶Justice will dwell in the desert
and righteousness live in the fertile
field.
¹⁷The fruit of righteousness will be
peace;
the effect of righteousness will be
quietness and confidence for
ever.
¹⁸My people will live in peaceful
dwelling-places,
in secure homes,
in undisturbed places of rest.
¹⁹Though hail flattens the forest
and the city is levelled completely,
²⁰how blessed you will be,
sowing your seed by every stream,
and letting your cattle and donkeys
range free.

Distress and Help

33 Woe to you, O destroyer,
    you who have not been destroyed!
Woe to you, O traitor,
    you who have not been betrayed!
When you stop destroying,
    you will be destroyed;
when you stop betraying,
    you will be betrayed.

²O LORD, be gracious to us;
    we long for you.
Be our strength every morning,
    our salvation in time of distress.
³At the thunder of your voice, the
        peoples flee;
    when you rise up, the nations scatter.
⁴Your plunder, O nations, is harvested
        as by young locusts;
    like a swarm of locusts men pounce
        on it.

⁵The LORD is exalted, for he dwells on
        high;
    he will fill Zion with justice and
        righteousness.
⁶He will be the sure foundation for your
        times,
    a rich store of salvation and wisdom
        and knowledge;
    the fear of the LORD is the key to this
        treasure.ᵃ

⁷Look, their brave men cry aloud in the
        streets;
    the envoys of peace weep bitterly.
⁸The highways are deserted,
    no travellers are on the roads.
The treaty is broken,
    its witnessesᵇ are despised,
    no-one is respected.
⁹The land mournsᶜ and wastes away,
    Lebanon is ashamed and withers;
Sharon is like the Arabah,
    and Bashan and Carmel drop their
        leaves.

¹⁰"Now will I arise," says the LORD.
    "Now will I be exalted;
    now will I be lifted up.
¹¹You conceive chaff,
    you give birth to straw;
    your breath is a fire that consumes
        you.
¹²The peoples will be burned as if to lime;
    like cut thornbushes they will be set
        ablaze."

¹³You who are far away, hear what I have
        done;
    you who are near, acknowledge my
        power!
¹⁴The sinners in Zion are terrified;
    trembling grips the godless:
"Who of us can dwell with the
        consuming fire?
Who of us can dwell with everlasting
        burning?"
¹⁵He who walks righteously
    and speaks what is right,
who rejects gain from extortion
    and keeps his hand from accepting
        bribes,
who stops his ears against plots of
        murder
    and shuts his eyes against
        contemplating evil—
¹⁶this is the man who will dwell on the
        heights,
    whose refuge will be the mountain
        fortress.
His bread will be supplied,
    and water will not fail him.

¹⁷Your eyes will see the king in his beauty
    and view a land that stretches afar.
¹⁸In your thoughts you will ponder the
        former terror:
    "Where is that chief officer?
Where is the one who took the
        revenue?
Where is the officer in charge of the
        towers?"
¹⁹You will see those arrogant people no
        more,
    those people of an obscure speech,
    with their strange, incomprehensible
        tongue.

²⁰Look upon Zion, the city of our
        festivals;
    your eyes will see Jerusalem,
    a peaceful abode, a tent that will not
        be moved;

ᵃ6 Or *is a treasure from him*   ᵇ8 Dead Sea Scrolls; Masoretic Text / *the cities*   ᶜ9 Or *dries up*

its stakes will never be pulled up,
  nor any of its ropes broken.
21There the LORD will be our Mighty One.
  It will be like a place of broad rivers
    and streams.
No galley with oars will ride them,
  no mighty ship will sail them.
22For the LORD is our judge,
  the LORD is our lawgiver,
the LORD is our king;
  it is he who will save us.

23Your rigging hangs loose:
  The mast is not held secure,
    the sail is not spread.
Then an abundance of spoils will be
    divided
  and even the lame will carry off
    plunder.
24No-one living in Zion will say, "I am
    ill";
  and the sins of those who dwell there
    will be forgiven.

Judgment Against the Nations

34 Come near, you nations, and
    listen;
  pay attention, you peoples!
Let the earth hear, and all that is in it,
  the world, and all that comes out
    of it!
2The LORD is angry with all nations;
  his wrath is upon all their armies.
He will totally destroy[a] them,
  he will give them over to slaughter.
3Their slain will be thrown out,
  their dead bodies will send up a
    stench;
  the mountains will be soaked with
    their blood.
4All the stars of the heavens will be
    dissolved
  and the sky rolled up like a scroll;
all the starry host will fall
  like withered leaves from the vine,
  like shrivelled figs from the fig-tree.

5My sword'has drunk its fill in the
    heavens;

see, it descends in judgment on
    Edom,
  the people I have totally destroyed.
6The sword of the LORD is bathed in
    blood,
  it is covered with fat—
the blood of lambs and goats,
  fat from the kidneys of rams.
For the LORD has a sacrifice in Bozrah
  and a great slaughter in Edom.
7And the wild oxen will fall with them,
  the bull calves and the great bulls.
Their land will be drenched with blood,
  and the dust will be soaked with fat.

8For the LORD has a day of vengeance,
  a year of retribution, to uphold
    Zion's cause.
9Edom's streams will be turned into pitch,
  her dust into burning sulphur;
  her land will become blazing pitch!
10It will not be quenched night and day;
  its smoke will rise for ever.
From generation to generation it will lie
    desolate;
  no-one will ever pass through it again.
11The desert owl[b] and screech owl[b] will
    possess it;
  the great owl[b] and the raven will nest
    there.
God will stretch out over Edom
  the measuring line of chaos
  and the plumb-line of desolation.
12Her nobles will have nothing there to be
    called a kingdom,
  all her princes will vanish away.
13Thorns will overrun her citadels,
  nettles and brambles her strongholds.
She will become a haunt for jackals,
  a home for owls.
14Desert creatures will meet with hyenas,
  and wild goats will bleat to each other;
  there the night creatures will also repose
  and find for themselves places of rest.
15The owl will nest there and lay eggs,
  she will hatch them, and care for her
    young under the shadow of her
    wings;
  there also the falcons will gather,
  each with its mate.

---

a2 The Hebrew term refers to the irrevocable giving over of things or persons to the LORD, often by totally destroying them; also in verse 5.   *b11* The precise identification of these birds is uncertain.

¹⁶Look in the scroll of the LORD and read:

None of these will be missing,
  not one will lack her mate.
For it is his mouth that has given the
    order,
  and his Spirit will gather them
    together.
¹⁷He allots their portions;
  his hand distributes them by
    measure.
They will possess it for ever
  and dwell there from generation to
    generation.

Joy of the Redeemed

35 The desert and the parched land
  will be glad;
  the wilderness will rejoice and
    blossom.
Like the crocus, ²it will burst into
    bloom;
  it will rejoice greatly and shout for
    joy.
The glory of Lebanon will be given to it,
  the splendour of Carmel and Sharon;
they will see the glory of the LORD,
  the splendour of our God.

³Strengthen the feeble hands,
  steady the knees that give way;
⁴say to those with fearful hearts,
  "Be strong, do not fear;
your God will come,
  he will come with vengeance;
with divine retribution
  he will come to save you."

⁵Then will the eyes of the blind be
    opened
  and the ears of the deaf unstopped.
⁶Then will the lame leap like a deer,
  and the mute tongue shout for joy.
Water will gush forth in the wilderness
  and streams in the desert.
⁷The burning sand will become a pool,
  the thirsty ground bubbling springs.
In the haunts where jackals once lay,
  grass and reeds and papyrus will grow.

⁸And a highway will be there;
  it will be called the Way of Holiness.
The unclean will not journey on it;
  it will be for those who walk in that
    Way;
  wicked fools will not go about on it.ᵃ
⁹No lion will be there,
  nor will any ferocious beast get up on
    it;
  they will not be found there.
But only the redeemed will walk there,
¹⁰ and the ransomed of the LORD will
    return.
They will enter Zion with singing;
  everlasting joy will crown their
    heads.
Gladness and joy will overtake them,
  and sorrow and sighing will flee away.

Sennacherib Threatens Jerusalem

36 In the fourteenth year of King
  Hezekiah's reign, Sennacherib
king of Assyria attacked all the fortified
cities of Judah and captured them. ²Then
the king of Assyria sent his field commander with a large army from Lachish to
King Hezekiah at Jerusalem. When the
commander stopped at the aqueduct of
the Upper Pool, on the road to the
Washerman's Field, ³Eliakim son of
Hilkiah the palace administrator, Shebna
the secretary, and Joah son of Asaph the
recorder went out to him.

⁴The field commander said to them,
"Tell Hezekiah,

"'This is what the great king, the
king of Assyria, says: On what are
you basing this confidence of yours?
⁵You say you have strategy and military strength—but you speak only
empty words. On whom are you depending, that you rebel against me?
⁶Look now, you are depending on
Egypt, that splintered reed of a staff,
which pierces a man's hand and
wounds him if he leans on it! Such is
Pharaoh king of Egypt to all who
depend on him. ⁷And if you say to
me, "We are depending on the LORD

ᵃ8 Or / the simple will not stray from it

our God"—isn't he the one whose high places and altars Hezekiah removed, saying to Judah and Jerusalem, "You must worship before this altar"?

⁸"'Come now, make a bargain with my master, the king of Assyria: I will give you two thousand horses—if you can put riders on them! ⁹How then can you repulse one officer of the least of my master's officials, even though you are depending on Egypt for chariots and horsemen? ¹⁰Furthermore, have I come to attack and destroy this land without the LORD? The LORD himself told me to march against this country and destroy it.'"

¹¹Then Eliakim, Shebna and Joah said to the field commander, "Please speak to your servants in Aramaic, since we understand it. Don't speak to us in Hebrew in the hearing of the people on the wall."

¹²But the commander replied, "Was it only to your master and you that my master sent me to say these things, and not to the men sitting on the wall—who, like you, will have to eat their own filth and drink their own urine?"

¹³Then the commander stood and called out in Hebrew, "Hear the words of the great king, the king of Assyria! ¹⁴This is what the king says: Do not let Hezekiah deceive you. He cannot deliver you! ¹⁵Do not let Hezekiah persuade you to trust in the LORD when he says, 'The LORD will surely deliver us; this city will not be given into the hand of the king of Assyria.'

¹⁶"Do not listen to Hezekiah. This is what the king of Assyria says: Make peace with me and come out to me. Then every one of you will eat from his own vine and fig-tree and drink water from his own cistern, ¹⁷until I come and take you to a land like your own—a land of corn and new wine, a land of bread and vineyards.

¹⁸"Do not let Hezekiah mislead you when he says, 'The LORD will deliver us.' Has the god of any nation ever delivered his land from the hand of the king of Assyria? ¹⁹Where are the gods of Hamath and Arpad? Where are the gods of

Sepharvaim? Have they rescued Samaria from my hand? ²⁰Who of all the gods of these countries has been able to save his land from me? How then can the LORD deliver Jerusalem from my hand?"

²¹But the people remained silent and said nothing in reply, because the king had commanded, "Do not answer him."

²²Then Eliakim son of Hilkiah the palace administrator, Shebna the secretary, and Joah son of Asaph the recorder went to Hezekiah, with their clothes torn, and told him what the field commander had said.

Jerusalem's Deliverance Foretold

37 When King Hezekiah heard this, he tore his clothes and put on sackcloth and went into the temple of the LORD. ²He sent Eliakim the palace administrator, Shebna the secretary, and the leading priests, all wearing sackcloth, to the prophet Isaiah son of Amoz. ³They told him, "This is what Hezekiah says: This day is a day of distress and rebuke and disgrace, as when children come to the point of birth and there is no strength to deliver them. ⁴It may be that the LORD your God will hear the words of the field commander, whom his master, the king of Assyria, has sent to ridicule the living God, and that he will rebuke him for the words the LORD your God has heard. Therefore pray for the remnant that still survives."

⁵When King Hezekiah's officials came to Isaiah, ⁶Isaiah said to them, "Tell your master, 'This is what the LORD says: Do not be afraid of what you have heard—those words with which the underlings of the king of Assyria have blasphemed me. ⁷Listen! I am going to put a spirit in him so that when he hears a certain report, he will return to his own country, and there I will have him cut down with the sword.'"

⁸When the field commander heard that the king of Assyria had left Lachish, he withdrew and found the king fighting against Libnah.

⁹Now Sennacherib received a report

that Tirhakah, the Cushite[a] king ⌐of Egypt⌐, was marching out to fight against him. When he heard it, he sent messengers to Hezekiah with this word: [10]"Say to Hezekiah king of Judah: Do not let the god you depend on deceive you when he says, 'Jerusalem will not be handed over to the king of Assyria.' [11]Surely you have heard what the kings of Assyria have done to all the countries, destroying them completely. And will you be delivered? [12]Did the gods of the nations that were destroyed by my forefathers deliver them— the gods of Gozan, Haran, Rezeph and the people of Eden who were in Tel Assar? [13]Where is the king of Hamath, the king of Arpad, the king of the city of Sepharvaim, or of Hena or Ivvah?"

Hezekiah's Prayer

[14]Hezekiah received the letter from the messengers and read it. Then he went up to the temple of the LORD and spread it out before the LORD. [15]And Hezekiah prayed to the LORD: [16]"O LORD Almighty, God of Israel, enthroned between the cherubim, you alone are God over all the kingdoms of the earth. You have made heaven and earth. [17]Give ear, O LORD, and hear; open your eyes, O LORD, and see; listen to all the words Sennacherib has sent to insult the living God.

[18]"It is true, O LORD, that the Assyrian kings have laid waste all these peoples and their lands. [19]They have thrown their gods into the fire and destroyed them, for they were not gods but only wood and stone, fashioned by human hands. [20]Now, O LORD our God, deliver us from his hand, so that all kingdoms on earth may know that you alone, O LORD, are God."[b]

Sennacherib's Fall

[21]Then Isaiah son of Amoz sent a message to Hezekiah: "This is what the LORD, the God of Israel, says: Because you have prayed to me concerning Sennacherib king of Assyria, [22]this is the word the LORD has spoken against him:

"The Virgin Daughter of Zion
    despises and mocks you.
The Daughter of Jerusalem
    tosses her head as you flee.
[23]Who is it you have insulted and
        blasphemed?
    Against whom have you raised your
        voice
and lifted your eyes in pride?
    Against the Holy One of Israel!
[24]By your messengers
    you have heaped insults on the Lord.
And you have said,
    'With my many chariots
I have ascended the heights of the
        mountains,
    the utmost heights of Lebanon.
I have cut down its tallest cedars,
    the choicest of its pines.
I have reached its remotest heights,
    the finest of its forests.
[25]I have dug wells in foreign lands[c]
    and drunk the water there.
With the soles of my feet
    I have dried up all the streams of
        Egypt.'

[26]"Have you not heard?
    Long ago I ordained it.
In days of old I planned it;
    now I have brought it to pass,
that you have turned fortified cities
    into piles of stone.
[27]Their people, drained of power,
    are dismayed and put to shame.
They are like plants in the field,
    like tender green shoots,
like grass sprouting on the roof,
    scorched[d] before it grows up.

[28]"But I know where you stay
    and when you come and go
    and how you rage against me.
[29]Because you rage against me
    and because your insolence has
        reached my ears,

a9 That is, from the upper Nile region
b20 Dead Sea Scrolls (see also 2 Kings 19:19); Masoretic Text alone are the LORD
c25 Dead Sea Scrolls (see also 2 Kings 19:24); Masoretic Text does not have in foreign lands.
d27 Some manuscripts of the Masoretic Text, Dead Sea Scrolls and some Septuagint manuscripts (see also 2 Kings 19:26); most manuscripts of the Masoretic Text roof / and terraced fields

I will put my hook in your nose
    and my bit in your mouth,
and I will make you return
    by the way you came.

30"This will be the sign for you, O
Hezekiah:

"This year you will eat what grows by
    itself,
    and the second year what springs
        from that.
But in the third year sow and reap,
    plant vineyards and eat their fruit.
31Once more a remnant of the house of
    Judah
will take root below and bear fruit
    above.
32For out of Jerusalem will come a
    remnant,
    and out of Mount Zion a band of
        survivors.
The zeal of the LORD Almighty
    will accomplish this.

33"Therefore this is what the LORD says
concerning the king of Assyria:

"He will not enter this city
    or shoot an arrow here.
He will not come before it with shield
    or build a siege ramp against it.
34By the way that he came he will
    return;
    he will not enter this city,"
                    declares the LORD.
35"I will defend this city and save it,
    for my sake and for the sake of David
        my servant!"

36Then the angel of the LORD went out
and put to death a hundred and eighty-five
thousand men in the Assyrian camp.
When the people got up the next morning—there were all the dead bodies! 37So
Sennacherib king of Assyria broke camp
and withdrew. He returned to Nineveh
and stayed there.

38One day, while he was worshiping in
the temple of his god Nisroch, his sons
Adrammelech and Sharezer cut him down

with the sword, and they escaped to the
land of Ararat. And Esarhaddon his son
succeeded him as king.

Hezekiah's Illness

38 In those days Hezekiah became ill
and was at the point of death. The
prophet Isaiah son of Amoz went to him
and said, "This is what the LORD says: Put
your house in order, because you are
going to die; you will not recover."

2Hezekiah turned his face to the wall
and prayed to the LORD, 3"Remember, O
LORD, how I have walked before you faithfully and with wholehearted devotion and
have done what is good in your eyes."
And Hezekiah wept bitterly.

4Then the word of the LORD came to
Isaiah: 5"Go and tell Hezekiah, 'This is
what the LORD, the God of your father
David, says: I have heard your prayer and
seen your tears; I will add fifteen years to
your life. 6And I will deliver you and this
city from the hand of the king of Assyria. I
will defend this city.

7"'This is the LORD's sign to you that the
LORD will do what he has promised: 8I will
make the shadow cast by the sun go back
the ten steps it has gone down on the
stairway of Ahaz.'" So the sunlight went
back the ten steps it had gone down.

9A writing of Hezekiah king of Judah
after his illness and recovery:

10I said, "In the prime of my life
    must I go through the gates of death*a*
    and be robbed of the rest of my
        years?"
11I said, "I will not again see the LORD,
    the LORD, in the land of the living;
no longer will I look on mankind,
    or be with those who now dwell in
        this world.*b*
12Like a shepherd's tent my house
    has been pulled down and taken from
        me.
Like a weaver I have rolled up my life,
    and he has cut me off from the loom;

day and night you made an end of
me.
[13]I waited patiently till dawn,
but like a lion he broke all my bones;
day and night you made an end of
me.
[14]I cried like a swift or thrush,
I moaned like a mourning dove.
My eyes grew weak as I looked to the
heavens.
I am troubled; O Lord, come to my
aid!"

[15]But what can I say?
He has spoken to me, and he himself
has done this.
I will walk humbly all my years
because of this anguish of my
soul.
[16]Lord, by such things men live;
and my spirit finds life in them
too.
You restored me to health
and let me live.
[17]Surely it was for my benefit
that I suffered such anguish.
In your love you kept me
from the pit of destruction;
you have put all my sins
behind your back.
[18]For the grave[c] cannot praise you,
death cannot sing your praise;
those who go down to the pit
cannot hope for your faithfulness.
[19]The living, the living—they praise you,
as I am doing today;
fathers tell their children
about your faithfulness.

[20]The LORD will save me,
and we will sing with stringed
instruments
all the days of our lives
in the temple of the LORD.

[21]Isaiah had said, "Prepare a poultice of
figs and apply it to the boil, and he will
recover."
[22]Hezekiah had asked, "What will be
the sign that I will go up to the temple of
the LORD?"

Envoys From Babylon

39 At that time Merodach-Baladan
son of Baladan king of Babylon
sent Hezekiah letters and a gift, because
he had heard of his illness and recovery.
[2]Hezekiah received the envoys gladly and
showed them what was in his storehouses—the silver, the gold, the spices,
the fine oil, his entire armoury and everything found among his treasures. There
was nothing in his palace or in all his kingdom that Hezekiah did not show them.
[3]Then Isaiah the prophet went to King
Hezekiah and asked, "What did those
men say, and where did they come from?"
"From a distant land," Hezekiah replied. "They came to me from Babylon."
[4]The prophet asked, "What did they see
in your palace?"
"They saw everything in my palace,"
Hezekiah said. "There is nothing among
my treasures that I did not show them."
[5]Then Isaiah said to Hezekiah, "Hear
the word of the LORD Almighty: [6]The time
will surely come when everything in your
palace, and all that your fathers have
stored up until this day, will be carried off
to Babylon. Nothing will be left, says the
LORD. [7]And some of your descendants,
your own flesh and blood who will be born
to you, will be taken away, and they will
become eunuchs in the palace of the king
of Babylon."
[8]"The word of the LORD you have
spoken is good," Hezekiah replied. For he
thought, "There will be peace and security
in my lifetime."

Comfort for God's People

40 Comfort, comfort my people,
says your God.
[2]Speak tenderly to Jerusalem,
and proclaim to her
that her hard service has been
completed,
that her sin has been paid for,
that she has received from the LORD's
hand
double for all her sins.

[c]18 Hebrew *Sheol*

³A voice of one calling:
"In the desert prepare
  the way for the Lord;^{*a*}
make straight in the wilderness
  a highway for our God.^{*b*}
⁴Every valley shall be raised up,
  every mountain and hill made low;
the rough ground shall become level,
  the rugged places a plain.
⁵And the glory of the Lord will be
    revealed,
  and all mankind together will see it.
      For the mouth of the Lord has
          spoken."

⁶A voice says, "Cry out."
  And I said, "What shall I cry?"

"All men are like grass,
  and all their glory is like the flowers
    of the field.
⁷The grass withers and the flowers fall,
  because the breath of the Lord blows
    on them.
  Surely the people are grass.
⁸The grass withers and the flowers fall,
  but the word of our God stands for
    ever."

⁹You who bring good tidings to Zion,
  go up on a high mountain.
You who bring good tidings to
    Jerusalem,^{*c*}
lift up your voice with a shout,
lift it up, do not be afraid;
  say to the towns of Judah,
  "Here is your God!"
¹⁰See, the Sovereign Lord comes with
    power,
  and his arm rules for him.
  See, his reward is with him,
  and his recompense accompanies him.
¹¹He tends his flock like a shepherd:
  He gathers the lambs in his arms
and carries them close to his heart;
  he gently leads those that have young.

¹²Who has measured the waters in the
  hollow of his hand,
or with the breadth of his hand
  marked off the heavens?
Who has held the dust of the earth in a
  basket,
  or weighed the mountains on the
    scales
  and the hills in a balance?
¹³Who has understood the mind^{*d*} of the
  Lord,
  or instructed him as his counsellor?
¹⁴Whom did the Lord consult to
  enlighten him,
  and who taught him the right way?
Who was it that taught him knowledge
  or showed him the path of
    understanding?

¹⁵Surely the nations are like a drop in a
  bucket;
  they are regarded as dust on the
    scales;
he weighs the islands as though they
  were fine dust.
¹⁶Lebanon is not sufficient for altar fires,
  nor its animals enough for burnt
    offerings.
¹⁷Before him all the nations are as
  nothing;
  they are regarded by him as worthless
  and less than nothing.

¹⁸To whom, then, will you compare God?
  What image will you compare him
    to?
¹⁹As for an idol, a craftsman casts it,
  and a goldsmith overlays it with gold
  and fashions silver chains for it.
²⁰A man too poor to present such an
    offering
  selects wood that will not rot.
He looks for a skilled craftsman
  to set up an idol that will not topple.

²¹Do you not know?
  Have you not heard?
Has it not been told you from the
  beginning?
  Have you not understood since the
  earth was founded?

---

a3 Or *A voice of one calling in the desert:* / *"Prepare the way for the Lord*
b3 Hebrew; Septuagint *make straight the paths of our God*
c9 Or *O Zion, bringer of good tidings,* / *go up on a high mountain.* / *O Jerusalem, bringer of good tidings*
d13 Or *Spirit;* or *spirit*

²²He sits enthroned above the circle of
the earth,
  and its people are like grasshoppers.
He stretches out the heavens like a
canopy,
  and spreads them out like a tent to
live in.
²³He brings princes to naught
  and reduces the rulers of this world to
nothing.
²⁴No sooner are they planted,
  no sooner are they sown,
  no sooner do they take root in the
ground,
than he blows on them and they wither,
  and a whirlwind sweeps them away
like chaff.

²⁵"To whom will you compare me?
  Or who is my equal?" says the Holy
One.
²⁶Lift your eyes and look to the heavens:
  Who created all these?
He who brings out the starry host one
by one,
  and calls them each by name.
Because of his great power and mighty
strength,
  not one of them is missing.

²⁷Why do you say, O Jacob,
  and complain, O Israel,
"My way is hidden from the LORD;
  my cause is disregarded by my
God"?
²⁸Do you not know?
  Have you not heard?
The LORD is the everlasting God,
  the Creator of the ends of the earth.
He will not grow tired or weary,
  and his understanding no-one can
fathom.
²⁹He gives strength to the weary
  and increases the power of the weak.
³⁰Even youths grow tired and weary,
  and young men stumble and fall;
³¹but those who hope in the LORD
  will renew their strength.
They will soar on wings like eagles;
  they will run and not grow weary,
  they will walk and not be faint.

The Helper of Israel

41 "Be silent before me, you islands!
  Let the nations renew their
strength!
Let them come forward and speak;
  let us meet together at the place of
judgment.

²"Who has stirred up one from the east,
  calling him in righteousness to his
service?ᵃ
He hands nations over to him
  and subdues kings before him.
He turns them to dust with his sword,
  to wind-blown chaff with his bow.
³He pursues them and moves on
unscathed,
  by a path his feet have not travelled
before.
⁴Who has done this and carried it
through,
  calling forth the generations from the
beginning?
I, the LORD—with the first of them
  and with the last—I am he."

⁵The islands have seen it and fear;
  the ends of the earth tremble.
They approach and come forward;
6   each helps the other
  and says to his brother, "Be strong!"
⁷The craftsman encourages the
goldsmith,
  and he who smooths with the
hammer
spurs on him who strikes the anvil.
He says of the welding, "It is good."
  He nails down the idol so that it will
not topple.

⁸"But you, O Israel, my servant,
  Jacob, whom I have chosen,
  you descendants of Abraham my
friend,
⁹I took you from the ends of the earth,
  from its farthest corners I called
you.
I said, 'You are my servant';
  I have chosen you and have not
rejected you.

ᵃ2 Or / *whom victory meets at every step*

¹⁰So do not fear, for I am with you;
do not be dismayed, for I am your
God.
I will strengthen you and help you;
I will uphold you with my righteous
right hand.

¹¹"All who rage against you
will surely be ashamed and
disgraced;
those who oppose you
will be as nothing and perish.
¹²Though you search for your enemies,
you will not find them.
Those who wage war against you
will be as nothing at all.
¹³For I am the LORD, your God,
who takes hold of your right hand
and says to you, Do not fear;
I will help you.
¹⁴Do not be afraid, O worm Jacob,
O little Israel,
for I myself will help you," declares the
LORD,
your Redeemer, the Holy One of
Israel.
¹⁵"See, I will make you into a
threshing-sledge,
new and sharp, with many teeth.
You will thresh the mountains and
crush them,
and reduce the hills to chaff.
¹⁶You will winnow them, the wind will
pick them up,
and a gale will blow them away.
But you will rejoice in the LORD
and glory in the Holy One of Israel.

¹⁷"The poor and needy search for water,
but there is none;
their tongues are parched with thirst.
But I the LORD will answer them;
I, the God of Israel, will not forsake
them.
¹⁸I will make rivers flow on barren
heights,
and springs within the valleys.
I will turn the desert into pools of
water,
and the parched ground into springs.
¹⁹I will put in the desert
the cedar and the acacia, the myrtle
and the olive.

I will set pines in the wasteland,
the fir and the cypress together,
²⁰so that people may see and know,
may consider and understand,
that the hand of the LORD has done this,
that the Holy One of Israel has
created it.

²¹"Present your case," says the LORD.
"Set forth your arguments," says
Jacob's King.
²²"Bring in ⌐your idols⌐ to tell us
what is going to happen.
Tell us what the former things were,
so that we may consider them
and know their final outcome.
Or declare to us the things to come,
²³ tell us what the future holds,
so that we may know you are gods.
Do something, whether good or bad,
so that we will be dismayed and filled
with fear.
²⁴But you are less than nothing
and your works are utterly worthless;
he who chooses you is detestable.

²⁵"I have stirred up one from the north,
and he comes—
one from the rising sun who calls on
my name.
He treads on rulers as if they were
mortar,
as if he were a potter treading the
clay.
²⁶Who told of this from the beginning, so
that we could know,
or beforehand, so that we could say,
'He was right'?
No-one told of this,
no-one foretold it,
no-one heard any words from you.
²⁷I was the first to tell Zion, 'Look, here
they are!'
I gave to Jerusalem a messenger of
good tidings.
²⁸I look but there is no-one—
no-one among them to give counsel,
no-one to give answer when I ask
them.
²⁹See, they are all false!
Their deeds amount to nothing;
their images are but wind and
confusion.

The Servant of the LORD

42 "Here is my servant, whom I uphold,
my chosen one in whom I delight;
I will put my Spirit on him
and he will bring justice to the
nations.
²He will not shout or cry out,
or raise his voice in the streets.
³A bruised reed he will not break,
and a smouldering wick he will not
snuff out.
In faithfulness he will bring forth
justice;
⁴ he will not falter or be discouraged
till he establishes justice on earth.
In his law the islands will put their
hope."

⁵This is what God the LORD says—
he who created the heavens and
stretched them out,
who spread out the earth and all that
comes out of it,
who gives breath to its people,
and life to those who walk on it:
⁶"I, the LORD, have called you in
righteousness;
I will take hold of your hand.
I will keep you and will make you
to be a covenant for the people
and a light for the Gentiles,
⁷to open eyes that are blind,
to free captives from prison
and to release from the dungeon
those who sit in darkness.

⁸"I am the LORD; that is my name!
I will not give my glory to another
or my praise to idols.
⁹See, the former things have taken
place,
and new things I declare;
before they spring into being
I announce them to you."

Song of Praise to the LORD

¹⁰Sing to the LORD a new song,
his praise from the ends of the earth,
you who go down to the sea, and all that
is in it,
you islands, and all who live in them.
¹¹Let the desert and its towns raise their
voices;
let the settlements where Kedar lives
rejoice.
Let the people of Sela sing for joy;
let them shout from the
mountaintops.
¹²Let them give glory to the LORD
and proclaim his praise in the islands.
¹³The LORD will march out like a mighty
man,
like a warrior he will stir up his zeal;
with a shout he will raise the battle cry
and will triumph over his enemies.

¹⁴"For a long time I have kept silent,
I have been quiet and held myself
back.
But now, like a woman in childbirth,
I cry out, I gasp and pant.
¹⁵I will lay waste the mountains and hills
and dry up all their vegetation;
I will turn rivers into islands
and dry up the pools.
¹⁶I will lead the blind by ways they have
not known,
along unfamiliar paths I will guide
them;
I will turn the darkness into light before
them
and make the rough places smooth.
These are the things I will do;
I will not forsake them.
¹⁷But those who trust in idols,
who say to images, 'You are our gods,'
will be turned back in utter shame.

Israel Blind and Deaf

¹⁸"Hear, you deaf;
look, you blind, and see!
¹⁹Who is blind but my servant,
and deaf like the messenger I send?
Who is blind like the one committed to
me,
blind like the servant of the LORD?
²⁰You have seen many things, but have
paid no attention;
your ears are open, but you hear
nothing."
²¹It pleased the LORD
for the sake of his righteousness

to make his law great and glorious.
22But this is a people plundered and
      looted,
   all of them trapped in pits
   or hidden away in prisons.
They have become plunder,
   with no-one to rescue them;
they have been made loot,
   with no-one to say, "Send them back."

23Which of you will listen to this
   or pay close attention in time to
      come?
24Who handed Jacob over to become
      loot,
   and Israel to the plunderers?
Was it not the LORD,
   against whom we have sinned?
For they would not follow his ways;
   they did not obey his law.
25So he poured out on them his burning
      anger,
   the violence of war.
It enveloped them in flames, yet they
      did not understand;
   it consumed them, but they did not
      take it to heart.

Israel's Only Saviour

43 But now, this is what the LORD
      says—
   he who created you, O Jacob,
   he who formed you, O Israel:
"Fear not, for I have redeemed you;
   I have summoned you by name; you
      are mine.
2When you pass through the waters,
   I will be with you;
and when you pass through the rivers,
   they will not sweep over you.
When you walk through the fire,
   you will not be burned;
   the flames will not set you ablaze.
3For I am the LORD, your God,
   the Holy One of Israel, your Saviour;
I give Egypt for your ransom,
   Cush*a* and Seba in your stead.
4Since you are precious and honoured in
      my sight,
   and because I love you,
I will give men in exchange for you,

and people in exchange for your life.
5Do not be afraid, for I am with you;
   I will bring your children from the east
   and gather you from the west.
6I will say to the north, 'Give them up!'
   and to the south, 'Do not hold them
      back.'
Bring my sons from afar
   and my daughters from the ends of
      the earth—
7everyone who is called by my name,
   whom I created for my glory,
   whom I formed and made."

8Lead out those who have eyes but are
      blind,
   who have ears but are deaf.
9All the nations gather together
   and the peoples assemble.
Which of them foretold this
   and proclaimed to us the former
      things?
Let them bring in their witnesses to
      prove they were right,
   so that others may hear and say, "It is
      true."
10"You are my witnesses," declares the
      LORD,
   "and my servant whom I have
      chosen,
so that you may know and believe me
   and understand that I am he.
Before me no god was formed,
   nor will there be one after me.
11I, even I, am the LORD,
   and apart from me there is no
      saviour.
12I have revealed and saved and
      proclaimed—
   I, and not some foreign god among
      you.
You are my witnesses," declares the
      LORD, "that I am God.
13   Yes, and from ancient days I am he.
No-one can deliver out of my hand.
   When I act, who can reverse it?"

God's Mercy and Israel's Unfaithfulness

14This is what the LORD says—
   your Redeemer, the Holy One of
      Israel:

a3 That is, the upper Nile region

"For your sake I will send to Babylon
and bring down as fugitives all the
Babylonians,*b*
in the ships in which they took pride.
¹⁵I am the LORD, your Holy One,
Israel's Creator, your King."

¹⁶This is what the LORD says—
he who made a way through the sea,
a path through the mighty waters,
¹⁷who drew out the chariots and horses,
the army and reinforcements
together,
and they lay there, never to rise again,
extinguished, snuffed out like a wick:
¹⁸"Forget the former things;
do not dwell on the past.
¹⁹See, I am doing a new thing!
Now it springs up; do you not
perceive it?
I am making a way in the desert
and streams in the wasteland.
²⁰The wild animals honour me,
the jackals and the owls,
because I provide water in the desert
and streams in the wasteland,
to give drink to my people, my chosen,
²¹ the people I formed for myself
that they may proclaim my praise.

²²"Yet you have not called upon me, O
Jacob,
you have not wearied yourselves for
me, O Israel.
²³You have not brought me sheep for
burnt offerings,
nor honoured me with your sacrifices.
I have not burdened you with grain
offerings
nor wearied you with demands for
incense.
²⁴You have not bought any fragrant
calamus for me,
or lavished on me the fat of your
sacrifices.
But you have burdened me with your
sins
and wearied me with your offences.

²⁵"I, even I, am he who blots out

your transgressions, for my own sake,
and remembers your sins no more.
²⁶Review the past for me,
let us argue the matter together;
state the case for your innocence.
²⁷Your first father sinned;
your spokesmen rebelled against me.
²⁸So I will disgrace the dignitaries of your
temple,
and I will consign Jacob to
destruction*c*
and Israel to scorn.

Israel the Chosen

44 "But now listen, O Jacob, my
servant,
Israel, whom I have chosen.
²This is what the LORD says—
he who made you, who formed you in
the womb,
and who will help you:
Do not be afraid, O Jacob, my servant,
Jeshurun, whom I have chosen.
³For I will pour water on the thirsty land,
and streams on the dry ground;
I will pour out my Spirit on your
offspring,
and my blessing on your descendants.
⁴They will spring up like grass in a
meadow,
like poplar trees by flowing streams.
⁵One will say, 'I belong to the LORD';
another will call himself by the name
of Jacob;
still another will write on his hand, 'The
LORD's',
and will take the name Israel.

The LORD, Not Idols

⁶"This is what the LORD says—
Israel's King and Redeemer, the
LORD Almighty:
I am the first and I am the last;
apart from me there is no God.
⁷Who then is like me? Let him proclaim
it.
Let him declare and lay out before
me

---

b14 Or *Chaldeans*
c28 The Hebrew term refers to the irrevocable giving over of things or persons to the LORD, often by totally destroying
them.

what has happened since I established
    my ancient people,
  and what is yet to come—
  yes, let him foretell what will come.
8Do not tremble, do not be afraid.
    Did I not proclaim this and foretell it
      long ago?
  You are my witnesses. Is there any God
    besides me?
  No, there is no other Rock; I know
    not one."

9All who make idols are nothing,
  and the things they treasure are
    worthless.
  Those who would speak up for them are
    blind;
  they are ignorant, to their own
    shame.
10Who shapes a god and casts an idol,
  which can profit him nothing?
11He and his kind will be put to shame;
  craftsmen are nothing but men.
  Let them all come together and take
    their stand;
  they will be brought down to terror
    and infamy.

12The blacksmith takes a tool
  and works with it in the coals;
  he shapes an idol with hammers,
    he forges it with the might of his arm.
  He gets hungry and loses his strength;
    he drinks no water and grows faint.
13The carpenter measures with a line
  and makes an outline with a marker;
  he roughs it out with chisels
    and marks it with compasses.
  He shapes it in the form of man,
    of man in all his glory,
    that it may dwell in a shrine.
14He cut down cedars,
  or perhaps took a cypress or oak.
  He let it grow among the trees of the
    forest,
  or planted a pine, and the rain made
    it grow.
15It is man's fuel for burning;
  some of it he takes and warms himself,
  he kindles a fire and bakes bread.
  But he also fashions a god and worships
    it;
  he makes an idol and bows down to it.

16Half of the wood he burns in the fire;
  over it he prepares his meal,
  he roasts his meat and eats his fill.
  He also warms himself and says,
    "Ah! I am warm; I see the fire."
17From the rest he makes a god, his idol;
  he bows down to it and worships.
  He prays to it and says,
    "Save me; you are my god."
18They know nothing, they understand
    nothing;
  their eyes are plastered over so that
    they cannot see,
  and their minds closed so that they
    cannot understand.
19No-one stops to think,
  no-one has the knowledge or
    understanding to say,
  "Half of it I used for fuel;
    I even baked bread over its coals,
    I roasted meat and I ate.
  Shall I make a detestable thing from
    what is left?
  Shall I bow down to a block of
    wood?"
20He feeds on ashes, a deluded heart
    misleads him;
  he cannot save himself, or say,
    "Is not this thing in my right hand a
    lie?"

21"Remember these things, O Jacob,
  for you are my servant, O Israel.
  I have made you, you are my servant;
    O Israel, I will not forget you.
22I have swept away your offences like a
    cloud,
  your sins like the morning mist.
  Return to me,
    for I have redeemed you."

23Sing for joy, O heavens, for the LORD
    has done this;
  shout aloud, O earth beneath.
  Burst into song, you mountains,
    you forests and all your trees,
  for the LORD has redeemed Jacob,
    he displays his glory in Israel.

Jerusalem to Be Inhabited

24"This is what the LORD says—
  your Redeemer, who formed you in
    the womb:

I am the LORD,
who has made all things,
who alone stretched out the heavens,
who spread out the earth by myself,

²⁵who foils the signs of false prophets
   and makes fools of diviners,
who overthrows the learning of the wise
   and turns it into nonsense,
²⁶who carries out the words of his
      servants
   and fulfils the predictions of his
      messengers,

who says of Jerusalem, 'It shall be
      inhabited,'
   of the towns of Judah, 'They shall be
      built,'
   and of their ruins, 'I will restore
      them,'
²⁷who says to the watery deep, 'Be dry,
   and I will dry up your streams,'
²⁸who says of Cyrus, 'He is my shepherd
   and will accomplish all that I please;
   he will say of Jerusalem, "Let it be
      rebuilt,"
   and of the temple, "Let its
      foundations be laid." '

45 "This is what the LORD says to his
      anointed,
   to Cyrus, whose right hand I take
      hold of
to subdue nations before him
   and to strip kings of their armour,
to open doors before him
   so that gates will not be shut:
²I will go before you
   and will level the mountains;^a
I will break down gates of bronze
   and cut through bars of iron.
³I will give you the treasures of darkness,
   riches stored in secret places,
so that you may know that I am the
      LORD,
   the God of Israel, who summons you
      by name.
⁴For the sake of Jacob my servant,
   of Israel my chosen,
I summon you by name
   and bestow on you a title of honour,

though you do not acknowledge me.
⁵I am the LORD, and there is no other;
   apart from me there is no God.
I will strengthen you,
   though you have not acknowledged
      me,
⁶so that from the rising of the sun
   to the place of its setting
men may know there is none besides
      me.
I am the LORD, and there is no other.
⁷I form the light and create darkness,
   I bring prosperity and create disaster;
   I, the LORD, do all these things.

⁸"You heavens above, rain down
      righteousness;
   let the clouds shower it down.
Let the earth open wide,
   let salvation spring up,
let righteousness grow with it;
   I, the LORD, have created it.

⁹"Woe to him who quarrels with his
      Maker,
   to him who is but a potsherd among
      the potsherds on the ground.
Does the clay say to the potter,
   'What are you making?'
Does your work say,
   'He has no hands'?
¹⁰Woe to him who says to his father,
   'What have you begotten?'
or to his mother,
   'What have you brought to birth?'

¹¹"This is what the LORD says—
   the Holy One of Israel, and its
      Maker:
Concerning things to come,
   do you question me about my
      children,
   or give me orders about the work of
      my hands?
¹²It is I who made the earth
   and created mankind upon it.
My own hands stretched out the
      heavens;
   I marshalled their starry hosts.
¹³I will raise up Cyrus^b in my
      righteousness:

---

^a2 Dead Sea Scrolls and Septuagint; the meaning of the word in the Masoretic Text is uncertain.
^b13 Hebrew *him*

I will make all his ways straight.
He will rebuild my city
and set my exiles free,
but not for a price or reward,
says the LORD Almighty."

14This is what the LORD says:

"The products of Egypt and the
merchandise of Cush,c
and those tall Sabeans—
they will come over to you
and will be yours;
they will trudge behind you,
coming over to you in chains.
They will bow down before you
and plead with you, saying,
'Surely God is with you, and there is no
other;
there is no other god.'"

15Truly you are a God who hides
himself,
O God and Saviour of Israel.
16All the makers of idols will be put to
shame and disgraced;
they will go off into disgrace
together.
17But Israel will be saved by the LORD
with an everlasting salvation;
you will never be put to shame or
disgraced,
to ages everlasting.

18For this is what the LORD says—
he who created the heavens,
he is God;
he who fashioned and made the earth,
he founded it;
he did not create it to be empty,
but formed it to be inhabited—
he says:
"I am the LORD,
and there is no other.
19I have not spoken in secret,
from somewhere in a land of
darkness;
I have not said to Jacob's descendants,
'Seek me in vain.'
I, the LORD, speak the truth;
I declare what is right.

20"Gather together and come;
assemble, you fugitives from the
nations.
Ignorant are those who carry about
idols of wood,
who pray to gods that cannot save.
21Declare what is to be, present it—
let them take counsel together.
Who foretold this long ago,
who declared it from the distant past?
Was it not I, the LORD?
And there is no God apart from me,
a righteous God and a Saviour;
there is none but me.

22"Turn to me and be saved,
all you ends of the earth;
for I am God, and there is no other.
23By myself I have sworn,
my mouth has uttered in all integrity
a word that will not be revoked:
Before me every knee will bow;
by me every tongue will swear.
24They will say of me, 'In the LORD alone
are righteousness and strength.'"
All who have raged against him
will come to him and be put to
shame.
25But in the LORD all the descendants of
Israel
will be found righteous and will exult.

Gods of Babylon

46 Bel bows down, Nebo stoops low;
their idols are borne by beasts
of burden.a
The images that are carried about are
burdensome,
a burden for the weary.
2They stoop and bow down together;
unable to rescue the burden,
they themselves go off into captivity.

3"Listen to me, O house of Jacob,
all you who remain of the house of
Israel,
you whom I have upheld since you were
conceived,
and have carried since your birth.
4Even to your old age and grey hairs

---

c14 That is, the upper Nile region   a1 Or are but beasts and cattle

I am he, I am he who will sustain you.
I have made you and I will carry you;
  I will sustain you and I will rescue you.

5"To whom will you compare me or
    count me equal?
  To whom will you liken me that we
    may be compared?
6Some pour out gold from their bags
  and weigh out silver on the scales;
they hire a goldsmith to make it into a
    god,
  and they bow down and worship it.
7They lift it to their shoulders and carry it;
  they set it up in its place, and there it
    stands.
  From that spot it cannot move.
Though one cries out to it, it does not
    answer;
  it cannot save him from his troubles.

8"Remember this, fix it in mind,
  take it to heart, you rebels.
9Remember the former things, those of
    long ago;
I am God, and there is no other;
  I am God, and there is none like me.
10I make known the end from the
    beginning,
  from ancient times, what is still to
    come.
I say: My purpose will stand,
  and I will do all that I please.
11From the east I summon a bird of prey;
  from a far-off land, a man to fulfil my
    purpose.
  What I have said, that will I bring about;
  what I have planned, that will I do.
12Listen to me, you stubborn-hearted,
  you who are far from righteousness.
13I am bringing my righteousness near,
  it is not far away;
  and my salvation will not be delayed.
I will grant salvation to Zion,
  my splendour to Israel.

The Fall of Babylon

47   "Go down, sit in the dust,
      Virgin Daughter of Babylon;
  sit on the ground without a throne,

Daughter of the Babylonians.[a]
No more will you be called
  tender or delicate.
2Take millstones and grind flour;
  take off your veil.
Lift up your skirts, bare your legs,
  and wade through the streams.
3Your nakedness will be exposed
  and your shame uncovered.
I will take vengeance;
  I will spare no-one."

4Our Redeemer—the Lord Almighty is
    his name—
  is the Holy One of Israel.

5"Sit in silence, go into darkness,
  Daughter of the Babylonians;
no more will you be called
  queen of kingdoms.
6I was angry with my people
  and desecrated my inheritance;
I gave them into your hand,
  and you showed them no mercy.
Even on the aged
  you laid a very heavy yoke.
7You said, 'I will continue for ever—
  the eternal queen!'
But you did not consider these things
  or reflect on what might happen.

8"Now then, listen, you wanton
    creature,
  lounging in your security
and saying to yourself,
  'I am, and there is none besides me.
I will never be a widow
  or suffer the loss of children.'
9Both of these will overtake you
  in a moment, on a single day:
  loss of children and widowhood.
They will come upon you in full
    measure,
  in spite of your many sorceries
  and all your potent spells.
10You have trusted in your wickedness
  and have said, 'No-one sees me.'
Your wisdom and knowledge mislead
    you
  when you say to yourself,
  'I am, and there is none besides me.'

a1 Or Chaldeans; also in verse 5

¹¹Disaster will come upon you,
  and you will not know how to conjure
    it away.
A calamity will fall upon you
  that you cannot ward off with a
    ransom;
a catastrophe you cannot foresee
  will suddenly come upon you.

¹²"Keep on, then, with your magic spells
  and with your many sorceries,
  which you have laboured at since
    childhood.
Perhaps you will succeed,
  perhaps you will cause terror.
¹³All the counsel you have received has
    only worn you out!
Let your astrologers come forward,
  those stargazers who make predictions
    month by month,
  let them save you from what is
    coming upon you.
¹⁴Surely they are like stubble;
  the fire will burn them up.
They cannot even save themselves
  from the power of the flame.
Here are no coals to warm anyone;
  here is no fire to sit by.
¹⁵That is all they can do for you—
  these you have laboured with
  and trafficked with since childhood.
Each of them goes on in his error;
  there is not one that can save you.

Stubborn Israel

48 "Listen to this, O house of Jacob,
   you who are called by the name of
     Israel
  and come from the line of Judah,
you who take oaths in the name of the
    LORD
  and invoke the God of Israel—
  but not in truth or righteousness—
²you who call yourselves citizens of the
    holy city
  and rely on the God of Israel—
  the LORD Almighty is his name:
³I foretold the former things long ago,
  my mouth announced them and I
    made them known;
  then suddenly I acted, and they came
    to pass.

⁴For I knew how stubborn you were;
  the sinews of your neck were iron,
  your forehead was bronze.
⁵Therefore I told you these things long
    ago;
  before they happened I announced
    them to you
so that you could not say,
  'My idols did them;
  my wooden image and metal god
    ordained them.'
⁶You have heard these things; look at
    them all.
  Will you not admit them?

"From now on I will tell you of new
    things,
  of hidden things unknown to you.
⁷They are created now, and not long
    ago;
  you have not heard of them before
    today.
So you cannot say,
  'Yes, I knew of them.'
⁸You have neither heard nor
    understood;
  from of old your ear has not been
    open.
Well do I know how treacherous you
    are;
  you were called a rebel from birth.
⁹For my own name's sake I delay my
    wrath;
  for the sake of my praise I hold it
    back from you,
  so as not to cut you off.
¹⁰See, I have refined you, though not as
    silver;
  I have tested you in the furnace of
    affliction.
¹¹For my own sake, for my own sake, I do
    this.
  How can I let myself be defamed?
  I will not yield my glory to another.

Israel Freed

¹²"Listen to me, O Jacob,
  Israel, whom I have called:
I am he;
  I am the first and I am the last.
¹³My own hand laid the foundations of
    the earth,

and my right hand spread out the
heavens;
when I summon them,
they all stand up together.

¹⁴"Come together, all of you, and listen:
Which of ⌞the idols⌟ has foretold
these things?
The LORD's chosen ally
will carry out his purpose against
Babylon;
his arm will be against the
Babylonians.^a
¹⁵I, even I, have spoken;
yes, I have called him.
I will bring him,
and he will succeed in his mission.

¹⁶"Come near me and listen to this:

"From the first announcement I have
not spoken in secret;
at the time it happens, I am there."

And now the Sovereign LORD has sent
me,
with his Spirit.

¹⁷This is what the LORD says—
your Redeemer, the Holy One of
Israel:
"I am the LORD your God,
who teaches you what is best for you,
who directs you in the way you
should go.
¹⁸If only you had paid attention to my
commands,
your peace would have been like a
river,
your righteousness like the waves of
the sea.
¹⁹Your descendants would have been like
the sand,
your children like its numberless
grains;
their name would never be cut off
nor destroyed from before me."

²⁰Leave Babylon,
flee from the Babylonians!
Announce this with shouts of joy
and proclaim it.
Send it out to the ends of the earth;

say, "The LORD has redeemed his
servant Jacob."
²¹They did not thirst when he led them
through the deserts;
he made water flow for them from the
rock;
he split the rock
and water gushed out.

²²"There is no peace," says the LORD,
"for the wicked."

The Servant of the LORD

49 Listen to me, you islands;
hear this, you distant nations:
Before I was born the LORD called me;
from my birth he has made mention
of my name.
²He made my mouth like a sharpened
sword,
in the shadow of his hand he hid me;
he made me into a polished arrow
and concealed me in his quiver.
³He said to me, "You are my servant,
Israel, in whom I will display my
splendour."
⁴But I said, "I have laboured to no
purpose;
I have spent my strength in vain and
for nothing.
Yet what is due to me is in the LORD's
hand,
and my reward is with my God."

⁵And now the LORD says—
he who formed me in the womb to be
his servant
to bring Jacob back to him
and gather Israel to himself,
for I am honoured in the eyes of the
LORD
and my God has been my strength—
⁶he says:
"It is too small a thing for you to be my
servant
to restore the tribes of Jacob
and bring back those of Israel I have
kept.
I will also make you a light for the
Gentiles,
that you may bring my salvation to
the ends of the earth."

---

^a14 Or *Chaldeans*; also in verse 20

7This is what the LORD says—
  the Redeemer and Holy One of
    Israel—
to him who was despised and abhorred
    by the nation,
  to the servant of rulers:
"Kings will see you and rise up,
  princes will see and bow down,
because of the LORD, who is faithful,
  the Holy One of Israel, who has
    chosen you."

Restoration of Israel

  8This is what the LORD says:

"In the time of my favour I will answer
    you,
  and in the day of salvation I will help
    you;
I will keep you and will make you
  to be a covenant for the people,
to restore the land
  and to reassign its desolate
    inheritances,
9to say to the captives, 'Come out,'
  and to those in darkness, 'Be free!'

"They will feed beside the roads
  and find pasture on every barren
    hill.
10They will neither hunger nor thirst,
  nor will the desert heat or the sun
    beat upon them.
He who has compassion on them will
    guide them
  and lead them beside springs of
    water.
11I will turn all my mountains into roads,
  and my highways will be raised up.
12See, they will come from afar—
  some from the north, some from the
    west,
  some from the region of Aswan."*a*

13Shout for joy, O heavens;
  rejoice, O earth;
  burst into song, O mountains!
For the LORD comforts his people
  and will have compassion on his
    afflicted ones.

14But Zion said, "The LORD has forsaken
    me,
  the Lord has forgotten me."

15"Can a mother forget the baby at her
    breast
  and have no compassion on the child
    she has borne?
Though she may forget,
  I will not forget you!
16See, I have engraved you on the palms
    of my hands;
  your walls are ever before me.
17Your sons hasten back,
  and those who laid you waste depart
    from you.
18Lift up your eyes and look around;
  all your sons gather and come to you.
As surely as I live," declares the LORD,
  "you will wear them all as ornaments;
  you will put them on, like a bride.

19"Though you were ruined and made
    desolate
  and your land laid waste,
now you will be too small for your
    people,
  and those who devoured you will be
    far away.
20The children born during your
    bereavement
  will yet say in your hearing,
'This place is too small for us;
  give us more space to live in.'
21Then you will say in your heart,
  'Who bore me these?
I was bereaved and barren;
  I was exiled and rejected.
  Who brought these up?
I was left all alone,
  but these—where have they come
    from?'"

  22This is what the Sovereign LORD says:

"See, I will beckon to the Gentiles,
  I will lift up my banner to the
    peoples;
they will bring your sons in their arms
  and carry your daughters on their
    shoulders.

a12 Dead Sea Scrolls; Masoretic Text Sinim

²³Kings will be your foster fathers,
  and their queens your nursing
    mothers.
They will bow down before you with
    their faces to the ground;
  they will lick the dust at your feet.
Then you will know that I am the LORD;
  those who hope in me will not be
    disappointed."

²⁴Can plunder be taken from warriors,
  or captives rescued from the fierce?^b

²⁵But this is what the LORD says:

"Yes, captives will be taken from
    warriors,
  and plunder retrieved from the
    fierce;
I will contend with those who
    contend with you,
  and your children I will save.
²⁶I will make your oppressors eat their
    own flesh;
  they will be drunk on their own
    blood, as with wine.
Then all mankind will know
  that I, the LORD, am your Saviour,
  your Redeemer, the Mighty One of
    Jacob."

Israel's Sin and the Servant's Obedience

50

This is what the LORD says:

"Where is your mother's certificate of
    divorce
  with which I sent her away?
Or to which of my creditors
  did I sell you?
Because of your sins you were sold;
  because of your transgressions your
    mother was sent away.
²When I came, why was there no-one?
  When I called, why was there no-one
    to answer?
Was my arm too short to ransom you?
  Do I lack the strength to rescue you?
By a mere rebuke I dry up the sea,
  I turn rivers into a desert;
their fish rot for lack of water
  and die of thirst.

³I clothe the sky with darkness
  and make sackcloth its covering."

⁴The Sovereign LORD has given me an
    instructed tongue,
  to know the word that sustains the
    weary.
He wakens me morning by morning,
  wakens my ear to listen like one
    being taught.
⁵The Sovereign LORD has opened my
    ears,
  and I have not been rebellious;
  I have not drawn back.
⁶I offered my back to those who beat
    me,
  my cheeks to those who pulled out
    my beard;
I did not hide my face
  from mocking and spitting.
⁷Because the Sovereign LORD helps me,
  I will not be disgraced.
Therefore have I set my face like flint,
  and I know I will not be put to
    shame.
⁸He who vindicates me is near.
  Who then will bring charges against
    me?
  Let us face each other!
Who is my accuser?
  Let him confront me!
⁹It is the Sovereign LORD who helps me.
  Who is he who will condemn me?
They will all wear out like a garment;
  the moths will eat them up.

¹⁰Who among you fears the LORD
  and obeys the word of his servant?
Let him who walks in the dark,
  who has no light,
trust in the name of the LORD
  and rely on his God.
¹¹But now, all you who light fires
  and provide yourselves with flaming
    torches,
go, walk in the light of your fires
  and of the torches you have set
    ablaze.
This is what you shall receive from my
    hand:
  You will lie down in torment.

^b24 Dead Sea Scrolls, Vulgate and Syriac (see also Septuagint and verse 25); Masoretic Text *righteous*

Everlasting Salvation for Zion

51

"Listen to me, you who pursue righteousness
and who seek the LORD:
Look to the rock from which you were cut
and to the quarry from which you were hewn;
2look to Abraham, your father,
and to Sarah, who gave you birth.
When I called him he was but one,
and I blessed him and made him many.
3The LORD will surely comfort Zion
and will look with compassion on all her ruins;
he will make her deserts like Eden,
her wastelands like the garden of the LORD.
Joy and gladness will be found in her,
thanksgiving and the sound of singing.

4"Listen to me, my people;
hear me, my nation:
The law will go out from me;
my justice will become a light to the nations.
5My righteousness draws near speedily,
my salvation is on the way,
and my arm will bring justice to the nations.
The islands will look to me
and wait in hope for my arm.
6Lift up your eyes to the heavens,
look at the earth beneath;
the heavens will vanish like smoke,
the earth will wear out like a garment
and its inhabitants die like flies.
But my salvation will last for ever,
my righteousness will never fail.

7"Hear me, you who know what is right,
you people who have my law in your hearts:
Do not fear the reproach of men
or be terrified by their insults.
8For the moth will eat them up like a garment;
the worm will devour them like wool.
But my righteousness will last for ever,

my salvation through all generations."

9Awake, awake! Clothe yourself with strength,
O arm of the LORD;
awake, as in days gone by,
as in generations of old.
Was it not you who cut Rahab to pieces,
who pierced that monster through?
10Was it not you who dried up the sea,
the waters of the great deep,
who made a road in the depths of the sea
so that the redeemed might cross over?
11The ransomed of the LORD will return.
They will enter Zion with singing;
everlasting joy will crown their heads.
Gladness and joy will overtake them,
and sorrow and sighing will flee away.

12"I, even I, am he who comforts you.
Who are you that you fear mortal men,
the sons of men, who are but grass,
13that you forget the LORD your Maker,
who stretched out the heavens
and laid the foundations of the earth,
that you live in constant terror every day
because of the wrath of the oppressor,
who is bent on destruction?
For where is the wrath of the oppressor?
14 The cowering prisoners will soon be set free;
they will not die in their dungeon,
nor will they lack bread.
15For I am the LORD your God,
who churns up the sea so that its waves roar—
the LORD Almighty is his name.
16I have put my words in your mouth
and covered you with the shadow of my hand—
I who set the heavens in place,
who laid the foundations of the earth,
and who say to Zion, 'You are my people.'"

The Cup of the LORD's Wrath

17Awake, awake!
    Rise up, O Jerusalem,
you who have drunk from the hand of
        the LORD
    the cup of his wrath,
you who have drained to its dregs
    the goblet that makes men stagger.
18Of all the sons she bore
    there was none to guide her;
of all the sons she brought up
    there was none to take her by the
        hand.
19These double calamities have come
        upon you—
    who can comfort you?—
ruin and destruction, famine and
        sword—
    who can*a* console you?
20Your sons have fainted;
    they lie at the head of every street,
    like antelope caught in a net.
They are filled with the wrath of the
        LORD
    and the rebuke of your God.

21Therefore hear this, you afflicted one,
    made drunk, but not with wine.
22This is what your Sovereign LORD says,
    your God, who defends his people:
"See, I have taken out of your hand
    the cup that made you stagger;
from that cup, the goblet of my wrath,
    you will never drink again.
23I will put it into the hands of your
        tormentors,
    who said to you,
    'Fall prostrate that we may walk over
        you.'
And you made your back like the
        ground,
    like a street to be walked over."

52 Awake, awake, O Zion,
    clothe yourself with strength.
Put on your garments of splendour,
    O Jerusalem, the holy city.
The uncircumcised and defiled
    will not enter you again.
2Shake off your dust;

rise up, sit enthroned, O Jerusalem.
Free yourself from the chains on your
        neck,
    O captive Daughter of Zion.

3For this is what the LORD says:

"You were sold for nothing,
    and without money you will be
        redeemed."

4For this is what the Sovereign LORD
says:

"At first my people went down to Egypt
        to live;
    lately, Assyria has oppressed them.

5"And now what do I have here?" declares the LORD.

"For my people have been taken away
        for nothing,
    and those who rule them mock,"*a*
                        declares the LORD.
"And all day long
    my name is constantly blasphemed.
6Therefore my people will know my
        name;
    therefore in that day they will know
    that it is I who foretold it.
    Yes, it is I."

7How beautiful on the mountains
    are the feet of those who bring good
        news,
who proclaim peace,
    who bring good tidings,
    who proclaim salvation,
who say to Zion,
    "Your God reigns!"
8Listen! Your watchmen lift up their
        voices;
    together they shout for joy.
When the LORD returns to Zion,
    they will see it with their own eyes.
9Burst into songs of joy together,
    you ruins of Jerusalem,
for the LORD has comforted his people,
    he has redeemed Jerusalem.

*a*19 Dead Sea Scrolls, Septuagint, Vulgate and Syriac; Masoretic Text / *how can I*
*a*5 Dead Sea Scrolls and Vulgate; Masoretic Text *wail*

¹⁰The LORD will lay bare his holy arm
in the sight of all the nations,
and all the ends of the earth will see
the salvation of our God.

¹¹Depart, depart, go out from there!
Touch no unclean thing!
Come out from it and be pure,
you who carry the vessels of the
LORD.
¹²But you will not leave in haste
or go in flight;
for the LORD will go before you,
the God of Israel will be your rear
guard.

The Suffering and Glory of the Servant

¹³See, my servant will act wisely;[b]
he will be raised and lifted up and
highly exalted.
¹⁴Just as there were many who were
appalled at him[c]—
his appearance was so disfigured
beyond that of any man
and his form marred beyond human
likeness—
¹⁵so will he sprinkle many nations,[d]
and kings will shut their mouths
because of him.
For what they were not told, they will
see,
and what they have not heard, they
will understand.

53 Who has believed our message
and to whom has the arm of the
LORD been revealed?
²He grew up before him like a tender
shoot,
and like a root out of dry ground.
He had no beauty or majesty to attract
us to him,
nothing in his appearance that we
should desire him.
³He was despised and rejected by men,
a man of sorrows, and familiar with
suffering.
Like one from whom men hide their
faces

he was despised, and we esteemed
him not.

⁴Surely he took up our infirmities
and carried our sorrows,
yet we considered him stricken by God,
smitten by him, and afflicted.
⁵But he was pierced for our
transgressions,
he was crushed for our iniquities;
the punishment that brought us peace
was upon him,
and by his wounds we are healed.
⁶We all, like sheep, have gone astray,
each of us has turned to his own way;
and the LORD has laid on him
the iniquity of us all.

⁷He was oppressed and afflicted,
yet he did not open his mouth;
he was led like a lamb to the slaughter,
and as a sheep before her shearers is
silent,
so he did not open his mouth.
⁸By oppression[a] and judgment he was
taken away.
And who can speak of his
descendants?
For he was cut off from the land of the
living;
for the transgression of my people he
was stricken.[b]
⁹He was assigned a grave with the
wicked,
and with the rich in his death,
though he had done no violence,
nor was any deceit in his mouth.

¹⁰Yet it was the LORD's will to crush him
and cause him to suffer,
and though the LORD makes[c] his life a
guilt offering,
he will see his offspring and prolong his
days,
and the will of the LORD will prosper
in his hand.
¹¹After the suffering of his soul,
he will see the light ⌊of life⌋[d] and be
satisfied;[e]

---

b13 Or will prosper   c14 Hebrew you   d15 Hebrew; Septuagint so will many nations marvel at him
a8 Or From arrest   b8 Or away. / Yet who of his generation considered / that he was cut off from the land of the living /
for the transgression of my people, / to whom the blow was due?   c10 Hebrew though you make
d11 Dead Sea Scrolls (see also Septuagint); Masoretic Text does not have the light ⌊of life⌋.
e11 Or (with Masoretic Text) 11He will see the result of the suffering of his soul / and be satisfied

by his knowledge ^{f} my righteous servant
　　will justify many,
　and he will bear their iniquities.
^{12}Therefore I will give him a portion
　　among the great,^{g}
　and he will divide the spoils with the
　　strong,^{h}
because he poured out his life unto
　　death,
　and was numbered with the
　　transgressors.
For he bore the sin of many,
　and made intercession for the
　　transgressors.

The Future Glory of Zion

54 "Sing, O barren woman,
　　you who never bore a child;
burst into song, shout for joy,
　you who were never in labour;
because more are the children of the
　　desolate woman
　than of her who has a husband,"
　　　　　　　　says the LORD.
^{2}"Enlarge the place of your tent,
　stretch your tent curtains wide,
　　do not hold back;
lengthen your cords,
　strengthen your stakes.
^{3}For you will spread out to the right and
　　to the left;
　your descendants will dispossess
　　nations
　and settle in their desolate cities.

^{4}"Do not be afraid; you will not suffer
　　shame.
　Do not fear disgrace; you will not be
　　humiliated.
You will forget the shame of your youth
　and remember no more the reproach
　　of your widowhood.
^{5}For your Maker is your husband—
　the LORD Almighty is his name—
the Holy One of Israel is your
　　Redeemer;
　he is called the God of all the earth.
^{6}The LORD will call you back
　as if you were a wife deserted and
　　distressed in spirit—

a wife who married young,
　only to be rejected," says your God.
^{7}"For a brief moment I abandoned you,
　but with deep compassion I will bring
　　you back.
^{8}In a surge of anger
　I hid my face from you for a moment,
but with everlasting kindness
　I will have compassion on you,"
　says the LORD your Redeemer.

^{9}"To me this is like the days of Noah,
　　when I swore that the waters of Noah
　　　would never again cover the
　　　earth.
So now I have sworn not to be angry
　　with you,
　never to rebuke you again.
^{10}Though the mountains be shaken
　　and the hills be removed,
yet my unfailing love for you will not be
　　shaken
　nor my covenant of peace be
　　removed,"
　says the LORD, who has compassion
　　on you.

^{11}"O afflicted city, lashed by storms and
　　not comforted,
　I will build you with stones of
　　turquoise,^{a}
　your foundations with sapphires.^{b}
^{12}I will make your battlements of rubies,
　your gates of sparkling jewels,
　and all your walls of precious stones.
^{13}All your sons will be taught by the
　　LORD,
　and great will be your children's
　　peace.
^{14}In righteousness you will be
　　established:
　Tyranny will be far from you;
　　you will have nothing to fear.
Terror will be far removed;
　it will not come near you.
^{15}If anyone does attack you, it will not be
　　my doing;
　whoever attacks you will surrender to
　　you.

^{16}"See, it is I who created the blacksmith
　who fans the coals into flame

---

f11 Or by knowledge of him　　*812 Or many*　　*h12 Or numerous*
a11 The meaning of the Hebrew for this word is uncertain.　　*b11 Or lapis lazuli*

and forges a weapon fit for its work.
And it is I who have created the
  destroyer to work havoc;
17 no weapon forged against you will
  prevail,
  and you will refute every tongue that
    accuses you.
This is the heritage of the servants of
  the LORD,
  and this is their vindication from me,"
                    declares the LORD.

Invitation to the Thirsty

55 "Come, all you who are thirsty,
  come to the waters;
and you who have no money,
  come, buy and eat!
Come, buy wine and milk
  without money and without cost.
2Why spend money on what is not bread,
  and your labour on what does not
    satisfy?
Listen, listen to me, and eat what is
  good,
  and your soul will delight in the
    richest of fare.
3Give ear and come to me;
  hear me, that your soul may live.
I will make an everlasting covenant with
  you,
  my faithful love promised to David.
4See, I have made him a witness to the
  peoples,
  a leader and commander of the
    peoples.
5Surely you will summon nations you
  know not,
  and nations that do not know you will
    hasten to you,
because of the LORD your God,
  the Holy One of Israel,
  for he has endowed you with
    splendour."

6Seek the LORD while he may be found;
  call on him while he is near.
7Let the wicked forsake his way
  and the evil man his thoughts.
Let him turn to the LORD, and he will
  have mercy on him,
  and to our God, for he will freely
    pardon.

8"For my thoughts are not your
  thoughts,
  neither are your ways my ways,"
                    declares the LORD.
9"As the heavens are higher than the
  earth,
  so are my ways higher than your ways
  and my thoughts than your thoughts.
10As the rain and the snow
  come down from heaven,
  and do not return to it
  without watering the earth
  and making it bud and flourish,
  so that it yields seed for the sower
    and bread for the eater,
11so is my word that goes out from my
  mouth:
  It will not return to me empty,
  but will accomplish what I desire
    and achieve the purpose for which I
      sent it.
12You will go out in joy
  and be led forth in peace;
the mountains and hills
  will burst into song before you,
  and all the trees of the field
    will clap their hands.
13Instead of the thornbush will grow the
  pine tree,
  and instead of briers the myrtle will
    grow.
This will be for the LORD's renown,
  for an everlasting sign,
  which will not be destroyed."

Salvation for Others

56 This is what the LORD says:
  "Maintain justice
    and do what is right,
  for my salvation is close at hand
    and my righteousness will soon be
      revealed.
2Blessed is the man who does this,
  the man who holds it fast,
who keeps the Sabbath without
  desecrating it,
  and keeps his hand from doing any
    evil."

3Let no foreigner who has bound himself
  to the LORD say,

"The LORD will surely exclude me
    from his people."
And let not any eunuch complain,
    "I am only a dry tree."

⁴For this is what the LORD says:

"To the eunuchs who keep my
        Sabbaths,
    who choose what pleases me
    and hold fast to my covenant—
⁵to them I will give within my temple and
        its walls
    a memorial and a name
    better than sons and daughters;
I will give them an everlasting name
    that will not be cut off.
⁶And foreigners who bind themselves to
        the LORD
    to serve him,
to love the name of the LORD,
    and to worship him,
all who keep the Sabbath without
        desecrating it
    and who hold fast to my covenant—
⁷these I will bring to my holy mountain
    and give them joy in my house of
        prayer.
Their burnt offerings and sacrifices
    will be accepted on my altar;
for my house will be called
    a house of prayer for all nations."
⁸The Sovereign LORD declares—
    he who gathers the exiles of Israel:
"I will gather still others to them
    besides those already gathered."

God's Accusation Against the Wicked

⁹Come, all you beasts of the field,
    come and devour, all you beasts of
        the forest!
¹⁰Israel's watchmen are blind,
    they all lack knowledge;
they are all mute dogs,
    they cannot bark;
they lie around and dream,
    they love to sleep.
¹¹They are dogs with mighty appetites;
    they never have enough.
They are shepherds who lack
        understanding;
    they all turn to their own way,

each seeks his own gain.
¹²"Come," each one cries, "let me get
        wine!
    Let us drink our fill of beer!
And tomorrow will be like today,
    or even far better."

57 The righteous perish,
        and no-one ponders it in his
        heart;
devout men are taken away,
    and no-one understands
that the righteous are taken away
    to be spared from evil.
²Those who walk uprightly
    enter into peace;
    they find rest as they lie in death.

³"But you—come here, you sons of a
        sorceress,
    you offspring of adulterers and
        prostitutes!
⁴Whom are you mocking?
    At whom do you sneer
    and stick out your tongue?
Are you not a brood of rebels,
    the offspring of liars?
⁵You burn with lust among the oaks
    and under every spreading tree;
you sacrifice your children in the
        ravines
    and under the overhanging crags.
⁶⌐The idols⌐ among the smooth stones of
        the ravines are your portion;
    they, they are your lot.
Yes, to them you have poured out drink
        offerings
    and offered grain offerings.
    In the light of these things, should I
        relent?
⁷You have made your bed on a high and
        lofty hill;
    there you went up to offer your
        sacrifices.
⁸Behind your doors and your
        doorposts
    you have put your pagan symbols.
Forsaking me, you uncovered your bed,
    you climbed into it and opened it
        wide;
you made a pact with those whose beds
        you love,
    and you looked on their nakedness.

⁹You went to Molech*ᵃ* with olive oil
and increased your perfumes.
You sent your ambassadors*ᵇ* far away;
you descended to the grave*ᶜ* itself!
¹⁰You were wearied by all your ways,
but you would not say, 'It is
hopeless.'
You found renewal of your strength,
and so you did not faint.

¹¹"Whom have you so dreaded and
feared
that you have been false to me,
and have neither remembered me
nor pondered this in your hearts?
Is it not because I have long been silent
that you do not fear me?
¹²I will expose your righteousness and
your works,
and they will not benefit you.
¹³When you cry out for help,
let your collection ⌊of idols⌋ save you!
The wind will carry all of them off,
a mere breath will blow them away.
But the man who makes me his refuge
will inherit the land
and possess my holy mountain."

Comfort for the Contrite

¹⁴And it will be said:

"Build up, build up, prepare the road!
Remove the obstacles out of the way
of my people."
¹⁵For this is what the high and lofty One
says—
he who lives for ever, whose name is
holy:
"I live in a high and holy place,
but also with him who is contrite and
lowly in spirit,
to revive the spirit of the lowly
and to revive the heart of the
contrite.
¹⁶I will not accuse for ever,
nor will I always be angry,
for then the spirit of man would grow
faint before me—
the breath of man that I have created.
¹⁷I was enraged by his sinful greed;

I punished him, and hid my face in
anger,
yet he kept on in his wilful ways.
¹⁸I have seen his ways, but I will heal
him;
I will guide him and restore comfort
to him,
¹⁹ creating praise on the lips of the
mourners in Israel.
Peace, peace, to those far and near,"
says the LORD. "And I will heal
them."
²⁰But the wicked are like the tossing sea,
which cannot rest,
whose waves cast up mire and mud.
²¹"There is no peace," says my God, "for
the wicked."

True Fasting

58

"Shout it aloud, do not hold back.
Raise your voice like a trumpet.
Declare to my people their rebellion
and to the house of Jacob their sins.
²For day after day they seek me out;
they seem eager to know my ways,
as if they were a nation that does what is
right
and has not forsaken the commands
of its God.
They ask me for just decisions
and seem eager for God to come near
them.
³'Why have we fasted,' they say,
'and you have not seen it?
Why have we humbled ourselves,
and you have not noticed?'

"Yet on the day of your fasting, you do
as you please
and exploit all your workers.
⁴Your fasting ends in quarrelling and
strife,
and in striking each other with
wicked fists.
You cannot fast as you do today
and expect your voice to be heard on
high.
⁵Is this the kind of fast I have chosen,
only a day for a man to humble
himself?

ᵃ9 Or *to the king*   *ᵇ9* Or *idols*   *ᶜ9* Hebrew *Sheol*

Is it only for bowing one's head like a
  reed
  and for lying on sackcloth and ashes?
Is that what you call a fast,
  a day acceptable to the LORD?

⁶"Is not this the kind of fasting I have
  chosen:
to loose the chains of injustice
  and untie the cords of the yoke,
to set the oppressed free
  and break every yoke?
⁷Is it not to share your food with the
  hungry
  and to provide the poor wanderer
    with shelter—
when you see the naked, to clothe him,
  and not to turn away from your own
    flesh and blood?
⁸Then your light will break forth like the
  dawn,
  and your healing will quickly appear;
then your righteousness*a* will go before
  you,
  and the glory of the LORD will be your
    rear guard.
⁹Then you will call, and the LORD will
  answer;
  you will cry for help, and he will say:
    Here am I.

"If you do away with the yoke of
  oppression,
  with the pointing finger and malicious
    talk,
¹⁰and if you spend yourselves on behalf of
  the hungry
  and satisfy the needs of the oppressed,
then your light will rise in the darkness,
  and your night will become like the
    noonday.
¹¹The LORD will guide you always;
  he will satisfy your needs in a
    sun-scorched land
  and will strengthen your frame.
You will be like a well-watered garden,
  like a spring whose waters never fail.
¹²Your people will rebuild the ancient
  ruins
  and will raise up the age-old
    foundations;

you will be called Repairer of Broken
  Walls,
  Restorer of Streets with Dwellings.

¹³"If you keep your feet from breaking
  the Sabbath
  and from doing as you please on my
    holy day,
if you call the Sabbath a delight
  and the LORD's holy day honourable,
and if you honour it by not going your
  own way
  and not doing as you please or
    speaking idle words,
¹⁴then you will find your joy in the LORD,
  and I will cause you to ride on the
    heights of the land
  and to feast on the inheritance of
    your father Jacob."
              The mouth of the LORD
                        has spoken.

Sin, Confession and Redemption

59 Surely the arm of the LORD is not
      too short to save,
  nor his ear too dull to hear.
²But your iniquities have separated
    you from your God;
  your sins have hidden his face from you,
    so that he will not hear.
³For your hands are stained with blood,
    your fingers with guilt.
Your lips have spoken lies,
    and your tongue mutters wicked
      things.
⁴No-one calls for justice;
    no-one pleads his case with integrity.
They rely on empty arguments and
    speak lies;
  they conceive trouble and give birth
    to evil.
⁵They hatch the eggs of vipers
    and spin a spider's web.
Whoever eats their eggs will die,
  and when one is broken, an adder is
    hatched.
⁶Their cobwebs are useless for clothing;
  they cannot cover themselves with
    what they make.
Their deeds are evil deeds,

a8 Or *your righteous One*

and acts of violence are in their
   hands.
7Their feet rush into sin;
   they are swift to shed innocent blood.
Their thoughts are evil thoughts;
   ruin and destruction mark their ways.
8The way of peace they do not know;
   there is no justice in their paths.
They have turned them into crooked
   roads;
   no-one who walks in them will know
    peace.

9So justice is far from us,
   and righteousness does not reach us.
We look for light, but all is darkness;
   for brightness, but we walk in deep
    shadows.
10Like the blind we grope along the wall,
   feeling our way like men without
    eyes.
At midday we stumble as if it were
   twilight;
   among the strong, we are like the
    dead.
11We all growl like bears;
   we moan mournfully like doves.
We look for justice, but find none;
   for deliverance, but it is far away.

12For our offences are many in your sight,
   and our sins testify against us.
Our offences are ever with us,
   and we acknowledge our iniquities:
13rebellion and treachery against the
   LORD,
   turning our backs on our God,
   fomenting oppression and revolt,
   uttering lies our hearts have
    conceived.
14So justice is driven back,
   and righteousness stands at a
    distance;
truth has stumbled in the streets,
   honesty cannot enter.
15Truth is nowhere to be found,
   and whoever shuns evil becomes a
    prey.

The LORD looked and was displeased
   that there was no justice.

16He saw that there was no-one,
   he was appalled that there was
    no-one to intervene;
so his own arm worked salvation for him,
   and his own righteousness sustained
    him.
17He put on righteousness as his
   breastplate,
   and the helmet of salvation on his
    head;
he put on the garments of vengeance
   and wrapped himself in zeal as in a
    cloak.
18According to what they have done,
   so will he repay
wrath to his enemies
   and retribution to his foes;
   he will repay the islands their due.
19From the west, men will fear the name
   of the LORD,
   and from the rising of the sun, they
    will revere his glory.
For he will come like a pent-up flood
   that the breath of the LORD drives
    along.[a]

20"The Redeemer will come to Zion,
   to those in Jacob who repent of their
    sins,"
              declares the LORD.

21"As for me, this is my covenant with
them," says the LORD. "My Spirit, who is
on you, and my words that I have put in
your mouth will not depart from your
mouth, or from the mouths of your children, or from the mouths of their descendants from this time on and for ever," says
the LORD.

The Glory of Zion

60 "Arise, shine, for your light has
   come,
   and the glory of the LORD rises upon
    you.
2See, darkness covers the earth
   and thick darkness is over the
    peoples,
but the LORD rises upon you
   and his glory appears over you.

a19 Or When the enemy comes in like a flood, / the Spirit of the LORD will put him to flight

³Nations will come to your light,
 and kings to the brightness of your
  dawn.

⁴"Lift up your eyes and look about you:
 All assemble and come to you;
your sons come from afar,
 and your daughters are carried on the
  arm.
⁵Then you will look and be radiant,
 your heart will throb and swell with
  joy;
the wealth on the seas will be brought to
  you,
 to you the riches of the nations will
  come.
⁶Herds of camels will cover your land,
 young camels of Midian and Ephah.
And all from Sheba will come,
 bearing gold and incense
 and proclaiming the praise of the
  LORD.
⁷All Kedar's flocks will be gathered to
  you,
 the rams of Nebaioth will serve you;
they will be accepted as offerings on my
  altar,
 and I will adorn my glorious temple.

⁸"Who are these that fly along like
  clouds,
 like doves to their nests?
⁹Surely the islands look to me;
 in the lead are the ships of Tarshish,ᵃ
bringing your sons from afar,
 with their silver and gold,
to the honour of the LORD your God,
 the Holy One of Israel,
 for he has endowed you with
  splendour.

¹⁰"Foreigners will rebuild your walls,
 and their kings will serve you.
Though in anger I struck you,
 in favour I will show you compassion.
¹¹Your gates will always stand open,
 they will never be shut, day or night,
so that men may bring you the wealth of
  the nations—
 their kings led in triumphal
  procession.

¹²For the nation or kingdom that will not
  serve you will perish;
 it will be utterly ruined.

¹³"The glory of Lebanon will come to
  you,
 the pine, the fir and the cypress
  together,
to adorn the place of my sanctuary;
 and I will glorify the place of my feet.
¹⁴The sons of your oppressors will come
  bowing before you;
 all who despise you will bow down at
  your feet
and will call you the City of the LORD,
 Zion of the Holy One of Israel.

¹⁵"Although you have been forsaken and
  hated,
 with no-one travelling through,
I will make you the everlasting pride
 and the joy of all generations.
¹⁶You will drink the milk of nations
 and be nursed at royal breasts.
Then you will know that I, the LORD,
  am your Saviour,
 your Redeemer, the Mighty One of
  Jacob.
¹⁷Instead of bronze I will bring you gold,
 and silver in place of iron.
Instead of wood I will bring you bronze,
 and iron in place of stones.
I will make peace your governor
 and righteousness your ruler.
¹⁸No longer will violence be heard in your
  land,
 nor ruin or destruction within your
  borders,
but you will call your walls Salvation
 and your gates Praise.
¹⁹The sun will no more be your light by
  day,
 nor will the brightness of the moon
  shine on you,
for the LORD will be your everlasting
  light,
 and your God will be your glory.
²⁰Your sun will never set again,
 and your moon will wane no more;
the LORD will be your everlasting light,
 and your days of sorrow will end.

ᵃ9 Or the trading ships

²¹Then will all your people be righteous
and they will possess the land for
ever.
They are the shoot I have planted,
the work of my hands,
for the display of my splendour.
²²The least of you will become a
thousand,
the smallest a mighty nation.
I am the LORD;
in its time I will do this swiftly."

The Year of the LORD's Favour

61 The Spirit of the Sovereign LORD
is on me,
because the LORD has anointed me
to preach good news to the poor.
He has sent me to bind up the
broken-hearted,
to proclaim freedom for the captives
and release from darkness for the
prisoners,ᵃ
²to proclaim the year of the LORD's
favour
and the day of vengeance of our God,
to comfort all who mourn,
3   and provide for those who grieve in
Zion—
to bestow on them a crown of beauty
instead of ashes,
the oil of gladness
instead of mourning,
and a garment of praise
instead of a spirit of despair.
They will be called oaks of
righteousness,
a planting of the LORD
for the display of his splendour.

⁴They will rebuild the ancient ruins
and restore the places long
devastated;
they will renew the ruined cities
that have been devastated for
generations.
⁵Aliens will shepherd your flocks;
foreigners will work your fields and
vineyards.
⁶And you will be called priests of the
LORD,

you will be named ministers of our
God.
You will feed on the wealth of nations,
and in their riches you will boast.

⁷Instead of their shame
my people will receive a double
portion,
and instead of disgrace
they will rejoice in their inheritance;
and so they will inherit a double portion
in their land,
and everlasting joy will be theirs.

⁸"For I, the LORD, love justice;
I hate robbery and iniquity.
In my faithfulness I will reward them
and make an everlasting covenant
with them.
⁹Their descendants will be known
among the nations
and their offspring among the peoples.
All who see them will acknowledge
that they are a people the LORD has
blessed."

¹⁰I delight greatly in the LORD;
my soul rejoices in my God.
For he has clothed me with garments of
salvation
and arrayed me in a robe of
righteousness,
as a bridegroom adorns his head like a
priest,
and as a bride adorns herself with her
jewels.
¹¹For as the soil makes the young plant
come up
and a garden causes seeds to grow,
so the Sovereign LORD will make
righteousness and praise
spring up before all nations.

Zion's New Name

62 For Zion's sake I will not keep
silent,
for Jerusalem's sake I will not remain
quiet,
till her righteousness shines out like the
dawn,

ᵃ1 Hebrew; Septuagint the blind

her salvation like a blazing torch.
²The nations will see your righteousness,
and all kings your glory;
you will be called by a new name
that the mouth of the LORD will
bestow.
³You will be a crown of splendour in the
LORD's hand,
a royal diadem in the hand of your
God.
⁴No longer will they call you Deserted,
or name your land Desolate.
But you will be called Hephzibah,ᵃ
and your land Beulah;ᵇ
for the LORD will take delight in you,
and your land will be married.
⁵As a young man marries a maiden,
so will your sonsᶜ marry you;
as a bridegroom rejoices over his bride,
so will your God rejoice over you.

⁶I have posted watchmen on your walls,
O Jerusalem;
they will never be silent day or night.
You who call on the LORD,
give yourselves no rest,
⁷and give him no rest till he establishes
Jerusalem
and makes her the praise of the earth.

⁸The LORD has sworn by his right hand
and by his mighty arm:
"Never again will I give your grain
as food for your enemies,
and never again will foreigners drink
the new wine
for which you have toiled;
⁹but those who harvest it will eat it
and praise the LORD,
and those who gather the grapes will
drink it
in the courts of my sanctuary."

¹⁰Pass through, pass through the gates!
Prepare the way for the people.
Build up, build up the highway!
Remove the stones.
Raise a banner for the nations.

¹¹The LORD has made proclamation
to the ends of the earth:

"Say to the Daughter of Zion,
'See, your Saviour comes!
See, his reward is with him,
and his recompense accompanies
him.'"
¹²They will be called the Holy People,
the Redeemed of the LORD;
and you will be called Sought After,
the City No Longer Deserted.

God's Day of Vengeance and Redemption

63 Who is this coming from Edom,
from Bozrah, with his garments
stained crimson?
Who is this, robed in splendour,
striding forward in the greatness of
his strength?

"It is I, speaking in righteousness,
mighty to save."

²Why are your garments red,
like those of one treading the
winepress?

³"I have trodden the winepress alone;
from the nations no-one was with me.
I trampled them in my anger
and trod them down in my wrath;
their blood spattered my garments,
and I stained all my clothing.
⁴For the day of vengeance was in my
heart,
and the year of my redemption has
come.
⁵I looked, but there was no-one to help,
I was appalled that no-one gave
support;
so my own arm worked salvation for
me,
and my own wrath sustained me.
⁶I trampled the nations in my anger;
in my wrath I made them drunk
and poured their blood on the
ground."

Praise and Prayer

⁷I will tell of the kindnesses of the LORD,
the deeds for which he is to be
praised,

ᵃ4 *Hephzibah* means *my delight is in her.*   ᵇ4 *Beulah* means *married.*   ᶜ5 Or *Builder*

according to all the LORD has done
for us—
yes, the many good things he has done
for the house of Israel,
according to his compassion and
many kindnesses.
8He said, "Surely they are my people,
sons who will not be false to me";
and so he became their Saviour.
9In all their distress he too was
distressed,
and the angel of his presence saved
them.
In his love and mercy he redeemed
them;
he lifted them up and carried them
all the days of old.
10Yet they rebelled
and grieved his Holy Spirit.
So he turned and became their enemy
and he himself fought against them.

11Then his people recalled[a] the days of
old,
the days of Moses and his people—
where is he who brought them through
the sea,
with the shepherd of his flock?
Where is he who set
his Holy Spirit among them,
12who sent his glorious arm of power
to be at Moses' right hand,
who divided the waters before them,
to gain for himself everlasting
renown,
13who led them through the depths?
Like a horse in open country,
they did not stumble;
14like cattle that go down to the plain,
they were given rest by the Spirit of
the LORD.
This is how you guided your people
to make for yourself a glorious name.

15Look down from heaven and see
from your lofty throne, holy and
glorious.
Where are your zeal and your might?
Your tenderness and compassion are
withheld from us.
16But you are our Father,

though Abraham does not know us
or Israel acknowledge us;
you, O LORD, are our Father,
our Redeemer from of old is your
name.
17Why, O LORD, do you make us wander
from your ways
and harden our hearts so that we do
not revere you?
Return for the sake of your servants,
the tribes that are your inheritance.
18For a little while your people possessed
your holy place,
but now our enemies have trampled
down your sanctuary.
19We are yours from of old;
but you have not ruled over them,
they have not been called by your
name.[b]

64 Oh, that you would rend
the heavens and come down,
that the mountains would tremble
before you!
2As when fire sets twigs ablaze
and causes water to boil,
come down to make your name known
to your enemies
and cause the nations to quake before
you!
3For when you did awesome things that
we did not expect,
you came down, and the mountains
trembled before you.
4Since ancient times no-one has heard,
no ear has perceived,
no eye has seen any God besides you,
who acts on behalf of those who wait
for him.
5You come to the help of those who
gladly do right,
who remember your ways.
But when we continued to sin against
them,
you were angry.
How then can we be saved?
6All of us have become like one who is
unclean,
and all our righteous acts are like
filthy rags;
we all shrivel up like a leaf,

a11 Or But may he recall   _b19 Or We are like those you have never ruled, / like those never called by your name_

and like the wind our sins sweep us
away.
⁷No-one calls on your name
or strives to lay hold of you;
for you have hidden your face from us
and made us waste away because of
our sins.

⁸Yet, O LORD, you are our Father.
We are the clay, you are the potter;
we are all the work of your hand.
⁹Do not be angry beyond measure, O
LORD;
do not remember our sins for ever.
Oh, look upon us we pray,
for we are all your people.
¹⁰Your sacred cities have become a
desert;
even Zion is a desert, Jerusalem a
desolation.
¹¹Our holy and glorious temple, where
our fathers praised you,
has been burned with fire,
and all that we treasured lies in ruins.
¹²After all this, O LORD, will you hold
yourself back?
Will you keep silent and punish us
beyond measure?

Judgment and Salvation

65 "I revealed myself to those
who did not ask for me;
I was found by those who did not
seek me.
To a nation that did not call on my
name,
I said, 'Here am I, here am I.'
²All day long I have held out my hands
to an obstinate people,
who walk in ways not good,
pursuing their own imaginations—
³a people who continually provoke me
to my very face,
offering sacrifices in gardens
and burning incense on altars of
brick;
⁴who sit among the graves
and spend their nights keeping secret
vigil;
who eat the flesh of pigs,
and whose pots hold broth of unclean
meat;

⁵who say, 'Keep away; don't come near
me,
for I am too sacred for you!'
Such people are smoke in my nostrils,
a fire that keeps burning all day.

⁶"See, it stands written before me;
I will not keep silent but will pay back
in full;
I will pay it back into their laps—
⁷both your sins and the sins of your
fathers,"
says the LORD.
"Because they burned sacrifices on the
mountains
and defied me on the hills,
I will measure into their laps
the full payment for their former
deeds."

⁸This is what the LORD says:

"As when juice is still found in a cluster
of grapes
and men say, 'Don't destroy it,
there is yet some good in it,'
so will I do on behalf of my
servants;
I will not destroy them all.
⁹I will bring forth descendants from
Jacob,
and from Judah those who will
possess my mountains;
my chosen people will inherit them,
and there will my servants live.
¹⁰Sharon will become a pasture for
flocks,
and the Valley of Achor a resting
place for herds,
for my people who seek me.

¹¹"But as for you who forsake the LORD
and forget my holy mountain,
who spread a table for Fortune
and fill bowls of mixed wine for
Destiny,
¹²I will destine you for the sword,
and you will all bend down for the
slaughter;
for I called but you did not answer,
I spoke but you did not listen.
You did evil in my sight
and chose what displeases me."

¹³Therefore this is what the Sovereign
LORD says:

"My servants will eat,
  but you will go hungry;
my servants will drink,
  but you will go thirsty;
my servants will rejoice,
  but you will be put to shame.
¹⁴My servants will sing
  out of the joy of their hearts,
but you will cry out
  from anguish of heart
  and wail in brokenness of spirit.
¹⁵You will leave your name
  to my chosen ones as a curse;
the Sovereign LORD will put you to
    death,
  but to his servants he will give
    another name.
¹⁶Whoever invokes a blessing in the land
  will do so by the God of truth;
he who takes an oath in the land
  will swear by the God of truth.
For the past troubles will be forgotten
  and hidden from my eyes.

New Heavens and a New Earth

¹⁷"Behold, I will create
  new heavens and a new earth.
The former things will not be
    remembered,
  nor will they come to mind.
¹⁸But be glad and rejoice for ever
  in what I will create,
for I will create Jerusalem to be a delight
  and its people a joy.
¹⁹I will rejoice over Jerusalem
  and take delight in my people;
the sound of weeping and of crying
  will be heard in it no more.

²⁰"Never again will there be in it
  an infant who lives but a few days,
  or an old man who does not live out
    his years;
he who dies at a hundred
  will be thought a mere youth;
he who fails to reach*ᵃ* a hundred
  will be considered accursed.

²¹They will build houses and dwell in
    them;
  they will plant vineyards and eat their
    fruit.
²²No longer will they build houses and
    others live in them,
  or plant and others eat.
For as the days of a tree,
  so will be the days of my people;
my chosen ones will long enjoy
  the works of their hands.
²³They will not toil in vain
  or bear children doomed to
    misfortune;
for they will be a people blessed by the
    LORD,
  they and their descendants with
    them.
²⁴Before they call I will answer;
  while they are still speaking I will
    hear.
²⁵The wolf and the lamb will feed
    together,
  and the lion will eat straw like the ox,
  but dust will be the serpent's food.
They will neither harm nor destroy
  on all my holy mountain,"
                         says the LORD.

Judgment and Hope

66

This is what the LORD says:

"Heaven is my throne,
  and the earth is my footstool.
Where is the house you will build for
    me?
  Where will my resting place be?
²Has not my hand made all these
    things,
  and so they came into being?"
                       declares the LORD.

"This is the one I esteem:
  he who is humble and contrite in
    spirit,
  and trembles at my word.
³But whoever sacrifices a bull
  is like one who kills a man,
and whoever offers a lamb,
  like one who breaks a dog's neck;

ᵃ20 Or / the sinner who reaches

whoever makes a grain offering
    is like one who presents pig's blood,
and whoever burns memorial incense,
    like one who worships an idol.
They have chosen their own ways,
    and their souls delight in their
      abominations;
[4]so I also will choose harsh treatment for
    them
    and will bring upon them what they
      dread.
For when I called, no-one answered,
    when I spoke, no-one listened.
They did evil in my sight
    and chose what displeases me."

[5]Hear the word of the LORD,
    you who tremble at his word;
"Your brothers who hate you,
    and exclude you because of my name,
      have said,
'Let the LORD be glorified,
    that we may see your joy!'
Yet they will be put to shame.
[6]Hear that uproar from the city,
    hear that noise from the temple!
It is the sound of the LORD
    repaying his enemies all they deserve.

[7]"Before she goes into labour,
    she gives birth;
before the pains come upon her,
    she delivers a son.
[8]Who has ever heard of such a thing?
    Who has ever seen such things?
Can a country be born in a day
    or a nation be brought forth in a
      moment?
Yet no sooner is Zion in labour
    than she gives birth to her children.
[9]Do I bring to the moment of birth
    and not give delivery?" says the
      LORD.
"Do I close up the womb
    when I bring to delivery?" says your
      God.
[10]"Rejoice with Jerusalem and be glad
    for her,
    all you who love her;
rejoice greatly with her,
    all you who mourn over her.

[11]For you will nurse and be satisfied
    at her comforting breasts;
you will drink deeply
    and delight in her overflowing
      abundance."

[12]For this is what the LORD says:

"I will extend peace to her like a river,
    and the wealth of nations like a
      flooding stream;
you will nurse and be carried on her
    arm
    and dandled on her knees.
[13]As a mother comforts her child,
    so will I comfort you;
and you will be comforted over
      Jerusalem."

[14]When you see this, your heart will
    rejoice
    and you will flourish like grass;
the hand of the LORD will be made
      known to his servants,
    but his fury will be shown to his foes.
[15]See, the LORD is coming with fire,
    and his chariots are like a whirlwind;
he will bring down his anger with fury,
    and his rebuke with flames of fire.
[16]For with fire and with his sword
    the LORD will execute judgment upon
      all men,
    and many will be those slain by the
      LORD.

[17]"Those who consecrate and purify themselves to go into the gardens, following the one in the midst of[a] those who eat the flesh of pigs and rats and other abominable things—they will meet their end together," declares the LORD.

[18]"And I, because of their actions and their imaginations, am about to come[b] and gather all nations and tongues, and they will come and see my glory.

[19]"I will set a sign among them, and I will send some of those who survive to the nations—to Tarshish, to the Libyans[c] and Lydians (famous as archers), to Tubal and Greece, and to the distant islands that have not heard of my fame or seen my

[a]17 Or gardens behind one of your temples, and   [b]18 The meaning of the Hebrew for this clause is uncertain.
[c]19 Some Septuagint manuscripts Put (Libyans); Hebrew Pul

glory. They will proclaim my glory among the nations. 20And they will bring all your brothers, from all the nations, to my holy mountain in Jerusalem as an offering to the LORD—on horses, in chariots and wagons, and on mules and camels," says the LORD. "They will bring them, as the Israelites bring their grain offerings, to the temple of the LORD in ceremonially clean vessels. 21And I will select some of them also to be priests and Levites," says the LORD.

22"As the new heavens and the new earth that I make will endure before me," declares the LORD, "so will your name and descendants endure. 23From one New Moon to another and from one Sabbath to another, all mankind will come and bow down before me," says the LORD. 24"And they will go out and look upon the dead bodies of those who rebelled against me; their worm will not die, nor will their fire be quenched, and they will be loathsome to all mankind."

Jeremiah

1 The words of Jeremiah son of Hilkiah, one of the priests at Anathoth in the territory of Benjamin. ²The word of the LORD came to him in the thirteenth year of the reign of Josiah son of Amon king of Judah, ³and through the reign of Jehoiakim son of Josiah king of Judah, down to the fifth month of the eleventh year of Zedekiah son of Josiah king of Judah, when the people of Jerusalem went into exile.

The Call of Jeremiah

⁴The word of the LORD came to me, saying,

⁵"Before I formed you in the womb I
    knew*ᵃ* you,
  before you were born I set you apart;
  I appointed you as a prophet to the
    nations."

⁶"Ah, Sovereign LORD," I said, "I do not know how to speak; I am only a child."

⁷But the LORD said to me, "Do not say, 'I am only a child.' You must go to everyone I send you to and say whatever I command you. ⁸Do not be afraid of them, for I am with you and will rescue you," declares the LORD.

⁹Then the LORD reached out his hand and touched my mouth and said to me, "Now, I have put my words in your mouth. ¹⁰See, today I appoint you over nations and kingdoms to uproot and tear down, to destroy and overthrow, to build and to plant."

¹¹The word of the LORD came to me: "What do you see, Jeremiah?"

"I see the branch of an almond tree," I replied.

¹²The LORD said to me, "You have seen correctly, for I am watching*ᵇ* to see that my word is fulfilled."

¹³The word of the LORD came to me again: "What do you see?"

"I see a boiling pot, tilting away from the north," I answered.

¹⁴The LORD said to me, "From the north disaster will be poured out on all who live in the land. ¹⁵I am about to summon all the peoples of the northern kingdoms," declares the LORD.

"Their kings will come and set up their
    thrones
  in the entrance of the gates of
    Jerusalem;
they will come against all her
    surrounding walls
  and against all the towns of Judah.
¹⁶I will pronounce my judgments on my
    people
  because of their wickedness in
    forsaking me,
in burning incense to other gods
  and in worshipping what their hands
    have made.

¹⁷"Get yourself ready! Stand up and say to them whatever I command you. Do not be terrified by them, or I will terrify you before them. ¹⁸Today I have made you a fortified city, an iron pillar and a bronze wall to stand against the whole land—

ᵃ5 Or *chose*   *ᵇ12* The Hebrew for *watching* sounds like the Hebrew for *almond tree.*

against the kings of Judah, its officials, its priests and the people of the land. ¹⁹They will fight against you but will not overcome you, for I am with you and will rescue you," declares the LORD.

Israel Forsakes God

2 The word of the LORD came to me: ²"Go and proclaim in the hearing of Jerusalem:

"'I remember the devotion of your
     youth,
   how as a bride you loved me
and followed me through the desert,
   through a land not sown.
³Israel was holy to the LORD,
   the firstfruits of his harvest;
all who devoured her were held guilty,
   and disaster overtook them,'"
                    declares the LORD.

⁴Hear the word of the LORD, O house of
     Jacob,
   all you clans of the house of Israel.

⁵This is what the LORD says:

"What fault did your fathers find in me,
   that they strayed so far from me?
They followed worthless idols
   and became worthless themselves.
⁶They did not ask, 'Where is the LORD,
   who brought us up out of Egypt
and led us through the barren
     wilderness,
   through a land of deserts and rifts,
a land of drought and darkness,ᵃ
   a land where no-one travels and
     no-one lives?'
⁷I brought you into a fertile land
   to eat its fruit and rich produce.
But you came and defiled my land
   and made my inheritance detestable.
⁸The priests did not ask,
   'Where is the LORD?'
Those who deal with the law did not
     know me;

the leaders rebelled against me.
The prophets prophesied by Baal,
   following worthless idols.

⁹"Therefore I bring charges against you
     again,"
                    declares the LORD.
"And I will bring charges against
   your children's children.
¹⁰Cross over to the coasts of Kittimᵇ and
     look,
   send to Kedarᶜ and observe closely;
   see if there has ever been anything
     like this:
¹¹Has a nation ever changed its gods?
   (Yet they are not gods at all.)
But my people have exchanged theirᵈ
     Glory
   for worthless idols.
¹²Be appalled at this, O heavens,
   and shudder with great horror,"
                    declares the LORD.
¹³"My people have committed two sins:
They have forsaken me,
   the spring of living water,
and have dug their own cisterns,
   broken cisterns that cannot hold
     water.
¹⁴Is Israel a servant, a slave by birth?
   Why then has he become plunder?
¹⁵Lions have roared;
   they have growled at him.
They have laid waste his land;
   his towns are burned and deserted.
¹⁶Also, the men of Memphisᵉ and
     Tahpanhes
   have shaved the crown of your head.ᶠ
¹⁷Have you not brought this on
     yourselves
   by forsaking the LORD your God
   when he led you in the way?
¹⁸Now why go to Egypt
   to drink water from the Shihor?ᵍ
And why go to Assyria
   to drink water from the River?ʰ
¹⁹Your wickedness will punish you;
   your backsliding will rebuke you.
Consider then and realise
   how evil and bitter it is for you

ᵃ6 Or *and the shadow of death*   ᵇ10 That is, Cyprus and western coastlands
ᶜ10 The home of Bedouin tribes in the Syro-Arabian desert
ᵈ11 Masoretic Text; an ancient Hebrew scribal tradition *my*   ᵉ16 Hebrew *Noph*
ᶠ16 Or *have cracked your skull*   ᵍ18 That is, a branch of the Nile   ʰ18 That is, the Euphrates

when you forsake the LORD your God
  and have no awe of me,"
                    declares the Lord,
                        the LORD Almighty.

20"Long ago you broke off your yoke
  and tore off your bonds;
  you said, 'I will not serve you!'
Indeed, on every high hill
  and under every spreading tree
  you lay down as a prostitute.
21I had planted you like a choice vine
  of sound and reliable stock.
How then did you turn against me
  into a corrupt, wild vine?
22Although you wash yourself with soda
  and use an abundance of soap,
  the stain of your guilt is still before
    me,"
                declares the Sovereign LORD.
23"How can you say, 'I am not defiled;
  I have not run after the Baals'?
See how you behaved in the valley;
  consider what you have done.
You are a swift she-camel
  running here and there,
24a wild donkey accustomed to the desert,
  sniffing the wind in her craving—
  in her heat who can restrain her?
Any males that pursue her need not tire
    themselves;
  at mating time they will find her.
25Do not run until your feet are bare
  and your throat is dry.
But you said, 'It's no use!
  I love foreign gods,
  and I must go after them.'

26"As a thief is disgraced when he is
    caught,
  so the house of Israel is disgraced—
they, their kings and their officials,
  their priests and their prophets.
27They say to wood, 'You are my father,'
  and to stone, 'You gave me birth.'
They have turned their backs to me
  and not their faces;
yet when they are in trouble, they say,
  'Come and save us!'
28Where then are the gods you made for
    yourselves?
  Let them come if they can save you
    when you are in trouble!

For you have as many gods
  as you have towns, O Judah.

29"Why do you bring charges against me?
  You have all rebelled against me,"
                        declares the LORD.
30"In vain I punished your people;
  they did not respond to correction.
Your sword has devoured your
    prophets
  like a ravening lion.

31"You of this generation, consider the
word of the LORD:

"Have I been a desert to Israel
  or a land of great darkness?
Why do my people say, 'We are free to
    roam;
  we will come to you no more'?
32Does a maiden forget her jewellery,
  a bride her wedding ornaments?
Yet my people have forgotten me,
  days without number.
33How skilled you are at pursuing love!
  Even the worst of women can learn
    from your ways.
34On your clothes men find
  the lifeblood of the innocent poor,
  though you did not catch them
    breaking in.
Yet in spite of all this
35   you say, 'I am innocent;
  he is not angry with me.'
But I will pass judgment on you
  because you say, 'I have not
    sinned.'
36Why do you go about so much,
  changing your ways?
You will be disappointed by Egypt
  as you were by Assyria.
37You will also leave that place
  with your hands on your head,
for the LORD has rejected those you
    trust;
  you will not be helped by them.

3 "If a man divorces his wife
    and she leaves him and marries
    another man,
  should he return to her again?
  Would not the land be completely
    defiled?

But you have lived as a prostitute with
  many lovers—
  would you now return to me?"
              declares the LORD.
2"Look up to the barren heights and see.
  Is there any place where you have not
    been ravished?
By the roadside you sat waiting for
  lovers,
  sat like a nomad[a] in the desert.
You have defiled the land
  with your prostitution and
    wickedness.
3Therefore the showers have been
  withheld,
  and no spring rains have fallen.
Yet you have the brazen look of a
  prostitute;
  you refuse to blush with shame.
4Have you not just called to me:
  'My Father, my friend from my youth,
5will you always be angry?
  Will your wrath continue for ever?'
This is how you talk,
  but you do all the evil you can."

Unfaithful Israel

6During the reign of King Josiah, the
LORD said to me, "Have you seen what
faithless Israel has done? She has gone up
on every high hill and under every spreading tree and has committed adultery there.
7I thought that after she had done all this
she would return to me but she did not,
and her unfaithful sister Judah saw it. 8I
gave faithless Israel her certificate of divorce and sent her away because of all her
adulteries. Yet I saw that her unfaithful
sister Judah had no fear; she also went out
and committed adultery. 9Because Israel's
immorality mattered so little to her, she
defiled the land and committed adultery
with stone and wood. 10In spite of all this,
her unfaithful sister Judah did not return
to me with all her heart, but only in pretence," declares the LORD.

11The LORD said to me, "Faithless Israel
is more righteous than unfaithful Judah.
12Go, proclaim this message towards the
north:

"'Return, faithless Israel,' declares the
  LORD,
'I will frown on you no longer,
for I am merciful,' declares the LORD,
'I will not be angry for ever.
13Only acknowledge your guilt—
  you have rebelled against the LORD
    your God,
you have scattered your favours to
  foreign gods
  under every spreading tree,
  and have not obeyed me,'"
              declares the LORD.

14"Return, faithless people," declares
the LORD, "for I am your husband. I will
choose you—one from a town and two
from a clan—and bring you to Zion.
15Then I will give you shepherds after my
own heart, who will lead you with knowledge and understanding. 16In those days,
when your numbers have increased greatly in the land," declares the LORD, "men
will no longer say, 'The ark of the covenant of the LORD.' It will never enter their
minds or be remembered; it will not be
missed, nor will another one be made.
17At that time they will call Jerusalem The
Throne of the LORD, and all nations will
gather in Jerusalem to honour the name of
the LORD. No longer will they follow the
stubbornness of their evil hearts. 18In
those days the house of Judah will join the
house of Israel, and together they will
come from a northern land to the land I
gave your forefathers as an inheritance.

19"I myself said,

"'How gladly would I treat you like
  sons
  and give you a desirable land,
  the most beautiful inheritance of any
    nation.'
I thought you would call me 'Father'
  and not turn away from following
    me.
20But like a woman unfaithful to her
  husband,
  so you have been unfaithful to me, O
    house of Israel,"
              declares the LORD.

---

a2 Or an Arab

21A cry is heard on the barren heights,
　　the weeping and pleading of the
　　　　people of Israel,
　　because they have perverted their ways
　　　and have forgotten the LORD their
　　　　God.

22"Return, faithless people;
　　I will cure you of backsliding."

　　"Yes, we will come to you,
　　　for you are the LORD our God.
23Surely the ⌐idolatrous⌐ commotion on
　　　the hills
　　and mountains is a deception;
　　surely in the LORD our God
　　　is the salvation of Israel.
24From our youth shameful gods have
　　　consumed
　　the fruits of our fathers' labour—
　　their flocks and herds,
　　　their sons and daughters.
25Let us lie down in our shame,
　　and let our disgrace cover us.
　　We have sinned against the LORD our
　　　God,
　　both we and our fathers;
　　from our youth till this day
　　　we have not obeyed the LORD our
　　　　God."

4 "If you will return, O Israel,
　　return to me,"
　　　　　　　　declares the LORD.
　　"If you put your detestable idols out of
　　　my sight
　　and no longer go astray,
2and if in a truthful, just and righteous
　　　way
　　you swear, 'As surely as the LORD
　　　lives,'
　　then the nations will be blessed by him
　　and in him they will glory."

3This is what the LORD says to the men of
Judah and to Jerusalem:

　　"Break up your unploughed ground
　　and do not sow among thorns.
4Circumcise yourselves to the LORD,
　　circumcise your hearts,

　　you men of Judah and people of
　　　Jerusalem,
　　or my wrath will break out and burn
　　　like fire
　　because of the evil you have done—
　　burn with no-one to quench it.

Disaster From the North

5"Announce in Judah and proclaim in
　　Jerusalem and say:
　　'Sound the trumpet throughout the
　　　land!'
　　Cry aloud and say:
　　'Gather together!
　　Let us flee to the fortified cities!'
6Raise the signal to go to Zion!
　　Flee for safety without delay!
　　For I am bringing disaster from the
　　　north,
　　even terrible destruction."

7A lion has come out of his lair;
　　a destroyer of nations has set out.
　　He has left his place
　　to lay waste your land.
　　Your towns will lie in ruins
　　without inhabitant.
8So put on sackcloth,
　　lament and wail,
　　for the fierce anger of the LORD
　　has not turned away from us.

9"In that day," declares the LORD,
　　"the king and the officials will lose
　　　heart,
　　the priests will be horrified,
　　and the prophets will be appalled."

10Then I said, "Ah, Sovereign LORD,
how completely you have deceived this
people and Jerusalem by saying, 'You will
have peace,' when the sword is at our
throats."

11At that time this people and Jerusalem will be told, "A scorching wind
from the barren heights in the desert
blows towards my people, but not to winnow or cleanse; 12a wind too strong for
that comes from me.*a* Now I pronounce
my judgments against them."

---

a12 Or *comes at my command*

¹³Look! He advances like the clouds,
  his chariots come like a whirlwind,
his horses are swifter than eagles.
  Woe to us! We are ruined!
¹⁴O Jerusalem, wash the evil from your
  heart and be saved.
  How long will you harbour wicked
    thoughts?
¹⁵A voice is announcing from Dan,
  proclaiming disaster from the hills of
    Ephraim.
¹⁶"Tell this to the nations,
  proclaim it to Jerusalem:
'A besieging army is coming from a
  distant land,
  raising a war cry against the cities of
    Judah.
¹⁷They surround her like men guarding a
  field,
  because she has rebelled against
    me,'"
                declares the LORD.
¹⁸"Your own conduct and actions
  have brought this upon you.
This is your punishment.
  How bitter it is!
  How it pierces to the heart!"

¹⁹Oh, my anguish, my anguish!
  I writhe in pain.
Oh, the agony of my heart!
  My heart pounds within me,
  I cannot keep silent.
For I have heard the sound of the
  trumpet;
  I have heard the battle cry.
²⁰Disaster follows disaster;
  the whole land lies in ruins.
In an instant my tents are destroyed,
  my shelter in a moment.
²¹How long must I see the battle standard
  and hear the sound of the trumpet?

²²"My people are fools;
  they do not know me.
They are senseless children;
  they have no understanding.
They are skilled in doing evil;
  they know not how to do good."

²³I looked at the earth,
  and it was formless and empty;
and at the heavens,

  and their light was gone.
²⁴I looked at the mountains,
  and they were quaking;
  all the hills were swaying.
²⁵I looked, and there were no people;
  every bird in the sky had flown away.
²⁶I looked, and the fruitful land was a
  desert;
  all its towns lay in ruins
  before the LORD, before his fierce
    anger.

²⁷This is what the LORD says:

"The whole land will be ruined,
  though I will not destroy it
    completely.
²⁸Therefore the earth will mourn
  and the heavens above grow dark,
because I have spoken and will not
  relent,
  I have decided and will not turn
    back."

²⁹At the sound of horsemen and archers
  every town takes to flight.
Some go into the thickets;
  some climb up among the rocks.
All the towns are deserted;
  no-one lives in them.

³⁰What are you doing, O devastated one?
  Why dress yourself in scarlet
  and put on jewels of gold?
Why shade your eyes with paint?
  You adorn yourself in vain.
Your lovers despise you;
  they seek your life.

³¹I hear a cry as of a woman in labour,
  a groan as of one bearing her first
    child—
the cry of the Daughter of Zion
    gasping for breath,
  stretching out her hands and saying,
"Alas! I am fainting;
  my life is given over to murderers."

Not One Is Upright

5 "Go up and down the streets of
    Jerusalem
  look around and consider,

search through her squares.
If you can find but one person
   who deals honestly and seeks the
      truth,
   I will forgive this city.
²Although they say, 'As surely as the
      LORD lives,'
   still they are swearing falsely."

³O LORD, do not your eyes look for
      truth?
   You struck them, but they felt no
      pain;
   you crushed them but they refused
      correction.
They made their faces harder than
      stone
   and refused to repent.
⁴I thought, "These are only the poor;
   they are foolish,
for they do not know the way of the
      LORD,
   the requirements of their God.
⁵So I will go to the leaders
   and speak to them;
surely they know the way of the LORD,
   the requirements of their God."
But with one accord they too had
      broken off the yoke
   and torn off the bonds.
⁶Therefore a lion from the forest will
      attack them,
   a wolf from the desert will ravage
      them,
a leopard will lie in wait near their
      towns
   to tear to pieces any who venture out,
for their rebellion is great
   and their backslidings many.

⁷"Why should I forgive you?
   Your children have forsaken me
   and sworn by gods that are not gods.
I supplied all their needs,
   yet they committed adultery
   and thronged to the houses of
      prostitutes.
⁸They are well-fed, lusty stallions,
   each neighing for another man's wife.
⁹Should I not punish them for this?"
   declares the LORD.
"Should I not avenge myself
   on such a nation as this?

¹⁰"Go through her vineyards and ravage
      them,
   but do not destroy them completely.
Strip off her branches,
   for these people do not belong to the
      LORD.
¹¹The house of Israel and the house of
      Judah
   have been utterly unfaithful to me,"
                     declares the LORD.

¹²They have lied about the LORD;
   they said, "He will do nothing!
No harm will come to us;
   we will never see sword or famine.
¹³The prophets are but wind
   and the word is not in them;
   so let what they say be done to them."

¹⁴Therefore this is what the LORD God
Almighty says:

   "Because the people have spoken these
      words,
   I will make my words in your mouth a
      fire
   and these people the wood it
      consumes.
¹⁵O house of Israel," declares the LORD,
   "I am bringing a distant nation
      against you—
an ancient and enduring nation,
   a people whose language you do not
      know,
   whose speech you do not understand.
¹⁶Their quivers are like an open grave;
   all of them are mighty warriors.
¹⁷They will devour your harvests and
      food,
   devour your sons and daughters;
they will devour your flocks and herds,
   devour your vines and fig-trees.
With the sword they will destroy
   the fortified cities in which you trust.

¹⁸"Yet even in those days," declares the
LORD, "I will not destroy you completely.
¹⁹And when the people ask, 'Why has the
LORD our God done all this to us?' you will
tell them, 'As you have forsaken me and
served foreign gods in your own land, so
now you will serve foreigners in a land not
your own.'

20"Announce this to the house of Jacob
and proclaim it in Judah:
21Hear this, you foolish and senseless
people,
who have eyes but do not see,
who have ears but do not hear:
22Should you not fear me?" declares the
LORD.
"Should you not tremble in my
presence?
I made the sand a boundary for the sea,
an everlasting barrier it cannot
cross.
The waves may roll, but they cannot
prevail;
they may roar, but they cannot cross
it.
23But these people have stubborn and
rebellious hearts;
they have turned aside and gone
away.
24They do not say to themselves,
'Let us fear the LORD our God,
who gives autumn and spring rains in
season,
who assures us of the regular weeks
of harvest.'
25Your wrongdoings have kept these
away;
your sins have deprived you of
good.

26"Among my people are wicked men
who lie in wait like men who snare
birds
and like those who set traps to catch
men.
27Like cages full of birds,
their houses are full of deceit;
they have become rich and powerful
28 and have grown fat and sleek.
Their evil deeds have no limit;
they do not plead the case of the
fatherless to win it,
they do not defend the rights of the
poor.
29Should I not punish them for this?"
declares the LORD.
"Should I not avenge myself
on such a nation as this?

30"A horrible and shocking thing
has happened in the land:

31The prophets prophesy lies,
the priests rule by their own
authority,
and my people love it this way.
But what will you do in the end?

Jerusalem Under Siege

6 "Flee for safety, people of
Benjamin!
Flee from Jerusalem!
Sound the trumpet in Tekoa!
Raise the signal over Beth
Hakkerem!
For disaster looms out of the north,
even terrible destruction.
2I will destroy the Daughter of Zion,
so beautiful and delicate.
3Shepherds with their flocks will come
against her;
they will pitch their tents round her,
each tending his own portion."

4"Prepare for battle against her!
Arise, let us attack at noon!
But, alas, the daylight is fading,
and the shadows of evening grow
long.
5So arise, let us attack at night
and destroy her fortresses!"

6This is what the LORD Almighty says:

"Cut down the trees
and build siege ramps against
Jerusalem.
This city must be punished;
it is filled with oppression.
7As a well pours out its water,
so she pours out her wickedness.
Violence and destruction resound in
her;
her sickness and wounds are ever
before me.
8Take warning, O Jerusalem,
or I will turn away from you
and make your land desolate
so that no-one can live in it."

9This is what the LORD Almighty says:

"Let them glean the remnant of Israel
as thoroughly as a vine;

pass your hand over the branches again,
   like one gathering grapes."

¹⁰To whom can I speak and give warning?
   Who will listen to me?
Their ears are closed[a]
   so that they cannot hear.
The word of the LORD is offensive to
   them;
   they find no pleasure in it.
¹¹But I am full of the wrath of the LORD,
   and I cannot hold it in.

"Pour it out on the children in the street
   and on the young men gathered
     together;
both husband and wife will be caught
   in it,
   and the old, those weighed down with
     years.
¹²Their houses will be turned over to
     others,
   together with their fields and their
     wives,
when I stretch out my hand
   against those who live in the land,"
              declares the LORD.
¹³"From the least to the greatest,
   all are greedy for gain;
prophets and priests alike,
   all practise deceit.
¹⁴They dress the wound of my people
   as though it were not serious.
'Peace, peace,' they say,
   when there is no peace.
¹⁵Are they ashamed of their loathsome
     conduct?
   No, they have no shame at all;
   they do not even know how to blush.
So they will fall among the fallen;
   they will be brought down when I
     punish them,"
             says the LORD.

¹⁶This is what the LORD says:

"Stand at the crossroads and look;
   ask for the ancient paths,
ask where the good way is, and walk
     in it,
   and you will find rest for your souls.
   But you said, 'We will not walk in it.'

¹⁷I appointed watchmen over you and
     said,
   'Listen to the sound of the trumpet!'
   But you said, 'We will not listen.'
¹⁸Therefore hear, O nations;
   observe, O witnesses,
   what will happen to them.
¹⁹Hear, O earth:
   I am bringing disaster on this people,
   the fruit of their schemes,
because they have not listened to my
     words
   and have rejected my law.
²⁰What do I care about incense from
     Sheba
   or sweet calamus from a distant land?
Your burnt offerings are not
     acceptable;
   your sacrifices do not please me."

²¹Therefore this is what the LORD says:

"I will put obstacles before this people.
   Fathers and sons alike will stumble
     over them;
   neighbours and friends will perish."

²²This is what the LORD says:

"Look, an army is coming
   from the land of the north;
a great nation is being stirred up
   from the ends of the earth.
²³They are armed with bow and spear;
   they are cruel and show no mercy.
They sound like the roaring sea
   as they ride on their horses;
they come like men in battle formation
   to attack you, O Daughter of Zion."

²⁴We have heard reports about them,
   and our hands hang limp.
Anguish has gripped us,
   pain like that of a woman in labour.
²⁵Do not go out to the fields
   or walk on the roads,
for the enemy has a sword,
   and there is terror on every
     side.
²⁶O my people, put on sackcloth
   and roll in ashes;

mourn with bitter wailing
as for an only son,
for suddenly the destroyer
will come upon us.

27"I have made you a tester of metals
and my people the ore,
that you may observe
and test their ways.
28They are all hardened rebels,
going about to slander.
They are bronze and iron;
they all act corruptly.
29The bellows blow fiercely
to burn away the lead with fire,
but the refining goes on in vain;
the wicked are not purged out.
30They are called rejected silver,
because the LORD has rejected
them."

False Religion Worthless

7 This is the word that came to Jeremiah from the LORD: 2"Stand at the gate of the LORD's house and there proclaim this message:

"'Hear the word of the LORD, all you people of Judah who come through these gates to worship the LORD. 3This is what the LORD Almighty, the God of Israel, says: Reform your ways and your actions, and I will let you live in this place. 4Do not trust in deceptive words and say, "This is the temple of the LORD, the temple of the LORD, the temple of the LORD!" 5If you really change your ways and your actions and deal with each other justly, 6if you do not oppress the alien, the fatherless or the widow and do not shed innocent blood in this place, and if you do not follow other gods to your own harm, 7then I will let you live in this place, in the land I gave to your forefathers for ever and ever. 8But look, you are trusting in deceptive words that are worthless.

9"'Will you steal and murder, commit adultery and perjury,[a] burn incense to Baal and follow other gods you have not known, 10and then come and stand before me in this house, which bears my Name, and say, "We are safe"—safe to do all these detestable things? 11Has this house, which bears my Name, become a den of robbers to you? But I have been watching! declares the LORD.

12"'Go now to the place in Shiloh where I first made a dwelling for my Name, and see what I did to it because of the wickedness of my people Israel. 13While you were doing all these things, declares the LORD, I spoke to you again and again, but you did not listen; I called you, but you did not answer. 14Therefore, what I did to Shiloh I will now do to the house that bears my Name, the temple you trust in, the place I gave to you and your fathers. 15I will thrust you from my presence, just as I did all your brothers, the people of Ephraim.'

16"So do not pray for this people nor offer any plea or petition for them; do not plead with me, for I will not listen to you. 17Do you not see what they are doing in the towns of Judah and in the streets of Jerusalem? 18The children gather wood, the fathers light the fire, and the women knead the dough and make cakes of bread for the Queen of Heaven. They pour out drink offerings to other gods to provoke me to anger. 19But am I the one they are provoking? declares the LORD. Are they not rather harming themselves, to their own shame?

20"'Therefore this is what the Sovereign LORD says: My anger and my wrath will be poured out on this place, on man and beast, on the trees of the field and on the fruit of the ground, and it will burn and not be quenched.

21"'This is what the LORD Almighty, the God of Israel, says: Go ahead, add your burnt offerings to your other sacrifices and eat the meat yourselves! 22For when I brought your forefathers out of Egypt and spoke to them, I did not just give them commands about burnt offerings and sacrifices, 23but I gave them this command: Obey me, and I will be your God and you will be my people. Walk in all the ways I command you, that it may go well with you. 24But they did not listen or pay attention; instead, they followed the stubborn

a9 Or and swear by false gods

inclinations of their evil hearts. They went backward and not forward. ²⁵From the time your forefathers left Egypt until now, day after day, again and again I sent you my servants the prophets. ²⁶But they did not listen to me or pay attention. They were stiff-necked and did more evil than their forefathers.'

²⁷"When you tell them all this, they will not listen to you; when you call to them, they will not answer. ²⁸Therefore say to them, 'This is the nation that has not obeyed the LORD its God or responded to correction. Truth has perished; it has vanished from their lips. ²⁹Cut off your hair and throw it away; take up a lament on the barren heights, for the LORD has rejected and abandoned this generation that is under his wrath.

The Valley of Slaughter

³⁰"'The people of Judah have done evil in my eyes, declares the LORD. They have set up their detestable idols in the house that bears my Name and have defiled it. ³¹They have built the high places of Topheth in the Valley of Ben Hinnom to burn their sons and daughters in the fire—something I did not command, nor did it enter my mind. ³²So beware, the days are coming, declares the LORD, when people will no longer call it Topheth or the Valley of Ben Hinnom, but the Valley of Slaughter, for they will bury the dead in Topheth until there is no more room. ³³Then the carcasses of this people will become food for the birds of the air and the beasts of the earth, and there will be no-one to frighten them away. ³⁴I will bring an end to the sounds of joy and gladness and to the voices of bride and bridegroom in the towns of Judah and the streets of Jerusalem, for the land will become desolate.

8 "'At that time, declares the LORD, the bones of the kings and officials of Judah, the bones of the priests and prophets, and the bones of the people of Jerusalem will be removed from their graves. ²They will be exposed to the sun and the moon and all the stars of the heavens, which they have loved and served and which they have followed and consulted and worshipped. They will not be gathered up or buried, but will be like refuse lying on the ground. ³Wherever I banish them, all the survivors of this evil nation will prefer death to life, declares the LORD Almighty.'

Sin and Punishment

⁴"Say to them, 'This is what the LORD says:

"'When men fall down, do they not get
        up?
    When a man turns away, does he not
        return?
⁵Why then have these people turned
        away?
    Why does Jerusalem always turn
        away?
They cling to deceit;
    they refuse to return.
⁶I have listened attentively,
    but they do not say what is right.
No-one repents of his wickedness,
    saying, "What have I done?"
Each pursues his own course
    like a horse charging into battle.
⁷Even the stork in the sky
    knows her appointed seasons,
and the dove, the swift and the thrush
    observe the time of their migration.
But my people do not know
    the requirements of the LORD.

⁸"'How can you say, "We are wise,
    for we have the law of the LORD,"
when actually the lying pen of the
        scribes
    has handled it falsely?
⁹The wise will be put to shame;
    they will be dismayed and trapped.
Since they have rejected the word of the
        LORD,
    what kind of wisdom do they have?
¹⁰Therefore I will give their wives to
        other men
    and their fields to new owners.
From the least to the greatest,
    all are greedy for gain;
prophets and priests alike,
    all practise deceit.
¹¹They dress the wound of my people

as though it were not serious.
"Peace, peace," they say,
    when there is no peace.
12Are they ashamed of their loathsome
    conduct?
No, they have no shame at all;
    they do not even know how to
        blush.
So they will fall among the fallen;
    they will be brought down when they
        are punished,
                    says the LORD.

13" 'I will take away their harvest,
                    declares the LORD.
There will be no grapes on the vine.
There will be no figs on the tree,
    and their leaves will wither.
What I have given them
    will be taken from them.' "*a*

14"Why are we sitting here?
    Gather together!
Let us flee to the fortified cities
    and perish there!
For the LORD our God has doomed us to
        perish
    and given us poisoned water to drink,
    because we have sinned against him.
15We hoped for peace
    but no good has come,
for a time of healing
    but there was only terror.
16The snorting of the enemy's horses
    is heard from Dan;
at the neighing of their stallions
    the whole land trembles.
They have come to devour
    the land and everything in it,
    the city and all who live there."

17"See, I will send venomous snakes
        among you,
    vipers that cannot be charmed,
    and they will bite you,"
                    declares the LORD.

18O my Comforter*b* in sorrow,
    my heart is faint within me.
19Listen to the cry of my people

from a land far away:
"Is the LORD not in Zion?
    Is her King no longer there?"

"Why have they provoked me to anger
        with their images,
    with their worthless foreign idols?"

20"The harvest is past,
    the summer has ended,
    and we are not saved."

21Since my people are crushed, I am
        crushed;
    I mourn, and horror grips me.
22Is there no balm in Gilead?
    Is there no physician there?
Why then is there no healing
    for the wound of my people?

9 1Oh, that my head were a spring of
        water
    and my eyes a fountain of tears!
I would weep day and night
    for the slain of my people.
2Oh, that I had in the desert
    a lodging place for travellers,
so that I might leave my people
    and go away from them;
for they are all adulterers,
    a crowd of unfaithful people.

3"They make ready their tongue
    like a bow, to shoot lies;
it is not by truth
    that they triumph*a* in the land.
They go from one sin to another;
    they do not acknowledge me,"
                    declares the LORD.
4"Beware of your friends;
    do not trust your brothers.
For every brother is a deceiver,*b*
    and every friend a slanderer.
5Friend deceives friend,
    and no-one speaks the truth.
They have taught their tongues to lie;
    they weary themselves with sinning.
6You*c* live in the midst of deception;
    in their deceit they refuse to
        acknowledge me,"
                    declares the LORD.

a13 The meaning of the Hebrew for this sentence is uncertain.
b18 The meaning of the Hebrew for this word is uncertain.
b4 Or *a deceiving Jacob*   *c6* That is, Jeremiah (the Hebrew is singular)
a3 Or *lies; / they are not valiant for truth*

[7]Therefore this is what the LORD Almighty says:

"See, I will refine and test them,
  for what else can I do
  because of the sin of my people?
[8]Their tongue is a deadly arrow;
  it speaks with deceit.
With his mouth each speaks cordially to
    his neighbour,
  but in his heart he sets a trap for him.
[9]Should I not punish them for this?"
    declares the LORD.
"Should I not avenge myself
  on such a nation as this?"

[10]I will weep and wail for the mountains
  and take up a lament concerning the
    desert pastures.
They are desolate and untravelled,
  and the lowing of cattle is not heard.
The birds of the air have fled
  and the animals are gone.

[11]"I will make Jerusalem a heap of ruins,
  a haunt of jackals;
and I will lay waste the towns of Judah
  so that no-one can live there."

[12]What man is wise enough to understand this? Who has been instructed by the LORD and can explain it? Why has the land been ruined and laid waste like a desert that no-one can cross?

[13]The LORD said, "It is because they have forsaken my law, which I set before them; they have not obeyed me or followed my law. [14]Instead, they have followed the stubbornness of their hearts; they have followed the Baals, as their fathers taught them." [15]Therefore, this is what the LORD Almighty, the God of Israel, says: "See, I will make this people eat bitter food and drink poisoned water. [16]I will scatter them among nations that neither they nor their fathers have known, and I will pursue them with the sword until I have destroyed them."

[17]This is what the LORD Almighty says:

"Consider now! Call for the wailing
    women to come;

send for the most skilful of them.
[18]Let them come quickly
  and wail over us
till our eyes overflow with tears
  and water streams from our eyelids.
[19]The sound of wailing is heard from
    Zion:
  'How ruined we are!
  How great is our shame!
We must leave our land
  because our houses are in ruins.'"

[20]Now, O women, hear the word of the
    LORD;
  open your ears to the words of his
    mouth.
Teach your daughters how to wail;
  teach one another a lament.
[21]Death has climbed in through our
    windows
  and has entered our fortresses;
it has cut off the children from the
    streets
  and the young men from the public
    squares.

[22]Say, "This is what the LORD declares:

"'The dead bodies of men will lie
  like refuse on the open field,
like cut corn behind the reaper,
  with no-one to gather them.'"

[23]This is what the LORD says:

"Let not the wise man boast of his
    wisdom
  or the strong man boast of his
    strength
  or the rich man boast of his riches,
[24]but let him who boasts boast about
    this:
  that he understands and knows me,
that I am the LORD, who exercises
    kindness,
  justice and righteousness on earth,
  for in these I delight,"
                        declares the LORD.

[25]"The days are coming," declares the LORD, "when I will punish all who are circumcised only in the flesh—[26]Egypt, Judah, Edom, Ammon, Moab and all who

live in the desert in distant places.*d* For all these nations are really uncircumcised, and even the whole house of Israel is uncircumcised in heart."

God and Idols

10
Hear what the LORD says to you, O house of Israel. [2]This is what the LORD says:

"Do not learn the ways of the nations
    or be terrified by signs in the sky,
    though the nations are terrified by
        them.
[3]For the customs of the peoples are
        worthless;
    they cut a tree out of the forest,
    and a craftsman shapes it with his
        chisel.
[4]They adorn it with silver and gold;
    they fasten it with hammer and nails
    so that it will not totter.
[5]Like a scarecrow in a melon patch,
    their idols cannot speak;
they must be carried
    because they cannot walk.
Do not fear them;
    they can do no harm
    nor can they do any good."

[6]No-one is like you, O LORD;
    you are great,
    and your name is mighty in power.
[7]Who should not revere you,
    O King of the nations?
    This is your due.
Among all the wise men of the nations
    and in all their kingdoms,
    there is no-one like you.
[8]They are all senseless and foolish;
    they are taught by worthless wooden
        idols.
[9]Hammered silver is brought from
        Tarshish
    and gold from Uphaz.
What the craftsman and goldsmith have
        made
    is then dressed in blue and purple—
    all made by skilled workers.
[10]But the LORD is the true God;

he is the living God, the eternal King.
When he is angry, the earth trembles;
    the nations cannot endure his wrath.

[11]"Tell them this: 'These gods, who did not make the heavens and the earth, will perish from the earth and from under the heavens.'"*a*

[12]But God made the earth by his power;
    he founded the world by his wisdom
    and stretched out the heavens by his
        understanding.
[13]When he thunders, the waters in the
        heavens roar;
    he makes clouds rise from the ends of
        the earth.
He sends lightning with the rain
    and brings out the wind from his
        storehouses.

[14]Everyone is senseless and without
        knowledge;
    every goldsmith is shamed by his
        idols.
His images are a fraud;
    they have no breath in them.
[15]They are worthless, the objects of
        mockery;
    when their judgment comes, they will
        perish.
[16]He who is the Portion of Jacob is not
        like these,
    for he is the Maker of all things,
    including Israel, the tribe of his
        inheritance—
    the LORD Almighty is his name.

Coming Destruction

[17]Gather up your belongings to leave the
        land,
    you who live under siege.
[18]For this is what the LORD says:
    "At this time I will hurl out
        those who live in this land;
    I will bring distress on them
        so that they may be captured."

[19]Woe to me because of my injury!
    My wound is incurable!

---

d26 Or desert and who clip the hair by their foreheads   *a11 The text of this verse is in Aramaic.*

Yet I said to myself,
"This is my sickness, and I must
endure it."
20My tent is destroyed;
all its ropes are snapped.
My sons are gone from me and are no
more;
no-one is left now to pitch my tent
or to set up my shelter.
21The shepherds are senseless
and do not enquire of the LORD;
so they do not prosper
and all their flock is scattered.
22Listen! The report is coming—
a great commotion from the land of
the north!
It will make the towns of Judah
desolate,
a haunt of jackals.

Jeremiah's Prayer

23I know, O LORD, that a man's life is not
his own;
it is not for man to direct his steps.
24Correct me, LORD, but only with
justice—
not in your anger,
lest you reduce me to nothing.
25Pour out your wrath on the nations
that do not acknowledge you,
on the peoples who do not call on
your name.
For they have devoured Jacob;
they have devoured him completely
and destroyed his homeland.

The Covenant Is Broken

11 This is the word that came to Jeremiah from the LORD: 2"Listen to the terms of this covenant and tell them to the people of Judah and to those who live in Jerusalem. 3Tell them that this is what the LORD, the God of Israel, says: 'Cursed is the man who does not obey the terms of this covenant—4the terms I commanded your forefathers when I brought them out of Egypt, out of the iron-smelting furnace.' I said, 'Obey me and do everything I command you, and you will be my people, and I will be your God, 5Then I will fulfil the oath I swore to your forefathers, to give them a land flowing with milk and honey'—the land you possess today."

I answered, "Amen, LORD."

6The LORD said to me, "Proclaim all these words in the towns of Judah and in the streets of Jerusalem: 'Listen to the terms of this covenant and follow them. 7From the time I brought your forefathers up from Egypt until today, I warned them again and again, saying, "Obey me." 8But they did not listen or pay attention; instead, they followed the stubbornness of their evil hearts. So I brought on them all the curses of the covenant I had commanded them to follow but that they did not keep.'"

9Then the LORD said to me, "There is a conspiracy among the people of Judah and those who live in Jerusalem. 10They have returned to the sins of their forefathers, who refused to listen to my words. They have followed other gods to serve them. Both the house of Israel and the house of Judah have broken the covenant I made with their forefathers. 11Therefore this is what the LORD says: 'I will bring on them a disaster they cannot escape. Although they cry out to me, I will not listen to them. 12The towns of Judah and the people of Jerusalem will go and cry out to the gods to whom they burn incense, but they will not help them at all when disaster strikes. 13You have as many gods as you have towns, O Judah; and the altars you have set up to burn incense to that shameful god Baal are as many as the streets of Jerusalem.'

14"Do not pray for this people nor offer any plea or petition for them, because I will not listen when they call to me in the time of their distress.

15"What is my beloved doing in my
temple
as she works out her evil schemes
with many?
Can consecrated meat avert ⌐your
punishment⌐?
When you engage in your wickedness,
then you rejoice."*a*

---

*a*15 Or *Could consecrated meat avert your punishment? / Then you would rejoice*

16The LORD called you a thriving olive
tree
  with fruit beautiful in form.
But with the roar of a mighty storm
  he will set it on fire,
  and its branches will be broken.

17The LORD Almighty, who planted you,
has decreed disaster for you, because the
house of Israel and the house of Judah
have done evil and provoked me to anger
by burning incense to Baal.

Plot Against Jeremiah

18Because the LORD revealed their plot
to me, I knew it, for at that time he showed
me what they were doing. 19I had been like
a gentle lamb led to the slaughter; I did not
realise that they had plotted against me,
saying,

"Let us destroy the tree and its fruit;
  let us cut him off from the land of the
    living,
  that his name be remembered no
    more."
20But, O LORD Almighty, you who judge
  righteously
  and test the heart and mind,
let me see your vengeance upon them,
  for to you I have committed my
    cause.

21"Therefore this is what the LORD says
about the men of Anathoth who are seeking your life and saying, 'Do not prophesy
in the name of the LORD or you will die by
our hands'— 22therefore this is what the
LORD Almighty says: 'I will punish them.
Their young men will die by the sword,
their sons and daughters by famine. 23Not
even a remnant will be left to them, because I will bring disaster on the men of
Anathoth in the year of their punishment.'"

Jeremiah's Complaint

12 You are always righteous, O
LORD,
  when I bring a case before you.

Yet I would speak with you about your
  justice:
  Why does the way of the wicked
    prosper?
  Why do all the faithless live at ease?
2You have planted them, and they have
    taken root;
  they grow and bear fruit.
You are always on their lips
  but far from their hearts.
3Yet you know me, O LORD;
  you see me and test my thoughts
    about you.
Drag them off like sheep to be
    butchered!
  Set them apart for the day of
    slaughter!
4How long will the land lie parched[a]
  and the grass in every field be
    withered?
Because those who live in it are wicked,
  the animals and birds have perished.
Moreover, the people are saying,
  "He will not see what happens to us."

God's Answer

5"If you have raced with men on foot
  and they have worn you out,
  how can you compete with horses?
If you stumble in safe country,[b]
  how will you manage in the thickets
    by[c] the Jordan?
6Your brothers, your own family—
  even they have betrayed you;
  they have raised a loud cry against
    you.
Do not trust them,
  though they speak well of you.

7"I will forsake my house,
  abandon my inheritance;
I will give the one I love
  into the hands of her enemies.
8My inheritance has become to me
  like a lion in the forest.
She roars at me;
  therefore I hate her.
9Has not my inheritance become to me
  like a speckled bird of prey
  that other birds of prey surround and
    attack?

---

*a*4 Or *land mourn*   *b*5 Or *If you put your trust in a land of safety*   *c*5 Or *the flooding of*

Go and gather all the wild beasts;
    bring them to devour.
¹⁰Many shepherds will ruin my vineyard
    and trample down my field;
they will turn my pleasant field
    into a desolate wasteland.
¹¹It will be made a wasteland,
    parched and desolate before me;
the whole land will be laid waste
    because there is no-one who cares.
¹²Over all the barren heights in the desert
    destroyers will swarm,
for the sword of the LORD will devour
    from one end of the land to the other;
    no-one will be safe.
¹³They will sow wheat but reap thorns;
    they will wear themselves out but
      gain nothing.
So bear the shame of your harvest
    because of the LORD's fierce anger."

¹⁴This is what the LORD says: "As for all my wicked neighbours who seize the inheritance I gave to my people Israel, I will uproot them from their lands and I will uproot the house of Judah from among them. ¹⁵But after I uproot them, I will again have compassion and will bring each of them back to his own inheritance and his own country. ¹⁶And if they learn well the ways of my people and swear by my name, saying, 'As surely as the LORD lives'—even as they once taught my people to swear by Baal—then they will be established among my people. ¹⁷But if any nation does not listen, I will completely uproot and destroy it," declares the LORD.

A Linen Belt

13 This is what the LORD said to me: "Go and buy a linen belt and put it round your waist, but do not let it touch water." ²So I bought a belt, as the LORD directed, and put it round my waist.

³Then the word of the LORD came to me a second time: ⁴"Take the belt you bought and are wearing round your waist, and go now to Perath^a and hide it there in a crevice in the rocks." ⁵So I went and hid it at Perath, as the LORD told me.

⁶Many days later the LORD said to me, "Go now to Perath and get the belt I told you to hide there." ⁷So I went to Perath and dug up the belt and took it from the place where I had hidden it, but now it was ruined and completely useless.

⁸Then the word of the LORD came to me: ⁹"This is what the LORD says: 'In the same way I will ruin the pride of Judah and the great pride of Jerusalem. ¹⁰These wicked people, who refuse to listen to my words, who follow the stubbornness of their hearts and go after other gods to serve and worship them, will be like this belt—completely useless! ¹¹For as a belt is bound round a man's waist, so I bound the whole house of Israel and the whole house of Judah to me,' declares the LORD, 'to be my people for my renown and praise and honour. But they have not listened.'

Wineskins

¹²"Say to them: 'This is what the LORD, the God of Israel, says: Every wineskin should be filled with wine.' And if they say to you, 'Don't we know that every wineskin should be filled with wine?' ¹³then tell them, 'This is what the LORD says: I am going to fill with drunkenness all who live in this land, including the kings who sit on David's throne, the priests, the prophets and all those living in Jerusalem. ¹⁴I will smash them one against the other, fathers and sons alike, declares the LORD. I will allow no pity or mercy or compassion to keep me from destroying them.' "

Threat of Captivity

¹⁵Hear and pay attention,
    do not be arrogant,
    for the LORD has spoken.
¹⁶Give glory to the LORD your God
    before he brings the darkness,
before your feet stumble
    on the darkening hills.
You hope for light,
    but he will turn it to thick darkness
    and change it to deep gloom.
¹⁷But if you do not listen,

I will weep in secret
because of your pride;
my eyes will weep bitterly,
overflowing with tears,
because the LORD's flock will be taken
captive.

¹⁸Say to the king and to the queen
mother,
"Come down from your thrones,
for your glorious crowns
will fall from your heads."
¹⁹The cities in the Negev will be shut up,
and there will be no-one to open
them.
All Judah will be carried into exile,
carried completely away.

²⁰Lift up your eyes and see
those who are coming from the north.
Where is the flock that was entrusted to
you,
the sheep of which you boasted?
²¹What will you say when ⌊the LORD⌋ sets
over you
those you cultivated as your special
allies?
Will not pain grip you
like that of a woman in labour?
²²And if you ask yourself,
"Why has this happened to me?"—
it is because of your many sins
that your skirts have been torn off
and your body ill-treated.
²³Can the Ethiopianᵇ change his skin
or the leopard its spots?
Neither can you do good
who are accustomed to doing evil.

²⁴"I will scatter you like chaff
driven by the desert wind.
²⁵This is your lot,
the portion I have decreed for you,"
declares the LORD,
"because you have forgotten me
and trusted in false gods.
²⁶I will pull up your skirts over your face
that your shame may be seen—
²⁷your adulteries and lustful neighings,
your shameless prostitution!
I have seen your detestable acts

on the hills and in the fields.
Woe to you, O Jerusalem!
How long will you be unclean?"

Drought, Famine, Sword

14 This is the word of the LORD to
Jeremiah concerning the drought:

²"Judah mourns,
her cities languish;
they wail for the land,
and a cry goes up from Jerusalem.
³The nobles send their servants for
water;
they go to the cisterns
but find no water.
They return with their jars unfilled;
dismayed and despairing,
they cover their heads.
⁴The ground is cracked
because there is no rain in the land;
the farmers are dismayed
and cover their heads.
⁵Even the doe in the field
deserts her newborn fawn
because there is no grass.
⁶Wild donkeys stand on the barren
heights
and pant like jackals;
their eyesight fails
for lack of pasture."

⁷Although our sins testify against us,
O LORD, do something for the sake of
your name.
For our backsliding is great;
we have sinned against you.
⁸O Hope of Israel,
its Saviour in times of distress,
why are you like a stranger in the land,
like a traveller who stays only a night?
⁹Why are you like a man taken by
surprise,
like a warrior powerless to save?
You are among us, O LORD,
and we bear your name;
do not forsake us!

¹⁰This is what the LORD says about this
people:

ᵇ23 Hebrew *Cushite* (probably a person from the upper Nile region)

"They greatly love to wander;
  they do not restrain their feet.
So the LORD does not accept them;
  he will now remember their
      wickedness
  and punish them for their sins."

¹¹Then the LORD said to me, "Do not pray for the well-being of this people. ¹²Although they fast, I will not listen to their cry; though they offer burnt offerings and grain offerings, I will not accept them. Instead, I will destroy them with the sword, famine and plague."

¹³But I said, "Ah, Sovereign LORD, the prophets keep telling them, 'You will not see the sword or suffer famine. Indeed, I will give you lasting peace in this place.'"

¹⁴Then the LORD said to me, "The prophets are prophesying lies in my name. I have not sent them or appointed them or spoken to them. They are prophesying to you false visions, divinations, idolatries*a* and the delusions of their own minds. ¹⁵Therefore, this is what the LORD says about the prophets who are prophesying in my name: I did not send them, yet they are saying, 'No sword or famine will touch this land.' Those same prophets will perish by sword and famine. ¹⁶And the people they are prophesying to will be thrown out into the streets of Jerusalem because of the famine and sword. There will be no-one to bury them or their wives, their sons or their daughters. I will pour out on them the calamity they deserve.

¹⁷"Speak this word to them:

" 'Let my eyes overflow with tears
    night and day without ceasing;
for my virgin daughter—my people—
    has suffered a grievous wound,
    a crushing blow.
¹⁸If I go into the country,
    I see those slain by the sword;
if I go into the city,
    I see the ravages of famine.
Both prophet and priest
    have gone to a land they know
      not.'"

¹⁹Have you rejected Judah completely?
    Do you despise Zion?
Why have you afflicted us
    so that we cannot be healed?
We hoped for peace
    but no good has come,
for a time of healing
    but there is only terror.
²⁰O LORD, we acknowledge our
      wickedness
    and the guilt of our fathers;
    we have indeed sinned against you.
²¹For the sake of your name do not
      despise us;
    do not dishonour your glorious
      throne.
Remember your covenant with us
    and do not break it.
²²Do any of the worthless idols of the
      nations bring rain?
    Do the skies themselves send down
      showers?
No, it is you, O LORD our God.
    Therefore our hope is in you,
    for you are the one who does all this.

15 Then the LORD said to me: "Even if Moses and Samuel were to stand before me, my heart would not go out to this people. Send them away from my presence! Let them go! ²And if they ask you, 'Where shall we go?' tell them, 'This is what the LORD says:

" 'Those destined for death, to death;
  those for the sword, to the sword;
  those for starvation, to starvation;
  those for captivity, to captivity.'

³"I will send four kinds of destroyers against them," declares the LORD, "the sword to kill and the dogs to drag away and the birds of the air and the beasts of the earth to devour and destroy. ⁴I will make them abhorrent to all the kingdoms of the earth because of what Manasseh son of Hezekiah king of Judah did in Jerusalem.

⁵"Who will have pity on you, O
    Jerusalem?

---

a14 Or visions, worthless divinations

Who will mourn·for you?
Who will stop to ask how you are?
⁶"You have rejected me," declares the
LORD.
"You keep on backsliding.
So I will lay hands on you and destroy
      you;
   I can no longer show compassion.
⁷I will winnow them with a winnowing
      fork
   at the city gates of the land.
I will bring bereavement and
      destruction on my people,
   for they have not changed their ways.
⁸I will make their widows more
      numerous
   than the sand of the sea.
At midday I will bring a destroyer
   against the mothers of their young
      men;
suddenly I will bring down on them
   anguish and terror.
⁹The mother of seven will grow faint
   and breathe her last.
Her sun will set while it is still day;
   she will be disgraced and humiliated.
I will put the survivors to the sword
   before their enemies,"
                    declares the LORD.

¹⁰Alas, my mother, that you gave me
      birth,
   a man with whom the whole land
      strives and contends!
I have neither lent nor borrowed,
   yet everyone curses me.

   ¹¹The LORD said,

"Surely I will deliver you for a good
      purpose;
   surely I will make your enemies plead
      with you
   in times of disaster and times of
      distress.

¹²"Can a man break iron—
   iron from the north— or bronze?
¹³Your wealth and your treasures
   I will give as plunder, without charge,
because of all your sins

throughout your country.
¹⁴I will enslave you to your enemies
   inᵃ a land you do not know,
for my anger will kindle a fire
   that will burn against you."

¹⁵You understand, O LORD;
   remember me and care for me.
   Avenge me on my persecutors.
You are long-suffering—do not take me
      away;
   think of how I suffer reproach for
      your sake.
¹⁶When your words came, I ate them;
   they were my joy and my heart's
      delight,
for I bear your name,
   O LORD God Almighty.
¹⁷I never sat in the company of revellers,
   never made merry with them;
I sat alone because your hand was on
      me
   and you had filled me with
      indignation.
¹⁸Why is my pain unending
   and my wound grievous and
      incurable?
Will you be to me like a deceptive
      brook,
   like a spring that fails?

   ¹⁹Therefore this is what the LORD says:

"If you repent, I will restore you
   that you may serve me;
if you utter worthy, not worthless,
      words,
   you will be my spokesman.
Let this people turn to you,
   but you must not turn to them.
²⁰I will make you a wall to this people,
   a fortified wall of bronze;
they will fight against you
   but will not overcome you,
for I am with you
   to rescue and save you,"
                    declares the LORD.
²¹"I will save you from the hands of the
      wicked
   and redeem you from the grasp of the
      cruel."

ᵃ14 Some Hebrew manuscripts, Septuagint and Syriac (see also Jer. 17:4); most Hebrew manuscripts *I will cause your enemies to bring you* / *into*

Day of Disaster

16 Then the word of the LORD came to me: ²"You must not marry and have sons or daughters in this place." ³For this is what the LORD says about the sons and daughters born in this land and about the women who are their mothers and the men who are their fathers: ⁴"They will die of deadly diseases. They will not be mourned or buried but will be like refuse lying on the ground. They will perish by sword and famine, and their dead bodies will become food for the birds of the air and the beasts of the earth."

⁵For this is what the LORD says: "Do not enter a house where there is a funeral meal; do not go to mourn or show sympathy, because I have withdrawn my blessing, my love and my pity from this people," declares the LORD. ⁶"Both high and low will die in this land. They will not be buried or mourned, and no-one will cut himself or shave his head for them. ⁷No-one will offer food to comfort those who mourn for the dead—not even for a father or a mother—nor will anyone give them a drink to console them.

⁸"And do not enter a house where there is feasting and sit down to eat and drink. ⁹For this is what the LORD Almighty, the God of Israel, says: Before your eyes and in your days I will bring an end to the sounds of joy and gladness and to the voices of bride and bridegroom in this place.

¹⁰"When you tell these people all this and they ask you, 'Why has the LORD decreed such a great disaster against us? What wrong have we done? What sin have we committed against the LORD our God?' ¹¹then say to them, 'It is because your fathers forsook me,' declares the LORD, 'and followed other gods and served and worshipped them. They forsook me and did not keep my law. ¹²But you have behaved more wickedly than your fathers. See how each of you is following the stubbornness of his evil heart instead of obeying me. ¹³So I will throw you out of this land into a land neither you nor your fathers have known, and there you will serve other gods day and night, for I will show you no favour.'

¹⁴"However, the days are coming," declares the LORD, "when men will no longer say, 'As surely as the LORD lives, who brought the Israelites up out of Egypt,' ¹⁵but they will say, 'As surely as the LORD lives, who brought the Israelites up out of the land of the north and out of all the countries where he had banished them.' For I will restore them to the land I gave to their forefathers.

¹⁶"But now I will send for many fishermen," declares the LORD, "and they will catch them. After that I will send for many hunters, and they will hunt them down on every mountain and hill and from the crevices of the rocks. ¹⁷My eyes are on all their ways; they are not hidden from me, nor is their sin concealed from my eyes. ¹⁸I will repay them double for their wickedness and their sin, because they have defiled my land with the lifeless forms of their vile images and have filled my inheritance with their detestable idols."

¹⁹O LORD, my strength and my fortress,
my refuge in time of distress,
to you the nations will come
from the ends of the earth and say,
"Our fathers possessed nothing but
false gods,
worthless idols that did them no
good.
²⁰Do men make their own gods?
Yes, but they are not gods!"

²¹"Therefore I will teach them—
this time I will teach them
my power and might.
Then they will know
that my name is the LORD.

17 "Judah's sin is engraved with an iron tool,
inscribed with a flint point,
on the tablets of their hearts
and on the horns of their altars.
²Even their children remember
their altars and Asherah poles[a]

a2 That is, symbols of the goddess Asherah

beside the spreading trees
and on the high hills.
³My mountain in the land
and your[b] wealth and all your
treasures
I will give away as plunder,
together with your high places,
because of sin throughout your
country.
⁴Through your own fault you will lose
the inheritance I gave you.
I will enslave you to your enemies
in a land you do not know,
for you have kindled my anger,
and it will burn for ever."

⁵This is what the LORD says:

"Cursed is the one who trusts in man,
who depends on flesh for his strength
and whose heart turns away from the
LORD.
⁶He will be like a bush in the wastelands;
he will not see prosperity when it
comes.
He will dwell in the parched places of
the desert,
in a salt land where no-one lives.

⁷"But blessed is the man who trusts in
the LORD,
whose confidence is in him.
⁸He will be like a tree planted by the
water
that sends out its roots by the
stream.
It does not fear when heat comes;
its leaves are always green.
It has no worries in a year of drought
and never fails to bear fruit."

⁹The heart is deceitful above all things
and beyond cure.
Who can understand it?

¹⁰"I the LORD search the heart
and examine the mind,
to reward a man according to his
conduct,
according to what his deeds
deserve."

¹¹Like a partridge that hatches eggs it did
not lay
is the man who gains riches by unjust
means.
When his life is half gone, they will
desert him,
and in the end he will prove to be a
fool.

¹²A glorious throne, exalted from the
beginning,
is the place of our sanctuary.
¹³O LORD, the hope of Israel,
all who forsake you will be put to
shame.
Those who turn away from you will be
written in the dust
because they have forsaken the LORD,
the spring of living water.

¹⁴Heal me, O LORD, and I shall be healed;
save me and I shall be saved,
for you are the one I praise.
¹⁵They keep saying to me,
"Where is the word of the LORD?
Let it now be fulfilled!"
¹⁶I have not run away from being your
shepherd;
you know I have not desired the day
of despair.
What passes my lips is open before
you.
¹⁷Do not be a terror to me;
you are my refuge in the day of
disaster.
¹⁸Let my persecutors be put to shame,
but keep me from shame;
let them be terrified,
but keep me from terror.
Bring on them the day of disaster;
destroy them with double
destruction.

Keeping the Sabbath Holy

¹⁹This is what the LORD said to me: "Go
and stand at the gate of the people,
through which the kings of Judah go in and
out; stand also at all the other gates of
Jerusalem. ²⁰Say to them, 'Hear the word
of the LORD, O kings of Judah and all

---

b2, 3 Or hills / ³ and the mountains of the land. / Your

people of Judah and everyone living in Jerusalem who come through these gates. 21This is what the LORD says: Be careful not to carry a load on the Sabbath day or bring it through the gates of Jerusalem. 22Do not bring a load out of your houses or do any work on the Sabbath, but keep the Sabbath day holy, as I commanded your forefathers. 23Yet they did not listen or pay attention; they were stiff-necked and would not listen or respond to discipline. 24But if you are careful to obey me, declares the LORD, and bring no load through the gates of this city on the Sabbath, but keep the Sabbath day holy by not doing any work on it, 25then kings who sit on David's throne will come through the gates of this city with their officials. They and their officials will come riding in chariots and on horses, accompanied by the men of Judah and those living in Jerusalem, and this city will be inhabited for ever. 26People will come from the towns of Judah and the villages around Jerusalem, from the territory of Benjamin and the western foothills, from the hill country and the Negev, bringing burnt offerings and sacrifices, grain offerings, incense and thank-offerings to the house of the LORD. 27But if you do not obey me to keep the Sabbath day holy by not carrying any load as you come through the gates of Jerusalem on the Sabbath day, then I will kindle an unquenchable fire in the gates of Jerusalem that will consume her fortresses.'"

At the Potter's House

18 This is the word that came to Jeremiah from the LORD: 2"Go down to the potter's house, and there I will give you my message." 3So I went down to the potter's house, and I saw him working at the wheel. 4But the pot he was shaping from the clay was marred in his hands; so the potter formed it into another pot, shaping it as seemed best to him.

5Then the word of the LORD came to me: 6"O house of Israel, can I not do with you as this potter does?" declares the LORD.

"Like clay in the hand of the potter, so are you in my hand, O house of Israel. 7If at any time I announce that a nation or kingdom is to be uprooted, torn down and destroyed, 8and if that nation I warned repents of its evil, then I will relent and not inflict on it the disaster I had planned. 9And if at another time I announce that a nation or kingdom is to be built up and planted, 10and if it does evil in my sight and does not obey me, then I will reconsider the good I had intended to do for it.

11"Now therefore say to the people of Judah and those living in Jerusalem, 'This is what the LORD says: Look! I am preparing a disaster for you and devising a plan against you. So turn from your evil ways, each one of you, and reform your ways and your actions.' 12But they will reply, 'It's no use. We will continue with our own plans; each of us will follow the stubbornness of his evil heart.'"

13Therefore this is what the LORD says:

"Enquire among the nations:
　　Who has ever heard anything like
　　　this?
A most horrible thing has been done
　　by Virgin Israel.
14Does the snow of Lebanon
　　ever vanish from its rocky slopes?
Do its cool waters from distant sources
　　ever cease to flow?[a]
15Yet my people have forgotten me;
　　they burn incense to worthless idols,
which made them stumble in their ways
　　and in the ancient paths.
They made them walk in bypaths
　　and on roads not built up.
16Their land will be laid waste,
　　an object of lasting scorn;
all who pass by will be appalled
　　and will shake their heads.
17Like a wind from the east,
　　I will scatter them before their
　　　enemies;
I will show them my back and not my
　　face
　　in the day of their disaster."

---

[a]14 The meaning of the Hebrew for this sentence is uncertain.

[18]They said, "Come, let's make plans against Jeremiah; for the teaching of the law by the priest will not be lost, nor will counsel from the wise, nor the word from the prophets. So come, let's attack him with our tongues and pay no attention to anything he says."

[19]Listen to me, O LORD;
hear what my accusers are saying!
[20]Should good be repaid with evil?
Yet they have dug a pit for me.
Remember that I stood before you
and spoke on their behalf
to turn your wrath away from them.
[21]So give their children over to famine;
hand them over to the power of the
sword.
Let their wives be made childless and
widows;
let their men be put to death,
their young men slain by the sword in
battle.
[22]Let a cry be heard from their houses
when you suddenly bring invaders
against them,
for they have dug a pit to capture me
and have hidden snares for my feet.
[23]But you know, O LORD,
all their plots to kill me.
Do not forgive their crimes
or blot out their sins from your sight.
Let them be overthrown before you;
deal with them in the time of your
anger.

19 This is what the LORD says: "Go and buy a clay jar from a potter. Take along some of the elders of the people and of the priests [2]and go out to the Valley of Ben Hinnom, near the entrance of the Potsherd Gate. There proclaim the words I tell you, [3]and say, 'Hear the word of the LORD, O kings of Judah and people of Jerusalem. This is what the LORD Almighty, the God of Israel, says: Listen! I am going to bring a disaster on this place that will make the ears of everyone who hears of it tingle. [4]For they have forsaken me and made this a place of foreign gods; they have burned sacrifices in it to gods that neither they nor their fathers nor the kings of Judah ever knew, and they have filled this place with the blood of the innocent. [5]They have built the high places of Baal to burn their sons in the fire as offerings to Baal—something I did not command or mention, nor did it enter my mind. [6]So beware, the days are coming, declares the LORD, when people will no longer call this place Topheth or the Valley of Ben Hinnom, but the Valley of Slaughter.

[7]"'In this place I will ruin[a] the plans of Judah and Jerusalem. I will make them fall by the sword before their enemies, at the hands of those who seek their lives, and I will give their carcasses as food to the birds of the air and the beasts of the earth. [8]I will devastate this city and make it an object of scorn; all who pass by will be appalled and will scoff because of all its wounds. [9]I will make them eat the flesh of their sons and daughters, and they will eat one another's flesh during the stress of the siege imposed on them by the enemies who seek their lives.'

[10]"Then break the jar while those who go with you are watching, [11]and say to them, 'This is what the LORD Almighty says: I will smash this nation and this city just as this potter's jar is smashed and cannot be repaired. They will bury the dead in Topheth until there is no more room. [12]This is what I will do to this place and to those who live here, declares the LORD. I will make this city like Topheth. [13]The houses in Jerusalem and those of the kings of Judah will be defiled like this place, Topheth—all the houses where they burned incense on the roofs to all the starry hosts and poured out drink offerings to other gods.'"

[14]Jeremiah then returned from Topheth, where the LORD had sent him to prophesy, and stood in the court of the LORD's temple and said to all the people, [15]"This is what the LORD Almighty, the God of Israel, says: 'Listen! I am going to bring on this city and the villages around it every disaster I pronounced against them, because they were stiff-necked and would not listen to my words.'"

---

[a]7 The Hebrew for *ruin* sounds like the Hebrew for *jar* (see verses 1 and 10).

Jeremiah and Pashhur

20 When the priest Pashhur son of Immer, the chief officer in the temple of the LORD, heard Jeremiah prophesying these things, ²he had Jeremiah the prophet beaten and put in the stocks at the Upper Gate of Benjamin at the LORD's temple. ³The next day, when Pashhur released him from the stocks, Jeremiah said to him, "The LORD's name for you is not Pashhur, but Magor-Missabib.*a* ⁴For this is what the LORD says: 'I will make you a terror to yourself and to all your friends; with your own eyes you will see them fall by the sword of their enemies. I will hand all Judah over to the king of Babylon, who will carry them away to Babylon or put them to the sword. ⁵I will hand over to their enemies all the wealth of this city—all its products, all its valuables and all the treasures of the kings of Judah. They will take it away as plunder and carry it off to Babylon. ⁶And you, Pashhur, and all who live in your house will go into exile to Babylon. There you will die and be buried, you and all your friends to whom you have prophesied lies.'"

Jeremiah's Complaint

⁷O LORD, you deceived*b* me, and I was deceived;*b*
  you overpowered me and prevailed.
 I am ridiculed all day long;
  everyone mocks me.
⁸Whenever I speak, I cry out
  proclaiming violence and destruction.
 So the word of the LORD has brought me
  insult and reproach all day long.
⁹But if I say, "I will not mention him
  or speak any more in his name,"
 his word is in my heart like a fire,
  a fire shut up in my bones.
 I am weary of holding it in;
  indeed, I cannot.
¹⁰I hear many whispering,
  "Terror on every side!
  Report him! Let's report him!"

All my friends
  are waiting for me to slip, saying,
 "Perhaps he will be deceived;
  then we will prevail over him
  and take our revenge on him."

¹¹But the LORD is with me like a mighty warrior;
  so my persecutors will stumble and not prevail.
 They will fail and be thoroughly disgraced;
  their dishonour will never be forgotten.
¹²O LORD Almighty, you who examine the righteous
  and probe the heart and mind,
 let me see your vengeance upon them,
  for to you I have committed my cause.

¹³Sing to the LORD!
  Give praise to the LORD!
 He rescues the life of the needy
  from the hands of the wicked.

¹⁴Cursed be the day I was born!
  May the day my mother bore me not be blessed!
¹⁵Cursed be the man who brought my father the news,
  who made him very glad, saying,
  "A child is born to you—a son!"
¹⁶May that man be like the towns
  the LORD overthrew without pity.
 May he hear wailing in the morning,
  a battle cry at noon.
¹⁷For he did not kill me in the womb,
  with my mother as my grave,
  her womb enlarged for ever.
¹⁸Why did I ever come out of the womb
  to see trouble and sorrow
  and to end my days in shame?

God Rejects Zedekiah's Request

21 The word came to Jeremiah from the LORD when King Zedekiah sent to him Pashhur son of Malkijah and the priest Zephaniah son of Maaseiah. They said: ²"Enquire now of the LORD for

---

a3 Magor-Missabib means *terror on every side.*   *b7* Or *persuaded* us because Nebuchadnezzar[a] king of Babylon is attacking us. Perhaps the LORD will perform wonders for us as in times past so that he will withdraw from us."

³But Jeremiah answered them, "Tell Zedekiah, ⁴'This is what the LORD, the God of Israel, says: I am about to turn against you the weapons of war that are in your hands, which you are using to fight the king of Babylon and the Babylonians[b] who are outside the wall besieging you. And I will gather them inside this city. ⁵I myself will fight against you with an outstretched hand and a mighty arm in anger and fury and great wrath. ⁶I will strike down those who live in this city—both men and animals—and they will die of a terrible plague. ⁷After that, declares the LORD, I will hand over Zedekiah king of Judah, his officials and the people in this city who survive the plague, sword and famine, to Nebuchadnezzar king of Babylon and to their enemies who seek their lives. He will put them to the sword; he will show them no mercy or pity or compassion.'

⁸"Furthermore, tell the people, 'This is what the LORD says: See, I am setting before you the way of life and the way of death. ⁹Whoever stays in this city will die by the sword, famine or plague. But whoever goes out and surrenders to the Babylonians who are besieging you will live; he will escape with his life. ¹⁰I have determined to do this city harm and not good, declares the LORD. It will be given into the hands of the king of Babylon, and he will destroy it with fire.'

¹¹"Moreover, say to the royal house of Judah, 'Hear the word of the LORD; ¹²O house of David, this is what the LORD says:

"'Administer justice every morning;
    rescue from the hand of his oppressor
    the one who has been robbed,
or my wrath will break out and burn
    like fire
    because of the evil you have done—
    burn with no-one to quench it.

¹³I am against you, ⌊Jerusalem,⌋
    you who live above this valley
    on the rocky plateau,
                    declares the LORD—
you who say, "Who can come against
    us?
    Who can enter our refuge?"
¹⁴I will punish you as your deeds deserve,
                    declares the LORD.
I will kindle a fire in your forests
    that will consume everything around
    you.'"

Judgment Against Evil Kings

22 This is what the LORD says: "Go down to the palace of the king of Judah and proclaim this message there: ²'Hear the word of the LORD, O king of Judah, you who sit on David's throne—you, your officials and your people who come through these gates. ³This is what the LORD says: Do what is just and right. Rescue from the hand of his oppressor the one who has been robbed. Do no wrong or violence to the alien, the fatherless or the widow, and do not shed innocent blood in this place. ⁴For if you are careful to carry out these commands, then kings who sit on David's throne will come through the gates of this palace, riding in chariots and on horses, accompanied by their officials and their people. ⁵But if you do not obey these commands, declares the LORD, I swear by myself that this palace will become a ruin.'"

⁶For this is what the LORD says about the palace of the king of Judah:

"Though you are like Gilead to me,
    like the summit of Lebanon,
I will surely make you like a desert,
    like towns not inhabited.
⁷I will send destroyers against you,
    each man with his weapons,
and they will cut up your fine cedar
    beams
    and throw them into the fire.

⁸"People from many nations will pass by this city and will ask one another, 'Why

---

[a]2 Hebrew *Nebuchadrezzar*, of which *Nebuchadnezzar* is a variant; here and often in Jeremiah and Ezekiel
[b]4 Or *Chaldeans*; also in verse 9

has the LORD done such a thing to this great city?' ⁹And the answer will be: 'Because they have forsaken the covenant of the LORD their God and have worshipped and served other gods.'"

¹⁰Do not weep for the dead ⌐king⌐ or
     mourn his loss;
   rather, weep bitterly for him who is
     exiled,
because he will never return
   nor see his native land again.

¹¹For this is what the LORD says about Shallum*ᵃ* son of Josiah, who succeeded his father as king of Judah but has gone from this place: "He will never return. ¹²He will die in the place where they have led him captive; he will not see this land again."

¹³"Woe to him who builds his palace by
     unrighteousness,
   his upper rooms by injustice,
making his countrymen work for
     nothing,
   not paying them for their labour.
¹⁴He says, 'I will build myself a great
     palace
   with spacious upper rooms.'
So he makes large windows in it,
   panels it with cedar
   and decorates it in red.

¹⁵Does it make you a king
   to have more and more cedar?
Did not your father have food and
     drink?
   He did what was right and just,
     so all went well with him.
¹⁶He defended the cause of the poor and
     needy,
   and so all went well.
Is that not what it means to know me?"
   declares the LORD.
¹⁷"But your eyes and your heart
   are set only on dishonest gain,
on shedding innocent blood
   and on oppression and extortion."

¹⁸Therefore this is what the LORD says about Jehoiakim son of Josiah king of Judah:

"They will not mourn for him:
   'Alas, my brother! Alas, my sister!'
They will not mourn for him:
   'Alas, my master! Alas, his
     splendour!'
¹⁹He will have the burial of a donkey—
   dragged away and thrown
   outside the gates of Jerusalem."

²⁰"Go up to Lebanon and cry out,
   let your voice be heard in Bashan,
cry out from Abarim,
   for all your allies are crushed.
²¹I warned you when you felt secure,
   but you said, 'I will not listen!'
This has been your way from your
     youth;
   you have not obeyed me.
²²The wind will drive all your shepherds
     away,
   and your allies will go into exile.
Then you will be ashamed and
     disgraced
   because of all your wickedness.
²³You who live in 'Lebanon',*ᵇ*
   who are nestled in cedar buildings,
how you will groan when pangs come
     upon you,
   pain like that of a woman in labour!

²⁴"As surely as I live," declares the LORD, "even if you, Jehoiachin*ᶜ* son of Jehoiakim king of Judah, were a signet ring on my right hand, I would still pull you off. ²⁵I will hand you over to those who seek your life, those you fear—to Nebuchadnezzar king of Babylon and to the Babylonians.*ᵈ* ²⁶I will hurl you and the mother who gave you birth into another country, where neither of you was born, and there you both will die. ²⁷You will never come back to the land you long to return to."

²⁸Is this man Jehoiachin a despised,
     broken pot,
   an object no-one wants?
Why will he and his children be hurled
     out,
   cast into a land they do not know?

ᵃ11 Also called *Jehoahaz*   *ᵇ23* That is, the palace in Jerusalem (see 1 Kings 7:2)
ᶜ24 Hebrew *Coniah*, a variant of *Jehoiachin*; also in verse 28   *ᵈ25* Or *Chaldeans*

²⁹O land, land, land,
  hear the word of the LORD!
³⁰This is what the LORD says:

"Record this man as if childless,
  a man who will not prosper in his
    lifetime,
for none of his offspring will prosper,
  none will sit on the throne of David
  or rule any more in Judah."

The Righteous Branch

23 "Woe to the shepherds who are destroying and scattering the sheep of my pasture!" declares the LORD. ²Therefore this is what the LORD, the God of Israel, says to the shepherds who tend my people: "Because you have scattered my flock and driven them away and have not bestowed care on them, I will bestow punishment on you for the evil you have done," declares the LORD. ³"I myself will gather the remnant of my flock out of all the countries where I have driven them and will bring them back to their pasture, where they will be fruitful and increase in number. ⁴I will place shepherds over them who will tend them, and they will no longer be afraid or terrified, nor will any be missing," declares the LORD.

⁵"The days are coming," declares the
  LORD,
  "when I will raise up to David^a a
    righteous Branch,
  a King who will reign wisely
  and do what is just and right in the
    land.
⁶In his days Judah will be saved
  and Israel will live in safety.
This is the name by which he will be
    called:
  The LORD Our Righteousness.

⁷"So then, the days are coming," declares the LORD, "when people will no longer say, 'As surely as the LORD lives, who brought the Israelites up out of Egypt,' ⁸but they will say, 'As surely as the LORD lives, who brought the descendants of Israel up out of the land of the north and out of all the countries where he had banished them.' Then they will live in their own land."

Lying Prophets

⁹Concerning the prophets:

My heart is broken within me;
  all my bones tremble.
I am like a drunken man,
  like a man overcome by wine,
because of the LORD
  and his holy words.
¹⁰The land is full of adulterers;
  because of the curse^b the land lies
    parched^c
  and the pastures in the desert are
    withered.
The ⌊prophets⌋ follow an evil course
  and use their power unjustly.

¹¹"Both prophet and priest are godless;
  even in my temple I find their
    wickedness,"
                        declares the LORD.
¹²"Therefore their path will become
    slippery;
  they will be banished to darkness
  and there they will fall.
I will bring disaster on them
  in the year they are punished,"
                        declares the LORD.

¹³"Among the prophets of Samaria
  I saw this repulsive thing:
They prophesied by Baal
  and led my people Israel astray.
¹⁴And among the prophets of Jerusalem
  I have seen something horrible:
  They commit adultery and live a lie.
They strengthen the hands of
    evildoers,
  so that no-one turns from his
    wickedness.
They are all like Sodom to me;
  the people of Jerusalem are like
    Gomorrah."

¹⁵Therefore, this is what the LORD Almighty says concerning the prophets:

---

^a5 Or *up from David's line*   ^b10 Or *because of these things*   ^c10 Or *land mourns*

"I will make them eat bitter food
  and drink poisoned water,
because from the prophets of Jerusalem
  ungodliness has spread throughout
    the land.''

16This is what the LORD Almighty
says:

"Do not listen to what the prophets are
  prophesying to you;
  they fill you with false hopes.
They speak visions from their own
  minds,
  not from the mouth of the LORD.
17They keep saying to those who despise
  me,
  'The LORD says: You will have
    peace.'
And to all who follow the stubbornness
  of their hearts
-they say, 'No harm will come to you.'
18But which of them has stood in the
  council of the LORD
  to see or to hear his word?
  Who has listened and heard his
    word?
19See, the storm of the LORD
  will burst out in wrath,
  a whirlwind swirling down
    on the heads of the wicked.
20The anger of the LORD will not turn
  back
  until he fully accomplishes
  the purposes of his heart.
In days to come
  you will understand it clearly.
21I did not send these prophets,
  yet they have run with their message;
I did not speak to them,
  yet they have prophesied.
22But if they had stood in my council,
  they would have proclaimed my
    words to my people
and would have turned them from their
  evil ways
  and from their evil deeds.

23"Am I only a God nearby,"
          declares the LORD,
  "and not a God far away?

24Can anyone hide in secret places
  so that I cannot see him?''
          declares the LORD.
"Do not I fill heaven and earth?''
          declares the LORD.

25"I have heard what the prophets say
who prophesy lies in my name. They say,
'I had a dream! I had a dream!' 26How long
will this continue in the hearts of these
lying prophets, who prophesy the delusions of their own minds? 27They think the
dreams they tell one another will make my
people forget my name, just as their
fathers forgot my name through Baal
worship. 28Let the prophet who has a
dream tell his dream, but let the one who
has my word speak it faithfully. For what
has straw to do with grain?" declares the
LORD. 29"Is not my word like fire," declares the LORD, "and like a hammer that
breaks a rock in pieces?

30"Therefore," declares the LORD, "I
am against the prophets who steal from
one another words supposedly from me.
31Yes," declares the LORD, "I am against
the prophets who wag their own tongues
and yet declare, 'The LORD declares.'
32Indeed, I am against those who prophesy false dreams," declares the LORD.
"They tell them and lead my people astray
with their reckless lies, yet I did not send
or appoint them. They do not benefit
these people in the least," declares the
LORD.

False Oracles and False Prophets

33"When these people, or a prophet or a
priest, ask you, 'What is the oracled of the
LORD?' say to them, 'What oracle?e I will
forsake you, declares the LORD.' 34If a
prophet or a priest or anyone else claims,
'This is the oracle of the LORD,' I will
punish that man and his household. 35This
is what each of you keeps on saying to his
friend or relative: 'What is the LORD's
answer?' or 'What has the LORD spoken?'
36But you must not mention 'the oracle of
the LORD' again, because every man's own
word becomes his oracle and so you distort

---

d33 Or *burden* (see Septuagint and Vulgate)
e33 Hebrew; Septuagint and Vulgate '*You are the burden*'; the Hebrew for *oracle* and *burden* is the same.

the words of the living God, the LORD Almighty, our God. ³⁷This is what you keep saying to a prophet: 'What is the LORD's answer to you?' or 'What has the LORD spoken?' ³⁸Although you claim, 'This is the oracle of the LORD,' this is what the LORD says: You used the words, 'This is the oracle of the LORD,' even though I told you that you must not claim, 'This is the oracle of the LORD.' ³⁹Therefore, I will surely forget you and cast you out of my presence along with the city I gave to you and your fathers. ⁴⁰I will bring upon you everlasting disgrace—everlasting shame that will not be forgotten."

Two Baskets of Figs

24 After Jehoiachin*ᵃ* son of Jehoiakim king of Judah and the officials, the craftsmen and the artisans of Judah were carried into exile from Jerusalem to Babylon by Nebuchadnezzar king of Babylon, the LORD showed me two baskets of figs placed in front of the temple of the LORD. ²One basket had very good figs, like those that ripen early; the other basket had very poor figs, so bad that they could not be eaten.

³Then the LORD asked me, "What do you see, Jeremiah?"

"Figs," I answered. "The good ones are very good, but the poor ones are so bad that they cannot be eaten."

⁴Then the word of the LORD came to me: ⁵"This is what the LORD, the God of Israel, says: 'Like these good figs, I regard as good the exiles from Judah, whom I sent away from this place to the land of the Babylonians.*ᵇ* ⁶My eyes will watch over them for their good, and I will bring them back to this land. I will build them up and not tear them down; I will plant them and not uproot them. ⁷I will give them a heart to know me, that I am the LORD. They will be my people, and I will be their God, for they will return to me with all their heart.

⁸"But like the poor figs, which are so bad that they cannot be eaten,' says the LORD, 'so will I deal with Zedekiah king of Judah, his officials and the survivors from Jerusalem, whether they remain in this land or live in Egypt. ⁹I will make them abhorrent and an offence to all the kingdoms of the earth, a reproach and a byword, an object of ridicule and cursing, wherever I banish them. ¹⁰I will send the sword, famine and plague against them until they are destroyed from the land I gave to them and their fathers.'"

Seventy Years of Captivity

25 The word came to Jeremiah concerning all the people of Judah in the fourth year of Jehoiakim son of Josiah king of Judah, which was the first year of Nebuchadnezzar king of Babylon. ²So Jeremiah the prophet said to all the people of Judah and to all those living in Jerusalem: ³For twenty-three years—from the thirteenth year of Josiah son of Amon king of Judah until this very day—the word of the LORD has come to me and I have spoken to you again and again, but you have not listened.

⁴And though the LORD has sent all his servants the prophets to you again and again, you have not listened or paid any attention. ⁵They said, "Turn now, each of you, from your evil ways and your evil practices, and you can stay in the land the LORD gave to you and your fathers for ever and ever. ⁶Do not follow other gods to serve and worship them; do not provoke me to anger with what your hands have made. Then I will not harm you."

⁷"But you did not listen to me," declares the LORD, "and you have provoked me with what your hands have made, and you have brought harm to yourselves."

⁸Therefore the LORD Almighty says this: "Because you have not listened to my words, ⁹I will summon all the peoples of the north and my servant Nebuchadnezzar king of Babylon," declares the LORD, "and I will bring them against this land and its inhabitants and against all the surrounding nations. I will completely destroy*ᵃ* them and make them an object of horror and scorn, and an everlasting ruin. ¹⁰I will banish from them the sounds of joy

---

ᵃ1 Hebrew *Jeconiah*, a variant of *Jehoiachin*　　*ᵇ5* Or *Chaldeans*
ᵃ9 The Hebrew term refers to the irrevocable giving over of things or persons to the LORD, often by totally destroying them.

and gladness, the voices of bride and bridegroom, the sound of millstones and the light of the lamp. [11]This whole country will become a desolate wasteland, and these nations will serve the king of Babylon for seventy years.

[12]"But when the seventy years are fulfilled, I will punish the king of Babylon and his nation, the land of the Babylonians,[b] for their guilt," declares the LORD, "and will make it desolate for ever. [13]I will bring upon that land all the things I have spoken against it, all that are written in this book and prophesied by Jeremiah against all the nations. [14]They themselves will be enslaved by many nations and great kings; I will repay them according to their deeds and the work of their hands."

The Cup of God's Wrath

[15]This is what the LORD, the God of Israel, said to me: "Take from my hand this cup filled with the wine of my wrath and make all the nations to whom I send you drink it. [16]When they drink it, they will stagger and go mad because of the sword I will send among them."

[17]So I took the cup from the LORD's hand and made all the nations to whom he sent me drink it: [18]Jerusalem and the towns of Judah, its kings and officials, to make them a ruin and an object of horror and scorn and cursing, as they are today; [19]Pharaoh king of Egypt, his attendants, his officials and all his people, [20]and all the foreign people there; all the kings of Uz; all the kings of the Philistines (those of Ashkelon, Gaza, Ekron, and the people left at Ashdod); [21]Edom, Moab and Ammon; [22]all the kings of Tyre and Sidon; the kings of the coastlands across the sea; [23]Dedan, Tema, Buz and all who are in distant places;[c] [24]all the kings of Arabia and all the kings of the foreign people who live in the desert; [25]all the kings of Zimri, Elam and Media; [26]and all the kings of the north, near and far, one after the other— all the kingdoms on the face of the earth. And after all of them, the king of Sheshach[d] will drink it too.

[27]"Then tell them, 'This is what the LORD Almighty, the God of Israel, says: Drink, get drunk and vomit, and fall to rise no more because of the sword I will send among you.' [28]But if they refuse to take the cup from your hand and drink, tell them, 'This is what the LORD Almighty says: You must drink it! [29]See, I am beginning to bring disaster on the city that bears my Name, and will you indeed go unpunished? You will not go unpunished, for I am calling down a sword upon all who live on the earth, declares the LORD Almighty.'

[30]"Now prophesy all these words against them and say to them:

" 'The LORD will roar from on high;
    he will thunder from his holy dwelling
    and roar mightily against his land.
He will shout like those who tread the grapes,
    shout against all who live on the earth.
[31]The tumult will resound to the ends of the earth,
    for the LORD will bring charges against the nations;
he will bring judgment on all mankind
    and put the wicked to the sword,' "
                              declares the LORD.

[32]This is what the LORD Almighty says:

"Look! Disaster is spreading
    from nation to nation;
a mighty storm is rising
    from the ends of the earth."

[33]At that time those slain by the LORD will be everywhere—from one end of the earth to the other. They will not be mourned or gathered up or buried, but will be like refuse lying on the ground.

[34]Weep and wail, you shepherds;
    roll in the dust, you leaders of the flock.
For your time to be slaughtered has come;

---

b12 Or *Chaldeans*   *c23* Or *who clip the hair by their foreheads*   *d26 Sheshach* is a cryptogram for Babylon.

you will fall and be shattered like fine
pottery.
35The shepherds will have nowhere to
flee,
the leaders of the flock no place to
escape.
36Hear the cry of the shepherds,
the wailing of the leaders of the flock,
for the LORD is destroying their
pasture.
37The peaceful meadows will be laid
waste
because of the fierce anger of the
LORD.
38Like a lion he will leave his lair,
and their land will become desolate
because of the sword*e* of the oppressor
and because of the LORD's fierce
anger.

Jeremiah Threatened With Death

26 Early in the reign of Jehoiakim son
of Josiah king of Judah, this word
came from the LORD: 2"This is what the
LORD says: Stand in the courtyard of the
LORD's house and speak to all the people
of the towns of Judah who come to
worship in the house of the LORD. Tell
them everything I command you; do not
omit a word. 3Perhaps they will listen and
each will turn from his evil way. Then I
will relent and not bring on them the
disaster I was planning because of the evil
they have done. 4Say to them, 'This is
what the LORD says: If you do not listen to
me and follow my law, which I have set
before you, 5and if you do not listen to the
words of my servants the prophets, whom
I have sent to you again and again (though
you have not listened), 6then I will make
this house like Shiloh and this city an
object of cursing among all the nations of
the earth.'"

7The priests, the prophets and all the
people heard Jeremiah speak these words
in the house of the LORD. 8But as soon as
Jeremiah finished telling all the people
everything the LORD had commanded him
to say, the priests, the prophets and all the
people seized him and said, "You must

die! 9Why do you prophesy in the LORD's
name that this house will be like Shiloh
and this city will be desolate and deserted?" And all the people crowded
around Jeremiah in the house of the LORD.

10When the officials of Judah heard
about these things, they went up from the
royal palace to the house of the LORD and
took their places at the entrance of the
New Gate of the LORD's house. 11Then the
priests and the prophets said to the officials and all the people, "This man
should be sentenced to death because he
has prophesied against this city. You have
heard it with your own ears!"

12Then Jeremiah said to all the officials
and all the people: "The LORD sent me to
prophesy against this house and this city
all the things you have heard. 13Now reform your ways and your actions and obey
the LORD your God. Then the LORD will
relent and not bring the disaster he has
pronounced against you. 14As for me, I am
in your hands; do with me whatever you
think is good and right. 15Be assured,
however, that if you put me to death, you
will bring the guilt of innocent blood on
yourselves and on this city and on those
who live in it, for in truth the LORD has sent
me to you to speak all these words in your
hearing."

16Then the officials and all the people
said to the priests and the prophets, "This
man should not be sentenced to death! He
has spoken to us in the name of the LORD
our God."

17Some of the elders of the land stepped
forward and said to the entire assembly of
people, 18"Micah of Moresheth prophesied in the days of Hezekiah king of Judah.
He told all the people of Judah, 'This is
what the LORD Almighty says:

"'Zion will be ploughed like a field,
Jerusalem will become a heap of
rubble,
the temple hill a mound overgrown
with thickets.'*a*

19"Did Hezekiah king of Judah or anyone
else in Judah put him to death? Did not

---

e38 Some Hebrew manuscripts and Septuagint (see also Jer. 46:16 and 50:16); most Hebrew manuscripts *anger*
a18 Micah 3:12

Hezekiah fear the LORD and seek his favour? And did not the LORD relent, so that he did not bring the disaster he pronounced against them? We are about to bring a terrible disaster on ourselves!''

²⁰(Now Uriah son of Shemaiah from Kiriath Jearim was another man who prophesied in the name of the LORD; he prophesied the same things against this city and this land as Jeremiah did. ²¹When King Jehoiakim and all his officers and officials heard his words, the king sought to put him to death. But Uriah heard of it and fled in fear to Egypt. ²²King Jehoiakim, however, sent Elnathan son of Acbor to Egypt, along with some other men. ²³They brought Uriah out of Egypt and took him to King Jehoiakim, who had him struck down with a sword and his body thrown into the burial place of the common people.)

²⁴Furthermore, Ahikam son of Shaphan supported Jeremiah, and so he was not handed over to the people to be put to death.

Judah to Serve Nebuchadnezzar

27 Early in the reign of Zedekiah[a] son of Josiah king of Judah, this word came to Jeremiah from the LORD: ²This is what the LORD said to me: "Make a yoke out of straps and crossbars and put it on your neck. ³Then send word to the kings of Edom, Moab, Ammon, Tyre and Sidon through the envoys who have come to Jerusalem to Zedekiah king of Judah. ⁴Give them a message for their masters and say, 'This is what the LORD Almighty, the God of Israel, says: "Tell this to your masters: ⁵With my great power and outstretched arm I made the earth and its people and the animals that are on it, and I give it to anyone I please. ⁶Now I will hand all your countries over to my servant Nebuchadnezzar king of Babylon; I will make even the wild animals subject to him. ⁷All nations will serve him and his son and his grandson until the time for his land comes; then many nations and great kings will subjugate him.

⁸'''If, however, any nation or kingdom will not serve Nebuchadnezzar king of Babylon or bow its neck under his yoke, I will punish that nation with the sword, famine and plague, declares the LORD, until I destroy it by his hand. ⁹So do not listen to your prophets, your diviners, your interpreters of dreams, your mediums or your sorcerers who tell you, 'You will not serve the king of Babylon.' ¹⁰They prophesy lies to you that will only serve to remove you far from your lands; I will banish you and you will perish. ¹¹But if any nation will bow its neck under the yoke of the king of Babylon and serve him, I will let that nation remain in its own land to till it and to live there, declares the LORD.'''''

¹²I gave the same message to Zedekiah king of Judah. I said, "Bow your neck under the yoke of the king of Babylon; serve him and his people, and you will live. ¹³Why will you and your people die by the sword, famine and plague with which the LORD has threatened any nation that will not serve the king of Babylon? ¹⁴Do not listen to the words of the prophets who say to you, 'You will not serve the king of Babylon,' for they are prophesying lies to you. ¹⁵'I have not sent them,' declares the LORD. 'They are prophesying lies in my name. Therefore, I will banish you and you will perish, both you and the prophets who prophesy to you.'''

¹⁶Then I said to the priests and all these people, "This is what the LORD says: Do not listen to the prophets who say, 'Very soon now the articles from the LORD's house will be brought back from Babylon.' They are prophesying lies to you. ¹⁷Do not listen to them. Serve the king of Babylon, and you will live. Why should this city become a ruin? ¹⁸If they are prophets and have the word of the LORD, let them plead with the LORD Almighty that the furnishings remaining in the house of the LORD and in the palace of the king of Judah and in Jerusalem not be taken to Babylon. ¹⁹For this is what the LORD Almighty says about the pillars, the

---

a1 A few Hebrew manuscripts and Syriac (see also Jer. 27:3, 12 and 28:1); most Hebrew manuscripts *Jehoiakim* (most Septuagint manuscripts do not have this verse.)

Sea, the movable stands and the other furnishings that are left in this city, [20]which Nebuchadnezzar king of Babylon did not take away when he carried Jehoiachin[b] son of Jehoiakim king of Judah into exile from Jerusalem to Babylon, along with all the nobles of Judah and Jerusalem—[21]yes, this is what the LORD Almighty, the God of Israel, says about the things that are left in the house of the LORD and in the palace of the king of Judah and in Jerusalem: [22]'They will be taken to Babylon and there they will remain until the day I come for them,' declares the LORD. 'Then I will bring them back and restore them to this place.'"

The False Prophet Hananiah

28 In the fifth month of that same year, the fourth year, early in the reign of Zedekiah king of Judah, the prophet Hananiah son of Azzur, who was from Gibeon, said to me in the house of the LORD in the presence of the priests and all the people: [2]"This is what the LORD Almighty, the God of Israel, says: 'I will break the yoke of the king of Babylon. [3]Within two years I will bring back to this place all the articles of the LORD's house that Nebuchadnezzar king of Babylon removed from here and took to Babylon. [4]I will also bring back to this place Jehoiachin son of Jehoiakim king of Judah and all the other exiles from Judah who went to Babylon,' declares the LORD, 'for I will break the yoke of the king of Babylon.'"

[5]Then the prophet Jeremiah replied to the prophet Hananiah before the priests and all the people who were standing in the house of the LORD. [6]He said, "Amen! May the LORD do so! May the LORD fulfil the words you have prophesied by bringing the articles of the LORD's house and all the exiles back to this place from Babylon. [7]Nevertheless, listen to what I have to say in your hearing and in the hearing of all the people: [8]From early times the prophets who preceded you and me have prophesied war, disaster and plague against many countries and great kingdoms. [9]But the prophet who prophesies peace will be recognised as one truly sent by the LORD only if his prediction comes true."

[10]Then the prophet Hananiah took the yoke off the neck of the prophet Jeremiah and broke it, [11]and he said before all the people, "This is what the LORD says: 'In the same way will I break the yoke of Nebuchadnezzar king of Babylon off the neck of all the nations within two years.'" At this, the prophet Jeremiah went on his way.

[12]Shortly after the prophet Hananiah had broken the yoke off the neck of the prophet Jeremiah, the word of the LORD came to Jeremiah: [13]"Go and tell Hananiah, 'This is what the LORD says: You have broken a wooden yoke, but in its place you will get a yoke of iron. [14]This is what the LORD Almighty, the God of Israel, says: I will put an iron yoke on the necks of all these nations to make them serve Nebuchadnezzar king of Babylon, and they will serve him. I will even give him control over the wild animals.'"

[15]Then the prophet Jeremiah said to Hananiah the prophet, "Listen, Hananiah! The LORD has not sent you, yet you have persuaded this nation to trust in lies. [16]Therefore, this is what the LORD says: 'I am about to remove you from the face of the earth. This very year you are going to die, because you have preached rebellion against the LORD.'"

[17]In the seventh month of that same year, Hananiah the prophet died.

A Letter to the Exiles

29 This is the text of the letter that the prophet Jeremiah sent from Jerusalem to the surviving elders among the exiles and to the priests, the prophets and all the other people Nebuchadnezzar had carried into exile from Jerusalem to Babylon. [2](This was after King Jehoiachin and the queen mother, the court officials and the leaders of Judah and Jerusalem, the craftsmen and the artisans had gone into exile from Jerusalem.) [3]He entrusted the

---

b20 Hebrew Jeconiah, a variant of Jehoiachin; also in 28:4 and 29:2 letter to Elasah son of Shaphan and to Gemariah son of Hilkiah, whom Zedekiah king of Judah sent to King Nebuchadnezzar in Babylon. It said:

⁴This is what the LORD Almighty, the God of Israel, says to all those I carried into exile from Jerusalem to Babylon: ⁵"Build houses and settle down; plant gardens and eat what they produce. ⁶Marry and have sons and daughters; find wives for your sons and give your daughters in marriage, so that they too may have sons and daughters. Increase in number there; do not decrease. ⁷Also, seek the peace and prosperity of the city to which I have carried you into exile. Pray to the LORD for it, because if it prospers, you too will prosper." ⁸Yes, this is what the LORD Almighty, the God of Israel, says: "Do not let the prophets and diviners among you deceive you. Do not listen to the dreams you encourage them to have. ⁹They are prophesying lies to you in my name. I have not sent them," declares the LORD.

¹⁰This is what the LORD says: "When seventy years are completed for Babylon, I will come to you and fulfil my gracious promise to bring you back to this place. ¹¹For I know the plans I have for you," declares the LORD, "plans to prosper you and not to harm you, plans to give you hope and a future. ¹²Then you will call upon me and come and pray to me, and I will listen to you. ¹³You will seek me and find me when you seek me with all your heart. ¹⁴I will be found by you," declares the LORD, "and will bring you back from captivity.ᵃ I will gather you from all the nations and places where I have banished you," declares the LORD, "and will bring you back to the place from which I carried you into exile."

¹⁵You may say, "The LORD has raised up prophets for us in Babylon," ¹⁶but this is what the LORD says about the king who sits on David's throne and all the people who remain in this city, your countrymen who did not go with you into exile—¹⁷yes, this is what the LORD Almighty says: "I will send the sword, famine and plague against them and I will make them like poor figs that are so bad they cannot be eaten. ¹⁸I will pursue them with the sword, famine and plague and will make them abhorrent to all the kingdoms of the earth and an object of cursing and horror, of scorn and reproach, among all the nations where I drive them. ¹⁹For they have not listened to my words," declares the LORD, "words that I sent to them again and again by my servants the prophets. And you exiles have not listened either," declares the LORD.

²⁰Therefore, hear the word of the LORD, all you exiles whom I have sent away from Jerusalem to Babylon. ²¹This is what the LORD Almighty, the God of Israel, says about Ahab son of Kolaiah and Zedekiah son of Maaseiah, who are prophesying lies to you in my name: "I will hand them over to Nebuchadnezzar king of Babylon, and he will put them to death before your very eyes. ²²Because of them, all the exiles from Judah who are in Babylon will use this curse: 'The LORD treat you like Zedekiah and Ahab, whom the king of Babylon burned in the fire.' ²³For they have done outrageous things in Israel; they have committed adultery with their neighbours' wives and in my name have spoken lies, which I did not tell them to do. I know it and am a witness to it," declares the LORD.

Message to Shemaiah

²⁴Tell Shemaiah the Nehelamite, ²⁵"This is what the LORD Almighty, the God of Israel, says: You sent letters in your own name to all the people in Jerusalem, to Zephaniah son of Maaseiah the

ᵃ14 Or will restore your fortunes

priest, and to all the other priests. You said to Zephaniah, 26'The LORD has appointed you priest in place of Jehoiada to be in charge of the house of the LORD; you should put any madman who acts like a prophet into the stocks and neck-irons. 27So why have you not reprimanded Jeremiah from Anathoth, who poses as a prophet among you? 28He has sent this message to us in Babylon: It will be a long time. Therefore build houses and settle down; plant gardens and eat what they produce.'"

29Zephaniah the priest, however, read the letter to Jeremiah the prophet. 30Then the word of the LORD came to Jeremiah: 31"Send this message to all the exiles: 'This is what the LORD says about Shemaiah the Nehelamite: Because Shemaiah has prophesied to you, even though I did not send him, and has led you to believe a lie, 32this is what the LORD says: I will surely punish Shemaiah the Nehelamite and his descendants. He will have no-one left among this people, nor will he see the good things I will do for my people, declares the LORD, because he has preached rebellion against me.'"

Restoration of Israel

30 This is the word that came to Jeremiah from the LORD: 2"This is what the LORD, the God of Israel, says: 'Write in a book all the words I have spoken to you. 3The days are coming,' declares the LORD, 'when I will bring my people Israel and Judah back from captivity*a* and restore them to the land I gave to their forefathers to possess,' says the LORD."

4These are the words the LORD spoke concerning Israel and Judah: 5"This is what the LORD says:

"'Cries of fear are heard—
    terror, not peace.
6Ask and see:
    Can a man bear children?
Then why do I see every strong man
    with his hands on his stomach like a
    woman in labour,

every face turned deathly pale?
7How awful that day will be!
    None will be like it.
It will be a time of trouble for Jacob,
    but he will be saved out of it.

8"'In that day,' declares the LORD
        Almighty,
    'I will break the yoke off their necks
and will tear off their bonds;
    no longer will foreigners enslave
        them.
9Instead, they will serve the LORD their
        God
    and David their king,
    whom I will raise up for them.

10"'So do not fear, O Jacob my servant;
    do not be dismayed, O Israel,'
                declares the LORD.
'I will surely save you out of a distant
        place,
    your descendants from the land of
        their exile.
Jacob will again have peace and
        security,
    and no-one will make him afraid.
11I am with you and will save you,'
    declares the LORD.
'Though I completely destroy all the
        nations
    among which I scatter you,
    I will not completely destroy
        you.
I will discipline you but only with
        justice;
    I will not let you go entirely
        unpunished.'

12"This is what the LORD says:

"'Your wound is incurable,
    your injury beyond healing.
13There is no-one to plead your cause,
    no remedy for your sore,
    no healing for you.
14All your allies have forgotten you;
    they care nothing for you.
I have struck you as an enemy would
    and punished you as would the cruel,
because your guilt is so great
    and your sins so many.

a3 Or *will restore the fortunes of my people Israel and Judah*

¹⁵Why do you cry out over your wound,
   your pain that has no cure?
Because of your great guilt and many
      sins
   I have done these things to you.

¹⁶"'But all who devour you will be
      devoured;
   all your enemies will go into exile.
Those who plunder you will be
      plundered;
   all who make spoil of you I will
      despoil.
¹⁷But I will restore you to health
   and heal your wounds,'
                        declares the LORD,
'because you are called an outcast,
   Zion for whom no-one cares.'

¹⁸"This is what the LORD says:

"'I will restore the fortunes of Jacob's
      tents
   and have compassion on his
      dwellings;
the city will be rebuilt on her ruins,
   and the palace will stand in its proper
      place.
¹⁹From them will come songs of
      thanksgiving
   and the sound of rejoicing.
I will add to their numbers,
   and they will not be decreased;
I will bring them honour,
   and they will not be disdained.
²⁰Their children will be as in days of old,
   and their community will be
      established before me;
I will punish all who oppress them.
²¹Their leader will be one of their own;
   their ruler will arise from among
      them.
I will bring him near and he will come
      close to me,
   for who is he who will devote himself
      to be close to me?'
                        declares the LORD.
²²"'So you will be my people,
   and I will be your God.'"

²³See, the storm of the LORD
   will burst out in wrath,

a driving wind swirling down
   on the heads of the wicked.
²⁴The fierce anger of the LORD will not
      turn back
   until he fully accomplishes
   the purposes of his heart.
In days to come
   you will understand this.

31 "At that time," declares the LORD,
      "I will be the God of all the clans
of Israel, and they will be my people."
   ²This is what the LORD says:

"The people who survive the sword
   will find favour in the desert;
   I will come to give rest to Israel."

³The LORD appeared to us in the past,ᵃ
saying:

"I have loved you with an everlasting
      love;
   I have drawn you with
      loving-kindness.
⁴I will build you up again
   and you will be rebuilt, O Virgin
      Israel.
Again you will take up your
      tambourines
   and go out to dance with the joyful.
⁵Again you will plant vineyards
   on the hills of Samaria;
the farmers will plant them
   and enjoy their fruit.
⁶There will be a day when watchmen cry
      out
   on the hills of Ephraim,
'Come, let us go up to Zion,
   to the LORD our God.'"

⁷This is what the LORD says:

"Sing with joy for Jacob;
   shout for the foremost of the nations.
Make your praises heard, and say,
   'O LORD, save your people,
   the remnant of Israel.'
⁸See, I will bring them from the land of
      the north
   and gather them from the ends of the
      earth.

ᵃ3 Or LORD has appeared to us from afar

Among them will be the blind and the
 lame,
 expectant mothers and women in
 labour;
 a great throng will return.
9They will come with weeping;
 they will pray as I bring them back.
I will lead them beside streams of water
 on a level path where they will not
 stumble,
because I am Israel's father,
 and Ephraim is my firstborn son.

10"Hear the word of the LORD, O nations;
 proclaim it in distant coastlands:
'He who scattered Israel will gather
 them
 and will watch over his flock like a
 shepherd.'
11For the LORD will ransom Jacob
 and redeem them from the hand of
 those stronger than they.
12They will come and shout for joy on the
 heights of Zion;
 they will rejoice in the bounty of the
 LORD—
the grain, the new wine and the oil,
 the young of the flocks and herds.
They will be like a well-watered garden,
 and they will sorrow no more.
13Then maidens will dance and be glad,
 young men and old as well.
I will turn their mourning into gladness;
 I will give them comfort and joy
 instead of sorrow.
14I will satisfy the priests with abundance,
 and my people will be filled with my
 bounty,"
                    declares the LORD.

15This is what the LORD says:

"A voice is heard in Ramah,
 mourning and great weeping,
Rachel weeping for her children
 and refusing to be comforted,
 because her children are no more."

16This is what the LORD says:

"Restrain your voice from weeping
 and your eyes from tears,

for your work will be rewarded,"
                    declares the LORD.
"They will return from the land of the
 enemy.
17So there is hope for your future,"
                    declares the LORD.
"Your children will return to their
 own land.

18"I have surely heard Ephraim's
 moaning:
'You disciplined me like an unruly
 calf,
 and I have been disciplined.
Restore me, and I will return,
 because you are the LORD my God.
19After I strayed,
 I repented;
after I came to understand,
 I beat my breast.
I was ashamed and humiliated
 because I bore the disgrace of my
 youth.'
20Is not Ephraim my dear son,
 the child in whom I delight?
Though I often speak against him,
 I still remember him.
Therefore my heart yearns for him;
 I have great compassion for him,"
                    declares the LORD.

21"Set up road signs;
 put up guideposts.
Take note of the highway,
 the road that you take.
Return, O Virgin Israel,
 return to your towns.
22How long will you wander,
 O unfaithful daughter?
The LORD will create a new thing on
 earth—
 a woman will surround*b* a man."

23This is what the LORD Almighty, the
God of Israel, says: "When I bring them
back from captivity,*c* the people in the
land of Judah and in its towns will once
again use these words: 'The LORD bless
you, O righteous dwelling, O sacred
mountain.' 24People will live together in
Judah and all its towns—farmers and

---

b22 Or will go about ⌐seeking⌐; or will protect   *c23 Or I restore their fortunes* those who move about with their flocks. [25]I will refresh the weary and satisfy the faint."

[26]At this I awoke and looked around. My sleep had been pleasant to me.

[27]"The days are coming," declares the LORD, "when I will plant the house of Israel and the house of Judah with the offspring of men and of animals. [28]Just as I watched over them to uproot and tear down, and to overthrow, destroy and bring disaster, so I will watch over them to build and to plant," declares the LORD. [29]"In those days people will no longer say,

'The fathers have eaten sour grapes,
    and the children's teeth are set on
        edge.'

[30]Instead, everyone will die for his own sin; whoever eats sour grapes—his own teeth will be set on edge.

[31]"The time is coming," declares the
    LORD,
    "when I will make a new covenant
with the house of Israel
    and with the house of Judah.
[32]It will not be like the covenant
    I made with their forefathers
when I took them by the hand
    to lead them out of Egypt,
because they broke my covenant,
    though I was a husband to[d] them,"[e]
                        declares the LORD.
[33]"This is the covenant that I will make
    with the house of Israel
after that time," declares the LORD.
"I will put my law in their minds
    and write it on their hearts.
I will be their God,
    and they will be my people.
[34]No longer will a man teach his
        neighbour,
    or a man his brother, saying, 'Know
        the LORD,'
because they will all know me,
    from the least of them to the
        greatest,"
                    declares the LORD.

"For I will forgive their wickedness
    and will remember their sins no
        more."

[35]This is what the LORD says,

he who appoints the sun
    to shine by day,
who decrees the moon and stars
    to shine by night,
who stirs up the sea
    so that its waves roar—
    the LORD Almighty is his name:
[36]"Only if these decrees vanish from my
        sight,"
    declares the LORD,
"will the descendants of Israel ever
        cease
    to be a nation before me."

[37]This is what the LORD says:

"Only if the heavens above can be
        measured
    and the foundations of the earth
        below be searched out
will I reject all the descendants of Israel
    because of all they have done,"
                        declares the LORD.

[38]"The days are coming," declares the LORD, "when this city will be rebuilt for me from the Tower of Hananel to the Corner Gate. [39]The measuring line will stretch from there straight to the hill of Gareb and then turn to Goah. [40]The whole valley where dead bodies and ashes are thrown, and all the terraces out to the Kidron Valley on the east as far as the corner of the Horse Gate, will be holy to the LORD. The city will never again be uprooted or demolished."

Jeremiah Buys a Field

32 This is the word that came to Jeremiah from the LORD in the tenth year of Zedekiah king of Judah, which was the eighteenth year of Nebuchadnezzar. [2]The army of the king of Babylon was then besieging Jerusalem, and Jeremiah

---

[d]32 Hebrew; Septuagint and Syriac *covenant, / and I turned away from*   [e]32 Or *was their master*

the prophet was confined in the courtyard of the guard in the royal palace of Judah.

3Now Zedekiah king of Judah had imprisoned him there, saying, "Why do you prophesy as you do? You say, 'This is what the LORD says: I am about to hand this city over to the king of Babylon, and he will capture it. 4Zedekiah king of Judah will not escape out of the hands of the Babylonians*a* but will certainly be handed over to the king of Babylon, and will speak with him face to face and see him with his own eyes. 5He will take Zedekiah to Babylon, where he will remain until I deal with him, declares the LORD. If you fight against the Babylonians, you will not succeed.'"

6Jeremiah said, "The word of the LORD came to me: 7Hanamel son of Shallum your uncle is going to come to you and say, 'Buy my field at Anathoth, because as nearest relative it is your right and duty to buy it.'

8"Then, just as the LORD had said, my cousin Hanamel came to me in the courtyard of the guard and said, 'Buy my field at Anathoth in the territory of Benjamin. Since it is your right to redeem it and possess it, buy it for yourself.'

"I knew that this was the word of the LORD; 9so I bought the field at Anathoth from my cousin Hanamel and weighed out for him seventeen shekels*b* of silver. 10I signed and sealed the deed, had it witnessed, and weighed out the silver on the scales. 11I took the deed of purchase—the sealed copy containing the terms and conditions, as well as the unsealed copy—12and I gave this deed to Baruch son of Neriah, the son of Mahseiah, in the presence of my cousin Hanamel and of the witnesses who had signed the deed and of all the Jews sitting in the courtyard of the guard.

13"In their presence I gave Baruch these instructions: 14'This is what the LORD Almighty, the God of Israel, says: Take these documents, both the sealed and unsealed copies of the deed of purchase, and put them in a clay jar so that they will last a long time. 15For this is what the LORD Almighty, the God of Israel, says:

Houses, fields and vineyards will again be bought in this land.'

16"After I had given the deed of purchase to Baruch son of Neriah, I prayed to the LORD:

17"Ah, Sovereign LORD, you have made the heavens and the earth by your great power and outstretched arm. Nothing is too hard for you. 18You show love to thousands but bring the punishment for the fathers' sins into the laps of their children after them. O great and powerful God, whose name is the LORD Almighty, 19great are your purposes and mighty are your deeds. Your eyes are open to all the ways of men; you reward everyone according to his conduct and as his deeds deserve. 20You performed miraculous signs and wonders in Egypt and have continued them to this day, both in Israel and among all mankind, and have gained the renown that is still yours. 21You brought your people Israel out of Egypt with signs and wonders, by a mighty hand and an outstretched arm and with great terror. 22You gave them this land you had sworn to give to their forefathers, a land flowing with milk and honey. 23They came in and took possession of it, but they did not obey you or follow your law; they did not do what you commanded them to do. So you brought all this disaster upon them.

24"See how the siege ramps are built up to take the city. Because of the sword, famine and plague, the city will be handed over to the Babylonians who are attacking it. What you said has happened, as you now see. 25And though the city will be handed over to the Babylonians, you, O Sovereign LORD, say to me, 'Buy the field with silver and have the transaction witnessed.'"

26Then the word of the LORD came to Jeremiah: 27"I am the LORD, the God of all

a4 Or *Chaldeans*; also in verses 5, 24, 25, 28, 29 and 43
b9 That is, about 7 ounces (about 200 grams)

mankind. Is anything too hard for me? [28]Therefore, this is what the LORD says: I am about to hand this city over to the Babylonians and to Nebuchadnezzar king of Babylon, who will capture it. [29]The Babylonians who are attacking this city will come in and set it on fire; they will burn it down, along with the houses where the people provoked me to anger by burning incense on the roofs to Baal and by pouring out drink offerings to other gods.

[30]"The people of Israel and Judah have done nothing but evil in my sight from their youth; indeed, the people of Israel have done nothing but provoke me with what their hands have made, declares the LORD. [31]From the day it was built until now, this city has so aroused my anger and wrath that I must remove it from my sight. [32]The people of Israel and Judah have provoked me by all the evil they have done—they, their kings and officials, their priests and prophets, the men of Judah and the people of Jerusalem. [33]They turned their backs to me and not their faces; though I taught them again and again, they would not listen or respond to discipline. [34]They set up their abominable idols in the house that bears my Name and defiled it. [35]They built high places for Baal in the Valley of Ben Hinnom to sacrifice their sons and daughters[c] to Molech, though I never commanded, nor did it enter my mind, that they should do such a detestable thing and so make Judah sin.

[36]"You are saying about this city, 'By the sword, famine and plague it will be handed over to the king of Babylon'; but this is what the LORD, the God of Israel, says: [37]I will surely gather them from all the lands where I banish them in my furious anger and great wrath; I will bring them back to this place and let them live in safety. [38]They will be my people, and I will be their God. [39]I will give them singleness of heart and action, so that they will always fear me for their own good and the good of their children after them. [40]I will make an everlasting covenant with them: I will never stop doing good to them, and I will inspire them to fear me, so that they

will never turn away from me. [41]I will rejoice in doing them good and will assuredly plant them in this land with all my heart and soul.

[42]"This is what the LORD says: As I have brought all this great calamity on this people, so I will give them all the prosperity I have promised them. [43]Once more fields will be bought in this land of which you say, 'It is a desolate waste, without men or animals, for it has been handed over to the Babylonians.' [44]Fields will be bought for silver, and deeds will be signed, sealed and witnessed in the territory of Benjamin, in the villages around Jerusalem, in the towns of Judah and in the towns of the hill country, of the western foothills and of the Negev, because I will restore their fortunes,[d] declares the LORD."

Promise of Restoration

33 While Jeremiah was still confined in the courtyard of the guard, the word of the LORD came to him a second time: [2]"This is what the LORD says, he who made the earth, the LORD who formed it and established it—the LORD is his name: [3]'Call to me and I will answer you and tell you great and unsearchable things you do not know.' [4]For this is what the LORD, the God of Israel, says about the houses in this city and the royal palaces of Judah that have been torn down to be used against the siege ramps and the sword [5]in the fight with the Babylonians:[a] 'They will be filled with the dead bodies of the men I will slay in my anger and wrath. I will hide my face from this city because of all its wickedness.

[6]"'Nevertheless, I will bring health and healing to it; I will heal my people and will let them enjoy abundant peace and security. [7]I will bring Judah and Israel back from captivity[b] and will rebuild them as they were before. [8]I will cleanse them from all the sin they have committed against me and will forgive all their sins of rebellion against me. [9]Then this city will bring me renown, joy, praise and honour before all nations on earth that hear of all

[c]35 Or to make their sons and daughters pass through ⌐the fire⌐   [d]44 Or will bring them back from captivity
[a]5 Or Chaldeans   [b]7 Or will restore the fortunes of Judah and Israel

the good things I do for it; and they will be in awe and will tremble at the abundant prosperity and peace I provide for it.'

10"This is what the LORD says: 'You say about this place, "It is a desolate waste, without men or animals." Yet in the towns of Judah and the streets of Jerusalem that are deserted, inhabited by neither men nor animals, there will be heard once more 11the sounds of joy and gladness, the voices of bride and bridegroom, and the voices of those who bring thank-offerings to the house of the LORD, saying,

"Give thanks to the LORD Almighty,
    for the LORD is good;
    his love endures for ever."

For I will restore the fortunes of the land as they were before,' says the LORD.

12"This is what the LORD Almighty says: 'In this place, desolate and without men or animals—in all its towns there will again be pastures for shepherds to rest their flocks. 13In the towns of the hill country, of the western foothills and of the Negev, in the territory of Benjamin, in the villages around Jerusalem and in the towns of Judah, flocks will again pass under the hand of the one who counts them,' says the LORD.

14"'The days are coming,' declares the LORD, 'when I will fulfil the gracious promise I made to the house of Israel and to the house of Judah.

15"'In those days and at that time
    I will make a righteous Branch sprout
        from David's line;
    he will do what is just and right in the
        land.
16In those days Judah will be saved
    and Jerusalem will live in safety.
This is the name by which it[c] will be
        called:
    The LORD Our Righteousness.'

17For this is what the LORD says: 'David will never fail to have a man to sit on the throne of the house of Israel, 18nor will the priests, who are Levites, ever fail to have a

man to stand before me continually to offer burnt offerings, to burn grain offerings and to present sacrifices.'"

19The word of the LORD came to Jeremiah: 20"This is what the LORD says: 'If you can break my covenant with the day and my covenant with the night, so that day and night no longer come at their appointed time, 21then my covenant with David my servant—and my covenant with the Levites who are priests ministering before me—can be broken and David will no longer have a descendant to reign on his throne. 22I will make the descendants of David my servant and the Levites who minister before me as countless as the stars of the sky and as measureless as the sand on the seashore.'"

23The word of the LORD came to Jeremiah: 24"Have you not noticed that these people are saying, 'The LORD has rejected the two kingdoms[d] he chose'? So they despise my people and no longer regard them as a nation. 25This is what the LORD says: 'If I have not established my covenant with day and night and the fixed laws of heaven and earth, 26then I will reject the descendants of Jacob and David my servant and will not choose one of his sons to rule over the descendants of Abraham, Isaac and Jacob. For I will restore their fortunes[e] and have compassion on them.'"

Warning to Zedekiah

34 While Nebuchadnezzar king of Babylon and all his army and all the kingdoms and peoples in the empire he ruled were fighting against Jerusalem and all its surrounding towns, this word came to Jeremiah from the LORD: 2"This is what the LORD, the God of Israel, says: Go to Zedekiah king of Judah and tell him, 'This is what the LORD says: I am about to hand this city over to the king of Babylon, and he will burn it down. 3You will not escape from his grasp but will surely be captured and handed over to him. You will see the king of Babylon with your own eyes, and he will speak with you face to face. And you will go to Babylon.

---

c16 Or *he*   *d24* Or *families*   *e26* Or *will bring them back from captivity*

[4]"'Yet hear the promise of the LORD, O Zedekiah king of Judah. This is what the LORD says concerning you: You will not die by the sword; [5]you will die peacefully. As people made a funeral fire in honour of your fathers, the former kings who preceded you, so they will make a fire in your honour and lament, "Alas, O master!" I myself make this promise, declares the LORD.'"

[6]Then Jeremiah the prophet told all this to Zedekiah king of Judah, in Jerusalem, [7]while the army of the king of Babylon was fighting against Jerusalem and the other cities of Judah that were still holding out—Lachish and Azekah. These were the only fortified cities left in Judah.

Freedom for Slaves

[8]The word came to Jeremiah from the LORD after King Zedekiah had made a covenant with all the people in Jerusalem to proclaim freedom for the slaves. [9]Everyone was to free his Hebrew slaves, both male and female; no-one was to hold a fellow Jew in bondage. [10]So all the officials and people who entered into this covenant agreed that they would free their male and female slaves and no longer hold them in bondage. They agreed, and set them free. [11]But afterwards they changed their minds and took back the slaves they had freed and enslaved them again.

[12]Then the word of the LORD came to Jeremiah: [13]"This is what the LORD, the God of Israel, says: I made a covenant with your forefathers when I brought them out of Egypt, out of the land of slavery. I said, [14]'Every seventh year each of you must free any fellow Hebrew who has sold himself to you. After he has served you for six years, you must let him go free.'[a] Your fathers, however, did not listen to me or pay attention to me. [15]Recently you repented and did what is right in my sight: Each of you proclaimed freedom to his countrymen. You even made a covenant before me in the house that bears my Name. [16]But now you have turned round and profaned my name;

each of you has taken back the male and female slaves you had set free to go where they wished. You have forced them to become your slaves again.

[17]"Therefore, this is what the LORD says: You have not obeyed me; you have not proclaimed freedom for your fellow countrymen. So I now proclaim 'freedom' for you, declares the LORD—'freedom' to fall by the sword, plague and famine. I will make you abhorrent to all the kingdoms of the earth. [18]The men who have violated my covenant and have not fulfilled the terms of the covenant they made before me, I will treat like the calf they cut in two and then walked between its pieces. [19]The leaders of Judah and Jerusalem, the court officials, the priests and all the people of the land who walked between the pieces of the calf, [20]I will hand over to their enemies who seek their lives. Their dead bodies will become food for the birds of the air and the beasts of the earth.

[21]"I will hand Zedekiah king of Judah and his officials over to their enemies who seek their lives, to the army of the king of Babylon, which has withdrawn from you. [22]I am going to give the order, declares the LORD, and I will bring them back to this city. They will fight against it, take it and burn it down. And I will lay waste the towns of Judah so that no-one can live there."

The Recabites

35 This is the word that came to Jeremiah from the LORD during the reign of Jehoiakim son of Josiah king of Judah: [2]"Go to the Recabite family and invite them to come to one of the side rooms of the house of the LORD and give them wine to drink."

[3]So I went to get Jaazaniah son of Jeremiah, the son of Habazziniah, and his brothers and all his sons—the whole family of the Recabites. [4]I brought them into the house of the LORD, into the room of the sons of Hanan son of Igdaliah the man of God. It was next to the room of the officials, which was over that of Maaseiah son of Shallum the door-keeper. [5]Then I

[a]14 Deut. 15:12

set bowls full of wine and some cups before the men of the Recabite family and said to them, "Drink some wine."

6But they replied, "We do not drink wine, because our forefather Jonadab son of Recab gave us this command: 'Neither you nor your descendants must ever drink wine. 7Also you must never build houses, sow seed or plant vineyards; you must never have any of these things, but must always live in tents. Then you will live a long time in the land where you are nomads.' 8We have obeyed everything our forefather Jonadab son of Recab commanded us. Neither we nor our wives nor our sons and daughters have ever drunk wine 9or built houses to live in or had vineyards, fields or crops. 10We have lived in tents and have fully obeyed everything our forefather Jonadab commanded us. 11But when Nebuchadnezzar king of Babylon invaded this land, we said, 'Come, we must go to Jerusalem to escape the Babylonian*a* and Aramean armies.' So we have remained in Jerusalem."

12Then the word of the LORD came to Jeremiah, saying: 13"This is what the LORD Almighty, the God of Israel, says: Go and tell the men of Judah and the people of Jerusalem, 'Will you not learn a lesson and obey my words?' declares the LORD. 14'Jonadab son of Recab ordered his sons not to drink wine and this command has been kept. To this day they do not drink wine, because they obey their forefather's command. But I have spoken to you again and again, yet you have not obeyed me. 15Again and again I sent all my servants the prophets to you. They said, "Each of you must turn from your wicked ways and reform your actions; do not follow other gods to serve them. Then you shall live in the land I have given to you and your fathers." But you have not paid attention or listened to me. 16The descendants of Jonadab son of Recab have carried out the command their forefather gave them, but these people have not obeyed me.'

17"Therefore, this is what the LORD God Almighty, the God of Israel, says: 'Listen! I am going to bring on Judah and on everyone living in Jerusalem every disaster I pronounced against them. I spoke to them, but they did not listen; I called to them, but they did not answer.'"

18Then Jeremiah said to the family of the Recabites, "This is what the LORD Almighty, the God of Israel, says: 'You have obeyed the command of your forefather Jonadab and have followed all his instructions and have done everything he ordered.' 19Therefore, this is what the LORD Almighty, the God of Israel, says: 'Jonadab son of Recab shall never fail to have a man to serve me.'"

Jehoiakim Burns Jeremiah's Scroll

36 In the fourth year of Jehoiakim son of Josiah king of Judah, this word came to Jeremiah from the LORD: 2"Take a scroll and write on it all the words I have spoken to you concerning Israel, Judah and all the other nations from the time I began speaking to you in the reign of Josiah till now. 3Perhaps when the people of Judah hear about every disaster I plan to inflict on them, each of them will turn from his wicked way; then I will forgive their wickedness and their sin."

4So Jeremiah called Baruch son of Neriah, and while Jeremiah dictated all the words the LORD had spoken to him, Baruch wrote them on the scroll. 5Then Jeremiah told Baruch, "I am restricted; I cannot go to the LORD's temple. 6So you go to the house of the LORD on a day of fasting and read to the people from the scroll the words of the LORD that you wrote as I dictated. Read them to all the people of Judah who come in from their towns. 7Perhaps they will bring their petition before the LORD, and each will turn from his wicked ways, for the anger and wrath pronounced against this people by the LORD are great."

8Baruch son of Neriah did everything Jeremiah the prophet told him to do; at the LORD's temple he read the words of the LORD from the scroll. 9In the ninth month of the fifth year of Jehoiakim son of Josiah king of Judah, a time of fasting before the LORD was proclaimed for all the people in

a11 Or Chaldean

Jerusalem and those who had come from the towns of Judah. [10]From the room of Gemariah son of Shaphan the secretary, which was in the upper courtyard at the entrance of the New Gate of the temple, Baruch read to all the people at the LORD's temple the words of Jeremiah from the scroll.

[11]When Micaiah son of Gemariah, the son of Shaphan, heard all the words of the LORD from the scroll, [12]he went down to the secretary's room in the royal palace, where all the officials were sitting: Elishama the secretary, Delaiah son of Shemaiah, Elnathan son of Acbor, Gemariah son of Shaphan, Zedekiah son of Hananiah, and all the other officials. [13]After Micaiah told them everything he had heard Baruch read to the people from the scroll, [14]all the officials sent Jehudi son of Nethaniah, the son of Shelemiah, the son of Cushi, to say to Baruch, "Bring the scroll from which you have read to the people and come." So Baruch son of Neriah went to them with the scroll in his hand. [15]They said to him, "Sit down, please, and read it to us."

So Baruch read it to them. [16]When they heard all these words, they looked at each other in fear and said to Baruch, "We must report all these words to the king." [17]Then they asked Baruch, "Tell us, how did you come to write all this? Did Jeremiah dictate it?"

[18]"Yes," Baruch replied, "he dictated all these words to me, and I wrote them in ink on the scroll."

[19]Then the officials said to Baruch, "You and Jeremiah, go and hide. Don't let anyone know where you are."

[20]After they put the scroll in the room of Elishama the secretary, they went to the king in the courtyard and reported everything to him. [21]The king sent Jehudi to get the scroll, and Jehudi brought it from the room of Elishama the secretary and read it to the king and all the officials standing beside him. [22]It was the ninth month and the king was sitting in the winter apartment, with a fire burning in the brazier in front of him. [23]Whenever Jehudi had read

three or four columns of the scroll, the king cut them off with a scribe's knife and threw them into the brazier, until the entire scroll was burned in the fire. [24]The king and all his attendants who heard all these words showed no fear, nor did they tear their clothes. [25]Even though Elnathan, Delaiah and Gemariah urged the king not to burn the scroll, he would not listen to them. [26]Instead, the king commanded Jerahmeel, a son of the king, Seraiah son of Azriel and Shelemiah son of Abdeel to arrest Baruch the scribe and Jeremiah the prophet. But the LORD had hidden them.

[27]After the king burned the scroll containing the words that Baruch had written at Jeremiah's dictation, the word of the LORD came to Jeremiah: [28]"Take another scroll and write on it all the words that were on the first scroll, which Jehoiakim king of Judah burned up. [29]Also tell Jehoiakim king of Judah, 'This is what the LORD says: You burned that scroll and said, "Why did you write on it that the king of Babylon would certainly come and destroy this land and cut off both men and animals from it?" [30]Therefore, this is what the LORD says about Jehoiakim king of Judah: He will have no-one to sit on the throne of David; his body will be thrown out and exposed to the heat by day and the frost by night. [31]I will punish him and his children and his attendants for their wickedness; I will bring on them and those living in Jerusalem and the people of Judah every disaster I pronounced against them, because they have not listened.'"

[32]So Jeremiah took another scroll and gave it to the scribe Baruch son of Neriah, and as Jeremiah dictated, Baruch wrote on it all the words of the scroll that Jehoiakim king of Judah had burned in the fire. And many similar words were added to them.

Jeremiah in Prison

37 Zedekiah son of Josiah was made king of Judah by Nebuchadnezzar king of Babylon; he reigned in place of Jehoiachin[a] son of Jehoiakim. [2]Neither he

---

[a]1 Hebrew *Coniah*, a variant of *Jehoiachin*

nor his attendants nor the people of the land paid any attention to the words the LORD had spoken through Jeremiah the prophet.

³King Zedekiah, however, sent Jehucal son of Shelemiah with the priest Zephaniah son of Maaseiah to Jeremiah the prophet with this message: "Please pray to the LORD our God for us."

⁴Now Jeremiah was free to come and go among the people, for he had not yet been put in prison. ⁵Pharaoh's army had marched out of Egypt, and when the Babylonians*b* who were besieging Jerusalem heard the report about them, they withdrew from Jerusalem.

⁶Then the word of the LORD came to Jeremiah the prophet: ⁷"This is what the LORD, the God of Israel, says: Tell the king of Judah, who sent you to enquire of me, 'Pharaoh's army, which has marched out to support you, will go back to its own land, to Egypt. ⁸Then the Babylonians will return and attack this city; they will capture it and burn it down.'

⁹"This is what the LORD says: Do not deceive yourselves, thinking, 'The Babylonians will surely leave us.' They will not! ¹⁰Even if you were to defeat the entire Babylonian*c* army that is attacking you and you only wounded men were left in their tents, they would come out and burn this city down."

¹¹After the Babylonian army had withdrawn from Jerusalem because of Pharaoh's army, ¹²Jeremiah started to leave the city to go to the territory of Benjamin to get his share of the property among the people there. ¹³But when he reached the Benjamin Gate, the captain of the guard, whose name was Irijah son of Shelemiah, the son of Hananiah, arrested him and said, "You are deserting to the Babylonians!"

¹⁴"That's not true!" Jeremiah said. "I am not deserting to the Babylonians." But Irijah would not listen to him; instead, he arrested Jeremiah and brought him to the officials. ¹⁵They were angry with Jeremiah and had him beaten and imprisoned in the house of Jonathan the secretary, which they had made into a prison.

¹⁶Jeremiah was put into a vaulted cell in a dungeon, where he remained a long time. ¹⁷Then King Zedekiah sent for him and had him brought to the palace, where he asked him privately, "Is there any word from the LORD?"

"Yes," Jeremiah replied, "you will be handed over to the king of Babylon."

¹⁸Then Jeremiah said to King Zedekiah, "What crime have I committed against you or your officials or this people, that you have put me in prison? ¹⁹Where are your prophets who prophesied to you, 'The king of Babylon will not attack you or this land'? ²⁰But now, my lord the king, please listen. Let me bring my petition before you: Do not send me back to the house of Jonathan the secretary, or I shall die there."

²¹King Zedekiah then gave orders for Jeremiah to be placed in the courtyard of the guard and given bread from the street of the bakers each day until all the bread in the city was gone. So Jeremiah remained in the courtyard of the guard.

Jeremiah Thrown Into a Cistern

38 Shephatiah son of Mattan, Gedaliah son of Pashhur, Jehucal*a* son of Shelemiah, and Pashhur son of Malkijah heard what Jeremiah was telling all the people when he said, ²"This is what the LORD says: 'Whoever stays in this city will die by the sword, famine or plague, but whoever goes over to the Babylonians*b* will live. He will escape with his life; he will live.' ³And this is what the LORD says: 'This city will certainly be handed over to the army of the king of Babylon, who will capture it.'"

⁴Then the officials said to the king, "This man should be put to death. He is discouraging the soldiers who are left in this city, as well as all the people, by the things he is saying to them. This man is not seeking the good of these people but their ruin."

---

b5 Or *Chaldeans*; also in verses 8, 9, 13 and 14   *c10* Or *Chaldean*; also in verse 11
a1 Hebrew *Jucal*, a variant of *Jehucal*   *b2* Or *Chaldeans*; also in verses 18, 19 and 23

[5]"He is in your hands," King Zedekiah answered. "The king can do nothing to oppose you."

[6]So they took Jeremiah and put him into the cistern of Malkijah, the king's son, which was in the courtyard of the guard. They lowered Jeremiah by ropes into the cistern; it had no water in it, only mud, and Jeremiah sank down into the mud.

[7]But Ebed-Melech, a Cushite,[c] an official[d] in the royal palace, heard that they had put Jeremiah into the cistern. While the king was sitting in the Benjamin Gate, [8]Ebed-Melech went out of the palace and said to him, [9]"My lord the king, these men have acted wickedly in all they have done to Jeremiah the prophet. They have thrown him into a cistern, where he will starve to death when there is no longer any bread in the city."

[10]Then the king commanded Ebed-Melech the Cushite, "Take thirty men from here with you and lift Jeremiah the prophet out of the cistern before he dies."

[11]So Ebed-Melech took the men with him and went to a room under the treasury in the palace. He took some old rags and worn-out clothes from there and let them down with ropes to Jeremiah in the cistern. [12]Ebed-Melech the Cushite said to Jeremiah, "Put these old rags and worn-out clothes under your arms to pad the ropes." Jeremiah did so, [13]and they pulled him up with the ropes and lifted him out of the cistern. And Jeremiah remained in the courtyard of the guard.

Zedekiah Questions Jeremiah Again

[14]Then King Zedekiah sent for Jeremiah the prophet and had him brought to the third entrance to the temple of the LORD. "I am going to ask you something," the king said to Jeremiah. "Do not hide anything from me."

[15]Jeremiah said to Zedekiah, "If I give you an answer, will you not kill me? Even if I did give you counsel, you would not listen to me."

[16]But King Zedekiah swore this oath secretly to Jeremiah: "As surely as the LORD lives, who has given us breath, I will neither kill you nor hand you over to those who are seeking your life."

[17]Then Jeremiah said to Zedekiah, "This is what the LORD God Almighty, the God of Israel, says: 'If you surrender to the officers of the king of Babylon, your life will be spared and this city will not be burned down; you and your family will live. [18]But if you will not surrender to the officers of the king of Babylon, this city will be handed over to the Babylonians and they will burn it down; you yourself will not escape from their hands.'"

[19]King Zedekiah said to Jeremiah, "I am afraid of the Jews who have gone over to the Babylonians, for the Babylonians may hand me over to them and they will ill-treat me."

[20]"They will not hand you over," Jeremiah replied. "Obey the LORD by doing what I tell you. Then it will go well with you, and your life will be spared. [21]But if you refuse to surrender, this is what the LORD has revealed to me: [22]All the women left in the palace of the king of Judah will be brought out to the officials of the king of Babylon. Those women will say to you:

"'They misled you and overcame you—
    those trusted friends of yours.
Your feet are sunk in the mud;
    your friends have deserted you.'

[23]"All your wives and children will be brought out to the Babylonians. You yourself will not escape from their hands but will be captured by the king of Babylon; and this city will[e] be burned down."

[24]Then Zedekiah said to Jeremiah, "Do not let anyone know about this conversation, or you may die. [25]If the officials hear that I talked with you, and they come to you and say, 'Tell us what you said to the king and what the king said to you; do not hide it from us or we will kill you,' [26]then tell them, 'I was pleading with the king not to send me back to Jonathan's house to die there.'"

[27]All the officials did come to Jeremiah and question him, and he told them

---

[c]7 Probably from the upper Nile region   [d]7 Or a eunuch   [e]23 Or and you will cause this city to

everything the king had ordered him to say. So they said no more to him, for no-one had heard his conversation with the king.

²⁸And Jeremiah remained in the courtyard of the guard until the day Jerusalem was captured.

The Fall of Jerusalem

39 This is how Jerusalem was taken: ¹In the ninth year of Zedekiah king of Judah, in the tenth month, Nebuchadnezzar king of Babylon marched against Jerusalem with his whole army and laid siege to it. ²And on the ninth day of the fourth month of Zedekiah's eleventh year, the city wall was broken through. ³Then all the officials of the king of Babylon came and took seats in the Middle Gate: Nergal-Sharezer of Samgar, Nebo-Sarsekim*a* a chief officer, Nergal-Sharezer a high official and all the other officials of the king of Babylon. ⁴When Zedekiah king of Judah and all the soldiers saw them, they fled; they left the city at night by way of the king's garden, through the gate between the two walls, and headed towards the Arabah.*b*

⁵But the Babylonian*c* army pursued them and overtook Zedekiah in the plains of Jericho. They captured him and took him to Nebuchadnezzar king of Babylon at Riblah in the land of Hamath, where he pronounced sentence on him. ⁶There at Riblah the king of Babylon slaughtered the sons of Zedekiah before his eyes and also killed all the nobles of Judah. ⁷Then he put out Zedekiah's eyes and bound him with bronze shackles to take him to Babylon.

⁸The Babylonians*d* set fire to the royal palace and the houses of the people and broke down the walls of Jerusalem. ⁹Nebuzaradan commander of the imperial guard carried into exile to Babylon the people who remained in the city, along with those who had gone over to him, and the rest of the people. ¹⁰But Nebuzaradan the commander of the guard left behind in the land of Judah some of the poor people, who owned nothing; and at that time he gave them vineyards and fields.

¹¹Now Nebuchadnezzar king of Babylon had given these orders about Jeremiah through Nebuzaradan commander of the imperial guard: ¹²"Take him and look after him; don't harm him but do for him whatever he asks." ¹³So Nebuzaradan the commander of the guard, Nebushazban a chief officer, Nergal-Sharezer a high official and all the other officers of the king of Babylon ¹⁴sent and had Jeremiah taken out of the courtyard of the guard. They handed him over to Gedaliah son of Ahikam, the son of Shaphan, to take him back to his home. So he remained among his own people.

¹⁵While Jeremiah had been confined in the courtyard of the guard, the word of the LORD came to him: ¹⁶"Go and tell Ebed-Melech the Cushite, 'This is what the LORD Almighty, the God of Israel, says: I am about to fulfil my words against this city through disaster, not prosperity. At that time they will be fulfilled before your eyes. ¹⁷But I will rescue you on that day, declares the LORD; you will not be handed over to those you fear. ¹⁸I will save you; you will not fall by the sword but will escape with your life, because you trust in me, declares the LORD.'"

Jeremiah Freed

40 The word came to Jeremiah from the LORD after Nebuzaradan commander of the imperial guard had released him at Ramah. He had found Jeremiah bound in chains among all the captives from Jerusalem and Judah who were being carried into exile to Babylon. ²When the commander of the guard found Jeremiah, he said to him, "The LORD your God decreed this disaster for this place. ³And now the LORD has brought it about; he has done just as he said he would. All this happened because you people sinned against the LORD and did not obey him. ⁴But today I am freeing you from the chains on your wrists. Come with me to Babylon, if you like, and I will look after you; but if you do not want to, then don't come. Look, the whole country lies before you; go wherever you please." ⁵However,

---

*a*3 Or *Nergal-Sharezer, Samgar-Nebo, Sarsekim* *b*4 Or *the Jordan Valley* *c*5 Or *Chaldean* *d*8 Or *Chaldeans* before Jeremiah turned to go,[a] Nebuzaradan added, "Go back to Gedaliah son of Ahikam, the son of Shaphan, whom the king of Babylon has appointed over the towns of Judah, and live with him among the people, or go anywhere else you please."

Then the commander gave him provisions and a present and let him go. [6]So Jeremiah went to Gedaliah son of Ahikam at Mizpah and stayed with him among the people who were left behind in the land.

Gedaliah Assassinated

[7]When all the army officers and their men who were still in the open country heard that the king of Babylon had appointed Gedaliah son of Ahikam as governor over the land and had put him in charge of the men, women and children who were the poorest in the land and who had not been carried into exile to Babylon, [8]they came to Gedaliah at Mizpah— Ishmael son of Nethaniah, Johanan and Jonathan the sons of Kareah, Seraiah son of Tanhumeth, the sons of Ephai the Netophathite, and Jaazaniah[b] the son of the Maacathite, and their men. [9]Gedaliah son of Ahikam, the son of Shaphan, took an oath to reassure them and their men. "Do not be afraid to serve the Babylonians,"[c] he said. "Settle down in the land and serve the king of Babylon, and it will go well with you. [10]I myself will stay in Mizpah to represent you before the Babylonians who come to us, but you are to harvest the wine, summer fruit and oil, and put them in your storage jars, and live in the towns you have taken over."

[11]When all the Jews in Moab, Ammon, Edom and all the other countries heard that the king of Babylon had left a remnant in Judah and had appointed Gedaliah son of Ahikam, the son of Shaphan, as governor over them, [12]they all came back to the land of Judah, to Gedaliah at Mizpah, from all the countries where they had been scattered. And they harvested an abundance of wine and summer fruit.

[13]Johanan son of Kareah and all the army officers still in the open country came to Gedaliah at Mizpah [14]and said to him, "Don't you know that Baalis king of the Ammonites has sent Ishmael son of Nethaniah to take your life?" But Gedaliah son of Ahikam did not believe them.

[15]Then Johanan son of Kareah said privately to Gedaliah in Mizpah, "Let me go and kill Ishmael son of Nethaniah, and no-one will know it. Why should he take your life and cause all the Jews who are gathered around you to be scattered and the remnant of Judah to perish?"

[16]But Gedaliah son of Ahikam said to Johanan son of Kareah, "Don't do such a thing! What you are saying about Ishmael is not true."

41 In the seventh month Ishmael son of Nethaniah, the son of Elishama, who was of royal blood and had been one of the king's officers, came with ten men to Gedaliah son of Ahikam at Mizpah. While they were eating together there, [2]Ishmael son of Nethaniah and the ten men who were with him got up and struck down Gedaliah son of Ahikam, the son of Shaphan, with the sword, killing the one whom the king of Babylon had appointed as governor over the land. [3]Ishmael also killed all the Jews who were with Gedaliah at Mizpah, as well as the Babylonian[a] soldiers who were there.

[4]The day after Gedaliah's assassination, before anyone knew about it, [5]eighty men who had shaved off their beards, torn their clothes and cut themselves came from Shechem, Shiloh and Samaria, bringing grain offerings and incense with them to the house of the LORD. [6]Ishmael son of Nethaniah went out from Mizpah to meet them, weeping as he went. When he met them, he said, "Come to Gedaliah son of Ahikam." [7]When they went into the city, Ishmael son of Nethaniah and the men who were with him slaughtered them and threw them into a cistern. [8]But ten of them said to Ishmael, "Don't kill us! We have wheat and barley, oil and honey, hidden in a field." So he let them alone and did not kill them with the others. [9]Now the cistern where he threw all the bodies of the men

---

[a]5 Or *Jeremiah answered*   [b]8 Hebrew *Jezaniah*, a variant of *Jaazaniah*   [c]9 Or *Chaldeans*; also in verse 10
[a]3 Or *Chaldean*

he had killed along with Gedaliah was the one King Asa had made as part of his defence against Baasha king of Israel. Ishmael son of Nethaniah filled it with the dead.

[10]Ishmael made captives of all the rest of the people who were in Mizpah—the king's daughters along with all the others who were left there, over whom Nebuzaradan commander of the imperial guard had appointed Gedaliah son of Ahikam. Ishmael son of Nethaniah took them captive and set out to cross over to the Ammonites.

[11]When Johanan son of Kareah and all the army officers who were with him heard about all the crimes Ishmael son of Nethaniah had committed, [12]they took all their men and went to fight Ishmael son of Nethaniah. They caught up with him near the great pool in Gibeon. [13]When all the people Ishmael had with him saw Johanan son of Kareah and the army officers who were with him, they were glad. [14]All the people Ishmael had taken captive at Mizpah turned and went over to Johanan son of Kareah. [15]But Ishmael son of Nethaniah and eight of his men escaped from Johanan and fled to the Ammonites.

Flight to Egypt

[16]Then Johanan son of Kareah and all the army officers who were with him led away all the survivors from Mizpah whom he had recovered from Ishmael son of Nethaniah after he had assassinated Gedaliah son of Ahikam: the soldiers, women, children and court officials he had brought from Gibeon. [17]And they went on, stopping at Geruth Kimham near Bethlehem on their way to Egypt [18]to escape the Babylonians.*b* They were afraid of them because Ishmael son of Nethaniah had killed Gedaliah son of Ahikam, whom the king of Babylon had appointed as governor over the land.

42 Then all the army officers, including Johanan son of Kareah and Jezaniah*a* son of Hoshaiah, and all the people from the least to the greatest

approached [2]Jeremiah the prophet and said to him, "Please hear our petition and pray to the LORD your God for this entire remnant. For as you now see, though we were once many, now only a few are left. [3]Pray that the LORD your God will tell us where we should go and what we should do."

[4]"I have heard you," replied Jeremiah the prophet. "I will certainly pray to the LORD your God as you have requested; I will tell you everything the LORD says and will keep nothing back from you."

[5]Then they said to Jeremiah, "May the LORD be a true and faithful witness against us if we do not act in accordance with everything the LORD your God sends you to tell us. [6]Whether it is favourable or unfavourable, we will obey the LORD our God, to whom we are sending you, so that it will go well with us, for we will obey the LORD our God."

[7]Ten days later the word of the LORD came to Jeremiah. [8]So he called together Johanan son of Kareah and all the army officers who were with him and all the people from the least to the greatest. [9]He said to them, "This is what the LORD, the God of Israel, to whom you sent me to present your petition, says: [10]'If you stay in this land, I will build you up and not tear you down; I will plant you and not uproot you, for I am grieved over the disaster I have inflicted on you. [11]Do not be afraid of the king of Babylon, whom you now fear. Do not be afraid of him, declares the LORD, for I am with you and will save you and deliver you from his hands. [12]I will show you compassion so that he will have compassion on you and restore you to your land.'

[13]"However, if you say, 'We will not stay in this land,' and so disobey the LORD your God, [14]and if you say, 'No, we will go and live in Egypt, where we will not see war or hear the trumpet or be hungry for bread,' [15]then hear the word of the LORD, O remnant of Judah. This is what the LORD Almighty, the God of Israel, says: 'If you are determined to go to Egypt and you do go to settle there, [16]then the sword you

b18 Or *Chaldeans*   *a1* Hebrew; Septuagint (see also 43:2) *Azariah* fear will overtake you there, and the famine you dread will follow you into Egypt, and there you will die. ¹⁷Indeed, all who are determined to go to Egypt to settle there will die by the sword, famine and plague; not one of them will survive or escape the disaster I will bring on them.' ¹⁸This is what the LORD Almighty, the God of Israel, says: 'As my anger and wrath have been poured out on those who lived in Jerusalem, so will my wrath be poured out on you when you go to Egypt. You will be an object of cursing and horror, of condemnation and reproach; you will never see this place again.'

¹⁹"O remnant of Judah, the LORD has told you, 'Do not go to Egypt.' Be sure of this: I warn you today ²⁰that you made a fatal mistake^b when you sent me to the LORD your God and said, 'Pray to the LORD our God for us; tell us everything he says and we will do it.' ²¹I have told you today, but you still have not obeyed the LORD your God in all he sent me to tell you. ²²So now, be sure of this: You will die by the sword, famine and plague in the place where you want to go to settle."

43 When Jeremiah finished telling the people all the words of the LORD their God—everything the LORD had sent him to tell them— ²Azariah son of Hoshaiah and Johanan son of Kareah and all the arrogant men said to Jeremiah, "You are lying! The LORD our God has not sent you to say, 'You must not go to Egypt to settle there.' ³But Baruch son of Neriah is inciting you against us to hand us over to the Babylonians,^a so that they may kill us or carry us into exile to Babylon."

⁴So Johanan son of Kareah and all the army officers and all the people disobeyed the LORD's command to stay in the land of Judah. ⁵Instead, Johanan son of Kareah and all the army officers led away all the remnant of Judah who had come back to live in the land of Judah from all the nations where they had been scattered. ⁶They also led away all the men, women and children and the king's daughters whom Nebuzaradan commander of the imperial guard had left with Gedaliah son

of Ahikam, the son of Shaphan, and Jeremiah the prophet and Baruch son of Neriah. ⁷So they entered Egypt in disobedience to the LORD and went as far as Tahpanhes.

⁸In Tahpanhes the word of the LORD came to Jeremiah: ⁹"While the Jews are watching, take some large stones with you and bury them in clay in the brick pavement at the entrance to Pharaoh's palace in Tahpanhes. ¹⁰Then say to them, 'This is what the LORD Almighty, the God of Israel, says: I will send for my servant Nebuchadnezzar king of Babylon, and I will set his throne over these stones I have buried here; he will spread his royal canopy above them. ¹¹He will come and attack Egypt, bringing death to those destined for death, captivity to those destined for captivity, and the sword to those destined for the sword. ¹²He^b will set fire to the temples of the gods of Egypt; he will burn their temples and take their gods captive. As a shepherd wraps his garment round him, so will he wrap Egypt round himself and depart from there unscathed. ¹³There in the temple of the sun^c in Egypt he will demolish the sacred pillars and will burn down the temples of the gods of Egypt.'"

Disaster Because of Idolatry

44 This word came to Jeremiah concerning all the Jews living in Lower Egypt—in Migdol, Tahpanhes and Memphis^a—and in Upper Egypt:^b ²"This is what the LORD Almighty, the God of Israel, says: You saw the great disaster I brought on Jerusalem and on all the towns of Judah. Today they lie deserted and in ruins ³because of the evil they have done. They provoked me to anger by burning incense and by worshipping other gods that neither they nor you nor your fathers ever knew. ⁴Again and again I sent my servants the prophets, who said, 'Do not do this detestable thing that I hate!' ⁵But they did not listen or pay attention; they did not turn from their wickedness or stop burning incense to other gods.

---

^b20 Or *you erred in your hearts*   ^a3 Or *Chaldeans*
^a1 Hebrew *Noph*   ^b1 Hebrew *in Pathros*
^b12 Or *I*   ^c13 Or *in Heliopolis*

6Therefore, my fierce anger was poured out; it raged against the towns of Judah and the streets of Jerusalem and made them the desolate ruins they are today.

7"Now this is what the LORD God Almighty, the God of Israel, says: Why bring such great disaster on yourselves by cutting off from Judah the men and women, the children and infants, and so leave yourselves without a remnant? 8Why provoke me to anger with what your hands have made, burning incense to other gods in Egypt, where you have come to live? You will destroy yourselves and make yourselves an object of cursing and reproach among all the nations on earth. 9Have you forgotten the wickedness committed by your fathers and by the kings and queens of Judah and the wickedness committed by you and your wives in the land of Judah and the streets of Jerusalem? 10To this day they have not humbled themselves or shown reverence, nor have they followed my law and the decrees I set before you and your fathers.

11"Therefore, this is what the LORD Almighty, the God of Israel, says: I am determined to bring disaster on you and to destroy all Judah. 12I will take away the remnant of Judah who were determined to go to Egypt to settle there. They will all perish in Egypt; they will fall by the sword or die from famine. From the least to the greatest, they will die by sword or famine. They will become an object of cursing and horror, of condemnation and reproach. 13I will punish those who live in Egypt with the sword, famine and plague, as I punished Jerusalem. 14None of the remnant of Judah who have gone to live in Egypt will escape or survive to return to the land of Judah, to which they long to return and live; none will return except a few fugitives."

15Then all the men who knew that their wives were burning incense to other gods, along with all the women who were present—a large assembly—and all the people living in Lower and Upper Egypt,c said to Jeremiah, 16"We will not listen to the message you have spoken to us in the name of the LORD! 17We will certainly do everything we said we would: We will burn incense to the Queen of Heaven and will pour out drink offerings to her just as we and our fathers, our kings and our officials did in the towns of Judah and in the streets of Jerusalem. At that time we had plenty of food and were well off and suffered no harm. 18But ever since we stopped burning incense to the Queen of Heaven and pouring out drink offerings to her, we have had nothing and have been perishing by sword and famine."

19The women added, "When we burned incense to the Queen of Heaven and poured out drink offerings to her, did not our husbands know that we were making cakes like her image and pouring out drink offerings to her?"

20Then Jeremiah said to all the people, both men and women, who were answering him, 21"Did not the LORD remember and think about the incense burned in the towns of Judah and the streets of Jerusalem by you and your fathers, your kings and your officials and the people of the land? 22When the LORD could no longer endure your wicked actions and the detestable things you did, your land became an object of cursing and a desolate waste without inhabitants, as it is today. 23Because you have burned incense and have sinned against the LORD and have not obeyed him or followed his law or his decrees or his stipulations, this disaster has come upon you, as you now see."

24Then Jeremiah said to all the people, including the women, "Hear the word of the LORD, all you people of Judah in Egypt. 25This is what the LORD Almighty, the God of Israel, says: You and your wives have shown by your actions what you promised when you said, 'We will certainly carry out the vows we made to burn incense and pour out drink offerings to the Queen of Heaven.'

"Go ahead then, do what you promised! Keep your vows! 26But hear the word of the LORD, all Jews living in Egypt: 'I swear by my great name,' says the LORD, 'that no-one from Judah living anywhere

c15 Hebrew in Egypt and Pathros

in Egypt shall ever again invoke my name or swear, "As surely as the Sovereign LORD lives." ²⁷For I am watching over them for harm, not for good; the Jews in Egypt will perish by sword and famine until they are all destroyed. ²⁸Those who escape the sword and return to the land of Judah from Egypt will be very few. Then the whole remnant of Judah who came to live in Egypt will know whose word will stand—mine or theirs.

²⁹"'This will be the sign to you that I will punish you in this place,' declares the LORD, 'so that you will know that my threats of harm against you will surely stand.' ³⁰This is what the LORD says: 'I am going to hand Pharaoh Hophra king of Egypt over to his enemies who seek his life, just as I handed Zedekiah king of Judah over to Nebuchadnezzar king of Babylon, the enemy who was seeking his life.'"

A Message to Baruch

45 This is what Jeremiah the prophet told Baruch son of Neriah in the fourth year of Jehoiakim son of Josiah king of Judah, after Baruch had written on a scroll the words Jeremiah was then dictating: ²"This is what the LORD, the God of Israel, says to you, Baruch: ³You said, 'Woe to me! The LORD has added sorrow to my pain; I am worn out with groaning and find no rest.'"

⁴⌐The LORD said,⌐ "Say this to him: 'This is what the LORD says: I will overthrow what I have built and uproot what I have planted, throughout the land. ⁵Should you then seek great things for yourself? Seek them not. For I will bring disaster on all people, declares the LORD, but wherever you go I will let you escape with your life.'"

A Message About Egypt

46 This is the word of the LORD that came to Jeremiah the prophet concerning the nations:

²Concerning Egypt:

This is the message against the army of Pharaoh Neco king of Egypt, which was defeated at Carchemish on the Euphrates River by Nebuchadnezzar king of Babylon in the fourth year of Jehoiakim son of Josiah king of Judah:

³"Prepare your shields, both large and
  small,
  and march out for battle!
⁴Harness the horses,
  mount the steeds!
Take your positions
  with helmets on!
Polish your spears,
  put on your armour!
⁵What do I see?
  They are terrified,
  they are retreating,
  their warriors are defeated.
They flee in haste
  without looking back,
  and there is terror on every side,"
                    declares the LORD.
⁶"The swift cannot flee
  nor the strong escape.
In the north by the River Euphrates
  they stumble and fall.

⁷"Who is this that rises like the Nile,
  like rivers of surging waters?
⁸Egypt rises like the Nile,
  like rivers of surging waters.
She says, 'I will rise and cover the
  earth;
  I will destroy cities and their people.'
⁹Charge, O horses!
  Drive furiously, O charioteers!
March on, O warriors—
  men of Cushᵃ and Put who carry
  shields,
  men of Lydia who draw the bow.
¹⁰But that day belongs to the Lord, the
  LORD Almighty—
  a day of vengeance, for vengeance on
  his foes.
The sword will devour till it is satisfied,
  till it has quenched its thirst with
  blood.

ᵃ9 That is, the upper Nile region

For the Lord, the LORD Almighty, will
    offer sacrifice
in the land of the north by the River
    Euphrates.

11"Go up to Gilead and get balm,
    O Virgin Daughter of Egypt.
But you multiply remedies in vain;
    there is no healing for you.
12The nations will hear of your shame;
    your cries will fill the earth.
One warrior will stumble over another;
    both will fall down together."

13This is the message the LORD spoke to
Jeremiah the prophet about the coming of
Nebuchadnezzar king of Babylon to
attack Egypt:

14"Announce this in Egypt, and proclaim
    it in Migdol;
    proclaim it also in Memphis*b* and
      Tahpanhes:
'Take your positions and get ready,
    for the sword devours those around
      you.'
15Why will your warriors be laid low?
    They cannot stand, for the LORD will
      push them down.
16They will stumble repeatedly;
    they will fall over each other.
They will say, 'Get up, let us go back
    to our own people and our native
      lands,
away from the sword of the
      oppressor.'
17There they will exclaim,
'Pharaoh king of Egypt is only a loud
    noise;
he has missed his opportunity.'

18"As surely as I live," declares the
    King,
    whose name is the LORD Almighty,
"one will come who is like Tabor
    among the mountains,
like Carmel by the sea.
19Pack your belongings for exile,
    you who live in Egypt,
for Memphis will be laid waste
    and lie in ruins without inhabitant.

20"Egypt is a beautiful heifer,
    but a gadfly is coming
    against her from the north.
21The mercenaries in her ranks
    are like fattened calves.
They too will turn and flee together,
    they will not stand their ground,
for the day of disaster is coming upon
    them,
the time for them to be punished.
22Egypt will hiss like a fleeing serpent
    as the enemy advances in force;
they will come against her with axes,
    like men who cut down trees.
23They will chop down her forest,"
               declares the LORD,
"dense though it be.
They are more numerous than locusts,
    they cannot be counted.
24The Daughter of Egypt will be put to
    shame,
handed over to the people of the
      north."

25The LORD Almighty, the God of
Israel, says: "I am about to bring punishment on Amon god of Thebes,*c* on Pharaoh, on Egypt and her gods and her kings,
and on those who rely on Pharaoh. 26I will
hand them over to those who seek their
lives, to Nebuchadnezzar king of Babylon
and his officers. Later, however, Egypt
will be inhabited as in times past," declares the LORD.

27"Do not fear, O Jacob my servant;
    do not be dismayed, O Israel.
I will surely save you out of a distant
    place,
    and your descendants from the land
      of their exile.
Jacob will again have peace and
    security,
    and no-one will make him afraid.
28Do not fear, O Jacob my servant,
    for I am with you," declares the
      LORD.
"Though I completely destroy all the
    nations
    among which I scatter you,
I will not completely destroy you.

I will discipline you but only with
justice;
I will not let you go entirely
unpunished."

A Message About the Philistines

47 This is the word of the LORD that
came to Jeremiah the prophet concerning the Philistines before Pharaoh
attacked Gaza:

²This is what the LORD says:

"See how the waters are rising in the
north;
they will become an overflowing
torrent.
They will overflow the land and
everything in it,
the towns and those who live in them.
The people will cry out;
all who dwell in the land will wail
³at the sound of the hoofs of galloping
steeds,
at the noise of enemy chariots
and the rumble of their wheels.
Fathers will not turn to help their
children;
their hands will hang limp.
⁴For the day has come
to destroy all the Philistines
and to cut off all survivors
who could help Tyre and Sidon.
The LORD is about to destroy the
Philistines,
the remnant from the coasts of
Caphtor.*a*
⁵Gaza will shave her head in mourning;
Ashkelon will be silenced.
O remnant on the plain,
how long will you cut yourselves?

⁶"'Ah, sword of the LORD,' ⌐you cry,⌐
'how long till you rest?
Return to your scabbard;
cease and be still.'
⁷But how can it rest
when the LORD has commanded it,
when he has ordered it
to attack Ashkelon and the coast?''

A Message About Moab

48 Concerning Moab:

This is what the LORD Almighty, the
God of Israel, says:

"Woe to Nebo, for it will be ruined.
Kiriathaim will be disgraced and
captured;
the stronghold*a* will be disgraced and
shattered.
²Moab will be praised no more;
in Heshbon*b* men will plot her
downfall:
'Come, let us put an end to that
nation.'
You too, O Madmen,*c* will be silenced:
the sword will pursue you.
³Listen to the cries from Horonaim,
cries of great havoc and destruction.
⁴Moab will be broken;
her little ones will cry out.*d*
⁵They go up the way to Luhith,
weeping bitterly as they go;
on the road down to Horonaim
anguished cries over the destruction
are heard.
⁶Flee! Run for your lives;
become like a bush*e* in the desert.
⁷Since you trust in your deeds and
riches,
you too will be taken captive,
and Chemosh will go into exile,
together with his priests and officials.
⁸The destroyer will come against every
town,
and not a town will escape.
The valley will be ruined
and the plateau destroyed,
because the LORD has spoken.
⁹Put salt on Moab,
for she will be laid waste;*f*
her towns will become desolate,
with no-one to live in them.

¹⁰"A curse on him who is lax in doing the
LORD's work!
A curse on him who keeps his sword
from bloodshed!

---

a4 That is, Crete   *a1* Or / *Misgab*   *b2* The Hebrew for *Heshbon* sounds like the Hebrew for *plot.*
c2 The name of the Moabite town Madmen sounds like the Hebrew for *be silenced.*
d4 Hebrew; Septuagint / *proclaim it to Zoar*   *e6* Or *like Aroer*   *f9* Or *Give wings to Moab, / for she will fly away*

11"Moab has been at rest from youth,
   like wine left on its dregs,
not poured from one jar to another—
   she has not gone into exile.
So she tastes as she did,
   and her aroma is unchanged.
12But days are coming,"
   declares the LORD,
"when I will send men who pour from
   jars,
and they will pour her out;
they will empty her jars
   and smash her jugs.
13Then Moab will be ashamed of
   Chemosh,
as the house of Israel was ashamed
   when they trusted in Bethel.

14"How can you say, 'We are warriors,
   men valiant in battle'?
15Moab will be destroyed and her towns
   invaded;
her finest young men will go down in
   the slaughter,"
declares the King, whose name is the
   LORD Almighty.
16"The fall of Moab is at hand;
   her calamity will come quickly.
17Mourn for her, all who live around her,
   all who know her fame;
say, 'How broken is the mighty sceptre,
   how broken the glorious staff!'

18"Come down from your glory
   and sit on the parched ground,
O inhabitants of the Daughter of
   Dibon,
for he who destroys Moab
   will come up against you
   and ruin your fortified cities.
19Stand by the road and watch,
   you who live in Aroer.
Ask the man fleeing and the woman
   escaping,
   ask them, 'What has happened?'
20Moab is disgraced, for she is shattered.
   Wail and cry out!
Announce by the Arnon
   that Moab is destroyed.
21Judgment has come to the plateau—
   to Holon, Jahzah and Mephaath,

22 to Dibon, Nebo and Beth
    Diblathaim,
23 to Kiriathaim, Beth Gamul and Beth
    Meon,
24 to Kerioth and Bozrah—
    to all the towns of Moab, far and
    near.
25Moab's horn[g] is cut off;
   her arm is broken,"
            declares the LORD.

26"Make her drunk,
   for she has defied the LORD.
Let Moab wallow in her vomit;
   let her be an object of ridicule.
27Was not Israel the object of your
   ridicule?
Was she caught among thieves,
that you shake your head in scorn
   whenever you speak of her?
28Abandon your towns and dwell among
   the rocks,
   you who live in Moab.
Be like a dove that makes its nest
   at the mouth of a cave.

29"We have heard of Moab's pride—
   her overweening pride and conceit,
her pride and arrogance
   and the haughtiness of her heart.
30I know her insolence but it is futile,"
          declares the LORD,
"and her boasts accomplish nothing.
31Therefore I wail over Moab,
   for all Moab I cry out,
I moan for the men of Kir Hareseth.
32I weep for you, as Jazer weeps,
   O vines of Sibmah.
Your branches spread as far as the sea;
   they reached as far as the sea of
   Jazer.
The destroyer has fallen
   on your ripened fruit and grapes.
33Joy and gladness are gone
   from the orchards and fields of Moab.
I have stopped the flow of wine from
   the presses;
no-one treads them with shouts of
   joy.
Although there are shouts,
   they are not shouts of joy.

---

825 Horn here symbolises strength.

34"The sound of their cry rises
   from Heshbon to Elealeh and Jahaz,
from Zoar as far as Horonaim and
   Eglath Shelishiyah,
   for even the waters of Nimrim are
     dried up.
35In Moab I will put an end
   to those who make offerings on the
     high places
   and burn incense to their gods,"
               declares the LORD.
36"So my heart laments for Moab like a
     flute;
   it laments like a flute for the men of
     Kir Hareseth.
   The wealth they acquired is gone.
37Every head is shaved
   and every beard cut off;
every hand is slashed
   and every waist is covered with
     sackcloth.
38On all the roofs in Moab
   and in the public squares
there is nothing but mourning,
   for I have broken Moab
   like a jar that no-one wants,"
               declares the LORD.
39"How shattered she is! How they wail!
   How Moab turns her back in shame!
Moab has become an object of
     ridicule,
   an object of horror to all those
     around her."

40This is what the LORD says:

"Look! An eagle is swooping down,
   spreading its wings over Moab.
41Kerioth[h] will be captured
   and the strongholds taken.
In that day the hearts of Moab's
     warriors
   will be like the heart of a woman in
     labour.
42Moab will be destroyed as a nation
   because she defied the LORD.
43Terror and pit and snare await you,
   O people of Moab,"
               declares the LORD.
44"Whoever flees from the terror
   will fall into a pit,

whoever climbs out of the pit
   will be caught in a snare;
for I will bring upon Moab
   the year of her punishment,"
               declares the LORD.

45"In the shadow of Heshbon
   the fugitives stand helpless,
for a fire has gone out from Heshbon,
   a blaze from the midst of Sihon;
it burns the foreheads of Moab,
   the skulls of the noisy boasters.
46Woe to you, O Moab!
   The people of Chemosh are
     destroyed;
your sons are taken into exile
   and your daughters into captivity.

47"Yet I will restore the fortunes of Moab
   in days to come,"
               declares the LORD.

Here ends the judgment on Moab.

A Message About Ammon

49

Concerning the Ammonites:

This is what the LORD says:

"Has Israel no sons?
   Has she no heirs?
Why then has Molech[a] taken possession
   of Gad?
   Why do his people live in its towns?
2But the days are coming,"
   declares the LORD,
"when I will sound the battle cry
   against Rabbah of the Ammonites;
it will become a mound of ruins,
   and its surrounding villages will be set
     on fire.
Then Israel will drive out
   those who drove her out,"
               says the LORD.
3"Wail, O Heshbon, for Ai is destroyed!
   Cry out, O inhabitants of Rabbah!
Put on sackcloth and mourn;
   rush here and there inside the walls,
for Molech will go into exile,
   together with his priests and officials.

h41 Or *The cities*   a1 Or *their king*; Hebrew *malcam*; also in verse 3

⁴Why do you boast of your valleys,
    boast of your valleys so fruitful?
O unfaithful daughter,
    you trust in your riches and say,
    'Who will attack me?'
⁵I will bring terror on you
    from all those around you,"
            declares the Lord,
                the LORD Almighty.
"Every one of you will be driven away,
    and no-one will gather the fugitives.

⁶"Yet afterwards, I will restore the
    fortunes of the Ammonites,"
                declares the LORD.

A Message About Edom

⁷Concerning Edom:

This is what the LORD Almighty says:

"Is there no longer wisdom in Teman?
    Has counsel perished from the
        prudent?
    Has their wisdom decayed?
⁸Turn and flee, hide in deep caves,
    you who live in Dedan,
for I will bring disaster on Esau
    at the time I punish him.
⁹If grape-pickers came to you,
    would they not leave a few grapes?
If thieves came during the night,
    would they not steal only as much as
        they wanted?
¹⁰But I will strip Esau bare;
    I will uncover his hiding-places,
    so that he cannot conceal himself.
His children, relatives and neighbours
        will perish,
    and he will be no more.
¹¹Leave your orphans; I will protect their
        lives.
    Your widows too can trust in me."

¹²This is what the LORD says: "If those
who do not deserve to drink the cup must
drink it, why should you go unpunished?
You will not go unpunished, but must
drink it. ¹³I swear by myself," declares the
LORD, "that Bozrah will become a ruin
and an object of horror, of reproach and

of cursing; and all its towns will be in ruins
for ever."

¹⁴I have heard a message from the LORD:
    An envoy was sent to the nations to
        say,
    "Assemble yourselves to attack it!
        Rise up for battle!"

¹⁵"Now I will make you small among the
        nations,
    despised among men.
¹⁶The terror you inspire
    and the pride of your heart have
        deceived you,
you who live in the clefts of the rocks,
    who occupy the heights of the hill.
Though you build your nest as high as
        the eagle's,
    from there I will bring you down,"
                declares the LORD.
¹⁷"Edom will become an object of
        horror;
    all who pass by will be appalled and
        will scoff
    because of all its wounds.
¹⁸As Sodom and Gomorrah were
        overthrown,
    along with their neighbouring
        towns,"
                    says the LORD,
    "so no-one will live there;
    no man will dwell in it.

¹⁹"Like a lion coming up from Jordan's
        thickets
    to a rich pasture-land,
I will chase Edom from its land in an
        instant.
    Who is the chosen one I will appoint
        for this?
Who is like me and who can challenge
        me?
    And what shepherd can stand against
        me?"
²⁰Therefore, hear what the LORD has
        planned against Edom,
    what he has purposed against those
        who live in Teman:
The young of the flock will be dragged
        away;
    he will completely destroy their
        pasture because of them.

²¹At the sound of their fall the earth will
　　tremble;
　　their cry will resound to the Red
　　　Sea.*b*
²²Look! An eagle will soar and swoop
　　down,
　　spreading its wings over Bozrah.
In that day the hearts of Edom's
　　warriors
　　will be like the heart of a woman in
　　labour.

A Message About Damascus

²³Concerning Damascus:

"Hamath and Arpad are dismayed,
　　for they have heard bad news.
They are disheartened,
　　troubled like*c* the restless sea.
²⁴Damascus has become feeble,
　　she has turned to flee
　　and panic has gripped her;
anguish and pain have seized her,
　　pain like that of a woman in labour.
²⁵Why has the city of renown not been
　　abandoned,
　　the town in which I delight?
²⁶Surely, her young men will fall in the
　　streets;
　　all her soldiers will be silenced in that
　　day,"
　　　　　　declares the LORD Almighty.
²⁷"I will set fire to the walls of Damascus;
　　it will consume the fortresses of
　　　Ben-Hadad."

A Message About Kedar and Hazor

²⁸Concerning Kedar and the kingdoms
of Hazor, which Nebuchadnezzar king of
Babylon attacked:

This is what the LORD says:

"Arise, and attack Kedar
　　and destroy the people of the East.
²⁹Their tents and their flocks will be
　　taken;
　　their shelters will be carried off
with all their goods and camels.

Men will shout to them,
　　'Terror on every side!'

³⁰"Flee quickly away!
　　Stay in deep caves, you who live in
　　　Hazor,"
　　　　　　　　　　declares the LORD.
"Nebuchadnezzar king of Babylon has
　　plotted against you;
　　he has devised a plan against you.

³¹"Arise and attack a nation at ease,
　　which lives in confidence,"
　　　　　　　　　declares the LORD,
"a nation that has neither gates nor
　　bars;
　　its people live alone.
³²Their camels will become plunder,
　　and their large herds will be booty.
I will scatter to the winds those who are
　　in distant places*d*
　　and will bring disaster on them from
　　every side,"
　　　　　　　　　　declares the LORD.
³³"Hazor will become a haunt of jackals,
　　a desolate place for ever.
No-one will live there;
　　no man will dwell in it."

A Message About Elam

³⁴This is the word of the LORD that came
to Jeremiah the prophet concerning Elam,
early in the reign of Zedekiah king of
Judah:

³⁵This is what the LORD Almighty says:

"See, I will break the bow of Elam,
　　the mainstay of their might.
³⁶I will bring against Elam the four winds
　　from the four quarters of the
　　　heavens;
I will scatter them to the four winds,
　　and there will not be a nation
　　where Elam's exiles do not go.
³⁷I will shatter Elam before their foes,
　　before those who seek their lives;
I will bring disaster upon them,
　　even my fierce anger,"
　　　　　　　　　　declares the LORD.

b21 Hebrew *Yam Suph*; that is, Sea of Reeds　　　*c23* Hebrew *on* or *by*　　　*d32* Or *who clip the hair by their foreheads*

"I will pursue them with the sword
    until I have made an end of them.
³⁸I will set my throne in Elam
    and destroy her king and officials,"
                            declares the LORD.

³⁹"Yet I will restore the fortunes of Elam
    in days to come,"
                            declares the LORD.

A Message About Babylon

50 This is the word the LORD spoke
      through Jeremiah the prophet
concerning Babylon and the land of the
Babylonians:ᵃ

²"Announce and proclaim among the
        nations,
    lift up a banner and proclaim it;
    keep nothing back, but say,
'Babylon will be captured;
    Bel will be put to shame,
    Marduk filled with terror.
Her images will be put to shame
    and her idols filled with terror.'
³A nation from the north will attack her
    and lay waste her land.
No-one will live in it;
    both men and animals will flee away.

⁴"In those days, at that time,"
        declares the LORD,
    "the people of Israel and the people of
        Judah together
    will go in tears to seek the LORD their
        God.
⁵They will ask the way to Zion
    and turn their faces towards it.
They will come and bind themselves to
        the LORD
    in an everlasting covenant
    that will not be forgotten.

⁶"My people have been lost sheep;
    their shepherds have led them astray
    and caused them to roam on the
        mountains.
They wandered over mountain and hill
    and forgot their own resting place.
⁷Whoever found them devoured them;

their enemies said, 'We are not
        guilty,
for they sinned against the LORD, their
        true pasture,
    the LORD, the hope of their fathers.'

⁸"Flee out of Babylon;
    leave the land of the Babylonians,
    and be like the goats that lead the
        flock.
⁹For I will stir up and bring against
        Babylon
    an alliance of great nations from the
        land of the north.
They will take up their positions against
        her,
    and from the north she will be
        captured.
Their arrows will be like skilled
        warriors
    who do not return empty-handed.
¹⁰So Babyloniaᵇ will be plundered;
    all who plunder her will have their
        fill,"
                            declares the LORD.

¹¹"Because you rejoice and are glad,
    you who pillage my inheritance,
because you frolic like a heifer
        threshing corn
    and neigh like stallions,
¹²your mother will be greatly ashamed;
    she who gave you birth will be
        disgraced.
She will be the least of the nations—
    a wilderness, a dry land, a desert.
¹³Because of the LORD's anger she will not
        be inhabited
    but will be completely desolate.
All who pass Babylon will be horrified
        and scoff
    because of all her wounds.

¹⁴"Take up your positions round
        Babylon,
    all you who draw the bow.
Shoot at her! Spare no arrows,
    for she has sinned against the LORD.
¹⁵Shout against her on every side!
    She surrenders, her towers fall,
    her walls are torn down.

ᵃ1 Or *Chaldeans*; also in verses 8, 25, 35 and 45   ᵇ10 Or *Chaldea*

Since this is the vengeance of the LORD,
    take vengeance on her;
    do to her as she has done to others.
[16]Cut off from Babylon the sower,
    and the reaper with his sickle at
        harvest.
Because of the sword of the oppressor
    let everyone return to his own people,
    let everyone flee to his own land.

[17]"Israel is a scattered flock
    that lions have chased away.
The first to devour him
    was the king of Assyria;
the last to crush his bones
    was Nebuchadnezzar king of
        Babylon."

[18]Therefore this is what the LORD
Almighty, the God of Israel, says:

"I will punish the king of Babylon and
        his land
    as I punished the king of Assyria.
[19]But I will bring Israel back to his own
        pasture
    and he will graze on Carmel and
        Bashan;
his appetite will be satisfied
    on the hills of Ephraim and Gilead.
[20]In those days, at that time,"
    declares the LORD,
"search will be made for Israel's guilt,
    but there will be none,
and for the sins of Judah,
    but none will be found,
    for I will forgive the remnant I spare.

[21]"Attack the land of Merathaim
    and those who live in Pekod.
Pursue, kill and completely destroy[c]
    them,"
                declares the LORD.
"Do everything I have commanded
    you.
[22]The noise of battle is in the land,
    the noise of great destruction!
[23]How broken and shattered
    is the hammer of the whole earth!
How desolate is Babylon
    among the nations!

[24]I set a trap for you, O Babylon,
    and you were caught before you
        knew it;
you were found and captured
    because you opposed the LORD.
[25]The LORD has opened his arsenal
    and brought out the weapons of his
        wrath,
for the Sovereign LORD Almighty has
        work to do
    in the land of the Babylonians.
[26]Come against her from afar.
    Break open her granaries;
    pile her up like heaps of grain.
Completely destroy her
    and leave her no remnant.
[27]Kill all her young bulls;
    let them go down to the slaughter!
Woe to them! For their day has come,
    the time for them to be punished.
[28]Listen to the fugitives and refugees
        from Babylon
    declaring in Zion
how the LORD our God has taken
        vengeance,
    vengeance for his temple.

[29]"Summon archers against Babylon,
    all those who draw the bow.
Encamp all round her;
    let no-one escape.
Repay her for her deeds;
    do to her as she has done.
For she defied the LORD,
    the Holy One of Israel.
[30]Therefore, her young men will fall in
        the streets;
    all her soldiers will be silenced in that
        day,"
                declares the LORD.
[31]"See, I am against you, O arrogant
        one,"
    declares the Lord, the LORD
        Almighty,
"for your day has come,
    the time for you to be punished.
[32]The arrogant one will stumble and fall
    and no-one will help her up;
I will kindle a fire in her towns
    that will consume all who are around
        her."

[c]21 The Hebrew term refers to the irrevocable giving over of things or persons to the LORD, often by totally destroying them; also in verse 26.

³³This is what the LORD Almighty says:

"The people of Israel are oppressed,
     and the people of Judah as well.
All their captors hold them fast,
     refusing to let them go.
³⁴Yet their Redeemer is strong;
     the LORD Almighty is his name.
He will vigorously defend their cause
     so that he may bring rest to their
          land,
     but unrest to those who live in
          Babylon.

³⁵"A sword against the Babylonians!"
     declares the LORD—
"against those who live in Babylon
     and against her officials and wise
          men!
³⁶A sword against her false prophets!
     They will become fools.
A sword against her warriors!
     They will be filled with terror.
³⁷A sword against her horses and chariots
     and all the foreigners in her ranks!
     They will become women.
A sword against her treasures!
     They will be plundered.
³⁸A drought on*d* her waters!
     They will dry up.
For it is a land of idols,
     idols that will go mad with terror.

³⁹"So desert creatures and hyenas will
     live there,
     and there the owl will dwell.
It will never again be inhabited
     or lived in from generation to
          generation.
⁴⁰As God overthrew Sodom and
     Gomorrah
     along with their neighbouring
          towns,"
                    declares the LORD,
"so no-one will live there;
     no man will dwell in it.

⁴¹"Look! An army is coming from the
     north;
     a great nation and many kings
are being stirred up from the ends of
     the earth.
⁴²They are armed with bows and spears;
     they are cruel and without mercy.
They sound like the roaring sea
     as they ride on their horses;
they come like men in battle formation
     to attack you, O Daughter of
          Babylon.
⁴³The king of Babylon has heard reports
     about them,
     and his hands hang limp.
Anguish has gripped him,
     pain like that of a woman in labour.
⁴⁴Like a lion coming up from Jordan's
     thickets
     to a rich pasture-land,
I will chase Babylon from its land in an
     instant.
     Who is the chosen one I will appoint
          for this?
Who is like me and who can challenge
     me?
     And what shepherd can stand against
          me?"
⁴⁵Therefore, hear what the LORD has
     planned against Babylon,
     what he has purposed against the
          land of the Babylonians:
The young of the flock will be dragged
     away;
     he will completely destroy their
          pasture because of them.
⁴⁶At the sound of Babylon's capture the
     earth will tremble;
     its cry will resound among the
          nations.

51   This is what the LORD says:

"See, I will stir up the spirit of a
     destroyer
     against Babylon and the people of
          Leb Kamai.*a*
²I will send foreigners to Babylon
     to winnow her and to devastate her
          land;
they will oppose her on every side
     in the day of her disaster.
³Let not the archer string his bow,
     nor let him put on his armour.

Do not spare her young men;
  completely destroy[b] her army.
⁴They will fall down slain in Babylon,[c]
  fatally wounded in her streets.
⁵For Israel and Judah have not been
    forsaken
  by their God, the LORD Almighty,
though their land[d] is full of guilt
  before the Holy One of Israel.

⁶"Flee from Babylon!
    Run for your lives!
    Do not be destroyed because of her
      sins.
  It is time for the LORD's vengeance;
    he will pay her what she deserves.
⁷Babylon was a gold cup in the LORD's
    hand;
  she made the whole earth drunk.
The nations drank her wine;
  therefore they have now gone mad.
⁸Babylon will suddenly fall and be
    broken.
  Wail over her!
Get balm for her pain;
  perhaps she can be healed.

⁹"'We would have healed Babylon,
  but she cannot be healed;
let us leave her and each go to his own
    land,
  for her judgment reaches to the skies,
  it rises as high as the clouds.'

¹⁰"'The LORD has vindicated us;
  come, let us tell in Zion
  what the LORD our God has done.'

¹¹"Sharpen the arrows,
    take up the shields!
  The LORD has stirred up the kings of the
    Medes,
    because his purpose is to destroy
      Babylon.
  The LORD will take vengeance,
    vengeance for his temple.
¹²Lift up a banner against the walls of
    Babylon!
  Reinforce the guard,
  station the watchmen,
    prepare an ambush!

The LORD will carry out his purpose,
  his decree against the people of
    Babylon.
¹³You who live by many waters
  and are rich in treasures,
your end has come,
  the time for you to be cut off.
¹⁴The LORD Almighty has sworn by
    himself:
  I will surely fill you with men, as with
    a swarm of locusts,
  and they will shout in triumph over
    you.

¹⁵"He made the earth by his power;
  he founded the world by his wisdom
  and stretched out the heavens by his
    understanding.
¹⁶When he thunders, the waters in the
    heavens roar;
  he makes clouds rise from the ends of
    the earth.
He sends lightning with the rain
  and brings out the wind from his
    storehouses.

¹⁷"Every man is senseless and without
    knowledge;
  every goldsmith is shamed by his
    idols.
His images are a fraud;
  they have no breath in them.
¹⁸They are worthless, the objects of
    mockery;
  when their judgment comes, they will
    perish.
¹⁹He who is the Portion of Jacob is not
    like these,
  for he is the Maker of all things,
including the tribe of his inheritance—
  the LORD Almighty is his name.

²⁰"You are my war club,
    my weapon for battle—
  with you I shatter nations,
  with you I destroy kingdoms,
²¹with you I shatter horse and rider,
  with you I shatter chariot and driver,
²²with you I shatter man and woman,
  with you I shatter old man and
    youth,

---

b3 The Hebrew term refers to the irrevocable giving over of things or persons to the LORD, often by totally destroying them.   *c4* Or *Chaldea*   *d5* Or / *and the land ˻of the Babylonians˼*

with you I shatter young man and
maiden,
23with you I shatter shepherd and flock,
with you I shatter farmer and oxen,
with you I shatter governors and
officials.

24"Before your eyes I will repay Babylon and all who live in Babylonia*e* for all
the wrong they have done in Zion," declares the LORD.

25"I am against you, O destroying
mountain,
you who destroy the whole earth,"
declares the LORD.
"I will stretch out my hand against you,
roll you off the cliffs,
and make you a burnt-out mountain.
26No rock will be taken from you for a
cornerstone,
nor any stone for a foundation,
for you will be desolate for ever,"
declares the LORD.

27"Lift up a banner in the land!
Blow the trumpet among the nations!
Prepare the nations for battle against
her;
summon against her these kingdoms:
Ararat, Minni and Ashkenaz.
Appoint a commander against her;
send up horses like a swarm of
locusts.
28Prepare the nations for battle against
her—
the kings of the Medes,
their governors and all their officials,
and all the countries they rule.
29The land trembles and writhes,
for the LORD's purposes against
Babylon stand—
to lay waste the land of Babylon
so that no-one will live there.
30Babylon's warriors have stopped
fighting;
they remain in their strongholds.
Their strength is exhausted;
they have become like women.
Her dwellings are set on fire;
the bars of her gates are broken.

31One courier follows another
and messenger follows messenger
to announce to the king of Babylon
that his entire city is captured,
32the river crossings seized,
the marshes set on fire,
and the soldiers terrified."

33This is what the LORD Almighty, the
God of Israel, says:

"The Daughter of Babylon is like a
threshing-floor
at the time it is trampled;
the time to harvest her will soon
come."

34"Nebuchadnezzar king of Babylon has
devoured us,
he has thrown us into confusion,
he has made us an empty jar.
Like a serpent he has swallowed us
and filled his stomach with our
delicacies,
and then has spewed us out.
35May the violence done to our flesh*f* be
upon Babylon,"
say the inhabitants of Zion.
"May our blood be on those who live in
Babylonia,"
says Jerusalem.

36Therefore, this is what the LORD
says:

"See, I will defend your cause
and avenge you;
I will dry up her sea
and make her springs dry.
37Babylon will be a heap of ruins,
a haunt of jackals,
an object of horror and scorn,
a place where no-one lives.
38Her people all roar like young lions,
they growl like lion cubs.
39But while they are aroused,
I will set out a feast for them
and make them drunk,
so that they shout with laughter—
then sleep for ever and not awake,"
declares the LORD.

e24 Or *Chaldea*; also in verse 35   *f35* Or *done to us and to our children*

40"I will bring them down
   like lambs to the slaughter,
   like rams and goats.

41"How Sheshach[g] will be captured,
   the boast of the whole earth seized!
What a horror Babylon will be
   among the nations!
42The sea will rise over Babylon;
   its roaring waves will cover her.
43Her towns will be desolate,
   a dry and desert land,
a land where no-one lives,
   through which no man travels.
44I will punish Bel in Babylon
   and make him spew out what he has
      swallowed.
The nations will no longer stream to him.
And the wall of Babylon will fall.

45"Come out of her, my people!
   Run for your lives!
   Run from the fierce anger of the
      LORD.
46Do not lose heart or be afraid
   when rumours are heard in the land;
one rumour comes this year, another
      the next,
   rumours of violence in the land
   and of ruler against ruler.
47For the time will surely come
   when I will punish the idols of
      Babylon;
   her whole land will be disgraced
   and her slain will all lie fallen within
      her.
48Then heaven and earth and all that is in
      them
   will shout for joy over Babylon,
for out of the north
   destroyers will attack her,"
                  declares the LORD.

49"Babylon must fall because of Israel's
      slain,
   just as the slain in all the earth
   have fallen because of Babylon.
50You who have escaped the sword,
   leave and do not linger!
Remember the LORD in a distant land,
   and think on Jerusalem."

51"We are disgraced,
   for we have been insulted
   and shame covers our faces,
because foreigners have entered
   the holy places of the LORD's house."

52"But days are coming," declares the
      LORD,
   "when I will punish her idols,
and throughout her land
   the wounded will groan.
53Even if Babylon reaches the sky
   and fortifies her lofty stronghold,
I will send destroyers against her,"
                  declares the LORD.

54"The sound of a cry comes from
      Babylon,
   the sound of great destruction
   from the land of the Babylonians.[h]
55The LORD will destroy Babylon;
   he will silence her noisy din.
Waves ⌊of enemies⌋ will rage like great
      waters;
   the roar of their voices will resound.
56A destroyer will come against Babylon;
   her warriors will be captured,
   and their bows will be broken.
For the LORD is a God of retribution;
   he will repay in full.
57I will make her officials and wise men
      drunk,
   her governors, officers and warriors
      as well;
they will sleep for ever and not awake,"
   declares the King, whose name is the
      LORD Almighty.

58This is what the LORD Almighty says:

"Babylon's thick wall will be levelled
   and her high gates set on fire;
the peoples exhaust themselves for
      nothing,
   the nations' labour is only fuel for the
      flames."

59This is the message Jeremiah gave to
the staff officer Seraiah son of Neriah, the
son of Mahseiah, when he went to Babylon with Zedekiah king of Judah in the

---

g41 Sheshach is a cryptogram for Babylon.   *h54* Or *Chaldeans* fourth year of his reign. 60Jeremiah had written on a scroll about all the disasters that would come upon Babylon—all that had been recorded concerning Babylon. 61He said to Seraiah, "When you get to Babylon, see that you read all these words aloud. 62Then say, 'O LORD, you have said you will destroy this place, so that neither man nor animal will live in it; it will be desolate for ever.' 63When you finish reading this scroll, tie a stone to it and throw it into the Euphrates. 64Then say, 'So will Babylon sink to rise no more because of the disaster I will bring upon her. And her people will fall.'"

The words of Jeremiah end here.

The Fall of Jerusalem

52 Zedekiah was twenty-one years old when he became king, and he reigned in Jerusalem for eleven years. His mother's name was Hamutal daughter of Jeremiah; she was from Libnah. 2He did evil in the eyes of the LORD, just as Jehoiakim had done. 3It was because of the LORD's anger that all this happened to Jerusalem and Judah, and in the end he thrust them from his presence.

Now Zedekiah rebelled against the king of Babylon.

4So in the ninth year of Zedekiah's reign, on the tenth day of the tenth month, Nebuchadnezzar king of Babylon marched against Jerusalem with his whole army. They camped outside the city and built siege works all around it. 5The city was kept under siege until the eleventh year of King Zedekiah.

6By the ninth day of the fourth month the famine in the city had become so severe that there was no food for the people to eat. 7Then the city wall was broken through, and the whole army fled. They left the city at night through the gate between the two walls near the king's garden, though the Babylonians*a* were surrounding the city. They fled towards the Arabah,*b* 8but the Babylonian*c* army

pursued King Zedekiah and overtook him in the plains of Jericho. All his soldiers were separated from him and scattered, 9and he was captured.

He was taken to the king of Babylon at Riblah in the land of Hamath, where he pronounced sentence on him. 10There at Riblah the king of Babylon slaughtered the sons of Zedekiah before his eyes; he also killed all the officials of Judah. 11Then he put out Zedekiah's eyes, bound him with bronze shackles and took him to Babylon, where he put him in prison till the day of his death.

12On the tenth day of the fifth month, in the nineteenth year of Nebuchadnezzar king of Babylon, Nebuzaradan commander of the imperial guard, who served the king of Babylon, came to Jerusalem. 13He set fire to the temple of the LORD, the royal palace and all the houses of Jerusalem. Every important building he burned down. 14The whole Babylonian army under the commander of the imperial guard broke down all the walls around Jerusalem. 15Nebuzaradan the commander of the guard carried into exile some of the poorest people and those who remained in the city, along with the rest of the craftsmen*d* and those who had gone over to the king of Babylon. 16But Nebuzaradan left behind the rest of the poorest people of the land to work the vineyards and fields.

17The Babylonians broke up the bronze pillars, the movable stands and the bronze Sea that were at the temple of the LORD and they carried all the bronze to Babylon. 18They also took away the pots, shovels, wick trimmers, sprinkling bowls, dishes and all the bronze articles used in the temple service. 19The commander of the imperial guard took away the basins, censers, sprinkling bowls, pots, lampstands, dishes and bowls used for drink offerings—all that were made of pure gold or silver.

20The bronze from the two pillars, the Sea and the twelve bronze bulls under it, and the movable stands, which King

a7 Or *Chaldeans*; also in verse 17   *b7* Or *the Jordan Valley*   *c8* Or *Chaldean*; also in verse 14
d15 Or *populace*

Solomon had made for the temple of the LORD, was more than could be weighed. [21]Each of the pillars was eighteen cubits high and twelve cubits in circumference;[e] each was four fingers thick, and hollow. [22]The bronze capital on the top of the one pillar was five cubits[f] high and was decorated with a network and pomegranates of bronze all around. The other pillar, with its pomegranates, was similar. [23]There were ninety-six pomegranates on the sides; the total number of pomegranates above the surrounding network was a hundred.

[24]The commander of the guard took as prisoners Seraiah the chief priest, Zephaniah the priest next in rank and the three doorkeepers. [25]Of those still in the city, he took the officer in charge of the fighting men, and seven royal advisers. He also took the secretary who was chief officer in charge of conscripting the people of the land and sixty of his men who were found in the city. [26]Nebuzaradan the commander took them all and brought them to the king of Babylon at Riblah. [27]There at Riblah, in the land of Hamath, the king had them executed.

So Judah went into captivity, away from her land. [28]This is the number of the people Nebuchadnezzar carried into exile:

in the seventh year, 3,023 Jews;
[29]in Nebuchadnezzar's eighteenth year,
   832 people from Jerusalem;
[30]in his twenty-third year,
   745 Jews taken into exile by
      Nebuzaradan the commander of
      the imperial guard.
There were 4,600 people in all.

Jehoiachin Released

[31]In the thirty-seventh year of the exile of Jehoiachin king of Judah, in the year Evil-Merodach[g] became king of Babylon, he released Jehoiachin king of Judah and freed him from prison on the twenty-fifth day of the twelfth month. [32]He spoke kindly to him and gave him a seat of honour higher than those of the other kings who were with him in Babylon. [33]So Jehoiachin put aside his prison clothes and for the rest of his life ate regularly at the king's table. [34]Day by day the king of Babylon gave Jehoiachin a regular allowance as long as he lived, till the day of his death.

---

e21 That is, about 27 feet (about 8.1 metres) high and 18 feet (about 5.5 metres) in circumference
f22 That is, about 7½ feet (about 2.3 metres)   *g31* Also called *Amel-Marduk*

Lamentations

1 *a* How deserted lies the city,
   once so full of people!
How like a widow is she,
   who once was great among the
      nations!
She who was queen among the
      provinces
   has now become a slave.

2 Bitterly she weeps at night,
   tears are upon her cheeks.
Among all her lovers
   there is none to comfort her.
All her friends have betrayed her;
   they have become her enemies.

3 After affliction and harsh labour,
   Judah has gone into exile.
She dwells among the nations;
   she finds no resting place.
All who pursue her have overtaken her
   in the midst of her distress.

4 The roads to Zion mourn,
   for no-one comes to her appointed
      feasts.
All her gateways are desolate,
   her priests groan,
her maidens grieve,
   and she is in bitter anguish.

5 Her foes have become her masters;
   her enemies are at ease.
The LORD has brought her grief
   because of her many sins.
Her children have gone into exile,
   captive before the foe.

6 All the splendour has departed
   from the Daughter of Zion.
Her princes are like deer
   that find no pasture;
in weakness they have fled
   before the pursuer.

7 In the days of her affliction and
      wandering
   Jerusalem remembers all the
      treasures
   that were hers in days of old.
When her people fell into enemy hands,
   there was no-one to help her.
Her enemies looked at her
   and laughed at her destruction.

8 Jerusalem has sinned greatly
   and so has become unclean.
All who honoured her despise her,
   for they have seen her nakedness;
she herself groans
   and turns away.

9 Her filthiness clung to her skirts;
   she did not consider her future.
Her fall was astounding;
   there was none to comfort her.
"Look, O LORD, on my affliction,
   for the enemy has triumphed."

10 The enemy laid hands
   on all her treasures;
she saw pagan nations
   enter her sanctuary—
those you had forbidden
   to enter your assembly.

a This chapter is an acrostic poem, the verses of which begin with the successive letters of the Hebrew alphabet.

¹¹All her people groan
  as they search for bread;
they barter their treasures for food
  to keep themselves alive.
"Look, O LORD, and consider,
  for I am despised."

¹²"Is it nothing to you, all you who pass
    by?
  Look around and see.
Is any suffering like my suffering
  that was inflicted on me,
that the LORD brought on me
  in the day of his fierce anger?

¹³"From on high he sent fire,
  sent it down into my bones.
He spread a net for my feet
  and turned me back.
He made me desolate,
  faint all the day long.

¹⁴"My sins have been bound into a yoke;*b*
  by his hands they were woven
    together.
They have come upon my neck
  and the Lord has sapped my strength.
He has handed me over
  to those I cannot withstand.

¹⁵"The Lord has rejected
  all the warriors in my midst;
he has summoned an army against me
  to*c* crush my young men.
In his winepress the Lord has trampled
  the Virgin Daughter of Judah.

¹⁶"This is why I weep
  and my eyes overflow with tears.
No-one is near to comfort me,
  no-one to restore my spirit.
My children are destitute
  because the enemy has prevailed."

¹⁷Zion stretches out her hands,
  but there is no-one to comfort her.
The LORD has decreed for Jacob
  that his neighbours become his foes;
Jerusalem has become
  an unclean thing among them.

¹⁸"The LORD is righteous,
  yet I rebelled against his command.
Listen, all you peoples;
  look upon my suffering.
My young men and maidens
  have gone into exile.

¹⁹"I called to my allies
  but they betrayed me.
My priests and my elders
  perished in the city
while they searched for food
  to keep themselves alive.

²⁰"See, O LORD, how distressed I am!
  I am in torment within,
and in my heart I am disturbed,
  for I have been most rebellious.
Outside, the sword bereaves;
  inside, there is only death.

²¹"People have heard my groaning,
  but there is no-one to comfort me.
All my enemies have heard of my
    distress;
  they rejoice at what you have done.
May you bring the day you have
    announced
  so that they may become like me.

²²"Let all their wickedness come before
    you;
  deal with them
as you have dealt with me
  because of all my sins.
My groans are many
  and my heart is faint."

2*a* How the Lord has covered the
    Daughter of Zion
  with the cloud of his anger!*b*
He has hurled down the splendour of
    Israel
  from heaven to earth;
he has not remembered his footstool
  in the day of his anger.

²Without pity the Lord has swallowed up
  all the dwellings of Jacob;

---

b14 Most Hebrew manuscripts; Septuagint *He kept watch over my sins*   *c15* Or *has set a time for me / when he will*
*a*This chapter is an acrostic poem, the verses of which begin with the successive letters of the Hebrew alphabet.
b1 Or *How the LORD in his anger / has treated the Daughter of Zion with contempt!*

in his wrath he has torn down
  the strongholds of the Daughter of
    Judah.
He has brought her kingdom and its
  princes
down to the ground in dishonour.

3In fierce anger he has cut off
  every horn[c] of Israel.
He has withdrawn his right hand
  at the approach of the enemy.
He has burned in Jacob like a flaming
  fire
that consumes everything around it.

4Like an enemy he has strung his bow;
  his right hand is ready.
Like a foe he has slain
  all who were pleasing to the eye;
he has poured out his wrath like fire
  on the tent of the Daughter of Zion.

5The Lord is like an enemy;
  he has swallowed up Israel.
He has swallowed up all her palaces
  and destroyed her strongholds.
He has multiplied mourning and
  lamentation
for the Daughter of Judah.

6He has laid waste his dwelling like a
  garden;
  he has destroyed his place of
    meeting.
The LORD has made Zion forget
  her appointed feasts and her
    Sabbaths;
in his fierce anger he has spurned
  both king and priest.

7The Lord has rejected his altar
  and abandoned his sanctuary.
He has handed over to the enemy
  the walls of her palaces;
they have raised a shout in the house of
  the LORD
as on the day of an appointed feast.

8The LORD determined to tear down
  the wall around the Daughter of
    Zion.

He stretched out a measuring line
  and did not withhold his hand from
    destroying.
He made ramparts and walls lament;
  together they wasted away.

9Her gates have sunk into the ground;
  their bars he has broken and
    destroyed.
Her king and her princes are exiled
  among the nations,
  the law is no more,
and her prophets no longer find
  visions from the LORD.

10The elders of the Daughter of Zion
  sit on the ground in silence;
they have sprinkled dust on their heads
  and put on sackcloth.
The young women of Jerusalem
  have bowed their heads to the
    ground.

11My eyes fail from weeping,
  I am in torment within,
my heart is poured out on the ground
  because my people are destroyed,
because children and infants faint
  in the streets of the city.

12They say to their mothers,
  "Where is bread and wine?"
as they faint like wounded men
  in the streets of the city,
as their lives ebb away
  in their mothers' arms.

13What can I say for you?
  With what can I compare
    you,
O Daughter of Jerusalem?
To what can I liken you,
  that I may comfort you,
O Virgin Daughter of Zion?
Your wound is as deep as the sea.
  Who can heal you?

14The visions of your prophets
  were false and worthless;
they did not expose your sin
  to ward off your captivity.

---

[c]3 Or / all the strength; or every king; horn here symbolises strength.

The oracles they gave you
  were false and misleading.

¹⁵All who pass your way
  clap their hands at you;
they scoff and shake their heads
  at the Daughter of Jerusalem:
"Is this the city that was called
  the perfection of beauty,
  the joy of the whole earth?"

¹⁶All your enemies open their mouths
  wide against you;
they scoff and gnash their teeth
  and say, "We have swallowed her up.
This is the day we have waited for;
  we have lived to see it."

¹⁷The LORD has done what he planned;
  he has fulfilled his word,
  which he decreed long ago.
He has overthrown you without pity,
  he has let the enemy gloat over you,
  he has exalted the horn[d] of your
    foes.

¹⁸The hearts of the people
  cry out to the Lord.
O wall of the Daughter of Zion,
  let your tears flow like a river
  day and night;
give yourself no relief,
  your eyes no rest.

¹⁹Arise, cry out in the night,
  as the watches of the night begin;
pour out your heart like water
  in the presence of the Lord.
Lift up your hands to him
  for the lives of your children,
who faint from hunger
  at the head of every street.

²⁰"Look, O LORD, and consider:
  Whom have you ever treated like
    this?
Should women eat their offspring,
  the children they have cared for?
Should priest and prophet be killed
  in the sanctuary of the Lord?

²¹"Young and old lie together
  in the dust of the streets;
my young men and maidens
  have fallen by the sword.
You have slain them in the day of your
    anger;
you have slaughtered them without
    pity.

²²"As you summon to a feast day,
  so you summoned against me terrors
    on every side.
In the day of the LORD's anger
  no-one escaped or survived;
those I cared for and reared,
  my enemy has destroyed."

3[a] I am the man who has seen affliction
  by the rod of his wrath.
²He has driven me away and made me
  walk
  in darkness rather than light;
³indeed, he has turned his hand against
  me
  again and again, all day long.

⁴He has made my skin and my flesh grow
  old
  and has broken my bones.
⁵He has besieged me and surrounded me
  with bitterness and hardship.
⁶He has made me dwell in darkness
  like those long dead.

⁷He has walled me in so that I cannot
    escape;
  he has weighed me down with chains.
⁸Even when I call out or cry for help,
  he shuts out my prayer.
⁹He has barred my way with blocks of
    stone;
  he has made my paths crooked.

¹⁰Like a bear lying in wait,
  like a lion in hiding,
¹¹he dragged me from the path and
    mangled me
  and left me without help.
¹²He drew his bow
  and made me the target for his arrows.

---

d17 Horn here symbolises strength.
*a*This chapter is an acrostic poem; the verses of each stanza begin with the successive letters of the Hebrew alphabet, and the verses within each stanza begin with the same letter.

13He pierced my heart
   with arrows from his quiver.
14I became the laughing-stock of all my
      people;
   they mock me in song all day long.
15He has filled me with bitter herbs
   and sated me with gall.

16He has broken my teeth with gravel;
   he has trampled me in the dust.
17I have been deprived of peace;
   I have forgotten what prosperity is.
18So I say, "My splendour is gone
   and all that I had hoped from the
      LORD."

19I remember my affliction and my
      wandering,
   the bitterness and the gall.
20I well remember them,
   and my soul is downcast within me.
21Yet this I call to mind
   and therefore I have hope:

22Because of the LORD's great love we are
      not consumed,
   for his compassions never fail.
23They are new every morning;
   great is your faithfulness.
24I say to myself, "The LORD is my
      portion;
   therefore I will wait for him."

25The LORD is good to those whose hope
      is in him,
   to the one who seeks him;
26it is good to wait quietly
   for the salvation of the LORD.
27It is good for a man to bear the yoke
   while he is young.

28Let him sit alone in silence,
   for the LORD has laid it on him.
29Let him bury his face in the dust—
   there may yet be hope.
30Let him offer his cheek to one who
      would strike him,
   and let him be filled with disgrace.

31For men are not cast off
   by the Lord for ever.
32Though he brings grief, he will show
      compassion,

so great is his unfailing love.
33For he does not willingly bring affliction
   or grief to the children of men.

34To crush underfoot
   all prisoners in the land,
35to deny a man his rights
   before the Most High,
36to deprive a man of justice—
   would not the Lord see such things?

37Who can speak and have it happen
   if the Lord has not decreed it?
38Is it not from the mouth of the Most
      High
   that both calamities and good things
      come?
39Why should any living man complain
   when punished for his sins?

40Let us examine our ways and test them,
   and let us return to the LORD.
41Let us lift up our hearts and our hands
   to God in heaven, and say:
42"We have sinned and rebelled
   and you have not forgiven.

43"You have covered yourself with anger
      and pursued us;
   you have slain without pity.
44You have covered yourself with a cloud
   so that no prayer can get through.
45You have made us scum and refuse
   among the nations.

46"All our enemies have opened their
      mouths
   wide against us.
47We have suffered terror and pitfalls,
   ruin and destruction."
48Streams of tears flow from my eyes
   because my people are destroyed.

49My eyes will flow unceasingly,
   without relief,
50until the LORD looks down
   from heaven and sees.
51What I see brings grief to my soul
   because of all the women of my
      city.

52Those who were my enemies without
      cause

hunted me like a bird.
⁵³They tried to end my life in a pit
and threw stones at me;
⁵⁴the waters closed over my head,
and I thought I was about to be cut
off.

⁵⁵I called on your name, O LORD,
from the depths of the pit.
⁵⁶You heard my plea: "Do not close your
ears
to my cry for relief."
⁵⁷You came near when I called you,
and you said, "Do not fear."

⁵⁸O Lord, you took up my case;
you redeemed my life.
⁵⁹You have seen, O LORD, the wrong
done to me.
Uphold my cause!
⁶⁰You have seen the depth of their
vengeance,
all their plots against me.

⁶¹O LORD, you have heard their insults,
all their plots against me—
⁶²what my enemies whisper and mutter
against me all day long.
⁶³Look at them! Sitting or standing,
they mock me in their songs.

⁶⁴Pay them back what they deserve, O
LORD,
for what their hands have done.
⁶⁵Put a veil over their hearts,
and may your curse be on them!
⁶⁶Pursue them in anger and destroy them
from under the heavens of the LORD.

4 ᵃ How the gold has lost its lustre,
the fine gold become dull!
The sacred gems are scattered
at the head of every street.

²How the precious sons of Zion,
once worth their weight in gold,
are now considered as pots of clay,
the work of a potter's hands!

³Even jackals offer their breasts
to nurse their young,

but my people have become heartless
like ostriches in the desert.

⁴Because of thirst the infant's tongue
sticks to the roof of its mouth;
the children beg for bread,
but no-one gives it to them.

⁵Those who once ate delicacies
are destitute in the streets.
Those nurtured in purple
now lie on ash heaps.

⁶The punishment of my people
is greater than that of Sodom,
which was overthrown in a moment
without a hand turned to help her.

⁷Their princes were brighter than snow
and whiter than milk,
their bodies more ruddy than rubies,
their appearance like sapphires.ᵇ

⁸But now they are blacker than soot;
they are not recognised in the
streets.
Their skin has shrivelled on their bones;
it has become as dry as a stick.

⁹Those killed by the sword are better off
than those who die of famine;
racked with hunger, they waste away
for lack of food from the field.

¹⁰With their own hands compassionate
women
have cooked their own children,
who became their food
when my people were destroyed.

¹¹The LORD has given full vent to his
wrath;
he has poured out his fierce anger.
He kindled a fire in Zion
that consumed her foundations.

¹²The kings of the earth did not believe,
nor did any of the world's people,
that enemies and foes could enter
the gates of Jerusalem.

ᵃThis chapter is an acrostic poem, the verses of which begin with the successive letters of the Hebrew
alphabet.   ᵇ7 Or *lapis lazuli*

13But it happened because of the sins of
her prophets
and the iniquities of her priests,
who shed within her
the blood of the righteous.

14Now they grope through the streets
like men who are blind.
They are so defiled with blood
that no-one dares to touch their
garments.

15"Go away! You are unclean!" men cry
to them.
"Away! Away! Don't touch us!"
When they flee and wander about,
people among the nations say,
"They can stay here no longer."

16The LORD himself has scattered them;
he no longer watches over them.
The priests are shown no honour,
the elders no favour.

17Moreover, our eyes failed,
looking in vain for help;
from our towers we watched
for a nation that could not save us.

18Men stalked us at every step,
so we could not walk in our
streets.
Our end was near, our days were
numbered,
for our end had come.

19Our pursuers were swifter
than eagles in the sky;
they chased us over the mountains
and lay in wait for us in the desert.

20The LORD's anointed, our very life
breath,
was caught in their traps.
We thought that under his shadow
we would live among the nations.

21Rejoice and be glad, O Daughter of
Edom,
you who live in the land of Uz.
But to you also the cup will be passed;
you will be drunk and stripped
naked.

22O Daughter of Zion, your punishment
will end;
he will not prolong your exile.
But, O Daughter of Edom, he will
punish your sin
and expose your wickedness.

5 Remember, O LORD, what has
happened to us;
look, and see our disgrace.
2Our inheritance has been turned over to
aliens,
our homes to foreigners.
3We have become orphans and
fatherless,
our mothers like widows.
4We must buy the water we drink;
our wood can be had only at a
price.
5Those who pursue us are at our heels;
we are weary and find no rest.
6We submitted to Egypt and Assyria
to get enough bread.
7Our fathers sinned and are no more,
and we bear their punishment.
8Slaves rule over us,
and there is none to free us from their
hands.
9We get our bread at the risk of our lives
because of the sword in the desert.
10Our skin is hot as an oven,
feverish from hunger.
11Women have been ravished in Zion,
and virgins in the towns of
Judah.
12Princes have been hung up by their
hands;
elders are shown no respect.
13Young men toil at the millstones;
boys stagger under loads of
wood.
14The elders are gone from the city gate;
the young men have stopped their
music.
15Joy is gone from our hearts;
our dancing has turned to mourning.
16The crown has fallen from our head.
Woe to us, for we have sinned!
17Because of this our hearts are faint;
because of these things our eyes grow
dim
18for Mount Zion, which lies desolate,
with jackals prowling over it.

¹⁹You, O Lord, reign for ever;
    your throne endures from
        generation to generation.
²⁰Why do you always forget us?
    Why do you forsake us so
        long?

²¹Restore us to yourself, O Lord, that we
    may return;
    renew our days as of old
²²unless you have utterly rejected us
    and are angry with us beyond
        measure.

Ezekiel

The Living Creatures and the Glory of the LORD

1 In the[a] thirtieth year, in the fourth month on the fifth day, while I was among the exiles by the Kebar River, the heavens were opened and I saw visions of God.

[2] On the fifth of the month—it was the fifth year of the exile of King Jehoiachin— [3] the word of the LORD came to Ezekiel the priest, the son of Buzi,[b] by the Kebar River in the land of the Babylonians.[c] There the hand of the LORD was upon him.

[4] I looked, and I saw a windstorm coming out of the north—an immense cloud with flashing lightning and surrounded by brilliant light. The centre of the fire looked like glowing metal, [5] and in the fire was what looked like four living creatures. In appearance their form was that of a man, [6] but each of them had four faces and four wings. [7] Their legs were straight; their feet were like those of a calf and gleamed like burnished bronze. [8] Under their wings on their four sides they had the hands of a man. All four of them had faces and wings, [9] and their wings touched one another. Each one went straight ahead; they did not turn as they moved.

[10] Their faces looked like this: Each of the four had the face of a man, and on the right side each had the face of a lion, and on the left the face of an ox; each also had the face of an eagle. [11] Such were their faces. Their wings were spread out upwards; each had two wings, one touching the wing of another creature on either side, and two wings covering its body. [12] Each one went straight ahead. Wherever the spirit would go, they would go, without turning as they went. [13] The appearance of the living creatures was like burning coals of fire or like torches. Fire moved back and forth among the creatures; it was bright, and lightning flashed out of it. [14] The creatures sped back and forth like flashes of lightning.

[15] As I looked at the living creatures, I saw a wheel on the ground beside each creature with its four faces. [16] This was the appearance and structure of the wheels: They sparkled like chrysolite, and all four looked alike. Each appeared to be made like a wheel intersecting a wheel. [17] As they moved, they would go in any one of the four directions the creatures faced; the wheels did not turn about[d] as the creatures went. [18] Their rims were high and awesome, and all four rims were full of eyes all around.

[19] When the living creatures moved, the wheels beside them moved; and when the living creatures rose from the ground, the wheels also rose. [20] Wherever the spirit would go, they would go, and the wheels would rise along with them, because the spirit of the living creatures was in the wheels. [21] When the creatures moved, they also moved; when the creatures stood still, they also stood still; and when the creatures rose from the ground, the wheels rose along with them, because the spirit of the living creatures was in the wheels.

---

a1 Or ⌞my⌟   b3 Or *Ezekiel son of Buzi the priest*   c3 Or *Chaldeans*   d17 Or *aside*

²²Spread out above the heads of the living creatures was what looked like an expanse, sparkling like ice, and awesome. ²³Under the expanse their wings were stretched out one towards the other, and each had two wings covering its body. ²⁴When the creatures moved, I heard the sound of their wings, like the roar of rushing waters, like the voice of the Almighty,ᵉ like the tumult of an army. When they stood still, they lowered their wings.

²⁵Then there came a voice from above the expanse over their heads as they stood with lowered wings. ²⁶Above the expanse over their heads was what looked like a throne of sapphire,ᶠ and high above on the throne was a figure like that of a man. ²⁷I saw that from what appeared to be his waist up he looked like glowing metal, as if full of fire, and that from there down he looked like fire; and brilliant light surrounded him. ²⁸Like the appearance of a rainbow in the clouds on a rainy day, so was the radiance around him.

This was the appearance of the likeness of the glory of the LORD. When I saw it, I fell face down, and I heard the voice of one speaking.

Ezekiel's Call

2 He said to me, "Son of man, stand up on your feet and I will speak to you." ²As he spoke, the Spirit came into me and raised me to my feet, and I heard him speaking to me.

³He said: "Son of man, I am sending you to the Israelites, to a rebellious nation that has rebelled against me; they and their fathers have been in revolt against me to this very day. ⁴The people to whom I am sending you are obstinate and stubborn. Say to them, 'This is what the Sovereign LORD says.' ⁵And whether they listen or fail to listen—for they are a rebellious house—they will know that a prophet has been among them. ⁶And you, son of man, do not be afraid of them or their words. Do not be afraid, though briers and thorns are all around you and

you live among scorpions. Do not be afraid of what they say or terrified by them, though they are a rebellious house. ⁷You must speak my words to them, whether they listen or fail to listen, for they are rebellious. ⁸But you, son of man, listen to what I say to you. Do not rebel like that rebellious house; open your mouth and eat what I give you."

⁹Then I looked, and I saw a hand stretched out to me. In it was a scroll, ¹⁰which he unrolled before me. On both sides of it were written words of lament and mourning and woe.

3 And he said to me, "Son of man, eat what is before you, eat this scroll; then go and speak to the house of Israel." ²So I opened my mouth, and he gave me the scroll to eat.

³Then he said to me, "Son of man, eat this scroll I am giving you and fill your stomach with it." So I ate it, and it tasted as sweet as honey in my mouth.

⁴He then said to me: "Son of man, go now to the house of Israel and speak my words to them. ⁵You are not being sent to a people of obscure speech and difficult language, but to the house of Israel—⁶not to many peoples of obscure speech and difficult language, whose words you cannot understand. Surely if I had sent you to them, they would have listened to you. ⁷But the house of Israel is not willing to listen to you because they are not willing to listen to me, for the whole house of Israel is hardened and obstinate. ⁸But I will make you as unyielding and hardened as they are. ⁹I will make your forehead like the hardest stone, harder than flint. Do not be afraid of them or terrified by them, though they are a rebellious house."

¹⁰And he said to me, "Son of man, listen carefully and take to heart all the words I speak to you. ¹¹Go now to your countrymen in exile and speak to them. Say to them, 'This is what the Sovereign LORD says,' whether they listen or fail to listen."

¹²Then the Spirit lifted me up, and I heard behind me a loud rumbling sound—May the glory of the LORD be praised in his dwelling-place!—¹³the sound of the wings

---

ᵉ24 Hebrew *Shaddai*   ᶠ26 Or *lapis lazuli*

of the living creatures brushing against each other and the sound of the wheels beside them, a loud rumbling sound. [14]The Spirit then lifted me up and took me away, and I went in bitterness and in the anger of my spirit, with the strong hand of the LORD upon me. [15]I came to the exiles who lived at Tel Abib near the Kebar River. And there, where they were living, I sat among them for seven days—overwhelmed.

Warning to Israel

[16]At the end of seven days the word of the LORD came to me: [17]"Son of man, I have made you a watchman for the house of Israel; so hear the word I speak and give them warning from me. [18]When I say to a wicked man, 'You will surely die,' and you do not warn him or speak out to dissuade him from his evil ways in order to save his life, that wicked man will die for[a] his sin, and I will hold you accountable for his blood. [19]But if you do warn the wicked man and he does not turn from his wickedness or from his evil ways, he will die for his sin; but you will have saved yourself.

[20]"Again, when a righteous man turns from his righteousness and does evil, and I put a stumbling-block before him, he will die. Since you did not warn him, he will die for his sin. The righteous things he did will not be remembered, and I will hold you accountable for his blood. [21]But if you do warn the righteous man not to sin and he does not sin, he will surely live because he took warning, and you will have saved yourself."

[22]The hand of the LORD was upon me there, and he said to me, "Get up and go out to the plain, and there I will speak to you." [23]So I got up and went out to the plain. And the glory of the LORD was standing there, like the glory I had seen by the Kebar River, and I fell face down. [24]Then the Spirit came into me and raised me to my feet. He spoke to me and said: "Go, shut yourself inside your house. [25]And you, son of man, they will tie with ropes; you will be bound so that you

cannot go out among the people. [26]I will make your tongue stick to the roof of your mouth so that you will be silent and unable to rebuke them, though they are a rebellious house. [27]But when I speak to you, I will open your mouth and you shall say to them, 'This is what the Sovereign LORD says.' Whoever will listen let him listen, and whoever will refuse let him refuse; for they are a rebellious house.

Siege of Jerusalem Symbolised

4 "Now, son of man, take a clay tablet, put it in front of you and draw the city of Jerusalem on it. [2]Then lay siege to it: Erect siege works against it, build a ramp up to it, set up camps against it and put battering-rams around it. [3]Then take an iron pan, place it as an iron wall between you and the city and turn your face towards it. It will be under siege, and you shall besiege it. This will be a sign to the house of Israel.

[4]"Then lie on your left side and put the sin of the house of Israel upon yourself.[a] You are to bear their sin for the number of days you lie on your side. [5]I have assigned you the same number of days as the years of their sin. So for 390 days you will bear the sin of the house of Israel.

[6]"After you have finished this, lie down again, this time on your right side, and bear the sin of the house of Judah. I have assigned you 40 days, a day for each year. [7]Turn your face towards the siege of Jerusalem and with bared arm prophesy against her. [8]I will tie you up with ropes so that you cannot turn from one side to the other until you have finished the days of your siege.

[9]"Take wheat and barley, beans and lentils, millet and spelt; put them in a storage jar and use them to make bread for yourself. You are to eat it during the 390 days you lie on your side. [10]Weigh out twenty shekels[b] of food to eat each day and eat it at set times. [11]Also measure out a sixth of a hin[c] of water and drink it at set times. [12]Eat the food as you would a barley cake; bake it in the sight of the people,

---

[a]18 Or in; also in verses 19 and 20   [a]4 Or your side
[b]10 That is, about 8 ounces (about 0.2 kilogram)   [c]11 That is, about 1 pint (about 0.6 litre)

using human excrement for fuel." ¹³The
Lord said, "In this way the people of
Israel will eat defiled food among the na-
tions where I will drive them."

¹⁴Then I said, "Not so, Sovereign Lord!
I have never defiled myself. From my
youth until now I have never eaten anything found dead or torn by wild animals.
No unclean meat has ever entered my
mouth."

¹⁵"Very well," he said, "I will let you
bake your bread over cow manure instead
of human excrement."

¹⁶He then said to me: "Son of man, I will
cut off the supply of food in Jerusalem.
The people will eat rationed food in anxiety and drink rationed water in despair,
¹⁷for food and water will be scarce. They
will be appalled at the sight of each other
and will waste away because of*d* their sin.

5 "Now, son of man, take a sharp
sword and use it as a barber's razor to
shave your head and your beard. Then
take a set of scales and divide up the hair.
²When the days of your siege come to an
end, burn a third of the hair with fire inside
the city. Take a third and strike it with the
sword all around the city. And scatter a
third to the wind. For I will pursue them
with drawn sword. ³But take a few strands
of hair and tuck them away in the folds of
your garment. ⁴Again, take a few of these
and throw them into the fire and burn
them up. A fire will spread from there to
the whole house of Israel.

⁵"This is what the Sovereign Lord says:
This is Jerusalem, which I have set in the
centre of the nations, with countries all
around her. ⁶Yet in her wickedness she
has rebelled against my laws and decrees
more than the nations and countries
around her. She has rejected my laws and
has not followed my decrees.

⁷"Therefore this is what the Sovereign
Lord says: You have been more unruly
than the nations around you and have not
followed my decrees or kept my laws. You
have not even*a* conformed to the standards of the nations around you.

⁸"Therefore this is what the Sovereign
Lord says: I myself am against you,

Jerusalem, and I will inflict punishment
on you in the sight of the nations. ⁹Because of all your detestable idols, I will do
to you what I have never done before and
will never do again. ¹⁰Therefore in your
midst fathers will eat their children,
and children will eat their fathers. I will
inflict punishment on you and will scatter
all your survivors to the winds. ¹¹Therefore
as surely as I live, declares the Sovereign
Lord, because you have defiled my sanctuary with all your vile images and detestable practices, I myself will withdraw my
favour; I will not look on you with pity
or spare you. ¹²A third of your people
will die of the plague or perish by famine
inside you; a third will fall by the sword outside your walls; and a third I will scatter to
the winds and pursue with drawn sword.

¹³"Then my anger will cease and my
wrath against them will subside, and I will
be avenged. And when I have spent my
wrath upon them, they will know that I the
Lord have spoken in my zeal.

¹⁴"I will make you a ruin and a reproach
among the nations around you, in the sight
of all who pass by. ¹⁵You will be a reproach and a taunt, a warning and an
object of horror to the nations around you
when I inflict punishment on you in anger
and in wrath and with stinging rebuke. I
the Lord have spoken. ¹⁶When I shoot at
you with my deadly and destructive
arrows of famine, I will shoot to destroy
you. I will bring more and more famine
upon you and cut off your supply of food.
¹⁷I will send famine and wild beasts against
you, and they will leave you childless.
Plague and bloodshed will sweep through
you, and I will bring the sword against
you. I the Lord have spoken."

*A Prophecy Against the Mountains of
Israel*

6 The word of the Lord came to me:
²"Son of man, set your face against
the mountains of Israel; prophesy against
them ³and say: 'O mountains of Israel,
hear the word of the Sovereign Lord. This
is what the Sovereign Lord says to the

d17 Or away in   a7 Most Hebrew manuscripts; some Hebrew manuscripts and Syriac You have mountains and hills, to the ravines and valleys: I am about to bring a sword against you, and I will destroy your high places. ⁴Your altars will be demolished and your incense altars will be smashed; and I will slay your people in front of your idols. ⁵I will lay the dead bodies of the Israelites in front of their idols, and I will scatter your bones around your altars. ⁶Wherever you live, the towns will be laid waste and the high places demolished, so that your altars will be laid waste and devastated, your idols smashed and ruined, your incense altars broken down, and what you have made wiped out. ⁷Your people will fall slain among you, and you will know that I am the LORD.

⁸"But I will spare some, for some of you will escape the sword when you are scattered among the lands and nations. ⁹Then in the nations where they have been carried captive, those who escape will remember me—how I have been grieved by their adulterous hearts, which have turned away from me, and by their eyes, which have lusted after their idols. They will loathe themselves for the evil they have done and for all their detestable practices. ¹⁰And they will know that I am the LORD; I did not threaten in vain to bring this calamity on them.

¹¹"This is what the Sovereign LORD says: Strike your hands together and stamp your feet and cry out "Alas!" because of all the wicked and detestable practices of the house of Israel, for they will fall by the sword, famine and plague. ¹²He that is far away will die of the plague, and he that is near will fall by the sword, and he that survives and is spared will die of famine. So will I spend my wrath upon them. ¹³And they will know that I am the LORD, when their people lie slain among their idols around their altars, on every high hill and on all the mountaintops, under every spreading tree and every leafy oak—places where they offered fragrant incense to all their idols. ¹⁴And I will stretch out my hand against them and make the land a desolate waste from the desert to Diblah[a]—wherever they live. Then they will know that I am the LORD.'"

The End Has Come

7 The word of the LORD came to me: ²"Son of man, this is what the Sovereign LORD says to the land of Israel: The end! The end has come upon the four corners of the land. ³The end is now upon you and I will unleash my anger against you. I will judge you according to your conduct and repay you for all your detestable practices. ⁴I will not look on you with pity or spare you; I will surely repay you for your conduct and the detestable practices among you. Then you will know that I am the LORD.

⁵"This is what the Sovereign LORD says: Disaster! An unheard-of[a] disaster is coming. ⁶The end has come! The end has come! It has roused itself against you. It has come! ⁷Doom has come upon you—you who dwell in the land. The time has come, the day is near; there is panic, not joy, upon the mountains. ⁸I am about to pour out my wrath on you and spend my anger against you; I will judge you according to your conduct and repay you for all your detestable practices. ⁹I will not look on you with pity or spare you; I will repay you in accordance with your conduct and the detestable practices among you. Then you will know that it is I the LORD who strikes the blow.

¹⁰"The day is here! It has come! Doom has burst forth, the rod has budded, arrogance has blossomed! ¹¹Violence has grown into[b] a rod to punish wickedness; none of the people will be left, none of that crowd—no wealth, nothing of value. ¹²The time has come, the day has arrived. Let not the buyer rejoice nor the seller grieve, for wrath is upon the whole crowd. ¹³The seller will not recover the land he has sold as long as both of them live, for the vision concerning the whole crowd will not be reversed. Because of their sins, not one of them will preserve his life. ¹⁴Though they blow the trumpet and get

---

a14 Most Hebrew manuscripts; a few Hebrew manuscripts *Riblah*
a5 Most Hebrew manuscripts; some Hebrew manuscripts and Syriac *Disaster after*
b11 Or *The violent one has become*

everything ready, no-one will go into battle, for my wrath is upon the whole crowd.

15"Outside is the sword, inside is plague and famine; those in the country will die by the sword, and those in the city will be devoured by famine and plague. 16All who survive and escape will be in the mountains, moaning like doves of the valleys, each because of his sins. 17Every hand will go limp, and every knee will become as weak as water. 18They will put on sackcloth and be clothed with terror. Their faces will be covered with shame and their heads will be shaved. 19They will throw their silver into the streets, and their gold will be an unclean thing. Their silver and gold will not be able to save them in the day of the LORD's wrath. They will not satisfy their hunger or fill their stomachs with it, for it has made them stumble into sin. 20They were proud of their beautiful jewellery and used it to make their detestable idols and vile images. Therefore I will turn these into an unclean thing for them. 21I will hand it all over as plunder to foreigners and as loot to the wicked of the earth, and they will defile it. 22I will turn my face away from them, and they will desecrate my treasured place; robbers will enter it and desecrate it.

23"Prepare chains, because the land is full of bloodshed and the city is full of violence. 24I will bring the most wicked of the nations to take possession of their houses; I will put an end to the pride of the mighty, and their sanctuaries will be desecrated. 25When terror comes, they will seek peace, but there will be none. 26Calamity upon calamity will come, and rumour upon rumour. They will try to get a vision from the prophet; the teaching of the law by the priest will be lost, as will the counsel of the elders. 27The king will mourn, the prince will be clothed with despair, and the hands of the people of the land will tremble. I will deal with them according to their conduct, and by their own standards I will judge them. Then they will know that I am the LORD."

Idolatry in the Temple

8 In the sixth year, in the sixth month on the fifth day, while I was sitting in my house and the elders of Judah were sitting before me, the hand of the Sovereign LORD came upon me there. 2I looked, and I saw a figure like that of a man.*a* From what appeared to be his waist down he was like fire, and from there up his appearance was as bright as glowing metal. 3He stretched out what looked like a hand and took me by the hair of my head. The Spirit lifted me up between earth and heaven and in visions of God he took me to Jerusalem, to the entrance to the north gate of the inner court, where the idol that provokes to jealousy stood. 4And there before me was the glory of the God of Israel, as in the vision I had seen in the plain.

5Then he said to me, "Son of man, look towards the north." So I looked, and in the entrance north of the gate of the altar I saw this idol of jealousy.

6And he said to me, "Son of man, do you see what they are doing—the utterly detestable things the house of Israel is doing here, things that will drive me far from my sanctuary? But you will see things that are even more detestable."

7Then he brought me to the entrance to the court. I looked, and I saw a hole in the wall. 8He said to me, "Son of man, now dig into the wall." So I dug into the wall and saw a doorway there.

9And he said to me, "Go in and see the wicked and detestable things they are doing here." 10So I went in and looked, and I saw portrayed all over the walls all kinds of crawling things and detestable animals and all the idols of the house of Israel. 11In front of them stood seventy elders of the house of Israel, and Jaazaniah son of Shaphan was standing among them. Each had a censer in his hand, and a fragrant cloud of incense was rising.

12He said to me, "Son of man, have you seen what the elders of the house of Israel are doing in the darkness, each at the shrine of his own idol? They say, 'The LORD does not see us; the LORD has

*a*2 Or *saw a fiery figure*

forsaken the land.'" ¹³Again, he said, "You will see them doing things that are even more detestable."

¹⁴Then he brought me to the entrance to the north gate of the house of the LORD, and I saw women sitting there, mourning for Tammuz. ¹⁵He said to me, "Do you see this, son of man? You will see things that are even more detestable than this."

¹⁶He then brought me into the inner court of the house of the LORD, and there at the entrance to the temple, between the portico and the altar, were about twenty-five men. With their backs towards the temple of the LORD and their faces towards the east, they were bowing down to the sun in the east.

¹⁷He said to me, "Have you seen this, son of man? Is it a trivial matter for the house of Judah to do the detestable things they are doing here? Must they also fill the land with violence and continually provoke me to anger? Look at them putting the branch to their nose! ¹⁸Therefore I will deal with them in anger; I will not look on them with pity or spare them. Although they shout in my ears, I will not listen to them."

Idolaters Killed

9 Then I heard him call out in a loud voice, "Bring the guards of the city here, each with a weapon in his hand." ²And I saw six men coming from the direction of the upper gate, which faces north, each with a deadly weapon in his hand. With them was a man clothed in linen who had a writing kit at his side. They came in and stood beside the bronze altar.

³Now the glory of the God of Israel went up from above the cherubim, where it had been, and moved to the threshold of the temple. Then the LORD called to the man clothed in linen who had the writing kit at his side ⁴and said to him, "Go throughout the city of Jerusalem and put a mark on the foreheads of those who grieve and lament over all the detestable things that are done in it."

⁵As I listened, he said to the others, "Follow him through the city and kill, without showing pity or compassion. ⁶Slaughter old men, young men and maidens, women and children, but do not touch anyone who has the mark. Begin at my sanctuary." So they began with the elders who were in front of the temple.

⁷Then he said to them, "Defile the temple and fill the courts with the slain. Go!" So they went out and began killing throughout the city. ⁸While they were killing and I was left alone, I fell face down, crying out, "Ah, Sovereign LORD! Are you going to destroy the entire remnant of Israel in this outpouring of your wrath on Jerusalem?"

⁹He answered me, "The sin of the house of Israel and Judah is exceedingly great; the land is full of bloodshed and the city is full of injustice. They say, 'The LORD has forsaken the land; the LORD does not see.' ¹⁰So I will not look on them with pity or spare them, but I will bring down on their own heads what they have done."

¹¹Then the man in linen with the writing kit at his side brought back word, saying, "I have done as you commanded."

The Glory Departs From the Temple

10 I looked, and I saw the likeness of a throne of sapphire[a] above the expanse that was over the heads of the cherubim. ²The LORD said to the man clothed in linen, "Go in among the wheels beneath the cherubim. Fill your hands with burning coals from among the cherubim and scatter them over the city." And as I watched, he went in.

³Now the cherubim were standing on the south side of the temple when the man went in, and a cloud filled the inner court. ⁴Then the glory of the LORD rose from above the cherubim and moved to the threshold of the temple. The cloud filled the temple, and the court was full of the radiance of the glory of the LORD. ⁵The sound of the wings of the cherubim could be heard as far away as the outer court, like the voice of God Almighty[b] when he speaks.

⁶When the LORD commanded the man

---

a1 Or *lapis lazuli*   *b5* Hebrew *El-Shaddai*

in linen, "Take fire from among the wheels, from among the cherubim," the man went in and stood beside a wheel. [7]Then one of the cherubim reached out his hand to the fire that was among them. He took up some of it and put it into the hands of the man in linen, who took it and went out. [8](Under the wings of the cherubim could be seen what looked like the hands of a man.)

[9]I looked, and I saw beside the cherubim four wheels, one beside each of the cherubim; the wheels sparkled like chrysolite. [10]As for their appearance, the four of them looked alike; each was like a wheel intersecting a wheel. [11]As they moved, they would go in any one of the four directions the cherubim faced; the wheels did not turn about[c] as the cherubim went. The cherubim went in whatever direction the head faced, without turning as they went. [12]Their entire bodies, including their backs, their hands and their wings, were completely full of eyes, as were their four wheels. [13]I heard the wheels being called "the whirling wheels". [14]Each of the cherubim had four faces: One face was that of a cherub, the second the face of a man, the third the face of a lion, and the fourth the face of an eagle.

[15]Then the cherubim rose upwards. These were the living creatures I had seen by the Kebar River. [16]When the cherubim moved, the wheels beside them moved; and when the cherubim spread their wings to rise from the ground, the wheels did not leave their side. [17]When the cherubim stood still, they also stood still; and when the cherubim rose, they rose with them, because the spirit of the living creatures was in them.

[18]Then the glory of the LORD departed from over the threshold of the temple and stopped above the cherubim. [19]While I watched, the cherubim spread their wings and rose from the ground, and as they went, the wheels went with them. They stopped at the entrance to the east gate of the LORD's house, and the glory of the God of Israel was above them.

[20]These were the living creatures I had seen beneath the God of Israel by the Kebar River, and I realised that they were cherubim. [21]Each had four faces and four wings, and under their wings were what looked like the hands of a man. [22]Their faces had the same appearance as those I had seen by the Kebar River. Each one went straight ahead.

Judgment on Israel's Leaders

11 Then the Spirit lifted me up and brought me to the gate of the house of the LORD that faces east. There at the entrance to the gate were twenty-five men, and I saw among them Jaazaniah son of Azzur and Pelatiah son of Benaiah, leaders of the people. [2]The LORD said to me, "Son of man, these are the men who are plotting evil and giving wicked advice in this city. [3]They say, 'Will it not soon be time to build houses?[a] This city is a cooking pot, and we are the meat.' [4]Therefore prophesy against them; prophesy, son of man."

[5]Then the Spirit of the LORD came upon me, and he told me to say: "This is what the LORD says: That is what you are saying, O house of Israel, but I know what is going through your mind. [6]You have killed many people in this city and filled its streets with the dead.

[7]"Therefore this is what the Sovereign LORD says: The bodies you have thrown there are the meat and this city is the pot, but I will drive you out of it. [8]You fear the sword, and the sword is what I will bring against you, declares the Sovereign LORD. [9]I will drive you out of the city and hand you over to foreigners and inflict punishment on you. [10]You will fall by the sword, and I will execute judgment on you at the borders of Israel. Then you will know that I am the LORD. [11]This city will not be a pot for you, nor will you be the meat in it; I will execute judgment on you at the borders of Israel. [12]And you will know that I am the LORD, for you have not followed my decrees or kept my laws but have conformed to the standards of the nations around you."

[c]11 Or aside   [a]3 Or *This is not the time to build houses.*

¹³Now as I was prophesying, Pelatiah son of Benaiah died. Then I fell face down and cried out in a loud voice, "Ah, Sovereign LORD! Will you completely destroy the remnant of Israel?"

¹⁴The word of the LORD came to me: ¹⁵"Son of man, your brothers—your brothers who are your blood-relatives[b] and the whole house of Israel—are those of whom the people of Jerusalem have said, 'They are[c] far away from the LORD; this land was given to us as our possession.'

Promised Return of Israel

¹⁶"Therefore say: 'This is what the Sovereign LORD says: Although I sent them far away among the nations and scattered them among the countries, yet for a little while I have been a sanctuary for them in the countries where they have gone.'

¹⁷"Therefore say: 'This is what the Sovereign LORD says: I will gather you from the nations and bring you back from the countries where you have been scattered, and I will give you back the land of Israel again.'

¹⁸"They will return to it and remove all its vile images and detestable idols. ¹⁹I will give them an undivided heart and put a new spirit in them; I will remove from them their heart of stone and give them a heart of flesh. ²⁰Then they will follow my decrees and be careful to keep my laws. They will be my people, and I will be their God. ²¹But as for those whose hearts are devoted to their vile images and detestable idols, I will bring down on their own heads what they have done, declares the Sovereign LORD."

²²Then the cherubim, with the wheels beside them, spread their wings, and the glory of the God of Israel was above them. ²³The glory of the LORD went up from within the city and stopped above the mountain east of it. ²⁴The Spirit lifted me up and brought me to the exiles in Babylonia[d] in the vision given by the Spirit of God.

Then the vision I had seen went up from me, ²⁵and I told the exiles everything the LORD had shown me.

The Exile Symbolised

12 The word of the LORD came to me: ²"Son of man, you are living among a rebellious people. They have eyes to see but do not see and ears to hear but do not hear, for they are a rebellious people.

³"Therefore, son of man, pack your belongings for exile and in the daytime, as they watch, set out and go from where you are to another place. Perhaps they will understand, though they are a rebellious house. ⁴During the daytime, while they watch, bring out your belongings packed for exile. Then in the evening, while they are watching, go out like those who go into exile. ⁵While they watch, dig through the wall and take your belongings out through it. ⁶Put them on your shoulder as they are watching and carry them out at dusk. Cover your face so that you cannot see the land, for I have made you a sign to the house of Israel."

⁷So I did as I was commanded. During the day I brought out my things packed for exile. Then in the evening I dug through the wall with my hands. I took my belongings out at dusk, carrying them on my shoulders while they watched.

⁸In the morning the word of the LORD came to me: ⁹"Son of man, did not that rebellious house of Israel ask you, 'What are you doing?'

¹⁰"Say to them, 'This is what the Sovereign LORD says: This oracle concerns the prince in Jerusalem and the whole house of Israel who are there.' ¹¹Say to them, 'I am a sign to you.'

"As I have done, so it will be done to them. They will go into exile as captives.

¹²"The prince among them will put his things on his shoulder at dusk and leave, and a hole will be dug in the wall for him to go through. He will cover his face so that he cannot see the land. ¹³I will spread my net for him, and he will be caught in my

---

b15 Or are in exile with you (see Septuagint and Syriac)
c15 Or those to whom the people of Jerusalem have said, 'Stay
d24 Or Chaldea

snare; I will bring him to Babylonia, the land of the Chaldeans, but he will not see it, and there he will die. ¹⁴I will scatter to the winds all those around him—his staff and all his troops—and I will pursue them with drawn sword.

¹⁵"They will know that I am the LORD, when I disperse them among the nations and scatter them through the countries. ¹⁶But I will spare a few of them from the sword, famine and plague, so that in the nations where they go they may acknowledge all their detestable practices. Then they will know that I am the LORD."

¹⁷The word of the LORD came to me: ¹⁸"Son of man, tremble as you eat your food, and shudder in fear as you drink your water. ¹⁹Say to the people of the land: 'This is what the Sovereign LORD says about those living in Jerusalem and in the land of Israel: They will eat their food in anxiety and drink their water in despair, for their land will be stripped of everything in it because of the violence of all who live there. ²⁰The inhabited towns will be laid waste and the land will be desolate. Then you will know that I am the LORD.'"

²¹The word of the LORD came to me: ²²"Son of man, what is this proverb you have in the land of Israel: 'The days go by and every vision comes to nothing'? ²³Say to them, 'This is what the Sovereign LORD says: I am going to put an end to this proverb, and they will no longer quote it in Israel.' Say to them, 'The days are near when every vision will be fulfilled. ²⁴For there will be no more false visions or flattering divinations among the people of Israel. ²⁵But I the LORD will speak what I will, and it shall be fulfilled without delay. For in your days, you rebellious house, I will fulfil whatever I say, declares the Sovereign LORD.'"

²⁶The word of the LORD came to me: ²⁷"Son of man, the house of Israel is saying, 'The vision he sees is for many years from now, and he prophesies about the distant future.'

²⁸"Therefore say to them, 'This is what the Sovereign LORD says: None of my words will be delayed any longer;

ᵃ3 Or *wicked*

whatever I say will be fulfilled, declares the Sovereign LORD.'"

False Prophets Condemned

13 The word of the LORD came to me: ²"Son of man, prophesy against the prophets of Israel who are now prophesying. Say to those who prophesy out of their own imagination: 'Hear the word of the LORD! ³This is what the Sovereign LORD says: Woe to the foolishᵃ prophets who follow their own spirit and have seen nothing! ⁴Your prophets, O Israel, are like jackals among ruins. ⁵You have not gone up to the breaks in the wall to repair it for the house of Israel so that it will stand firm in the battle on the day of the LORD. ⁶Their visions are false and their divinations a lie. They say, "The LORD declares", when the LORD has not sent them; yet they expect their words to be fulfilled. ⁷Have you not seen false visions and uttered lying divinations when you say, "The LORD declares", though I have not spoken?

⁸"'Therefore this is what the Sovereign LORD says: Because of your false words and lying visions, I am against you, declares the Sovereign LORD. ⁹My hand will be against the prophets who see false visions and utter lying divinations. They will not belong to the council of my people or be listed in the records of the house of Israel, nor will they enter the land of Israel. Then you will know that I am the Sovereign LORD.

¹⁰"'Because they lead my people astray, saying, "Peace", when there is no peace, and because, when a flimsy wall is built, they cover it with whitewash, ¹¹therefore tell those who cover it with whitewash that it is going to fall. Rain will come in torrents, and I will send hailstones hurtling down, and violent winds will burst forth. ¹²When the wall collapses, will people not ask you, "Where is the whitewash you covered it with?"

¹³"'Therefore this is what the Sovereign LORD says: In my wrath I will unleash a violent wind, and in my anger hailstones and torrents of rain will fall with destructive

fury. [14]I will tear down the wall you have covered with whitewash and will level it to the ground so that its foundation will be laid bare. When it[b] falls, you will be destroyed in it; and you will know that I am the LORD. [15]So I will spend my wrath against the wall and against those who covered it with whitewash. I will say to you, "The wall is gone and so are those who whitewashed it, [16]those prophets of Israel who prophesied to Jerusalem and saw visions of peace for her when there was no peace, declares the Sovereign LORD."'

[17]"Now, son of man, set your face against the daughters of your people who prophesy out of their own imagination. Prophesy against them [18]and say, 'This is what the Sovereign LORD says: Woe to the women who sew magic charms on all their wrists and make veils of various lengths for their heads in order to ensnare people. Will you ensnare the lives of my people but preserve your own? [19]You have profaned me among my people for a few handfuls of barley and scraps of bread. By lying to my people, who listen to lies, you have killed those who should not have died and have spared those who should not live.

[20]"'Therefore this is what the Sovereign LORD says: I am against your magic charms with which you ensnare people like birds and I will tear them from your arms; I will set free the people that you ensnare like birds. [21]I will tear off your veils and save my people from your hands, and they will no longer fall prey to your power. Then you will know that I am the LORD. [22]Because you disheartened the righteous with your lies, when I had brought them no grief, and because you encouraged the wicked not to turn from their evil ways and so save their lives, [23]therefore you will no longer see false visions or practise divination. I will save my people from your hands. And then you will know that I am the LORD.'"

Idolaters Condemned

14 Some of the elders of Israel came to me and sat down in front of me. [2]Then the word of the LORD came to me:

[3]"Son of man, these men have set up idols in their hearts and put wicked stumbling-blocks before their faces. Should I let them enquire of me at all? [4]Therefore speak to them and tell them, 'This is what the Sovereign LORD says: When any Israelite sets up idols in his heart and puts a wicked stumbling-block before his face and then goes to a prophet, I the LORD will answer him myself in keeping with his great idolatry. [5]I will do this to recapture the hearts of the people of Israel, who have all deserted me for their idols.'

[6]"Therefore say to the house of Israel, 'This is what the Sovereign LORD says: Repent! Turn from your idols and renounce all your detestable practices!

[7]"'When any Israelite or any alien living in Israel separates himself from me and sets up idols in his heart and puts a wicked stumbling-block before his face and then goes to a prophet to enquire of me, I the LORD will answer him myself. [8]I will set my face against that man and make him an example and a byword. I will cut him off from my people. Then you will know that I am the LORD.

[9]"'And if the prophet is enticed to utter a prophecy, I the LORD have enticed that prophet, and I will stretch out my hand against him and destroy him from among my people Israel. [10]They will bear their guilt—the prophet will be as guilty as the one who consults him. [11]Then the people of Israel will no longer stray from me, nor will they defile themselves any more with all their sins. They will be my people, and I will be their God, declares the Sovereign LORD.'"

Judgment Inescapable

[12]The word of the LORD came to me: [13]"Son of man, if a country sins against me by being unfaithful and I stretch out my hand against it to cut off its food supply and send famine upon it and kill its men and their animals, [14]even if these three men—Noah, Daniel[a] and Job—were in it, they could save only themselves by their righteousness, declares the Sovereign LORD.

---

[b]14 Or *the city*
[a]14 Or *Danel*; the Hebrew spelling may suggest a person other than the prophet Daniel; also in verse 20.

¹⁵"Or if I send wild beasts through that country and they leave it childless and it becomes desolate so that no-one can pass through it because of the beasts, ¹⁶as surely as I live, declares the Sovereign LORD, even if these three men were in it, they could not save their own sons or daughters. They alone would be saved, but the land would be desolate.

¹⁷"Or if I bring a sword against that country and say, 'Let the sword pass throughout the land,' and I kill its men and their animals, ¹⁸as surely as I live, declares the Sovereign LORD, even if these three men were in it, they could not save their own sons or daughters. They alone would be saved.

¹⁹"Or if I send a plague into that land and pour out my wrath upon it through bloodshed, killing its men and their animals, ²⁰as surely as I live, declares the Sovereign LORD, even if Noah, Daniel and Job were in it, they could save neither son nor daughter. They would save only themselves by their righteousness.

²¹"For this is what the Sovereign LORD says: How much worse will it be when I send against Jerusalem my four dreadful judgments—sword and famine and wild beasts and plague—to kill its men and their animals! ²²Yet there will be some survivors—sons and daughters who will be brought out of it. They will come to you, and when you see their conduct and their actions, you will be consoled regarding the disaster I have brought upon Jerusalem—every disaster I have brought upon it. ²³You will be consoled when you see their conduct and their actions, for you will know that I have done nothing in it without cause, declares the Sovereign LORD."

Jerusalem, a Useless Vine

15 The word of the LORD came to me: ²"Son of man, how is the wood of a vine better than that of a branch on any of the trees in the forest? ³Is wood ever taken from it to make anything useful? Do they make pegs from it to hang things on? ⁴And after it is thrown on the fire as fuel and the fire burns both ends and chars the middle, is it then useful for anything? ⁵If it was not useful for anything when it was whole, how much less can it be made into something useful when the fire has burned it and it is charred?

⁶"Therefore this is what the Sovereign LORD says: As I have given the wood of the vine among the trees of the forest as fuel for the fire, so will I treat the people living in Jerusalem. ⁷I will set my face against them. Although they have come out of the fire, the fire will yet consume them. And when I set my face against them, you will know that I am the LORD. ⁸I will make the land desolate because they have been unfaithful, declares the Sovereign LORD."

An Allegory of Unfaithful Jerusalem

16 The word of the LORD came to me: ²"Son of man, confront Jerusalem with her detestable practices ³and say, 'This is what the Sovereign LORD says to Jerusalem: Your ancestry and birth were in the land of the Canaanites; your father was an Amorite and your mother a Hittite. ⁴On the day you were born your cord was not cut, nor were you washed with water to make you clean, nor were you rubbed with salt or wrapped in cloths. ⁵No-one looked on you with pity or had compassion enough to do any of these things for you. Rather, you were thrown out into the open field, for on the day you were born you were despised.

⁶"Then I passed by and saw you kicking about in your blood, and as you lay there in your blood I said to you, "Live!"ᵃ ⁷I made you grow like a plant of the field. You grew up and developed and became the most beautiful of jewels.ᵇ Your breasts were formed and your hair grew, you who were naked and bare.

⁸"Later I passed by, and when I looked at you and saw that you were old enough for love, I spread the corner of my garment over you and covered your nakedness. I gave you my solemn oath and entered into a covenant with you, declares

---

ᵃ6 A few Hebrew manuscripts, Septuagint and Syriac; most Hebrew manuscripts *"Live!" And as you lay there in your blood I said to you, "Live!"*　　ᵇ7 Or *became mature* the Sovereign LORD, and you became mine.

9 "'I bathed^c you with water and washed the blood from you and put ointments on you. 10I clothed you with an embroidered dress and put leather sandals on you. I dressed you in fine linen and covered you with costly garments. 11I adorned you with jewellery: I put bracelets on your arms and a necklace around your neck, 12and I put a ring on your nose, ear-rings on your ears and a beautiful crown on your head. 13So you were adorned with gold and silver; your clothes were of fine linen and costly fabric and embroidered cloth. Your food was fine flour, honey and olive oil. You became very beautiful and rose to be a queen. 14And your fame spread among the nations on account of your beauty, because the splendour I had given you made your beauty perfect, declares the Sovereign LORD.

15 "'But you trusted in your beauty and used your fame to become a prostitute. You lavished your favours on anyone who passed by and your beauty became his.^{d} 16You took some of your garments to make gaudy high places, where you carried on your prostitution. Such things should not happen, nor should they ever occur. 17You also took the fine jewellery I gave you, the jewellery made of my gold and silver, and you made for yourself male idols and engaged in prostitution with them. 18And you took your embroidered clothes to put on them, and you offered my oil and incense before them. 19Also the food I provided for you—the fine flour, olive oil and honey I gave you to eat—you offered as fragrant incense before them. That is what happened, declares the Sovereign LORD.

20 "'And you took your sons and daughters whom you bore to me and sacrificed them as food to the idols. Was your prostitution not enough? 21You slaughtered my children and sacrificed them^e to the idols. 22In all your detestable practices and your prostitution you did not remember the days of your youth, when you were naked and bare, kicking about in your blood.

23 "'Woe! Woe to you, declares the Sovereign LORD. In addition to all your other wickedness, 24you built a mound for yourself and made a lofty shrine in every public square. 25At the head of every street you built your lofty shrines and degraded your beauty, offering your body with increasing promiscuity to anyone who passed by. 26You engaged in prostitution with the Egyptians, your lustful neighbours, and provoked me to anger with your increasing promiscuity. 27So I stretched out my hand against you and reduced your territory; I gave you over to the greed of your enemies, the daughters of the Philistines, who were shocked by your lewd conduct. 28You engaged in prostitution with the Assyrians too, because you were insatiable; and even after that, you still were not satisfied. 29Then you increased your promiscuity to include Babylonia,^{f} a land of merchants, but even with this you were not satisfied.

30 "'How weak-willed you are, declares the Sovereign LORD, when you do all these things, acting like a brazen prostitute! 31When you built your mounds at the head of every street and made your lofty shrines in every public square, you were unlike a prostitute, because you scorned payment.

32 "'You adulterous wife! You prefer strangers to your own husband! 33Every prostitute receives a fee, but you give gifts to all your lovers, bribing them to come to you from everywhere for your illicit favours. 34So in your prostitution you are the opposite of others; no-one runs after you for your favours. You are the opposite, for you give payment and none is given to you.

35 "'Therefore, you prostitute, hear the word of the LORD! 36This is what the Sovereign LORD says: Because you poured out your wealth^g and exposed your nakedness in your promiscuity with your lovers, and because of all your detestable idols, and because you gave them your

^{d}15 Most Hebrew manuscripts; one Hebrew manuscript (see some Septuagint manuscripts) by. Such a thing should not happen ^{e}21 Or and made them pass through ⌊the fire⌋ ^{f}29 Or Chaldea ^{g}36 Or lust children's blood, ³⁷therefore I am going to gather all your lovers, with whom you found pleasure, those you loved as well as those you hated. I will gather them against you from all around and will strip you in front of them, and they will see all your nakedness. ³⁸I will sentence you to the punishment of women who commit adultery and who shed blood; I will bring upon you the blood vengeance of my wrath and jealous anger. ³⁹Then I will hand you over to your lovers, and they will tear down your mounds and destroy your lofty shrines. They will strip you of your clothes and take your fine jewellery and leave you naked and bare. ⁴⁰They will bring a mob against you, who will stone you and hack you to pieces with their swords. ⁴¹They will burn down your houses and inflict punishment on you in the sight of many women. I will put a stop to your prostitution, and you will no longer pay your lovers. ⁴²Then my wrath against you will subside and my jealous anger will turn away from you; I will be calm and no longer angry.

⁴³"Because you did not remember the days of your youth but enraged me with all these things, I will surely bring down on your head what you have done, declares the Sovereign LORD. Did you not add lewdness to all your other detestable practices?

⁴⁴"Everyone who quotes proverbs will quote this proverb about you: "Like mother, like daughter." ⁴⁵You are a true daughter of your mother, who despised her husband and her children; and you are a true sister of your sisters, who despised their husbands and their children. Your mother was a Hittite and your father an Amorite. ⁴⁶Your older sister was Samaria, who lived to the north of you with her daughters; and your younger sister, who lived to the south of you with her daughters, was Sodom. ⁴⁷You not only walked in their ways and copied their detestable practices, but in all your ways you soon became more depraved than they. ⁴⁸As surely as I live, declares the Sovereign LORD, your sister Sodom and her

daughters never did what you and your daughters have done.

⁴⁹"'Now this was the sin of your sister Sodom: She and her daughters were arrogant, overfed and unconcerned; they did not help the poor and needy. ⁵⁰They were haughty and did detestable things before me. Therefore I did away with them as you have seen. ⁵¹Samaria did not commit half the sins you did. You have done more detestable things than they, and have made your sisters seem righteous by all these things you have done. ⁵²Bear your disgrace, for you have furnished some justification for your sisters. Because your sins were more vile than theirs, they appear more righteous than you. So then, be ashamed and bear your disgrace, for you have made your sisters appear righteous.

⁵³"'However, I will restore the fortunes of Sodom and her daughters and of Samaria and her daughters, and your fortunes along with them, ⁵⁴so that you may bear your disgrace and be ashamed of all you have done in giving them comfort. ⁵⁵And your sisters, Sodom with her daughters and Samaria with her daughters, will return to what they were before; and you and your daughters will return to what you were before. ⁵⁶You would not even mention your sister Sodom in the day of your pride, ⁵⁷before your wickedness was uncovered. Even so, you are now scorned by the daughters of Edom[h] and all her neighbours and the daughters of the Philistines—all those around you who despise you. ⁵⁸You will bear the consequences of your lewdness and your detestable practices, declares the LORD.

⁵⁹"'This is what the Sovereign LORD says: I will deal with you as you deserve, because you have despised my oath by breaking the covenant. ⁶⁰Yet I will remember the covenant I made with you in the days of your youth, and I will establish an everlasting covenant with you. ⁶¹Then you will remember your ways and be ashamed when you receive your sisters, both those who are older than you and those who are younger. I will give them to

[h]57 Many Hebrew manuscripts and Syriac; most Hebrew manuscripts, Septuagint and Vulgate *Aram*

you as daughters, but not on the basis of my covenant with you. 62So I will establish my covenant with you, and you will know that I am the LORD. 63Then, when I make atonement for you for all you have done, you will remember and be ashamed and never again open your mouth because of your humiliation, declares the Sovereign LORD.'"

Two Eagles and a Vine

17 The word of the LORD came to me: 2"Son of man, set forth an allegory and tell the house of Israel a parable. 3Say to them, 'This is what the Sovereign LORD says: A great eagle with powerful wings, long feathers and full plumage of varied colours came to Lebanon. Taking hold of the top of a cedar, 4he broke off its topmost shoot and carried it away to a land of merchants, where he planted it in a city of traders.

5"'He took some of the seed of your land and put it in fertile soil. He planted it like a willow by abundant water, 6and it sprouted and became a low, spreading vine. Its branches turned towards him, but its roots remained under it. So it became a vine and produced branches and put out leafy boughs.

7"'But there was another great eagle with powerful wings and full plumage. The vine now sent out its roots towards him from the plot where it was planted and stretched out its branches to him for water. 8It had been planted in good soil by abundant water so that it would produce branches, bear fruit and become a splendid vine.'

9"Say to them, 'This is what the Sovereign LORD says: Will it thrive? Will it not be uprooted and stripped of its fruit so that it withers? All its new growth will wither. It will not take a strong arm or many people to pull it up by the roots. 10Even if it is transplanted, will it thrive? Will it not wither completely when the east wind strikes it—wither away in the plot where it grew?'"

11Then the word of the LORD came to me: 12"Say to this rebellious house, 'Do you not know what these things mean?'

Say to them: 'The king of Babylon went to Jerusalem and carried off her king and her nobles, bringing them back with him to Babylon. 13Then he took a member of the royal family and made a treaty with him, putting him under oath. He also carried away the leading men of the land, 14so that the kingdom would be brought low, unable to rise again, surviving only by keeping his treaty. 15But the king rebelled against him by sending his envoys to Egypt to get horses and a large army. Will he succeed? Will he who does such things escape? Will he break the treaty and yet escape?

16"'As surely as I live, declares the Sovereign LORD, he shall die in Babylon, in the land of the king who put him on the throne, whose oath he despised and whose treaty he broke. 17Pharaoh with his mighty army and great horde will be of no help to him in war, when ramps are built and siege works erected to destroy many lives. 18He despised the oath by breaking the covenant. Because he had given his hand in pledge and yet did all these things, he shall not escape.

19"'Therefore this is what the Sovereign LORD says: As surely as I live, I will bring down on his head my oath that he despised and my covenant that he broke. 20I will spread my net for him, and he will be caught in my snare. I will bring him to Babylon and execute judgment upon him there because he was unfaithful to me. 21All his fleeing troops will fall by the sword, and the survivors will be scattered to the winds. Then you will know that I the LORD have spoken.

22"'This is what the Sovereign LORD says: I myself will take a shoot from the very top of a cedar and plant it; I will break off a tender sprig from its topmost shoots and plant it on a high and lofty mountain. 23On the mountain heights of Israel I will plant it; it will produce branches and bear fruit and become a splendid cedar. Birds of every kind will nest in it; they will find shelter in the shade of its branches. 24All the trees of the field will know that I the LORD bring down the tall tree and make the low tree grow tall. I dry up the green tree and make the dry tree flourish.

" 'I the LORD have spoken, and I will do it.' "

The Soul Who Sins Will Die

18 The word of the LORD came to me: 2"What do you people mean by quoting this proverb about the land of Israel:

" 'The fathers eat sour grapes,
    and the children's teeth are set on
      edge'?

3"As surely as I live, declares the Sovereign LORD, you will no longer quote this proverb in Israel. 4For every living soul belongs to me, the father as well as the son—both alike belong to me. The soul who sins is the one who will die.

5"Suppose there is a righteous man
    who does what is just and right.
6He does not eat at the mountain shrines
    or look to the idols of the house of
      Israel.
He does not defile his neighbour's wife
    or lie with a woman during her period.
7He does not oppress anyone,
    but returns what he took in pledge for
      a loan.
He does not commit robbery,
    but gives his food to the hungry
    and provides clothing for the naked.
8He does not lend at usury
    or take excessive interest.*a*
He withholds his hand from doing
      wrong
    and judges fairly between man and
      man.
9He follows my decrees
    and faithfully keeps my laws.
That man is righteous;
    he will surely live,
          declares the Sovereign LORD.

10"Suppose he has a violent son, who sheds blood or does any of these other things*b* 11(though the father has done none of them):

"He eats at the mountain shrines.
He defiles his neighbour's wife.
12He oppresses the poor and needy.
He commits robbery.
He does not return what he took in
    pledge.
He looks to the idols.
He does detestable things.
13He lends at usury and takes excessive
    interest.

Will such a man live? He will not! Because he has done all these detestable things, he will surely be put to death and his blood will be on his own head.

14"But suppose this son has a son who sees all the sins his father commits, and though he sees them, he does not do such things:

15"He does not eat at the mountain
      shrines
    or look to the idols of the house of
      Israel.
He does not defile his neighbour's
      wife.
16He does not oppress anyone
    or require a pledge for a loan.
He does not commit robbery,
    but gives his food to the hungry
    and provides clothing for the
      naked.
17He withholds his hand from sin*c*
    and takes no usury or excessive
      interest.
He keeps my laws and follows my
      decrees.

He will not die for his father's sin; he will surely live. 18But his father will die for his own sin, because he practised extortion, robbed his brother and did what was wrong among his people.

19"Yet you ask, 'Why does the son not share the guilt of his father?' Since the son has done what is just and right and has been careful to keep all my decrees, he will surely live. 20The soul who sins is the one who will die. The son will not share the guilt of the father, nor will the father

---

*a*8 Or *take interest*; similarly in verses 13 and 17   *b*10 Or *things to a brother*
*c*17 Septuagint (see also verse 8); Hebrew *from the poor*

share the guilt of the son. The righteousness of the righteous man will be credited to him, and the wickedness of the wicked will be charged against him.

21"But if a wicked man turns away from all the sins he has committed and keeps all my decrees and does what is just and right, he will surely live; he will not die. 22None of the offences he has committed will be remembered against him. Because of the righteous things he has done, he will live. 23Do I take any pleasure in the death of the wicked? declares the Sovereign LORD. Rather, am I not pleased when they turn from their ways and live?

24"But if a righteous man turns from his righteousness and commits sin and does the same detestable things the wicked man does, will he live? None of the righteous things he has done will be remembered. Because of the unfaithfulness he is guilty of and because of the sins he has committed, he will die. 25"Yet you say, 'The way of the Lord is not just.' Hear, O house of Israel: Is my way unjust? Is it not your ways that are unjust? 26If a righteous man turns from his righteousness and commits sin, he will die for it; because of the sin he has committed he will die. 27But if a wicked man turns away from the wickedness he has committed and does what is just and right, he will save his life. 28Because he considers all the offences he has committed and turns away from them, he will surely live; he will not die. 29Yet the house of Israel says, 'The way of the Lord is not just.' Are my ways unjust, O house of Israel? Is it not your ways that are unjust?

30"Therefore, O house of Israel, I will judge you, each one according to his ways, declares the Sovereign LORD. Repent! Turn away from all your offences; then sin will not be your downfall. 31Rid yourselves of all the offences you have committed, and get a new heart and a new spirit. Why will you die, O house of Israel? 32For I take no pleasure in the death of anyone, declares the Sovereign LORD. Repent and live!

A Lament for Israel's Princes

19 "Take up a lament concerning the princes of Israel 2and say:

"'What a lioness was your mother
    among the lions!
She lay down among the young lions
    and reared her cubs.
3She brought up one of her cubs,
    and he became a strong lion.
He learned to tear the prey
    and he devoured men.
4The nations heard about him,
    and he was trapped in their pit.
They led him with hooks
    to the land of Egypt.

5"'When she saw her hope unfulfilled,
    her expectation gone,
she took another of her cubs
    and made him a strong lion.
6He prowled among the lions,
    for he was now a strong lion.
He learned to tear the prey
    and he devoured men.
7He broke down[a] their strongholds
    and devastated their towns.
The land and all who were in it
    were terrified by his roaring.
8Then the nations came against him,
    those from regions round about.
They spread their net for him,
    and he was trapped in their pit.
9With hooks they pulled him into a cage
    and brought him to the king of
      Babylon.
They put him in prison,
    so his roar was heard no longer
    on the mountains of Israel.

10"'Your mother was like a vine in your
      vineyard[b]
  planted by the water;
it was fruitful and full of branches
    because of abundant water.
11Its branches were strong,
    fit for a ruler's sceptre.
It towered high
    above the thick foliage,

---

[a]7 Targum (see Septuagint); Hebrew He knew
[b]10 Two Hebrew manuscripts; most Hebrew manuscripts your blood

conspicuous for its height
  and for its many branches.
¹²But it was uprooted in fury
  and thrown to the ground.
The east wind made it shrivel,
  it was stripped of its fruit;
its strong branches withered
  and fire consumed them.
¹³Now it is planted in the desert,
  in a dry and thirsty land.
¹⁴Fire spread from one of its main^c
     branches
  and consumed its fruit.
No strong branch is left on it
  fit for a ruler's sceptre.'

This is a lament and is to be used as a
lament."

Rebellious Israel

20 In the seventh year, in the fifth month on the tenth day, some of the elders of Israel came to enquire of the LORD, and they sat down in front of me.

²Then the word of the LORD came to me: ³"Son of man, speak to the elders of Israel and say to them, 'This is what the Sovereign LORD says: Have you come to enquire of me? As surely as I live, I will not let you enquire of me, declares the Sovereign LORD.'

⁴"Will you judge them? Will you judge them, son of man? Then confront them with the detestable practices of their fathers ⁵and say to them: 'This is what the Sovereign LORD says: On the day I chose Israel, I swore with uplifted hand to the descendants of the house of Jacob and revealed myself to them in Egypt. With uplifted hand I said to them, "I am the LORD your God." ⁶On that day I swore to them that I would bring them out of Egypt into a land I had searched out for them, a land flowing with milk and honey, the most beautiful of all lands. ⁷And I said to them, "Each of you, get rid of the vile images you have set your eyes on, and do not defile yourselves with the idols of Egypt. I am the LORD your God."

⁸"But they rebelled against me and would not listen to me; they did not get rid of the vile images they had set their eyes on, nor did they forsake the idols of Egypt. So I said I would pour out my wrath on them and spend my anger against them in Egypt. ⁹But for the sake of my name I did what would keep it from being profaned in the eyes of the nations they lived among and in whose sight I had revealed myself to the Israelites by bringing them out of Egypt. ¹⁰Therefore I led them out of Egypt and brought them into the desert. ¹¹I gave them my decrees and made known to them my laws, for the man who obeys them will live by them. ¹²Also I gave them my Sabbaths as a sign between us, so they would know that I the LORD made them holy.

¹³"Yet the people of Israel rebelled against me in the desert. They did not follow my decrees but rejected my laws—although the man who obeys them will live by them—and they utterly desecrated my Sabbaths. So I said I would pour out my wrath on them and destroy them in the desert. ¹⁴But for the sake of my name I did what would keep it from being profaned in the eyes of the nations in whose sight I had brought them out. ¹⁵Also with uplifted hand I swore to them in the desert that I would not bring them into the land I had given them—a land flowing with milk and honey, most beautiful of all lands— ¹⁶because they rejected my laws and did not follow my decrees and desecrated my Sabbaths. For their hearts were devoted to their idols. ¹⁷Yet I looked on them with pity and did not destroy them or put an end to them in the desert. ¹⁸I said to their children in the desert, "Do not follow the statutes of your fathers or keep their laws or defile yourselves with their idols. ¹⁹I am the LORD your God; follow my decrees and be careful to keep my laws. ²⁰Keep my Sabbaths holy, that they may be a sign between us. Then you will know that I am the LORD your God."

²¹"But the children rebelled against me: They did not follow my decrees, they were not careful to keep my laws—although the man who obeys them will live by them—and they desecrated my Sabbaths. So I said I would pour out my wrath

^c14 Or *from under its*

on them and spend my anger against them in the desert. ²²But I withheld my hand, and for the sake of my name I did what would keep it from being profaned in the eyes of the nations in whose sight I had brought them out. ²³Also with uplifted hand I swore to them in the desert that I would disperse them among the nations and scatter them through the countries, ²⁴because they had not obeyed my laws but had rejected my decrees and desecrated my Sabbaths, and their eyes ₋lusted₋ after their fathers' idols. ²⁵I also gave them over to statutes that were not good and laws they could not live by; ²⁶I let them become defiled through their gifts—the sacrifice of every firstborn^a—that I might fill them with horror so that they would know that I am the LORD.'

²⁷"Therefore, son of man, speak to the people of Israel and say to them, 'This is what the Sovereign LORD says: In this also your fathers blasphemed me by forsaking me: ²⁸When I brought them into the land I had sworn to give them and they saw any high hill or any leafy tree, there they offered their sacrifices, made offerings that provoked me to anger, presented their fragrant incense and poured out their drink offerings. ²⁹Then I said to them: What is this high place you go to?'" (It is called Bamah^b to this day.)

Judgment and Restoration

³⁰"Therefore say to the house of Israel: 'This is what the Sovereign LORD says: Will you defile yourselves the way your fathers did and lust after their vile images? ³¹When you offer your gifts—the sacrifice of your sons in^c the fire—you continue to defile yourselves with all your idols to this day. Am I to let you enquire of me, O house of Israel? As surely as I live, declares the Sovereign LORD, I will not let you enquire of me.

³²"'You say, "We want to be like the nations, like the peoples of the world, who serve wood and stone." But what you have in mind will never happen. ³³As surely as I live, declares the Sovereign LORD, I

will rule over you with a mighty hand and an outstretched arm and with outpoured wrath. ³⁴I will bring you from the nations and gather you from the countries where you have been scattered—with a mighty hand and an outstretched arm and with outpoured wrath. ³⁵I will bring you into the desert of the nations and there, face to face, I will execute judgment upon you. ³⁶As I judged your fathers in the desert of the land of Egypt, so I will judge you, declares the Sovereign LORD. ³⁷I will take note of you as you pass under my rod, and I will bring you into the bond of the covenant. ³⁸I will purge you of those who revolt and rebel against me. Although I will bring them out of the land where they are living, yet they will not enter the land of Israel. Then you will know that I am the LORD.

³⁹"'As for you, O house of Israel, this is what the Sovereign LORD says: Go and serve your idols, every one of you! But afterwards you will surely listen to me and no longer profane my holy name with your gifts and idols. ⁴⁰For on my holy mountain, the high mountain of Israel, declares the Sovereign LORD, there in the land the entire house of Israel will serve me, and there I will accept them. There I will require your offerings and your choice gifts,^d along with all your holy sacrifices. ⁴¹I will accept you as fragrant incense when I bring you out from the nations and gather you from the countries where you have been scattered, and I will show myself holy among you in the sight of the nations. ⁴²Then you will know that I am the LORD, when I bring you into the land of Israel, the land I had sworn with uplifted hand to give to your fathers. ⁴³There you will remember your conduct and all the actions by which you have defiled yourselves, and you will loathe yourselves for all the evil you have done. ⁴⁴You will know that I am the LORD, when I deal with you for my name's sake and not according to your evil ways and your corrupt practices, O house of Israel, declares the Sovereign LORD.'"

---

^a26 Or—making every firstborn pass through ₋the fire₋   ^b29 Bamah means high place.
^c31 Or—making your sons pass through   ^d40 Or and the gifts of your firstfruits

Prophecy Against the South

[45]The word of the LORD came to me: [46]"Son of man, set your face towards the south; preach against the south and prophesy against the forest of the southland. [47]Say to the southern forest: 'Hear the word of the LORD. This is what the Sovereign LORD says: I am about to set fire to you, and it will consume all your trees, both green and dry. The blazing flame will not be quenched, and every face from south to north will be scorched by it. [48]Everyone will see that I the LORD have kindled it; it will not be quenched.'"

[49]Then I said, "Ah, Sovereign LORD! They are saying of me, 'Isn't he just telling parables?'"

Babylon, God's Sword of Judgment

21 The word of the LORD came to me: [2]"Son of man, set your face against Jerusalem and preach against the sanctuary. Prophesy against the land of Israel [3]and say to her: 'This is what the LORD says: I am against you. I will draw my sword from its scabbard and cut off from you both the righteous and the wicked. [4]Because I am going to cut off the righteous and the wicked, my sword will be unsheathed against everyone from south to north. [5]Then all people will know that I the LORD have drawn my sword from its scabbard; it will not return again.'

[6]"Therefore groan, son of man! Groan before them with broken heart and bitter grief. [7]And when they ask you, 'Why are you groaning?' you shall say, 'Because of the news that is coming. Every heart will melt and every hand go limp; every spirit will become faint and every knee become as weak as water.' It is coming! It will surely take place, declares the Sovereign LORD."

[8]The word of the LORD came to me: [9]"Son of man, prophesy and say, 'This is what the Lord says:

"'A sword, a sword,
   sharpened and polished—

[10]sharpened for the slaughter,
   polished to flash like lightning!

"'Shall we rejoice in the sceptre of my son ⌊Judah⌋? The sword despises every such stick.

[11]"'The sword is appointed to be
   polished,
  to be grasped with the hand;
it is sharpened and polished,
  made ready for the hand of the slayer.
[12]Cry out and wail, son of man,
  for it is against my people;
  it is against all the princes of Israel.
They are thrown to the sword
  along with my people.
Therefore beat your breast.

[13]"'Testing will surely come. And what if the sceptre ⌊of Judah⌋, which the sword despises, does not continue? declares the Sovereign LORD.'

[14]"So then, son of man, prophesy
  and strike your hands together.
Let the sword strike twice,
  even three times.
It is a sword for slaughter—
  a sword for great slaughter,
  closing in on them from every side.
[15]So that hearts may melt
  and the fallen be many,
I have stationed the sword for
   slaughter[a]
  at all their gates.
Oh! It is made to flash like lightning,
  it is grasped for slaughter.
[16]O sword, slash to the right,
  then to the left,
  wherever your blade is turned.
[17]I too will strike my hands together,
  and my wrath will subside.
I the LORD have spoken."

[18]The word of the LORD came to me: [19]"Son of man, mark out two roads for the sword of the king of Babylon to take, both starting from the same country. Make a signpost where the road branches off to the city. [20]Mark out one road for the

---

[a]15 Septuagint; the meaning of the Hebrew for this word is uncertain.

sword to come against Rabbah of the Ammonites and another against Judah and fortified Jerusalem. ²¹For the king of Babylon will stop at the fork in the road, at the junction of the two roads, to seek an omen: He will cast lots with arrows, he will consult his idols, he will examine the liver. ²²Into his right hand will come the lot for Jerusalem, where he is to set up battering-rams, to give the command to slaughter, to sound the battle cry, to set battering-rams against the gates, to build a ramp and to erect siege works. ²³It will seem like a false omen to those who have sworn allegiance to him, but he will remind them of their guilt and take them captive.

²⁴"Therefore this is what the Sovereign LORD says: 'Because you people have brought to mind your guilt by your open rebellion, revealing your sins in all that you do—because you have done this, you will be taken captive.

²⁵"'O profane and wicked prince of Israel, whose day has come, whose time of punishment has reached its climax, ²⁶this is what the Sovereign LORD says: Take off the turban, remove the crown. It will not be as it was: The lowly will be exalted and the exalted will be brought low. ²⁷A ruin! A ruin! I will make it a ruin! It will not be restored until he comes to whom it rightfully belongs; to him I will give it.'

²⁸"And you, son of man, prophesy and say, 'This is what the Sovereign LORD says about the Ammonites and their insults:

"'A sword, a sword,
    drawn for the slaughter,
polished to consume
    and to flash like lightning!
²⁹Despite false visions concerning you
    and lying divinations about you,
it will be laid on the necks
    of the wicked who are to be slain,
whose day has come,
    whose time of punishment has
        reached its climax.
³⁰Return the sword to its scabbard.
    In the place where you were created,
    in the land of your ancestry,
        I will judge you.
³¹I will pour out my wrath upon you

and breathe out my fiery anger
    against you;
I will hand you over to brutal men,
    men skilled in destruction.
³²You will be fuel for the fire,
    your blood will be shed in your land,
    you will be remembered no more;
    for I the LORD have spoken.'"

Jerusalem's Sins

22 The word of the LORD came to me: ²"Son of man, will you judge her? Will you judge this city of bloodshed? Then confront her with all her detestable practices ³and say: 'This is what the Sovereign LORD says: O city that brings on herself doom by shedding blood in her midst and defiles herself by making idols, ⁴you have become guilty because of the blood you have shed and have become defiled by the idols you have made. You have brought your days to a close, and the end of your years has come. Therefore I will make you an object of scorn to the nations and a laughing-stock to all the countries. ⁵Those who are near and those who are far away will mock you, O infamous city, full of turmoil.

⁶"See how each of the princes of Israel who are in you uses his power to shed blood. ⁷In you they have treated father and mother with contempt; in you they have oppressed the alien and ill-treated the fatherless and the widow. ⁸You have despised my holy things and desecrated my Sabbaths. ⁹In you are slanderous men bent on shedding blood; in you are those who eat at the mountain shrines and commit lewd acts. ¹⁰In you are those who dishonour their fathers' bed; in you are those who violate women during their period, when they are ceremonially unclean. ¹¹In you one man commits a detestable offence with his neighbour's wife, another shamefully defiles his daughter-in-law, and another violates his sister, his own father's daughter. ¹²In you men accept bribes to shed blood; you take usury and excessive interest[a] and make unjust gain from your neighbours by

---

[a]12 Or usury and interest

extortion. And you have forgotten me, declares the Sovereign LORD.

13"'I will surely strike my hands together at the unjust gain you have made and at the blood you have shed in your midst. 14Will your courage endure or your hands be strong in the day I deal with you? I the LORD have spoken, and I will do it. 15I will disperse you among the nations and scatter you through the countries; and I will put an end to your uncleanness. 16When you have been defiled[b] in the eyes of the nations, you will know that I am the LORD.'"

17Then the word of the LORD came to me: 18"Son of man, the house of Israel has become dross to me; all of them are the copper, tin, iron and lead left inside a furnace. They are but the dross of silver. 19Therefore this is what the Sovereign LORD says: 'Because you have all become dross, I will gather you into Jerusalem. 20As men gather silver, copper, iron, lead and tin into a furnace to melt it with a fiery blast, so will I gather you in my anger and my wrath and put you inside the city and melt you. 21I will gather you and I will blow on you with my fiery wrath, and you will be melted inside her. 22As silver is melted in a furnace, so you will be melted inside her, and you will know that I the LORD have poured out my wrath upon you.'"

23Again the word of the LORD came to me: 24"Son of man, say to the land, 'You are a land that has had no rain or showers[c] in the day of wrath.' 25There is a conspiracy of her princes[d] within her like a roaring lion tearing its prey; they devour people, take treasures and precious things and make many widows within her. 26Her priests do violence to my law and profane my holy things; they do not distinguish between the holy and the common; they teach that there is no difference between the unclean and the clean; and they shut their eyes to the keeping of my Sabbaths, so that I am profaned among them. 27Her officials within her are like wolves tearing their prey; they shed blood and kill people to make unjust gain. 28Her prophets

whitewash these deeds for them by false visions and lying divinations. They say, 'This is what the Sovereign LORD says'— when the LORD has not spoken. 29The people of the land practise extortion and commit robbery; they oppress the poor and needy and ill-treat the alien, denying them justice.

30"I looked for a man among them who would build up the wall and stand before me in the gap on behalf of the land so that I would not have to destroy it, but I found none. 31So I will pour out my wrath on them and consume them with my fiery anger, bringing down on their own heads all they have done, declares the Sovereign LORD."

Two Adulterous Sisters

23 The word of the LORD came to me: 2"Son of man, there were two women, daughters of the same mother. 3They became prostitutes in Egypt, engaging in prostitution from their youth. In that land their breasts were fondled and their virgin bosoms caressed. 4The older was named Oholah, and her sister was Oholibah. They were mine and gave birth to sons and daughters. Oholah is Samaria, and Oholibah is Jerusalem.

5"Oholah engaged in prostitution while she was still mine; and she lusted after her lovers, the Assyrians—warriors 6clothed in blue, governors and commanders, all of them handsome young men, and mounted horsemen. 7She gave herself as a prostitute to all the elite of the Assyrians and defiled herself with all the idols of everyone she lusted after. 8She did not give up the prostitution she began in Egypt, when during her youth men slept with her, caressed her virgin bosom and poured out their lust upon her.

9"Therefore I handed her over to her lovers, the Assyrians, for whom she lusted. 10They stripped her naked, took away her sons and daughters and killed her with the sword. She became a byword among women, and punishment was inflicted on her.

b16 Or When I have allotted you your inheritance   c24 Septuagint; Hebrew has not been cleansed or rained on   d25 Septuagint; Hebrew prophets

11"Her sister Oholibah saw this, yet in her lust and prostitution she was more depraved than her sister. 12She too lusted after the Assyrians—governors and commanders, warriors in full dress, mounted horsemen, all handsome young men. 13I saw that she too defiled herself; both of them went the same way.

14"But she carried her prostitution still further. She saw men portrayed on a wall, figures of Chaldeans*a* portrayed in red, 15with belts round their waists and flowing turbans on their heads; all of them looked like Babylonian chariot officers, natives of Chaldea.*b* 16As soon as she saw them, she lusted after them and sent messengers to them in Chaldea. 17Then the Babylonians came to her, to the bed of love, and in their lust they defiled her. After she had been defiled by them, she turned away from them in disgust. 18When she carried on her prostitution openly and exposed her nakedness, I turned away from her in disgust, just as I had turned away from her sister. 19Yet she became more and more promiscuous as she recalled the days of her youth, when she was a prostitute in Egypt. 20There she lusted after her lovers, whose genitals were like those of donkeys and whose emission was like that of horses. 21So you longed for the lewdness of your youth, when in Egypt your bosom was caressed and your young breasts fondled.*c*

22"Therefore, Oholibah, this is what the Sovereign LORD says: I will stir up your lovers against you, those you turned away from in disgust, and I will bring them against you from every side—23the Babylonians and all the Chaldeans, the men of Pekod and Shoa and Koa, and all the Assyrians with them, handsome young men, all of them governors and commanders, chariot officers and men of high rank, all mounted on horses. 24They will come against you with weapons,*d* chariots and wagons and with a throng of people; they will take up positions against you on every side with large and small shields and with helmets. I will turn you over to them

for punishment, and they will punish you according to their standards. 25I will direct my jealous anger against you, and they will deal with you in fury. They will cut off your noses and your ears, and those of you who are left will fall by the sword. They will take away your sons and daughters, and those of you who are left will be consumed by fire. 26They will also strip you of your clothes and take your fine jewellery. 27So I will put a stop to the lewdness and prostitution you began in Egypt. You will not look on these things with longing or remember Egypt any more.

28"For this is what the Sovereign LORD says: I am about to hand you over to those you hate, to those you turned away from in disgust. 29They will deal with you in hatred and take away everything you have worked for. They will leave you naked and bare, and the shame of your prostitution will be exposed. Your lewdness and promiscuity 30have brought this upon you, because you lusted after the nations and defiled yourself with their idols. 31You have gone the way of your sister; so I will put her cup into your hand.

32"This is what the Sovereign LORD says:

"You will drink your sister's cup,
    a cup large and deep;
it will bring scorn and derision,
    for it holds so much.
33You will be filled with drunkenness and
        sorrow,
    the cup of ruin and desolation,
    the cup of your sister Samaria.
34You will drink it and drain it dry;
    you will dash it to pieces
    and tear your breasts.

I have spoken, declares the Sovereign LORD.

35"Therefore this is what the Sovereign LORD says: Since you have forgotten me and thrust me behind your back, you must bear the consequences of your lewdness and prostitution."

a14 Or Babylonians   b15 Or Babylonia; also in verse 16
c21 Syriac (see also verse 3); Hebrew caressed because of your young breasts
d24 The meaning of the Hebrew for this word is uncertain.

³⁶The Lord said to me: "Son of man, will you judge Oholah and Oholibah? Then confront them with their detestable practices, ³⁷for they have committed adultery and blood is on their hands. They committed adultery with their idols; they even sacrificed their children, whom they bore to me,^e as food for them. ³⁸They have also done this to me: At that same time they defiled my sanctuary and desecrated my Sabbaths. ³⁹On the very day they sacrificed their children to their idols, they entered my sanctuary and desecrated it. That is what they did in my house.

⁴⁰"They even sent messengers for men who came from far away, and when they arrived you bathed yourself for them, painted your eyes and put on your jewellery. ⁴¹You sat on an elegant couch, with a table spread before it on which you had placed the incense and oil that belonged to me.

⁴²"The noise of a carefree crowd was around her; Sabeans^f were brought from the desert along with men from the rabble, and they put bracelets on the arms of the woman and her sister and beautiful crowns on their heads. ⁴³Then I said about the one worn out by adultery, 'Now let them use her as a prostitute, for that is all she is.' ⁴⁴And they slept with her. As men sleep with a prostitute, so they slept with those lewd women, Oholah and Oholibah. ⁴⁵But righteous men will sentence them to the punishment of women who commit adultery and shed blood, because they are adulterous and blood is on their hands.

⁴⁶"This is what the Sovereign Lord says: Bring a mob against them and give them over to terror and plunder. ⁴⁷The mob will stone them and cut them down with their swords; they will kill their sons and daughters and burn down their houses.

⁴⁸"So I will put an end to lewdness in the land, that all women may take warning and not imitate you. ⁴⁹You will suffer the penalty for your lewdness and bear the consequences of your sins of idolatry. Then you will know that I am the Sovereign Lord."

The Cooking Pot

24 In the ninth year, in the tenth month on the tenth day, the word of the Lord came to me: ²"Son of man, record this date, this very date, because the king of Babylon has laid siege to Jerusalem this very day. ³Tell this rebellious house a parable and say to them: 'This is what the Sovereign Lord says:

"'Put on the cooking pot; put it on
  and pour water into it.
⁴Put into it the pieces of meat,
  all the choice pieces—the leg and the
    shoulder.
Fill it with the best of these bones;
⁵ take the pick of the flock.
Pile wood beneath it for the bones;
  bring it to the boil
  and cook the bones in it.

⁶"'For this is what the Sovereign Lord says:

"'Woe to the city of bloodshed,
  to the pot now encrusted,
  whose deposit will not go away!
Empty it piece by piece
  without casting lots for them.

⁷"'For the blood she shed is in her midst:
  She poured it on the bare rock;
she did not pour it on the ground,
  where the dust would cover it.
⁸To stir up wrath and take revenge
  I put her blood on the bare rock,
  so that it would not be covered.

⁹"'Therefore this is what the Sovereign Lord says:

"'Woe to the city of bloodshed!
  I, too, will pile the wood high.
¹⁰So heap on the wood
  and kindle the fire.
Cook the meat well,
  mixing in the spices;
  and let the bones be charred.
¹¹Then set the empty pot on the coals
  till it becomes hot and its copper
    glows

---

^e37 Or *even made the children they bore to me pass through ⌊the fire⌋*   ^f42 Or *drunkards*

so its impurities may be melted
and its deposit burned away.
12It has frustrated all efforts;
its heavy deposit has not been
removed,
not even by fire.

13"'Now your impurity is lewdness. Because I tried to cleanse you but you would not be cleansed from your impurity, you will not be clean again until my wrath against you has subsided.

14"'I the LORD have spoken. The time has come for me to act. I will not hold back; I will not have pity, nor will I relent. You will be judged according to your conduct and your actions, declares the Sovereign LORD.'"

Ezekiel's Wife Dies

15The word of the LORD came to me: 16"Son of man, with one blow I am about to take away from you the delight of your eyes. Yet do not lament or weep or shed any tears. 17Groan quietly; do not mourn for the dead. Keep your turban fastened and your sandals on your feet; do not cover the lower part of your face or eat the customary food ⌊of mourners⌋."

18So I spoke to the people in the morning, and in the evening my wife died. The next morning I did as I had been commanded.

19Then the people asked me, "Won't you tell us what these things have to do with us?"

20So I said to them, "The word of the LORD came to me: 21Say to the house of Israel, 'This is what the Sovereign LORD says: I am about to desecrate my sanctuary—the stronghold in which you take pride, the delight of your eyes, the object of your affection. The sons and daughters you left behind will fall by the sword. 22And you will do as I have done. You will not cover the lower part of your face or eat the customary food ⌊of mourners⌋. 23You will keep your turbans on your heads and your sandals on your feet. You will not

mourn or weep but will waste away because of[a] your sins and groan among yourselves. 24Ezekiel will be a sign to you; you will do just as he has done. When this happens, you will know that I am the Sovereign LORD.'

25"And you, son of man, on the day I take away their stronghold, their joy and glory, the delight of their eyes, their heart's desire, and their sons and daughters as well—26on that day a fugitive will come to tell you the news. 27At that time your mouth will be opened; you will speak with him and will no longer be silent. So you will be a sign to them, and they will know that I am the LORD."

A Prophecy Against Ammon

25 The word of the LORD came to me: 2"Son of man, set your face against the Ammonites and prophesy against them. 3Say to them, 'Hear the word of the Sovereign LORD. This is what the Sovereign LORD says: Because you said "Aha!" over my sanctuary when it was desecrated and over the land of Israel when it was laid waste and over the people of Judah when they went into exile, 4therefore I am going to give you to the people of the East as a possession. They will set up their camps and pitch their tents among you; they will eat your fruit and drink your milk. 5I will turn Rabbah into a pasture for camels and Ammon into a resting place for sheep. Then you will know that I am the LORD. 6For this is what the Sovereign LORD says: Because you have clapped your hands and stamped your feet, rejoicing with all the malice of your heart against the land of Israel, 7therefore I will stretch out my hand against you and give you as plunder to the nations. I will cut you off from the nations and exterminate you from the countries. I will destroy you, and you will know that I am the LORD.'"

A Prophecy Against Moab

8"This is what the Sovereign LORD says: 'Because Moab and Seir said, "Look, the house of Judah has become like all the other nations," ⁹therefore I will expose the flank of Moab, beginning at its frontier towns—Beth Jeshimoth, Baal Meon and Kiriathaim—the glory of that land. ¹⁰I will give Moab along with the Ammonites to the people of the East as a possession, so that the Ammonites will not be remembered among the nations; ¹¹and I will inflict punishment on Moab. Then they will know that I am the LORD.' "

A Prophecy Against Edom

¹²"This is what the Sovereign LORD says: 'Because Edom took revenge on the house of Judah and became very guilty by doing so, ¹³therefore this is what the Sovereign LORD says: I will stretch out my hand against Edom and kill its men and their animals. I will lay it waste, and from Teman to Dedan they will fall by the sword. ¹⁴I will take vengeance on Edom by the hand of my people Israel, and they will deal with Edom in accordance with my anger and my wrath; they will know my vengeance, declares the Sovereign LORD.' "

A Prophecy Against Philistia

¹⁵"This is what the Sovereign LORD says: 'Because the Philistines acted in vengeance and took revenge with malice in their hearts, and with ancient hostility sought to destroy Judah, ¹⁶therefore this is what the Sovereign LORD says: I am about to stretch out my hand against the Philistines, and I will cut off the Kerethites and destroy those remaining along the coast. ¹⁷I will carry out great vengeance on them and punish them in my wrath. Then they will know that I am the LORD, when I take vengeance on them.' "

A Prophecy Against Tyre

26 In the eleventh year, on the first day of the month, the word of the LORD came to me: ²"Son of man, because

Tyre has said of Jerusalem, 'Aha! The gate to the nations is broken, and its doors have swung open to me; now that she lies in ruins I will prosper,' ³therefore this is what the Sovereign LORD says: I am against you, O Tyre, and I will bring many nations against you, like the sea casting up its waves. ⁴They will destroy the walls of Tyre and pull down her towers; I will scrape away her rubble and make her a bare rock. ⁵Out in the sea she will become a place to spread fishing nets, for I have spoken, declares the Sovereign LORD. She will become plunder for the nations, ⁶and her settlements on the mainland will be ravaged by the sword. Then they will know that I am the LORD.

⁷"For this is what the Sovereign LORD says: From the north I am going to bring against Tyre Nebuchadnezzar[a] king of Babylon, king of kings, with horses and chariots, with horsemen and a great army. ⁸He will ravage your settlements on the mainland with the sword; he will set up siege works against you, build a ramp up to your walls and raise his shields against you. ⁹He will direct the blows of his battering-rams against your walls and demolish your towers with his weapons. ¹⁰His horses will be so many that they will cover you with dust. Your walls will tremble at the noise of the war horses, wagons and chariots when he enters your gates as men enter a city whose walls have been broken through. ¹¹The hoofs of his horses will trample all your streets; he will kill your people with the sword, and your strong pillars will fall to the ground. ¹²They will plunder your wealth and loot your merchandise; they will break down your walls and demolish your fine houses and throw your stones, timber and rubble into the sea. ¹³I will put an end to your noisy songs, and the music of your harps will be heard no more. ¹⁴I will make you a bare rock, and you will become a place to spread fishing nets. You will never be rebuilt, for I the LORD have spoken, declares the Sovereign LORD.

¹⁵"This is what the Sovereign LORD says to Tyre: Will not the coastlands tremble at

---

a7 Hebrew *Nebuchadrezzar*, of which *Nebuchadnezzar* is a variant; here and often in Ezekiel and Jeremiah the sound of your fall, when the wounded groan and the slaughter takes place in you? ¹⁶Then all the princes of the coast will step down from their thrones and lay aside their robes and take off their embroidered garments. Clothed with terror, they will sit on the ground, trembling every moment, appalled at you. ¹⁷Then they will take up a lament concerning you and say to you:

> "'How you are destroyed, O city of renown,
> peopled by men of the sea!
> You were a power on the seas,
> you and your citizens;
> you put your terror
> on all who lived there.
> ¹⁸Now the coastlands tremble
> on the day of your fall;
> the islands in the sea
> are terrified at your collapse.'

¹⁹"This is what the Sovereign LORD says: When I make you a desolate city, like cities no longer inhabited, and when I bring the ocean depths over you and its vast waters cover you, ²⁰then I will bring you down with those who go down to the pit, to the people of long ago. I will make you dwell in the earth below, as in ancient ruins, with those who go down to the pit, and you will not return or take your place^b in the land of the living. ²¹I will bring you to a horrible end and you will be no more. You will be sought, but you will never again be found, declares the Sovereign LORD."

A Lament for Tyre

27 The word of the LORD came to me: ²"Son of man, take up a lament concerning Tyre. ³Say to Tyre, situated at the gateway to the sea, merchant of peoples on many coasts, 'This is what the Sovereign LORD says:

> "'You say, O Tyre,
> "I am perfect in beauty."

⁴Your domain was on the high seas;
your builders brought your beauty to perfection.
⁵They made all your timbers
of pine trees from Senir;^a
they took a cedar from Lebanon
to make a mast for you.
⁶Of oaks from Bashan
they made your oars;
of cypress wood^b from the coasts of Cyprus^c
they made your deck, inlaid with ivory.
⁷Fine embroidered linen from Egypt was your sail
and served as your banner;
your awnings were of blue and purple
from the coasts of Elishah.
⁸Men of Sidon and Arvad were your oarsmen;
your skilled men, O Tyre, were aboard as your seamen.
⁹Veteran craftsmen of Gebal^d were on board
as shipwrights to caulk your seams.
All the ships of the sea and their sailors
came alongside to trade for your wares.

¹⁰"'Men of Persia, Lydia and Put
served as soldiers in your army.
They hung their shields and helmets on your walls,
bringing you splendour.
¹¹Men of Arvad and Helech
manned your walls on every side;
men of Gammad
were in your towers.
They hung their shields around your walls;
they brought your beauty to perfection.

¹²"'Tarshish did business with you because of your great wealth of goods; they exchanged silver, iron, tin and lead for your merchandise.
¹³"'Greece, Tubal and Meshech traded

with you; they exchanged slaves and articles of bronze for your wares.

[14]" 'Men of Beth Togarmah exchanged work horses, war horses and mules for your merchandise.

[15]" 'The men of Rhodes[e] traded with you, and many coastlands were your customers; they paid you with ivory tusks and ebony.

[16]" 'Aram[f] did business with you because of your many products; they exchanged turquoise, purple fabric, embroidered work, fine linen, coral and rubies for your merchandise.

[17]" 'Judah and Israel traded with you; they exchanged wheat from Minnith and confections,[g] honey, oil and balm for your wares.

[18]" 'Damascus, because of your many products and great wealth of goods, did business with you in wine from Helbon and wool from Zahar.

[19]" 'Danites and Greeks from Uzal bought your merchandise; they exchanged wrought iron, cassia and calamus for your wares.

[20]" 'Dedan traded in saddle blankets with you.

[21]" 'Arabia and all the princes of Kedar were your customers; they did business with you in lambs, rams and goats.

[22]" 'The merchants of Sheba and Raamah traded with you; for your merchandise they exchanged the finest of all kinds of spices and precious stones, and gold.

[23]" 'Haran, Canneh and Eden and merchants of Sheba, Asshur and Kilmad traded with you. [24]In your market-place they traded with you beautiful garments, blue fabric, embroidered work and multi-coloured rugs with cords twisted and tightly knotted.

[25]" 'The ships of Tarshish serve
as carriers for your wares.
You are filled with heavy cargo
in the heart of the sea.
[26]Your oarsmen take you
out to the high seas.

But the east wind will break you to
pieces
in the heart of the sea.
[27]Your wealth, merchandise and wares,
your mariners, seamen and
shipwrights,
your merchants and all your soldiers,
and everyone else on board
will sink into the heart of the
sea
on the day of your shipwreck.
[28]The shorelands will quake
when your seamen cry out.
[29]All who handle the oars
will abandon their ships;
the mariners and all the seamen
will stand on the shore.
[30]They will raise their voice
and cry bitterly over you;
they will sprinkle dust on their heads
and roll in ashes.
[31]They will shave their heads because of
you
and will put on sackcloth.
They will weep over you with anguish of
soul
and with bitter mourning.
[32]As they wail and mourn over you,
they will take up a lament concerning
you:
"Who was ever silenced like Tyre,
surrounded by the sea?"
[33]When your merchandise went out on
the seas,
you satisfied many nations;
with your great wealth and your wares
you enriched the kings of the
earth.
[34]Now you are shattered by the sea
in the depths of the waters;
your wares and all your company
have gone down with you.
[35]All who live in the coastlands
are appalled at you;
their kings shudder with horror
and their faces are distorted with
fear.
[36]The merchants among the nations hiss
at you;
you have come to a horrible end
and will be no more.' "

---

[e]15 Septuagint; Hebrew *Dedan*   [f]16 Most Hebrew manuscripts; some Hebrew manuscripts and Syriac *Edom*
[g]17 The meaning of the Hebrew for this word is uncertain.

A Prophecy Against the King of Tyre

28 The word of the LORD came to me: [2]"Son of man, say to the ruler of Tyre, 'This is what the Sovereign LORD says:

"'In the pride of your heart
    you say, "I am a god;
I sit on the throne of a god
    in the heart of the seas."
But you are a man and not a god,
    though you think you are as wise as a
        god.
[3]Are you wiser than Daniel?[a]
    Is no secret hidden from you?
[4]By your wisdom and understanding
    you have gained wealth for yourself
and amassed gold and silver
    in your treasuries.
[5]By your great skill in trading
    you have increased your wealth,
and because of your wealth
    your heart has grown proud.

[6]"'Therefore this is what the Sovereign LORD says:

"'Because you think you are wise,
    as wise as a god,
[7]I am going to bring foreigners against
        you,
    the most ruthless of nations;
they will draw their swords against your
        beauty and wisdom
    and pierce your shining splendour.
[8]They will bring you down to the pit,
    and you will die a violent death
    in the heart of the seas.
[9]Will you then say, "I am a god,"
    in the presence of those who kill you?
You will be but a man, not a god,
    in the hands of those who slay you.
[10]You will die the death of the
        uncircumcised
    at the hands of foreigners.

I have spoken, declares the Sovereign LORD.'"

[11]The word of the LORD came to me: [12]"Son of man, take up a lament concerning the king of Tyre and say to him: 'This is what the Sovereign LORD says:

"'You were the model of perfection,
    full of wisdom and perfect in beauty.
[13]You were in Eden,
    the garden of God;
every precious stone adorned you:
    ruby, topaz and emerald,
    chrysolite, onyx and jasper,
    sapphire,[b] turquoise and beryl.[c]
Your settings and mountings[d] were
        made of gold;
    on the day you were created they
        were prepared.
[14]You were anointed as a guardian
        cherub,
    for so I ordained you.
You were on the holy mount of God;
    you walked among the fiery stones.
[15]You were blameless in your ways
    from the day you were created
    till wickedness was found in you.
[16]Through your widespread trade
    you were filled with violence,
        and you sinned.
So I drove you in disgrace from the
        mount of God,
    and I expelled you, O guardian
        cherub,
    from among the fiery stones.
[17]Your heart became proud
    on account of your beauty,
and you corrupted your wisdom
    because of your splendour.
So I threw you to the earth;
    I made a spectacle of you before
        kings.
[18]By your many sins and dishonest trade
    you have desecrated your
        sanctuaries.
So I made a fire come out from you,
    and it consumed you,
and I reduced you to ashes on the
        ground
    in the sight of all who were
        watching.

---

a3 Or *Danel*; the Hebrew spelling may suggest a person other than the prophet Daniel.   *b13* Or *lapis lazuli*
c13 The precise identification of some of these precious stones is uncertain.
d13 The meaning of the Hebrew for this phrase is uncertain.

[19]All the nations who knew you
    are appalled at you;
you have come to a horrible end
    and will be no more.'"

A Prophecy Against Sidon

[20]The word of the LORD came to me:
[21]"Son of man, set your face against
Sidon; prophesy against her [22]and say:
'This is what the Sovereign LORD says:

"'I am against you, O Sidon,
    and I will gain glory within you.
They will know that I am the LORD,
    when I inflict punishment on her
    and show myself holy within her.
[23]I will send a plague upon her
    and make blood flow in her streets.
The slain will fall within her,
    with the sword against her on every
      side.
Then they will know that I am the
    LORD.

[24]"'No longer will the people of Israel
have malicious neighbours who are painful briers and sharp thorns. Then they will
know that I am the Sovereign LORD.

[25]"'This is what the Sovereign LORD
says: When I gather the people of Israel
from the nations where they have been
scattered, I will show myself holy among
them in the sight of the nations. Then they
will live in their own land, which I gave to
my servant Jacob. [26]They will live there in
safety and will build houses and plant
vineyards; they will live in safety when I
inflict punishment on all their neighbours
who maligned them. Then they will know
that I am the LORD their God.'"

A Prophecy Against Egypt

29 In the tenth year, in the tenth
month on the twelfth day, the
word of the LORD came to me: [2]"Son of
man, set your face against Pharaoh king of
Egypt and prophesy against him and
against all Egypt. [3]Speak to him and say:
'This is what the Sovereign LORD says:

"'I am against you, Pharaoh king of
    Egypt,
you great monster lying among your
    streams.
You say, "The Nile is mine;
    I made it for myself."
[4]But I will put hooks in your jaws
    and make the fish of your streams
      stick to your scales.
I will pull you out from among your
    streams,
    with all the fish sticking to your
      scales.
[5]I will leave you in the desert,
    you and all the fish of your streams.
You will fall on the open field
    and not be gathered or picked up.
I will give you as food
    to the beasts of the earth and the
      birds of the air.

[6]Then all who live in Egypt will know that
I am the LORD.

"'You have been a staff of reed for the
house of Israel. [7]When they grasped you
with their hands, you splintered and you
tore open their shoulders; when they
leaned on you, you broke and their backs
were wrenched.[a]

[8]"'Therefore this is what the Sovereign
LORD says: I will bring a sword against you
and kill your men and their animals.
[9]Egypt will become a desolate wasteland.
Then they will know that I am the LORD.

"'Because you said, "The Nile is mine;
I made it," [10]therefore I am against you
and against your streams, and I will make
the land of Egypt a ruin and a desolate
waste from Migdol to Aswan, as far as the
border of Cush.[b] [11]No foot of man or
animal will pass through it; no-one will
live there for forty years. [12]I will make the
land of Egypt desolate among devastated
lands, and her cities will lie desolate for
forty years among ruined cities. And I will
disperse the Egyptians among the nations
and scatter them through the countries.

[13]"'Yet this is what the Sovereign LORD
says: At the end of forty years I will gather
the Egyptians from the nations where they

[a]7 Syriac (see also Septuagint and Vulgate); Hebrew *and you caused their backs to stand*
[b]10 That is, the upper Nile region

were scattered. [14]I will bring them back from captivity and return them to Upper Egypt,[c] the land of their ancestry. There they will be a lowly kingdom. [15]It will be the lowliest of kingdoms and will never again exalt itself above the other nations. I will make it so weak that it will never again rule over the nations. [16]Egypt will no longer be a source of confidence for the people of Israel but will be a reminder of their sin in turning to her for help. Then they will know that I am the Sovereign LORD.'"

[17]In the twenty-seventh year, in the first month on the first day, the word of the LORD came to me: [18]"Son of man, Nebuchadnezzar king of Babylon drove his army in a hard campaign against Tyre; every head was rubbed bare and every shoulder made raw. Yet he and his army got no reward from the campaign he led against Tyre. [19]Therefore this is what the Sovereign LORD says: I am going to give Egypt to Nebuchadnezzar king of Babylon, and he will carry off its wealth. He will loot and plunder the land as pay for his army. [20]I have given him Egypt as a reward for his efforts because he and his army did it for me, declares the Sovereign LORD.

[21]"On that day I will make a horn[d] grow for the house of Israel, and I will open your mouth among them. Then they will know that I am the LORD."

A Lament for Egypt

30 The word of the LORD came to me: [2]"Son of man, prophesy and say: 'This is what the Sovereign LORD says:

"'Wail and say,
  "Alas for that day!"
[3]For the day is near,
  the day of the LORD is near—
a day of clouds,
  a time of doom for the nations.
[4]A sword will come against Egypt,
  and anguish will come upon Cush.[a]

When the slain fall in Egypt,
  her wealth will be carried away
  and her foundations torn down.

[5]Cush and Put, Lydia and all Arabia, Libya[b] and the people of the covenant land will fall by the sword along with Egypt.

[6]"This is what the LORD says:

"'The allies of Egypt will fall
  and her proud strength will fail.
From Migdol to Aswan
  they will fall by the sword within her,
    declares the Sovereign LORD.
[7]"They will be desolate
  among desolate lands,
  and their cities will lie
  among ruined cities.
[8]Then they will know that I am the
    LORD,
  when I set fire to Egypt
  and all her helpers are crushed.

[9]"'On that day messengers will go out from me in ships to frighten Cush out of her complacency. Anguish will take hold of them on the day of Egypt's doom, for it is sure to come.

[10]"This is what the Sovereign LORD says:

"'I will put an end to the hordes of
    Egypt
  by the hand of Nebuchadnezzar king
    of Babylon
[11]He and his army—the most ruthless of
    nations—
  will be brought in to destroy the land.
They will draw their swords against
    Egypt
  and fill the land with the slain.
[12]I will dry up the streams of the Nile
  and sell the land to evil men;
  by the hand of foreigners
  I will lay waste the land and
    everything in it.

I the LORD have spoken.

---

c14 Hebrew *to Pathros*   *d21* *Horn* here symbolises strength.
a4 That is, the upper Nile region; also in verses 5 and 9   *b5* Hebrew *Cub*

13"'This is what the Sovereign LORD says:

"'I will destroy the idols
and put an end to the images in
Memphis.*c*
No longer will there be a prince in
Egypt,
and I will spread fear throughout the
land.
14I will lay waste Upper Egypt,*d*
set fire to Zoan
and inflict punishment on Thebes.*e*
15I will pour out my wrath on Pelusium,*f*
the stronghold of Egypt,
and cut off the hordes of Thebes.
16I will set fire to Egypt;
Pelusium will writhe in agony.
Thebes will be taken by storm;
Memphis will be in constant distress.
17The young men of Heliopolis*g* and
Bubastis*h*
will fall by the sword,
and the cities themselves will go into
captivity.
18Dark will be the day at Tahpanhes
when I break the yoke of Egypt;
there her proud strength will come to
an end.
She will be covered with clouds,
and her villages will go into captivity.
19So I will inflict punishment on Egypt,
and they will know that I am the
LORD.'"

20In the eleventh year, in the first month
on the seventh day, the word of the LORD
came to me: 21"Son of man, I have broken
the arm of Pharaoh king of Egypt. It has
not been bound up for healing or put in a
splint so as to become strong enough to
hold a sword. 22Therefore this is what the
Sovereign LORD says: I am against Pharaoh king of Egypt. I will break both his
arms, the good arm as well as the broken
one, and make the sword fall from his
hand. 23I will disperse the Egyptians
among the nations and scatter them
through the countries. 24I will strengthen
the arms of the king of Babylon and put
my sword in his hand, but I will break the

arms of Pharaoh, and he will groan before
him like a mortally wounded man. 25I will
strengthen the arms of the king of Babylon, but the arms of Pharaoh will fall limp.
Then they will know that I am the LORD,
when I put my sword into the hand of the
king of Babylon and he brandishes it
against Egypt. 26I will disperse the Egyptians among the nations and scatter them
through the countries. Then they will
know that I am the LORD."

A Cedar in Lebanon

31 In the eleventh year, in the third
month on the first day, the word of
the LORD came to me: 2"Son of man, say to
Pharaoh king of Egypt and to his hordes:

"'Who can be compared with you in
majesty?
3Consider Assyria, once a cedar in
Lebanon,
with beautiful branches
overshadowing the forest;
it towered on high,
its top above the thick foliage.
4The waters nourished it,
deep springs made it grow tall;
their streams flowed
all around its base
and sent their channels
to all the trees of the field.
5So it towered higher
than all the trees of the field;
its boughs increased
and its branches grew long,
spreading because of abundant
waters.
6All the birds of the air
nested in its boughs,
all the beasts of the field
gave birth under its branches;
all the great nations
lived in its shade.
7It was majestic in beauty,
with its spreading boughs,
for its roots went down
to abundant waters.
8The cedars in the garden of God
could not rival it,

---

c13 Hebrew *Noph*; also in verse 16   *d14* Hebrew *waste Pathros*   *e14* Hebrew *No*; also in verses 15 and 16
f15 Hebrew *Sin*; also in verse 16   *g17* Hebrew *Awen* (or *On*)   *h17* Hebrew *Pi Beseth*

nor could the pine trees
   equal its boughs,
nor could the plane trees
   compare with its branches—
no tree in the garden of God
   could match its beauty.
⁹I made it beautiful
   with abundant branches,
the envy of all the trees of Eden
   in the garden of God.

¹⁰"'Therefore this is what the Sovereign LORD says: Because it towered on high, lifting its top above the thick foliage, and because it was proud of its height, ¹¹I handed it over to the ruler of the nations, for him to deal with according to its wickedness. I cast it aside, ¹²and the most ruthless of foreign nations cut it down and left it. Its boughs fell on the mountains and in all the valleys; its branches lay broken in all the ravines of the land. All the nations of the earth came out from under its shade and left it. ¹³All the birds of the air settled on the fallen tree, and all the beasts of the field were among its branches. ¹⁴Therefore no other trees by the waters are ever to tower proudly on high, lifting their tops above the thick foliage. No other trees so well-watered are ever to reach such a height; they are all destined for death, for the earth below, among mortal men, with those who go down to the pit.

¹⁵"'This is what the Sovereign LORD says: On the day it was brought down to the grave[a] I covered the deep springs with mourning for it; I held back its streams, and its abundant waters were restrained. Because of it I clothed Lebanon with gloom, and all the trees of the field withered away. ¹⁶I made the nations tremble at the sound of its fall when I brought it down to the grave with those who go down to the pit. Then all the trees of Eden, the choicest and best of Lebanon, all the trees that were well-watered, were consoled in the earth below. ¹⁷Those who lived in its shade, its allies among the nations, had also gone down to the grave with it, joining those killed by the sword.

¹⁸"'Which of the trees of Eden can be compared with you in splendour and majesty? Yet you, too, will be brought down with the trees of Eden to the earth below; you will lie among the uncircumcised, with those killed by the sword.

"'This is Pharaoh and all his hordes, declares the Sovereign LORD.'"

A Lament for Pharaoh

32 In the twelfth year, in the twelfth month on the first day, the word of the LORD came to me: ²"Son of man, take up a lament concerning Pharaoh king of Egypt and say to him:

"'You are like a lion among the
   nations;
   you are like a monster in the seas
thrashing about in your streams,
   churning the water with your feet
   and muddying the streams.

³"'This is what the Sovereign LORD says:

"'With a great throng of people
   I will cast my net over you,
   and they will haul you up in my net.
⁴I will throw you on the land
   and hurl you on the open field.
I will let all the birds of the air settle on
   you
   and all the beasts of the earth gorge
   themselves on you.
⁵I will spread your flesh on the
   mountains
   and fill the valleys with your remains.
⁶I will drench the land with your flowing
   blood
   all the way to the mountains,
   and the ravines will be filled with
   your flesh.
⁷When I snuff you out, I will cover the
   heavens
   and darken their stars;
I will cover the sun with a cloud,
   and the moon will not give its
   light.
⁸All the shining lights in the heavens
   I will darken over you;

<hr>

a15 Hebrew *Sheol*; also in verses 16 and 17

I will bring darkness over your land,
   declares the Sovereign LORD.
⁹I will trouble the hearts of many
      peoples
   when I bring about your destruction
      among the nations,
   among[a] lands you have not known.
¹⁰I will cause many peoples to be appalled
      at you,
   and their kings will shudder with
      horror because of you
   when I brandish my sword before
      them.
On the day of your downfall
   each of them will tremble
   every moment for his life.

¹¹" 'For this is what the Sovereign LORD
says:

" 'The sword of the king of Babylon
   will come against you.
¹²I will cause your hordes to fall
   by the swords of mighty men—
   the most ruthless of all nations.
They will shatter the pride of Egypt,
   and all her hordes will be
      overthrown.
¹³I will destroy all her cattle
   from beside abundant waters
no longer to be stirred by the foot of
      man
   or muddied by the hoofs of cattle.
¹⁴Then I will let her waters settle
   and make her streams flow like oil,
      declares the Sovereign LORD.
¹⁵When I make Egypt desolate
   and strip the land of everything in it,
   when I strike down all who live there,
      then they will know that I am the
      LORD.'

¹⁶"This is the lament they will chant for
her. The daughters of the nations will
chant it; for Egypt and all her hordes they
will chant it, declares the Sovereign
LORD."

¹⁷In the twelfth year, on the fifteenth
day of the month, the word of the LORD
came to me: ¹⁸"Son of man, wail for the
hordes of Egypt and consign to the earth
below both her and the daughters of
mighty nations, with those who go down
to the pit. ¹⁹Say to them, 'Are you more
favoured than others? Go down and be
laid among the uncircumcised.' ²⁰They
will fall among those killed by the sword.
The sword is drawn; let her be dragged off
with all her hordes. ²¹From within the
grave[b] the mighty leaders will say of Egypt
and her allies, 'They have come down and
they lie with the uncircumcised, with those
killed by the sword.'

²²"Assyria is there with her whole army;
she is surrounded by the graves of all her
slain, all who have fallen by the sword.
²³Their graves are in the depths of the pit
and her army lies around her grave. All
who had spread terror in the land of the
living are slain, fallen by the sword.

²⁴"Elam is there, with all her hordes
around her grave. All of them are slain,
fallen by the sword. All who had spread
terror in the land of the living went down
uncircumcised to the earth below. They
bear their shame with those who go down
to the pit. ²⁵A bed is made for her among
the slain, with all her hordes around her
grave. All of them are uncircumcised,
killed by the sword. Because their terror
had spread in the land of the living, they
bear their shame with those who go down
to the pit; they are laid among the slain.

²⁶"Meshech and Tubal are there, with
all their hordes around their graves. All of
them are uncircumcised, killed by the
sword because they spread their terror in
the land of the living. ²⁷Do they not lie
with the other uncircumcised warriors
who have fallen, who went down to the
grave with their weapons of war, whose
swords were placed under their heads?
The punishment for their sins rested on
their bones, though the terror of these
warriors had stalked through the land of
the living.

²⁸"You too, O Pharaoh, will be broken
and will lie among the uncircumcised, with
those killed by the sword.

²⁹"Edom is there, her kings and all her
princes; despite their power, they are laid

---

a9 Hebrew; Septuagint *bring you into captivity among the nations, / to*   *b21* Hebrew *Sheol*; also in verse 27 with those killed by the sword. They lie with the uncircumcised, with those who go down to the pit.

30"All the princes of the north and all the Sidonians are there; they went down with the slain in disgrace despite the terror caused by their power. They lie uncircumcised with those killed by the sword and bear their shame with those who go down to the pit.

31"Pharaoh—he and all his army—will see them and he will be consoled for all his hordes that were killed by the sword, declares the Sovereign LORD. 32Although I had him spread terror in the land of the living, Pharaoh and all his hordes will be laid among the uncircumcised, with those killed by the sword, declares the Sovereign LORD."

Ezekiel a Watchman

33 The word of the LORD came to me: 2"Son of man, speak to your countrymen and say to them: 'When I bring the sword against a land, and the people of the land choose one of their men and make him their watchman, 3and he sees the sword coming against the land and blows the trumpet to warn the people, 4then if anyone hears the trumpet but does not take warning and the sword comes and takes his life, his blood will be on his own head. 5Since he heard the sound of the trumpet but did not take warning, his blood will be on his own head. If he had taken warning, he would have saved himself. 6But if the watchman sees the sword coming and does not blow the trumpet to warn the people and the sword comes and takes the life of one of them, that man will be taken away because of his sin, but I will hold the watchman accountable for his blood.'

7"Son of man, I have made you a watchman for the house of Israel; so hear the word I speak and give them warning from me. 8When I say to the wicked, 'O wicked man, you will surely die,' and you do not speak out to dissuade him from his ways, that wicked man will die for[a] his sin, and I will hold you accountable for his blood.

9But if you do warn the wicked man to turn from his ways and he does not do so, he will die for his sin, but you will be saved yourself.

10"Son of man, say to the house of Israel, 'This is what you are saying: "Our offences and sins weigh us down, and we are wasting away because of[b] them. How then can we live?"' 11Say to them, 'As surely as I live, declares the Sovereign LORD, I take no pleasure in the death of the wicked, but rather that they turn from their ways and live. Turn! Turn from your evil ways! Why will you die, O house of Israel?'

12"Therefore, son of man, say to your countrymen, 'The righteousness of the righteous man will not save him when he disobeys, and the wickedness of the wicked man will not cause him to fall when he turns from it. The righteous man, if he sins, will not be allowed to live because of his former righteousness.' 13If I tell the righteous man that he will surely live, but then he trusts in his righteousness and does evil, none of the righteous things he has done will be remembered; he will die for the evil he has done. 14And if I say to the wicked man, 'You will surely die,' but he then turns away from his sin and does what is just and right—15if he gives back what he took in pledge for a loan, returns what he has stolen, follows the decrees that give life, and does no evil, he will surely live; he will not die. 16None of the sins he has committed will be remembered against him. He has done what is just and right; he will surely live.

17"Yet your countrymen say, 'The way of the Lord is not just.' But it is their way that is not just. 18If a righteous man turns from his righteousness and does evil, he will die for it. 19And if a wicked man turns away from his wickedness and does what is just and right, he will live by doing so. 20Yet, O house of Israel, you say, 'The way of the Lord is not just.' But I will judge each of you according to his own ways."

Jerusalem's Fall Explained

21In the twelfth year of our exile, in the tenth month on the fifth day, a man who

a8 Or in; also in verse 9   b10 Or away in

had escaped from Jerusalem came to me and said, "The city has fallen!" 22Now the evening before the man arrived, the hand of the LORD was upon me, and he opened my mouth before the man came to me in the morning. So my mouth was opened and I was no longer silent.

23Then the word of the LORD came to me: 24"Son of man, the people living in those ruins in the land of Israel are saying, 'Abraham was only one man, yet he possessed the land. But we are many; surely the land has been given to us as our possession.' 25Therefore say to them, 'This is what the Sovereign LORD says: Since you eat meat with the blood still in it and look to your idols and shed blood, should you then possess the land? 26You rely on your sword, you do detestable things, and each of you defiles his neighbour's wife. Should you then possess the land?'

27"Say this to them: 'This is what the Sovereign LORD says: As surely as I live, those who are left in the ruins will fall by the sword, those out in the country I will give to the wild animals to be devoured, and those in strongholds and caves will die of a plague. 28I will make the land a desolate waste, and her proud strength will come to an end, and the mountains of Israel will become desolate so that no-one will cross them. 29Then they will know that I am the LORD, when I have made the land a desolate waste because of all the detestable things they have done.'

30"As for you, son of man, your countrymen are talking together about you by the walls and at the doors of the houses, saying to each other, 'Come and hear the message that has come from the LORD.' 31My people come to you, as they usually do, and sit before you to listen to your words, but they do not put them into practice. With their mouths they express devotion, but their hearts are greedy for unjust gain. 32Indeed, to them you are nothing more than one who sings love songs with a beautiful voice and plays an instrument well, for they hear your words but do not put them into practice.

33"When all this comes true—and it surely will—then they will know that a prophet has been among them."

Shepherds and Sheep

34 The word of the LORD came to me: 2"Son of man, prophesy against the shepherds of Israel; prophesy and say to them: 'This is what the Sovereign LORD says: Woe to the shepherds of Israel who only take care of themselves! Should not shepherds take care of the flock? 3You eat the curds, clothe yourselves with the wool and slaughter the choice animals, but you do not take care of the flock. 4You have not strengthened the weak or healed the sick or bound up the injured. You have not brought back the strays or searched for the lost. You have ruled them harshly and brutally. 5So they were scattered because there was no shepherd, and when they were scattered they became food for all the wild animals. 6My sheep wandered over all the mountains and on every high hill. They were scattered over the whole earth, and no-one searched or looked for them.

7"'Therefore, you shepherds, hear the word of the LORD: 8As surely as I live, declares the Sovereign LORD, because my flock lacks a shepherd and so has been plundered and has become food for all the wild animals, and because my shepherds did not search for my flock but cared for themselves rather than for my flock, 9therefore, O shepherds, hear the word of the LORD: 10This is what the Sovereign LORD says: I am against the shepherds and will hold them accountable for my flock. I will remove them from tending the flock so that the shepherds can no longer feed themselves. I will rescue my flock from their mouths, and it will no longer be food for them.

11"'For this is what the Sovereign LORD says: I myself will search for my sheep and look after them. 12As a shepherd looks after his scattered flock when he is with them, so will I look after my sheep. I will rescue them from all the places where they were scattered on a day of clouds and darkness. 13I will bring them out from the nations and gather them from the countries, and I will bring them into their own land. I will pasture them on the mountains of Israel, in the ravines and in all the settlements in the land. [14]I will tend them in a good pasture, and the mountain heights of Israel will be their grazing land. There they will lie down in good grazing land, and there they will feed in a rich pasture on the mountains of Israel. [15]I myself will tend my sheep and make them lie down, declares the Sovereign LORD. [16]I will search for the lost and bring back the strays. I will bind up the injured and strengthen the weak, but the sleek and the strong I will destroy. I will shepherd the flock with justice.

[17]"'As for you, my flock, this is what the Sovereign LORD says: I will judge between one sheep and another, and between rams and goats. [18]Is it not enough for you to feed on the good pasture? Must you also trample the rest of your pasture with your feet? Is it not enough for you to drink clear water? Must you also muddy the rest with your feet? [19]Must my flock feed on what you have trampled and drink what you have muddied with your feet?

[20]"'Therefore this is what the Sovereign LORD says to them: See, I myself will judge between the fat sheep and the lean sheep. [21]Because you shove with flank and shoulder, butting all the weak sheep with your horns until you have driven them away, [22]I will save my flock, and they will no longer be plundered. I will judge between one sheep and another. [23]I will place over them one shepherd, my servant David, and he will tend them; he will tend them and be their shepherd. [24]I the LORD will be their God, and my servant David will be prince among them. I the LORD have spoken.

[25]"'I will make a covenant of peace with them and rid the land of wild beasts so that they may live in the desert and sleep in the forests in safety. [26]I will bless them and the places surrounding my hill.[a] I will send down showers in season; there will be showers of blessing. [27]The trees of the field will yield their fruit and the ground will yield its crops; the people will be secure in their land. They will know that I am the LORD, when I break the bars of their yoke and rescue them from the hands

of those who enslaved them. [28]They will no longer be plundered by the nations, nor will wild animals devour them. They will live in safety, and no-one will make them afraid. [29]I will provide for them a land renowned for its crops, and they will no longer be victims of famine in the land or bear the scorn of the nations. [30]Then they will know that I, the LORD their God, am with them and that they, the house of Israel, are my people, declares the Sovereign LORD. [31]You my sheep, the sheep of my pasture, are people, and I am your God, declares the Sovereign LORD.'"

A Prophecy Against Edom

35 The word of the LORD came to me: [2]"Son of man, set your face against Mount Seir; prophesy against it [3]and say: 'This is what the Sovereign LORD says: I am against you, Mount Seir, and I will stretch out my hand against you and make you a desolate waste. [4]I will turn your towns into ruins and you will be desolate. Then you will know that I am the LORD.

[5]"'Because you harboured an ancient hostility and delivered the Israelites over to the sword at the time of their calamity, the time their punishment reached its climax, [6]therefore as surely as I live, declares the Sovereign LORD, I will give you over to bloodshed and it will pursue you. Since you did not hate bloodshed, bloodshed will pursue you. [7]I will make Mount Seir a desolate waste and cut off from it all who come and go. [8]I will fill your mountains with the slain; those killed by the sword will fall on your hills and in your valleys and in all your ravines. [9]I will make you desolate for ever; your towns will not be inhabited. Then you will know that I am the LORD.

[10]"'Because you have said, "These two nations and countries will be ours and we will take possession of them," even though I the LORD was there, [11]therefore as surely as I live, declares the Sovereign LORD, I will treat you in accordance with the anger and jealousy you showed in your

---

[a]26 Or I will make them and the places surrounding my hill a blessing

hatred of them and I will make myself known among them when I judge you. [12]Then you will know that I the LORD have heard all the contemptible things you have said against the mountains of Israel. You said, "They have been laid waste and have been given over to us to devour." [13]You boasted against me and spoke against me without restraint, and I heard it. [14]This is what the Sovereign LORD says: While the whole earth rejoices, I will make you desolate. [15]Because you rejoiced when the inheritance of the house of Israel became desolate, that is how I will treat you. You will be desolate, O Mount Seir, you and all of Edom. Then they will know that I am the LORD.'"

A Prophecy to the Mountains of Israel

36 "Son of man, prophesy to the mountains of Israel and say, 'O mountains of Israel, hear the word of the LORD. [2]This is what the Sovereign LORD says: The enemy said of you, "Aha! The ancient heights have become our possession."' [3]Therefore prophesy and say, 'This is what the Sovereign LORD says: Because they ravaged and hounded you from every side so that you became the possession of the rest of the nations and the object of people's malicious talk and slander, [4]therefore, O mountains of Israel, hear the word of the Sovereign LORD: This is what the Sovereign LORD says to the mountains and hills, to the ravines and valleys, to the desolate ruins and the deserted towns that have been plundered and ridiculed by the rest of the nations around you—[5]this is what the Sovereign LORD says: In my burning zeal I have spoken against the rest of the nations, and against Edom, for with glee and with malice in their hearts they made my land their own possession so that they might plunder its pasture-land.' [6]Therefore prophesy concerning the land of Israel and say to the mountains and hills, to the ravines and valleys: 'This is what the Sovereign LORD says: I speak in my jealous wrath because you have suffered the scorn of the nations. [7]Therefore this is what the Sovereign LORD says: I

swear with uplifted hand that the nations around you will also suffer scorn.

[8]"'But you, O mountains of Israel, will produce branches and fruit for my people Israel, for they will soon come home. [9]I am concerned for you and will look on you with favour; you will be ploughed and sown, [10]and I will multiply the number of people upon you, even the whole house of Israel. The towns will be inhabited and the ruins rebuilt. [11]I will increase the number of men and animals upon you, and they will be fruitful and become numerous. I will settle people on you as in the past and will make you prosper more than before. Then you will know that I am the LORD. [12]I will cause people, my people Israel, to walk upon you. They will possess you, and you will be their inheritance; you will never again deprive them of their children.

[13]"'This is what the Sovereign LORD says: Because people say to you, "You devour men and deprive your nation of its children," [14]therefore you will no longer devour men or make your nation childless, declares the Sovereign LORD. [15]No longer will I make you hear the taunts of the nations, and no longer will you suffer the scorn of the peoples or cause your nation to fall, declares the Sovereign LORD.'"

[16]Again the word of the LORD came to me: [17]"Son of man, when the people of Israel were living in their own land, they defiled it by their conduct and their actions. Their conduct was like a woman's monthly uncleanness in my sight. [18]So I poured out my wrath on them because they had shed blood in the land and because they had defiled it with their idols. [19]I dispersed them among the nations, and they were scattered through the countries; I judged them according to their conduct and their actions. [20]And wherever they went among the nations they profaned my holy name, for it was said of them, 'These are the LORD's people, and yet they had to leave his land.' [21]I had concern for my holy name, which the house of Israel profaned among the nations where they had gone.

[22]"Therefore say to the house of Israel, 'This is what the Sovereign LORD says: It is

not for your sake, O house of Israel, that I am going to do these things, but for the sake of my holy name, which you have profaned among the nations where you have gone. 23I will show the holiness of my great name, which has been profaned among the nations, the name you have profaned among them. Then the nations will know that I am the LORD, declares the Sovereign LORD, when I show myself holy through you before their eyes.

24"'For I will take you out of the nations; I will gather you from all the countries and bring you back into your own land. 25I will sprinkle clean water on you, and you will be clean; I will cleanse you from all your impurities and from all your idols. 26I will give you a new heart and put a new spirit in you; I will remove from you your heart of stone and give you a heart of flesh. 27And I will put my Spirit in you and move you to follow my decrees and be careful to keep my laws. 28You will live in the land I gave your forefathers; you will be my people, and I will be your God. 29I will save you from all your uncleanness. I will call for the corn and make it plentiful and will not bring famine upon you. 30I will increase the fruit of the trees and the crops of the field, so that you will no longer suffer disgrace among the nations because of famine. 31Then you will remember your evil ways and wicked deeds, and you will loathe yourselves for your sins and detestable practices. 32I want you to know that I am not doing this for your sake, declares the Sovereign LORD. Be ashamed and disgraced for your conduct, O house of Israel!

33"'This is what the Sovereign LORD says: On the day I cleanse you from all your sins, I will resettle your towns, and the ruins will be rebuilt. 34The desolate land will be cultivated instead of lying desolate in the sight of all who pass through it. 35They will say, "This land that was laid waste has become like the garden of Eden; the cities that were lying in ruins, desolate and destroyed, are now fortified and inhabited." 36Then the nations around you that remain will know that I

the LORD have rebuilt what was destroyed and have replanted what was desolate. I the LORD have spoken, and I will do it.'

37"This is what the Sovereign LORD says: Once again I will yield to the plea of the house of Israel and do this for them: I will make their people as numerous as sheep, 38as numerous as the flocks for offerings at Jerusalem during her appointed feasts. So will the ruined cities be filled with flocks of people. Then they will know that I am the LORD."

The Valley of Dry Bones

37 The hand of the LORD was upon me, and he brought me out by the Spirit of the LORD and set me in the middle of a valley; it was full of bones. 2He led me to and fro among them, and I saw a great many bones on the floor of the valley, bones that were very dry. 3He asked me, "Son of man, can these bones live?"

I said, "O Sovereign LORD, you alone know."

4Then he said to me, "Prophesy to these bones and say to them, 'Dry bones, hear the word of the LORD! 5This is what the Sovereign LORD says to these bones: I will make breath*a* enter you, and you will come to life. 6I will attach tendons to you and make flesh come upon you and cover you with skin; I will put breath in you, and you will come to life. Then you will know that I am the LORD.'"

7So I prophesied as I was commanded. And as I was prophesying, there was a noise, a rattling sound, and the bones came together, bone to bone. 8I looked, and tendons and flesh appeared on them and skin covered them, but there was no breath in them.

9Then he said to me, "Prophesy to the breath; prophesy, son of man, and say to it, 'This is what the Sovereign LORD says: Come from the four winds, O breath, and breathe into these slain, that they may live.'" 10So I prophesied as he commanded me, and breath entered them; they came to life and stood up on their feet—a vast army.

---

*a*5 The Hebrew for this word can also mean *wind* or *spirit* (see verses 6–14).

¹¹Then he said to me: "Son of man, these bones are the whole house of Israel. They say, 'Our bones are dried up and our hope is gone; we are cut off.' ¹²Therefore prophesy and say to them: 'This is what the Sovereign LORD says: O my people, I am going to open your graves and bring you up from them; I will bring you back to the land of Israel. ¹³Then you, my people, will know that I am the LORD, when I open your graves and bring you up from them. ¹⁴I will put my Spirit in you and you will live, and I will settle you in your own land. Then you will know that I the LORD have spoken, and I have done it, declares the LORD.' "

One Nation Under One King

¹⁵The word of the LORD came to me: ¹⁶"Son of man, take a stick of wood and write on it, 'Belonging to Judah and the Israelites associated with him.' Then take another stick of wood, and write on it, 'Ephraim's stick, belonging to Joseph and all the house of Israel associated with him.' ¹⁷Join them together into one stick so that they will become one in your hand. ¹⁸"When your countrymen ask you, 'Won't you tell us what you mean by this?' ¹⁹say to them, 'This is what the Sovereign LORD says: I am going to take the stick of Joseph—which is in Ephraim's hand—and of the Israelite tribes associated with him, and join it to Judah's stick, making them a single stick of wood, and they will become one in my hand.' ²⁰Hold before their eyes the sticks you have written on ²¹and say to them, 'This is what the Sovereign LORD says: I will take the Israelites out of the nations where they have gone. I will gather them from all around and bring them back into their own land. ²²I will make them one nation in the land, on the mountains of Israel. There will be one king over all of them and they will never again be two nations or be divided into two kingdoms. ²³They will no longer defile themselves with their idols and vile images or with any of their offences, for I will save them from all their sinful backsliding,ᵇ

and I will cleanse them. They will be my people, and I will be their God. ²⁴"'My servant David will be king over them, and they will all have one shepherd. They will follow my laws and be careful to keep my decrees. ²⁵They will live in the land I gave to my servant Jacob, the land where your fathers lived. They and their children and their children's children will live there for ever, and David my servant will be their prince for ever. ²⁶I will make a covenant of peace with them; it will be an everlasting covenant. I will establish them and increase their numbers, and I will put my sanctuary among them for ever. ²⁷My dwelling-place will be with them; I will be their God, and they will be my people. ²⁸Then the nations will know that I the LORD make Israel holy, when my sanctuary is among them for ever.' "

A Prophecy Against Gog

38 The word of the LORD came to me: ²"Son of man, set your face against Gog, of the land of Magog, the chief prince ofᵃ Meshech and Tubal; prophesy against him ³and say: 'This is what the Sovereign LORD says: I am against you, O Gog, chief prince ofᵇ Meshech and Tubal. ⁴I will turn you around, put hooks in your jaws and bring you out with your whole army—your horses, your horsemen fully armed, and a great horde with large and small shields, all of them brandishing their swords. ⁵Persia, Cushᶜ and Put will be with them, all with shields and helmets, ⁶also Gomer with all its troops, and Beth Togarmah from the far north with all its troops—the many nations with you.

⁷"'Get ready; be prepared, you and all the hordes gathered about you, and take command of them. ⁸After many days you will be called to arms. In future years you will invade a land that has recovered from war, whose people were gathered from many nations to the mountains of Israel, which had long been desolate. They had been brought out from the nations, and now all of them live in safety. ⁹You and all

---

ᵇ²³ Many Hebrew manuscripts (see also Septuagint); most Hebrew manuscripts *all their dwelling-places where they sinned*
ᵃ² Or *the prince of Rosh,*   ᵇ³ Or *Gog, prince of Rosh,*   ᶜ⁵ That is, the upper Nile region

your troops and the many nations with you will go up, advancing like a storm; you will be like a cloud covering the land.

10"This is what the Sovereign LORD says: On that day thoughts will come into your mind and you will devise an evil scheme. 11You will say, "I will invade a land of unwalled villages; I will attack a peaceful and unsuspecting people—all of them living without walls and without gates and bars. 12I will plunder and loot and turn my hand against the resettled ruins and the people gathered from the nations, rich in livestock and goods, living at the centre of the land." 13Sheba and Dedan and the merchants of Tarshish and all her villages*d* will say to you, "Have you come to plunder? Have you gathered your hordes to loot, to carry off silver and gold, to take away livestock and goods and to seize much plunder?"'

14"Therefore, son of man, prophesy and say to Gog: 'This is what the Sovereign LORD says: In that day, when my people Israel are living in safety, will you not take notice of it? 15You will come from your place in the far north, you and many nations with you, all of them riding on horses, a great horde, a mighty army. 16You will advance against my people Israel like a cloud that covers the land. In days to come, O Gog, I will bring you against my land, so that the nations may know me when I show myself holy through you before their eyes.

17"'This is what the Sovereign LORD says: Are you not the one I spoke of in former days by my servants the prophets of Israel? At that time they prophesied for years that I would bring you against them. 18This is what will happen in that day: When Gog attacks the land of Israel, my hot anger will be aroused, declares the Sovereign LORD. 19In my zeal and fiery wrath I declare that at that time there shall be a great earthquake in the land of Israel. 20The fish of the sea, the birds of the air, the beasts of the field, every creature that moves along the ground, and all the people on the face of the earth will tremble at my presence. The mountains will be overturned, the cliffs will crumble and every wall will fall to the ground. 21I will summon a sword against Gog on all my mountains, declares the Sovereign LORD. Every man's sword will be against his brother. 22I will execute judgment upon him with plague and bloodshed; I will pour down torrents of rain, hailstones and burning sulphur on him and on his troops and on the many nations with him. 23And so I will show my greatness and my holiness, and I will make myself known in the sight of many nations. Then they will know that I am the LORD.'

39 "Son of man, prophesy against Gog and say: 'This is what the Sovereign LORD says: I am against you, O Gog, chief prince of*a* Meshech and Tubal. 2I will turn you around and drag you along. I will bring you from the far north and send you against the mountains of Israel. 3Then I will strike your bow from your left hand and make your arrows drop from your right hand. 4On the mountains of Israel you will fall, you and all your troops and the nations with you. I will give you as food to all kinds of carrion birds and to the wild animals. 5You will fall in the open field, for I have spoken, declares the Sovereign LORD. 6I will send fire on Magog and on those who live in safety in the coastlands, and they will know that I am the LORD.

7"'I will make known my holy name among my people Israel. I will no longer let my holy name be profaned, and the nations will know that I the LORD am the Holy One in Israel. 8It is coming! It will surely take place, declares the Sovereign LORD. This is the day I have spoken of.

9"'Then those who live in the towns of Israel will go out and use the weapons for fuel and burn them up—the small and large shields, the bows and arrows, the war clubs and spears. For seven years they will use them for fuel. 10They will not need to gather wood from the fields or cut it from the forests, because they will use the weapons for fuel. And they will plunder those who plundered them and loot those

---

*d*13 Or *her strong lions*   *a*1 Or *Gog, prince of Rosh,* who looted them, declares the Sovereign LORD.

11"'On that day I will give Gog a burial place in Israel, in the valley of those who travel east towards[b] the Sea.[c] It will block the way of travellers, because Gog and all his hordes will be buried there. So it will be called the Valley of Hamon Gog.[d]

12"'For seven months the house of Israel will be burying them in order to cleanse the land. 13All the people of the land will bury them, and the day I am glorified will be a memorable day for them, declares the Sovereign LORD.

14"'Men will be regularly employed to cleanse the land. Some will go throughout the land and, in addition to them, others will bury those that remain on the ground. At the end of the seven months they will begin their search. 15As they go through the land and one of them sees a human bone, he will set up a marker beside it until the gravediggers have buried it in the Valley of Hamon Gog. 16(Also a town called Hamonah[e] will be there.) And so they will cleanse the land.'

17"Son of man, this is what the Sovereign LORD says: Call out to every kind of bird and all the wild animals: 'Assemble and come together from all around to the sacrifice I am preparing for you, the great sacrifice on the mountains of Israel. There you will eat flesh and drink blood. 18You will eat the flesh of mighty men and drink the blood of the princes of the earth as if they were rams and lambs, goats and bulls—all of them fattened animals from Bashan. 19At the sacrifice I am preparing for you, you will eat fat till you are glutted and drink blood till you are drunk. 20At my table you will eat your fill of horses and riders, mighty men and soldiers of every kind,' declares the Sovereign LORD.

21"I will display my glory among the nations, and all the nations will see the punishment I inflict and the hand I lay upon them. 22From that day forward the house of Israel will know that I am the LORD their God. 23And the nations will

know that the people of Israel went into exile for their sin, because they were unfaithful to me. So I hid my face from them and handed them over to their enemies, and they all fell by the sword. 24I dealt with them according to their uncleanness and their offences, and I hid my face from them.

25"Therefore this is what the Sovereign LORD says: I will now bring Jacob back from captivity[f] and will have compassion on all the people of Israel, and I will be zealous for my holy name. 26They will forget their shame and all the unfaithfulness they showed towards me when they lived in safety in their land with no-one to make them afraid. 27When I have brought them back from the nations and have gathered them from the countries of their enemies, I will show myself holy through them in the sight of many nations. 28Then they will know that I am the LORD their God, for though I sent them into exile among the nations, I will gather them to their own land, not leaving any behind. 29I will no longer hide my face from them, for I will pour out my Spirit on the house of Israel, declares the Sovereign LORD."

The New Temple Area

40 In the twenty-fifth year of our exile, at the beginning of the year, on the tenth of the month, in the fourteenth year after the fall of the city—on that very day the hand of the LORD was upon me and he took me there. 2In visions of God he took me to the land of Israel and set me on a very high mountain, on whose south side were some buildings that looked like a city. 3He took me there, and I saw a man whose appearance was like bronze; he was standing in the gateway with a linen cord and a measuring rod in his hand. 4The man said to me, "Son of man, look with your eyes and hear with your ears and pay attention to everything I am going to show you, for that is why you have been brought here. Tell the house of Israel everything you see."

---

b11 Or *of*   *c11* That is, the Dead Sea
d11 Hamon Gog means *hordes of Gog.*   *e16 Hamonah* means *horde.*   *f25* Or *now restore the fortunes of Jacob*

The East Gate to the Outer Court

⁵I saw a wall completely surrounding the temple area. The length of the measuring rod in the man's hand was six long cubits, each of which was a cubit*a* and a handbreadth.*b* He measured the wall; it was one measuring rod thick and one rod high.

⁶Then he went to the gate facing east. He climbed its steps and measured the threshold of the gate; it was one rod deep.*c* ⁷The alcoves for the guards were one rod long and one rod wide, and the projecting walls between the alcoves were five cubits thick. And the threshold of the gate next to the portico facing the temple was one rod deep.

⁸Then he measured the portico of the gateway; ⁹it*d* was eight cubits deep and its jambs were two cubits thick. The portico of the gateway faced the temple.

¹⁰Inside the east gate were three alcoves on each side; the three had the same measurements, and the faces of the projecting walls on each side had the same measurements. ¹¹Then he measured the width of the entrance to the gateway; it was ten cubits and its length was thirteen cubits. ¹²In front of each alcove was a wall one cubit high, and the alcoves were six cubits square. ¹³Then he measured the gateway from the top of the rear wall of one alcove to the top of the opposite one; the distance was twenty-five cubits from one parapet opening to the opposite one. ¹⁴He measured along the faces of the projecting walls all around the inside of the gateway—sixty cubits. The measurement was up to the portico*e* facing the courtyard.*f* ¹⁵The distance from the entrance of the gateway to the far end of its portico was fifty cubits. ¹⁶The alcoves and the projecting walls inside the gateway were surmounted by narrow parapet openings all round, as was the portico; the openings all round faced inward. The faces of the projecting walls were decorated with palm trees.

The Outer Court

¹⁷Then he brought me into the outer court. There I saw some rooms and a pavement that had been constructed all round the court; there were thirty rooms along the pavement. ¹⁸It abutted the sides of the gateways and was as wide as they were long; this was the lower pavement. ¹⁹Then he measured the distance from the inside of the lower gateway to the outside of the inner court; it was a hundred cubits on the east side as well as on the north.

The North Gate

²⁰Then he measured the length and width of the gate facing north, leading into the outer court. ²¹Its alcoves—three on each side—its projecting walls and its portico had the same measurements as those of the first gateway. It was fifty cubits long and twenty-five cubits wide. ²²Its openings, its portico and its palm tree decorations had the same measurements as those of the gate facing east. Seven steps led up to it, with its portico opposite them. ²³There was a gate to the inner court facing the north gate, just as there was on the east. He measured from one gate to the opposite one; it was a hundred cubits.

The South Gate

²⁴Then he led me to the south side and I saw a gate facing south. He measured its jambs and its portico, and they had the same measurements as the others. ²⁵The gateway and its portico had narrow openings all round, like the openings of the others. It was fifty cubits long and twenty-five cubits wide. ²⁶Seven steps led up to it, with its portico opposite them; it had palm tree decorations on the faces of the projecting walls on each side. ²⁷The inner court also had a gate facing south, and he measured from this gate to the outer gate on the south side; it was a hundred cubits.

---

a5 The common cubit was about 1½ feet (about 0.5 metre).   *b5* That is, about 3 inches (about 8 centimetres) *c6* Septuagint; Hebrew *deep, the first threshold, one rod deep* *d8, 9* Many Hebrew manuscripts, Septuagint, Vulgate and Syriac; most Hebrew manuscripts *gateway facing the temple; it was one rod deep.* *⁹Then he measured the portico of the gateway; it*   *e14* Septuagint; Hebrew *projecting wall* *f14* The meaning of the Hebrew for this verse is uncertain.

Gates to the Inner Court

²⁸Then he brought me into the inner court through the south gate, and he measured the south gate; it had the same measurements as the others. ²⁹Its alcoves, its projecting walls and its portico had the same measurements as the others. The gateway and its portico had openings all round. It was fifty cubits long and twenty-five cubits wide. ³⁰(The porticoes of the gateways around the inner court were twenty-five cubits wide and five cubits deep.) ³¹Its portico faced the outer court; palm trees decorated its jambs, and eight steps led up to it.

³²Then he brought me to the inner court on the east side, and he measured the gateway; it had the same measurements as the others. ³³Its alcoves, its projecting walls and its portico had the same measurements as the others. The gateway and its portico had openings all round. It was fifty cubits long and twenty-five cubits wide. ³⁴Its portico faced the outer court; palm trees decorated the jambs on either side, and eight steps led up to it.

³⁵Then he brought me to the north gate and measured it. It had the same measurements as the others, ³⁶as did its alcoves, its projecting walls and its portico, and it had openings all round. It was fifty cubits long and twenty-five cubits wide. ³⁷Its portico*g* faced the outer court; palm trees decorated the jambs on either side, and eight steps led up to it.

The Rooms for Preparing Sacrifices

³⁸A room with a doorway was by the portico in each of the inner gateways, where the burnt offerings were washed. ³⁹In the portico of the gateway were two tables on each side, on which the burnt offerings, sin offerings and guilt offerings were slaughtered. ⁴⁰By the outside wall of the portico of the gateway, near the steps at the entrance to the north gateway were two tables, and on the other side of the steps were two tables. ⁴¹So there were four tables on one side of the gateway and four on the other—eight tables in all—on which the sacrifices were slaughtered. ⁴²There were also four tables of dressed stone for the burnt offerings, each a cubit and a half long, a cubit and a half wide and a cubit high. On them were placed the utensils for slaughtering the burnt offerings and the other sacrifices. ⁴³And double-pronged hooks, each a handbreadth long, were attached to the wall all around. The tables were for the flesh of the offerings.

Rooms for the Priests

⁴⁴Outside the inner gate, within the inner court, were two rooms, one*h* at the side of the north gate and facing south, and another at the side of the south*i* gate and facing north. ⁴⁵He said to me, "The room facing south is for the priests who have charge of the temple, ⁴⁶and the room facing north is for the priests who have charge of the altar. These are the sons of Zadok, who are the only Levites who may draw near to the LORD to minister before him."

⁴⁷Then he measured the court: It was square—a hundred cubits long and a hundred cubits wide. And the altar was in front of the temple.

The Temple

⁴⁸He brought me to the portico of the temple and measured the jambs of the portico; they were five cubits wide on either side. The width of the entrance was fourteen cubits and its projecting walls were*j* three cubits wide on either side. ⁴⁹The portico was twenty cubits wide, and twelve*k* cubits from front to back. It was reached by a flight of stairs,*l* and there were pillars on each side of the jambs.

41 Then the man brought me to the outer sanctuary and measured the jambs; the width of the jambs was six cubits*a* on each side.*b* ²The entrance was ten cubits wide, and the projecting walls

837 Septuagint (see also verses 31 and 34); Hebrew *jambs*   *h44* Septuagint; Hebrew *were rooms for singers, which were*
i44 Septuagint; Hebrew *east*   *j48* Septuagint; Hebrew *entrance was*   *k49* Septuagint; Hebrew *eleven*
l49 Hebrew; Septuagint *Ten steps led up to it*   *a1* The common cubit was about 1½ feet (about 0.5 metre).
b1 One Hebrew manuscript and Septuagint; most Hebrew manuscripts *side, the width of the tent*

on each side of it were five cubits wide. He also measured the outer sanctuary; it was forty cubits long and twenty cubits wide.

³Then he went into the inner sanctuary and measured the jambs of the entrance; each was two cubits wide. The entrance was six cubits wide, and the projecting walls on each side of it were seven cubits wide. ⁴And he measured the length of the inner sanctuary; it was twenty cubits, and its width was twenty cubits across the end of the outer sanctuary. He said to me, "This is the Most Holy Place."

⁵Then he measured the wall of the temple; it was six cubits thick, and each side room round the temple was four cubits wide. ⁶The side rooms were on three levels, one above another, thirty on each level. There were ledges all round the wall of the temple to serve as supports for the side rooms, so that the supports were not inserted into the wall of the temple. ⁷The side rooms all round the temple were wider at each successive level. The structure surrounding the temple was built in ascending stages, so that the rooms widened as one went upward. A stairway went up from the lowest floor to the top floor through the middle floor.

⁸I saw that the temple had a raised base all round it, forming the foundation of the side rooms. It was the length of the rod, six long cubits. ⁹The outer wall of the side rooms was five cubits thick. The open area between the side rooms of the temple ¹⁰and the ⌊priests'⌋ rooms was twenty cubits wide all round the temple. ¹¹There were entrances to the side rooms from the open area, one on the north and another on the south; and the base adjoining the open area was five cubits wide all round.

¹²The building facing the temple courtyard on the west side was seventy cubits wide. The wall of the building was five cubits thick all round, and its length was ninety cubits.

¹³Then he measured the temple; it was a hundred cubits long, and the temple courtyard and the building with its walls were also a hundred cubits long. ¹⁴The width of the temple courtyard on the east, including the front of the temple, was a hundred cubits.

¹⁵Then he measured the length of the building facing the courtyard at the rear of the temple, including its galleries on each side; it was a hundred cubits.

The outer sanctuary, the inner sanctuary and the portico facing the court, ¹⁶as well as the thresholds and the narrow windows and galleries round the three of them—everything beyond and including the threshold was covered with wood. The floor, the wall up to the windows, and the windows were covered. ¹⁷In the space above the outside of the entrance to the inner sanctuary and on the walls at regular intervals all round the inner and outer sanctuary ¹⁸were carved cherubim and palm trees. Palm trees alternated with cherubim. Each cherub had two faces: ¹⁹the face of a man towards the palm tree on one side and the face of a lion towards the palm tree on the other. They were carved all round the whole temple. ²⁰From the floor to the area above the entrance, cherubim and palm trees were carved on the wall of the outer sanctuary.

²¹The outer sanctuary had a rectangular door-frame, and the one at the front of the Most Holy Place was similar. ²²There was a wooden altar three cubits high and two cubits square;ᶜ its corners, its baseᵈ and its sides were of wood. The man said to me, "This is the table that is before the LORD." ²³Both the outer sanctuary and the Most Holy Place had double doors. ²⁴Each door had two leaves—two hinged leaves for each door. ²⁵And on the doors of the outer sanctuary were carved cherubim and palm trees like those carved on the walls, and there was a wooden overhang on the front of the portico. ²⁶On the side walls of the portico were narrow windows with palm trees carved on each side. The side rooms of the temple also had overhangs.

Rooms for the Priests

42 Then the man led me northward into the outer court and brought me to the rooms opposite the temple courtyard and opposite the outer wall on the north side. ²The building whose door faced north was a hundred cubits*a* long and fifty cubits wide. ³Both in the section twenty cubits from the inner court and in the section opposite the pavement of the outer court, gallery faced gallery at the three levels. ⁴In front of the rooms was an inner passageway ten cubits wide and a hundred cubits*b* long. Their doors were on the north. ⁵Now the upper rooms were narrower, for the galleries took more space from them than from the rooms on the lower and middle floors of the building. ⁶The rooms on the third floor had no pillars, as the courts had; so they were smaller in floor space than those on the lower and middle floors. ⁷There was an outer wall parallel to the rooms and the outer court; it extended in front of the rooms for fifty cubits. ⁸While the row of rooms on the side next to the outer court was fifty cubits long, the row on the side nearest the sanctuary was a hundred cubits long. ⁹The lower rooms had an entrance on the east side as one enters them from the outer court.

¹⁰On the south side*c* along the length of the wall of the outer court, adjoining the temple courtyard and opposite the outer wall, were rooms ¹¹with a passageway in front of them. These were like the rooms on the north; they had the same length and width, with similar exits and dimensions. Similar to the doorways on the north ¹²were the doorways of the rooms on the south. There was a doorway at the beginning of the passageway that was parallel to the corresponding wall extending eastward, by which one enters the rooms.

¹³Then he said to me, "The north and south rooms facing the temple courtyard are the priests' rooms, where the priests who approach the LORD will eat the most holy offerings. There they will put the most holy offerings—the grain offerings, the sin offerings and the guilt offerings—for the place is holy. ¹⁴Once the priests enter the holy precincts, they are not to go into the outer court until they leave behind the garments in which they minister, for these are holy. They are to put on other clothes before they go near the places that are for the people."

¹⁵When he had finished measuring what was inside the temple area, he led me out by the east gate and measured the area all around: ¹⁶He measured the east side with the measuring rod; it was five hundred cubits.*d* ¹⁷He measured the north side; it was five hundred cubits*e* by the measuring rod. ¹⁸He measured the south side; it was five hundred cubits by the measuring rod. ¹⁹Then he turned to the west side and measured; it was five hundred cubits by the measuring rod. ²⁰So he measured the area on all four sides. It had a wall round it, five hundred cubits long and five hundred cubits wide, to separate the holy from the common.

The Glory Returns to the Temple

43 Then the man brought me to the gate facing east, ²and I saw the glory of the God of Israel coming from the east. His voice was like the roar of rushing waters, and the land was radiant with his glory. ³The vision I saw was like the vision I had seen when he*a* came to destroy the city and like the visions I had seen by the Kebar River, and I fell face down. ⁴The glory of the LORD entered the temple through the gate facing east. ⁵Then the Spirit lifted me up and brought me into the inner court, and the glory of the LORD filled the temple.

⁶While the man was standing beside me, I heard someone speaking to me from inside the temple. ⁷He said: "Son of man, this is the place of my throne and the place for the soles of my feet. This is where I will live among the Israelites for ever. The house of Israel will never again defile my holy name—neither they nor their kings—by their prostitution*b* and the lifeless idols*c* of their kings at their high places. ⁸When they placed their threshold next to my

a2 The common cubit was about 1½ feet (about 0.5 metre).   *b4* Septuagint and Syriac; Hebrew *and one cubit*
c10 Septuagint; Hebrew *Eastward*   *d16* See Septuagint of verse 17; Hebrew *rods*; also in verses 18 and 19.
e17 Septuagint; Hebrew *rods*   *a3* Some Hebrew manuscripts and Vulgate; most Hebrew manuscripts *I*
b7 Or *their spiritual adultery*; also in verse 9   *c7* Or *the corpses*; also in verse 9

threshold and their doorposts beside my doorposts, with only a wall between me and them, they defiled my holy name by their detestable practices. So I destroyed them in my anger. ⁹Now let them put away from me their prostitution and the lifeless idols of their kings, and I will live among them for ever.

¹⁰"Son of man, describe the temple to the people of Israel, that they may be ashamed of their sins. Let them consider the plan, ¹¹and if they are ashamed of all they have done, make known to them the design of the temple—its arrangement, its exits and entrances—its whole design and all its regulations*d* and laws. Write these down before them so that they may be faithful to its design and follow all its regulations.

¹²"This is the law of the temple: All the surrounding area on top of the mountain will be most holy. Such is the law of the temple.

The Altar

¹³"These are the measurements of the altar in long cubits, that cubit being a cubit*e* and a handbreadth:*f* Its gutter is a cubit deep and a cubit wide, with a rim of one span*g* around the edge. And this is the height of the altar: ¹⁴From the gutter on the ground up to the lower ledge it is two cubits high and a cubit wide, and from the smaller ledge up to the larger ledge it is four cubits high and a cubit wide. ¹⁵The altar hearth is four cubits high, and four horns project upward from the hearth. ¹⁶The altar hearth is square, twelve cubits long and twelve cubits wide. ¹⁷The upper ledge also is square, fourteen cubits long and fourteen cubits wide, with a rim of half a cubit and a gutter of a cubit all round. The steps of the altar face east."

¹⁸Then he said to me, "Son of man, this is what the Sovereign LORD says: These will be the regulations for sacrificing burnt offerings and sprinkling blood upon the altar when it is built: ¹⁹You are to give a young bull as a sin offering to the priests,

who are Levites, of the family of Zadok, who come near to minister before me, declares the Sovereign LORD. ²⁰You are to take some of its blood and put it on the four horns of the altar and on the four corners of the upper ledge and all round the rim, and so purify the altar and make atonement for it. ²¹You are to take the bull for the sin offering and burn it in the designated part of the temple area outside the sanctuary.

²²"On the second day you are to offer a male goat without defect for a sin offering, and the altar is to be purified as it was purified with the bull. ²³When you have finished purifying it, you are to offer a young bull and a ram from the flock, both without defect. ²⁴You are to offer them before the LORD, and the priests are to sprinkle salt on them and sacrifice them as a burnt offering to the LORD.

²⁵"For seven days you are to provide a male goat daily for a sin offering; you are also to provide a young bull and a ram from the flock, both without defect. ²⁶For seven days they are to make atonement for the altar and cleanse it; thus they will dedicate it. ²⁷At the end of these days, from the eighth day on, the priests are to present your burnt offerings and fellowship offerings*h* on the altar. Then I will accept you, declares the Sovereign LORD."

The Prince, the Levites, the Priests

44 Then the man brought me back to the outer gate of the sanctuary, the one facing east, and it was shut. ²The LORD said to me, "This gate is to remain shut. It must not be opened; no-one may enter through it. It is to remain shut because the LORD, the God of Israel, has entered through it. ³The prince himself is the only one who may sit inside the gateway to eat in the presence of the LORD. He is to enter by way of the portico of the gateway and go out the same way."

⁴Then the man brought me by way of the north gate to the front of the temple. I

---

d11 Some Hebrew manuscripts and Septuagint; most Hebrew manuscripts *regulations and its whole design*
e13 The common cubit was about 1½ feet (about 0.5 metre).   *f13* That is, about 3 inches (about 8 centimetres)
g13 That is, about 9 inches (about 23 centimetres)   *h27* Traditionally *peace offerings*

looked and saw the glory of the LORD filling the temple of the LORD, and I fell face down.

⁵The LORD said to me, "Son of man, look carefully, listen closely and give attention to everything I tell you concerning all the regulations regarding the temple of the LORD. Give attention to the entrance of the temple and all the exits of the sanctuary. ⁶Say to the rebellious house of Israel, 'This is what the Sovereign LORD says: Enough of your detestable practices, O house of Israel! ⁷In addition to all your other detestable practices, you brought foreigners uncircumcised in heart and flesh into my sanctuary, desecrating my temple while you offered me food, fat and blood, and you broke my covenant. ⁸Instead of carrying out your duty in regard to my holy things, you put others in charge of my sanctuary. ⁹This is what the Sovereign LORD says: No foreigner uncircumcised in heart and flesh is to enter my sanctuary, not even the foreigners who live among the Israelites.

¹⁰ "The Levites who went far from me when Israel went astray and who wandered from me after their idols must bear the consequences of their sin. ¹¹They may serve in my sanctuary, having charge of the gates of the temple and serving in it; they may slaughter the burnt offerings and sacrifices for the people and stand before the people and serve them. ¹²But because they served them in the presence of their idols and made the house of Israel fall into sin, therefore I have sworn with uplifted hand that they must bear the consequences of their sin, declares the Sovereign LORD. ¹³They are not to come near to serve me as priests or come near any of my holy things or my most holy offerings; they must bear the shame of their detestable practices. ¹⁴Yet I will put them in charge of the duties of the temple and all the work that is to be done in it.

¹⁵ "But the priests, who are Levites and descendants of Zadok and who faithfully carried out the duties of my sanctuary when the Israelites went astray from me, are to come near to minister before me; they are to stand before me to offer

sacrifices of fat and blood, declares the Sovereign LORD. ¹⁶They alone are to enter my sanctuary; they alone are to come near my table to minister before me and perform my service.

¹⁷ "When they enter the gates of the inner court, they are to wear linen clothes; they must not wear any woollen garment while ministering at the gates of the inner court or inside the temple. ¹⁸They are to wear linen turbans on their heads and linen undergarments round their waists. They must not wear anything that makes them perspire. ¹⁹When they go out into the outer court where the people are, they are to take off the clothes they have been ministering in and leave them in the sacred rooms, and put on other clothes, so that they do not consecrate the people by means of their garments.

²⁰ "They must not shave their heads or let their hair grow long, but they are to keep the hair of their heads trimmed. ²¹No priest is to drink wine when he enters the inner court. ²²They must not marry widows or divorced women; they may marry only virgins of Israelite descent or widows of priests. ²³They are to teach my people the difference between the holy and the common and show them how to distinguish between the unclean and the clean.

²⁴ "In any dispute, the priests are to serve as judges and decide it according to my ordinances. They are to keep my laws and my decrees for all my appointed feasts, and they are to keep my Sabbaths holy.

²⁵ "A priest must not defile himself by going near a dead person; however, if the dead person was his father or mother, son or daughter, brother or unmarried sister, then he may defile himself. ²⁶After he is cleansed, he must wait seven days. ²⁷On the day he goes into the inner court of the sanctuary to minister in the sanctuary, he is to offer a sin offering for himself, declares the Sovereign LORD.

²⁸ "I am to be the only inheritance the priests have. You are to give them no possession in Israel; I will be their possession. ²⁹They will eat the grain offerings, the sin offerings and the guilt offerings;

and everything in Israel devoted[a] to the LORD will belong to them. [30]The best of all the firstfruits and of all your special gifts will belong to the priests. You are to give them the first portion of your ground meal so that a blessing may rest on your household. [31]The priests must not eat anything, bird or animal, found dead or torn by wild animals.

Division of the Land

45 "'When you allot the land as an inheritance, you are to present to the LORD a portion of the land as a sacred district, 25,000 cubits long and 20,000[a] cubits wide; the entire area will be holy. [2]Of this, a section 500 cubits square is to be for the sanctuary, with 50 cubits around it for open land. [3]In the sacred district, measure off a section 25,000 cubits[b] long and 10,000 cubits[c] wide. In it will be the sanctuary, the Most Holy Place. [4]It will be the sacred portion of the land for the priests, who minister in the sanctuary and who draw near to minister before the LORD. It will be a place for their houses as well as a holy place for the sanctuary. [5]An area 25,000 cubits long and 10,000 cubits wide will belong to the Levites, who serve in the temple, as their possession for towns to live in.[d]

[6]"'You are to give the city as its property an area 5,000 cubits wide and 25,000 cubits long, adjoining the sacred portion; it will belong to the whole house of Israel.

[7]"'The prince will have the land bordering each side of the area formed by the sacred district and the property of the city. It will extend westward from the west side and eastward from the east side, running lengthwise from the western to the eastern border parallel to one of the tribal portions. [8]This land will be his possession in Israel. And my princes will no longer oppress my people but will allow the house of Israel to possess the land according to their tribes.

[9]"'This is what the Sovereign LORD says: You have gone far enough, O princes of Israel! Give up your violence and oppression and do what is just and right. Stop dispossessing my people, declares the Sovereign LORD. [10]You are to use accurate scales, an accurate ephah[e] and an accurate bath.[f] [11]The ephah and the bath are to be the same size, the bath containing a tenth of a homer[g] and the ephah a tenth of a homer; the homer is to be the standard measure for both. [12]The shekel[h] is to consist of twenty gerahs. Twenty shekels plus twenty-five shekels plus fifteen shekels equal one mina.[i]

Offerings and Holy Days

[13]"'This is the special gift you are to offer: a sixth of an ephah from each homer of wheat and a sixth of an ephah from each homer of barley. [14]The prescribed portion of oil, measured by the bath, is a tenth of a bath from each cor (which consists of ten baths or one homer, for ten baths are equivalent to a homer). [15]Also one sheep is to be taken from every flock of two hundred from the well-watered pastures of Israel. These will be used for the grain offerings, burnt offerings and fellowship offerings[j] to make atonement for the people, declares the Sovereign LORD. [16]All the people of the land will participate in this special gift for the use of the prince in Israel. [17]It will be the duty of the prince to provide the burnt offerings, grain offerings and drink offerings at the festivals, the New Moons and the Sabbaths—at all the appointed feasts of the house of Israel. He will provide the sin offerings, grain offerings, burnt offerings and fellowship offerings to make atonement for the house of Israel.

[18]"'This is what the Sovereign LORD

---

a29 The Hebrew term refers to the irrevocable giving over of things or persons to the LORD.
a1 Septuagint (see also verses 3 and 5 and 48:9); Hebrew *10,000*   *b3* That is, about 7 miles (about 11 kilometres)
c3 That is, about 3 miles (about 5 kilometres)
d5 Septuagint; Hebrew *temple; they will have as their possession 20 rooms*   *e10* An ephah was a dry measure.
f10 A bath was a liquid measure.   *g11* A homer was a dry measure.
h12 A shekel weighed about ⅔ ounce (about 11.5 grams).   *i12* That is, 60 shekels; the common mina was 50 shekels.
j15 Traditionally *peace offerings*; also in verse 17

says: In the first month on the first day you are to take a young bull without defect and purify the sanctuary. [19]The priest is to take some of the blood of the sin offering and put it on the doorposts of the temple, on the four corners of the upper ledge of the altar and on the gateposts of the inner court. [20]You are to do the same on the seventh day of the month for anyone who sins unintentionally or through ignorance; so you are to make atonement for the temple.

[21]"'In the first month on the fourteenth day you are to observe the Passover, a feast lasting seven days, during which you shall eat bread made without yeast. [22]On that day the prince is to provide a bull as a sin offering for himself and for all the people of the land. [23]Every day during the seven days of the Feast he is to provide seven bulls and seven rams without defect as a burnt offering to the LORD, and a male goat for a sin offering. [24]He is to provide as a grain offering an ephah for each bull and an ephah for each ram, along with a hin[k] of oil for each ephah.

[25]"'During the seven days of the Feast, which begins in the seventh month on the fifteenth day, he is to make the same provision for sin offerings, burnt offerings, grain offerings and oil.

46

"'This is what the Sovereign LORD says: The gate of the inner court facing east is to be shut on the six working days, but on the Sabbath day and on the day of the New Moon it is to be opened. [2]The prince is to enter from the outside through the portico of the gateway and stand by the gatepost. The priests are to sacrifice his burnt offering and his fellowship offerings.[a] He is to worship at the threshold of the gateway and then go out, but the gate will not be shut until evening. [3]On the Sabbaths and New Moons the people of the land are to worship in the presence of the LORD at the entrance to that gateway. [4]The burnt offering the prince brings to the LORD on the Sabbath day is to be six male lambs and a ram, all without defect. [5]The grain offering given

with the ram is to be an ephah,[b] and the grain offering with the lambs is to be as much as he pleases, along with a hin[c] of oil for each ephah. [6]On the day of the New Moon he is to offer a young bull, six lambs and a ram, all without defect. [7]He is to provide as a grain offering one ephah with the bull, one ephah with the ram, and with the lambs as much as he wants to give, along with a hin of oil with each ephah. [8]When the prince enters, he is to go in through the portico of the gateway, and he is to come out the same way.

[9]"'When the people of the land come before the LORD at the appointed feasts, whoever enters by the north gate to worship is to go out by the south gate; and whoever enters by the south gate is to go out by the north gate. No-one is to return through the gate by which he entered, but each is to go out by the opposite gate. [10]The prince is to be among them, going in when they go in and going out when they go out.

[11]"'At the festivals and the appointed feasts, the grain offering is to be an ephah with a bull, an ephah with a ram, and with the lambs as much as one pleases, along with a hin of oil for each ephah. [12]When the prince provides a freewill offering to the LORD—whether a burnt offering or fellowship offerings—the gate facing east is to be opened for him. He shall offer his burnt offering or his fellowship offerings as he does on the Sabbath day. Then he shall go out, and after he has gone out, the gate will be shut.

[13]"'Every day you are to provide a year-old lamb without defect for a burnt offering to the LORD; morning by morning you shall provide it. [14]You are also to provide with it morning by morning a grain offering, consisting of a sixth of an ephah with a third of a hin of oil to moisten the flour. The presenting of this grain offering to the LORD is a lasting ordinance. [15]So the lamb and the grain offering and the oil shall be provided morning by morning for a regular burnt offering.

[16]"'This is what the Sovereign LORD

---

[k]24 That is, probably about 6 pints (about 4 litres)
[b]5 That is, probably about ⅗ bushel (about 22 litres)

[a]2 Traditionally peace offerings; also in verse 12
[c]5 That is, probably about 6 pints (about 4 litres)

says: If the prince makes a gift from his inheritance to one of his sons, it will also belong to his descendants; it is to be their property by inheritance. [17]If, however, he makes a gift from his inheritance to one of his servants, the servant may keep it until the year of freedom; then it will revert to the prince. His inheritance belongs to his sons only; it is theirs. [18]The prince must not take any of the inheritance of the people, driving them off their property. He is to give his sons their inheritance out of his own property, so that none of my people will be separated from his property.'"

[19]Then the man brought me through the entrance at the side of the gate to the sacred rooms facing north, which belonged to the priests, and showed me a place at the western end. [20]He said to me, "This is the place where the priests will cook the guilt offering and the sin offering and bake the grain offering, to avoid bringing them into the outer court and consecrating the people."

[21]He then brought me to the outer court and led me round to its four corners, and I saw in each corner another court. [22]In the four corners of the outer court were enclosed[d] courts, forty cubits long and thirty cubits wide; each of the courts in the four corners was the same size. [23]Around the inside of each of the four courts was a ledge of stone, with places for fire built all round under the ledge. [24]He said to me, "These are the kitchens where those who minister at the temple will cook the sacrifices of the people."

The River From the Temple

47 The man brought me back to the entrance of the temple, and I saw water coming out from under the threshold of the temple towards the east (for the temple faced east). The water was coming down from under the south side of the temple, south of the altar. [2]He then brought me out through the north gate and led me round the outside to the outer

gate facing east, and the water was flowing from the south side.

[3]As the man went eastward with a measuring line in his hand, he measured off a thousand cubits[a] and then led me through water that was ankle-deep. [4]He measured off another thousand cubits and led me through water that was knee-deep. He measured off another thousand and led me through water that was up to the waist. [5]He measured off another thousand, but now it was a river that I could not cross, because the water had risen and was deep enough to swim in—a river that no-one could cross. [6]He asked me, "Son of man, do you see this?"

Then he led me back to the bank of the river. [7]When I arrived there, I saw a great number of trees on each side of the river. [8]He said to me, "This water flows towards the eastern region and goes down into the Arabah,[b] where it enters the Sea.[c] When it empties into the Sea,[c] the water there becomes fresh. [9]Swarms of living creatures will live wherever the river flows. There will be large numbers of fish, because this water flows there and makes the salt water fresh; so where the river flows everything will live. [10]Fishermen will stand along the shore; from En Gedi to En Eglaim there will be places for spreading nets. The fish will be of many kinds—like the fish of the Great Sea.[d] [11]But the swamps and marshes will not become fresh; they will be left for salt. [12]Fruit trees of all kinds will grow on both banks of the river. Their leaves will not wither, nor will their fruit fail. Every month they will bear, because the water from the sanctuary flows to them. Their fruit will serve for food and their leaves for healing."

The Boundaries of the Land

[13]This is what the Sovereign LORD says: "These are the boundaries by which you are to divide the land for an inheritance among the twelve tribes of Israel, with two portions for Joseph. [14]You are to divide it equally among them. Because I swore

d22 The meaning of the Hebrew for this word is uncertain.
a3 That is, about 1,500 feet (about 460 metres)   b8 Or the Jordan Valley   c8 That is, the Dead Sea
d10 That is, the Mediterranean; also in verses 15, 19 and 20

with uplifted hand to give it to your forefathers, this land will become your inheritance.

¹⁵"This is to be the boundary of the land:

"On the north side it will run from the Great Sea by the Hethlon road past Lebo*ᵉ* Hamath to Zedad, ¹⁶Berothah*ᶠ* and Sibraim (which lies on the border between Damascus and Hamath), as far as Hazer Hatticon, which is on the border of Hauran. ¹⁷The boundary will extend from the sea to Hazar Enan,*ᵍ* along the northern border of Damascus, with the border of Hamath to the north. This will be the north boundary.

¹⁸"On the east side the boundary will run between Hauran and Damascus, along the Jordan between Gilead and the land of Israel, to the eastern sea and as far as Tamar.*ʰ* This will be the east boundary.

¹⁹"On the south side it will run from Tamar as far as the waters of Meribah Kadesh, then along the Wadi ⌐of Egypt⌐ to the Great Sea. This will be the south boundary.

²⁰"On the west side, the Great Sea will be the boundary to a point opposite Lebo*ⁱ* Hamath. This will be the west boundary.

²¹"You are to distribute this land among yourselves according to the tribes of Israel. ²²You are to allot it as an inheritance for yourselves and for the aliens who have settled among you and who have children. You are to consider them as native-born Israelites; along with you they are to be allotted an inheritance among the tribes of Israel. ²³In whatever tribe the alien settles, there you are to give him his inheritance," declares the Sovereign LORD.

The Division of the Land

48 "These are the tribes, listed by name: At the northern frontier, Dan will have one portion; it will follow the Hethlon road to Lebo*ᵃ* Hamath; Hazar Enan and the northern border of Damascus next to Hamath will be part of its border from the east side to the west side.

²"Asher will have one portion; it will border the territory of Dan from east to west.

³"Naphtali will have one portion; it will border the territory of Asher from east to west.

⁴"Manasseh will have one portion; it will border the territory of Naphtali from east to west.

⁵"Ephraim will have one portion; it will border the territory of Manasseh from east to west.

⁶"Reuben will have one portion; it will border the territory of Ephraim from east to west.

⁷"Judah will have one portion; it will border the territory of Reuben from east to west.

⁸"Bordering the territory of Judah from east to west will be the portion you are to present as a special gift. It will be 25,000 cubits*ᵇ* wide, and its length from east to west will equal one of the tribal portions; the sanctuary will be in the centre of it.

⁹"The special portion you are to offer to the LORD will be 25,000 cubits long and 10,000 cubits*ᶜ* wide. ¹⁰This will be the sacred portion for the priests. It will be 25,000 cubits long on the north side, 10,000 cubits wide on the west side, 10,000 cubits wide on the east side and 25,000 cubits long on the south side. In the centre of it will be the sanctuary of the LORD. ¹¹This will be for the consecrated priests, the Zadokites, who were faithful in serving me and did not go astray as the Levites did when the Israelites went astray. ¹²It will be a special gift to them from the

*ᵉ*15 Or *past the entrance to*
*ᶠ*15, 16 See Septuagint and Ezekiel 48:1; Hebrew *road to go into Zedad,* ¹⁶*Hamath, Berothah*
*ᵍ*17 Hebrew *Enon,* a variant of *Enan*   *ʰ*18 Septuagint and Syriac; Hebrew *Israel. You will measure to the eastern sea*
*ⁱ*20 Or *opposite the entrance to*   *ᵃ*1 Or *to the entrance to*   *ᵇ*8 That is, about 7 miles (about 11 kilometres)
*ᶜ*9 That is, about 3 miles (about 5 kilometres)

sacred portion of the land, a most holy portion, bordering the territory of the Levites.

¹³"Alongside the territory of the priests, the Levites will have an allotment 25,000 cubits long and 10,000 cubits wide. Its total length will be 25,000 cubits and its width 10,000 cubits. ¹⁴They must not sell or exchange any of it. This is the best of the land, and must not pass into other hands, because it is holy to the LORD.

¹⁵"The remaining area, 5,000 cubits wide and 25,000 cubits long, will be for the common use of the city, for houses and for pasture-land. The city will be in the centre of it ¹⁶and will have these measurements: the north side 4,500 cubits, the south side 4,500 cubits, the east side 4,500 cubits, and the west side 4,500 cubits. ¹⁷The pasture-land for the city will be 250 cubits on the north, 250 cubits on the south, 250 cubits on the east, and 250 cubits on the west. ¹⁸What remains of the area, bordering on the sacred portion and running the length of it, will be 10,000 cubits on the east side and 10,000 cubits on the west side. Its produce will supply food for the workers of the city. ¹⁹The workers from the city who farm it will come from all the tribes of Israel. ²⁰The entire portion will be a square, 25,000 cubits on each side. As a special gift you will set aside the sacred portion, along with the property of the city.

²¹"What remains on both sides of the area formed by the sacred portion and the city property will belong to the prince. It will extend eastward from the 25,000 cubits of the sacred portion to the eastern border, and westward from the 25,000 cubits to the western border. Both these areas running the length of the tribal portions will belong to the prince, and the sacred portion with the temple sanctuary will be in the centre of them. ²²So the property of the Levites and the property of the city will lie in the centre of the area that belongs to the prince. The area belonging to the prince will lie between the border of Judah and the border of Benjamin.

²³"As for the rest of the tribes: Benjamin will have one portion; it will extend from the east side to the west side.

²⁴"Simeon will have one portion; it will border the territory of Benjamin from east to west.

²⁵"Issachar will have one portion; it will border the territory of Simeon from east to west.

²⁶"Zebulun will have one portion; it will border the territory of Issachar from east to west.

²⁷"Gad will have one portion; it will border the territory of Zebulun from east to west.

²⁸"The southern boundary of Gad will run south from Tamar to the waters of Meribah Kadesh, then along the Wadi ⌐of Egypt⌐ to the Great Sea.ᵈ

²⁹"This is the land you are to allot as an inheritance to the tribes of Israel, and these will be their portions," declares the Sovereign LORD.

The Gates of the City

³⁰"These will be the exits of the city: Beginning on the north side, which is 4,500 cubits long, ³¹the gates of the city will be named after the tribes of Israel. The three gates on the north side will be the gate of Reuben, the gate of Judah and the gate of Levi.

³²"On the east side, which is 4,500 cubits long, will be three gates: the gate of Joseph, the gate of Benjamin and the gate of Dan.

³³"On the south side, which measures 4,500 cubits, will be three gates: the gate of Simeon, the gate of Issachar and the gate of Zebulun.

³⁴"On the west side, which is 4,500 cubits long, will be three gates: the gate of Gad, the gate of Asher and the gate of Naphtali.

³⁵"The distance all around will be 18,000 cubits.

"And the name of the city from that time on will be:

THE LORD IS THERE."

---

d28 That is, the Mediterranean

Daniel

Daniel's Training in Babylon

1 In the third year of the reign of Jehoiakim king of Judah, Nebuchadnezzar king of Babylon came to Jerusalem and besieged it. ²And the Lord delivered Jehoiakim king of Judah into his hand, along with some of the articles from the temple of God. These he carried off to the temple of his god in Babylonia*ᵃ* and put in the treasure-house of his god.

³Then the king ordered Ashpenaz, chief of his court officials, to bring in some of the Israelites from the royal family and the nobility—⁴young men without any physical defect, handsome, showing aptitude for every kind of learning, well informed, quick to understand, and qualified to serve in the king's palace. He was to teach them the language and literature of the Babylonians.*ᵇ* ⁵The king assigned them a daily amount of food and wine from the king's table. They were to be trained for three years, and after that they were to enter the king's service.

⁶Among these were some from Judah: Daniel, Hananiah, Mishael and Azariah. ⁷The chief official gave them new names: to Daniel, the name Belteshazzar; to Hananiah, Shadrach; to Mishael, Meshach; and to Azariah, Abednego.

⁸But Daniel resolved not to defile himself with the royal food and wine, and he asked the chief official for permission not to defile himself in this way. ⁹Now God had caused the official to show favour and sympathy to Daniel, ¹⁰but the official told Daniel, "I am afraid of my lord the king, who has assigned your*ᶜ* food and drink. Why should he see you looking worse than the other young men of your age? The king would then have my head because of you."

¹¹Daniel then said to the guard whom the chief official had appointed over Daniel, Hananiah, Mishael and Azariah, ¹²"Please test your servants for ten days: Give us nothing but vegetables to eat and water to drink. ¹³Then compare our appearance with that of the young men who eat the royal food, and treat your servants in accordance with what you see." ¹⁴So he agreed to this and tested them for ten days.

¹⁵At the end of the ten days they looked healthier and better nourished than any of the young men who ate the royal food. ¹⁶So the guard took away their choice food and the wine they were to drink and gave them vegetables instead.

¹⁷To these four young men God gave knowledge and understanding of all kinds of literature and learning. And Daniel could understand visions and dreams of all kinds.

¹⁸At the end of the time set by the king to bring them in, the chief official presented them to Nebuchadnezzar. ¹⁹The king talked with them, and he found none equal to Daniel, Hananiah, Mishael and Azariah; so they entered the king's service. ²⁰In every matter of wisdom and understanding about which the king questioned them, he found them ten times

---

*ᵃ*2 Hebrew *Shinar*   *ᵇ*4 Or *Chaldeans*   *ᶜ*10 The Hebrew for *your* and *you* in this verse is plural.

better than all the magicians and enchanters in his whole kingdom.

²¹And Daniel remained there until the first year of King Cyrus.

Nebuchadnezzar's Dream

2 In the second year of his reign, Nebuchadnezzar had dreams; his mind was troubled and he could not sleep. ²So the king summoned the magicians, enchanters, sorcerers and astrologers*ᵃ* to tell him what he had dreamed. When they came in and stood before the king, ³he said to them, "I have had a dream that troubles me and I want to know what it means."*ᵇ*

⁴Then the astrologers answered the king in Aramaic,*ᶜ* "O king, live for ever! Tell your servants the dream, and we will interpret it."

⁵The king replied to the astrologers, "This is what I have firmly decided: If you do not tell me what my dream was and interpret it, I will have you cut into pieces and your houses turned into piles of rubble. ⁶But if you tell me the dream and explain it, you will receive from me gifts and rewards and great honour. So tell me the dream and interpret it for me."

⁷Once more they replied, "Let the king tell his servants the dream, and we will interpret it."

⁸Then the king answered, "I am certain that you are trying to gain time, because you realise that this is what I have firmly decided: ⁹If you do not tell me the dream, there is just one penalty for you. You have conspired to tell me misleading and wicked things, hoping the situation will change. So then, tell me the dream, and I will know that you can interpret it for me."

¹⁰The astrologers answered the king, "There is not a man on earth who can do what the king asks! No king, however great and mighty, has ever asked such a thing of any magician or enchanter or astrologer. ¹¹What the king asks is too difficult. No-one can reveal it to the king except the gods, and they do not live among men."

¹²This made the king so angry and furious that he ordered the execution of all the wise men of Babylon. ¹³So the decree was issued to put the wise men to death, and men were sent to look for Daniel and his friends to put them to death.

¹⁴When Arioch, the commander of the king's guard, had gone out to put to death the wise men of Babylon, Daniel spoke to him with wisdom and tact. ¹⁵He asked the king's officer, "Why did the king issue such a harsh decree?" Arioch then explained the matter to Daniel. ¹⁶At this, Daniel went in to the king and asked for time, so that he might interpret the dream for him.

¹⁷Then Daniel returned to his house and explained the matter to his friends Hananiah, Mishael and Azariah. ¹⁸He urged them to plead for mercy from the God of heaven concerning this mystery, so that he and his friends might not be executed with the rest of the wise men of Babylon. ¹⁹During the night the mystery was revealed to Daniel in a vision. Then Daniel praised the God of heaven ²⁰and said:

"Praise be to the name of God for ever
    and ever;
  wisdom and power are his.
²¹He changes times and seasons;
  he sets up kings and deposes them.
He gives wisdom to the wise
  and knowledge to the discerning.
²²He reveals deep and hidden things;
  he knows what lies in darkness,
  and light dwells with him.
²³I thank and praise you, O God of my
    fathers:
  You have given me wisdom and
    power,
you have made known to me what we
    asked of you,
  you have made known to us the
    dream of the king."

Daniel Interprets the Dream

²⁴Then Daniel went to Arioch, whom the king had appointed to execute the wise men of Babylon, and said to him, "Do not execute the wise men of Babylon. Take

---

*ᵃ*2 Or *Chaldeans*; also in verses 4, 5 and 10   *ᵇ*3 Or *was*   *ᶜ*4 The text from here through chapter 7 is in Aramaic.

me to the king, and I will interpret his dream for him."

25Arioch took Daniel to the king at once and said, "I have found a man among the exiles from Judah who can tell the king what his dream means."

26The king asked Daniel (also called Belteshazzar), "Are you able to tell me what I saw in my dream and interpret it?"

27Daniel replied, "No wise man, enchanter, magician or diviner can explain to the king the mystery he has asked about, 28but there is a God in heaven who reveals mysteries. He has shown King Nebuchadnezzar what will happen in days to come. Your dream and the visions that passed through your mind as you lay on your bed are these:

29"As you were lying there, O king, your mind turned to things to come, and the revealer of mysteries showed you what is going to happen. 30As for me, this mystery has been revealed to me, not because I have greater wisdom than other living men, but so that you, O king, may know the interpretation and that you may understand what went through your mind.

31"You looked, O king, and there before you stood a large statue—an enormous, dazzling statue, awesome in appearance. 32The head of the statue was made of pure gold, its chest and arms of silver, its belly and thighs of bronze, 33its legs of iron, its feet partly of iron and partly of baked clay. 34While you were watching, a rock was cut out, but not by human hands. It struck the statue on its feet of iron and clay and smashed them. 35Then the iron, the clay, the bronze, the silver and the gold were broken to pieces at the same time and became like chaff on a threshing-floor in the summer. The wind swept them away without leaving a trace. But the rock that struck the statue became a huge mountain and filled the whole earth.

36"This was the dream, and now we will interpret it to the king. 37You, O king, are the king of kings. The God of heaven has given you dominion and power and might and glory; 38in your hands he has placed mankind and the beasts of the field and the birds of the air. Wherever they live, he has made you ruler over them all. You are that head of gold.

39"After you, another kingdom will rise, inferior to yours. Next, a third kingdom, one of bronze, will rule over the whole earth. 40Finally, there will be a fourth kingdom, strong as iron—for iron breaks and smashes everything—and as iron breaks things to pieces, so it will crush and break all the others. 41Just as you saw that the feet and toes were partly of baked clay and partly of iron, so this will be a divided kingdom; yet it will have some of the strength of iron in it, even as you saw iron mixed with clay. 42As the toes were partly iron and partly clay, so this kingdom will be partly strong and partly brittle. 43And just as you saw the iron mixed with baked clay, so the people will be a mixture and will not remain united, any more than iron mixes with clay.

44"In the time of those kings, the God of heaven will set up a kingdom that will never be destroyed, nor will it be left to another people. It will crush all those kingdoms and bring them to an end, but it will itself endure for ever. 45This is the meaning of the vision of the rock cut out of a mountain, but not by human hands—a rock that broke the iron, the bronze, the clay, the silver and the gold to pieces.

"The great God has shown the king what will take place in the future. The dream is true and the interpretation is trustworthy."

46Then King Nebuchadnezzar fell prostrate before Daniel and paid him honour and ordered that an offering and incense be presented to him. 47The king said to Daniel, "Surely your God is the God of gods and the Lord of kings and a revealer of mysteries, for you were able to reveal this mystery."

48Then the king placed Daniel in a high position and lavished many gifts on him. He made him ruler over the entire province of Babylon and placed him in charge of all its wise men. 49Moreover, at Daniel's request the king appointed Shadrach, Meshach and Abednego administrators over the province of Babylon, while Daniel himself remained at the royal court.

The Image of Gold and the Fiery Furnace

3 King Nebuchadnezzar made an image of gold, ninety feet high and nine feet[a] wide, and set it up on the plain of Dura in the province of Babylon. ²He then summoned the satraps, prefects, governors, advisers, treasurers, judges, magistrates and all the other provincial officials to come to the dedication of the image he had set up. ³So the satraps, prefects, governors, advisers, treasurers, judges, magistrates and all the other provincial officials assembled for the dedication of the image that King Nebuchadnezzar had set up, and they stood before it.

⁴Then the herald loudly proclaimed, "This is what you are commanded to do, O peoples, nations and men of every language: ⁵As soon as you hear the sound of the horn, flute, zither, lyre, harp, pipes and all kinds of music, you must fall down and worship the image of gold that King Nebuchadnezzar has set up. ⁶Whoever does not fall down and worship will immediately be thrown into a blazing furnace."

⁷Therefore, as soon as they heard the sound of the horn, flute, zither, lyre, harp and all kinds of music, all the peoples, nations and men of every language fell down and worshipped the image of gold that King Nebuchadnezzar had set up.

⁸At this time some astrologers[b] came forward and denounced the Jews. ⁹They said to King Nebuchadnezzar, "O king, live for ever! ¹⁰You have issued a decree, O king, that everyone who hears the sound of the horn, flute, zither, lyre, harp, pipes and all kinds of music must fall down and worship the image of gold, ¹¹and that whoever does not fall down and worship will be thrown into a blazing furnace. ¹²But there are some Jews whom you have set over the affairs of the province of Babylon—Shadrach, Meshach and Abednego—who pay no attention to you, O king. They neither serve your gods nor worship the image of gold you have set up."

¹³Furious with rage, Nebuchadnezzar summoned Shadrach, Meshach and Abednego. So these men were brought before the king, ¹⁴and Nebuchadnezzar said to them, "Is it true, Shadrach, Meshach and Abednego, that you do not serve my gods or worship the image of gold I have set up? ¹⁵Now when you hear the sound of the horn, flute, zither, lyre, harp, pipes and all kinds of music, if you are ready to fall down and worship the image I made, very good. But if you do not worship it, you will be thrown immediately into a blazing furnace. Then what god will be able to rescue you from my hand?"

¹⁶Shadrach, Meshach and Abednego replied to the king, "O Nebuchadnezzar, we do not need to defend ourselves before you in this matter. ¹⁷If we are thrown into the blazing furnace, the God we serve is able to save us from it, and he will rescue us from your hand, O king. ¹⁸But even if he does not, we want you to know, O king, that we will not serve your gods or worship the image of gold you have set up."

¹⁹Then Nebuchadnezzar was furious with Shadrach, Meshach and Abednego, and his attitude towards them changed. He ordered the furnace to be heated seven times hotter than usual ²⁰and commanded some of the strongest soldiers in his army to tie up Shadrach, Meshach and Abednego and throw them into the blazing furnace. ²¹So these men, wearing their robes, trousers, turbans and other clothes, were bound and thrown into the blazing furnace. ²²The king's command was so urgent and the furnace so hot that the flames of the fire killed the soldiers who took up Shadrach, Meshach and Abednego, ²³and these three men, firmly tied, fell into the blazing furnace.

²⁴Then King Nebuchadnezzar leaped to his feet in amazement and asked his advisers, "Weren't there three men that we tied up and threw into the fire?"

They replied, "Certainly, O king."

²⁵He said, "Look! I see four men walking around in the fire, unbound and unharmed, and the fourth looks like a son of the gods."

---

a1 Aramaic *sixty cubits high and six cubits wide* (about 27 metres high and 2.7 metres wide)   *b8* Or *Chaldeans*

²⁶Nebuchadnezzar then approached the opening of the blazing furnace and shouted, "Shadrach, Meshach and Abednego, servants of the Most High God, come out! Come here!"

So Shadrach, Meshach and Abednego came out of the fire, ²⁷and the satraps, prefects, governors and royal advisers crowded around them. They saw that the fire had not harmed their bodies, nor was a hair of their heads singed; their robes were not scorched, and there was no smell of fire on them.

²⁸Then Nebuchadnezzar said, "Praise be to the God of Shadrach, Meshach and Abednego, who has sent his angel and rescued his servants! They trusted in him and defied the king's command and were willing to give up their lives rather than serve or worship any god except their own God. ²⁹Therefore I decree that the people of any nation or language who say anything against the God of Shadrach, Meshach and Abednego be cut into pieces and their houses be turned into piles of rubble, for no other god can save in this way."

³⁰Then the king promoted Shadrach, Meshach and Abednego in the province of Babylon.

Nebuchadnezzar's Dream of a Tree

4 King Nebuchadnezzar,

To the peoples, nations and men of every language, who live in all the world:

May you prosper greatly!

²It is my pleasure to tell you about the miraculous signs and wonders that the Most High God has performed for me.

3 How great are his signs,
      how mighty his wonders!
   His kingdom is an eternal kingdom;
      his dominion endures from
         generation to generation.

⁴I, Nebuchadnezzar, was at home in my palace, contented and prosperous. ⁵I had a dream that made me afraid. As I was lying in my bed, the images and visions that passed through my mind terrified me. ⁶So I commanded that all the wise men of Babylon be brought before me to interpret the dream for me. ⁷When the magicians, enchanters, astrologers*ᵃ* and diviners came, I told them the dream, but they could not interpret it for me. ⁸Finally, Daniel came into my presence and I told him the dream. (He is called Belteshazzar, after the name of my god, and the spirit of the holy gods is in him.)

⁹I said, "Belteshazzar, chief of the magicians, I know that the spirit of the holy gods is in you, and no mystery is too difficult for you. Here is my dream; interpret it for me. ¹⁰These are the visions I saw while lying in my bed: I looked, and there before me stood a tree in the middle of the land. Its height was enormous. ¹¹The tree grew large and strong and its top touched the sky; it was visible to the ends of the earth. ¹²Its leaves were beautiful, its fruit abundant, and on it was food for all. Under it the beasts of the field found shelter, and the birds of the air lived in its branches; from it every creature was fed.

¹³"In the visions I saw while lying in my bed, I looked, and there before me was a messenger,*ᵇ* a holy one, coming down from heaven. ¹⁴He called ed in a loud voice: 'Cut down the tree and trim off its branches; strip off its leaves and scatter its fruit. Let the animals flee from under it and the birds from its branches. ¹⁵But let the stump and its roots, bound with iron and bronze, remain in the ground, in the grass of the field.

"'Let him be drenched with the dew of heaven, and let him live with the animals among the plants of the earth. ¹⁶Let his mind be changed from that of a man and let him be given the

---

ᵃ7 Or *Chaldeans*   ᵇ13 Or *watchman*; also in verses 17 and 23 mind of an animal, till seven times[c] pass by for him.

[17]"'The decision is announced by messengers, the holy ones declare the verdict, so that the living may know that the Most High is sovereign over the kingdoms of men and gives them to anyone he wishes and sets over them the lowliest of men.'

[18]"This is the dream that I, King Nebuchadnezzar, had. Now, Belteshazzar, tell me what it means, for none of the wise men in my kingdom can interpret it for me. But you can, because the spirit of the holy gods is in you."

Daniel Interprets the Dream

[19]Then Daniel (also called Belteshazzar) was greatly perplexed for a time, and his thoughts terrified him. So the king said, "Belteshazzar, do not let the dream or its meaning alarm you."

Belteshazzar answered, "My lord, if only the dream applied to your enemies and its meaning to your adversaries! [20]The tree you saw, which grew large and strong, with its top touching the sky, visible to the whole earth, [21]with beautiful leaves and abundant fruit, providing food for all, giving shelter to the beasts of the field, and having nesting places in its branches for the birds of the air— [22]you, O king, are that tree! You have become great and strong; your greatness has grown until it reaches the sky, and your dominion extends to distant parts of the earth.

[23]"You, O king, saw a messenger, a holy one, coming down from heaven and saying, 'Cut down the tree and destroy it, but leave the stump, bound with iron and bronze, in the grass of the field, while its roots remain in the ground. Let him be drenched with the dew of heaven; let him live like the wild animals, until seven times pass by for him.'

[24]"This is the interpretation, O king, and this is the decree the Most High has issued against my lord the king: [25]You will be driven away from people and will live with the wild animals; you will eat grass like cattle and be drenched with the dew of heaven. Seven times will pass by for you until you acknowledge that the Most High is sovereign over the kingdoms of men and gives them to anyone he wishes. [26]The command to leave the stump of the tree with its roots means that your kingdom will be restored to you when you acknowledge that Heaven rules. [27]Therefore, O king, be pleased to accept my advice: Renounce your sins by doing what is right, and your wickedness by being kind to the oppressed. It may be that then your prosperity will continue."

The Dream Is Fulfilled

[28]All this happened to King Nebuchadnezzar. [29]Twelve months later, as the king was walking on the roof of the royal palace of Babylon, [30]he said, "Is not this the great Babylon I have built as the royal residence, by my mighty power and for the glory of my majesty?"

[31]The words were still on his lips when a voice came from heaven, "This is what is decreed for you, King Nebuchadnezzar: Your royal authority has been taken from you. [32]You will be driven away from people and will live with the wild animals; you will eat grass like cattle. Seven times will pass by for you until you acknowledge that the Most High is sovereign over the kingdoms of men and gives them to anyone he wishes."

[33]Immediately what had been said about Nebuchadnezzar was fulfilled. He was driven away from people and ate grass like cattle. His body was drenched with the dew of heaven until his hair grew like the feathers of an

[c]16 Or years; also in verses 23, 25 and 32

eagle and his nails like the claws of a bird.

³⁴At the end of that time, I, Nebuchadnezzar, raised my eyes towards heaven, and my sanity was restored. Then I praised the Most High; I honoured and glorified him who lives for ever.

His dominion is an eternal dominion;
his kingdom endures from
generation to generation.
³⁵ All the peoples of the earth
are regarded as nothing.
He does as he pleases
with the powers of heaven
and the peoples of the earth.
No-one can hold back his hand
or say to him: "What have you
done?"

³⁶At the same time that my sanity was restored, my honour and splendour were returned to me for the glory of my kingdom. My advisers and nobles sought me out, and I was restored to my throne and became even greater than before. ³⁷Now I, Nebuchadnezzar, praise and exalt and glorify the King of heaven, because everything he does is right and all his ways are just. And those who walk in pride he is able to humble.

The Writing on the Wall

5 King Belshazzar gave a great banquet for a thousand of his nobles and drank wine with them. ²While Belshazzar was drinking his wine, he gave orders to bring in the gold and silver goblets that Nebuchadnezzar his father*a* had taken from the temple in Jerusalem, so that the king and his nobles, his wives and his concubines might drink from them. ³So they brought in the gold goblets that had been taken from the temple of God in Jerusalem, and the king and his nobles, his wives and his concubines drank from them. ⁴As they drank the wine, they praised the gods of gold and silver, of bronze, iron, wood and stone.

⁵Suddenly the fingers of a human hand appeared and wrote on the plaster of the wall, near the lampstand in the royal palace. The king watched the hand as it wrote. ⁶His face turned pale and he was so frightened that his knees knocked together and his legs gave way.

⁷The king called out for the enchanters, astrologers*b* and diviners to be brought and said to these wise men of Babylon, "Whoever reads this writing and tells me what it means will be clothed in purple and have a gold chain placed around his neck, and he will be made the third highest ruler in the kingdom."

⁸Then all the king's wise men came in, but they could not read the writing or tell the king what it meant. ⁹So King Belshazzar became even more terrified and his face grew more pale. His nobles were baffled.

¹⁰The queen,*c* hearing the voices of the king and his nobles, came into the banquet hall. "O king, live for ever!" she said. "Don't be alarmed! Don't look so pale! ¹¹There is a man in your kingdom who has the spirit of the holy gods in him. In the time of your father he was found to have insight and intelligence and wisdom like that of the gods. King Nebuchadnezzar your father—your father the king, I say—appointed him chief of the magicians, enchanters, astrologers and diviners. ¹²This man Daniel, whom the king called Belteshazzar, was found to have a keen mind and knowledge and understanding, and also the ability to interpret dreams, explain riddles and solve difficult problems. Call for Daniel, and he will tell you what the writing means."

¹³So Daniel was brought before the king, and the king said to him, "Are you Daniel, one of the exiles my father the king brought from Judah? ¹⁴I have heard that the spirit of the gods is in you and that you have insight, intelligence and outstanding wisdom. ¹⁵The wise men and enchanters were brought before me to read this writing and tell me what it means, but

---

a2 Or *ancestor*; or *predecessor*; also in verses 11, 13 and 18   *b7* Or *Chaldeans*; also in verse 11
c10 Or *queen mother*

they could not explain it. ¹⁶Now I have heard that you are able to give interpretations and to solve difficult problems. If you can read this writing and tell me what it means, you will be clothed in purple and have a gold chain placed around your neck, and you will be made the third highest ruler in the kingdom."

¹⁷Then Daniel answered the king, "You may keep your gifts for yourself and give your rewards to someone else. Nevertheless, I will read the writing for the king and tell him what it means.

¹⁸"O king, the Most High God gave your father Nebuchadnezzar sovereignty and greatness and glory and splendour. ¹⁹Because of the high position he gave him, all the peoples and nations and men of every language dreaded and feared him. Those the king wanted to put to death, he put to death; those he wanted to spare, he spared; those he wanted to promote, he promoted; and those he wanted to humble, he humbled. ²⁰But when his heart became arrogant and hardened with pride, he was deposed from his royal throne and stripped of his glory. ²¹He was driven away from people and given the mind of an animal; he lived with the wild donkeys and ate grass like cattle; and his body was drenched with the dew of heaven, until he acknowledged that the Most High God is sovereign over the kingdoms of men and sets over them anyone he wishes.

²²"But you his son,*d* O Belshazzar, have not humbled yourself, though you knew all this. ²³Instead, you have set yourself up against the Lord of heaven. You had the goblets from his temple brought to you, and you and your nobles, your wives and your concubines drank wine from them. You praised the gods of silver and gold, of bronze, iron, wood and stone, which cannot see or hear or understand. But you did not honour the God who holds in his hand your life and all your ways. ²⁴Therefore he sent the hand that wrote the inscription.

²⁵"This is the inscription that was written:

MENE, MENE, TEKEL, PARSIN*e*

²⁶"This is what these words mean:

Mene f: God has numbered the days of your reign and brought it to an end.
²⁷*Tekel g*: You have been weighed on the scales and found wanting.
²⁸*Peres h*: Your kingdom is divided and given to the Medes and Persians."

²⁹Then at Belshazzar's command, Daniel was clothed in purple, a gold chain was placed around his neck, and he was proclaimed the third highest ruler in the kingdom. ³⁰That very night Belshazzar, king of the Babylonians,*i* was slain, ³¹and Darius the Mede took over the kingdom, at the age of sixty-two.

Daniel in the Den of Lions

6 It pleased Darius to appoint 120 satraps to rule throughout the kingdom, ²with three administrators over them, one of whom was Daniel. The satraps were made accountable to them so that the king might not suffer loss. ³Now Daniel so distinguished himself among the administrators and the satraps by his exceptional qualities that the king planned to set him over the whole kingdom. ⁴At this, the administrators and the satraps tried to find grounds for charges against Daniel in his conduct of government affairs, but they were unable to do so. They could find no corruption in him, because he was trustworthy and neither corrupt nor negligent. ⁵Finally these men said, "We will never find any basis for charges against this man Daniel unless it has something to do with the law of his God."

---

d22 Or descendant; or successor   e25 Aramaic UPARSIN (that is, AND PARSIN)
f26 Mene can mean numbered or mina (a unit of money).   g27 Tekel can mean weighed or shekel.
h28 Peres (the singular of Parsin) can mean divided or Persia or a half mina or a half shekel.   i30 Or Chaldeans

[6]So the administrators and the satraps went as a group to the king and said: "O King Darius, live for ever! [7]The royal administrators, prefects, satraps, advisers and governors have all agreed that the king should issue an edict and enforce the decree that anyone who prays to any god or man during the next thirty days, except to you, O king, shall be thrown into the lions' den. [8]Now, O king, issue the decree and put it in writing so that it cannot be altered—in accordance with the laws of the Medes and Persians, which cannot be repealed." [9]So King Darius put the decree in writing.

[10]Now when Daniel learned that the decree had been published, he went home to his upstairs room where the windows opened towards Jerusalem. Three times a day he got down on his knees and prayed, giving thanks to his God, just as he had done before. [11]Then these men went as a group and found Daniel praying and asking God for help. [12]So they went to the king and spoke to him about his royal decree: "Did you not publish a decree that during the next thirty days anyone who prays to any god or man except to you, O king, would be thrown into the lions' den?"

The king answered, "The decree stands—in accordance with the laws of the Medes and Persians, which cannot be repealed."

[13]Then they said to the king, "Daniel, who is one of the exiles from Judah, pays no attention to you, O king, or to the decree you put in writing. He still prays three times a day." [14]When the king heard this, he was greatly distressed; he was determined to rescue Daniel and made every effort until sundown to save him.

[15]Then the men went as a group to the king and said to him, "Remember, O king, that according to the law of the Medes and Persians no decree or edict that the king issues can be changed."

[16]So the king gave the order, and they brought Daniel and threw him into the lions' den. The king said to Daniel, "May your God, whom you serve continually, rescue you!"

[17]A stone was brought and placed over the mouth of the den, and the king sealed it with his own signet ring and with the rings of his nobles, so that Daniel's situation might not be changed. [18]Then the king returned to his palace and spent the night without eating and without any entertainment being brought to him. And he could not sleep.

[19]At the first light of dawn, the king got up and hurried to the lions' den. [20]When he came near the den, he called to Daniel in an anguished voice, "Daniel, servant of the living God, has your God, whom you serve continually, been able to rescue you from the lions?"

[21]Daniel answered, "O king, live for ever! [22]My God sent his angel, and he shut the mouths of the lions. They have not hurt me, because I was found innocent in his sight. Nor have I ever done any wrong before you, O king."

[23]The king was overjoyed and gave orders to lift Daniel out of the den. And when Daniel was lifted from the den, no wound was found on him, because he had trusted in his God.

[24]At the king's command, the men who had falsely accused Daniel were brought in and thrown into the lions' den, along with their wives and children. And before they reached the floor of the den, the lions overpowered them and crushed all their bones.

[25]Then King Darius wrote to all the peoples, nations and men of every language throughout the land:

"May you prosper greatly!

[26]"I issue a decree that in every part of my kingdom people must fear and reverence the God of Daniel.

"For he is the living God
and he endures for ever;
his kingdom will not be destroyed,
his dominion will never end.
[27] He rescues and he saves;
he performs signs and wonders
in the heavens and on the earth.
He has rescued Daniel
from the power of the lions."

28So Daniel prospered during the reign of Darius and the reign of Cyrus[a] the Persian.

Daniel's Dream of Four Beasts

7 In the first year of Belshazzar king of Babylon, Daniel had a dream, and visions passed through his mind as he was lying on his bed. He wrote down the substance of his dream.

2Daniel said: "In my vision at night I looked, and there before me were the four winds of heaven churning up the great sea. 3Four great beasts, each different from the others, came up out of the sea.

4"The first was like a lion, and it had the wings of an eagle. I watched until its wings were torn off and it was lifted from the ground so that it stood on two feet like a man, and the heart of a man was given to it.

5"And there before me was a second beast, which looked like a bear. It was raised up on one of its sides, and it had three ribs in its mouth between its teeth. It was told, 'Get up and eat your fill of flesh!'

6"After that, I looked, and there before me was another beast, one that looked like a leopard. And on its back it had four wings like those of a bird. This beast had four heads, and it was given authority to rule.

7"After that, in my vision at night I looked, and there before me was a fourth beast—terrifying and frightening and very powerful. It had large iron teeth; it crushed and devoured its victims and trampled underfoot whatever was left. It was different from all the former beasts, and it had ten horns.

8"While I was thinking about the horns, there before me was another horn, a little one, which came up among them; and three of the first horns were uprooted before it. This horn had eyes like the eyes of a man and a mouth that spoke boastfully.

9"As I looked,

"thrones were set in place,

and the Ancient of Days took his seat.
His clothing was as white as snow;
    the hair of his head was white like wool.
His throne was flaming with fire,
    and its wheels were all ablaze.
10A river of fire was flowing,
    coming out from before him.
Thousands upon thousands attended him;
    ten thousand times ten thousand stood before him.
The court was seated,
    and the books were opened.

11"Then I continued to watch because of the boastful words the horn was speaking. I kept looking until the beast was slain and its body destroyed and thrown into the blazing fire. 12(The other beasts had been stripped of their authority, but were allowed to live for a period of time.)

13"In my vision at night I looked, and there before me was one like a son of man, coming with the clouds of heaven. He approached the Ancient of Days and was led into his presence. 14He was given authority, glory and sovereign power; all peoples, nations and men of every language worshipped him. His dominion is an everlasting dominion that will not pass away, and his kingdom is one that will never be destroyed.

The Interpretation of the Dream

15"I, Daniel, was troubled in spirit, and the visions that passed through my mind disturbed me. 16I approached one of those standing there and asked him the true meaning of all this.

"So he told me and gave me the interpretation of these things: 17'The four great beasts are four kingdoms that will rise from the earth. 18But the saints of the Most High will receive the kingdom and will possess it for ever—yes, for ever and ever.'

19"Then I wanted to know the true meaning of the fourth beast, which was

a28 Or Darius, that is, the reign of Cyrus

different from all the others and most terrifying, with its iron teeth and bronze claws—the beast that crushed and devoured its victims and trampled underfoot whatever was left. ²⁰I also wanted to know about the ten horns on its head and about the other horn that came up, before which three of them fell—the horn that looked more imposing than the others and that had eyes and a mouth that spoke boastfully. ²¹As I watched, this horn was waging war against the saints and defeating them, ²²until the Ancient of Days came and pronounced judgment in favour of the saints of the Most High, and the time came when they possessed the kingdom.

²³"He gave me this explanation: 'The fourth beast is a fourth kingdom that will appear on earth. It will be different from all the other kingdoms and will devour the whole earth, trampling it down and crushing it. ²⁴The ten horns are ten kings who will come from this kingdom. After them another king will arise, different from the earlier ones; he will subdue three kings. ²⁵He will speak against the Most High and oppress his saints and try to change the set times and the laws. The saints will be handed over to him for a time, times and half a time.^{*a*}

²⁶"'But the court will sit, and his power will be taken away and completely destroyed for ever. ²⁷Then the sovereignty, power and greatness of the kingdoms under the whole heaven will be handed over to the saints, the people of the Most High. His kingdom will be an everlasting kingdom, and all rulers will worship and obey him.'

²⁸"This is the end of the matter. I, Daniel, was deeply troubled by my thoughts, and my face turned pale, but I kept the matter to myself."

Daniel's Vision of a Ram and a Goat

8 In the third year of King Belshazzar's reign, I, Daniel, had a vision, after the one that had already appeared to me. ²In my vision I saw myself in the citadel of Susa in the province of Elam; in the vision I was beside the Ulai Canal. ³I looked up, and there before me was a ram with two horns, standing beside the canal, and the horns were long. One of the horns was longer than the other but grew up later. ⁴I watched the ram as he charged towards the west and the north and the south. No animal could stand against him, and none could rescue from his power. He did as he pleased and became great.

⁵As I was thinking about this, suddenly a goat with a prominent horn between his eyes came from the west, crossing the whole earth without touching the ground. ⁶He came towards the two-horned ram I had seen standing beside the canal and charged at him in great rage. ⁷I saw him attack the ram furiously, striking the ram and shattering his two horns. The ram was powerless to stand against him; the goat knocked him to the ground and trampled on him, and none could rescue the ram from his power. ⁸The goat became very great, but at the height of his power his large horn was broken off, and in its place four prominent horns grew up towards the four winds of heaven.

⁹Out of one of them came another horn, which started small but grew in power to the south and to the east and towards the Beautiful Land. ¹⁰It grew until it reached the host of the heavens, and it threw some of the starry host down to the earth and trampled on them. ¹¹It set itself up to be as great as the Prince of the host; it took away the daily sacrifice from him, and the place of his sanctuary was brought low. ¹²Because of rebellion, the host ⌊of the saints⌋^{*a*} and the daily sacrifice were given over to it. It prospered in everything it did, and truth was thrown to the ground.

¹³Then I heard a holy one speaking, and another holy one said to him, "How long will it take for the vision to be fulfilled—the vision concerning the daily sacrifice, the rebellion that causes desolation, and the surrender of the sanctuary and of the host that will be trampled underfoot?"

¹⁴He said to me, "It will take 2,300 evenings and mornings; then the sanctuary will be reconsecrated."

^a25 Or for a year, two years and half a year   ^a12 Or rebellion, the armies

The Interpretation of the Vision

[15]While I, Daniel, was watching the vision and trying to understand it, there before me stood one who looked like a man. [16]And I heard a man's voice from the Ulai calling, "Gabriel, tell this man the meaning of the vision."

[17]As he came near the place where I was standing, I was terrified and fell prostrate. "Son of man," he said to me, "understand that the vision concerns the time of the end."

[18]While he was speaking to me, I was in a deep sleep, with my face to the ground. Then he touched me and raised me to my feet.

[19]He said: "I am going to tell you what will happen later in the time of wrath, because the vision concerns the appointed time of the end.[b] [20]The two-horned ram that you saw represents the kings of Media and Persia. [21]The shaggy goat is the king of Greece, and the large horn between his eyes is the first king. [22]The four horns that replaced the one that was broken off represent four kingdoms that will emerge from his nation but will not have the same power.

[23]"In the latter part of their reign, when rebels have become completely wicked, a stern-faced king, a master of intrigue, will arise. [24]He will become very strong, but not by his own power. He will cause astounding devastation and will succeed in whatever he does. He will destroy the mighty men and the holy people. [25]He will cause deceit to prosper, and he will consider himself superior. When they feel secure, he will destroy many and take his stand against the Prince of princes. Yet he will be destroyed, but not by human power.

[26]"The vision of the evenings and mornings that has been given you is true, but seal up the vision, for it concerns the distant future."

[27]I, Daniel, was exhausted and lay ill for several days. Then I got up and went about the king's business. I was appalled by the vision; it was beyond understanding.

Daniel's Prayer

9 In the first year of Darius son of Xerxes[a] (a Mede by descent), who was made ruler over the Babylonian[b] kingdom— [2]in the first year of his reign, I, Daniel, understood from the Scriptures, according to the word of the LORD given to Jeremiah the prophet, that the desolation of Jerusalem would last seventy years. [3]So I turned to the Lord God and pleaded with him in prayer and petition, in fasting, and in sackcloth and ashes.

[4]I prayed to the LORD my God and confessed:

"O Lord, the great and awesome God, who keeps his covenant of love with all who love him and obey his commands, [5]we have sinned and done wrong. We have been wicked and have rebelled; we have turned away from your commands and laws. [6]We have not listened to your servants the prophets, who spoke in your name to our kings, our princes and our fathers, and to all the people of the land.

[7]"Lord, you are righteous, but this day we are covered with shame—the men of Judah and people of Jerusalem and all Israel, both near and far, in all the countries where you have scattered us because of our unfaithfulness to you. [8]O LORD, we and our kings, our princes and our fathers are covered with shame because we have sinned against you. [9]The Lord our God is merciful and forgiving, even though we have rebelled against him; [10]we have not obeyed the LORD our God or kept the laws he gave us through his servants the prophets. [11]All Israel has transgressed your law and turned away, refusing to obey you.

"Therefore the curses and sworn judgments written in the Law of Moses, the servant of God, have been poured out on us, because we have sinned against you. [12]You have

---

b19 Or *because the end will be at the appointed time*   *a1* Hebrew *Ahasuerus*   *b1* Or *Chaldean* fulfilled the words spoken against us and against our rulers by bringing upon us great disaster. Under the whole heaven nothing has ever been done like what has been done to Jerusalem. [13]Just as it is written in the Law of Moses, all this disaster has come upon us, yet we have not sought the favour of the LORD our God by turning from our sins and giving attention to your truth. [14]The LORD did not hesitate to bring the disaster upon us, for the LORD our God is righteous in everything he does; yet we have not obeyed him.

[15]"Now, O Lord our God, who brought your people out of Egypt with a mighty hand and who made for yourself a name that endures to this day, we have sinned, we have done wrong. [16]O Lord, in keeping with all your righteous acts, turn away your anger and your wrath from Jerusalem, your city, your holy hill. Our sins and the iniquities of our fathers have made Jerusalem and your people an object of scorn to all those around us.

[17]"Now, our God, hear the prayers and petitions of your servant. For your sake, O Lord, look with favour on your desolate sanctuary. [18]Give ear, O God, and hear; open your eyes and see the desolation of the city that bears your Name. We do not make requests of you because we are righteous, but because of your great mercy. [19]O Lord, listen! O Lord, forgive! O Lord, hear and act! For your sake, O my God, do not delay, because your city and your people bear your Name."

The Seventy "Sevens"

[20]While I was speaking and praying, confessing my sin and the sin of my people Israel and making my request to the LORD my God for his holy hill—[21]while I was still in prayer, Gabriel, the man I had seen in the earlier vision, came to me in swift flight about the time of the evening sacrifice. [22]He instructed me and said to me, "Daniel, I have now come to give you insight and understanding. [23]As soon as you began to pray, an answer was given, which I have come to tell you, for you are highly esteemed. Therefore, consider the message and understand the vision:

[24]"Seventy 'sevens'[c] are decreed for your people and your holy city to finish[d] transgression, to put an end to sin, to atone for wickedness, to bring in everlasting righteousness, to seal up vision and prophecy and to anoint the most holy.[e]

[25]"Know and understand this: From the issuing of the decree[f] to restore and rebuild Jerusalem until the Anointed One,[g] the ruler, comes, there will be seven 'sevens', and sixty-two 'sevens'. It will be rebuilt with streets and a trench, but in times of trouble. [26]After the sixty-two 'sevens', the Anointed One will be cut off and will have nothing.[h] The people of the ruler who will come will destroy the city and the sanctuary. The end will come like a flood: War will continue until the end, and desolations have been decreed. [27]He will confirm a covenant with many for one 'seven'.[i] In the middle of the 'seven'[i] he will put an end to sacrifice and offering. And on a wing ⌊of the temple⌋ he will set up an abomination that causes desolation, until the end that is decreed is poured out on him.[j]"[k]

Daniel's Vision of a Man

10 In the third year of Cyrus king of Persia, a revelation was given to Daniel (who was called Belteshazzar). Its message was true and it concerned a great war.[a] The understanding of the message came to him in a vision.

[2]At that time I, Daniel, mourned for three weeks. [3]I ate no choice food; no

---

[c]24 Or 'weeks'; also in verses 25 and 26   [d]24 Or restrain   [e]24 Or Most Holy Place; or most holy One
[f]25 Or word   [g]25 Or an anointed one; also in verse 26
[h]26 Or off and will have no-one; or off, but not for himself   [i]27 Or 'week'   [i]27 Or it
[k]27 Or And one who causes desolation will come upon the pinnacle of the abominable ⌊temple⌋, until the end that is decreed is poured out on the desolated ⌊city⌋
[a]1 Or true and burdensome

meat or wine touched my lips; and I used no lotions at all until the three weeks were over.

⁴On the twenty-fourth day of the first month, as I was standing on the bank of the great river, the Tigris, ⁵I looked up and there before me was a man dressed in linen, with a belt of the finest gold round his waist. ⁶His body was like chrysolite, his face like lightning, his eyes like flaming torches, his arms and legs like the gleam of burnished bronze, and his voice like the sound of a multitude.

⁷I, Daniel, was the only one who saw the vision; the men with me did not see it, but such terror overwhelmed them that they fled and hid themselves. ⁸So I was left alone, gazing at this great vision; I had no strength left, my face turned deathly pale and I was helpless. ⁹Then I heard him speaking, and as I listened to him, I fell into a deep sleep, my face to the ground.

¹⁰A hand touched me and set me trembling on my hands and knees. ¹¹He said, "Daniel, you who are highly esteemed, consider carefully the words I am about to speak to you, and stand up, for I have now been sent to you." And when he said this to me, I stood up trembling.

¹²Then he continued, "Do not be afraid, Daniel. Since the first day that you set your mind to gain understanding and to humble yourself before your God, your words were heard, and I have come in response to them. ¹³But the prince of the Persian kingdom resisted me twenty-one days. Then Michael, one of the chief princes, came to help me, because I was detained there with the king of Persia. ¹⁴Now I have come to explain to you what will happen to your people in the future, for the vision concerns a time yet to come."

¹⁵While he was saying this to me, I bowed with my face towards the ground and was speechless. ¹⁶Then one who looked like a manᵇ touched my lips, and I opened my mouth and began to speak. I said to the one standing before me, "I am overcome with anguish because of the vision, my lord, and I am helpless. ¹⁷How can I, your servant, talk with you, my lord? My strength is gone and I can hardly breathe."

¹⁸Again the one who looked like a man touched me and gave me strength. ¹⁹"Do not be afraid, O man highly esteemed," he said. "Peace! Be strong now; be strong."

When he spoke to me, I was strengthened and said, "Speak, my lord, since you have given me strength."

²⁰So he said, "Do you know why I have come to you? Soon I will return to fight against the prince of Persia, and when I go, the prince of Greece will come; ²¹but first I will tell you what is written in the Book of Truth. (No-one supports me against them except Michael, your prince. ¹And in the first year of Darius the Mede, I took my stand to support and protect him.)

The Kings of the South and the North

²"Now then, I tell you the truth: Three more kings will appear in Persia, and then a fourth, who will be far richer than all the others. When he has gained power by his wealth, he will stir up everyone against the kingdom of Greece. ³Then a mighty king will appear, who will rule with great power and do as he pleases. ⁴After he has appeared, his empire will be broken up and parcelled out towards the four winds of heaven. It will not go to his descendants, nor will it have the power he exercised, because his empire will be uprooted and given to others.

⁵"The king of the South will become strong, but one of his commanders will become even stronger than he and will rule his own kingdom with great power. ⁶After some years, they will become allies. The daughter of the king of the South will go to the king of the North to make an alliance, but she will not retain her power, and he and his powerᵃ will not last. In those days she will be handed over, together with her royal escort and her fatherᵇ and the one who supported her. ⁷"One from her family line will arise to

---

ᵇ16 Most manuscripts of the Masoretic Text; one manuscript of the Masoretic Text, Dead Sea Scrolls and Septuagint *Then something that looked like a man's hand*   ᵃ6 Or *offspring*   ᵇ6 Or *child* (see Vulgate and Syriac) take her place. He will attack the forces of the king of the North and enter his fortress; he will fight against them and be victorious. [8]He will also seize their gods, their metal images and their valuable articles of silver and gold and carry them off to Egypt. For some years he will leave the king of the North alone. [9]Then the king of the North will invade the realm of the king of the South but will retreat to his own country. [10]His sons will prepare for war and assemble a great army, which will sweep on like an irresistible flood and carry the battle as far as his fortress.

[11]"Then the king of the South will march out in rage and fight against the king of the North, who will raise a large army, but it will be defeated. [12]When the army is carried off, the king of the South will be filled with pride and will slaughter many thousands, yet he will not remain triumphant. [13]For the king of the North will muster another army, larger than the first; and after several years, he will advance with a huge army fully equipped.

[14]"In those times many will rise against the king of the South. The violent men among your own people will rebel in fulfilment of the vision, but without success. [15]Then the king of the North will come and build up siege ramps and will capture a fortified city. The forces of the South will be powerless to resist; even their best troops will not have the strength to stand. [16]The invader will do as he pleases; no-one will be able to stand against him. He will establish himself in the Beautiful Land and will have the power to destroy it. [17]He will determine to come with the might of his entire kingdom and will make an alliance with the king of the South. And he will give him a daughter in marriage in order to overthrow the kingdom, but his plans[c] will not succeed or help him. [18]Then he will turn his attention to the coastlands and will take many of them, but a commander will put an end to his insolence and will turn his insolence back upon him. [19]After this, he will turn back towards the fortresses of his own country but will stumble and fall, to be seen no more.

[20]"His successor will send out a tax collector to maintain the royal splendour. In a few years, however, he will be destroyed, yet not in anger or in battle.

[21]"He will be succeeded by a contemptible person who has not been given the honour of royalty. He will invade the kingdom when its people feel secure, and he will seize it through intrigue. [22]Then an overwhelming army will be swept away before him; both it and a prince of the covenant will be destroyed. [23]After coming to an agreement with him, he will act deceitfully, and with only a few people he will rise to power. [24]When the richest provinces feel secure, he will invade them and will achieve what neither his fathers nor his forefathers did. He will distribute plunder, loot and wealth among his followers. He will plot the overthrow of fortresses—but only for a time.

[25]"With a large army he will stir up his strength and courage against the king of the South. The king of the South will wage war with a large and very powerful army, but he will not be able to stand because of the plots devised against him. [26]Those who eat from the king's provisions will try to destroy him; his army will be swept away, and many will fall in battle. [27]The two kings, with their hearts bent on evil, will sit at the same table and lie to each other, but to no avail, because an end will still come at the appointed time. [28]The king of the North will return to his own country with great wealth, but his heart will be set against the holy covenant. He will take action against it and then return to his own country.

[29]"At the appointed time he will invade the South again, but this time the outcome will be different from what it was before. [30]Ships of the western coastlands[d] will oppose him, and he will lose heart. Then he will turn back and vent his fury against the holy covenant. He will return and show favour to those who forsake the holy covenant.

[31]"His armed forces will rise up to desecrate the temple fortress and will abolish the daily sacrifice. Then they will set up

---

c17 Or *but she*   d30 Hebrew *of Kittim*

the abomination that causes desolation. ³²With flattery he will corrupt those who have violated the covenant, but the people who know their God will firmly resist him.

³³"Those who are wise will instruct many, though for a time they will fall by the sword or be burned or captured or plundered. ³⁴When they fall, they will receive a little help, and many who are not sincere will join them. ³⁵Some of the wise will stumble, so that they may be refined, purified and made spotless until the time of the end, for it will still come at the appointed time.

The King Who Exalts Himself

³⁶"The king will do as he pleases. He will exalt and magnify himself above every god and will say unheard-of things against the God of gods. He will be successful until the time of wrath is completed, for what has been determined must take place. ³⁷He will show no regard for the gods of his fathers or for the one desired by women, nor will he regard any god, but will exalt himself above them all. ³⁸Instead of them, he will honour a god of fortresses; a god unknown to his fathers he will honour with gold and silver, with precious stones and costly gifts. ³⁹He will attack the mightiest fortresses with the help of a foreign god and will greatly honour those who acknowledge him. He will make them rulers over many people and will distribute the land at a price.ᵉ

⁴⁰"At the time of the end the king of the South will engage him in battle, and the king of the North will storm out against him with chariots and cavalry and a great fleet of ships. He will invade many countries and sweep through them like a flood. ⁴¹He will also invade the Beautiful Land. Many countries will fall, but Edom, Moab and the leaders of Ammon will be delivered from his hand. ⁴²He will extend his power over many countries; Egypt will not escape. ⁴³He will gain control of the treasures of gold and silver and all the riches of Egypt, with the Libyans and Nubians in submission. ⁴⁴But reports from the east and the north will alarm him, and he will set out in a great rage to destroy and annihilate many. ⁴⁵He will pitch his royal tents between the seas atᶠ the beautiful holy mountain. Yet he will come to his end, and no-one will help him.

The End Times

12 "At that time Michael, the great prince who protects your people, will arise. There will be a time of distress such as has not happened from the beginning of nations until then. But at that time your people—everyone whose name is found written in the book—will be delivered. ²Multitudes who sleep in the dust of the earth will awake: some to everlasting life, others to shame and everlasting contempt. ³Those who are wiseᵃ will shine like the brightness of the heavens, and those who lead many to righteousness, like the stars for ever and ever. ⁴But you, Daniel, close up and seal the words of the scroll until the time of the end. Many will go here and there to increase knowledge."

⁵Then I, Daniel, looked, and there before me stood two others, one on this bank of the river and one on the opposite bank. ⁶One of them said to the man clothed in linen, who was above the waters of the river, "How long will it be before these astonishing things are fulfilled?"

⁷The man clothed in linen, who was above the waters of the river, lifted his right hand and his left hand towards heaven, and I heard him swear by him who lives for ever, saying, "It will be for a time, times and half a time.ᵇ When the power of the holy people has been finally broken, all these things will be completed."

⁸I heard, but I did not understand. So I asked, "My lord, what will the outcome of all this be?"

⁹He replied, "Go your way, Daniel,

ᵉ39 Or land for a reward   ᶠ45 Or the sea and   ᵃ3 Or who impart wisdom   ᵇ7 Or a year, two years and
half a year

because the words are closed up and sealed until the time of the end. [10]Many will be purified, made spotless and refined, but the wicked will continue to be wicked. None of the wicked will understand, but those who are wise will understand.

[11]"From the time that the daily sacrifice is abolished and the abomination that causes desolation is set up, there will be 1,290 days. [12]Blessed is the one who waits for and reaches the end of the 1,335 days.

[13]"As for you, go your way till the end. You will rest, and then at the end of the days you will rise to receive your allotted inheritance."

Hosea

1

¹ The word of the LORD that came to Hosea son of Beeri during the reigns of Uzziah, Jotham, Ahaz and Hezekiah, kings of Judah, and during the reign of Jeroboam son of Joash king of Israel:

Hosea's Wife and Children

²When the LORD began to speak through Hosea, the LORD said to him, "Go, take to yourself an adulterous wife and children of unfaithfulness, because the land is guilty of the vilest adultery in departing from the LORD." ³So he married Gomer daughter of Diblaim, and she conceived and bore him a son.

⁴Then the LORD said to Hosea, "Call him Jezreel, because I will soon punish the house of Jehu for the massacre at Jezreel, and I will put an end to the kingdom of Israel. ⁵In that day I will break Israel's bow in the Valley of Jezreel."

⁶Gomer conceived again and gave birth to a daughter. Then the LORD said to Hosea, "Call her Lo-Ruhamah,ᵃ for I will no longer show love to the house of Israel, that I should at all forgive them. ⁷Yet I will show love to the house of Judah; and I will save them—not by bow, sword or battle, or by horses and horsemen, but by the LORD their God."

⁸After she had weaned Lo-Ruhamah, Gomer had another son. ⁹Then the LORD said, "Call him Lo-Ammi,ᵇ for you are not my people, and I am not your God.

¹⁰"Yet the Israelites will be like the sand on the seashore, which cannot be measured or counted. In the place where it was said to them, 'You are not my people', they will be called 'sons of the living God'. ¹¹The people of Judah and the people of Israel will be reunited, and they will appoint one leader and will come up out of the land, for great will be the day of Jezreel.

2

"Say of your brothers, 'My people', and of your sisters, 'My loved one'.

Israel Punished and Restored

²"Rebuke your mother, rebuke her,
 for she is not my wife,
 and I am not her husband.
Let her remove the adulterous look
  from her face
 and the unfaithfulness from between
  her breasts.
³Otherwise I will strip her naked
 and make her as bare as on the day
  she was born;
 I will make her like a desert,
 turn her into a parched land,
 and slay her with thirst.
⁴I will not show my love to her children,
 because they are the children of
  adultery.
⁵Their mother has been unfaithful
 and has conceived them in disgrace.
 She said, 'I will go after my lovers,
 who give me my food and my water,
 my wool and my linen, my oil and my
  drink.'
⁶Therefore I will block her path with
 thornbushes;

ᵃ6 Lo-Ruhamah means *not loved*. ᵇ9 Lo-Ammi means *not my people*.

I will wall her in so that she cannot
   find her way.
7She will chase after her lovers but not
   catch them;
she will look for them but not find
   them.
Then she will say,
   'I will go back to my husband as at
      first,
   for then I was better off than now.'
8She has not acknowledged that I was
   the one
   who gave her the grain, the new wine
      and oil,
who lavished on her the silver and
   gold—
   which they used for Baal.

9"Therefore I will take away my grain
   when it ripens,
   and my new wine when it is ready.
I will take back my wool and my linen,
   intended to cover her nakedness.
10So now I will expose her lewdness
   before the eyes of her lovers;
   no-one will take her out of my hands.
11I will stop all her celebrations:
   her yearly festivals, her New Moons,
   her Sabbath days—all her appointed
      feasts.
12I will ruin her vines and her fig-trees,
   which she said were her pay from her
      lovers;
I will make them a thicket,
   and wild animals will devour them.
13I will punish her for the days
   she burned incense to the Baals;
she decked herself with rings and
      jewellery,
   and went after her lovers,
   but me she forgot,"
                                    declares the LORD.

14"Therefore I am now going to allure
      her;
   I will lead her into the desert
   and speak tenderly to her.
15There I will give her back her
      vineyards,
   and will make the Valley of Achor^a^ a
      door of hope.

There she will sing^b^ as in the days of her
      youth,
   as in the day she came up out of
      Egypt.

16"In that day," declares the LORD,
   "you will call me 'my husband';
   you will no longer call me 'my
      master'.^c^
17I will remove the names of the Baals
   from her lips;
   no longer will their names be
      invoked.
18In that day I will make a covenant for
      them
   with the beasts of the field and the
      birds of the air
   and the creatures that move along the
      ground.
Bow and sword and battle
   I will abolish from the land,
   so that all may lie down in
      safety.
19I will betroth you to me for ever;
   I will betroth you in^d^ righteousness
      and justice,
   in^e^ love and compassion.
20I will betroth you in faithfulness,
   and you will acknowledge the LORD.

21"In that day I will respond,"
   declares the LORD—
   "I will respond to the skies,
   and they will respond to the earth;
22and the earth will respond to the grain,
   the new wine and oil,
   and they will respond to Jezreel.^f^
23I will plant her for myself in the land;
   I will show my love to the one I called
      'Not my loved one'.^g^
I will say to those called 'Not my
   people',^h^ 'You are my people';
   and they will say, 'You are my
      God.'"

Hosea's Reconciliation With His Wife

3 The LORD said to me, "Go, show your
      love to your wife again, though she is
loved by another and is an adulteress.
Love her as the LORD loves the Israelites,

---

^a^15 *Achor* means trouble.   ^b^15 Or *respond*   ^c^16 Hebrew *baal*   ^d^19 Or *with*; also in verse 20
^e^19 Or *with*   ^f^22 *Jezreel* means *God plants*.   ^g^23 Hebrew *Lo-Ruhamah*   ^h^23 Hebrew *Lo-Ammi*

though they turn to other gods and love the sacred raisin cakes.''

[2]So I bought her for fifteen shekels[a] of silver and about a homer and a lethek[b] of barley. [3]Then I told her, "You are to live with[c] me for many days; you must not be a prostitute or be intimate with any man, and I will live with[c] you."

[4]For the Israelites will live for many days without king or prince, without sacrifice or sacred stones, without ephod or idol. [5]Afterwards the Israelites will return and seek the LORD their God and David their king. They will come trembling to the LORD and to his blessings in the last days.

The Charge Against Israel

4 Hear the word of the LORD,
    you Israelites,
  because the LORD has a charge to
      bring
  against you who live in the land:
"There is no faithfulness, no love,
    no acknowledgment of God in the
      land.
[2]There is only cursing,[a] lying and murder,
    stealing and adultery;
  they break all bounds,
    and bloodshed follows bloodshed.
[3]Because of this the land mourns,[b]
    and all who live in it waste away;
  the beasts of the field and the birds of
      the air
    and the fish of the sea are dying.

[4]"But let no man bring a charge,
    let no man accuse another,
  for your people are like those
    who bring charges against a priest.
[5]You stumble day and night,
    and the prophets stumble with you.
  So I will destroy your mother—
[6]   my people are destroyed from lack of
      knowledge.

  "Because you have rejected knowledge,
    I also reject you as my priests;

because you have ignored the law of
    your God,
  I also will ignore your children.
[7]The more the priests increased,
    the more they sinned against me;
  they exchanged[c] their[d] Glory for
    something disgraceful.
[8]They feed on the sins of my people
    and relish their wickedness.
[9]And it will be: Like people, like priests.
  I will punish both of them for their
      ways
    and repay them for their deeds.

[10]"They will eat but not have enough;
    they will engage in prostitution but
      not increase,
  because they have deserted the LORD
    to give themselves [11]to prostitution,
  to old wine and new,
    which take away the understanding
[12]of my people.
  They consult a wooden idol
    and are answered by a stick of wood.
  A spirit of prostitution leads them
      astray;
    they are unfaithful to their God.
[13]They sacrifice on the mountaintops
    and burn offerings on the hills,
  under oak, poplar and terebinth,
    where the shade is pleasant.
  Therefore your daughters turn to
      prostitution
    and your daughters-in-law to
      adultery.

[14]"I will not punish your daughters
    when they turn to prostitution,
  nor your daughters-in-law
    when they commit adultery,
  because the men themselves consort
      with harlots
    and sacrifice with shrine-prostitutes—
  a people without understanding will
    come to ruin!

[15]"Though you commit adultery, O
      Israel,
    let not Judah become guilty.

---

[a]2 That is, about 6 ounces (about 170 grams)   [b]2 That is, probably about 9 bushels (about 330 litres)
[c]3 Or *wait for*   [a]2 That is, to pronounce a curse upon   [b]3 Or *dries up*
[c]7 Syriac and an ancient Hebrew scribal tradition; Masoretic Text *I will exchange*
[d]7 Masoretic Text; an ancient Hebrew scribal tradition *my*

"Do not go to Gilgal;
do not go up to Beth Aven.[e]
And do not swear, 'As surely as the
LORD lives!'
[16]The Israelites are stubborn,
like a stubborn heifer.
How then can the LORD pasture them
like lambs in a meadow?
[17]Ephraim is joined to idols;
leave him alone!
[18]Even when their drinks are gone,
they continue their prostitution;
their rulers dearly love shameful
ways.
[19]A whirlwind will sweep them away,
and their sacrifices will bring them
shame.

Judgment Against Israel

5 "Hear this, you priests!
Pay attention, you Israelites!
Listen, O royal house!
This judgment is against you:
You have been a snare at Mizpah,
a net spread out on Tabor.
[2]The rebels are deep in slaughter.
I will discipline all of them.
[3]I know all about Ephraim;
Israel is not hidden from me.
Ephraim, you have now turned to
prostitution;
Israel is corrupt.

[4]"Their deeds do not permit them
to return to their God.
A spirit of prostitution is in their heart;
they do not acknowledge the LORD.
[5]Israel's arrogance testifies against them;
the Israelites, even Ephraim, stumble
in their sin;
Judah also stumbles with them.
[6]When they go with their flocks and
herds
to seek the LORD,
they will not find him;
he has withdrawn himself from them.
[7]They are unfaithful to the LORD;
they give birth to illegitimate
children.

Now their New Moon festivals
will devour them and their fields.

[8]"Sound the trumpet in Gibeah,
the horn in Ramah.
Raise the battle cry in Beth Aven;[a]
lead on, O Benjamin.
[9]Ephraim will be laid waste
on the day of reckoning.
Among the tribes of Israel
I proclaim what is certain.
[10]Judah's leaders are like those
who move boundary stones.
I will pour out my wrath on them
like a flood of water.
[11]Ephraim is oppressed,
trampled in judgment,
intent on pursuing idols.[b]
[12]I am like a moth to Ephraim,
like rot to the people of Judah.

[13]"When Ephraim saw his sickness,
and Judah his sores,
then Ephraim turned to Assyria,
and sent to the great king for help.
But he is not able to cure you,
not able to heal your sores.
[14]For I will be like a lion to Ephraim,
like a great lion to Judah.
I will tear them to pieces and go away;
I will carry them off, with no-one to
rescue them.
[15]Then I will go back to my place
until they admit their guilt.
And they will seek my face;
in their misery they will earnestly
seek me."

Israel Unrepentant

6 "Come, let us return to the
LORD.
He has torn us to pieces
but he will heal us;
he has injured us
but he will bind up our wounds.
[2]After two days he will revive us;
on the third day he will restore us,
that we may live in his presence.
[3]Let us acknowledge the LORD;
let us press on to acknowledge him.

---

[e]15 Beth Aven means *house of wickedness* (a name for Bethel, which means *house of God*).
[a]8 Beth Aven means *house of wickedness* (a name for Bethel, which means *house of God*).
[b]11 The meaning of the Hebrew for this word is uncertain.

As surely as the sun rises,
  he will appear;
he will come to us like the winter rains,
  like the spring rains that water the
    earth."

4"What can I do with you, Ephraim?
  What can I do with you, Judah?
Your love is like the morning mist,
  like the early dew that disappears.
5Therefore I cut you in pieces with my
    prophets,
  I killed you with the words of my
    mouth;
  my judgments flashed like lightning
    upon you.
6For I desire mercy, not sacrifice,
  and acknowledgment of God rather
    than burnt offerings.
7Like Adam,*a* they have broken the
    covenant—
  they were unfaithful to me there.
8Gilead is a city of wicked men,
  stained with footprints of blood.
9As marauders lie in ambush for a man,
  so do bands of priests;
they murder on the road to Shechem,
  committing shameful crimes.
10I have seen a horrible thing
  in the house of Israel.
There Ephraim is given to prostitution
  and Israel is defiled.

11"Also for you, Judah,
  a harvest is appointed.

"Whenever I would restore the fortunes
  of my people,
7 1whenever I would heal Israel,
  the sins of Ephraim are exposed
and the crimes of Samaria revealed.
They practise deceit,
  thieves break into houses,
  bandits rob in the streets;
2but they do not realise
  that I remember all their evil deeds.
Their sins engulf them;
  they are always before me.

3"They delight the king with their
    wickedness,

the princes with their lies.
4They are all adulterers,
  burning like an oven
whose fire the baker need not stir
  from the kneading of the dough till it
    rises.
5On the day of the festival of our king
  the princes become inflamed with
    wine,
  and he joins hands with the mockers.
6Their hearts are like an oven;
  they approach him with intrigue.
Their passion smoulders all night;
  in the morning it blazes like a flaming
    fire.
7All of them are hot as an oven;
  they devour their rulers.
All their kings fall,
  and none of them calls on me.

8"Ephraim mixes with the nations;
  Ephraim is a flat cake not turned
    over.
9Foreigners sap his strength,
  but he does not realise it.
His hair is sprinkled with grey,
  but he does not notice.
10Israel's arrogance testifies against him,
  but despite all this
he does not return to the LORD his God
  or search for him.

11"Ephraim is like a dove,
  easily deceived and senseless—
now calling to Egypt,
  now turning to Assyria.
12When they go, I will throw my net over
    them;
  I will pull them down like birds of the
    air.
When I hear them flocking together,
  I will catch them.
13Woe to them,
  because they have strayed from me!
Destruction to them,
  because they have rebelled against
    me!
I long to redeem them
  but they speak lies against me.
14They do not cry out to me from their
    hearts

---

*a*7 Or *As at Adam*; or *Like men*

but wail upon their beds.
They gather together[a] for grain and new
    wine
but turn away from me.
¹⁵I trained them and strengthened them,
    but they plot evil against me.
¹⁶They do not turn to the Most High;
    they are like a faulty bow.
Their leaders will fall by the sword
    because of their insolent words.
For this they will be ridiculed
    in the land of Egypt.

Israel to Reap the Whirlwind

8 "Put the trumpet to your lips!
  An eagle is over the house
    of the LORD
because the people have broken my
    covenant
    and rebelled against my law.
²Israel cries out to me,
    'O our God, we acknowledge you!'
³But Israel has rejected what is good;
    an enemy will pursue him.
⁴They set up kings without my consent;
    they choose princes without my
        approval.
With their silver and gold
    they make idols for themselves
    to their own destruction.
⁵Throw out your calf-idol, O Samaria!
    My anger burns against them.
How long will they be incapable of
    purity?
⁶   They are from Israel!
This calf—a craftsman has made it;
    it is not God.
It will be broken in pieces,
    that calf of Samaria.

⁷"They sow the wind
    and reap the whirlwind.
The stalk has no head;
    it will produce no flour.
Were it to yield grain,
    foreigners would swallow it up.
⁸Israel is swallowed up;
    now she is among the nations
    like a worthless thing.

⁹For they have gone up to Assyria
    like a wild donkey wandering alone.
Ephraim has sold herself to lovers.
¹⁰Although they have sold themselves
    among the nations,
    I will now gather them together.
They will begin to waste away
    under the oppression of the mighty
        king.

¹¹"Though Ephraim built many altars for
    sin offerings,
    these have become altars for sinning.
¹²I wrote for them the many things of my
    law,
    but they regarded them as something
        alien.
¹³They offer sacrifices given to me
    and they eat the meat,
    but the LORD is not pleased with
        them.
Now he will remember their wickedness
    and punish their sins:
    They will return to Egypt.
¹⁴Israel has forgotten his Maker
    and built palaces;
    Judah has fortified many towns.
But I will send fire upon their cities
    that will consume their fortresses."

Punishment for Israel

9 Do not rejoice, O Israel;
  do not be jubilant like the other
    nations.
For you have been unfaithful to your
    God;
    you love the wages of a prostitute
    at every threshing-floor.
²Threshing-floors and winepresses will
    not feed the people;
    the new wine will fail them.
³They will not remain in the LORD's land;
    Ephraim will return to Egypt
    and eat unclean[a] food in Assyria.
⁴They will not pour out wine offerings to
    the LORD,
    nor will their sacrifices please
        him.
Such sacrifices will be to them like the
    bread of mourners;

---

[a]14 Most Hebrew manuscripts; some Hebrew manuscripts and Septuagint *They slash themselves*
[a]3 That is, ceremonially unclean

all who eat them will be unclean.
This food will be for themselves;
  it will not come into the temple of the
    LORD.

⁵What will you do on the day of your
    appointed feasts,
  on the festival days of the LORD?
⁶Even if they escape from destruction,
    Egypt will gather them,
  and Memphis will bury them.
Their treasures of silver will be taken
    over by briers,
  and thorns will overrun their tents.
⁷The days of punishment are coming,
  the days of reckoning are at hand.
Let Israel know this.
Because your sins are so many
  and your hostility so great,
the prophet is considered a fool,
  the inspired man a maniac.
⁸The prophet, along with my God,
  is the watchman over Ephraim,ᵇ
yet snares await him on all his paths,
  and hostility in the house of his God.
⁹They have sunk deep into corruption,
  as in the days of Gibeah.
God will remember their wickedness
  and punish them for their sins.

¹⁰"When I found Israel,
  it was like finding grapes in the
    desert;
when I saw your fathers,
  it was like seeing the early fruit on the
    fig-tree.
But when they came to Baal Peor,
  they consecrated themselves to that
    shameful idol
  and became as vile as the thing they
    loved.
¹¹Ephraim's glory will fly away like a
    bird—
  no birth, no pregnancy, no
    conception.
¹²Even if they bring up children,
  I will bereave them of every one.
Woe to them
  when I turn away from them!
¹³I have seen Ephraim, like Tyre,
  planted in a pleasant place.

But Ephraim will bring out
  their children to the slayer."

¹⁴Give them, O LORD—
  what will you give them?
Give them wombs that miscarry
  and breasts that are dry.

¹⁵"Because of all their wickedness in
    Gilgal,
  I hated them there.
Because of their sinful deeds,
  I will drive them out of my house.
I will no longer love them;
  all their leaders are rebellious.
¹⁶Ephraim is blighted,
  their root is withered,
  they yield no fruit.
Even if they bear children,
  I will slay their cherished offspring."

¹⁷My God will reject them
  because they have not obeyed him;
they will be wanderers among the
    nations.

10 Israel was a spreading vine;
    he brought forth fruit for himself.
As his fruit increased,
  he built more altars;
as his land prospered,
  he adorned his sacred stones.
²Their heart is deceitful,
  and now they must bear their guilt.
The LORD will demolish their altars
  and destroy their sacred stones.

³Then they will say, "We have no king
  because we did not revere the
    LORD.
But even if we had a king,
  what could he do for us?"
⁴They make many promises,
  take false oaths
  and make agreements;
therefore lawsuits spring up
  like poisonous weeds in a ploughed
    field.
⁵The people who live in Samaria fear
  for the calf-idol of Beth Aven.ᵃ
Its people will mourn over it,

ᵇ8 Or *The prophet is the watchman over Ephraim, / the people of my God*
ᵃ5 *Beth Aven* means *house of wickedness* (a name for Bethel, which means *house of God*).

and so will its idolatrous priests,
those who had rejoiced over its
    splendour,
because it is taken from them into
    exile.
⁶It will be carried to Assyria
    as tribute for the great king.
Ephraim will be disgraced;
    Israel will be ashamed of its wooden
      idols.ᵇ
⁷Samaria and its king will float away
    like a twig on the surface of the
      waters.
⁸The high places of wickednessᶜ will be
    destroyed—
it is the sin of Israel.
Thorns and thistles will grow up
    and cover their altars.
Then they will say to the mountains,
    "Cover us!"
and to the hills, "Fall on us!"

⁹"Since the days of Gibeah, you have
    sinned, O Israel,
and there you have remained.ᵈ
Did not war overtake
    the evildoers in Gibeah?
¹⁰When I please, I will punish them;
    nations will be gathered against them
to put them in bonds for their double
    sin.
¹¹Ephraim is a trained heifer
    that loves to thresh;
so I will put a yoke
    on her fair neck.
I will drive Ephraim,
    Judah must plough,
and Jacob must break up the ground.
¹²Sow for yourselves righteousness,
    reap the fruit of unfailing love,
and break up your unploughed ground;
    for it is time to seek the LORD,
until he comes
    and showers righteousness on you.
¹³But you have planted wickedness,
    you have reaped evil,
you have eaten the fruit of
    deception.
Because you have depended on your
    own strength
and on your many warriors,

¹⁴the roar of battle will rise against your
    people,
so that all your fortresses will be
    devastated—
as Shalman devastated Beth Arbel on
    the day of battle,
when mothers were dashed to the
    ground with their children.
¹⁵Thus will it happen to you, O Bethel,
    because your wickedness is great.
When that day dawns,
    the king of Israel will be completely
      destroyed.

God's Love for Israel

11 "When Israel was a child, I loved
      him,
    and out of Egypt I called my son.
²But the more Iᵃ called Israel,
    the further they went from me.ᵇ
They sacrificed to the Baals
    and they burned incense to images.
³It was I who taught Ephraim to walk,
    taking them by the arms;
but they did not realise
    it was I who healed them.
⁴I led them with cords of human
    kindness,
    with ties of love;
I lifted the yoke from their neck
    and bent down to feed them.

⁵"Will they not return to Egypt
    and will not Assyria rule over them
because they refuse to repent?
⁶Swords will flash in their cities,
    will destroy the bars of their gates
and put an end to their plans.
⁷My people are determined to turn from
    me.
Even if they call to the Most High,
    he will by no means exalt them.

⁸"How can I give you up, Ephraim?
    How can I hand you over, Israel?
How can I treat you like Admah?
    How can I make you like Zeboiim?
My heart is changed within me;
    all my compassion is aroused.

ᵇ6 Or *its counsel*   ᶜ8 Hebrew *aven*, a reference to Beth Aven (a derogatory name for Bethel)
ᵈ9 Or *there a stand was taken*   ᵃ2 Some Septuagint manuscripts; Hebrew *they*   ᵇ2 Septuagint; Hebrew *them*

⁹I will not carry out my fierce anger,
nor will I turn and devastate Ephraim.
For I am God, and not man—
the Holy One among you.
I will not come in wrath.ᶜ
¹⁰They will follow the LORD;
he will roar like a lion.
When he roars,
his children will come trembling from the west.
¹¹They will come trembling
like birds from Egypt,
like doves from Assyria.
I will settle them in their homes,"
declares the LORD.

Israel's Sin

¹²Ephraim has surrounded me with lies,
the house of Israel with deceit.
And Judah is unruly against God,
even against the faithful Holy One.

12 ¹Ephraim feeds on the wind;
he pursues the east wind all day
and multiplies lies and violence.
He makes a treaty with Assyria
and sends olive oil to Egypt.
²The LORD has a charge to bring against Judah;
he will punish Jacobᵃ according to his ways
and repay him according to his deeds.
³In the womb he grasped his brother's heel;
as a man he struggled with God.
⁴He struggled with the angel and overcame him;
he wept and begged for his favour.
He found him at Bethel
and talked with him there—
⁵the LORD God Almighty,
the LORD is his name of renown!
⁶But you must return to your God;
maintain love and justice,
and wait for your God always.

⁷The merchant uses dishonest scales;
he loves to defraud.

⁸Ephraim boasts,
"I am very rich; I have become wealthy.
With all my wealth they will not find in me
any iniquity or sin."

⁹"I am the LORD your God,
who brought you out ofᵇ Egypt;
I will make you live in tents again,
as in the days of your appointed feasts.
¹⁰I spoke to the prophets,
gave them many visions
and told parables through them."

¹¹Is Gilead wicked?
Its people are worthless!
Do they sacrifice bulls in Gilgal?
Their altars will be like piles of stones
on a ploughed field.
¹²Jacob fled to the country of Aram;ᶜ
Israel served to get a wife,
and to pay for her he tended sheep.
¹³The LORD used a prophet to bring Israel up from Egypt,
by a prophet he cared for him.
¹⁴But Ephraim has bitterly provoked him to anger;
his Lord will leave upon him the guilt of his bloodshed
and will repay him for his contempt.

The LORD's Anger Against Israel

13 When Ephraim spoke, men trembled;
he was exalted in Israel.
But he became guilty of Baal worship and died.
²Now they sin more and more;
they make idols for themselves from their silver,
cleverly fashioned images,
all of them the work of craftsmen.
It is said of these people,
"They offer human sacrifice
and kissᵃ the calf-idols."
³Therefore they will be like the morning mist,

ᶜ9 Or *come against any city*   ᵃ2 *Jacob* means *he grasps the heel* (figuratively, *he deceives*).
ᵇ9 Or *God / ever since you were in*   ᶜ12 That is, North-west Mesopotamia
ᵃ2 Or *"Men who sacrifice / kiss*

like the early dew that disappears,
like chaff swirling from a
threshing-floor,
like smoke escaping through a
window.

4"But I am the LORD your God,
ʟwho brought youʟ out of[b] Egypt.
You shall acknowledge no God but
me,
no Saviour except me.
5I cared for you in the desert,
in the land of burning heat.
6When I fed them, they were satisfied;
when they were satisfied, they
became proud;
then they forgot me.
7So I will come upon them like a lion,
like a leopard I will lurk by the path.
8Like a bear robbed of her cubs,
I will attack them and rip them open.
Like a lion I will devour them;
a wild animal will tear them apart.

9"You are destroyed, O Israel,
because you are against me, against
your helper.
10Where is your king, that he may save
you?
Where are your rulers in all your
towns,
of whom you said,
'Give me a king and princes'?
11So in my anger I gave you a king,
and in my wrath I took him
away.
12The guilt of Ephraim is stored up,
his sins are kept on record.
13Pains as of a woman in childbirth come
to him,
but he is a child without wisdom;
when the time arrives,
he does not come to the opening of
the womb.

14"I will ransom them from the power of
the grave;[c]
I will redeem them from death.
Where, O death, are your plagues?
Where, O grave,[c] is your
destruction?

"I will have no compassion,
15   even though he thrives among his
brothers.
An east wind from the LORD will come,
blowing in from the desert;
his spring will fail
and his well dry up.
His storehouse will be plundered
of all its treasures.
16The people of Samaria must bear their
guilt,
because they have rebelled against
their God.
They will fall by the sword;
their little ones will be dashed to the
ground,
their pregnant women ripped open."

Repentance to Bring Blessing

14 Return, O Israel, to the LORD
your God.
Your sins have been your downfall!
2Take words with you
and return to the LORD.
Say to him:
"Forgive all our sins
and receive us graciously,
that we may offer the fruit of our
lips.[a]
3Assyria cannot save us;
we will not mount war-horses.
We will never again say 'Our gods'
to what our own hands have made,
for in you the fatherless find
compassion."

4"I will heal their waywardness
and love them freely,
for my anger has turned away from
them.
5I will be like the dew to Israel;
he will blossom like a lily.
Like a cedar of Lebanon
he will send down his roots;
6   his young shoots will grow.
His splendour will be like an olive tree,
his fragrance like a cedar of
Lebanon.
7Men will dwell again in his shade.
He will flourish like the corn.

---

b4 Or God I ever since you were in   *c14 Hebrew Sheol*   *a2 Or offer our lips as sacrifices of bulls*

He will blossom like a vine,
and his fame will be like the wine
from Lebanon.
[8]O Ephraim, what more have I[b] to do
with idols?
I will answer him and care for him.
I am like a green pine tree;
your fruitfulness comes from me."

[9]Who is wise? He will realise these
things.
Who is discerning? He will
understand them.
The ways of the LORD are right;
the righteous walk in them,
but the rebellious stumble in
them.

---

b8 Or *What more has Ephraim*

Joel

1 The word of the LORD that came to Joel son of Pethuel.

An Invasion of Locusts

²Hear this, you elders;
  listen, all who live in the land.
Has anything like this ever happened in
    your days
  or in the days of your forefathers?
³Tell it to your children,
  and let your children tell it to their
    children,
  and their children to the next
    generation.
⁴What the locust swarm has left
  the great locusts have eaten;
what the great locusts have left
  the young locusts have eaten;
what the young locusts have left
  other locusts*ᵃ* have eaten.

⁵Wake up, you drunkards, and weep!
  Wail, all you drinkers of wine;
wail because of the new wine,
  for it has been snatched from your
    lips.
⁶A nation has invaded my land,
  powerful and without number;
it has the teeth of a lion,
  the fangs of a lioness.
⁷It has laid waste my vines
  and ruined my fig-trees.
It has stripped off their bark
  and thrown it away,
  leaving their branches white.

⁸Mourn like a virgin*ᵇ* in sackcloth
  grieving for the husband*ᶜ* of her
    youth.
⁹Grain offerings and drink offerings
  are cut off from the house of the
    LORD.
The priests are in mourning,
  those who minister before the LORD.
¹⁰The fields are ruined,
  the ground is dried up;*ᵈ*
the grain is destroyed,
  the new wine is dried up,
  the oil fails.
¹¹Despair, you farmers,
  wail, you vine growers;
grieve for the wheat and the barley,
  because the harvest of the field is
    destroyed.
¹²The vine is dried up
  and the fig-tree is withered;
the pomegranate, the palm and the
    apple tree—
  all the trees of the field—are dried up.
Surely the joy of mankind
  is withered away.

A Call to Repentance

¹³Put on sackcloth, O priests, and mourn;
  wail, you who minister before the
    altar.
Come, spend the night in sackcloth,
  you who minister before my God;
for the grain offerings and drink
    offerings
  are withheld from the house of your
    God.

ᵃ4 The precise meaning of the four Hebrew words used here for locusts is uncertain.
ᵇ8 Or *young woman*   *ᶜ8* Or *betrothed*   *ᵈ10* Or *ground mourns*

14Declare a holy fast;
  call a sacred assembly.
Summon the elders
  and all who live in the land
to the house of the LORD your God,
  and cry out to the LORD.

15Alas for that day!
  For the day of the LORD is near;
  it will come like destruction from the
    Almighty.*e*

16Has not the food been cut off
  before our very eyes—
joy and gladness
  from the house of our God?
17The seeds are shrivelled
  beneath the clods.*f*
The storehouses are in ruins,
  the granaries have been broken
    down,
for the grain has dried up.
18How the cattle moan!
  The herds mill about
because they have no pasture;
  even the flocks of sheep are suffering.

19To you, O LORD, I call,
  for fire has devoured the open
    pastures
  and flames have burned up all the
    trees of the field.
20Even the wild animals pant for you;
  the streams of water have dried up
  and fire has devoured the open
    pastures.

An Army of Locusts

2 Blow the trumpet in Zion;
  sound the alarm on my holy hill.
Let all who live in the land tremble,
  for the day of the LORD is coming.
It is close at hand—
2   a day of darkness and gloom,
    a day of clouds and blackness.
Like dawn spreading across the
    mountains
  a large and mighty army comes,
such as never was of old
  nor ever will be in ages to come.

3Before them fire devours,
  behind them a flame blazes.
Before them the land is like the garden
    of Eden,
  behind them, a desert waste—
    nothing escapes them.
4They have the appearance of horses;
  they gallop along like cavalry.
5With a noise like that of chariots
  they leap over the mountaintops,
like a crackling fire consuming
    stubble,
  like a mighty army drawn up for
    battle.

6At the sight of them, nations are in
    anguish;
  every face turns pale.
7They charge like warriors;
  they scale walls like soldiers.
They all march in line,
  not swerving from their course.
8They do not jostle each other;
  each marches straight ahead.
They plunge through defences
  without breaking ranks.
9They rush upon the city;
  they run along the wall.
They climb into the houses;
  like thieves they enter through the
    windows.

10Before them the earth shakes,
  the sky trembles,
the sun and moon are darkened,
  and the stars no longer shine.
11The LORD thunders
  at the head of his army;
his forces are beyond number,
  and mighty are those who obey his
    command.
The day of the LORD is great;
  it is dreadful.
  Who can endure it?

Rend Your Heart

12"Even now," declares the LORD,
  "return to me with all your heart,
  with fasting and weeping and
    mourning."

¹³Rend your heart
    and not your garments.
Return to the LORD your God,
    for he is gracious and compassionate,
slow to anger and abounding in love,
    and he relents from sending calamity.
¹⁴Who knows? He may turn and have pity
    and leave behind a blessing—
grain offerings and drink offerings
    for the LORD your God.

¹⁵Blow the trumpet in Zion,
    declare a holy fast,
    call a sacred assembly.
¹⁶Gather the people,
    consecrate the assembly;
bring together the elders,
    gather the children,
    those nursing at the breast.
Let the bridegroom leave his room
    and the bride her chamber.
¹⁷Let the priests, who minister before the
    LORD,
    weep between the temple porch and
    the altar.
Let them say, "Spare your people, O
    LORD.
    Do not make your inheritance an
    object of scorn,
    a byword among the nations.
Why should they say among the
    peoples,
    'Where is their God?' "

The LORD's Answer

¹⁸Then the LORD will be jealous for his
    land
    and take pity on his people.

¹⁹The LORD will reply[a] to them:

"I am sending you grain, new wine and
    oil,
    enough to satisfy you fully;
never again will I make you
    an object of scorn to the nations.

²⁰"I will drive the northern army far from
    you,

pushing it into a parched and barren
    land,
with its front columns going into the
    eastern sea[b]
and those in the rear into the western
    sea.[c]
And its stench will go up;
    its smell will rise."

Surely he has done great things.[d]
²¹ Be not afraid, O land;
    be glad and rejoice.
Surely the LORD has done great
    things.
²² Be not afraid, O wild animals,
    for the open pastures are becoming
    green.
The trees are bearing their fruit;
    the fig-tree and the vine yield their
    riches.
²³Be glad, O people of Zion,
    rejoice in the LORD your God,
for he has given you
    the autumn rains in righteousness.[e]
He sends you abundant showers,
    both autumn and spring rains, as
    before.
²⁴The threshing-floors will be filled with
    grain;
    the vats will overflow with new wine
    and oil.

²⁵"I will repay you for the years the
    locusts have eaten—
    the great locust and the young locust,
    the other locusts and the locust
    swarm[f]—
my great army that I sent among
    you.
²⁶You will have plenty to eat, until you
    are full,
    and you will praise the name of the
    LORD your God,
who has worked wonders for you;
    never again will my people be shamed.
²⁷Then you will know that I am in Israel,
    that I am the LORD your God,
    and that there is no other;
never again will my people be shamed.

---

a18, 19 Or *LORD was jealous . . . / and took pity . . . / *¹⁹The LORD replied*   *b20* That is, the Dead Sea
c20 That is, the Mediterranean   *d20* Or *rise. / Surely it has done great things."*
e23 Or / *the teacher for righteousness:*
f25 The precise meaning of the four Hebrew words used here for locusts is uncertain.

The Day of the LORD

28"And afterwards,
    I will pour out my Spirit on all
        people.
    Your sons and daughters will prophesy,
        your old men will dream dreams,
        your young men will see visions.
29Even on my servants, both men and
    women,
        I will pour out my Spirit in those
            days.
30I will show wonders in the heavens
    and on the earth,
        blood and fire and billows of smoke.
31The sun will be turned to darkness
    and the moon to blood
        before the coming of the great and
            dreadful day of the LORD.
32And everyone who calls
    on the name of the LORD will be
        saved;
    for on Mount Zion and in Jerusalem
        there will be deliverance,
            as the LORD has said,
        among the survivors
            whom the LORD calls.

The Nations Judged

3 "In those days and at that time,
    when I restore the fortunes of
    Judah and Jerusalem,
2I will gather all nations
    and bring them down to the Valley of
        Jehoshaphat.a
    There I will enter into judgment against
        them
    concerning my inheritance, my
        people Israel,
    for they scattered my people among the
        nations
        and divided up my land.
3They cast lots for my people
    and traded boys for prostitutes;
    they sold girls for wine
        that they might drink.

4"Now what have you against me, O
Tyre and Sidon and all you regions of
Philistia? Are you repaying me for

something I have done? If you are paying
me back, I will swiftly and speedily return
on your own heads what you have done.
5For you took my silver and my gold and
carried off my finest treasures to your
temples. 6You sold the people of Judah
and Jerusalem to the Greeks, that you
might send them far from their homeland.

7"See, I am going to rouse them out of
the places to which you sold them, and I
will return on your own heads what you
have done. 8I will sell your sons and
daughters to the people of Judah, and they
will sell them to the Sabeans, a nation far
away." The LORD has spoken.

9Proclaim this among the nations:
    Prepare for war!
    Rouse the warriors!
        Let all the fighting men draw near
            and attack.
10Beat your ploughshares into swords
    and your pruning hooks into spears.
    Let the weakling say,
        "I am strong!"
11Come quickly, all you nations from
    every side,
        and assemble there.

    Bring down your warriors, O LORD!

12"Let the nations be roused;
    let them advance into the Valley of
        Jehoshaphat,
    for there I will sit
        to judge all the nations on every side.
13Swing the sickle,
    for the harvest is ripe.
    Come, trample the grapes,
        for the winepress is full
        and the vats overflow—
    so great is their wickedness!"

14Multitudes, multitudes
    in the valley of decision!
    For the day of the LORD is near
        in the valley of decision.
15The sun and moon will be darkened,
    and the stars no longer shine.
16The LORD will roar from Zion
    and thunder from Jerusalem;

---

a2 *Jehoshaphat* means *the LORD judges*; also in verse 12.

the earth and the sky will tremble.
But the LORD will be a refuge for his
    people,
    a stronghold for the people of Israel.

Blessings for God's People

17"Then you will know that I, the LORD
    your God,
    dwell in Zion, my holy hill.
Jerusalem will be holy;
    never again will foreigners invade
    her.

18"In that day the mountains will drip
    new wine,
    and the hills will flow with milk;
    all the ravines of Judah will run with
    water.

A fountain will flow out of the LORD's
    house
    and will water the valley of
    acacias.*b*
19But Egypt will be desolate,
    Edom a desert waste,
because of violence done to the people
    of Judah,
    in whose land they shed innocent
    blood.
20Judah will be inhabited for ever
    and Jerusalem through all
    generations.
21Their bloodguilt, which I have not
    pardoned,
    I will pardon."

The LORD dwells in Zion!

b18 Or Valley of Shittim

Amos

1 The words of Amos, one of the shepherds of Tekoa—what he saw concerning Israel two years before the earthquake, when Uzziah was king of Judah and Jeroboam son of Jehoash[a] was king of Israel.

²He said:

"The LORD roars from Zion
  and thunders from Jerusalem;
the pastures of the shepherds dry up,[b]
  and the top of Carmel withers."

Judgment on Israel's Neighbours

³This is what the LORD says:

"For three sins of Damascus,
  even for four, I will not turn back ⌐my
    wrath⌐.
Because she threshed Gilead
  with sledges having iron teeth,
⁴I will send fire upon the house of Hazael
  that will consume the fortresses of
    Ben-Hadad.
⁵I will break down the gate of Damascus;
  I will destroy the king who is in[c] the
    Valley of Aven[d]
and the one who holds the sceptre in
    Beth Eden.
  The people of Aram will go into exile
    to Kir,"

          says the LORD.

⁶This is what the LORD says:

"For three sins of Gaza,
  even for four, I will not turn back ⌐my
    wrath⌐.
Because she took captive whole
    communities
  and sold them to Edom,
⁷I will send fire upon the walls of Gaza
  that will consume her fortresses.
⁸I will destroy the king[e] of Ashdod
  and the one who holds the sceptre in
    Ashkelon.
I will turn my hand against Ekron,
  till the last of the Philistines is dead,"
          says the Sovereign LORD.

⁹This is what the LORD says:

"For three sins of Tyre,
  even for four, I will not turn back ⌐my
    wrath⌐.
Because she sold whole communities of
    captives to Edom,
  disregarding a treaty of brotherhood,
¹⁰I will send fire upon the walls of Tyre
  that will consume her fortresses."

¹¹This is what the LORD says:

"For three sins of Edom,
  even for four, I will not turn back ⌐my
    wrath⌐.
Because he pursued his brother with a
    sword,
  stifling all compassion,[f]
because his anger raged continually
  and his fury flamed unchecked,

a1 Hebrew Joash, a variant of Jehoash   b2 Or shepherds mourn   c5 Or the inhabitants of
d5 Aven means wickedness.   e8 Or inhabitants   f11 Or sword / and destroyed his allies

¹²I will send fire upon Teman
   that will consume the fortresses of
      Bozrah."

¹³This is what the LORD says:

"For three sins of Ammon,
   even for four, I will not turn back ⌐my
      wrath⌐.
Because he ripped open the pregnant
      women of Gilead
   in order to extend his borders,
¹⁴I will set fire to the walls of Rabbah
   that will consume her fortresses
amid war cries on the day of battle,
   amid violent winds on a stormy day.
¹⁵Her kingᵍ will go into exile,
   he and his officials together,"
                        says the LORD.

2 This is what the LORD says:

"For three sins of Moab,
   even for four, I will not turn back ⌐my
      wrath⌐.
Because he burned, as if to lime,
   the bones of Edom's king,
²I will send fire upon Moab
   that will consume the fortresses of
      Kerioth.ᵃ
Moab will go down in great tumult
   amid war cries and the blast of the
      trumpet.
³I will destroy her ruler
   and kill all her officials with him,"
                        says the LORD.

⁴This is what the LORD says:

"For three sins of Judah,
   even for four, I will not turn back ⌐my
      wrath⌐.
Because they have rejected the law of
      the LORD
   and have not kept his decrees,
because they have been led astray by
      false gods,ᵇ
   the godsᶜ their ancestors followed,
⁵I will send fire upon Judah
   that will consume the fortfesses of
      Jerusalem."

Judgment on Israel

⁶This is what the LORD says:

"For three sins of Israel,
   even for four, I will not turn back ⌐my
      wrath⌐.
They sell the righteous for silver,
   and the needy for a pair of sandals.
⁷They trample on the heads of the poor
   as upon the dust of the ground
   and deny justice to the oppressed.
Father and son use the same girl
   and so profane my holy name.
⁸They lie down beside every altar
   on garments taken in pledge.
In the house of their god
   they drink wine taken as fines.

⁹"I destroyed the Amorite before them,
   though he was tall as the cedars
   and strong as the oaks.
I destroyed his fruit above
   and his roots below.

¹⁰"I brought you up out of Egypt,
   and I led you for forty years in the
      desert
   to give you the land of the Amorites.
¹¹I also raised up prophets from among
      your sons
   and Nazirites from among your
      young men.
Is this not true, people of Israel?"
                     declares the LORD.
¹²"But you made the Nazirites drink wine
   and commanded the prophets not to
      prophesy.

¹³"Now then, I will crush you
   as a cart crushes when loaded with
      grain.
¹⁴The swift will not escape,
   the strong will not muster their
      strength,
   and the warrior will not save his life.
¹⁵The archer will not stand his ground,
   the fleet-footed soldier will not get
      away,
   and the horseman will not save his
      life.

815 Or *l Molech*; Hebrew *malcam*   *a2* Or *of her cities*   *b4* Or *by lies*   *c4* Or *lies*

¹⁶Even the bravest warriors
  will flee naked on that day,"
                declares the LORD.

Witnesses Summoned Against Israel

3 Hear this word the LORD has spoken
  against you, O people of Israel—
against the whole family I brought up out
of Egypt:

²"You only have I chosen
  of all the families of the earth;
therefore I will punish you
  for all your sins."

³Do two walk together
  unless they have agreed to do so?
⁴Does a lion roar in the thicket
  when he has no prey?
Does he growl in his den
  when he has caught nothing?
⁵Does a bird fall into a trap on the
    ground
  where no snare has been set?
Does a trap spring up from the earth
  when there is nothing to catch?
⁶When a trumpet sounds in a city,
  do not the people tremble?
When disaster comes to a city,
  has not the LORD caused it?

⁷Surely the Sovereign LORD does nothing
  without revealing his plan
  to his servants the prophets.

⁸The lion has roared—
  who will not fear?
The Sovereign LORD has spoken—
  who can but prophesy?

⁹Proclaim to the fortresses of Ashdod
  and to the fortresses of Egypt:
"Assemble yourselves on the
    mountains of Samaria;
  see the great unrest within her
  and the oppression among her
    people."

¹⁰"They do not know how to do right,"
  declares the LORD,

"who hoard plunder and loot in their
  fortresses."

¹¹Therefore this is what the Sovereign
LORD says:

"An enemy will overrun the land;
  he will pull down your strongholds
  and plunder your fortresses."

¹²This is what the LORD says:

"As a shepherd saves from the lion's
    mouth
  only two leg bones or a piece of an
    ear,
so will the Israelites be saved,
those who sit in Samaria
  on the edge of their beds
  and in Damascus on their couches."^a

¹³"Hear this and testify against the
house of Jacob," declares the Lord, the
LORD God Almighty.

¹⁴"On the day I punish Israel for her sins,
  I will destroy the altars of Bethel;
the horns of the altar will be cut off
  and fall to the ground.
¹⁵I will tear down the winter house
  along with the summer house;
the houses adorned with ivory will be
    destroyed
  and the mansions will be
    demolished,"
                declares the LORD.

Israel Has Not Returned to God

4 Hear this word, you cows of Bashan
  on Mount Samaria,
you women who oppress the poor
  and crush the needy
  and say to your husbands, "Bring us
    some drinks!"
²The Sovereign LORD has sworn by his
    holiness:
"The time will surely come
when you will be taken away with
    hooks,
  the last of you with fish-hooks.

---

^a12 The meaning of the Hebrew for this line is uncertain.

3You will each go straight out
  through breaks in the wall,
  and you will be cast out towards
    Harmon,"[a]
                              declares the LORD.
4"Go to Bethel and sin;
  go to Gilgal and sin yet more.
 Bring your sacrifices every morning,
  your tithes every three years.[b]
5Burn leavened bread as a
    thank-offering
  and brag about your freewill
    offerings—
 boast about them, you Israelites,
  for this is what you love to do,"
              declares the Sovereign LORD.

6"I gave you empty stomachs[c] in every
    city
  and lack of bread in every town,
  yet you have not returned to me,"
                      declares the LORD.

7"I also withheld rain from you
  when the harvest was still three
    months away.
 I sent rain on one town,
  but withheld it from another.
 One field had rain;
  another had none and dried up.
8People staggered from town to town for
    water
  but did not get enough to drink,
  yet you have not returned to me,"
                      declares the LORD.

9"Many times I struck your gardens and
    vineyards,
  I struck them with blight and mildew.
 Locusts devoured your fig and olive
    trees,
  yet you have not returned to me,"
                      declares the LORD.

10"I sent plagues among you
  as I did to Egypt.
 I killed your young men with the sword,
  along with your captured horses.
 I filled your nostrils with the stench of
    your camps,
  yet you have not returned to me,"
                      declares the LORD.

11"I overthrew some of you
  as I[d] overthrew Sodom and
    Gomorrah.
 You were like a burning stick snatched
    from the fire,
  yet you have not returned to me,"
                      declares the LORD.

12"Therefore this is what I will do to you,
    Israel,
  and because I will do this to you,
  prepare to meet your God, O Israel."

13He who forms the mountains,
  creates the wind,
  and reveals his thoughts to man,
 he who turns dawn to darkness,
  and treads the high places of the
    earth—
  the LORD God Almighty is his name.

A Lament and Call to Repentance

5 Hear this word, O house of Israel,
  this lament I take up concerning you:

2"Fallen is Virgin Israel,
  never to rise again,
 deserted in her own land,
  with no-one to lift her up."

3This is what the Sovereign LORD says:

"The city that marches out a thousand
    strong for Israel
  will have only a hundred left;
 the town that marches out a hundred
    strong
  will have only ten left."

4This is what the LORD says to the house
of Israel:

"Seek me and live;
 5 do not seek Bethel,
 do not go to Gilgal,
  do not journey to Beersheba.
 For Gilgal will surely go into exile,
  and Bethel will be reduced to
    nothing."[a]

a3 Masoretic Text; with a different word division of the Hebrew (see Septuagint) *out, O mountain of oppression*
b4 Or *tithes on the third day*   *c6* Hebrew *you cleanness of teeth*   *d11* Hebrew *God*
a5 Or *grief; or wickedness*; Hebrew *aven*, a reference to Beth Aven (a derogatory name for Bethel)

⁶Seek the LORD and live,
    or he will sweep through the house of
        Joseph like a fire;
it will devour,
    and Bethel will have no-one to
        quench it.

⁷You who turn justice into bitterness
    and cast righteousness to the ground
⁸(he who made the Pleiades and Orion,
    who turns blackness into dawn
    and darkens day into night,
who calls for the waters of the sea
    and pours them out over the face of
        the land—
    the LORD is his name—
⁹he flashes destruction on the stronghold
    and brings the fortified city to ruin),
¹⁰you hate the one who reproves in court
    and despise him who tells the truth.

¹¹You trample on the poor
    and force him to give you grain.
Therefore, though you have built stone
        mansions,
    you will not live in them;
though you have planted lush
        vineyards,
    you will not drink their wine.
¹²For I know how many are your offences
    and how great your sins.

    You oppress the righteous and take
        bribes
    and you deprive the poor of justice in
        the courts.
¹³Therefore the prudent man keeps quiet
        in such times,
    for the times are evil.

¹⁴Seek good, not evil,
    that you may live.
Then the LORD God Almighty will be
        with you,
    just as you say he is.
¹⁵Hate evil, love good;
    maintain justice in the courts.
Perhaps the LORD God Almighty will
        have mercy
    on the remnant of Joseph.

¹⁶Therefore this is what the Lord, the
LORD God Almighty, says:

"There will be wailing in all the streets
    and cries of anguish in every public
        square.
The farmers will be summoned to weep
    and the mourners to wail.
¹⁷There will be wailing in all the
        vineyards,
    for I will pass through your midst,"
                                    says the LORD.

The Day of the LORD

¹⁸Woe to you who long
    for the day of the LORD!
Why do you long for the day of the
        LORD?
    That day will be darkness, not light.
¹⁹It will be as though a man fled from a
        lion
    only to meet a bear,
as though he entered his house
    and rested his hand on the wall
    only to have a snake bite him.
²⁰Will not the day of the LORD be
        darkness, not light—
    pitch-dark, without a ray of
        brightness?

²¹"I hate, I despise your religious
        feasts;
    I cannot stand your assemblies.
²²Even though you bring me burnt
        offerings and grain offerings,
    I will not accept them.
Though you bring choice fellowship
        offerings,ᵇ
    I will have no regard for them.
²³Away with the noise of your songs!
    I will not listen to the music of your
        harps.
²⁴But let justice roll on like a river,
    righteousness like a never-failing
        stream!

²⁵"Did you bring me sacrifices and
        offerings
    for forty years in the desert, O house
        of Israel?

b22 Traditionally peace offerings

26You have lifted up the shrine of your
     king,
    the pedestal of your idols,
    the star of your god—*c*
    which you made for yourselves.
27Therefore I will send you into exile
     beyond Damascus,"
    says the LORD, whose name is God
     Almighty.

Woe to the Complacent

6 Woe to you who are complacent in
    Zion,
    and to you who feel secure on Mount
     Samaria,
  you notable men of the foremost
     nation,
    to whom the people of Israel come!
2Go to Calneh and look at it;
    go from there to great Hamath,
    and then go down to Gath in
     Philistia.
  Are they better off than your two
     kingdoms?
  Is their land larger than yours?
3You put off the evil day
    and bring near a reign of terror.
4You lie on beds inlaid with ivory
    and lounge on your couches.
  You dine on choice lambs
    and fattened calves.
5You strum away on your harps like
     David
    and improvise on musical
     instruments.
6You drink wine by the bowlful
    and use the finest lotions,
    but you do not grieve over the ruin of
     Joseph.
7Therefore you will be among the first to
     go into exile;
    your feasting and lounging will end.

The LORD Abhors the Pride of Israel

8The Sovereign LORD has sworn by himself—the LORD God Almighty declares:

  "I abhor the pride of Jacob
    and detest his fortresses;
  I will deliver up the city
    and everything in it."

9If ten men are left in one house, they
too will die. 10And if a relative who is to
burn the bodies comes to carry them out of
the house and asks anyone still hiding
there, "Is anyone with you?" and he says,
"No," then he will say, "Hush! We must
not mention the name of the LORD."

11For the LORD has given the command,
    and he will smash the great house
     into pieces
    and the small house into bits.

12Do horses run on the rocky crags?
    Does one plough there with oxen?
  But you have turned justice into poison
    and the fruit of righteousness into
     bitterness—
13you who rejoice in the conquest of Lo
     Debar*a*
    and say, "Did we not take Karnaim*b*
     by our own strength?"

14For the LORD God Almighty declares,
    "I will stir up a nation against you, O
     house of Israel,
  that will oppress you all the way
    from Lebo*c* Hamath to the valley of
     the Arabah."

Locusts, Fire and a Plumb-Line

7 This is what the Sovereign LORD
    showed me: He was preparing
swarms of locusts after the king's share
had been harvested and just as the second
crop was coming up. 2When they had
stripped the land clean, I cried out,
"Sovereign LORD, forgive! How can Jacob
survive? He is so small!"

3So the LORD relented.

"This will not happen," the LORD said.

4This is what the Sovereign LORD
showed me: The Sovereign LORD was

---

*c*26 Or *lifted up Sakkuth your king* / *and Kaiwan your idols,* / *your star-gods*; Septuagint *lifted up the shrine of Molech* / *and the star of your god Rephan,* / *their idols*   *a*13 *Lo Debar* means *nothing.*
*b*13 *Karnaim* means *horns*; *horn* here symbolises strength.   *c*14 Or *from the entrance to*

calling for judgment by fire; it dried up the great deep and devoured the land. ⁵Then I cried out, "Sovereign LORD, I beg you, stop! How can Jacob survive? He is so small!"

⁶So the LORD relented.

"This will not happen either," the Sovereign LORD said.

⁷This is what he showed me: the Lord was standing by a wall that had been built true to plumb, with a plumb-line in his hand. ⁸And the LORD asked me, "What do you see, Amos?"

"A plumb-line," I replied.

Then the Lord said, "Look, I am setting a plumb-line among my people Israel; I will spare them no longer.

⁹"The high places of Isaac will be destroyed
   and the sanctuaries of Israel will be ruined;
   with my sword I will rise against the house of Jeroboam."

Amos and Amaziah

¹⁰Then Amaziah the priest of Bethel sent a message to Jeroboam king of Israel: "Amos is raising a conspiracy against you in the very heart of Israel. The land cannot bear all his words. ¹¹For this is what Amos is saying:

"'Jeroboam will die by the sword,
   and Israel will surely go into exile,
   away from their native land.'"

¹²Then Amaziah said to Amos, "Get out, you seer! Go back to the land of Judah. Earn your bread there and do your prophesying there. ¹³Don't prophesy any more at Bethel, because this is the king's sanctuary and the temple of the kingdom."

¹⁴Amos answered Amaziah, "I was neither a prophet nor a prophet's son, but I was a shepherd, and I also took care of sycamore-fig trees. ¹⁵But the LORD took me from tending the flock and said to me,

'Go, prophesy to my people Israel.' ¹⁶Now then, hear the word of the LORD. You say,

"'Do not prophesy against Israel,
   and stop preaching against the house of Isaac.'

¹⁷"Therefore this is what the LORD says:

"'Your wife will become a prostitute in the city,
   and your sons and daughters will fall by the sword.
Your land will be measured and divided up,
   and you yourself will die in a pagan*ᵃ* country.
And Israel will certainly go into exile,
   away from their native land.'"

A Basket of Ripe Fruit

8 This is what the Sovereign LORD showed me: a basket of ripe fruit. ²"What do you see, Amos?" he asked.

"A basket of ripe fruit," I answered.

Then the LORD said to me, "The time is ripe for my people Israel; I will spare them no longer.

³"In that day," declares the Sovereign LORD, "the songs in the temple will turn to wailing.*ᵃ* Many, many bodies—flung everywhere! Silence!"

⁴Hear this, you who trample the needy
   and do away with the poor of the land,

⁵saying,

"When will the New Moon be over
   that we may sell grain,
and the Sabbath be ended
   that we may market wheat?"—
skimping the measure,
   boosting the price
   and cheating with dishonest scales,
⁶buying the poor with silver
   and the needy for a pair of sandals,

ᵃ17 Hebrew *an unclean*   *ᵃ3* Or *"the temple singers will wail"* selling even the sweepings with the wheat.

⁷The LORD has sworn by the Pride of Jacob: "I will never forget anything they have done.

⁸"Will not the land tremble for this,
    and all who live in it mourn?
The whole land will rise like the Nile;
    it will be stirred up and then sink
    like the river of Egypt.

⁹"In that day," declares the Sovereign LORD,

"I will make the sun go down at noon
    and darken the earth in broad
        daylight.
¹⁰I will turn your religious feasts into
        mourning
    and all your singing into weeping.
I will make all of you wear sackcloth
    and shave your heads.
I will make that time like mourning for
        an only son
    and the end of it like a bitter day.

¹¹"The days are coming," declares the
        Sovereign LORD,
    "when I will send a famine through
        the land—
not a famine of food or a thirst for
        water,
    but a famine of hearing the words of
        the LORD.
¹²Men will stagger from sea to sea
    and wander from north to east,
searching for the word of the LORD,
    but they will not find it.

¹³"In that day

"the lovely young women and strong
        young men
    will faint because of thirst.
¹⁴They who swear by the shame*b* of
        Samaria,
    or say, 'As surely as your god lives, O
        Dan',

or, 'As surely as the god*c* of
        Beersheba lives'—
they will fall,
    never to rise again."

Israel to Be Destroyed

9 I saw the Lord standing by the altar,
    and he said:

"Strike the tops of the pillars
    so that the thresholds shake.
Bring them down on the heads of all the
        people;
    those who are left I will kill with the
        sword.
Not one will get away,
    none will escape.
²Though they dig down to the depths of
        the grave,*a*
    from there my hand will take them.
Though they climb up to the heavens,
    from there I will bring them down.
³Though they hide themselves on the top
        of Carmel,
    there I will hunt them down and seize
        them.
Though they hide from me at the
        bottom of the sea,
    there I will command the serpent to
        bite them.
⁴Though they are driven into exile by
        their enemies,
    there I will command the sword to
        slay them.
I will fix my eyes upon them
    for evil and not for good."

⁵The Lord, the LORD Almighty,
    he who touches the earth and it melts,
    and all who live in it mourn—
the whole land rises like the Nile,
    then sinks like the river of Egypt—
⁶he who builds his lofty palace*b* in the
        heavens
    and sets its foundation*c* on the earth,
who calls for the waters of the sea
    and pours them out over the face of
        the land—
    the LORD is his name.

b14 Or *by Ashima;* or *by the idol*   *c14* Or *power*   *a2* Hebrew *to Sheol*
b6 The meaning of the Hebrew for this phrase is uncertain.
c6 The meaning of the Hebrew for this word is uncertain.

7"Are not you Israelites
  the same to me as the Cushites?"[d]
               declares the LORD.
"Did I not bring Israel up from Egypt,
  the Philistines from Caphtor[e]
  and the Arameans from Kir?

8"Surely the eyes of the Sovereign LORD
  are on the sinful kingdom.
I will destroy it
  from the face of the earth—
yet I will not totally destroy
  the house of Jacob,"
               declares the LORD.
9"For I will give the command,
  and I will shake the house of Israel
  among all the nations
as grain is shaken in a sieve,
  and not a pebble will reach the
    ground.
10All the sinners among my people
  will die by the sword,
all those who say,
  'Disaster will not overtake or meet
    us.'

Israel's Restoration

11"In that day I will restore
  David's fallen tent.
I will repair its broken places,

  restore its ruins,
  and build it as it used to be,
12so that they may possess the remnant of
    Edom
  and all the nations that bear my
    name,"[f]
               declares the LORD,
           who will do these things.

13"The days are coming," declares the
LORD,

"when the reaper will be overtaken by
    the ploughman
  and the planter by the one treading
    grapes.
New wine will drip from the mountains
  and flow from all the hills.
14I will bring back my exiled[g] people
    Israel;
  they will rebuild the ruined cities and
    live in them.
They will plant vineyards and drink
    their wine;
  they will make gardens and eat their
    fruit.
15I will plant Israel in their own land,
  never again to be uprooted
  from the land I have given them,"

            says the LORD your God.

---

[d]7 That is, people from the upper Nile region   [e]7 That is, Crete
[f]12 Hebrew; Septuagint *so that the remnant of men / and all the nations that bear my name may seek the Lord*
[g]14 Or *will restore the fortunes of my*

Obadiah

¹The vision of Obadiah.

This is what the Sovereign LORD says about Edom—

We have heard a message from the
  LORD:
  An envoy was sent to the nations to
    say,
  "Rise, and let us go against her for
    battle"—

²"See, I will make you small among the
    nations;
  you will be utterly despised.
³The pride of your heart has deceived
    you,
  you who live in the clefts of the rocks*a*
  and make your home on the heights,
you who say to yourself,
  'Who can bring me down to the
    ground?'
⁴Though you soar like the eagle
  and make your nest among the stars,
  from there I will bring you down,"
                    declares the LORD.
⁵"If thieves came to you,
  if robbers in the night—
Oh, what a disaster awaits you—
  would they not steal only as much as
    they wanted?
If grape pickers came to you,
  would they not leave a few grapes?
⁶But how Esau will be ransacked,
  his hidden treasures pillaged!
⁷All your allies will force you to the
    border;

your friends will deceive and
    overpower you;
those who eat your bread will set a trap
    for you,*b*
  but you will not detect it.

⁸"In that day," declares the LORD,
  "will I not destroy the wise men of
    Edom,
  men of understanding in the
    mountains of Esau?
⁹Your warriors, O Teman, will be
    terrified,
  and everyone in Esau's mountains
  will be cut down in the slaughter.
¹⁰Because of the violence against your
    brother Jacob,
  you will be covered with shame;
  you will be destroyed for ever.
¹¹On the day you stood aloof
  while strangers carried off his wealth
and foreigners entered his gates
  and cast lots for Jerusalem,
  you were like one of them.
¹²You should not look down on your
    brother
  in the day of his misfortune,
nor rejoice over the people of Judah
  in the day of their destruction,
nor boast so much
  in the day of their trouble.
¹³You should not march through the
    gates of my people
  in the day of their disaster,
nor look down on them in their calamity
  in the day of their disaster,
nor seize their wealth

---

a3 Or *of Sela*   *b7* The meaning of the Hebrew for this clause is uncertain.

in the day of their disaster.
¹⁴You should not wait at the crossroads
  to cut down their fugitives,
nor hand over their survivors
  in the day of their trouble.

¹⁵"The day of the LORD is near
  for all nations.
As you have done, it will be done to
    you;
  your deeds will return upon your own
    head.
¹⁶Just as you drank on my holy hill,
  so all the nations will drink
    continually;
they will drink and drink
  and be as if they had never been.
¹⁷But on Mount Zion will be deliverance;
  it will be holy,
and the house of Jacob
  will possess its inheritance.
¹⁸The house of Jacob will be a fire
  and the house of Joseph a flame;
the house of Esau will be stubble,

and they will set it on fire and
    consume it.
There will be no survivors
  from the house of Esau."
                        The LORD has spoken.

¹⁹People from the Negev will occupy
  the mountains of Esau,
and people from the foothills will
    possess
  the land of the Philistines.
They will occupy the fields of Ephraim
    and Samaria,
  and Benjamin will possess Gilead.
²⁰This company of Israelite exiles who are
    in Canaan
  will possess ˻the land˼ as far as
    Zarephath;
the exiles from Jerusalem who are in
    Sepharad
  will possess the towns of the Negev.
²¹Deliverers will go up onᶜ Mount Zion
  to govern the mountains of Esau.
  And the kingdom will be the LORD's.

ᶜ21 Or *from*

Jonah

Jonah Flees From the Lord

1 The word of the Lord came to Jonah son of Amittai: 2"Go to the great city of Nineveh and preach against it, because its wickedness has come up before me."

3But Jonah ran away from the Lord and headed for Tarshish. He went down to Joppa, where he found a ship bound for that port. After paying the fare, he went aboard and sailed for Tarshish to flee from the Lord.

4Then the Lord sent a great wind on the sea, and such a violent storm arose that the ship threatened to break up. 5All the sailors were afraid and each cried out to his own god. And they threw the cargo into the sea to lighten the ship.

But Jonah had gone below deck, where he lay down and fell into a deep sleep. 6The captain went to him and said, "How can you sleep? Get up and call on your god! Maybe he will take notice of us, and we will not perish."

7Then the sailors said to each other, "Come, let us cast lots to find out who is responsible for this calamity." They cast lots and the lot fell on Jonah.

8So they asked him, "Tell us, who is responsible for making all this trouble for us? What do you do? Where do you come from? What is your country? From what people are you?"

9He answered, "I am a Hebrew and I worship the Lord, the God of heaven, who made the sea and the land."

10This terrified them and they asked, "What have you done?" (They knew he was running away from the Lord, because he had already told them so.)

11The sea was getting rougher and rougher. So they asked him, "What should we do to you to make the sea calm down for us?"

12"Pick me up and throw me into the sea," he replied, "and it will become calm. I know that it is my fault that this great storm has come upon you."

13Instead, the men did their best to row back to land. But they could not, for the sea grew even wilder than before. 14Then they cried to the Lord, "O Lord, please do not let us die for taking this man's life. Do not hold us accountable for killing an innocent man, for you, O Lord, have done as you pleased." 15Then they took Jonah and threw him overboard, and the raging sea grew calm. 16At this the men greatly feared the Lord, and they offered a sacrifice to the Lord and made vows to him.

17But the Lord provided a great fish to swallow Jonah, and Jonah was inside the fish three days and three nights.

Jonah's Prayer

2 From inside the fish Jonah prayed to the Lord his God. 2He said:

"In my distress I called to the Lord,
    and he answered me.
From the depths of the grave*a* I called
    for help,

*a*2 Hebrew *Sheol*

and you listened to my cry.
³You hurled me into the deep,
    into the very heart of the seas,
        and the currents swirled about me;
all your waves and breakers
    swept over me.
⁴I said, 'I have been banished
    from your sight;
yet I will look again
    towards your holy temple.'
⁵The engulfing waters threatened me,*b*
    the deep surrounded me;
        seaweed was wrapped around my
            head.
⁶To the roots of the mountains I sank
    down;
    the earth beneath barred me in for
        ever.
But you brought my life up from the pit,
    O LORD my God.

⁷"When my life was ebbing away,
    I remembered you, LORD,
and my prayer rose to you,
    to your holy temple.

⁸"Those who cling to worthless idols
    forfeit the grace that could be theirs.
⁹But I, with a song of thanksgiving,
    will sacrifice to you.
What I have vowed I will make good.
    Salvation comes from the LORD.' "

¹⁰And the LORD commanded the fish, and it vomited Jonah onto dry land.

Jonah Goes to Nineveh

3 Then the word of the LORD came to Jonah a second time: ²"Go to the great city of Nineveh and proclaim to it the message I give you."

³Jonah obeyed the word of the LORD and went to Nineveh. Now Nineveh was a very important city—a visit required three days. ⁴On the first day, Jonah started into the city. He proclaimed: "Forty more days and Nineveh will be overturned." ⁵The Ninevites believed God. They declared a fast, and all of them, from the greatest to the least, put on sackcloth.

⁶When the news reached the king of Nineveh, he rose from his throne, took off his royal robes, covered himself with sackcloth and sat down in the dust. ⁷Then he issued a proclamation in Nineveh:

"By the decree of the king and his nobles:

Do not let any man or beast, herd or flock, taste anything; do not let them eat or drink. ⁸But let man and beast be covered with sackcloth. Let everyone call urgently on God. Let them give up their evil ways and their violence. ⁹Who knows? God may yet relent and with compassion turn from his fierce anger so that we will not perish."

¹⁰When God saw what they did and how they turned from their evil ways, he had compassion and did not bring upon them the destruction he had threatened.

Jonah's Anger at the LORD's Compassion

4 But Jonah was greatly displeased and became angry. ²He prayed to the LORD, "O LORD, is this not what I said when I was still at home? That is why I was so quick to flee to Tarshish. I knew that you are a gracious and compassionate God, slow to anger and abounding in love, a God who relents from sending calamity. ³Now, O LORD, take away my life, for it is better for me to die than to live."

⁴But the LORD replied, "Have you any right to be angry?"

⁵Jonah went out and sat down at a place east of the city. There he made himself a shelter, sat in its shade and waited to see what would happen to the city. ⁶Then the LORD God provided a vine and made it grow up over Jonah to give shade for his head to ease his discomfort, and Jonah was very happy about the vine. ⁷But at dawn the next day God provided a worm, which chewed the vine so that it withered. ⁸When the sun rose, God provided a scorching east wind, and the sun blazed on

---

b5 Or waters were at my throat

Jonah's head so that he grew faint. He wanted to die, and said, "It would be better for me to die than to live."

⁹But God said to Jonah, "Do you have a right to be angry about the vine?"

"I do," he said. "I am angry enough to die."

¹⁰But the LORD said, "You have been concerned about this vine, though you did not tend it or make it grow. It sprang up overnight and died overnight. ¹¹But Nineveh has more than a hundred and twenty thousand people who cannot tell their right hand from their left, and many cattle as well. Should I not be concerned about that great city?"

Micah

1 The word of the LORD that came to Micah of Moresheth during the reigns of Jotham, Ahaz and Hezekiah, kings of Judah—the vision he saw concerning Samaria and Jerusalem.

² Hear, O peoples, all of you,
  listen, O earth and all who are in it,
that the Sovereign LORD may witness
      against you,
  the Lord from his holy temple.

Judgment Against Samaria and Jerusalem

³ Look! The LORD is coming from his
      dwelling-place;
  he comes down and treads the high
      places of the earth.
⁴ The mountains melt beneath him
  and the valleys split apart,
like wax before the fire,
  like water rushing down a slope.
⁵ All this is because of Jacob's
      transgression,
  because of the sins of the house of
      Israel.
What is Jacob's transgression?
  Is it not Samaria?
What is Judah's high place?
  Is it not Jerusalem?

⁶ "Therefore I will make Samaria a heap
      of rubble,
  a place for planting vineyards.
I will pour her stones into the valley
  and lay bare her foundations.
⁷ All her idols will be broken to pieces;
  all her temple gifts will be burned
      with fire;
  I will destroy all her images.
Since she gathered her gifts from the
      wages of prostitutes,
  as the wages of prostitutes they will
      again be used."

Weeping and Mourning

⁸ Because of this I will weep and wail;
  I will go about barefoot and naked.
I will howl like a jackal
  and moan like an owl.
⁹ For her wound is incurable;
  it has come to Judah.
It*a* has reached the very gate of my
      people,
  even to Jerusalem itself.
¹⁰ Tell it not in Gath;*b*
  weep not at all.*c*
In Beth Ophrah*d*
  roll in the dust.
¹¹ Pass on in nakedness and shame,
  you who live in Shaphir.*e*
Those who live in Zaanan*f*
  will not come out.
Beth Ezel is in mourning;
  its protection is taken from you.
¹² Those who live in Maroth*g* writhe in
      pain,

---

a9 Or He   b10 Gath sounds like the Hebrew for tell.
c10 Hebrew; Septuagint may suggest not in Acco. The Hebrew for in Acco sounds like the Hebrew for weep.
d10 Beth Ophrah means house of dust.   e11 Shaphir means pleasant.
f11 Zaanan sounds like the Hebrew for come out.   g12 Maroth sounds like the Hebrew for bitter.

waiting for relief,
because disaster has come from the
    LORD,
even to the gate of Jerusalem.
¹³You who live in Lachish,ʰ
harness the team to the chariot.
You were the beginning of sin
    to the Daughter of Zion,
for the transgressions of Israel
    were found in you.
¹⁴Therefore you will give parting gifts
    to Moresheth Gath.
The town of Aczibⁱ will prove deceptive
    to the kings of Israel.
¹⁵I will bring a conqueror against you
    who live in Mareshah.ʲ
He who is the glory of Israel
    will come to Adullam.
¹⁶Shave your heads in mourning
    for the children in whom you
        delight;
make yourselves as bald as the vulture,
    for they will go from you into exile.

Man's Plans and God's

2 Woe to those who plan iniquity,
    to those who plot evil on their beds!
At morning's light they carry it out
    because it is in their power to do it.
²They covet fields and seize them,
    and houses, and take them.
They defraud a man of his home,
    a fellow-man of his inheritance.

³Therefore, the LORD says:

"I am planning disaster against this
        people,
    from which you cannot save
        yourselves.
You will no longer walk proudly,
    for it will be a time of calamity.
⁴In that day men will ridicule you;
    they will taunt you with this mournful
        song:
'We are utterly ruined;
    my people's possession is divided up.
He takes it from me!
    He assigns our fields to traitors.'"

⁵Therefore you will have no-one in the
        assembly of the LORD
    to divide the land by lot.

False Prophets

⁶"Do not prophesy," their prophets say.
    "Do not prophesy about these things;
    disgrace will not overtake us."
⁷Should it be said, O house of Jacob:
    "Is the Spirit of the LORD angry?
    Does he do such things?"

"Do not my words do good
    to him whose ways are upright?
⁸Lately my people have risen up
    like an enemy.
You strip off the rich robe
    from those who pass by without a
        care,
    like men returning from battle.
⁹You drive the women of my people
    from their pleasant homes.
You take away my blessing
    from their children for ever.
¹⁰Get up, go away!
    For this is not your resting place,
because it is defiled,
    it is ruined, beyond all remedy.
¹¹If a liar and deceiver comes and says,
    'I will prophesy for you plenty of
        wine and beer,'
    he would be just the prophet for this
        people!

Deliverance Promised

¹²"I will surely gather all of you, O Jacob;
    I will surely bring together the
        remnant of Israel.
I will bring them together like sheep in
        a pen,
    like a flock in its pasture;
    the place will throng with people.
¹³One who breaks open the way will go
        up before them;
    they will break through the gate and
        go out.
Their king will pass through before
        them,
    the LORD at their head."

ʰ13 Lachish sounds like the Hebrew for *team*.   ⁱ14 Aczib means *deception*.
ʲ15 Mareshah sounds like the Hebrew for *conqueror*.

Leaders and Prophets Rebuked

3 Then I said,

"Listen, you leaders of Jacob,
  you rulers of the house of Israel.
Should you not know justice,
² you who hate good and love evil;
who tear the skin from my people
  and the flesh from their bones;
³who eat my people's flesh,
  strip off their skin
  and break their bones in pieces;
who chop them up like meat for the
    pan,
  like flesh for the pot."

⁴Then they will cry out to the LORD,
  but he will not answer them.
At that time he will hide his face from
    them
  because of the evil they have done.

⁵This is what the LORD says:

"As for the prophets
  who lead my people astray,
if one feeds them,
  they proclaim 'peace';
if he does not,
  they prepare to wage war against
    him.
⁶Therefore night will come over you,
    without visions,
  and darkness, without divination.
The sun will set for the prophets,
  and the day will go dark for them.
⁷The seers will be ashamed
  and the diviners disgraced.
They will all cover their faces
  because there is no answer from
    God."

⁸But as for me, I am filled with power,
  with the Spirit of the LORD,
  and with justice and might,
to declare to Jacob his transgression,
  to Israel his sin.
⁹Hear this, you leaders of the house of
    Jacob,
  you rulers of the house of Israel,
who despise justice
  and distort all that is right;
¹⁰who build Zion with bloodshed,
  and Jerusalem with wickedness.
¹¹Her leaders judge for a bribe,
  her priests teach for a price,
  and her prophets tell fortunes for
    money.
Yet they lean upon the LORD and say,
  "Is not the LORD among us?
  No disaster will come upon us."
¹²Therefore because of you,
  Zion will be ploughed like a field,
Jerusalem will become a heap of
    rubble,
  the temple hill a mound overgrown
    with thickets.

The Mountain of the LORD

4 In the last days

the mountain of the LORD's temple will
    be established
  as chief among the mountains;
it will be raised above the hills,
  and peoples will stream to it.

²Many nations will come and say,

"Come, let us go up to the mountain of
    the LORD,
  to the house of the God of Jacob.
He will teach us his ways,
  so that we may walk in his paths."
The law will go out from Zion,
  the word of the LORD from
    Jerusalem.
³He will judge between many peoples
  and will settle disputes for strong
    nations far and wide.
They will beat their swords into
    ploughshares
  and their spears into pruning hooks.
Nation will not take up sword against
    nation,
  nor will they train for war any more.
⁴Every man will sit under his own vine
  and under his own fig-tree,
  and no-one will make them afraid,
    for the LORD Almighty has spoken.

[5]All the nations may walk
    in the name of their gods;
we will walk in the name of the LORD
    our God for ever and ever.

The LORD's Plan

[6]"In that day," declares the LORD,

"I will gather the lame;
    I will assemble the exiles
    and those I have brought to grief.
[7]I will make the lame a remnant,
    those driven away a strong nation.
The LORD will rule over them in Mount
        Zion
    from that day and for ever.
[8]As for you, O watchtower of the flock,
    O stronghold[a] of the Daughter of
        Zion,
    the former dominion will be restored to
        you;
    kingship will come to the Daughter of
        Jerusalem."

[9]Why do you now cry aloud—
    have you no king?
Has your counsellor perished,
    that pain seizes you like that of a
        woman in labour?
[10]Writhe in agony, O Daughter of Zion,
    like a woman in labour,
for now you must leave the city
    to camp in the open field.
You will go to Babylon;
    there you will be rescued.
There the LORD will redeem you
    out of the hand of your enemies.

[11]But now many nations
    are gathered against you.
They say, "Let her be defiled,
    let our eyes gloat over Zion!"
[12]But they do not know
    the thoughts of the LORD;
they do not understand his plan,
    he who gathers them like sheaves to
        the threshing-floor.

[13]"Rise and thresh, O Daughter of Zion,
    for I will give you horns of iron;

I will give you hoofs of bronze
    and you will break to pieces many
        nations."

You will devote their ill-gotten gains to
        the LORD,
    their wealth to the Lord of all the
        earth.

A Promised Ruler From Bethlehem

5   Marshal your troops, O city of
        troops,[a]
    for a siege is laid against us.
They will strike Israel's ruler
    on the cheek with a rod.

[2]"But you, Bethlehem Ephrathah,
    though you are small among the
        clans[b] of Judah,
out of you will come for me
    one who will be ruler over Israel,
whose origins[c] are from of old,
    from ancient times."[d]

[3]Therefore Israel will be abandoned
    until the time when she who is in
        labour gives birth
and the rest of his brothers return
    to join the Israelites.

[4]He will stand and shepherd his flock
    in the strength of the LORD,
    in the majesty of the name of the
        LORD his God.
And they will live securely, for then his
        greatness
    will reach to the ends of the earth.
[5]   And he will be their peace.

Deliverance and Destruction

When the Assyrian invades our land
    and marches through our fortresses,
we will raise against him seven
        shepherds,
    even eight leaders of men.
[6]They will rule[e] the land of Assyria with
        the sword,
    the land of Nimrod with drawn
        sword.[f]

---

a8 Or hill   a1 Or Strengthen your walls, O walled city   b2 Or rulers   c2 Hebrew goings out
d2 Or from days of eternity   e6 Or crush   f6 Or Nimrod in its gates

He will deliver us from the Assyrian
  when he invades our land
  and marches into our borders.

⁷The remnant of Jacob will be
  in the midst of many peoples
like dew from the LORD,
  like showers on the grass,
which do not wait for man
  or linger for mankind.
⁸The remnant of Jacob will be among the
    nations,
  in the midst of many peoples,
like a lion among the beasts of the
    forest,
  like a young lion among flocks of
    sheep,
which mauls and mangles as it goes,
  and no-one can rescue.
⁹Your hand will be lifted up in triumph
    over your enemies,
  and all your foes will be destroyed.

¹⁰"In that day," declares the LORD,

"I will destroy your horses from among
    you
  and demolish your chariots.
¹¹I will destroy the cities of your land
  and tear down all your strongholds.
¹²I will destroy your witchcraft
  and you will no longer cast spells.
¹³I will destroy your carved images
  and your sacred stones from among
    you;
you will no longer bow down
  to the work of your hands.
¹⁴I will uproot from among you your
    Asherah poles*g*
  and demolish your cities.
¹⁵I will take vengeance in anger and wrath
  upon the nations that have not
    obeyed me."

The LORD's Case Against Israel

6

Listen to what the LORD says:

"Stand up, plead your case before the
    mountains;
  let the hills hear what you have to
    say.

²Hear, O mountains, the LORD's
    accusation;
  listen, you everlasting foundations of
    the earth.
For the LORD has a case against his
    people;
  he is lodging a charge against Israel.

³"My people, what have I done to you?
  How have I burdened you? Answer
    me.
⁴I brought you up out of Egypt
  and redeemed you from the land of
    slavery.
I sent Moses to lead you,
  also Aaron and Miriam.
⁵My people, remember
  what Balak king of Moab counselled
  and what Balaam son of Beor
    answered.
Remember ⌐your journey⌐ from Shittim
    to Gilgal,
  that you may know the righteous acts
    of the LORD."

⁶With what shall I come before the LORD
  and bow down before the exalted
    God?
Shall I come before him with burnt
    offerings,
  with calves a year old?
⁷Will the LORD be pleased with
    thousands of rams,
  with ten thousand rivers of oil?
Shall I offer my firstborn for my
    transgression,
  the fruit of my body for the sin of my
    soul?
⁸He has showed you, O man, what is
    good.
  And what does the LORD require of
    you?
To act justly and to love mercy
  and to walk humbly with your God.

Israel's Guilt and Punishment

⁹Listen! The LORD is calling to the city—
  and to fear your name is wisdom—
  "Heed the rod and the One who
    appointed it.*a*

---

g14 That is, symbols of the goddess Asherah   *a9* The meaning of the Hebrew for this line is uncertain.

¹⁰Am I still to forget, O wicked house,
  your ill-gotten treasures
  and the short ephah,ᵇ which is
      accursed?
¹¹Shall I acquit a man with dishonest
      scales,
  with a bag of false weights?
¹²Her rich men are violent;
  her people are liars
  and their tongues speak deceitfully.
¹³Therefore, I have begun to destroy you,
  to ruin you because of your sins.
¹⁴You will eat but not be satisfied;
  your stomach will still be empty.ᶜ
  You will store up but save nothing,
  because what you save I will give to
      the sword.
¹⁵You will plant but not harvest;
  you will press olives but not use the
      oil on yourselves,
  you will crush grapes but not drink
      the wine.
¹⁶You have observed the statutes of Omri
  and all the practices of Ahab's house,
  and you have followed their
      traditions.
  Therefore I will give you over to ruin
  and your people to derision;
  you will bear the scorn of the
      nations."ᵈ

Israel's Misery

7 What misery is mine!
  I am like one who gathers summer
      fruit
  at the gleaning of the vineyard;
  there is no cluster of grapes to eat,
  none of the early figs that I crave.
²The godly have been swept from the
      land;
  not one upright man remains.
  All men lie in wait to shed blood;
  each hunts his brother with a net.
³Both hands are skilled in doing evil;
  the ruler demands gifts,
  the judge accepts bribes,
  the powerful dictate what they
      desire—
  they all conspire together.

⁴The best of them is like a brier,
  the most upright worse than a thorn
      hedge.
  The day of your watchmen has come,
  the day God visits you.
  Now is the time of their confusion.
⁵Do not trust a neighbour;
  put no confidence in a friend.
  Even with her who lies in your embrace
  be careful of your words.
⁶For a son dishonours his father,
  a daughter rises up against her
      mother,
  a daughter-in-law against her
      mother-in-law—
  a man's enemies are the members of
      his own household.

⁷But as for me, I watch in hope for the
      LORD,
  I wait for God my Saviour;
  my God will hear me.

Israel Will Rise

⁸Do not gloat over me, my enemy!
  Though I have fallen, I will rise.
  Though I sit in darkness,
  the LORD will be my light.
⁹Because I have sinned against him,
  I will bear the LORD's wrath,
  until he pleads my case
  and establishes my right.
  He will bring me out into the
      light;
  I will see his righteousness.
¹⁰Then my enemy will see it
  and will be covered with
      shame,
  she who said to me,
  "Where is the LORD your God?"
  My eyes will see her downfall;
  even now she will be trampled
      underfoot
  like mire in the streets.

¹¹The day for building your walls will
      come,
  the day for extending your
      boundaries.

ᵇ10 An ephah was a dry measure.   ᶜ14 The meaning of the Hebrew for this word is uncertain.
ᵈ16 Septuagint; Hebrew *scorn due to my people*

¹²In that day people will come to you
 from Assyria and the cities of Egypt,
 even from Egypt to the Euphrates
 and from sea to sea
 and from mountain to mountain.
¹³The earth will become desolate because
   of its inhabitants,
 as the result of their deeds.

Prayer and Praise

¹⁴Shepherd your people with your staff,
 the flock of your inheritance,
 which lives by itself in a forest,
 in fertile pasture-lands.^a
 Let them feed in Bashan and Gilead
 as in days long ago.

¹⁵"As in the days when you came out of
   Egypt,
 I will show them my wonders."

¹⁶Nations will see and be ashamed,
 deprived of all their power.
 They will lay their hands on their
   mouths
 and their ears will become deaf.
¹⁷They will lick dust like a snake,
 like creatures that crawl on the
   ground.
 They will come trembling out of their
   dens;
 they will turn in fear to the LORD our
   God
 and will be afraid of you.
¹⁸Who is a God like you,
 who pardons sin and forgives the
   transgression
 of the remnant of his inheritance?
 You do not stay angry for ever
 but delight to show mercy.
¹⁹You will again have compassion on us;
 you will tread our sins underfoot
 and hurl all our iniquities into the
   depths of the sea.
²⁰You will be true to Jacob,
 and show mercy to Abraham,
 as you pledged on oath to our fathers
 in days long ago.

---

^a14 Or *in the middle of Carmel*

Nahum

1

An oracle concerning Nineveh. The book of the vision of Nahum the Elkoshite.

The Lord's Anger Against Nineveh

²The Lord is a jealous and avenging God;
 the Lord takes vengeance and is filled with wrath.
The Lord takes vengeance on his foes
 and maintains his wrath against his enemies.
³The Lord is slow to anger and great in power;
 the Lord will not leave the guilty unpunished.
His way is in the whirlwind and the storm,
 and clouds are the dust of his feet.
⁴He rebukes the sea and dries it up;
 he makes all the rivers run dry.
Bashan and Carmel wither
 and the blossoms of Lebanon fade.
⁵The mountains quake before him
 and the hills melt away.
The earth trembles at his presence,
 the world and all who live in it.
⁶Who can withstand his indignation?
 Who can endure his fierce anger?
His wrath is poured out like fire;
 the rocks are shattered before him.

⁷The Lord is good,
 a refuge in times of trouble.
He cares for those who trust in him,
⁸ but with an overwhelming flood
he will make an end of ⌐Nineveh⌐;
 he will pursue his foes into darkness.

⁹Whatever they plot against the Lord
 he*ᵃ* will bring to an end;
 trouble will not come a second time.
¹⁰They will be entangled among thorns
 and drunk from their wine;
 they will be consumed like dry stubble.*ᵇ*
¹¹From you, ⌐O Nineveh,⌐ has one come forth
 who plots evil against the Lord
 and counsels wickedness.

¹²This is what the Lord says:

"Although they have allies and are numerous,
 they will be cut off and pass away.
Although I have afflicted you, ⌐O Judah,⌐
 I will afflict you no more.
¹³Now I will break their yoke from your neck
 and tear your shackles away."

¹⁴The Lord has given a command
 concerning you, ⌐Nineveh⌐:
 "You will have no descendants to bear your name.
I will destroy the carved images and cast idols
 that are in the temple of your gods.
I will prepare your grave,
 for you are vile."

ᵃ9 Or *What do you foes plot against the Lord? / He*   *ᵇ10* The meaning of the Hebrew for this verse is uncertain.

¹⁵Look, there on the mountains,
the feet of one who brings good news,
who proclaims peace!
Celebrate your festivals, O Judah,
and fulfil your vows.
No more will the wicked invade you;
they will be completely destroyed.

Nineveh to Fall

2 An attacker advances against you,
⌊Nineveh⌋.
Guard the fortress,
watch the road,
brace yourselves,
marshal all your strength!

²The LORD will restore the splendour of
Jacob
like the splendour of Israel,
though destroyers have laid them waste
and have ruined their vines.

³The shields of his soldiers are red;
the warriors are clad in scarlet.
The metal on the chariots flashes
on the day they are made ready;
the spears of pine are brandished.^a
⁴The chariots storm through the streets,
rushing back and forth through the
squares.
They look like flaming torches;
they dart about like lightning.

⁵He summons his picked troops,
yet they stumble on their way.
They dash to the city wall;
the protective shield is put in place.
⁶The river gates are thrown open
and the palace collapses.
⁷It is decreed^b that ⌊the city⌋
be exiled and carried away.
Its slave girls moan like doves
and beat upon their breasts.
⁸Nineveh is like a pool,
and its water is draining away.
"Stop! Stop!" they cry,
but no-one turns back.
⁹Plunder the silver!
Plunder the gold!

The supply is endless,
the wealth from all its treasures!
¹⁰She is pillaged, plundered, stripped!
Hearts melt, knees give way,
bodies tremble, every face grows
pale.

¹¹Where now is the lions' den,
the place where they fed their young,
where the lion and lioness went,
and the cubs, with nothing to fear?
¹²The lion killed enough for his cubs
and strangled the prey for his mate,
filling his lairs with the kill
and his dens with the prey.

¹³"I am against you,"
declares the LORD Almighty.
"I will burn up your chariots in smoke,
and the sword will devour your young
lions.
I will leave you no prey on the earth.
The voices of your messengers
will no longer be heard."

Woe to Nineveh

3 Woe to the city of blood,
full of lies,
full of plunder,
never without victims!
²The crack of whips,
the clatter of wheels,
galloping horses
and jolting chariots!
³Charging cavalry,
flashing swords
and glittering spears!
Many casualties,
piles of dead,
bodies without number,
people stumbling over the corpses—
⁴all because of the wanton lust of a
harlot,
alluring, the mistress of sorceries,
who enslaved nations by her
prostitution
and peoples by her witchcraft.

⁵"I am against you," declares the LORD
Almighty.

---

^a3 Hebrew; Septuagint and Syriac / *the horsemen rush to and fro*
^b7 The meaning of the Hebrew for this word is uncertain.

"I will lift your skirts over your face.
I will show the nations your nakedness
    and the kingdoms your shame.
⁶I will pelt you with filth,
    I will treat you with contempt
    and make you a spectacle.
⁷All who see you will flee from you and
        say,
    'Nineveh is in ruins—who will mourn
        for her?'
    Where can I find anyone to comfort
        you?"

⁸Are you better than Thebes,ᵃ
    situated on the Nile,
    with water around her?
The river was her defence,
    the waters her wall.
⁹Cushᵇ and Egypt were her boundless
        strength;
    Put and Libya were among her allies.
¹⁰Yet she was taken captive
    and went into exile.
Her infants were dashed to pieces
    at the head of every street.
Lots were cast for her nobles,
    and all her great men were put in
        chains.
¹¹You too will become drunk;
    you will go into hiding
    and seek refuge from the enemy.

¹²All your fortresses are like fig-trees
    with their first ripe fruit;
when they are shaken,
    the figs fall into the mouth of the
        eater.
¹³Look at your troops—
    they are all women!

The gates of your land
    are wide open to your enemies;
    fire has consumed their bars.

¹⁴Draw water for the siege,
    strengthen your defences!
Work the clay,
    tread the mortar,
    repair the brickwork!
¹⁵There the fire will devour you;
    the sword will cut you down
    and, like grasshoppers, consume you.
Multiply like grasshoppers,
    multiply like locusts!
¹⁶You have increased the number of your
        merchants
    till they are more than the stars of the
        sky,
but like locusts they strip the land
    and then fly away.
¹⁷Your guards are like locusts,
    your officials like swarms of locusts
    that settle in the walls on a cold day—
but when the sun appears they fly away,
    and no-one knows where.

¹⁸O king of Assyria, your shepherdsᶜ
        slumber;
    your nobles lie down to rest.
Your people are scattered on the
        mountains
    with no-one to gather them.
¹⁹Nothing can heal your wound;
    your injury is fatal.
Everyone who hears the news about
        you
    claps his hands at your fall,
for who has not felt
    your endless cruelty?

ᵃ8 Hebrew No Amon   ᵇ9 That is, the upper Nile region   ᶜ18 Or rulers

Habakkuk

1 The oracle that Habakkuk the prophet received.

Habakkuk's Complaint

[2]How long, O LORD, must I call for help,
  but you do not listen?
Or cry out to you, "Violence!"
  but you do not save?
[3]Why do you make me look at injustice?
  Why do you tolerate wrong?
Destruction and violence are before
    me;
  there is strife, and conflict abounds.
[4]Therefore the law is paralysed,
  and justice never prevails.
The wicked hem in the righteous,
  so that justice is perverted.

The LORD's Answer

[5]"Look at the nations and watch—
  and be utterly amazed.
For I am going to do something in your
    days
  that you would not believe,
  even if you were told.
[6]I am raising up the Babylonians,[a]
  that ruthless and impetuous people,
who sweep across the whole earth
  to seize dwelling-places not their
    own.
[7]They are a feared and dreaded people;
  they are a law to themselves
  and promote their own honour.
[8]Their horses are swifter than leopards,
  fiercer than wolves at dusk.
Their cavalry gallops headlong;
  their horsemen come from afar.
They fly like a vulture swooping to
    devour;
[9] they all come bent on violence.
Their hordes[b] advance like a desert
    wind
  and gather prisoners like sand.
[10]They deride kings
  and scoff at rulers.
They laugh at all fortified cities;
  they build earthen ramps and capture
    them.
[11]Then they sweep past like the wind and
    go on—
  guilty men, whose own strength is
    their god."

Habakkuk's Second Complaint

[12]O LORD, are you not from everlasting?
  My God, my Holy One, we will not
    die.
O LORD, you have appointed them to
    execute judgment;
  O Rock, you have ordained them to
    punish.
[13]Your eyes are too pure to look on
    evil;
  you cannot tolerate wrong.
Why then do you tolerate the
    treacherous?
  Why are you silent while the wicked
swallow up those more righteous than
    themselves?
[14]You have made men like fish in the sea,
  like sea creatures that have no ruler.

¹⁵The wicked foe pulls all of them up with
     hooks,
  he catches them in his net,
he gathers them up in his drag-net;
  and so he rejoices and is glad.
¹⁶Therefore he sacrifices to his net
     and burns incense to his drag-net,
for by his net he lives in luxury
     and enjoys the choicest food.
¹⁷Is he to keep on emptying his net,
     destroying nations without mercy?

2 I will stand at my watch
     and station myself on the
     ramparts;
  I will look to see what he will say to me,
     and what answer I am to give to this
     complaint.^a

The Lord's Answer

²Then the Lord replied:

"Write down the revelation
     and make it plain on tablets
  so that a herald^b may run with it.
³For the revelation awaits an appointed
     time;
  it speaks of the end
     and will not prove false.
Though it linger, wait for it;
  it^c will certainly come and will not
     delay.

⁴"See, he is puffed up;
     his desires are not upright—
  but the righteous will live by his
     faith—^d
⁵indeed, wine betrays him;
  he is arrogant and never at rest.
Because he is as greedy as the grave^e
     and like death is never satisfied,
he gathers to himself all the nations
     and takes captive all the peoples.

⁶"Will not all of them taunt him with
ridicule and scorn, saying,

"'Woe to him who piles up stolen goods
     and makes himself wealthy by
     extortion!

How long must this go on?'
⁷Will not your debtors^f suddenly arise?
  Will they not wake up and make you
     tremble?
Then you will become their victim.
⁸Because you have plundered many
     nations,
  the peoples who are left will plunder
     you.
For you have shed man's blood;
  you have destroyed lands and cities
     and everyone in them.

⁹"Woe to him who builds his realm by
     unjust gain
  to set his nest on high,
  to escape the clutches of ruin!
¹⁰You have plotted the ruin of many
     peoples,
  shaming your own house and
     forfeiting your life.
¹¹The stones of the wall will cry out,
  and the beams of the woodwork will
     echo it.

¹²"Woe to him who builds a city with
     bloodshed
  and establishes a town by crime!
¹³Has not the Lord Almighty determined
  that the people's labour is only fuel
     for the fire,
  that nations exhaust themselves for
     nothing?
¹⁴For the earth will be filled with the
     knowledge of the glory of the
     Lord,
  as the waters cover the sea.

¹⁵"Woe to him who gives drink to his
     neighbours,
  pouring it from the wineskin till they
     are drunk,
  so that he can gaze on their naked
     bodies.
¹⁶You will be filled with shame instead of
     glory.
  Now it is your turn! Drink and be
     exposed!^g
The cup from the Lord's right hand is
     coming round to you,

---

^a1 Or *and what to answer when I am rebuked*   ^b2 Or *so that whoever reads it*
^c3 Or *Though he linger, wait for him; / he*   ^d4 Or *faithfulness*   ^e5 Hebrew *Sheol*   ^f7 Or *creditors*
^g16 Masoretic Text; Dead Sea Scrolls, Aquila, Vulgate and Syriac (see also Septuagint) *and stagger*

and disgrace will cover your glory.
17The violence you have done to Lebanon
    will overwhelm you,
  and your destruction of animals will
    terrify you.
  For you have shed man's blood;
    you have destroyed lands and cities
    and everyone in them.

18"Of what value is an idol, since a man
    has carved it?
  Or an image that teaches lies?
  For he who makes it trusts in his own
    creation;
    he makes idols that cannot speak.
19Woe to him who says to wood, 'Come
    to life!'
  Or to lifeless stone, 'Wake up!'
  Can it give guidance?
    It is covered with gold and silver;
    there is no breath in it.
20But the LORD is in his holy temple;
    let all the earth be silent before
    him."

Habakkuk's Prayer

3 A prayer of Habakkuk the prophet.
  On *shigionoth*.[a]

2LORD, I have heard of your fame;
  I stand in awe of your deeds,
    O LORD.
  Renew them in our day,
    in our time make them known;
    in wrath remember mercy.

3God came from Teman,
  the Holy One from Mount Paran.
                                    Selah[b]
  His glory covered the heavens
    and his praise filled the earth.
4His splendour was like the sunrise;
    rays flashed from his hand,
    where his power was hidden.
5Plague went before him;
    pestilence followed his steps.
6He stood, and shook the earth;
  he looked, and made the nations
    tremble.

The ancient mountains crumbled
    and the age-old hills collapsed.
  His ways are eternal.
7I saw the tents of Cushan in distress,
    the dwellings of Midian in anguish.

8Were you angry with the rivers, O
    LORD?
  Was your wrath against the
    streams?
  Did you rage against the sea
    when you rode with your horses
    and your victorious chariots?
9You uncovered your bow,
    you called for many arrows.   *Selah*
  You split the earth with rivers;
10 the mountains saw you and writhed.
  Torrents of water swept by;
    the deep roared
    and lifted its waves on high.

11Sun and moon stood still in the heavens
    at the glint of your flying arrows,
    at the lightning of your flashing
    spear.
12In wrath you strode through the earth
    and in anger you threshed the
    nations.
13You came out to deliver your people,
    to save your anointed one.
  You crushed the leader of the land of
    wickedness,
    you stripped him from head to foot.
                                    Selah
14With his own spear you pierced his head
    when his warriors stormed out to
    scatter us,
  gloating as though about to devour
    the wretched who were in hiding.
15You trampled the sea with your
    horses,
    churning the great waters.

16I heard and my heart pounded,
    my lips quivered at the sound;
  decay crept into my bones,
    and my legs trembled.
  Yet I will wait patiently for the day of
    calamity
    to come on the nation invading us.

---

a1 Probably a literary or musical term
b3 A word of uncertain meaning; possibly a musical term; also in verses 9 and 13

17Though the fig-tree does not bud
and there are no grapes on the vines,
though the olive crop fails
and the fields produce no food,
though there are no sheep in the pen
and no cattle in the stalls,
18yet I will rejoice in the LORD,
I will be joyful in God my Saviour.

19The Sovereign LORD is my strength;
he makes my feet like the feet of a
deer,
he enables me to go on the
heights.

For the director of music. On my
stringed instruments.

Zephaniah

1 The word of the LORD that came to
Zephaniah son of Cushi, the son of
Gedaliah, the son of Amariah, the son of
Hezekiah, during the reign of Josiah son
of Amon king of Judah:

Warning of Coming Destruction

2"I will sweep away everything
    from the face of the earth,"
            declares the LORD.
3"I will sweep away both men and
        animals;
    I will sweep away the birds of the air
    and the fish of the sea.
The wicked will have only heaps of
        rubble*a*
    when I cut off man from the face of
        the earth,"
            declares the LORD.

Against Judah

4"I will stretch out my hand against
        Judah
    and against all who live in Jerusalem.
I will cut off from this place every
        remnant of Baal,
    the names of the pagan and the
        idolatrous priests—
5those who bow down on the roofs
    to worship the starry host,
    those who bow down and swear by the
        LORD
    and who also swear by Molech,*b*
6those who turn back from following the
        LORD

and neither seek the LORD nor
    enquire of him.
7Be silent before the Sovereign LORD,
    for the day of the LORD is near.
The LORD has prepared a sacrifice;
    he has consecrated those he has
        invited.
8On the day of the LORD's sacrifice
    I will punish the princes
    and the king's sons
and all those clad
    in foreign clothes.
9On that day I will punish
    all who avoid stepping on the
        threshold,*c*
who fill the temple of their gods
    with violence and deceit.

10"On that day," declares the LORD,
    "a cry will go up from the Fish Gate,
    wailing from the New Quarter,
    and a loud crash from the hills.
11Wail, you who live in the market
        district;*d*
    all your merchants will be wiped out,
    all who trade with*e* silver will be
        ruined.
12At that time I will search Jerusalem
        with lamps
    and punish those who are
        complacent,
    who are like wine left on its dregs,
    who think, 'The LORD will do nothing,
        either good or bad.'
13Their wealth will be plundered,
    their houses demolished.
They will build houses

---

a3 The meaning of the Hebrew for this line is uncertain.   *b5* Hebrew *Malcam*, that is, Milcom
c9 See 1 Samuel 5:5.   *d11* Or *the Mortar*   *e11* Or *in*

but not live in them;
they will plant vineyards
but not drink the wine.

The Great Day of the LORD

14"The great day of the LORD is near—
near and coming quickly.
Listen! The cry on the day of the LORD
will be bitter,
the shouting of the warrior
there.
15That day will be a day of wrath,
a day of distress and anguish,
a day of trouble and ruin,
a day of darkness and gloom,
a day of clouds and blackness,
16a day of trumpet and battle cry
against the fortified cities
and against the corner towers.
17I will bring distress on the people
and they will walk like blind men,
because they have sinned against the
LORD.
Their blood will be poured out like dust
and their entrails like filth.
18Neither their silver nor their gold
will be able to save them
on the day of the LORD's
wrath.
In the fire of his jealousy
the whole world will be consumed,
for he will make a sudden end
of all who live in the earth."

2 Gather together, gather together,
O shameful nation,
2before the appointed time arrives
and that day sweeps on like chaff,
before the fierce anger of the LORD
comes upon you,
before the day of the LORD's wrath
comes upon you.
3Seek the LORD, all you humble of the
land,
you who do what he commands.
Seek righteousness, seek humility;
perhaps you will be sheltered
on the day of the LORD's
anger.

Against Philistia

4Gaza will be abandoned
and Ashkelon left in ruins.
At midday Ashdod will be emptied
and Ekron uprooted.
5Woe to you who live by the sea,
O Kerethite people;
the word of the LORD is against you,
O Canaan, land of the Philistines.

"I will destroy you,
and none will be left."

6The land by the sea, where the
Kerethites*a* dwell,
will be a place for shepherds and
sheep pens.
7It will belong to the remnant of the
house of Judah;
there they will find pasture.
In the evening they will lie down
in the houses of Ashkelon.
The LORD their God will care for them;
he will restore their fortunes.*b*

Against Moab and Ammon

8"I have heard the insults of Moab
and the taunts of the Ammonites,
who insulted my people
and made threats against their land.
9Therefore, as surely as I live,"
declares the LORD Almighty, the God
of Israel,
"surely Moab will become like Sodom,
the Ammonites like Gomorrah—
a place of weeds and salt pits,
a wasteland for ever.
The remnant of my people will plunder
them;
the survivors of my nation will inherit
their land."

10This is what they will get in return for
their pride,
for insulting and mocking the people
of the LORD Almighty.
11The LORD will be awesome to them
when he destroys all the gods of the
land.

*a*6 The meaning of the Hebrew for this word is uncertain.   *b*7 Or *will bring back their captives*

The nations on every shore will worship
    him,
    every one in its own land.

Against Cush

12"You too, O Cushites,*c*
    will be slain by my sword."

Against Assyria

13He will stretch out his hand against the
    north
    and destroy Assyria,
leaving Nineveh utterly desolate
    and dry as the desert.
14Flocks and herds will lie down there,
    creatures of every kind.
The desert owl and the screech owl
    will roost on her columns.
Their calls will echo through the
    windows,
    rubble will be in the doorways,
    the beams of cedar will be exposed.
15This is the carefree city
    that lived in safety.
She said to herself,
    "I am, and there is none besides me."
What a ruin she has become,
    a lair for wild beasts!
All who pass by her scoff
    and shake their fists.

The Future of Jerusalem

3 Woe to the city of oppressors,
    rebellious and defiled!
2She obeys no-one,
    she accepts no correction.
She does not trust in the LORD,
    she does not draw near to her God.
3Her officials are roaring lions,
    her rulers are evening wolves,
    who leave nothing for the morning.
4Her prophets are arrogant;
    they are treacherous men.
Her priests profane the sanctuary
    and do violence to the law.
5The LORD within her is righteous;
    he does no wrong.

Morning by morning he dispenses his
    justice,
    and every new day he does not fail,
    yet the unrighteous know no shame.

6"I have cut off nations;
    their strongholds are demolished.
I have left their streets deserted,
    with no-one passing through.
Their cities are destroyed;
    no-one will be left—no-one at all.
7I said to the city,
    'Surely you will fear me
    and accept correction!'
Then her dwelling would not be cut off,
    nor all my punishments come upon
    her.
But they were still eager
    to act corruptly in all they did.
8Therefore wait for me," declares the
    LORD,
    "for the day I will stand up to testify.*a*
I have decided to assemble the nations,
    to gather the kingdoms
and to pour out my wrath on them—
    all my fierce anger.
The whole world will be consumed
    by the fire of my jealous anger.

9"Then will I purify the lips of the
    peoples,
    that all of them may call on the name
    of the LORD
    and serve him shoulder to shoulder.
10From beyond the rivers of Cush*b*
    my worshippers, my scattered
    people,
    will bring me offerings.
11On that day you will not be put to
    shame
    for all the wrongs you have done to
    me,
because I will remove from this city
    those who rejoice in their pride.
Never again will you be haughty
    on my holy hill.
12But I will leave within you
    the meek and humble,
    who trust in the name of the LORD.
13The remnant of Israel will do no wrong;

---

*c*12 That is, people from the upper Nile region
*b*10 That is, the upper Nile region

*a*8 Septuagint and Syriac; Hebrew *will rise up to plunder*

they will speak no lies,
nor will deceit be found in their
   mouths.
They will eat and lie down
and no-one will make them afraid."

14Sing, O Daughter of Zion;
   shout aloud, O Israel!
Be glad and rejoice with all your
   heart,
   O Daughter of Jerusalem!
15The LORD has taken away your
   punishment,
   he has turned back your enemy.
The LORD, the King of Israel, is with
   you;
   never again will you fear any harm.
16On that day they will say to Jerusalem,
   "Do not fear, O Zion;
do not let your hands hang limp.
17The LORD your God is with you,
   he is mighty to save.
He will take great delight in you,

he will quiet you with his love,
he will rejoice over you with
   singing."

18"The sorrows for the appointed feasts
   I will remove from you;
   they are a burden and a reproach to
   you.c
19At that time I will deal
   with all who oppressed you;
I will rescue the lame
   and gather those who have been
   scattered.
I will give them praise and honour
   in every land where they were put to
   shame.
20At that time I will gather you;
   at that time I will bring you home.
I will give you honour and praise
   among all the peoples of the earth
when I restore your fortunesd
   before your very eyes,"
                  says the LORD.

c18 Or "I will gather you who mourn for the appointed feasts; / your reproach is a burden to you
d20 Or I bring back your captives

Haggai

A Call to Build the House of the LORD

1 In the second year of King Darius, on the first day of the sixth month, the word of the LORD came through the prophet Haggai to Zerubbabel son of Shealtiel, governor of Judah, and to Joshua*a* son of Jehozadak, the high priest:

2This is what the LORD Almighty says: "These people say, 'The time has not yet come for the LORD's house to be built.'"

3Then the word of the LORD came through the prophet Haggai: 4"Is it a time for you yourselves to be living in your panelled houses, while this house remains a ruin?"

5Now this is what the LORD Almighty says: "Give careful thought to your ways. 6You have planted much, but have harvested little. You eat, but never have enough. You drink, but never have your fill. You put on clothes, but are not warm. You earn wages, only to put them in a purse with holes in it."

7This is what the LORD Almighty says: "Give careful thought to your ways. 8Go up into the mountains and bring down timber and build the house, so that I may take pleasure in it and be honoured," says the LORD. 9"You expected much, but see, it turned out to be little. What you brought home, I blew away. Why?" declares the LORD Almighty. "Because of my house, which remains a ruin, while each of you is busy with his own house. 10Therefore, because of you the heavens have withheld their dew and the earth its crops. 11I called

for a drought on the fields and the mountains, on the grain, the new wine, the oil and whatever the ground produces, on men and cattle, and on the labour of your hands."

12Then Zerubbabel son of Shealtiel, Joshua son of Jehozadak, the high priest, and the whole remnant of the people obeyed the voice of the LORD their God and the message of the prophet Haggai, because the LORD their God had sent him. And the people feared the LORD.

13Then Haggai, the LORD's messenger, gave this message of the LORD to the people: "I am with you," declares the LORD. 14So the LORD stirred up the spirit of Zerubbabel son of Shealtiel, governor of Judah, and the spirit of Joshua son of Jehozadak, the high priest, and the spirit of the whole remnant of the people. They came and began work on the house of the LORD Almighty, their God, 15on the twenty-fourth day of the sixth month in the second year of King Darius.

The Promised Glory of the New House

2 On the twenty-first day of the seventh month, the word of the LORD came through the prophet Haggai: 2"Speak to Zerubbabel son of Shealtiel, governor of Judah, to Joshua son of Jehozadak, the high priest, and to the remnant of the people. Ask them, 3'Who of you is left who saw this house in its former glory? How does it look to you now? Does it not

a1 A variant of *Jeshua*; here and elsewhere in Haggai

seem to you like nothing? [4]But now be strong, O Zerubbabel,' declares the LORD. 'Be strong, O Joshua son of Jehozadak, the high priest. Be strong, all you people of the land,' declares the LORD, 'and work. For I am with you,' declares the LORD Almighty. [5]'This is what I covenanted with you when you came out of Egypt. And my Spirit remains among you. Do not fear.'

[6]"This is what the LORD Almighty says: 'In a little while I will once more shake the heavens and the earth, the sea and the dry land. [7]I will shake all nations, and the desired of all nations will come, and I will fill this house with glory,' says the LORD Almighty. [8]'The silver is mine and the gold is mine,' declares the LORD Almighty. [9]'The glory of this present house will be greater than the glory of the former house,' says the LORD Almighty. 'And in this place I will grant peace,' declares the LORD Almighty."

Blessings for a Defiled People

[10]On the twenty-fourth day of the ninth month, in the second year of Darius, the word of the LORD came to the prophet Haggai: [11]"This is what the LORD Almighty says: 'Ask the priests what the law says: [12]If a person carries consecrated meat in the fold of his garment, and that fold touches some bread or stew, some wine, oil or other food, does it become consecrated?'"

The priests answered, "No."

[13]Then Haggai said, "If a person defiled by contact with a dead body touches one of these things, does it become defiled?"

"Yes," the priests replied, "it becomes defiled."

[14]Then Haggai said, "'So it is with this people and this nation in my sight,' declares the LORD. 'Whatever they do and whatever they offer there is defiled.

[15]"'Now give careful thought to this from this day on[a]—consider how things were before one stone was laid on another in the LORD's temple. [16]When anyone came to a heap of twenty measures, there were only ten. When anyone went to a wine vat to draw fifty measures, there were only twenty. [17]I struck all the work of your hands with blight, mildew and hail, yet you did not turn to me,' declares the LORD. [18]'From this day on, from this twenty-fourth day of the ninth month, give careful thought to the day when the foundation of the LORD's temple was laid. Give careful thought: [19]Is there yet any seed left in the barn? Until now, the vine and the fig-tree, the pomegranate and the olive tree have not borne fruit.

"'From this day on I will bless you.'"

Zerubbabel the LORD's Signet Ring

[20]The word of the LORD came to Haggai a second time on the twenty-fourth day of the month: [21]"Tell Zerubbabel governor of Judah that I will shake the heavens and the earth. [22]I will overturn royal thrones and shatter the power of the foreign kingdoms. I will overthrow chariots and their drivers; horses and their riders will fall, each by the sword of his brother.

[23]"'On that day,' declares the LORD Almighty, 'I will take you, my servant Zerubbabel son of Shealtiel,' declares the LORD, 'and I will make you like my signet ring, for I have chosen you,' declares the LORD Almighty."

a15 Or to the days past

Zechariah

A Call to Return to the LORD

1 In the eighth month of the second year of Darius, the word of the LORD came to the prophet Zechariah son of Berekiah, the son of Iddo:

²The LORD was very angry with your forefathers. ³Therefore tell the people: This is what the LORD Almighty says: 'Return to me,' declares the LORD Almighty, 'and I will return to you,' says the LORD Almighty. ⁴Do not be like your forefathers, to whom the earlier prophets proclaimed: This is what the LORD Almighty says: 'Turn from your evil ways and your evil practices.' But they would not listen or pay attention to me, declares the LORD. ⁵Where are your forefathers now? And the prophets, do they live for ever? ⁶But did not my words and my decrees, which I commanded my servants the prophets, overtake your forefathers?

"Then they repented and said, 'The LORD Almighty has done to us what our ways and practices deserve, just as he determined to do.'"

The Man Among the Myrtle Trees

⁷On the twenty-fourth day of the eleventh month, the month of Shebat, in the second year of Darius, the word of the LORD came to the prophet Zechariah son of Berekiah, the son of Iddo.

⁸During the night I had a vision—and there before me was a man riding a red horse! He was standing among the myrtle trees in a ravine. Behind him were red, brown and white horses.

⁹I asked, "What are these, my lord?"

The angel who was talking with me answered, "I will show you what they are."

¹⁰Then the man standing among the myrtle trees explained, "They are the ones the LORD has sent to go throughout the earth."

¹¹And they reported to the angel of the LORD, who was standing among the myrtle trees, "We have gone throughout the earth and found the whole world at rest and in peace."

¹²Then the angel of the LORD said, "LORD Almighty, how long will you withhold mercy from Jerusalem and from the towns of Judah, which you have been angry with these seventy years?" ¹³So the LORD spoke kind and comforting words to the angel who talked with me.

¹⁴Then the angel who was speaking to me said, "Proclaim this word: This is what the LORD Almighty says: 'I am very jealous for Jerusalem and Zion, ¹⁵but I am very angry with the nations that feel secure. I was only a little angry, but they added to the calamity.'

¹⁶"Therefore, this is what the LORD says: 'I will return to Jerusalem with mercy, and there my house will be rebuilt. And the measuring line will be stretched out over Jerusalem,' declares the LORD Almighty.

¹⁷"Proclaim further: This is what the LORD Almighty says: 'My towns will again overflow with prosperity, and the LORD will again comfort Zion and choose Jerusalem.'"

Relating to Jesus

As you read this story **use your imagination** to picture the scene; the house and the room, the meal table and the food (its colour and smell), the distinctive smell of myrrh (the perfume mentioned), the conversations and the moods, attitudes and facial expressions of those in the room. Imagine the drama and impact of the woman's actions, the shock, horror and surprise of those who witnessed so many cultural violations.

How do you imagine Jesus felt?

Relationship with Jesus

This event in the life of Jesus illustrates two different types of relationship to God which existed at that time:

● *formal and official (similar to 'civic' religion) expecting Jesus to act in a certain way;*

● *genuine and sacrificial and recognising Jesus for who he was;*

✴ To fully understand the passage: What did it mean to be a Pharisee? Check out how they behaved and acted? What attitudes and values did they prize?

★ Also, try and fill in the blanks below:

Simon
saw in Jesus a......... to be.........
The woman
saw in Jesus a .... to be ....
Simon looked on the woman
as a .... to be ....
Jesus looked on the woman
as a .... to be ....

Here is an opportunity, as you reflect on this passage, to evaluate your relationship to Jesus, and also the way you see and value others. Fill in the blanks:

I look on Jesus
as a .... to be ....
I look on the woman
as a .... to be ....

Relationship with other people

Take a moment to think about the way you perceive and treat other people, especially those who are different to you, socially, racially, or economically. What criteria do you use and are you aware of the dangers of stereotyping? In all honesty do you ever show signs of pride or superiority? Should Christians have favourites? What do you learn here from the actions and attitudes of Jesus in this passage? What lessons and principles do you need to build into your discipleship? Is your relationship to Jesus, at this moment in time, more like Simon's, or the woman's?

*i*m**a**g**e** 1

Anon I find both men and women in my generation and younger are continually struggling nobody's got the answers.

Ann How often in church have we actually heard teaching on the image of God? As Christians have we countered this false media image?

YOUR IMAGE

Andrew Working in a design and marketing environment, I was ashamed when I went to college and started learning about the manipulative tricks that are played. For instance, advertising a car comes down to three things: fear, greed and lust.

DESIGN

Simon How are we going to explain that what society promotes as a normal lifestyle is actually not acceptable by God's standards?

LIFESTYLE

Emma Get people to read the Bible. Get people to realise that God loves them just the way they are and that they should love themselves and not try to be what they are not.

Anon Self-image and self-worth need addressing, our generation has to provide the answers. I'm not saying I don't like clothes and I don't like fashion but I'm not going to be forced into the position where I have to act macho (drink a lot and have big muscles). I've been there before where I've been down the gym all the time.

FASHION

Simon I get very upset about what is happening to my friends who are getting anorexia and that's the devil's work, I have to speak out and pray out against that. At the same time I believe in creativity. I believe that God has given us all these amazing gifts and although I'm not into fashion I can see that fashion is part of the gift of creativity.

WORTH

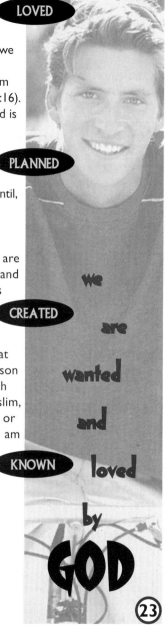

image

Simon We know it's there in the Bible that we are loved and wanted by God, that we were all individually planned by God (Psalm 8:4-6, Luke 15, John 3:16). The choosing of David is a classic example (1 Samuel 16:7), but I don't know how you make that awareness personal for somebody until, bang, it happens.

LOVED

PLANNED

Ann From reading the Bible, we know that we are created in God's image and that he loves us and has paid a price for us. I remember that, and it still blows me away. When I first realised that my life was worth God sending his only son to die for me I realised I had some worth whether I was pretty, or whether I was slim, whether I could speak another language, or whether I had friends or not, I was and I am worth something.

CREATED

KNOWN

we are wanted and loved by **GOD**

SO GOD CREATED MAN
IN HIS OWN IMAGE,
IN THE IMAGE OF GOD
HE CREATED HIM
MALE AND FEMALE
HE CREATED THEM.
GENESIS 1:27

(23)

ReLating to JeSUS

[part 2]

Forgiveness At the end of this passage Jesus declares that the woman's sins are forgiven. Notice Jesus does not forgive the attitude of Simon the Pharisee as well! What is Simon's attitude? What or who is a hypocrite? Have others ever called you a hypocrite? Were they justified? Where does that story and this story connect?

As shown by Jesus forgiveness means...

....

....

Recall a time when you found it hard to forgive. Why?

Which of the following would you find it most difficult to forgive? For what reasons?
a] Mrs Brown who steals food for her hungry family from the supermarket which dumps several tons each week
b] Liam who steals from his dad's wallet
c] Elizabeth who helps herself to small items of stationery from the office where she works
d] Damien who snatches the handbag of

an OAP just as she leaves the post office with her pension money
e] Mike who goes shoplifting with his mates, just for the thrill of it
f] Sue who sells her body to support her drug habit
What does this passage have to say about God's forgiveness and in what areas of

What does forgiveness mean to you ? Using your definition, how do you rate yourself on forgiving?	hopeless	OK	good	fantastic
family member	❏	❏	❏	❏
people in the community	❏	❏	❏	❏
fellow Christians	❏	❏	❏	❏
people who hurt you	❏	❏	❏	❏
companies that damage the environment	❏	❏	❏	❏
rich nations exploiting poorer ones	❏	❏	❏	❏

your life do you need to experience that power of Christ to forgive?

Reflection and prayer
Bring these thoughts and reflections together in a time of prayer. Confess and own up to those things that you know are wrong in your life. Accept God's forgiveness and start over.

Four Horns and Four Craftsmen

¹⁸Then I looked up—and there before me were four horns! ¹⁹I asked the angel who was speaking to me, "What are these?"

He answered me, "These are the horns that scattered Judah, Israel and Jerusalem."

²⁰Then the LORD showed me four craftsmen. ²¹I asked, "What are these coming to do?"

He answered, "These are the horns that scattered Judah so that no-one could raise his head, but the craftsmen have come to terrify them and throw down these horns of the nations who lifted up their horns against the land of Judah to scatter its people."

A Man With a Measuring Line

2 Then I looked up—and there before me was a man with a measuring line in his hand! ²I asked, "Where are you going?"

He answered me, "To measure Jerusalem, to find out how wide and how long it is."

³Then the angel who was speaking to me left, and another angel came to meet him ⁴and said to him: "Run, tell that young man, 'Jerusalem will be a city without walls because of the great number of men and livestock in it. ⁵And I myself will be a wall of fire around it,' declares the LORD, 'and I will be its glory within.'

⁶"Come! Come! Flee from the land of the north," declares the LORD, "for I have scattered you to the four winds of heaven," declares the LORD.

⁷"Come, O Zion! Escape, you who live in the Daughter of Babylon!" ⁸For this is what the LORD Almighty says: "After he has honoured me and has sent me against the nations that have plundered you—for whoever touches you touches the apple of his eye—⁹I will surely raise my hand against them so that their slaves will plunder them.ᵃ Then you will know that the LORD Almighty has sent me.

¹⁰"Shout and be glad, O Daughter of Zion. For I am coming, and I will live among you," declares the LORD. ¹¹"Many nations will be joined with the LORD in that day and will become my people. I will live among you and you will know that the LORD Almighty has sent me to you. ¹²The LORD will inherit Judah as his portion in the holy land and will again choose Jerusalem. ¹³Be still before the LORD, all mankind, because he has roused himself from his holy dwelling."

Clean Garments for the High Priest

3 Then he showed me Joshuaᵃ the high priest standing before the angel of the LORD, and Satanᵇ standing at his right side to accuse him. ²The LORD said to Satan, "The LORD rebuke you, Satan! The LORD, who has chosen Jerusalem, rebuke you! Is not this man a burning stick snatched from the fire?"

³Now Joshua was dressed in filthy clothes as he stood before the angel. ⁴The angel said to those who were standing before him, "Take off his filthy clothes."

Then he said to Joshua, "See, I have taken away your sin, and I will put rich garments on you."

⁵Then I said, "Put a clean turban on his head." So they put a clean turban on his head and clothed him, while the angel of the LORD stood by.

⁶The angel of the LORD gave this charge to Joshua: ⁷"This is what the LORD Almighty says: 'If you will walk in my ways and keep my requirements, then you will govern my house and have charge of my courts, and I will give you a place among these standing here.

⁸"'Listen, O high priest Joshua and your associates seated before you, who are men symbolic of things to come: I am going to bring my servant, the Branch. ⁹See, the stone I have set in front of Joshua! There are seven eyesᶜ on that one stone, and I will engrave an inscription on it,' says the LORD Almighty, 'and I will remove the sin of this land in a single day.

¹⁰"'In that day each of you will invite his

The Gold Lampstand and the Two Olive Trees

4 Then the angel who talked with me returned and wakened me, as a man is wakened from his sleep. [2]He asked me, "What do you see?"

I answered, "I see a solid gold lampstand with a bowl at the top and seven lights on it, with seven channels to the lights. [3]Also there are two olive trees by it, one on the right of the bowl and the other on its left."

[4]I asked the angel who talked with me, "What are these, my lord?"

[5]He answered, "Do you not know what these are?"

"No, my lord," I replied.

[6]So he said to me, "This is the word of the LORD to Zerubbabel: 'Not by might nor by power, but by my Spirit,' says the LORD Almighty.

[7]"What[a] are you, O mighty mountain? Before Zerubbabel you will become level ground. Then he will bring out the capstone to shouts of 'God bless it! God bless it!'"

[8]Then the word of the LORD came to me: [9]"The hands of Zerubbabel have laid the foundation of this temple; his hands will also complete it. Then you will know that the LORD Almighty has sent me to you.

[10]"Who despises the day of small things? Men will rejoice when they see the plumb-line in the hand of Zerubbabel.

"(These seven are the eyes of the LORD, which range throughout the earth.)"

[11]Then I asked the angel, "What are these two olive trees on the right and the left of the lampstand?"

[12]Again I asked him, "What are these two olive branches beside the two gold pipes that pour out golden oil?"

[13]He replied, "Do you not know what these are?"

"No, my lord," I said.

[14]So he said, "These are the two who are anointed to[b] serve the Lord of all the earth."

The Flying Scroll

5 I looked again—and there before me was a flying scroll!

[2]He asked me, "What do you see?"

I answered, "I see a flying scroll, thirty feet long and fifteen feet wide."[a]

[3]And he said to me, "This is the curse that is going out over the whole land; for according to what it says on one side, every thief will be banished, and according to what it says on the other, everyone who swears falsely will be banished. [4]The LORD Almighty declares, 'I will send it out, and it will enter the house of the thief and the house of him who swears falsely by my name. It will remain in his house and destroy it, both its timbers and its stones.'"

The Woman in a Basket

[5]Then the angel who was speaking to me came forward and said to me, "Look up and see what this is that is appearing."

[6]I asked, "What is it?"

He replied, "It is a measuring basket."[b] And he added, "This is the iniquity[c] of the people throughout the land."

[7]Then the cover of lead was raised, and there in the basket sat a woman! [8]He said, "This is wickedness," and he pushed her back into the basket and pushed the lead cover down over its mouth.

[9]Then I looked up—and there before me were two women, with the wind in their wings! They had wings like those of a stork, and they lifted up the basket between heaven and earth.

[10]"Where are they taking the basket?" I asked the angel who was speaking to me.

[11]He replied, "To the country of Babylonia[d] to build a house for it. When it is ready, the basket will be set there in its place."

---

a7 Or *Who*   *b14* Or *two who bring oil and*
a2 Hebrew *twenty cubits long and ten cubits wide* (about 9 metres long and 4.5 metres wide)
b6 Hebrew *an ephah*; also in verses 7–11   *c6* Or *appearance*   *d11* Hebrew *Shinar*

Four Chariots

6 I looked up again—and there before me were four chariots coming out from between two mountains—mountains of bronze! [2]The first chariot had red horses, the second black, [3]the third white, and the fourth dappled—all of them powerful. [4]I asked the angel who was speaking to me, "What are these, my lord?"

[5]The angel answered me, "These are the four spirits[a] of heaven, going out from standing in the presence of the Lord of the whole world. [6]The one with the black horses is going towards the north country, the one with the white horses towards the west,[b] and the one with the dappled horses towards the south."

[7]When the powerful horses went out, they were straining to go throughout the earth. And he said, "Go throughout the earth!" So they went throughout the earth.

[8]Then he called to me, "Look, those going towards the north country have given my Spirit[c] rest in the land of the north."

A Crown for Joshua

[9]The word of the Lord came to me: [10]"Take ⌐silver and gold⌐ from the exiles Heldai, Tobijah and Jedaiah, who have arrived from Babylon. Go the same day to the house of Josiah son of Zephaniah. [11]Take the silver and gold and make a crown, and set it on the head of the high priest, Joshua son of Jehozadak. [12]Tell him this is what the Lord Almighty says: 'Here is the man whose name is the Branch, and he will branch out from his place and build the temple of the Lord. [13]It is he who will build the temple of the Lord, and he will be clothed with majesty and will sit and rule on his throne. And he will be a priest on his throne. And there will be harmony between the two.' [14]The crown will be given to Heldai,[d] Tobijah, Jedaiah and Hen[e] son of Zephaniah as a memorial in the temple of the Lord.

[15]Those who are far away will come and help to build the temple of the Lord, and you will know that the Lord Almighty has sent me to you. This will happen if you diligently obey the Lord your God."

Justice and Mercy, Not Fasting

7 In the fourth year of King Darius, the word of the Lord came to Zechariah on the fourth day of the ninth month, the month of Kislev. [2]The people of Bethel had sent Sharezer and Regem-Melech, together with their men, to entreat the Lord [3]by asking the priests of the house of the Lord Almighty and the prophets, "Should I mourn and fast in the fifth month, as I have done for so many years?"

[4]Then the word of the Lord Almighty came to me: [5]"Ask all the people of the land and the priests, 'When you fasted and mourned in the fifth and seventh months for the past seventy years, was it really for me that you fasted? [6]And when you were eating and drinking, were you not just feasting for yourselves? [7]Are these not the words the Lord proclaimed through the earlier prophets when Jerusalem and its surrounding towns were at rest and prosperous, and the Negev and the western foothills were settled?'"

[8]And the word of the Lord came again to Zechariah: [9]"This is what the Lord Almighty says: 'Administer true justice; show mercy and compassion to one another. [10]Do not oppress the widow or the fatherless, the alien or the poor. In your hearts do not think evil of each other.'

[11]"But they refused to pay attention; stubbornly they turned their backs and stopped up their ears. [12]They made their hearts as hard as flint and would not listen to the law or to the words that the Lord Almighty had sent by his Spirit through the earlier prophets. So the Lord Almighty was very angry.

[13]"When I called, they did not listen; so when they called, I would not listen,' says the Lord Almighty. [14]I scattered them with a whirlwind among all the

---

[a]5 Or winds   [b]6 Or horses after them   [c]8 Or spirit   [d]14 Syriac; Hebrew Helem
[e]14 Or and the gracious one, the

nations, where they were strangers. The land was left so desolate behind them that no-one could come or go. This is how they made the pleasant land desolate.'"

The LORD Promises to Bless Jerusalem

8 Again the word of the LORD Almighty came to me. ²This is what the LORD Almighty says: "I am very jealous for Zion; I am burning with jealousy for her."

³This is what the LORD says: "I will return to Zion and dwell in Jerusalem. Then Jerusalem will be called the City of Truth, and the mountain of the LORD Almighty will be called the Holy Mountain."

⁴This is what the LORD Almighty says: "Once again men and women of ripe old age will sit in the streets of Jerusalem, each with cane in hand because of his age. ⁵The city streets will be filled with boys and girls playing there."

⁶This is what the LORD Almighty says: "It may seem marvellous to the remnant of this people at that time, but will it seem marvellous to me?" declares the LORD Almighty.

⁷This is what the LORD Almighty says: "I will save my people from the countries of the east and the west. ⁸I will bring them back to live in Jerusalem; they will be my people, and I will be faithful and righteous to them as their God."

⁹This is what the LORD Almighty says: "You who now hear these words spoken by the prophets who were there when the foundation was laid for the house of the LORD Almighty, let your hands be strong so that the temple may be built. ¹⁰Before that time there were no wages for man or beast. No-one could go about his business safely because of his enemy, for I had turned every man against his neighbour. ¹¹But now I will not deal with the remnant of this people as I did in the past," declares the LORD Almighty.

¹²"The seed will grow well, the vine will yield its fruit, the ground will produce its crops, and the heavens will drop their dew. I will give all these things as an inheritance to the remnant of this people. ¹³As you have been an object of cursing among the nations, O Judah and Israel, so will I save you, and you will be a blessing. Do not be afraid, but let your hands be strong."

¹⁴This is what the LORD Almighty says: "Just as I had determined to bring disaster upon you and showed no pity when your fathers angered me," says the LORD Almighty, ¹⁵"so now I have determined to do good again to Jerusalem and Judah. Do not be afraid. ¹⁶These are the things you are to do: Speak the truth to each other, and render true and sound judgment in your courts; ¹⁷do not plot evil against your neighbour, and do not love to swear falsely. I hate all this," declares the LORD.

¹⁸Again the word of the LORD Almighty came to me. ¹⁹This is what the LORD Almighty says: "The fasts of the fourth, fifth, seventh and tenth months will become joyful and glad occasions and happy festivals for Judah. Therefore love truth and peace."

²⁰This is what the LORD Almighty says: "Many peoples and the inhabitants of many cities will yet come, ²¹and the inhabitants of one city will go to another and say, 'Let us go at once to entreat the LORD and seek the LORD Almighty. I myself am going.' ²²And many peoples and powerful nations will come to Jerusalem to seek the LORD Almighty and to entreat him."

²³This is what the LORD Almighty says: "In those days ten men from all languages and nations will take firm hold of one Jew by the hem of his robe and say, 'Let us go with you, because we have heard that God is with you.'"

Judgment on Israel's Enemies

An Oracle

9 The word of the LORD is
against the land of Hadrach
and will rest upon Damascus—
for the eyes of men and all the tribes of
    Israel
are on the LORD—ᵃ

ᵃ1 Or *Damascus.* / *For the eye of the LORD is on all mankind,* / *as well as on the tribes of Israel.*

²and upon Hamath too, which borders
on it,
and upon Tyre and Sidon, though
they are very skilful.
³Tyre has built herself a stronghold;
she has heaped up silver like dust,
and gold like the dirt of the streets.
⁴But the Lord will take away her
possessions
and destroy her power on the sea,
and she will be consumed by fire.
⁵Ashkelon will see it and fear;
Gaza will writhe in agony,
and Ekron too, for her hope will
wither.
Gaza will lose her king
and Ashkelon will be deserted.
⁶Foreigners will occupy Ashdod,
and I will cut off the pride of the
Philistines.
⁷I will take the blood from their mouths,
the forbidden food from between
their teeth.
Those who are left will belong to our
God
and become leaders in Judah,
and Ekron will be like the Jebusites.
⁸But I will defend my house
against marauding forces.
Never again will an oppressor overrun
my people,
for now I am keeping watch.

The Coming of Zion's King

⁹Rejoice greatly, O Daughter of Zion!
Shout, Daughter of Jerusalem!
See, your kingᵇ comes to you,
righteous and having salvation,
gentle and riding on a donkey,
on a colt, the foal of a donkey.
¹⁰I will take away the chariots from
Ephraim
and the war-horses from Jerusalem,
and the battle-bow will be broken.
He will proclaim peace to the nations.
His rule will extend from sea to sea
and from the Riverᶜ to the ends of the
earth.ᵈ
¹¹As for you, because of the blood of my
covenant with you,

I will free your prisoners from the
waterless pit.
¹²Return to your fortress, O prisoners of
hope;
even now I announce that I will
restore twice as much to you.
¹³I will bend Judah as I bend my bow
and fill it with Ephraim.
I will rouse your sons, O Zion,
against your sons, O Greece,
and make you like a warrior's
sword.

The Lord Will Appear

¹⁴Then the Lord will appear over them;
his arrow will flash like lightning.
The Sovereign Lord will sound the
trumpet;
he will march in the storms of the
south,
15   and the Lord Almighty will shield
them.
They will destroy
and overcome with slingstones.
They will drink and roar as with wine;
they will be full like a bowl
used for sprinklingᵉ the corners of the
altar.
¹⁶The Lord their God will save them on
that day
as the flock of his people.
They will sparkle in his land
like jewels in a crown.
¹⁷How attractive and beautiful they will
be!
Grain will make the young men
thrive,
and new wine the young women.

The Lord Will Care for Judah

10 Ask the Lord for rain in the
springtime;
it is the Lord who makes the storm
clouds.
He gives showers of rain to men,
and plants of the field to
everyone.
²The idols speak deceit,
diviners see visions that lie;

ᵇ9 Or King   ᶜ10 That is, the Euphrates   ᵈ10 Or the end of the land   ᵉ15 Or bowl, / like

they tell dreams that are false,
   they give comfort in vain.
Therefore the people wander like sheep
   oppressed for lack of a shepherd.

3"My anger burns against the shepherds,
   and I will punish the leaders;
for the LORD Almighty will care
   for his flock, the house of Judah,
   and make them like a proud horse in
      battle.
4From Judah will come the cornerstone,
   from him the tent peg,
   from him the battle-bow,
   from him every ruler.
5Together they[a] will be like mighty men
   trampling the muddy streets in battle.
Because the LORD is with them,
   they will fight and overthrow the
      horsemen.

6"I will strengthen the house of Judah
   and save the house of Joseph.
I will restore them
   because I have compassion on them.
They will be as though
   I had not rejected them,
for I am the LORD their God
   and I will answer them.
7The Ephraimites will become like
      mighty men,
   and their hearts will be glad as with
      wine.
Their children will see it and be joyful;
   their hearts will rejoice in the LORD.
8I will signal for them
   and gather them in.
Surely I will redeem them;
   they will be as numerous as before.
9Though I scatter them among the
      peoples,
   yet in distant lands they will
      remember me.
They and their children will survive,
   and they will return.
10I will bring them back from Egypt
   and gather them from Assyria.
I will bring them to Gilead and
      Lebanon,
   and there will not be room enough
      for them.

11They will pass through the sea of
      trouble;
   the surging sea will be subdued
   and all the depths of the Nile will dry
      up.
Assyria's pride will be brought down
   and Egypt's sceptre will pass away.
12I will strengthen them in the LORD
   and in his name they will walk,"
               declares the LORD.

11 Open your doors, O
    Lebanon,
so that fire may devour your cedars!
2Wail, O pine tree, for the cedar has
      fallen;
   the stately trees are ruined!
Wail, oaks of Bashan;
   the dense forest has been cut down!
3Listen to the wail of the shepherds:
   their rich pastures are destroyed!
Listen to the roar of the lions;
   the lush thicket of the Jordan is
      ruined!

Two Shepherds

4This is what the LORD my God says:
"Pasture the flock marked for slaughter.
5Their buyers slaughter them and go unpunished. Those who sell them say,
'Praise the LORD, I am rich!' Their own
shepherds do not spare them. 6For I will
no longer have pity on the people of the
land," declares the LORD. "I will hand
everyone over to his neighbour and his
king. They will oppress the land, and I will
not rescue them from their hands."

7So I pastured the flock marked for
slaughter, particularly the oppressed of
the flock. Then I took two staffs and called
one Favour and the other Union, and I
pastured the flock. 8In one month I got rid
of the three shepherds.

The flock detested me, and I grew
weary of them 9and said, "I will not be
your shepherd. Let the dying die, and the
perishing perish. Let those who are left eat
one another's flesh."

10Then I took my staff called Favour
and broke it, revoking the covenant I had

made with all the nations. ¹¹It was revoked on that day, and so the afflicted of the flock who were watching me knew it was the word of the LORD.

¹²I told them, "If you think it best, give me my pay; but if not, keep it." So they paid me thirty pieces of silver.

¹³And the LORD said to me, "Throw it to the potter"—the handsome price at which they priced me! So I took the thirty pieces of silver and threw them into the house of the LORD to the potter.

¹⁴Then I broke my second staff called Union, breaking the brotherhood between Judah and Israel.

¹⁵Then the LORD said to me, "Take again the equipment of a foolish shepherd. ¹⁶For I am going to raise up a shepherd over the land who will not care for the lost, or seek the young, or heal the injured, or feed the healthy, but will eat the meat of the choice sheep, tearing off their hoofs.

¹⁷"Woe to the worthless shepherd,
who deserts the flock!
May the sword strike his arm and his
right eye!
May his arm be completely withered,
his right eye totally blinded!"

Jerusalem's Enemies to Be Destroyed

An Oracle

12 This is the word of the LORD concerning Israel. The LORD, who stretches out the heavens, who lays the foundation of the earth, and who forms the spirit of man within him, declares: ²"I am going to make Jerusalem a cup that sends all the surrounding peoples reeling. Judah will be besieged as well as Jerusalem. ³On that day, when all the nations of the earth are gathered against her, I will make Jerusalem an immovable rock for all the nations. All who try to move it will injure themselves. ⁴On that day I will strike every horse with panic and its rider with madness," declares the LORD. "I will keep a watchful eye over the house of Judah, but I will blind all the horses of the nations. ⁵Then the leaders of Judah will say in their hearts, 'The people of Jerusalem are strong, because the LORD Almighty is their God.'

⁶"On that day I will make the leaders of Judah like a brazier in a woodpile, like a flaming torch among sheaves. They will consume right and left all the surrounding peoples, but Jerusalem will remain intact in her place.

⁷"The LORD will save the dwellings of Judah first, so that the honour of the house of David and of Jerusalem's inhabitants may not be greater than that of Judah. ⁸On that day the LORD will shield those who live in Jerusalem, so that the feeblest among them will be like David, and the house of David will be like God, like the Angel of the LORD going before them. ⁹On that day I will set out to destroy all the nations that attack Jerusalem.

Mourning for the One They Pierced

¹⁰"And I will pour out on the house of David and the inhabitants of Jerusalem a spirit*a* of grace and supplication. They will look on*b* me, the one they have pierced, and they will mourn for him as one mourns for an only child, and grieve bitterly for him as one grieves for a firstborn son. ¹¹On that day the weeping in Jerusalem will be great, like the weeping of Hadad Rimmon in the plain of Megiddo. ¹²The land will mourn, each clan by itself, with their wives by themselves: the clan of the house of David and their wives, the clan of the house of Nathan and their wives, ¹³the clan of the house of Levi and their wives, the clan of Shimei and their wives, ¹⁴and all the rest of the clans and their wives.

Cleansing From Sin

13 "On that day a fountain will be opened to the house of David and the inhabitants of Jerusalem, to cleanse them from sin and impurity.

²"On that day, I will banish the names of the idols from the land, and they will be

remembered no more," declares the LORD Almighty. "I will remove both the prophets and the spirit of impurity from the land. ³And if anyone still prophesies, his father and mother, to whom he was born, will say to him, 'You must die, because you have told lies in the LORD's name.' When he prophesies, his own parents will stab him.

⁴"On that day every prophet will be ashamed of his prophetic vision. He will not put on a prophet's garment of hair in order to deceive. ⁵He will say, 'I am not a prophet. I am a farmer; the land has been my livelihood since my youth.'ᵃ ⁶If someone asks him, 'What are these wounds on your body?'ᵇ he will answer, 'The wounds I was given at the house of my friends.'

The Shepherd Struck, the Sheep Scattered

⁷"Awake, O sword, against my
    shepherd,
    against the man who is close to me!"
    declares the LORD Almighty.
"Strike the shepherd,
    and the sheep will be scattered,
    and I will turn my hand against the
    little ones.
⁸In the whole land," declares the LORD,
    "two-thirds will be struck down and
    perish;
    yet one-third will be left in it.
⁹This third I will bring into the fire;
    I will refine them like silver
    and test them like gold.
They will call on my name
    and I will answer them;
I will say, 'They are my people,'
    and they will say, 'The LORD is our
    God.'"

The LORD Comes and Reigns

14 A day of the LORD is coming when your plunder will be divided among you.

²I will gather all the nations to Jerusalem to fight against it; the city will be captured, the houses ransacked, and the women raped. Half of the city will go into exile, but the rest of the people will not be taken from the city.

³Then the LORD will go out and fight against those nations, as he fights in the day of battle. ⁴On that day his feet will stand on the Mount of Olives, east of Jerusalem, and the Mount of Olives will be split in two from east to west, forming a great valley, with half of the mountain moving north and half moving south. ⁵You will flee by my mountain valley, for it will extend to Azel. You will flee as you fled from the earthquakeᵃ in the days of Uzziah king of Judah. Then the LORD my God will come, and all the holy ones with him.

⁶On that day there will be no light, no cold or frost. ⁷It will be a unique day, without daytime or night-time—a day known to the LORD. When evening comes, there will be light.

⁸On that day living water will flow out from Jerusalem, half to the eastern seaᵇ and half to the western sea,ᶜ in summer and in winter.

⁹The LORD will be king over the whole earth. On that day there will be one LORD, and his name the only name.

¹⁰The whole land, from Geba to Rimmon, south of Jerusalem, will become like the Arabah. But Jerusalem will be raised up and remain in its place, from the Benjamin Gate to the site of the First Gate, to the Corner Gate, and from the Tower of Hananel to the royal winepresses. ¹¹It will be inhabited; never again will it be destroyed. Jerusalem will be secure.

¹²This is the plague with which the LORD will strike all the nations that fought against Jerusalem: Their flesh will rot while they are still standing on their feet, their eyes will rot in their sockets, and their tongues will rot in their mouths. ¹³On that day men will be stricken by the LORD with great panic. Each man will seize the hand of another, and they will attack each other. ¹⁴Judah too will fight at Jerusalem.

ᵃ5 Or *farmer; a man sold me in my youth*   ᵇ6 Or *wounds between your hands*
ᵃ5 Or ⁵*My mountain valley will be blocked and will extend to Azel. It will be blocked as it was blocked because of the earthquake*   ᵇ8 That is, the Dead Sea   ᶜ8 That is, the Mediterranean

The wealth of all the surrounding nations will be collected—great quantities of gold and silver and clothing. ¹⁵A similar plague will strike the horses and mules, the camels and donkeys, and all the animals in those camps.

¹⁶Then the survivors from all the nations that have attacked Jerusalem will go up year after year to worship the King, the LORD Almighty, and to celebrate the Feast of Tabernacles. ¹⁷If any of the peoples of the earth do not go up to Jerusalem to worship the King, the LORD Almighty, they will have no rain. ¹⁸If the Egyptian people do not go up and take part, they will have no rain. The LORD^d will bring on them the plague he inflicts on the nations that do not go up to celebrate the Feast of Tabernacles. ¹⁹This will be the punishment of Egypt and the punishment of all the nations that do not go up to celebrate the Feast of Tabernacles.

²⁰On that day HOLY TO THE LORD will be inscribed on the bells of the horses, and the cooking pots in the LORD's house will be like the sacred bowls in front of the altar. ²¹Every pot in Jerusalem and Judah will be holy to the LORD Almighty, and all who come to sacrifice will take some of the pots and cook in them. And on that day there will no longer be a Canaanite^e in the house of the LORD Almighty.

Malachi

An oracle: The word of the LORD to
Israel through Malachi.*a*

Jacob Loved, Esau Hated

²"I have loved you," says the LORD.

"But you ask, 'How have you loved us?'

"Was not Esau Jacob's brother?" the
LORD says. "Yet I have loved Jacob, ³but
Esau I have hated, and I have turned his
mountains into a wasteland and left his
inheritance to the desert jackals."

⁴Edom may say, "Though we have been
crushed, we will rebuild the ruins."

But this is what the LORD Almighty says:
"They may build, but I will demolish.
They will be called the Wicked Land, a
people always under the wrath of the
LORD. ⁵You will see it with your own eyes
and say, 'Great is the LORD—even beyond
the borders of Israel!'

Blemished Sacrifices

⁶"A son honours his father, and a servant his master. If I am a father, where is
the honour due to me? If I am a master,
where is the respect due to me?" says the
LORD Almighty. "It is you, O priests, who
show contempt for my name.

"But you ask, 'How have we shown
contempt for your name?'

⁷"You place defiled food on my altar.

"But you ask, 'How have we defiled
you?'

"By saying that the LORD's table is contemptible. ⁸When you bring blind animals
for sacrifice, is that not wrong? When you
sacrifice crippled or diseased animals, is
that not wrong? Try offering them to your
governor! Would he be pleased with you?
Would he accept you?" says the LORD
Almighty.

⁹"Now implore God to be gracious to
us. With such offerings from your hands,
will he accept you?"—says the LORD
Almighty.

¹⁰"Oh, that one of you would shut the
temple doors, so that you would not light
useless fires on my altar! I am not pleased
with you," says the LORD Almighty, "and I
will accept no offering from your hands.
¹¹My name will be great among the
nations, from the rising to the setting
of the sun. In every place incense and
pure offerings will be brought to my
name, because my name will be great
among the nations," says the LORD
Almighty.

¹²"But you profane it by saying of the
Lord's table, 'It is defiled', and of its food,
'It is contemptible.' ¹³And you say, 'What
a burden!' and you sniff at it contemptu-
ously," says the LORD Almighty.

"When you bring injured, crippled or
diseased animals and offer them as sacrifices, should I accept them from your
hands?" says the LORD. ¹⁴"Cursed is the
cheat who has an acceptable male in his
flock and vows to give it, but then sacrifices a blemished animal to the Lord.
For I am a great king," says the LORD
Almighty, "and my name is to be feared
among the nations.

a1 Malachi means my messenger.

Admonition for the Priests

2 "And now this admonition is for you, O priests. ²If you do not listen, and if you do not set your heart to honour my name," says the LORD Almighty, "I will send a curse upon you, and I will curse your blessings. Yes, I have already cursed them, because you have not set your heart to honour me.

³"Because of you I will rebuke*a* your descendants;*b* I will spread on your faces the offal from your festival sacrifices, and you will be carried off with it. ⁴And you will know that I have sent you this admonition so that my covenant with Levi may continue," says the LORD Almighty. ⁵"My covenant was with him, a covenant of life and peace, and I gave them to him; this called for reverence and he revered me and stood in awe of my name. ⁶True instruction was in his mouth and nothing false was found on his lips. He walked with me in peace and uprightness, and turned many from sin.

⁷"For the lips of a priest ought to preserve knowledge, and from his mouth men should seek instruction—because he is the messenger of the LORD Almighty. ⁸But you have turned from the way and by your teaching have caused many to stumble; you have violated the covenant with Levi," says the LORD Almighty. ⁹"So I have caused you to be despised and humiliated before all the people, because you have not followed my ways but have shown partiality in matters of the law."

Judah Unfaithful

¹⁰Have we not all one Father?*c* Did not one God create us? Why do we profane the covenant of our fathers by breaking faith with one another?

¹¹Judah has broken faith. A detestable thing has been committed in Israel and in Jerusalem: Judah has desecrated the sanctuary the LORD loves, by marrying the daughter of a foreign god. ¹²As for the

man who does this, whoever he may be, may the LORD cut him off from the tents of Jacob*d*—even though he brings offerings to the LORD Almighty.

¹³Another thing you do: You flood the LORD's altar with tears. You weep and wail because he no longer pays attention to your offerings or accepts them with pleasure from your hands. ¹⁴You ask, "Why?" It is because the LORD is acting as the witness between you and the wife of your youth, because you have broken faith with her, though she is your partner, the wife of your marriage covenant.

¹⁵Has not ⌊the LORD⌋ made them one? In flesh and spirit they are his. And why one? Because he was seeking godly offspring.*e* So guard yourself in your spirit, and do not break faith with the wife of your youth.

¹⁶"I hate divorce," says the LORD God of Israel, "and I hate a man's covering himself*f* with violence as well as with his garment," says the LORD Almighty.

So guard yourself in your spirit, and do not break faith.

The Day of Judgment

¹⁷You have wearied the LORD with your words.

"How have we wearied him?" you ask.

By saying, "All who do evil are good in the eyes of the LORD, and he is pleased with them" or "Where is the God of justice?"

3 "See, I will send my messenger, who will prepare the way before me. Then suddenly the Lord you are seeking will come to his temple; the messenger of the covenant, whom you desire, will come," says the Lord Almighty.

²But who can endure the day of his coming? Who can stand when he appears? For he will be like a refiner's fire or a launderer's soap. ³He will sit as a refiner and purifier of silver; he will purify the Levites and refine them like gold and silver. Then the LORD will have men who

---

*a*3 Or *cut off* (see Septuagint)   *b*3 Or *will blight your corn*   *c*10 Or *father*
*d*12 Or ¹²*May the LORD cut off from the tents of Jacob anyone who gives testimony on behalf of the man who does this*
*e*15 Or ¹⁵*But the one* ⌊*who is our father*⌋ *did not do this, not as long as life remained in him. And what was he seeking? An offspring from God*   *f*16 Or *his wife*

will bring offerings in righteousness, ⁴and the offerings of Judah and Jerusalem will be acceptable to the LORD, as in days gone by, as in former years.

⁵"So I will come near to you for judgment. I will be quick to testify against sorcerers, adulterers and perjurers, against those who defraud labourers of their wages, who oppress the widows and the fatherless, and deprive aliens of justice, but do not fear me," says the LORD Almighty.

Robbing God

⁶"I the LORD do not change. So you, O descendants of Jacob, are not destroyed. ⁷Ever since the time of your forefathers you have turned away from my decrees and have not kept them. Return to me, and I will return to you," says the LORD Almighty.

"But you ask, 'How are we to return?'

⁸"Will a man rob God? Yet you rob me.

"But you ask, 'How do we rob you?'

"In tithes and offerings. ⁹You are under a curse—the whole nation of you—because you are robbing me. ¹⁰Bring the whole tithe into the storehouse, that there may be food in my house. Test me in this," says the LORD Almighty, "and see if I will not throw open the floodgates of heaven and pour out so much blessing that you will not have room enough for it. ¹¹I will prevent pests from devouring your crops, and the vines in your fields will not cast their fruit," says the LORD Almighty. ¹²"Then all the nations will call you blessed, for yours will be a delightful land," says the LORD Almighty.

¹³"You have said harsh things against me," says the LORD.

"Yet you ask, 'What have we said against you?'

¹⁴"You have said, 'It is futile to serve God. What did we gain by carrying out his requirements and going about like mourners before the LORD Almighty? ¹⁵But now we call the arrogant blessed. Certainly the evildoers prosper, and even those who challenge God escape.'"

¹⁶Then those who feared the LORD talked with each other, and the LORD listened and heard. A scroll of remembrance was written in his presence concerning those who feared the LORD and honoured his name.

¹⁷"They will be mine," says the LORD Almighty, "in the day when I make up my treasured possession.ᵃ I will spare them, just as in compassion a man spares his son who serves him. ¹⁸And you will again see the distinction between the righteous and the wicked, between those who serve God and those who do not.

The Day of the LORD

4 "Surely the day is coming; it will burn like a furnace. All the arrogant and every evildoer will be stubble, and that day that is coming will set them on fire," says the LORD Almighty. "Not a root or a branch will be left to them. ²But for you who revere my name, the sun of righteousness will rise with healing in its wings. And you will go out and leap like calves released from the stall. ³Then you will trample down the wicked; they will be ashes under the soles of your feet on the day when I do these things," says the LORD Almighty.

⁴"Remember the law of my servant Moses, the decrees and laws I gave him at Horeb for all Israel.

⁵"See, I will send you the prophet Elijah before that great and dreadful day of the LORD comes. ⁶He will turn the hearts of the fathers to their children, and the hearts of the children to their fathers; or else I will come and strike the land with a curse."

ᵃ17 Or Almighty, "my treasured possession, in the day when I act

THE
NEW TESTAMENT

Matthew

The Genealogy of Jesus

1 A record of the genealogy of Jesus
Christ the son of David, the son of
Abraham:

²Abraham was the father of Isaac,
Isaac the father of Jacob,
Jacob the father of Judah and his
brothers,
³Judah the father of Perez and
Zerah, whose mother was
Tamar,
Perez the father of Hezron,
Hezron the father of Ram,
⁴Ram the father of Amminadab,
Amminadab the father of Nahshon,
Nahshon the father of Salmon,
⁵Salmon the father of Boaz, whose
mother was Rahab,
Boaz the father of Obed, whose
mother was Ruth,
Obed the father of Jesse,
⁶and Jesse the father of King David.

David was the father of Solomon,
whose mother had been Uriah's
wife,
⁷Solomon the father of Rehoboam,
Rehoboam the father of Abijah,
Abijah the father of Asa,
⁸Asa the father of Jehoshaphat,
Jehoshaphat the father of Jehoram,
Jehoram the father of Uzziah,
⁹Uzziah the father of Jotham,
Jotham the father of Ahaz,
Ahaz the father of Hezekiah,

¹⁰Hezekiah the father of Manasseh,
Manasseh the father of Amon,
Amon the father of Josiah,
¹¹and Josiah the father of Jeconiah*a*
and his brothers at the time of the
exile to Babylon.

¹²After the exile to Babylon:
Jeconiah was the father of Shealtiel,
Shealtiel the father of Zerubbabel,
¹³Zerubbabel the father of Abiud,
Abiud the father of Eliakim,
Eliakim the father of Azor,
¹⁴Azor the father of Zadok,
Zadok the father of Akim,
Akim the father of Eliud,
¹⁵Eliud the father of Eleazar,
Eleazar the father of Matthan,
Matthan the father of Jacob,
¹⁶and Jacob the father of Joseph, the
husband of Mary, of whom was
born Jesus, who is called Christ.

¹⁷Thus there were fourteen generations
in all from Abraham to David, fourteen
from David to the exile to Babylon, and
fourteen from the exile to the Christ.*b*

The Birth of Jesus Christ

¹⁸This is how the birth of Jesus Christ
came about: His mother Mary was
pledged to be married to Joseph, but before they came together, she was found to
be with child through the Holy Spirit.
¹⁹Because Joseph her husband was a righteous man and did not want to expose her

a11 That is, Jehoiachin; also in verse 12
b17 Or *Messiah*. "The Christ" (Greek) and "the Messiah" (Hebrew) both mean "the Anointed One".

to public disgrace, he had in mind to divorce her quietly.

²⁰But after he had considered this, an angel of the Lord appeared to him in a dream and said, "Joseph son of David, do not be afraid to take Mary home as your wife, because what is conceived in her is from the Holy Spirit. ²¹She will give birth to a son, and you are to give him the name Jesus,ᶜ because he will save his people from their sins."

²²All this took place to fulfil what the Lord had said through the prophet: ²³"The virgin will be with child and will give birth to a son, and they will call him Immanuel"ᵈ—which means, "God with us."

²⁴When Joseph woke up, he did what the angel of the Lord had commanded him and took Mary home as his wife. ²⁵But he had no union with her until she gave birth to a son. And he gave him the name Jesus.

The Visit of the Magi

2 After Jesus was born in Bethlehem in Judea, during the time of King Herod, Magiᵃ from the east came to Jerusalem ²and asked, "Where is the one who has been born king of the Jews? We saw his star in the eastᵇ and have come to worship him."

³When King Herod heard this he was disturbed, and all Jerusalem with him. ⁴When he had called together all the people's chief priests and teachers of the law, he asked them where the Christᶜ was to be born. ⁵"In Bethlehem in Judea," they replied, "for this is what the prophet has written:

⁶"'But you, Bethlehem, in the land of Judah,
  are by no means least among the rulers of Judah;
for out of you will come a ruler
  who will be the shepherd of my people Israel.'ᵈ"

⁷Then Herod called the Magi secretly and found out from them the exact time the star had appeared. ⁸He sent them to Bethlehem and said, "Go and make a careful search for the child. As soon as you find him, report to me, so that I too may go and worship him."

⁹After they had heard the king, they went on their way, and the star they had seen in the eastᵉ went ahead of them until it stopped over the place where the child was. ¹⁰When they saw the star, they were overjoyed. ¹¹On coming to the house, they saw the child with his mother Mary, and they bowed down and worshipped him. Then they opened their treasures and presented him with gifts of gold and of incense and of myrrh. ¹²And having been warned in a dream not to go back to Herod, they returned to their country by another route.

The Escape to Egypt

¹³When they had gone, an angel of the Lord appeared to Joseph in a dream. "Get up," he said, "take the child and his mother and escape to Egypt. Stay there until I tell you, for Herod is going to search for the child to kill him."

¹⁴So he got up, took the child and his mother during the night and left for Egypt, ¹⁵where he stayed until the death of Herod. And so was fulfilled what the Lord had said through the prophet: "Out of Egypt I called my son."ᶠ

¹⁶When Herod realised that he had been outwitted by the Magi, he was furious, and he gave orders to kill all the boys in Bethlehem and its vicinity who were two years old and under, in accordance with the time he had learned from the Magi. ¹⁷Then what was said through the prophet Jeremiah was fulfilled:

¹⁸"A voice is heard in Ramah,
  weeping and great mourning,
Rachel weeping for her children
  and refusing to be comforted,
because they are no more."ᵍ

ᶜ21 *Jesus* is the Greek form of *Joshua*, which means *the* LORD *saves.*   ᵈ23 Isaiah 7:14   ᵃ1 Traditionally *Wise Men*
ᵇ2 Or *star when it rose*   ᶜ4 Or *Messiah*   ᵈ6 Micah 5:2   ᵉ9 Or *seen when it rose*   ᶠ15 Hosea 11:1
ᵍ18 Jer. 31:15

The Return to Nazareth

¹⁹After Herod died, an angel of the Lord appeared in a dream to Joseph in Egypt ²⁰and said, "Get up, take the child and his mother and go to the land of Israel, for those who were trying to take the child's life are dead."

²¹So he got up, took the child and his mother and went to the land of Israel. ²²But when he heard that Archelaus was reigning in Judea in place of his father Herod, he was afraid to go there. Having been warned in a dream, he withdrew to the district of Galilee, ²³and he went and lived in a town called Nazareth. So was fulfilled what was said through the prophets: "He will be called a Nazarene."

John the Baptist Prepares the Way

3 In those days John the Baptist came, preaching in the Desert of Judea ²and saying, "Repent, for the kingdom of heaven is near." ³This is he who was spoken of through the prophet Isaiah:

"A voice of one calling in the desert,
'Prepare the way for the Lord,
    make straight paths for him.' "ᵃ

⁴John's clothes were made of camel's hair, and he had a leather belt round his waist. His food was locusts and wild honey. ⁵People went out to him from Jerusalem and all Judea and the whole region of the Jordan. ⁶Confessing their sins, they were baptised by him in the Jordan River.

⁷But when he saw many of the Pharisees and Sadducees coming to where he was baptising, he said to them: "You brood of vipers! Who warned you to flee from the coming wrath? ⁸Produce fruit in keeping with repentance. ⁹And do not think you can say to yourselves, 'We have Abraham as our father.' I tell you that out of these stones God can raise up children for Abraham. ¹⁰The axe is already at the root of the trees, and every tree that does not produce good fruit will be cut down and thrown into the fire.

¹¹"I baptise you withᵇ water for repentance. But after me will come one who is more powerful than I, whose sandals I am not fit to carry. He will baptise you with the Holy Spirit and with fire. ¹²His winnowing fork is in his hand, and he will clear his threshing-floor, gathering his wheat into the barn and burning up the chaff with unquenchable fire."

The Baptism of Jesus

¹³Then Jesus came from Galilee to the Jordan to be baptised by John. ¹⁴But John tried to deter him, saying, "I need to be baptised by you, and do you come to me?"

¹⁵Jesus replied, "Let it be so now; it is proper for us to do this to fulfil all righteousness." Then John consented.

¹⁶As soon as Jesus was baptised, he went up out of the water. At that moment heaven was opened, and he saw the Spirit of God descending like a dove and lighting on him. ¹⁷And a voice from heaven said, "This is my Son, whom I love; with him I am well pleased."

The Temptation of Jesus

4 Then Jesus was led by the Spirit into the desert to be tempted by the devil. ²After fasting for forty days and forty nights, he was hungry. ³The tempter came to him and said, "If you are the Son of God, tell these stones to become bread."

⁴Jesus answered, "It is written: 'Man does not live on bread alone, but on every word that comes from the mouth of God.'ᵃ"

⁵Then the devil took him to the holy city and had him stand on the highest point of the temple. ⁶"If you are the Son of God," he said, "throw yourself down. For it is written:

"'He will command his angels
        concerning you,
    and they will lift you up in their
        hands,

so that you will not strike your foot
　　against a stone.'*b*"

[7]Jesus answered him, "It is also written:
'Do not put the Lord your God to the
test.'*c*"

[8]Again, the devil took him to a very high
mountain and showed him all the kingdoms of the world and their splendour.
[9]"All this I will give you," he said, "if you
will bow down and worship me."

[10]Jesus said to him, "Away from me,
Satan! For it is written: 'Worship the Lord
your God, and serve him only.'*d*"

[11]Then the devil left him, and angels
came and attended him.

Jesus Begins to Preach

[12]When Jesus heard that John had been
put in prison, he returned to Galilee.
[13]Leaving Nazareth, he went and lived in
Capernaum, which was by the lake in the
area of Zebulun and Naphtali—[14]to fulfil
what was said through the prophet Isaiah:

[15]"Land of Zebulun and land of Naphtali,
　　the way to the sea, along the Jordan,
　　Galilee of the Gentiles—
[16]the people living in darkness
　　have seen a great light;
on those living in the land of the shadow
　　of death
　　a light has dawned."*e*

[17]From that time on Jesus began to
preach, "Repent, for the kingdom of
heaven is near."

The Calling of the First Disciples

[18]As Jesus was walking beside the Sea of
Galilee, he saw two brothers, Simon called Peter and his brother Andrew. They
were casting a net into the lake, for they
were fishermen. [19]"Come, follow me,"
Jesus said, "and I will make you fishers of
men." [20]At once they left their nets and
followed him.

[21]Going on from there, he saw two
other brothers, James son of Zebedee and
his brother John. They were in a boat with
their father Zebedee, preparing their

nets. Jesus called them, [22]and immediately they left the boat and their father and
followed him.

Jesus Heals the Sick

[23]Jesus went throughout Galilee,
teaching in their synagogues, preaching
the good news of the kingdom, and healing every disease and sickness among the
people. [24]News about him spread all over
Syria, and people brought to him all who
were ill with various diseases, those suffering severe pain, the demon-possessed,
those having seizures, and the paralysed,
and he healed them. [25]Large crowds from
Galilee, the Decapolis,*f* Jerusalem, Judea
and the region across the Jordan followed
him.

The Beatitudes

5 Now when he saw the crowds, he
went up on a mountainside and sat
down. His disciples came to him, [2]and he
began to teach them, saying:

[3]"Blessed are the poor in spirit,
　　for theirs is the kingdom of heaven.
[4]Blessed are those who mourn,
　　for they will be comforted.
[5]Blessed are the meek,
　　for they will inherit the earth.
[6]Blessed are those who hunger and thirst
　　　for righteousness,
　　for they will be filled.
[7]Blessed are the merciful,
　　for they will be shown mercy.
[8]Blessed are the pure in heart,
　　for they will see God.
[9]Blessed are the peacemakers,
　　for they will be called sons of God.
[10]Blessed are those who are persecuted
　　　because of righteousness,
　　for theirs is the kingdom of heaven.

[11]"Blessed are you when people insult
you, persecute you and falsely say all
kinds of evil against you because of me.
[12]Rejoice and be glad, because great is
your reward in heaven, for in the same
way they persecuted the prophets who
were before you.

---

*b*6 Psalm 91:11,12　　*c*7 Deut. 6:16　　*d*10 Deut. 6:13　　*e*16 Isaiah 9:1,2　　*f*25 That is, the Ten Cities

Salt and Light

[13]"You are the salt of the earth. But if the salt loses its saltiness, how can it be made salty again? It is no longer good for anything, except to be thrown out and trampled by men.

[14]"You are the light of the world. A city on a hill cannot be hidden. [15]Neither do people light a lamp and put it under a bowl. Instead they put it on its stand, and it gives light to everyone in the house. [16]In the same way, let your light shine before men, that they may see your good deeds and praise your Father in heaven.

The Fulfilment of the Law

[17]"Do not think that I have come to abolish the Law or the Prophets; I have not come to abolish them but to fulfil them. [18]I tell you the truth, until heaven and earth disappear, not the smallest letter, not the least stroke of a pen, will by any means disappear from the Law until everything is accomplished. [19]Anyone who breaks one of the least of these commandments and teaches others to do the same will be called least in the kingdom of heaven, but whoever practises and teaches these commands will be called great in the kingdom of heaven. [20]For I tell you that unless your righteousness surpasses that of the Pharisees and the teachers of the law, you will certainly not enter the kingdom of heaven.

Murder

[21]"You have heard that it was said to the people long ago, 'Do not murder,[a] and anyone who murders will be subject to judgment.' [22]But I tell you that anyone who is angry with his brother[b] will be subject to judgment. Again, anyone who says to his brother, 'Raca,'[c] is answerable to the Sanhedrin. But anyone who says, 'You fool!' will be in danger of the fire of hell.

[23]"Therefore, if you are offering your gift at the altar and there remember that your brother has something against you, [24]leave your gift there in front of the altar. First go and be reconciled to your brother; then come and offer your gift.

[25]"Settle matters quickly with your adversary who is taking you to court. Do it while you are still with him on the way, or he may hand you over to the judge, and the judge may hand you over to the officer, and you may be thrown into prison. [26]I tell you the truth, you will not get out until you have paid the last penny.[d]

Adultery

[27]"You have heard that it was said, 'Do not commit adultery.'[e] [28]But I tell you that anyone who looks at a woman lustfully has already committed adultery with her in his heart. [29]If your right eye causes you to sin, gouge it out and throw it away. It is better for you to lose one part of your body than for your whole body to be thrown into hell. [30]And if your right hand causes you to sin, cut it off and throw it away. It is better for you to lose one part of your body than for your whole body to go into hell.

Divorce

[31]"It has been said, 'Anyone who divorces his wife must give her a certificate of divorce.'[f] [32]But I tell you that anyone who divorces his wife, except for marital unfaithfulness, causes her to become an adulteress, and anyone who marries the divorced woman commits adultery.

Oaths

[33]"Again, you have heard that it was said to the people long ago, 'Do not break your oath, but keep the oaths you have made to the Lord.' [34]But I tell you, Do not swear at all: either by heaven, for it is God's throne; [35]or by the earth, for it is his footstool; or by Jerusalem, for it is the city of the Great King. [36]And do not swear by your head, for you cannot make even one hair white or black. [37]Simply let your 'Yes'

---

[a]21 Exodus 20:13   [b]22 Some manuscripts *brother without cause*   [c]22 An Aramaic term of contempt
[d]26 Greek *kodrantes*   [e]27 Exodus 20:14   [f]31 Deut. 24:1

be 'Yes', and your 'No', 'No'; anything beyond this comes from the evil one.

An Eye for an Eye

38"You have heard that it was said, 'Eye for eye, and tooth for tooth.'*g* 39But I tell you, Do not resist an evil person. If someone strikes you on the right cheek, turn to him the other also. 40And if someone wants to sue you and take your tunic, let him have your cloak as well. 41If someone forces you to go one mile, go with him two miles. 42Give to the one who asks you, and do not turn away from the one who wants to borrow from you.

Love for Enemies

43"You have heard that it was said, 'Love your neighbour*h* and hate your enemy.' 44But I tell you: Love your enemies*i* and pray for those who persecute you, 45that you may be sons of your Father in heaven. He causes his sun to rise on the evil and the good, and sends rain on the righteous and the unrighteous. 46If you love those who love you, what reward will you get? Are not even the tax collectors doing that? 47And if you greet only your brothers, what are you doing more than others? Do not even pagans do that? 48Be perfect, therefore, as your heavenly Father is perfect.

Giving to the Needy

6 "Be careful not to do your 'acts of righteousness' before men, to be seen by them. If you do, you will have no reward from your Father in heaven.

2"So when you give to the needy, do not announce it with trumpets, as the hypocrites do in the synagogues and on the streets, to be honoured by men. I tell you the truth, they have received their reward in full. 3But when you give to the needy, do not let your left hand know what your right hand is doing, 4so that your giving may be in secret. Then your Father, who

sees what is done in secret, will reward you.

Prayer

5"And when you pray, do not be like the hypocrites, for they love to pray standing in the synagogues and on the street corners to be seen by men. I tell you the truth, they have received their reward in full. 6But when you pray, go into your room, close the door and pray to your Father, who is unseen. Then your Father, who sees what is done in secret, will reward you. 7And when you pray, do not keep on babbling like pagans, for they think they will be heard because of their many words. 8Do not be like them, for your Father knows what you need before you ask him.

9"This, then, is how you should pray:

"'Our Father in heaven,
   hallowed be your name,
10your kingdom come,
   your will be done
      on earth as it is in heaven.
11Give us today our daily bread.
12Forgive us our debts,
      as we also have forgiven our debtors.
13And lead us not into temptation,
      but deliver us from the evil one.'*a*

14For if you forgive men when they sin against you, your heavenly Father will also forgive you. 15But if you do not forgive men their sins, your Father will not forgive your sins.

Fasting

16"When you fast, do not look sombre as the hypocrites do, for they disfigure their faces to show men they are fasting. I tell you the truth, they have received their reward in full. 17But when you fast, put oil on your head and wash your face, 18so that it will not be obvious to men that you are fasting, but only to your Father, who is unseen; and your Father, who sees what is done in secret, will reward you.

---

838 Exodus 21:24; Lev. 24:20 and Deut. 19:21   *h43* Lev. 19:18
i44 Some late manuscripts *enemies, bless those who curse you, do good to those who hate you*
a13 Or *from evil*; some late manuscripts *one, / for yours is the kingdom and the power and the glory for ever. Amen.*

Treasures in Heaven

19"Do not store up for yourselves treasures on earth, where moth and rust destroy, and where thieves break in and steal. 20But store up for yourselves treasures in heaven, where moth and rust do not destroy, and where thieves do not break in and steal. 21For where your treasure is, there your heart will be also.

22"The eye is the lamp of the body. If your eyes are good, your whole body will be full of light. 23But if your eyes are bad, your whole body will be full of darkness. If then the light within you is darkness, how great is that darkness!

24"No-one can serve two masters. Either he will hate the one and love the other, or he will be devoted to the one and despise the other. You cannot serve both God and Money.

Do Not Worry

25"Therefore I tell you, do not worry about your life, what you will eat or drink; or about your body, what you will wear. Is not life more important than food, and the body more important than clothes? 26Look at the birds of the air; they do not sow or reap or store away in barns, and yet your heavenly Father feeds them. Are you not much more valuable than they? 27Who of you by worrying can add a single hour to his life?*b* 28"And why do you worry about clothes? See how the lilies of the field grow. They do not labour or spin. 29Yet I tell you that not even Solomon in all his splendour was dressed like one of these. 30If that is how God clothes the grass of the field, which is here today and tomorrow is thrown into the fire, will he not much more clothe you, O you of little faith? 31So do not worry, saying, 'What shall we eat?' or 'What shall we drink?' or 'What shall we wear?' 32For the pagans run after all these things, and your heavenly Father knows that you need them. 33But seek first his kingdom and his righteousness, and all these things will be given to you as well.

34Therefore do not worry about tomorrow, for tomorrow will worry about itself. Each day has enough trouble of its own.

Judging Others

7 "Do not judge, or you too will be judged. 2For in the same way as you judge others, you will be judged, and with the measure you use, it will be measured to you.

3"Why do you look at the speck of sawdust in your brother's eye and pay no attention to the plank in your own eye? 4How can you say to your brother, 'Let me take the speck out of your eye,' when all the time there is a plank in your own eye? 5You hypocrite, first take the plank out of your own eye, and then you will see clearly to remove the speck from your brother's eye.

6"Do not give dogs what is sacred; do not throw your pearls to pigs. If you do, they may trample them under their feet, and then turn and tear you to pieces.

Ask, Seek, Knock

7"Ask and it will be given to you; seek and you will find; knock and the door will be opened to you. 8For everyone who asks receives; he who seeks finds; and to him who knocks, the door will be opened.

9"Which of you, if his son asks for bread, will give him a stone? 10Or if he asks for a fish, will give him a snake? 11If you, then, though you are evil, know how to give good gifts to your children, how much more will your Father in heaven give good gifts to those who ask him! 12So in everything, do to others what you would have them do to you, for this sums up the Law and the Prophets.

The Narrow and Wide Gates

13"Enter through the narrow gate. For wide is the gate and broad is the road that

b27 Or single cubit to his height

leads to destruction, and many enter through it. [14]But small is the gate and narrow the road that leads to life, and only a few find it.

A Tree and Its Fruit

[15]"Watch out for false prophets. They come to you in sheep's clothing, but inwardly they are ferocious wolves. [16]By their fruit you will recognise them. Do people pick grapes from thornbushes, or figs from thistles? [17]Likewise every good tree bears good fruit, but a bad tree bears bad fruit. [18]A good tree cannot bear bad fruit, and a bad tree cannot bear good fruit. [19]Every tree that does not bear good fruit is cut down and thrown into the fire. [20]Thus, by their fruit you will recognise them.

[21]"Not everyone who says to me, 'Lord, Lord,' will enter the kingdom of heaven, but only he who does the will of my Father who is in heaven. [22]Many will say to me on that day, 'Lord, Lord, did we not prophesy in your name, and in your name drive out demons and perform many miracles?' [23]Then I will tell them plainly, 'I never knew you. Away from me, you evildoers!'

The Wise and Foolish Builders

[24]"Therefore everyone who hears these words of mine and puts them into practice is like a wise man who built his house on the rock. [25]The rain came down, the streams rose, and the winds blew and beat against that house; yet it did not fall, because it had its foundation on the rock. [26]But everyone who hears these words of mine and does not put them into practice is like a foolish man who built his house on sand. [27]The rain came down, the streams rose, and the winds blew and beat against that house, and it fell with a great crash."

[28]When Jesus had finished saying these things, the crowds were amazed at his teaching, [29]because he taught as one who had authority, and not as their teachers of the law.

The Man With Leprosy

8 When he came down from the mountainside, large crowds followed him. [2]A man with leprosy[a] came and knelt before him and said, "Lord, if you are willing, you can make me clean."

[3]Jesus reached out his hand and touched the man. "I am willing," he said. "Be clean!" Immediately he was cured[b] of his leprosy. [4]Then Jesus said to him, "See that you don't tell anyone. But go, show yourself to the priest and offer the gift Moses commanded, as a testimony to them."

The Faith of the Centurion

[5]When Jesus had entered Capernaum, a centurion came to him, asking for help. [6]"Lord," he said, "my servant lies at home paralysed and in terrible suffering."

[7]Jesus said to him, "I will go and heal him."

[8]The centurion replied, "Lord, I do not deserve to have you come under my roof. But just say the word, and my servant will be healed. [9]For I myself am a man under authority, with soldiers under me. I tell this one, 'Go,' and he goes; and that one, 'Come,' and he comes. I say to my servant, 'Do this,' and he does it."

[10]When Jesus heard this, he was astonished and said to those following him, "I tell you the truth, I have not found anyone in Israel with such great faith. [11]I say to you that many will come from the east and the west, and will take their places at the feast with Abraham, Isaac and Jacob in the kingdom of heaven. [12]But the subjects of the kingdom will be thrown outside, into the darkness, where there will be weeping and gnashing of teeth."

[13]Then Jesus said to the centurion, "Go! It will be done just as you believed it would." And his servant was healed at that very hour.

Jesus Heals Many

[14]When Jesus came into Peter's house, he saw Peter's mother-in-law lying in bed

---

a2 The Greek word was used for various diseases affecting the skin—not necessarily leprosy.
b3 Greek made clean

with a fever. [15]He touched her hand and the fever left her, and she got up and began to wait on him.

[16]When evening came, many who were demon-possessed were brought to him, and he drove out the spirits with a word and healed all the sick. [17]This was to fulfil what was spoken through the prophet Isaiah:

"He took up our infirmities
and carried our diseases."[c]

The Cost of Following Jesus

[18]When Jesus saw the crowd around him, he gave orders to cross to the other side of the lake. [19]Then a teacher of the law came to him and said, "Teacher, I will follow you wherever you go."

[20]Jesus replied, "Foxes have holes and birds of the air have nests, but the Son of Man has nowhere to lay his head."

[21]Another disciple said to him, "Lord, first let me go and bury my father."

[22]But Jesus told him, "Follow me, and let the dead bury their own dead."

Jesus Calms the Storm

[23]Then he got into the boat and his disciples followed him. [24]Without warning, a furious storm came up on the lake, so that the waves swept over the boat. But Jesus was sleeping. [25]The disciples went and woke him, saying, "Lord, save us! We're going to drown!"

[26]He replied, "You of little faith, why are you so afraid?" Then he got up and rebuked the winds and the waves, and it was completely calm.

[27]The men were amazed and asked, "What kind of man is this? Even the winds and the waves obey him!"

The Healing of Two Demon-possessed Men

[28]When he arrived at the other side in the region of the Gadarenes,[d] two demon-possessed men coming from the tombs met him. They were so violent that no-one could pass that way. [29]"What do you want with us, Son of God?" they shouted. "Have you come here to torture us before the appointed time?"

[30]Some distance from them a large herd of pigs was feeding. [31]The demons begged Jesus, "If you drive us out, send us into the herd of pigs."

[32]He said to them, "Go!" So they came out and went into the pigs, and the whole herd rushed down the steep bank into the lake and died in the water. [33]Those tending the pigs ran off, went into the town and reported all this, including what had happened to the demon-possessed men. [34]Then the whole town went out to meet Jesus. And when they saw him, they pleaded with him to leave their region.

Jesus Heals a Paralytic

9 Jesus stepped into a boat, crossed over and came to his own town. [2]Some men brought to him a paralytic, lying on a mat. When Jesus saw their faith, he said to the paralytic, "Take heart, son; your sins are forgiven."

[3]At this, some of the teachers of the law said to themselves, "This fellow is blaspheming!"

[4]Knowing their thoughts, Jesus said, "Why do you entertain evil thoughts in your hearts? [5]Which is easier: to say, 'Your sins are forgiven,' or to say, 'Get up and walk'? [6]But so that you may know that the Son of Man has authority on earth to forgive sins. . . ." Then he said to the paralytic, "Get up, take your mat and go home." [7]And the man got up and went home. [8]When the crowd saw this, they were filled with awe; and they praised God, who had given such authority to men.

The Calling of Matthew

[9]As Jesus went on from there, he saw a man named Matthew sitting at the tax collector's booth. "Follow me," he told

---

[c]17 Isaiah 53:4   [d]28 Some manuscripts *Gergesenes*; others *Gerasenes*

him, and Matthew got up and followed him.

¹⁰While Jesus was having dinner at Matthew's house, many tax collectors and "sinners" came and ate with him and his disciples. ¹¹When the Pharisees saw this, they asked his disciples, "Why does your teacher eat with tax collectors and 'sinners'?"

¹²On hearing this, Jesus said, "It is not the healthy who need a doctor, but the sick. ¹³But go and learn what this means: 'I desire mercy, not sacrifice.'ᵃ For I have not come to call the righteous, but sinners."

Jesus Questioned About Fasting

¹⁴Then John's disciples came and asked him, "How is it that we and the Pharisees fast, but your disciples do not fast?"

¹⁵Jesus answered, "How can the guests of the bridegroom mourn while he is with them? The time will come when the bridegroom will be taken from them; then they will fast.

¹⁶"No-one sews a patch of unshrunk cloth on an old garment, for the patch will pull away from the garment, making the tear worse. ¹⁷Neither do men pour new wine into old wineskins. If they do, the skins will burst, the wine will run out and the wineskins will be ruined. No, they pour new wine into new wineskins, and both are preserved."

A Dead Girl and a Sick Woman

¹⁸While he was saying this, a ruler came and knelt before him and said, "My daughter has just died. But come and put your hand on her, and she will live." ¹⁹Jesus got up and went with him, and so did his disciples.

²⁰Just then a woman who had been subject to bleeding for twelve years came up behind him and touched the edge of his cloak. ²¹She said to herself, "If I only touch his cloak, I will be healed."

²²Jesus turned and saw her. "Take heart, daughter," he said, "your faith has healed you." And the woman was healed from that moment.

²³When Jesus entered the ruler's house and saw the flute players and the noisy crowd, ²⁴he said, "Go away. The girl is not dead but asleep." But they laughed at him. ²⁵After the crowd had been put outside, he went in and took the girl by the hand, and she got up. ²⁶News of this spread through all that region.

Jesus Heals the Blind and Mute

²⁷As Jesus went on from there, two blind men followed him, calling out, "Have mercy on us, Son of David!"

²⁸When he had gone indoors, the blind men came to him, and he asked them, "Do you believe that I am able to do this?"

"Yes, Lord," they replied.

²⁹Then he touched their eyes and said, "According to your faith will it be done to you"; ³⁰and their sight was restored. Jesus warned them sternly, "See that no-one knows about this." ³¹But they went out and spread the news about him all over that region.

³²While they were going out, a man who was demon-possessed and could not talk was brought to Jesus. ³³And when the demon was driven out, the man who had been mute spoke. The crowd was amazed and said, "Nothing like this has ever been seen in Israel."

³⁴But the Pharisees said, "It is by the prince of demons that he drives out demons."

The Workers Are Few

³⁵Jesus went through all the towns and villages, teaching in their synagogues, preaching the good news of the kingdom and healing every disease and sickness. ³⁶When he saw the crowds, he had compassion on them, because they were harassed and helpless, like sheep without a shepherd. ³⁷Then he said to his disciples, "The harvest is plentiful but the workers are few. ³⁸Ask the Lord of the harvest,

ᵃ13 Hosea 6:6

therefore, to send out workers into his harvest field."

Jesus Sends Out the Twelve

10 He called his twelve disciples to him and gave them authority to drive out evil*a* spirits and to heal every disease and sickness.

²These are the names of the twelve apostles: first, Simon (who is called Peter) and his brother Andrew; James son of Zebedee, and his brother John; ³Philip and Bartholomew; Thomas and Matthew the tax collector; James son of Alphaeus, and Thaddaeus; ⁴Simon the Zealot and Judas Iscariot, who betrayed him.

⁵These twelve Jesus sent out with the following instructions: "Do not go among the Gentiles or enter any town of the Samaritans. ⁶Go rather to the lost sheep of Israel. ⁷As you go, preach this message: 'The kingdom of heaven is near.' ⁸Heal the sick, raise the dead, cleanse those who have leprosy,*b* drive out demons. Freely you have received, freely give. ⁹Do not take along any gold or silver or copper in your belts; ¹⁰take no bag for the journey, or extra tunic, or sandals or a staff; for the worker is worth his keep.

¹¹"Whatever town or village you enter, search for some worthy person there and stay at his house until you leave. ¹²As you enter the home, give it your greeting. ¹³If the home is deserving, let your peace rest on it; if it is not, let your peace return to you. ¹⁴If anyone will not welcome you or listen to your words, shake the dust off your feet when you leave that home or town. ¹⁵I tell you the truth, it will be more bearable for Sodom and Gomorrah on the day of judgment than for that town. ¹⁶I am sending you out like sheep among wolves. Therefore be as shrewd as snakes and as innocent as doves.

¹⁷"Be on your guard against men; they will hand you over to the local councils and flog you in their synagogues. ¹⁸On my account you will be brought before governors and kings as witnesses to them and to the Gentiles. ¹⁹But when they arrest you, do not worry about what to say or how to say it. At that time you will be given what to say, ²⁰for it will not be you speaking, but the Spirit of your Father speaking through you.

²¹"Brother will betray brother to death, and a father his child; children will rebel against their parents and have them put to death. ²²All men will hate you because of me, but he who stands firm to the end will be saved. ²³When you are persecuted in one place, flee to another. I tell you the truth, you will not finish going through the cities of Israel before the Son of Man comes.

²⁴"A student is not above his teacher, nor a servant above his master. ²⁵It is enough for the student to be like his teacher, and the servant like his master. If the head of the house has been called Beelzebub,*c* how much more the members of his household!

²⁶"So do not be afraid of them. There is nothing concealed that will not be disclosed, or hidden that will not be made known. ²⁷What I tell you in the dark, speak in the daylight; what is whispered in your ear, proclaim from the roofs. ²⁸Do not be afraid of those who kill the body but cannot kill the soul. Rather, be afraid of the One who can destroy both soul and body in hell. ²⁹Are not two sparrows sold for a penny?*d* Yet not one of them will fall to the ground apart from the will of your Father. ³⁰And even the very hairs of your head are all numbered. ³¹So don't be afraid; you are worth more than many sparrows.

³²"Whoever acknowledges me before men, I will also acknowledge him before my Father in heaven. ³³But whoever disowns me before men, I will disown him before my Father in heaven.

³⁴"Do not suppose that I have come to bring peace to the earth. I did not come to

a1 Greek *unclean*
b8 The Greek word was used for various diseases affecting the skin—not necessarily leprosy.
c25 Greek *Beezeboul* or *Beelzeboul*   *d29* Greek *an assarion*

bring peace, but a sword. ³⁵For I have come to turn

> "'a man against his father,
>   a daughter against her mother,
>   a daughter-in-law against her
>   mother-in-law—
> ³⁶   a man's enemies will be the members
>   of his own household.'ᵉ

³⁷"Anyone who loves his father or mother more than me is not worthy of me; anyone who loves his son or daughter more than me is not worthy of me; ³⁸and anyone who does not take his cross and follow me is not worthy of me. ³⁹Whoever finds his life will lose it, and whoever loses his life for my sake will find it.

⁴⁰"He who receives you receives me, and he who receives me receives the one who sent me. ⁴¹Anyone who receives a prophet because he is a prophet will receive a prophet's reward, and anyone who receives a righteous man because he is a righteous man will receive a righteous man's reward. ⁴²And if anyone gives even a cup of cold water to one of these little ones because he is my disciple, I tell you the truth, he will certainly not lose his reward."

Jesus and John the Baptist

11 After Jesus had finished instructing his twelve disciples, he went on from there to teach and preach in the towns of Galilee.ᵃ

²When John heard in prison what Christ was doing, he sent his disciples ³to ask him, "Are you the one who was to come, or should we expect someone else?"

⁴Jesus replied, "Go back and report to John what you hear and see: ⁵The blind receive sight, the lame walk, those who have leprosyᵇ are cured, the deaf hear, the dead are raised, and the good news is preached to the poor. ⁶Blessed is the man who does not fall away on account of me."

⁷As John's disciples were leaving, Jesus began to speak to the crowd about John: "What did you go out into the desert to see? A reed swayed by the wind? ⁸If not,

what did you go out to see? A man dressed in fine clothes? No, those who wear fine clothes are in kings' palaces. ⁹Then what did you go out to see? A prophet? Yes, I tell you, and more than a prophet. ¹⁰This is the one about whom it is written:

> "'I will send my messenger ahead of
>   you,
>   who will prepare your way before
>   you.'ᶜ

¹¹I tell you the truth: Among those born of women there has not risen anyone greater than John the Baptist; yet he who is least in the kingdom of heaven is greater than he. ¹²From the days of John the Baptist until now, the kingdom of heaven has been forcefully advancing, and forceful men lay hold of it. ¹³For all the Prophets and the Law prophesied until John. ¹⁴And if you are willing to accept it, he is the Elijah who was to come. ¹⁵He who has ears, let him hear.

¹⁶"To what can I compare this generation? They are like children sitting in the market-places and calling out to others:

> ¹⁷"'We played the flute for you,
>   and you did not dance;
>   we sang a dirge,
>   and you did not mourn.'

¹⁸For John came neither eating nor drinking, and they say, 'He has a demon.' ¹⁹The Son of Man came eating and drinking, and they say, 'Here is a glutton and a drunkard, a friend of tax collectors and "sinners".' But wisdom is proved right by her actions."

Woe on Unrepentant Cities

²⁰Then Jesus began to denounce the cities in which most of his miracles had been performed, because they did not repent. ²¹"Woe to you, Korazin! Woe to you, Bethsaida! If the miracles that were performed in you had been performed in Tyre and Sidon, they would have repented long ago in sackcloth and ashes. ²²But I

ᵉ36 Micah 7:6   ᵃ1 Greek in their towns
ᵇ5 The Greek word was used for various diseases affecting the skin—not necessarily leprosy.   ᶜ10 Mal. 3:1

tell you, it will be more bearable for Tyre and Sidon on the day of judgment than for you. 23And you, Capernaum, will you be lifted up to the skies? No, you will go down to the depths.*d* If the miracles that were performed in you had been performed in Sodom, it would have remained to this day. 24But I tell you that it will be more bearable for Sodom on the day of judgment than for you.''

Rest for the Weary

25At that time Jesus said, ''I praise you, Father, Lord of heaven and earth, because you have hidden these things from the wise and learned, and revealed them to little children. 26Yes, Father, for this was your good pleasure.

27''All things have been committed to me by my Father. No-one knows the Son except the Father, and no-one knows the Father except the Son and those to whom the Son chooses to reveal him.

28''Come to me, all you who are weary and burdened, and I will give you rest. 29Take my yoke upon you and learn from me, for I am gentle and humble in heart, and you will find rest for your souls. 30For my yoke is easy and my burden is light.''

Lord of the Sabbath

12 At that time Jesus went through the cornfields on the Sabbath. His disciples were hungry and began to pick some ears of corn and eat them. 2When the Pharisees saw this, they said to him, ''Look! Your disciples are doing what is unlawful on the Sabbath.''

3He answered, ''Haven't you read what David did when he and his companions were hungry? 4He entered the house of God, and he and his companions ate the consecrated bread—which was not lawful for them to do, but only for the priests. 5Or haven't you read in the Law that on the Sabbath the priests in the temple desecrate the day and yet are innocent? 6I tell you that one*a* greater than the temple is here. 7If you had known what these words

mean, 'I desire mercy, not sacrifice,'*b* you would not have condemned the innocent. 8For the Son of Man is Lord of the Sabbath.''

9Going on from that place, he went into their synagogue, 10and a man with a shrivelled hand was there. Looking for a reason to accuse Jesus, they asked him, ''Is it lawful to heal on the Sabbath?''

11He said to them, ''If any of you has a sheep and it falls into a pit on the Sabbath, will you not take hold of it and lift it out? 12How much more valuable is a man than a sheep! Therefore it is lawful to do good on the Sabbath.''

13Then he said to the man, ''Stretch out your hand.'' So he stretched it out and it was completely restored, just as sound as the other. 14But the Pharisees went out and plotted how they might kill Jesus.

God's Chosen Servant

15Aware of this, Jesus withdrew from that place. Many followed him, and he healed all their sick, 16warning them not to tell who he was. 17This was to fulfil what was spoken through the prophet Isaiah:

18''Here is my servant whom I have
        chosen,
    the one I love, in whom I delight;
 I will put my Spirit on him,
        and he will proclaim justice to the
        nations.
19He will not quarrel or cry out;
        no-one will hear his voice in the
        streets.
20A bruised reed he will not break,
        and a smouldering wick he will not
        snuff out,
    till he leads justice to victory.
21 In his name the nations will put their
        hope.''*c*

Jesus and Beelzebub

22Then they brought him a demon-possessed man who was blind and mute, and Jesus healed him, so that he could both talk and see. 23All the people were

---

d23 Greek *Hades*   *a6* Or *something*; also in verses 41 and 42   *b7* Hosea 6:6   *c21* Isaiah 42:1–4 astonished and said, "Could this be the Son of David?"

24But when the Pharisees heard this, they said, "It is only by Beelzebub,*d* the prince of demons, that this fellow drives out demons."

25Jesus knew their thoughts and said to them, "Every kingdom divided against itself will be ruined, and every city or household divided against itself will not stand. 26If Satan drives out Satan, he is divided against himself. How then can his kingdom stand? 27And if I drive out demons by Beelzebub, by whom do your people drive them out? So then, they will be your judges. 28But if I drive out demons by the Spirit of God, then the kingdom of God has come upon you.

29"Or again, how can anyone enter a strong man's house and carry off his possessions unless he first ties up the strong man? Then he can rob his house.

30"He who is not with me is against me, and he who does not gather with me scatters. 31And so I tell you, every sin and blasphemy will be forgiven men, but the blasphemy against the Spirit will not be forgiven. 32Anyone who speaks a word against the Son of Man will be forgiven, but anyone who speaks against the Holy Spirit will not be forgiven, either in this age or in the age to come.

33"Make a tree good and its fruit will be good, or make a tree bad and its fruit will be bad, for a tree is recognised by its fruit. 34You brood of vipers, how can you who are evil say anything good? For out of the overflow of the heart the mouth speaks. 35The good man brings good things out of the good stored up in him, and the evil man brings evil things out of the evil stored up in him. 36But I tell you that men will have to give account on the day of judgment for every careless word they have spoken. 37For by your words you will be acquitted, and by your words you will be condemned."

The Sign of Jonah

38Then some of the Pharisees and teachers of the law said to him, "Teacher, we want to see a miraculous sign from you."

39He answered, "A wicked and adulterous generation asks for a miraculous sign! But none will be given it except the sign of the prophet Jonah. 40For as Jonah was three days and three nights in the belly of a huge fish, so the Son of Man will be three days and three nights in the heart of the earth. 41The men of Nineveh will stand up at the judgment with this generation and condemn it; for they repented at the preaching of Jonah, and now one*e* greater than Jonah is here. 42The Queen of the South will rise at the judgment with this generation and condemn it; for she came from the ends of the earth to listen to Solomon's wisdom, and now one greater than Solomon is here.

43"When an evil*f* spirit comes out of a man, it goes through arid places seeking rest and does not find it. 44Then it says, 'I will return to the house I left.' When it arrives, it finds the house unoccupied, swept clean and put in order. 45Then it goes and takes with it seven other spirits more wicked than itself, and they go in and live there. And the final condition of that man is worse than the first. That is how it will be with this wicked generation."

Jesus' Mother and Brothers

46While Jesus was still talking to the crowd, his mother and brothers stood outside, wanting to speak to him. 47Someone told him, "Your mother and brothers are standing outside, wanting to speak to you."*g*

48He replied to him, "Who is my mother, and who are my brothers?" 49Pointing to his disciples, he said, "Here are my mother and my brothers. 50For whoever does the will of my Father in heaven is my brother and sister and mother."

The Parable of the Sower

13 That same day Jesus went out of the house and sat by the lake. 2Such large crowds gathered round him

---

d24 Greek *Beezeboul* or *Beelzeboul*; also in verse 27   *e41* Or *something*; also in verse 42   *f43* Greek *unclean*
g47 Some manuscripts do not have verse 47.

that he got into a boat and sat in it, while all the people stood on the shore. ³Then he told them many things in parables, saying: "A farmer went out to sow his seed. ⁴As he was scattering the seed, some fell along the path, and the birds came and ate it up. ⁵Some fell on rocky places, where it did not have much soil. It sprang up quickly, because the soil was shallow. ⁶But when the sun came up, the plants were scorched, and they withered because they had no root. ⁷Other seed fell among thorns, which grew up and choked the plants. ⁸Still other seed fell on good soil, where it produced a crop—a hundred, sixty or thirty times what was sown. ⁹He who has ears, let him hear."

¹⁰The disciples came to him and asked, "Why do you speak to the people in parables?"

¹¹He replied, "The knowledge of the secrets of the kingdom of heaven has been given to you, but not to them. ¹²Whoever has will be given more, and he will have an abundance. Whoever does not have, even what he has will be taken from him. ¹³This is why I speak to them in parables:

"Though seeing, they do not see;
    though hearing, they do not hear or
        understand.

¹⁴In them is fulfilled the prophecy of Isaiah:

"'You will be ever hearing but never
        understanding;
    you will be ever seeing but never
        perceiving.
¹⁵For this people's heart has become
        calloused;
    they hardly hear with their ears,
    and they have closed their eyes.
Otherwise they might see with their
        eyes,
    hear with their ears,
    understand with their hearts
and turn, and I would heal them.'*ᵃ*

¹⁶"But blessed are your eyes because they see, and your ears because they hear. ¹⁷For I tell you the truth, many prophets and righteous men longed to see what you see but did not see it, and to hear what you hear but did not hear it.

¹⁸"Listen then to what the parable of the sower means: ¹⁹When anyone hears the message about the kingdom and does not understand it, the evil one comes and snatches away what was sown in his heart. This is the seed sown along the path. ²⁰The one who received the seed that fell on rocky places is the man who hears the word and at once receives it with joy. ²¹But since he has no root, he lasts only a short time. When trouble or persecution comes because of the word, he quickly falls away. ²²The one who received the seed that fell among the thorns is the man who hears the word, but the worries of this life and the deceitfulness of wealth choke it, making it unfruitful. ²³But the one who received the seed that fell on good soil is the man who hears the word and understands it. He produces a crop, yielding a hundred, sixty or thirty times what was sown."

The Parable of the Weeds

²⁴Jesus told them another parable: "The kingdom of heaven is like a man who sowed good seed in his field. ²⁵But while everyone was sleeping, his enemy came and sowed weeds among the wheat, and went away. ²⁶When the wheat sprouted and formed ears, then the weeds also appeared.

²⁷"The owner's servants came to him and said, 'Sir, didn't you sow good seed in your field? Where then did the weeds come from?'

²⁸"'An enemy did this,' he replied.

"The servants asked him, 'Do you want us to go and pull them up?'

²⁹"'No,' he answered, 'because while you are pulling the weeds, you may root up the wheat with them. ³⁰Let both grow together until the harvest. At that time I will tell the harvesters: First collect the weeds and tie them in bundles to be burned; then gather the wheat and bring it into my barn.'"

ᵃ15 Isaiah 6:9,10

The Parables of the Mustard Seed and the Yeast

[31]He told them another parable: "The kingdom of heaven is like a mustard seed, which a man took and planted in his field. [32]Though it is the smallest of all your seeds, yet when it grows, it is the largest of garden plants and becomes a tree, so that the birds of the air come and perch in its branches."

[33]He told them still another parable: "The kingdom of heaven is like yeast that a woman took and mixed into a large amount[b] of flour until it worked all through the dough."

[34]Jesus spoke all these things to the crowd in parables; he did not say anything to them without using a parable. [35]So was fulfilled what was spoken through the prophet:

"I will open my mouth in parables,
   I will utter things hidden since the
      creation of the world."[c]

The Parable of the Weeds Explained

[36]Then he left the crowd and went into the house. His disciples came to him and said, "Explain to us the parable of the weeds in the field."

[37]He answered, "The one who sowed the good seed is the Son of Man. [38]The field is the world, and the good seed stands for the sons of the kingdom. The weeds are the sons of the evil one, [39]and the enemy who sows them is the devil. The harvest is the end of the age, and the harvesters are angels.

[40]"As the weeds are pulled up and burned in the fire, so it will be at the end of the age. [41]The Son of Man will send out his angels, and they will weed out of his kingdom everything that causes sin and all who do evil. [42]They will throw them into the fiery furnace, where there will be weeping and gnashing of teeth. [43]Then the righteous will shine like the sun in the kingdom of their Father. He who has ears, let him hear.

The Parables of the Hidden Treasure and the Pearl

[44]"The kingdom of heaven is like treasure hidden in a field. When a man found it, he hid it again, and then in his joy went and sold all he had and bought that field.

[45]"Again, the kingdom of heaven is like a merchant looking for fine pearls. [46]When he found one of great value, he went away and sold everything he had and bought it.

The Parable of the Net

[47]"Once again, the kingdom of heaven is like a net that was let down into the lake and caught all kinds of fish. [48]When it was full, the fishermen pulled it up on the shore. Then they sat down and collected the good fish in baskets, but threw the bad away. [49]This is how it will be at the end of the age. The angels will come and separate the wicked from the righteous [50]and throw them into the fiery furnace, where there will be weeping and gnashing of teeth.

[51]"Have you understood all these things?" Jesus asked.

"Yes," they replied.

[52]He said to them, "Therefore every teacher of the law who has been instructed about the kingdom of heaven is like the owner of a house who brings out of his storeroom new treasures as well as old."

A Prophet Without Honour

[53]When Jesus had finished these parables, he moved on from there. [54]Coming to his home town, he began teaching the people in their synagogue, and they were amazed. "Where did this man get this wisdom and these miraculous powers?" they asked. [55]"Isn't this the carpenter's son? Isn't his mother's name Mary, and aren't his brothers James, Joseph, Simon and Judas? [56]Aren't all his sisters with us? Where then did this man get all these things?" [57]And they took offence at him.

But Jesus said to them, "Only in his

---

[b]33 Greek three satas (probably about ⅗ bushel or 22 litres)   [c]35 Psalm 78:2

home town and in his own house is a prophet without honour."

⁵⁸And he did not do many miracles there because of their lack of faith.

John the Baptist Beheaded

14 At that time Herod the tetrarch heard the reports about Jesus, ²and he said to his attendants, "This is John the Baptist; he has risen from the dead! That is why miraculous powers are at work in him."

³Now Herod had arrested John and bound him and put him in prison because of Herodias, his brother Philip's wife, ⁴for John had been saying to him: "It is not lawful for you to have her." ⁵Herod wanted to kill John, but he was afraid of the people, because they considered him a prophet.

⁶On Herod's birthday the daughter of Herodias danced for them and pleased Herod so much ⁷that he promised with an oath to give her whatever she asked. ⁸Prompted by her mother, she said, "Give me here on a platter the head of John the Baptist." ⁹The king was distressed, but because of his oaths and his dinner guests, he ordered that her request be granted ¹⁰and had John beheaded in the prison. ¹¹His head was brought in on a platter and given to the girl, who carried it to her mother. ¹²John's disciples came and took his body and buried it. Then they went and told Jesus.

Jesus Feeds the Five Thousand

¹³When Jesus heard what had happened, he withdrew by boat privately to a solitary place. Hearing of this, the crowds followed him on foot from the towns. ¹⁴When Jesus landed and saw a large crowd, he had compassion on them and healed their sick.

¹⁵As evening approached, the disciples came to him and said, "This is a remote place, and it's already getting late. Send the crowds away, so that they can go to the villages and buy themselves some food."

¹⁶Jesus replied, "They do not need to go away. You give them something to eat."

¹⁷"We have here only five loaves of bread and two fish," they answered.

¹⁸"Bring them here to me," he said. ¹⁹And he directed the people to sit down on the grass. Taking the five loaves and the two fish and looking up to heaven, he gave thanks and broke the loaves. Then he gave them to the disciples, and the disciples gave them to the people. ²⁰They all ate and were satisfied, and the disciples picked up twelve basketfuls of broken pieces that were left over. ²¹The number of those who ate was about five thousand men, besides women and children.

Jesus Walks on the Water

²²Immediately Jesus made the disciples get into the boat and go on ahead of him to the other side, while he dismissed the crowd. ²³After he had dismissed them, he went up on a mountainside by himself to pray. When evening came, he was there alone, ²⁴but the boat was already a considerable distance*ᵃ* from land, buffeted by the waves because the wind was against it.

²⁵During the fourth watch of the night Jesus went out to them, walking on the lake. ²⁶When the disciples saw him walking on the lake, they were terrified. "It's a ghost," they said, and cried out in fear.

²⁷But Jesus immediately said to them: "Take courage! It is I. Don't be afraid."

²⁸"Lord, if it's you," Peter replied, "tell me to come to you on the water."

²⁹"Come," he said.

Then Peter got down out of the boat, walked on the water and came towards Jesus. ³⁰But when he saw the wind, he was afraid and, beginning to sink, cried out, "Lord, save me!"

³¹Immediately Jesus reached out his hand and caught him. "You of little faith," he said, "why did you doubt?"

³²And when they climbed into the boat, the wind died down. ³³Then those who were in the boat worshipped him, saying, "Truly you are the Son of God."

³⁴When they had crossed over, they

ᵃ24 Greek many stadia

landed at Gennesaret. ³⁵And when the men of that place recognised Jesus, they sent word to all the surrounding country. People brought all their sick to him ³⁶and begged him to let the sick just touch the edge of his cloak, and all who touched him were healed.

Clean and Unclean

15 Then some Pharisees and teachers of the law came to Jesus from Jerusalem and asked, ²"Why do your disciples break the tradition of the elders? They don't wash their hands before they eat!"

³Jesus replied, "And why do you break the command of God for the sake of your tradition? ⁴For God said, 'Honour your father and mother'ᵃ and 'Anyone who curses his father or mother must be put to death.'ᵇ ⁵But you say that if a man says to his father or mother, 'Whatever help you might otherwise have received from me is a gift devoted to God,' ⁶he is not to 'honour his father'ᶜ with it. Thus you nullify the word of God for the sake of your tradition. ⁷You hypocrites! Isaiah was right when he prophesied about you:

⁸"'These people honour me with their lips,
  but their hearts are far from me.
⁹They worship me in vain;
  their teachings are but rules taught by men.'ᵈ"

¹⁰Jesus called the crowd to him and said, "Listen and understand. ¹¹What goes into a man's mouth does not make him 'unclean', but what comes out of his mouth, that is what makes him 'unclean'."

¹²Then the disciples came to him and asked, "Do you know that the Pharisees were offended when they heard this?"

¹³He replied, "Every plant that my heavenly Father has not planted will be pulled up by the roots. ¹⁴Leave them; they are blind guides.ᵉ If a blind man leads a blind man, both will fall into a pit."

¹⁵Peter said, "Explain the parable to us."

¹⁶"Are you still so dull?" Jesus asked them. ¹⁷"Don't you see that whatever enters the mouth goes into the stomach and then out of the body? ¹⁸But the things that come out of the mouth come from the heart, and these make a man 'unclean'. ¹⁹For out of the heart come evil thoughts, murder, adultery, sexual immorality, theft, false testimony, slander. ²⁰These are what make a man 'unclean'; but eating with unwashed hands does not make him 'unclean'."

The Faith of the Canaanite Woman

²¹Leaving that place, Jesus withdrew to the region of Tyre and Sidon. ²²A Canaanite woman from that vicinity came to him, crying out, "Lord, Son of David, have mercy on me! My daughter is suffering terribly from demon-possession."

²³Jesus did not answer a word. So his disciples came to him and urged him, "Send her away, for she keeps crying out after us."

²⁴He answered, "I was sent only to the lost sheep of Israel."

²⁵The woman came and knelt before him. "Lord, help me!" she said.

²⁶He replied, "It is not right to take the children's bread and toss it to their dogs."

²⁷"Yes, Lord," she said, "but even the dogs eat the crumbs that fall from their masters' table."

²⁸Then Jesus answered, "Woman, you have great faith! Your request is granted." And her daughter was healed from that very hour.

Jesus Feeds the Four Thousand

²⁹Jesus left there and went along the Sea of Galilee. Then he went up on a mountainside and sat down. ³⁰Great crowds came to him, bringing the lame, the blind, the crippled, the mute and many others, and laid them at his feet; and he healed them. ³¹The people were amazed when they saw the mute speaking, the crippled made well, the lame walking and the blind

ᵃ4 Exodus 20:12; Deut. 5:16   ᵇ4 Exodus 21:17; Lev. 20:9   ᶜ6 Some manuscripts *father or his mother*
ᵈ9 Isaiah 29:13   ᵉ14 Some manuscripts *guides of the blind*

seeing. And they praised the God of Israel.

³²Jesus called his disciples to him and said, "I have compassion for these people; they have already been with me three days and have nothing to eat. I do not want to send them away hungry, or they may collapse on the way."

³³His disciples answered, "Where could we get enough bread in this remote place to feed such a crowd?"

³⁴"How many loaves do you have?" Jesus asked.

"Seven," they replied, "and a few small fish."

³⁵He told the crowd to sit down on the ground. ³⁶Then he took the seven loaves and the fish, and when he had given thanks, he broke them and gave them to the disciples, and they in turn to the people. ³⁷They all ate and were satisfied. Afterwards the disciples picked up seven basketfuls of broken pieces that were left over. ³⁸The number of those who ate was four thousand, besides women and children. ³⁹After Jesus had sent the crowd away, he got into the boat and went to the vicinity of Magadan.

The Demand for a Sign

16 The Pharisees and Sadducees came to Jesus and tested him by asking him to show them a sign from heaven.

²He replied,ᵃ "When evening comes, you say, 'It will be fair weather, for the sky is red,' ³and in the morning, 'Today it will be stormy, for the sky is red and overcast.' You know how to interpret the appearance of the sky, but you cannot interpret the signs of the times. ⁴A wicked and adulterous generation looks for a miraculous sign, but none will be given it except the sign of Jonah." Jesus then left them and went away.

The Yeast of the Pharisees and Sadducees

⁵When they went across the lake, the disciples forgot to take bread. ⁶"Be careful," Jesus said to them. "Be on your guard against the yeast of the Pharisees and Sadducees."

⁷They discussed this among themselves and said, "It is because we didn't bring any bread."

⁸Aware of their discussion, Jesus asked, "You of little faith, why are you talking among yourselves about having no bread? ⁹Do you still not understand? Don't you remember the five loaves for the five thousand, and how many basketfuls you gathered? ¹⁰Or the seven loaves for the four thousand, and how many basketfuls you gathered? ¹¹How is it you don't understand that I was not talking to you about bread? But be on your guard against the yeast of the Pharisees and Sadducees."

¹²Then they understood that he was not telling them to guard against the yeast used in bread, but against the teaching of the Pharisees and Sadducees.

Peter's Confession of Christ

¹³When Jesus came to the region of Caesarea Philippi, he asked his disciples, "Who do people say the Son of Man is?"

¹⁴They replied, "Some say John the Baptist; others say Elijah; and still others, Jeremiah or one of the prophets."

¹⁵"But what about you?" he asked. "Who do you say I am?"

¹⁶Simon Peter answered, "You are the Christ,ᵇ the Son of the living God."

¹⁷Jesus replied, "Blessed are you, Simon son of Jonah, for this was not revealed to you by man, but by my Father in heaven. ¹⁸And I tell you that you are Peter,ᶜ and on this rock I will build my church, and the gates of Hadesᵈ will not overcome it.ᵉ ¹⁹I will give you the keys of the kingdom of heaven; whatever you bind on earth will beᶠ bound in heaven, and whatever you loose on earth will beᶠ loosed in heaven." ²⁰Then he warned his disciples not to tell anyone that he was the Christ.

ᵃ2 Some early manuscripts do not have the rest of verse 2 and all of verse 3.   ᵇ16 Or *Messiah*; also in verse 20
ᶜ18 *Peter* means *rock*.   ᵈ18 Or *hell*   ᵉ18 Or *not prove stronger than it*   ᶠ19 Or *have been*

Jesus Predicts His Death

21From that time on Jesus began to explain to his disciples that he must go to Jerusalem and suffer many things at the hands of the elders, chief priests and teachers of the law, and that he must be killed and on the third day be raised to life. 22Peter took him aside and began to rebuke him. "Never, Lord!" he said. "This shall never happen to you!"

23Jesus turned and said to Peter, "Get behind me, Satan! You are a stumbling-block to me; you do not have in mind the things of God, but the things of men."

24Then Jesus said to his disciples, "If anyone would come after me, he must deny himself and take up his cross and follow me. 25For whoever wants to save his life^g will lose it, but whoever loses his life for me will find it. 26What good will it be for a man if he gains the whole world, yet forfeits his soul? Or what can a man give in exchange for his soul? 27For the Son of Man is going to come in his Father's glory with his angels, and then he will reward each person according to what he has done. 28I tell you the truth, some who are standing here will not taste death before they see the Son of Man coming in his kingdom."

The Transfiguration

17 After six days Jesus took with him Peter, James and John the brother of James, and led them up a high mountain by themselves. 2There he was transfigured before them. His face shone like the sun, and his clothes became as white as the light. 3Just then there appeared before them Moses and Elijah, talking with Jesus.

4Peter said to Jesus, "Lord, it is good for us to be here. If you wish, I will put up three shelters—one for you, one for Moses and one for Elijah."

5While he was still speaking, a bright cloud enveloped them, and a voice from the cloud said, "This is my Son, whom I love; with him I am well pleased. Listen to him!"

6When the disciples heard this, they fell face down to the ground, terrified. 7But Jesus came and touched them. "Get up," he said. "Don't be afraid." 8When they looked up, they saw no-one except Jesus.

9As they were coming down the mountain, Jesus instructed them, "Don't tell anyone what you have seen, until the Son of Man has been raised from the dead."

10The disciples asked him, "Why then do the teachers of the law say that Elijah must come first?"

11Jesus replied, "To be sure, Elijah comes and will restore all things. 12But I tell you, Elijah has already come, and they did not recognise him, but have done to him everything they wished. In the same way the Son of Man is going to suffer at their hands." 13Then the disciples understood that he was talking to them about John the Baptist.

The Healing of a Boy With a Demon

14When they came to the crowd, a man approached Jesus and knelt before him. 15"Lord, have mercy on my son," he said. "He has seizures and is suffering greatly. He often falls into the fire or into the water. 16I brought him to your disciples, but they could not heal him."

17"O unbelieving and perverse generation," Jesus replied, "how long shall I stay with you? How long shall I put up with you? Bring the boy here to me." 18Jesus rebuked the demon, and it came out of the boy, and he was healed from that moment.

19Then the disciples came to Jesus in private and asked, "Why couldn't we drive it out?"

20He replied, "Because you have so little faith. I tell you the truth, if you have faith as small as a mustard seed, you can say to this mountain, 'Move from here to there' and it will move. Nothing will be impossible for you."^{a}

22When they came together in Galilee, he said to them, "The Son of Man is going to be betrayed into the hands of men. 23They will kill him, and on the third day

^{g}25 The Greek word means either *life* or *soul*; also in verse 26.
^{a}20 Some manuscripts *you.* ^{21}*But this kind does not go out except by prayer and fasting.*

he will be raised to life." And the disciples were filled with grief.

The Temple Tax

[24]After Jesus and his disciples arrived in Capernaum, the collectors of the two-drachma tax came to Peter and asked, "Doesn't your teacher pay the temple tax?"[b]

[25]"Yes, he does," he replied.

When Peter came into the house, Jesus was the first to speak. "What do you think, Simon?" he asked. "From whom do the kings of the earth collect duty and taxes—from their own sons or from others?"

[26]"From others," Peter answered.

"Then the sons are exempt," Jesus said to him. [27]"But so that we may not offend them, go to the lake and throw out your line. Take the first fish you catch; open its mouth and you will find a four-drachma coin. Take it and give it to them for my tax and yours."

The Greatest in the Kingdom of Heaven

18 At that time the disciples came to Jesus and asked, "Who is the greatest in the kingdom of heaven?"

[2]He called a little child and had him stand among them. [3]And he said: "I tell you the truth, unless you change and become like little children, you will never enter the kingdom of heaven. [4]Therefore, whoever humbles himself like this child is the greatest in the kingdom of heaven.

[5]"And whoever welcomes a little child like this in my name welcomes me. [6]But if anyone causes one of these little ones who believe in me to sin, it would be better for him to have a large millstone hung around his neck and to be drowned in the depths of the sea.

[7]"Woe to the world because of the things that cause people to sin! Such things must come, but woe to the man through whom they come! [8]If your hand or your foot causes you to sin, cut it off and throw it away. It is better for you to enter life maimed or crippled than to have two

hands or two feet and be thrown into eternal fire. [9]And if your eye causes you to sin, gouge it out and throw it away. It is better for you to enter life with one eye than to have two eyes and be thrown into the fire of hell.

The Parable of the Lost Sheep

[10]"See that you do not look down on one of these little ones. For I tell you that their angels in heaven always see the face of my Father in heaven.[a]

[12]"What do you think? If a man owns a hundred sheep, and one of them wanders away, will he not leave the ninety-nine on the hills and go to look for the one that wandered off? [13]And if he finds it, I tell you the truth, he is happier about that one sheep than about the ninety-nine that did not wander off. [14]In the same way your Father in heaven is not willing that any of these little ones should be lost.

A Brother Who Sins Against You

[15]"If your brother sins against you,[b] go and show him his fault, just between the two of you. If he listens to you, you have won your brother over. [16]But if he will not listen, take one or two others along, so that 'every matter may be established by the testimony of two or three witnesses.'[c] [17]If he refuses to listen to them, tell it to the church; and if he refuses to listen even to the church, treat him as you would a pagan or a tax collector.

[18]"I tell you the truth, whatever you bind on earth will be[d] bound in heaven, and whatever you loose on earth will be[d] loosed in heaven.

[19]"Again, I tell you that if two of you on earth agree about anything you ask for, it will be done for you by my Father in heaven. [20]For where two or three come together in my name, there am I with them."

The Parable of the Unmerciful Servant

[21]Then Peter came to Jesus and asked, "Lord, how many times shall I forgive my

---

b24 Greek *the two drachmas*   *a10* Some manuscripts *heaven.* [11]*The Son of Man came to save what was lost.*
b15 Some manuscripts do not have *against you.*   *c16* Deut. 19:15   *d18* Or *have been*

brother when he sins against me? Up to seven times?"

²²Jesus answered, "I tell you, not seven times, but seventy-seven times.ᵉ

²³"Therefore, the kingdom of heaven is like a king who wanted to settle accounts with his servants. ²⁴As he began the settlement, a man who owed him ten thousand talents*f* was brought to him. ²⁵Since he was not able to pay, the master ordered that he and his wife and his children and all that he had be sold to repay the debt.

²⁶"The servant fell on his knees before him. 'Be patient with me,' he begged, 'and I will pay back everything.' ²⁷The servant's master took pity on him, cancelled the debt and let him go.

²⁸"But when that servant went out, he found one of his fellow-servants who owed him a hundred denarii.*g* He grabbed him and began to choke him. 'Pay back what you owe me!' he demanded.

²⁹"His fellow-servant fell to his knees and begged him, 'Be patient with me, and I will pay you back.'

³⁰"But he refused. Instead, he went off and had the man thrown into prison until he could pay the debt. ³¹When the other servants saw what had happened, they were greatly distressed and went and told their master everything that had happened.

³²"Then the master called the servant in. 'You wicked servant,' he said, 'I cancelled all that debt of yours because you begged me to. ³³Shouldn't you have had mercy on your fellow-servant just as I had on you?' ³⁴In anger his master turned him over to the jailers to be tortured, until he should pay back all he owed.

³⁵"This is how my heavenly Father will treat each of you unless you forgive your brother from your heart."

Divorce

19 When Jesus had finished saying these things, he left Galilee and went into the region of Judea to the other

side of the Jordan. ²Large crowds followed him, and he healed them there.

³Some Pharisees came to him to test him. They asked, "Is it lawful for a man to divorce his wife for any and every reason?"

⁴"Haven't you read," he replied, "that at the beginning the Creator 'made them male and female',*a* ⁵and said, 'For this reason a man will leave his father and mother and be united to his wife, and the two will become one flesh'*b*? ⁶So they are no longer two, but one. Therefore what God has joined together, let man not separate."

⁷"Why then," they asked, "did Moses command that a man give his wife a certificate of divorce and send her away?"

⁸Jesus replied, "Moses permitted you to divorce your wives because your hearts were hard. But it was not this way from the beginning. ⁹I tell you that anyone who divorces his wife, except for marital unfaithfulness, and marries another woman commits adultery."

¹⁰The disciples said to him, "If this is the situation between a husband and wife, it is better not to marry."

¹¹Jesus replied, "Not everyone can accept this word, but only those to whom it has been given. ¹²For some are eunuchs because they were born that way; others were made that way by men; and others have renounced marriage*c* because of the kingdom of heaven. The one who can accept this should accept it."

The Little Children and Jesus

¹³Then little children were brought to Jesus for him to place his hands on them and pray for them. But the disciples rebuked those who brought them.

¹⁴Jesus said, "Let the little children come to me, and do not hinder them, for the kingdom of heaven belongs to such as these." ¹⁵When he had placed his hands on them, he went on from there.

---

e22 Or seventy times seven   f24 That is, millions of pounds   g28 That is, a few pounds
a4 Gen. 1:27   b5 Gen. 2:24   c12 Or have made themselves eunuchs

The Rich Young Man

16Now a man came up to Jesus and asked, "Teacher, what good thing must I do to get eternal life?"

17"Why do you ask me about what is good?" Jesus replied. "There is only One who is good. If you want to enter life, obey the commandments."

18"Which ones?" the man enquired.

Jesus replied, "'Do not murder, do not commit adultery, do not steal, do not give false testimony, 19honour your father and mother,'*d* and 'love your neighbour as yourself.'*e*"

20"All these I have kept," the young man said. "What do I still lack?"

21Jesus answered, "If you want to be perfect, go, sell your possessions and give to the poor, and you will have treasure in heaven. Then come, follow me."

22When the young man heard this, he went away sad, because he had great wealth.

23Then Jesus said to his disciples, "I tell you the truth, it is hard for a rich man to enter the kingdom of heaven. 24Again I tell you, it is easier for a camel to go through the eye of a needle than for a rich man to enter the kingdom of God."

25When the disciples heard this, they were greatly astonished and asked, "Who then can be saved?"

26Jesus looked at them and said, "With man this is impossible, but with God all things are possible."

27Peter answered him, "We have left everything to follow you! What then will there be for us?"

28Jesus said to them, "I tell you the truth, at the renewal of all things, when the Son of Man sits on his glorious throne, you who have followed me will also sit on twelve thrones, judging the twelve tribes of Israel. 29And everyone who has left houses or brothers or sisters or father or mother*f* or children or fields for my sake will receive a hundred times as much and will inherit eternal life. 30But many who are first will be last, and many who are last will be first.

The Parable of the Workers in the Vineyard

20 "For the kingdom of heaven is like a landowner who went out early in the morning to hire men to work in his vineyard. 2He agreed to pay them a denarius for the day and sent them into his vineyard.

3"About the third hour he went out and saw others standing in the market-place doing nothing. 4He told them, 'You also go and work in my vineyard, and I will pay you whatever is right.' 5So they went.

"He went out again about the sixth hour and the ninth hour and did the same thing. 6About the eleventh hour he went out and found still others standing around. He asked them, 'Why have you been standing here all day long doing nothing?'

7"'Because no-one has hired us,' they answered.

"He said to them, 'You also go and work in my vineyard.'

8"When evening came, the owner of the vineyard said to his foreman, 'Call the workers and pay them their wages, beginning with the last ones hired and going on to the first.'

9"The workers who were hired about the eleventh hour came and each received a denarius. 10So when those came who were hired first, they expected to receive more. But each one of them also received a denarius. 11When they received it, they began to grumble against the landowner. 12'These men who were hired last worked only one hour,' they said, 'and you have made them equal to us who have borne the burden of the work and the heat of the day.'

13"But he answered one of them, 'Friend, I am not being unfair to you. Didn't you agree to work for a denarius? 14Take your pay and go. I want to give the man who was hired last the same as I gave you. 15Don't I have the right to do what I want with my own money? Or are you envious because I am generous?'

16"So the last will be first, and the first will be last."

d19 Exodus 20:12–16; Deut. 5:16–20   *e19* Lev. 19:18   *f29* Some manuscripts *mother or wife*

Jesus Again Predicts His Death

17Now as Jesus was going up to Jerusalem, he took the twelve disciples aside and said to them, 18"We are going up to Jerusalem, and the Son of Man will be betrayed to the chief priests and the teachers of the law. They will condemn him to death 19and will turn him over to the Gentiles to be mocked and flogged and crucified. On the third day he will be raised to life!"

A Mother's Request

20Then the mother of Zebedee's sons came to Jesus with her sons and, kneeling down, asked a favour of him.

21"What is it you want?" he asked.

She said, "Grant that one of these two sons of mine may sit at your right and the other at your left in your kingdom."

22"You don't know what you are asking," Jesus said to them. "Can you drink the cup I am going to drink?"

"We can," they answered.

23Jesus said to them, "You will indeed drink from my cup, but to sit at my right or left is not for me to grant. These places belong to those for whom they have been prepared by my Father."

24When the ten heard about this, they were indignant with the two brothers. 25Jesus called them together and said, "You know that the rulers of the Gentiles lord it over them, and their high officials exercise authority over them. 26Not so with you. Instead, whoever wants to become great among you must be your servant, 27and whoever wants to be first must be your slave—28just as the Son of Man did not come to be served, but to serve, and to give his life as a ransom for many."

Two Blind Men Receive Sight

29As Jesus and his disciples were leaving Jericho, a large crowd followed him. 30Two blind men were sitting by the roadside, and when they heard that Jesus was going by, they shouted, "Lord, Son of David, have mercy on us!"

31The crowd rebuked them and told them to be quiet, but they shouted all the louder, "Lord, Son of David, have mercy on us!"

32Jesus stopped and called them. "What do you want me to do for you?" he asked.

33"Lord," they answered, "we want our sight."

34Jesus had compassion on them and touched their eyes. Immediately they received their sight and followed him.

The Triumphal Entry

21 As they approached Jerusalem and came to Bethphage on the Mount of Olives, Jesus sent two disciples, 2saying to them, "Go to the village ahead of you, and at once you will find a donkey tied there, with her colt by her. Untie them and bring them to me. 3If anyone says anything to you, tell him that the Lord needs them, and he will send them right away."

4This took place to fulfil what was spoken through the prophet:

5"Say to the Daughter of Zion,
    'See, your king comes to you,
gentle and riding on a donkey,
    on a colt, the foal of a donkey.'"*a*

6The disciples went and did as Jesus had instructed them. 7They brought the donkey and the colt, placed their cloaks on them, and Jesus sat on them. 8A very large crowd spread their cloaks on the road, while others cut branches from the trees and spread them on the road. 9The crowds that went ahead of him and those that followed shouted,

"Hosanna*b* to the Son of David!"

"Blessed is he who comes in the name of the Lord!"*c*

"Hosanna*b* in the highest!"

*a*5 Zech. 9:9   *b*9 A Hebrew expression meaning "Save!" which became an exclamation of praise; also in verse 15
*c*9 Psalm 118:26

[10]When Jesus entered Jerusalem, the whole city was stirred and asked, "Who is this?"

[11]The crowds answered, "This is Jesus, the prophet from Nazareth in Galilee."

Jesus at the Temple

[12]Jesus entered the temple area and drove out all who were buying and selling there. He overturned the tables of the money-changers and the benches of those selling doves. [13]"It is written," he said to them, " 'My house will be called a house of prayer,'[d] but you are making it a 'den of robbers'.[e]"

[14]The blind and the lame came to him at the temple, and he healed them. [15]But when the chief priests and the teachers of the law saw the wonderful things he did and the children shouting in the temple area, "Hosanna to the Son of David," they were indignant.

[16]"Do you hear what these children are saying?" they asked him.

"Yes," replied Jesus, "have you never read,

" 'From the lips of children and infants you have ordained praise'[f]?"

[17]And he left them and went out of the city to Bethany, where he spent the night.

The Fig-Tree Withers

[18]Early in the morning, as he was on his way back to the city, he was hungry. [19]Seeing a fig-tree by the road, he went up to it but found nothing on it except leaves. Then he said to it, "May you never bear fruit again!" Immediately the tree withered.

[20]When the disciples saw this, they were amazed. "How did the fig-tree wither so quickly?" they asked.

[21]Jesus replied, "I tell you the truth, if you have faith and do not doubt, not only can you do what was done to the fig-tree, but also you can say to this mountain, 'Go, throw yourself into the sea,' and it will be done. [22]If you believe, you will receive whatever you ask for in prayer."

The Authority of Jesus Questioned

[23]Jesus entered the temple courts, and, while he was teaching, the chief priests and the elders of the people came to him. "By what authority are you doing these things?" they asked. "And who gave you this authority?"

[24]Jesus replied, "I will also ask you one question. If you answer me, I will tell you by what authority I am doing these things. [25]John's baptism—where did it come from? Was it from heaven, or from men?"

They discussed it among themselves and said, "If we say, 'From heaven', he will ask, 'Then why didn't you believe him?' [26]But if we say, 'From men'—we are afraid of the people, for they all hold that John was a prophet."

[27]So they answered Jesus, "We don't know."

Then he said, "Neither will I tell you by what authority I am doing these things.

The Parable of the Two Sons

[28]"What do you think? There was a man who had two sons. He went to the first and said, 'Son, go and work today in the vineyard.'

[29]" 'I will not,' he answered, but later he changed his mind and went.

[30]"Then the father went to the other son and said the same thing. He answered, 'I will, sir,' but he did not go.

[31]"Which of the two did what his father wanted?"

"The first," they answered.

Jesus said to them, "I tell you the truth, the tax collectors and the prostitutes are entering the kingdom of God ahead of you. [32]For John came to you to show you the way of righteousness, and you did not believe him, but the tax collectors and the prostitutes did. And even after you saw this, you did not repent and believe him.

d13 Isaiah 56:7   *e13* Jer. 7:11   *f16* Psalm 8:2

The Parable of the Tenants

33"Listen to another parable: There was a landowner who planted a vineyard. He put a wall around it, dug a winepress in it and built a watchtower. Then he rented the vineyard to some farmers and went away on a journey. 34When the harvest time approached, he sent his servants to the tenants to collect his fruit.

35"The tenants seized his servants; they beat one, killed another, and stoned a third. 36Then he sent other servants to them, more than the first time, and the tenants treated them in the same way. 37Last of all, he sent his son to them. 'They will respect my son,' he said.

38"But when the tenants saw the son, they said to each other, 'This is the heir. Come, let's kill him and take his inheritance.' 39So they took him and threw him out of the vineyard and killed him.

40"Therefore, when the owner of the vineyard comes, what will he do to those tenants?"

41"He will bring those wretches to a wretched end," they replied, "and he will rent the vineyard to other tenants, who will give him his share of the crop at harvest time."

42Jesus said to them, "Have you never read in the Scriptures:

"'The stone the builders rejected
    has become the capstone;g
the Lord has done this,
    and it is marvellous in our eyes'h?

43"Therefore I tell you that the kingdom of God will be taken away from you and given to a people who will produce its fruit. 44He who falls on this stone will be broken to pieces, but he on whom it falls will be crushed."i

45When the chief priests and the Pharisees heard Jesus' parables, they knew he was talking about them. 46They looked for a way to arrest him, but they were afraid of the crowd because the people held that he was a prophet.

The Parable of the Wedding Banquet

22 Jesus spoke to them again in parables, saying: 2"The kingdom of heaven is like a king who prepared a wedding banquet for his son. 3He sent his servants to those who had been invited to the banquet to tell them to come, but they refused to come.

4"Then he sent some more servants and said, 'Tell those who have been invited that I have prepared my dinner: My oxen and fattened cattle have been slaughtered, and everything is ready. Come to the wedding banquet.'

5"But they paid no attention and went off—one to his field, another to his business. 6The rest seized his servants, ill-treated them and killed them. 7The king was enraged. He sent his army and destroyed those murderers and burned their city.

8"Then he said to his servants, 'The wedding banquet is ready, but those I invited did not deserve to come. 9Go to the street corners and invite to the banquet anyone you find.' 10So the servants went out into the streets and gathered all the people they could find, both good and bad, and the wedding hall was filled with guests.

11"But when the king came in to see the guests, he noticed a man there who was not wearing wedding clothes. 12'Friend,' he asked, 'how did you get in here without wedding clothes?' The man was speechless.

13"Then the king told the attendants, 'Tie him hand and foot, and throw him outside, into the darkness, where there will be weeping and gnashing of teeth.'

14"For many are invited, but few are chosen."

Paying Taxes to Caesar

15Then the Pharisees went out and laid plans to trap him in his words. 16They sent their disciples to him along with the Herodians. "Teacher," they said, "we know you are a man of integrity and that you

---

g42 Or cornerstone   h42 Psalm 118:22,23   i44 Some manuscripts do not have verse 44.

teach the way of God in accordance with the truth. You aren't swayed by men, because you pay no attention to who they are. [17]Tell us then, what is your opinion? Is it right to pay taxes to Caesar or not?"

[18]But Jesus, knowing their evil intent, said, "You hypocrites, why are you trying to trap me? [19]Show me the coin used for paying the tax." They brought him a denarius, [20]and he asked them, "Whose portrait is this? And whose inscription?"

[21]"Caesar's," they replied.

Then he said to them, "Give to Caesar what is Caesar's, and to God what is God's."

[22]When they heard this, they were amazed. So they left him and went away.

Marriage at the Resurrection

[23]That same day the Sadducees, who say there is no resurrection, came to him with a question. [24]"Teacher," they said, "Moses told us that if a man dies without having children, his brother must marry the widow and have children for him. [25]Now there were seven brothers among us. The first one married and died, and since he had no children, he left his wife to his brother. [26]The same thing happened to the second and third brother, right on down to the seventh. [27]Finally, the woman died. [28]Now then, at the resurrection, whose wife will she be of the seven, since all of them were married to her?"

[29]Jesus replied, "You are in error because you do not know the Scriptures or the power of God. [30]At the resurrection people will neither marry nor be given in marriage; they will be like the angels in heaven. [31]But about the resurrection of the dead—have you not read what God said to you, [32]'I am the God of Abraham, the God of Isaac, and the God of Jacob'[a]? He is not the God of the dead but of the living."

[33]When the crowds heard this, they were astonished at his teaching.

The Greatest Commandment

[34]Hearing that Jesus had silenced the Sadducees, the Pharisees got together. [35]One of them, an expert in the law, tested him with this question: [36]"Teacher, which is the greatest commandment in the Law?"

[37]Jesus replied: "'Love the Lord your God with all your heart and with all your soul and with all your mind.'[b] [38]This is the first and greatest commandment. [39]And the second is like it: 'Love your neighbour as yourself.'[c] [40]All the Law and the Prophets hang on these two commandments."

Whose Son Is the Christ?

[41]While the Pharisees were gathered together, Jesus asked them, [42]"What do you think about the Christ?[d] Whose son is he?"

"The son of David," they replied.

[43]He said to them, "How is it then that David, speaking by the Spirit, calls him 'Lord'? For he says,

[44]"'The Lord said to my Lord:
     "Sit at my right hand
until I put your enemies
     under your feet."'[e]

[45]If then David calls him 'Lord', how can he be his son?" [46]No-one could say a word in reply, and from that day on no-one dared to ask him any more questions.

Seven Woes

23 Then Jesus said to the crowds and to his disciples: [2]"The teachers of the law and the Pharisees sit in Moses' seat. [3]So you must obey them and do everything they tell you. But do not do what they do, for they do not practise what they preach. [4]They tie up heavy loads and put them on men's shoulders, but they themselves are not willing to lift a finger to move them.

[5]"Everything they do is done for men to see: They make their phylacteries[a] wide

---

[a]32 Exodus 3:6   [b]37 Deut. 6:5   [c]39 Lev. 19:18   [d]42 Or *Messiah*   [e]44 Psalm 110:1
[a]5 That is, boxes containing Scripture verses, worn on forehead and arm

and the tassels on their garments long; [6]they love the place of honour at banquets and the most important seats in the synagogues; [7]they love to be greeted in the market-places and to have men call them 'Rabbi'.

[8]"But you are not to be called 'Rabbi', for you have only one Master and you are all brothers. [9]And do not call anyone on earth 'father', for you have one Father, and he is in heaven. [10]Nor are you to be called 'teacher', for you have one Teacher, the Christ.[b] [11]The greatest among you will be your servant. [12]For whoever exalts himself will be humbled, and whoever humbles himself will be exalted.

[13]"Woe to you, teachers of the law and Pharisees, you hypocrites! You shut the kingdom of heaven in men's faces. You yourselves do not enter, nor will you let those enter who are trying to.[c]

[15]"Woe to you, teachers of the law and Pharisees, you hypocrites! You travel over land and sea to win a single convert, and when he becomes one, you make him twice as much a son of hell as you are.

[16]"Woe to you, blind guides! You say, 'If anyone swears by the temple, it means nothing; but if anyone swears by the gold of the temple, he is bound by his oath.' [17]You blind fools! Which is greater: the gold, or the temple that makes the gold sacred? [18]You also say, 'If anyone swears by the altar, it means nothing; but if anyone swears by the gift on it, he is bound by his oath.' [19]You blind men! Which is greater: the gift, or the altar that makes the gift sacred? [20]Therefore, he who swears by the altar swears by it and by everything on it. [21]And he who swears by the temple swears by it and by the one who dwells in it. [22]And he who swears by heaven swears by God's throne and by the one who sits on it.

[23]"Woe to you, teachers of the law and Pharisees, you hypocrites! You give a tenth of your spices—mint, dill and cummin. But you have neglected the more important matters of the law—justice, mercy and faithfulness. You should have practised the latter, without neglecting the former. [24]You blind guides! You strain out a gnat but swallow a camel.

[25]"Woe to you, teachers of the law and Pharisees, you hypocrites! You clean the outside of the cup and dish, but inside they are full of greed and self-indulgence. [26]Blind Pharisee! First clean the inside of the cup and dish, and then the outside also will be clean.

[27]"Woe to you, teachers of the law and Pharisees, you hypocrites! You are like whitewashed tombs, which look beautiful on the outside but on the inside are full of dead men's bones and everything unclean. [28]In the same way, on the outside you appear to people as righteous but on the inside you are full of hypocrisy and wickedness.

[29]"Woe to you, teachers of the law and Pharisees, you hypocrites! You build tombs for the prophets and decorate the graves of the righteous. [30]And you say, 'If we had lived in the days of our forefathers, we would not have taken part with them in shedding the blood of the prophets.' [31]So you testify against yourselves that you are the descendants of those who murdered the prophets. [32]Fill up, then, the measure of the sin of your forefathers!

[33]"You snakes! You brood of vipers! How will you escape being condemned to hell? [34]Therefore I am sending you prophets and wise men and teachers. Some of them you will kill and crucify; others you will flog in your synagogues and pursue from town to town. [35]And so upon you will come all the righteous blood that has been shed on earth, from the blood of righteous Abel to the blood of Zechariah son of Barakiah, whom you murdered between the temple and the altar. [36]I tell you the truth, all this will come upon this generation.

[37]"O Jerusalem, Jerusalem, you who kill the prophets and stone those sent to you, how often I have longed to gather your children together, as a hen gathers her chicks under her wings, but you were

---

b10 Or Messiah　　*c13 Some manuscripts to. [14]Woe to you, teachers of the law and Pharisees, you hypocrites! You devour widows' houses and for a show make lengthy prayers. Therefore you will be punished more severely.*

not willing. [38]Look, your house is left to you desolate. [39]For I tell you, you will not see me again until you say, 'Blessed is he who comes in the name of the Lord.'[d]"

Signs of the End of the Age

24 Jesus left the temple and was walking away when his disciples came up to him to call his attention to its buildings. [2]"Do you see all these things?" he asked. "I tell you the truth, not one stone here will be left on another; every one will be thrown down."

[3]As Jesus was sitting on the Mount of Olives, the disciples came to him privately. "Tell us," they said, "when will this happen, and what will be the sign of your coming and of the end of the age?"

[4]Jesus answered: "Watch out that no-one deceives you. [5]For many will come in my name, claiming, 'I am the Christ,'[a] and will deceive many. [6]You will hear of wars and rumours of wars, but see to it that you are not alarmed. Such things must happen, but the end is still to come. [7]Nation will rise against nation, and kingdom against kingdom. There will be famines and earthquakes in various places. [8]All these are the beginning of birth-pains.

[9]"Then you will be handed over to be persecuted and put to death, and you will be hated by all nations because of me. [10]At that time many will turn away from the faith and will betray and hate each other, [11]and many false prophets will appear and deceive many people. [12]Because of the increase of wickedness, the love of most will grow cold, [13]but he who stands firm to the end will be saved. [14]And this gospel of the kingdom will be preached in the whole world as a testimony to all nations, and then the end will come.

[15]"So when you see standing in the holy place 'the abomination that causes desolation',[b] spoken of through the prophet Daniel—let the reader understand— [16]then let those who are in Judea flee to the mountains. [17]Let no-one on the roof of his house go down to take anything out of

the house. [18]Let no-one in the field go back to get his cloak. [19]How dreadful it will be in those days for pregnant women and nursing mothers! [20]Pray that your flight will not take place in winter or on the Sabbath. [21]For then there will be great distress, unequalled from the beginning of the world until now—and never to be equalled again. [22]If those days had not been cut short, no-one would survive, but for the sake of the elect those days will be shortened. [23]At that time if anyone says to you, 'Look, here is the Christ!' or, 'There he is!' do not believe it. [24]For false Christs and false prophets will appear and perform great signs and miracles to deceive even the elect—if that were possible. [25]See, I have told you ahead of time.

[26]"So if anyone tells you, 'There he is, out in the desert,' do not go out; or, 'Here he is, in the inner rooms,' do not believe it. [27]For as lightning that comes from the east is visible even in the west, so will be the coming of the Son of Man. [28]Wherever there is a carcass, there the vultures will gather.

[29]"Immediately after the distress of those days

" 'the sun will be darkened,
    and the moon will not give its light;
the stars will fall from the sky,
    and the heavenly bodies will be
        shaken.'[c]

[30]"At that time the sign of the Son of Man will appear in the sky, and all the nations of the earth will mourn. They will see the Son of Man coming on the clouds of the sky, with power and great glory. [31]And he will send his angels with a loud trumpet call, and they will gather his elect from the four winds, from one end of the heavens to the other.

[32]"Now learn this lesson from the fig-tree: As soon as its twigs get tender and its leaves come out, you know that summer is near. [33]Even so, when you see all these things, you know that it[d] is near, right at the door. [34]I tell you the truth, this generation[e] will certainly not pass away until all

---

d39 Psalm 118:26   *a5* Or *Messiah*; also in verse 23   *b15* Daniel 9:27; 11:31; 12:11   *c29* Isaiah 13:10; 34:4
d33 Or *he*   *e34* Or *race*

these things have happened. ³⁵Heaven and earth will pass away, but my words will never pass away.

The Day and Hour Unknown

³⁶"No-one knows about that day or hour, not even the angels in heaven, nor the Son,ƒ but only the Father. ³⁷As it was in the days of Noah, so it will be at the coming of the Son of Man. ³⁸For in the days before the flood, people were eating and drinking, marrying and giving in marriage, up to the day Noah entered the ark; ³⁹and they knew nothing about what would happen until the flood came and took them all away. That is how it will be at the coming of the Son of Man. ⁴⁰Two men will be in the field; one will be taken and the other left. ⁴¹Two women will be grinding with a hand mill; one will be taken and the other left.

⁴²"Therefore keep watch, because you do not know on what day your Lord will come. ⁴³But understand this: If the owner of the house had known at what time of night the thief was coming, he would have kept watch and would not have let his house be broken into. ⁴⁴So you also must be ready, because the Son of Man will come at an hour when you do not expect him.

⁴⁵"Who then is the faithful and wise servant, whom the master has put in charge of the servants in his household to give them their food at the proper time? ⁴⁶It will be good for that servant whose master finds him doing so when he returns. ⁴⁷I tell you the truth, he will put him in charge of all his possessions. ⁴⁸But suppose that servant is wicked and says to himself, 'My master is staying away a long time,' ⁴⁹and he then begins to beat his fellow-servants and to eat and drink with drunkards. ⁵⁰The master of that servant will come on a day when he does not expect him and at an hour he is not aware of. ⁵¹He will cut him to pieces and assign him a place with the hypocrites, where there will be weeping and gnashing of teeth.

The Parable of the Ten Virgins

25 "At that time the kingdom of heaven will be like ten virgins who took their lamps and went out to meet the bridegroom. ²Five of them were foolish and five were wise. ³The foolish ones took their lamps but did not take any oil with them. ⁴The wise, however, took oil in jars along with their lamps. ⁵The bridegroom was a long time in coming, and they all became drowsy and fell asleep.

⁶"At midnight the cry rang out: 'Here's the bridegroom! Come out to meet him!'

⁷"Then all the virgins woke up and trimmed their lamps. ⁸The foolish ones said to the wise, 'Give us some of your oil; our lamps are going out.'

⁹"'No,' they replied, 'there may not be enough for both us and you. Instead, go to those who sell oil and buy some for yourselves.'

¹⁰"But while they were on their way to buy the oil, the bridegroom arrived. The virgins who were ready went in with him to the wedding banquet. And the door was shut.

¹¹"Later the others also came. 'Sir! Sir!' they said. 'Open the door for us!'

¹²"But he replied, 'I tell you the truth, I don't know you.'

¹³"Therefore keep watch, because you do not know the day or the hour.

The Parable of the Talents

¹⁴"Again, it will be like a man going on a journey, who called his servants and entrusted his property to them. ¹⁵To one he gave five talentsᵃ of money, to another two talents, and to another one talent, each according to his ability. Then he went on his journey. ¹⁶The man who had received the five talents went at once and put his money to work and gained five more. ¹⁷So also, the one with the two talents gained two more. ¹⁸But the man who had received the one talent went off, dug a hole in the ground and hid his master's money. ¹⁹"After a long time the master of those servants returned and settled accounts

---

ƒ36 Some manuscripts do not have *nor the Son*.   ᵃ15 A talent was worth several hundred pounds.

with them. 20The man who had received the five talents brought the other five. 'Master,' he said, 'you entrusted me with five talents. See, I have gained five more.'

21"His master replied, 'Well done, good and faithful servant! You have been faithful with a few things; I will put you in charge of many things. Come and share your master's happiness!'

22"The man with the two talents also came. 'Master,' he said, 'you entrusted me with two talents; see, I have gained two more.'

23"His master replied, 'Well done, good and faithful servant! You have been faithful with a few things; I will put you in charge of many things. Come and share your master's happiness!'

24"Then the man who had received the one talent came. 'Master,' he said, 'I knew that you are a hard man, harvesting where you have not sown and gathering where you have not scattered seed. 25So I was afraid and went out and hid your talent in the ground. See, here is what belongs to you.'

26"His master replied, 'You wicked, lazy servant! So you knew that I harvest where I have not sown and gather where I have not scattered seed? 27Well then, you should have put my money on deposit with the bankers, so that when I returned I would have received it back with interest.

28"'Take the talent from him and give it to the one who has the ten talents. 29For everyone who has will be given more, and he will have an abundance. Whoever does not have, even what he has will be taken from him. 30And throw that worthless servant outside, into the darkness, where there will be weeping and gnashing of teeth.'

The Sheep and the Goats

31"When the Son of Man comes in his glory, and all the angels with him, he will sit on his throne in heavenly glory. 32All the nations will be gathered before him, and he will separate the people one from another as a shepherd separates the sheep from the goats. 33He will put the sheep on his right and the goats on his left.

34"Then the King will say to those on his right, 'Come, you who are blessed by my Father; take your inheritance, the kingdom prepared for you since the creation of the world. 35For I was hungry and you gave me something to eat, I was thirsty and you gave me something to drink, I was a stranger and you invited me in, 36I needed clothes and you clothed me, I was sick and you looked after me, I was in prison and you came to visit me.'

37"Then the righteous will answer him, 'Lord, when did we see you hungry and feed you, or thirsty and give you something to drink? 38When did we see you a stranger and invite you in, or needing clothes and clothe you? 39When did we see you sick or in prison and go to visit you?'

40"The King will reply, 'I tell you the truth, whatever you did for one of the least of these brothers of mine, you did for me.'

41"Then he will say to those on his left, 'Depart from me, you who are cursed, into the eternal fire prepared for the devil and his angels. 42For I was hungry and you gave me nothing to eat, I was thirsty and you gave me nothing to drink, 43I was a stranger and you did not invite me in, I needed clothes and you did not clothe me, I was sick and in prison and you did not look after me.'

44"They also will answer, 'Lord, when did we see you hungry or thirsty or a stranger or needing clothes or sick or in prison, and did not help you?'

45"He will reply, 'I tell you the truth, whatever you did not do for one of the least of these, you did not do for me.'

46"Then they will go away to eternal punishment, but the righteous to eternal life."

The Plot Against Jesus

26 When Jesus had finished saying all these things, he said to his disciples, 2"As you know, the Passover is two days away—and the Son of Man will be handed over to be crucified."

3Then the chief priests and the elders of the people assembled in the palace of the high priest, whose name was Caiaphas, 4and they plotted to arrest Jesus in some sly way and kill him. 5"But not during the Feast," they said, "or there may be a riot among the people."

Jesus Anointed at Bethany

6While Jesus was in Bethany in the home of a man known as Simon the Leper, 7a woman came to him with an alabaster jar of very expensive perfume, which she poured on his head as he was reclining at the table.

8When the disciples saw this, they were indignant. "Why this waste?" they asked. 9"This perfume could have been sold at a high price and the money given to the poor."

10Aware of this, Jesus said to them, "Why are you bothering this woman? She has done a beautiful thing to me. 11The poor you will always have with you, but you will not always have me. 12When she poured this perfume on my body, she did it to prepare me for burial. 13I tell you the truth, wherever this gospel is preached throughout the world, what she has done will also be told, in memory of her."

Judas Agrees to Betray Jesus

14Then one of the Twelve—the one called Judas Iscariot—went to the chief priests 15and asked, "What are you willing to give me if I hand him over to you?" So they counted out for him thirty silver coins. 16From then on Judas watched for an opportunity to hand him over.

The Lord's Supper

17On the first day of the Feast of Unleavened Bread, the disciples came to Jesus and asked, "Where do you want us to make preparations for you to eat the Passover?"

18He replied, "Go into the city to a certain man and tell him, 'The Teacher says: My appointed time is near. I am going to celebrate the Passover with my disciples at your house.'" 19So the

disciples did as Jesus had directed them and prepared the Passover.

20When evening came, Jesus was reclining at the table with the Twelve. 21And while they were eating, he said, "I tell you the truth, one of you will betray me."

22They were very sad and began to say to him one after the other, "Surely not I, Lord?"

23Jesus replied, "The one who has dipped his hand into the bowl with me will betray me. 24The Son of Man will go just as it is written about him. But woe to that man who betrays the Son of Man! It would be better for him if he had not been born."

25Then Judas, the one who would betray him, said, "Surely not I, Rabbi?"

Jesus answered, "Yes, it is you."a

26While they were eating, Jesus took bread, gave thanks and broke it, and gave it to his disciples, saying, "Take and eat; this is my body."

27Then he took the cup, gave thanks and offered it to them, saying, "Drink from it, all of you. 28This is my blood of theb covenant, which is poured out for many for the forgiveness of sins. 29I tell you, I will not drink of this fruit of the vine from now on until that day when I drink it anew with you in my Father's kingdom."

30When they had sung a hymn, they went out to the Mount of Olives.

Jesus Predicts Peter's Denial

31Then Jesus told them, "This very night you will all fall away on account of me, for it is written:

"'I will strike the shepherd,
    and the sheep of the flock will be
        scattered.'c

32But after I have risen, I will go ahead of you into Galilee."

33Peter replied, "Even if all fall away on account of you, I never will."

34"I tell you the truth," Jesus answered, "this very night, before the cock crows, you will disown me three times."

a25 Or "You yourself have said it."   b28 Some manuscripts the new   c31 Zech. 13:7

[35]But Peter declared, "Even if I have to die with you, I will never disown you." And all the other disciples said the same.

Gethsemane

[36]Then Jesus went with his disciples to a place called Gethsemane, and he said to them, "Sit here while I go over there and pray." [37]He took Peter and the two sons of Zebedee along with him, and he began to be sorrowful and troubled. [38]Then he said to them, "My soul is overwhelmed with sorrow to the point of death. Stay here and keep watch with me."

[39]Going a little farther, he fell with his face to the ground and prayed, "My Father, if it is possible, may this cup be taken from me. Yet not as I will, but as you will."

[40]Then he returned to his disciples and found them sleeping. "Could you men not keep watch with me for one hour?" he asked Peter. [41]"Watch and pray so that you will not fall into temptation. The spirit is willing, but the body is weak."

[42]He went away a second time and prayed, "My Father, if it is not possible for this cup to be taken away unless I drink it, may your will be done."

[43]When he came back, he again found them sleeping, because their eyes were heavy. [44]So he left them and went away once more and prayed the third time, saying the same thing.

[45]Then he returned to the disciples and said to them, "Are you still sleeping and resting? Look, the hour is near, and the Son of Man is betrayed into the hands of sinners. [46]Rise, let us go! Here comes my betrayer!"

Jesus Arrested

[47]While he was still speaking, Judas, one of the Twelve, arrived. With him was a large crowd armed with swords and clubs, sent from the chief priests and the elders of the people. [48]Now the betrayer had arranged a signal with them: "The one I kiss is the man; arrest him." [49]Going at once to Jesus, Judas said, "Greetings, Rabbi!" and kissed him.

[50]Jesus replied, "Friend, do what you came for."[d]

Then the men stepped forward, seized Jesus and arrested him. [51]With that, one of Jesus' companions reached for his sword, drew it out and struck the servant of the high priest, cutting off his ear.

[52]"Put your sword back in its place," Jesus said to him, "for all who draw the sword will die by the sword. [53]Do you think I cannot call on my Father, and he will at once put at my disposal more than twelve legions of angels? [54]But how then would the Scriptures be fulfilled that say it must happen in this way?"

[55]At that time Jesus said to the crowd, "Am I leading a rebellion, that you have come out with swords and clubs to capture me? Every day I sat in the temple courts teaching, and you did not arrest me. [56]But this has all taken place that the writings of the prophets might be fulfilled." Then all the disciples deserted him and fled.

Before the Sanhedrin

[57]Those who had arrested Jesus took him to Caiaphas, the high priest, where the teachers of the law and the elders had assembled. [58]But Peter followed him at a distance, right up to the courtyard of the high priest. He entered and sat down with the guards to see the outcome.

[59]The chief priests and the whole Sanhedrin were looking for false evidence against Jesus so that they could put him to death. [60]But they did not find any, though many false witnesses came forward.

Finally two came forward [61]and declared, "This fellow said, 'I am able to destroy the temple of God and rebuild it in three days.'"

[62]Then the high priest stood up and said to Jesus, "Are you not going to answer? What is this testimony that these men are bringing against you?" [63]But Jesus remained silent.

The high priest said to him, "I charge you under oath by the living God: Tell us if you are the Christ,[e] the Son of God."

---

d50 Or *"Friend, why have you come?"*   e63 Or *Messiah*; also in verse 68

64"Yes, it is as you say," Jesus replied. "But I say to all of you: In the future you will see the Son of Man sitting at the right hand of the Mighty One and coming on the clouds of heaven."

65Then the high priest tore his clothes and said, "He has spoken blasphemy! Why do we need any more witnesses? Look, now you have heard the blasphemy. 66What do you think?"

"He is worthy of death," they answered.

67Then they spat in his face and struck him with their fists. Others slapped him 68and said, "Prophesy to us, Christ. Who hit you?"

Peter Disowns Jesus

69Now Peter was sitting out in the courtyard, and a servant girl came to him. "You also were with Jesus of Galilee," she said.

70But he denied it before them all. "I don't know what you're talking about," he said.

71Then he went out to the gateway, where another girl saw him and said to the people there, "This fellow was with Jesus of Nazareth."

72He denied it again, with an oath: "I don't know the man!"

73After a little while, those standing there went up to Peter and said, "Surely you are one of them, for your accent gives you away."

74Then he began to call down curses on himself and he swore to them, "I don't know the man!"

Immediately a cock crowed. 75Then Peter remembered the word Jesus had spoken: "Before the cock crows, you will disown me three times." And he went outside and wept bitterly.

Judas Hangs Himself

27 Early in the morning, all the chief priests and the elders of the people came to the decision to put Jesus to death.

2They bound him, led him away and handed him over to Pilate, the governor.

3When Judas, who had betrayed him, saw that Jesus was condemned, he was seized with remorse and returned the thirty silver coins to the chief priests and the elders. 4"I have sinned," he said "for I have betrayed innocent blood."

"What is that to us?" they replied. "That's your responsibility."

5So Judas threw the money into the temple and left. Then he went away and hanged himself.

6The chief priests picked up the coins and said, "It is against the law to put this into the treasury, since it is blood money." 7So they decided to use the money to buy the potter's field as a burial place for foreigners. 8That is why it has been called the Field of Blood to this day. 9Then what was spoken by Jeremiah the prophet was fulfilled: "They took the thirty silver coins, the price set on him by the people of Israel, 10and they used them to buy the potter's field, as the Lord commanded me."*a*

Jesus Before Pilate

11Meanwhile Jesus stood before the governor, and the governor asked him, "Are you the king of the Jews?"

"Yes, it is as you say," Jesus replied.

12When he was accused by the chief priests and the elders, he gave no answer. 13Then Pilate asked him, "Don't you hear the testimony they are bringing against you?" 14But Jesus made no reply, not even to a single charge—to the great amazement of the governor.

15Now it was the governor's custom at the Feast to release a prisoner chosen by the crowd. 16At that time they had a notorious prisoner, called Barabbas. 17So when the crowd had gathered, Pilate asked them, "Which one do you want me to release to you: Barabbas, or Jesus who is called Christ?" 18For he knew it was out of envy that they had handed Jesus over to him.

a10 See Zech. 11:12, 13; Jer. 19:1–13; 32:6–9.

[19]While Pilate was sitting on the judge's seat, his wife sent him this message: "Don't have anything to do with that innocent man, for I have suffered a great deal today in a dream because of him."

[20]But the chief priests and the elders persuaded the crowd to ask for Barabbas and to have Jesus executed.

[21]"Which of the two do you want me to release to you?" asked the governor.

"Barabbas," they answered.

[22]"What shall I do, then, with Jesus who is called Christ?" Pilate asked.

They all answered, "Crucify him!"

[23]"Why? What crime has he committed?" asked Pilate.

But they shouted all the louder, "Crucify him!"

[24]When Pilate saw that he was getting nowhere, but that instead an uproar was starting, he took water and washed his hands in front of the crowd. "I am innocent of this man's blood," he said. "It is your responsibility!"

[25]All the people answered, "Let his blood be on us and on our children!"

[26]Then he released Barabbas to them. But he had Jesus flogged, and handed him over to be crucified.

The Soldiers Mock Jesus

[27]Then the governor's soldiers took Jesus into the Praetorium and gathered the whole company of soldiers round him. [28]They stripped him and put a scarlet robe on him, [29]and then twisted together a crown of thorns and set it on his head. They put a staff in his right hand and knelt in front of him and mocked him. "Hail, king of the Jews!" they said. [30]They spat on him, and took the staff and struck him on the head again and again. [31]After they had mocked him, they took off the robe and put his own clothes on him. Then they led him away to crucify him.

The Crucifixion

[32]As they were going out, they met a man from Cyrene, named Simon, and

they forced him to carry the cross. [33]They came to a place called Golgotha (which means The Place of the Skull). [34]There they offered Jesus wine to drink, mixed with gall; but after tasting it, he refused to drink it. [35]When they had crucified him, they divided up his clothes by casting lots.[b] [36]And sitting down, they kept watch over him there. [37]Above his head they placed the written charge against him: THIS IS JESUS, THE KING OF THE JEWS. [38]Two robbers were crucified with him, one on his right and one on his left. [39]Those who passed by hurled insults at him, shaking their heads [40]and saying, "You who are going to destroy the temple and build it in three days, save yourself! Come down from the cross, if you are the Son of God!"

[41]In the same way the chief priests, the teachers of the law and the elders mocked him. [42]"He saved others," they said, "but he can't save himself! He's the King of Israel! Let him come down now from the cross, and we will believe in him. [43]He trusts in God. Let God rescue him now if he wants him, for he said, 'I am the Son of God.'" [44]In the same way the robbers who were crucified with him also heaped insults on him.

The Death of Jesus

[45]From the sixth hour until the ninth hour darkness came over all the land. [46]About the ninth hour Jesus cried out in a loud voice, "*Eloi, Eloi,[c] lama sabachthani?*"—which means, "My God, my God, why have you forsaken me?"[d]

[47]When some of those standing there heard this, they said, "He's calling Elijah."

[48]Immediately one of them ran and got a sponge. He filled it with wine vinegar, put it on a stick, and offered it to Jesus to drink. [49]The rest said, "Now leave him alone. Let's see if Elijah comes to save him."

[50]And when Jesus had cried out again in a loud voice, he gave up his spirit.

---

b35 A few late manuscripts lots that the word spoken by the prophet might be fulfilled: "They divided my garments among themselves and cast lots for my clothing." (Psalm 22:18)   c46 Some manuscripts Eli, Eli   d46 Psalm 22:1

[51]At that moment the curtain of the temple was torn in two from top to bottom. The earth shook and the rocks split. [52]The tombs broke open and the bodies of many holy people who had died were raised to life. [53]They came out of the tombs, and after Jesus' resurrection they went into the holy city and appeared to many people.

[54]When the centurion and those with him who were guarding Jesus saw the earthquake and all that had happened, they were terrified, and exclaimed, "Surely he was the Son[e] of God!"

[55]Many women were there, watching from a distance. They had followed Jesus from Galilee to care for his needs. [56]Among them were Mary Magdalene, Mary the mother of James and Joses, and the mother of Zebedee's sons.

The Burial of Jesus

[57]As evening approached, there came a rich man from Arimathea, named Joseph, who had himself become a disciple of Jesus. [58]Going to Pilate, he asked for Jesus' body, and Pilate ordered that it be given to him. [59]Joseph took the body, wrapped it in a clean linen cloth, [60]and placed it in his own new tomb that he had cut out of the rock. He rolled a big stone in front of the entrance to the tomb and went away. [61]Mary Magdalene and the other Mary were sitting there opposite the tomb.

The Guard at the Tomb

[62]The next day, the one after Preparation Day, the chief priests and the Pharisees went to Pilate. [63]"Sir," they said, "we remember that while he was still alive that deceiver said, 'After three days I will rise again.' [64]So give the order for the tomb to be made secure until the third day. Otherwise, his disciples may come and steal the body and tell the people that he has been raised from the dead. This last deception will be worse than the first."

[65]"Take a guard," Pilate answered. "Go, make the tomb as secure as you know how." [66]So they went and made the tomb secure by putting a seal on the stone and posting the guard.

The Resurrection

28 After the Sabbath, at dawn on the first day of the week, Mary Magdalene and the other Mary went to look at the tomb.

[2]There was a violent earthquake, for an angel of the Lord came down from heaven and, going to the tomb, rolled back the stone and sat on it. [3]His appearance was like lightning, and his clothes were white as snow. [4]The guards were so afraid of him that they shook and became like dead men.

[5]The angel said to the women, "Do not be afraid, for I know that you are looking for Jesus, who was crucified. [6]He is not here; he has risen, just as he said. Come and see the place where he lay. [7]Then go quickly and tell his disciples: 'He has risen from the dead and is going ahead of you into Galilee. There you will see him.' Now I have told you."

[8]So the women hurried away from the tomb, afraid yet filled with joy, and ran to tell his disciples. [9]Suddenly Jesus met them. "Greetings," he said. They came to him, clasped his feet and worshipped him. [10]Then Jesus said to them, "Do not be afraid. Go and tell my brothers to go to Galilee; there they will see me."

The Guards' Report

[11]While the women were on their way, some of the guards went into the city and reported to the chief priests everything that had happened. [12]When the chief priests had met with the elders and devised a plan, they gave the soldiers a large sum of money, [13]telling them, "You are to say, 'His disciples came during the night and stole him away while we were asleep.' [14]If this report gets to the governor, we

[e]54 Or a son

will satisfy him and keep you out of trouble." [15]So the soldiers took the money and did as they were instructed. And this story has been widely circulated among the Jews to this very day.

The Great Commission

[16]Then the eleven disciples went to Galilee, to the mountain where Jesus had told them to go. [17]When they saw him, they worshipped him; but some doubted. [18]Then Jesus came to them and said, "All authority in heaven and on earth has been given to me. [19]Therefore go and make disciples of all nations, baptising them in[a] the name of the Father and of the Son and of the Holy Spirit, [20]and teaching them to obey everything I have commanded you. And surely I am with you always, to the very end of the age."

[a]19 Or *into*; see Acts 8:16; 19:5; Rom. 6:3; I Cor. 1:13; 10:2 and Gal. 3:27.

Mark

John the Baptist Prepares the Way

1 The beginning of the gospel about Jesus Christ, the Son of God.[a]

[2]It is written in Isaiah the prophet:

"I will send my messenger ahead of
  you,
  who will prepare your way"[b]—
[3]"a voice of one calling in the desert,
 'Prepare the way for the Lord,
  make straight paths for him.'"[c]

[4]And so John came, baptising in the desert region and preaching a baptism of repentance for the forgiveness of sins. [5]The whole Judean countryside and all the people of Jerusalem went out to him. Confessing their sins, they were baptised by him in the Jordan River. [6]John wore clothing made of camel's hair, with a leather belt round his waist, and he ate locusts and wild honey. [7]And this was his message: "After me will come one more powerful than I, the thongs of whose sandals I am not worthy to stoop down and untie. [8]I baptise you with[d] water, but he will baptise you with the Holy Spirit."

The Baptism and Temptation of Jesus

[9]At that time Jesus came from Nazareth in Galilee and was baptised by John in the Jordan. [10]As Jesus was coming up out of the water, he saw heaven being torn open and the Spirit descending on him like a dove. [11]And a voice came from heaven: "You are my Son, whom I love; with you I am well pleased."

[12]At once the Spirit sent him out into the desert, [13]and he was in the desert for forty days, being tempted by Satan. He was with the wild animals, and angels attended him.

The Calling of the First Disciples

[14]After John was put in prison, Jesus went into Galilee, proclaiming the good news of God. [15]"The time has come," he said. "The kingdom of God is near. Repent and believe the good news!"

[16]As Jesus walked beside the Sea of Galilee, he saw Simon and his brother Andrew casting a net into the lake, for they were fishermen. [17]"Come, follow me," Jesus said, "and I will make you fishers of men." [18]At once they left their nets and followed him.

[19]When he had gone a little farther, he saw James son of Zebedee and his brother John in a boat, preparing their nets. [20]Without delay he called them, and they left their father Zebedee in the boat with the hired men and followed him.

Jesus Drives Out an Evil Spirit

[21]They went to Capernaum, and when the Sabbath came, Jesus went into the synagogue and began to teach. [22]The people were amazed at his teaching, because he taught them as one who had

---

a1 Some manuscripts do not have *the Son of God*.   *b2* Mal. 3:1   *c3* Isaiah 40:3   *d8* Or *in* authority, not as the teachers of the law. ²³Just then a man in their synagogue who was possessed by an evil^e spirit cried out, ²⁴"What do you want with us, Jesus of Nazareth? Have you come to destroy us? I know who you are—the Holy One of God!"

²⁵"Be quiet!" said Jesus sternly. "Come out of him!" ²⁶The evil spirit shook the man violently and came out of him with a shriek.

²⁷The people were all so amazed that they asked each other, "What is this? A new teaching—and with authority! He even gives orders to evil spirits and they obey him." ²⁸News about him spread quickly over the whole region of Galilee.

Jesus Heals Many

²⁹As soon as they left the synagogue, they went with James and John to the home of Simon and Andrew. ³⁰Simon's mother-in-law was in bed with a fever, and they told Jesus about her. ³¹So he went to her, took her hand and helped her up. The fever left her and she began to wait on them.

³²That evening after sunset the people brought to Jesus all the sick and demon-possessed. ³³The whole town gathered at the door, ³⁴and Jesus healed many who had various diseases. He also drove out many demons, but he would not let the demons speak because they knew who he was.

Jesus Prays in a Solitary Place

³⁵Very early in the morning, while it was still dark, Jesus got up, left the house and went off to a solitary place, where he prayed. ³⁶Simon and his companions went to look for him, ³⁷and when they found him, they exclaimed: "Everyone is looking for you!"

³⁸Jesus replied, "Let us go somewhere else—to the nearby villages—so that I can preach there also. That is why I have come." ³⁹So he travelled throughout Galilee, preaching in their synagogues and driving out demons.

A Man With Leprosy

⁴⁰A man with leprosy^f came to him and begged him on his knees, "If you are willing, you can make me clean."

⁴¹Filled with compassion, Jesus reached out his hand and touched the man. "I am willing," he said. "Be clean!" ⁴²Immediately the leprosy left him and he was cured.

⁴³Jesus sent him away at once with a strong warning: ⁴⁴"See that you don't tell this to anyone. But go, show yourself to the priest and offer the sacrifices that Moses commanded for your cleansing, as a testimony to them." ⁴⁵Instead he went out and began to talk freely, spreading the news. As a result, Jesus could no longer enter a town openly but stayed outside in lonely places. Yet the people still came to him from everywhere.

Jesus Heals a Paralytic

2 A few days later, when Jesus again entered Capernaum, the people heard that he had come home. ²So many gathered that there was no room left, not even outside the door, and he preached the word to them. ³Some men came, bringing to him a paralytic, carried by four of them. ⁴Since they could not get him to Jesus because of the crowd, they made an opening in the roof above Jesus and, after digging through it, lowered the mat the paralysed man was lying on. ⁵When Jesus saw their faith, he said to the paralytic, "Son, your sins are forgiven."

⁶Now some teachers of the law were sitting there, thinking to themselves, ⁷"Why does this fellow talk like that? He's blaspheming! Who can forgive sins but God alone?"

⁸Immediately Jesus knew in his spirit that this was what they were thinking in their hearts, and he said to them, "Why are you thinking these things? ⁹Which is easier: to say to the paralytic, 'Your sins are forgiven,' or to say, 'Get up, take your mat and walk'? ¹⁰But that you may know that the Son of Man has authority on earth

---

^e23 Greek *unclean*; also in verses 26 and 27
^f40 The Greek word was used for various diseases affecting the skin—not necessarily leprosy.

to forgive sins. . . ." He said to the paralytic, [11]"I tell you, get up, take your mat and go home." [12]He got up, took his mat and walked out in full view of them all. This amazed everyone and they praised God, saying, "We have never seen anything like this!"

The Calling of Levi

[13]Once again Jesus went out beside the lake. A large crowd came to him, and he began to teach them. [14]As he walked along, he saw Levi son of Alphaeus sitting at the tax collector's booth. "Follow me," Jesus told him, and Levi got up and followed him.

[15]While Jesus was having dinner at Levi's house, many tax collectors and "sinners" were eating with him and his disciples, for there were many who followed him. [16]When the teachers of the law who were Pharisees saw him eating with the "sinners" and tax collectors, they asked his disciples: "Why does he eat with tax collectors and 'sinners'?"

[17]On hearing this, Jesus said to them, "It is not the healthy who need a doctor, but the sick. I have not come to call the righteous, but sinners."

Jesus Questioned About Fasting

[18]Now John's disciples and the Pharisees were fasting. Some people came and asked Jesus, "How is it that John's disciples and the disciples of the Pharisees are fasting, but yours are not?"

[19]Jesus answered, "How can the guests of the bridegroom fast while he is with them? They cannot, so long as they have him with them. [20]But the time will come when the bridegroom will be taken from them, and on that day they will fast.

[21]"No-one sews a patch of unshrunk cloth on an old garment. If he does, the new piece will pull away from the old, making the tear worse. [22]And no-one pours new wine into old wineskins. If he does, the wine will burst the skins, and both the wine and the wineskins will be ruined. No, he pours new wine into new wineskins."

Lord of the Sabbath

[23]One Sabbath Jesus was going through the cornfields, and as his disciples walked along, they began to pick some ears of corn. [24]The Pharisees said to him, "Look, why are they doing what is unlawful on the Sabbath?"

[25]He answered, "Have you never read what David did when he and his companions were hungry and in need? [26]In the days of Abiathar the high priest, he entered the house of God and ate the consecrated bread, which is lawful only for priests to eat. And he also gave some to his companions."

[27]Then he said to them, "The Sabbath was made for man, not man for the Sabbath. [28]So the Son of Man is Lord even of the Sabbath."

3 Another time he went into the synagogue, and a man with a shrivelled hand was there. [2]Some of them were looking for a reason to accuse Jesus, so they watched him closely to see if he would heal him on the Sabbath. [3]Jesus said to the man with the shrivelled hand, "Stand up in front of everyone."

[4]Then Jesus asked them, "Which is lawful on the Sabbath: to do good or to do evil, to save life or to kill?" But they remained silent.

[5]He looked round at them in anger and, deeply distressed at their stubborn hearts, said to the man, "Stretch out your hand." He stretched it out, and his hand was completely restored. [6]Then the Pharisees went out and began to plot with the Herodians how they might kill Jesus.

Crowds Follow Jesus

[7]Jesus withdrew with his disciples to the lake, and a large crowd from Galilee followed. [8]When they heard all he was doing, many people came to him from Judea, Jerusalem, Idumea, and the regions across the Jordan and around Tyre and Sidon. [9]Because of the crowd he told his disciples to have a small boat ready for him, to keep the people from crowding him. [10]For he had healed many, so that those with diseases were pushing forward

to touch him. [11]Whenever the evil[a] spirits saw him, they fell down before him and cried out, "You are the Son of God." [12]But he gave them strict orders not to tell who he was.

The Appointing of the Twelve Apostles

[13]Jesus went up on a mountainside and called to him those he wanted, and they came to him. [14]He appointed twelve—designating them apostles[b]—that they might be with him and that he might send them out to preach [15]and to have authority to drive out demons. [16]These are the twelve he appointed: Simon (to whom he gave the name Peter); [17]James son of Zebedee and his brother John (to them he gave the name Boanerges, which means Sons of Thunder); [18]Andrew, Philip, Bartholomew, Matthew, Thomas, James son of Alphaeus, Thaddaeus, Simon the Zealot [19]and Judas Iscariot, who betrayed him.

Jesus and Beelzebub

[20]Then Jesus entered a house, and again a crowd gathered, so that he and his disciples were not even able to eat. [21]When his family heard about this, they went to take charge of him, for they said, "He is out of his mind."

[22]And the teachers of the law who came down from Jerusalem said, "He is possessed by Beelzebub![c] By the prince of demons he is driving out demons."

[23]So Jesus called them and spoke to them in parables: "How can Satan drive out Satan? [24]If a kingdom is divided against itself, that kingdom cannot stand. [25]If a house is divided against itself, that house cannot stand. [26]And if Satan opposes himself and is divided, he cannot stand; his end has come. [27]In fact, no-one can enter a strong man's house and carry off his possessions unless he first ties up the strong man. Then he can rob his house. [28]I tell you the truth, all the sins and blasphemies of men will be forgiven them. [29]But whoever blasphemes against

the Holy Spirit will never be forgiven; he is guilty of an eternal sin."

[30]He said this because they were saying, "He has an evil spirit."

Jesus' Mother and Brothers

[31]Then Jesus' mother and brothers arrived. Standing outside, they sent someone in to call him. [32]A crowd was sitting around him, and they told him, "Your mother and brothers are outside looking for you."

[33]"Who are my mother and my brothers?" he asked.

[34]Then he looked at those seated in a circle around him and said, "Here are my mother and my brothers! [35]Whoever does God's will is my brother and sister and mother."

The Parable of the Sower

4 Again Jesus began to teach by the lake. The crowd that gathered round him was so large that he got into a boat and sat in it out on the lake, while all the people were along the shore at the water's edge. [2]He taught them many things by parables, and in his teaching said: [3]"Listen! A farmer went out to sow his seed. [4]As he was scattering the seed, some fell along the path, and the birds came and ate it up. [5]Some fell on rocky places, where it did not have much soil. It sprang up quickly, because the soil was shallow. [6]But when the sun came up, the plants were scorched, and they withered because they had no root. [7]Other seed fell among thorns, which grew up and choked the plants, so that they did not bear grain. [8]Still other seed fell on good soil. It came up, grew and produced a crop, multiplying thirty, sixty, or even a hundred times."

[9]Then Jesus said, "He who has ears to hear, let him hear."

[10]When he was alone, the Twelve and the others around him asked him about the parables. [11]He told them, "The secret of the kingdom of God has been given to

---

you. But to those on the outside everything is said in parables 12so that,

"'they may be ever seeing but never
		perceiving,
	and ever hearing but never
		understanding;
	otherwise they might turn and be
		forgiven!'a"

13Then Jesus said to them, "Don't you understand this parable? How then will you understand any parable? 14The farmer sows the word. 15Some people are like seed along the path, where the word is sown. As soon as they hear it, Satan comes and takes away the word that was sown in them. 16Others, like seed sown on rocky places, hear the word and at once receive it with joy. 17But since they have no root, they last only a short time. When trouble or persecution comes because of the word, they quickly fall away. 18Still others, like seed sown among thorns, hear the word; 19but the worries of this life, the deceitfulness of wealth and the desires for other things come in and choke the word, making it unfruitful. 20Others, like seed sown on good soil, hear the word, accept it, and produce a crop—thirty, sixty or even a hundred times what was sown."

A Lamp on a Stand

21He said to them, "Do you bring in a lamp to put it under a bowl or a bed? Instead, don't you put it on its stand? 22For whatever is hidden is meant to be disclosed, and whatever is concealed is meant to be brought out into the open. 23If anyone has ears to hear, let him hear."

24"Consider carefully what you hear," he continued. "With the measure you use, it will be measured to you—and even more. 25Whoever has will be given more; whoever does not have, even what he has will be taken from him."

The Parable of the Growing Seed

26He also said, "This is what the kingdom of God is like. A man scatters seed on the ground. 27Night and day, whether he sleeps or gets up, the seed sprouts and grows, though he does not know how. 28All by itself the soil produces corn—first the stalk, then the ear, then the full grain in the ear. 29As soon as the grain is ripe, he puts the sickle to it, because the harvest has come."

The Parable of the Mustard Seed

30Again he said, "What shall we say the kingdom of God is like, or what parable shall we use to describe it? 31It is like a mustard seed, which is the smallest seed you plant in the ground. 32Yet when planted, it grows and becomes the largest of all garden plants, with such big branches that the birds of the air can perch in its shade."

33With many similar parables Jesus spoke the word to them, as much as they could understand. 34He did not say anything to them without using a parable. But when he was alone with his own disciples, he explained everything.

Jesus Calms the Storm

35That day when evening came, he said to his disciples, "Let us go over to the other side." 36Leaving the crowd behind, they took him along, just as he was, in the boat. There were also other boats with him. 37A furious squall came up, and the waves broke over the boat, so that it was nearly swamped. 38Jesus was in the stern, sleeping on a cushion. The disciples woke him and said to him, "Teacher, don't you care if we drown?"

39He got up, rebuked the wind and said to the waves, "Quiet! Be still!" Then the wind died down and it was completely calm.

40He said to his disciples, "Why are you so afraid? Do you still have no faith?"

41They were terrified and asked each other, "Who is this? Even the wind and the waves obey him!"

a12 Isaiah 6:9,10

The Healing of a Demon-possessed Man

5 They went across the lake to the region of the Gerasenes.[a] 2When Jesus got out of the boat, a man with an evil[b] spirit came from the tombs to meet him. 3This man lived in the tombs, and no-one could bind him any more, not even with a chain. 4For he had often been chained hand and foot, but he tore the chains apart and broke the irons on his feet. No-one was strong enough to subdue him. 5Night and day among the tombs and in the hills he would cry out and cut himself with stones.

6When he saw Jesus from a distance, he ran and fell on his knees in front of him. 7He shouted at the top of his voice, "What do you want with me, Jesus, Son of the Most High God? Swear to God that you won't torture me!" 8For Jesus had said to him, "Come out of this man, you evil spirit!"

9Then Jesus asked him, "What is your name?"

"My name is Legion," he replied, "for we are many." 10And he begged Jesus again and again not to send them out of the area.

11A large herd of pigs was feeding on the nearby hillside. 12The demons begged Jesus, "Send us among the pigs; allow us to go into them." 13He gave them permission, and the evil spirits came out and went into the pigs. The herd, about two thousand in number, rushed down the steep bank into the lake and were drowned.

14Those tending the pigs ran off and reported this in the town and countryside, and the people went out to see what had happened. 15When they came to Jesus, they saw the man who had been possessed by the legion of demons, sitting there, dressed and in his right mind; and they were afraid. 16Those who had seen it told the people what had happened to the demon-possessed man—and told about the pigs as well. 17Then the people began to plead with Jesus to leave their region.

18As Jesus was getting into the boat, the man who had been demon-possessed begged to go with him. 19Jesus did not let him, but said, "Go home to your family and tell them how much the Lord has done for you, and how he has had mercy on you." 20So the man went away and began to tell in the Decapolis[c] how much Jesus had done for him. And all the people were amazed.

A Dead Girl and a Sick Woman

21When Jesus had again crossed over by boat to the other side of the lake, a large crowd gathered round him while he was by the lake. 22Then one of the synagogue rulers, named Jairus, came there. Seeing Jesus, he fell at his feet 23and pleaded earnestly with him, "My little daughter is dying. Please come and put your hands on her so that she will be healed and live." 24So Jesus went with him.

A large crowd followed and pressed around him. 25And a woman was there who had been subject to bleeding for twelve years. 26She had suffered a great deal under the care of many doctors and had spent all she had, yet instead of getting better she grew worse. 27When she heard about Jesus, she came up behind him in the crowd and touched his cloak, 28because she thought, "If I just touch his clothes, I will be healed." 29Immediately her bleeding stopped and she felt in her body that she was freed from her suffering.

30At once Jesus realised that power had gone out from him. He turned around in the crowd and asked, "Who touched my clothes?"

31"You see the people crowding against you," his disciples answered, "and yet you can ask, 'Who touched me?'"

32But Jesus kept looking around to see who had done it. 33Then the woman, knowing what had happened to her, came and fell at his feet and, trembling with fear, told him the whole truth. 34He said to her, "Daughter, your faith has healed you. Go in peace and be freed from your suffering."

---

[a]1 Some manuscripts *Gadarenes*; other manuscripts *Gergesenes*   [b]2 Greek *unclean*; also in verses 8 and 13
[c]20 That is, the Ten Cities

³⁵While Jesus was still speaking, some men came from the house of Jairus, the synagogue ruler. "Your daughter is dead," they said. "Why bother the teacher any more?"

³⁶Ignoring what they said, Jesus told the synagogue ruler, "Don't be afraid; just believe."

³⁷He did not let anyone follow him except Peter, James and John the brother of James. ³⁸When they came to the home of the synagogue ruler, Jesus saw a commotion, with people crying and wailing loudly. ³⁹He went in and said to them, "Why all this commotion and wailing? The child is not dead but asleep." ⁴⁰But they laughed at him.

After he put them all out, he took the child's father and mother and the disciples who were with him, and went in where the child was. ⁴¹He took her by the hand and said to her, *"Talitha koum!"* (which means, "Little girl, I say to you, get up!"). ⁴²Immediately the girl stood up and walked around (she was twelve years old). At this they were completely astonished. ⁴³He gave strict orders not to let anyone know about this, and told them to give her something to eat.

A Prophet Without Honour

6 Jesus left there and went to his home town, accompanied by his disciples. ²When the Sabbath came, he began to teach in the synagogue, and many who heard him were amazed.

"Where did this man get these things?" they asked. "What's this wisdom that has been given him, that he even does miracles! ³Isn't this the carpenter? Isn't this Mary's son and the brother of James, Joseph,^a Judas and Simon? Aren't his sisters here with us?" And they took offence at him.

⁴Jesus said to them, "Only in his home town, among his relatives and in his own house is a prophet without honour." ⁵He could not do any miracles there, except lay his hands on a few sick people and heal

them. ⁶And he was amazed at their lack of faith.

Jesus Sends Out the Twelve

Then Jesus went round teaching from village to village. ⁷Calling the Twelve to him, he sent them out two by two and gave them authority over evil^b spirits.

⁸These were his instructions: "Take nothing for the journey except a staff—no bread, no bag, no money in your belts. ⁹Wear sandals but not an extra tunic. ¹⁰Whenever you enter a house, stay there until you leave that town. ¹¹And if any place will not welcome you or listen to you, shake the dust off your feet when you leave, as a testimony against them."

¹²They went out and preached that people should repent. ¹³They drove out many demons and anointed many sick people with oil and healed them.

John the Baptist Beheaded

¹⁴King Herod heard about this, for Jesus' name had become well known. Some were saying,^c "John the Baptist has been raised from the dead, and that is why miraculous powers are at work in him."

¹⁵Others said, "He is Elijah."

And still others claimed, "He is a prophet, like one of the prophets of long ago."

¹⁶But when Herod heard this, he said, "John, the man I beheaded, has been raised from the dead!"

¹⁷For Herod himself had given orders to have John arrested, and he had him bound and put in prison. He did this because of Herodias, his brother Philip's wife, whom he had married. ¹⁸For John had been saying to Herod, "It is not lawful for you to have your brother's wife." ¹⁹So Herodias nursed a grudge against John and wanted to kill him. But she was not able to, ²⁰because Herod feared John and protected him, knowing him to be a righteous and holy man. When Herod heard John, he was greatly puzzled;^d yet he liked to listen to him.

---

^a3 Greek *Joses*, a variant of *Joseph*   ^b7 Greek *unclean*   ^c14 Some early manuscripts *He was saying*
^d20 Some early manuscripts *he did many things*

[21]Finally the opportune time came. On his birthday Herod gave a banquet for his high officials and military commanders and the leading men of Galilee. [22]When the daughter of Herodias came in and danced, she pleased Herod and his dinner guests.

The king said to the girl, "Ask me for anything you want, and I'll give it to you." [23]And he promised her with an oath, "Whatever you ask I will give you, up to half my kingdom."

[24]She went out and said to her mother, "What shall I ask for?"

"The head of John the Baptist," she answered.

[25]At once the girl hurried in to the king with the request: "I want you to give me right now the head of John the Baptist on a platter."

[26]The king was greatly distressed, but because of his oaths and his dinner guests, he did not want to refuse her. [27]So he immediately sent an executioner with orders to bring John's head. The man went, beheaded John in the prison, [28]and brought back his head on a platter. He presented it to the girl, and she gave it to her mother. [29]On hearing of this, John's disciples came and took his body and laid it in a tomb.

Jesus Feeds the Five Thousand

[30]The apostles gathered round Jesus and reported to him all they had done and taught. [31]Then, because so many people were coming and going that they did not even have a chance to eat, he said to them, "Come with me by yourselves to a quiet place and get some rest."

[32]So they went away by themselves in a boat to a solitary place. [33]But many who saw them leaving recognised them and ran on foot from all the towns and got there ahead of them. [34]When Jesus landed and saw a large crowd, he had compassion on them, because they were like sheep without a shepherd. So he began teaching them many things.

[35]By this time it was late in the day, so his disciples came to him. "This is a

remote place," they said, "and it's already very late. [36]Send the people away so that they can go to the surrounding countryside and villages and buy themselves something to eat."

[37]But he answered, "You give them something to eat."

They said to him, "That would take eight months of a man's wages![e] Are we to go and spend that much on bread and give it to them to eat?"

[38]"How many loaves do you have?" he asked. "Go and see."

When they found out, they said, "Five—and two fish."

[39]Then Jesus directed them to have all the people sit down in groups on the green grass. [40]So they sat down in groups of hundreds and fifties. [41]Taking the five loaves and the two fish and looking up to heaven, he gave thanks and broke the loaves. Then he gave them to his disciples to set before the people. He also divided the two fish among them all. [42]They all ate and were satisfied, [43]and the disciples picked up twelve basketfuls of broken pieces of bread and fish. [44]The number of the men who had eaten was five thousand.

Jesus Walks on the Water

[45]Immediately Jesus made his disciples get into the boat and go on ahead of him to Bethsaida, while he dismissed the crowd. [46]After leaving them, he went up on a mountainside to pray.

[47]When evening came, the boat was in the middle of the lake, and he was alone on land. [48]He saw the disciples straining at the oars, because the wind was against them. About the fourth watch of the night he went out to them, walking on the lake. He was about to pass by them, [49]but when they saw him walking on the lake, they thought he was a ghost. They cried out, [50]because they all saw him and were terrified.

Immediately he spoke to them and said, "Take courage! It is I. Don't be afraid." [51]Then he climbed into the boat with them, and the wind died down. They were completely amazed, [52]for they had not

[e]37 Greek *take two hundred denarii*

understood about the loaves; their hearts were hardened.

53When they had crossed over, they landed at Gennesaret and anchored there. 54As soon as they got out of the boat, people recognised Jesus. 55They ran throughout that whole region and carried the sick on mats to wherever they heard he was. 56And wherever he went—into villages, towns or countryside—they placed the sick in the market-places. They begged him to let them touch even the edge of his cloak, and all who touched him were healed.

Clean and Unclean

7 The Pharisees and some of the teachers of the law who had come from Jerusalem gathered round Jesus and 2saw some of his disciples eating food with hands that were "unclean", that is, unwashed. 3(The Pharisees and all the Jews do not eat unless they give their hands a ceremonial washing, holding to the tradition of the elders. 4When they come from the market-place they do not eat unless they wash. And they observe many other traditions, such as the washing of cups, pitchers and kettles.a)

5So the Pharisees and teachers of the law asked Jesus, "Why don't your disciples live according to the tradition of the elders instead of eating their food with 'unclean' hands?"

6He replied, "Isaiah was right when he prophesied about you hypocrites; as it is written:

"'These people honour me with their
   lips,
but their hearts are far from me.
7They worship me in vain;
   their teachings are but rules taught by
   men.'b

8You have let go of the commands of God and are holding on to the traditions of men."

9And he said to them: "You have a fine way of setting aside the commandsc of God in order to observe your own traditions! 10For Moses said, 'Honour your father and your mother,'d and, 'Anyone who curses his father or mother must be put to death.'e 11But you say that if a man says to his father or mother: 'Whatever help you might otherwise have received from me is Corban' (that is, a gift devoted to God), 12then you no longer let him do anything for his father or mother. 13Thus you nullify the word of God by your tradition that you have handed down. And you do many things like that."

14Again Jesus called the crowd to him and said, "Listen to me, everyone, and understand this. 15Nothing outside a man can make him 'unclean' by going into him. Rather, it is what comes out of a man that makes him 'unclean'."f

17After he had left the crowd and entered the house, his disciples asked him about this parable. 18"Are you so dull?" he asked. "Don't you see that nothing that enters a man from the outside can make him 'unclean'? 19For it doesn't go into his heart but into his stomach, and then out of his body." (In saying this, Jesus declared all foods "clean".)

20He went on: "What comes out of a man is what makes him 'unclean'. 21For from within, out of men's hearts, come evil thoughts, sexual immorality, theft, murder, adultery, 22greed, malice, deceit, lewdness, envy, slander, arrogance and folly. 23All these evils come from inside and make a man 'unclean'."

The Faith of a Syro-Phoenician Woman

24Jesus left that place and went to the vicinity of Tyre.g He entered a house and did not want anyone to know it; yet he could not keep his presence secret. 25In fact, as soon as she heard about him, a woman whose little daughter was possessed by an evilh spirit came and fell at his feet. 26The woman was a Greek, born in

---

a4 Some early manuscripts *pitchers, kettles and dining couches*   b6,7 Isaiah 29:13   c9 Some manuscripts *set up*
d10 Exodus 20:12; Deut. 5:16   e10 Exodus 21:17; Lev. 20:9
f15 Some early manuscripts *'unclean'.* 16*If anyone has ears to hear, let him hear."*
g24 Many early manuscripts *Tyre and Sidon*   h25 Greek *unclean*

Syrian Phoenicia. She begged Jesus to drive the demon out of her daughter.

27"First let the children eat all they want," he told her, "for it is not right to take the children's bread and toss it to their dogs."

28"Yes, Lord," she replied, "but even the dogs under the table eat the children's crumbs."

29Then he told her, "For such a reply, you may go; the demon has left your daughter."

30She went home and found her child lying on the bed, and the demon gone.

The Healing of a Deaf and Mute Man

31Then Jesus left the vicinity of Tyre and went through Sidon, down to the Sea of Galilee and into the region of the Decapolis.*i* 32There some people brought to him a man who was deaf and could hardly talk, and they begged him to place his hand on the man.

33After he took him aside, away from the crowd, Jesus put his fingers into the man's ears. Then he spat and touched the man's tongue. 34He looked up to heaven and with a deep sigh said to him, *"Ephphatha!"* (which means, "Be opened!"). 35At this, the man's ears were opened, his tongue was loosened and he began to speak plainly.

36Jesus commanded them not to tell anyone. But the more he did so, the more they kept talking about it. 37People were overwhelmed with amazement. "He has done everything well," they said. "He even makes the deaf hear and the mute speak."

Jesus Feeds the Four Thousand

8 During those days another large crowd gathered. Since they had nothing to eat, Jesus called his disciples to him and said, 2"I have compassion for these people; they have already been with me three days and have nothing to eat. 3If I send them home hungry, they will collapse on the way, because some of them have come a long distance."

4His disciples answered, "But where in this remote place can anyone get enough bread to feed them?"

5"How many loaves do you have?" Jesus asked.

"Seven," they replied.

6He told the crowd to sit down on the ground. When he had taken the seven loaves and given thanks, he broke them and gave them to his disciples to set before the people, and they did so. 7They had a few small fish as well; he gave thanks for them also and told the disciples to distribute them. 8The people ate and were satisfied. Afterwards the disciples picked up seven basketfuls of broken pieces that were left over. 9About four thousand men were present. And having sent them away, 10he got into the boat with his disciples and went to the region of Dalmanutha.

11The Pharisees came and began to question Jesus. To test him, they asked him for a sign from heaven. 12He sighed deeply and said, "Why does this generation ask for a miraculous sign? I tell you the truth, no sign will be given to it." 13Then he left them, got back into the boat and crossed to the other side.

The Yeast of the Pharisees and Herod

14The disciples had forgotten to bring bread, except for one loaf they had with them in the boat. 15"Be careful," Jesus warned them. "Watch out for the yeast of the Pharisees and that of Herod."

16They discussed this with one another and said, "It is because we have no bread."

17Aware of their discussion, Jesus asked them: "Why are you talking about having no bread? Do you still not see or understand? Are your hearts hardened? 18Do you have eyes but fail to see, and ears but fail to hear? And don't you remember? 19When I broke the five loaves for the five thousand, how many basketfuls of pieces did you pick up?"

i31 That is, the Ten Cities

"Twelve," they replied.

²⁰"And when I broke the seven loaves for the four thousand, how many basketfuls of pieces did you pick up?"

They answered, "Seven."

²¹He said to them, "Do you still not understand?"

The Healing of a Blind Man at Bethsaida

²²They came to Bethsaida, and some people brought a blind man and begged Jesus to touch him. ²³He took the blind man by the hand and led him outside the village. When he had spat on the man's eyes and put his hands on him, Jesus asked, "Do you see anything?"

²⁴He looked up and said, "I see people; they look like trees walking around."

²⁵Once more Jesus put his hands on the man's eyes. Then his eyes were opened, his sight was restored, and he saw everything clearly. ²⁶Jesus sent him home, saying, "Don't go into the village."ᵃ

Peter's Confession of Christ

²⁷Jesus and his disciples went on to the villages around Caesarea Philippi. On the way he asked them, "Who do people say I am?"

²⁸They replied, "Some say John the Baptist; others say Elijah; and still others, one of the prophets."

²⁹"But what about you?" he asked. "Who do you say I am?"

Peter answered, "You are the Christ."ᵇ

³⁰Jesus warned them not to tell anyone about him.

Jesus Predicts His Death

³¹He then began to teach them that the Son of Man must suffer many things and be rejected by the elders, chief priests and teachers of the law, and that he must be killed and after three days rise again. ³²He spoke plainly about this, and Peter took him aside and began to rebuke him.

³³But when Jesus turned and looked at his disciples, he rebuked Peter. "Get behind me, Satan!" he said. "You do not have in mind the things of God, but the things of men."

³⁴Then he called the crowd to him along with his disciples and said: "If anyone would come after me, he must deny himself and take up his cross and follow me. ³⁵For whoever wants to save his lifeᶜ will lose it, but whoever loses his life for me and for the gospel will save it. ³⁶What good is it for a man to gain the whole world, yet forfeit his soul? ³⁷Or what can a man give in exchange for his soul? ³⁸If anyone is ashamed of me and my words in this adulterous and sinful generation, the Son of Man will be ashamed of him when he comes in his Father's glory with the holy angels."

9 And he said to them, "I tell you the truth, some who are standing here will not taste death before they see the kingdom of God come with power."

The Transfiguration

²After six days Jesus took Peter, James and John with him and led them up a high mountain, where they were all alone. There he was transfigured before them. ³His clothes became dazzling white, whiter than anyone in the world could bleach them. ⁴And there appeared before them Elijah and Moses, who were talking with Jesus.

⁵Peter said to Jesus, "Rabbi, it is good for us to be here. Let us put up three shelters—one for you, one for Moses and one for Elijah." ⁶(He did not know what to say, they were so frightened.)

⁷Then a cloud appeared and enveloped them, and a voice came from the cloud: "This is my Son, whom I love. Listen to him!"

⁸Suddenly, when they looked round, they no longer saw anyone with them except Jesus.

⁹As they were coming down the mountain, Jesus gave them orders not to tell anyone what they had seen until the Son of

---

ᵃ26 Some manuscripts Don't go and tell anyone in the village
ᵇ29 Or Messiah. "The Christ" (Greek) and "the Messiah" (Hebrew) both mean "the Anointed One".
ᶜ35 The Greek word means either life or soul; also in verse 36.

Man had risen from the dead. [10]They kept the matter to themselves, discussing what "rising from the dead" meant.

[11]And they asked him, "Why do the teachers of the law say that Elijah must come first?"

[12]Jesus replied, "To be sure, Elijah does come first, and restores all things. Why then is it written that the Son of Man must suffer much and be rejected? [13]But I tell you, Elijah has come, and they have done to him everything they wished, just as it is written about him."

The Healing of a Boy With an Evil Spirit

[14]When they came to the other disciples, they saw a large crowd around them and the teachers of the law arguing with them. [15]As soon as all the people saw Jesus, they were overwhelmed with wonder and ran to greet him.

[16]"What are you arguing with them about?" he asked.

[17]A man in the crowd answered, "Teacher, I brought you my son, who is possessed by a spirit that has robbed him of speech. [18]Whenever it seizes him, it throws him to the ground. He foams at the mouth, gnashes his teeth and becomes rigid. I asked your disciples to drive out the spirit, but they could not."

[19]"O unbelieving generation," Jesus replied, "how long shall I stay with you? How long shall I put up with you? Bring the boy to me."

[20]So they brought him. When the spirit saw Jesus, it immediately threw the boy into a convulsion. He fell to the ground and rolled around, foaming at the mouth.

[21]Jesus asked the boy's father, "How long has he been like this?"

"From childhood," he answered. [22]"It has often thrown him into fire or water to kill him. But if you can do anything, take pity on us and help us."

[23]"'If you can'?" said Jesus. "Everything is possible for him who believes."

[24]Immediately the boy's father exclaimed, "I do believe; help me overcome my unbelief!"

[25]When Jesus saw that a crowd was running to the scene, he rebuked the evil[a] spirit. "You deaf and mute spirit," he said, "I command you, come out of him and never enter him again."

[26]The spirit shrieked, convulsed him violently and came out. The boy looked so much like a corpse that many said, "He's dead." [27]But Jesus took him by the hand and lifted him to his feet, and he stood up.

[28]After Jesus had gone indoors, his disciples asked him privately, "Why couldn't we drive it out?"

[29]He replied, "This kind can come out only by prayer."[b]

[30]They left that place and passed through Galilee. Jesus did not want anyone to know where they were, [31]because he was teaching his disciples. He said to them, "The Son of Man is going to be betrayed into the hands of men. They will kill him, and after three days he will rise." [32]But they did not understand what he meant and were afraid to ask him about it.

Who Is the Greatest?

[33]They came to Capernaum. When he was in the house, he asked them, "What were you arguing about on the road?" [34]But they kept quiet because on the way they had argued about who was the greatest.

[35]Sitting down, Jesus called the Twelve and said, "If anyone wants to be first, he must be the very last, and the servant of all."

[36]He took a little child and had him stand among them. Taking him in his arms, he said to them, [37]"Whoever welcomes one of these little children in my name welcomes me; and whoever welcomes me does not welcome me but the one who sent me."

Whoever Is Not Against Us Is for Us

[38]"Teacher," said John, "we saw a man driving out demons in your name and we told him to stop, because he was not one of us."

---

[a]25 Greek unclean   [b]29 Some manuscripts prayer and fasting

[39]"Do not stop him," Jesus said. "No-one who does a miracle in my name can in the next moment say anything bad about me, [40]for whoever is not against us is for us. [41]I tell you the truth, anyone who gives you a cup of water in my name because you belong to Christ will certainly not lose his reward.

Causing to Sin

[42]"And if anyone causes one of these little ones who believe in me to sin, it would be better for him to be thrown into the sea with a large millstone tied around his neck. [43]If your hand causes you to sin, cut it off. It is better for you to enter life maimed than with two hands to go into hell, where the fire never goes out.[c] [45]And if your foot causes you to sin, cut it off. It is better for you to enter life crippled than to have two feet and be thrown into hell.[d] [47]And if your eye causes you to sin, pluck it out. It is better for you to enter the kingdom of God with one eye than to have two eyes and be thrown into hell, [48]where

"'their worm does not die,
    and the fire is not quenched.'[e]

[49]Everyone will be salted with fire.
[50]"Salt is good, but if it loses its saltiness, how can you make it salty again? Have salt in yourselves, and be at peace with each other."

Divorce

10 Jesus then left that place and went into the region of Judea and across the Jordan. Again crowds of people came to him, and as was his custom, he taught them.

[2]Some Pharisees came and tested him by asking, "Is it lawful for a man to divorce his wife?"

[3]"What did Moses command you?" he replied.

[4]They said, "Moses permitted a man to write a certificate of divorce and send her away."

[5]"It was because your hearts were hard that Moses wrote you this law," Jesus replied. [6]"But at the beginning of creation God 'made them male and female'.[a] [7]For this reason a man will leave his father and mother and be united to his wife,[b] [8]and the two will become one flesh.'[c] So they are no longer two, but one. [9]Therefore what God has joined together, let man not separate."

[10]When they were in the house again, the disciples asked Jesus about this. [11]He answered, "Anyone who divorces his wife and marries another woman commits adultery against her. [12]And if she divorce her husband and marries another man she commits adultery."

The Little Children and Jesus

[13]People were bringing little children to Jesus to have him touch them, but the disciples rebuked them. [14]When Jesus saw this, he was indignant. He said to them, "Let the little children come to me, and do not hinder them, for the kingdom of God belongs to such as these. [15]I tell you the truth, anyone who will not receive the kingdom of God like a little child will never enter it." [16]And he took the children in his arms, put his hands on them and blessed them.

The Rich Young Man

[17]As Jesus started on his way, a man ran up to him and fell on his knees before him "Good teacher," he asked, "what must I do to inherit eternal life?"

[18]"Why do you call me good?" Jesus answered. "No-one is good—except God alone. [19]You know the commandments 'Do not murder, do not commit adultery, do not steal, do not give false testimony, do not defraud, honour your father and mother.'[d]"

---

[c]43 Some manuscripts out, [44]where / "'their worm does not die, / and the fire is not quenched.'
[d]45 Some manuscripts hell, [46]where / "'their worm does not die, / and the fire is not quenched.'
[e]48 Isaiah 66:24   [a]6 Gen. 1:27   [b]7 Some early manuscripts do not have and be united to his wife.
[c]8 Gen. 2:24   [d]19 Exodus 20:12–16; Deut. 5:16–20

being Jesus to others

[John 13:1-21]

Biblical background
Jesus often taught the disciples as they ate together. After a long journey, travellers' feet were dirty so the host would provide water as a sign of hospitality and welcome. Jesus violated several cultural norms by washing the disciples' feet to the extent that even Peter found his actions unthinkable. Foot washing was a servile task for a servant or a submissive wife. Even taking off his outer garment was a sign of great humility, as was going to the outside of the circle to wash their feet (couches were arranged around tables with the upper part of the body facing the food and the feet turned away). Jesus applies a spiritual meaning to the physical act (v 10). Lastly, (v15) disciples generally served their teachers and learnt by imitating them.

Picture yourself in the situation (you are a disciple): how would you have reacted? What feelings would you have experienced: joy, shame, a desire to hide in the corner? Be honest and take a moment to list those feelings. Why those feelings not others? Is it possible to identify how your upbringing, cultural conditioning and education have helped to shape those feelings? As Jesus comes to you how does he treat you? What does he say? As well as clean feet, what are your needs just now? Would you share them with Jesus? Imagine he takes your hand and reminds you that he loves you no matter what happens?

Recreate the scene in your mind: the room's ambience and atmosphere, its furnishings, the expressions and reactions of the disciples. How animated is the discussion and what are they talking about? Do you think the mood changed as Jesus took the towel and the basin?

Listen to and contemplate your feelings. Do not rush on and forego this opportunity. Put your thoughts and reflections into an expression of prayer, praise and thanksgiving.

(25)

the church

Why do Christians go to church?

Pat I quite resent it when people tell me that you don't have to go to church as a Christian. I think it is fundamental because it's an opportunity to meet with other Christians, to share the faith, to bounce ideas off each other, to sing, to have a cry, to have a laugh together. To look at the world go by and ask 'what are we doing about it?' If you don't do that you dry up.

Jonathan I think fellowship is really, really important just to keep you going because if you think you're on your own, it gets really hard. When you know there are all these other people going through the same kind of troubles as you, it helps. The breadth of knowledge helps as well. It's like the whole being greater than the sum of its parts, see Romans 12:4-5.

Ann In a very large church it is so easy to be lost, to go unnoticed so that you don't turn up. I go to my (big) church but the only way to get to know people there is to join a Bible study or a homegroup and I would recommend that for any new

A church should be lots of things:

Bible-based

focused on the Trinity *

centred on Jesus

visionary

somewhere you can be yourself

full of people of different ages

somewhere with a social conscience

open to you getting involved

* see jargonbuster

Christian because you get a cross-section of people there and you'll also get weekly teaching.

Penny There are about fifty of us in our church, and we have small groups which we see as the critical part of church. We're thinking of doing away with Sunday meetings for a while to focus on the small groups.

Paul I've seen so many people who have just got lost in this thing called 'church' and have lost their relationship with God. I've been in danger of that myself, one of my friends said to me, 'Do you realise all you ever talk about is church, you never talk about God?'

Anon Sometimes we misuse what church should be. Jesus walked around the community and said, 'Follow me.' We often say, 'Come here and watch me.'

follow me

Christian belief and church attendance
World statistics show that virtually everyone in South America says they are Christian (96%), and over three-quarters (76%) in North America. Oceania comes next with almost two-thirds (65%), followed by Europe with three in five (60%), along with a third of the African peoples. It is in Asia where three-fifths (60%) of the world's population live, that the Christian percentage is lowest (8%).

The numbers who claim to be Christian do not necessarily match the numbers who actually attend church, however. In England about one–fifth (19%) of the adult population say they go to church each week, though in practice only 8% are observed to do so. Also, church attendance and profession of a Christian faith do not necessarily correlate with church membership which, in Britain, is expected to decrease by 21% during the period 1980 and 2000.

(Statistics taken from UKCH: Religious Trends No. 1 1998/99 Edition, Edited by Dr Peter Brierley, Christian Research and Paternoster Publishing.)

being Jesus to others

[John 13:1-12 part 2]

As you return to the story, ask yourself why Jesus acted like he did and at that particular moment in his ministry.

Was it:

to show how much he cared for the disciples?

to teach them a profound lesson in servanthood?

to show what he meant by leadership?

to reveal an essential tool in building community?

something else altogether? (See Isaiah 53, p.740-1)

Are there people you need to serve?

Would it be a risk to help them? Dare you take that risk?
What do you find most difficult when thinking about serving others?

Do you:

feel you have nothing to offer?

sense that people don't need help?

feel too shy?

want to stay in the background?

get embarrassed easily?

Think about the following barriers to service:
- people are too self reliant and hate to depend on anyone
- no-one knows (or wants to know) the real needs of others
- mostly we experience relationships in only a superficial way
- people are too busy to get to know each other at a deeply personal level
- other

....
....

28

[20]"Teacher," he declared, "all these I have kept since I was a boy."

[21]Jesus looked at him and loved him. "One thing you lack," he said. "Go, sell everything you have and give to the poor, and you will have treasure in heaven. Then come, follow me."

[22]At this the man's face fell. He went away sad, because he had great wealth.

[23]Jesus looked around and said to his disciples, "How hard it is for the rich to enter the kingdom of God!"

[24]The disciples were amazed at his words. But Jesus said again, "Children, how hard it is[e] to enter the kingdom of God! [25]It is easier for a camel to go through the eye of a needle than for a rich man to enter the kingdom of God."

[26]The disciples were even more amazed, and said to each other, "Who then can be saved?"

[27]Jesus looked at them and said, "With man this is impossible, but not with God; all things are possible with God."

[28]Peter said to him, "We have left everything to follow you!"

[29]"I tell you the truth," Jesus replied, "no-one who has left home or brothers or sisters or mother or father or children or fields for me and the gospel [30]will fail to receive a hundred times as much in this present age (homes, brothers, sisters, mothers, children and fields—and with them, persecutions) and in the age to come, eternal life. [31]But many who are first will be last, and the last first."

Jesus Again Predicts His Death

[32]They were on their way up to Jerusalem, with Jesus leading the way, and the disciples were astonished, while those who followed were afraid. Again he took the Twelve aside and told them what was going to happen to him. [33]"We are going up to Jerusalem," he said, "and the Son of Man will be betrayed to the chief priests and teachers of the law. They will condemn him to death and will hand him over to the Gentiles, [34]who will mock him and spit on him, flog him and kill him. Three days later he will rise."

The Request of James and John

[35]Then James and John, the sons of Zebedee, came to him. "Teacher," they said, "we want you to do for us whatever we ask."

[36]"What do you want me to do for you?" he asked.

[37]They replied, "Let one of us sit at your right and the other at your left in your glory."

[38]"You don't know what you are asking," Jesus said. "Can you drink the cup I drink or be baptised with the baptism I am baptised with?"

[39]"We can," they answered.

Jesus said to them, "You will drink the cup I drink and be baptised with the baptism I am baptised with, [40]but to sit at my right or left is not for me to grant. These places belong to those for whom they have been prepared."

[41]When the ten heard about this, they became indignant with James and John. [42]Jesus called them together and said, "You know that those who are regarded as rulers of the Gentiles lord it over them, and their high officials exercise authority over them. [43]Not so with you. Instead, whoever wants to become great among you must be your servant, [44]and whoever wants to be first must be slave of all. [45]For even the Son of Man did not come to be served, but to serve, and to give his life as a ransom for many."

Blind Bartimaeus Receives His Sight

[46]Then they came to Jericho. As Jesus and his disciples, together with a large crowd, were leaving the city, a blind man, Bartimaeus (that is, the Son of Timaeus), was sitting by the roadside begging. [47]When he heard that it was Jesus of Nazareth, he began to shout, "Jesus, Son of David, have mercy on me!"

[48]Many rebuked him and told him to be quiet, but he shouted all the more, "Son of David, have mercy on me!"

[49]Jesus stopped and said, "Call him."

So they called to the blind man, "Cheer up! On your feet! He's calling you."

---

[e]24 Some manuscripts *is for those who trust in riches*

⁵⁰Throwing his cloak aside, he jumped to his feet and came to Jesus.

⁵¹"What do you want me to do for you?" Jesus asked him.

The blind man said, "Rabbi, I want to see."

⁵²"Go," said Jesus, "your faith has healed you." Immediately he received his sight and followed Jesus along the road.

The Triumphal Entry

11 As they approached Jerusalem and came to Bethphage and Bethany at the Mount of Olives, Jesus sent two of his disciples, ²saying to them, "Go to the village ahead of you, and just as you enter it, you will find a colt tied there, which no-one has ever ridden. Untie it and bring it here. ³If anyone asks you, 'Why are you doing this?' tell him, 'The Lord needs it and will send it back here shortly.'"

⁴They went and found a colt outside in the street, tied at a doorway. As they untied it, ⁵some people standing there asked, "What are you doing, untying that colt?" ⁶They answered as Jesus had told them to, and the people let them go. ⁷When they brought the colt to Jesus and threw their cloaks over it, he sat on it. ⁸Many people spread their cloaks on the road, while others spread branches they had cut in the fields. ⁹Those who went ahead and those who followed shouted,

"Hosanna!"*a*

"Blessed is he who comes in the name of the Lord!"*b*

¹⁰"Blessed is the coming kingdom of our father David!"

"Hosanna in the highest!"

¹¹Jesus entered Jerusalem and went to the temple. He looked around at everything, but since it was already late, he went out to Bethany with the Twelve.

Jesus Clears the Temple

¹²The next day as they were leaving Bethany, Jesus was hungry. ¹³Seeing in the distance a fig-tree in leaf, he went to find out if it had any fruit. When he reached it, he found nothing but leaves, because it was not the season for figs. ¹⁴Then he said to the tree, "May no-one ever eat fruit from you again." And his disciples heard him say it.

¹⁵On reaching Jerusalem, Jesus entered the temple area and began driving out those who were buying and selling there. He overturned the tables of the money-changers and the benches of those selling doves, ¹⁶and would not allow anyone to carry merchandise through the temple courts. ¹⁷And as he taught them, he said, "Is it not written:

"'My house will be called
    a house of prayer for all nations'*c*?

But you have made it 'a den of robbers'.*d*"

¹⁸The chief priests and the teachers of the law heard this and began looking for a way to kill him, for they feared him, because the whole crowd was amazed at his teaching.

¹⁹When evening came, they*e* went out of the city.

The Withered Fig-Tree

²⁰In the morning, as they went along, they saw the fig-tree withered from the roots. ²¹Peter remembered and said to Jesus, "Rabbi, look! The fig-tree you cursed has withered!"

²²"Have*f* faith in God," Jesus answered. ²³"I tell you the truth, if anyone says to this mountain, 'Go, throw yourself into the sea,' and does not doubt in his heart but believes that what he says will happen, it will be done for him. ²⁴Therefore I tell you, whatever you ask for in prayer, believe that you have received it, and it will be yours. ²⁵And when you stand praying, if you hold anything

a9 A Hebrew expression meaning "Save!" which became an exclamation of praise; also in verse 10.
b9 Psalm 118:25,26   *c17* Isaiah 56:7   *d17* Jer. 7:11   *e19* Some early manuscripts *he*
f22 Some early manuscripts *If you have*

against anyone, forgive him, so that your Father in heaven may forgive you your sins."[g]

The Authority of Jesus Questioned

[27]They arrived again in Jerusalem, and while Jesus was walking in the temple courts, the chief priests, the teachers of the law and the elders came to him. [28]"By what authority are you doing these things?" they asked. "And who gave you authority to do this?"

[29]Jesus replied, "I will ask you one question. Answer me, and I will tell you by what authority I am doing these things. [30]John's baptism—was it from heaven, or from men? Tell me!"

[31]They discussed it among themselves and said, "If we say, 'From heaven', he will ask, 'Then why didn't you believe him?' [32]But if we say, 'From men'. . . ." (They feared the people, for everyone held that John really was a prophet.)

[33]So they answered Jesus, "We don't know."

Jesus said, "Neither will I tell you by what authority I am doing these things."

The Parable of the Tenants

12 He then began to speak to them in parables: "A man planted a vineyard. He put a wall around it, dug a pit for the winepress and built a watchtower. Then he rented the vineyard to some farmers and went away on a journey. [2]At harvest time he sent a servant to the tenants to collect from them some of the fruit of the vineyard. [3]But they seized him, beat him and sent him away empty-handed. [4]Then he sent another servant to them; they struck this man on the head and treated him shamefully. [5]He sent still another, and that one they killed. He sent many others; some of them they beat, others they killed.

[6]"He had one left to send, a son, whom he loved. He sent him last of all, saying, 'They will respect my son.'

[7]"But the tenants said to one another, 'This is the heir. Come, let's kill him, and the inheritance will be ours.' [8]So they took him and killed him, and threw him out of the vineyard.

[9]"What then will the owner of the vineyard do? He will come and kill those tenants and give the vineyard to others. [10]Haven't you read this scripture:

" 'The stone the builders rejected
   has become the capstone;[a]
[11]the Lord has done this,
   and it is marvellous in our eyes'[b]?"

[12]Then they looked for a way to arrest him because they knew he had spoken the parable against them. But they were afraid of the crowd; so they left him and went away.

Paying Taxes to Caesar

[13]Later they sent some of the Pharisees and Herodians to Jesus to catch him in his words. [14]They came to him and said, "Teacher, we know you are a man of integrity. You aren't swayed by men, because you pay no attention to who they are; but you teach the way of God in accordance with the truth. Is it right to pay taxes to Caesar or not? [15]Should we pay or shouldn't we?"

But Jesus knew their hypocrisy. "Why are you trying to trap me?" he asked. "Bring me a denarius and let me look at it." [16]They brought the coin, and he asked them, "Whose portrait is this? And whose inscription?"

"Caesar's," they replied.

[17]Then Jesus said to them, "Give to Caesar what is Caesar's and to God what is God's."

And they were amazed at him.

Marriage at the Resurrection

[18]Then the Sadducees, who say there is no resurrection, came to him with a question. [19]"Teacher," they said, "Moses

---

[g]25 Some manuscripts sins. [26]But if you do not forgive, neither will your Father who is in heaven forgive your sins.
[a]10 Or cornerstone   [b]11 Psalm 118:22,23

wrote for us that if a man's brother dies and leaves a wife but no children, the man must marry the widow and have children for his brother. ²⁰Now there were seven brothers. The first one married and died without leaving any children. ²¹The second one married the widow, but he also died, leaving no child. It was the same with the third. ²²In fact, none of the seven left any children. Last of all, the woman died too. ²³At the resurrection[c] whose wife will she be, since the seven were married to her?"

²⁴Jesus replied, "Are you not in error because you do not know the Scriptures or the power of God? ²⁵When the dead rise, they will neither marry nor be given in marriage; they will be like the angels in heaven. ²⁶Now about the dead rising— have you not read in the book of Moses, in the account of the bush, how God said to him, 'I am the God of Abraham, the God of Isaac, and the God of Jacob'[d]? ²⁷He is not the God of the dead, but of the living. You are badly mistaken!"

The Greatest Commandment

²⁸One of the teachers of the law came and heard them debating. Noticing that Jesus had given them a good answer, he asked him, "Of all the commandments, which is the most important?"

²⁹"The most important one," answered Jesus, "is this: 'Hear, O Israel, the Lord our God, the Lord is one.[e] ³⁰Love the Lord your God with all your heart and with all your soul and with all your mind and with all your strength.'[f] ³¹The second is this: 'Love your neighbour as yourself.'[g] There is no commandment greater than these."

³²"Well said, teacher," the man replied. "You are right in saying that God is one and there is no other but him. ³³To love him with all your heart, with all your understanding and with all your strength, and to love your neighbour as yourself is more important than all burnt offerings and sacrifices."

³⁴When Jesus saw that he had answered wisely, he said to him, "You are not far from the kingdom of God." And from then on no-one dared ask him any more questions.

Whose Son Is the Christ?

³⁵While Jesus was teaching in the temple courts, he asked, "How is it that the teachers of the law say that the Christ[h] is the son of David? ³⁶David himself, speaking by the Holy Spirit, declared:

" 'The Lord said to my Lord:
   "Sit at my right hand
until I put your enemies
   under your feet." '[i]

³⁷David himself calls him 'Lord'. How then can he be his son?"

The large crowd listened to him with delight.

³⁸As he taught, Jesus said, "Watch out for the teachers of the law. They like to walk around in flowing robes and be greeted in the market-places, ³⁹and have the most important seats in the synagogues and the places of honour at banquets. ⁴⁰They devour widows' houses and for a show make lengthy prayers. Such men will be punished most severely."

The Widow's Offering

⁴¹Jesus sat down opposite the place where the offerings were put and watched the crowd putting their money into the temple treasury. Many rich people threw in large amounts. ⁴²But a poor widow came and put in two very small copper coins,[j] worth only a fraction of a penny.[k]

⁴³Calling his disciples to him, Jesus said, "I tell you the truth, this poor widow has put more into the treasury than all the others. ⁴⁴They all gave out of their wealth; but she, out of her poverty, put in everything—all she had to live on."

---

[c]23 Some manuscripts *resurrection, when men rise from the dead,*   [d]26 Exodus 3:6
[e]29 Or *the Lord our God is one Lord*   [f]30 Deut. 6:4,5   [g]31 Lev. 19:18   [h]35 Or *Messiah*
[i]36 Psalm 110:1   [j]42 Greek *two lepta*   [k]42 Greek *kodrantes*

Signs of the End of the Age

13 As he was leaving the temple, one of his disciples said to him, "Look, Teacher! What massive stones! What magnificent buildings!"

2"Do you see all these great buildings?" replied Jesus. "Not one stone here will be left on another; every one will be thrown down."

3As Jesus was sitting on the Mount of Olives opposite the temple, Peter, James, John and Andrew asked him privately, 4"Tell us, when will these things happen? And what will be the sign that they are all about to be fulfilled?"

5Jesus said to them: "Watch out that no-one deceives you. 6Many will come in my name, claiming, 'I am he,' and will deceive many. 7When you hear of wars and rumours of wars, do not be alarmed. Such things must happen, but the end is still to come. 8Nation will rise against nation, and kingdom against kingdom. There will be earthquakes in various places, and famines. These are the beginning of birth-pains.

9"You must be on your guard. You will be handed over to the local councils and flogged in the synagogues. On account of me you will stand before governors and kings as witnesses to them. 10And the gospel must first be preached to all nations. 11Whenever you are arrested and brought to trial, do not worry beforehand about what to say. Just say whatever is given you at the time, for it is not you speaking, but the Holy Spirit.

12"Brother will betray brother to death, and a father his child. Children will rebel against their parents and have them put to death. 13All men will hate you because of me, but he who stands firm to the end will be saved.

14"When you see 'the abomination that causes desolation'*a* standing where it*b* does not belong—let the reader understand—then let those who are in Judea flee to the mountains. 15Let no-one on the roof of his house go down or enter the house to take anything out. 16Let no-one

in the field go back to get his cloak. 17How dreadful it will be in those days for pregnant women and nursing mothers! 18Pray that this will not take place in winter, 19because those will be days of distress unequalled from the beginning, when God created the world, until now—and never to be equalled again. 20If the Lord had not cut short those days, no-one would survive. But for the sake of the elect, whom he has chosen, he has shortened them. 21At that time if anyone says to you, 'Look, here is the Christ!'*c* or, 'Look, there he is!' do not believe it. 22For false Christs and false prophets will appear and perform signs and miracles to deceive the elect—if that were possible. 23So be on your guard; I have told you everything ahead of time.

24"But in those days, following that distress,

" 'the sun will be darkened,
  and the moon will not give its light;
25the stars will fall from the sky,
  and the heavenly bodies will be
    shaken.'*d*

26"At that time men will see the Son of Man coming in clouds with great power and glory. 27And he will send his angels and gather his elect from the four winds, from the ends of the earth to the ends of the heavens.

28"Now learn this lesson from the fig-tree: As soon as its twigs get tender and its leaves come out, you know that summer is near. 29Even so, when you see these things happening, you know that it is near, right at the door. 30I tell you the truth, this generation*e* will certainly not pass away until all these things have happened. 31Heaven and earth will pass away, but my words will never pass away.

The Day and Hour Unknown

32"No-one knows about that day or hour, not even the angels in heaven, nor the Son, but only the Father. 33Be on guard! Be alert!*f* You do not know when

---

a14 Daniel 9:27; 11:31; 12:11   *b14* Or *he*; also in verse 29   *c21* Or *Messiah*   *d25* Isaiah 13:10; 34:4
e30 Or *race*   *f33* Some manuscripts *alert and pray*

that time will come. [34]It's like a man going away: He leaves his house and puts his servants in charge, each with his assigned task, and tells the one at the door to keep watch.

[35]"Therefore keep watch because you do not know when the owner of the house will come back—whether in the evening, or at midnight, or when the cock crows, or at dawn. [36]If he comes suddenly, do not let him find you sleeping. [37]What I say to you, I say to everyone: 'Watch!'"

Jesus Anointed at Bethany

14 Now the Passover and the Feast of Unleavened Bread were only two days away, and the chief priests and the teachers of the law were looking for some sly way to arrest Jesus and kill him. [2]"But not during the Feast," they said, "or the people may riot."

[3]While he was in Bethany, reclining at the table in the home of a man known as Simon the Leper, a woman came with an alabaster jar of very expensive perfume, made of pure nard. She broke the jar and poured the perfume on his head.

[4]Some of those present were saying indignantly to one another, "Why this waste of perfume? [5]It could have been sold for more than a year's wages[a] and the money given to the poor." And they rebuked her harshly.

[6]"Leave her alone," said Jesus. "Why are you bothering her? She has done a beautiful thing to me. [7]The poor you will always have with you, and you can help them any time you want. But you will not always have me. [8]She did what she could. She poured perfume on my body beforehand to prepare for my burial. [9]I tell you the truth, wherever the gospel is preached throughout the world, what she has done will also be told, in memory of her."

[10]Then Judas Iscariot, one of the Twelve, went to the chief priests to betray Jesus to them. [11]They were delighted to hear this and promised to give him money. So he watched for an opportunity to hand him over.

The Lord's Supper

[12]On the first day of the Feast of Unleavened Bread, when it was customary to sacrifice the Passover lamb, Jesus' disciples asked him, "Where do you want us to go and make preparations for you to eat the Passover?"

[13]So he sent two of his disciples, telling them, "Go into the city, and a man carrying a jar of water will meet you. Follow him. [14]Say to the owner of the house he enters, 'The Teacher asks: Where is my guest room, where I may eat the Passover with my disciples?' [15]He will show you a large upper room, furnished and ready. Make preparations for us there."

[16]The disciples left, went into the city and found things just as Jesus had told them. So they prepared the Passover.

[17]When evening came, Jesus arrived with the Twelve. [18]While they were reclining at the table eating, he said, "I tell you the truth, one of you will betray me—one who is eating with me."

[19]They were saddened, and one by one they said to him, "Surely not I?"

[20]"It is one of the Twelve," he replied, "one who dips bread into the bowl with me. [21]The Son of Man will go just as it is written about him. But woe to that man who betrays the Son of Man! It would be better for him if he had not been born."

[22]While they were eating, Jesus took bread, gave thanks and broke it, and gave it to his disciples, saying, "Take it; this is my body."

[23]Then he took the cup, gave thanks and offered it to them, and they all drank from it.

[24]"This is my blood of the[b] covenant, which is poured out for many," he said to them. [25]"I tell you the truth, I will not drink again of the fruit of the vine until that day when I drink it anew in the kingdom of God."

[26]When they had sung a hymn, they went out to the Mount of Olives.

---

[a]5 Greek *than three hundred denarii*   [b]24 Some manuscripts *the new*

Jesus Predicts Peter's Denial

[27] "You will all fall away," Jesus told them, "for it is written:

" 'I will strike the shepherd,
and the sheep will be scattered.'[c]

[28] But after I have risen, I will go ahead of you into Galilee."

[29] Peter declared, "Even if all fall away, I will not."

[30] "I tell you the truth," Jesus answered, "today—yes, tonight—before the cock crows twice[d] you yourself will disown me three times."

[31] But Peter insisted emphatically, "Even if I have to die with you, I will never disown you." And all the others said the same.

Gethsemane

[32] They went to a place called Gethsemane, and Jesus said to his disciples, "Sit here while I pray." [33] He took Peter, James and John along with him, and he began to be deeply distressed and troubled. [34] "My soul is overwhelmed with sorrow to the point of death," he said to them. "Stay here and keep watch."

[35] Going a little farther, he fell to the ground and prayed that if possible the hour might pass from him. [36] "*Abba*,[e] Father," he said, "everything is possible for you. Take this cup from me. Yet not what I will, but what you will."

[37] Then he returned to his disciples and found them sleeping. "Simon," he said to Peter, "are you asleep? Could you not keep watch for one hour? [38] Watch and pray so that you will not fall into temptation. The spirit is willing, but the body is weak."

[39] Once more he went away and prayed the same thing. [40] When he came back, he again found them sleeping, because their eyes were heavy. They did not know what to say to him.

[41] Returning the third time, he said to them, "Are you still sleeping and resting? Enough! The hour has come. Look, the Son of Man is betrayed into the hands of sinners. [42] Rise! Let us go! Here comes my betrayer!"

Jesus Arrested

[43] Just as he was speaking, Judas, one of the Twelve, appeared. With him was a crowd armed with swords and clubs, sent from the chief priests, the teachers of the law, and the elders. [44] Now the betrayer had arranged a signal with them: "The one I kiss is the man; arrest him and lead him away under guard." [45] Going at once to Jesus, Judas said, "Rabbi!" and kissed him. [46] The men seized Jesus and arrested him. [47] Then one of those standing near drew his sword and struck the servant of the high priest, cutting off his ear.

[48] "Am I leading a rebellion," said Jesus, "that you have come out with swords and clubs to capture me? [49] Every day I was with you, teaching in the temple courts, and you did not arrest me. But the Scriptures must be fulfilled." [50] Then everyone deserted him and fled.

[51] A young man, wearing nothing but a linen garment, was following Jesus. When they seized him, [52] he fled naked, leaving his garment behind.

Before the Sanhedrin

[53] They took Jesus to the high priest, and all the chief priests, elders and teachers of the law came together. [54] Peter followed him at a distance, right into the courtyard of the high priest. There he sat with the guards and warmed himself at the fire.

[55] The chief priests and the whole Sanhedrin were looking for evidence against Jesus so that they could put him to death, but they did not find any. [56] Many testified falsely against him, but their statements did not agree.

[57] Then some stood up and gave this false testimony against him: [58] "We heard him say, 'I will destroy this man-made temple and in three days will build

---

[c]27 Zech. 13:7   [d]30 Some early manuscripts do not have *twice*.   [e]36 Aramaic for *Father*

another, not made by man.'" ⁵⁹Yet even then their testimony did not agree.

⁶⁰Then the high priest stood up before them and asked Jesus, "Are you not going to answer? What is this testimony that these men are bringing against you?" ⁶¹But Jesus remained silent and gave no answer.

Again the high priest asked him, "Are you the Christ,ᶠ the Son of the Blessed One?"

⁶²"I am," said Jesus. "And you will see the Son of Man sitting at the right hand of the Mighty One and coming on the clouds of heaven."

⁶³The high priest tore his clothes. "Why do we need any more witnesses?" he asked. ⁶⁴"You have heard the blasphemy. What do you think?"

They all condemned him as worthy of death. ⁶⁵Then some began to spit at him; they blindfolded him, struck him with their fists, and said, "Prophesy!" And the guards took him and beat him.

Peter Disowns Jesus

⁶⁶While Peter was below in the courtyard, one of the servant girls of the high priest came by. ⁶⁷When she saw Peter warming himself, she looked closely at him.

"You also were with that Nazarene, Jesus," she said.

⁶⁸But he denied it. "I don't know or understand what you're talking about," he said, and went out into the entrance.ᵍ

⁶⁹When the servant girl saw him there, she said again to those standing around, "This fellow is one of them." ⁷⁰Again he denied it.

After a little while, those standing near said to Peter, "Surely you are one of them, for you are a Galilean."

⁷¹He began to call down curses on himself, and he swore to them, "I don't know this man you're talking about."

⁷²Immediately the cock crowed the second time.ʰ Then Peter remembered the word Jesus had spoken to him: "Before the cock crows twiceⁱ you will disown

me three times." And he broke down and wept.

Jesus Before Pilate

15 Very early in the morning, the chief priests, with the elders, the teachers of the law and the whole Sanhedrin, reached a decision. They bound Jesus, led him away and turned him over to Pilate.

²"Are you the king of the Jews?" asked Pilate.

"Yes, it is as you say," Jesus replied.

³The chief priests accused him of many things. ⁴So again Pilate asked him, "Aren't you going to answer? See how many things they are accusing you of."

⁵But Jesus still made no reply, and Pilate was amazed.

⁶Now it was the custom at the Feast to release a prisoner whom the people requested. ⁷A man called Barabbas was in prison with the insurrectionists who had committed murder in the uprising. ⁸The crowd came up and asked Pilate to do for them what he usually did.

⁹"Do you want me to release to you the king of the Jews?" asked Pilate, ¹⁰knowing it was out of envy that the chief priests had handed Jesus over to him. ¹¹But the chief priests stirred up the crowd to have Pilate release Barabbas instead.

¹²"What shall I do, then, with the one you call the king of the Jews?" Pilate asked them.

¹³"Crucify him!" they shouted.

¹⁴"Why? What crime has he committed?" asked Pilate.

But they shouted all the louder, "Crucify him!"

¹⁵Wanting to satisfy the crowd, Pilate released Barabbas to them. He had Jesus flogged, and handed him over to be crucified.

The Soldiers Mock Jesus

¹⁶The soldiers led Jesus away into the palace (that is, the Praetorium) and called together the whole company of soldiers.

---

*f*61 Or *Messiah* *g*68 Some early manuscripts *entrance and the cock crowed*
*h*72 Some early manuscripts do not have *the second time.* *i*72 Some early manuscripts do not have *twice.*

[17]They put a purple robe on him, then twisted together a crown of thorns and set it on him. [18]And they began to call out to him, "Hail, king of the Jews!" [19]Again and again they struck him on the head with a staff and spat on him. Falling on their knees, they paid homage to him. [20]And when they had mocked him, they took off the purple robe and put his own clothes on him. Then they led him out to crucify him.

The Crucifixion

[21]A certain man from Cyrene, Simon, the father of Alexander and Rufus, was passing by on his way in from the country, and they forced him to carry the cross. [22]They brought Jesus to the place called Golgotha (which means The Place of the Skull). [23]Then they offered him wine mixed with myrrh, but he did not take it. [24]And they crucified him. Dividing up his clothes, they cast lots to see what each would get.

[25]It was the third hour when they crucified him. [26]The written notice of the charge against him read: THE KING OF THE JEWS. [27]They crucified two robbers with him, one on his right and one on his left.[a] [29]Those who passed by hurled insults at him, shaking their heads and saying, "So! You who are going to destroy the temple and build it in three days, [30]come down from the cross and save yourself!"

[31]In the same way the chief priests and the teachers of the law mocked him among themselves. "He saved others," they said, "but he can't save himself! [32]Let this Christ,[b] this King of Israel, come down now from the cross, that we may see and believe." Those crucified with him also heaped insults on him.

The Death of Jesus

[33]At the sixth hour darkness came over the whole land until the ninth hour. [34]And at the ninth hour Jesus cried out in a loud voice, *"Eloi, Eloi, lama sabachthani?"*—which means, "My God, my God, why have you forsaken me?"[c]

[35]When some of those standing near heard this, they said, "Listen, he's calling Elijah."

[36]One man ran, filled a sponge with wine vinegar, put it on a stick, and offered it to Jesus to drink. "Now leave him alone. Let's see if Elijah comes to take him down," he said.

[37]With a loud cry, Jesus breathed his last.

[38]The curtain of the temple was torn in two from top to bottom. [39]And when the centurion, who stood there in front of Jesus, heard his cry and[d] saw how he died, he said, "Surely this man was the Son[e] of God!"

[40]Some women were watching from a distance. Among them were Mary Magdalene, Mary the mother of James the younger and of Joses, and Salome. [41]In Galilee these women had followed him and cared for his needs. Many other women who had come up with him to Jerusalem were also there.

The Burial of Jesus

[42]It was Preparation Day (that is, the day before the Sabbath). So as evening approached, [43]Joseph of Arimathea, a prominent member of the Council, who was himself waiting for the kingdom of God, went boldly to Pilate and asked for Jesus' body. [44]Pilate was surprised to hear that he was already dead. Summoning the centurion, he asked him if Jesus had already died. [45]When he learned from the centurion that it was so, he gave the body to Joseph. [46]So Joseph bought some linen cloth, took down the body, wrapped it in the linen, and placed it in a tomb cut out of rock. Then he rolled a stone against the entrance of the tomb. [47]Mary Magdalene and Mary the mother of Joses saw where he was laid.

---

[a]27 Some manuscripts *left,* [28]*and the scripture was fulfilled which says, "He was counted with the lawless ones"* (Isaiah 53:12)   [b]32 Or *Messiah*   [c]34 Psalm 22:1   [d]39 Some manuscripts do not have *heard his cry and.*   [e]39 Or *a son*

The Resurrection

16 When the Sabbath was over, Mary Magdalene, Mary the mother of James, and Salome bought spices so that they might go to anoint Jesus' body. ²Very early on the first day of the week, just after sunrise, they were on their way to the tomb ³and they asked each other, "Who will roll the stone away from the entrance of the tomb?"

⁴But when they looked up, they saw that the stone, which was very large, had been rolled away. ⁵As they entered the tomb, they saw a young man dressed in a white robe sitting on the right side, and they were alarmed.

⁶"Don't be alarmed," he said. "You are looking for Jesus the Nazarene, who was crucified. He has risen! He is not here. See the place where they laid him. ⁷But go, tell his disciples and Peter, 'He is going ahead of you into Galilee. There you will see him, just as he told you.'"

⁸Trembling and bewildered, the women went out and fled from the tomb. They said nothing to anyone, because they were afraid.

[The earliest manuscripts and some other ancient witnesses do not have Mark 16:9–20]

⁹When Jesus rose early on the first day of the week, he appeared first to Mary Magdalene, out of whom he had driven seven demons. ¹⁰She went and told those who had been with him and who were mourning and weeping. ¹¹When they heard that Jesus was alive and that she had seen him, they did not believe it.

¹²Afterwards Jesus appeared in a different form to two of them while they were walking in the country. ¹³These returned and reported it to the rest; but they did not believe them either.

¹⁴Later Jesus appeared to the Eleven as they were eating; he rebuked them for their lack of faith and their stubborn refusal to believe those who had seen him after he had risen.

¹⁵He said to them, "Go into all the world and preach the good news to all creation. ¹⁶Whoever believes and is baptised will be saved, but whoever does not believe will be condemned. ¹⁷And these signs will accompany those who believe: In my name they will drive out demons; they will speak in new tongues; ¹⁸they will pick up snakes with their hands; and when they drink deadly poison, it will not hurt them at all; they will place their hands on sick people, and they will get well."

¹⁹After the Lord Jesus had spoken to them, he was taken up into heaven and he sat at the right hand of God. ²⁰Then the disciples went out and preached everywhere, and the Lord worked with them and confirmed his word by the signs that accompanied it.

Luke

Introduction

1 Many have undertaken to draw up an account of the things that have been fulfilled[a] among us, [2]just as they were handed down to us by those who from the first were eye-witnesses and servants of the word. [3]Therefore, since I myself have carefully investigated everything from the beginning, it seemed good also to me to write an orderly account for you, most excellent Theophilus, [4]so that you may know the certainty of the things you have been taught.

The Birth of John the Baptist Foretold

[5]In the time of Herod king of Judea there was a priest named Zechariah, who belonged to the priestly division of Abijah; his wife Elizabeth was also a descendant of Aaron. [6]Both of them were upright in the sight of God, observing all the Lord's commandments and regulations blamelessly. [7]But they had no children, because Elizabeth was barren; and they were both well on in years.

[8]Once when Zechariah's division was on duty and he was serving as priest before God, [9]he was chosen by lot, according to the custom of the priesthood, to go into the temple of the Lord and burn incense. [10]And when the time for the burning of incense came, all the assembled worshippers were praying outside.

[11]Then an angel of the Lord appeared to him, standing at the right side of the altar of incense. [12]When Zechariah saw him, he was startled and was gripped with fear. [13]But the angel said to him: "Do not be afraid, Zechariah; your prayer has been heard. Your wife Elizabeth will bear you a son, and you are to give him the name John. [14]He will be a joy and delight to you, and many will rejoice because of his birth, [15]for he will be great in the sight of the Lord. He is never to take wine or other fermented drink, and he will be filled with the Holy Spirit even from birth.[b] [16]Many of the people of Israel will he bring back to the Lord their God. [17]And he will go on before the Lord, in the spirit and power of Elijah, to turn the hearts of the fathers to their children and the disobedient to the wisdom of the righteous—to make ready a people prepared for the Lord."

[18]Zechariah asked the angel, "How can I be sure of this? I am an old man and my wife is well on in years."

[19]The angel answered, "I am Gabriel. I stand in the presence of God, and I have been sent to speak to you and to tell you this good news. [20]And now you will be silent and not able to speak until the day this happens, because you did not believe my words, which will come true at their proper time."

[21]Meanwhile, the people were waiting for Zechariah and wondering why he stayed so long in the temple. [22]When he came out, he could not speak to them. They realised he had seen a vision in the temple, for he kept making signs to them but remained unable to speak.

²³When his time of service was completed, he returned home. ²⁴After this his wife Elizabeth became pregnant and for five months remained in seclusion. ²⁵"The Lord has done this for me," she said. "In these days he has shown his favour and taken away my disgrace among the people."

The Birth of Jesus Foretold

²⁶In the sixth month, God sent the angel Gabriel to Nazareth, a town in Galilee, ²⁷to a virgin pledged to be married to a man named Joseph, a descendant of David. The virgin's name was Mary. ²⁸The angel went to her and said, "Greetings, you who are highly favoured! The Lord is with you."

²⁹Mary was greatly troubled at his words and wondered what kind of greeting this might be. ³⁰But the angel said to her, "Do not be afraid, Mary, you have found favour with God. ³¹You will be with child and give birth to a son, and you are to give him the name Jesus. ³²He will be great and will be called the Son of the Most High. The Lord God will give him the throne of his father David, ³³and he will reign over the house of Jacob for ever; his kingdom will never end."

³⁴"How will this be," Mary asked the angel, "since I am a virgin?"

³⁵The angel answered, "The Holy Spirit will come upon you, and the power of the Most High will overshadow you. So the holy one to be born will be called[c] the Son of God. ³⁶Even Elizabeth your relative is going to have a child in her old age, and she who was said to be barren is in her sixth month. ³⁷For nothing is impossible with God."

³⁸"I am the Lord's servant," Mary answered. "May it be to me as you have said." Then the angel left her.

Mary Visits Elizabeth

³⁹At that time Mary got ready and hurried to a town in the hill country of Judea,

⁴⁰where she entered Zechariah's home and greeted Elizabeth. ⁴¹When Elizabeth heard Mary's greeting, the baby leaped in her womb, and Elizabeth was filled with the Holy Spirit. ⁴²In a loud voice she exclaimed: "Blessed are you among women, and blessed is the child you will bear! ⁴³But why am I so favoured, that the mother of my Lord should come to me? ⁴⁴As soon as the sound of your greeting reached my ears, the baby in my womb leaped for joy. ⁴⁵Blessed is she who has believed that what the Lord has said to her will be accomplished!"

Mary's Song

⁴⁶And Mary said:

"My soul glorifies the Lord
⁴⁷   and my spirit rejoices in God my
        Saviour,
⁴⁸for he has been mindful
    of the humble state of his servant.
From now on all generations will call
        me blessed,
⁴⁹   for the Mighty One has done great
        things for me—
    holy is his name.
⁵⁰His mercy extends to those who fear
        him,
    from generation to generation.
⁵¹He has performed mighty deeds with
        his arm;
    he has scattered those who are proud
        in their inmost thoughts.
⁵²He has brought down rulers from their
        thrones
    but has lifted up the humble.
⁵³He has filled the hungry with good
        things
    but has sent the rich away empty.
⁵⁴He has helped his servant Israel,
    remembering to be merciful
⁵⁵to Abraham and his descendants for
        ever,
    even as he said to our fathers."

⁵⁶Mary stayed with Elizabeth for about three months and then returned home.

c35 Or So the child to be born will be called holy,

The Birth of John the Baptist

⁵⁷When it was time for Elizabeth to have her baby, she gave birth to a son. ⁵⁸Her neighbours and relatives heard that the Lord had shown her great mercy, and they shared her joy.

⁵⁹On the eighth day they came to circumcise the child, and they were going to name him after his father Zechariah, ⁶⁰but his mother spoke up and said, "No! He is to be called John."

⁶¹They said to her, "There is no-one among your relatives who has that name."

⁶²Then they made signs to his father, to find out what he would like to name the child. ⁶³He asked for a writing tablet, and to everyone's astonishment he wrote, "His name is John." ⁶⁴Immediately his mouth was opened and his tongue was loosed, and he began to speak, praising God. ⁶⁵The neighbours were all filled with awe, and throughout the hill country of Judea people were talking about all these things. ⁶⁶Everyone who heard this wondered about it, asking, "What then is this child going to be?" For the Lord's hand was with him.

Zechariah's Song

⁶⁷His father Zechariah was filled with the Holy Spirit and prophesied:

⁶⁸"Praise be to the Lord, the God of Israel,
  because he has come and has redeemed his people.
⁶⁹He has raised up a horn*d* of salvation for us
  in the house of his servant David
⁷⁰(as he said through his holy prophets of long ago),
⁷¹salvation from our enemies
  and from the hand of all who hate us—
⁷²to show mercy to our fathers
  and to remember his holy covenant,
⁷³ the oath he swore to our father Abraham:
⁷⁴to rescue us from the hand of our enemies,
  and to enable us to serve him without fear
⁷⁵ in holiness and righteousness before him all our days.

⁷⁶And you, my child, will be called a prophet of the Most High;
  for you will go on before the Lord to prepare the way for him,
⁷⁷to give his people the knowledge of salvation
  through the forgiveness of their sins,
⁷⁸because of the tender mercy of our God,
  by which the rising sun will come to us from heaven
⁷⁹to shine on those living in darkness and in the shadow of death,
  to guide our feet into the path of peace."

⁸⁰And the child grew and became strong in spirit; and he lived in the desert until he appeared publicly to Israel.

The Birth of Jesus

2 In those days Caesar Augustus issued a decree that a census should be taken of the entire Roman world. (²This was the first census that took place while Quirinius was governor of Syria.) ³And everyone went to his own town to register.

⁴So Joseph also went up from the town of Nazareth in Galilee to Judea, to Bethlehem the town of David, because he belonged to the house and line of David. ⁵He went there to register with Mary, who was pledged to be married to him and was expecting a child. ⁶While they were there, the time came for the baby to be born, ⁷and she gave birth to her firstborn, a son. She wrapped him in cloths and placed him in a manger, because there was no room for them in the inn.

The Shepherds and the Angels

⁸And there were shepherds living out in the fields near by, keeping watch over their flocks at night. ⁹An angel of the Lord

d69 Horn here symbolises strength.

appeared to them, and the glory of the Lord shone around them, and they were terrified. [10]But the angel said to them, "Do not be afraid. I bring you good news of great joy that will be for all the people. [11]Today in the town of David a Saviour has been born to you; he is Christ[a] the Lord. [12]This will be a sign to you: You will find a baby wrapped in cloths and lying in a manger."

[13]Suddenly a great company of the heavenly host appeared with the angel, praising God and saying,

[14]"Glory to God in the highest,
and on earth peace to men on whom his favour rests."

[15]When the angels had left them and gone into heaven, the shepherds said to one another, "Let's go to Bethlehem and see this thing that has happened, which the Lord has told us about."

[16]So they hurried off and found Mary and Joseph, and the baby, who was lying in the manger. [17]When they had seen him, they spread the word concerning what had been told them about this child, [18]and all who heard it were amazed at what the shepherds said to them. [19]But Mary treasured up all these things and pondered them in her heart. [20]The shepherds returned, glorifying and praising God for all the things they had heard and seen, which were just as they had been told.

Jesus Presented in the Temple

[21]On the eighth day, when it was time to circumcise him, he was named Jesus, the name the angel had given him before he had been conceived.

[22]When the time of their purification according to the Law of Moses had been completed, Joseph and Mary took him to Jerusalem to present him to the Lord [23](as it is written in the Law of the Lord, "Every firstborn male is to be consecrated to the Lord"[b]), [24]and to offer a sacrifice in keeping with what is said in the Law of the

Lord: "a pair of doves or two young pigeons".[c]

[25]Now there was a man in Jerusalem called Simeon, who was righteous and devout. He was waiting for the consolation of Israel, and the Holy Spirit was upon him. [26]It had been revealed to him by the Holy Spirit that he would not die before he had seen the Lord's Christ. [27]Moved by the Spirit, he went into the temple courts. When the parents brought in the child Jesus to do for him what the custom of the Law required, [28]Simeon took him in his arms and praised God, saying:

[29]"Sovereign Lord, as you have promised,
you now dismiss[d] your servant in peace.
[30]For my eyes have seen your salvation,
[31]   which you have prepared in the sight of all people,
[32]a light for revelation to the Gentiles and for glory to your people Israel."

[33]The child's father and mother marvelled at what was said about him. [34]Then Simeon blessed them and said to Mary, his mother: "This child is destined to cause the falling and rising of many in Israel, and to be a sign that will be spoken against, [35]so that the thoughts of many hearts will be revealed. And a sword will pierce your own soul too."

[36]There was also a prophetess, Anna, the daughter of Phanuel, of the tribe of Asher. She was very old; she had lived with her husband seven years after her marriage, [37]and then was a widow until she was eighty-four.[e] She never left the temple but worshipped night and day, fasting and praying. [38]Coming up to them at that very moment, she gave thanks to God and spoke about the child to all who were looking forward to the redemption of Jerusalem.

[39]When Joseph and Mary had done everything required by the Law of the Lord, they returned to Galilee to their

---

[a]11 Or Messiah. "The Christ" (Greek) and "the Messiah" (Hebrew) both mean "the Anointed One"; also in verse 26.
[b]23 Exodus 13:2,12   [c]24 Lev. 12:8   [d]29 Or promised, / now dismiss
[e]37 Or widow for eighty-four years

own town of Nazareth. ⁴⁰And the child grew and became strong; he was filled with wisdom, and the grace of God was upon him.

The Boy Jesus at the Temple

⁴¹Every year his parents went to Jerusalem for the Feast of the Passover. ⁴²When he was twelve years old, they went up to the Feast, according to the custom. ⁴³After the Feast was over, while his parents were returning home, the boy Jesus stayed behind in Jerusalem, but they were unaware of it. ⁴⁴Thinking he was in their company, they travelled on for a day. Then they began looking for him among their relatives and friends. ⁴⁵When they did not find him, they went back to Jerusalem to look for him. ⁴⁶After three days they found him in the temple courts, sitting among the teachers, listening to them and asking them questions. ⁴⁷Everyone who heard him was amazed at his understanding and his answers. ⁴⁸When his parents saw him, they were astonished. His mother said to him, "Son, why have you treated us like this? Your father and I have been anxiously searching for you."

⁴⁹"Why were you searching for me?" he asked. "Didn't you know I had to be in my Father's house?" ⁵⁰But they did not understand what he was saying to them.

⁵¹Then he went down to Nazareth with them and was obedient to them. But his mother treasured all these things in her heart. ⁵²And Jesus grew in wisdom and stature, and in favour with God and men.

John the Baptist Prepares the Way

3 In the fifteenth year of the reign of Tiberius Caesar—when Pontius Pilate was governor of Judea, Herod tetrarch of Galilee, his brother Philip tetrarch of Iturea and Traconitis, and Lysanias tetrarch of Abilene—²during the high priesthood of Annas and Caiaphas, the word of God came to John son of Zechariah in the desert. ³He went into all the country around the Jordan, preaching a baptism of repentance for the forgiveness of sins. ⁴As is written in the book of the words of Isaiah the prophet:

"A voice of one calling in the desert,
'Prepare the way for the Lord,
    make straight paths for him.
⁵Every valley shall be filled in,
    every mountain and hill made low.
The crooked roads shall become
        straight,
    the rough ways smooth.
⁶And all mankind will see God's
        salvation.'"ᵃ

⁷John said to the crowds coming out to be baptised by him, "You brood of vipers! Who warned you to flee from the coming wrath? ⁸Produce fruit in keeping with repentance. And do not begin to say to yourselves, 'We have Abraham as our father.' For I tell you that out of these stones God can raise up children for Abraham. ⁹The axe is already at the root of the trees, and every tree that does not produce good fruit will be cut down and thrown into the fire."

¹⁰"What should we do then?" the crowd asked.

¹¹John answered, "The man with two tunics should share with him who has none, and the one who has food should do the same."

¹²Tax collectors also came to be baptised. "Teacher," they asked, "what should we do?"

¹³"Don't collect any more than you are required to," he told them.

¹⁴Then some soldiers asked him, "And what should we do?"

He replied, "Don't extort money and don't accuse people falsely—be content with your pay."

¹⁵The people were waiting expectantly and were all wondering in their hearts if John might possibly be the Christ.ᵇ ¹⁶John answered them all, "I baptise you withᶜ water. But one more powerful than I will come, the thongs of whose sandals I am not worthy to untie. He will baptise you with the Holy Spirit and with fire. ¹⁷His

ᵃ6 Isaiah 40:3–5   ᵇ15 Or *Messiah*   ᶜ16 Or *in*

winnowing fork is in his hand to clear his threshing-floor and to gather the wheat into his barn, but he will burn up the chaff with unquenchable fire." 18And with many other words John exhorted the people and preached the good news to them.

19But when John rebuked Herod the tetrarch because of Herodias, his brother's wife, and all the other evil things he had done, 20Herod added this to them all: He locked John up in prison.

The Baptism and Genealogy of Jesus

21When all the people were being baptised, Jesus was baptised too. And as he was praying, heaven was opened 22and the Holy Spirit descended on him in bodily form like a dove. And a voice came from heaven: "You are my Son, whom I love; with you I am well pleased."

23Now Jesus himself was about thirty years old when he began his ministry. He was the son, so it was thought, of Joseph,

the son of Heli, 24the son of Matthat,
the son of Levi, the son of Melki,
the son of Jannai, the son of Joseph,
25the son of Mattathias, the son of Amos,
the son of Nahum, the son of Esli,
the son of Naggai, 26the son of Maath,
the son of Mattathias, the son of
    Semein,
the son of Josech, the son of Joda,
27the son of Joanan, the son of Rhesa,
the son of Zerubbabel, the son of
    Shealtiel,
the son of Neri, 28the son of Melki,
the son of Addi, the son of Cosam,
the son of Elmadam, the son of Er,
29the son of Joshua, the son of Eliezer,
the son of Jorim, the son of Matthat,
the son of Levi, 30the son of Simeon,
the son of Judah, the son of Joseph,
the son of Jonam, the son of Eliakim,
31the son of Melea, the son of Menna,
the son of Mattatha, the son of Nathan,
the son of David, 32the son of Jesse,
the son of Obed, the son of Boaz,
the son of Salmon,d the son of
    Nahshon,

33the son of Amminadab, the son of
    Ram,e
the son of Hezron, the son of Perez,
the son of Judah, 34the son of Jacob,
the son of Isaac, the son of Abraham,
the son of Terah, the son of Nahor,
35the son of Serug, the son of Reu,
the son of Peleg, the son of Eber,
the son of Shelah, 36the son of Cainan,
the son of Arphaxad, the son of Shem,
the son of Noah, the son of Lamech,
37the son of Methuselah, the son of
    Enoch,
the son of Jared, the son of Mahalalel,
the son of Kenan, 38the son of Enosh,
the son of Seth, the son of Adam,
the son of God.

The Temptation of Jesus

4 Jesus, full of the Holy Spirit, returned from the Jordan and was led by the Spirit in the desert, 2where for forty days he was tempted by the devil. He ate nothing during those days, and at the end of them he was hungry.

3The devil said to him, "If you are the Son of God, tell this stone to become bread."

4Jesus answered, "It is written: 'Man does not live on bread alone.'a"

5The devil led him up to a high place and showed him in an instant all the kingdoms of the world. 6And he said to him, "I will give you all their authority and splendour, for it has been given to me, and I can give it to anyone I want to. 7So if you worship me, it will all be yours."

8Jesus answered, "It is written: 'Worship the Lord your God and serve him only.'b"

9The devil led him to Jerusalem and had him stand on the highest point of the temple. "If you are the Son of God," he said, "throw yourself down from here. 10For it is written:

"'He will command his angels
    concerning you
    to guard you carefully;

d32 Some early manuscripts Sala
e33 Some manuscripts Amminadab, the son of Admin, the son of Arni; other manuscripts vary widely.
a4 Deut. 8:3   b8 Deut. 6:13

[11]they will lift you up in their hands,
so that you will not strike your foot
against a stone.'[c]"

[12]Jesus answered, "It says: 'Do not put the Lord your God to the test.'[d]"

[13]When the devil had finished all this tempting, he left him until an opportune time.

Jesus Rejected at Nazareth

[14]Jesus returned to Galilee in the power of the Spirit, and news about him spread through the whole countryside. [15]He taught in their synagogues, and everyone praised him.

[16]He went to Nazareth, where he had been brought up, and on the Sabbath day he went into the synagogue, as was his custom. And he stood up to read. [17]The scroll of the prophet Isaiah was handed to him. Unrolling it, he found the place where it is written:

[18]"The Spirit of the Lord is on me,
because he has anointed me
to preach good news to the poor.
He has sent me to proclaim freedom for
the prisoners
and recovery of sight for the blind,
to release the oppressed,
[19]   to proclaim the year of the Lord's
favour."[e]

[20]Then he rolled up the scroll, gave it back to the attendant and sat down. The eyes of everyone in the synagogue were fastened on him, [21]and he began by saying to them, "Today this scripture is fulfilled in your hearing."

[22]All spoke well of him and were amazed at the gracious words that came from his lips. "Isn't this Joseph's son?" they asked.

[23]Jesus said to them, "Surely you will quote this proverb to me: 'Physician, heal yourself! Do here in your home town what we have heard that you did in Capernaum.'"

[24]"I tell you the truth," he continued, "no prophet is accepted in his home town. [25]I assure you that there were many widows in Israel in Elijah's time, when the sky was shut for three and a half years and there was a severe famine throughout the land. [26]Yet Elijah was not sent to any of them, but to a widow in Zarephath in the region of Sidon. [27]And there were many in Israel with leprosy[f] in the time of Elisha the prophet, yet not one of them was cleansed—only Naaman the Syrian."

[28]All the people in the synagogue were furious when they heard this. [29]They got up, drove him out of the town, and took him to the brow of the hill on which the town was built, in order to throw him down the cliff. [30]But he walked right through the crowd and went on his way.

Jesus Drives Out an Evil Spirit

[31]Then he went down to Capernaum, a town in Galilee, and on the Sabbath began to teach the people. [32]They were amazed at his teaching, because his message had authority.

[33]In the synagogue there was a man possessed by a demon, an evil[g] spirit. He cried out at the top of his voice, [34]"Ha! What do you want with us, Jesus of Nazareth? Have you come to destroy us? I know who you are—the Holy One of God!"

[35]"Be quiet!" Jesus said sternly. "Come out of him!" Then the demon threw the man down before them all and came out without injuring him.

[36]All the people were amazed and said to each other, "What is this teaching? With authority and power he gives orders to evil spirits and they come out!" [37]And the news about him spread throughout the surrounding area.

Jesus Heals Many

[38]Jesus left the synagogue and went to the home of Simon. Now Simon's mother-in-law was suffering from a high fever, and

---

[c]11 Psalm 91:11,12   [d]12 Deut. 6:16   [e]19 Isaiah 61:1,2
[f]27 The Greek word was used for various diseases affecting the skin—not necessarily leprosy.
[g]33 Greek *unclean*; also in verse 36

they asked Jesus to help her. ³⁹So he bent over her and rebuked the fever, and it left her. She got up at once and began to wait on them.

⁴⁰When the sun was setting, the people brought to Jesus all who had various kinds of sickness, and laying his hands on each one, he healed them. ⁴¹Moreover, demons came out of many people, shouting, "You are the Son of God!" But he rebuked them and would not allow them to speak, because they knew he was the Christ.ʰ

⁴²At daybreak Jesus went out to a solitary place. The people were looking for him and when they came to where he was, they tried to keep him from leaving them. ⁴³But he said, "I must preach the good news of the kingdom of God to the other towns also, because that is why I was sent." ⁴⁴And he kept on preaching in the synagogues of Judea.ⁱ

The Calling of the First Disciples

5 One day as Jesus was standing by the Lake of Gennesaret,ᵃ with the people crowding round him and listening to the word of God, ²he saw at the water's edge two boats, left there by the fishermen, who were washing their nets. ³He got into one of the boats, the one belonging to Simon, and asked him to put out a little from shore. Then he sat down and taught the people from the boat.

⁴When he had finished speaking, he said to Simon, "Put out into deep water, and let downᵇ the nets for a catch."

⁵Simon answered, "Master, we've worked hard all night and haven't caught anything. But because you say so, I will let down the nets."

⁶When they had done so, they caught such a large number of fish that their nets began to break. ⁷So they signalled to their partners in the other boat to come and help them, and they came and filled both boats so full that they began to sink.

⁸When Simon Peter saw this, he fell at Jesus' knees and said, "Go away from me, Lord; I am a sinful man!" ⁹For he and all his companions were astonished at the catch of fish they had taken, ¹⁰and so were James and John, the sons of Zebedee, Simon's partners.

Then Jesus said to Simon, "Don't be afraid; from now on you will catch men." ¹¹So they pulled their boats up on shore, left everything and followed him.

The Man With Leprosy

¹²While Jesus was in one of the towns, a man came along who was covered with leprosy.ᶜ When he saw Jesus, he fell with his face to the ground and begged him, "Lord, if you are willing, you can make me clean."

¹³Jesus reached out his hand and touched the man. "I am willing," he said. "Be clean!" And immediately the leprosy left him.

¹⁴Then Jesus ordered him, "Don't tell anyone, but go, show yourself to the priest and offer the sacrifices that Moses commanded for your cleansing, as a testimony to them."

¹⁵Yet the news about him spread all the more, so that crowds of people came to hear him and to be healed of their sicknesses. ¹⁶But Jesus often withdrew to lonely places and prayed.

Jesus Heals a Paralytic

¹⁷One day as he was teaching, Pharisees and teachers of the law, who had come from every village of Galilee and from Judea and Jerusalem, were sitting there. And the power of the Lord was present for him to heal the sick. ¹⁸Some men came carrying a paralytic on a mat and tried to take him into the house to lay him before Jesus. ¹⁹When they could not find a way to do this because of the crowd, they went up on the roof and lowered him on his mat through the tiles into the middle of the crowd, right in front of Jesus.

²⁰When Jesus saw their faith, he said, "Friend, your sins are forgiven."

²¹The Pharisees and the teachers of the law began thinking to themselves, "Who

ʰ41 Or Messiah   ⁱ44 Or the land of the Jews; some manuscripts Galilee
ᵃ1 That is, Sea of Galilee   ᵇ4 The Greek verb is plural.
ᶜ12 The Greek word was used for various diseases affecting the skin—not necessarily leprosy.

is this fellow who speaks blasphemy? Who can forgive sins but God alone?''

²²Jesus knew what they were thinking and asked, "Why are you thinking these things in your hearts? ²³Which is easier: to say, 'Your sins are forgiven,' or to say, 'Get up and walk'? ²⁴But that you may know that the Son of Man has authority on earth to forgive sins. . . ." He said to the paralysed man, "I tell you, get up, take your mat and go home." ²⁵Immediately he stood up in front of them, took what he had been lying on and went home praising God. ²⁶Everyone was amazed and gave praise to God. They were filled with awe and said, "We have seen remarkable things today."

The Calling of Levi

²⁷After this, Jesus went out and saw a tax collector by the name of Levi sitting at his tax booth. "Follow me," Jesus said to him, ²⁸and Levi got up, left everything and followed him.

²⁹Then Levi held a great banquet for Jesus at his house, and a large crowd of tax collectors and others were eating with them. ³⁰But the Pharisees and the teachers of the law who belonged to their sect complained to his disciples, "Why do you eat and drink with tax collectors and 'sinners'?''

³¹Jesus answered them, "It is not the healthy who need a doctor, but the sick. ³²I have not come to call the righteous, but sinners to repentance."

Jesus Questioned About Fasting

³³They said to him, "John's disciples often fast and pray, and so do the disciples of the Pharisees, but yours go on eating and drinking."

³⁴Jesus answered, "Can you make the guests of the bridegroom fast while he is with them? ³⁵But the time will come when the bridegroom will be taken from them; in those days they will fast."

³⁶He told them this parable: "No-one tears a patch from a new garment and sews it on an old one. If he does, he will have torn the new garment, and the patch from

the new will not match the old. ³⁷And no-one pours new wine into old wineskins. If he does, the new wine will burst the skins, the wine will run out and the wineskins will be ruined. ³⁸No, new wine must be poured into new wineskins. ³⁹And no-one after drinking old wine wants the new, for he says, 'The old is better.'''

Lord of the Sabbath

6 One Sabbath Jesus was going through the cornfields, and his disciples began to pick some ears of corn, rub them in their hands and eat the grain. ²Some of the Pharisees asked, "Why are you doing what is unlawful on the Sabbath?"

³Jesus answered them, "Have you never read what David did when he and his companions were hungry? ⁴He entered the house of God, and taking the consecrated bread, he ate what is lawful only for priests to eat. And he also gave some to his companions." ⁵Then Jesus said to them, "The Son of Man is Lord of the Sabbath."

⁶On another Sabbath he went into the synagogue and was teaching, and a man was there whose right hand was shrivelled. ⁷The Pharisees and the teachers of the law were looking for a reason to accuse Jesus, so they watched him closely to see if he would heal on the Sabbath. ⁸But Jesus knew what they were thinking and said to the man with the shrivelled hand, "Get up and stand in front of everyone." So he got up and stood there.

⁹Then Jesus said to them, "I ask you, which is lawful on the Sabbath: to do good or to do evil, to save life or to destroy it?"

¹⁰He looked round at them all, and then said to the man, "Stretch out your hand." He did so, and his hand was completely restored. ¹¹But they were furious and began to discuss with one another what they might do to Jesus.

The Twelve Apostles

¹²One of those days Jesus went out to a mountainside to pray, and spent the night praying to God. ¹³When morning came, he called his disciples to him and chose

twelve of them, whom he also designated apostles: [14]Simon (whom he named Peter), his brother Andrew, James, John, Philip, Bartholomew, [15]Matthew, Thomas, James son of Alphaeus, Simon who was called the Zealot, [16]Judas son of James, and Judas Iscariot, who became a traitor.

Blessings and Woes

[17]He went down with them and stood on a level place. A large crowd of his disciples was there and a great number of people from all over Judea, from Jerusalem, and from the coast of Tyre and Sidon, [18]who had come to hear him and to be healed of their diseases. Those troubled by evil[a] spirits were cured, [19]and the people all tried to touch him, because power was coming from him and healing them all.

[20]Looking at his disciples, he said:

"Blessed are you who are poor,
    for yours is the kingdom of God.
[21]Blessed are you who hunger now,
    for you will be satisfied.
Blessed are you who weep now,
    for you will laugh.
[22]Blessed are you when men hate you,
    when they exclude you and insult you
    and reject your name as evil,
    because of the Son of Man.

[23]"Rejoice in that day and leap for joy, because great is your reward in heaven. For that is how their fathers treated the prophets.

[24]"But woe to you who are rich,
    for you have already received your
        comfort.
[25]Woe to you who are well fed now,
    for you will go hungry.
Woe to you who laugh now,
    for you will mourn and weep.
[26]Woe to you when all men speak well of
        you,
    for that is how their fathers treated
        the false prophets.

Love for Enemies

[27]"But I tell you who hear me: Love your enemies, do good to those who hate you, [28]bless those who curse you, pray for those who ill-treat you. [29]If someone strikes you on one cheek, turn to him the other also. If someone takes your cloak, do not stop him from taking your tunic. [30]Give to everyone who asks you, and if anyone takes what belongs to you, do not demand it back. [31]Do to others as you would have them do to you.

[32]"If you love those who love you, what credit is that to you? Even 'sinners' love those who love them. [33]And if you do good to those who are good to you, what credit is that to you? Even 'sinners' do that. [34]And if you lend to those from whom you expect repayment, what credit is that to you? Even 'sinners' lend to 'sinners', expecting to be repaid in full. [35]But love your enemies, do good to them, and lend to them without expecting to get anything back. Then your reward will be great, and you will be sons of the Most High, because he is kind to the ungrateful and wicked. [36]Be merciful, just as your Father is merciful.

Judging Others

[37]"Do not judge, and you will not be judged. Do not condemn, and you will not be condemned. Forgive, and you will be forgiven. [38]Give, and it will be given to you. A good measure, pressed down, shaken together and running over, will be poured into your lap. For with the measure you use, it will be measured to you."

[39]He also told them this parable: "Can a blind man lead a blind man? Will they not both fall into a pit? [40]A student is not above his teacher, but everyone who is fully trained will be like his teacher.

[41]"Why do you look at the speck of sawdust in your brother's eye and pay no attention to the plank in your own eye? [42]How can you say to your brother, 'Brother, let me take the speck out of your eye,' when you yourself fail to see the

[a]18 Greek unclean

plank in your own eye? You hypocrite, first take the plank out of your eye, and then you will see clearly to remove the speck from your brother's eye.

A Tree and Its Fruit

43"No good tree bears bad fruit, nor does a bad tree bear good fruit. 44Each tree is recognised by its own fruit. People do not pick figs from thorn-bushes, or grapes from briers. 45The good man brings good things out of the good stored up in his heart, and the evil man brings evil things out of the evil stored up in his heart. For out of the overflow of his heart his mouth speaks.

The Wise and Foolish Builders

46"Why do you call me, 'Lord, Lord,' and do not do what I say? 47I will show you what he is like who comes to me and hears my words and puts them into practice. 48He is like a man building a house, who dug down deep and laid the foundation on rock. When the flood came, the torrent struck that house but could not shake it, because it was well built. 49But the one who hears my words and does not put them into practice is like a man who built a house on the ground without a foundation. The moment the torrent struck that house, it collapsed and its destruction was complete."

The Faith of the Centurion

7 When Jesus had finished saying all this in the hearing of the people, he entered Capernaum. 2There a centurion's servant, whom his master valued highly, was sick and about to die. 3The centurion heard of Jesus and sent some elders of the Jews to him, asking him to come and heal his servant. 4When they came to Jesus, they pleaded earnestly with him, "This man deserves to have you do this, 5because he loves our nation and has built our synagogue." 6So Jesus went with them.

He was not far from the house when the centurion sent friends to say to him: "Lord, don't trouble yourself, for I do not deserve to have you come under my roof. 7That is why I did not even consider myself worthy to come to you. But say the word, and my servant will be healed. 8For I myself am a man under authority, with soldiers under me. I tell this one, 'Go', and he goes; and that one, 'Come', and he comes. I say to my servant, 'Do this', and he does it."

9When Jesus heard this, he was amazed at him, and turning to the crowd following him, he said, "I tell you, I have not found such great faith even in Israel." 10Then the men who had been sent returned to the house and found the servant well.

Jesus Raises a Widow's Son

11Soon afterwards, Jesus went to a town called Nain, and his disciples and a large crowd went along with him. 12As he approached the town gate, a dead person was being carried out—the only son of his mother, and she was a widow. And a large crowd from the town was with her. 13When the Lord saw her, his heart went out to her and he said, "Don't cry."

14Then he went up and touched the coffin, and those carrying it stood still. He said, "Young man, I say to you, get up!" 15The dead man sat up and began to talk, and Jesus gave him back to his mother.

16They were all filled with awe and praised God. "A great prophet has appeared among us," they said. "God has come to help his people." 17This news about Jesus spread throughout Judea[a] and the surrounding country.

Jesus and John the Baptist

18John's disciples told him about all these things. Calling two of them, 19he sent them to the Lord to ask, "Are you the one who was to come, or should we expect someone else?"

20When the men came to Jesus, they said, "John the Baptist sent us to you to

---

a17 Or the land of the Jews

ask, 'Are you the one who was to come, or should we expect someone else?'"

²¹At that very time Jesus cured many who had diseases, sicknesses and evil spirits, and gave sight to many who were blind. ²²So he replied to the messengers, "Go back and report to John what you have seen and heard: The blind receive sight, the lame walk, those who have leprosy*ᵇ* are cured, the deaf hear, the dead are raised, and the good news is preached to the poor. ²³Blessed is the man who does not fall away on account of me."

²⁴After John's messengers left, Jesus began to speak to the crowd about John: "What did you go out into the desert to see? A reed swayed by the wind? ²⁵If not, what did you go out to see? A man dressed in fine clothes? No, those who wear expensive clothes and indulge in luxury are in palaces. ²⁶But what did you go out to see? A prophet? Yes, I tell you, and more than a prophet. ²⁷This is the one about whom it is written:

"'I will send my messenger ahead of you,
　who will prepare your way before
　　you.'*ᶜ*

²⁸I tell you, among those born of women there is no-one greater than John; yet the one who is least in the kingdom of God is greater than he."

(²⁹All the people, even the tax collectors, when they heard Jesus' words, acknowledged that God's way was right, because they had been baptised by John. ³⁰But the Pharisees and experts in the law rejected God's purpose for themselves, because they had not been baptised by John.)

³¹"To what, then, can I compare the people of this generation? What are they like? ³²They are like children sitting in the market-place and calling out to each other:

"'We played the flute for you,
　and you did not dance;
we sang a dirge,
　and you did not cry.'

³³For John the Baptist came neither eating bread nor drinking wine, and you say, 'He has a demon.' ³⁴The Son of Man came eating and drinking, and you say, 'Here is a glutton and a drunkard, a friend of tax collectors and "sinners".' ³⁵But wisdom is proved right by all her children."

Jesus Anointed by a Sinful Woman

³⁶Now one of the Pharisees invited Jesus to have dinner with him, so he went to the Pharisee's house and reclined at the table. ³⁷When a woman who had lived a sinful life in that town learned that Jesus was eating at the Pharisee's house, she brought an alabaster jar of perfume, ³⁸and as she stood behind him at his feet weeping, she began to wet his feet with her tears. Then she wiped them with her hair, kissed them and poured perfume on them.

³⁹When the Pharisee who had invited him saw this, he said to himself, "If this man were a prophet, he would know who is touching him and what kind of woman she is—that she is a sinner."

⁴⁰Jesus answered him, "Simon, I have something to tell you."

"Tell me, teacher," he said.

⁴¹"Two men owed money to a certain money-lender. One owed him five hundred denarii,*ᵈ* and the other fifty. ⁴²Neither of them had the money to pay him back, so he cancelled the debts of both. Now which of them will love him more?"

⁴³Simon replied, "I suppose the one who had the bigger debt cancelled."

"You have judged correctly," Jesus said.

⁴⁴Then he turned towards the woman and said to Simon, "Do you see this woman? I came into your house. You did not give me any water for my feet, but she wet my feet with her tears and wiped them with her hair. ⁴⁵You did not give me a kiss, but this woman, from the time I entered, has not stopped kissing my feet. ⁴⁶You did not put oil on my head, but she has poured

---

b22 The Greek word was used for various diseases affecting the skin—not necessarily leprosy.
c27 Mal. 3:1　　*d41* A denarius was a coin worth about a day's wages.

perfume on my feet. [47]Therefore, I tell you, her many sins have been forgiven— for she loved much. But he who has been forgiven little loves little."

[48]Then Jesus said to her, "Your sins are forgiven."

[49]The other guests began to say among themselves, "Who is this who even forgives sins?"

[50]Jesus said to the woman, "Your faith has saved you; go in peace."

The Parable of the Sower

8 After this, Jesus travelled about from one town and village to another, proclaiming the good news of the kingdom of God. The Twelve were with him, [2]and also some women who had been cured of evil spirits and diseases: Mary (called Magdalene) from whom seven demons had come out; [3]Joanna the wife of Chuza, the manager of Herod's household; Susanna; and many others. These women were helping to support them out of their own means.

[4]While a large crowd was gathering and people were coming to Jesus from town after town, he told this parable: [5]"A farmer went out to sow his seed. As he was scattering the seed, some fell along the path; it was trampled on, and the birds of the air ate it up. [6]Some fell on rock, and when it came up, the plants withered because they had no moisture. [7]Other seed fell among thorns, which grew up with it and choked the plants. [8]Still other seed fell on good soil. It came up and yielded a crop, a hundred times more than was sown."

When he said this, he called out, "He who has ears to hear, let him hear."

[9]His disciples asked him what this parable meant. [10]He said, "The knowledge of the secrets of the kingdom of God has been given to you, but to others I speak in parables, so that,

"'though seeing, they may not see;
  though hearing, they may not
    understand.'[a]

[11]"This is the meaning of the parable: The seed is the word of God. [12]Those along the path are the ones who hear, and then the devil comes and takes away the word from their hearts, so that they may not believe and be saved. [13]Those on the rock are the ones who receive the word with joy when they hear it, but they have no root. They believe for a while, but in the time of testing they fall away. [14]The seed that fell among thorns stands for those who hear, but as they go on their way they are choked by life's worries, riches and pleasures, and they do not mature. [15]But the seed on good soil stands for those with a noble and good heart, who hear the word, retain it, and by persevering produce a crop.

A Lamp on a Stand

[16]"No-one lights a lamp and hides it in a jar or puts it under a bed. Instead, he puts it on a stand, so that those who come in can see the light. [17]For there is nothing hidden that will not be disclosed, and nothing concealed that will not be known or brought out into the open. [18]Therefore consider carefully how you listen. Whoever has will be given more; whoever does not have, even what he thinks he has will be taken from him."

Jesus' Mother and Brothers

[19]Now Jesus' mother and brothers came to see him, but they were not able to get near him because of the crowd. [20]Someone told him, "Your mother and brothers are standing outside, wanting to see you."

[21]He replied, "My mother and brothers are those who hear God's word and put it into practice."

Jesus Calms the Storm

[22]One day Jesus said to his disciples, "Let's go over to the other side of the lake." So they got into a boat and set out. [23]As they sailed, he fell asleep. A squall

[a]10 Isaiah 6:9

came down on the lake, so that the boat was being swamped, and they were in great danger.

²⁴The disciples went and woke him, saying, "Master, Master, we're going to drown!"

He got up and rebuked the wind and the raging waters; the storm subsided, and all was calm. ²⁵"Where is your faith?" he asked his disciples.

In fear and amazement they asked one another, "Who is this? He commands even the winds and the water, and they obey him."

The Healing of a Demon-possessed Man

²⁶They sailed to the region of the Gerasenes,^b which is across the lake from Galilee. ²⁷When Jesus stepped ashore, he was met by a demon-possessed man from the town. For a long time this man had not worn clothes or lived in a house, but had lived in the tombs. ²⁸When he saw Jesus, he cried out and fell at his feet, shouting at the top of his voice, "What do you want with me, Jesus, Son of the Most High God? I beg you, don't torture me!" ²⁹For Jesus had commanded the evil^c spirit to come out of the man. Many times it had seized him, and though he was chained hand and foot and kept under guard, he had broken his chains and had been driven by the demon into solitary places.

³⁰Jesus asked him, "What is your name?"

"Legion," he replied, because many demons had gone into him. ³¹And they begged him repeatedly not to order them to go into the Abyss.

³²A large herd of pigs was feeding there on the hillside. The demons begged Jesus to let them go into them, and he gave them permission. ³³When the demons came out of the man, they went into the pigs, and the herd rushed down the steep bank into the lake and was drowned.

³⁴When those tending the pigs saw what had happened, they ran off and reported this in the town and countryside, ³⁵and the people went out to see what had

happened. When they came to Jesus, they found the man from whom the demons had gone out, sitting at Jesus' feet, dressed and in his right mind; and they were afraid. ³⁶Those who had seen it told the people how the demon-possessed man had been cured. ³⁷Then all the people of the region of the Gerasenes asked Jesus to leave them, because they were overcome with fear. So he got into the boat and left.

³⁸The man from whom the demons had gone out begged to go with him, but Jesus sent him away, saying, ³⁹"Return home and tell how much God has done for you." So the man went away and told all over the town how much Jesus had done for him.

A Dead Girl and a Sick Woman

⁴⁰Now when Jesus returned, a crowd welcomed him, for they were all expecting him. ⁴¹Then a man named Jairus, a ruler of the synagogue, came and fell at Jesus' feet, pleading with him to come to his house ⁴²because his only daughter, a girl of about twelve, was dying.

As Jesus was on his way, the crowds almost crushed him. ⁴³And a woman was there who had been subject to bleeding for twelve years,^d but no-one could heal her. ⁴⁴She came up behind him and touched the edge of his cloak, and immediately her bleeding stopped.

⁴⁵"Who touched me?" Jesus asked.

When they all denied it, Peter said, "Master, the people are crowding and pressing against you."

⁴⁶But Jesus said, "Someone touched me; I know that power has gone out from me."

⁴⁷Then the woman, seeing that she could not go unnoticed, came trembling and fell at his feet. In the presence of all the people, she told why she had touched him and how she had been instantly healed. ⁴⁸Then he said to her, "Daughter, your faith has healed you. Go in peace."

⁴⁹While Jesus was still speaking, someone came from the house of Jairus, the synagogue ruler. "Your daughter is dead," he said. "Don't bother the teacher any more."

---

b26 Some manuscripts *Gadarenes*; other manuscripts *Gergesenes*; also in verse 37
c29 Greek *unclean*   d43 Many manuscripts *years, and she had spent all she had on doctors*

⁵⁰Hearing this, Jesus said to Jairus, "Don't be afraid; just believe, and she will be healed."

⁵¹When he arrived at the house of Jairus, he did not let anyone go in with him except Peter, John and James, and the child's father and mother. ⁵²Meanwhile, all the people were wailing and mourning for her. "Stop wailing," Jesus said. "She is not dead but asleep."

⁵³They laughed at him, knowing that she was dead. ⁵⁴But he took her by the hand and said, "My child, get up!" ⁵⁵Her spirit returned, and at once she stood up. Then Jesus told them to give her something to eat. ⁵⁶Her parents were astonished, but he ordered them not to tell anyone what had happened.

Jesus Sends Out the Twelve

9 When Jesus had called the Twelve together, he gave them power and authority to drive out all demons and to cure diseases, ²and he sent them out to preach the kingdom of God and to heal the sick. ³He told them: "Take nothing for the journey—no staff, no bag, no bread, no money, no extra tunic. ⁴Whatever house you enter, stay there until you leave that town. ⁵If people do not welcome you, shake the dust off your feet when you leave their town, as a testimony against them." ⁶So they set out and went from village to village, preaching the gospel and healing people everywhere.

⁷Now Herod the tetrarch heard about all that was going on. And he was perplexed, because some were saying that John had been raised from the dead, ⁸others that Elijah had appeared, and still others that one of the prophets of long ago had come back to life. ⁹But Herod said, "I beheaded John. Who, then, is this I hear such things about?" And he tried to see him.

Jesus Feeds the Five Thousand

¹⁰When the apostles returned, they reported to Jesus what they had done. Then he took them with him and they withdrew by themselves to a town called Bethsaida, ¹¹but the crowds learned about it and followed him. He welcomed them and spoke to them about the kingdom of God, and healed those who needed healing.

¹²Late in the afternoon the Twelve came to him and said, "Send the crowd away so they can go to the surrounding villages and countryside and find food and lodging, because we are in a remote place here."

¹³He replied, "You give them something to eat."

They answered, "We have only five loaves of bread and two fish—unless we go and buy food for all this crowd." ¹⁴(About five thousand men were there.)

But he said to his disciples, "Make them sit down in groups of about fifty each." ¹⁵The disciples did so, and everybody sat down. ¹⁶Taking the five loaves and the two fish and looking up to heaven, he gave thanks and broke them. Then he gave them to the disciples to set before the people. ¹⁷They all ate and were satisfied, and the disciples picked up twelve basketfuls of broken pieces that were left over.

Peter's Confession of Christ

¹⁸Once when Jesus was praying in private and his disciples were with him, he asked them, "Who do the crowds say I am?"

¹⁹They replied, "Some say John the Baptist; others say Elijah; and still others, that one of the prophets of long ago has come back to life."

²⁰"But what about you?" he asked. "Who do you say I am?"

Peter answered, "The Christ*a* of God."

²¹Jesus strictly warned them not to tell this to anyone. ²²And he said, "The Son of Man must suffer many things and be rejected by the elders, chief priests and teachers of the law, and he must be killed and on the third day be raised to life."

²³Then he said to them all: "If anyone would come after me, he must deny himself and take up his cross daily and follow me. ²⁴For whoever wants to save his life

a20 Or Messiah

will lose it, but whoever loses his life for me will save it. 25What good is it for a man to gain the whole world, and yet lose or forfeit his very self? 26If anyone is ashamed of me and my words, the Son of Man will be ashamed of him when he comes in his glory and in the glory of the Father and of the holy angels. 27I tell you the truth, some who are standing here will not taste death before they see the kingdom of God."

The Transfiguration

28About eight days after Jesus said this, he took Peter, John and James with him and went up onto a mountain to pray. 29As he was praying, the appearance of his face changed, and his clothes became as bright as a flash of lightning. 30Two men, Moses and Elijah, 31appeared in glorious splendour, talking with Jesus. They spoke about his departure, which he was about to bring to fulfilment at Jerusalem. 32Peter and his companions were very sleepy, but when they became fully awake, they saw his glory and the two men standing with him. 33As the men were leaving Jesus, Peter said to him, "Master, it is good for us to be here. Let us put up three shelters—one for you, one for Moses and one for Elijah." (He did not know what he was saying.)

34While he was speaking, a cloud appeared and enveloped them, and they were afraid as they entered the cloud. 35A voice came from the cloud, saying, "This is my Son, whom I have chosen; listen to him." 36When the voice had spoken, they found that Jesus was alone. The disciples kept this to themselves, and told no-one at that time what they had seen.

The Healing of a Boy With an Evil Spirit

37The next day, when they came down from the mountain, a large crowd met him. 38A man in the crowd called out, "Teacher, I beg you to look at my son, for he is my only child. 39A spirit seizes him and he suddenly screams; it throws him into convulsions so that he foams at the

mouth. It scarcely ever leaves him and is destroying him. 40I begged your disciples to drive it out, but they could not."

41"O unbelieving and perverse generation," Jesus replied, "how long shall I stay with you and put up with you? Bring your son here."

42Even while the boy was coming, the demon threw him to the ground in a convulsion. But Jesus rebuked the evil*b* spirit, healed the boy and gave him back to his father. 43And they were all amazed at the greatness of God.

While everyone was marvelling at all that Jesus did, he said to his disciples, 44"Listen carefully to what I am about to tell you: The Son of Man is going to be betrayed into the hands of men." 45But they did not understand what this meant. It was hidden from them, so that they did not grasp it, and they were afraid to ask him about it.

Who Will Be the Greatest?

46An argument started among the disciples as to which of them would be the greatest. 47Jesus, knowing their thoughts, took a little child and made him stand beside him. 48Then he said to them, "Whoever welcomes this little child in my name welcomes me; and whoever welcomes me welcomes the one who sent me. For he who is least among you all—he is the greatest."

49"Master," said John, "we saw a man driving out demons in your name and we tried to stop him, because he is not one of us."

50"Do not stop him," Jesus said, "for whoever is not against you is for you."

Samaritan Opposition

51As the time approached for him to be taken up to heaven, Jesus resolutely set out for Jerusalem. 52And he sent messengers on ahead, who went into a Samaritan village to get things ready for him; 53but the people there did not welcome him, because he was heading for Jerusalem. 54When the disciples James and John saw this, they asked, "Lord, do you want us to call fire down from heaven to destroy them?"*c* 55But Jesus turned and rebuked them, 56and*d* they went to another village.

The Cost of Following Jesus

57As they were walking along the road, a man said to him, "I will follow you wherever you go."

58Jesus replied, "Foxes have holes and birds of the air have nests, but the Son of Man has nowhere to lay his head."

59He said to another man, "Follow me."

But the man replied, "Lord, first let me go and bury my father."

60Jesus said to him, "Let the dead bury their own dead, but you go and proclaim the kingdom of God."

61Still another said, "I will follow you, Lord; but first let me go back and say good-bye to my family."

62Jesus replied, "No-one who puts his hand to the plough and looks back is fit for service in the kingdom of God."

Jesus Sends Out the Seventy-two

10 After this the Lord appointed seventy-two*a* others and sent them two by two ahead of him to every town and place where he was about to go. 2He told them, "The harvest is plentiful, but the workers are few. Ask the Lord of the harvest, therefore, to send out workers into his harvest field. 3Go! I am sending you out like lambs among wolves. 4Do not take a purse or bag or sandals; and do not greet anyone on the road.

5"When you enter a house, first say, 'Peace to this house.' 6If a man of peace is there, your peace will rest on him; if not, it will return to you. 7Stay in that house, eating and drinking whatever they give you, for the worker deserves his wages. Do not move around from house to house.

8"When you enter a town and are welcomed, eat what is set before you. 9Heal the sick who are there and tell them, 'The kingdom of God is near you.' 10But when you enter a town and are not welcomed, go into its streets and say, 11'Even the dust of your town that sticks to our feet we wipe off against you. Yet be sure of this: The kingdom of God is near.' 12I tell you, it will be more bearable on that day for Sodom than for that town.

13"Woe to you, Korazin! Woe to you, Bethsaida! For if the miracles that were performed in you had been performed in Tyre and Sidon, they would have repented long ago, sitting in sackcloth and ashes. 14But it will be more bearable for Tyre and Sidon at the judgment than for you. 15And you, Capernaum, will you be lifted up to the skies? No, you will go down to the depths.*b*

16"He who listens to you listens to me; he who rejects you rejects me; but he who rejects me rejects him who sent me."

17The seventy-two returned with joy and said, "Lord, even the demons submit to us in your name."

18He replied, "I saw Satan fall like lightning from heaven. 19I have given you authority to trample on snakes and scorpions and to overcome all the power of the enemy; nothing will harm you. 20However, do not rejoice that the spirits submit to you, but rejoice that your names are written in heaven."

21At that time Jesus, full of joy through the Holy Spirit, said, "I praise you, Father, Lord of heaven and earth, because you have hidden these things from the wise and learned, and revealed them to little children. Yes, Father, for this was your good pleasure.

22"All things have been committed to me by my Father. No-one knows who the Son is except the Father, and no-one knows who the Father is except the Son and those to whom the Son chooses to reveal him."

23Then he turned to his disciples and said privately, "Blessed are the eyes that see what you see. 24For I tell you that

---

c54 Some manuscripts *them, even as Elijah did*
d55,56 Some manuscripts *them. And he said, "You do not know what kind of spirit you are of, for the Son of Man did not come to destroy men's lives, but to save them." 56And*   *a1* Some manuscripts *seventy*; also in verse 17
b15 Greek *Hades*

many prophets and kings wanted to see what you see but did not see it, and to hear what you hear but did not hear it."

The Parable of the Good Samaritan

²⁵On one occasion an expert in the law stood up to test Jesus. "Teacher," he asked, "what must I do to inherit eternal life?"

²⁶"What is written in the Law?" he replied. "How do you read it?"

²⁷He answered: "'Love the Lord your God with all your heart and with all your soul and with all your strength and with all your mind';*c* and, 'Love your neighbour as yourself.'*d*"

²⁸"You have answered correctly," Jesus replied. "Do this and you will live."

²⁹But he wanted to justify himself, so he asked Jesus, "And who is my neighbour?"

³⁰In reply Jesus said: "A man was going down from Jerusalem to Jericho, when he fell into the hands of robbers. They stripped him of his clothes, beat him and went away, leaving him half-dead. ³¹A priest happened to be going down the same road, and when he saw the man, he passed by on the other side. ³²So too, a Levite, when he came to the place and saw him, passed by on the other side. ³³But a Samaritan, as he travelled, came where the man was; and when he saw him, he took pity on him. ³⁴He went to him and bandaged his wounds, pouring on oil and wine. Then he put the man on his own donkey, brought him to an inn and took care of him. ³⁵The next day he took out two silver coins*e* and gave them to the innkeeper. 'Look after him,' he said, 'and when I return, I will reimburse you for any extra expense you may have.'

³⁶"Which of these three do you think was a neighbour to the man who fell into the hands of robbers?"

³⁷The expert in the law replied, "The one who had mercy on him."

Jesus told him, "Go and do likewise."

At the Home of Martha and Mary

³⁸As Jesus and his disciples were on their way, he came to a village where a woman named Martha opened her home to him. ³⁹She had a sister called Mary, who sat at the Lord's feet listening to what he said. ⁴⁰But Martha was distracted by all the preparations that had to be made. She came to him and asked, "Lord, don't you care that my sister has left me to do the work by myself? Tell her to help me!"

⁴¹"Martha, Martha," the Lord answered, "you are worried and upset about many things, ⁴²but only one thing is needed.*f* Mary has chosen what is better, and it will not be taken away from her."

Jesus' Teaching on Prayer

11 One day Jesus was praying in a certain place. When he finished, one of his disciples said to him, "Lord, teach us to pray, just as John taught his disciples."

²He said to them, "When you pray, say:

"'Father,*a*
hallowed be your name,
your kingdom come.*b*
³Give us each day our daily bread.
⁴Forgive us our sins,
    for we also forgive everyone who sins
        against us.*c*
And lead us not into temptation.'"*d*

⁵Then he said to them, "Suppose one of you has a friend, and he goes to him at midnight and says, 'Friend, lend me three loaves of bread, ⁶because a friend of mine on a journey has come to me, and I have nothing to set before him.'

⁷"Then the one inside answers, 'Don't bother me. The door is already locked, and my children are with me in bed. I can't get up and give you anything.' ⁸I tell you, though he will not get up and give him the bread because he is his friend, yet because of the man's boldness*e* he will get up and give him as much as he needs.

---

c27 Deut. 6:5   *d27* Lev. 19:18   *e35* Greek *two denarii*
f42 Some manuscripts *but few things are needed—or only one*   *a2* Some manuscripts *Our Father in heaven*
b2 Some manuscripts *come. May your will be done on earth as it is in heaven.*   *c4* Greek *everyone who is indebted to us*
d4 Some manuscripts *temptation but deliver us from the evil one*   *e8* Or *persistence*

9"So I say to you: Ask and it will be given to you; seek and you will find; knock and the door will be opened to you. 10For everyone who asks receives; he who seeks finds; and to him who knocks, the door will be opened.

11"Which of you fathers, if your son asks for*f* a fish, will give him a snake instead? 12Or if he asks for an egg, will give him a scorpion? 13If you then, though you are evil, know how to give good gifts to your children, how much more will your Father in heaven give the Holy Spirit to those who ask him!"

Jesus and Beelzebub

14Jesus was driving out a demon that was mute. When the demon left, the man who had been mute spoke, and the crowd was amazed. 15But some of them said, "By Beelzebub,*g* the prince of demons, he is driving out demons." 16Others tested him by asking for a sign from heaven.

17Jesus knew their thoughts and said to them: "Any kingdom divided against itself will be ruined, and a house divided against itself will fall. 18If Satan is divided against himself, how can his kingdom stand? I say this because you claim that I drive out demons by Beelzebub. 19Now if I drive out demons by Beelzebub, by whom do your followers drive them out? So then, they will be your judges. 20But if I drive out demons by the finger of God, then the kingdom of God has come to you.

21"When a strong man, fully armed, guards his own house, his possessions are safe. 22But when someone stronger attacks and overpowers him, he takes away the armour in which the man trusted and divides up the spoils.

23"He who is not with me is against me, and he who does not gather with me, scatters.

24"When an evil*h* spirit comes out of a man, it goes through arid places seeking rest and does not find it. Then it says, 'I will return to the house I left.' 25When it arrives, it finds the house swept clean and put in order. 26Then it goes and takes seven other spirits more wicked than itself, and they go in and live there. And the final condition of that man is worse than the first."

27As Jesus was saying these things, a woman in the crowd called out, "Blessed is the mother who gave you birth and nursed you."

28He replied, "Blessed rather are those who hear the word of God and obey it."

The Sign of Jonah

29As the crowds increased, Jesus said, "This is a wicked generation. It asks for a miraculous sign, but none will be given it except the sign of Jonah. 30For as Jonah was a sign to the Ninevites, so also will the Son of Man be to this generation. 31The Queen of the South will rise at the judgment with the men of this generation and condemn them; for she came from the ends of the earth to listen to Solomon's wisdom, and now one*i* greater than Solomon is here. 32The men of Nineveh will stand up at the judgment with this generation and condemn it; for they repented at the preaching of Jonah, and now one greater than Jonah is here.

The Lamp of the Body

33"No-one lights a lamp and puts it in a place where it will be hidden, or under a bowl. Instead he puts it on its stand, so that those who come in may see the light. 34Your eye is the lamp of your body. When your eyes are good, your whole body also is full of light. But when they are bad, your body also is full of darkness. 35See to it, then, that the light within you is not darkness. 36Therefore, if your whole body is full of light, and no part of it dark, it will be completely lighted, as when the light of a lamp shines on you."

Six Woes

37When Jesus had finished speaking, a Pharisee invited him to eat with him; so he

---

f11 Some manuscripts *for bread, will give him a stone; or if he asks for*
g15 Greek *Beezeboul* or *Beelzeboul*; also in verses 18 and 19   *h24* Greek *unclean*
i31 Or *something*; also in verse 32

went in and reclined at the table. ³⁸But the Pharisee, noticing that Jesus did not first wash before the meal, was surprised.

³⁹Then the Lord said to him, "Now then, you Pharisees clean the outside of the cup and dish, but inside you are full of greed and wickedness. ⁴⁰You foolish people! Did not the one who made the outside make the inside also? ⁴¹But give what is inside ˻the dish˼ʲ to the poor, and everything will be clean for you.

⁴²"Woe to you Pharisees, because you give God a tenth of your mint, rue and all other kinds of garden herbs, but you neglect justice and the love of God. You should have practised the latter without leaving the former undone.

⁴³"Woe to you Pharisees, because you love the most important seats in the synagogues and greetings in the marketplaces.

⁴⁴"Woe to you, because you are like unmarked graves, which men walk over without knowing it."

⁴⁵One of the experts in the law answered him, "Teacher, when you say these things, you insult us also."

⁴⁶Jesus replied, "And you experts in the law, woe to you, because you load people down with burdens they can hardly carry, and you yourselves will not lift one finger to help them.

⁴⁷"Woe to you, because you build tombs for the prophets, and it was your forefathers who killed them. ⁴⁸So you testify that you approve of what your forefathers did; they killed the prophets, and you build their tombs. ⁴⁹Because of this, God in his wisdom said, 'I will send them prophets and apostles, some of whom they will kill and others they will persecute.' ⁵⁰Therefore this generation will be held responsible for the blood of all the prophets that has been shed since the beginning of the world, ⁵¹from the blood of Abel to the blood of Zechariah, who was killed between the altar and the sanctuary. Yes, I tell you, this generation will be held responsible for it all.

⁵²"Woe to you experts in the law, because you have taken away the key to knowledge. You yourselves have not entered, and you have hindered those who were entering."

⁵³When Jesus left there, the Pharisees and the teachers of the law began to oppose him fiercely and to besiege him with questions, ⁵⁴waiting to catch him in something he might say.

Warnings and Encouragements

12 Meanwhile, when a crowd of many thousands had gathered, so that they were trampling on one another, Jesus began to speak first to his disciples, saying: "Be on your guard against the yeast of the Pharisees, which is hypocrisy. ²There is nothing concealed that will not be disclosed, or hidden that will not be made known. ³What you have said in the dark will be heard in the daylight, and what you have whispered in the ear in the inner rooms will be proclaimed from the roofs.

⁴"I tell you, my friends, do not be afraid of those who kill the body and after that can do no more. ⁵But I will show you whom you should fear: Fear him who, after the killing of the body, has power to throw you into hell. Yes, I tell you, fear him. ⁶Are not five sparrows sold for two pennies?ᵃ Yet not one of them is forgotten by God. ⁷Indeed, the very hairs of your head are all numbered. Don't be afraid; you are worth more than many sparrows.

⁸"I tell you, whoever acknowledges me before men, the Son of Man will also acknowledge him before the angels of God. ⁹But he who disowns me before men will be disowned before the angels of God. ¹⁰And everyone who speaks a word against the Son of Man will be forgiven, but anyone who blasphemes against the Holy Spirit will not be forgiven.

¹¹"When you are brought before synagogues, rulers and authorities, do not worry about how you will defend yourselves or what you will say, ¹²for the Holy Spirit will teach you at that time what you should say."

ʲ41 Or what you have   ᵃ6 Greek two assaria

The Parable of the Rich Fool

13Someone in the crowd said to him, "Teacher, tell my brother to divide the inheritance with me."

14Jesus replied, "Man, who appointed me a judge or an arbiter between you?" 15Then he said to them, "Watch out! Be on your guard against all kinds of greed; a man's life does not consist in the abundance of his possessions."

16And he told them this parable: "The ground of a certain rich man produced a good crop. 17He thought to himself, 'What shall I do? I have no place to store my crops.'

18"Then he said, 'This is what I'll do. I will tear down my barns and build bigger ones, and there I will store all my grain and my goods. 19And I'll say to myself, "You have plenty of good things laid up for many years. Take life easy; eat, drink and be merry."'

20"But God said to him, 'You fool! This very night your life will be demanded from you. Then who will get what you have prepared for yourself?'

21"This is how it will be with anyone who stores up things for himself but is not rich towards God."

Do Not Worry

22Then Jesus said to his disciples: "Therefore I tell you, do not worry about your life, what you will eat; or about your body, what you will wear. 23Life is more than food, and the body more than clothes. 24Consider the ravens: They do not sow or reap, they have no storeroom or barn; yet God feeds them. And how much more valuable you are than birds! 25Who of you by worrying can add a single hour to his life?b 26Since you cannot do this very little thing, why do you worry about the rest?

27"Consider how the lilies grow. They do not labour or spin. Yet I tell you, not even Solomon in all his splendour was dressed like one of these. 28If that is how God clothes the grass of the field, which is

here today, and tomorrow is thrown into the fire, how much more will he clothe you, O you of little faith! 29And do not set your heart on what you will eat or drink; do not worry about it. 30For the pagan world runs after all such things, and your Father knows that you need them. 31But seek his kingdom, and these things will be given to you as well.

32"Do not be afraid, little flock, for your Father has been pleased to give you the kingdom. 33Sell your possessions and give to the poor. Provide purses for yourselves that will not wear out, a treasure in heaven that will not be exhausted, where no thief comes near and no moth destroys. 34For where your treasure is, there your heart will be also.

Watchfulness

35"Be dressed ready for service and keep your lamps burning, 36like men waiting for their master to return from a wedding banquet, so that when he comes and knocks they can immediately open the door for him. 37It will be good for those servants whose master finds them watching when he comes. I tell you the truth, he will dress himself to serve, will have them recline at the table and will come and wait on them. 38It will be good for those servants whose master finds them ready, even if he comes in the second or third watch of the night. 39But understand this: If the owner of the house had known at what hour the thief was coming, he would not have let his house be broken into. 40You also must be ready, because the Son of Man will come at an hour when you do not expect him."

41Peter asked, "Lord, are you telling this parable to us, or to everyone?"

42The Lord answered, "Who then is the faithful and wise manager, whom the master puts in charge of his servants to give them their food allowance at the proper time? 43It will be good for that servant whom the master finds doing so when he returns. 44I tell you the truth, he will put him in charge of all his possessions. 45But

---

b25 Or *single cubit to his height*

suppose the servant says to himself, 'My master is taking a long time in coming,' and he then begins to beat the menservants and maidservants and to eat and drink and get drunk. ⁴⁶The master of that servant will come on a day when he does not expect him and at an hour he is not aware of. He will cut him to pieces and assign him a place with the unbelievers.

⁴⁷"That servant who knows his master's will and does not get ready or does not do what his master wants will be beaten with many blows. ⁴⁸But the one who does not know and does things deserving punishment will be beaten with few blows. From everyone who has been given much, much will be demanded; and from the one who has been entrusted with much, much more will be asked.

Not Peace but Division

⁴⁹"I have come to bring fire on the earth, and how I wish it were already kindled! ⁵⁰But I have a baptism to undergo, and how distressed I am until it is completed! ⁵¹Do you think I came to bring peace on earth? No, I tell you, but division. ⁵²From now on there will be five in one family divided against each other, three against two and two against three. ⁵³They will be divided, father against son and son against father, mother against daughter and daughter against mother, mother-in-law against daughter-in-law and daughter-in-law against mother-in-law."

Interpreting the Times

⁵⁴He said to the crowd: "When you see a cloud rising in the west, immediately you say, 'It's going to rain,' and it does. ⁵⁵And when the south wind blows, you say, 'It's going to be hot,' and it is. ⁵⁶Hypocrites! You know how to interpret the appearance of the earth and the sky. How is it that you don't know how to interpret this present time?

⁵⁷"Why don't you judge for yourselves what is right? ⁵⁸As you are going with your adversary to the magistrate, try hard to be reconciled to him on the way, or he may drag you off to the judge, and the judge turn you over to the officer, and the officer throw you into prison. ⁵⁹I tell you, you will not get out until you have paid the last penny."ᶜ

Repent or Perish

13 Now there were some present at that time who told Jesus about the Galileans whose blood Pilate had mixed with their sacrifices. ²Jesus answered, "Do you think that these Galileans were worse sinners than all the other Galileans because they suffered this way? ³I tell you, no! But unless you repent, you too will all perish. ⁴Or those eighteen who died when the tower in Siloam fell on them—do you think they were more guilty than all the others living in Jerusalem? ⁵I tell you, no! But unless you repent, you too will all perish."

⁶Then he told this parable: "A man had a fig-tree, planted in his vineyard, and he went to look for fruit on it, but did not find any. ⁷So he said to the man who took care of the vineyard, 'For three years now I've been coming to look for fruit on this fig-tree and haven't found any. Cut it down! Why should it use up the soil?'

⁸"'Sir,' the man replied, 'leave it alone for one more year, and I'll dig round it and fertilise it. ⁹If it bears fruit next year, fine! If not, then cut it down.'"

A Crippled Woman Healed on the Sabbath

¹⁰On a Sabbath Jesus was teaching in one of the synagogues, ¹¹and a woman was there who had been crippled by a spirit for eighteen years. She was bent over and could not straighten up at all. ¹²When Jesus saw her, he called her forward and said to her, "Woman, you are set free from your infirmity." ¹³Then he put his hands on her, and immediately she straightened up and praised God.

¹⁴Indignant because Jesus had healed

ᶜ59 Greek lepton

on the Sabbath, the synagogue ruler said to the people, "There are six days for work. So come and be healed on those days, not on the Sabbath."

[15]The Lord answered him, "You hypocrites! Doesn't each of you on the Sabbath untie his ox or donkey from the stall and lead it out to give it water? [16]Then should not this woman, a daughter of Abraham, whom Satan has kept bound for eighteen long years, be set free on the Sabbath day from what bound her?"

[17]When he said this, all his opponents were humiliated, but the people were delighted with all the wonderful things he was doing.

The Parables of the Mustard Seed and the Yeast

[18]Then Jesus asked, "What is the kingdom of God like? What shall I compare it to? [19]It is like a mustard seed, which a man took and planted in his garden. It grew and became a tree, and the birds of the air perched in its branches."

[20]Again he asked, "What shall I compare the kingdom of God to? [21]It is like yeast that a woman took and mixed into a large amount[a] of flour until it worked all through the dough."

The Narrow Door

[22]Then Jesus went through the towns and villages, teaching as he made his way to Jerusalem. [23]Someone asked him, "Lord, are only a few people going to be saved?"

He said to them, [24]"Make every effort to enter through the narrow door, because many, I tell you, will try to enter and will not be able to. [25]Once the owner of the house gets up and closes the door, you will stand outside knocking and pleading, 'Sir, open the door for us.'

"But he will answer, 'I don't know you or where you come from.'

[26]"Then you will say, 'We ate and drank with you, and you taught in our streets.'

[27]"But he will reply, 'I don't know you or where you come from. Away from me, all you evildoers!'

[28]"There will be weeping there, and gnashing of teeth, when you see Abraham, Isaac and Jacob and all the prophets in the kingdom of God, but you yourselves thrown out. [29]People will come from east and west and north and south, and will take their places at the feast in the kingdom of God. [30]Indeed there are those who are last who will be first, and first who will be last."

Jesus' Sorrow for Jerusalem

[31]At that time some Pharisees came to Jesus and said to him, "Leave this place and go somewhere else. Herod wants to kill you."

[32]He replied, "Go tell that fox, 'I will drive out demons and heal people today and tomorrow, and on the third day I will reach my goal.' [33]In any case, I must keep going today and tomorrow and the next day—for surely no prophet can die outside Jerusalem!

[34]"O Jerusalem, Jerusalem, you who kill the prophets and stone those sent to you, how often I have longed to gather your children together, as a hen gathers her chicks under her wings, but you were not willing! [35]Look, your house is left to you desolate. I tell you, you will not see me again until you say, 'Blessed is he who comes in the name of the Lord.'[b]"

Jesus at a Pharisee's House

14 One Sabbath, when Jesus went to eat in the house of a prominent Pharisee, he was being carefully watched. [2]There in front of him was a man suffering from dropsy. [3]Jesus asked the Pharisees and experts in the law, "Is it lawful to heal on the Sabbath or not?" [4]But they remained silent. So taking hold of the man, he healed him and sent him away.

[5]Then he asked them, "If one of you has a son[a] or an ox that falls into a well on the Sabbath day, will you not immediately pull him out?" [6]And they had nothing to say.

[7]When he noticed how the guests picked

---

[a]21 Greek *three satas* (probably about ⅗ bushel or 22 litres)   [b]35 Psalm 118:26   [a]5 Some manuscripts *donkey*

the places of honour at the table, he told them this parable: 8"When someone invites you to a wedding feast, do not take the place of honour, for a person more distinguished than you may have been invited. 9If so, the host who invited both of you will come and say to you, 'Give this man your seat.' Then, humiliated, you will have to take the least important place. 10But when you are invited, take the lowest place, so that when your host comes, he will say to you, 'Friend, move up to a better place.' Then you will be honoured in the presence of all your fellow guests. 11For everyone who exalts himself will be humbled, and he who humbles himself will be exalted."

12Then Jesus said to his host, "When you give a luncheon or dinner, do not invite your friends, your brothers or relatives, or your rich neighbours; if you do, they may invite you back and so you will be repaid. 13But when you give a banquet, invite the poor, the crippled, the lame, the blind, 14and you will be blessed. Although they cannot repay you, you will be repaid at the resurrection of the righteous."

The Parable of the Great Banquet

15When one of those at the table with him heard this, he said to Jesus, "Blessed is the man who will eat at the feast in the kingdom of God."

16Jesus replied: "A certain man was preparing a great banquet and invited many guests. 17At the time of the banquet he sent his servant to tell those who had been invited, 'Come, for everything is now ready.'

18"But they all alike began to make excuses. The first said, 'I have just bought a field, and I must go and see it. Please excuse me.'

19"Another said, 'I have just bought five yoke of oxen, and I'm on my way to try them out. Please excuse me.'

20"Still another said, 'I have just got married, so I can't come.'

21"The servant came back and reported this to his master. Then the owner of the house became angry and ordered his servant, 'Go out quickly into the streets and alleys of the town and bring in the poor, the crippled, the blind and the lame.'

22"'Sir,' the servant said, 'what you ordered has been done, but there is still room.'

23"Then the master told his servant, 'Go out to the roads and country lanes and make them come in, so that my house will be full. 24I tell you, not one of those men who were invited will get a taste of my banquet.'"

The Cost of Being a Disciple

25Large crowds were travelling with Jesus, and turning to them he said: 26"If anyone comes to me and does not hate his father and mother, his wife and children, his brothers and sisters—yes, even his own life—he cannot be my disciple. 27And anyone who does not carry his cross and follow me cannot be my disciple.

28"Suppose one of you wants to build a tower. Will he not first sit down and estimate the cost to see if he has enough money to complete it? 29For if he lays the foundation and is not able to finish it, everyone who sees it will ridicule him, 30saying, 'This fellow began to build and was not able to finish.'

31"Or suppose a king is about to go to war against another king. Will he not first sit down and consider whether he is able with ten thousand men to oppose the one coming against him with twenty thousand? 32If he is not able, he will send a delegation while the other is still a long way off and will ask for terms of peace. 33In the same way, any of you who does not give up everything he has cannot be my disciple.

34"Salt is good, but if it loses its saltiness, how can it be made salty again? 35It is fit neither for the soil nor for the manure heap; it is thrown out.

"He who has ears to hear, let him hear."

The Parable of the Lost Sheep

15 Now the tax collectors and "sinners" were all gathering round to hear him. 2But the Pharisees and the

teachers of the law muttered, "This man welcomes sinners, and eats with them."

³Then Jesus told them this parable: ⁴"Suppose one of you has a hundred sheep and loses one of them. Does he not leave the ninety-nine in the open country and go after the lost sheep until he finds it? ⁵And when he finds it, he joyfully puts it on his shoulders ⁶and goes home. Then he calls his friends and neighbours together and says, 'Rejoice with me; I have found my lost sheep.' ⁷I tell you that in the same way there will be more rejoicing in heaven over one sinner who repents than over ninety-nine righteous persons who do not need to repent.

The Parable of the Lost Coin

⁸"Or suppose a woman has ten silver coins*ᵃ* and loses one. Does she not light a lamp, sweep the house and search carefully until she finds it? ⁹And when she finds it, she calls her friends and neighbours together and says, 'Rejoice with me; I have found my lost coin.' ¹⁰In the same way, I tell you, there is rejoicing in the presence of the angels of God over one sinner who repents."

The Parable of the Lost Son

¹¹Jesus continued: "There was a man who had two sons. ¹²The younger one said to his father, 'Father, give me my share of the estate.' So he divided his property between them.

¹³"Not long after that, the younger son got together all he had, set off for a distant country and there squandered his wealth in wild living. ¹⁴After he had spent everything, there was a severe famine in that whole country, and he began to be in need. ¹⁵So he went and hired himself out to a citizen of that country, who sent him to his fields to feed pigs. ¹⁶He longed to fill his stomach with the pods that the pigs were eating, but no-one gave him anything.

¹⁷"When he came to his senses, he said,

'How many of my father's hired men have food to spare, and here I am starving to death! ¹⁸I will set out and go back to my father and say to him: Father, I have sinned against heaven and against you. ¹⁹I am no longer worthy to be called your son; make me like one of your hired men.' ²⁰So he got up and went to his father.

"But while he was still a long way off, his father saw him and was filled with compassion for him; he ran to his son, threw his arms around him and kissed him.

²¹"The son said to him, 'Father, I have sinned against heaven and against you. I am no longer worthy to be called your son.'*ᵇ*

²²"But the father said to his servants, 'Quick! Bring the best robe and put it on him. Put a ring on his finger and sandals on his feet. ²³Bring the fattened calf and kill it. Let's have a feast and celebrate. ²⁴For this son of mine was dead and is alive again; he was lost and is found.' So they began to celebrate.

²⁵"Meanwhile, the older son was in the field. When he came near the house, he heard music and dancing. ²⁶So he called one of the servants and asked him what was going on. ²⁷'Your brother has come,' he replied, 'and your father has killed the fattened calf because he has him back safe and sound.'

²⁸"The older brother became angry and refused to go in. So his father went out and pleaded with him. ²⁹But he answered his father, 'Look! All these years I've been slaving for you and never disobeyed your orders. Yet you never gave me even a young goat so I could celebrate with my friends. ³⁰But when this son of yours who has squandered your property with prostitutes comes home, you kill the fattened calf for him!'

³¹"'My son,' the father said, 'you are always with me, and everything I have is yours. ³²But we had to celebrate and be glad, because this brother of yours was dead and is alive again; he was lost and is found.'"

ᵃ8 Greek *ten drachmas*, each worth about a day's wages
ᵇ21 Some early manuscripts *son. Make me like one of your hired men.*

The Parable of the Shrewd Manager

16 Jesus told his disciples: "There was a rich man whose manager was accused of wasting his possessions. ²So he called him in and asked him, 'What is this I hear about you? Give an account of your management, because you cannot be manager any longer.'

³"The manager said to himself, 'What shall I do now? My master is taking away my job. I'm not strong enough to dig, and I'm ashamed to beg— ⁴I know what I'll do so that, when I lose my job here, people will welcome me into their houses.'

⁵"So he called in each one of his master's debtors. He asked the first, 'How much do you owe my master?'

⁶"'Eight hundred gallons*ᵃ* of olive oil,' he replied.

"The manager told him, 'Take your bill, sit down quickly, and make it four hundred.'

⁷"Then he asked the second, 'And how much do you owe?'

"'A thousand bushels*ᵇ* of wheat,' he replied.

"He told him, 'Take your bill and make it eight hundred.'

⁸"The master commended the dishonest manager because he had acted shrewdly. For the people of this world are more shrewd in dealing with their own kind than are the people of the light. ⁹I tell you, use worldly wealth to gain friends for yourselves, so that when it is gone, you will be welcomed into eternal dwellings.

¹⁰"Whoever can be trusted with very little can also be trusted with much, and whoever is dishonest with very little will also be dishonest with much. ¹¹So if you have not been trustworthy in handling worldly wealth, who will trust you with true riches? ¹²And if you have not been trustworthy with someone else's property, who will give you property of your own?

¹³"No servant can serve two masters. Either he will hate the one and love the other, or he will be devoted to the one and despise the other. You cannot serve both God and Money."

¹⁴The Pharisees, who loved money, heard all this and were sneering at Jesus. ¹⁵He said to them, "You are the ones who justify yourselves in the eyes of men, but God knows your hearts. What is highly valued among men is detestable in God's sight.

Additional Teachings

¹⁶"The Law and the Prophets were proclaimed until John. Since that time, the good news of the kingdom of God is being preached, and everyone is forcing his way into it. ¹⁷It is easier for heaven and earth to disappear than for the least stroke of a pen to drop out of the Law.

¹⁸"Anyone who divorces his wife and marries another woman commits adultery, and the man who marries a divorced woman commits adultery.

The Rich Man and Lazarus

¹⁹"There was a rich man who was dressed in purple and fine linen and lived in luxury every day. ²⁰At his gate was laid a beggar named Lazarus, covered with sores ²¹and longing to eat what fell from the rich man's table. Even the dogs came and licked his sores.

²²"The time came when the beggar died and the angels carried him to Abraham's side. The rich man also died and was buried. ²³In hell,*ᶜ* where he was in torment, he looked up and saw Abraham far away, with Lazarus by his side. ²⁴So he called to him, 'Father Abraham, have pity on me and send Lazarus to dip the tip of his finger in water and cool my tongue, because I am in agony in this fire.'

²⁵"But Abraham replied, 'Son, remember that in your lifetime you received your good things, while Lazarus received bad things, but now he is comforted here and you are in agony. ²⁶And besides all this, between us and you a great chasm has been fixed, so that those who want to go

---

ᵃ6 Greek *one hundred batous* (probably about 3 kilolitres)
ᵇ7 Greek *one hundred korous* (probably about 35 kilolitres)   *ᶜ23* Greek *Hades*

from here to you cannot, nor can anyone cross over from there to us.'

²⁷"He answered, 'Then I beg you, father, send Lazarus to my father's house, ²⁸for I have five brothers. Let him warn them, so that they will not also come to this place of torment.'

²⁹"Abraham replied, 'They have Moses and the Prophets; let them listen to them.'

³⁰"'No, father Abraham,' he said, 'but if someone from the dead goes to them, they will repent.'

³¹"He said to him, 'If they do not listen to Moses and the Prophets, they will not be convinced even if someone rises from the dead.'"

Sin, Faith, Duty

17 Jesus said to his disciples: "Things that cause people to sin are bound to come, but woe to that person through whom they come. ²It would be better for him to be thrown into the sea with a millstone tied round his neck than for him to cause one of these little ones to sin. ³So watch yourselves.

"If your brother sins, rebuke him, and if he repents, forgive him. ⁴If he sins against you seven times in a day, and seven times comes back to you and says, 'I repent,' forgive him."

⁵The apostles said to the Lord, "Increase our faith!"

⁶He replied, "If you have faith as small as a mustard seed, you can say to this mulberry tree, 'Be uprooted and planted in the sea,' and it will obey you.

⁷"Suppose one of you had a servant ploughing or looking after the sheep. Would he say to the servant when he comes in from the field, 'Come along now and sit down to eat'? ⁸Would he not rather say, 'Prepare my supper, get yourself ready and wait on me while I eat and drink; after that you may eat and drink'? ⁹Would he thank the servant because he did what he was told to do? ¹⁰So you also, when you have done everything you were

told to do, should say, 'We are unworthy servants; we have only done our duty.'"

Ten Healed of Leprosy

¹¹Now on his way to Jerusalem, Jesus travelled along the border between Samaria and Galilee. ¹²As he was going into a village, ten men who had leprosy*ᵃ* met him. They stood at a distance ¹³and called out in a loud voice, "Jesus, Master, have pity on us!"

¹⁴When he saw them, he said, "Go, show yourselves to the priests." And as they went, they were cleansed.

¹⁵One of them, when he saw he was healed, came back, praising God in a loud voice. ¹⁶He threw himself at Jesus' feet and thanked him—and he was a Samaritan.

¹⁷Jesus asked, "Were not all ten cleansed? Where are the other nine? ¹⁸Was no-one found to return and give praise to God except this foreigner?" ¹⁹Then he said to him, "Rise and go; your faith has made you well."

The Coming of the Kingdom of God

²⁰Once, having been asked by the Pharisees when the kingdom of God would come, Jesus replied, "The kingdom of God does not come with your careful observation, ²¹nor will people say, 'Here it is,' or 'There it is,' because the kingdom of God is within*ᵇ* you."

²²Then he said to his disciples, "The time is coming when you will long to see one of the days of the Son of Man, but you will not see it. ²³Men will tell you, 'There he is!' or 'Here he is!' Do not go running off after them. ²⁴For the Son of Man in his day*ᶜ* will be like the lightning, which flashes and lights up the sky from one end to the other. ²⁵But first he must suffer many things and be rejected by this generation.

²⁶"Just as it was in the days of Noah, so also will it be in the days of the Son of Man. ²⁷People were eating, drinking,

---

ᵃ12 The Greek word was used for various diseases affecting the skin—not necessarily leprosy.
ᵇ21 Or *among*   *ᶜ24* Some manuscripts do not have *in his day.*

marrying and being given in marriage up to the day Noah entered the ark. Then the flood came and destroyed them all.

²⁸"It was the same in the days of Lot. People were eating and drinking, buying and selling, planting and building. ²⁹But the day Lot left Sodom, fire and sulphur rained down from heaven and destroyed them all.

³⁰"It will be just like this on the day the Son of Man is revealed. ³¹On that day no-one who is on the roof of his house, with his goods inside, should go down to get them. Likewise, no-one in the field should go back for anything. ³²Remember Lot's wife! ³³Whoever tries to keep his life will lose it, and whoever loses his life will preserve it. ³⁴I tell you, on that night two people will be in one bed; one will be taken and the other left. ³⁵Two women will be grinding grain together; one will be taken and the other left."*d*

³⁷"Where, Lord?" they asked.

He replied, "Where there is a dead body, there the vultures will gather."

The Parable of the Persistent Widow

18 Then Jesus told his disciples a parable to show them that they should always pray and not give up. ²He said: "In a certain town there was a judge who neither feared God nor cared about men. ³And there was a widow in that town who kept coming to him with the plea, 'Grant me justice against my adversary.'

⁴"For some time he refused. But finally he said to himself, 'Even though I don't fear God or care about men, ⁵yet because this widow keeps bothering me, I will see that she gets justice, so that she won't eventually wear me out with her coming!'"

⁶And the Lord said, "Listen to what the unjust judge says. ⁷And will not God bring about justice for his chosen ones, who cry out to him day and night? Will he keep putting them off? ⁸I tell you, he will see that they get justice, and quickly. However, when the Son of Man comes, will he find faith on the earth?"

The Parable of the Pharisee and the Tax Collector

⁹To some who were confident of their own righteousness and looked down on everybody else, Jesus told this parable: ¹⁰"Two men went up to the temple to pray, one a Pharisee and the other a tax collector. ¹¹The Pharisee stood up and prayed about*a* himself: 'God, I thank you that I am not like other men—robbers, evildoers, adulterers—or even like this tax collector. ¹²I fast twice a week and give a tenth of all I get.'

¹³"But the tax collector stood at a distance. He would not even look up to heaven, but beat his breast and said, 'God, have mercy on me, a sinner.'

¹⁴"I tell you that this man, rather than the other, went home justified before God. For everyone who exalts himself will be humbled, and he who humbles himself will be exalted."

The Little Children and Jesus

¹⁵People were also bringing babies to Jesus to have him touch them. When the disciples saw this, they rebuked them. ¹⁶But Jesus called the children to him and said, "Let the little children come to me, and do not hinder them, for the kingdom of God belongs to such as these. ¹⁷I tell you the truth, anyone who will not receive the kingdom of God like a little child will never enter it."

The Rich Ruler

¹⁸A certain ruler asked him, "Good teacher, what must I do to inherit eternal life?"

¹⁹"Why do you call me good?" Jesus answered. "No-one is good—except God alone. ²⁰You know the commandments: 'Do not commit adultery, do not murder, do not steal, do not give false testimony, honour your father and mother.'*b*"

²¹"All these I have kept since I was a boy," he said.

²²When Jesus heard this, he said to him,

---

d35 Some manuscripts *left.* ³⁶*Two men will be in the field; one will be taken and the other left.*
a11 Or *to*   *b20* Exodus 20:12–16; Deut. 5:16–20

"You still lack one thing. Sell everything you have and give to the poor, and you will have treasure in heaven. Then come, follow me."

²³When he heard this, he became very sad, because he was a man of great wealth. ²⁴Jesus looked at him and said, "How hard it is for the rich to enter the kingdom of God! ²⁵Indeed, it is easier for a camel to go through the eye of a needle than for a rich man to enter the kingdom of God."

²⁶Those who heard this asked, "Who then can be saved?"

²⁷Jesus replied, "What is impossible with men is possible with God."

²⁸Peter said to him, "We have left all we had to follow you!"

²⁹"I tell you the truth," Jesus said to them, "no-one who has left home or wife or brothers or parents or children for the sake of the kingdom of God ³⁰will fail to receive many times as much in this age and, in the age to come, eternal life."

Jesus Again Predicts His Death

³¹Jesus took the Twelve aside and told them, "We are going up to Jerusalem, and everything that is written by the prophets about the Son of Man will be fulfilled. ³²He will be turned over to the Gentiles. They will mock him, insult him, spit on him, flog him and kill him. ³³On the third day he will rise again."

³⁴The disciples did not understand any of this. Its meaning was hidden from them, and they did not know what he was talking about.

A Blind Beggar Receives His Sight

³⁵As Jesus approached Jericho, a blind man was sitting by the roadside begging. ³⁶When he heard the crowd going by, he asked what was happening. ³⁷They told him, "Jesus of Nazareth is passing by."

³⁸He called out, "Jesus, Son of David, have mercy on me!"

³⁹Those who led the way rebuked him and told him to be quiet, but he shouted all the more, "Son of David, have mercy on me!"

⁴⁰Jesus stopped and ordered the man to be brought to him. When he came near, Jesus asked him, ⁴¹"What do you want me to do for you?"

"Lord, I want to see," he replied.

⁴²Jesus said to him, "Receive your sight; your faith has healed you." ⁴³Immediately he received his sight and followed Jesus, praising God. When all the people saw it, they also praised God.

Zacchaeus the Tax Collector

19 Jesus entered Jericho and was passing through. ²A man was there by the name of Zacchaeus; he was a chief tax collector and was wealthy. ³He wanted to see who Jesus was, but being a short man he could not, because of the crowd. ⁴So he ran ahead and climbed a sycamore-fig tree to see him, since Jesus was coming that way.

⁵When Jesus reached the spot, he looked up and said to him, "Zacchaeus, come down immediately. I must stay at your house today." ⁶So he came down at once and welcomed him gladly.

⁷All the people saw this and began to mutter, "He has gone to be the guest of a 'sinner'."

⁸But Zacchaeus stood up and said to the Lord, "Look, Lord! Here and now I give half of my possessions to the poor, and if I have cheated anybody out of anything, I will pay back four times the amount."

⁹Jesus said to him, "Today salvation has come to this house, because this man, too, is a son of Abraham. ¹⁰For the Son of Man came to seek and to save what was lost."

The Parable of the Ten Minas

¹¹While they were listening to this, he went on to tell them a parable, because he was near Jerusalem and the people thought that the kingdom of God was going to appear at once. ¹²He said: "A man of noble birth went to a distant country to have himself appointed king and then to return. ¹³So he called ten of his servants and gave them ten minas.ᵃ 'Put

---

ᵃ13 A mina was about three months' wages.

this money to work,' he said, 'until I come back.'

¹⁴"But his subjects hated him and sent a delegation after him to say, 'We don't want this man to be our king.'

¹⁵"He was made king, however, and returned home. Then he sent for the servants to whom he had given the money, in order to find out what they had gained with it.

¹⁶"The first one came and said, 'Sir, your mina has earned ten more.'

¹⁷"'Well done, my good servant!' his master replied. 'Because you have been trustworthy in a very small matter, take charge of ten cities.'

¹⁸"The second came and said, 'Sir, your mina has earned five more.'

¹⁹"His master answered, 'You take charge of five cities.'

²⁰"Then another servant came and said, 'Sir, here is your mina; I have kept it laid away in a piece of cloth. ²¹I was afraid of you, because you are a hard man. You take out what you did not put in and reap what you did not sow.'

²²"His master replied, 'I will judge you by your own words, you wicked servant! You knew, did you, that I am a hard man, taking out what I did not put in, and reaping what I did not sow? ²³Why then didn't you put my money on deposit, so that when I came back, I could have collected it with interest?'

²⁴"Then he said to those standing by, 'Take his mina away from him and give it to the one who has ten minas.'

²⁵"'Sir,' they said, 'he already has ten!'

²⁶"He replied, 'I tell you that to everyone who has, more will be given, but as for the one who has nothing, even what he has will be taken away. ²⁷But those enemies of mine who did not want me to be a king over them—bring them here and kill them in front of me.'"

The Triumphal Entry

²⁸After Jesus had said this, he went on ahead, going up to Jerusalem. ²⁹As he approached Bethphage and Bethany at the hill called the Mount of Olives, he sent two of his disciples, saying to them, ³⁰"Go to the village ahead of you, and as you enter it, you will find a colt tied there, which no-one has ever ridden. Untie it and bring it here. ³¹If anyone asks you, 'Why are you untying it?' tell him, 'The Lord needs it.'"

³²Those who were sent ahead went and found it just as he had told them. ³³As they were untying the colt, its owners asked them, "Why are you untying the colt?"

³⁴They replied, "The Lord needs it."

³⁵They brought it to Jesus, threw their cloaks on the colt and put Jesus on it. ³⁶As he went along, people spread their cloaks on the road.

³⁷When he came near the place where the road goes down the Mount of Olives, the whole crowd of disciples began joyfully to praise God in loud voices for all the miracles they had seen:

³⁸"Blessed is the king who comes in the name of the Lord!"ᵇ

"Peace in heaven and glory in the highest!"

³⁹Some of the Pharisees in the crowd said to Jesus, "Teacher, rebuke your disciples!"

⁴⁰"I tell you," he replied, "if they keep quiet, the stones will cry out."

⁴¹As he approached Jerusalem and saw the city, he wept over it ⁴²and said, "If you, even you, had only known on this day what would bring you peace—but now it is hidden from your eyes. ⁴³The days will come upon you when your enemies will build an embankment against you and encircle you and hem you in on every side. ⁴⁴They will dash you to the ground, you and the children within your walls. They will not leave one stone on another, because you did not recognise the time of God's coming to you."

Jesus at the Temple

⁴⁵Then he entered the temple area and began driving out those who were selling.

[46]"It is written," he said to them, " 'My house will be a house of prayer';[c] but you have made it 'a den of robbers'.[d]"

[47]Every day he was teaching at the temple. But the chief priests, the teachers of the law and the leaders among the people were trying to kill him. [48]Yet they could not find any way to do it, because all the people hung on his words.

The Authority of Jesus Questioned

20 One day as he was teaching the people in the temple courts and preaching the gospel, the chief priests and the teachers of the law, together with the elders, came up to him. [2]"Tell us by what authority you are doing these things," they said. "Who gave you this authority?"

[3]He replied, "I will also ask you a question. Tell me, [4]John's baptism—was it from heaven, or from men?"

[5]They discussed it among themselves and said, "If we say, 'From heaven', he will ask, 'Why didn't you believe him?' [6]But if we say, 'From men', all the people will stone us, because they are persuaded that John was a prophet."

[7]So they answered, "We don't know where it was from."

[8]Jesus said, "Neither will I tell you by what authority I am doing these things."

The Parable of the Tenants

[9]He went on to tell the people this parable: "A man planted a vineyard, rented it to some farmers and went away for a long time. [10]At harvest time he sent a servant to the tenants so they would give him some of the fruit of the vineyard. But the tenants beat him and sent him away empty-handed. [11]He sent another servant, but that one also they beat and treated shamefully and sent away empty-handed. [12]He sent still a third, and they wounded him and threw him out.

[13]"Then the owner of the vineyard said, 'What shall I do? I will send my son, whom I love; perhaps they will respect him.'

[14]"But when the tenants saw him, they talked the matter over. 'This is the heir,' they said. 'Let's kill him, and the inheritance will be ours.' [15]So they threw him out of the vineyard and killed him.

"What then will the owner of the vineyard do to them? [16]He will come and kill those tenants and give the vineyard to others."

When the people heard this, they said, "May this never be!"

[17]Jesus looked directly at them and asked, "Then what is the meaning of that which is written:

" 'The stone the builders rejected
    has become the capstone'[a,b]?

[18]Everyone who falls on that stone will be broken to pieces, but he on whom it falls will be crushed."

[19]The teachers of the law and the chief priests looked for a way to arrest him immediately, because they knew he had spoken this parable against them. But they were afraid of the people.

Paying Taxes to Caesar

[20]Keeping a close watch on him, they sent spies, who pretended to be honest. They hoped to catch Jesus in something he said so that they might hand him over to the power and authority of the governor. [21]So the spies questioned him: "Teacher, we know that you speak and teach what is right, and that you do not show partiality but teach the way of God in accordance with the truth. [22]Is it right for us to pay taxes to Caesar or not?"

[23]He saw through their duplicity and said to them, [24]"Show me a denarius. Whose portrait and inscription are on it?"

[25]"Caesar's," they replied.

He said to them, "Then give to Caesar what is Caesar's, and to God what is God's."

[26]They were unable to trap him in what he had said there in public. And astonished by his answer, they became silent.

---

[c]46 Isaiah 56:7   [d]46 Jer. 7:11   [a]17 Or cornerstone   [b]17 Psalm 118:22

The Resurrection and Marriage

27Some of the Sadducees, who say there is no resurrection, came to Jesus with a question. 28"Teacher," they said, "Moses wrote for us that if a man's brother dies and leaves a wife but no children, the man must marry the widow and have children for his brother. 29Now there were seven brothers. The first one married a woman and died childless. 30The second 31and then the third married her, and in the same way the seven died, leaving no children. 32Finally, the woman died too. 33Now then, at the resurrection whose wife will she be, since the seven were married to her?"

34Jesus replied, "The people of this age marry and are given in marriage. 35But those who are considered worthy of taking part in that age and in the resurrection from the dead will neither marry nor be given in marriage, 36and they can no longer die; for they are like the angels. They are God's children, since they are children of the resurrection. 37But in the account of the bush, even Moses showed that the dead rise, for he calls the Lord 'the God of Abraham, and the God of Isaac, and the God of Jacob'.*c* 38He is not the God of the dead, but of the living, for to him all are alive."

39Some of the teachers of the law responded, "Well said, teacher!" 40And no-one dared to ask him any more questions.

Whose Son Is the Christ?

41Then Jesus said to them, "How is it that they say the Christ*d* is the Son of David? 42David himself declares in the Book of Psalms:

" 'The Lord said to my Lord:
"Sit at my right hand
43until I make your enemies
　a footstool for your feet." '*e*

44David calls him 'Lord'. How then can he be his son?"

45While all the people were listening,

Jesus said to his disciples, 46"Beware of the teachers of the law. They like to walk around in flowing robes and love to be greeted in the market-places and have the most important seats in the synagogues and the places of honour at banquets. 47They devour widows' houses and for a show make lengthy prayers. Such men will be punished most severely."

The Widow's Offering

21 As he looked up, Jesus saw the rich putting their gifts into the temple treasury. 2He also saw a poor widow put in two very small copper coins.*a* 3"I tell you the truth," he said, "this poor widow has put in more than all the others. 4All these people gave their gifts out of their wealth; but she out of her poverty put in all she had to live on."

Signs of the End of the Age

5Some of his disciples were remarking about how the temple was adorned with beautiful stones and with gifts dedicated to God. But Jesus said, 6"As for what you see here, the time will come when not one stone will be left on another; every one of them will be thrown down."

7"Teacher," they asked, "when will these things happen? And what will be the sign that they are about to take place?"

8He replied: "Watch out that you are not deceived. For many will come in my name, claiming, 'I am he,' and 'The time is near.' Do not follow them. 9When you hear of wars and revolutions, do not be frightened. These things must happen first, but the end will not come right away."

10Then he said to them: "Nation will rise against nation, and kingdom against kingdom. 11There will be great earthquakes, famines and pestilences in various places, and fearful events and great signs from heaven.

12"But before all this, they will lay hands on you and persecute you. They will deliver you to synagogues and prisons, and you will be brought before kings and governors, and all on account of my name. [13]This will result in your being witnesses to them. [14]But make up your mind not to worry beforehand how you will defend yourselves. [15]For I will give you words and wisdom that none of your adversaries will be able to resist or contradict. [16]You will be betrayed even by parents, brothers, relatives and friends, and they will put some of you to death. [17]All men will hate you because of me. [18]But not a hair of your head will perish. [19]By standing firm you will gain life.

[20]"When you see Jerusalem being surrounded by armies, you will know that its desolation is near. [21]Then let those who are in Judea flee to the mountains, let those in the city get out, and let those in the country not enter the city. [22]For this is the time of punishment in fulfilment of all that has been written. [23]How dreadful it will be in those days for pregnant women and nursing mothers! There will be great distress in the land and wrath against this people. [24]They will fall by the sword and will be taken as prisoners to all the nations. Jerusalem will be trampled on by the Gentiles until the times of the Gentiles are fulfilled.

[25]"There will be signs in the sun, moon and stars. On the earth, nations will be in anguish and perplexity at the roaring and tossing of the sea. [26]Men will faint from terror, apprehensive of what is coming on the world, for the heavenly bodies will be shaken. [27]At that time they will see the Son of Man coming in a cloud with power and great glory. [28]When these things begin to take place, stand up and lift up your heads, because your redemption is drawing near."

[29]He told them this parable: "Look at the fig-tree and all the trees. [30]When they sprout leaves, you can see for yourselves and know that summer is near. [31]Even so, when you see these things happening, you know that the kingdom of God is near.

[32]"I tell you the truth, this generation[b] will certainly not pass away until all these things have happened. [33]Heaven and earth will pass away, but my words will never pass away.

[34]"Be careful, or your hearts will be weighed down with dissipation, drunkenness and the anxieties of life, and that day will close on you unexpectedly like a trap. [35]For it will come upon all those who live on the face of the whole earth. [36]Be always on the watch, and pray that you may be able to escape all that is about to happen, and that you may be able to stand before the Son of Man."

[37]Each day Jesus was teaching at the temple, and each evening he went out to spend the night on the hill called the Mount of Olives, [38]and all the people came early in the morning to hear him at the temple.

Judas Agrees to Betray Jesus

22 Now the Feast of Unleavened Bread, called the Passover, was approaching, [2]and the chief priests and the teachers of the law were looking for some way to get rid of Jesus, for they were afraid of the people. [3]Then Satan entered Judas, called Iscariot, one of the Twelve. [4]And Judas went to the chief priests and the officers of the temple guard and discussed with them how he might betray Jesus. [5]They were delighted and agreed to give him money. [6]He consented, and watched for an opportunity to hand Jesus over to them when no crowd was present.

The Last Supper

[7]Then came the day of Unleavened Bread on which the Passover lamb had to be sacrificed. [8]Jesus sent Peter and John, saying, "Go and make preparations for us to eat the Passover."

[9]"Where do you want us to prepare for it?" they asked.

[10]He replied, "As you enter the city, a man carrying a jar of water will meet you. Follow him to the house that he enters, [11]and say to the owner of the house, 'The Teacher asks: Where is the guest room, where I may eat the Passover with my

b32 Or race

disciples?' ¹²He will show you a large upper room, all furnished. Make preparations there."

¹³They left and found things just as Jesus had told them. So they prepared the Passover.

¹⁴When the hour came, Jesus and his apostles reclined at the table. ¹⁵And he said to them, "I have eagerly desired to eat this Passover with you before I suffer. ¹⁶For I tell you, I will not eat it again until it finds fulfilment in the kingdom of God."

¹⁷After taking the cup, he gave thanks and said, "Take this and divide it among you. ¹⁸For I tell you I will not drink again of the fruit of the vine until the kingdom of God comes."

¹⁹And he took bread, gave thanks and broke it, and gave it to them, saying, "This is my body given for you; do this in remembrance of me."

²⁰In the same way, after the supper he took the cup, saying, "This cup is the new covenant in my blood, which is poured out for you. ²¹But the hand of him who is going to betray me is with mine on the table. ²²The Son of Man will go as it has been decreed, but woe to that man who betrays him." ²³They began to question among themselves which of them it might be who would do this.

²⁴Also a dispute arose among them as to which of them was considered to be greatest. ²⁵Jesus said to them, "The kings of the Gentiles lord it over them; and those who exercise authority over them call themselves Benefactors. ²⁶But you are not to be like that. Instead, the greatest among you should be like the youngest, and the one who rules like the one who serves. ²⁷For who is greater, the one who is at the table or the one who serves? Is it not the one who is at the table? But I am among you as one who serves. ²⁸You are those who have stood by me in my trials. ²⁹And I confer on you a kingdom, just as my Father conferred one on me, ³⁰so that you may eat and drink at my table in my kingdom and sit on thrones, judging the twelve tribes of Israel.

³¹"Simon, Simon, Satan has asked to sift you*a* as wheat. ³²But I have prayed for you, Simon, that your faith may not fail. And when you have turned back, strengthen your brothers."

³³But he replied, "Lord, I am ready to go with you to prison and to death."

³⁴Jesus answered, "I tell you, Peter, before the cock crows today, you will deny three times that you know me."

³⁵Then Jesus asked them, "When I sent you without purse, bag or sandals, did you lack anything?"

"Nothing," they answered.

³⁶He said to them, "But now if you have a purse, take it, and also a bag; and if you don't have a sword, sell your cloak and buy one. ³⁷It is written: 'And he was numbered with the transgressors';*b* and I tell you that this must be fulfilled in me. Yes, what is written about me is reaching its fulfilment."

³⁸The disciples said, "See, Lord, here are two swords."

"That is enough," he replied.

Jesus Prays on the Mount of Olives

³⁹Jesus went out as usual to the Mount of Olives, and his disciples followed him. ⁴⁰On reaching the place, he said to them, "Pray that you will not fall into temptation." ⁴¹He withdrew about a stone's throw beyond them, knelt down and prayed, ⁴²"Father, if you are willing, take this cup from me; yet not my will, but yours be done." ⁴³An angel from heaven appeared to him and strengthened him. ⁴⁴And being in anguish, he prayed more earnestly, and his sweat was like drops of blood falling to the ground.*c*

⁴⁵When he rose from prayer and went back to the disciples, he found them asleep, exhausted from sorrow. ⁴⁶"Why are you sleeping?" he asked them. "Get up and pray so that you will not fall into temptation."

Jesus Arrested

⁴⁷While he was still speaking a crowd came up, and the man who was called Judas, one of the Twelve, was leading

---

a31 The Greek is plural.   *b37* Isaiah 53:12   *c44* Some early manuscripts do not have verses 43 and 44.

them. He approached Jesus to kiss him, [48]but Jesus asked him, "Judas, are you betraying the Son of Man with a kiss?"

[49]When Jesus' followers saw what was going to happen, they said, "Lord, should we strike with our swords?" [50]And one of them struck the servant of the high priest, cutting off his right ear.

[51]But Jesus answered, "No more of this!" And he touched the man's ear and healed him.

[52]Then Jesus said to the chief priests, the officers of the temple guard, and the elders, who had come for him, "Am I leading a rebellion, that you have come with swords and clubs? [53]Every day I was with you in the temple courts, and you did not lay a hand on me. But this is your hour—when darkness reigns."

Peter Disowns Jesus

[54]Then seizing him, they led him away and took him into the house of the high priest. Peter followed at a distance. [55]But when they had kindled a fire in the middle of the courtyard and had sat down together, Peter sat down with them. [56]A servant girl saw him seated there in the firelight. She looked closely at him and said, "This man was with him."

[57]But he denied it. "Woman, I don't know him," he said.

[58]A little later someone else saw him and said, "You also are one of them."

"Man, I am not!" Peter replied.

[59]About an hour later another asserted, "Certainly this fellow was with him, for he is a Galilean."

[60]Peter replied, "Man, I don't know what you're talking about!" Just as he was speaking, the cock crowed. [61]The Lord turned and looked straight at Peter. Then Peter remembered the word the Lord had spoken to him: "Before the cock crows today, you will disown me three times." [62]And he went outside and wept bitterly.

The Guards Mock Jesus

[63]The men who were guarding Jesus began mocking and beating him. [64]They blindfolded him and demanded, "Prophesy! Who hit you?" [65]And they said many other insulting things to him.

Jesus Before Pilate and Herod

[66]At daybreak the council of the elders of the people, both the chief priests and teachers of the law, met together, and Jesus was led before them. [67]"If you are the Christ,"[d] they said, "tell us."

Jesus answered, "If I tell you, you will not believe me, [68]and if I asked you, you would not answer. [69]But from now on, the Son of Man will be seated at the right hand of the mighty God."

[70]They all asked, "Are you then the Son of God?"

He replied, "You are right in saying I am."

[71]Then they said, "Why do we need any more testimony? We have heard it from his own lips."

23 Then the whole assembly rose and led him off to Pilate. [2]And they began to accuse him, saying, "We have found this man subverting our nation. He opposes payment of taxes to Caesar and claims to be Christ,[a] a king."

[3]So Pilate asked Jesus, "Are you the king of the Jews?"

"Yes, it is as you say," Jesus replied.

[4]Then Pilate announced to the chief priests and the crowd, "I find no basis for a charge against this man."

[5]But they insisted, "He stirs up the people all over Judea[b] by his teaching. He started in Galilee and has come all the way here."

[6]On hearing this, Pilate asked if the man was a Galilean. [7]When he learned that Jesus was under Herod's jurisdiction, he sent him to Herod, who was also in Jerusalem at that time.

[8]When Herod saw Jesus, he was greatly pleased, because for a long time he had been wanting to see him. From what he had heard about him, he hoped to see him perform some miracle. [9]He plied him with many questions, but Jesus gave him no answer. [10]The chief priests and the

---

d67 Or Messiah   *a2 Or Messiah; also in verses 35 and 39*   *b5 Or over the land of the Jews* teachers of the law were standing there, vehemently accusing him. [11]Then Herod and his soldiers ridiculed and mocked him. Dressing him in an elegant robe, they sent him back to Pilate. [12]That day Herod and Pilate became friends—before this they had been enemies.

[13]Pilate called together the chief priests, the rulers and the people, [14]and said to them, "You brought me this man as one who was inciting the people to rebellion. I have examined him in your presence and have found no basis for your charges against him. [15]Neither has Herod, for he sent him back to us; as you can see, he has done nothing to deserve death. [16]Therefore, I will punish him and then release him."[c]

[18]With one voice they cried out, "Away with this man! Release Barabbas to us!" ([19]Barabbas had been thrown into prison for an insurrection in the city, and for murder.)

[20]Wanting to release Jesus, Pilate appealed to them again. [21]But they kept shouting, "Crucify him! Crucify him!"

[22]For the third time he spoke to them: "Why? What crime has this man committed? I have found in him no grounds for the death penalty. Therefore I will have him punished and then release him."

[23]But with loud shouts they insistently demanded that he be crucified, and their shouts prevailed. [24]So Pilate decided to grant their demand. [25]He released the man who had been thrown into prison for insurrection and murder, the one they asked for, and surrendered Jesus to their will.

The Crucifixion

[26]As they led him away, they seized Simon from Cyrene, who was on his way in from the country, and put the cross on him and made him carry it behind Jesus. [27]A large number of people followed him, including women who mourned and wailed for him. [28]Jesus turned and said to them, "Daughters of Jerusalem, do not weep for me; weep for yourselves and for your children. [29]For the time will come when you will say, 'Blessed are the barren women, the wombs that never bore and the breasts that never nursed!' [30]Then

> " 'they will say to the mountains, "Fall
>   on us!"
>   and to the hills "Cover us!" ' [d]

[31]For if men do these things when the tree is green, what will happen when it is dry?"

[32]Two other men, both criminals, were also led out with him to be executed. [33]When they came to the place called the Skull, there they crucified him, along with the criminals—one on his right, the other on his left. [34]Jesus said, "Father, forgive them, for they do not know what they are doing."[e] And they divided up his clothes by casting lots.

[35]The people stood watching, and the rulers even sneered at him. They said, "He saved others; let him save himself if he is the Christ of God, the Chosen One."

[36]The soldiers also came up and mocked him. They offered him wine vinegar [37]and said, "If you are the king of the Jews, save yourself."

[38]There was a written notice above him, which read: THIS IS THE KING OF THE JEWS.

[39]One of the criminals who hung there hurled insults at him: "Aren't you the Christ? Save yourself and us!"

[40]But the other criminal rebuked him. "Don't you fear God," he said, "since you are under the same sentence? [41]We are punished justly, for we are getting what our deeds deserve. But this man has done nothing wrong."

[42]Then he said, "Jesus, remember me when you come into your kingdom.[f]"

[43]Jesus answered him, "I tell you the truth, today you will be with me in paradise."

Jesus' Death

[44]It was now about the sixth hour, and darkness came over the whole land until

---

[c]16 Some manuscripts *him.*" [17]*Now he was obliged to release one man to them at the Feast.*   [d]30 Hosea 10:8
[e]34 Some early manuscripts do not have this sentence.   [f]42 Some manuscripts *come with your kingly power*

the ninth hour, [45]for the sun stopped shining. And the curtain of the temple was torn in two. [46]Jesus called out with a loud voice, "Father, into your hands I commit my spirit." When he had said this, he breathed his last.

[47]The centurion, seeing what had happened, praised God and said, "Surely this was a righteous man." [48]When all the people who had gathered to witness this sight saw what took place, they beat their breasts and went away. [49]But all those who knew him, including the women who had followed him from Galilee, stood at a distance, watching these things.

Jesus' Burial

[50]Now there was a man named Joseph, a member of the Council, a good and upright man, [51]who had not consented to their decision and action. He came from the Judean town of Arimathea and he was waiting for the kingdom of God. [52]Going to Pilate, he asked for Jesus' body. [53]Then he took it down, wrapped it in linen cloth and placed it in a tomb cut in the rock, one in which no-one had yet been laid. [54]It was Preparation Day, and the Sabbath was about to begin.

[55]The women who had come with Jesus from Galilee followed Joseph and saw the tomb and how his body was laid in it. [56]Then they went home and prepared spices and perfumes. But they rested on the Sabbath in obedience to the commandment.

The Resurrection

24 On the first day of the week, very early in the morning, the women took the spices they had prepared and went to the tomb. [2]They found the stone rolled away from the tomb, [3]but when they entered, they did not find the body of the Lord Jesus. [4]While they were wondering about this, suddenly two men in clothes that gleamed like lightning stood beside them. [5]In their fright the women bowed down with their faces to the

ground, but the men said to them, "Why do you look for the living among the dead? [6]He is not here; he has risen! Remember how he told you, while he was still with you in Galilee: [7]'The Son of Man must be delivered into the hands of sinful men, be crucified and on the third day be raised again.'" [8]Then they remembered his words.

[9]When they came back from the tomb, they told all these things to the Eleven and to all the others. [10]It was Mary Magdalene, Joanna, Mary the mother of James, and the others with them who told this to the apostles. [11]But they did not believe the women, because their words seemed to them like nonsense. [12]Peter, however, got up and ran to the tomb. Bending over, he saw the strips of linen lying by themselves, and he went away, wondering to himself what had happened.

On the Road to Emmaus

[13]Now that same day two of them were going to a village called Emmaus, about seven miles[a] from Jerusalem. [14]They were talking with each other about everything that had happened. [15]As they talked and discussed these things with each other, Jesus himself came up and walked along with them; [16]but they were kept from recognising him.

[17]He asked them, "What are you discussing together as you walk along?"

They stood still, their faces downcast. [18]One of them, named Cleopas, asked him, "Are you only a visitor to Jerusalem and do not know the things that have happened there in these days?"

[19]"What things?" he asked.

"About Jesus of Nazareth," they replied. "He was a prophet, powerful in word and deed before God and all the people. [20]The chief priests and our rulers handed him over to be sentenced to death, and they crucified him; [21]but we had hoped that he was the one who was going to redeem Israel. And what is more, it is the third day since all this took place. [22]In addition, some of our women amazed us.

---

[a]13 Greek *sixty stadia* (about 11 kilometres)

They went to the tomb early this morning [23]but didn't find his body. They came and told us that they had seen a vision of angels, who said he was alive. [24]Then some of our companions went to the tomb and found it just as the women had said, but him they did not see."

[25]He said to them, "How foolish you are, and how slow of heart to believe all that the prophets have spoken! [26]Did not the Christ[b] have to suffer these things and then enter his glory?" [27]And beginning with Moses and all the Prophets, he explained to them what was said in all the Scriptures concerning himself.

[28]As they approached the village to which they were going, Jesus acted as if he were going further. [29]But they urged him strongly, "Stay with us, for it is nearly evening; the day is almost over." So he went in to stay with them.

[30]When he was at the table with them, he took bread, gave thanks, broke it and began to give it to them. [31]Then their eyes were opened and they recognised him, and he disappeared from their sight. [32]They asked each other, "Were not our hearts burning within us while he talked with us on the road and opened the Scriptures to us?"

[33]They got up and returned at once to Jerusalem. There they found the Eleven and those with them, assembled together [34]and saying, "It is true! The Lord has risen and has appeared to Simon." [35]Then the two told what had happened on the way, and how Jesus was recognised by them when he broke the bread.

Jesus Appears to the Disciples

[36]While they were still talking about this, Jesus himself stood among them and said to them, "Peace be with you."

[37]They were startled and frightened, thinking they saw a ghost. [38]He said to them, "Why are you troubled, and why do doubts rise in your minds? [39]Look at my hands and my feet. It is I myself! Touch me and see; a ghost does not have flesh and bones, as you see I have."

[40]When he had said this, he showed them his hands and feet. [41]And while they still did not believe it because of joy and amazement, he asked them, "Do you have anything here to eat?" [42]They gave him a piece of broiled fish, [43]and he took it and ate it in their presence.

[44]He said to them, "This is what I told you while I was still with you: Everything must be fulfilled that is written about me in the Law of Moses, the Prophets and the Psalms."

[45]Then he opened their minds so they could understand the Scriptures. [46]He told them, "This is what is written: The Christ will suffer and rise from the dead on the third day, [47]and repentance and forgiveness of sins will be preached in his name to all nations, beginning at Jerusalem. [48]You are witnesses of these things. [49]I am going to send you what my Father has promised; but stay in the city until you have been clothed with power from on high."

The Ascension

[50]When he had led them out to the vicinity of Bethany, he lifted up his hands and blessed them. [51]While he was blessing them, he left them and was taken up into heaven. [52]Then they worshipped him and returned to Jerusalem with great joy. [53]And they stayed continually at the temple, praising God.

[b]26 Or *Messiah*; also in verse 46

John

The Word Became Flesh

1 In the beginning was the Word, and the Word was with God, and the Word was God. ²He was with God in the beginning.

³Through him all things were made; without him nothing was made that has been made. ⁴In him was life, and that life was the light of men. ⁵The light shines in the darkness, but the darkness has not understood[a] it.

⁶There came a man who was sent from God; his name was John. ⁷He came as a witness to testify concerning that light, so that through him all men might believe. ⁸He himself was not the light; he came only as a witness to the light. ⁹The true light that gives light to every man was coming into the world.[b]

¹⁰He was in the world, and though the world was made through him, the world did not recognise him. ¹¹He came to that which was his own, but his own did not receive him. ¹²Yet to all who received him, to those who believed in his name, he gave the right to become children of God—¹³children born not of natural descent,[c] nor of human decision or a husband's will, but born of God.

¹⁴The Word became flesh and made his dwelling among us. We have seen his glory, the glory of the One and Only,[d] who came from the Father, full of grace and truth.

¹⁵John testifies concerning him. He cries out, saying, "This was he of whom I said, 'He who comes after me has surpassed me because he was before me.'" ¹⁶From the fulness of his grace we have all received one blessing after another. ¹⁷For the law was given through Moses; grace and truth came through Jesus Christ. ¹⁸No-one has ever seen God, but God the One and Only,[e,f] who is at the Father's side, has made him known.

John the Baptist Denies Being the Christ

¹⁹Now this was John's testimony when the Jews of Jerusalem sent priests and Levites to ask him who he was. ²⁰He did not fail to confess, but confessed freely, "I am not the Christ."[g]

²¹They asked him, "Then who are you? Are you Elijah?"

He said, "I am not."

"Are you the Prophet?"

He answered, "No."

²²Finally they said, "Who are you? Give us an answer to take back to those who sent us. What do you say about yourself?"

²³John replied in the words of Isaiah the prophet, "I am the voice of one calling in the desert, 'Make straight the way for the Lord.'[h]"

²⁴Now some Pharisees who had been sent ²⁵questioned him, "Why then do you baptise if you are not the Christ, nor Elijah, nor the Prophet?"

---

a5 Or *darkness, and the darkness has not overcome*
b9 Or *This was the true light that gives light to every man who comes into the world*   *c13* Greek *of bloods*
d14 Or *the Only Begotten*   *e18* Or *the Only Begotten*   *f18* Some manuscripts *but the only* (or *only begotten*) *Son*
g20 Or *Messiah.* "The Christ" (Greek) and "the Messiah" (Hebrew) both mean "the Anointed One"; also in verse 25.
h23 Isaiah 40:3

²⁶"I baptise with*ⁱ* water," John replied, "but among you stands one you do not know. ²⁷He is the one who comes after me, the thongs of whose sandals I am not worthy to untie."

²⁸This all happened at Bethany on the other side of the Jordan, where John was baptising.

Jesus the Lamb of God

²⁹The next day John saw Jesus coming towards him and said, "Look, the Lamb of God, who takes away the sin of the world! ³⁰This is the one I meant when I said, 'A man who comes after me has surpassed me because he was before me.' ³¹I myself did not know him, but the reason I came baptising with water was that he might be revealed to Israel."

³²Then John gave this testimony: "I saw the Spirit come down from heaven as a dove and remain on him. ³³I would not have known him, except that the one who sent me to baptise with water told me, 'The man on whom you see the Spirit come down and remain is he who will baptise with the Holy Spirit.' ³⁴I have seen and I testify that this is the Son of God."

Jesus' First Disciples

³⁵The next day John was there again with two of his disciples. ³⁶When he saw Jesus passing by, he said, "Look, the Lamb of God!"

³⁷When the two disciples heard him say this, they followed Jesus. ³⁸Turning round, Jesus saw them following and asked, "What do you want?"

They said, "Rabbi" (which means Teacher), "where are you staying?"

³⁹"Come," he replied, "and you will see."

So they went and saw where he was staying, and spent that day with him. It was about the tenth hour.

⁴⁰Andrew, Simon Peter's brother, was one of the two who heard what John had said and who had followed Jesus. ⁴¹The first thing Andrew did was to find his brother Simon and tell him, "We have found the Messiah" (that is, the Christ). ⁴²And he brought him to Jesus.

Jesus looked at him and said, "You are Simon son of John. You will be called Cephas" (which, when translated, is Peter*ʲ*).

Jesus Calls Philip and Nathanael

⁴³The next day Jesus decided to leave for Galilee. Finding Philip, he said to him, "Follow me."

⁴⁴Philip, like Andrew and Peter, was from the town of Bethsaida. ⁴⁵Philip found Nathanael and told him, "We have found the one Moses wrote about in the Law, and about whom the prophets also wrote—Jesus of Nazareth, the son of Joseph."

⁴⁶"Nazareth! Can anything good come from there?" Nathanael asked.

"Come and see," said Philip.

⁴⁷When Jesus saw Nathanael approaching, he said of him, "Here is a true Israelite, in whom there is nothing false."

⁴⁸"How do you know me?" Nathanael asked.

Jesus answered, "I saw you while you were still under the fig-tree before Philip called you."

⁴⁹Then Nathanael declared, "Rabbi, you are the Son of God; you are the King of Israel."

⁵⁰Jesus said, "You believe*ᵏ* because I told you I saw you under the fig-tree. You shall see greater things than that." ⁵¹He then added, "I tell you*ˡ* the truth, you*ˡ* shall see heaven open, and the angels of God ascending and descending on the Son of Man."

Jesus Changes Water to Wine

2 On the third day a wedding took place at Cana in Galilee. Jesus' mother was there, ²and Jesus and his disciples had also been invited to the wedding. ³When the wine was gone, Jesus'

---

i26 Or *in;* also in verses 31 and 33   *j42* Both *Cephas* (Aramaic) and *Peter* (Greek) mean *rock.*
k50 Or *Do you believe . . . ?*   *l51* The Greek is plural.

mother said to him, "They have no more wine."

⁴"Dear woman, why do you involve me?" Jesus replied, "My time has not yet come."

⁵His mother said to the servants, "Do whatever he tells you."

⁶Nearby stood six stone water jars, the kind used by the Jews for ceremonial washing, each holding from twenty to thirty gallons.ᵃ

⁷Jesus said to the servants, "Fill the jars with water"; so they filled them to the brim.

⁸Then he told them, "Now draw some out and take it to the master of the banquet."

They did so, ⁹and the master of the banquet tasted the water that had been turned into wine. He did not realise where it had come from, though the servants who had drawn the water knew. Then he called the bridegroom aside ¹⁰and said, "Everyone brings out the choice wine first and then the cheaper wine after the guests have had too much to drink; but you have saved the best till now."

¹¹This, the first of his miraculous signs, Jesus performed at Cana in Galilee. He thus revealed his glory, and his disciples put their faith in him.

Jesus Clears the Temple

¹²After this he went down to Capernaum with his mother and brothers and his disciples. There they stayed for a few days.

¹³When it was almost time for the Jewish Passover, Jesus went up to Jerusalem. ¹⁴In the temple courts he found men selling cattle, sheep and doves, and others sitting at tables exchanging money. ¹⁵So he made a whip out of cords, and drove all from the temple area, both sheep and cattle; he scattered the coins of the money-changers and overturned their tables. ¹⁶To those who sold doves he said, "Get these out of here! How dare you turn my Father's house into a market!"

¹⁷His disciples remembered that it is written, "Zeal for your house will consume me."ᵇ

¹⁸Then the Jews demanded of him, "What miraculous sign can you show us to prove your authority to do all this?"

¹⁹Jesus answered them, "Destroy this temple, and I will raise it again in three days."

²⁰The Jews replied, "It has taken forty-six years to build this temple, and you are going to raise it in three days?" ²¹But the temple he had spoken of was his body. ²²After he was raised from the dead, his disciples recalled what he had said. Then they believed the Scripture and the words that Jesus had spoken.

²³Now while he was in Jerusalem at the Passover Feast, many people saw the miraculous signs he was doing and believed in his name.ᶜ ²⁴But Jesus would not entrust himself to them, for he knew all men. ²⁵He did not need man's testimony about man, for he knew what was in a man.

Jesus Teaches Nicodemus

3 ¹Now there was a man of the Pharisees named Nicodemus, a member of the Jewish ruling council. ²He came to Jesus at night and said, "Rabbi, we know you are a teacher who has come from God. For no-one could perform the miraculous signs you are doing if God were not with him."

³In reply Jesus declared, "I tell you the truth, no-one can see the kingdom of God unless he is born again."ᵃ

⁴"How can a man be born when he is old?" Nicodemus asked. "Surely he cannot enter a second time into his mother's womb to be born!"

⁵Jesus answered, "I tell you the truth, no-one can enter the kingdom of God unless he is born of water and the Spirit. ⁶Flesh gives birth to flesh, but the Spiritᵇ gives birth to spirit. ⁷You should not be surprised at my saying, 'Youᶜ must be born again.' ⁸The wind blows wherever it pleases. You hear its sound, but you cannot tell where it comes from or where

---

ᵃ6 Greek *two to three metretes* (probably about 75 to 115 litres)   ᵇ17 Psalm 69:9   ᶜ23 Or *and believed in him*
ᵃ3 Or *born from above*; also in verse 7   ᵇ6 Or *but spirit*   ᶜ7 The Greek is plural.

it is going. So it is with everyone born of the Spirit.''

9''How can this be?'' Nicodemus asked.

10''You are Israel's teacher,'' said Jesus, ''and do you not understand these things? 11I tell you the truth, we speak of what we know, and we testify to what we have seen, but still you people do not accept our testimony. 12I have spoken to you of earthly things and you do not believe; how then will you believe if I speak of heavenly things? 13No-one has ever gone into heaven except the one who came from heaven—the Son of Man.*d* 14Just as Moses lifted up the snake in the desert, so the Son of Man must be lifted up, 15that everyone who believes in him may have eternal life.*e*

16''For God so loved the world that he gave his one and only Son,*f* that whoever believes in him shall not perish but have eternal life. 17For God did not send his Son into the world to condemn the world, but to save the world through him. 18Whoever believes in him is not condemned, but whoever does not believe stands condemned already because he has not believed in the name of God's one and only Son.*g* 19This is the verdict: Light has come into the world, but men loved darkness instead of light because their deeds were evil. 20Everyone who does evil hates the light, and will not come into the light for fear that his deeds will be exposed. 21But whoever lives by the truth comes into the light, so that it may be seen plainly that what he has done has been done through God.''*h*

John the Baptist's Testimony About Jesus

22After this, Jesus and his disciples went out into the Judean countryside, where he spent some time with them, and baptised. 23Now John also was baptising at Aenon near Salim, because there was plenty of water, and people were constantly coming to be baptised. 24(This was before John was put in prison.) 25An argument developed between some of John's disciples and a certain Jew*i* over the matter of ceremonial washing. 26They came to John and said to him, ''Rabbi, that man who was with you on the other side of the Jordan—the one you testified about—well, he is baptising, and everyone is going to him.''

27To this John replied, ''A man can receive only what is given him from heaven. 28You yourselves can testify that I said, 'I am not the Christ*j* but am sent ahead of him.' 29The bride belongs to the bridegroom. The friend who attends the bridegroom waits and listens for him, and is full of joy when he hears the bridegroom's voice. That joy is mine, and it is now complete. 30He must become greater; I must become less.

31''The one who comes from above is above all; the one who is from the earth belongs to the earth, and speaks as one from the earth. The one who comes from heaven is above all. 32He testifies to what he has seen and heard, but no-one accepts his testimony. 33The man who has accepted it has certified that God is truthful. 34For the one whom God has sent speaks the words of God, for God*k* gives the Spirit without limit. 35The Father loves the Son and has placed everything in his hands. 36Whoever believes in the Son has eternal life, but whoever rejects the Son will not see life, for God's wrath remains on him.''*l*

Jesus Talks With a Samaritan Woman

4 The Pharisees heard that Jesus was gaining and baptising more disciples than John, 2although in fact it was not Jesus who baptised, but his disciples. 3When the Lord learned of this, he left Judea and went back once more to Galilee.

4Now he had to go through Samaria. 5So he came to a town in Samaria called Sychar, near the plot of ground Jacob had given to his son Joseph. 6Jacob's well was there, and Jesus, tired as he was from the

---

d13 Some manuscripts *Man, who is in heaven*   *e15* Or *believes may have eternal life in him*
f16 Or *his only begotten Son*   *g18* Or *God's only begotten Son*
h21 Some interpreters end the quotation after verse 15.   *i25* Some manuscripts *and certain Jews*
j28 Or *Messiah*   *k34* Greek *he*   *l36* Some interpreters end the quotation after verse 30.

journey, sat down by the well. It was about the sixth hour.

[7]When a Samaritan woman came to draw water, Jesus said to her, "Will you give me a drink?" [8](His disciples had gone into the town to buy food.)

[9]The Samaritan woman said to him, "You are a Jew and I am a Samaritan woman. How can you ask me for a drink?" (For Jews do not associate with Samaritans.[a])

[10]Jesus answered her, "If you knew the gift of God and who it is that asks you for a drink, you would have asked him and he would have given you living water."

[11]"Sir," the woman said, "you have nothing to draw with and the well is deep. Where can you get this living water? [12]Are you greater than our father Jacob, who gave us the well and drank from it himself, as did also his sons and his flocks and herds?"

[13]Jesus answered, "Everyone who drinks this water will be thirsty again, [14]but whoever drinks the water I give him will never thirst. Indeed, the water I give him will become in him a spring of water welling up to eternal life."

[15]The woman said to him, "Sir, give me this water so that I won't get thirsty and have to keep coming here to draw water."

[16]He told her, "Go, call your husband and come back."

[17]"I have no husband," she replied.

Jesus said to her, "You are right when you say you have no husband. [18]The fact is, you have had five husbands, and the man you now have is not your husband. What you have just said is quite true."

[19]"Sir," the woman said, "I can see that you are a prophet. [20]Our fathers worshipped on this mountain, but you Jews claim that the place where we must worship is in Jerusalem."

[21]Jesus declared, "Believe me, woman, a time is coming when you will worship the Father neither on this mountain nor in Jerusalem. [22]You Samaritans worship what you do not know; we worship what we do know, for salvation is from the Jews. [23]Yet a time is coming and has now come when the true worshippers will worship the Father in spirit and truth, for they are the kind of worshippers the Father seeks. [24]God is spirit, and his worshippers must worship in spirit and in truth."

[25]The woman said, "I know that Messiah" (called Christ) "is coming. When he comes, he will explain everything to us."

[26]Then Jesus declared, "I who speak to you am he."

The Disciples Rejoin Jesus

[27]Just then his disciples returned and were surprised to find him talking with a woman. But no-one asked, "What do you want?" or "Why are you talking with her?"

[28]Then, leaving her water jar, the woman went back to the town and said to the people, [29]"Come, see a man who told me everything I ever did. Could this be the Christ?"[b] [30]They came out of the town and made their way towards him.

[31]Meanwhile his disciples urged him, "Rabbi, eat something."

[32]But he said to them, "I have food to eat that you know nothing about."

[33]Then his disciples said to each other, "Could someone have brought him food?"

[34]"My food," said Jesus, "is to do the will of him who sent me and to finish his work. [35]Do you not say, 'Four months more and then the harvest'? I tell you, open your eyes and look at the fields! They are ripe for harvest. [36]Even now the reaper draws his wages, even now he harvests the crop for eternal life, so that the sower and the reaper may be glad together. [37]Thus the saying 'One sows and another reaps' is true. [38]I sent you to reap what you have not worked for. Others have done the hard work, and you have reaped the benefits of their labour."

Many Samaritans Believe

[39]Many of the Samaritans from that town believed in him because of the woman's testimony, "He told me

---

a9 Or *do not use dishes Samaritans have used*   *b29* Or *Messiah* everything I ever did." [40]So when the Samaritans came to him, they urged him to stay with them, and he stayed two days. [41]And because of his words many more became believers.

[42]They said to the woman, "We no longer believe just because of what you said; now we have heard for ourselves, and we know that this man really is the Saviour of the world."

Jesus Heals the Official's Son

[43]After the two days he left for Galilee. [44](Now Jesus himself had pointed out that a prophet has no honour in his own country.) [45]When he arrived in Galilee, the Galileans welcomed him. They had seen all that he had done in Jerusalem at the Passover Feast, for they also had been there.

[46]Once more he visited Cana in Galilee, where he had turned the water into wine. And there was a certain royal official whose son lay sick at Capernaum. [47]When this man heard that Jesus had arrived in Galilee from Judea, he went to him and begged him to come and heal his son, who was close to death.

[48]"Unless you people see miraculous signs and wonders," Jesus told him, "you will never believe."

[49]The royal official said, "Sir, come down before my child dies."

[50]Jesus replied, "You may go. Your son will live."

The man took Jesus at his word and departed. [51]While he was still on the way, his servants met him with the news that his boy was living. [52]When he enquired as to the time when his son got better, they said to him, "The fever left him yesterday at the seventh hour."

[53]Then the father realised that this was the exact time at which Jesus had said to him, "Your son will live." So he and all his household believed.

[54]This was the second miraculous sign that Jesus performed, having come from Judea to Galilee.

The Healing at the Pool

5 Some time later, Jesus went up to Jerusalem for a feast of the Jews. [2]Now there is in Jerusalem near the Sheep Gate a pool, which in Aramaic is called Bethesda[a] and which is surrounded by five covered colonnades. [3]Here a great number of disabled people used to lie—the blind, the lame, the paralysed.[b] [5]One who was there had been an invalid for thirty-eight years. [6]When Jesus saw him lying there and learned that he had been in this condition for a long time, he asked him, "Do you want to get well?"

[7]"Sir," the invalid replied, "I have no-one to help me into the pool when the water is stirred. While I am trying to get in, someone else goes down ahead of me."

[8]Then Jesus said to him, "Get up! Pick up your mat and walk." [9]At once the man was cured; he picked up his mat and walked.

The day on which this took place was a Sabbath, [10]and so the Jews said to the man who had been healed, "It is the Sabbath; the law forbids you to carry your mat."

[11]But he replied, "The man who made me well said to me, 'Pick up your mat and walk.'"

[12]So they asked him, "Who is this fellow who told you to pick it up and walk?"

[13]The man who was healed had no idea who it was, for Jesus had slipped away into the crowd that was there.

[14]Later Jesus found him at the temple and said to him, "See, you are well again. Stop sinning or something worse may happen to you." [15]The man went away and told the Jews that it was Jesus who had made him well.

Life Through the Son

[16]So, because Jesus was doing these things on the Sabbath, the Jews persecuted him. [17]Jesus said to them, "My Father is always at his work to this very

---

[a]2 Some manuscripts *Bethzatha*; other manuscripts *Bethsaida*
[b]3 Some less important manuscripts *paralysed—and they waited for the moving of the waters. [4]From time to time an angel of the Lord would come down and stir up the waters. The first one into the pool after each such disturbance would be cured of whatever disease he had.*

day, and I, too, am working." [18]For this reason the Jews tried all the harder to kill him; not only was he breaking the Sabbath, but he was even calling God his own Father, making himself equal with God.

[19]Jesus gave them this answer: "I tell you the truth, the Son can do nothing by himself; he can do only what he sees his Father doing, because whatever the Father does the Son also does. [20]For the Father loves the Son and shows him all he does. Yes, to your amazement he will show him even greater things than these. [21]For just as the Father raises the dead and gives them life, even so the Son gives life to whom he is pleased to give it. [22]Moreover, the Father judges no-one, but has entrusted all judgment to the Son, [23]that all may honour the Son just as they honour the Father. He who does not honour the Son does not honour the Father, who sent him.

[24]"I tell you the truth, whoever hears my word and believes him who sent me has eternal life and will not be condemned; he has crossed over from death to life. [25]I tell you the truth, a time is coming and has now come when the dead will hear the voice of the Son of God and those who hear will live. [26]For as the Father has life in himself, so he has granted the Son to have life in himself. [27]And he has given him authority to judge because he is the Son of Man.

[28]"Do not be amazed at this, for a time is coming when all who are in their graves will hear his voice [29]and come out—those who have done good will rise to live, and those who have done evil will rise to be condemned. [30]By myself I can do nothing; I judge only as I hear, and my judgment is just, for I seek not to please myself but him who sent me.

Testimonies About Jesus

[31]"If I testify about myself, my testimony is not valid. [32]There is another who testifies in my favour, and I know that his testimony about me is valid. [33]"You have sent to John and he has testified to the truth. [34]Not that I accept human testimony; but I mention it that you may be saved. [35]John was a lamp that burned and gave light, and you chose for a time to enjoy his light.

[36]"I have testimony weightier than that of John. For the very work that the Father has given me to finish, and which I am doing, testifies that the Father has sent me. [37]And the Father who sent me has himself testified concerning me. You have never heard his voice nor seen his form, [38]nor does his word dwell in you, for you do not believe the one he sent. [39]You diligently study[c] the Scriptures because you think that by them you possess eternal life. These are the Scriptures that testify about me, [40]yet you refuse to come to me to have life.

[41]"I do not accept praise from men, [42]but I know you. I know that you do not have the love of God in your hearts. [43]I have come in my Father's name, and you do not accept me; but if someone else comes in his own name, you will accept him. [44]How can you believe if you accept praise from one another, yet make no effort to obtain the praise that comes from the only God?[d]

[45]"But do not think I will accuse you before the Father. Your accuser is Moses, on whom your hopes are set. [46]If you believed Moses, you would believe me, for he wrote about me. [47]But since you do not believe what he wrote, how are you going to believe what I say?"

Jesus Feeds the Five Thousand

6 Some time after this, Jesus crossed to the far shore of the Sea of Galilee (that is, the Sea of Tiberias), [2]and a great crowd of people followed him because they saw the miraculous signs he had performed on the sick. [3]Then Jesus went up on a mountainside and sat down with his disciples. [4]The Jewish Passover Feast was near.

[5]When Jesus looked up and saw a great crowd coming towards him, he said to

[c]39 Or *Study diligently* (the imperative)   [d]44 Some early manuscripts *the Only One*

Philip, "Where shall we buy bread for these people to eat?" [6]He asked this only to test him, for he already had in mind what he was going to do.

[7]Philip answered him, "Eight months' wages[a] would not buy enough bread for each one to have a bite!"

[8]Another of his disciples, Andrew, Simon Peter's brother, spoke up, [9]"Here is a boy with five small barley loaves and two small fish, but how far will they go among so many?"

[10]Jesus said, "Make the people sit down." There was plenty of grass in that place, and the men sat down, about five thousand of them. [11]Jesus then took the loaves, gave thanks, and distributed to those who were seated as much as they wanted. He did the same with the fish.

[12]When they had all had enough to eat, he said to his disciples, "Gather the pieces that are left over. Let nothing be wasted." [13]So they gathered them and filled twelve baskets with the pieces of the five barley loaves left over by those who had eaten.

[14]After the people saw the miraculous sign that Jesus did, they began to say, "Surely this is the Prophet who is to come into the world." [15]Jesus, knowing that they intended to come and make him king by force, withdrew again to a mountain by himself.

Jesus Walks on the Water

[16]When evening came, his disciples went down to the lake, [17]where they got into a boat and set off across the lake for Capernaum. By now it was dark, and Jesus had not yet joined them. [18]A strong wind was blowing and the waters grew rough. [19]When they had rowed three or three and a half miles,[b] they saw Jesus approaching the boat, walking on the water; and they were terrified. [20]But he said to them, "It is I; don't be afraid." [21]Then they were willing to take him into the boat, and immediately the boat reached the shore where they were heading.

[22]The next day the crowd that had stayed on the opposite shore of the lake realised that only one boat had been there, and that Jesus had not entered it with his disciples, but that they had gone away alone. [23]Then some boats from Tiberias landed near the place where the people had eaten the bread after the Lord had given thanks. [24]Once the crowd realised that neither Jesus nor his disciples were there, they got into the boats and went to Capernaum in search of Jesus.

Jesus the Bread of Life

[25]When they found him on the other side of the lake, they asked him, "Rabbi, when did you get here?"

[26]Jesus answered, "I tell you the truth, you are looking for me, not because you saw miraculous signs but because you ate the loaves and had your fill. [27]Do not work for food that spoils, but for food that endures to eternal life, which the Son of Man will give you. On him God the Father has placed his seal of approval."

[28]Then they asked him, "What must we do to do the works God requires?"

[29]Jesus answered, "The work of God is this: to believe in the one he has sent."

[30]So they asked him, "What miraculous sign then will you give that we may see it and believe you? What will you do? [31]Our forefathers ate the manna in the desert; as it is written: 'He gave them bread from heaven to eat.'[c]"

[32]Jesus said to them, "I tell you the truth, it is not Moses who has given you the bread from heaven, but it is my Father who gives you the true bread from heaven. [33]For the bread of God is he who comes down from heaven and gives life to the world."

[34]"Sir," they said, "from now on give us this bread."

[35]Then Jesus declared, "I am the bread of life. He who comes to me will never go hungry, and he who believes in me will never be thirsty. [36]But as I told you, you have seen me and still you do not believe. [37]All that the Father gives me will come to me, and whoever comes to me I will never

drive away. [38]For I have come down from heaven not to do my will but to do the will of him who sent me. [39]And this is the will of him who sent me, that I shall lose none of all that he has given me, but raise them up at the last day. [40]For my Father's will is that everyone who looks to the Son and believes in him shall have eternal life, and I will raise him up at the last day."

[41]At this the Jews began to grumble about him because he said, "I am the bread that came down from heaven." [42]They said, "Is this not Jesus, the son of Joseph, whose father and mother we know? How can he now say, 'I came down from heaven'?"

[43]"Stop grumbling among yourselves," Jesus answered. [44]"No-one can come to me unless the Father who sent me draws him, and I will raise him up at the last day. [45]It is written in the Prophets: 'They will all be taught by God.'[d] Everyone who listens to the Father and learns from him comes to me. [46]No-one has seen the Father except the one who is from God; only he has seen the Father. [47]I tell you the truth, he who believes has everlasting life. [48]I am the bread of life. [49]Your forefathers ate the manna in the desert, yet they died. [50]But here is the bread that comes down from heaven, which a man may eat and not die. [51]I am the living bread that came down from heaven. If anyone eats of this bread, he will live for ever. This bread is my flesh, which I will give for the life of the world."

[52]Then the Jews began to argue sharply among themselves, "How can this man give us his flesh to eat?"

[53]Jesus said to them, "I tell you the truth, unless you can eat the flesh of the Son of Man and drink his blood, you have no life in you. [54]Whoever eats my flesh and drinks my blood has eternal life, and I will raise him up at the last day. [55]For my flesh is real food and my blood is real drink. [56]Whoever eats my flesh and drinks my blood remains in me, and I in him. [57]Just as the living Father sent me and I live because of the Father, so the one who feeds on me will live because of me. [58]This is the bread that came down from heaven. Your forefathers ate manna and died, but he who feeds on this bread will live for ever." [59]He said this while teaching in the synagogue in Capernaum.

Many Disciples Desert Jesus

[60]On hearing it, many of his disciples said, "This is a hard teaching. Who can accept it?"

[61]Aware that his disciples were grumbling about this, Jesus said to them, "Does this offend you? [62]What if you see the Son of Man ascend to where he was before! [63]The Spirit gives life; the flesh counts for nothing. The words I have spoken to you are spirit[e] and they are life. [64]Yet there are some of you who do not believe." For Jesus had known from the beginning which of them did not believe and who would betray him. [65]He went on to say, "This is why I told you that no-one can come to me unless the Father has enabled him."

[66]From this time many of his disciples turned back and no longer followed him.

[67]"You do not want to leave too, do you?" Jesus asked the Twelve.

[68]Simon Peter answered him, "Lord, to whom shall we go? You have the words of eternal life. [69]We believe and know that you are the Holy One of God."

[70]Then Jesus replied, "Have I not chosen you, the Twelve? Yet one of you is a devil!" [71](He meant Judas, the son of Simon Iscariot, who, though one of the Twelve, was later to betray him.)

Jesus Goes to the Feast of Tabernacles

7 After this, Jesus went around in Galilee, purposely staying away from Judea because the Jews there were waiting to take his life. [2]But when the Jewish Feast of Tabernacles was near, [3]Jesus' brothers said to him, "You ought to leave here and go to Judea, so that your disciples may see the miracles you do. [4]No-one who wants to become a public figure acts in secret. Since you are doing these things, show

---

d45 Isaiah 54:13   *e63 Or Spirit*

yourself to the world." ⁵For even his own brothers did not believe in him.

⁶Therefore Jesus told them, "The right time for me has not yet come; for you any time is right. ⁷The world cannot hate you, but it hates me because I testify that what it does is evil. ⁸You go to the Feast. I am not yet*a* going up to this Feast, because for me the right time has not yet come." ⁹Having said this, he stayed in Galilee.

¹⁰However, after his brothers had left for the Feast, he went also, not publicly, but in secret. ¹¹Now at the Feast the Jews were watching for him and asking, "Where is that man?"

¹²Among the crowds there was widespread whispering about him. Some said, "He is a good man."

Others replied, "No, he deceives the people." ¹³But no-one would say anything publicly about him for fear of the Jews.

Jesus Teaches at the Feast

¹⁴Not until halfway through the Feast did Jesus go up to the temple courts and begin to teach. ¹⁵The Jews were amazed and asked, "How did this man get such learning without having studied?"

¹⁶Jesus answered, "My teaching is not my own. It comes from him who sent me. ¹⁷If anyone chooses to do God's will, he will find out whether my teaching comes from God or whether I speak on my own. ¹⁸He who speaks on his own does so to gain honour for himself, but he who works for the honour of the one who sent him is a man of truth; there is nothing false about him. ¹⁹Has not Moses given you the law? Yet not one of you keeps the law. Why are you trying to kill me?"

²⁰"You are demon-possessed," the crowd answered. "Who is trying to kill you?"

²¹Jesus said to them, "I did one miracle, and you are all astonished. ²²Yet, because Moses gave you circumcision (though actually it did not come from Moses, but from the patriarchs), you circumcise a child on the Sabbath. ²³Now if a child can be circumcised on the Sabbath so that the

law of Moses may not be broken, why are you angry with me for healing the whole man on the Sabbath? ²⁴Stop judging by mere appearances, and make a right judgment."

Is Jesus the Christ?

²⁵At that point some of the people of Jerusalem began to ask, "Isn't this the man they are trying to kill? ²⁶Here he is, speaking publicly, and they are not saying a word to him. Have the authorities really concluded that he is the Christ?*b* ²⁷But we know where this man is from; when the Christ comes, no-one will know where he is from."

²⁸Then Jesus, still teaching in the temple courts, cried out, "Yes, you know me, and you know where I am from. I am not here on my own, but he who sent me is true. You do not know him, ²⁹but I know him because I am from him and he sent me."

³⁰At this they tried to seize him, but no-one laid a hand on him, because his time had not yet come. ³¹Still, many in the crowd put their faith in him. They said, "When the Christ comes, will he do more miraculous signs than this man?"

³²The Pharisees heard the crowd whispering such things about him. Then the chief priests and the Pharisees sent temple guards to arrest him.

³³Jesus said, "I am with you for only a short time, and then I go to the one who sent me. ³⁴You will look for me, but you will not find me; and where I am, you cannot come."

³⁵The Jews said to one another, "Where does this man intend to go that we cannot find him? Will he go where our people live scattered among the Greeks, and teach the Greeks? ³⁶What did he mean when he said, 'You will look for me, but you will not find me,' and 'Where I am, you cannot come'?"

³⁷On the last and greatest day of the Feast, Jesus stood and said in a loud voice, "If anyone is thirsty, let him come to me and drink. ³⁸Whoever believes in me, as*c* the Scripture has said, streams of living

a8 Some early manuscripts do not have yet.   *b26 Or Messiah; also in verses 27, 31, 41, and 42*
c37,38 Or If anyone is thirsty, let him come to me. / And let him drink, ³⁸who believes in me. / As

water will flow from within him." [39]By this he meant the Spirit, whom those who believed in him were later to receive. Up to that time the Spirit had not been given, since Jesus had not yet been glorified.

[40]On hearing his words, some of the people said, "Surely this man is the Prophet."

[41]Others said, "He is the Christ."

Still others asked, "How can the Christ come from Galilee? [42]Does not the Scripture say that the Christ will come from David's family[d] and from Bethlehem, the town where David lived?" [43]Thus the people were divided because of Jesus. [44]Some wanted to seize him, but no-one laid a hand on him.

Unbelief of the Jewish Leaders

[45]Finally the temple guards went back to the chief priests and Pharisees, who asked them, "Why didn't you bring him in?"

[46]"No-one ever spoke the way this man does," the guards declared.

[47]"You mean he has deceived you also?" the Pharisees retorted. [48]"Has any of the rulers or of the Pharisees believed in him? [49]No! But this mob that knows nothing of the law—there is a curse on them."

[50]Nicodemus, who had gone to Jesus earlier and who was one of their own number, asked, [51]"Does our law condemn a man without first hearing him to find out what he is doing?"

[52]They replied, "Are you from Galilee, too? Look into it, and you will find that a prophet[e] does not come out of Galilee."

[The earliest manuscripts and other ancient witnesses do not have John 7:53–8:11]

[53]Then each went to his own home.

8 But Jesus went to the Mount of Olives. [2]At dawn he appeared again in the temple courts, where all the people gathered round him, and he sat down to teach them. [3]The teachers of the law and the Pharisees brought in a woman caught in adultery. They made her stand before the group [4]and said to Jesus, "Teacher, this woman was caught in the act of adultery. [5]In the Law Moses commanded us to stone such women. Now what do you say?" [6]They were using this question as a trap, in order to have a basis for accusing him.

But Jesus bent down and started to write on the ground with his finger. [7]When they kept on questioning him, he straightened up and said to them, "If any one of you is without sin, let him be the first to throw a stone at her." [8]Again he stooped down and wrote on the ground.

[9]At this, those who heard began to go away one at a time, the older ones first, until only Jesus was left, with the woman still standing there. [10]Jesus straightened up and asked her, "Woman, where are they? Has no-one condemned you?"

[11]"No-one, sir," she said.

"Then neither do I condemn you," Jesus declared. "Go now and leave your life of sin."

The Validity of Jesus' Testimony

[12]When Jesus spoke again to the people, he said, "I am the light of the world. Whoever follows me will never walk in darkness, but will have the light of life."

[13]The Pharisees challenged him, "Here you are, appearing as your own witness; your testimony is not valid."

[14]Jesus answered, "Even if I testify on my own behalf, my testimony is valid, for I know where I came from and where I am going. But you have no idea where I come from or where I am going. [15]You judge by human standards; I pass judgment on no-one. [16]But if I do judge, my decisions are right, because I am not alone. I stand with the Father, who sent me. [17]In your own Law it is written that the testimony of two men is valid. [18]I am one who testifies for myself; my other witness is the Father, who sent me."

d42 Greek *seed*　　e52 Two early manuscripts *the Prophet*

¹⁹Then they asked him, "Where is your father?"

"You do not know me or my Father," Jesus replied. "If you knew me, you would know my Father also." ²⁰He spoke these words while teaching in the temple area near the place where the offerings were put. Yet no-one seized him, because his time had not yet come.

²¹Once more Jesus said to them, "I am going away, and you will look for me, and you will die in your sin. Where I go, you cannot come."

²²This made the Jews ask, "Will he kill himself? Is that why he says, 'Where I go, you cannot come'?"

²³But he continued, "You are from below; I am from above. You are of this world; I am not of this world. ²⁴I told you that you would die in your sins; if you do not believe that I am ˌthe one I claim to be˩,ᵃ you will indeed die in your sins."

²⁵"Who are you?" they asked.

"Just what I have been claiming all along," Jesus replied. ²⁶"I have much to say in judgment of you. But he who sent me is reliable, and what I have heard from him I tell the world."

²⁷They did not understand that he was telling them about his Father. ²⁸So Jesus said, "When you have lifted up the Son of Man, then you will know that I am ˌthe one I claim to be˩, and that I do nothing on my own but speak just what the Father has taught me. ²⁹The one who sent me is with me; he has not left me alone, for I always do what pleases him." ³⁰Even as he spoke, many put their faith in him.

The Children of Abraham

³¹To the Jews who had believed him, Jesus said, "If you hold to my teaching, you are really my disciples. ³²Then you will know the truth, and the truth will set you free."

³³They answered him, "We are Abraham's descendantsᵇ and have never been slaves of anyone. How can you say that we shall be set free?"

³⁴Jesus replied, "I tell you the truth, everyone who sins is a slave to sin. ³⁵Now a slave has no permanent place in the family, but a son belongs to it for ever. ³⁶So if the Son sets you free, you will be free indeed. ³⁷I know you are Abraham's descendants. Yet you are ready to kill me, because you have no room for my word. ³⁸I am telling you what I have seen in the Father's presence, and you do what you have heard from your father."ᶜ

³⁹"Abraham is our father," they answered.

"If you were Abraham's children," said Jesus, "then you wouldᵈ do the things Abraham did. ⁴⁰As it is, you are determined to kill me, a man who has told you the truth that I heard from God. Abraham did not do such things. ⁴¹You are doing the things your own father does."

"We are not illegitimate children," they protested. "The only Father we have is God himself."

The Children of the Devil

⁴²Jesus said to them, "If God were your Father, you would love me, for I came from God and now am here. I have not come on my own; but he sent me. ⁴³Why is my language not clear to you? Because you are unable to hear what I say. ⁴⁴You belong to your father, the devil, and you want to carry out your father's desire. He was a murderer from the beginning, not holding to the truth, for there is no truth in him. When he lies, he speaks his native language, for he is a liar and the father of lies. ⁴⁵Yet because I tell the truth, you do not believe me! ⁴⁶Can any of you prove me guilty of sin? If I am telling the truth, why don't you believe me? ⁴⁷He who belongs to God hears what God says. The reason you do not hear is that you do not belong to God."

The Claims of Jesus About Himself

⁴⁸The Jews answered him, "Aren't we right in saying that you are a Samaritan and demon-possessed?"

ᵃ24 Or *I am he*; also in verse 28   ᵇ33 Greek *seed*; also in verse 37
ᶜ38 Or *presence. Therefore do what you have heard from the Father.*
ᵈ39 Some early manuscripts *"If you are Abraham's children," said Jesus, "then*

⁴⁹"I am not possessed by a demon," said Jesus, "but I honour my Father and you dishonour me. ⁵⁰I am not seeking glory for myself; but there is one who seeks it, and he is the judge. ⁵¹I tell you the truth, if anyone keeps my word, he will never see death."

⁵²At this the Jews exclaimed, "Now we know that you are demon-possessed! Abraham died and so did the prophets, yet you say that if anyone keeps your word, he will never taste death. ⁵³Are you greater than our father Abraham? He died, and so did the prophets. Who do you think you are?"

⁵⁴Jesus replied, "If I glorify myself, my glory means nothing. My Father, whom you claim as your God, is the one who glorifies me. ⁵⁵Though you do not know him, I know him. If I said I did not, I would be a liar like you, but I do know him and keep his word. ⁵⁶Your father Abraham rejoiced at the thought of seeing my day; he saw it and was glad."

⁵⁷"You are not yet fifty years old," the Jews said to him, "and you have seen Abraham!"

⁵⁸"I tell you the truth," Jesus answered, "before Abraham was born, I am!" ⁵⁹At this, they picked up stones to stone him, but Jesus hid himself, slipping away from the temple grounds.

Jesus Heals a Man Born Blind

9 As he went along, he saw a man blind from birth. ²His disciples asked him, "Rabbi, who sinned, this man or his parents, that he was born blind?"

³"Neither this man nor his parents sinned," said Jesus, "but this happened so that the work of God might be displayed in his life. ⁴As long as it is day, we must do the work of him who sent me. Night is coming, when no-one can work. ⁵While I am in the world, I am the light of the world."

⁶Having said this, he spat on the ground, made some mud with the saliva, and put it on the man's eyes. ⁷"Go," he told him, "wash in the Pool of Siloam" (this word means Sent). So the man went and washed, and came home seeing.

⁸His neighbours and those who had formerly seen him begging asked, "Isn't this the same man who used to sit and beg?" ⁹Some claimed that he was.

Others said, "No, he only looks like him."

But he himself insisted, "I am the man."

¹⁰"How then were your eyes opened?" they demanded.

¹¹He replied, "The man they call Jesus made some mud and put it on my eyes. He told me to go to Siloam and wash. So I went and washed, and then I could see."

¹²"Where is this man?" they asked him. "I don't know," he said.

The Pharisees Investigate the Healing

¹³They brought to the Pharisees the man who had been blind. ¹⁴Now the day on which Jesus had made the mud and opened the man's eyes was a Sabbath. ¹⁵Therefore the Pharisees also asked him how he had received his sight. "He put mud on my eyes," the man replied, "and I washed, and now I see."

¹⁶Some of the Pharisees said, "This man is not from God, for he does not keep the Sabbath."

But others asked, "How can a sinner do such miraculous signs?" So they were divided.

¹⁷Finally they turned again to the blind man, "What have you to say about him? It was your eyes he opened."

The man replied, "He is a prophet."

¹⁸The Jews still did not believe that he had been blind and had received his sight until they sent for the man's parents. ¹⁹"Is this your son?" they asked. "Is this the one you say was born blind? How is it that now he can see?"

²⁰"We know he is our son," the parents answered, "and we know he was born blind. ²¹But how he can see now, or who opened his eyes, we don't know. Ask him. He is of age; he will speak for himself." ²²His parents said this because they were afraid of the Jews, for already the Jews had decided that anyone who acknowledged that Jesus was the Christ[a] would

be put out of the synagogue. ²³That was why his parents said, "He is of age; ask him."

²⁴A second time they summoned the man who had been blind. "Give glory to God,"*b* they said. "We know this man is a sinner."

²⁵He replied, "Whether he is a sinner or not, I don't know. One thing I do know. I was blind but now I see!"

²⁶Then they asked him, "What did he do to you? How did he open your eyes?"

²⁷He answered, "I have told you already and you did not listen. Why do you want to hear it again? Do you want to become his disciples, too?"

²⁸Then they hurled insults at him and said, "You are this fellow's disciple! We are disciples of Moses! ²⁹We know that God spoke to Moses, but as for this fellow, we don't even know where he comes from."

³⁰The man answered, "Now that is remarkable! You don't know where he comes from, yet he opened my eyes. ³¹We know that God does not listen to sinners. He listens to the godly man who does his will. ³²Nobody has ever heard of opening the eyes of a man born blind. ³³If this man were not from God, he could do nothing."

³⁴To this they replied, "You were steeped in sin at birth; how dare you lecture us!" And they threw him out.

Spiritual Blindness

³⁵Jesus heard that they had thrown him out, and when he found him, he said, "Do you believe in the Son of Man?"

³⁶"Who is he, sir?" the man asked. "Tell me so that I may believe in him."

³⁷Jesus said, "You have now seen him; in fact, he is the one speaking with you."

³⁸Then the man said, "Lord, I believe," and he worshipped him.

³⁹Jesus said, "For judgment I have come into this world, so that the blind will see and those who see will become blind."

⁴⁰Some Pharisees who were with him heard him say this and asked, "What? Are we blind too?"

⁴¹Jesus said, "If you were blind, you would not be guilty of sin; but now that you claim you can see, your guilt remains.

The Shepherd and His Flock

10 "I tell you the truth, the man who does not enter the sheep pen by the gate, but climbs in by some other way, is a thief and a robber. ²The man who enters by the gate is the shepherd of his sheep. ³The watchman opens the gate for him, and the sheep listen to his voice. He calls his own sheep by name and leads them out. ⁴When he has brought out all his own, he goes on ahead of them, and his sheep follow him because they know his voice. ⁵But they will never follow a stranger; in fact, they will run away from him because they do not recognise a stranger's voice." ⁶Jesus used this figure of speech, but they did not understand what he was telling them.

⁷Therefore Jesus said again, "I tell you the truth, I am the gate for the sheep. ⁸All who ever came before me were thieves and robbers, but the sheep did not listen to them. ⁹I am the gate; whoever enters through me will be saved.*a* He will come in and go out, and find pasture. ¹⁰The thief comes only to steal and kill and destroy; I have come that they may have life, and have it to the full.

¹¹"I am the good shepherd. The good shepherd lays down his life for the sheep. ¹²The hired hand is not the shepherd who owns the sheep. So when he sees the wolf coming, he abandons the sheep and runs away. Then the wolf attacks the flock and scatters it. ¹³The man runs away because he is a hired hand and cares nothing for the sheep.

¹⁴"I am the good shepherd; I know my sheep and my sheep know me—¹⁵just as the Father knows me and I know the Father—and I lay down my life for the sheep. ¹⁶I have other sheep that are not of this sheep pen. I must bring them also. They too will listen to my voice, and there shall be one flock and one shepherd. ¹⁷The reason my Father loves me is that I lay

---

a22 Or Messiah   b24 A solemn charge to tell the truth (see Joshua 7:19)   a9 Or kept safe down my life—only to take it up again. [18]No-one takes it from me, but I lay it down of my own accord. I have authority to lay it down and authority to take it up again. This command I received from my Father."

[19]At these words the Jews were again divided. [20]Many of them said, "He is demon-possessed and raving mad. Why listen to him?"

[21]But others said, "These are not the sayings of a man possessed by a demon. Can a demon open the eyes of the blind?"

The Unbelief of the Jews

[22]Then came the Feast of Dedication[b] at Jerusalem. It was winter, [23]and Jesus was in the temple area walking in Solomon's Colonnade. [24]The Jews gathered round him, saying, "How long will you keep us in suspense? If you are the Christ,[c] tell us plainly."

[25]Jesus answered, "I did tell you, but you do not believe. The miracles I do in my Father's name speak for me, [26]but you do not believe because you are not my sheep. [27]My sheep listen to my voice; I know them, and they follow me. [28]I give them eternal life, and they shall never perish; no-one can snatch them out of my hand. [29]My Father, who has given them to me, is greater than all;[d] no-one can snatch them out of my Father's hand. [30]I and the Father are one."

[31]Again the Jews picked up stones to stone him, [32]but Jesus said to them, "I have shown you many great miracles from the Father. For which of these do you stone me?"

[33]"We are not stoning you for any of these," replied the Jews, "but for blasphemy, because you, a mere man, claim to be God."

[34]Jesus answered them, "Is it not written in your Law, 'I have said you are gods'[e]? [35]If he called them 'gods', to whom the word of God came—and the Scripture cannot be broken—[36]what about the one whom the Father set apart as his very own and sent into the world? Why then do you

accuse me of blasphemy because I said, 'I am God's Son'? [37]Do not believe me unless I do what my Father does. [38]But if I do it, even though you do not believe me, believe the miracles, that you may know and understand that the Father is in me, and I in the Father." [39]Again they tried to seize him, but he escaped their grasp.

[40]Then Jesus went back across the Jordan to the place where John had been baptising in the early days. Here he stayed [41]and many people came to him. They said, "Though John never performed a miraculous sign, all that John said about this man was true." [42]And in that place many believed in Jesus.

The Death of Lazarus

11 Now a man named Lazarus was sick. He was from Bethany, the village of Mary and her sister Martha. [2]This Mary, whose brother Lazarus now lay sick, was the same one who poured perfume on the Lord and wiped his feet with her hair. [3]So the sisters sent word to Jesus, "Lord, the one you love is sick."

[4]When he heard this, Jesus said, "This sickness will not end in death. No, it is for God's glory so that God's Son may be glorified through it." [5]Jesus loved Martha and her sister and Lazarus. [6]Yet when he heard that Lazarus was sick, he stayed where he was two more days.

[7]Then he said to his disciples, "Let us go back to Judea."

[8]"But Rabbi," they said, "a short while ago the Jews tried to stone you, and yet you are going back there?"

[9]Jesus answered, "Are there not twelve hours of daylight? A man who walks by day will not stumble, for he sees by this world's light. [10]It is when he walks by night that he stumbles, for he has no light."

[11]After he had said this, he went on to tell them, "Our friend Lazarus has fallen asleep; but I am going there to wake him up."

[12]His disciples replied, "Lord, if he sleeps, he will get better." [13]Jesus had been speaking of his death, but his

---

[b]22 That is, Hanukkah　　[c]24 Or Messiah
[d]29 Many early manuscripts What my Father has given me is greater than all　　[e]34 Psalm 82:6

disciples thought he meant natural sleep.
[14]So then he told them plainly, "Lazarus is dead, [15]and for your sake I am glad I was not there, so that you may believe. But let us go to him."

[16]Then Thomas (called Didymus) said to the rest of the disciples, "Let us also go, that we may die with him."

Jesus Comforts the Sisters

[17]On his arrival, Jesus found that Lazarus had already been in the tomb for four days. [18]Bethany was less than two miles[a] from Jerusalem, [19]and many Jews had come to Martha and Mary to comfort them in the loss of their brother. [20]When Martha heard that Jesus was coming, she went out to meet him, but Mary stayed at home.

[21]"Lord," Martha said to Jesus, "if you had been here, my brother would not have died. [22]But I know that even now God will give you whatever you ask."

[23]Jesus said to her, "Your brother will rise again."

[24]Martha answered, "I know he will rise again in the resurrection at the last day."

[25]Jesus said to her, "I am the resurrection and the life. He who believes in me will live, even though he dies; [26]and whoever lives and believes in me will never die. Do you believe this?"

[27]"Yes, Lord," she told him, "I believe that you are the Christ,[b] the Son of God, who was to come into the world."

[28]And after she had said this, she went back and called her sister Mary aside. "The Teacher is here," she said, "and is asking for you." [29]When Mary heard this, she got up quickly and went to him. [30]Now Jesus had not yet entered the village, but was still at the place where Martha had met him. [31]When the Jews who had been with Mary in the house, comforting her, noticed how quickly she got up and went out, they followed her, supposing she was going to the tomb to mourn there.

[32]When Mary reached the place where Jesus was and saw him, she fell at his feet and said, "Lord, if you had been here, my brother would not have died."

[33]When Jesus saw her weeping, and the Jews who had come along with her also weeping, he was deeply moved in spirit and troubled. [34]"Where have you laid him?" he asked.

"Come and see, Lord," they replied.

[35]Jesus wept.

[36]Then the Jews said, "See how he loved him!"

[37]But some of them said, "Could not he who opened the eyes of the blind man have kept this man from dying?"

Jesus Raises Lazarus From the Dead

[38]Jesus, once more deeply moved, came to the tomb. It was a cave with a stone laid across the entrance. [39]"Take away the stone," he said.

"But, Lord," said Martha, the sister of the dead man, "by this time there is a bad odour, for he has been there four days."

[40]Then Jesus said, "Did I not tell you that if you believed, you would see the glory of God?"

[41]So they took away the stone. Then Jesus looked up and said, "Father, I thank you that you have heard me. [42]I knew that you always hear me, but I said this for the benefit of the people standing here, that they may believe that you sent me."

[43]When he had said this, Jesus called in a loud voice, "Lazarus, come out!" [44]The dead man came out, his hands and feet wrapped with strips of linen, and a cloth around his face.

Jesus said to them, "Take off the grave clothes and let him go."

The Plot to Kill Jesus

[45]Therefore many of the Jews who had come to visit Mary, and had seen what Jesus did, put their faith in him. [46]But some of them went to the Pharisees and told them what Jesus had done. [47]Then the chief priests and the Pharisees called a meeting of the Sanhedrin.

"What are we accomplishing?" they asked. "Here is this man performing many miraculous signs. [48]If we let him go on like this, everyone will believe in him, and

---

[a]18 Greek *fifteen stadia* (about 3 kilometres)   [b]27 Or *Messiah*

then the Romans will come and take away both our place*c* and our nation."

49Then one of them, named Caiaphas, who was high priest that year, spoke up, "You know nothing at all! 50You do not realise that it is better for you that one man die for the people than that the whole nation perish."

51He did not say this on his own, but as high priest that year he prophesied that Jesus would die for the Jewish nation, 52and not only for that nation but also for the scattered children of God, to bring them together and make them one. 53So from that day on they plotted to take his life.

54Therefore Jesus no longer moved about publicly among the Jews. Instead he withdrew to a region near the desert, to a village called Ephraim, where he stayed with his disciples.

55When it was almost time for the Jewish Passover, many went up from the country to Jerusalem for their ceremonial cleansing before the Passover. 56They kept looking for Jesus, and as they stood in the temple area they asked one another, "What do you think? Isn't he coming to the Feast at all?" 57But the chief priests and Pharisees had given orders that if anyone found out where Jesus was, he should report it so that they might arrest him.

Jesus Anointed at Bethany

12 Six days before the Passover, Jesus arrived at Bethany, where Lazarus lived, whom Jesus had raised from the dead. 2Here a dinner was given in Jesus' honour. Martha served, while Lazarus was among those reclining at the table with him. 3Then Mary took about a pint*a* of pure nard, an expensive perfume; she poured it on Jesus' feet and wiped his feet with her hair. And the house was filled with the fragrance of the perfume.

4But one of his disciples, Judas Iscariot, who was later to betray him, objected, 5"Why wasn't this perfume sold and the money given to the poor? It was worth a year's wages."*b* 6He did not say this because he cared about the poor but because he was a thief; as keeper of the money bag, he used to help himself to what was put into it.

7"Leave her alone," Jesus replied. "⌐It was intended⌐ that she should save this perfume for the day of my burial. 8You will always have the poor among you, but you will not always have me."

9Meanwhile a large crowd of Jews found out that Jesus was there and came, not only because of him but also to see Lazarus, whom he had raised from the dead. 10So the chief priests made plans to kill Lazarus as well, 11for on account of him many of the Jews were going over to Jesus and putting their faith in him.

The Triumphal Entry

12The next day the great crowd that had come for the Feast heard that Jesus was on his way to Jerusalem. 13They took palm branches and went out to meet him, shouting,

"Hosanna!"*c*

"Blessed is he who comes in the name
     of the Lord!"*d*

"Blessed is the King of Israel!"

14Jesus found a young donkey and sat upon it, as it is written,

15"Do not be afraid, O Daughter of Zion;
     see, your king is coming,
     seated on a donkey's colt."*e*

16At first his disciples did not understand all this. Only after Jesus was glorified did they realise that these things had been written about him and that they had done these things to him. 17Now the crowd that was with him when he called Lazarus from the tomb and raised him from the dead continued to spread the word. 18Many people, because they had heard that he had given this miraculous sign, went out to meet him.

---

c48 Or *temple*   *a3* Greek a litra (probably about 0.5 litre)   *b5* Greek *three hundred denarii*
c13 A Hebrew expression meaning "Save!" which became an exclamation of praise   *d13* Psalm 118:25,26
e15 Zech. 9:9

19So the Pharisees said to one another, "See, this is getting us nowhere. Look how the whole world has gone after him!"

Jesus Predicts His Death

20Now there were some Greeks among those who went up to worship at the Feast. 21They came to Philip, who was from Bethsaida in Galilee, with a request. "Sir," they said, "we would like to see Jesus." 22Philip went to tell Andrew; Andrew and Philip in turn told Jesus.

23Jesus replied, "The hour has come for the Son of Man to be glorified. 24I tell you the truth, unless a grain of wheat falls to the ground and dies, it remains only a single seed. But if it dies, it produces many seeds. 25The man who loves his life will lose it, while the man who hates his life in this world will keep it for eternal life. 26Whoever serves me must follow me; and where I am, my servant also will be. My Father will honour the one who serves me.

27"Now my heart is troubled, and what shall I say? 'Father, save me from this hour'? No, it was for this very reason I came to this hour. 28Father, glorify your name!"

Then a voice came from heaven, "I have glorified it, and will glorify it again." 29The crowd that was there and heard it said it had thundered; others said an angel had spoken to him.

30Jesus said, "This voice was for your benefit, not mine. 31Now is the time for judgment on this world; now the prince of this world will be driven out. 32But I, when I am lifted up from the earth, will draw all men to myself." 33He said this to show the kind of death he was going to die.

34The crowd spoke up, "We have heard from the Law that the Christ*f* will remain for ever, so how can you say, 'The Son of Man must be lifted up'? Who is this 'Son of Man'?"

35Then Jesus told them, "You are going to have the light just a little while longer. Walk while you have the light, before darkness overtakes you. The man who walks in the dark does not know where he is going. 36Put your trust in the light while you have it, so that you may become sons of light." When he had finished speaking, Jesus left and hid himself from them.

The Jews Continue in Their Unbelief

37Even after Jesus had done all these miraculous signs in their presence, they still would not believe in him. 38This was to fulfil the word of Isaiah the prophet:

"Lord, who has believed our message
    and to whom has the arm of the Lord
        been revealed?"*g*

39For this reason they could not believe, because, as Isaiah says elsewhere:

40"He has blinded their eyes
    and deadened their hearts,
so they can neither see with their eyes,
    nor understand with their hearts,
    nor turn—and I would heal them."*h*

41Isaiah said this because he saw Jesus' glory and spoke about him.

42Yet at the same time many even among the leaders believed in him. But because of the Pharisees they would not confess their faith for fear they would be put out of the synagogue; 43for they loved praise from men more than praise from God.

44Then Jesus cried out, "When a man believes in me, he does not believe in me only, but in the one who sent me. 45When he looks at me, he sees the one who sent me. 46I have come into the world as a light, so that no-one who believes in me should stay in darkness.

47"As for the person who hears my words but does not keep them, I do not judge him. For I did not come to judge the world, but to save it. 48There is a judge for the one who rejects me and does not accept my words; that very word which I spoke will condemn him at the last day. 49For I did not speak of my own accord, but the Father who sent me commanded me what to say and how to say it. [50]I know that his command leads to eternal life. So whatever I say is just what the Father has told me to say."

Jesus Washes His Disciples' Feet

13 It was just before the Passover Feast. Jesus knew that the time had come for him to leave this world and go to the Father. Having loved his own who were in the world, he now showed them the full extent of his love.[a]

[2]The evening meal was being served, and the devil had already prompted Judas Iscariot, son of Simon, to betray Jesus. [3]Jesus knew that the Father had put all things under his power, and that he had come from God and was returning to God; [4]so he got up from the meal, took off his outer clothing, and wrapped a towel round his waist. [5]After that, he poured water into a basin and began to wash his disciples' feet, drying them with the towel that was wrapped round him.

[6]He came to Simon Peter, who said to him, "Lord, are you going to wash my feet?"

[7]Jesus replied, "You do not realise now what I am doing, but later you will understand."

[8]"No," said Peter, "you shall never wash my feet."

Jesus answered, "Unless I wash you, you have no part with me."

[9]"Then, Lord," Simon Peter replied, "not just my feet but my hands and my head as well!"

[10]Jesus answered, "A person who has had a bath needs only to wash his feet; his whole body is clean. And you are clean, though not every one of you." [11]For he knew who was going to betray him, and that was why he said not every one was clean.

[12]When he had finished washing their feet, he put on his clothes and returned to his place. "Do you understand what I have done for you?" he asked them. [13]"You call me 'Teacher' and 'Lord', and rightly so, for that is what I am. [14]Now that I, your

Lord and Teacher, have washed your feet, you also should wash one another's feet. [15]I have set you an example that you should do as I have done for you. [16]I tell you the truth, no servant is greater than his master, nor is a messenger greater than the one who sent him. [17]Now that you know these things, you will be blessed if you do them.

Jesus Predicts His Betrayal

[18]"I am not referring to all of you; I know those I have chosen. But this is to fulfil the scripture: 'He who shares my bread has lifted up his heel against me.'[b]

[19]"I am telling you now before it happens, so that when it does happen you will believe that I am He. [20]I tell you the truth, whoever accepts anyone I send accepts me; and whoever accepts me accepts the one who sent me."

[21]After he had said this, Jesus was troubled in spirit and testified, "I tell you the truth, one of you is going to betray me."

[22]His disciples stared at one another, at a loss to know which of them he meant. [23]One of them, the disciple whom Jesus loved, was reclining next to him. [24]Simon Peter motioned to this disciple and said, "Ask him which one he means."

[25]Leaning back against Jesus, he asked him, "Lord, who is it?"

[26]Jesus answered, "It is the one to whom I will give this piece of bread when I have dipped it in the dish." Then, dipping the piece of bread, he gave it to Judas Iscariot, son of Simon. [27]As soon as Judas took the bread, Satan entered into him.

"What you are about to do, do quickly," Jesus told him, [28]but no-one at the meal understood why Jesus said this to him. [29]Since Judas had charge of the money, some thought Jesus was telling him to buy what was needed for the Feast, or to give something to the poor. [30]As soon as Judas had taken the bread, he went out. And it was night.

---

a1 Or *he loved them to the last*   *b18* Psalm 41:9

Jesus Predicts Peter's Denial

[31] When he was gone, Jesus said, "Now is the Son of Man glorified and God is glorified in him. [32] If God is glorified in him,[c] God will glorify the Son in himself, and will glorify him at once.

[33] "My children, I will be with you only a little longer. You will look for me, and just as I told the Jews, so I tell you now: Where I am going, you cannot come.

[34] "A new command I give you: Love one another. As I have loved you, so you must love one another. [35] By this all men will know that you are my disciples, if you love one another."

[36] Simon Peter asked him, "Lord, where are you going?"

Jesus replied, "Where I am going, you cannot follow now, but you will follow later."

[37] Peter asked, "Lord, why can't I follow you now? I will lay down my life for you."

[38] Then Jesus answered, "Will you really lay down your life for me? I tell you the truth, before the cock crows, you will disown me three times!

Jesus Comforts His Disciples

14 "Do not let your hearts be troubled. Trust in God;[a] trust also in me. [2] In my Father's house are many rooms; if it were not so, I would have told you. I am going there to prepare a place for you. [3] And if I go and prepare a place for you, I will come back and take you to be with me that you also may be where I am. [4] You know the way to the place where I am going."

Jesus the Way to the Father

[5] Thomas said to him, "Lord, we don't know where you are going, so how can we know the way?"

[6] Jesus answered, "I am the way and the truth and the life. No-one comes to the Father except through me. [7] If you really knew me, you would know[b] my Father as well. From now on, you do know him and have seen him."

[8] Philip said, "Lord, show us the Father and that will be enough for us."

[9] Jesus answered: "Don't you know me, Philip, even after I have been among you such a long time? Anyone who has seen me has seen the Father. How can you say, 'Show us the Father'? [10] Don't you believe that I am in the Father, and that the Father is in me? The words I say to you are not just my own. Rather, it is the Father, living in me, who is doing his work. [11] Believe me when I say that I am in the Father and the Father is in me; or at least believe on the evidence of the miracles themselves. [12] I tell you the truth, anyone who has faith in me will do what I have been doing. He will do even greater things than these, because I am going to the Father. [13] And I will do whatever you ask in my name, so that the Son may bring glory to the Father. [14] You may ask me for anything in my name, and I will do it.

Jesus Promises the Holy Spirit

[15] "If you love me, you will obey what I command. [16] And I will ask the Father, and he will give you another Counsellor to be with you for ever—[17] the Spirit of truth. The world cannot accept him, because it neither sees him nor knows him. But you know him, for he lives with you and will be[c] in you. [18] I will not leave you as orphans; I will come to you. [19] Before long, the world will not see me any more, but you will see me. Because I live, you also will live. [20] On that day you will realise that I am in my Father, and you are in me, and I am in you. [21] Whoever has my commands and obeys them, he is the one who loves me. He who loves me will be loved by my Father, and I too will love him and show myself to him."

[22] Then Judas (not Judas Iscariot) said, "But, Lord, why do you intend to show yourself to us and not to the world?"

[23] Jesus replied, "If anyone loves me, he will obey my teaching. My Father will love him, and we will come to him and make our home with him. [24] He who does not

---

c32 Many early manuscripts do not have *If God is glorified in him.*
b7 Some early manuscripts *If you really have known me, you will know*
a1 Or *You trust in God*
c17 Some early manuscripts *and is*

love me will not obey my teaching. These words you hear are not my own; they belong to the Father who sent me.

²⁵"All this I have spoken while still with you. ²⁶But the Counsellor, the Holy Spirit, whom the Father will send in my name, will teach you all things and will remind you of everything I have said to you. ²⁷Peace I leave with you; my peace I give you. I do not give to you as the world gives. Do not let your hearts be troubled and do not be afraid.

²⁸"You heard me say, 'I am going away and I am coming back to you.' If you loved me, you would be glad that I am going to the Father, for the Father is greater than I. ²⁹I have told you now before it happens, so that when it does happen you will believe. ³⁰I will not speak with you much longer, for the prince of this world is coming. He has no hold on me, ³¹but the world must learn that I love the Father and that I do exactly what my Father has commanded me.

"Come now; let us leave.

The Vine and the Branches

15 "I am the true vine, and my Father is the gardener. ²He cuts off every branch in me that bears no fruit, while every branch that does bear fruit he prunes[a] so that it will be even more fruitful. ³You are already clean because of the word I have spoken to you. ⁴Remain in me, and I will remain in you. No branch can bear fruit by itself; it must remain in the vine. Neither can you bear fruit unless you remain in me.

⁵"I am the vine; you are the branches. If a man remains in me and I in him, he will bear much fruit; apart from me you can do nothing. ⁶If anyone does not remain in me, he is like a branch that is thrown away and withers; such branches are picked up, thrown into the fire and burned. ⁷If you remain in me and my words remain in you, ask whatever you wish, and it will be given you. ⁸This is to my Father's glory, that you bear much fruit, showing yourselves to be my disciples.

⁹"As the Father has loved me, so have I loved you. Now remain in my love. ¹⁰If you obey my commands, you will remain in my love, just as I have obeyed my Father's commands and remain in his love. ¹¹I have told you this so that my joy may be in you and that your joy may be complete. ¹²My command is this: Love each other as I have loved you. ¹³Greater love has no-one than this, that he lay down his life for his friends. ¹⁴You are my friends if you do what I command. ¹⁵I no longer call you servants, because a servant does not know his master's business. Instead, I have called you friends, for everything that I learned from my Father I have made known to you. ¹⁶You did not choose me, but I chose you and appointed you to go and bear fruit—fruit that will last. Then the Father will give you whatever you ask in my name. ¹⁷This is my command: Love each other.

The World Hates the Disciples

¹⁸"If the world hates you, keep in mind that it hated me first. ¹⁹If you belonged to the world, it would love you as its own. As it is, you do not belong to the world, but I have chosen you out of the world. That is why the world hates you. ²⁰Remember the words I spoke to you: 'No servant is greater than his master.'[b] If they persecuted me, they will persecute you also. If they obeyed my teaching, they will obey yours also. ²¹They will treat you this way because of my name, for they do not know the One who sent me. ²²If I had not come and spoken to them, they would not be guilty of sin. Now, however, they have no excuse for their sin. ²³He who hates me hates my Father as well. ²⁴If I had not done among them what no-one else did, they would not be guilty of sin. But now they have seen these miracles, and yet they have hated both me and my Father. ²⁵But this is to fulfil what is written in their Law: 'They hated me without reason.'[c]

²⁶"When the Counsellor comes, whom I will send to you from the Father, the Spirit of truth who goes out from the Father, he

^a2 The Greek for *prunes* also means *cleans*.   ^b20 John 13:16   ^c25 Psalms 35:19; 69:4

will testify about me. 27And you also must testify, for you have been with me from the beginning.

16 "All this I have told you so that you will not go astray. 2They will put you out of the synagogue; in fact, a time is coming when anyone who kills you will think he is offering a service to God. 3They will do such things because they have not known the Father or me. 4I have told you this, so that when the time comes you will remember that I warned you. I did not tell you this at first because I was with you.

The Work of the Holy Spirit

5"Now I am going to him who sent me, yet none of you asks me, 'Where are you going?' 6Because I have said these things, you are filled with grief. 7But I tell you the truth: It is for your good that I am going away. Unless I go away, the Counsellor will not come to you; but if I go, I will send him to you. 8When he comes, he will convict the world of guilt*a* in regard to sin and righteousness and judgment: 9in regard to sin, because men do not believe in me; 10in regard to righteousness, because I am going to the Father, where you can see me no longer; 11and in regard to judgment, because the prince of this world now stands condemned.

12"I have much more to say to you, more than you can now bear. 13But when he, the Spirit of truth, comes, he will guide you into all truth. He will not speak on his own; he will speak only what he hears, and he will tell you what is yet to come. 14He will bring glory to me by taking from what is mine and making it known to you. 15All that belongs to the Father is mine. That is why I said the Spirit will take from what is mine and make it known to you.

16"In a little while you will see me no more, and then after a little while you will see me."

The Disciples' Grief Will Turn to Joy

17Some of his disciples said to one another, "What does he mean by saying,

'In a little while you will see me no more, and then after a little while you will see me,' and 'Because I am going to the Father'?" 18They kept asking, "What does he mean by 'a little while'? We don't understand what he is saying."

19Jesus saw that they wanted to ask him about this, so he said to them, "Are you asking one another what I meant when I said, 'In a little while you will see me no more, and then after a little while you will see me'? 20I tell you the truth, you will weep and mourn while the world rejoices. You will grieve, but your grief will turn to joy. 21A woman giving birth to a child has pain because her time has come; but when her baby is born she forgets the anguish because of her joy that a child is born into the world. 22So with you: Now is your time of grief, but I will see you again and you will rejoice, and no-one will take away your joy. 23In that day you will no longer ask me anything. I tell you the truth, my Father will give you whatever you ask in my name. 24Until now you have not asked for anything in my name. Ask and you will receive, and your joy will be complete.

25"Though I have been speaking figuratively, a time is coming when I will no longer use this kind of language but will tell you plainly about my Father. 26In that day you will ask in my name. I am not saying that I will ask the Father on your behalf. 27No, the Father himself loves you because you have loved me and have believed that I came from God. 28I came from the Father and entered the world; now I am leaving the world and going back to the Father."

29Then Jesus' disciples said, "Now you are speaking clearly and without figures of speech. 30Now we can see that you know all things and that you do not even need to have anyone ask you questions. This makes us believe that you came from God."

31"You believe at last!"*b* Jesus answered. 32"But a time is coming, and has come, when you will be scattered, each to his own home. You will leave me all alone. Yet I am not alone, for my Father is with me.

---

a8 Or *will expose the guilt of the world*   *b31* Or *"Do you now believe?"*

³³"I have told you these things, so that in me you may have peace. In this world you will have trouble. But take heart! I have overcome the world."

Jesus Prays for Himself

17 After Jesus said this, he looked towards heaven and prayed:

"Father, the time has come. Glorify your Son, that your Son may glorify you. ²For you granted him authority over all people that he might give eternal life to all those you have given him. ³Now this is eternal life: that they may know you, the only true God, and Jesus Christ, whom you have sent. ⁴I have brought you glory on earth by completing the work you gave me to do. ⁵And now, Father, glorify me in your presence with the glory I had with you before the world began.

Jesus Prays for His Disciples

⁶"I have revealed you^a to those whom you gave me out of the world. They were yours; you gave them to me and they have obeyed your word. ⁷Now they know that everything you have given me comes from you. ⁸For I gave them the words you gave me and they accepted them. They knew with certainty that I came from you, and they believed that you sent me. ⁹I pray for them. I am not praying for the world, but for those you have given me, for they are yours. ¹⁰All I have is yours, and all you have is mine. And glory has come to me through them. ¹¹I will remain in the world no longer, but they are still in the world, and I am coming to you. Holy Father, protect them by the power of your name—the name you gave me—so that they may be one as we are one. ¹²While I was with them, I protected them and kept them safe by that name you gave me. None has

been lost except the one doomed to destruction so that Scripture would be fulfilled.

¹³"I am coming to you now, but I say these things while I am still in the world, so that they may have the full measure of my joy within them. ¹⁴I have given them your word and the world has hated them, for they are not of the world any more than I am of the world. ¹⁵My prayer is not that you take them out of the world but that you protect them from the evil one. ¹⁶They are not of the world, even as I am not of it. ¹⁷Sanctify^b them by the truth; your word is truth. ¹⁸As you sent me into the world, I have sent them into the world. ¹⁹For them I sanctify myself, that they too may be truly sanctified.

Jesus Prays for All Believers

²⁰"My prayer is not for them alone. I pray also for those who will believe in me through their message, ²¹that all of them may be one, Father, just as you are in me and I am in you. May they also be in us so that the world may believe that you have sent me. ²²I have given them the glory that you gave me, that they may be one as we are one: ²³I in them and you in me. May they be brought to complete unity to let the world know that you sent me and have loved them even as you have loved me.

²⁴"Father, I want those you have given me to be with me where I am, and to see my glory, the glory you have given me because you loved me before the creation of the world.

²⁵"Righteous Father, though the world does not know you, I know you, and they know that you have sent me. ²⁶I have made you known to them, and will continue to make you known in order that the love you have for me may be in them and that I myself may be in them."

Jesus Arrested

18 When he had finished praying, Jesus left with his disciples and crossed the Kidron Valley. On the other side there was an olive grove, and he and his disciples went into it.

²Now Judas, who betrayed him, knew the place, because Jesus had often met there with his disciples. ³So Judas came to the grove, guiding a detachment of soldiers and some officials from the chief priests and Pharisees. They were carrying torches, lanterns and weapons.

⁴Jesus, knowing all that was going to happen to him, went out and asked them, "Who is it you want?"

⁵"Jesus of Nazareth," they replied.

"I am he," Jesus said. (And Judas the traitor was standing there with them.) ⁶When Jesus said, "I am he," they drew back and fell to the ground.

⁷Again he asked them, "Who is it you want?"

And they said, "Jesus of Nazareth."

⁸"I told you that I am he," Jesus answered. "If you are looking for me, then let these men go." ⁹This happened so that the words he had spoken would be fulfilled: "I have not lost one of those you gave me."ᵃ

¹⁰Then Simon Peter, who had a sword, drew it and struck the high priest's servant, cutting off his right ear. (The servant's name was Malchus.)

¹¹Jesus commanded Peter, "Put your sword away! Shall I not drink the cup the Father has given me?"

Jesus Taken to Annas

¹²Then the detachment of soldiers with its commander and the Jewish officials arrested Jesus. They bound him ¹³and brought him first to Annas, who was the father-in-law of Caiaphas, the high priest that year. ¹⁴Caiaphas was the one who had advised the Jews that it would be good if one man died for the people.

Peter's First Denial

¹⁵Simon Peter and another disciple were following Jesus. Because this disciple was known to the high priest, he went with Jesus into the high priest's courtyard, ¹⁶but Peter had to wait outside at the door. The other disciple, who was known to the high priest, came back, spoke to the girl on duty there and brought Peter in.

¹⁷"You are not one of his disciples, are you?" the girl at the door asked Peter.

He replied, "I am not."

¹⁸It was cold, and the servants and officials stood round a fire they had made to keep warm. Peter also was standing with them, warming himself.

The High Priest Questions Jesus

¹⁹Meanwhile, the high priest questioned Jesus about his disciples and his teaching.

²⁰"I have spoken openly to the world," Jesus replied. "I always taught in synagogues or at the temple, where all the Jews come together. I said nothing in secret. ²¹Why question me? Ask those who heard me. Surely they know what I said."

²²When Jesus said this, one of the officials near by struck him in the face. "Is this the way you answer the high priest?" he demanded.

²³"If I said something wrong," Jesus replied, "testify as to what is wrong. But if I spoke the truth, why did you strike me?" ²⁴Then Annas sent him, still bound, to Caiaphas the high priest.ᵇ

Peter's Second and Third Denials

²⁵As Simon Peter stood warming himself, he was asked, "You are not one of his disciples, are you?"

He denied it, saying, "I am not."

²⁶One of the high priest's servants, a relative of the man whose ear Peter had cut off, challenged him, "Didn't I see you

ᵃ9 John 6:39   ᵇ24 Or (Now Annas had sent him, still bound, to Caiaphas the high priest.)

with him in the olive grove?" ²⁷Again Peter denied it, and at that moment a cock began to crow.

Jesus Before Pilate

²⁸Then the Jews led Jesus from Caiaphas to the palace of the Roman governor. By now it was early morning, and to avoid ceremonial uncleanness the Jews did not enter the palace; they wanted to be able to eat the Passover. ²⁹So Pilate came out to them and asked, "What charges are you bringing against this man?"

³⁰"If he were not a criminal," they replied, "we would not have handed him over to you."

³¹Pilate said, "Take him yourselves and judge him by your own law."

"But we have no right to execute anyone," the Jews objected. ³²This happened so that the words Jesus had spoken indicating the kind of death he was going to die would be fulfilled.

³³Pilate then went back inside the palace, summoned Jesus and asked him, "Are you the king of the Jews?"

³⁴"Is that your own idea," Jesus asked, "or did others talk to you about me?"

³⁵"Am I a Jew?" Pilate replied. "It was your people and your chief priests who handed you over to me. What is it you have done?"

³⁶Jesus said, "My kingdom is not of this world. If it were, my servants would fight to prevent my arrest by the Jews. But now my kingdom is from another place."

³⁷"You are a king, then!" said Pilate.

Jesus answered, "You are right in saying I am a king. In fact, for this reason I was born, and for this I came into the world, to testify to the truth. Everyone on the side of truth listens to me."

³⁸"What is truth?" Pilate asked. With this he went out again to the Jews and said, "I find no basis for a charge against him. ³⁹But it is your custom for me to release to you one prisoner at the time of the Passover. Do you want me to release 'the king of the Jews'?"

⁴⁰They shouted back, "No, not him! Give us Barabbas!" Now Barabbas had taken part in a rebellion.

Jesus Sentenced to be Crucified

19 Then Pilate took Jesus and had him flogged. ²The soldiers twisted together a crown of thorns and put it on his head. They clothed him in a purple robe ³and went up to him again and again, saying, "Hail, king of the Jews!" And they struck him in the face.

⁴Once more Pilate came out and said to the Jews, "Look, I am bringing him out to you to let you know that I find no basis for a charge against him." ⁵When Jesus came out wearing the crown of thorns and the purple robe, Pilate said to them, "Here is the man!"

⁶As soon as the chief priests and their officials saw him, they shouted, "Crucify! Crucify!"

But Pilate answered, "You take him and crucify him. As for me, I find no basis for a charge against him."

⁷The Jews insisted, "We have a law, and according to that law he must die, because he claimed to be the Son of God."

⁸When Pilate heard this, he was even more afraid, ⁹and he went back inside the palace. "Where do you come from?" he asked Jesus, but Jesus gave him no answer. ¹⁰"Do you refuse to speak to me?" Pilate said. "Don't you realise I have power either to free you or to crucify you?"

¹¹Jesus answered, "You would have no power over me if it were not given to you from above. Therefore the one who handed me over to you is guilty of a greater sin."

¹²From then on, Pilate tried to set Jesus free, but the Jews kept shouting, "If you let this man go, you are no friend of Caesar. Anyone who claims to be a king opposes Caesar."

¹³When Pilate heard this, he brought Jesus out and sat down on the judge's seat at a place known as the Stone Pavement (which in Aramaic is Gabbatha). ¹⁴It was the day of Preparation of Passover Week, about the sixth hour.

"Here is your king," Pilate said to the Jews.

¹⁵But they shouted, "Take him away! Take him away! Crucify him!"

"Shall I crucify your king?" Pilate asked.

"We have no king but Caesar," the chief priests answered.

[16]Finally Pilate handed him over to them to be crucified.

The Crucifixion

So the soldiers took charge of Jesus. [17]Carrying his own cross, he went out to the place of the Skull (which in Aramaic is called Golgotha). [18]Here they crucified him, and with him two others—one on each side and Jesus in the middle.

[19]Pilate had a notice prepared and fastened to the cross. It read: JESUS OF NAZARETH, THE KING OF THE JEWS. [20]Many of the Jews read this sign, for the place where Jesus was crucified was near the city, and the sign was written in Aramaic, Latin and Greek. [21]The chief priests of the Jews protested to Pilate, "Do not write 'The King of the Jews', but that this man claimed to be king of the Jews."

[22]Pilate answered, "What I have written, I have written."

[23]When the soldiers crucified Jesus, they took his clothes, dividing them into four shares, one for each of them, with the undergarment remaining. This garment was seamless, woven in one piece from top to bottom.

[24]"Let's not tear it," they said to one another. "Let's decide by lot who will get it."

This happened that the scripture might be fulfilled which said,

"They divided my garments among
　　them
and cast lots for my clothing."[a]

So this is what the soldiers did.

[25]Near the cross of Jesus stood his mother, his mother's sister, Mary the wife of Clopas, and Mary Magdalene. [26]When Jesus saw his mother there, and the disciple whom he loved standing near by, he said to his mother, "Dear woman, here is your son," [27]and to the disciple, "Here is

your mother." From that time on, this disciple took her into his home.

The Death of Jesus

[28]Later, knowing that all was now completed, and so that the Scripture would be fulfilled, Jesus said, "I am thirsty." [29]A jar of wine vinegar was there, so they soaked a sponge in it, put the sponge on a stalk of the hyssop plant, and lifted it to Jesus' lips. [30]When he had received the drink, Jesus said, "It is finished." With that, he bowed his head and gave up his spirit.

[31]Now it was the day of Preparation, and the next day was to be a special Sabbath. Because the Jews did not want the bodies left on the crosses during the Sabbath, they asked Pilate to have the legs broken and the bodies taken down. [32]The soldiers therefore came and broke the legs of the first man who had been crucified with Jesus, and then those of the other. [33]But when they came to Jesus and found that he was already dead, they did not break his legs. [34]Instead, one of the soldiers pierced Jesus' side with a spear, bringing a sudden flow of blood and water. [35]The man who saw it has given testimony, and his testimony is true. He knows that he tells the truth, and he testifies so that you also may believe. [36]These things happened so that the scripture would be fulfilled: "Not one of his bones will be broken,"[b] [37]and, as another scripture says, "They will look on the one they have pierced."[c]

The Burial of Jesus

[38]Later, Joseph of Arimathea asked Pilate for the body of Jesus. Now Joseph was a disciple of Jesus, but secretly because he feared the Jews. With Pilate's permission, he came and took the body away. [39]He was accompanied by Nicodemus, the man who earlier had visited Jesus at night. Nicodemus brought a mixture of myrrh and aloes, about seventy-five pounds.[d] [40]Taking Jesus' body, the two of them wrapped it, with the spices, in strips of linen. This was in

---

[a]24 Psalm 22:18　　[b]36 Exodus 12:46; Num. 9:12; Psalm 34:20　　[c]37 Zech. 12:10
[d]39 Greek a hundred litrai (about 34 kilograms)

accordance with Jewish burial customs. ⁴¹At the place where Jesus was crucified, there was a garden, and in the garden a new tomb, in which no-one had ever been laid. ⁴²Because it was the Jewish day of Preparation and since the tomb was near by, they laid Jesus there.

The Empty Tomb

20 Early on the first day of the week, while it was still dark, Mary Magdalene went to the tomb and saw that the stone had been removed from the entrance. ²So she came running to Simon Peter and the other disciple, the one Jesus loved, and said, "They have taken the Lord out of the tomb, and we don't know where they have put him!"

³So Peter and the other disciple started for the tomb. ⁴Both were running, but the other disciple outran Peter and reached the tomb first. ⁵He bent over and looked in at the strips of linen lying there but did not go in. ⁶Then Simon Peter, who was behind him, arrived and went into the tomb. He saw the strips of linen lying there, ⁷as well as the burial cloth that had been around Jesus' head. The cloth was folded up by itself, separate from the linen. ⁸Finally the other disciple, who had reached the tomb first, also went inside. He saw and believed. ⁹(They still did not understand from Scripture that Jesus had to rise from the dead.)

Jesus Appears to Mary Magdalene

¹⁰Then the disciples went back to their homes, ¹¹but Mary stood outside the tomb crying. As she wept, she bent over to look into the tomb ¹²and saw two angels in white, seated where Jesus' body had been, one at the head and the other at the foot.

¹³They asked her, "Woman, why are you crying?"

"They have taken my Lord away," she said, "and I don't know where they have put him." ¹⁴At this, she turned round and saw Jesus standing there, but she did not realise that it was Jesus.

¹⁵"Woman," he said, "why are you crying? Who is it you are looking for?"

Thinking he was the gardener, she said, "Sir, if you have carried him away, tell me where you have put him, and I will get him."

¹⁶Jesus said to her, "Mary."

She turned towards him and cried out in Aramaic, "Rabboni!" (which means Teacher).

¹⁷Jesus said, "Do not hold on to me, for I have not yet returned to the Father. Go instead to my brothers and tell them, 'I am returning to my Father and your Father, to my God and your God.'"

¹⁸Mary Magdalene went to the disciples with the news: "I have seen the Lord!" And she told them that he had said these things to her.

Jesus Appears to His Disciples

¹⁹On the evening of that first day of the week, when the disciples were together, with the doors locked for fear of the Jews, Jesus came and stood among them and said, "Peace be with you!" ²⁰After he said this, he showed them his hands and side. The disciples were overjoyed when they saw the Lord.

²¹Again Jesus said, "Peace be with you! As the Father has sent me, I am sending you." ²²And with that he breathed on them and said, "Receive the Holy Spirit. ²³If you forgive anyone his sins, they are forgiven; if you do not forgive them, they are not forgiven."

Jesus Appears to Thomas

²⁴Now Thomas (called Didymus), one of the Twelve, was not with the disciples when Jesus came. ²⁵So the other disciples told him, "We have seen the Lord!"

But he said to them, "Unless I see the nail marks in his hands and put my finger where the nails were, and put my hand into his side, I will not believe it."

²⁶A week later his disciples were in the house again, and Thomas was with them. Though the doors were locked, Jesus came and stood among them and said, "Peace be with you!" ²⁷Then he said to Thomas, "Put your finger here; see my

hands. Reach out your hand and put it into my side. Stop doubting and believe."

28Thomas said to him, "My Lord and my God!"

29Then Jesus told him, "Because you have seen me, you have believed; blessed are those who have not seen and yet have believed."

30Jesus did many other miraculous signs in the presence of his disciples, which are not recorded in this book. 31But these are written that you may*a* believe that Jesus is the Christ, the Son of God, and that by believing you may have life in his name.

Jesus and the Miraculous Catch of Fish

21 Afterwards Jesus appeared again to his disciples, by the Sea of Tiberias.*a* It happened this way: 2Simon Peter, Thomas (called Didymus), Nathanael from Cana in Galilee, the sons of Zebedee, and two other disciples were together. 3"I'm going out to fish," Simon Peter told them, and they said, "We'll go with you." So they went out and got into the boat, but that night they caught nothing.

4Early in the morning, Jesus stood on the shore, but the disciples did not realise that it was Jesus.

5He called out to them, "Friends, haven't you any fish?"

"No," they answered.

6He said, "Throw your net on the right side of the boat and you will find some." When they did, they were unable to haul the net in because of the large number of fish.

7Then the disciple whom Jesus loved said to Peter, "It is the Lord!" As soon as Simon Peter heard him say, "It is the Lord," he wrapped his outer garment around him (for he had taken it off) and jumped into the water. 8The other disciples followed in the boat, towing the net full of fish, for they were not far from shore, about a hundred yards.*b* 9When they landed, they saw a fire of burning coals there with fish on it, and some bread.

10Jesus said to them, "Bring some of the fish you have just caught."

11Simon Peter climbed aboard and dragged the net ashore. It was full of large fish, 153, but even with so many the net was not torn. 12Jesus said to them, "Come and have breakfast." None of the disciples dared ask him, "Who are you?" They knew it was the Lord. 13Jesus came, took the bread and gave it to them, and did the same with the fish. 14This was now the third time Jesus appeared to his disciples after he was raised from the dead.

Jesus Reinstates Peter

15When they had finished eating, Jesus said to Simon Peter, "Simon son of John, do you truly love me more than these?"

"Yes, Lord," he said, "you know that I love you."

Jesus said, "Feed my lambs."

16Again Jesus said, "Simon son of John, do you truly love me?"

He answered, "Yes, Lord, you know that I love you."

Jesus said, "Take care of my sheep."

17The third time he said to him, "Simon son of John, do you love me?"

Peter was hurt because Jesus asked him the third time, "Do you love me?" He said, "Lord, you know all things; you know that I love you."

Jesus said, "Feed my sheep. 18I tell you the truth, when you were younger you dressed yourself and went where you wanted; but when you are old you will stretch out your hands, and someone else will dress you and lead you where you do not want to go." 19Jesus said this to indicate the kind of death by which Peter would glorify God. Then he said to him, "Follow me!"

20Peter turned and saw that the disciple whom Jesus loved was following them. (This was the one who had leaned back against Jesus at the supper and had said, "Lord, who is going to betray you?") 21When Peter saw him, he asked, "Lord, what about him?"

---

*a*31 Some manuscripts *may continue to*
*b*8 Greek *about two hundred cubits* (about 90 metres)

*a*1 That is, Sea of Galilee

22Jesus answered, "If I want him to remain alive until I return, what is that to you? You must follow me." 23Because of this, the rumour spread among the brothers that this disciple would not die. But Jesus did not say that he would not die; he only said, "If I want him to remain alive until I return, what is that to you?"

24This is the disciple who testifies to these things and who wrote them down. We know that his testimony is true.

25Jesus did many other things as well. If every one of them were written down, I suppose that even the whole world would not have room for the books that would be written.

Acts

same Jesus, who has been taken from you into heaven, will come back in the same way you have seen him go into heaven."

Jesus Taken Up Into Heaven

1 In my former book, Theophilus, I wrote about all that Jesus began to do and to teach ²until the day he was taken up to heaven, after giving instructions through the Holy Spirit to the apostles he had chosen. ³After his suffering, he showed himself to these men and gave many convincing proofs that he was alive. He appeared to them over a period of forty days and spoke about the kingdom of God. ⁴On one occasion, while he was eating with them, he gave them this command: "Do not leave Jerusalem, but wait for the gift my Father promised, which you have heard me speak about. ⁵For John baptised with*ᵃ* water, but in a few days you will be baptised with the Holy Spirit."

⁶So when they met together, they asked him, "Lord, are you at this time going to restore the kingdom to Israel?"

⁷He said to them: "It is not for you to know the times or dates the Father has set by his own authority. ⁸But you will receive power when the Holy Spirit comes on you; and you will be my witnesses in Jerusalem, and in all Judea and Samaria, and to the ends of the earth."

⁹After he said this, he was taken up before their very eyes, and a cloud hid him from their sight.

¹⁰They were looking intently up into the sky as he was going, when suddenly two men dressed in white stood beside them. ¹¹"Men of Galilee," they said, "why do you stand here looking into the sky? This same Jesus, who has been taken from you into heaven, will come back in the same way you have seen him go into heaven."

Matthias Chosen to Replace Judas

¹²Then they returned to Jerusalem from the hill called the Mount of Olives, a Sabbath day's walk*ᵇ* from the city. ¹³When they arrived, they went upstairs to the room where they were staying. Those present were Peter, John, James and Andrew; Philip and Thomas, Bartholomew and Matthew; James son of Alphaeus and Simon the Zealot, and Judas son of James. ¹⁴They all joined together constantly in prayer, along with the women and Mary the mother of Jesus, and with his brothers.

¹⁵In those days Peter stood up among the believers*ᶜ* (a group numbering about a hundred and twenty) ¹⁶and said, "Brothers, the Scripture had to be fulfilled which the Holy Spirit spoke long ago through the mouth of David concerning Judas, who served as guide for those who arrested Jesus—¹⁷he was one of our number and shared in this ministry."

¹⁸(With the reward he got for his wickedness, Judas bought a field; there he fell headlong, his body burst open and all his intestines spilled out. ¹⁹Everyone in Jerusalem heard about this, so they called that field in their language Akeldama, that is, Field of Blood.)

²⁰"For," said Peter, "it is written in the Book of Psalms,

ᵃ5 Or in   *ᵇ12 That is, about ¾ of a mile (about 1,100 metres)*   *ᶜ15 Greek brothers*

"'May his place be deserted;
    let there be no-one to dwell in it,'*d*

and,

    "'May another take his place of
        leadership.'*e*

21Therefore it is necessary to choose one
of the men who have been with us the
whole time the Lord Jesus went in and out
among us, 22beginning from John's baptism to the time when Jesus was taken up
from us. For one of these must become a
witness with us of his resurrection."

23So they proposed two men: Joseph
called Barsabbas (also known as Justus)
and Matthias. 24Then they prayed, "Lord,
you know everyone's heart. Show us
which of these two you have chosen 25to
take over this apostolic ministry, which
Judas left to go where he belongs." 26Then
they cast lots, and the lot fell to Matthias;
so he was added to the eleven apostles.

The Holy Spirit Comes at Pentecost

2 When the day of Pentecost came,
    they were all together in one place.
2Suddenly a sound like the blowing of a
violent wind came from heaven and filled
the whole house where they were sitting.
3They saw what seemed to be tongues of
fire that separated and came to rest on
each of them. 4All of them were filled with
the Holy Spirit and began to speak in
other tongues*a* as the Spirit enabled them.

5Now there were staying in Jerusalem
God-fearing Jews from every nation
under heaven. 6When they heard this
sound, a crowd came together in bewilder-
ment, because each one heard them
speaking in his own language. 7Utterly
amazed, they asked: "Are not all these
men who are speaking Galileans? 8Then
how is it that each of us hears them in his
own native language? 9Parthians, Medes
and Elamites; residents of Mesopotamia,
Judea and Cappadocia, Pontus and Asia,
10Phrygia and Pamphylia, Egypt and the
parts of Libya near Cyrene; visitors from

Rome 11(both Jews and converts to Judaism); Cretans and Arabs—we hear them
declaring the wonders of God in our own
tongues!" 12Amazed and perplexed, they
asked one another, "What does this
mean?"

13Some, however, made fun of them
and said, "They have had too much
wine."*b*

Peter Addresses the Crowd

14Then Peter stood up with the Eleven,
raised his voice and addressed the crowd:
"Fellow Jews and all of you who live in
Jerusalem, let me explain this to you;
listen carefully to what I say. 15These men
are not drunk, as you suppose. It's only
nine in the morning! 16No, this is what was
spoken by the prophet Joel:

17"'In the last days, God says,
    I will pour out my Spirit on all
        people.
  Your sons and daughters will prophesy,
    your young men will see visions,
    your old men will dream dreams.
18Even on my servants, both men and
        women,
    I will pour out my Spirit in those
        days,
    and they will prophesy.
19I will show wonders in the heaven
        above
    and signs on the earth below,
    blood and fire and billows of smoke.
20The sun will be turned to darkness
    and the moon to blood
    before the coming of the great and
        glorious day of the Lord.
21And everyone who calls
    on the name of the Lord will be
        saved.'*c*

22"Men of Israel, listen to this: Jesus of
Nazareth was a man accredited by God to
you by miracles, wonders and signs, which
God did among you through him, as you
yourselves know. 23This man was handed
over to you by God's set purpose and
foreknowledge; and you, with the help of

d20 Psalm 69:25   *e20* Psalm 109:8
a4 Or *languages*; also in verse 11   *b13* Or *sweet wine*   *c21* Joel 2:28–32

wicked men,*d* put him to death by nailing him to the cross. 24But God raised him from the dead, freeing him from the agony of death, because it was impossible for death to keep its hold on him. 25David said about him:

"'I saw the Lord always before me.
     Because he is at my right hand,
     I will not be shaken.
26Therefore my heart is glad and my
          tongue rejoices;
     my body also will live in hope,
27because you will not abandon me to the
          grave,
     nor will you let your Holy One see
          decay.
28You have made known to me the paths
          of life;
     you will fill me with joy in your
          presence.'*e*

29"Brothers, I can tell you confidently that the patriarch David died and was buried, and his tomb is here to this day. 30But he was a prophet and knew that God had promised him on oath that he would place one of his descendants on his throne. 31Seeing what was ahead, he spoke of the resurrection of the Christ,*f* that he was not abandoned to the grave, nor did his body see decay. 32God has raised this Jesus to life, and we are all witnesses of the fact. 33Exalted to the right hand of God, he has received from the Father the promised Holy Spirit and has poured out what you now see and hear. 34For David did not ascend to heaven, and yet he said,

"'The Lord said to my Lord:
     "Sit at my right hand
35until I make your enemies
     a footstool for your feet."'*g*

36"Therefore let all Israel be assured of this: God has made this Jesus, whom you crucified, both Lord and Christ."

37When the people heard this, they were cut to the heart and said to Peter and the other apostles, "Brothers, what shall we do?"

38Peter replied, "Repent and be baptised, every one of you, in the name of Jesus Christ for the forgiveness of your sins. And you will receive the gift of the Holy Spirit. 39The promise is for you and your children and for all who are far off— for all whom the Lord our God will call." 40With many other words he warned them; and he pleaded with them, "Save yourselves from this corrupt generation." 41Those who accepted his message were baptised, and about three thousand were added to their number that day.

The Fellowship of the Believers

42They devoted themselves to the apostles' teaching and to the fellowship, to the breaking of bread and to prayer. 43Everyone was filled with awe, and many wonders and miraculous signs were done by the apostles. 44All the believers were together and had everything in common. 45Selling their possessions and goods, they gave to anyone as he had need. 46Every day they continued to meet together in the temple courts. They broke bread in their homes and ate together with glad and sincere hearts, 47praising God and enjoying the favour of all the people. And the Lord added to their number daily those who were being saved.

Peter Heals the Crippled Beggar

3 One day Peter and John were going up to the temple at the time of prayer—at three in the afternoon. 2Now a man crippled from birth was being carried to the temple gate called Beautiful, where he was put every day to beg from those going into the temple courts. 3When he saw Peter and John about to enter, he asked them for money. 4Peter looked straight at him, as did John. Then Peter said, "Look at us!" 5So the man gave them his attention, expecting to get something from them.

d23 Or of those not having the law (that is, Gentiles)   *e28 Psalm 16:8–11*
f31 Or Messiah. "The Christ" (Greek) and "the Messiah" (Hebrew) both mean "the Anointed One"; also in verse 36.
g35 Psalm 110:1

[6]Then Peter said, "Silver or gold I do not have, but what I have I give you. In the name of Jesus Christ of Nazareth, walk." [7]Taking him by the right hand, he helped him up, and instantly the man's feet and ankles became strong. [8]He jumped to his feet and began to walk. Then he went with them into the temple courts, walking and jumping, and praising God. [9]When all the people saw him walking and praising God, [10]they recognised him as the same man who used to sit begging at the temple gate called Beautiful, and they were filled with wonder and amazement at what had happened to him.

Peter Speaks to the Onlookers

[11]While the beggar held on to Peter and John, all the people were astonished and came running to them in the place called Solomon's Colonnade. [12]When Peter saw this, he said to them: "Men of Israel, why does this surprise you? Why do you stare at us as if by our own power or godliness we had made this man walk? [13]The God of Abraham, Isaac and Jacob, the God of our fathers, has glorified his servant Jesus. You handed him over to be killed, and you disowned him before Pilate, though he had decided to let him go. [14]You disowned the Holy and Righteous One and asked that a murderer be released to you. [15]You killed the author of life, but God raised him from the dead. We are witnesses of this. [16]By faith in the name of Jesus, this man whom you see and know was made strong. It is Jesus' name and the faith that comes through him that has given this complete healing to him, as you can all see.

[17]"Now, brothers, I know that you acted in ignorance, as did your leaders. [18]But this is how God fulfilled what he had foretold through all the prophets, saying that his Christ[a] would suffer. [19]Repent, then, and turn to God, so that your sins may be wiped out, that times of refreshing may come from the Lord, [20]and that he may send the Christ, who has been appointed for you—even Jesus. [21]He must remain in heaven until the time comes for God to restore everything, as he promised long ago through his holy prophets. [22]For Moses said, 'The Lord your God will raise up for you a prophet like me from among your own people; you must listen to everything he tells you. [23]Anyone who does not listen to him will be completely cut off from among his people.'[b]

[24]"Indeed, all the prophets from Samuel on, as many as have spoken, have foretold these days. [25]And you are heirs of the prophets and of the covenant God made with your fathers. He said to Abraham, 'Through your offspring all peoples on earth will be blessed.'[c] [26]When God raised up his servant, he sent him first to you to bless you by turning each of you from your wicked ways."

Peter and John Before the Sanhedrin

4 The priests and the captain of the temple guard and the Sadducees came up to Peter and John while they were speaking to the people. [2]They were greatly disturbed because the apostles were teaching the people and proclaiming in Jesus the resurrection of the dead. [3]They seized Peter and John, and because it was evening, they put them in jail until the next day. [4]But many who heard the message believed, and the number of men grew to about five thousand.

[5]The next day the rulers, elders and teachers of the law met in Jerusalem. [6]Annas the high priest was there, and so were Caiaphas, John, Alexander and the other men of the high priest's family. [7]They had Peter and John brought before them and began to question them: "By what power or what name did you do this?"

[8]Then Peter, filled with the Holy Spirit, said to them: "Rulers and elders of the people! [9]If we are being called to account today for an act of kindness shown to a cripple and are asked how he was healed, [10]then know this, you and all the people of Israel: It is by the name of Jesus Christ of Nazareth, whom you crucified but whom

---

[a]18 Or *Messiah*; also in verse 20   [b]23 Deut. 18:15,18,19   [c]25 Gen. 22:18; 26:4

God raised from the dead, that this man stands before you healed. [11]He is

> "'the stone you builders rejected,
> which has become the capstone.'[a, b]

[12]Salvation is found in no-one else, for there is no other name under heaven given to men by which we must be saved."

[13]When they saw the courage of Peter and John and realised that they were un-schooled, ordinary men, they were astonished and they took note that these men had been with Jesus. [14]But since they could see the man who had been healed standing there with them, there was nothing they could say. [15]So they ordered them to withdraw from the Sanhedrin and then conferred together. [16]"What are we going to do with these men?" they asked. "Everybody living in Jerusalem knows they have done an outstanding miracle, and we cannot deny it. [17]But to stop this thing from spreading any further among the people, we must warn these men to speak no longer to anyone in this name."

[18]Then they called them in again and commanded them not to speak or teach at all in the name of Jesus. [19]But Peter and John replied, "Judge for yourselves whether it is right in God's sight to obey you rather than God. [20]For we cannot help speaking about what we have seen and heard."

[21]After further threats they let them go. They could not decide how to punish them, because all the people were praising God for what had happened. [22]For the man who was miraculously healed was over forty years old.

The Believers' Prayer

[23]On their release, Peter and John went back to their own people and reported all that the chief priests and elders had said to them. [24]When they heard this, they raised their voices together in prayer to God. "Sovereign Lord," they said, "you made the heaven and the earth and the sea, and everything in them. [25]You spoke by the Holy Spirit through the mouth of your servant, our father David:

> "'Why do the nations rage
> and the peoples plot in vain?
> [26]The kings of the earth take their stand
> and the rulers gather together
> against the Lord
> and against his Anointed One.'[c, d]

[27]Indeed Herod and Pontius Pilate met together with the Gentiles and the people[e] of Israel in this city to conspire against your holy servant Jesus, whom you anointed. [28]They did what your power and will had decided beforehand should happen. [29]Now, Lord, consider their threats and enable your servants to speak your word with great boldness. [30]Stretch out your hand to heal and perform miraculous signs and wonders through the name of your holy servant Jesus."

[31]After they prayed, the place where they were meeting was shaken. And they were all filled with the Holy Spirit and spoke the word of God boldly.

The Believers Share Their Possessions

[32]All the believers were one in heart and mind. No-one claimed that any of his possessions was his own, but they shared everything they had. [33]With great power the apostles continued to testify to the resurrection of the Lord Jesus, and much grace was upon them all. [34]There were no needy persons among them. For from time to time those who owned lands or houses sold them, brought the money from the sales [35]and put it at the apostles' feet, and it was distributed to anyone as he had need.

[36]Joseph, a Levite from Cyprus, whom the apostles called Barnabas (which means Son of Encouragement), [37]sold a field he owned and brought the money and put it at the apostles' feet.

Ananias and Sapphira

5 Now a man named Ananias, together with his wife Sapphira, also sold a piece of property. [2]With his wife's full

---

[a]11 Or cornerstone   [b]11 Psalm 118:22   [c]26 That is, Christ or Messiah   [d]26 Psalm 2:1,2
[e]27 The Greek is plural.

knowledge he kept back part of the money for himself, but brought the rest and put it at the apostles' feet.

³Then Peter said, "Ananias, how is it that Satan has so filled your heart that you have lied to the Holy Spirit and have kept for yourself some of the money you received for the land? ⁴Didn't it belong to you before it was sold? And after it was sold, wasn't the money at your disposal? What made you think of doing such a thing? You have not lied to men but to God."

⁵When Ananias heard this, he fell down and died. And great fear seized all who heard what had happened. ⁶Then the young men came forward, wrapped up his body, and carried him out and buried him.

⁷About three hours later his wife came in, not knowing what had happened. ⁸Peter asked her, "Tell me, is this the price you and Ananias got for the land?"

"Yes," she said, "that is the price."

⁹Peter said to her, "How could you agree to test the Spirit of the Lord? Look! The feet of the men who buried your husband are at the door, and they will carry you out also."

¹⁰At that moment she fell down at his feet and died. Then the young men came in and, finding her dead, carried her out and buried her beside her husband. ¹¹Great fear seized the whole church and all who heard about these events.

The Apostles Heal Many

¹²The apostles performed many miraculous signs and wonders among the people. And all the believers used to meet together in Solomon's Colonnade. ¹³No-one else dared join them, even though they were highly regarded by the people. ¹⁴Nevertheless, more and more men and women believed in the Lord and were added to their number. ¹⁵As a result, people brought the sick into the streets and laid them on beds and mats so that at least Peter's shadow might fall on some of them as he passed by. ¹⁶Crowds gathered also from the towns around Jerusalem,

bringing their sick and those tormented by evil*a* spirits, and all of them were healed.

The Apostles Persecuted

¹⁷Then the high priest and all his associates, who were members of the party of the Sadducees, were filled with jealousy. ¹⁸They arrested the apostles and put them in the public jail. ¹⁹But during the night an angel of the Lord opened the doors of the jail and brought them out. ²⁰"Go, stand in the temple courts," he said, "and tell the people the full message of this new life."

²¹At daybreak they entered the temple courts, as they had been told, and began to teach the people.

When the high priest and his associates arrived, they called together the Sanhedrin—the full assembly of the elders of Israel—and sent to the jail for the apostles. ²²But on arriving at the jail, the officers did not find them there. So they went back and reported, ²³"We found the jail securely locked, with the guards standing at the doors; but when we opened them, we found no-one inside." ²⁴On hearing this report, the captain of the temple guard and the chief priests were puzzled, wondering what would come of this.

²⁵Then someone came and said, "Look! The men you put in jail are standing in the temple courts teaching the people." ²⁶At that, the captain went with his officers and brought the apostles. They did not use force, because they feared that the people would stone them.

²⁷Having brought the apostles, they made them appear before the Sanhedrin to be questioned by the high priest. ²⁸"We gave you strict orders not to teach in this name," he said. "Yet you have filled Jerusalem with your teaching and are determined to make us guilty of this man's blood."

²⁹Peter and the other apostles replied: "We must obey God rather than men! ³⁰The God of our fathers raised Jesus from the dead—whom you had killed by hanging him on a tree. ³¹God exalted him to his own right hand as Prince and Saviour that

a16 Greek *unclean*

he might give repentance and forgiveness of sins to Israel. ³²We are witnesses of these things, and so is the Holy Spirit, whom God has given to those who obey him."

³³When they heard this, they were furious and wanted to put them to death. ³⁴But a Pharisee named Gamaliel, a teacher of the law, who was honoured by all the people, stood up in the Sanhedrin and ordered that the men be put outside for a little while. ³⁵Then he addressed them: "Men of Israel, consider carefully what you intend to do to these men. ³⁶Some time ago Theudas appeared, claiming to be somebody, and about four hundred men rallied to him. He was killed, all his followers were dispersed, and it all came to nothing. ³⁷After him, Judas the Galilean appeared in the days of the census and led a band of people in revolt. He too was killed, and all his followers were scattered. ³⁸Therefore, in the present case I advise you: Leave these men alone! Let them go! For if their purpose or activity is of human origin, it will fail. ³⁹But if it is from God, you will not be able to stop these men; you will only find yourselves fighting against God."

⁴⁰His speech persuaded them. They called the apostles in and had them flogged. Then they ordered them not to speak in the name of Jesus, and let them go.

⁴¹The apostles left the Sanhedrin, rejoicing because they had been counted worthy of suffering disgrace for the Name. ⁴²Day after day, in the temple courts and from house to house, they never stopped teaching and proclaiming the good news that Jesus is the Christ.ᵇ

The Choosing of the Seven

6 In those days when the number of disciples was increasing, the Grecian Jews among them complained against the Hebraic Jews because their widows were being overlooked in the daily distribution of food. ²So the Twelve gathered all the disciples together and

said, "It would not be right for us to neglect the ministry of the word of God in order to wait on tables. ³Brothers, choose seven men from among you who are known to be full of the Spirit and wisdom. We will turn this responsibility over to them ⁴and will give our attention to prayer and the ministry of the word."

⁵This proposal pleased the whole group. They chose Stephen, a man full of faith and of the Holy Spirit; also Philip, Procorus, Nicanor, Timon, Parmenas, and Nicolas from Antioch, a convert to Judaism. ⁶They presented these men to the apostles, who prayed and laid their hands on them.

⁷So the word of God spread. The number of disciples in Jerusalem increased rapidly, and a large number of priests became obedient to the faith.

Stephen Seized

⁸Now Stephen, a man full of God's grace and power, did great wonders and miraculous signs among the people. ⁹Opposition arose, however, from members of the Synagogue of the Freedmen (as it was called)—Jews of Cyrene and Alexandria as well as the provinces of Cilicia and Asia. These men began to argue with Stephen, ¹⁰but they could not stand up against his wisdom or the Spirit by whom he spoke.

¹¹Then they secretly persuaded some men to say, "We have heard Stephen speak words of blasphemy against Moses and against God."

¹²So they stirred up the people and the elders and the teachers of the law. They seized Stephen and brought him before the Sanhedrin. ¹³They produced false witnesses, who testified, "This fellow never stops speaking against this holy place and against the law. ¹⁴For we have heard him say that this Jesus of Nazareth will destroy this place and change the customs Moses handed down to us."

¹⁵All who were sitting in the Sanhedrin looked intently at Stephen, and they saw that his face was like the face of an angel.

ᵇ42 Or Messiah

Stephen's Speech to the Sanhedrin

7 Then the high priest asked him, "Are these charges true?"

²To this he replied: "Brothers and fathers, listen to me! The God of glory appeared to our father Abraham while he was still in Mesopotamia, before he lived in Haran. ³'Leave your country and your people,' God said, 'and go to the land I will show you.'ᵃ

⁴"So he left the land of the Chaldeans and settled in Haran. After the death of his father, God sent him to this land where you are now living. ⁵He gave him no inheritance here, not even a foot of ground. But God promised him that he and his descendants after him would possess the land, even though at that time Abraham had no child. ⁶God spoke to him in this way: 'Your descendants will be strangers in a country not their own, and they will be enslaved and ill-treated for four hundred years. ⁷But I will punish the nation they serve as slaves,' God said, 'and afterwards they will come out of that country and worship me in this place.'ᵇ ⁸Then he gave Abraham the covenant of circumcision. And Abraham became the father of Isaac and circumcised him eight days after his birth. Later Isaac became the father of Jacob, and Jacob became the father of the twelve patriarchs.

⁹"Because the patriarchs were jealous of Joseph, they sold him as a slave into Egypt. But God was with him ¹⁰and rescued him from all his troubles. He gave Joseph wisdom and enabled him to gain the goodwill of Pharaoh king of Egypt; so he made him ruler over Egypt and all his palace.

¹¹"Then a famine struck all Egypt and Canaan, bringing great suffering, and our fathers could not find food. ¹²When Jacob heard that there was grain in Egypt, he sent our fathers on their first visit. ¹³On their second visit, Joseph told his brothers who he was, and Pharaoh learned about Joseph's family. ¹⁴After this, Joseph sent for his father Jacob and his whole family, seventy-five in all. ¹⁵Then Jacob went down to Egypt, where he and our fathers died. ¹⁶Their bodies were brought back to Shechem and placed in the tomb that Abraham had bought from the sons of Hamor at Shechem for a certain sum of money.

¹⁷"As the time drew near for God to fulfil his promise to Abraham, the number of our people in Egypt greatly increased. ¹⁸Then another king, who knew nothing about Joseph, became ruler of Egypt. ¹⁹He dealt treacherously with our people and oppressed our forefathers by forcing them to throw out their newborn babies so that they would die.

²⁰"At that time Moses was born, and he was no ordinary child.ᶜ For three months he was cared for in his father's house. ²¹When he was placed outside, Pharaoh's daughter took him and brought him up as her own son. ²²Moses was educated in all the wisdom of the Egyptians and was powerful in speech and action.

²³"When Moses was forty years old, he decided to visit his fellow Israelites. ²⁴He saw one of them being ill-treated by an Egyptian, so he went to his defence and avenged him by killing the Egyptian. ²⁵Moses thought that his own people would realise that God was using him to rescue them, but they did not. ²⁶The next day Moses came upon two Israelites who were fighting. He tried to reconcile them by saying, 'Men, you are brothers; why do you want to hurt each other?'

²⁷"But the man who was ill-treating the other pushed Moses aside and said, 'Who made you ruler and judge over us? ²⁸Do you want to kill me as you killed the Egyptian yesterday?'ᵈ ²⁹When Moses heard this, he fled to Midian, where he settled as a foreigner and had two sons.

³⁰"After forty years had passed, an angel appeared to Moses in the flames of a burning bush in the desert near Mount Sinai. ³¹When he saw this, he was amazed at the sight. As he went over to look more closely, he heard the Lord's voice: ³²'I am the God of your fathers, the God of Abraham, Isaac and Jacob.'ᵉ Moses trembled with fear and did not dare to look.

---

a3 Gen. 12:1   *b7* Gen. 15:13,14   *c20* Or *was fair in the sight of God*   *d28* Exodus 2:14
e32 Exodus 3:6

33"Then the Lord said to him, 'Take off your sandals; the place where you are standing is holy ground. 34I have indeed seen the oppression of my people in Egypt. I have heard their groaning and have come down to set them free. Now come, I will send you back to Egypt.'*f*

35"This is the same Moses whom they had rejected with the words, 'Who made you ruler and judge?' He was sent to be their ruler and deliverer by God himself, through the angel who appeared to him in the bush. 36He led them out of Egypt and did wonders and miraculous signs in Egypt, at the Red Sea*g* and for forty years in the desert.

37"This is that Moses who told the Israelites, 'God will send you a prophet like me from your own people.'*h* 38He was in the assembly in the desert, with the angel who spoke to him on Mount Sinai, and with our fathers; and he received living words to pass on to us.

39"But our fathers refused to obey him. Instead, they rejected him and in their hearts turned back to Egypt. 40They told Aaron, 'Make us gods who will go before us. As for this fellow Moses who led us out of Egypt—we don't know what has happened to him!'*i* 41That was the time they made an idol in the form of a calf. They brought sacrifices to it and held a celebration in honour of what their hands had made. 42But God turned away and gave them over to the worship of the heavenly bodies. This agrees with what is written in the book of the prophets:

" 'Did you bring me sacrifices and
offerings
for forty years in the desert, O house
of Israel?
43You have lifted up the shrine of Molech
and the star of your god Rephan,
the idols you made to worship.
Therefore I will send you into exile'*j*
beyond Babylon.

44"Our forefathers had the tabernacle of the Testimony with them in the desert.

It had been made as God directed Moses, according to the pattern he had seen. 45Having received the tabernacle, our fathers under Joshua brought it with them when they took the land from the nations God drove out before them. It remained in the land until the time of David, 46who enjoyed God's favour and asked that he might provide a dwelling-place for the God of Jacob.*k* 47But it was Solomon who built the house for him.

48"However, the Most High does not live in houses made by men. As the prophet says:

49" 'Heaven is my throne,
and the earth is my footstool.
What kind of house will you build for
me?
says the Lord.
Or where will my resting place be?
50Has not my hand made all these
things?'*l*

51"You stiff-necked people, with uncircumcised hearts and ears! You are just like your fathers: You always resist the Holy Spirit! 52Was there ever a prophet your fathers did not persecute? They even killed those who predicted the coming of the Righteous One. And now you have betrayed and murdered him—53you who have received the law that was put into effect through angels but have not obeyed it."

The Stoning of Stephen

54When they heard this, they were furious and gnashed their teeth at him. 55But Stephen, full of the Holy Spirit, looked up to heaven and saw the glory of God, and Jesus standing at the right hand of God. 56"Look," he said, "I see heaven open and the Son of Man standing at the right hand of God."

57At this they covered their ears and, yelling at the top of their voices, they all rushed at him, 58dragged him out of the city and began to stone him. Meanwhile,

f34 Exodus 3:5,7,8,10   *g36* That is, Sea of Reeds   *h37* Deut. 18:15   *i40* Exodus 32:1
j43 Amos 5:25–27   *k46* Some early manuscripts *the house of Jacob*   *l50* Isaiah 66:1,2

the witnesses laid their clothes at the feet of a young man named Saul.

[59]While they were stoning him, Stephen prayed, "Lord Jesus, receive my spirit." [60]Then he fell on his knees and cried out, "Lord, do not hold this sin against them." When he had said this, he fell asleep.

8 And Saul was there, giving approval to his death.

The Church Persecuted and Scattered

On that day a great persecution broke out against the church at Jerusalem, and all except the apostles were scattered throughout Judea and Samaria. [2]Godly men buried Stephen and mourned deeply for him. [3]But Saul began to destroy the church. Going from house to house, he dragged off men and women and put them in prison.

Philip in Samaria

[4]Those who had been scattered preached the word wherever they went. [5]Philip went down to a city in Samaria and proclaimed the Christ[a] there. [6]When the crowds heard Philip and saw the miraculous signs he did, they all paid close attention to what he said. [7]With shrieks, evil[b] spirits came out of many, and many paralytics and cripples were healed. [8]So there was great joy in that city.

Simon the Sorcerer

[9]Now for some time a man named Simon had practised sorcery in the city and amazed all the people of Samaria. He boasted that he was someone great, [10]and all the people, both high and low, gave him their attention and exclaimed, "This man is the divine power known as the Great Power." [11]They followed him because he had amazed them for a long time with his magic. [12]But when they believed Philip as he preached the good news of the kingdom of God and the name of Jesus

Christ, they were baptised, both men and women. [13]Simon himself believed and was baptised. And he followed Philip everywhere, astonished by the great signs and miracles he saw.

[14]When the apostles in Jerusalem heard that Samaria had accepted the word of God, they sent Peter and John to them. [15]When they arrived, they prayed for them that they might receive the Holy Spirit, [16]because the Holy Spirit had not yet come upon any of them; they had simply been baptised into[c] the name of the Lord Jesus. [17]Then Peter and John placed their hands on them, and they received the Holy Spirit.

[18]When Simon saw that the Spirit was given at the laying on of the apostles' hands, he offered them money [19]and said, "Give me also this ability so that everyone on whom I lay my hands may receive the Holy Spirit."

[20]Peter answered: "May your money perish with you, because you thought you could buy the gift of God with money! [21]You have no part or share in this ministry, because your heart is not right before God. [22]Repent of this wickedness and pray to the Lord. Perhaps he will forgive you for having such a thought in your heart. [23]For I see that you are full of bitterness and captive to sin."

[24]Then Simon answered, "Pray to the Lord for me so that nothing you have said may happen to me."

[25]When they had testified and proclaimed the word of the Lord, Peter and John returned to Jerusalem, preaching the gospel in many Samaritan villages.

Philip and the Ethiopian

[26]Now an angel of the Lord said to Philip, "Go south to the road—the desert road—that goes down from Jerusalem to Gaza." [27]So he started out, and on his way he met an Ethiopian[d] eunuch, an important official in charge of all the treasury of Candace, queen of the Ethiopians. This man had gone to Jerusalem to worship, [28]and on his way home was sitting in his

---

[a]5 Or *Messiah*   [b]7 Greek *unclean*   [c]16 Or *in*   [d]27 That is, from the upper Nile region

chariot reading the book of Isaiah the prophet. [29]The Spirit told Philip, "Go to that chariot and stay near it."

[30]Then Philip ran up to the chariot and heard the man reading Isaiah the prophet. "Do you understand what you are reading?" Philip asked.

[31]"How can I," he said, "unless someone explains it to me?" So he invited Philip to come up and sit with him.

[32]The eunuch was reading this passage of Scripture:

"He was led like a sheep to the
    slaughter,
and as a lamb before the shearer is
    silent,
so he did not open his mouth.
[33]In his humiliation he was deprived of
    justice.
Who can speak of his descendants?
For his life was taken from the
    earth."[e]

[34]The eunuch asked Philip, "Tell me, please, who is the prophet talking about, himself or someone else?" [35]Then Philip began with that very passage of Scripture and told him the good news about Jesus.

[36]As they travelled along the road, they came to some water and the eunuch said, "Look, here is water. Why shouldn't I be baptised?"[f] [38]And he gave orders to stop the chariot. Then both Philip and the eunuch went down into the water and Philip baptised him. [39]When they came up out of the water, the Spirit of the Lord suddenly took Philip away, and the eunuch did not see him again, but went on his way rejoicing. [40]Philip, however, appeared at Azotus and travelled about, preaching the gospel in all the towns until he reached Caesarea.

Saul's Conversion

9 Meanwhile, Saul was still breathing out murderous threats against the Lord's disciples. He went to the high priest [2]and asked him for letters to the synagogues in Damascus, so that if he found any there who belonged to the Way,

whether men or women, he might take them as prisoners to Jerusalem. [3]As he neared Damascus on his journey, suddenly a light from heaven flashed around him. [4]He fell to the ground and heard a voice say to him, "Saul, Saul, why do you persecute me?"

[5]"Who are you, Lord?" Saul asked.

"I am Jesus, whom you are persecuting," he replied. [6]"Now get up and go into the city, and you will be told what you must do."

[7]The men travelling with Saul stood there speechless; they heard the sound but did not see anyone. [8]Saul got up from the ground, but when he opened his eyes he could see nothing. So they led him by the hand into Damascus. [9]For three days he was blind, and did not eat or drink anything.

[10]In Damascus there was a disciple named Ananias. The Lord called to him in a vision, "Ananias!"

"Yes, Lord," he answered.

[11]The Lord told him, "Go to the house of Judas on Straight Street and ask for a man from Tarsus named Saul, for he is praying. [12]In a vision he has seen a man named Ananias come and place his hands on him to restore his sight."

[13]"Lord," Ananias answered, "I have heard many reports about this man and all the harm he has done to your saints in Jerusalem. [14]And he has come here with authority from the chief priests to arrest all who call on your name."

[15]But the Lord said to Ananias, "Go! This man is my chosen instrument to carry my name before the Gentiles and their kings and before the people of Israel. [16]I will show him how much he must suffer for my name."

[17]Then Ananias went to the house and entered it. Placing his hands on Saul, he said, "Brother Saul, the Lord—Jesus, who appeared to you on the road as you were coming here—has sent me so that you may see again and be filled with the Holy Spirit." [18]Immediately, something like scales fell from Saul's eyes, and he

---

[e]33 Isaiah 53:7,8
[f]36 Some late manuscripts *baptised?"* [37]*Philip said, "If you believe with all your heart, you may." The eunuch answered, "I believe that Jesus Christ is the Son of God."*

could see again. He got up and was baptised, [19]and after taking some food, he regained his strength.

Saul in Damascus and Jerusalem

Saul spent several days with the disciples in Damascus. [20]At once he began to preach in the synagogues that Jesus is the Son of God. [21]All those who heard him were astonished and asked, "Isn't he the man who caused havoc in Jerusalem among those who call on this name? And hasn't he come here to take them as prisoners to the chief priests?" [22]Yet Saul grew more and more powerful and baffled the Jews living in Damascus by proving that Jesus is the Christ.[a]

[23]After many days had gone by, the Jews conspired to kill him, [24]but Saul learned of their plan. Day and night they kept close watch on the city gates in order to kill him. [25]But his followers took him by night and lowered him in a basket through an opening in the wall.

[26]When he came to Jerusalem, he tried to join the disciples, but they were all afraid of him, not believing that he really was a disciple. [27]But Barnabas took him and brought him to the apostles. He told them how Saul on his journey had seen the Lord and that the Lord had spoken to him, and how in Damascus he had preached fearlessly in the name of Jesus. [28]So Saul stayed with them and moved about freely in Jerusalem, speaking boldly in the name of the Lord. [29]He talked and debated with the Grecian Jews, but they tried to kill him. [30]When the brothers learned of this, they took him down to Caesarea and sent him off to Tarsus.

[31]Then the church throughout Judea, Galilee and Samaria enjoyed a time of peace. It was strengthened; and encouraged by the Holy Spirit, it grew in numbers, living in the fear of the Lord.

Aeneas and Dorcas

[32]As Peter travelled about the country, he went to visit the saints in Lydda. [33]There he found a man named Aeneas, a paralytic who had been bedridden for eight years. [34]"Aeneas," Peter said to him, "Jesus Christ heals you. Get up and tidy up your mat." Immediately Aeneas got up. [35]All those who lived in Lydda and Sharon saw him and turned to the Lord.

[36]In Joppa there was a disciple named Tabitha (which, when translated, is Dorcas[b]), who was always doing good and helping the poor. [37]About that time she became sick and died, and her body was washed and placed in an upstairs room. [38]Lydda was near Joppa; so when the disciples heard that Peter was in Lydda, they sent two men to him and urged him, "Please come at once!"

[39]Peter went with them, and when he arrived he was taken upstairs to the room. All the widows stood around him, crying and showing him the robes and other clothing that Dorcas had made while she was still with them.

[40]Peter sent them all out of the room; then he got down on his knees and prayed. Turning towards the dead woman, he said, "Tabitha, get up." She opened her eyes, and seeing Peter she sat up. [41]He took her by the hand and helped her to her feet. Then he called the believers and the widows and presented her to them alive. [42]This became known all over Joppa, and many people believed in the Lord. [43]Peter stayed in Joppa for some time with a tanner named Simon.

Cornelius Calls for Peter

10 At Caesarea there was a man named Cornelius, a centurion in what was known as the Italian Regiment. [2]He and all his family were devout and God-fearing; he gave generously to those in need and prayed to God regularly. [3]One day at about three in the afternoon he had a vision. He distinctly saw an angel of God, who came to him and said, "Cornelius!"

[4]Cornelius stared at him in fear. "What is it, Lord?" he asked.

The angel answered, "Your prayers and gifts to the poor have come up as a memorial offering before God. [5]Now send men

---

[a]22 Or *Messiah*   [b]36 Both *Tabitha* (Aramaic) and *Dorcas* (Greek) mean *gazelle.*

to Joppa to bring back a man named Simon who is called Peter. ⁶He is staying with Simon the tanner, whose house is by the sea.''

⁷When the angel who spoke to him had gone, Cornelius called two of his servants and a devout soldier who was one of his attendants. ⁸He told them everything that had happened and sent them to Joppa.

Peter's Vision

⁹About noon the following day as they were on their journey and approaching the city, Peter went up on the roof to pray. ¹⁰He became hungry and wanted something to eat, and while the meal was being prepared, he fell into a trance. ¹¹He saw heaven opened and something like a large sheet being let down to earth by its four corners. ¹²It contained all kinds of four-footed animals, as well as reptiles of the earth and birds of the air. ¹³Then a voice told him, "Get up, Peter. Kill and eat.''

¹⁴"Surely not, Lord!'' Peter replied. "I have never eaten anything impure or unclean.''

¹⁵The voice spoke to him a second time, "Do not call anything impure that God has made clean.''

¹⁶This happened three times, and immediately the sheet was taken back to heaven.

¹⁷While Peter was wondering about the meaning of the vision, the men sent by Cornelius found out where Simon's house was and stopped at the gate. ¹⁸They called out, asking if Simon who was known as Peter was staying there.

¹⁹While Peter was still thinking about the vision, the Spirit said to him, "Simon, three^a men are looking for you. ²⁰So get up and go downstairs. Do not hesitate to go with them, for I have sent them.''

²¹Peter went down and said to the men, "I'm the one you're looking for. Why have you come?''

²²The men replied, "We have come from Cornelius the centurion. He is a righteous and God-fearing man, who is respected by all the Jewish people. A holy

angel told him to have you come to his house so that he could hear what you have to say.'' ²³Then Peter invited the men into the house to be his guests.

Peter at Cornelius' House

The next day Peter started out with them, and some of the brothers from Joppa went along. ²⁴The following day he arrived in Caesarea. Cornelius was expecting them and had called together his relatives and close friends. ²⁵As Peter entered the house, Cornelius met him and fell at his feet in reverence. ²⁶But Peter made him get up. "Stand up,'' he said, "I am only a man myself.''

²⁷Talking with him, Peter went inside and found a large gathering of people. ²⁸He said to them: "You are well aware that it is against our law for a Jew to associate with a Gentile or visit him. But God has shown me that I should not call any man impure or unclean. ²⁹So when I was sent for, I came without raising any objection. May I ask why you sent for me?''

³⁰Cornelius answered: "Four days ago I was in my house praying at this hour, at three in the afternoon. Suddenly a man in shining clothes stood before me ³¹and said, 'Cornelius, God has heard your prayer and remembered your gifts to the poor. ³²Send to Joppa for Simon who is called Peter. He is a guest in the home of Simon the tanner, who lives by the sea.' ³³So I sent for you immediately, and it was good of you to come. Now we are all here in the presence of God to listen to everything the Lord has commanded you to tell us.''

³⁴Then Peter began to speak: "I now realise how true it is that God does not show favouritism ³⁵but accepts men from every nation who fear him and do what is right. ³⁶You know the message God sent to the people of Israel, telling the good news of peace through Jesus Christ, who is Lord of all. ³⁷You know what has happened throughout Judea, beginning in Galilee after the baptism that John

---

^{a}19 One early manuscript two; other manuscripts do not have the number.

preached—[38]how God anointed Jesus of Nazareth with the Holy Spirit and power, and how he went around doing good and healing all who were under the power of the devil, because God was with him.

[39]"We are witnesses of everything he did in the country of the Jews and in Jerusalem. They killed him by hanging him on a tree, [40]but God raised him from the dead on the third day and caused him to be seen. [41]He was not seen by all the people, but by witnesses whom God had already chosen—by us who ate and drank with him after he rose from the dead. [42]He commanded us to preach to the people and to testify that he is the one whom God appointed as judge of the living and the dead. [43]All the prophets testify about him that everyone who believes in him receives forgiveness of sins through his name."

[44]While Peter was still speaking these words, the Holy Spirit came on all who heard the message. [45]The circumcised believers who had come with Peter were astonished that the gift of the Holy Spirit had been poured out even on the Gentiles. [46]For they heard them speaking in tongues[b] and praising God.

Then Peter said, [47]"Can anyone keep these people from being baptised with water? They have received the Holy Spirit just as we have." [48]So he ordered that they be baptised in the name of Jesus Christ. Then they asked Peter to stay with them for a few days.

Peter Explains His Actions

11 The apostles and the brothers throughout Judea heard that the Gentiles also had received the word of God. [2]So when Peter went up to Jerusalem, the circumcised believers criticised him [3]and said, "You went into the house of uncircumcised men and ate with them."

[4]Peter began and explained everything to them precisely as it had happened: [5]"I was in the city of Joppa praying, and in a trance I saw a vision. I saw something like a large sheet being let down from heaven by its four corners, and it came down to where I was. [6]I looked into it and saw four-footed animals of the earth, wild beasts, reptiles, and birds of the air. [7]Then I heard a voice telling me, 'Get up, Peter. Kill and eat.'

[8]"I replied, 'Surely not, Lord! Nothing impure or unclean has ever entered my mouth.'

[9]"The voice spoke from heaven a second time, 'Do not call anything impure that God has made clean.' [10]This happened three times, and then it was pulled up to heaven again.

[11]"Right then three men who had been sent to me from Caesarea stopped at the house where I was staying. [12]The Spirit told me to have no hesitation about going with them. These six brothers also went with me, and we entered the man's house. [13]He told us how he had seen an angel appear in his house and say, 'Send to Joppa for Simon who is called Peter. [14]He will bring you a message through which you and all your household will be saved.'

[15]"As I began to speak, the Holy Spirit came on them as he had come on us at the beginning. [16]Then I remembered what the Lord had said: 'John baptised with[a] water, but you will be baptised with the Holy Spirit.' [17]So if God gave them the same gift as he gave us, who believed in the Lord Jesus Christ, who was I to think that I could oppose God?"

[18]When they heard this, they had no further objections and praised God, saying, "So then, God has granted even the Gentiles repentance unto life."

The Church in Antioch

[19]Now those who had been scattered by the persecution in connection with Stephen travelled as far as Phoenicia, Cyprus and Antioch, telling the message only to Jews. [20]Some of them, however, men from Cyprus and Cyrene, went to Antioch and began to speak to Greeks also, telling them the good news about the Lord Jesus. [21]The Lord's hand was with

them, and a great number of people believed and turned to the Lord.

22News of this reached the ears of the church at Jerusalem, and they sent Barnabas to Antioch. 23When he arrived and saw the evidence of the grace of God, he was glad and encouraged them all to remain true to the Lord with all their hearts. 24He was a good man, full of the Holy Spirit and faith, and a great number of people were brought to the Lord.

25Then Barnabas went to Tarsus to look for Saul, 26and when he found him, he brought him to Antioch. So for a whole year Barnabas and Saul met with the church and taught great numbers of people. The disciples were called Christians first at Antioch.

27During this time some prophets came down from Jerusalem to Antioch. 28One of them, named Agabus, stood up and through the Spirit predicted that a severe famine would spread over the entire Roman world. (This happened during the reign of Claudius.) 29The disciples, each according to his ability, decided to provide help for the brothers living in Judea. 30This they did, sending their gift to the elders by Barnabas and Saul.

Peter's Miraculous Escape From Prison

12 It was about this time that King Herod arrested some who belonged to the church, intending to persecute them. 2He had James, the brother of John, put to death with the sword. 3When he saw that this pleased the Jews, he proceeded to seize Peter also. This happened during the Feast of Unleavened Bread. 4After arresting him, he put him in prison, handing him over to be guarded by four squads of four soldiers each. Herod intended to bring him out for public trial after the Passover.

5So Peter was kept in prison, but the church was earnestly praying to God for him.

6The night before Herod was to bring him to trial, Peter was sleeping between two soldiers, bound with two chains, and sentries stood guard at the entrance. 7Suddenly an angel of the Lord appeared and a light shone in the cell. He struck

Peter on the side and woke him up. "Quick, get up!" he said, and the chains fell off Peter's wrists.

8Then the angel said to him, "Put on your clothes and sandals." And Peter did so. "Wrap your cloak around you and follow me," the angel told him. 9Peter followed him out of the prison, but he had no idea that what the angel was doing was really happening; he thought he was seeing a vision. 10They passed the first and second guards and came to the iron gate leading to the city. It opened for them by itself, and they went through it. When they had walked the length of one street, suddenly the angel left him.

11Then Peter came to himself and said, "Now I know without a doubt that the Lord sent his angel and rescued me from Herod's clutches and from everything the Jewish people were anticipating."

12When this had dawned on him, he went to the house of Mary the mother of John, also called Mark, where many people had gathered and were praying. 13Peter knocked at the outer entrance, and a servant girl named Rhoda came to answer the door. 14When she recognised Peter's voice, she was so overjoyed she ran back without opening it and exclaimed, "Peter is at the door!"

15"You're out of your mind," they told her. When she kept insisting that it was so, they said, "It must be his angel."

16But Peter kept on knocking, and when they opened the door and saw him, they were astonished. 17Peter motioned with his hand for them to be quiet and described how the Lord had brought him out of prison. "Tell James and the brothers about this," he said, and then he left for another place.

18In the morning, there was no small commotion among the soldiers as to what had become of Peter. 19After Herod had a thorough search made for him and did not find him, he cross-examined the guards and ordered that they be executed.

Herod's Death

Then Herod went from Judea to Caesarea and stayed there a while. 20He had been quarrelling with the people of Tyre and Sidon; they now joined together and sought an audience with him. Having secured the support of Blastus, a trusted personal servant of the king, they asked for peace, because they depended on the king's country for their food supply.

²¹On the appointed day Herod, wearing his royal robes, sat on his throne and delivered a public address to the people. ²²They shouted, "This is the voice of a god, not of a man." ²³Immediately, because Herod did not give praise to God, an angel of the Lord struck him down, and he was eaten by worms and died.

²⁴But the word of God continued to increase and spread.

²⁵When Barnabas and Saul had finished their mission, they returned from*a* Jerusalem, taking with them John, also called Mark.

Barnabas and Saul Sent Off

13 In the church at Antioch there were prophets and teachers: Barnabas, Simeon called Niger, Lucius of Cyrene, Manaen (who had been brought up with Herod the tetrarch) and Saul. ²While they were worshiping the Lord and fasting, the Holy Spirit said, "Set apart for me Barnabas and Saul for the work to which I have called them." ³So after they had fasted and prayed, they placed their hands on them and sent them off.

On Cyprus

⁴The two of them, sent on their way by the Holy Spirit, went down to Seleucia and sailed from there to Cyprus. ⁵When they arrived at Salamis, they proclaimed the word of God in the Jewish synagogues. John was with them as their helper.

⁶They travelled through the whole island until they came to Paphos. There they met a Jewish sorcerer and false prophet named Bar-Jesus, ⁷who was an attendant of the proconsul, Sergius Paulus. The proconsul, an intelligent

man, sent for Barnabas and Saul because he wanted to hear the word of God. ⁸But Elymas the sorcerer (for that is what his name means) opposed them and tried to turn the proconsul from the faith. ⁹Then Saul, who was also called Paul, filled with the Holy Spirit, looked straight at Elymas and said, ¹⁰"You are a child of the devil and an enemy of everything that is right! You are full of all kinds of deceit and trickery. Will you never stop perverting the right ways of the Lord? ¹¹Now the hand of the Lord is against you. You are going to be blind, and for a time you will be unable to see the light of the sun."

Immediately mist and darkness came over him, and he groped about, seeking someone to lead him by the hand. ¹²When the proconsul saw what had happened, he believed, for he was amazed at the teaching about the Lord.

In Pisidian Antioch

¹³From Paphos, Paul and his companions sailed to Perga in Pamphylia, where John left them to return to Jerusalem. ¹⁴From Perga they went on to Pisidian Antioch. On the Sabbath they entered the synagogue and sat down. ¹⁵After the reading from the Law and the Prophets, the synagogue rulers sent word to them, saying, "Brothers, if you have a message of encouragement for the people, please speak."

¹⁶Standing up, Paul motioned with his hand and said: "Men of Israel and you Gentiles who worship God, listen to me! ¹⁷The God of the people of Israel chose our fathers; he made the people prosper during their stay in Egypt, with mighty power he led them out of that country, ¹⁸he endured their conduct*a* for about forty years in the desert, ¹⁹he overthrew seven nations in Canaan and gave their land to his people as their inheritance. ²⁰All this took about 450 years.

"After this, God gave them judges until the time of Samuel the prophet. ²¹Then the people asked for a king, and he gave them Saul son of Kish, of the tribe of

---

*a*25 Some manuscripts *to*   *a*18 Some manuscripts *and cared for them*

Benjamin, who ruled for forty years. [22]After removing Saul, he made David their king. He testified concerning him: 'I have found David son of Jesse a man after my own heart; he will do everything I want him to do.'

[23]"From this man's descendants God has brought to Israel the Saviour Jesus, as he promised. [24]Before the coming of Jesus, John preached repentance and baptism to all the people of Israel. [25]As John was completing his work, he said: 'Who do you think I am? I am not that one. No, but he is coming after me, whose sandals I am not worthy to untie.'

[26]"Brothers, children of Abraham, and you God-fearing Gentiles, it is to us that this message of salvation has been sent. [27]The people of Jerusalem and their rulers did not recognise Jesus, yet in condemning him they fulfilled the words of the prophets that are read every Sabbath. [28]Though they found no proper ground for a death sentence, they asked Pilate to have him executed. [29]When they had carried out all that was written about him, they took him down from the tree and laid him in a tomb. [30]But God raised him from the dead, [31]and for many days he was seen by those who had travelled with him from Galilee to Jerusalem. They are now his witnesses to our people.

[32]"We tell you the good news: What God promised our fathers [33]he has fulfilled for us, their children, by raising up Jesus. As it is written in the second Psalm:

"'You are my Son;
     today I have become your Father.'[b, c]

[34]The fact that God raised him from the dead, never to decay, is stated in these words:

"'I will give you the holy and sure
     blessings promised to David.'[d]

[35]So it is stated elsewhere:

"'You will not let your Holy One see
     decay.'[e]

[36]"For when David had served God's purpose in his own generation, he fell asleep; he was buried with his fathers and his body decayed. [37]But the one whom God raised from the dead did not see decay.

[38]"Therefore, my brothers, I want you to know that through Jesus the forgiveness of sins is proclaimed to you. [39]Through him everyone who believes is justified from everything you could not be justified from by the law of Moses. [40]Take care that what the prophets have said does not happen to you:

[41]"'Look, you scoffers,
     wonder and perish,
for I am going to do something in your
     days
     that you would never believe,
     even if someone told you.'[f]"

[42]As Paul and Barnabas were leaving the synagogue, the people invited them to speak further about these things on the next Sabbath. [43]When the congregation was dismissed, many of the Jews and devout converts to Judaism followed Paul and Barnabas, who talked with them and urged them to continue in the grace of God.

[44]On the next Sabbath almost the whole city gathered to hear the word of the Lord. [45]When the Jews saw the crowds, they were filled with jealousy and talked abusively against what Paul was saying.

[46]Then Paul and Barnabas answered them boldly: "We had to speak the word of God to you first. Since you reject it and do not consider yourselves worthy of eternal life, we now turn to the Gentiles. [47]For this is what the Lord has commanded us:

"'I have made you[g] a light for the
     Gentiles,
that you[g] may bring salvation to the
     ends of the earth.'[h]"

[48]When the Gentiles heard this, they were glad and honoured the word of the

---

b33 Or *have begotten you*   *c33* Psalm 2:7   *d34* Isaiah 55:3   *e35* Psalm 16:10   *f41* Hab. 1:5
g47 The Greek is singular.   *h47* Isaiah 49:6

Lord; and all who were appointed for eternal life believed.

⁴⁹The word of the Lord spread through the whole region. ⁵⁰But the Jews incited the God-fearing women of high standing and the leading men of the city. They stirred up persecution against Paul and Barnabas, and expelled them from their region. ⁵¹So they shook the dust from their feet in protest against them and went to Iconium. ⁵²And the disciples were filled with joy and with the Holy Spirit.

In Iconium

14 At Iconium Paul and Barnabas went as usual into the Jewish synagogue. There they spoke so effectively that a great number of Jews and Gentiles believed. ²But the Jews who refused to believe stirred up the Gentiles and poisoned their minds against the brothers. ³So Paul and Barnabas spent considerable time there, speaking boldly for the Lord, who confirmed the message of his grace by enabling them to do miraculous signs and wonders. ⁴The people of the city were divided; some sided with the Jews, others with the apostles. ⁵There was a plot afoot among the Gentiles and Jews, together with their leaders, to ill-treat them and stone them. ⁶But they found out about it and fled to the Lycaonian cities of Lystra and Derbe and to the surrounding country, ⁷where they continued to preach the good news.

In Lystra and Derbe

⁸In Lystra there sat a man crippled in his feet, who was lame from birth and had never walked. ⁹He listened to Paul as he was speaking. Paul looked directly at him, saw that he had faith to be healed ¹⁰and called out, "Stand up on your feet!" At that, the man jumped up and began to walk.

¹¹When the crowd saw what Paul had done, they shouted in the Lycaonian language, "The gods have come down to us

in human form!" ¹²Barnabas they called Zeus, and Paul they called Hermes because he was the chief speaker. ¹³The priest of Zeus, whose temple was just outside the city, brought bulls and wreaths to the city gates because he and the crowd wanted to offer sacrifices to them.

¹⁴But when the apostles Barnabas and Paul heard of this, they tore their clothes and rushed out into the crowd, shouting: ¹⁵"Men, why are you doing this? We too are only men, human like you. We are bringing you good news, telling you to turn from these worthless things to the living God, who made heaven and earth and sea and everything in them. ¹⁶In the past, he let all nations go their own way. ¹⁷Yet he has not left himself without testimony: He has shown kindness by giving you rain from heaven and crops in their seasons; he provides you with plenty of food and fills your hearts with joy." ¹⁸Even with these words, they had difficulty keeping the crowd from sacrificing to them.

¹⁹Then some Jews came from Antioch and Iconium and won the crowd over. They stoned Paul and dragged him outside the city, thinking he was dead. ²⁰But after the disciples had gathered round him, he got up and went back into the city. The next day he and Barnabas left for Derbe.

The Return to Antioch in Syria

²¹They preached the good news in that city and won a large number of disciples. Then they returned to Lystra, Iconium and Antioch, ²²strengthening the disciples and encouraging them to remain true to the faith. "We must go through many hardships to enter the kingdom of God," they said. ²³Paul and Barnabas appointed elders*ᵃ* for them in each church and, with prayer and fasting, committed them to the Lord, in whom they had put their trust. ²⁴After going through Pisidia, they came into Pamphylia, ²⁵and when they had preached the word in Perga, they went down to Attalia.

²⁶From Attalia they sailed back to

ᵃ23 Or Barnabas ordained elders; or Barnabas had elders elected

Antioch, where they had been committed to the grace of God for the work they had now completed. [27]On arriving there, they gathered the church together and reported all that God had done through them and how he had opened the door of faith to the Gentiles. [28]And they stayed there a long time with the disciples.

The Council at Jerusalem

15 Some men came down from Judea to Antioch and were teaching the brothers: "Unless you are circumcised, according to the custom taught by Moses, you cannot be saved." [2]This brought Paul and Barnabas into sharp dispute and debate with them. So Paul and Barnabas were appointed, along with some other believers, to go up to Jerusalem to see the apostles and elders about this question. [3]The church sent them on their way, and as they travelled through Phoenicia and Samaria, they told how the Gentiles had been converted. This news made all the brothers very glad. [4]When they came to Jerusalem, they were welcomed by the church and the apostles and elders, to whom they reported everything God had done through them.

[5]Then some of the believers who belonged to the party of the Pharisees stood up and said, "The Gentiles must be circumcised and required to obey the law of Moses."

[6]The apostles and elders met to consider this question. [7]After much discussion, Peter got up and addressed them: "Brothers, you know that some time ago God made a choice among you that the Gentiles might hear from my lips the message of the gospel and believe. [8]God, who knows the heart, showed that he accepted them by giving the Holy Spirit to them, just as he did to us. [9]He made no distinction between us and them, for he purified their hearts by faith. [10]Now then, why do you try to test God by putting on the necks of the disciples a yoke that neither we nor our fathers have been able to bear? [11]No! We believe it is through the grace of our

Lord Jesus that we are saved, just as they are."

[12]The whole assembly became silent as they listened to Barnabas and Paul telling about the miraculous signs and wonders God had done among the Gentiles through them. [13]When they finished, James spoke up: "Brothers, listen to me. [14]Simon[a] has described to us how God at first showed his concern by taking from the Gentiles a people for himself. [15]The words of the prophets are in agreement with this, as it is written:

[16]" 'After this I will return
    and rebuild David's fallen tent.
  Its ruins I will rebuild,
    and I will restore it,
[17]that the remnant of men may seek the
      Lord,
    and all the Gentiles who bear my
      name,
  says the Lord, who does these things'[b]
[18] that have been known for ages.[c]

[19]"It is my judgment, therefore, that we should not make it difficult for the Gentiles who are turning to God. [20]Instead we should write to them, telling them to abstain from food polluted by idols, from sexual immorality, from the meat of strangled animals and from blood. [21]For Moses has been preached in every city from the earliest times and is read in the synagogues on every Sabbath."

The Council's Letter to Gentile Believers

[22]Then the apostles and elders, with the whole church, decided to choose some of their own men and send them to Antioch with Paul and Barnabas. They chose Judas (called Barsabbas) and Silas, two men who were leaders among the brothers. [23]With them they sent the following letter:

The apostles and elders, your brothers,

To the Gentile believers in Antioch, Syria and Cilicia:

---

[a]14 Greek *Simeon*, a variant of *Simon*; that is, Peter   [b]17 Amos 9:11,12
[c]17,18 Some manuscripts *things'—* / [18]*known to the Lord for ages is his work*

Greetings.

24We have heard that some went out from us without our authorisation and disturbed you, troubling your minds by what they said. 25So we all agreed to choose some men and send them to you with our dear friends Barnabas and Paul—26men who have risked their lives for the name of our Lord Jesus Christ. 27Therefore we are sending Judas and Silas to confirm by word of mouth what we are writing. 28It seemed good to the Holy Spirit and to us not to burden you with anything beyond the following requirements: 29You are to abstain from food sacrificed to idols, from blood, from the meat of strangled animals and from sexual immorality. You will do well to avoid these things.

Farewell.

30The men were sent off and went down to Antioch, where they gathered the church together and delivered the letter. 31The people read it and were glad for its encouraging message. 32Judas and Silas, who themselves were prophets, said much to encourage and strengthen the brothers. 33After spending some time there, they were sent off by the brothers with the blessing of peace to return to those who had sent them.*d* 35But Paul and Barnabas remained in Antioch, where they and many others taught and preached the word of the Lord.

Disagreement Between Paul and Barnabas

36Some time later Paul said to Barnabas, "Let us go back and visit the brothers in all the towns where we preached the word of the Lord and see how they are doing." 37Barnabas wanted to take John, also called Mark, with them, 38but Paul did not think it wise to take him, because he had deserted them in Pamphylia and had not continued with them in the work.

39They had such a sharp disagreement that they parted company. Barnabas took Mark and sailed for Cyprus, 40but Paul chose Silas and left, commended by the brothers to the grace of the Lord. 41He went through Syria and Cilicia, strengthening the churches.

Timothy Joins Paul and Silas

16 He came to Derbe and then to Lystra, where a disciple named Timothy lived, whose mother was a Jewess and a believer, but whose father was a Greek. 2The brothers at Lystra and Iconium spoke well of him. 3Paul wanted to take him along on the journey, so he circumcised him because of the Jews who lived in that area, for they all knew that his father was a Greek. 4As they travelled from town to town, they delivered the decisions reached by the apostles and elders in Jerusalem for the people to obey. 5So the churches were strengthened in the faith and grew daily in numbers.

Paul's Vision of the Man of Macedonia

6Paul and his companions travelled throughout the region of Phrygia and Galatia, having been kept by the Holy Spirit from preaching the word in the province of Asia. 7When they came to the border of Mysia, they tried to enter Bithynia, but the Spirit of Jesus would not allow them to. 8So they passed by Mysia and went down to Troas. 9During the night Paul had a vision of a man of Macedonia standing and begging him, "Come over to Macedonia and help us." 10After Paul had seen the vision, we got ready at once to leave for Macedonia, concluding that God had called us to preach the gospel to them.

Lydia's Conversion in Philippi

11From Troas we put out to sea and sailed straight for Samothrace, and the next day on to Neapolis. 12From there we travelled to Philippi, a Roman colony and

---

d33 Some manuscripts them, 34 *but Silas decided to remain there* the leading city of that district of Macedonia. And we stayed there several days.

[13]On the Sabbath we went outside the city gate to the river, where we expected to find a place of prayer. We sat down and began to speak to the women who had gathered there. [14]One of those listening was a woman named Lydia, a dealer in purple cloth from the city of Thyatira, who was a worshipper of God. The Lord opened her heart to respond to Paul's message. [15]When she and the members of her household were baptised, she invited us to her home. "If you consider me a believer in the Lord," she said, "come and stay at my house." And she persuaded us.

Paul and Silas in Prison

[16]Once when we were going to the place of prayer, we were met by a slave girl who had a spirit by which she predicted the future. She earned a great deal of money for her owners by fortune-telling. [17]This girl followed Paul and the rest of us, shouting, "These men are servants of the Most High God, who are telling you the way to be saved." [18]She kept this up for many days. Finally Paul became so troubled that he turned round and said to the spirit, "In the name of Jesus Christ I command you to come out of her!" At that moment the spirit left her.

[19]When the owners of the slave girl realised that their hope of making money was gone, they seized Paul and Silas and dragged them into the market-place to face the authorities. [20]They brought them before the magistrates and said, "These men are Jews, and are throwing our city into an uproar [21]by advocating customs unlawful for us Romans to accept or practise."

[22]The crowd joined in the attack against Paul and Silas, and the magistrates ordered them to be stripped and beaten. [23]After they had been severely flogged, they were thrown into prison, and the jailer was commanded to guard them carefully. [24]Upon receiving such orders, he put them in the inner cell and fastened their feet in the stocks.

[25]About midnight Paul and Silas were praying and singing hymns to God, and the other prisoners were listening to them. [26]Suddenly there was such a violent earthquake that the foundations of the prison were shaken. At once all the prison doors flew open, and everybody's chains came loose. [27]The jailer woke up, and when he saw the prison doors open, he drew his sword and was about to kill himself because he thought the prisoners had escaped. [28]But Paul shouted, "Don't harm yourself! We are all here!"

[29]The jailer called for lights, rushed in and fell trembling before Paul and Silas. [30]He then brought them out and asked, "Sirs, what must I do to be saved?"

[31]They replied, "Believe in the Lord Jesus, and you will be saved—you and your household." [32]Then they spoke the word of the Lord to him and to all the others in his house. [33]At that hour of the night the jailer took them and washed their wounds; then immediately he and all his family were baptised. [34]The jailer brought them into his house and set a meal before them; he was filled with joy because he had come to believe in God—he and his whole family.

[35]When it was daylight, the magistrates sent their officers to the jailer with the order: "Release those men." [36]The jailer told Paul, "The magistrates have ordered that you and Silas be released. Now you can leave. Go in peace."

[37]But Paul said to the officers: "They beat us publicly without a trial, even though we are Roman citizens, and threw us into prison. And now do they want to get rid of us quietly? No! Let them come themselves and escort us out."

[38]The officers reported this to the magistrates, and when they heard that Paul and Silas were Roman citizens, they were alarmed. [39]They came to appease them and escorted them from the prison, requesting them to leave the city. [40]After Paul and Silas came out of the prison, they went to Lydia's house, where they met with the brothers and encouraged them. Then they left.

In Thessalonica

17 When they had passed through Amphipolis and Apollonia, they came to Thessalonica, where there was a Jewish synagogue. [2]As his custom was, Paul went into the synagogue, and on three Sabbath days he reasoned with them from the Scriptures, [3]explaining and proving that the Christ[a] had to suffer and rise from the dead. "This Jesus I am proclaiming to you is the Christ,"[a] he said. [4]Some of the Jews were persuaded and joined Paul and Silas, as did a large number of God-fearing Greeks and not a few prominent women.

[5]But the Jews were jealous; so they rounded up some bad characters from the market-place, formed a mob and started a riot in the city. They rushed to Jason's house in search of Paul and Silas in order to bring them out to the crowd.[b] [6]But when they did not find them, they dragged Jason and some other brothers before the city officials, shouting: "These men who have caused trouble all over the world have now come here, [7]and Jason has welcomed them into his house. They are all defying Caesar's decrees, saying that there is another king, one called Jesus." [8]When they heard this, the crowd and the city officials were thrown into turmoil. [9]Then they put Jason and the others on bail and let them go.

In Berea

[10]As soon as it was night, the brothers sent Paul and Silas away to Berea. On arriving there, they went to the Jewish synagogue. [11]Now the Bereans were of more noble character than the Thessalonians, for they received the message with great eagerness and examined the Scriptures every day to see if what Paul said was true. [12]Many of the Jews believed, as did also a number of prominent Greek women and many Greek men.

[13]When the Jews in Thessalonica learned that Paul was preaching the word of God at Berea, they went there too, agitating the crowds and stirring them up.

[14]The brothers immediately sent Paul to the coast, but Silas and Timothy stayed at Berea. [15]The men who escorted Paul brought him to Athens and then left with instructions for Silas and Timothy to join him as soon as possible.

In Athens

[16]While Paul was waiting for them in Athens, he was greatly distressed to see that the city was full of idols. [17]So he reasoned in the synagogue with the Jews and the God-fearing Greeks, as well as in the market-place day by day with those who happened to be there. [18]A group of Epicurean and Stoic philosophers began to dispute with him. Some of them asked, "What is this babbler trying to say?" Others remarked, "He seems to be advocating foreign gods." They said this because Paul was preaching the good news about Jesus and the resurrection. [19]Then they took him and brought him to a meeting of the Areopagus, where they said to him, "May we know what this new teaching is that you are presenting? [20]You are bringing some strange ideas to our ears, and we want to know what they mean." [21](All the Athenians and the foreigners who lived there spent their time doing nothing but talking about and listening to the latest ideas.)

[22]Paul then stood up in the meeting of the Areopagus and said: "Men of Athens! I see that in every way you are very religious. [23]For as I walked around and looked carefully at your objects of worship, I even found an altar with this inscription: TO AN UNKNOWN GOD. Now what you worship as something unknown I am going to proclaim to you.

[24]"The God who made the world and everything in it is the Lord of heaven and earth and does not live in temples built by hands. [25]And he is not served by human hands, as if he needed anything, because he himself gives all men life and breath and everything else. [26]From one man he made every nation of men, that they should inhabit the whole earth; and he

---

a3 Or Messiah   *b5 Or the assembly of the people*

determined the times set for them and the exact places where they should live. ²⁷God did this so that men would seek him and perhaps reach out for him and find him, though he is not far from each one of us. ²⁸'For in him we live and move and have our being.' As some of your own poets have said, 'We are his offspring.'

²⁹"Therefore since we are God's offspring, we should not think that the divine being is like gold or silver or stone—an image made by man's design and skill. ³⁰In the past God overlooked such ignorance, but now he commands all people everywhere to repent. ³¹For he has set a day when he will judge the world with justice by the man he has appointed. He has given proof of this to all men by raising him from the dead."

³²When they heard about the resurrection of the dead, some of them sneered, but others said, "We want to hear you again on this subject." ³³At that, Paul left the Council. ³⁴A few men became followers of Paul and believed. Among them was Dionysius, a member of the Areopagus, also a woman named Damaris, and a number of others.

In Corinth

18 After this, Paul left Athens and went to Corinth. ²There he met a Jew named Aquila, a native of Pontus, who had recently come from Italy with his wife Priscilla, because Claudius had ordered all the Jews to leave Rome. Paul went to see them, ³and because he was a tentmaker as they were, he stayed and worked with them. ⁴Every Sabbath he reasoned in the synagogue, trying to persuade Jews and Greeks.

⁵When Silas and Timothy came from Macedonia, Paul devoted himself exclusively to preaching, testifying to the Jews that Jesus was the Christ.^a ⁶But when the Jews opposed Paul and became abusive, he shook out his clothes in protest and said to them, "Your blood be on your own heads! I am clear of my responsibility. From now on I will go to the Gentiles."

⁷Then Paul left the synagogue and went next door to the house of Titius Justus, a worshipper of God. ⁸Crispus, the synagogue ruler, and his entire household believed in the Lord; and many of the Corinthians who heard him believed and were baptised.

⁹One night the Lord spoke to Paul in a vision: "Do not be afraid; keep on speaking, do not be silent. ¹⁰For I am with you, and no-one is going to attack and harm you, because I have many people in this city." ¹¹So Paul stayed for a year and a half, teaching them the word of God.

¹²While Gallio was proconsul of Achaia, the Jews made a united attack on Paul and brought him into court. ¹³"This man," they charged, "is persuading the people to worship God in ways contrary to the law."

¹⁴Just as Paul was about to speak, Gallio said to the Jews, "If you Jews were making a complaint about some misdemeanour or serious crime, it would be reasonable for me to listen to you. ¹⁵But since it involves questions about words and names and your own law—settle the matter yourselves. I will not be a judge of such things." ¹⁶So he had them ejected from the court. ¹⁷Then they all turned on Sosthenes the synagogue ruler and beat him in front of the court. But Gallio showed no concern whatever.

Priscilla, Aquila and Apollos

¹⁸Paul stayed on in Corinth for some time. Then he left the brothers and sailed for Syria, accompanied by Priscilla and Aquila. Before he sailed, he had his hair cut off at Cenchrea because of a vow he had taken. ¹⁹They arrived at Ephesus, where Paul left Priscilla and Aquila. He himself went into the synagogue and reasoned with the Jews. ²⁰When they asked him to spend more time with them, he declined. ²¹But as he left, he promised, "I will come back if it is God's will." Then he set sail from Ephesus. ²²When he landed at Caesarea, he went up and greeted the church and then went down to Antioch.

^a5 Or *Messiah*; also in verse 28

[23]After spending some time in Antioch, Paul set out from there and travelled from place to place throughout the region of Galatia and Phrygia, strengthening all the disciples.

[24]Meanwhile a Jew named Apollos, a native of Alexandria, came to Ephesus. He was a learned man, with a thorough knowledge of the Scriptures. [25]He had been instructed in the way of the Lord, and he spoke with great fervour[b] and taught about Jesus accurately, though he knew only the baptism of John. [26]He began to speak boldly in the synagogue. When Priscilla and Aquila heard him, they invited him to their home and explained to him the way of God more adequately.

[27]When Apollos wanted to go to Achaia, the brothers encouraged him and wrote to the disciples there to welcome him. On arriving, he was a great help to those who by grace had believed. [28]For he vigorously refuted the Jews in public debate, proving from the Scriptures that Jesus was the Christ.

Paul in Ephesus

19 While Apollos was at Corinth, Paul took the road through the interior and arrived at Ephesus. There he found some disciples [2]and asked them, "Did you receive the Holy Spirit when[a] you believed?"

They answered, "No, we have not even heard that there is a Holy Spirit."

[3]So Paul asked, "Then what baptism did you receive?"

"John's baptism," they replied.

[4]Paul said, "John's baptism was a baptism of repentance. He told the people to believe in the one coming after him, that is, in Jesus." [5]On hearing this, they were baptised into[b] the name of the Lord Jesus. [6]When Paul placed his hands on them, the Holy Spirit came on them, and they spoke in tongues[c] and prophesied. [7]There were about twelve men in all.

[8]Paul entered the synagogue and spoke boldly there for three months, arguing persuasively about the kingdom of God. [9]But some of them became obstinate; they refused to believe and publicly maligned the Way. So Paul left them. He took the disciples with him and had discussions daily in the lecture hall of Tyrannus. [10]This went on for two years, so that all the Jews and Greeks who lived in the province of Asia heard the word of the Lord.

[11]God did extraordinary miracles through Paul, [12]so that even handkerchiefs and aprons that had touched him were taken to the sick, and their illnesses were cured and the evil spirits left them.

[13]Some Jews who went around driving out evil spirits tried to invoke the name of the Lord Jesus over those who were demon-possessed. They would say, "In the name of Jesus, whom Paul preaches, I command you to come out." [14]Seven sons of Sceva, a Jewish chief priest, were doing this. [15]⌊One day⌋ the evil spirit answered them, "Jesus I know, and I know about Paul, but who are you?" [16]Then the man who had the evil spirit jumped on them and overpowered them all. He gave them such a beating that they ran out of the house naked and bleeding.

[17]When this became known to the Jews and Greeks living in Ephesus, they were all seized with fear, and the name of the Lord Jesus was held in high honour. [18]Many of those who believed now came and openly confessed their evil deeds. [19]A number who had practised sorcery brought their scrolls together and burned them publicly. When they calculated the value of the scrolls, the total came to fifty thousand drachmas.[d] [20]In this way the word of the Lord spread widely and grew in power.

[21]After all this had happened, Paul decided to go to Jerusalem, passing through Macedonia and Achaia. "After I have been there," he said, "I must visit Rome also." [22]He sent two of his helpers, Timothy and Erastus, to Macedonia, while he stayed in the province of Asia a little longer.

---

b25 Or *with fervour in the Spirit*   *a2* Or *after*   *b5* Or *in*   *c6* Or *other languages*
d19 A drachma was a silver coin worth about a day's wages.

The Riot in Ephesus

23About that time there arose a great disturbance about the Way. 24A silversmith named Demetrius, who made silver shrines of Artemis, brought in no little business for the craftsmen. 25He called them together, along with the workmen in related trades, and said: "Men, you know we receive a good income from this business. 26And you see and hear how this fellow Paul has convinced and led astray large numbers of people here in Ephesus and in practically the whole province of Asia. He says that man-made gods are no gods at all. 27There is danger not only that our trade will lose its good name, but also that the temple of the great goddess Artemis will be discredited, and the goddess herself, who is worshipped throughout the province of Asia and the world, will be robbed of her divine majesty."

28When they heard this, they were furious and began shouting: "Great is Artemis of the Ephesians!" 29Soon the whole city was in an uproar. The people seized Gaius and Aristarchus, Paul's travelling companions from Macedonia, and rushed as one man into the theatre. 30Paul wanted to appear before the crowd, but the disciples would not let him. 31Even some of the officials of the province, friends of Paul, sent him a message begging him not to venture into the theatre.

32The assembly was in confusion: Some were shouting one thing, some another. Most of the people did not even know why they were there. 33The Jews pushed Alexander to the front, and some of the crowd shouted instructions to him. He motioned for silence in order to make a defence before the people. 34But when they realised he was a Jew, they all shouted in unison for about two hours: "Great is Artemis of the Ephesians!"

35The city clerk quietened the crowd and said: "Men of Ephesus, doesn't all the world know that the city of Ephesus is the guardian of the temple of the great Artemis and of her image, which fell from heaven? 36Therefore, since these facts are undeniable, you ought to be quiet and not do anything rash. 37You have brought these men here, though they have neither robbed temples nor blasphemed our goddess. 38If, then, Demetrius and his fellow craftsmen have a grievance against anybody, the courts are open and there are proconsuls. They can press charges. 39If there is anything further you want to bring up, it must be settled in a legal assembly. 40As it is, we are in danger of being charged with rioting because of today's events. In that case we would not be able to account for this commotion, since there is no reason for it." 41After he had said this, he dismissed the assembly.

Through Macedonia and Greece

20 When the uproar had ended, Paul sent for the disciples and, after encouraging them, said good-bye and set out for Macedonia. 2He travelled through that area, speaking many words of encouragement to the people, and finally arrived in Greece, 3where he stayed three months. Because the Jews made a plot against him just as he was about to sail for Syria, he decided to go back through Macedonia. 4He was accompanied by Sopater son of Pyrrhus from Berea, Aristarchus and Secundus from Thessalonica, Gaius from Derbe, Timothy also, and Tychicus and Trophimus from the province of Asia. 5These men went on ahead and waited for us at Troas. 6But we sailed from Philippi after the Feast of Unleavened Bread, and five days later joined the others at Troas, where we stayed seven days.

Eutychus Raised From the Dead at Troas

7On the first day of the week we came together to break bread. Paul spoke to the people and, because he intended to leave the next day, kept on talking until midnight. 8There were many lamps in the upstairs room where we were meeting. 9Seated in a window was a young man named Eutychus, who was sinking into a deep sleep as Paul talked on and on. When he was sound asleep, he fell to the ground from the third storey and was picked up dead. 10Paul went down, threw himself on the young man and put his arms around him. "Don't be alarmed," he said. "He's alive!" [11]Then he went upstairs again and broke bread and ate. After talking until daylight, he left. [12]The people took the young man home alive and were greatly comforted.

Paul's Farewell to the Ephesian Elders

[13]We went on ahead to the ship and sailed for Assos, where we were going to take Paul aboard. He had made this arrangement because he was going there on foot. [14]When he met us at Assos, we took him aboard and went on to Mitylene. [15]The next day we set sail from there and arrived off Kios. The day after that we crossed over to Samos, and on the following day arrived at Miletus. [16]Paul had decided to sail past Ephesus to avoid spending time in the province of Asia, for he was in a hurry to reach Jerusalem, if possible, by the day of Pentecost.

[17]From Miletus, Paul sent to Ephesus for the elders of the church. [18]When they arrived, he said to them: "You know how I lived the whole time I was with you, from the first day I came into the province of Asia. [19]I served the Lord with great humility and with tears, although I was severely tested by the plots of the Jews. [20]You know that I have not hesitated to preach anything that would be helpful to you but have taught you publicly and from house to house. [21]I have declared to both Jews and Greeks that they must turn to God in repentance and have faith in our Lord Jesus.

[22]"And now, compelled by the Spirit, I am going to Jerusalem, not knowing what will happen to me there. [23]I only know that in every city the Holy Spirit warns me that prison and hardships are facing me. [24]However, I consider my life worth nothing to me, if only I may finish the race and complete the task the Lord Jesus has given me—the task of testifying to the gospel of God's grace.

[25]"Now I know that none of you among whom I have gone about preaching the kingdom will ever see me again.

[26]Therefore, I declare to you today that I am innocent of the blood of all men. [27]For I have not hesitated to proclaim to you the whole will of God. [28]Keep watch over yourselves and all the flock of which the Holy Spirit has made you overseers.[a] Be shepherds of the church of God,[b] which he bought with his own blood. [29]I know that after I leave, savage wolves will come in among you and will not spare the flock. [30]Even from your own number men will arise and distort the truth in order to draw away disciples after them. [31]So be on your guard! Remember that for three years I never stopped warning each of you night and day with tears.

[32]"Now I commit you to God and to the word of his grace, which can build you up and give you an inheritance among all those who are sanctified. [33]I have not coveted anyone's silver or gold or clothing. [34]You yourselves know that these hands of mine have supplied my own needs and the needs of my companions. [35]In everything I did, I showed you that by this kind of hard work we must help the weak, remembering the words the Lord Jesus himself said: 'It is more blessed to give than to receive.'"

[36]When he had said this, he knelt down with all of them and prayed. [37]They all wept as they embraced him and kissed him. [38]What grieved them most was his statement that they would never see his face again. Then they accompanied him to the ship.

On to Jerusalem

21 After we had torn ourselves away from them, we put out to sea and sailed straight to Cos. The next day we went to Rhodes and from there to Patara. [2]We found a ship crossing over to Phoenicia, went on board and set sail. [3]After sighting Cyprus and passing to the south of it, we sailed on to Syria. We landed at Tyre, where our ship was to unload its cargo. [4]Finding the disciples there, we stayed with them seven days. Through the Spirit they urged Paul not to go on to

---

[a]28 Traditionally *bishops*   [b]28 Many manuscripts *of the Lord*

Jerusalem. 5But when our time was up, we left and continued on our way. All the disciples and their wives and children accompanied us out of the city, and there on the beach we knelt to pray. 6After saying good-bye to each other, we went aboard the ship, and they returned home.

7We continued our voyage from Tyre and landed at Ptolemais, where we greeted the brothers and stayed with them for a day. 8Leaving the next day, we reached Caesarea and stayed at the house of Philip the evangelist, one of the Seven. 9He had four unmarried daughters who prophesied.

10After we had been there a number of days, a prophet named Agabus came down from Judea. 11Coming over to us, he took Paul's belt, tied his own hands and feet with it and said, "The Holy Spirit says, 'In this way the Jews of Jerusalem will bind the owner of this belt and will hand him over to the Gentiles.'"

12When we heard this, we and the people there pleaded with Paul not to go up to Jerusalem. 13Then Paul answered, "Why are you weeping and breaking my heart? I am ready not only to be bound, but also to die in Jerusalem for the name of the Lord Jesus." 14When he would not be dissuaded, we gave up and said, "The Lord's will be done."

15After this, we got ready and went up to Jerusalem. 16Some of the disciples from Caesarea accompanied us and brought us to the home of Mnason, where we were to stay. He was a man from Cyprus and one of the early disciples.

Paul's Arrival at Jerusalem

17When we arrived at Jerusalem, the brothers received us warmly. 18The next day Paul and the rest of us went to see James, and all the elders were present. 19Paul greeted them and reported in detail what God had done among the Gentiles through his ministry.

20When they heard this, they praised God. Then they said to Paul: "You see, brother, how many thousands of Jews have believed, and all of them are zealous for the law. 21They have been informed that you teach all the Jews who live among the Gentiles to turn away from Moses, telling them not to circumcise their children or live according to our customs. 22What shall we do? They will certainly hear that you have come, 23so do what we tell you. There are four men with us who have made a vow. 24Take these men, join in their purification rites and pay their expenses, so that they can have their heads shaved. Then everybody will know there is no truth in these reports about you, but that you yourself are living in obedience to the law. 25As for the Gentile believers, we have written to them our decision that they should abstain from food sacrificed to idols, from blood, from the meat of strangled animals and from sexual immorality."

26The next day Paul took the men and purified himself along with them. Then he went to the temple to give notice of the date when the days of purification would end and the offering would be made for each of them.

Paul Arrested

27When the seven days were nearly over, some Jews from the province of Asia saw Paul at the temple. They stirred up the whole crowd and seized him, 28shouting, "Men of Israel, help us! This is the man who teaches all men everywhere against our people and our law and this place. And besides, he has brought Greeks into the temple area and defiled this holy place." 29(They had previously seen Trophimus the Ephesian in the city with Paul and assumed that Paul had brought him into the temple area.)

30The whole city was aroused, and the people came running from all directions. Seizing Paul, they dragged him from the temple, and immediately the gates were shut. 31While they were trying to kill him, news reached the commander of the Roman troops that the whole city of Jerusalem was in an uproar. 32He at once took some officers and soldiers and ran down to the crowd. When the rioters saw the commander and his soldiers, they stopped beating Paul.

[33]The commander came up and arrested him and ordered him to be bound with two chains. Then he asked who he was and what he had done. [34]Some in the crowd shouted one thing and some another, and since the commander could not get at the truth because of the uproar, he ordered that Paul be taken into the barracks. [35]When Paul reached the steps, the violence of the mob was so great he had to be carried by the soldiers. [36]The crowd that followed kept shouting, "Away with him!"

Paul Speaks to the Crowd

[37]As the soldiers were about to take Paul into the barracks, he asked the commander, "May I say something to you?"

"Do you speak Greek?" he replied. [38]"Aren't you the Egyptian who started a revolt and led four thousand terrorists out into the desert some time ago?"

[39]Paul answered, "I am a Jew, from Tarsus in Cilicia, a citizen of no ordinary city. Please let me speak to the people."

[40]Having received the commander's permission, Paul stood on the steps and motioned to the crowd. When they were all silent, he said to them in Aramaic[a]:

22 [1]"Brothers and fathers, listen now to my defence."

[2]When they heard him speak to them in Aramaic, they became very quiet.

Then Paul said: [3]"I am a Jew, born in Tarsus of Cilicia, but brought up in this city. Under Gamaliel I was thoroughly trained in the law of our fathers and was just as zealous for God as any of you are today. [4]I persecuted the followers of this Way to their death, arresting both men and women and throwing them into prison, [5]as also the high priest and all the Council can testify. I even obtained letters from them to their brothers in Damascus, and went there to bring these people as prisoners to Jerusalem to be punished.

[6]"About noon as I came near Damascus, suddenly a bright light from heaven flashed around me. [7]I fell to the ground and heard a voice say to me, 'Saul! Saul! Why do you persecute me?'

[8]"'Who are you, Lord?' I asked.

"'I am Jesus of Nazareth, whom you are persecuting,' he replied. [9]My companions saw the light, but they did not understand the voice of him who was speaking to me.

[10]"'What shall I do, Lord?' I asked.

"'Get up,' the Lord said, 'and go into Damascus. There you will be told all that you have been assigned to do.' [11]My companions led me by the hand into Damascus, because the brilliance of the light had blinded me.

[12]"A man named Ananias came to see me. He was a devout observer of the law and highly respected by all the Jews living there. [13]He stood beside me and said, 'Brother Saul, receive your sight!' And at that very moment I was able to see him.

[14]"Then he said: 'The God of our fathers has chosen you to know his will and to see the Righteous One and to hear words from his mouth. [15]You will be his witness to all men of what you have seen and heard. [16]And now what are you waiting for? Get up, be baptised and wash your sins away, calling on his name.'

[17]"When I returned to Jerusalem and was praying at the temple, I fell into a trance [18]and saw the Lord speaking. 'Quick!' he said to me. 'Leave Jerusalem immediately, because they will not accept your testimony about me.'

[19]"'Lord,' I replied, 'these men know that I went from one synagogue to another to imprison and beat those who believe in you. [20]And when the blood of your martyr[a] Stephen was shed, I stood there giving my approval and guarding the clothes of those who were killing him.'

[21]"Then the Lord said to me, 'Go; I will send you far away to the Gentiles.'"

Paul the Roman Citizen

[22]The crowd listened to Paul until he said this. Then they raised their voices and shouted, "Rid the earth of him! He's not fit to live!"

[23]As they were shouting and throwing off their cloaks and flinging dust into the air, [24]the commander ordered Paul to be taken into the barracks. He directed that he be flogged and questioned in order to find out why the people were shouting at

---

[a]40 Or possibly *Hebrew*; also in 22:2   [a]20 Or *witness*

him like this. 25As they stretched him out to flog him, Paul said to the centurion standing there, "Is it legal for you to flog a Roman citizen who hasn't even been found guilty?"

26When the centurion heard this, he went to the commander and reported it. "What are you going to do?" he asked. "This man is a Roman citizen."

27The commander went to Paul and asked, "Tell me, are you a Roman citizen?"

"Yes, I am," he answered.

28Then the commander said, "I had to pay a big price for my citizenship."

"But I was born a citizen," Paul replied.

29Those who were about to question him withdrew immediately. The commander himself was alarmed when he realised that he had put Paul, a Roman citizen, in chains.

Before the Sanhedrin

30The next day, since the commander wanted to find out exactly why Paul was being accused by the Jews, he released him and ordered the chief priests and all the Sanhedrin to assemble. Then he brought Paul and had him stand before them.

23 Paul looked straight at the Sanhedrin and said, "My brothers, I have fulfilled my duty to God in all good conscience to this day." 2At this the high priest Ananias ordered those standing near Paul to strike him on the mouth. 3Then Paul said to him, "God will strike you, you whitewashed wall! You sit there to judge me according to the law, yet you yourself violate the law by commanding that I be struck!"

4Those who were standing near Paul said, "You dare to insult God's high priest?"

5Paul replied, "Brothers, I did not realise that he was the high priest; for it is written: 'Do not speak evil about the ruler of your people.'*a*"

6Then Paul, knowing that some of them were Sadducees and the others Pharisees,

called out in the Sanhedrin, "My brothers, I am a Pharisee, the son of a Pharisee. I stand on trial because of my hope in the resurrection of the dead." 7When he said this, a dispute broke out between the Pharisees and the Sadducees, and the assembly was divided. 8(The Sadducees say that there is no resurrection, and that there are neither angels nor spirits, but the Pharisees acknowledge them all.)

9There was a great uproar, and some of the teachers of the law who were Pharisees stood up and argued vigorously. "We find nothing wrong with this man," they said. "What if a spirit or an angel has spoken to him?" 10The dispute became so violent that the commander was afraid Paul would be torn to pieces by them. He ordered the troops to go down and take him away from them by force and bring him into the barracks.

11The following night the Lord stood near Paul and said, "Take courage! As you have testified about me in Jerusalem, so you must also testify in Rome."

The Plot to Kill Paul

12The next morning the Jews formed a conspiracy and bound themselves with an oath not to eat or drink until they had killed Paul. 13More than forty men were involved in this plot. 14They went to the chief priests and elders and said, "We have taken a solemn oath not to eat anything until we have killed Paul. 15Now then, you and the Sanhedrin petition the commander to bring him before you on the pretext of wanting more accurate information about his case. We are ready to kill him before he gets here."

16But when the son of Paul's sister heard of this plot, he went into the barracks and told Paul.

17Then Paul called one of the centurions and said, "Take this young man to the commander; he has something to tell him." 18So he took him to the commander.

The centurion said, "Paul, the prisoner, sent for me and asked me to bring this young man to you because he has something to tell you."

¹⁹The commander took the young man by the hand, drew him aside and asked, "What is it you want to tell me?"

²⁰He said: "The Jews have agreed to ask you to bring Paul before the Sanhedrin tomorrow on the pretext of wanting more accurate information about him. ²¹Don't give in to them, because more than forty of them are waiting in ambush for him. They have taken an oath not to eat or drink until they have killed him. They are ready now, waiting for your consent to their request."

²²The commander dismissed the young man and cautioned him, "Don't tell anyone that you have reported this to me."

Paul Transferred to Caesarea

²³Then he called two of his centurions and ordered them, "Get ready a detachment of two hundred soldiers, seventy horsemen and two hundred spearmen*b* to go to Caesarea at nine tonight. ²⁴Provide mounts for Paul so that he may be taken safely to Governor Felix."

²⁵He wrote a letter as follows:

²⁶Claudius Lysias,

To His Excellency, Governor Felix:

Greetings.

²⁷This man was seized by the Jews and they were about to kill him, but I came with my troops and rescued him, for I had learned that he is a Roman citizen. ²⁸I wanted to know why they were accusing him, so I brought him to their Sanhedrin. ²⁹I found that the accusation had to do with questions about their law, but there was no charge against him that deserved death or imprisonment. ³⁰When I was informed of a plot to be carried out against the man, I sent him to you at once. I also ordered his accusers to present to you their case against him.

³¹So the soldiers, carrying out their orders, took Paul with them during the night and brought him as far as Antipatris. ³²The next day they let the cavalry go on with him, while they returned to the barracks. ³³When the cavalry arrived in Caesarea, they delivered the letter to the governor and handed Paul over to him. ³⁴The governor read the letter and asked what province he was from. Learning that he was from Cilicia, ³⁵he said, "I will hear your case when your accusers get here." Then he ordered that Paul be kept under guard in Herod's palace.

The Trial Before Felix

24 Five days later the high priest Ananias went down to Caesarea with some of the elders and a lawyer named Tertullus, and they brought their charges against Paul before the governor. ²When Paul was called in, Tertullus presented his case before Felix: "We have enjoyed a long period of peace under you, and your foresight has brought about reforms in this nation. ³Everywhere and in every way, most excellent Felix, we acknowledge this with profound gratitude. ⁴But in order not to weary you further, I would request that you be kind enough to hear us briefly.

⁵"We have found this man to be a troublemaker, stirring up riots among the Jews all over the world. He is a ringleader of the Nazarene sect ⁶and even tried to desecrate the temple; so we seized him. ⁸By*a* examining him yourself you will be able to learn the truth about all these charges we are bringing against him."

⁹The Jews joined in the accusation, asserting that these things were true.

¹⁰When the governor motioned for him to speak, Paul replied: "I know that for a number of years you have been a judge over this nation; so I gladly make my defence. ¹¹You can easily verify that no

more than twelve days ago I went up to Jerusalem to worship. [12]My accusers did not find me arguing with anyone at the temple, or stirring up a crowd in the synagogues or anywhere else in the city. [13]And they cannot prove to you the charges they are now making against me. [14]However, I admit that I worship the God of our fathers as a follower of the Way, which they call a sect. I believe everything that agrees with the Law and that is written in the Prophets, [15]and I have the same hope in God as these men, that there will be a resurrection of both the righteous and the wicked. [16]So I strive always to keep my conscience clear before God and man.

[17]"After an absence of several years, I came to Jerusalem to bring my people gifts for the poor and to present offerings. [18]I was ceremonially clean when they found me in the temple courts doing this. There was no crowd with me, nor was I involved in any disturbance. [19]But there are some Jews from the province of Asia, who ought to be here before you and bring charges if they have anything against me. [20]Or these who are here should state what crime they found in me when I stood before the Sanhedrin—[21]unless it was this one thing I shouted as I stood in their presence: 'It is concerning the resurrection of the dead that I am on trial before you today.'"

[22]Then Felix, who was well acquainted with the Way, adjourned the proceedings. "When Lysias the commander comes," he said, "I will decide your case." [23]He ordered the centurion to keep Paul under guard but to give him some freedom and permit his friends to take care of his needs.

[24]Several days later Felix came with his wife Drusilla, who was a Jewess. He sent for Paul and listened to him as he spoke about faith in Christ Jesus. [25]As Paul discoursed on righteousness, self-control and the judgment to come, Felix was afraid and said, "That's enough for now! You may leave. When I find it convenient, I will send for you." [26]At the same time he was hoping that Paul would offer him a bribe, so he sent for him frequently and talked with him.

[27]When two years had passed, Felix was succeeded by Porcius Festus, but because Felix wanted to grant a favour to the Jews, he left Paul in prison.

The Trial Before Festus

25 Three days after arriving in the province, Festus went up from Caesarea to Jerusalem, [2]where the chief priests and Jewish leaders appeared before him and presented the charges against Paul. [3]They urgently requested Festus, as a favour to them, to have Paul transferred to Jerusalem, for they were preparing an ambush to kill him along the way. [4]Festus answered, "Paul is being held at Caesarea, and I myself am going there soon. [5]Let some of your leaders come with me and press charges against the man there, if he has done anything wrong."

[6]After spending eight or ten days with them, he went down to Caesarea, and the next day he convened the court and ordered that Paul be brought before him. [7]When Paul appeared, the Jews who had come down from Jerusalem stood around him, bringing many serious charges against him, which they could not prove.

[8]Then Paul made his defence: "I have done nothing wrong against the law of the Jews or against the temple or against Caesar."

[9]Festus, wishing to do the Jews a favour, said to Paul, "Are you willing to go up to Jerusalem and stand trial before me there on these charges?"

[10]Paul answered: "I am now standing before Caesar's court, where I ought to be tried. I have not done any wrong to the Jews, as you yourself know very well. [11]If, however, I am guilty of doing anything deserving death, I do not refuse to die. But if the charges brought against me by these Jews are not true, no-one has the right to hand me over to them. I appeal to Caesar!"

[12]After Festus had conferred with his council, he declared: "You have appealed to Caesar. To Caesar you will go!"

Festus Consults King Agrippa

[13]A few days later King Agrippa and Bernice arrived at Caesarea to pay their respects to Festus. [14]Since they were spending many days there, Festus discussed Paul's case with the king. He said: "There is a man here whom Felix left as a prisoner. [15]When I went to Jerusalem, the chief priests and elders of the Jews brought charges against him and asked that he be condemned.

[16]"I told them that it is not the Roman custom to hand over any man before he has faced his accusers and has had an opportunity to defend himself against their charges. [17]When they came here with me, I did not delay the case, but convened the court the next day and ordered the man to be brought in. [18]When his accusers got up to speak, they did not charge him with any of the crimes I had expected. [19]Instead, they had some points of dispute with him about their own religion and about a dead man named Jesus whom Paul claimed was alive. [20]I was at a loss how to investigate such matters; so I asked if he would be willing to go to Jerusalem and stand trial there on these charges. [21]When Paul made his appeal to be held over for the Emperor's decision, I ordered him to be held until I could send him to Caesar."

[22]Then Agrippa said to Festus, "I would like to hear this man myself."

He replied, "Tomorrow you will hear him."

Paul Before Agrippa

[23]The next day Agrippa and Bernice came with great pomp and entered the audience room with the high ranking officers and the leading men of the city. At the command of Festus, Paul was brought in. [24]Festus said: "King Agrippa, and all who are present with us, you see this man! The whole Jewish community has petitioned me about him in Jerusalem and here in Caesarea, shouting that he ought not to live any longer. [25]I found he had done nothing deserving of death, but because he made his appeal to the Emperor I decided to send him to Rome. [26]But I have nothing definite to write to His Majesty about him. Therefore I have brought him before all of you, and especially before you, King Agrippa, so that as a result of this investigation I may have something to write. [27]For I think it is unreasonable to send on a prisoner without specifying the charges against him."

26 Then Agrippa said to Paul, "You have permission to speak for yourself."

So Paul motioned with his hand and began his defence: [2]"King Agrippa, I consider myself fortunate to stand before you today as I make my defence against all the accusations of the Jews, [3]and especially so because you are well acquainted with all the Jewish customs and controversies. Therefore, I beg you to listen to me patiently.

[4]"The Jews all know the way I have lived ever since I was a child, from the beginning of my life in my own country, and also in Jerusalem. [5]They have known me for a long time and can testify, if they are willing, that according to the strictest sect of our religion, I lived as a Pharisee. [6]And now it is because of my hope in what God has promised our fathers that I am on trial today. [7]This is the promise our twelve tribes are hoping to see fulfilled as they earnestly serve God day and night. O King, it is because of this hope that the Jews are accusing me. [8]Why should any of you consider it incredible that God raises the dead?

[9]"I too was convinced that I ought to do all that was possible to oppose the name of Jesus of Nazareth. [10]And that is just what I did in Jerusalem. On the authority of the chief priests I put many of the saints in prison, and when they were put to death, I cast my vote against them. [11]Many a time I went from one synagogue to another to have them punished, and I tried to force them to blaspheme. In my obsession against them, I even went to foreign cities to persecute them.

[12]"On one of these journeys I was going to Damascus with the authority and commission of the chief priests. [13]About noon, O King, as I was on the road, I saw a light from heaven, brighter than the sun, blazing around me and my companions. [14]We

all fell to the ground, and I heard a voice saying to me in Aramaic,*a* 'Saul, Saul, why do you persecute me? It is hard for you to kick against the goads.'

15"Then I asked, 'Who are you, Lord?'

"'I am Jesus, whom you are persecuting,' the Lord replied. 16'Now get up and stand on your feet. I have appeared to you to appoint you as a servant and as a witness of what you have seen of me and what I will show you. 17I will rescue you from your own people and from the Gentiles. I am sending you to them 18to open their eyes and turn them from darkness to light, and from the power of Satan to God, so that they may receive forgiveness of sins and a place among those who are sanctified by faith in me.'

19"So then, King Agrippa, I was not disobedient to the vision from heaven. 20First to those in Damascus, then to those in Jerusalem and in all Judea, and to the Gentiles also, I preached that they should repent and turn to God and prove their repentance by their deeds. 21That is why the Jews seized me in the temple courts and tried to kill me. 22But I have had God's help to this very day, and so I stand here and testify to small and great alike. I am saying nothing beyond what the prophets and Moses said would happen— 23that the Christ*b* would suffer and, as the first to rise from the dead, would proclaim light to his own people and to the Gentiles."

24At this point Festus interrupted Paul's defence. "You are out of your mind, Paul!" he shouted. "Your great learning is driving you insane."

25"I am not insane, most excellent Festus," Paul replied. "What I am saying is true and reasonable. 26The king is familiar with these things, and I can speak freely to him. I am convinced that none of this has escaped his notice, because it was not done in a corner. 27King Agrippa, do you believe the prophets? I know you do."

28Then Agrippa said to Paul, "Do you think that in such a short time you can persuade me to be a Christian?"

29Paul replied, "Short time or long—I pray God that not only you but all who are listening to me today may become what I am, except for these chains."

30The king rose, and with him the governor and Bernice and those sitting with them. 31They left the room, and while talking with one another, they said, "This man is not doing anything that deserves death or imprisonment."

32Agrippa said to Festus, "This man could have been set free if he had not appealed to Caesar."

Paul Sails for Rome

27 When it was decided that we would sail for Italy, Paul and some other prisoners were handed over to a centurion named Julius, who belonged to the Imperial Regiment. 2We boarded a ship from Adramyttium about to sail for ports along the coast of the province of Asia, and we put out to sea. Aristarchus, a Macedonian from Thessalonica, was with us.

3The next day we landed at Sidon; and Julius, in kindness to Paul, allowed him to go to his friends so they might provide for his needs. 4From there we put out to sea again and passed to the lee of Cyprus because the winds were against us. 5When we had sailed across the open sea off the coast of Cilicia and Pamphylia, we landed at Myra in Lycia. 6There the centurion found an Alexandrian ship sailing for Italy and put us on board. 7We made slow headway for many days and had difficulty arriving off Cnidus. When the wind did not allow us to hold our course, we sailed to the lee of Crete, opposite Salmone. 8We moved along the coast with difficulty and came to a place called Fair Havens, near the town of Lasea.

9Much time had been lost, and sailing had already become dangerous because by now it was after the Fast.*a* So Paul warned them, 10"Men, I can see that our voyage is going to be disastrous and bring great loss to ship and cargo, and to our own lives also." 11But the centurion, instead of listening to what Paul said, followed the advice of the pilot and of the

---

a14 Or Hebrew   *b23 Or Messiah*   *a9 That is, the Day of Atonement (Yom Kippur)* owner of the ship. [12]Since the harbour was unsuitable to winter in, the majority decided that we should sail on, hoping to reach Phoenix and winter there. This was a harbour in Crete, facing both south-west and north-west.

The Storm

[13]When a gentle south wind began to blow, they thought they had obtained what they wanted; so they weighed anchor and sailed along the shore of Crete. [14]Before very long, a wind of hurricane force, called the "north-easter", swept down from the island. [15]The ship was caught by the storm and could not head into the wind; so we gave way to it and were driven along. [16]As we passed to the lee of a small island called Cauda, we were hardly able to make the lifeboat secure. [17]When the men had hoisted it aboard, they passed ropes under the ship itself to hold it together. Fearing that they would run aground on the sand-bars of Syrtis, they lowered the sea anchor and let the ship be driven along. [18]We took such a violent battering from the storm that the next day they began to throw the cargo overboard. [19]On the third day, they threw the ship's tackle overboard with their own hands. [20]When neither sun nor stars appeared for many days and the storm continued raging, we finally gave up all hope of being saved.

[21]After the men had gone a long time without food, Paul stood up before them and said: "Men, you should have taken my advice not to sail from Crete; then you would have spared yourselves this damage and loss. [22]But now I urge you to keep up your courage, because not one of you will be lost; only the ship will be destroyed. [23]Last night an angel of the God whose I am and whom I serve stood beside me [24]and said, 'Do not be afraid, Paul. You must stand trial before Caesar; and God has graciously given you the lives of all who sail with you.' [25]So keep up your courage, men, for I have faith in God that

it will happen just as he told me. [26]Nevertheless, we must run aground on some island."

The Shipwreck

[27]On the fourteenth night we were still being driven across the Adriatic[b] Sea, when about midnight the sailors sensed they were approaching land. [28]They took soundings and found that the water was one hundred and twenty feet[c] deep. A short time later they took soundings again and found it was ninety feet[d] deep. [29]Fearing that we would be dashed against the rocks, they dropped four anchors from the stern and prayed for daylight. [30]In an attempt to escape from the ship, the sailors let the lifeboat down into the sea, pretending they were going to lower some anchors from the bow. [31]Then Paul said to the centurion and the soldiers, "Unless these men stay with the ship, you cannot be saved." [32]So the soldiers cut the ropes that held the lifeboat and let it fall away.

[33]Just before dawn Paul urged them all to eat. "For the last fourteen days," he said, "you have been in constant suspense and have gone without food—you haven't eaten anything. [34]Now I urge you to take some food. You need it to survive. Not one of you will lose a single hair from his head." [35]After he said this, he took some bread and gave thanks to God in front of them all. Then he broke it and began to eat. [36]They were all encouraged and ate some food themselves. [37]Altogether there were 276 of us on board. [38]When they had eaten as much as they wanted, they lightened the ship by throwing the grain into the sea.

[39]When daylight came, they did not recognise the land, but they saw a bay with a sandy beach, where they decided to run the ship aground if they could. [40]Cutting loose the anchors, they left them in the sea and at the same time untied the ropes that held the rudders. Then they hoisted the foresail to the wind and made for the beach. [41]But the ship struck a sand-bar

---

[b]27 In ancient times the name referred to an area extending well south of Italy.
[c]28 Greek *twenty orguias* (about 37 metres)   [d]28 Greek *fifteen orguias* (about 27 metres)

and ran aground. The bow stuck fast and would not move, and the stern was broken to pieces by the pounding of the surf.

⁴²The soldiers planned to kill the prisoners to prevent any of them from swimming away and escaping. ⁴³But the centurion wanted to spare Paul's life and kept them from carrying out their plan. He ordered those who could swim to jump overboard first and get to land. ⁴⁴The rest were to get there on planks or on pieces of the ship. In this way everyone reached land in safety.

Ashore on Malta

28 Once safely on shore, we found out that the island was called Malta. ²The islanders showed us unusual kindness. They built a fire and welcomed us all because it was raining and cold. ³Paul gathered a pile of brushwood and, as he put it on the fire, a viper, driven out by the heat, fastened itself on his hand. ⁴When the islanders saw the snake hanging from his hand, they said to each other, "This man must be a murderer; for though he escaped from the sea, Justice has not allowed him to live." ⁵But Paul shook the snake off into the fire and suffered no ill effects. ⁶The people expected him to swell up or suddenly fall dead, but after waiting a long time and seeing nothing unusual happen to him, they changed their minds and said he was a god.

⁷There was an estate near by that belonged to Publius, the chief official of the island. He welcomed us to his home and for three days entertained us hospitably. ⁸His father was sick in bed, suffering from fever and dysentery. Paul went in to see him and, after prayer, placed his hands on him and healed him. ⁹When this had happened, the rest of the sick on the island came and were cured. ¹⁰They honoured us in many ways and when we were ready to sail, they furnished us with the supplies we needed.

Arrival at Rome

¹¹After three months we put out to sea in a ship that had wintered in the island. It was an Alexandrian ship with the figurehead of the twin gods Castor and Pollux. ¹²We put in at Syracuse and stayed there three days. ¹³From there we set sail and arrived at Rhegium. The next day the south wind came up, and on the following day we reached Puteoli. ¹⁴There we found some brothers who invited us to spend a week with them. And so we came to Rome. ¹⁵The brothers there had heard that we were coming, and they travelled as far as the Forum of Appius and the Three Taverns to meet us. At the sight of these men Paul thanked God and was encouraged. ¹⁶When we got to Rome, Paul was allowed to live by himself, with a soldier to guard him.

Paul Preaches at Rome Under Guard

¹⁷Three days later he called together the leaders of the Jews. When they had assembled, Paul said to them: "My brothers, although I have done nothing against our people or against the customs of our ancestors, I was arrested in Jerusalem and handed over to the Romans. ¹⁸They examined me and wanted to release me, because I was not guilty of any crime deserving death. ¹⁹But when the Jews objected, I was compelled to appeal to Caesar—not that I had any charge to bring against my own people. ²⁰For this reason I have asked to see you and talk with you. It is because of the hope of Israel that I am bound with this chain."

²¹They replied, "We have not received any letters from Judea concerning you, and none of the brothers who have come from there has reported or said anything bad about you. ²²But we want to hear what your views are, for we know that people everywhere are talking against this sect."

²³They arranged to meet Paul on a certain day, and came in even larger numbers to the place where he was staying. From morning till evening he explained and declared to them the kingdom of God and tried to convince them about Jesus from the Law of Moses and from the Prophets. ²⁴Some were convinced by what he said, but others would not believe. ²⁵They disagreed among themselves and began to leave after Paul had made this final

statement: "The Holy Spirit spoke the truth to your forefathers when he said through Isaiah the prophet:

26"'Go to this people and say,
  "You will be ever hearing but never
    understanding;
    you will be ever seeing but never
      perceiving."
27For this people's heart has become
    calloused;
  they hardly hear with their ears,
  and they have closed their eyes.
  Otherwise they might see with their eyes,

hear with their ears,
  understand with their hearts
and turn, and I would heal
    them.'[a]

28"Therefore I want you to know that God's salvation has been sent to the Gentiles, and they will listen!"[b]

30For two whole years Paul stayed there in his own rented house and welcomed all who came to see him. 31Boldly and without hindrance he preached the kingdom of God and taught about the Lord Jesus Christ.

---

[a]27 Isaiah 6:9,10
[b]28 Some manuscripts *listen!"* 29*After he said this, the Jews left, arguing vigorously among themselves.*

Romans

1 Paul, a servant of Christ Jesus, called to be an apostle and set apart for the gospel of God—²the gospel he promised beforehand through his prophets in the Holy Scriptures ³regarding his Son, who as to his human nature was a descendant of David, ⁴and who through the Spirit[a] of holiness was declared with power to be the Son of God,[b] by his resurrection from the dead: Jesus Christ our Lord. ⁵Through him and for his name's sake, we received grace and apostleship to call people from among all the Gentiles to the obedience that comes from faith. ⁶And you also are among those who are called to belong to Jesus Christ.

⁷To all in Rome who are loved by God and called to be saints:

Grace and peace to you from God our Father and from the Lord Jesus Christ.

Paul's Longing to Visit Rome

⁸First, I thank my God through Jesus Christ for all of you, because your faith is being reported all over the world. ⁹God, whom I serve with my whole heart in preaching the gospel of his Son, is my witness how constantly I remember you ¹⁰in my prayers at all times; and I pray that now at last by God's will the way may be opened for me to come to you. ¹¹I long to see you so that I may impart to you some spiritual gift to make you strong—¹²that is, that you and I may be mutually encouraged by each other's faith. ¹³I do not want you to be unaware, brothers, that I planned many times to come to you (but have been prevented from doing so until now) in order that I might have a harvest among you, just as I have had among the other Gentiles.

¹⁴I am bound both to Greeks and non-Greeks, both to the wise and the foolish. ¹⁵That is why I am so eager to preach the gospel also to you who are at Rome.

¹⁶I am not ashamed of the gospel, because it is the power of God for the salvation of everyone who believes: first for the Jew, then for the Gentile. ¹⁷For in the gospel a righteousness from God is revealed, a righteousness that is by faith from first to last,[c] just as it is written: "The righteous will live by faith."[d]

God's Wrath Against Mankind

¹⁸The wrath of God is being revealed from heaven against all the godlessness and wickedness of men who suppress the truth by their wickedness, ¹⁹since what may be known about God is plain to them, because God has made it plain to them. ²⁰For since the creation of the world God's invisible qualities—his eternal power and divine nature—have been clearly seen, being understood from what has been made, so that men are without excuse.

²¹For although they knew God, they neither glorified him as God nor gave thanks to him, but their thinking became

---

a4 Or *who as to his spirit*   *b4* Or *was appointed to be the Son of God with power*
c17 Or *is from faith to faith*   *d17* Hab. 2:4

futile and their foolish hearts were darkened. [22]Although they claimed to be wise, they became fools [23]and exchanged the glory of the immortal God for images made to look like mortal man and birds and animals and reptiles.

[24]Therefore God gave them over in the sinful desires of their hearts to sexual impurity for the degrading of their bodies with one another. [25]They exchanged the truth of God for a lie, and worshipped and served created things rather than the Creator—who is for ever praised. Amen.

[26]Because of this, God gave them over to shameful lusts. Even their women exchanged natural relations for unnatural ones. [27]In the same way the men also abandoned natural relations with women and were inflamed with lust for one another. Men committed indecent acts with other men, and received in themselves the due penalty for their perversion.

[28]Furthermore, since they did not think it worth while to retain the knowledge of God, he gave them over to a depraved mind, to do what ought not to be done. [29]They have become filled with every kind of wickedness, evil, greed and depravity. They are full of envy, murder, strife, deceit and malice. They are gossips, [30]slanderers, God-haters, insolent, arrogant and boastful; they invent ways of doing evil; they disobey their parents; [31]they are senseless, faithless, heartless, ruthless. [32]Although they know God's righteous decree that those who do such things deserve death, they not only continue to do these very things but also approve of those who practise them.

God's Righteous Judgment

2 You, therefore, have no excuse, you who pass judgment on someone else, for at whatever point you judge the other, you are condemning yourself, because you who pass judgment do the same things. [2]Now we know that God's judgment against those who do such things is based on truth. [3]So when you, a mere man, pass judgment on them and yet do the same things, do you think you will escape God's judgment? [4]Or do you show contempt for the riches of his kindness, tolerance and patience, not realising that God's kindness leads you towards repentance?

[5]But because of your stubbornness and your unrepentant heart, you are storing up wrath against yourself for the day of God's wrath, when his righteous judgment will be revealed. [6]God "will give to each person according to what he has done".[a] [7]To those who by persistence in doing good seek glory, honour and immortality, he will give eternal life. [8]But for those who are self-seeking and who reject the truth and follow evil, there will be wrath and anger. [9]There will be trouble and distress for every human being who does evil: first for the Jew, then for the Gentile; [10]but glory, honour and peace for everyone who does good: first for the Jew, then for the Gentile. [11]For God does not show favouritism.

[12]All who sin apart from the law will also perish apart from the law, and all who sin under the law will be judged by the law. [13]For it is not those who hear the law who are righteous in God's sight, but it is those who obey the law who will be declared righteous. [14](Indeed, when Gentiles, who do not have the law, do by nature things required by the law, they are a law for themselves, even though they do not have the law, [15]since they show that the requirements of the law are written on their hearts, their consciences also bearing witness, and their thoughts now accusing, now even defending them.) [16]This will take place on the day when God will judge men's secrets through Jesus Christ, as my gospel declares.

The Jews and the Law

[17]Now you, if you call yourself a Jew; if you rely on the law and brag about your relationship to God; [18]if you know his will and approve of what is superior because you are instructed by the law; [19]if you are

[a]6 Psalm 62:12; Prov. 24:12

convinced that you are a guide for the blind, a light for those who are in the dark, [20]an instructor of the foolish, a teacher of infants, because you have in the law the embodiment of knowledge and truth— [21]you, then, who teach others, do you not teach yourself? You who preach against stealing, do you steal? [22]You who say that people should not commit adultery, do you commit adultery? You who abhor idols, do you rob temples? [23]You who brag about the law, do you dishonour God by breaking the law? [24]As it is written: "God's name is blasphemed among the Gentiles because of you."[b]

[25]Circumcision has value if you observe the law, but if you break the law, you have become as though you had not been circumcised. [26]If those who are not circumcised keep the law's requirements, will they not be regarded as though they were circumcised? [27]The one who is not circumcised physically and yet obeys the law will condemn you who, even though you have the[c] written code and circumcision, are a law-breaker.

[28]A man is not a Jew if he is only one outwardly, nor is circumcision merely outward and physical. [29]No, a man is a Jew if he is one inwardly; and circumcision is circumcision of the heart, by the Spirit, not by the written code. Such a man's praise is not from men, but from God.

God's Faithfulness

3 What advantage, then, is there in being a Jew, or what value is there in circumcision? [2]Much in every way! First of all, they have been entrusted with the very words of God.

[3]What if some did not have faith? Will their lack of faith nullify God's faithfulness? [4]Not at all! Let God be true, and every man a liar. As it is written:

"So that you may be proved right when you speak and prevail when you judge."[a]

[5]But if our unrighteousness brings out God's righteousness more clearly, what shall we say? That God is unjust in bringing his wrath on us? (I am using a human argument.) [6]Certainly not! If that were so, how could God judge the world? [7]Someone might argue, "If my falsehood enhances God's truthfulness and so increases his glory, why am I still condemned as a sinner?" [8]Why not say—as we are being slanderously reported as saying and as some claim that we say— "Let us do evil that good may result"? Their condemnation is deserved.

No-one Is Righteous

[9]What shall we conclude then? Are we any better?[b] Not at all! We have already made the charge that Jews and Gentiles alike are all under sin. [10]As it is written:

"There is no-one righteous, not even one;
11 there is no-one who understands, no-one who seeks God.
[12]All have turned away, they have together become worthless;
there is no-one who does good, not even one."[c]
[13]"Their throats are open graves; their tongues practise deceit."[d]
"The poison of vipers is on their lips."[e]
14 "Their mouths are full of cursing and bitterness."[f]
[15]"Their feet are swift to shed blood;
16 ruin and misery mark their ways,
17and the way of peace they do not know."[g]
18 "There is no fear of God before their eyes."[h]

[19]Now we know that whatever the law says, it says to those who are under the law, so that every mouth may be silenced and the whole world held accountable to God. [20]Therefore no-one will be declared righteous in his sight by observing the law; rather, through the law we become conscious of sin.

b24 Isaiah 52:5; Ezek. 36:22   c27 Or who, by means of a
c12 Psalms 14:1–3; 53:1–3; Eccles. 7:20   d13 Psalm 5:9
g17 Isaiah 59:7,8   h18 Psalm 36:1   a4 Psalm 51:4   e13 Psalm 140:3   b9 Or worse   f14 Psalm 10:7

Righteousness Through Faith

²¹But now a righteousness from God, apart from law, has been made known, to which the Law and the Prophets testify. ²²This righteousness from God comes through faith in Jesus Christ to all who believe. There is no difference, ²³for all have sinned and fall short of the glory of God, ²⁴and are justified freely by his grace through the redemption that came by Christ Jesus. ²⁵God presented him as a sacrifice of atonement,*ⁱ* through faith in his blood. He did this to demonstrate his justice, because in his forbearance he had left the sins committed beforehand unpunished ²⁶—he did it to demonstrate his justice at the present time, so as to be just and the one who justifies those who have faith in Jesus.

²⁷Where, then, is boasting? It is excluded. On what principle? On that of observing the law? No, but on that of faith. ²⁸For we maintain that a man is justified by faith apart from observing the law. ²⁹Is God the God of Jews only? Is he not the God of Gentiles too? Yes, of Gentiles too, ³⁰since there is only one God, who will justify the circumcised by faith and the uncircumcised through that same faith. ³¹Do we, then, nullify the law by this faith? Not at all! Rather, we uphold the law.

Abraham Justified by Faith

4 What then shall we say that Abraham, our forefather, discovered in this matter? ²If, in fact, Abraham was justified by works, he had something to boast about—but not before God. ³What does the Scripture say? "Abraham believed God, and it was credited to him as righteousness."*ᵃ*

⁴Now when a man works, his wages are not credited to him as a gift, but as an obligation. ⁵However, to the man who does not work but trusts God who justifies the wicked, his faith is credited as righteousness. ⁶David says the same thing when he speaks of the blessedness of the

man to whom God credits righteousness apart from works:

⁷"Blessed are they
  whose transgressions are forgiven,
  whose sins are covered.
⁸Blessed is the man
  whose sin the Lord will never count
    against him."*ᵇ*

⁹Is this blessedness only for the circumcised, or also for the uncircumcised? We have been saying that Abraham's faith was credited to him as righteousness. ¹⁰Under what circumstances was it credited? Was it after he was circumcised, or before? It was not after, but before! ¹¹And he received the sign of circumcision, a seal of the righteousness that he had by faith while he was still uncircumcised. So then, he is the father of all who believe but have not been circumcised, in order that righteousness might be credited to them. ¹²And he is also the father of the circumcised who not only are circumcised but who also walk in the footsteps of the faith that our father Abraham had before he was circumcised.

¹³It was not through law that Abraham and his offspring received the promise that he would be heir of the world, but through the righteousness that comes by faith. ¹⁴For if those who live by law are heirs, faith has no value and the promise is worthless, ¹⁵because law brings wrath. And where there is no law there is no transgression.

¹⁶Therefore, the promise comes by faith, so that it may be by grace and may be guaranteed to all Abraham's offspring—not only to those who are of the law but also to those who are of the faith of Abraham. He is the father of us all. ¹⁷As it is written: "I have made you a father of many nations."*ᶜ* He is our father in the sight of God, in whom he believed—the God who gives life to the dead and calls things that are not as though they were.

¹⁸Against all hope, Abraham in hope believed and so became the father of many nations, just as it had been said to him,

---

ⁱ25 Or *as the one who would turn aside his wrath, taking away sin*   *ᵃ3* Gen. 15:6; also in verse 22
ᵇ8 Psalm 32:1,2   *ᶜ17* Gen. 17:5

"So shall your offspring be."[d] [19]Without weakening in his faith, he faced the fact that his body was as good as dead—since he was about a hundred years old—and that Sarah's womb was also dead. [20]Yet he did not waver through unbelief regarding the promise of God, but was strengthened in his faith and gave glory to God, [21]being fully persuaded that God had power to do what he had promised. [22]This is why "it was credited to him as righteousness." [23]The words "it was credited to him" were written not for him alone, [24]but also for us, to whom God will credit righteousness— for us who believe in him who raised Jesus our Lord from the dead. [25]He was delivered over to death for our sins and was raised to life for our justification.

Peace and Joy

5 Therefore, since we have been justified through faith, we[a] have peace with God through our Lord Jesus Christ, [2]through whom we have gained access by faith into this grace in which we now stand. And we[a] rejoice in the hope of the glory of God. [3]Not only so, but we[a] also rejoice in our sufferings, because we know that suffering produces perseverance; [4]perseverance, character; and character, hope. [5]And hope does not disappoint us, because God has poured out his love into our hearts by the Holy Spirit, whom he has given us.

[6]You see, at just the right time, when we were still powerless, Christ died for the ungodly. [7]Very rarely will anyone die for a righteous man, though for a good man someone might possibly dare to die. [8]But God demonstrates his own love for us in this: While we were still sinners, Christ died for us.

[9]Since we have now been justified by his blood, how much more shall we be saved from God's wrath through him! [10]For if, when we were God's enemies, we were reconciled to him through the death of his Son, how much more, having been reconciled, shall we be saved through his life! [11]Not only is this so, but we also rejoice in God through our Lord Jesus Christ,

through whom we have now received reconciliation.

Death Through Adam, Life Through Christ

[12]Therefore, just as sin entered the world through one man, and death through sin, and in this way death came to all men, because all sinned—[13]for before the law was given, sin was in the world. But sin is not taken into account when there is no law. [14]Nevertheless, death reigned from the time of Adam to the time of Moses, even over those who did not sin by breaking a command, as did Adam, who was a pattern of the one to come.

[15]But the gift is not like the trespass. For if the many died by the trespass of the one man, how much more did God's grace and the gift that came by the grace of the one man, Jesus Christ, overflow to the many! [16]Again, the gift of God is not like the result of the one man's sin: The judgment followed one sin and brought condemnation, but the gift followed many trespasses and brought justification. [17]For if, by the trespass of the one man, death reigned through that one man, how much more will those who receive God's abundant provision of grace and of the gift of righteousness reign in life through the one man, Jesus Christ.

[18]Consequently, just as the result of one trespass was condemnation for all men, so also the result of one act of righteousness was justification that brings life for all men. [19]For just as through the disobedience of the one man the many were made sinners, so also through the obedience of the one man the many will be made righteous.

[20]The law was added so that the trespass might increase. But where sin increased, grace increased all the more, [21]so that, just as sin reigned in death, so also grace might reign through righteousness to bring eternal life through Jesus Christ our Lord.

Dead to Sin, Alive in Christ

6 What shall we say, then? Shall we go on sinning, so that grace may increase? [2]By no means! We died to sin; how

can we live in it any longer? [3]Or don't you know that all of us who were baptised into Christ Jesus were baptised into his death? [4]We were therefore buried with him through baptism into death in order that, just as Christ was raised from the dead through the glory of the Father, we too may live a new life.

[5]If we have been united with him like this in his death, we will certainly also be united with him in his resurrection. [6]For we know that our old self was crucified with him so that the body of sin might be done away with,[a] that we should no longer be slaves to sin—[7]because anyone who has died has been freed from sin.

[8]Now if we died with Christ, we believe that we will also live with him. [9]For we know that since Christ was raised from the dead, he cannot die again; death no longer has mastery over him. [10]The death he died, he died to sin once for all; but the life he lives, he lives to God.

[11]In the same way, count yourselves dead to sin but alive to God in Christ Jesus. [12]Therefore do not let sin reign in your mortal body so that you obey its evil desires. [13]Do not offer the parts of your body to sin, as instruments of wickedness, but rather offer yourselves to God, as those who have been brought from death to life; and offer the parts of your body to him as instruments of righteousness. [14]For sin shall not be your master, because you are not under law, but under grace.

Slaves to Righteousness

[15]What then? Shall we sin because we are not under law but under grace? By no means! [16]Don't you know that when you offer yourselves to someone to obey him as slaves, you are slaves to the one whom you obey—whether you are slaves to sin, which leads to death, or to obedience, which leads to righteousness? [17]But thanks be to God that, though you used to be slaves to sin, you wholeheartedly obeyed the form of teaching to which you were entrusted. [18]You have been set free from sin and have become slaves to righteousness.

[19]I put this in human terms because you are weak in your natural selves. Just as you used to offer the parts of your body in slavery to impurity and to ever-increasing wickedness, so now offer them in slavery to righteousness leading to holiness. [20]When you were slaves to sin, you were free from the control of righteousness. [21]What benefit did you reap at that time from the things you are now ashamed of? Those things result in death! [22]But now that you have been set free from sin and have become slaves to God, the benefit you reap leads to holiness, and the result is eternal life. [23]For the wages of sin is death, but the gift of God is eternal life in[b] Christ Jesus our Lord.

An Illustration From Marriage

7 Do you not know, brothers—for I am speaking to men who know the law—that the law has authority over a man only as long as he lives? [2]For example, by law a married woman is bound to her husband as long as he is alive, but if her husband dies, she is released from the law of marriage. [3]So then, if she marries another man while her husband is still alive, she is called an adulteress. But if her husband dies, she is released from that law and is not an adulteress, even though she marries another man.

[4]So, my brothers, you also died to the law through the body of Christ, that you might belong to another, to him who was raised from the dead, in order that we might bear fruit to God. [5]For when we were controlled by the sinful nature,[a] the sinful passions aroused by the law were at work in our bodies, so that we bore fruit for death. [6]But now, by dying to what once bound us, we have been released from the law so that we serve in the new way of the Spirit, and not in the old way of the written code.

Struggling With Sin

[7]What shall we say, then? Is the law sin? Certainly not! Indeed I would not have known what sin was except through the

---

[a]6 Or *be rendered powerless*   [b]23 Or *through*   [a]5 Or *the flesh*; also in verse 25

law. For I would not have known what coveting really was if the law had not said, "Do not covet."[b] [8]But sin, seizing the opportunity afforded by the commandment, produced in me every kind of covetous desire. For apart from law, sin is dead. [9]Once I was alive apart from law; but when the commandment came, sin sprang to life and I died. [10]I found that the very commandment that was intended to bring life actually brought death. [11]For sin, seizing the opportunity afforded by the commandment, deceived me, and through the commandment put me to death. [12]So then, the law is holy, and the commandment is holy, righteous and good.

[13]Did that which is good, then, become death to me? By no means! But in order that sin might be recognised as sin, it produced death in me through what was good, so that through the commandment sin might become utterly sinful.

[14]We know that the law is spiritual; but I am unspiritual, sold as a slave to sin. [15]I do not understand what I do. For what I want to do I do not do, but what I hate I do. [16]And if I do what I do not want to do, I agree that the law is good. [17]As it is, it is no longer I myself who do it, but it is sin living in me. [18]I know that nothing good lives in me, that is, in my sinful nature.[c] For I have the desire to do what is good, but I cannot carry it out. [19]For what I do is not the good I want to do; no, the evil I do not want to do—this I keep on doing. [20]Now if I do what I do not want to do, it is no longer I who do it, but it is sin living in me that does it.

[21]So I find this law at work: When I want to do good, evil is right there with me. [22]For in my inner being I delight in God's law; [23]but I see another law at work in the members of my body, waging war against the law of my mind and making me a prisoner of the law of sin at work within my members. [24]What a wretched man I am! Who will rescue me from this body of death? [25]Thanks be to God—through Jesus Christ our Lord!

So then, I myself in my mind am a slave to God's law, but in the sinful nature a slave to the law of sin.

Life Through the Spirit

8 Therefore, there is now no condemnation for those who are in Christ Jesus,[a] [2]because through Christ Jesus the law of the Spirit of life set me free from the law of sin and death. [3]For what the law was powerless to do in that it was weakened by the sinful nature,[b] God did by sending his own Son in the likeness of sinful man to be a sin offering.[c] And so he condemned sin in sinful man,[d] [4]in order that the righteous requirements of the law might be fully met in us, who do not live according to the sinful nature but according to the Spirit.

[5]Those who live according to the sinful nature have their minds set on what that nature desires; but those who live in accordance with the Spirit have their minds set on what the Spirit desires. [6]The mind of sinful man[e] is death, but the mind controlled by the Spirit is life and peace; [7]the sinful mind[f] is hostile to God. It does not submit to God's law, nor can it do so. [8]Those controlled by the sinful nature cannot please God.

[9]You, however, are controlled not by the sinful nature but by the Spirit, if the Spirit of God lives in you. And if anyone does not have the Spirit of Christ, he does not belong to Christ. [10]But if Christ is in you, your body is dead because of sin, yet your spirit is alive because of righteousness. [11]And if the Spirit of him who raised Jesus from the dead is living in you, he who raised Christ from the dead will also give life to your mortal bodies through his Spirit, who lives in you.

[12]Therefore, brothers, we have an obligation—but it is not to the sinful nature, to live according to it. [13]For if you live according to the sinful nature, you will die; but if by the Spirit you put to death the misdeeds of the body, you will live, [14]because those who are led by the Spirit

---

[b]7 Exodus 20:17; Deut. 5:21   [c]18 Or *my flesh*
[a]1 Some later manuscripts *Jesus, who do not live according to the sinful nature but according to the Spirit,*
[b]3 Or *the flesh*; also in verses 4, 5, 8, 9, 12 and 13   [c]3 Or *man, for sin*   [d]3 Or *in the flesh*
[e]6 Or *mind set on the flesh*   [f]7 Or *The mind set on the flesh*

of God are sons of God. [15]For you did not receive a spirit that makes you a slave again to fear, but you received the Spirit of sonship.[g] And by him we cry, "*Abba,*[h] Father." [16]The Spirit himself testifies with our spirit that we are God's children. [17]Now if we are children, then we are heirs—heirs of God and co-heirs with Christ, if indeed we share in his sufferings in order that we may also share in his glory.

Future Glory

[18]I consider that our present sufferings are not worth comparing with the glory that will be revealed in us. [19]The creation waits in eager expectation for the sons of God to be revealed. [20]For the creation was subjected to frustration, not by its own choice, but by the will of the one who subjected it, in hope [21]that[i] the creation itself will be liberated from its bondage to decay and brought into the glorious freedom of the children of God.

[22]We know that the whole creation has been groaning as in the pains of childbirth right up to the present time. [23]Not only so, but we ourselves, who have the firstfruits of the Spirit, groan inwardly as we wait eagerly for our adoption as sons, the redemption of our bodies. [24]For in this hope we were saved. But hope that is seen is no hope at all. Who hopes for what he already has? [25]But if we hope for what we do not yet have, we wait for it patiently.

[26]In the same way, the Spirit helps us in our weakness. We do not know what we ought to pray for, but the Spirit himself intercedes for us with groans that words cannot express. [27]And he who searches our hearts knows the mind of the Spirit, because the Spirit intercedes for the saints in accordance with God's will.

More Than Conquerors

[28]And we know that in all things God works for the good of those who love him,[j] who[k] have been called according to his purpose. [29]For those God foreknew he also predestined to be conformed to the likeness of his Son, that he might be the firstborn among many brothers. [30]And those he predestined, he also called; those he called, he also justified; those he justified, he also glorified.

[31]What, then, shall we say in response to this? If God is for us, who can be against us? [32]He who did not spare his own Son, but gave him up for us all—how will he not also, along with him, graciously give us all things? [33]Who will bring any charge against those whom God has chosen? It is God who justifies. [34]Who is he that condemns? Christ Jesus, who died—more than that, who was raised to life—is at the right hand of God and is also interceding for us. [35]Who shall separate us from the love of Christ? Shall trouble or hardship or persecution or famine or nakedness or danger or sword? [36]As it is written:

"For your sake we face death all day
    long;
  we are considered as sheep to be
    slaughtered."[l]

[37]No, in all these things we are more than conquerors through him who loved us. [38]For I am convinced that neither death nor life, neither angels nor demons,[m] neither the present nor the future, nor any powers, [39]neither height nor depth, nor anything else in all creation, will be able to separate us from the love of God that is in Christ Jesus our Lord.

God's Sovereign Choice

9 I speak the truth in Christ—I am not lying, my conscience confirms it in the Holy Spirit—[2]I have great sorrow and unceasing anguish in my heart. [3]For I could wish that I myself were cursed and cut off from Christ for the sake of my brothers, those of my own race, [4]the people of Israel. Theirs is the adoption as sons; theirs the divine glory, the

---

g15 Or *adoption*   *h15* Aramaic for *Father*   *i20,21* Or *subjected it in hope.* [21]*For*
j28 Some manuscripts *And we know that all things work together for good to those who love God*
k28 Or *works together with those who love him to bring about what is good—with those who*
l36 Psalm 44:22   *m38* Or *nor heavenly rulers*

covenants, the receiving of the law, the temple worship and the promises. [5]Theirs are the patriarchs, and from them is traced the human ancestry of Christ, who is God over all, for ever praised![a] Amen.

[6]It is not as though God's word had failed. For not all who are descended from Israel are Israel. [7]Nor because they are his descendants are they all Abraham's children. On the contrary, "It is through Isaac that your offspring will be reckoned."[b] [8]In other words, it is not the natural children who are God's children, but it is the children of the promise who are regarded as Abraham's offspring. [9]For this was how the promise was stated: "At the appointed time I will return, and Sarah will have a son."[c]

[10]Not only that, but Rebekah's children had one and the same father, our father Isaac. [11]Yet, before the twins were born or had done anything good or bad—in order that God's purpose in election might stand: [12]not by works but by him who calls—she was told, "The older will serve the younger."[d] [13]Just as it is written: "Jacob I loved, but Esau I hated."[e]

[14]What then shall we say? Is God unjust? Not at all! [15]For he says to Moses,

"I will have mercy on whom I have
        mercy,
    and I will have compassion on whom
        I have compassion."[f]

[16]It does not, therefore, depend on man's desire or effort, but on God's mercy. [17]For the Scripture says to Pharaoh: "I raised you up for this very purpose, that I might display my power in you and that my name might be proclaimed in all the earth."[g] [18]Therefore God has mercy on whom he wants to have mercy, and he hardens whom he wants to harden.

[19]One of you will say to me: "Then why does God still blame us? For who resists his will?" [20]But who are you, O man, to talk back to God? "Shall what is formed say to him who formed it, 'Why did you

make me like this?' "[h] [21]Does not the potter have the right to make out of the same lump of clay some pottery for noble purposes and some for common use?

[22]What if God, choosing to show his wrath and make his power known, bore with great patience the objects of his wrath—prepared for destruction? [23]What if he did this to make the riches of his glory known to the objects of his mercy, whom he prepared in advance for glory—[24]even us, whom he also called, not only from the Jews but also from the Gentiles? [25]As he says in Hosea:

"I will call them 'my people' who are
        not my people;
    and I will call her 'my loved one' who
        is not my loved one,"[i]

[26]and,

"It will happen that in the very place
        where it was said to them,
    'You are not my people,'
they will be called 'sons of the living
        God'."[j]

[27]Isaiah cries out concerning Israel:

"Though the number of the Israelites
        be like the sand by the sea,
    only the remnant will be saved.
[28]For the Lord will carry out
    his sentence on earth with speed and
        finality."[k]

[29]It is just as Isaiah said previously:

"Unless the Lord Almighty
    had left us descendants,
we would have become like Sodom,
    we would have been like
        Gomorrah."[l]

Israel's Unbelief

[30]What then shall we say? That the Gentiles, who did not pursue righteousness,

a5 Or *Christ, who is over all. God be for ever praised!* Or *Christ. God who is over all be for ever praised!*
b7 Gen. 21:12   *c9* Gen. 18:10,14   *d12* Gen. 25:23   *e13* Mal. 1:2,3   *f15* Exodus 33:19
g17 Exodus 9:16   *h20* Isaiah 29:16; 45:9   *i25* Hosea 2:23   *j26* Hosea 1:10   *k28* Isaiah 10:22,23
l29 Isaiah 1:9

have obtained it, a righteousness that is by faith; [31]but Israel, who pursued a law of righteousness, has not attained it. [32]Why not? Because they pursued it not by faith but as if it were by works. They stumbled over the "stumbling-stone". [33]As it is written:

> "See, I lay in Zion a stone that causes men to stumble
> and a rock that makes them fall,
> and the one who trusts in him will never be put to shame." [m]

10 Brothers, my heart's desire and prayer to God for the Israelites is that they may be saved. [2]For I can testify about them that they are zealous for God, but their zeal is not based on knowledge. [3]Since they did not know the righteousness that comes from God and sought to establish their own, they did not submit to God's righteousness. [4]Christ is the end of the law so that there may be righteousness for everyone who believes.

[5]Moses describes in this way the righteousness that is by the law: "The man who does these things will live by them." [a] [6]But the righteousness that is by faith says: "Do not say in your heart, 'Who will ascend into heaven?' [b]" (that is, to bring Christ down) [7]"or 'Who will descend into the deep?' [c]" (that is, to bring Christ up from the dead). [8]But what does it say? "The word is near you; it is in your mouth and in your heart," [d] that is, the word of faith we are proclaiming: [9]That if you confess with your mouth, "Jesus is Lord," and believe in your heart that God raised him from the dead, you will be saved. [10]For it is with your heart that you believe and are justified, and it is with your mouth that you confess and are saved. [11]As the Scripture says, "Anyone who trusts in him will never be put to shame." [e] [12]For there is no difference between Jew and Gentile—the same Lord is Lord of all and richly blesses all who call on him, [13]for, "Everyone who calls on the name of the Lord will be saved." [f]

[14]How, then, can they call on the one they have not believed in? And how can they believe in the one of whom they have not heard? And how can they hear without someone preaching to them? [15]And how can they preach unless they are sent? As it is written, "How beautiful are the feet of those who bring good news!" [g]

[16]But not all the Israelites accepted the good news. For Isaiah says, "Lord, who has believed our message?" [h] [17]Consequently, faith comes from hearing the message, and the message is heard through the word of Christ. [18]But I ask: Did they not hear? Of course they did:

> "Their voice has gone out into all the earth,
> their words to the ends of the world." [i]

[19]Again I ask: Did Israel not understand? First, Moses says,

> "I will make you envious by those who are not a nation;
> I will make you angry by a nation that has no understanding." [j]

[20]And Isaiah boldly says,

> "I was found by those who did not seek me;
> I revealed myself to those who did not ask for me." [k]

[21]But concerning Israel he says,

> "All day long I have held out my hands to a disobedient and obstinate people." [l]

The Remnant of Israel

11 I ask then: Did God reject his people? By no means! I am an Israelite myself, a descendant of Abraham, from the tribe of Benjamin. [2]God did not reject his people, whom he foreknew. Don't you know what the Scripture

---

[m]33 Isaiah 8:14; 28:16   [a]5 Lev. 18:5   [b]6 Deut. 30:12   [c]7 Deut. 30:13   [d]8 Deut. 30:14
[e]11 Isaiah 28:16   [f]13 Joel 2:32   [g]15 Isaiah 52:7   [h]16 Isaiah 53:1   [i]18 Psalm 19:4
[j]19 Deut. 32:21   [k]20 Isaiah 65:1   [l]21 Isaiah 65:2

says in the passage about Elijah—how he appealed to God against Israel: [3]"Lord, they have killed your prophets and torn down your altars; I am the only one left, and they are trying to kill me"[a]? [4]And what was God's answer to him? "I have reserved for myself seven thousand who have not bowed the knee to Baal."[b] [5]So too, at the present time there is a remnant chosen by grace. [6]And if by grace, then it is no longer by works; if it were, grace would no longer be grace.[c]

[7]What then? What Israel sought so earnestly it did not obtain, but the elect did. The others were hardened, [8]as it is written:

> "God gave them a spirit of stupor,
>   eyes so that they could not see
>   and ears so that they could not hear,
> to this very day."[d]

[9]And David says:

> "May their table become a snare and a trap,
>   a stumbling-block and a retribution for them.
> [10]May their eyes be darkened so they cannot see,
>   and their backs be bent for ever."[e]

Ingrafted Branches

[11]Again I ask: Did they stumble so as to fall beyond recovery? Not at all! Rather, because of their transgression, salvation has come to the Gentiles to make Israel envious. [12]But if their transgression means riches for the world, and their loss means riches for the Gentiles, how much greater riches will their fulness bring!

[13]I am talking to you Gentiles. Inasmuch as I am the apostle to the Gentiles, I make much of my ministry [14]in the hope that I may somehow arouse my own people to envy and save some of them. [15]For if their rejection is the reconciliation of the world, what will their acceptance be

but life from the dead? [16]If the part of the dough offered as firstfruits is holy, then the whole batch is holy; if the root is holy, so are the branches.

[17]If some of the branches have been broken off, and you, though a wild olive shoot, have been grafted in among the others and now share in the nourishing sap from the olive root, [18]do not boast over those branches. If you do, consider this: You do not support the root, but the root supports you. [19]You will say then, "Branches were broken off so that I could be grafted in." [20]Granted. But they were broken off because of unbelief, and you stand by faith. Do not be arrogant, but be afraid. [21]For if God did not spare the natural branches, he will not spare you either.

[22]Consider therefore the kindness and sternness of God: sternness to those who fell, but kindness to you, provided that you continue in his kindness. Otherwise, you also will be cut off. [23]And if they do not persist in unbelief, they will be grafted in, for God is able to graft them in again. [24]After all, if you were cut out of an olive tree that is wild by nature, and contrary to nature were grafted into a cultivated olive tree, how much more readily will these, the natural branches, be grafted into their own olive tree!

All Israel Will Be Saved

[25]I do not want you to be ignorant of this mystery, brothers, so that you may not be conceited: Israel has experienced a hardening in part until the full number of the Gentiles has come in. [26]And so all Israel will be saved, as it is written:

> "The deliverer will come from Zion;
>   he will turn godlessness away from Jacob.
> [27]And this is[f] my covenant with them
>   when I take away their sins."[g]

[a]3 1 Kings 19:10,14   [b]4 1 Kings 19:18
[c]6 Some manuscripts *by grace. But if by works, then it is no longer grace; if it were, work would no longer be work.*
[d]8 Deut. 29:4; Isaiah 29:10   [e]10 Psalm 69:22,23   [f]27 Or *will be*
[g]27 Isaiah 59:20,21; 27:9; Jer. 31:33,34

[28]As far as the gospel is concerned, they are enemies on your account; but as far as election is concerned, they are loved on account of the patriarchs, [29]for God's gifts and his call are irrevocable. [30]Just as you who were at one time disobedient to God have now received mercy as a result of their disobedience, [31]so they too have now become disobedient in order that they too may now[h] receive mercy as a result of God's mercy to you. [32]For God has bound all men over to disobedience so that he may have mercy on them all.

Doxology

[33]Oh, the depth of the riches of the
wisdom and[i] knowledge of God!
How unsearchable his judgments,
and his paths beyond tracing out!
[34]"Who has known the mind of the Lord?
Or who has been his counsellor?"[j]
[35]"Who has ever given to God,
that God should repay him?"[k]
[36]For from him and through him and to
him are all things.
To him be the glory for ever! Amen.

Living Sacrifices

12 Therefore, I urge you, brothers, in view of God's mercy, to offer your bodies as living sacrifices, holy and pleasing to God—this is your spiritual[a] act of worship. [2]Do not conform any longer to the pattern of this world, but be transformed by the renewing of your mind. Then you will be able to test and approve what God's will is—his good, pleasing and perfect will.

[3]For by the grace given me I say to every one of you: Do not think of yourself more highly than you ought, but rather think of yourself with sober judgment, in accordance with the measure of faith God has given you. [4]Just as each of us has one body with many members, and these members do not all have the same function, [5]so in Christ we who are many form one body,

and each member belongs to all the others. [6]We have different gifts, according to the grace given us. If a man's gift is prophesying, let him use it in proportion to his[b] faith. [7]If it is serving, let him serve; if it is teaching, let him teach; [8]if it is encouraging, let him encourage; if it is contributing to the needs of others, let him give generously; if it is leadership, let him govern diligently; if it is showing mercy, let him do it cheerfully.

Love

[9]Love must be sincere. Hate what is evil; cling to what is good. [10]Be devoted to one another in brotherly love. Honour one another above yourselves. [11]Never be lacking in zeal, but keep your spiritual fervour, serving the Lord. [12]Be joyful in hope, patient in affliction, faithful in prayer. [13]Share with God's people who are in need. Practise hospitality.

[14]Bless those who persecute you; bless and do not curse. [15]Rejoice with those who rejoice; mourn with those who mourn. [16]Live in harmony with one another. Do not be proud, but be willing to associate with people of low position.[c] Do not be conceited.

[17]Do not repay anyone evil for evil. Be careful to do what is right in the eyes of everybody. [18]If it is possible, as far as it depends on you, live at peace with everyone. [19]Do not take revenge, my friends, but leave room for God's wrath, for it is written: "It is mine to avenge; I will repay,"[d] says the Lord. [20]On the contrary:

"If your enemy is hungry, feed him;
if he is thirsty, give him something to drink.
In doing this, you will heap burning coals on his head."[e]

[21]Do not be overcome by evil, but overcome evil with good.

---

h31 Some manuscripts do not have *now*. *i33* Or *riches and the wisdom and the* *j34* Isaiah 40:13
k35 Job 41:11 *a1* Or *reasonable* *b6* Or *in agreement with the* *c16* Or *willing to do menial work*
d19 Deut. 32:35 *e20* Prov. 25:21,22

Submission to the Authorities

13 Everyone must submit himself to the governing authorities, for there is no authority except that which God has established. The authorities that exist have been established by God. ²Consequently, he who rebels against the authority is rebelling against what God has instituted, and those who do so will bring judgment on themselves. ³For rulers hold no terror for those who do right, but for those who do wrong. Do you want to be free from fear of the one in authority? Then do what is right and he will commend you. ⁴For he is God's servant to do you good. But if you do wrong, be afraid, for he does not bear the sword for nothing. He is God's servant, an agent of wrath to bring punishment on the wrongdoer. ⁵Therefore, it is necessary to submit to the authorities, not only because of possible punishment but also because of conscience.

⁶This is also why you pay taxes, for the authorities are God's servants, who give their full time to governing. ⁷Give everyone what you owe him: If you owe taxes, pay taxes; if revenue, then revenue; if respect, then respect; if honour, then honour.

Love, for the Day Is Near

⁸Let no debt remain outstanding, except the continuing debt to love one another, for he who loves his fellow-man has fulfilled the law. ⁹The commandments, "Do not commit adultery," "Do not murder," "Do not steal," "Do not covet,"*a* and whatever other commandment there may be, are summed up in this one rule: "Love your neighbour as yourself."*b* ¹⁰Love does no harm to its neighbour. Therefore love is the fulfilment of the law.

¹¹And do this, understanding the present time. The hour has come for you to wake up from your slumber, because our salvation is nearer now than when we first believed. ¹²The night is nearly over; the day is almost here. So let us put aside the deeds of darkness and put on the armour of light. ¹³Let us behave decently, as in the daytime, not in orgies and drunkenness, not in sexual immorality and debauchery, not in dissension and jealousy. ¹⁴Rather, clothe yourselves with the Lord Jesus Christ, and do not think about how to gratify the desires of the sinful nature.*c*

The Weak and the Strong

14 Accept him whose faith is weak, without passing judgment on disputable matters. ²One man's faith allows him to eat everything, but another man, whose faith is weak, eats only vegetables. ³The man who eats everything must not look down on him who does not, and the man who does not eat everything must not condemn the man who does, for God has accepted him. ⁴Who are you to judge someone else's servant? To his own master he stands or falls. And he will stand, for the Lord is able to make him stand.

⁵One man considers one day more sacred than another; another man considers every day alike. Each one should be fully convinced in his own mind. ⁶He who regards one day as special, does so to the Lord. He who eats meat, eats to the Lord, for he gives thanks to God; and he who abstains, does so to the Lord and gives thanks to God. ⁷For none of us lives to himself alone and none of us dies to himself alone. ⁸If we live, we live to the Lord; and if we die, we die to the Lord. So, whether we live or die, we belong to the Lord.

⁹For this very reason, Christ died and returned to life so that he might be the Lord of both the dead and the living. ¹⁰You, then, why do you judge your brother? Or why do you look down on your brother? For we will all stand before God's judgment seat. ¹¹It is written:

"'As surely as I live,' says the Lord,
'Every knee will bow before me;
every tongue will confess to God.'"*a*

a9 Exodus 20:13–15,17; Deut. 5:17–19,21   *b9* Lev. 19:18   *c14* Or *the flesh*   *a11* Isaiah 45:23

¹²So then, each of us will give an account of himself to God.

¹³Therefore let us stop passing judgment on one another. Instead, make up your mind not to put any stumbling-block or obstacle in your brother's way. ¹⁴As one who is in the Lord Jesus, I am fully convinced that no food*b* is unclean in itself. But if anyone regards something as unclean, then for him it is unclean. ¹⁵If your brother is distressed because of what you eat, you are no longer acting in love. Do not by your eating destroy your brother for whom Christ died. ¹⁶Do not allow what you consider good to be spoken of as evil. ¹⁷For the kingdom of God is not a matter of eating and drinking, but of righteousness, peace and joy in the Holy Spirit, ¹⁸because anyone who serves Christ in this way is pleasing to God and approved by men.

¹⁹Let us therefore make every effort to do what leads to peace and to mutual edification. ²⁰Do not destroy the work of God for the sake of food. All food is clean, but it is wrong for a man to eat anything that causes someone else to stumble. ²¹It is better not to eat meat or drink wine or to do anything else that will cause your brother to fall.

²²So whatever you believe about these things keep between yourself and God. Blessed is the man who does not condemn himself by what he approves. ²³But the man who has doubts is condemned if he eats, because his eating is not from faith; and everything that does not come from faith is sin.

15

We who are strong ought to bear with the failings of the weak and not to please ourselves. ²Each of us should please his neighbour for his good, to build him up. ³For even Christ did not please himself but, as it is written: "The insults of those who insult you have fallen on me."*a* ⁴For everything that was written in the past was written to teach us, so that through endurance and the encouragement of the Scriptures we might have hope.

⁵May the God who gives endurance and encouragement give you a spirit of unity among yourselves as you follow Christ Jesus, ⁶so that with one heart and mouth you may glorify the God and Father of our Lord Jesus Christ.

⁷Accept one another, then, just as Christ accepted you, in order to bring praise to God. ⁸For I tell you that Christ has become a servant of the Jews*b* on behalf of God's truth, to confirm the promises made to the patriarchs ⁹so that the Gentiles may glorify God for his mercy, as it is written:

> "Therefore I will praise you among the
>   Gentiles;
> I will sing hymns to your name."*c*

¹⁰Again, it says,

> "Rejoice, O Gentiles, with his
>   people."*d*

¹¹And again,

> "Praise the Lord, all you Gentiles,
>   and sing praises to him, all you
>   peoples."*e*

¹²And again, Isaiah says,

> "The Root of Jesse will spring up,
>   one who will arise to rule over the
>   nations;
> the Gentiles will hope in him."*f*

¹³May the God of hope fill you with all joy and peace as you trust in him, so that you may overflow with hope by the power of the Holy Spirit.

Paul the Minister to the Gentiles

¹⁴I myself am convinced, my brothers, that you yourselves are full of goodness, complete in knowledge and competent to instruct one another. ¹⁵I have written to you quite boldly on some points, as if to remind you of them again, because of the grace God gave me ¹⁶to be a minister of

---

b14 Or *that nothing*   *a3* Psalm 69:9   *b8* Greek *circumcision*   *c9* 2 Samuel 22:50; Psalm 18:49
d10 Deut. 32:43   *e11* Psalm 117:1   *f12* Isaiah 11:10

Christ Jesus to the Gentiles with the priestly duty of proclaiming the gospel of God, so that the Gentiles might become an offering acceptable to God, sanctified by the Holy Spirit.

[17]Therefore I glory in Christ Jesus in my service to God. [18]I will not venture to speak of anything except what Christ has accomplished through me in leading the Gentiles to obey God by what I have said and done—[19]by the power of signs and miracles, through the power of the Spirit. So from Jerusalem all the way round to Illyricum, I have fully proclaimed the gospel of Christ. [20]It has always been my ambition to preach the gospel where Christ was not known, so that I would not be building on someone else's foundation. [21]Rather, as it is written:

> "Those who were not told about him
>   will see,
> and those who have not heard will
>   understand."[g]

[22]This is why I have often been hindered from coming to you.

Paul's Plan to Visit Rome

[23]But now that there is no more place for me to work in these regions, and since I have been longing for many years to see you, [24]I plan to do so when I go to Spain. I hope to visit you while passing through and to have you assist me on my journey there, after I have enjoyed your company for a while. [25]Now, however, I am on my way to Jerusalem in the service of the saints there. [26]For Macedonia and Achaia were pleased to make a contribution for the poor among the saints in Jerusalem. [27]They were pleased to do it, and indeed they owe it to them. For if the Gentiles have shared in the Jews' spiritual blessings, they owe it to the Jews to share with them their material blessings. [28]So after I have completed this task and have made sure that they have received this fruit, I will go to Spain and visit you on the way. [29]I know that when I come to you, I will come in the full measure of the blessing of Christ.

[30]I urge you, brothers, by our Lord Jesus Christ and by the love of the Spirit, to join me in my struggle by praying to God for me. [31]Pray that I may be rescued from the unbelievers in Judea and that my service in Jerusalem may be acceptable to the saints there, [32]so that by God's will I may come to you with joy and together with you be refreshed. [33]The God of peace be with you all. Amen.

Personal Greetings

16 I commend to you our sister Phoebe, a servant[a] of the church in Cenchrea. [2]I ask you to receive her in the Lord in a way worthy of the saints and to give her any help she may need from you, for she has been a great help to many people, including me.

[3]Greet Priscilla[b] and Aquila, my fellow workers in Christ Jesus. [4]They risked their lives for me. Not only I but all the churches of the Gentiles are grateful to them.

[5]Greet also the church that meets at their house.

Greet my dear friend Epenetus, who was the first convert to Christ in the province of Asia.

[6]Greet Mary, who worked very hard for you.

[7]Greet Andronicus and Junias, my relatives who have been in prison with me. They are outstanding among the apostles, and they were in Christ before I was.

[8]Greet Ampliatus, whom I love in the Lord.

[9]Greet Urbanus, our fellow-worker in Christ, and my dear friend Stachys.

[10]Greet Apelles, tested and approved in Christ.

Greet those who belong to the household of Aristobulus.

[11]Greet Herodion, my relative.

Greet those in the household of Narcissus who are in the Lord.

Spiritual growth

[John21:1-19 (p1090)]

You are an expert in your field, a professional with hands-on life-time experience. As you struggle to undertake a particular task an apparent stranger leans over and says **'Try it this way...'** *How do you react? Do you tell them where to go, ignore the remark or start a discussion?*

Read through this story (you may want to read from chapter 18, p1086, first) and note the reaction of the disciples to the suggestion from a 'stranger on the shore', telling them how to catch fish.

As you read the narrative consider these questions:

- Why did Simon Peter feel the need to go fishing?
- Is fishing ever as easy as it is in this story?
- How did John (the disciple whom Jesus loved) realise it was Jesus?
- Why did Jesus ask Peter the same question three times?
- Recall the events and trauma which the disciples had just lived through. The entry into Jerusalem, the meal together, the arrest, trial, crucifixion of Jesus. The end of all they had been getting excited about. Imagine their confusion, and then take the story a little further to the empty tomb and Jesus' reappearance here when he invites them to come and eat.

- If Jesus had given you the invitation 'Come and have breakfast' how would you have reacted?

A difficult question

Jesus gets to the point. Looking at Peter he asks, three times, 'Do you love me?' How do you react if you're asked the same question more than once? Do you get angry, go quiet, refuse to answer, feel hurt? Write out Jesus' question 'Simon Peter do you love me?', but insert your name at the beginning:

.... **do you love me ?**

> **What do you reply? Why?**
> Is this the first time you have admitted that you love Jesus? If it's not the first time, can you honestly say that you love Jesus all or most of the time?

A difficult request

Now comes the next 'crunch' moment as Jesus asks Peter to 'Feed my sheep'. We are all 'sheep' (Psalm 100:3) and have been called by God into a unique and special relationship, in and through Christ. Jesus asks you to 'feed my sheep'. What does that mean for you? What is God asking you to do? You may not be sure, meanwhile ask yourself these questions;

- Do you feel that you are living up to all that God demands of you as a disciple?
- Should you make changes to your lifestyle, your priorities, desires, dreams and relationships in order to take this request seriously?
- What support might you need in order to be able to make those changes?

(29)

Stocktaking time

Read through chapter 11 (p1209) first as its themes of faith, journey, witness and perseverance provide the context for these verses. The image in the passage is that of runners training and disciplining themselves for the race. Modern training methods and lycra clothing have not removed the need for fitness and discipline if you want to be a winning athlete.

In Graeco-Roman literature the image of running a race was often used to describe the moral battle waged by a wise person in the world. Discipline, v5ff, is not a favourite word today and given the choice most people prefer not to be disciplined, or even to discipline others.

> *Hebrews 12:3* '*Consider him who endured such opposition from sinful men, so that you will not* **grow weary** *and lose heart.*'

> *Hebrews 12:5*
> '*And you have forgotten that word of encouragement that addresses you as sons:* "*My son, do not make light of the Lord's discipline, and do not lose heart when he rebukes you,...*"'

The verbs in v3 translated 'grow weary' (discouraged) and 'lose heart' (give up) were sometimes used for the exhaustion a runner would face. The call to endure in v1 reflects the language of a long distance race. The Christian life is not a short sprint, it is a lifelong, long-term journey of discipleship, learning and discovery. Paul reminds God's people that being a Christian is anything but easy (see Ephesians 6:12ff). Complacency, indiscipline and compromise are ever-present dangers.

These verses provide a useful opportunity for taking an honest look at your Christian life and evaluating its liveliness, authenticity and reality. Unless you're perfect (!) you'll need to act on what you find, see the table of priorities below.

30

HoW you WoULd grade yourseLF?

On a scale of 1 to 10 (1 = poor, 10 = excellent), grade yourself
on these aspects of your Christian and spiritual experience:

- ❑ **your relationship with Jesus**
- ❑ your prayer life
- ❑ **your interaction with and study of the Bible**
- ❑ your desire to understand and work out God's intentions for your life
- ❑ **your witness to Jesus and sharing of the good news**
- ❑ your relationships with others within and outside the church
- ❑ **your sensitivity and awareness of others**
- ❑ your behaviour, attitudes, values and lifestyle
- ❑ **the way you are using your God-given gifts, money and time**
- ❑ your concern for the poor, the dispossessed, the marginalised and excluded

Grade the following statements in order of importance depending on the action needed after your stocktake:

- ❑ I need to listen more to what God is saying
- ❑ When I care for others I am showing them Jesus
- ❑ Knowing God is different from knowing about God

I need to change my attitudes and practice in relation to:

- ❑ prayer
- ❑ Bible reading
- ❑ church
- ❑ worship
- ❑ witnessing
- ❑ politics
- ❑ social action

I need to be more disciplined in my Christian life with respect to:

- ❑ prayer
- ❑ Bible reading
- ❑ church
- ❑ worship
- ❑ witnessing
- ❑ politics
- ❑ social action

- ❑ I am still excited by the fact that God loves me as I am

- ❑ I have learnt that growth can arise from pain or suffering

**Use the above as a guide to prayer,
and pray in particular about those things which
God has brought to your attention.**

(31)

On the spot with Jonathan Edwards

AGE 32

OCCUPATION Athlete

BIGGEST ACHIEVEMENT Breaking the world record for the triple jump

FAVOURITE TELEVISION PROGRAMMES ER, Question of Sport

SCARIEST FAIRGROUND RIDE The Revolution at Blackpool Pleasure Beach

SADDEST THING? That people turn their backs to God

I was raised in a strong Christian home and have always been aware of God and wanted to serve him. My mum and dad probably bought me my first Bible. I like reading the Bible in my study in a seat by the window. The Bible is God's primary way of speaking to me. Not to rule out that God can speak in other ways, but primarily a Christian's focus must be on knowing God's word and applying it.

Of all the characters in the Bible, I most identify with Daniel in Babylon, because he had the courage to stand up for what he believed in and the courage not to compromise. I would like to be like that too.

HEART'S DESIRE To please God

I like going to church because I like sharing my life with other people. The most important person in my life (apart from God) is my wife and then my two boys.

[12]Greet Tryphena and Tryphosa, those women who work hard in the Lord.

Greet my dear friend Persis, another woman who has worked very hard in the Lord. [13]Greet Rufus, chosen in the Lord, and his mother, who has been a mother to me, too. [14]Greet Asyncritus, Phlegon, Hermes, Patrobas, Hermas and the brothers with them. [15]Greet Philologus, Julia, Nereus and his sister, and Olympas and all the saints with them. [16]Greet one another with a holy kiss.

All the churches of Christ send greetings.

[17]I urge you, brothers, to watch out for those who cause divisions and put obstacles in your way that are contrary to the teaching you have learned. Keep away from them. [18]For such people are not serving our Lord Christ, but their own appetites. By smooth talk and flattery they deceive the minds of naïve people. [19]Everyone has heard about your obedience, so I am full of joy over you; but I want you to be wise about what is good, and innocent about what is evil.

[20]The God of peace will soon crush Satan under your feet.

The grace of our Lord Jesus be with you.

[21]Timothy, my fellow-worker, sends his greetings to you, as do Lucius, Jason and Sosipater, my relatives.

[22]I, Tertius, who wrote down this letter, greet you in the Lord.

[23]Gaius, whose hospitality I and the whole church here enjoy, sends you his greetings.

Erastus, who is the city's director of public works, and our brother Quartus send you their greetings.[c]

[25]Now to him who is able to establish you by my gospel and the proclamation of Jesus Christ, according to the revelation of the mystery hidden for long ages past, [26]but now revealed and made known through the prophetic writings by the command of the eternal God, so that all nations might believe and obey him—[27]to the only wise God be glory for ever through Jesus Christ! Amen.

[c]23 Some manuscripts *their greetings.* [24]*May the grace of our Lord Jesus Christ be with all of you. Amen.*

1 Corinthians

1 Paul, called to be an apostle of Christ Jesus by the will of God, and our brother Sosthenes,

[2]To the church of God in Corinth, to those sanctified in Christ Jesus and called to be holy, together with all those everywhere who call on the name of our Lord Jesus Christ—their Lord and ours:

[3]Grace and peace to you from God our Father and the Lord Jesus Christ.

Thanksgiving

[4]I always thank God for you because of his grace given you in Christ Jesus. [5]For in him you have been enriched in every way—in all your speaking and in all your knowledge—[6]because our testimony about Christ was confirmed in you. [7]Therefore you do not lack any spiritual gift as you eagerly wait for our Lord Jesus Christ to be revealed. [8]He will keep you strong to the end, so that you will be blameless on the day of our Lord Jesus Christ. [9]God, who has called you into fellowship with his Son Jesus Christ our Lord, is faithful.

Divisions in the Church

[10]I appeal to you, brothers, in the name of our Lord Jesus Christ, that all of you agree with one another so that there may be no divisions among you and that you may be perfectly united in mind and thought. [11]My brothers, some from Chloe's household have informed me that there are quarrels among you. [12]What I mean is this: One of you says, "I follow Paul"; another, "I follow Apollos"; another, "I follow Cephas";[a] still another, "I follow Christ."

[13]Is Christ divided? Was Paul crucified for you? Were you baptised into[b] the name of Paul? [14]I am thankful that I did not baptise any of you except Crispus and Gaius, [15]so that no-one can say that you were baptised into my name. ([16]Yes, I also baptised the household of Stephanas; beyond that, I don't remember if I baptised anyone else.) [17]For Christ did not send me to baptise, but to preach the gospel—not with words of human wisdom, lest the cross of Christ be emptied of its power.

Christ the Wisdom and Power of God

[18]For the message of the cross is foolishness to those who are perishing, but to us who are being saved it is the power of God. [19]For it is written:

"I will destroy the wisdom of the wise;
the intelligence of the intelligent I
will frustrate."[c]

[20]Where is the wise man? Where is the scholar? Where is the philosopher of this age? Has not God made foolish the wisdom of the world? [21]For since in the wisdom of God the world through its wisdom did not know him, God was pleased

---

[a]12 That is, Peter   [b]13 Or in; also in verse 15   [c]19 Isaiah 29:14

through the foolishness of what was preached to save those who believe. [22]Jews demand miraculous signs and Greeks look for wisdom, [23]but we preach Christ crucified: a stumbling-block to Jews and foolishness to Gentiles, [24]but to those whom God has called, both Jews and Greeks, Christ the power of God and the wisdom of God. [25]For the foolishness of God is wiser than man's wisdom, and the weakness of God is stronger than man's strength.

[26]Brothers, think of what you were when you were called. Not many of you were wise by human standards; not many were influential; not many were of noble birth. [27]But God chose the foolish things of the world to shame the wise; God chose the weak things of the world to shame the strong. [28]He chose the lowly things of this world and the despised things—and the things that are not—to nullify the things that are, [29]so that no-one may boast before him. [30]It is because of him that you are in Christ Jesus, who has become for us wisdom from God—that is, our righteousness, holiness and redemption. [31]Therefore, as it is written: "Let him who boasts boast in the Lord."[d]

2 When I came to you, brothers, I did not come with eloquence or superior wisdom as I proclaimed to you the testimony about God.[a] [2]For I resolved to know nothing while I was with you except Jesus Christ and him crucified. [3]I came to you in weakness and fear, and with much trembling. [4]My message and my preaching were not with wise and persuasive words, but with a demonstration of the Spirit's power, [5]so that your faith might not rest on men's wisdom, but on God's power.

Wisdom From the Spirit

[6]We do, however, speak a message of wisdom among the mature, but not the wisdom of this age or of the rulers of this age, who are coming to nothing. [7]No, we speak of God's secret wisdom, a wisdom that has been hidden and that God destined for our glory before time began.

[8]None of the rulers of this age understood it, for if they had, they would not have crucified the Lord of glory. [9]However, as it is written:

> "No eye has seen,
> no ear has heard,
> no mind has conceived
> what God has prepared for those who
> love him"[b]—

[10]but God has revealed it to us by his Spirit.

The Spirit searches all things, even the deep things of God. [11]For who among men knows the thoughts of a man except the man's spirit within him? In the same way no-one knows the thoughts of God except the Spirit of God. [12]We have not received the spirit of the world but the Spirit who is from God, that we may understand what God has freely given us. [13]This is what we speak, not in words taught us by human wisdom but in words taught by the Spirit, expressing spiritual truths in spiritual words.[c] [14]The man without the Spirit does not accept the things that come from the Spirit of God, for they are foolishness to him, and he cannot understand them, because they are spiritually discerned. [15]The spiritual man makes judgments about all things, but he himself is not subject to any man's judgment:

> [16]"For who has known the mind of the
> Lord
> that he may instruct him?"[d]

But we have the mind of Christ.

On Divisions in the Church

3 Brothers, I could not address you as spiritual but as worldly—mere infants in Christ. [2]I gave you milk, not solid food, for you were not yet ready for it. Indeed, you are still not ready. [3]You are still worldly. For since there is jealousy and quarrelling among you, are you not worldly? Are you not acting like mere

---

[d]31 Jer. 9:24　　[a]1 Some manuscripts *as I proclaimed to you God's mystery*　　[b]9 Isaiah 64:4
[c]13 Or *Spirit, interpreting spiritual truths to spiritual men*　　[d]16 Isaiah 40:13

men? ⁴For when one says, "I follow Paul," and another, "I follow Apollos," are you not mere men?

⁵What, after all, is Apollos? And what is Paul? Only servants, through whom you came to believe—as the Lord has assigned to each his task. ⁶I planted the seed, Apollos watered it, but God made it grow. ⁷So neither he who plants nor he who waters is anything, but only God, who makes things grow. ⁸The man who plants and the man who waters have one purpose, and each will be rewarded according to his own labour. ⁹For we are God's fellow-workers; you are God's field, God's building.

¹⁰By the grace God has given me, I laid a foundation as an expert builder, and someone else is building on it. But each one should be careful how he builds. ¹¹For no-one can lay any foundation other than the one already laid, which is Jesus Christ. ¹²If any man builds on this foundation using gold, silver, costly stones, wood, hay or straw, ¹³his work will be shown for what it is, because the Day will bring it to light. It will be revealed with fire, and the fire will test the quality of each man's work. ¹⁴If what he has built survives, he will receive his reward. ¹⁵If it is burned up, he will suffer loss; he himself will be saved, but only as one escaping through the flames.

¹⁶Don't you know that you yourselves are God's temple and that God's Spirit lives in you? ¹⁷If anyone destroys God's temple, God will destroy him; for God's temple is sacred, and you are that temple.

¹⁸Do not deceive yourselves. If any one of you thinks he is wise by the standards of this age, he should become a "fool" so that he may become wise. ¹⁹For the wisdom of this world is foolishness in God's sight. As it is written: "He catches the wise in their craftiness";ᵃ ²⁰and again, "The Lord knows that the thoughts of the wise are futile."ᵇ ²¹So then, no more boasting about men! All things are yours, ²²whether Paul or Apollos or Cephasᶜ or the world or life or death or the present or the future—all are yours, ²³and you are of Christ, and Christ is of God.

Apostles of Christ

4 So then, men ought to regard us as servants of Christ and as those entrusted with the secret things of God. ²Now it is required that those who have been given a trust must prove faithful. ³I care very little if I am judged by you or by any human court; indeed, I do not even judge myself. ⁴My conscience is clear, but that does not make me innocent. It is the Lord who judges me. ⁵Therefore judge nothing before the appointed time; wait till the Lord comes. He will bring to light what is hidden in darkness and will expose the motives of men's hearts. At that time each will receive his praise from God.

⁶Now, brothers, I have applied these things to myself and Apollos for your benefit, so that you may learn from us the meaning of the saying, "Do not go beyond what is written." Then you will not take pride in one man over against another. ⁷For who makes you different from anyone else? What do you have that you did not receive? And if you did receive it, why do you boast as though you did not?

⁸Already you have all you want! Already you have become rich! You have become kings—and that without us! How I wish that you really had become kings so that we might be kings with you! ⁹For it seems to me that God has put us apostles on display at the end of the procession, like men condemned to die in the arena. We have been made a spectacle to the whole universe, to angels as well as to men. ¹⁰We are fools for Christ, but you are so wise in Christ! We are weak, but you are strong! You are honoured, we are dishonoured! ¹¹To this very hour we go hungry and thirsty, we are in rags, we are brutally treated, we are homeless. ¹²We work hard with our own hands. When we are cursed, we bless; when we are persecuted, we endure it; ¹³when we are slandered, we answer kindly. Up to this moment we have become the scum of the earth, the refuse of the world.

¹⁴I am not writing this to shame you, but to warn you, as my dear children. ¹⁵Even

---

ᵃ19 Job 5:13   ᵇ20 Psalm 94:11   ᶜ22 That is, Peter

though you have ten thousand guardians in Christ, you do not have many fathers, for in Christ Jesus I became your father through the gospel. [16]Therefore I urge you to imitate me. [17]For this reason I am sending to you Timothy, my son whom I love, who is faithful in the Lord. He will remind you of my way of life in Christ Jesus, which agrees with what I teach everywhere in every church.

[18]Some of you have become arrogant, as if I were not coming to you. [19]But I will come to you very soon, if the Lord is willing, and then I will find out not only how these arrogant people are talking, but what power they have. [20]For the kingdom of God is not a matter of talk but of power. [21]What do you prefer? Shall I come to you with a whip, or in love and with a gentle spirit?

Expel the Immoral Brother!

5 It is actually reported that there is sexual immorality among you, and of a kind that does not occur even among pagans: A man has his father's wife. [2]And you are proud! Shouldn't you rather have been filled with grief and have put out of your fellowship the man who did this? [3]Even though I am not physically present, I am with you in spirit. And I have already passed judgment on the one who did this, just as if I were present. [4]When you are assembled in the name of our Lord Jesus and I am with you in spirit, and the power of our Lord Jesus is present, [5]hand this man over to Satan, so that the sinful nature[a] may be destroyed and his spirit saved on the day of the Lord.

[6]Your boasting is not good. Don't you know that a little yeast works through the whole batch of dough? [7]Get rid of the old yeast that you may be a new batch without yeast—as you really are. For Christ, our Passover lamb, has been sacrificed. [8]Therefore let us keep the Festival, not with the old yeast, the yeast of malice and wickedness, but with bread without yeast, the bread of sincerity and truth.

[9]I have written to you in my letter not to associate with sexually immoral people— [10]not at all meaning the people of this world who are immoral, or the greedy and swindlers, or idolaters. In that case you would have to leave this world. [11]But now I am writing to you that you must not associate with anyone who calls himself a brother but is sexually immoral or greedy, an idolater or a slanderer, a drunkard or a swindler. With such a man do not even eat.

[12]What business is it of mine to judge those outside the church? Are you not to judge those inside? [13]God will judge those outside. "Expel the wicked man from among you."[b]

Lawsuits Among Believers

6 If any of you has a dispute with another, dare he take it before the ungodly for judgment instead of before the saints? [2]Do you not know that the saints will judge the world? And if you are to judge the world, are you not competent to judge trivial cases? [3]Do you not know that we will judge angels? How much more the things of this life! [4]Therefore, if you have disputes about such matters, appoint as judges even men of little account in the church![a] [5]I say this to shame you. Is it possible that there is nobody among you wise enough to judge a dispute between believers? [6]But instead, one brother goes to law against another—and this in front of unbelievers!

[7]The very fact that you have lawsuits among you means you have been completely defeated already. Why not rather be wronged? Why not rather be cheated? [8]Instead, you yourselves cheat and do wrong, and you do this to your brothers.

[9]Do you not know that the wicked will not inherit the kingdom of God? Do not be deceived: Neither the sexually immoral nor idolaters nor adulterers nor male prostitutes nor homosexual offenders [10]nor thieves nor the greedy nor drunkards nor slanderers nor swindlers will

---

[a]5 Or that his body; or that the flesh   [b]13 Deut. 17:7; 19:19; 21:21; 22:21,24; 24:7
[a]4 Or matters, do you appoint as judges men of little account in the church?

inherit the kingdom of God. [11]And that is what some of you were. But you were washed, you were sanctified, you were justified in the name of the Lord Jesus Christ and by the Spirit of our God.

Sexual Immorality

[12]"Everything is permissible for me"—but not everything is beneficial. "Everything is permissible for me"—but I will not be mastered by anything. [13]"Food for the stomach and the stomach for food"—but God will destroy them both. The body is not meant for sexual immorality, but for the Lord, and the Lord for the body. [14]By his power God raised the Lord from the dead, and he will raise us also. [15]Do you not know that your bodies are members of Christ himself? Shall I then take the members of Christ and unite them with a prostitute? Never! [16]Do you not know that he who unites himself with a prostitute is one with her in body? For it is said, "The two will become one flesh."[b] [17]But he who unites himself with the Lord is one with him in spirit.

[18]Flee from sexual immorality. All other sins a man commits are outside his body, but he who sins sexually sins against his own body. [19]Do you not know that your body is a temple of the Holy Spirit, who is in you, whom you have received from God? You are not your own; [20]you were bought at a price. Therefore honour God with your body.

Marriage

7 Now for the matters you wrote about: It is good for a man not to marry.[a] [2]But since there is so much immorality, each man should have his own wife, and each woman her own husband. [3]The husband should fulfil his marital duty to his wife, and likewise the wife to her husband. [4]The wife's body does not belong to her alone but also to her husband. In the same way, the husband's body does not belong to him alone but also to his wife. [5]Do not deprive each other except by mutual consent and for a time, so that you may devote yourselves to prayer. Then come together again so that Satan will not tempt you because of your lack of self-control. [6]I say this as a concession, not as a command. [7]I wish that all men were as I am. But each man has his own gift from God; one has this gift, another has that.

[8]Now to the unmarried and the widows I say: It is good for them to stay unmarried, as I am. [9]But if they cannot control themselves, they should marry, for it is better to marry than to burn with passion.

[10]To the married I give this command (not I, but the Lord): A wife must not separate from her husband. [11]But if she does, she must remain unmarried or else be reconciled to her husband. And a husband must not divorce his wife.

[12]To the rest I say this (I, not the Lord): If any brother has a wife who is not a believer and she is willing to live with him, he must not divorce her. [13]And if a woman has a husband who is not a believer and he is willing to live with her, she must not divorce him. [14]For the unbelieving husband has been sanctified through his wife, and the unbelieving wife has been sanctified through her believing husband. Otherwise your children would be unclean, but as it is, they are holy.

[15]But if the unbeliever leaves, let him do so. A believing man or woman is not bound in such circumstances; God has called us to live in peace. [16]How do you know, wife, whether you will save your husband? Or, how do you know, husband, whether you will save your wife?

[17]Nevertheless, each one should retain the place in life that the Lord assigned to him and to which God has called him. This is the rule I lay down in all the churches. [18]Was a man already circumcised when he was called? He should not become uncircumcised. Was a man uncircumcised when he was called? He should not be circumcised. [19]Circumcision is nothing and uncircumcision is nothing. Keeping God's commands is what counts. [20]Each one should remain in the situation which he was in when God called him. [21]Were you a slave

---

b16 Gen. 2:24   a1 Or "It is good for a man not to have sexual relations with a woman."

when you were called? Don't let it trouble you—although if you can gain your freedom, do so. [22]For he who was a slave when he was called by the Lord is the Lord's freedman; similarly, he who was a free man when he was called is Christ's slave. [23]You were bought at a price; do not become slaves of men. [24]Brothers, each man, as responsible to God, should remain in the situation God called him to.

[25]Now about virgins: I have no command from the Lord, but I give a judgment as one who by the Lord's mercy is trustworthy. [26]Because of the present crisis, I think that it is good for you to remain as you are. [27]Are you married? Do not seek a divorce. Are you unmarried? Do not look for a wife. [28]But if you do marry, you have not sinned; and if a virgin marries, she has not sinned. But those who marry will face many troubles in this life, and I want to spare you this.

[29]What I mean, brothers, is that the time is short. From now on those who have wives should live as if they had none; [30]those who mourn, as if they did not; those who are happy, as if they were not; those who buy something, as if it were not theirs to keep; [31]those who use the things of the world, as if not engrossed in them. For this world in its present form is passing away.

[32]I would like you to be free from concern. An unmarried man is concerned about the Lord's affairs—how he can please the Lord. [33]But a married man is concerned about the affairs of this world—how he can please his wife—[34]and his interests are divided. An unmarried woman or virgin is concerned about the Lord's affairs: Her aim is to be devoted to the Lord in both body and spirit. But a married woman is concerned about the affairs of this world—how she can please her husband. [35]I am saying this for your own good, not to restrict you, but that you may live in a right way in undivided devotion to the Lord.

[36]If anyone thinks he is acting improperly towards the virgin he is engaged to, and if she is getting on in years and he feels he ought to marry, he should do as he wants. He is not sinning. They should get married. [37]But the man who has settled the matter in his own mind, who is under no compulsion but has control over his own will, and who has made up his mind not to marry the virgin—this man also does the right thing. [38]So then, he who marries the virgin does right, but he who does not marry her does even better.[b]

[39]A woman is bound to her husband as long as he lives. But if her husband dies, she is free to marry anyone she wishes, but he must belong to the Lord. [40]In my judgment, she is happier if she stays as she is—and I think that I too have the Spirit of God.

Food Sacrificed to Idols

8 Now about food sacrificed to idols: We know that we all possess knowledge.[a] Knowledge puffs up, but love builds up. [2]The man who thinks he knows something does not yet know as he ought to know. [3]But the man who loves God is known by God.

[4]So then, about eating food sacrificed to idols: We know that an idol is nothing at all in the world and that there is no God but one. [5]For even if there are so-called gods, whether in heaven or on earth (as indeed there are many "gods" and many "lords"), [6]yet for us there is but one God, the Father, from whom all things came and for whom we live; and there is but one Lord, Jesus Christ, through whom all things came and through whom we live.

[7]But not everyone knows this. Some people are still so accustomed to idols that when they eat such food they think of it as having been sacrificed to an idol, and since their conscience is weak, it is defiled. [8]But food does not bring us near to God; we are

---

[b]36-38 Or [36]If anyone thinks he is not treating his daughter properly, and if she is getting on in years, and he feels she ought to marry, he should do as he wants. He is not sinning. He should let her get married. [37]But the man who has settled the matter in his own mind, who is under no compulsion but has control over his own will, and who has made up his mind to keep the virgin unmarried—this man also does the right thing. [38]So then, he who gives his virgin in marriage does right, but he who does not give her in marriage does even better.   [a]1 Or "We all possess knowledge," as you say

no worse if we do not eat, and no better if we do.

⁹Be careful, however, that the exercise of your freedom does not become a stumbling-block to the weak. ¹⁰For if anyone with a weak conscience sees you who have this knowledge eating in an idol's temple, won't he be emboldened to eat what has been sacrificed to idols? ¹¹So this weak brother, for whom Christ died, is destroyed by your knowledge. ¹²When you sin against your brothers in this way and wound their weak conscience, you sin against Christ. ¹³Therefore, if what I eat causes my brother to fall into sin, I will never eat meat again, so that I will not cause him to fall.

The Rights of an Apostle

9 Am I not free? Am I not an apostle? Have I not seen Jesus our Lord? Are you not the result of my work in the Lord? ²Even though I may not be an apostle to others, surely I am to you! For you are the seal of my apostleship in the Lord.

³This is my defence to those who sit in judgment on me. ⁴Don't we have the right to food and drink? ⁵Don't we have the right to take a believing wife along with us, as do the other apostles and the Lord's brothers and Cephas?ᵃ ⁶Or is it only I and Barnabas who must work for a living?

⁷Who serves as a soldier at his own expense? Who plants a vineyard and does not eat of its grapes? Who tends a flock and does not drink of the milk? ⁸Do I say this merely from a human point of view? Doesn't the Law say the same thing? ⁹For it is written in the Law of Moses: "Do not muzzle an ox while it is treading out the grain."ᵇ Is it about oxen that God is concerned? ¹⁰Surely he says this for us, doesn't he? Yes, this was written for us, because when the ploughman ploughs and the thresher threshes, they ought to do so in the hope of sharing in the harvest. ¹¹If we have sown spiritual seed among you, is it too much if we reap a material harvest from you? ¹²If others have this right of support from you, shouldn't we have it all the more?

But we did not use this right. On the contrary, we put up with anything rather than hinder the gospel of Christ. ¹³Don't you know that those who work in the temple get their food from the temple, and those who serve at the altar share in what is offered on the altar? ¹⁴In the same way, the Lord has commanded that those who preach the gospel should receive their living from the gospel.

¹⁵But I have not used any of these rights. And I am not writing this in the hope that you will do such things for me. I would rather die than have anyone deprive me of this boast. ¹⁶Yet when I preach the gospel, I cannot boast, for I am compelled to preach. Woe to me if I do not preach the gospel! ¹⁷If I preach voluntarily, I have a reward; if not voluntarily, I am simply discharging the trust committed to me. ¹⁸What then is my reward? Just this: that in preaching the gospel I may offer it free of charge, and so not make use of my rights in preaching it.

¹⁹Though I am free and belong to no man, I make myself a slave to everyone, to win as many as possible. ²⁰To the Jews I became like a Jew, to win the Jews. To those under the law I became like one under the law (though I myself am not under the law), so as to win those under the law. ²¹To those not having the law I became like one not having the law (though I am not free from God's law but am under Christ's law), so as to win those not having the law. ²²To the weak I became weak, to win the weak. I have become all things to all men so that by all possible means I might save some. ²³I do all this for the sake of the gospel, that I may share in its blessings.

²⁴Do you not know that in a race all the runners run, but only one gets the prize? Run in such a way as to get the prize. ²⁵Everyone who competes in the games goes into strict training. They do it to get a crown that will not last; but we do it to get a crown that will last for ever. ²⁶Therefore I do not run like a man running aimlessly; I do not fight like a man beating the air. ²⁷No, I beat my body and make it my slave so that after I have preached to others, I

ᵃ5 That is, Peter   ᵇ9 Deut. 25:4

myself will not be disqualified for the prize.

Warnings From Israel's History

10 For I do not want you to be ignorant of the fact, brothers, that our forefathers were all under the cloud and that they all passed through the sea. [2]They were all baptised into Moses in the cloud and in the sea. [3]They all ate the same spiritual food [4]and drank the same spiritual drink; for they drank from the spiritual rock that accompanied them, and that rock was Christ. [5]Nevertheless, God was not pleased with most of them; their bodies were scattered over the desert.

[6]Now these things occurred as examples[a] to keep us from setting our hearts on evil things as they did. [7]Do not be idolaters, as some of them were; as it is written: "The people sat down to eat and drink and got up to indulge in pagan revelry."[b] [8]We should not commit sexual immorality, as some of them did—and in one day twenty-three thousand of them died. [9]We should not test the Lord, as some of them did—and were killed by snakes. [10]And do not grumble, as some of them did—and were killed by the destroying angel.

[11]These things happened to them as examples and were written down as warnings for us, on whom the fulfilment of the ages has come. [12]So, if you think you are standing firm, be careful that you don't fall! [13]No temptation has seized you except what is common to man. And God is faithful; he will not let you be tempted beyond what you can bear. But when you are tempted, he will also provide a way out so that you can stand up under it.

Idol Feasts and the Lord's Supper

[14]Therefore, my dear friends, flee from idolatry. [15]I speak to sensible people; judge for yourselves what I say. [16]Is not the cup of thanksgiving for which we give thanks a participation in the blood of Christ? And is not the bread that we break a participation in the body of Christ? [17]Because there is one loaf, we, who are many, are one body, for we all partake of the one loaf.

[18]Consider the people of Israel: Do not those who eat the sacrifices participate in the altar? [19]Do I mean then that a sacrifice offered to an idol is anything, or that an idol is anything? [20]No, but the sacrifices of pagans are offered to demons, not to God, and I do not want you to be participants with demons. [21]You cannot drink the cup of the Lord and the cup of demons too; you cannot have a part in both the Lord's table and the table of demons. [22]Are we trying to arouse the Lord's jealousy? Are we stronger than he?

The Believer's Freedom

[23]"Everything is permissible"—but not everything is beneficial. "Everything is permissible"—but not everything is constructive. [24]Nobody should seek his own good, but the good of others.

[25]Eat anything sold in the meat market without raising questions of conscience, [26]for, "The earth is the Lord's, and everything in it."[c]

[27]If some unbeliever invites you to a meal and you want to go, eat whatever is put before you without raising questions of conscience. [28]But if anyone says to you, "This has been offered in sacrifice," then do not eat it, both for the sake of the man who told you and for conscience' sake[d]— [29]the other man's conscience, I mean, not yours. For why should my freedom be judged by another's conscience? [30]If I take part in the meal with thankfulness, why am I denounced because of something I thank God for?

[31]So whether you eat or drink or whatever you do, do it all for the glory of God. [32]Do not cause anyone to stumble, whether Jews, Greeks or the church of God—[33]even as I try to please everybody in every way. For I am not seeking my own good but the good of many, so

11 that they may be saved. [1]Follow my example, as I follow the example of Christ.

[a]6 Or *types*; also in verse 11   [b]7 Exodus 32:6   [c]26 Psalm 24:1
[d]28 Some manuscripts *conscience' sake, for "the earth is the Lord's and everything in it"*

Propriety in Worship

[2]I praise you for remembering me in everything and for holding to the teachings,[a] just as I passed them on to you.

[3]Now I want you to realise that the head of every man is Christ, and the head of the woman is man, and the head of Christ is God. [4]Every man who prays or prophesies with his head covered dishonours his head. [5]And every woman who prays or prophesies with her head uncovered dishonours her head—it is just as though her head were shaved. [6]If a woman does not cover her head, she should have her hair cut off; and if it is a disgrace for a woman to have her hair cut or shaved off, she should cover her head. [7]A man ought not to cover his head,[b] since he is the image and glory of God; but the woman is the glory of man. [8]For man did not come from woman, but woman from man; [9]neither was man created for woman, but woman for man. [10]For this reason, and because of the angels, the woman ought to have a sign of authority on her head.

[11]In the Lord, however, woman is not independent of man, nor is man independent of woman. [12]For as woman came from man, so also man is born of woman. But everything comes from God. [13]Judge for yourselves: Is it proper for a woman to pray to God with her head uncovered? [14]Does not the very nature of things teach you that if a man has long hair, it is a disgrace to him, [15]but that if a woman has long hair, it is her glory? For long hair is given to her as a covering. [16]If anyone wants to be contentious about this, we have no other practice—nor do the churches of God.

The Lord's Supper

[17]In the following directives I have no praise for you, for your meetings do more harm than good. [18]In the first place, I hear that when you come together as a church, there are divisions among you, and to

some extent I believe it. [19]No doubt there have to be differences among you to show which of you have God's approval. [20]When you come together, it is not the Lord's Supper you eat, [21]for as you eat, each of you goes ahead without waiting for anybody else. One remains hungry, another gets drunk. [22]Don't you have homes to eat and drink in? Or do you despise the church of God and humiliate those who have nothing? What shall I say to you? Shall I praise you for this? Certainly not!

[23]For I received from the Lord what I also passed on to you: The Lord Jesus, on the night he was betrayed, took bread, [24]and when he had given thanks, he broke it and said, "This is my body, which is for you; do this in remembrance of me." [25]In the same way, after supper he took the cup, saying, "This cup is the new covenant in my blood; do this, whenever you drink it, in remembrance of me." [26]For whenever you eat this bread and drink this cup, you proclaim the Lord's death until he comes.

[27]Therefore, whoever eats the bread or drinks the cup of the Lord in an unworthy manner will be guilty of sinning against the body and blood of the Lord. [28]A man ought to examine himself before he eats of the bread and drinks of the cup. [29]For anyone who eats and drinks without recognising the body of the Lord eats and drinks judgment on himself. [30]That is why many among you are weak and sick, and a number of you have fallen asleep. [31]But if we judged ourselves, we would not come under judgment. [32]When we are judged by the Lord, we are being disciplined so that we will not be condemned with the world.

[33]So then, my brothers, when you come together to eat, wait for each other. [34]If anyone is hungry, he should eat at home, so that when you meet together it may not result in judgment.

And when I come I will give further directions.

---

[a]2 Or *traditions*

[b]4-7 Or [4]*Every man who prays or prophesies with long hair dishonours his head.* [5]*And every woman who prays or prophesies with no covering of hair on her head dishonours her head—she is just like one of the "shorn women."* [6]*If a woman has no covering, let her be for now with short hair, but since it is a disgrace for a woman to have her hair shorn or shaved, she should grow it again.* [7]*A man ought not to have long hair*

Spiritual Gifts

12 Now about spiritual gifts, brothers, I do not want you to be ignorant. ²You know that when you were pagans, somehow or other you were influenced and led astray to mute idols. ³Therefore I tell you that no-one who is speaking by the Spirit of God says, "Jesus be cursed," and no-one can say, "Jesus is Lord," except by the Holy Spirit.

⁴There are different kinds of gifts, but the same Spirit. ⁵There are different kinds of service, but the same Lord. ⁶There are different kinds of working, but the same God works all of them in all men.

⁷Now to each one the manifestation of the Spirit is given for the common good. ⁸To one there is given through the Spirit the message of wisdom, to another the message of knowledge by means of the same Spirit, ⁹to another faith by the same Spirit, to another gifts of healing by that one Spirit, ¹⁰to another miraculous powers, to another prophecy, to another distinguishing between spirits, to another speaking in different kinds of tongues,*a* and to still another the interpretation of tongues.*a* ¹¹All these are the work of one and the same Spirit, and he gives them to each one, just as he determines.

One Body, Many Parts

¹²The body is a unit, though it is made up of many parts; and though all its parts are many, they form one body. So it is with Christ. ¹³For we were all baptised by*b* one Spirit into one body—whether Jews or Greeks, slave or free—and we were all given the one Spirit to drink.

¹⁴Now the body is not made up of one part but of many. ¹⁵If the foot should say, "Because I am not a hand, I do not belong to the body," it would not for that reason cease to be part of the body. ¹⁶And if the ear should say, "Because I am not an eye, I do not belong to the body," it would not for that reason cease to be part of the body. ¹⁷If the whole body were an eye, where would the sense of hearing be? If the whole body were an ear, where would the sense of smell be? ¹⁸But in fact God has arranged the parts in the body, every one of them, just as he wanted them to be. ¹⁹If they were all one part, where would the body be? ²⁰As it is, there are many parts, but one body.

²¹The eye cannot say to the hand, "I don't need you!" And the head cannot say to the feet, "I don't need you!" ²²On the contrary, those parts of the body that seem to be weaker are indispensable, ²³and the parts that we think are less honourable we treat with special honour. And the parts that are unpresentable are treated with special modesty, ²⁴while our presentable parts need no special treatment. But God has combined the members of the body and has given greater honour to the parts that lacked it, ²⁵so that there should be no division in the body, but that its parts should have equal concern for each other. ²⁶If one part suffers, every part suffers with it; if one part is honoured, every part rejoices with it.

²⁷Now you are the body of Christ, and each one of you is a part of it. ²⁸And in the church God has appointed first of all apostles, second prophets, third teachers, then workers of miracles, also those having gifts of healing, those able to help others, those with gifts of administration, and those speaking in different kinds of tongues. ²⁹Are all apostles? Are all prophets? Are all teachers? Do all work miracles? ³⁰Do all have gifts of healing? Do all speak in tongues?*c* Do all interpret? ³¹But eagerly desire*d* the greater gifts.

Love

And now I will show you the most excellent way.

13 If I speak in the tongues*a* of men and of angels, but have not love, I am only a resounding gong or a clanging cymbal. ²If I have the gift of prophecy and can fathom all mysteries and all knowledge, and if I have a faith that can move mountains, but have not love, I am

---

a10 Or *languages*; also in verse 28   *b13* Or *with*; or *in*   *c30* Or *other languages*
d31 Or *But you are eagerly desiring*   *a1* Or *languages*

nothing. ³If I give all I possess to the poor and surrender my body to the flames,*b* but have not love, I gain nothing.

⁴Love is patient, love is kind. It does not envy, it does not boast, it is not proud. ⁵It is not rude, it is not self-seeking, it is not easily angered, it keeps no record of wrongs. ⁶Love does not delight in evil but rejoices with the truth. ⁷It always protects, always trusts, always hopes, always perseveres.

⁸Love never fails. But where there are prophecies, they will cease; where there are tongues, they will be stilled; where there is knowledge, it will pass away. ⁹For we know in part and we prophesy in part, ¹⁰but when perfection comes, the imperfect disappears. ¹¹When I was a child, I talked like a child, I thought like a child, I reasoned like a child. When I became a man, I put childish ways behind me. ¹²Now we see but a poor reflection as in a mirror; then we shall see face to face. Now I know in part; then I shall know fully, even as I am fully known.

¹³And now these three remain: faith, hope and love. But the greatest of these is love.

Gifts of Prophecy and Tongues

14 Follow the way of love and eagerly desire spiritual gifts, especially the gift of prophecy. ²For anyone who speaks in a tongue*a* does not speak to men but to God. Indeed, no-one understands him; he utters mysteries with his spirit.*b* ³But everyone who prophesies speaks to men for their strengthening, encouragement and comfort. ⁴He who speaks in a tongue edifies himself, but he who prophesies edifies the church. ⁵I would like every one of you to speak in tongues,*c* but I would rather have you prophesy. He who prophesies is greater than one who speaks in tongues,*c* unless he interprets, so that the church may be edified.

⁶Now, brothers, if I come to you and speak in tongues, what good will I be to you, unless I bring you some revelation or

knowledge or prophecy or word of instruction? ⁷Even in the case of lifeless things that make sounds, such as the flute or harp, how will anyone know what tune is being played unless there is a distinction in the notes? ⁸Again, if the trumpet does not sound a clear call, who will get ready for battle? ⁹So it is with you. Unless you speak intelligible words with your tongue, how will anyone know what you are saying? You will just be speaking into the air. ¹⁰Undoubtedly there are all sorts of languages in the world, yet none of them is without meaning. ¹¹If then I do not grasp the meaning of what someone is saying, I am a foreigner to the speaker, and he is a foreigner to me. ¹²So it is with you. Since you are eager to have spiritual gifts, try to excel in gifts that build up the church.

¹³For this reason anyone who speaks in a tongue should pray that he may interpret what he says. ¹⁴For if I pray in a tongue, my spirit prays, but my mind is unfruitful. ¹⁵So what shall I do? I will pray with my spirit, but I will also pray with my mind; I will sing with my spirit, but I will also sing with my mind. ¹⁶If you are praising God with your spirit, how can one who finds himself among those who do not understand*d* say "Amen" to your thanksgiving, since he does not know what you are saying? ¹⁷You may be giving thanks well enough, but the other man is not edified.

¹⁸I thank God that I speak in tongues more than all of you. ¹⁹But in the church I would rather speak five intelligible words to instruct others than ten thousand words in a tongue.

²⁰Brothers, stop thinking like children. In regard to evil be infants, but in your thinking be adults. ²¹In the Law it is written:

"Through men of strange tongues
    and through the lips of foreigners
I will speak to this people,
    but even then they will not listen to
    me,"*e*
says the Lord.

---

b3 Some early manuscripts *body that I may boast*   *a2* Or *another language*; also in verses 4, 13, 14, 19, 26 and 27
b2 Or *by the Spirit*   *c5* Or *other languages*; also in verses 6, 18, 22, 23 and 39   *d16* Or *among the enquirers*
e21 Isaiah 28:11,12

22Tongues, then, are a sign, not for believers but for unbelievers; prophecy, however, is for believers, not for unbelievers. 23So if the whole church comes together and everyone speaks in tongues, and some who do not understand*f* or some unbelievers come in, will they not say that you are out of your mind? 24But if an unbeliever or someone who does not understand*g* comes in while everybody is prophesying, he will be convinced by all that he is a sinner and will be judged by all, 25and the secrets of his heart will be laid bare. So he will fall down and worship God, exclaiming, "God is really among you!"

Orderly Worship

26What then shall we say, brothers? When you come together, everyone has a hymn, or a word of instruction, a revelation, a tongue or an interpretation. All of these must be done for the strengthening of the church. 27If anyone speaks in a tongue, two—or at the most three—should speak, one at a time, and someone must interpret. 28If there is no interpreter, the speaker should keep quiet in the church and speak to himself and God.

29Two or three prophets should speak, and the others should weigh carefully what is said. 30And if a revelation comes to someone who is sitting down, the first speaker should stop. 31For you can all prophesy in turn so that everyone may be instructed and encouraged. 32The spirits of prophets are subject to the control of prophets. 33For God is not a God of disorder but of peace.

As in all the congregations of the saints, 34women should remain silent in the churches. They are not allowed to speak, but must be in submission, as the Law says. 35If they want to enquire about something, they should ask their own husbands at home; for it is disgraceful for a woman to speak in the church.

36Did the word of God originate with you? Or are you the only people it has

reached? 37If anybody thinks he is a prophet or spiritually gifted, let him acknowledge that what I am writing to you is the Lord's command. 38If he ignores this, he himself will be ignored.*h*

39Therefore, my brothers, be eager to prophesy, and do not forbid speaking in tongues. 40But everything should be done in a fitting and orderly way.

The Resurrection of Christ

15 Now, brothers, I want to remind you of the gospel I preached to you, which you received and on which you have taken your stand. 2By this gospel you are saved, if you hold firmly to the word I preached to you. Otherwise, you have believed in vain.

3For what I received I passed on to you as of first importance:*a* that Christ died for our sins according to the Scriptures, 4that he was buried, that he was raised on the third day according to the Scriptures, 5and that he appeared to Peter,*b* and then to the Twelve. 6After that, he appeared to more than five hundred of the brothers at the same time, most of whom are still living, though some have fallen asleep. 7Then he appeared to James, then to all the apostles, 8and last of all he appeared to me also, as to one abnormally born.

9For I am the least of the apostles and do not even deserve to be called an apostle, because I persecuted the church of God. 10But by the grace of God I am what I am, and his grace to me was not without effect. No, I worked harder than all of them—yet not I, but the grace of God that was with me. 11Whether, then, it was I or they, this is what we preach, and this is what you believed.

The Resurrection of the Dead

12But if it is preached that Christ has been raised from the dead, how can some of you say that there is no resurrection of the dead? 13If there is no resurrection of the dead, then not even Christ has been

f23 Or *some enquirers*   *g24* Or *or some enquirer*
h38 Some manuscripts *If he is ignorant of this, let him be ignorant*   *a3* Or *you at the first*
b5 Greek *Cephas*

raised. [14]And if Christ has not been raised, our preaching is useless and so is your faith. [15]More than that, we are then found to be false witnesses about God, for we have testified about God that he raised Christ from the dead. But he did not raise him if in fact the dead are not raised. [16]For if the dead are not raised, then Christ has not been raised either. [17]And if Christ has not been raised, your faith is futile; you are still in your sins. [18]Then those also who have fallen asleep in Christ are lost. [19]If only for this life we have hope in Christ, we are to be pitied more than all men.

[20]But Christ has indeed been raised from the dead, the firstfruits of those who have fallen asleep. [21]For since death came through a man, the resurrection of the dead comes also through a man. [22]For as in Adam all die, so in Christ all will be made alive. [23]But each in his own turn: Christ, the firstfruits; then, when he comes, those who belong to him. [24]Then the end will come, when he hands over the kingdom to God the Father after he has destroyed all dominion, authority and power. [25]For he must reign until he has put all his enemies under his feet. [26]The last enemy to be destroyed is death. [27]For he "has put everything under his feet".[c] Now when it says that "everything" has been put under him, it is clear that this does not include God himself, who put everything under Christ. [28]When he has done this, then the Son himself will be made subject to him who put everything under him, so that God may be all in all.

[29]Now if there is no resurrection, what will those do who are baptised for the dead? If the dead are not raised at all, why are people baptised for them? [30]And as for us, why do we endanger ourselves every hour? [31]I die every day—I mean that, brothers—just as surely as I glory over you in Christ Jesus our Lord. [32]If I fought with wild beasts in Ephesus for merely human reasons, what have I gained? If the dead are not raised,

"Let us eat and drink,
for tomorrow we die."[d]

[33]Do not be misled: "Bad company corrupts good character." [34]Come back to your senses as you ought, and stop sinning; for there are some who are ignorant of God—I say this to your shame.

The Resurrection Body

[35]But someone may ask, "How are the dead raised? With what kind of body will they come?" [36]How foolish! What you sow does not come to life unless it dies. [37]When you sow, you do not plant the body that will be, but just a seed, perhaps of wheat or of something else. [38]But God gives it a body as he has determined, and to each kind of seed he gives its own body. [39]All flesh is not the same: Men have one kind of flesh, animals have another, birds another and fish another. [40]There are also heavenly bodies and there are earthly bodies; but the splendour of the heavenly bodies is one kind, and the splendour of the earthly bodies is another. [41]The sun has one kind of splendour, the moon another and the stars another; and star differs from star in splendour.

[42]So will it be with the resurrection of the dead. The body that is sown is perishable, it is raised imperishable; [43]it is sown in dishonour, it is raised in glory; it is sown in weakness, it is raised in power; [44]it is sown a natural body, it is raised a spiritual body.

If there is a natural body, there is also a spiritual body. [45]So it is written: "The first man Adam became a living being";[e] the last Adam, a life-giving spirit. [46]The spiritual did not come first, but the natural, and after that the spiritual. [47]The first man was of the dust of the earth, the second man from heaven. [48]As was the earthly man, so are those who are of the earth; and as is the man from heaven, so also are those who are of heaven. [49]And just as we have borne the likeness of the earthly man, so shall we[f] bear the likeness of the man from heaven.

[50]I declare to you, brothers, that flesh and blood cannot inherit the kingdom of God, nor does the perishable inherit the

[c]27 Psalm 8:6   [d]32 Isaiah 22:13   [e]45 Gen. 2:7   [f]49 Some early manuscripts *so let us*

imperishable. [51]Listen, I tell you a mystery: We will not all sleep, but we will all be changed—[52]in a flash, in the twinkling of an eye, at the last trumpet. For the trumpet will sound, the dead will be raised imperishable, and we will be changed. [53]For the perishable must clothe itself with the imperishable, and the mortal with immortality. [54]When the perishable has been clothed with the imperishable, and the mortal with immortality, then the saying that is written will come true: "Death has been swallowed up in victory."[g]

[55]"Where, O death, is your victory?
    Where, O death, is your sting?"[h]

[56]The sting of death is sin, and the power of sin is the law. [57]But thanks be to God! He gives us the victory through our Lord Jesus Christ.

[58]Therefore, my dear brothers, stand firm. Let nothing move you. Always give yourselves fully to the work of the Lord, because you know that your labour in the Lord is not in vain.

The Collection for God's People

16 Now about the collection for God's people: Do what I told the Galatian churches to do. [2]On the first day of every week, each one of you should set aside a sum of money in keeping with his income, saving it up, so that when I come no collections will have to be made. [3]Then, when I arrive, I will give letters of introduction to the men you approve and send them with your gift to Jerusalem. [4]If it seems advisable for me to go also, they will accompany me.

Personal Requests

[5]After I go through Macedonia, I will come to you—for I will be going through Macedonia. [6]Perhaps I will stay with you awhile, or even spend the winter, so that you can help me on my journey, wherever I go. [7]I do not want to see you now and

make only a passing visit; I hope to spend some time with you, if the Lord permits. [8]But I will stay on at Ephesus until Pentecost, [9]because a great door for effective work has opened to me, and there are many who oppose me.

[10]If Timothy comes, see to it that he has nothing to fear while he is with you, for he is carrying on the work of the Lord, just as I am. [11]No-one, then, should refuse to accept him. Send him on his way in peace so that he may return to me. I am expecting him along with the brothers.

[12]Now about our brother Apollos: I strongly urged him to go to you with the brothers. He was quite unwilling to go now, but he will go when he has the opportunity.

[13]Be on your guard; stand firm in the faith; be men of courage; be strong. [14]Do everything in love.

[15]You know that the household of Stephanas were the first converts in Achaia, and they have devoted themselves to the service of the saints. I urge you, brothers, [16]to submit to such as these and to everyone who joins in the work, and labours at it. [17]I was glad when Stephanas, Fortunatus and Achaicus arrived, because they have supplied what was lacking from you. [18]For they refreshed my spirit and yours also. Such men deserve recognition.

Final Greetings

[19]The churches in the province of Asia send you greetings. Aquila and Priscilla[a] greet you warmly in the Lord, and so does the church that meets at their house. [20]All the brothers here send you greetings. Greet one another with a holy kiss.

[21]I, Paul, write this greeting in my own hand.

[22]If anyone does not love the Lord—a curse be on him. Come, O Lord![b]

[23]The grace of the Lord Jesus be with you.

[24]My love to all of you in Christ Jesus. Amen.[c]

---

[g]54 Isaiah 25:8   [h]55 Hosea 13:14   [a]19 Greek *Prisca*, a variant of *Priscilla*
[b]22 In Aramaic the expression *Come, O Lord* is *Marana tha*.   [c]24 Some manuscripts do not have *Amen*.

2 Corinthians

1

Paul, an apostle of Christ Jesus by the will of God, and Timothy our brother,

To the church of God in Corinth, together with all the saints throughout Achaia:

2Grace and peace to you from God our Father and the Lord Jesus Christ.

The God of All Comfort

3Praise be to the God and Father of our Lord Jesus Christ, the Father of compassion and the God of all comfort, 4who comforts us in all our troubles, so that we can comfort those in any trouble with the comfort we ourselves have received from God. 5For just as the sufferings of Christ flow over into our lives, so also through Christ our comfort overflows. 6If we are distressed, it is for your comfort and salvation; if we are comforted, it is for your comfort, which produces in you patient endurance of the same sufferings we suffer. 7And our hope for you is firm, because we know that just as you share in our sufferings, so also you share in our comfort.

8We do not want you to be uninformed, brothers, about the hardships we suffered in the province of Asia. We were under great pressure, far beyond our ability to endure, so that we despaired even of life. 9Indeed, in our hearts we felt the sentence of death. But this happened that we might not rely on ourselves but on God, who raises the dead. 10He has delivered us from such a deadly peril, and he will deliver us. On him we have set our hope that he will continue to deliver us, 11as you help us by your prayers. Then many will give thanks on our*a* behalf for the gracious favour granted us in answer to the prayers of many.

Paul's Change of Plans

12Now this is our boast: Our conscience testifies that we have conducted ourselves in the world, and especially in our relations with you, in the holiness and sincerity that are from God. We have done so not according to worldly wisdom but according to God's grace. 13For we do not write to you anything you cannot read or understand. And I hope that, 14as you have understood us in part, you will come to understand fully that you can boast of us just as we will boast of you in the day of the Lord Jesus.

15Because I was confident of this, I planned to visit you first so that you might benefit twice. 16I planned to visit you on my way to Macedonia and to come back to you from Macedonia, and then to have you send me on my way to Judea. 17When I planned this, did I do it lightly? Or do I make my plans in a worldly manner so that in the same breath I say, "Yes, yes" and "No, no"?

18But as surely as God is faithful, our message to you is not "Yes" and "No".

[19]For the Son of God, Jesus Christ, who was preached among you by me and Silas[b] and Timothy, was not "Yes" and "No", but in him it has always been "Yes". [20]For no matter how many promises God has made, they are "Yes" in Christ. And so through him the "Amen" is spoken by us to the glory of God. [21]Now it is God who makes both us and you stand firm in Christ. He anointed us, [22]set his seal of ownership on us, and put his Spirit in our hearts as a deposit, guaranteeing what is to come.

[23]I call God as my witness that it was in order to spare you that I did not return to Corinth. [24]Not that we lord it over your faith, but we work with you for your joy, because it is by faith you stand firm. [1]So I made up my mind that I would not make another painful visit to you. [2]For if I grieve you, who is left to make me glad but you whom I have grieved? [3]I wrote as I did so that when I came I should not be distressed by those who ought to make me rejoice. I had confidence in all of you, that you would all share my joy. [4]For I wrote to you out of great distress and anguish of heart and with many tears, not to grieve you but to let you know the depth of my love for you.

Forgiveness for the Sinner

[5]If anyone has caused grief, he has not so much grieved me as he has grieved all of you, to some extent—not to put it too severely. [6]The punishment inflicted on him by the majority is sufficient for him. [7]Now instead, you ought to forgive and comfort him, so that he will not be overwhelmed by excessive sorrow. [8]I urge you, therefore, to reaffirm your love for him. [9]The reason I wrote to you was to see if you would stand the test and be obedient in everything. [10]If you forgive anyone, I also forgive him. And what I have forgiven—if there was anything to forgive—I have forgiven in the sight of Christ for your sake, [11]in order that Satan might not outwit us. For we are not unaware of his schemes.

Ministers of the New Covenant

[12]Now when I went to Troas to preach the gospel of Christ and found that the Lord had opened a door for me, [13]I still had no peace of mind, because I did not find my brother Titus there. So I said good-bye to them and went on to Macedonia.

[14]But thanks be to God, who always leads us in triumphal procession in Christ and through us spreads everywhere the fragrance of the knowledge of him. [15]For we are to God the aroma of Christ among those who are being saved and those who are perishing. [16]To the one we are the smell of death; to the other, the fragrance of life. And who is equal to such a task? [17]Unlike so many, we do not peddle the word of God for profit. On the contrary, in Christ we speak before God with sincerity, like men sent from God.

[1]Are we beginning to commend ourselves again? Or do we need, like some people, letters of recommendation to you or from you? [2]You yourselves are our letter, written on our hearts, known and read by everybody. [3]You show that you are a letter from Christ, the result of our ministry, written not with ink but with the Spirit of the living God, not on tablets of stone but on tablets of human hearts.

[4]Such confidence as this is ours through Christ before God. [5]Not that we are competent in ourselves to claim anything for ourselves, but our competence comes from God. [6]He has made us competent as ministers of a new covenant—not of the letter but of the Spirit; for the letter kills, but the Spirit gives life.

The Glory of the New Covenant

[7]Now if the ministry that brought death, which was engraved in letters on stone, came with glory, so that the Israelites could not look steadily at the face of Moses because of its glory, fading though it was, [8]will not the ministry of the Spirit be even more glorious? [9]If the ministry that condemns men is glorious, how much

more glorious is the ministry that brings righteousness! [10]For what was glorious has no glory now in comparison with the surpassing glory. [11]And if what was fading away came with glory, how much greater is the glory of that which lasts!

[12]Therefore, since we have such a hope, we are very bold. [13]We are not like Moses, who would put a veil over his face to keep the Israelites from gazing at it while the radiance was fading away. [14]But their minds were made dull, for to this day the same veil remains when the old covenant is read. It has not been removed, because only in Christ is it taken away. [15]Even to this day when Moses is read, a veil covers their hearts. [16]But whenever anyone turns to the Lord, the veil is taken away. [17]Now the Lord is the Spirit, and where the Spirit of the Lord is, there is freedom. [18]And we, who with unveiled faces all reflect[a] the Lord's glory, are being transformed into his likeness with ever-increasing glory, which comes from the Lord, who is the Spirit.

Treasures in Jars of Clay

4 Therefore, since through God's mercy we have this ministry, we do not lose heart. [2]Rather, we have renounced secret and shameful ways; we do not use deception, nor do we distort the word of God. On the contrary, by setting forth the truth plainly we commend ourselves to every man's conscience in the sight of God. [3]And even if our gospel is veiled, it is veiled to those who are perishing. [4]The god of this age has blinded the minds of unbelievers, so that they cannot see the light of the gospel of the glory of Christ, who is the image of God. [5]For we do not preach ourselves, but Jesus Christ as Lord, and ourselves as your servants for Jesus' sake. [6]For God, who said, "Let light shine out of darkness,"[a] made his light shine in our hearts to give us the light of the knowledge of the glory of God in the face of Christ.

[7]But we have this treasure in jars of clay to show that this all-surpassing power is from God and not from us. [8]We are hard pressed on every side, but not crushed; perplexed, but not in despair; [9]persecuted, but not abandoned; struck down, but not destroyed. [10]We always carry around in our body the death of Jesus, so that the life of Jesus may also be revealed in our body. [11]For we who are alive are always being given over to death for Jesus' sake, so that his life may be revealed in our mortal body. [12]So then, death is at work in us, but life is at work in you.

[13]It is written: "I believed; therefore I have spoken."[b] With that same spirit of faith we also believe and therefore speak, [14]because we know that the one who raised the Lord Jesus from the dead will also raise us with Jesus and present us with you in his presence. [15]All this is for your benefit, so that the grace that is reaching more and more people may cause thanksgiving to overflow to the glory of God.

[16]Therefore we do not lose heart. Though outwardly we are wasting away, yet inwardly we are being renewed day by day. [17]For our light and momentary troubles are achieving for us an eternal glory that far outweighs them all. [18]So we fix our eyes not on what is seen, but on what is unseen. For what is seen is temporary, but what is unseen is eternal.

Our Heavenly Dwelling

5 Now we know that if the earthly tent we live in is destroyed, we have a building from God, an eternal house in heaven, not built by human hands. [2]Meanwhile we groan, longing to be clothed with our heavenly dwelling, [3]because when we are clothed, we will not be found naked. [4]For while we are in this tent, we groan and are burdened, because we do not wish to be unclothed but to be clothed with our heavenly dwelling, so that what is mortal may be swallowed up by life. [5]Now it is God who has made us for this very purpose and has given us the Spirit as a deposit, guaranteeing what is to come.

[6]Therefore we are always confident and

---

know that as long as we are at home in the body we are away from the Lord. [7]We live by faith, not by sight. [8]We are confident, I say, and would prefer to be away from the body and at home with the Lord. [9]So we make it our goal to please him, whether we are at home in the body or away from it. [10]For we must all appear before the judgment seat of Christ, that each one may receive what is due to him for the things done while in the body, whether good or bad.

The Ministry of Reconciliation

[11]Since, then, we know what it is to fear the Lord, we try to persuade men. What we are is plain to God, and I hope it is also plain to your conscience. [12]We are not trying to commend ourselves to you again, but are giving you an opportunity to take pride in us, so that you can answer those who take pride in what is seen rather than in what is in the heart. [13]If we are out of our mind, it is for the sake of God; if we are in our right mind, it is for you. [14]For Christ's love compels us, because we are convinced that one died for all, and therefore all died. [15]And he died for all, that those who live should no longer live for themselves but for him who died for them and was raised again.

[16]So from now on we regard no-one from a worldly point of view. Though we once regarded Christ in this way, we do so no longer. [17]Therefore, if anyone is in Christ, he is a new creation; the old has gone, the new has come! [18]All this is from God, who reconciled us to himself through Christ and gave us the ministry of reconciliation: [19]that God was reconciling the world to himself in Christ, not counting men's sins against them. And he has committed to us the message of reconciliation. [20]We are therefore Christ's ambassadors, as though God were making his appeal through us. We implore you on Christ's behalf: Be reconciled to God. [21]God made him who had no sin to be sin[a] for us, so that in him we might become the righteousness of God.

[6] As God's fellow-workers we urge you not to receive God's grace in vain. [2]For he says,

> "In the time of my favour I heard you,
> and in the day of salvation I helped
> you."[a]

I tell you, now is the time of God's favour, now is the day of salvation.

Paul's Hardships

[3]We put no stumbling-block in anyone's path, so that our ministry will not be discredited. [4]Rather, as servants of God we commend ourselves in every way: in great endurance; in troubles, hardships and distresses; [5]in beatings, imprisonments and riots; in hard work, sleepless nights and hunger; [6]in purity, understanding, patience and kindness; in the Holy Spirit and in sincere love; [7]in truthful speech and in the power of God; with weapons of righteousness in the right hand and in the left; [8]through glory and dishonour, bad report and good report; genuine, yet regarded as impostors; [9]known, yet regarded as unknown; dying, and yet we live on; beaten, and yet not killed; [10]sorrowful, yet always rejoicing; poor, yet making many rich; having nothing, and yet possessing everything.

[11]We have spoken freely to you, Corinthians, and opened wide our hearts to you. [12]We are not withholding our affection from you, but you are withholding yours from us. [13]As a fair exchange—I speak as to my children—open wide your hearts also.

Do Not Be Yoked With Unbelievers

[14]Do not be yoked together with unbelievers. For what do righteousness and wickedness have in common? Or what fellowship can light have with darkness? [15]What harmony is there between Christ and Belial?[b] What does a believer have in common with an unbeliever? [16]What

---

[a]21 Or *be a sin offering*   [a]2 Isaiah 49:8   [b]15 Greek *Beliar*, a variant of *Belial*

agreement is there between the temple of God and idols? For we are the temple of the living God. As God has said: "I will live with them and walk among them, and I will be their God, and they will be my people."[c]

[17]"Therefore come out from them
  and be separate,
                                says the Lord.
  Touch no unclean thing,
    and I will receive you."[d]
[18]"I will be a Father to you,
    and you will be my sons and
      daughters,
                  says the Lord Almighty."[e]

7 Since we have these promises, dear friends, let us purify ourselves from everything that contaminates body and spirit, perfecting holiness out of reverence for God.

Paul's Joy

[2]Make room for us in your hearts. We have wronged no-one, we have corrupted no-one, we have exploited no-one. [3]I do not say this to condemn you; I have said before that you have such a place in our hearts that we would live or die with you. [4]I have great confidence in you; I take great pride in you. I am greatly encouraged; in all our troubles my joy knows no bounds.

[5]For when we came into Macedonia, this body of ours had no rest, but we were harassed at every turn—conflicts on the outside, fears within. [6]But God, who comforts the downcast, comforted us by the coming of Titus, [7]and not only by his coming but also by the comfort you had given him. He told us about your longing for me, your deep sorrow, your ardent concern for me, so that my joy was greater than ever.

[8]Even if I caused you sorrow by my letter, I do not regret it. Though I did regret it—I see that my letter hurt you, but only for a little while—[9]yet now I am happy, not because you were made sorry, but because your sorrow led you to repentance. For you became sorrowful as God intended and so were not harmed in any way by us. [10]Godly sorrow brings repentance that leads to salvation and leaves no regret, but worldly sorrow brings death. [11]See what this godly sorrow has produced in you: what earnestness, what eagerness to clear yourselves, what indignation, what alarm, what longing, what concern, what readiness to see justice done. At every point you have proved yourselves to be innocent in this matter. [12]So even though I wrote to you, it was not on account of the one who did the wrong or of the injured party, but rather that before God you could see for yourselves how devoted to us you are. [13]By all this we are encouraged.

In addition to our own encouragement, we were especially delighted to see how happy Titus was, because his spirit has been refreshed by all of you. [14]I had boasted to him about you, and you have not embarrassed me. But just as everything we said to you was true, so our boasting about you to Titus has proved to be true as well. [15]And his affection for you is all the greater when he remembers that you were all obedient, receiving him with fear and trembling. [16]I am glad I can have complete confidence in you.

Generosity Encouraged

8 And now, brothers, we want you to know about the grace that God has given the Macedonian churches. [2]Out of the most severe trial, their overflowing joy and their extreme poverty welled up in rich generosity. [3]For I testify that they gave as much as they were able, and even beyond their ability. Entirely on their own, [4]they urgently pleaded with us for the privilege of sharing in this service to the saints. [5]And they did not do as we expected, but they gave themselves first to the Lord and then to us in keeping with God's will. [6]So we urged Titus, since he had earlier made a beginning, to bring also to completion this act of grace on your

---

[c]16 Lev. 26:12; Jer. 32:38; Ezek. 37:27   [d]17 Isaiah 52:11; Ezek. 20:34,41   [e]18 2 Samuel 7:14; 7:8

part. [7]But just as you excel in everything— in faith, in speech, in knowledge, in complete earnestness and in your love for us[a]—see that you also excel in this grace of giving.

[8]I am not commanding you, but I want to test the sincerity of your love by comparing it with the earnestness of others. [9]For you know the grace of our Lord Jesus Christ, that though he was rich, yet for your sakes he became poor, so that you through his poverty might become rich.

[10]And here is my advice about what is best for you in this matter: Last year you were the first not only to give but also to have the desire to do so. [11]Now finish the work, so that your eager willingness to do it may be matched by your completion of it, according to your means. [12]For if the willingness is there, the gift is acceptable according to what one has, not according to what he does not have.

[13]Our desire is not that others might be relieved while you are hard pressed, but that there might be equality. [14]At the present time your plenty will supply what they need, so that in turn their plenty will supply what you need. Then there will be equality, [15]as it is written: "He who gathered much did not have too much, and he who gathered little did not have too little."[b]

Titus Sent to Corinth

[16]I thank God, who put into the heart of Titus the same concern I have for you. [17]For Titus not only welcomed our appeal, but he is coming to you with much enthusiasm and on his own initiative. [18]And we are sending along with him the brother who is praised by all the churches for his service to the gospel. [19]What is more, he was chosen by the churches to accompany us as we carry the offering, which we administer in order to honour the Lord himself and to show our eagerness to help. [20]We want to avoid any criticism of the way we administer this liberal gift. [21]For we are taking pains to do what is right, not only in the eyes of the Lord but also in the eyes of men.

[22]In addition, we are sending with them our brother who has often proved to us in many ways that he is zealous, and now even more so because of his great confidence in you. [23]As for Titus, he is my partner and fellow-worker among you; as for our brothers, they are representatives of the churches and an honour to Christ. [24]Therefore show these men the proof of your love and the reason for our pride in you, so that the churches can see it.

9 There is no need for me to write to you about this service to the saints. [2]For I know your eagerness to help, and I have been boasting about it to the Macedonians, telling them that since last year you in Achaia were ready to give; and your enthusiasm has stirred most of them to action. [3]But I am sending the brothers in order that our boasting about you in this matter should not prove hollow, but that you may be ready, as I said you would be. [4]For if any Macedonians come with me and find you unprepared, we—not to say anything about you—would be ashamed of having been so confident. [5]So I thought it necessary to urge the brothers to visit you in advance and finish the arrangements for the generous gift you had promised. Then it will be ready as a generous gift, not as one grudgingly given.

Sowing Generously

[6]Remember this: Whoever sows sparingly will also reap sparingly, and whoever sows generously will also reap generously. [7]Each man should give what he has decided in his heart to give, not reluctantly or under compulsion, for God loves a cheerful giver. [8]And God is able to make all grace abound to you, so that in all things at all times, having all that you need, you will abound in every good work. [9]As it is written:

> "He has scattered abroad his gifts to the poor;
> his righteousness endures for ever."[a]

---

[a]7 Some manuscripts *in our love for you*   [b]15 Exodus 16:18   [a]9 Psalm 112:9

¹⁰Now he who supplies seed to the sower and bread for food will also supply and increase your store of seed and will enlarge the harvest of your righteousness. ¹¹You will be made rich in every way so that you can be generous on every occasion, and through us your generosity will result in thanksgiving to God.

¹²This service that you perform is not only supplying the needs of God's people but is also overflowing in many expressions of thanks to God. ¹³Because of the service by which you have proved yourselves, men will praise God for the obedience that accompanies your confession of the gospel of Christ, and for your generosity in sharing with them and with everyone else. ¹⁴And in their prayers for you their hearts will go out to you, because of the surpassing grace God has given you. ¹⁵Thanks be to God for his indescribable gift!

Paul's Defence of His Ministry

10 By the meekness and gentleness of Christ, I appeal to you—I, Paul, who am "timid" when face to face with you, but "bold" when away! ²I beg you that when I come I may not have to be as bold as I expect to be towards some people who think that we live by the standards of this world. ³For though we live in the world, we do not wage war as the world does. ⁴The weapons we fight with are not the weapons of the world. On the contrary, they have divine power to demolish strongholds. ⁵We demolish arguments and every pretension that sets itself up against the knowledge of God, and we take captive every thought to make it obedient to Christ. ⁶And we will be ready to punish every act of disobedience, once your obedience is complete.

⁷You are looking only on the surface of things.ᵃ If anyone is confident that he belongs to Christ, he should consider again that we belong to Christ just as much as he. ⁸For even if I boast somewhat freely about the authority the Lord gave us for building you up rather than pulling you down, I will not be ashamed of it. ⁹I do not want to seem to be trying to frighten you with my letters. ¹⁰For some say, "His letters are weighty and forceful, but in person he is unimpressive and his speaking amounts to nothing." ¹¹Such people should realise that what we are in our letters when we are absent, we will be in our actions when we are present.

¹²We do not dare to classify or compare ourselves with some who commend themselves. When they measure themselves by themselves and compare themselves with themselves, they are not wise. ¹³We, however, will not boast beyond proper limits, but will confine our boasting to the field God has assigned to us, a field that reaches even to you. ¹⁴We are not going too far in our boasting, as would be the case if we had not come to you, for we did get as far as you with the gospel of Christ. ¹⁵Neither do we go beyond our limits by boasting of work done by others.ᵇ Our hope is that, as your faith continues to grow, our area of activity among you will greatly expand, ¹⁶so that we can preach the gospel in the regions beyond you. For we do not want to boast about work already done in another man's territory. ¹⁷But, "Let him who boasts boast in the Lord."ᶜ ¹⁸For it is not the one who commends himself who is approved, but the one whom the Lord commends.

Paul and the False Apostles

11 I hope you will put up with a little of my foolishness; but you are already doing that. ²I am jealous for you with a godly jealousy. I promised you to one husband, to Christ, so that I might present you as a pure virgin to him. ³But I am afraid that just as Eve was deceived by the serpent's cunning, your minds may somehow be led astray from your sincere and pure devotion to Christ. ⁴For if someone comes to you and preaches a Jesus

---

ᵃ7 Or *Look at the obvious facts*
ᵇ13–15 Or ¹³*We, however, will not boast about things that cannot be measured, but we will boast according to the standard of measurement that the God of measure has assigned us—a measurement that relates even to you.* ¹⁴. . . ¹⁵*Neither do we boast about things that cannot be measured in regard to the work done by others.*   ᶜ17 Jer. 9:24

other than the Jesus we preached, or if you receive a different spirit from the one you received, or a different gospel from the one you accepted, you put up with it easily enough. [5]But I do not think I am in the least inferior to those "super-apostles". [6]I may not be a trained speaker, but I do have knowledge. We have made this perfectly clear to you in every way.

[7]Was it a sin for me to lower myself in order to elevate you by preaching the gospel of God to you free of charge? [8]I robbed other churches by receiving support from them so as to serve you. [9]And when I was with you and needed something, I was not a burden to anyone, for the brothers who came from Macedonia supplied what I needed. I have kept myself from being a burden to you in any way, and will continue to do so. [10]As surely as the truth of Christ is in me, nobody in the regions of Achaia will stop this boasting of mine. [11]Why? Because I do not love you? God knows I do! [12]And I will keep on doing what I am doing in order to cut the ground from under those who want an opportunity to be considered equal with us in the things they boast about.

[13]For such men are false apostles, deceitful workmen, masquerading as apostles of Christ. [14]And no wonder, for Satan himself masquerades as an angel of light. [15]It is not surprising, then, if his servants masquerade as servants of righteousness. Their end will be what their actions deserve.

Paul Boasts About His Sufferings

[16]I repeat: Let no-one take me for a fool. But if you do, then receive me just as you would a fool, so that I may do a little boasting. [17]In this self-confident boasting I am not talking as the Lord would, but as a fool. [18]Since many are boasting in the way the world does, I too will boast. [19]You gladly put up with fools since you are so wise! [20]In fact, you even put up with anyone who enslaves you or exploits you or takes advantage of you or pushes himself forward or slaps you in the face. [21]To my shame I admit that we were too weak for that!

What anyone else dares to boast about —I am speaking as a fool—I also dare to boast about. [22]Are they Hebrews? So am I. Are they Israelites? So am I. Are they Abraham's descendants? So am I. [23]Are they servants of Christ? (I am out of my mind to talk like this.) I am more. I have worked much harder, been in prison more frequently, been flogged more severely, and been exposed to death again and again. [24]Five times I received from the Jews the forty lashes minus one. [25]Three times I was beaten with rods, once I was stoned, three times I was shipwrecked, I spent a night and a day in the open sea, [26]I have been constantly on the move. I have been in danger from rivers, in danger from bandits, in danger from my own countrymen, in danger from Gentiles; in danger in the city, in danger in the country, in danger at sea; and in danger from false brothers. [27]I have laboured and toiled and have often gone without sleep; I have known hunger and thirst and have often gone without food; I have been cold and naked. [28]Besides everything else, I face daily the pressure of my concern for all the churches. [29]Who is weak, and I do not feel weak? Who is led into sin, and I do not inwardly burn?

[30]If I must boast, I will boast of the things that show my weakness. [31]The God and Father of the Lord Jesus, who is to be praised for ever, knows that I am not lying. [32]In Damascus the governor under King Aretas had the city of the Damascenes guarded in order to arrest me. [33]But I was lowered in a basket from a window in the wall and slipped through his hands.

Paul's Vision and His Thorn

12 I must go on boasting. Although there is nothing to be gained, I will go on to visions and revelations from the Lord. [2]I know a man in Christ who fourteen years ago was caught up to the third heaven. Whether it was in the body or out of the body I do not know—God knows. [3]And I know that this man—whether in

the body or apart from the body I do not know, but God knows—⁴was caught up to paradise. He heard inexpressible things, things that man is not permitted to tell. ⁵I will boast about a man like that, but I will not boast about myself, except about my weaknesses. ⁶Even if I should choose to boast, I would not be a fool, because I would be speaking the truth. But I refrain, so no-one will think more of me than is warranted by what I do or say.

⁷To keep me from becoming conceited because of these surpassingly great revelations, there was given me a thorn in my flesh, a messenger of Satan, to torment me. ⁸Three times I pleaded with the Lord to take it away from me. ⁹But he said to me, "My grace is sufficient for you, for my power is made perfect in weakness." Therefore I will boast all the more gladly about my weaknesses, so that Christ's power may rest on me. ¹⁰That is why, for Christ's sake, I delight in weaknesses, in insults, in hardships, in persecutions, in difficulties. For when I am weak, then I am strong.

Paul's Concern for the Corinthians

¹¹I have made a fool of myself, but you drove me to it. I ought to have been commended by you, for I am not in the least inferior to the "super-apostles", even though I am nothing. ¹²The things that mark an apostle—signs, wonders and miracles—were done among you with great perseverance. ¹³How were you inferior to the other churches, except that I was never a burden to you? Forgive me this wrong!

¹⁴Now I am ready to visit you for the third time, and I will not be a burden to you, because what I want is not your possessions but you. After all, children should not have to save up for their parents, but parents for their children. ¹⁵So I will very gladly spend for you everything I have and expend myself as well. If I love you more, will you love me less? ¹⁶Be that as it may, I have not been a burden to you.

Yet, crafty fellow that I am, I caught you by trickery! ¹⁷Did I exploit you through any of the men I sent you? ¹⁸I urged Titus to go to you and I sent our brother with him. Titus did not exploit you, did he? Did we not act in the same spirit and follow the same course?

¹⁹Have you been thinking all along that we have been defending ourselves to you? We have been speaking in the sight of God as those in Christ; and everything we do, dear friends, is for your strengthening. ²⁰For I am afraid that when I come I may not find you as I want you to be, and you may not find me as you want me to be. I fear that there may be quarrelling, jealousy, outbursts of anger, factions, slander, gossip, arrogance and disorder. ²¹I am afraid that when I come again my God will humble me before you, and I will be grieved over many who have sinned earlier and have not repented of the impurity, sexual sin and debauchery in which they have indulged.

Final Warnings

13 This will be my third visit to you. "Every matter must be established by the testimony of two or three witnesses."*ᵃ* ²I already gave you a warning when I was with you the second time. I now repeat it while absent: On my return I will not spare those who sinned earlier or any of the others, ³since you are demanding proof that Christ is speaking through me. He is not weak in dealing with you, but is powerful among you. ⁴For to be sure, he was crucified in weakness, yet he lives by God's power. Likewise, we are weak in him, yet by God's power we will live with him to serve you.

⁵Examine yourselves to see whether you are in the faith; test yourselves. Do you not realise that Christ Jesus is in you— unless, of course, you fail the test? ⁶And I trust that you will discover that we have not failed the test. ⁷Now we pray to God that you will not do anything wrong. Not that people will see that we have stood the

ᵃ1 Deut. 19:15

test but that you will do what is right even though we may seem to have failed. [8]For we cannot do anything against the truth, but only for the truth. [9]We are glad whenever we are weak but you are strong; and our prayer is for your perfection. [10]This is why I write these things when I am absent, that when I come I may not have to be harsh in my use of authority—the authority the Lord gave me for building you up, not for tearing you down.

Final Greetings

[11]Finally, brothers, good-bye. Aim for perfection, listen to my appeal, be of one mind, live in peace. And the God of love and peace will be with you.

[12]Greet one another with a holy kiss. [13]All the saints send their greetings.

[14]May the grace of the Lord Jesus Christ, and the love of God, and the fellowship of the Holy Spirit be with you all.

Galatians

1

¹ Paul, an apostle—sent not from men nor by man, but by Jesus Christ and God the Father, who raised him from the dead—²and all the brothers with me,

To the churches in Galatia:

³Grace and peace to you from God our Father and the Lord Jesus Christ, ⁴who gave himself for our sins to rescue us from the present evil age, according to the will of our God and Father, ⁵to whom be glory for ever and ever. Amen.

No Other Gospel

⁶I am astonished that you are so quickly deserting the one who called you by the grace of Christ and are turning to a different gospel—⁷which is really no gospel at all. Evidently some people are throwing you into confusion and are trying to pervert the gospel of Christ. ⁸But even if we or an angel from heaven should preach a gospel other than the one we preached to you, let him be eternally condemned! ⁹As we have already said, so now I say again: If anybody is preaching to you a gospel other than what you accepted, let him be eternally condemned!

¹⁰Am I now trying to win the approval of men, or of God? Or am I trying to please men? If I were still trying to please men, I would not be a servant of Christ.

Paul Called by God

¹¹I want you to know, brothers, that the gospel I preached is not something that man made up. ¹²I did not receive it from any man, nor was I taught it; rather, I received it by revelation from Jesus Christ.

¹³For you have heard of my previous way of life in Judaism, how intensely I persecuted the church of God and tried to destroy it. ¹⁴I was advancing in Judaism beyond many Jews of my own age and was extremely zealous for the traditions of my fathers. ¹⁵But when God, who set me apart from birth*a* and called me by his grace, was pleased ¹⁶to reveal his Son in me so that I might preach him among the Gentiles, I did not consult any man, ¹⁷nor did I go up to Jerusalem to see those who were apostles before I was, but I went immediately into Arabia and later returned to Damascus.

¹⁸Then after three years, I went up to Jerusalem to get acquainted with Peter*b* and stayed with him fifteen days. ¹⁹I saw none of the other apostles—only James, the Lord's brother. ²⁰I assure you before God that what I am writing to you is no lie. ²¹Later I went to Syria and Cilicia. ²²I was personally unknown to the churches of Judea that are in Christ. ²³They only heard the report: "The man who formerly persecuted us is now preaching the faith he once tried to destroy." ²⁴And they praised God because of me.

Paul Accepted by the Apostles

2

Fourteen years later I went up again to Jerusalem, this time with Barnabas. I took Titus along also. ²I went in

a15 Or from my mother's womb   *b18 Greek Cephas*

response to a revelation and set before them the gospel that I preach among the Gentiles. But I did this privately to those who seemed to be leaders, for fear that I was running or had run my race in vain. ³Yet not even Titus, who was with me, was compelled to be circumcised, even though he was a Greek. ⁴ˌThis matter aroseˌ because some false brothers had infiltrated our ranks to spy on the freedom we have in Christ Jesus and to make us slaves. ⁵We did not give in to them for a moment, so that the truth of the gospel might remain with you.

⁶As for those who seemed to be important—whatever they were makes no difference to me; God does not judge by external appearance—those men added nothing to my message. ⁷On the contrary, they saw that I had been entrusted with the task of preaching the gospel to the Gentiles,ᵃ just as Peter had been to the Jews.ᵇ ⁸For God, who was at work in the ministry of Peter as an apostle to the Jews, was also at work in my ministry as an apostle to the Gentiles. ⁹James, Peterᶜ and John, those reputed to be pillars, gave me and Barnabas the right hand of fellowship when they recognised the grace given to me. They agreed that we should go to the Gentiles, and they to the Jews. ¹⁰All they asked was that we should continue to remember the poor, the very thing I was eager to do.

Paul Opposes Peter

¹¹When Peter came to Antioch, I opposed him to his face, because he was clearly in the wrong. ¹²Before certain men came from James, he used to eat with the Gentiles. But when they arrived, he began to draw back and separate himself from the Gentiles because he was afraid of those who belonged to the circumcision group. ¹³The other Jews joined him in his hypocrisy, so that by their hypocrisy even Barnabas was led astray.

¹⁴When I saw that they were not acting in line with the truth of the gospel, I said to Peter in front of them all, "You are a Jew,

yet you live like a Gentile and not like a Jew. How is it, then, that you force Gentiles to follow Jewish customs?

¹⁵"We who are Jews by birth and not 'Gentile sinners' ¹⁶know that a man is not justified by observing the law, but by faith in Jesus Christ. So we, too, have put our faith in Christ Jesus that we may be justified by faith in Christ and not by observing the law, because by observing the law no-one will be justified.

¹⁷"If, while we seek to be justified in Christ, it becomes evident that we ourselves are sinners, does that mean that Christ promotes sin? Absolutely not! ¹⁸If I rebuild what I destroyed, I prove that I am a law-breaker. ¹⁹For through the law I died to the law so that I might live for God. ²⁰I have been crucified with Christ and I no longer live, but Christ lives in me. The life I live in the body, I live by faith in the Son of God, who loved me and gave himself for me. ²¹I do not set aside the grace of God, for if righteousness could be gained through the law, Christ died for nothing!"ᵈ

Faith or Observance of the Law

3 You foolish Galatians! Who has bewitched you? Before your very eyes Jesus Christ was clearly portrayed as crucified. ²I would like to learn just one thing from you: Did you receive the Spirit by observing the law, or by believing what you heard? ³Are you so foolish? After beginning with the Spirit, are you now trying to attain your goal by human effort? ⁴Have you suffered so much for nothing— if it really was for nothing? ⁵Does God give you his Spirit and work miracles among you because you observe the law, or because you believe what you heard?

⁶Consider Abraham: "He believed God, and it was credited to him as righteousness."ᵃ ⁷Understand, then, that those who believe are children of Abraham. ⁸The Scripture foresaw that God would justify the Gentiles by faith, and announced the gospel in advance to Abraham: "All nations will be blessed

---

ᵃ7 Greek *uncircumcised*   ᵇ7 Greek *circumcised*; also in verses 8 and 9
ᶜ9 Greek *Cephas*; also in verses 11 and 14   ᵈ21 Some interpreters end the quotation after verse 14.   ᵃ6 Gen. 15:6

through you."*b* 9So those who have faith are blessed along with Abraham, the man of faith.

10All who rely on observing the law are under a curse, for it is written: "Cursed is everyone who does not continue to do everything written in the Book of the Law."*c* 11Clearly no-one is justified before God by the law, because, "The righteous will live by faith."*d* 12The law is not based on faith; on the contrary, "The man who does these things will live by them."*e* 13Christ redeemed us from the curse of the law by becoming a curse for us, for it is written: "Cursed is everyone who is hung on a tree."*f* 14He redeemed us in order that the blessing given to Abraham might come to the Gentiles through Christ Jesus, so that by faith we might receive the promise of the Spirit.

The Law and the Promise

15Brothers, let me take an example from everyday life. Just as no-one can set aside or add to a human covenant that has been duly established, so it is in this case. 16The promises were spoken to Abraham and to his seed. The Scripture does not say "and to seeds", meaning many people, but "and to your seed",*g* meaning one person, who is Christ. 17What I mean is this: The law, introduced 430 years later, does not set aside the covenant previously established by God and thus do away with the promise. 18For if the inheritance depends on the law, then it no longer depends on a promise; but God in his grace gave it to Abraham through a promise.

19What, then, was the purpose of the law? It was added because of transgressions until the Seed to whom the promise referred had come. The law was put into effect through angels by a mediator. 20A mediator, however, does not represent just one party; but God is one.

21Is the law, therefore, opposed to the promises of God? Absolutely not! For if a law had been given that could impart life, then righteousness would certainly have come by the law. 22But the Scripture

declares that the whole world is a prisoner of sin, so that what was promised, being given through faith in Jesus Christ, might be given to those who believe.

23Before this faith came, we were held prisoners by the law, locked up until faith should be revealed. 24So the law was put in charge to lead us to Christ*h* that we might be justified by faith. 25Now that faith has come, we are no longer under the supervision of the law.

Sons of God

26You are all sons of God through faith in Christ Jesus, 27for all of you who were baptised into Christ have clothed yourselves with Christ. 28There is neither Jew nor Greek, slave nor free, male nor female, for you are all one in Christ Jesus. 29If you belong to Christ, then you are Abraham's seed, and heirs according to the promise.

4 What I am saying is that as long as the heir is a child, he is no different from a slave, although he owns the whole estate. 2He is subject to guardians and trustees until the time set by his father. 3So also, when we were children, we were in slavery under the basic principles of the world. 4But when the time had fully come, God sent his Son, born of a woman, born under law, 5to redeem those under law, that we might receive the full rights of sons. 6Because you are sons, God sent the Spirit of his Son into our hearts, the Spirit who calls out, "*Abba*,*a* Father." 7So you are no longer a slave, but a son; and since you are a son, God has made you also an heir.

Paul's Concern for the Galatians

8Formerly, when you did not know God, you were slaves to those who by nature are not gods. 9But now that you know God—or rather are known by God—how is it that you are turning back to those weak and miserable principles? Do you wish to be enslaved by them all over again? 10You are observing special

b8 Gen. 12:3; 18:18; 22:18   *c10* Deut. 27:26   *d11* Hab. 2:4   *e12* Lev. 18:5   *f13* Deut. 21:23
g16 Gen. 12:7; 13:15; 24:7   *h24* Or *charge until Christ came*   *a6* Aramaic for *Father*

days and months and seasons and years! [11]I fear for you, that somehow I have wasted my efforts on you.

[12]I plead with you, brothers, become like me, for I became like you. You have done me no wrong. [13]As you know, it was because of an illness that I first preached the gospel to you. [14]Even though my illness was a trial to you, you did not treat me with contempt or scorn. Instead, you welcomed me as if I were an angel of God, as if I were Christ Jesus himself. [15]What has happened to all your joy? I can testify that, if you could have done so, you would have torn out your eyes and given them to me. [16]Have I now become your enemy by telling you the truth?

[17]Those people are zealous to win you over, but for no good. What they want is to alienate you ⌊from us⌋, so that you may be zealous for them. [18]It is fine to be zealous, provided the purpose is good, and to be so always and not just when I am with you. [19]My dear children, for whom I am again in the pains of childbirth until Christ is formed in you, [20]how I wish I could be with you now and change my tone, because I am perplexed about you!

Hagar and Sarah

[21]Tell me, you who want to be under the law, are you not aware of what the law says? [22]For it is written that Abraham had two sons, one by the slave woman and the other by the free woman. [23]His son by the slave woman was born in the ordinary way; but his son by the free woman was born as the result of a promise.

[24]These things may be taken figuratively, for the women represent two covenants. One covenant is from Mount Sinai and bears children who are to be slaves: This is Hagar. [25]Now Hagar stands for Mount Sinai in Arabia and corresponds to the present city of Jerusalem, because she is in slavery with her children. [26]But the Jerusalem that is above is free, and she is our mother. [27]For it is written:

"Be glad, O barren woman,
   who bears no children;
break forth and cry aloud,
   you who have no labour pains;
because more are the children of the
     desolate woman
   than of her who has a husband."[b]

[28]Now you, brothers, like Isaac, are children of promise. [29]At that time the son born in the ordinary way persecuted the son born by the power of the Spirit. It is the same now. [30]But what does the Scripture say? "Get rid of the slave woman and her son, for the slave woman's son will never share in the inheritance with the free woman's son."[c] [31]Therefore, brothers, we are not children of the slave woman, but of the free woman.

Freedom in Christ

5 It is for freedom that Christ has set us free. Stand firm, then, and do not let yourselves be burdened again by a yoke of slavery.

[2]Mark my words! I, Paul, tell you that if you let yourselves be circumcised, Christ will be of no value to you at all. [3]Again I declare to every man who lets himself be circumcised that he is required to obey the whole law. [4]You who are trying to be justified by law have been alienated from Christ; you have fallen away from grace. [5]But by faith we eagerly await through the Spirit the righteousness for which we hope. [6]For in Christ Jesus neither circumcision nor uncircumcision has any value. The only thing that counts is faith expressing itself through love.

[7]You were running a good race. Who cut in on you and kept you from obeying the truth? [8]That kind of persuasion does not come from the one who calls you. [9]"A little yeast works through the whole batch of dough." [10]I am confident in the Lord that you will take no other view. The one who is throwing you into confusion will pay the penalty, whoever he may be. [11]Brothers, if I am still preaching

circumcision, why am I still being persecuted? In that case the offence of the cross has been abolished. [12]As for those agitators, I wish they would go the whole way and emasculate themselves!

[13]You, my brothers, were called to be free. But do not use your freedom to indulge the sinful nature;[a] rather, serve one another in love. [14]The entire law is summed up in a single command: "Love your neighbour as yourself."[b] [15]If you keep on biting and devouring each other, watch out or you will be destroyed by each other.

Life by the Spirit

[16]So I say, live by the Spirit, and you will not gratify the desires of the sinful nature. [17]For the sinful nature desires what is contrary to the Spirit, and the Spirit what is contrary to the sinful nature. They are in conflict with each other, so that you do not do what you want. [18]But if you are led by the Spirit, you are not under law.

[19]The acts of the sinful nature are obvious: sexual immorality, impurity and debauchery; [20]idolatry and witchcraft; hatred, discord, jealousy, fits of rage, selfish ambition, dissensions, factions [21]and envy; drunkenness, orgies, and the like. I warn you, as I did before, that those who live like this will not inherit the kingdom of God.

[22]But the fruit of the Spirit is love, joy, peace, patience, kindness, goodness, faithfulness, [23]gentleness and self-control. Against such things there is no law. [24]Those who belong to Christ Jesus have crucified the sinful nature with its passions and desires. [25]Since we live by the Spirit, let us keep in step with the Spirit. [26]Let us not become conceited, provoking and envying each other.

Doing Good to All

6 Brothers, if someone is caught in a sin, you who are spiritual should restore him gently. But watch yourself, or you also may be tempted. [2]Carry each other's burdens, and in this way you will fulfil the law of Christ. [3]If anyone thinks he is something when he is nothing, he deceives himself. [4]Each one should test his own actions. Then he can take pride in himself, without comparing himself to somebody else, [5]for each one should carry his own load.

[6]Anyone who receives instruction in the word must share all good things with his instructor.

[7]Do not be deceived: God cannot be mocked. A man reaps what he sows. [8]The one who sows to please his sinful nature, from that nature[a] will reap destruction; the one who sows to please the Spirit, from the Spirit will reap eternal life. [9]Let us not become weary in doing good, for at the proper time we will reap a harvest if we do not give up. [10]Therefore, as we have opportunity, let us do good to all people, especially to those who belong to the family of believers.

Not Circumcision but a New Creation

[11]See what large letters I use as I write to you with my own hand!

[12]Those who want to make a good impression outwardly are trying to compel you to be circumcised. The only reason they do this is to avoid being persecuted for the cross of Christ. [13]Not even those who are circumcised obey the law, yet they want you to be circumcised that they may boast about your flesh. [14]May I never boast except in the cross of our Lord Jesus Christ, through which[b] the world has been crucified to me, and I to the world. [15]Neither circumcision nor uncircumcision means anything; what counts is a new creation. [16]Peace and mercy to all who follow this rule, even to the Israel of God.

[17]Finally, let no-one cause me trouble, for I bear on my body the marks of Jesus.

[18]The grace of our Lord Jesus Christ be with your spirit, brothers. Amen.

---

[a]13 Or *the flesh*; also in verses 16, 17, 19 and 24   [b]14 Lev. 19:18   [a]8 Or *his flesh, from the flesh*
[b]14 Or *whom*

Ephesians

1 Paul, an apostle of Christ Jesus by the will of God,

To the saints in Ephesus,*a* the faithful*b* in Christ Jesus:

²Grace and peace to you from God our Father and the Lord Jesus Christ.

Spiritual Blessings in Christ

³Praise be to the God and Father of our Lord Jesus Christ, who has blessed us in the heavenly realms with every spiritual blessing in Christ. ⁴For he chose us in him before the creation of the world to be holy and blameless in his sight. In love ⁵he*c* predestined us to be adopted as his sons through Jesus Christ, in accordance with his pleasure and will—⁶to the praise of his glorious grace, which he has freely given us in the One he loves. ⁷In him we have redemption through his blood, the forgiveness of sins, in accordance with the riches of God's grace ⁸that he lavished on us with all wisdom and understanding. ⁹And he*d* made known to us the mystery of his will according to his good pleasure, which he purposed in Christ, ¹⁰to be put into effect when the times will have reached their fulfilment—to bring all things in heaven and on earth together under one head, even Christ.

¹¹In him we were also chosen,*e* having been predestined according to the plan of him who works out everything in conformity with the purpose of his will, ¹²in order that we, who were the first to hope in Christ, might be for the praise of his glory. ¹³And you also were included in Christ when you heard the word of truth, the gospel of your salvation. Having believed, you were marked in him with a seal, the promised Holy Spirit, ¹⁴who is a deposit guaranteeing our inheritance until the redemption of those who are God's possession—to the praise of his glory.

Thanksgiving and Prayer

¹⁵For this reason, ever since I heard about your faith in the Lord Jesus and your love for all the saints, ¹⁶I have not stopped giving thanks for you, remembering you in my prayers. ¹⁷I keep asking that the God of our Lord Jesus Christ, the glorious Father, may give you the Spirit*f* of wisdom and revelation, so that you may know him better. ¹⁸I pray also that the eyes of your heart may be enlightened in order that you may know the hope to which he has called you, the riches of his glorious inheritance in the saints, ¹⁹and his incomparably great power for us who believe. That power is like the working of his mighty strength, ²⁰which he exerted in Christ when he raised him from the dead and seated him at his right hand in the heavenly realms, ²¹far above all rule and authority, power and dominion, and every title that can be given, not only in the present age but also in the one to come. ²²And God placed all things under his feet

---

a1 Some early manuscripts do not have *in Ephesus.*
b1 Or *believers who are*
c4, 5 Or *sight in love.* ⁵*He*
d8, 9 Or *us. With all wisdom and understanding,* ⁹*he*
e11 Or *were made heirs*
f17 Or *a spirit*

and appointed him to be head over everything for the church, [23]which is his body, the fulness of him who fills everything in every way.

Made Alive in Christ

2 As for you, you were dead in your transgressions and sins, [2]in which you used to live when you followed the ways of this world and of the ruler of the kingdom of the air, the spirit who is now at work in those who are disobedient. [3]All of us also lived among them at one time, gratifying the cravings of our sinful nature*a* and following its desires and thoughts. Like the rest, we were by nature objects of wrath. [4]But because of his great love for us, God, who is rich in mercy, [5]made us alive with Christ even when we were dead in transgressions—it is by grace you have been saved. [6]And God raised us up with Christ and seated us with him in the heavenly realms in Christ Jesus, [7]in order that in the coming ages he might show the incomparable riches of his grace, expressed in his kindness to us in Christ Jesus. [8]For it is by grace you have been saved, through faith—and this not from yourselves, it is the gift of God—[9]not by works, so that no-one can boast. [10]For we are God's workmanship, created in Christ Jesus to do good works, which God prepared in advance for us to do.

One in Christ

[11]Therefore, remember that formerly you who are Gentiles by birth and called "uncircumcised" by those who call themselves "the circumcision" (that done in the body by the hands of men)—[12]remember that at that time you were separate from Christ, excluded from citizenship in Israel and foreigners to the covenants of the promise, without hope and without God in the world. [13]But now in Christ Jesus you who once were far away have been brought near through the blood of Christ. [14]For he himself is our peace, who has made the two one and has destroyed the barrier, the dividing wall of hostility, [15]by abolishing in his flesh the law with its commandments and regulations. His purpose was to create in himself one new man out of the two, thus making peace, [16]and in this one body to reconcile both of them to God through the cross, by which he put to death their hostility. [17]He came and preached peace to you who were far away and peace to those who were near. [18]For through him we both have access to the Father by one Spirit.

[19]Consequently, you are no longer foreigners and aliens, but fellow-citizens with God's people and members of God's household, [20]built on the foundation of the apostles and prophets, with Christ Jesus himself as the chief cornerstone. [21]In him the whole building is joined together and rises to become a holy temple in the Lord. [22]And in him you too are being built together to become a dwelling in which God lives by his Spirit.

Paul the Preacher to the Gentiles

3 For this reason I, Paul, the prisoner of Christ Jesus for the sake of you Gentiles—

[2]Surely you have heard about the administration of God's grace that was given to me for you, [3]that is, the mystery made known to me by revelation, as I have already written briefly. [4]In reading this, then, you will be able to understand my insight into the mystery of Christ, [5]which was not made known to men in other generations as it has now been revealed by the Spirit to God's holy apostles and prophets. [6]This mystery is that through the gospel the Gentiles are heirs together with Israel, members together of one body, and sharers together in the promise in Christ Jesus.

[7]I became a servant of this gospel by the gift of God's grace given me through the working of his power. [8]Although I am less than the least of all God's people, this grace was given me: to preach to the Gentiles the unsearchable riches of Christ, [9]and to make plain to everyone the

a3 Or our flesh

administration of this mystery, which for ages past was kept hidden in God, who created all things. [10]His intent was that now, through the church, the manifold wisdom of God should be made known to the rulers and authorities in the heavenly realms, [11]according to his eternal purpose which he accomplished in Christ Jesus our Lord. [12]In him and through faith in him we may approach God with freedom and confidence. [13]I ask you, therefore, not to be discouraged because of my sufferings for you, which are your glory.

A Prayer for the Ephesians

[14]For this reason I kneel before the Father, [15]from whom his whole family[a] in heaven and on earth derives its name. [16]I pray that out of his glorious riches he may strengthen you with power through his Spirit in your inner being, [17]so that Christ may dwell in your hearts through faith. And I pray that you, being rooted and established in love, [18]may have power, together with all the saints, to grasp how wide and long and high and deep is the love of Christ, [19]and to know this love that surpasses knowledge—that you may be filled to the measure of all the fulness of God.

[20]Now to him who is able to do immeasurably more than all we ask or imagine, according to his power that is at work within us, [21]to him be glory in the church and in Christ Jesus throughout all generations, for ever and ever! Amen.

Unity in the Body of Christ

4 As a prisoner for the Lord, then, I urge you to live a life worthy of the calling you have received. [2]Be completely humble and gentle; be patient, bearing with one another in love. [3]Make every effort to keep the unity of the Spirit through the bond of peace. [4]There is one body and one Spirit—just as you were called to one hope when you were called— [5]one Lord, one faith, one baptism; [6]one

God and Father of all, who is over all and through all and in all.

[7]But to each one of us grace has been given as Christ apportioned it. [8]This is why it[a] says:

"When he ascended on high,
 he led captives in his train
 and gave gifts to men."[b]

[9](What does "he ascended" mean except that he also descended to the lower, earthly regions?[c] [10]He who descended is the very one who ascended higher than all the heavens, in order to fill the whole universe.) [11]It was he who gave some to be apostles, some to be prophets, some to be evangelists, and some to be pastors and teachers, [12]to prepare God's people for works of service, so that the body of Christ may be built up [13]until we all reach unity in the faith and in the knowledge of the Son of God and become mature, attaining to the whole measure of the fulness of Christ.

[14]Then we will no longer be infants, tossed back and forth by the waves, and blown here and there by every wind of teaching and by the cunning and craftiness of men in their deceitful scheming. [15]Instead, speaking the truth in love, we will in all things grow up into him who is the Head, that is, Christ. [16]From him the whole body, joined and held together by every supporting ligament, grows and builds itself up in love, as each part does its work.

Living as Children of Light

[17]So I tell you this, and insist on it in the Lord, that you must no longer live as the Gentiles do, in the futility of their thinking. [18]They are darkened in their understanding and separated from the life of God because of the ignorance that is in them due to the hardening of their hearts. [19]Having lost all sensitivity, they have given themselves over to sensuality so as to indulge in every kind of impurity, with a continual lust for more.

---

[a]15 Or whom all fatherhood   [a]8 Or God   [b]8 Psalm 68:18   [c]9 Or the depths of the earth

20You, however, did not come to know Christ that way. 21Surely you heard of him and were taught in him in accordance with the truth that is in Jesus. 22You were taught, with regard to your former way of life, to put off your old self, which is being corrupted by its deceitful desires; 23to be made new in the attitude of your minds; 24and to put on the new self, created to be like God in true righteousness and holiness.

25Therefore each of you must put off falsehood and speak truthfully to his neighbour, for we are all members of one body. 26"In your anger do not sin"d: Do not let the sun go down while you are still angry, 27and do not give the devil a foothold. 28He who has been stealing must steal no longer, but must work, doing something useful with his own hands, that he may have something to share with those in need.

29Do not let any unwholesome talk come out of your mouths, but only what is helpful for building others up according to their needs, that it may benefit those who listen. 30And do not grieve the Holy Spirit of God, with whom you were sealed for the day of redemption. 31Get rid of all bitterness, rage and anger, brawling and slander, along with every form of malice. 32Be kind and compassionate to one another, forgiving each other, just as in Christ God forgave you.

5 Be imitators of God, therefore, as dearly loved children 2and live a life of love, just as Christ loved us and gave himself up for us as a fragrant offering and sacrifice to God.

3But among you there must not be even a hint of sexual immorality, or of any kind of impurity, or of greed, because these are improper for God's holy people. 4Nor should there be obscenity, foolish talk or coarse joking, which are out of place, but rather thanksgiving. 5For of this you can be sure: No immoral, impure or greedy person—such a man is an idolater—has any inheritance in the kingdom of Christ and of God.a 6Let no-one deceive you with empty words, for because of such things

God's wrath comes on those who are disobedient. 7Therefore do not be partners with them.

8For you were once darkness, but now you are light in the Lord. Live as children of light 9(for the fruit of the light consists in all goodness, righteousness and truth) 10and find out what pleases the Lord. 11Have nothing to do with the fruitless deeds of darkness, but rather expose them. 12For it is shameful even to mention what the disobedient do in secret. 13But everything exposed by the light becomes visible, 14for it is light that makes everything visible. This is why it is said:

"Wake up, O sleeper,
    rise from the dead,
    and Christ will shine on you."

15Be very careful, then, how you live— not as unwise but as wise, 16making the most of every opportunity, because the days are evil. 17Therefore do not be foolish, but understand what the Lord's will is. 18Do not get drunk on wine, which leads to debauchery. Instead, be filled with the Spirit. 19Speak to one another with psalms, hymns and spiritual songs. Sing and make music in your heart to the Lord, 20always giving thanks to God the Father for everything, in the name of our Lord Jesus Christ.

21Submit to one another out of reverence for Christ.

Wives and Husbands

22Wives, submit to your husbands as to the Lord. 23For the husband is the head of the wife as Christ is the head of the church, his body, of which he is the Saviour. 24Now as the church submits to Christ, so also wives should submit to their husbands in everything.

25Husbands, love your wives, just as Christ loved the church and gave himself up for her 26to make her holy, cleansingb her by the washing with water through the word, 27and to present her to himself as a radiant church, without stain or wrinkle or

---

d26 Psalm 4:4   a5 Or kingdom of the Christ and God   b26 Or having cleansed any other blemish, but holy and blameless. 28In this same way, husbands ought to love their wives as their own bodies. He who loves his wife loves himself. 29After all, no-one ever hated his own body, but he feeds and cares for it, just as Christ does the church—30for we are members of his body. 31"For this reason a man will leave his father and mother and be united to his wife, and the two will become one flesh."*c* 32This is a profound mystery—but I am talking about Christ and the church. 33However, each one of you also must love his wife as he loves himself, and the wife must respect her husband.

Children and Parents

6 Children, obey your parents in the Lord, for this is right. 2"Honour your father and mother"—which is the first commandment with a promise—3 "that it may go well with you and that you may enjoy long life on the earth."*a*

4Fathers, do not exasperate your children; instead, bring them up in the training and instruction of the Lord.

Slaves and Masters

5Slaves, obey your earthly masters with respect and fear, and with sincerity of heart, just as you would obey Christ. 6Obey them not only to win their favour when their eye is on you, but like slaves of Christ, doing the will of God from your heart. 7Serve wholeheartedly, as if you were serving the Lord, not men, 8because you know that the Lord will reward everyone for whatever good he does, whether he is slave or free.

9And masters, treat your slaves in the same way. Do not threaten them, since you know that he who is both their Master and yours is in heaven, and there is no favouritism with him.

The Armour of God

10Finally, be strong in the Lord and in his mighty power. 11Put on the full armour of God so that you can take your stand against the devil's schemes. 12For our struggle is not against flesh and blood, but against the rulers, against the authorities, against the powers of this dark world and against the spiritual forces of evil in the heavenly realms. 13Therefore put on the full armour of God, so that when the day of evil comes, you may be able to stand your ground, and after you have done everything, to stand. 14Stand firm then, with the belt of truth buckled round your waist, with the breastplate of righteousness in place, 15and with your feet fitted with the readiness that comes from the gospel of peace. 16In addition to all this, take up the shield of faith, with which you can extinguish all the flaming arrows of the evil one. 17Take the helmet of salvation and the sword of the Spirit, which is the word of God. 18And pray in the Spirit on all occasions with all kinds of prayers and requests. With this in mind, be alert and always keep on praying for all the saints.

19Pray also for me, that whenever I open my mouth, words may be given me so that I will fearlessly make known the mystery of the gospel, 20for which I am an ambassador in chains. Pray that I may declare it fearlessly, as I should.

Final Greetings

21Tychicus, the dear brother and faithful servant in the Lord, will tell you everything, so that you also may know how I am and what I am doing. 22I am sending him to you for this very purpose, that you may know how we are, and that he may encourage you.

23Peace to the brothers, and love with faith from God the Father and the Lord Jesus Christ. 24Grace to all who love our Lord Jesus Christ with an undying love.

c31 Gen. 2:24   *a3* Deut. 5:16

Philippians

1

1 Paul and Timothy, servants of Christ Jesus,

To all the saints in Christ Jesus at Philippi, together with the overseers[a] and deacons:

2Grace and peace to you from God our Father and the Lord Jesus Christ.

Thanksgiving and Prayer

3I thank my God every time I remember you. 4In all my prayers for all of you, I always pray with joy 5because of your partnership in the gospel from the first day until now, 6being confident of this, that he who began a good work in you will carry it on to completion until the day of Christ Jesus.

7It is right for me to feel this way about all of you, since I have you in my heart; for whether I am in chains or defending and confirming the gospel, all of you share in God's grace with me. 8God can testify how I long for all of you with the affection of Christ Jesus.

9And this is my prayer: that your love may abound more and more in knowledge and depth of insight, 10so that you may be able to discern what is best and may be pure and blameless until the day of Christ, 11filled with the fruit of righteousness that comes through Jesus Christ—to the glory and praise of God.

Paul's Chains Advance the Gospel

12Now I want you to know, brothers, that what has happened to me has really served to advance the gospel. 13As a result, it has become clear throughout the whole palace guard[b] and to everyone else that I am in chains for Christ. 14Because of my chains, most of the brothers in the Lord have been encouraged to speak the word of God more courageously and fearlessly.

15It is true that some preach Christ out of envy and rivalry, but others out of goodwill. 16The latter do so in love, knowing that I am put here for the defence of the gospel. 17The former preach Christ out of selfish ambition, not sincerely, supposing that they can stir up trouble for me while I am in chains.[c] 18But what does it matter? The important thing is that in every way, whether from false motives or true, Christ is preached. And because of this I rejoice.

Yes, and I will continue to rejoice, 19for I know that through your prayers and the help given by the Spirit of Jesus Christ, what has happened to me will turn out for my deliverance.[d] 20I eagerly expect and hope that I will in no way be ashamed, but will have sufficient courage so that now as always Christ will be exalted in my body, whether by life or by death. 21For to me, to live is Christ and to die is gain. 22If I am to go on living in the body, this will mean fruitful labour for me. Yet what shall I choose? I do not know! [23]I am torn between the two: I desire to depart and be with Christ, which is better by far; [24]but it is more necessary for you that I remain in the body. [25]Convinced of this, I know that I will remain, and I will continue with all of you for your progress and joy in the faith, [26]so that through my being with you again your joy in Christ Jesus will overflow on account of me.

[27]Whatever happens, conduct yourselves in a manner worthy of the gospel of Christ. Then, whether I come and see you or only hear about you in my absence, I will know that you stand firm in one spirit, contending as one man for the faith of the gospel [28]without being frightened in any way by those who oppose you. This is a sign to them that they will be destroyed, but that you will be saved—and that by God. [29]For it has been granted to you on behalf of Christ not only to believe on him, but also to suffer for him, [30]since you are going through the same struggle you saw I had, and now hear that I still have.

Imitating Christ's Humility

2 If you have any encouragement from being united with Christ, if any comfort from his love, if any fellowship with the Spirit, if any tenderness and compassion, [2]then make my joy complete by being like-minded, having the same love, being one in spirit and purpose. [3]Do nothing out of selfish ambition or vain conceit, but in humility consider others better than yourselves. [4]Each of you should look not only to your own interests, but also to the interests of others.

[5]Your attitude should be the same as that of Christ Jesus:

[6]Who, being in very nature[a] God,
  did not consider equality with God
    something to be grasped,
[7]but made himself nothing,
  taking the very nature[b] of a servant,
  being made in human likeness.
[8]And being found in appearance as a
  man,

he humbled himself
  and became obedient to death—even
    death on a cross!
[9]Therefore God exalted him to the
  highest place
  and gave him the name that is above
    every name,
[10]that at the name of Jesus every knee
  should bow,
  in heaven and on earth and under the
    earth,
[11]and every tongue confess that Jesus
  Christ is Lord,
  to the glory of God the Father.

Shining as Stars

[12]Therefore, my dear friends, as you have always obeyed—not only in my presence, but now much more in my absence—continue to work out your salvation with fear and trembling, [13]for it is God who works in you to will and to act according to his good purpose.

[14]Do everything without complaining or arguing, [15]so that you may become blameless and pure, children of God without fault in a crooked and depraved generation, in which you shine like stars in the universe [16]as you hold out[c] the word of life—in order that I may boast on the day of Christ that I did not run or labour for nothing. [17]But even if I am being poured out like a drink offering on the sacrifice and service coming from your faith, I am glad and rejoice with all of you. [18]So you too should be glad and rejoice with me.

Timothy and Epaphroditus

[19]I hope in the Lord Jesus to send Timothy to you soon, that I also may be cheered when I receive news about you. [20]I have no-one else like him, who takes a genuine interest in your welfare. [21]For everyone looks out for his own interests, not those of Jesus Christ. [22]But you know that Timothy has proved himself, because as a son with his father he has served with me in the work of the gospel. [23]I hope, therefore, to send him as soon as I see how

---

[a]6 Or *in the form of*   [b]7 Or *the form*   [c]16 Or *hold on to*

things go with me. 24And I am confident in the Lord that I myself will come soon.

25But I think it is necessary to send back to you Epaphroditus, my brother, fellow-worker and fellow-soldier, who is also your messenger, whom you sent to take care of my needs. 26For he longs for all of you and is distressed because you heard he was ill. 27Indeed he was ill, and almost died. But God had mercy on him, and not on him only but also on me, to spare me sorrow upon sorrow. 28Therefore I am all the more eager to send him, so that when you see him again you may be glad and I may have less anxiety. 29Welcome him in the Lord with great joy, and honour men like him, 30because he almost died for the work of Christ, risking his life to make up for the help you could not give me.

No Confidence in the Flesh

3 Finally, my brothers, rejoice in the Lord! It is no trouble for me to write the same things to you again, and it is a safeguard for you.

2Watch out for those dogs, those men who do evil, those mutilators of the flesh. 3For it is we who are the circumcision, we who worship by the Spirit of God, who glory in Christ Jesus, and who put no confidence in the flesh—4though I myself have reasons for such confidence.

If anyone else thinks he has reasons to put confidence in the flesh, I have more: 5circumcised on the eighth day, of the people of Israel, of the tribe of Benjamin, a Hebrew of Hebrews; in regard to the law, a Pharisee; 6as for zeal, persecuting the church; as for legalistic righteousness, faultless.

7But whatever was to my profit I now consider loss for the sake of Christ. 8What is more, I consider everything a loss compared to the surpassing greatness of knowing Christ Jesus my Lord, for whose sake I have lost all things. I consider them rubbish, that I may gain Christ 9and be found in him, not having a righteousness of my own that comes from the law, but that which is through faith in Christ—the righteousness that comes from God and is by

faith. 10I want to know Christ and the power of his resurrection and the fellowship of sharing in his sufferings, becoming like him in his death, 11and so, somehow, to attain to the resurrection from the dead.

Pressing on Towards the Goal

12Not that I have already obtained all this, or have already been made perfect, but I press on to take hold of that for which Christ Jesus took hold of me. 13Brothers, I do not consider myself yet to have taken hold of it. But one thing I do: Forgetting what is behind and straining towards what is ahead, 14I press on towards the goal to win the prize for which God has called me heavenwards in Christ Jesus.

15All of us who are mature should take such a view of things. And if on some point you think differently, that too God will make clear to you. 16Only let us live up to what we have already attained.

17Join with others in following my example, brothers, and take note of those who live according to the pattern we gave you. 18For, as I have often told you before and now say again even with tears, many live as enemies of the cross of Christ. 19Their destiny is destruction, their god is their stomach, and their glory is in their shame. Their mind is on earthly things. 20But our citizenship is in heaven. And we eagerly await a Saviour from there, the Lord Jesus Christ, 21who, by the power that enables him to bring everything under his control, will transform our lowly bodies so that they will be like his glorious body.

4 Therefore, my brothers, you whom I love and long for, my joy and crown, that is how you should stand firm in the Lord, dear friends!

Exhortations

2I plead with Euodia and I plead with Syntyche to agree with each other in the Lord. 3Yes, and I ask you, loyal yoke-fellow,[a] help these women who have contended at my side in the cause of the

a3 Or loyal Syzygus

gospel, along with Clement and the rest of my fellow-workers, whose names are in the book of life.

[4]Rejoice in the Lord always. I will say it again: Rejoice! [5]Let your gentleness be evident to all. The Lord is near. [6]Do not be anxious about anything, but in everything, by prayer and petition, with thanksgiving, present your requests to God. [7]And the peace of God, which transcends all understanding, will guard your hearts and your minds in Christ Jesus.

[8]Finally, brothers, whatever is true, whatever is noble, whatever is right, whatever is pure, whatever is lovely, whatever is admirable—if anything is excellent or praiseworthy—think about such things. [9]Whatever you have learned or received or heard from me, or seen in me—put it into practice. And the God of peace will be with you.

Thanks for Their Gifts

[10]I rejoice greatly in the Lord that at last you have renewed your concern for me. Indeed, you have been concerned, but you had no opportunity to show it. [11]I am not saying this because I am in need, for I have learned to be content whatever the circumstances. [12]I know what it is to be in need, and I know what it is to have plenty. I have learned the secret of being content in any and every situation, whether well fed or hungry, whether living in plenty or in want. [13]I can do everything through him who gives me strength.

[14]Yet it was good of you to share in my troubles. [15]Moreover, as you Philippians know, in the early days of your acquaintance with the gospel, when I set out from Macedonia, not one church shared with me in the matter of giving and receiving, except you only; [16]for even when I was in Thessalonica, you sent me aid again and again when I was in need. [17]Not that I am looking for a gift, but I am looking for what may be credited to your account. [18]I have received full payment and even more; I am amply supplied, now that I have received from Epaphroditus the gifts you sent. They are a fragrant offering, an acceptable sacrifice, pleasing to God. [19]And my God will meet all your needs according to his glorious riches in Christ Jesus.

[20]To our God and Father be glory for ever and ever. Amen.

Final Greetings

[21]Greet all the saints in Christ Jesus. The brothers who are with me send greetings. [22]All the saints send you greetings, especially those who belong to Caesar's household.

[23]The grace of the Lord Jesus Christ be with your spirit. Amen.*b*

---

b23 Some manuscripts do not have *Amen.*

Colossians

1

¹ Paul, an apostle of Christ Jesus by the will of God, and Timothy our brother,

² To the holy and faithful*a* brothers in Christ at Colosse:

Grace and peace to you from God our Father.*b*

Thanksgiving and Prayer

³ We always thank God, the Father of our Lord Jesus Christ, when we pray for you, ⁴ because we have heard of your faith in Christ Jesus and of the love you have for all the saints—⁵ the faith and love that spring from the hope that is stored up for you in heaven and that you have already heard about in the word of truth, the gospel ⁶ that has come to you. All over the world this gospel is bearing fruit and growing, just as it has been doing among you since the day you heard it and understood God's grace in all its truth. ⁷ You learned it from Epaphras, our dear fellow-servant, who is a faithful minister of Christ on our*c* behalf, ⁸ and who also told us of your love in the Spirit.

⁹ For this reason, since the day we heard about you, we have not stopped praying for you and asking God to fill you with the knowledge of his will through all spiritual wisdom and understanding. ¹⁰ And we pray this in order that you may live a life worthy of the Lord and may please him in every way: bearing fruit in every good work, growing in the knowledge of God, ¹¹ being strengthened with all power according to his glorious might so that you may have great endurance and patience, and joyfully ¹² giving thanks to the Father, who has qualified you*d* to share in the inheritance of the saints in the kingdom of light. ¹³ For he has rescued us from the dominion of darkness and brought us into the kingdom of the Son he loves, ¹⁴ in whom we have redemption,*e* the forgiveness of sins.

The Supremacy of Christ

¹⁵ He is the image of the invisible God, the firstborn over all creation. ¹⁶ For by him all things were created: things in heaven and on earth, visible and invisible, whether thrones or powers or rulers or authorities; all things were created by him and for him. ¹⁷ He is before all things, and in him all things hold together. ¹⁸ And he is the head of the body, the church; he is the beginning and the firstborn from among the dead, so that in everything he might have the supremacy. ¹⁹ For God was pleased to have all his fulness dwell in him, ²⁰ and through him to reconcile to himself all things, whether things on earth or things in heaven, by making peace through his blood, shed on the cross. ²¹ Once you were alienated from God and were enemies in your minds because of*f* your evil behaviour. ²² But now he has reconciled you by Christ's physical body through death to present you holy in his

---

*a*2 Or *believing*   *b*2 Some manuscripts *Father and the Lord Jesus Christ*   *c*7 Some manuscripts *your*
*d*12 Some manuscripts *us*   *e*14 A few late manuscripts *redemption through his blood*
*f*21 Or *minds, as shown by*

sight, without blemish and free from accusation—²³if you continue in your faith, established and firm, not moved from the hope held out in the gospel. This is the gospel that you heard and that has been proclaimed to every creature under heaven, and of which I, Paul, have become a servant.

Paul's Labour for the Church

²⁴Now I rejoice in what was suffered for you, and I fill up in my flesh what is still lacking in regard to Christ's afflictions, for the sake of his body, which is the church. ²⁵I have become its servant by the commission God gave me to present to you the word of God in its fulness—²⁶the mystery that has been kept hidden for ages and generations, but is now disclosed to the saints. ²⁷To them God has chosen to make known among the Gentiles the glorious riches of this mystery, which is Christ in you, the hope of glory.

²⁸We proclaim him, admonishing and teaching everyone with all wisdom, so that we may present everyone perfect in Christ. ²⁹To this end I labour, struggling with all his energy, which so powerfully works in me.

2 I want you to know how much I am struggling for you and for those at Laodicea, and for all who have not met me personally. ²My purpose is that they may be encouraged in heart and united in love, so that they may have the full riches of complete understanding, in order that they may know the mystery of God, namely, Christ, ³in whom are hidden all the treasures of wisdom and knowledge. ⁴I tell you this so that no-one may deceive you by fine-sounding arguments. ⁵For though I am absent from you in body, I am present with you in spirit and delight to see how orderly you are and how firm your faith in Christ is.

Freedom From Human Regulations Through Life With Christ

⁶So then, just as you received Christ Jesus as Lord, continue to live in him,

⁷rooted and built up in him, strengthened in the faith as you were taught, and overflowing with thankfulness.

⁸See to it that no-one takes you captive through hollow and deceptive philosophy, which depends on human tradition and the basic principles of this world rather than on Christ.

⁹For in Christ all the fulness of the Deity lives in bodily form, ¹⁰and you have been given fulness in Christ, who is the Head over every power and authority. ¹¹In him you were also circumcised, in the putting off of the sinful nature,ᵃ not with a circumcision done by the hands of men but with the circumcision done by Christ, ¹²having been buried with him in baptism and raised with him through your faith in the power of God, who raised him from the dead.

¹³When you were dead in your sins and in the uncircumcision of your sinful nature,ᵇ God made youᶜ alive with Christ. He forgave us all our sins, ¹⁴having cancelled the written code, with its regulations, that was against us and that stood opposed to us; he took it away, nailing it to the cross. ¹⁵And having disarmed the powers and authorities, he made a public spectacle of them, triumphing over them by the cross.ᵈ

¹⁶Therefore do not let anyone judge you by what you eat or drink, or with regard to a religious festival, a New Moon celebration or a Sabbath day. ¹⁷These are a shadow of the things that were to come; the reality, however, is found in Christ. ¹⁸Do not let anyone who delights in false humility and the worship of angels disqualify you for the prize. Such a person goes into great detail about what he has seen, and his unspiritual mind puffs him up with idle notions. ¹⁹He has lost connection with the Head, from whom the whole body, supported and held together by its ligaments and sinews, grows as God causes it to grow.

²⁰Since you died with Christ to the basic principles of this world, why, as though you still belonged to it, do you submit to its rules: ²¹"Do not handle! Do not taste! Do not touch!"? ²²These are all destined

---

ᵃ11 Or *the flesh*   ᵇ13 Or *your flesh*   ᶜ13 Some manuscripts *us*   ᵈ15 Or *them in him* to perish with use, because they are based on human commands and teachings. [23]Such regulations indeed have an appearance of wisdom, with their self-imposed worship, their false humility and their harsh treatment of the body, but they lack any value in restraining sensual indulgence.

Rules for Holy Living

3 Since, then, you have been raised with Christ, set your hearts on things above, where Christ is seated at the right hand of God. [2]Set your minds on things above, not on earthly things. [3]For you died, and your life is now hidden with Christ in God. [4]When Christ, who is your[a] life, appears, then you also will appear with him in glory.

[5]Put to death, therefore, whatever belongs to your earthly nature: sexual immorality, impurity, lust, evil desires and greed, which is idolatry. [6]Because of these, the wrath of God is coming.[b] [7]You used to walk in these ways, in the life you once lived. [8]But now you must rid yourselves of all such things as these: anger, rage, malice, slander and filthy language from your lips. [9]Do not lie to each other, since you have taken off your old self with its practices [10]and have put on the new self, which is being renewed in knowledge in the image of its Creator. [11]Here there is no Greek or Jew, circumcised or uncircumcised, barbarian, Scythian, slave or free, but Christ is all, and is in all.

[12]Therefore, as God's chosen people, holy and dearly loved, clothe yourselves with compassion, kindness, humility, gentleness and patience. [13]Bear with each other and forgive whatever grievances you may have against one another. Forgive as the Lord forgave you. [14]And over all these virtues put on love, which binds them all together in perfect unity.

[15]Let the peace of Christ rule in your hearts, since as members of one body you were called to peace. And be thankful. [16]Let the word of Christ dwell in you richly as you teach and admonish one another with all wisdom, and as you sing psalms, hymns and spiritual songs with gratitude in your hearts to God. [17]And whatever you do, whether in word or deed, do it all in the name of the Lord Jesus, giving thanks to God the Father through him.

Rules for Christian Households

[18]Wives, submit to your husbands, as is fitting in the Lord.

[19]Husbands, love your wives and do not be harsh with them.

[20]Children, obey your parents in everything, for this pleases the Lord.

[21]Fathers, do not embitter your children, or they will become discouraged.

[22]Slaves, obey your earthly masters in everything; and do it, not only when their eye is on you and to win their favour, but with sincerity of heart and reverence for the Lord. [23]Whatever you do, work at it with all your heart, as working for the Lord, not for men, [24]since you know that you will receive an inheritance from the Lord as a reward. It is the Lord Christ you are serving. [25]Anyone who does wrong will be repaid for his wrong, and there is no favouritism.

4 Masters, provide your slaves with what is right and fair, because you know that you also have a Master in heaven.

Further Instructions

[2]Devote yourselves to prayer, being watchful and thankful. [3]And pray for us, too, that God may open a door for our message, so that we may proclaim the mystery of Christ, for which I am in chains. [4]Pray that I may proclaim it clearly, as I should. [5]Be wise in the way you act towards outsiders; make the most of every opportunity. [6]Let your conversation be always full of grace, seasoned with salt, so that you may know how to answer everyone.

---

*a*4 Some manuscripts *our*　　　*b*6 Some early manuscripts *coming on those who are disobedient*

Final Greetings

[7]Tychicus will tell you all the news about me. He is a dear brother, a faithful minister and fellow-servant in the Lord. [8]I am sending him to you for the express purpose that you may know about our[a] circumstances and that he may encourage your hearts. [9]He is coming with Onesimus, our faithful and dear brother, who is one of you. They will tell you everything that is happening here.

[10]My fellow-prisoner Aristarchus sends you his greetings, as does Mark, the cousin of Barnabas. (You have received instructions about him; if he comes to you, welcome him.) [11]Jesus, who is called Justus, also sends greetings. These are the only Jews among my fellow-workers for the kingdom of God, and they have proved a comfort to me. [12]Epaphras, who is one of you and a servant of Christ Jesus, sends greetings. He is always wrestling in prayer for you, that you may stand firm in all the will of God, mature and fully assured. [13]I vouch for him that he is working hard for you and for those at Laodicea and Hierapolis. [14]Our dear friend Luke, the doctor, and Demas send greetings. [15]Give my greetings to the brothers at Laodicea, and to Nympha and the church in her house.

[16]After this letter has been read to you, see that it is also read in the church of the Laodiceans and that you in turn read the letter from Laodicea.

[17]Tell Archippus: "See to it that you complete the work you have received in the Lord."

[18]I, Paul, write this greeting in my own hand. Remember my chains. Grace be with you.

---

*a*8 Some manuscripts *that he may know about your*

1 Thessalonians

1

Paul, Silas[a] and Timothy,

To the church of the Thessalonians in God the Father and the Lord Jesus Christ:

Grace and peace to you.[b]

Thanksgiving for the Thessalonians' Faith

[2]We always thank God for all of you, mentioning you in our prayers. [3]We continually remember before our God and Father your work produced by faith, your labour prompted by love, and your endurance inspired by hope in our Lord Jesus Christ.

[4]For we know, brothers loved by God, that he has chosen you, [5]because our gospel came to you not simply with words, but also with power, with the Holy Spirit and with deep conviction. You know how we lived among you for your sake. [6]You became imitators of us and of the Lord; in spite of severe suffering, you welcomed the message with the joy given by the Holy Spirit. [7]And so you became a model to all the believers in Macedonia and Achaia. [8]The Lord's message rang out from you not only in Macedonia and Achaia—your faith in God has become known everywhere. Therefore we do not need to say anything about it, [9]for they themselves report what kind of reception you gave us. They tell how you turned to God from idols to serve the living and true God, [10]and to wait for his Son from heaven, whom he raised from the dead—Jesus, who rescues us from the coming wrath.

Paul's Ministry in Thessalonica

2

You know, brothers, that our visit to you was not a failure. [2]We had previously suffered and been insulted in Philippi, as you know, but with the help of our God we dared to tell you his gospel in spite of strong opposition. [3]For the appeal we make does not spring from error or impure motives, nor are we trying to trick you. [4]On the contrary, we speak as men approved by God to be entrusted with the gospel. We are not trying to please men but God, who tests our hearts. [5]You know we never used flattery, nor did we put on a mask to cover up greed—God is our witness. [6]We were not looking for praise from men, not from you or anyone else.

As apostles of Christ we could have been a burden to you, [7]but we were gentle among you, like a mother caring for her little children. [8]We loved you so much that we were delighted to share with you not only the gospel of God but our lives as well, because you had become so dear to us. [9]Surely you remember, brothers, our toil and hardship; we worked night and day in order not to be a burden to anyone while we preached the gospel of God to you.

[10]You are witnesses, and so is God, of how holy, righteous and blameless we were among you who believed. [11]For you know that we dealt with each of you as

---

[a]1 Greek Silvanus, a variant of Silas   [b]1 Some early manuscripts you from God our Father and the Lord Jesus Christ

a father deals with his own children, [12]encouraging, comforting and urging you to live lives worthy of God, who calls you into his kingdom and glory.

[13]And we also thank God continually because, when you received the word of God, which you heard from us, you accepted it not as the word of men, but as it actually is, the word of God, which is at work in you who believe. [14]For you, brothers, became imitators of God's churches in Judea, which are in Christ Jesus: You suffered from your own countrymen the same things those churches suffered from the Jews, [15]who killed the Lord Jesus and the prophets and also drove us out. They displease God and are hostile to all men [16]in their effort to keep us from speaking to the Gentiles so that they may be saved. In this way they always heap up their sins to the limit. The wrath of God has come upon them at last.[a]

Paul's Longing to See the Thessalonians

[17]But, brothers, when we were torn away from you for a short time (in person, not in thought), out of our intense longing we made every effort to see you. [18]For we wanted to come to you—certainly I, Paul, did, again and again—but Satan stopped us. [19]For what is our hope, our joy, or the crown in which we will glory in the presence of our Lord Jesus Christ when he comes? Is it not you? [20]Indeed, you are our glory and joy.

3 So when we could stand it no longer, we thought it best to be left by ourselves in Athens. [2]We sent Timothy, who is our brother and God's fellow-worker[a] in spreading the gospel of Christ, to strengthen and encourage you in your faith, [3]so that no-one would be unsettled by these trials. You know quite well that we were destined for them. [4]In fact, when we were with you, we kept telling you that we would be persecuted. And it turned out that way, as you well know. [5]For this reason, when I could stand it no longer, I sent to find out about your faith. I was afraid that in some way the tempter might have tempted you and our efforts might have been useless.

Timothy's Encouraging Report

[6]But Timothy has just now come to us from you and has brought good news about your faith and love. He has told us that you always have pleasant memories of us and that you long to see us, just as we also long to see you. [7]Therefore, brothers, in all our distress and persecution we were encouraged about you because of your faith. [8]For now we really live, since you are standing firm in the Lord. [9]How can we thank God enough for you in return for all the joy we have in the presence of our God because of you? [10]Night and day we pray most earnestly that we may see you again and supply what is lacking in your faith.

[11]Now may our God and Father himself and our Lord Jesus clear the way for us to come to you. [12]May the Lord make your love increase and overflow for each other and for everyone else, just as ours does for you. [13]May he strengthen your hearts so that you will be blameless and holy in the presence of our God and Father when our Lord Jesus comes with all his holy ones.

Living to Please God

4 Finally, brothers, we instructed you how to live in order to please God, as in fact you are living. Now we ask you and urge you in the Lord Jesus to do this more and more. [2]For you know what instructions we gave you by the authority of the Lord Jesus.

[3]It is God's will that you should be sanctified: that you should avoid sexual immorality; [4]that each of you should learn to control his own body[a] in a way that is holy and honourable, [5]not in passionate lust like the heathen, who do not know God; [6]and that in this matter no-one should wrong his brother or take advantage of him. The Lord will punish men for

---

a16 Or them fully   a2 Some manuscripts brother and fellow-worker; other manuscripts brother and God's servant
a4 Or learn to live with his own wife; or learn to acquire a wife

all such sins, as we have already told you and warned you. [7]For God did not call us to be impure, but to live a holy life. [8]Therefore, he who rejects this instruction does not reject man but God, who gives you his Holy Spirit.

[9]Now about brotherly love we do not need to write to you, for you yourselves have been taught by God to love each other. [10]And in fact, you do love all the brothers throughout Macedonia. Yet we urge you, brothers, to do so more and more.

[11]Make it your ambition to lead a quiet life, to mind your own business and to work with your hands, just as we told you, [12]so that your daily life may win the respect of outsiders and so that you will not be dependent on anybody.

The Coming of the Lord

[13]Brothers, we do not want you to be ignorant about those who fall asleep, or to grieve like the rest of men, who have no hope. [14]We believe that Jesus died and rose again and so we believe that God will bring with Jesus those who have fallen asleep in him. [15]According to the Lord's own word, we tell you that we who are still alive, who are left till the coming of the Lord, will certainly not precede those who have fallen asleep. [16]For the Lord himself will come down from heaven, with a loud command, with the voice of the archangel and with the trumpet call of God, and the dead in Christ will rise first. [17]After that, we who are still alive and are left will be caught up together with them in the clouds to meet the Lord in the air. And so we will be with the Lord for ever. [18]Therefore encourage each other with these words.

5 Now, brothers, about times and dates we do not need to write to you, [2]for you know very well that the day of the Lord will come like a thief in the night. [3]While people are saying, "Peace and safety", destruction will come on them suddenly, as labour pains on a pregnant woman, and they will not escape.

[4]But you, brothers, are not in darkness so that this day should surprise you like a thief. [5]You are all sons of the light and sons of the day. We do not belong to the night or to the darkness. [6]So then, let us not be like others, who are asleep, but let us be alert and self-controlled. [7]For those who sleep, sleep at night, and those who get drunk, get drunk at night. [8]But since we belong to the day, let us be self-controlled, putting on faith and love as a breastplate, and the hope of salvation as a helmet. [9]For God did not appoint us to suffer wrath but to receive salvation through our Lord Jesus Christ. [10]He died for us so that, whether we are awake or asleep, we may live together with him. [11]Therefore encourage one another and build each other up, just as in fact you are doing.

Final Instructions

[12]Now we ask you, brothers, to respect those who work hard among you, who are over you in the Lord and who admonish you. [13]Hold them in the highest regard in love because of their work. Live in peace with each other. [14]And we urge you, brothers, warn those who are idle, encourage the timid, help the weak, be patient with everyone. [15]Make sure that nobody pays back wrong for wrong, but always try to be kind to each other and to everyone else.

[16]Be joyful always; [17]pray continually; [18]give thanks in all circumstances, for this is God's will for you in Christ Jesus.

[19]Do not put out the Spirit's fire; [20]do not treat prophecies with contempt. [21]Test everything. Hold on to the good. [22]Avoid every kind of evil.

[23]May God himself, the God of peace, sanctify you through and through. May your whole spirit, soul and body be kept blameless at the coming of our Lord Jesus Christ. [24]The one who calls you is faithful and he will do it.

[25]Brothers, pray for us. [26]Greet all the brothers with a holy kiss. [27]I charge you before the Lord to have this letter read to all the brothers.

[28]The grace of our Lord Jesus Christ be with you.

2 Thessalonians

1

Paul, Silas*a* and Timothy,

To the church of the Thessalonians in God our Father and the Lord Jesus Christ:

²Grace and peace to you from God the Father and the Lord Jesus Christ.

Thanksgiving and Prayer

³We ought always to thank God for you, brothers, and rightly so, because your faith is growing more and more, and the love every one of you has for each other is increasing. ⁴Therefore, among God's churches we boast about your perseverance and faith in all the persecutions and trials you are enduring.

⁵All this is evidence that God's judgment is right, and as a result you will be counted worthy of the kingdom of God, for which you are suffering. ⁶God is just: He will pay back trouble to those who trouble you ⁷and give relief to you who are troubled, and to us as well. This will happen when the Lord Jesus is revealed from heaven in blazing fire with his powerful angels. ⁸He will punish those who do not know God and do not obey the gospel of our Lord Jesus. ⁹They will be punished with everlasting destruction and shut out from the presence of the Lord and from the majesty of his power ¹⁰on the day he comes to be glorified in his holy people and to be marvelled at among all those who have believed. This includes you, because you believed our testimony to you.

¹¹With this in mind, we constantly pray for you, that our God may count you worthy of his calling, and that by his power he may fulfil every good purpose of yours and every act prompted by your faith. ¹²We pray this so that the name of our Lord Jesus may be glorified in you, and you in him, according to the grace of our God and the Lord Jesus Christ.*b*

The Man of Lawlessness

2

Concerning the coming of our Lord Jesus Christ and our being gathered to him, we ask you, brothers, ²not to become easily unsettled or alarmed by some prophecy, report or letter supposed to have come from us, saying that the day of the Lord has already come. ³Don't let anyone deceive you in any way, for ⌊that day will not come⌋ until the rebellion occurs and the man of lawlessness*a* is revealed, the man doomed to destruction. ⁴He will oppose and will exalt himself over everything that is called God or is worshipped, so that he sets himself up in God's temple, proclaiming himself to be God.

⁵Don't you remember that when I was with you I used to tell you these things? ⁶And now you know what is holding him back, so that he may be revealed at the proper time. ⁷For the secret power of lawlessness is already at work; but the one who now holds it back will continue to do so till he is taken out of the way. ⁸And then the lawless one will be revealed, whom the

---

a1 Greek *Silvanus*, a variant of *Silas*   *b12* Or *God and Lord, Jesus Christ*   *a3* Some manuscripts *sin*

Lord Jesus will overthrow with the breath of his mouth and destroy by the splendour of his coming. [9]The coming of the lawless one will be in accordance with the work of Satan displayed in all kinds of counterfeit miracles, signs and wonders, [10]and in every sort of evil that deceives those who are perishing. They perish because they refused to love the truth and so be saved. [11]For this reason God sends them a powerful delusion so that they will believe the lie [12]and so that all will be condemned who have not believed the truth but have delighted in wickedness.

Stand Firm

[13]But we ought always to thank God for you, brothers loved by the Lord, because from the beginning God chose you[b] to be saved through the sanctifying work of the Spirit and through belief in the truth. [14]He called you to this through our gospel, that you might share in the glory of our Lord Jesus Christ. [15]So then, brothers, stand firm and hold to the teachings[c] we passed on to you, whether by word of mouth or by letter.

[16]May our Lord Jesus Christ himself and God our Father, who loved us and by his grace gave us eternal encouragement and good hope, [17]encourage your hearts and strengthen you in every good deed and word.

Request for Prayer

3 Finally, brothers, pray for us that the message of the Lord may spread rapidly and be honoured, just as it was with you. [2]And pray that we may be delivered from wicked and evil men, for not everyone has faith. [3]But the Lord is faithful, and he will strengthen and protect you from the evil one. [4]We have confidence in the Lord that you are doing and will continue to do the things we command. [5]May

the Lord direct your hearts into God's love and Christ's perseverance.

Warning Against Idleness

[6]In the name of the Lord Jesus Christ, we command you, brothers, to keep away from every brother who is idle and does not live according to the teaching[a] you received from us. [7]For you yourselves know how you ought to follow our example. We were not idle when we were with you, [8]nor did we eat anyone's food without paying for it. On the contrary, we worked night and day, labouring and toiling so that we would not be a burden to any of you. [9]We did this, not because we do not have the right to such help, but in order to make ourselves a model for you to follow. [10]For even when we were with you, we gave you this rule: "If a man will not work, he shall not eat."

[11]We hear that some among you are idle. They are not busy; they are busybodies. [12]Such people we command and urge in the Lord Jesus Christ to settle down and earn the bread they eat. [13]And as for you, brothers, never tire of doing what is right.

[14]If anyone does not obey our instruction in this letter, take special note of him. Do not associate with him, in order that he may feel ashamed. [15]Yet do not regard him as an enemy, but warn him as a brother.

Final Greetings

[16]Now may the Lord of peace himself give you peace at all times and in every way. The Lord be with all of you.

[17]I, Paul, write this greeting in my own hand, which is the distinguishing mark in all my letters. This is how I write.

[18]The grace of our Lord Jesus Christ be with you all.

---

[b]13 Some manuscripts *because God chose you as his firstfruits*   [c]15 Or *traditions*   [a]6 Or *tradition*

1 Timothy

1 Paul, an apostle of Christ Jesus by the command of God our Saviour and of Christ Jesus our hope,

²To Timothy my true son in the faith:

Grace, mercy and peace from God the Father and Christ Jesus our Lord.

Warning Against False Teachers of the Law

³As I urged you when I went into Macedonia, stay there in Ephesus so that you may command certain men not to teach false doctrines any longer ⁴nor to devote themselves to myths and endless genealogies. These promote controversies rather than God's work—which is by faith. ⁵The goal of this command is love, which comes from a pure heart and a good conscience and a sincere faith. ⁶Some have wandered away from these and turned to meaningless talk. ⁷They want to be teachers of the law, but they do not know what they are talking about or what they so confidently affirm.

⁸We know that the law is good if one uses it properly. ⁹We also know that law*ᵃ* is made not for the righteous but for lawbreakers and rebels, the ungodly and sinful, the unholy and irreligious; for those who kill their fathers or mothers, for murderers, ¹⁰for adulterers and perverts, for slave traders and liars and perjurers— and for whatever else is contrary to the sound doctrine ¹¹that conforms to the glorious gospel of the blessed God, which he entrusted to me.

The Lord's Grace to Paul

¹²I thank Christ Jesus our Lord, who has given me strength, that he considered me faithful, appointing me to his service. ¹³Even though I was once a blasphemer and a persecutor and a violent man, I was shown mercy because I acted in ignorance and unbelief. ¹⁴The grace of our Lord was poured out on me abundantly, along with the faith and love that are in Christ Jesus.

¹⁵Here is a trustworthy saying that deserves full acceptance: Christ Jesus came into the world to save sinners—of whom I am the worst. ¹⁶But for that very reason I was shown mercy so that in me, the worst of sinners, Christ Jesus might display his unlimited patience as an example for those who would believe on him and receive eternal life. ¹⁷Now to the King eternal, immortal, invisible, the only God, be honour and glory for ever and ever. Amen.

¹⁸Timothy, my son, I give you this instruction in keeping with the prophecies once made about you, so that by following them you may fight the good fight, ¹⁹holding on to faith and a good conscience. Some have rejected these and so have shipwrecked their faith. ²⁰Among them are Hymenaeus and Alexander, whom I have handed over to Satan to be taught not to blaspheme.

ᵃ9 Or that the law

Instructions on Worship

2 I urge, then, first of all, that requests, prayers, intercession and thanksgiving be made for everyone—²for kings and all those in authority, that we may live peaceful and quiet lives in all godliness and holiness. ³This is good, and pleases God our Saviour, ⁴who wants all men to be saved and to come to a knowledge of the truth. ⁵For there is one God and one mediator between God and men, the man Christ Jesus, ⁶who gave himself as a ransom for all men—the testimony given in its proper time. ⁷And for this purpose I was appointed a herald and an apostle—I am telling the truth, I am not lying—and a teacher of the true faith to the Gentiles.

⁸I want men everywhere to lift up holy hands in prayer, without anger or disputing.

⁹I also want women to dress modestly, with decency and propriety, not with braided hair or gold or pearls or expensive clothes, ¹⁰but with good deeds, appropriate for women who profess to worship God.

¹¹A woman should learn in quietness and full submission. ¹²I do not permit a woman to teach or to have authority over a man; she must be silent. ¹³For Adam was formed first, then Eve. ¹⁴And Adam was not the one deceived; it was the woman who was deceived and became a sinner. ¹⁵But women*a* will be saved*b* through childbearing—if they continue in faith, love and holiness with propriety.

Overseers and Deacons

3 Here is a trustworthy saying: If anyone sets his heart on being an overseer,*a* he desires a noble task. ²Now the overseer must be above reproach, the husband of but one wife, temperate, self-controlled, respectable, hospitable, able to teach, ³not given to drunkenness, not violent but gentle, not quarrelsome, not a lover of money. ⁴He must manage his own family well and see that his children obey him with proper respect. ⁵(If anyone does

not know how to manage his own family, how can he take care of God's church?) ⁶He must not be a recent convert, or he may become conceited and fall under the same judgment as the devil. ⁷He must also have a good reputation with outsiders, so that he will not fall into disgrace and into the devil's trap.

⁸Deacons, likewise, are to be men worthy of respect, sincere, not indulging in much wine, and not pursuing dishonest gain. ⁹They must keep hold of the deep truths of the faith with a clear conscience. ¹⁰They must first be tested; and then if there is nothing against them, let them serve as deacons.

¹¹In the same way, their wives*b* are to be women worthy of respect, not malicious talkers but temperate and trustworthy in everything.

¹²A deacon must be the husband of but one wife and must manage his children and his household well. ¹³Those who have served well gain an excellent standing and great assurance in their faith in Christ Jesus.

¹⁴Although I hope to come to you soon, I am writing you these instructions so that, ¹⁵if I am delayed, you will know how people ought to conduct themselves in God's household, which is the church of the living God, the pillar and foundation of the truth. ¹⁶Beyond all question, the mystery of godliness is great:

He*c* appeared in a body,*d*
  was vindicated by the Spirit,
  was seen by angels,
  was preached among the nations,
was believed on in the world,
  was taken up in glory.

Instructions to Timothy

4 The Spirit clearly says that in later times some will abandon the faith and follow deceiving spirits and things taught by demons. ²Such teachings come through hypocritical liars, whose consciences have been seared as with a hot iron. ³They forbid people to marry and order them to

---

abstain from certain foods, which God created to be received with thanksgiving by those who believe and who know the truth. ⁴For everything God created is good, and nothing is to be rejected if it is received with thanksgiving, ⁵because it is consecrated by the word of God and prayer.

⁶If you point these things out to the brothers, you will be a good minister of Christ Jesus, brought up in the truths of the faith and of the good teaching that you have followed. ⁷Have nothing to do with godless myths and old wives' tales; rather, train yourself to be godly. ⁸For physical training is of some value, but godliness has value for all things, holding promise for both the present life and the life to come.

⁹This is a trustworthy saying that deserves full acceptance ¹⁰(and for this we labour and strive), that we have put our hope in the living God, who is the Saviour of all men, and especially of those who believe.

¹¹Command and teach these things. ¹²Don't let anyone look down on you because you are young, but set an example for the believers in speech, in life, in love, in faith and in purity. ¹³Until I come, devote yourself to the public reading of Scripture, to preaching and to teaching. ¹⁴Do not neglect your gift, which was given you through a prophetic message when the body of elders laid their hands on you.

¹⁵Be diligent in these matters; give yourself wholly to them, so that everyone may see your progress. ¹⁶Watch your life and doctrine closely. Persevere in them, because if you do, you will save both yourself and your hearers.

Advice About Widows, Elders and Slaves

5 Do not rebuke an older man harshly, but exhort him as if he were your father. Treat younger men as brothers, ²older women as mothers, and younger women as sisters, with absolute purity.

³Give proper recognition to those widows who are really in need. ⁴But if a widow has children or grandchildren, these should learn first of all to put their religion into practice by caring for their own family and so repaying their parents and grandparents, for this is pleasing to God. ⁵The widow who is really in need and left all alone puts her hope in God and continues night and day to pray and to ask God for help. ⁶But the widow who lives for pleasure is dead even while she lives. ⁷Give the people these instructions, too, so that no-one may be open to blame. ⁸If anyone does not provide for his relatives, and especially for his immediate family, he has denied the faith and is worse than an unbeliever.

⁹No widow may be put on the list of widows unless she is over sixty, has been faithful to her husband,ᵃ ¹⁰and is well known for her good deeds, such as bringing up children, showing hospitality, washing the feet of the saints, helping those in trouble and devoting herself to all kinds of good deeds.

¹¹As for younger widows, do not put them on such a list. For when their sensual desires overcome their dedication to Christ, they want to marry. ¹²Thus they bring judgment on themselves, because they have broken their first pledge. ¹³Besides, they get into the habit of being idle and going about from house to house. And not only do they become idlers, but also gossips and busybodies, saying things they ought not to. ¹⁴So I counsel younger widows to marry, to have children, to manage their homes and to give the enemy no opportunity for slander. ¹⁵Some have in fact already turned away to follow Satan.

¹⁶If any woman who is a believer has widows in her family, she should help them and not let the church be burdened with them, so that the church can help those widows who are really in need.

¹⁷The elders who direct the affairs of the church well are worthy of double honour, especially those whose work is preaching and teaching. ¹⁸For the Scripture says, "Do not muzzle the ox while it is treading out the grain,"ᵇ and "The worker

---

ᵃ9 Or *has had but one husband*   *ᵇ18* Deut. 25:4

deserves his wages."[c] [19]Do not entertain an accusation against an elder unless it is brought by two or three witnesses. [20]Those who sin are to be rebuked publicly, so that the others may take warning.

[21]I charge you, in the sight of God and Christ Jesus and the elect angels, to keep these instructions without partiality, and to do nothing out of favouritism.

[22]Do not be hasty in the laying on of hands, and do not share in the sins of others. Keep yourself pure.

[23]Stop drinking only water, and use a little wine because of your stomach and your frequent illnesses.

[24]The sins of some men are obvious, reaching the place of judgment ahead of them; the sins of others trail behind them. [25]In the same way, good deeds are obvious, and even those that are not cannot be hidden.

6 All who are under the yoke of slavery should consider their masters worthy of full respect, so that God's name and our teaching may not be slandered. [2]Those who have believing masters are not to show less respect for them because they are brothers. Instead, they are to serve them even better, because those who benefit from their service are believers, and dear to them. These are the things you are to teach and urge on them.

Love of Money

[3]If anyone teaches false doctrines and does not agree to the sound instruction of our Lord Jesus Christ and to godly teaching, [4]he is conceited and understands nothing. He has an unhealthy interest in controversies and quarrels about words that result in envy, strife, malicious talk, evil suspicions [5]and constant friction between men of corrupt mind, who have been robbed of the truth and who think that godliness is a means to financial gain.

[6]But godliness with contentment is great gain. [7]For we brought nothing into the world, and we can take nothing out of it. [8]But if we have food and clothing, we will be content with that. [9]People who

want to get rich fall into temptation and a trap and into many foolish and harmful desires that plunge men into ruin and destruction. [10]For the love of money is a root of all kinds of evil. Some people, eager for money, have wandered from the faith and pierced themselves with many griefs.

Paul's Charge to Timothy

[11]But you, man of God, flee from all this, and pursue righteousness, godliness, faith, love, endurance and gentleness. [12]Fight the good fight of the faith. Take hold of the eternal life to which you were called when you made your good confession in the presence of many witnesses. [13]In the sight of God, who gives life to everything, and of Christ Jesus, who while testifying before Pontius Pilate made the good confession, I charge you [14]to keep this command without spot or blame until the appearing of our Lord Jesus Christ, [15]which God will bring about in his own time—God, the blessed and only Ruler, the King of kings and Lord of lords, [16]who alone is immortal and who lives in unapproachable light, whom no-one has seen or can see. To him be honour and might for ever. Amen.

[17]Command those who are rich in this present world not to be arrogant nor to put their hope in wealth, which is so uncertain, but to put their hope in God, who richly provides us with everything for our enjoyment. [18]Command them to do good, to be rich in good deeds, and to be generous and willing to share. [19]In this way they will lay up treasure for themselves as a firm foundation for the coming age, so that they may take hold of the life that is truly life.

[20]Timothy, guard what has been entrusted to your care. Turn away from godless chatter and the opposing ideas of what is falsely called knowledge, [21]which some have professed and in so doing have wandered from the faith.

Grace be with you.

[c]18 Luke 10:7

2 Timothy

1 Paul, an apostle of Christ Jesus by the will of God, according to the promise of life that is in Christ Jesus,

²To Timothy, my dear son:

Grace, mercy and peace from God the Father and Christ Jesus our Lord.

Encouragement to Be Faithful

³I thank God, whom I serve, as my forefathers did, with a clear conscience, as night and day I constantly remember you in my prayers. ⁴Recalling your tears, I long to see you, so that I may be filled with joy. ⁵I have been reminded of your sincere faith, which first lived in your grandmother Lois and in your mother Eunice and, I am persuaded, now lives in you also. ⁶For this reason I remind you to fan into flame the gift of God, which is in you through the laying on of my hands. ⁷For God did not give us a spirit of timidity, but a spirit of power, of love and of self-discipline.

⁸So do not be ashamed to testify about our Lord, or ashamed of me his prisoner. But join with me in suffering for the gospel, by the power of God, ⁹who has saved us and called us to a holy life—not because of anything we have done but because of his own purpose and grace. This grace was given us in Christ Jesus before the beginning of time, ¹⁰but it has now been revealed through the appearing of our Saviour, Christ Jesus, who has destroyed death and has brought life and immortality to light through the gospel. ¹¹And of

this gospel I was appointed a herald and an apostle and a teacher. ¹²That is why I am suffering as I am. Yet I am not ashamed, because I know whom I have believed, and am convinced that he is able to guard what I have entrusted to him for that day.

¹³What you heard from me, keep as the pattern of sound teaching, with faith and love in Christ Jesus. ¹⁴Guard the good deposit that was entrusted to you—guard it with the help of the Holy Spirit who lives in us.

¹⁵You know that everyone in the province of Asia has deserted me, including Phygelus and Hermogenes.

¹⁶May the Lord show mercy to the household of Onesiphorus, because he often refreshed me and was not ashamed of my chains. ¹⁷On the contrary, when he was in Rome, he searched hard for me until he found me. ¹⁸May the Lord grant that he will find mercy from the Lord on that day! You know very well in how many ways he helped me in Ephesus.

2 You then, my son, be strong in the grace that is in Christ Jesus. ²And the things you have heard me say in the presence of many witnesses entrust to reliable men who will also be qualified to teach others. ³Endure hardship with us like a good soldier of Christ Jesus. ⁴No-one serving as a soldier gets involved in civilian affairs—he wants to please his commanding officer. ⁵Similarly, if anyone competes as an athlete, he does not receive the victor's crown unless he competes according to the rules. ⁶The hardworking farmer should be the first to receive a share of the

crops. [7]Reflect on what I am saying, for the Lord will give you insight into all this.

[8]Remember Jesus Christ, raised from the dead, descended from David. This is my gospel, [9]for which I am suffering even to the point of being chained like a criminal. But God's word is not chained. [10]Therefore I endure everything for the sake of the elect, that they too may obtain the salvation that is in Christ Jesus, with eternal glory.

[11]Here is a trustworthy saying:

If we died with him,
    we will also live with him;
[12]if we endure,
    we will also reign with him.
If we disown him,
    he will also disown us;
[13]if we are faithless,
    he will remain faithful,
    for he cannot disown himself.

A Workman Approved by God

[14]Keep reminding them of these things. Warn them before God against quarrelling about words; it is of no value, and only ruins those who listen. [15]Do your best to present yourself to God as one approved, a workman who does not need to be ashamed and who correctly handles the word of truth. [16]Avoid godless chatter, because those who indulge in it will become more and more ungodly. [17]Their teaching will spread like gangrene. Among them are Hymenaeus and Philetus, [18]who have wandered away from the truth. They say that the resurrection has already taken place, and they destroy the faith of some. [19]Nevertheless, God's solid foundation stands firm, sealed with this inscription: "The Lord knows those who are his,"[a] and, "Everyone who confesses the name of the Lord must turn away from wickedness."

[20]In a large house there are articles not only of gold and silver, but also of wood and clay; some are for noble purposes and some for ignoble. [21]If a man cleanses himself from the latter, he will be an instrument for noble purposes, made holy, useful to the Master and prepared to do any good work.

[22]Flee the evil desires of youth, and pursue righteousness, faith, love and peace, along with those who call on the Lord out of a pure heart. [23]Don't have anything to do with foolish and stupid arguments, because you know they produce quarrels. [24]And the Lord's servant must not quarrel; instead, he must be kind to everyone, able to teach, not resentful. [25]Those who oppose him he must gently instruct, in the hope that God will grant them repentance leading them to a knowledge of the truth, [26]and that they will come to their senses and escape from the trap of the devil, who has taken them captive to do his will.

Godlessness in the Last Days

3 But mark this: There will be terrible times in the last days. [2]People will be lovers of themselves, lovers of money, boastful, proud, abusive, disobedient to their parents, ungrateful, unholy, [3]without love, unforgiving, slanderous, without self-control, brutal, not lovers of the good, [4]treacherous, rash, conceited, lovers of pleasure rather than lovers of God—[5]having a form of godliness but denying its power. Have nothing to do with them.

[6]They are the kind who worm their way into homes and gain control over weak-willed women, who are loaded down with sins and are swayed by all kinds of evil desires, [7]always learning but never able to acknowledge the truth. [8]Just as Jannes and Jambres opposed Moses, so also these men oppose the truth—men of depraved minds, who, as far as the faith is concerned, are rejected. [9]But they will not get very far because, as in the case of those men, their folly will be clear to everyone.

Paul's Charge to Timothy

[10]You, however, know all about my teaching, my way of life, my purpose,

faith, patience, love, endurance, [11]persecutions, sufferings—what kinds of things happened to me in Antioch, Iconium and Lystra, the persecutions I endured. Yet the Lord rescued me from all of them. [12]In fact, everyone who wants to live a godly life in Christ Jesus will be persecuted, [13]while evil men and impostors will go from bad to worse, deceiving and being deceived. [14]But as for you, continue in what you have learned and have become convinced of, because you know those from whom you learned it, [15]and how from infancy you have known the holy Scriptures, which are able to make you wise for salvation through faith in Christ Jesus. [16]All Scripture is God-breathed and is useful for teaching, rebuking, correcting and training in righteousness, [17]so that the man of God may be thoroughly equipped for every good work.

4 In the presence of God and of Christ Jesus, who will judge the living and the dead, and in view of his appearing and his kingdom, I give you this charge: [2]Preach the Word; be prepared in season and out of season; correct, rebuke and encourage—with great patience and careful instruction. [3]For the time will come when men will not put up with sound doctrine. Instead, to suit their own desires, they will gather around them a great number of teachers to say what their itching ears want to hear. [4]They will turn their ears away from the truth and turn aside to myths. [5]But you, keep your head in all situations, endure hardship, do the work of an evangelist, discharge all the duties of your ministry.

[6]For I am already being poured out like a drink offering, and the time has come for my departure. [7]I have fought the good fight, I have finished the race, I have kept the faith. [8]Now there is in store for me the crown of righteousness, which the Lord,

the righteous Judge, will award to me on that day—and not only to me, but also to all who have longed for his appearing.

Personal Remarks

[9]Do your best to come to me quickly, [10]for Demas, because he loved this world, has deserted me and has gone to Thessalonica. Crescens has gone to Galatia, and Titus to Dalmatia. [11]Only Luke is with me. Get Mark and bring him with you, because he is helpful to me in my ministry. [12]I sent Tychicus to Ephesus. [13]When you come, bring the cloak that I left with Carpus at Troas, and my scrolls, especially the parchments.

[14]Alexander the metalworker did me a great deal of harm. The Lord will repay him for what he has done. [15]You too should be on your guard against him, because he strongly opposed our message.

[16]At my first defence, no-one came to my support, but everyone deserted me. May it not be held against them. [17]But the Lord stood at my side and gave me strength, so that through me the message might be fully proclaimed and all the Gentiles might hear it. And I was delivered from the lion's mouth. [18]The Lord will rescue me from every evil attack and will bring me safely to his heavenly kingdom. To him be glory for ever and ever. Amen.

Final Greetings

[19]Greet Priscilla[a] and Aquila and the household of Onesiphorus. [20]Erastus stayed in Corinth, and I left Trophimus sick in Miletus. [21]Do your best to get here before winter. Eubulus greets you, and so do Pudens, Linus, Claudia and all the brothers.

[22]The Lord be with your spirit. Grace be with you.

---

[a]19 Greek *Prisca*, a variant of *Priscilla*

Titus

1 Paul, a servant of God and an apostle of Jesus Christ for the faith of God's elect and the knowledge of the truth that leads to godliness—²a faith and knowledge resting on the hope of eternal life, which God, who does not lie, promised before the beginning of time, ³and at his appointed season he brought his word to light through the preaching entrusted to me by the command of God our Saviour,

⁴To Titus, my true son in our common faith:

Grace and peace from God the Father and Christ Jesus our Saviour.

Titus' Task on Crete

⁵The reason I left you in Crete was that you might straighten out what was left unfinished and appoint*ᵃ* elders in every town, as I directed you. ⁶An elder must be blameless, the husband of but one wife, a man whose children believe and are not open to the charge of being wild and disobedient. ⁷Since an overseer*ᵇ* is entrusted with God's work, he must be blameless— not overbearing, not quick-tempered, not given to drunkenness, not violent, not pursuing dishonest gain. ⁸Rather he must be hospitable, one who loves what is good, who is self-controlled, upright, holy and disciplined. ⁹He must hold firmly to the trustworthy message as it has been taught, so that he can encourage others by sound doctrine and refute those who oppose it.

¹⁰For there are many rebellious people, mere talkers and deceivers, especially those of the circumcision group. ¹¹They must be silenced, because they are ruining whole households by teaching things they ought not to teach—and that for the sake of dishonest gain. ¹²Even one of their own prophets has said, "Cretans are always liars, evil brutes, lazy gluttons." ¹³This testimony is true. Therefore, rebuke them sharply, so that they will be sound in the faith ¹⁴and will pay no attention to Jewish myths or to the commands of those who reject the truth. ¹⁵To the pure, all things are pure, but to those who are corrupted and do not believe, nothing is pure. In fact, both their minds and consciences are corrupted. ¹⁶They claim to know God, but by their actions they deny him. They are detestable, disobedient and unfit for doing anything good.

What Must Be Taught to Various Groups

2 You must teach what is in accord with sound doctrine. ²Teach the older men to be temperate, worthy of respect, self-controlled, and sound in faith, in love and in endurance.

³Likewise, teach the older women to be reverent in the way they live, not to be slanderers or addicted to much wine, but to teach what is good. ⁴Then they can train the younger women to love their husbands and children, ⁵to be self-controlled and pure, to be busy at home, to be kind, and

---

*ᵃ*5 Or *ordain*   *ᵇ*7 Traditionally *bishop*

to be subject to their husbands, so that no-one will malign the word of God.

[6]Similarly, encourage the young men to be self-controlled. [7]In everything set them an example by doing what is good. In your teaching show integrity, seriousness [8]and soundness of speech that cannot be condemned, so that those who oppose you may be ashamed because they have nothing bad to say about us.

[9]Teach slaves to be subject to their masters in everything, to try to please them, not to talk back to them, [10]and not to steal from them, but to show that they can be fully trusted, so that in every way they will make the teaching about God our Saviour attractive.

[11]For the grace of God that brings salvation has appeared to all men. [12]It teaches us to say "No" to ungodliness and worldly passions, and to live self-controlled, upright and godly lives in this present age, [13]while we wait for the blessed hope—the glorious appearing of our great God and Saviour, Jesus Christ, [14]who gave himself for us to redeem us from all wickedness and to purify for himself a people that are his very own, eager to do what is good.

[15]These, then, are the things you should teach. Encourage and rebuke with all authority. Do not let anyone despise you.

Doing What is Good

3 Remind the people to be subject to rulers and authorities, to be obedient, to be ready to do whatever is good, [2]to slander no-one, to be peaceable and considerate, and to show true humility towards all men.

[3]At one time we too were foolish, disobedient, deceived and enslaved by all kinds of passions and pleasures. We lived in malice and envy, being hated and hating one another. [4]But when the kindness and love of God our Saviour appeared, [5]he saved us, not because of righteous things we had done, but because of his mercy. He saved us through the washing of rebirth and renewal by the Holy Spirit, [6]whom he poured out on us generously through Jesus Christ our Saviour, [7]so that, having been justified by his grace, we might become heirs having the hope of eternal life. [8]This is a trustworthy saying. And I want you to stress these things, so that those who have trusted in God may be careful to devote themselves to doing what is good. These things are excellent and profitable for everyone.

[9]But avoid foolish controversies and genealogies and arguments and quarrels about the law, because these are unprofitable and useless. [10]Warn a divisive person once, and then warn him a second time. After that, have nothing to do with him. [11]You may be sure that such a man is warped and sinful; he is self-condemned.

Final Remarks

[12]As soon as I send Artemas or Tychicus to you, do your best to come to me at Nicopolis, because I have decided to winter there. [13]Do everything you can to help Zenas the lawyer and Apollos on their way and see that they have everything they need. [14]Our people must learn to devote themselves to doing what is good, in order that they may provide for daily necessities and not live unproductive lives.

[15]Everyone with me sends you greetings. Greet those who love us in the faith.

Grace be with you all.

Philemon

¹Paul, a prisoner of Christ Jesus, and Timothy our brother,

To Philemon our dear friend and fellow-worker, ²to Apphia our sister, to Archippus our fellow-soldier and to the church that meets in your home:

³Grace to you and peace from God our Father and the Lord Jesus Christ.

Thanksgiving and Prayer

⁴I always thank my God as I remember you in my prayers, ⁵because I hear about your faith in the Lord Jesus and your love for all the saints. ⁶I pray that you may be active in sharing your faith, so that you will have a full understanding of every good thing we have in Christ. ⁷Your love has given me great joy and encouragement, because you, brother, have refreshed the hearts of the saints.

Paul's Plea for Onesimus

⁸Therefore, although in Christ I could be bold and order you to do what you ought to do, ⁹yet I appeal to you on the basis of love. I then, as Paul—an old man and now also a prisoner of Christ Jesus— ¹⁰I appeal to you for my son Onesimus,^a who became my son while I was in chains. ¹¹Formerly he was useless to you, but now he has become useful both to you and to me.

¹²I am sending him—who is my very heart—back to you. ¹³I would have liked to keep him with me so that he could take your place in helping me while I am in chains for the gospel. ¹⁴But I did not want to do anything without your consent, so that any favour you do will be spontaneous and not forced. ¹⁵Perhaps the reason he was separated from you for a little while was that you might have him back for good—¹⁶no longer as a slave, but better than a slave, as a dear brother. He is very dear to me but even dearer to you, both as a man and as a brother in the Lord.

¹⁷So if you consider me a partner, welcome him as you would welcome me. ¹⁸If he has done you any wrong or owes you anything, charge it to me. ¹⁹I, Paul, am writing this with my own hand. I will pay it back—not to mention that you owe me your very self. ²⁰I do wish, brother, that I may have some benefit from you in the Lord; refresh my heart in Christ. ²¹Confident of your obedience, I write to you, knowing that you will do even more than I ask.

²²And one thing more: Prepare a guest room for me, because I hope to be restored to you in answer to your prayers.

²³Epaphras, my fellow-prisoner in Christ Jesus, sends you greetings. ²⁴And so do Mark, Aristarchus, Demas and Luke, my fellow-workers.

²⁵The grace of the Lord Jesus Christ be with your spirit.

^a10 Onesimus means useful.

Hebrews

The Son Superior to Angels

1 In the past God spoke to our fore-fathers through the prophets at many times and in various ways, [2]but in these last days he has spoken to us by his Son, whom he appointed heir of all things, and through whom he made the universe. [3]The Son is the radiance of God's glory and the exact representation of his being, sustaining all things by his powerful word. After he had provided purification for sins, he sat down at the right hand of the Majesty in heaven. [4]So he became as much superior to the angels as the name he has inherited is superior to theirs.

[5]For to which of the angels did God ever say,

"You are my Son;
    today I have become your
        Father"[a,b]?

Or again,

"I will be his Father,
    and he will be my Son"[c]?

[6]And again, when God brings his firstborn into the world, he says,

"Let all God's angels worship him."[d]

[7]In speaking of the angels he says,

"He makes his angels winds,
    his servants flames of fire."[e]

[8]But about the Son he says,

"Your throne, O God, will last for ever
        and ever,
    and righteousness will be the sceptre
        of your kingdom.
[9]You have loved righteousness and
        hated wickedness;
    therefore God, your God, has set you
        above your companions
    by anointing you with the oil of joy."[f]

[10]He also says,

"In the beginning, O Lord, you laid the
        foundations of the earth,
    and the heavens are the work of your
        hands.
[11]They will perish, but you remain;
    they will all wear out like a garment.
[12]You will roll them up like a robe;
    like a garment they will be changed.
But you remain the same,
    and your years will never end."[g]

[13]To which of the angels did God ever say,

"Sit at my right hand
until I make your enemies
    a footstool for your feet"[h]?

[14]Are not all angels ministering spirits sent to serve those who will inherit salvation?

Warning to Pay Attention

2 We must pay more careful attention, therefore, to what we have heard, so that we do not drift away. [2]For if the

a5 Or *have begotten you*   *b5* Psalm 2:7   *c5* 2 Samuel 7:14; 1 Chron. 17:13
d6 Deut. 32:43 (see Dead Sea Scrolls and Septuagint)   *e7* Psalm 104:4   *f9* Psalm 45:6,7
g12 Psalm 102:25-27   *h13* Psalm 110:1

message spoken by angels was binding, and every violation and disobedience received its just punishment, ³how shall we escape if we ignore such a great salvation? This salvation, which was first announced by the Lord, was confirmed to us by those who heard him. ⁴God also testified to it by signs, wonders and various miracles, and gifts of the Holy Spirit distributed according to his will.

Jesus Made Like His Brothers

⁵It is not to angels that he has subjected the world to come, about which we are speaking. ⁶But there is a place where someone has testified:

"What is man that you are mindful of
    him,
    the son of man that you care for him?
⁷You made him a little*a* lower than the
    angels;
    you crowned him with glory and
    honour
⁸   and put everything under his feet."*b*

In putting everything under him, God left nothing that is not subject to him. Yet at present we do not see everything subject to him. ⁹But we see Jesus, who was made a little lower than the angels, now crowned with glory and honour because he suffered death, so that by the grace of God he might taste death for everyone.

¹⁰In bringing many sons to glory, it was fitting that God, for whom and through whom everything exists, should make the author of their salvation perfect through suffering. ¹¹Both the one who makes men holy and those who are made holy are of the same family. So Jesus is not ashamed to call them brothers. ¹²He says,

"I will declare your name to my
    brothers;
    in the presence of the congregation I
    will sing your praises."*c*

¹³And again,

"I will put my trust in him."*d*

And again he says,

"Here am I, and the children God has
    given me."*e*

¹⁴Since the children have flesh and blood, he too shared in their humanity so that by his death he might destroy him who holds the power of death—that is, the devil—¹⁵and free those who all their lives were held in slavery by their fear of death. ¹⁶For surely it is not angels he helps, but Abraham's descendants. ¹⁷For this reason he had to be made like his brothers in every way, in order that he might become a merciful and faithful high priest in service to God, and that he might make atonement for*f* the sins of the people. ¹⁸Because he himself suffered when he was tempted, he is able to help those who are being tempted.

Jesus Greater Than Moses

3 Therefore, holy brothers, who share in the heavenly calling, fix your thoughts on Jesus, the apostle and high priest whom we confess. ²He was faithful to the one who appointed him, just as Moses was faithful in all God's house. ³Jesus has been found worthy of greater honour than Moses, just as the builder of a house has greater honour than the house itself. ⁴For every house is built by someone, but God is the builder of everything. ⁵Moses was faithful as a servant in all God's house, testifying to what would be said in the future. ⁶But Christ is faithful as a son over God's house. And we are his house, if we hold on to our courage and the hope of which we boast.

Warning Against Unbelief

⁷So, as the Holy Spirit says:

"Today, if you hear his voice,
⁸   do not harden your hearts
    as you did in the rebellion,
    during the time of testing in the
        desert,

---

*a*7 Or *him for a little while*; also in verse 9   *b*8 Psalm 8:4–6   *c*12 Psalm 22:22   *d*13 Isaiah 8:17
*e*13 Isaiah 8:18   *f*17 Or *and that he might turn aside God's wrath, taking away*

⁹where your fathers tested and tried me
    and for forty years saw what I did.
¹⁰That is why I was angry with that
        generation,
    and I said, 'Their hearts are always
        going astray,
    and they have not known my ways.'
¹¹So I declared on oath in my anger,
    'They shall never enter my rest.'"ᵃ

¹²See to it, brothers, that none of you
has a sinful, unbelieving heart that turns
away from the living God. ¹³But encourage one another daily, as long as it is called
Today, so that none of you may be hardened by sin's deceitfulness. ¹⁴We have
come to share in Christ if we hold firmly
till the end the confidence we had at first.
¹⁵As has just been said:

"Today, if you hear his voice,
    do not harden your hearts
as you did in the rebellion."ᵇ

¹⁶Who were they who heard and rebelled? Were they not all those Moses led out
of Egypt? ¹⁷And with whom was he angry
for forty years? Was it not with those who
sinned, whose bodies fell in the desert?
¹⁸And to whom did God swear that they
would never enter his rest if not to those
who disobeyed?ᶜ ¹⁹So we see that they
were not able to enter, because of their
unbelief.

A Sabbath-rest for the People of God

4 Therefore, since the promise of en-
    tering his rest still stands, let us be
careful that none of you be found to have
fallen short of it. ²For we also have had the
gospel preached to us, just as they did; but
the message they heard was of no value to
them, because those who heard did not
combine it with faith.ᵃ ³Now we who have
believed enter that rest, just as God has
said,

"So I declared on oath in my anger,
    'They shall never enter my rest.'"ᵇ

And yet his work has been finished since
the creation of the world. ⁴For somewhere
he has spoken about the seventh day in
these words: "And on the seventh day
God rested from all his work."ᶜ ⁵And
again in the passage above he says, "They
shall never enter my rest."

⁶It still remains that some will enter that
rest, and those who formerly had the gospel preached to them did not go in, because of their disobedience. ⁷Therefore
God again set a certain day, calling it
Today, when a long time later he spoke
through David, as was said before:

"Today, if you hear his voice,
    do not harden your hearts."ᵈ

⁸For if Joshua had given them rest, God
would not have spoken later about
another day. ⁹There remains, then, a
Sabbath-rest for the people of God; ¹⁰for
anyone who enters God's rest also rests
from his own work, just as God did from
his. ¹¹Let us, therefore, make every effort
to enter that rest, so that no-one will fall
by following their example of disobedience.

¹²For the word of God is living and
active. Sharper than any double-edged
sword, it penetrates even to dividing soul
and spirit, joints and marrow; it judges the
thoughts and attitudes of the heart.
¹³Nothing in all creation is hidden from
God's sight. Everything is uncovered and
laid bare before the eyes of him to whom
we must give account.

Jesus the Great High Priest

¹⁴Therefore, since we have a great high
priest who has gone through the heavens,ᵉ
Jesus the Son of God, let us hold firmly to
the faith we profess. ¹⁵For we do not have
a high priest who is unable to sympathise
with our weaknesses, but we have one
who has been tempted in every way, just
as we are—yet was without sin. ¹⁶Let us

ᵃ11 Psalm 95:7–11   ᵇ15 Psalm 95:7,8   ᶜ18 Or disbelieved
ᵃ2 Many manuscripts because they did not share in the faith of those who obeyed   ᵇ3 Psalm 95:11; also in verse 5
ᶜ4 Gen. 2:2   ᵈ7 Psalm 95:7,8   ᵉ14 Or gone into heaven

then approach the throne of grace with confidence, so that we may receive mercy and find grace to help us in our time of need.

5 Every high priest is selected from among men and is appointed to represent them in matters related to God, to offer gifts and sacrifices for sins. [2]He is able to deal gently with those who are ignorant and are going astray, since he himself is subject to weakness. [3]This is why he has to offer sacrifices for his own sins, as well as for the sins of the people.

[4]No-one takes this honour upon himself; he must be called by God, just as Aaron was. [5]So Christ also did not take upon himself the glory of becoming a high priest. But God said to him,

"You are my Son;
    today I have become your Father."[a,b]

[6]And he says in another place,

"You are a priest for ever,
    in the order of Melchizedek."[c]

[7]During the days of Jesus' life on earth, he offered up prayers and petitions with loud cries and tears to the one who could save him from death, and he was heard because of his reverent submission. [8]Although he was a son, he learned obedience from what he suffered [9]and, once made perfect, he became the source of eternal salvation for all who obey him [10]and was designated by God to be high priest in the order of Melchizedek.

Warning Against Falling Away

[11]We have much to say about this, but it is hard to explain because you are slow to learn. [12]In fact, though by this time you ought to be teachers, you need someone to teach you the elementary truths of God's word all over again. You need milk, not solid food! [13]Anyone who lives on milk, being still an infant, is not acquainted with the teaching about righteousness. [14]But solid food is for the mature, who by constant use have trained themselves to distinguish good from evil.

6 Therefore let us leave the elementary teachings about Christ and go on to maturity, not laying again the foundation of repentance from acts that lead to death,[a] and of faith in God, [2]instruction about baptisms, the laying on of hands, the resurrection of the dead, and eternal judgment. [3]And God permitting, we will do so.

[4]It is impossible for those who have once been enlightened, who have tasted the heavenly gift, who have shared in the Holy Spirit, [5]who have tasted the goodness of the word of God and the powers of the coming age, [6]if they fall away, to be brought back to repentance, because[b] to their loss they are crucifying the Son of God all over again and subjecting him to public disgrace.

[7]Land that drinks in the rain often falling on it and that produces a crop useful to those for whom it is farmed receives the blessing of God. [8]But land that produces thorns and thistles is worthless and is in danger of being cursed. In the end it will be burned.

[9]Even though we speak like this, dear friends, we are confident of better things in your case—things that accompany salvation. [10]God is not unjust; he will not forget your work and the love you have shown him as you have helped his people and continue to help them. [11]We want each of you to show this same diligence to the very end, in order to make your hope sure. [12]We do not want you to become lazy, but to imitate those who through faith and patience inherit what has been promised.

The Certainty of God's Promise

[13]When God made his promise to Abraham, since there was no-one greater for him to swear by, he swore by himself, [14]saying, "I will surely bless you and give you many descendants."[c] [15]And so after waiting patiently, Abraham received what was promised.

---

[a]5 Or *have begotten you*   [b]5 Psalm 2:7   [c]6 Psalm 110:4   [a]1 Or *from useless rituals*
[b]6 Or *repentance while*   [c]14 Gen. 22:17

[16]Men swear by someone greater than themselves, and the oath confirms what is said and puts an end to all argument. [17]Because God wanted to make the unchanging nature of his purpose very clear to the heirs of what was promised, he confirmed it with an oath. [18]God did this so that, by two unchangeable things in which it is impossible for God to lie, we who have fled to take hold of the hope offered to us may be greatly encouraged. [19]We have this hope as an anchor for the soul, firm and secure. It enters the inner sanctuary behind the curtain, [20]where Jesus, who went before us, has entered on our behalf. He has become a high priest for ever, in the order of Melchizedek.

Melchizedek the Priest

7 This Melchizedek was king of Salem and priest of God Most High. He met Abraham returning from the defeat of the kings and blessed him, [2]and Abraham gave him a tenth of everything. First, his name means "king of righteousness"; then also, "king of Salem" means "king of peace". [3]Without father or mother, without genealogy, without beginning of days or end of life, like the Son of God he remains a priest for ever.

[4]Just think how great he was: Even the patriarch Abraham gave him a tenth of the plunder! [5]Now the law requires the descendants of Levi who become priests to collect a tenth from the people—that is, their brothers—even though their brothers are descended from Abraham. [6]This man, however, did not trace his descent from Levi, yet he collected a tenth from Abraham and blessed him who had the promises. [7]And without doubt the lesser person is blessed by the greater. [8]In the one case, the tenth is collected by men who die; but in the other case, by him who is declared to be living. [9]One might even say that Levi, who collects the tenth, paid the tenth through Abraham, [10]because when Melchizedek met Abraham, Levi was still in the body of his ancestor.

Jesus Like Melchizedek

[11]If perfection could have been attained through the Levitical priesthood (for on the basis of it the law was given to the people), why was there still need for another priest to come—one in the order of Melchizedek, not in the order of Aaron? [12]For when there is a change of the priesthood, there must also be a change of the law. [13]He of whom these things are said belonged to a different tribe, and no-one from that tribe has ever served at the altar. [14]For it is clear that our Lord descended from Judah, and in regard to that tribe Moses said nothing about priests. [15]And what we have said is even more clear if another priest like Melchizedek appears, [16]one who has become a priest not on the basis of a regulation as to his ancestry but on the basis of the power of an indestructible life. [17]For it is declared:

"You are a priest for ever,
    in the order of Melchizedek."[a]

[18]The former regulation is set aside because it was weak and useless [19](for the law made nothing perfect), and a better hope is introduced, by which we draw near to God.

[20]And it was not without an oath! Others became priests without any oath, [21]but he became a priest with an oath when God said to him:

"The Lord has sworn
    and will not change his mind:
'You are a priest for ever.'"[b]

[22]Because of this oath, Jesus has become the guarantee of a better covenant.

[23]Now there have been many of those priests, since death prevented them from continuing in office; [24]but because Jesus lives for ever, he has a permanent priesthood. [25]Therefore he is able to save completely[c] those who come to God through him, because he always lives to intercede for them.

---

[a]17 Psalm 110:4   [b]21 Psalm 110:4   [c]25 Or *for ever*

26Such a high priest meets our need—one who is holy, blameless, pure, set apart from sinners, exalted above the heavens. 27Unlike the other high priests, he does not need to offer sacrifices day after day, first for his own sins, and then for the sins of the people. He sacrificed for their sins once for all when he offered himself. 28For the law appoints as high priests men who are weak; but the oath, which came after the law, appointed the Son, who has been made perfect for ever.

The High Priest of a New Covenant

8 The point of what we are saying is this: We do have such a high priest, who sat down at the right hand of the throne of the Majesty in heaven, 2and who serves in the sanctuary, the true tabernacle set up by the Lord, not by man.

3Every high priest is appointed to offer both gifts and sacrifices, and so it was necessary for this one also to have something to offer. 4If he were on earth, he would not be a priest, for there are already men who offer the gifts prescribed by the law. 5They serve at a sanctuary that is a copy and shadow of what is in heaven. This is why Moses was warned when he was about to build the tabernacle: "See to it that you make everything according to the pattern shown you on the mountain."a 6But the ministry Jesus has received is as superior to theirs as the covenant of which he is mediator is superior to the old one, and it is founded on better promises.

7For if there had been nothing wrong with that first covenant, no place would have been sought for another. 8But God found fault with the people and said:b

"The time is coming, declares the Lord,
    when I will make a new covenant
with the house of Israel
    and with the house of Judah.
9It will not be like the covenant
    I made with their forefathers
when I took them by the hand
    to lead them out of Egypt,

because they did not remain faithful to
    my covenant,
and I turned away from them,
                    declares the Lord.
10This is the covenant I will make with the
    house of Israel
after that time, declares the Lord.
I will put my laws in their minds
    and write them on their hearts.
I will be their God,
    and they will be my people.
11No longer will a man teach his
    neighbour,
    or a man his brother, saying, 'Know
    the Lord,'
because they will all know me,
    from the least of them to the greatest.
12For I will forgive their wickedness
    and will remember their sins no
        more."c

13By calling this covenant "new", he has made the first one obsolete; and what is obsolete and ageing will soon disappear.

Worship in the Earthly Tabernacle

9 Now the first covenant had regulations for worship and also an earthly sanctuary. 2A tabernacle was set up. In its first room were the lampstand, the table and the consecrated bread; this was called the Holy Place. 3Behind the second curtain was a room called the Most Holy Place, 4which had the golden altar of incense and the gold-covered ark of the covenant. This ark contained the gold jar of manna, Aaron's staff that had budded, and the stone tablets of the covenant. 5Above the ark were the cherubim of the Glory, overshadowing the atonement cover.a But we cannot discuss these things in detail now.

6When everything had been arranged like this, the priests entered regularly into the outer room to carry on their ministry. 7But only the high priest entered the inner room, and that only once a year, and never without blood, which he offered for himself and for the sins the people had

a5 Exodus 25:40   b8 Some manuscripts may be translated *fault and said to the people.*   c12 Jer. 31:31–34
a5 Traditionally *the mercy seat*

committed in ignorance. [8]The Holy Spirit was showing by this that the way into the Most Holy Place had not yet been disclosed as long as the first tabernacle was still standing. [9]This is an illustration for the present time, indicating that the gifts and sacrifices being offered were not able to clear the conscience of the worshipper. [10]They are only a matter of food and drink and various ceremonial washings—external regulations applying until the time of the new order.

The Blood of Christ

[11]When Christ came as high priest of the good things that are already here,[b] he went through the greater and more perfect tabernacle that is not man-made, that is to say, not a part of this creation. [12]He did not enter by means of the blood of goats and calves; but he entered the Most Holy Place once for all by his own blood, having obtained eternal redemption. [13]The blood of goats and bulls and the ashes of a heifer sprinkled on those who are ceremonially unclean sanctify them so that they are outwardly clean. [14]How much more, then, will the blood of Christ, who through the eternal Spirit offered himself unblemished to God, cleanse our consciences from acts that lead to death,[c] so that we may serve the living God!

[15]For this reason Christ is the mediator of a new covenant, that those who are called may receive the promised eternal inheritance—now that he has died as a ransom to set them free from the sins committed under the first covenant.

[16]In the case of a will,[d] it is necessary to prove the death of the one who made it, [17]because a will is in force only when somebody has died; it never takes effect while the one who made it is living. [18]This is why even the first covenant was not put into effect without blood. [19]When Moses had proclaimed every commandment of the law to all the people, he took the blood of calves, together with water, scarlet wool and branches of hyssop, and sprinkled the scroll and all the people.

[20]He said, "This is the blood of the covenant, which God has commanded you to keep."[e] [21]In the same way, he sprinkled with the blood both the tabernacle and everything used in its ceremonies. [22]In fact, the law requires that nearly everything be cleansed with blood, and without the shedding of blood there is no forgiveness.

[23]It was necessary, then, for the copies of the heavenly things to be purified with these sacrifices, but the heavenly things themselves with better sacrifices than these. [24]For Christ did not enter a man-made sanctuary that was only a copy of the true one; he entered heaven itself, now to appear for us in God's presence. [25]Nor did he enter heaven to offer himself again and again, the way the high priest enters the Most Holy Place every year with blood that is not his own. [26]Then Christ would have had to suffer many times since the creation of the world. But now he has appeared once for all at the end of the ages to do away with sin by the sacrifice of himself. [27]Just as man is destined to die once, and after that to face judgment, [28]so Christ was sacrificed once to take away the sins of many people; and he will appear a second time, not to bear sin, but to bring salvation to those who are waiting for him.

Christ's Sacrifice Once for All

10 The law is only a shadow of the good things that are coming—not the realities themselves. For this reason it can never, by the same sacrifices repeated endlessly year after year, make perfect those who draw near to worship. [2]If it could, would they not have stopped being offered? For the worshippers would have been cleansed once for all, and would no longer have felt guilty for their sins. [3]But those sacrifices are an annual reminder of sins, [4]because it is impossible for the blood of bulls and goats to take away sins.

[5]Therefore, when Christ came into the world, he said:

---

b11 Some early manuscripts *are to come*   *c14* Or *from useless rituals*
d16 Same Greek word as *covenant*; also in verse 17   *e20* Exodus 24:8

"Sacrifice and offering you did not
    desire,
but a body you prepared for me;
[6]with burnt offerings and sin offerings
    you were not pleased.
[7]Then I said, 'Here I am—it is written
    about me in the scroll—
I have come to do your will, O
    God.' "[a]

[8]First he said, "Sacrifices and offerings,
burnt offerings and sin offerings you did
not desire, nor were you pleased with
them" (although the law required them to
be made). [9]Then he said, "Here I am, I
have come to do your will." He sets aside
the first to establish the second. [10]And by
that will, we have been made holy through
the sacrifice of the body of Jesus Christ
once for all.

[11]Day after day every priest stands and
performs his religious duties; again and
again he offers the same sacrifices, which
can never take away sins. [12]But when this
priest had offered for all time one sacrifice
for sins, he sat down at the right hand of
God. [13]Since that time he waits for his
enemies to be made his footstool,
[14]because by one sacrifice he has made
perfect for ever those who are being made
holy.

[15]The Holy Spirit also testifies to us
about this. First he says:

[16]"This is the covenant I will make with
    them
after that time, says the Lord.
I will put my laws in their hearts,
    and I will write them on their
    minds."[b]

[17]Then he adds:

"Their sins and lawless acts
    I will remember no more."[c]

[18]And where these have been forgiven,
there is no longer any sacrifice for sin.

A Call to Persevere

[19]Therefore, brothers, since we have
confidence to enter the Most Holy Place
by the blood of Jesus, [20]by a new and living
way opened for us through the curtain,
that is, his body, [21]and since we have a
great priest over the house of God, [22]let us
draw near to God with a sincere heart in
full assurance of faith, having our hearts
sprinkled to cleanse us from a guilty conscience and having our bodies washed
with pure water. [23]Let us hold unswerv-
ingly to the hope we profess, for he who
promised is faithful. [24]And let us consider
how we may spur one another on towards
love and good deeds. [25]Let us not give up
meeting together, as some are in the habit
of doing, but let us encourage one
another—and all the more as you see the
Day approaching.

[26]If we deliberately keep on sinning
after we have received the knowledge of
the truth, no sacrifice for sins is left, [27]but
only a fearful expectation of judgment and
of raging fire that will consume the enemies of God. [28]Anyone who rejected the
law of Moses died without mercy on the
testimony of two or three witnesses.
[29]How much more severely do you think a
man deserves to be punished who has
trampled the Son of God under foot, who
has treated as an unholy thing the blood of
the covenant that sanctified him, and who
has insulted the Spirit of grace? [30]For we
know him who said, "It is mine to avenge;
I will repay,"[d] and again, "The Lord will
judge his people."[e] [31]It is a dreadful thing
to fall into the hands of the living God.

[32]Remember those earlier days after
you had received the light, when you
stood your ground in a great contest in the
face of suffering. [33]Sometimes you were
publicly exposed to insult and persecution; at other times you stood side by side
with those who were so treated. [34]You
sympathised with those in prison and
joyfully accepted the confiscation of your
property, because you knew that you
yourselves had better and lasting possessions.

a7 Psalm 40:6–8 (see Septuagint)   *b16* Jer. 31:33   *c17* Jer. 31:34   *d30* Deut. 32:35
e30 Deut. 32:36; Psalm 135:14

[35] So do not throw away your confidence; it will be richly rewarded. [36] You need to persevere so that when you have done the will of God, you will receive what he has promised. [37] For in just a very little while,

"He who is coming will come and will not delay.
[38]   But my righteous one[f] will live by faith.
And if he shrinks back,
     I will not be pleased with him."[g]

[39] But we are not of those who shrink back and are destroyed, but of those who believe and are saved.

By Faith

11 Now faith is being sure of what we hope for and certain of what we do not see. [2] This is what the ancients were commended for.

[3] By faith we understand that the universe was formed at God's command, so that what is seen was not made out of what was visible.

[4] By faith Abel offered God a better sacrifice than Cain did. By faith he was commended as a righteous man, when God spoke well of his offerings. And by faith he still speaks, even though he is dead.

[5] By faith Enoch was taken from this life, so that he did not experience death; he could not be found, because God had taken him away. For before he was taken, he was commended as one who pleased God. [6] And without faith it is impossible to please God, because anyone who comes to him must believe that he exists and that he rewards those who earnestly seek him.

[7] By faith Noah, when warned about things not yet seen, in holy fear built an ark to save his family. By his faith he condemned the world and became heir of the righteousness that comes by faith.

[8] By faith Abraham, when called to go to a place he would later receive as his inheritance, obeyed and went, even though he did not know where he was going. [9] By faith he made his home in the promised land like a stranger in a foreign country; he lived in tents, as did Isaac and Jacob, who were heirs with him of the same promise. [10] For he was looking forward to the city with foundations, whose architect and builder is God.

[11] By faith Abraham, even though he was past age—and Sarah herself was barren—was enabled to become a father because he[a] considered him faithful who had made the promise. [12] And so from this one man, and he as good as dead, came descendants as numerous as the stars in the sky and as countless as the sand on the seashore.

[13] All these people were still living by faith when they died. They did not receive the things promised; they only saw them and welcomed them from a distance. And they admitted that they were aliens and strangers on earth. [14] People who say such things show that they are looking for a country of their own. [15] If they had been thinking of the country they had left, they would have had opportunity to return. [16] Instead, they were longing for a better country—a heavenly one. Therefore God is not ashamed to be called their God, for he has prepared a city for them.

[17] By faith Abraham, when God tested him, offered Isaac as a sacrifice. He who had received the promises was about to sacrifice his one and only son, [18] even though God had said to him, "It is through Isaac that your offspring[b] will be reckoned."[c] [19] Abraham reasoned that God could raise the dead, and figuratively speaking, he did receive Isaac back from death.

[20] By faith Isaac blessed Jacob and Esau in regard to their future.

[21] By faith Jacob, when he was dying, blessed each of Joseph's sons, and worshipped as he leaned on the top of his staff.

[22] By faith Joseph, when his end was

---

[f]38 One early manuscript *But the righteous*   [g]38 Hab. 2:3,4
[a]11 Or *By faith even Sarah, who was past age, was enabled to bear children because she*
[b]18 Greek *seed*   [c]18 Gen. 21:12

near, spoke about the exodus of the Israelites from Egypt and gave instructions about his bones.

23By faith Moses' parents hid him for three months after he was born, because they saw he was no ordinary child, and they were not afraid of the king's edict.

24By faith Moses, when he had grown up, refused to be known as the son of Pharaoh's daughter. 25He chose to be ill-treated along with the people of God rather than to enjoy the pleasures of sin for a short time. 26He regarded disgrace for the sake of Christ as of greater value than the treasures of Egypt, because he was looking ahead to his reward. 27By faith he left Egypt, not fearing the king's anger; he persevered because he saw him who is invisible. 28By faith he kept the Passover and the sprinkling of blood, so that the destroyer of the firstborn would not touch the firstborn of Israel.

29By faith the people passed through the Red Sea*d* as on dry land; but when the Egyptians tried to do so, they were drowned.

30By faith the walls of Jericho fell, after the people had marched around them for seven days.

31By faith the prostitute Rahab, because she welcomed the spies, was not killed with those who were disobedient.*e*

32And what more shall I say? I do not have time to tell about Gideon, Barak, Samson, Jephthah, David, Samuel and the prophets, 33who through faith conquered kingdoms, administered justice, and gained what was promised; who shut the mouths of lions, 34quenched the fury of the flames, and escaped the edge of the sword; whose weakness was turned to strength; and who became powerful in battle and routed foreign armies. 35Women received back their dead, raised to life again. Others were tortured and refused to be released, so that they might gain a better resurrection. 36Some faced jeers and flogging, while still others were chained and put in prison. 37They were stoned;*f* they were sawn in two; they were put to death by the sword. They went

about in sheepskins and goatskins, destitute, persecuted and ill-treated—38the world was not worthy of them. They wandered in deserts and mountains, and in caves and holes in the ground.

39These were all commended for their faith, yet none of them received what had been promised. 40God had planned something better for us so that only together with us would they be made perfect.

God Disciplines His Sons

12 Therefore, since we are surrounded by such a great cloud of witnesses, let us throw off everything that hinders and the sin that so easily entangles, and let us run with perseverance the race marked out for us. 2Let us fix our eyes on Jesus, the author and perfecter of our faith, who for the joy set before him endured the cross, scorning its shame, and sat down at the right hand of the throne of God. 3Consider him who endured such opposition from sinful men, so that you will not grow weary and lose heart.

4In your struggle against sin, you have not yet resisted to the point of shedding your blood. 5And you have forgotten that word of encouragement that addresses you as sons:

"My son, do not make light of the
    Lord's discipline,
and do not lose heart when he
    rebukes you,
6because the Lord disciplines those he
    loves,
and he punishes everyone he accepts
    as a son."*a*

7Endure hardship as discipline; God is treating you as sons. For what son is not disciplined by his father? 8If you are not disciplined (and everyone undergoes discipline), then you are illegitimate children and not true sons. 9Moreover, we have all had human fathers who disciplined us and we respected them for it. How much more should we submit to the Father of our spirits and live! 10Our fathers disciplined

d29 That is, Sea of Reeds   e31 Or unbelieving   f37 Some early manuscripts stoned; they were put to the test;   a6 Prov. 3:11,12 us for a little while as they thought best; but God disciplines us for our good, that we may share in his holiness. ¹¹No discipline seems pleasant at the time, but painful. Later on, however, it produces a harvest of righteousness and peace for those who have been trained by it.

¹²Therefore, strengthen your feeble arms and weak knees! ¹³"Make level paths for your feet,"*b* so that the lame may not be disabled, but rather healed.

Warning Against Refusing God

¹⁴Make every effort to live in peace with all men and to be holy; without holiness no-one will see the Lord. ¹⁵See to it that no-one misses the grace of God and that no bitter root grows up to cause trouble and defile many. ¹⁶See that no-one is sexually immoral, or is godless like Esau, who for a single meal sold his inheritance rights as the oldest son. ¹⁷Afterwards, as you know, when he wanted to inherit this blessing, he was rejected. He could bring about no change of mind, though he sought the blessing with tears.

¹⁸You have not come to a mountain that can be touched and that is burning with fire; to darkness, gloom and storm; ¹⁹to a trumpet blast or to such a voice speaking words that those who heard it begged that no further word be spoken to them, ²⁰because they could not bear what was commanded: "If even an animal touches the mountain, it must be stoned."*c* ²¹The sight was so terrifying that Moses said, "I am trembling with fear."*d*

²²But you have come to Mount Zion, to the heavenly Jerusalem, the city of the living God. You have come to thousands upon thousands of angels in joyful assembly, ²³to the church of the firstborn, whose names are written in heaven. You have come to God, the judge of all men, to the spirits of righteous men made perfect, ²⁴to Jesus the mediator of a new covenant, and to the sprinkled blood that speaks a better word than the blood of Abel.

²⁵See to it that you do not refuse him who speaks. If they did not escape when they refused him who warned them on earth, how much less will we, if we turn away from him who warns us from heaven? ²⁶At that time his voice shook the earth, but now he has promised, "Once more I will shake not only the earth but also the heavens."*e* ²⁷The words "once more" indicate the removing of what can be shaken—that is, created things—so that what cannot be shaken may remain.

²⁸Therefore, since we are receiving a kingdom that cannot be shaken, let us be thankful, and so worship God acceptably with reverence and awe, ²⁹for our "God is a consuming fire."*f*

Concluding Exhortations

13 Keep on loving each other as brothers. ²Do not forget to entertain strangers, for by so doing some people have entertained angels without knowing it. ³Remember those in prison as if you were their fellow-prisoners, and those who are ill-treated as if you yourselves were suffering.

⁴Marriage should be honoured by all, and the marriage bed kept pure, for God will judge the adulterer and all the sexually immoral. ⁵Keep your lives free from the love of money and be content with what you have, because God has said,

"Never will I leave you;
    never will I forsake you."*a*

⁶So we say with confidence,

"The Lord is my helper; I will not be
    afraid.
What can man do to me?"*b*

⁷Remember your leaders, who spoke the word of God to you. Consider the outcome of their way of life and imitate their faith. ⁸Jesus Christ is the same yesterday and today and for ever.

⁹Do not be carried away by all kinds of strange teachings. It is good for our hearts

---

b13 Prov. 4:26   *c20* Exodus 19:12,13   *d21* Deut. 9:19   *e26* Haggai 2:6   *f29* Deut. 4:24
a5 Deut. 31:6   *b6* Psalm 118:6,7

to be strengthened by grace, not by ceremonial foods, which are of no value to those who eat them. [10]We have an altar from which those who minister at the tabernacle have no right to eat.

[11]The high priest carries the blood of animals into the Most Holy Place as a sin offering, but the bodies are burned outside the camp. [12]And so Jesus also suffered outside the city gate to make the people holy through his own blood. [13]Let us, then, go to him outside the camp, bearing the disgrace he bore. [14]For here we do not have an enduring city, but we are looking for the city that is to come.

[15]Through Jesus, therefore, let us continually offer to God a sacrifice of praise—the fruit of lips that confess his name. [16]And do not forget to do good and to share with others, for with such sacrifices God is pleased.

[17]Obey your leaders and submit to their authority. They keep watch over you as men who must give an account. Obey them so that their work will be a joy, not a burden, for that would be of no advantage to you.

[18]Pray for us. We are sure that we have a clear conscience and desire to live honourably in every way. [19]I particularly urge you to pray so that I may be restored to you soon.

[20]May the God of peace, who through the blood of the eternal covenant brought back from the dead our Lord Jesus, that great Shepherd of the sheep, [21]equip you with everything good for doing his will, and may he work in us what is pleasing to him, through Jesus Christ, to whom be glory for ever and ever. Amen.

[22]Brothers, I urge you to bear with my word of exhortation, for I have written you only a short letter.

[23]I want you to know that our brother Timothy has been released. If he arrives soon, I will come with him to see you.

[24]Greet all your leaders and all God's people. Those from Italy send you their greetings.

[25]Grace be with you all.

James

1 James, a servant of God and of the Lord Jesus Christ,

To the twelve tribes scattered among the nations:

Greetings.

Trials and Temptations

²Consider it pure joy, my brothers, whenever you face trials of many kinds, ³because you know that the testing of your faith develops perseverance. ⁴Perseverance must finish its work so that you may be mature and complete, not lacking anything. ⁵If any of you lacks wisdom, he should ask God, who gives generously to all without finding fault, and it will be given to him. ⁶But when he asks, he must believe and not doubt, because he who doubts is like a wave of the sea, blown and tossed by the wind. ⁷That man should not think he will receive anything from the Lord; ⁸he is a double-minded man, unstable in all he does.

⁹The brother in humble circumstances ought to take pride in his high position. ¹⁰But the one who is rich should take pride in his low position, because he will pass away like a wild flower. ¹¹For the sun rises with scorching heat and withers the plant; its blossom falls and its beauty is destroyed. In the same way, the rich man will fade away even while he goes about his business.

¹²Blessed is the man who perseveres under trial, because when he has stood the test, he will receive the crown of life that God has promised to those who love him. ¹³When tempted, no-one should say, "God is tempting me." For God cannot be tempted by evil, nor does he tempt anyone; ¹⁴but each one is tempted when, by his own evil desire, he is dragged away and enticed. ¹⁵Then, after desire has conceived, it gives birth to sin; and sin, when it is full-grown, gives birth to death.

¹⁶Don't be deceived, my dear brothers. ¹⁷Every good and perfect gift is from above, coming down from the Father of the heavenly lights, who does not change like shifting shadows. ¹⁸He chose to give us birth through the word of truth, that we might be a kind of firstfruits of all he created.

Listening and Doing

¹⁹My dear brothers, take note of this: Everyone should be quick to listen, slow to speak and slow to become angry, ²⁰for man's anger does not bring about the righteous life that God desires. ²¹Therefore, get rid of all moral filth and the evil that is so prevalent, and humbly accept the word planted in you, which can save you.

²²Do not merely listen to the word, and so deceive yourselves. Do what it says. ²³Anyone who listens to the word but does not do what it says is like a man who looks at his face in a mirror ²⁴and, after looking at himself, goes away and immediately forgets what he looks like. ²⁵But the man who looks intently into the perfect law that gives freedom, and continues to do this, not forgetting what he has heard, but

doing it—he will be blessed in what he does.

²⁶If anyone considers himself religious and yet does not keep a tight rein on his tongue, he deceives himself and his religion is worthless. ²⁷Religion that God our Father accepts as pure and faultless is this: to look after orphans and widows in their distress and to keep oneself from being polluted by the world.

Favouritism Forbidden

2 My brothers, as believers in our glorious Lord Jesus Christ, don't show favouritism. ²Suppose a man comes into your meeting wearing a gold ring and fine clothes, and a poor man in shabby clothes also comes in. ³If you show special attention to the man wearing fine clothes and say, "Here's a good seat for you," but say to the poor man, "You stand there" or "Sit on the floor by my feet," ⁴have you not discriminated among yourselves and become judges with evil thoughts?

⁵Listen, my dear brothers: Has not God chosen those who are poor in the eyes of the world to be rich in faith and to inherit the kingdom he promised those who love him? ⁶But you have insulted the poor. Is it not the rich who are exploiting you? Are they not the ones who are dragging you into court? ⁷Are they not the ones who are slandering the noble name of him to whom you belong?

⁸If you really keep the royal law found in Scripture, "Love your neighbour as yourself,"ᵃ you are doing right. ⁹But if you show favouritism, you sin and are convicted by the law as law-breakers. ¹⁰For whoever keeps the whole law and yet stumbles at just one point is guilty of breaking all of it. ¹¹For he who said, "Do not commit adultery,"ᵇ also said, "Do not murder."ᶜ If you do not commit adultery but do commit murder, you have become a law-breaker.

¹²Speak and act as those who are going to be judged by the law that gives freedom, ¹³because judgment without mercy will be shown to anyone who has not been merciful. Mercy triumphs over judgment!

Faith and Deeds

¹⁴What good is it, my brothers, if a man claims to have faith but has no deeds? Can such faith save him? ¹⁵Suppose a brother or sister is without clothes and daily food. ¹⁶If one of you says to him, "Go, I wish you well; keep warm and well fed," but does nothing about his physical needs, what good is it? ¹⁷In the same way, faith by itself, if it is not accompanied by action, is dead.

¹⁸But someone will say, "You have faith; I have deeds."

Show me your faith without deeds, and I will show you my faith by what I do. ¹⁹You believe that there is one God. Good! Even the demons believe that— and shudder.

²⁰You foolish man, do you want evidence that faith without deeds is useless?ᵈ ²¹Was not our ancestor Abraham considered righteous for what he did when he offered his son Isaac on the altar? ²²You see that his faith and his actions were working together, and his faith was made complete by what he did. ²³And the scripture was fulfilled that says, "Abraham believed God, and it was credited to him as righteousness,"ᵉ and he was called God's friend. ²⁴You see that a person is justified by what he does and not by faith alone.

²⁵In the same way, was not even Rahab the prostitute considered righteous for what she did when she gave lodging to the spies and sent them off in a different direction? ²⁶As the body without the spirit is dead, so faith without deeds is dead.

Taming the Tongue

3 Not many of you should presume to be teachers, my brothers, because you know that we who teach will be judged more strictly. ²We all stumble in many ways. If anyone is never at fault in

---

ᵃ8 Lev. 19:18   ᵇ11 Exodus 20:14; Deut. 5:18   ᶜ11 Exodus 20:13; Deut. 5:17
ᵈ20 Some early manuscripts dead   ᵉ23 Gen. 15:6

what he says, he is a perfect man, able to keep his whole body in check.

³When we put bits into the mouths of horses to make them obey us, we can turn the whole animal. ⁴Or take ships as an example. Although they are so large and are driven by strong winds, they are steered by a very small rudder wherever the pilot wants to go. ⁵Likewise the tongue is a small part of the body, but it makes great boasts. Consider what a great forest is set on fire by a small spark. ⁶The tongue also is a fire, a world of evil among the parts of the body. It corrupts the whole person, sets the whole course of his life on fire, and is itself set on fire by hell.

⁷All kinds of animals, birds, reptiles and creatures of the sea are being tamed and have been tamed by man, ⁸but no man can tame the tongue. It is a restless evil, full of deadly poison.

⁹With the tongue we praise our Lord and Father, and with it we curse men, who have been made in God's likeness. ¹⁰Out of the same mouth come praise and cursing. My brothers, this should not be. ¹¹Can both fresh water and salt*ᵃ* water flow from the same spring? ¹²My brothers, can a fig-tree bear olives, or a grapevine bear figs? Neither can a salt spring produce fresh water.

Two Kinds of Wisdom

¹³Who is wise and understanding among you? Let him show it by his good life, by deeds done in the humility that comes from wisdom. ¹⁴But if you harbour bitter envy and selfish ambition in your hearts, do not boast about it or deny the truth. ¹⁵Such "wisdom" does not come down from heaven but is earthly, unspiritual, of the devil. ¹⁶For where you have envy and selfish ambition, there you find disorder and every evil practice.

¹⁷But the wisdom that comes from heaven is first of all pure; then peace-loving, considerate, submissive, full of mercy and good fruit, impartial and sincere. ¹⁸Peacemakers who sow in peace raise a harvest of righteousness.

Submit Yourselves to God

4 What causes fights and quarrels among you? Don't they come from your desires that battle within you? ²You want something but don't get it. You kill and covet, but you cannot have what you want. You quarrel and fight. You do not have, because you do not ask God. ³When you ask, you do not receive, because you ask with wrong motives, that you may spend what you get on your pleasures.

⁴You adulterous people, don't you know that friendship with the world is hatred towards God? Anyone who chooses to be a friend of the world becomes an enemy of God. ⁵Or do you think Scripture says without reason that the spirit he caused to live in us envies intensely?*ᵃ* ⁶But he gives us more grace. That is why Scripture says:

"God opposes the proud
    but gives grace to the humble."*ᵇ*

⁷Submit yourselves, then, to God. Resist the devil, and he will flee from you. ⁸Come near to God and he will come near to you. Wash your hands, you sinners, and purify your hearts, you double-minded. ⁹Grieve, mourn and wail. Change your laughter to mourning and your joy to gloom. ¹⁰Humble yourselves before the Lord, and he will lift you up.

¹¹Brothers, do not slander one another. Anyone who speaks against his brother or judges him speaks against the law and judges it. When you judge the law, you are not keeping it, but sitting in judgment on it. ¹²There is only one Lawgiver and Judge, the one who is able to save and destroy. But you—who are you to judge your neighbour?

Boasting About Tomorrow

¹³Now listen, you who say, "Today or tomorrow we will go to this or that city, spend a year there, carry on business and make money." ¹⁴Why, you do not even know what will happen tomorrow. What is

---

ᵃ11 Greek bitter (see also verse 14)
ᵃ5 Or that God jealously longs for the spirit that he made to live in us; or that the Spirit he caused to live in us longs jealously
ᵇ6 Prov. 3:34

your life? You are a mist that appears for a little while and then vanishes. ¹⁵Instead, you ought to say, "If it is the Lord's will, we will live and do this or that." ¹⁶As it is, you boast and brag. All such boasting is evil. ¹⁷Anyone, then, who knows the good he ought to do and doesn't do it, sins.

Warning to Rich Oppressors

5 Now listen, you rich people, weep and wail because of the misery that is coming upon you. ²Your wealth has rotted, and moths have eaten your clothes. ³Your gold and silver are corroded. Their corrosion will testify against you and eat your flesh like fire. You have hoarded wealth in the last days. ⁴Look! The wages you failed to pay the workmen who mowed your fields are crying out against you. The cries of the harvesters have reached the ears of the Lord Almighty. ⁵You have lived on earth in luxury and self-indulgence. You have fattened yourselves in the day of slaughter.ᵃ ⁶You have condemned and murdered innocent men, who were not opposing you.

Patience in Suffering

⁷Be patient, then, brothers, until the Lord's coming. See how the farmer waits for the land to yield its valuable crop and how patient he is for the autumn and spring rains. ⁸You too, be patient and stand firm, because the Lord's coming is near. ⁹Don't grumble against each other, brothers, or you will be judged. The Judge is standing at the door!

¹⁰Brothers, as an example of patience in the face of suffering, take the prophets who spoke in the name of the Lord. ¹¹As you know, we consider blessed those who have persevered. You have heard of Job's perseverance and have seen what the Lord finally brought about. The Lord is full of compassion and mercy.

¹²Above all, my brothers, do not swear—not by heaven or by earth or by anything else. Let your "Yes" be yes, and your "No", no, or you will be condemned.

The Prayer of Faith

¹³Is any one of you in trouble? He should pray. Is anyone happy? Let him sing songs of praise. ¹⁴Is any one of you sick? He should call the elders of the church to pray over him and anoint him with oil in the name of the Lord. ¹⁵And the prayer offered in faith will make the sick person well; the Lord will raise him up. If he has sinned, he will be forgiven. ¹⁶Therefore confess your sins to each other and pray for each other so that you may be healed. The prayer of a righteous man is powerful and effective.

¹⁷Elijah was a man just like us. He prayed earnestly that it would not rain, and it did not rain on the land for three and a half years. ¹⁸Again he prayed, and the heavens gave rain, and the earth produced its crops.

¹⁹My brothers, if one of you should wander from the truth and someone should bring him back, ²⁰remember this: Whoever turns a sinner from the error of his way will save him from death and cover over a multitude of sins.

ᵃ5 Or yourselves as in a day of feasting

1 Peter

1 Peter, an apostle of Jesus Christ,

To God's elect, strangers in the world, scattered throughout Pontus, Galatia, Cappadocia, Asia and Bithynia, ²who have been chosen according to the foreknowledge of God the Father, through the sanctifying work of the Spirit, for obedience to Jesus Christ and sprinkling by his blood:

Grace and peace be yours in abundance.

Praise to God for a Living Hope

³Praise be to the God and Father of our Lord Jesus Christ! In his great mercy he has given us new birth into a living hope through the resurrection of Jesus Christ from the dead, ⁴and into an inheritance that can never perish, spoil or fade—kept in heaven for you, ⁵who through faith are shielded by God's power until the coming of the salvation that is ready to be revealed in the last time. ⁶In this you greatly rejoice, though now for a little while you may have had to suffer grief in all kinds of trials. ⁷These have come so that your faith—of greater worth than gold, which perishes even though refined by fire—may be proved genuine and may result in praise, glory and honour when Jesus Christ is revealed. ⁸Though you have not seen him, you love him; and even though you do not see him now, you believe in him and are filled with an inexpressible and glorious joy, ⁹for you are receiving the goal of your faith, the salvation of your souls.

¹⁰Concerning this salvation, the prophets, who spoke of the grace that was to come to you, searched intently and with the greatest care, ¹¹trying to find out the time and circumstances to which the Spirit of Christ in them was pointing when he predicted the sufferings of Christ and the glories that would follow. ¹²It was revealed to them that they were not serving themselves but you, when they spoke of the things that have now been told you by those who have preached the gospel to you by the Holy Spirit sent from heaven. Even angels long to look into these things.

Be Holy

¹³Therefore, prepare your minds for action; be self-controlled; set your hope fully on the grace to be given you when Jesus Christ is revealed. ¹⁴As obedient children, do not conform to the evil desires you had when you lived in ignorance. ¹⁵But just as he who called you is holy, so be holy in all you do; ¹⁶for it is written: "Be holy, because I am holy."*a*

¹⁷Since you call on a Father who judges each man's work impartially, live your lives as strangers here in reverent fear. ¹⁸For you know that it was not with perishable things such as silver or gold that you were redeemed from the empty way of life handed down to you from your forefathers, ¹⁹but with the precious blood of

a16 Lev. 11:44,45; 19:2; 20:7

Christ, a lamb without blemish or defect. [20]He was chosen before the creation of the world, but was revealed in these last times for your sake. [21]Through him you believe in God, who raised him from the dead and glorified him, and so your faith and hope are in God.

[22]Now that you have purified yourselves by obeying the truth so that you have sincere love for your brothers, love one another deeply, from the heart.[b] [23]For you have been born again, not of perishable seed, but of imperishable, through the living and enduring word of God. [24]For,

"All men are like grass,
   and all their glory is like the flowers of the field;
the grass withers and the flowers fall,
[25]   but the word of the Lord stands for ever."[c]

And this is the word that was preached to you.

2 Therefore, rid yourselves of all malice and all deceit, hypocrisy, envy, and slander of every kind. [2]Like newborn babies, crave pure spiritual milk, so that by it you may grow up in your salvation, [3]now that you have tasted that the Lord is good.

The Living Stone and a Chosen People

[4]As you come to him, the living Stone—rejected by men but chosen by God and precious to him—[5]you also, like living stones, are being built into a spiritual house to be a holy priesthood, offering spiritual sacrifices acceptable to God through Jesus Christ. [6]For in Scripture it says:

"See, I lay a stone in Zion,
   a chosen and precious cornerstone,
   and the one who trusts in him
   will never be put to shame."[a]

[7]Now to you who believe, this stone is precious. But to those who do not believe,

"The stone the builders rejected
   has become the capstone,"[b,c]

[8]and,

"A stone that causes men to stumble
   and a rock that makes them fall."[d]

They stumble because they disobey the message—which is also what they were destined for.

[9]But you are a chosen people, a royal priesthood, a holy nation, a people belonging to God, that you may declare the praises of him who called you out of darkness into his wonderful light. [10]Once you were not a people, but now you are the people of God; once you had not received mercy, but now you have received mercy.

[11]Dear friends, I urge you, as aliens and strangers in the world, to abstain from sinful desires, which war against your soul. [12]Live such good lives among the pagans that, though they accuse you of doing wrong, they may see your good deeds and glorify God on the day he visits us.

Submission to Rulers and Masters

[13]Submit yourselves for the Lord's sake to every authority instituted among men: whether to the king, as the supreme authority, [14]or to governors, who are sent by him to punish those who do wrong and to commend those who do right. [15]For it is God's will that by doing good you should silence the ignorant talk of foolish men. [16]Live as free men, but do not use your freedom as a cover-up for evil; live as servants of God. [17]Show proper respect to everyone: Love the brotherhood of believers, fear God, honour the king.

[18]Slaves, submit yourselves to your masters with all respect, not only to those who are good and considerate, but also to those who are harsh. [19]For it is commendable if a man bears up under the pain of unjust suffering because he is conscious of God. [20]But how is it to your credit if you receive a beating for doing wrong and

---

b22 Some early manuscripts *from a pure heart*   *c25* Isaiah 40:6-8   *a6* Isaiah 28:16   *b7* Or *cornerstone*
c7 Psalm 118:22   *d8* Isaiah 8:14

endure it? But if you suffer for doing good and you endure it, this is commendable before God. [21]To this you were called, because Christ suffered for you, leaving you an example, that you should follow in his steps.

[22]"He committed no sin,
    and no deceit was found in his
       mouth."[e]

[23]When they hurled their insults at him, he did not retaliate; when he suffered, he made no threats. Instead, he entrusted himself to him who judges justly. [24]He himself bore our sins in his body on the tree, so that we might die to sins and live for righteousness; by his wounds you have been healed. [25]For you were like sheep going astray, but now you have returned to the Shepherd and Overseer of your souls.

Wives and Husbands

3 Wives, in the same way be submissive to your husbands so that, if any of them do not believe the word, they may be won over without words by the behaviour of their wives, [2]when they see the purity and reverence of your lives. [3]Your beauty should not come from outward adornment, such as braided hair and the wearing of gold jewellery and fine clothes. [4]Instead, it should be that of your inner self, the unfading beauty of a gentle and quiet spirit, which is of great worth in God's sight. [5]For this is the way the holy women of the past who put their hope in God used to make themselves beautiful. They were submissive to their own husbands, [6]like Sarah, who obeyed Abraham and called him her master. You are her daughters if you do what is right and do not give way to fear.

[7]Husbands, in the same way be considerate as you live with your wives, and treat them with respect as the weaker partner and as heirs with you of the gracious gift of life, so that nothing will hinder your prayers.

Suffering for Doing Good

[8]Finally, all of you, live in harmony with one another; be sympathetic, love as brothers, be compassionate and humble. [9]Do not repay evil with evil or insult with insult, but with blessing, because to this you were called so that you may inherit a blessing. [10]For,

"Whoever would love life
    and see good days
must keep his tongue from evil
    and his lips from deceitful speech.
[11]He must turn from evil and do good;
    he must seek peace and pursue it.
[12]For the eyes of the Lord are on the
       righteous
    and his ears are attentive to their
       prayer,
but the face of the Lord is against those
    who do evil."[a]

[13]Who is going to harm you if you are eager to do good? [14]But even if you should suffer for what is right, you are blessed. "Do not fear what they fear;[b] do not be frightened."[c] [15]But in your hearts set apart Christ as Lord. Always be prepared to give an answer to everyone who asks you to give the reason for the hope that you have. But do this with gentleness and respect, [16]keeping a clear conscience, so that those who speak maliciously against your good behaviour in Christ may be ashamed of their slander. [17]It is better, if it is God's will, to suffer for doing good than for doing evil. [18]For Christ died for sins once for all, the righteous for the unrighteous, to bring you to God. He was put to death in the body but made alive by the Spirit, [19]through whom[d] also he went and preached to the spirits in prison [20]who disobeyed long ago when God waited patiently in the days of Noah while the ark was being built. In it only a few people, eight in all, were saved through water, [21]and this water symbolises baptism that now saves you also—not the removal of dirt from the body but the pledge[e] of a good conscience towards God. It saves

---

[e]22 Isaiah 53:9   [a]12 Psalm 34:12–16   [b]14 Or *not fear their threats*   [c]14 Isaiah 8:12
[d]18,19 Or *alive in the spirit*, [19]*through which*   [e]21 Or *response*

you by the resurrection of Jesus Christ, [22]who has gone into heaven and is at God's right hand—with angels, authorities and powers in submission to him.

Living for God

4 Therefore, since Christ suffered in his body, arm yourselves also with the same attitude, because he who has suffered in his body is done with sin. [2]As a result, he does not live the rest of his earthly life for evil human desires, but rather for the will of God. [3]For you have spent enough time in the past doing what pagans choose to do—living in debauchery, lust, drunkenness, orgies, carousing and detestable idolatry. [4]They think it strange that you do not plunge with them into the same flood of dissipation, and they heap abuse on you. [5]But they will have to give account to him who is ready to judge the living and the dead. [6]For this is the reason the gospel was preached even to those who are now dead, so that they might be judged according to men in regard to the body, but live according to God in regard to the spirit.

[7]The end of all things is near. Therefore be clear minded and self-controlled so that you can pray. [8]Above all, love each other deeply, because love covers over a multitude of sins. [9]Offer hospitality to one another without grumbling. [10]Each one should use whatever gift he has received to serve others, faithfully administering God's grace in its various forms. [11]If anyone speaks, he should do it as one speaking the very words of God. If anyone serves, he should do it with the strength God provides, so that in all things God may be praised through Jesus Christ. To him be the glory and the power for ever and ever. Amen.

Suffering for Being a Christian

[12]Dear friends, do not be surprised at the painful trial you are suffering, as though something strange were happening to you. [13]But rejoice that you participate in the sufferings of Christ, so that you may be overjoyed when his glory is revealed. [14]If you are insulted because of the name of Christ, you are blessed, for the Spirit of glory and of God rests on you. [15]If you suffer, it should not be as a murderer or thief or any other kind of criminal, or even as a meddler. [16]However, if you suffer as a Christian, do not be ashamed, but praise God that you bear that name. [17]For it is time for judgment to begin with the family of God; and if it begins with us, what will the outcome be for those who do not obey the gospel of God? [18]And,

> "If it is hard for the righteous to be
>   saved,
>   what will become of the ungodly and
>   the sinner?"[a]

[19]So then, those who suffer according to God's will should commit themselves to their faithful Creator and continue to do good.

To Elders and Young Men

5 To the elders among you, I appeal as a fellow-elder, a witness of Christ's sufferings and one who also will share in the glory to be revealed: [2]Be shepherds of God's flock that is under your care, serving as overseers—not because you must, but because you are willing, as God wants you to be; not greedy for money, but eager to serve; [3]not lording it over those entrusted to you, but being examples to the flock. [4]And when the Chief Shepherd appears, you will receive the crown of glory that will never fade away.

[5]Young men, in the same way be submissive to those who are older. All of you, clothe yourselves with humility towards one another, because,

> "God opposes the proud
>   but gives grace to the humble."[a]

[6]Humble yourselves, therefore, under God's mighty hand, that he may lift you up in due time. [7]Cast all your anxiety on him because he cares for you.

[a]18 Prov. 11:31   [a]5 Prov. 3:34

[8]Be self-controlled and alert. Your enemy the devil prowls around like a roaring lion looking for someone to devour. [9]Resist him, standing firm in the faith, because you know that your brothers throughout the world are undergoing the same kind of sufferings.

[10]And the God of all grace, who called you to his eternal glory in Christ, after you have suffered a little while, will himself restore you and make you strong, firm and steadfast. [11]To him be the power for ever and ever. Amen.

Final Greetings

[12]With the help of Silas,[b] whom I regard as a faithful brother, I have written to you briefly, encouraging you and testifying that this is the true grace of God. Stand fast in it.

[13]She who is in Babylon, chosen together with you, sends you her greetings, and so does my son Mark. [14]Greet one another with a kiss of love.

Peace to all of you who are in Christ.

---

b12 Greek *Silvanus*, a variant of *Silas*

2 Peter

1 Simon Peter, a servant and apostle of Jesus Christ,

To those who through the righteousness of our God and Saviour Jesus Christ have received a faith as precious as ours:

²Grace and peace be yours in abundance through the knowledge of God and of Jesus our Lord.

Making One's Calling and Election Sure

³His divine power has given us everything we need for life and godliness through our knowledge of him who called us by his own glory and goodness. ⁴Through these he has given us his very great and precious promises, so that through them you may participate in the divine nature and escape the corruption in the world caused by evil desires.

⁵For this very reason, make every effort to add to your faith goodness; and to goodness, knowledge; ⁶and to knowledge, self-control; and to self-control, perseverance; and to perseverance, godliness; ⁷and to godliness, brotherly kindness; and to brotherly kindness, love. ⁸For if you possess these qualities in increasing measure, they will keep you from being ineffective and unproductive in your knowledge of our Lord Jesus Christ. ⁹But if anyone does not have them, he is short-sighted and blind, and has forgotten that he has been cleansed from his past sins.

¹⁰Therefore, my brothers, be all the more eager to make your calling and election sure. For if you do these things, you will never fall, ¹¹and you will receive a rich welcome into the eternal kingdom of our Lord and Saviour Jesus Christ.

Prophecy of Scripture

¹²So I will always remind you of these things, even though you know them and are firmly established in the truth you now have. ¹³I think it is right to refresh your memory as long as I live in the tent of this body, ¹⁴because I know that I will soon put it aside, as our Lord Jesus Christ has made clear to me. ¹⁵And I will make every effort to see that after my departure you will always be able to remember these things.

¹⁶We did not follow cleverly invented stories when we told you about the power and coming of our Lord Jesus Christ, but we were eye-witnesses of his majesty. ¹⁷For he received honour and glory from God the Father when the voice came to him from the Majestic Glory, saying, "This is my Son, whom I love; with him I am well pleased."*a* ¹⁸We ourselves heard this voice that came from heaven when we were with him on the sacred mountain.

¹⁹And we have the word of the prophets made more certain, and you will do well to pay attention to it, as to a light shining in a dark place, until the day dawns and the morning star rises in your hearts. ²⁰Above all, you must understand that no prophecy of Scripture came about by the prophet's own interpretation. ²¹For prophecy never

*a*17 Matt. 17:5; Mark 9:7; Luke 9:35

had its origin in the will of man, but men spoke from God as they were carried along by the Holy Spirit.

False Teachers and Their Destruction

2 But there were also false prophets among the people, just as there will be false teachers among you. They will secretly introduce destructive heresies, even denying the sovereign Lord who bought them—bringing swift destruction on themselves. [2]Many will follow their shameful ways and will bring the way of truth into disrepute. [3]In their greed these teachers will exploit you with stories they have made up. Their condemnation has long been hanging over them, and their destruction has not been sleeping.

[4]For if God did not spare angels when they sinned, but sent them to hell,[a] putting them into gloomy dungeons[b] to be held for judgment; [5]if he did not spare the ancient world when he brought the flood on its ungodly people, but protected Noah, a preacher of righteousness, and seven others; [6]if he condemned the cities of Sodom and Gomorrah by burning them to ashes, and made them an example of what is going to happen to the ungodly; [7]and if he rescued Lot, a righteous man, who was distressed by the filthy lives of lawless men [8](for that righteous man, living among them day after day, was tormented in his righteous soul by the lawless deeds he saw and heard)—[9]if this is so, then the Lord knows how to rescue godly men from trials and to hold the unrighteous for the day of judgment, while continuing their punishment.[c] [10]This is especially true of those who follow the corrupt desire of the sinful nature[d] and despise authority.

Bold and arrogant, these men are not afraid to slander celestial beings; [11]yet even angels, although they are stronger and more powerful, do not bring slanderous accusations against such beings in the presence of the Lord. [12]But these men blaspheme in matters they do not understand. They are like brute beasts, creatures of instinct, born only to be caught and destroyed, and like beasts they too will perish.

[13]They will be paid back with harm for the harm they have done. Their idea of pleasure is to carouse in broad daylight. They are blots and blemishes, revelling in their pleasures while they feast with you.[e] [14]With eyes full of adultery, they never stop sinning; they seduce the unstable; they are experts in greed—an accursed brood! [15]They have left the straight way and wandered off to follow the way of Balaam son of Beor, who loved the wages of wickedness. [16]But he was rebuked for his wrongdoing by a donkey—a beast without speech—who spoke with a man's voice and restrained the prophet's madness.

[17]These men are springs without water and mists driven by a storm. Blackest darkness is reserved for them. [18]For they mouth empty, boastful words and, by appealing to the lustful desires of sinful human nature, they entice people who are just escaping from those who live in error. [19]They promise them freedom, while they themselves are slaves of depravity—for a man is a slave to whatever has mastered him. [20]If they have escaped the corruption of the world by knowing our Lord and Saviour Jesus Christ and are again entangled in it and overcome, they are worse off at the end than they were at the beginning. [21]It would have been better for them not to have known the way of righteousness, than to have known it and then to turn their backs on the sacred command that was passed on to them. [22]Of them the proverbs are true: "A dog returns to its vomit,"[f] and, "A sow that is washed goes back to her wallowing in the mud."

The Day of the Lord

3 Dear friends, this is now my second letter to you. I have written both of them as reminders to stimulate you to wholesome thinking. [2]I want you to recall the words spoken in the past by the

---

[a]4 Greek *Tartarus*　　[b]4 Some manuscripts *into chains of darkness*
[c]9 Or *unrighteous for punishment until the day of judgment*　　[d]10 Or *the flesh*
[e]13 Some manuscripts *in their love feasts*　　[f]22 Prov. 26:11

holy prophets and the command given by our Lord and Saviour through your apostles.

³First of all, you must understand that in the last days scoffers will come, scoffing and following their own evil desires. ⁴They will say, "Where is this 'coming' he promised? Ever since our fathers died, everything goes on as it has since the beginning of creation." ⁵But they deliberately forget that long ago by God's word the heavens existed and the earth was formed out of water and by water. ⁶By these waters also the world of that time was deluged and destroyed. ⁷By the same word the present heavens and earth are reserved for fire, being kept for the day of judgment and destruction of ungodly men.

⁸But do not forget this one thing, dear friends: With the Lord a day is like a thousand years, and a thousand years are like a day. ⁹The Lord is not slow in keeping his promise, as some understand slowness. He is patient with you, not wanting anyone to perish, but everyone to come to repentance.

¹⁰But the day of the Lord will come like a thief. The heavens will disappear with a roar; the elements will be destroyed by fire, and the earth and everything in it will be laid bare.ᵃ

¹¹Since everything will be destroyed in this way, what kind of people ought you to be? You ought to live holy and godly lives ¹²as you look forward to the day of God and speed its coming.ᵇ That day will bring about the destruction of the heavens by fire, and the elements will melt in the heat. ¹³But in keeping with his promise we are looking forward to a new heaven and a new earth, the home of righteousness.

¹⁴So then, dear friends, since you are looking forward to this, make every effort to be found spotless, blameless and at peace with him. ¹⁵Bear in mind that our Lord's patience means salvation, just as our dear brother Paul also wrote to you with the wisdom that God gave him. ¹⁶He writes the same way in all his letters, speaking in them of these matters. His letters contain some things that are hard to understand, which ignorant and unstable people distort, as they do the other Scriptures, to their own destruction.

¹⁷Therefore, dear friends, since you already know this, be on your guard so that you may not be carried away by the error of lawless men and fall from your secure position. ¹⁸But grow in the grace and knowledge of our Lord and Saviour Jesus Christ. To him be glory both now and for ever! Amen.

1 John

The Word of Life

1 That which was from the beginning, which we have heard, which we have seen with our eyes, which we have looked at and our hands have touched—this we proclaim concerning the Word of life. ²The life appeared; we have seen it and testify to it, and we proclaim to you the eternal life, which was with the Father and has appeared to us. ³We proclaim to you what we have seen and heard, so that you also may have fellowship with us. And our fellowship is with the Father and with his Son, Jesus Christ. ⁴We write this to make our*a* joy complete.

Walking in the Light

⁵This is the message we have heard from him and declare to you: God is light; in him there is no darkness at all. ⁶If we claim to have fellowship with him yet walk in the darkness, we lie and do not live by the truth. ⁷But if we walk in the light, as he is in the light, we have fellowship with one another, and the blood of Jesus, his Son, purifies us from all*b* sin.

⁸If we claim to be without sin, we deceive ourselves and the truth is not in us. ⁹If we confess our sins, he is faithful and just and will forgive us our sins and purify us from all unrighteousness. ¹⁰If we claim we have not sinned, we make him out to be a liar and his word has no place in our lives.

2 My dear children, I write this to you so that you will not sin. But if anybody does sin, we have one who speaks to the Father in our defence—Jesus Christ, the Righteous One. ²He is the atoning sacrifice for our sins, and not only for ours but also for*a* the sins of the whole world.

³We know that we have come to know him if we obey his commands. ⁴The man who says, "I know him," but does not do what he commands is a liar, and the truth is not in him. ⁵But if anyone obeys his word, God's love*b* is truly made complete in him. This is how we know we are in him: ⁶Whoever claims to live in him must walk as Jesus did.

⁷Dear friends, I am not writing you a new command but an old one, which you have had since the beginning. This old command is the message you have heard. ⁸Yet I am writing you a new command; its truth is seen in him and you, because the darkness is passing and the true light is already shining.

⁹Anyone who claims to be in the light but hates his brother is still in the darkness. ¹⁰Whoever loves his brother lives in the light, and there is nothing in him*c* to make him stumble. ¹¹But whoever hates his brother is in the darkness and walks around in the darkness; he does not know where he is going, because the darkness has blinded him.

¹²I write to you, dear children,
    because your sins have been forgiven
        on account of his name.

---

*a*4 Some manuscripts *your*   *b*7 Or *every*
*a*2 Or *He is the one who turns aside God's wrath, taking away our sins, and not only ours but also*
*b*5 Or *word, love for God*   *c*10 Or *it*

¹³I write to you, fathers,
because you have known him who is
from the beginning.
I write to you, young men,
because you have overcome the evil
one.
I write to you, dear children,
because you have known the Father.
¹⁴I write to you, fathers,
because you have known him who is
from the beginning.
I write to you, young men,
because you are strong,
and the word of God lives in you,
and you have overcome the evil one.

Do Not Love the World

¹⁵Do not love the world or anything in
the world. If anyone loves the world, the
love of the Father is not in him. ¹⁶For
everything in the world—the cravings of
sinful man, the lust of his eyes and the
boasting of what he has and does—comes
not from the Father but from the world.
¹⁷The world and its desires pass away, but
the man who does the will of God lives for
ever.

Warning Against Antichrists

¹⁸Dear children, this is the last hour;
and as you have heard that the antichrist is
coming, even now many antichrists have
come. This is how we know it is the last
hour. ¹⁹They went out from us, but they
did not really belong to us. For if they had
belonged to us, they would have remained
with us; but their going showed that none
of them belonged to us.

²⁰But you have an anointing from the
Holy One, and all of you know the truth.^d
²¹I do not write to you because you do not
know the truth, but because you do know
it and because no lie comes from the truth.
²²Who is the liar? It is the man who denies
that Jesus is the Christ. Such a man is the
antichrist—he denies the Father and the
Son. ²³No-one who denies the Son has the
Father; whoever acknowledges the Son
has the Father also.

²⁴See that what you have heard from the
beginning remains in you. If it does, you
also will remain in the Son and in the
Father. ²⁵And this is what he promised
us—even eternal life.

²⁶I am writing these things to you about
those who are trying to lead you astray.
²⁷As for you, the anointing you received
from him remains in you, and you do not
need anyone to teach you. But as his
anointing teaches you about all things and
as that anointing is real, not counterfeit—
just as it has taught you, remain in him.

Children of God

²⁸And now, dear children, continue in
him, so that when he appears we may be
confident and unashamed before him at
his coming.

²⁹If you know that he is righteous, you
know that everyone who does what is right
has been born of him.

3 How great is the love the Father has
lavished on us, that we should be
called children of God! And that is what
we are! The reason the world does not
know us is that it did not know him. ²Dear
friends, now we are children of God, and
what we will be has not yet been made
known. But we know that when he
appears,^a we shall be like him, for we shall
see him as he is. ³Everyone who has this
hope in him purifies himself, just as he is
pure.

⁴Everyone who sins breaks the law; in
fact, sin is lawlessness. ⁵But you know that
he appeared so that he might take away
our sins. And in him is no sin. ⁶No-one
who lives in him keeps on sinning. No-one
who continues to sin has either seen him or
known him.

⁷Dear children, do not let anyone lead
you astray. He who does what is right is
righteous, just as he is righteous. ⁸He who
does what is sinful is of the devil, because
the devil has been sinning from the beginning. The reason the Son of God appeared
was to destroy the devil's work. ⁹No-one
who is born of God will continue to sin,
because God's seed remains in him; he

cannot go on sinning, because he has been born of God. [10]This is how we know who the children of God are and who the children of the devil are: Anyone who does not do what is right is not a child of God; nor is anyone who does not love his brother.

Love One Another

[11]This is the message you heard from the beginning: We should love one another. [12]Do not be like Cain, who belonged to the evil one and murdered his brother. And why did he murder him? Because his own actions were evil and his brother's were righteous. [13]Do not be surprised, my brothers, if the world hates you. [14]We know that we have passed from death to life, because we love our brothers. Anyone who does not love remains in death. [15]Anyone who hates his brother is a murderer, and you know that no murderer has eternal life in him.

[16]This is how we know what love is: Jesus Christ laid down his life for us. And we ought to lay down our lives for our brothers. [17]If anyone has material possessions and sees his brother in need but has no pity on him, how can the love of God be in him? [18]Dear children, let us not love with words or tongue but with actions and in truth. [19]This then is how we know that we belong to the truth, and how we set our hearts at rest in his presence [20]whenever our hearts condemn us. For God is greater than our hearts, and he knows everything.

[21]Dear friends, if our hearts do not condemn us, we have confidence before God [22]and receive from him anything we ask, because we obey his commands and do what pleases him. [23]And this is his command: to believe in the name of his Son, Jesus Christ, and to love one another as he commanded us. [24]Those who obey his commands live in him, and he in them. And this is how we know that he lives in us: We know it by the Spirit he gave us.

Test the Spirits

4 Dear friends, do not believe every spirit, but test the spirits to see whether they are from God, because many false prophets have gone out into the world. [2]This is how you can recognise the Spirit of God: Every spirit that acknowledges that Jesus Christ has come in the flesh is from God, [3]but every spirit that does not acknowledge Jesus is not from God. This is the spirit of the antichrist, which you have heard is coming and even now is already in the world.

[4]You, dear children, are from God and have overcome them, because the one who is in you is greater than the one who is in the world. [5]They are from the world and therefore speak from the viewpoint of the world, and the world listens to them. [6]We are from God, and whoever knows God listens to us; but whoever is not from God does not listen to us. This is how we recognise the Spirit[a] of truth and the spirit of falsehood.

God's Love and Ours

[7]Dear friends, let us love one another, for love comes from God. Everyone who loves has been born of God and knows God. [8]Whoever does not love does not know God, because God is love. [9]This is how God showed his love among us: He sent his one and only Son[b] into the world that we might live through him. [10]This is love: not that we loved God, but that he loved us and sent his Son as an atoning sacrifice for[c] our sins. [11]Dear friends, since God so loved us, we also ought to love one another. [12]No-one has ever seen God; but if we love one another, God lives in us and his love is made complete in us.

[13]We know that we live in him and he in us, because he has given us of his Spirit. [14]And we have seen and testify that the Father has sent his Son to be the Saviour of the world. [15]If anyone acknowledges that Jesus is the Son of God, God lives in him and he in God. [16]And so we know and

[a]6 Or spirit   [b]9 Or his only begotten Son   [c]10 Or as the one who would turn aside his wrath, taking away

rely on the love God has for us.

God is love. Whoever lives in love lives in God, and God in him. [17]In this way, love is made complete among us so that we will have confidence on the day of judgment, because in this world we are like him. [18]There is no fear in love. But perfect love drives out fear, because fear has to do with punishment. The one who fears is not made perfect in love.

[19]We love because he first loved us. [20]If anyone says, "I love God," yet hates his brother, he is a liar. For anyone who does not love his brother, whom he has seen, cannot love God, whom he has not seen. [21]And he has given us this command: Whoever loves God must also love his brother.

Faith in the Son of God

5 Everyone who believes that Jesus is the Christ is born of God, and everyone who loves the father loves his child as well. [2]This is how we know that we love the children of God: by loving God and carrying out his commands. [3]This is love for God: to obey his commands. And his commands are not burdensome, [4]for everyone born of God overcomes the world. This is the victory that has overcome the world, even our faith. [5]Who is it that overcomes the world? Only he who believes that Jesus is the Son of God.

[6]This is the one who came by water and blood—Jesus Christ. He did not come by water only, but by water and blood. And it is the Spirit who testifies, because the Spirit is the truth. [7]For there are three that testify: [8]the[a] Spirit, the water and the blood; and the three are in agreement. [9]We accept man's testimony, but God's testimony is greater because it is the testimony of God, which he has given about

his Son. [10]Anyone who believes in the Son of God has this testimony in his heart. Anyone who does not believe God has made him out to be a liar, because he has not believed the testimony God has given about his Son. [11]And this is the testimony: God has given us eternal life, and this life is in his Son. [12]He who has the Son has life; he who does not have the Son of God does not have life.

Concluding Remarks

[13]I write these things to you who believe in the name of the Son of God so that you may know that you have eternal life. [14]This is the confidence we have in approaching God: that if we ask anything according to his will, he hears us. [15]And if we know that he hears us—whatever we ask—we know that we have what we asked of him.

[16]If anyone sees his brother commit a sin that does not lead to death, he should pray and God will give him life. I refer to those whose sin does not lead to death. There is a sin that leads to death. I am not saying that he should pray about that. [17]All wrongdoing is sin, and there is sin that does not lead to death.

[18]We know that anyone born of God does not continue to sin; the one who was born of God keeps him safe, and the evil one cannot harm him. [19]We know that we are children of God, and that the whole world is under the control of the evil one. [20]We know also that the Son of God has come and has given us understanding, so that we may know him who is true. And we are in him who is true—even in his Son Jesus Christ. He is the true God and eternal life.

[21]Dear children, keep yourselves from idols.

---

[a]7, 8 Late manuscripts of the Vulgate *testify in heaven: the Father, the Word and the Holy Spirit, and these three are one.* [8]*And there are three that testify on earth: the* (not found in any Greek manuscript before the sixteenth century)

2 John

¹The elder,

To the chosen lady and her children, whom I love in the truth—and not I only, but also all who know the truth—²because of the truth, which lives in us and will be with us for ever:

³Grace, mercy and peace from God the Father and from Jesus Christ, the Father's Son, will be with us in truth and love.

⁴It has given me great joy to find some of your children walking in the truth, just as the Father commanded us. ⁵And now, dear lady, I am not writing you a new command but one we have had from the beginning. I ask that we love one another. ⁶And this is love: that we walk in obedience to his commands. As you have heard from the beginning, his command is that you walk in love.

⁷Many deceivers, who do not acknowledge Jesus Christ as coming in the flesh, have gone out into the world. Any such person is the deceiver and the antichrist. ⁸Watch out that you do not lose what you have worked for, but that you may be rewarded fully. ⁹Anyone who runs ahead and does not continue in the teaching of Christ does not have God; whoever continues in the teaching has both the Father and the Son. ¹⁰If anyone comes to you and does not bring this teaching, do not take him into your house or welcome him. ¹¹Anyone who welcomes him shares in his wicked work.

¹²I have much to write to you, but I do not want to use paper and ink. Instead, I hope to visit you and talk with you face to face, so that our joy may be complete.

¹³The children of your chosen sister send their greetings.

3 John

¹The elder,

To my dear friend Gaius, whom I love in the truth.

²Dear friend, I pray that you may enjoy good health and that all may go well with you, even as your soul is getting along well. ³It gave me great joy to have some brothers come and tell about your faithfulness to the truth and how you continue to walk in the truth. ⁴I have no greater joy than to hear that my children are walking in the truth.

⁵Dear friend, you are faithful in what you are doing for the brothers, even though they are strangers to you. ⁶They have told the church about your love. You will do well to send them on their way in a manner worthy of God. ⁷It was for the sake of the Name that they went out, receiving no help from the pagans. ⁸We ought therefore to show hospitality to such men so that we may work together for the truth.

⁹I wrote to the church, but Diotrephes, who loves to be first, will have nothing to do with us. ¹⁰So if I come, I will call attention to what he is doing, gossiping maliciously about us. Not satisfied with that, he refuses to welcome the brothers. He also stops those who want to do so and puts them out of the church.

¹¹Dear friend, do not imitate what is evil but what is good. Anyone who does what is good is from God. Anyone who does what is evil has not seen God. ¹²Demetrius is well spoken of by everyone—and even by the truth itself. We also speak well of him, and you know that our testimony is true.

¹³I have much to write to you, but I do not want to do so with pen and ink. ¹⁴I hope to see you soon, and we will talk face to face.

Peace to you. The friends here send their greetings. Greet the friends there by name.

Jude

¹Jude, a servant of Jesus Christ and a brother of James,

To those who have been called, who are loved by God the Father and kept by*ᵃ* Jesus Christ:

²Mercy, peace and love be yours in abundance.

The Sin and Doom of Godless Men

³Dear friends, although I was very eager to write to you about the salvation we share, I felt I had to write and urge you to contend for the faith that was once for all entrusted to the saints. ⁴For certain men whose condemnation was written about*ᵇ* long ago have secretly slipped in among you. They are godless men, who change the grace of our God into a licence for immorality and deny Jesus Christ our only Sovereign and Lord.

⁵Though you already know all this, I want to remind you that the Lord*ᶜ* delivered his people out of Egypt, but later destroyed those who did not believe. ⁶And the angels who did not keep their positions of authority but abandoned their own home—these he has kept in darkness, bound with everlasting chains for judgment on the great Day. ⁷In a similar way, Sodom and Gomorrah and the surrounding towns gave themselves up to sexual immorality and perversion. They serve as an example of those who suffer the punishment of eternal fire.

⁸In the very same way, these dreamers pollute their own bodies, reject authority and slander celestial beings. ⁹But even the archangel Michael, when he was disputing with the devil about the body of Moses, did not dare to bring a slanderous accusation against him, but said, "The Lord rebuke you!" ¹⁰Yet these men speak abusively against whatever they do not understand; and what things they do understand by instinct, like unreasoning animals— these are the very things that destroy them.

¹¹Woe to them! They have taken the way of Cain; they have rushed for profit into Balaam's error; they have been destroyed in Korah's rebellion.

¹²These men are blemishes at your love feasts, eating with you without the slightest qualm—shepherds who feed only themselves. They are clouds without rain, blown along by the wind; autumn trees, without fruit and uprooted—twice dead. ¹³They are wild waves of the sea, foaming up their shame; wandering stars, for whom blackest darkness has been reserved for ever.

¹⁴Enoch, the seventh from Adam, prophesied about these men: "See, the Lord is coming with thousands upon thousands of his holy ones ¹⁵to judge everyone, and to convict all the ungodly of all the ungodly acts they have done in the ungodly way, and of all the harsh words ungodly sinners have spoken against him." ¹⁶These men are grumblers and fault-finders; they follow their own evil

---

ᵃ1 Or *for*; or *in*   *ᵇ4* Or *men who were marked out for condemnation*   *ᶜ5* Some early manuscripts *Jesus* desires; they boast about themselves and flatter others for their own advantage.

A Call to Persevere

[17]But, dear friends, remember what the apostles of our Lord Jesus Christ foretold. [18]They said to you, "In the last times there will be scoffers who will follow their own ungodly desires." [19]These are the men who divide you, who follow mere natural instincts and do not have the Spirit.

[20]But you, dear friends, build yourselves up in your most holy faith and pray in the Holy Spirit. [21]Keep yourselves in God's love as you wait for the mercy of our Lord Jesus Christ to bring you to eternal life.

[22]Be merciful to those who doubt; [23]snatch others from the fire and save them; to others show mercy, mixed with fear—hating even the clothing stained by corrupted flesh.

Doxology

[24]To him who is able to keep you from falling and to present you before his glorious presence without fault and with great joy—[25]to the only God our Saviour be glory, majesty, power and authority, through Jesus Christ our Lord, before all ages, now and for evermore! Amen.

Revelation

Prologue

Prologue

1 The revelation of Jesus Christ, which God gave him to show his servants what must soon take place. He made it known by sending his angel to his servant John, ²who testifies to everything he saw—that is, the word of God and the testimony of Jesus Christ. ³Blessed is the one who reads the words of this prophecy, and blessed are those who hear it and take to heart what is written in it, because the time is near.

Greetings and Doxology

⁴John,

To the seven churches in the province of Asia:

Grace and peace to you from him who is, and who was, and who is to come, and from the seven spirits*ᵃ* before his throne, ⁵and from Jesus Christ, who is the faithful witness, the firstborn from the dead, and the ruler of the kings of the earth.

To him who loves us and has freed us from our sins by his blood, ⁶and has made us to be a kingdom and priests to serve his God and Father—to him be glory and power for ever and ever! Amen.

⁷Look, he is coming with the clouds,
    and every eye will see him,
    even those who pierced him;

and all the peoples of the earth will
    mourn because of him.
                So shall it be! Amen.

⁸"I am the Alpha and the Omega," says the Lord God, "who is, and who was, and who is to come, the Almighty."

One Like a Son of Man

⁹I, John, your brother and companion in the suffering and kingdom and patient endurance that are ours in Jesus, was on the island of Patmos because of the word of God and the testimony of Jesus. ¹⁰On the Lord's Day I was in the Spirit, and I heard behind me a loud voice like a trumpet, ¹¹which said: "Write on a scroll what you see and send it to the seven churches: to Ephesus, Smyrna, Pergamum, Thyatira, Sardis, Philadelphia and Laodicea."

¹²I turned round to see the voice that was speaking to me. And when I turned I saw seven golden lampstands, ¹³and among the lampstands was someone "like a son of man",*ᵇ* dressed in a robe reaching down to his feet and with a golden sash round his chest. ¹⁴His head and hair were white like wool, as white as snow, and his eyes were like blazing fire. ¹⁵His feet were like bronze glowing in a furnace, and his voice was like the sound of rushing waters. ¹⁶In his right hand he held seven stars, and out of his mouth came a sharp double-edged sword. His face was like the sun shining in all its brilliance.

17When I saw him, I fell at his feet as though dead. Then he placed his right hand on me and said: "Do not be afraid. I am the First and the Last. 18I am the Living One; I was dead, and behold I am alive for ever and ever! And I hold the keys of death and Hades.

19"Write, therefore, what you have seen, what is now and what will take place later. 20The mystery of the seven stars that you saw in my right hand and of the seven golden lampstands is this: The seven stars are the angels*c* of the seven churches, and the seven lampstands are the seven churches.

To the Church in Ephesus

2 "To the angel*a* of the church in Ephesus write:

These are the words of him who holds the seven stars in his right hand and walks among the seven golden lampstands: 2I know your deeds, your hard work and your perseverance. I know that you cannot tolerate wicked men, that you have tested those who claim to be apostles but are not, and have found them false. 3You have persevered and have endured hardships for my name, and have not grown weary.

4Yet I hold this against you: You have forsaken your first love. 5Remember the height from which you have fallen! Repent and do the things you did at first. If you do not repent, I will come to you and remove your lampstand from its place. 6But you have this in your favour: You hate the practices of Nicolaitans, which I also hate.

7He who has an ear, let him hear what the Spirit says to the churches. To him who overcomes, I will give the right to eat from the tree of life, which is in the paradise of God.

To the Church in Smyrna

8"To the angel of the church in Smyrna write:

These are the words of him who is the First and the Last, who died and came to life again. 9I know your afflictions and your poverty—yet you are rich! I know the slander of those who say they are Jews and are not, but are a synagogue of Satan. 10Do not be afraid of what you are about to suffer. I tell you, the devil will put some of you in prison to test you, and you will suffer persecution for ten days. Be faithful, even to the point of death, and I will give you the crown of life.

11He who has an ear, let him hear what the Spirit says to the churches. He who overcomes will not be hurt at all by the second death.

To the Church in Pergamum

12"To the angel of the church in Pergamum write:

These are the words of him who has the sharp, double-edged sword. 13I know where you live—where Satan has his throne. Yet you remain true to my name. You did not renounce your faith in me, even in the days of Antipas, my faithful witness, who was put to death in your city—where Satan lives.

14Nevertheless, I have a few things against you: You have people there who hold to the teaching of Balaam, who taught Balak to entice the Israelites to sin by eating food sacrificed to idols and by committing sexual immorality. 15Likewise you also have those who hold to the teaching of the Nicolaitans. 16Repent therefore! Otherwise, I will soon come to you and will fight against them with the sword of my mouth.

17He who has an ear, let him hear what the Spirit says to the churches. To him who overcomes, I will give some of the hidden manna. I will also give him a white stone with a new name written on it, known only to him who receives it.

c20 Or *messengers*   *a1* Or *messenger*; also in verses 8, 12 and 18

To the Church in Thyatira

18"To the angel of the church in Thyatira write:

These are the words of the Son of God, whose eyes are like blazing fire and whose feet are like burnished bronze. 19I know your deeds, your love and faith, your service and perseverance, and that you are now doing more than you did at first.

20Nevertheless, I have this against you: You tolerate that woman Jezebel, who calls herself a prophetess. By her teaching she misleads my servants into sexual immorality and the eating of food sacrificed to idols. 21I have given her time to repent of her immorality, but she is unwilling. 22So I will cast her on a bed of suffering, and I will make those who commit adultery with her suffer intensely, unless they repent of her ways. 23I will strike her children dead. Then all the churches will know that I am he who searches hearts and minds, and I will repay each of you according to your deeds. 24Now I say to the rest of you in Thyatira, to you who do not hold to her teaching and have not learned Satan's so-called deep secrets (I will not impose any other burden on you): 25Only hold on to what you have until I come.

26To him who overcomes and does my will to the end, I will give authority over the nations—

27'He will rule them with an iron
      sceptre;
   he will dash them to pieces like
      pottery'b—

just as I have received authority from my Father. 28I will also give him the morning star. 29He who has an ear, let him hear what the Spirit says to the churches.

To the Church in Sardis

3 "To the angela of the church in Sardis write:

These are the words of him who holds the seven spiritsb of God and the seven stars. I know your deeds; you have a reputation of being alive, but you are dead. 2Wake up! Strengthen what remains and is about to die, for I have not found your deeds complete in the sight of my God. 3Remember, therefore, what you have received and heard; obey it, and repent. But if you do not wake up, I will come like a thief, and you will not know at what time I will come to you.

4Yet you have a few people in Sardis who have not soiled their clothes. They will walk with me, dressed in white, for they are worthy. 5He who overcomes will, like them, be dressed in white. I will never blot out his name from the book of life, but will acknowledge his name before my Father and his angels. 6He who has an ear, let him hear what the Spirit says to the churches.

To the Church in Philadelphia

7"To the angel of the church in Philadelphia write:

These are the words of him who is holy and true, who holds the key of David. What he opens no-one can shut, and what he shuts no-one can open. 8I know your deeds. See, I have placed before you an open door that no-one can shut. I know that you have little strength, yet you have kept my word and have not denied my name. 9I will make those who are of the synagogue of Satan, who claim to be Jews though they are not, but are liars—I will make them come and fall down at your feet and acknowledge that I have loved you. 10Since you have kept my command to endure

---

b27 Psalm 2:9   a1 Or *messenger*; also in verses 7 and 14   b1 Or *the sevenfold Spirit* patiently, I will also keep you from the hour of trial that is going to come upon the whole world to test those who live on the earth.

¹¹I am coming soon. Hold on to what you have, so that no-one will take your crown. ¹²Him who overcomes I will make a pillar in the temple of my God. Never again will he leave it. I will write on him the name of my God and the name of the city of my God, the new Jerusalem, which is coming down out of heaven from my God; and I will also write on him my new name. ¹³He who has an ear, let him hear what the Spirit says to the churches.

To the Church in Laodicea

¹⁴"To the angel of the church in Laodicea write:

These are the words of the Amen, the faithful and true witness, the ruler of God's creation. ¹⁵I know your deeds, that you are neither cold nor hot. I wish you were either one or the other! ¹⁶So, because you are luke-warm—neither hot nor cold—I am about to spit you out of my mouth. ¹⁷You say, 'I am rich; I have acquired wealth and do not need a thing.' But you do not realise that you are wretched, pitiful, poor, blind and naked. ¹⁸I counsel you to buy from me gold refined in the fire, so that you can become rich; and white clothes to wear, so that you can cover your shameful nakedness; and salve to put on your eyes, so that you can see.

¹⁹Those whom I love I rebuke and discipline. So be earnest, and repent. ²⁰Here I am! I stand at the door and knock. If anyone hears my voice and opens the door, I will come in and eat with him, and he with me.

²¹To him who overcomes, I will give the right to sit with me on my throne, just as I overcame and sat

down with my Father on his throne. ²²He who has an ear, let him hear what the Spirit says to the churches."

The Throne in Heaven

4 After this I looked, and there before me was a door standing open in heaven. And the voice I had first heard speaking to me like a trumpet said, "Come up here, and I will show you what must take place after this." ²At once I was in the Spirit, and there before me was a throne in heaven with someone sitting on it. ³And the one who sat there had the appearance of jasper and carnelian. A rainbow, resembling an emerald, encircled the throne. ⁴Surrounding the throne were twenty-four other thrones, and seated on them were twenty-four elders. They were dressed in white and had crowns of gold on their heads. ⁵From the throne came flashes of lightning, rumblings and peals of thunder. Before the throne, seven lamps were blazing. These are the seven spirits*a* of God. ⁶Also before the throne there was what looked like a sea of glass, clear as crystal.

In the centre, around the throne, were four living creatures, and they were covered with eyes, in front and behind. ⁷The first living creature was like a lion, the second was like an ox, the third had a face like a man, the fourth was like a flying eagle. ⁸Each of the four living creatures had six wings and was covered with eyes all around, even under his wings. Day and night they never stop saying:

"Holy, holy, holy
is the Lord God Almighty,
who was, and is, and is to come."

⁹Whenever the living creatures give glory, honour and thanks to him who sits on the throne and who lives for ever and ever, ¹⁰the twenty-four elders fall down before him who sits on the throne, and worship him who lives for ever and ever. They lay their crowns before the throne and say:

---

*a*5 Or *the sevenfold Spirit*

[11]"You are worthy, our Lord and God,
   to receive glory and honour and
      power,
for you created all things,
   and by your will they were created
   and have their being."

The Scroll and the Lamb

5 Then I saw in the right hand of him who sat on the throne a scroll with writing on both sides and sealed with seven seals. [2]And I saw a mighty angel proclaiming in a loud voice, "Who is worthy to break the seals and open the scroll?" [3]But no-one in heaven or on earth or under the earth could open the scroll or even look inside it. [4]I wept and wept because no-one was found who was worthy to open the scroll or look inside. [5]Then one of the elders said to me, "Do not weep! See, the Lion of the tribe of Judah, the Root of David, has triumphed. He is able to open the scroll and its seven seals."

[6]Then I saw a Lamb, looking as if it had been slain, standing in the centre of the throne, encircled by the four living creatures and the elders. He had seven horns and seven eyes, which are the seven spirits[a] of God sent out into all the earth. [7]He came and took the scroll from the right hand of him who sat on the throne. [8]And when he had taken it, the four living creatures and the twenty-four elders fell down before the Lamb. Each one had a harp and they were holding golden bowls full of incense, which are the prayers of the saints. [9]And they sang a new song:

"You are worthy to take the scroll
   and to open its seals,
because you were slain,
   and with your blood you purchased
      men for God
   from every tribe and language and
      people and nation.
[10]You have made them to be a kingdom
   and priests to serve our God,
   and they will reign on the earth."

[11]Then I looked and heard the voice of many angels, numbering thousands upon thousands, and ten thousand times ten thousand. They encircled the throne and the living creatures and the elders. [12]In a loud voice they sang:

"Worthy is the Lamb, who was slain,
to receive power and wealth and
      wisdom and strength
and honour and glory and praise!"

[13]Then I heard every creature in heaven and on earth and under the earth and on the sea, and all that is in them, singing:

"To him who sits on the throne and to
      the Lamb
be praise and honour and glory and
      power,
      for ever and ever!"

[14]The four living creatures said, "Amen", and the elders fell down and worshipped.

The Seals

6 I watched as the Lamb opened the first of the seven seals. Then I heard one of the four living creatures say in a voice like thunder, "Come!" [2]I looked, and there before me was a white horse! Its rider held a bow, and he was given a crown, and he rode out as a conqueror bent on conquest.

[3]When the Lamb opened the second seal, I heard the second living creature say, "Come!" [4]Then another horse came out, a fiery red one. Its rider was given power to take peace from the earth and to make men slay each other. To him was given a large sword.

[5]When the Lamb opened the third seal, I heard the third living creature say, "Come!" I looked, and there before me was a black horse! Its rider was holding a pair of scales in his hand. [6]Then I heard what sounded like a voice among the four living creatures, saying, "A quart[a] of wheat for a day's wages,[b] and three quarts of barley for a day's wages,[b] and do not damage the oil and the wine!"

[7]When the Lamb opened the fourth seal, I heard the voice of the fourth living

---

a6 Or the sevenfold Spirit   *a6 Greek a choinix (probably about a litre)*   *b6 Greek a denarius* creature say, "Come!" [8]I looked, and there before me was a pale horse! Its rider was named Death, and Hades was following close behind him. They were given power over a fourth of the earth to kill by sword, famine and plague, and by the wild beasts of the earth.

[9]When he opened the fifth seal, I saw under the altar the souls of those who had been slain because of the word of God and the testimony they had maintained. [10]They called out in a loud voice, "How long, Sovereign Lord, holy and true, until you judge the inhabitants of the earth and avenge our blood?" [11]Then each of them was given a white robe, and they were told to wait a little longer, until the number of their fellow-servants and brothers who were to be killed as they had been was completed.

[12]I watched as he opened the sixth seal. There was a great earthquake. The sun turned black like sackcloth made of goat hair, the whole moon turned blood red, [13]and the stars in the sky fell to earth, as late figs drop from a fig-tree when shaken by a strong wind. [14]The sky receded like a scroll, rolling up, and every mountain and island was removed from its place.

[15]Then the kings of the earth, the princes, the generals, the rich, the mighty, and every slave and every free man hid in caves and among the rocks of the mountains. [16]They called to the mountains and the rocks, "Fall on us and hide us from the face of him who sits on the throne and from the wrath of the Lamb! [17]For the great day of their wrath has come, and who can stand?"

144,000 Sealed

7 After this I saw four angels standing at the four corners of the earth, holding back the four winds of the earth to prevent any wind from blowing on the land or on the sea or on any tree. [2]Then I saw another angel coming up from the east, having the seal of the living God. He called out in a loud voice to the four angels who had been given power to harm the land and the sea: [3]"Do not harm the land or the sea or the trees until we put a seal on the foreheads of the servants of our God." [4]Then I heard the number of those who were sealed: 144,000 from all the tribes of Israel.

[5]From the tribe of Judah 12,000 were sealed,
  from the tribe of Reuben 12,000,
  from the tribe of Gad 12,000,
[6]from the tribe of Asher 12,000,
  from the tribe of Naphtali 12,000,
  from the tribe of Manasseh 12,000,
[7]from the tribe of Simeon 12,000,
  from the tribe of Levi 12,000,
  from the tribe of Issachar 12,000,
[8]from the tribe of Zebulun 12,000,
  from the tribe of Joseph 12,000,
  from the tribe of Benjamin 12,000.

The Great Multitude in White Robes

[9]After this I looked and there before me was a great multitude that no-one could count, from every nation, tribe, people and language, standing before the throne and in front of the Lamb. They were wearing white robes and were holding palm branches in their hands. [10]And they cried out in a loud voice:

"Salvation belongs to our God,
who sits on the throne,
and to the Lamb."

[11]All the angels were standing round the throne and around the elders and the four living creatures. They fell down on their faces before the throne and worshipped God, [12]saying:

"Amen!
Praise and glory
and wisdom and thanks and honour
and power and strength
be to our God for ever and ever.
Amen!"

[13]Then one of the elders asked me, "These in white robes—who are they, and where did they come from?"

[14]I answered, "Sir, you know."

And he said, "These are they who have come out of the great tribulation; they have washed their robes and made them white in the blood of the Lamb. ¹⁵Therefore,

"they are before the throne of God
    and serve him day and night in his
    temple;
and he who sits on the throne will
    spread his tent over them.
¹⁶Never again will they hunger;
    never again will they thirst.
The sun will not beat upon them,
    nor any scorching heat.
¹⁷For the Lamb at the centre of the
    throne will be their shepherd;
he will lead them to springs of living
    water.
And God will wipe away every tear
    from their eyes."

The Seventh Seal and the Golden Censer

8 When he opened the seventh seal, there was silence in heaven for about half an hour.

²And I saw the seven angels who stand before God, and to them were given seven trumpets.

³Another angel, who had a golden censer, came and stood at the altar. He was given much incense to offer, with the prayers of all the saints, on the golden altar before the throne. ⁴The smoke of the incense, together with the prayers of the saints, went up before God from the angel's hand. ⁵Then the angel took the censer, filled it with fire from the altar, and hurled it on the earth; and there came peals of thunder, rumblings, flashes of lightning and an earthquake.

The Trumpets

⁶Then the seven angels who had the seven trumpets prepared to sound them.

⁷The first angel sounded his trumpet, and there came hail and fire mixed with blood, and it was hurled down upon the earth. A third of the earth was burned up, a third of the trees were burned up, and all the green grass was burned up.

⁸The second angel sounded his trumpet, and something like a huge mountain, all ablaze, was thrown into the sea. A third of the sea turned into blood, ⁹a third of the living creatures in the sea died, and a third of the ships were destroyed.

¹⁰The third angel sounded his trumpet, and a great star, blazing like a torch, fell from the sky on a third of the rivers and on the springs of water—¹¹the name of the star is Wormwood.ᵃ A third of the waters turned bitter, and many people died from the waters that had become bitter.

¹²The fourth angel sounded his trumpet, and a third of the sun was struck, a third of the moon, and a third of the stars, so that a third of them turned dark. A third of the day was without light, and also a third of the night.

¹³As I watched, I heard an eagle that was flying in mid-air call out in a loud voice: "Woe! Woe! Woe to the inhabitants of the earth, because of the trumpet blasts about to be sounded by the other three angels!"

9 The fifth angel sounded his trumpet, and I saw a star that had fallen from the sky to the earth. The star was given the key to the shaft of the Abyss. ²When he opened the Abyss, smoke rose from it like the smoke from a gigantic furnace. The sun and sky were darkened by the smoke from the Abyss. ³And out of the smoke locusts came down upon the earth and were given power like that of scorpions of the earth. ⁴They were told not to harm the grass of the earth or any plant or tree, but only those people who did not have the seal of God on their foreheads. ⁵They were not given power to kill them, but only to torture them for five months. And the agony they suffered was like that of the sting of a scorpion when it strikes a man. ⁶During those days men will seek death, but will not find it; they will long to die, but death will elude them.

⁷The locusts looked like horses prepared for battle. On their heads they wore something like crowns of gold, and their faces resembled human faces. ⁸Their hair was like women's hair, and their teeth

ᵃ11 That is, Bitterness

were like lions' teeth. [9]They had breast-plates like breastplates of iron, and the sound of their wings was like the thundering of many horses and chariots rushing into battle. [10]They had tails and stings like scorpions, and in their tails they had power to torment people for five months. [11]They had as king over them the angel of the Abyss, whose name in Hebrew is Abaddon, and in Greek, Apollyon.[a]

[12]The first woe is past; two other woes are yet to come.

[13]The sixth angel sounded his trumpet, and I heard a voice coming from the horns[b] of the golden altar that is before God. [14]It said to the sixth angel who had the trumpet, "Release the four angels who are bound at the great river Euphrates." [15]And the four angels who had been kept ready for this very hour and day and month and year were released to kill a third of mankind. [16]The number of the mounted troops was two hundred million. I heard their number.

[17]The horses and riders I saw in my vision looked like this: Their breastplates were fiery red, dark blue, and yellow as sulphur. The heads of the horses resembled the heads of lions, and out of their mouths came fire, smoke and sulphur. [18]A third of mankind was killed by the three plagues of fire, smoke and sulphur that came out of their mouths. [19]The power of the horses was in their mouths and in their tails; for their tails were like snakes, having heads with which they inflict injury.

[20]The rest of mankind that were not killed by these plagues still did not repent of the work of their hands; they did not stop worshipping demons, and idols of gold, silver, bronze, stone and wood—idols that cannot see or hear or walk. [21]Nor did they repent of their murders, their magic arts, their sexual immorality or their thefts.

The Angel and the Little Scroll

10 Then I saw another mighty angel coming down from heaven. He was robed in a cloud, with a rainbow above his head; his face was like the sun, and his legs were like fiery pillars. [2]He was holding a little scroll, which lay open in his hand. He planted his right foot on the sea and his left foot on the land, [3]and he gave a loud shout like the roar of a lion. When he shouted, the voices of the seven thunders spoke. [4]And when the seven thunders spoke, I was about to write; but I heard a voice from heaven say, "Seal up what the seven thunders have said and do not write it down."

[5]Then the angel I had seen standing on the sea and on the land raised his right hand to heaven. [6]And he swore by him who lives for ever and ever, who created the heavens and all that is in them, the earth and all that is in it, and the sea and all that is in it, and said, "There will be no more delay! [7]But in the days when the seventh angel is about to sound his trumpet, the mystery of God will be accomplished, just as he announced to his servants the prophets."

[8]Then the voice that I had heard from heaven spoke to me once more: "Go, take the scroll that lies open in the hand of the angel who is standing on the sea and on the land."

[9]So I went to the angel and asked him to give me the little scroll. He said to me, "Take it and eat it. It will turn your stomach sour, but in your mouth it will be as sweet as honey." [10]I took the little scroll from the angel's hand and ate it. It tasted as sweet as honey in my mouth, but when I had eaten it, my stomach turned sour. [11]Then I was told, "You must prophesy again about many peoples, nations, languages and kings."

The Two Witnesses

11 I was given a reed like a measuring rod and was told, "Go and measure the temple of God and the altar, and count the worshippers there. [2]But exclude the outer court; do not measure it, because it has been given to the Gentiles. They will trample on the holy city for 42 months. [3]And I will give power to my two witnesses, and they will prophesy for 1,260 days, clothed in sackcloth." ⁴These are the two olive trees and the two lampstands that stand before the Lord of the earth. ⁵If anyone tries to harm them, fire comes from their mouths and devours their enemies. This is how anyone who wants to harm them must die. ⁶These men have power to shut up the sky so that it will not rain during the time they are prophesying; and they have power to turn the waters into blood and to strike the earth with every kind of plague as often as they want.

⁷Now when they have finished their testimony, the beast that comes up from the Abyss will attack them, and overpower and kill them. ⁸Their bodies will lie in the street of the great city, which is figuratively called Sodom and Egypt, where also their Lord was crucified. ⁹For three and a half days men from every people, tribe, language and nation will gaze on their bodies and refuse them burial. ¹⁰The inhabitants of the earth will gloat over them and will celebrate by sending each other gifts, because these two prophets had tormented those who live on earth.

¹¹But after the three and a half days a breath of life from God entered them, and they stood on their feet, and terror struck those who saw them. ¹²Then they heard a loud voice from heaven saying to them, "Come up here " And they went up to heaven in a cloud, while their enemies looked on.

¹³At that very hour there was a severe earthquake and a tenth of the city collapsed. Seven thousand people were killed in the earthquake, and the survivors were terrified and gave glory to the God of heaven.

¹⁴The second woe has passed; the third woe is coming soon.

The Seventh Trumpet

¹⁵The seventh angel sounded his trumpet, and there were loud voices in heaven, which said:

"The kingdom of the world has become the kingdom of our Lord and of his Christ,
and he will reign for ever and ever."

¹⁶And the twenty-four elders, who were seated on their thrones before God, fell on their faces and worshipped God, ¹⁷saying:

"We give thanks to you, Lord God Almighty,
the One who is and who was,
because you have taken your great power
and have begun to reign.
¹⁸The nations were angry;
and your wrath has come.
The time has come for judging the dead,
and for rewarding your servants the prophets
and your saints and those who reverence your name,
both small and great—
and for destroying those who destroy the earth."

¹⁹Then God's temple in heaven was opened, and within his temple was seen the ark of his covenant. And there came flashes of lightning, rumblings, peals of thunder, an earthquake and a great hailstorm.

The Woman and the Dragon

12 A great and wondrous sign appeared in heaven: a woman clothed with the sun, with the moon under her feet and a crown of twelve stars on her head. ²She was pregnant and cried out in pain as she was about to give birth. ³Then another sign appeared in heaven: an enormous red dragon with seven heads and ten horns and seven crowns on his heads. ⁴His tail swept a third of the stars out of the sky and flung them to the earth. The dragon stood in front of the woman who was about to give birth, so that he might devour her child the moment it was born. ⁵She gave birth to a son, a male child, who will rule all the nations with an iron sceptre. And her child was snatched up to God and to his throne. ⁶The woman fled

into the desert to a place prepared for her by God, where she might be taken care of for 1,260 days.

[7]And there was war in heaven. Michael and his angels fought against the dragon, and the dragon and his angels fought back. [8]But he was not strong enough, and they lost their place in heaven. [9]The great dragon was hurled down—that ancient serpent called the devil, or Satan, who leads the whole world astray. He was hurled to the earth, and his angels with him.

[10]Then I heard a loud voice in heaven say:

"Now have come the salvation and the
    power and the kingdom of our
    God,
and the authority of his Christ.
For the accuser of our brothers,
    who accuses them before our God
        day and night,
    has been hurled down.
[11]They overcame him
    by the blood of the Lamb
    and by the word of their testimony;
they did not love their lives so much
    as to shrink from death.
[12]Therefore rejoice, you heavens
    and you who dwell in them!
But woe to the earth and the sea,
    because the devil has gone down to
        you!
He is filled with fury,
    because he knows that his time is
        short."

[13]When the dragon saw that he had been hurled to the earth, he pursued the woman who had given birth to the male child. [14]The woman was given the two wings of a great eagle, so that she might fly to the place prepared for her in the desert, where she would be taken care of for a time, times and half a time, out of the serpent's reach. [15]Then from his mouth the serpent spewed water like a river, to overtake the woman and sweep her away with the torrent. [16]But the earth helped the woman by opening its mouth and

swallowing the river that the dragon had spewed out of his mouth. [17]Then the dragon was enraged at the woman and went off to make war against the rest of her offspring—those who obey God's commandments and hold to the testimony of Jesus. [1]And the dragon[a] stood on the shore of the sea.

13

The Beast out of the Sea

And I saw a beast coming out of the sea. He had ten horns and seven heads, with ten crowns on his horns, and on each head a blasphemous name. [2]The beast I saw resembled a leopard, but had feet like those of a bear and a mouth like that of a lion. The dragon gave the beast his power and his throne and great authority. [3]One of the heads of the beast seemed to have had a fatal wound, but the fatal wound had been healed. The whole world was astonished and followed the beast. [4]Men worshipped the dragon because he had given authority to the beast, and they also worshipped the beast and asked, "Who is like the beast? Who can make war against him?"

[5]The beast was given a mouth to utter proud words and blasphemies and to exercise his authority for forty-two months. [6]He opened his mouth to blaspheme God, and to slander his name and his dwellingplace and those who live in heaven. [7]He was given power to make war against the saints and to conquer them. And he was given authority over every tribe, people, language and nation. [8]All inhabitants of the earth will worship the beast—all whose names have not been written in the book of life belonging to the Lamb that was slain from the creation of the world.[b]

[9]He who has an ear, let him hear.

[10]If anyone is to go into captivity,
    into captivity he will go.
If anyone is to be killed[c] with the sword,
    with the sword he will be killed.

This calls for patient endurance and faithfulness on the part of the saints.

---

[a]1 Some late manuscripts *And I*
[b]8 Or *written from the creation of the world in the book of life belonging to the Lamb that was slain*
[c]10 Some manuscripts *anyone kills*

"'Woe! Woe, O great city,
> dressed in fine linen, purple and
> scarlet,
> and glittering with gold, precious
> stones and pearls!
17In one hour such great wealth has been
brought to ruin!'

"Every sea captain, and all who travel
by ship, the sailors, and all who earn their
living from the sea, will stand far off.
18When they see the smoke of her burning, they will exclaim, 'Was there ever a
city like this great city?' 19They will throw
dust on their heads, and with weeping and
mourning cry out:

"'Woe! Woe, O great city,
> where all who had ships on the sea
> became rich through her wealth!
> In one hour she has been brought to
> ruin!
20Rejoice over her, O heaven!
> Rejoice, saints and apostles and
> prophets!
> God has judged her for the way she
> treated you.'"

21Then a mighty angel picked up a boul-
der the size of a large millstone and threw
it into the sea, and said:

"With such violence
> the great city of Babylon will be
> thrown down,
> never to be found again.
22The music of harpists and musicians,
> flute players and trumpeters,
> will never be heard in you again.
No workman of any trade
> will ever be found in you again.
The sound of a millstone
> will never be heard in you again.
23The light of a lamp
> will never shine in you again.
The voice of bridegroom and bride
> will never be heard in you again.
Your merchants were the world's great
> men.
By your magic spell all the nations
> were led astray.
24In her was found the blood of prophets
> and of the saints,

and of all who have been killed on the
earth."

Hallelujah!

19 After this I heard what sounded
like the roar of a great multitude in
heaven shouting:

"Hallelujah!
Salvation and glory and power belong
> to our God,
2   for true and just are his judgments.
He has condemned the great prostitute
> who corrupted the earth by her
> adulteries.
He has avenged on her the blood of his
> servants."

3And again they shouted:

"Hallelujah!
The smoke from her goes up for ever
> and ever."

4The twenty-four elders and the four
living creatures fell down and worshipped
God, who was seated on the throne. And
they cried:

"Amen, Hallelujah!"

5Then a voice came from the throne,
saying:

"Praise our God,
> all you his servants,
you who fear him,
> both small and great!"

6Then I heard what sounded like a great
multitude, like the roar of rushing waters
and like loud peals of thunder, shouting:

"Hallelujah!
For our Lord God Almighty reigns.
7Let us rejoice and be glad
> and give him glory!
For the wedding of the Lamb has come,
> and his bride has made herself
> ready.
8Fine linen, bright and clean,
> was given her to wear."

(Fine linen stands for the righteous acts of the saints.)

⁹Then the angel said to me, "Write: 'Blessed are those who are invited to the wedding supper of the Lamb!'" And he added, "These are the true words of God."

¹⁰At this I fell at his feet to worship him. But he said to me, "Do not do it! I am a fellow-servant with you and with your brothers who hold to the testimony of Jesus. Worship God! For the testimony of Jesus is the spirit of prophecy."

The Rider on the White Horse

¹¹I saw heaven standing open and there before me was a white horse, whose rider is called Faithful and True. With justice he judges and makes war. ¹²His eyes are like blazing fire, and on his head are many crowns. He has a name written on him that no-one knows but he himself. ¹³He is dressed in a robe dipped in blood, and his name is the Word of God. ¹⁴The armies of heaven were following him, riding on white horses and dressed in fine linen, white and clean. ¹⁵Out of his mouth comes a sharp sword with which to strike down the nations. "He will rule them with an iron sceptre."[a] He treads the winepress of the fury of the wrath of God Almighty. ¹⁶On his robe and on his thigh he has this name written:

KING OF KINGS AND LORD OF LORDS.

¹⁷And I saw an angel standing in the sun, who cried in a loud voice to all the birds flying in mid-air, "Come, gather together for the great supper of God, ¹⁸so that you may eat the flesh of kings, generals, and mighty men, of horses and their riders, and the flesh of all people, free and slave, small and great."

¹⁹Then I saw the beast and the kings of the earth and their armies gathered together to make war against the rider on the horse and his army. ²⁰But the beast was captured, and with him the false prophet who had performed the miraculous signs on his behalf. With these signs he had deluded those who had received the mark of the beast and worshipped his image. The two of them were thrown alive into the fiery lake of burning sulphur. ²¹The rest of them were killed with the sword that came out of the mouth of the rider on the horse, and all the birds gorged themselves on their flesh.

The Thousand Years

20 And I saw an angel coming down out of heaven, having the key to the Abyss and holding in his hand a great chain. ²He seized the dragon, that ancient serpent, who is the devil, or Satan, and bound him for a thousand years. ³He threw him into the Abyss, and locked and sealed it over him, to keep him from deceiving the nations any more until the thousand years were ended. After that, he must be set free for a short time.

⁴I saw thrones on which were seated those who had been given authority to judge. And I saw the souls of those who had been beheaded because of their testimony for Jesus and because of the word of God. They had not worshipped the beast or his image and had not received his mark on their foreheads or their hands. They came to life and reigned with Christ for a thousand years. ⁵(The rest of the dead did not come to life until the thousand years were ended.) This is the first resurrection. ⁶Blessed and holy are those who have part in the first resurrection. The second death has no power over them, but they will be priests of God and of Christ and will reign with him for a thousand years.

Satan's Doom

⁷When the thousand years are over, Satan will be released from his prison ⁸and will go out to deceive the nations in the four corners of the earth—Gog and Magog—to gather them for battle. In number they are like the sand on the seashore. ⁹They marched across the

breadth of the earth and surrounded the camp of God's people, the city he loves. But fire came down from heaven and devoured them. [10]And the devil, who deceived them, was thrown into the lake of burning sulphur, where the beast and the false prophet had been thrown. They will be tormented day and night for ever and ever.

The Dead Are Judged

[11]Then I saw a great white throne and him who was seated on it. Earth and sky fled from his presence, and there was no place for them. [12]And I saw the dead, great and small, standing before the throne, and books were opened. Another book was opened, which is the book of life. The dead were judged according to what they had done as recorded in the books. [13]The sea gave up the dead that were in it, and death and Hades gave up the dead that were in them, and each person was judged according to what he had done. [14]Then death and Hades were thrown into the lake of fire. The lake of fire is the second death. [15]If anyone's name was not found written in the book of life, he was thrown into the lake of fire.

The New Jerusalem

21 Then I saw a new heaven and a new earth, for the first heaven and the first earth had passed away, and there was no longer any sea. [2]I saw the Holy City, the new Jerusalem, coming down out of heaven from God, prepared as a bride beautifully dressed for her husband. [3]And I heard a loud voice from the throne saying, "Now the dwelling of God is with men, and he will live with them. They will be his people, and God himself will be with them and be their God. [4]He will wipe every tear from their eyes. There will be no more death or mourning or crying or pain, for the old order of things has passed away."

[5]He who was seated on the throne said,

"I am making everything new!" Then he said, "Write this down, for these words are trustworthy and true."

[6]He said to me: "It is done. I am the Alpha and the Omega, the Beginning and the End. To him who is thirsty I will give to drink without cost from the spring of the water of life. [7]He who overcomes will inherit all this, and I will be his God and he will be my son. [8]But the cowardly, the unbelieving, the vile, the murderers, the sexually immoral, those who practise magic arts, the idolaters and all liars—their place will be in the fiery lake of burning sulphur. This is the second death."

[9]One of the seven angels who had the seven bowls full of the seven last plagues came and said to me, "Come, I will show you the bride, the wife of the Lamb." [10]And he carried me away in the Spirit to a mountain great and high, and showed me the Holy City, Jerusalem, coming down out of heaven from God. [11]It shone with the glory of God, and its brilliance was like that of a very precious jewel, like a jasper, clear as crystal. [12]It had a great, high wall with twelve gates, and with twelve angels at the gates. On the gates were written the names of the twelve tribes of Israel. [13]There were three gates on the east, three on the north, three on the south and three on the west. [14]The wall of the city had twelve foundations, and on them were the names of the twelve apostles of the Lamb.

[15]The angel who talked with me had a measuring rod of gold to measure the city, its gates and its walls. [16]The city was laid out like a square, as long as it was wide. He measured the city with the rod and found it to be 12,000 stadia[a] in length, and as wide and high as it is long. [17]He measured its wall and it was 144 cubits[b] thick,[c] by man's measurement, which the angel was using. [18]The wall was made of jasper, and the city of pure gold, as pure as glass. [19]The foundations of the city walls were decorated with every kind of precious stone. The first foundation was jasper, the second sapphire, the third chalcedony, the

---

a16 That is, about 1,400 miles (about 2,200 kilometres)   *b17* That is, about 200 feet (about 65 metres)
c17 Or *high*

fourth emerald, 20the fifth sardonyx, the sixth carnelian, the seventh chrysolite, the eighth beryl, the ninth topaz, the tenth chrysoprase, the eleventh jacinth, and the twelfth amethyst.*d* 21The twelve gates were twelve pearls, each gate made of a single pearl. The great street of the city was of pure gold, like transparent glass.

22I did not see a temple in the city, because the Lord God Almighty and the Lamb are its temple. 23The city does not need the sun or the moon to shine on it, for the glory of God gives it light, and the Lamb is its lamp. 24The nations will walk by its light, and the kings of the earth will bring their splendour into it. 25On no day will its gates ever be shut, for there will be no night there. 26The glory and honour of the nations will be brought into it. 27Nothing impure will ever enter it, nor will anyone who does what is shameful or deceitful, but only those whose names are written in the Lamb's book of life.

The River of Life

22 Then the angel showed me the river of the water of life, as clear as crystal, flowing from the throne of God and of the Lamb 2down the middle of the great street of the city. On each side of the river stood the tree of life, bearing twelve crops of fruit, yielding its fruit every month. And the leaves of the tree are for the healing of the nations. 3No longer will there be any curse. The throne of God and of the Lamb will be in the city, and his servants will serve him. 4They will see his face, and his name will be on their foreheads. 5There will be no more night. They will not need the light of a lamp or the light of the sun, for the Lord God will give them light. And they will reign for ever and ever.

6The angel said to me, "These words are trustworthy and true. The Lord, the God of the spirits of the prophets, sent his angel to show his servants the things that must soon take place."

Jesus Is Coming

7"Behold, I am coming soon! Blessed is he who keeps the words of the prophecy in this book."

8I, John, am the one who heard and saw these things. And when I had heard and seen them, I fell down to worship at the feet of the angel who had been showing them to me. 9But he said to me, "Do not do it! I am a fellow-servant with you and with your brothers the prophets and of all who keep the words of this book. Worship God!"

10Then he told me, "Do not seal up the words of the prophecy of this book, because the time is near. 11Let him who does wrong continue to do wrong; let him who is vile continue to be vile; let him who does right continue to do right; and let him who is holy continue to be holy."

12"Behold, I am coming soon! My reward is with me, and I will give to everyone according to what he has done. 13I am the Alpha and the Omega, the First and the Last, the Beginning and the End. 14"Blessed are those who wash their robes, that they may have the right to the tree of life and may go through the gates into the city. 15Outside are the dogs, those who practise magic arts, the sexually immoral, the murderers, the idolaters and everyone who loves and practises falsehood.

16"I, Jesus, have sent my angel to give you*a* this testimony for the churches. I am the Root and the Offspring of David, and the bright Morning Star."

17The Spirit and the bride say, "Come!" And let him who hears say, "Come!" Whoever is thirsty, let him come; and whoever wishes, let him take the free gift of the water of life.

18I warn everyone who hears the words of the prophecy of this book: If anyone adds anything to them, God will add to him the plagues described in this book.

---

d20 The precise identification of some of these precious stones is uncertain.   *a16* The Greek is plural.

[19]And if anyone takes words away from this book of prophecy, God will take away from him his share in the tree of life and in the holy city, which are described in this book.

[20]He who testifies to these things says, "Yes, I am coming soon."

Amen. Come, Lord Jesus.

[21]The grace of the Lord Jesus be with God's people. Amen.

Table of Weights and Measures

BIBLICAL UNIT		APPROXIMATE IMPERIAL EQUIVALENT	APPROXIMATE METRIC EQUIVALENT
WEIGHTS			
talent	(60 minas)	75 pounds	34 kilograms
mina	(50 shekels)	1¼ pounds	0.6 kilogram
shekel	(2 bekas)	⅖ ounce	11.5 grams
pim	(⅔ shekel)	¼ ounce	7.7 grams
beka	(10 gerahs)	⅕ ounce	5.8 grams
gerah		⅟₅₀ ounce	0.6 gram
LENGTH			
cubit		18 inches	0.5 metre
span		9 inches	23 centimetres
handbreadth		3 inches	8 centimetres
CAPACITY			
Dry Measure			
cor [homer]	(10 ephahs)	6 bushels	220 litres
lethek	(5 ephahs)	3 bushels	110 litres
ephah	(10 omers)	⅗ bushel	22 litres
seah	(⅓ ephah)	13 pints	7.3 litres
omer	(⅟₁₀ ephah)	4 pints	2 litres
cab	(⅟₁₈ ephah)	2 pints	1 litre
Liquid Measure			
bath	(1 ephah)	5 gallons	22 litres
hin	(⅙ bath)	7 pints	4 litres
log	(⅟₇₂ bath)	½ pint	0.3 litre

The figures of the table are calculated on the basis of a shekel equalling 11.5 grams, a cubit equalling 18 inches and an ephah equalling 22 litres. It is based upon the best available information, but it is not intended to be mathematically precise; like the measurement equivalents in the footnotes, it merely gives approximate amounts and distances. Weights and measures differed somewhat at various times and places in the ancient world. There is uncertainty particularly about the ephah and the bath; further discoveries may give more light on these units of capacity.

The Deep End

The

THE

Deep

DEEP

End

END

The Deep End

contents

5-Day Plans

Welcome On the following pages you will find a number of short and simple reading plans which will help you learn more about what the Bible says on particular issues and will help you get closer to God. We have set out the readings as 5-day plans because we reckon you can do one each day Monday to Friday and then have the weekend off. They are not necessarily meant to be used one after the other, although you could certainly do that if you wanted to.

Thinking about Faith

Gives you the opportunity to look into what the Bible says about what Christians believe. It covers questions such as: **'Who was Jesus?'** and **'What happens when I die?'**

Big Issues

Will help you look into what the Bible says about some of the issues we all think about, such as **'What does God think about sex?'** and **'Would God vote Socialist?'**

Going Deeper

Has been written for you if you want to learn to use the Bible to get closer to God.

Each day you will be able to: read a passage from the Bible; read a short paragraph from this section relating to it; answer a question or do something in response to what you have read. If you only read the Bible passage, it shouldn't take you very long at all. If you choose to respond to the readings as suggested, it will take a little longer. The longest of all will be if you only read the comments as you need to read the Bible passage before the comments and suggestions will make sense! *(Also, do read as much of the Bible passage surrounding the day's reading as you need to for understanding.)*

Thinking about faith

GOD AND THE WORLD

These five days are for you to think about God's relationship with the created universe. We all have a certain image of what God might be like, but the best way to relate to him is to think about him as we experience him in the world.

WEEK 1

Day 1 - Genesis 1:1-10 (p.3)

God made the world
You've probably read or heard these words before, but try to forget that. Forget big bangs, atoms and stuff, because the Bible isn't going to tell you exactly what happened on day one. Instead, just imagine God making the universe and saying, 'That's good!'

action *Bring it all closer to home by imagining yourself, in the area where you live, and hear God saying, 'That's good! I made that!'* ❏

Day 2 - Genesis 6:11-21 (p.8)

Did God make a big mistake?
Something went wrong. We know it. We can all feel it. The world is in a mess and nobody seems to be able to do anything about it. When everything first began to go wrong, God came close to wiping the slate clean altogether. But, he didn't because there was one man (Noah) trying to do good. It's difficult to imagine what God felt like: he had created this beautiful world and 'all the people on earth' v12 had corrupted it.

action *Why not spend some time saying sorry for the times you have contributed to the mess the world is in, and pray that God will help you to be more like Noah in v9.* ❏

Day 3 - Psalm 104 (p. 606)

Our provider This Psalm is a song of thanksgiving for all the good things in the world. It's worth reminding ourselves regularly that the world isn't all bad, that there are many wonderful things that God has made.

action *If you can, why not go to a place that makes you aware of how good the world is: it could be out in the countryside, or an art gallery . . . go and thank God for all that he has given you. And if you can't go today, go soon!* ❏

Day 4 - John 3:16-21 (p.1029)

How much does God love us?
This is a famous passage, which is often used to tell us about Jesus. Yet it really tells us about God the Father and how much he loves us. Because the world is in a mess and none of us are perfect, we might sometimes think of God as a school head teacher who will tell us off when they find out what we've done. Yet we learn here that God doesn't want to condemn us at all, but wants to bring us back into friendship with him through the death of his Son, Jesus Christ.

action *Spend time today being quiet and ask God to show you how much he loves you. Read this passage through a few times and marvel!* ❑

Day 5 - Romans 8:18-25 (p. 1135)

Where's the world going?
If we believe that God has created the universe, then we can also believe that he will restore it one day. This passage is describing Paul's understanding about the way the world is: that some of the troubles that we encounter are part of the straining of creation to be restored. It's a powerful image.

action *As you think about your week ahead, ask God to show you what he is doing in the world. Praying every morning (or evening) that you will see what God is up to can make a huge difference to your life!* ❑

GOD'S LAW

The law is an important part of Christian history. Today we tend to see laws as bad, but in the Bible the law is God's way of letting people know that they are special and that he wants them to relate to him and to each other in a certain way.

Day 1 - Deuteronomy 4:1-14 (p.182)

For life Here Moses is reminding the Israelites of why God gave them the Ten Commandments. In the Old Testament the Law of Moses was a whole way of life for the individual and for society. God didn't just make up rules for the sake of it. For us today, there is a principle at stake: can we acknowledge that God knows better than we do how we should live?

action *Read through the first two verses again and tell God how you feel.* ❑

Day 2 - Joshua 1:1-9 (p. 216)

Living in a dangerous land

'Be strong and very courageous.' That's fine, if you know what you're doing. The book of Joshua is all about Joshua's ability to hear from God and do what God asked. Right at the start God reminds Joshua that one of the important things he has to do is to obey the new Law that has been given to the people through Moses. The Israelites were entering a new territory and they were in danger of losing their identity.

action *What situations are there in your life where you need to obey God and 'go against the flow'? Talk to God about them and ask for his help.* ❑

Day 3 - Psalm 119:97-104 (p. 620)

Passionate about the Bible?

'Oh how I love your law!' Can you imagine a criminal approaching a judge in court and saying that? Yet here we have someone saying that they love the law so much that they will spend hours studying it. Perhaps with the Bible it's no good waiting to fall in love with it: we need to get to know it and learn to love it that way.

action *Sometimes when you are reading the Bible you know that God is speaking to you through it. Pray for more of those times.* ❑

Day 4 - Matthew 22:34-40 (p. 991)

The real meaning of the law

It is easy to forget what Christianity is all about. If you were to ask the average person in the street what being a Christian meant, you would probably get a wide variety of answers, with many talking about 'doing good' or 'going to church'.

action *What do you think it's all about? And where do you think is the best place to find the answer?* ❑

Day 5 - Galatians 5:16-25 (p. 1172)

Not under law

We're coming in halfway through an argument here, about whether non-Jews who accept Jesus need to be circumcised. Paul is arguing that although the law is good, we now have a new way of knowing what we should do: knowing Jesus. In some ways this new way is harder, because when you have detailed rules, you know exactly what you're supposed to do and not to do. Following Jesus means trying to work out what he would do.

action *Are there issues in your life where you're not sure what God wants you to do? Talk to God about it: Paul says you are now 'led by the Spirit' (v18).* ❑

JESUS THE MAN

The first thing everyone could see about Jesus just by looking at him was that he was a regular guy. It would have taken a long time for anyone to realise just who he was until they spoke to him or spent time with him. So what was he like?

Day 1 - Luke 2:41-52
(p.1029)

The precocious kid This is the only story about Jesus' childhood which has come down to us within the Bible. There are other stories about Jesus as a child, but none of them have the ring of truth like this one. Jesus would have been about thirteen and just beginning to find his feet as an adult.

action *Try to imagine how the different people in the story would have felt: Jesus, Mary, the religious leaders . . .* ❑

Day 2 - Matthew 9:35-38
(p. 974)

Compassionate When you think of Jesus, what do you see? Probably a gentle-looking man in a funny white outfit. The real Jesus almost certainly didn't wear white, because it would have got dirty very quickly in the places he went to teaching, preaching, healing etc.

action *Think about a situation where you need to care more than you are able. Perhaps you have an ageing relative who needs your time, or there is someone you don't like but need to get on with: bring them before God and ask him for some of his compassion.* ❑

Day 3 - Luke 19:41-46
(p.1054)

Anger and frustration These are not feelings that one associates with the son of God, but here we see them displayed very vividly. Sometimes we need to feel the same anger and frustration if we are to fight for justice and try and change the wrong we see in the world.

action *Think of something that you know is wrong and try to do some small thing to change matters: even writing a letter can make a difference!* ❑

Day 4 - Mark 14:32-43
(p.1021)

Alone Compassion we expect and anger we can cope with, but Jesus sad and lonely? Most of us feel alone at some time in our lives, although probably not quite as alone as Jesus did on that night, knowing, as he did, what was to come.

action *If you are feeling isolated, or you know someone who is, thank God that he knows how you/they feel, and pray for his love to come visiting.* ❏

Day 5 - Hebrews 2:10-18
(p. 1202)

Our brother Jesus came to be with us for many reasons. One reason is probably to show us what being human is all about. After all, he could just have popped down, died, risen again and that would have been it. But no, he was born as a real child and became an adult who was around for over 30 years. He's our brother, he understands everything.

action *Perhaps you've never talked to Jesus like he was your brother. Try thinking of him in that way and pray accordingly.* ❏

JESUS THE SON

Over the next five days you'll be able to find out why Christians call Jesus 'the Son of God'. Of all the things that we can learn about Jesus, the fact that he was God on earth is perhaps the most important.

Day 1 - Philippians 2:5-12
(p. 1179)

The pre-existent one In his letter to the people of Philippi, Paul talks about what makes for a godly way of life and he reminds his fellow Christians of what Jesus did for them.

Paul says that Jesus is an amazing person worthy to be praised and adored, and he is amazing because he gave up all his status as God to be with us as the man Jesus and to die for us.

Isn't that amazing! ❏

Day 2 - Matthew 3:13-17
(p. 967)

Approved by God Here, God makes known that he has big plans for his son and he lets Jesus know how much he loves him. There are many passages in the Old Testament which serve the same function of letting us know that God had a plan for Jesus.

action *Read Isaiah 53:1-6 to see one of the amazing prophecies that Jesus fulfilled.* ❏

Day 3 - Mark 2:1-12 (p.1003)

A man of authority This story describes the time when Jesus really started to irritate the religious leaders of the day. In the passage they argue that only God can forgive sins, but really they are probably upset more because Jesus' action might put people off from coming to their temple and paying to make a sacrifice for their sins to be forgiven. Perhaps the most important thing Jesus is saying here is that God's forgiveness is directly available through Jesus. A direct relationship with God is possible.

action *A prayer to help you do this appears on the last page of this Bible.* ❑

Day 4 - Luke 24:1-12 (p.1061)

Alive The resurrection of Jesus is a point at which it really becomes clear who he is. Right at the beginning of his work, Jesus was blessed by God and called his son, so here, right at the end of Luke's Gospel (and there are similar accounts in the other Gospels), God gives Jesus the ultimate stamp of approval. The resurrection makes Jesus totally different from any other prophet, priest or religious leader.

action *Spend a minute thinking about what it means if Jesus is still alive today and then why not ask him to show you that he is still alive?* ❑

Day 5 - Mark 8:27-31 (p.1012)

The Christ/Messiah
Jesus was human, he was not so amazing that he walked on air every day and didn't need to eat or sleep. Probably because of this humanity, it took the disciples quite a long time to realise who Jesus was. Jesus' question here is the biggest question in history.

action *Don't just accept Peter's answer, continue to read the Bible and listen to Jesus asking you the question, 'who do you say I am?'* ❑

GOD WITH US TODAY

This week looks at the work of the Holy Spirit, third person of the trinity we meet when God appears in our daily lives.

Day 1 - Genesis 1:1-3 (p. 3)

Over us You may have read this passage before, but think about it again: the image of the Spirit, hovering over the waters. It's beautiful.

action *Spend a minute or so in quiet and imagine that the Spirit is hovering over you right now, ready to create light. What dark corners do you need to deal with? Why wait?* ❑

Day 2 - Exodus 35:30-36:1
(p. 95)

In us This is an early mention of the Holy Spirit giving special abilities to people, this is a regular occurrence as the story of God develops. Everything you can do is a gift from God, but perhaps there is something particular that you can or want to do for him. As here in the book of Exodus, the gifts God gives are so we can worship him.

action *What can you give back to God as an act of worship?* ❏

Day 3 - Ezekiel 36:24-32
(p. 868)

Breaking us This is a very beautiful passage in which God promises to restore Israel. But it's tough work! Are you willing to have your heart removed by God and replaced with one that beats to his tune? The only way that the Spirit can live in you is if you give your whole life to him.

action *Consider whether you are ready to give your life to God.* ❏

Day 4 - Joel 2:28-30
(p. 914)

Leading us This passage is from a description of what the prophet Joel saw as being the end times, yet Peter in Acts 2 says that everyone born since Jesus' death and resurrection is living in such times (are those things evident?). Jesus said that he wouldn't leave us alone, that he would send us a helper (John 16:7). Thank goodness!

action *If you feel able to, ask God to speak to you as he did to Joel and the other prophets in the Bible. Take your time, and talk to friends about it, but listen out for him . . .* ❏

Day 5 - 1Corinthians 12:1-11 (p.1153)

For us God sends his Holy Spirit to us individually so that we can all join together and do the things he wants us to do.

action *If you have time, carry on reading the passage to the end of the chapter. Over the last few days you may have begun to think about this, continue to think and pray about whether to join a local church or whether to become a more active member of your present church, empowered by the Holy Spirit.* ❏

WHAT IS SIN?
WHAT CAN WE DO ABOUT IT?

Sin is a small word with big consequences in the Bible.
You won't get far in reading the Bible or coming to know God until
you have some understanding of what it means.

Day 1 - Genesis 3 (p. 5)

The big questions The story of the creation and of Adam and Eve is important because it helps us answer the big questions: How did we get here? Who are we? Why is the world in such a mess? It's clear from Genesis 3 that no-one can say of their actions, 'It's OK I'm not hurting anyone'. Sin has eternal mega-consequences. It's said that sin is a small word with 'I' in the middle of it, and that's the problem.

action *Why not spend some time saying sorry to God for the times you've put yourself first.* ❑

Day 2 - 2 Samuel 12:1-13 (p. 315)

King-sized sin Over the next two days we're going to look at the story of David and Bathsheba. The background to this story (see 2 Samuel 11): David had seen Bathsheba bathing (tut, tut) and found her very attractive. Learning that she was married to one of his own army officers, Uriah, David eventually ordered that Uriah be put into the most dangerous spot in the current fighting. Sure enough, Uriah died and David took Bathsheba as his wife. And that's where God's prophet, Nathan, came in, to point out David's sin.

action *What is it you want most in life? What would you do to get it? Talk to God about it.* ❑

Day 3 - Psalm 51 (p. 573)

Royal repentance As you read yesterday, David realised the error of his ways. This psalm is widely thought to have been written as a direct response to the events read yesterday. Use it as a prayer, whenever you need to.

action *Perhaps you feel that David's gone a bit over the top about his sin, but one day you will feel like that too. Pick a verse that you can identify with and carry it around with you in your mind for the day and whenever you remember it, try saying: 'Restore to me the joy of your salvation and grant me a willing spirit, to sustain me.'* ❑

Day 4 - John 8:1-11 (p. 1073)

The meaning of forgiveness
This story speaks for itself: ' ...neither do I condemn you, now go and sin no more.' The gospel is made up of both elements: forgiveness of God; our desire to change.

action *Take time to imagine yourself as this woman, and how it must have felt to be in her position: the accusing faces, the tension as Jesus sits there scribbling in the dirt, and then . . . the blessing.*

❏

Day 5 - Ephesians 2:1-10 (p. 1174)

God's gift Someone clever once helped to explain the meaning of GRACE: 'God's Riches At Christ's Expense'. The bad news about sin is that we are all guilty, the good news is that it is God's will that we are all forgiven. All we need to do is accept God's great gift of forgiveness and agree to live for him.

action *If you've already done that, thank God for your forgiveness. If you haven't, there's a prayer on the last page of this Bible that may help you.*

❏

THE END OF THE WORLD

This subject is one that many Christians talk about a lot. These five passages will give you a picture of what both Jesus and Paul thought about the last days of this world.

Day 1 - Matthew 24:36-44 (p. 994)

Get ready This passage is part of a huge chunk of stuff Jesus says about the future. If you have time, try reading the whole chapter – with a commentary! In this section Jesus gives us some very sound advice as we look at this subject: firstly, that setting dates for his return is not appropriate and never going to work; secondly, that we should live as though he is going to return tomorrow.

action *Spend some time thinking about how ready you would be if Jesus did return tomorrow.*

❏

Day 2 - Matthew 25:31-46 (p. 995)

Judgment day This story is very frightening! It describes Jesus' return (Jesus used to call himself 'the son of man' because it had lots of meaning for the people at the time) and he isn't quite as 'cuddly' as we might expect. Clearly the way that we live our lives today will have an effect on our eternal destiny.

action *Think about all the people that you see regularly and ask Jesus to show you how you can serve him by serving them.* ❑

Day 3 - 1 Corinthians 15:12-19, 35-41
(pp. 1155-1156)

We'll be there Key questions today are the same as those for the early Christians: Are we really going to be resurrected?; If I'm going to get raised from the dead, what will I be like? This passage contains Paul's answers.

action *Read the whole chapter if you have time, but before you do that, ask God any questions you might have. He's not afraid of your questions, and he wants you to know the answers. If you have difficulties, try talking to a Christian friend.* ❑

Day 4 - Revelation 5
(p. 1237)

The biggest party in the universe John saw Jesus through a special revelation which he wrote down in the book named after that revelation. It is not clear what is written on the scroll that Jesus ('the lamb who was slain') has, but it seems to be the trigger for the unfolding events throughout the book. What is clear though is that Jesus is the key to the future, and the amazing creatures that John sees in his vision worship him as central to the completion of history.

action *Read the hymns that are contained in this chapter and imagine you are there, singing along.* ❑

Day 5 - Matthew 28:18-20
(p. 1001)

There's work to be done If the world is going to end in such an amazing way as we have been reading, we've got work to do! In his last moments, Jesus gave everyone this challenge. In the NIV, 'all nations' means, 'every kind of people'. That means the people **you** know!

action *Take some time to pray for friends and relatives who aren't yet Christians, and ask God what he wants you to do to help them becomes disciples.* ❑

HEAVEN AND HELL

So, the day of judgment has arrived, and then what?
And what is heaven anyway?

Day 1 - Philippians 3:17-21
(p. 1180)

Citizens of heaven The first thing to know is that Christians are, in a mysterious way, in heaven already. Paul refers to the destruction that is to come for those that don't know Jesus, but for Christians, they are already part of the new world that God is preparing.

action *Thank God if you are a citizen of heaven and pray for new citizens! Or, you could seriously consider making that step, see the prayer on the last page of this Bible.* ❏

Day 2 - Matthew 16:15-19
(p. 983)

Heavenly consequences Here Jesus makes reference to both Hades (the world of the dead) and heaven (the place of God). It's clear from this passage that heaven isn't a place that will be created after we die, but it's where God is today, what you might call 'the spiritual dimension'. Jesus says that our actions here on earth can have heavenly consequences. That sin is important and baptising people to live a new life.

action *Take a minute to review your day and imagine what impression your actions and words may have had from a heavenly perspective. If you can celebrate, do so. If you need to say sorry, do that too.* ❏

Day 3 - Luke 6:17-31 (p.1034)

Blessings and woes This passage describes both present and future blessings and woes. One of the big questions people have about God is that he seems to save up rewards and blessings for the future rather than sharing them round right now. This passage seems to indicate that it's our job to do good on earth now, and it's God's to bring us home when the time is right.

consider *God is challenging us to live heavenly lives here on earth. What will you do?* ❏

Day 4 - 2 Thessalonians 1:5-10
(p. 1189)

Destruction and glory The idea that God is going to let the people he created and called 'good' be destroyed is a hard one to accept today. Yet there's no getting away from the word 'punish' in the passage. This is an aspect of God's justice which should not be ignored. If someone chooses to live their life without God, their decision will be honoured - for ever.

action *Express your feelings to God: are you angry? Fearful for your friends? Unsure about him. Tell him.* ❏

Day 5 - Revelation 21:1-4 (p. 1249)

A new creation The book of Revelation is often very difficult to understand, particularly if taken too literally. But here we can see something clearly: 'heaven', meaning the place we'll (hopefully!) go to when we die, will be a new creation, not just a strange ethereal spiritual realm (although see Day 2 when we said that heaven already exists now). There'll be a new earth as well as a new heaven. That's great news! But it means that the earth as well as individuals is bound up in judgment.

consider *Think how you can bring heavenly values to the world in which you live.* ❏

JUSTICE AND MERCY

These five studies are to help you look at two aspects of God's character which are sometimes said to conflict. Both are vital parts of the Bible's testimony about God.

Day 1 - Isaiah 58:1-10 (p.744)

Real Justice Justice isn't merely making sure the law is kept. God suggests here that someone who has no interest in seeing justice done in the world is not truly following or worshipping him. Justice is about ensuring that everyone gets looked after as well as ensuring that criminals are dealt with. God is saying, 'If you are not into justice I don't want to listen to your lovely worship songs, however good they sound'.

consider *Will you respond to God's challenge?* ❏

Day 2 - Romans 2:1-8 (p.1129)

Judgment This passage tells us another important truth: being a judge is part of who God is. Christians are often the first to judge but Paul warns us about judging others when we are equally deserving of judgment. He goes on to say that part of God's justice is that those who refuse to see things

God's way are 'storing up wrath' against themselves.

action *Are you guilty of judging others? If so, say sorry to God. If you have judged someone harshly, say sorry to them.* ❑

Day 3 - Psalm 103 (p. 605)

The Father This is a wonderful psalm of praise to a compassionate and loving God who is 'slow to anger'.

action *Read through this psalm. Take your time, and use it to worship God.* ❑

Day 4 - James 2:8-13 (p.1214)

The royal law James here reminds us of two wonderful aspects of Christianity: first, the law of God is really about love and second, mercy gets the upper hand over justice.

action *Remember that mercy will be shown to those who have given their lives to Jesus. Does that apply to you? If so, be thankful. If not, read and pray some more...* ❑

Day 5 - 1 Timothy 1:15-17 (p.1191)

Real mercy Some of Shakespeare's words about mercy are well-known, but long before he lived, Paul knew the significance of mercy. Instead of worrying about our future, we can fall on God's mercy and be saved from our sinfulness. Paul acknowledges his weakness as a way of giving glory to God.

consider *How could you honour God more than yourself in the place you work, study or live?* ❑

FOLLOWING JESUS

When Jesus said, 'Follow me', his disciples didn't know what to expect on an individual basis. Neither do we, but we have plenty of clues from what happened to Jesus' earliest followers.

Day 1 - Mark 1:14-20 (p.1002)

Will you? The most amazing thing about this story is the way that Simon, Andrew, James and John dropped everything to follow Jesus. They probably knew a little bit about him, but what was it that made them do this?

action *Spend some time going over what you know about Jesus (if you don't know much, try the two 5-day plans on Jesus), and think about what you'd be willing to do* for him. **Try writing Jesus a letter. Imagine he's written to you asking** you to follow him. How would you reply? ❑

Day 2 - Mark 8:34-38
(p. 1012)

The cost Giving up everything is very difficult, and if you know anyone who has chosen to live more simply, you'll know that it makes them look out of place. But, Jesus challenges us to give up everything and be proud of it at the same time.

action *Are you embarrassed about being a Christian? Talk to Jesus about why it might be hard to follow him. Talk to friends about how you can follow him in a way that makes you proud to be a Christian.* ❑

Day 3 - Luke 14:25-33
(p. 1048)

Scary stuff Jesus challenges us saying: 'Following me isn't easy. Are you sure you know what you're getting into?' When people have a difficult decision to make, they often write down the 'pros' and 'cons' to help them make up their minds.

action *Why not try that? Write down the reasons why you should follow Jesus and then write down the things that put you off following him or continuing to follow him. Take some time to pray on your own or with a friend about your two lists.* ❑

Day 4 - Luke 18:18-25 (p.1052)

Things that get in the way Jesus knew exactly what this guy's problem was. If you've managed to get this far through these studies without thinking about something (or some-one) that might get between you and God, do it now.

action *A helpful exercise is to imagine Jesus coming towards you and then to ask God to reveal anything that might stand between you and Jesus. If you need to deal with anything that is in the way, then do it straight away.* ❑

Day 5 - Romans 15:5-9
(p. 1141)

You made it! This has probably been a hard week! Jesus asks for our whole lives to be given to him, if you have done so, you are part of the worldwide movement known as the Church, and you now belong to God!

action *Listen to Paul's prayer for you: you mustn't follow Jesus on your own, make sure you are part of a community of Christians who can help you.* ❑

REAL LOVE

English-speakers generally use one word to cover many different kinds of feelings. In the Hebrew and Greek there are plenty of words for love. These five studies will help you to understand what God means by love, (which is slightly different from what you might hear from the latest pop stars).

Day 1 - Psalm 146:6-9
(p. 632)

Who do you love? The first thing to realise about God's love is how unconditional it is. God loves everyone! In fact, if he shows any kind of preference, it's for the people that no-one else loves. We would expect God to love the righteous (verse 8), but he also loves refugees and single parent families (verse 9), folk who don't always get a fair look-in when it comes to love. The psalmist recognises and recalls God's love.

action *Do that now, and say thank you to God for loving you.* ❏

Day 2 - Matthew 22:34-40
(p. 991)

Love is the Law This short passage speaks for itself, its message is important.

action *Why not think about how you could do something today that would let someone know that you love them. Go on!* ❏

Day 3 - Romans 5:6-8 (p. 1132)

What is love? (part 1)
Verse 8 says it all.

action *Meditate on that verse:* *learn it and then spend five minutes (or more!) just letting it really sink in! Recite it a few times and try and remember it.* ❏

Day 4 - 1 Corinthians 13
(p. 1153)

What is love? (part 2)
You've probably heard this passage read out at a wedding, but it's not only about the love between a husband and wife. It's about the love we need to share as Christian brothers and sisters. It is certainly a tough proposition, but obviously important: Paul interrupts a big discussion about how the church in Corinth should be run to remind his readers of how they should be

treating each other.

action *Why not pray for your local* church, *that all its members may be able to live together in love (but not in-love necessarily).* ☐

Day 5 - 1 John 3:16-20
(p. 1227)

What is love? (part 3) Love has very practical consequences: if you love someone, you will go out of your way to help them. God's love, which he wants to put in our hearts, is for everyone. That means a lot of helping!

Hopefully earlier this week you showed someone that you loved them.

action *Now try that again with someone you know less well. In showing kindness to someone society shuns, you are bringing God's love into being before your very eyes!* ☐

FORGIVENESS

Forgiveness is a big issue today. When someone is murdered, one of the first things the victim's family is asked is, 'will you forgive the murderer?' What does God say?

Day 1 - Psalm 32:1-5
(p.560)

The need for forgiveness 'Blessed is he whose transgressions are forgiven.' Why? This passage says that one reason why forgiveness is key is because our sins always find us out.

Forgiveness is our way back to relationship with God. It's something we need to seek regularly by confession and repentance.

action *Have a look at the prayer on the last page of this Bible, you might like to pray it.* ☐

Day 2 - Matthew 6:9-15
(p. 970)

The Prayer Many people know the Lord's Prayer but, how many of us try and forget a section of it? God says that we have the same duty to forgive as he does. God obviously cares as much about our relationships with each other as he does about

our relationship with him.

action *Make sure you're in a quiet place and think if there is anyone you need to forgive. If there is someone you need to make peace with, resolve to do what you can to make it happen. Talking to a friend about it may help.* ☐

Day 3 - Luke 15 (p. 1048)

God loves forgiving If you read the story of the prodigal son in isolation it's easy to think that the son is at the centre of the story, but read the whole of chapter 15 and you'll see that Jesus is talking about parties, 'forgiveness-parties'! Every time someone comes to God for forgiveness there's a party in heaven!

action *Remember the day you decied that you were going to follow Jesus for the rest of your life (or a day when you made a special commitment) and imagine the event from God's perspective: God cheering, all the angels dancing! All for you! (If you have not made that commitment, it's worth considering again, go to the last page)* ❏

Day 4 - Matthew 26:27-29 (p. 996)

Forgiveness costs The story of Jesus' last hours is a heart-rending one, yet it is clear that Jesus wasn't just thinking about himself as his death approached. Jesus knew that he would die so that people could be forgiven, and he instituted what is now called Holy Communion as a way for us to remember his death and its significance.

action *Spend some time on that now. Perhaps you could keep reading through Matthew if you can make the time.* ❏

Day 5 - Colossians 2:13-15 (p. 1183)

The cosmic view Read this passage and remember that after his death, Jesus was raised from the dead. Our forgiveness is a result of God's victory over evil. Yesterday you remembered Jesus' suffering on your behalf.

action *Today, remember that he won a victory over death and is still alive! In whatever way seems appropriate, celebrate the fact that you are forgiven and that Jesus is here with you now to celebrate.* ❏

Big Issues

WHAT GOD REALLY THINKS OF YOU

If you feel like no-one loves you, including God, these five readings are for you.

Day 1 - Exodus 34:4-7 (p. 93)

What is God like? The moment that Moses met God on a mountain, what did he learn about God? He learnt that God was: compassionate; gracious; slow to anger; abounding in love; faithful; forgiving of sin; just.

action *Spend some time thinking about God. Can you believe he is all these things? Talk to him about it.* ❑

Day 2 - Psalm 139 (p. 628)

Closer than breathing God knows every one of us and everything about us, yet, he still loves us.

consider *Think about that.* ❑

Day 3 - Isaiah 43:1-7 (p.728)

Afraid This passage was originally written to a nation, but let God speak to you through it: 'Do not be afraid, for I am with you'.

action *Ask God to let you know over the next few days that he is with you.* ❑

Day 4 - Galatians 2:20 (p. 1169)

It's not my life Read this verse as many times as you can cope with, or until you can remember and recite it. You belong to Jesus.

action *Remember that throughout the day.* ❑

Day 5 - 1 John 4:7-21 (p.1227)

It's there to be shared God loves you, but that's not all: you are not alone. Everything you have is for sharing.

action *If God has given you anything this week, think about how you can share it with others.* ❑

SOUL FOOD

By using five consecutive psalms, we're going to look at things that will help you stay in touch with God. This list is not exhaustive, but if you are feeling cut off from God, the first thing to do is check these five things.

Day 1 - Psalm 22 (p. 554)

Honesty The first place to start with God is exactly where you are. One thing Jesus was really against was hypocrisy, when someone pretends to be something they're not. Don't bother pretending, be honest. In this psalm we read that David (later quoted by Jesus on the cross) feels completely abandoned by God, yet he still acknowledges him as Lord.

action *Think about whether or not you are a 'fair-weather friend' to God and spend some time praising him no matter how you feel.* ❏

Day 2 - Psalm 23 (p. 555)

Trust The reason David was able to praise God despite his apparent depression in Psalm 22 is revealed in the following psalm: he was secure in his faith in God. 'Even though' says David, 'I will' David doesn't expect God to take away all his troubles, but he trusts that God will be with him in them. Sometimes trust has to be unquestioning.

consider *How would living as a person who completely trusts God change your life?* ❏

Day 3 - Psalm 24 (p. 555)

Sacrifice When the psalmist calls God 'The Almighty', what does he mean? Is it just a name? In this Psalm we read about a King who is able to rejoice in the fact that nothing belongs to him because everything belongs to God. David sees that his task is to remain pure and to worship God.

action *Can you list all your most treasured possessions (and the people who are important to you) and say, 'all this belongs to God'?* ❏

Day 4 - Psalm 25 (p. 556)

Submission Not only does David acknowledge that his possessions are not really his, but he asks God to show him how he can let go of his life too. Submission can be a negative word as it seems to imply humiliation. David knew better than that: 'Show me your ways', he says, 'for you are God my Saviour.'

action *Spend some time before God remembering that your life* now belongs to him. Give it back to him if you need to. ❏

Day 5 - Psalm 26 (p. 556)

Holiness David was king of a country surrounded on all sides by countries which worshipped other gods. He knew that if he was to remain faithful to God, he would need to keep himself safe from the many influences that surrounded him. This didn't mean that he hid in Jerusalem and never ventured outside for fear of being 'contaminated', but it did mean he knew where to draw the line.

action *Is there any situation in your life where you need to draw the line to protect yourself from losing your way?* ❏

DOES GOD CARE WHEN I'M HURTING?

These five readings are all from Paul's second letter to the Corinthians, in which he describes (quite vividly) his own sufferings. Through his own experiences, he can shed some light on this thorny question, but for many of us, there may be no complete answer until we meet Jesus face to face.

Day 1 - 2 Corinthians 1:3-7 (p. 1158)

You're not alone The early church knew a lot about suffering as it suffered periodic religious persecution. Paul opens his letter with praise to God because he comforts us in our troubles. I must admit, when I'm feeling down the last things I care about are other peoples problems. Yet here, right at the start, Paul reminds us of the greatest resource we have when we are hurting: each other. Paul's point is this: anyone who has been through hard times can help others or sympathise with them when they suffer.

action *Do you have a friend you can talk to in person, on the phone, or on the internet (see the Youth Bible Forum on the internet), is there someone in your family or local church you could talk to?* ❏

Day 2 - 2 Corinthians 1:8-11 (p. 1158)

The sentence of death I have never experienced the 'sentence of death', but I know some individuals who reached the point where they felt that life was no longer worth living. It amazes me how upbeat Paul is about this experience, although I suspect that at the time he was not so upbeat. Indeed, Paul was killed ultimately and in his later letters (1 and 2 Timothy and Titus) we begin to see the effect of this sentence of death. That said, here we find Paul able to say what many Christians over the centuries have echoed: as soon as there is no human hope, God steps in.

action *Spend time now asking God to bring you deliverance from whatever makes you suffer right now.*

❏

Day 3
2 Corinthians 4:16-18 (p.1160)

Secret renewal One of the hardest things to say to someone who is going through a really difficult time is something like, 'Well, I'm sure you'll learn something through it.' Yet, this is absolutely true.

action *Ask God to show you what inner renewal might be happening even though you might be outwardly 'wasting away'. Take your time, and ask a friend if you feel you can: friends can often see things about us that we don't even notice.* ❏

Day 4
2 Corinthians 11:21b-33
(p. 1165)

Suffering for Jesus Paul is in the middle of an argument about his authority as an apostle, and he jokingly starts 'boasting' about how much he has suffered for Jesus. In his own way, he seems to enjoy the privilege! If you feel that part of your own pain is because of your faith, it may be cold comfort but you are part of a great tradition. Jesus himself called you blessed (Matthew 5:11)!

action *I can't tell you to rejoice in your sufferings, but try telling yourself a few good things about God that you know to be true.* ❏

Day 5
2 Corinthians 12:7-10 (p.1166)

Power in weakness We do not know what Paul's 'thorn in the flesh' was: some suggest an actual physical handicap, others a psychological problem. What is clear is that Paul was resolved to living an imperfect life within an imperfect body. He doesn't feel far from God because of it, but feels that his own weakness gives God more room to do his work. Why not pray today that you will be able to feel strong through God's strength and not your own?

❏

WHY DOESN'T GOD STOP DISASTERS?

We can probably all agree that most human suffering is caused by selfish people, but not all of it is. We know the world is morally in a mess, but why is the world physically in a mess?

Day 1 - Genesis 3:16-19 (p. 5-6)

Big consequences Nobody warned Adam and Eve that disobeying God would have profound physical consequences. Up to this point there had been no sign of pain or even hard work: suddenly, as sin comes into the world, there are these amazing physical results. This short story gives us a brief picture of our own connectedness with the rest of creation: as the image of God in creation, our actions have global significance. As humans, we still have to bear a lot of the blame for the state of the environment on our planet.

consider *Think about how you could be good for the earth.* ❑

Day 2 - Job 1:1-12 (p. 509)

There is a devil Job helps us work through the issue of how God relates to suffering. The story starts with a picture of heaven, with the devil being given permission by God to test Job. This picture communicates two things: first, that there is undoubtedly a force for evil which is alive and kicking; second, that God allows this force some power. Job spends a long time asking God why he does this, without getting a clear answer.

action *If you have a spare day, you could try reading the book of Job, if you don't have time, do what Job did: cry out to God and ask 'why?'* ❑

Day 3 - Isaiah 53 (p.740)

God suffers One of the things that people say about God is that he doesn't understand what humans go through. Isaiah's prophecy of the suffering servant, which is seen to be about Jesus, tells us that this is not true. In a time when there is constant war across the globe, it is good to know that God not only understands our suffering, but has already experienced more suffering than we can each imagine.

action *Spend some time in quiet, and ask God to let you know a little bit of how he feels when there is a famine in Africa or a flood in Bangladesh.* ❑

Day 4 - Luke 17:22-37
(p.1051)

Signs of the future (part 1)
Jesus tells us that the world is basically an unstable place, and as God brings about the end of the universe, there will be physical signs that something is up. Global warming and other climate changes and global events may be signs that this world is approaching its end.

consider *Jesus' challenge is that we be ready. Are you?* ❑

Day 5 - Romans 8:18-25
(p. 1135)

Signs of the future (part 2)
Paul uses a more positive image: that of childbirth. Perhaps we should see the world's sufferings not as signs of impending doom but of impending rebirth. Paul and Jesus are not in disagreement but the contexts in which they speak demand different emphases. Paul interprets the end times optimistically.

action *Pray today that people will see what God is doing in the world and turn to him.* ❑

GOING TO WORK

Paid work is often something that dominates our lives but is a place not occupied by God. We tend to expect God to stay at home, keeping us spiritual in our spare time. After all, what does God have to do with fixing the photocopier? See pp C6-7 where some young people discuss this subject.

Day 1 - Proverbs 2:1-15 (p.636)

Wisdom What are your ambitions? What would you really like to achieve in your life? Probably not many of us would say that we pursue wisdom above all things, but when choosing a career or making career decisions, wouldn't we all like a bit of wisdom?

action *Use this passage as a prayer to start the week.* ❑

Day 2 - Ecclesiastes 2:4-11
(p. 669)

A warning Perhaps you haven't yet got to that point in life when you realise that what you do and what you acquire will never make you happy, but many people have.

action *Evaluate the importance in your life that career and social status have for you (either now or in the* future). *Let God speak to you and challenge you. Where are your priorities?* ❏

Day 3 - Ezra 3:8-13 (p. 475)

Joyful work I don't know about you, but I've heard more crying than shouting for joy at my various places of work. What was so special about this particular job? Well, there was the obvious thing: they were rebuilding the temple of God. But perhaps there's another lesson here for us: they were where God wanted them to be, doing what he wanted them to do. Not everyone had the best job, but everyone was needed in God's plan.

action *Do you know if you are where God wants you to be, doing what God wants you to do? It may be that God is happy for you to be where you are but that you need to speak out there about something that's not quite right. Think about how you could know that you are being the person God wants you to be.* ❏

Day 4 - Colossians 3:23-24 (p. 1184)

Working for God Perhaps you feel that the work you do has no value before God, perhaps it is not paid work or there are no prospects. Even if you don't feel that your current role is the one God has planned for you, do your work for him anyway! If you get up every morning and do everything as if for him, it is his work.

action *Try getting together with Christians who are in a similar situation to yourself and praying together.* ❏

Day 5
2 Thessalonians 3:6-13
(p. 1190)

And the bad news The Bible tells us about God's love for the poor, which we should follow. This does not mean we should condone people who can work not doing so. Paul, despite being a travelling evangelist, worked part time making tents in order to set a good example to his fellow Christians. Work is about taking responsibility for ourselves and our families.

consider *Are you thinking in these terms as well?* ❏

FALLING IN LOVE (or not)

Through these five readings we're going to look at male/female relationships mentioned in the Bible, but also (briefly) at the issue of singleness.

Day 1 - Judges 14:1-7 (p.257)

Desire Looked at from the turn of a new millennium, this story can seem either quaint or sexist depending on your point of view. It's the closest we get to dating in the Bible, apart from the verbal foreplay of the Song of Songs. There are two things to think about here: one is that although the Jewish society strongly encouraged arranged marriages, 'love' was allowed to blossom. The other is that God was involved, and wanted this marriage to take place. Read on to find out why!

action *Remember that God invented love, and if you find 'the right person', he is happy! Thank him for that!* ❑

Day 2 - Ruth 4:1-12 (p. 269)

Romance If you have time, read the story of Ruth: it's almost a biblical Jane Austen, all understated skirt-bustling and mysterious social conventions. In this episode Boaz, the local lord, has ensured that he gets the widow Ruth's hand in marriage. The theological centre of the story is how Ruth is faithful to God, despite the fact that she is a Gentile. The romantic subtext is a very pleasant diversion, showing that you can follow God and still get your man!

action *Take time to tell God of your desires for your life, including relationships. Give him time to speak to you as well.* ❑

Day 3
Songs of Songs 1:2-4 (p. 678)

Promise The song of songs was probably written for a royal wedding and describes the eager expectation of the soon-to-be-married couple for physical union. Sexual attraction is one of the hardest things to deal with as a Christian in a largely secular society because the norm is now to wait a long time after puberty before marriage. The Song of Songs clearly indicates that God blesses sex.

action *If you are married, take time to remember the gift of your spouse and perhaps make even more of an effort for them today. If you are single, pray that God and your friends will help you find ways of remaining a sexual being without being sexually active, and read on.* ❑

Day 4
1 Corinthians 7:1-11 (p.1148)

Better off single? We have to remind ourselves that the two most important human beings in the New Testament, Jesus and Paul, were not married. It's not just that they were 'called to be single', it's simply about the best use of time: Paul felt that marriage was a distraction from the work of the kingdom. While this is no comfort to the single person who wants to be married, and too late for the married person who thinks they should be single, it reminds us again that God's will for us is important in these matters and that his will for us may be different to his will for someone else.

consider *Are you seeking God's will for you? Or do you keep going solo?* ❑

Day 5 - Ephesians 5:25-33 (p.1176)

How to be married These verses come as part of a long section of a letter describing how we all need to love each other and not to dominate each other. The husband's duty to love his wife is likened to the love Jesus has for his wife (the church). So, if you are thinking of getting married, remember what it means: sacrifice. If you are single, are you ready to make the kind of commitment needed to make a marriage work? If you are married, what are you doing to love your spouse Jesus-style? ❑

WOULD GOD VOTE SOCIALIST?

Of course he does (not). Choose your answer, but don't be too sure. God doesn't vote, but one day he will be holding politicians to account for how each of them has looked after God's people. These five readings will help you ponder what God thinks about politics, but they won't tell you how to vote.

Day 1 - Habakkuk 1:1-6 (p.940)

The cry for justice In these verses, the prophet Habakkuk called out to God asking what he was going to do to 'sort out' the rulers of his country. He didn't get the response he wanted: God replied that he was going to destroy Judah and its people would be taken off into exile. Lesson one: God's solutions may not be the obvious ones. Lesson two: don't cry out for God to change things unless you really want him to.

action *What do you want to shout at God for? Do it now.* ❑

Day 2 - Ezekiel 16:49-52
(p. 843)

What is political sin?
Sodom and Gomorrah are famous as cities destroyed by God in the time of Abraham (Genesis 13–19). They are linked even now with sexual immorality. The prophet Ezekiel reveals that Sodom as a city was arrogant and ignored the needs of the poor.

action *In what ways does this describe the country you live in? You may like to plead with God as Abraham did, or may try and do something about a particular situation. Your local church may have details of various ways in which you can help the poor in your locality or in the country.*

❏

Day 3 - Matthew 22:15-22
(p. 990)

Do religion and politics mix?
The Pharisees are out to trap Jesus, to make him say something politically incorrect so that they can arrest and crucify him. Jesus' statement baffles to this day, so it is difficult to do more than ask the question: what belongs to Caesar (ie to the government)? What belongs to God?

action *Think about your answer to this question and try and live accordingly.*

❏

Day 4 - Romans 13:1-7
(p. 1140)

Government from God
This passage is a very difficult one, not least because it has been used to quell many a rebellion against a corrupt government. Indeed, the Roman Empire (about which Paul is speaking and of which he was a citizen) was not known for its kindness to Christians. Think about how you should participate in your own government if it is actually part of God's purpose in your country. You will certainly pay taxes at some point, so will you care what that income is spent on? What do you need to do to ensure that your government (local or national) is acting as God's instrument?

❏

Day 5 - Revelation 13:1b-9
(p. 1242)

The other side of the coin
Don't worry if you can't understand this! This passage, written probably 30 years after Paul wrote his letter to the Romans, describes that same Roman Empire as an evil beast. Using symbolism that would have been clear to all his readers, the writer John, who was a Roman prisoner on the island of Patmos, makes it clear what God thinks of the Roman government. It is clear that God's hand of blessing over a government is also judging, just as it was over

Israel and Judah in the Old Testament.

action Do you need to pronounce God's judgment on your government? How could you do that in a way that would ensure that you were listened to? ❏

THE MEDIA

Music, newspapers, magazines, television, the internet all impact on our lives in unknown ways every day. How should we be in control of the media, rather than having the media tell us how to live?

Day 1 - Psalm 1 (p. 543)

Which way now? It's a good first principle to remember what judgment is. So much of what's on the TV or in the movies requires us to suspend our judgment so that we are in danger of forgetting to use it at all. How do you decide what is fruitful media for you and what is just like chaff?

action If you've never thought about it before, why not start thinking of a few guidelines about what you should be 'consuming' on a regular basis. ❏

Day 2 - Jeremiah 1:4-10 (p. 755)

The great commission Christians often see the media as an enemy rather than a friend, yet it is clearly the most effective way of getting news around the world that has ever been invented. Just imagine if Jeremiah had been able to appear on satellite TV! We need to think very seriously about how we can use the media effectively.

action Pray today for anyone you know in the media who is a Christian, they might be a pop star, TV presenter or producer, or someone behind the scenes. These people need our help: they are doing the work of the kingdom in a dangerous place.

❏

Day 3 - Romans 12:1-2 (p. 1139)

Get your head straight These two verses could easily be entitled: 'How to be a Christian'. When you are wondering what God wants you to do with your life, remember these verses: in order to know God's will, you must first allow your mind to be renewed so that you can live in complete obedience and service to God as a 'living sacrifice'.

action *Think about how the world describes itself through the media, and how different that is to the world we know through the Bible. Spend* *time with God asking him to renew your mind so that you can hear his will for you out of all the background noise.* ❏

Day 4 - Colossians 3:5-17 (p. 1184)

Us against and for the world
This passage is an amazing collection of sayings from Paul, starting off with a list of things we need to kill the urge for (which, let's face it, rules out most TV after 9pm), but then goes on to talk about the kind of lives we can live in a positive way to show people what we're about. You will need to decide how you take Paul's instructions to stay pure in the face of all the muck that gets thrown at you, but the main part of Paul's message is that if we lived as Jesus lived, we would be the ones making positive headlines on the evening news.

action *Take one thing from this passage which has challenged you and try and do something about it over the next week.* ❏

Day 5 - Psalm 19:1-4 (p. 552)

Where is God? Sometimes we forget that God likes creativity: he is a creator God. We must remember that the natural world, creation, is very eloquent about God and it is in our nature to be the same. Think of something that someone has made, a poem, or a song, a TV programme or a book, that made you more aware of God, and thank God for it. ❏

SEX AND ALL THAT

Over these five days we are going to have a very brief look at some of the big issues that surround sex. Please don't take any of these as the definitive word: as with anything else, it's important to sit down with a wise Christian friend or family member (who has some experience) and talk it through. But, to get you thinking . . .

Day 1 - Genesis 1:26-27 (p.4)

Marriage Sex (meaning both the sex act and gender) is a vital part of being human. Being single doesn't stop you from being a man or a woman, or from having sexual feelings. But in some mysterious way, it is generic man + woman that makes humanity. This union is what societies all over the world call marriage.

action *If you are married, thank God for your marriage. If you are single, pray for marriages around the world, that they will be places where God's image can be seen clearly.* ❏

Day 2 - 1 Corinthians 6:9-20
(p. 1147)

When it goes wrong This is a frightening passage. Paul talks about various sins, including sex outside marriage and homosexual sex, but includes them in a list of other, 'nicer' sins like greed or slander. Then he comes back to the sexual sins and declares that something special is going on when two people have sex. Sinning sexually is a spiritual act unlike any other, says Paul. Nearly all of us struggle with our sexual desires in one way or another, so it is good news that Paul reminds us that Christians have been 'washed', meaning cleansed and forgiven, from sin (verse 11).

action *If you need to be washed again, come to God, confess your sin and give your life back to him. (See the last page)* ❏

Day 3 - Malachi 2:13-16
(p. 961)

Divorce There's no arguing with God on this one. The context explains God's anger a little: not only were the Jews leaving the wives of their youth, they were leaving Jewish wives to marry Gentile women. But this hardly takes the edge off a very black-and-white statement: 'I hate divorce'. It's clear from other Bible passages that while God hates divorce, he does not completely forbid it. There can be no doubting the damage that marriage breakdown and divorce are causing our society.

action *Pray for legislators and politicians to create or uphold laws that protect individuals within families but also protect society itself by supporting families.* ❏

Day 4 - Psalm 139:14-16
(p. 628)

Abortion The Bible clearly teaches here and elsewhere that human beings do not just appear at birth, they are created in the womb. This means that every foetus that is aborted is a person that is killed.

action *Pray for all the people around the world that have gone through the trauma of abortion. Pray for Christians who stand up for the truth while offering a positive alternative at the same time.* ❏

Day 5 - Mark 1:40-42 (p.1003)

AIDS It is sad when it is only some-one in the public eye, such as the late Princess Diana, that can wake up a civilisation to the prejudice that exists against AIDS victims. We need look no further than Jesus to see how Christians should be treating these 'new lepers'. Remember that however a person becomes HIV positive, Jesus excluded no-one from his company.

action *How can you respond to the need for healing between the church and the outcast?* ❑

MONEY

Love it or hate it, you can't get to work without it (unless you work round the corner, but then you'd still need to buy clothes and food and pay taxes to have the roads maintained...).

Day 1 - Deuteronomy 28:1-8 (p. 205)

The big blessing People seem to forget that blessings can be material as well as spiritual. There is nothing wrong with having good things in your life. God wants everyone to be blessed with wonderful things.

action *Write down the possessions you have which give you most pleasure. Thank God for all of them.* ❑

Day 2 - Psalm 24 (p. 555)

Who owns what? In theory, we may be able to say 'the earth is the LORD's'. But does it really make a difference? If the car you drive or the CD player you use belonged to someone else, wouldn't you treat it differently?

action *Take the list you made yesterday and pray over it for a while. How should you treat your possessions differently?* ❑

Day 3 - Matthew 6:19-21 (p. 971)

Buried Treasure Now that you have looked at your possessions and thought about whether they belong to you or God, you need to think about how important they are to you. This is really a question of investment. Jesus seems to be saying that £100 into a pension plan may give you less return (eternally) than £100 given to someone who needs it.

action *What are you investing in? Are you concerned with today, tomorrow* or for ever? Do you need to change any of your spending plans? ❏

Day 4 - Matthew 6:24-34
(p. 971)

Worry? Me? Jesus takes things one step further: forget trusting me for the future, what about trusting me today? Will I not ensure that you are provided for?

action *Take time today to talk to God about what really worries you about your financial situation. Leave room for him to respond to you.* ❏

Day 5 - John 12:1-8 (p.1079)

Giving beautifully This passage has caused much thought over the years. Jesus did so much to alleviate poverty and suffering, so why would he seem to sanction leaving people in poverty? It would seem Jesus felt that life wasn't only about helping the poor: Mary's gift was indeed expensive, but it was an act of worship. The famous Old Testament tithe, where everyone had to give one tenth of their produce to the temple, was used for the worship of God.

action *A question you need to ask yourself is this: 'How much of my income am I using to alleviate poverty and how much am I using to worship God?' Where is your treasure (Matthew 6:19-21)?* ❏

Going Deeper

MEETING GOD

Over these five days you will read about five different people who met God in unique circumstances. Each day, try to use your imagination to picture the scene. Get your mind full of the ways in which the writers describe God. The God who met them in Bible times is the God who wants to meet with you. Ask God to come close to you and meet with you.

Day 1 - Genesis 28:10-22
(p. 30)

Jacob Jacob is on the run from his brother who wants to kill him for cheating him out of his birth-right and their father's blessing (it's all a bit like a Mafia story). He is on his own for the first time, in a strange place. God speaks to him in a dream, and shows him how close at hand heaven (the kingdom of God) always is. How does Jacob react to this meeting with God?

consider *How does knowing that God is close by help you when you are afraid?* ❑

Day 2 - 1 Kings 19:3-15 (p. 361)

Elijah Elijah is also fleeing for his life, not because he has done anything wrong, but because the local tyrants Ahab and Jezebel object to his habit of telling everyone how evil they are, and killing off their henchmen and false prophets. He is God's man, doing God's business, but he's got to the end of his tether. He's fed up and has given up. God's answer to this is to 'pass by', to meet with Elijah.

consider *How do you think this experience of the presence of God changed things for Elijah? What does focusing on God's presence do when you are fed up?* ❑

Day 3 - Luke 5:1-11 (p. 1032)

Simon Peter Simon (also called Peter) is just getting on with the daily grind, when Jesus asks him for a favour. In return, Jesus offers Simon the fisherman advice about fishing. Simon Peter could have resented his advice, but instead he takes it and acts on it. The miraculous results make him look at Jesus in a new light, and look at himself in a true light.

consider *Why do you think he left everything to follow Jesus from that day onwards? What would make you or does make you follow Jesus?* ❑

If you have time, look at another occasion Jesus gave Simon Peter fishing advice (John 21:1-19). This is after Simon Peter has denied three times ever knowing Jesus in order to save his own skin. Why do you think Jesus keeps asking the same question?

Day 4 - John 4:7-29 (p. 1067)

Samaritan woman This woman was used to being ignored or looked down upon, because of her background, race, gender and her relationships. She is surprised and intrigued by Jesus who treats her like a human being, someone worth talking to about things that matter. She is even more surprised by his intimate knowledge of her life and her situation, and that he still wants to know her, even though he knows all about her. Jesus very rarely comes right out and tells people that he is the Saviour (or Messiah).

consider *Why do you think he tells this woman? Do you think there is any reason why Jesus wouldn't want to know you?* ❑

Day 5 - Revelation 1:9-18
(p. 1233)

John John is a prisoner on a prison island, when the Holy Spirit gives him a vision (or revelation) of Jesus in heaven. He describes the weird and wonderful things he sees, trying to put into words the indescribable.

consider *How do you think John felt, seeing Jesus in this vision? Try to describe a time you have felt close to God (perhaps in worship).* ❏

If you have time, look at another description John gives of God in heaven (Revelation 4:1-11). John is meeting God on his home patch. What do these descriptions tell you about God?

PRAYING

Over the next five days, you will read five unique prayers offered up to God by different people in the Bible. Read each prayer, and then have a go at a prayer of your own. Offer your prayer up to God, and try to wait for a response. This might be a change in how you feel, a change in the situation, or an answer from God in some form (for example as an image or words from God directly to you, or through somebody else).

Day 1 - Jonah 3:10-4:4
(p. 928)

Jonah's prayer Jonah is angry with God. God has not done what Jonah wanted. Jonah wanted God to punish the people of Nineveh, but God gave them a chance to repent and turn from their evil ways, they did so and God forgave them. Jonah knew God's character all along, but he wished God

wasn't so compassionate to others. So he prays for his own death!

consider *What do you think of God's answer to Jonah?* ❏

If you have time, read the whole book of Jonah (it's not very long), and see how earlier on in the story Jonah was glad that God forgives when he needed that forgiveness himself.

Day 2 - Nehemiah 1:4-11
(p. 485)

Nehemiah's prayer Nehemiah has just heard some bad news. His fellow countrymen (the people of Israel) are

in a bad way, their capital city is in ruins, the people are living as refugees and prisoners. Nehemiah is a long way away, but wants to do something to help. So he prays. He prays about who God is and what God has promised. He prays for himself and for the people, asking for forgiveness, and asking for help.

consider *Do you pray if you hear bad news (for example things on the news)?* ❏

If you want to know God's answer to Nehemiah, read 2:1-18.

Day 3 - Exodus 33:12-20 (p. 92)

Moses' prayer Moses has some questions for God. He wants to know how he can do the things God is asking him to do (to lead the people of Israel). What help is God going to give him? How will people know God is on his side and the people's side? So he prays.

consider *What is God asking you to do? Ask God for whatever help you need.* ❏

Day 4 - Ephesians 3:14-21 (p. 1175)

Paul's prayer Paul has some friends that he cares about. So he prays for them. He wants them to know how huge God's love is. He asks God to give them strength, faith, and insight, and to fill them with the Holy Spirit.

consider *Who do you want to pray for? What do you want God to do for them? What do they need to know about God?* ❏

Day 5 - Acts 4:23-31 (p. 1096)

Peter and John's prayer Peter and John are celebrating with the other believers. The have just been let out of prison, after being arrested for telling people about Jesus. They have been released with a warning not to teach any more. So they pray. They remind themselves and God about who is more powerful - God or the people telling them what to do. They ask God to show his power, to do amazing things. They ask God to use them. God responds by filling them with his Holy Spirit.

consider *Do you need to see God's power winning through in some situation? Do you believe that God can do miraculous things?* ❏

DAVID'S SONGS

David was God's choice as king for his people (see 1 Samuel 16ff). He knew God well, and wrote lots of songs (or psalms) to God and about God. Each day, read the song-words through a few times, and then try using them as a prayer yourself. Find a phrase or two from the song that expresses something you would like to say. (You can change some of the words to fit your situation better.) And then just say (or sing!) the words to God - out loud or in your head. That's one way of praying!

Day 1 - Psalm 13 (p. 548)

David is having a hard time. He feels overwhelmed by his troubles, and can't think of a way out. Yet he holds on to his trust in God, his belief that God loves him even though it doesn't feel that way right then. He pours out his frustration to God and he affirms his faith in this song.

consider *What things overwhelm you? How can you hold on to God through those times?* ❏

Day 2 - Psalm 8 (p. 546)

Imagine David looking up at the clear night sky, and just being wowed. The vastness and beauty of the universe make him think of two things. First how big and wonderful the God who created all this must be. And second how small and insignificant people are. So he writes these words of praise to God.

consider *What makes you go 'wow' about God?* ❏

Day 3 - Psalm 70 (p. 584)

David calls this song a petition. People petition the government to change the law, because they know only the government has the power to do that. David is asking and pleading with God for help because he knows God has the power to help. In fact he calls God his 'help' and 'deliverer'.

consider *What names or words do you call God?* ❏

Day 4 - Psalm 30 (p. 558)

David is remembering the bad times, his prayers then and the ways God has answered them. So he writes a song of thanks.

consider *Look back over the time you have known God. Remember the prayers you have made, and the* ways that God has answered them. If you don't know God, take a look at the prayer of the back of this Bible ☐

Day 5 - Psalm 103 (p. 605)

This is a song of praise. David is praising God, giving God the credit for all the things he has done and continues to do. Very often, we forget to give God the credit, or we give the credit to other things or other people.

action *Try making a list of all the things you can give God credit for.* ☐

JESUS & PRAYER

Jesus was a man of prayer. He was always in close contact with his heavenly Father through prayer. He taught his followers how to pray, and what prayer is like. He also prayed some amazing prayers.

Day 1 - Matthew 6:5-8 (p. 970)

How to pray Jesus tells us to focus on who we are praying to, God, rather than using prayer as a way to tell people what to do or to impress them. Secondly, to realise that we can't tell God anything he doesn't already know. Prayer is how we communicate with God - who we can't see, but who sees us.

consider *How do you talk to the unseen God?* ☐

Day 2 - Luke 11:1-4 (p. 1042)

The Lord's Prayer The prayer that Jesus taught his followers is used today by Christians all round the world. This simple prayer helps us to praise God, pray for God's concerns, ask for things we need, focus on forgiveness, and on how easily we are tempted. It can be helpful to have a prayer you know by heart to use when you are finding it hard to pray.

action *Try praying this slowly, pausing to think about every word.* ☐

Day 3 - Luke 11:5-13 (p. 1042)

Ask, seek, knock Jesus tells us to pester God with our prayers. We are to go to God with needs and questions for ourselves and for others because we know he can help - just like the man in the story. But we are to keep on asking boldly. And we can be sure God will only give us good things in response.

consider *Think of things you have been prepared to pester other* people for. What do you need to pester God about? Don't give up, keep at him! ❏

If you have time, look at another story, or parable, Jesus told to keep his followers pestering God, Luke 18:1-8 (p. 1052)

Day 4 - Luke 22:41-44
(p.1058)

Jesus prays on the Mount of Olives Jesus knows what is about to happen. He knows that he has been betrayed, and will die at the hands of unjust rulers. He also knows that through this, God will offer forgiveness to all people. But that still doesn't make it easy for Jesus to give up his life. So he prays. He asks God to spare him this anguish. But more than that, he wants to do what God the Father wants. He prays one of the toughest prayers: 'not my will, but yours be done'.

consider *Is this a prayer you can offer to God?* ❏

Day 5 - Luke 23:32-34
(p. 1060)

Jesus prays on the cross Jesus is dying, nailed to a wooden cross in the heat of the day. Yet his concern is not for himself. He is concerned for those people who are killing him, for those who are jeering at him, for those who are just letting it happen. So he prays. When we feel we are suffering, or are victims of other people's action or inaction, it is easy to be concerned only for ourselves. Jesus prays one of the toughest prayers: 'Father, forgive them'.

consider *Is this a prayer you can offer to God?* ❏

THINGS JESUS NEVER SAID

Some well-known sayings are not as biblical as we think and can even stop us from really getting to know God because they give us a false idea of him. As we read the Bible more it becomes easier to spot the things that Jesus would never have said, because we get to know him better.

Day 1 - Mark 7:14-23
(p. 1010)

'Cleanliness is next to godliness' Jesus is not particularly bothered about personal hygiene, tidiness or clean food. He's much more concerned with inner cleanness - how clean or wholesome our thoughts, desires and motives are. We read in I Samuel 16:7 that 'the LORD does not look at the things man looks at. Man looks at the outward appearance, but the LORD looks at the heart'.

consider *Are you more concerned with what you look like, or what you are like?* ❑

Day 2 - Luke 14:7-11
(p.1047)

'God helps those who help themselves' Jesus was never impressed with people who helped themselves, be it to the best seats, other people's things, other people's husbands and wives, or just to whatever was up for grabs. Helping ourselves in this sense means putting ourselves first. If we have an inflated view of ourselves, God will soon put us in our place. But if we have a humble view of ourselves, we will think more of others and put them first. Then we will find that God will help us as we help others.

consider *When do you 'help yourself' rather than others? How could you act differently?* ❑

Day 3 - Matthew 6:19-21
(p. 971)

'Money is the root of all evil' Paul nearly says this, (see 1 Timothy 6:6-10) but he says that it is the love of money that is the problem. Jesus makes the point that whatever we desire and value most is our 'treasure'. It captivates us. We keep thinking and dreaming about it. We put our time and energy into getting it. So Jesus suggests we should choose our treasure carefully.

action *Read verse 24 and ask youself who you are serving?* ❑

Day 4 - Matthew 5:43-48
(p. 970)

'Charity begins at home' Jesus says that charity, being generous with our love and belongings, doesn't really count among people who will do the same for us. After all, its easy to be nice to someone who's nice back. Anyone can do that. It's being generous to those who won't or can't repay us that is real charity, real love. Giving to those who don't seem to deserve it. After all, do we deserve God's love and forgiveness?

action *Read Luke 14:12-14, who could you invite to something who could not repay you?* ❑

Day 5 - Luke 9:23-25
(p.1039)

'Being a Christian makes life easy' Jesus never promised an easy life! In fact life sometimes gets even harder. For starters, we don't suddenly turn perfect when we become a Christian, and neither does the world around us. So we (and others) still mess up and have to deal with the consequences. Becoming one of Jesus' followers means we attract the attention of his enemy, the devil. This enemy is trying to make life tough for us, to make us give up. And sometimes God in his wisdom thinks we'll learn more by going through something tough rather than avoiding it. But becoming a Christian does mean that life's biggest problems are dealt with.

consider *What do you think those are?* ☐

QUESTIONS GOD ASKS

In the Bible, God asks people certain questions. These tell us things about God and help us to know him better. They are questions God still asks today.

Day 1 - Jeremiah 1:11-14 (p. 755)

'What do you see?' God often wants to show us something. So he asks us what we can see, then he tells us what it means. What you see may be something in front of your eyes at the time, or it may be something you see in your imagination. Read Jeremiah 18:1-6 for an example of Jeremiah seeing something, and God using it to tell him something about God.

action *Listen for God at different times asking you what you see. Tell him what you see with your eyes or your mind's eye, and wait for God to show you what it means.* ☐

Day 2 - Genesis 4:8-12 (p. 6)

'Where is your brother? What have you done?' God asks Cain this question, knowing very well what Cain has done. Yet God prefers to ask the question rather than just launch into Cain. Why do you think this is? He seems to be giving Cain a chance to own up, and say he is sorry. God would always rather forgive than punish, but he can only forgive us if we ask him to. And that means taking responsibility for things we have done (or should have done but haven't), and especially for the things we do that effect others. How different might things have been if Cain had answered God in this way?

action *Listen for God asking you what you have done. Take the opportunity to tell him, being honest with yourself and God (after all, he already knows the truth). Ask for his forgiveness.* ☐

Day 3 - John 5:1-9 (p. 1068)

'Do you want to get well?'
This might sound a stupid question to ask an invalid. Of course he wants to get better! But he doesn't give a straight answer. He lists the reasons why he can't get well, or gives excuses for why he hasn't been healed already. We can all be like this. We say we want to change in some way (perhaps our habits, behaviour or thoughts), but actually we give ourselves lots of reasons why we can't, or excuses why it hasn't happened yet.

consider *What excuses or reasons do you give yourself that Jesus' question sees straight through?* ❏

Day 4 - Mark 4:35-41 (p. 1006)

'Why are you so afraid?'
Jesus contrasts being afraid with having faith. He is asking us what we are actually afraid of, what ultimately it is that scares us. Being scared distracts us from God. Being scared is a way of giving something power over us: our fears can rule our lives.

consider *What are you afraid of? How can you enable Jesus, not fear, to rule your life?* ❏

Read Matthew 10:28-31. Jesus is pointing out that there is no-one or nothing of which we should be afraid, as long as we fear God. 'Fear of God' doesn't mean being scared of him. It means knowing just how awesome and powerful God is, and giving him rightful respect. We should fear God because we know he is worth fearing.

Day 5 - Isaiah 6:1-8 (p. 690)

'Who will go for us?'
God wants volunteers! In this weird and wonderful passage we get a glimpse of God on a recruitment drive. Isaiah goes on to be one of the most important prophets, or spokesperson for God in the whole Bible. God has work to be done, good news to be spread, people to set free. And he wants to involve his people in all of this. But he wants willing volunteers.

consider *What is he asking you to help with? If you have time, read Luke 4:14-21. This prophecy was written about Jesus, but it is also true of everyone who responds to God's call for volunteers. That's encouraging, isn't it!* ❏

RELATING TO JESUS

Jesus wants us to know him. Each of the next five readings will focus on one of the ways in which Jesus wants us to relate to him.

Day 1 - Mark 3:31-35
(p.1005)

As family This might look as though Jesus was being rude to his family. But actually, he was saying that being like him was more important than being related to him. Jesus spent his whole earthly life doing God's will. If we do God's will, then there will be a family-likeness between Jesus and us. And Jesus will call us his brother or sister.

consider *In what ways do you show a family-likeness?* ❏

Day 2 - John 13:3-5,12-17
(p.1081)

As a servant Jesus reminds us that he wants us to be people who serve. People who serve others, and people who serve him. Jesus is the boss or VIP and he wants us to be the servants. How often we get this basic relationship mixed up, and think Jesus is there to serve us, to do our bidding! We need to get things in perspective, and remember who is God. When we do serve him, Jesus says 'Well done, good and faithful servant!' (Matthew 25:21).

consider *Ask Jesus to show you when you do and when you don't serve him.* ❏

Day 3 - Matthew 11:25-30
(p. 977)

As a student Jesus is a good teacher, but if we want to learn from him, we have to be his student or apprentice. It means admitting that we have a lot to learn! God doesn't teach the 'know-alls', but rather those who feel like they are struggling. And Jesus doesn't teach us by making us swot for exams, but by being alongside us and pointing things out to us as we read his word and get to know him. He also teaches by showing us by example, so we learn by copying him.

consider *In what ways are you imitating Jesus?* ❏

Day 4 - John 15:9-14
(p. 1083)

As a friend Your family are a gift, your boss comes with the job, but you can choose your friends. Jesus invites us to be his friends. He does this by dying for us. His death on the cross and his new life give us the chance to be God's friend rather than his enemy. Jesus says we are his friend if we do what he commands.

consider *What does he command? Are you a friend of God?* ❏

Day 5 - 2 Corinthians 5:18-21 (p. 1161)

As a messenger Jesus sends us out as his representatives, not with something to sell, but with something to give away (the NIV uses the term 'ambassador' but some translations use the word 'messenger'). He trusts us with the message, the good news, that people can get right with God through him. He wants us to be messengers who know that the message is more important that we are. This is a close relationship - Jesus says that how we are treated as his messengers is how he, the one who sends us, is treated (see Luke 10:16).

consider *When are you a messenger for Jesus?* ❏

GETTING CLOSER

Jesus always wants us to be even closer to him than we are. Over these five days we are going to explore five things that can help us to achieve that.

Day 1 - Luke 6:46-49 (p.1035)

Obedience Nothing seems to frustrate Jesus more than people who think they know him, but ignore what he tells them! They are on dodgy ground. John the disciple puts it this way: 'We know that we have come to know him if we obey his commands' (1 John 2:3). If we are going to call Jesus our Lord and God, then we must do what he says (its no good joining the army but refusing to obey orders or joining a club and breaking all the rules!)

consider *Of the things Jesus says, which do you find hardest to do?* ❏

Day 2 - Matthew 25:34-46 (p. 995)

Caring for others Jesus challenges us to really care for others, to actually do things to help. We can show our love for Christ by treating everyone we meet as though they were Jesus himself. As John urges us, 'let us not love with words or tongue but with actions and in truth' (1 John 3:18).

action *Today, try to treat people as you would want to treat Jesus.* ❏

Day 3 - Mark 14:3-9 (p.1020)

Worship Jesus praises this woman for doing something beautiful. Other people present think she has done something stupid, embarrassing, wasteful and over the top. She sees Jesus as the wonderful, loving Son of God that he is, and has to do something that recognises this. Giving ourselves in worship can easily look goofy to an on-looker. But to Jesus it will always be beautiful.

consider *How do you worship Jesus?* ❏

Day 4 - Luke 18:18-25 (p1052)

Removing obstacles It is hard to get close to Jesus if there is something in the way. That something can be almost anything - it is whatever we find hardest to give up and leave behind in order to follow Jesus. It might be friends, a hobby, a way of behaving, our reputation, a habit, or almost anything.

consider *What do you find it hard to give up?* ❏

Day 5 - Matthew 5:23-24 (p. 969)

Repairing relationships Jesus is saying that we can't get close to God if we are distant from people we know. This is especially true if it is our fault that we are not getting on with someone. Making our peace with people is part of living in the peace that Jesus gives us (John 14:27).

consider *Are there any relationships that you need to put right?* ❏

Jargonbuster

Key Concepts and Big Words

If you want to find out about a religious or biblical word, look it up here in the jargonbuster which lists words alphabetically. The Bible references give you examples of each jargonword. Don't feel you have to restrict yourself to reading only the particular verse or sentence in which the jargonword appears, read as much of the context as you need for a full understanding. Words **HIGHLIGHTED** like this have their own entry in the jargonbuster. If you want even more information about a word, try using a Bible dictionary or Bible concordance.

B.C. Before Christ's birth   **OT** Old Testament   **NT** New Testament

Aaron **MOSES'** brother and spokesman (*Exodus 7:1*) who became the first high **PRIEST**. *Exodus 28:1*

Abba The Aramaic for 'Daddy', an intimate word used by **JESUS** to address **GOD** the Father. *Mark 14:36; Romans 8:15*

Abraham, Abram A traveller, he was called by **GOD** to enter into a **COVENANT** relationship with him (*Genesis 15:17-21*). Miraculously given a son **ISAAC**, whom God challenged him to sacrifice (*Genesis 22:1-14*). Seen as the 'father of **ISRAEL**' and subsequently viewed by the **CHRISTIAN CHURCH** as a model of Christian **FAITH**. *Galatians 3:6-9*

Adam The personal name for the first man created by **GOD** *Genesis 2:7*

and also means 'mankind' or 'humanity' in general.

Almighty Sometimes an adjective which simply means 'very powerful', but sometimes a name of **GOD**: 'the Almighty'... ie, the big one! *Genesis 17:1*

altar Normally a stone or table where people **WORSHIPPED** or **SACRIFICED** offerings to **GOD**. There are few mentions in the NT (except in the vision of **REVELATION**), but they are mentioned a lot in the OT. *Genesis 22:9; 2 Kings 23:15*

Amen A **HEBREW** word which means 'surely' or 'so be it'. *Revelation 22:21*

anoint, A-ed One Literally means, 'to pour'. In the OT, anointing with oil was a sign of being specially set apart for **GOD. JESUS** is the Anointed One. *2 Samuel 16:12; Luke 4:18*

angel A messenger of **GOD**. Angels appear to be special 'envoys' who God sometimes uses to communicate with the human race. They seem to be frightening or bring frightening messages as they often begin by saying, 'Don't be afraid!' *Exodus 23:23; Luke 1:30*

antichrist These people are referred to only in the letters of John. However, the idea of an antichrist - a person who will oppose Jesus during the last days - is a very popular image. John tells us that this person is not **SATAN**, but that he comes 'by the activity of Satan'. *1 John 2:22; 2 John 7*

apostle A Greek word meaning 'sent one' and implying leadership and teaching. *Matthew 10:2; 1 Corinthians 9:1*

ark Literally means 'chest' or 'box'.
ark, Noah's The big boat that **GOD** commanded Noah to go to sea in!
ark of the covenant A special box covered in gold where the **ISRAELITES** stored their holy treasures, including the two stone tablets of the **TEN COMMANDMENTS.** *Genesis 6:14; 2 Samuel 6:3*

ascension, the JESUS' return to his Father in order to establish his **KINGDOM.** *Mark 16:19, Acts 1:9-11*

atonement Means what it says: 'making at one'. The word describes the work of reconciliation between **GOD** and the human race, both in the OT through **SACRIFICE** and in the NT through the death and **RESURRECTION** of **JESUS**. *Exodus 29:36; Romans 3:25*

Baal. A name given to the local god of the **CANAANITES**. When the **ISRAELITES** rebelled against **GOD**, they made **IDOLS** so that they could worship Baal. *Number 25:3-5; 2 Chronicles 28:1-2*

Babylon, -ian Empire A city that would now be in modern Iraq, it was the capital city of the Empire of Babylonia. A dominant power, it was always a big enemy of **ISRAEL**, and eventually invaded and sent nearly all the Israelites into Exile (*see* the book of **DANIEL**). In the NT, the term signifies 'the world' in opposition to **GOD**. *Revelation 14:8*

baptism Originally an act of ceremonial cleansing for **JEWS**, baptism was transformed by John the Baptist and is used by the **CHURCH** as a sign of cleansing and **SALVATION** that is open to all who **BELIEVE**. *Romans 6:3; Ephesians 4:5*

Beelzebub A Hebrew pun on **BAAL**, it means, 'the Lord of the Flies'. It came to mean lord of the **DEMONS** (*Matthew 10:25*), and was eventually used as a name for **SATAN** (*Luke 11:14-20*).

Bethlehem Famous as the City of **DAVID** (*2 Samuel 5:7*), and the birthplace of **JESUS** (*Luke 2:4*).

believe, -ing In the Bible, believing is not just mentally accepting something as true: believing in **JESUS** is about trusting him with your whole life and responding to what he says. *Psalm 119:66; Romans 10:9*

blasphemy When a person dishonours or offends **GOD**, they commit blasphemy. In the NT, blasphemy includes insulting God's people. *Ezekiel 20:39; Matthew 12:31*

bless, -ing To bless someone is to wish good on them, both spiritually and materially. *Numbers 6:24-26; Romans 12:14*

Blood The symbol of life, blood was shed at all the major **JEWISH** ceremonies. This sacrificial giving up of life reaches its climax in the **CRUCIFIXION** of **JESUS**, which is remembered in the **LAST SUPPER**. *Numbers 18:17; Romans 3:25*

Born again *See* New birth

Bride of Christ One of the descriptions of the church in the NT with **JESUS** as the bridegroom. *Mark 2:20; John 3:29*

Caesar AUGUSTUS The ruler of the **ROMAN EMPIRE** in Jesus' time. *Luke 2:1*

Canaan, -ites Today, an area called Palestine occupying the coastal areas of modern **ISRAEL**, Syria and inland areas across to the **RIVER JORDAN** and the Dead Sea. In the Bible, it signifies the promised land given by **GOD** to the people of **ISRAEL**. *Joshua 1:2-3, 6*

child, -ren of God Through faith, believers have God as Father who they are encouraged by Scripture to imitate in their daily lives. *John 1:12-13; Romans 8:15; Ephesians 1:5*

Christ The Greek word for **MESSIAH** or '**ANOINTED ONE**'. Priests, kings and prophets were anointed with oil in the OT as a setting apart for their important work. Jesus was anointed with the Holy Spirit in a unique way for the work he came to do. *Mark 8:29; Luke 4:17-21; Romans 1:1*

Christian This word was first used to refer to Christian believers by those outside the **CHURCH**, and means 'a person who belongs to **CHRIST**'. *Acts 11:26; 1 Peter 4:16*

church The word in the NT which we translate as 'church' means 'the gathering'. So it really is the people (also called the body of **CHRIST'**) and not the building that makes the church! *1 Corinthians 1:2, 12:27-31, 1 Thessalonians 2:14*

circumcision This was a special ritual ordained by **GOD** to set the **JEWS** apart from other peoples in Palestine (*see* **CANAAN**): every male child had to have his foreskin removed. *Genesis 17:10*

Ten Commandments When the word 'commandment' is used rather than 'command', it tends to mean that this is a command of highest importance and should be observed for all time. Thus the Ten Commandments are still the basis for modern-day morality even in the largely non-**CHRISTIAN** and non-**JEWISH** west. *Exodus 10:1-7, 34:28; Matthew 22:36*

confess Confession has two meanings. To confess your **FAITH** means to openly acknowledge that you are a **CHRISTIAN**. To confess your **SINS** means to acknowledge before **GOD** that you have wronged him. *Romans 10:9; James 5:16*

convert Literally means, 'to turn' or 'to return'. Used as a noun of a person who becomes a **CHRISTIAN**. *Romans 16:5*

covenant A special agreement, a contract, showing a close relationship between two parties. Important early covenants were made between **GOD** and **ABRAHAM** (*Genesis 15:18*) and between God and **ISRAEL** (*Genesis 35:9-12*). When **JESUS** shared the **LAST SUPPER** with the **DISCIPLES** he said that he had instituted a new covenant. *Genesis 6:18; Matthew 26:28*

cross, the **JESUS'** death on the cross is central to the **CHRISTIAN** faith. Through **JESUS' DEATH**, sinners are reconciled to **GOD**. *Matthew 27:32-56; Mark 15:21-41; Luke 23:26-49; John 19:16-37; Acts 2:23; Ephesians 2:13-17*

crucifixion In the Roman Empire, crucifixion (being nailed to a cross) was used as a way of torturing and executing criminals, especially political rebels. It was a particularly nasty way to kill someone. *John 19:16-37*

curse The opposite of **BLESSING**: a wish of evil on a person, nation or thing. *Genesis 3:17; James 3:9-12*

Daniel A **JEW** who became a leading official in the **BABYLONIAN EMPIRE** (*see* the book of Daniel). As a prophet, **GOD** used him and gave him dreams and visions about the end of the world.

David One of the most famous of

the Kings of **ISRAEL**. David made serious mistakes *(2 Samuel 11)*, but he was at heart a godly man, favoured by **GOD** and king at a time when Israel was at its peak *(1 Samuel 13:14)*. God's covenant with David had messianic implications and **JESUS**, born in David's City (**BETHLEHEM**) fulfilled these expectations *(Luke 18:35-38)*.

deacon Literally means 'servant'. It was first used to describe those who fed the widows in the Jerusalem **CHURCH**, but soon came to refer to a particular office in the church. *1 Timothy 3:8*

death The end of a person's life in the present world which comes to everyone as a result of sin *(Genesis 3)*. Believers will then live in the joy of God's presence. *Psalm 39:5; Luke 23:43; Romans 6:23*

deliverance Rescue, which **GOD'S** people often cry out for when suffering oppression. This is also the term used to describe someone's release from demonic forces *(see* **DEMONS**). *Psalm 3:7; Joel 2:32*

demon, -s, -ic. Evil spiritual forces. There is some indication in the Bible that **ANGELS** have free will like humans and can therefore **SIN**. It is thought that demons may be fallen angels led astray by **SATAN**. *Matthew 12:24-28; Romans 8:38*

devil *See* **SATAN**.

discernment A gift of the **HOLY SPIRIT** which helps people to distinguish good from bad, true from false. *Proverbs 28:11; 1 Corinthians 12:7-11*

disciple Someone who followed the teachings of a particular **RABBI**. Used in the **GOSPELS** of one of those who followed Jesus (also often known as The Twelve). Now refers to a person who follows Jesus. *Luke 5:33; John 13:35*

divine **HOLY**, or of **GOD**. *Isaiah 35:4; Romans 1:20*

doctrine The beliefs that we have about who **GOD** is, who **JESUS** is, and what the human race is like. *1 Timothy 4:16; Titus 1:9*

edify Literally means, 'to build up', as in strengthening believers in their faith. *Romans 14:19; 1 Corinthians 14:4*

Egypt, -ian Highly significant in the Bible, particularly as the empire in which **JOSEPH** served *(Genesis 37:36, 39 – 47)*, and from which **MOSES** led his people out of captivity *(Exodus)*.

elder A special position of leadership in the early **CHURCH** not necessarily held exclusively by the old. *Titus 1:6*

Elijah A PROPHET who was used by GOD to combat the worship of BAAL and who opposed the SIN and injustices of various kings and queens in ISRAEL. *1 Kings 17 – 2 Kings 2*

ephod A special kind of vest, worn originally by the high PRIEST in the TEMPLE. *Exodus 28:6; 2 Samuel 6:14*

Esau Brother of JACOB. Famous for being hairy! *Genesis 25:19-33*

eternal Means 'existing always', 'for ever', 'without end'. A quality or characteristic of GOD. *Genesis 21:33; John 3:16*

evangelise Means 'to tell people the good news about Jesus'. *2 Timothy 4:5*

evil Is it just the absence of good or something more active? The Bible's teaching on the existence of SATAN certainly implies that there is an active force in the world today which is evil. *Proverbs 12:13; Romans 12:9*

exalt Means 'to make great' or 'to acknowledge something as great'. In the Bible, GOD is exalted. *Psalm 30:1; Luke 14:11*

exile Exiles are people who live away from their own country, normally because they have been forced to leave. The exile was the time when CANAAN was invaded by the BABYLONIAN EMPIRE and the JEWS were relocated to other parts of the empire. *Jeremiah 1:3; Ezekiel 1:1*

exodus Literally means, 'the departure'. The exodus was the event in history when Jewish slaves, led by MOSES, left EGYPT to return home to the PROMISED LAND. Exodus (the whole book!)

faith The Bible itself defines this: 'Faith is being sure of what we hope for and certain of what we do not see.' *Romans 5:1; Hebrews 11:1*

fall *Genesis 3* describes the 'fall' of the human race, the time when GOD's perfect creation was spoilt by the disobedience of Adam and Eve.

fast Fasting in the Bible usually involves giving up food for a long period of time, often to focus on GOD or to show him that he is worth any SACRIFICE. *Esther 4:16; Isaiah 58*

fellowship In the OT, the ISRAELITES often made fellowship SACRIFICES as a sign of being close to GOD. In the NT the Greek word 'fellowship' means something like 'sharing in a common life', implying a relationship of mutual commitment. *Leviticus 3:1; 1 John 1:7*

festival, feast A time of celebration. The **JEWS** still have three main religious festivals each year: **PASSOVER**, **PENTECOST** and Tabernacles. They are based on the agricultural year, and reaffirm **GOD**'s central place in their lives and the importance of receiving God's **FORGIVENESS**. *Leviticus 23:39; 1 Corinthians 5:8*

forgive To pardon or to let someone off from being punished for doing wrong. Forgiveness is two-sided: **GOD** forgives us (once we have repented of our sins); and **JESUS** commands us to forgive others as God has forgiven us. See also **ATONEMENT**. *Psalm 103:3; Ephesians 4:32*

Galilee The northern area of modern **ISRAEL** and the scene of much of Jesus' life and ministry as recorded in the Gospels.

Gentile The main word used in the Bible to describe people who are not **JEWS**. *Acts 15:23*

glorify Has the sense of 'to revel in the beauty of' something. It also means 'to praise' and 'to make something more splendid'. *Psalm 34:3; John 12:23*

glory The word in **HEBREW** comes from a word meaning 'heavy' and originally described that part of a person's character which impresses most. In the Bible it is often used to describe the presence of **GOD**, his power and character, or some event (such as Jesus' **CRUCIFIXION**) which points to God. *Exodus 33:18; Ezekiel 1:28*

God The Creator and Redeemer or Saviour of the world. God has many names in the Bible, but the most important one is Yahweh, translated as LORD in the NIV, but which really means simply 'I am' (*Exodus 3:14*).

gods There are many 'gods' in the Bible, but these are clearly very different from the God of the Bible who is the source of all being. *1 Kings 18:18; 1 Corinthians 8:5-6*

gospel Literally means, 'good news' and concerns the **SALVATION** of **SINFUL** humanity through the life, **DEATH** and **RESURRECTION** of **JESUS CHRIST**. *Mark 1:1; 1 Corinthians 9:16*

Gospel John's etc. Four separate accounts of the life of **JESUS** which appear as the first four books in the NT.

grace The undeserved favour of God, expressed most fully in the forgiveness of sinners through faith in **JESUS CHRIST**. *John 1:4, 16-17; Ephesians 2:4-9; Titus 3:4-7*

Hades *See* **HELL**

Hallelujah Means '**PRAISE** the LORD' in **HEBREW**. *Revelation 19*

healing Making physically or spiritually healthy. The Bible is full of stories of people being supernaturally healed by **GOD**. What is clear is that even if someone is recognised as a **PROPHET** or healer, it is still **GOD** - and not the person themself - who performs the healing. *Matthew 10:1; James 5:16*

heathen Although the word now has very negative connotations, it really just means the same as 'GENTILE', ie not a **JEW**. *1 Thessalonians 4:5*

heaven The first use of the word heaven in the Bible is to describe the sky, but it also describes the place where **GOD** lives, his 'home'. The main biblical view of heaven seems to be commonly accepted today as being the spiritual dimension of the universe. **REVELATION** tells us that when **JESUS** returns there will be 'a new heaven and a new earth'. *Genesis 1:1, Psalm 2:4; Revelation 21:1*

Hebrew The language spoken by the **JEWS** during the time the OT was written.
Hebrews, the Describes the **JEWISH** people in the OT. *2 Chronicles 32:18; Jonah 1:9*

hell Primarily, a place of punishment and separation from **GOD**, in contrast with **HEAVEN**. The OT word *Sheol* refers to the place of the dead without reference to punishment (*Psalm 30:3* 'the grave'); the Greek word *Hades* is also a neutral reference to the place of the dead as somewhere they remain until judgment day (*Matthew 16:18; Revelation 20:13*). *Gehenna* is used to refer to the strongly negative aspects of hell, the idea of punishment (fire) and separation from God. (*Matthew 5:22*) *Tartaroo* (*2 Peter 2:4*) is the place in Greek mythology where **EVIL GODS** were sent for **ETERNITY** (*see* **ETERNAL**).

Herod In Palestine at the time of **JESUS**, the Herodian rulers were puppet Kings under the **ROMANS**. Herod the Great was king of **JUDAH** when Jesus was a child (*Matthew 2:1-12*) and Herod Antipas was ruler of **GALILEE** when he was an adult (*Luke 23:6-12*).

holy, -iness Comes from a root word meaning, 'set apart, different'. **GOD** is holy because he is pure and morally A+++ in a class of his own. We grow in holiness and become more like God as we dedicate ourselves to serving God (and are therefore set apart from the world). *Exodus 3:5; Psalm 71:22; Mark 1:24*

Holy Spirit, the third person of the **TRINITY**. The Spirit is seen as having a creative and sustaining role (the Spirit was 'hovering over the waters' at creation, *Genesis 1:2*). The Spirit inspired Scripture

(*2 Timothy 3:16*) and is here today as God present with us on earth (*John 16:7*) and in us (*Acts 1:8*).

hope A confident expectation for the future which motivates Christians even in the face of hardship and doubt. *Psalm 71:5; Romans 5:3-5*

Hosanna A HEBREW word meaning, 'Save us' which came to be a word in its own right like HALLELUJAH. *Matthew 21:9*

hymn Another word for song, specifically a song of PRAISE to God in worship. *Psalm 40:3; 1 Corinthians 14:26*

idol In the Bible an idol is a statue of a false GOD, but today the word is used to mean anything that someone holds as the most important thing in their life, more important than GOD. *Exodus 20:4; 1 Corinthians 8:4*

image The Bible uses the word image to mean a close likeness of something. We are made in the image of GOD, an image which was damaged in the FALL, but may be restored through Jesus. *Genesis 1:26; 1 Corinthians 11:7*

Immanuel Literally means, 'GOD with us' and refers to Jesus. *Isaiah 7:14; Mark 1:23*

iniquity Another word for SIN. *Psalm 51:2; Micah 2:1*

Isaac Son of ABRAHAM and Sarah and father of JACOB. His birth was seen as a fulfilment of the promise to Abraham that he would be the father of many nations. *Genesis 17*

Ishmael ISAAC's older half-brother (*Genesis 25:12-18*) who was banished. Muslims claim him as their ancestor.

Israel, -ites GOD's special name for JACOB (*Genesis 32:28*), Israel also became the name of God's people. Its most famous kings were SAUL, DAVID and SOLOMON (*see* 1&2 Kings). At one time, Israel was the name of the northern kingdom and JUDAH the southern kingdom (*2 Samuel 2:10*), but today Israel is the name of the whole JEWISH nation in Palestine.

Jacob The son of ISAAC and twin brother of ESAU. Jacob stole a blessing from his father (*Genesis 27*) but God used him to found a nation. His twelve sons became the twelve tribes of ISRAEL.

Jerusalem An ancient city, perhaps five thousand years old, captured by the ISRAELITES and used as their capital. Much of the drama of the Bible focuses around this city which had theological significance as the location for God's temple and the place for sacrificial worship. Jerusalem is sacred to Jews, Christians and Muslims.

Jesus A name meaning 'God saves'. It is the Greek version of the **HEBREW** 'Joshua'.

Jew, -ish A designation arising from around 800-600 B.C. for descendants of the people from the kingdom of Judah and also for those from other nations who followed their religion. The term is often used in place of **'ISRAELITES'** meaning the OT people of God as opposed to non-**JEWS** or **GENTILES**. *Jeremiah 40:11-12; Mark 7:3; Romans 11:25-32*

River Jordan in the Middle East running from the Sea of **GALILEE** to the Dead Sea.

Joseph Eleventh son of **JACOB**, Joseph was abducted by his brothers and sold into slavery in **EGYPT**, where he prospered and was eventually reconciled to his family *(Genesis 37—50)*.

Joshua Led the Israelites into **CANAAN** (the promised land) after the death of **MOSES** (book of *Joshua*).

joy A profound kind of happiness, joy is associated in the Bible with God's people who rejoice at all that he has done for them. Joy is also associated with more ordinary things, such as having children and working. *1 Chronicles 29:22; Nehemiah 8:10; Philippians 1:4; Hebrews 13:17*

Jubilee, Year of Means literally, 'the blowing of the ram's horn' and was instituted by **GOD** as a time when debts would be cancelled and property redistributed. This was supposed to happen every fifty years throughout Israel. *Leviticus 25–27*

Judah Also known as Judea. The southern Kingdom with its capital at **JERUSALEM**.

Judas One of **JESUS'** twelve **DISCIPLES**, he betrayed Jesus to the Jewish authorities. *Matthew 26:14-16, 27:1-9*

Judge Generally, someone responsible for administering justice and government. The OT records a time in Jewish history when **GOD** sent special 'judges' to restore **ISRAEL** to God, often in battle. God is the supreme judge and Jesus is presented in the NT as a judge appointed by God. *Judges; Psalm 7:8; John 5:27*

judgment day The Bible clearly speaks of a time when everyone who has lived will come before **GOD** and be judged according to their actions and their relationship with **JESUS**. *Hebrews 10:27; 2 Peter 3:7*

justice The main use of the word 'justice' in the Bible is the honest practice of the law, so that **GOD**'s people could rely on their legal system, but God also began to demand justice from individuals, particularly in regard to the poor. Justice is seen as one of God's most important attributes. *Psalm 101:1; Amos 5:24*

kingdom of God/heaven This term is vital to an understanding of the message of **JESUS**. It means the place where **GOD** rules, but implies that there are places where God doesn't fully rule. Jesus spoke both of an element of the kingdom that is already here, and an element to come. *Mark 1:15; Luke 13:18-21*

Lamb In the OT, a young sheep was a good sacrifice to **GOD**. **JESUS** was called 'the Lamb of God' by John the Baptist and after his death, the **CHURCH** used the image of the lamb to symbolise his death as an **ATONEMENT** for **SIN**. *Leviticus 3:7; John 1:29; Revelation 5:6*

Last Supper, the In the last days of his life, **JESUS** ate a **PASSOVER** meal with his disciples and encouraged them to remember him and his death every time they had the meal. This is what we now call 'Holy Communion' or 'Eucharist'. *Mark 14:12-26*

Law Directions from God on our right behaviour towards him and towards each other. The Israelites (later called **JEWS**) believed that their Law, received via **MOSES**, was from **GOD**. The NT indicates that Jesus is the fulfilment of the Law so that blind adherence to it is not enough. Not that the rules can be thrown out, but that the motivation behind them is key. *Psalm 119:44; Matthew 5:17; Romans 8:3*

Levite The name given to a descendant of Levi. The Levites became a special tribe of **PRIESTS** in the **TABERNACLE** and **TEMPLE**. *Deuteronomy 10:8; Nehemiah 8:9*

LORD Look out for this version of Lord: it is used as a translation of YHWH (*Yahweh*, or sometimes *Jehovah*). The Hebrew name for **GOD** (meaning 'I am') which **JESUS** took for himself. *John 8:58-59, 11:25, 15:1*
Lord. Another name for God which is frequently used of Jesus in the NT. *John 20:28*

love A caring commitment including affection and fondness. When the first **CHRISTIANS** tried to describe the love that they had between them, they adopted a little-used word, *agapé*. In most instances in the NT, it is this special word which describes God's sacrificial love for us and Christian love for each other. Love is perhaps the most important aspect of **GOD'S** character as revealed in the Bible. *Matthew 3:17; John 3:16, 13:35*

Manger A feeding trough for domestic or farm animals such as sheep or donkeys. Where **JESUS** was put shortly after his birth, according to Luke's Gospel. *Luke 2:7*

manna Literally means, 'What is it?'. Manna was a form of food provided by **GOD** during the time of the **EXODUS**. *Exodus 16*

Mary The mother of **JESUS** *(Matthew 1:18)*. Another Mary was a close follower of Jesus *(Mark 16:1)*. Mary, sister of Martha and Lazarus was close to Jesus *(John 11)*.

meek Meekness is not the same as weakness, but rather it suggests a humble ability to survive life's ups and downs with an even temper. It is used to describe **JESUS** *(2 Corinthians 10:1)*. *Psalm 37:11; Matthew 5:5*

mercy An important attribute of **GOD**'s character, mercy is God's ability to override his **JUSTICE** and **FORGIVE** our wrongdoing. **JESUS**' death is the means by which God demonstrates his mercy. Christians are urged to be merciful to one another. *Psalm 51:1; Micah 6:8; Ephesians 2:4-5*

Messiah Literally means, 'the **ANOINTED ONE**' who was anointed by **GOD** to deliver and **REDEEM** his people. The OT looked ahead to the coming of such a figure, the NT sees that expectation fulfilled in **JESUS**. *Isaiah 45:1; John 1:41.* *See also* **CHRIST**

miracle A miracle is something that does not conform to the normal laws of nature. This could be a healing or a dramatic weather change that has no ordinary explanation. It is clear from the Bible that **GOD** is into miracles. Jesus performed miracles and the disciples did so after his death by the power of the **HOLY SPIRIT**. *Psalm 77:14; Mark 6:2; 1 Corinthians 12:28*

Moses A **HEBREW PROPHET** brought up in an **EGYPTIAN** household, Moses led the **ISRAELITES** out of **EGYPT** and to the **PROMISED LAND** *(Exodus)*. While in the wilderness, **GOD** revealed to Moses the **TEN COMMANDMENTS** *(Exodus 20:1-17)*.

Nazareth A small village in south-west **GALILEE**, the home of **JESUS** until around his thirtieth birthday. *Matthew 26:71*

Nebuchadnezzar Babylonian King in the time of **DANIEL**. *2 Kings 24:1; Daniel 1:1*

new birth The radical renewal of a person's inner being by the work of the **HOLY SPIRIT**. Sometimes likened to becoming a child of God. *John 1:12-13, 3:5-8*

offering Nowadays this word describes the money we give in a church service. Originally it meant a SACRIFICE to GOD, normally the burning of an animal on an ALTAR. *Leviticus 1:2; 2 Corinthians 8:19*

Pagan Another word for 'GENTILE', originally it didn't have such a negative meaning as today. *2 Kings 23:5; Luke 12:30*

Palestine *See* Canaan

parable A Greek word meaning 'something put alongside' using one thing to explain another. JESUS is famous for his stories, known as parables. *Ezekiel 20:49; Luke 15:3*

paradise A word from Persia, that originally described a park or pleasure garden. It was used by the JEWS to describe the Garden of Eden and the future blessed state in HEAVEN. *Luke 23:43; Revelation 2:7*

Passover The FESTIVAL of Passover celebrated the time when, just before the EXODUS, the ANGEL of death passed over (ie spared from death) the ISRAELITES and killed only EGYPTIANS. It was an important time every year when JEWS would come from all over the world to JERUSALEM to celebrate GOD's liberation of his people. *Exodus 12; Luke 22:15*

Paul Originally named SAUL *(Acts 9:1-30)*, Paul wrote more than half the books in the NT (see *Romans, Corinthians* for example). He is widely credited with spreading the GOSPEL of Jesus throughout the Roman empire *(Acts 16–28)*.

peace The HEBREW word for peace, *shalom*, means a complete wholeness and is much broader and more positive than the current meaning of the word, which tends to be 'no war'. *Joshua 9:15; Isaiah 9:6*

Pentecost This was the equivalent of the harvest FESTIVAL for the JEWS. It is also known as the Feast of Weeks and is often called the 'birthday of the CHURCH' because it was at a Pentecost celebration that GOD gave the HOLY SPIRIT to the first DISCIPLES. *Leviticus 23:15-21; Acts 2:1*

Peter Originally called Simon, JESUS renamed him Peter 'the Rock'. Although a DISCIPLE of Jesus, Peter denied even knowing him *(Luke 22:54-62)*. The resurrected Jesus gave him the task of establishing the CHRISTIAN CHURCH *(John 21:15-17)*.

Pharaoh The name given to the rulers of the EGYPTIAN empire.

Pharisees The Pharisees were an influential religious group among the JEWS of JESUS' time. PAUL was himself a Pharisee *(Philippians 3:3-5)*, and it is quite likely that Jesus was taught his religion by Pharisees. They were a renewal movement within Judaism, but their passion for strict adherence to the law brought them into conflict with Jesus, who criticised them for their lack of compassion *(Matthew 9:11-13)*.

Pilate Full name Pontius Pilate, he was governor of **JUDAH** when **JESUS** was crucified *(see* **CRUCIFIXION***)*. *Matthew 27:2, 11-26*

praise A general term which describes anything (words or actions) which acknowledges or **EXALTS** God or a great deed or person. *Psalm 52:9; 1 Peter 1:3*

prayer Our varied communication with **GOD** which can be talking and listening to God, worshipping God, shouting at God, singing, **FASTING** . . . If you have ever spoken to God or heard from him, you have prayed. **JESUS** also prayed to God and taught the **DISCIPLES** the Lord's Prayer. *2 Chronicles 7:14; Luke 6:12, 11:2-4*

preaching The NT describes this as a special gift from **GOD**: the ability, given by the **HOLY SPIRIT**, to speak out in public about what God has done. *Isaiah 61:1; Luke 9:6, 24:46-47*

priest In the OT the priest's function was to represent **GOD** to people and people to God. The priest performed all the most important rituals

on behalf of the people. In the NT **JESUS** is described as high priest and all believers now have a priestly role to play. *Exodus 28:3; Hebrews 6:20; 1 Peter 2:9*

promised land *See* **CANAAN**

prophecy What **GOD** speaks to his people through a particular individual, a **PROPHET**. Sometimes a prophecy tells of what God is going to do in the future, sometimes it is instruction for the present. *Jeremiah 1:5; 2 Peter 1:19-21*

prophet Someone who speaks for **GOD**, receives and delivers messages from him. Some prophets wrote down their prophecies, others did not. The most famous prophets include **MOSES, ELIJAH, DANIEL.**

psalm A Greek word for a song. In the Bible the book of Psalms consists of 150 psalms in five collections or books. Many of these are believed to have been written by King **DAVID**. Some psalms are particularly psalms (or songs) of **PRAISE**, others are psalms of petition (ie requests to God). *See also* **DAVID.**

purification The **JEWS** laid great emphasis on ritual washing or cleansing because they wanted always to be **HOLY**. Thus anything which might cause them to be tainted (touching **BLOOD** for example) would necessitate acts of purification. In the NT, the blood of Christ provides purification for sin. *Numbers 8:5ff; Hebrews 1:3*

Rabbi HEBREW for 'teacher'. The Rabbi was normally the person who taught the **LAW,** so when the DISCIPLES call **JESUS** Rabbi they are likening him to other, often travelling, preachers (*see* **PREACHING**). *Mark 9:5*

redeem, redemption When you redeem a book token at the local bookshop you exchange your token for the book you want. In the same way, redemption is a kind of trading, though not as basic. In the OT, slaves could redeem themselves out of slavery or be redeemed by someone else by means of a payment to the slave's owner. It is this image that the NT picks up on: **JESUS**' death paid the price for our **SIN** so we are free and no longer slaves to **DEATH.** *Exodus 6:6; Ephesians 1:7*

rejoice Literally means, 'to take **JOY** in something'. *Psalm 31:7; Proverbs 5:18; Romans 5:2*

religion This word describes activities (**BELIEF, WORSHIP, RITUAL, PRAYER,** morality) by which people express their belief in **GOD.** The term is sometimes used negatively in the Bible because of Christianity's strong statement that religious activity will never earn us **SALVATION.** Only God's activity can save. *Amos 5:21; James 1:27*

repent, -ed, -ance Literally means, 'to turn around', 'to change one's mind', which leads to a change of action. It particularly concerns turning away from **SIN**. *Jeremiah 15:19; Matthew 3:2*

resurrection Coming back to life after death. The resurrection of **JESUS** is of central importance in the NT. Believers in him will one day be raised to life and be with him for ever. *Romans 1:4; 1 Corinthians 15:12ff*

revelation Based on the word 'reveal', as well as being the last book in the Bible, revelation means 'making something known'. Our knowledge of **GOD** is revealed to us by him. *Proverbs 29:18; Ephesians 3:3*

righteous, -ness Includes both doing the right thing and having right relationships and attitudes. It is most often used to describe **GOD'S** character and activity in the world, but **CHRISTIANS** are also called to be righteous in their actions and relationships. *Genesis 15:6; Psalm 145:17; Zephaniah 2:3; Romans 1:17*

ritual Although this word does not appear in the Bible, it is an important concept. It speaks of the connection between the physical and spiritual parts of life which is acknowledged in religious actions or ceremonies. Holy Communion (the **LAST SUPPER**) is a ritual or rite, as was an OT SACRIFICE. *Acts 21:24*

Rome Capital City of the Roman empire, seat of power and military might in JESUS' day.

sackcloth Cloth used to make sacks. This was the coarsest kind of material available to the JEWS, so when they wanted to show mourning, REPENTANCE or to FAST, they would dress in sackcloth and ashes as a sign of their willingness to suffer to see GOD's will done. *2 Samuel 3:31; Esther 4:1*

sacred Another word for HOLY. *Romans 14:5; 1 Corinthians 3:17*

sacrifice The idea of giving an offering to GOD is an important one throughout the Bible, as it was throughout the Near East at that time. ABRAHAM's near-sacrifice of ISAAC *(Genesis 22:1-14)* and ELIJAH's sacrifice 'competition' with the prophets of BAAL *(1 Kings 18:16-39)* are good examples of famous sacrifices, but the sacrifice of animals took place every day in the TEMPLE in JERUSALEM. JESUS' death was a sacrifice of ATONEMENT. *1 Kings 8:63; 1 John 2:2*

saints Literally means, 'HOLY ones', is used in the NT as a description for CHRISTIANS. *Ephesians 1:1; Revelation 5:8*

salvation In the NT one of the major images of becoming a CHRISTIAN is that of being 'saved'. Salvation is the process of being saved from sin and its punishment in order to live for GOD. Salvation is grounded in the life, DEATH and RESURRECTION of JESUS. *Exodus 15:2; Acts 4:12*

Samaria, –itans A town in central Israel once the capital of the northern kingdom of ISRAEL. Samaritans were despised by JEWS because they had married outside their own race. They feature favourably in the NT (the woman at the well *John 4:4-30*; the parable of the good Samaritan *Luke 10:30-37*; the healing of ten lepers *Luke 17:11-19*).

Samuel A PROPHET of GOD, Samuel appointed and counselled SAUL and DAVID, two of ISRAEL's most successful Kings *(see Samuel)*.

sanctuary A HOLY place. It normally means the special place in the TABERNACLE or TEMPLE. *Exodus 25:8; Psalm 150:1*

Sanhedrin The JEWISH council of ELDERS during the time of the ROMAN Empire. *Mark 15:1; Acts 6:12*

Satan Another name for the devil or the Prince of evil *(Revelation 12:9)*. The word means 'adversary'. In addition to the RELIGIOUS and political leaders of the time who acted against Jesus, it is clear that **JESUS** saw Satan as his true enemy (*Matthew 4:1-11; Luke 10:17-20*).

Saul The first king of **ISRAEL**, appointed by **GOD** through **SAMUEL**. He eventually became corrupted and was defeated in battle (*1 Samuel 9—31:5*).

Saviour A title of **JESUS**, meaning, 'the one who saves'. *Psalm 18:46; 2 Peter 1:1*

Scripture Literally means, 'writings', but is used exclusively in the Bible to mean writings that have special authority because they are inspired by **GOD**. *Daniel 9:2; 2 Timothy 3:16*

scroll Before books, people wrote on one long piece of parchment which they rolled up into a scroll. *Exodus 17:14; Revelation 1:11*

Seer Another word for **PROPHET** (*see* **PROPHECY**). *2 Samuel 15:27; Isaiah 30:10*

Simon *See* **PETER**.

sin, -ful The word has two related meanings: primarily, it describes the fact that we are in a wrong relationship with **GOD** and we rebel against him. It also describes individual acts of rebellion. *Psalm 51:9; Romans 6:23*

Son of Man A term found in Daniel to describe the **MESSIAH** as coming in

judgment and with authority. It was also used simply to mean 'man' and thus emphasises the servant role and humanity of **JESUS** when he applies the term to himself. *Daniel 7:13; Luke 6:5*

Solomon Son of **DAVID**, Solomon completed his father's work by building the great **TEMPLE** in **JERUSALEM**. Solomon was famous throughout the near East for his wisdom and also his love of women (*1 Kings 1–11*), hence his many foreign wives who influenced him to turn away from God to idolatry.

soul The biblical description of our personality or inner being. It is unclear exactly how the soul is viewed (see the **PSALMIST** telling his soul to praise the **LORD**, *Psalm 103:1*). *Psalm 62:1; Matthew 10:28. See also* **SPIRIT**.

spirit Sometimes seen as synonym for **SOUL**, the spirit of a person seems to be the part that connects with **GOD**. *Job 17:1; Hebrews 4:12*

spiritual warfare The struggle against Satan and evil forces opposed to **GOD**. *Ephesians 6:12*

synagogue As the **JEWS** began to live farther away from the **TEMPLE**, lots of local places of worship (synagogues) began to spring up so that people could continue to **WORSHIP GOD**. *Mark 1:21; Acts 18:4*

tabernacle The tabernacle was a tent used in the desert during the time of the **Exodus** as the first sanctuary, where the **ARK OF THE COVENANT** remained. It was eventually surpassed by the **TEMPLE**. *Exodus 25:9; Psalm 27:6*

Tabernacles, Feast of This celebrated the beginning of the harvest and **GOD**'s provision for his people in the wilderness after the **EXODUS** from **EGYPT**. *Exodus 23:16*

temple When the **ISRAELITES** finally settled in the promised land they built a **TEMPLE** in **JERUSALEM** where the **ARK OF THE COVENANT** would rest. The first temple built by **SOLOMON** was destroyed by the **BABYLONIANS**. It was rebuilt after the exile, then rebuilt again in a grand manner by **HEROD** around the time of **JESUS**' birth. This third temple was destroyed in A.D. 70, as prophesied by Jesus. *1 Kings 5:1-13; Ezra 3:12; John 2:19-22*

temptation The word means 'test' or 'trial', and in the Bible it is clear that both **GOD** and **SATAN** test the faith of believers (but for different reasons). *Matthew 6:13; 1 Corinthians 10:13*

Testament Another word for **COVENANT**, it has come to be used to describe the two parts of the Bible, which record **GOD**'s relationship with his people.

tithe A tenth. It was Jewish **LAW** that a tenth of everyone's produce be given to the **TEMPLE** for **WORSHIP** and **SACRIFICE**. Many people today give a tithe to their church. *Leviticus 27:30; Malachi 3:10*

transgression Another word for **SIN**. *Isaiah 53:8*

Trinity Although the word does not appear in the Bible, the idea that **GOD** is one *and* three is very much part of the NT's teaching. The three persons that make up God are God the Father, **JESUS** (God the Son) and the **HOLY SPIRIT**. In Genesis God says 'Let us . . .', implying that God has always been three persons in relationship. *Genesis 1:26; Matthew 28:19; 2 Corinthians 13:14*

worship The honour, reverence, **PRAISE** and adoration given to **GOD** for his love, greatness and saving acts. Worship is a celebration of the worthiness of God who alone is worthy of worship. Acts of worship can be private and public and can vary in style from one occasion to another. *Jonah 1:9; John 4:23*

wrath Anger. Used to describe both human and **DIVINE** anger. *Deuteronomy 9:8; Hosea 5:10; Romans 1:18*

zealous To say zealous means 'keen' is to understate its meaning, but words like 'fanatical' have too many negative connotations. In **JESUS'** day, the Zealots were a terrorist group who were trying to eject the **ROMANS** by force. It is unclear whether Simon the Zealot was just keen, or belonged to this group. *Numbers 25:13; Luke 6:15*

Zion The mountain on which **JERUSALEM** (and therefore the **TEMPLE**) is built *(2 Samuel 5:7)*. The term is symbolic of many things: the people of **GOD**; God's presence; dwelling-place of the future **MESSIAH**; the new **ISRAEL**. *Psalm 9:11; Isaiah 52:1-3.*

BIBLE INSTANTS 1

First Aid

afraid

I know that you are pleased with me, for my enemy does not triumph over me. Psalm 41:11 (p. 567) *and* Joshua 1:6-9; Psalm 34

anxious

Cast all your anxiety on him because he cares for you. 1 Peter 5:7 (p. 1220) *and* Psalm 46; Isaiah 43:1-3; Matthew 6:25-34; Philippians 4:6-7

bitter or critical

When my heart was grieved and my spirit embittered, I was senseless and ignorant; I was a brute beast before you. Psalm 73:21-22 (p. 587) *and* Psalm 73; 1 Corinthians 13

danger, in

I will say of the Lord, 'He is my refuge and my fortress, my God, in whom I trust.' Psalm 91:2 (p. 600) *and* Psalm 91; Proverbs 18:10

depressed

We are hard pressed on every side, but not crushed; perplexed, but not in despair, persecuted, but not abandoned; struck down, but not destroyed. 2 Corinthians 4:8-9 (p. 1160) and 2 Corinthians 4:16-18; Hebrews 12:1-3

directionless

I will instruct you and teach you in the way you should go; I will counsel you and watch over you. Psalm 32:8 (p. 560) *and* Psalm 30:19-21, 32:8-10

guilt, full of

'Neither do I condemn you,' Jesus declared. 'Go now and leave your life of sin.' John 8:11 (p. 1073) *and* Psalm 51; Luke 7: 36-50; John 3:16-17, 8:1-11; Romans 8:1-2; Hebrews 10:22-23

God is far away

For you created my innermost being; you knit me together in my mother's womb. I praise you because I am fearfully and wonderfully made. Psalm 139:13-14 (p. 628) *and* Psalm 139:1-18; Isaiah 55

ill

The prayer offered in faith will make the sick person well; the Lord will raise him up. If he has sinned, he will be forgiven. James 5:15 (p. 1216) *and* Psalm 103:1-6; 2 Corinthians 12:9-10; James 5:13-15

failure

In all these things we are more than conquerors through him who loved us. Romans 8:37 (p. 1135) *and* Psalm 77; Romans 8:28-39

faith, lacking in

I do believe! Help me overcome my unbelief! Mark 9:24 (p. 1013) *and* Mark 9:23-24; John 20:24-29; Romans 4:5; Hebrews 11; 1 John 4:15-16

let down

In my integrity you uphold me and set me in your presence for ever. Psalm 41:12 (p. 567) *and* Psalm 27:10-14, 41; 2 Timothy 4:16-18

lonely

I will not leave you as orphans; I will come to you. John 14:18 (p. 1082) *and* Psalm 23; John 14:15-21

tempted

Because he himself suffered when he was tempted, he is able to help those who are being tempted. Hebrews 2:18 (p. 1202) *and* Matthew 4:1-10;

1 Corinthians 10:12-13; Hebrews 4:15-16; 1 Peter 5:8-10

tired

Come to me; all you who are weary and burdened, and I will give you rest. Matthew 11:28 (p. 977) *and* Psalm 116:5-14; Isaiah 40:28-31; Matthew 11:28-30

unhappy, restless

Let the peace of Christ rule in your hearts. Colossians 3:15 (p. 1184) *and* Matthew 11:25-30; John 14:21; Romans 5:1-5; Philippians 4:4-7; Colossians 3:12-17

unloved

This is how God showed his love among us: he sent his one and only son into the world that we might live through him. 1 John 4:9 (p. 1227) *and* Matthew 10:30-31; John 3:16

worried

Don't worry about tomorrow, for tomorow will worry about itself. Matthew 7:34 (p. 973) *and* Matthew 7:19-34

BIBLE INSTANTS II

General

anger: 2 Chronicles 36:14-21; Psalm 4; Matthew 5:21-24; John 2:12-22; Ephesians 4:26-27; James 1:19-21

celebration: 2 Samuel 6:16-23; Psalm 81:1-10; Isaiah 40:1-11; Jeremiah 31:1-17; John 21:1-14

church: John 13:1-17; Acts 2:36-47; 1 Corinthians 12:12-27; Ephesians 4:1-6; Hebrews 10:19-39

conflict: Matthew 18:15-17; Galatians 2:11-14; 2 Timothy 2:23-24; James 4:1-12

death: 2 Samuel 1:17-27; Romans 14:7-9; 2 Corinthians 5:1-10; 1 Thessalonians 4:13-18; Revelation 21:1-6

decisions: Deuteronomy 30:11-20; Job 28:20-28; Jeremiah 17:5-8; Luke 9:57-62

depression: Genesis 15:1-6; 1 Kings 19:3-18; Psalm 73; Lamentations 3:1-20; Isaiah 35; Ezekiel 37:1-14

discipleship: John 15:1-8; Acts 11:19-26; 1 Peter 2:21-25

doubt: Judges 6:33-40; Psalm 13; John 14:1-14, 20:24-29

ecology and environment: Genesis 2:4-17; Job 38 – 41; Proverbs 8:22-31; Joel 2:21-27

evil: Genesis 6:5 – 7:24; Psalm 97; Mark 3:20-30; 1 Peter 5:8-9

faith: Matthew 16:13-20; Mark 11:22-24; Romans 5:1-2; 2 Corinthians 4:13-18; Hebrews 11:1 – 12:2
- sharing your faith:
Matthew 5:13-16; Acts 4:1-13; Acts 17:22-31; Romans 10:8-18; 2 Corinthians 2:14-16; 2 Timothy 1:3-14

family: Genesis 25:19-34; Ruth 1:11-17; Psalm 127; Proverbs 22:6; Luke 2:22-52

fear: Psalm 27; Matthew 14:22-33; John 18:1-27

forgiveness: Psalm 32:1-2, 51; Jonah 3:1-10; Ephesians 4:31-32

freedom: Exodus 14:19-31; Matthew 2:13-23; Mark 2:23 – 3:6; Romans 6:1-12; 1 Corinthians 8:1-13

friends: Ruth 1:1-19; Psalm 69:6-15; John 15:12-17; Romans 5:1-19; Philemon 4-21

fruit, spiritual: Matthew 7:17-20; John 15:1-8; Galatians 5:22-23

gifts: Romans 12:3-8; 1 Corinthians 12:1-11; Ephesians 4:11-13

giving: Isaiah 58; Malachi 3:10-12; Mark 12:38-44

God's love: Genesis 18:20 – 19:29; Psalm 103; Isaiah 66:10-14; Luke 15:11-24; Romans 5:8

God's will: Exodus 20:1-20; Matthew 26:36-42; Acts 16:6-10; 1 Thessalonians 5:16-18; James 4:13-17

gratitude: Luke 17:17-18; Colossians 3:15-17

guilt: Hosea 5:15; Zechariah 3:3-4; John 16:7-11

happiness: Psalm 23; Zephaniah 3:14-18; Matthew 5:1-12; 1 Peter 1:3-9

heaven: Matthew 25:31-40; I Peter 1:3-4; Revelation 21 – 22

hell: Matthew 25:41-46; 2 Thessalonians 1:7-9

Holy Spirit: Luke 19:1-10; John 14:16-18; Acts 2:1-21

honesty: Psalm 112; Ezekiel 3:16-21; I John 1:1 – 2:2

humility: Luke 22:24-27; John 13:1-17; Philippians 2:3-11; I Peter 5:5-7

hypocrisy: Isaiah 58:3-9; Amos 5:18-24; Matthew 23:25-28; Mark 7:1-23; I Thessalonians 2:3-6

jealousy: Nahum 1:2-6; Luke 15:25-32; I Corinthians 3:3-9; Galatians 5:19-26

Jesus: Isaiah 52:13 – 53:12; John 10:10; John 14:6; I Peter 3:18

judging others: Matthew 7:1-5; Romans 14:4-13; James 4:11-12

justice: Isaiah 9:1-7; Amos 8:4-8; Micah 6:8; Matthew 20:1-16; Luke 4:16-30

leadership: I Samuel 16:1-13; Micah 5:2-4; I Timothy 5:17-18

leisure: Mark 7:24; John 2:1-12

life: Genesis 1:1-31; Luke 24:1-11; John 5:24; I John 5:12

love: Matthew 5:43-48; I Corinthians 13; I Peter 1:17-23; I John 4:7-12 *See also* **God's love**

marriage: Genesis 2:18-24; Mark 10:2-12; Ephesians 5:21-33

money: Proverbs 10:16, 22; Zephaniah 1:17-18; Luke 16:1-13; I Timothy 6:6-16

non-Christians: Matthew 9:9-13; Luke 7:36-50, 15:1-10; John 13:34-35; I Corinthians 5:9-13; I Corinthians 7:10-16; Titus 2:11 – 3:7

patience: Habakkuk 2:13; James 5:7-11; 2 Peter 3:8-9

peace: Matthew 5:9; John 14:27; James 3:17-18

peer pressure: Psalm 1; Jeremiah 26:8-15; Daniel 1; John 13:31-35; Romans 12:1-2

perseverance: Isaiah 40: 27-31; Luke 18:1-8; Hebrews 12:1-3; Jude 17-25

praise: Psalm 18; Hebrews 13:15; I Peter 1:3-7

prayer: 2 Chronicles 7:14; Matthew 6:5-13; Luke 6:12-13; John 14:13-14; Hebrews 4:14-16; I Timothy 2:1-4

pride: Genesis 11:1-9; Luke 18:9-14; James 3:13-18

rejection: Mark 15:34; Romans 15:7; James 2:1-9

relationships: Judges 14:1-2; Song of Songs 2:10-17; 2 Corinthians 6:14

relationship with God: 1 Samuel 3:1-20; Matthew 14:22-23; 1 John 3:1-14

religion, false: Matthew 5:13-16; Acts 4:1-13, 17:22-31; Romans 10:8-18; 2 Corinthians 2:14-16; 2 Timothy 1:3-14

self-esteem: Psalm 139; Isaiah 44:1-8; Jeremiah 1:4-10; Amos 6:1-7; Matthew 10:24-33; Titus 2:1—3:7; 1 Peter 2:2-10

selfishness: 2 Corinthians 3:5-6; 2 Timothy 3:1-4

serving others: Isaiah 42:1-9; Micah 6:1-8; Matthew 20:20-28; John 12:1-11; Hebrews 13:1-8; James 2:14-17

sex: 2 Samuel 11:1-15; Song of Songs 5:2-6; John 8:1-11; Hebrews 13:4

sin: Psalm 130; Isaiah 59:1-2; Malachi 4:1-2; Romans 3:23

spiritual maturity: Romans 8:6-17; Philippians 2:12-16; 1 Timothy 6:11-12; 2 Peter 1:3-8

spiritual warfare: Ephesians 6:10-18; 1 Peter 5:8-9

suffering: Lamentations 3:1-24; Obadiah 11-14; Luke 13:1-5, 22:63-71; 2 Corinthians 6:3-10; 1 Peter 4:12-19

temptation: 1 Corinthians 10:13; Hebrews 2:18; James 1:12-15

truth: Joshua 23:14-16; Psalm 33:4; Psalm 119:151, John 15:1 — 17:3; Acts 11:23

work: Ezra 3:8-13; Proverbs 2:1-10; Ecclesiastes 2:4-11

worry: Matthew 6:25-34; Philippians 4:4-7

worship: 2 Samuel 6:12-22; Psalm 47; 1 Corinthians 14:26-33; Ephesians 5:15-20; Revelation 5:11-14

THE BIBLE IN ONE YEAR

I - Year Bible Reading Plan

This reading plan divides the complete Bible into 365 portions, dated for every day of the year. Each section offers a reading from the Old Testament, the New Testament, and from Psalms or Proverbs. The Old Testament is in broadly chronological order; otherwise, traditional Bible order is maintained.

The names of the books of the Bible are abbreviated as follows:

The Old Testament

Genesis	**Ge**
Exodus	**Ex**
Leviticus	**Lev**
Numbers	**Nu**
Deuteronomy	**Dt**
Joshua	**Jos**
Judges	**Jdg**
Ruth	**Ru**
I Samuel	**ISa**
2 Samuel	**2Sa**
I Kings	**IKi**
2 Kings	**2Ki**
I Chronicles	**ICh**
2 Chronicles	**2Ch**
Ezra	**Ezr**
Nehemiah	**Ne**
Esther	**Est**
Job	**Job**
Psalms	**Ps**
Proverbs	**Pr**
Ecclesiastes	**Ecc**
Song of Songs	**SS**
Isaiah	**Isa**
Jeremiah	**Jer**
Lamentations	**Lam**
Ezekiel	**Eze**
Daniel	**Dan**
Hosea	**Hos**
Joel	**Joel**
Amos	**Am**
Obadiah	**Ob**
Jonah	**Jnh**
Micah	**Mic**
Nahum	**Na**
Habakkuk	**Hab**
Zephaniah	**Zep**
Haggai	**Hag**
Zechariah	**Zec**
Malachi	**Mal**

The New Testament

Matthew	**Mt**
Mark	**Mk**
Luke	**Lk**
John	**Jn**
Acts	**Ac**
Romans	**Ro**
I Corinthians	**ICo**
2 Corinthians	**2Co**
Galatians	**Gal**
Ephesians	**Eph**
Philippians	**Php**
Colossians	**Col**
I Thessalonians	**ITh**
2 Thessalonians	**2Th**
I Timothy	**ITi**
2 Timothy	**2Ti**
Titus	**Tit**
Philemon	**Phm**
Hebrews	**Heb**
James	**Jas**
I Peter	**IPe**
2 Peter	**2Pe**
I John	**IJn**
2 John	**2Jn**
3 John	**3Jn**
Jude	**Jude**
Revelation	**Rev**

1	Ge 1:1—2:17	Mt 1:1-17	Ps 1:1-6	❏
2	Ge 2:18—4:16	Mt 1:18—2:18	Ps 2:1-12	❏
3	Ge 4:17—6:22	Mt 2:19—3:17	Ps 3:1-8	❏
4	Ge 7:1—9:17	Mt 4:1-22	Pr 1:1-7	❏
5	Ge 9:18—11:9	Mt 4:23—5:20	Ps 4:1-8	❏
6	Ge 11:10—13:18	Mt 5:21-42	Ps 5:1-12	❏
7	Ge 14:1—16:16	Mt 5:43—6:24	Ps 6:1-10	❏
8	Ge 17:1—18:33	Mt 6:25—7:23	Pr 1:8-19	❏
9	Ge 19:1—20:18	Mt 7:24—8:22	Ps 7:1-9	❏
10	Ge 21:1—23:20	Mt 8:23—9:13	Ps 7:10-17	❏
11	Ge 24:1-67	Mt 9:14-38	Ps 8:1-9	❏
12	Ge 25:1—26:35	Mt 10:1-31	Pr 1:20-33	❏
13	Ge 27:1—28:22	Mt 10:32—11:10	Ps 9:1-6	❏
14	Ge 29:1—30:43	Mt 11:11-30	Ps 9:7-12	❏
15	Ge 31:1-55	Mt 12:1-21	Ps 9:13-20	❏
16	Ge 32:1—33:20	Mt 12:22-45	Pr 2:1-11	❏
17	Ge 34:1—35:29	Mt 12:46—13:17	Ps 10:1-11	❏
18	Ge 36:1—37:36	Mt 13:18-35	Ps 10:12-18	❏
19	Ge 38:1—39:23	Mt 13:36-58	Ps 11:1-7	❏
20	Ge 40:1—41:40	Mt 14:1-21	Pr 2:12-22	❏
21	Ge 41:41—42:38	Mt 14:22—15:9	Ps 12:1-8	❏
22	Ge 43:1—44:34	Mt 15:10-39	Ps 13:1-6	❏
23	Ge 45:1—46:34	Mt 16:1-20	Ps 14:1-7	❏
24	Ge 47:1—48:22	Mt 16:21—17:13	Pr 3:1-10	❏
25	Ge 49:1—50:26	Mt 17:14—18:9	Ps 15:1-5	❏
26	Job 1:1—4:11	Mt 18:10-35	Ps 16:1-11	❏
27	Job 4:12—7:21	Mt 19:1-15	Ps 17:1-5	❏
28	Job 8:1—10:22	Mt 19:16-30	Pr 3:11-20	❏
29	Job 11:1—14:22	Mt 20:1-19	Ps 17:6-12	❏
30	Job 15:1—18:21	Mt 20:20-34	Ps 17:13-15	❏
31	Job 19:1—21:34	Mt 21:1-17	Ps 18:1-6	❏

1	Job 22:1—24:25	Mt 21:18-32	Pr 3:21-35	❏
2	Job 25:1—29:25	Mt 21:33—22:14	Ps 18:7-15	❏
3	Job 30:1—32:22	Mt 22:15-45	Ps 18:16-24	❏
4	Job 33:1—35:16	Mt 23:1-39	Ps 18:25-36	❏
5	Job 36:1—38:41	Mt 24:1-31	Pr 4:1-9	❏
6	Job 39:1—42:17	Mt 24:32—25:13	Ps 18:37-42	❏
7	Ex 1:1—2:25	Mt 25:14-46	Ps 18:43-50	❏
8	Ex 3:1—4:31	Mt 26:1-30	Ps 19:1-6	❏
9	Ex 5:1—6:27	Mt 26:31-46	Pr 4:10-19	❏
10	Ex 6:28—8:32	Mt 26:47-68	Ps 19:7-14	❏
11	Ex 9:1—10:29	Mt 26:69—27:10	Ps 20:1-9	❏
12	Ex 11:1—12:51	Mt 27:11-44	Ps 21:1-7	❏
13	Ex 13:1—14:31	Mt 27:45-66	Pr 4:20-27	❏
14	Ex 15:1—16:36	Mt 28:1-20	Ps 21:8-13	❏
15	Ex 17:1—18:27	Mk 1:1-28	Ps 22:1-11	❏
16	Ex 19:1—20:26	Mk 1:29—2:17	Ps 22:12-21	❏

17	Ex 21:1—22:31	Mk 2:18—3:30	Pr 5:1-14	❏
18	Ex 23:1—24:18	Mk 3:31—4:29	Ps 22:22-31	❏
19	Ex 25:1—26:37	Mk 4:30—5:20	Ps 23:1-6	❏
20	Ex 27:1—28:43	Mk 5:21—6:6a	Ps 24:1-10	❏
21	Ex 29:1—30:38	Mk 6:6b-29	Pr 5:15-23	❏
22	Ex 31:1—33:6	Mk 6:30-56	Ps 25:1-7	❏
23	Ex 33:7—34:35	Mk 7:1-30	Ps 25:8-15	❏
24	Ex 35:1—36:38	Mk 7:31—8:13	Ps 25:16-22	❏
25	Ex 37:1—38:31	Mk 8:14—9:1	Pr 6:1-11	❏
26	Ex 39:1—40:38	Mk 9:2-32	Ps 26:1-12	❏
27	Lev 1:1—2:16	Mk 9:33—10:12	Ps 27:1-6	❏
28	Lev 3:1—4:35	Mk 10:13-31	Ps 27:7-14	❏

MARCH

1	Lev 5:1—7:10	Mk 10:32-52	Pr 6:12-19	❏
2	Lev 7:11—8:36	Mk 11:1-26	Ps 28:1-9	❏
3	Lev 9:1—10:20	Mk 11:27—12:12	Ps 29:1-11	❏
4	Lev 11:1—12:9	Mk 12:13-27	Ps 30:1-7	❏
5	Lev 13:1-59	Mk 12:28-44	Pr 6:20-29	❏
6	Lev 14:1-57	Mk 13:1-31	Ps 30:8-12	❏
7	Lev 15:1—16:34	Mk 13:32—14:16	Ps 31:1-8	❏
8	Lev 17:1—18:30	Mk 14:17-42	Ps 31:9-18	❏
9	Lev 19:1—20:27	Mk 14:43-72	Pr 6:30-35	❏
10	Lev 21:1—22:33	Mk 15:1-32	Ps 31:19-24	❏
11	Lev 23:1—24:23	Mk 15:33-47	Ps 32:1-11	❏
12	Lev 25:1—26:13	Mk 16:1-20	Ps 33:1-11	❏
13	Lev 26:14—27:34	Lk 1:1-25	Pr 7:1-9	❏
14	Nu 1:1-29	Lk 1:26-38	Ps 33:12-22	❏
15	Nu 2:10—3:51	Lk 1:39-56	Ps 34:1-10	❏
16	Nu 4:1—5:10	Lk 1:57-80	Ps 34:11-22	❏
17	Nu 5:11—6:27	Lk 2:1-20	Pr 7:10-20	❏
18	Nu 7:1-65	Lk 2:21-40	Ps 35:1-10	❏
19	Nu 7:66—9:14	Lk 2:41-52	Ps 35:11-18	❏
20	Nu 9:15—11:23	Lk 3:1-22	Ps 35:19-28	❏
21	Nu 11:24—13:33	Lk 3:23—4:13	Pr 7:21-27	❏
22	Nu 14:1—15:21	Lk 4:14-37	Ps 36:1-12	❏
23	Nu 15:22—16:35	Lk 4:38—5:16	Ps 37:1-9	❏
24	Nu 16:36—18:32	Lk 5:17-32	Ps 37:10-20	❏
25	Nu 19:1—21:3	Lk 5:33—6:11	Pr 8:1-11	❏
26	Nu 21:4—22:20	Lk 6:12-36	Ps 37:21-31	❏
27	Nu 22:21—23:30	Lk 6:37—7:10	Ps 37:32-40	❏
28	Nu 24:1—26:11	Lk 7:11-35	Ps 38:1-12	❏
29	Nu 26:12—27:11	Lk 7:36-50	Pr 8:12-21	❏
30	Nu 27:12—29:11	Lk 8:1-18	Ps 38:13-22	❏
31	Nu 29:12—31:24	Lk 8:19-39	Ps 39:1-13	❏

APRIL

1	Nu 31:25—32:42	Lk 8:40—9:9	Ps 40:1-8	❏
2	Nu 33:1—34:29	Lk 9:10-27	Pr 8:22-31	❏
3	Nu 35:1—36:13	Lk 9:28-56	Ps 40:9-17	❏

4	Dt 1:1—2:37	Lk 9:57—10:24	Ps 41:1-6	❏
5	Dt 3:1—4:49	Lk 10:25—11:4	Ps 41:7-13	❏
6	Dt 5:1—6:25	Lk 11:5-32	Pr 8:32-36	❏
7	Dt 7:1—8:20	Lk 11:33-54	Ps 42:1-6a	❏
8	Dt 9:1—10:22	Lk 12:1-34	Ps 42:6b-11	❏
9	Dt 11:1—12:32	Lk 12:35-59	Ps 43:1-5	❏
10	Dt 13:1—14:29	Lk 13:1-30	Pr 9:1-12	❏
11	Dt 15:1—16:20	Lk 13:31—14:14	Ps 44:1-12	❏
12	Dt 16:21—18:22	Lk 14:15-35	Ps 44:13-26	❏
13	Dt 19:1—20:20	Lk 15:1-32	Ps 45:1-9	❏
14	Dt 21:1—22:30	Lk 16:1-18	Pr 9:13-18	❏
15	Dt 23:1—25:19	Lk 16:19—17:10	Ps 45:10-17	❏
16	Dt 26:1—28:14	Lk 17:11-37	Ps 46:1-11	❏
17	Dt 28:15-68	Lk 18:1-30	Ps 47:1-9	❏
18	Dt 29:1—30:10	Lk 18:31—19:10	Pr 10:1-10	❏
19	Dt 30:11—31:30	Lk 19:11-44	Ps 48:1-8	❏
20	Dt 32:1-52	Lk 19:45—20:26	Ps 48:9-14	❏
21	Dt 33:1—34:12	Lk 20:27—21:4	Ps 49:1-20	❏
22	Jos 1:1—2:24	Lk 21:5-38	Pr 10:11-20	❏
23	Jos 3:1—5:12	Lk 22:1-38	Ps 50:1-15	❏
24	Jos 5:13—7:26	Lk 22:39-62	Ps 50:16-23	❏
25	Jos 8:1—9:15	Lk 22:63—23:25	Ps 51:1-9	❏
26	Jos 9:16—10:43	Lk 23:26-56	Pr 10:21-30	❏
27	Jos 11:1—12:24	Lk 24:1-35	Ps 51:10-19	❏
28	Jos 13:1—14:15	Lk 24:36-53	Ps 52:1-9	❏
29	Jos 15:1-63	Jn 1:1-28	Ps 53:1-6	❏
30	Jos 16:1—18:28	Jn 1:29-51	Pr 10:31—11:8	❏

MAY

1	Jos 19:1—20:9	Jn 2:1-25	Ps 54:1-7	❏
2	Jos 21:1—22:34	Jn 3:1-21	Ps 55:1-11	❏
3	Jos 23:1—24:33	Jn 3:22-36	Ps 55:12-23	❏
4	Jdg 1:1—2:5	Jn 4:1-26	Pr 11:9-18	❏
5	Jdg 2:6—3:31	Jn 4:27-42	Ps 56:1-13	❏
6	Jdg 4:1—5:31	Jn 4:43—5:15	Ps 57:1-6	❏
7	Jdg 6:1—7:8a	Jn 5:16-30	Ps 57:7-11	❏
8	Jdg 7:8b—8:35	Jn 5:31-47	Pr 11:19-28	❏
9	Jdg 9:1-57	Jn 6:1-24	Ps 58:1-11	❏
10	Jdg 10:1—11:28	Jn 6:25-59	Ps 59:1-8	❏
11	Jdg 11:29—13:25	Jn 6:60—7:13	Ps 59:9-17	❏
12	Jdg 14:1—15:20	Jn 7:14-44	Pr 11:29—12:7	❏
13	Jdg 16:1—17:13	Jn 7:45—8:11	Ps 60:1-4	❏
14	Jdg 18:1—19:30	Jn 8:12-30	Ps 60:5-12	❏
15	Jdg 20:1—21:25	Jn 8:31-59	Ps 61:1-8	❏
16	Ru 1:1—2:23	Jn 9:1-34	Pr 12:8-17	❏
17	Ru 3:1—4:22	Jn 9:35—10:21	Ps 62:1-12	❏
18	1Sa 1:1—2:26	Jn 10:22-42	Ps 63:1-11	❏
19	1Sa 2:27—4:22	Jn 11:1-44	Ps 64:1-10	❏
20	1Sa 5:1—7:17	Jn 11:45—12:11	Pr 12:18-27	❏
21	1Sa 8:1—10:8	Jn 12:12-36	Ps 65:1-13	❏

22	1Sa 10:9—12:25	Jn 12:37—13:17	Ps 66:1-12	❏
23	1Sa 13:1—14:23	Jn 13:18-38	Ps 66:13-20	❏
24	1Sa 14:24—15:35	Jn 14:1-31	Pr 12:28—13:9	❏
25	1Sa 16:1—17:37	Jn 15:1—16:4	Ps 67:1-7	❏
26	1Sa 17:38—18:30	Jn 16:5—17:5	Ps 68:1-6	❏
27	1Sa 19:1—20:42	Jn 17:6-26	Ps 68:7-14	❏
28	1Sa 21:1—23:29	Jn 18:1-24	Pr 13:10-19	❏
29	1Sa 24:1—25:44	Jn 18:25-40	Ps 68:15-20	❏
30	1Sa 26:1—28:25	Jn 19:1-27	Ps 68:21-27	❏
31	1Sa 29:1—31:13	Jn 19:28—20:9	Ps 68:28-35	❏

JUNE

1	2Sa 1:1—2:7	Jn 20:10-31	Pr 13:20—14:4	❏
2	2Sa 2:8—3:21	Jn 21:1-25	Ps 69:1-12	❏
3	2Sa 3:22—5:16	Ac 1:1-22	Ps 69:13-28	❏
4	2Sa 5:17—6:23	Ac 1:23—2:21	Ps 69:29-36	❏
5	2Sa 7:1—8:18	Ac 2:22-47	Pr 14:5-14	❏
6	2Sa 9:1—10:19	Ac 3:1-26	Ps 70:1-5	❏
7	2Sa 11:1—12:31	Ac 4:1-22	Ps 71:1-8	❏
8	2Sa 13:1-39	Ac 4:23—5:11	Ps 71:9-18	❏
9	2Sa 14:1—15:12	Ac 5:12-42	Pr 14:15-24	❏
10	2Sa 15:13—16:23	Ac 6:1—7:19	Ps 71:19-24	❏
11	2Sa 17:1—18:18	Ac 7:20-43	Ps 72:1-20	❏
12	2Sa 18:19—19:43	Ac 7:44—8:3	Ps 73:1-14	❏
13	2Sa 20:1—21:22	Ac 8:4-40	Pr 14:25-35	❏
14	2Sa 22:1—23:7	Ac 9:1-31	Ps 73:15-28	❏
15	2Sa 23:8—24:25	Ac 9:32—10:23a	Ps 74:1-9	❏
16	1Ki 1:1—2:12	Ac 10:23b—11:18	Ps 74:10-17	❏
17	1Ki 2:13—3:15	Ac 11:19—12:19a	Pr 15:1-10	❏
18	1Ki 3:16—5:18	Ac 12:19b—13:15	Ps 74:18-23	❏
19	1Ki 6:1—7:22	Ac 13:16-41	Ps 75:1-10	❏
20	1Ki 7:23—8:21	Ac 13:42—14:7	Ps 76:1-12	❏
21	1Ki 8:22—9:9	Ac 14:8-28	Pr 15:11-20	❏
22	1Ki 9:10—11:13	Ac 15:1-21	Ps 77:1-9	❏
23	1Ki 11:14—12:24	Ac 15:22-41	Ps 77:10-20	❏
24	1Ki 12:25—14:20	Ac 16:1-15	Ps 78:1-8	❏
25	1Ki 14:21—16:7	Ac 16:16-40	Pr 15:21-30	❏
26	1Ki 16:8—18:15	Ac 17:1-21	Ps 78:9-16	❏
27	1Ki 18:16—19:21	Ac 17:22—18:8	Ps 78:17-31	❏
28	1Ki 20:1—21:29	Ac 18:9-28	Ps 78:32-39	❏
29	1Ki 22:1-53	Ac 19:1-41	Pr 15:31—16:7	❏
30	2Ki 1:1—2:25	Ac 20:1-38	Ps 78:40-55	❏

JULY

1	2Ki 3:1—4:37	Ac 21:1-26	Ps 78:56-72	❏
2	2Ki 4:38—6:23	Ac 21:27—22:16	Ps 79:1-13	❏
3	2Ki 6:24—8:15	Ac 22:17—23:11	Pr 16:8-17	❏
4	2Ki 8:16—9:37	Ac 23:12-35	Ps 80:1-7	❏
5	2Ki 10:1—11:21	Ac 24:1-27	Ps 80:8-19	❏
6	2Ki 12:1—14:22	Ac 25:1-22	Ps 81:1-7	❏

7	2Ki 14:23—15:38	Ac 25:23—26:23	Pr 16:18-27	❏
8	2Ki 16:1—17:41	Ac 26:24—27:12	Ps 81:8-16	❏
9	2Ki 18:1—19:13	Ac 27:13-32	Ps 82:1-8	❏
10	2Ki 19:14—20:21	Ac 27:33—28:16	Ps 83:1-18	❏
11	2Ki 21:1—23:7	Ac 28:17-31	Pr 16:28—17:4	❏
12	2Ki 23:8—24:17	Ro 1:1-17	Ps 84:1-7	❏
13	2Ki 24:18—25:30	Ro 1:18-32	Ps 84:8-12	❏
14	Jnh 1:1—4:11	Ro 2:1-24	Ps 85:1-7	❏
15	Am 1:1—2:16	Ro 2:25—3:8	Pr 17:5-14	❏
16	Am 3:1—4:13	Ro 3:9-31	Ps 85:8-13	❏
17	Am 5:1-27	Ro 4:1-15	Ps 86:1-10	❏
18	Am 6:1—7:17	Ro 4:16—5:11	Ps 86:11-17	❏
19	Am 8:1—9:15	Ro 5:12—6:10	Pr 17:15-24	❏
20	Hos 1:1—2:23	Ro 6:11-23	Ps 87:1-7	❏
21	Hos 3:1—5:15	Ro 7:1-13	Ps 88:1-9a	❏
22	Hos 6:1—7:16	Ro 7:14—8:8	Ps 88:9b-18	❏
23	Hos 8:1—9:17	Ro 8:9-27	Pr 17:25—18:6	❏
24	Hos 10:1—11:11	Ro 8:28-39	Ps 89:1-8	❏
25	Hos 11:12—14:9	Ro 9:1-21	Ps 89:9-13	❏
26	1Ch 1:1—2:17	Ro 9:22—10:4	Ps 89:14-18	❏
27	1Ch 2:18—4:8	Ro 10:5—11:10	Pr 18:7-16	❏
28	1Ch 4:9—5:26	Ro 11:11-32	Ps 89:19-29	❏
29	1Ch 6:1-81	Ro 11:33—12:21	Ps 89:30-37	❏
30	1Ch 7:1—8:28	Ro 13:1-14	Ps 89:38-45	❏
31	1Ch 8:29—10:14	Ro 14:1-18	Pr 18:17—19:2	❏

AUGUST

1	1Ch 11:1—12:18	Ro 14:19—15:13	Ps 89:46-52	❏
2	1Ch 12:19—14:17	Ro 15:14-33	Ps 90:1-10	❏
3	1Ch 15:1—16:36	Ro 16:1-27	Ps 90:11-17	❏
4	1Ch 16:37—18:17	1Co 1:1-17	Pr 19:3-12	❏
5	1Ch 19:1—22:1	1Co 1:18—2:5	Ps 91:1-8	❏
6	1Ch 22:2—23:32	1Co 2:6-16	Ps 91:9-16	❏
7	1Ch 24:1—26:13	1Co 3:1-23	Ps 92:1-15	❏
8	1Ch 26:14—27:34	1Co 4:1-21	Pr 19:13-22	❏
9	1Ch 28:1—29:30	1Co 5:1-13	Ps 93:1-5	❏
10	2Ch 1:1-17	1Co 6:1-20	Ps 94:1-11	❏
11	Ecc 1:1—3:22	1Co 7:1-16	Ps 94:12-23	❏
12	Ecc 4:1—6:12	1Co 7:17-31	Pr 19:23—20:4	❏
13	Ecc 7:1—9:12	1Co 7:32—8:13	Ps 95:1-11	❏
14	Ecc 9:13—12:14	1Co 9:1-18	Ps 96:1-13	❏
15	2Ch 2:1—5:1	1Co 9:19—10:13	Ps 97:1-12	❏
16	2Ch 5:2—7:10	1Co 10:14—11:1	Pr 20:5-14	❏
17	2Ch 7:11—9:31	1Co 11:2-34	Ps 98:1-9	❏
18	SS 1:1—4:16	1Co 12:1-26	Ps 99:1-9	❏
19	SS 5:1—8:14	1Co 12:27—13:13	Ps 100:1-5	❏
20	2Ch 10:1—12:16	1Co 14:1-17	Pr 20:15-24	❏
21	2Ch 13:1—15:19	1Co 14:18-40	Ps 101:1-8	❏
22	2Ch 16:1—18:27	1Co 15:1-34	Ps 102:1-11	❏
23	2Ch 18:28—21:3	1Co 15:35-49	Ps 102:12-17	❏

24	2Ch 21:4—23:21	1Co 15:50—16:4	Pr 20:25—21:4	❏
25	2Ch 24:1—25:28	1Co 16:5-24	Ps 102:18-28	❏
26	2Ch 26:1—28:27	2Co 1:1-11	Ps 103:1-12	❏
27	2Ch 29:1—31:1	2Co 1:12-22	Ps 103:13-22	❏
28	2Ch 31:2—33:20	2Co 1:23—2:11	Pr 21:5-16	❏
29	2Ch 33:21—35:19	2Co 2:12—3:6	Ps 104:1-18	❏
30	2Ch 35:20—36:23	2Co 3:7-18	Ps 104:19-30	❏
31	Mic 1:1—4:13	2Co 4:1-18	Ps 104:31-35	❏

S E P T E M B E R

1	Mic 5:1—7:20	2Co 5:1-10	Pr 21:17-26	❏
2	Isa 1:1—2:22	2Co 5:11—6:2	Ps 105:1-11	❏
3	Isa 3:1—5:7	2Co 6:3—7:1	Ps 105:12-22	❏
4	Isa 5:8—8:10	2Co 7:2-16	Ps 105:23-36	❏
5	Isa 8:11—10:19	2Co 8:1-15	Pr 21:27—22:6	❏
6	Isa 10:20—13:22	2Co 8:16—9:5	Ps 105:37-45	❏
7	Isa 14:1—16:14	2Co 9:6-15	Ps 106:1-15	❏
8	Isa 17:1—19:25	2Co 10:1-18	Ps 106:16-31	❏
9	Isa 20:1—23:18	2Co 11:1-15	Pr 22:7-16	❏
10	Isa 24:1—26:21	2Co 11:16-33	Ps 106:32-39	❏
11	Isa 27:1—28:29	2Co 12:1-10	Ps 106:40-48	❏
12	Isa 29:1—30:18	2Co 12:11-21	Ps 107:1-9	❏
13	Isa 30:19—32:20	2Co 13:1-14	Pr 22:17-27	❏
14	Isa 33:1—35:10	Gal 1:1-24	Ps 107:10-22	❏
15	Isa 36:1—37:38	Gal 2:1-10	Ps 107:23-32	❏
16	Isa 38:1—40:31	Gal 2:11—3:9	Ps 107:33-43	❏
17	Isa 41:1—42:25	Gal 3:10-25	Pr 22:28—23:9	❏
18	Isa 43:1—44:23	Gal 3:26—4:20	Ps 108:1-5	❏
19	Isa 44:24—46:13	Gal 4:21—5:6	Ps 108:6-13	❏
20	Isa 47:1—49:7	Gal 5:7-26	Ps 109:1-20	❏
21	Isa 49:8—51:16	Gal 6:1-18	Pr 23:10-18	❏
22	Isa 51:17—54:17	Eph 1:1-23	Ps 109:21-31	❏
23	Isa 55:1—57:13	Eph 2:1-22	Ps 110:1-7	❏
24	Isa 57:14—59:21	Eph 3:1-21	Ps 111:1-10	❏
25	Isa 60:1—62:12	Eph 4:1-16	Pr 23:19-28	❏
26	Isa 63:1—65:16	Eph 4:17—5:7	Ps 112:1-10	❏
27	Isa 65:17—66:24	Eph 5:8-33	Ps 113:1-9	❏
28	Na 1:1—3:19	Eph 6:1-24	Ps 114:1-8	❏
29	Zep 1:1—3:20	Php 1:1-26	Pr 23:29—24:4	❏
30	Jer 1:1—2:30	Php 1:27—2:11	Ps 115:1-11	. ❏

O C T O B E R

1	Jer 2:31—4:9	Php 2:12-30	Ps 115:12-18	❏
2	Jer 4:10—5:31	Php 3:1—4:1	Ps 116:1-11	❏
3	Jer 6:1—7:29	Php 4:2-23	Pr 24:5-14	❏
4	Jer 7:30—9:16	Col 1:1-23	Ps 116:12-19	❏
5	Jer 9:17—11:13	Col 1:24—2:5	Ps 117:1-2	❏
6	Jer 11:14—13:27	Col 2:6-23	Ps 118:1-16	❏
7	Jer 14:1—15:21	Col 3:1—4:1	Pr 24:15-22	❏
8	Jer 16:1—17:27	Col 4:2-18	Ps 118:17-29	❏

9	Jer 18:1—20:18	1Th 1:1—2:16	Ps 119:1-8	❏
10	Jer 21:1—23:8	1Th 2:17—3:13	Ps 119:9-16	❏
11	Jer 23:9—25:14	1Th 4:1-18	Pr 24:23-34	❏
12	Jer 25:15—26:24	1Th 5:1-28	Ps 119:17-24	❏
13	Jer 27:1—29:23	2Th 1:1-12	Ps 119:25-32	❏
14	Jer 29:24—31:14	2Th 2:1-17	Ps 119:33-40	❏
15	Jer 31:15—32:25	2Th 3:1-18	Pr 25:1-10	❏
16	Jer 32:26—34:22	1Ti 1:1-20	Ps 119:41-48	❏
17	Jer 35:1—37:21	1Ti 2:1-15	Ps 119:49-56	❏
18	Jer 38:1—40:6	1Ti 3:1-16	Ps 119:57-64	❏
19	Jer 40:7—42:22	1Ti 4:1-16	Pr 25:11-20	❏
20	Jer 43:1—45:5	1Ti 5:1—6:2	Ps 119:65-72	❏
21	Jer 46:1—47:7	1Ti 6:3-21	Ps 119:73-80	❏
22	Jer 48:1—49:6	2Ti 1:1-18	Ps 119:81-88	❏
23	Jer 49:7—50:10	2Ti 2:1-26	Pr 25:21—26:2	❏
24	Jer 50:11—51:14	2Ti 3:1-17	Ps 119:89-96	❏
25	Jer 51:15-64	2Ti 4:1-22	Ps 119:97-104	❏
26	Jer 52:1-34	Tit 1:1-16	Ps 119:105-112	❏
27	Hab 1:1—3:19	Tit 2:1-15	Pr 26:3-12	❏
28	La 1:1—2:6	Tit 3:1-15	Ps 119:113-120	❏
29	La 2:7—3:39	Phm 1-25	Ps 119:121-128	❏
30	La 3:40—5:22	Heb 1:1-14	Ps119:129-136	❏
31	Ob 1-21	Heb 2:1-18	Pr 26:13-22	❏

N O V E M B E R

1	Joel 1:1—2:17	Heb 3:1-19	Ps 119:137-144	❏
2	Joel 2:18—3:21	Heb 4:1-13	Ps 119:145-152	❏
3	Eze 1:1—3:27	Heb 4:14—5:10	Ps119:153-160	❏
4	Eze 4:1—6:14	Heb 5:11—6:12	Pr 26:23—27:4	❏
5	Eze 7:1—9:11	Heb 6:13—7:10	Ps 119:161-168	❏
6	Eze 10:1—12:28	Heb 7:11-28	Ps 119 169-176	❏
7	Eze 13:1—15:18	Heb 8:1-13	Ps 120:1-7	❏
8	Eze 16:1-63	Heb 9:1-15	Pr 27:5-14	❏
9	Eze 17:1—18:32	Heb 9:16-28	Ps 121:1-8	❏
10	Eze 19:1—20:44	Heb 10:1-18	Ps 122:1-9	❏
11	Eze 20:45—22:22	Heb 10:19-39	Ps 123:1-4	❏
12	Eze 22:23—23:49	Heb 11:1-16	Pr 27:15-22	❏
13	Eze 24:1—25:17	Heb 11:17-40	Ps 124:1-8	❏
14	Eze 26:1—27:36	Heb 12:1-13	Ps 125:1-5	❏
15	Eze 28:1—29:21	Heb 12:14-29	Ps 126:1-6	❏
16	Eze 30:1—31:18	Heb 13:1-25	Pr 27:23—28:6	❏
17	Eze 32:1—33:20	Jas 1:1-27	Ps 127:1-5	❏
18	Eze 33:21—34:31	Jas 2:1-26	Ps 128:1-6	❏
19	Eze 35:1—37:14	Jas 3:1-18	Ps 129:1-8	❏
20	Eze 37:15—39:20	Jas 4:1-17	Pr 28:7-17	❏
21	Eze 39:21—40:49	Jas 5:1-20	Ps 130:1-8	❏
22	Eze 41:1—42:20	1Pe 1:1—2:3	Ps 131:1-3	❏
23	Eze 43:1—44:31	1Pe 2:4-25	Ps 132:1-18	❏
24	Eze 45:1—46:24	1Pe 3:1-22	Pr 28:18-28	❏
25	Eze 47:1—48:35	1Pe 4:1-19	Ps 133:1-3	❏

26	Da 1:1—2:23	1Pe 5:1-14	Ps 134:1-3	❏
27	Da 2:24—3:12	2Pe 1:1-21	Ps 135:1-12	❏
28	Da 3:13—4:18	2Pe 2:1-22	Pr 29:1-9	❏
29	Da 4:19—5:16	2Pe 3:1-18	Ps 135:13-21	❏
30	Da 5:17—6:28	1Jn 1:1—2:1	Ps 136:1-12	❏

DECEMBER

1	Da 7:1—8:14	1Jn 2:12-27	Ps 136:13-26	❏
2	Da 8:15—9:19	1Jn 2:28—3:10	Pr 29:10-18	❏
3	Da 9:20—11:1	1Jn 3:11—4:6	Ps 137:1-9	❏
4	Da 11:2-35	1Jn 4:7-21	Ps 138:1-8	❏
5	Da 11:36—12:13	1Jn 5:1-21	Ps 139:1-10	❏
6	Hag 1:1—2:23	2Jn 1-13	Ps 139:11-16	❏
7	Zec 1:1—4:14	3Jn 1-14	Ps 139:11-16	❏
8	Zec 5:1—8:23	Jude 1-25	Ps 139:17-24	❏
9	Zec 9:1—11:17	Rev 1:1-20	Ps 140:1-5	❏
10	Zec 12:1—14:21	Rev 2:1-17	Pr 30:1-10	❏
11	Est 1:1—2:18	Rev 2:18—3:6	Ps 140:6-13	❏
12	Est 2:19—5:14	Rev 3:7-22	Ps 141:1-10	❏
13	Est 6:1—8:17	Rev 4:1—5:5	Ps 142:1-7	❏
14	Est 9:1—10:3	Rev 5:6-14	Pr 30:11-23	❏
15	Mal 1:1—2:16	Rev 6:1-17	Ps 143:1-12	❏
16	Mal 2:17—4:6	Rev 7:1-17	Ps 144:1-8	❏
17	Ezr 1:1—2:67	Rev 8:1—9:12	Ps 144:9-15	❏
18	Ezr 2:68—4:5	Rev 9:13—10:11	Pr 30:24-33	❏
19	Ezr 4:6—5:17	Rev 11:1-19	Ps 145:1-7	❏
20	Ezr 6:1—7:10	Rev 12:1—13:1a	Ps 145:8-13a	❏
21	Ezr 7:11—8:14	Rev 13:1b-18	Ps 145:13b-21	❏
22	Ezr 8:15—9:15	Rev 14:1-13	Pr 31:1-9	❏
23	Ezr 10:1-44	Rev 14:14—15:8	Ps 146:1-10	❏
24	Ne 1:1—2:20	Rev 16:1-21	Ps 147:1-11	❏
25	Ne 3:1—4:23	Rev 17:1-18	Ps 147:12-20	❏
26	Ne 5:1—7:3	Rev 18:1-17a	Pr 31:10-20	❏
27	Ne 7:4—8:18	Rev 18:17b—19:10	Ps 148:1-6	❏
28	Ne 9:1-37	Rev 19:11—20:6	Ps 148:7-14	❏
29	Ne 9:38—11:21	Rev 20:7—21:4	Ps 149:1-9	❏
30	Ne 11:22—12:47	Rev 21:5-27	Pr 31:21-31	❏
31	Ne 13:1-31	Rev 22:1-21	Ps 150:1-6	❏

God, my father in heaven,

I'm coming before you now
confessing my weakness,
my sin,
my selfishness.

I need you.
I give up everything I am
and say, 'I am yours.'

I want to leave behind all that has gone before,
please wipe the slate clean,
help me to start again.

I call out to your Son Jesus to bring your forgiveness to me;
I call out to your Holy Spirit to bring your power to me;
I call out to you, Father God, to love me.

I am yours,
you are mine.

I thank you that Jesus died for me
so that I can live a new life.
I will do that now
with your help.

Amen